MW01227810

STATS™ 1996 Pro Football Handbook

STATS, Inc.

STATS
PUBLISHING

Published by STATS Publishing
A division of Sports Team Analysis & Tracking Systems, Inc.
Dr. Richard Cramer, Chairman • John Dewan, President

Cover by Excel Marketing, Schaumburg, Illinois

Photo by Ponzini Photography

© Copyright 1996 by STATS, Inc.

All rights reserved. No information contained in this book nor any part of this book may be used, reproduced or transmitted for commercial use in any form without express written consent of STATS, Inc., 8131 Monticello, Skokie, Illinois 60076. (847) 676-3322. STATS is a trademark of Sports Team Analysis and Tracking Systems, Inc.

First Edition: February, 1996

Printed in the United States of America

ISBN 1-884064-24-8

Acknowledgments

When a team wins the Super Bowl, it's not just the players who get the pretty rings. Everyone else in the organization gets one, too, from the junior equipment manager to the team receptionist to the part-time scout. Why? Because to accomplish something so fantastic takes the contributions of many people who never set foot on the field.

The numbers you'll see in this book are presented courtesy of our Operations Department, led by Steve Moyer. Allan Spear is personally responsible for the collection of our football data, as he oversees our dedicated scorers. Kenn Ruby and Mike Hammer share the title of "Guys Who Stay Until 6am Monday Morning to Make Sure Our Numbers are Perfect." Peter Woelflein, Ethan Cooperson, and Jason Kinsey also assist with football when they aren't consumed with baseball, basketball and hockey.

Producing a book like this in roughly two weeks is an awesome task, and we couldn't do it without computers. That, of course, means we need somebody to work the darned things, and our programmers are the best. Sue Dewan and Mike Canter oversee the Systems Department. Dave Mundo and Jeff Schinski worked specifically on this book, with help from Jim Guthrie, Stefan Kretschmann and David Pinto. Art Ashley ensures quality control over the whole operation, and Pat Quinn serves as our Product Manager of On-line Services.

The Department of Finances and Human Resources, headed by Bob Meyerhoff, processes the orders, handles the paperwork, and makes sure our books get to you. Bob's staff consists of Ginny Hamill, Tim Harbert, Marge Morra, Betty Moy, Brynne Orlando, Jim Osborne and Leena Sheth. Stephanie Seburn is our Assistant Director of Marketing Support and Administration, and Buffy Cramer-Hammann serves as John Dewan's assistant.

The Marketing Department gets the STATS word to the public. Our fine group includes Kristen Beauregard, Drew Faust, Ron Freer, Chuck Miller and Jim Musso. Jim Capuano serves as our Director of National Sales.

Don Zminda is the guiding force behind the Publications Department, and for that we're all grateful. Scott McDevitt and Jim Henzler both joined us last year, and their dedication has energized all of our books.

That STATS exists in its present form is primarily due to Dick Cramer, Chairman and founder, and John Dewan, President and CEO. They've set the standards for an entire industry.

— Rob Neyer

This book is for the 1995 Northwestern football team,
which will produce its share of doctors, teachers, world leaders. . .
and football players.

— Kenn Ruby

Table of Contents

Foreword

by Gene Upshaw

I've been involved with professional football for nearly 30 years. During that period, first as an offensive lineman with the Oakland Raiders and now as the chairman of National Football League Players Incorporated, statistics have always played an important role in my career. When I played for the Raiders, I used them to prepare myself for the games on Sunday. Knowing which statistics were important and how to read them was extremely important in helping me gain an edge over the competition. Now, although I don't use statistics to prepare for gameday anymore, they are still very useful and important to me at NFL Players Inc.

In fact, statistics have become so important to our business that we recently began a search to find our own statistics service. That search led us to STATS, Inc., pro football's premier statistical service.

Considering that we represent all of the players in the NFL, it is important that we have comprehensive statistical information on every active NFL player. This book has that. Actually, it's the only book in which you can find statistics for every NFL player who appeared in a game in 1995. And not only is the information comprehensive, it's also valuable and easily understood.

Equally important in compiling NFL statistics is the timeliness of the information. STATS, Inc. is simply unparalleled in this regard. Not only do they compile the best statistics, they publish them first. They are so timely, in fact, that we use them to regularly update our website, www.nflplayers.com.

Another perspective not to be overlooked are the details. No other publication gives you more details and in-depth information than does the *Pro Football Handbook*. Player performance is described game by game, on grass and turf, on various downs and even in different formations.

As professional football becomes ever more complex and sophisticated, the fan's need for comprehensive statistical data continues to increase. Game plans that were once shown to players on chalk boards and printed in manuals are now displayed via computer systems. Soon, even that information may be brought to your home, and game and player statistics won't be far behind. It's quite likely that the company bringing you those statistics will be STATS, Inc., the "official statistical service of the NFL Players."

Introduction

You ever heard that advice about buying a car? "Never buy a brand-new model in its first year," they say. "Wait a year, because then they'll have all the bugs worked out." Well, a lot of you didn't follow that advice when it came to the *Pro Football Handbook* last year. The very first edition sold so well that we were (happily) forced to a second printing. We got the message loud and clear: You want lots of stats, and you want them fast.

You should be very happy this year. The second edition of the *Pro Football Handbook* has even more stats. One new feature is active career leaders in a number of statistical categories. Another first: we've created a new position for the book, "long snapper" (LS). Finally, Ed Brady (page 32) gets his due. Also new is complete sack data for every active quarterback. That information, like much of what you'll find here, simply isn't available anywhere else. (By the way, for the most amazing stat in the book, check out Randall Cunningham's 1986 sack numbers on page 64.) And the best news of all for numbers-lovers: two new teams in 1995 means lots more players, lots more pages, and lots more stats.

For you new readers, there isn't space here to list all the stuff you'll find here that you've never seen before, but here's a flavor: sacks allowed by individual linemen, directional running and passing numbers, dropped passes, field-goal data by distance, more punting stats than you could ever want, game-by-game logs for all significant players. . . . . and that's just a flavor. Take the book wherever you go, spend some time with it; before you know it, the *Football Handbook* will be one of your best friends.

You want your stats fast? *Fast?* This book was available just *days* after the Super Bowl, as compared to mid-summer releases for the other record books.

As always, we welcome your comments on the book, and we thank you for reading.

— Rob Neyer

A Note on the Numbers

This year's book was sent to press more than a month prior to the release of the official NFL stats to the media. We are confident that there will be very few differences between the stats found here and the official ones. With the exception of the Kerry Collins pass attempt (more on that below), the discrepancies reported here are minor differences.

We would, however, like to point out several differences between our stats and those reported by the NFL and published in *USA Today* late in December. We have reviewed each of these plays and are confident that STATS' data are correct.

Panthers vs. Rams, 11/12/95

With 1:22 to play in the 2nd quarter, the Panthers had the ball 1st and 10 on the Ram 21 yardline. Panthers tight end Pete Metzelaars jumped offside and whistles sounded stopping play, but Kerry Collins threw the ball incomplete to Eric Guliford. The Ram coaching staff hastily declined the penalty before realizing the play had been whistled dead. The following play was also 1st-and-10 on the Ram 21, confirming that the previous incomplete pass play didn't actually count. STATS therefore reports Kerry Collins with 432 pass attempts, while the NFL still listed him with 433 when this book went to press. The Elias Sports Bureau reports that the play will be reviewed.

Packers vs. Browns, 11/19/95

With 11 minutes to play in the 3rd quarter, the Browns had the ball 2nd-and-6 on the Packer 30 following a 4-yard pass to Brad Kinchen. The original play-by-play reported the situation as 2nd- and-5 on the 30 yardline. So when the Packers jumped offsides for a 5-yard penalty, the Browns were credited with a first down on the stat sheet. But in reality, the next play was 2nd-and-1 on the Packer 25. The Browns did pick up a first down on that play, which meant they were credited with two first downs instead of the correct figure, one. Therefore, STATS reports 292 first downs for the Browns, while the NFL reports 293 first downs.

Cowboys vs. Raiders, 11/19/95

With 11:40 to play in the 1st quarter, Raiders WR Raghib Ismail ran for 13 yards on an end-around play, but Tim Brown was called for holding downfield. The penalty was marked from the point of the infraction, resulting in a net gain of 3 yards. The down was replayed so no first-down rushing should have been credited. STATS has 316 first downs for the Raiders, while the NFL reported 317 first downs.

— Mike Hammer

Final 1995 NFL Standings

American Conference

East

East	W	L	T	PF	PA	vs AFC	vs Div
Buffalo	10	6	0	350	335	7 - 5 - 0	5 - 3 - 0
Indianapolis	9	7	0	331	316	7 - 5 - 0	6 - 2 - 0
Miami	9	7	0	398	332	7 - 5 - 0	3 - 5 - 0
New England	6	10	0	294	377	6 - 6 - 0	5 - 3 - 0
New York	3	13	0	233	384	3 - 9 - 0	1 - 7 - 0

Central

Central	W	L	T	PF	PA	vs AFC	vs Div
Pittsburgh	11	5	0	407	327	9 - 3 - 0	6 - 2 - 0
Cincinnati	7	9	0	349	374	5 - 7 - 0	4 - 4 - 0
Houston	7	9	0	348	324	6 - 6 - 0	3 - 5 - 0
Cleveland	5	11	0	289	356	4 - 8 - 0	3 - 5 - 0
Jacksonville	4	12	0	275	404	4 - 8 - 0	4 - 4 - 0

West

West	W	L	T	PF	PA	vs AFC	vs Div
Kansas City	13	3	0	358	241	10 - 2 - 0	8 - 0 - 0
San Diego	9	7	0	321	323	6 - 6 - 0	4 - 4 - 0
Seattle	8	8	0	363	366	5 - 7 - 0	3 - 5 - 0
Denver	8	8	0	388	345	6 - 6 - 0	3 - 5 - 0
Oakland	8	8	0	348	332	5 - 7 - 0	2 - 6 - 0

National Conference

East

East	W	L	T	PF	PA	vs NFC	vs Div
Dallas	12	4	0	435	291	8 - 4 - 0	5 - 3 - 0
Philadelphia	10	6	0	318	338	9 - 3 - 0	7 - 1 - 0
Washington	6	10	0	326	359	6 - 6 - 0	3 - 5 - 0
New York	5	11	0	290	340	5 - 7 - 0	4 - 4 - 0
Arizona	4	12	0	275	422	3 - 9 - 0	1 - 7 - 0

Central

Central	W	L	T	PF	PA	vs NFC	vs Div
Green Bay	11	5	0	404	314	7 - 5 - 0	5 - 3 - 0
Detroit	10	6	0	436	336	7 - 5 - 0	6 - 2 - 0
Chicago	9	7	0	392	360	7 - 5 - 0	4 - 4 - 0
Minnesota	8	8	0	412	385	5 - 7 - 0	3 - 5 - 0
Tampa Bay	7	9	0	238	335	5 - 7 - 0	2 - 6 - 0

West

West	W	L	T	PF	PA	vs NFC	vs Div
San Francisco	11	5	0	457	258	8 - 4 - 0	5 - 3 - 0
Atlanta	9	7	0	362	349	7 - 5 - 0	5 - 3 - 0
St. Louis	7	9	0	309	418	6 - 6 - 0	4 - 4 - 0
Carolina	7	9	0	289	325	4 - 8 - 0	3 - 5 - 0
New Orleans	7	9	0	319	348	3 - 9 - 0	3 - 5 - 0

Wild Card Games

Saturday, December 30, 1995
Buffalo 37, Miami 22
Philadelphia 58, Detroit 37

Sunday, December 31, 1995
Green Bay 37, Atlanta 20
Indianapolis 35, San Diego 20

Conference Semifinals

Saturday, January 6, 1996
Pittsburgh 40, Buffalo 21
Green Bay 27, San Francisco 17

Sunday, January 7, 1996
Dallas 30, Philadelphia 11
Indianapolis 10, Kansas City 7

Conference Finals

Sunday, January 14, 1996
Pittsburgh 20, Indianapolis 16
Dallas 38, Green Bay 27

Super Bowl XXX

at Sun Devil Stadium, Tempe, Arizona
Sunday, January 28, 1996
Dallas 27, Pittsburgh 17

Career Statistics

The following section includes the records of all players who saw NFL action in 1995, plus two others—Johnny Johnson and Barry Foster—who missed the entire season but might well return in 1996.

Abbreviations: You're probably familiar with most of the abbreviations, but below are all of them and what they stand for. Details on the various categories ("What's the difference between Net Punts and Total Punts?") may be found in the Glossary.

Age is seasonal age, based on November 1, 1996, approximate mid-point of the season.

For ALL PLAYERS, **G** = Games Played; **GS** = Games Started; **Att** = Attempts; **Rec** = Receptions; **Yds** = Yards; **Avg** = Average; **TD** = Touchdowns; **Int** = Passes Intercepted; **Lg** = Long; **Fum** = Fumbles; **Rcvr** = Fumbles Recovered.

For PASSERS, **Com** = Completions; **Pct** = Percentage of Passes Completed; **Rtng** = Quarterback Rating; **Sckd** = Times Sacked.

For DEFENSIVE PLAYERS, **Tk** = Tackles; **Ast** = Assists; **FF** = Fumbles Forced; **FR** = Fumbles Recovered; **Blk** = Punts and Place Kicks Blocked.

For PUNTERS, **In20** = Inside 20; **TotPunts** = Total Punts; **TB** = Touchbacks; **Blkd** = Punts Blocked; **OppRet** = Punts Returned; **RetYds** = Return Yards; **NetAvg** = Net Punting Average.

Profiles: For many offensive and defensive players, and all regular kickers and punters, you will see a note just above the age, "(statistical profile on page 357)," for example. This directs you to the Profiles sections, where you'll find detailed situational break-downs for the player's 1995 campaign.

Two-Team Seasons: If a player saw action with more than one NFL team in a season, his stats for each team in the season(s) in question appear just above the career-totals line at the bottom of each entry. The teams are listed in the correct order.

Sacks and Sacked: Sacks for individual defensive players were not an official stat until 1982. A few players in this book were active before then, and you'll see some sack data for them. This information has been collected from team sources, and is unofficial. All such sack data is italicized here, and does not count in the career total.

League Leaders: Throughout the career statistics, any stat which led the NFL in a given season will be in bold face and slightly larger than normal. All categories are eligible for this treatment except: Games, Games Started, Fumble Yards, Tackles, Assists, Fumbles Forced, Blocks, Safeties, Miscellaneous TDs. We should also note that for kickers, one might lead the league in 50+ yard field goals made, but not attempted (or vice versa).

Rather than spend much time here on qualifications, we direct you to the Leader Boards later in the book. There, you'll find the minimum numbers required to qualify for leadership in any percentage category. For the seasons in this book which didn't consist of 16 games (pre-1978, 1982 and 1987), the minimums are prorated.

Draft: Above his statistics, each player here has a note describing when he was drafted. After "**Rnd:**" you'll find a number for whatever round the player was drafted in. If the player was drafted in the first round of the regular draft, a number in parentheses tells you in what order he was picked. If an "(S)" appears after a number, that means the players was acquired in one of the NFL's supplemental drafts. And if the player entered the NFL as a free agent, "FA" is listed.

A Lengthy Note on Tackles: Nearly all of the numbers in the career section are official NFL statistics. However, tackle data is *not* official, so we had to decide whether or not to list them. Once we decided to do so, we still had to decide *which* data to use, and we had plenty of options. You see, there is lots of different tackle data. There's the stuff released in the NFL's game summaries shortly after games are completed. There are the numbers released months later, after the coaches have reviewed film. And there are the data painstakingly recorded by STATS reporters.

You might say (as we did), "The answer is obvious. Just use tackles as determined by the coaching staffs. They're more qualified than anyone." But there is one big problem with doing that: teams vary wildly in giving credit, especially for assists. What's more, some teams don't conduct tape review at all. The results are things like this: in 1993, Charger defenders were credited with 123 assists. That same season, Atlanta defenders racked up *602* assists.

So for the sake of consistency, we've decided to go with the NFL game summaries, figuring that the standards used in crediting tackles and assists are at least relatively uniform among the stat crews at the game sites. However, for seasons before 1994 we are listing the team-supplied totals because that's all we have. For this reason, many regular defenders show substantially lower assists in 1994 and 1995 than in previous seasons. To alert you that 1994 and 1995 tackle/assist totals come from a different source than previous seasons, that data is italicized. One more thing: A few teams have never listed assists, instead folding them in with overall tackles. The result was initially a bunch of zeroes in the assists column for some players, which suggested that those players never assisted on tackles. To alert you to these players, we've inserted a dash in all instances in which a player was credited with at least 10 tackles, but zero assists. In other words, he probably had some assists, but no one knows how many.

Rob Neyer

Clifton Abraham

Pos: CB/S **Rnd:** 5 **College:** Florida State **Ht:** 5' 9" **Wt:** 184 **Born:** 12/9/71 **Age:** 24

Year	Team	G	GS	Tackles Tk	Ast	Sack	Misc. FF	FR	TD	Blk	Int. Int	Yds	Avg	TD	Totals Sfty	TD	Pts
1995	Tampa Bay Buccaneers	6	0	3	0	0.0	0	0	0	0	0	0	-	0	0	0	0

Bobby Abrams

Pos: LB **Rnd:** FA **College:** Michigan **Ht:** 6' 3" **Wt:** 240 **Born:** 4/12/67 **Age:** 29

Year	Team	G	GS	Tackles Tk	Ast	Sack	Misc. FF	FR	TD	Blk	Int. Int	Yds	Avg	TD	Totals Sfty	TD	Pts
1990	New York Giants	16	0	11	2	0.0	0	0	0	0	0	0	-	0	0	0	0
1991	New York Giants	16	2	18	2	0.0	1	0	0	0	0	0	-	0	0	0	0
1992	Dal - Cle - NYN	8	0	2	0	0.0	0	0	0	0	0	0	-	0	0	0	0
1993	Dal - Min	9	0	2	0	0.0	0	0	0	0	0	0	-	0	0	0	0
1994	Minnesota Vikings	16	0	1	0	0.0	0	0	0	0	0	0	-	0	0	0	0
1995	New England Patriots	9	1	2	0	0.0	0	0	0	0	0	0	-	0	0	0	0
1992	Dallas Cowboys	4	0	0	0	0.0	0	0	0	0	0	0	-	0	0	0	0
	Cleveland Browns	3	0	0	0	0.0	0	0	0	0	0	0	-	0	0	0	0
	New York Giants	1	0	0	0	0.0	0	0	0	0	0	0	-	0	0	0	0
1993	Dallas Cowboys	5	0	0	0	0.0	0	0	0	0	0	0	-	0	0	0	0
	Minnesota Vikings	4	0	2	0	0.0	0	0	0	0	0	0	-	0	0	0	0
	6 NFL Seasons	74	3	34	4	0.0	1	0	0	0	0	0	-	0	0	0	0

Sam Adams

Pos: DT **Rnd:** 1 (8) **College:** Texas A&M **Ht:** 6' 3" **Wt:** 285 **Born:** 6/13/73 **Age:** 23

Year	Team	G	GS	Tackles Tk	Ast	Sack	Misc. FF	FR	TD	Blk	Int. Int	Yds	Avg	TD	Totals Sfty	TD	Pts
1994	Seattle Seahawks	12	7	20	7	4.0	0	0	0	0	0	0	-	0	0	0	0
1995	Seattle Seahawks	16	5	16	10	3.5	0	0	0	0	0	0	-	0	1	0	2
	2 NFL Seasons	28	12	36	17	7.5	0	0	0	0	0	0	-	0	1	0	2

Scott Adams

Pos: T **Rnd:** FA **College:** Georgia **Ht:** 6' 5" **Wt:** 305 **Born:** 9/28/66 **Age:** 30

Year	Team	G	GS	Year	Team	G	GS	Year	Team	G	GS	Year	Team	G	GS
1992	Minnesota Vikings	15	0	1993	Minnesota Vikings	15	10	1994	New Orleans Saints	11	0	1995	Chicago Bears	4	0
													4 NFL Seasons	45	10

Other Statistics: 1992–returned 1 kickoff for 0 yards; fumbled 1 time for 0 yards. 1994–recovered 1 fumble for 0 yards.

Theo Adams

Pos: G **Rnd:** FA **College:** Hawaii **Ht:** 6' 5" **Wt:** 300 **Born:** 4/24/66 **Age:** 30

Year	Team	G	GS	Year	Team	G	GS	Year	Team	G	GS			G	GS
1992	Seattle Seahawks	10	0	1993	Tampa Bay Buccaneers	7	0	1995	Philadelphia Eagles	1	0		3 NFL Seasons	18	0

Vashone Adams

Pos: S **Rnd:** FA **College:** Eastern Michigan **Ht:** 5' 10" **Wt:** 196 **Born:** 9/12/73 **Age:** 23

Year	Team	G	GS	Tackles Tk	Ast	Sack	Misc. FF	FR	TD	Blk	Int. Int	Yds	Avg	TD	Totals Sfty	TD	Pts
1995	Cleveland Browns	8	6	23	12	0.0	0	0	0	0	0	0	-	0	0	0	0

Mel Agee

Pos: DT **Rnd:** 6 **College:** Illinois **Ht:** 6' 5" **Wt:** 300 **Born:** 11/22/68 **Age:** 27

Year	Team	G	GS	Tackles Tk	Ast	Sack	Misc. FF	FR	TD	Blk	Int. Int	Yds	Avg	TD	Totals Sfty	TD	Pts
1991	Indianapolis Colts	16	2	29	-	0.0	1	0	0	0	0	0	-	0	0	0	0
1992	Indianapolis Colts	1	0	0	0	0.0	0	0	0	0	0	0	-	0	0	0	0
1993	Atlanta Falcons	11	7	23	20	2.5	1	0	0	0	0	0	-	0	0	0	0
1994	Atlanta Falcons	16	6	24	8	0.0	0	0	0	0	0	0	-	0	0	0	0
1995	Atlanta Falcons	10	1	7	0	0.0	0	0	0	0	0	0	-	0	0	0	0
	5 NFL Seasons	54	16	83	28	2.5	2	0	0	0	0	0	-	0	0	0	0

Ray Agnew

Pos: DT **Rnd:** 1 (10) **College:** North Carolina State **Ht:** 6' 3" **Wt:** 285 **Born:** 12/9/67 **Age:** 28

Year	Team	G	GS	Tackles Tk	Ast	Sack	Misc. FF	FR	TD	Blk	Int. Int	Yds	Avg	TD	Totals Sfty	TD	Pts
1990	New England Patriots	12	9	38	14	2.5	0	1	0	0	0	0	-	0	0	0	0
1991	New England Patriots	13	10	22	14	2.0	0	0	0	0	0	0	-	0	0	0	0

Year	Team	G	GS	Tackles			Miscellaneous				Interceptions				Totals		
				Tk	Ast	Sack	FF	FR	TD	Blk	Int	Yds	Avg	TD	Sfty	TD	Pts
1992	New England Patriots	14	14	44	17	1.0	0	1	0	0	0	0	-	0	0	0	0
1993	New England Patriots	16	1	29	16	1.5	0	0	0	0	0	0	-	0	0	0	0
1994	New England Patriots	11	3	14	8	0.5	0	0	0	0	0	0	-	0	0	0	0
1995	New York Giants	16	15	47	18	1.0	2	1	0	0	0	0	-	0	0	0	0
	6 NFL Seasons	82	52	194	87	8.5	2	3	0	0	0	0	-	0	0	0	0

Louis Aguiar

(statistical profile on page 466)

Pos: P **Rnd:** FA **College:** Utah State **Ht:** 6' 2" **Wt:** 219 **Born:** 6/30/66 **Age:** 30

Year	Team	G	Punting						TotPunts	TB	Blocks	OppRet	RetYds	NetAvg	Field Goals			Passing			
			NetPunts	Yards	Avg	Long	In20	In20%							Overall	Pct	Long	Att	Com	Yds	Int
1991	New York Jets	16	64	2521	39.4	61	14	21.9	64	7	0	29	164	34.6	1-2	50.0	23	0	0	0	0
1992	New York Jets	16	73	2993	41.0	65	21	28.8	73	3	0	26	189	37.6	0-0	-	-	0	0	0	0
1993	New York Jets	16	73	2806	38.4	71	21	28.8	73	7	0	26	156	34.4	0-0	-	-	2	0	0	1
1994	Kansas City Chiefs	16	85	3582	42.1	61	15	17.6	85	7	0	50	506	34.5	0-0	-	-	0	0	0	0
1995	Kansas City Chiefs	16	91	3990	43.8	65	29	31.9	91	12	0	42	433	36.5	0-0	-	-	0	0	0	0
	5 NFL Seasons	80	386	15892	41.2	71	100	25.9	386	36	0	173	1448	35.6	1-2	50.0	23	2	0	0	1

Other Statistics: 1991–recovered 1 fumble for 0 yards; rushed 1 time for 18 yards. 1993–recovered 1 fumble for -10 yards; rushed 3 times for -27 yards; fumbled 2 times.

Chidi Ahanotu

Pos: DE **Rnd:** 6 **College:** California **Ht:** 6' 2" **Wt:** 288 **Born:** 10/11/70 **Age:** 26

Year	Team	G	GS	Tackles			Miscellaneous				Interceptions				Totals		
				Tk	Ast	Sack	FF	FR	TD	Blk	Int	Yds	Avg	TD	Sfty	TD	Pts
1993	Tampa Bay Buccaneers	16	10	15	16	1.5	1	0	0	0	0	0	-	0	0	0	0
1994	Tampa Bay Buccaneers	16	16	31	15	1.0	0	0	0	0	0	0	-	0	0	0	0
1995	Tampa Bay Buccaneers	16	15	36	12	3.0	0	0	0	0	0	0	-	0	0	0	0
	3 NFL Seasons	48	41	82	43	5.5	1	0	0	0	0	0	-	0	0	0	0

Troy Aikman

(statistical profile on page 278)

Pos: QB **Rnd:** 1 (1) **College:** UCLA **Ht:** 6' 4" **Wt:** 228 **Born:** 11/21/66 **Age:** 29

Year	Team	G	GS	Passing										Rushing					Miscellaneous			
				Att	Com	Pct	Yards	Yds/Att	Lg	TD	Int	Int%	Rating	Att	Yds	Avg	Lg	TD	Sckd	Yds	Fum	Recv Yds	Pts
1989	Dallas Cowboys	11	11	293	155	52.9	1749	5.97	t75	9	18	6.1	55.7	38	302	7.9	25	0	19	155	6	3	0	0
1990	Dallas Cowboys	15	15	399	226	56.6	2579	6.46	t61	11	18	4.5	66.6	40	172	4.3	20	1	39	288	5	1	0	6
1991	Dallas Cowboys	12	12	363	237	65.3	2754	7.59	61	11	10	2.8	86.7	16	5	0.3	9	1	32	224	4	0	0	6
1992	Dallas Cowboys	16	16	473	302	63.8	3445	7.28	t87	23	14	3.0	89.5	37	105	2.8	19	1	23	112	4	1	0	6
1993	Dallas Cowboys	14	14	392	271	69.1	3100	7.91	t80	15	6	1.5	99.0	32	125	3.9	20	0	26	153	7	3	-3	0
1994	Dallas Cowboys	14	14	361	233	64.5	2676	7.41	90	13	12	3.3	84.9	30	62	2.1	13	1	14	59	2	2	0	6
1995	Dallas Cowboys	16	16	432	280	64.8	3304	7.65	50	16	7	1.6	93.6	21	32	1.5	12	1	14	89	5	2	-15	6
	7 NFL Seasons	98	98	2713	1704	62.8	19607	7.23	90	98	85	3.1	83.5	214	803	3.8	25	5	167	1080	33	12	-18	30

Other Statistics: 1989–caught 1 pass for -13 yards. 1991–caught 1 pass for -6 yards.

Trev Alberts

Pos: LB/DE **Rnd:** 1 (5) **College:** Nebraska **Ht:** 6' 4" **Wt:** 245 **Born:** 8/8/70 **Age:** 26

Year	Team	G	GS	Tackles			Miscellaneous				Interceptions				Totals		
				Tk	Ast	Sack	FF	FR	TD	Blk	Int	Yds	Avg	TD	Sfty	TD	Pts
1994	Indianapolis Colts	5	0	5	0	2.0	1	0	0	0	0	0	-	0	0	0	0
1995	Indianapolis Colts	15	3	25	12	2.0	2	0	0	0	0	0	-	0	0	0	0
	2 NFL Seasons	20	3	30	12	4.0	3	0	0	0	0	0	-	0	0	0	0

Ethan Albright

Pos: T/G **Rnd:** FA **College:** North Carolina **Ht:** 6' 5" **Wt:** 292 **Born:** 5/1/71 **Age:** 25

Year	Team	G	GS				G	GS
1995	Miami Dolphins	10	0		1 NFL Season		10	0

Allen Aldridge

(statistical profile on page 393)

Pos: LB **Rnd:** 2 **College:** Houston **Ht:** 6' 1" **Wt:** 245 **Born:** 5/30/72 **Age:** 24

Year	Team	G	GS	Tackles			Miscellaneous				Interceptions				Totals		
				Tk	Ast	Sack	FF	FR	TD	Blk	Int	Yds	Avg	TD	Sfty	TD	Pts
1994	Denver Broncos	16	2	1	0	0.0	0	0	0	0	0	0	-	0	0	0	0
1995	Denver Broncos	16	12	65	24	1.5	0	1	0	0	0	0	-	0	0	0	0
	2 NFL Seasons	32	14	66	24	1.5	0	1	0	0	0	0	-	0	0	0	0

Melvin Aldridge

Pos: S **Rnd:** FA **College:** Murray State **Ht:** 6' 2" **Wt:** 195 **Born:** 7/22/70 **Age:** 26

Year	Team	G	GS	Tackles			Miscellaneous				Interceptions				Totals		
				Tk	Ast	Sack	FF	FR	TD	Blk	Int	Yds	Avg	TD	Sfty	TD	Pts
1993	Houston Oilers	1	0	0	0	0.0	0	0	0	0	0	0	-	0	0	0	0
1995	Arizona Cardinals	2	0	0	0	0.0	0	0	0	0	0	0	-	0	0	0	0
	2 NFL Seasons	3	0	0	0	0.0	0	0	0	0	0	0	-	0	0	0	0

Keith Alex

Pos: G **Rnd:** 9 **College:** Texas A&M **Ht:** 6' 4" **Wt:** 307 **Born:** 6/9/69 **Age:** 27

Year	Team	G	GS	Year	Team	G	GS			G	GS
1993	Atlanta Falcons	14	0	1995	Minnesota Vikings	1	0		2 NFL Seasons	15	0

Brent Alexander

(statistical profile on page 393)

Pos: S/CB **Rnd:** FA **College:** Tennessee State **Ht:** 5' 10" **Wt:** 184 **Born:** 7/10/70 **Age:** 26

Year	Team	G	GS	Tackles			Miscellaneous				Interceptions				Totals		
				Tk	Ast	Sack	FF	FR	TD	Blk	Int	Yds	Avg	TD	Sfty	TD	Pts
1994	Arizona Cardinals	16	7	26	10	0.0	0	0	0	0	0	0	-	0	0	0	0
1995	Arizona Cardinals	16	13	51	17	0.5	2	1	0	0	2	14	7.0	0	0	0	0
	2 NFL Seasons	32	20	77	27	0.5	2	1	0	0	2	14	7.0	0	0	0	0

Derrick Alexander

Pos: KR/WR **Rnd:** 1 (29) **College:** Michigan **Ht:** 6' 2" **Wt:** 195 **Born:** 11/6/71 **Age:** 24

Year	Team	G	GS	Rushing					Receiving					Punt Returns				Kickoff Returns				Totals		
				Att	Yds	Avg	Lg	TD	Rec	Yds	Avg	Lg	TD	Num	Yds	Avg	TD	Num	Yds	Avg	TD	Fum	TD	Pts
1994	Cleveland Browns	14	12	4	38	9.5	25	0	48	828	17.3	t81	2	0	0	-	0	0	0	-	0	2	2	14
1995	Cleveland Browns	14	2	1	29	29.0	29	0	15	216	14.4	40	0	9	122	13.6	1	21	419	20.0	0	3	1	6
	2 NFL Seasons	28	14	5	67	13.4	29	0	63	1044	16.6	t81	2	9	122	13.6	1	21	419	20.0	0	5	3	20

Other Statistics: 1994–scored 1 two-point conversion. 1995–recovered 1 fumble for 0 yards.

Derrick Alexander

Pos: DE **Rnd:** 1 (11) **College:** Florida State **Ht:** 6' 4" **Wt:** 276 **Born:** 11/3/73 **Age:** 22

Year	Team	G	GS	Tackles			Miscellaneous				Interceptions				Totals		
				Tk	Ast	Sack	FF	FR	TD	Blk	Int	Yds	Avg	TD	Sfty	TD	Pts
1995	Minnesota Vikings	15	12	22	12	2.0	2	1	0	0	0	0	-	0	0	0	0

Elijah Alexander

Pos: LB **Rnd:** 10 **College:** Kansas State **Ht:** 6' 2" **Wt:** 230 **Born:** 8/8/70 **Age:** 26

Year	Team	G	GS	Tackles			Miscellaneous				Interceptions				Totals		
				Tk	Ast	Sack	FF	FR	TD	Blk	Int	Yds	Avg	TD	Sfty	TD	Pts
1992	Tampa Bay Buccaneers	12	0	0	0	0.0	0	0	0	0	0	0	-	0	0	0	0
1993	Denver Broncos	16	0	8	2	0.0	0	0	0	0	0	0	-	0	0	0	0
1994	Denver Broncos	16	16	88	24	1.0	0	1	0	0	1	0	0.0	0	0	0	0
1995	Denver Broncos	9	8	22	6	0.5	0	0	0	0	2	5	2.5	0	0	0	0
	4 NFL Seasons	53	24	118	32	1.5	0	1	0	0	3	5	1.7	0	0	0	0

Tuineau Alipate

Pos: LB **Rnd:** FA **College:** Washington State **Ht:** 6' 2" **Wt:** 245 **Born:** 8/21/67 **Age:** 29

Year	Team	G	GS	Tackles			Miscellaneous				Interceptions				Totals		
				Tk	Ast	Sack	FF	FR	TD	Blk	Int	Yds	Avg	TD	Sfty	TD	Pts
1994	New York Jets	9	0	0	0	0.0	0	1	0	0	0	0	-	0	0	0	0
1995	Minnesota Vikings	16	0	3	1	0.0	0	0	0	0	0	0	-	0	0	0	0
	2 NFL Seasons	25	0	3	1	0.0	0	1	0	0	0	0	-	0	0	0	0

Derek Allen

Pos: G **Rnd:** FA **College:** Illinois **Ht:** 6' 4" **Wt:** 290 **Born:** 1/30/71 **Age:** 25

Year	Team	G	GS				G	GS
1995	New York Giants	1	0		1 NFL Season		1	0

Eric Allen

(statistical profile on page 393)

Pos: CB **Rnd:** 2 **College:** Arizona State **Ht:** 5' 10" **Wt:** 180 **Born:** 11/22/65 **Age:** 30

Year	Team	G	GS	Tackles			Miscellaneous				Interceptions				Punt Returns				Kickoff Returns				Totals	
				Tk	Ast	Sack	FF	FR	TD	Blk	Int	Yds	Avg	TD	Num	Yds	Avg	TD	Num	Yds	Avg	TD	TD	Fum
1988	Philadelphia Eagles	16	16	57	8	0.0	0	0	0	0	5	76	15.2	0	0	0	-	0	0	0	-	0	0	0
1989	Philadelphia Eagles	15	15	38	10	0.0	0	0	0	0	8	38	4.8	0	0	0	-	0	0	0	-	0	0	1

Year	Team	G	GS	Tackles			Miscellaneous				Interceptions				Punt Returns				Kickoff Returns				Totals	
				Tk	Ast	Sack	FF	FR	TD	Blk	Int	Yds	Avg	TD	Num	Yds	Avg	TD	Num	Yds	Avg	TD	TD	Fum
1990	Philadelphia Eagles	16	15	56	7	0.0	0	1	0	0	3	37	12.3	1	0	0	-	0	1	2	2.0	0	1	0
1991	Philadelphia Eagles	16	16	27	12	0.0	0	1	0	0	5	20	4.0	0	0	0	-	0	0	0	-	0	0	0
1992	Philadelphia Eagles	16	16	42	30	0.0	1	2	0	0	4	49	12.3	0	0	0	-	0	0	0	-	0	0	0
1993	Philadelphia Eagles	16	16	42	22	2.0	3	0	0	0	6	201	33.5	4	0	0	-	0	0	0	-	0	4	0
1994	Philadelphia Eagles	16	16	46	11	0.0	0	1	0	0	3	61	20.3	0	0	0	-	0	0	0	-	0	0	0
1995	New Orleans Saints	16	16	44	15	0.0	0	0	0	0	2	28	14.0	0	0	0	-	0	0	0	-	0	0	0
	8 NFL Seasons	127	126	352	115	2.0	4	5	0	0	36	510	14.2	5	0	0	-	0	1	2	2.0	0	5	1

Larry Allen

Pos: G   **Rnd:** 2   **College:** Sonoma State   **Ht:** 6' 3"   **Wt:** 325   **Born:** 11/27/71   **Age:** 24

Year	Team	G	GS	Year	Team	G	GS				G	GS
1994	Dallas Cowboys	16	10	1995	Dallas Cowboys	16	16		2 NFL Seasons		32	26

Other Statistics: 1995–recovered 1 fumble for 0 yards.

Marcus Allen

(statistical profile on page 278)

Pos: RB   **Rnd:** 1 (10)   **College:** Southern California   **Ht:** 6' 2"   **Wt:** 210   **Born:** 3/26/60   **Age:** 36

Year	Team	G	GS	Rushing					Receiving					Kickoff Returns				Passing				Totals		
				Att	Yds	Avg	Lg	TD	Rec	Yds	Avg	Lg	TD	Num	Yds	Avg	TD	Att	Com	Yds	Int	Fum	TD	Pts
1982	Los Angeles Raiders	9	9	160	697	4.4	53	11	38	401	10.6	t51	3	0	0	-	0	4	1	47	0	5	14	84
1983	Los Angeles Raiders	15	14	266	1014	3.8	19	9	68	590	8.7	36	2	0	0	-	0	7	4	111	0	14	12	72
1984	Los Angeles Raiders	16	16	275	1168	4.2	t52	13	64	758	11.8	92	5	0	0	-	0	4	1	38	0	8	18	108
1985	Los Angeles Raiders	16	16	380	1759	4.6	t61	11	67	555	8.3	44	3	0	0	-	0	2	1	16	0	3	14	84
1986	Los Angeles Raiders	13	10	208	759	3.6	t28	5	46	453	9.8	36	2	0	0	-	0	0	0	0	0	7	7	42
1987	Los Angeles Raiders	12	12	200	754	3.8	44	5	51	410	8.0	39	0	0	0	-	0	2	1	23	0	3	5	30
1988	Los Angeles Raiders	15	15	223	831	3.7	32	7	34	303	8.9	t30	1	0	0	-	0	2	1	21	0	5	8	48
1989	Los Angeles Raiders	8	5	69	293	4.2	15	2	20	191	9.6	26	0	0	0	-	0	0	0	0	0	2	2	12
1990	Los Angeles Raiders	16	15	179	682	3.8	28	12	15	189	12.6	30	1	0	0	-	0	1	0	0	1	2	13	78
1991	Los Angeles Raiders	8	2	63	287	4.6	26	2	15	131	8.7	25	0	0	0	-	0	2	1	11	0	1	2	12
1992	Los Angeles Raiders	16	0	67	301	4.5	21	2	28	277	9.9	40	1	0	0	-	0	0	0	0	0	1	3	18
1993	Kansas City Chiefs	16	10	206	764	3.7	39	12	34	238	7.0	t18	3	0	0	-	0	0	0	0	0	4	15	90
1994	Kansas City Chiefs	13	13	189	709	3.8	t36	7	42	349	8.3	38	0	0	0	-	0	0	0	0	0	3	7	44
1995	Kansas City Chiefs	16	15	207	890	4.3	38	5	27	210	7.8	20	0	0	0	-	0	0	0	0	0	2	5	30
	14 NFL Seasons	189	152	2692	10908	4.1	t61	103	549	5055	9.2	92	21	0	0	-	0	24	10	267	1	59	125	752

Other Statistics: 1982–recovered 2 fumbles for 0 yards. 1983–recovered 2 fumbles for 0 yards and 1 touchdown; passed for 3 touchdowns. 1984–recovered 3 fumbles for 0 yards. 1985–recovered 2 fumbles for 0 yards. 1986–recovered 1 fumble for 0 yards. 1990–recovered 1 fumble for 0 yards. 1991–passed for 1 touchdown. 1993–recovered 1 fumble for 0 yards. 1994–scored 1 two-point conversion. 1995–recovered 1 fumble for 0 yards.

Terry Allen

(statistical profile on page 279)

Pos: RB   **Rnd:** 9   **College:** Clemson   **Ht:** 5' 10"   **Wt:** 207   **Born:** 2/21/68   **Age:** 28

Year	Team	G	GS	Rushing					Receiving					Punt Returns				Kickoff Returns				Totals		
				Att	Yds	Avg	Lg	TD	Rec	Yds	Avg	Lg	TD	Num	Yds	Avg	TD	Num	Yds	Avg	TD	Fum	TD	Pts
1991	Minnesota Vikings	15	6	120	563	4.7	t55	2	6	49	8.2	21	1	0	0	-	0	1	14	14.0	0	4	3	18
1992	Minnesota Vikings	16	16	266	1201	4.5	51	13	49	478	9.8	t36	2	0	0	-	0	0	0	-	0	9	15	90
1994	Minnesota Vikings	16	16	255	1031	4.0	45	8	17	148	8.7	31	0	0	0	-	0	0	0	-	0	3	8	50
1995	Washington Redskins	16	16	338	1309	3.9	28	10	31	232	7.5	24	1	0	0	-	0	0	0	-	0	6	11	66
	4 NFL Seasons	63	54	979	4104	4.2	t55	33	103	907	8.8	t36	4	0	0	-	0	1	14	14.0	0	22	37	224

Other Statistics: 1991–recovered 1 fumble for 0 yards. 1992–recovered 2 fumbles for 0 yards. 1994–recovered 2 fumbles for 4 yards; scored 1 two-point conversion. 1995–recovered 1 fumble for 0 yards.

John Alt

Pos: T   **Rnd:** 1 (21)   **College:** Iowa   **Ht:** 6' 8"   **Wt:** 307   **Born:** 5/30/62   **Age:** 34

Year	Team	G	GS	Year	Team	G	GS	Year	Team	G	GS	Year	Team	G	GS
1984	Kansas City Chiefs	15	1	1987	Kansas City Chiefs	9	9	1990	Kansas City Chiefs	16	16	1993	Kansas City Chiefs	16	16
1985	Kansas City Chiefs	13	6	1988	Kansas City Chiefs	14	13	1991	Kansas City Chiefs	16	16	1994	Kansas City Chiefs	13	13
1986	Kansas City Chiefs	7	0	1989	Kansas City Chiefs	16	16	1992	Kansas City Chiefs	16	16	1995	Kansas City Chiefs	16	16
													12 NFL Seasons	167	138

Ashley Ambrose

Pos: DB/CB   **Rnd:** 2   **College:** Mississippi Valley State   **Ht:** 5' 10"   **Wt:** 192   **Born:** 9/17/70   **Age:** 26

Year	Team	G	GS	Tackles			Miscellaneous				Interceptions				Punt Returns				Kickoff Returns				Totals	
				Tk	Ast	Sack	FF	FR	TD	Blk	Int	Yds	Avg	TD	Num	Yds	Avg	TD	Num	Yds	Avg	TD	TD	Fum
1992	Indianapolis Colts	10	2	6	2	0.0	0	0	0	0	0	0	-	0	0	0	-	0	8	126	15.8	0	0	2
1993	Indianapolis Colts	14	9	36	8	0.0	0	0	0	0	0	0	-	0	0	0	-	0	0	0	-	0	0	0
1994	Indianapolis Colts	16	4	31	4	0.0	0	1	0	0	2	50	25.0	0	0	0	-	0	0	0	-	0	0	0
1995	Indianapolis Colts	16	0	11	3	0.0	1	0	0	0	3	12	4.0	0	0	0	-	0	0	0	-	0	0	0

11

Year Team	G	GS	Tackles			Miscellaneous				Interceptions				Punt Returns				Kickoff Returns				Totals	
			Tk	Ast	Sack	FF	FR	TD	Blk	Int	Yds	Avg	TD	Num	Yds	Avg	TD	Num	Yds	Avg	TD	TD	Fum
4 NFL Seasons	56	12	84	17	0.0	1	1	0	0	5	62	12.4	0	0	0	-	0	8	126	15.8	0	0	2

Kimble Anders

Pos: RB **Rnd:** FA **College:** Houston **Ht:** 5' 11" **Wt:** 230 **Born:** 9/10/66 **Age:** 30

Year Team	G	GS	Rushing					Receiving					Punt Returns				Kickoff Returns				Totals		
			Att	Yds	Avg	Lg	TD	Rec	Yds	Avg	Lg	TD	Num	Yds	Avg	TD	Num	Yds	Avg	TD	Fum	TD	Pts
1991 Kansas City Chiefs	2	0	0	0	-	-	0	2	30	15.0	23	0	0	0	-	0	0	0	-	0	0	0	0
1992 Kansas City Chiefs	11	2	1	1	1.0	1	0	5	65	13.0	28	0	0	0	-	0	1	20	20.0	0	1	0	0
1993 Kansas City Chiefs	16	13	75	291	3.9	18	0	40	326	8.2	27	1	0	0	-	0	1	47	47.0	0	1	1	6
1994 Kansas City Chiefs	16	13	62	231	3.7	19	2	67	525	7.8	30	1	0	0	-	0	2	36	18.0	0	1	3	18
1995 Kansas City Chiefs	16	13	58	398	6.9	44	2	55	349	6.3	28	1	0	0	-	0	0	0	-	0	1	3	18
5 NFL Seasons	61	41	196	921	4.7	44	4	169	1295	7.7	30	3	0	0	-	0	4	103	25.8	0	4	7	42

Other Statistics: 1994–recovered 2 fumbles for 1 yard.

Morten Andersen

(statistical profile on page 466)

Pos: K **Rnd:** 4 **College:** Michigan State **Ht:** 6' 2" **Wt:** 221 **Born:** 8/19/60 **Age:** 36

Year Team	G	Field Goals												PAT		Tot
		1-29 Yds	Pct	30-39 Yds	Pct	40-49 Yds	Pct	50+ Yds	Pct	Overall	Pct	Long	Made	Att	Pts
1982 New Orleans Saints	8	0-0	-	1-1	100.0	1-3	33.3	0-1	0.0	2-5	40.0	45	6	6	12
1983 New Orleans Saints	16	10-10	100.0	3-4	75.0	2-6	33.3	3-4	75.0	18-24	75.0	52	37	38	91
1984 New Orleans Saints	16	9-9	100.0	4-5	80.0	5-10	50.0	2-3	66.7	20-27	74.1	53	34	34	94
1985 New Orleans Saints	16	4-5	80.0	13-14	92.9	11-12	91.7	3-4	75.0	31-35	88.6	55	27	29	120
1986 New Orleans Saints	16	12-12	100.0	6-7	85.7	6-6	100.0	2-5	40.0	26-30	86.7	53	30	30	108
1987 New Orleans Saints	12	9-9	100.0	9-9	100.0	8-12	66.7	2-6	33.3	28-36	77.8	52	37	37	121
1988 New Orleans Saints	16	12-13	92.3	8-11	72.7	5-8	62.5	1-4	25.0	26-36	72.2	51	32	33	110
1989 New Orleans Saints	16	7-8	87.5	10-11	90.9	3-6	50.0	0-4	0.0	20-29	69.0	49	44	45	104
1990 New Orleans Saints	16	5-5	100.0	5-6	83.3	8-12	66.7	3-4	75.0	21-27	77.8	52	29	29	92
1991 New Orleans Saints	16	6-6	100.0	11-13	84.6	6-9	66.7	2-4	50.0	25-32	78.1	60	38	38	113
1992 New Orleans Saints	16	10-10	100.0	8-10	80.0	8-11	72.7	3-3	100.0	29-34	85.3	52	33	34	120
1993 New Orleans Saints	16	10-10	100.0	7-7	100.0	11-14	78.6	1-5	20.0	28-35	80.0	56	33	33	117
1994 New Orleans Saints	16	9-9	100.0	11-14	78.6	8-10	80.0	0-6	0.0	28-39	71.8	48	32	32	116
1995 Atlanta Falcons	16	9-9	100.0	11-11	100.0	3-8	37.5	8-9	88.9	31-37	83.8	59	29	30	122
14 NFL Seasons	212	112-115	97.4	107-123	87.0	85-127	66.9	30-62	48.4	333-426	78.2	60	441	448	1440

Darren Anderson

Pos: CB **Rnd:** 4 **College:** Toledo **Ht:** 5' 10" **Wt:** 187 **Born:** 1/11/69 **Age:** 27

Year Team	G	GS	Tackles			Miscellaneous				Interceptions				Totals		
			Tk	Ast	Sack	FF	FR	TD	Blk	Int	Yds	Avg	TD	Sfty	TD	Pts
1992 NE - TB	2	0	0	0	0.0	0	0	0	0	0	0	-	0	0	0	0
1993 Tampa Bay Buccaneers	14	1	12	5	0.0	0	0	0	0	1	6	6.0	0	0	0	0
1994 Kansas City Chiefs	15	1	9	1	0.0	0	1	0	0	0	0	-	0	0	0	0
1995 Kansas City Chiefs	16	0	6	0	0.0	0	0	0	0	0	0	-	0	0	0	0
1992 New England Patriots	1	0	0	0	0.0	0	0	0	0	0	0	-	0	0	0	0
Tampa Bay Buccaneers	1	0	0	0	0.0	0	0	0	0	0	0	-	0	0	0	0
4 NFL Seasons	47	2	27	6	0.0	0	1	0	0	1	6	6.0	0	0	0	0

Eddie Anderson

(statistical profile on page 394)

Pos: S **Rnd:** 6 **College:** Fort Valley State **Ht:** 6' 1" **Wt:** 210 **Born:** 7/22/63 **Age:** 33

Year Team	G	GS	Tackles			Miscellaneous				Interceptions				Totals		
			Tk	Ast	Sack	FF	FR	TD	Blk	Int	Yds	Avg	TD	Sfty	TD	Pts
1986 Seattle Seahawks	5	0	0	-	0.0	0	0	0	0	0	0	-	0	0	0	0
1987 Los Angeles Raiders	13	3	52	-	0.0	0	1	0	0	1	58	58.0	0	0	0	0
1988 Los Angeles Raiders	16	5	91	-	0.0	0	0	0	0	2	-6	-3.0	0	0	0	0
1989 Los Angeles Raiders	15	10	88	-	0.0	0	0	0	0	5	233	46.6	2	0	2	12
1990 Los Angeles Raiders	16	16	92	-	0.0	0	1	0	0	3	49	16.3	0	0	0	0
1991 Los Angeles Raiders	16	16	118	-	0.0	0	1	0	0	2	14	7.0	0	0	0	0
1992 Los Angeles Raiders	16	16	85	-	1.0	0	0	0	0	2	131	43.7	1	0	1	6
1993 Los Angeles Raiders	16	16	61	16	1.0	1	1	0	0	2	52	26.0	0	0	0	0
1994 Los Angeles Raiders	14	14	65	23	2.0	0	1	0	0	0	0	-	0	0	0	0
1995 Oakland Raiders	14	14	60	17	0.0	3	2	0	0	1	0	0.0	0	0	0	0
10 NFL Seasons	141	110	712	56	4.0	4	7	0	0	19	531	27.9	3	0	3	18

Flipper Anderson

Pos: WR **Rnd:** 2 **College:** UCLA **Ht:** 6' 0" **Wt:** 176 **Born:** 3/7/65 **Age:** 31

				Rushing					Receiving					Punt Returns				Kickoff Returns				Totals		
Year	Team	G	GS	Att	Yds	Avg	Lg	TD	Rec	Yds	Avg	Lg	TD	Num	Yds	Avg	TD	Num	Yds	Avg	TD	Fum	TD	Pts
1988	Los Angeles Rams	16	1	0	0	-	-	0	11	319	29.0	56	0	0	0	-	0	0	0	-	0	0	0	0
1989	Los Angeles Rams	16	13	1	-1	-1.0	-1	0	44	1146	26.0	t78	5	0	0	-	0	0	0	-	0	0	5	30
1990	Los Angeles Rams	16	10	1	13	13.0	13	0	51	1097	21.5	t55	4	0	0	-	0	0	0	-	0	0	4	24
1991	Los Angeles Rams	12	10	0	0	-	-	0	32	530	16.6	54	1	0	0	-	0	0	0	-	0	2	1	6
1992	Los Angeles Rams	15	8	0	0	-	-	0	38	657	17.3	51	7	0	0	-	0	1	9	9.0	0	1	7	42
1993	Los Angeles Rams	15	15	0	0	-	-	0	37	552	14.9	t56	4	0	0	-	0	0	0	-	0	0	4	24
1994	Los Angeles Rams	16	16	1	11	11.0	11	0	46	945	20.5	t72	5	0	0	-	0	0	0	-	0	0	5	30
1995	Indianapolis Colts	2	2	0	0	-	-	0	8	111	13.9	28	2	0	0	-	0	0	0	-	0	0	2	12
	8 NFL Seasons	108	75	3	23	7.7	13	0	267	5357	20.1	t78	28	0	0	-	0	1	9	9.0	0	3	28	168

Other Statistics: 1990–recovered 1 fumble for 0 yards. 1991–recovered 1 fumble for 0 yards. 1993–recovered 1 fumble for 0 yards. 1994–recovered 1 fumble for 7 yards.

Gary Anderson

(statistical profile on page 466)

Pos: K **Rnd:** 7 **College:** Syracuse **Ht:** 5' 11" **Wt:** 179 **Born:** 7/16/59 **Age:** 37

							Field Goals								PAT		Tot
Year	Team	G	1-29 Yds	Pct	30-39 Yds	Pct	40-49 Yds	Pct	50+ Yds	Pct	Overall	Pct	Long	Made	Att	Pts
1982	Pittsburgh Steelers	9	4-4	100.0	1-2	50.0	5-5	100.0	0-1	0.0	10-12	83.3	48	22	22	52
1983	Pittsburgh Steelers	16	10-11	90.9	9-10	90.0	8-10	80.0	0-0	-	27-31	87.1	49	38	39	119
1984	Pittsburgh Steelers	16	8-9	88.9	6-9	66.7	8-11	72.7	2-3	66.7	24-32	75.0	55	45	45	117
1985	Pittsburgh Steelers	16	13-14	92.9	14-15	93.3	5-9	55.6	1-4	25.0	33-42	78.6	52	40	40	139
1986	Pittsburgh Steelers	16	6-8	75.0	6-7	85.7	9-14	64.3	0-3	0.0	21-32	65.6	45	32	32	95
1987	Pittsburgh Steelers	12	8-9	88.9	5-5	100.0	7-11	63.6	2-2	100.0	22-27	81.5	52	21	21	87
1988	Pittsburgh Steelers	16	12-12	100.0	9-10	90.0	6-12	50.0	1-2	50.0	28-36	77.8	52	34	35	118
1989	Pittsburgh Steelers	16	7-7	100.0	5-8	62.5	9-15	60.0	0-0	-	21-30	70.0	49	28	28	91
1990	Pittsburgh Steelers	16	4-4	100.0	8-8	100.0	8-11	72.7	0-2	0.0	20-25	80.0	48	32	32	92
1991	Pittsburgh Steelers	16	8-10	80.0	9-11	81.8	5-6	83.3	1-6	16.7	23-33	69.7	54	31	31	100
1992	Pittsburgh Steelers	16	12-13	92.3	12-15	80.0	4-6	66.7	0-2	0.0	28-36	77.8	49	29	31	113
1993	Pittsburgh Steelers	16	9-10	90.0	14-14	100.0	5-6	83.3	0-0	-	28-30	93.3	46	32	32	116
1994	Pittsburgh Steelers	16	8-9	88.9	8-9	88.9	7-9	77.8	1-2	50.0	24-29	82.8	50	32	32	104
1995	Philadelphia Eagles	16	5-5	100.0	9-10	90.0	8-12	66.7	0-3	0.0	22-30	73.3	43	32	33	98
	14 NFL Seasons	213	114-125	91.2	115-133	86.5	94-137	68.6	8-30	26.7	331-425	77.9	55	448	453	1441

Other Statistics: 1994–rushed 1 time for 3 yards.

Jamal Anderson

Pos: RB/KR **Rnd:** 7 **College:** Utah **Ht:** 5' 10" **Wt:** 240 **Born:** 3/6/72 **Age:** 24

				Rushing					Receiving					Punt Returns				Kickoff Returns				Totals		
Year	Team	G	GS	Att	Yds	Avg	Lg	TD	Rec	Yds	Avg	Lg	TD	Num	Yds	Avg	TD	Num	Yds	Avg	TD	Fum	TD	Pts
1994	Atlanta Falcons	4	0	2	-1	-0.5	0	0	0	0	-	-	0	0	0	-	0	1	11	11.0	0	0	0	0
1995	Atlanta Falcons	16	0	39	161	4.1	13	1	4	42	10.5	17	0	0	0	-	0	24	541	22.5	0	0	1	6
	2 NFL Seasons	20	0	41	160	3.9	13	1	4	42	10.5	17	0	0	0	-	0	25	552	22.1	0	0	1	6

Richie Anderson

Pos: RB **Rnd:** 6 **College:** Penn State **Ht:** 6' 2" **Wt:** 225 **Born:** 9/13/71 **Age:** 25

				Rushing					Receiving					Kickoff Returns				Passing				Totals		
Year	Team	G	GS	Att	Yds	Avg	Lg	TD	Rec	Yds	Avg	Lg	TD	Num	Yds	Avg	TD	Att	Com	Yds	Int	Fum	TD	Pts
1993	New York Jets	7	0	0	0	-	-	0	0	0	-	-	0	4	66	16.5	0	0	0	0	0	1	0	0
1994	New York Jets	13	5	43	207	4.8	55	1	25	212	8.5	t27	1	3	43	14.3	0	0	0	0	0	1	2	12
1995	New York Jets	10	0	5	17	3.4	10	0	5	26	5.2	9	0	0	0	-	0	1	0	0	0	2	0	0
	3 NFL Seasons	30	5	48	224	4.7	55	1	30	238	7.9	t27	1	7	109	15.6	0	1	0	0	0	4	2	12

Other Statistics: 1993–recovered 1 fumble for 0 yards. 1994–recovered 1 fumble for 0 yards.

Stevie Anderson

Pos: WR **Rnd:** 8 **College:** Grambling **Ht:** 6' 5" **Wt:** 215 **Born:** 5/12/70 **Age:** 26

				Rushing					Receiving					Punt Returns				Kickoff Returns				Totals		
Year	Team	G	GS	Att	Yds	Avg	Lg	TD	Rec	Yds	Avg	Lg	TD	Num	Yds	Avg	TD	Num	Yds	Avg	TD	Fum	TD	Pts
1994	New York Jets	10	0	0	0	-	-	0	9	90	10.0	17	0	0	0	-	0	0	0	-	0	0	0	0
1995	Arizona Cardinals	6	0	0	0	-	-	0	3	34	11.3	18	1	0	0	-	0	1	17	17.0	0	0	1	10
	2 NFL Seasons	16	0	0	0	-	-	0	12	124	10.3	18	1	0	0	-	0	1	17	17.0	0	0	1	10

Other Statistics: 1995–scored 2 two-point conversions.

Charles Arbuckle

Pos: TE **Rnd:** 5 **College:** UCLA **Ht:** 6' 3" **Wt:** 248 **Born:** 9/13/68 **Age:** 28

Year	Team	G	GS	Rushing Att	Yds	Avg	Lg	TD	Receiving Rec	Yds	Avg	Lg	TD	Punt Returns Num	Yds	Avg	TD	Kickoff Returns Num	Yds	Avg	TD	Totals Fum	TD	Pts
1992	Indianapolis Colts	16	3	0	0	-	-	0	13	152	11.7	t23	1	0	0	-	0	0	0	-	0	0	1	6
1993	Indianapolis Colts	16	2	0	0	-	-	0	15	90	6.0	23	0	0	0	-	0	0	0	-	0	1	0	0
1994	Indianapolis Colts	7	0	0	0	-	-	0	1	7	7.0	7	0	0	0	-	0	0	0	-	0	0	0	0
1995	Indianapolis Colts	3	3	0	0	-	-	0	4	33	8.3	12	0	0	0	-	0	0	0	-	0	0	0	0
	4 NFL Seasons	42	8	0	0	-	-	0	33	282	8.5	t23	1	0	0	-	0	0	0	-	0	1	1	6

Lester Archambeau

Pos: DE/DT **Rnd:** 7 **College:** Stanford **Ht:** 6' 5" **Wt:** 275 **Born:** 6/27/67 **Age:** 29

Year	Team	G	GS	Tackles Tk	Ast	Sack	Miscellaneous FF	FR	TD	Blk	Interceptions Int	Yds	Avg	TD	Totals Sfty	TD	Pts
1990	Green Bay Packers	4	0	0	0	0.0	0	0	0	0	0	0	-	0	0	0	0
1991	Green Bay Packers	16	0	20	4	4.5	0	0	0	0	0	0	-	0	0	0	0
1992	Green Bay Packers	16	0	20	9	1.0	0	0	0	0	0	0	-	0	0	0	0
1993	Atlanta Falcons	15	11	45	22	0.0	1	0	0	0	0	0	-	0	0	0	0
1994	Atlanta Falcons	16	12	24	3	2.0	1	0	0	1	0	0	-	0	0	0	0
1995	Atlanta Falcons	16	7	15	3	3.0	1	1	0	0	0	0	-	0	0	0	0
	6 NFL Seasons	83	30	124	41	10.5	3	1	0	1	0	0	-	0	0	0	0

Justin Armour

Pos: WR/RB **Rnd:** 4 **College:** Stanford *(statistical profile on page 279)* **Ht:** 6' 4" **Wt:** 221 **Born:** 1/1/73 **Age:** 23

Year	Team	G	GS	Rushing Att	Yds	Avg	Lg	TD	Receiving Rec	Yds	Avg	Lg	TD	Kickoff Returns Num	Yds	Avg	TD	Passing Att	Com	Yds	Int	Totals Fum	TD	Pts
1995	Buffalo Bills	15	9	4	-5	-1.3	6	0	26	300	11.5	t28	3	0	0	-	0	1	0	0	0	1	3	18

Other Statistics: 1995–recovered 2 fumbles for 0 yards.

Jesse Armstead

Pos: LB **Rnd:** 8 **College:** Miami (FL) **Ht:** 6' 1" **Wt:** 232 **Born:** 10/26/70 **Age:** 26

Year	Team	G	GS	Tackles Tk	Ast	Sack	Miscellaneous FF	FR	TD	Blk	Interceptions Int	Yds	Avg	TD	Totals Sfty	TD	Pts
1993	New York Giants	16	0	28	3	0.0	1	0	0	0	1	0	0.0	0	0	0	0
1994	New York Giants	16	0	33	8	3.0	1	0	0	0	1	0	0.0	0	1	0	2
1995	New York Giants	16	2	36	10	0.5	0	1	0	0	1	58	58.0	1	0	1	6
	3 NFL Seasons	48	2	97	21	3.5	2	1	0	0	3	58	19.3	1	1	1	8

Antonio Armstrong

Pos: LB **Rnd:** 6 **College:** Texas A&M **Ht:** 6' 1" **Wt:** 234 **Born:** 10/15/73 **Age:** 23

Year	Team	G	GS	Tackles Tk	Ast	Sack	Miscellaneous FF	FR	TD	Blk	Interceptions Int	Yds	Avg	TD	Totals Sfty	TD	Pts
1995	Miami Dolphins	4	0	0	0	0.0	0	0	0	0	0	0	-	0	0	0	0

Bruce Armstrong

Pos: T **Rnd:** 1 (23) **College:** Louisville **Ht:** 6' 4" **Wt:** 295 **Born:** 9/7/65 **Age:** 31

Year	Team	G	GS	Year	Team	G	GS	Year	Team	G	GS		G	GS
1987	New England Patriots	12	12	1990	New England Patriots	16	16	1993	New England Patriots	16	16			
1988	New England Patriots	16	16	1991	New England Patriots	16	16	1994	New England Patriots	16	16			
1989	New England Patriots	16	16	1992	New England Patriots	8	8	1995	New England Patriots	16	16	9 NFL Seasons	132	132

Other Statistics: 1990–recovered 2 fumbles for 4 yards. 1992–recovered 1 fumble for 0 yards. 1993–recovered 1 fumble for 0 yards. 1995–recovered 1 fumble for 0 yards.

Trace Armstrong

Pos: DE **Rnd:** 1 (12) **College:** Florida **Ht:** 6' 4" **Wt:** 265 **Born:** 10/5/65 **Age:** 31

Year	Team	G	GS	Tackles Tk	Ast	Sack	Miscellaneous FF	FR	TD	Blk	Interceptions Int	Yds	Avg	TD	Totals Sfty	TD	Pts
1989	Chicago Bears	15	15	37	43	5.0	1	1	0	0	0	0	-	0	0	0	0
1990	Chicago Bears	16	16	33	49	10.0	2	2	0	0	0	0	-	0	0	0	0
1991	Chicago Bears	12	12	26	30	1.5	0	0	0	0	0	0	-	0	0	0	0
1992	Chicago Bears	14	14	40	35	6.5	1	1	0	0	0	0	-	0	0	0	0
1993	Chicago Bears	16	16	34	24	11.5	3	3	0	0	0	0	-	0	0	0	0
1994	Chicago Bears	15	15	31	10	7.5	0	0	0	1	0	0	-	0	0	0	0
1995	Miami Dolphins	15	0	21	5	4.5	2	1	0	0	0	0	-	0	0	0	0
	7 NFL Seasons	103	88	222	196	46.5	9	8	0	1	0	0	-	0	0	0	0

Tyji Armstrong

Pos: TE **Rnd:** 3 **College:** Mississippi **Ht:** 6' 4" **Wt:** 262 **Born:** 10/3/70 **Age:** 26

Year Team	G	GS	Rushing Att	Yds	Avg	Lg	TD	Receiving Rec	Yds	Avg	Lg	TD	Punt Returns Num	Yds	Avg	TD	Kickoff Returns Num	Yds	Avg	TD	Totals Fum	TD	Pts
1992 Tampa Bay Buccaneers	15	7	0	0	-	-	0	7	138	19.7	t81	1	0	0	-	0	0	0	-	0	0	1	6
1993 Tampa Bay Buccaneers	12	7	2	5	2.5	4	0	9	86	9.6	29	1	0	0	-	0	0	0	-	0	0	1	6
1994 Tampa Bay Buccaneers	16	9	1	-1	-1.0	-1	0	22	265	12.0	29	1	0	0	-	0	1	6	6.0	0	2	1	6
1995 Tampa Bay Buccaneers	16	3	0	0	-	-	0	7	68	9.7	29	0	0	0	-	0	1	6	6.0	0	1	0	0
4 NFL Seasons	59	26	3	4	1.3	4	0	45	557	12.4	t81	3	0	0	-	0	2	12	6.0	0	3	3	18

Other Statistics: 1994–recovered 1 fumble for 0 yards. 1995–recovered 1 fumble for 0 yards.

Mike Arthur

Pos: C **Rnd:** 5 **College:** Texas A&M **Ht:** 6' 3" **Wt:** 280 **Born:** 5/7/68 **Age:** 28

Year	Team	G	GS	Year	Team	G	GS	Year	Team	G	GS			G	GS
1991	Cincinnati Bengals	7	3	1993	New England Patriots	13	11	1995	Green Bay Packers	11	0				
1992	Cincinnati Bengals	16	13	1994	New England Patriots	12	11						5 NFL Seasons	59	38

Other Statistics: 1991–recovered 1 fumble for 0 yards. 1992–fumbled 4 times for -33 yards. 1993–recovered 1 fumble for 0 yards. 1994–recovered 1 fumble for -2 yards; fumbled 1 time. 1995–returned 1 kickoff for 10 yards.

Herman Arvie

Pos: T/G **Rnd:** 5 **College:** Grambling **Ht:** 6' 4" **Wt:** 305 **Born:** 10/12/70 **Age:** 26

Year	Team	G	GS	Year	Team	G	GS	Year	Team	G	GS			G	GS
1993	Cleveland Browns	16	0	1994	Cleveland Browns	16	1	1995	Cleveland Browns	15	2		3 NFL Seasons	47	3

Jamie Asher

Pos: TE **Rnd:** 5 **College:** Louisville **Ht:** 6' 3" **Wt:** 243 **Born:** 10/31/72 **Age:** 24

Year Team	G	GS	Rushing Att	Yds	Avg	Lg	TD	Receiving Rec	Yds	Avg	Lg	TD	Punt Returns Num	Yds	Avg	TD	Kickoff Returns Num	Yds	Avg	TD	Totals Fum	TD	Pts
1995 Washington Redskins	7	1	0	0	-	-	0	14	172	12.3	20	0	0	0	-	0	1	13	13.0	0	0	0	0

Darryl Ashmore

Pos: T **Rnd:** 7 **College:** Northwestern **Ht:** 6' 7" **Wt:** 300 **Born:** 11/1/69 **Age:** 27

Year	Team	G	GS	Year	Team	G	GS	Year	Team	G	GS			G	GS
1993	Los Angeles Rams	9	7	1994	Los Angeles Rams	11	3	1995	St. Louis Rams	16	15		3 NFL Seasons	36	25

Joe Aska

Pos: RB **Rnd:** 3 **College:** Central Oklahoma **Ht:** 5' 10" **Wt:** 230 **Born:** 7/14/72 **Age:** 24

Year Team	G	GS	Rushing Att	Yds	Avg	Lg	TD	Receiving Rec	Yds	Avg	Lg	TD	Punt Returns Num	Yds	Avg	TD	Kickoff Returns Num	Yds	Avg	TD	Totals Fum	TD	Pts
1995 Oakland Raiders	1	0	0	0	-	-	0	0	0	-	-	0	0	0	-	0	0	0	-	0	0	0	0

Gene Atkins

Pos: S **Rnd:** 7 **College:** Florida A&M **Ht:** 5' 11" **Wt:** 201 **Born:** 11/22/64 **Age:** 31

Year Team	G	GS	Tackles Tk	Ast	Sack	Misc. FF	FR	TD	Blk	Int	Yds	Avg	TD	Punt Returns Num	Yds	Avg	TD	Kickoff Returns Num	Yds	Avg	TD	Totals TD	Fum
1987 New Orleans Saints	13	5	28	8	0.0	0	1	0	0	3	12	4.0	0	0	0	-	0	0	0	-	0	0	0
1988 New Orleans Saints	16	6	39	11	0.0	1	2	0	0	4	42	10.5	0	0	0	-	0	20	424	21.2	0	0	1
1989 New Orleans Saints	14	12	62	14	0.0	0	2	0	0	1	-2	-2.0	0	0	0	-	0	12	245	20.4	0	0	1
1990 New Orleans Saints	16	16	54	12	3.0	3	3	0	0	2	15	7.5	0	0	0	-	0	19	471	24.8	0	0	0
1991 New Orleans Saints	16	16	67	8	3.0	4	2	0	0	5	198	39.6	0	0	0	-	0	20	368	18.4	0	0	0
1992 New Orleans Saints	16	16	67	17	0.0	1	1	0	0	3	0	0.0	0	0	0	-	0	0	0	-	0	0	0
1993 New Orleans Saints	16	16	51	24	1.0	0	2	0	0	3	59	19.7	0	0	0	-	0	0	0	-	0	0	0
1994 Miami Dolphins	15	15	54	10	1.0	3	0	0	0	3	24	8.0	0	0	0	-	0	0	0	-	0	0	0
1995 Miami Dolphins	16	11	54	14	0.0	1	1	0	0	1	0	0.0	0	0	0	-	0	0	0	-	0	0	0
9 NFL Seasons	138	113	476	118	8.0	15	14	0	0	25	348	13.9	0	0	0	-	0	71	1508	21.2	0	0	3

James Atkins

Pos: T **Rnd:** FA **College:** Southwestern Louisiana **Ht:** 6' 6" **Wt:** 303 **Born:** 1/28/70 **Age:** 26

Year	Team	G	GS	Year	Team	G	GS			G	GS
1994	Seattle Seahawks	4	2	1995	Seattle Seahawks	16	16		2 NFL Seasons	20	18

Other Statistics: 1995–recovered 1 fumble for 0 yards.

Steve Atwater

(statistical profile on page 394)

Pos: S   **Rnd:** 1 (20)   **College:** Arkansas   **Ht:** 6' 3"   **Wt:** 217   **Born:** 10/28/66   **Age:** 30

Year	Team	G	GS	Tk	Ast	Sack	FF	FR	TD	Blk	Int	Yds	Avg	TD	Num	Yds	Avg	TD	Num	Yds	Avg	TD	TD	Fum
															Punt Returns				**Kickoff Returns**				**Totals**	
1989	Denver Broncos	16	16	86	43	0.0	0	1	0	0	3	34	11.3	0	0	0	-	0	0	0	-	0	0	0
1990	Denver Broncos	15	15	112	61	1.0	2	0	0	0	2	32	16.0	0	0	0	-	0	1	0	0.0	0	0	0
1991	Denver Broncos	16	16	83	67	1.0	1	1	0	0	5	104	20.8	0	0	0	-	0	0	0	-	0	0	0
1992	Denver Broncos	15	15	73	78	1.0	2	2	0	0	2	22	11.0	0	0	0	-	0	0	0	-	0	0	0
1993	Denver Broncos	16	16	80	61	1.0	2	0	0	0	2	81	40.5	0	0	0	-	0	0	0	-	0	0	0
1994	Denver Broncos	15	14	52	22	0.0	1	2	0	0	1	24	24.0	0	0	0	-	0	0	0	-	0	0	0
1995	Denver Broncos	16	16	82	21	0.0	2	0	0	0	3	54	18.0	0	0	0	-	0	0	0	-	0	0	0
	7 NFL Seasons	109	108	568	353	4.0	10	6	0	0	18	351	19.5	0	0	0	-	0	1	0	0.0	0	0	0

Troy Auzenne

Pos: T   **Rnd:** 2   **College:** California   **Ht:** 6' 7"   **Wt:** 305   **Born:** 6/26/69   **Age:** 27

Year	Team	G	GS	Year	Team	G	GS	Year	Team	G	GS	Year	Team	G	GS
1992	Chicago Bears	16	16	1993	Chicago Bears	11	11	1994	Chicago Bears	11	3	1995	Chicago Bears	12	0
													4 NFL Seasons	50	30

Other Statistics: 1992–recovered 1 fumble for 0 yards.

Steve Avery

Pos: RB   **Rnd:** FA   **College:** Northern Michigan   **Ht:** 6' 2"   **Wt:** 226   **Born:** 8/18/66   **Age:** 30

Year	Team	G	GS	Att	Yds	Avg	Lg	TD	Rec	Yds	Avg	Lg	TD	Num	Yds	Avg	TD	Num	Yds	Avg	TD	Fum	TD	Pts
				Rushing					**Receiving**					**Punt Returns**				**Kickoff Returns**				**Totals**		
1989	Houston Oilers	1	0	0	0	-	-	0	0	0	-	-	0	0	0	-	0	0	0	-	0	0	0	0
1991	Green Bay Packers	1	0	0	0	-	-	0	0	0	-	-	0	0	0	-	0	0	0	-	0	0	0	0
1994	Pittsburgh Steelers	14	1	2	4	2.0	5	0	1	2	2.0	2	0	0	0	-	0	0	0	-	0	0	0	0
1995	Pittsburgh Steelers	12	2	1	3	3.0	3	0	11	82	7.5	t18	1	0	0	-	0	0	0	-	0	0	1	6
	4 NFL Seasons	28	3	3	7	2.3	5	0	12	84	7.0	t18	1	0	0	-	0	0	0	-	0	0	1	6

Matt Bahr

(statistical profile on page 467)

Pos: K   **Rnd:** 6   **College:** Penn State   **Ht:** 5' 10"   **Wt:** 175   **Born:** 7/6/56   **Age:** 40

Year	Team	G	1-29 Yds	Pct	30-39 Yds	Pct	40-49 Yds	Pct	50+ Yds	Pct	Overall	Pct	Long	Made	Att	Pts
					Field Goals									**PAT**		**Tot**
1979	Pittsburgh Steelers	16	5-5	100.0	6-11	54.5	7-13	53.8	0-1	0.0	18-30	60.0	47	50	52	104
1980	Pittsburgh Steelers	16	10-11	90.9	7-10	70.0	2-6	33.3	0-1	0.0	19-28	67.9	48	39	42	96
1981	SF - Cle	15	8-10	80.0	5-10	50.0	2-5	40.0	0-1	0.0	15-26	57.7	47	34	34	79
1982	Cleveland Browns	9	4-5	80.0	1-3	33.3	2-7	28.6	0-0	-	7-15	46.7	46	17	17	38
1983	Cleveland Browns	16	10-10	100.0	5-6	83.3	6-7	85.7	0-1	0.0	21-24	87.5	47	38	40	101
1984	Cleveland Browns	16	15-15	100.0	2-7	28.6	6-9	66.7	1-1	100.0	24-32	75.0	50	25	25	97
1985	Cleveland Browns	16	3-3	100.0	8-9	88.9	3-5	60.0	0-1	0.0	14-18	77.8	45	35	35	77
1986	Cleveland Browns	12	11-13	84.6	7-8	87.5	1-2	50.0	1-3	33.3	20-26	76.9	52	30	30	90
1987	Cleveland Browns	3	2-2	100.0	2-3	66.7	0-0	-	0-0	-	4-5	80.0	31	9	10	21
1988	Cleveland Browns	16	11-13	84.6	8-10	80.0	5-6	83.3	0-0	-	24-29	82.8	47	32	33	104
1989	Cleveland Browns	16	5-5	100.0	6-8	75.0	4-9	44.4	1-2	50.0	16-24	66.7	50	40	40	88
1990	New York Giants	13	9-9	100.0	3-3	100.0	5-9	55.6	0-2	0.0	17-23	73.9	49	29	30	80
1991	New York Giants	13	6-6	100.0	6-8	75.0	9-12	75.0	1-3	33.3	22-29	75.9	54	24	25	90
1992	New York Giants	12	3-3	100.0	10-11	90.9	3-5	60.0	0-2	0.0	16-21	76.2	47	29	29	77
1993	Phi - NE	14	6-8	75.0	5-5	100.0	2-5	40.0	0-0	-	13-18	72.2	48	28	29	67
1994	New England Patriots	16	14-14	100.0	9-12	75.0	4-8	50.0	0-0	-	27-34	79.4	48	36	36	117
1995	New England Patriots	16	13-14	92.9	3-7	42.9	5-7	71.4	2-5	40.0	23-33	69.7	55	27	27	96
1981	San Francisco 49ers	4	0-2	0.0	0-1	0.0	2-3	66.7	0-0	-	2-6	33.3	47	12	12	18
	Cleveland Browns	11	8-8	100.0	5-9	55.6	0-2	0.0	0-1	0.0	13-20	65.0	0	22	22	61
1993	Philadelphia Eagles	11	4-6	66.7	2-2	100.0	2-5	40.0	0-0	-	8-13	61.5	48	18	19	42
	New England Patriots	3	2-2	100.0	3-3	100.0	0-0	-	0-0	-	5-5	100.0	37	10	10	25
	17 NFL Seasons	235	135-146	92.5	93-131	71.0	66-115	57.4	6-23	26.1	300-415	72.3	55	522	534	1422

Other Statistics: 1988–rushed 1 time for -8 yards. 1995–punted 1 time for 29 yards.

Aaron Bailey

Pos: WR/KR   **Rnd:** FA   **College:** Louisville   **Ht:** 5' 10"   **Wt:** 184   **Born:** 10/24/71   **Age:** 25

Year	Team	G	GS	Att	Yds	Avg	Lg	TD	Rec	Yds	Avg	Lg	TD	Num	Yds	Avg	TD	Num	Yds	Avg	TD	Fum	TD	Pts
				Rushing					**Receiving**					**Punt Returns**				**Kickoff Returns**				**Totals**		
1994	Indianapolis Colts	12	0	0	0	-	-	0	2	30	15.0	23	0	0	0	-	0	0	0	-	0	0	0	0
1995	Indianapolis Colts	15	3	1	34	34.0	34	0	21	379	18.0	45	3	0	0	-	0	21	495	23.6	1	0	4	24
	2 NFL Seasons	27	3	1	34	34.0	34	0	23	409	17.8	45	3	0	0	-	0	21	495	23.6	1	0	4	24

Other Statistics: 1995–recovered 1 fumble for 0 yards.

Carlton Bailey

(statistical profile on page 394)

Pos: LB **Rnd:** 9 **College:** North Carolina **Ht:** 6' 3" **Wt:** 235 **Born:** 12/15/64 **Age:** 31

Year Team	G	GS	Tackles			Miscellaneous				Interceptions				Totals		
			Tk	Ast	Sack	FF	FR	TD	Blk	Int	Yds	Avg	TD	Sfty	TD	Pts
1988 Buffalo Bills	6	0	6	0	0.0	0	0	0	0	0	0	-	0	0	0	0
1989 Buffalo Bills	16	0	16	11	0.0	0	0	0	0	1	16	16.0	0	0	0	0
1990 Buffalo Bills	16	6	38	19	2.0	0	1	0	0	0	0	-	0	0	0	0
1991 Buffalo Bills	16	16	61	32	0.0	1	1	0	0	0	0	-	0	0	0	0
1992 Buffalo Bills	16	10	44	21	1.0	1	0	0	0	0	0	-	0	0	0	0
1993 New York Giants	16	16	96	40	1.5	2	1	0	0	0	0	-	0	0	0	0
1994 New York Giants	16	11	47	23	0.0	0	1	0	0	0	0	-	0	0	0	0
1995 Carolina Panthers	16	14	75	24	3.0	1	0	0	0	0	0	-	0	0	0	0
8 NFL Seasons	118	73	383	170	7.5	5	4	0	0	1	16	16.0	0	0	0	0

Other Statistics: 1993–fumbled 1 time.

Johnny Bailey

(statistical profile on page 280)

Pos: RB **Rnd:** 9 **College:** Texas A&I **Ht:** 5' 8" **Wt:** 180 **Born:** 3/17/67 **Age:** 29

Year Team	G	GS	Rushing					Receiving					Punt Returns				Kickoff Returns				Totals		
			Att	Yds	Avg	Lg	TD	Rec	Yds	Avg	Lg	TD	Num	Yds	Avg	TD	Num	Yds	Avg	TD	Fum	TD	Pts
1990 Chicago Bears	16	1	26	86	3.3	9	0	0	0	-	-	0	36	399	11.1	1	23	363	15.8	0	8	1	6
1991 Chicago Bears	14	0	15	43	2.9	11	1	0	0	-	-	0	36	281	7.8	0	16	311	19.4	0	4	1	6
1992 Phoenix Cardinals	12	2	52	233	4.5	15	1	33	331	10.0	34	1	20	263	13.2	0	28	690	24.6	0	2	2	12
1993 Phoenix Cardinals	13	0	49	253	5.2	31	1	32	243	7.6	30	0	35	282	8.1	1	31	699	22.5	0	4	2	12
1994 Los Angeles Rams	14	0	11	35	3.2	9	1	58	516	8.9	28	0	19	153	8.1	0	12	260	21.7	0	2	1	6
1995 St. Louis Rams	12	1	36	182	5.1	17	2	38	265	7.0	25	0	2	42	21.0	0	5	97	19.4	0	1	2	14
6 NFL Seasons	81	4	189	832	4.4	31	6	161	1355	8.4	34	1	148	1420	9.6	2	115	2420	21.0	0	21	9	56

Other Statistics: 1990–recovered 4 fumbles for 0 yards; attempted 1 pass with 1 completion for 22 yards. 1991–recovered 2 fumbles for 0 yards. 1992–recovered 2 fumbles for 0 yards. 1995–recovered 1 fumble for 0 yards; scored 1 two-point conversion.

Robert Bailey

Pos: CB **Rnd:** 4 **College:** Miami (FL) **Ht:** 5' 9" **Wt:** 176 **Born:** 9/3/68 **Age:** 28

Year Team	G	GS	Tackles			Miscellaneous				Interceptions				Punt Returns				Kickoff Returns				Totals	
			Tk	Ast	Sack	FF	FR	TD	Blk	Int	Yds	Avg	TD	Num	Yds	Avg	TD	Num	Yds	Avg	TD	TD	Fum
1991 Los Angeles Rams	6	0	1	0	0.0	0	0	0	0	0	0	-	0	0	0	-	0	0	0	-	0	0	0
1992 Los Angeles Rams	16	7	41	2	0.0	0	0	0	0	3	61	20.3	1	0	0	-	0	0	0	-	0	1	0
1993 Los Angeles Rams	9	3	15	3	0.0	0	0	0	0	2	41	20.5	0	0	0	-	0	0	0	-	0	0	0
1994 Los Angeles Rams	16	1	25	2	0.0	0	1	0	0	0	0	-	0	1	103	103.0	1	0	0	-	0	1	0
1995 Was - Dal	13	0	7	3	0.0	0	0	0	0	0	0	-	0	0	0	-	0	0	0	-	0	0	0
1995 Washington Redskins	4	0	0	1	0.0	0	0	0	0	0	0	-	0	0	0	-	0	0	0	-	0	0	0
Dallas Cowboys	9	0	7	2	0.0	0	0	0	0	0	0	-	0	0	0	-	0	0	0	-	0	0	0
5 NFL Seasons	60	11	89	10	0.0	0	1	0	0	5	102	20.4	1	1	103	103.0	1	0	0	-	0	2	0

Thomas Bailey

Pos: WR **Rnd:** FA **College:** Auburn **Ht:** 6' 0" **Wt:** 196 **Born:** 12/6/71 **Age:** 24

Year Team	G	GS	Rushing					Receiving					Punt Returns				Kickoff Returns				Totals		
			Att	Yds	Avg	Lg	TD	Rec	Yds	Avg	Lg	TD	Num	Yds	Avg	TD	Num	Yds	Avg	TD	Fum	TD	Pts
1995 Cincinnati Bengals	1	0	0	0	-	-	0	0	0	-	-	0	0	0	-	0	0	0	-	0	0	0	0

Jon Baker

Pos: K **Rnd:** FA **College:** Arizona State **Ht:** 6' 1" **Wt:** 170 **Born:** 8/13/72 **Age:** 24

Year Team	G	Field Goals										PAT		Tot
		1-29 Yds	Pct	30-39 Yds	Pct	40-49 Yds	Pct	50+ Yds	Pct	Overall	Pct	Long	Made	Att	Pts
1995 Dallas Cowboys	3	0-0	-	0-0	-	0-0	-	0-0	-	0-0	-	-	0	0	0

Myron Baker

Pos: LB **Rnd:** 4 **College:** Louisiana Tech **Ht:** 6' 1" **Wt:** 232 **Born:** 1/6/71 **Age:** 25

Year Team	G	GS	Tackles			Miscellaneous				Interceptions				Totals		
			Tk	Ast	Sack	FF	FR	TD	Blk	Int	Yds	Avg	TD	Sfty	TD	Pts
1993 Chicago Bears	16	0	10	13	0.0	0	2	2	0	0	0	-	0	0	2	12
1994 Chicago Bears	16	3	15	6	0.0	0	0	0	0	0	0	-	0	0	0	0
1995 Chicago Bears	16	0	1	0	0.0	0	0	0	0	0	0	-	0	0	0	0
3 NFL Seasons	48	3	26	19	0.0	0	2	2	0	0	0	-	0	0	2	12

Randy Baldwin

Pos: RB/KR **Rnd:** 4   **College:** Mississippi   **Ht:** 5' 10" **Wt:** 216   **Born:** 8/19/67   **Age:** 29

Year	Team	G	GS	Rushing					Receiving					Punt Returns				Kickoff Returns				Totals		
				Att	Yds	Avg	Lg	TD	Rec	Yds	Avg	Lg	TD	Num	Yds	Avg	TD	Num	Yds	Avg	TD	Fum	TD	Pts
1991	Minnesota Vikings	4	0	0	0	-	-	0	0	0	-	-	0	0	0	-	0	1	14	14.0	0	0	0	0
1992	Cleveland Browns	15	0	10	31	3.1	11	0	2	30	15.0	20	0	0	0	-	0	30	675	22.5	0	1	0	0
1993	Cleveland Browns	14	0	18	61	3.4	11	0	1	5	5.0	15	1	0	0	-	0	24	444	18.5	0	2	1	6
1994	Cleveland Browns	16	0	23	78	3.4	16	0	3	15	5.0	15	0	0	0	-	0	28	753	26.9	1	1	1	6
1995	Carolina Panthers	7	2	23	61	2.7	9	0	0	0	-	-	0	0	0	-	0	14	316	22.6	0	1	0	0
	5 NFL Seasons	56	2	74	231	3.1	16	0	6	50	8.3	20	1	0	0	-	0	97	2202	22.7	1	5	2	12

Other Statistics: 1993–recovered 1 fumble for 0 yards. 1994–recovered 1 fumble for 0 yards.

Eric Ball

Pos: RB **Rnd:** 2   **College:** UCLA   **Ht:** 6' 2" **Wt:** 225   **Born:** 7/1/66   **Age:** 30

Year	Team	G	GS	Rushing					Receiving					Punt Returns				Kickoff Returns				Totals		
				Att	Yds	Avg	Lg	TD	Rec	Yds	Avg	Lg	TD	Num	Yds	Avg	TD	Num	Yds	Avg	TD	Fum	TD	Pts
1989	Cincinnati Bengals	15	9	98	391	4.0	27	3	6	44	7.3	15	0	0	0	-	0	1	19	19.0	0	3	3	18
1990	Cincinnati Bengals	13	1	22	72	3.3	15	1	2	46	23.0	t48	1	0	0	-	0	16	366	22.9	0	1	2	12
1991	Cincinnati Bengals	6	4	10	21	2.1	10	1	3	17	5.7	9	0	0	0	-	0	13	262	20.2	0	1	1	6
1992	Cincinnati Bengals	16	14	16	55	3.4	17	2	6	66	11.0	t35	2	0	0	-	0	20	411	20.6	0	1	4	24
1993	Cincinnati Bengals	15	1	8	37	4.6	18	1	4	39	9.8	24	0	0	0	-	0	23	501	21.8	0	0	1	6
1994	Cincinnati Bengals	16	0	2	0	0.0	1	0	1	4	4.0	4	0	0	0	-	0	42	915	21.8	0	1	0	0
1995	Oakland Raiders	16	0	2	10	5.0	10	0	0	0	-	-	0	0	0	-	0	0	0	-	0	0	0	0
	7 NFL Seasons	97	29	158	586	3.7	27	8	22	216	9.8	t48	3	0	0	-	0	115	2474	21.5	0	7	11	66

Other Statistics: 1992–recovered 2 fumbles for -6 yards. 1994–recovered 1 fumble for 0 yards.

Jerry Ball

Pos: DT **Rnd:** 3   **College:** Southern Methodist   **Ht:** 6' 1" **Wt:** 315   **Born:** 12/15/64 **Age:** 31

Year	Team	G	GS	Tackles			Miscellaneous				Interceptions				Punt Returns				Kickoff Returns				Totals	
				Tk	Ast	Sack	FF	FR	TD	Blk	Int	Yds	Avg	TD	Num	Yds	Avg	TD	Num	Yds	Avg	TD	TD	Fum
1987	Detroit Lions	12	12	27	9	1.0	0	0	0	0	0	0	-	0	0	0	-	0	2	23	11.5	0	0	0
1988	Detroit Lions	16	16	49	19	2.0	0	0	0	0	0	0	-	0	0	0	-	0	0	0	-	0	0	0
1989	Detroit Lions	16	16	62	11	9.0	0	3	0	0	0	0	-	0	0	0	-	0	0	0	-	0	0	0
1990	Detroit Lions	15	15	38	12	2.0	0	0	0	0	0	0	-	0	0	0	-	0	0	0	-	0	0	0
1991	Detroit Lions	13	13	31	5	2.0	1	0	0	0	0	0	-	0	0	0	-	0	0	0	-	0	0	0
1992	Detroit Lions	12	12	31	12	2.5	0	3	1	0	0	0	-	0	0	0	-	0	0	0	-	0	1	0
1993	Cleveland Browns	16	7	24	22	3.0	2	0	0	0	0	0	-	0	0	0	-	0	0	0	-	0	0	0
1994	Los Angeles Raiders	16	13	44	8	3.0	0	0	0	0	0	0	-	0	0	0	-	0	0	0	-	0	0	0
1995	Oakland Raiders	15	15	33	8	3.0	1	0	0	0	0	0	-	0	0	0	-	0	0	0	-	0	0	0
	9 NFL Seasons	131	119	339	106	27.5	4	9	1	0	0	0	-	0	0	0	-	0	2	23	11.5	0	1	0

Other Statistics: 1991–credited with 1 safety.

Howard Ballard

Pos: T **Rnd:** 11   **College:** Alabama A&M   **Ht:** 6' 6" **Wt:** 332   **Born:** 11/3/63   **Age:** 32

Year	Team	G	GS	Year	Team	G	GS	Year	Team	G	GS	Year	Team	G	GS
1988	Buffalo Bills	16	0	1990	Buffalo Bills	16	16	1992	Buffalo Bills	16	16	1994	Seattle Seahawks	16	16
1989	Buffalo Bills	16	16	1991	Buffalo Bills	16	16	1993	Buffalo Bills	16	16	1995	Seattle Seahawks	16	16
													8 NFL Seasons	128	112

Romeo Bandison

Pos: DT **Rnd:** 3   **College:** Oregon   **Ht:** 6' 5" **Wt:** 290   **Born:** 2/12/71   **Age:** 25

Year	Team	G	GS	Tackles			Miscellaneous				Interceptions				Totals		
				Tk	Ast	Sack	FF	FR	TD	Blk	Int	Yds	Avg	TD	Sfty	TD	Pts
1995	Washington Redskins	4	0	1	1	0.0	0	0	0	0	0	0	-	0	0	0	0

Carl Banks

Pos: LB **Rnd:** 1 (3)   **College:** Michigan State   **Ht:** 6' 4" **Wt:** 235   **Born:** 8/29/62   **Age:** 34

Year	Team	G	GS	Tackles			Miscellaneous				Interceptions				Totals		
				Tk	Ast	Sack	FF	FR	TD	Blk	Int	Yds	Avg	TD	Sfty	TD	Pts
1984	New York Giants	16	4	29	8	3.0	0	1	0	0	0	0	-	0	0	0	0
1985	New York Giants	12	5	25	6	3.0	0	1	0	0	0	0	-	0	0	0	0
1986	New York Giants	16	16	81	32	6.5	0	2	0	0	0	0	-	0	0	0	0
1987	New York Giants	12	12	85	16	9.0	0	0	0	0	1	0	0.0	0	0	0	0
1988	New York Giants	14	14	51	11	1.5	0	0	0	0	1	15	15.0	1	0	1	6
1989	New York Giants	16	16	71	18	4.0	0	1	1	0	1	6	6.0	0	0	1	6
1990	New York Giants	9	8	35	15	1.0	0	1	0	0	0	0	-	0	0	0	0

Year Team	G	GS	Tackles			Miscellaneous				Interceptions				Totals		
			Tk	Ast	Sack	FF	FR	TD	Blk	Int	Yds	Avg	TD	Sfty	TD	Pts
1991 New York Giants	15	15	68	16	4.0	0	0	0	0	0	0	-	0	0	0	0
1992 New York Giants	15	15	43	17	4.0	0	0	0	0	0	0	-	0	0	0	0
1993 Washington Redskins	15	15	57	45	1.0	0	0	0	0	0	0	-	0	0	0	0
1994 Cleveland Browns	16	15	56	17	1.5	0	0	0	0	0	0	-	0	0	0	0
1995 Cleveland Browns	16	16	41	17	1.0	1	0	0	0	0	0	-	0	0	0	0
12 NFL Seasons	172	151	642	218	39.5	1	6	1	0	3	21	7.0	1	0	2	12

Other Statistics: 1989–caught 1 pass for 22 yards and 1 touchdown.

Michael Bankston
(statistical profile on page 395)

Pos: DE/DT **Rnd:** 4 **College:** Sam Houston State **Ht:** 6' 3" **Wt:** 280 **Born:** 3/12/70 **Age:** 26

Year Team	G	GS	Tackles			Miscellaneous				Interceptions				Totals		
			Tk	Ast	Sack	FF	FR	TD	Blk	Int	Yds	Avg	TD	Sfty	TD	Pts
1992 Phoenix Cardinals	16	6	14	10	2.0	0	0	0	0	0	0	-	0	0	0	0
1993 Phoenix Cardinals	16	12	43	27	3.0	2	5	0	0	0	0	-	0	0	0	0
1994 Arizona Cardinals	16	16	56	29	6.5	0	1	0	0	0	0	-	0	0	0	0
1995 Arizona Cardinals	16	16	56	24	2.0	0	0	0	0	1	28	28.0	0	0	0	0
4 NFL Seasons	64	50	169	90	13.5	2	6	0	0	1	28	28.0	0	0	0	0

Other Statistics: 1995–fumbled 1 time for 0 yards.

Bradford Banta

Pos: TE/WR **Rnd:** 4 **College:** Southern California **Ht:** 6' 6" **Wt:** 257 **Born:** 12/14/70 **Age:** 25

Year Team	G	GS	Rushing					Receiving					Punt Returns				Kickoff Returns				Totals		
			Att	Yds	Avg	Lg	TD	Rec	Yds	Avg	Lg	TD	Num	Yds	Avg	TD	Num	Yds	Avg	TD	Fum	TD	Pts
1994 Indianapolis Colts	16	0	0	0	-	0	0	0	-	0	0	0	0	-	0	0	0	0	-	0	0	0	0
1995 Indianapolis Colts	16	2	0	0	-	0	0	1	6	6.0	6	0	0	0	-	0	0	0	0	-	0	0	0	0
2 NFL Seasons	32	2	0	0	-	0	0	1	6	6.0	6	0	0	0	-	0	0	0	0	-	0	0	0	0

Kurt Barber

Pos: DE **Rnd:** 2 **College:** Southern California **Ht:** 6' 4" **Wt:** 260 **Born:** 1/5/69 **Age:** 27

Year Team	G	GS	Tackles			Miscellaneous				Interceptions				Totals		
			Tk	Ast	Sack	FF	FR	TD	Blk	Int	Yds	Avg	TD	Sfty	TD	Pts
1992 New York Jets	16	0	8	6	0.5	0	0	0	0	0	0	-	0	0	0	0
1993 New York Jets	13	0	0	0	0.0	0	0	0	0	0	0	-	0	0	0	0
1994 New York Jets	15	0	6	2	1.0	0	0	0	0	0	0	-	0	0	0	0
1995 New York Jets	6	0	7	0	2.0	0	0	0	0	0	0	-	0	0	0	0
4 NFL Seasons	50	0	21	8	3.5	0	0	0	0	0	0	-	0	0	0	0

Michael Barber

Pos: LB **Rnd:** FA **College:** Clemson **Ht:** 6' 1" **Wt:** 247 **Born:** 11/9/71 **Age:** 24

Year Team	G	GS	Tackles			Miscellaneous				Interceptions				Totals		
			Tk	Ast	Sack	FF	FR	TD	Blk	Int	Yds	Avg	TD	Sfty	TD	Pts
1995 Seattle Seahawks	2	0	0	0	0.0	0	0	0	0	0	0	-	0	0	0	0

Bryan Barker
(statistical profile on page 467)

Pos: P **Rnd:** FA **College:** Santa Clara **Ht:** 6' 2" **Wt:** 189 **Born:** 6/28/64 **Age:** 32

Year Team	G	Punting											Rushing		Passing			
		NetPunts	Yards	Avg	Long	In20	In20%	TotPunts	TB	Blocks	OppRet	RetYds	NetAvg	Att	Yards	Att	Com	Yards	Int
1990 Kansas City Chiefs	13	64	2479	38.7	56	16	25.0	64	1	0	38	324	33.4	0	0	0	0	0	0
1991 Kansas City Chiefs	16	57	2303	40.4	57	11	19.3	57	6	0	27	190	35.0	0	0	0	0	0	0
1992 Kansas City Chiefs	15	75	3245	43.3	65	16	21.3	76	13	1	35	300	35.3	0	0	0	0	0	0
1993 Kansas City Chiefs	16	76	3240	42.6	59	19	25.0	77	8	1	43	352	35.4	0	0	0	0	0	0
1994 Philadelphia Eagles	11	66	2696	40.0	67	20	30.3	66	7	0	37	158	36.3	0	0	0	0	0	0
1995 Jacksonville Jaguars	16	82	3591	43.8	63	19	23.2	82	5	0	45	323	35.6	0	0	0	0	0	0
6 NFL Seasons	87	420	17554	41.8	67	101	24.0	422	40	2	225	1647	35.8	0	0	0	0	0	0

Roy Barker

Pos: DE **Rnd:** 4 **College:** North Carolina **Ht:** 6' 4" **Wt:** 285 **Born:** 2/14/69 **Age:** 27

Year Team	G	GS	Tackles			Miscellaneous				Interceptions				Totals		
			Tk	Ast	Sack	FF	FR	TD	Blk	Int	Yds	Avg	TD	Sfty	TD	Pts
1992 Minnesota Vikings	9	0	0	0	0.0	0	0	0	0	0	0	-	0	0	0	0
1993 Minnesota Vikings	16	16	40	7	6.0	3	1	0	0	0	0	-	0	0	0	0
1994 Minnesota Vikings	16	15	30	12	3.5	1	1	0	0	0	0	-	0	0	0	0
1995 Minnesota Vikings	16	16	36	9	3.0	0	0	0	0	1	-2	-2.0	0	0	0	0
4 NFL Seasons	57	47	106	28	12.5	4	2	0	0	1	-2	-2.0	0	0	0	0

Johnnie Barnes

Pos: WR **Rnd:** 9 **College:** Hampton **Ht:** 6' 1" **Wt:** 180 **Born:** 7/21/68 **Age:** 28

Year Team	G	GS	Rushing Att	Yds	Avg	Lg	TD	Receiving Rec	Yds	Avg	Lg	TD	Punt Returns Num	Yds	Avg	TD	Kickoff Returns Num	Yds	Avg	TD	Totals Fum	TD	Pts
1992 San Diego Chargers	1	0	0	0	-	-	0	0	0	-	-	0	0	0	-	0	0	0	-	0	0	0	0
1993 San Diego Chargers	14	0	0	0	-	-	0	10	137	13.7	21	0	0	0	-	0	0	0	-	0	0	0	0
1994 San Diego Chargers	11	0	0	0	-	-	0	1	6	6.0	6	0	0	0	-	0	0	0	-	0	0	0	0
1995 Pittsburgh Steelers	3	0	0	0	-	-	0	3	48	16.0	25	0	0	0	-	0	0	0	-	0	0	0	0
4 NFL Seasons	29	0	0	0	-	-	0	14	191	13.6	25	0	0	0	-	0	0	0	-	0	0	0	0

Reggie Barnes

Pos: LB **Rnd:** FA **College:** Oklahoma **Ht:** 6' 1" **Wt:** 240 **Born:** 10/23/69 **Age:** 27

Year Team	G	GS	Tackles Tk	Ast	Sack	Miscellaneous FF	FR	TD	Blk	Interceptions Int	Yds	Avg	TD	Totals Sfty	TD	Pts
1993 Pittsburgh Steelers	16	0	4	8	0.0	0	0	0	0	0	0	-	0	0	0	0
1995 Dallas Cowboys	7	0	4	0	0.0	0	1	0	0	0	0	-	0	0	0	0
2 NFL Seasons	23	0	8	8	0.0	0	1	0	0	0	0	-	0	0	0	0

Tomur Barnes

Pos: CB **Rnd:** FA **College:** North Texas **Ht:** 5' 10" **Wt:** 188 **Born:** 9/8/70 **Age:** 26

Year Team	G	GS	Tackles Tk	Ast	Sack	Misc FF	FR	TD	Blk	Int	Yds	Avg	TD	PR Num	Yds	Avg	TD	KR Num	Yds	Avg	TD	Totals TD	Fum
1994 Houston Oilers	1	0	0	0	0.0	0	0	0	0	0	0	-	0	0	0	-	0	0	0	-	0	0	0
1995 Houston Oilers	15	0	21	2	0.0	1	1	0	0	2	6	3.0	0	0	0	-	0	1	-4	-4.0	0	0	0
2 NFL Seasons	16	0	21	2	0.0	1	1	0	0	2	6	3.0	0	0	0	-	0	1	-4	-4.0	0	0	0

Fred Barnett

(statistical profile on page 280)

Pos: WR **Rnd:** 3 **College:** Arkansas State **Ht:** 6' 0" **Wt:** 200 **Born:** 6/17/66 **Age:** 30

Year Team	G	GS	Rushing Att	Yds	Avg	Lg	TD	Receiving Rec	Yds	Avg	Lg	TD	Punt Returns Num	Yds	Avg	TD	Kickoff Returns Num	Yds	Avg	TD	Totals Fum	TD	Pts
1990 Philadelphia Eagles	16	11	2	13	6.5	12	0	36	721	20.0	t95	8	0	0	-	0	4	65	16.3	0	0	8	48
1991 Philadelphia Eagles	15	15	1	0	0.0	0	0	62	948	15.3	t75	4	0	0	-	0	0	0	-	0	2	4	24
1992 Philadelphia Eagles	16	16	1	-15	-15.0	-15	0	67	1083	16.2	t71	6	0	0	-	0	0	0	-	0	1	6	36
1993 Philadelphia Eagles	4	4	0	0	-	-	0	17	170	10.0	21	0	0	0	-	0	0	0	-	0	1	0	0
1994 Philadelphia Eagles	16	16	0	0	-	-	0	78	1127	14.4	54	5	0	0	-	0	0	0	-	0	1	5	30
1995 Philadelphia Eagles	14	14	0	0	-	-	0	48	585	12.2	33	5	0	0	-	0	0	0	-	0	0	5	32
6 NFL Seasons	81	76	4	-2	-0.5	12	0	308	4634	15.0	t95	28	0	0	-	0	4	65	16.3	0	5	28	170

Other Statistics: 1991–recovered 1 fumble for 0 yards. 1995–recovered 1 fumble for 0 yards; scored 1 two-point conversion.

Harlon Barnett

Pos: S **Rnd:** 4 **College:** Michigan State **Ht:** 5' 11" **Wt:** 200 **Born:** 1/2/67 **Age:** 29

Year Team	G	GS	Tackles Tk	Ast	Sack	Misc FF	FR	TD	Blk	Int	Yds	Avg	TD	PR Num	Yds	Avg	TD	KR Num	Yds	Avg	TD	Totals TD	Fum
1990 Cleveland Browns	6	0	1	1	0.0	0	0	0	0	0	0	-	0	0	0	-	0	1	15	15.0	0	0	0
1991 Cleveland Browns	16	10	37	23	1.0	0	0	0	0	0	0	-	0	0	0	-	0	0	0	-	0	0	0
1992 Cleveland Browns	16	0	4	0	0.0	0	0	0	0	0	0	-	0	0	0	-	0	0	0	-	0	0	0
1993 New England Patriots	14	12	54	23	0.0	0	0	0	0	1	40	40.0	0	0	0	-	0	0	0	-	0	0	0
1994 New England Patriots	16	16	43	19	0.0	2	2	0	0	3	51	17.0	0	0	0	-	0	0	0	-	0	0	0
1995 Minnesota Vikings	15	12	30	5	0.0	0	0	0	0	0	0	-	0	0	0	-	0	0	0	-	0	0	0
6 NFL Seasons	83	50	169	71	1.0	2	2	0	0	4	91	22.8	0	0	0	-	0	1	15	15.0	0	0	0

Oliver Barnett

Pos: DE **Rnd:** 3 **College:** Kentucky **Ht:** 6' 3" **Wt:** 285 **Born:** 4/9/66 **Age:** 30

Year Team	G	GS	Tackles Tk	Ast	Sack	Misc FF	FR	TD	Blk	Int	Yds	Avg	TD	PR Num	Yds	Avg	TD	KR Num	Yds	Avg	TD	Totals TD	Fum
1990 Atlanta Falcons	15	1	10	11	0.0	0	0	0	0	0	0	-	0	0	0	-	0	0	0	-	0	0	0
1991 Atlanta Falcons	15	2	21	26	1.0	0	1	1	0	0	0	-	0	0	0	-	0	0	0	-	0	1	0
1992 Atlanta Falcons	16	7	24	30	0.0	0	0	0	0	0	0	-	0	0	0	-	0	1	13	13.0	0	0	0
1993 Buffalo Bills	16	6	26	10	2.0	0	0	0	0	0	0	-	0	0	0	-	0	0	0	-	0	0	0
1994 Buffalo Bills	16	2	14	5	1.0	1	0	0	1	0	0	-	0	0	0	-	0	0	0	-	0	0	0
1995 San Francisco 49ers	6	0	5	0	1.0	0	0	0	0	0	0	-	0	0	0	-	0	0	0	-	0	0	0
6 NFL Seasons	84	18	100	82	5.0	1	1	1	1	0	0	-	0	0	0	-	0	1	13	13.0	0	1	0

Troy Barnett

Pos: DE **Rnd:** FA **College:** North Carolina **Ht:** 6' 5" **Wt:** 293 **Born:** 5/24/71 **Age:** 25

			Tackles			Miscellaneous				Interceptions				Totals		
Year Team	G	GS	Tk	Ast	Sack	FF	FR	TD	Blk	Int	Yds	Avg	TD	Sfty	TD	Pts
1994 New England Patriots	14	0	7	6	1.0	0	0	0	1	0	0	-	0	0	0	0
1995 New England Patriots	16	15	34	19	2.0	0	1	0	2	0	0	-	0	0	0	0
2 NFL Seasons	30	15	41	25	3.0	0	1	0	3	0	0	-	0	0	0	0

Tommy Barnhardt

(statistical profile on page 467)

Pos: P **Rnd:** 9 **College:** North Carolina **Ht:** 6' 2" **Wt:** 207 **Born:** 6/11/63 **Age:** 33

						Punting							Rushing		Passing			
Year Team	G	NetPunts	Yards	Avg	Long	In20	In20%	TotPunts	TB	Blocks	OppRet	RetYds	NetAvg	Att	Yards	Att	Com	Yards	Int
1987 NO - Chi	5	17	719	42.3	52	6	35.3	17	1	0	9	100	35.2	1	-13	0	0	0	0
1988 Washington Redskins	4	15	628	41.9	55	1	6.7	15	2	0	9	74	34.3	0	0	0	0	0	0
1989 New Orleans Saints	11	55	2179	39.6	56	17	30.9	55	4	0	28	174	35.0	0	0	0	0	0	0
1990 New Orleans Saints	16	70	2990	42.7	65	20	28.6	71	6	1	43	302	36.2	0	0	0	0	0	0
1991 New Orleans Saints	16	86	**3743**	43.5	61	20	23.3	87	10	1	**50**	470	35.3	1	0	0	0	0	0
1992 New Orleans Saints	16	67	2947	44.0	62	19	28.4	67	10	0	31	218	37.7	4	-2	0	0	0	0
1993 New Orleans Saints	16	77	3356	43.6	58	26	33.8	77	6	0	36	348	37.5	1	18	1	1	7	0
1994 New Orleans Saints	16	67	2920	43.6	57	14	20.9	67	9	0	40	495	33.5	1	21	1	0	0	0
1995 Carolina Panthers	16	95	3906	41.1	54	27	28.4	95	11	0	39	342	35.2	0	0	0	0	0	0
1987 New Orleans Saints	3	11	483	43.9	52	4	36.4	11	1	0	6	64	36.3	1	-13	0	0	0	0
Chicago Bears	2	6	236	39.3	50	2	33.3	6	0	0	3	36	33.3	0	0	0	0	0	0
9 NFL Seasons	116	549	23388	42.6	65	150	27.3	551	59	2	285	2523	35.7	8	24	2	1	7	0

Other Statistics: 1992–fumbled 2 times for -16 yards.

Dave Barr

Pos: QB **Rnd:** 4 **College:** California **Ht:** 6' 3" **Wt:** 205 **Born:** 5/9/72 **Age:** 24

			Passing									Rushing				Miscellaneous			
Year Team	G	GS	Att	Com	Pct	Yards	Yds/Att	Lg	TD	Int	Int%	Rating	Att	Yds	Avg	Lg	TD	Sckd	Yds	Fum	Recv	Yds	Pts
1995 St. Louis Rams	2	0	9	5	55.6	42	4.67	18	0	0	0.0	67.8	1	5	5.0	5	0	1	4	0	0	0	0

Sebastian Barrie

Pos: DT **Rnd:** FA **College:** Liberty **Ht:** 6' 2" **Wt:** 280 **Born:** 5/26/70 **Age:** 26

			Tackles			Miscellaneous				Interceptions				Totals		
Year Team	G	GS	Tk	Ast	Sack	FF	FR	TD	Blk	Int	Yds	Avg	TD	Sfty	TD	Pts
1992 Green Bay Packers	3	0	2	1	0.0	0	0	0	0	0	0	-	0	0	0	0
1994 Arizona Cardinals	10	0	6	0	0.0	0	0	0	0	0	0	-	0	0	0	0
1995 San Diego Chargers	7	0	2	0	0.0	0	0	0	0	0	0	-	0	0	0	0
3 NFL Seasons	20	0	10	1	0.0	0	0	0	0	0	0	-	0	0	0	0

Micheal Barrow

(statistical profile on page 395)

Pos: LB **Rnd:** 2 **College:** Miami (FL) **Ht:** 6' 1" **Wt:** 236 **Born:** 4/19/70 **Age:** 26

			Tackles			Miscellaneous				Interceptions				Totals		
Year Team	G	GS	Tk	Ast	Sack	FF	FR	TD	Blk	Int	Yds	Avg	TD	Sfty	TD	Pts
1993 Houston Oilers	16	0	21	5	1.0	1	0	0	0	0	0	-	0	0	0	0
1994 Houston Oilers	16	16	57	37	2.5	0	0	0	0	0	0	-	0	0	0	0
1995 Houston Oilers	13	12	54	32	3.0	2	1	0	0	0	0	-	0	0	0	0
3 NFL Seasons	45	28	132	74	6.5	3	1	0	0	0	0	-	0	0	0	0

Harris Barton

Pos: T **Rnd:** 1 (22) **College:** North Carolina **Ht:** 6' 4" **Wt:** 280 **Born:** 4/19/64 **Age:** 32

Year Team	G	GS	Year Team	G	GS	Year Team	G	GS		G	GS
1987 San Francisco 49ers	12	9	1990 San Francisco 49ers	16	16	1993 San Francisco 49ers	15	15			
1988 San Francisco 49ers	16	15	1991 San Francisco 49ers	16	16	1994 San Francisco 49ers	0	0			
1989 San Francisco 49ers	16	16	1992 San Francisco 49ers	13	13	1995 San Francisco 49ers	12	12	9 NFL Seasons	125	121

Other Statistics: 1987–recovered 1 fumble for 0 yards. 1991–recovered 1 fumble for 0 yards.

Mike Bartrum

Pos: LS/TE **Rnd:** FA **College:** Marshall **Ht:** 6' 5" **Wt:** 243 **Born:** 6/23/70 **Age:** 26

			Rushing				Receiving					Punt Returns				Kickoff Returns				Totals		
Year Team	G	GS	Att	Yds	Avg	Lg	TD	Rec	Yds	Avg	Lg	TD	Num	Yds	Avg	TD	Num	Yds	Avg	TD	Fum	TD	Pts
1993 Kansas City Chiefs	3	0	0	0	-	-	0	0	0	-	-	0	0	0	-	0	0	0	-	0	0	0	0
1995 Green Bay Packers	4	0	0	0	-	-	0	0	0	-	-	0	0	0	-	0	0	0	-	0	0	0	0
2 NFL Seasons	7	0	0	0	-	-	0	0	0	-	-	0	0	0	-	0	0	0	-	0	0	0	0

Robert Bass

Pos: LB **Rnd:** FA **College:** Miami (FL) **Ht:** 6' 1" **Wt:** 239 **Born:** 11/10/70 **Age:** 25

Year Team	G	GS	Tk	Ast	Sack	FF	FR	TD	Blk	Int	Yds	Avg	TD	Sfty	TD	Pts
			Tackles			**Miscellaneous**				**Interceptions**				**Totals**		
1995 Chicago Bears	2	0	0	0	0.0	0	0	0	0	0	0	-	0	0	0	0

Bill Bates

Pos: S **Rnd:** FA **College:** Tennessee **Ht:** 6' 1" **Wt:** 210 **Born:** 6/6/61 **Age:** 35

Year Team	G	GS	Tk	Ast	Sack	FF	FR	TD	Blk	Int	Yds	Avg	TD	Num	Yds	Avg	TD	Num	Yds	Avg	TD	TD	Fum
			Tackles			**Miscellaneous**				**Interceptions**				**Punt Returns**				**Kickoff Returns**				**Totals**	
1983 Dallas Cowboys	16	1	54	30	4.0	0	2	0	0	1	29	29.0	0	0	0	-	0	0	0	-	0	0	1
1984 Dallas Cowboys	12	2	38	14	5.0	0	1	0	0	1	3	3.0	0	0	0	-	0	0	0	-	0	0	0
1985 Dallas Cowboys	16	0	38	13	1.0	0	0	0	0	4	15	3.8	0	22	152	6.9	0	0	0	-	0	0	0
1986 Dallas Cowboys	15	15	50	37	2.5	0	0	0	0	0	0	-	0	0	0	-	0	0	0	-	0	0	0
1987 Dallas Cowboys	12	11	46	35	3.0	0	0	0	0	3	28	9.3	0	0	0	-	0	0	0	-	0	0	0
1988 Dallas Cowboys	16	16	85	39	0.5	0	1	0	0	1	0	0.0	0	0	0	-	0	0	0	-	0	0	0
1989 Dallas Cowboys	16	0	24	10	0.0	0	0	0	0	1	18	18.0	0	0	0	-	0	0	0	-	0	0	0
1990 Dallas Cowboys	16	0	29	22	0.0	0	0	0	0	1	4	4.0	0	0	0	-	0	0	0	-	0	0	0
1991 Dallas Cowboys	16	0	28	5	0.0	1	2	0	0	0	0	-	0	0	0	-	0	0	0	-	0	0	0
1992 Dallas Cowboys	6	0	5	6	0.0	0	0	0	0	0	0	-	0	0	0	-	0	0	0	-	0	0	0
1993 Dallas Cowboys	16	0	19	9	0.0	0	1	0	0	2	25	12.5	0	0	0	-	0	0	0	-	0	0	0
1994 Dallas Cowboys	15	0	8	1	1.0	0	0	0	0	0	0	-	0	0	0	-	0	0	0	-	0	0	0
1995 Dallas Cowboys	16	0	11	5	0.0	0	0	0	0	0	0	-	0	0	0	-	0	0	0	-	0	0	0
13 NFL Seasons	188	45	435	226	17.0	1	7	0	0	14	122	8.7	0	22	152	6.9	0	0	0	-	0	0	1

Other Statistics: 1989–rushed 1 time for 0 yards. 1990–rushed 1 time for 4 yards.

Mario Bates

Pos: RB **Rnd:** 2 **College:** Arizona State *(statistical profile on page 281)* **Ht:** 6' 1" **Wt:** 217 **Born:** 1/16/73 **Age:** 23

Year Team	G	GS	Att	Yds	Avg	Lg	TD	Rec	Yds	Avg	Lg	TD	Num	Yds	Avg	TD	Num	Yds	Avg	TD	Fum	TD	Pts
			Rushing					**Receiving**					**Punt Returns**				**Kickoff Returns**				**Totals**		
1994 New Orleans Saints	11	7	151	579	3.8	40	6	8	62	7.8	14	0	0	0	-	0	1	20	20.0	0	3	6	36
1995 New Orleans Saints	16	16	244	951	3.9	t66	7	18	114	6.3	26	0	0	0	-	0	0	0	-	0	2	7	42
2 NFL Seasons	27	23	395	1530	3.9	t66	13	26	176	6.8	26	0	0	0	-	0	1	20	20.0	0	5	13	78

Other Statistics: 1994–recovered 1 fumble for 0 yards. 1995–recovered 1 fumble for 0 yards.

Michael Bates

Pos: WR **Rnd:** 6 **College:** Arizona **Ht:** 5' 10" **Wt:** 196 **Born:** 12/19/69 **Age:** 26

Year Team	G	GS	Att	Yds	Avg	Lg	TD	Rec	Yds	Avg	Lg	TD	Num	Yds	Avg	TD	Num	Yds	Avg	TD	Fum	TD	Pts
			Rushing					**Receiving**					**Punt Returns**				**Kickoff Returns**				**Totals**		
1993 Seattle Seahawks	16	1	2	12	6.0	6	0	1	6	6.0	6	0	0	0	-	0	30	603	20.1	0	1	0	0
1994 Seattle Seahawks	15	0	2	-4	-2.0	7	0	5	112	22.4	t40	1	0	0	-	0	26	508	19.5	0	3	1	6
1995 Cleveland Browns	13	0	0	0	-	0		0	0	-	0		0	0	-	0	9	176	19.6	0	0	0	0
3 NFL Seasons	44	1	4	8	2.0	7	0	6	118	19.7	t40	1	0	0	-	0	65	1287	19.8	0	4	1	6

Other Statistics: 1993–recovered 2 fumbles for 3 yards.

Michael Batiste

Pos: G **Rnd:** FA **College:** Tulane **Ht:** 6' 3" **Wt:** 295 **Born:** 12/24/70 **Age:** 25

Year Team	G	GS			G	GS
1995 Dallas Cowboys	2	0		1 NFL Season	2	0

Brad Baxter

Pos: RB **Rnd:** 11 **College:** Alabama State *(statistical profile on page 281)* **Ht:** 6' 1" **Wt:** 235 **Born:** 5/5/67 **Age:** 29

Year Team	G	GS	Att	Yds	Avg	Lg	TD	Rec	Yds	Avg	Lg	TD	Num	Yds	Avg	TD	Num	Yds	Avg	TD	Fum	TD	Pts
			Rushing					**Receiving**					**Punt Returns**				**Kickoff Returns**				**Totals**		
1989 New York Jets	1	0	0	0	-	0		0	0	-	0		0	0	-	0	0	0	-	0	0	0	0
1990 New York Jets	16	10	124	539	4.3	t28	6	8	73	9.1	22	0	0	0	-	0	0	0	-	0	4	6	36
1991 New York Jets	16	15	184	666	3.6	31	11	12	124	10.3	34	0	0	0	-	0	0	0	-	0	6	11	66
1992 New York Jets	15	15	152	698	4.6	30	6	4	32	8.0	12	0	0	0	-	0	0	0	-	0	3	6	36
1993 New York Jets	16	13	174	559	3.2	16	7	20	158	7.9	24	0	0	0	-	0	0	0	-	0	3	7	42
1994 New York Jets	15	9	60	170	2.8	13	4	10	40	4.0	7	0	0	0	-	0	0	0	-	0	0	4	24
1995 New York Jets	15	13	85	296	3.5	26	1	26	160	6.2	20	0	0	0	-	0	0	0	-	0	0	1	6
7 NFL Seasons	94	75	779	2928	3.8	31	35	80	587	7.3	34	0	0	0	-	0	0	0	-	0	16	35	210

Other Statistics: 1990–recovered 1 fumble for 0 yards. 1991–recovered 1 fumble for 0 yards. 1992–recovered 1 fumble for 0 yards. 1993–recovered 2 fumbles for 0 yards.

Fred Baxter

Pos: TE **Rnd:** 5 **College:** Auburn **Ht:** 6' 3" **Wt:** 260 **Born:** 6/14/71 **Age:** 25

Year	Team	G	GS	Rushing Att	Yds	Avg	Lg	TD	Receiving Rec	Yds	Avg	Lg	TD	Punt Returns Num	Yds	Avg	TD	Kickoff Returns Num	Yds	Avg	TD	Totals Fum	TD	Pts
1993	New York Jets	7	0	0	0	-	-	0	3	48	16.0	25	1	0	0	-	0	0	0	-	0	0	1	6
1994	New York Jets	12	1	0	0	-	-	0	3	11	3.7	6	1	0	0	-	0	1	20	20.0	0	0	1	6
1995	New York Jets	15	3	0	0	-	-	0	18	222	12.3	32	1	0	0	-	0	6	36	6.0	0	1	1	6
	3 NFL Seasons	34	4	0	0	-	-	0	24	281	11.7	32	3	0	0	-	0	7	56	8.0	0	1	3	18

Other Statistics: 1994–recovered 1 fumble for 0 yards. 1995–recovered 2 fumbles for 8 yards.

Martin Bayless

Pos: S **Rnd:** 4 **College:** Bowling Green **Ht:** 6' 2" **Wt:** 219 **Born:** 10/11/62 **Age:** 34

Year	Team	G	GS	Tackles Tk	Ast	Sack	Miscellaneous FF	FR	TD	Blk	Interceptions Int	Yds	Avg	TD	Totals Sfty	TD	Pts
1984	StL - Buf	16	1	6	1	0.0	0	0	0	0	0	0	-	0	0	0	0
1985	Buffalo Bills	12	11	43	22	0.0	0	1	0	0	2	10	5.0	0	0	0	0
1986	Buffalo Bills	16	15	68	34	1.0	0	0	0	0	1	0	0.0	0	0	0	0
1987	San Diego Chargers	12	11	44	22	2.5	0	0	0	0	0	0	-	0	0	0	0
1988	San Diego Chargers	15	11	28	3	1.0	0	0	0	0	0	0	-	0	0	0	0
1989	San Diego Chargers	16	16	49	12	1.0	0	1	0	0	1	0	0.0	0	0	0	0
1990	San Diego Chargers	14	14	60	16	3.0	0	1	0	0	1	0	0.0	0	0	0	0
1991	San Diego Chargers	16	11	46	11	0.0	0	1	0	0	1	0	0.0	0	0	0	0
1992	Kansas City Chiefs	16	16	57	32	0.0	0	0	0	0	1	0	0.0	0	0	0	0
1993	Kansas City Chiefs	16	10	53	37	1.0	2	0	0	0	2	14	7.0	0	0	0	0
1994	Washington Redskins	16	15	67	11	0.0	0	1	1	0	3	38	12.7	0	0	1	6
1995	Kansas City Chiefs	12	0	35	3	1.0	0	1	0	0	0	0	-	0	0	0	0
1984	St. Louis Cardinals	3	0	2	0	0.0	0	0	0	0	0	0	-	0	0	0	0
	Buffalo Bills	13	1	4	1	0.0	0	0	0	0	0	0	-	0	0	0	0
	12 NFL Seasons	177	131	556	204	10.5	2	6	1	0	12	62	5.2	0	0	1	6

Willie Beamon

Pos: CB **Rnd:** FA **College:** Northern Iowa **Ht:** 5' 11" **Wt:** 178 **Born:** 6/14/70 **Age:** 26

Year	Team	G	GS	Tackles Tk	Ast	Sack	Miscellaneous FF	FR	TD	Blk	Interceptions Int	Yds	Avg	TD	Totals Sfty	TD	Pts
1993	New York Giants	13	0	16	2	0.0	0	0	0	0	1	0	0.0	0	0	0	0
1994	New York Giants	15	0	23	3	1.0	0	2	0	0	0	0	-	0	0	0	0
1995	New York Giants	16	0	30	2	0.0	0	0	0	0	0	0	-	0	0	0	0
	3 NFL Seasons	44	0	69	7	1.0	0	2	0	0	1	0	0.0	0	0	0	0

Aubrey Beavers

Pos: LB **Rnd:** 2 **College:** Oklahoma **Ht:** 6' 3" **Wt:** 231 **Born:** 8/30/71 **Age:** 25

Year	Team	G	GS	Tackles Tk	Ast	Sack	Miscellaneous FF	FR	TD	Blk	Interceptions Int	Yds	Avg	TD	Totals Sfty	TD	Pts
1994	Miami Dolphins	16	10	36	12	0.0	0	0	0	0	2	0	0.0	0	0	0	0
1995	Miami Dolphins	16	1	7	4	0.0	0	0	0	0	1	8	8.0	0	0	0	0
	2 NFL Seasons	32	11	43	16	0.0	0	0	0	0	3	8	2.7	0	0	0	0

Ian Beckles

Pos: G **Rnd:** 5 **College:** Indiana **Ht:** 6' 1" **Wt:** 304 **Born:** 7/20/67 **Age:** 29

Year	Team	G	GS	Year	Team	G	GS	Year	Team	G	GS		G	GS
1990	Tampa Bay Buccaneers	16	16	1992	Tampa Bay Buccaneers	11	7	1994	Tampa Bay Buccaneers	16	16			
1991	Tampa Bay Buccaneers	16	16	1993	Tampa Bay Buccaneers	14	14	1995	Tampa Bay Buccaneers	15	15	6 NFL Seasons	88	84

Other Statistics: 1993–recovered 1 fumble for 0 yards. 1994–recovered 2 fumbles for 0 yards. 1995–recovered 2 fumbles for 0 yards.

Don Beebe

Pos: WR **Rnd:** 3 **College:** Chadron State **Ht:** 5' 11" **Wt:** 183 **Born:** 12/10/64 **Age:** 31

Year	Team	G	GS	Rushing Att	Yds	Avg	Lg	TD	Receiving Rec	Yds	Avg	Lg	TD	Punt Returns Num	Yds	Avg	TD	Kickoff Returns Num	Yds	Avg	TD	Totals Fum	TD	Pts
1989	Buffalo Bills	14	0	0	0	-	-	0	17	317	18.6	t63	2	0	0	-	0	16	353	22.1	0	1	2	12
1990	Buffalo Bills	12	4	1	23	23.0	23	0	11	221	20.1	49	1	0	0	-	0	6	119	19.8	0	0	1	6
1991	Buffalo Bills	11	7	0	0	-	-	0	32	414	12.9	t34	6	0	0	-	0	7	121	17.3	0	3	6	36
1992	Buffalo Bills	12	8	1	-6	-6.0	-6	0	33	554	16.8	t65	2	0	0	-	0	0	0	-	0	1	2	12
1993	Buffalo Bills	14	14	0	0	-	-	0	31	504	16.3	t65	3	0	0	-	0	10	160	16.0	0	1	3	18
1994	Buffalo Bills	13	11	2	11	5.5	6	0	40	527	13.2	t72	4	0	0	-	0	12	230	19.2	0	3	4	24
1995	Carolina Panthers	14	1	0	0	-	-	0	14	152	10.9	24	1	0	0	-	0	9	215	23.9	0	0	1	6
	7 NFL Seasons	90	45	4	28	7.0	23	0	178	2689	15.1	t72	19	0	0	-	0	60	1198	20.0	0	9	19	114

Other Statistics: 1993–recovered 1 fumble for 0 yards.

Thomas Beer

Pos: RB/LB **Rnd:** 7 **College:** Wayne State (MI) **Ht:** 6' 2" **Wt:** 237 **Born:** 3/27/69 **Age:** 27

Year	Team	G	GS	Rushing					Receiving					Punt Returns				Kickoff Returns				Totals		
				Att	Yds	Avg	Lg	TD	Rec	Yds	Avg	Lg	TD	Num	Yds	Avg	TD	Num	Yds	Avg	TD	Fum	TD	Pts
1994	Detroit Lions	9	0	0	0	-	-	0	0	0	-	-	0	0	0	-	0	0	0	-	0	0	0	0
1995	Detroit Lions	16	0	0	0	-	-	0	0	0	-	-	0	0	0	-	0	0	0	-	0	0	0	0
	2 NFL Seasons	25	0	0	0	-	-	0	0	0	-	-	0	0	0	-	0	0	0	-	0	0	0	0

Chuck Belin

Pos: G **Rnd:** 5 **College:** Wisconsin **Ht:** 6' 2" **Wt:** 312 **Born:** 10/27/70 **Age:** 26

Year	Team	G	GS	Year	Team	G	GS			Team	G	GS
1994	Los Angeles Rams	14	6	1995	St. Louis Rams	6	0		2 NFL Seasons		20	6

Other Statistics: 1994–recovered 1 fumble for 0 yards.

Coleman Bell

Pos: TE/WR **Rnd:** FA **College:** Miami (FL) **Ht:** 6' 2" **Wt:** 232 **Born:** 4/22/70 **Age:** 26

Year	Team	G	GS	Rushing					Receiving					Punt Returns				Kickoff Returns				Totals		
				Att	Yds	Avg	Lg	TD	Rec	Yds	Avg	Lg	TD	Num	Yds	Avg	TD	Num	Yds	Avg	TD	Fum	TD	Pts
1995	Washington Redskins	11	1	0	0	-	-	0	14	166	11.9	t29	1	0	0	-	0	0	0	-	0	1	1	6

Myron Bell

Pos: S **Rnd:** 5 **College:** Michigan State **Ht:** 5' 11" **Wt:** 203 **Born:** 9/15/71 **Age:** 25

Year	Team	G	GS	Tackles			Miscellaneous				Interceptions				Totals		
				Tk	Ast	Sack	FF	FR	TD	Blk	Int	Yds	Avg	TD	Sfty	TD	Pts
1994	Pittsburgh Steelers	15	0	4	0	0.0	0	0	0	0	0	0	-	0	0	0	0
1995	Pittsburgh Steelers	16	9	25	11	0.0	2	1	0	0	2	4	2.0	0	0	0	0
	2 NFL Seasons	31	9	29	11	0.0	2	1	0	0	2	4	2.0	0	0	0	0

William Bell

Pos: RB **Rnd:** FA **College:** Georgia Tech **Ht:** 5' 11" **Wt:** 203 **Born:** 7/22/71 **Age:** 25

Year	Team	G	GS	Rushing					Receiving					Punt Returns				Kickoff Returns				Totals		
				Att	Yds	Avg	Lg	TD	Rec	Yds	Avg	Lg	TD	Num	Yds	Avg	TD	Num	Yds	Avg	TD	Fum	TD	Pts
1994	Washington Redskins	8	0	0	0	-	-	0	0	0	-	-	0	0	0	-	0	2	43	21.5	0	0	0	0
1995	Washington Redskins	16	0	4	13	3.3	5	0	0	0	-	-	0	0	0	-	0	8	121	15.1	0	0	0	0
	2 NFL Seasons	24	0	4	13	3.3	5	0	0	0	-	-	0	0	0	-	0	10	164	16.4	0	0	0	0

Jay Bellamy

Pos: S **Rnd:** FA **College:** Rutgers **Ht:** 5' 11" **Wt:** 193 **Born:** 7/8/72 **Age:** 24

Year	Team	G	GS	Tackles			Miscellaneous				Interceptions				Totals		
				Tk	Ast	Sack	FF	FR	TD	Blk	Int	Yds	Avg	TD	Sfty	TD	Pts
1994	Seattle Seahawks	3	0	0	0	0.0	0	0	0	0	0	0	-	0	0	0	0
1995	Seattle Seahawks	14	0	2	1	0.0	1	0	0	0	0	0	-	0	0	0	0
	2 NFL Seasons	17	0	2	1	0.0	1	0	0	0	0	0	-	0	0	0	0

Jason Belser

(statistical profile on page 395)

Pos: S **Rnd:** 8 **College:** Oklahoma **Ht:** 5' 9" **Wt:** 185 **Born:** 5/28/70 **Age:** 26

Year	Team	G	GS	Tackles			Miscellaneous				Interceptions				Punt Returns				Kickoff Returns				Totals	
				Tk	Ast	Sack	FF	FR	TD	Blk	Int	Yds	Avg	TD	Num	Yds	Avg	TD	Num	Yds	Avg	TD	TD	Fum
1992	Indianapolis Colts	16	2	55	-	0.0	0	2	0	0	3	27	9.0	0	0	0	-	0	0	0	-	0	0	1
1993	Indianapolis Colts	16	16	94	33	0.0	0	3	0	0	1	14	14.0	0	0	0	-	0	0	0	-	0	0	0
1994	Indianapolis Colts	13	12	43	25	0.0	0	0	0	0	1	31	31.0	0	0	0	-	0	0	0	-	0	0	0
1995	Indianapolis Colts	16	16	63	13	0.0	1	2	0	0	1	0	-	0	0	0	-	0	1	15	15.0	0	0	0
	4 NFL Seasons	61	46	255	71	0.0	1	7	0	0	6	72	12.0	0	0	0	-	0	1	15	15.0	0	0	1

Lou Benfatti

Pos: DT **Rnd:** 3 **College:** Penn State **Ht:** 6' 4" **Wt:** 278 **Born:** 3/9/71 **Age:** 25

Year	Team	G	GS	Tackles			Miscellaneous				Interceptions				Punt Returns				Kickoff Returns				Totals	
				Tk	Ast	Sack	FF	FR	TD	Blk	Int	Yds	Avg	TD	Num	Yds	Avg	TD	Num	Yds	Avg	TD	TD	Fum
1994	New York Jets	7	0	1	3	0.0	0	0	0	0	0	0	-	0	0	0	-	0	0	0	-	0	0	0
1995	New York Jets	12	0	13	4	0.0	0	0	0	0	0	0	-	0	0	0	-	0	1	25	25.0	0	0	0
	2 NFL Seasons	19	0	14	7	0.0	0	0	0	0	0	0	-	0	0	0	-	0	1	25	25.0	0	0	0

Cornelius Bennett

(statistical profile on page 396)

Pos: LB **Rnd:** 1 (2) **College:** Alabama **Ht:** 6' 2" **Wt:** 238 **Born:** 8/25/65 **Age:** 31

Year Team	G	GS	Tackles			Miscellaneous				Interceptions				Totals		
			Tk	Ast	Sack	FF	FR	TD	Blk	Int	Yds	Avg	TD	Sfty	TD	Pts
1987 Buffalo Bills	8	7	54	15	8.5	5	0	0	0	0	0	-	0	0	0	0
1988 Buffalo Bills	16	16	85	18	9.5	3	3	0	0	2	30	15.0	0	0	0	0
1989 Buffalo Bills	12	12	43	11	5.5	1	2	0	0	2	5	2.5	0	0	0	0
1990 Buffalo Bills	16	16	71	25	4.0	3	2	1	0	0	0	-	0	0	1	6
1991 Buffalo Bills	16	16	84	23	9.0	4	2	1	0	0	0	-	0	0	1	6
1992 Buffalo Bills	15	15	61	20	4.0	2	3	0	0	0	0	-	0	0	0	0
1993 Buffalo Bills	16	16	81	21	5.0	2	2	0	0	1	5	5.0	0	0	0	0
1994 Buffalo Bills	16	16	58	19	5.0	1	3	0	0	0	0	-	0	0	0	0
1995 Buffalo Bills	14	14	81	23	2.0	1	2	0	0	1	69	69.0	1	0	1	6
9 NFL Seasons	129	128	618	175	52.5	22	19	2	0	6	109	18.2	1	0	3	18

Other Statistics: 1993–fumbled 1 time.

Darren Bennett

(statistical profile on page 468)

Pos: P **Rnd:** FA **College:** None **Ht:** 6' 5" **Wt:** 235 **Born:** 1/9/65 **Age:** 31

Year Team	G	Punting												Rushing		Passing			
		NetPunts	Yards	Avg	Long	In20	In20%	TotPunts	TB	Blocks	OppRet	RetYds	NetAvg	Att	Yards	Att	Com	Yards	Int
1995 San Diego Chargers	16	72	3221	44.7	66	28	38.9	72	8	0	35	429	36.6	0	0	0	0	0	0

Donnell Bennett

(statistical profile on page 468)

Pos: RB **Rnd:** 2 **College:** Miami (FL) **Ht:** 6' 0" **Wt:** 241 **Born:** 9/14/72 **Age:** 24

Year Team	G	GS	Rushing					Receiving					Punt Returns				Kickoff Returns				Totals		
			Att	Yds	Avg	Lg	TD	Rec	Yds	Avg	Lg	TD	Num	Yds	Avg	TD	Num	Yds	Avg	TD	Fum	TD	Pts
1994 Kansas City Chiefs	15	0	46	178	3.9	17	2	7	53	7.6	15	0	0	0	-	0	1	12	12.0	0	2	2	12
1995 Kansas City Chiefs	3	1	7	11	1.6	11	0	1	12	12.0	12	0	0	0	-	0	0	0	-	0	0	0	0
2 NFL Seasons	18	1	53	189	3.6	17	2	8	65	8.1	15	0	0	0	-	0	1	12	12.0	0	2	2	12

Other Statistics: 1994–recovered 1 fumble for 0 yards.

Edgar Bennett

(statistical profile on page 282)

Pos: RB **Rnd:** 4 **College:** Florida State **Ht:** 6' 0" **Wt:** 224 **Born:** 2/15/69 **Age:** 27

Year Team	G	GS	Rushing					Receiving					Punt Returns				Kickoff Returns				Totals		
			Att	Yds	Avg	Lg	TD	Rec	Yds	Avg	Lg	TD	Num	Yds	Avg	TD	Num	Yds	Avg	TD	Fum	TD	Pts
1992 Green Bay Packers	16	2	61	214	3.5	18	0	13	93	7.2	22	0	0	0	-	0	5	104	20.8	0	2	0	0
1993 Green Bay Packers	16	14	159	550	3.5	19	9	59	457	7.7	t39	1	0	0	-	0	0	0	-	0	0	10	60
1994 Green Bay Packers	16	15	178	623	3.5	t39	5	78	546	7.0	40	4	0	0	-	0	0	0	-	0	1	9	54
1995 Green Bay Packers	16	16	316	1067	3.4	23	3	61	648	10.6	35	4	0	0	-	0	0	0	-	0	2	7	42
4 NFL Seasons	64	47	714	2454	3.4	t39	17	211	1744	8.3	40	9	0	0	-	0	5	104	20.8	0	5	26	156

Other Statistics: 1993–recovered 1 fumble for 0 yards. 1994–recovered 1 fumble for 0 yards. 1995–recovered 1 fumble for 0 yards.

Tony Bennett

(statistical profile on page 396)

Pos: DE **Rnd:** 1 (18) **College:** Mississippi **Ht:** 6' 2" **Wt:** 242 **Born:** 7/1/67 **Age:** 29

Year Team	G	GS	Tackles			Miscellaneous				Interceptions				Totals		
			Tk	Ast	Sack	FF	FR	TD	Blk	Int	Yds	Avg	TD	Sfty	TD	Pts
1990 Green Bay Packers	14	0	8	5	3.0	1	1	0	0	0	0	-	0	0	0	0
1991 Green Bay Packers	16	16	70	41	13.0	3	0	0	0	0	0	-	0	0	0	0
1992 Green Bay Packers	16	16	52	39	13.5	4	3	1	0	0	0	-	0	0	1	6
1993 Green Bay Packers	10	7	25	11	6.5	1	0	0	0	0	0	-	0	0	0	0
1994 Indianapolis Colts	16	15	42	20	9.0	2	1	1	0	0	0	-	0	0	1	6
1995 Indianapolis Colts	16	16	47	10	10.5	3	1	1	0	0	0	-	0	1	1	8
6 NFL Seasons	88	70	244	126	55.5	14	6	3	0	0	0	-	0	1	3	20

Darren Benson

Pos: DT **Rnd:** FA **College:** Trinity Valley C.C. **Ht:** 6' 7" **Wt:** 305 **Born:** 8/25/74 **Age:** 22

Year Team	G	GS	Tackles			Miscellaneous				Interceptions				Totals		
			Tk	Ast	Sack	FF	FR	TD	Blk	Int	Yds	Avg	TD	Sfty	TD	Pts
1995 Dallas Cowboys	6	0	2	1	0.0	0	0	0	0	0	0	-	0	0	0	0

Pete Bercich

Pos: LB **Rnd:** 7 **College:** Notre Dame **Ht:** 6' 1" **Wt:** 240 **Born:** 12/23/71 **Age:** 24

Year Team	G	GS	Tackles			Miscellaneous				Interceptions				Totals		
			Tk	Ast	Sack	FF	FR	TD	Blk	Int	Yds	Avg	TD	Sfty	TD	Pts
1995 Minnesota Vikings	9	0	1	1	0.0	0	0	0	0	0	0	-	0	0	0	0

Rod Bernstine

Pos: RB   **Rnd:** 1 (24)   **College:** Texas A&M   **Ht:** 6' 3" **Wt:** 238 **Born:** 2/8/65 **Age:** 31

Year	Team	G	GS	Rushing					Receiving					Kickoff Returns				Passing				Totals		
				Att	Yds	Avg	Lg	TD	Rec	Yds	Avg	Lg	TD	Num	Yds	Avg	TD	Att	Com	Yds	Int	Fum	TD	Pts
1987	San Diego Chargers	10	2	1	9	9.0	9	0	10	76	7.6	15	1	1	13	13.0	0	0	0	0	0	0	1	6
1988	San Diego Chargers	14	13	2	7	3.5	5	0	29	340	11.7	59	0	0	0	-	0	0	0	0	0	0	0	0
1989	San Diego Chargers	5	0	15	137	9.1	t32	1	21	222	10.6	36	1	0	0	-	0	0	0	0	0	0	2	12
1990	San Diego Chargers	12	1	124	589	4.8	t40	4	8	40	5.0	11	0	0	0	-	0	0	0	0	0	1	4	24
1991	San Diego Chargers	13	8	159	766	4.8	t63	8	11	124	11.3	25	0	1	7	7.0	0	1	1	11	0	1	8	48
1992	San Diego Chargers	9	1	106	499	4.7	t25	4	12	86	7.2	16	0	0	0	-	0	0	0	0	0	2	4	24
1993	Denver Broncos	15	14	223	816	3.7	24	4	44	372	8.5	41	0	0	0	-	0	0	0	0	0	3	4	24
1994	Denver Broncos	3	3	17	91	5.4	24	0	9	70	7.8	16	0	0	0	-	0	0	0	0	0	0	0	0
1995	Denver Broncos	3	3	23	76	3.3	18	1	5	54	10.8	38	0	0	0	-	0	0	0	0	0	0	1	6
	9 NFL Seasons	84	45	670	2990	4.5	t63	22	149	1384	9.3	59	2	2	20	10.0	0	1	1	11	0	7	24	144

Other Statistics: 1987–recovered 1 fumble for 0 yards. 1991–passed for 1 touchdown. 1993–recovered 1 fumble for 0 yards. 1995–recovered 1 fumble for 0 yards.

Tony Berti

Pos: T   **Rnd:** 6   **College:** Colorado   **Ht:** 6' 5" **Wt:** 287 **Born:** 6/21/72 **Age:** 24

Year	Team	G	GS			G	GS
1995	San Diego Chargers	1	0		1 NFL Season	1	0

Jerome Bettis

(statistical profile on page 282)

Pos: RB   **Rnd:** 1 (10)   **College:** Notre Dame   **Ht:** 5' 11" **Wt:** 243 **Born:** 2/16/72 **Age:** 24

Year	Team	G	GS	Rushing					Receiving					Punt Returns				Kickoff Returns				Totals		
				Att	Yds	Avg	Lg	TD	Rec	Yds	Avg	Lg	TD	Num	Yds	Avg	TD	Num	Yds	Avg	TD	Fum	TD	Pts
1993	Los Angeles Rams	16	12	294	1429	4.9	t71	7	26	244	9.4	28	0	0	0	-	0	0	0	-	0	4	7	42
1994	Los Angeles Rams	16	16	319	1025	3.2	19	3	31	293	9.5	34	1	0	0	-	0	0	0	-	0	5	4	28
1995	St. Louis Rams	15	13	183	637	3.5	41	3	18	106	5.9	19	0	0	0	-	0	0	0	-	0	4	3	18
	3 NFL Seasons	47	41	796	3091	3.9	t71	13	75	643	8.6	34	1	0	0	-	0	0	0	-	0	13	14	88

Other Statistics: 1994–recovered 3 fumbles for 0 yards; scored 2 two-point conversions. 1995–recovered 2 fumbles for 0 yards.

Steve Beuerlein

(statistical profile on page 283)

Pos: QB   **Rnd:** 4   **College:** Notre Dame   **Ht:** 6' 3" **Wt:** 220 **Born:** 3/7/65 **Age:** 31

Year	Team	G	GS	Passing										Rushing					Miscellaneous				
				Att	Com	Pct	Yards	Yds/Att	Lg	TD	Int	Int%	Rating	Att	Yds	Avg	Lg	TD	Sckd	Yds	Fum	Recv	Yds	Pts
1988	Los Angeles Raiders	10	8	238	105	44.1	1643	6.90	57	8	7	2.9	66.6	30	35	1.2	20	0	26	215	6	2	-1	0
1989	Los Angeles Raiders	10	7	217	108	49.8	1677	7.73	t67	13	9	4.1	78.4	16	39	2.4	10	0	22	175	6	3	-8	0
1991	Dallas Cowboys	7	4	137	68	49.6	909	6.64	t66	5	2	1.5	77.2	7	-14	-2.0	-1	0	6	49	0	0	0	0
1992	Dallas Cowboys	16	0	18	12	66.7	152	8.44	27	0	1	5.6	69.7	4	-7	-1.8	-1	0	0	0	0	0	0	0
1993	Phoenix Cardinals	16	14	418	258	61.7	3164	7.57	t65	18	17	4.1	82.5	22	45	2.0	20	0	29	206	8	2	0	0
1994	Arizona Cardinals	9	7	255	130	51.0	1545	6.06	63	5	9	3.5	61.6	22	39	1.8	19	1	20	129	8	3	-2	6
1995	Jacksonville Jaguars	7	6	142	71	50.0	952	6.70	t71	4	7	4.9	60.5	5	32	6.4	13	0	17	103	3	0	0	0
	7 NFL Seasons	75	46	1425	752	52.8	10042	7.05	t71	53	52	3.6	72.6	106	169	1.6	20	1	120	877	31	10	-11	6

Other Statistics: 1988–caught 1 pass for 21 yards.

Dean Biasucci

(statistical profile on page 468)

Pos: K   **Rnd:** FA   **College:** Western Carolina   **Ht:** 6' 0" **Wt:** 190 **Born:** 7/25/62 **Age:** 34

Year	Team	G	Field Goals										PAT		Tot
			1-29 Yds	Pct	30-39 Yds	Pct	40-49 Yds	Pct	50+ Yds	Pct	Overall	Pct	Long	Made	Att	Pts
1984	Indianapolis Colts	15	1-1	100.0	0-0	-	1-1	100.0	1-3	33.3	3-5	60.0	50	13	14	22
1986	Indianapolis Colts	16	4-4	100.0	2-5	40.0	5-8	62.5	2-8	25.0	13-25	52.0	52	26	27	65
1987	Indianapolis Colts	12	5-6	83.3	12-12	100.0	6-7	85.7	1-2	50.0	24-27	88.9	50	24	24	96
1988	Indianapolis Colts	16	8-8	100.0	5-6	83.3	6-10	60.0	6-8	75.0	25-32	78.1	53	39	40	114
1989	Indianapolis Colts	16	8-8	100.0	9-10	90.0	3-5	60.0	1-4	25.0	21-27	77.8	55	31	32	94
1990	Indianapolis Colts	16	6-7	85.7	7-8	87.5	2-4	50.0	2-5	40.0	17-24	70.8	55	32	33	83
1991	Indianapolis Colts	16	6-6	100.0	3-4	75.0	5-13	38.5	1-3	33.3	15-26	57.7	54	14	14	59
1992	Indianapolis Colts	16	3-3	100.0	6-11	54.5	6-12	50.0	1-3	33.3	16-29	55.2	52	24	24	72
1993	Indianapolis Colts	16	15-15	100.0	7-8	87.5	3-6	50.0	1-2	50.0	26-31	83.9	53	15	16	93
1994	Indianapolis Colts	16	6-6	100.0	3-7	42.9	5-9	55.6	2-2	100.0	16-24	66.7	50	37	37	85
1995	St. Louis Rams	8	4-4	100.0	3-4	75.0	1-1	100.0	1-3	33.3	9-12	75.0	51	13	14	40
	11 NFL Seasons	163	66-68	97.1	57-75	76.0	43-76	56.6	19-43	44.2	185-262	70.6	55	268	275	823

Other Statistics: 1988–recovered 1 fumble for 0 yards.

Duane Bickett

Pos: LB **Rnd:** 1 (5) **College:** Southern California   **Ht:** 6' 5" **Wt:** 251 **Born:** 12/1/62 **Age:** 33

Year	Team	G	GS	Tk	Ast	Sack	FF	FR	TD	Blk	Int	Yds	Avg	TD	Sfty	TD	Pts
				Tackles			**Miscellaneous**				**Interceptions**				**Totals**		
1985	Indianapolis Colts	16	16	87	54	6.0	1	2	0	0	1	0	0.0	0	0	0	0
1986	Indianapolis Colts	16	16	104	40	5.0	1	1	0	0	2	10	5.0	0	0	0	0
1987	Indianapolis Colts	12	12	74	39	8.0	2	2	0	0	0	0	-	0	0	0	0
1988	Indianapolis Colts	16	16	83	43	3.5	1	1	0	0	3	7	2.3	0	0	0	0
1989	Indianapolis Colts	16	16	83	17	8.0	0	3	0	0	1	6	6.0	0	0	0	0
1990	Indianapolis Colts	15	15	84	33	4.5	1	2	0	0	1	9	9.0	0	0	0	0
1991	Indianapolis Colts	16	16	82	43	5.0	1	2	0	0	0	0	-	0	0	0	0
1992	Indianapolis Colts	15	15	62	27	6.5	1	2	0	0	1	14	14.0	0	0	0	0
1993	Indianapolis Colts	15	15	61	36	3.5	0	1	0	0	0	0	-	0	0	0	0
1994	Seattle Seahawks	7	1	7	1	0.0	0	0	0	0	0	0	-	0	0	0	0
1995	Seattle Seahawks	13	0	5	2	1.0	1	0	0	0	0	0	-	0	0	0	0
	11 NFL Seasons	157	138	732	335	51.0	9	14	0	0	9	46	5.1	0	0	0	0

Other Statistics: 1987–fumbled 1 time.

Greg Biekert

Pos: LB **Rnd:** 7 **College:** Colorado   **Ht:** 6' 3" **Wt:** 240 **Born:** 3/14/69 **Age:** 27   *(statistical profile on page 396)*

Year	Team	G	GS	Tk	Ast	Sack	FF	FR	TD	Blk	Int	Yds	Avg	TD	Sfty	TD	Pts
				Tackles			**Miscellaneous**				**Interceptions**				**Totals**		
1993	Los Angeles Raiders	16	0	8	2	0.0	0	0	0	0	0	0	-	0	0	0	0
1994	Los Angeles Raiders	16	14	75	25	1.5	2	0	0	0	1	11	11.0	0	0	0	0
1995	Oakland Raiders	16	14	69	16	1.0	2	0	0	0	0	0	-	0	0	0	0
	3 NFL Seasons	48	28	152	43	2.5	4	0	0	0	1	11	11.0	0	0	0	0

Eric Bieniemy

Pos: RB **Rnd:** 2 **College:** Colorado   **Ht:** 5' 7" **Wt:** 198 **Born:** 8/15/69 **Age:** 27   *(statistical profile on page 283)*

Year	Team	G	GS	Att	Yds	Avg	Lg	TD	Rec	Yds	Avg	Lg	TD	Num	Yds	Avg	TD	Num	Yds	Avg	TD	Fum	TD	Pts
				Rushing					**Receiving**					**Punt Returns**				**Kickoff Returns**				**Totals**		
1991	San Diego Chargers	15	0	3	17	5.7	15	0	0	0	-	-	0	0	0	-	0	0	0	-	0	0	0	0
1992	San Diego Chargers	15	0	74	264	3.6	21	3	5	49	9.8	25	0	30	229	7.6	0	15	257	17.1	0	4	3	18
1993	San Diego Chargers	16	0	33	135	4.1	12	1	1	0	0.0	0	0	0	0	-	0	7	110	15.7	0	1	1	6
1994	San Diego Chargers	16	0	73	295	4.0	36	0	5	48	9.6	25	0	0	0	-	0	0	0	-	0	0	0	0
1995	Cincinnati Bengals	16	1	98	381	3.9	27	3	43	424	9.9	33	0	7	47	6.7	0	8	168	21.0	0	1	3	18
	5 NFL Seasons	78	1	281	1092	3.9	36	7	54	521	9.6	33	0	37	276	7.5	0	30	535	17.8	0	7	7	42

Other Statistics: 1992–recovered 1 fumble for 0 yards. 1994–recovered 1 fumble for 0 yards. 1995–recovered 1 fumble for 0 yards; attempted 2 passes with 0 completions for 0 yards.

David Binn

Pos: TE/C **Rnd:** FA **College:** California   **Ht:** 6' 3" **Wt:** 240 **Born:** 2/6/72 **Age:** 24

Year	Team	G	GS	Att	Yds	Avg	Lg	TD	Rec	Yds	Avg	Lg	TD	Num	Yds	Avg	TD	Num	Yds	Avg	TD	Fum	TD	Pts
				Rushing					**Receiving**					**Punt Returns**				**Kickoff Returns**				**Totals**		
1994	San Diego Chargers	16	0	0	0	-	-	0	0	0	-	-	0	0	0	-	0	0	0	-	0	0	0	0
1995	San Diego Chargers	16	0	0	0	-	-	0	0	0	-	-	0	0	0	-	0	0	0	-	0	0	0	0
	2 NFL Seasons	32	0	0	0	-	-	0	0	0	-	-	0	0	0	-	0	0	0	-	0	0	0	0

J.J. Birden

Pos: WR **Rnd:** 8 **College:** Oregon   **Ht:** 5' 9" **Wt:** 170 **Born:** 6/16/65 **Age:** 31   *(statistical profile on page 284)*

Year	Team	G	GS	Att	Yds	Avg	Lg	TD	Rec	Yds	Avg	Lg	TD	Num	Yds	Avg	TD	Num	Yds	Avg	TD	Fum	TD	Pts
				Rushing					**Receiving**					**Punt Returns**				**Kickoff Returns**				**Totals**		
1990	Kansas City Chiefs	11	0	0	0	-	-	0	15	352	23.5	t90	3	10	72	7.2	0	1	14	14.0	0	1	3	18
1991	Kansas City Chiefs	15	0	0	0	-	-	0	27	465	17.2	t57	2	0	0	-	0	0	0	-	0	1	2	12
1992	Kansas City Chiefs	16	11	0	0	-	-	0	42	644	15.3	t72	3	0	0	-	0	0	0	-	0	3	3	18
1993	Kansas City Chiefs	16	16	0	0	-	-	0	51	721	14.1	t50	2	5	43	8.6	0	0	0	-	0	1	2	12
1994	Kansas City Chiefs	13	13	0	0	-	-	0	48	637	13.3	44	4	0	0	-	0	0	0	-	0	1	4	26
1995	Atlanta Falcons	10	10	0	0	-	-	0	31	303	9.8	24	1	0	0	-	0	0	0	-	0	0	1	6
	6 NFL Seasons	81	50	0	0	-	-	0	214	3122	14.6	t90	15	15	115	7.7	0	1	14	14.0	0	7	15	92

Other Statistics: 1992–recovered 1 fumble for 0 yards. 1994–recovered 1 fumble for 0 yards; scored 1 two-point conversion. 1995–recovered 1 fumble for 0 yards.

Blaine Bishop

Pos: S **Rnd:** 8 **College:** Ball State   **Ht:** 5' 9" **Wt:** 197 **Born:** 7/24/70 **Age:** 26   *(statistical profile on page 397)*

Year	Team	G	GS	Tk	Ast	Sack	FF	FR	TD	Blk	Int	Yds	Avg	TD	Num	Yds	Avg	TD	Num	Yds	Avg	TD	TD	Fum
				Tackles			**Miscellaneous**				**Interceptions**				**Punt Returns**				**Kickoff Returns**				**Totals**	
1993	Houston Oilers	16	2	24	3	1.0	2	1	0	0	1	1	1.0	0	0	0	-	0	0	0	-	0	0	1
1994	Houston Oilers	16	13	76	36	1.5	0	1	0	0	1	21	21.0	0	0	0	-	0	2	18	9.0	0	0	0

			Tackles			Miscellaneous				Interceptions				Punt Returns				Kickoff Returns				Totals	
Year Team	G	GS	Tk	Ast	Sack	FF	FR	TD	Blk	Int	Yds	Avg	TD	Num	Yds	Avg	TD	Num	Yds	Avg	TD	TD	Fum
1995 Houston Oilers	16	16	75	22	1.5	3	4	0	0	1	62	62.0	1	0	0	0	-	0	0	0	0	-	0	1	0
3 NFL Seasons	48	31	175	61	4.0	5	6	0	0	3	84	28.0	1	0	0	-	0	2	18	9.0	0	1	1

Greg Bishop

Pos: G **Rnd:** 4 **College:** Pacific **Ht:** 6' 5" **Wt:** 296 **Born:** 5/2/71 **Age:** 25

Year	Team	G	GS	Year	Team	G	GS	Year	Team	G	GS		G	GS
1993	New York Giants	8	0	1994	New York Giants	16	1	1995	New York Giants	16	16	3 NFL Seasons	40	17

Other Statistics: 1994–recovered 2 fumbles for 0 yards. 1995–recovered 1 fumble for 0 yards.

Harold Bishop

Pos: TE **Rnd:** 3 **College:** Louisiana State **Ht:** 6' 4" **Wt:** 250 **Born:** 4/8/70 **Age:** 26

			Rushing				Receiving				Punt Returns				Kickoff Returns				Totals		
Year Team	G	GS	Att	Yds	Avg	Lg	TD	Rec	Yds	Avg	Lg	TD	Num	Yds	Avg	TD	Num	Yds	Avg	TD	Fum	TD	Pts
1994 Tampa Bay Buccaneers	7	0	0	0	-	0	0	0	0	-	0	0	0	0	-	0	0	0	-	0	0	0	0
1995 Cleveland Browns	13	3	0	0	-	0	0	16	135	8.4	21	0	0	0	-	0	0	0	-	0	0	0	0
2 NFL Seasons	20	3	0	0	-	0	0	16	135	8.4	21	0	0	0	-	0	0	0	-	0	0	0	0

Eric Bjornson

Pos: TE **Rnd:** 4 **College:** Washington **Ht:** 6' 4" **Wt:** 215 **Born:** 12/15/71 **Age:** 24

			Rushing				Receiving				Punt Returns				Kickoff Returns				Totals		
Year Team	G	GS	Att	Yds	Avg	Lg	TD	Rec	Yds	Avg	Lg	TD	Num	Yds	Avg	TD	Num	Yds	Avg	TD	Fum	TD	Pts
1995 Dallas Cowboys	14	1	0	0	-	0	0	7	53	7.6	16	0	0	0	-	0	0	0	-	0	0	0	0

Robert Blackmon

(statistical profile on page 397)

Pos: S **Rnd:** 2 **College:** Baylor **Ht:** 6' 0" **Wt:** 203 **Born:** 5/12/67 **Age:** 29

			Tackles			Miscellaneous				Interceptions				Totals		
Year Team	G	GS	Tk	Ast	Sack	FF	FR	TD	Blk	Int	Yds	Avg	TD	Sfty	TD	Pts
1990 Seattle Seahawks	15	5	36	5	0.0	0	1	0	0	0	0	-	0	0	0	0
1991 Seattle Seahawks	16	16	52	12	1.0	0	0	0	0	3	59	19.7	0	0	0	0
1992 Seattle Seahawks	15	15	51	16	3.5	0	1	0	0	1	69	69.0	0	0	0	0
1993 Seattle Seahawks	16	16	55	19	0.0	0	1	1	0	2	0	0.0	0	0	1	6
1994 Seattle Seahawks	15	15	49	20	0.0	1	3	0	0	1	24	24.0	0	0	0	0
1995 Seattle Seahawks	13	13	49	11	1.0	1	0	0	0	5	46	9.2	0	0	0	0
6 NFL Seasons	90	80	292	83	5.5	2	7	1	0	12	198	16.5	0	0	1	6

Jeff Blackshear

Pos: G **Rnd:** 8 **College:** Northeast Louisiana **Ht:** 6' 6" **Wt:** 323 **Born:** 3/29/69 **Age:** 27

Year	Team	G	GS	Year	Team	G	GS	Year	Team	G	GS		G	GS
1993	Seattle Seahawks	15	2	1994	Seattle Seahawks	16	16	1995	Seattle Seahawks	16	3	3 NFL Seasons	47	21

Bennie Blades

(statistical profile on page 397)

Pos: S/LB **Rnd:** 1 (3) **College:** Miami (FL) **Ht:** 6' 1" **Wt:** 221 **Born:** 9/3/66 **Age:** 30

			Tackles			Miscellaneous				Interceptions				Totals		
Year Team	G	GS	Tk	Ast	Sack	FF	FR	TD	Blk	Int	Yds	Avg	TD	Sfty	TD	Pts
1988 Detroit Lions	15	14	86	16	1.0	3	4	0	0	2	12	6.0	0	0	0	0
1989 Detroit Lions	16	16	81	19	0.0	2	1	0	0	0	0	-	0	0	0	0
1990 Detroit Lions	12	12	61	22	1.0	1	1	0	0	2	25	12.5	0	0	0	0
1991 Detroit Lions	16	16	65	28	0.0	2	3	0	0	1	14	14.0	0	0	0	0
1992 Detroit Lions	16	16	62	33	0.0	1	0	1	0	3	56	18.7	0	0	1	6
1993 Detroit Lions	4	4	15	8	0.0	0	0	0	0	0	0	-	0	0	0	0
1994 Detroit Lions	16	16	71	19	1.0	0	2	0	0	1	0	0.0	0	0	0	0
1995 Detroit Lions	16	16	69	29	1.0	0	0	0	0	1	0	0.0	0	1	0	2
8 NFL Seasons	111	110	510	174	4.0	9	11	1	0	10	107	10.7	0	1	1	8

Brian Blades

(statistical profile on page 284)

Pos: WR **Rnd:** 2 **College:** Miami (FL) **Ht:** 5' 11" **Wt:** 186 **Born:** 7/24/65 **Age:** 31

			Rushing				Receiving				Punt Returns				Kickoff Returns				Totals		
Year Team	G	GS	Att	Yds	Avg	Lg	TD	Rec	Yds	Avg	Lg	TD	Num	Yds	Avg	TD	Num	Yds	Avg	TD	Fum	TD	Pts
1988 Seattle Seahawks	16	7	5	24	4.8	12	0	40	682	17.1	55	8	0	0	-	0	0	0	-	0	1	8	48
1989 Seattle Seahawks	16	14	1	3	3.0	3	0	77	1063	13.8	t60	5	0	0	-	0	0	0	-	0	3	5	30
1990 Seattle Seahawks	16	16	3	19	6.3	12	0	49	525	10.7	24	3	0	0	-	0	0	0	-	0	0	3	18
1991 Seattle Seahawks	16	16	2	17	8.5	11	0	70	1003	14.3	52	2	0	0	-	0	0	0	-	0	1	2	12
1992 Seattle Seahawks	6	5	1	5	5.0	5	0	19	256	13.5	37	1	0	0	-	0	0	0	-	0	1	1	6
1993 Seattle Seahawks	16	14	5	52	10.4	26	0	80	945	11.8	41	3	0	0	-	0	0	0	-	0	1	3	18

Year	Team	G	GS	Rushing					Receiving					Punt Returns				Kickoff Returns				Totals		
				Att	Yds	Avg	Lg	TD	Rec	Yds	Avg	Lg	TD	Num	Yds	Avg	TD	Num	Yds	Avg	TD	Fum	TD	Pts
1994	Seattle Seahawks	16	16	2	32	16.0	40	0	81	1086	13.4	45	4	0	0	-	0	0	0	-	0	1	4	26
1995	Seattle Seahawks	16	16	2	4	2.0	4	0	77	1001	13.0	49	4	0	0	-	0	0	0	-	0	0	4	24
	8 NFL Seasons	118	104	21	156	7.4	40	0	493	6561	13.3	t60	30	0	0	-	0	0	0	-	0	8	30	182

Other Statistics: 1988–recovered 1 fumble for 0 yards. 1989–recovered 1 fumble for 0 yards. 1994–recovered 2 fumbles for 0 yards; scored 1 two-point conversion.

Jeff Blake

(statistical profile on page 285)

Pos: QB **Rnd:** 6 **College:** East Carolina **Ht:** 6' 0" **Wt:** 202 **Born:** 12/4/70 **Age:** 25

Year	Team	G	GS	Passing									Rushing					Miscellaneous			
				Att	Com	Pct	Yards	Yds/Att	Lg	TD	Int	Int%	Rating	Att	Yds	Avg	Lg	TD	Sckd	Yds	Fum Recv	Yds	Pts
1992	New York Jets	3	0	9	4	44.4	40	4.44	19	0	1	11.1	18.1	2	-2	-1.0	1	0	2	7	1	0	0
1994	Cincinnati Bengals	10	9	306	156	51.0	2154	7.04	76	14	9	2.9	76.9	37	204	5.5	16	1	19	120	6	0	-3	8
1995	Cincinnati Bengals	16	16	567	326	57.5	3822	6.74	t88	28	17	3.0	82.1	53	309	5.8	30	2	24	152	10	0	-7	14
	3 NFL Seasons	29	25	882	486	55.1	6016	6.82	t88	42	27	3.1	79.5	92	511	5.6	30	3	45	279	17	0	-10	22

Other Statistics: 1994–scored 1 two-point conversion. 1995–scored 1 two-point conversion.

Cary Blanchard

(statistical profile on page 468)

Pos: K **Rnd:** FA **College:** Oklahoma State **Ht:** 6' 1" **Wt:** 225 **Born:** 11/5/68 **Age:** 27

Year	Team	G	Field Goals												PAT		Tot
			1-29 Yds	Pct	30-39 Yds	Pct	40-49 Yds	Pct	50+ Yds	Pct	Overall	Pct	Long	Made	Att	Pts
1992	New York Jets	11	4-5	80.0	5-7	71.4	7-9	77.8	0-1	0.0	16-22	72.7	47	17	17	65
1993	New York Jets	16	8-9	88.9	4-5	80.0	5-10	50.0	0-2	0.0	17-26	65.4	45	31	31	82
1995	Indianapolis Colts	12	5-5	100.0	6-8	75.0	7-10	70.0	1-1	100.0	19-24	79.2	50	25	25	82
	3 NFL Seasons	39	17-19	89.5	15-20	75.0	19-29	65.5	1-4	25.0	52-72	72.2	50	73	73	229

Drew Bledsoe

(statistical profile on page 285)

Pos: QB **Rnd:** 1 (1) **College:** Washington State **Ht:** 6' 5" **Wt:** 233 **Born:** 2/14/72 **Age:** 24

Year	Team	G	GS	Passing									Rushing					Miscellaneous			
				Att	Com	Pct	Yards	Yds/Att	Lg	TD	Int	Int%	Rating	Att	Yds	Avg	Lg	TD	Sckd	Yds	Fum Recv	Yds	Pts
1993	New England Patriots	13	12	429	214	49.9	2494	5.81	t54	15	15	3.5	65.0	32	82	2.6	15	0	16	99	8	5	-23	0
1994	New England Patriots	16	16	691	400	57.9	4555	6.59	t62	25	27	3.9	73.6	44	40	0.9	7	0	22	139	9	3	-5	0
1995	New England Patriots	15	15	636	323	50.8	3507	5.51	t47	13	16	2.5	63.7	20	28	1.4	15	0	23	170	11	1	-8	0
	3 NFL Seasons	44	43	1756	937	53.4	10556	6.01	t62	53	58	3.3	67.9	96	150	1.6	15	0	61	408	28	9	-36	0

Other Statistics: 1995–caught 1 pass for -9 yards.

Harry Boatswain

Pos: G/T **Rnd:** 5 **College:** New Haven **Ht:** 6' 4" **Wt:** 295 **Born:** 6/26/69 **Age:** 27

Year	Team	G	GS	Year	Team	G	GS	Year	Team	G	GS	Year	Team	G	GS
1992	San Francisco 49ers	16	2	1993	San Francisco 49ers	16	2	1994	San Francisco 49ers	13	4	1995	Philadelphia Eagles	13	7
													4 NFL Seasons	58	15

Other Statistics: 1995–recovered 1 fumble for 0 yards.

John Bock

Pos: C/G **Rnd:** FA **College:** Indiana State **Ht:** 6' 3" **Wt:** 275 **Born:** 2/11/71 **Age:** 25

Year	Team	G	GS											G	GS
1995	New York Jets	10	7										1 NFL Season	10	7

Other Statistics: 1995–fumbled 1 time for 0 yards.

Shane Bonham

Pos: DT/DE **Rnd:** 3 **College:** Tennessee **Ht:** 6' 2" **Wt:** 275 **Born:** 10/18/70 **Age:** 26

Year	Team	G	GS	Tackles			Miscellaneous				Interceptions				Totals		
				Tk	Ast	Sack	FF	FR	TD	Blk	Int	Yds	Avg	TD	Sfty	TD	Pts
1994	Detroit Lions	15	1	1	2	0.0	0	0	0	0	0	0	-	0	0	0	0
1995	Detroit Lions	15	0	7	6	1.0	0	0	0	0	0	0	-	0	0	0	0
	2 NFL Seasons	30	1	8	8	1.0	0	0	0	0	0	0	-	0	0	0	0

Chris Boniol

(statistical profile on page 469)

Pos: K **Rnd:** FA **College:** Louisiana Tech **Ht:** 5' 11" **Wt:** 159 **Born:** 12/9/71 **Age:** 24

Year	Team	G	Field Goals												PAT		Tot
			1-29 Yds	Pct	30-39 Yds	Pct	40-49 Yds	Pct	50+ Yds	Pct	Overall	Pct	Long	Made	Att	Pts
1994	Dallas Cowboys	16	6-7	85.7	10-12	83.3	6-9	66.7	0-1	0.0	22-29	75.9	47	48	48	114
1995	Dallas Cowboys	16	11-12	91.7	13-13	100.0	3-3	100.0	0-0	-	27-28	96.4	45	46	48	127
	2 NFL Seasons	32	17-19	89.5	23-25	92.0	9-12	75.0	0-1	0.0	49-57	86.0	47	94	96	241

Other Statistics: 1995–punted 2 times for 77 yards.

Steve Bono

(statistical profile on page 286)

Pos: QB **Rnd:** 6 **College:** UCLA   **Ht:** 6' 4" **Wt:** 215 **Born:** 5/11/62 **Age:** 34

Year	Team	G	GS	Att	Com	Pct	Yards	Yds/Att	Lg	TD	Int	Int%	Rating	Att	Yds	Avg	Lg	TD	Sckd	Yds	Fum	Recv	Yds	Pts
1985	Minnesota Vikings	1	0	10	1	10.0	5	0.50	5	0	0	0.0	39.6	0	0	-	-	0	2	13	0	0	0	0
1986	Minnesota Vikings	1	0	1	1	100.0	3	3.00	3	0	0	0.0	79.2	0	0	-	-	0	0	0	0	0	0	0
1987	Pittsburgh Steelers	3	3	74	34	45.9	438	5.92	57	5	2	2.7	76.3	8	27	3.4	23	1	6	30	5	3	0	6
1988	Pittsburgh Steelers	2	0	35	10	28.6	110	3.14	15	1	2	5.7	25.9	0	0	-	-	0	1	8	0	0	0	0
1989	San Francisco 49ers	1	0	5	4	80.0	62	12.40	t45	1	0	0.0	157.9	0	0	-	-	0	0	0	0	0	0	0
1991	San Francisco 49ers	9	6	237	141	59.5	1617	6.82	78	11	4	1.7	88.5	17	46	2.7	18	0	11	91	7	0	-8	0
1992	San Francisco 49ers	16	0	56	36	64.3	463	8.27	36	2	2	3.6	87.1	15	23	1.5	19	0	2	14	2	1	-3	0
1993	San Francisco 49ers	8	0	61	39	63.9	416	6.82	33	0	1	1.6	76.9	12	14	1.2	10	1	4	18	0	0	0	6
1994	Kansas City Chiefs	7	2	117	66	56.4	796	6.80	t62	4	4	3.4	74.6	4	-1	-0.3	2	0	0	0	0	0	0	0
1995	Kansas City Chiefs	16	16	520	293	56.3	3121	6.00	t60	21	10	1.9	79.5	28	113	4.0	t76	5	21	158	10	1	-5	30
	10 NFL Seasons	64	27	1116	625	56.0	7031	6.30	78	45	25	2.2	79.1	84	222	2.6	t76	7	47	332	24	5	-16	42

Other Statistics: 1987–caught 1 pass for 2 yards.

Vaughn Booker

Pos: DE **Rnd:** FA **College:** Cincinnati   **Ht:** 6' 5" **Wt:** 293 **Born:** 2/24/68 **Age:** 28

Year	Team	G	GS	Tk	Ast	Sack	FF	FR	TD	Blk	Int	Yds	Avg	TD	Num	Yds	Avg	TD	Num	Yds	Avg	TD	TD	Fum
1994	Kansas City Chiefs	15	0	13	2	0.0	1	2	0	0	0	0	-	0	0	0	-	0	2	10	5.0	0	0	0
1995	Kansas City Chiefs	16	10	27	5	1.5	0	1	1	0	0	0	-	0	0	0	-	0	0	0	-	0	1	0
	2 NFL Seasons	31	10	40	7	1.5	1	3	1	0	0	0	-	0	0	0	-	0	2	10	5.0	0	1	0

Isaac Booth

Pos: DB/CB **Rnd:** 5 **College:** California   **Ht:** 6' 3" **Wt:** 190 **Born:** 5/23/71 **Age:** 25

Year	Team	G	GS	Tk	Ast	Sack	FF	FR	TD	Blk	Int	Yds	Avg	TD	Sfty	TD	Pts
1994	Cleveland Browns	16	1	24	3	0.0	1	0	0	0	1	4	4.0	0	0	0	0
1995	Cleveland Browns	9	1	10	0	0.0	0	0	0	0	1	11	11.0	0	0	0	0
	2 NFL Seasons	25	2	34	3	0.0	1	0	0	0	2	15	7.5	0	0	0	0

John Booty

Pos: S **Rnd:** 10 **College:** Texas Christian   **Ht:** 6' 0" **Wt:** 180 **Born:** 10/9/65 **Age:** 31

Year	Team	G	GS	Tk	Ast	Sack	FF	FR	TD	Blk	Int	Yds	Avg	TD	Num	Yds	Avg	TD	Num	Yds	Avg	TD	TD	Fum
1988	New York Jets	16	0	11	5	0.0	0	2	0	0	3	0	0.0	0	0	0	-	0	0	0	-	0	0	0
1989	New York Jets	9	1	17	3	0.0	0	0	0	0	1	13	13.0	0	0	0	-	0	0	0	-	0	0	0
1990	New York Jets	13	1	22	5	0.0	0	0	0	0	0	0	-	0	0	0	-	0	0	0	-	0	0	0
1991	Philadelphia Eagles	13	1	13	11	1.0	0	1	0	0	1	24	24.0	0	0	0	-	0	0	0	-	0	0	0
1992	Philadelphia Eagles	16	11	48	49	0.0	0	1	0	0	3	22	7.3	0	0	0	-	0	1	11	11.0	0	0	0
1993	Phoenix Cardinals	12	12	59	16	3.0	0	0	0	0	2	24	12.0	0	0	0	-	0	0	0	-	0	0	0
1994	New York Giants	16	9	43	16	0.0	0	2	0	0	3	95	31.7	0	0	0	-	0	0	0	-	0	0	0
1995	Tampa Bay Buccaneers	8	2	6	3	0.0	0	0	0	0	1	21	21.0	0	0	0	-	0	0	0	-	0	0	0
	8 NFL Seasons	103	37	219	108	4.0	0	6	0	0	14	199	14.2	0	0	0	-	0	1	11	11.0	0	0	0

Other Statistics: 1995–caught 1 pass for 48 yards.

Jocelyn Borgella

Pos: CB **Rnd:** 6 **College:** Cincinnati   **Ht:** 5' 10" **Wt:** 180 **Born:** 8/26/71 **Age:** 25

Year	Team	G	GS	Tk	Ast	Sack	FF	FR	TD	Blk	Int	Yds	Avg	TD	Sfty	TD	Pts
1994	Detroit Lions	4	0	0	0	0.0	0	0	0	0	0	0	-	0	0	0	0
1995	Detroit Lions	1	0	0	0	0.0	0	0	0	0	0	0	-	0	0	0	0
	2 NFL Seasons	5	0	0	0	0.0	0	0	0	0	0	0	-	0	0	0	0

Dirk Borgognone

Pos: K **Rnd:** FA **College:** Pacific   **Ht:** 6' 2" **Wt:** 221 **Born:** 1/9/68 **Age:** 28

Year	Team	G	1-29 Yds	Pct	30-39 Yds	Pct	40-49 Yds	Pct	50+ Yds	Pct	Overall	Pct	Long	Made	Att	Pts
1995	Green Bay Packers	2	0-0	-	0-0	-	0-0	-	0-0	-	0-0	-	-	0	0	0

Tony Boselli

Pos: T **Rnd:** 1 (2) **College:** Southern California   **Ht:** 6' 7" **Wt:** 323 **Born:** 4/17/72 **Age:** 24

Year	Team	G	GS					G	GS
1995	Jacksonville Jaguars	13	12				1 NFL Season	13	12

Kirk Botkin

Pos: LS/TE **Rnd:** FA   **College:** Arkansas   **Ht:** 6' 3" **Wt:** 245 **Born:** 3/19/71 **Age:** 25

Year Team	G	GS	Rushing Att	Yds	Avg	Lg	TD	Receiving Rec	Yds	Avg	Lg	TD	Punt Returns Num	Yds	Avg	TD	Kickoff Returns Num	Yds	Avg	TD	Totals Fum	TD	Pts
1994 New Orleans Saints	3	0	0	0	-	-	0	0	0	-	-	0	0	0	-	0	0	0	-	0	0	0	0
1995 New Orleans Saints	16	0	0	0	-	-	0	1	8	8.0	8	0	0	0	-	0	0	0	-	0	0	0	0
2 NFL Seasons	19	0	0	0	-	-	0	1	8	8.0	8	0	0	0	-	0	0	0	-	0	0	0	0

Tony Bouie

Pos: S   **Rnd:** FA   **College:** Arizona   **Ht:** 5' 10" **Wt:** 187 **Born:** 8/7/72 **Age:** 24

Year Team	G	GS	Tackles Tk	Ast	Sack	Miscellaneous FF	FR	TD	Blk	Interceptions Int	Yds	Avg	TD	Totals Sfty	TD	Pts
1995 Tampa Bay Buccaneers	9	3	11	8	0.0	0	0	0	0	1	19	19.0	0	0	0	0

Marc Boutte

Pos: DT   **Rnd:** 3   **College:** Louisiana State   **Ht:** 6' 4" **Wt:** 296 **Born:** 7/26/69 **Age:** 27

Year Team	G	GS	Tackles Tk	Ast	Sack	Miscellaneous FF	FR	TD	Blk	Interceptions Int	Yds	Avg	TD	Totals Sfty	TD	Pts
1992 Los Angeles Rams	16	15	25	7	1.0	4	0	0	0	0	0	-	0	0	0	0
1993 Los Angeles Rams	16	16	29	10	1.0	0	1	0	0	0	0	-	0	0	0	0
1994 Washington Redskins	10	3	8	1	0.0	0	0	0	0	0	0	-	0	0	0	0
1995 Washington Redskins	16	16	30	12	2.0	0	1	0	0	0	0	-	0	0	0	0
4 NFL Seasons	58	50	92	30	4.0	4	2	0	0	0	0	-	0	0	0	0

Shawn Bouwens

Pos: G   **Rnd:** 9   **College:** Nebraska Wesleyan   **Ht:** 6' 5" **Wt:** 293 **Born:** 5/25/68 **Age:** 28

Year	Team	G	GS	Year	Team	G	GS	Year	Team	G	GS		G	GS
1991	Detroit Lions	16	0	1993	Detroit Lions	16	1	1995	Jacksonville Jaguars	10	9			
1992	Detroit Lions	16	16	1994	Detroit Lions	16	16					5 NFL Seasons	74	42

Other Statistics: 1992–recovered 1 fumble for 0 yards. 1994–recovered 3 fumbles for 0 yards; fumbled 1 time.

Joe Bowden

Pos: LB   **Rnd:** 5   **College:** Oklahoma   **Ht:** 5' 11" **Wt:** 230 **Born:** 2/25/70 **Age:** 26

Year Team	G	GS	Tackles Tk	Ast	Sack	Misc FF	FR	TD	Blk	Interceptions Int	Yds	Avg	TD	Punt Returns Num	Yds	Avg	TD	Kickoff Returns Num	Yds	Avg	TD	Totals TD	Fum
1992 Houston Oilers	14	0	4	5	0.0	0	0	0	0	0	0	-	0	0	0	-	0	0	0	-	0	0	0
1993 Houston Oilers	16	6	19	9	1.0	0	1	0	0	0	0	-	0	0	0	-	0	0	0	-	0	0	0
1994 Houston Oilers	13	1	7	6	0.0	0	0	0	0	0	0	-	0	0	0	-	0	0	0	-	0	0	0
1995 Houston Oilers	16	14	38	13	1.0	3	1	0	0	0	0	-	0	0	0	-	0	1	6	6.0	0	0	0
4 NFL Seasons	59	21	68	33	2.0	3	2	0	0	0	0	-	0	0	0	-	0	1	6	6.0	0	0	0

Tim Bowens

Pos: DT   **Rnd:** 1 (20)   **College:** Mississippi   **Ht:** 6' 4" **Wt:** 310 **Born:** 2/7/73 **Age:** 23

Year Team	G	GS	Tackles Tk	Ast	Sack	Miscellaneous FF	FR	TD	Blk	Interceptions Int	Yds	Avg	TD	Totals Sfty	TD	Pts
1994 Miami Dolphins	16	15	44	8	3.0	2	1	0	0	0	0	-	0	0	0	0
1995 Miami Dolphins	16	16	34	7	2.0	2	2	0	0	0	0	-	0	0	0	0
2 NFL Seasons	32	31	78	15	5.0	4	3	0	0	0	0	-	0	0	0	0

Fabien Bownes

Pos: WR   **Rnd:** FA   **College:** Western Illinois   **Ht:** 5' 11" **Wt:** 180 **Born:** 2/29/72 **Age:** 24

Year Team	G	GS	Rushing Att	Yds	Avg	Lg	TD	Receiving Rec	Yds	Avg	Lg	TD	Punt Returns Num	Yds	Avg	TD	Kickoff Returns Num	Yds	Avg	TD	Totals Fum	TD	Pts
1995 Chicago Bears	1	0	0	0	-	-	0	0	0	-	-	0	0	0	-	0	0	0	-	0	0	0	0

Stephen Boyd

Pos: LB   **Rnd:** 5   **College:** Boston College   **Ht:** 6' 1" **Wt:** 247 **Born:** 8/22/72 **Age:** 24

Year Team	G	GS	Tackles Tk	Ast	Sack	Miscellaneous FF	FR	TD	Blk	Interceptions Int	Yds	Avg	TD	Totals Sfty	TD	Pts
1995 Detroit Lions	16	0	1	0	1.0	0	0	0	0	0	0	-	0	0	0	0

Brant Boyer

Pos: LB   **Rnd:** 6   **College:** Arizona   **Ht:** 6' 1"   **Wt:** 235   **Born:** 6/27/71   **Age:** 25

Year	Team	G	GS	Tackles			Miscellaneous				Interceptions				Totals		
				Tk	Ast	Sack	FF	FR	TD	Blk	Int	Yds	Avg	TD	Sfty	TD	Pts
1994	Miami Dolphins	14	0	1	1	0.0	0	0	0	0	0	0	-	0	0	0	0
1995	Jacksonville Jaguars	2	0	0	0	0.0	0	0	0	0	0	0	-	0	0	0	0
	2 NFL Seasons	16	0	1	1	0.0	0	0	0	0	0	0	-	0	0	0	0

Deral Boykin

Pos: S   **Rnd:** 6   **College:** Louisville   **Ht:** 5' 11"   **Wt:** 198   **Born:** 9/2/70   **Age:** 26

Year	Team	G	GS	Tackles			Miscellaneous				Interceptions				Punt Returns				Kickoff Returns				Totals	
				Tk	Ast	Sack	FF	FR	TD	Blk	Int	Yds	Avg	TD	Num	Yds	Avg	TD	Num	Yds	Avg	TD	TD	Fum
1993	Los Angeles Rams	16	0	3	2	0.0	1	2	1	0	0	0	-	0	0	0	-	0	13	216	16.6	0	1	1
1994	Washington Redskins	12	0	4	3	0.0	0	0	0	0	0	0	-	0	0	0	-	0	0	0	-	0	0	0
1995	Jacksonville Jaguars	5	0	1	0	0.0	0	0	0	0	0	0	-	0	0	0	-	0	0	0	-	0	0	0
	3 NFL Seasons	33	0	8	5	0.0	1	2	1	0	0	0	-	0	0	0	-	0	13	216	16.6	0	1	1

Ronnie Bradford

Pos: CB   **Rnd:** 4   **College:** Colorado   **Ht:** 5' 10"   **Wt:** 188   **Born:** 10/1/70   **Age:** 26

Year	Team	G	GS	Tackles			Miscellaneous				Interceptions				Punt Returns				Kickoff Returns				Totals	
				Tk	Ast	Sack	FF	FR	TD	Blk	Int	Yds	Avg	TD	Num	Yds	Avg	TD	Num	Yds	Avg	TD	TD	Fum
1993	Denver Broncos	10	3	10	3	0.0	0	0	0	0	1	0	0.0	0	1	0	0.0	0	0	0	-	0	0	1
1994	Denver Broncos	12	1	20	2	1.0	0	2	0	0	0	0	-	0	0	0	-	0	0	0	-	0	0	0
1995	Denver Broncos	4	0	2	0	0.0	0	0	0	0	0	0	-	0	0	0	-	0	0	0	-	0	0	0
	3 NFL Seasons	26	4	32	5	1.0	0	2	0	0	1	0	0.0	0	1	0	0.0	0	0	0	-	0	0	1

Donny Brady

Pos: DB   **Rnd:** FA   **College:** Wisconsin   **Ht:** 6' 2"   **Wt:** 195   **Born:** 11/24/73   **Age:** 22

Year	Team	G	GS	Tackles			Miscellaneous				Interceptions				Totals		
				Tk	Ast	Sack	FF	FR	TD	Blk	Int	Yds	Avg	TD	Sfty	TD	Pts
1995	Cleveland Browns	2	0	0	0	0.0	0	0	0	0	0	0	-	0	0	0	0

Ed Brady

Pos: LS   **Rnd:** 8   **College:** Illinois   **Ht:** 6' 2"   **Wt:** 238   **Born:** 6/17/62   **Age:** 34

Year	Team	G	GS	Tackles			Miscellaneous				Interceptions				Totals		
				Tk	Ast	Sack	FF	FR	TD	Blk	Int	Yds	Avg	TD	Sfty	TD	Pts
1984	Los Angeles Rams	16	0	0	0	0.0	0	0	0	0	0	0	-	0	0	0	0
1985	Los Angeles Rams	16	0	0	0	0.0	0	1	0	0	0	0	-	0	0	0	0
1986	Cincinnati Bengals	16	0	0	0	0.0	0	0	0	0	0	0	-	0	0	0	0
1987	Cincinnati Bengals	12	0	0	0	0.0	0	1	0	0	0	0	-	0	0	0	0
1988	Cincinnati Bengals	16	0	1	0	0.0	0	0	0	0	0	0	-	0	0	0	0
1989	Cincinnati Bengals	16	0	0	0	0.0	0	0	0	0	0	0	-	0	0	0	0
1990	Cincinnati Bengals	16	0	0	0	0.0	0	1	0	0	0	0	-	0	0	0	0
1991	Cincinnati Bengals	16	0	0	0	0.0	0	0	0	0	0	0	-	0	0	0	0
1992	Tampa Bay Buccaneers	16	0	0	0	0.0	0	1	0	0	0	0	-	0	0	0	0
1993	Tampa Bay Buccaneers	16	0	0	0	0.0	0	0	0	0	0	0	-	0	0	0	0
1994	Tampa Bay Buccaneers	16	0	0	0	0.0	0	1	0	0	0	0	-	0	0	0	0
1995	Tampa Bay Buccaneers	16	0	0	0	0.0	0	0	0	0	0	0	-	0	0	0	0
	12 NFL Seasons	188	0	1	0	0.0	0	5	0	0	0	0	-	0	0	0	0

Other Statistics: 1986–fumbled 1 time for -7 yards. 1995–fumbled 1 time for -18 yards.

Jeff Brady

Pos: LB   **Rnd:** 12   **College:** Kentucky   **Ht:** 6' 1"   **Wt:** 238   **Born:** 11/9/68   **Age:** 27

Year	Team	G	GS	Tackles			Miscellaneous				Interceptions				Totals		
				Tk	Ast	Sack	FF	FR	TD	Blk	Int	Yds	Avg	TD	Sfty	TD	Pts
1991	Pittsburgh Steelers	16	0	9	2	0.0	0	0	0	0	0	0	-	0	0	0	0
1992	Green Bay Packers	8	0	3	4	0.0	0	0	0	0	0	0	-	0	0	0	0
1993	LAN - SD	9	0	0	0	0.0	0	1	0	0	0	0	-	0	0	0	0
1994	Tampa Bay Buccaneers	16	0	13	3	0.0	0	0	0	0	0	0	-	0	0	0	0
1995	Minnesota Vikings	16	7	43	11	3.0	0	2	0	0	2	7	3.5	0	0	0	0
1993	Los Angeles Rams	6	0	0	0	0.0	0	0	0	0	0	0	-	0	0	0	0
	San Diego Chargers	3	0	0	0	0.0	0	1	0	0	0	0	-	0	0	0	0
	5 NFL Seasons	65	7	68	20	3.0	0	3	0	0	2	7	3.5	0	0	0	0

Kyle Brady

(statistical profile on page 286)

Pos: TE   **Rnd:** 1 (9)   **College:** Penn State   **Ht:** 6' 6"   **Wt:** 260   **Born:** 1/14/72   **Age:** 24

			Rushing					Receiving					Punt Returns				Kickoff Returns				Totals		
Year Team	G	GS	Att	Yds	Avg	Lg	TD	Rec	Yds	Avg	Lg	TD	Num	Yds	Avg	TD	Num	Yds	Avg	TD	Fum	TD	Pts
1995 New York Jets	15	11	0	0	-	-	0	26	252	9.7	29	2	0	0	-	0	2	25	12.5	0	0	2	12

David Brandon

Pos: LB   **Rnd:** 3   **College:** Memphis   **Ht:** 6' 4"   **Wt:** 240   **Born:** 2/9/65   **Age:** 31

			Tackles			Miscellaneous				Interceptions				Totals		
Year Team	G	GS	Tk	Ast	Sack	FF	FR	TD	Blk	Int	Yds	Avg	TD	Sfty	TD	Pts
1987 San Diego Chargers	8	1	4	0	0.0	0	0	1	0	0	0	-	0	0	1	6
1988 San Diego Chargers	8	1	6	0	0.0	0	0	0	0	0	0	-	0	0	0	0
1989 San Diego Chargers	13	0	8	1	0.0	0	0	0	0	0	0	-	0	0	0	0
1991 Cleveland Browns	16	8	35	16	3.0	0	0	0	0	2	70	35.0	1	0	1	6
1992 Cleveland Browns	16	13	31	17	1.0	0	3	1	0	2	123	61.5	1	0	2	12
1993 Cle - Sea	13	3	10	12	0.0	1	0	0	0	0	0	-	0	0	0	0
1994 Seattle Seahawks	13	0	4	5	0.0	0	0	0	0	0	0	-	0	0	0	0
1995 San Diego Chargers	15	1	5	1	1.0	0	0	0	0	0	0	-	0	0	0	0
1993 Cleveland Browns	6	3	10	12	0.0	1	0	0	0	0	0	-	0	0	0	0
Seattle Seahawks	7	0	0	0	0.0	0	0	0	0	0	0	-	0	0	0	0
8 NFL Seasons	102	27	103	52	5.0	1	3	2	0	4	193	48.3	2	0	4	24

Michael Brandon

Pos: DE   **Rnd:** 12   **College:** Florida   **Ht:** 6' 4"   **Wt:** 290   **Born:** 7/30/68   **Age:** 28

			Tackles			Miscellaneous				Interceptions				Totals		
Year Team	G	GS	Tk	Ast	Sack	FF	FR	TD	Blk	Int	Yds	Avg	TD	Sfty	TD	Pts
1993 Indianapolis Colts	15	0	16	9	0.0	1	0	0	0	0	0	-	0	0	0	0
1994 Arizona Cardinals	1	0	0	0	0.0	0	0	0	0	0	0	-	0	0	0	0
1995 San Francisco 49ers	12	0	1	0	0.0	0	0	0	0	0	0	-	0	0	0	0
3 NFL Seasons	28	0	17	9	0.0	1	0	0	0	0	0	-	0	0	0	0

Chad Bratzke

Pos: LS/DE   **Rnd:** 5   **College:** Eastern Kentucky   **Ht:** 6' 4"   **Wt:** 270   **Born:** 9/15/71   **Age:** 25

			Tackles			Miscellaneous				Interceptions				Totals		
Year Team	G	GS	Tk	Ast	Sack	FF	FR	TD	Blk	Int	Yds	Avg	TD	Sfty	TD	Pts
1994 New York Giants	2	0	0	0	0.0	0	0	0	0	0	0	-	0	0	0	0
1995 New York Giants	6	0	2	3	0.0	0	0	0	0	0	0	-	0	0	0	0
2 NFL Seasons	8	0	2	3	0.0	0	0	0	0	0	0	-	0	0	0	0

Tyrone Braxton

(statistical profile on page 398)

Pos: S   **Rnd:** 12   **College:** North Dakota State   **Ht:** 5' 11"   **Wt:** 185   **Born:** 12/17/64   **Age:** 31

			Tackles			Miscellaneous				Interceptions				Punt Returns				Kickoff Returns				Totals	
Year Team	G	GS	Tk	Ast	Sack	FF	FR	TD	Blk	Int	Yds	Avg	TD	Num	Yds	Avg	TD	Num	Yds	Avg	TD	TD	Fum
1987 Denver Broncos	2	0	0	0	0.0	0	0	0	0	0	0	-	0	0	0	-	0	0	0	-	0	0	0
1988 Denver Broncos	16	0	28	11	1.0	0	1	0	0	2	6	3.0	0	0	0	-	0	0	0	-	0	0	0
1989 Denver Broncos	16	16	77	34	0.0	0	2	0	0	6	103	17.2	1	0	0	-	0	0	0	-	0	1	0
1990 Denver Broncos	3	2	11	6	0.0	0	0	0	0	1	10	10.0	0	0	0	-	0	0	0	-	0	0	0
1991 Denver Broncos	16	15	57	35	1.0	0	1	0	0	4	55	13.8	1	0	0	-	0	0	0	-	0	1	1
1992 Denver Broncos	16	14	56	43	0.0	0	0	0	0	2	54	27.0	0	0	0	-	0	0	0	-	0	0	0
1993 Denver Broncos	16	16	79	32	0.0	2	2	0	0	3	37	12.3	0	0	0	-	0	0	0	-	0	0	0
1994 Miami Dolphins	16	0	2	2	0.0	0	0	0	0	2	3	1.5	0	0	0	-	0	1	34	34.0	0	0	0
1995 Denver Broncos	16	16	70	23	0.0	1	0	0	0	2	36	18.0	0	0	0	-	0	0	0	-	0	0	0
9 NFL Seasons	117	79	380	186	2.0	3	6	0	0	22	304	13.8	2	0	0	-	0	1	34	34.0	0	2	1

Alundis Brice

Pos: CB   **Rnd:** 4   **College:** Mississippi   **Ht:** 5' 10"   **Wt:** 178   **Born:** 5/1/70   **Age:** 26

			Tackles			Miscellaneous				Interceptions				Totals		
Year Team	G	GS	Tk	Ast	Sack	FF	FR	TD	Blk	Int	Yds	Avg	TD	Sfty	TD	Pts
1995 Dallas Cowboys	11	1	7	1	0.0	0	0	0	0	1	2	2.0	0	0	0	0

Doug Brien

(statistical profile on page 469)

Pos: K   **Rnd:** 3   **College:** California   **Ht:** 5' 11"   **Wt:** 177   **Born:** 11/24/70   **Age:** 25

			Field Goals										PAT		Tot
Year Team	G	1-29 Yds	Pct	30-39 Yds	Pct	40-49 Yds	Pct	50+ Yds	Pct	Overall	Pct	Long	Made	Att	Pts
1994 San Francisco 49ers	16	5-5	100.0	5-6	83.3	5-8	62.5	0-1	0.0	15-20	75.0	48	60	62	105

			Field Goals												PAT		Tot
Year	Team	G	1-29 Yds	Pct	30-39 Yds	Pct	40-49 Yds	Pct	50+ Yds	Pct	Overall	Pct	Long	Made	Att	Pts
1995	SF - NO	14	8-8	100.0	4-7	57.1	6-12	50.0	1-2	50.0	19-29	65.5	51	35	35	92
1995	San Francisco 49ers	6	4-4	100.0	0-1	0.0	2-6	33.3	1-1	100.0	7-12	58.3	51	19	19	40
	New Orleans Saints	8	4-4	100.0	4-6	66.7	4-6	66.7	0-1	0.0	12-17	70.6	47	16	16	52
	2 NFL Seasons	30	13-13	100.0	9-13	69.2	11-20	55.0	1-3	33.3	34-49	69.4	51	95	97	197

Greg Briggs

Pos: S **Rnd:** FA **College:** Texas Southern **Ht:** 6' 3" **Wt:** 212 **Born:** 10/1/68 **Age:** 28

				Tackles			Miscellaneous				Interceptions				Totals		
Year	Team	G	GS	Tk	Ast	Sack	FF	FR	TD	Blk	Int	Yds	Avg	TD	Sfty	TD	Pts
1995	Dallas Cowboys	11	0	0	0	0.0	0	0	0	0	0	0	-	0	0	0	0

Darrick Brilz

Pos: C **Rnd:** FA **College:** Oregon State **Ht:** 6' 4" **Wt:** 287 **Born:** 2/14/64 **Age:** 32

Year	Team	G	GS	Year	Team	G	GS	Year	Team	G	GS			G	GS
1987	Washington Redskins	7	4	1990	Seattle Seahawks	16	5	1993	Seattle Seahawks	16	16				
1988	San Diego Chargers	14	0	1991	Seattle Seahawks	16	7	1994	Cincinnati Bengals	15	15				
1989	Seattle Seahawks	14	0	1992	Seattle Seahawks	16	16	1995	Cincinnati Bengals	16	16	9 NFL Seasons		130	79

Other Statistics: 1991–recovered 1 fumble for 0 yards. 1994–recovered 1 fumble for 0 yards.

Mike Brim

Pos: CB **Rnd:** 4 **College:** Virginia Union **Ht:** 6' 0" **Wt:** 192 **Born:** 1/23/66 **Age:** 30

				Tackles			Miscellaneous				Interceptions				Totals		
Year	Team	G	GS	Tk	Ast	Sack	FF	FR	TD	Blk	Int	Yds	Avg	TD	Sfty	TD	Pts
1988	Phoenix Cardinals	4	0	9	0	0.0	0	0	0	0	0	0	-	0	0	0	0
1989	Det - Min	14	0	14	-	0.0	0	0	0	0	0	0	-	0	0	0	0
1990	Minnesota Vikings	16	2	16	-	0.0	0	0	0	0	2	11	5.5	0	0	0	0
1991	New York Jets	16	12	70	-	1.0	0	1	0	0	4	52	13.0	0	0	0	0
1992	New York Jets	16	16	40	14	0.0	0	0	0	0	6	139	23.2	1	0	1	6
1993	Cincinnati Bengals	16	16	48	8	0.0	2	2	0	0	3	74	24.7	1	0	1	6
1994	Cincinnati Bengals	16	16	44	4	0.0	0	1	0	0	2	72	36.0	0	0	0	0
1995	Cincinnati Bengals	1	0	2	0	0.0	0	0	0	0	0	0	-	0	0	0	0
1989	Detroit Lions	7	0	7	0	0.0	0	0	0	0	0	0	-	0	0	0	0
	Minnesota Vikings	7	0	7	0	0.0	0	0	0	0	0	0	-	0	0	0	0
	8 NFL Seasons	99	62	243	26	1.0	2	4	0	0	17	348	20.5	2	0	2	12

Vincent Brisby

(statistical profile on page 287)

Pos: WR **Rnd:** 2 **College:** Northeast Louisiana **Ht:** 6' 2" **Wt:** 188 **Born:** 1/25/71 **Age:** 25

				Rushing					Receiving					Punt Returns				Kickoff Returns				Totals		
Year	Team	G	GS	Att	Yds	Avg	Lg	TD	Rec	Yds	Avg	Lg	TD	Num	Yds	Avg	TD	Num	Yds	Avg	TD	Fum	TD	Pts
1993	New England Patriots	16	12	0	0	-	-	0	45	626	13.9	39	2	0	0	-	0	0	0	-	0	1	2	12
1994	New England Patriots	14	11	0	0	-	-	0	58	904	15.6	43	5	0	0	-	0	0	0	-	0	1	5	30
1995	New England Patriots	16	16	0	0	-	-	0	66	974	14.8	72	3	0	0	-	0	0	0	-	0	0	3	18
	3 NFL Seasons	46	39	0	0	-	-	0	169	2504	14.8	72	10	0	0	-	0	0	0	-	0	2	10	60

Other Statistics: 1993–recovered 1 fumble for 0 yards.

Bubby Brister

(statistical profile on page 287)

Pos: QB **Rnd:** 3 **College:** Northeast Louisiana **Ht:** 6' 3" **Wt:** 207 **Born:** 8/15/62 **Age:** 34

				Passing										Rushing					Miscellaneous				
Year	Team	G	GS	Att	Com	Pct	Yards	Yds/Att	Lg	TD	Int	Int%	Rating	Att	Yds	Avg	Lg	TD	Sckd	Yds	Fum	Recv	Yds	Pts
1986	Pittsburgh Steelers	2	2	60	21	35.0	291	4.85	58	0	2	3.3	37.6	6	10	1.7	9	1	6	57	1	0	0	6
1987	Pittsburgh Steelers	2	0	12	4	33.3	20	1.67	10	0	3	25.0	2.8	0	0	-	-	0	2	14	0	0	0	0
1988	Pittsburgh Steelers	13	13	370	175	47.3	2634	7.12	t89	11	14	3.8	65.3	45	209	4.6	20	6	36	292	8	2	0	36
1989	Pittsburgh Steelers	14	14	342	187	54.7	2365	6.92	t79	9	10	2.9	73.1	27	25	0.9	15	0	45	452	4	1	0	0
1990	Pittsburgh Steelers	16	16	387	223	57.6	2725	7.04	90	20	14	3.6	81.6	25	64	2.6	11	0	28	213	9	4	-28	0
1991	Pittsburgh Steelers	8	8	190	103	54.2	1350	7.11	t65	9	9	4.7	72.9	11	17	1.5	8	0	15	145	4	2	0	0
1992	Pittsburgh Steelers	6	4	116	63	54.3	719	6.20	42	2	5	4.3	61.0	10	16	1.6	8	0	13	88	2	2	-2	0
1993	Philadelphia Eagles	10	8	309	181	58.6	1905	6.17	58	14	5	1.6	84.9	20	39	2.0	13	0	19	148	3	0	0	0
1994	Philadelphia Eagles	8	2	76	51	67.1	507	6.67	53	2	1	1.3	89.1	1	7	7.0	7	0	5	39	0	0	0	0
1995	New York Jets	9	4	170	93	54.7	726	4.27	32	4	8	4.7	53.7	16	18	1.1	7	0	16	122	4	3	-9	0
	10 NFL Seasons	88	71	2032	1101	54.2	13242	6.52	90	71	71	3.5	71.5	161	405	2.5	20	7	185	1570	35	14	-39	42

Other Statistics: 1989–caught 1 pass for -10 yards. 1995–caught 1 pass for 2 yards.

Matt Brock

(statistical profile on page 398)

Pos: DT   **Rnd:** 3   **College:** Oregon   **Ht:** 6' 5"   **Wt:** 290   **Born:** 1/14/66   **Age:** 30

Year	Team	G	GS	Tk	Ast	Sack	FF	FR	TD	Blk	Int	Yds	Avg	TD	Sfty	TD	Pts
1989	Green Bay Packers	7	0	3	0	0.0	0	0	0	0	0	0	-	0	0	0	0
1990	Green Bay Packers	16	16	35	24	4.0	0	0	0	0	0	0	-	0	0	0	0
1991	Green Bay Packers	16	16	35	22	2.5	0	0	0	0	0	0	-	0	0	0	0
1992	Green Bay Packers	16	16	38	18	4.0	0	2	0	0	0	0	-	0	0	0	0
1993	Green Bay Packers	16	13	17	10	2.0	0	1	0	0	1	0	0.0	0	0	0	0
1994	Green Bay Packers	5	0	1	1	0.0	0	0	0	0	0	0	-	0	0	0	0
1995	New York Jets	16	15	46	20	5.0	1	2	1	0	1	9	9.0	0	0	1	6
	7 NFL Seasons	92	76	175	95	17.5	1	5	1	0	2	9	4.5	0	0	1	6

Stan Brock

Pos: T   **Rnd:** 1 (12)   **College:** Colorado   **Ht:** 6' 6"   **Wt:** 295   **Born:** 6/8/58   **Age:** 38

Year	Team	G	GS	Year	Team	G	GS	Year	Team	G	GS	Year	Team	G	GS
1980	New Orleans Saints	16	12	1984	New Orleans Saints	14	14	1988	New Orleans Saints	7	7	1992	New Orleans Saints	16	16
1981	New Orleans Saints	16	16	1985	New Orleans Saints	16	16	1989	New Orleans Saints	16	16	1993	San Diego Chargers	16	16
1982	New Orleans Saints	9	9	1986	New Orleans Saints	16	16	1990	New Orleans Saints	16	16	1994	San Diego Chargers	16	16
1983	New Orleans Saints	16	16	1987	New Orleans Saints	12	12	1991	New Orleans Saints	16	16	1995	San Diego Chargers	16	9
													16 NFL Seasons	234	223

Other Statistics: 1980–recovered 1 fumble for 0 yards. 1981–recovered 2 fumbles for 0 yards; returned 2 kickoffs for 18 yards. 1983–recovered 1 fumble for 0 yards; returned 1 kickoff for 15 yards. 1985–recovered 1 fumble for 0 yards. 1987–returned 1 kickoff for 11 yards. 1989–recovered 1 fumble for 0 yards. 1990–recovered 1 fumble for 0 yards.

Blake Brockermeyer

Pos: T   **Rnd:** 1 (29)   **College:** Texas   **Ht:** 6' 4"   **Wt:** 305   **Born:** 4/11/73   **Age:** 23

Year	Team	G	GS								
1995	Carolina Panthers	16	16				1 NFL Season			16	16

Ben Bronson

Pos: PR/KR   **Rnd:** FA   **College:** Baylor   **Ht:** 5' 10"   **Wt:** 165   **Born:** 9/9/72   **Age:** 24

Year	Team	G	GS	Att	Yds	Avg	Lg	TD	Rec	Yds	Avg	Lg	TD	Num	Yds	Avg	TD	Num	Yds	Avg	TD	Fum	TD	Pts
1995	Indianapolis Colts	9	0	0	0	-	-	0	0	0	-	-	0	13	79	6.1	0	1	31	31.0	0	2	0	0

Barrett Brooks

Pos: T   **Rnd:** 2   **College:** Kansas State   **Ht:** 6' 4"   **Wt:** 309   **Born:** 5/5/72   **Age:** 24

Year	Team	G	GS								
1995	Philadelphia Eagles	16	16				1 NFL Season			16	16

Bill Brooks

(statistical profile on page 288)

Pos: WR   **Rnd:** 4   **College:** Boston University   **Ht:** 6' 0"   **Wt:** 188   **Born:** 4/6/64   **Age:** 32

Year	Team	G	GS	Att	Yds	Avg	Lg	TD	Rec	Yds	Avg	Lg	TD	Num	Yds	Avg	TD	Num	Yds	Avg	TD	Fum	TD	Pts
1986	Indianapolis Colts	16	12	4	5	1.3	12	0	65	1131	17.4	t84	8	18	141	7.8	0	8	143	17.9	0	2	8	48
1987	Indianapolis Colts	12	12	2	-2	-1.0	1	0	51	722	14.2	t52	3	22	136	6.2	0	0	0	-	0	3	3	18
1988	Indianapolis Colts	16	16	5	62	12.4	38	0	54	867	16.1	t53	3	3	15	5.0	0	0	0	-	0	1	3	18
1989	Indianapolis Colts	16	16	2	-3	-1.5	0	0	63	919	14.6	t55	4	0	0	-	0	0	0	-	0	1	4	24
1990	Indianapolis Colts	16	16	0	0	-	0	0	62	823	13.3	75	5	0	0	-	0	0	0	-	0	0	5	30
1991	Indianapolis Colts	16	16	0	0	-	0	0	72	888	12.3	46	4	0	0	-	0	0	0	-	0	0	4	24
1992	Indianapolis Colts	14	10	2	14	7.0	8	0	44	468	10.6	26	1	0	0	-	0	0	0	-	0	0	1	6
1993	Buffalo Bills	16	13	3	30	10.0	15	0	60	714	11.9	32	5	1	3	3.0	0	0	0	-	0	0	5	30
1994	Buffalo Bills	16	9	0	0	-	0	0	42	482	11.5	32	2	0	0	-	0	0	0	-	0	1	2	12
1995	Buffalo Bills	15	10	3	7	2.3	9	0	53	763	14.4	t51	11	6	35	5.8	0	0	0	-	0	0	11	66
	10 NFL Seasons	153	130	21	113	5.4	38	0	566	7777	13.7	t84	46	50	330	6.6	0	8	143	17.9	0	8	46	276

Other Statistics: 1986–recovered 1 fumble for 0 yards. 1988–recovered 2 fumbles for 0 yards. 1991–recovered 1 fumble for 0 yards. 1992–recovered 1 fumble for 0 yards.

Carlos Brooks

Pos: CB   **Rnd:** FA   **College:** Bowling Green   **Ht:** 6' 0"   **Wt:** 200   **Born:** 5/8/71   **Age:** 25

Year	Team	G	GS	Tk	Ast	Sack	FF	FR	TD	Blk	Int	Yds	Avg	TD	Sfty	TD	Pts
1995	Arizona Cardinals	7	0	8	4	0.0	0	0	0	0	0	0	-	0	0	0	0

Derrick Brooks

(statistical profile on page 398)

Pos: LB **Rnd:** 1 (28) **College:** Florida State **Ht:** 6' 0" **Wt:** 229 **Born:** 4/18/73 **Age:** 23

Year Team	G	GS	Tackles			Miscellaneous				Interceptions				Totals		
			Tk	Ast	Sack	FF	FR	TD	Blk	Int	Yds	Avg	TD	Sfty	TD	Pts
1995 Tampa Bay Buccaneers	16	13	60	19	1.0	2	0	0	0	0	0	-	0	0	0	0

Michael Brooks

(statistical profile on page 399)

Pos: LB **Rnd:** 3 **College:** Louisiana State **Ht:** 6' 1" **Wt:** 236 **Born:** 10/2/64 **Age:** 32

Year Team	G	GS	Tackles			Miscellaneous				Interceptions				Totals		
			Tk	Ast	Sack	FF	FR	TD	Blk	Int	Yds	Avg	TD	Sfty	TD	Pts
1987 Denver Broncos	12	0	5	3	1.0	1	1	0	0	0	0	-	0	0	0	0
1988 Denver Broncos	16	4	39	10	0.0	0	0	0	0	0	0	-	0	0	0	0
1989 Denver Broncos	16	16	66	57	1.0	1	2	0	0	0	0	-	0	1	0	2
1990 Denver Broncos	16	16	102	73	2.0	2	0	0	0	0	0	-	0	0	0	0
1991 Denver Broncos	14	14	96	57	0.0	0	0	0	0	2	7	3.5	0	0	0	0
1992 Denver Broncos	15	14	109	61	0.0	3	2	1	0	1	17	17.0	0	0	1	6
1993 New York Giants	13	13	73	19	1.0	2	1	0	0	0	0	-	0	0	0	0
1994 New York Giants	16	16	91	27	1.0	0	3	0	0	1	10	10.0	0	0	0	0
1995 New York Giants	16	16	95	21	1.0	0	0	0	0	0	0	-	0	0	0	0
9 NFL Seasons	134	109	676	328	7.0	9	9	1	0	4	34	8.5	0	1	1	8

Other Statistics: 1994–fumbled 1 time.

Reggie Brooks

Pos: RB **Rnd:** 2 **College:** Notre Dame **Ht:** 5' 8" **Wt:** 211 **Born:** 1/19/71 **Age:** 25

Year Team	G	GS	Rushing					Receiving					Punt Returns				Kickoff Returns				Totals		
			Att	Yds	Avg	Lg	TD	Rec	Yds	Avg	Lg	TD	Num	Yds	Avg	TD	Num	Yds	Avg	TD	Fum	TD	Pts
1993 Washington Redskins	16	11	223	1063	4.8	t85	3	21	186	8.9	43	0	0	0	-	0	1	12	12.0	0	4	3	18
1994 Washington Redskins	12	5	100	297	3.0	15	2	13	68	5.2	16	0	0	0	-	0	0	0	-	0	3	2	12
1995 Washington Redskins	1	0	2	-2	-1.0	-1	0	0	0	-	-	0	0	0	-	0	0	0	-	0	0	0	0
3 NFL Seasons	29	16	325	1358	4.2	t85	5	34	254	7.5	43	0	0	0	-	0	1	12	12.0	0	7	5	30

Other Statistics: 1993–recovered 1 fumble for 0 yards.

Robert Brooks

(statistical profile on page 288)

Pos: WR **Rnd:** 3 **College:** South Carolina **Ht:** 6' 0" **Wt:** 180 **Born:** 6/23/70 **Age:** 26

Year Team	G	GS	Rushing					Receiving					Punt Returns				Kickoff Returns				Totals		
			Att	Yds	Avg	Lg	TD	Rec	Yds	Avg	Lg	TD	Num	Yds	Avg	TD	Num	Yds	Avg	TD	Fum	TD	Pts
1992 Green Bay Packers	16	1	2	14	7.0	8	0	12	126	10.5	18	1	11	102	9.3	0	18	338	18.8	0	0	1	6
1993 Green Bay Packers	14	0	3	17	5.7	21	0	20	180	9.0	25	0	16	135	8.4	0	23	611	26.6	1	1	1	6
1994 Green Bay Packers	16	16	1	0	0.0	0	0	58	648	11.2	35	4	40	352	8.8	1	9	260	28.9	1	4	6	36
1995 Green Bay Packers	16	15	4	21	5.3	21	0	102	1497	14.7	t99	13	0	0	-	0	1	28	28.0	0	0	13	78
4 NFL Seasons	62	32	10	52	5.2	21	0	192	2451	12.8	t99	18	67	589	8.8	1	51	1237	24.3	2	5	21	126

Other Statistics: 1993–recovered 1 fumble for 0 yards. 1994–recovered 1 fumble for 0 yards.

Bern Brostek

Pos: C **Rnd:** 1 (23) **College:** Washington **Ht:** 6' 3" **Wt:** 300 **Born:** 9/11/66 **Age:** 30

Year	Team	G	GS	Year	Team	G	GS	Year	Team	G	GS			G	GS
1990	Los Angeles Rams	16	2	1992	Los Angeles Rams	16	16	1994	Los Angeles Rams	11	10				
1991	Los Angeles Rams	14	8	1993	Los Angeles Rams	16	16	1995	St. Louis Rams	16	16	6 NFL Seasons		89	68

Other Statistics: 1992–recovered 1 fumble for 0 yards. 1993–fumbled 1 time for 0 yards.

Willie Broughton

Pos: NT/DE **Rnd:** 4 **College:** Miami (FL) **Ht:** 6' 5" **Wt:** 295 **Born:** 9/9/64 **Age:** 32

Year Team	G	GS	Tackles			Miscellaneous				Interceptions				Totals		
			Tk	Ast	Sack	FF	FR	TD	Blk	Int	Yds	Avg	TD	Sfty	TD	Pts
1985 Indianapolis Colts	15	1	0	-	1.0	0	0	0	0	0	0	-	0	0	0	0
1986 Indianapolis Colts	15	8	0	-	1.0	0	1	0	0	0	0	-	0	0	0	0
1989 Dallas Cowboys	16	14	92	-	3.0	0	0	0	0	0	0	-	0	0	0	0
1990 Dallas Cowboys	4	0	0	-	0.0	0	0	0	0	0	0	-	0	0	0	0
1992 Los Angeles Raiders	16	8	47	-	1.0	0	0	0	0	0	0	-	0	0	0	0
1993 Los Angeles Raiders	15	0	8	2	1.0	0	0	0	0	0	0	-	0	0	0	0
1995 New Orleans Saints	16	11	23	8	2.0	0	0	0	0	0	0	-	0	0	0	0
7 NFL Seasons	97	42	170	10	9.0	0	1	0	0	0	0	-	0	0	0	0

Steve Broussard

Pos: RB/KR **Rnd:** 1 (20) **College:** Washington State   **Ht:** 5' 7" **Wt:** 201 **Born:** 2/22/67 **Age:** 29

Year	Team	G	GS	Rushing					Receiving					Kickoff Returns				Passing				Totals		
				Att	Yds	Avg	Lg	TD	Rec	Yds	Avg	Lg	TD	Num	Yds	Avg	TD	Att	Com	Yds	Int	Fum	TD	Pts
1990	Atlanta Falcons	13	10	126	454	3.6	t50	4	24	160	6.7	18	0	3	45	15.0	0	0	0	0	0	6	4	24
1991	Atlanta Falcons	14	5	99	449	4.5	36	4	12	120	10.0	t25	1	0	0	-	0	0	0	0	0	1	5	30
1992	Atlanta Falcons	15	1	84	363	4.3	27	1	11	96	8.7	24	1	0	0	-	0	0	0	0	0	3	2	12
1993	Atlanta Falcons	8	0	39	206	5.3	26	1	1	4	4.0	4	0	0	0	-	0	0	0	0	0	0	1	6
1994	Cincinnati Bengals	14	3	94	403	4.3	t37	2	34	218	6.4	25	0	7	115	16.4	0	1	0	0	0	5	2	14
1995	Seattle Seahawks	15	1	46	222	4.8	t21	1	10	94	9.4	25	0	43	1064	24.7	0	0	0	0	0	4	1	6
	6 NFL Seasons	79	20	488	2097	4.3	t50	13	92	692	7.5	t25	2	53	1224	23.1	0	1	0	0	0	19	15	92

Other Statistics: 1992–recovered 1 fumble for -2 yards. 1994–recovered 1 fumble for 0 yards; scored 1 two-point conversion. 1995–recovered 1 fumble for 0 yards.

Anthony Brown

Pos: T/G **Rnd:** FA **College:** Utah   **Ht:** 6' 5" **Wt:** 310 **Born:** 11/6/72 **Age:** 23

Year	Team	G	GS			G	GS
1995	Cincinnati Bengals	6	2		1 NFL Season	6	2

Chad Brown

Pos: LB **Rnd:** 2 **College:** Colorado   **Ht:** 6' 2" **Wt:** 240 **Born:** 7/12/70 **Age:** 26

Year	Team	G	GS	Tackles			Miscellaneous				Interceptions				Totals		
				Tk	Ast	Sack	FF	FR	TD	Blk	Int	Yds	Avg	TD	Sfty	TD	Pts
1993	Pittsburgh Steelers	16	9	43	26	3.0	2	0	0	0	0	0	-	0	0	0	0
1994	Pittsburgh Steelers	16	16	90	29	8.5	2	0	0	0	1	9	9.0	0	0	0	0
1995	Pittsburgh Steelers	10	10	20	10	5.5	0	0	0	0	0	0	-	0	0	0	0
	3 NFL Seasons	42	35	153	65	17.0	4	0	0	0	1	9	9.0	0	0	0	0

Chadrick Brown

Pos: DE **Rnd:** 7 **College:** Mississippi   **Ht:** 6' 7" **Wt:** 265 **Born:** 7/9/71 **Age:** 25

Year	Team	G	GS	Tackles			Miscellaneous				Interceptions				Totals		
				Tk	Ast	Sack	FF	FR	TD	Blk	Int	Yds	Avg	TD	Sfty	TD	Pts
1993	Phoenix Cardinals	5	0	1	0	0.0	0	0	0	0	0	0	-	0	0	0	0
1994	Arizona Cardinals	8	2	5	5	0.0	0	0	0	0	0	0	-	0	0	0	0
1995	Arizona Cardinals	6	4	7	7	0.5	0	0	0	0	0	0	-	0	0	0	0
	3 NFL Seasons	19	6	13	12	0.5	0	0	0	0	0	0	-	0	0	0	0

Corwin Brown

Pos: S **Rnd:** 4 **College:** Michigan   **Ht:** 6' 1" **Wt:** 200 **Born:** 4/25/70 **Age:** 26

Year	Team	G	GS	Tackles			Miscellaneous				Interceptions				Totals		
				Tk	Ast	Sack	FF	FR	TD	Blk	Int	Yds	Avg	TD	Sfty	TD	Pts
1993	New England Patriots	15	12	33	23	0.0	0	1	0	0	0	0	-	0	0	0	0
1994	New England Patriots	16	0	9	4	0.0	0	0	0	0	0	0	-	0	0	0	0
1995	New England Patriots	16	2	19	1	0.0	0	1	0	0	0	0	-	0	0	0	0
	3 NFL Seasons	47	14	61	28	0.0	0	2	0	0	0	0	-	0	0	0	0

Dave Brown

(statistical profile on page 289)

Pos: QB **Rnd:** 1(S) **College:** Duke   **Ht:** 6' 5" **Wt:** 224 **Born:** 2/25/70 **Age:** 26

Year	Team	G	GS	Passing										Rushing					Miscellaneous					
				Att	Com	Pct	Yards	Yds/Att	Lg	TD	Int	Int%	Rating	Att	Yds	Avg	Lg	TD	Sckd	Yds	Fum	Recv	Yds	Pts
1992	New York Giants	2	0	7	4	57.1	21	3.00	8	0	0	0.0	62.2	2	-1	-0.5	1	0	4	19	0	0	0	0
1993	New York Giants	1	0	0	0	-	0	-	0	0	-	0.0		3	-4	-1.3	-1	0	0	0	0	0	0	0
1994	New York Giants	15	15	350	201	57.4	2536	7.25	53	12	16	4.6	72.5	60	196	3.3	21	2	42	248	11	4	-11	12
1995	New York Giants	16	16	456	254	55.7	2814	6.17	t57	11	10	2.2	73.1	45	228	5.1	23	4	44	206	10	2	-8	24
	4 NFL Seasons	34	31	813	459	56.5	5371	6.61	t57	23	26	3.2	72.8	110	419	3.8	23	6	90	473	21	6	-19	36

Other Statistics: 1994–punted 2 times for 57 yards. 1995–punted 1 time for 15 yards.

Dennis Brown

Pos: DE **Rnd:** 2 **College:** Washington   **Ht:** 6' 4" **Wt:** 285 **Born:** 11/6/67 **Age:** 28

Year	Team	G	GS	Tackles			Miscellaneous				Interceptions				Totals		
				Tk	Ast	Sack	FF	FR	TD	Blk	Int	Yds	Avg	TD	Sfty	TD	Pts
1990	San Francisco 49ers	15	0	8	1	6.0	0	0	0	0	0	0	-	0	0	0	0
1991	San Francisco 49ers	16	4	26	12	3.0	0	0	0	0	0	0	-	0	0	0	0
1992	San Francisco 49ers	16	3	27	9	3.5	0	0	0	0	1	0	0.0	0	0	0	0
1993	San Francisco 49ers	16	16	49	9	5.5	2	0	0	0	0	0	-	0	0	0	0
1994	San Francisco 49ers	16	14	19	5	3.0	1	0	0	0	1	0	0.0	0	0	0	0
1995	San Francisco 49ers	16	16	29	8	1.5	0	2	0	0	0	0	-	0	0	0	0

Year Team	G	GS	Tk	Ast	Sack	FF	FR	TD	Blk	Int	Yds	Avg	TD	Sfty	TD	Pts
			Tackles			**Miscellaneous**				**Interceptions**				**Totals**		
6 NFL Seasons	95	53	158	44	22.5	3	2	0	0	2	0	0.0	0	0	0	0

Derek Brown

(statistical profile on page 289)

Pos: RB **Rnd:** 4 **College:** Nebraska **Ht:** 5' 9" **Wt:** 197 **Born:** 4/15/71 **Age:** 25

Year Team	G	GS	Att	Yds	Avg	Lg	TD	Rec	Yds	Avg	Lg	TD	Num	Yds	Avg	TD	Num	Yds	Avg	TD	Fum	TD	Pts
			Rushing					**Receiving**					**Punt Returns**				**Kickoff Returns**				**Totals**		
1993 New Orleans Saints	13	12	180	705	3.9	60	2	21	170	8.1	19	1	0	0	-	0	3	58	19.3	0	1	3	18
1994 New Orleans Saints	16	9	146	489	3.3	16	3	44	428	9.7	37	1	0	0	-	0	1	3	3.0	0	4	4	24
1995 New Orleans Saints	16	0	49	159	3.2	t35	1	35	266	7.6	19	1	0	0	-	0	0	0	-	0	0	2	12
3 NFL Seasons	45	21	375	1353	3.6	60	6	100	864	8.6	37	3	0	0	-	0	4	61	15.3	0	5	9	54

Other Statistics: 1994–recovered 2 fumbles for 0 yards.

Gary Brown

Pos: T **Rnd:** 5 **College:** Georgia Tech **Ht:** 6' 4" **Wt:** 315 **Born:** 6/25/71 **Age:** 25

Year	Team	G	GS	Year	Team	G	GS		G	GS
1994	Green Bay Packers	1	0	1995	Green Bay Packers	16	0	2 NFL Seasons	17	0

Gary Brown

(statistical profile on page 290)

Pos: RB **Rnd:** 8 **College:** Penn State **Ht:** 5' 11" **Wt:** 233 **Born:** 7/1/69 **Age:** 27

Year Team	G	GS	Att	Yds	Avg	Lg	TD	Rec	Yds	Avg	Lg	TD	Num	Yds	Avg	TD	Num	Yds	Avg	TD	Fum	TD	Pts
			Rushing					**Receiving**					**Punt Returns**				**Kickoff Returns**				**Totals**		
1991 Houston Oilers	11	0	8	85	10.6	t39	1	2	1	0.5	4	0	0	0	-	0	3	30	10.0	0	0	1	6
1992 Houston Oilers	16	0	19	87	4.6	26	1	1	5	5.0	5	0	0	0	-	0	1	15	15.0	0	0	1	6
1993 Houston Oilers	16	8	195	1002	5.1	26	6	21	240	11.4	t38	2	0	0	-	0	2	29	14.5	0	4	8	48
1994 Houston Oilers	12	8	169	648	3.8	18	4	18	194	10.8	24	1	0	0	-	0	0	0	-	0	6	5	30
1995 Houston Oilers	9	4	86	293	3.4	21	0	6	16	2.7	7	0	0	0	-	0	0	0	-	0	2	0	0
5 NFL Seasons	64	20	477	2115	4.4	t39	12	48	456	9.5	t38	3	0	0	-	0	6	74	12.3	0	12	15	90

Other Statistics: 1992–recovered 1 fumble for 0 yards. 1993–recovered 2 fumbles for 4 yards. 1995–recovered 1 fumble for 0 yards.

Gilbert Brown

Pos: DT/NT **Rnd:** 3 **College:** Kansas **Ht:** 6' 2" **Wt:** 325 **Born:** 2/22/71 **Age:** 25

Year Team	G	GS	Tk	Ast	Sack	FF	FR	TD	Blk	Int	Yds	Avg	TD	Sfty	TD	Pts
			Tackles			**Miscellaneous**				**Interceptions**				**Totals**		
1993 Green Bay Packers	2	0	1	0	0.0	0	0	0	0	0	0	-	0	0	0	0
1994 Green Bay Packers	13	1	25	6	3.0	0	0	0	0	0	0	-	0	0	0	0
1995 Green Bay Packers	13	7	17	6	0.0	0	0	0	0	0	0	-	0	0	0	0
3 NFL Seasons	28	8	43	12	3.0	0	0	0	0	0	0	-	0	0	0	0

J.B. Brown

Pos: CB **Rnd:** 12 **College:** Maryland **Ht:** 6' 0" **Wt:** 191 **Born:** 1/5/67 **Age:** 29

Year Team	G	GS	Tk	Ast	Sack	FF	FR	TD	Blk	Int	Yds	Avg	TD	Sfty	TD	Pts
			Tackles			**Miscellaneous**				**Interceptions**				**Totals**		
1989 Miami Dolphins	16	0	7	2	0.0	0	0	0	0	0	0	-	0	0	0	0
1990 Miami Dolphins	16	16	43	5	1.0	0	0	0	0	0	0	-	0	0	0	0
1991 Miami Dolphins	15	11	50	5	0.0	0	0	0	0	1	0	0.0	0	0	0	0
1992 Miami Dolphins	16	16	48	8	0.0	0	1	0	0	4	119	29.8	1	0	1	6
1993 Miami Dolphins	16	16	60	12	0.0	1	0	0	0	5	43	8.6	0	0	0	0
1994 Miami Dolphins	16	16	66	10	0.0	1	0	0	0	3	82	27.3	0	0	0	0
1995 Miami Dolphins	13	12	44	3	0.0	2	2	0	0	2	20	10.0	0	0	0	0
7 NFL Seasons	108	87	318	45	1.0	4	3	0	0	15	264	17.6	1	0	1	6

Other Statistics: 1993–fumbled 1 time for 0 yards. 1995–fumbled 1 time.

James Brown

Pos: T **Rnd:** 3 **College:** Virginia State **Ht:** 6' 6" **Wt:** 329 **Born:** 1/3/70 **Age:** 26

Year	Team	G	GS	Year	Team	G	GS	Year	Team	G	GS		G	GS
1993	New York Jets	13	1	1994	New York Jets	16	6	1995	New York Jets	14	12	3 NFL Seasons	43	19

Other Statistics: 1994–recovered 1 fumble for 0 yards.

Jamie Brown

Pos: T **Rnd:** 4 **College:** Florida A&M **Ht:** 6' 8" **Wt:** 320 **Born:** 4/24/72 **Age:** 24

Year	Team	G	GS						G	GS
1995	Denver Broncos	6	0					1 NFL Season	6	0

Ken Brown

Pos: LB **Rnd:** 4 **College:** Virginia Tech **Ht:** 6' 1" **Wt:** 235 **Born:** 5/5/71 **Age:** 25

Year Team	G	GS	Tackles Tk	Ast	Sack	Misc. FF	FR	TD	Blk	Int Int	Yds	Avg	TD	Totals Sfty	TD	Pts
1995 Denver Broncos	2	0	0	0	0.0	0	0	0	0	0	0	-	0	0	0	0

Lance Brown

Pos: DB/CB **Rnd:** 5 **College:** Indiana **Ht:** 6' 0" **Wt:** 200 **Born:** 2/2/72 **Age:** 24

Year Team	G	GS	Tackles Tk	Ast	Sack	Misc. FF	FR	TD	Blk	Int Int	Yds	Avg	TD	Totals Sfty	TD	Pts
1995 Arizona Cardinals	11	5	22	3	0.0	0	1	0	0	0	0	-	0	0	0	0

Larry Brown

(statistical profile on page 399)

Pos: CB **Rnd:** 12 **College:** Texas Christian **Ht:** 5' 11" **Wt:** 186 **Born:** 11/30/69 **Age:** 26

Year Team	G	GS	Tackles Tk	Ast	Sack	Misc. FF	FR	TD	Blk	Int Int	Yds	Avg	TD	Totals Sfty	TD	Pts
1991 Dallas Cowboys	16	13	55	13	0.0	0	1	0	0	2	31	15.5	0	0	0	0
1992 Dallas Cowboys	16	15	45	16	0.0	0	1	0	0	1	30	30.0	0	0	0	0
1993 Dallas Cowboys	16	16	46	17	0.0	1	0	0	0	0	0	-	0	0	0	0
1994 Dallas Cowboys	15	15	43	8	0.0	0	0	0	0	4	21	5.3	0	0	0	0
1995 Dallas Cowboys	16	15	43	4	0.0	0	0	0	0	6	124	20.7	2	0	2	12
5 NFL Seasons	79	74	232	58	0.0	1	2	0	0	13	206	15.8	2	0	2	12

Lomas Brown

Pos: T **Rnd:** 1 (6) **College:** Florida **Ht:** 6' 4" **Wt:** 275 **Born:** 3/30/63 **Age:** 33

Year	Team	G	GS	Year	Team	G	GS	Year	Team	G	GS	Year	Team	G	GS
1985	Detroit Lions	16	16	1988	Detroit Lions	16	16	1991	Detroit Lions	15	15	1994	Detroit Lions	16	16
1986	Detroit Lions	16	16	1989	Detroit Lions	16	16	1992	Detroit Lions	16	16	1995	Detroit Lions	15	14
1987	Detroit Lions	11	11	1990	Detroit Lions	16	16	1993	Detroit Lions	11	11		11 NFL Seasons	164	163

Other Statistics: 1989–recovered 1 fumble for 0 yards; rushed 1 time for 3 yards. 1991–recovered 1 fumble for 0 yards.

Monty Brown

Pos: LB **Rnd:** FA **College:** Ferris State **Ht:** 6' 0" **Wt:** 233 **Born:** 4/13/70 **Age:** 26

Year Team	G	GS	Tackles Tk	Ast	Sack	Misc. FF	FR	TD	Blk	Int Int	Yds	Avg	TD	Totals Sfty	TD	Pts
1993 Buffalo Bills	13	0	2	1	0.0	0	0	0	0	0	0	-	0	0	0	0
1994 Buffalo Bills	3	0	0	0	0.0	0	0	0	0	0	0	-	0	0	0	0
1995 Buffalo Bills	16	6	45	24	0.0	0	0	0	0	0	0	-	0	0	0	0
3 NFL Seasons	32	6	47	25	0.0	0	0	0	0	0	0	-	0	0	0	0

Orlando Brown

Pos: T **Rnd:** FA **College:** South Carolina State **Ht:** 6' 7" **Wt:** 340 **Born:** 12/12/70 **Age:** 25

Year	Team	G	GS	Year	Team	G	GS							G	GS
1994	Cleveland Browns	14	8	1995	Cleveland Browns	16	16						2 NFL Seasons	30	24

Other Statistics: 1995–recovered 1 fumble for 0 yards.

Ray Brown

Pos: G **Rnd:** 8 **College:** Arkansas State **Ht:** 6' 5" **Wt:** 312 **Born:** 12/12/62 **Age:** 33

Year	Team	G	GS	Year	Team	G	GS	Year	Team	G	GS	Year	Team	G	GS
1986	St. Louis Cardinals	11	4	1988	Phoenix Cardinals	15	1	1992	Washington Redskins	16	8	1994	Washington Redskins	16	15
1987	St. Louis Cardinals	7	3	1989	Washington Redskins	7	0	1993	Washington Redskins	16	14	1995	Washington Redskins	16	16
													8 NFL Seasons	104	61

Richard Brown

Pos: LB **Rnd:** FA **College:** San Diego State **Ht:** 6' 3" **Wt:** 240 **Born:** 9/21/65 **Age:** 31

Year Team	G	GS	Tk	Ast	Sack	FF	FR	TD	Blk	Int	Yds	Avg	TD	Num	Yds	Avg	TD	Num	Yds	Avg	TD	TD	Fum
1987 Los Angeles Rams	8	0	2	0	0.0	0	0	0	0	0	0	-	0	0	0	-	0	1	15	15.0	0	0	0
1989 Los Angeles Rams	13	2	14	-	0.0	0	2	0	0	0	0	-	0	0	0	-	0	0	0	-	0	0	0
1990 San Diego Chargers	11	0	5	0	0.0	0	1	0	0	0	0	-	0	0	0	-	0	0	0	-	0	0	0
1991 Cleveland Browns	16	12	77	49	0.5	1	0	0	0	1	19	19.0	0	0	0	-	0	0	0	-	0	0	0
1992 Cleveland Browns	10	0	5	2	1.0	0	1	0	0	0	0	-	0	0	0	-	0	0	0	-	0	0	0
1994 Minnesota Vikings	3	0	0	0	0.0	0	1	0	0	0	0	-	0	0	0	-	0	0	0	-	0	0	0
1995 Minnesota Vikings	16	0	3	0	0.0	0	0	0	0	0	0	-	0	0	0	-	0	0	0	-	0	0	0
7 NFL Seasons	77	14	106	51	1.5	0	5	0	0	1	19	19.0	0	0	0	-	0	1	15	15.0	0	0	0

Ruben Brown

Pos: G   **Rnd:** 1 (14)   **College:** Pittsburgh   **Ht:** 6' 3"   **Wt:** 304   **Born:** 2/13/72   **Age:** 24

Year	Team	G	GS					G	GS
1995	Buffalo Bills	16	16			1 NFL Season		16	16

Tim Brown

(statistical profile on page 290)

Pos: WR/PR   **Rnd:** 1 (6)   **College:** Notre Dame   **Ht:** 6' 0"   **Wt:** 195   **Born:** 7/22/66   **Age:** 30

Year	Team	G	GS	Rushing					Receiving					Punt Returns				Kickoff Returns				Totals		
				Att	Yds	Avg	Lg	TD	Rec	Yds	Avg	Lg	TD	Num	Yds	Avg	TD	Num	Yds	Avg	TD	Fum	TD	Pts
1988	Los Angeles Raiders	16	9	14	50	3.6	12	1	43	725	16.9	t65	5	49	444	9.1	0	41	1098	26.8	1	5	7	42
1989	Los Angeles Raiders	1	1	0	0	-	-	0	1	8	8.0	8	0	4	43	10.8	0	3	63	21.0	0	1	0	0
1990	Los Angeles Raiders	16	9	0	0	-	-	0	18	265	14.7	51	3	34	295	8.7	0	0	0	-	0	3	3	18
1991	Los Angeles Raiders	16	1	5	16	3.2	9	0	36	554	15.4	t78	5	29	330	11.4	1	1	29	29.0	0	1	6	36
1992	Los Angeles Raiders	15	12	3	-4	-1.3	3	0	49	693	14.1	t68	7	37	383	10.4	0	2	14	7.0	0	6	7	42
1993	Los Angeles Raiders	16	16	2	7	3.5	14	0	80	1180	14.8	t71	7	40	465	11.6	1	0	0	-	0	1	8	48
1994	Los Angeles Raiders	16	16	0	0	-	-	0	89	1309	14.7	t77	9	40	**487**	12.2	0	0	0	-	0	3	9	54
1995	Oakland Raiders	16	16	0	0	-	-	0	89	1342	15.1	t80	10	36	364	10.1	0	0	0	-	0	0	10	60
	8 NFL Seasons	112	80	24	69	2.9	14	1	405	6076	15.0	t80	46	269	2811	10.4	2	47	1204	25.6	1	20	50	300

Other Statistics: 1988–recovered 7 fumbles for 0 yards. 1992–recovered 1 fumble for 0 yards. 1995–recovered 1 fumble for 3 yards.

Tony Brown

Pos: CB   **Rnd:** 5   **College:** Fresno State   **Ht:** 5' 9"   **Wt:** 183   **Born:** 5/15/70   **Age:** 26

Year	Team	G	GS	Tackles			Miscellaneous				Interceptions				Totals		
				Tk	Ast	Sack	FF	FR	TD	Blk	Int	Yds	Avg	TD	Sfty	TD	Pts
1992	Houston Oilers	12	1	6	3	0.0	0	0	0	0	0	0	-	0	0	0	0
1993	Houston Oilers	16	0	4	0	0.0	0	0	0	0	0	0	-	0	0	0	0
1994	Seattle Seahawks	13	5	30	11	0.0	1	0	0	0	0	0	-	0	0	0	0
1995	Seattle Seahawks	16	0	15	0	0.0	0	0	0	0	0	0	-	0	0	0	0
	4 NFL Seasons	57	6	55	14	0.0	1	0	0	0	0	0	-	0	0	0	0

Troy Brown

Pos: KR/WR   **Rnd:** 8   **College:** Marshall   **Ht:** 5' 9"   **Wt:** 190   **Born:** 7/2/71   **Age:** 25

Year	Team	G	GS	Rushing					Receiving					Punt Returns				Kickoff Returns				Totals		
				Att	Yds	Avg	Lg	TD	Rec	Yds	Avg	Lg	TD	Num	Yds	Avg	TD	Num	Yds	Avg	TD	Fum	TD	Pts
1993	New England Patriots	12	0	0	0	-	-	0	2	22	11.0	14	0	25	224	9.0	0	15	243	16.2	0	2	0	0
1994	New England Patriots	9	0	0	0	-	-	0	0	0	-	-	0	24	202	8.4	0	1	14	14.0	0	2	0	0
1995	New England Patriots	16	0	0	0	-	-	0	14	159	11.4	31	0	0	0	-	0	31	672	21.7	0	1	1	6
	3 NFL Seasons	37	0	0	0	-	-	0	16	181	11.3	31	0	49	426	8.7	0	47	929	19.8	0	5	1	6

Other Statistics: 1993–recovered 1 fumble for 0 yards. 1994–recovered 2 fumbles for 0 yards. 1995–recovered 1 fumble for 75 yards and 1 touchdown.

Tyrone Brown

Pos: WR   **Rnd:** FA   **College:** Toledo   **Ht:** 5' 11"   **Wt:** 164   **Born:** 1/3/73   **Age:** 23

Year	Team	G	GS	Rushing					Receiving					Punt Returns				Kickoff Returns				Totals		
				Att	Yds	Avg	Lg	TD	Rec	Yds	Avg	Lg	TD	Num	Yds	Avg	TD	Num	Yds	Avg	TD	Fum	TD	Pts
1995	Atlanta Falcons	6	5	0	0	-	-	0	17	198	11.6	26	0	0	0	-	0	0	0	-	0	1	0	0

Vincent Brown

(statistical profile on page 399)

Pos: LB   **Rnd:** 2   **College:** Mississippi Valley State   **Ht:** 6' 2"   **Wt:** 245   **Born:** 1/9/65   **Age:** 31

Year	Team	G	GS	Tackles			Miscellaneous				Interceptions				Totals		
				Tk	Ast	Sack	FF	FR	TD	Blk	Int	Yds	Avg	TD	Sfty	TD	Pts
1988	New England Patriots	16	3	21	14	0.0	0	0	0	0	0	0	-	0	0	0	0
1989	New England Patriots	14	10	47	31	4.0	1	2	0	0	1	-1	-1.0	0	0	0	0
1990	New England Patriots	16	14	57	30	2.5	1	0	0	0	0	0	-	0	0	0	0
1991	New England Patriots	16	15	96	21	3.0	2	1	0	0	0	0	-	0	0	0	0
1992	New England Patriots	13	13	78	25	0.5	0	2	1	0	1	49	49.0	1	0	2	12
1993	New England Patriots	16	16	104	54	1.0	1	0	0	0	1	24	24.0	0	0	0	0
1994	New England Patriots	16	16	82	36	1.5	0	1	0	0	3	22	7.3	0	0	0	0
1995	New England Patriots	16	16	77	38	4.0	1	1	0	0	4	1	0.3	0	0	0	0
	8 NFL Seasons	123	103	562	249	16.5	6	7	1	0	10	95	9.5	1	0	2	12

Darrick Brownlow

Pos: LB   **Rnd:** 5   **College:** Illinois   **Ht:** 6' 0"   **Wt:** 260   **Born:** 12/28/68   **Age:** 27

Year	Team	G	GS	Tackles			Miscellaneous				Interceptions				Punt Returns				Kickoff Returns				Totals	
				Tk	Ast	Sack	FF	FR	TD	Blk	Int	Yds	Avg	TD	Num	Yds	Avg	TD	Num	Yds	Avg	TD	TD	Fum
1991	Dallas Cowboys	16	0	3	1	0.0	0	0	0	0	0	0	-	0	1	0	0.0	0	0	0	-	0	0	0
1992	Tampa Bay Buccaneers	16	4	14	6	0.0	0	0	0	0	0	0	-	0	0	0	-	0	0	0	-	0	0	0

Year Team	G	GS	Tackles			Miscellaneous				Interceptions				Punt Returns				Kickoff Returns				Totals	
			Tk	Ast	Sack	FF	FR	TD	Blk	Int	Yds	Avg	TD	Num	Yds	Avg	TD	Num	Yds	Avg	TD	TD	Fum
1993 Tampa Bay Buccaneers	15	0	1	8	0.0	0	0	0	0	0	0	-	0	0	0	-	0	0	0	-	0	0	0
1994 Dallas Cowboys	16	0	6	1	0.0	0	0	0	0	0	0	-	0	0	0	-	0	0	0	-	0	0	0
1995 Washington Redskins	16	0	0	0	0.0	0	0	0	1	0	0	-	0	0	0	-	0	0	0	-	0	0	0
5 NFL Seasons	79	4	24	16	0.0	0	0	0	1	0	0	-	0	1	0	0.0	0	0	0	-	0	0	0

Aundray Bruce

Pos: DE **Rnd:** 1 (1) **College:** Auburn **Ht:** 6' 5" **Wt:** 265 **Born:** 4/30/66 **Age:** 30

Year Team	G	GS	Tackles			Miscellaneous				Interceptions				Punt Returns				Kickoff Returns				Totals	
			Tk	Ast	Sack	FF	FR	TD	Blk	Int	Yds	Avg	TD	Num	Yds	Avg	TD	Num	Yds	Avg	TD	TD	Fum
1988 Atlanta Falcons	16	16	70	-	6.0	2	1	0	0	2	10	5.0	0	0	0	-	0	0	0	-	0	0	0
1989 Atlanta Falcons	16	13	66	-	6.0	2	0	0	0	1	0	0.0	0	0	0	-	0	1	15	15.0	0	0	0
1990 Atlanta Falcons	16	3	40	-	4.0	4	0	0	0	0	0	-	0	0	0	-	0	0	0	-	0	0	0
1991 Atlanta Falcons	14	3	0	0	0.0	0	0	0	0	0	0	-	0	0	0	-	0	0	0	-	0	0	0
1992 Los Angeles Raiders	16	4	23	-	3.5	0	0	0	0	0	0	-	0	0	0	-	0	0	0	-	0	0	0
1993 Los Angeles Raiders	16	0	10	1	2.0	0	1	0	0	0	0	-	0	0	0	-	0	0	0	-	0	0	0
1994 Los Angeles Raiders	16	0	4	1	0.0	0	0	0	0	0	0	-	0	0	0	-	0	0	0	-	0	0	0
1995 Oakland Raiders	14	0	25	5	5.5	1	0	0	0	1	1	1.0	1	0	0	-	0	0	0	-	0	1	0
8 NFL Seasons	124	39	238	7	27.0	9	2	0	0	4	11	2.8	1	0	0	-	0	1	15	15.0	0	1	0

Other Statistics: 1991–caught 1 pass for 11 yards.

Isaac Bruce

(statistical profile on page 291)

Pos: WR **Rnd:** 2 **College:** Memphis **Ht:** 6' 0" **Wt:** 178 **Born:** 11/10/72 **Age:** 23

Year Team	G	GS	Rushing					Receiving					Punt Returns				Kickoff Returns				Totals		
			Att	Yds	Avg	Lg	TD	Rec	Yds	Avg	Lg	TD	Num	Yds	Avg	TD	Num	Yds	Avg	TD	Fum	TD	Pts
1994 Los Angeles Rams	12	0	1	2	2.0	2	0	21	272	13.0	t34	3	0	0	-	0	0	0	-	0	0	3	18
1995 St. Louis Rams	16	16	3	17	5.7	12	0	119	1781	15.0	72	13	0	52	-	0	0	0	-	0	2	13	80
2 NFL Seasons	28	16	4	19	4.8	12	0	140	2053	14.7	72	16	0	52	-	0	0	0	-	0	2	16	98

Other Statistics: 1995–recovered 1 fumble for 0 yards; scored 1 two-point conversion.

Mark Bruener

(statistical profile on page 291)

Pos: TE **Rnd:** 1 (27) **College:** Washington **Ht:** 6' 4" **Wt:** 250 **Born:** 9/16/72 **Age:** 24

Year Team	G	GS	Rushing					Receiving					Punt Returns				Kickoff Returns				Totals		
			Att	Yds	Avg	Lg	TD	Rec	Yds	Avg	Lg	TD	Num	Yds	Avg	TD	Num	Yds	Avg	TD	Fum	TD	Pts
1995 Pittsburgh Steelers	16	13	0	0	-	-	0	26	238	9.2	29	3	0	0	-	0	2	19	9.5	0	0	3	18

Scott Brumfield

Pos: G/T **Rnd:** FA **College:** Brigham Young **Ht:** 6' 8" **Wt:** 320 **Born:** 8/19/70 **Age:** 26

Year Team	G	GS	Year Team	G	GS	Year Team	G	GS		G	GS
1993 Cincinnati Bengals	16	7	1994 Cincinnati Bengals	2	0	1995 Cincinnati Bengals	13	11	3 NFL Seasons	31	18

Mark Brunell

(statistical profile on page 292)

Pos: QB **Rnd:** 5 **College:** Washington **Ht:** 6' 0" **Wt:** 217 **Born:** 9/17/70 **Age:** 26

Year Team	G	GS	Passing										Rushing				Miscellaneous			
			Att	Com	Pct	Yards	Yds/Att	Lg	TD	Int	Int%	Rating	Att	Yds	Avg	Lg	TD	Sckd	Yds	Fum Recv	Yds	Pts
1994 Green Bay Packers	2	0	27	12	44.4	95	3.52	25	0	0	0.0	53.8	6	7	1.2	t5	1	2	16	1	0	6
1995 Jacksonville Jaguars	13	10	346	201	58.1	2168	6.27	45	15	7	2.0	82.6	67	480	7.2	t27	4	39	238	5	3	0	24
2 NFL Seasons	15	10	373	213	57.1	2263	6.07	45	15	7	1.9	80.5	73	487	6.7	t27	5	41	254	6	3	0	30

Junior Bryant

Pos: DE/DT **Rnd:** FA **College:** Notre Dame **Ht:** 6' 4" **Wt:** 275 **Born:** 1/16/71 **Age:** 25

Year Team	G	GS	Tackles			Miscellaneous				Interceptions				Totals		
			Tk	Ast	Sack	FF	FR	TD	Blk	Int	Yds	Avg	TD	Sfty	TD	Pts
1995 San Francisco 49ers	16	4	26	1	1.0	1	0	0	0	0	0	-	0	0	0	0

Ray Buchanan

(statistical profile on page 400)

Pos: CB/PR **Rnd:** 3 **College:** Louisville **Ht:** 5' 9" **Wt:** 189 **Born:** 9/29/71 **Age:** 25

Year Team	G	GS	Tackles			Miscellaneous				Interceptions				Punt Returns				Kickoff Returns				Totals	
			Tk	Ast	Sack	FF	FR	TD	Blk	Int	Yds	Avg	TD	Num	Yds	Avg	TD	Num	Yds	Avg	TD	TD	Fum
1993 Indianapolis Colts	16	5	44	21	0.0	0	0	0	0	4	45	11.3	0	0	0	-	0	0	0	-	0	0	0
1994 Indianapolis Colts	16	16	76	24	1.0	0	1	0	0	8	221	27.6	3	0	0	-	0	0	0	-	0	3	0
1995 Indianapolis Colts	16	16	68	15	1.0	0	2	0	0	2	60	30.0	0	16	113	7.1	0	1	22	22.0	0	0	1
3 NFL Seasons	48	37	188	60	2.0	0	3	0	0	14	326	23.3	3	16	113	7.1	0	1	22	22.0	0	3	1

Mike Buck

Pos: QB **Rnd:** 6 **College:** Maine **Ht:** 6' 3" **Wt:** 227 **Born:** 4/22/67 **Age:** 29

Year	Team	G	GS	Passing										Rushing					Miscellaneous				
				Att	Com	Pct	Yards	Yds/Att	Lg	TD	Int	Int%	Rating	Att	Yds	Avg	Lg	TD	Sckd	Yds	Fum	Recv	Yds	Pts
1991	New Orleans Saints	2	0	2	1	50.0	61	30.50	61	0	1	50.0	56.3	0	0	-	-	0	0	0	0	0	0	0
1992	New Orleans Saints	2	0	4	2	50.0	10	2.50	10	0	0	0.0	56.3	3	-4	-1.3	-1	0	0	0	0	0	0	0
1993	New Orleans Saints	4	1	54	32	59.3	448	8.30	t63	4	3	5.6	87.6	1	0	0.0	0	0	3	17	2	0	-8	0
1995	Arizona Cardinals	6	0	32	20	62.5	271	8.47	28	1	0	0.0	99.9	1	0	0.0	0	0	2	10	1	1	0	0
	4 NFL Seasons	14	1	92	55	59.8	790	8.59	t63	5	4	4.3	87.7	5	-4	-0.8	0	0	5	27	3	1	-8	0

Vince Buck

(statistical profile on page 400)

Pos: S **Rnd:** 2 **College:** Central State **Ht:** 6' 0" **Wt:** 198 **Born:** 1/12/68 **Age:** 28

Year	Team	G	GS	Tackles			Miscellaneous				Interceptions				Punt Returns				Kickoff Returns				Totals	
				Tk	Ast	Sack	FF	FR	TD	Blk	Int	Yds	Avg	TD	Num	Yds	Avg	TD	Num	Yds	Avg	TD	TD	Fum
1990	New Orleans Saints	16	1	35	3	0.0	0	2	0	0	0	0	-	0	37	305	8.2	0	3	38	12.7	0	0	2
1991	New Orleans Saints	13	13	43	2	0.0	0	3	0	0	5	12	2.4	0	31	260	8.4	0	0	0	-	0	0	0
1992	New Orleans Saints	10	5	27	7	0.5	0	0	0	0	2	51	25.5	1	2	4	2.0	0	0	0	-	0	1	0
1993	New Orleans Saints	16	16	59	14	3.0	1	2	0	0	2	28	14.0	0	0	0	-	0	0	0	-	0	0	0
1994	New Orleans Saints	16	16	65	23	1.0	0	1	0	0	1	0	0.0	0	0	0	-	0	0	0	-	0	0	0
1995	New Orleans Saints	13	13	51	15	0.0	0	4	0	0	0	0	-	0	0	0	-	0	0	0	-	0	0	1
	6 NFL Seasons	84	64	280	64	4.5	1	12	0	0	10	91	9.1	1	70	569	8.1	0	3	38	12.7	0	1	3

Curtis Buckley

Pos: S **Rnd:** FA **College:** East Texas State **Ht:** 6' 0" **Wt:** 191 **Born:** 9/25/70 **Age:** 26

Year	Team	G	GS	Tackles			Miscellaneous				Interceptions				Punt Returns				Kickoff Returns				Totals	
				Tk	Ast	Sack	FF	FR	TD	Blk	Int	Yds	Avg	TD	Num	Yds	Avg	TD	Num	Yds	Avg	TD	TD	Fum
1993	Tampa Bay Buccaneers	10	2	0	0	0.0	0	0	0	0	0	0	-	0	0	0	-	0	0	0	-	0	0	0
1994	Tampa Bay Buccaneers	13	0	0	0	0.0	0	2	0	0	0	0	-	0	0	0	-	0	8	177	22.1	0	0	1
1995	Tampa Bay Buccaneers	15	0	0	0	0.0	0	0	0	2	0	0	-	0	0	0	-	0	2	29	14.5	0	0	0
	3 NFL Seasons	38	2	0	0	0.0	0	2	0	2	0	0	-	0	0	0	-	0	10	206	20.6	0	0	1

Marcus Buckley

Pos: LB **Rnd:** 3 **College:** Texas A&M **Ht:** 6' 3" **Wt:** 240 **Born:** 2/3/71 **Age:** 25

Year	Team	G	GS	Tackles			Miscellaneous				Interceptions				Totals		
				Tk	Ast	Sack	FF	FR	TD	Blk	Int	Yds	Avg	TD	Sfty	TD	Pts
1993	New York Giants	16	2	9	2	0.0	0	1	0	0	0	0	-	0	0	0	0
1994	New York Giants	16	1	11	4	0.0	0	0	0	0	0	0	-	0	0	0	0
1995	New York Giants	16	5	14	6	0.0	1	1	0	0	0	0	-	0	0	0	0
	3 NFL Seasons	48	8	34	12	0.0	1	2	0	0	0	0	-	0	0	0	0

Terrell Buckley

Pos: CB **Rnd:** 1 (5) **College:** Florida State **Ht:** 5' 9" **Wt:** 178 **Born:** 6/7/71 **Age:** 25

Year	Team	G	GS	Tackles			Miscellaneous				Interceptions				Punt Returns				Kickoff Returns				Totals	
				Tk	Ast	Sack	FF	FR	TD	Blk	Int	Yds	Avg	TD	Num	Yds	Avg	TD	Num	Yds	Avg	TD	TD	Fum
1992	Green Bay Packers	14	12	30	2	0.0	0	4	0	0	3	33	11.0	0	21	211	10.0	1	0	0	-	0	2	7
1993	Green Bay Packers	16	16	47	1	0.0	0	0	0	0	2	31	15.5	0	11	76	6.9	0	0	0	-	0	0	1
1994	Green Bay Packers	16	16	48	11	0.0	3	1	0	0	5	38	7.6	0	0	0	-	0	0	0	-	0	0	0
1995	Miami Dolphins	16	4	23	3	0.0	0	0	0	0	1	0	0.0	0	0	0	-	0	1	16	16.0	0	0	0
	4 NFL Seasons	62	48	148	17	0.0	3	5	0	0	11	102	9.3	1	32	287	9.0	1	1	16	16.0	0	2	8

Brentson Buckner

Pos: DE/NT **Rnd:** 2 **College:** Clemson **Ht:** 6' 2" **Wt:** 310 **Born:** 9/30/71 **Age:** 25

Year	Team	G	GS	Tackles			Miscellaneous				Interceptions				Totals		
				Tk	Ast	Sack	FF	FR	TD	Blk	Int	Yds	Avg	TD	Sfty	TD	Pts
1994	Pittsburgh Steelers	12	5	13	5	2.0	0	1	0	1	0	0	-	0	0	0	0
1995	Pittsburgh Steelers	16	16	29	19	3.0	1	1	1	0	0	0	-	0	0	1	6
	2 NFL Seasons	28	21	42	24	5.0	1	2	1	1	0	0	-	0	0	1	6

Todd Burger

Pos: G **Rnd:** FA **College:** Penn State **Ht:** 6' 3" **Wt:** 301 **Born:** 3/20/70 **Age:** 26

Year	Team	G	GS	Year	Team	G	GS		G	GS
1994	Chicago Bears	4	0	1995	Chicago Bears	16	1	2 NFL Seasons	20	1

John Burke

Pos: TE **Rnd:** 4 **College:** Virginia Tech **Ht:** 6' 2" **Wt:** 258 **Born:** 9/7/71 **Age:** 25

			Rushing					Receiving					Punt Returns				Kickoff Returns				Totals		
Year Team	G	GS	Att	Yds	Avg	Lg	TD	Rec	Yds	Avg	Lg	TD	Num	Yds	Avg	TD	Num	Yds	Avg	TD	Fum	TD	Pts
1994 New England Patriots	16	6	0	0	-	-	0	9	86	9.6	17	0	0	0	-	0	3	11	3.7	0	0	0	0
1995 New England Patriots	16	4	0	0	-	-	0	15	136	9.1	21	0	0	0	-	0	1	7	7.0	0	0	0	0
2 NFL Seasons	32	10	0	0	-	-	0	24	222	9.3	21	0	0	0	-	0	4	18	4.5	0	0	0	0

Other Statistics: 1995–recovered 1 fumble for 0 yards.

Rob Burnett

(statistical profile on page 400)

Pos: DE **Rnd:** 5 **College:** Syracuse **Ht:** 6' 4" **Wt:** 280 **Born:** 8/27/67 **Age:** 29

			Tackles			Miscellaneous				Interceptions				Totals		
Year Team	G	GS	Tk	Ast	Sack	FF	FR	TD	Blk	Int	Yds	Avg	TD	Sfty	TD	Pts
1990 Cleveland Browns	16	6	38	19	2.0	0	0	0	0	0	0	-	0	0	0	0
1991 Cleveland Browns	13	8	17	14	3.0	0	1	0	0	0	0	-	0	0	0	0
1992 Cleveland Browns	16	16	37	23	9.0	0	2	0	0	0	0	-	0	0	0	0
1993 Cleveland Browns	16	16	39	37	9.0	0	2	0	0	0	0	-	0	0	0	0
1994 Cleveland Browns	16	16	41	13	10.0	2	1	0	0	0	0	-	0	0	0	0
1995 Cleveland Browns	16	16	40	15	7.5	0	1	0	2	0	0	-	0	0	0	0
6 NFL Seasons	93	78	212	121	40.5	2	7	0	2	0	0	-	0	0	0	0

Jason Burns

Pos: RB **Rnd:** FA **College:** Wisconsin **Ht:** 5' 7" **Wt:** 185 **Born:** 11/27/72 **Age:** 23

			Rushing					Receiving					Punt Returns				Kickoff Returns				Totals		
Year Team	G	GS	Att	Yds	Avg	Lg	TD	Rec	Yds	Avg	Lg	TD	Num	Yds	Avg	TD	Num	Yds	Avg	TD	Fum	TD	Pts
1995 Cincinnati Bengals	1	0	1	1	1.0	1	0	0	0	-	-	0	0	0	-	0	0	0	-	0	0	0	0

Keith Burns

Pos: LB **Rnd:** 7 **College:** Oklahoma State **Ht:** 6' 1" **Wt:** 233 **Born:** 5/16/72 **Age:** 24

			Tackles			Miscellaneous				Interceptions				Punt Returns				Kickoff Returns				Totals	
Year Team	G	GS	Tk	Ast	Sack	FF	FR	TD	Blk	Int	Yds	Avg	TD	Num	Yds	Avg	TD	Num	Yds	Avg	TD	TD	Fum
1994 Denver Broncos	12	1	15	3	0.0	0	0	0	0	0	0	-	0	0	0	-	0	0	0	-	0	0	0
1995 Denver Broncos	16	0	10	3	1.5	0	2	0	0	0	0	-	0	0	0	-	0	1	5	5.0	0	0	0
2 NFL Seasons	28	1	25	6	1.5	0	2	0	0	0	0	-	0	0	0	-	0	1	5	5.0	0	0	0

Jeff Burris

Pos: CB/PR **Rnd:** 1 (27) **College:** Notre Dame **Ht:** 5' 10" **Wt:** 191 **Born:** 6/7/72 **Age:** 24

			Tackles			Miscellaneous				Interceptions				Punt Returns				Kickoff Returns				Totals	
Year Team	G	GS	Tk	Ast	Sack	FF	FR	TD	Blk	Int	Yds	Avg	TD	Num	Yds	Avg	TD	Num	Yds	Avg	TD	TD	Fum
1994 Buffalo Bills	16	0	13	3	0.0	0	1	0	0	2	24	12.0	0	32	332	10.4	0	0	0	-	0	0	2
1995 Buffalo Bills	9	9	28	6	0.0	0	0	0	0	1	19	19.0	0	20	229	11.5	0	0	0	-	0	0	0
2 NFL Seasons	25	9	41	9	0.0	0	1	0	0	3	43	14.3	0	52	561	10.8	0	0	0	-	0	0	2

John Burrough

Pos: DT/DE **Rnd:** 7 **College:** Wyoming **Ht:** 6' 5" **Wt:** 265 **Born:** 5/17/72 **Age:** 24

			Tackles			Miscellaneous				Interceptions				Totals		
Year Team	G	GS	Tk	Ast	Sack	FF	FR	TD	Blk	Int	Yds	Avg	TD	Sfty	TD	Pts
1995 Atlanta Falcons	16	0	4	1	0.0	0	0	0	0	0	0	-	0	0	0	0

James Burton

Pos: CB **Rnd:** 5 **College:** Fresno State **Ht:** 5' 9" **Wt:** 181 **Born:** 4/22/71 **Age:** 25

			Tackles			Miscellaneous				Interceptions				Totals		
Year Team	G	GS	Tk	Ast	Sack	FF	FR	TD	Blk	Int	Yds	Avg	TD	Sfty	TD	Pts
1994 Chicago Bears	10	1	7	0	0.0	0	0	0	0	0	0	-	0	0	0	0
1995 Chicago Bears	11	2	19	1	0.0	0	0	0	0	0	0	-	0	0	0	0
2 NFL Seasons	24	3	26	1	0.0	0	0	0	0	0	0	-	0	0	0	0

Devin Bush

Pos: S **Rnd:** 1 (26) **College:** Florida State **Ht:** 5' 11" **Wt:** 205 **Born:** 7/3/73 **Age:** 23

			Tackles			Miscellaneous				Interceptions				Totals		
Year Team	G	GS	Tk	Ast	Sack	FF	FR	TD	Blk	Int	Yds	Avg	TD	Sfty	TD	Pts
1995 Atlanta Falcons	11	5	21	14	0.0	0	1	0	0	1	0	0.0	0	0	0	0

Lewis Bush

Pos: LB **Rnd:** 4 **College:** Washington State **Ht:** 6' 2" **Wt:** 245 **Born:** 12/21/69 **Age:** 26

			Tackles			Miscellaneous				Interceptions				Totals		
Year	Team	G	GS	Tk	Ast	Sack	FF	FR	TD	Blk	Int	Yds	Avg	TD	Sfty	TD	Pts
1993	San Diego Chargers	16	0	1	1	0.0	0	0	0	0	0	0	-	0	0	0	0
1994	San Diego Chargers	16	0	3	0	0.0	0	1	0	0	0	0	-	0	0	0	0
1995	San Diego Chargers	16	15	45	11	0.0	2	2	0	0	1	0	0.0	0	0	0	0
	3 NFL Seasons	48	15	49	12	0.0	2	3	0	0	1	0	0.0	0	0	0	0

Barney Bussey

Pos: S **Rnd:** 5 **College:** South Carolina State **Ht:** 6' 0" **Wt:** 215 **Born:** 5/20/62 **Age:** 34

				Tackles			Miscellaneous				Interceptions				Punt Returns				Kickoff Returns				Totals	
Year	Team	G	GS	Tk	Ast	Sack	FF	FR	TD	Blk	Int	Yds	Avg	TD	Num	Yds	Avg	TD	Num	Yds	Avg	TD	TD	Fum
1986	Cincinnati Bengals	16	0	19	5	1.0	0	0	0	0	1	19	19.0	0	0	0	-	0	0	0	-	0	0	0
1987	Cincinnati Bengals	12	1	26	13	2.0	0	0	0	0	1	0	0.0	0	0	0	-	0	21	406	19.3	0	0	1
1988	Cincinnati Bengals	16	0	21	4	4.0	0	1	0	0	0	0	-	0	0	0	-	0	7	83	11.9	0	0	1
1989	Cincinnati Bengals	16	1	20	5	2.5	0	1	0	1	1	0	0.0	0	0	0	-	0	0	0	-	0	1	0
1990	Cincinnati Bengals	16	5	47	9	2.0	0	1	1	0	4	37	9.3	0	0	0	-	0	0	0	-	0	1	0
1991	Cincinnati Bengals	12	7	29	8	0.0	0	1	0	0	2	18	9.0	0	0	0	-	0	0	0	-	0	0	0
1992	Cincinnati Bengals	16	4	24	8	0.0	0	1	0	0	1	3	3.0	0	0	0	-	0	1	18	18.0	0	0	0
1993	Tampa Bay Buccaneers	16	7	33	20	0.0	1	1	0	0	0	0	-	0	0	0	-	0	0	0	-	0	0	0
1994	Tampa Bay Buccaneers	16	15	53	19	1.5	0	1	0	0	0	0	-	0	0	0	-	0	0	0	-	0	0	0
1995	Tampa Bay Buccaneers	8	5	23	9	0.0	0	1	0	0	0	0	-	0	0	0	-	0	0	0	-	0	0	0
	10 NFL Seasons	144	45	295	100	13.0	1	6	2	0	10	77	7.7	0	0	0	-	0	29	507	17.5	0	2	2

Paul Butcher

Pos: LB **Rnd:** FA **College:** Wayne State (MI) **Ht:** 6' 0" **Wt:** 240 **Born:** 11/8/63 **Age:** 32

				Tackles			Miscellaneous				Interceptions				Punt Returns				Kickoff Returns				Totals	
Year	Team	G	GS	Tk	Ast	Sack	FF	FR	TD	Blk	Int	Yds	Avg	TD	Num	Yds	Avg	TD	Num	Yds	Avg	TD	TD	Fum
1986	Detroit Lions	12	0	7	1	0.0	0	0	0	0	0	0	-	0	0	0	-	0	0	0	-	0	0	0
1987	Detroit Lions	12	0	10	1	0.0	0	1	0	0	0	0	-	0	0	0	-	0	0	0	-	0	0	0
1988	Detroit Lions	16	0	17	1	0.0	0	0	0	0	0	0	-	0	0	0	-	0	0	0	-	0	0	0
1990	Los Angeles Rams	16	1	9	3	0.0	0	0	0	0	0	0	-	0	0	0	-	0	0	0	-	0	0	0
1991	Los Angeles Rams	16	3	13	2	0.0	0	1	0	0	0	0	-	0	0	0	-	0	0	0	-	0	0	0
1992	Los Angeles Rams	1	1	0	0	0.0	0	0	0	0	0	0	-	0	0	0	-	0	0	0	-	0	0	0
1993	Indianapolis Colts	16	0	1	0	0.0	0	0	0	0	0	0	-	0	0	0	-	0	2	2	1.0	0	0	0
1994	Indianapolis Colts	13	0	1	0	0.0	0	0	0	0	0	0	-	0	0	0	-	0	0	0	-	0	0	0
1995	Carolina Panthers	16	0	3	0	0.0	0	0	0	0	0	0	-	0	0	0	-	0	1	5	5.0	0	0	0
	9 NFL Seasons	118	5	61	8	0.0	0	2	0	0	0	0	-	0	0	0	-	0	3	7	2.3	0	0	0

Kevin Butler

(statistical profile on page 469)

Pos: K **Rnd:** 4 **College:** Georgia **Ht:** 6' 1" **Wt:** 205 **Born:** 7/24/62 **Age:** 34

			Field Goals											PAT		Tot
Year	Team	G	1-29 Yds	Pct	30-39 Yds	Pct	40-49 Yds	Pct	50+ Yds	Pct	Overall	Pct	Long	Made	Att	Pts
1985	Chicago Bears	16	15-15	100.0	13-14	92.9	3-6	50.0	0-2	0.0	31-37	83.8	46	51	51	144
1986	Chicago Bears	16	12-15	80.0	9-12	75.0	6-8	75.0	1-6	16.7	28-41	68.3	52	36	37	120
1987	Chicago Bears	12	11-11	100.0	5-5	100.0	1-6	16.7	2-6	33.3	19-28	67.9	52	28	30	85
1988	Chicago Bears	16	5-5	100.0	7-8	87.5	3-5	50.0	0-0	-	15-19	78.9	45	37	38	82
1989	Chicago Bears	16	6-6	100.0	6-7	85.7	3-5	60.0	0-1	0.0	15-19	78.9	46	43	45	88
1990	Chicago Bears	16	9-9	100.0	5-8	62.5	8-13	61.5	4-7	57.1	26-37	70.3	52	36	37	114
1991	Chicago Bears	16	10-12	83.3	3-5	60.0	5-9	55.6	1-3	33.3	19-29	65.5	50	32	34	89
1992	Chicago Bears	16	9-9	100.0	9-10	90.0	0-4	0.0	1-3	33.3	19-26	73.1	50	34	34	91
1993	Chicago Bears	16	7-8	87.5	12-13	92.3	3-7	42.9	5-8	62.5	27-36	75.0	52	21	22	102
1994	Chicago Bears	15	8-8	100.0	6-9	66.7	5-8	62.5	2-4	50.0	21-29	72.4	52	24	24	87
1995	Chicago Bears	16	16-19	84.2	5-6	83.3	2-4	50.0	0-2	0.0	23-31	74.2	47	45	45	114
	11 NFL Seasons	171	108-117	92.3	80-97	82.5	39-76	51.3	16-42	38.1	243-332	73.2	55	387	397	1116

Leroy Butler

(statistical profile on page 401)

Pos: S **Rnd:** 2 **College:** Florida State **Ht:** 6' 0" **Wt:** 200 **Born:** 7/19/68 **Age:** 28

				Tackles			Miscellaneous				Interceptions				Totals		
Year	Team	G	GS	Tk	Ast	Sack	FF	FR	TD	Blk	Int	Yds	Avg	TD	Sfty	TD	Pts
1990	Green Bay Packers	16	0	18	1	0.0	1	0	0	0	3	42	14.0	0	0	0	0
1991	Green Bay Packers	16	16	53	10	0.0	1	1	0	0	3	6	2.0	0	0	0	0
1992	Green Bay Packers	15	15	56	18	0.0	1	1	0	0	1	0	0.0	0	0	0	0
1993	Green Bay Packers	16	16	69	21	1.0	2	1	1	0	6	131	21.8	0	0	1	6
1994	Green Bay Packers	13	13	47	16	1.0	1	0	0	0	3	68	22.7	0	0	0	0
1995	Green Bay Packers	16	16	82	20	1.0	1	0	0	0	5	105	21.0	0	0	0	0

Year Team	G	GS	Tackles			Miscellaneous				Interceptions				Totals		
			Tk	Ast	Sack	FF	FR	TD	Blk	Int	Yds	Avg	TD	Sfty	TD	Pts
6 NFL Seasons	92	76	325	86	3.0	7	3	1	0	21	352	16.8	0	0	1	6

Marion Butts

Pos: RB **Rnd:** 7 **College:** Florida State **Ht:** 6' 1" **Wt:** 248 **Born:** 8/1/66 **Age:** 30

Year Team	G	GS	Rushing					Receiving					Punt Returns				Kickoff Returns				Totals		
			Att	Yds	Avg	Lg	TD	Rec	Yds	Avg	Lg	TD	Num	Yds	Avg	TD	Num	Yds	Avg	TD	Fum	TD	Pts
1989 San Diego Chargers	15	5	170	683	4.0	t50	9	7	21	3.0	8	0	0	0	-	0	0	0	-	0	2	9	54
1990 San Diego Chargers	14	13	265	1225	4.6	52	8	16	117	7.3	26	0	0	0	-	0	0	0	-	0	0	8	48
1991 San Diego Chargers	16	8	193	834	4.3	44	6	10	91	9.1	46	1	0	0	-	0	1	0	0.0	0	3	7	42
1992 San Diego Chargers	15	15	218	809	3.7	22	4	9	73	8.1	22	0	0	0	-	0	0	0	-	0	4	4	24
1993 San Diego Chargers	16	16	185	746	4.0	27	4	15	105	7.0	23	0	0	0	-	0	0	0	-	0	0	4	24
1994 New England Patriots	16	15	243	703	2.9	26	8	9	54	6.0	15	0	0	0	-	0	0	0	-	0	1	8	48
1995 Houston Oilers	12	2	71	185	2.6	9	4	2	10	5.0	10	0	0	0	-	0	2	14	7.0	0	0	4	24
7 NFL Seasons	104	74	1345	5185	3.9	52	43	68	471	6.9	46	1	0	0	-	0	3	14	4.7	0	10	44	264

Other Statistics: 1989–recovered 1 fumble for 0 yards. 1990–recovered 1 fumble for 0 yards. 1992–recovered 1 fumble for 0 yards. 1994–recovered 1 fumble for 0 yards.

Butler By'Not'e

Pos: CB/KR **Rnd:** 7 **College:** Ohio State **Ht:** 5' 9" **Wt:** 190 **Born:** 9/29/72 **Age:** 24

Year Team	G	GS	Tackles			Miscellaneous				Interceptions				Punt Returns				Kickoff Returns				Totals	
			Tk	Ast	Sack	FF	FR	TD	Blk	Int	Yds	Avg	TD	Num	Yds	Avg	TD	Num	Yds	Avg	TD	TD	Fum
1994 Denver Broncos	10	0	1	0	0.0	0	0	0	0	0	0	-	0	0	0	-	0	24	545	22.7	0	0	0
1995 Carolina Panthers	7	0	0	0	0.0	0	0	0	0	0	0	-	0	0	0	-	0	18	335	18.6	0	0	0
2 NFL Seasons	17	0	1	0	0.0	0	0	0	0	0	0	-	0	0	0	-	0	42	880	21.0	0	0	0

Keith Byars

(statistical profile on page 292)

Pos: RB **Rnd:** 1 (10) **College:** Ohio State **Ht:** 6' 1" **Wt:** 255 **Born:** 10/14/63 **Age:** 33

Year Team	G	GS	Rushing					Receiving					Kickoff Returns				Passing				Totals		
			Att	Yds	Avg	Lg	TD	Rec	Yds	Avg	Lg	TD	Num	Yds	Avg	TD	Att	Com	Yds	Int	Fum	TD	Pts
1986 Philadelphia Eagles	16	8	177	577	3.3	32	1	11	44	4.0	17	0	2	47	23.5	0	2	1	55	0	3	1	6
1987 Philadelphia Eagles	10	8	116	426	3.7	30	3	21	177	8.4	30	1	0	0	-	0	0	0	0	0	3	4	24
1988 Philadelphia Eagles	16	16	152	517	3.4	52	6	72	705	9.8	t37	4	2	20	10.0	0	2	0	0	0	5	10	60
1989 Philadelphia Eagles	16	15	133	452	3.4	t16	5	68	721	10.6	60	0	1	27	27.0	0	0	0	0	0	4	5	30
1990 Philadelphia Eagles	16	15	37	141	3.8	23	0	81	819	10.1	54	3	0	0	-	0	4	4	53	0	4	3	18
1991 Philadelphia Eagles	16	16	94	383	4.1	28	1	62	564	9.1	37	3	0	0	-	0	2	0	0	1	5	4	24
1992 Philadelphia Eagles	15	15	41	176	4.3	23	1	56	502	9.0	46	2	0	0	-	0	1	0	0	0	1	3	18
1993 Miami Dolphins	16	16	64	269	4.2	t77	3	61	613	10.0	27	3	0	0	-	0	2	1	11	0	3	6	36
1994 Miami Dolphins	9	9	19	64	3.4	12	2	49	418	8.5	34	5	0	0	-	0	0	0	0	0	0	7	42
1995 Miami Dolphins	16	16	15	44	2.9	15	1	51	362	7.1	26	2	0	0	-	0	0	0	0	0	0	3	18
10 NFL Seasons	146	134	848	3049	3.6	t77	23	532	4925	9.3	60	23	5	94	18.8	0	13	6	119	1	28	46	276

Other Statistics: 1986–recovered 2 fumbles for 0 yards; passed for 1 touchdown. 1987–recovered 2 fumbles for 0 yards. 1988–recovered 2 fumbles for 14 yards. 1989–recovered 4 fumbles for 6 yards. 1990–recovered 1 fumble for 0 yards; passed for 4 touchdowns. 1992–recovered 1 fumble for 0 yards. 1993–passed for 1 touchdown.

Earnest Byner

(statistical profile on page 293)

Pos: RB **Rnd:** 10 **College:** East Carolina **Ht:** 5' 10" **Wt:** 215 **Born:** 9/15/62 **Age:** 34

Year Team	G	GS	Rushing					Receiving					Kickoff Returns				Passing				Totals		
			Att	Yds	Avg	Lg	TD	Rec	Yds	Avg	Lg	TD	Num	Yds	Avg	TD	Att	Com	Yds	Int	Fum	TD	Pts
1984 Cleveland Browns	16	3	72	426	5.9	54	2	11	118	10.7	26	0	22	415	18.9	0	0	0	0	0	3	3	18
1985 Cleveland Browns	16	13	244	1002	4.1	36	8	45	460	10.2	31	2	0	0	-	0	0	0	0	0	5	10	60
1986 Cleveland Browns	7	7	94	277	2.9	37	2	37	328	8.9	40	2	0	0	-	0	0	0	0	0	1	4	24
1987 Cleveland Browns	12	12	105	432	4.1	21	8	52	552	10.6	37	2	1	2	2.0	0	0	0	0	0	5	10	60
1988 Cleveland Browns	16	16	157	576	3.7	t27	3	59	576	9.8	t39	2	0	0	-	0	0	0	0	0	5	5	30
1989 Washington Redskins	16	13	134	580	4.3	24	7	54	458	8.5	27	2	0	0	-	0	1	0	0	0	2	9	54
1990 Washington Redskins	16	16	297	1219	4.1	22	6	31	279	9.0	19	1	0	0	-	0	2	1	31	0	2	7	42
1991 Washington Redskins	16	16	274	1048	3.8	32	5	34	308	9.1	31	0	0	0	-	0	4	1	18	0	3	5	30
1992 Washington Redskins	16	16	262	998	3.8	23	6	39	338	8.7	29	1	0	0	-	0	3	1	41	0	1	7	42
1993 Washington Redskins	16	3	23	105	4.6	16	1	27	194	7.2	20	0	0	0	-	0	0	0	0	0	0	1	6
1994 Cleveland Browns	16	1	75	219	2.9	15	2	11	102	9.3	30	0	0	0	-	0	0	0	0	0	0	2	12
1995 Cleveland Browns	16	2	115	432	3.8	23	2	61	494	8.1	t29	2	5	98	19.6	0	0	0	0	0	1	4	24
12 NFL Seasons	179	118	1852	7314	3.9	54	52	461	4207	9.1	40	14	28	515	18.4	0	10	3	90	0	28	67	402

Other Statistics: 1984–recovered 2 fumbles for 55 yards and 1 touchdown. 1985–recovered 4 fumbles for 0 yards. 1987–recovered 1 fumble for 0 yards. 1988–recovered 2 fumbles for 0 yards. 1989–recovered 2 fumbles for 0 yards. 1990–recovered 1 fumble for 0 yards; passed for 1 touchdown. 1991–recovered 1 fumble for 0 yards; passed for 1 touchdown. 1992–passed for 1 touchdown. 1993–recovered 1 fumble for 0 yards. 1995–recovered 1 fumble for 0 yards.

Israel Byrd

Pos: CB **Rnd:** FA **College:** Utah State **Ht:** 5' 11" **Wt:** 184 **Born:** 2/1/71 **Age:** 25

Year	Team	G	GS	Tackles			Miscellaneous				Interceptions				Totals		
				Tk	Ast	Sack	FF	FR	TD	Blk	Int	Yds	Avg	TD	Sfty	TD	Pts
1994	New Orleans Saints	3	0	0	0	0.0	0	0	0	0	0	0	-	0	0	0	0
1995	New Orleans Saints	4	0	0	0	0.0	0	0	0	0	0	0	-	0	0	0	0
	2 NFL Seasons	7	0	0	0	0.0	0	0	0	0	0	0	-	0	0	0	0

Eddie Cade

Pos: S **Rnd:** FA **College:** Arizona State **Ht:** 6' 1" **Wt:** 206 **Born:** 8/4/73 **Age:** 23

Year	Team	G	GS	Tackles			Miscellaneous				Interceptions				Totals		
				Tk	Ast	Sack	FF	FR	TD	Blk	Int	Yds	Avg	TD	Sfty	TD	Pts
1995	New England Patriots	10	0	0	0	0.0	0	0	0	0	0	0	-	0	0	0	0

Glenn Cadrez

Pos: LB **Rnd:** 6 **College:** Houston **Ht:** 6' 3" **Wt:** 245 **Born:** 1/2/70 **Age:** 26

Year	Team	G	GS	Tackles			Miscellaneous				Interceptions				Punt Returns				Kickoff Returns				Totals	
				Tk	Ast	Sack	FF	FR	TD	Blk	Int	Yds	Avg	TD	Num	Yds	Avg	TD	Num	Yds	Avg	TD	TD	Fum
1992	New York Jets	16	0	1	0	0.0	0	1	0	0	0	0	-	0	0	0	-	0	0	0	-	0	0	0
1993	New York Jets	16	0	5	1	0.0	0	0	0	0	0	0	-	0	0	0	-	0	0	0	-	0	0	0
1994	New York Jets	16	0	0	0	0.0	0	1	0	0	0	0	-	0	0	0	-	0	1	10	10.0	0	0	0
1995	NYA - Den	11	7	20	4	2.0	0	1	0	0	0	0	-	0	0	0	-	0	0	0	-	0	0	0
1995	New York Jets	1	0	0	0	0.0	0	0	0	0	0	0	-	0	0	0	-	0	0	0	-	0	0	0
	Denver Broncos	10	7	20	4	2.0	0	1	0	0	0	0	-	0	0	0	-	0	0	0	-	0	0	0
	4 NFL Seasons	59	7	26	5	2.0	0	3	0	0	0	0	-	0	0	0	-	0	1	10	10.0	0	0	0

Joe Cain

(statistical profile on page 401)

Pos: LB **Rnd:** 8 **College:** Oregon Tech **Ht:** 6' 1" **Wt:** 239 **Born:** 6/11/65 **Age:** 31

Year	Team	G	GS	Tackles			Miscellaneous				Interceptions				Totals		
				Tk	Ast	Sack	FF	FR	TD	Blk	Int	Yds	Avg	TD	Sfty	TD	Pts
1989	Seattle Seahawks	9	0	10	-	0.0	0	0	0	0	0	0	-	0	0	0	0
1990	Seattle Seahawks	16	5	29	-	0.0	0	0	0	0	0	0	-	0	0	0	0
1991	Seattle Seahawks	16	0	14	-	0.0	0	0	0	0	1	5	5.0	0	0	0	0
1992	Seattle Seahawks	16	8	43	19	0.0	0	1	0	0	2	3	1.5	0	0	0	0
1993	Chicago Bears	15	15	63	45	0.0	1	0	0	0	0	0	-	0	0	0	0
1994	Chicago Bears	16	15	72	21	0.0	1	1	0	0	0	0	-	0	0	0	0
1995	Chicago Bears	16	16	60	19	0.0	0	0	0	0	0	0	-	0	0	0	0
	7 NFL Seasons	104	59	291	104	0.0	2	2	0	0	3	8	2.7	0	0	0	0

Mike Caldwell

Pos: LB **Rnd:** 3 **College:** Middle Tennessee State **Ht:** 6' 2" **Wt:** 235 **Born:** 8/31/71 **Age:** 25

Year	Team	G	GS	Tackles			Miscellaneous				Interceptions				Punt Returns				Kickoff Returns				Totals	
				Tk	Ast	Sack	FF	FR	TD	Blk	Int	Yds	Avg	TD	Num	Yds	Avg	TD	Num	Yds	Avg	TD	TD	Fum
1993	Cleveland Browns	15	1	13	29	0.0	0	1	0	0	0	0	-	0	0	0	-	0	0	0	-	0	0	0
1994	Cleveland Browns	16	1	30	10	0.0	1	0	0	0	1	0	0.0	0	1	2	2.0	0	0	0	-	0	0	0
1995	Cleveland Browns	16	6	58	12	0.0	0	0	0	0	2	24	12.0	1	0	0	-	0	0	0	-	0	1	0
	3 NFL Seasons	47	8	101	51	0.0	1	1	0	0	3	24	8.0	1	1	2	2.0	0	0	0	-	0	1	0

Mike Caldwell

Pos: WR **Rnd:** FA **College:** California **Ht:** 6' 2" **Wt:** 200 **Born:** 3/28/71 **Age:** 25

Year	Team	G	GS	Rushing					Receiving					Punt Returns				Kickoff Returns				Totals		
				Att	Yds	Avg	Lg	TD	Rec	Yds	Avg	Lg	TD	Num	Yds	Avg	TD	Num	Yds	Avg	TD	Fum	TD	Pts
1995	San Francisco 49ers	2	0	0	0	-	-	0	0	0	-	-	0	0	0	-	0	2	40	20.0	0	0	0	0

Chris Calloway

(statistical profile on page 293)

Pos: WR **Rnd:** 4 **College:** Michigan **Ht:** 5' 10" **Wt:** 188 **Born:** 3/29/68 **Age:** 28

Year	Team	G	GS	Rushing					Receiving					Punt Returns				Kickoff Returns				Totals		
				Att	Yds	Avg	Lg	TD	Rec	Yds	Avg	Lg	TD	Num	Yds	Avg	TD	Num	Yds	Avg	TD	Fum	TD	Pts
1990	Pittsburgh Steelers	16	2	0	0	-	-	0	10	124	12.4	t20	1	0	0	-	0	0	0	-	0	0	1	6
1991	Pittsburgh Steelers	12	0	0	0	-	-	0	15	254	16.9	t33	1	0	0	-	0	0	0	-	0	0	1	6
1992	New York Giants	16	1	0	0	-	-	0	27	335	12.4	28	1	0	0	-	0	2	29	14.5	0	0	1	6
1993	New York Giants	16	8	0	0	-	-	0	35	513	14.7	47	3	0	0	-	0	6	89	14.8	0	0	3	18
1994	New York Giants	16	14	8	77	9.6	20	0	43	666	15.5	t51	2	0	0	-	0	0	0	-	0	1	2	12
1995	New York Giants	16	15	2	-9	-4.5	-3	0	56	796	14.2	49	3	0	0	-	0	0	0	-	0	0	3	18
	6 NFL Seasons	92	40	10	68	6.8	20	0	186	2688	14.5	t51	11	0	0	-	0	8	118	14.8	0	1	11	66

Other Statistics: 1991–recovered 1 fumble for 0 yards. 1993–recovered 1 fumble for 0 yards.

Rich Camarillo
(statistical profile on page 470)

Pos: P **Rnd:** FA **College:** Washington **Ht:** 5' 11" **Wt:** 202 **Born:** 11/29/59 **Age:** 36

Year Team	G	Punting NetPunts	Yards	Avg	Long	In20	In20%	TotPunts	TB	Blocks	OppRet	RetYds	NetAvg	Rushing Att	Yards	Passing Att	Com	Yards	Int
1981 New England Patriots	9	47	1959	41.7	75	12	25.5	47	9	0	20	209	33.4	0	0	0	0	0	0
1982 New England Patriots	9	49	2140	43.7	76	10	20.4	49	5	0	26	191	37.7	0	0	0	0	0	0
1983 New England Patriots	16	81	3615	44.6	70	25	30.9	81	11	0	48	392	37.1	0	0	0	0	0	0
1984 New England Patriots	7	48	2020	42.1	61	12	25.0	48	7	0	24	214	34.7	0	0	0	0	0	0
1985 New England Patriots	16	92	3953	43.0	75	16	17.4	92	13	0	56	598	33.6	0	0	0	0	0	0
1986 New England Patriots	16	89	3746	42.1	64	16	18.0	92	7	3	60	565	33.1	0	0	0	0	0	0
1987 New England Patriots	12	62	2489	40.1	73	14	22.6	63	8	1	34	333	31.7	1	0	0	0	0	0
1988 Los Angeles Rams	9	40	1579	39.5	57	11	27.5	40	2	0	26	145	34.9	0	0	0	0	0	0
1989 Phoenix Cardinals	15	76	3298	43.4	58	21	27.6	76	6	0	42	330	37.5	0	0	1	1	0	0
1990 Phoenix Cardinals	16	67	2865	42.8	63	16	23.9	67	5	0	41	258	37.4	1	-11	0	0	0	0
1991 Phoenix Cardinals	16	76	3445	45.3	60	19	25.0	77	7	1	48	313	38.9	0	0	1	0	0	0
1992 Phoenix Cardinals	15	54	2317	42.9	73	23	42.6	54	2	0	22	141	39.6	0	0	0	0	0	0
1993 Phoenix Cardinals	16	73	3189	43.7	61	23	31.5	73	8	0	30	267	37.8	1	0	0	0	0	0
1994 Houston Oilers	16	96	4115	42.9	58	34	35.4	96	9	0	50	438	36.4	0	0	1	0	0	0
1995 Houston Oilers	16	77	3165	41.1	60	26	33.8	78	8	1	35	288	34.8	0	0	1	0	0	0
15 NFL Seasons	204	1027	43895	42.7	76	278	27.1	1033	107	6	562	4682	35.9	3	-11	4	1	0	0

Other Statistics: 1981–recovered 1 fumble for 0 yards; fumbled 1 time. 1990–fumbled 1 time for 0 yards. 1991–recovered 1 fumble for 0 yards. 1992–converted 0 of 1 extra-point attempts. 1993–recovered 1 fumble for 0 yards. 1994–recovered 1 fumble for 0 yards; fumbled 1 time. 1995–recovered 1 fumble for 0 yards; fumbled 1 time.

Jesse Campbell
(statistical profile on page 401)

Pos: S **Rnd:** 2 **College:** North Carolina State **Ht:** 6' 1" **Wt:** 215 **Born:** 4/11/69 **Age:** 27

Year Team	G	GS	Tackles Tk	Ast	Sack	Miscellaneous FF	FR	TD	Blk	Interceptions Int	Yds	Avg	TD	Totals Sfty	TD	Pts
1992 New York Giants	11	0	2	0	0.0	0	1	0	0	0	0	-	0	0	0	0
1993 New York Giants	16	0	3	1	0.0	0	0	0	0	1	0	0.0	0	0	0	0
1994 New York Giants	14	10	62	24	0.0	2	2	0	0	2	3	1.5	0	0	0	0
1995 New York Giants	16	16	72	28	0.0	1	0	0	0	0	0	-	0	0	0	0
4 NFL Seasons	57	26	139	53	0.0	3	3	0	0	3	3	1.0	0	0	0	0

Matthew Campbell

Pos: TE **Rnd:** FA **College:** South Carolina **Ht:** 6' 4" **Wt:** 270 **Born:** 7/14/72 **Age:** 24

Year Team	G	GS	Rushing Att	Yds	Avg	Lg	TD	Receiving Rec	Yds	Avg	Lg	TD	Punt Returns Num	Yds	Avg	TD	Kickoff Returns Num	Yds	Avg	TD	Totals Fum	TD	Pts
1995 Carolina Panthers	10	1	0	0	-	-	0	3	32	10.7	12	0	0	0	-	0	0	0	-	0	1	0	0

John Carney
(statistical profile on page 470)

Pos: K **Rnd:** FA **College:** Notre Dame **Ht:** 5' 11" **Wt:** 170 **Born:** 4/20/64 **Age:** 32

Year Team	G	Field Goals 1-29 Yds	Pct	30-39 Yds	Pct	40-49 Yds	Pct	50+ Yds	Pct	Overall	Pct	Long	PAT Made	Att	Tot Pts
1988 Tampa Bay Buccaneers	4	2-3	66.7	0-1	0.0	0-1	0.0	0-0	-	2-5	40.0	29	6	6	12
1989 Tampa Bay Buccaneers	1	0-0	-	0-0	-	0-0	-	0-0	-	0-0	-	-	0	0	0
1990 LAN - SD	13	10-10	100.0	6-7	85.7	3-3	100.0	0-1	0.0	19-21	90.5	43	27	28	84
1991 San Diego Chargers	16	7-7	100.0	6-8	75.0	4-9	44.4	2-4	50.0	19-29	65.5	54	31	31	88
1992 San Diego Chargers	16	13-14	92.9	5-7	71.4	7-8	87.5	1-3	33.3	26-32	81.3	50	35	35	113
1993 San Diego Chargers	16	8-8	100.0	14-17	82.4	7-12	58.3	2-3	66.7	31-40	77.5	51	31	33	124
1994 San Diego Chargers	16	12-12	100.0	15-15	100.0	5-9	55.6	2-2	100.0	34-38	89.5	50	33	33	135
1995 San Diego Chargers	16	8-8	100.0	10-11	90.9	3-5	60.0	0-2	0.0	21-26	80.8	45	32	33	95
1990 Los Angeles Rams	1	0-0	-	0-0	-	0-0	-	0-0	-	0-0	-	-	0	0	0
San Diego Chargers	12	10-10	100.0	6-7	85.7	3-3	100.0	0-1	0.0	19-21	90.5	43	27	28	84
8 NFL Seasons	98	60-62	96.8	56-66	84.8	29-47	61.7	7-15	46.7	152-191	79.6	54	195	199	651

Other Statistics: 1993–punted 4 times for 155 yards.

Brett Carolan

Pos: TE **Rnd:** FA **College:** Washington State **Ht:** 6' 3" **Wt:** 241 **Born:** 10/16/71 **Age:** 25

Year Team	G	GS	Rushing Att	Yds	Avg	Lg	TD	Receiving Rec	Yds	Avg	Lg	TD	Punt Returns Num	Yds	Avg	TD	Kickoff Returns Num	Yds	Avg	TD	Totals Fum	TD	Pts
1994 San Francisco 49ers	5	0	0	0	-	-	0	2	10	5.0	6	0	0	0	-	0	0	0	-	0	0	0	0
1995 San Francisco 49ers	14	0	0	0	-	-	0	1	3	3.0	3	0	0	0	-	0	0	0	-	0	0	0	0
2 NFL Seasons	19	0	0	0	-	-	0	3	13	4.3	6	0	0	0	-	0	0	0	-	0	0	0	0

Rob Carpenter

Pos: WR/PR **Rnd:** 4 **College:** Syracuse   *(statistical profile on page 294)*   **Ht:** 6' 2" **Wt:** 190 **Born:** 8/1/68 **Age:** 28

Year	Team	G	GS	Rushing					Receiving					Punt Returns				Passing				Totals		
				Att	Yds	Avg	Lg	TD	Rec	Yds	Avg	Lg	TD	Num	Yds	Avg	TD	Att	Com	Yds	Int	Fum	TD	Pts
1991	New England Patriots	8	1	0	0	-	-	0	3	45	15.0	23	0	0	0	-	0	0	0	0	0	0	0	0
1992	New York Jets	16	0	1	2	2.0	2	0	13	161	12.4	51	1	28	208	7.4	0	1	0	0	0	3	1	6
1993	New York Jets	16	0	0	0	-	-	0	6	83	13.8	18	0	0	0	-	0	0	0	0	0	0	0	0
1994	New York Jets	3	0	0	0	-	-	0	0	0	-	-	0	0	0	-	0	0	0	0	0	0	0	0
1995	Philadelphia Eagles	16	4	0	0	-	-	0	29	318	11.0	29	0	12	79	6.6	0	0	0	0	0	2	0	0
	5 NFL Seasons	59	5	1	2	2.0	2	0	51	607	11.9	51	1	40	287	7.2	0	1	0	0	0	5	1	6

Other Statistics: 1995–recovered 1 fumble for 0 yards.

Ron Carpenter

Pos: S/KR **Rnd:** FA **College:** Miami (OH)   **Ht:** 6' 1" **Wt:** 189 **Born:** 1/20/70 **Age:** 26

Year	Team	G	GS	Tackles			Miscellaneous				Interceptions				Punt Returns				Kickoff Returns				Totals	
				Tk	Ast	Sack	FF	FR	TD	Blk	Int	Yds	Avg	TD	Num	Yds	Avg	TD	Num	Yds	Avg	TD	TD	Fum
1993	Min - Cin	13	0	1	0	0.0	0	0	0	0	0	0	-	0	0	0	-	0	0	0	-	0	0	0
1995	New York Jets	13	4	17	8	0.0	1	0	0	0	0	0	-	0	0	0	-	0	21	553	26.3	0	0	3
1993	Minnesota Vikings	7	0	0	0	0.0	0	0	0	0	0	0	-	0	0	0	-	0	0	0	-	0	0	0
	Cincinnati Bengals	6	0	1	0	0.0	0	0	0	0	0	0	-	0	0	0	-	0	0	0	-	0	0	0
	2 NFL Seasons	26	4	18	8	0.0	1	0	0	0	0	0	-	0	0	0	-	0	21	553	26.3	0	0	3

Mark Carrier

Pos: WR **Rnd:** 3 **College:** Nicholls State   *(statistical profile on page 294)*   **Ht:** 6' 0" **Wt:** 185 **Born:** 10/28/65 **Age:** 31

Year	Team	G	GS	Rushing					Receiving					Punt Returns				Kickoff Returns				Totals		
				Att	Yds	Avg	Lg	TD	Rec	Yds	Avg	Lg	TD	Num	Yds	Avg	TD	Num	Yds	Avg	TD	Fum	TD	Pts
1987	Tampa Bay Buccaneers	10	5	0	0	-	-	0	26	423	16.3	38	3	0	0	-	0	1	0	0.0	0	0	3	18
1988	Tampa Bay Buccaneers	16	16	0	0	-	-	0	57	970	17.0	t59	5	0	0	-	0	0	0	-	0	2	5	30
1989	Tampa Bay Buccaneers	16	15	0	0	-	-	0	86	1422	16.5	t78	9	0	0	-	0	0	0	-	0	1	9	54
1990	Tampa Bay Buccaneers	16	16	0	0	-	-	0	49	813	16.6	t68	4	0	0	-	0	0	0	-	0	0	4	24
1991	Tampa Bay Buccaneers	16	16	0	0	-	-	0	47	698	14.9	35	2	0	0	-	0	0	0	-	0	2	2	12
1992	Tampa Bay Buccaneers	14	12	0	0	-	-	0	56	692	12.4	40	4	0	0	-	0	0	0	-	0	1	4	24
1993	Cleveland Browns	16	16	4	26	6.5	t15	1	43	746	17.3	55	3	6	92	15.3	1	0	0	-	0	0	5	30
1994	Cleveland Browns	16	6	1	14	14.0	t14	1	29	452	15.6	43	5	9	112	12.4	0	0	0	-	0	1	6	36
1995	Carolina Panthers	16	15	3	-4	-1.3	4	0	66	1002	15.2	t66	3	6	25	4.2	0	0	0	-	0	0	3	18
	9 NFL Seasons	136	117	8	36	4.5	t15	2	459	7218	15.7	t78	38	21	229	10.9	1	1	0	0.0	0	7	41	246

Other Statistics: 1991–recovered 1 fumble for 0 yards. 1995–recovered 1 fumble for 0 yards.

Mark Carrier

Pos: S **Rnd:** 1 (6) **College:** Southern California   *(statistical profile on page 402)*   **Ht:** 6' 1" **Wt:** 190 **Born:** 4/28/68 **Age:** 28

Year	Team	G	GS	Tackles			Miscellaneous				Interceptions				Totals		
				Tk	Ast	Sack	FF	FR	TD	Blk	Int	Yds	Avg	TD	Sfty	TD	Pts
1990	Chicago Bears	16	16	55	67	0.0	5	2	0	0	10	39	3.9	0	0	0	0
1991	Chicago Bears	16	16	41	52	0.0	1	1	0	0	2	54	27.0	0	0	0	0
1992	Chicago Bears	16	14	43	46	0.0	1	2	0	0	0	0	-	0	0	0	0
1993	Chicago Bears	16	16	47	44	0.0	1	0	0	0	4	94	23.5	1	0	1	6
1994	Chicago Bears	16	15	53	16	0.0	1	0	0	0	2	10	5.0	0	0	0	0
1995	Chicago Bears	16	15	64	8	0.0	0	1	0	0	0	0	-	0	0	0	0
	6 NFL Seasons	96	92	303	233	0.0	9	6	0	0	18	197	10.9	1	0	1	6

Darren Carrington

Pos: S **Rnd:** 5 **College:** Northern Arizona   **Ht:** 6' 2" **Wt:** 204 **Born:** 10/10/66 **Age:** 30

Year	Team	G	GS	Tackles			Miscellaneous				Interceptions				Punt Returns				Kickoff Returns				Totals	
				Tk	Ast	Sack	FF	FR	TD	Blk	Int	Yds	Avg	TD	Num	Yds	Avg	TD	Num	Yds	Avg	TD	TD	Fum
1989	Denver Broncos	16	0	11	5	0.0	0	0	0	0	1	2	2.0	0	1	0	0.0	0	6	152	25.3	0	0	1
1990	Detroit Lions	12	0	12	-	0.0	0	1	0	0	0	0	-	0	0	0	-	0	0	0	-	0	0	0
1991	San Diego Chargers	16	1	17	-	0.0	0	0	0	0	3	30	10.0	0	0	0	-	0	0	24	-	0	0	0
1992	San Diego Chargers	16	4	26	3	0.0	0	0	0	0	6	152	25.3	1	0	0	-	0	0	0	-	0	1	0
1993	San Diego Chargers	16	14	67	12	1.0	0	1	0	0	7	104	14.9	0	0	0	-	0	0	0	-	0	0	1
1994	San Diego Chargers	16	16	66	20	0.0	1	2	0	0	3	51	17.0	0	0	0	-	0	0	0	-	0	0	0
1995	Jacksonville Jaguars	6	2	12	6	0.0	0	0	0	0	1	17	17.0	0	0	0	-	0	0	0	-	0	0	0
	7 NFL Seasons	98	37	211	46	1.0	3	5	0	0	21	356	17.0	1	1	0	0.0	0	6	176	29.3	0	1	2

Dwayne Carswell

Pos: TE **Rnd:** FA **College:** Liberty **Ht:** 6' 3" **Wt:** 261 **Born:** 1/18/72 **Age:** 24

			Rushing					Receiving					Punt Returns				Kickoff Returns				Totals		
Year Team	G	GS	Att	Yds	Avg	Lg	TD	Rec	Yds	Avg	Lg	TD	Num	Yds	Avg	TD	Num	Yds	Avg	TD	Fum	TD	Pts
1994 Denver Broncos	4	0	0	0	-	-	0	0	0	-	-	0	0	0	-	0	1	0	0.0	0	0	0	0
1995 Denver Broncos	9	2	0	0	-	-	0	3	37	12.3	23	0	0	0	-	0	0	0	-	0	0	0	0
2 NFL Seasons	13	2	0	0	-	-	0	3	37	12.3	23	0	0	0	-	0	1	0	0.0	0	0	0	0

Other Statistics: 1994–recovered 1 fumble for 0 yards.

Anthony Carter

Pos: WR **Rnd:** 12 **College:** Michigan **Ht:** 5' 11" **Wt:** 181 **Born:** 9/17/60 **Age:** 36

			Rushing					Receiving					Punt Returns				Kickoff Returns				Totals		
Year Team	G	GS	Att	Yds	Avg	Lg	TD	Rec	Yds	Avg	Lg	TD	Num	Yds	Avg	TD	Num	Yds	Avg	TD	Fum	TD	Pts
1985 Minnesota Vikings	16	15	0	0	-	-	0	43	821	19.1	t57	8	9	117	13.0	0	0	0	-	0	1	8	48
1986 Minnesota Vikings	12	10	1	12	12.0	12	0	38	686	18.1	t60	7	0	0	-	0	0	0	-	0	1	7	42
1987 Minnesota Vikings	12	11	0	0	-	-	0	38	922	24.3	t73	7	3	40	13.3	0	0	0	-	0	0	7	42
1988 Minnesota Vikings	16	16	4	41	10.3	21	0	72	1225	17.0	t67	6	1	3	3.0	0	1	0	0.0	0	1	6	36
1989 Minnesota Vikings	16	16	3	18	6.0	17	0	65	1066	16.4	50	4	1	2	2.0	0	1	19	19.0	0	0	4	24
1990 Minnesota Vikings	15	15	3	16	5.3	11	0	70	1008	14.4	t56	8	0	0	-	0	0	0	-	0	2	8	48
1991 Minnesota Vikings	15	15	13	117	9.0	32	1	51	553	10.8	t46	5	0	0	-	0	0	0	-	0	0	6	36
1992 Minnesota Vikings	16	14	16	66	4.1	14	1	41	580	14.1	54	2	0	0	-	0	0	0	-	0	1	3	18
1993 Minnesota Vikings	15	14	7	19	2.7	9	0	60	775	12.9	39	5	0	0	-	0	0	0	-	0	1	5	30
1994 Detroit Lions	4	1	0	0	-	-	0	8	97	12.1	18	3	0	0	-	0	0	0	-	0	0	3	18
1995 Detroit Lions	3	0	0	0	-	-	0	0	0	-	-	0	1	3	3.0	0	2	46	23.0	0	0	0	0
11 NFL Seasons	140	127	47	289	6.1	32	2	486	7733	15.9	t73	55	15	165	11.0	0	4	65	16.3	0	7	57	342

Other Statistics: 1985–recovered 1 fumble for 0 yards. 1988–recovered 1 fumble for 0 yards. 1989–recovered 1 fumble for 0 yards. 1992–attempted 1 pass with 0 completions for 0 yards.

Bernard Carter

Pos: LB **Rnd:** 6 **College:** East Carolina **Ht:** 6' 2" **Wt:** 245 **Born:** 8/22/71 **Age:** 25

			Tackles			Miscellaneous				Interceptions				Totals		
Year Team	G	GS	Tk	Ast	Sack	FF	FR	TD	Blk	Int	Yds	Avg	TD	Sfty	TD	Pts
1995 Jacksonville Jaguars	5	0	2	2	0.0	0	0	0	0	0	0	-	0	0	0	0

Cris Carter

(statistical profile on page 295)

Pos: WR **Rnd:** 4(S) **College:** Ohio State **Ht:** 6' 3" **Wt:** 202 **Born:** 11/25/65 **Age:** 30

			Rushing					Receiving					Kickoff Returns				Passing				Totals		
Year Team	G	GS	Att	Yds	Avg	Lg	TD	Rec	Yds	Avg	Lg	TD	Num	Yds	Avg	TD	Att	Com	Yds	Int	Fum	TD	Pts
1987 Philadelphia Eagles	9	0	0	0	-	-	0	5	84	16.8	25	2	12	241	20.1	0	1	0	0	0	0	2	12
1988 Philadelphia Eagles	16	16	1	1	1.0	1	0	39	761	19.5	t80	6	0	0	-	0	0	0	0	0	0	7	42
1989 Philadelphia Eagles	16	15	2	16	8.0	11	0	45	605	13.4	42	11	0	0	-	0	0	0	0	0	1	11	66
1990 Minnesota Vikings	16	5	2	6	3.0	8	0	27	413	15.3	t78	3	0	0	-	0	0	0	0	0	0	3	18
1991 Minnesota Vikings	16	16	0	0	-	-	0	72	962	13.4	50	5	0	0	-	0	0	0	0	0	1	5	30
1992 Minnesota Vikings	12	12	5	15	3.0	6	0	53	681	12.8	44	6	0	0	-	0	0	0	0	0	1	6	36
1993 Minnesota Vikings	16	16	0	0	-	-	0	86	1071	12.5	58	9	0	0	-	0	0	0	0	0	0	9	54
1994 Minnesota Vikings	16	16	0	0	-	-	0	122	1256	10.3	t65	7	0	0	-	0	0	0	0	0	4	7	46
1995 Minnesota Vikings	16	16	1	0	0.0	0	0	122	1371	11.2	t60	17	0	0	-	0	0	0	0	0	0	17	102
9 NFL Seasons	133	112	11	38	3.5	11	0	571	7204	12.6	t80	66	12	241	20.1	0	1	0	0	0	7	67	406

Other Statistics: 1988–recovered 1 fumble for 0 yards and 1 touchdown. 1989–recovered 1 fumble for 0 yards. 1993–recovered 1 fumble for 0 yards. 1994–scored 2 two-point conversions.

Dale Carter

(statistical profile on page 402)

Pos: CD **Rnd:** 1 (20) **College:** Tennessee **Ht:** 6' 1" **Wt:** 188 **Born:** 11/28/69 **Age:** 26

			Tackles			Miscellaneous				Interceptions				Punt Returns				Kickoff Returns				Totals	
Year Team	G	GS	Tk	Ast	Sack	FF	FR	TD	Blk	Int	Yds	Avg	TD	Num	Yds	Avg	TD	Num	Yds	Avg	TD	TD	Fum
1992 Kansas City Chiefs	16	9	39	16	0.0	0	2	0	0	7	65	9.3	1	38	398	10.5	2	11	190	17.3	0	3	7
1993 Kansas City Chiefs	15	11	43	15	0.0	1	2	0	0	1	0	0.0	0	27	247	9.1	0	0	0	-	0	0	4
1994 Kansas City Chiefs	16	16	78	3	0.0	2	1	0	0	2	24	12.0	0	16	124	7.8	0	0	0	-	0	0	1
1995 Kansas City Chiefs	16	14	48	5	0.0	0	2	0	0	4	45	11.3	0	0	0	-	0	0	0	-	0	0	0
4 NFL Seasons	63	50	208	39	0.0	3	7	0	0	14	134	9.6	1	81	769	9.5	2	11	190	17.3	0	3	12

Other Statistics: 1993–rushed 1 time for 2 yards.

Dexter Carter

Pos: KR/PR **Rnd:** 1 (25) **College:** Florida State   **Ht:** 5' 9" **Wt:** 175 **Born:** 9/15/67 **Age:** 29

Year Team	G	GS	Rushing Att	Yds	Avg	Lg	TD	Receiving Rec	Yds	Avg	Lg	TD	Punt Returns Num	Yds	Avg	TD	Kickoff Returns Num	Yds	Avg	TD	Totals Fum	TD	Pts
1990 San Francisco 49ers	16	5	114	460	4.0	t74	1	25	217	8.7	26	0	0	0	-	0	41	783	19.1	0	8	1	6
1991 San Francisco 49ers	16	15	85	379	4.5	t53	2	23	253	11.0	26	1	0	0	-	0	37	839	22.7	1	5	4	24
1992 San Francisco 49ers	3	0	4	9	2.3	6	0	1	43	43.0	t43	1	0	0	-	0	2	55	27.5	0	0	1	6
1993 San Francisco 49ers	16	0	10	72	7.2	t50	1	3	40	13.3	14	0	34	411	12.1	1	25	494	19.8	0	5	2	12
1994 San Francisco 49ers	16	0	8	34	4.3	18	0	7	99	14.1	44	0	38	321	8.4	0	48	1105	23.0	1	2	1	6
1995 NYA - SF	17	0	7	22	3.1	15	0	2	4	2.0	4	0	30	309	10.3	1	56	1227	21.9	0	8	1	6
1995 New York Jets	10	0	0	0	-	-	0	1	0	0.0	0	0	21	145	6.9	0	33	705	21.4	0	7	0	0
San Francisco 49ers	7	0	7	22	3.1	15	0	1	4	4.0	4	0	9	164	18.2	1	23	522	22.7	0	1	1	6
6 NFL Seasons	84	20	228	976	4.3	t74	4	61	656	10.8	44	2	102	1041	10.2	2	209	4503	21.5	2	28	10	60

Other Statistics: 1990–recovered 2 fumbles for 0 yards. 1991–recovered 1 fumble for 0 yards. 1993–recovered 1 fumble for 0 yards. 1994–recovered 2 fumbles for 0 yards. 1995–recovered 4 fumbles for 0 yards.

Kevin Carter

(statistical profile on page 402)

Pos: DE **Rnd:** 1 (6) **College:** Florida   **Ht:** 6' 5" **Wt:** 275 **Born:** 9/21/73 **Age:** 23

Year Team	G	GS	Tackles Tk	Ast	Sack	Miscellaneous FF	FR	TD	Blk	Interceptions Int	Yds	Avg	TD	Totals Sfty	TD	Pts
1995 St. Louis Rams	16	16	33	4	6.0	1	1	0	0	0	0	-	0	1	0	2

Marty Carter

(statistical profile on page 403)

Pos: S **Rnd:** 8 **College:** Middle Tennessee State   **Ht:** 6' 1" **Wt:** 209 **Born:** 12/17/69 **Age:** 26

Year Team	G	GS	Tackles Tk	Ast	Sack	Misc FF	FR	TD	Blk	Interceptions Int	Yds	Avg	TD	Punt Returns Num	Yds	Avg	TD	Kickoff Returns Num	Yds	Avg	TD	Totals TD	Fum
1991 Tampa Bay Buccaneers	14	11	41	21	0.0	0	0	0	0	1	5	5.0	0	0	0	-	0	0	0	-	0	0	0
1992 Tampa Bay Buccaneers	16	16	78	40	2.0	0	0	0	0	3	1	0.3	0	0	0	-	0	0	0	-	0	0	0
1993 Tampa Bay Buccaneers	16	14	94	36	0.0	1	2	0	0	1	0	0.0	0	0	0	-	0	0	0	-	0	0	0
1994 Tampa Bay Buccaneers	16	14	74	19	1.0	1	0	0	0	0	0	-	0	0	0	-	0	1	0	0.0	0	0	0
1995 Chicago Bears	16	16	80	15	0.0	2	1	0	0	2	20	10.0	0	0	0	-	0	0	0	-	0	0	0
5 NFL Seasons	78	71	367	131	3.0	4	3	0	0	7	26	3.7	0	0	0	-	0	1	0	0.0	0	0	0

Other Statistics: 1994–caught 1 pass for 21 yards.

Pat Carter

Pos: TE/RB **Rnd:** 2 **College:** Florida State   **Ht:** 6' 4" **Wt:** 258 **Born:** 8/1/66 **Age:** 30

Year Team	G	GS	Rushing Att	Yds	Avg	Lg	TD	Receiving Rec	Yds	Avg	Lg	TD	Punt Returns Num	Yds	Avg	TD	Kickoff Returns Num	Yds	Avg	TD	Totals Fum	TD	Pts
1988 Detroit Lions	15	14	0	0	-	-	0	13	145	11.2	31	0	0	0	-	0	0	0	-	0	0	0	0
1989 Los Angeles Rams	16	0	0	0	-	-	0	0	0	-	-	0	0	0	-	0	0	0	-	0	0	0	0
1990 Los Angeles Rams	16	4	0	0	-	-	0	8	58	7.3	16	0	0	0	-	0	0	0	-	0	0	0	0
1991 Los Angeles Rams	16	5	0	0	-	-	0	8	69	8.6	t18	2	0	0	-	0	1	18	18.0	0	1	2	12
1992 Los Angeles Rams	16	16	0	0	-	-	0	20	232	11.6	25	3	0	0	-	0	0	0	-	0	0	3	18
1993 Los Angeles Rams	11	10	0	0	-	-	0	14	166	11.9	38	1	0	0	-	0	0	0	-	0	0	1	6
1994 Houston Oilers	16	12	0	0	-	-	0	11	74	6.7	19	1	0	0	-	0	0	0	-	0	0	1	6
1995 St. Louis Rams	16	5	0	0	-	-	0	0	0	-	-	0	0	0	-	0	0	0	-	0	0	0	0
8 NFL Seasons	122	66	0	0	-	-	0	74	744	10.1	38	7	0	0	-	0	1	18	18.0	0	1	7	42

Perry Carter

Pos: CB **Rnd:** 4 **College:** Southern Mississippi   **Ht:** 5' 11" **Wt:** 206 **Born:** 8/15/71 **Age:** 25

Year Team	G	GS	Tackles Tk	Ast	Sack	Miscellaneous FF	FR	TD	Blk	Interceptions Int	Yds	Avg	TD	Totals Sfty	TD	Pts
1995 Kansas City Chiefs	2	0	0	0	0.0	0	0	0	0	0	0	-	0	0	0	0

Tom Carter

(statistical profile on page 403)

Pos: CB **Rnd:** 1 (17) **College:** Notre Dame   **Ht:** 6' 0" **Wt:** 181 **Born:** 9/5/72 **Age:** 24

Year Team	G	GS	Tackles Tk	Ast	Sack	Miscellaneous FF	FR	TD	Blk	Interceptions Int	Yds	Avg	TD	Totals Sfty	TD	Pts
1993 Washington Redskins	14	11	31	7	0.0	0	0	0	0	6	54	9.0	0	0	0	0
1994 Washington Redskins	16	16	38	5	0.0	0	0	0	0	3	58	19.3	0	0	0	0
1995 Washington Redskins	16	16	74	4	0.0	1	0	0	0	4	116	29.0	1	0	1	6
3 NFL Seasons	46	43	143	16	0.0	1	0	0	0	13	228	17.5	1	0	1	6

Tony Carter

(statistical profile on page 295)

Pos: RB **Rnd:** FA **College:** Minnesota **Ht:** 5' 11" **Wt:** 232 **Born:** 8/23/72 **Age:** 24

			Rushing					Receiving					Punt Returns				Kickoff Returns				Totals		
Year Team	G	GS	Att	Yds	Avg	Lg	TD	Rec	Yds	Avg	Lg	TD	Num	Yds	Avg	TD	Num	Yds	Avg	TD	Fum	TD	Pts
1994 Chicago Bears	14	0	0	0	-	-	0	1	24	24.0	24	0	0	0	-	0	6	99	16.5	0	0	0	0
1995 Chicago Bears	16	11	10	34	3.4	7	0	40	329	8.2	27	1	0	0	-	0	3	24	8.0	0	1	1	6
2 NFL Seasons	30	11	10	34	3.4	7	0	41	353	8.6	27	1	0	0	-	0	9	123	13.7	0	1	1	6

Shante Carver

Pos: DE **Rnd:** 1 (23) **College:** Arizona State **Ht:** 6' 5" **Wt:** 242 **Born:** 2/12/71 **Age:** 25

			Tackles			Miscellaneous				Interceptions				Totals		
Year Team	G	GS	Tk	Ast	Sack	FF	FR	TD	Blk	Int	Yds	Avg	TD	Sfty	TD	Pts
1994 Dallas Cowboys	7	0	2	0	0.0	0	0	0	0	0	0	-	0	0	0	0
1995 Dallas Cowboys	15	3	8	2	2.5	0	1	0	0	0	0	-	0	0	0	0
2 NFL Seasons	22	3	10	2	2.5	0	1	0	0	0	0	-	0	0	0	0

Chad Cascadden

Pos: LB **Rnd:** FA **College:** Wisconsin **Ht:** 6' 1" **Wt:** 225 **Born:** 5/14/72 **Age:** 24

			Tackles			Miscellaneous				Interceptions				Totals		
Year Team	G	GS	Tk	Ast	Sack	FF	FR	TD	Blk	Int	Yds	Avg	TD	Sfty	TD	Pts
1995 New York Jets	12	0	0	0	0.0	0	0	0	0	0	0	-	0	0	0	0

Scott Case

Pos: S **Rnd:** 2 **College:** Oklahoma **Ht:** 6' 1" **Wt:** 188 **Born:** 5/17/62 **Age:** 34

			Tackles			Miscellaneous				Interceptions				Punt Returns				Kickoff Returns				Totals	
Year Team	G	GS	Tk	Ast	Sack	FF	FR	TD	Blk	Int	Yds	Avg	TD	Num	Yds	Avg	TD	Num	Yds	Avg	TD	TD	Fum
1984 Atlanta Falcons	16	0	28	14	0.0	0	0	0	0	0	0	-	0	0	0	-	0	0	0	-	0	0	0
1985 Atlanta Falcons	14	13	58	37	1.0	0	1	0	0	4	78	19.5	0	0	0	-	0	0	0	-	0	0	0
1986 Atlanta Falcons	16	15	42	27	0.0	0	0	0	0	4	41	10.3	0	0	0	-	0	0	0	-	0	0	0
1987 Atlanta Falcons	11	10	41	11	0.0	0	0	0	0	1	12	12.0	0	0	0	-	0	0	0	-	0	0	0
1988 Atlanta Falcons	16	15	34	31	1.0	0	0	0	0	10	47	4.7	0	0	0	-	0	0	0	-	0	0	0
1989 Atlanta Falcons	14	7	27	11	1.0	0	0	0	0	2	13	6.5	0	0	0	-	0	0	0	-	0	0	0
1990 Atlanta Falcons	16	16	78	92	3.0	0	2	0	0	3	38	12.7	1	0	0	-	0	1	13	13.0	0	1	0
1991 Atlanta Falcons	16	16	68	94	0.0	0	2	0	0	2	23	11.5	0	0	0	-	0	0	0	-	0	0	0
1992 Atlanta Falcons	12	11	51	51	0.0	0	2	0	0	2	0	0.0	0	0	0	-	0	0	0	-	0	0	0
1993 Atlanta Falcons	16	16	60	63	1.5	0	0	0	0	0	3	-	0	0	0	-	0	0	0	-	0	0	0
1994 Atlanta Falcons	14	3	28	13	0.0	0	0	0	0	2	12	6.0	0	0	0	-	0	0	0	-	0	0	0
1995 Dallas Cowboys	15	1	14	3	0.0	0	0	0	0	0	0	-	0	0	0	-	0	0	0	-	0	0	0
12 NFL Seasons	176	123	529	447	7.5	0	7	0	0	30	267	8.9	1	0	0	-	0	1	13	13.0	0	1	0

Other Statistics: 1984–credited with 1 safety.

Stoney Case

Pos: QB **Rnd:** 3 **College:** New Mexico **Ht:** 6' 2" **Wt:** 206 **Born:** 7/7/72 **Age:** 24

			Passing										Rushing				Miscellaneous			
Year Team	G	GS	Att	Com	Pct	Yards	Yds/Att	Lg	TD	Int	Int%	Rating	Att	Yds	Avg	Lg	TD	Sckd	Yds	Fum Rec	Yds	Pts
1995 Arizona Cardinals	3	0	2	1	50.0	19	9.50	19	0	1	50.0	43.8	1	4	4.0	4	0	0	0	0	0	0

Keith Cash

(statistical profile on page 296)

Pos: TE **Rnd:** 7 **College:** Texas **Ht:** 6' 4" **Wt:** 242 **Born:** 8/7/69 **Age:** 27

			Rushing					Receiving					Punt Returns				Kickoff Returns				Totals		
Year Team	G	GS	Att	Yds	Avg	Lg	TD	Rec	Yds	Avg	Lg	TD	Num	Yds	Avg	TD	Num	Yds	Avg	TD	Fum	TD	Pts
1991 Pittsburgh Steelers	5	2	0	0	-	-	0	7	90	12.9	20	1	1	6	6.0	0	0	0	-	0	0	1	6
1992 Kansas City Chiefs	15	8	0	0	-	-	0	12	113	9.4	19	2	0	0	-	0	1	36	36.0	0	0	2	12
1993 Kansas City Chiefs	15	0	1	0	0.0	0	0	24	242	10.1	24	4	0	0	-	0	0	0	-	0	1	4	24
1994 Kansas City Chiefs	6	5	0	0	-	-	0	19	192	10.1	31	2	0	0	-	0	0	0	-	0	0	2	12
1995 Kansas City Chiefs	14	14	0	0	-	-	0	42	419	10.0	t38	1	0	0	-	0	0	0	-	0	0	1	6
5 NFL Seasons	55	29	1	0	0.0	0	0	104	1056	10.2	t38	10	1	6	6.0	0	1	36	36.0	0	1	10	60

Other Statistics: 1992–recovered 1 fumble for 0 yards. 1993–recovered 2 fumbles for 0 yards. 1995–recovered 1 fumble for 0 yards.

Kerry Cash

(statistical profile on page 296)

Pos: TE **Rnd:** 5 **College:** Texas **Ht:** 6' 4" **Wt:** 245 **Born:** 8/7/69 **Age:** 27

			Rushing					Receiving					Punt Returns				Kickoff Returns				Totals		
Year Team	G	GS	Att	Yds	Avg	Lg	TD	Rec	Yds	Avg	Lg	TD	Num	Yds	Avg	TD	Num	Yds	Avg	TD	Fum	TD	Pts
1991 Indianapolis Colts	4	2	0	0	-	-	0	1	18	18.0	18	0	0	0	-	0	0	0	-	0	0	0	0
1992 Indianapolis Colts	16	16	0	0	-	-	0	43	521	12.1	41	3	0	0	-	0	0	0	-	0	0	3	18

			Rushing					Receiving					Punt Returns				Kickoff Returns				Totals		
Year Team	G	GS	Att	Yds	Avg	Lg	TD	Rec	Yds	Avg	Lg	TD	Num	Yds	Avg	TD	Num	Yds	Avg	TD	Fum	TD	Pts
1993 Indianapolis Colts	16	14	0	0	-	-	0	43	402	9.3	37	3	0	0	-	0	1	11	11.0	0	2	3	18
1994 Indianapolis Colts	16	16	0	0	-	-	0	16	190	11.9	24	1	0	0	-	0	0	0	-	0	1	1	6
1995 Oakland Raiders	16	10	0	0	-	-	0	25	254	10.2	23	2	0	0	-	0	0	0	-	0	2	2	12
5 NFL Seasons	68	58	0	0	-	-	0	128	1385	10.8	41	9	0	0	-	0	1	11	11.0	0	5	9	54

Other Statistics: 1992–recovered 2 fumbles for 0 yards. 1993–recovered 1 fumble for 0 yards. 1994–recovered 1 fumble for 0 yards. 1995–recovered 2 fumbles for 3 yards.

Tony Casillas

Pos: DT   **Rnd:** 1 (2)   **College:** Oklahoma   **Ht:** 6' 3"   **Wt:** 278   **Born:** 10/26/63   **Age:** 33

			Tackles			Miscellaneous				Interceptions				Totals		
Year Team	G	GS	Tk	Ast	Sack	FF	FR	TD	Blk	Int	Yds	Avg	TD	Sfty	TD	Pts
1986 Atlanta Falcons	16	16	55	56	1.0	2	1	0	0	0	0	-	0	0	0	0
1987 Atlanta Falcons	9	9	38	34	2.0	1	1	0	0	0	0	-	0	0	0	0
1988 Atlanta Falcons	16	16	62	49	2.0	3	1	0	0	0	0	-	0	0	0	0
1989 Atlanta Falcons	16	16	98	54	2.0	2	3	0	0	0	0	-	0	0	0	0
1990 Atlanta Falcons	9	0	18	14	1.0	0	0	0	0	0	0	-	0	0	0	0
1991 Dallas Cowboys	16	16	23	38	2.5	1	1	0	0	0	0	-	0	0	0	0
1992 Dallas Cowboys	15	15	28	27	3.0	0	1	0	0	0	0	-	0	0	0	0
1993 Dallas Cowboys	15	14	28	26	2.0	1	1	0	0	0	0	-	0	0	0	0
1994 New York Jets	13	11	23	12	1.5	0	0	0	0	0	0	-	0	0	0	0
1995 New York Jets	11	5	20	10	3.0	0	0	0	0	0	0	-	0	0	0	0
10 NFL Seasons	136	118	393	320	20.0	9	9	0	0	0	0	-	0	0	0	0

Eric Castle

Pos: S   **Rnd:** 6   **College:** Oregon   **Ht:** 6' 3"   **Wt:** 212   **Born:** 3/15/70   **Age:** 26

			Tackles			Miscellaneous				Interceptions				Totals		
Year Team	G	GS	Tk	Ast	Sack	FF	FR	TD	Blk	Int	Yds	Avg	TD	Sfty	TD	Pts
1993 San Diego Chargers	5	0	0	0	0.0	0	0	0	0	0	0	-	0	0	0	0
1994 San Diego Chargers	16	1	8	2	0.0	0	0	0	0	0	0	-	0	0	0	0
1995 San Diego Chargers	16	0	2	0	0.0	0	0	0	0	0	0	-	0	0	0	0
3 NFL Seasons	37	1	10	2	0.0	0	0	0	0	0	0	-	0	0	0	0

Alcides Catanho

Pos: LB   **Rnd:** FA   **College:** Rutgers   **Ht:** 6' 3"   **Wt:** 216   **Born:** 1/20/72   **Age:** 24

			Tackles			Miscellaneous				Interceptions				Totals		
Year Team	G	GS	Tk	Ast	Sack	FF	FR	TD	Blk	Int	Yds	Avg	TD	Sfty	TD	Pts
1995 New England Patriots	12	0	0	0	0.0	0	1	0	0	0	0	-	0	0	0	0

Curtis Ceaser

Pos: WR   **Rnd:** 7   **College:** Grambling   **Ht:** 6' 2"   **Wt:** 190   **Born:** 8/11/72   **Age:** 24

			Rushing					Receiving					Punt Returns				Kickoff Returns				Totals		
Year Team	G	GS	Att	Yds	Avg	Lg	TD	Rec	Yds	Avg	Lg	TD	Num	Yds	Avg	TD	Num	Yds	Avg	TD	Fum	TD	Pts
1995 New York Jets	4	0	0	0	-	-	0	0	0	-	-	0	0	0	-	0	0	0	-	0	0	0	0

Chuck Cecil

(statistical profile on page 403)

Pos: S   **Rnd:** 4   **College:** Arizona   **Ht:** 6' 0"   **Wt:** 185   **Born:** 11/8/64   **Age:** 31

			Tackles			Miscellaneous				Interceptions				Punt Returns				Kickoff Returns				Totals	
Year Team	G	GS	Tk	Ast	Sack	FF	FR	TD	Blk	Int	Yds	Avg	TD	Num	Yds	Avg	TD	Num	Yds	Avg	TD	TD	Fum
1988 Green Bay Packers	16	2	32	7	0.0	0	1	0	0	4	56	14.0	0	0	0	-	0	0	0	-	0	0	0
1989 Green Bay Packers	9	0	25	13	0.0	0	0	0	0	1	16	16.0	0	0	0	-	0	0	0	-	0	0	0
1990 Green Bay Packers	9	8	36	15	0.0	0	0	0	0	1	0	0	0	0	0	-	0	0	0	-	0	0	0
1991 Green Bay Packers	16	16	82	28	0.0	0	0	0	0	3	76	25.3	0	0	0	-	0	0	0	-	0	0	0
1992 Green Bay Packers	16	16	82	20	0.0	0	0	0	0	4	52	13.0	0	1	0	0.0	0	0	0	-	0	0	1
1993 Phoenix Cardinals	15	7	43	18	0.0	0	0	0	0	0	0	-	0	0	0	-	0	0	0	-	0	0	0
1995 Houston Oilers	14	12	44	16	0.0	0	0	0	0	3	35	11.7	1	0	0	-	0	0	0	-	0	1	0
7 NFL Seasons	95	61	344	117	0.0	0	1	0	0	16	235	14.7	1	1	0	0.0	0	0	0	-	0	1	1

Larry Centers

(statistical profile on page 297)

Pos: RB   **Rnd:** 5   **College:** Stephen F. Austin   **Ht:** 5' 11"   **Wt:** 215   **Born:** 6/1/68   **Age:** 28

			Rushing					Receiving					Punt Returns				Kickoff Returns				Totals		
Year Team	G	GS	Att	Yds	Avg	Lg	TD	Rec	Yds	Avg	Lg	TD	Num	Yds	Avg	TD	Num	Yds	Avg	TD	Fum	TD	Pts
1990 Phoenix Cardinals	6	0	0	0	-	-	0	0	0	-	-	0	0	0	-	0	16	272	17.0	0	1	0	0
1991 Phoenix Cardinals	9	2	14	44	3.1	8	0	19	176	9.3	23	0	5	30	6.0	0	16	330	20.6	0	4	0	0
1992 Phoenix Cardinals	16	1	37	139	3.8	28	0	50	417	8.3	26	2	0	0	-	0	0	0	-	0	1	2	12
1993 Phoenix Cardinals	16	9	25	152	6.1	33	0	66	603	9.1	29	3	0	0	-	0	0	0	-	0	1	3	18

52

Year Team	G	GS	Rushing Att	Yds	Avg	Lg	TD	Receiving Rec	Yds	Avg	Lg	TD	Punt Returns Num	Yds	Avg	TD	Kickoff Returns Num	Yds	Avg	TD	Totals Fum	TD	Pts
1994 Arizona Cardinals	16	8	115	336	2.9	17	5	77	647	8.4	36	2	0	0	-	0	0	0	-	0	2	7	42
1995 Arizona Cardinals	16	10	78	254	3.3	20	2	101	962	9.5	32	2	0	0	-	0	1	15	15.0	0	2	4	24
6 NFL Seasons	79	30	269	925	3.4	33	7	313	2805	9.0	36	9	5	30	6.0	0	33	617	18.7	0	11	16	96

Other Statistics: 1991–recovered 2 fumbles for 0 yards. 1993–recovered 2 fumbles for 0 yards. 1994–recovered 2 fumbles for 27 yards. 1995–recovered 1 fumble for 2 yards; attempted 1 pass with 0 completions for 0 yards and 1 interception.

Mike Chalenski

Pos: DT/DE **Rnd:** FA **College:** UCLA **Ht:** 6' 5" **Wt:** 285 **Born:** 1/28/70 **Age:** 26

Year Team	G	GS	Tackles Tk	Ast	Sack	Miscellaneous FF	FR	TD	Blk	Interceptions Int	Yds	Avg	TD	Totals Sfty	TD	Pts
1993 Philadelphia Eagles	15	0	1	0	0.0	0	0	0	0	0	0	-	0	0	0	0
1995 Philadelphia Eagles	9	0	4	0	0.0	0	0	0	0	0	0	-	0	0	0	0
2 NFL Seasons	24	0	5	0	0.0	0	0	0	0	0	0	-	0	0	0	0

Byron Chamberlain

Pos: TE/WR **Rnd:** 7 **College:** Wayne State (NE) **Ht:** 6' 1" **Wt:** 225 **Born:** 10/17/71 **Age:** 25

Year Team	G	GS	Rushing Att	Yds	Avg	Lg	TD	Receiving Rec	Yds	Avg	Lg	TD	Punt Returns Num	Yds	Avg	TD	Kickoff Returns Num	Yds	Avg	TD	Totals Fum	TD	Pts
1995 Denver Broncos	5	0	0	0	-	-	0	1	11	11.0	11	0	0	0	-	0	0	0	-	0	0	0	0

Chris Chandler

(statistical profile on page 297)

Pos: QB **Rnd:** 3 **College:** Washington **Ht:** 6' 4" **Wt:** 225 **Born:** 10/12/65 **Age:** 31

Year Team	G	GS	Passing Att	Com	Pct	Yards	Yds/Att	Lg	TD	Int	Int%	Rating	Rushing Att	Yds	Avg	Lg	TD	Miscellaneous Sckd	Yds	Fum	Recv	Yds	Pts
1988 Indianapolis Colts	15	13	233	129	55.4	1619	6.95	54	8	12	5.2	67.2	46	139	3.0	t29	3	18	128	8	5	-6	18
1989 Indianapolis Colts	3	3	80	39	48.8	537	6.71	23	2	3	3.8	63.4	7	57	8.1	23	1	3	17	0	0	0	6
1990 Tampa Bay Buccaneers	7	3	83	42	50.6	464	5.59	t68	1	6	7.2	41.4	13	71	5.5	18	1	15	103	5	1	-2	6
1991 TB - Pho	9	5	154	78	50.6	846	5.49	t45	5	10	6.5	50.9	26	111	4.3	12	0	17	134	6	2	-7	0
1992 Phoenix Cardinals	15	13	413	245	59.3	2832	6.86	t72	15	15	3.6	77.1	36	149	4.1	18	1	29	226	9	2	-11	6
1993 Phoenix Cardinals	4	2	103	52	50.5	471	4.57	t27	3	2	1.9	64.8	3	2	0.7	1	0	4	25	2	0	0	0
1994 Los Angeles Rams	12	6	176	108	61.4	1352	7.68	t72	7	2	1.1	93.8	18	61	3.4	22	1	7	46	3	0	-2	6
1995 Houston Oilers	13	13	356	225	63.2	2460	6.91	t76	17	10	2.8	87.8	28	58	2.1	9	2	21	173	12	5	-6	14
1991 Tampa Bay Buccaneers	6	3	104	53	51.0	557	5.36	35	4	8	7.7	47.6	18	79	4.4	12	0	10	76	3	1	0	0
Phoenix Cardinals	3	2	50	25	50.0	289	5.78	t45	1	2	4.0	57.8	8	32	4.0	12	0	7	58	3	1	-7	0
8 NFL Seasons	78	58	1598	918	57.4	10581	6.62	t82	58	60	3.8	74.0	177	648	3.7	t29	9	114	852	45	15	-34	56

Other Statistics: 1995–scored 1 two-point conversion.

Ray Childress

Pos: DT **Rnd:** 1 (3) **College:** Texas A&M **Ht:** 6' 6" **Wt:** 272 **Born:** 10/20/62 **Age:** 34

Year Team	G	GS	Tackles Tk	Ast	Sack	Miscellaneous FF	FR	TD	Blk	Interceptions Int	Yds	Avg	TD	Totals Sfty	TD	Pts
1985 Houston Oilers	16	16	71	64	3.5	2	1	0	0	0	0	-	0	0	0	0
1986 Houston Oilers	16	16	67	105	5.0	1	1	0	0	0	0	-	0	0	0	0
1987 Houston Oilers	13	13	44	25	6.0	2	1	0	0	0	0	-	0	0	0	0
1988 Houston Oilers	16	16	45	15	8.5	1	7	0	0	0	0	-	0	0	0	0
1989 Houston Oilers	14	14	38	19	8.5	1	1	0	0	0	0	-	0	0	0	0
1990 Houston Oilers	16	16	65	20	8.0	1	0	0	0	0	0	-	0	1	0	2
1991 Houston Oilers	15	15	55	20	7.0	3	1	0	0	0	0	-	0	0	0	0
1992 Houston Oilers	16	16	64	26	13.0	3	2	1	0	0	0	-	0	0	1	6
1993 Houston Oilers	16	16	45	13	9.0	1	3	1	0	0	0	-	0	0	1	6
1994 Houston Oilers	16	16	49	19	6.0	3	0	0	0	0	0	-	0	0	0	0
1995 Houston Oilers	6	6	8	7	1.0	1	1	0	0	0	0	-	0	0	0	0
11 NFL Seasons	160	160	551	333	75.5	19	19	2	0	0	0	-	0	1	2	14

Ron Childs

Pos: LB **Rnd:** FA **College:** Washington State **Ht:** 5' 11" **Wt:** 212 **Born:** 9/18/71 **Age:** 25

Year Team	G	GS	Tackles Tk	Ast	Sack	Miscellaneous FF	FR	TD	Blk	Interceptions Int	Yds	Avg	TD	Totals Sfty	TD	Pts
1995 New Orleans Saints	9	0	0	0	0.0	0	0	0	0	0	0	-	0	0	0	0

Mark Chmura

(statistical profile on page 298)

Pos: TE/LS **Rnd:** 6 **College:** Boston College **Ht:** 6' 5" **Wt:** 250 **Born:** 2/22/69 **Age:** 27

Year	Team	G	GS	Rushing					Receiving					Punt Returns				Kickoff Returns				Totals		
				Att	Yds	Avg	Lg	TD	Rec	Yds	Avg	Lg	TD	Num	Yds	Avg	TD	Num	Yds	Avg	TD	Fum	TD	Pts
1993	Green Bay Packers	14	0	0	0	-	-	0	2	13	6.5	7	0	0	0	-	0	1	0	0.0	0	1	0	0
1994	Green Bay Packers	15	4	0	0	-	-	0	14	165	11.8	27	0	0	0	-	0	0	0	-	0	0	0	0
1995	Green Bay Packers	16	15	0	0	-	-	0	54	679	12.6	33	7	0	0	-	0	0	0	-	0	0	7	44
	3 NFL Seasons	45	19	0	0	-	-	0	70	857	12.2	33	7	0	0	-	0	1	0	0.0	0	1	7	44

Other Statistics: 1993–recovered 1 fumble for 0 yards. 1995–scored 1 two-point conversion.

Wayne Chrebet

(statistical profile on page 298)

Pos: WR **Rnd:** FA **College:** Hofstra **Ht:** 5' 10" **Wt:** 180 **Born:** 8/14/73 **Age:** 23

Year	Team	G	GS	Rushing					Receiving					Punt Returns				Kickoff Returns				Totals		
				Att	Yds	Avg	Lg	TD	Rec	Yds	Avg	Lg	TD	Num	Yds	Avg	TD	Num	Yds	Avg	TD	Fum	TD	Pts
1995	New York Jets	16	16	1	1	1.0	1	0	66	726	11.0	32	4	0	0	-	0	0	0	-	0	1	4	24

Bob Christian

(statistical profile on page 299)

Pos: RB **Rnd:** 12 **College:** Northwestern **Ht:** 5' 10" **Wt:** 225 **Born:** 11/14/68 **Age:** 27

Year	Team	G	GS	Rushing					Receiving					Punt Returns				Kickoff Returns				Totals		
				Att	Yds	Avg	Lg	TD	Rec	Yds	Avg	Lg	TD	Num	Yds	Avg	TD	Num	Yds	Avg	TD	Fum	TD	Pts
1992	Chicago Bears	2	0	0	0	-	-	0	0	0	-	-	0	0	0	-	0	0	0	-	0	0	0	0
1993	Chicago Bears	14	1	8	19	2.4	12	0	16	160	10.0	36	0	0	0	-	0	0	0	-	0	0	0	0
1994	Chicago Bears	12	0	7	29	4.1	8	0	2	30	15.0	21	0	0	0	-	0	0	0	-	0	0	0	0
1995	Carolina Panthers	14	12	41	158	3.9	17	0	29	255	8.8	23	1	0	0	-	0	0	0	-	0	1	1	8
	4 NFL Seasons	42	13	56	206	3.7	17	0	47	445	9.5	36	1	0	0	-	0	0	0	-	0	1	1	8

Other Statistics: 1995–recovered 1 fumble for 0 yards; scored 1 two-point conversion.

Steve Christie

(statistical profile on page 470)

Pos: K **Rnd:** FA **College:** William & Mary **Ht:** 6' 0" **Wt:** 185 **Born:** 11/13/67 **Age:** 28

Year	Team	G	1-29 Yds	Pct	30-39 Yds	Pct	40-49 Yds	Pct	50+ Yds	Pct	Overall	Pct	Long	PAT Made	Att	Tot Pts
1990	Tampa Bay Buccaneers	16	7-7	100.0	10-13	76.9	4-5	80.0	2-2	100.0	23-27	85.2	54	27	27	96
1991	Tampa Bay Buccaneers	16	5-5	100.0	7-11	63.6	3-4	75.0	0-0	-	15-20	75.0	49	22	22	67
1992	Buffalo Bills	16	11-11	100.0	3-6	50.0	7-8	87.5	3-5	60.0	24-30	80.0	54	43	44	115
1993	Buffalo Bills	16	4-5	80.0	12-12	100.0	6-9	66.7	1-6	16.7	23-32	71.9	59	36	37	105
1994	Buffalo Bills	16	11-12	91.7	6-7	85.7	5-7	71.4	2-2	100.0	24-28	85.7	52	38	38	110
1995	Buffalo Bills	16	13-14	92.9	13-15	86.7	3-6	50.0	2-5	40.0	31-40	77.5	51	33	35	126
	6 NFL Seasons	96	51-54	94.4	51-64	79.7	28-39	71.8	10-20	50.0	140-177	79.1	59	199	203	619

Other Statistics: 1994–recovered 1 fumble for 0 yards.

Ryan Christopherson

Pos: RB **Rnd:** 5 **College:** Wyoming **Ht:** 5' 11" **Wt:** 237 **Born:** 7/26/72 **Age:** 24

Year	Team	G	GS	Rushing					Receiving					Punt Returns				Kickoff Returns				Totals		
				Att	Yds	Avg	Lg	TD	Rec	Yds	Avg	Lg	TD	Num	Yds	Avg	TD	Num	Yds	Avg	TD	Fum	TD	Pts
1995	Jacksonville Jaguars	11	0	16	16	1.0	10	1	1	-1	-1.0	-1	0	0	0	-	0	0	0	-	0	1	1	6

Jeff Christy

Pos: C **Rnd:** 4 **College:** Pittsburgh **Ht:** 6' 3" **Wt:** 290 **Born:** 2/3/69 **Age:** 27

Year	Team	G	GS	Year	Team	G	GS	Year	Team	G	GS		G	GS
1993	Minnesota Vikings	9	0	1994	Minnesota Vikings	16	16	1995	Minnesota Vikings	16	16	3 NFL Seasons	41	32

Eugene Chung

Pos: G/T **Rnd:** 1 (13) **College:** Virginia Tech **Ht:** 6' 5" **Wt:** 311 **Born:** 6/14/69 **Age:** 27

Year	Team	G	GS	Year	Team	G	GS	Year	Team	G	GS	Year	Team	G	GS
1992	New England Patriots	15	14	1993	New England Patriots	16	16	1994	New England Patriots	4	0	1995	Jacksonville Jaguars	11	0
													4 NFL Seasons	46	30

Gary Clark

(statistical profile on page 299)

Pos: WR **Rnd:** 2(S) **College:** James Madison **Ht:** 5' 9" **Wt:** 175 **Born:** 5/1/62 **Age:** 34

Year	Team	G	GS	Rushing					Receiving					Punt Returns				Kickoff Returns				Totals		
				Att	Yds	Avg	Lg	TD	Rec	Yds	Avg	Lg	TD	Num	Yds	Avg	TD	Num	Yds	Avg	TD	Fum	TD	Pts
1985	Washington Redskins	16	10	2	10	5.0	7	0	72	926	12.9	55	5	0	0	-	0	0	0	-	0	0	5	30
1986	Washington Redskins	15	15	0	0	-	0	0	74	1265	17.1	55	7	1	14	14.0	0	0	0	-	0	1	7	42
1987	Washington Redskins	12	11	1	0	0.0	0	0	56	1066	19.0	t84	7	0	0	-	0	0	0	-	0	3	7	42

Year	Team	G	GS	Att	Rushing Yds	Avg	Lg	TD	Rec	Receiving Yds	Avg	Lg	TD	Num	Punt Returns Yds	Avg	TD	Num	Kickoff Returns Yds	Avg	TD	Fum	Totals TD	Pts
1988	Washington Redskins	16	13	2	6	3.0	4	0	59	892	15.1	t60	7	8	48	6.0	0	0	0	-	0	2	7	42
1989	Washington Redskins	15	12	2	19	9.5	11	0	79	1229	15.6	t80	9	0	0	-	0	0	0	-	0	1	9	54
1990	Washington Redskins	16	16	1	1	1.0	1	0	75	1112	14.8	t53	8	0	0	-	0	0	0	-	0	0	8	48
1991	Washington Redskins	16	16	1	0	0.0	0	0	70	1340	19.1	t82	10	0	0	-	0	0	0	-	0	0	10	60
1992	Washington Redskins	16	14	2	18	9.0	12	0	64	912	14.3	47	5	0	0	-	0	0	0	-	0	1	5	30
1993	Phoenix Cardinals	14	10	0	0	-	-	0	63	818	13.0	55	4	0	0	-	0	0	0	-	0	1	4	24
1994	Arizona Cardinals	15	2	0	0	-	-	0	50	771	15.4	45	1	0	0	-	0	0	0	-	0	0	1	6
1995	Miami Dolphins	16	0	0	0	-	-	0	37	525	14.2	t42	2	0	0	-	0	0	0	-	0	0	2	12
	11 NFL Seasons	167	119	11	54	4.9	12	0	699	10856	15.5	t84	65	9	62	6.9	0	0	0	-	0	9	65	390

Other Statistics: 1986--recovered 1 fumble for 0 yards.

Reggie Clark

Pos: LB **Rnd:** FA **College:** North Carolina **Ht:** 6' 3" **Wt:** 245 **Born:** 10/17/67 **Age:** 29

Year	Team	G	GS	Tackles Tk	Ast	Sack	Miscellaneous FF	FR	TD	Blk	Interceptions Int	Yds	Avg	TD	Totals Sfty	TD	Pts
1994	Pittsburgh Steelers	5	0	0	0	0.0	0	1	0	0	0	0	-	0	0	0	0
1995	Jacksonville Jaguars	5	0	0	2	0.0	0	1	0	0	0	0	-	0	0	0	0
	2 NFL Seasons	10	0	0	2	0.0	0	2	0	0	0	0	-	0	0	0	0

Vinnie Clark

(statistical profile on page 404)

Pos: CB **Rnd:** 1 (19) **College:** Ohio State **Ht:** 6' 0" **Wt:** 204 **Born:** 1/22/69 **Age:** 27

Year	Team	G	GS	Tackles Tk	Ast	Sack	FF	Miscellaneous FR	TD	Blk	Int	Interceptions Yds	Avg	TD	Num	Punt Returns Yds	Avg	TD	Num	Kickoff Returns Yds	Avg	TD	Totals TD	Fum
1991	Green Bay Packers	16	4	27	3	0.0	0	0	0	0	2	42	21.0	0	0	0	-	0	0	0	-	0	0	0
1992	Green Bay Packers	16	11	38	-	0.0	0	0	0	0	2	70	35.0	0	1	0	0.0	0	0	0	-	0	0	0
1993	Atlanta Falcons	15	9	43	13	0.0	1	1	1	0	2	59	29.5	0	1	0	0.0	0	0	0	-	0	1	1
1994	Atl - NO	16	15	64	9	0.0	2	0	0	0	5	149	29.8	0	0	0	-	0	0	0	-	0	0	0
1995	Jacksonville Jaguars	16	16	56	10	0.0	0	0	0	0	1	0	0.0	0	0	0	-	0	0	0	-	0	0	0
1994	Atlanta Falcons	11	11	45	7	0.0	2	0	0	0	4	119	29.8	0	0	0	-	0	0	0	-	0	0	0
	New Orleans Saints	5	4	19	2	0.0	0	0	0	0	1	30	30.0	0	0	0	-	0	0	0	-	0	0	0
	5 NFL Seasons	79	55	228	35	0.0	3	1	1	0	12	320	26.7	0	2	0	0.0	0	0	0	-	0	1	1

Willie Clark

Pos: CB **Rnd:** 3 **College:** Notre Dame **Ht:** 5' 10" **Wt:** 186 **Born:** 1/6/72 **Age:** 24

Year	Team	G	GS	Tackles Tk	Ast	Sack	Miscellaneous FF	FR	TD	Blk	Interceptions Int	Yds	Avg	TD	Totals Sfty	TD	Pts
1994	San Diego Chargers	6	0	11	2	0.0	0	0	0	0	0	0	-	0	0	0	0
1995	San Diego Chargers	16	2	26	5	0.0	1	1	0	0	2	14	7.0	0	0	0	0
	2 NFL Seasons	22	2	37	7	0.0	1	1	0	0	2	14	7.0	0	0	0	0

Conrad Clarks

Pos: S **Rnd:** FA **College:** Northeast Louisiana **Ht:** 5' 10" **Wt:** 212 **Born:** 4/21/69 **Age:** 27

Year	Team	G	GS	Tackles Tk	Ast	Sack	Miscellaneous FF	FR	TD	Blk	Interceptions Int	Yds	Avg	TD	Totals Sfty	TD	Pts
1995	Indianapolis Colts	6	0	0	0	0.0	0	0	0	0	0	0	-	0	0	0	0

Shannon Clavelle

Pos: DE **Rnd:** 6 **College:** Colorado **Ht:** 6' 2" **Wt:** 283 **Born:** 12/12/73 **Age:** 22

Year	Team	G	GS	Tackles Tk	Ast	Sack	Miscellaneous FF	FR	TD	Blk	Interceptions Int	Yds	Avg	TD	Totals Sfty	TD	Pts
1995	Green Bay Packers	1	0	0	0	0.0	0	0	0	0	0	0	-	0	0	0	0

Willie Clay

(statistical profile on page 404)

Pos: S **Rnd:** 8 **College:** Georgia Tech **Ht:** 5' 9" **Wt:** 184 **Born:** 9/5/70 **Age:** 26

Year	Team	G	GS	Tackles Tk	Ast	Sack	FF	Miscellaneous FR	TD	Blk	Int	Interceptions Yds	Avg	TD	Num	Punt Returns Yds	Avg	TD	Num	Kickoff Returns Yds	Avg	TD	Totals TD	Fum
1992	Detroit Lions	6	0	4	2	0.0	0	0	0	0	0	0	-	0	0	0	-	0	0	0	-	0	0	0
1993	Detroit Lions	16	1	22	2	1.0	1	2	2	0	0	0	-	0	0	0	-	0	2	34	17.0	0	2	0
1994	Detroit Lions	16	16	59	17	0.0	3	0	0	0	3	54	18.0	1	3	20	6.7	0	0	0	-	0	1	0
1995	Detroit Lions	16	16	50	16	0.0	0	0	0	0	8	**173**	21.6	0	5	49	9.8	0	0	0	-	0	0	0
	4 NFL Seasons	54	33	135	37	1.0	4	2	2	0	11	227	20.6	1	8	69	8.6	0	2	34	17.0	0	3	0

Kyle Clifton

Pos: LB **Rnd:** 3   **College:** Texas Christian   **Ht:** 6' 4" **Wt:** 236 **Born:** 8/23/62 **Age:** 34

			Tackles			Miscellaneous				Interceptions				Punt Returns				Kickoff Returns				Totals	
Year Team	G	GS	Tk	Ast	Sack	FF	FR	TD	Blk	Int	Yds	Avg	TD	Num	Yds	Avg	TD	Num	Yds	Avg	TD	TD	Fum
1984 New York Jets	16	9	66	47	0.0	0	1	0	0	1	0	0.0	0	0	0	-	0	0	0	-	0	0	0
1985 New York Jets	16	16	99	61	0.0	2	2	0	0	3	10	3.3	0	0	0	-	0	0	0	-	0	0	0
1986 New York Jets	16	16	108	66	0.0	1	1	0	0	2	8	4.0	0	0	0	-	0	0	0	-	0	0	0
1987 New York Jets	12	8	37	14	0.0	0	0	0	0	0	0	-	0	0	0	-	0	0	0	-	0	0	0
1988 New York Jets	16	15	116	46	0.0	0	2	0	0	0	0	-	0	0	0	-	0	0	0	-	0	0	0
1989 New York Jets	16	16	106	56	2.0	2	1	0	0	0	0	-	0	0	0	-	0	0	0	-	0	0	0
1990 New York Jets	16	16	142	57	0.5	1	1	0	0	3	49	16.3	0	0	0	-	0	0	0	-	0	0	0
1991 New York Jets	16	16	62	84	1.0	2	0	0	0	1	3	3.0	0	0	0	-	0	0	0	-	0	0	0
1992 New York Jets	16	16	50	88	1.0	3	4	0	0	1	1	1.0	0	0	0	-	0	0	0	-	0	0	0
1993 New York Jets	16	16	91	52	1.0	2	2	0	0	1	3	3.0	0	0	0	-	0	0	0	-	0	0	0
1994 New York Jets	16	5	19	13	0.0	0	1	0	0	0	0	-	0	0	0	-	0	1	13	13.0	0	0	0
1995 New York Jets	16	0	1	3	0.0	0	0	0	0	0	0	-	0	0	0	-	0	0	0	-	0	0	0
12 NFL Seasons	188	149	897	587	5.5	13	15	0	0	12	74	6.2	0	0	0	-	0	1	13	13.0	0	0	0

Tony Cline

Pos: TE **Rnd:** 4   **College:** Stanford   **Ht:** 6' 4" **Wt:** 251 **Born:** 11/24/71 **Age:** 24

			Rushing					Receiving					Punt Returns				Kickoff Returns				Totals		
Year Team	G	GS	Att	Yds	Avg	Lg	TD	Rec	Yds	Avg	Lg	TD	Num	Yds	Avg	TD	Num	Yds	Avg	TD	Fum	TD	Pts
1995 Buffalo Bills	16	1	0	0	-	-	0	8	64	8.0	17	0	0	0	-	0	1	11	11.0	0	0	0	0

Ben Coates

(statistical profile on page 300)

Pos: TE **Rnd:** 5   **College:** Livingstone College   **Ht:** 6' 5" **Wt:** 245 **Born:** 8/16/69 **Age:** 27

			Rushing					Receiving					Punt Returns				Kickoff Returns				Totals		
Year Team	G	GS	Att	Yds	Avg	Lg	TD	Rec	Yds	Avg	Lg	TD	Num	Yds	Avg	TD	Num	Yds	Avg	TD	Fum	TD	Pts
1991 New England Patriots	16	2	1	-6	-6.0	-6	0	10	95	9.5	17	1	0	0	-	0	1	6	6.0	0	0	1	6
1992 New England Patriots	16	2	1	2	2.0	2	0	20	171	8.6	t22	3	0	0	-	0	0	0	-	0	1	3	18
1993 New England Patriots	16	10	0	0	-	-	0	53	659	12.4	t54	8	0	0	-	0	0	0	-	0	0	8	48
1994 New England Patriots	16	16	1	0	0.0	0	0	96	1174	12.2	t62	7	0	0	-	0	0	0	-	0	2	7	42
1995 New England Patriots	16	15	0	0	-	-	0	84	915	10.9	35	6	0	0	-	0	0	0	-	0	4	6	36
5 NFL Seasons	80	45	3	-4	-1.3	2	0	263	3014	11.5	t62	25	0	0	-	0	1	6	6.0	0	7	25	150

Other Statistics: 1994–recovered 2 fumbles for 0 yards.

Reggie Cobb

Pos: WR **Rnd:** 2   **College:** Tennessee   **Ht:** 6' 1" **Wt:** 221 **Born:** 7/7/68 **Age:** 28

			Rushing					Receiving					Punt Returns				Kickoff Returns				Totals		
Year Team	G	GS	Att	Yds	Avg	Lg	TD	Rec	Yds	Avg	Lg	TD	Num	Yds	Avg	TD	Num	Yds	Avg	TD	Fum	TD	Pts
1990 Tampa Bay Buccaneers	16	13	151	480	3.2	17	2	39	299	7.7	17	0	0	0	-	0	11	223	20.3	0	8	2	12
1991 Tampa Bay Buccaneers	16	11	196	752	3.8	t59	7	15	111	7.4	21	0	0	0	-	0	2	15	7.5	0	3	7	42
1992 Tampa Bay Buccaneers	16	13	310	1171	3.8	25	9	21	156	7.4	27	0	0	0	-	0	0	0	-	0	3	9	54
1993 Tampa Bay Buccaneers	12	10	221	658	3.0	16	3	9	61	6.8	19	1	0	0	-	0	0	0	-	0	5	4	24
1994 Green Bay Packers	16	13	153	579	3.8	30	3	35	299	8.5	t37	1	0	0	-	0	0	0	-	0	1	4	24
1995 Jacksonville Jaguars	1	0	9	18	2.0	5	0	0	0	-	-	0	0	0	-	0	0	0	-	0	1	0	0
6 NFL Seasons	77	60	1040	3658	3.5	t59	24	119	926	7.8	t37	2	0	0	-	0	13	238	18.3	0	21	26	156

Other Statistics: 1990–recovered 6 fumbles for 0 yards. 1992–recovered 1 fumble for 0 yards. 1993–recovered 1 fumble for 0 yards.

Joe Cocozzo

Pos: G **Rnd:** 3   **College:** Michigan   **Ht:** 6' 4" **Wt:** 300 **Born:** 8/7/70 **Age:** 26

Year	Team	G	GS	Year	Team	G	GS	Year	Team	G	GS		G	GS
1993	San Diego Chargers	16	5	1994	San Diego Chargers	13	13	1995	San Diego Chargers	15	7	3 NFL Seasons	44	25

Mike Cofer

(statistical profile on page 471)

Pos: K **Rnd:** FA   **College:** North Carolina State   **Ht:** 6' 1" **Wt:** 195 **Born:** 2/19/64 **Age:** 32

		Field Goals											PAT		Tot
Year Team	G	1-29 Yds	Pct	30-39 Yds	Pct	40-49 Yds	Pct	50+ Yds	Pct	Overall	Pct	Long	Made	Att	Pts
1987 New Orleans Saints	2	1-1	100.0	0-0	-	0-0	-	0-0	-	1-1	100.0	27	5	7	8
1988 San Francisco 49ers	16	10-11	90.9	9-11	81.8	7-11	63.6	1-5	20.0	27-38	71.1	52	40	41	121
1989 San Francisco 49ers	16	11-11	100.0	8-9	88.9	10-15	66.7	0-1	0.0	29-36	80.6	47	49	51	136
1990 San Francisco 49ers	16	9-9	100.0	7-9	77.8	6-12	50.0	2-6	33.3	24-36	66.7	56	39	39	111
1991 San Francisco 49ers	16	5-5	100.0	3-9	33.3	4-10	40.0	2-3	66.7	14-28	50.0	50	49	50	91
1992 San Francisco 49ers	16	7-8	87.5	5-8	62.5	6-10	60.0	0-1	0.0	18-27	66.7	46	53	54	107
1993 San Francisco 49ers	16	7-9	77.8	5-7	71.4	4-7	57.1	0-3	0.0	16-26	61.5	46	59	61	107
1995 Indianapolis Colts	4	2-2	100.0	0-4	0.0	1-2	50.0	1-1	100.0	4-9	44.4	52	9	9	21

Year Team	G	1-29 Yds	Pct	30-39 Yds	Pct	40-49 Yds	Pct	50+ Yds	Pct	Overall	Pct	Long	Made	Att	Pts
						Field Goals							**PAT**		**Tot**
8 NFL Seasons	102	52-56	92.9	37-57	64.9	38-67	56.7	6-20	30.0	133-201	66.2	56	303	312	702

Other Statistics: 1990–recovered 2 fumbles for 0 yards.

Andre Coleman

Pos: KR/PR **Rnd:** 3   **College:** Kansas State   **Ht:** 5' 9" **Wt:** 165 **Born:** 1/18/71 **Age:** 25

Year Team	G	GS	Att	Yds	Avg	Lg	TD	Rec	Yds	Avg	Lg	TD	Num	Yds	Avg	TD	Num	Yds	Avg	TD	Fum	TD	Pts
			Rushing					**Receiving**					**Punt Returns**				**Kickoff Returns**				**Totals**		
1994 San Diego Chargers	13	0	0	0	-	-	0	0	0	-	-	0	0	0	-	0	49	1293	26.4	2	3	2	12
1995 San Diego Chargers	15	0	0	0	-	-	0	4	78	19.5	41	0	28	326	11.6	1	62	1411	22.8	2	10	3	18
2 NFL Seasons	28	0	0	0	-	-	0	4	78	19.5	41	0	28	326	11.6	1	111	2704	24.4	4	13	5	30

Other Statistics: 1994–recovered 1 fumble for 0 yards. 1995–recovered 3 fumbles for 0 yards.

Ben Coleman

Pos: G/T **Rnd:** 2   **College:** Wake Forest   **Ht:** 6' 6" **Wt:** 335 **Born:** 5/18/71 **Age:** 25

Year	Team	G	GS	Year	Team	G	GS	Year	Team	G	GS	Year	Team	G	GS
1993	Phoenix Cardinals	12	0	1994	Arizona Cardinals	15	13	1995	Arizona Cardinals	3	0	1995	Jacksonville Jaguars	10	5
													3 NFL Seasons	40	18

Other Statistics: 1995–recovered 1 fumble for 0 yards.

Marco Coleman

(statistical profile on page 404)

Pos: DE **Rnd:** 1 (12) **College:** Georgia Tech   **Ht:** 6' 3" **Wt:** 267 **Born:** 12/18/69 **Age:** 26

Year Team	G	GS	Tk	Ast	Sack	FF	FR	TD	Blk	Int	Yds	Avg	TD	Sfty	TD	Pts
			Tackles			**Miscellaneous**				**Interceptions**				**Totals**		
1992 Miami Dolphins	16	15	61	23	6.0	1	0	0	0	0	0	-	0	0	0	0
1993 Miami Dolphins	15	15	35	19	5.5	2	0	0	0	0	0	-	0	0	0	0
1994 Miami Dolphins	16	16	34	9	6.0	3	1	0	0	0	0	-	0	0	0	0
1995 Miami Dolphins	16	16	33	12	6.5	0	0	0	0	0	0	-	0	0	0	0
4 NFL Seasons	63	62	163	63	24.0	6	1	0	0	0	0	-	0	0	0	0

Andre Collins

Pos: LB **Rnd:** 2   **College:** Penn State   **Ht:** 6' 1" **Wt:** 231 **Born:** 5/4/68 **Age:** 28

Year Team	G	GS	Tk	Ast	Sack	FF	FR	TD	Blk	Int	Yds	Avg	TD	Num	Yds	Avg	TD	Num	Yds	Avg	TD	TD	Fum
			Tackles			**Miscellaneous**				**Interceptions**				**Punt Returns**				**Kickoff Returns**				**Totals**	
1990 Washington Redskins	16	16	54	39	6.0	0	0	0	0	0	0	-	0	0	0	-	0	0	0	-	0	0	0
1991 Washington Redskins	16	16	91	60	3.0	0	0	0	2	2	33	16.5	1	0	0	-	0	0	0	-	0	1	1
1992 Washington Redskins	14	14	61	55	2.0	0	1	0	0	1	59	59.0	0	0	0	-	0	0	0	-	0	0	0
1993 Washington Redskins	13	13	64	48	6.0	2	0	0	0	1	5	5.0	0	0	0	-	0	0	0	-	0	0	0
1994 Washington Redskins	16	16	107	21	1.5	1	1	0	0	4	150	37.5	2	0	0	-	0	1	0	0.0	0	2	0
1995 Cincinnati Bengals	16	6	50	12	4.0	0	0	0	0	2	3	1.5	0	0	0	-	0	1	-3	-3.0	0	0	0
6 NFL Seasons	91	81	427	235	22.5	3	2	0	0	10	250	25.0	3	0	0	-	0	2	-3	-1.5	0	3	1

Gerald Collins

Pos: LB **Rnd:** FA   **College:** Vanderbilt   **Ht:** 6' 3" **Wt:** 250 **Born:** 2/13/71 **Age:** 25

Year Team	G	GS	Tk	Ast	Sack	FF	FR	TD	Blk	Int	Yds	Avg	TD	Sfty	TD	Pts
			Tackles			**Miscellaneous**				**Interceptions**				**Totals**		
1995 Cincinnati Bengals	3	0	0	0	0.0	0	0	0	0	0	0	-	0	0	0	0

Kerry Collins

(statistical profile on page 300)

Pos: QB **Rnd:** 1 (5)   **College:** Penn State   **Ht:** 6' 5" **Wt:** 240 **Born:** 12/30/72 **Age:** 23

Year Team	G	GS	Att	Com	Pct	Yards	Yds/Att	Lg	TD	Int	Int%	Rating	Att	Yds	Avg	Lg	TD	Sckd	Yds	Fum	Recv	Yds	Pts
			Passing										**Rushing**					**Miscellaneous**					
1995 Carolina Panthers	15	13	433	214	49.5	2717	6.29	t89	14	19	4.4	62.0	42	74	1.8	10	3	24	150	13	4	-7	18

Mark Collins

(statistical profile on page 405)

Pos: S/CB **Rnd:** 2   **College:** California State-Fullerton   **Ht:** 5' 10" **Wt:** 196 **Born:** 1/16/64 **Age:** 32

Year Team	G	GS	Tk	Ast	Sack	FF	FR	TD	Blk	Int	Yds	Avg	TD	Num	Yds	Avg	TD	Num	Yds	Avg	TD	TD	Fum
			Tackles			**Miscellaneous**				**Interceptions**				**Punt Returns**				**Kickoff Returns**				**Totals**	
1986 New York Giants	15	9	45	15	0.0	1	3	0	0	1	0	0.0	0	3	11	3.7	0	11	204	18.5	0	0	2
1987 New York Giants	11	11	44	5	1.5	0	0	0	0	2	28	14.0	0	0	0	-	0	0	0	-	0	0	0
1988 New York Giants	11	11	54	2	0.0	0	0	0	0	1	13	13.0	0	0	0	-	0	4	67	16.8	0	0	0
1989 New York Giants	16	16	72	9	1.0	0	2	0	0	2	12	6.0	0	0	0	-	0	1	0	0.0	0	0	0
1990 New York Giants	13	12	45	6	0.0	1	0	0	0	2	0	0.0	0	0	0	-	0	0	0	-	0	0	0
1991 New York Giants	16	15	62	18	0.0	1	2	0	0	4	77	19.3	0	0	0	-	0	0	0	-	0	0	0

Year	Team	G	GS	Tackles Tk	Ast	Sack	Miscellaneous FF	FR	TD	Blk	Interceptions Int	Yds	Avg	TD	Punt Returns Num	Yds	Avg	TD	Kickoff Returns Num	Yds	Avg	TD	Totals TD	Fum
1992	New York Giants	14	14	62	5	0.0	1	0	0	0	1	0	0.0	0	0	0	-	0	0	0	-	0	0	0
1993	New York Giants	16	16	61	10	1.0	0	0	0	0	4	77	19.3	1	0	0	-	0	0	0	-	0	1	0
1994	Kansas City Chiefs	14	13	50	6	2.0	0	2	0	0	2	83	41.5	1	0	0	-	0	0	0	-	0	1	0
1995	Kansas City Chiefs	16	15	65	8	0.0	3	1	1	0	1	8	8.0	0	0	0	-	0	0	0	-	0	1	1
	10 NFL Seasons	142	132	560	84	5.5	7	10	1	0	20	298	14.9	2	3	11	3.7	0	16	271	16.9	0	3	3

Other Statistics: 1988–credited with 1 safety.

Todd Collins

Pos: QB **Rnd:** 2 **College:** Michigan **Ht:** 6' 4" **Wt:** 224 **Born:** 11/5/71 **Age:** 24

Year	Team	G	GS	Passing Att	Com	Pct	Yards	Yds/Att	Lg	TD	Int	Int%	Rating	Rushing Att	Yds	Avg	Lg	TD	Miscellaneous Sckd	Yds	Fum Recv	Yds	Pts
1995	Buffalo Bills	7	1	29	14	48.3	112	3.86	18	0	1	3.4	44.0	9	23	2.6	10	0	6	43	0	0	0

Ferric Collons

Pos: DE/DT **Rnd:** FA **College:** California **Ht:** 6' 6" **Wt:** 295 **Born:** 12/4/69 **Age:** 26

Year	Team	G	GS	Tackles Tk	Ast	Sack	Miscellaneous FF	FR	TD	Blk	Interceptions Int	Yds	Avg	TD	Totals Sfty	TD	Pts
1995	New England Patriots	16	4	18	3	4.0	0	0	0	0	0	0	-	0	0	0	0

Harry Colon

(statistical profile on page 405)

Pos: S **Rnd:** 8 **College:** Missouri **Ht:** 6' 0" **Wt:** 203 **Born:** 2/14/69 **Age:** 27

Year	Team	G	GS	Tackles Tk	Ast	Sack	Miscellaneous FF	FR	TD	Blk	Interceptions Int	Yds	Avg	TD	Totals Sfty	TD	Pts
1991	New England Patriots	16	14	27	18	0.0	0	2	0	0	0	0	-	0	0	0	0
1992	Detroit Lions	16	0	18	-	0.0	0	2	0	0	0	0	-	0	0	0	0
1993	Detroit Lions	15	11	27	19	1.0	3	0	0	0	2	28	14.0	0	0	0	0
1994	Detroit Lions	16	0	16	1	0.0	0	0	0	0	1	3	3.0	0	0	0	0
1995	Jacksonville Jaguars	16	16	55	24	0.0	3	0	0	0	3	46	15.3	0	0	0	0
	5 NFL Seasons	79	41	143	62	1.0	6	4	0	0	6	77	12.8	0	0	0	0

Mike Compton

Pos: G/T **Rnd:** 3 **College:** West Virginia **Ht:** 6' 6" **Wt:** 297 **Born:** 9/18/70 **Age:** 26

Year	Team	G	GS	Year	Team	G	GS	Year	Team	G	GS		G	GS
1993	Detroit Lions	8	0	1994	Detroit Lions	3	0	1995	Detroit Lions	16	8	3 NFL Seasons	27	8

Cary Conklin

Pos: QB **Rnd:** 4 **College:** Washington **Ht:** 6' 4" **Wt:** 215 **Born:** 2/29/68 **Age:** 28

Year	Team	G	GS	Passing Att	Com	Pct	Yards	Yds/Att	Lg	TD	Int	Int%	Rating	Rushing Att	Yds	Avg	Lg	TD	Miscellaneous Sckd	Yds	Fum Recv	Yds	Pts
1992	Washington Redskins	1	0	2	2	100.0	16	8.00	110	1	0	0.0	139.6	3	-4	-1.3	-1	0	0	0	0	0	0
1993	Washington Redskins	4	2	87	46	52.9	496	5.70	t34	4	3	3.4	70.9	2	-2	-1.0	-1	0	8	45	1	0	0
1995	San Francisco 49ers	3	0	12	4	33.3	48	4.00	28	0	0	0.0	46.5	0	0	-	-	0	2	20	0	0	0
	3 NFL Seasons	8	2	101	52	51.5	560	5.54	t34	5	3	3.0	72.2	5	-6	-1.2	-1	0	10	65	1	0	0

Shane Conlan

Pos: LB **Rnd:** 1 (8) **College:** Penn State **Ht:** 6' 3" **Wt:** 235 **Born:** 3/4/64 **Age:** 32

Year	Team	G	GS	Tackles Tk	Ast	Sack	Miscellaneous FF	FR	TD	Blk	Interceptions Int	Yds	Avg	TD	Totals Sfty	TD	Pts
1987	Buffalo Bills	12	11	72	42	0.5	1	0	0	0	0	0	-	0	0	0	0
1988	Buffalo Bills	13	13	60	24	1.5	1	1	0	0	1	0	0.0	0	0	0	0
1989	Buffalo Bills	10	9	37	13	1.0	1	0	0	0	1	0	0.0	0	0	0	0
1990	Buffalo Bills	16	16	72	21	1.0	0	0	0	0	0	0	-	0	0	0	0
1991	Buffalo Bills	16	15	82	40	0.0	1	2	0	0	0	0	-	0	0	0	0
1992	Buffalo Bills	13	12	61	21	2.0	0	0	0	0	1	7	7.0	0	0	0	0
1993	Los Angeles Rams	12	11	56	19	0.0	0	0	0	0	1	28	28.0	0	0	0	0
1994	Los Angeles Rams	15	15	84	24	1.0	1	0	0	0	0	0	-	0	0	0	0
1995	St. Louis Rams	13	11	47	8	0.0	1	2	0	0	1	1	1.0	0	0	0	0
	9 NFL Seasons	120	113	571	212	7.0	6	5	0	0	5	36	7.2	0	0	0	0

Darion Conner

(statistical profile on page 405)

Pos: LB **Rnd:** 2 **College:** Jackson State **Ht:** 6' 2" **Wt:** 242 **Born:** 9/28/67 **Age:** 29

Year	Team	G	GS	Tackles Tk	Ast	Sack	Miscellaneous FF	FR	TD	Blk	Interceptions Int	Yds	Avg	TD	Totals Sfty	TD	Pts
1990	Atlanta Falcons	16	7	87	46	2.0	0	0	0	0	0	0	-	0	0	0	0

				Tackles			Miscellaneous				Interceptions				Totals		
Year	Team	G	GS	Tk	Ast	Sack	FF	FR	TD	Blk	Int	Yds	Avg	TD	Sfty	TD	Pts
1991	Atlanta Falcons	15	14	44	61	3.5	0	1	0	0	0	0	-	0	0	0	0
1992	Atlanta Falcons	16	16	60	56	7.0	0	0	0	0	0	0	-	0	0	0	0
1993	Atlanta Falcons	14	10	28	23	1.5	1	0	0	0	0	0	-	0	0	0	0
1994	New Orleans Saints	16	13	40	14	10.5	3	1	0	0	1	56	56.0	0	0	0	0
1995	Carolina Panthers	16	16	41	11	7.0	1	0	0	0	0	0	-	0	0	0	0
	6 NFL Seasons	93	76	300	211	31.5	5	2	0	0	1	56	56.0	0	0	0	0

Other Statistics: 1991–fumbled 1 time.

Scott Conover

Pos: T **Rnd:** 5 **College:** Purdue **Ht:** 6' 4" **Wt:** 276 **Born:** 9/27/68 **Age:** 28

Year	Team	G	GS	Year	Team	G	GS	Year	Team	G	GS		G	GS
1991	Detroit Lions	16	3	1993	Detroit Lions	1	0	1995	Detroit Lions	14	2			
1992	Detroit Lions	15	15	1994	Detroit Lions	12	0		5 NFL Seasons				58	20

Other Statistics: 1994–caught 1 pass for 1 yard and 1 touchdown.

Curtis Conway

(statistical profile on page 301)

Pos: WR **Rnd:** 1 (7) **College:** Southern California **Ht:** 6' 0" **Wt:** 193 **Born:** 3/13/71 **Age:** 25

				Rushing					Receiving					Punt Returns				Kickoff Returns				Totals		
Year	Team	G	GS	Att	Yds	Avg	Lg	TD	Rec	Yds	Avg	Lg	TD	Num	Yds	Avg	TD	Num	Yds	Avg	TD	Fum	TD	Pts
1993	Chicago Bears	16	6	5	44	8.8	18	0	19	231	12.2	t38	2	0	0	-	0	21	450	21.4	0	1	2	12
1994	Chicago Bears	13	12	6	31	5.2	12	0	39	546	14.0	t85	2	8	63	7.9	0	10	228	22.8	0	2	2	14
1995	Chicago Bears	16	16	5	77	15.4	20	0	62	1037	16.7	t76	12	0	0	-	0	0	0	-	0	0	12	72
	3 NFL Seasons	45	34	16	152	9.5	20	0	120	1814	15.1	t85	16	8	63	7.9	0	31	678	21.9	0	3	16	98

Other Statistics: 1994–recovered 1 fumble for 0 yards; attempted 1 pass with 1 completion for 23 yards and 1 touchdown; scored 1 two-point conversion. 1995–attempted 1 pass with 0 completions for 0 yards.

Anthony Cook

Pos: DE **Rnd:** 2 **College:** South Carolina State **Ht:** 6' 3" **Wt:** 293 **Born:** 5/30/72 **Age:** 24

				Tackles			Miscellaneous				Interceptions				Totals		
Year	Team	G	GS	Tk	Ast	Sack	FF	FR	TD	Blk	Int	Yds	Avg	TD	Sfty	TD	Pts
1995	Houston Oilers	11	5	15	7	4.5	0	0	0	0	0	0	-	0	1	0	2

Marv Cook

(statistical profile on page 301)

Pos: TE **Rnd:** 3 **College:** Iowa **Ht:** 6' 4" **Wt:** 241 **Born:** 2/24/66 **Age:** 30

				Rushing					Receiving					Punt Returns				Kickoff Returns				Totals		
Year	Team	G	GS	Att	Yds	Avg	Lg	TD	Rec	Yds	Avg	Lg	TD	Num	Yds	Avg	TD	Num	Yds	Avg	TD	Fum	TD	Pts
1989	New England Patriots	16	0	0	0	-	-	0	3	13	4.3	5	0	0	0	-	0	0	0	-	0	0	0	0
1990	New England Patriots	16	16	0	0	-	-	0	51	455	8.9	t35	5	0	0	-	0	0	0	-	0	2	5	30
1991	New England Patriots	16	16	0	0	-	-	0	82	808	9.9	49	3	0	0	-	0	0	0	-	0	2	3	18
1992	New England Patriots	15	15	0	0	-	-	0	52	413	7.9	27	2	0	0	-	0	0	0	-	0	3	2	12
1993	New England Patriots	16	12	0	0	-	-	0	22	154	7.0	17	1	0	0	-	0	1	8	8.0	0	1	1	6
1994	Chicago Bears	16	8	0	0	-	-	0	21	212	10.1	34	1	0	0	-	0	0	0	-	0	0	1	6
1995	St. Louis Rams	16	10	0	0	-	-	0	26	135	5.2	16	1	0	0	-	0	0	0	-	0	1	1	6
	7 NFL Seasons	112	77	0	0	-	-	0	257	2190	8.5	49	13	0	0	-	0	1	8	8.0	0	9	13	78

Other Statistics: 1991–recovered 2 fumbles for 0 yards. 1992–recovered 1 fumble for -26 yards. 1994–recovered 1 fumble for 0 yards.

Toi Cook

Pos: CB **Rnd:** 8 **College:** Stanford **Ht:** 5' 11" **Wt:** 188 **Born:** 12/3/64 **Age:** 31

				Tackles			Miscellaneous				Interceptions				Punt Returns				Kickoff Returns				Totals	
Year	Team	G	GS	Tk	Ast	Sack	FF	FR	TD	Blk	Int	Yds	Avg	TD	Num	Yds	Avg	TD	Num	Yds	Avg	TD	TD	Fum
1987	New Orleans Saints	7	0	3	1	0.0	0	0	0	0	0	0	-	0	1	3	3.0	0	0	0	-	0	0	0
1988	New Orleans Saints	16	0	12	-	0.0	0	0	0	0	1	0	0.0	0	0	0	-	0	0	0	-	0	0	0
1989	New Orleans Saints	16	14	45	11	1.0	0	0	0	0	3	81	27.0	1	0	0	-	0	0	0	-	0	1	1
1990	New Orleans Saints	16	16	66	7	1.0	0	0	0	0	2	55	27.5	0	0	0	-	0	0	0	-	0	0	0
1991	New Orleans Saints	14	14	35	1	0.0	0	0	0	0	3	54	18.0	0	0	0	-	0	0	0	-	0	0	0
1992	New Orleans Saints	16	15	48	15	1.0	0	0	0	0	6	90	15.0	1	0	0	-	0	0	0	-	0	1	0
1993	New Orleans Saints	16	16	42	8	1.0	0	0	0	0	1	0	0.0	0	0	0	-	0	0	0	-	0	0	0
1994	San Francisco 49ers	16	2	25	1	0.0	0	0	0	0	1	18	18.0	0	0	0	-	0	0	0	-	0	0	0
1995	San Francisco 49ers	2	0	1	0	0.0	0	0	0	0	0	0	-	0	0	0	-	0	0	0	-	0	0	0
	9 NFL Seasons	119	77	277	44	4.0	1	3	0	0	17	298	17.5	2	1	3	3.0	0	0	0	-	0	2	1

Other Statistics: 1989–caught 1 pass for 8 yards.

Rob Coons

Pos: TE **Rnd:** FA **College:** Pittsburgh **Ht:** 6' 5" **Wt:** 249 **Born:** 9/18/69 **Age:** 27

			Rushing					Receiving					Punt Returns				Kickoff Returns				Totals		
Year Team	G	GS	Att	Yds	Avg	Lg	TD	Rec	Yds	Avg	Lg	TD	Num	Yds	Avg	TD	Num	Yds	Avg	TD	Fum	TD	Pts
1995 Buffalo Bills	4	0	0	0	-	-	0	3	28	9.3	13	0	0	0	-	0	0	0	-	0	0	0	0

Adrian Cooper

Pos: TE **Rnd:** 4 **College:** Oklahoma **Ht:** 6' 5" **Wt:** 268 **Born:** 4/27/68 **Age:** 28

			Rushing					Receiving					Punt Returns				Kickoff Returns				Totals		
Year Team	G	GS	Att	Yds	Avg	Lg	TD	Rec	Yds	Avg	Lg	TD	Num	Yds	Avg	TD	Num	Yds	Avg	TD	Fum	TD	Pts
1991 Pittsburgh Steelers	16	8	0	0	-	-	0	11	147	13.4	t47	2	0	0	-	0	0	0	-	0	0	2	12
1992 Pittsburgh Steelers	16	15	0	0	-	-	0	16	197	12.3	27	3	0	0	-	0	1	8	8.0	0	1	3	18
1993 Pittsburgh Steelers	14	3	0	0	-	-	0	9	112	12.4	38	0	0	0	-	0	1	2	2.0	0	1	0	0
1994 Minnesota Vikings	12	11	0	0	-	-	0	32	363	11.3	34	0	0	0	-	0	0	0	-	0	2	0	0
1995 Minnesota Vikings	13	13	0	0	-	-	0	18	207	11.5	41	0	0	0	-	0	0	0	-	0	0	0	0
5 NFL Seasons	71	50	0	0	-	-	0	86	1026	11.9	t47	5	0	0	-	0	2	10	5.0	0	4	5	30

Other Statistics: 1994–recovered 1 fumble for 0 yards. 1995–recovered 1 fumble for 0 yards.

Richard Cooper

Pos: T **Rnd:** FA **College:** Tennessee **Ht:** 6' 5" **Wt:** 290 **Born:** 11/1/64 **Age:** 32

Year	Team	G	GS	Year	Team	G	GS	Year	Team	G	GS		G	GS
1990	New Orleans Saints	2	1	1992	New Orleans Saints	16	16	1994	New Orleans Saints	14	14			
1991	New Orleans Saints	15	11	1993	New Orleans Saints	16	16	1995	New Orleans Saints	14	14	6 NFL Seasons	77	72

Other Statistics: 1991–recovered 1 fumble for 0 yards. 1992–recovered 1 fumble for 0 yards; caught 0 passes for 20 yards. 1993–recovered 1 fumble for 0 yards. 1995–recovered 1 fumble for 0 yards.

Horace Copeland

(statistical profile on page 302)

Pos: WR **Rnd:** 4 **College:** Miami (FL) **Ht:** 6' 3" **Wt:** 202 **Born:** 1/2/71 **Age:** 25

			Rushing					Receiving					Punt Returns				Kickoff Returns				Totals		
Year Team	G	GS	Att	Yds	Avg	Lg	TD	Rec	Yds	Avg	Lg	TD	Num	Yds	Avg	TD	Num	Yds	Avg	TD	Fum	TD	Pts
1993 Tampa Bay Buccaneers	14	8	3	34	11.3	22	0	30	633	21.1	t67	4	0	0	-	0	0	0	-	0	0	4	24
1994 Tampa Bay Buccaneers	16	2	0	0	-	-	0	17	308	18.1	65	0	0	0	-	0	0	0	-	0	0	0	2
1995 Tampa Bay Buccaneers	15	7	0	0	-	-	0	35	605	17.3	t64	2	0	0	-	0	0	0	-	0	0	2	12
3 NFL Seasons	45	17	3	34	11.3	22	0	82	1546	18.9	t67	6	0	0	-	0	0	0	-	0	0	6	38

Other Statistics: 1994–scored 1 two-point conversion.

John Copeland

(statistical profile on page 406)

Pos: DE **Rnd:** 1 (5) **College:** Alabama **Ht:** 6' 3" **Wt:** 286 **Born:** 9/20/70 **Age:** 26

			Tackles			Miscellaneous				Interceptions				Totals		
Year Team	G	GS	Tk	Ast	Sack	FF	FR	TD	Blk	Int	Yds	Avg	TD	Sfty	TD	Pts
1993 Cincinnati Bengals	14	14	43	5	2.0	2	0	0	0	0	0	-	0	0	0	0
1994 Cincinnati Bengals	12	12	36	5	1.0	1	0	0	0	0	0	-	0	0	0	0
1995 Cincinnati Bengals	16	16	55	8	9.0	2	0	0	1	0	0	-	0	0	0	0
3 NFL Seasons	42	42	134	18	13.0	5	0	0	1	0	0	-	0	0	0	0

Russell Copeland

(statistical profile on page 302)

Pos: WR **Rnd:** 4 **College:** Memphis **Ht:** 6' 1" **Wt:** 200 **Born:** 11/4/71 **Age:** 24

			Rushing					Receiving					Punt Returns				Kickoff Returns				Totals		
Year Team	G	GS	Att	Yds	Avg	Lg	TD	Rec	Yds	Avg	Lg	TD	Num	Yds	Avg	TD	Num	Yds	Avg	TD	Fum	TD	Pts
1993 Buffalo Bills	16	2	0	0	-	-	0	13	242	18.6	60	0	31	274	8.8	1	24	436	18.2	0	1	1	6
1994 Buffalo Bills	15	4	1	-7	-7.0	-7	0	21	255	12.1	35	1	1	11	11.0	0	12	232	19.3	0	0	1	6
1995 Buffalo Bills	16	15	1	-1	-1.0	-1	0	42	646	15.4	t77	1	2	8	4.0	0	0	0	-	0	1	1	6
3 NFL Seasons	47	21	2	-8	-4.0	-1	0	76	1143	15.0	t77	2	34	293	8.6	1	36	668	18.6	0	2	3	18

Other Statistics: 1995–recovered 1 fumble for 0 yards.

Frank Cornish

Pos: C **Rnd:** 6 **College:** UCLA **Ht:** 6' 4" **Wt:** 287 **Born:** 9/24/67 **Age:** 29

Year	Team	G	GS	Year	Team	G	GS	Year	Team	G	GS	Year	Team	G	GS
1990	San Diego Chargers	16	16	1992	Dallas Cowboys	11	2	1994	Minnesota Vikings	7	0	1995	Philadelphia Eagles	2	0
1991	San Diego Chargers	16	0	1993	Dallas Cowboys	14	3	1995	Jacksonville Jaguars	3	0		6 NFL Seasons	69	21

60

Quentin Coryatt
(statistical profile on page 406)

Pos: LB   **Rnd:** 1 (2)   **College:** Texas A&M   **Ht:** 6' 3" **Wt:** 246   **Born:** 8/1/70   **Age:** 26

Year Team	G	GS	Tackles			Miscellaneous				Interceptions				Totals		
			Tk	Ast	Sack	FF	FR	TD	Blk	Int	Yds	Avg	TD	Sfty	TD	Pts
1992 Indianapolis Colts	7	7	41	13	2.0	2	1	0	0	0	0	-	0	0	0	0
1993 Indianapolis Colts	16	16	96	54	1.0	1	0	0	0	0	0	-	0	0	0	0
1994 Indianapolis Colts	16	15	59	34	1.0	0	1	1	0	0	0	-	0	0	1	6
1995 Indianapolis Colts	16	16	87	21	2.5	1	3	0	0	1	6	6.0	0	0	0	0
4 NFL Seasons	55	54	283	122	6.5	4	5	1	0	1	6	6.0	0	0	1	6

Chad Cota

Pos: S   **Rnd:** 7   **College:** Oregon   **Ht:** 6' 1" **Wt:** 195   **Born:** 8/13/71   **Age:** 25

Year Team	G	GS	Tackles			Miscellaneous				Interceptions				Totals		
			Tk	Ast	Sack	FF	FR	TD	Blk	Int	Yds	Avg	TD	Sfty	TD	Pts
1995 Carolina Panthers	16	0	4	0	0.0	0	1	0	0	0	0	-	0	0	0	0

Jeff Cothran

Pos: RB   **Rnd:** 3   **College:** Ohio State   **Ht:** 6' 1" **Wt:** 240   **Born:** 6/28/71   **Age:** 25

Year Team	G	GS	Rushing					Receiving					Punt Returns				Kickoff Returns				Totals		
			Att	Yds	Avg	Lg	TD	Rec	Yds	Avg	Lg	TD	Num	Yds	Avg	TD	Num	Yds	Avg	TD	Fum	TD	Pts
1994 Cincinnati Bengals	14	4	26	85	3.3	13	0	4	24	6.0	8	1	0	0	-	0	0	0	-	0	0	1	6
1995 Cincinnati Bengals	15	13	16	62	3.9	15	0	8	44	5.5	15	0	0	0	-	0	0	0	-	0	1	0	0
2 NFL Seasons	29	17	42	147	3.5	15	0	12	68	5.7	15	1	0	0	-	0	0	0	-	0	1	1	6

Damien Covington

Pos: LB   **Rnd:** 3   **College:** North Carolina State   **Ht:** 5' 11" **Wt:** 236   **Born:** 12/4/72   **Age:** 23

Year Team	G	GS	Tackles			Miscellaneous				Interceptions				Totals		
			Tk	Ast	Sack	FF	FR	TD	Blk	Int	Yds	Avg	TD	Sfty	TD	Pts
1995 Buffalo Bills	12	1	9	6	0.0	0	0	0	0	0	0	-	0	0	0	0

Tony Covington

Pos: S   **Rnd:** 4   **College:** Virginia   **Ht:** 5' 11" **Wt:** 193   **Born:** 12/26/67   **Age:** 28

Year Team	G	GS	Tackles			Miscellaneous				Interceptions				Totals		
			Tk	Ast	Sack	FF	FR	TD	Blk	Int	Yds	Avg	TD	Sfty	TD	Pts
1991 Tampa Bay Buccaneers	16	12	64	20	1.0	0	1	0	0	3	21	7.0	0	0	0	0
1992 Tampa Bay Buccaneers	1	1	2	2	0.0	0	0	0	0	0	0	-	0	0	0	0
1994 Tampa Bay Buccaneers	13	2	26	7	0.0	0	0	0	0	1	38	38.0	0	0	0	0
1995 Seattle Seahawks	11	0	0	3	0.0	0	0	0	0	0	0	-	0	0	0	0
4 NFL Seasons	41	15	92	32	1.0	0	1	0	0	4	59	14.8	0	0	0	0

Bryan Cox
(statistical profile on page 406)

Pos: LB   **Rnd:** 5   **College:** Western Illinois   **Ht:** 6' 4" **Wt:** 248   **Born:** 2/17/68   **Age:** 28

Year Team	G	GS	Tackles			Miscellaneous				Interceptions				Totals		
			Tk	Ast	Sack	FF	FR	TD	Blk	Int	Yds	Avg	TD	Sfty	TD	Pts
1991 Miami Dolphins	13	13	51	10	2.0	0	0	0	0	0	0	-	0	0	0	0
1992 Miami Dolphins	16	16	84	43	14.0	5	1	0	0	1	0	0.0	0	0	0	0
1993 Miami Dolphins	16	16	87	35	5.0	4	4	0	0	1	26	26.0	0	0	0	0
1994 Miami Dolphins	16	16	75	25	3.0	2	0	0	0	0	0	-	0	0	0	0
1995 Miami Dolphins	16	16	95	24	7.5	3	1	0	0	1	12	12.0	0	0	0	0
5 NFL Seasons	77	77	392	137	31.5	14	6	0	0	3	38	12.7	0	0	0	0

Ron Cox

Pos: LB   **Rnd:** 2   **College:** Fresno State   **Ht:** 6' 2" **Wt:** 240   **Born:** 2/27/68   **Age:** 28

Year Team	G	GS	Tackles			Miscellaneous				Interceptions				Totals		
			Tk	Ast	Sack	FF	FR	TD	Blk	Int	Yds	Avg	TD	Sfty	TD	Pts
1990 Chicago Bears	13	0	15	13	3.0	0	0	0	0	0	0	-	0	0	0	0
1991 Chicago Bears	6	0	5	1	1.0	0	0	0	0	0	0	-	0	0	0	0
1992 Chicago Bears	16	3	23	33	1.0	0	1	0	0	0	0	-	0	0	0	0
1993 Chicago Bears	16	1	21	12	2.0	2	1	0	0	0	0	-	0	0	0	0
1994 Chicago Bears	15	3	24	6	0.0	0	0	0	0	0	0	-	0	0	0	0
1995 Chicago Bears	16	13	41	11	0.0	0	0	0	0	1	1	1.0	0	0	0	0
6 NFL Seasons	82	20	129	76	7.0	2	2	0	0	1	1	1.0	0	0	0	0

Aaron Craver

(statistical profile on page 303)

Pos: RB **Rnd:** 3 **College:** Fresno State **Ht:** 6' 0" **Wt:** 220 **Born:** 12/18/68 **Age:** 27

Year Team	G	GS	Rushing Att	Yds	Avg	Lg	TD	Receiving Rec	Yds	Avg	Lg	TD	Punt Returns Num	Yds	Avg	TD	Kickoff Returns Num	Yds	Avg	TD	Totals Fum	TD	Pts
1991 Miami Dolphins	14	0	20	58	2.9	t7	1	8	67	8.4	25	0	0	0	-	0	32	615	19.2	0	2	1	6
1992 Miami Dolphins	6	0	3	9	3.0	8	0	0	0	-	-	0	0	0	-	0	8	174	21.8	0	0	0	0
1994 Miami Dolphins	8	0	6	43	7.2	19	0	24	237	9.9	28	0	0	0	-	0	0	0	-	0	1	0	2
1995 Denver Broncos	16	10	73	333	4.6	23	5	43	369	8.6	32	1	0	0	-	0	7	50	7.1	0	1	6	36
4 NFL Seasons	44	10	102	443	4.3	23	6	75	673	9.0	32	1	0	0	-	0	47	839	17.9	0	4	7	44

Other Statistics: 1991–recovered 2 fumbles for 0 yards. 1994–recovered 1 fumble for 0 yards; scored 1 two-point conversion. 1995–recovered 1 fumble for 0 yards.

Keith Crawford

Pos: CB **Rnd:** FA **College:** Howard Payne **Ht:** 6' 2" **Wt:** 198 **Born:** 11/21/70 **Age:** 25

Year Team	G	GS	Tackles Tk	Ast	Sack	Miscellaneous FF	FR	TD	Blk	Interceptions Int	Yds	Avg	TD	Totals Sfty	TD	Pts
1993 New York Giants	7	0	0	0	0.0	0	0	0	0	0	0	-	0	0	0	0
1995 Green Bay Packers	13	0	20	3	0.0	0	0	0	0	0	0	-	0	0	0	0
2 NFL Seasons	20	0	20	3	0.0	0	0	0	0	0	0	-	0	0	0	0

Other Statistics: 1993–caught 1 pass for 6 yards.

Terry Crews

Pos: DE/LB **Rnd:** 11 **College:** Western Michigan **Ht:** 6' 2" **Wt:** 245 **Born:** 7/30/68 **Age:** 28

Year Team	G	GS	Tackles Tk	Ast	Sack	Miscellaneous FF	FR	TD	Blk	Interceptions Int	Yds	Avg	TD	Totals Sfty	TD	Pts
1991 Los Angeles Rams	6	0	0	0	0.0	0	0	0	0	0	0	-	0	0	0	0
1993 San Diego Chargers	10	0	1	0	0.0	0	0	0	0	0	0	-	0	0	0	0
1995 Washington Redskins	16	0	1	1	0.0	0	0	0	0	0	0	-	0	0	0	0
3 NFL Seasons	32	0	2	1	0.0	0	0	0	0	0	0	-	0	0	0	0

Jeff Criswell

Pos: T **Rnd:** FA **College:** Graceland College **Ht:** 6' 7" **Wt:** 294 **Born:** 3/7/64 **Age:** 32

Year	Team	G	GS	Year	Team	G	GS	Year	Team	G	GS		G	GS
1987	Indianapolis Colts	3	3	1990	New York Jets	16	16	1993	New York Jets	16	16			
1988	New York Jets	15	12	1991	New York Jets	16	16	1994	New York Jets	15	15			
1989	New York Jets	16	16	1992	New York Jets	14	13	1995	Kansas City Chiefs	15	4	9 NFL Seasons	126	111

Other Statistics: 1989–recovered 1 fumble for 0 yards. 1990–recovered 1 fumble for 0 yards. 1994–recovered 1 fumble for 0 yards.

Ray Crockett

(statistical profile on page 407)

Pos: CB **Rnd:** 4 **College:** Baylor **Ht:** 5' 10" **Wt:** 185 **Born:** 1/5/67 **Age:** 29

Year Team	G	GS	Tackles Tk	Ast	Sack	Misc. FF	FR	TD	Blk	Interceptions Int	Yds	Avg	TD	Punt Returns Num	Yds	Avg	TD	Kickoff Returns Num	Yds	Avg	TD	Totals TD	Fum
1989 Detroit Lions	16	0	34	12	0.0	1	1	0	0	1	5	5.0	0	0	0	-	0	1	8	8.0	0	0	0
1990 Detroit Lions	16	6	62	29	1.0	2	2	1	0	3	17	5.7	0	0	0	-	0	0	0	-	0	1	0
1991 Detroit Lions	16	16	74	12	1.0	1	0	0	0	6	141	23.5	1	0	0	-	0	0	0	-	0	1	0
1992 Detroit Lions	15	15	41	11	1.0	1	1	0	0	4	50	12.5	0	0	0	-	0	0	0	-	0	0	0
1993 Detroit Lions	16	16	57	11	1.0	1	1	0	0	2	31	15.5	0	0	0	-	0	0	0	-	0	0	0
1994 Denver Broncos	14	14	58	6	0.0	0	2	0	0	2	6	3.0	0	0	0	-	0	0	0	-	0	0	0
1995 Denver Broncos	16	16	60	12	3.0	1	1	1	0	0	0	-	0	0	4	-	0	0	0	-	0	1	0
7 NFL Seasons	109	83	386	93	7.0	7	8	2	0	18	250	13.9	1	0	4	-	0	1	8	8.0	0	3	0

Zack Crockett

Pos: RB **Rnd:** 3 **College:** Florida State **Ht:** 6' 2" **Wt:** 241 **Born:** 12/2/72 **Age:** 23

Year Team	G	GS	Rushing Att	Yds	Avg	Lg	TD	Receiving Rec	Yds	Avg	Lg	TD	Punt Returns Num	Yds	Avg	TD	Kickoff Returns Num	Yds	Avg	TD	Totals Fum	TD	Pts
1995 Indianapolis Colts	16	0	1	0	0.0	0	0	2	35	17.5	19	0	0	0	-	0	0	0	-	0	0	0	0

Mike Croel

Pos: LB **Rnd:** 1 (4) **College:** Nebraska **Ht:** 6' 3" **Wt:** 240 **Born:** 6/6/69 **Age:** 27

Year Team	G	GS	Tackles Tk	Ast	Sack	Miscellaneous FF	FR	TD	Blk	Interceptions Int	Yds	Avg	TD	Totals Sfty	TD	Pts
1991 Denver Broncos	13	10	55	29	10.0	0	0	0	0	0	0	-	0	0	0	0
1992 Denver Broncos	16	16	66	31	5.0	0	1	0	0	0	0	-	0	0	0	0
1993 Denver Broncos	16	16	79	31	5.0	1	2	0	0	1	22	22.0	1	0	1	6
1994 Denver Broncos	13	12	29	10	0.0	1	0	0	0	0	0	-	0	0	0	0
1995 New York Giants	16	14	38	17	1.0	1	0	0	0	0	0	-	0	0	0	0

Year Team	G	GS	Tk	Ast	Sack	FF	FR	TD	Blk	Int	Yds	Avg	TD	Sfty	TD	Pts
			Tackles			**Miscellaneous**				**Interceptions**				**Totals**		
5 NFL Seasons	74	68	267	118	21.0	3	3	0	0	1	22	22.0	1	0	1	6

Corey Croom

Pos: RB **Rnd:** FA **College:** Ball State **Ht:** 5' 11" **Wt:** 208 **Born:** 5/22/71 **Age:** 25

Year Team	G	GS	Att	Yds	Avg	Lg	TD	Rec	Yds	Avg	Lg	TD	Num	Yds	Avg	TD	Num	Yds	Avg	TD	Fum	TD	Pts
			Rushing					**Receiving**					**Punt Returns**				**Kickoff Returns**				**Totals**		
1993 New England Patriots	14	1	60	198	3.3	22	1	8	92	11.5	21	0	0	0	-	0	0	0	-	0	1	1	6
1994 New England Patriots	16	0	0	0	-	-	0	0	0	-	-	0	0	0	-	0	10	172	17.2	0	1	0	0
1995 New England Patriots	13	1	13	54	4.2	12	0	1	8	8.0	8	0	0	0	-	0	0	0	-	0	0	0	0
3 NFL Seasons	43	2	73	252	3.5	22	1	9	100	11.1	21	0	0	0	-	0	10	172	17.2	0	2	1	6

Howard Cross

Pos: TE **Rnd:** 6 **College:** Alabama **Ht:** 6' 5" **Wt:** 260 **Born:** 8/8/67 **Age:** 29

Year Team	G	GS	Att	Yds	Avg	Lg	TD	Rec	Yds	Avg	Lg	TD	Num	Yds	Avg	TD	Num	Yds	Avg	TD	Fum	TD	Pts
			Rushing					**Receiving**					**Punt Returns**				**Kickoff Returns**				**Totals**		
1989 New York Giants	16	4	0	0	-	-	0	6	107	17.8	27	1	0	0	-	0	0	0	-	0	1	1	6
1990 New York Giants	16	8	0	0	-	-	0	8	106	13.3	21	0	0	0	-	0	1	10	10.0	0	0	0	0
1991 New York Giants	16	16	0	0	-	-	0	20	283	14.2	30	2	0	0	-	0	1	11	11.0	0	1	2	12
1992 New York Giants	16	16	0	0	-	-	0	27	357	13.2	29	2	0	0	-	0	0	0	-	0	2	2	12
1993 New York Giants	16	16	0	0	-	-	0	21	272	13.0	32	5	0	0	-	0	2	15	7.5	0	0	5	30
1994 New York Giants	16	16	0	0	-	-	0	31	364	11.7	40	4	0	0	-	0	0	0	-	0	0	4	24
1995 New York Giants	15	15	0	0	-	-	0	18	197	10.9	26	0	0	0	-	0	0	0	-	0	0	0	0
7 NFL Seasons	111	91	0	0	-	-	0	131	1686	12.9	40	14	0	0	-	0	4	36	9.0	0	4	14	84

Other Statistics: 1992–recovered 1 fumble for 0 yards. 1993–recovered 1 fumble for 0 yards. 1994–recovered 1 fumble for 1 yard.

Jeff Cross

(statistical profile on page 407)

Pos: DE **Rnd:** 9 **College:** Missouri **Ht:** 6' 4" **Wt:** 280 **Born:** 3/25/66 **Age:** 30

Year Team	G	GS	Tk	Ast	Sack	FF	FR	TD	Blk	Int	Yds	Avg	TD	Sfty	TD	Pts
			Tackles			**Miscellaneous**				**Interceptions**				**Totals**		
1988 Miami Dolphins	16	1	8	3	0.0	0	0	0	0	0	0	-	0	0	0	0
1989 Miami Dolphins	16	16	50	9	10.0	1	0	0	0	0	0	-	0	0	0	0
1990 Miami Dolphins	16	16	51	9	11.5	3	2	0	0	0	0	-	0	0	0	0
1991 Miami Dolphins	16	16	38	4	7.0	1	0	0	0	0	0	-	0	0	0	0
1992 Miami Dolphins	16	16	33	13	5.0	1	0	0	0	0	0	-	0	0	0	0
1993 Miami Dolphins	16	16	64	29	10.5	2	2	0	0	0	0	-	0	0	0	0
1994 Miami Dolphins	13	10	23	5	9.5	1	1	0	0	1	0	0.0	0	0	0	0
1995 Miami Dolphins	16	16	31	7	6.0	1	2	0	0	0	0	-	0	0	0	0
8 NFL Seasons	125	107	298	79	59.5	10	7	0	0	1	0	0.0	0	0	0	0

Other Statistics: 1995–fumbled 1 time.

Carlester Crumpler

Pos: TE **Rnd:** 7 **College:** East Carolina **Ht:** 6' 6" **Wt:** 255 **Born:** 9/5/71 **Age:** 25

Year Team	G	GS	Att	Yds	Avg	Lg	TD	Rec	Yds	Avg	Lg	TD	Num	Yds	Avg	TD	Num	Yds	Avg	TD	Fum	TD	Pts
			Rushing					**Receiving**					**Punt Returns**				**Kickoff Returns**				**Totals**		
1994 Seattle Seahawks	9	4	0	0	-	-	0	2	19	9.5	12	0	0	0	-	0	0	0	-	0	0	0	0
1995 Seattle Seahawks	16	7	0	0	-	-	0	23	254	11.0	24	1	0	0	-	0	0	0	-	0	1	1	6
2 NFL Seasons	25	11	0	0	-	-	0	25	273	10.9	24	1	0	0	-	0	0	0	-	0	1	1	6

Brad Culpepper

Pos: DT **Rnd:** 10 **College:** Florida **Ht:** 6' 1" **Wt:** 270 **Born:** 5/8/69 **Age:** 27

Year Team	G	GS	Tk	Ast	Sack	FF	FR	TD	Blk	Int	Yds	Avg	TD	Num	Yds	Avg	TD	Num	Yds	Avg	TD	TD	Fum
			Tackles			**Miscellaneous**				**Interceptions**				**Punt Returns**				**Kickoff Returns**				**Totals**	
1992 Minnesota Vikings	11	2	4	6	0.0	0	0	0	0	0	0	-	0	0	0	-	0	0	0	-	0	0	0
1993 Minnesota Vikings	15	0	7	2	0.0	0	0	0	0	0	0	-	0	0	0	-	0	0	0	-	0	0	0
1994 Tampa Bay Buccaneers	16	15	47	14	4.0	2	1	0	0	0	0	-	0	0	0	-	0	2	30	15.0	0	0	0
1995 Tampa Bay Buccaneers	16	4	16	7	4.0	1	1	0	0	0	0	-	0	0	0	-	0	0	0	-	0	0	0
4 NFL Seasons	58	21	74	29	8.0	3	2	0	0	0	0	-	0	0	0	-	0	2	30	15.0	0	0	0

Rodney Culver

Pos: RB **Rnd:** 4 **College:** Notre Dame **Ht:** 5' 9" **Wt:** 224 **Born:** 12/23/69 **Age:** 26

Year Team	G	GS	Att	Yds	Avg	Lg	TD	Rec	Yds	Avg	Lg	TD	Num	Yds	Avg	TD	Num	Yds	Avg	TD	Fum	TD	Pts
			Rushing					**Receiving**					**Punt Returns**				**Kickoff Returns**				**Totals**		
1992 Indianapolis Colts	16	2	121	321	2.7	t36	7	26	210	8.1	27	2	0	0	-	0	0	0	-	0	2	9	54
1993 Indianapolis Colts	16	1	65	150	2.3	9	3	11	112	10.2	26	1	0	0	-	0	3	51	17.0	0	3	5	30

Year	Team	G	GS	Att	Rushing Yds	Avg	Lg	TD	Rec	Receiving Yds	Avg	Lg	TD	Num	Punt Returns Yds	Avg	TD	Num	Kickoff Returns Yds	Avg	TD	Fum	Totals TD	Pts
1994	San Diego Chargers	3	0	8	63	7.9	22	0	0	0	-	-	0	0	0	-	0	0	0	-	0	0	0	0
1995	San Diego Chargers	8	2	47	155	3.3	17	3	5	21	4.2	12	0	0	0	-	0	0	0	-	0	0	3	18
	4 NFL Seasons	43	5	241	689	2.9	t36	13	42	343	8.2	27	3	0	0	-	0	3	51	17.0	0	5	17	102

Other Statistics: 1992–recovered 1 fumble for 0 yards. 1993–recovered 2 fumbles for 56 yards and 1 touchdown.

Ed Cunningham

Pos: C **Rnd:** 3 **College:** Washington **Ht:** 6' 3" **Wt:** 285 **Born:** 8/17/69 **Age:** 27

Year	Team	G	GS	Year	Team	G	GS	Year	Team	G	GS	Year	Team	G	GS
1992	Phoenix Cardinals	10	5	1993	Phoenix Cardinals	15	15	1994	Arizona Cardinals	16	16	1995	Arizona Cardinals	9	8
													4 NFL Seasons	50	44

Other Statistics: 1995–fumbled 1 time for -25 yards.

Randall Cunningham

(statistical profile on page 303)

Pos: QB **Rnd:** 2 **College:** UNLV **Ht:** 6' 4" **Wt:** 205 **Born:** 3/27/63 **Age:** 33

Year	Team	G	GS	Att	Com	Passing Pct	Yards	Yds/Att	Lg	TD	Int	Int%	Rating	Att	Rushing Yds	Avg	Lg	TD	Sckd	Miscellaneous Yds	Fum	Recv	Yds	Pts
1985	Philadelphia Eagles	6	4	81	34	42.0	548	6.77	69	1	8	9.9	29.8	29	205	7.1	37	0	20	150	3	0	0	0
1986	Philadelphia Eagles	15	5	209	111	53.1	1391	6.66	t75	8	7	3.3	72.9	66	540	8.2	20	5	72	489	7	4	0	30
1987	Philadelphia Eagles	12	12	406	223	54.9	2786	6.86	t70	23	12	3.0	83.0	76	505	6.6	45	3	54	380	12	6	-7	18
1988	Philadelphia Eagles	16	16	560	301	53.8	3808	6.80	t80	24	16	2.9	77.6	93	624	6.7	t33	6	57	442	12	6	0	36
1989	Philadelphia Eagles	16	16	532	290	54.5	3400	6.39	t66	21	15	2.8	75.5	104	621	6.0	51	4	45	343	17	4	-6	24
1990	Philadelphia Eagles	16	16	465	271	58.3	3466	7.45	t95	30	13	2.8	91.6	118	942	8.0	t52	5	49	431	9	3	-4	30
1991	Philadelphia Eagles	1	1	4	1	25.0	19	4.75	19	0	0	0.0	46.9	0	0	-	-	0	2	16	0	0	0	0
1992	Philadelphia Eagles	15	15	384	233	60.7	2775	7.23	t75	19	11	2.9	87.3	87	549	6.3	30	5	60	437	13	3	0	30
1993	Philadelphia Eagles	4	4	110	76	69.1	850	7.73	t80	5	5	4.5	88.1	18	110	6.1	26	1	7	33	3	0	0	6
1994	Philadelphia Eagles	14	14	490	265	54.1	3229	6.59	93	16	13	2.7	74.4	65	288	4.4	22	3	43	333	10	2	0	18
1995	Philadelphia Eagles	7	4	121	69	57.0	605	5.00	33	3	5	4.1	61.5	21	98	4.7	20	0	13	79	3	1	-5	0
	11 NFL Seasons	122	107	3362	1874	55.7	22877	6.80	t95	150	105	3.1	78.7	677	4482	6.6	t52	32	422	3133	89	29	-22	192

Other Statistics: 1986–punted 2 times for 54 yards. 1987–caught 1 pass for -3 yards. 1988–punted 3 times for 167 yards. 1989–punted 6 times for 319 yards. 1994–punted 1 time for 80 yards.

Rick Cunningham

Pos: T **Rnd:** 4 **College:** Texas A&M **Ht:** 6' 6" **Wt:** 307 **Born:** 1/4/67 **Age:** 29

Year	Team	G	GS	Year	Team	G	GS	Year	Team	G	GS	Year	Team	G	GS
1992	Phoenix Cardinals	8	6	1993	Phoenix Cardinals	16	16	1994	Arizona Cardinals	12	10	1995	Minnesota Vikings	11	1
													4 NFL Seasons	47	33

Other Statistics: 1993–recovered 1 fumble for 0 yards. 1995–recovered 1 fumble for 0 yards.

Eric Curry

Pos: DE **Rnd:** 1 (6) **College:** Alabama **Ht:** 6' 5" **Wt:** 270 **Born:** 2/3/70 **Age:** 26

Year	Team	G	GS	Tk	Tackles Ast	Sack	FF	Miscellaneous FR	TD	Blk	Int	Interceptions Yds	Avg	TD	Sfty	Totals TD	Pts
1993	Tampa Bay Buccaneers	10	10	16	5	5.0	3	1	0	0	0	0	-	0	0	0	0
1994	Tampa Bay Buccaneers	15	14	18	6	3.0	2	0	0	0	0	0	-	0	0	0	0
1995	Tampa Bay Buccaneers	16	16	25	4	2.0	1	1	0	0	0	0	-	0	0	0	0
	3 NFL Seasons	41	40	59	15	10.0	6	2	0	0	0	0	-	0	0	0	0

Bernard Dafney

Pos: G/T **Rnd:** 9 **College:** Tennessee **Ht:** 6' 5" **Wt:** 329 **Born:** 11/1/68 **Age:** 28

Year	Team	G	GS	Year	Team	G	GS	Year	Team	G	GS	Year	Team	G	GS
1992	Minnesota Vikings	2	0	1993	Minnesota Vikings	16	4	1994	Minnesota Vikings	16	16	1995	Arizona Cardinals	12	8
													4 NFL Seasons	46	28

Other Statistics: 1994–recovered 1 fumble for 0 yards.

Bob Dahl

Pos: G **Rnd:** 3 **College:** Notre Dame **Ht:** 6' 5" **Wt:** 310 **Born:** 11/5/68 **Age:** 27

Year	Team	G	GS	Year	Team	G	GS	Year	Team	G	GS	Year	Team	G	GS
1992	Cleveland Browns	9	9	1993	Cleveland Browns	16	16	1994	Cleveland Browns	15	15	1995	Cleveland Browns	16	16
													4 NFL Seasons	56	56

Other Statistics: 1993–recovered 1 fumble for 0 yards.

Chris Dalman

Pos: G/C **Rnd:** 6   **College:** Stanford   **Ht:** 6' 3" **Wt:** 285 **Born:** 3/15/70 **Age:** 26

Year	Team	G	GS	Year	Team	G	GS	Year	Team	G	GS			G	GS
1993	San Francisco 49ers	15	0	1994	San Francisco 49ers	16	4	1995	San Francisco 49ers	15	1		3 NFL Seasons	46	5

Other Statistics: 1993–recovered 1 fumble for 0 yards. 1994–fumbled 1 time for -3 yards. 1995–recovered 1 fumble for 0 yards; caught 1 pass for -1 yard; returned 3 kickoffs for 29 yards.

Brad Daluiso

(statistical profile on page 471)

Pos: K **Rnd:** FA   **College:** UCLA   **Ht:** 6' 2" **Wt:** 215 **Born:** 12/31/67 **Age:** 28

Year	Team	G	1-29 Yds	Pct	30-39 Yds	Pct	40-49 Yds	Pct	50+ Yds	Pct	Overall	Pct	Long	Made	Att	Pts
							Field Goals							**PAT**		**Tot**
1991	Atl - Buf	16	2-3	66.7	0-0	-	0-0	-	0-0	-	2-3	66.7	23	2	2	8
1992	Denver Broncos	16	0-0	-	0-0	-	0-0	-	0-1	0.0	0-1	0.0	-	0	0	0
1993	New York Giants	15	0-0	-	0-0	-	0-0	-	1-3	33.3	1-3	33.3	54	0	0	3
1994	New York Giants	16	3-3	100.0	5-5	**100.0**	2-2	100.0	1-1	100.0	11-11	100.0	52	5	5	38
1995	New York Giants	16	7-7	**100.0**	9-10	90.0	2-9	22.2	2-2	**100.0**	20-28	71.4	51	28	28	88
1991	Atlanta Falcons	2	2-3	66.7	0-0	-	0-0	-	0-0	-	2-3	66.7	23	2	2	8
	Buffalo Bills	14	0-0	-	0-0	-	0-0	-	0-0	-	0-0	-	-	0	0	0
	5 NFL Seasons	79	12-13	92.3	14-15	93.3	4-11	36.4	4-7	57.1	34-46	73.9	54	35	35	137

Other Statistics: 1992–punted 10 times for 467 yards.

Eugene Daniel

(statistical profile on page 407)

Pos: CB **Rnd:** 8   **College:** Louisiana State   **Ht:** 5' 11" **Wt:** 180 **Born:** 5/4/61 **Age:** 35

Year	Team	G	GS	Tk	Ast	Sack	FF	FR	TD	Blk	Int	Yds	Avg	TD	Num	Yds	Avg	TD	Num	Yds	Avg	TD	TD	Fum
					Tackles			**Miscellaneous**				**Interceptions**				**Punt Returns**				**Kickoff Returns**			**Totals**	
1984	Indianapolis Colts	15	13	45	17	0.0	0	0	0	0	6	25	4.2	0	0	0	-	0	0	0	-	0	0	0
1985	Indianapolis Colts	16	16	65	9	0.0	0	3	0	0	8	53	6.6	0	1	6	6.0	0	0	0	-	0	0	1
1986	Indianapolis Colts	15	15	52	17	0.0	0	1	1	0	3	11	3.7	0	0	0	-	0	0	0	-	0	1	0
1987	Indianapolis Colts	12	11	30	9	0.0	0	0	0	0	2	34	17.0	0	0	0	-	0	0	0	-	0	0	0
1988	Indianapolis Colts	16	16	52	13	0.0	0	0	0	0	2	44	22.0	1	0	0	-	0	0	0	-	0	1	0
1989	Indianapolis Colts	15	14	41	10	0.0	0	1	0	0	1	34	34.0	0	0	0	-	0	0	0	-	0	0	0
1990	Indianapolis Colts	15	15	48	11	0.0	0	0	0	0	0	0	-	0	1	0	0.0	0	0	0	-	0	0	0
1991	Indianapolis Colts	16	16	38	20	0.0	0	0	0	0	3	22	7.3	0	0	0	-	0	0	0	-	0	0	0
1992	Indianapolis Colts	14	13	49	7	2.0	0	0	0	0	1	0	0.0	0	0	0	-	0	0	0	-	0	0	0
1993	Indianapolis Colts	16	16	47	16	0.0	0	0	0	0	1	17	17.0	0	0	0	-	0	0	0	-	0	0	0
1994	Indianapolis Colts	16	15	65	12	0.0	1	0	0	0	2	6	3.0	0	0	0	-	0	0	0	-	0	0	0
1995	Indianapolis Colts	16	16	28	7	0.0	0	0	0	0	3	142	47.3	1	0	0	-	0	0	0	-	0	1	0
	12 NFL Seasons	182	175	560	148	2.0	1	5	1	0	32	388	12.1	2	2	6	3.0	0	0	0	-	0	3	1

Kirby Dar Dar

Pos: WR **Rnd:** FA   **College:** Syracuse   **Ht:** 5' 9" **Wt:** 183 **Born:** 3/27/72 **Age:** 24

Year	Team	G	GS	Att	Yds	Avg	Lg	TD	Rec	Yds	Avg	Lg	TD	Num	Yds	Avg	TD	Num	Yds	Avg	TD	Fum	TD	Pts
					Rushing					**Receiving**					**Punt Returns**				**Kickoff Returns**				**Totals**	
1995	Miami Dolphins	1	0	0	0	-	-	0	0	0	-	-	0	0	0	-	0	1	22	22.0	0	0	0	0

Matt Darby

Pos: S **Rnd:** 5   **College:** UCLA   **Ht:** 6' 1" **Wt:** 200 **Born:** 11/19/68 **Age:** 27

Year	Team	G	GS	Tk	Ast	Sack	FF	FR	TD	Blk	Int	Yds	Avg	TD	Sfty	TD	Pts
					Tackles			**Miscellaneous**				**Interceptions**				**Totals**	
1992	Buffalo Bills	16	1	15	8	0.0	0	1	0	0	0	0	-	0	0	0	0
1993	Buffalo Bills	16	3	39	14	0.0	1	1	0	0	2	32	16.0	0	0	0	0
1994	Buffalo Bills	16	16	52	14	0.0	0	0	0	0	4	20	5.0	0	0	0	0
1995	Buffalo Bills	7	3	14	2	0.0	0	0	0	0	2	37	18.5	0	0	0	0
	4 NFL Seasons	55	23	120	53	0.0	1	2	0	0	8	89	11.1	0	0	0	0

Don Davey

Pos: DT/DE **Rnd:** 3   **College:** Wisconsin   **Ht:** 6' 4" **Wt:** 275 **Born:** 4/8/68 **Age:** 28

Year	Team	G	GS	Tk	Ast	Sack	FF	FR	TD	Blk	Int	Yds	Avg	TD	Num	Yds	Avg	TD	Num	Yds	Avg	TD	TD	Fum
					Tackles			**Miscellaneous**				**Interceptions**				**Punt Returns**				**Kickoff Returns**			**Totals**	
1991	Green Bay Packers	16	0	0	0	0.0	0	0	0	0	0	0	-	0	0	0	-	0	1	8	8.0	0	0	0
1992	Green Bay Packers	9	0	4	1	0.0	0	0	0	0	0	0	-	0	0	0	-	0	1	8	8.0	0	0	0
1993	Green Bay Packers	9	0	2	0	0.0	0	0	0	0	0	0	-	0	0	0	-	0	0	0	-	0	0	0
1994	Green Bay Packers	16	2	11	5	1.5	0	0	0	0	0	0	-	0	0	0	-	0	1	6	6.0	0	0	0
1995	Jacksonville Jaguars	16	16	32	17	3.0	0	0	0	0	0	0	-	0	0	0	-	0	0	0	-	0	0	0
	5 NFL Seasons	66	18	49	23	4.5	0	0	0	0	0	0	-	0	0	0	-	0	3	22	7.3	0	0	0

Kenny Davidson

Pos: DE/DT **Rnd:** 2 **College:** Louisiana State **Ht:** 6' 5" **Wt:** 288 **Born:** 8/17/67 **Age:** 29

Year	Team	G	GS	Tk	Tackles Ast	Sack	FF	FR	Miscellaneous TD	Blk	Int	Yds	Interceptions Avg	TD	Sfty	Totals TD	Pts
1990	Pittsburgh Steelers	14	0	21	1	3.5	0	0	0	0	0	0	-	0	0	0	0
1991	Pittsburgh Steelers	13	1	8	5	0.0	0	0	0	0	0	0	-	0	0	0	0
1992	Pittsburgh Steelers	16	13	18	15	2.0	0	0	0	0	0	0	-	0	0	0	0
1993	Pittsburgh Steelers	16	9	26	25	2.5	0	1	1	0	1	6	6.0	0	0	1	6
1994	Houston Oilers	16	16	47	20	6.0	0	0	0	0	0	0	-	0	0	0	0
1995	Houston Oilers	15	12	16	16	2.0	1	1	0	0	1	3	3.0	0	0	0	0
	6 NFL Seasons	90	51	136	82	16.0	1	2	1	0	2	9	4.5	0	0	1	6

Anthony Davis

Pos: LB **Rnd:** 11 **College:** Utah **Ht:** 6' 0" **Wt:** 231 **Born:** 3/7/69 **Age:** 27

Year	Team	G	GS	Tk	Tackles Ast	Sack	FF	FR	Miscellaneous TD	Blk	Int	Yds	Interceptions Avg	TD	Sfty	Totals TD	Pts
1993	Seattle Seahawks	10	0	0	0	0.0	0	0	0	0	0	0	-	0	0	0	0
1994	Kansas City Chiefs	5	0	0	0	0.0	0	0	0	0	0	0	-	0	0	0	0
1995	Kansas City Chiefs	16	2	51	6	2.0	0	0	0	0	1	11	11.0	0	0	0	0
	3 NFL Seasons	31	2	51	6	2.0	0	0	0	0	1	11	11.0	0	0	0	0

Antone Davis

Pos: T **Rnd:** 1 (9) **College:** Tennessee **Ht:** 6' 4" **Wt:** 335 **Born:** 2/28/67 **Age:** 29

Year	Team	G	GS	Year	Team	G	GS	Year	Team	G	GS			G	GS
1991	Philadelphia Eagles	16	15	1993	Philadelphia Eagles	16	16	1995	Philadelphia Eagles	15	14				
1992	Philadelphia Eagles	15	15	1994	Philadelphia Eagles	16	14						5 NFL Seasons	78	74

Billy Davis

Pos: WR **Rnd:** FA **College:** Pittsburgh **Ht:** 6' 1" **Wt:** 199 **Born:** 7/6/72 **Age:** 24

Year	Team	G	GS	Att	Rushing Yds	Avg	Lg	TD	Rec	Receiving Yds	Avg	Lg	TD	Num	Punt Returns Yds	Avg	TD	Num	Kickoff Returns Yds	Avg	TD	Fum	Totals TD	Pts
1995	Dallas Cowboys	16	0	0	0	-	-	0	0	0	-	-	0	0	0	-	0	0	0	-	0	0	0	0

Dexter Davis

Pos: CB **Rnd:** 4 **College:** Clemson **Ht:** 5' 10" **Wt:** 185 **Born:** 3/20/70 **Age:** 26

Year	Team	G	GS	Tk	Tackles Ast	Sack	FF	FR	Miscellaneous TD	Blk	Int	Yds	Interceptions Avg	TD	Sfty	Totals TD	Pts
1991	Phoenix Cardinals	11	0	4	1	0.0	0	2	0	0	0	0	-	0	0	0	0
1992	Phoenix Cardinals	16	2	22	3	0.0	0	0	0	0	2	27	13.5	0	0	0	0
1993	Pho - LAN	12	4	17	2	0.0	0	0	0	0	0	0	-	0	0	0	0
1994	Los Angeles Rams	4	0	1	0	0.0	0	1	0	0	0	0	-	0	0	0	0
1995	St. Louis Rams	16	0	6	2	1.0	0	1	0	0	0	0	-	0	0	0	0
1993	Phoenix Cardinals	6	1	3	0	0.0	0	0	0	0	0	0	-	0	0	0	0
	Los Angeles Rams	6	3	14	2	0.0	0	0	0	0	0	0	-	0	0	0	0
	5 NFL Seasons	59	6	50	8	1.0	0	4	0	0	2	27	13.5	0	0	0	0

Eric Davis

(statistical profile on page 408)

Pos: CB **Rnd:** 2 **College:** Jacksonville State **Ht:** 5' 11" **Wt:** 178 **Born:** 1/26/68 **Age:** 28

Year	Team	G	GS	Tk	Tackles Ast	Sack	FF	FR	TD	Blk	Int	Yds	Interceptions Avg	TD	Num	Punt Returns Yds	Avg	TD	Num	Kickoff Returns Yds	Avg	TD	Totals TD	Fum
1990	San Francisco 49ers	16	0	20	1	0.0	2	1	0	0	1	13	13.0	0	5	38	7.6	0	0	0	-	0	0	0
1991	San Francisco 49ers	2	2	9	1	0.0	0	0	0	0	0	0	-	0	0	0	-	0	0	0	-	0	0	0
1992	San Francisco 49ers	16	16	58	3	0.0	0	2	0	0	3	52	17.3	0	0	0	-	0	0	0	-	0	0	0
1993	San Francisco 49ers	16	16	63	6	0.0	1	1	1	0	4	45	11.3	1	0	0	-	0	0	0	-	0	2	0
1994	San Francisco 49ers	16	16	68	6	0.0	1	2	0	0	1	8	8.0	0	0	0	-	0	0	0	-	0	0	1
1995	San Francisco 49ers	15	15	43	8	1.0	2	0	0	0	3	84	28.0	1	0	0	-	0	0	0	-	0	1	0
	6 NFL Seasons	81	65	261	25	1.0	6	6	1	0	12	202	16.8	2	5	38	7.6	0	0	0	-	0	3	1

Greg Davis

(statistical profile on page 471)

Pos: K **Rnd:** 9 **College:** The Citadel **Ht:** 6' 0" **Wt:** 205 **Born:** 10/29/65 **Age:** 31

Year	Team	G	1-29 Yds	Pct	30-39 Yds	Pct	40-49 Yds	Pct	50+ Yds	Pct	Overall	Pct	Long	PAT Made	Att	Tot Pts
1987	Atlanta Falcons	3	1-1	100.0	1-1	100.0	1-2	50.0	0-0	-	3-4	75.0	42	6	6	15
1988	Atlanta Falcons	16	4-5	80.0	6-9	66.7	8-12	66.7	1-4	25.0	19-30	63.3	52	25	27	82
1989	NE - Atl	15	6-6	100.0	8-12	66.7	7-14	50.0	2-2	100.0	23-34	67.6	52	25	28	94
1990	Atlanta Falcons	16	6-6	100.0	8-9	88.9	6-13	46.2	2-5	40.0	22-33	66.7	53	40	40	106

Year	Team	G	1-29 Yds	Pct	30-39 Yds	Pct	40-49 Yds	Pct	50+ Yds	Pct	Overall	Pct	Long	Made	Att	Pts
							Field Goals							**PAT**		**Tot**
1991	Phoenix Cardinals	16	6-6	100.0	7-7	100.0	5-10	50.0	3-7	42.9	21-30	70.0	52	19	19	82
1992	Phoenix Cardinals	16	6-10	60.0	3-4	75.0	4-9	44.4	0-3	0.0	13-26	50.0	49	28	28	67
1993	Phoenix Cardinals	16	12-12	100.0	1-1	100.0	4-10	40.0	4-5	80.0	21-28	75.0	55	37	37	100
1994	Arizona Cardinals	14	10-11	90.9	3-4	75.0	6-7	85.7	1-4	25.0	20-26	76.9	51	17	17	77
1995	Arizona Cardinals	16	14-15	93.3	9-10	90.0	6-8	75.0	1-6	16.7	30-39	76.9	55	19	19	109
1989	New England Patriots	9	3-3	100.0	6-9	66.7	5-9	55.6	2-2	100.0	16-23	69.6	52	13	16	61
	Atlanta Falcons	6	3-3	100.0	2-3	66.7	2-5	40.0	0-0	-	7-11	63.6	46	12	12	33
	9 NFL Seasons	128	65-72	90.3	46-57	80.7	47-85	55.3	14-36	38.9	172-250	68.8	55	216	221	732

Other Statistics: 1987–punted 6 times for 191 yards. 1992–punted 4 times for 167 yards.

Isaac Davis

Pos: G   **Rnd:** 2   **College:** Arkansas   **Ht:** 6' 3" **Wt:** 325 **Born:** 4/8/72 **Age:** 24

Year	Team	G	GS	Year	Team	G	GS				G	GS
1994	San Diego Chargers	13	2	1995	San Diego Chargers	16	10		2 NFL Seasons		29	12

Mike Davis

Pos: CB   **Rnd:** 4   **College:** Cincinnati   **Ht:** 6' 0" **Wt:** 195 **Born:** 1/14/72 **Age:** 24

Year	Team	G	GS	Tk	Ast	Sack	FF	FR	TD	Blk	Int	Yds	Avg	TD	Sfty	TD	Pts
				Tackles			**Miscellaneous**				**Interceptions**				**Totals**		
1994	Houston Oilers	16	0	2	0	0.0	0	0	0	0	0	0	-	0	0	0	0
1995	Cleveland Browns	3	0	0	0	0.0	0	0	0	0	0	0	-	0	0	0	0
	2 NFL Seasons	19	0	2	0	0.0	0	0	0	0	0	0	-	0	0	0	0

Paschall Davis

Pos: LB   **Rnd:** FA   **College:** Texas A&I   **Ht:** 6' 2" **Wt:** 225 **Born:** 7/5/69 **Age:** 27

Year	Team	G	GS	Tk	Ast	Sack	FF	FR	TD	Blk	Int	Yds	Avg	TD	Sfty	TD	Pts
				Tackles			**Miscellaneous**				**Interceptions**				**Totals**		
1995	St. Louis Rams	3	0	0	0	0.0	0	0	0	0	0	0	-	0	0	0	0

Reuben Davis

Pos: DT   **Rnd:** 9   **College:** North Carolina   **Ht:** 6' 5" **Wt:** 320 **Born:** 5/7/65 **Age:** 31

Year	Team	G	GS	Tk	Ast	Sack	FF	FR	TD	Blk	Int	Yds	Avg	TD	Sfty	TD	Pts
				Tackles			**Miscellaneous**				**Interceptions**				**Totals**		
1988	Tampa Bay Buccaneers	16	13	44	17	3.0	0	0	0	0	0	0	-	0	0	0	0
1989	Tampa Bay Buccaneers	16	15	52	9	3.0	0	2	0	0	1	13	13.0	1	0	1	6
1990	Tampa Bay Buccaneers	16	16	43	19	1.0	0	1	0	0	0	0	-	0	0	0	0
1991	Tampa Bay Buccaneers	12	11	34	6	3.5	0	0	0	0	0	0	-	0	0	0	0
1992	TB - Pho	16	5	16	4	2.0	0	0	0	0	0	0	-	0	0	0	0
1993	Phoenix Cardinals	16	15	28	21	1.0	1	1	0	0	0	0	-	0	0	0	0
1994	San Diego Chargers	16	16	29	9	0.5	0	1	0	0	0	0	-	0	0	0	0
1995	San Diego Chargers	16	16	37	11	3.5	0	0	0	0	0	0	-	0	1	0	2
1992	Tampa Bay Buccaneers	5	0	3	0	0.0	0	0	0	0	0	0	-	0	0	0	0
	Phoenix Cardinals	11	5	13	4	2.0	0	0	0	0	0	0	-	0	0	0	0
	8 NFL Seasons	124	107	283	96	17.5	1	5	0	0	1	13	13.0	1	1	1	8

Ron Davis

Pos: CB   **Rnd:** 2   **College:** Tennessee   **Ht:** 5' 10" **Wt:** 190 **Born:** 2/24/72 **Age:** 24

Year	Team	G	GS	Tk	Ast	Sack	FF	FR	TD	Blk	Int	Yds	Avg	TD	Sfty	TD	Pts
				Tackles			**Miscellaneous**				**Interceptions**				**Totals**		
1995	Atlanta Falcons	12	5	25	2	0.0	0	1	0	0	0	0	-	0	0	0	0

Terrell Davis

(statistical profile on page 304)

Pos: RB   **Rnd:** 6   **College:** Georgia   **Ht:** 5' 11" **Wt:** 200 **Born:** 10/28/72 **Age:** 24

Year	Team	G	GS	Att	Yds	Avg	Lg	TD	Rec	Yds	Avg	Lg	TD	Num	Yds	Avg	TD	Num	Yds	Avg	TD	Fum	TD	Pts
				Rushing					**Receiving**					**Punt Returns**				**Kickoff Returns**				**Totals**		
1995	Denver Broncos	14	14	237	1117	4.7	t60	7	49	367	7.5	31	1	0	0	-	0	0	0	-	0	5	8	48

Other Statistics: 1995–recovered 1 fumble for 0 yards.

Travis Davis

Pos: S   **Rnd:** 7   **College:** Notre Dame   **Ht:** 6' 0" **Wt:** 200 **Born:** 1/10/73 **Age:** 23

Year	Team	G	GS	Tk	Ast	Sack	FF	FR	TD	Blk	Int	Yds	Avg	TD	Sfty	TD	Pts
				Tackles			**Miscellaneous**				**Interceptions**				**Totals**		
1995	Jacksonville Jaguars	9	5	26	7	0.0	0	1	0	0	0	0	-	0	0	0	0

Tyree Davis

Pos: WR   **Rnd:** 7   **College:** Central Arkansas   **Ht:** 5' 9" **Wt:** 175   **Born:** 9/28/70   **Age:** 26

Year Team	G	GS	Att	Yds	Avg	Lg	TD	Rec	Yds	Avg	Lg	TD	Num	Yds	Avg	TD	Num	Yds	Avg	TD	Fum	TD	Pts
				Rushing					Receiving					Punt Returns				Kickoff Returns				Totals	
1995 Tampa Bay Buccaneers	1	0	0	0	-	-	0	0	0	-	-	0	0	0	-	0	0	0	-	0	0	0	0

Tyrone Davis

Pos: WR   **Rnd:** 4   **College:** Virginia   **Ht:** 6' 4" **Wt:** 229   **Born:** 6/30/72   **Age:** 24

Year Team	G	GS	Att	Yds	Avg	Lg	TD	Rec	Yds	Avg	Lg	TD	Num	Yds	Avg	TD	Num	Yds	Avg	TD	Fum	TD	Pts
				Rushing					Receiving					Punt Returns				Kickoff Returns				Totals	
1995 New York Jets	4	0	0	0	-	-	0	1	9	9.0	9	0	0	0	-	0	0	0	-	0	0	0	0

Willie Davis

(statistical profile on page 304)

Pos: WR   **Rnd:** FA   **College:** Central Arkansas   **Ht:** 6' 0" **Wt:** 181   **Born:** 10/10/67   **Age:** 29

Year Team	G	GS	Att	Yds	Avg	Lg	TD	Rec	Yds	Avg	Lg	TD	Num	Yds	Avg	TD	Num	Yds	Avg	TD	Fum	TD	Pts
				Rushing					Receiving					Punt Returns				Kickoff Returns				Totals	
1991 Kansas City Chiefs	1	0	0	0	-	-	0	0	0	-	-	0	0	0	-	0	0	0	-	0	0	0	0
1992 Kansas City Chiefs	16	14	1	-11	-11.0	-11	0	36	756	21.0	t74	3	0	0	-	0	0	0	-	0	0	3	18
1993 Kansas City Chiefs	16	15	0	0	-	-	0	52	909	17.5	t66	7	0	0	-	0	0	0	-	0	0	7	42
1994 Kansas City Chiefs	14	13	0	0	-	-	0	51	822	16.1	t62	5	0	0	-	0	0	0	-	0	0	5	32
1995 Kansas City Chiefs	16	16	0	0	-	-	0	33	527	16.0	t60	5	0	0	-	0	0	0	-	0	0	5	30
5 NFL Seasons	63	58	1	-11	-11.0	-11	0	172	3014	17.5	t74	20	0	0	-	0	0	0	-	0	1	20	122

Other Statistics: 1994–scored 1 two-point conversion.

Sean Dawkins

(statistical profile on page 305)

Pos: WR   **Rnd:** 1 (16)   **College:** California   **Ht:** 6' 4" **Wt:** 211   **Born:** 2/3/71   **Age:** 25

Year Team	G	GS	Att	Yds	Avg	Lg	TD	Rec	Yds	Avg	Lg	TD	Num	Yds	Avg	TD	Num	Yds	Avg	TD	Fum	TD	Pts
				Rushing					Receiving					Punt Returns				Kickoff Returns				Totals	
1993 Indianapolis Colts	16	7	0	0	-	-	0	26	430	16.5	68	1	0	0	-	0	0	0	-	0	0	1	6
1994 Indianapolis Colts	16	16	0	0	-	-	0	51	742	14.5	49	5	0	0	-	0	0	0	-	0	1	5	30
1995 Indianapolis Colts	16	13	0	0	-	-	0	52	784	15.1	52	3	0	0	-	0	0	0	-	0	1	3	18
3 NFL Seasons	48	36	0	0	-	-	0	129	1956	15.2	68	9	0	0	-	0	0	0	-	0	2	9	54

Lawrence Dawsey

(statistical profile on page 305)

Pos: WR   **Rnd:** 3   **College:** Florida State   **Ht:** 6' 0" **Wt:** 192   **Born:** 11/16/67   **Age:** 28

Year Team	G	GS	Att	Yds	Avg	Lg	TD	Rec	Yds	Avg	Lg	TD	Num	Yds	Avg	TD	Num	Yds	Avg	TD	Fum	TD	Pts
				Rushing					Receiving					Punt Returns				Kickoff Returns				Totals	
1991 Tampa Bay Buccaneers	16	10	1	9	9.0	t9	1	55	818	14.9	t65	3	0	0	-	0	0	0	-	0	0	4	24
1992 Tampa Bay Buccaneers	15	12	0	0	-	-	0	60	776	12.9	41	1	0	0	-	0	0	0	-	0	1	1	6
1993 Tampa Bay Buccaneers	4	4	0	0	-	-	0	15	203	13.5	24	0	0	0	-	0	0	0	-	0	0	0	0
1994 Tampa Bay Buccaneers	10	5	0	0	-	-	0	46	673	14.6	46	1	0	0	-	0	0	0	-	0	0	1	6
1995 Tampa Bay Buccaneers	12	10	0	0	-	-	0	30	372	12.4	26	0	0	0	-	0	0	0	-	0	0	0	0
5 NFL Seasons	57	41	1	9	9.0	t9	1	206	2842	13.8	t65	5	0	0	-	0	0	0	-	0	1	6	36

Other Statistics: 1992–recovered 1 fumble for 0 yards.

Dermontti Dawson

Pos: C   **Rnd:** 2   **College:** Kentucky   **Ht:** 6' 2" **Wt:** 286   **Born:** 6/17/65   **Age:** 31

Year	Team	G	GS	Year	Team	G	GS	Year	Team	G	GS	Year	Team	G	GS
1988	Pittsburgh Steelers	8	5	1990	Pittsburgh Steelers	16	16	1992	Pittsburgh Steelers	16	16	1994	Pittsburgh Steelers	16	16
1989	Pittsburgh Steelers	16	16	1991	Pittsburgh Steelers	16	16	1993	Pittsburgh Steelers	16	16	1995	Pittsburgh Steelers	16	16
													8 NFL Seasons	120	117

Other Statistics: 1991–recovered 1 fumble for 2 yards; fumbled 2 times. 1993–fumbled 1 time for 0 yards.

Lake Dawson

(statistical profile on page 306)

Pos: WR   **Rnd:** 3   **College:** Notre Dame   **Ht:** 6' 1" **Wt:** 207   **Born:** 1/2/72   **Age:** 24

Year Team	G	GS	Att	Yds	Avg	Lg	TD	Rec	Yds	Avg	Lg	TD	Num	Yds	Avg	TD	Num	Yds	Avg	TD	Fum	TD	Pts
				Rushing					Receiving					Punt Returns				Kickoff Returns				Totals	
1994 Kansas City Chiefs	12	6	3	24	8.0	13	0	37	537	14.5	50	2	0	0	-	0	0	0	-	0	1	2	12
1995 Kansas City Chiefs	16	9	1	-9	-9.0	-9	0	40	513	12.8	t45	5	0	0	-	0	0	0	-	0	0	5	30
2 NFL Seasons	28	15	4	15	3.8	13	0	77	1050	13.6	50	7	0	0	-	0	0	0	-	0	1	7	42

Derrick Deese

Pos: G   **Rnd:** FA   **College:** Southern California   **Ht:** 6' 3" **Wt:** 275   **Born:** 5/17/70   **Age:** 26

Year	Team	G	GS	Year	Team	G	GS
1994	San Francisco 49ers	16	15	1995	San Francisco 49ers	2	2
				2 NFL Seasons		18	17

Al Del Greco

(statistical profile on page 472)

Pos: K   **Rnd:** FA   **College:** Auburn   **Ht:** 5' 10" **Wt:** 200   **Born:** 3/2/62   **Age:** 34

Year	Team	G	1-29 Yds	Pct	30-39 Yds	Pct	40-49 Yds	Pct	50+ Yds	Pct	Overall	Pct	Long	Made	Att	Pts
1984	Green Bay Packers	9	2-2	100.0	3-4	75.0	4-5	80.0	0-1	0.0	9-12	75.0	45	34	34	61
1985	Green Bay Packers	16	10-12	83.3	4-4	100.0	5-9	55.6	0-1	0.0	19-26	73.1	46	38	40	95
1986	Green Bay Packers	16	8-8	100.0	4-6	66.7	3-9	33.3	2-4	50.0	17-27	63.0	50	29	29	80
1987	GB - StL	8	3-5	60.0	4-6	66.7	2-4	50.0	0-0	-	9-15	60.0	47	19	20	46
1988	Phoenix Cardinals	16	5-7	71.4	3-3	100.0	3-9	33.3	1-2	50.0	12-21	57.1	51	42	44	78
1989	Phoenix Cardinals	16	7-7	100.0	5-6	83.3	5-11	45.5	1-2	50.0	18-26	69.2	50	28	29	82
1990	Phoenix Cardinals	16	5-5	100.0	7-10	70.0	3-6	50.0	2-6	33.3	17-27	63.0	50	31	31	82
1991	Houston Oilers	7	5-6	83.3	2-3	66.7	2-3	66.7	1-1	100.0	10-13	76.9	52	16	16	46
1992	Houston Oilers	16	11-12	91.7	5-6	83.3	4-8	50.0	1-1	100.0	21-27	77.8	54	41	41	104
1993	Houston Oilers	16	13-13	100.0	8-9	88.9	4-5	80.0	4-7	57.1	29-34	85.3	52	39	40	126
1994	Houston Oilers	16	4-5	80.0	4-4	100.0	7-8	87.5	1-3	33.3	16-20	80.0	50	18	18	66
1995	Houston Oilers	16	6-6	100.0	8-8	100.0	10-12	83.3	3-5	60.0	27-31	87.1	53	33	33	114
1987	Green Bay Packers	5	1-2	50.0	2-4	50.0	2-4	50.0	0-0	-	5-10	50.0	47	11	11	26
	St. Louis Cardinals	3	2-3	66.7	2-2	100.0	0-0	-	0-0	-	4-5	80.0	37	8	9	20
	12 NFL Seasons	168	79-88	89.8	57-69	82.6	52-89	58.4	16-33	48.5	204-279	73.1	54	368	375	980

Other Statistics: 1988–rushed 1 time for 8 yards. 1990–recovered 1 fumble for 0 yards. 1995–punted 1 time for 15 yards.

Jack Del Rio

Pos: LB   **Rnd:** 3   **College:** Southern California   **Ht:** 6' 4" **Wt:** 246   **Born:** 4/4/63   **Age:** 33

Year	Team	G	GS	Tk	Ast	Sack	FF	FR	TD	Blk	Int	Yds	Avg	TD	Num	Yds	Avg	TD	Num	Yds	Avg	TD	TD	Fum
1985	New Orleans Saints	16	9	51	17	0.0	3	5	1	0	2	13	6.5	0	0	0	-	0	0	0	-	0	1	0
1986	New Orleans Saints	16	1	14	6	0.0	3	0	0	0	0	0	-	0	0	0	-	0	0	0	-	0	0	0
1987	Kansas City Chiefs	10	7	32	12	3.0	1	0	0	0	0	0	-	0	0	0	-	0	0	0	-	0	0	0
1988	Kansas City Chiefs	15	10	45	32	1.0	0	1	0	0	1	0	0.0	0	0	0	-	0	0	0	-	0	0	0
1989	Dallas Cowboys	14	12	40	18	0.0	0	2	1	0	0	0	-	0	0	0	-	0	0	0	-	0	1	0
1990	Dallas Cowboys	16	16	48	56	1.5	1	0	0	0	0	0	-	0	0	0	-	0	0	0	-	0	0	0
1991	Dallas Cowboys	16	16	77	53	0.0	1	0	0	0	0	0	-	0	0	0	-	0	0	0	-	0	1	0
1992	Minnesota Vikings	16	16	113	40	2.0	1	2	0	0	2	92	46.0	1	0	0	-	0	0	0	-	0	1	0
1993	Minnesota Vikings	16	16	108	61	0.5	1	0	0	0	4	3	0.8	0	0	0	-	0	1	4	4.0	0	0	0
1994	Minnesota Vikings	16	16	86	43	2.0	1	2	0	0	3	5	1.7	0	0	0	-	0	0	0	-	0	0	0
1995	Minnesota Vikings	9	9	32	21	3.0	0	1	0	0	1	15	15.0	0	0	0	-	0	0	0	-	0	0	0
	11 NFL Seasons	160	128	646	359	13.0	12	14	2	0	13	128	9.8	1	0	0	-	0	1	4	4.0	0	3	0

Other Statistics: 1986–rushed 1 time for 16 yards.

Jeff Dellenbach

Pos: C   **Rnd:** 4   **College:** Wisconsin   **Ht:** 6' 6" **Wt:** 300   **Born:** 2/14/63   **Age:** 33

Year	Team	G	GS	Year	Team	G	GS	Year	Team	G	GS	Year	Team	G	GS
1985	Miami Dolphins	11	1	1988	Miami Dolphins	16	16	1991	Miami Dolphins	15	2	1994	Miami Dolphins	16	16
1986	Miami Dolphins	13	6	1989	Miami Dolphins	16	16	1992	Miami Dolphins	16	8	1995	New England Patriots	15	5
1987	Miami Dolphins	11	6	1990	Miami Dolphins	15	0	1993	Miami Dolphins	16	16		11 NFL Seasons	160	92

Other Statistics: 1987–fumbled 1 time for -13 yards. 1988–fumbled 1 time for -9 yards. 1991–returned 1 kickoff for 0 yards. 1992–recovered 1 fumble for 0 yards. 1993–recovered 1 fumble for -6 yards; fumbled 1 time. 1994–fumbled 1 time for -11 yards.

Greg DeLong

Pos: TE   **Rnd:** FA   **College:** North Carolina   **Ht:** 6' 4" **Wt:** 245   **Born:** 4/3/73   **Age:** 23

Year	Team	G	GS	Att	Yds	Avg	Lg	TD	Rec	Yds	Avg	Lg	TD	Num	Yds	Avg	TD	Num	Yds	Avg	TD	Fum	TD	Pts
1995	Minnesota Vikings	2	2	0	0	-	-	0	6	38	6.3	9	0	0	0	-	0	0	0	-	0	0	0	0

Brian DeMarco

Pos: T   **Rnd:** 2   **College:** Michigan State   **Ht:** 6' 5" **Wt:** 314   **Born:** 4/0/72   **Age:** 24

Year	Team	G	GS						G	GS
1995	Jacksonville Jaguars	16	16				1 NFL Season		16	16

Mark Dennis

Pos: T   **Rnd:** 8   **College:** Illinois   **Ht:** 6' 6" **Wt:** 296   **Born:** 4/15/65   **Age:** 31

Year	Team	G	GS	Year	Team	G	GS	Year	Team	G	GS			G	GS
1987	Miami Dolphins	5	2	1990	Miami Dolphins	16	16	1993	Miami Dolphins	16	0				
1988	Miami Dolphins	13	7	1991	Miami Dolphins	16	16	1994	Cincinnati Bengals	6	1				
1989	Miami Dolphins	8	1	1992	Miami Dolphins	16	8	1995	Carolina Panthers	12	9	9 NFL Seasons		108	60

Other Statistics: 1991–recovered 1 fumble for 0 yards. 1993–recovered 1 fumble for 0 yards. 1995–caught 1 pass for 3 yards.

Richard Dent

Pos: DE/DT **Rnd:** 8   **College:** Tennessee State   **Ht:** 6' 5" **Wt:** 265 **Born:** 12/13/60 **Age:** 35

Year Team	G	GS	Tackles			Miscellaneous				Interceptions				Totals		
			Tk	Ast	Sack	FF	FR	TD	Blk	Int	Yds	Avg	TD	Sfty	TD	Pts
1983 Chicago Bears	16	3	9	3	3.0	1	0	0	0	0	0	-	0	0	0	0
1984 Chicago Bears	16	10	31	8	17.5	4	1	0	0	0	0	-	0	0	0	0
1985 Chicago Bears	16	16	33	5	17.0	7	2	0	0	2	10	5.0	1	0	1	6
1986 Chicago Bears	15	14	30	45	11.5	4	0	0	0	0	0	-	0	0	0	0
1987 Chicago Bears	12	12	18	16	12.5	4	2	0	0	0	0	-	0	0	0	0
1988 Chicago Bears	13	13	31	30	10.5	3	1	0	0	0	0	-	0	0	0	0
1989 Chicago Bears	15	15	37	33	9.0	2	2	0	0	1	30	30.0	0	0	0	0
1990 Chicago Bears	16	16	43	38	12.0	2	3	1	0	3	21	7.0	0	0	1	6
1991 Chicago Bears	16	16	50	34	10.5	0	1	0	0	1	4	4.0	0	0	0	0
1992 Chicago Bears	16	16	46	36	8.5	6	1	0	0	0	0	-	0	0	0	0
1993 Chicago Bears	16	16	43	21	12.5	1	0	0	0	1	24	24.0	0	0	0	0
1994 San Francisco 49ers	2	2	7	1	2.0	0	0	0	0	0	0	-	0	0	0	0
1995 Chicago Bears	3	1	1	0	0.0	0	0	0	0	0	0	-	0	0	0	0
13 NFL Seasons	172	150	379	270	126.5	34	13	1	0	8	89	11.1	1	0	2	12

Steve DeOssie

Pos: LS **Rnd:** 4   **College:** Boston College   **Ht:** 6' 2" **Wt:** 248 **Born:** 11/22/62 **Age:** 33

Year Team	G	GS	Tackles			Miscellaneous				Interceptions				Punt Returns				Kickoff Returns				Totals	
			Tk	Ast	Sack	FF	FR	TD	Blk	Int	Yds	Avg	TD	Num	Yds	Avg	TD	Num	Yds	Avg	TD	TD	Fum
1984 Dallas Cowboys	16	0	4	4	0.0	0	0	0	0	0	0	-	0	0	0	-	0	0	0	-	0	0	0
1985 Dallas Cowboys	16	0	3	3	0.0	0	0	0	0	0	0	-	0	0	0	-	0	0	0	-	0	0	0
1986 Dallas Cowboys	16	0	4	3	0.0	0	0	0	0	0	0	-	0	0	0	-	0	0	0	-	0	0	0
1987 Dallas Cowboys	11	2	15	11	0.0	0	0	0	0	0	0	-	0	0	0	-	0	0	0	-	0	0	0
1988 Dallas Cowboys	16	1	12	11	0.0	0	0	0	0	0	0	-	0	0	0	-	0	0	0	-	0	0	0
1989 New York Giants	9	3	17	2	0.0	0	0	0	0	1	10	10.0	0	0	0	-	0	0	0	-	0	0	0
1990 New York Giants	16	13	36	17	0.0	0	1	0	0	0	0	-	0	0	0	-	0	0	0	-	0	0	0
1991 New York Giants	16	2	7	2	0.0	0	0	0	0	0	0	-	0	0	0	-	0	0	0	-	0	0	0
1992 New York Giants	12	11	33	10	0.0	0	0	0	0	0	0	-	0	0	0	-	0	0	0	-	0	0	0
1993 NYN - NYA	15	0	0	0	0.0	0	0	0	0	0	0	-	0	0	0	-	0	0	0	-	0	0	0
1994 New England Patriots	16	0	0	0	0.0	0	0	0	0	0	0	-	0	0	0	-	0	1	14	14.0	0	0	0
1995 New England Patriots	16	0	0	0	0.0	0	0	0	0	0	0	-	0	0	0	-	0	0	0	-	0	0	0
1993 New York Giants	8	0	0	0	0.0	0	0	0	0	0	0	-	0	0	0	-	0	0	0	-	0	0	0
New York Jets	7	0	0	0	0.0	0	0	0	0	0	0	-	0	0	0	-	0	0	0	-	0	0	0
12 NFL Seasons	175	32	131	63	0.0	0	1	0	0	1	10	10.0	0	0	0	-	0	1	14	14.0	0	0	0

Lee DeRamus

Pos: WR   **Rnd:** 6   **College:** Wisconsin   **Ht:** 6' 0" **Wt:** 191 **Born:** 8/24/72 **Age:** 24

Year Team	G	GS	Rushing					Receiving					Punt Returns				Kickoff Returns				Totals		
			Att	Yds	Avg	Lg	TD	Rec	Yds	Avg	Lg	TD	Num	Yds	Avg	TD	Num	Yds	Avg	TD	Fum	TD	Pts
1995 New Orleans Saints	8	0	0	0	-	-	0	6	76	12.7	27	0	0	0	-	0	0	0	-	0	0	0	0

Ty Detmer

Pos: QB   **Rnd:** 9   **College:** Brigham Young   **Ht:** 6' 0" **Wt:** 194 **Born:** 10/30/67 **Age:** 29

Year Team	G	GS	Passing										Rushing					Miscellaneous				
			Att	Com	Pct	Yards	Yds/Att	Lg	TD	Int	Int%	Rating	Att	Yds	Avg	Lg	TD	Sckd	Yds	Fum Rec	Yds	Pts
1993 Green Bay Packers	3	0	5	3	60.0	26	5.20	25	0	0	0.0	73.8	1	-2	-2.0	-2	0	0	0	0	0	0
1995 Green Bay Packers	4	0	16	8	50.0	81	5.06	25	1	1	6.3	59.6	3	3	1.0	5	0	0	0	1	1	0
2 NFL Seasons	7	0	21	11	52.4	107	5.10	25	1	1	4.8	63.0	4	1	0.3	5	0	0	0	1	1	0

Mike Devlin

Pos: C/G   **Rnd:** 5   **College:** Iowa   **Ht:** 6' 2" **Wt:** 300 **Born:** 11/16/69 **Age:** 26

Year Team	G	GS	Year Team	G	GS	Year Team	G	GS		G	GS
1993 Buffalo Bills	12	0	1994 Buffalo Bills	16	0	1995 Buffalo Bills	16	0	3 NFL Seasons	44	0

Jed Devries

Pos: T   **Rnd:** FA   **College:** Utah State   **Ht:** 6' 6" **Wt:** 300 **Born:** 1/6/71 **Age:** 25

Year Team	G	GS		G	GS
1995 Cleveland Browns	3	0	1 NFL Season	3	0

Bryan Dickerson

Pos: RB **Rnd:** FA **College:** Eastern Kentucky **Ht:** 6' 1" **Wt:** 260 **Born:** 3/22/71 **Age:** 25

			Rushing					Receiving					Punt Returns				Kickoff Returns				Totals		
Year Team	G	GS	Att	Yds	Avg	Lg	TD	Rec	Yds	Avg	Lg	TD	Num	Yds	Avg	TD	Num	Yds	Avg	TD	Fum	TD	Pts
1995 Jacksonville Jaguars	1	0	0	0	-	-	0	0	0	-	-	0	0	0	-	0	0	0	-	0	0	0	0

Trent Dilfer

(statistical profile on page 306)

Pos: QB **Rnd:** 1 (6) **College:** Fresno State **Ht:** 6' 4" **Wt:** 235 **Born:** 3/13/72 **Age:** 24

			Passing									Rushing				Miscellaneous			
Year Team	G	GS	Att	Com	Pct	Yards	Yds/Att	Lg	TD	Int	Int%	Rating	Att	Yds	Avg	Lg	TD	Sckd	Yds	Fum	Recv	Yds	Pts
1994 Tampa Bay Buccaneers	5	2	82	38	46.3	433	5.28	42	1	6	7.3	36.3	2	27	13.5	15	0	8	42	2	0	0	0
1995 Tampa Bay Buccaneers	16	16	415	224	54.0	2774	6.68	t64	4	18	4.3	60.1	23	115	5.0	t21	2	47	331	13	1	-9	12
2 NFL Seasons	21	18	497	262	52.7	3207	6.45	t64	5	24	4.8	56.1	25	142	5.7	t21	2	55	373	15	1	-9	12

Ken Dilger

(statistical profile on page 307)

Pos: TE **Rnd:** 2 **College:** Illinois **Ht:** 6' 5" **Wt:** 256 **Born:** 2/2/71 **Age:** 25

			Rushing					Receiving					Punt Returns				Kickoff Returns				Totals		
Year Team	G	GS	Att	Yds	Avg	Lg	TD	Rec	Yds	Avg	Lg	TD	Num	Yds	Avg	TD	Num	Yds	Avg	TD	Fum	TD	Pts
1995 Indianapolis Colts	16	13	0	0	-	-	0	42	635	15.1	42	4	0	0	-	0	0	0	-	0	0	4	24

Scott Dill

Pos: T **Rnd:** 9 **College:** Memphis **Ht:** 6' 5" **Wt:** 295 **Born:** 4/5/66 **Age:** 30

Year	Team	G	GS	Year	Team	G	GS	Year	Team	G	GS	Year	Team	G	GS
1988	Phoenix Cardinals	13	0	1990	Tampa Bay Buccaneers	3	2	1992	Tampa Bay Buccaneers	4	0	1994	Tampa Bay Buccaneers	16	16
1989	Phoenix Cardinals	16	0	1991	Tampa Bay Buccaneers	8	0	1993	Tampa Bay Buccaneers	16	16	1995	Tampa Bay Buccaneers	12	12
													8 NFL Seasons	88	46

Other Statistics: 1989–recovered 1 fumble for 0 yards. 1993–recovered 1 fumble for 0 yards.

Stacey Dillard

Pos: DT **Rnd:** 6 **College:** Oklahoma **Ht:** 6' 5" **Wt:** 290 **Born:** 9/17/68 **Age:** 28

			Tackles			Miscellaneous				Interceptions				Totals		
Year Team	G	GS	Tk	Ast	Sack	FF	FR	TD	Blk	Int	Yds	Avg	TD	Sfty	TD	Pts
1992 New York Giants	12	0	1	1	0.0	0	0	0	0	0	0	-	0	0	0	0
1993 New York Giants	16	16	24	8	3.0	0	0	0	0	0	0	-	0	0	0	0
1994 New York Giants	16	0	22	2	1.5	1	0	0	0	0	0	-	0	0	0	0
1995 New York Giants	15	3	22	11	1.0	0	0	0	0	0	0	-	0	0	0	0
4 NFL Seasons	59	19	69	22	5.5	1	0	0	0	0	0	-	0	0	0	0

Charles Dimry

(statistical profile on page 408)

Pos: CB **Rnd:** 5 **College:** UNLV **Ht:** 6' 1" **Wt:** 176 **Born:** 1/31/66 **Age:** 30

			Tackles			Miscellaneous				Interceptions				Punt Returns				Kickoff Returns				Totals	
Year Team	G	GS	Tk	Ast	Sack	FF	FR	TD	Blk	Int	Yds	Avg	TD	Num	Yds	Avg	TD	Num	Yds	Avg	TD	TD	Fum
1988 Atlanta Falcons	16	1	15	5	0.0	0	0	0	0	0	0	-	0	0	0	-	0	0	0	-	0	0	0
1989 Atlanta Falcons	16	4	26	5	1.0	0	0	0	0	2	72	36.0	0	0	0	-	0	0	0	-	0	0	0
1990 Atlanta Falcons	16	12	41	14	0.0	0	0	0	0	3	16	5.3	0	0	0	-	0	0	0	-	0	0	0
1991 Denver Broncos	16	1	21	17	0.0	0	1	0	0	3	35	11.7	1	0	0	-	0	0	0	-	0	1	0
1992 Denver Broncos	16	6	47	12	0.0	0	0	0	0	1	2	2.0	0	1	4	4.0	0	0	0	-	0	0	0
1993 Denver Broncos	12	11	30	21	0.0	0	0	0	0	1	0	0.0	0	0	0	-	0	0	0	-	0	0	0
1994 Tampa Bay Buccaneers	16	16	54	6	0.0	0	1	0	0	1	0	0.0	0	0	0	-	0	0	0	-	0	0	0
1995 Tampa Bay Buccaneers	16	16	63	14	0.0	0	2	0	0	1	0	0.0	0	0	0	-	0	0	0	-	0	1	0
8 NFL Seasons	124	67	297	94	1.0	0	4	0	0	12	125	10.4	1	1	4	4.0	0	0	0	-	0	1	0

Nate Dingle

Pos: LB **Rnd:** FA **College:** Cincinnati **Ht:** 6' 3" **Wt:** 254 **Born:** 7/23/71 **Age:** 25

			Tackles			Miscellaneous				Interceptions				Totals		
Year Team	G	GS	Tk	Ast	Sack	FF	FR	TD	Blk	Int	Yds	Avg	TD	Sfty	TD	Pts
1995 Philadelphia Eagles	6	0	0	0	0.0	0	0	0	0	0	0	-	0	0	0	0

Cris Dishman

(statistical profile on page 408)

Pos: CB **Rnd:** 5 **College:** Purdue **Ht:** 6' 0" **Wt:** 188 **Born:** 8/13/65 **Age:** 31

			Tackles			Miscellaneous				Interceptions				Punt Returns				Kickoff Returns				Totals	
Year Team	G	GS	Tk	Ast	Sack	FF	FR	TD	Blk	Int	Yds	Avg	TD	Num	Yds	Avg	TD	Num	Yds	Avg	TD	TD	Fum
1988 Houston Oilers	15	2	21	-	0.0	1	1	1	0	0	0	-	0	0	0	-	0	0	0	-	0	1	0
1989 Houston Oilers	16	0	31	6	0.0	1	1	1	0	4	31	7.8	0	0	0	-	0	0	0	-	0	1	0
1990 Houston Oilers	16	14	45	17	0.0	1	0	0	0	4	50	12.5	0	0	0	-	0	0	0	-	0	0	0

Year Team	G	GS	Tackles Tk	Ast	Sack	Miscellaneous FF	FR	TD	Blk	Interceptions Int	Yds	Avg	TD	Punt Returns Num	Yds	Avg	TD	Kickoff Returns Num	Yds	Avg	TD	Totals TD	Fum
1991 Houston Oilers	15	15	53	13	0.0	2	3	1	0	6	61	10.2	0	0	0	-	0	0	0	-	0	1	0
1992 Houston Oilers	15	15	27	13	0.0	1	0	0	0	3	34	11.3	0	0	0	-	0	0	0	-	0	1	0
1993 Houston Oilers	16	16	68	10	0.0	4	2	1	0	6	74	12.3	0	0	0	-	0	0	0	-	0	1	0
1994 Houston Oilers	16	16	53	13	0.0	0	1	0	0	4	74	18.5	1	1	0	0.0	0	0	0	-	0	1	0
1995 Houston Oilers	15	15	48	10	0.0	1	2	0	0	3	17	5.7	0	0	0	-	0	0	0	-	0	0	0
8 NFL Seasons	124	93	346	82	0.0	11	10	4	0	30	341	11.4	1	1	0	0.0	0	0	0	-	0	5	0

Cal Dixon

Pos: C/G **Rnd:** 5 **College:** Florida   **Ht:** 6' 4" **Wt:** 302 **Born:** 10/11/69 **Age:** 27

Year	Team	G	GS	Year	Team	G	GS	Year	Team	G	GS	Year	Team	G	GS
1992	New York Jets	11	0	1993	New York Jets	16	0	1994	New York Jets	15	0	1995	New York Jets	13	12
													4 NFL Seasons	55	12

Other Statistics: 1992–returned 1 kickoff for 6 yards. 1995–recovered 1 fumble for 0 yards.

David Dixon

Pos: G **Rnd:** 9 **College:** Arizona State   **Ht:** 6' 5" **Wt:** 354 **Born:** 1/5/69 **Age:** 27

Year	Team	G	GS	Year	Team	G	GS			G	GS
1994	Minnesota Vikings	1	0	1995	Minnesota Vikings	15	6	2 NFL Seasons		16	6

Ernest Dixon

Pos: LB/DE **Rnd:** FA **College:** South Carolina   **Ht:** 6' 1" **Wt:** 240 **Born:** 10/17/71 **Age:** 25

Year Team	G	GS	Tackles Tk	Ast	Sack	Miscellaneous FF	FR	TD	Blk	Interceptions Int	Yds	Avg	TD	Totals Sfty	TD	Pts
1994 New Orleans Saints	15	1	3	0	0.0	0	0	0	0	0	0	-	0	0	0	0
1995 New Orleans Saints	16	5	26	6	4.0	2	0	0	0	2	17	8.5	0	0	0	0
2 NFL Seasons	31	6	29	6	4.0	2	0	0	0	2	17	8.5	0	0	0	0

Other Statistics: 1995–fumbled 1 time for 0 yards.

Gerald Dixon

Pos: LB **Rnd:** 3 **College:** South Carolina   **Ht:** 6' 3" **Wt:** 250 **Born:** 6/20/69 **Age:** 27

Year Team	G	GS	Tackles Tk	Ast	Sack	Miscellaneous FF	FR	TD	Blk	Interceptions Int	Yds	Avg	TD	Punt Returns Num	Yds	Avg	TD	Kickoff Returns Num	Yds	Avg	TD	Totals TD	Fum
1993 Cleveland Browns	11	0	0	0	0.0	0	0	0	0	0	0	-	0	0	0	-	0	0	0	-	0	0	0
1994 Cleveland Browns	16	0	1	1	1.0	0	0	0	1	0	0	-	0	0	0	-	0	0	0	-	0	0	0
1995 Cleveland Browns	16	9	44	14	0.0	0	1	0	0	2	48	24.0	1	0	0	-	0	1	10	10.0	0	1	0
3 NFL Seasons	43	9	45	15	1.0	0	1	0	1	2	48	24.0	1	0	0	-	0	1	10	10.0	0	1	0

Randy Dixon

Pos: G **Rnd:** 4 **College:** Pittsburgh   **Ht:** 6' 3" **Wt:** 305 **Born:** 3/12/65 **Age:** 31

Year	Team	G	GS	Year	Team	G	GS	Year	Team	G	GS			G	GS
1987	Indianapolis Colts	3	0	1990	Indianapolis Colts	15	14	1993	Indianapolis Colts	15	15				
1988	Indianapolis Colts	16	16	1991	Indianapolis Colts	12	11	1994	Indianapolis Colts	14	14				
1989	Indianapolis Colts	16	16	1992	Indianapolis Colts	15	15	1995	Indianapolis Colts	12	9	9 NFL Seasons		118	110

Other Statistics: 1989–recovered 1 fumble for 0 yards and 1 touchdown. 1991–recovered 1 fumble for 0 yards.

Ronnie Dixon

Pos: DT **Rnd:** 6 **College:** Cincinnati   **Ht:** 6' 3" **Wt:** 292 **Born:** 5/10/71 **Age:** 25

Year Team	G	GS	Tackles Tk	Ast	Sack	Miscellaneous FF	FR	TD	Blk	Interceptions Int	Yds	Avg	TD	Totals Sfty	TD	Pts
1993 New Orleans Saints	2	0	0	0	0.0	0	0	0	0	0	0	-	0	0	0	0
1995 Philadelphia Eagles	16	10	22	7	0.0	0	0	0	0	0	0	-	0	0	0	0
2 NFL Seasons	18	10	22	7	0.0	0	0	0	0	0	0	-	0	0	0	0

Dedrick Dodge

Pos: S **Rnd:** FA **College:** Florida State   **Ht:** 6' 2" **Wt:** 184 **Born:** 6/14/67 **Age:** 29

Year Team	G	GS	Tackles Tk	Ast	Sack	Miscellaneous FF	FR	TD	Blk	Interceptions Int	Yds	Avg	TD	Totals Sfty	TD	Pts
1991 Seattle Seahawks	11	0	6	1	0.0	0	0	0	0	0	0	-	0	0	0	0
1992 Seattle Seahawks	14	0	14	2	1.0	0	0	0	0	1	13	13.0	0	0	0	0
1994 San Francisco 49ers	15	0	8	0	0.0	0	0	0	0	0	0	-	0	0	0	0
1995 San Francisco 49ers	16	0	16	0	0.0	1	0	0	0	1	13	13.0	0	0	0	0
4 NFL Seasons	56	0	44	3	1.0	1	0	0	0	2	26	13.0	0	0	0	0

Chris Doleman

(statistical profile on page 409)

Pos: DE **Rnd:** 1 (4) **College:** Pittsburgh **Ht:** 6' 5" **Wt:** 275 **Born:** 10/16/61 **Age:** 35

			Tackles			Miscellaneous				Interceptions				Totals		
Year	Team	G	GS	Tk	Ast	Sack	FF	FR	TD	Blk	Int	Yds	Avg	TD	Sfty	TD	Pts
1985	Minnesota Vikings	16	13	69	44	0.5	0	3	0	0	1	5	5.0	0	0	0	0
1986	Minnesota Vikings	16	9	42	7	3.0	2	0	0	0	1	59	59.0	1	0	1	6
1987	Minnesota Vikings	12	12	38	19	11.0	6	0	0	0	0	0	-	0	0	0	0
1988	Minnesota Vikings	16	16	42	16	8.0	2	0	0	0	0	0	-	0	0	0	0
1989	Minnesota Vikings	16	16	68	26	**21.0**	5	5	0	0	0	0	-	0	0	0	0
1990	Minnesota Vikings	16	16	66	26	11.0	4	0	0	0	1	30	30.0	0	1	0	2
1991	Minnesota Vikings	16	16	56	45	7.0	1	2	0	0	0	0	-	0	0	0	0
1992	Minnesota Vikings	16	16	49	15	14.5	6	3	0	0	1	27	27.0	1	1	1	8
1993	Minnesota Vikings	16	16	59	9	12.5	3	1	0	0	1	-3	-3.0	0	0	0	0
1994	Atlanta Falcons	14	7	*26*	*4*	7.0	1	0	0	0	1	2	2.0	0	0	0	0
1995	Atlanta Falcons	16	16	*36*	*15*	9.0	1	2	0	0	0	0	-	0	0	0	0
	11 NFL Seasons	170	153	551	226	104.5	31	16	0	0	6	120	20.0	2	2	2	16

Jim Dombrowski

Pos: G **Rnd:** 1 (6) **College:** Virginia **Ht:** 6' 5" **Wt:** 300 **Born:** 10/19/63 **Age:** 33

Year	Team	G	GS	Year	Team	G	GS	Year	Team	G	GS	Year	Team	G	GS
1986	New Orleans Saints	3	3	1989	New Orleans Saints	16	16	1992	New Orleans Saints	16	16	1995	New Orleans Saints	16	16
1987	New Orleans Saints	10	10	1990	New Orleans Saints	16	16	1993	New Orleans Saints	16	2				
1988	New Orleans Saints	16	16	1991	New Orleans Saints	16	16	1994	New Orleans Saints	16	16		10 NFL Seasons	141	127

Other Statistics: 1988–recovered 1 fumble for 0 yards. 1989–recovered 1 fumble for 0 yards. 1992–recovered 1 fumble for 0 yards.

Ray Donaldson

Pos: C **Rnd:** 2 **College:** Georgia **Ht:** 6' 3" **Wt:** 300 **Born:** 5/18/58 **Age:** 38

Year	Team	G	GS	Year	Team	G	GS	Year	Team	G	GS	Year	Team	G	GS
1980	Baltimore Colts	16	0	1984	Indianapolis Colts	16	16	1988	Indianapolis Colts	16	16	1992	Indianapolis Colts	16	16
1981	Baltimore Colts	16	16	1985	Indianapolis Colts	16	16	1989	Indianapolis Colts	16	16	1993	Seattle Seahawks	16	16
1982	Baltimore Colts	9	9	1986	Indianapolis Colts	16	16	1990	Indianapolis Colts	16	16	1994	Seattle Seahawks	16	16
1983	Baltimore Colts	16	16	1987	Indianapolis Colts	12	12	1991	Indianapolis Colts	3	3	1995	Dallas Cowboys	12	12
													16 NFL Seasons	228	212

Other Statistics: 1981–recovered 1 fumble for 0 yards. 1982–recovered 1 fumble for 0 yards. 1983–fumbled 1 time for 0 yards. 1985–recovered 1 fumble for 0 yards. 1986–fumbled 2 times for -4 yards. 1988–caught 1 pass for -3 yards. 1989–recovered 1 fumble for -22 yards; fumbled 1 time. 1991–recovered 1 fumble for 0 yards. 1992–fumbled 1 time for -17 yards. 1993–fumbled 1 time for -7 yards. 1994–fumbled 2 times for -3 yards.

Kevin Donnalley

Pos: G **Rnd:** 3 **College:** North Carolina **Ht:** 6' 5" **Wt:** 305 **Born:** 6/10/68 **Age:** 28

Year	Team	G	GS	Year	Team	G	GS	Year	Team	G	GS			G	GS
1991	Houston Oilers	16	0	1993	Houston Oilers	16	6	1995	Houston Oilers	16	16				
1992	Houston Oilers	16	2	1994	Houston Oilers	13	11						5 NFL Seasons	77	35

Other Statistics: 1995–recovered 1 fumble for 0 yards.

Torin Dorn

Pos: CB **Rnd:** 4 **College:** North Carolina **Ht:** 6' 0" **Wt:** 190 **Born:** 2/29/68 **Age:** 28

			Tackles			Miscellaneous				Interceptions				Totals		
Year	Team	G	GS	Tk	Ast	Sack	FF	FR	TD	Blk	Int	Yds	Avg	TD	Sfty	TD	Pts
1990	Los Angeles Raiders	16	0	0	-	0.0	0	0	0	0	0	0	-	0	0	0	0
1991	Los Angeles Raiders	16	1	0	-	0.0	0	1	0	0	0	0	-	0	1	0	2
1992	Los Angeles Raiders	15	0	28	-	0.0	0	0	0	0	1	7	7.0	0	0	0	0
1993	Los Angeles Raiders	15	0	18	2	0.0	1	0	0	0	0	0	-	0	0	0	0
1995	St. Louis Rams	12	3	*9*	*2*	0.0	0	1	1	0	1	24	24.0	1	0	2	12
	5 NFL Seasons	74	4	55	4	0.0	1	2	1	0	2	31	15.5	1	1	2	14

Matthew Dorsett

Pos: CB **Rnd:** FA **College:** Southern **Ht:** 5' 11" **Wt:** 187 **Born:** 8/23/73 **Age:** 23

			Tackles			Miscellaneous				Interceptions				Totals		
Year	Team	G	GS	Tk	Ast	Sack	FF	FR	TD	Blk	Int	Yds	Avg	TD	Sfty	TD	Pts
1995	Green Bay Packers	10	0	*0*	*0*	0.0	0	0	0	0	0	0	-	0	0	0	0

Dewayne Dotson

Pos: LB **Rnd:** 4 **College:** Mississippi **Ht:** 6' 1" **Wt:** 256 **Born:** 6/10/71 **Age:** 25

			Tackles			Miscellaneous				Interceptions				Totals		
Year	Team	G	GS	Tk	Ast	Sack	FF	FR	TD	Blk	Int	Yds	Avg	TD	Sfty	TD	Pts
1995	Miami Dolphins	15	0	*0*	*0*	0.0	0	1	0	0	0	0	-	0	0	0	0

Earl Dotson

Pos: T **Rnd:** 3 **College:** Texas A&I **Ht:** 6' 3" **Wt:** 310 **Born:** 12/17/70 **Age:** 25

Year	Team	G	GS	Year	Team	G	GS	Year	Team	G	GS			G	GS
1993	Green Bay Packers	13	0	1994	Green Bay Packers	4	0	1995	Green Bay Packers	16	16	3 NFL Seasons		33	16

Santana Dotson

Pos: DT **Rnd:** 5 **College:** Baylor **Ht:** 6' 5" **Wt:** 276 **Born:** 12/19/69 **Age:** 26

Year	Team	G	GS	Tackles			Miscellaneous				Interceptions				Totals		
				Tk	Ast	Sack	FF	FR	TD	Blk	Int	Yds	Avg	TD	Sfty	TD	Pts
1992	Tampa Bay Buccaneers	16	16	57	14	10.0	2	2	1	0	0	0	-	0	0	1	6
1993	Tampa Bay Buccaneers	16	13	41	22	5.0	3	0	0	0	0	0	-	0	0	0	0
1994	Tampa Bay Buccaneers	16	9	18	5	3.0	0	0	0	0	0	0	-	0	0	0	0
1995	Tampa Bay Buccaneers	16	8	24	14	5.0	0	2	0	0	0	0	-	0	0	0	0
	4 NFL Seasons	64	46	140	55	23.0	5	4	1	0	0	0	-	0	0	1	6

Hugh Douglas

Pos: DE **Rnd:** 1 (16) **College:** Central State **Ht:** 6' 2" **Wt:** 265 **Born:** 8/23/71 **Age:** 25

Year	Team	G	GS	Tackles			Miscellaneous				Interceptions				Totals		
				Tk	Ast	Sack	FF	FR	TD	Blk	Int	Yds	Avg	TD	Sfty	TD	Pts
1995	New York Jets	15	3	25	8	10.0	0	2	0	1	0	0	-	0	0	0	0

Omar Douglas

Pos: WR **Rnd:** FA **College:** Minnesota **Ht:** 5' 10" **Wt:** 180 **Born:** 6/3/72 **Age:** 24

Year	Team	G	GS	Rushing					Receiving					Punt Returns				Kickoff Returns				Totals		
				Att	Yds	Avg	Lg	TD	Rec	Yds	Avg	Lg	TD	Num	Yds	Avg	TD	Num	Yds	Avg	TD	Fum	TD	Pts
1994	New York Giants	7	0	0	0	-	-	0	0	0	-	-	0	0	0	-	0	0	0	-	0	0	0	0
1995	New York Giants	8	1	0	0	-	-	0	2	15	7.5	11	0	0	0	-	0	1	13	13.0	0	1	1	6
	2 NFL Seasons	15	1	0	0	-	-	0	2	15	7.5	11	0	0	0	-	0	1	13	13.0	0	1	1	6

Other Statistics: 1995–recovered 2 fumbles for 41 yards and 1 touchdown.

Maurice Douglass

Pos: S **Rnd:** 8 **College:** Kentucky **Ht:** 5' 11" **Wt:** 203 **Born:** 2/12/64 **Age:** 32

Year	Team	G	GS	Tackles			Miscellaneous				Interceptions				Totals		
				Tk	Ast	Sack	FF	FR	TD	Blk	Int	Yds	Avg	TD	Sfty	TD	Pts
1986	Chicago Bears	4	0	0	4	0.0	0	0	0	0	0	0	-	0	0	0	0
1987	Chicago Bears	12	1	10	3	0.0	0	1	0	0	2	0	0.0	0	0	0	0
1988	Chicago Bears	15	9	43	33	0.0	0	3	0	0	1	35	35.0	0	0	0	0
1989	Chicago Bears	10	1	12	11	0.0	0	1	0	0	1	0	0.0	0	0	0	0
1990	Chicago Bears	11	0	1	0	0.0	0	1	0	0	0	0	-	0	0	0	0
1991	Chicago Bears	16	0	8	9	0.0	0	2	0	0	0	0	-	0	0	0	0
1992	Chicago Bears	16	0	3	0	0.0	0	0	0	0	0	0	-	0	0	0	0
1993	Chicago Bears	16	1	39	23	0.0	0	0	0	0	0	0	-	0	0	0	0
1994	Chicago Bears	16	4	47	10	1.5	1	1	0	0	1	18	18.0	0	0	0	0
1995	New York Giants	8	0	5	1	1.0	0	2	0	0	0	0	-	0	0	0	0
	10 NFL Seasons	124	16	168	94	2.5	2	11	0	0	5	53	10.6	0	0	0	0

Other Statistics: 1988–fumbled 1 time.

Marcus Dowdell

Pos: KR/WR **Rnd:** 10 **College:** Tennessee State **Ht:** 5' 10" **Wt:** 179 **Born:** 5/22/70 **Age:** 26

Year	Team	G	GS	Rushing					Receiving					Punt Returns				Kickoff Returns				Totals		
				Att	Yds	Avg	Lg	TD	Rec	Yds	Avg	Lg	TD	Num	Yds	Avg	TD	Num	Yds	Avg	TD	Fum	TD	Pts
1992	New Orleans Saints	4	0	0	0	-	-	0	1	6	6.0	6	0	12	37	3.1	0	0	0	-	0	4	0	0
1993	New Orleans Saints	9	1	0	0	-	-	0	6	46	7.7	t11	1	0	0	-	0	0	52	-	0	1	1	6
1995	Arizona Cardinals	13	0	0	0	-	-	0	10	96	9.6	23	0	1	0	0.0	0	18	344	19.1	0	1	0	0
	3 NFL Seasons	26	1	0	0	-	-	0	17	148	8.7	23	1	13	37	2.8	0	18	396	22.0	0	6	1	6

Other Statistics: 1992–recovered 3 fumbles for 0 yards. 1995–recovered 1 fumble for 0 yards.

Gary Downs

Pos: RB **Rnd:** 3 **College:** North Carolina State **Ht:** 6' 0" **Wt:** 212 **Born:** 6/28/71 **Age:** 25

Year	Team	G	GS	Rushing					Receiving					Punt Returns				Kickoff Returns				Totals		
				Att	Yds	Avg	Lg	TD	Rec	Yds	Avg	Lg	TD	Num	Yds	Avg	TD	Num	Yds	Avg	TD	Fum	TD	Pts
1994	New York Giants	14	0	15	51	3.4	8	0	2	15	7.5	10	0	0	0	-	0	0	0	-	0	1	0	0
1995	Denver Broncos	1	0	0	0	-	-	0	0	0	-	-	0	0	0	-	0	0	0	-	0	0	0	0
	2 NFL Seasons	15	0	15	51	3.4	8	0	2	15	7.5	10	0	0	0	-	0	0	0	-	0	1	0	0

Jerry Drake

Pos: T/DE **Rnd:** FA **College:** Hastings College   **Ht:** 6' 4" **Wt:** 292 **Born:** 7/9/69 **Age:** 27

Year	Team	G	GS												G	GS
1995	Arizona Cardinals	2	0							1 NFL Season					2	0

Troy Drake

Pos: T **Rnd:** FA **College:** Indiana   **Ht:** 6' 6" **Wt:** 289 **Born:** 5/15/72 **Age:** 24

Year	Team	G	GS												G	GS
1995	Philadelphia Eagles	1	0							1 NFL Season					1	0

Tyronne Drakeford

Pos: CB **Rnd:** 2 **College:** Virginia Tech   **Ht:** 5' 9" **Wt:** 185 **Born:** 6/21/71 **Age:** 25

				Tackles			Miscellaneous				Interceptions				Totals		
Year	Team	G	GS	Tk	Ast	Sack	FF	FR	TD	Blk	Int	Yds	Avg	TD	Sfty	TD	Pts
1994	San Francisco 49ers	13	0	7	1	0.0	0	0	0	0	1	6	6.0	0	0	0	0
1995	San Francisco 49ers	16	2	38	3	1.0	1	1	0	0	5	54	10.8	0	0	0	0
	2 NFL Seasons	29	2	45	4	1.0	1	1	0	0	6	60	10.0	0	0	0	0

Other Statistics: 1995–fumbled 1 time.

Troy Drayton

(statistical profile on page 307)

Pos: TE/WR **Rnd:** 2 **College:** Penn State   **Ht:** 6' 3" **Wt:** 255 **Born:** 6/29/70 **Age:** 26

				Rushing					Receiving					Punt Returns				Kickoff Returns				Totals		
Year	Team	G	GS	Att	Yds	Avg	Lg	TD	Rec	Yds	Avg	Lg	TD	Num	Yds	Avg	TD	Num	Yds	Avg	TD	Fum	TD	Pts
1993	Los Angeles Rams	16	2	1	7	7.0	7	0	27	319	11.8	27	4	0	0	-	0	1	-15	-15.0	0	1	4	24
1994	Los Angeles Rams	16	16	1	4	4.0	4	0	32	276	8.6	t22	6	0	0	-	0	0	0	-	0	0	6	36
1995	St. Louis Rams	16	16	0	0	-	-	0	47	458	9.7	31	4	0	0	-	0	0	0	-	0	2	4	24
	3 NFL Seasons	48	34	2	11	5.5	7	0	106	1053	9.9	31	14	0	0	-	0	1	-15	-15.0	0	3	14	84

Shane Dronett

Pos: DE/DT **Rnd:** 2 **College:** Texas   **Ht:** 6' 5" **Wt:** 275 **Born:** 1/12/71 **Age:** 25

				Tackles			Miscellaneous				Interceptions				Totals		
Year	Team	G	GS	Tk	Ast	Sack	FF	FR	TD	Blk	Int	Yds	Avg	TD	Sfty	TD	Pts
1992	Denver Broncos	16	2	30	23	6.5	1	2	0	0	0	0	-	0	0	0	0
1993	Denver Broncos	16	16	32	17	7.0	1	0	0	0	2	13	6.5	0	0	0	0
1994	Denver Broncos	16	15	30	6	6.0	1	0	0	3	0	0	-	0	0	0	0
1995	Denver Broncos	13	2	6	3	2.0	0	0	0	0	0	0	-	0	0	0	0
	4 NFL Seasons	61	35	98	49	21.5	3	2	0	3	2	13	6.5	0	0	0	0

Demetrius DuBose

Pos: LB **Rnd:** 2 **College:** Notre Dame   **Ht:** 6' 1" **Wt:** 240 **Born:** 3/23/71 **Age:** 25

				Tackles			Miscellaneous				Interceptions				Totals		
Year	Team	G	GS	Tk	Ast	Sack	FF	FR	TD	Blk	Int	Yds	Avg	TD	Sfty	TD	Pts
1993	Tampa Bay Buccaneers	15	4	16	18	0.0	0	0	0	0	0	0	-	0	0	0	0
1994	Tampa Bay Buccaneers	16	1	12	4	0.0	0	0	0	0	0	0	-	0	0	0	0
1995	Tampa Bay Buccaneers	15	0	6	1	0.0	0	0	0	0	0	0	-	0	0	0	0
	3 NFL Seasons	46	5	34	23	0.0	0	0	0	0	0	0	-	0	0	0	0

Jamal Duff

Pos: DE **Rnd:** 6 **College:** San Diego State   **Ht:** 6' 7" **Wt:** 259 **Born:** 3/11/72 **Age:** 24

				Tackles			Miscellaneous				Interceptions				Totals		
Year	Team	G	GS	Tk	Ast	Sack	FF	FR	TD	Blk	Int	Yds	Avg	TD	Sfty	TD	Pts
1995	New York Giants	15	2	10	5	4.0	0	0	0	0	0	0	-	0	0	0	0

Roger Duffy

Pos: G/LS **Rnd:** 8 **College:** Penn State   **Ht:** 6' 3" **Wt:** 311 **Born:** 7/16/67 **Age:** 29

Year	Team	G	GS	Year	Team	G	GS	Year	Team	G	GS			G	GS
1990	New York Jets	16	2	1992	New York Jets	16	6	1994	New York Jets	16	14			92	39
1991	New York Jets	12	0	1993	New York Jets	16	1	1995	New York Jets	16	16	6 NFL Seasons			

Other Statistics: 1990–returned 1 kickoff for 8 yards. 1992–recovered 1 fumble for 0 yards; returned 1 kickoff for 7 yards. 1993–recovered 1 fumble for 0 yards. 1995–recovered 2 fumbles for 0 yards.

Jamie Dukes

Pos: C **Rnd:** FA **College:** Florida State   **Ht:** 6' 1" **Wt:** 285 **Born:** 6/14/64 **Age:** 32

Year	Team	G	GS	Year	Team	G	GS	Year	Team	G	GS	Year	Team	G	GS
1986	Atlanta Falcons	14	4	1989	Atlanta Falcons	16	16	1992	Atlanta Falcons	16	16	1995	Arizona Cardinals	9	8

Year	Team	G	GS	Year	Team	G	GS	Year	Team	G	GS	Year	Team	G	GS
1987	Atlanta Falcons	5	0	1990	Atlanta Falcons	16	16	1993	Atlanta Falcons	16	16				
1988	Atlanta Falcons	12	5	1991	Atlanta Falcons	16	16	1994	Green Bay Packers	6	6	10 NFL Seasons		126	103

Other Statistics: 1986–recovered 1 fumble for 0 yards. 1988–returned 1 kickoff for 13 yards. 1990–recovered 1 fumble for -6 yards; fumbled 1 time. 1991–recovered 1 fumble for 0 yards. 1992–recovered 2 fumbles for 0 yards. 1993–recovered 1 fumble for 0 yards.

Mike Dumas

Pos: S **Rnd:** 2 **College:** Indiana **Ht:** 5' 11" **Wt:** 198 **Born:** 3/18/69 **Age:** 27

				Tackles			Miscellaneous				Interceptions				Totals		
Year	Team	G	GS	Tk	Ast	Sack	FF	FR	TD	Blk	Int	Yds	Avg	TD	Sfty	TD	Pts
1991	Houston Oilers	13	0	10	7	0.0	0	3	1	0	1	19	19.0	0	0	1	6
1992	Houston Oilers	16	1	23	9	0.0	0	1	0	0	1	0	0.0	0	0	0	0
1994	Buffalo Bills	14	0	0	0	0.0	0	2	0	0	0	0	-	0	0	0	0
1995	Jacksonville Jaguars	14	8	33	12	0.0	0	2	0	1	1	0	0.0	0	0	0	0
	4 NFL Seasons	57	9	66	28	0.0	0	8	1	1	3	19	6.3	0	0	1	6

Karl Dunbar

Pos: DT/DE **Rnd:** 8 **College:** Louisiana State **Ht:** 6' 4" **Wt:** 275 **Born:** 5/18/67 **Age:** 29

				Tackles			Miscellaneous				Interceptions				Totals		
Year	Team	G	GS	Tk	Ast	Sack	FF	FR	TD	Blk	Int	Yds	Avg	TD	Sfty	TD	Pts
1993	New Orleans Saints	13	1	14	10	0.0	0	0	0	0	0	0	-	0	0	0	0
1994	Arizona Cardinals	3	0	1	0	0.0	0	0	0	0	0	0	-	0	0	0	0
1995	Arizona Cardinals	5	0	2	0	0.0	0	0	0	0	0	0	-	0	0	0	0
	3 NFL Seasons	21	1	17	10	0.0	0	0	0	0	0	0	-	0	0	0	0

Vaughn Dunbar

(statistical profile on page 308)

Pos: RB **Rnd:** 1 (21) **College:** Indiana **Ht:** 5' 10" **Wt:** 204 **Born:** 9/4/68 **Age:** 28

				Rushing					Receiving					Punt Returns				Kickoff Returns				Totals		
Year	Team	G	GS	Att	Yds	Avg	Lg	TD	Rec	Yds	Avg	Lg	TD	Num	Yds	Avg	TD	Num	Yds	Avg	TD	Fum	TD	Pts
1992	New Orleans Saints	16	8	154	565	3.7	25	3	9	62	6.9	13	0	0	0	-	0	10	187	18.7	0	3	3	18
1994	New Orleans Saints	8	0	3	9	3.0	3	0	0	0	-	-	0	0	0	-	0	1	28	28.0	0	0	0	0
1995	NO - Jac	15	7	110	361	3.3	26	2	2	11	5.5	8	0	0	0	-	0	2	32	16.0	0	0	2	12
1995	New Orleans Saints	1	0	0	0	-	-	0	0	0	-	-	0	0	0	-	0	0	0	-	0	0	0	0
	Jacksonville Jaguars	14	7	110	361	3.3	26	2	2	11	5.5	8	0	0	0	-	0	2	32	16.0	0	0	2	12
	3 NFL Seasons	39	15	267	935	3.5	26	5	11	73	6.6	13	0	0	0	-	0	13	247	19.0	0	3	5	30

David Dunn

Pos: KR/WR **Rnd:** 5 **College:** Fresno State **Ht:** 6' 3" **Wt:** 210 **Born:** 6/10/72 **Age:** 24

				Rushing					Receiving					Kickoff Returns				Passing					Totals		
Year	Team	G	GS	Att	Yds	Avg	Lg	TD	Rec	Yds	Avg	Lg	TD	Num	Yds	Avg	TD	Att	Com	Yds	Int	Fum	TD	Pts
1995	Cincinnati Bengals	16	0	1	-13	-13.0	-13	0	17	209	12.3	37	1	50	1092	21.8	0	1	0	0	0	2	1	6

Ernest Dye

Pos: T **Rnd:** 1 (18) **College:** South Carolina **Ht:** 6' 6" **Wt:** 325 **Born:** 7/15/71 **Age:** 25

Year	Team	G	GS	Year	Team	G	GS	Year	Team	G	GS		G	GS
1993	Phoenix Cardinals	7	1	1994	Arizona Cardinals	16	16	1995	Arizona Cardinals	6	6	3 NFL Seasons	29	23

Other Statistics: 1994–recovered 1 fumble for 0 yards.

Matt Dyson

Pos: DT **Rnd:** 5 **College:** Michigan **Ht:** 6' 3" **Wt:** 265 **Born:** 8/1/72 **Age:** 24

				Tackles			Miscellaneous				Interceptions				Totals		
Year	Team	G	GS	Tk	Ast	Sack	FF	FR	TD	Blk	Int	Yds	Avg	TD	Sfty	TD	Pts
1995	Oakland Raiders	4	0	0	0	0.0	0	0	0	0	0	0	-	0	0	0	0

Quinn Early

(statistical profile on page 308)

Pos: WR **Rnd:** 3 **College:** Iowa **Ht:** 6' 0" **Wt:** 190 **Born:** 4/13/65 **Age:** 31

				Rushing					Receiving					Punt Returns				Kickoff Returns				Totals		
Year	Team	G	GS	Att	Yds	Avg	Lg	TD	Rec	Yds	Avg	Lg	TD	Num	Yds	Avg	TD	Num	Yds	Avg	TD	Fum	TD	Pts
1988	San Diego Chargers	16	10	7	63	9.0	37	0	29	375	12.9	t38	4	0	0	-	0	0	0	-	0	1	4	24
1989	San Diego Chargers	6	3	1	19	19.0	19	0	11	126	11.5	21	0	0	0	-	0	0	0	-	0	0	0	0
1990	San Diego Chargers	14	4	0	0	-	0	0	15	238	15.9	t45	1	0	0	-	0	0	0	-	0	1	1	6
1991	New Orleans Saints	15	12	3	13	4.3	6	0	32	541	16.9	52	2	0	0	-	0	9	168	18.7	0	2	2	12
1992	New Orleans Saints	16	16	3	-1	-0.3	7	0	30	566	18.9	t59	5	0	0	-	0	0	0	-	0	5	5	30
1993	New Orleans Saints	16	15	2	32	16.0	26	0	45	670	14.9	t63	6	0	0	-	0	0	0	-	0	1	6	36
1994	New Orleans Saints	16	13	2	10	5.0	8	0	82	894	10.9	33	4	0	0	-	0	0	0	-	0	4	4	24
1995	New Orleans Saints	16	15	2	-3	-1.5	9	0	81	1087	13.4	t70	8	0	0	-	0	0	0	-	0	1	8	48

Year Team	G	GS	Rushing Att	Yds	Avg	Lg	TD	Receiving Rec	Yds	Avg	Lg	TD	Punt Returns Num	Yds	Avg	TD	Kickoff Returns Num	Yds	Avg	TD	Totals Fum	TD	Pts
8 NFL Seasons	115	88	20	133	6.7	37	0	325	4497	13.8	t70	30	0	0	-	0	9	168	18.7	0	5	30	180

Irv Eatman

Pos: T   **Rnd:** 8   **College:** UCLA   **Ht:** 6' 7" **Wt:** 305   **Born:** 1/1/61   **Age:** 35

Year	Team	G	GS	Year	Team	G	GS	Year	Team	G	GS	Year	Team	G	GS
1986	Kansas City Chiefs	16	16	1989	Kansas City Chiefs	13	13	1992	New York Jets	12	12	1995	Houston Oilers	16	7
1987	Kansas City Chiefs	12	8	1990	Kansas City Chiefs	12	0	1993	Los Angeles Rams	16	16				
1988	Kansas City Chiefs	16	14	1991	New York Jets	16	16	1994	Atlanta Falcons	4	0		10 NFL Seasons	133	102

Other Statistics: 1989–recovered 1 fumble for 0 yards. 1991–recovered 1 fumble for 0 yards. 1993–recovered 1 fumble for 0 yards. 1995–recovered 1 fumble for 0 yards.

Bobby Joe Edmonds

Pos: KR/PR **Rnd:** 5   **College:** Arkansas   **Ht:** 5' 11" **Wt:** 190   **Born:** 9/26/64   **Age:** 32

Year Team	G	GS	Rushing Att	Yds	Avg	Lg	TD	Receiving Rec	Yds	Avg	Lg	TD	Punt Returns Num	Yds	Avg	TD	Kickoff Returns Num	Yds	Avg	TD	Totals Fum	TD	Pts
1986 Seattle Seahawks	15	0	1	-11	-11.0	-11	0	0	0	-	0	0	34	419	12.3	1	34	764	22.5	0	4	1	6
1987 Seattle Seahawks	11	0	0	0	-	-	0	0	0	-	-	0	20	251	12.6	0	27	564	20.9	0	1	0	0
1988 Seattle Seahawks	16	0	0	0	-	-	0	0	0	-	-	0	35	340	9.7	0	40	900	22.5	0	2	0	0
1989 Los Angeles Raiders	7	0	0	0	-	-	0	0	0	-	-	0	16	168	10.5	0	14	271	19.4	0	0	0	0
1995 Tampa Bay Buccaneers	16	0	5	28	5.6	9	0	1	8	8.0	8	0	29	293	10.1	0	58	1147	19.8	0	1	0	0
5 NFL Seasons	65	0	6	17	2.8	9	0	1	8	8.0	8	0	134	1471	11.0	1	173	3646	21.1	0	8	1	6

Other Statistics: 1986–recovered 1 fumble for 0 yards. 1987–recovered 1 fumble for 0 yards. 1988–recovered 1 fumble for 0 yards. 1995–recovered 1 fumble for 0 yards.

Anthony Edwards

(statistical profile on page 309)

Pos: WR/PR **Rnd:** FA   **College:** New Mexico Highlands   **Ht:** 5' 10" **Wt:** 190   **Born:** 5/26/66   **Age:** 30

Year Team	G	GS	Rushing Att	Yds	Avg	Lg	TD	Receiving Rec	Yds	Avg	Lg	TD	Punt Returns Num	Yds	Avg	TD	Kickoff Returns Num	Yds	Avg	TD	Totals Fum	TD	Pts
1989 Philadelphia Eagles	9	0	0	0	-	-	0	2	74	37.0	66	0	7	64	9.1	0	3	23	7.7	0	2	0	0
1990 Philadelphia Eagles	5	0	0	0	-	-	0	0	0	-	-	0	8	60	7.5	0	3	36	12.0	0	2	0	0
1991 Phoenix Cardinals	12	0	0	0	-	-	0	0	0	-	-	0	1	7	7.0	0	13	261	20.1	0	0	0	0
1992 Phoenix Cardinals	16	0	0	0	-	-	0	14	147	10.5	t25	1	0	0	-	0	8	143	17.9	0	0	1	6
1993 Phoenix Cardinals	16	0	0	0	-	-	0	13	326	25.1	t65	1	3	12	4.0	0	3	51	17.0	0	0	1	6
1995 Arizona Cardinals	15	0	0	0	-	-	0	29	417	14.4	t28	2	18	131	7.3	0	3	50	16.7	0	0	2	12
6 NFL Seasons	73	0	0	0	-	-	0	58	964	16.6	66	4	37	274	7.4	0	33	564	17.1	0	4	4	24

Other Statistics: 1989–recovered 1 fumble for 0 yards. 1995–recovered 1 fumble for 0 yards.

Antonio Edwards

Pos: DE   **Rnd:** 8   **College:** Valdosta State   **Ht:** 6' 3" **Wt:** 270   **Born:** 3/10/70   **Age:** 26

Year Team	G	GS	Tackles Tk	Ast	Sack	Miscellaneous FF	FR	TD	Blk	Interceptions Int	Yds	Avg	TD	Totals Sfty	TD	Pts
1993 Seattle Seahawks	9	0	6	1	3.0	0	0	0	0	0	0	-	0	1	0	2
1994 Seattle Seahawks	15	13	24	13	2.5	0	0	0	0	0	0	-	0	1	0	2
1995 Seattle Seahawks	13	8	23	9	5.5	0	1	1	0	0	0	-	0	0	1	6
3 NFL Seasons	37	21	53	23	11.0	0	1	1	0	0	0	-	0	2	1	10

Brad Edwards

Pos: S   **Rnd:** 2   **College:** South Carolina   **Ht:** 6' 2" **Wt:** 207   **Born:** 3/22/66   **Age:** 30

Year Team	G	GS	Tackles Tk	Ast	Sack	Miscellaneous FF	FR	TD	Blk	Interceptions Int	Yds	Avg	TD	Totals Sfty	TD	Pts
1988 Minnesota Vikings	16	6	27	9	0.0	0	0	0	0	2	47	23.5	1	0	1	6
1989 Minnesota Vikings	9	1	13	8	0.0	0	0	0	0	1	18	18.0	0	0	0	0
1990 Washington Redskins	16	1	25	20	0.0	0	0	0	0	2	33	16.5	0	0	0	0
1991 Washington Redskins	16	16	70	65	0.0	0	0	0	0	4	52	13.0	0	0	0	0
1992 Washington Redskins	16	16	82	60	0.0	0	0	0	0	6	157	26.2	1	0	1	6
1993 Washington Redskins	16	16	89	61	0.0	0	1	0	0	1	17	17.0	0	0	0	0
1994 Atlanta Falcons	4	0	5	4	0.0	0	0	0	0	0	0	-	0	0	0	0
1995 Atlanta Falcons	13	0	3	2	0.0	0	0	0	0	0	0	-	0	0	0	0
8 NFL Seasons	106	56	314	255	0.0	0	1	0	0	16	324	20.3	2	0	2	12

Dixon Edwards

Pos: LB   **Rnd:** 2   **College:** Michigan State   **Ht:** 6' 1" **Wt:** 225   **Born:** 3/25/68   **Age:** 28

Year Team	G	GS	Tackles Tk	Ast	Sack	Misc FF	FR	TD	Blk	Interceptions Int	Yds	Avg	TD	Punt Returns Num	Yds	Avg	TD	Kickoff Returns Num	Yds	Avg	TD	Totals TD	Fum
1991 Dallas Cowboys	12	1	10	8	0.0	0	0	0	0	1	36	36.0	1	0	0	-	0	0	0	-	0	1	0
1992 Dallas Cowboys	16	1	5	5	0.0	0	0	0	0	0	0	-	0	0	0	-	0	1	0	0.0	0	0	0

Year	Team	G	GS	Tackles			Miscellaneous				Interceptions				Punt Returns				Kickoff Returns				Totals	
				Tk	Ast	Sack	FF	FR	TD	Blk	Int	Yds	Avg	TD	Num	Yds	Avg	TD	Num	Yds	Avg	TD	TD	Fum
1993	Dallas Cowboys	16	15	42	40	1.5	2	1	0	0	0	0	-	0	0	0	-	0	0	0	-	0	0	0
1994	Dallas Cowboys	16	15	59	15	1.0	1	1	0	0	0	0	-	0	0	0	-	0	0	0	-	0	0	0
1995	Dallas Cowboys	15	15	47	15	0.0	0	0	0	0	0	0	-	0	0	0	-	0	0	0	-	0	0	0
	5 NFL Seasons	75	47	163	83	2.5	3	2	0	0	1	36	36.0	1	0	0	-	0	1	0	0.0	0	1	0

Pat Eilers

Pos: S   **Rnd:** FA   **College:** Notre Dame   **Ht:** 5' 11"   **Wt:** 195   **Born:** 9/3/66   **Age:** 30

Year	Team	G	GS	Tackles			Miscellaneous				Interceptions				Punt Returns				Kickoff Returns				Totals	
				Tk	Ast	Sack	FF	FR	TD	Blk	Int	Yds	Avg	TD	Num	Yds	Avg	TD	Num	Yds	Avg	TD	TD	Fum
1990	Minnesota Vikings	8	0	8	3	0.0	0	1	0	0	0	0	-	0	0	0	-	0	0	0	-	0	0	0
1991	Minnesota Vikings	16	0	3	7	0.0	0	2	0	0	0	0	-	0	0	0	-	0	5	99	19.8	0	0	0
1992	Washington Redskins	1	0	0	0	0.0	0	0	0	0	0	0	-	0	0	0	-	0	0	0	-	0	0	0
1993	Washington Redskins	11	0	6	6	0.0	0	3	0	0	0	0	-	0	0	0	-	0	0	0	-	0	0	0
1994	Washington Redskins	16	0	0	0	0.0	0	0	0	0	0	0	-	0	0	0	-	0	0	0	-	0	0	0
1995	Chicago Bears	9	0	1	0	0.0	0	1	0	0	0	0	-	0	0	0	-	0	0	0	-	0	0	0
	6 NFL Seasons	61	0	18	16	0.0	0	7	0	0	0	0	-	0	0	0	-	0	5	99	19.8	0	0	0

Hicham El-Mashtoub

Pos: C   **Rnd:** 6   **College:** Arizona   **Ht:** 6' 2"   **Wt:** 288   **Born:** 5/11/72   **Age:** 24

Year	Team	G	GS		Year	Team	G	GS
1995	Houston Oilers	2	0			1 NFL Season	2	0

Jason Elam

(statistical profile on page 472)

Pos: K   **Rnd:** 3   **College:** Hawaii   **Ht:** 5' 11"   **Wt:** 192   **Born:** 3/8/70   **Age:** 26

Year	Team	G	Field Goals										Overall	Pct	Long	PAT		Tot
			1-29 Yds	Pct	30-39 Yds	Pct	40-49 Yds	Pct	50+ Yds	Pct						Made	Att	Pts
1993	Denver Broncos	16	11-12	91.7	7-7	100.0	4-10	40.0	4-6	66.7			26-35	74.3	54	41	42	119
1994	Denver Broncos	16	11-11	100.0	11-11	100.0	7-12	58.3	1-3	33.3			30-37	81.1	54	29	29	119
1995	Denver Broncos	16	7-9	77.8	14-15	93.3	5-7	71.4	5-7	71.4			31-38	81.6	56	39	39	132
	3 NFL Seasons	48	29-32	90.6	32-33	97.0	16-29	55.2	10-16	62.5			87-110	79.1	56	109	110	370

Other Statistics: 1995–punted 1 time for 17 yards.

Mo Elewonibi

Pos: T   **Rnd:** 3   **College:** Brigham Young   **Ht:** 6' 4"   **Wt:** 286   **Born:** 12/16/65   **Age:** 30

Year	Team	G	GS	Year	Team	G	GS	Year	Team	G	GS			G	GS
1992	Washington Redskins	5	4	1993	Washington Redskins	15	15	1995	Philadelphia Eagles	6	0		3 NFL Seasons	26	19

Other Statistics: 1993–recovered 2 fumbles for 10 yards. 1995–recovered 1 fumble for 0 yards.

Keith Elias

Pos: RB   **Rnd:** FA   **College:** Princeton   **Ht:** 5' 9"   **Wt:** 200   **Born:** 2/3/72   **Age:** 24

Year	Team	G	GS	Rushing					Receiving					Punt Returns				Kickoff Returns				Totals		
				Att	Yds	Avg	Lg	TD	Rec	Yds	Avg	Lg	TD	Num	Yds	Avg	TD	Num	Yds	Avg	TD	Fum	TD	Pts
1994	New York Giants	2	0	2	4	2.0	5	0	0	0	-	-	0	0	0	-	0	0	0	-	0	0	0	0
1995	New York Giants	15	0	10	44	4.4	8	0	9	69	7.7	18	0	0	0	-	0	0	0	-	0	0	0	0
	2 NFL Seasons	17	0	12	48	4.0	8	0	9	69	7.7	18	0	0	0	-	0	0	0	-	0	0	0	0

Henry Ellard

(statistical profile on page 309)

Pos: WR   **Rnd:** 2   **College:** Fresno State   **Ht:** 5' 11"   **Wt:** 185   **Born:** 7/21/61   **Age:** 35

Year	Team	G	GS	Rushing					Receiving					Punt Returns				Kickoff Returns				Totals		
				Att	Yds	Avg	Lg	TD	Rec	Yds	Avg	Lg	TD	Num	Yds	Avg	TD	Num	Yds	Avg	TD	Fum	TD	Pts
1983	Los Angeles Rams	12	0	3	7	2.3	12	0	16	268	16.8	44	0	16	217	13.6	1	15	314	20.9	0	2	1	6
1984	Los Angeles Rams	16	16	3	-5	-1.7	5	0	34	622	18.3	t63	6	30	403	13.4	2	2	24	12.0	0	4	8	48
1985	Los Angeles Rams	16	16	3	8	2.7	16	0	54	811	15.0	t64	5	37	501	13.5	1	0	0	-	0	3	6	36
1986	Los Angeles Rams	9	8	1	-15	-15.0	-15	0	34	447	13.1	t34	4	14	127	9.1	0	1	18	18.0	0	3	4	24
1987	Los Angeles Rams	12	12	1	4	4.0	4	0	51	799	15.7	t81	3	15	107	7.1	0	1	8	8.0	0	3	3	18
1988	Los Angeles Rams	16	16	1	7	7.0	7	0	86	1414	16.4	68	10	17	119	7.0	0	0	0	-	0	3	10	60
1989	Los Angeles Rams	14	12	2	10	5.0	6	0	70	1382	19.7	53	8	2	20	10.0	0	0	0	-	0	4	8	48
1990	Los Angeles Rams	15	15	2	21	10.5	13	0	76	1294	17.0	t50	4	2	15	7.5	0	0	0	-	0	4	4	24
1991	Los Angeles Rams	16	16	0	0	-	-	0	64	1052	16.4	38	3	0	0	-	0	0	0	-	0	1	3	18
1992	Los Angeles Rams	16	16	0	0	-	-	0	47	727	15.5	t33	3	0	0	-	0	0	0	-	0	0	3	18
1993	Los Angeles Rams	16	16	2	18	9.0	16	0	61	945	15.5	54	2	2	18	9.0	0	0	0	-	0	0	2	12
1994	Washington Redskins	16	16	1	-5	-5.0	-5	0	74	1397	18.9	t73	6	0	0	-	0	0	0	-	0	1	6	36
1995	Washington Redskins	15	15	0	0	-	-	0	56	1005	17.9	59	5	0	0	-	0	0	0	-	0	1	5	30
	13 NFL Seasons	189	174	19	50	2.6	16	0	723	12163	16.8	t81	59	135	1527	11.3	4	19	364	19.2	0	25	63	378

Other Statistics: 1983–recovered 2 fumbles for 0 yards. 1984–recovered 2 fumbles for 0 yards. 1985–recovered 5 fumbles for 0 yards. 1986–recovered 1 fumble for 0 yards. 1987–recovered 1 fumble for 0 yards. 1991–recovered 1 fumble for 0 yards.

John Elliott

Pos: T   **Rnd:** 2   **College:** Michigan   **Ht:** 6' 7" **Wt:** 308 **Born:** 4/1/65 **Age:** 31

Year	Team	G	GS	Year	Team	G	GS	Year	Team	G	GS	Year	Team	G	GS
1988	New York Giants	16	5	1990	New York Giants	8	8	1992	New York Giants	16	16	1994	New York Giants	16	15
1989	New York Giants	13	11	1991	New York Giants	16	16	1993	New York Giants	11	11	1995	New York Giants	16	16
													8 NFL Seasons	112	98

Other Statistics: 1988–recovered 1 fumble for 0 yards.

Lin Elliott

(statistical profile on page 472)

Pos: K   **Rnd:** FA   **College:** Texas Tech   **Ht:** 6' 0" **Wt:** 182 **Born:** 11/11/68 **Age:** 27

			Field Goals													PAT		Tot
Year	Team	G	1-29 Yds	Pct	30-39 Yds	Pct	40-49 Yds	Pct	50+ Yds	Pct	Overall	Pct	Long	Made	Att	Pts
1992	Dallas Cowboys	16	6-7	85.7	10-14	71.4	5-10	50.0	3-4	75.0	24-35	68.6	53	47	48	119
1993	Dallas Cowboys	2	1-1	100.0	0-1	0.0	1-2	50.0	0-0	-	2-4	50.0	43	2	3	8
1994	Kansas City Chiefs	16	**18-20**	90.0	4-6	66.7	3-4	75.0	0-0	-	25-30	83.3	49	30	30	105
1995	Kansas City Chiefs	16	10-11	90.9	7-9	77.8	7-10	70.0	0-0	-	24-30	80.0	49	34	37	106
	4 NFL Seasons	50	35-39	89.7	21-30	70.0	16-26	61.5	3-4	75.0	75-99	75.8	53	113	118	338

Other Statistics: 1994–recovered 1 fumble for 0 yards.

Matt Elliott

Pos: G   **Rnd:** 12   **College:** Michigan   **Ht:** 6' 3" **Wt:** 294 **Born:** 10/1/68 **Age:** 28

Year	Team	G	GS	Year	Team	G	GS			G	GS
1992	Washington Redskins	16	2	1995	Carolina Panthers	15	14	2 NFL Seasons		31	16

'OMar Ellison

Pos: WR   **Rnd:** 5   **College:** Florida State   **Ht:** 6' 1" **Wt:** 200 **Born:** 10/8/71 **Age:** 25

				Rushing				Receiving					Punt Returns				Kickoff Returns				Totals		
Year	Team	G	GS	Att	Yds	Avg	Lg TD	Rec	Yds	Avg	Lg TD	Num	Yds	Avg TD	Num	Yds	Avg TD	Fum	TD	Pts
1995	San Diego Chargers	2	0	0	0	-	0	1	6	6.0	6 0	0	0	- 0	0	0	- 0	0	0	0

Jerry Ellison

Pos: RB/KR   **Rnd:** FA   **College:** Tennessee-Chattanooga   **Ht:** 5' 10" **Wt:** 194 **Born:** 12/20/71 **Age:** 24

				Rushing				Receiving					Punt Returns				Kickoff Returns				Totals		
Year	Team	G	GS	Att	Yds	Avg	Lg TD	Rec	Yds	Avg	Lg TD	Num	Yds	Avg TD	Num	Yds	Avg TD	Fum	TD	Pts
1995	Tampa Bay Buccaneers	16	3	26	218	8.4	75 5	7	44	6.3	14 0	0	0	- 0	15	261	17.4 0	0	5	30

Other Statistics: 1995–recovered 1 fumble for 0 yards.

Luther Elliss

Pos: DE   **Rnd:** 1 (20)   **College:** Utah   **Ht:** 6' 5" **Wt:** 291 **Born:** 3/22/73 **Age:** 23

				Tackles			Miscellaneous				Interceptions				Totals		
Year	Team	G	GS	Tk	Ast	Sack	FF	FR	TD	Blk	Int	Yds	Avg	TD	Sfty	TD	Pts
1995	Detroit Lions	16	16	9	10	0.0	0	0	0	0	0	0	-	0	0	0	0

John Elway

(statistical profile on page 310)

Pos: QB   **Rnd:** 1 (1)   **College:** Stanford   **Ht:** 6' 3" **Wt:** 215 **Born:** 6/28/60 **Age:** 36

				Passing									Rushing					Miscellaneous			
Year	Team	G	GS	Att	Com	Pct	Yards	Yds/Att	Lg	TD	Int	Int%	Rating	Att	Yds	Avg	Lg TD	Sckd	Yds	Fum Recv	Yds	Pts
1983	Denver Broncos	11	10	259	123	47.5	1663	6.42	t49	7	14	5.4	54.9	28	146	5.2	23 1	28	218	6 3	0	6
1984	Denver Broncos	15	14	380	214	56.3	2598	6.84	73	18	15	3.9	76.8	56	237	4.2	21 1	24	158	14 5	-10	6
1985	Denver Broncos	16	16	**605**	327	54.0	3891	6.43	t65	22	23	3.8	70.2	51	253	5.0	22 0	38	307	7 2	-35	0
1986	Denver Broncos	16	16	504	280	55.6	3485	6.91	53	19	13	2.6	79.0	52	257	4.9	24 1	32	233	8 1	-13	12
1987	Denver Broncos	12	12	410	224	54.6	3198	7.80	t72	19	12	2.9	83.4	66	304	4.6	29 4	20	138	2 0	-1	24
1988	Denver Broncos	15	15	496	274	55.2	3309	6.67	86	17	19	3.8	71.4	54	234	4.3	26 1	30	237	7 5	-9	6
1989	Denver Broncos	15	15	416	223	53.6	3051	7.33	69	18	18	4.3	73.7	48	244	5.1	31 3	35	290	9 0	4	18
1990	Denver Broncos	16	16	502	294	58.6	3526	7.02	66	15	14	2.8	78.5	50	258	5.2	21 3	43	311	8 1	-3	18
1991	Denver Broncos	16	16	451	242	53.7	3253	7.21	71	13	12	2.7	75.4	55	255	4.6	t17 6	45	305	**12** 2	0	36
1992	Denver Broncos	12	12	316	174	55.1	2242	7.09	t80	10	17	5.4	65.7	34	94	2.8	9 2	36	272	12 1	0	12
1993	Denver Broncos	16	16	551	348	63.2	**4030**	7.31	63	25	10	1.8	92.8	44	153	3.5	18 0	39	293	8 5	-5	0
1994	Denver Broncos	14	14	494	307	62.1	3490	7.06	63	16	10	2.0	85.7	58	235	4.1	22 4	**46**	303	11 2	-5	24
1995	Denver Broncos	16	16	542	316	58.3	3970	7.32	t62	26	14	2.6	86.4	41	176	4.3	25 1	22	180	9 1	-7	8
	13 NFL Seasons	190	188	5926	3346	56.5	41706	7.04	86	225	191	3.2	77.7	637	2846	4.5	31 27	438	3253	113 30	-92	170

Other Statistics: 1986–caught 1 pass for 23 yards and 1 touchdown. 1987–punted 1 time for 31 yards. 1988–punted 3 times for 117 yards. 1989–punted 1 time for 34 yards. 1990–punted 1 time for 37 yards. 1991–caught 1 pass for 24 yards; punted 1 time for 34 yards. 1995–scored 1 two-point conversion.

Bert Emanuel

Pos: WR   **Rnd:** 2   **College:** Rice   *(statistical profile on page 310)*   **Ht:** 5' 10" **Wt:** 180 **Born:** 10/27/70 **Age:** 26

Year	Team	G	GS	Rushing Att	Yds	Avg	Lg	TD	Receiving Rec	Yds	Avg	Lg	TD	Kickoff Returns Num	Yds	Avg	TD	Passing Att	Com	Yds	Int	Totals Fum	TD	Pts
1994	Atlanta Falcons	16	16	2	4	2.0	2	0	46	649	14.1	t85	4	0	0	-	0	1	0	0	1	0	4	24
1995	Atlanta Falcons	16	16	1	0	0.0	0	0	74	1039	14.0	52	5	0	0	-	0	0	0	0	0	2	5	30
	2 NFL Seasons	32	32	3	4	1.3	2	0	120	1688	14.1	t85	9	0	0	-	0	1	0	0	1	2	9	54

Steve Emtman

Pos: DT   **Rnd:** 1 (1)   **College:** Washington   **Ht:** 6' 4" **Wt:** 284 **Born:** 4/16/70 **Age:** 26

Year	Team	G	GS	Tackles Tk	Ast	Sack	Miscellaneous FF	FR	TD	Blk	Interceptions Int	Yds	Avg	TD	Totals Sfty	TD	Pts
1992	Indianapolis Colts	9	9	33	16	3.0	1	0	0	0	1	90	90.0	1	0	1	6
1993	Indianapolis Colts	5	5	16	6	1.0	0	0	0	0	0	0	-	0	0	0	0
1994	Indianapolis Colts	4	0	3	1	1.0	0	1	0	0	0	0	-	0	0	0	0
1995	Miami Dolphins	16	1	10	4	1.0	0	1	0	0	0	0	-	0	0	0	0
	4 NFL Seasons	34	15	62	27	6.0	1	2	0	0	1	90	90.0	1	0	1	6

Greg Engel

Pos: C   **Rnd:** FA   **College:** Illinois   **Ht:** 6' 3" **Wt:** 285 **Born:** 1/18/71 **Age:** 25

Year	Team	G	GS					G	GS
1995	San Diego Chargers	10	0				1 NFL Season	10	0

Other Statistics: 1995--returned 0 kickoffs for 1 yard.

Eric England

Pos: DE   **Rnd:** 3   **College:** Texas A&M   **Ht:** 6' 2" **Wt:** 283 **Born:** 3/25/71 **Age:** 25

Year	Team	G	GS	Tackles Tk	Ast	Sack	Miscellaneous FF	FR	TD	Blk	Interceptions Int	Yds	Avg	TD	Totals Sfty	TD	Pts
1994	Arizona Cardinals	10	1	2	1	0.0	0	0	0	0	0	0	-	0	0	0	0
1995	Arizona Cardinals	15	0	4	4	0.0	0	2	0	0	0	0	-	0	0	0	0
	2 NFL Seasons	25	1	6	5	0.0	0	2	0	0	0	0	-	0	0	0	0

Tory Epps

Pos: DT/NT   **Rnd:** 8   **College:** Memphis   **Ht:** 6' 1" **Wt:** 280 **Born:** 5/28/67 **Age:** 29

Year	Team	G	GS	Tackles Tk	Ast	Sack	Miscellaneous FF	FR	TD	Blk	Interceptions Int	Yds	Avg	TD	Totals Sfty	TD	Pts
1990	Atlanta Falcons	16	15	39	45	3.0	0	0	0	0	0	0	-	0	0	0	0
1991	Atlanta Falcons	16	2	26	34	1.5	0	1	0	0	0	0	-	0	0	0	0
1992	Atlanta Falcons	16	5	16	38	0.0	1	1	0	0	0	0	-	0	0	0	0
1993	Atl - Chi	5	0	0	0	0.0	0	0	0	0	0	0	-	0	0	0	0
1994	Chicago Bears	5	0	3	2	1.0	0	0	0	0	0	0	-	0	0	0	0
1995	New Orleans Saints	11	0	6	0	0.0	0	0	0	0	0	0	-	0	0	0	0
1993	Atlanta Falcons	2	0	0	0	0.0	0	0	0	0	0	0	-	0	0	0	0
	Chicago Bears	3	0	0	0	0.0	0	0	0	0	0	0	-	0	0	0	0
	6 NFL Seasons	69	22	90	119	5.5	1	2	0	0	0	0	-	0	0	0	0

Craig Erickson

Pos: QB   **Rnd:** 5   **College:** Miami (FL)   *(statistical profile on page 311)*   **Ht:** 6' 2" **Wt:** 205 **Born:** 5/17/69 **Age:** 27

Year	Team	G	GS	Passing Att	Com	Pct	Yards	Yds/Att	Lg	TD	Int	Int%	Rating	Rushing Att	Yds	Avg	Lg	TD	Miscellaneous Sckd	Yds	Fum	Recv	Yds	Pts
1992	Tampa Bay Buccaneers	6	0	26	15	57.7	121	4.65	24	0	0	0.0	69.6	1	-1	-1.0	-1	0	2	9	0	0	0	0
1993	Tampa Bay Buccaneers	16	15	457	233	51.0	3054	6.68	t67	18	21	4.6	66.4	26	96	3.7	15	0	35	236	9	6	-2	0
1994	Tampa Bay Buccaneers	15	14	399	225	56.4	2919	7.32	t71	16	10	2.5	82.5	26	68	2.6	17	1	22	129	6	1	-1	6
1995	Indianapolis Colts	6	3	83	50	60.2	586	7.06	39	3	4	4.8	73.7	9	14	1.6	15	0	10	68	2	0	-3	0
	4 NFL Seasons	43	32	965	523	54.2	6680	6.92	t71	37	35	3.6	73.8	62	177	2.9	17	1	69	442	17	7	-6	6

Ricky Ervins

Pos: RB   **Rnd:** 3   **College:** Southern California   **Ht:** 5' 7" **Wt:** 195 **Born:** 12/7/68 **Age:** 27

Year	Team	G	GS	Rushing Att	Yds	Avg	Lg	TD	Receiving Rec	Yds	Avg	Lg	TD	Punt Returns Num	Yds	Avg	TD	Kickoff Returns Num	Yds	Avg	TD	Totals Fum	TD	Pts
1991	Washington Redskins	15	0	145	680	4.7	t65	3	16	181	11.3	28	1	0	0	-	0	11	232	21.1	0	1	4	24
1992	Washington Redskins	16	0	151	495	3.3	25	2	32	252	7.9	19	0	0	0	-	0	0	0	-	0	1	2	12
1993	Washington Redskins	15	1	50	201	4.0	18	0	16	123	7.7	20	0	0	0	-	0	2	29	14.5	0	2	0	0
1994	Washington Redskins	16	10	185	650	3.5	49	3	51	293	5.7	21	1	0	0	-	0	1	17	17.0	0	1	4	24
1995	San Francisco 49ers	14	0	23	88	3.8	13	0	2	21	10.5	11	0	0	0	-	0	5	32	6.4	0	0	0	0
	5 NFL Seasons	76	11	554	2114	3.8	t65	8	117	870	7.4	28	2	0	0	-	0	19	310	16.3	0	5	10	60

Other Statistics: 1991--recovered 1 fumble for 0 yards. 1992--recovered 1 fumble for 0 yards.

80

Boomer Esiason

(statistical profile on page 311)

Pos: QB **Rnd:** 2 **College:** Maryland **Ht:** 6' 5" **Wt:** 224 **Born:** 4/17/61 **Age:** 35

Year Team	G	GS	Passing Att	Com	Pct	Yards	Yds/Att	Lg	TD	Int	Int%	Rating	Rushing Att	Yds	Avg	Lg	TD	Misc. Sckd	Yds	Fum	Recv	Yds	Pts
1984 Cincinnati Bengals	10	4	102	51	50.0	530	5.20	36	3	3	2.9	62.9	19	63	3.3	9	2	5	52	4	2	-2	12
1985 Cincinnati Bengals	15	14	431	251	58.2	3443	7.99	t68	27	12	2.8	93.2	33	79	2.4	20	1	32	289	9	4	-5	6
1986 Cincinnati Bengals	16	16	469	273	58.2	3959	**8.44**	57	24	17	3.6	87.7	44	146	3.3	23	1	26	194	12	5	-10	6
1987 Cincinnati Bengals	12	12	440	240	54.5	3321	7.55	t61	16	19	4.3	73.1	52	241	4.6	19	0	26	209	10	4	-8	0
1988 Cincinnati Bengals	16	16	388	223	57.5	3572	**9.21**	t86	28	14	3.6	**97.4**	43	248	5.8	24	1	30	245	5	4	0	6
1989 Cincinnati Bengals	16	15	455	258	56.7	3525	7.75	t74	28	11	2.4	92.1	47	278	5.9	24	0	36	288	8	2	-4	0
1990 Cincinnati Bengals	16	16	402	224	55.7	3031	7.54	53	24	**22**	5.5	77.0	49	157	3.2	21	0	31	198	11	2	-23	0
1991 Cincinnati Bengals	14	14	413	233	56.4	2883	6.98	53	13	16	3.9	72.5	24	66	2.8	16	0	25	190	10	3	-5	0
1992 Cincinnati Bengals	12	11	278	144	51.8	1407	5.06	38	11	15	5.4	57.0	21	66	3.1	15	0	19	150	12	6	-9	0
1993 New York Jets	16	16	473	288	60.9	3421	7.23	77	16	11	2.3	84.5	45	118	2.6	17	1	18	139	13	5	-10	6
1994 New York Jets	15	14	440	255	58.0	2782	6.32	69	17	13	3.0	77.3	28	59	2.1	15	0	19	134	11	3	-10	0
1995 New York Jets	12	12	389	221	56.8	2275	5.85	t43	16	15	3.9	71.4	19	14	0.7	19	0	27	198	12	4	-17	0
12 NFL Seasons	170	160	4680	2661	56.9	34149	7.30	t86	223	168	3.6	80.8	424	1535	3.6	24	6	294	2286	117	44	-103	36

Other Statistics: 1986–punted 1 time for 31 yards. 1987–punted 2 times for 68 yards. 1988–punted 1 time for 21 yards. 1993–caught 1 pass for -8 yards.

Charles Evans

Pos: RB **Rnd:** 11 **College:** Clark Atlanta **Ht:** 6' 1" **Wt:** 232 **Born:** 4/16/67 **Age:** 29

Year Team	G	GS	Rushing Att	Yds	Avg	Lg	TD	Receiving Rec	Yds	Avg	Lg	TD	Punt Returns Num	Yds	Avg	TD	Kickoff Returns Num	Yds	Avg	TD	Totals Fum	TD	Pts
1993 Minnesota Vikings	3	0	14	32	2.3	5	0	4	39	9.8	21	0	0	0	-	0	1	11	11.0	0	0	0	0
1994 Minnesota Vikings	14	0	6	20	3.3	8	0	1	2	2.0	2	0	0	0	-	0	1	4	4.0	0	0	0	0
1995 Minnesota Vikings	16	7	19	59	3.1	12	1	18	119	6.6	24	1	0	0	-	0	0	0	-	0	0	2	12
3 NFL Seasons	33	7	39	111	2.8	12	1	23	160	7.0	24	1	0	0	-	0	2	15	7.5	0	0	2	12

Donald Evans

Pos: DE **Rnd:** 2 **College:** Winston-Salem State **Ht:** 6' 2" **Wt:** 282 **Born:** 3/14/64 **Age:** 32

Year Team	G	GS	Tackles Tk	Ast	Sack	Misc. FF	FR	TD	Blk	Int. Int	Yds	Avg	TD	Totals Sfty	TD	Pts
1987 Los Angeles Rams	1	0	0	0	0.0	0	0	0	0	0	0	-	0	0	0	0
1988 Philadelphia Eagles	5	0	0	0	0.0	0	0	0	0	0	0	-	0	0	0	0
1990 Pittsburgh Steelers	16	16	21	5	3.0	0	3	0	0	0	0	-	0	0	0	0
1991 Pittsburgh Steelers	16	14	26	9	2.0	0	1	0	0	0	0	-	0	0	0	0
1992 Pittsburgh Steelers	16	16	40	48	3.0	0	2	0	0	0	0	-	0	0	0	0
1993 Pittsburgh Steelers	16	16	40	44	6.5	0	0	0	0	0	0	-	0	0	0	0
1994 New York Jets	16	16	49	30	0.5	0	1	0	0	0	0	-	0	0	0	0
1995 New York Jets	4	4	10	5	2.0	0	1	0	0	0	0	-	0	0	0	0
8 NFL Seasons	90	82	186	141	17.0	0	8	0	0	0	0	-	0	0	0	0

Other Statistics: 1987–rushed 3 times for 10 yards.

Doug Evans

(statistical profile on page 409)

Pos: CB **Rnd:** 6 **College:** Louisiana Tech **Ht:** 6' 0" **Wt:** 190 **Born:** 5/13/70 **Age:** 26

Year Team	G	GS	Tackles Tk	Ast	Sack	Misc. FF	FR	TD	Blk	Int. Int	Yds	Avg	TD	Punt Returns Num	Yds	Avg	TD	Kickoff Returns Num	Yds	Avg	TD	Totals TD	Fum
1993 Green Bay Packers	16	0	9	5	0.0	2	2	0	0	1	0	0.0	0	0	0	-	0	0	0	-	0	0	0
1994 Green Bay Packers	16	15	46	12	1.0	2	1	0	0	1	0	0.0	0	0	0	-	0	0	0	-	0	0	0
1995 Green Bay Packers	16	16	74	15	1.0	0	0	0	0	2	24	12.0	0	1	0	0.0	0	0	0	-	0	0	1
3 NFL Seasons	48	31	129	32	2.0	4	3	0	0	4	24	6.0	0	1	0	0.0	0	0	0	-	0	0	1

Greg Evans

Pos: S **Rnd:** FA **College:** Texas Christian **Ht:** 6' 1" **Wt:** 205 **Born:** 6/28/71 **Age:** 25

Year Team	G	GS	Tackles Tk	Ast	Sack	Misc. FF	FR	TD	Blk	Int. Int	Yds	Avg	TD	Totals Sfty	TD	Pts
1995 Buffalo Bills	16	4	18	7	0.0	0	1	0	0	1	18	18.0	0	0	0	0

Jerry Evans

Pos: TE **Rnd:** 8 **College:** Toledo **Ht:** 6' 5" **Wt:** 260 **Born:** 9/28/68 **Age:** 28

Year Team	G	GS	Rushing Att	Yds	Avg	Lg	TD	Receiving Rec	Yds	Avg	Lg	TD	Punt Returns Num	Yds	Avg	TD	Kickoff Returns Num	Yds	Avg	TD	Totals Fum	TD	Pts
1993 Denver Broncos	14	2	0	0	-	-	0	0	0	-	-	0	0	0	-	0	0	0	-	0	0	0	0
1994 Denver Broncos	16	10	0	0	-	-	0	13	127	9.8	t20	2	0	0	-	0	1	6	6.0	0	0	2	12
1995 Denver Broncos	13	4	0	0	-	-	0	12	124	10.3	22	1	0	0	-	0	0	0	-	0	1	1	6
3 NFL Seasons	43	16	0	0	-	-	0	25	251	10.0	22	3	0	0	-	0	1	6	6.0	0	1	3	18

Josh Evans

Pos: DT **Rnd:** FA **College:** Alabama-Birmingham **Ht:** 6' 2" **Wt:** 283 **Born:** 9/6/72 **Age:** 24

Year Team	G	GS	Tackles			Miscellaneous				Interceptions				Totals		
			Tk	Ast	Sack	FF	FR	TD	Blk	Int	Yds	Avg	TD	Sfty	TD	Pts
1995 Houston Oilers	7	0	2	1	0.0	0	0	0	0	0	0	-	0	0	0	0

Vince Evans

(statistical profile on page 312)

Pos: QB **Rnd:** 6 **College:** Southern California **Ht:** 6' 2" **Wt:** 215 **Born:** 6/14/55 **Age:** 41

Year Team	G	GS	Passing										Rushing					Miscellaneous				
			Att	Com	Pct	Yards	Yds/Att	Lg	TD	Int	Int%	Rating	Att	Yds	Avg	Lg	TD	Sckd	Yds	Fum	Recv	Yds	Pts
1977 Chicago Bears	13	0	0	0	-	0	-	-	0	0	-	0.0	1	0	0.0	0	0	0	0	3	2	0	0
1978 Chicago Bears	3	0	3	1	33.3	38	12.67	38	0	1	33.3	42.4	6	23	3.8	13	0	2	25	0	0	0	0
1979 Chicago Bears	4	3	63	32	50.8	508	8.06	t65	4	5	7.9	66.1	12	72	6.0	17	1	8	75	1	0	-2	6
1980 Chicago Bears	13	10	278	148	53.2	2039	7.33	t89	11	16	5.8	66.2	60	306	5.1	58	8	26	205	4	0	-3	48
1981 Chicago Bears	16	16	436	195	44.7	2354	5.40	t85	11	20	4.6	51.1	43	218	5.1	25	3	23	173	13	2	-10	18
1982 Chicago Bears	4	0	28	12	42.9	125	4.46	19	0	4	14.3	16.8	2	0	0.0	6	0	2	17	1	0	-24	0
1983 Chicago Bears	9	3	145	76	52.4	1108	7.64	t72	5	7	4.8	69.0	22	142	6.5	27	1	11	92	0	0	0	6
1987 Los Angeles Raiders	3	3	83	39	47.0	630	7.59	47	5	4	4.8	72.9	11	144	13.1	24	1	7	38	0	0	0	6
1989 Los Angeles Raiders	1	0	2	2	100.0	50	25.00	40	0	0	0.0	118.8	1	16	16.0	16	0	2	19	1	0	0	0
1990 Los Angeles Raiders	5	0	1	1	100.0	36	36.00	36	0	0	0.0	118.8	1	-2	-2.0	-2	0	0	0	0	0	0	0
1991 Los Angeles Raiders	4	0	14	6	42.9	127	9.07	t80	1	2	14.3	59.8	8	20	2.5	11	0	2	20	0	0	0	0
1992 Los Angeles Raiders	5	0	53	29	54.7	372	7.02	50	4	3	5.7	78.5	11	79	7.2	16	0	3	26	1	0	0	0
1993 Los Angeles Raiders	8	1	76	45	59.2	640	8.42	t68	3	4	5.3	77.7	14	51	3.6	17	0	12	87	4	0	0	0
1994 Los Angeles Raiders	9	0	33	18	54.5	222	6.73	t65	2	0	0.0	95.8	6	24	4.0	23	0	9	57	2	1	0	0
1995 Oakland Raiders	9	3	175	100	57.1	1236	7.06	t73	6	8	4.6	71.5	14	36	2.6	11	0	11	70	5	0	-4	0
14 NFL Seasons	106	39	1390	704	50.6	9485	6.82	t89	52	74	5.3	63.0	212	1129	5.4	58	14	118	904	39	5	-43	84

Other statistics: 1977–returned 13 kickoffs for 253 yards.

Jim Everett

(statistical profile on page 312)

Pos: QB **Rnd:** 1 (3) **College:** Purdue **Ht:** 6' 5" **Wt:** 212 **Born:** 1/3/63 **Age:** 33

Year Team	G	GS	Passing										Rushing					Miscellaneous				
			Att	Com	Pct	Yards	Yds/Att	Lg	TD	Int	Int%	Rating	Att	Yds	Avg	Lg	TD	Sckd	Yds	Fum	Recv	Yds	Pts
1986 Los Angeles Rams	6	5	147	73	49.7	1018	6.93	t60	8	8	5.4	67.8	16	46	2.9	14	1	8	50	2	0	-2	6
1987 Los Angeles Rams	11	11	302	162	53.6	2064	6.83	t81	10	13	4.3	68.4	18	83	4.6	16	1	17	139	2	1	0	6
1988 Los Angeles Rams	16	16	517	308	59.6	3964	7.67	t69	31	18	3.5	89.2	34	104	3.1	19	0	28	197	7	0	-17	0
1989 Los Angeles Rams	16	16	518	304	58.7	4310	8.32	t78	29	17	3.3	90.6	25	31	1.2	t13	1	29	214	4	4	-1	6
1990 Los Angeles Rams	16	16	554	307	55.4	3989	7.20	t55	23	17	3.1	79.3	20	31	1.6	15	1	30	198	4	0	-12	6
1991 Los Angeles Rams	16	16	490	277	56.5	3438	7.02	78	11	20	4.1	68.9	27	44	1.6	10	0	30	200	12	1	-4	0
1992 Los Angeles Rams	16	16	475	281	59.2	3323	7.00	t67	22	18	3.8	80.2	32	133	4.2	22	0	26	204	5	0	-9	0
1993 Los Angeles Rams	10	9	274	135	49.3	1652	6.03	t60	8	12	4.4	59.7	19	38	2.0	14	0	18	125	7	1	-1	0
1994 New Orleans Saints	16	16	540	346	64.1	3855	7.14	t78	22	18	3.3	84.9	15	35	2.3	14	0	21	164	3	0	-2	0
1995 New Orleans Saints	16	16	567	345	60.8	3970	7.00	t70	26	14	2.5	87.0	24	42	1.8	9	0	27	210	6	0	-5	0
10 NFL Seasons	139	137	4384	2538	57.9	31583	7.20	t81	190	155	3.5	80.1	230	587	2.6	22	4	234	1701	52	7	-53	24

Thomas Everett

Pos: S **Rnd:** 4 **College:** Baylor **Ht:** 5' 9" **Wt:** 190 **Born:** 11/21/64 **Age:** 31

Year Team	G	GS	Tackles			Miscellaneous				Interceptions				Punt Returns				Kickoff Returns				Totals	
			Tk	Ast	Sack	FF	FR	TD	Blk	Int	Yds	Avg	TD	Num	Yds	Avg	TD	Num	Yds	Avg	TD	TD	Fum
1987 Pittsburgh Steelers	12	9	59	13	0.0	1	2	0	0	3	22	7.3	0	4	22	5.5	0	0	0	-	0	0	1
1988 Pittsburgh Steelers	14	12	49	11	0.0	0	2	0	0	3	31	10.3	0	0	0	-	0	0	0	-	0	0	1
1989 Pittsburgh Steelers	16	16	63	18	0.0	0	1	0	0	3	68	22.7	0	0	0	-	0	0	0	-	0	0	0
1990 Pittsburgh Steelers	15	14	28	7	0.0	0	0	0	0	3	2	0.7	0	0	0	-	0	0	0	-	0	0	0
1991 Pittsburgh Steelers	16	16	47	20	0.0	1	2	0	0	4	53	13.3	0	0	0	-	0	0	0	-	0	0	0
1992 Dallas Cowboys	11	9	27	31	0.0	0	2	0	0	2	28	14.0	0	0	0	-	0	0	0	-	0	0	0
1993 Dallas Cowboys	16	16	54	43	0.0	0	0	0	0	2	25	12.5	0	0	0	-	0	0	0	-	0	0	0
1994 Tampa Bay Buccaneers	15	15	53	12	0.0	0	1	0	0	1	26	26.0	0	2	2	1.0	0	0	0	-	0	0	0
1995 Tampa Bay Buccaneers	13	10	42	12	1.0	0	1	0	0	0	0	-	0	0	0	-	0	0	0	-	0	0	0
9 NFL Seasons	128	117	422	167	1.0	4	11	0	0	21	255	12.1	0	6	24	4.0	0	0	0	-	0	0	2

Steve Everitt

Pos: C/LS **Rnd:** 1 (14) **College:** Michigan **Ht:** 6' 5" **Wt:** 290 **Born:** 8/21/70 **Age:** 26

Year Team	G	GS	Year Team	G	GS	Year Team	G	GS		G	GS
1993 Cleveland Browns	16	16	1994 Cleveland Browns	15	15	1995 Cleveland Browns	15	14	3 NFL Seasons	46	45

Other Statistics: 1993–recovered 2 fumbles for 0 yards. 1995–recovered 1 fumble for 0 yards.

Chad Fann

Pos: TE **Rnd:** FA   **College:** Florida A&M   **Ht:** 6' 3" **Wt:** 250 **Born:** 6/7/70 **Age:** 26

Year Team	G	GS	Att	Yds	Avg	Lg	TD	Rec	Yds	Avg	Lg	TD	Num	Yds	Avg	TD	Num	Yds	Avg	TD	Fum	TD	Pts
				Rushing					Receiving					Punt Returns				Kickoff Returns				Totals	
1993 Phoenix Cardinals	1	0	0	0	-	-	0	0	0	-	-	0	0	0	-	0	0	0	-	0	0	0	0
1994 Arizona Cardinals	16	7	0	0	-	-	0	12	96	8.0	16	0	0	0	-	0	0	0	-	0	1	0	0
1995 Arizona Cardinals	16	3	0	0	-	-	0	5	41	8.2	13	0	0	0	-	0	0	0	-	0	1	0	0
3 NFL Seasons	33	10	0	0	-	-	0	17	137	8.1	16	0	0	0	-	0	0	0	-	0	2	0	0

D'Marco Farr

(statistical profile on page 409)

Pos: DT **Rnd:** FA   **College:** Washington   **Ht:** 6' 1" **Wt:** 270 **Born:** 6/9/71 **Age:** 25

Year Team	G	GS	Tk	Ast	Sack	FF	FR	TD	Blk	Int	Yds	Avg	TD	Num	Yds	Avg	TD	Num	Yds	Avg	TD	TD	Fum
				Tackles			Miscellaneous				Interceptions				Punt Returns				Kickoff Returns				Totals
1994 Los Angeles Rams	10	3	9	2	1.0	0	0	0	0	0	0	-	0	0	0	-	0	1	16	16.0	0	0	0
1995 St. Louis Rams	16	16	48	2	11.5	5	0	0	1	1	5	5.0	0	0	0	-	0	0	0	-	0	0	0
2 NFL Seasons	26	19	57	4	12.5	5	0	0	1	1	5	5.0	0	0	0	-	0	1	16	16.0	0	0	0

Brett Faryniarz

Pos: LB **Rnd:** FA   **College:** San Diego State   **Ht:** 6' 3" **Wt:** 230 **Born:** 7/23/65 **Age:** 31

Year Team	G	GS	Tk	Ast	Sack	FF	FR	TD	Blk	Int	Yds	Avg	TD	Sfty	TD	Pts
				Tackles			Miscellaneous				Interceptions				Totals	
1988 Los Angeles Rams	15	0	14	1	1.0	0	0	0	0	0	0	-	0	0	0	0
1989 Los Angeles Rams	16	0	24	4	3.0	0	2	0	0	0	0	-	0	0	0	0
1990 Los Angeles Rams	16	3	27	1	2.0	0	0	0	0	0	0	-	0	0	0	0
1991 Los Angeles Rams	12	7	21	5	0.0	0	1	0	0	0	0	-	0	0	0	0
1993 San Francisco 49ers	2	0	0	0	0.0	0	0	0	0	0	0	-	0	0	0	0
1994 Houston Oilers	16	0	1	0	0.0	0	0	0	0	0	0	-	0	0	0	0
1995 Carolina Panthers	15	1	5	1	0.0	0	0	0	0	0	0	-	0	0	0	0
7 NFL Seasons	92	11	92	12	6.0	0	0	0	0	0	0	-	0	0	0	0

Marshall Faulk

(statistical profile on page 313)

Pos: RB **Rnd:** 1 (2)   **College:** San Diego State   **Ht:** 5' 10" **Wt:** 205 **Born:** 2/26/73 **Age:** 23

Year Team	G	GS	Att	Yds	Avg	Lg	TD	Rec	Yds	Avg	Lg	TD	Num	Yds	Avg	TD	Num	Yds	Avg	TD	Fum	TD	Pts
				Rushing					Receiving					Punt Returns				Kickoff Returns				Totals	
1994 Indianapolis Colts	16	16	314	1282	4.1	52	11	52	522	10.0	t85	1	0	0	-	0	0	0	-	0	5	12	72
1995 Indianapolis Colts	16	16	289	1078	3.7	40	11	56	475	8.5	34	3	0	0	-	0	0	0	-	0	8	14	84
2 NFL Seasons	32	32	603	2360	3.9	52	22	108	997	9.2	t85	4	0	0	-	0	0	0	-	0	13	26	156

Other Statistics: 1994–recovered 1 fumble for 0 yards. 1995–recovered 1 fumble for 0 yards.

Mike Faulkerson

Pos: RB **Rnd:** FA   **College:** North Carolina   **Ht:** 6' 0" **Wt:** 237 **Born:** 9/9/70 **Age:** 26

Year Team	G	GS	Att	Yds	Avg	Lg	TD	Rec	Yds	Avg	Lg	TD	Num	Yds	Avg	TD	Num	Yds	Avg	TD	Fum	TD	Pts
				Rushing					Receiving					Punt Returns				Kickoff Returns				Totals	
1995 Chicago Bears	5	1	0	0	-	-	0	2	22	11.0	12	0	0	0	-	0	0	0	-	0	0	0	0

Ta'ase Faumui

Pos: DE **Rnd:** 4   **College:** Hawaii   **Ht:** 6' 3" **Wt:** 271 **Born:** 3/19/71 **Age:** 25

Year Team	G	GS	Tk	Ast	Sack	FF	FR	TD	Blk	Int	Yds	Avg	TD	Sfty	TD	Pts
				Tackles			Miscellaneous				Interceptions				Totals	
1994 Pittsburgh Steelers	5	0	2	0	0.0	0	0	0	0	0	0	-	0	0	0	0
1995 Pittsburgh Steelers	2	0	0	0	0.0	0	0	0	0	0	0	-	0	0	0	0
2 NFL Seasons	7	0	2	0	0.0	0	0	0	0	0	0	-	0	0	0	0

Christian Fauria

Pos: TE **Rnd:** 2   **College:** Colorado   **Ht:** 6' 5" **Wt:** 245 **Born:** 9/22/71 **Age:** 25

Year Team	G	GS	Att	Yds	Avg	Lg	TD	Rec	Yds	Avg	Lg	TD	Num	Yds	Avg	TD	Num	Yds	Avg	TD	Fum	TD	Pts
				Rushing					Receiving					Punt Returns				Kickoff Returns				Totals	
1995 Seattle Seahawks	14	9	0	0	-	-	0	17	181	10.6	t20	1	0	0	-	0	0	0	-	0	0	1	6

Brett Favre

(statistical profile on page 313)

Pos: QB **Rnd:** 2   **College:** Southern Mississippi   **Ht:** 6' 2" **Wt:** 220 **Born:** 10/10/69 **Age:** 27

Year Team	G	GS	Att	Com	Pct	Yards	Yds/Att	Lg	TD	Int	Int%	Rating	Att	Yds	Avg	Lg	TD	Sckd	Yds	Fum	Recv	Yds	Pts
				Passing										Rushing					Miscellaneous			
1991 Atlanta Falcons	2	0	5	0	0.0	0	0.00	0	0	2	40.0	0.0	0	0	-	-	0	1	11	0	0	0	0
1992 Green Bay Packers	15	13	471	302	64.1	3227	6.85	t76	18	13	2.8	85.3	47	198	4.2	19	1	34	208	12	3	-12	6

Year	Team	G	GS	Att	Com	Pct	Yards	Yds/Att	Lg	TD	Int	Int%	Rating	Att	Yds	Avg	Lg	TD	Sckd	Yds	Fum	Recv	Yds	Pts
1993	Green Bay Packers	16	16	522	318	60.9	3303	6.33	t66	19	24	4.6	72.2	58	216	3.7	27	1	30	199	14	2	-1	6
1994	Green Bay Packers	16	16	582	363	62.4	3882	6.67	49	33	14	2.4	90.7	42	202	4.8	t36	2	31	188	7	1	0	12
1995	Green Bay Packers	16	16	570	359	63.0	4413	7.74	t99	38	13	2.3	99.5	39	181	4.6	40	3	33	217	8	0	0	18
	5 NFL Seasons	65	61	2150	1342	62.4	14825	6.90	t99	108	66	3.1	86.8	186	797	4.3	40	7	129	823	41	6	-13	42

Other Statistics: 1992–caught 1 pass for -7 yards.

Jeff Feagles

(statistical profile on page 473)

Pos: P   **Rnd:** FA   **College:** Miami (FL)   **Ht:** 6' 1"   **Wt:** 205   **Born:** 3/7/66   **Age:** 30

Year	Team	G	NetPunts	Yards	Avg	Long	In20	In20%	TotPunts	TB	Blocks	OppRet	RetYds	NetAvg	Att	Yards	Att	Com	Yards	Int
1988	New England Patriots	16	91	3482	38.3	74	24	26.4	91	8	0	37	217	34.1	1	0	0	0	0	0
1989	New England Patriots	16	63	2392	38.0	64	13	20.6	64	2	1	38	346	31.3	0	0	2	0	0	0
1990	Philadelphia Eagles	16	72	3026	42.0	60	20	27.8	74	3	2	37	338	35.5	2	3	1	0	0	0
1991	Philadelphia Eagles	16	87	3640	41.8	77	29	33.3	88	11	1	42	431	34.0	3	-1	0	0	0	0
1992	Philadelphia Eagles	16	82	3459	42.2	68	26	31.7	82	7	0	36	295	36.9	0	0	0	0	0	0
1993	Philadelphia Eagles	16	83	3323	40.0	60	31	37.3	83	4	0	35	311	35.3	2	6	0	0	0	0
1994	Arizona Cardinals	16	98	3997	40.8	54	33	33.7	98	10	0	40	270	36.0	2	8	0	0	0	0
1995	Arizona Cardinals	16	72	3150	43.8	60	20	27.8	72	8	0	32	242	38.2	2	4	0	0	0	0
	8 NFL Seasons	128	648	26469	40.8	77	196	30.2	652	53	4	297	2450	35.2	12	20	3	0	0	0

Other Statistics: 1988–recovered 1 fumble for 0 yards. 1989–recovered 1 fumble for 0 yards; fumbled 1 time. 1991–recovered 1 fumble for 0 yards; fumbled 1 time. 1993–recovered 1 fumble for 0 yards. 1995–fumbled 1 time for -22 yards.

Derrick Fenner

(statistical profile on page 314)

Pos: RB   **Rnd:** 10   **College:** North Carolina   **Ht:** 6' 3"   **Wt:** 240   **Born:** 4/6/67   **Age:** 29

Year	Team	G	GS	Att	Yds	Avg	Lg	TD	Rec	Yds	Avg	Lg	TD	Num	Yds	Avg	TD	Num	Yds	Avg	TD	Fum	TD	Pts
1989	Seattle Seahawks	5	1	11	41	3.7	9	1	3	23	7.7	9	0	0	0	-	0	0	0	-	0	1	1	6
1990	Seattle Seahawks	16	15	215	859	4.0	36	14	17	143	8.4	50	1	0	0	-	0	0	0	-	0	3	15	90
1991	Seattle Seahawks	11	7	91	267	2.9	15	4	11	72	6.5	15	0	0	0	-	0	0	0	-	0	2	4	24
1992	Cincinnati Bengals	16	1	112	500	4.5	t35	7	7	41	5.9	15	1	0	0	-	0	2	38	19.0	0	1	8	48
1993	Cincinnati Bengals	15	14	121	482	4.0	26	1	48	427	8.9	40	0	0	0	-	0	0	0	-	0	1	1	6
1994	Cincinnati Bengals	16	12	141	468	3.3	21	1	36	276	7.7	29	1	0	0	-	0	0	0	-	0	6	2	12
1995	Oakland Raiders	16	13	39	110	2.8	10	0	35	252	7.2	23	3	0	0	-	0	0	0	-	0	2	3	18
	7 NFL Seasons	95	63	730	2727	3.7	36	28	157	1234	7.9	50	6	0	0	-	0	2	38	19.0	0	15	34	204

Other Statistics: 1990–recovered 1 fumble for 0 yards. 1992–recovered 1 fumble for 0 yards. 1993–recovered 2 fumbles for 0 yards. 1994–recovered 1 fumble for 0 yards. 1995–recovered 2 fumbles for 0 yards.

Jay Fiedler

Pos: QB   **Rnd:** FA   **College:** Dartmouth   **Ht:** 6' 1"   **Wt:** 214   **Born:** 12/29/71   **Age:** 24

Year	Team	G	GS	Att	Com	Pct	Yards	Yds/Att	Lg	TD	Int	Int%	Rating	Att	Yds	Avg	Lg	TD	Sckd	Yds	Fum	Recv	Yds	Pts
1994	Philadelphia Eagles	1	0	0	0	-	0	-	0	0	0	-	0.0	0	0	-	0	0	0	0	0	0	0	0
1995	Philadelphia Eagles	1	0	0	0	-	0	-	0	0	0	-	0.0	0	0	-	0	0	0	0	0	0	0	0
	2 NFL Seasons	2	0	0	0	-	0	-	0	0	0	-	0.0	0	0	-	0	0	0	0	0	0	0	0

Anthony Fieldings

Pos: LB   **Rnd:** FA   **College:** Morningside College   **Ht:** 6' 1"   **Wt:** 237   **Born:** 7/9/71   **Age:** 25

Year	Team	G	GS	Tk	Ast	Sack	FF	FR	TD	Blk	Int	Yds	Avg	TD	Sfty	TD	Pts
1995	Dallas Cowboys	4	0	0	1	0.0	0	0	0	0	0	0	-	0	0	0	0

Jeff Fields

Pos: NT   **Rnd:** 9   **College:** Arkansas State   **Ht:** 6' 3"   **Wt:** 320   **Born:** 7/3/67   **Age:** 29

Year	Team	G	GS	Tk	Ast	Sack	FF	FR	TD	Blk	Int	Yds	Avg	TD	Sfty	TD	Pts
1995	Carolina Panthers	2	0	0	0	0.0	0	0	0	0	0	0	-	0	0	0	0

Mark Fields

Pos: LB   **Rnd:** 1 (13)   **College:** Washington State   **Ht:** 6' 2"   **Wt:** 244   **Born:** 11/9/72   **Age:** 23

Year	Team	G	GS	Tk	Ast	Sack	FF	FR	TD	Blk	Int	Yds	Avg	TD	Sfty	TD	Pts
1995	New Orleans Saints	16	3	31	9	1.0	0	0	0	0	0	0	-	0	0	0	0

Cedric Figaro

Pos: LB **Rnd:** 6 **College:** Notre Dame **Ht:** 6' 3" **Wt:** 258 **Born:** 8/17/66 **Age:** 30

				Tackles			Miscellaneous				Interceptions				Punt Returns				Kickoff Returns				Totals	
Year	Team	G	GS	Tk	Ast	Sack	FF	FR	TD	Blk	Int	Yds	Avg	TD	Num	Yds	Avg	TD	Num	Yds	Avg	TD	TD	Fum
1988	San Diego Chargers	6	5	24	11	0.0	0	0	0	0	0	0	-	0	0	0	-	0	0	0	-	0	0	0
1989	San Diego Chargers	16	14	54	10	0.0	0	1	0	0	1	2	2.0	0	1	0	0.0	0	1	21	21.0	0	0	0
1990	San Diego Chargers	16	1	5	3	0.0	0	0	0	0	0	0	-	0	0	0	-	0	0	0	-	0	0	0
1991	Ind - Cle	13	0	18	16	0.0	2	1	0	0	1	9	9.0	0	0	0	-	0	0	0	-	0	0	0
1992	Cleveland Browns	16	0	3	3	0.0	0	1	0	0	0	0	-	0	0	0	-	0	0	0	-	0	0	0
1995	St. Louis Rams	16	1	*11*	*2*	1.0	1	1	0	0	0	0	-	0	0	0	-	0	0	0	-	0	0	0
1991	Indianapolis Colts	1	0	0	0	0.0	0	0	0	0	0	0	-	0	0	0	-	0	0	0	-	0	0	0
	Cleveland Browns	12	0	18	16	0.0	2	1	0	0	1	9	9.0	0	0	0	-	0	0	0	-	0	0	0
	6 NFL Seasons	83	21	115	45	1.0	3	4	0	0	2	11	5.5	0	1	0	0.0	0	1	21	21.0	0	0	0

Deon Figures

Pos: CB **Rnd:** 1 (23) **College:** Colorado **Ht:** 6' 0" **Wt:** 200 **Born:** 1/20/70 **Age:** 26

				Tackles			Miscellaneous				Interceptions				Punt Returns				Kickoff Returns				Totals	
Year	Team	G	GS	Tk	Ast	Sack	FF	FR	TD	Blk	Int	Yds	Avg	TD	Num	Yds	Avg	TD	Num	Yds	Avg	TD	TD	Fum
1993	Pittsburgh Steelers	15	4	34	4	0.0	1	2	0	0	1	78	78.0	0	5	15	3.0	0	0	0	-	0	0	2
1994	Pittsburgh Steelers	16	15	*56*	*14*	1.0	1	1	0	0	0	0	-	0	0	0	-	0	0	0	-	0	0	0
1995	Pittsburgh Steelers	14	1	*10*	*0*	0.0	0	0	0	0	0	0	-	0	0	0	-	0	0	0	-	0	0	0
	3 NFL Seasons	45	20	100	18	1.0	2	3	0	0	1	78	78.0	0	5	15	3.0	0	0	0	-	0	0	2

John Fina

Pos: T **Rnd:** 1 (27) **College:** Arizona **Ht:** 6' 4" **Wt:** 287 **Born:** 3/11/69 **Age:** 27

Year	Team	G	GS	Year	Team	G	GS	Year	Team	G	GS	Year	Team	G	GS
1992	Buffalo Bills	16	0	1993	Buffalo Bills	16	16	1994	Buffalo Bills	12	12	1995	Buffalo Bills	16	16
													4 NFL Seasons	60	44

Other Statistics: 1992–caught 1 pass for 1 yard and 1 touchdown. 1993–rushed 1 time for -2 yards.

Jason Fisk

Pos: DT **Rnd:** 7 **College:** Stanford **Ht:** 6' 3" **Wt:** 286 **Born:** 9/4/72 **Age:** 24

				Tackles			Miscellaneous				Interceptions				Totals		
Year	Team	G	GS	Tk	Ast	Sack	FF	FR	TD	Blk	Int	Yds	Avg	TD	Sfty	TD	Pts
1995	Minnesota Vikings	8	0	*0*	*0*	0.0	0	0	0	0	0	0	-	0	0	0	0

Jim Flanigan

(statistical profile on page 410)

Pos: DT **Rnd:** 3 **College:** Notre Dame **Ht:** 6' 2" **Wt:** 280 **Born:** 8/27/71 **Age:** 25

				Tackles			Miscellaneous				Interceptions				Punt Returns				Kickoff Returns				Totals	
Year	Team	G	GS	Tk	Ast	Sack	FF	FR	TD	Blk	Int	Yds	Avg	TD	Num	Yds	Avg	TD	Num	Yds	Avg	TD	TD	Fum
1994	Chicago Bears	14	0	*10*	*1*	0.0	0	0	0	0	0	0	-	0	0	0	-	0	2	26	13.0	0	0	0
1995	Chicago Bears	16	12	*39*	*10*	11.0	0	1	2	0	0	0	-	0	0	0	-	0	0	0	-	0	2	0
	2 NFL Seasons	30	12	49	11	11.0	0	1	2	0	0	0	-	0	0	0	-	0	2	26	13.0	0	2	0

Other Statistics: 1995–rushed 1 time for 0 yards; caught 2 passes for 6 yards and 2 touchdowns.

Cory Fleming

Pos: WR **Rnd:** 3 **College:** Tennessee **Ht:** 6' 1" **Wt:** 216 **Born:** 3/19/71 **Age:** 25

				Rushing					Receiving					Punt Returns				Kickoff Returns				Totals		
Year	Team	G	GS	Att	Yds	Avg	Lg	TD	Rec	Yds	Avg	Lg	TD	Num	Yds	Avg	TD	Num	Yds	Avg	TD	Fum	TD	Pts
1994	Dallas Cowboys	2	0	0	0	-	-	0	0	0	-	-	0	0	0	-	0	0	0	-	0	0	0	0
1995	Dallas Cowboys	14	0	0	0	-	-	0	6	83	13.8	16	0	0	0	-	0	0	0	-	0	0	0	0
	2 NFL Seasons	16	0	0	0	-	-	0	6	83	13.8	16	0	0	0	-	0	0	0	-	0	0	0	0

Simon Fletcher

(statistical profile on page 410)

Pos: DE **Rnd:** 2 **College:** Houston **Ht:** 6' 0" **Wt:** 240 **Born:** 2/18/62 **Age:** 34

				Tackles			Miscellaneous				Interceptions				Totals		
Year	Team	G	GS	Tk	Ast	Sack	FF	FR	TD	Blk	Int	Yds	Avg	TD	Sfty	TD	Pts
1985	Denver Broncos	16	1	12	5	1.0	0	0	0	0	0	0	-	0	0	0	0
1986	Denver Broncos	16	2	26	17	5.5	0	2	0	0	0	0	-	0	0	0	0
1987	Denver Broncos	12	12	49	21	4.0	0	1	0	0	0	0	-	0	0	0	0
1988	Denver Broncos	16	16	79	36	9.0	0	1	0	0	1	4	4.0	0	0	0	0
1989	Denver Broncos	16	16	61	44	12.0	3	1	0	0	0	0	-	0	0	0	0
1990	Denver Broncos	16	16	55	42	11.0	4	1	0	0	0	0	-	0	1	0	2
1991	Denver Broncos	16	16	46	43	13.5	2	1	0	0	0	0	-	0	0	0	0
1992	Denver Broncos	16	16	64	35	16.0	5	0	0	0	0	0	-	0	0	0	0
1993	Denver Broncos	16	16	62	37	13.5	3	1	0	0	0	0	-	0	0	0	0

Year	Team	G	GS	Tackles			Miscellaneous				Interceptions				Totals		
				Tk	Ast	Sack	FF	FR	TD	Blk	Int	Yds	Avg	TD	Sfty	TD	Pts
1994	Denver Broncos	16	16	38	12	7.0	1	2	0	0	1	4	4.0	0	0	0	0
1995	Denver Broncos	16	16	36	8	5.0	2	0	0	0	0	0	-	0	0	0	0
	11 NFL Seasons	172	143	528	300	97.5	20	10	0	0	2	8	4.0	0	1	0	2

Terrell Fletcher

Pos: RB **Rnd:** 2 **College:** Wisconsin **Ht:** 5' 8" **Wt:** 196 **Born:** 9/14/73 **Age:** 23

Year	Team	G	GS	Rushing					Receiving					Punt Returns				Kickoff Returns				Totals		
				Att	Yds	Avg	Lg	TD	Rec	Yds	Avg	Lg	TD	Num	Yds	Avg	TD	Num	Yds	Avg	TD	Fum	TD	Pts
1995	San Diego Chargers	16	0	26	140	5.4	46	1	3	26	8.7	15	0	3	12	4.0	0	4	65	16.3	0	2	1	6

Other Statistics: 1995–recovered 2 fumbles for 0 yards.

Mike Flores

Pos: DE **Rnd:** 11 **College:** Louisville **Ht:** 6' 3" **Wt:** 256 **Born:** 12/1/66 **Age:** 29

Year	Team	G	GS	Tackles			Miscellaneous				Interceptions				Totals		
				Tk	Ast	Sack	FF	FR	TD	Blk	Int	Yds	Avg	TD	Sfty	TD	Pts
1991	Philadelphia Eagles	5	0	1	0	0.0	0	0	0	0	0	0	-	0	0	0	0
1992	Philadelphia Eagles	15	0	1	1	0.0	0	0	0	0	0	0	-	0	0	0	0
1993	Philadelphia Eagles	16	11	40	9	3.0	1	1	0	0	0	0	-	0	1	0	2
1994	Philadelphia Eagles	15	2	10	4	2.0	0	1	0	0	0	0	-	0	0	0	0
1995	Was - SF	11	0	8	0	1.0	1	0	0	0	0	0	-	0	0	0	0
1995	Washington Redskins	10	0	8	0	1.0	1	0	0	0	0	0	-	0	0	0	0
	San Francisco 49ers	1	0	0	0	0.0	0	0	0	0	0	0	-	0	0	0	0
	5 NFL Seasons	62	13	60	14	6.0	2	2	0	0	0	0	-	0	1	0	2

Lethon Flowers

Pos: DB/CB **Rnd:** 5 **College:** Georgia Tech **Ht:** 6' 0" **Wt:** 202 **Born:** 1/14/73 **Age:** 23

Year	Team	G	GS	Tackles			Miscellaneous				Interceptions				Totals		
				Tk	Ast	Sack	FF	FR	TD	Blk	Int	Yds	Avg	TD	Sfty	TD	Pts
1995	Pittsburgh Steelers	10	0	0	0	0.0	0	0	0	0	0	0	-	0	0	0	0

Eric Floyd

Pos: G **Rnd:** FA **College:** Auburn **Ht:** 6' 5" **Wt:** 310 **Born:** 10/28/65 **Age:** 31

Year	Team	G	GS	Year	Team	G	GS	Year	Team	G	GS			G	GS
1990	San Diego Chargers	16	6	1992	Philadelphia Eagles	16	16	1995	Arizona Cardinals	1	0				
1991	San Diego Chargers	2	0	1993	Philadelphia Eagles	3	3						5 NFL Seasons	38	25

Other Statistics: 1993–recovered 1 fumble for 5 yards.

William Floyd

(statistical profile on page 314)

Pos: RB **Rnd:** 1 (28) **College:** Florida State **Ht:** 6' 1" **Wt:** 230 **Born:** 2/17/72 **Age:** 24

Year	Team	G	GS	Rushing					Receiving					Punt Returns				Kickoff Returns				Totals		
				Att	Yds	Avg	Lg	TD	Rec	Yds	Avg	Lg	TD	Num	Yds	Avg	TD	Num	Yds	Avg	TD	Fum	TD	Pts
1994	San Francisco 49ers	16	11	87	305	3.5	26	6	19	145	7.6	15	0	0	0	-	0	0	0	-	0	0	6	36
1995	San Francisco 49ers	8	8	64	237	3.7	23	2	47	348	7.4	23	1	0	0	-	0	0	0	-	0	1	3	18
	2 NFL Seasons	24	19	151	542	3.6	26	8	66	493	7.5	23	1	0	0	-	0	0	0	-	0	1	9	54

Glenn Foley

Pos: QB **Rnd:** 7 **College:** Boston College **Ht:** 6' 2" **Wt:** 210 **Born:** 10/10/70 **Age:** 26

Year	Team	G	GS	Passing										Rushing				Miscellaneous			
				Att	Com	Pct	Yards	Yds/Att	Lg	TD	Int	Int%	Rating	Att	Yds	Avg	Lg TD	Sckd Yds	Fum Recv Yds		Pts
1994	New York Jets	1	0	8	5	62.5	45	5.63	16	0	1	12.5	38.0	0	0	-	0	0 0	0 0 0		0
1995	New York Jets	1	0	29	16	55.2	128	4.41	32	0	1	3.4	52.1	1	9	9.0	9 0	4 21	0 0 0		0
	2 NFL Seasons	2	0	37	21	56.8	173	4.68	32	0	2	5.4	46.3	1	9	9.0	9 0	4 21	0 0 0		0

Other Statistics: 1995–caught 1 pass for -9 yards.

James Folston

Pos: LB **Rnd:** 2 **College:** Northeast Louisiana **Ht:** 6' 3" **Wt:** 235 **Born:** 8/14/71 **Age:** 25

Year	Team	G	GS	Tackles			Miscellaneous				Interceptions				Totals		
				Tk	Ast	Sack	FF	FR	TD	Blk	Int	Yds	Avg	TD	Sfty	TD	Pts
1994	Los Angeles Raiders	7	0	0	0	0.0	0	0	0	0	0	0	-	0	0	0	0
1995	Oakland Raiders	15	0	3	1	0.0	0	0	0	0	0	0	-	0	0	0	0
	2 NFL Seasons	22	0	3	1	0.0	0	0	0	0	0	0	-	0	0	0	0

Al Fontenot

Pos: DE   **Rnd:** 4   **College:** Baylor   **Ht:** 6' 4" **Wt:** 275 **Born:** 9/17/70 **Age:** 26

			Tackles			Miscellaneous				Interceptions				Punt Returns				Kickoff Returns				Totals	
Year Team	G	GS	Tk	Ast	Sack	FF	FR	TD	Blk	Int	Yds	Avg	TD	Num	Yds	Avg	TD	Num	Yds	Avg	TD	TD	Fum
1993 Chicago Bears	16	0	2	2	1.0	1	0	0	0	0	0	-	0	0	0	-	0	1	8	8.0	0	0	0
1994 Chicago Bears	16	8	24	10	4.0	0	0	0	1	0	0	-	0	0	0	-	0	0	0	-	0	0	0
1995 Chicago Bears	13	5	10	6	2.5	0	1	0	1	0	0	-	0	0	0	-	0	0	0	-	0	0	0
3 NFL Seasons	45	13	36	18	7.5	1	1	0	2	0	0	-	0	0	0	-	0	1	8	8.0	0	0	0

Other Statistics: 1995–credited with 1 safety.

Jerry Fontenot

Pos: C   **Rnd:** 3   **College:** Texas A&M   **Ht:** 6' 3" **Wt:** 300 **Born:** 11/21/66 **Age:** 29

Year Team	G	GS	Year Team	G	GS	Year Team	G	GS	Year Team	G	GS
1989 Chicago Bears	16	0	1991 Chicago Bears	16	7	1993 Chicago Bears	16	16	1995 Chicago Bears	16	16
1990 Chicago Bears	16	2	1992 Chicago Bears	16	16	1994 Chicago Bears	16	16	7 NFL Seasons	112	73

Other Statistics: 1989–recovered 1 fumble for 0 yards. 1990–fumbled 1 time for 0 yards. 1992–fumbled 1 time for -2 yards. 1993–recovered 1 fumble for 0 yards.

Dan Footman

(statistical profile on page 410)

Pos: DT   **Rnd:** 2   **College:** Florida State   **Ht:** 6' 5" **Wt:** 290 **Born:** 1/13/69 **Age:** 27

			Tackles			Miscellaneous				Interceptions				Totals		
Year Team	G	GS	Tk	Ast	Sack	FF	FR	TD	Blk	Int	Yds	Avg	TD	Sfty	TD	Pts
1993 Cleveland Browns	8	0	1	0	1.0	0	0	0	0	0	0	-	0	0	0	0
1994 Cleveland Browns	16	2	16	4	2.5	0	0	0	0	0	0	-	0	0	0	0
1995 Cleveland Browns	16	16	33	6	5.0	0	1	0	0	0	0	-	0	0	0	0
3 NFL Seasons	40	18	50	10	8.5	0	1	0	0	0	0	-	0	0	0	0

Cole Ford

(statistical profile on page 473)

Pos: K   **Rnd:** 7   **College:** Southern California   **Ht:** 6' 2" **Wt:** 195 **Born:** 12/31/72 **Age:** 23

								Field Goals							PAT		Tot
Year Team	G	1-29 Yds	Pct	30-39 Yds	Pct	40-49 Yds	Pct	50+ Yds	Pct	Overall	Pct	Long	Made	Att	Pts
1995 Oakland Raiders	5	4-4	100.0	3-3	100.0	1-1	100.0	0-1	0.0	8-9	88.9	46	17	18	41

Henry Ford

(statistical profile on page 411)

Pos: DE   **Rnd:** 1 (26)   **College:** Arkansas   **Ht:** 6' 3" **Wt:** 284 **Born:** 10/30/71 **Age:** 25

			Tackles			Miscellaneous				Interceptions				Totals		
Year Team	G	GS	Tk	Ast	Sack	FF	FR	TD	Blk	Int	Yds	Avg	TD	Sfty	TD	Pts
1994 Houston Oilers	13	0	10	1	0.0	0	0	0	0	0	0	-	0	0	0	0
1995 Houston Oilers	16	16	27	16	4.5	0	0	0	0	0	0	-	0	0	0	0
2 NFL Seasons	29	16	37	17	4.5	0	0	0	0	0	0	-	0	0	0	0

Roman Fortin

Pos: C   **Rnd:** 8   **College:** San Diego State   **Ht:** 6' 5" **Wt:** 295 **Born:** 2/26/67 **Age:** 29

Year Team	G	GS	Year Team	G	GS	Year Team	G	GS		G	GS
1991 Detroit Lions	16	2	1993 Atlanta Falcons	16	1	1995 Atlanta Falcons	16	15			
1992 Atlanta Falcons	16	1	1994 Atlanta Falcons	16	16				5 NFL Seasons	80	35

Other Statistics: 1991–caught 1 pass for 4 yards. 1992–recovered 1 fumble for 0 yards; returned 1 kickoff for 5 yards. 1995–fumbled 2 times for -6 yards.

Barry Foster

Pos: RB   **Rnd:** 5   **College:** Arkansas   **Ht:** 5' 10" **Wt:** 218 **Born:** 12/8/68 **Age:** 27

			Rushing					Receiving					Kickoff Returns				Passing				Totals		
Year Team	G	GS	Att	Yds	Avg	Lg	TD	Rec	Yds	Avg	Lg	TD	Num	Yds	Avg	TD	Att	Com	Yds	Int	Fum	TD	Pts
1990 Pittsburgh Steelers	16	1	36	203	5.6	38	1	1	2	2.0	2	0	3	29	9.7	0	0	0	0	0	2	1	6
1991 Pittsburgh Steelers	10	9	96	488	5.1	t56	1	9	117	13.0	31	1	0	0	-	0	0	0	0	0	5	2	12
1992 Pittsburgh Steelers	16	15	390	1690	4.3	69	11	36	344	9.6	42	0	0	0	-	0	1	0	0	0	9	11	66
1993 Pittsburgh Steelers	9	9	177	711	4.0	38	8	27	217	8.0	21	1	0	0	-	0	0	0	0	0	3	9	54
1994 Pittsburgh Steelers	11	10	216	851	3.9	t29	5	20	124	6.2	27	0	0	0	-	0	0	0	0	0	0	5	30
5 NFL Seasons	62	44	915	3943	4.3	69	26	93	804	8.6	42	2	3	29	9.7	0	1	0	0	0	19	28	168

Other Statistics: 1990–recovered 1 fumble for 0 yards. 1991–recovered 1 fumble for 1 yard. 1992–recovered 2 fumbles for -20 yards.

Jamal Fountaine

Pos: DE   **Rnd:** FA   **College:** Washington   **Ht:** 6' 3" **Wt:** 240 **Born:** 1/29/71 **Age:** 25

			Tackles			Miscellaneous				Interceptions				Totals		
Year Team	G	GS	Tk	Ast	Sack	FF	FR	TD	Blk	Int	Yds	Avg	TD	Sfty	TD	Pts
1995 San Francisco 49ers	7	0	1	0	1.0	0	0	0	0	0	0	-	0	0	0	0

Mike Fox

(statistical profile on page 411)

Pos: DE   **Rnd:** 2   **College:** West Virginia   **Ht:** 6' 8"   **Wt:** 288   **Born:** 8/5/67   **Age:** 29

Year Team	G	GS	Tackles Tk	Ast	Sack	Miscellaneous FF	FR	TD	Blk	Interceptions Int	Yds	Avg	TD	Totals Sfty	TD	Pts
1990 New York Giants	16	0	4	2	1.5	1	0	0	0	0	0	-	0	0	0	0
1991 New York Giants	15	5	11	3	0.0	0	0	0	0	0	0	-	0	0	0	0
1992 New York Giants	16	4	18	6	2.5	0	0	0	0	0	0	-	0	0	0	0
1993 New York Giants	16	16	22	10	4.5	0	1	0	0	0	0	-	0	0	0	0
1994 New York Giants	16	16	29	11	1.0	1	0	0	0	0	0	-	0	0	0	0
1995 Carolina Panthers	16	16	42	11	4.5	0	0	0	0	0	0	-	0	0	0	0
6 NFL Seasons	95	57	126	43	14.0	2	1	0	0	0	0	-	0	0	0	0

Dion Foxx

Pos: LB   **Rnd:** FA   **College:** James Madison   **Ht:** 6' 3"   **Wt:** 250   **Born:** 6/11/71   **Age:** 25

Year Team	G	GS	Tackles Tk	Ast	Sack	Miscellaneous FF	FR	TD	Blk	Interceptions Int	Yds	Avg	TD	Totals Sfty	TD	Pts
1994 Miami Dolphins	16	0	0	0	0.0	0	0	0	0	0	0	-	0	0	0	0
1995 Mia - Was	4	0	0	1	0.5	0	0	0	0	0	0	-	0	0	0	0
1995 Miami Dolphins	2	0	0	1	0.5	0	0	0	0	0	0	-	0	0	0	0
Washington Redskins	2	0	0	0	0.0	0	0	0	0	0	0	-	0	0	0	0
2 NFL Seasons	20	0	0	1	0.5	0	0	0	0	0	0	-	0	0	0	0

James Francis

Pos: LB   **Rnd:** 1 (12)   **College:** Baylor   **Ht:** 6' 5"   **Wt:** 252   **Born:** 8/4/68   **Age:** 28

Year Team	G	GS	Tackles Tk	Ast	Sack	Miscellaneous FF	FR	TD	Blk	Interceptions Int	Yds	Avg	TD	Totals Sfty	TD	Pts
1990 Cincinnati Bengals	16	16	63	15	8.0	0	0	0	0	1	17	17.0	1	1	1	8
1991 Cincinnati Bengals	16	16	50	18	3.0	0	1	0	0	1	0	0.0	0	0	0	0
1992 Cincinnati Bengals	14	13	33	6	6.0	4	2	0	0	3	108	36.0	1	0	1	6
1993 Cincinnati Bengals	14	12	35	6	2.0	0	1	0	0	2	12	6.0	0	0	0	0
1994 Cincinnati Bengals	16	16	87	14	4.5	2	0	0	0	0	0	-	0	0	0	0
1995 Cincinnati Bengals	11	11	55	10	3.0	1	0	0	0	0	0	-	0	0	0	0
6 NFL Seasons	87	84	323	69	26.5	7	4	0	0	7	137	19.6	2	1	2	14

Donald Frank

Pos: CB   **Rnd:** FA   **College:** Winston-Salem State   **Ht:** 6' 0"   **Wt:** 192   **Born:** 10/24/65   **Age:** 31

Year Team	G	GS	Tackles Tk	Ast	Sack	Misc FF	FR	TD	Blk	Interceptions Int	Yds	Avg	TD	Punt Returns Num	Yds	Avg	TD	Kickoff Returns Num	Yds	Avg	TD	Totals TD	Fum
1990 San Diego Chargers	16	2	25	2	0.0	0	0	0	0	2	8	4.0	0	0	0	-	0	8	172	21.5	0	0	0
1991 San Diego Chargers	16	1	40	1	0.0	0	0	0	0	1	71	71.0	1	0	0	-	0	0	0	-	0	1	0
1992 San Diego Chargers	16	0	26	3	0.0	0	0	0	0	4	37	9.3	0	0	0	-	0	0	0	-	0	0	0
1993 San Diego Chargers	16	16	65	8	0.0	0	0	0	0	3	119	39.7	1	0	0	-	0	0	0	-	0	1	0
1994 Los Angeles Raiders	16	0	7	0	0.0	0	1	0	0	1	8	8.0	0	0	0	-	0	0	0	-	0	0	0
1995 Minnesota Vikings	12	5	31	2	0.0	0	0	0	0	3	72	24.0	0	0	0	-	0	0	0	-	0	0	0
6 NFL Seasons	92	24	194	16	0.0	0	1	0	0	14	315	22.5	2	0	0	-	0	8	172	21.5	0	2	0

Keith Franklin

Pos: LB   **Rnd:** FA   **College:** South Carolina   **Ht:** 6' 2"   **Wt:** 230   **Born:** 3/4/70   **Age:** 26

Year Team	G	GS	Tackles Tk	Ast	Sack	Miscellaneous FF	FR	TD	Blk	Interceptions Int	Yds	Avg	TD	Totals Sfty	TD	Pts
1995 Oakland Raiders	2	0	0	0	0.0	0	0	0	0	0	0	-	0	0	0	0

Paul Frase

Pos: DE/DT   **Rnd:** 6   **College:** Syracuse   **Ht:** 6' 5"   **Wt:** 276   **Born:** 5/5/65   **Age:** 31

Year Team	G	GS	Tackles Tk	Ast	Sack	Miscellaneous FF	FR	TD	Blk	Interceptions Int	Yds	Avg	TD	Totals Sfty	TD	Pts
1988 New York Jets	16	7	23	8	1.0	0	0	0	0	0	0	-	0	0	0	0
1989 New York Jets	16	14	46	13	2.0	0	0	0	0	0	0	-	0	0	0	0
1991 New York Jets	16	2	15	3	0.0	0	0	0	0	0	0	-	0	0	0	0
1992 New York Jets	16	12	34	13	5.0	0	0	0	0	0	0	-	0	0	0	0
1993 New York Jets	16	4	27	13	1.0	1	2	0	0	0	0	-	0	0	0	0
1994 New York Jets	16	5	14	2	1.0	0	1	0	0	0	0	-	0	0	0	0
1995 Jacksonville Jaguars	9	5	12	5	1.0	2	0	0	0	0	0	-	0	0	0	0
7 NFL Seasons	105	49	171	57	11.0	3	3	0	0	0	0	-	0	0	0	0

Other Statistics: 1991–fumbled 1 time for 0 yards.

Derrick Frazier

Pos: CB **Rnd:** 3 **College:** Texas A&M **Ht:** 5' 10" **Wt:** 172 **Born:** 4/29/70 **Age:** 26

Year Team	G	GS	Tackles			Miscellaneous				Interceptions				Totals		
			Tk	Ast	Sack	FF	FR	TD	Blk	Int	Yds	Avg	TD	Sfty	TD	Pts
1994 Philadelphia Eagles	13	0	1	2	0.0	0	1	0	0	0	0	-	0	0	0	0
1995 Philadelphia Eagles	7	4	23	3	0.0	0	0	0	0	1	3	3.0	0	0	0	0
2 NFL Seasons	20	4	24	5	0.0	0	1	0	0	1	3	3.0	0	0	0	0

Mike Frederick

Pos: DE **Rnd:** 3 **College:** Virginia **Ht:** 6' 5" **Wt:** 280 **Born:** 8/6/72 **Age:** 24

Year Team	G	GS	Tackles			Miscellaneous				Interceptions				Punt Returns				Kickoff Returns				Totals	
			Tk	Ast	Sack	FF	FR	TD	Blk	Int	Yds	Avg	TD	Num	Yds	Avg	TD	Num	Yds	Avg	TD	TD	Fum
1995 Cleveland Browns	16	0	8	4	1.5	0	0	0	0	0	0	-	0	0	0	-	0	2	16	8.0	0	0	0

Rob Fredrickson

(statistical profile on page 411)

Pos: LB **Rnd:** 1 (22) **College:** Michigan State **Ht:** 6' 4" **Wt:** 240 **Born:** 5/13/71 **Age:** 25

Year Team	G	GS	Tackles			Miscellaneous				Interceptions				Totals		
			Tk	Ast	Sack	FF	FR	TD	Blk	Int	Yds	Avg	TD	Sfty	TD	Pts
1994 Los Angeles Raiders	16	12	58	23	3.0	1	0	0	0	0	0	-	0	0	0	0
1995 Oakland Raiders	16	15	71	14	0.0	0	4	1	0	1	14	14.0	0	0	1	6
2 NFL Seasons	32	27	129	37	3.0	1	4	1	0	1	14	14.0	0	0	1	6

Antonio Freeman

Pos: PR/KR **Rnd:** 3 **College:** Virginia Tech **Ht:** 6' 0" **Wt:** 187 **Born:** 5/27/72 **Age:** 24

Year Team	G	GS	Rushing					Receiving					Punt Returns				Kickoff Returns				Totals		
			Att	Yds	Avg	Lg	TD	Rec	Yds	Avg	Lg	TD	Num	Yds	Avg	TD	Num	Yds	Avg	TD	Fum	TD	Pts
1995 Green Bay Packers	11	0	0	0	-	-	0	8	106	13.3	28	1	37	292	7.9	0	24	556	23.2	0	7	1	6

Other Statistics: 1995–recovered 4 fumbles for 0 yards.

Russell Freeman

Pos: T **Rnd:** FA **College:** Georgia Tech **Ht:** 6' 7" **Wt:** 290 **Born:** 9/2/69 **Age:** 27

Year	Team	G	GS	Year	Team	G	GS	Year	Team	G	GS	Year	Team	G	GS
1992	Denver Broncos	16	16	1993	Denver Broncos	14	14	1994	Denver Broncos	13	7	1995	Oakland Raiders	15	1
													4 NFL Seasons	58	38

Gus Frerotte

(statistical profile on page 315)

Pos: QB **Rnd:** 7 **College:** Tulsa **Ht:** 6' 2" **Wt:** 221 **Born:** 7/31/71 **Age:** 25

Year Team	G	GS	Passing										Rushing					Miscellaneous			
			Att	Com	Pct	Yards	Yds/Att	Lg	TD	Int	Int%	Rating	Att	Yds	Avg	Lg	TD	Sckd	Yds	Fum	Recv	Yds	Pts
1994 Washington Redskins	5	4	100	46	46.0	600	6.00	51	5	5	5.0	61.3	4	1	0.3	10	1	3	18	4	2	-4	0
1995 Washington Redskins	16	11	396	199	50.3	2751	6.95	t73	13	13	3.3	70.2	22	16	0.7	10	1	23	192	7	4	-3	6
2 NFL Seasons	21	15	496	245	49.4	3351	6.76	t73	18	18	3.6	68.4	26	17	0.7	10	1	26	210	11	6	-7	6

John Friesz

(statistical profile on page 315)

Pos: QB **Rnd:** 6 **College:** Idaho **Ht:** 6' 4" **Wt:** 220 **Born:** 5/19/67 **Age:** 29

Year Team	G	GS	Passing										Rushing					Miscellaneous			
			Att	Com	Pct	Yards	Yds/Att	Lg	TD	Int	Int%	Rating	Att	Yds	Avg	Lg	TD	Sckd	Yds	Fum	Recv	Yds	Pts
1990 San Diego Chargers	1	1	22	11	50.0	98	4.45	17	1	1	4.5	58.5	1	3	3.0	3	0	1	7	0	0	0	0
1991 San Diego Chargers	16	16	487	262	53.8	2896	5.95	58	12	15	3.1	67.1	10	18	1.8	11	0	32	214	10	2	-21	0
1993 San Diego Chargers	12	6	238	128	53.8	1402	5.89	t66	6	4	1.7	72.8	10	3	0.3	2	0	14	98	2	1	-3	0
1994 Washington Redskins	15	4	180	105	58.3	1266	7.03	t73	10	9	5.0	77.7	1	1	1.0	1	0	6	45	2	1	0	0
1995 Seattle Seahawks	6	3	120	64	53.3	795	6.63	t43	6	3	2.5	80.4	11	0	0.0	2	0	3	12	2	1	-3	0
5 NFL Seasons	50	30	1047	570	54.4	6457	6.17	t73	35	32	3.1	71.6	33	25	0.8	11	0	56	376	16	5	-27	0

David Frisch

Pos: TE **Rnd:** FA **College:** Colorado State **Ht:** 6' 7" **Wt:** 260 **Born:** 6/22/70 **Age:** 26

Year Team	G	GS	Rushing					Receiving					Punt Returns				Kickoff Returns				Totals		
			Att	Yds	Avg	Lg	TD	Rec	Yds	Avg	Lg	TD	Num	Yds	Avg	TD	Num	Yds	Avg	TD	Fum	TD	Pts
1993 Cincinnati Bengals	11	2	0	0	-	-	0	6	43	7.2	12	0	0	0	-	0	0	0	-	0	0	0	0
1994 Cincinnati Bengals	16	0	0	0	-	-	0	0	0	-	-	0	0	0	-	0	0	0	-	0	0	0	0
1995 New England Patriots	2	0	0	0	-	-	0	0	0	-	-	0	0	0	-	0	1	8	8.0	0	0	0	0
3 NFL Seasons	29	2	0	0	-	-	0	6	43	7.2	12	0	0	0	-	0	1	8	8.0	0	0	0	0

Irving Fryar

(statistical profile on page 316)

Pos: WR   **Rnd:** 1 (1)   **College:** Nebraska   **Ht:** 6' 0"   **Wt:** 200   **Born:** 9/28/62   **Age:** 34

				Rushing					Receiving					Punt Returns				Kickoff Returns				Totals		
Year	Team	G	GS	Att	Yds	Avg	Lg	TD	Rec	Yds	Avg	Lg	TD	Num	Yds	Avg	TD	Num	Yds	Avg	TD	Fum	TD	Pts
1984	New England Patriots	14	2	2	-11	-5.5	0	0	11	164	14.9	26	1	36	347	9.6	0	5	95	19.0	0	4	1	6
1985	New England Patriots	16	14	7	27	3.9	13	1	39	670	17.2	56	7	37	520	14.1	2	3	39	13.0	0	4	10	60
1986	New England Patriots	14	13	4	80	20.0	31	0	43	737	17.1	t69	6	35	366	10.5	1	10	192	19.2	0	4	7	42
1987	New England Patriots	12	12	9	52	5.8	16	0	31	467	15.1	40	5	18	174	9.7	0	6	119	19.8	0	2	5	30
1988	New England Patriots	15	14	6	12	2.0	6	0	33	490	14.8	t80	5	38	398	10.5	0	1	3	3.0	0	2	5	30
1989	New England Patriots	11	5	2	15	7.5	11	0	29	537	18.5	52	3	12	107	8.9	0	1	47	47.0	0	2	3	18
1990	New England Patriots	16	15	2	-4	-2.0	-1	0	54	856	15.9	56	4	28	133	4.8	0	0	0	-	0	1	4	24
1991	New England Patriots	16	15	2	11	5.5	9	0	68	1014	14.9	t56	3	2	10	5.0	0	0	0	-	0	2	3	18
1992	New England Patriots	15	14	1	6	6.0	8	0	55	791	14.4	t54	4	0	0	-	0	0	0	-	0	0	4	24
1993	Miami Dolphins	16	16	3	-4	-1.3	2	0	64	1010	15.8	t65	5	0	0	-	0	1	10	10.0	0	0	5	30
1994	Miami Dolphins	16	16	0	0	-	-	0	73	1270	17.4	t54	7	0	0	-	0	0	0	-	0	0	7	46
1995	Miami Dolphins	16	16	0	0	-	-	0	62	910	14.7	t67	8	0	0	-	0	0	0	-	0	0	8	48
	12 NFL Seasons	177	152	38	184	4.8	31	1	562	8916	15.9	t80	58	206	2055	10.0	3	27	505	18.7	0	21	62	376

Other Statistics: 1984–recovered 1 fumble for 0 yards. 1986–recovered 1 fumble for 0 yards. 1990–recovered 1 fumble for 0 yards. 1991–attempted 1 pass with 0 completions for 0 yards. 1994–recovered 1 fumble for 7 yards; scored 2 two-point conversions.

Corey Fuller

(statistical profile on page 412)

Pos: CB   **Rnd:** 2   **College:** Florida State   **Ht:** 5' 10"   **Wt:** 197   **Born:** 5/11/71   **Age:** 25

				Tackles			Miscellaneous				Interceptions				Totals		
Year	Team	G	GS	Tk	Ast	Sack	FF	FR	TD	Blk	Int	Yds	Avg	TD	Sfty	TD	Pts
1995	Minnesota Vikings	16	11	57	9	0.5	2	1	1	0	1	0	0.0	0	0	1	6

Randy Fuller

(statistical profile on page 412)

Pos: DB/CB   **Rnd:** 4   **College:** Tennessee State   **Ht:** 5' 9"   **Wt:** 173   **Born:** 6/2/70   **Age:** 26

				Tackles			Miscellaneous				Interceptions				Totals		
Year	Team	G	GS	Tk	Ast	Sack	FF	FR	TD	Blk	Int	Yds	Avg	TD	Sfty	TD	Pts
1994	Denver Broncos	10	1	15	2	0.0	0	0	0	0	0	0	-	0	0	0	0
1995	Pittsburgh Steelers	13	0	7	1	0.0	0	0	0	0	0	0	-	0	0	0	0
	2 NFL Seasons	23	1	22	3	0.0	0	0	0	0	0	0	-	0	0	0	0

William Fuller

(statistical profile on page 412)

Pos: DE   **Rnd:** 1(S)   **College:** North Carolina   **Ht:** 6' 3"   **Wt:** 280   **Born:** 3/8/62   **Age:** 34

				Tackles			Miscellaneous				Interceptions				Punt Returns				Kickoff Returns				Totals	
Year	Team	G	GS	Tk	Ast	Sack	FF	FR	TD	Blk	Int	Yds	Avg	TD	Num	Yds	Avg	TD	Num	Yds	Avg	TD	TD	Fum
1986	Houston Oilers	13	0	9	13	1.0	0	0	0	0	0	0	-	0	0	0	-	0	0	0	-	0	0	0
1987	Houston Oilers	12	1	13	9	2.0	0	1	0	0	0	0	-	0	0	0	-	0	1	0	0.0	0	0	0
1988	Houston Oilers	16	15	40	16	8.5	2	0	0	0	1	9	9.0	0	0	0	-	0	0	0	-	0	0	0
1989	Houston Oilers	15	8	31	11	6.5	1	0	0	0	0	0	-	0	0	0	-	0	0	0	-	0	0	0
1990	Houston Oilers	16	16	31	19	8.0	0	1	0	0	0	0	-	0	0	0	-	0	0	0	-	0	0	0
1991	Houston Oilers	16	16	40	14	15.0	1	2	0	0	0	0	-	0	0	0	-	0	0	0	-	0	0	0
1992	Houston Oilers	15	14	42	10	8.0	1	1	1	0	0	0	-	0	0	0	-	0	0	0	-	0	0	0
1993	Houston Oilers	16	16	29	8	10.0	2	0	0	0	0	0	-	0	0	0	-	0	0	0	-	0	0	1
1994	Philadelphia Eagles	16	16	44	6	10.5	4	1	0	0	0	0	-	0	0	0	-	0	0	0	-	0	0	0
1995	Philadelphia Eagles	14	13	35	11	13.0	5	1	0	0	0	0	-	0	0	0	-	0	0	0	-	0	0	0
	10 NFL Seasons	149	115	314	117	82.5	16	7	1	0	1	9	9.0	0	0	0	-	0	1	0	0.0	0	1	0

Other Statistics: 1994–credited with 1 safety.

Will Furrer

(statistical profile on page 316)

Pos: QB   **Rnd:** 4   **College:** Virginia Tech   **Ht:** 6' 3"   **Wt:** 210   **Born:** 2/5/68   **Age:** 28

				Passing										Rushing					Miscellaneous			
Year	Team	G	GS	Att	Com	Pct	Yards	Yds/Att	Lg	TD	Int	Int%	Rating	Att	Yds	Avg	Lg	TD	Sckd	Yds	Fum Recv	Yds	Pts
1992	Chicago Bears	2	1	25	9	36.0	89	3.56	16	0	3	12.0	7.3	0	0	-	0	4	39	1	0	0	0
1994	Denver Broncos	1	0	0	0	-	0	-	-	0	0	-	0.0	0	0	-	0	0	0	0	0	0	0
1995	Houston Oilers	7	1	99	48	48.5	483	4.88	48	2	7	7.1	40.1	8	20	2.5	11	0	5	35	3	0	0
	3 NFL Seasons	10	2	124	57	46.0	572	4.61	48	2	10	8.1	31.4	8	20	2.5	11	0	9	74	4	0	0

Wendall Gaines

Pos: TE   **Rnd:** FA   **College:** Oklahoma State   **Ht:** 6' 4"   **Wt:** 293   **Born:** 1/17/72   **Age:** 24

				Rushing					Receiving					Punt Returns				Kickoff Returns				Totals		
Year	Team	G	GS	Att	Yds	Avg	Lg	TD	Rec	Yds	Avg	Lg	TD	Num	Yds	Avg	TD	Num	Yds	Avg	TD	Fum	TD	Pts
1995	Arizona Cardinals	16	11	0	0	-	-	0	14	117	8.4	t22	2	0	0	-	0	0	0	-	0	0	2	12

Other Statistics: 1995–recovered 1 fumble for 0 yards.

William Gaines

Pos: DT **Rnd:** 5 **College:** Florida **Ht:** 6' 5" **Wt:** 294 **Born:** 6/20/71 **Age:** 25

Year Team	G	GS	Tackles Tk	Ast	Sack	Miscellaneous FF	FR	TD	Blk	Interceptions Int	Yds	Avg	TD	Totals Sfty	TD	Pts
1994 Miami Dolphins	8	0	2	0	0.0	0	0	0	0	0	0	-	0	0	0	0
1995 Washington Redskins	15	11	21	2	2.0	0	0	0	0	0	0	-	0	0	0	0
2 NFL Seasons	23	11	23	2	2.0	0	0	0	0	0	0	-	0	0	0	0

Scott Galbraith

Pos: TE **Rnd:** 7 **College:** Southern California **Ht:** 6' 2" **Wt:** 255 **Born:** 1/7/67 **Age:** 29

Year Team	G	GS	Rushing Att	Yds	Avg	Lg	TD	Receiving Rec	Yds	Avg	Lg	TD	Punt Returns Num	Yds	Avg	TD	Kickoff Returns Num	Yds	Avg	TD	Totals Fum	TD	Pts
1990 Cleveland Browns	16	1	0	0	-	-	0	4	62	15.5	28	0	0	0	-	0	3	16	5.3	0	0	0	0
1991 Cleveland Browns	16	13	0	0	-	-	0	27	328	12.1	42	0	0	0	-	0	2	13	6.5	0	0	0	0
1992 Cleveland Browns	14	2	0	0	-	-	0	4	63	15.8	28	1	0	0	-	0	0	0	-	0	0	1	6
1993 Dallas Cowboys	7	0	0	0	-	-	0	1	1	1.0	t1	1	0	0	-	0	0	0	-	0	0	1	6
1994 Dallas Cowboys	15	2	0	0	-	-	0	4	31	7.8	15	0	0	0	-	0	0	0	-	0	0	0	0
1995 Washington Redskins	16	16	0	0	-	-	0	10	80	8.0	25	2	0	0	-	0	0	0	-	0	0	2	12
6 NFL Seasons	84	34	0	0	-	-	0	50	565	11.3	42	4	0	0	-	0	5	29	5.8	0	0	4	24

Other Statistics: 1990–recovered 1 fumble for 0 yards. 1991–recovered 1 fumble for 0 yards.

Harry Galbreath

Pos: G **Rnd:** 8 **College:** Tennessee **Ht:** 6' 1" **Wt:** 295 **Born:** 1/1/65 **Age:** 31

Year	Team	G	GS	Year	Team	G	GS	Year	Team	G	GS	Year	Team	G	GS
1988	Miami Dolphins	16	13	1990	Miami Dolphins	16	16	1992	Miami Dolphins	16	16	1994	Green Bay Packers	16	16
1989	Miami Dolphins	14	16	1991	Miami Dolphins	16	16	1993	Green Bay Packers	16	16	1995	Green Bay Packers	16	16
													8 NFL Seasons	126	125

Other Statistics: 1989–recovered 1 fumble for 0 yards.

Joey Galloway

(statistical profile on page 317)

Pos: WR/PR **Rnd:** 1 (8) **College:** Ohio State **Ht:** 5' 11" **Wt:** 188 **Born:** 11/20/71 **Age:** 24

Year Team	G	GS	Rushing Att	Yds	Avg	Lg	TD	Receiving Rec	Yds	Avg	Lg	TD	Punt Returns Num	Yds	Avg	TD	Kickoff Returns Num	Yds	Avg	TD	Totals Fum	TD	Pts
1995 Seattle Seahawks	16	16	11	154	14.0	t86	1	67	1039	15.5	t59	7	36	360	10.0	1	2	30	15.0	0	1	9	54

Kendall Gammon

Pos: C/LS **Rnd:** 11 **College:** Pittsburg State **Ht:** 6' 4" **Wt:** 286 **Born:** 10/23/68 **Age:** 28

Year	Team	G	GS	Year	Team	G	GS	Year	Team	G	GS	Year	Team	G	GS
1992	Pittsburgh Steelers	16	0	1993	Pittsburgh Steelers	16	0	1994	Pittsburgh Steelers	16	0	1995	Pittsburgh Steelers	16	0
													4 NFL Seasons	64	0

Wayne Gandy

Pos: T **Rnd:** 1 (15) **College:** Auburn **Ht:** 6' 4" **Wt:** 289 **Born:** 6/29/70 **Age:** 26

Year	Team	G	GS	Year	Team	G	GS			G	GS
1994	Los Angeles Rams	16	9	1995	St. Louis Rams	16	16				
									2 NFL Seasons	32	25

Rich Gannon

Pos: QB **Rnd:** 4 **College:** Delaware **Ht:** 6' 3" **Wt:** 208 **Born:** 12/20/65 **Age:** 30

Year Team	G	GS	Passing Att	Com	Pct	Yards	Yds/Att	Lg	TD	Int	Int%	Rating	Rushing Att	Yds	Avg	Lg	TD	Miscellaneous Sckd	Yds	Fum	Recv	Yds	Pts
1987 Minnesota Vikings	5	0	6	2	33.3	18	3.00	12	0	1	16.7	2.8	0	0	-	-	0	0	0	0	0	0	0
1988 Minnesota Vikings	3	0	15	7	46.7	90	6.00	19	0	0	0.0	66.0	4	29	7.3	15	0	3	22	0	0	0	0
1990 Minnesota Vikings	14	1	349	182	52.1	2278	6.53	78	16	16	4.6	68.9	52	268	5.2	21	1	34	188	10	6	-3	6
1991 Minnesota Vikings	15	11	354	211	59.6	2166	6.12	50	12	6	1.7	81.5	43	236	5.5	42	2	19	91	2	0	0	12
1992 Minnesota Vikings	12	12	279	159	57.0	1905	6.83	t60	12	13	4.7	72.9	45	187	4.2	14	0	£5	177	5	0	0	0
1993 Washington Redskins	8	4	125	74	59.2	704	5.63	54	3	7	5.6	59.5	21	88	4.2	12	1	16	87	3	1	0	6
1995 Kansas City Chiefs	2	0	11	7	63.6	57	5.18	18	0	0	0.0	76.7	8	25	3.1	t12	1	0	0	0	0	0	6
7 NFL Seasons	59	28	1139	642	56.4	7218	6.34	t78	43	43	3.8	72.3	173	833	4.8	42	5	97	565	20	7	-3	30

Other Statistics: 1991–caught 1 pass for 0 yards.

Kenneth Gant

Pos: S **Rnd:** 9 **College:** Albany State **Ht:** 5' 11" **Wt:** 189 **Born:** 4/18/67 **Age:** 29

Year Team	G	GS	Tackles Tk	Ast	Sack	Miscellaneous FF	FR	TD	Blk	Interceptions Int	Yds	Avg	TD	Punt Returns Num	Yds	Avg	TD	Kickoff Returns Num	Yds	Avg	TD	Totals TD	Fum
1990 Dallas Cowboys	12	0	9	0	0.0	0	0	0	0	1	26	26.0	0	0	0	-	0	0	0	-	0	0	0

Year	Team	G	GS	Tackles			Miscellaneous				Interceptions				Punt Returns				Kickoff Returns			Totals	
				Tk	Ast	Sack	FF	FR	TD	Blk	Int	Yds	Avg	TD	Num	Yds	Avg	TD	Num	Yds	Avg TD	TD	Fum
1991	Dallas Cowboys	16	1	9	5	0.0	0	1	0	0	1	0	0.0	0	0	0	-	0	6	114	19.0 0	0	0
1992	Dallas Cowboys	16	4	33	21	3.0	0	1	0	0	3	19	6.3	0	0	0	-	0	0	0	- 0	0	0
1993	Dallas Cowboys	12	1	25	18	0.0	1	0	0	0	1	0	0.0	0	0	0	-	0	1	18	18.0 0	0	0
1994	Dallas Cowboys	16	0	10	1	0.0	0	0	0	0	1	0	0.0	0	0	0	-	0	0	0	- 0	0	0
1995	Tampa Bay Buccaneers	16	3	22	6	0.0	0	1	0	0	0	0	-	0	0	0	-	0	0	0	- 0	0	0
	6 NFL Seasons	88	9	108	51	3.0	1	3	0	0	7	45	6.4	0	0	0	-	0	7	132	18.9 0	0	0

Frank Garcia

Pos: G/C **Rnd:** 4 **College:** Washington   **Ht:** 6' 1" **Wt:** 290 **Born:** 1/28/72 **Age:** 24

Year	Team	G	GS										
1995	Carolina Panthers	15	14							1 NFL Season		G 15	GS 14

Other Statistics: 1995–recovered 1 fumble for 10 yards; fumbled 1 time.

Carwell Gardner

Pos: RB **Rnd:** 2 **College:** Louisville   **Ht:** 6' 2" **Wt:** 240 **Born:** 11/27/66 **Age:** 29

Year	Team	G	GS	Rushing					Receiving					Punt Returns				Kickoff Returns				Totals		
				Att	Yds	Avg	Lg	TD	Rec	Yds	Avg	Lg	TD	Num	Yds	Avg	TD	Num	Yds	Avg	TD	Fum	TD	Pts
1990	Buffalo Bills	7	0	15	41	2.7	14	0	0	0	-	-	0	0	0	-	0	0	0	-	0	0	0	0
1991	Buffalo Bills	16	5	42	146	3.5	18	4	3	20	6.7	11	0	0	0	-	0	1	10	10.0	0	4	4	24
1992	Buffalo Bills	16	7	40	166	4.2	19	2	7	67	9.6	17	0	0	0	-	0	0	0	-	0	2	2	12
1993	Buffalo Bills	13	2	20	56	2.8	8	0	4	50	12.5	22	1	0	0	-	0	0	0	-	0	1	1	6
1994	Buffalo Bills	16	7	41	135	3.3	13	4	11	89	8.1	21	0	0	0	-	0	1	6	6.0	0	1	4	24
1995	Buffalo Bills	15	4	20	77	3.9	17	0	2	17	8.5	13	0	0	0	-	0	0	0	-	0	0	1	8
	6 NFL Seasons	83	25	178	621	3.5	19	10	27	243	9.0	22	1	0	0	-	0	2	16	8.0	0	6	12	74

Other Statistics: 1991–recovered 3 fumbles for 0 yards. 1992–recovered 2 fumbles for 0 yards. 1995–recovered 2 fumbles for 0 yards and 1 touchdown; scored 1 two-point conversion.

Moe Gardner

Pos: DT **Rnd:** 4 **College:** Illinois   **Ht:** 6' 2" **Wt:** 265 **Born:** 8/10/68 **Age:** 28

Year	Team	G	GS	Tackles			Miscellaneous				Interceptions				Totals		
				Tk	Ast	Sack	FF	FR	TD	Blk	Int	Yds	Avg	TD	Sfty	TD	Pts
1991	Atlanta Falcons	16	13	51	45	3.0	0	0	0	0	0	0	-	0	0	0	0
1992	Atlanta Falcons	16	14	47	64	4.5	0	0	0	0	0	0	-	0	0	0	0
1993	Atlanta Falcons	16	16	63	65	2.0	1	0	0	0	0	0	-	0	0	0	0
1994	Atlanta Falcons	16	16	36	14	0.0	0	1	0	0	0	0	-	0	0	0	0
1995	Atlanta Falcons	16	15	28	10	0.5	0	0	0	0	0	0	-	0	0	0	0
	5 NFL Seasons	80	74	225	198	10.0	1	1	0	0	0	0	-	0	0	0	0

Chris Gardocki

(statistical profile on page 473)

Pos: P **Rnd:** 3 **College:** Clemson   **Ht:** 6' 1" **Wt:** 199 **Born:** 2/7/70 **Age:** 26

Year	Team	G	Punting												Rushing		Passing			
			NetPunts	Yards	Avg	Long	In20	In20%	TotPunts	TB	Blocks	OppRet	RetYds	NetAvg	Att	Yards	Att	Com	Yards	Int
1991	Chicago Bears	4	0	0	-	-	-	-	0	-	0	0	0	-	0	0	0	0	0	0
1992	Chicago Bears	16	79	3393	42.9	61	19	24.1	79	9	0	38	351	36.2	0	0	3	1	43	0
1993	Chicago Bears	16	80	3080	38.5	58	28	35.0	80	2	0	22	115	36.6	0	0	2	0	0	0
1994	Chicago Bears	16	76	2871	37.8	57	23	30.3	76	9	0	26	225	32.4	0	0	0	0	0	0
1995	Indianapolis Colts	16	63	2681	42.6	69	16	25.4	63	7	0	37	436	33.4	0	0	1	0	0	0
	5 NFL Seasons	68	298	12025	40.4	69	86	28.9	298	27	0	123	1127	34.8	0	0	6	1	43	0

Other Statistics: 1992–recovered 1 fumble for 0 yards. 1993–recovered 1 fumble for 0 yards; fumbled 1 time.

Charlie Garner

(statistical profile on page 317)

Pos: RB/KR **Rnd:** 2 **College:** Tennessee   **Ht:** 5' 9" **Wt:** 187 **Born:** 2/13/72 **Age:** 24

Year	Team	G	GS	Rushing					Receiving					Punt Returns				Kickoff Returns				Totals		
				Att	Yds	Avg	Lg	TD	Rec	Yds	Avg	Lg	TD	Num	Yds	Avg	TD	Num	Yds	Avg	TD	Fum	TD	Pts
1994	Philadelphia Eagles	10	8	109	399	3.7	t28	3	8	74	9.3	28	0	0	0	-	0	0	0	-	0	3	3	18
1995	Philadelphia Eagles	15	2	108	588	5.4	t55	6	10	61	6.1	29	0	0	0	-	0	29	590	20.3	0	2	6	36
	2 NFL Seasons	25	10	217	987	4.5	t55	9	18	135	7.5	29	0	0	0	-	0	29	590	20.3	0	5	9	54

Dave Garnett

Pos: LB **Rnd:** FA **College:** Stanford   **Ht:** 6' 2" **Wt:** 219 **Born:** 12/6/70 **Age:** 25

Year	Team	G	GS	Tackles			Miscellaneous				Interceptions				Punt Returns				Kickoff Returns				Totals	
				Tk	Ast	Sack	FF	FR	TD	Blk	Int	Yds	Avg	TD	Num	Yds	Avg	TD	Num	Yds	Avg	TD	TD	Fum
1993	Minnesota Vikings	16	0	6	5	0.0	0	0	0	0	0	0	-	0	0	0	-	0	0	0	-	0	0	0
1994	Minnesota Vikings	9	0	5	2	0.0	0	2	0	0	0	0	-	0	0	0	-	0	1	0	0.0	0	0	0
1995	Denver Broncos	3	0	2	1	0.0	0	0	0	0	0	0	-	0	0	0	-	0	0	0	-	0	0	0

Year	Team	G	GS	Tackles Tk	Ast	Sack	Miscellaneous FF	FR	TD	Blk	Interceptions Int	Yds	Avg	TD	Punt Returns Num	Yds	Avg	TD	Kickoff Returns Num	Yds	Avg	TD	Totals TD	Fum
	3 NFL Seasons	28	0	13	8	0.0	0	2	0	0	0	0	-	0	0	0	-	0	1	0	0.0	0	0	0

Jason Garrett

Pos: QB **Rnd:** FA **College:** Princeton **Ht:** 6' 2" **Wt:** 195 **Born:** 3/28/66 **Age:** 30

Year	Team	G	GS	Passing Att	Com	Pct	Yards	Yds/Att	Lg	TD	Int	Int%	Rating	Rushing Att	Yds	Avg	Lg	TD	Miscellaneous Sckd	Yds	Fum	Recv	Yds	Pts
1993	Dallas Cowboys	5	1	19	9	47.4	61	3.21	16	0	0	0.0	54.9	8	-8	-1.0	0	0	1	6	1	0	-2	0
1994	Dallas Cowboys	2	1	31	16	51.6	315	10.16	68	2	1	3.2	95.5	3	-2	-0.7	0	0	2	13	0	1	0	0
1995	Dallas Cowboys	1	0	5	4	80.0	46	9.20	24	1	0	0.0	144.6	1	-1	-1.0	-1	0	0	0	0	0	0	0
	3 NFL Seasons	8	2	55	29	52.7	422	7.67	68	3	1	1.8	88.6	12	-11	-0.9	0	0	3	19	1	1	-2	0

Sam Gash

(statistical profile on page 318)

Pos: RB **Rnd:** 8 **College:** Penn State **Ht:** 5' 11" **Wt:** 224 **Born:** 3/7/69 **Age:** 27

Year	Team	G	GS	Rushing Att	Yds	Avg	Lg	TD	Receiving Rec	Yds	Avg	Lg	TD	Punt Returns Num	Yds	Avg	TD	Kickoff Returns Num	Yds	Avg	TD	Totals Fum	TD	Pts
1992	New England Patriots	15	0	5	7	1.4	4	1	0	0	-	0	0	0	0	-	0	0	0	-	0	1	1	6
1993	New England Patriots	15	4	48	149	3.1	14	1	14	93	6.6	15	0	0	0	-	0	0	0	-	0	1	1	6
1994	New England Patriots	13	6	30	86	2.9	10	0	9	61	6.8	19	0	0	0	-	0	1	9	9.0	0	1	0	6
1995	New England Patriots	15	12	8	24	3.0	9	0	26	242	9.3	30	1	0	0	-	0	0	0	-	0	0	1	6
	4 NFL Seasons	58	22	91	266	2.9	14	2	49	396	8.1	30	1	0	0	-	0	1	9	9.0	0	3	3	18

Other Statistics: 1992–recovered 2 fumbles for 0 yards. 1994–recovered 1 fumble for 0 yards.

Shaun Gayle

(statistical profile on page 412)

Pos: S **Rnd:** 10 **College:** Ohio State **Ht:** 5' 11" **Wt:** 202 **Born:** 3/8/62 **Age:** 34

Year	Team	G	GS	Tackles Tk	Ast	Sack	Miscellaneous FF	FR	TD	Blk	Interceptions Int	Yds	Avg	TD	Totals Sfty	TD	Pts
1984	Chicago Bears	15	6	14	5	0.0	0	0	0	0	1	-1	-1.0	0	0	0	0
1985	Chicago Bears	16	0	16	2	0.0	0	1	0	0	1	0	-	0	0	0	0
1986	Chicago Bears	16	0	9	5	0.0	1	1	0	0	1	13	13.0	0	0	0	0
1987	Chicago Bears	8	0	1	8	0.0	0	0	0	0	1	20	20.0	1	0	1	6
1988	Chicago Bears	4	4	11	11	0.0	0	0	0	0	1	0	0.0	0	0	0	0
1989	Chicago Bears	14	14	60	48	0.0	1	2	0	0	3	39	13.0	0	0	0	0
1990	Chicago Bears	16	16	73	52	1.0	4	3	0	0	2	5	2.5	0	0	0	0
1991	Chicago Bears	12	9	37	30	0.0	1	0	0	0	1	11	11.0	0	0	0	0
1992	Chicago Bears	11	11	48	52	0.0	0	3	0	0	2	39	19.5	0	0	0	0
1993	Chicago Bears	16	16	79	45	1.0	2	0	0	0	2	33	16.5	0	0	0	0
1994	Chicago Bears	16	16	65	14	0.0	2	1	0	0	2	33	16.5	0	0	0	0
1995	San Diego Chargers	16	16	73	12	0.0	0	1	1	0	2	99	49.5	1	0	2	12
	12 NFL Seasons	160	108	486	284	2.0	11	12	1	0	16	258	16.1	2	0	3	18

Jumpy Geathers

Pos: DT **Rnd:** 2 **College:** Wichita State **Ht:** 6' 7" **Wt:** 300 **Born:** 6/26/60 **Age:** 36

Year	Team	G	GS	Tackles Tk	Ast	Sack	Miscellaneous FF	FR	TD	Blk	Interceptions Int	Yds	Avg	TD	Totals Sfty	TD	Pts
1984	New Orleans Saints	16	0	10	1	6.0	0	0	0	0	0	0	-	0	0	0	0
1985	New Orleans Saints	16	0	25	4	6.5	0	0	0	0	0	0	-	0	0	0	0
1986	New Orleans Saints	16	2	24	8	9.0	0	1	0	0	0	0	-	0	0	0	0
1987	New Orleans Saints	1	0	1	0	0.0	0	0	0	0	0	0	-	0	0	0	0
1988	New Orleans Saints	16	6	26	7	3.5	0	3	0	0	0	0	-	0	0	0	0
1989	New Orleans Saints	15	15	16	7	1.0	0	5	0	0	0	0	-	0	0	0	0
1990	Washington Redskins	9	1	2	1	3.0	0	0	0	0	0	0	-	0	0	0	0
1991	Washington Redskins	16	0	15	6	4.5	0	0	0	0	0	0	-	0	0	0	0
1992	Washington Redskins	16	0	4	10	5.0	0	0	0	0	0	0	-	0	0	0	0
1993	Atlanta Falcons	13	0	16	11	3.5	1	0	0	0	0	0	-	0	0	0	0
1994	Atlanta Falcons	16	1	27	6	8.0	2	0	0	0	0	0	-	0	0	0	0
1995	Atlanta Falcons	16	2	26	4	7.0	2	0	0	0	0	0	-	0	0	0	0
	12 NFL Seasons	166	27	192	65	57.0	5	9	0	0	0	0	-	0	0	0	0

Chris Gedney

Pos: TE/LS **Rnd:** 3 **College:** Syracuse **Ht:** 6' 5" **Wt:** 265 **Born:** 8/9/70 **Age:** 26

Year	Team	G	GS	Rushing Att	Yds	Avg	Lg	TD	Receiving Rec	Yds	Avg	Lg	TD	Punt Returns Num	Yds	Avg	TD	Kickoff Returns Num	Yds	Avg	TD	Totals Fum	TD	Pts
1993	Chicago Bears	7	3	0	0	-	0	0	10	98	9.8	24	0	0	0	-	0	0	0	-	0	1	0	0
1994	Chicago Bears	7	7	0	0	-	0	0	13	157	12.1	t37	3	0	0	-	0	0	0	-	0	1	3	18
1995	Chicago Bears	14	1	0	0	-	0	0	5	52	10.4	15	0	0	0	-	0	0	0	-	0	0	0	0

		G	GS	Rushing					Receiving					Punt Returns				Kickoff Returns				Totals		
Year	Team			Att	Yds	Avg	Lg	TD	Rec	Yds	Avg	Lg	TD	Num	Yds	Avg	TD	Num	Yds	Avg	TD	Fum	TD	Pts
	3 NFL Seasons	28	11	0	0	-	-	0	28	307	11.0	t37	3	0	0	0	-	0	0	0	-	0	2	3	18

Jeff George

(statistical profile on page 318)

Pos: QB **Rnd:** 1 (1) **College:** Illinois **Ht:** 6' 4" **Wt:** 215 **Born:** 12/8/67 **Age:** 28

		G	GS	Passing									Rushing					Miscellaneous		
Year	Team			Att	Com	Pct	Yards	Yds/Att	Lg	TD	Int	Int%	Rating	Att	Yds	Avg	Lg	TD	Sckd	Yds	Fum	Recv	Yds	Pts
1990	Indianapolis Colts	13	12	334	181	54.2	2152	6.44	75	16	13	3.9	73.8	11	2	0.2	6	1	37	320	4	2	0	6
1991	Indianapolis Colts	16	16	485	292	60.2	2910	6.00	t49	10	12	2.5	73.8	16	36	2.3	13	0	56	481	8	2	-4	0
1992	Indianapolis Colts	10	10	306	167	54.6	1963	6.42	t57	7	15	4.9	61.5	14	26	1.9	13	1	27	188	6	1	-2	6
1993	Indianapolis Colts	13	11	407	234	57.5	2526	6.21	t72	8	6	1.5	76.3	13	39	3.0	14	0	26	190	4	0	-1	0
1994	Atlanta Falcons	16	16	524	322	61.5	3734	7.13	t85	23	18	3.4	83.3	30	66	2.2	10	0	32	206	12	6	-10	0
1995	Atlanta Falcons	16	16	557	336	60.3	4143	7.44	t62	24	11	2.0	89.5	27	17	0.6	6	0	43	270	6	2	-15	0
	6 NFL Seasons	84	81	2613	1532	58.6	17428	6.67	t85	88	75	2.9	78.0	111	186	1.7	14	2	221	1655	40	13	-32	12

Ron George

Pos: LB **Rnd:** 5 **College:** Stanford **Ht:** 6' 2" **Wt:** 235 **Born:** 3/20/70 **Age:** 26

		G	GS	Tackles			Miscellaneous				Interceptions				Punt Returns				Kickoff Returns				Totals	
Year	Team			Tk	Ast	Sack	FF	FR	TD	Blk	Int	Yds	Avg	TD	Num	Yds	Avg	TD	Num	Yds	Avg	TD	TD	Fum
1993	Atlanta Falcons	12	4	25	18	1.0	0	0	0	0	0	0	-	0	0	0	-	0	0	0	-	0	0	0
1994	Atlanta Falcons	16	9	31	6	0.0	0	1	0	0	0	0	-	0	0	0	-	0	0	0	-	0	0	0
1995	Atlanta Falcons	16	0	1	0	0.0	0	0	0	0	0	0	-	0	0	0	-	0	3	45	15.0	0	0	0
	3 NFL Seasons	44	13	57	24	1.0	0	1	0	0	0	0	-	0	0	0	-	0	3	45	15.0	0	0	0

John Gerak

Pos: G/TE **Rnd:** 3 **College:** Penn State **Ht:** 6' 3" **Wt:** 284 **Born:** 1/6/70 **Age:** 26

Year	Team	G	GS	Year	Team	G	GS	Year	Team	G	GS		G	GS
1993	Minnesota Vikings	4	0	1994	Minnesota Vikings	13	3	1995	Minnesota Vikings	15	6	3 NFL Seasons	32	9

Other Statistics: 1995–caught 1 pass for 3 yards; returned 1 kickoff for 19 yards.

John Gesek

Pos: C/G **Rnd:** 10 **College:** Sacramento State **Ht:** 6' 5" **Wt:** 282 **Born:** 2/18/63 **Age:** 33

Year	Team	G	GS	Year	Team	G	GS	Year	Team	G	GS		G	GS
1987	Los Angeles Raiders	3	1	1990	Dallas Cowboys	15	12	1993	Dallas Cowboys	14	0			
1988	Los Angeles Raiders	12	6	1991	Dallas Cowboys	16	15	1994	Washington Redskins	15	12			
1989	Los Angeles Raiders	16	16	1992	Dallas Cowboys	16	16	1995	Washington Redskins	16	16	9 NFL Seasons	123	94

Other Statistics: 1988–fumbled 1 time for 0 yards. 1990–recovered 2 fumbles for 0 yards. 1992–caught 1 pass for 4 yards; fumbled 1 time for 0 yards. 1994–recovered 1 fumble for 0 yards.

Dennis Gibson

(statistical profile on page 413)

Pos: LB **Rnd:** 8 **College:** Iowa State **Ht:** 6' 2" **Wt:** 240 **Born:** 2/8/64 **Age:** 32

		G	GS	Tackles			Miscellaneous				Interceptions				Totals		
Year	Team			Tk	Ast	Sack	FF	FR	TD	Blk	Int	Yds	Avg	TD	Sfty	TD	Pts
1987	Detroit Lions	12	12	68	14	1.0	0	0	0	0	1	5	5.0	0	0	0	0
1988	Detroit Lions	16	16	89	27	0.5	0	1	0	0	0	0	-	0	0	0	0
1989	Detroit Lions	6	6	25	4	0.0	0	3	0	0	1	10	10.0	0	0	0	0
1990	Detroit Lions	11	11	60	8	0.0	0	1	0	0	0	0	-	0	0	0	0
1991	Detroit Lions	16	16	36	26	0.0	0	0	0	0	0	0	-	0	0	0	0
1992	Detroit Lions	16	16	39	21	0.0	0	0	0	0	0	0	-	0	0	0	0
1993	Detroit Lions	15	15	38	21	1.0	1	1	0	0	1	0	0.0	0	0	0	0
1994	San Diego Chargers	16	15	51	17	0.0	0	0	0	0	0	0	-	0	0	0	0
1995	San Diego Chargers	13	13	55	14	0.0	0	0	0	0	0	0	-	0	0	0	0
	9 NFL Seasons	121	120	461	152	2.5	1	6	0	0	3	15	5.0	0	0	0	0

Oliver Gibson

Pos: DT **Rnd:** 4 **College:** Notre Dame **Ht:** 6' 2" **Wt:** 283 **Born:** 3/15/72 **Age:** 24

		G	GS	Tackles			Miscellaneous				Interceptions				Punt Returns				Kickoff Returns				Totals	
Year	Team			Tk	Ast	Sack	FF	FR	TD	Blk	Int	Yds	Avg	TD	Num	Yds	Avg	TD	Num	Yds	Avg	TD	TD	Fum
1995	Pittsburgh Steelers	12	0	1	1	0.0	0	0	0	0	0	0	-	0	0	0	-	0	1	10	10.0	0	0	0

Gale Gilbert

(statistical profile on page 319)

Pos: QB **Rnd:** FA **College:** California **Ht:** 6' 3" **Wt:** 209 **Born:** 12/20/61 **Age:** 34

		G	GS	Passing									Rushing					Miscellaneous		
Year	Team			Att	Com	Pct	Yards	Yds/Att	Lg	TD	Int	Int%	Rating	Att	Yds	Avg	Lg	TD	Sckd	Yds	Fum	Recv	Yds	Pts
1985	Seattle Seahawks	9	0	40	19	47.5	218	5.45	t37	1	2	5.0	51.9	7	4	0.6	8	0	1	9	1	1	-5	0

Year	Team	G	GS	Att	Com	Pct	Yards	Yds/Att	Lg	TD	Int	Int%	Rating	Att	Yds	Avg	Lg	TD	Sckd	Yds	Fum	Recv	Yds	Pts
								Passing								Rushing					Miscellaneous			
1986	Seattle Seahawks	16	2	76	42	55.3	485	6.38	t38	3	3	3.9	71.4	3	8	2.7	12	0	4	34	1	0	0	0
1990	Buffalo Bills	1	0	15	8	53.3	106	7.07	23	2	2	13.3	76.0	0	0	-	-	0	1	9	0	0	0	0
1993	Buffalo Bills	1	0	0	0	-	0	-	-	0	0	-	0.0	0	0	-	-	0	0	0	0	0	0	0
1994	San Diego Chargers	16	1	67	41	61.2	410	6.12	26	3	1	1.5	87.3	8	-3	-0.4	5	0	4	28	0	0	0	0
1995	San Diego Chargers	16	1	61	36	59.0	325	5.33	41	0	4	6.6	46.1	6	11	1.8	8	0	9	43	2	0	0	0
	6 NFL Seasons	59	4	259	146	56.4	1544	5.96	41	9	12	4.6	66.2	24	20	0.8	12	0	19	123	4	1	-5	0

Sean Gilbert

(statistical profile on page 413)

Pos: DE **Rnd:** 1 (3) **College:** Pittsburgh **Ht:** 6' 4" **Wt:** 315 **Born:** 4/10/70 **Age:** 26

Year	Team	G	GS	Tk	Ast	Sack	FF	FR	TD	Blk	Int	Yds	Avg	TD	Sfty	TD	Pts
					Tackles			Miscellaneous				Interceptions				Totals	
1992	Los Angeles Rams	16	16	46	8	5.0	1	1	0	0	0	0	-	0	0	0	0
1993	Los Angeles Rams	16	16	54	27	10.5	1	0	0	0	0	0	-	0	0	0	0
1994	Los Angeles Rams	14	14	36	11	3.0	1	0	0	0	0	0	-	0	1	0	2
1995	St. Louis Rams	14	14	24	9	6.5	2	1	0	0	0	0	-	0	0	0	0
	4 NFL Seasons	60	60	160	55	25.0	5	2	0	0	0	0	-	0	1	0	2

Jason Gildon

Pos: LB **Rnd:** 3 **College:** Oklahoma State **Ht:** 6' 3" **Wt:** 235 **Born:** 7/31/72 **Age:** 24

Year	Team	G	GS	Tk	Ast	Sack	FF	FR	TD	Blk	Int	Yds	Avg	TD	Sfty	TD	Pts
					Tackles			Miscellaneous				Interceptions				Totals	
1994	Pittsburgh Steelers	16	1	4	0	2.0	0	0	0	0	0	0	-	0	0	0	0
1995	Pittsburgh Steelers	16	0	8	4	3.0	2	1	0	0	0	0	-	0	0	0	0
	2 NFL Seasons	32	1	12	4	5.0	2	1	0	0	0	0	-	0	0	0	0

Mike Gisler

Pos: C **Rnd:** 11 **College:** Houston **Ht:** 6' 4" **Wt:** 300 **Born:** 8/26/69 **Age:** 27

Year	Team	G	GS	Year	Team	G	GS	Year	Team	G	GS			G	GS
1993	New England Patriots	12	0	1994	New England Patriots	14	5	1995	New England Patriots	16	0	3 NFL Seasons		42	5

Other Statistics: 1995–returned 2 kickoffs for 19 yards; fumbled 1 time for 0 yards.

Ernest Givins

(statistical profile on page 319)

Pos: WR **Rnd:** 2 **College:** Louisville **Ht:** 5' 10" **Wt:** 181 **Born:** 9/3/64 **Age:** 32

Year	Team	G	GS	Att	Yds	Avg	Lg	TD	Rec	Yds	Avg	Lg	TD	Num	Yds	Avg	TD	Att	Com	Yds	Int	Fum	TD	Pts
					Rushing					Receiving					Punt Returns				Passing				Totals	
1986	Houston Oilers	15	15	9	148	16.4	t43	1	61	1062	17.4	60	3	8	80	10.0	0	2	0	0	0	0	4	24
1987	Houston Oilers	12	12	1	-13	-13.0	-13	0	53	933	17.6	t83	6	0	0	-	0	0	0	0	0	2	6	36
1988	Houston Oilers	16	16	4	26	6.5	10	0	60	976	16.3	46	5	0	0	-	0	0	0	0	0	1	5	30
1989	Houston Oilers	15	15	0	0	-	-	0	55	794	14.4	48	3	0	0	-	0	0	0	0	0	0	3	18
1990	Houston Oilers	16	16	3	65	21.7	31	0	72	979	13.6	t80	9	0	0	-	0	0	0	0	0	1	9	54
1991	Houston Oilers	16	16	4	30	7.5	23	0	70	996	14.2	49	5	11	107	9.7	0	0	0	0	0	3	5	30
1992	Houston Oilers	16	16	7	75	10.7	44	0	67	787	11.7	41	10	0	0	-	0	0	0	0	0	3	10	60
1993	Houston Oilers	16	16	6	19	3.2	16	0	68	887	13.0	t80	4	0	0	-	0	0	0	0	0	2	4	24
1994	Houston Oilers	16	16	1	-5	-5.0	-5	0	36	521	14.5	t76	1	37	210	5.7	1	0	0	0	0	3	2	12
1995	Jacksonville Jaguars	9	9	0	0	-	-	0	29	280	9.7	18	3	2	-7	-3.5	0	0	0	0	0	1	3	18
	10 NFL Seasons	147	147	35	345	9.9	44	1	571	8215	14.4	t83	49	58	390	6.7	1	2	0	0	0	16	51	306

Other Statistics: 1989–recovered 1 fumble for 0 yards. 1992–recovered 1 fumble for 0 yards. 1994–recovered 3 fumbles for 0 yards; returned 1 kickoff for 27 yards.

Aaron Glenn

Pos: CB **Rnd:** 1 (12) **College:** Texas A&M **Ht:** 5' 9" **Wt:** 185 **Born:** 7/16/72 **Age:** 24

Year	Team	G	GS	Tk	Ast	Sack	FF	FR	TD	Blk	Int	Yds	Avg	TD	Num	Yds	Avg	TD	Num	Yds	Avg	TD	TD	Fum
					Tackles			Miscellaneous				Interceptions				Punt Returns				Kickoff Returns			Totals	
1994	New York Jets	15	15	58	9	0.0	2	1	0	0	0	0	-	0	0	0	-	0	27	582	21.6	0	0	2
1995	New York Jets	16	16	42	10	0.0	1	1	0	0	1	17	17.0	0	0	0	-	0	1	12	12.0	0	0	0
	2 NFL Seasons	31	31	100	19	0.0	3	2	0	0	1	17	17.0	0	0	0	-	0	28	594	21.2	0	0	2

Vencie Glenn

(statistical profile on page 413)

Pos: S **Rnd:** 2 **College:** Indiana State **Ht:** 6' 0" **Wt:** 189 **Born:** 10/26/64 **Age:** 32

Year	Team	G	GS	Tk	Ast	Sack	FF	FR	TD	Blk	Int	Yds	Avg	TD	Num	Yds	Avg	TD	Num	Yds	Avg	TD	TD	Fum
					Tackles			Miscellaneous				Interceptions				Punt Returns				Kickoff Returns			Totals	
1986	NE - SD	16	7	34	8	0.0	0	2	0	0	2	31	15.5	0	0	0	-	0	0	0	-	0	0	0
1987	San Diego Chargers	12	12	57	9	0.5	0	1	0	0	4	166	41.5	1	0	0	-	0	0	0	-	0	1	0
1988	San Diego Chargers	16	16	73	17	0.0	0	2	0	0	4	52	13.0	0	0	0	-	0	0	0	-	0	0	0
1989	San Diego Chargers	16	16	55	13	1.0	0	1	1	0	4	52	13.0	0	0	0	-	0	0	0	-	0	1	0

95

Year	Team	G	GS	Tackles			Miscellaneous				Interceptions				Punt Returns				Kickoff Returns				Totals	
				Tk	Ast	Sack	FF	FR	TD	Blk	Int	Yds	Avg	TD	Num	Yds	Avg	TD	Num	Yds	Avg	TD	TD	Fum
1990	San Diego Chargers	14	14	45	9	0.0	0	0	0	0	1	0	0.0	0	0	0	-	0	0	0	-	0	0	0
1991	New Orleans Saints	16	1	26	4	0.0	1	1	0	0	4	35	8.8	0	0	0	-	0	1	10	10.0	0	0	0
1992	Minnesota Vikings	16	3	34	16	0.0	0	0	0	0	5	65	13.0	0	0	0	-	0	0	0	-	0	0	0
1993	Minnesota Vikings	16	16	51	25	0.0	1	0	0	0	5	49	9.8	0	0	0	-	0	0	0	-	0	0	0
1994	Minnesota Vikings	16	16	58	23	1.0	0	0	0	0	4	55	13.8	0	0	0	-	0	0	0	-	0	0	0
1995	New York Giants	15	15	67	18	0.0	3	2	0	0	5	91	18.2	1	0	0	-	0	0	0	-	0	1	0
1986	New England Patriots	4	0	5	4	0.0	0	0	0	0	0	0	-	0	0	0	-	0	0	0	-	0	0	0
	San Diego Chargers	12	7	29	4	0.0	0	2	0	0	2	31	15.5	0	0	0	-	0	0	0	-	0	0	0
	10 NFL Seasons	153	116	500	142	3.5	5	9	1	0	35	544	15.5	2	0	0	-	0	1	10	10.0	0	3	0

Andrew Glover

(statistical profile on page 320)

Pos: TE **Rnd:** 10 **College:** Grambling **Ht:** 6' 6" **Wt:** 250 **Born:** 8/12/67 **Age:** 29

Year	Team	G	GS	Rushing					Receiving					Punt Returns				Kickoff Returns				Totals		
				Att	Yds	Avg	Lg	TD	Rec	Yds	Avg	Lg	TD	Num	Yds	Avg	TD	Num	Yds	Avg	TD	Fum	TD	Pts
1991	Los Angeles Raiders	16	1	0	0	-	0	0	5	45	9.0	18	3	0	0	-	0	0	0	-	0	0	3	18
1992	Los Angeles Raiders	16	2	0	0	-	0	0	15	178	11.9	30	1	0	0	-	0	0	0	-	0	1	1	6
1993	Los Angeles Raiders	15	0	0	0	-	0	0	4	55	13.8	26	1	0	0	-	0	0	0	-	0	0	1	6
1994	Los Angeles Raiders	16	16	0	0	-	0	0	33	371	11.2	t27	2	0	0	-	0	0	0	-	0	0	2	12
1995	Oakland Raiders	16	7	0	0	-	0	0	26	220	8.5	25	3	0	0	-	0	0	0	-	0	0	3	18
	5 NFL Seasons	79	26	0	0	-	0	0	83	869	10.5	30	10	0	0	-	0	0	0	-	0	1	10	60

Other Statistics: 1992–recovered 1 fumble for 0 yards.

Kevin Glover

Pos: C **Rnd:** 2 **College:** Maryland **Ht:** 6' 2" **Wt:** 282 **Born:** 6/17/63 **Age:** 33

Year	Team	G	GS	Year	Team	G	GS	Year	Team	G	GS	Year	Team	G	GS
1985	Detroit Lions	10	0	1988	Detroit Lions	16	16	1991	Detroit Lions	16	16	1994	Detroit Lions	16	16
1986	Detroit Lions	4	1	1989	Detroit Lions	16	16	1992	Detroit Lions	7	7	1995	Detroit Lions	16	16
1987	Detroit Lions	12	9	1990	Detroit Lions	16	16	1993	Detroit Lions	16	16		11 NFL Seasons	145	129

Other Statistics: 1987–returned 1 kickoff for 19 yards. 1988–recovered 2 fumbles for 0 yards. 1990–recovered 1 fumble for 0 yards. 1992–recovered 1 fumble for 0 yards. 1995–recovered 1 fumble for -14 yards; fumbled 2 times.

Tim Goad

Pos: DT **Rnd:** 4 **College:** North Carolina **Ht:** 6' 3" **Wt:** 280 **Born:** 2/28/66 **Age:** 30

Year	Team	G	GS	Tackles			Miscellaneous				Interceptions				Totals		
				Tk	Ast	Sack	FF	FR	TD	Blk	Int	Yds	Avg	TD	Sfty	TD	Pts
1988	New England Patriots	16	14	32	10	2.0	0	0	0	0	0	0	-	0	0	0	0
1989	New England Patriots	16	16	43	19	1.0	0	0	0	0	0	0	-	0	0	0	0
1990	New England Patriots	16	16	53	36	2.5	0	1	0	0	0	0	-	0	0	0	0
1991	New England Patriots	16	15	31	14	0.0	0	0	0	0	0	0	-	0	0	0	0
1992	New England Patriots	16	16	44	28	2.5	0	1	1	0	0	0	-	0	0	1	6
1993	New England Patriots	16	15	52	25	0.5	0	1	0	0	0	0	-	0	0	0	0
1994	New England Patriots	13	13	47	27	3.0	1	1	0	0	0	0	-	0	0	0	0
1995	Cleveland Browns	16	13	38	11	0.0	0	2	0	0	0	0	-	0	0	0	0
	8 NFL Seasons	125	118	340	170	11.5	1	6	1	0	0	0	-	0	0	1	6

Leo Goeas

Pos: G/T **Rnd:** 3 **College:** Hawaii **Ht:** 6' 4" **Wt:** 292 **Born:** 8/15/66 **Age:** 30

Year	Team	G	GS	Year	Team	G	GS	Year	Team	G	GS			G	GS
1990	San Diego Chargers	15	9	1992	San Diego Chargers	16	5	1994	Los Angeles Rams	13	13				
1991	San Diego Chargers	9	4	1993	Los Angeles Rams	16	16	1995	St. Louis Rams	15	14		6 NFL Seasons	84	61

Other Statistics: 1990–recovered 1 fumble for 0 yards. 1992–recovered 1 fumble for 0 yards. 1994–recovered 1 fumble for 0 yards.

Robert Goff

Pos: NT/DT **Rnd:** 4 **College:** Auburn **Ht:** 6' 3" **Wt:** 280 **Born:** 10/2/65 **Age:** 31

Year	Team	G	GS	Tackles			Miscellaneous				Interceptions				Totals		
				Tk	Ast	Sack	FF	FR	TD	Blk	Int	Yds	Avg	TD	Sfty	TD	Pts
1988	Tampa Bay Buccaneers	16	6	17	7	2.0	0	3	0	0	0	0	-	0	0	0	0
1989	Tampa Bay Buccaneers	12	12	22	9	4.0	0	1	0	0	0	0	-	0	0	0	0
1990	New Orleans Saints	15	10	19	3	0.0	0	1	0	0	0	0	-	0	0	0	0
1991	New Orleans Saints	15	0	14	5	2.0	0	0	0	0	0	0	-	0	0	0	0
1992	New Orleans Saints	16	0	9	0	0.0	0	3	2	0	0	0	-	0	0	2	12
1993	New Orleans Saints	16	9	33	16	2.0	0	0	0	0	0	0	-	0	0	0	0
1994	New Orleans Saints	16	0	13	7	0.0	0	0	0	0	0	0	-	0	0	0	0
1995	New Orleans Saints	11	6	15	5	1.5	0	0	0	0	0	0	-	0	0	0	0
	8 NFL Seasons	117	43	142	52	11.5	0	8	2	0	0	0	-	0	0	2	12

Kevin Gogan

Pos: G **Rnd:** 8 **College:** Washington **Ht:** 6' 7" **Wt:** 320 **Born:** 11/2/64 **Age:** 31

Year	Team	G	GS	Year	Team	G	GS	Year	Team	G	GS			G	GS
1987	Dallas Cowboys	11	10	1990	Dallas Cowboys	16	4	1993	Dallas Cowboys	16	16				
1988	Dallas Cowboys	15	15	1991	Dallas Cowboys	16	16	1994	Los Angeles Raiders	16	16				
1989	Dallas Cowboys	13	13	1992	Dallas Cowboys	16	1	1995	Oakland Raiders	16	16	9 NFL Seasons		135	107

Other Statistics: 1987–recovered 1 fumble for 0 yards. 1990–recovered 1 fumble for 0 yards.

Keith Goganious

(statistical profile on page 414)

Pos: LB **Rnd:** 3 **College:** Penn State **Ht:** 6' 3" **Wt:** 244 **Born:** 12/7/68 **Age:** 27

				Tackles			Miscellaneous				Interceptions				Totals		
Year	Team	G	GS	Tk	Ast	Sack	FF	FR	TD	Blk	Int	Yds	Avg	TD	Sfty	TD	Pts
1992	Buffalo Bills	13	0	2	2	0.0	0	0	0	0	0	0	-	0	0	0	0
1993	Buffalo Bills	16	7	37	18	1.0	0	1	0	0	0	0	-	0	0	0	0
1994	Buffalo Bills	16	1	16	5	0.0	0	0	0	0	0	0	-	0	0	0	0
1995	Jacksonville Jaguars	16	15	56	27	0.0	0	0	0	0	2	11	5.5	0	0	0	0
	4 NFL Seasons	61	23	111	52	1.0	0	1	0	0	2	11	5.5	0	0	0	0

Dwayne Gordon

Pos: LB **Rnd:** 8 **College:** New Hampshire **Ht:** 6' 1" **Wt:** 240 **Born:** 11/2/69 **Age:** 26

				Tackles			Miscellaneous				Interceptions				Totals		
Year	Team	G	GS	Tk	Ast	Sack	FF	FR	TD	Blk	Int	Yds	Avg	TD	Sfty	TD	Pts
1993	Atlanta Falcons	5	0	0	1	0.0	0	0	0	0	0	0	-	0	0	0	0
1994	Atlanta Falcons	16	0	6	2	0.0	0	0	0	0	0	0	-	0	0	0	0
1995	San Diego Chargers	15	3	18	2	1.0	1	1	0	0	0	0	-	0	0	0	0
	3 NFL Seasons	36	3	24	5	1.0	1	1	0	0	0	0	-	0	0	0	0

Other Statistics: 1993–fumbled 1 time for 0 yards.

Antonio Goss

Pos: LB **Rnd:** 12 **College:** North Carolina **Ht:** 6' 4" **Wt:** 228 **Born:** 8/11/66 **Age:** 30

				Tackles			Miscellaneous				Interceptions				Totals		
Year	Team	G	GS	Tk	Ast	Sack	FF	FR	TD	Blk	Int	Yds	Avg	TD	Sfty	TD	Pts
1989	San Francisco 49ers	8	0	4	1	0.0	0	1	0	0	0	0	-	0	0	0	0
1991	San Francisco 49ers	14	0	11	1	0.0	0	0	0	0	0	0	-	0	0	0	0
1992	San Francisco 49ers	16	0	14	4	0.0	0	0	0	0	0	0	-	0	0	0	0
1993	San Francisco 49ers	14	1	7	1	0.0	0	0	0	0	0	0	-	0	0	0	0
1994	San Francisco 49ers	16	1	2	1	0.0	0	0	0	0	0	0	-	0	0	0	0
1995	San Francisco 49ers	16	0	1	0	0.0	0	0	0	0	0	0	-	0	0	0	0
	6 NFL Seasons	84	2	39	8	0.0	0	1	0	0	0	0	-	0	0	0	0

Jeff Gossett

(statistical profile on page 474)

Pos: P **Rnd:** FA **College:** Eastern Illinois **Ht:** 6' 2" **Wt:** 195 **Born:** 1/25/57 **Age:** 39

				Punting											Rushing		Passing			
Year	Team	G	NetPunts	Yards	Avg	Long	In20	In20%	TotPunts	TB	Blocks	OppRet	RetYds	NetAvg	Att	Yards	Att	Com	Yards	Int
1981	Kansas City Chiefs	7	29	1141	39.3	55	4	13.8	29	3	0	20	128	32.9	0	0	0	0	0	0
1982	Kansas City Chiefs	8	33	1366	41.4	56	6	18.2	33	5	0	20	247	30.9	0	0	0	0	0	0
1983	Cleveland Browns	16	70	2854	40.8	60	17	24.3	70	8	0	30	309	34.1	0	0	0	0	0	0
1985	Cleveland Browns	16	81	3261	40.3	64	18	22.2	81	8	0	36	304	34.5	0	0	1	0	0	0
1986	Cleveland Browns	16	83	3423	41.2	61	21	25.3	83	10	0	44	268	35.6	0	0	2	1	30	1
1987	Cle - Hou	9	44	1777	40.4	55	4	9.1	45	6	1	23	234	31.6	0	0	0	0	0	0
1988	Los Angeles Raiders	16	91	3804	41.8	58	27	29.7	91	8	0	47	397	35.7	0	0	0	0	0	0
1989	Los Angeles Raiders	16	67	2711	40.5	60	12	17.9	67	7	0	41	301	33.9	0	0	1	0	0	0
1990	Los Angeles Raiders	16	60	2315	38.6	57	19	31.7	62	4	2	24	153	33.6	0	0	0	0	0	0
1991	Los Angeles Raiders	16	67	2961	44.2	61	26	38.8	67	2	0	41	341	38.5	0	0	1	1	34	0
1992	Los Angeles Raiders	16	77	3255	42.3	56	17	22.1	77	3	0	40	385	36.5	1	-12	0	0	0	0
1993	Los Angeles Raiders	16	71	2971	41.8	61	19	26.8	71	9	0	35	301	35.1	1	-10	0	0	0	0
1994	Los Angeles Raiders	16	77	3377	43.9	65	19	24.7	77	14	0	38	366	35.5	0	0	0	0	0	0
1995	Oakland Raiders	16	75	3089	41.2	60	22	29.3	76	8	1	38	294	34.7	0	0	0	0	0	0
1987	Cleveland Browns	5	19	769	40.5	55	4	21.1	19	4	0	6	43	34.0	0	0	0	0	0	0
	Houston Oilers	4	25	1008	40.3	53	0	0.0	26	2	1	17	191	29.9	0	0	0	0	0	0
	14 NFL Seasons	200	925	38305	41.4	65	231	25.0	929	95	4	477	4028	34.9	2	-22	5	2	64	1

Other Statistics: 1982–recovered 1 fumble for 0 yards. 1992–fumbled 1 time for 0 yards.

Kurt Gouveia

(statistical profile on page 414)

Pos: LB **Rnd:** 8 **College:** Brigham Young **Ht:** 6' 1" **Wt:** 240 **Born:** 9/14/64 **Age:** 32

Year	Team	G	GS	Tackles			Miscellaneous				Interceptions				Punt Returns				Kickoff Returns				Totals	
				Tk	Ast	Sack	FF	FR	TD	Blk	Int	Yds	Avg	TD	Num	Yds	Avg	TD	Num	Yds	Avg	TD	TD	Fum
1987	Washington Redskins	12	1	20	7	0.0	0	0	0	0	0	0	-	0	0	0	-	0	0	0	-	0	0	0
1988	Washington Redskins	16	0	12	9	0.0	0	0	0	0	0	0	-	0	0	0	-	0	0	0	-	0	0	0
1989	Washington Redskins	15	1	32	5	0.0	0	0	0	0	1	1	1.0	0	0	0	-	0	1	0	0.0	0	0	0
1990	Washington Redskins	16	7	45	31	1.0	0	1	1	0	0	0	-	0	0	0	-	0	2	23	11.5	0	1	0
1991	Washington Redskins	14	1	26	16	0.0	0	0	0	0	1	22	22.0	0	0	0	-	0	3	12	4.0	0	0	0
1992	Washington Redskins	16	14	94	75	1.0	0	0	0	0	3	43	14.3	0	0	0	-	0	1	7	7.0	0	0	0
1993	Washington Redskins	16	16	83	88	1.5	2	0	0	0	1	59	59.0	1	0	0	-	0	0	0	-	0	1	0
1994	Washington Redskins	14	1	27	3	0.0	0	0	0	0	1	7	7.0	0	0	0	-	0	0	0	-	0	0	0
1995	Philadelphia Eagles	16	16	88	18	0.0	1	1	0	0	1	20	20.0	0	0	0	-	0	0	0	-	0	0	0
	9 NFL Seasons	135	57	427	252	3.5	3	2	1	0	8	152	19.0	1	0	0	-	0	7	42	6.0	0	2	0

Scott Gragg

Pos: T **Rnd:** 2 **College:** Montana **Ht:** 6' 8" **Wt:** 316 **Born:** 2/28/72 **Age:** 24

Year	Team	G	GS
1995	New York Giants	13	0
	1 NFL Season	13	0

Derrick Graham

Pos: T **Rnd:** 5 **College:** Appalachian State **Ht:** 6' 4" **Wt:** 315 **Born:** 3/18/67 **Age:** 29

Year	Team	G	GS	Year	Team	G	GS	Year	Team	G	GS
1990	Kansas City Chiefs	6	0	1992	Kansas City Chiefs	2	2	1994	Kansas City Chiefs	16	11
1991	Kansas City Chiefs	16	1	1993	Kansas City Chiefs	11	2	1995	Carolina Panthers	11	7
									6 NFL Seasons	62	23

Hason Graham

Pos: WR **Rnd:** FA **College:** Georgia **Ht:** 5' 10" **Wt:** 176 **Born:** 3/21/71 **Age:** 25

Year	Team	G	GS	Rushing					Receiving					Punt Returns				Kickoff Returns				Totals		
				Att	Yds	Avg	Lg	TD	Rec	Yds	Avg	Lg	TD	Num	Yds	Avg	TD	Num	Yds	Avg	TD	Fum	TD	Pts
1995	New England Patriots	10	1	0	0	-	-	0	10	156	15.6	t37	2	0	0	-	0	0	0	-	0	0	2	12

Jeff Graham

(statistical profile on page 320)

Pos: WR/PR **Rnd:** 2 **College:** Ohio State **Ht:** 6' 2" **Wt:** 200 **Born:** 2/14/69 **Age:** 27

Year	Team	G	GS	Rushing					Receiving					Punt Returns				Kickoff Returns				Totals		
				Att	Yds	Avg	Lg	TD	Rec	Yds	Avg	Lg	TD	Num	Yds	Avg	TD	Num	Yds	Avg	TD	Fum	TD	Pts
1991	Pittsburgh Steelers	13	1	0	0	-	-	0	2	21	10.5	15	0	8	46	5.8	0	3	48	16.0	0	0	0	0
1992	Pittsburgh Steelers	14	10	0	0	-	-	0	49	711	14.5	51	0	0	0	-	0	0	0	-	0	0	1	6
1993	Pittsburgh Steelers	15	12	0	0	-	-	0	38	579	15.2	51	0	0	0	-	0	0	0	-	0	0	0	0
1994	Chicago Bears	16	15	0	0	-	-	0	68	944	13.9	t76	4	15	140	9.3	1	0	0	-	0	1	5	32
1995	Chicago Bears	16	16	0	0	-	-	0	82	1301	15.9	51	4	23	183	8.0	0	1	12	12.0	0	3	4	24
	5 NFL Seasons	74	54	0	0	-	-	0	239	3556	14.9	t76	9	46	369	8.0	1	4	60	15.0	0	4	10	62

Other Statistics: 1994–recovered 1 fumble for 0 yards; scored 1 two-point conversion.

Kent Graham

Pos: QB **Rnd:** 8 **College:** Ohio State **Ht:** 6' 5" **Wt:** 236 **Born:** 11/1/68 **Age:** 28

Year	Team	G	GS	Passing										Rushing					Miscellaneous					
				Att	Com	Pct	Yards	Yds/Att	Lg	TD	Int	Int%	Rating	Att	Yds	Avg	Lg	TD	Sckd	Yds	Fum	Recv	Yds	Pts
1992	New York Giants	6	3	97	42	43.3	470	4.85	44	1	4	4.1	44.6	6	36	6.0	15	0	7	49	1	1	0	0
1993	New York Giants	9	0	22	8	36.4	79	3.59	18	0	0	0.0	47.3	2	-3	-1.5	-1	0	3	28	0	0	0	0
1994	New York Giants	13	1	53	24	45.3	295	5.57	55	3	2	3.8	66.2	2	11	5.5	9	0	2	22	2	1	0	0
1995	Detroit Lions	2	0	0	0	-	0	-	-	0	0		0.0	0	0	-	0	0	0	0	0	0	0	0
	4 NFL Seasons	30	4	172	74	43.0	844	4.91	55	4	6	3.5	51.6	10	44	4.4	15	0	12	99	3	2	0	0

Scottie Graham

(statistical profile on page 321)

Pos: RB **Rnd:** 7 **College:** Ohio State **Ht:** 5' 9" **Wt:** 217 **Born:** 3/28/69 **Age:** 27

Year	Team	G	GS	Rushing					Receiving					Punt Returns				Kickoff Returns				Totals		
				Att	Yds	Avg	Lg	TD	Rec	Yds	Avg	Lg	TD	Num	Yds	Avg	TD	Num	Yds	Avg	TD	Fum	TD	Pts
1992	New York Jets	2	0	14	29	2.1	6	0	0	0	-	-	0	0	0	-	0	0	0	-	0	0	0	0
1993	Minnesota Vikings	7	3	118	488	4.1	31	3	7	46	6.6	11	0	0	0	-	0	1	16	16.0	0	0	3	18
1994	Minnesota Vikings	16	0	64	207	3.2	11	2	1	1	1.0	1	0	0	0	-	0	0	0	-	0	0	2	12
1995	Minnesota Vikings	16	6	110	406	3.7	26	2	4	30	7.5	11	0	0	0	-	0	0	0	-	0	0	2	12
	4 NFL Seasons	41	9	306	1130	3.7	31	7	12	77	6.4	11	0	0	0	-	0	1	16	16.0	0	0	7	42

Rupert Grant

Pos: RB **Rnd:** FA **College:** Howard **Ht:** 6' 1" **Wt:** 233 **Born:** 11/5/73 **Age:** 22

Year Team	G	GS	Rushing Att	Yds	Avg	Lg	TD	Receiving Rec	Yds	Avg	Lg	TD	Punt Returns Num	Yds	Avg	TD	Kickoff Returns Num	Yds	Avg	TD	Totals Fum	TD	Pts
1995 New England Patriots	7	1	0	0	-	-	0	1	4	4.0	4	0	0	0	-	0	1	7	7.0	0	0	0	0

Other Statistics: 1995–recovered 1 fumble for 0 yards.

Stephen Grant

(statistical profile on page 414)

Pos: LB **Rnd:** 10 **College:** West Virginia **Ht:** 6' 0" **Wt:** 240 **Born:** 12/23/69 **Age:** 26

Year Team	G	GS	Tackles Tk	Ast	Sack	Miscellaneous FF	FR	TD	Blk	Interceptions Int	Yds	Avg	TD	Totals Sfty	TD	Pts
1992 Indianapolis Colts	16	0	5	4	0.0	0	0	0	0	0	0	-	0	0	0	0
1993 Indianapolis Colts	16	0	1	0	0.0	0	0	0	0	0	0	-	0	0	0	0
1994 Indianapolis Colts	16	12	68	39	0.0	2	1	0	0	0	0	-	0	0	0	0
1995 Indianapolis Colts	15	15	76	31	2.0	0	3	0	0	1	9	9.0	0	0	0	0
4 NFL Seasons	63	27	150	74	2.0	2	4	0	0	1	9	9.0	0	0	0	0

Carlton Gray

(statistical profile on page 415)

Pos: CB **Rnd:** 2 **College:** UCLA **Ht:** 6' 0" **Wt:** 196 **Born:** 6/26/71 **Age:** 25

Year Team	G	GS	Tackles Tk	Ast	Sack	Miscellaneous FF	FR	TD	Blk	Interceptions Int	Yds	Avg	TD	Totals Sfty	TD	Pts
1993 Seattle Seahawks	10	2	21	6	1.0	0	0	0	0	3	33	11.0	0	0	0	0
1994 Seattle Seahawks	11	11	45	5	0.0	0	0	0	0	2	0	0.0	0	0	0	0
1995 Seattle Seahawks	16	16	68	5	0.0	0	0	0	0	4	45	11.3	0	0	0	0
3 NFL Seasons	37	29	134	13	1.0	0	0	0	0	9	78	8.7	0	0	0	0

Other Statistics: 1995–fumbled 1 time for 0 yards.

Cecil Gray

Pos: T **Rnd:** 9 **College:** North Carolina **Ht:** 6' 4" **Wt:** 305 **Born:** 2/16/68 **Age:** 28

Year	Team	G	GS	Year	Team	G	GS	Year	Team	G	GS		G	GS
1990	Philadelphia Eagles	12	1	1992	Green Bay Packers	2	0	1994	Indianapolis Colts	16	5			
1991	Philadelphia Eagles	2	2	1993	Indianapolis Colts	6	2	1995	Arizona Cardinals	7	4	6 NFL Seasons	45	14

Chris Gray

Pos: G **Rnd:** 5 **College:** Auburn **Ht:** 6' 4" **Wt:** 292 **Born:** 6/19/70 **Age:** 26

Year	Team	G	GS	Year	Team	G	GS	Year	Team	G	GS		G	GS
1993	Miami Dolphins	5	0	1994	Miami Dolphins	16	2	1995	Miami Dolphins	10	10	3 NFL Seasons	31	12

Other Statistics: 1994–recovered 1 fumble for 0 yards.

Derwin Gray

Pos: DB/S **Rnd:** 4 **College:** Brigham Young **Ht:** 5' 11" **Wt:** 203 **Born:** 4/9/71 **Age:** 25

Year Team	G	GS	Tackles Tk	Ast	Sack	Miscellaneous FF	FR	TD	Blk	Interceptions Int	Yds	Avg	TD	Totals Sfty	TD	Pts
1993 Indianapolis Colts	11	0	0	0	0.0	0	1	0	0	0	0	-	0	0	0	0
1994 Indianapolis Colts	16	2	15	2	0.0	0	0	0	0	0	0	-	0	0	0	0
1995 Indianapolis Colts	16	0	10	4	0.0	1	1	0	0	1	10	10.0	0	0	0	0
3 NFL Seasons	43	2	25	6	0.0	1	2	0	0	1	10	10.0	0	0	0	0

Mel Gray

Pos: KR/PR **Rnd:** FA **College:** Purdue **Ht:** 5' 9" **Wt:** 171 **Born:** 3/16/61 **Age:** 35

Year Team	G	GS	Rushing Att	Yds	Avg	Lg	TD	Receiving Rec	Yds	Avg	Lg	TD	Punt Returns Num	Yds	Avg	TD	Kickoff Returns Num	Yds	Avg	TD	Totals Fum	TD	Pts
1986 New Orleans Saints	16	0	6	29	4.8	11	0	2	45	22.5	38	0	0	0	-	0	31	866	27.9	1	0	1	6
1987 New Orleans Saints	12	1	8	37	4.0	12	1	6	30	5.0	12	0	24	352	14.7	0	30	636	21.2	0	3	1	6
1988 New Orleans Saints	14	0	0	0	-	-	0	0	0	-	-	0	25	305	12.2	1	32	670	20.9	0	5	1	6
1989 Detroit Lions	10	1	3	22	7.3	14	0	2	47	23.5	30	0	11	76	6.9	0	24	640	26.7	0	0	0	0
1990 Detroit Lions	16	0	0	0	-	-	0	0	0	-	-	0	34	361	10.6	0	41	939	22.9	0	4	0	0
1991 Detroit Lions	16	0	2	11	5.5	6	0	3	42	14.0	31	0	25	385	15.4	1	36	929	25.8	0	3	1	6
1992 Detroit Lions	15	0	0	0	-	-	0	0	0	-	-	0	18	175	9.7	1	42	1006	24.0	0	0	2	12
1993 Detroit Lions	11	0	0	0	-	-	0	0	0	-	-	0	23	197	8.6	0	28	688	24.6	1	3	1	6
1994 Detroit Lions	16	0	0	0	-	-	0	0	0	-	-	0	21	233	11.1	0	45	1276	28.4	3	3	3	18
1995 Houston Oilers	15	0	0	0	-	-	0	0	0	-	-	0	30	303	10.1	0	53	1183	22.3	0	5	0	0
10 NFL Seasons	141	2	19	99	5.2	14	1	13	164	12.6	38	0	211	2387	11.3	3	362	8833	24.4	6	26	10	60

Other Statistics: 1987–recovered 1 fumble for 0 yards. 1988–recovered 2 fumbles for 0 yards. 1990–recovered 3 fumbles for 0 yards. 1991–recovered 2 fumbles for 0 yards. 1994–recovered 2 fumbles for 0 yards. 1995–recovered 1 fumble for 0 yards.

Elvis Grbac

(statistical profile on page 321)

Pos: QB **Rnd:** 8 **College:** Michigan **Ht:** 6' 5" **Wt:** 231 **Born:** 8/13/70 **Age:** 26

Year Team	G	GS	Passing										Rushing					Miscellaneous					
			Att	Com	Pct	Yards	Yds/Att	Lg	TD	Int	Int%	Rating	Att	Yds	Avg	Lg	TD	Sckd	Yds	Fum	Recv	Yds	Pts
1994 San Francisco 49ers	12	0	50	35	70.0	393	7.86	42	2	1	2.0	98.2	13	1	0.1	6	0	4	36	5	0	-2	0
1995 San Francisco 49ers	16	5	183	127	69.4	1469	8.03	t81	8	5	2.7	96.6	20	33	1.7	11	2	6	36	2	2	-1	12
2 NFL Seasons	28	5	233	162	69.5	1862	7.99	t81	10	6	2.6	96.9	33	34	1.0	11	2	10	72	7	2	-3	12

Chris Green

Pos: S **Rnd:** 7 **College:** Illinois **Ht:** 5' 11" **Wt:** 198 **Born:** 2/26/68 **Age:** 28

Year Team	G	GS	Tackles			Miscellaneous				Interceptions				Punt Returns				Kickoff Returns				Totals	
			Tk	Ast	Sack	FF	FR	TD	Blk	Int	Yds	Avg	TD	Num	Yds	Avg	TD	Num	Yds	Avg	TD	TD	Fum
1991 Miami Dolphins	16	0	20	3	0.0	0	0	0	0	0	0	-	0	0	0	-	0	0	0	-	0	0	0
1992 Miami Dolphins	4	2	8	2	0.0	0	0	0	0	0	0	-	0	0	0	-	0	0	0	-	0	0	0
1993 Miami Dolphins	14	0	15	4	0.0	0	0	0	0	2	0	0.0	0	0	0	-	0	0	0	-	0	0	0
1994 Miami Dolphins	16	1	15	5	0.0	0	0	0	0	0	0	-	0	0	0	-	0	0	0	-	0	0	0
1995 Buffalo Bills	16	1	9	3	0.0	0	0	0	0	0	0	-	0	0	0	-	0	2	37	18.5	0	0	0
5 NFL Seasons	66	4	67	17	0.0	0	0	0	0	2	0	0.0	0	0	0	-	0	2	37	18.5	0	0	0

Darrell Green

(statistical profile on page 415)

Pos: CB **Rnd:** 1 (28) **College:** Texas A&I **Ht:** 5' 9" **Wt:** 182 **Born:** 2/15/60 **Age:** 36

Year Team	G	GS	Tackles			Miscellaneous				Interceptions				Punt Returns				Kickoff Returns				Totals	
			Tk	Ast	Sack	FF	FR	TD	Blk	Int	Yds	Avg	TD	Num	Yds	Avg	TD	Num	Yds	Avg	TD	TD	Fum
1983 Washington Redskins	16	16	79	30	0.0	0	1	0	0	2	7	3.5	0	4	29	7.3	0	0	0	-	0	0	1
1984 Washington Redskins	16	16	69	19	0.0	0	0	0	0	5	91	18.2	1	2	13	6.5	0	0	0	-	0	1	0
1985 Washington Redskins	16	16	60	24	0.0	0	1	0	0	2	0	0.0	0	16	214	13.4	0	0	0	-	0	0	2
1986 Washington Redskins	16	15	58	12	0.0	0	1	0	0	5	9	1.8	0	12	120	10.0	0	0	0	-	0	0	0
1987 Washington Redskins	12	12	38	10	0.0	0	1	0	0	3	65	21.7	0	5	53	10.6	0	0	0	-	0	1	0
1988 Washington Redskins	15	15	50	13	1.0	0	1	0	0	1	12	12.0	0	9	103	11.4	0	0	0	-	0	0	1
1989 Washington Redskins	7	7	21	8	0.0	0	1	0	0	2	0	0.0	0	1	11	11.0	0	0	0	-	0	0	1
1990 Washington Redskins	16	16	56	22	0.0	0	1	0	0	4	20	5.0	1	1	6	6.0	0	0	0	-	0	1	0
1991 Washington Redskins	16	16	64	15	0.0	0	1	0	0	5	47	9.4	0	0	0	-	0	0	0	-	0	1	0
1992 Washington Redskins	8	7	25	10	0.0	0	1	0	0	1	15	15.0	0	0	0	-	0	0	0	-	0	0	0
1993 Washington Redskins	16	16	71	18	0.0	0	2	1	0	4	10	2.5	0	1	27	27.0	0	0	0	-	0	1	0
1994 Washington Redskins	16	16	52	3	0.0	0	0	0	0	3	32	10.7	1	0	0	-	0	0	0	-	0	1	0
1995 Washington Redskins	16	16	48	5	0.0	0	0	0	0	3	42	14.0	0	0	0	-	0	0	0	-	0	1	0
13 NFL Seasons	186	184	691	189	1.0	0	8	2	0	40	350	8.8	4	51	576	11.3	0	0	0	-	0	6	6

Other Statistics: 1985–rushed 1 time for 6 yards.

David Green

Pos: RB **Rnd:** FA **College:** Boston College **Ht:** 5' 11" **Wt:** 193 **Born:** 4/18/72 **Age:** 24

Year Team	G	GS	Rushing					Receiving					Punt Returns				Kickoff Returns				Totals		
			Att	Yds	Avg	Lg	TD	Rec	Yds	Avg	Lg	TD	Num	Yds	Avg	TD	Num	Yds	Avg	TD	Fum	TD	Pts
1995 New England Patriots	2	0	0	0	-	-	0	0	0	-	-	0	0	0	-	0	0	0	-	0	0	0	0

Eric Green

(statistical profile on page 322)

Pos: TE **Rnd:** 1 (21) **College:** Liberty **Ht:** 6' 5" **Wt:** 280 **Born:** 6/22/67 **Age:** 29

Year Team	G	GS	Rushing					Receiving					Punt Returns				Kickoff Returns				Totals		
			Att	Yds	Avg	Lg	TD	Rec	Yds	Avg	Lg	TD	Num	Yds	Avg	TD	Num	Yds	Avg	TD	Fum	TD	Pts
1990 Pittsburgh Steelers	13	7	0	0	-	-	0	34	387	11.4	46	7	0	0	-	0	1	16	16.0	0	1	7	42
1991 Pittsburgh Steelers	11	11	0	0	-	-	0	41	582	14.2	49	6	0	0	-	0	0	0	-	0	2	6	36
1992 Pittsburgh Steelers	7	5	0	0	-	-	0	14	152	10.9	24	2	0	0	-	0	0	0	-	0	0	2	12
1993 Pittsburgh Steelers	16	16	0	0	-	-	0	63	942	15.0	t71	5	0	0	-	0	0	0	-	0	3	5	30
1994 Pittsburgh Steelers	15	14	0	0	-	-	0	46	618	13.4	46	4	0	0	-	0	0	0	-	0	2	4	24
1995 Miami Dolphins	14	14	0	0	-	-	0	43	499	11.6	t31	3	0	0	-	0	0	0	-	0	0	3	20
6 NFL Seasons	76	67	0	0	-	-	0	241	3180	13.2	t71	27	0	0	-	0	1	16	16.0	0	8	27	164

Other Statistics: 1990–recovered 1 fumble for 0 yards. 1995–scored 1 two-point conversion.

Harold Green

(statistical profile on page 322)

Pos: RB **Rnd:** 2 **College:** South Carolina **Ht:** 6' 2" **Wt:** 222 **Born:** 1/29/68 **Age:** 28

Year Team	G	GS	Rushing					Receiving					Punt Returns				Kickoff Returns				Totals		
			Att	Yds	Avg	Lg	TD	Rec	Yds	Avg	Lg	TD	Num	Yds	Avg	TD	Num	Yds	Avg	TD	Fum	TD	Pts
1990 Cincinnati Bengals	12	9	83	353	4.3	39	1	12	90	7.5	22	1	0	0	-	0	0	0	-	0	2	2	12
1991 Cincinnati Bengals	14	10	158	731	4.6	t75	2	16	136	8.5	18	0	0	0	-	0	4	66	16.5	0	2	2	12
1992 Cincinnati Bengals	16	16	265	1170	4.4	53	2	41	214	5.2	19	0	0	0	-	0	0	0	-	0	1	2	12
1993 Cincinnati Bengals	15	15	215	589	2.7	25	0	22	115	5.2	16	0	0	0	-	0	0	0	-	0	3	0	0

Year Team	G	GS	Rushing					Receiving					Punt Returns				Kickoff Returns				Totals		
			Att	Yds	Avg	Lg	TD	Rec	Yds	Avg	Lg	TD	Num	Yds	Avg	TD	Num	Yds	Avg	TD	Fum	TD	Pts
1994 Cincinnati Bengals	14	11	76	223	2.9	22	1	27	267	9.9	34	1	0	0	-	0	5	113	22.6	0	1	2	12
1995 Cincinnati Bengals	15	15	171	661	3.9	t23	2	27	182	6.7	24	1	0	0	-	0	0	0	-	0	2	3	18
6 NFL Seasons	86	75	968	3727	3.9	t75	8	145	1004	6.9	34	3	0	0	-	0	9	179	19.9	0	11	11	66

Other Statistics: 1990–recovered 2 fumbles for 0 yards. 1992–recovered 1 fumble for 0 yards. 1994–recovered 1 fumble for 0 yards. 1995–recovered 1 fumble for 0 yards.

Robert Green

(statistical profile on page 323)

Pos: RB **Rnd:** FA **College:** William & Mary **Ht:** 5' 8" **Wt:** 212 **Born:** 9/10/70 **Age:** 26

Year Team	G	GS	Rushing					Receiving					Punt Returns				Kickoff Returns				Totals		
			Att	Yds	Avg	Lg	TD	Rec	Yds	Avg	Lg	TD	Num	Yds	Avg	TD	Num	Yds	Avg	TD	Fum	TD	Pts
1992 Washington Redskins	15	0	8	46	5.8	23	0	1	5	5.0	5	0	0	0	-	0	1	9	9.0	0	0	0	0
1993 Chicago Bears	16	0	15	29	1.9	10	0	13	63	4.8	9	0	0	0	-	0	9	141	15.7	0	0	0	0
1994 Chicago Bears	15	0	25	122	4.9	14	0	24	199	8.3	t39	2	0	0	-	0	6	77	12.8	0	1	2	12
1995 Chicago Bears	12	3	107	570	5.3	38	3	28	246	8.8	28	0	0	0	-	0	3	29	9.7	0	2	3	18
4 NFL Seasons	58	3	155	767	4.9	38	3	66	513	7.8	t39	2	0	0	-	0	19	256	13.5	0	3	5	30

Other Statistics: 1994–recovered 1 fumble for 0 yards. 1995–recovered 1 fumble for 0 yards.

Rogerick Green

Pos: CB **Rnd:** 5 **College:** Kansas State **Ht:** 5' 11" **Wt:** 187 **Born:** 12/15/69 **Age:** 26

Year Team	G	GS	Tackles			Miscellaneous				Interceptions				Punt Returns				Kickoff Returns				Totals	
			Tk	Ast	Sack	FF	FR	TD	Blk	Int	Yds	Avg	TD	Num	Yds	Avg	TD	Num	Yds	Avg	TD	TD	Fum
1992 Tampa Bay Buccaneers	1	1	0	0	0.0	0	0	0	0	0	0	-	0	0	0	-	0	0	0	-	0	0	0
1994 Tampa Bay Buccaneers	11	0	7	0	0.0	0	0	0	1	0	0	-	0	0	0	-	0	2	33	16.5	0	0	0
1995 Jacksonville Jaguars	14	0	3	1	0.0	0	0	0	0	0	0	-	0	0	0	-	0	0	0	-	0	0	0
3 NFL Seasons	26	1	10	1	0.0	0	0	0	1	0	0	-	0	0	0	-	0	2	33	16.5	0	0	0

Victor Green

(statistical profile on page 415)

Pos: S/CB **Rnd:** FA **College:** Akron **Ht:** 5' 9" **Wt:** 195 **Born:** 12/8/69 **Age:** 26

Year Team	G	GS	Tackles			Miscellaneous				Interceptions				Totals		
			Tk	Ast	Sack	FF	FR	TD	Blk	Int	Yds	Avg	TD	Sfty	TD	Pts
1993 New York Jets	11	0	0	0	0.0	0	0	0	0	0	0	-	0	0	0	0
1994 New York Jets	16	0	16	1	1.0	0	1	0	0	0	0	-	0	0	0	0
1995 New York Jets	16	12	103	34	2.0	0	1	0	0	1	2	2.0	0	0	0	0
3 NFL Seasons	43	12	119	35	3.0	0	2	0	0	1	2	2.0	0	0	0	0

Willie Green

(statistical profile on page 323)

Pos: WR **Rnd:** 8 **College:** Mississippi **Ht:** 6' 4" **Wt:** 188 **Born:** 4/2/66 **Age:** 30

Year Team	G	GS	Rushing					Receiving					Punt Returns				Kickoff Returns				Totals		
			Att	Yds	Avg	Lg	TD	Rec	Yds	Avg	Lg	TD	Num	Yds	Avg	TD	Num	Yds	Avg	TD	Fum	TD	Pts
1991 Detroit Lions	16	15	0	0	-	-	0	39	592	15.2	t73	7	0	0	-	0	0	0	-	0	0	7	42
1992 Detroit Lions	15	13	0	0	-	-	0	33	586	17.8	t73	5	0	0	-	0	0	0	-	0	1	5	30
1993 Detroit Lions	16	6	0	0	-	-	0	28	462	16.5	47	2	0	0	-	0	0	0	-	0	0	2	12
1994 Tampa Bay Buccaneers	5	0	0	0	-	-	0	9	150	16.7	28	0	0	0	-	0	0	0	-	0	0	0	0
1995 Carolina Panthers	16	7	0	0	-	-	0	47	882	18.8	t89	6	0	0	-	0	0	0	-	0	1	6	36
5 NFL Seasons	68	41	0	0	-	-	0	156	2672	17.1	t89	20	0	0	-	0	0	0	-	0	2	20	120

Andrew Greene

Pos: G **Rnd:** 2 **College:** Indiana **Ht:** 6' 3" **Wt:** 304 **Born:** 9/24/69 **Age:** 27

Year Team	G	GS
1995 Miami Dolphins	6	1
1 NFL Season	6	1

Kevin Greene

(statistical profile on page 416)

Pos: LB **Rnd:** 5 **College:** Auburn **Ht:** 6' 3" **Wt:** 249 **Born:** 7/31/62 **Age:** 34

Year Team	G	GS	Tackles			Miscellaneous				Interceptions				Totals		
			Tk	Ast	Sack	FF	FR	TD	Blk	Int	Yds	Avg	TD	Sfty	TD	Pts
1985 Los Angeles Rams	15	0	11	4	0.0	0	0	0	0	0	0	-	0	0	0	0
1986 Los Angeles Rams	16	0	29	4	7.0	0	1	0	0	0	0	-	0	0	0	0
1987 Los Angeles Rams	9	0	12	2	6.5	0	0	0	0	1	25	25.0	1	0	1	6
1988 Los Angeles Rams	16	14	47	4	16.5	2	0	0	0	1	10	10.0	0	1	0	2
1989 Los Angeles Rams	16	16	58	6	16.5	3	2	0	0	0	0	-	0	0	0	0
1990 Los Angeles Rams	15	15	52	9	13.0	4	4	0	0	0	0	-	0	0	0	0
1991 Los Angeles Rams	16	16	41	9	3.0	1	0	0	0	0	0	-	0	1	0	2
1992 Los Angeles Rams	16	16	75	12	10.0	3	4	0	0	0	0	-	0	1	0	2
1993 Pittsburgh Steelers	16	16	48	19	12.5	3	3	0	0	0	0	-	0	0	0	0
1994 Pittsburgh Steelers	16	16	53	16	14.0	1	3	0	0	0	0	-	0	0	0	0

Year Team	G	GS	Tackles			Miscellaneous				Interceptions				Totals		
			Tk	Ast	Sack	FF	FR	TD	Blk	Int	Yds	Avg	TD	Sfty	TD	Pts
1995 Pittsburgh Steelers	16	16	34	14	9.0	2	0	0	0	1	0	0.0	0	0	0	0
11 NFL Seasons	167	125	460	99	108.0	19	17	0	0	3	35	11.7	1	3	1	12

Tracy Greene

Pos: TE **Rnd:** 7 **College:** Grambling **Ht:** 6' 5" **Wt:** 282 **Born:** 11/5/72 **Age:** 23

Year Team	G	GS	Rushing					Receiving					Punt Returns				Kickoff Returns				Totals		
			Att	Yds	Avg	Lg	TD	Rec	Yds	Avg	Lg	TD	Num	Yds	Avg	TD	Num	Yds	Avg	TD	Fum	TD	Pts
1994 Kansas City Chiefs	7	1	0	0	-	-	0	6	69	11.5	20	1	0	0	-	0	0	0	-	0	0	1	6
1995 Pittsburgh Steelers	16	0	0	0	-	-	0	0	0	-	-	0	0	0	-	0	1	7	7.0	0	0	0	0
2 NFL Seasons	23	1	0	0	-	-	0	6	69	11.5	20	1	0	0	-	0	1	7	7.0	0	0	1	6

Carl Greenwood

Pos: CB **Rnd:** 5 **College:** UCLA **Ht:** 5' 11" **Wt:** 186 **Born:** 3/11/72 **Age:** 24

Year Team	G	GS	Tackles			Miscellaneous				Interceptions				Totals		
			Tk	Ast	Sack	FF	FR	TD	Blk	Int	Yds	Avg	TD	Sfty	TD	Pts
1995 New York Jets	10	0	6	1	0.0	0	0	0	0	0	0	-	0	0	0	0

Don Griffin

Pos: CB **Rnd:** 6 **College:** Middle Tennessee State **Ht:** 6' 0" **Wt:** 176 **Born:** 3/17/64 **Age:** 32

Year Team	G	GS	Tackles			Miscellaneous				Interceptions				Punt Returns				Kickoff Returns				Totals	
			Tk	Ast	Sack	FF	FR	TD	Blk	Int	Yds	Avg	TD	Num	Yds	Avg	TD	Num	Yds	Avg	TD	TD	Fum
1986 San Francisco 49ers	16	15	62	10	1.0	0	2	0	0	3	0	0.0	0	38	377	9.9	1	5	97	19.4	0	1	3
1987 San Francisco 49ers	12	10	22	1	0.0	0	1	0	0	5	1	0.2	0	9	79	8.8	0	0	0	-	0	0	0
1988 San Francisco 49ers	10	6	22	-	1.0	0	0	0	0	0	0	-	0	4	28	7.0	0	0	0	-	0	0	0
1989 San Francisco 49ers	16	16	45	2	0.0	0	1	0	0	2	6	3.0	0	1	9	9.0	0	0	0	-	0	0	0
1990 San Francisco 49ers	16	16	32	3	0.0	0	2	0	0	3	32	10.7	0	16	105	6.6	0	1	15	15.0	0	0	1
1991 San Francisco 49ers	16	16	47	10	0.0	0	3	1	0	1	0	0.0	0	0	0	-	0	0	0	-	0	1	0
1992 San Francisco 49ers	16	16	53	7	0.0	0	0	0	0	5	4	0.8	0	6	69	11.5	0	0	0	-	0	0	1
1993 San Francisco 49ers	12	12	22	-	0.0	0	0	0	0	3	6	2.0	0	0	0	-	0	0	0	-	0	0	1
1994 Cleveland Browns	15	15	59	8	4.0	1	3	0	0	2	2	1.0	0	0	0	-	0	0	0	-	0	0	1
1995 Cleveland Browns	16	16	48	7	0.0	1	0	0	0	1	0	0.0	0	0	0	-	0	0	0	-	0	0	0
10 NFL Seasons	145	138	412	48	6.0	2	12	1	0	25	51	2.0	0	74	667	9.0	1	6	112	18.7	0	2	6

Howard Griffith

Pos: RB **Rnd:** 9 **College:** Illinois **Ht:** 6' 0" **Wt:** 226 **Born:** 11/17/67 **Age:** 28

Year Team	G	GS	Rushing					Receiving					Punt Returns				Kickoff Returns				Totals		
			Att	Yds	Avg	Lg	TD	Rec	Yds	Avg	Lg	TD	Num	Yds	Avg	TD	Num	Yds	Avg	TD	Fum	TD	Pts
1993 Los Angeles Rams	15	0	0	0	-	-	0	0	0	-	-	0	0	0	-	0	8	169	21.1	0	0	0	0
1994 Los Angeles Rams	16	10	9	30	3.3	7	0	16	113	7.1	13	1	0	0	-	0	2	35	17.5	0	0	1	6
1995 Carolina Panthers	15	7	65	197	3.0	15	1	11	63	5.7	15	1	0	0	-	0	0	0	-	0	1	2	12
3 NFL Seasons	46	17	74	227	3.1	15	1	27	176	6.5	15	2	0	0	-	0	10	204	20.4	0	1	3	18

Other Statistics: 1995–recovered 1 fumble for 0 yards.

Rich Griffith

Pos: TE/LS **Rnd:** 5 **College:** Arizona **Ht:** 6' 5" **Wt:** 256 **Born:** 7/31/69 **Age:** 27

Year Team	G	GS	Rushing					Receiving					Punt Returns				Kickoff Returns				Totals		
			Att	Yds	Avg	Lg	TD	Rec	Yds	Avg	Lg	TD	Num	Yds	Avg	TD	Num	Yds	Avg	TD	Fum	TD	Pts
1993 New England Patriots	3	0	0	0	-	-	0	0	0	-	-	0	0	0	-	0	0	0	-	0	0	0	0
1995 Jacksonville Jaguars	16	15	0	0	-	-	0	16	243	15.2	39	0	0	0	-	0	1	9	9.0	0	0	0	0
2 NFL Seasons	19	15	0	0	-	-	0	16	243	15.2	39	0	0	0	-	0	1	9	9.0	0	0	0	0

Robert Griffith

Pos: S **Rnd:** FA **College:** San Diego State **Ht:** 5' 11" **Wt:** 189 **Born:** 11/30/70 **Age:** 25

Year Team	G	GS	Tackles			Miscellaneous				Interceptions				Totals		
			Tk	Ast	Sack	FF	FR	TD	Blk	Int	Yds	Avg	TD	Sfty	TD	Pts
1994 Minnesota Vikings	15	0	8	3	0.0	0	0	0	0	0	0	-	0	0	0	0
1995 Minnesota Vikings	16	0	30	8	0.5	0	0	0	0	0	0	-	0	0	0	0
2 NFL Seasons	31	0	38	11	0.5	0	0	0	0	0	0	-	0	0	0	0

Ryan Grigson

Pos: G **Rnd:** 6 **College:** Purdue **Ht:** 6' 6" **Wt:** 290 **Born:** 2/23/72 **Age:** 24

Year Team	G	GS
1995 Detroit Lions	1	0
1 NFL Season	1	0

Clif Groce

Pos: RB **Rnd:** FA **College:** Texas A&M **Ht:** 5' 11" **Wt:** 244 **Born:** 7/30/72 **Age:** 24

Year Team	G	GS	Rushing Att	Yds	Avg	Lg	TD	Receiving Rec	Yds	Avg	Lg	TD	Punt Returns Num	Yds	Avg	TD	Kickoff Returns Num	Yds	Avg	TD	Totals Fum	TD	Pts
1995 Indianapolis Colts	1	0	0	0	-	-	0	0	0	-	-	0	0	0	-	0	0	0	-	0	0	0	0

Monty Grow

Pos: S **Rnd:** FA **College:** Florida **Ht:** 6' 4" **Wt:** 214 **Born:** 9/4/71 **Age:** 25

Year Team	G	GS	Tackles Tk	Ast	Sack	Miscellaneous FF	FR	TD	Blk	Interceptions Int	Yds	Avg	TD	Totals Sfty	TD	Pts
1994 Kansas City Chiefs	15	0	7	1	0.0	1	0	0	0	1	21	21.0	0	0	0	0
1995 Jacksonville Jaguars	4	1	5	1	0.0	0	0	0	0	1	2	2.0	0	0	0	0
2 NFL Seasons	19	1	12	2	0.0	1	0	0	0	2	23	11.5	0	0	0	0

Other Statistics: 1994–fumbled 1 time for 0 yards.

Paul Gruber

Pos: T **Rnd:** 1 (4) **College:** Wisconsin **Ht:** 6' 5" **Wt:** 296 **Born:** 2/24/65 **Age:** 31

Year	Team	G	GS	Year	Team	G	GS	Year	Team	G	GS	Year	Team	G	GS
1988	Tampa Bay Buccaneers	16	16	1990	Tampa Bay Buccaneers	16	16	1992	Tampa Bay Buccaneers	16	16	1994	Tampa Bay Buccaneers	16	16
1989	Tampa Bay Buccaneers	16	16	1991	Tampa Bay Buccaneers	16	16	1993	Tampa Bay Buccaneers	10	10	1995	Tampa Bay Buccaneers	16	16
													8 NFL Seasons	122	122

Other Statistics: 1988–recovered 2 fumbles for 0 yards. 1990–recovered 1 fumble for 0 yards. 1991–recovered 1 fumble for 0 yards. 1992–recovered 1 fumble for 0 yards. 1994–recovered 1 fumble for 0 yards. 1995–recovered 2 fumbles for 0 yards.

Tim Grunhard

Pos: C **Rnd:** 2 **College:** Notre Dame **Ht:** 6' 2" **Wt:** 299 **Born:** 5/17/68 **Age:** 28

Year	Team	G	GS	Year	Team	G	GS	Year	Team	G	GS		G	GS
1990	Kansas City Chiefs	14	9	1992	Kansas City Chiefs	12	12	1994	Kansas City Chiefs	16	16			
1991	Kansas City Chiefs	16	16	1993	Kansas City Chiefs	16	16	1995	Kansas City Chiefs	16	16	6 NFL Seasons	90	85

Other Statistics: 1991–recovered 1 fumble for 0 yards. 1992–recovered 2 fumbles for 0 yards. 1993–fumbled 1 time for -1 yard. 1995–recovered 1 fumble for 0 yards.

Eric Guliford

(statistical profile on page 324)

Pos: PR/WR **Rnd:** FA **College:** Arizona State **Ht:** 5' 8" **Wt:** 165 **Born:** 10/25/69 **Age:** 27

Year Team	G	GS	Rushing Att	Yds	Avg	Lg	TD	Receiving Rec	Yds	Avg	Lg	TD	Punt Returns Num	Yds	Avg	TD	Kickoff Returns Num	Yds	Avg	TD	Totals Fum	TD	Pts
1993 Minnesota Vikings	10	0	0	0	-	-	0	1	45	45.0	45	0	29	212	7.3	0	5	101	20.2	0	1	0	0
1994 Minnesota Vikings	7	1	0	0	-	-	0	0	0	-	-	0	5	14	2.8	0	0	0	-	0	1	0	0
1995 Carolina Panthers	14	9	2	2	1.0	1	0	29	444	15.3	49	1	43	475	11.0	1	0	0	-	0	1	2	12
3 NFL Seasons	31	10	2	2	1.0	1	0	30	489	16.3	49	1	77	701	9.1	1	5	101	20.2	0	3	2	12

Other Statistics: 1995–recovered 1 fumble for 0 yards; attempted 2 passes with 1 completion for 46 yards and 1 interception.

Mark Gunn

Pos: DE/DT **Rnd:** 4 **College:** Pittsburgh **Ht:** 6' 5" **Wt:** 297 **Born:** 7/24/68 **Age:** 28

Year Team	G	GS	Tackles Tk	Ast	Sack	Miscellaneous FF	FR	TD	Blk	Interceptions Int	Yds	Avg	TD	Totals Sfty	TD	Pts
1991 New York Jets	15	1	2	2	0.0	0	0	0	0	0	0	-	0	0	0	0
1992 New York Jets	16	12	29	24	2.0	0	0	0	0	0	0	-	0	0	0	0
1993 New York Jets	12	0	6	2	0.0	0	0	0	0	0	0	-	0	0	0	0
1994 New York Jets	3	0	0	0	0.0	0	0	0	0	0	0	-	0	0	0	0
1995 Philadelphia Eagles	12	6	8	5	0.5	0	1	0	0	0	0	-	0	0	0	0
5 NFL Seasons	58	19	45	33	2.5	0	1	0	0	0	0	-	0	0	0	0

Myron Guyton

(statistical profile on page 416)

Pos: S **Rnd:** 8 **College:** Eastern Kentucky **Ht:** 6' 1" **Wt:** 205 **Born:** 8/26/67 **Age:** 29

Year Team	G	GS	Tackles Tk	Ast	Sack	Miscellaneous FF	FR	TD	Blk	Interceptions Int	Yds	Avg	TD	Punt Returns Num	Yds	Avg	TD	Kickoff Returns Num	Yds	Avg	TD	Totals TD	Fum
1989 New York Giants	16	15	75	23	0.0	0	3	0	0	2	27	13.5	0	0	0	-	0	0	0	-	0	0	0
1990 New York Giants	16	16	59	16	0.0	1	2	0	0	1	0	0.0	0	0	0	-	0	0	0	-	0	0	0
1991 New York Giants	16	16	60	15	0.0	0	1	0	0	0	0	-	0	0	0	-	0	0	0	-	0	0	0
1992 New York Giants	4	4	14	5	0.0	0	0	0	0	0	0	-	0	0	0	-	0	0	0	-	0	0	0
1993 New York Giants	16	16	59	18	0.0	0	1	0	0	2	34	17.0	0	0	0	-	0	0	0	-	0	0	0
1994 New England Patriots	16	16	63	18	0.0	0	3	0	0	2	18	9.0	0	0	0	-	0	1	-1	-1.0	0	0	0
1995 New England Patriots	14	14	60	14	0.0	1	1	0	0	3	68	22.7	0	0	0	-	0	0	0	-	0	0	1
7 NFL Seasons	98	97	390	109	0.0	2	11	0	0	10	147	14.7	0	0	0	-	0	1	-1	-1.0	0	0	1

103

Brian Habib

Pos: G   **Rnd:** 10   **College:** Washington   **Ht:** 6' 7"   **Wt:** 299   **Born:** 12/2/64   **Age:** 31

Year	Team	G	GS	Year	Team	G	GS	Year	Team	G	GS	Year	Team	G	GS
1989	Minnesota Vikings	16	0	1991	Minnesota Vikings	16	8	1993	Denver Broncos	16	16	1995	Denver Broncos	16	16
1990	Minnesota Vikings	16	0	1992	Minnesota Vikings	16	15	1994	Denver Broncos	16	16		7 NFL Seasons	112	71

Other Statistics: 1994–recovered 1 fumble for 0 yards.

Britt Hager

Pos: LB   **Rnd:** 3   **College:** Texas   **Ht:** 6' 1"   **Wt:** 225   **Born:** 2/20/66   **Age:** 30

Year	Team	G	GS	Tackles			Miscellaneous				Interceptions				Punt Returns				Kickoff Returns				Totals	
				Tk	Ast	Sack	FF	FR	TD	Blk	Int	Yds	Avg	TD	Num	Yds	Avg	TD	Num	Yds	Avg	TD	TD	Fum
1989	Philadelphia Eagles	16	0	7	4	0.0	0	2	0	0	0	0	-	0	0	0	-	0	0	0	-	0	0	0
1990	Philadelphia Eagles	16	1	3	4	0.0	0	0	0	0	0	0	-	0	0	0	-	0	1	0	0.0	0	0	0
1991	Philadelphia Eagles	16	0	6	9	0.0	0	1	0	0	0	0	-	0	0	0	-	0	0	0	-	0	0	0
1992	Philadelphia Eagles	10	0	12	4	0.0	0	0	0	0	0	0	-	0	0	0	-	0	0	0	-	0	0	0
1993	Philadelphia Eagles	16	7	55	23	1.0	0	0	0	0	1	19	19.0	0	0	0	-	0	0	0	-	0	0	0
1994	Philadelphia Eagles	16	5	41	9	1.0	0	1	0	0	0	0	0.0	0	0	0	-	0	0	0	-	0	0	0
1995	Denver Broncos	16	5	30	9	0.0	1	0	0	0	1	19	19.0	0	0	0	-	0	0	0	-	0	0	0
	7 NFL Seasons	106	18	154	62	2.0	1	4	0	0	3	38	12.7	0	0	0	-	0	1	0	0.0	0	0	0

Charles Haley

(statistical profile on page 416)

Pos: DE   **Rnd:** 4   **College:** James Madison   **Ht:** 6' 5"   **Wt:** 255   **Born:** 1/6/64   **Age:** 32

Year	Team	G	GS	Tackles			Miscellaneous				Interceptions				Totals		
				Tk	Ast	Sack	FF	FR	TD	Blk	Int	Yds	Avg	TD	Sfty	TD	Pts
1986	San Francisco 49ers	16	1	49	10	12.0	4	2	0	0	1	8	8.0	0	0	0	0
1987	San Francisco 49ers	12	2	21	4	6.5	1	0	0	0	0	0	-	0	0	0	0
1988	San Francisco 49ers	16	14	50	19	11.5	1	2	0	0	0	0	-	0	1	0	2
1989	San Francisco 49ers	16	16	43	14	10.5	3	1	1	0	0	0	-	0	0	1	6
1990	San Francisco 49ers	16	16	52	6	16.0	3	1	0	0	0	0	-	0	0	0	0
1991	San Francisco 49ers	14	14	46	7	7.0	2	1	0	0	0	0	-	0	0	0	0
1992	Dallas Cowboys	15	13	21	18	6.0	2	0	0	0	0	0	-	0	0	0	0
1993	Dallas Cowboys	14	11	30	11	4.0	3	1	0	0	0	0	-	0	0	0	0
1994	Dallas Cowboys	16	16	42	9	12.5	3	0	0	0	1	1	1.0	0	0	0	0
1995	Dallas Cowboys	13	11	31	3	10.5	3	0	0	0	0	0	-	0	0	0	0
	10 NFL Seasons	148	114	385	101	96.5	25	8	1	0	2	9	4.5	0	1	1	8

Other Statistics: 1986–fumbled 1 time.

Courtney Hall

Pos: C   **Rnd:** 2   **College:** Rice   **Ht:** 6' 2"   **Wt:** 281   **Born:** 8/26/68   **Age:** 28

Year	Team	G	GS	Year	Team	G	GS	Year	Team	G	GS	Year	Team	G	GS
1989	San Diego Chargers	16	16	1991	San Diego Chargers	16	16	1993	San Diego Chargers	16	16	1995	San Diego Chargers	16	16
1990	San Diego Chargers	16	16	1992	San Diego Chargers	16	16	1994	San Diego Chargers	15	15		7 NFL Seasons	111	111

Other Statistics: 1989–fumbled 1 time for -29 yards. 1991–recovered 2 fumbles for 0 yards. 1995–recovered 1 fumble for 0 yards.

Dana Hall

Pos: S   **Rnd:** 1 (18)   **College:** Washington   **Ht:** 6' 2"   **Wt:** 206   **Born:** 7/8/69   **Age:** 27

Year	Team	G	GS	Tackles			Miscellaneous				Interceptions				Totals		
				Tk	Ast	Sack	FF	FR	TD	Blk	Int	Yds	Avg	TD	Sfty	TD	Pts
1992	San Francisco 49ers	15	15	40	8	1.0	0	1	0	0	2	34	17.0	0	0	0	0
1993	San Francisco 49ers	13	7	22	6	0.0	0	0	0	0	0	0	-	0	0	0	0
1994	San Francisco 49ers	16	4	24	8	0.0	0	0	0	0	2	0	0.0	0	0	0	0
1995	Cleveland Browns	15	2	26	7	1.0	0	0	0	0	2	41	20.5	0	0	0	0
	4 NFL Seasons	59	28	112	29	2.0	0	1	0	0	6	75	12.5	0	0	0	0

Darryl Hall

Pos: CB/S   **Rnd:** FA   **College:** Washington   **Ht:** 6' 2"   **Wt:** 210   **Born:** 8/1/66   **Age:** 30

Year	Team	G	GS	Tackles			Miscellaneous				Interceptions				Totals		
				Tk	Ast	Sack	FF	FR	TD	Blk	Int	Yds	Avg	TD	Sfty	TD	Pts
1993	Denver Broncos	16	2	34	36	0.0	0	0	0	0	1	0	0.0	0	0	0	0
1994	Denver Broncos	16	3	22	3	0.0	0	0	0	0	0	0	-	0	0	0	0
1995	San Francisco 49ers	12	0	3	0	0.0	0	0	0	0	0	0	-	0	0	0	0
	3 NFL Seasons	44	5	59	39	0.0	0	0	0	0	1	0	0.0	0	0	0	0

Lemanski Hall

Pos: LB **Rnd:** 7 **College:** Alabama **Ht:** 6' 0" **Wt:** 229 **Born:** 11/24/70 **Age:** 25

Year Team	G	GS	Tackles			Miscellaneous				Interceptions				Totals		
			Tk	Ast	Sack	FF	FR	TD	Blk	Int	Yds	Avg	TD	Sfty	TD	Pts
1994 Houston Oilers	1	0	0	0	0.0	0	0	0	0	0	0	-	0	0	0	0
1995 Houston Oilers	12	0	1	1	0.0	0	0	0	0	0	0	-	0	0	0	0
2 NFL Seasons	13	0	1	1	0.0	0	0	0	0	0	0	-	0	0	0	0

Ray Hall

Pos: DT **Rnd:** FA **College:** Washington State **Ht:** 6' 4" **Wt:** 294 **Born:** 3/2/71 **Age:** 25

Year Team	G	GS	Tackles			Miscellaneous				Interceptions				Totals		
			Tk	Ast	Sack	FF	FR	TD	Blk	Int	Yds	Avg	TD	Sfty	TD	Pts
1995 Jacksonville Jaguars	12	0	4	0	0.0	0	0	0	0	0	0	-	0	0	0	0

Rhett Hall

Pos: DT **Rnd:** 6 **College:** California **Ht:** 6' 2" **Wt:** 276 **Born:** 12/5/68 **Age:** 27

Year Team	G	GS	Tackles			Miscellaneous				Interceptions				Totals		
			Tk	Ast	Sack	FF	FR	TD	Blk	Int	Yds	Avg	TD	Sfty	TD	Pts
1991 Tampa Bay Buccaneers	16	0	15	2	1.0	0	0	0	0	0	0	-	0	0	0	0
1992 Tampa Bay Buccaneers	4	0	1	0	0.0	0	0	0	0	0	0	-	0	0	0	0
1993 Tampa Bay Buccaneers	1	0	0	0	0.0	0	0	0	0	0	0	-	0	0	0	0
1994 San Francisco 49ers	12	2	9	3	4.0	0	1	0	0	0	0	-	0	0	0	0
1995 Philadelphia Eagles	3	1	5	3	1.0	0	0	0	0	0	0	-	0	0	0	0
5 NFL Seasons	36	3	30	8	6.0	0	1	0	0	0	0	-	0	0	0	0

Ron Hall

Pos: TE **Rnd:** 4 **College:** Hawaii **Ht:** 6' 4" **Wt:** 245 **Born:** 3/15/64 **Age:** 32

Year Team	G	GS	Rushing					Receiving					Punt Returns				Kickoff Returns				Totals		
			Att	Yds	Avg	Lg	TD	Rec	Yds	Avg	Lg	TD	Num	Yds	Avg	TD	Num	Yds	Avg	TD	Fum	TD	Pts
1987 Tampa Bay Buccaneers	11	3	0	0	-	-	0	16	169	10.6	29	1	0	0	-	0	0	0	-	0	0	1	6
1988 Tampa Bay Buccaneers	15	14	0	0	-	-	0	39	555	14.2	37	0	0	0	-	0	0	0	-	0	0	0	0
1989 Tampa Bay Buccaneers	16	15	0	0	-	-	0	30	331	11.0	32	2	0	0	-	0	0	0	-	0	0	2	12
1990 Tampa Bay Buccaneers	16	16	0	0	-	-	0	31	464	15.0	t54	2	0	0	-	0	1	0	0.0	0	0	2	12
1991 Tampa Bay Buccaneers	15	15	0	0	-	-	0	31	284	9.2	24	0	0	0	-	0	1	1	1.0	0	1	0	0
1992 Tampa Bay Buccaneers	12	11	0	0	-	-	0	39	351	9.0	32	4	0	0	-	0	0	0	-	0	0	4	24
1993 Tampa Bay Buccaneers	16	16	0	0	-	-	0	23	268	11.7	t37	1	0	0	-	0	0	0	-	0	0	1	6
1994 Detroit Lions	12	10	0	0	-	-	0	10	106	10.6	18	0	0	0	-	0	0	0	-	0	1	0	0
1995 Detroit Lions	6	6	0	0	-	-	0	11	81	7.4	15	0	0	0	-	0	0	0	-	0	0	0	0
9 NFL Seasons	119	106	0	0	-	-	0	230	2609	11.3	t54	10	0	0	-	0	2	1	0.5	0	2	10	60

Other Statistics: 1989–recovered 1 fumble for 0 yards.

Travis Hall

Pos: DE **Rnd:** 6 **College:** Brigham Young **Ht:** 6' 5" **Wt:** 278 **Born:** 8/3/72 **Age:** 24

Year Team	G	GS	Tackles			Miscellaneous				Interceptions				Totals		
			Tk	Ast	Sack	FF	FR	TD	Blk	Int	Yds	Avg	TD	Sfty	TD	Pts
1995 Atlanta Falcons	1	0	0	0	0.0	0	0	0	0	0	0	-	0	0	0	0

Alan Haller

Pos: CB **Rnd:** 5 **College:** Michigan State **Ht:** 5' 11" **Wt:** 186 **Born:** 8/9/70 **Age:** 26

Year Team	G	GS	Tackles			Miscellaneous				Interceptions				Totals		
			Tk	Ast	Sack	FF	FR	TD	Blk	Int	Yds	Avg	TD	Sfty	TD	Pts
1992 Pit - Cle	6	0	0	0	0.0	0	0	0	0	0	0	-	0	0	0	0
1993 Pittsburgh Steelers	4	0	0	0	0.0	0	0	0	0	0	0	-	0	0	0	0
1995 Carolina Panthers	2	0	0	0	0.0	0	0	0	0	0	0	-	0	0	0	0
1992 Pittsburgh Steelers	3	0	0	0	0.0	0	0	0	0	0	0	-	0	0	0	0
Cleveland Browns	3	0	0	0	0.0	0	0	0	0	0	0	-	0	0	0	0
3 NFL Seasons	12	0	0	0	0.0	0	0	0	0	0	0	-	0	0	0	0

Keith Hamilton

Pos: DT **Rnd:** 4 **College:** Pittsburgh **Ht:** 6' 6" **Wt:** 290 **Born:** 5/25/71 **Age:** 25

Year Team	G	GS	Tackles			Miscellaneous				Interceptions				Totals		
			Tk	Ast	Sack	FF	FR	TD	Blk	Int	Yds	Avg	TD	Sfty	TD	Pts
1992 New York Giants	16	0	15	6	3.5	3	1	0	0	0	0	-	0	0	0	0
1993 New York Giants	16	16	40	11	11.5	2	1	0	0	0	0	-	0	1	0	2
1994 New York Giants	15	15	27	14	6.5	0	3	0	0	0	0	-	0	0	0	0
1995 New York Giants	14	14	29	13	2.0	1	3	0	0	0	0	-	0	0	0	0

Year Team	G	GS	Tackles			Miscellaneous				Interceptions				Totals		
			Tk	Ast	Sack	FF	FR	TD	Blk	Int	Yds	Avg	TD	Sfty	TD	Pts
4 NFL Seasons	61	45	111	44	23.5	6	8	0	0	0	0	-	0	1	0	2

Other Statistics: 1995–fumbled 1 time.

Shelly Hammonds

Pos: CB/S   **Rnd:** 5   **College:** Penn State   **Ht:** 5' 10"   **Wt:** 187   **Born:** 2/13/71   **Age:** 25

Year Team	G	GS	Tackles			Miscellaneous				Interceptions				Totals		
			Tk	Ast	Sack	FF	FR	TD	Blk	Int	Yds	Avg	TD	Sfty	TD	Pts
1995 Minnesota Vikings	2	0	2	1	0.0	0	0	0	0	0	0	-	0	0	0	0

Rodney Hampton   *(statistical profile on page 324)*

Pos: RB   **Rnd:** 1 (24)   **College:** Georgia   **Ht:** 5' 11"   **Wt:** 230   **Born:** 4/3/69   **Age:** 27

Year Team	G	GS	Rushing					Receiving					Punt Returns				Kickoff Returns				Totals		
			Att	Yds	Avg	Lg	TD	Rec	Yds	Avg	Lg	TD	Num	Yds	Avg	TD	Num	Yds	Avg	TD	Fum	TD	Pts
1990 New York Giants	15	2	109	455	4.2	41	2	32	274	8.6	t27	2	0	0	-	0	20	340	17.0	0	2	4	24
1991 New York Giants	14	14	256	1059	4.1	44	10	43	283	6.6	19	0	0	0	-	0	10	204	20.4	0	5	10	60
1992 New York Giants	16	16	257	1141	4.4	t63	14	28	215	7.7	31	0	0	0	-	0	0	0	-	0	1	14	84
1993 New York Giants	12	10	292	1077	3.7	20	5	18	210	11.7	62	0	0	0	-	0	0	0	-	0	2	5	30
1994 New York Giants	14	13	327	1075	3.3	t27	6	14	103	7.4	17	0	0	0	-	0	0	0	-	0	0	6	38
1995 New York Giants	16	15	306	1182	3.9	32	10	24	142	5.9	18	0	0	0	-	0	0	0	-	0	5	10	62
6 NFL Seasons	87	70	1547	5989	3.9	t63	47	159	1227	7.7	62	2	0	0	-	0	30	544	18.1	0	15	49	298

Other Statistics: 1991–recovered 1 fumble for 0 yards. 1992–recovered 2 fumbles for 0 yards. 1993–recovered 1 fumble for 0 yards. 1994–recovered 1 fumble for 0 yards; scored 1 two-point conversion. 1995–recovered 1 fumble for 0 yards; scored 1 two-point conversion.

Merton Hanks   *(statistical profile on page 417)*

Pos: S   **Rnd:** 5   **College:** Iowa   **Ht:** 6' 2"   **Wt:** 185   **Born:** 3/12/68   **Age:** 28

Year Team	G	GS	Tackles			Miscellaneous				Interceptions				Punt Returns				Kickoff Returns				Totals	
			Tk	Ast	Sack	FF	FR	TD	Blk	Int	Yds	Avg	TD	Num	Yds	Avg	TD	Num	Yds	Avg	TD	TD	Fum
1991 San Francisco 49ers	13	8	34	3	0.0	1	2	0	0	0	0	-	0	0	0	-	0	0	0	-	0	0	0
1992 San Francisco 49ers	16	5	53	11	0.0	0	0	0	0	2	5	2.5	0	1	48	48.0	1	0	0	-	0	1	0
1993 San Francisco 49ers	16	14	61	6	0.0	0	1	0	0	3	104	34.7	1	0	0	-	0	0	0	-	0	1	0
1994 San Francisco 49ers	16	16	65	7	0.5	0	2	0	0	7	93	13.3	0	0	0	-	0	0	0	-	0	0	1
1995 San Francisco 49ers	16	16	54	9	0.0	0	2	1	0	5	31	6.2	0	1	0	0.0	0	0	0	-	0	1	0
5 NFL Seasons	77	59	267	36	0.5	1	7	1	0	17	233	13.7	1	2	48	24.0	1	0	0	-	0	3	1

Travis Hannah

Pos: WR   **Rnd:** 4   **College:** Southern California   **Ht:** 5' 7"   **Wt:** 161   **Born:** 1/31/70   **Age:** 26

Year Team	G	GS	Rushing					Receiving					Punt Returns				Kickoff Returns				Totals		
			Att	Yds	Avg	Lg	TD	Rec	Yds	Avg	Lg	TD	Num	Yds	Avg	TD	Num	Yds	Avg	TD	Fum	TD	Pts
1993 Houston Oilers	12	0	0	0	-	-	0	0	0	-	-	0	0	0	-	0	0	0	-	0	0	0	0
1994 Houston Oilers	8	0	0	0	-	-	0	3	24	8.0	11	0	9	58	6.4	0	5	116	23.2	0	1	0	0
1995 Houston Oilers	16	1	1	5	5.0	5	0	10	142	14.2	42	0	5	36	7.2	0	0	0	-	0	0	0	0
3 NFL Seasons	36	1	1	5	5.0	5	0	13	166	12.8	42	0	14	94	6.7	0	5	116	23.2	0	1	0	0

Other Statistics: 1995–recovered 1 fumble for 0 yards.

Brian Hansen   *(statistical profile on page 474)*

Pos: P   **Rnd:** 9   **College:** Sioux Falls College   **Ht:** 6' 4"   **Wt:** 215   **Born:** 10/26/60   **Age:** 36

Year Team	G	Punting												Rushing		Passing			
		NetPunts	Yards	Avg	Long	In20	In20%	TotPunts	TB	Blocks	OppRet	RetYds	NetAvg	Att	Yards	Att	Com	Yards	Int
1984 New Orleans Saints	16	69	3020	43.8	66	9	13.0	70	7	1	47	550	33.3	2	-27	0	0	0	0
1985 New Orleans Saints	16	89	3763	42.3	58	14	15.7	89	6	0	45	397	36.5	0	0	1	1	8	0
1986 New Orleans Saints	16	81	3456	42.7	66	17	21.0	82	11	1	37	234	36.6	1	0	0	0	0	0
1987 New Orleans Saints	12	52	2104	40.5	60	19	36.5	52	6	0	23	135	35.6	2	-6	0	0	0	0
1988 New Orleans Saints	16	72	2913	40.5	64	19	26.4	73	8	1	39	248	34.3	1	10	0	0	0	0
1990 New England Patriots	16	90	3752	41.7	69	18	20.0	92	8	2	50	503	33.6	1	0	0	0	0	0
1991 Cleveland Browns	16	80	3397	42.5	65	20	25.0	80	6	0	40	388	36.1	2	-3	1	1	11	0
1992 Cleveland Browns	16	74	3083	41.7	73	28	37.8	75	7	1	27	234	36.1	0	0	0	0	0	0
1993 Cleveland Browns	16	82	3632	44.3	72	15	18.3	84	10	2	49	438	35.6	0	0	0	0	0	0
1994 New York Jets	16	84	3534	42.1	64	25	29.8	84	12	0	38	260	36.1	0	0	0	0	0	0
1995 New York Jets	16	99	4090	41.3	67	23	23.2	100	10	1	59	703	31.9	0	0	0	0	0	0
11 NFL Seasons	172	872	36744	42.1	73	207	23.7	881	91	9	454	4090	35.0	9	-26	2	2	19	0

Other Statistics: 1986–recovered 1 fumble for 0 yards; fumbled 1 time. 1990–recovered 2 fumbles for -18 yards; fumbled 1 time. 1991–recovered 1 fumble for 0 yards; passed for 1 touchdown. 1992–recovered 1 fumble for 0 yards; fumbled 1 time.

Phil Hansen

(statistical profile on page 417)

Pos: DE **Rnd:** 2 **College:** North Dakota State **Ht:** 6' 5" **Wt:** 278 **Born:** 5/20/68 **Age:** 28

Year	Team	G	GS	Tk	Ast	Sack	FF	FR	TD	Blk	Int	Yds	Avg	TD	Sfty	TD	Pts
1991	Buffalo Bills	14	10	29	11	2.0	0	1	0	0	0	0	-	0	0	0	0
1992	Buffalo Bills	16	16	47	17	8.0	0	0	0	0	0	0	-	0	0	0	0
1993	Buffalo Bills	11	9	31	12	3.5	2	0	0	0	0	0	-	0	0	0	0
1994	Buffalo Bills	16	16	55	16	5.5	2	0	0	0	0	0	-	0	0	0	0
1995	Buffalo Bills	16	16	53	23	10.0	0	1	0	0	0	0	-	0	0	0	0
	5 NFL Seasons	73	67	215	79	29.0	4	2	0	0	0	0	-	0	0	0	0

Jason Hanson

(statistical profile on page 474)

Pos: K **Rnd:** 2 **College:** Washington State **Ht:** 5' 11" **Wt:** 183 **Born:** 6/17/70 **Age:** 26

Year	Team	G	1-29 Yds	Pct	30-39 Yds	Pct	40-49 Yds	Pct	50+ Yds	Pct	Overall	Pct	Long	Made	Att	Pts
1992	Detroit Lions	16	5-5	100.0	10-10	100.0	4-6	66.7	2-5	40.0	21-26	80.8	52	30	30	93
1993	Detroit Lions	16	9-9	100.0	15-15	100.0	7-12	58.3	3-7	42.9	34-43	79.1	53	28	28	130
1994	Detroit Lions	16	6-7	85.7	7-7	100.0	5-8	62.5	0-5	0.0	18-27	66.7	49	39	40	93
1995	Detroit Lions	16	6-6	100.0	16-17	94.1	5-10	50.0	1-1	100.0	28-34	82.4	56	48	48	132
	4 NFL Seasons	64	26-27	96.3	48-49	98.0	21-36	58.3	6-18	33.3	101-130	77.7	56	145	146	448

Other Statistics: 1995–punted 1 time for 34 yards.

Jim Harbaugh

(statistical profile on page 325)

Pos: QB **Rnd:** 1 (26) **College:** Michigan **Ht:** 6' 3" **Wt:** 215 **Born:** 12/23/63 **Age:** 32

Year	Team	G	GS	Att	Com	Pct	Yards	Yds/Att	Lg	TD	Int	Int%	Rating	Att	Yds	Avg	Lg	TD	Sckd	Yds	Fum	Recv	Yds	Pts
1987	Chicago Bears	6	0	11	8	72.7	62	5.64	21	0	0	0.0	86.2	4	15	3.8	9	0	4	45	0	0	0	0
1988	Chicago Bears	10	2	97	47	48.5	514	5.30	56	0	2	2.1	55.9	19	110	5.8	19	1	6	49	1	0	-1	6
1989	Chicago Bears	12	5	178	111	62.4	1204	6.76	t49	5	9	5.1	70.5	45	276	6.1	t26	3	18	106	2	0	0	18
1990	Chicago Bears	14	14	312	180	57.7	2178	6.98	t80	10	6	1.9	81.9	51	321	6.3	17	4	31	206	8	3	-4	24
1991	Chicago Bears	16	16	478	275	57.5	3121	6.53	t84	15	16	3.3	73.7	70	338	4.8	20	2	24	163	6	0	-3	12
1992	Chicago Bears	16	13	358	202	56.4	2486	6.94	t83	13	12	3.4	76.2	47	272	5.8	17	1	31	167	6	3	0	6
1993	Chicago Bears	15	15	325	200	61.5	2002	6.16	48	7	11	3.4	72.1	60	277	4.6	25	4	43	210	15	4	-1	24
1994	Indianapolis Colts	12	9	202	125	61.9	1440	7.13	t85	9	6	3.0	85.8	39	223	5.7	41	0	17	72	1	0	0	0
1995	Indianapolis Colts	15	12	314	200	63.7	2575	8.20	52	17	5	1.6	100.7	52	235	4.5	21	2	36	219	4	1	-20	12
	9 NFL Seasons	116	86	2275	1348	59.3	15582	6.85	t85	76	67	2.9	78.9	387	2067	5.3	41	17	210	1237	43	11	-29	102

Other Statistics: 1993–caught 1 pass for 1 yard. 1995–caught 1 pass for -9 yards.

Adrian Hardy

Pos: CB **Rnd:** 2 **College:** Northwestern Louisiana **Ht:** 5' 11" **Wt:** 194 **Born:** 8/16/70 **Age:** 26

Year	Team	G	GS	Tk	Ast	Sack	FF	FR	TD	Blk	Int	Yds	Avg	TD	Num	Yds	Avg	TD	Num	Yds	Avg	TD	TD	Fum
1993	San Francisco 49ers	10	0	3	0	0.0	0	0	0	0	0	0	-	0	0	0	-	0	0	0	-	0	0	0
1994	SF - Cin	16	0	0	0	0.0	0	1	0	1	0	0	-	0	0	0	-	0	8	185	23.1	0	0	0
1995	Cincinnati Bengals	10	0	3	0	0.0	0	0	0	0	0	0	-	0	0	0	-	0	0	0	-	0	0	0
1994	San Francisco 49ers	2	0	0	0	0.0	0	0	0	0	0	0	-	0	0	0	-	0	0	0	-	0	0	0
	Cincinnati Bengals	14	0	0	0	0.0	0	1	0	1	0	0	-	0	0	0	-	0	8	185	23.1	0	0	0
	3 NFL Seasons	36	0	6	0	0.0	0	1	0	1	0	0	-	0	0	0	-	0	8	185	23.1	0	0	0

Darryl Hardy

Pos: LB **Rnd:** FA **College:** Tennessee **Ht:** 6' 2" **Wt:** 220 **Born:** 11/22/68 **Age:** 27

Year	Team	G	GS	Tk	Ast	Sack	FF	FR	TD	Blk	Int	Yds	Avg	TD	Sfty	TD	Pts
1995	Ari - Dal	8	0	0	0	0.0	0	0	0	0	0	0	-	0	0	0	0
1995	Arizona Cardinals	4	0	0	0	0.0	0	0	0	0	0	0	-	0	0	0	0
	Dallas Cowboys	4	0	0	0	0.0	0	0	0	0	0	0	-	0	0	0	0

Pat Harlow

Pos: T **Rnd:** 1 (11) **College:** Southern California **Ht:** 6' 6" **Wt:** 290 **Born:** 3/16/69 **Age:** 27

Year	Team	G	GS	Year	Team	G	GS	Year	Team	G	GS		G	GS
1991	New England Patriots	16	16	1993	New England Patriots	16	16	1995	New England Patriots	10	0			
1992	New England Patriots	16	16	1994	New England Patriots	16	16					5 NFL Seasons	74	64

Andy Harmon

(statistical profile on page 417)

Pos: DT   **Rnd:** 6   **College:** Kent State   **Ht:** 6' 4"   **Wt:** 278   **Born:** 4/6/69   **Age:** 27

Year	Team	G	GS	Tackles			Miscellaneous				Interceptions				Totals		
				Tk	Ast	Sack	FF	FR	TD	Blk	Int	Yds	Avg	TD	Sfty	TD	Pts
1991	Philadelphia Eagles	16	0	2	0	0.0	0	0	0	0	0	0	-	0	0	0	0
1992	Philadelphia Eagles	16	13	36	29	7.0	1	1	0	0	0	0	-	0	0	0	0
1993	Philadelphia Eagles	15	15	60	29	11.5	2	2	0	0	0	0	-	0	0	0	0
1994	Philadelphia Eagles	16	16	48	18	9.0	1	2	0	0	1	0	0.0	0	0	0	0
1995	Philadelphia Eagles	15	15	56	7	11.0	3	1	0	0	0	0	-	0	0	0	0
	5 NFL Seasons	78	59	202	83	38.5	7	6	0	0	1	0	0.0	0	0	0	0

Ronnie Harmon

(statistical profile on page 325)

Pos: RB   **Rnd:** 1 (16)   **College:** Iowa   **Ht:** 5' 11"   **Wt:** 200   **Born:** 5/7/64   **Age:** 32

Year	Team	G	GS	Rushing					Receiving					Punt Returns				Kickoff Returns				Totals		
				Att	Yds	Avg	Lg	TD	Rec	Yds	Avg	Lg	TD	Num	Yds	Avg	TD	Num	Yds	Avg	TD	Fum	TD	Pts
1986	Buffalo Bills	14	2	54	172	3.2	38	0	22	185	8.4	27	1	0	0	-	0	18	321	17.8	0	2	1	6
1987	Buffalo Bills	12	10	116	485	4.2	21	2	56	477	8.5	42	2	0	0	-	0	1	30	30.0	0	2	4	24
1988	Buffalo Bills	16	1	57	212	3.7	32	1	37	427	11.5	36	3	0	0	-	0	11	249	22.6	0	2	4	24
1989	Buffalo Bills	15	2	17	99	5.8	24	0	29	363	12.5	t42	4	0	0	-	0	18	409	22.7	0	2	4	24
1990	San Diego Chargers	16	2	66	363	5.5	41	0	46	511	11.1	t36	2	0	0	-	0	0	0	-	0	1	2	12
1991	San Diego Chargers	16	0	89	544	6.1	33	1	59	555	9.4	36	1	0	0	-	0	2	25	12.5	0	2	2	12
1992	San Diego Chargers	16	2	55	235	4.3	33	3	79	914	11.6	55	1	0	0	-	0	7	96	13.7	0	4	4	24
1993	San Diego Chargers	16	1	46	216	4.7	19	0	73	671	9.2	37	2	0	0	-	0	1	18	18.0	0	0	2	12
1994	San Diego Chargers	16	0	25	94	3.8	t15	1	58	615	10.6	35	1	0	0	-	0	9	157	17.4	0	0	2	18
1995	San Diego Chargers	16	1	51	187	3.7	t48	1	62	662	10.7	44	5	0	0	-	0	4	25	6.3	0	1	6	36
	10 NFL Seasons	153	21	576	2607	4.5	t48	9	521	5380	10.3	55	22	0	0	-	0	71	1330	18.7	0	16	31	192

Other Statistics: 1992–recovered 2 fumbles for 0 yards. 1994–recovered 1 fumble for 0 yards; scored 3 two-point conversions.

Alvin Harper

(statistical profile on page 326)

Pos: WR   **Rnd:** 1 (12)   **College:** Tennessee   **Ht:** 6' 4"   **Wt:** 214   **Born:** 7/6/68   **Age:** 28

Year	Team	G	GS	Rushing					Receiving					Kickoff Returns				Passing				Totals		
				Att	Yds	Avg	Lg	TD	Rec	Yds	Avg	Lg	TD	Num	Yds	Avg	TD	Att	Com	Yds	Int	Fum	TD	Pts
1991	Dallas Cowboys	15	5	0	0	-	-	0	20	326	16.3	39	1	0	0	-	0	0	0	0	0	0	1	6
1992	Dallas Cowboys	16	13	1	15	15.0	15	0	35	562	16.1	52	4	0	0	-	0	0	0	0	0	1	4	24
1993	Dallas Cowboys	16	15	0	0	-	-	0	36	777	21.6	t80	5	0	0	-	0	1	1	46	0	1	5	30
1994	Dallas Cowboys	16	14	0	0	-	-	0	33	821	24.9	90	8	0	0	-	0	0	0	0	0	2	8	48
1995	Tampa Bay Buccaneers	13	13	0	0	-	-	0	46	633	13.8	49	2	0	0	-	0	0	0	0	0	0	2	12
	5 NFL Seasons	76	60	1	15	15.0	15	0	170	3119	18.3	90	20	0	0	-	0	1	1	46	0	4	20	120

Other Statistics: 1992–intercepted 1 pass for 1 yard.

Dwayne Harper

(statistical profile on page 418)

Pos: CB   **Rnd:** 11   **College:** South Carolina State   **Ht:** 5' 11"   **Wt:** 174   **Born:** 3/29/66   **Age:** 30

Year	Team	G	GS	Tackles			Miscellaneous				Interceptions				Punt Returns				Kickoff Returns				Totals	
				Tk	Ast	Sack	FF	FR	TD	Blk	Int	Yds	Avg	TD	Num	Yds	Avg	TD	Num	Yds	Avg	TD	TD	Fum
1988	Seattle Seahawks	16	1	29	5	1.0	0	1	0	0	0	0	-	0	0	0	-	0	0	0	-	0	0	0
1989	Seattle Seahawks	16	13	44	5	0.0	0	1	0	0	2	15	7.5	0	0	0	-	0	0	0	-	0	0	0
1990	Seattle Seahawks	16	16	62	9	0.0	0	0	0	0	3	69	23.0	0	0	0	-	0	0	0	-	0	0	0
1991	Seattle Seahawks	16	16	58	11	0.0	0	0	0	0	4	84	21.0	0	1	5	5.0	0	0	0	-	0	0	0
1992	Seattle Seahawks	16	16	51	14	0.0	0	2	1	0	3	74	24.7	0	0	0	-	0	0	0	-	0	1	1
1993	Seattle Seahawks	14	14	60	6	0.0	1	1	0	0	1	0	0.0	0	0	0	-	0	0	0	-	0	0	0
1994	San Diego Chargers	16	16	56	10	0.0	0	0	0	0	3	28	9.3	0	0	0	-	0	0	0	-	0	0	0
1995	San Diego Chargers	16	16	61	15	0.0	0	1	0	0	4	12	3.0	0	0	0	-	0	0	0	-	0	0	0
	8 NFL Seasons	126	108	421	75	1.0	1	6	1	0	20	282	14.1	0	1	5	5.0	0	0	0	-	0	1	1

Roger Harper

Pos: S   **Rnd:** 2   **College:** Ohio State   **Ht:** 6' 2"   **Wt:** 225   **Born:** 10/26/70   **Age:** 26

Year	Team	G	GS	Tackles			Miscellaneous				Interceptions				Totals		
				Tk	Ast	Sack	FF	FR	TD	Blk	Int	Yds	Avg	TD	Sfty	TD	Pts
1993	Atlanta Falcons	16	12	52	60	0.0	0	1	0	0	0	0	-	0	0	0	0
1994	Atlanta Falcons	10	10	37	11	1.0	2	0	0	0	1	22	22.0	0	0	0	0
1995	Atlanta Falcons	16	12	48	17	0.0	1	0	0	1	1	0	0.0	0	0	0	0
	3 NFL Seasons	42	34	137	88	1.0	3	1	0	1	2	22	11.0	0	0	0	0

Other Statistics: 1993–fumbled 1 time.

Shawn Harper

Pos: T **Rnd:** 4 **College:** Indiana **Ht:** 6' 4" **Wt:** 290 **Born:** 7/9/68 **Age:** 28

Year	Team	G	GS
1995	Indianapolis Colts	8	0
	1 NFL Season	8	0

Gary Harrell

Pos: PR/KR **Rnd:** FA **College:** Howard **Ht:** 5' 7" **Wt:** 170 **Born:** 1/23/72 **Age:** 24

Year	Team	G	GS	Rushing					Receiving					Punt Returns				Kickoff Returns				Totals		
				Att	Yds	Avg	Lg	TD	Rec	Yds	Avg	Lg	TD	Num	Yds	Avg	TD	Num	Yds	Avg	TD	Fum	TD	Pts
1995	New York Giants	4	0	0	0	-	-	0	0	0	-	-	0	12	76	6.3	0	1	23	23.0	0	0	0	0

Bernardo Harris

Pos: LB **Rnd:** FA **College:** North Carolina **Ht:** 6' 2" **Wt:** 243 **Born:** 10/15/71 **Age:** 25

Year	Team	G	GS	Tackles			Miscellaneous				Interceptions				Totals		
				Tk	Ast	Sack	FF	FR	TD	Blk	Int	Yds	Avg	TD	Sfty	TD	Pts
1995	Green Bay Packers	11	0	4	1	0.0	0	0	0	0	0	0	-	0	0	0	0

Corey Harris

(statistical profile on page 418)

Pos: CB/KR **Rnd:** 3 **College:** Vanderbilt **Ht:** 5' 11" **Wt:** 195 **Born:** 10/25/69 **Age:** 27

Year	Team	G	GS	Tackles			Miscellaneous				Interceptions				Punt Returns				Kickoff Returns				Totals	
				Tk	Ast	Sack	FF	FR	TD	Blk	Int	Yds	Avg	TD	Num	Yds	Avg	TD	Num	Yds	Avg	TD	TD	Fum
1992	Hou - GB	15	0	0	0	0.0	0	0	0	0	0	0	-	0	6	17	2.8	0	33	691	20.9	0	0	0
1993	Green Bay Packers	11	0	4	0	0.0	1	0	0	0	0	0	-	0	0	0	-	0	16	482	30.1	0	0	0
1994	Green Bay Packers	16	2	32	6	0.0	1	1	0	0	0	0	-	0	0	0	-	0	29	618	21.3	0	0	1
1995	Seattle Seahawks	16	16	76	9	0.0	1	1	1	0	3	-5	-1.7	0	0	0	-	0	19	397	20.9	0	1	0
1992	Houston Oilers	5	0	0	0	0.0	0	0	0	0	0	0	-	0	6	17	2.8	0	10	206	20.6	0	0	0
	Green Bay Packers	10	0	0	0	0.0	0	0	0	0	0	0	-	0	0	0	-	0	23	485	21.1	0	0	0
	4 NFL Seasons	58	18	112	15	0.0	3	2	1	0	3	-5	-1.7	0	6	17	2.8	0	97	2188	22.6	0	1	1

Other Statistics: 1992–rushed 2 times for 10 yards. 1993–caught 2 passes for 11 yards.

Jackie Harris

(statistical profile on page 326)

Pos: TE **Rnd:** 4 **College:** Northeast Louisiana **Ht:** 6' 4" **Wt:** 248 **Born:** 1/4/68 **Age:** 28

Year	Team	G	GS	Rushing					Receiving					Punt Returns				Kickoff Returns				Totals		
				Att	Yds	Avg	Lg	TD	Rec	Yds	Avg	Lg	TD	Num	Yds	Avg	TD	Num	Yds	Avg	TD	Fum	TD	Pts
1990	Green Bay Packers	16	3	0	0	-	-	0	12	157	13.1	26	0	0	0	-	0	0	0	-	0	0	0	0
1991	Green Bay Packers	16	6	1	1	1.0	1	0	24	264	11.0	35	3	0	0	-	0	0	0	-	0	1	3	18
1992	Green Bay Packers	16	11	0	0	-	-	0	55	595	10.8	40	2	0	0	-	0	0	0	-	0	1	2	12
1993	Green Bay Packers	12	12	0	0	-	-	0	42	604	14.4	t66	4	0	0	-	0	0	0	-	0	0	4	24
1994	Tampa Bay Buccaneers	9	9	0	0	-	-	0	26	337	13.0	t48	3	0	0	-	0	0	0	-	0	3	3	20
1995	Tampa Bay Buccaneers	16	16	0	0	-	-	0	62	751	12.1	33	1	0	0	-	0	0	0	-	0	2	1	6
	6 NFL Seasons	85	57	1	1	1.0	1	0	221	2708	12.3	t66	13	0	0	-	0	0	0	-	0	4	13	80

Other Statistics: 1991–recovered 1 fumble for 0 yards. 1994–scored 1 two-point conversion.

James Harris

Pos: DE **Rnd:** FA **College:** Temple **Ht:** 6' 6" **Wt:** 255 **Born:** 5/13/68 **Age:** 28

Year	Team	G	GS	Tackles			Miscellaneous				Interceptions				Totals		
				Tk	Ast	Sack	FF	FR	TD	Blk	Int	Yds	Avg	TD	Sfty	TD	Pts
1993	Minnesota Vikings	6	0	0	1	0.0	0	0	0	0	0	0	-	0	0	0	0
1994	Minnesota Vikings	16	16	28	8	3.0	1	3	1	0	1	21	21.0	0	0	1	6
1995	Minnesota Vikings	12	3	4	0	1.0	0	1	0	0	0	0	-	0	0	0	0
	3 NFL Seasons	34	19	32	9	4.0	1	4	1	0	1	21	21.0	0	0	1	6

Other Statistics: 1994–fumbled 2 times.

Odie Harris

Pos: CB/S **Rnd:** FA **College:** Sam Houston State **Ht:** 6' 0" **Wt:** 190 **Born:** 4/1/66 **Age:** 30

Year	Team	G	GS	Tackles			Miscellaneous				Interceptions				Totals		
				Tk	Ast	Sack	FF	FR	TD	Blk	Int	Yds	Avg	TD	Sfty	TD	Pts
1988	Tampa Bay Buccaneers	16	7	37	9	0.0	0	1	0	0	2	26	13.0	0	0	0	0
1989	Tampa Bay Buccaneers	16	2	5	5	0.0	0	0	0	0	1	19	19.0	0	0	0	0
1990	Tampa Bay Buccaneers	16	0	5	2	0.0	0	0	0	0	0	0	-	0	0	0	0
1991	Cleveland Browns	16	0	1	2	0.0	0	0	0	0	0	0	-	0	0	0	0
1992	Cle - Pho	12	0	1	2	0.0	0	0	0	0	0	0	-	0	0	0	0
1993	Phoenix Cardinals	16	0	0	0	0.0	0	0	0	0	0	0	-	0	0	0	0
1994	Arizona Cardinals	13	0	2	0	0.0	0	1	0	0	0	0	-	0	0	0	0
1995	Houston Oilers	16	2	10	9	0.0	0	0	0	0	2	0	0.0	0	0	0	0

Year Team	G	GS	Tk	Ast	Sack	FF	FR	TD	Blk	Int	Yds	Avg	TD	Sfty	TD	Pts
1992 Cleveland Browns	4	0	0	0	0.0	0	0	0	0	0	0	-	0	0	0	0
Phoenix Cardinals	8	0	1	2	0.0	0	0	0	0	0	0	-	0	0	0	0
8 NFL Seasons	121	11	61	29	0.0	0	3	0	0	5	45	9.0	0	0	0	0

Raymont Harris

Pos: RB **Rnd:** 4 **College:** Ohio State **Ht:** 6' 0" **Wt:** 225 **Born:** 12/23/70 **Age:** 25

Year Team	G	GS	Att	Yds	Avg	Lg	TD	Rec	Yds	Avg	Lg	TD	Num	Yds	Avg	TD	Num	Yds	Avg	TD	Fum	TD	Pts
			Rushing					Receiving					Punt Returns				Kickoff Returns				Totals		
1994 Chicago Bears	16	11	123	464	3.8	13	1	39	236	6.1	18	0	0	0	-	0	1	18	18.0	0	1	1	6
1995 Chicago Bears	2	1	0	0	-	0	0	1	4	4.0	4	0	0	0	-	0	0	0	-	0	0	0	0
2 NFL Seasons	18	12	123	464	3.8	13	1	40	240	6.0	18	0	0	0	-	0	1	18	18.0	0	1	1	6

Other Statistics: 1994–recovered 3 fumbles for 5 yards.

Robert Harris

(statistical profile on page 418)

Pos: DE **Rnd:** 2 **College:** Southern **Ht:** 6' 4" **Wt:** 290 **Born:** 6/13/69 **Age:** 27

Year Team	G	GS	Tk	Ast	Sack	FF	FR	TD	Blk	Int	Yds	Avg	TD	Sfty	TD	Pts
1992 Minnesota Vikings	7	0	1	3	0.0	0	0	0	0	0	0	-	0	0	0	0
1993 Minnesota Vikings	16	0	10	4	1.0	1	0	0	0	0	0	-	0	0	0	0
1994 Minnesota Vikings	11	1	6	2	2.0	0	0	0	0	0	0	-	0	0	0	0
1995 New York Giants	15	15	34	7	5.0	2	2	0	0	0	0	-	0	0	0	0
4 NFL Seasons	49	16	51	16	8.0	3	2	0	0	0	0	-	0	0	0	0

Ronnie Harris

Pos: WR **Rnd:** FA **College:** Oregon **Ht:** 5' 11" **Wt:** 180 **Born:** 6/4/70 **Age:** 26

Year Team	G	GS	Att	Yds	Avg	Lg	TD	Rec	Yds	Avg	Lg	TD	Num	Yds	Avg	TD	Num	Yds	Avg	TD	Fum	TD	Pts
			Rushing					Receiving					Punt Returns				Kickoff Returns				Totals		
1993 New England Patriots	5	0	0	0	-	0	0	0	0	-	0	0	23	201	8.7	0	6	90	15.0	0	2	0	0
1994 NE - Sea	2	0	0	0	-	0	0	1	11	11.0	11	0	3	26	8.7	0	0	0	-	0	1	0	0
1995 Seattle Seahawks	13	0	0	0	-	0	0	0	0	-	0	0	3	23	7.7	0	1	29	29.0	0	0	0	0
1994 New England Patriots	1	0	0	0	-	0	0	1	11	11.0	11	0	3	26	8.7	0	0	0	-	0	1	0	0
Seattle Seahawks	1	0	0	0	-	0	0	0	0	-	0	0	0	0	-	0	0	0	-	0	0	0	0
3 NFL Seasons	20	0	0	0	-	0	0	1	11	11.0	11	0	29	250	8.6	0	7	119	17.0	0	3	0	0

Other Statistics: 1993–recovered 1 fumble for 0 yards.

Sean Harris

Pos: LB **Rnd:** 3 **College:** Arizona **Ht:** 6' 3" **Wt:** 244 **Born:** 2/25/72 **Age:** 24

Year Team	G	GS	Tk	Ast	Sack	FF	FR	TD	Blk	Int	Yds	Avg	TD	Sfty	TD	Pts
1995 Chicago Bears	11	0	0	0	0.0	0	0	0	0	0	0	-	0	0	0	0

Tim Harris

Pos: DE **Rnd:** 4 **College:** Memphis **Ht:** 6' 6" **Wt:** 265 **Born:** 9/10/64 **Age:** 32

Year Team	G	GS	Tk	Ast	Sack	FF	FR	TD	Blk	Int	Yds	Avg	TD	Sfty	TD	Pts
1986 Green Bay Packers	16	10	51	16	8.0	0	1	0	0	0	0	-	0	0	0	0
1987 Green Bay Packers	12	12	55	14	7.0	0	0	0	0	0	0	-	0	0	0	0
1988 Green Bay Packers	16	16	83	28	13.5	0	0	1	0	0	0	-	0	2	1	10
1989 Green Bay Packers	16	16	45	41	19.5	0	3	0	0	0	0	-	0	0	0	0
1990 Green Bay Packers	16	16	54	36	7.0	0	2	0	0	0	0	-	0	0	0	0
1991 San Francisco 49ers	11	5	28	7	3.0	0	1	0	0	0	0	-	0	0	0	0
1992 San Francisco 49ers	16	14	56	8	17.0	0	1	0	0	0	0	-	0	0	0	0
1993 Philadelphia Eagles	4	3	2	4	0.0	1	0	0	0	0	0	-	0	0	0	0
1994 San Francisco 49ers	5	1	2	1	2.0	0	0	0	0	0	0	-	0	0	0	0
1995 San Francisco 49ers	10	0	8	0	4.0	1	0	0	0	0	0	-	0	0	0	0
10 NFL Seasons	122	93	384	155	81.0	2	8	1	0	0	0	-	0	2	1	10

Martin Harrison

Pos: DE **Rnd:** 10 **College:** Washington **Ht:** 6' 6" **Wt:** 263 **Born:** 9/20/67 **Age:** 29

Year Team	G	GS	Tk	Ast	Sack	FF	FR	TD	Blk	Int	Yds	Avg	TD	Sfty	TD	Pts
1990 San Francisco 49ers	2	0	4	0	0.0	0	0	0	0	0	0	-	0	0	0	0
1992 San Francisco 49ers	16	1	11	1	3.5	0	0	0	0	0	0	-	0	0	0	0
1993 San Francisco 49ers	11	1	21	2	6.0	2	0	0	0	0	0	-	0	0	0	0

Year Team	G	GS	Tackles			Miscellaneous				Interceptions				Totals		
			Tk	Ast	Sack	FF	FR	TD	Blk	Int	Yds	Avg	TD	Sfty	TD	Pts
1994 Minnesota Vikings	13	0	2	1	0.0	0	0	0	0	0	0	-	0	0	0	0
1995 Minnesota Vikings	11	0	10	4	4.5	0	0	0	0	1	15	15.0	0	0	0	0
5 NFL Seasons	53	2	48	8	14.0	2	0	0	0	1	15	15.0	0	0	0	0

Nolan Harrison

Pos: DE/DT **Rnd:** 6 **College:** Indiana **Ht:** 6' 5" **Wt:** 280 **Born:** 1/25/69 **Age:** 27

Year Team	G	GS	Tackles			Miscellaneous				Interceptions				Totals		
			Tk	Ast	Sack	FF	FR	TD	Blk	Int	Yds	Avg	TD	Sfty	TD	Pts
1991 Los Angeles Raiders	12	3	18	-	1.0	0	0	0	0	0	0	-	0	0	0	0
1992 Los Angeles Raiders	14	14	38	-	2.5	0	0	0	0	0	0	-	0	1	0	2
1993 Los Angeles Raiders	16	14	33	15	3.0	1	1	0	0	0	0	-	0	0	0	0
1994 Los Angeles Raiders	16	16	35	12	5.0	1	2	0	0	0	0	-	0	0	0	0
1995 Oakland Raiders	7	6	10	4	0.0	1	0	0	0	0	0	-	0	0	0	0
5 NFL Seasons	65	53	134	31	11.5	3	3	0	0	0	0	-	0	1	0	2

Rodney Harrison

Pos: S **Rnd:** 5 **College:** Western Illinois **Ht:** 6' 0" **Wt:** 201 **Born:** 12/15/72 **Age:** 23

Year Team	G	GS	Tackles			Miscellaneous				Interceptions				Totals		
			Tk	Ast	Sack	FF	FR	TD	Blk	Int	Yds	Avg	TD	Sfty	TD	Pts
1994 San Diego Chargers	15	0	0	0	0.0	0	1	0	0	0	0	-	0	0	0	0
1995 San Diego Chargers	11	0	21	3	0.0	0	0	0	0	5	22	4.4	0	0	0	0
2 NFL Seasons	26	0	21	3	0.0	0	1	0	0	5	22	4.4	0	0	0	0

Frank Hartley

Pos: TE **Rnd:** FA **College:** Illinois **Ht:** 6' 2" **Wt:** 268 **Born:** 12/15/67 **Age:** 28

Year Team	G	GS	Rushing					Receiving					Punt Returns				Kickoff Returns				Totals		
			Att	Yds	Avg	Lg	TD	Rec	Yds	Avg	Lg	TD	Num	Yds	Avg	TD	Num	Yds	Avg	TD	Fum	TD	Pts
1994 Cleveland Browns	10	5	0	0	-	-	0	3	13	4.3	8	0	0	0	-	0	0	0	-	0	0	1	6
1995 Cleveland Browns	15	13	0	0	-	-	0	11	137	12.5	23	1	0	0	-	0	0	0	-	0	1	1	6
2 NFL Seasons	25	18	0	0	-	-	0	14	150	10.7	23	2	0	0	-	0	0	0	-	0	1	2	12

Other Statistics: 1995–recovered 1 fumble for 0 yards.

Ken Harvey

(statistical profile on page 419)

Pos: LB **Rnd:** 1 (12) **College:** California **Ht:** 6' 2" **Wt:** 245 **Born:** 5/6/65 **Age:** 31

Year Team	G	GS	Tackles			Miscellaneous				Interceptions				Totals		
			Tk	Ast	Sack	FF	FR	TD	Blk	Int	Yds	Avg	TD	Sfty	TD	Pts
1988 Phoenix Cardinals	16	0	33	3	6.0	0	0	0	0	0	0	-	0	1	0	2
1989 Phoenix Cardinals	16	16	87	33	7.0	0	0	0	0	0	0	-	0	0	0	0
1990 Phoenix Cardinals	16	16	60	39	10.0	0	1	0	0	0	0	-	0	0	0	0
1991 Phoenix Cardinals	16	16	48	31	9.0	0	2	0	0	0	0	-	0	0	0	0
1992 Phoenix Cardinals	10	10	39	12	6.0	0	2	0	0	0	0	-	0	0	0	0
1993 Phoenix Cardinals	16	6	32	20	9.5	2	0	0	0	0	0	-	0	0	0	0
1994 Washington Redskins	16	16	80	18	13.5	4	1	0	0	0	0	-	0	0	0	0
1995 Washington Redskins	16	16	78	6	7.5	5	2	0	0	0	0	-	0	0	0	0
8 NFL Seasons	122	96	457	162	68.5	11	8	0	0	0	0	-	0	1	0	2

Richard Harvey

(statistical profile on page 419)

Pos: LB **Rnd:** 11 **College:** Tulane **Ht:** 6' 1" **Wt:** 242 **Born:** 9/11/66 **Age:** 30

Year Team	G	GS	Tackles			Miscellaneous				Interceptions				Totals		
			Tk	Ast	Sack	FF	FR	TD	Blk	Int	Yds	Avg	TD	Sfty	TD	Pts
1990 New England Patriots	16	9	33	19	0.0	0	0	0	0	0	0	-	0	0	0	0
1991 New England Patriots	1	0	0	0	0.0	0	0	0	0	0	0	-	0	0	0	0
1992 Buffalo Bills	12	0	4	2	0.0	0	1	0	0	0	0	-	0	0	0	0
1993 Buffalo Bills	15	0	2	2	0.0	1	0	0	0	0	0	-	0	0	0	0
1994 Denver Broncos	16	1	4	2	0.0	0	1	0	0	0	0	-	0	0	0	0
1995 New Orleans Saints	16	14	85	27	2.0	1	0	0	0	0	0	-	0	0	0	0
6 NFL Seasons	76	24	128	52	2.0	2	2	0	0	0	0	-	0	0	0	0

Carlton Haselrig

Pos: G **Rnd:** 12 **College:** Pittsburgh-Johnstown **Ht:** 6' 1" **Wt:** 290 **Born:** 1/22/66 **Age:** 30

Year	Team	G	GS	Year	Team	G	GS	Year	Team	G	GS		G	GS
1990	Pittsburgh Steelers	16	0	1992	Pittsburgh Steelers	16	16	1995	New York Jets	11	11			
1991	Pittsburgh Steelers	16	16	1993	Pittsburgh Steelers	9	4					5 NFL Seasons	68	47

Other Statistics: 1991–recovered 1 fumble for 2 yards. 1992–recovered 1 fumble for 4 yards.

Harald Hasselbach

Pos: DE **Rnd:** FA **College:** Washington **Ht:** 6' 6" **Wt:** 280 **Born:** 9/22/67 **Age:** 29

			Tackles			Miscellaneous				Interceptions				Totals		
Year	Team	G	GS	Tk	Ast	Sack	FF	FR	TD	Blk	Int	Yds	Avg	TD	Sfty	TD	Pts
1994	Denver Broncos	16	8	33	8	2.0	1	0	0	0	0	0	-	0	0	0	0
1995	Denver Broncos	16	10	21	7	4.0	0	4	0	0	0	0	-	0	0	0	0
	2 NFL Seasons	32	18	54	15	6.0	1	4	0	0	0	0	-	0	0	0	0

Andre Hastings

(statistical profile on page 327)

Pos: WR/PR **Rnd:** 3 **College:** Georgia **Ht:** 6' 1" **Wt:** 188 **Born:** 11/7/70 **Age:** 25

				Rushing				Receiving				Punt Returns			Kickoff Returns			Totals		
Year	Team	G	GS	Att	Yds	Avg	Lg	TD	Rec	Yds	Avg	Lg	TD	Num	Yds	Avg	TD	Num	Yds	Avg	TD	Fum	TD	Pts
1993	Pittsburgh Steelers	6	0	0	0	-	-	0	3	44	14.7	18	0	0	0	-	0	12	177	14.8	0	0	0	0
1994	Pittsburgh Steelers	16	8	0	0	-	-	0	20	281	14.1	46	2	2	15	7.5	0	0	0	-	0	0	2	12
1995	Pittsburgh Steelers	16	0	1	14	14.0	14	0	48	502	10.5	36	1	48	474	9.9	1	0	0	-	0	1	2	12
	3 NFL Seasons	38	8	1	14	14.0	14	0	71	827	11.6	46	3	50	489	9.8	1	12	177	14.8	0	1	4	24

James Hasty

(statistical profile on page 419)

Pos: CB **Rnd:** 3 **College:** Washington State **Ht:** 6' 0" **Wt:** 201 **Born:** 5/23/65 **Age:** 31

				Tackles			Miscellaneous				Interceptions				Punt Returns			Kickoff Returns			Totals	
Year	Team	G	GS	Tk	Ast	Sack	FF	FR	TD	Blk	Int	Yds	Avg	TD	Num	Yds	Avg	TD	Num	Yds	Avg	TD	TD	Fum
1988	New York Jets	15	15	45	13	1.0	0	3	0	0	5	20	4.0	0	0	0	-	0	0	0	-	0	0	0
1989	New York Jets	16	16	51	12	0.0	0	2	0	0	5	62	12.4	1	0	0	-	0	0	0	-	0	1	1
1990	New York Jets	16	16	49	17	0.0	1	3	0	0	2	0	0.0	0	1	0	0.0	0	0	0	-	0	0	1
1991	New York Jets	16	16	65	29	0.0	0	4	0	0	3	39	13.0	0	0	0	-	0	0	0	-	0	0	0
1992	New York Jets	16	16	43	22	0.0	2	2	0	0	2	18	9.0	0	0	0	-	0	0	0	-	0	0	0
1993	New York Jets	16	16	49	19	0.0	1	2	0	0	2	22	11.0	0	0	0	-	0	0	0	-	0	0	0
1994	New York Jets	16	16	77	11	3.0	2	2	0	0	5	90	18.0	0	0	0	-	0	0	0	-	0	0	0
1995	Kansas City Chiefs	16	16	72	3	0.0	1	1	0	0	3	89	29.7	1	0	0	-	0	0	0	-	0	1	0
	8 NFL Seasons	127	127	451	126	4.0	7	19	0	0	27	340	12.6	2	1	0	0.0	0	0	0	-	0	2	2

Tim Hauck

Pos: S **Rnd:** FA **College:** Montana **Ht:** 5' 10" **Wt:** 187 **Born:** 12/20/66 **Age:** 29

				Tackles			Miscellaneous				Interceptions				Punt Returns			Kickoff Returns			Totals	
Year	Team	G	GS	Tk	Ast	Sack	FF	FR	TD	Blk	Int	Yds	Avg	TD	Num	Yds	Avg	TD	Num	Yds	Avg	TD	TD	Fum
1990	New England Patriots	10	0	3	1	0.0	0	0	0	0	0	0	-	0	0	0	-	0	0	0	-	0	0	0
1991	Green Bay Packers	16	0	6	1	0.0	0	1	0	0	0	0	-	0	0	0	-	0	0	0	-	0	0	0
1992	Green Bay Packers	16	0	15	-	0.0	1	0	0	0	0	0	-	0	1	2	2.0	0	0	0	-	0	0	0
1993	Green Bay Packers	13	0	0	2	0.0	0	1	0	0	0	0	-	0	0	0	-	0	0	0	-	0	0	0
1994	Green Bay Packers	13	3	28	12	0.0	1	0	0	0	0	0	-	0	0	0	-	0	0	0	-	0	0	0
1995	Denver Broncos	16	0	12	2	0.0	0	0	0	0	0	0	-	0	0	0	-	0	0	0	-	0	0	0
	6 NFL Seasons	84	3	64	18	0.0	2	2	0	0	0	0	-	0	1	2	2.0	0	0	0	-	0	0	0

Courtney Hawkins

(statistical profile on page 327)

Pos: WR **Rnd:** 2 **College:** Michigan State **Ht:** 5' 9" **Wt:** 183 **Born:** 12/12/69 **Age:** 26

				Rushing				Receiving				Punt Returns			Kickoff Returns			Totals		
Year	Team	G	GS	Att	Yds	Avg	Lg	TD	Rec	Yds	Avg	Lg	TD	Num	Yds	Avg	TD	Num	Yds	Avg	TD	Fum	TD	Pts
1992	Tampa Bay Buccaneers	16	5	0	0	-	-	0	20	336	16.8	49	2	13	53	4.1	0	9	118	13.1	0	2	2	12
1993	Tampa Bay Buccaneers	16	12	0	0	-	-	0	62	933	15.0	67	5	15	166	11.1	0	0	0	-	0	2	5	30
1994	Tampa Bay Buccaneers	13	12	0	0	-	-	0	37	438	11.8	32	5	5	28	5.6	0	0	0	-	0	0	5	30
1995	Tampa Bay Buccaneers	16	3	4	5	1.3	11	0	41	493	12.0	47	0	0	0	-	0	0	0	-	0	1	0	0
	4 NFL Seasons	61	32	4	5	1.3	11	0	160	2200	13.8	67	12	33	247	7.5	0	9	118	13.1	0	5	12	72

Other Statistics: 1992–recovered 1 fumble for 0 yards.

Garland Hawkins

Pos: DE **Rnd:** FA **College:** Syracuse **Ht:** 6' 3" **Wt:** 253 **Born:** 2/19/70 **Age:** 26

				Tackles			Miscellaneous				Interceptions				Totals		
Year	Team	G	GS	Tk	Ast	Sack	FF	FR	TD	Blk	Int	Yds	Avg	TD	Sfty	TD	Pts
1995	Chicago Bears	1	0	1	0	0.0	0	0	0	0	0	0	-	0	0	0	0

Ed Hawthorne

Pos: WR **Rnd:** FA **College:** Minnesota **Ht:** 6' 1" **Wt:** 305 **Born:** 7/30/70 **Age:** 26

				Rushing				Receiving				Punt Returns			Kickoff Returns			Totals		
Year	Team	G	GS	Att	Yds	Avg	Lg	TD	Rec	Yds	Avg	Lg	TD	Num	Yds	Avg	TD	Num	Yds	Avg	TD	Fum	TD	Pts
1995	Miami Dolphins	1	0	0	0	-	-	0	0	0	-	-	0	0	0	-	0	0	0	-	0	0	0	0

Aaron Hayden

(statistical profile on page 328)

Pos: RB **Rnd:** 4 **College:** Tennessee **Ht:** 6' 0" **Wt:** 218 **Born:** 4/13/73 **Age:** 23

Year	Team	G	GS	Rushing					Receiving					Punt Returns				Kickoff Returns				Totals		
				Att	Yds	Avg	Lg	TD	Rec	Yds	Avg	Lg	TD	Num	Yds	Avg	TD	Num	Yds	Avg	TD	Fum	TD	Pts
1995	San Diego Chargers	7	4	128	470	3.7	20	3	5	53	10.6	16	0	0	0	-	0	0	0	-	0	0	3	18

Jonathan Hayes

Pos: TE **Rnd:** 2 **College:** Iowa **Ht:** 6' 5" **Wt:** 248 **Born:** 8/11/62 **Age:** 34

Year	Team	G	GS	Rushing					Receiving					Punt Returns				Kickoff Returns				Totals		
				Att	Yds	Avg	Lg	TD	Rec	Yds	Avg	Lg	TD	Num	Yds	Avg	TD	Num	Yds	Avg	TD	Fum	TD	Pts
1985	Kansas City Chiefs	16	0	0	0	-	0	0	5	39	7.8	12	1	0	0	-	0	1	0	0.0	0	0	1	6
1986	Kansas City Chiefs	16	4	0	0	-	0	0	8	69	8.6	16	0	0	0	-	0	0	0	-	0	0	0	0
1987	Kansas City Chiefs	12	8	0	0	-	0	0	21	272	13.0	33	2	0	0	-	0	0	0	-	0	0	2	12
1988	Kansas City Chiefs	16	9	0	0	-	0	0	22	233	10.6	25	1	0	0	-	0	0	0	-	0	0	1	6
1989	Kansas City Chiefs	16	16	0	0	-	0	0	18	229	12.7	23	2	0	0	-	0	0	0	-	0	1	2	12
1990	Kansas City Chiefs	12	11	0	0	-	0	0	9	83	9.2	21	1	0	0	-	0	0	0	-	0	0	1	6
1991	Kansas City Chiefs	16	16	0	0	-	0	0	19	208	10.9	23	2	0	0	-	0	0	0	-	0	1	2	12
1992	Kansas City Chiefs	16	16	0	0	-	0	0	9	77	8.6	21	2	0	0	-	0	0	0	-	0	1	2	12
1993	Kansas City Chiefs	16	16	0	0	-	0	0	24	331	13.8	49	1	0	0	-	0	0	0	-	0	1	1	6
1994	Pittsburgh Steelers	16	6	0	0	-	0	0	5	50	10.0	17	1	0	0	-	0	0	0	-	0	1	1	6
1995	Pittsburgh Steelers	16	6	0	0	-	0	0	11	113	10.3	32	0	0	0	-	0	0	0	-	0	0	0	0
	11 NFL Seasons	168	108	0	0	-	-	0	151	1704	11.3	49	13	0	0	-	0	1	0	0.0	0	4	13	78

Other Statistics: 1987–recovered 1 fumble for 0 yards.

Melvin Hayes

Pos: T **Rnd:** 4 **College:** Mississippi State **Ht:** 6' 6" **Wt:** 329 **Born:** 4/28/73 **Age:** 23

Year	Team	G	GS				G	GS
1995	New York Jets	3	0			1 NFL Season	3	0

Michael Haynes

(statistical profile on page 328)

Pos: WR **Rnd:** 7 **College:** Northern Arizona **Ht:** 6' 0" **Wt:** 184 **Born:** 12/24/65 **Age:** 30

Year	Team	G	GS	Rushing					Receiving					Punt Returns				Kickoff Returns				Totals		
				Att	Yds	Avg	Lg	TD	Rec	Yds	Avg	Lg	TD	Num	Yds	Avg	TD	Num	Yds	Avg	TD	Fum	TD	Pts
1988	Atlanta Falcons	15	5	0	0	-	0	0	13	232	17.8	t49	4	0	0	-	0	6	113	18.8	0	0	4	24
1989	Atlanta Falcons	13	11	4	35	8.8	21	0	40	681	17.0	t72	4	0	0	-	0	0	0	-	0	0	4	24
1990	Atlanta Falcons	13	10	0	0	-	0	0	31	445	14.4	60	0	0	0	-	0	0	0	-	0	0	0	0
1991	Atlanta Falcons	16	16	0	0	-	0	0	50	1122	22.4	t80	11	0	0	-	0	0	0	-	0	0	11	66
1992	Atlanta Falcons	14	14	0	0	-	0	0	48	808	16.8	t89	10	0	0	-	0	0	0	-	0	0	10	60
1993	Atlanta Falcons	16	16	0	0	-	0	0	72	778	10.8	t98	4	0	0	-	0	0	0	-	0	1	4	24
1994	New Orleans Saints	16	16	4	43	10.8	15	0	77	985	12.8	t78	5	0	0	-	0	0	0	-	0	1	5	30
1995	New Orleans Saints	16	15	0	0	-	0	0	41	597	14.6	48	4	0	0	-	0	0	0	-	0	0	4	24
	8 NFL Seasons	119	103	8	78	9.8	21	0	372	5648	15.2	t98	42	0	0	-	0	6	113	18.8	0	2	42	252

Tracy Hayworth

Pos: LB **Rnd:** 7 **College:** Tennessee **Ht:** 6' 3" **Wt:** 250 **Born:** 12/18/67 **Age:** 28

Year	Team	G	GS	Tackles			Miscellaneous				Interceptions				Totals		
				Tk	Ast	Sack	FF	FR	TD	Blk	Int	Yds	Avg	TD	Sfty	TD	Pts
1990	Detroit Lions	16	0	18	3	4.0	0	1	0	0	0	0	-	0	0	0	0
1991	Detroit Lions	16	14	26	17	2.0	0	2	1	0	1	0	0.0	0	0	1	6
1992	Detroit Lions	4	0	2	0	0.0	0	0	0	0	0	0	-	0	0	0	0
1993	Detroit Lions	11	2	6	2	2.0	0	0	0	0	0	0	-	0	0	0	0
1994	Detroit Lions	9	1	7	1	1.0	0	0	0	0	0	0	-	0	0	0	0
1995	Detroit Lions	16	14	23	8	1.0	1	1	0	0	0	0	-	0	0	0	0
	6 NFL Seasons	72	31	82	31	10.0	1	4	1	0	1	0	0.0	0	0	1	6

Garrison Hearst

(statistical profile on page 329)

Pos: RB **Rnd:** 1 (3) **College:** Georgia **Ht:** 5' 11" **Wt:** 215 **Born:** 1/4/71 **Age:** 25

Year	Team	G	GS	Rushing					Receiving					Kickoff Returns				Passing				Totals		
				Att	Yds	Avg	Lg	TD	Rec	Yds	Avg	Lg	TD	Num	Yds	Avg	TD	Att	Com	Yds	Int	Fum	TD	Pts
1993	Phoenix Cardinals	6	5	76	264	3.5	57	1	6	18	3.0	9	0	0	0	-	0	1	0	0	1	2	1	6
1994	Arizona Cardinals	9	0	37	169	4.6	36	1	6	49	8.2	29	0	0	0	-	0	1	1	10	0	0	1	6
1995	Arizona Cardinals	16	15	284	1070	3.8	38	1	29	243	8.4	39	1	0	0	-	0	2	1	16	0	12	2	12
	3 NFL Seasons	31	20	397	1503	3.8	57	3	41	310	7.6	39	1	0	0	-	0	4	2	26	1	14	4	24

Other Statistics: 1994–passed for 1 touchdown. 1995–recovered 2 fumbles for 0 yards.

Bobby Hebert

Pos: QB **Rnd:** FA **College:** Northwestern Louisiana **Ht:** 6' 4" **Wt:** 215 **Born:** 8/19/60 **Age:** 36

					Passing								Rushing					Miscellaneous				
Year	Team	G	GS	Att	Com	Pct	Yards	Yds/Att	Lg	TD	Int	Int%	Rating	Att	Yds	Avg	Lg	TD	Sckd	Yds	Fum	Recv	Yds	Pts
1985	New Orleans Saints	6	6	181	97	53.6	1208	6.67	t76	5	4	2.2	74.6	12	26	2.2	8	0	17	150	1	1	0	6
1986	New Orleans Saints	5	3	79	41	51.9	498	6.30	84	2	8	10.1	40.5	5	14	2.8	7	0	5	34	3	0	0	0
1987	New Orleans Saints	12	12	294	164	55.8	2119	7.21	67	15	9	3.1	82.9	13	95	7.3	19	0	20	119	4	2	0	0
1988	New Orleans Saints	16	16	478	280	58.6	3156	6.60	t40	20	15	3.1	79.3	37	79	2.1	16	0	24	171	9	1	0	0
1989	New Orleans Saints	14	13	353	222	62.9	2686	7.61	t54	15	15	4.2	82.7	25	87	3.5	11	0	22	171	2	0	0	0
1991	New Orleans Saints	9	9	248	149	60.1	1676	6.76	t65	9	8	3.2	79.0	18	56	3.1	16	0	16	134	5	2	-19	0
1992	New Orleans Saints	16	16	422	249	59.0	3287	7.79	t72	19	16	3.8	82.9	32	95	3.0	18	0	15	119	3	1	0	0
1993	Atlanta Falcons	14	12	430	263	61.2	2978	6.93	t98	24	17	4.0	84.0	24	49	2.0	14	0	29	190	11	3	-9	0
1994	Atlanta Falcons	10	0	103	52	50.5	610	5.92	40	2	6	5.8	51.0	9	43	4.8	20	0	3	17	2	0	-5	0
1995	Atlanta Falcons	4	0	45	28	62.2	313	6.96	t37	2	1	2.2	88.5	5	-1	-0.2	2	0	0	0	0	0	0	0
	10 NFL Seasons	106	87	2633	1545	58.7	18531	7.04	t98	113	99	3.8	78.9	180	543	3.0	20	0	151	1105	40	10	-33	6

Other Statistics: 1985–caught 1 pass for 7 yards and 1 touchdown. 1986–caught 1 pass for 1 yard. 1988–caught 2 passes for 0 yards.

Andy Heck

Pos: T **Rnd:** 1 (15) **College:** Notre Dame **Ht:** 6' 6" **Wt:** 296 **Born:** 1/1/67 **Age:** 29

Year	Team	G	GS	Year	Team	G	GS	Year	Team	G	GS	Year	Team	G	GS
1989	Seattle Seahawks	16	9	1991	Seattle Seahawks	16	16	1993	Seattle Seahawks	16	16	1995	Chicago Bears	16	16
1990	Seattle Seahawks	16	16	1992	Seattle Seahawks	13	13	1994	Chicago Bears	14	14		7 NFL Seasons	107	100

Other Statistics: 1989–recovered 1 fumble for 0 yards. 1990–recovered 1 fumble for 0 yards. 1993–recovered 2 fumbles for 0 yards.

Ron Heller

Pos: T **Rnd:** 4 **College:** Penn State **Ht:** 6' 6" **Wt:** 290 **Born:** 8/25/62 **Age:** 34

Year	Team	G	GS	Year	Team	G	GS	Year	Team	G	GS	Year	Team	G	GS
1984	Tampa Bay Buccaneers	14	14	1987	Tampa Bay Buccaneers	12	10	1990	Philadelphia Eagles	16	14	1993	Miami Dolphins	16	16
1985	Tampa Bay Buccaneers	16	16	1988	Philadelphia Eagles	15	15	1991	Philadelphia Eagles	16	14	1994	Miami Dolphins	16	16
1986	Tampa Bay Buccaneers	16	16	1989	Philadelphia Eagles	16	16	1992	Philadelphia Eagles	12	12	1995	Miami Dolphins	7	7
													12 NFL Seasons	172	166

Other Statistics: 1986–recovered 1 fumble for 0 yards; caught 1 pass for 1 yard and 1 touchdown. 1988–recovered 2 fumbles for 0 yards. 1991–recovered 1 fumble for 0 yards. 1992–recovered 2 fumbles for 0 yards. 1993–recovered 1 fumble for 0 yards.

Dale Hellestrae

Pos: C/G **Rnd:** 4 **College:** Southern Methodist **Ht:** 6' 5" **Wt:** 286 **Born:** 7/11/62 **Age:** 34

Year	Team	G	GS	Year	Team	G	GS	Year	Team	G	GS			G	GS
1985	Buffalo Bills	4	0	1990	Dallas Cowboys	16	0	1993	Dallas Cowboys	16	0				
1986	Buffalo Bills	8	0	1991	Dallas Cowboys	16	0	1994	Dallas Cowboys	16	0				
1988	Buffalo Bills	16	2	1992	Dallas Cowboys	16	0	1995	Dallas Cowboys	16	0		9 NFL Seasons	124	2

Other Statistics: 1986–fumbled 1 time for -14 yards.

Hessley Hempstead

Pos: G/C **Rnd:** 7 **College:** Kansas **Ht:** 6' 1" **Wt:** 295 **Born:** 1/29/72 **Age:** 24

Year	Team	G	GS											G	GS
1995	Detroit Lions	3	0										1 NFL Season	3	0

Jerome Henderson

Pos: CB **Rnd:** 2 **College:** Clemson **Ht:** 5' 10" **Wt:** 188 **Born:** 8/8/69 **Age:** 27

				Tackles			Miscellaneous				Interceptions				Punt Returns				Kickoff Returns				Totals	
Year	Team	G	GS	Tk	Ast	Sack	FF	FR	TD	Blk	Int	Yds	Avg	TD	Num	Yds	Avg	TD	Num	Yds	Avg	TD	TD	Fum
1991	New England Patriots	16	1	31	10	0.0	0	1	0	0	2	2	1.0	0	27	201	7.4	0	0	0	-	0	0	2
1992	New England Patriots	16	9	39	21	0.0	0	0	0	0	3	43	14.3	0	0	0	-	0	0	0	-	0	0	0
1993	NE - Buf	3	0	0	0	0.0	0	0	0	0	0	0	-	0	0	0	-	0	0	0	-	0	0	0
1994	Buffalo Bills	12	0	2	0	0.0	0	0	0	0	0	0	-	0	0	0	-	0	0	0	-	0	0	0
1995	Philadelphia Eagles	15	0	16	0	0.0	0	1	1	0	0	0	-	0	0	0	-	0	0	0	-	0	1	0
1993	New England Patriots	1	0	0	0	0.0	0	0	0	0	0	0	-	0	0	0	-	0	0	0	-	0	0	0
	Buffalo Bills	2	0	0	0	0.0	0	1	0	0	0	0	-	0	0	0	-	0	0	0	-	0	0	0
	5 NFL Seasons	62	10	88	31	0.0	0	3	1	0	5	45	9.0	0	27	201	7.4	0	0	0	-	0	1	2

William Henderson

Pos: RB/WR **Rnd:** 3 **College:** North Carolina **Ht:** 6' 1" **Wt:** 248 **Born:** 2/19/71 **Age:** 25

				Rushing					Receiving					Punt Returns				Kickoff Returns				Totals		
Year	Team	G	GS	Att	Yds	Avg	Lg	TD	Rec	Yds	Avg	Lg	TD	Num	Yds	Avg	TD	Num	Yds	Avg	TD	Fum	TD	Pts
1995	Green Bay Packers	15	2	7	35	5.0	17	0	3	21	7.0	9	0	0	0	-	0	0	0	-	0	0	0	0

Steve Hendrickson

Pos: RB/LB **Rnd:** 6 **College:** California **Ht:** 6' 0" **Wt:** 250 **Born:** 8/30/66 **Age:** 30

Year	Team	G	GS	Rushing Att	Yds	Avg	Lg	TD	Receiving Rec	Yds	Avg	Lg	TD	Punt Returns Num	Yds	Avg	TD	Kickoff Returns Num	Yds	Avg	TD	Totals Fum	TD	Pts
1989	SF - Dal	15	0	0	0	-	-	0	0	0	-	-	0	0	0	-	0	0	0	-	0	0	0	0
1990	San Diego Chargers	14	0	0	0	-	-	0	1	12	12.0	12	0	0	0	-	0	0	0	-	0	0	0	0
1991	San Diego Chargers	15	4	1	3	3.0	t3	1	4	36	9.0	20	1	0	0	-	0	0	0	-	0	0	2	12
1992	San Diego Chargers	16	2	0	0	-	-	0	0	0	-	-	0	0	0	-	0	2	14	7.0	0	0	0	0
1993	San Diego Chargers	16	10	1	0	0.0	0	0	0	0	-	-	0	0	0	-	0	2	25	12.5	0	0	0	0
1994	San Diego Chargers	16	0	1	3	3.0	3	0	0	0	-	-	0	0	0	-	0	0	0	-	0	0	0	0
1995	Phi - Hou	8	1	0	0	-	-	0	0	0	-	-	0	0	0	-	0	0	0	-	0	0	0	0
1989	San Francisco 49ers	11	0	0	0	-	-	0	0	0	-	-	0	0	0	-	0	0	0	-	0	0	0	0
	Dallas Cowboys	4	0	0	0	-	-	0	0	0	-	-	0	0	0	-	0	0	0	-	0	0	0	0
1995	Philadelphia Eagles	3	0	0	0	-	-	0	0	0	-	-	0	0	0	-	0	0	0	-	0	0	0	0
	Houston Oilers	5	1	0	0	-	-	0	0	0	-	-	0	0	0	-	0	0	0	-	0	0	0	0
	7 NFL Seasons	100	17	3	6	2.0	t3	1	5	48	9.6	20	1	0	0	-	0	4	39	9.8	0	0	2	12

Other Statistics: 1991–recovered 1 fumble for 0 yards. 1993–intercepted 1 pass for 16 yards; recovered 1 fumble for 0 yards. 1994–recovered 1 fumble for 0 yards.

David Hendrix

Pos: S **Rnd:** FA **College:** Georgia Tech **Ht:** 6' 1" **Wt:** 213 **Born:** 5/29/72 **Age:** 24

Year	Team	G	GS	Tackles Tk	Ast	Sack	Miscellaneous FF	FR	TD	Blk	Interceptions Int	Yds	Avg	TD	Totals Sfty	TD	Pts
1995	San Diego Chargers	5	0	0	0	0.0	0	0	0	0	0	0	-	0	0	0	0

Chad Hennings

Pos: DT **Rnd:** 11 **College:** Air Force **Ht:** 6' 6" **Wt:** 288 **Born:** 10/20/65 **Age:** 31

Year	Team	G	GS	Tackles Tk	Ast	Sack	Miscellaneous FF	FR	TD	Blk	Interceptions Int	Yds	Avg	TD	Punt Returns Num	Yds	Avg	TD	Kickoff Returns Num	Yds	Avg	TD	Totals TD	Fum
1992	Dallas Cowboys	8	0	1	0	0.0	0	0	0	0	0	0	-	0	0	0	-	0	0	0	-	0	0	0
1993	Dallas Cowboys	13	0	6	11	0.0	0	0	0	0	0	0	-	0	0	0	-	0	1	7	7.0	0	0	0
1994	Dallas Cowboys	16	0	19	4	7.0	1	1	0	0	0	0	-	0	0	0	-	0	0	0	-	0	0	0
1995	Dallas Cowboys	16	7	32	10	5.5	0	1	0	0	0	0	-	0	0	0	-	0	0	0	-	0	0	0
	4 NFL Seasons	53	7	58	25	12.5	1	2	0	0	0	0	-	0	0	0	-	0	1	7	7.0	0	0	0

Kevin Henry

Pos: DE **Rnd:** 4 **College:** Mississippi State **Ht:** 6' 4" **Wt:** 275 **Born:** 10/23/68 **Age:** 28

Year	Team	G	GS	Tackles Tk	Ast	Sack	Miscellaneous FF	FR	TD	Blk	Interceptions Int	Yds	Avg	TD	Totals Sfty	TD	Pts
1993	Pittsburgh Steelers	12	1	4	3	1.0	0	0	0	0	1	10	10.0	0	0	0	0
1994	Pittsburgh Steelers	16	5	12	5	0.0	0	1	0	0	0	0	-	0	0	0	0
1995	Pittsburgh Steelers	13	5	12	3	2.0	0	0	0	0	0	0	-	0	0	0	0
	3 NFL Seasons	41	11	28	11	3.0	0	1	0	0	1	10	10.0	0	0	0	0

Craig Hentrich

(statistical profile on page 475)

Pos: P **Rnd:** 8 **College:** Notre Dame **Ht:** 6' 3" **Wt:** 200 **Born:** 5/18/71 **Age:** 25

Year	Team	G	Punting NetPunts	Yards	Avg	Long	In20	In20%	TotPunts	TB	Blocks	OppRet	RetYds	NetAvg	Rushing Att	Yards	Field Goals Overall	Pct	Long
1994	Green Bay Packers	16	81	3351	41.4	70	24	29.6	81	10	0	36	272	35.5	0	0	0-0	-	-
1995	Green Bay Packers	16	65	2740	42.2	61	26	40.0	67	7	2	36	279	34.6	0	0	3-5	60.0	49
	2 NFL Seasons	32	146	6091	41.7	70	50	34.2	148	17	2	72	551	35.1	0	0	3-5	60.0	49

Other Statistics: 1995–converted 5 of 5 extra-point attempts.

Jeff Herrod

(statistical profile on page 420)

Pos: LB **Rnd:** 9 **College:** Mississippi **Ht:** 6' 0" **Wt:** 245 **Born:** 7/29/66 **Age:** 30

Year	Team	G	GS	Tackles Tk	Ast	Sack	Miscellaneous FF	FR	TD	Blk	Interceptions Int	Yds	Avg	TD	Totals Sfty	TD	Pts
1988	Indianapolis Colts	16	0	18	4	1.0	0	0	0	0	0	0	-	0	0	0	0
1989	Indianapolis Colts	15	14	104	50	2.0	2	0	0	0	0	0	-	0	0	0	0
1990	Indianapolis Colts	13	13	95	60	4.0	1	0	0	0	1	12	12.0	0	0	0	0
1991	Indianapolis Colts	14	14	105	55	2.5	0	3	0	0	1	25	25.0	0	0	0	0
1992	Indianapolis Colts	16	16	99	39	2.0	0	0	0	0	1	4	4.0	0	0	0	0
1993	Indianapolis Colts	14	14	94	48	2.0	0	1	1	0	1	29	29.0	0	0	1	6
1994	Indianapolis Colts	15	15	99	39	1.0	1	0	0	0	0	0	-	0	0	0	0
1995	Indianapolis Colts	16	16	82	42	0.0	2	0	0	0	0	0	-	0	0	0	0
	8 NFL Seasons	119	102	696	337	14.5	6	4	1	0	4	70	17.5	0	0	1	6

Jessie Hester

(statistical profile on page 329)

Pos: WR **Rnd:** 1 (23) **College:** Florida State **Ht:** 5' 11" **Wt:** 175 **Born:** 1/21/63 **Age:** 33

Year Team	G	GS	Rushing					Receiving					Punt Returns				Kickoff Returns				Totals		
			Att	Yds	Avg	Lg	TD	Rec	Yds	Avg	Lg	TD	Num	Yds	Avg	TD	Num	Yds	Avg	TD	Fum	TD	Pts
1985 Los Angeles Raiders	16	16	1	13	13.0	t13	1	32	665	20.8	59	4	0	0	-	0	0	0	-	0	0	5	30
1986 Los Angeles Raiders	13	1	0	0	-	-	0	23	632	27.5	t81	6	0	0	-	0	0	0	-	0	0	6	36
1987 Los Angeles Raiders	10	0	0	0	-	-	0	1	30	30.0	30	0	0	0	-	0	0	0	-	0	0	0	0
1988 Atlanta Falcons	16	3	1	3	3.0	3	0	12	176	14.7	41	0	0	0	-	0	0	0	-	0	1	0	0
1990 Indianapolis Colts	16	14	4	9	2.3	10	0	54	924	17.1	t64	6	0	0	-	0	0	0	-	0	0	6	36
1991 Indianapolis Colts	16	16	0	0	-	-	0	60	753	12.6	t49	5	0	0	-	0	0	0	-	0	3	5	30
1992 Indianapolis Colts	16	16	0	0	-	-	0	52	792	15.2	81	1	0	0	-	0	0	0	-	0	0	1	6
1993 Indianapolis Colts	16	16	0	0	-	-	0	64	835	13.0	58	1	0	0	-	0	0	0	-	0	1	1	6
1994 Los Angeles Rams	16	15	2	28	14.0	24	0	45	644	14.3	41	3	0	0	-	0	0	0	-	0	1	3	18
1995 St. Louis Rams	12	7	0	0	-	-	0	30	399	13.3	t38	3	0	0	-	0	0	0	-	0	0	3	18
10 NFL Seasons	147	104	8	53	6.6	24	1	373	5850	15.7	81	29	0	0	-	0	0	0	-	0	6	30	180

Other Statistics: 1985–recovered 1 fumble for 0 yards. 1990–recovered 2 fumbles for 0 yards. 1991–recovered 1 fumble for 0 yards.

Craig Heyward

(statistical profile on page 330)

Pos: RB **Rnd:** 1 (24) **College:** Pittsburgh **Ht:** 5' 11" **Wt:** 260 **Born:** 9/26/66 **Age:** 30

Year Team	G	GS	Rushing					Receiving					Kickoff Returns				Passing				Totals		
			Att	Yds	Avg	Lg	TD	Rec	Yds	Avg	Lg	TD	Num	Yds	Avg	TD	Att	Com	Yds	Int	Fum	TD	Pts
1988 New Orleans Saints	11	8	74	355	4.8	t73	1	13	105	8.1	18	0	0	0	-	0	0	0	0	0	0	1	6
1989 New Orleans Saints	16	6	49	183	3.7	15	1	13	69	5.3	12	0	0	0	-	0	0	0	0	0	2	1	6
1990 New Orleans Saints	16	15	129	599	4.6	t47	4	18	121	6.7	12	0	1	12	12.0	0	1	0	0	1	3	4	24
1991 New Orleans Saints	7	4	76	260	3.4	15	4	4	34	8.5	t22	1	0	0	-	0	1	1	44	0	0	5	30
1992 New Orleans Saints	16	13	104	416	4.0	23	3	19	159	8.4	21	0	1	14	14.0	0	0	0	0	0	1	3	18
1993 Chicago Bears	16	14	68	206	3.0	11	0	16	132	8.3	20	0	1	12	12.0	0	0	0	0	0	1	0	0
1994 Atlanta Falcons	16	11	183	779	4.3	17	7	32	335	10.5	34	1	1	7	7.0	0	0	0	0	0	5	8	48
1995 Atlanta Falcons	16	16	236	1083	4.6	31	6	37	350	9.5	25	2	0	0	-	0	0	0	0	0	3	8	48
8 NFL Seasons	114	87	919	3881	4.2	t73	26	152	1305	8.6	34	4	4	45	11.3	0	2	1	44	1	15	30	180

Other Statistics: 1988–recovered 1 fumble for 0 yards. 1989–recovered 1 fumble for 0 yards. 1992–recovered 1 fumble for 0 yards. 1994–recovered 2 fumbles for 0 yards. 1995–recovered 3 fumbles for 0 yards.

Kevin Hickman

Pos: TE **Rnd:** 6 **College:** Navy **Ht:** 6' 4" **Wt:** 258 **Born:** 8/20/71 **Age:** 25

Year Team	G	GS	Rushing					Receiving					Punt Returns				Kickoff Returns				Totals		
			Att	Yds	Avg	Lg	TD	Rec	Yds	Avg	Lg	TD	Num	Yds	Avg	TD	Num	Yds	Avg	TD	Fum	TD	Pts
1995 Detroit Lions	7	0	0	0	-	-	0	0	0	-	-	0	0	0	-	0	0	0	-	0	0	0	0

Clifford Hicks

Pos: CB **Rnd:** 3 **College:** Oregon **Ht:** 5' 9" **Wt:** 190 **Born:** 8/18/64 **Age:** 32

Year Team	G	GS	Tackles			Miscellaneous				Interceptions				Punt Returns				Kickoff Returns				Totals	
			Tk	Ast	Sack	FF	FR	TD	Blk	Int	Yds	Avg	TD	Num	Yds	Avg	TD	Num	Yds	Avg	TD	TD	Fum
1987 Los Angeles Rams	11	0	9	1	0.0	0	0	0	0	1	9	9.0	0	13	110	8.5	0	4	119	29.8	0	0	1
1988 Los Angeles Rams	7	0	1	0	0.0	0	0	0	0	0	0	-	0	25	144	5.8	0	0	0	-	0	0	1
1989 Los Angeles Rams	15	6	18	4	0.0	0	0	0	0	2	27	13.5	0	4	39	9.8	0	0	0	-	0	0	0
1990 LAN - Buf	5	0	11	3	1.0	0	0	0	0	1	0	0.0	0	0	0	-	0	0	0	-	0	0	0
1991 Buffalo Bills	16	0	11	6	0.0	0	0	0	0	1	0	0.0	0	12	203	16.9	0	0	0	-	0	0	1
1992 Buffalo Bills	12	2	6	0	1.0	0	0	0	0	0	0	-	0	29	289	10.0	0	1	5	5.0	0	0	2
1993 New York Jets	10	0	8	2	0.0	0	1	0	0	0	0	-	0	17	157	9.2	0	0	0	-	0	0	2
1994 New York Jets	16	0	*0*	*0*	0.0	0	0	0	0	0	0	-	0	38	342	9.0	0	2	30	15.0	0	0	5
1995 Denver Broncos	6	0	*0*	*0*	0.0	0	0	0	0	0	0	-	0	0	0	-	0	0	0	-	0	0	0
1990 Los Angeles Rams	1	0	0	0	0.0	0	0	0	0	0	0	-	0	0	0	-	0	0	0	-	0	0	0
Buffalo Bills	4	0	11	3	1.0	0	0	0	0	1	0	0.0	0	0	0	-	0	0	0	-	0	0	0
9 NFL Seasons	98	8	64	16	2.0	0	3	0	0	5	36	7.2	0	138	1284	9.3	0	7	154	22.0	0	0	12

Mark Higgs

Pos: RB **Rnd:** 8 **College:** Kentucky **Ht:** 5' 7" **Wt:** 199 **Born:** 4/11/66 **Age:** 30

Year Team	G	GS	Rushing					Receiving					Punt Returns				Kickoff Returns				Totals		
			Att	Yds	Avg	Lg	TD	Rec	Yds	Avg	Lg	TD	Num	Yds	Avg	TD	Num	Yds	Avg	TD	Fum	TD	Pts
1988 Dallas Cowboys	5	0	0	0	-	-	0	0	0	-	-	0	0	0	-	0	2	31	15.5	0	0	0	0
1989 Philadelphia Eagles	15	1	49	184	3.8	13	0	3	9	3.0	8	0	0	0	-	0	16	293	18.3	0	3	0	0
1990 Miami Dolphins	12	0	10	67	6.7	27	0	0	0	-	-	0	0	0	-	0	10	210	21.0	0	1	1	6
1991 Miami Dolphins	14	10	231	905	3.9	24	4	11	80	7.3	13	0	0	0	-	0	0	0	-	0	3	4	24
1992 Miami Dolphins	16	15	256	915	3.6	23	7	16	142	8.9	21	0	0	0	-	0	0	0	-	0	5	7	42
1993 Miami Dolphins	16	8	186	693	3.7	31	3	10	72	7.2	15	0	0	0	-	0	0	0	-	0	1	3	18
1994 Mia - Ari	11	1	62	195	3.1	21	0	0	0	-	-	0	0	0	-	0	2	25	12.5	0	1	0	0

Year Team	G	GS	Rushing Att	Yds	Avg	Lg	TD	Receiving Rec	Yds	Avg	Lg	TD	Punt Returns Num	Yds	Avg	TD	Kickoff Returns Num	Yds	Avg	TD	Totals Fum	TD	Pts
1995 Arizona Cardinals	3	0	0	0	-	-	0	0	0	-	-	0	0	0	-	0	2	26	13.0	0	0	0	0
1994 Miami Dolphins	5	1	19	68	3.6	21	0	0	0	-	-	0	0	0	-	0	0	0	-	0	1	0	0
Arizona Cardinals	6	0	43	127	3.0	16	0	0	0	-	-	0	0	0	-	0	2	25	12.5	0	0	0	0
8 NFL Seasons	92	35	794	2959	3.7	31	14	40	303	7.6	21	0	0	0	-	0	32	585	18.3	0	14	15	90

Other Statistics: 1989–recovered 1 fumble for 0 yards.

Eric Hill

(statistical profile on page 420)

Pos: LB   **Rnd:** 1 (10)   **College:** Louisiana State   **Ht:** 6' 2"   **Wt:** 255   **Born:** 11/14/66   **Age:** 29

Year Team	G	GS	Tackles Tk	Ast	Sack	Miscellaneous FF	FR	TD	Blk	Interceptions Int	Yds	Avg	TD	Totals Sfty	TD	Pts
1989 Phoenix Cardinals	15	14	58	33	1.0	1	1	0	0	0	0	-	0	0	0	0
1990 Phoenix Cardinals	16	16	61	35	1.5	1	0	0	0	0	0	-	0	0	0	0
1991 Phoenix Cardinals	16	15	62	46	1.0	1	1	1	0	0	0	-	0	0	1	6
1992 Phoenix Cardinals	16	16	68	35	0.0	0	1	0	0	0	0	-	0	0	0	0
1993 Phoenix Cardinals	13	12	59	33	1.0	2	1	0	0	0	0	-	0	0	0	0
1994 Arizona Cardinals	16	15	79	41	1.5	0	0	0	1	0	0	-	0	0	0	0
1995 Arizona Cardinals	15	14	89	29	2.0	2	0	0	0	0	0	-	0	0	0	0
7 NFL Seasons	107	102	476	252	8.0	7	4	1	1	0	0	-	0	0	1	6

Other Statistics: 1992–fumbled 1 time.

Greg Hill

(statistical profile on page 330)

Pos: RB   **Rnd:** 1 (25)   **College:** Texas A&M   **Ht:** 5' 11"   **Wt:** 209   **Born:** 2/23/72   **Age:** 24

Year Team	G	GS	Rushing Att	Yds	Avg	Lg	TD	Receiving Rec	Yds	Avg	Lg	TD	Punt Returns Num	Yds	Avg	TD	Kickoff Returns Num	Yds	Avg	TD	Totals Fum	TD	Pts
1994 Kansas City Chiefs	16	2	141	574	4.1	20	1	16	92	5.8	21	0	0	0	-	0	0	0	-	0	1	1	6
1995 Kansas City Chiefs	16	1	155	667	4.3	27	1	7	45	6.4	13	0	0	0	-	0	0	0	-	0	2	1	6
2 NFL Seasons	32	3	296	1241	4.2	27	2	23	137	6.0	21	0	0	0	-	0	0	0	-	0	3	2	12

Jeff Hill

Pos: KR/WR   **Rnd:** FA   **College:** Purdue   **Ht:** 5' 11"   **Wt:** 178   **Born:** 9/24/72   **Age:** 24

Year Team	G	GS	Rushing Att	Yds	Avg	Lg	TD	Receiving Rec	Yds	Avg	Lg	TD	Punt Returns Num	Yds	Avg	TD	Kickoff Returns Num	Yds	Avg	TD	Totals Fum	TD	Pts
1994 Cincinnati Bengals	1	0	0	0	-	-	0	0	0	-	-	0	0	0	-	0	4	97	24.3	0	0	0	0
1995 Cincinnati Bengals	16	1	1	-3	-3.0	-3	0	4	44	11.0	18	0	0	0	-	0	17	454	26.7	0	0	0	0
2 NFL Seasons	17	1	1	-3	-3.0	-3	0	4	44	11.0	18	0	0	0	-	0	21	551	26.2	0	0	0	0

Randal Hill

Pos: WR/KR   **Rnd:** 1 (23)   **College:** Miami (FL)   **Ht:** 5' 11"   **Wt:** 180   **Born:** 9/21/69   **Age:** 27

Year Team	G	GS	Rushing Att	Yds	Avg	Lg	TD	Receiving Rec	Yds	Avg	Lg	TD	Punt Returns Num	Yds	Avg	TD	Kickoff Returns Num	Yds	Avg	TD	Totals Fum	TD	Pts
1991 Mia - Pho	16	4	0	0	-	-	0	43	495	11.5	t31	1	0	0	-	0	9	146	16.2	0	0	1	6
1992 Phoenix Cardinals	16	14	1	4	4.0	4	0	58	861	14.8	49	3	0	0	-	0	0	0	-	0	2	3	18
1993 Phoenix Cardinals	16	9	0	0	-	-	0	35	519	14.8	t58	4	0	0	-	0	0	0	-	0	0	4	24
1994 Arizona Cardinals	14	14	0	0	-	-	0	38	544	14.3	51	0	0	0	-	0	0	0	-	0	0	0	0
1995 Miami Dolphins	12	0	0	0	-	-	0	12	260	21.7	58	0	0	0	-	0	12	287	23.9	0	0	0	0
1991 Miami Dolphins	1	0	0	0	-	-	0	0	0	-	-	0	0	0	-	0	1	33	33.0	0	0	0	0
Phoenix Cardinals	15	4	0	0	-	-	0	43	495	11.5	t31	1	0	0	-	0	8	113	14.1	0	0	1	6
5 NFL Seasons	74	41	1	4	4.0	4	0	186	2679	14.4	t58	8	0	0	-	0	21	433	20.6	0	2	8	48

Sean Hill

Pos: CB   **Rnd:** 7   **College:** Montana State   **Ht:** 5' 10"   **Wt:** 179   **Born:** 8/14/71   **Age:** 25

Year Team	G	GS	Tackles Tk	Ast	Sack	Miscellaneous FF	FR	TD	Blk	Interceptions Int	Yds	Avg	TD	Punt Returns Num	Yds	Avg	TD	Kickoff Returns Num	Yds	Avg	TD	Totals TD	Fum
1994 Miami Dolphins	16	1	12	-	0.0	0	0	0	0	0	0	-	0	0	0	-	0	0	0	-	0	0	0
1995 Miami Dolphins	16	0	3	0	0.0	0	0	0	0	0	0	-	0	0	0	-	0	1	38	38.0	0	0	0
2 NFL Seasons	32	1	15	0	0.0	0	0	0	0	0	0	-	0	0	0	-	0	1	38	38.0	0	0	0

Travis Hill

Pos: LB   **Rnd:** 7   **College:** Nebraska   **Ht:** 6' 2"   **Wt:** 240   **Born:** 10/3/69   **Age:** 27

Year Team	G	GS	Tackles Tk	Ast	Sack	Miscellaneous FF	FR	TD	Blk	Interceptions Int	Yds	Avg	TD	Totals Sfty	TD	Pts
1994 Cleveland Browns	14	0	0	1	0.0	0	0	1	0	0	0	-	0	0	1	6
1995 Car - Cle	7	0	1	0	0.0	0	0	0	0	0	0	-	0	0	0	0
1995 Carolina Panthers	3	0	1	0	0.0	0	0	0	0	0	0	-	0	0	0	0

Year	Team	G	GS	Tk	Ast	Sack	FF	FR	TD	Blk	Int	Yds	Avg	TD	Sfty	TD	Pts
	Cleveland Browns	4	0	0	0	0.0	0	0	0	0	0	0	-	0	0	0	0
2 NFL Seasons		21	0	1	1	0.0	0	0	1	0	0	0	-	0	0	1	6

Randy Hilliard

Pos: CB **Rnd:** 6 **College:** Northwestern Louisiana **Ht:** 5' 11" **Wt:** 170 **Born:** 2/6/67 **Age:** 29

				Tackles			Miscellaneous				Interceptions				Totals		
Year	Team	G	GS	Tk	Ast	Sack	FF	FR	TD	Blk	Int	Yds	Avg	TD	Sfty	TD	Pts
1990	Cleveland Browns	15	0	2	0	0.0	0	0	0	0	0	0	-	0	0	0	0
1991	Cleveland Browns	14	10	44	15	2.0	0	1	0	0	1	19	19.0	0	0	0	0
1992	Cleveland Browns	16	4	14	13	1.0	0	1	0	0	0	0	-	0	0	0	0
1993	Cleveland Browns	12	5	26	15	0.0	0	0	0	0	1	54	54.0	0	0	0	0
1994	Denver Broncos	15	4	40	4	0.0	1	0	0	0	2	8	4.0	0	0	0	0
1995	Denver Broncos	12	0	17	1	0.0	0	0	0	0	0	0	-	0	0	0	0
6 NFL Seasons		84	23	143	48	3.0	1	2	0	0	4	81	20.3	0	0	0	0

Chris Hinton

Pos: G **Rnd:** 1 (4) **College:** Northwestern **Ht:** 6' 4" **Wt:** 300 **Born:** 7/31/61 **Age:** 35

Year	Team	G	GS	Year	Team	G	GS	Year	Team	G	GS	Year	Team	G	GS
1983	Baltimore Colts	16	15	1987	Indianapolis Colts	12	12	1991	Atlanta Falcons	16	16	1995	Minnesota Vikings	4	4
1984	Indianapolis Colts	6	6	1988	Indianapolis Colts	14	14	1992	Atlanta Falcons	16	16				
1985	Indianapolis Colts	16	16	1989	Indianapolis Colts	14	14	1993	Atlanta Falcons	16	16				
1986	Indianapolis Colts	16	16	1990	Atlanta Falcons	16	12	1994	Minnesota Vikings	16	16	13 NFL Seasons		178	173

Other Statistics: 1983–recovered 1 fumble for 0 yards. 1986–recovered 2 fumbles for 0 yards. 1987–recovered 1 fumble for 0 yards. 1988–caught 1 pass for 1 yard. 1989–recovered 2 fumbles for 0 yards. 1990–recovered 1 fumble for 0 yards. 1992–caught 1 pass for -2 yards. 1993–caught 1 pass for -8 yards.

Jimmy Hitchcock

Pos: CB **Rnd:** 3 **College:** North Carolina **Ht:** 5' 10" **Wt:** 188 **Born:** 11/9/71 **Age:** 24

				Tackles			Miscellaneous				Interceptions				Totals		
Year	Team	G	GS	Tk	Ast	Sack	FF	FR	TD	Blk	Int	Yds	Avg	TD	Sfty	TD	Pts
1995	New England Patriots	8	0	4	0	0.0	0	0	0	0	0	0	-	0	0	0	0

Terry Hoage

Pos: S **Rnd:** 3 **College:** Georgia **Ht:** 6' 2" **Wt:** 203 **Born:** 4/11/62 **Age:** 34

				Tackles			Miscellaneous				Interceptions				Totals		
Year	Team	G	GS	Tk	Ast	Sack	FF	FR	TD	Blk	Int	Yds	Avg	TD	Sfty	TD	Pts
1984	New Orleans Saints	14	0	11	16	0.0	0	1	0	0	0	0	-	0	0	0	0
1985	New Orleans Saints	16	13	70	22	1.0	0	2	0	0	4	79	19.8	1	0	1	6
1986	Philadelphia Eagles	16	12	83	29	0.0	0	2	0	0	1	18	18.0	0	0	0	0
1987	Philadelphia Eagles	11	11	70	30	1.0	0	2	0	0	2	3	1.5	0	0	0	0
1988	Philadelphia Eagles	16	0	23	8	2.0	0	0	1	0	8	116	14.5	0	0	1	6
1989	Philadelphia Eagles	6	0	4	3	0.0	0	0	0	0	0	0	-	0	0	0	0
1990	Philadelphia Eagles	16	3	28	10	1.0	0	0	0	0	1	0	0.0	0	0	0	0
1991	Washington Redskins	6	0	3	8	0.0	0	0	0	0	0	0	-	0	0	0	0
1993	SF - Hou	7	0	4	1	0.0	0	0	0	0	0	0	-	0	0	0	0
1994	Arizona Cardinals	16	16	63	22	1.0	1	2	0	0	3	64	21.3	0	0	0	0
1995	Arizona Cardinals	13	7	39	13	1.0	0	2	0	0	2	0	0.0	0	0	0	0
1993	San Francisco 49ers	4	0	1	1	0.0	0	0	0	0	0	0	-	0	0	0	0
	Houston Oilers	3	0	3	0	0.0	0	0	0	0	0	0	-	0	0	0	0
11 NFL Seasons		137	62	398	162	7.0	1	11	1	0	21	280	13.3	1	0	2	12

Other Statistics: 1988–rushed 1 time for 38 yards and 1 touchdown.

Leroy Hoard

(statistical profile on page 331)

Pos: RB **Rnd:** 2 **College:** Michigan **Ht:** 5' 11" **Wt:** 225 **Born:** 5/5/68 **Age:** 28

				Rushing					Receiving					Kickoff Returns				Passing				Totals		
Year	Team	G	GS	Att	Yds	Avg	Lg	TD	Rec	Yds	Avg	Lg	TD	Num	Yds	Avg	TD	Att	Com	Yds	Int	Fum	TD	Pts
1990	Cleveland Browns	14	5	58	149	2.6	42	3	10	73	7.3	17	0	2	18	9.0	0	0	0	0	0	6	3	18
1991	Cleveland Browns	16	9	37	154	4.2	52	2	48	567	11.8	t71	9	0	0	-	0	0	0	0	0	1	11	66
1992	Cleveland Browns	16	9	54	236	4.4	37	0	26	310	11.9	t46	1	2	34	17.0	0	0	0	0	0	3	1	6
1993	Cleveland Browns	16	7	56	227	4.1	30	0	35	351	10.0	41	0	13	286	22.0	0	1	0	0	0	4	0	0
1994	Cleveland Browns	16	12	209	890	4.3	39	5	45	445	9.9	t65	4	2	30	15.0	0	0	0	0	0	8	9	54
1995	Cleveland Browns	12	12	136	547	4.0	25	0	13	103	7.9	24	0	1	13	13.0	0	0	0	0	0	5	0	0
6 NFL Seasons		90	54	550	2203	4.0	52	10	177	1849	10.4	t71	14	20	381	19.1	0	1	0	0	0	27	24	144

Other Statistics: 1991–recovered 1 fumble for 4 yards. 1992–recovered 1 fumble for 0 yards.

Daryl Hobbs

(statistical profile on page 331)

Pos: WR **Rnd:** FA **College:** Pacific **Ht:** 6' 2" **Wt:** 180 **Born:** 5/23/68 **Age:** 28

Year Team	G	GS	Rushing Att	Yds	Avg	Lg	TD	Receiving Rec	Yds	Avg	Lg	TD	Punt Returns Num	Yds	Avg	TD	Kickoff Returns Num	Yds	Avg	TD	Totals Fum	TD	Pts
1993 Los Angeles Raiders	3	0	0	0	-	-	0	0	0	-	-	0	0	0	-	0	0	0	-	0	0	0	0
1994 Los Angeles Raiders	10	0	0	0	-	-	0	5	52	10.4	14	0	0	0	-	0	0	0	-	0	0	0	0
1995 Oakland Raiders	16	1	0	0	-	-	0	38	612	16.1	t54	3	1	10	10.0	0	1	20	20.0	0	0	3	18
3 NFL Seasons	29	1	0	0	-	-	0	43	664	15.4	t54	3	1	10	10.0	0	1	20	20.0	0	0	3	18

Other Statistics: 1995–attempted 1 pass with 0 completions for 0 yards.

Billy Joe Hobert

(statistical profile on page 332)

Pos: QB **Rnd:** 3 **College:** Washington **Ht:** 6' 3" **Wt:** 230 **Born:** 1/8/71 **Age:** 25

Year Team	G	GS	Passing Att	Com	Pct	Yards	Yds/Att	Lg	TD	Int	Int%	Rating	Rushing Att	Yds	Avg	Lg	TD	Miscellaneous Sckd	Yds	Fum Recv	Yds	Pts
1995 Oakland Raiders	4	2	80	44	55.0	540	6.75	t80	6	4	5.0	80.2	3	5	1.7	6	0	3	11	0	0	0

Tom Hodson

Pos: QB **Rnd:** 3 **College:** Louisiana State **Ht:** 6' 3" **Wt:** 195 **Born:** 1/28/67 **Age:** 29

Year Team	G	GS	Passing Att	Com	Pct	Yards	Yds/Att	Lg	TD	Int	Int%	Rating	Rushing Att	Yds	Avg	Lg	TD	Miscellaneous Sckd	Yds	Fum Recv	Yds	Pts
1990 New England Patriots	7	6	156	85	54.5	968	6.21	56	4	5	3.2	68.5	12	79	6.6	23	0	20	147	5	0	0
1991 New England Patriots	16	3	68	36	52.9	345	5.07	32	1	4	5.9	47.7	4	0	0.0	1	0	9	57	2	0	0
1992 New England Patriots	9	3	91	50	54.9	496	5.45	t54	2	2	2.2	68.8	5	11	2.2	5	0	12	96	2	1	0	0
1995 New Orleans Saints	4	0	5	3	60.0	14	2.80	9	0	0	0.0	64.6	0	0	-	0	0	0	0	0	0	0
4 NFL Seasons	36	12	320	174	54.4	1823	5.70	56	7	11	3.4	64.1	21	90	4.3	23	0	41	300	9	1	0

Other Statistics: 1992–caught 1 pass for -6 yards.

John Holecek

Pos: LB **Rnd:** 5 **College:** Illinois **Ht:** 6' 2" **Wt:** 238 **Born:** 5/7/72 **Age:** 24

Year Team	G	GS	Tackles Tk	Ast	Sack	Miscellaneous FF	FR	TD	Blk	Interceptions Int	Yds	Avg	TD	Totals Sfty	TD	Pts
1995 Buffalo Bills	1	0	3	2	0.0	0	0	0	0	0	0	-	0	0	0	0

Darius Holland

Pos: DT **Rnd:** 3 **College:** Colorado **Ht:** 6' 4" **Wt:** 305 **Born:** 11/10/73 **Age:** 22

Year Team	G	GS	Tackles Tk	Ast	Sack	Miscellaneous FF	FR	TD	Blk	Interceptions Int	Yds	Avg	TD	Totals Sfty	TD	Pts
1995 Green Bay Packers	14	4	9	8	1.5	0	0	0	0	0	0	-	0	0	0	0

Corey Holliday

Pos: WR **Rnd:** FA **College:** North Carolina **Ht:** 6' 2" **Wt:** 208 **Born:** 1/31/71 **Age:** 25

Year Team	G	GS	Rushing Att	Yds	Avg	Lg	TD	Receiving Rec	Yds	Avg	Lg	TD	Punt Returns Num	Yds	Avg	TD	Kickoff Returns Num	Yds	Avg	TD	Totals Fum	TD	Pts
1995 Pittsburgh Steelers	3	0	0	0	-	-	0	0	0	-	-	0	0	0	-	0	0	0	-	0	0	0	0

Dwight Hollier

Pos: LB **Rnd:** 4 **College:** North Carolina **Ht:** 6' 2" **Wt:** 250 **Born:** 4/21/69 **Age:** 27

Year Team	G	GS	Tackles Tk	Ast	Sack	Miscellaneous FF	FR	TD	Blk	Interceptions Int	Yds	Avg	TD	Totals Sfty	TD	Pts
1992 Miami Dolphins	16	5	30	10	1.0	0	3	0	0	0	0	-	0	0	0	0
1993 Miami Dolphins	16	10	70	24	0.0	0	1	0	0	0	0	-	0	0	0	0
1994 Miami Dolphins	10	7	34	9	0.0	0	0	0	0	1	36	36.0	0	0	0	0
1995 Miami Dolphins	16	14	36	11	0.0	0	1	0	0	0	0	-	0	0	0	0
4 NFL Seasons	58	36	170	54	1.0	0	5	0	0	1	36	36.0	0	0	0	0

Mike Hollis

(statistical profile on page 475)

Pos: K **Rnd:** FA **College:** Idaho **Ht:** 5' 7" **Wt:** 180 **Born:** 5/22/72 **Age:** 24

Year Team	G	Field Goals 1-29 Yds	Pct	30-39 Yds	Pct	40-49 Yds	Pct	50+ Yds	Pct	Overall	Pct	Long	PAT Made	Att	Tot Pts
1995 Jacksonville Jaguars	16	7-9	77.8	7-8	87.5	4-7	57.1	2-3	66.7	20-27	74.1	53	27	28	87

Rodney Holman

Pos: TE **Rnd:** 3 **College:** Tulane **Ht:** 6'3" **Wt:** 238 **Born:** 4/20/60 **Age:** 36

Year	Team	G	GS	Rushing Att	Yds	Avg	Lg	TD	Receiving Rec	Yds	Avg	Lg	TD	Punt Returns Num	Yds	Avg	TD	Kickoff Returns Num	Yds	Avg	TD	Totals Fum	TD	Pts
1982	Cincinnati Bengals	9	0	0	0	-	-	0	3	18	6.0	10	1	0	0	-	0	0	0	-	0	0	1	6
1983	Cincinnati Bengals	16	0	0	0	-	-	0	2	15	7.5	10	0	0	0	-	0	0	0	-	0	0	0	0
1984	Cincinnati Bengals	16	2	0	0	-	-	0	21	239	11.4	27	1	0	0	-	0	0	0	-	0	0	1	6
1985	Cincinnati Bengals	16	16	0	0	-	-	0	38	479	12.6	t64	7	0	0	-	0	0	0	-	0	1	7	42
1986	Cincinnati Bengals	16	16	0	0	-	-	0	40	570	14.3	t34	2	0	0	-	0	1	18	18.0	0	1	2	12
1987	Cincinnati Bengals	12	12	0	0	-	-	0	28	438	15.6	t61	2	0	0	-	0	0	0	-	0	0	2	12
1988	Cincinnati Bengals	16	16	0	0	-	-	0	39	527	13.5	33	3	0	0	-	0	0	0	-	0	2	3	18
1989	Cincinnati Bengals	16	15	0	0	-	-	0	50	736	14.7	t73	9	0	0	-	0	0	0	-	0	0	9	54
1990	Cincinnati Bengals	16	15	0	0	-	-	0	40	596	14.9	53	5	0	0	-	0	0	0	-	0	1	5	30
1991	Cincinnati Bengals	16	15	0	0	-	-	0	31	445	14.4	39	2	0	0	-	0	1	15	15.0	0	1	2	12
1992	Cincinnati Bengals	16	13	0	0	-	-	0	26	266	10.2	t26	2	0	0	-	0	0	0	-	0	0	2	12
1993	Detroit Lions	16	16	0	0	-	-	0	25	244	9.8	t28	2	0	0	-	0	0	0	-	0	1	2	12
1994	Detroit Lions	15	7	0	0	-	-	0	17	163	9.6	18	0	0	0	-	0	0	0	-	0	1	0	0
1995	Detroit Lions	16	3	0	0	-	-	0	5	35	7.0	9	0	0	0	-	0	0	0	-	0	0	0	0
	14 NFL Seasons	212	146	0	0	-	-	0	365	4771	13.1	t73	36	0	0	-	0	2	33	16.5	0	8	36	216

Other Statistics: 1984–recovered 1 fumble for 0 yards. 1985–recovered 1 fumble for 0 yards. 1987–recovered 1 fumble for 0 yards. 1988–recovered 1 fumble for 0 yards. 1994–recovered 2 fumbles for -4 yards.

Rob Holmberg

Pos: LB **Rnd:** 7 **College:** Penn State **Ht:** 6'3" **Wt:** 225 **Born:** 5/6/71 **Age:** 25

Year	Team	G	GS	Tackles Tk	Ast	Sack	Miscellaneous FF	FR	TD	Blk	Interceptions Int	Yds	Avg	TD	Totals Sfty	TD	Pts
1994	Los Angeles Raiders	16	0	1	0	0.0	0	0	0	0	0	0	-	0	0	0	0
1995	Oakland Raiders	16	0	2	1	1.0	0	1	0	0	0	0	-	0	0	0	0
	2 NFL Seasons	32	0	3	1	1.0	0	1	0	0	0	0	-	0	0	0	0

Clayton Holmes

Pos: CB **Rnd:** 3 **College:** Carson-Newman **Ht:** 5'10" **Wt:** 181 **Born:** 8/23/69 **Age:** 27

Year	Team	G	GS	Tackles Tk	Ast	Sack	Misc FF	FR	TD	Blk	Interceptions Int	Yds	Avg	TD	Punt Returns Num	Yds	Avg	TD	Kickoff Returns Num	Yds	Avg	TD	Totals TD	Fum
1992	Dallas Cowboys	15	0	1	0	0.0	0	1	0	0	0	0	-	0	0	0	-	0	3	70	23.3	0	0	0
1994	Dallas Cowboys	15	1	7	3	0.0	0	0	0	0	0	3	-	0	5	55	11.0	0	4	89	22.3	0	0	1
1995	Dallas Cowboys	8	6	27	3	0.0	0	1	0	1	1	0	0.0	0	4	35	8.8	0	5	134	26.8	0	0	1
	3 NFL Seasons	38	7	35	6	0.0	0	2	0	1	1	3	3.0	0	9	90	10.0	0	12	293	24.4	0	0	2

Darick Holmes

Pos: RB/KR **Rnd:** 7 **College:** Portland State *(statistical profile on page 332)* **Ht:** 6'0" **Wt:** 226 **Born:** 7/1/71 **Age:** 25

Year	Team	G	GS	Rushing Att	Yds	Avg	Lg	TD	Receiving Rec	Yds	Avg	Lg	TD	Punt Returns Num	Yds	Avg	TD	Kickoff Returns Num	Yds	Avg	TD	Totals Fum	TD	Pts
1995	Buffalo Bills	16	2	172	698	4.1	t38	4	24	214	8.9	47	0	0	0	-	0	39	799	20.5	0	4	4	24

Other Statistics: 1995–recovered 2 fumbles for 0 yards.

Lester Holmes

Pos: T **Rnd:** 1 (19) **College:** Jackson State **Ht:** 6'3" **Wt:** 305 **Born:** 9/27/69 **Age:** 27

Year	Team	G	GS	Year	Team	G	GS	Year	Team	G	GS			G	GS
1993	Philadelphia Eagles	12	6	1994	Philadelphia Eagles	16	16	1995	Philadelphia Eagles	2	2		3 NFL Seasons	30	24

Other Statistics: 1993–recovered 1 fumble for 0 yards. 1994–recovered 3 fumbles for 0 yards.

Pierce Holt

Pos: DT **Rnd:** 2 **College:** Angelo State **Ht:** 6'4" **Wt:** 275 **Born:** 1/1/62 **Age:** 34

Year	Team	G	GS	Tackles Tk	Ast	Sack	Miscellaneous FF	FR	TD	Blk	Interceptions Int	Yds	Avg	TD	Totals Sfty	TD	Pts
1988	San Francisco 49ers	9	0	13	2	5.0	0	1	0	0	0	0	-	0	0	0	0
1989	San Francisco 49ers	16	11	43	5	10.5	1	1	0	0	0	0	-	0	0	0	0
1990	San Francisco 49ers	16	16	40	11	5.5	0	2	0	0	0	0	-	0	0	0	0
1991	San Francisco 49ers	13	11	35	9	3.0	0	0	0	0	0	0	-	0	0	0	0
1992	San Francisco 49ers	16	16	41	14	5.5	1	0	0	0	0	0	-	0	0	0	0
1993	Atlanta Falcons	16	15	44	35	6.5	1	0	0	0	0	0	-	0	0	0	0
1994	Atlanta Falcons	12	12	22	7	0.0	0	1	0	0	0	0	-	0	0	0	0
1995	Atlanta Falcons	11	10	22	7	1.0	0	0	0	0	0	0	-	0	0	0	0
	8 NFL Seasons	109	91	260	90	37.0	3	5	0	0	0	0	-	0	0	0	0

Thomas Homco

Pos: LB **Rnd:** FA **College:** Northwestern **Ht:** 6' 0" **Wt:** 245 **Born:** 1/8/70 **Age:** 26

Year	Team	G	GS	Tackles			Miscellaneous				Interceptions				Totals		
				Tk	Ast	Sack	FF	FR	TD	Blk	Int	Yds	Avg	TD	Sfty	TD	Pts
1993	Los Angeles Rams	16	3	20	13	0.0	1	0	0	0	1	6	6.0	0	0	0	0
1994	Los Angeles Rams	15	0	6	2	0.0	0	0	0	0	0	0	-	0	0	0	0
1995	St. Louis Rams	11	0	2	0	0.0	0	0	0	0	0	0	-	0	0	0	0
	3 NFL Seasons	42	3	28	15	0.0	1	0	0	0	1	6	6.0	0	0	0	0

Brad Hopkins

Pos: T **Rnd:** 1 (13) **College:** Illinois **Ht:** 6' 3" **Wt:** 306 **Born:** 9/5/70 **Age:** 26

Year	Team	G	GS	Year	Team	G	GS	Year	Team	G	GS		G	GS
1993	Houston Oilers	16	11	1994	Houston Oilers	16	15	1995	Houston Oilers	16	16	3 NFL Seasons	48	42

Other Statistics: 1994–recovered 1 fumble for 0 yards. 1995–recovered 3 fumbles for 0 yards.

Mike Horan

(statistical profile on page 475)

Pos: P **Rnd:** 9 **College:** Long Beach State **Ht:** 5' 11" **Wt:** 188 **Born:** 2/1/59 **Age:** 37

Year	Team	G	Punting											Rushing		Passing			
			NetPunts	Yards	Avg	Long	In20	In20%	TotPunts	TB	Blocks	OppRet	RetYds	NetAvg	Att	Yards	Att Com	Yards	Int
1984	Philadelphia Eagles	16	92	3880	42.2	69	21	22.8	92	6	0	58	486	35.6	0	0	0 0	0	0
1985	Philadelphia Eagles	16	91	3777	41.5	75	20	22.0	91	10	0	41	462	34.2	1	12	0 0	0	0
1986	Denver Broncos	4	21	864	41.1	50	8	38.1	21	2	0	11	99	34.5	1	0	0 0	0	0
1987	Denver Broncos	12	44	1807	41.1	61	11	25.0	46	5	2	22	186	33.1	0	0	0 0	0	0
1988	Denver Broncos	16	65	2861	44.0	70	19	29.2	65	2	0	33	364	37.8	0	0	0 0	0	0
1989	Denver Broncos	16	77	3111	40.4	63	24	31.2	77	5	0	28	370	34.3	0	0	0 0	0	0
1990	Denver Broncos	15	58	2575	44.4	67	14	24.1	59	6	1	22	159	38.9	0	0	0 0	0	0
1991	Denver Broncos	16	72	3012	41.8	71	24	33.3	73	8	1	28	170	36.7	2	9	0 0	0	0
1992	Denver Broncos	7	37	1681	45.4	62	7	18.9	38	1	1	14	132	40.2	0	0	0 0	0	0
1993	New York Giants	8	44	1882	42.8	60	13	29.5	44	1	0	25	107	39.9	0	0	0 0	0	0
1994	New York Giants	16	85	3521	41.4	63	25	29.4	87	7	2	39	307	35.3	0	0	0 0	0	0
1995	New York Giants	16	72	3063	42.5	60	15	20.8	72	8	0	34	297	36.2	1	0	0 0	0	0
	12 NFL Seasons	158	758	32034	42.3	75	201	26.5	765	61	7	355	3139	36.2	5	21	0 0	0	0

Other Statistics: 1986–recovered 1 fumble for -12 yards; fumbled 1 time. 1991–recovered 1 fumble for 0 yards. 1995–recovered 1 fumble for -18 yards; fumbled 1 time.

Derrick Hoskins

(statistical profile on page 420)

Pos: S **Rnd:** 5 **College:** Southern Mississippi **Ht:** 6' 2" **Wt:** 210 **Born:** 11/14/70 **Age:** 25

Year	Team	G	GS	Tackles			Miscellaneous				Interceptions				Totals		
				Tk	Ast	Sack	FF	FR	TD	Blk	Int	Yds	Avg	TD	Sfty	TD	Pts
1992	Los Angeles Raiders	16	0	0	0	0.0	0	0	0	0	0	0	-	0	0	0	0
1993	Los Angeles Raiders	16	16	68	20	0.0	0	1	0	0	2	34	17.0	0	0	0	0
1994	Los Angeles Raiders	15	9	51	24	0.0	2	1	0	0	0	0	-	0	0	0	0
1995	Oakland Raiders	13	13	54	12	0.0	1	0	0	0	1	26	26.0	0	0	0	0
	4 NFL Seasons	60	38	173	56	0.0	3	2	0	0	3	60	20.0	0	0	0	0

Jeff Hostetler

(statistical profile on page 333)

Pos: QB **Rnd:** 3 **College:** West Virginia **Ht:** 6' 3" **Wt:** 215 **Born:** 4/22/61 **Age:** 35

Year	Team	G	GS	Passing										Rushing				Miscellaneous			
				Att	Com	Pct	Yards	Yds/Att	Lg	TD	Int	Int%	Rating	Att	Yds	Avg	Lg TD	Sckd Yds	Fum Recv	Yds	Pts
1985	New York Giants	5	0	0	0	-	0	-	-	0	0	0.0	0.0	0	0	-	- 0	0 0	0	0	0
1986	New York Giants	13	0	0	0	-	0	-	-	0	0	0.0	0.0	1	1	1.0	1 0	- -	0	0	0
1988	New York Giants	16	1	29	16	55.2	244	8.41	t85	1	2	6.9	65.9	5	-3	-0.6	0 0	5 31	1 1	0	0
1989	New York Giants	16	1	39	20	51.3	294	7.54	t35	3	2	5.1	80.5	11	71	6.5	t19 0	6 37	2 1	0	12
1990	New York Giants	16	2	87	47	54.0	614	7.06	t44	3	1	1.1	83.2	39	190	4.9	30 2	9 38	4 5	-4	12
1991	New York Giants	12	12	285	179	62.8	2032	7.13	55	5	4	1.4	84.1	42	273	6.5	t47 2	20 100	7 6	-9	12
1992	New York Giants	13	9	192	103	53.6	1225	6.38	46	8	3	1.6	80.8	35	172	4.9	27 3	24 148	6 0	-3	18
1993	Los Angeles Raiders	15	15	419	236	56.3	3242	7.74	t74	14	10	2.4	82.5	55	202	3.7	19 5	39 206	6 2	1	30
1994	Los Angeles Raiders	16	16	455	263	57.8	3334	7.33	t77	20	16	3.5	80.8	46	159	3.5	14 2	41 232	10 0	-9	12
1995	Oakland Raiders	11	11	286	172	60.1	1998	6.99	t80	12	9	3.1	82.2	31	119	3.8	18 0	22 133	5 1	0	0
	10 NFL Seasons	133	67	1792	1036	57.8	12983	7.24	t85	66	47	2.6	81.8	265	1184	4.5	t47 16	165 925	41 16	-26	96

Other Statistics: 1988–caught 1 pass for 10 yards.

Bobby Houston

Pos: LB **Rnd:** 3 **College:** North Carolina State **Ht:** 6' 2" **Wt:** 245 **Born:** 10/26/67 **Age:** 29

Year	Team	G	GS	Tackles			Miscellaneous				Interceptions				Totals		
				Tk	Ast	Sack	FF	FR	TD	Blk	Int	Yds	Avg	TD	Sfty	TD	Pts
1990	Green Bay Packers	1	0	0	0	0.0	0	0	0	0	0	0	-	0	0	0	0

Year	Team	G	GS	Tackles			Miscellaneous				Interceptions				Totals		
				Tk	Ast	Sack	FF	FR	TD	Blk	Int	Yds	Avg	TD	Sfty	TD	Pts
1991	New York Jets	14	0	2	1	1.0	0	1	0	0	0	0	-	0	0	0	0
1992	New York Jets	16	15	31	20	4.0	0	0	0	0	1	20	20.0	1	0	1	6
1993	New York Jets	16	15	38	30	3.0	2	1	0	0	1	0	0.0	0	0	0	0
1994	New York Jets	16	16	53	30	3.5	1	1	0	0	0	0	-	0	0	0	0
1995	New York Jets	16	15	35	19	3.0	2	3	0	0	0	0	-	0	0	0	0
	6 NFL Seasons	79	61	159	100	14.5	5	6	0	0	2	20	10.0	1	0	1	6

Dana Howard

Pos: LB **Rnd:** 5 **College:** Illinois **Ht:** 6' 0" **Wt:** 238 **Born:** 2/25/72 **Age:** 24

Year	Team	G	GS	Tackles			Miscellaneous				Interceptions				Totals		
				Tk	Ast	Sack	FF	FR	TD	Blk	Int	Yds	Avg	TD	Sfty	TD	Pts
1995	St. Louis Rams	16	0	1	0	0.0	0	1	0	0	0	0	-	0	0	0	0

Desmond Howard

(statistical profile on page 333)

Pos: WR/PR **Rnd:** 1 (4) **College:** Michigan **Ht:** 5' 10" **Wt:** 180 **Born:** 5/15/70 **Age:** 26

Year	Team	G	GS	Rushing					Receiving					Punt Returns				Kickoff Returns				Totals		
				Att	Yds	Avg	Lg	TD	Rec	Yds	Avg	Lg	TD	Num	Yds	Avg	TD	Num	Yds	Avg	TD	Fum	TD	Pts
1992	Washington Redskins	16	1	3	14	4.7	7	0	3	20	6.7	8	0	6	84	14.0	1	22	462	21.0	0	1	1	6
1993	Washington Redskins	16	5	2	17	8.5	9	0	23	286	12.4	27	0	4	25	6.3	0	21	405	19.3	0	0	0	0
1994	Washington Redskins	16	15	1	4	4.0	4	0	40	727	18.2	t81	5	0	0	-	0	0	0	-	0	0	5	32
1995	Jacksonville Jaguars	13	7	1	8	8.0	8	0	26	276	10.6	24	1	24	246	10.3	0	10	178	17.8	0	0	1	6
	4 NFL Seasons	61	28	7	43	6.1	9	0	92	1309	14.2	t81	6	34	355	10.4	1	53	1045	19.7	0	1	7	44

Other Statistics: 1994–scored 1 two-point conversion.

Erik Howard

Pos: DE/DT **Rnd:** 2 **College:** Washington State **Ht:** 6' 4" **Wt:** 275 **Born:** 11/12/64 **Age:** 31

Year	Team	G	GS	Tackles			Miscellaneous				Interceptions				Totals		
				Tk	Ast	Sack	FF	FR	TD	Blk	Int	Yds	Avg	TD	Sfty	TD	Pts
1986	New York Giants	8	2	6	3	2.0	0	0	0	0	0	0	-	0	0	0	0
1987	New York Giants	12	5	21	6	5.5	0	1	0	0	0	0	-	0	0	0	0
1988	New York Giants	16	4	22	2	3.0	0	2	0	0	0	0	-	0	0	0	0
1989	New York Giants	16	16	52	17	5.5	1	1	0	0	0	0	-	0	0	0	0
1990	New York Giants	16	16	49	18	3.0	0	0	0	0	0	0	-	0	0	0	0
1991	New York Giants	6	4	19	6	1.5	0	1	0	0	0	0	-	0	0	0	0
1992	New York Giants	16	15	38	14	0.0	0	3	0	0	0	0	-	0	0	0	0
1993	New York Giants	16	0	26	7	3.5	1	0	0	0	0	0	-	0	0	0	0
1994	New York Giants	16	16	37	7	6.5	0	1	0	0	0	0	-	0	0	0	0
1995	New York Jets	16	16	33	19	2.5	0	1	0	0	0	0	-	0	1	0	2
	10 NFL Seasons	138	94	303	99	33.0	2	10	0	0	0	0	-	0	1	0	2

Chris Hudson

Pos: S **Rnd:** 3 **College:** Colorado **Ht:** 5' 9" **Wt:** 195 **Born:** 10/6/71 **Age:** 25

Year	Team	G	GS	Tackles			Miscellaneous				Interceptions				Totals		
				Tk	Ast	Sack	FF	FR	TD	Blk	Int	Yds	Avg	TD	Sfty	TD	Pts
1995	Jacksonville Jaguars	1	0	0	0	0.0	0	0	0	0	0	0	-	0	0	0	0

John Hudson

Pos: C/G **Rnd:** 11 **College:** Auburn **Ht:** 6' 2" **Wt:** 276 **Born:** 1/29/68 **Age:** 28

Year	Team	G	GS	Year	Team	G	GS	Year	Team	G	GS		G	GS
1991	Philadelphia Eagles	16	0	1993	Philadelphia Eagles	16	0	1995	Philadelphia Eagles	16	0			
1992	Philadelphia Eagles	3	0	1994	Philadelphia Eagles	16	0					5 NFL Seasons	67	0

Other Statistics: 1991–fumbled 1 time for 0 yards. 1993–fumbled 1 time for -14 yards.

Danan Hughes

Pos: WR **Rnd:** 7 **College:** Iowa **Ht:** 6' 1" **Wt:** 211 **Born:** 12/11/70 **Age:** 25

Year	Team	G	GS	Rushing					Receiving					Punt Returns				Kickoff Returns				Totals		
				Att	Yds	Avg	Lg	TD	Rec	Yds	Avg	Lg	TD	Num	Yds	Avg	TD	Num	Yds	Avg	TD	Fum	TD	Pts
1993	Kansas City Chiefs	6	0	0	0	-	-	0	0	0	-	-	0	3	49	16.3	0	14	266	19.0	0	0	0	0
1994	Kansas City Chiefs	16	0	0	0	-	-	0	7	80	11.4	22	0	27	192	7.1	0	9	190	21.1	0	0	0	0
1995	Kansas City Chiefs	16	0	1	5	5.0	5	0	14	103	7.4	16	1	3	9	3.0	0	1	18	18.0	0	0	1	6
	3 NFL Seasons	38	0	1	5	5.0	5	0	21	183	8.7	22	1	33	250	7.6	0	24	474	19.8	0	0	1	6

Tyrone Hughes

Pos: CB/KR **Rnd:** 5 **College:** Nebraska **Ht:** 5' 9" **Wt:** 175 **Born:** 1/14/70 **Age:** 26

			Tackles			Miscellaneous				Interceptions				Punt Returns				Kickoff Returns				Totals	
Year Team	G	GS	Tk	Ast	Sack	FF	FR	TD	Blk	Int	Yds	Avg	TD	Num	Yds	Avg	TD	Num	Yds	Avg	TD	TD	Fum
1993 New Orleans Saints	16	0	0	0	0.0	0	0	0	0	0	0	-	0	37	**503**	**13.6**	**2**	30	753	25.1	**1**	3	0
1994 New Orleans Saints	15	5	*31*	*5*	0.0	0	3	2	0	2	31	15.5	0	21	143	6.8	0	**63**	**1556**	24.7	2	4	7
1995 New Orleans Saints	16	2	*17*	*1*	0.0	0	0	0	0	2	19	9.5	0	28	262	9.4	0	**66**	**1617**	24.5	0	0	2
3 NFL Seasons	47	7	48	6	0.0	0	3	2	0	4	50	12.5	0	86	908	10.6	2	159	3926	24.7	3	7	9

Other Statistics: 1994–rushed 2 times for 6 yards.

Kent Hull

Pos: C **Rnd:** FA **College:** Mississippi State **Ht:** 6' 5" **Wt:** 284 **Born:** 1/13/61 **Age:** 35

Year	Team	G	GS	Year	Team	G	GS	Year	Team	G	GS	Year	Team	G	GS
1986	Buffalo Bills	16	16	1989	Buffalo Bills	16	16	1992	Buffalo Bills	16	16	1995	Buffalo Bills	16	16
1987	Buffalo Bills	12	12	1990	Buffalo Bills	16	16	1993	Buffalo Bills	14	13				
1988	Buffalo Bills	16	16	1991	Buffalo Bills	16	16	1994	Buffalo Bills	16	16		10 NFL Seasons	154	153

Other Statistics: 1989–recovered 2 fumbles for 0 yards. 1991–recovered 1 fumble for 0 yards. 1992–recovered 2 fumbles for 0 yards. 1994–fumbled 1 time for -19 yards. 1995–recovered 1 fumble for -1 yard; fumbled 1 time.

Ronald Humphrey

Pos: KR/RB **Rnd:** 8 **College:** Mississippi Valley State **Ht:** 5' 10" **Wt:** 211 **Born:** 3/3/69 **Age:** 27

			Rushing					Receiving					Punt Returns				Kickoff Returns				Totals		
Year Team	G	GS	Att	Yds	Avg	Lg	TD	Rec	Yds	Avg	Lg	TD	Num	Yds	Avg	TD	Num	Yds	Avg	TD	Fum	TD	Pts
1994 Indianapolis Colts	15	0	18	85	4.7	27	0	3	19	6.3	12	0	0	0	-	0	35	783	22.4	1	4	1	6
1995 Indianapolis Colts	11	0	2	6	3.0	5	0	2	11	5.5	6	0	0	0	-	0	21	453	21.6	0	1	0	0
2 NFL Seasons	26	0	20	91	4.6	27	0	5	30	6.0	12	0	0	0	-	0	56	1236	22.1	1	5	1	6

Other Statistics: 1994–recovered 1 fumble for 0 yards.

Stan Humphries

(statistical profile on page 334)

Pos: QB **Rnd:** 6 **College:** Northeast Louisiana **Ht:** 6' 2" **Wt:** 223 **Born:** 4/14/65 **Age:** 31

			Passing										Rushing					Miscellaneous					
Year Team	G	GS	Att	Com	Pct	Yards	Yds/Att	Lg	TD	Int	Int%	Rating	Att	Yds	Avg	Lg	TD	Sckd	Yds	Fum	Recv	Yds	Pts
1989 Washington Redskins	2	0	10	5	50.0	91	9.10	39	1	1	10.0	75.4	5	10	2.0	9	0	3	9	1	1	0	0
1990 Washington Redskins	7	5	156	91	58.3	1015	6.51	44	3	10	6.4	57.5	23	106	4.6	17	2	9	62	0	0	0	12
1992 San Diego Chargers	16	15	454	263	57.9	3356	7.39	t67	16	18	4.0	76.4	28	79	2.8	25	4	28	218	9	3	0	24
1993 San Diego Chargers	12	10	324	173	53.4	1981	6.11	t48	12	10	3.1	71.5	8	37	4.6	27	0	18	142	2	1	0	0
1994 San Diego Chargers	15	15	453	264	58.3	3209	7.08	**t99**	17	12	2.6	81.6	19	19	1.0	8	0	25	223	6	2	-9	0
1995 San Diego Chargers	15	15	478	282	59.0	3381	7.07	t51	17	14	2.9	80.4	33	53	1.6	18	1	23	197	9	7	-6	6
6 NFL Seasons	67	60	1875	1078	57.5	13033	6.95	t99	66	65	3.5	76.2	116	304	2.6	27	7	106	851	27	14	-15	42

Other Statistics: 1995–caught 1 pass for -4 yards.

Earnest Hunter

Pos: RB/KR **Rnd:** FA **College:** Southeast Oklahoma State **Ht:** 5' 8" **Wt:** 201 **Born:** 12/21/70 **Age:** 25

			Rushing					Receiving					Punt Returns				Kickoff Returns				Totals		
Year Team	G	GS	Att	Yds	Avg	Lg	TD	Rec	Yds	Avg	Lg	TD	Num	Yds	Avg	TD	Num	Yds	Avg	TD	Fum	TD	Pts
1995 Cleveland Browns	10	0	30	100	3.3	15	0	5	42	8.4	17	0	3	40	13.3	0	23	508	22.1	0	4	0	0

Patrick Hunter

Pos: CB **Rnd:** 3 **College:** Nevada **Ht:** 5' 11" **Wt:** 186 **Born:** 10/24/64 **Age:** 32

			Tackles			Miscellaneous				Interceptions				Punt Returns				Kickoff Returns				Totals	
Year Team	G	GS	Tk	Ast	Sack	FF	FR	TD	Blk	Int	Yds	Avg	TD	Num	Yds	Avg	TD	Num	Yds	Avg	TD	TD	Fum
1986 Seattle Seahawks	16	0	33	10	0.0	1	0	0	0	0	0	-	0	0	0	-	0	0	0	-	0	0	0
1987 Seattle Seahawks	11	11	24	3	0.0	0	0	0	0	1	3	3.0	0	0	0	-	0	0	0	-	0	0	0
1988 Seattle Seahawks	10	7	23	5	0.0	1	0	0	0	0	0	-	0	1	0	0.0	0	0	0	-	0	0	1
1989 Seattle Seahawks	16	14	49	4	1.0	0	0	0	0	0	0		0	0	0	-	0	0	0	-	0	0	0
1990 Seattle Seahawks	16	10	50	8	0.0	0	1	0	0	1	0	0.0	0	0	0	-	0	0	0	-	0	0	0
1991 Seattle Seahawks	15	15	37	10	0.0	0	0	0	0	1	32	32.0	1	0	0	-	0	0	0	-	0	1	0
1992 Seattle Seahawks	16	16	58	12	0.0	0	1	0	0	2	0	0.0	0	0	0	-	0	0	0	-	0	0	0
1993 Seattle Seahawks	15	15	51	7	0.0	0	3	0	0	4	54	13.5	0	0	0	-	0	0	0	-	0	0	0
1994 Seattle Seahawks	5	5	*11*	*5*	0.0	0	0	0	0	3	85	28.3	0	0	0	-	0	0	0	-	0	0	0
1995 Arizona Cardinals	5	5	*14*	*0*	0.0	1	0	0	0	2	21	10.5	0	0	0	-	0	0	0	-	0	0	0
10 NFL Seasons	125	104	350	64	1.0	3	5	0	0	14	195	13.9	1	1	0	0.0	0	0	0	-	0	1	1

Torey Hunter

Pos: CB **Rnd:** 3 **College:** Washington State **Ht:** 5' 9" **Wt:** 176 **Born:** 2/10/72 **Age:** 24

Year Team	G	GS	Tackles			Miscellaneous				Interceptions				Totals		
			Tk	Ast	Sack	FF	FR	TD	Blk	Int	Yds	Avg	TD	Sfty	TD	Pts
1995 Houston Oilers	11	0	6	0	0.0	0	0	0	0	0	0	-	0	0	0	0

Greg Huntington

Pos: G **Rnd:** 5 **College:** Penn State **Ht:** 6' 4" **Wt:** 293 **Born:** 9/22/70 **Age:** 26

Year	Team	G	GS	Year	Team	G	GS			G	GS
1993	Washington Redskins	9	0	1995	Jacksonville Jaguars	4	0		2 NFL Seasons	13	0

Maurice Hurst

Pos: CB **Rnd:** 4 **College:** Southern **Ht:** 5' 10" **Wt:** 185 **Born:** 9/17/67 **Age:** 29

Year Team	G	GS	Tackles			Miscellaneous				Interceptions				Punt Returns				Kickoff Returns				Totals	
			Tk	Ast	Sack	FF	FR	TD	Blk	Int	Yds	Avg	TD	Num	Yds	Avg	TD	Num	Yds	Avg	TD	TD	Fum
1989 New England Patriots	16	14	48	11	0.0	0	0	0	0	5	31	6.2	1	1	6	6.0	0	0	0	-	0	1	0
1990 New England Patriots	16	16	32	12	0.0	1	0	0	0	4	61	15.3	0	0	0	-	0	0	0	-	0	0	1
1991 New England Patriots	15	14	44	7	0.0	0	0	0	0	3	21	7.0	0	0	0	-	0	0	0	-	0	0	0
1992 New England Patriots	16	16	49	14	0.0	1	0	0	0	3	29	9.7	0	0	0	-	0	0	0	-	0	0	0
1993 New England Patriots	16	16	50	11	1.0	1	0	0	0	4	53	13.3	0	0	0	-	0	0	0	-	0	0	0
1994 New England Patriots	16	16	53	13	2.0	1	0	0	0	7	68	9.7	0	0	0	-	0	0	0	-	0	0	0
1995 New England Patriots	10	10	34	8	0.0	0	0	0	0	1	0	0.0	0	0	0	-	0	0	0	-	0	0	0
7 NFL Seasons	105	102	310	76	3.0	4	0	0	0	27	263	9.7	1	1	6	6.0	0	0	0	-	0	1	1

Michael Husted

(statistical profile on page 476)

Pos: K **Rnd:** FA **College:** Virginia **Ht:** 6' 0" **Wt:** 188 **Born:** 6/16/70 **Age:** 26

Year Team	G	Field Goals													PAT		Tot
		1-29 Yds	Pct	30-39 Yds	Pct	40-49 Yds	Pct	50+ Yds	Pct	Overall	Pct	Long	Made	Att		Pts
1993 Tampa Bay Buccaneers	16	5-5	100.0	5-6	83.3	3-6	50.0	3-5	60.0	16-22	72.7	57	27	27		75
1994 Tampa Bay Buccaneers	16	8-8	100.0	10-12	83.3	4-10	40.0	1-5	20.0	23-35	65.7	53	20	20		89
1995 Tampa Bay Buccaneers	16	6-7	85.7	5-7	71.4	5-9	55.6	3-3	100.0	19-26	73.1	53	25	25		82
3 NFL Seasons	48	19-20	95.0	20-25	80.0	12-25	48.0	7-13	53.8	58-83	69.9	57	72	72		246

Other Statistics: 1994–punted 2 times for 53 yards.

Tom Hutton

(statistical profile on page 476)

Pos: P **Rnd:** FA **College:** Tennessee **Ht:** 6' 1" **Wt:** 193 **Born:** 7/8/72 **Age:** 24

Year Team	G	Punting											Rushing		Passing			
		NetPunts	Yards	Avg	Long	In20	In20%	TotPunts	TB	Blocks	OppRet	RetYds	NetAvg	Att	Yards	Att	Com	Yards	Int
1995 Philadelphia Eagles	16	85	3682	43.3	63	20	23.5	86	13	1	38	527	33.7	1	0	0	0	0	0

Other Statistics: 1995–fumbled 1 time for -19 yards.

Mark Ingram

(statistical profile on page 334)

Pos: WR **Rnd:** 1 (28) **College:** Michigan State **Ht:** 5' 11" **Wt:** 194 **Born:** 8/23/65 **Age:** 31

Year Team	G	GS	Rushing					Receiving					Punt Returns				Kickoff Returns				Totals		
			Att	Yds	Avg	Lg	TD	Rec	Yds	Avg	Lg	TD	Num	Yds	Avg	TD	Num	Yds	Avg	TD	Fum	TD	Pts
1987 New York Giants	9	0	0	0	-	-	0	2	32	16.0	18	0	0	0	-	0	6	114	19.0	0	0	0	0
1988 New York Giants	7	4	0	0	-	-	0	13	158	12.2	32	1	0	0	-	0	8	129	16.1	0	0	1	6
1989 New York Giants	16	3	1	1	1.0	1	0	17	290	17.1	t41	1	0	0	-	0	22	332	15.1	0	2	1	6
1990 New York Giants	16	14	1	4	4.0	4	0	26	499	19.2	t57	5	0	0	-	0	3	42	14.0	0	1	5	30
1991 New York Giants	16	13	0	0	-	-	0	51	824	16.2	41	3	8	49	6.1	0	8	125	15.6	0	3	3	18
1992 New York Giants	12	12	0	0	-	-	0	27	408	15.1	34	1	0	0	-	0	0	0	-	0	0	1	6
1993 Miami Dolphins	16	16	0	0	-	-	0	44	707	16.1	t77	6	0	0	-	0	0	0	-	0	3	6	36
1994 Miami Dolphins	15	13	0	0	-	-	0	44	506	11.5	t64	6	0	0	-	0	1	0	0.0	0	1	6	36
1995 Green Bay Packers	16	9	1	-3	-3.0	-3	0	39	469	12.0	29	3	1	0	0.0	0	0	0	-	0	1	3	18
9 NFL Seasons	123	84	3	2	0.7	4	0	263	3893	14.8	t77	26	9	49	5.4	0	48	742	15.5	0	11	26	156

Other Statistics: 1989–recovered 2 fumbles for 0 yards. 1991–recovered 1 fumble for 0 yards; attempted 1 pass with 0 completions for 0 yards. 1992–recovered 1 fumble for 0 yards. 1993–recovered 1 fumble for 0 yards. 1994–recovered 1 fumble for 0 yards.

Stephen Ingram

Pos: T/G **Rnd:** 7 **College:** Maryland **Ht:** 6' 4" **Wt:** 311 **Born:** 5/8/71 **Age:** 25

Year	Team	G	GS			G	GS
1995	Tampa Bay Buccaneers	2	0		1 NFL Season	2	0

Darwin Ireland

Pos: LB **Rnd:** FA **College:** Arkansas   **Ht:** 5' 11" **Wt:** 240 **Born:** 5/26/71 **Age:** 25

			Tackles			Miscellaneous				Interceptions				Totals		
Year	Team	G	GS	Tk	Ast	Sack	FF	FR	TD	Blk	Int	Yds	Avg	TD	Sfty	TD	Pts
1994	Chicago Bears	2	0	0	0	0.0	0	0	0	0	0	0	-	0	0	0	0
1995	Chicago Bears	1	0	0	0	0.0	0	0	0	0	0	0	-	0	0	0	0
	2 NFL Seasons	3	0	0	0	0.0	0	0	0	0	0	0	-	0	0	0	0

Ken Irvin

Pos: CB **Rnd:** 4 **College:** Memphis   **Ht:** 5' 10" **Wt:** 182 **Born:** 7/11/72 **Age:** 24

				Tackles			Miscellaneous				Interceptions				Punt Returns				Kickoff Returns				Totals	
Year	Team	G	GS	Tk	Ast	Sack	FF	FR	TD	Blk	Int	Yds	Avg	TD	Num	Yds	Avg	TD	Num	Yds	Avg	TD	TD	Fum
1995	Buffalo Bills	16	3	18	2	0.0	0	0	0	0	0	0	-	0	0	0	-	0	1	12	12.0	0	0	0

Michael Irvin

(statistical profile on page 335)

Pos: WR **Rnd:** 1 (11) **College:** Miami (FL)   **Ht:** 6' 2" **Wt:** 205 **Born:** 3/5/66 **Age:** 30

				Rushing					Receiving					Punt Returns				Kickoff Returns				Totals		
Year	Team	G	GS	Att	Yds	Avg	Lg	TD	Rec	Yds	Avg	Lg	TD	Num	Yds	Avg	TD	Num	Yds	Avg	TD	Fum	TD	Pts
1988	Dallas Cowboys	14	10	1	2	2.0	2	0	32	654	20.4	t61	5	0	0	-	0	0	0	-	0	0	5	30
1989	Dallas Cowboys	6	6	1	6	6.0	6	0	26	378	14.5	t65	2	0	0	-	0	0	0	-	0	0	2	12
1990	Dallas Cowboys	12	7	0	0	-	-	0	20	413	20.7	t61	5	0	0	-	0	0	0	-	0	0	5	30
1991	Dallas Cowboys	16	16	0	0	-	-	0	93	1523	16.4	t66	8	0	0	-	0	0	0	-	0	3	8	48
1992	Dallas Cowboys	16	14	1	-9	-9.0	-9	0	78	1396	17.9	t87	7	0	0	-	0	0	0	-	0	1	7	42
1993	Dallas Cowboys	16	16	2	6	3.0	9	0	88	1330	15.1	t61	7	0	0	-	0	0	0	-	0	0	7	42
1994	Dallas Cowboys	16	16	0	0	-	-	0	79	1241	15.7	t65	6	0	0	-	0	0	0	-	0	0	6	36
1995	Dallas Cowboys	16	16	0	0	-	-	0	111	1603	14.4	50	10	0	0	-	0	0	0	-	0	1	10	60
	8 NFL Seasons	112	101	5	5	1.0	9	0	527	8538	16.2	t87	50	0	0	-	0	0	0	-	0	5	50	300

Other Statistics: 1989–recovered 1 fumble for 0 yards. 1991–recovered 1 fumble for 0 yards. 1992–recovered 1 fumble for 0 yards.

Terry Irving

Pos: LB **Rnd:** 4 **College:** McNeese State   **Ht:** 6' 0" **Wt:** 224 **Born:** 7/3/71 **Age:** 25

				Tackles			Miscellaneous				Interceptions				Totals		
Year	Team	G	GS	Tk	Ast	Sack	FF	FR	TD	Blk	Int	Yds	Avg	TD	Sfty	TD	Pts
1994	Arizona Cardinals	16	0	8	5	0.0	1	1	0	0	0	0	-	0	0	0	0
1995	Arizona Cardinals	16	8	49	10	1.0	1	3	0	0	0	0	-	0	0	0	0
	2 NFL Seasons	32	8	57	15	1.0	2	4	0	0	0	0	-	0	0	0	0

Qadry Ismail

(statistical profile on page 335)

Pos: KR/WR **Rnd:** 2 **College:** Syracuse   **Ht:** 6' 0" **Wt:** 191 **Born:** 11/8/70 **Age:** 25

				Rushing					Receiving					Punt Returns				Kickoff Returns				Totals		
Year	Team	G	GS	Att	Yds	Avg	Lg	TD	Rec	Yds	Avg	Lg	TD	Num	Yds	Avg	TD	Num	Yds	Avg	TD	Fum	TD	Pts
1993	Minnesota Vikings	15	3	3	14	4.7	6	0	19	212	11.2	37	1	0	0	-	0	42	902	21.5	0	1	1	6
1994	Minnesota Vikings	16	3	0	0	-	-	0	45	696	15.5	t65	5	0	0	-	0	35	807	23.1	0	2	5	30
1995	Minnesota Vikings	16	2	1	7	7.0	7	0	32	597	18.7	t85	3	0	0	-	0	42	1037	24.7	0	3	3	18
	3 NFL Seasons	47	8	4	21	5.3	7	0	96	1505	15.7	t85	9	0	0	-	0	119	2746	23.1	0	6	9	54

Other Statistics: 1994–recovered 1 fumble for 1 yard.

Raghib Ismail

(statistical profile on page 336)

Pos: KR/WR **Rnd:** 4 **College:** Notre Dame   **Ht:** 5' 11" **Wt:** 175 **Born:** 11/18/69 **Age:** 26

				Rushing					Receiving					Punt Returns				Kickoff Returns				Totals		
Year	Team	G	GS	Att	Yds	Avg	Lg	TD	Rec	Yds	Avg	Lg	TD	Num	Yds	Avg	TD	Num	Yds	Avg	TD	Fum	TD	Pts
1993	Los Angeles Raiders	13	0	4	-5	-1.3	10	0	26	353	13.6	t43	1	0	0	-	0	25	605	24.2	0	0	1	6
1994	Los Angeles Raiders	16	0	4	31	7.8	13	0	34	513	15.1	42	5	0	0	-	0	43	923	21.5	0	0	5	30
1995	Oakland Raiders	16	16	6	29	4.8	13	0	28	491	17.5	t73	3	0	0	-	0	36	706	19.6	0	4	3	18
	3 NFL Seasons	45	16	14	55	3.9	13	0	88	1357	15.4	t70	9	0	0	-	0	104	2234	21.5	0	4	9	54

Other Statistics: 1993–recovered 1 fumble for 0 yards. 1995–recovered 1 fumble for 0 yards.

Steve Israel

Pos: CB **Rnd:** 2 **College:** Pittsburgh   **Ht:** 5' 11" **Wt:** 186 **Born:** 3/16/69 **Age:** 27

				Tackles			Miscellaneous				Interceptions				Punt Returns				Kickoff Returns				Totals	
Year	Team	G	GS	Tk	Ast	Sack	FF	FR	TD	Blk	Int	Yds	Avg	TD	Num	Yds	Avg	TD	Num	Yds	Avg	TD	TD	Fum
1992	Los Angeles Rams	16	2	25	2	0.0	0	1	0	0	0	0	-	0	0	0	-	0	1	-3	-3.0	0	0	0
1993	Los Angeles Rams	16	12	31	4	0.0	0	0	0	0	0	0	-	0	0	0	-	0	5	92	18.4	0	0	0
1994	Los Angeles Rams	10	2	22	-	0.0	0	0	0	0	0	0	-	0	0	0	-	0	0	0	-	0	0	0
1995	San Francisco 49ers	8	0	1	0	0.0	0	0	0	0	0	0	-	0	0	0	-	0	0	0	-	0	0	0

Year	Team	G	GS	Tk	Ast	Sack	FF	FR	TD	Blk	Int	Yds	Avg	TD	Num	Yds	Avg	TD	Num	Yds	Avg	TD	TD	Fum
	4 NFL Seasons	50	16	79	6	0.0	0	1	0	0	0	0	-	0	0	0	-	0	6	89	14.8	0	0	0

Chris Jacke

(statistical profile on page 476)

Pos: K   **Rnd:** 6   **College:** Texas-El Paso   **Ht:** 6' 0" **Wt:** 205   **Born:** 3/12/66   **Age:** 30

Year	Team	G	1-29 Yds	Pct	30-39 Yds	Pct	40-49 Yds	Pct	50+ Yds	Pct	Overall	Pct	Long	Made	Att	Pts
1989	Green Bay Packers	16	10-10	**100.0**	4-6	66.7	7-9	77.8	1-3	33.3	22-28	78.6	52	42	42	108
1990	Green Bay Packers	16	9-9	**100.0**	10-13	76.9	2-4	50.0	2-4	50.0	23-30	76.7	53	28	29	97
1991	Green Bay Packers	16	9-9	**100.0**	4-5	80.0	4-9	44.4	1-1	100.0	18-24	75.0	53	31	31	85
1992	Green Bay Packers	16	5-7	71.4	9-10	90.0	6-9	66.7	2-3	66.7	22-29	75.9	53	30	30	96
1993	Green Bay Packers	16	13-13	**100.0**	6-10	60.0	6-7	85.7	**6-7**	85.7	31-37	83.8	54	35	35	128
1994	Green Bay Packers	16	12-12	**100.0**	4-6	66.7	2-5	40.0	1-3	33.3	19-26	73.1	50	41	43	98
1995	Green Bay Packers	14	6-7	85.7	0-2	0.0	8-10	80.0	3-4	75.0	17-23	73.9	51	43	43	94
	7 NFL Seasons	110	64-67	95.5	37-52	71.2	35-53	66.0	16-25	64.0	152-197	77.2	54	250	253	706

Alfred Jackson

Pos: CB   **Rnd:** 5   **College:** San Diego State   **Ht:** 6' 0" **Wt:** 185   **Born:** 7/10/67   **Age:** 29

Year	Team	G	GS	Tk	Ast	Sack	FF	FR	TD	Blk	Int	Yds	Avg	TD	Sfty	TD	Pts
1989	Los Angeles Rams	7	0	2	0	0.0	0	0	0	0	0	0	-	0	0	0	0
1990	Los Angeles Rams	5	0	3	1	0.0	0	0	0	0	0	0	-	0	0	0	0
1991	Cleveland Browns	6	1	8	2	0.0	0	2	0	0	1	0	0.0	0	0	0	0
1992	Cleveland Browns	5	0	2	1	0.0	0	0	0	0	0	0	-	0	0	0	0
1995	Minnesota Vikings	8	1	20	1	0.0	0	0	0	0	2	46	23.0	1	0	1	6
	5 NFL Seasons	31	2	35	5	0.0	0	2	0	0	3	46	15.3	1	0	1	6

Calvin Jackson

Pos: CB   **Rnd:** FA   **College:** Auburn   **Ht:** 5' 9" **Wt:** 185   **Born:** 10/28/72   **Age:** 24

Year	Team	G	GS	Tk	Ast	Sack	FF	FR	TD	Blk	Int	Yds	Avg	TD	Sfty	TD	Pts
1994	Miami Dolphins	2	0	0	0	0.0	0	0	0	0	0	0	-	0	0	0	0
1995	Miami Dolphins	9	1	12	0	0.0	0	0	0	0	1	23	23.0	0	0	0	0
	2 NFL Seasons	11	1	12	0	0.0	0	0	0	0	1	23	23.0	0	0	0	0

Greg Jackson

(statistical profile on page 421)

Pos: S   **Rnd:** 3   **College:** Louisiana State   **Ht:** 6' 1" **Wt:** 204   **Born:** 8/20/66   **Age:** 30

Year	Team	G	GS	Tk	Ast	Sack	FF	FR	TD	Blk	Int	Yds	Avg	TD	Sfty	TD	Pts
1989	New York Giants	16	1	17	2	0.0	1	1	0	0	0	0	-	0	0	0	0
1990	New York Giants	14	14	64	19	4.0	0	0	0	0	5	8	1.6	0	0	0	0
1991	New York Giants	13	12	50	9	0.0	0	0	0	0	1	3	3.0	0	0	0	0
1992	New York Giants	16	16	67	12	0.0	0	1	0	0	4	71	17.8	0	0	0	0
1993	New York Giants	16	16	51	20	0.0	1	3	0	0	4	32	8.0	0	0	0	0
1994	Philadelphia Eagles	16	16	65	16	0.0	2	0	0	0	6	86	14.3	1	0	1	6
1995	Philadelphia Eagles	16	16	56	14	0.0	3	3	1	0	1	18	18.0	0	0	1	6
	7 NFL Seasons	107	91	370	92	4.0	7	8	1	0	21	218	10.4	1	0	2	12

Other Statistics: 1991–fumbled 1 time for 0 yards.

John Jackson

Pos: T   **Rnd:** 10   **College:** Eastern Kentucky   **Ht:** 6' 6" **Wt:** 293   **Born:** 1/4/65   **Age:** 31

Year	Team	G	GS	Year	Team	G	GS	Year	Team	G	GS	Year	Team	G	GS
1988	Pittsburgh Steelers	16	0	1990	Pittsburgh Steelers	16	16	1992	Pittsburgh Steelers	16	13	1994	Pittsburgh Steelers	16	16
1989	Pittsburgh Steelers	14	12	1991	Pittsburgh Steelers	16	16	1993	Pittsburgh Steelers	16	16	1995	Pittsburgh Steelers	11	9
													8 NFL Seasons	121	98

Other Statistics: 1988–returned 1 kickoff for 10 yards. 1991–recovered 1 fumble for 0 yards. 1993–recovered 1 fumble for 0 yards. 1994–recovered 2 fumbles for 0 yards.

Keith Jackson

Pos: TE   **Rnd:** 1 (13)   **College:** Oklahoma   **Ht:** 6' 2" **Wt:** 258   **Born:** 4/19/65   **Age:** 31

Year	Team	G	GS	Att	Yds	Avg	Lg	TD	Rec	Yds	Avg	Lg	TD	Num	Yds	Avg	TD	Num	Yds	Avg	TD	Fum	TD	Pts
1988	Philadelphia Eagles	16	15	0	0	-	-	0	81	869	10.7	41	6	0	0	-	0	0	0	-	0	3	6	36
1989	Philadelphia Eagles	14	12	0	0	-	-	0	63	648	10.3	33	3	0	0	-	0	0	0	-	0	1	3	18
1990	Philadelphia Eagles	14	14	0	0	-	-	0	50	670	13.4	t37	6	0	0	-	0	0	0	-	0	1	6	36
1991	Philadelphia Eagles	16	16	0	0	-	-	0	48	569	11.9	t73	5	0	0	-	0	0	0	-	0	2	5	30

Year Team	G	GS	Rushing					Receiving					Punt Returns				Kickoff Returns				Totals		
			Att	Yds	Avg	Lg	TD	Rec	Yds	Avg	Lg	TD	Num	Yds	Avg	TD	Num	Yds	Avg	TD	Fum	TD	Pts
1992 Miami Dolphins	13	11	0	0	-	-	0	48	594	12.4	42	5	0	0	-	0	0	0	-	0	2	5	30
1993 Miami Dolphins	15	15	0	0	-	-	0	39	613	15.7	t57	6	0	0	-	0	0	0	-	0	2	6	36
1994 Miami Dolphins	16	16	0	0	-	-	0	59	673	11.4	35	7	0	0	-	0	0	0	-	0	2	7	44
1995 Green Bay Packers	9	1	0	0	-	-	0	13	142	10.9	22	1	0	0	-	0	0	0	-	0	0	1	6
8 NFL Seasons	113	100	0	0	-	-	0	401	4778	11.9	t73	39	0	0	-	0	0	0	-	0	13	39	236

Other Statistics: 1994–recovered 1 fumble for 0 yards; scored 1 two-point conversion.

Michael Jackson

(statistical profile on page 336)

Pos: WR   Rnd: 6   College: Southern Mississippi   Ht: 6' 4"   Wt: 195   Born: 4/12/69   Age: 27

Year Team	G	GS	Rushing					Receiving					Kickoff Returns				Passing				Totals		
			Att	Yds	Avg	Lg	TD	Rec	Yds	Avg	Lg	TD	Num	Yds	Avg	TD	Att	Com	Yds	Int	Fum	TD	Pts
1991 Cleveland Browns	16	7	0	0	-	-	0	17	268	15.8	t65	2	0	0	-	0	0	0	0	0	0	2	12
1992 Cleveland Browns	16	14	1	21	21.0	21	0	47	755	16.1	t69	7	0	0	-	0	0	0	0	0	0	7	42
1993 Cleveland Browns	15	11	1	1	1.0	1	0	41	756	18.4	t62	8	0	0	-	0	1	1	25	0	1	8	48
1994 Cleveland Browns	9	7	0	0	-	-	0	21	304	14.5	30	2	0	0	-	0	2	0	0	0	0	2	12
1995 Cleveland Browns	13	10	0	0	-	-	0	44	714	16.2	t70	9	0	0	-	0	1	0	0	1	1	9	54
5 NFL Seasons	69	49	2	22	11.0	21	0	170	2797	16.5	t70	28	0	0	-	0	4	1	25	1	2	28	168

Other Statistics: 1993–recovered 1 fumble for 0 yards. 1995–recovered 1 fumble for 0 yards.

Rickey Jackson

(statistical profile on page 421)

Pos: DE   Rnd: 2   College: Pittsburgh   Ht: 6' 2"   Wt: 245   Born: 3/20/58   Age: 38

Year Team	G	GS	Tackles			Miscellaneous				Interceptions				Totals		
			Tk	Ast	Sack	FF	FR	TD	Blk	Int	Yds	Avg	TD	Sfty	TD	Pts
1981 New Orleans Saints	16	16	85	40	8.0	2	1	0	0	0	0	-	0	0	0	0
1982 New Orleans Saints	9	9	32	15	4.5	1	2	0	0	1	32	32.0	0	0	0	0
1983 New Orleans Saints	16	16	67	35	12.0	0	2	0	0	1	0	0.0	0	0	0	0
1984 New Orleans Saints	16	16	97	27	12.0	4	4	0	0	1	14	14.0	0	0	0	0
1985 New Orleans Saints	16	16	69	38	11.0	0	0	0	0	0	0	-	0	0	0	0
1986 New Orleans Saints	16	16	85	29	9.0	6	1	0	0	1	1	1.0	0	0	0	0
1987 New Orleans Saints	12	12	57	17	9.5	3	0	0	0	2	4	2.0	0	0	0	0
1988 New Orleans Saints	16	16	71	21	7.0	2	0	0	0	1	16	16.0	0	1	0	2
1989 New Orleans Saints	14	14	40	7	7.5	3	0	0	0	0	0	-	0	0	0	0
1990 New Orleans Saints	16	16	49	19	6.0	0	7	0	0	0	0	-	0	0	0	0
1991 New Orleans Saints	16	16	47	12	11.5	3	4	0	0	0	0	-	0	0	0	0
1992 New Orleans Saints	16	16	56	10	13.5	6	3	0	0	0	0	-	0	0	0	0
1993 New Orleans Saints	16	16	67	12	11.5	4	3	0	0	0	0	-	0	0	0	0
1994 San Francisco 49ers	16	14	37	3	3.5	2	2	0	0	0	0	-	0	0	0	0
1995 San Francisco 49ers	16	16	32	4	9.5	0	0	0	0	1	1	1.0	0	0	0	0
15 NFL Seasons	227	225	891	289	128.0	40	29	0	0	8	68	8.5	0	1	0	2

Other Statistics: 1983–fumbled 1 time. 1984–fumbled 1 time.

Steve Jackson

Pos: CB   Rnd: 3   College: Purdue   Ht: 5' 8"   Wt: 182   Born: 4/8/69   Age: 27

Year Team	G	GS	Tackles			Miscellaneous				Interceptions				Punt Returns				Kickoff Returns				Totals	
			Tk	Ast	Sack	FF	FR	TD	Blk	Int	Yds	Avg	TD	Num	Yds	Avg	TD	Num	Yds	Avg	TD	TD	Fum
1991 Houston Oilers	15	2	26	8	1.0	0	2	0	0	0	0	-	0	1	0	0.0	0	0	0	-	0	0	1
1992 Houston Oilers	16	1	27	14	1.0	0	0	0	0	3	18	6.0	0	0	0	-	0	0	0	-	0	0	0
1993 Houston Oilers	16	12	45	10	0.0	1	0	0	0	5	54	10.8	1	0	0	-	0	0	0	-	0	1	0
1994 Houston Oilers	12	0	10	2	0.0	0	0	0	0	1	0	0.0	0	0	0	-	0	14	285	20.4	0	0	0
1995 Houston Oilers	10	1	17	4	1.0	0	0	0	0	2	0	0.0	0	0	0	-	0	0	0	-	0	0	0
5 NFL Seasons	69	16	125	38	4.0	1	2	0	0	11	72	6.5	1	1	0	0.0	0	14	285	20.4	0	1	1

Willie Jackson

(statistical profile on page 337)

Pos: WR/KR   Rnd: 4   College: Florida   Ht: 6' 1"   Wt: 203   Born: 0/10/71   Age: 25

Year Team	G	GS	Rushing					Receiving					Punt Returns				Kickoff Returns				Totals		
			Att	Yds	Avg	Lg	TD	Rec	Yds	Avg	Lg	TD	Num	Yds	Avg	TD	Num	Yds	Avg	TD	Fum	TD	Pts
1994 Dallas Cowboys	1	0	0	0	-	-	0	0	0	-	-	0	0	0	-	0	0	0	-	0	0	0	0
1995 Jacksonville Jaguars	14	10	0	0	-	-	0	53	589	11.1	45	5	1	-2	-2.0	0	19	404	21.3	0	2	5	32
2 NFL Seasons	15	10	0	0	-	-	0	53	589	11.1	45	5	1	-2	-2.0	0	19	404	21.3	0	2	5	32

Other Statistics: 1995–recovered 1 fumble for 0 yards; scored 1 two-point conversion.

Ray Jacobs

Pos: LB **Rnd:** FA **College:** North Carolina **Ht:** 6' 2" **Wt:** 244 **Born:** 8/18/72 **Age:** 24

Year	Team	G	GS	Tackles			Miscellaneous				Interceptions				Totals		
				Tk	Ast	Sack	FF	FR	TD	Blk	Int	Yds	Avg	TD	Sfty	TD	Pts
1994	Denver Broncos	16	0	0	0	0.0	0	0	0	0	0	0	-	0	0	0	0
1995	Denver Broncos	15	0	0	0	0.0	0	1	0	0	0	0	-	0	0	0	0
	2 NFL Seasons	31	0	0	0	0.0	0	1	0	0	0	0	-	0	0	0	0

Tim Jacobs

Pos: CB **Rnd:** FA **College:** Delaware **Ht:** 5' 10" **Wt:** 185 **Born:** 4/5/70 **Age:** 26

Year	Team	G	GS	Tackles			Miscellaneous				Interceptions				Totals		
				Tk	Ast	Sack	FF	FR	TD	Blk	Int	Yds	Avg	TD	Sfty	TD	Pts
1993	Cleveland Browns	2	0	0	1	0.0	0	0	0	0	0	0	-	0	0	0	0
1994	Cleveland Browns	10	1	6	2	0.0	0	0	0	0	2	9	4.5	0	0	0	0
1995	Cleveland Browns	14	0	23	1	0.0	0	0	0	0	0	0	-	0	0	0	0
	3 NFL Seasons	26	1	29	4	0.0	0	0	0	0	2	9	4.5	0	0	0	0

Jeff Jaeger

(statistical profile on page 477)

Pos: K **Rnd:** 3 **College:** Washington **Ht:** 5' 11" **Wt:** 195 **Born:** 11/26/64 **Age:** 31

Year	Team	G	Field Goals												PAT		Tot
			1-29 Yds	Pct	30-39 Yds	Pct	40-49 Yds	Pct	50+ Yds	Pct	Overall	Pct	Long		Made	Att	Pts
1987	Cleveland Browns	10	6-6	100.0	3-6	50.0	5-9	55.6	0-1	0.0	14-22	63.6	48		33	33	75
1989	Los Angeles Raiders	16	9-11	81.8	8-9	88.9	5-12	41.7	1-2	50.0	23-34	67.6	50		34	34	103
1990	Los Angeles Raiders	16	6-6	100.0	2-3	66.7	6-9	66.7	1-2	50.0	15-20	75.0	50		40	42	85
1991	Los Angeles Raiders	16	10-10	100.0	10-13	76.9	7-7	100.0	2-4	50.0	29-34	85.3	53		29	30	116
1992	Los Angeles Raiders	16	3-5	60.0	4-6	66.7	5-9	55.6	3-6	50.0	15-26	57.7	54		28	28	73
1993	Los Angeles Raiders	16	12-12	100.0	13-15	86.7	6-10	60.0	4-7	57.1	35-44	79.5	53		27	29	132
1994	Los Angeles Raiders	16	6-6	100.0	6-9	66.7	8-11	72.7	2-2	100.0	22-28	78.6	51		31	31	97
1995	Oakland Raiders	11	4-5	80.0	6-7	85.7	3-5	60.0	0-1	0.0	13-18	72.2	46		22	22	61
	8 NFL Seasons	117	56-61	91.8	52-68	76.5	45-72	62.5	13-25	52.0	166-226	73.5	54		244	249	742

Other Statistics: 1987–recovered 1 fumble for 0 yards; attempted 1 pass with 0 completions for 0 yards.

Jesse James

Pos: T/G **Rnd:** 2 **College:** Mississippi State **Ht:** 6' 4" **Wt:** 318 **Born:** 9/16/71 **Age:** 25

Year	Team	G	GS			G	GS
1995	St. Louis Rams	2	0		1 NFL Season	2	0

George Jamison

Pos: LB **Rnd:** 2(S) **College:** Cincinnati **Ht:** 6' 1" **Wt:** 235 **Born:** 9/30/62 **Age:** 34

Year	Team	G	GS	Tackles			Miscellaneous				Interceptions				Punt Returns				Kickoff Returns				Totals	
				Tk	Ast	Sack	FF	FR	TD	Blk	Int	Yds	Avg	TD	Num	Yds	Avg	TD	Num	Yds	Avg	TD	TD	Fum
1987	Detroit Lions	12	0	11	5	1.0	0	0	0	0	0	0	-	0	0	0	-	0	0	0	-	0	0	0
1988	Detroit Lions	16	11	66	11	5.5	0	3	1	0	3	56	18.7	1	0	0	-	0	0	0	-	0	2	0
1989	Detroit Lions	11	6	27	6	2.0	0	0	0	0	0	0	-	0	0	0	-	0	0	0	-	0	0	0
1990	Detroit Lions	14	7	39	4	2.0	0	1	0	0	0	0	-	0	0	0	-	0	0	0	-	0	0	0
1991	Detroit Lions	16	16	67	19	4.0	0	1	0	0	3	52	17.3	0	0	0	-	0	0	0	-	0	0	1
1992	Detroit Lions	16	16	80	31	2.0	0	1	0	0	0	0	-	0	0	0	-	0	0	0	-	0	0	0
1993	Detroit Lions	16	16	63	14	2.0	1	0	0	0	2	48	24.0	1	0	0	-	0	1	0	0.0	0	1	0
1994	Kansas City Chiefs	13	12	56	9	1.0	2	3	0	0	0	0	-	0	0	0	-	0	0	0	-	0	0	0
1995	Kansas City Chiefs	14	14	31	8	0.0	0	0	0	0	0	0	-	0	0	0	-	0	0	0	-	0	0	0
	9 NFL Seasons	128	98	440	107	19.5	3	11	1	0	8	156	19.5	2	0	0	-	0	1	0	0.0	0	3	1

Other Statistics: 1987–credited with 1 safety.

Garth Jax

Pos: LB **Rnd:** 11 **College:** Florida State **Ht:** 6' 2" **Wt:** 250 **Born:** 9/16/63 **Age:** 33

Year	Team	G	GS	Tackles			Miscellaneous				Interceptions				Punt Returns				Kickoff Returns				Totals	
				Tk	Ast	Sack	FF	FR	TD	Blk	Int	Yds	Avg	TD	Num	Yds	Avg	TD	Num	Yds	Avg	TD	TD	Fum
1986	Dallas Cowboys	16	0	1	0	0.0	0	0	0	0	0	0	-	0	0	0	-	0	0	0	-	0	0	0
1987	Dallas Cowboys	3	0	0	0	0.0	0	0	0	0	0	0	-	0	0	0	-	0	0	0	-	0	0	0
1988	Dallas Cowboys	16	2	7	6	0.0	0	1	0	0	0	0	-	0	0	0	-	0	0	0	-	0	0	0
1989	Phoenix Cardinals	16	0	2	2	0.0	0	0	0	0	0	0	-	0	0	0	-	0	0	0	-	0	0	0
1990	Phoenix Cardinals	16	12	47	23	3.0	0	0	0	0	2	5	2.5	0	0	0	-	0	2	17	8.5	0	0	0
1991	Phoenix Cardinals	12	9	33	19	0.0	0	0	0	0	0	0	-	0	0	0	-	0	0	0	-	0	0	0
1992	Phoenix Cardinals	16	0	2	2	0.0	0	0	0	0	0	0	-	0	0	0	-	0	0	0	-	0	0	0
1993	Phoenix Cardinals	16	0	1	0	0.0	0	0	0	0	0	0	-	0	0	0	-	0	0	0	-	0	0	0
1994	Arizona Cardinals	16	0	3	1	0.0	0	0	0	0	0	0	-	0	0	0	-	0	0	0	-	0	0	0

Year Team	G	GS	Tackles Tk	Ast	Sack	Miscellaneous FF	FR	TD	Blk	Interceptions Int	Yds	Avg	TD	Punt Returns Num	Yds	Avg	TD	Kickoff Returns Num	Yds	Avg	TD	Totals TD	Fum
1995 Arizona Cardinals	16	5	24	6	0.0	0	0	0	0	0	0	-	0	0	0	-	0	0	0	-	0	0	0
10 NFL Seasons	143	28	120	59	3.0	0	1	0	0	2	5	2.5	0	0	0	-	0	2	17	8.5	0	0	0

Jim Jeffcoat

Pos: DE/NT **Rnd:** 1 (23) **College:** Arizona State **Ht:** 6' 5" **Wt:** 280 **Born:** 4/1/61 **Age:** 35

Year Team	G	GS	Tackles Tk	Ast	Sack	Miscellaneous FF	FR	TD	Blk	Interceptions Int	Yds	Avg	TD	Totals Sfty	TD	Pts
1983 Dallas Cowboys	16	0	3	0	2.0	0	0	0	0	0	0	-	0	0	0	0
1984 Dallas Cowboys	16	16	50	32	11.5	1	1	1	0	0	0	-	0	0	1	6
1985 Dallas Cowboys	16	16	50	27	12.0	1	2	0	0	1	65	65.0	1	0	1	6
1986 Dallas Cowboys	16	16	46	19	14.0	1	2	0	0	0	0	-	0	0	0	0
1987 Dallas Cowboys	12	12	30	14	5.0	1	2	0	0	1	26	26.0	1	0	1	6
1988 Dallas Cowboys	16	15	52	28	6.5	4	0	0	0	0	0	-	0	0	0	0
1989 Dallas Cowboys	16	16	65	35	11.5	0	3	1	0	0	0	-	0	0	1	6
1990 Dallas Cowboys	16	13	42	23	3.5	1	1	0	0	0	0	-	0	0	0	0
1991 Dallas Cowboys	16	16	36	34	4.0	2	0	0	0	0	0	-	0	0	0	0
1992 Dallas Cowboys	16	3	23	19	10.5	3	0	0	0	0	0	-	0	0	0	0
1993 Dallas Cowboys	16	3	23	18	6.0	1	0	0	0	0	0	-	0	0	0	0
1994 Dallas Cowboys	16	1	21	6	8.0	1	0	0	0	0	0	-	0	0	0	0
1995 Buffalo Bills	16	2	9	5	2.5	2	0	0	0	0	0	-	0	0	0	0
13 NFL Seasons	204	129	450	260	97.0	18	11	2	0	2	91	45.5	2	0	4	24

Greg Jefferson

Pos: DE **Rnd:** 3 **College:** Central Florida **Ht:** 6' 3" **Wt:** 257 **Born:** 8/31/71 **Age:** 25

Year Team	G	GS	Tackles Tk	Ast	Sack	Miscellaneous FF	FR	TD	Blk	Interceptions Int	Yds	Avg	TD	Totals Sfty	TD	Pts
1995 Philadelphia Eagles	3	0	0	0	0.0	0	0	0	0	0	0	-	0	0	0	0

Kevin Jefferson

Pos: LB **Rnd:** FA **College:** Lehigh **Ht:** 6' 2" **Wt:** 232 **Born:** 1/14/74 **Age:** 22

Year Team	G	GS	Tackles Tk	Ast	Sack	Miscellaneous FF	FR	TD	Blk	Interceptions Int	Yds	Avg	TD	Totals Sfty	TD	Pts
1994 Cincinnati Bengals	6	0	0	0	0.0	0	0	0	0	0	0	-	0	0	0	0
1995 Cincinnati Bengals	16	0	1	0	0.0	0	1	0	0	0	0	-	0	0	0	0
2 NFL Seasons	22	0	1	0	0.0	0	1	0	0	0	0	-	0	0	0	0

Shawn Jefferson

(statistical profile on page 337)

Pos: WR **Rnd:** 9 **College:** Central Florida **Ht:** 5' 11" **Wt:** 172 **Born:** 2/22/69 **Age:** 27

Year Team	G	GS	Rushing Att	Yds	Avg	Lg	TD	Receiving Rec	Yds	Avg	Lg	TD	Punt Returns Num	Yds	Avg	TD	Kickoff Returns Num	Yds	Avg	TD	Fum	TD	Pts
1991 San Diego Chargers	16	3	1	27	27.0	27	0	12	125	10.4	29	1	0	0	-	0	0	0	-	0	0	1	6
1992 San Diego Chargers	16	1	0	0	-	-	0	29	377	13.0	51	2	0	0	-	0	0	0	-	0	0	2	12
1993 San Diego Chargers	16	4	5	53	10.6	33	0	30	391	13.0	t39	2	0	0	-	0	0	0	-	0	0	2	12
1994 San Diego Chargers	16	16	3	40	13.3	22	0	43	627	14.6	t52	3	0	0	-	0	0	0	-	0	0	3	18
1995 San Diego Chargers	16	15	2	1	0.5	11	0	48	621	12.9	45	2	0	0	-	0	0	0	-	0	0	2	12
5 NFL Seasons	80	39	11	121	11.0	33	0	162	2141	13.2	t52	10	0	0	-	0	0	0	-	0	0	10	60

Haywood Jeffires

(statistical profile on page 338)

Pos: WR **Rnd:** 1 (20) **College:** North Carolina State **Ht:** 6' 2" **Wt:** 201 **Born:** 12/12/64 **Age:** 31

Year Team	G	GS	Rushing Att	Yds	Avg	Lg	TD	Receiving Rec	Yds	Avg	Lg	TD	Punt Returns Num	Yds	Avg	TD	Kickoff Returns Num	Yds	Avg	TD	Fum	TD	Pts
1987 Houston Oilers	9	1	0	0	-	-	0	7	89	12.7	23	0	0	0	-	0	0	0	-	0	0	0	0
1988 Houston Oilers	2	0	0	0	-	-	0	2	49	24.5	42	1	0	0	-	0	0	0	-	0	0	1	6
1989 Houston Oilers	16	4	0	0	-	-	0	47	619	13.2	t45	2	0	0	-	0	0	0	-	0	0	2	12
1990 Houston Oilers	16	16	0	0	-	-	0	74	1048	14.2	t87	8	0	0	-	0	0	0	-	0	0	8	48
1991 Houston Oilers	16	16	0	0	-	-	0	100	1181	11.8	44	7	0	0	-	0	0	0	-	0	3	7	42
1992 Houston Oilers	16	16	0	0	-	-	0	90	913	10.1	47	9	0	0	-	0	0	0	-	0	1	9	54
1993 Houston Oilers	16	16	0	0	-	-	0	66	753	11.4	t66	6	0	0	-	0	0	0	-	0	5	6	36
1994 Houston Oilers	16	16	0	0	-	-	0	68	783	11.5	50	6	0	0	-	0	0	0	-	0	0	6	42
1995 Houston Oilers	16	16	0	0	-	-	0	61	684	11.2	t35	8	0	0	-	0	0	0	-	0	0	8	48
9 NFL Seasons	123	101	0	0	-	-	0	515	6119	11.9	t87	47	0	0	-	0	0	0	-	0	9	47	288

Other Statistics: 1991–recovered 1 fumble for 0 yards. 1994–scored 3 two-point conversions.

Dameian Jeffries

Pos: DE **Rnd:** 4 **College:** Alabama **Ht:** 6' 4" **Wt:** 277 **Born:** 5/7/73 **Age:** 23

Year	Team	G	GS	Tackles			Miscellaneous				Interceptions				Totals		
				Tk	Ast	Sack	FF	FR	TD	Blk	Int	Yds	Avg	TD	Sfty	TD	Pts
1995	New Orleans Saints	3	0	0	1	0.0	0	0	0	0	0	0	-	0	0	0	0

Greg Jeffries

Pos: CB **Rnd:** 6 **College:** Virginia **Ht:** 5' 9" **Wt:** 184 **Born:** 10/16/71 **Age:** 25

Year	Team	G	GS	Tackles			Miscellaneous				Interceptions				Totals		
				Tk	Ast	Sack	FF	FR	TD	Blk	Int	Yds	Avg	TD	Sfty	TD	Pts
1993	Detroit Lions	7	0	0	0	0.0	0	1	0	0	0	0	-	0	0	0	0
1994	Detroit Lions	16	1	36	8	0.0	1	0	0	0	0	0	-	0	0	0	0
1995	Detroit Lions	14	0	13	1	0.5	0	0	0	0	0	0	-	0	0	0	0
	3 NFL Seasons	37	1	49	9	0.5	1	1	0	0	0	0	-	0	0	0	0

Carlos Jenkins

(statistical profile on page 421)

Pos: LB **Rnd:** 3 **College:** Michigan State **Ht:** 6' 3" **Wt:** 217 **Born:** 7/12/68 **Age:** 28

Year	Team	G	GS	Tackles			Miscellaneous				Interceptions				Totals		
				Tk	Ast	Sack	FF	FR	TD	Blk	Int	Yds	Avg	TD	Sfty	TD	Pts
1991	Minnesota Vikings	3	0	0	0	0.0	0	0	0	0	0	0	-	0	0	0	0
1992	Minnesota Vikings	16	12	54	19	4.0	1	1	1	0	1	19	19.0	1	0	2	12
1993	Minnesota Vikings	16	16	58	30	2.5	3	1	0	0	2	7	3.5	0	0	0	0
1994	Minnesota Vikings	16	16	56	29	1.0	0	2	0	0	0	0	-	0	0	0	0
1995	St. Louis Rams	16	13	51	7	1.5	1	1	0	0	0	0	-	0	0	0	0
	5 NFL Seasons	67	57	219	85	9.0	5	5	1	0	3	26	8.7	1	0	2	12

James Jenkins

Pos: TE/RB **Rnd:** FA **College:** Rutgers **Ht:** 6' 2" **Wt:** 241 **Born:** 8/17/67 **Age:** 29

Year	Team	G	GS	Rushing					Receiving					Punt Returns				Kickoff Returns				Totals		
				Att	Yds	Avg	Lg	TD	Rec	Yds	Avg	Lg	TD	Num	Yds	Avg	TD	Num	Yds	Avg	TD	Fum	TD	Pts
1991	Washington Redskins	4	0	0	0	-	-	0	0	0	-	-	0	0	0	-	0	0	0	-	0	0	0	0
1992	Washington Redskins	5	1	0	0	-	-	0	0	0	-	-	0	0	0	-	0	0	0	-	0	0	0	0
1993	Washington Redskins	15	5	0	0	-	-	0	0	0	-	-	0	0	0	-	0	0	0	-	0	0	0	0
1994	Washington Redskins	16	3	0	0	-	-	0	8	32	4.0	9	4	0	0	-	0	1	4	4.0	0	0	4	24
1995	Washington Redskins	16	5	0	0	-	-	0	1	2	2.0	2	0	0	0	-	0	1	12	12.0	0	0	0	0
	5 NFL Seasons	56	14	0	0	-	-	0	9	34	3.8	9	4	0	0	-	0	2	16	8.0	0	0	4	24

Other Statistics: 1995–recovered 1 fumble for 0 yards.

Robert Jenkins

Pos: T **Rnd:** 6 **College:** UCLA **Ht:** 6' 5" **Wt:** 295 **Born:** 12/30/63 **Age:** 32

Year	Team	G	GS	Year	Team	G	GS	Year	Team	G	GS		G	GS
1987	Los Angeles Rams	10	0	1990	Los Angeles Rams	11	0	1993	Los Angeles Rams	8	1			
1988	Los Angeles Rams	16	0	1991	Los Angeles Rams	12	8	1994	Los Angeles Raiders	10	4			
1989	Los Angeles Rams	16	2	1992	Los Angeles Rams	9	0	1995	Oakland Raiders	15	13	9 NFL Seasons	107	28

Other Statistics: 1987–returned 1 kickoff for 12 yards.

Trezelle Jenkins

Pos: T **Rnd:** 1 (31) **College:** Michigan **Ht:** 6' 7" **Wt:** 323 **Born:** 3/13/73 **Age:** 23

Year	Team	G	GS					G	GS
1995	Kansas City Chiefs	1	0						
						1 NFL Season		1	0

Keith Jennings

(statistical profile on page 338)

Pos: TE **Rnd:** 5 **College:** Clemson **Ht:** 6' 4" **Wt:** 270 **Born:** 5/19/66 **Age:** 30

Year	Team	G	GS	Rushing					Receiving					Punt Returns				Kickoff Returns				Totals		
				Att	Yds	Avg	Lg	TD	Rec	Yds	Avg	Lg	TD	Num	Yds	Avg	TD	Num	Yds	Avg	TD	Fum	TD	Pts
1989	Dallas Cowboys	10	0	0	0	-	-	0	6	47	7.8	14	0	0	0	-	0	0	0	-	0	0	0	0
1991	Chicago Bears	10	3	0	0	-	-	0	8	109	13.6	19	0	0	0	-	0	0	0	-	0	0	0	0
1992	Chicago Bears	16	14	0	0	-	-	0	23	264	11.5	23	1	0	0	-	0	0	0	-	0	0	1	6
1993	Chicago Bears	13	11	0	0	-	-	0	14	150	10.7	29	0	0	0	-	0	0	0	-	0	1	0	0
1994	Chicago Bears	9	1	0	0	-	-	0	11	75	6.8	t23	3	0	0	-	0	0	0	-	0	0	3	18
1995	Chicago Bears	16	16	0	0	-	-	0	25	217	8.7	20	6	0	0	-	0	0	0	-	0	0	6	36
	6 NFL Seasons	74	45	0	0	-	-	0	87	862	9.9	29	10	0	0	-	0	0	0	-	0	1	10	60

Other Statistics: 1993–recovered 1 fumble for 0 yards.

Travis Jervey

Pos: RB **Rnd:** 5 **College:** Citadel **Ht:** 5' 11" **Wt:** 225 **Born:** 5/5/72 **Age:** 24

Year Team	G	GS	Rushing Att	Yds	Avg	Lg	TD	Receiving Rec	Yds	Avg	Lg	TD	Punt Returns Num	Yds	Avg	TD	Kickoff Returns Num	Yds	Avg	TD	Totals Fum	TD	Pts
1995 Green Bay Packers	16	0	0	0	-	-	0	0	0	-	-	0	0	0	-	0	8	165	20.6	0	0	0	0

Other Statistics: 1995–recovered 1 fumble for 0 yards.

James Jett

Pos: WR **Rnd:** FA **College:** West Virginia **Ht:** 5' 10" **Wt:** 165 **Born:** 12/28/70 **Age:** 25

Year Team	G	GS	Rushing Att	Yds	Avg	Lg	TD	Receiving Rec	Yds	Avg	Lg	TD	Punt Returns Num	Yds	Avg	TD	Kickoff Returns Num	Yds	Avg	TD	Totals Fum	TD	Pts
1993 Los Angeles Raiders	16	1	1	0	0.0	0	0	33	771	23.4	t74	3	0	0	-	0	0	0	-	0	1	3	18
1994 Los Angeles Raiders	16	1	0	0	-	-	0	15	253	16.9	54	0	0	0	-	0	0	0	-	0	0	0	0
1995 Oakland Raiders	16	0	0	0	-	-	0	13	179	13.8	t26	1	0	0	-	0	0	0	-	0	1	1	6
3 NFL Seasons	48	2	1	0	0.0	0	0	61	1203	19.7	t74	4	0	0	-	0	0	0	-	0	2	4	24

Other Statistics: 1994–recovered 2 fumbles for 15 yards.

John Jett

(statistical profile on page 477)

Pos: P **Rnd:** FA **College:** East Carolina **Ht:** 6' 0" **Wt:** 194 **Born:** 11/11/68 **Age:** 27

Year Team	G	Punting NetPunts	Yards	Avg	Long	In20	In20%	TotPunts	TB	Blocks	OppRet	RetYds	NetAvg	Rushing Att	Yards	Passing Att	Com	Yards	Int
1993 Dallas Cowboys	16	56	2342	41.8	59	22	39.3	56	3	0	32	169	37.7	0	0	0	0	0	0
1994 Dallas Cowboys	16	70	2935	41.9	58	27	38.6	70	4	0	36	378	35.4	0	0	0	0	0	0
1995 Dallas Cowboys	16	53	2166	40.9	58	17	32.1	53	6	0	22	216	34.5	0	0	0	0	0	0
3 NFL Seasons	48	179	7443	41.6	59	66	36.9	179	13	0	90	763	35.9	0	0	0	0	0	0

A.J. Johnson

Pos: CB **Rnd:** 6 **College:** Southwest Texas State **Ht:** 5' 8" **Wt:** 175 **Born:** 6/22/67 **Age:** 29

Year Team	G	GS	Tackles Tk	Ast	Sack	Misc FF	FR	TD	Blk	Int Int	Yds	Avg	TD	Punt Returns Num	Yds	Avg	TD	Kickoff Returns Num	Yds	Avg	TD	Totals TD	Fum
1989 Washington Redskins	16	8	46	9	0.0	0	0	0	0	4	94	23.5	1	0	0	-	0	24	504	21.0	0	1	0
1990 Washington Redskins	5	0	7	2	0.0	0	0	0	0	1	0	0.0	0	0	0	-	0	0	0	-	0	0	0
1991 Washington Redskins	11	0	21	7	1.0	0	1	0	0	0	0	-	0	0	0	-	0	0	0	-	0	0	0
1992 Washington Redskins	14	11	51	19	0.0	0	0	0	0	3	38	12.7	0	0	0	-	0	0	0	-	0	0	0
1993 Washington Redskins	13	3	22	12	0.0	0	1	0	0	1	69	69.0	1	0	0	-	0	0	0	-	0	1	0
1994 Washington Redskins	12	0	1	0	0.0	0	0	0	0	0	0	-	0	0	0	-	0	0	0	-	0	0	0
1995 San Diego Chargers	1	0	0	0	0.0	0	0	0	0	0	0	-	0	0	0	-	0	0	0	-	0	0	0
7 NFL Seasons	72	22	148	49	1.0	0	2	0	0	9	201	22.3	2	0	0	-	0	24	504	21.0	0	2	0

Anthony Johnson

(statistical profile on page 339)

Pos: RB **Rnd:** 2 **College:** Notre Dame **Ht:** 6' 0" **Wt:** 222 **Born:** 10/25/67 **Age:** 29

Year Team	G	GS	Rushing Att	Yds	Avg	Lg	TD	Receiving Rec	Yds	Avg	Lg	TD	Punt Returns Num	Yds	Avg	TD	Passing Att	Com	Yds	Int	Totals Fum	TD	Pts
1990 Indianapolis Colts	16	0	0	0	-	-	0	5	32	6.4	t15	2	0	0	-	0	0	0	0	0	0	2	12
1991 Indianapolis Colts	9	6	22	94	4.3	15	0	42	344	8.2	24	0	0	0	-	0	0	0	0	0	2	0	0
1992 Indianapolis Colts	15	13	178	592	3.3	19	0	49	517	10.6	t57	3	0	0	-	0	1	0	0	0	6	3	18
1993 Indianapolis Colts	13	8	95	331	3.5	14	1	55	443	8.1	36	0	0	0	-	0	1	0	0	1	5	1	6
1994 New York Jets	15	0	5	12	2.4	5	0	5	31	6.2	9	0	1	3	3.0	0	0	0	0	0	0	0	0
1995 Chi - Car	15	0	30	140	4.7	t23	1	29	207	7.1	37	0	0	0	-	0	0	0	0	0	2	1	6
1995 Chicago Bears	8	0	6	30	5.0	11	0	13	86	6.6	18	0	0	0	-	0	0	0	0	0	2	0	0
Carolina Panthers	7	0	24	110	4.6	t23	1	16	121	7.6	37	0	0	0	-	0	0	0	0	0	0	1	6
6 NFL Seasons	83	27	330	1169	3.5	t23	2	185	1574	8.5	t57	5	1	3	3.0	0	2	0	0	1	15	7	42

Other Statistics: 1992–recovered 4 fumbles for 0 yards. 1993–recovered 2 fumbles for 0 yards.

Barry Johnson

Pos: WR **Rnd:** FA **College:** Maryland **Ht:** 6' 2" **Wt:** 197 **Born:** 2/1/68 **Age:** 28

Year Team	G	GS	Rushing Att	Yds	Avg	Lg	TD	Receiving Rec	Yds	Avg	Lg	TD	Punt Returns Num	Yds	Avg	TD	Kickoff Returns Num	Yds	Avg	TD	Totals Fum	TD	Pts
1991 Denver Broncos	4	0	0	0	-	-	0	1	13	13.0	13	0	0	0	-	0	0	0	-	0	0	0	0

Bill Johnson

Pos: DT **Rnd:** 3 **College:** Michigan State **Ht:** 6' 4" **Wt:** 290 **Born:** 12/9/68 **Age:** 27

Year Team	G	GS	Tackles Tk	Ast	Sack	Misc FF	FR	TD	Blk	Int Int	Yds	Avg	TD	Totals Sfty	TD	Pts
1992 Cleveland Browns	15	3	16	9	2.0	0	0	0	0	0	0	-	0	0	0	0

Year Team	G	GS	Tackles			Miscellaneous				Interceptions				Totals		
			Tk	Ast	Sack	FF	FR	TD	Blk	Int	Yds	Avg	TD	Sfty	TD	Pts
1993 Cleveland Browns	10	0	19	20	1.0	0	0	0	0	0	0	-	0	0	0	0
1994 Cleveland Browns	14	13	34	9	1.0	0	1	0	0	0	0	-	0	0	0	0
1995 Pittsburgh Steelers	9	0	9	2	0.0	0	1	0	0	0	0	-	0	0	0	0
4 NFL Seasons	48	16	78	40	4.0	0	2	0	0	0	0	-	0	0	0	0

Brad Johnson

Pos: QB **Rnd:** 9 **College:** Florida State **Ht:** 6' 5" **Wt:** 221 **Born:** 9/13/68 **Age:** 28

Year Team	G	GS	Passing									Rushing					Miscellaneous			
			Att	Com	Pct	Yards	Yds/Att	Lg	TD	Int	Int%	Rating	Att	Yds	Avg	Lg	TD	Sckd	Yds	Fum Recv	Yds	Pts
1994 Minnesota Vikings	4	0	37	22	59.5	150	4.05	15	0	0	0.0	68.5	2	-2	-1.0	-1	0	1	5	0	0	0	0
1995 Minnesota Vikings	5	0	36	25	69.4	272	7.56	39	0	2	5.6	68.3	9	-9	-1.0	3	0	2	18	2	0	0	0
2 NFL Seasons	9	0	73	47	64.4	422	5.78	39	0	2	2.7	68.4	11	-11	-1.0	3	0	3	23	2	0	0	0

Charles Johnson

(statistical profile on page 339)

Pos: WR **Rnd:** 1 (17) **College:** Colorado **Ht:** 6' 0" **Wt:** 189 **Born:** 1/3/72 **Age:** 24

Year Team	G	GS	Rushing					Receiving					Punt Returns				Kickoff Returns				Totals		
			Att	Yds	Avg	Lg	TD	Rec	Yds	Avg	Lg	TD	Num	Yds	Avg	TD	Num	Yds	Avg	TD	Fum	TD	Pts
1994 Pittsburgh Steelers	16	9	4	-1	-0.3	7	0	38	577	15.2	t84	3	15	90	6.0	0	16	345	21.6	0	2	3	18
1995 Pittsburgh Steelers	14	12	1	-10	-10.0	-10	0	38	432	11.4	33	0	0	0	-	0	2	47	23.5	0	0	0	0
2 NFL Seasons	30	21	5	-11	-2.2	7	0	76	1009	13.3	t84	3	15	90	6.0	0	18	392	21.8	0	2	3	18

Other Statistics: 1995–recovered 1 fumble for 0 yards.

D.J. Johnson

(statistical profile on page 422)

Pos: CB **Rnd:** 7 **College:** Kentucky **Ht:** 6' 0" **Wt:** 190 **Born:** 7/14/66 **Age:** 30

Year Team	G	GS	Tackles			Miscellaneous				Interceptions				Totals		
			Tk	Ast	Sack	FF	FR	TD	Blk	Int	Yds	Avg	TD	Sfty	TD	Pts
1989 Pittsburgh Steelers	16	0	12	-	0.0	0	0	0	0	1	0	0.0	0	0	0	0
1990 Pittsburgh Steelers	16	15	59	10	0.0	0	1	0	0	2	60	30.0	1	0	1	6
1991 Pittsburgh Steelers	16	16	67	7	0.0	0	0	0	0	1	0	0.0	0	0	0	0
1992 Pittsburgh Steelers	16	15	51	5	0.0	0	2	0	0	5	67	13.4	0	0	0	0
1993 Pittsburgh Steelers	16	15	59	3	0.0	1	0	0	0	3	51	17.0	0	0	0	0
1994 Atlanta Falcons	16	16	66	6	0.0	0	2	0	0	5	0	0.0	0	0	0	0
1995 Atlanta Falcons	13	12	60	9	0.0	0	0	0	0	2	4	2.0	0	0	0	0
7 NFL Seasons	109	89	374	40	0.0	1	5	0	0	19	182	9.6	1	0	1	6

Ellis Johnson

Pos: DT/DE **Rnd:** 1 (15) **College:** Florida **Ht:** 6' 2" **Wt:** 298 **Born:** 10/30/73 **Age:** 23

Year Team	G	GS	Tackles			Miscellaneous				Interceptions				Totals		
			Tk	Ast	Sack	FF	FR	TD	Blk	Int	Yds	Avg	TD	Sfty	TD	Pts
1995 Indianapolis Colts	16	2	15	3	4.5	0	0	0	0	0	0	-	0	0	0	0

Filmel Johnson

Pos: CB **Rnd:** 7 **College:** Illinois **Ht:** 5' 10" **Wt:** 187 **Born:** 12/24/70 **Age:** 25

Year Team	G	GS	Tackles			Miscellaneous				Interceptions				Totals		
			Tk	Ast	Sack	FF	FR	TD	Blk	Int	Yds	Avg	TD	Sfty	TD	Pts
1995 Buffalo Bills	2	0	5	0	0.0	0	0	0	0	0	0	-	0	0	0	0

Jimmie Johnson

Pos: TE **Rnd:** 12 **College:** Howard **Ht:** 6' 2" **Wt:** 248 **Born:** 10/6/66 **Age:** 30

Year Team	G	GS	Rushing					Receiving					Punt Returns				Kickoff Returns				Totals		
			Att	Yds	Avg	Lg	TD	Rec	Yds	Avg	Lg	TD	Num	Yds	Avg	TD	Num	Yds	Avg	TD	Fum	TD	Pts
1989 Washington Redskins	16	0	0	0	-	-	0	4	84	21.0	39	0	0	0	-	0	0	0	-	0	0	0	0
1990 Washington Redskins	16	5	0	0	-	-	0	15	218	14.5	35	2	0	0	-	0	0	0	-	0	1	2	12
1991 Washington Redskins	6	0	0	0	-	-	0	3	7	2.3	t4	2	0	0	-	0	0	0	-	0	0	2	12
1992 Detroit Lions	16	5	0	0	-	-	0	6	34	5.7	9	0	0	0	-	0	1	0	0.0	0	0	0	0
1993 Detroit Lions	6	5	0	0	-	-	0	2	18	9.0	9	0	0	0	-	0	0	0	-	0	0	0	0
1994 Kansas City Chiefs	7	1	0	0	-	-	0	2	7	3.5	5	0	0	0	-	0	0	0	-	0	0	0	0
1995 Philadelphia Eagles	16	1	0	0	-	-	0	6	37	6.2	9	0	0	0	-	0	0	0	-	0	0	0	0
7 NFL Seasons	83	17	0	0	-	-	0	38	405	10.7	39	4	0	0	-	0	1	0	0.0	0	1	4	24

Joe Johnson
(statistical profile on page 422)

Pos: DE/DT **Rnd:** 1 (13) **College:** Louisville **Ht:** 6' 4" **Wt:** 285 **Born:** 7/11/72 **Age:** 24

Year Team	G	GS	Tackles			Miscellaneous				Interceptions				Totals		
			Tk	Ast	Sack	FF	FR	TD	Blk	Int	Yds	Avg	TD	Sfty	TD	Pts
1994 New Orleans Saints	15	14	36	10	1.5	2	1	0	1	0	0	-	0	0	0	0
1995 New Orleans Saints	14	14	36	14	5.5	1	0	0	0	0	0	-	0	0	0	0
2 NFL Seasons	29	28	72	24	7.0	3	1	0	1	0	0	-	0	0	0	0

John Johnson

Pos: LB **Rnd:** 2 **College:** Clemson **Ht:** 6' 3" **Wt:** 247 **Born:** 5/8/68 **Age:** 28

Year Team	G	GS	Tackles			Miscellaneous				Interceptions				Totals		
			Tk	Ast	Sack	FF	FR	TD	Blk	Int	Yds	Avg	TD	Sfty	TD	Pts
1991 San Francisco 49ers	9	0	3	2	0.0	0	0	0	0	0	0	-	0	0	0	0
1992 San Francisco 49ers	16	2	13	6	1.0	0	0	0	0	1	56	56.0	1	0	1	6
1993 San Francisco 49ers	15	12	32	14	2.0	3	1	0	0	1	0	0.0	0	0	0	0
1994 Cincinnati Bengals	5	0	3	1	0.0	0	0	0	0	0	0	-	0	0	0	0
1995 New Orleans Saints	1	0	0	0	0.0	0	0	0	0	0	0	-	0	0	0	0
5 NFL Seasons	46	14	51	23	3.0	3	1	0	0	2	56	28.0	1	0	1	6

Keshon Johnson

Pos: CB **Rnd:** 7 **College:** Arizona **Ht:** 5' 10" **Wt:** 183 **Born:** 7/17/70 **Age:** 26

Year Team	G	GS	Tackles			Miscellaneous				Interceptions				Totals		
			Tk	Ast	Sack	FF	FR	TD	Blk	Int	Yds	Avg	TD	Sfty	TD	Pts
1993 Chicago Bears	15	0	3	2	0.0	0	0	0	0	0	0	-	0	0	0	0
1994 Chi - GB	13	0	2	0	0.0	0	1	0	0	1	3	3.0	0	0	0	0
1995 Chicago Bears	12	0	1	0	0.0	0	0	0	0	0	0	-	0	0	0	0
1994 Chicago Bears	6	0	2	0	0.0	0	0	0	0	0	0	-	0	0	0	0
Green Bay Packers	7	0	0	0	0.0	0	1	0	0	1	3	3.0	0	0	0	0
3 NFL Seasons	40	0	6	2	0.0	0	1	0	0	1	3	3.0	0	0	0	0

Kevin Johnson

Pos: DT **Rnd:** 4 **College:** Texas Southern **Ht:** 6' 1" **Wt:** 310 **Born:** 10/30/70 **Age:** 26

Year Team	G	GS	Tackles			Miscellaneous				Interceptions				Totals		
			Tk	Ast	Sack	FF	FR	TD	Blk	Int	Yds	Avg	TD	Sfty	TD	Pts
1995 Philadelphia Eagles	11	1	19	0	6.0	1	1	1	0	0	0	-	0	0	1	6

Lee Johnson
(statistical profile on page 477)

Pos: P **Rnd:** 5 **College:** Brigham Young **Ht:** 6' 2" **Wt:** 200 **Born:** 11/27/61 **Age:** 34

Year Team	G	Punting							Punting							Field Goals			Passing			
		NetPunts	Yards	Avg	Long	In20	In20%	TotPunts	TB	Blocks	OppRet	RetYds	NetAvg	Overall	Pct	Long	Att	Com	Yds	Int
1985 Houston Oilers	16	83	3464	41.7	65	22	26.5	83	8	0	45	345	35.7	0-0	-	-	0	0	0	0
1986 Houston Oilers	16	88	3623	41.2	66	26	29.5	88	9	0	40	303	35.7	0-0	-	-	0	0	0	0
1987 Hou - Cle	12	50	1969	39.4	66	8	16.0	50	4	0	25	249	32.8	0-0	-	-	0	0	0	0
1988 Cle - Cin	15	31	1237	39.9	61	10	32.3	31	2	0	15	163	33.4	1-2	50.0	50	0	0	0	0
1989 Cincinnati Bengals	16	61	2446	40.1	62	14	23.0	63	11	2	33	323	30.2	0-0	-	-	0	0	0	0
1990 Cincinnati Bengals	16	64	2705	42.3	70	12	18.8	64	8	0	36	352	34.3	0-1	0.0	-	1	1	4	0
1991 Cincinnati Bengals	16	64	2795	43.7	62	15	23.4	64	6	0	38	456	34.7	1-3	33.3	53	1	1	3	0
1992 Cincinnati Bengals	16	76	3196	42.1	64	15	19.0	76	9	0	32	284	35.9	0-1	0.0	-	1	0	0	0
1993 Cincinnati Bengals	16	90	3954	43.9	60	24	26.7	90	12	0	47	416	36.6	0-0	-	-	1	0	0	0
1994 Cincinnati Bengals	16	79	3461	43.8	64	19	24.1	80	9	1	43	459	35.3	0-0	-	-	1	1	7	0
1995 Cincinnati Bengals	16	68	2861	42.1	61	26	38.2	68	4	0	27	154	38.6	0-0	-	-	1	1	5	0
1987 Houston Oilers	9	41	1652	40.3	59	5	12.2	41	3	0	22	238	33.0	0-0	-	-	0	0	0	0
Cleveland Browns	3	9	317	35.2	66	3	33.3	9	1	0	3	11	31.8	0-0	-	-	0	0	0	0
1988 Cleveland Browns	3	17	643	37.8	61	6	35.3	17	1	0	7	103	30.6	0-0	-	-	0	0	0	0
Cincinnati Bengals	12	14	594	42.4	52	4	28.6	14	1	0	8	60	36.7	1-2	50.0	50	0	0	0	0
11 NFL Seasons	171	754	31711	42.1	70	191	25.3	757	82	3	381	3504	35.1	2-7	28.6	53	5	4	19	0

Other Statistics: 1985–recovered 1 fumble for 7 yards; rushed 1 time for 0 yards, fumbled 2 times. 1989–converted 0 of 1 extra-point attempts; rushed 1 time for -7 yards. 1990–passed for 1 touchdown. 1991–rushed 1 time for -2 yards; fumbled 1 time for 0 yards. 1994–passed for 1 touchdown. 1995–rushed 1 time for -16 yards; fumbled 1 time for 0 yards.

LeShon Johnson

Pos: KR/RB **Rnd:** 3 **College:** Northern Illinois **Ht:** 5' 11" **Wt:** 195 **Born:** 1/15/71 **Age:** 25

Year Team	G	GS	Rushing					Receiving					Punt Returns				Kickoff Returns				Totals		
			Att	Yds	Avg	Lg	TD	Rec	Yds	Avg	Lg	TD	Num	Yds	Avg	TD	Num	Yds	Avg	TD	Fum	TD	Pts
1994 Green Bay Packers	12	0	26	99	3.8	43	0	13	168	12.9	33	0	0	0	-	0	0	0	-	0	0	0	0
1995 GB - Ari	6	0	2	-2	-1.0	0	0	0	0	-	-	0	0	0	-	0	11	259	23.5	0	1	0	0
1995 Green Bay Packers	2	0	2	-2	-1.0	0	0	0	0	-	-	0	0	0	-	0	0	0	-	0	0	0	0

Year Team	G	GS	Rushing Att	Yds	Avg	Lg	TD	Receiving Rec	Yds	Avg	Lg	TD	Punt Returns Num	Yds	Avg	TD	Kickoff Returns Num	Yds	Avg	TD	Totals Fum	TD	Pts
Arizona Cardinals	4	0	0	0	-	-	0	0	0	-	-	0	0	0	-	0	11	259	23.5	0	1	0	0
2 NFL Seasons	18	0	28	97	3.5	43	0	13	168	12.9	33	0	0	0	-	0	11	259	23.5	0	1	0	0

Other Statistics: 1995–recovered 1 fumble for 0 yards.

Lonnie Johnson

(statistical profile on page 340)

Pos: TE/WR **Rnd:** 2　**College:** Florida State　**Ht:** 6' 3" **Wt:** 232 **Born:** 2/14/71 **Age:** 25

Year Team	G	GS	Rushing Att	Yds	Avg	Lg	TD	Receiving Rec	Yds	Avg	Lg	TD	Punt Returns Num	Yds	Avg	TD	Kickoff Returns Num	Yds	Avg	TD	Totals Fum	TD	Pts
1994 Buffalo Bills	10	1	0	0	-	-	0	3	42	14.0	21	0	0	0	-	0	0	0	-	0	0	0	0
1995 Buffalo Bills	16	16	0	0	-	-	0	49	504	10.3	52	1	0	0	-	0	0	0	-	0	0	1	6
2 NFL Seasons	26	17	0	0	-	-	0	52	546	10.5	52	1	0	0	-	0	0	0	-	0	0	1	6

Other Statistics: 1995–recovered 1 fumble for 0 yards.

Melvin Johnson

Pos: S　**Rnd:** 2　**College:** Kentucky　**Ht:** 6' 0" **Wt:** 195 **Born:** 4/15/72 **Age:** 24

Year Team	G	GS	Tackles Tk	Ast	Sack	Miscellaneous FF	FR	TD	Blk	Interceptions Int	Yds	Avg	TD	Totals Sfty	TD	Pts
1995 Tampa Bay Buccaneers	11	3	20	6	0.0	0	0	0	0	1	0	0.0	0	0	0	0

Mike Johnson

(statistical profile on page 422)

Pos: LB　**Rnd:** 1(S)　**College:** Virginia Tech　**Ht:** 6' 1" **Wt:** 230 **Born:** 11/26/62 **Age:** 33

Year Team	G	GS	Tackles Tk	Ast	Sack	Miscellaneous FF	FR	TD	Blk	Interceptions Int	Yds	Avg	TD	Totals Sfty	TD	Pts
1986 Cleveland Browns	16	0	36	20	0.0	3	2	0	0	0	0	-	0	0	0	0
1987 Cleveland Browns	11	10	65	33	2.0	3	1	0	0	1	3	3.0	0	0	0	0
1988 Cleveland Browns	16	16	88	44	0.0	1	0	0	0	2	36	18.0	0	0	0	0
1989 Cleveland Browns	16	16	89	44	1.0	3	0	0	0	3	43	14.3	0	0	0	0
1990 Cleveland Browns	16	15	123	38	2.0	3	0	0	0	1	64	64.0	1	0	1	6
1991 Cleveland Browns	5	4	23	14	0.0	1	0	0	0	1	0	0.0	0	0	0	0
1992 Cleveland Browns	16	16	114	62	2.0	4	5	1	0	1	0	0.0	0	0	1	6
1993 Cleveland Browns	16	16	81	100	4.0	2	0	0	0	1	0	0.0	0	0	0	0
1994 Detroit Lions	16	16	92	42	1.5	4	1	0	0	1	48	48.0	1	0	1	6
1995 Detroit Lions	16	16	80	36	2.0	2	4	0	0	2	23	11.5	0	0	0	0
10 NFL Seasons	144	125	791	433	14.5	26	13	1	0	13	217	16.7	2	0	3	18

Norm Johnson

(statistical profile on page 478)

Pos: K　**Rnd:** FA　**College:** UCLA　**Ht:** 6' 2" **Wt:** 202 **Born:** 5/31/60 **Age:** 36

Year Team	G	Field Goals 1-29 Yds	Pct	30-39 Yds	Pct	40-49 Yds	Pct	50+ Yds	Pct	Overall	Pct	Long	PAT Made	Att	Tot Pts
1982 Seattle Seahawks	9	3-4	75.0	5-6	83.3	2-3	66.7	0-1	0.0	10-14	71.4	48	13	14	43
1983 Seattle Seahawks	16	5-5	100.0	4-7	57.1	8-10	80.0	1-3	33.3	18-25	72.0	54	49	50	103
1984 Seattle Seahawks	16	9-10	90.0	4-4	100.0	6-7	85.7	1-3	33.3	20-24	83.3	50	50	51	110
1985 Seattle Seahawks	16	5-5	100.0	7-9	77.8	1-8	12.5	1-3	33.3	14-25	56.0	51	40	41	82
1986 Seattle Seahawks	16	6-8	75.0	8-9	88.9	3-11	27.3	5-7	71.4	22-35	62.9	54	42	42	108
1987 Seattle Seahawks	13	7-7	100.0	4-7	57.1	4-5	80.0	0-1	0.0	15-20	75.0	49	40	40	85
1988 Seattle Seahawks	16	5-5	100.0	7-9	77.8	10-14	71.4	0-0	-	22-28	78.6	47	39	39	105
1989 Seattle Seahawks	16	7-8	87.5	3-4	75.0	4-8	50.0	1-5	20.0	15-25	60.0	50	27	27	72
1990 Seattle Seahawks	16	9-9	100.0	8-14	57.1	5-6	83.3	1-3	33.3	23-32	71.9	51	33	34	102
1991 Atlanta Falcons	14	9-9	100.0	4-4	100.0	5-8	62.5	1-2	50.0	19-23	82.6	50	38	39	95
1992 Atlanta Falcons	16	6-6	100.0	4-5	80.0	4-7	57.1	4-4	100.0	18-22	81.8	54	39	39	93
1993 Atlanta Falcons	15	8-8	100.0	9-10	90.0	7-7	100.0	2-2	100.0	26-27	96.3	54	34	34	112
1994 Atlanta Falcons	16	9-9	100.0	7-7	100.0	4-4	100.0	1-5	20.0	21-25	84.0	50	32	32	95
1995 Pittsburgh Steelers	16	11-11	100.0	14-16	87.5	8-13	61.5	1-1	100.0	34-41	82.9	50	39	39	141
14 NFL Seasons	211	99-104	95.2	88-111	79.3	71-111	64.0	19-40	47.5	277-366	75.7	54	515	521	1346

Other Statistics: 1982–attempted 1 pass with 1 completion for 27 yards. 1991–punted 1 time for 21 yards. 1992–punted 1 time for 37 yards.

Pat Johnson

Pos: S　**Rnd:** FA　**College:** Purdue　**Ht:** 6' 1" **Wt:** 204 **Born:** 6/10/72 **Age:** 24

Year Team	G	GS	Tackles Tk	Ast	Sack	Miscellaneous FF	FR	TD	Blk	Interceptions Int	Yds	Avg	TD	Totals Sfty	TD	Pts
1995 Miami Dolphins	14	0	0	0	0.0	0	1	1	0	0	0	-	0	0	1	6

Pepper Johnson
(statistical profile on page 423)

Pos: LB **Rnd:** 2 **College:** Ohio State **Ht:** 6' 3" **Wt:** 248 **Born:** 6/29/64 **Age:** 32

			Tackles			Miscellaneous				Interceptions				Totals		
Year Team	G	GS	Tk	Ast	Sack	FF	FR	TD	Blk	Int	Yds	Avg	TD	Sfty	TD	Pts
1986 New York Giants	16	0	15	8	2.0	0	0	0	0	1	13	13.0	0	0	0	0
1987 New York Giants	12	12	63	11	1.0	2	1	0	0	0	0	-	0	0	0	0
1988 New York Giants	16	15	64	23	4.0	2	1	0	0	1	33	33.0	1	0	1	6
1989 New York Giants	14	4	48	13	1.0	0	1	0	0	3	60	20.0	1	0	1	6
1990 New York Giants	16	16	80	35	3.5	3	1	0	0	1	0	0.0	0	0	0	0
1991 New York Giants	16	16	71	33	6.5	1	0	0	0	2	5	2.5	0	0	0	0
1992 New York Giants	16	16	81	34	1.0	1	2	0	0	2	42	21.0	0	0	0	0
1993 Cleveland Browns	16	11	45	42	1.0	0	0	0	0	0	0	-	0	0	0	0
1994 Cleveland Browns	16	16	95	27	2.5	0	1	0	0	0	0	-	0	0	0	0
1995 Cleveland Browns	16	16	100	30	2.0	2	0	0	0	2	22	11.0	0	0	0	0
10 NFL Seasons	154	122	662	256	24.5	11	7	0	0	12	175	14.6	2	0	2	12

Other Statistics: 1992–fumbled 1 time.

Raylee Johnson

Pos: DE **Rnd:** 4 **College:** Arkansas **Ht:** 6' 3" **Wt:** 265 **Born:** 6/1/70 **Age:** 26

			Tackles			Miscellaneous				Interceptions				Totals		
Year Team	G	GS	Tk	Ast	Sack	FF	FR	TD	Blk	Int	Yds	Avg	TD	Sfty	TD	Pts
1993 San Diego Chargers	9	0	0	1	0.0	0	0	0	0	0	0	-	0	0	0	0
1994 San Diego Chargers	15	0	4	2	1.5	0	0	0	0	0	0	-	0	0	0	0
1995 San Diego Chargers	16	1	14	1	3.0	1	0	0	0	0	0	-	0	0	0	0
3 NFL Seasons	40	1	18	4	4.5	1	0	0	0	0	0	-	0	0	0	0

Reggie Johnson

Pos: TE **Rnd:** 2 **College:** Florida State **Ht:** 6' 2" **Wt:** 255 **Born:** 1/27/68 **Age:** 28

			Rushing					Receiving					Punt Returns				Kickoff Returns				Totals		
Year Team	G	GS	Att	Yds	Avg	Lg	TD	Rec	Yds	Avg	Lg	TD	Num	Yds	Avg	TD	Num	Yds	Avg	TD	Fum	TD	Pts
1991 Denver Broncos	16	3	0	0	-	-	0	6	73	12.2	31	1	0	0	-	0	0	0	-	0	0	1	6
1992 Denver Broncos	15	7	2	7	3.5	8	0	10	139	13.9	48	1	0	0	-	0	2	47	23.5	0	0	1	6
1993 Denver Broncos	13	12	0	0	-	-	0	20	243	12.2	38	1	0	0	-	0	0	0	-	0	1	1	6
1994 Green Bay Packers	9	2	0	0	-	-	0	7	79	11.3	24	0	0	0	-	0	0	0	-	0	0	0	0
1995 Philadelphia Eagles	9	2	0	0	-	-	0	5	68	13.6	33	2	0	0	-	0	0	0	-	0	0	2	12
5 NFL Seasons	62	26	2	7	3.5	8	0	48	602	12.5	48	5	0	0	-	0	2	47	23.5	0	1	5	30

Other Statistics: 1991–recovered 1 fumble for 0 yards. 1992–recovered 1 fumble for 0 yards.

Rob Johnson

Pos: QB **Rnd:** 4 **College:** Southern California **Ht:** 6' 3" **Wt:** 220 **Born:** 3/18/73 **Age:** 23

			Passing									Rushing					Miscellaneous			
Year Team	G	GS	Att	Com	Pct	Yards	Yds/Att	Lg	TD	Int	Int%	Rating	Att	Yds	Avg	Lg	TD	Sckd	Yds	Fum Recv	Yds	Pts
1995 Jacksonville Jaguars	1	0	7	3	42.9	24	3.43	19	0	1	14.3	12.5	3	17	5.7	7	0	1	13	0	0	0

Ted Johnson

Pos: LB **Rnd:** 2 **College:** Colorado **Ht:** 6' 3" **Wt:** 240 **Born:** 12/4/72 **Age:** 23

			Tackles			Miscellaneous				Interceptions				Totals		
Year Team	G	GS	Tk	Ast	Sack	FF	FR	TD	Blk	Int	Yds	Avg	TD	Sfty	TD	Pts
1995 New England Patriots	12	11	41	28	0.5	0	2	0	0	0	0	-	0	0	0	0

Tim Johnson

Pos: DT/DE **Rnd:** 6 **College:** Penn State **Ht:** 6' 3" **Wt:** 286 **Born:** 1/29/65 **Age:** 31

			Tackles			Miscellaneous				Interceptions				Totals		
Year Team	G	GS	Tk	Ast	Sack	FF	FR	TD	Blk	Int	Yds	Avg	TD	Sfty	TD	Pts
1987 Pittsburgh Steelers	12	0	5	0	0.0	0	0	0	0	0	0	-	0	0	0	0
1988 Pittsburgh Steelers	15	12	25	9	4.0	0	0	0	0	0	0	-	0	0	0	0
1989 Pittsburgh Steelers	14	14	33	2	4.5	1	0	0	0	0	0	-	0	0	0	0
1990 Washington Redskins	16	2	12	14	3.0	1	1	0	0	0	0	-	0	0	0	0
1991 Washington Redskins	16	16	50	32	3.5	0	0	0	0	1	14	14.0	0	0	0	0
1992 Washington Redskins	16	16	52	27	6.0	0	1	0	0	0	0	-	0	0	0	0
1993 Washington Redskins	15	15	49	49	4.0	1	1	0	0	0	0	-	0	0	0	0
1994 Washington Redskins	14	13	46	9	1.0	0	0	0	0	0	0	-	0	0	0	0
1995 Washington Redskins	14	5	23	2	3.0	1	1	0	0	0	0	-	0	0	0	0
9 NFL Seasons	132	93	295	144	29.0	4	4	0	0	1	14	14.0	0	0	0	0

Tommy Johnson

Pos: CB **Rnd:** FA **College:** Alabama   **Ht:** 5' 10" **Wt:** 180 **Born:** 12/5/71 **Age:** 24

Year	Team	G	GS	Tackles			Miscellaneous				Interceptions				Totals		
				Tk	Ast	Sack	FF	FR	TD	Blk	Int	Yds	Avg	TD	Sfty	TD	Pts
1995	Jacksonville Jaguars	1	0	0	0	0.0	0	0	0	0	0	0	-	0	0	0	0

Tracy Johnson

Pos: RB **Rnd:** 10 **College:** Clemson   **Ht:** 6' 0" **Wt:** 242 **Born:** 11/29/66 **Age:** 29

Year	Team	G	GS	Rushing					Receiving					Punt Returns				Kickoff Returns				Totals		
				Att	Yds	Avg	Lg	TD	Rec	Yds	Avg	Lg	TD	Num	Yds	Avg	TD	Num	Yds	Avg	TD	Fum	TD	Pts
1989	Houston Oilers	16	0	4	16	4.0	8	0	1	8	8.0	8	0	0	0	-	0	13	224	17.2	0	1	0	0
1990	Atlanta Falcons	16	4	30	106	3.5	12	3	10	79	7.9	16	1	0	0	-	0	2	2	1.0	0	1	4	24
1991	Atlanta Falcons	16	5	8	26	3.3	6	0	3	27	9.0	13	0	0	0	-	0	0	0	-	0	0	0	0
1992	Seattle Seahawks	16	0	3	26	8.7	19	0	0	0	-	-	0	0	0	-	0	1	15	15.0	0	0	0	0
1993	Seattle Seahawks	16	1	2	8	4.0	5	0	3	15	5.0	8	1	0	0	-	0	0	0	-	0	0	1	6
1994	Seattle Seahawks	16	11	12	44	3.7	14	2	10	91	9.1	17	0	0	0	-	0	0	0	-	0	1	2	12
1995	Seattle Seahawks	15	4	1	2	2.0	t2	1	1	-2	-2.0	-2	0	0	0	-	0	0	0	-	0	0	1	6
	7 NFL Seasons	111	25	60	228	3.8	19	6	28	218	7.8	17	2	0	0	-	0	16	241	15.1	0	3	8	48

Other Statistics: 1991–recovered 1 fumble for 0 yards. 1992–recovered 1 fumble for 10 yards.

Tre Johnson

Pos: G **Rnd:** 2 **College:** Temple   **Ht:** 6' 2" **Wt:** 338 **Born:** 8/30/71 **Age:** 25

Year	Team	G	GS	Year	Team	G	GS			G	GS
1994	Washington Redskins	14	1	1995	Washington Redskins	10	9		2 NFL Seasons	24	10

Other Statistics: 1994–returned 2 kickoffs for 4 yards.

Vance Johnson

Pos: WR **Rnd:** 2 **College:** Arizona   **Ht:** 5' 11" **Wt:** 185 **Born:** 3/13/63 **Age:** 33

Year	Team	G	GS	Rushing					Receiving					Punt Returns				Kickoff Returns				Totals		
				Att	Yds	Avg	Lg	TD	Rec	Yds	Avg	Lg	TD	Num	Yds	Avg	TD	Num	Yds	Avg	TD	Fum	TD	Pts
1985	Denver Broncos	16	7	10	36	3.6	14	0	51	721	14.1	t63	3	30	260	8.7	0	30	740	24.7	0	5	3	18
1986	Denver Broncos	12	7	5	15	3.0	6	0	31	363	11.7	t34	2	3	36	12.0	0	2	21	10.5	0	1	2	12
1987	Denver Broncos	11	9	1	-8	-8.0	-8	0	42	684	16.3	t59	7	1	9	9.0	0	7	140	20.0	0	1	7	42
1988	Denver Broncos	16	13	1	1	1.0	1	0	68	896	13.2	86	5	0	0	-	0	0	0	-	0	0	5	30
1989	Denver Broncos	16	16	0	0	-	-	0	76	1095	14.4	69	7	12	118	9.8	0	0	0	-	0	0	7	42
1990	Denver Broncos	16	13	0	0	-	-	0	54	747	13.8	49	3	11	92	8.4	0	6	126	21.0	0	1	3	18
1991	Denver Broncos	10	0	0	0	-	-	0	21	208	9.9	22	3	24	174	7.3	0	0	0	-	0	1	3	18
1992	Denver Broncos	11	6	0	0	-	-	0	24	294	12.3	40	2	0	0	-	0	0	0	-	0	1	2	12
1993	Denver Broncos	10	8	0	0	-	-	0	36	517	14.4	56	5	0	0	-	0	0	0	-	0	0	5	30
1995	Denver Broncos	10	1	0	0	-	-	0	12	170	14.2	23	0	0	0	-	0	0	0	-	0	0	0	0
	10 NFL Seasons	128	80	17	44	2.6	14	0	415	5695	13.7	86	37	81	689	8.5	0	45	1027	22.8	0	10	37	222

Other Statistics: 1985–recovered 2 fumbles for 0 yards; attempted 1 pass with 0 completions for 0 yards. 1986–attempted 1 pass with 0 completions for 0 yards. 1987–attempted 1 pass with 0 completions for 0 yards. 1989–attempted 1 pass with 0 completions for 0 yards. 1991–recovered 1 fumble for 0 yards.

Daryl Johnston

(statistical profile on page 340)

Pos: RB **Rnd:** 2 **College:** Syracuse   **Ht:** 6' 2" **Wt:** 242 **Born:** 2/10/66 **Age:** 30

Year	Team	G	GS	Rushing					Receiving					Punt Returns				Kickoff Returns				Totals		
				Att	Yds	Avg	Lg	TD	Rec	Yds	Avg	Lg	TD	Num	Yds	Avg	TD	Num	Yds	Avg	TD	Fum	TD	Pts
1989	Dallas Cowboys	16	10	67	212	3.2	13	0	16	133	8.3	28	3	0	0	-	0	0	0	-	0	3	3	18
1990	Dallas Cowboys	16	0	10	35	3.5	8	1	14	148	10.6	26	1	0	0	-	0	0	0	-	0	1	2	12
1991	Dallas Cowboys	16	14	17	54	3.2	10	0	28	244	8.7	22	1	0	0	-	0	0	0	-	0	0	1	6
1992	Dallas Cowboys	16	16	17	61	3.6	14	0	32	249	7.8	18	2	0	0	-	0	0	0	-	0	0	2	12
1993	Dallas Cowboys	16	16	24	74	3.1	11	3	50	372	7.4	20	1	0	0	-	0	0	0	-	0	1	4	24
1994	Dallas Cowboys	16	16	40	138	3.5	t9	2	44	325	7.4	24	2	0	0	-	0	0	0	-	0	2	4	24
1995	Dallas Cowboys	16	16	25	111	4.4	18	2	30	248	8.3	24	1	0	0	-	0	0	0	-	0	1	3	18
	7 NFL Seasons	112	88	200	685	3.4	18	8	214	1719	8.0	28	11	0	0	-	0	0	0	-	0	8	19	114

Other Statistics: 1990–recovered 1 fumble for 0 yards. 1992–recovered 1 fumble for 0 yards. 1993–recovered 1 fumble for 0 yards. 1995–recovered 1 fumble for 0 yards.

Aaron Jones

Pos: DE **Rnd:** 1 (18) **College:** Eastern Kentucky   **Ht:** 6' 5" **Wt:** 267 **Born:** 12/18/66 **Age:** 29

Year	Team	G	GS	Tackles			Miscellaneous				Interceptions				Totals		
				Tk	Ast	Sack	FF	FR	TD	Blk	Int	Yds	Avg	TD	Sfty	TD	Pts
1988	Pittsburgh Steelers	15	12	16	4	1.5	0	0	0	0	0	0	-	0	0	0	0
1989	Pittsburgh Steelers	16	2	16	5	2.0	0	0	0	0	0	0	-	0	0	0	0
1990	Pittsburgh Steelers	7	1	7	3	2.0	0	1	0	0	1	3	3.0	0	0	0	0
1991	Pittsburgh Steelers	16	7	25	5	2.0	0	0	0	0	0	0	-	0	0	0	0

Year Team	G	GS	Tackles			Miscellaneous				Interceptions				Totals		
			Tk	Ast	Sack	FF	FR	TD	Blk	Int	Yds	Avg	TD	Sfty	TD	Pts
1992 Pittsburgh Steelers	13	0	19	14	2.0	0	1	0	0	0	0	-	0	0	0	0
1993 New England Patriots	11	1	10	7	3.5	0	0	0	0	0	0	-	0	0	0	0
1994 New England Patriots	16	0	14	6	4.0	1	3	0	0	0	0	-	0	0	0	0
1995 New England Patriots	10	0	5	2	1.0	0	0	0	0	0	0	-	0	0	0	0
8 NFL Seasons	104	23	112	46	18.0	1	5	0	0	1	3	3.0	0	0	0	0

Other Statistics: 1994–fumbled 1 time.

Brent Jones

(statistical profile on page 341)

Pos: TE **Rnd:** 5 **College:** Santa Clara **Ht:** 6' 4" **Wt:** 230 **Born:** 2/12/63 **Age:** 33

Year Team	G	GS	Rushing					Receiving					Punt Returns				Kickoff Returns				Totals		
			Att	Yds	Avg	Lg	TD	Rec	Yds	Avg	Lg	TD	Num	Yds	Avg	TD	Num	Yds	Avg	TD	Fum	TD	Pts
1987 San Francisco 49ers	4	0	0	0	-	-	0	2	35	17.5	22	0	0	0	-	0	0	0	-	0	0	0	0
1988 San Francisco 49ers	11	0	0	0	-	-	0	8	57	7.1	t18	2	0	0	-	0	0	0	-	0	2	2	12
1989 San Francisco 49ers	16	16	0	0	-	-	0	40	500	12.5	t36	4	0	0	-	0	0	0	-	0	4	4	24
1990 San Francisco 49ers	16	16	0	0	-	-	0	56	747	13.3	t67	5	0	0	-	0	0	0	-	0	2	5	30
1991 San Francisco 49ers	10	9	0	0	-	-	0	27	417	15.4	41	0	0	0	-	0	0	0	-	0	2	0	0
1992 San Francisco 49ers	15	15	0	0	-	-	0	45	628	14.0	43	4	0	0	-	0	0	0	-	0	1	4	24
1993 San Francisco 49ers	16	16	0	0	-	-	0	68	735	10.8	29	3	0	0	-	0	0	0	-	0	2	3	18
1994 San Francisco 49ers	15	15	0	0	-	-	0	49	670	13.7	t69	9	0	0	-	0	0	0	-	0	1	9	56
1995 San Francisco 49ers	16	16	0	0	-	-	0	60	595	9.9	39	3	0	0	-	0	0	0	-	0	3	3	18
9 NFL Seasons	119	103	0	0	-	-	0	355	4384	12.3	t69	30	0	0	-	0	0	0	-	0	11	30	182

Other Statistics: 1990–recovered 2 fumbles for 0 yards. 1991–recovered 1 fumble for 0 yards. 1993–recovered 2 fumbles for 0 yards. 1994–recovered 1 fumble for 0 yards; scored 1 two-point conversion. 1995–recovered 1 fumble for 0 yards.

Brian Jones

Pos: LB **Rnd:** 8 **College:** Texas **Ht:** 6' 1" **Wt:** 250 **Born:** 1/22/68 **Age:** 28

Year Team	G	GS	Tackles			Miscellaneous				Interceptions				Totals		
			Tk	Ast	Sack	FF	FR	TD	Blk	Int	Yds	Avg	TD	Sfty	TD	Pts
1991 Indianapolis Colts	11	1	5	2	0.0	0	0	0	0	0	0	-	0	0	0	0
1995 New Orleans Saints	16	7	36	11	1.0	1	1	0	0	0	0	-	0	0	0	0
2 NFL Seasons	27	8	41	13	1.0	1	1	0	0	0	0	-	0	0	0	0

Calvin Jones

Pos: RB **Rnd:** 3 **College:** Nebraska **Ht:** 5' 11" **Wt:** 205 **Born:** 11/27/70 **Age:** 25

Year Team	G	GS	Rushing					Receiving					Punt Returns				Kickoff Returns				Totals		
			Att	Yds	Avg	Lg	TD	Rec	Yds	Avg	Lg	TD	Num	Yds	Avg	TD	Num	Yds	Avg	TD	Fum	TD	Pts
1994 Los Angeles Raiders	7	0	22	93	4.2	10	0	2	6	3.0	4	0	0	0	-	0	0	0	-	0	0	0	0
1995 Oakland Raiders	9	0	5	19	3.8	15	0	0	0	-	-	0	0	0	-	0	5	92	18.4	0	1	0	0
2 NFL Seasons	16	0	27	112	4.1	15	0	2	6	3.0	4	0	0	0	-	0	5	92	18.4	0	1	0	0

Chris T. Jones

Pos: WR **Rnd:** 3 **College:** Miami (FL) **Ht:** 6' 3" **Wt:** 209 **Born:** 8/7/71 **Age:** 25

Year Team	G	GS	Rushing					Receiving					Punt Returns				Kickoff Returns				Totals		
			Att	Yds	Avg	Lg	TD	Rec	Yds	Avg	Lg	TD	Num	Yds	Avg	TD	Num	Yds	Avg	TD	Fum	TD	Pts
1995 Philadelphia Eagles	13	0	0	0	-	-	0	5	61	12.2	17	0	0	0	-	0	2	46	23.0	0	0	0	0

Clarence Jones

Pos: T **Rnd:** 4 **College:** Maryland **Ht:** 6' 6" **Wt:** 280 **Born:** 5/6/68 **Age:** 28

Year Team	G	GS	Year Team	G	GS	Year Team	G	GS		G	GS
1991 New York Giants	3	0	1993 New York Giants	4	0	1995 St. Louis Rams	13	0			
1992 New York Giants	3	0	1994 Los Angeles Rams	16	16				5 NFL Seasons	39	16

Dan Jones

Pos: T/G **Rnd:** FA **College:** Maine **Ht:** 6' 7" **Wt:** 298 **Born:** 7/22/70 **Age:** 26

Year Team	G	GS	Year Team	G	GS	Year Team	G	GS		G	GS
1993 Cincinnati Bengals	15	5	1994 Cincinnati Bengals	14	0	1995 Cincinnati Bengals	5	0	3 NFL Seasons	34	5

Dante Jones

Pos: LB **Rnd:** 2 **College:** Oklahoma **Ht:** 6' 2" **Wt:** 235 **Born:** 3/23/65 **Age:** 31

Year Team	G	GS	Tackles			Miscellaneous				Interceptions				Totals		
			Tk	Ast	Sack	FF	FR	TD	Blk	Int	Yds	Avg	TD	Sfty	TD	Pts
1988 Chicago Bears	15	1	10	6	0.0	0	0	0	0	0	0	-	0	0	0	0
1989 Chicago Bears	10	1	14	14	0.0	0	0	0	0	0	0	-	0	0	0	0
1990 Chicago Bears	2	0	6	3	2.0	1	0	0	0	0	0	-	0	0	0	0

Year	Team	G	GS	Tk	Ast	Sack	FF	FR	TD	Blk	Int	Yds	Avg	TD	Sfty	TD	Pts
1991	Chicago Bears	16	0	16	12	0.0	1	0	0	0	0	0	-	0	0	0	0
1992	Chicago Bears	13	0	16	13	0.0	0	0	0	0	0	0	-	0	0	0	0
1993	Chicago Bears	16	16	117	72	1.0	1	3	1	0	4	52	13.0	0	0	1	6
1994	Chicago Bears	15	11	61	18	0.0	0	2	0	0	0	0	-	0	0	0	0
1995	Denver Broncos	5	5	13	5	0.0	0	0	0	0	0	0	-	0	0	0	0
	8 NFL Seasons	92	34	253	143	3.0	3	5	1	0	4	52	13.0	0	0	1	6

Other Statistics: 1993–fumbled 1 time.

Donta Jones

Pos: LB **Rnd:** 4 **College:** Nebraska **Ht:** 6' 2" **Wt:** 226 **Born:** 8/27/72 **Age:** 24

Year	Team	G	GS	Tk	Ast	Sack	FF	FR	TD	Blk	Int	Yds	Avg	TD	Sfty	TD	Pts
1995	Pittsburgh Steelers	16	0	2	0	0.0	0	0	0	0	0	0	-	0	0	0	0

Ernie Jones

Pos: DE **Rnd:** 3 **College:** Oregon **Ht:** 6' 2" **Wt:** 270 **Born:** 4/1/71 **Age:** 25

Year	Team	G	GS	Tk	Ast	Sack	FF	FR	TD	Blk	Int	Yds	Avg	TD	Sfty	TD	Pts
1995	New Orleans Saints	1	0	0	0	0.0	0	0	0	0	0	0	-	0	0	0	0

Gary Jones

Pos: S **Rnd:** 9 **College:** Texas A&M **Ht:** 6' 1" **Wt:** 217 **Born:** 11/30/67 **Age:** 28

Year	Team	G	GS	Tk	Ast	Sack	FF	FR	TD	Blk	Int	Yds	Avg	TD	Sfty	TD	Pts
1990	Pittsburgh Steelers	16	1	9	0	0.0	0	0	0	0	0	0	-	0	0	0	0
1991	Pittsburgh Steelers	9	1	14	2	0.0	0	0	0	0	1	0	0.0	0	0	0	0
1993	Pittsburgh Steelers	13	2	24	10	0.0	0	1	0	0	2	11	5.5	0	0	0	0
1994	Pittsburgh Steelers	14	0	13	6	0.0	0	1	0	0	1	0	0.0	0	0	0	0
1995	New York Jets	11	8	28	13	0.0	0	0	0	0	2	51	25.5	1	0	1	6
	5 NFL Seasons	63	12	88	31	0.0	0	2	0	0	6	62	10.3	1	0	1	6

Henry Jones

(statistical profile on page 423)

Pos: S **Rnd:** 1 (26) **College:** Illinois **Ht:** 5' 11" **Wt:** 197 **Born:** 12/29/67 **Age:** 28

Year	Team	G	GS	Tk	Ast	Sack	FF	FR	TD	Blk	Int	Yds	Avg	TD	Sfty	TD	Pts
1991	Buffalo Bills	15	0	8	0	0.0	0	1	0	0	0	0	-	0	0	0	0
1992	Buffalo Bills	16	16	75	17	0.0	2	2	0	0	8	263	32.9	2	0	2	12
1993	Buffalo Bills	16	16	67	16	2.0	3	2	0	0	2	92	46.0	1	1	1	8
1994	Buffalo Bills	16	16	61	20	1.0	1	1	0	0	2	45	22.5	0	0	0	0
1995	Buffalo Bills	13	13	57	21	0.0	0	1	0	1	1	10	10.0	0	0	0	0
	5 NFL Seasons	76	61	268	74	3.0	6	7	0	1	13	410	31.5	3	1	3	20

James Jones

Pos: DT **Rnd:** 3 **College:** Northern Iowa **Ht:** 6' 2" **Wt:** 290 **Born:** 2/6/69 **Age:** 27

Year	Team	G	GS	Tk	Ast	Sack	FF	FR	TD	Blk	Int	Yds	Avg	TD	Sfty	TD	Pts
1991	Cleveland Browns	16	16	34	17	1.0	0	3	0	0	1	20	20.0	1	1	1	8
1992	Cleveland Browns	16	16	31	14	4.0	0	1	1	0	0	0	-	0	0	1	6
1993	Cleveland Browns	16	12	22	17	5.5	0	0	1	0	0	0	-	0	0	1	6
1994	Cleveland Browns	16	5	25	5	3.0	1	2	0	0	0	0	-	0	0	0	0
1995	Denver Broncos	16	16	23	8	1.0	0	2	0	0	0	0	-	0	0	0	0
	5 NFL Seasons	80	65	135	61	14.5	1	8	2	0	1	20	20.0	1	1	3	20

Other Statistics: 1992–caught 1 pass for 1 yard and 1 touchdown. 1993–rushed 2 times for 2 yards and 1 touchdown. 1994–rushed 1 time for 0 yards; caught 1 pass for 1 yard.

Jeff Jones

Pos: T **Rnd:** FA **College:** Texas A&M **Ht:** 6' 6" **Wt:** 310 **Born:** 5/30/72 **Age:** 24

Year	Team	G	GS					G	GS
1995	Detroit Lions	2	0				1 NFL Season	2	0

Jimmie Jones

Pos: NT/DT **Rnd:** 3 **College:** Miami (FL) **Ht:** 6' 4" **Wt:** 276 **Born:** 1/9/66 **Age:** 30

Year	Team	G	GS	Tk	Ast	Sack	FF	FR	TD	Blk	Int	Yds	Avg	TD	Sfty	TD	Pts
1990	Dallas Cowboys	16	6	34	26	7.5	0	0	0	0	0	0	-	0	0	0	0

Year Team	G	GS	Tackles			Miscellaneous				Interceptions				Totals		
			Tk	Ast	Sack	FF	FR	TD	Blk	Int	Yds	Avg	TD	Sfty	TD	Pts
1991 Dallas Cowboys	16	6	24	9	2.0	0	2	0	0	0	0	-	0	0	0	0
1992 Dallas Cowboys	16	2	14	9	4.0	0	0	0	0	0	0	-	0	0	0	0
1993 Dallas Cowboys	15	2	12	12	5.5	0	0	0	0	0	0	-	0	0	0	0
1994 Los Angeles Rams	14	14	34	11	5.0	1	1	0	0	0	0	-	0	0	0	0
1995 St. Louis Rams	16	16	31	9	0.0	0	0	0	0	0	0	-	0	0	0	0
6 NFL Seasons	93	46	149	76	24.0	1	3	0	0	0	0	-	0	0	0	0

Marvin Jones

Pos: LB **Rnd:** 1 (4) **College:** Florida State **Ht:** 6' 2" **Wt:** 249 **Born:** 6/28/72 **Age:** 24

Year Team	G	GS	Tackles			Miscellaneous				Interceptions				Totals		
			Tk	Ast	Sack	FF	FR	TD	Blk	Int	Yds	Avg	TD	Sfty	TD	Pts
1993 New York Jets	9	0	22	8	0.0	0	1	0	0	0	0	-	0	0	0	0
1994 New York Jets	15	11	60	26	0.5	1	0	0	0	0	0	-	0	0	0	0
1995 New York Jets	10	10	59	33	1.5	1	0	0	0	0	0	-	0	0	0	0
3 NFL Seasons	34	21	141	67	2.0	2	1	0	0	0	0	-	0	0	0	0

Mike Jones

(statistical profile on page 423)

Pos: LB **Rnd:** FA **College:** Missouri **Ht:** 6' 1" **Wt:** 230 **Born:** 4/15/69 **Age:** 27

Year Team	G	GS	Tackles			Miscellaneous				Interceptions				Totals		
			Tk	Ast	Sack	FF	FR	TD	Blk	Int	Yds	Avg	TD	Sfty	TD	Pts
1991 Los Angeles Raiders	16	0	0	0	0.0	0	0	0	0	0	0	-	0	0	0	0
1992 Los Angeles Raiders	16	0	0	0	0.0	0	0	0	0	0	0	-	0	0	0	0
1993 Los Angeles Raiders	16	2	44	5	0.0	0	0	0	0	0	0	-	0	0	0	0
1994 Los Angeles Raiders	16	2	23	3	0.0	0	0	0	0	0	0	-	0	0	0	0
1995 Oakland Raiders	16	16	84	17	0.0	1	2	1	0	1	23	23.0	0	0	1	6
5 NFL Seasons	80	20	151	25	0.0	1	2	1	0	1	23	23.0	0	0	1	6

Mike Jones

Pos: DE/NT **Rnd:** 2 **College:** North Carolina State **Ht:** 6' 4" **Wt:** 295 **Born:** 8/25/69 **Age:** 27

Year Team	G	GS	Tackles			Miscellaneous				Interceptions				Totals		
			Tk	Ast	Sack	FF	FR	TD	Blk	Int	Yds	Avg	TD	Sfty	TD	Pts
1991 Phoenix Cardinals	16	1	13	8	0.0	0	0	0	0	0	0	-	0	0	0	0
1992 Phoenix Cardinals	15	15	26	11	6.0	0	0	0	0	0	0	-	0	0	0	0
1993 Phoenix Cardinals	16	3	13	11	3.0	1	0	0	0	0	0	-	0	0	0	0
1994 New England Patriots	16	16	26	19	6.0	0	1	0	0	0	0	-	0	0	0	0
1995 New England Patriots	13	3	17	6	3.0	1	0	0	0	0	0	-	0	0	0	0
5 NFL Seasons	76	38	95	55	18.0	2	1	0	0	0	0	-	0	0	0	0

Reggie Jones

Pos: WR **Rnd:** FA **College:** Louisiana State **Ht:** 6' 0" **Wt:** 175 **Born:** 5/5/71 **Age:** 25

Year Team	G	GS	Rushing					Receiving					Punt Returns				Kickoff Returns				Totals		
			Att	Yds	Avg	Lg	TD	Rec	Yds	Avg	Lg	TD	Num	Yds	Avg	TD	Num	Yds	Avg	TD	Fum	TD	Pts
1995 Carolina Panthers	1	0	0	0	-	-	0	0	0	-	-	0	0	0	-	0	0	0	-	0	0	0	0

Robert Jones

(statistical profile on page 424)

Pos: LB **Rnd:** 1 (24) **College:** East Carolina **Ht:** 6' 2" **Wt:** 237 **Born:** 9/27/69 **Age:** 27

Year Team	G	GS	Tackles			Miscellaneous				Interceptions				Punt Returns				Kickoff Returns				Totals	
			Tk	Ast	Sack	FF	FR	TD	Blk	Int	Yds	Avg	TD	Num	Yds	Avg	TD	Num	Yds	Avg	TD	TD	Fum
1992 Dallas Cowboys	15	13	55	53	1.0	0	1	0	0	0	0	-	0	0	0	-	0	0	0	-	0	0	0
1993 Dallas Cowboys	13	3	16	20	0.0	0	0	0	0	0	0	-	0	0	0	-	0	1	12	12.0	0	0	0
1994 Dallas Cowboys	16	16	84	34	0.0	0	1	0	0	0	0	-	0	0	0	-	0	1	8	8.0	0	0	0
1995 Dallas Cowboys	12	12	55	17	1.0	0	0	0	0	0	0	-	0	0	0	-	0	0	0	-	0	0	0
4 NFL Seasons	56	44	210	124	2.0	0	2	0	0	0	0	-	0	0	0	-	0	2	20	10.0	0	0	0

Rod Jones

Pos: CB **Rnd:** 1 (25) **College:** Southern Methodist **Ht:** 6' 0" **Wt:** 185 **Born:** 3/31/64 **Age:** 32

Year Team	G	GS	Tackles			Miscellaneous				Interceptions				Totals		
			Tk	Ast	Sack	FF	FR	TD	Blk	Int	Yds	Avg	TD	Sfty	TD	Pts
1986 Tampa Bay Buccaneers	16	16	80	-	0.0	0	1	0	0	1	0	0.0	0	0	0	0
1987 Tampa Bay Buccaneers	11	11	47	-	0.0	0	1	0	0	2	9	4.5	0	0	0	0
1988 Tampa Bay Buccaneers	14	1	20	-	0.0	0	0	0	0	1	0	0.0	0	0	0	0
1989 Tampa Bay Buccaneers	16	16	92	-	0.0	0	0	0	0	0	0	-	0	0	0	0
1990 Cincinnati Bengals	16	6	38	8	0.0	0	1	0	0	0	0	-	0	0	0	0
1991 Cincinnati Bengals	4	2	9	0	0.0	0	0	0	0	0	0	-	0	0	0	0

Year	Team	G	GS	Tackles Tk	Ast	Sack	Miscellaneous FF	FR	TD	Blk	Interceptions Int	Yds	Avg	TD	Totals Sfty	TD	Pts
1992	Cincinnati Bengals	16	14	54	9	0.0	0	1	0	0	2	14	7.0	0	0	0	0
1993	Cincinnati Bengals	16	16	39	7	0.0	0	1	0	0	1	0	0.0	0	0	0	0
1994	Cincinnati Bengals	16	16	67	8	0.0	0	0	0	0	0	0	-	0	0	0	0
1995	Cincinnati Bengals	13	9	38	1	0.0	0	1	0	0	1	24	24.0	0	0	0	0
	10 NFL Seasons	138	107	484	33	0.0	0	6	0	0	8	47	5.9	0	0	0	0

Roger Jones

(statistical profile on page 424)

Pos: CB **Rnd:** FA **College:** Tennessee State **Ht:** 5' 9" **Wt:** 175 **Born:** 4/22/69 **Age:** 27

Year	Team	G	GS	Tackles Tk	Ast	Sack	Miscellaneous FF	FR	TD	Blk	Interceptions Int	Yds	Avg	TD	Punt Returns Num	Yds	Avg	TD	Kickoff Returns Num	Yds	Avg	TD	Totals TD	Fum
1991	Tampa Bay Buccaneers	6	0	6	1	0.0	0	1	0	0	0	0	-	0	0	0	-	0	0	0	-	0	0	0
1992	Tampa Bay Buccaneers	9	1	25	5	0.0	0	2	1	0	0	0	-	0	0	0	-	0	0	0	-	0	1	0
1993	Tampa Bay Buccaneers	16	5	39	5	0.0	1	3	0	0	0	0	-	0	0	0	-	0	0	0	-	0	0	0
1994	Cincinnati Bengals	16	0	5	2	1.5	1	0	0	0	0	0	-	0	1	0	0.0	0	0	0	-	0	0	1
1995	Cincinnati Bengals	16	15	75	11	2.0	2	0	0	0	1	17	17.0	1	0	0	-	0	0	0	-	0	1	0
	5 NFL Seasons	63	21	150	24	4.5	4	6	1	0	1	17	17.0	1	1	0	0.0	0	0	0	-	0	2	1

Rondell Jones

Pos: S **Rnd:** 3 **College:** North Carolina **Ht:** 6' 2" **Wt:** 210 **Born:** 5/7/71 **Age:** 25

Year	Team	G	GS	Tackles Tk	Ast	Sack	Miscellaneous FF	FR	TD	Blk	Interceptions Int	Yds	Avg	TD	Totals Sfty	TD	Pts
1993	Denver Broncos	16	0	4	2	0.0	0	0	0	0	0	0	-	0	0	0	0
1994	Denver Broncos	16	3	35	11	0.0	0	1	0	0	2	9	4.5	0	0	0	0
1995	Denver Broncos	14	0	9	0	0.0	0	0	0	0	0	0	-	0	0	0	0
	3 NFL Seasons	46	3	48	13	0.0	0	1	0	0	2	9	4.5	0	0	0	0

Sean Jones

(statistical profile on page 424)

Pos: DE **Rnd:** 2 **College:** Northeastern **Ht:** 6' 7" **Wt:** 283 **Born:** 12/19/62 **Age:** 33

Year	Team	G	GS	Tackles Tk	Ast	Sack	Miscellaneous FF	FR	TD	Blk	Interceptions Int	Yds	Avg	TD	Totals Sfty	TD	Pts
1984	Los Angeles Raiders	16	0	9	6	1.0	0	0	0	0	0	0	-	0	0	0	0
1985	Los Angeles Raiders	15	4	20	15	8.5	0	1	0	0	0	0	-	0	0	0	0
1986	Los Angeles Raiders	16	16	39	35	15.5	0	0	0	0	0	0	-	0	0	0	0
1987	Los Angeles Raiders	12	12	24	13	6.0	0	2	0	0	0	0	-	0	0	0	0
1988	Houston Oilers	16	0	22	15	7.5	0	0	0	0	0	0	-	0	0	0	0
1989	Houston Oilers	16	5	21	14	6.0	0	2	0	0	0	0	-	0	0	0	0
1990	Houston Oilers	16	16	34	22	12.5	1	1	0	0	0	0	-	0	0	0	0
1991	Houston Oilers	16	12	43	17	10.0	1	0	0	0	0	0	-	0	0	0	0
1992	Houston Oilers	15	15	34	19	8.5	2	0	0	0	1	0	0.0	0	0	0	0
1993	Houston Oilers	16	16	42	12	13.0	1	2	0	0	0	0	-	0	0	0	0
1994	Green Bay Packers	16	16	44	15	10.5	2	3	0	0	0	0	-	0	0	0	0
1995	Green Bay Packers	16	16	33	18	9.0	2	1	1	0	0	0	-	0	0	1	6
	12 NFL Seasons	186	128	365	201	108.0	9	12	1	0	1	0	0.0	0	0	1	6

Selwyn Jones

Pos: CB **Rnd:** 7 **College:** Colorado State **Ht:** 6' 0" **Wt:** 185 **Born:** 5/13/70 **Age:** 26

Year	Team	G	GS	Tackles Tk	Ast	Sack	Miscellaneous FF	FR	TD	Blk	Interceptions Int	Yds	Avg	TD	Totals Sfty	TD	Pts
1993	Cleveland Browns	11	2	15	9	0.0	0	1	0	0	3	0	0.0	0	0	0	0
1994	New Orleans Saints	5	1	9	2	0.0	0	0	0	0	0	0	-	0	0	0	0
1995	Seattle Seahawks	15	0	9	1	0.0	0	0	0	0	1	0	0.0	0	0	0	0
	3 NFL Seasons	31	3	33	12	0.0	0	1	0	0	4	0	0.0	0	0	0	0

Tony Jones

Pos: T **Rnd:** FA **College:** Western Carolina **Ht:** 6' 5" **Wt:** 295 **Born:** 5/24/66 **Age:** 30

Year	Team	G	GS	Year	Team	G	GS	Year	Team	G	GS	Year	Team	G	GS
1988	Cleveland Browns	4	0	1990	Cleveland Browns	16	16	1992	Cleveland Browns	16	16	1994	Cleveland Browns	16	16
1989	Cleveland Browns	8	3	1991	Cleveland Browns	16	16	1993	Cleveland Browns	16	16	1995	Cleveland Browns	16	16
													8 NFL Seasons	108	99

Other Statistics: 1989–recovered 1 fumble for 0 yards. 1991–recovered 1 fumble for 0 yards. 1994–recovered 1 fumble for 0 yards. 1995–recovered 1 fumble for 0 yards.

Tony Jones

Pos: S **Rnd:** FA **College:** Syracuse **Ht:** 6' 4" **Wt:** 200 **Born:** 3/2/72 **Age:** 24

Year Team	G	GS	Tackles			Miscellaneous				Interceptions				Totals		
			Tk	Ast	Sack	FF	FR	TD	Blk	Int	Yds	Avg	TD	Sfty	TD	Pts
1995 Arizona Cardinals	2	0	0	0	0.0	0	0	0	0	0	0	-	0	0	0	0

Andrew Jordan

(statistical profile on page 341)

Pos: TE **Rnd:** 6 **College:** Western Carolina **Ht:** 6' 4" **Wt:** 262 **Born:** 6/21/72 **Age:** 24

Year Team	G	GS	Rushing					Receiving					Punt Returns				Kickoff Returns				Totals		
			Att	Yds	Avg	Lg	TD	Rec	Yds	Avg	Lg	TD	Num	Yds	Avg	TD	Num	Yds	Avg	TD	Fum	TD	Pts
1994 Minnesota Vikings	16	12	0	0	-	-	0	35	336	9.6	25	0	0	0	-	0	1	8	8.0	0	1	0	2
1995 Minnesota Vikings	13	7	0	0	-	-	0	27	185	6.9	17	2	0	0	-	0	0	0	-	0	1	2	12
2 NFL Seasons	29	19	0	0	-	-	0	62	521	8.4	25	2	0	0	-	0	1	8	8.0	0	2	2	14

Other Statistics: 1994–recovered 1 fumble for 0 yards; scored 1 two-point conversion.

Charles Jordan

Pos: KR/PR **Rnd:** FA **College:** Long Beach City College **Ht:** 5' 10" **Wt:** 183 **Born:** 10/9/69 **Age:** 27

Year Team	G	GS	Rushing					Receiving					Punt Returns				Kickoff Returns				Totals		
			Att	Yds	Avg	Lg	TD	Rec	Yds	Avg	Lg	TD	Num	Yds	Avg	TD	Num	Yds	Avg	TD	Fum	TD	Pts
1994 Green Bay Packers	10	0	1	5	5.0	5	0	0	0	-	-	0	1	0	0.0	0	5	115	23.0	0	1	0	0
1995 Green Bay Packers	6	1	0	0	-	-	0	7	117	16.7	35	2	21	213	10.1	0	21	444	21.1	0	1	2	12
2 NFL Seasons	16	1	1	5	5.0	5	0	7	117	16.7	35	2	22	213	9.7	0	26	559	21.5	0	2	2	12

Other Statistics: 1995–recovered 1 fumble for 0 yards.

Randy Jordan

Pos: RB **Rnd:** FA **College:** North Carolina **Ht:** 5' 10" **Wt:** 216 **Born:** 6/6/70 **Age:** 26

Year Team	G	GS	Rushing					Receiving					Punt Returns				Kickoff Returns				Totals		
			Att	Yds	Avg	Lg	TD	Rec	Yds	Avg	Lg	TD	Num	Yds	Avg	TD	Num	Yds	Avg	TD	Fum	TD	Pts
1993 Los Angeles Raiders	10	2	12	33	2.8	12	0	4	42	10.5	33	0	0	0	-	0	0	0	-	0	2	0	0
1995 Jacksonville Jaguars	12	2	21	62	3.0	10	0	5	89	17.8	t71	1	0	0	-	0	2	41	20.5	0	0	1	6
2 NFL Seasons	22	4	33	95	2.9	12	0	9	131	14.6	t71	1	0	0	-	0	2	41	20.5	0	2	1	6

Dwayne Joseph

Pos: CB **Rnd:** FA **College:** Syracuse **Ht:** 5' 9" **Wt:** 188 **Born:** 6/2/72 **Age:** 24

Year Team	G	GS	Tackles			Miscellaneous				Interceptions				Totals		
			Tk	Ast	Sack	FF	FR	TD	Blk	Int	Yds	Avg	TD	Sfty	TD	Pts
1995 Chicago Bears	16	1	31	3	0.0	1	0	0	0	2	31	15.5	0	0	0	0

James Joseph

Pos: RB **Rnd:** 7 **College:** Auburn **Ht:** 6' 2" **Wt:** 222 **Born:** 10/28/67 **Age:** 29

Year Team	G	GS	Rushing					Receiving					Punt Returns				Kickoff Returns				Totals		
			Att	Yds	Avg	Lg	TD	Rec	Yds	Avg	Lg	TD	Num	Yds	Avg	TD	Num	Yds	Avg	TD	Fum	TD	Pts
1991 Philadelphia Eagles	16	3	135	440	3.3	24	3	10	64	6.4	13	0	0	0	-	0	0	0	-	0	2	3	18
1992 Philadelphia Eagles	16	0	0	0	-	-	0	0	0	-	-	0	0	0	-	0	0	0	-	0	0	0	0
1993 Philadelphia Eagles	16	5	39	140	3.6	12	0	29	291	10.0	48	1	0	0	-	0	0	0	-	0	1	1	6
1994 Philadelphia Eagles	14	6	60	203	3.4	t34	1	43	344	8.0	t35	2	0	0	-	0	1	11	11.0	0	1	3	18
1995 Cincinnati Bengals	16	1	16	40	2.5	8	0	20	118	5.9	13	0	0	0	-	0	1	17	17.0	0	1	0	0
5 NFL Seasons	78	15	250	823	3.3	t34	4	102	817	8.0	48	3	0	0	-	0	2	28	14.0	0	4	7	42

Other Statistics: 1994–recovered 1 fumble for 0 yards. 1995–recovered 3 fumbles for 0 yards.

Vance Joseph

Pos: CB **Rnd:** FA **College:** Colorado **Ht:** 6' 0" **Wt:** 202 **Born:** 9/20/72 **Age:** 24

Year Team	G	GS	Tackles			Miscellaneous				Interceptions				Totals		
			Tk	Ast	Sack	FF	FR	TD	Blk	Int	Yds	Avg	TD	Sfty	TD	Pts
1995 New York Jets	13	6	17	4	0.0	0	0	0	0	2	39	19.5	0	0	0	0

Yonel Jourdain

Pos: KR/RB **Rnd:** FA **College:** Southern Illinois **Ht:** 5' 11" **Wt:** 204 **Born:** 4/20/71 **Age:** 25

Year Team	G	GS	Rushing					Receiving					Punt Returns				Kickoff Returns				Totals		
			Att	Yds	Avg	Lg	TD	Rec	Yds	Avg	Lg	TD	Num	Yds	Avg	TD	Num	Yds	Avg	TD	Fum	TD	Pts
1994 Buffalo Bills	9	0	17	56	3.3	16	0	10	56	5.6	18	0	0	0	-	0	27	601	22.3	0	1	0	0
1995 Buffalo Bills	8	0	8	31	3.9	19	0	1	7	7.0	7	0	1	0	0.0	0	19	348	18.3	0	2	0	0
2 NFL Seasons	17	0	25	87	3.5	19	0	11	63	5.7	18	0	1	0	0.0	0	46	949	20.6	0	3	0	0

Other Statistics: 1995–recovered 2 fumbles for 0 yards.

Matt Joyce

Pos: G **Rnd:** FA **College:** Richmond **Ht:** 6' 7" **Wt:** 283 **Born:** 3/30/72 **Age:** 24

Year	Team	G	GS			G	GS
1995	Seattle Seahawks	16	13		1 NFL Season	16	13

Other Statistics: 1995–recovered 1 fumble for 0 yards.

Seth Joyner

(statistical profile on page 425)

Pos: LB/S **Rnd:** 8 **College:** Texas-El Paso **Ht:** 6' 2" **Wt:** 235 **Born:** 11/18/64 **Age:** 31

Year	Team	G	GS	Tk	Ast	Sack	FF	FR	TD	Blk	Int	Yds	Avg	TD	Sfty	TD	Pts
1986	Philadelphia Eagles	14	7	34	10	2.0	1	0	0	0	1	4	4.0	0	0	0	0
1987	Philadelphia Eagles	12	12	65	31	4.0	2	2	1	0	2	42	21.0	0	0	1	6
1988	Philadelphia Eagles	16	16	86	50	3.5	1	1	0	0	4	96	24.0	0	0	0	0
1989	Philadelphia Eagles	14	14	76	47	4.5	3	0	0	0	1	0	0.0	0	0	0	0
1990	Philadelphia Eagles	16	16	91	41	7.5	3	0	0	0	1	9	9.0	0	0	0	0
1991	Philadelphia Eagles	16	16	68	42	6.5	6	4	2	0	3	41	13.7	0	0	2	12
1992	Philadelphia Eagles	16	16	85	36	6.5	3	1	0	0	4	88	22.0	2	0	2	12
1993	Philadelphia Eagles	16	16	80	33	2.0	2	0	0	0	1	6	6.0	0	0	0	0
1994	Arizona Cardinals	16	16	38	15	6.0	3	0	0	1	3	2	0.7	0	0	0	0
1995	Arizona Cardinals	16	16	50	20	1.0	1	3	0	1	3	9	3.0	0	0	0	0
	10 NFL Seasons	152	145	673	325	43.5	25	11	3	2	23	297	12.9	2	0	5	30

Other Statistics: 1988–fumbled 1 time. 1990–fumbled 1 time for 0 yards. 1995–fumbled 1 time.

Trey Junkin

Pos: LS/TE **Rnd:** 4 **College:** Louisiana Tech **Ht:** 6' 2" **Wt:** 241 **Born:** 1/23/61 **Age:** 35

				Rushing					Receiving					Punt Returns				Kickoff Returns				Totals		
Year	Team	G	GS	Att	Yds	Avg	Lg	TD	Rec	Yds	Avg	Lg	TD	Num	Yds	Avg	TD	Num	Yds	Avg	TD	Fum	TD	Pts
1983	Buffalo Bills	16	0	0	0	-	-	0	0	0	-	-	0	0	0	-	0	0	0	-	0	0	0	0
1984	Buf - Was	14	0	0	0	-	-	0	0	0	-	-	0	0	0	-	0	0	0	-	0	0	0	0
1985	Los Angeles Raiders	16	0	0	0	-	-	0	2	8	4.0	5	1	0	0	-	0	0	0	-	0	0	1	6
1986	Los Angeles Raiders	3	0	0	0	-	-	0	2	38	19.0	19	0	0	0	-	0	0	0	-	0	0	0	0
1987	Los Angeles Raiders	12	1	0	0	-	-	0	2	15	7.5	8	0	0	0	-	0	0	0	-	0	0	0	0
1988	Los Angeles Raiders	16	1	0	0	-	-	0	4	25	6.3	9	2	0	0	-	0	0	0	-	0	0	2	12
1989	Los Angeles Raiders	16	0	0	0	-	-	0	3	32	10.7	28	2	0	0	-	0	1	0	0.0	0	0	2	12
1990	Seattle Seahawks	12	0	0	0	-	-	0	0	0	-	-	0	0	0	-	0	0	0	-	0	0	0	0
1991	Seattle Seahawks	16	0	0	0	-	-	0	0	0	-	-	0	0	0	-	0	0	0	-	0	0	0	0
1992	Seattle Seahawks	16	1	0	0	-	-	0	3	25	8.3	13	1	0	0	-	0	0	0	-	0	0	1	6
1993	Seattle Seahawks	16	1	0	0	-	-	0	0	0	-	-	0	0	0	-	0	0	0	-	0	0	0	0
1994	Seattle Seahawks	16	0	0	0	-	-	0	1	1	1.0	t1	1	0	0	-	0	0	0	-	0	0	1	6
1995	Seattle Seahawks	16	0	0	0	-	-	0	0	0	-	-	0	0	0	-	0	0	0	-	0	0	0	0
1984	Buffalo Bills	2	0	0	0	-	-	0	0	0	-	-	0	0	0	-	0	0	0	-	0	0	0	0
	Washington Redskins	12	0	0	0	-	-	0	0	0	-	-	0	0	0	-	0	0	0	-	0	0	0	0
	13 NFL Seasons	185	4	0	0	-	-	0	17	144	8.5	28	7	0	0	-	0	1	0	0.0	0	0	7	42

Other Statistics: 1983–recovered 1 fumble for 0 yards. 1984–recovered 1 fumble for 0 yards.

John Jurkovic

Pos: NT/DT **Rnd:** FA **College:** Eastern Illinois **Ht:** 6' 2" **Wt:** 295 **Born:** 8/18/67 **Age:** 29

				Tackles			Miscellaneous				Interceptions				Punt Returns				Kickoff Returns				Totals	
Year	Team	G	GS	Tk	Ast	Sack	FF	FR	TD	Blk	Int	Yds	Avg	TD	Num	Yds	Avg	TD	Num	Yds	Avg	TD	TD	Fum
1991	Green Bay Packers	5	0	1	0	0.0	0	0	0	0	0	0	-	0	0	0	-	0	0	0	-	0	0	0
1992	Green Bay Packers	16	12	22	12	2.0	0	0	0	0	0	0	-	0	0	0	-	0	3	39	13.0	0	0	0
1993	Green Bay Packers	16	12	30	10	5.5	1	0	0	0	0	0	-	0	0	0	-	0	2	22	11.0	0	0	0
1994	Green Bay Packers	16	15	41	11	0.0	0	0	0	0	0	0	-	0	0	0	-	0	4	57	14.3	0	0	0
1995	Green Bay Packers	16	14	28	8	0.0	0	0	0	0	0	0	-	0	0	0	-	0	1	17	17.0	0	0	0
	5 NFL Seasons	69	53	122	41	7.5	1	0	0	0	0	0	-	0	0	0	-	0	10	135	13.5	0	0	0

Paul Justin

Pos: QB **Rnd:** FA **College:** Arizona State **Ht:** 6' 4" **Wt:** 202 **Born:** 5/19/68 **Age:** 28

				Passing								Rushing					Miscellaneous			
Year	Team	G	GS	Att	Com	Pct	Yards	Yds/Att	Lg	TD	Int	Int%	Rating	Att	Yds	Avg	Lg	TD	Sckd Yds	Fum Recv Yds	Pts
1995	Indianapolis Colts	3	1	36	20	55.6	212	5.89	20	0	2	5.6	49.8	3	1	0.3	2	0	3 22	1 1 -1	0

Todd Kalis

Pos: G **Rnd:** 4 **College:** Arizona State **Ht:** 6' 6" **Wt:** 296 **Born:** 5/10/65 **Age:** 31

Year	Team	G	GS	Year	Team	G	GS	Year	Team	G	GS	Year	Team	G	GS
1988	Minnesota Vikings	14	0	1990	Minnesota Vikings	15	14	1993	Minnesota Vikings	16	7	1995	Cincinnati Bengals	16	11
1989	Minnesota Vikings	16	16	1991	Minnesota Vikings	16	8	1994	Pittsburgh Steelers	11	11		7 NFL Seasons	104	67

142

John Kasay

(statistical profile on page 478)

Pos: K **Rnd:** 4 **College:** Georgia **Ht:** 5' 10" **Wt:** 189 **Born:** 10/27/69 **Age:** 27

			Field Goals													PAT		Tot
Year	Team	G	1-29 Yds	Pct	30-39 Yds	Pct	40-49 Yds	Pct	50+ Yds	Pct	Overall	Pct	Long	Made	Att	Pts
1991	Seattle Seahawks	16	6-7	85.7	11-14	78.6	6-7	85.7	2-3	66.7	25-31	80.6	54	27	28	102
1992	Seattle Seahawks	16	4-5	80.0	8-11	72.7	2-6	33.3	0-0	-	14-22	63.6	43	14	14	56
1993	Seattle Seahawks	16	6-6	100.0	10-11	90.9	4-6	66.7	3-5	60.0	23-28	82.1	55	29	29	98
1994	Seattle Seahawks	16	2-2	100.0	11-11	100.0	6-9	66.7	1-2	50.0	20-24	83.3	50	25	26	85
1995	Carolina Panthers	16	6-6	100.0	10-14	71.4	9-12	75.0	1-1	100.0	26-33	78.8	52	27	28	105
	5 NFL Seasons	80	24-26	92.3	50-61	82.0	27-40	67.5	7-11	63.6	108-138	78.3	55	122	125	446

Other Statistics: 1993–recovered 1 fumble for 0 yards. 1995–punted 1 time for 32 yards.

Napoleon Kaufman

(statistical profile on page 342)

Pos: RB/KR **Rnd:** 1 (18) **College:** Washington **Ht:** 5' 9" **Wt:** 185 **Born:** 6/7/73 **Age:** 23

				Rushing					Receiving					Punt Returns				Kickoff Returns				Totals		
Year	Team	G	GS	Att	Yds	Avg	Lg	TD	Rec	Yds	Avg	Lg	TD	Num	Yds	Avg	TD	Num	Yds	Avg	TD	Fum	TD	Pts
1995	Oakland Raiders	16	1	108	490	4.5	28	1	9	62	6.9	18	0	0	0	-	0	22	572	26.0	1	0	2	12

Mike Keim

Pos: T **Rnd:** FA **College:** Brigham Young **Ht:** 6' 7" **Wt:** 302 **Born:** 11/12/65 **Age:** 30

Year	Team	G	GS	Year	Team	G	GS	Year	Team	G	GS			G	GS
1991	New Orleans Saints	1	0	1993	Seattle Seahawks	3	0	1995	Seattle Seahawks	6	0				
1992	Seattle Seahawks	1	0	1994	Seattle Seahawks	15	0						5 NFL Seasons	26	0

Craig Keith

Pos: TE/WR **Rnd:** 7 **College:** Lenoir-Rhyne **Ht:** 6' 3" **Wt:** 264 **Born:** 4/27/71 **Age:** 25

				Rushing					Receiving					Punt Returns				Kickoff Returns				Totals		
Year	Team	G	GS	Att	Yds	Avg	Lg	TD	Rec	Yds	Avg	Lg	TD	Num	Yds	Avg	TD	Num	Yds	Avg	TD	Fum	TD	Pts
1993	Pittsburgh Steelers	1	0	0	0	-	-	0	0	0	-	-	0	0	0	-	0	0	0	-	0	0	0	0
1994	Pittsburgh Steelers	16	1	0	0	-	-	0	1	2	2.0	2	0	0	0	-	0	0	0	-	0	0	0	0
1995	Jacksonville Jaguars	11	3	0	0	-	-	0	3	20	6.7	9	0	0	0	-	0	0	0	-	0	0	0	0
	3 NFL Seasons	28	4	0	0	-	-	0	4	22	5.5	9	0	0	0	-	0	0	0	-	0	0	0	0

Jim Kelly

(statistical profile on page 342)

Pos: QB **Rnd:** 1 (14) **College:** Miami (FL) **Ht:** 6' 3" **Wt:** 224 **Born:** 2/14/60 **Age:** 36

				Passing										Rushing					Miscellaneous			
Year	Team	G	GS	Att	Com	Pct	Yards	Yds/Att	Lg	TD	Int	Int%	Rating	Att	Yds	Avg	Lg	TD	Sckd	Yds	Fum Recv	Yds	Pts
1986	Buffalo Bills	16	16	480	285	59.4	3593	7.49	t84	22	17	3.5	83.3	41	199	4.9	20	0	43	330	7	2	0	0
1987	Buffalo Bills	12	12	419	250	59.7	2798	6.68	47	19	11	2.6	83.8	29	133	4.6	24	0	27	239	6	2	0	0
1988	Buffalo Bills	16	16	452	269	59.5	3380	7.48	t66	15	17	3.8	78.2	35	154	4.4	20	0	30	229	5	0	0	0
1989	Buffalo Bills	13	13	391	228	58.3	3130	8.01	t78	25	18	4.6	86.2	29	137	4.7	19	2	30	216	6	3	-6	12
1990	Buffalo Bills	14	14	346	219	63.3	2829	8.18	71	24	9	2.6	101.2	22	63	2.9	15	0	20	158	4	2	-8	0
1991	Buffalo Bills	15	15	474	304	64.1	3844	8.11	t77	33	17	3.6	97.6	20	45	2.3	12	1	31	227	6	2	-4	6
1992	Buffalo Bills	16	16	462	269	58.2	3457	7.48	t65	23	19	4.1	81.2	31	53	1.7	10	1	20	145	8	0	-18	6
1993	Buffalo Bills	16	16	470	288	61.3	3382	7.20	t65	18	18	3.8	79.9	36	102	2.8	17	0	25	171	7	3	-17	0
1994	Buffalo Bills	14	14	448	285	63.6	3114	6.95	t83	22	17	3.8	84.6	25	77	3.1	18	1	34	244	11	2	-19	6
1995	Buffalo Bills	15	15	458	255	55.7	3130	6.83	t77	22	13	2.8	81.1	17	20	1.2	17	0	26	181	7	2	0	0
	10 NFL Seasons	147	147	4400	2652	60.3	32657	7.42	t84	223	156	3.5	85.4	285	983	3.4	24	5	286	2140	67	18	-72	30

Other Statistics: 1987–caught 1 pass for 35 yards. 1988–caught 1 pass for 5 yards.

Joe Kelly

Pos: LB **Rnd:** 1 (11) **College:** Washington **Ht:** 6' 2" **Wt:** 235 **Born:** 12/11/64 **Age:** 31

				Tackles			Miscellaneous				Interceptions				Totals		
Year	Team	G	GS	Tk	Ast	Sack	FF	FR	TD	Blk	Int	Yds	Avg	TD	Sfty	TD	Pts
1986	Cincinnati Bengals	16	7	35	-	1.0	0	1	0	0	1	0	0.0	0	0	0	0
1987	Cincinnati Bengals	10	10	45	-	1.0	0	0	0	0	0	0	-	0	0	0	0
1988	Cincinnati Bengals	16	16	61	-	1.0	0	0	0	0	0	0	-	0	0	0	0
1989	Cincinnati Bengals	16	5	68	-	1.0	0	3	0	0	1	25	25.0	0	0	0	0
1990	New York Jets	12	11	74	-	0.0	0	1	0	0	0	0	-	0	0	0	0
1991	New York Jets	16	12	63	-	0.0	1	0	0	0	2	6	3.0	0	0	0	0
1992	New York Jets	9	0	0	0	0.0	0	0	0	0	0	0	-	0	0	0	0
1993	Los Angeles Raiders	16	14	79	18	1.0	0	1	0	0	0	0	-	0	0	0	0
1994	Los Angeles Rams	16	14	56	14	2.0	1	1	0	0	1	31	31.0	0	0	0	0
1995	Green Bay Packers	13	4	9	1	0.0	0	0	0	0	1	0	0.0	0	0	0	0
	10 NFL Seasons	140	93	490	33	6.0	2	7	0	0	6	68	11.3	0	0	0	0

Other Statistics: 1991–fumbled 1 time for 0 yards.

Todd Kelly

Pos: DE **Rnd:** 1 (27) **College:** Tennessee **Ht:** 6' 2" **Wt:** 259 **Born:** 11/27/70 **Age:** 25

Year	Team	G	GS	Tk	Ast	Sack	FF	FR	TD	Blk	Int	Yds	Avg	TD	Sfty	TD	Pts
1993	San Francisco 49ers	14	5	14	1	1.0	0	0	0	0	0	0	-	0	0	0	0
1994	San Francisco 49ers	11	1	7	2	3.5	2	0	0	0	0	0	-	0	0	0	0
1995	Cincinnati Bengals	16	0	3	0	1.0	0	1	0	0	0	0	-	0	0	0	0
	3 NFL Seasons	41	6	24	3	5.5	2	1	0	0	0	0	-	0	0	0	0

Derek Kennard

Pos: C/G **Rnd:** 2 **College:** Nevada **Ht:** 6' 3" **Wt:** 300 **Born:** 9/9/62 **Age:** 34

Year	Team	G	GS	Year	Team	G	GS	Year	Team	G	GS	Year	Team	G	GS
1986	St. Louis Cardinals	15	10	1989	Phoenix Cardinals	14	14	1992	New Orleans Saints	16	16	1995	Dallas Cowboys	8	4
1987	St. Louis Cardinals	12	11	1990	Phoenix Cardinals	16	16	1993	New Orleans Saints	16	16				
1988	Phoenix Cardinals	16	16	1991	New Orleans Saints	3	3	1994	Dallas Cowboys	16	16		10 NFL Seasons	132	122

Other Statistics: 1987–fumbled 2 times for -4 yards. 1992–recovered 1 fumble for 0 yards; returned 1 kickoff for 11 yards. 1994–caught 1 pass for -3 yards; fumbled 1 time for 0 yards. 1995–recovered 1 fumble for -1 yard; fumbled 1 time.

Cortez Kennedy

(statistical profile on page 425)

Pos: DT **Rnd:** 1 (3) **College:** Miami (FL) **Ht:** 6' 3" **Wt:** 293 **Born:** 8/23/68 **Age:** 28

Year	Team	G	GS	Tk	Ast	Sack	FF	FR	TD	Blk	Int	Yds	Avg	TD	Sfty	TD	Pts
1990	Seattle Seahawks	16	2	37	11	1.0	1	1	0	0	0	0	-	0	0	0	0
1991	Seattle Seahawks	16	16	64	9	6.5	1	1	0	0	0	0	-	0	0	0	0
1992	Seattle Seahawks	16	16	76	16	14.0	4	1	0	0	0	0	-	0	0	0	0
1993	Seattle Seahawks	16	16	60	17	6.5	1	1	0	0	0	0	-	0	0	0	0
1994	Seattle Seahawks	16	16	54	16	4.0	0	1	0	0	0	0	-	0	0	0	0
1995	Seattle Seahawks	16	16	40	14	6.5	1	0	0	0	0	0	-	0	0	0	0
	6 NFL Seasons	96	82	331	83	38.5	8	5	0	0	0	0	-	0	0	0	0

Other Statistics: 1992–fumbled 1 time.

Lincoln Kennedy

Pos: G/T **Rnd:** 1 (9) **College:** Washington **Ht:** 6' 6" **Wt:** 325 **Born:** 2/12/71 **Age:** 25

Year	Team	G	GS	Year	Team	G	GS	Year	Team	G	GS			G	GS
1993	Atlanta Falcons	16	16	1994	Atlanta Falcons	16	3	1995	Atlanta Falcons	16	4		3 NFL Seasons	48	23

Other Statistics: 1993–recovered 1 fumble for 0 yards. 1994–recovered 1 fumble for 0 yards.

Marlon Kerner

Pos: CB **Rnd:** 3 **College:** Ohio State **Ht:** 5' 10" **Wt:** 187 **Born:** 3/18/73 **Age:** 23

Year	Team	G	GS	Tk	Ast	Sack	FF	FR	TD	Blk	Int	Yds	Avg	TD	Sfty	TD	Pts
1995	Buffalo Bills	14	5	29	5	0.0	1	0	0	0	0	0	-	0	0	0	0

Carl Kidd

Pos: CB **Rnd:** FA **College:** Arkansas **Ht:** 6' 1" **Wt:** 205 **Born:** 6/14/73 **Age:** 23

Year	Team	G	GS	Tk	Ast	Sack	FF	FR	TD	Blk	Int	Yds	Avg	TD	Sfty	TD	Pts
1995	Oakland Raiders	13	0	1	0	0.0	0	0	0	0	0	0	-	0	0	0	0

John Kidd

(statistical profile on page 478)

Pos: P **Rnd:** 5 **College:** Northwestern **Ht:** 6' 3" **Wt:** 214 **Born:** 8/22/61 **Age:** 35

Year	Team	G	NetPunts	Yards	Avg	Long	In20	In20%	TotPunts	TB	Blocks	OppRet	RetYds	NetAvg	Att	Yards	Att	Com	Yards	Int
1984	Buffalo Bills	16	88	3696	42.0	63	16	18.2	90	8	2	52	597	32.7	0	0	0	0	0	0
1985	Buffalo Bills	16	92	3818	41.5	67	33	35.9	92	4	0	49	438	35.9	0	0	0	0	0	0
1986	Buffalo Bills	16	75	3031	40.4	57	14	18.7	75	9	0	32	260	34.5	1	0	0	0	0	0
1987	Buffalo Bills	12	64	2495	39.0	67	20	31.3	64	7	0	26	148	34.5	0	0	1	0	0	0
1988	Buffalo Bills	16	62	2451	39.5	60	13	21.0	62	2	0	36	222	35.3	0	0	0	0	0	0
1989	Buffalo Bills	16	65	2564	39.4	60	15	23.1	67	9	2	25	227	32.2	0	0	0	0	0	0
1990	San Diego Chargers	16	61	2442	40.0	59	14	23.0	62	2	1	28	131	36.6	0	0	0	0	0	0
1991	San Diego Chargers	16	76	3064	40.3	60	22	28.9	77	6	1	32	267	34.8	0	0	0	0	0	0
1992	San Diego Chargers	16	68	2899	42.6	65	22	32.4	68	9	0	24	244	36.4	2	-13	0	0	0	0
1993	San Diego Chargers	14	57	2431	42.6	67	16	28.1	57	7	0	28	243	35.9	3	-13	0	0	0	0
1994	SD - Mia	6	21	848	40.4	58	3	14.3	21	4	0	6	135	30.1	0	0	0	0	0	0
1995	Miami Dolphins	16	57	2433	42.7	56	15	26.3	57	5	0	35	265	36.3	0	0	0	0	0	0
1994	San Diego Chargers	2	7	246	35.1	53	1	14.3	7	1	0	0	0	32.3	0	0	0	0	0	0

Year Team	G	Punting												Rushing		Passing			
		NetPunts	Yards	Avg	Long	In20	In20%	TotPunts	TB	Blocks	OppRet	RetYds	NetAvg	Att	Yards	Att	Com	Yards	Int
Miami Dolphins	4	14	602	43.0	58	2	14.3	14	3	0	6	135	29.1	0	0	0	0	0	0
12 NFL Seasons	176	786	32172	40.9	67	203	25.8	792	72	6	373	3177	34.8	6	-26	1	0	0	0

Other Statistics: 1986–recovered 1 fumble for 0 yards. 1990–recovered 1 fumble for 0 yards; fumbled 1 time. 1992–recovered 1 fumble for -9 yards; fumbled 1 time.

Brian Kinchen

Pos: TE/LS **Rnd:** 12   **College:** Louisiana State   **Ht:** 6' 2" **Wt:** 240 **Born:** 8/6/65 **Age:** 31

Year Team	G	GS	Rushing					Receiving					Punt Returns				Kickoff Returns				Totals		
			Att	Yds	Avg	Lg	TD	Rec	Yds	Avg	Lg	TD	Num	Yds	Avg	TD	Num	Yds	Avg	TD	Fum	TD	Pts
1988 Miami Dolphins	16	0	0	0	-	-	0	1	3	3.0	3	0	0	0	-	0	0	0	-	0	0	0	0
1989 Miami Dolphins	16	0	0	0	-	-	0	1	12	12.0	12	0	0	0	-	0	2	26	13.0	0	2	0	0
1990 Miami Dolphins	4	0	0	0	-	-	0	0	0	-	-	0	0	0	-	0	1	16	16.0	0	0	0	0
1991 Cleveland Browns	14	0	0	0	-	-	0	0	0	-	-	0	0	0	-	0	0	0	-	0	1	0	0
1992 Cleveland Browns	16	0	0	0	-	-	0	0	0	-	-	0	0	0	-	0	0	0	-	0	0	0	0
1993 Cleveland Browns	16	15	0	0	-	-	0	29	347	12.0	40	2	0	0	-	0	1	0	0.0	0	1	2	12
1994 Cleveland Browns	16	11	0	0	-	-	0	24	232	9.7	38	1	0	0	-	0	3	38	12.7	0	1	1	6
1995 Cleveland Browns	13	12	0	0	-	-	0	20	216	10.8	41	0	0	0	-	0	0	0	-	0	1	0	0
8 NFL Seasons	111	38	0	0	-	-	0	75	810	10.8	41	3	0	0	-	0	7	80	11.4	0	6	3	18

Other Statistics: 1995–recovered 1 fumble for 0 yards.

Todd Kinchen   *(statistical profile on page 343)*

Pos: WR/TE **Rnd:** 3   **College:** Louisiana State   **Ht:** 5' 11" **Wt:** 187 **Born:** 1/7/69 **Age:** 27

Year Team	G	GS	Rushing					Receiving					Punt Returns				Kickoff Returns				Totals		
			Att	Yds	Avg	Lg	TD	Rec	Yds	Avg	Lg	TD	Num	Yds	Avg	TD	Num	Yds	Avg	TD	Fum	TD	Pts
1992 Los Angeles Rams	14	0	0	0	-	-	0	0	0	-	-	0	4	103	25.8	2	4	63	15.8	0	0	2	12
1993 Los Angeles Rams	6	1	2	10	5.0	8	0	8	137	17.1	t35	1	7	32	4.6	0	6	96	16.0	0	1	1	6
1994 Los Angeles Rams	13	0	1	44	44.0	t44	1	23	352	15.3	43	3	16	158	9.9	0	21	510	24.3	0	5	4	24
1995 St. Louis Rams	16	1	4	16	4.0	15	0	36	419	11.6	35	4	53	416	7.8	0	35	743	21.2	0	8	4	24
4 NFL Seasons	49	2	7	70	10.0	t44	1	67	908	13.6	43	8	80	709	8.9	2	66	1412	21.4	0	14	11	66

Other Statistics: 1995–recovered 1 fumble for 0 yards; attempted 1 pass with 0 completions for 0 yards.

Ed King

Pos: G **Rnd:** 2   **College:** Auburn   **Ht:** 6' 4" **Wt:** 300 **Born:** 12/3/69 **Age:** 26

Year	Team	G	GS	Year	Team	G	GS	Year	Team	G	GS	Year	Team	G	GS
1991	Cleveland Browns	16	15	1992	Cleveland Browns	16	15	1993	Cleveland Browns	6	3	1995	New Orleans Saints	1	0
													4 NFL Seasons	39	33

Other Statistics: 1991–recovered 1 fumble for 0 yards.

Joe King

Pos: S **Rnd:** FA   **College:** Oklahoma State   **Ht:** 6' 2" **Wt:** 195 **Born:** 5/7/68 **Age:** 28

Year Team	G	GS	Tackles			Miscellaneous				Interceptions				Punt Returns				Kickoff Returns				Totals	
			Tk	Ast	Sack	FF	FR	TD	Blk	Int	Yds	Avg	TD	Num	Yds	Avg	TD	Num	Yds	Avg	TD	TD	Fum
1991 Cin - Cle	13	0	2	1	0.0	0	0	0	0	0	0	-	0	0	0	-	0	3	34	11.3	0	0	0
1992 Tampa Bay Buccaneers	14	3	15	5	0.0	0	0	0	0	2	24	12.0	0	0	0	-	0	0	0	-	0	0	0
1993 Tampa Bay Buccaneers	15	10	37	9	0.0	1	2	0	0	3	29	9.7	0	0	0	-	0	0	0	-	0	0	0
1995 Oakland Raiders	16	2	13	6	0.0	1	0	0	0	0	0	-	0	0	0	-	0	0	0	-	0	0	0
1991 Cincinnati Bengals	6	0	0	0	0.0	0	0	0	0	0	0	-	0	0	0	-	0	3	34	11.3	0	0	0
Cleveland Browns	7	0	2	1	0.0	0	0	0	0	0	0	-	0	0	0	-	0	0	0	-	0	0	0
4 NFL Seasons	58	15	67	21	0.0	2	2	0	0	5	53	10.6	0	0	0	-	0	3	34	11.3	0	0	0

Shawn King

Pos: DE **Rnd:** 2   **College:** Northeast Louisiana   **Ht:** 6' 3" **Wt:** 279 **Born:** 6/24/72 **Age:** 24

Year Team	G	GS	Tackles			Miscellaneous				Interceptions				Totals		
			Tk	Ast	Sack	FF	FR	TD	Blk	Int	Yds	Avg	TD	Sfty	TD	Pts
1995 Carolina Panthers	13	0	6	2	2.0	0	0	0	0	0	0	-	0	0	0	0

Terry Kirby   *(statistical profile on page 343)*

Pos: RB **Rnd:** 3   **College:** Virginia   **Ht:** 6' 1" **Wt:** 218 **Born:** 1/20/70 **Age:** 26

Year Team	G	GS	Rushing					Receiving					Kickoff Returns				Passing				Totals		
			Att	Yds	Avg	Lg	TD	Rec	Yds	Avg	Lg	TD	Num	Yds	Avg	TD	Att	Com	Yds	Int	Fum	TD	Pts
1993 Miami Dolphins	16	8	119	390	3.3	20	3	75	874	11.7	47	3	4	85	21.3	0	0	0	0	0	5	6	36
1994 Miami Dolphins	4	4	60	233	3.9	30	2	14	154	11.0	26	0	0	0	-	0	0	0	0	0	2	2	14
1995 Miami Dolphins	16	4	108	414	3.8	38	4	66	618	9.4	46	3	0	0	-	0	1	1	31	0	2	7	42
3 NFL Seasons	36	16	287	1037	3.6	38	9	155	1646	10.6	47	6	4	85	21.3	0	1	1	31	0	9	15	92

Other Statistics: 1993–recovered 4 fumbles for 0 yards. 1994–scored 1 two-point conversion. 1995–passed for 1 touchdown.

Randy Kirk

Pos: LS **Rnd:** FA **College:** San Diego State **Ht:** 6' 2" **Wt:** 231 **Born:** 12/27/64 **Age:** 31

Year	Team	G	GS	Tackles Tk	Ast	Sack	Misc FF	FR	TD	Blk	Int	Yds	Avg	TD	PR Num	Yds	Avg	TD	KR Num	Yds	Avg	TD	Tot TD	Fum
1987	San Diego Chargers	13	1	11	4	1.0	0	1	0	0	0	0	-	0	0	0	-	0	3	15	5.00	0	0	1
1988	San Diego Chargers	16	0	0	1	0.0	0	1	0	0	0	0	-	0	0	0	-	0	0	0	-	0	0	0
1989	Phoenix Cardinals	6	0	2	0	0.0	0	0	0	0	0	0	-	0	0	0	-	0	0	0	-	0	0	0
1990	Washington Redskins	1	0	0	0	0.0	0	0	0	0	0	0	-	0	0	0	-	0	0	0	-	0	0	0
1991	Cle - SD	7	0	0	0	0.0	0	0	0	0	0	0	-	0	0	0	-	0	0	0	-	0	0	0
1992	Cincinnati Bengals	15	0	6	0	0.0	0	2	0	0	0	0	-	0	0	0	-	0	0	0	-	0	0	0
1993	Cincinnati Bengals	16	0	0	0	0.0	0	0	0	0	0	0	-	0	0	0	-	0	0	0	-	0	0	0
1994	Arizona Cardinals	16	0	0	0	0.0	0	0	0	0	0	0	-	0	0	0	-	0	0	0	-	0	0	0
1995	Arizona Cardinals	16	0	0	0	0.0	0	0	0	0	0	0	-	0	0	0	-	0	0	0	-	0	0	0
1991	Cleveland Browns	2	0	0	0	0.0	0	0	0	0	0	0	-	0	0	0	-	0	0	0	-	0	0	0
	San Diego Chargers	5	0	0	0	0.0	0	0	0	0	0	0	-	0	0	0	-	0	0	0	-	0	0	0
	9 NFL Seasons	106	1	19	5	1.0	0	4	0	0	0	0	-	0	0	0	-	0	3	15	5.00	0	0	1

Levon Kirkland

(statistical profile on page 425)

Pos: LB **Rnd:** 2 **College:** Clemson **Ht:** 6' 1" **Wt:** 255 **Born:** 2/17/69 **Age:** 27

Year	Team	G	GS	Tackles Tk	Ast	Sack	Misc FF	FR	TD	Blk	Int	Yds	Avg	TD	Sfty	TD	Pts
1992	Pittsburgh Steelers	16	0	1	4	0.0	0	0	0	0	0	0	-	0	0	0	0
1993	Pittsburgh Steelers	16	13	64	39	1.0	4	2	1	0	0	0	-	0	0	1	6
1994	Pittsburgh Steelers	16	15	70	30	3.0	0	0	0	0	2	0	0.0	0	0	0	0
1995	Pittsburgh Steelers	16	16	58	30	1.0	0	2	0	0	0	0	-	0	0	0	0
	4 NFL Seasons	64	44	193	103	5.0	4	4	1	0	2	0	0.0	0	0	1	6

Alan Kline

Pos: T **Rnd:** FA **College:** Ohio State **Ht:** 6' 5" **Wt:** 277 **Born:** 5/25/71 **Age:** 25

Year	Team	G	GS						G	GS
1995	New Orleans Saints	3	0				1 NFL Season		3	0

Chuck Klingbeil

Pos: NT/DT **Rnd:** FA **College:** Northern Michigan **Ht:** 6' 1" **Wt:** 288 **Born:** 11/2/65 **Age:** 30

Year	Team	G	GS	Tackles Tk	Ast	Sack	Misc FF	FR	TD	Blk	Int	Yds	Avg	TD	Sfty	TD	Pts
1991	Miami Dolphins	15	4	15	2	5.0	0	1	1	0	0	0	-	0	0	1	6
1992	Miami Dolphins	15	15	42	24	1.0	0	0	0	0	0	0	-	0	0	0	0
1993	Miami Dolphins	16	16	41	33	1.5	1	0	0	0	0	0	-	0	0	0	0
1994	Miami Dolphins	16	15	37	14	0.0	0	0	0	0	0	0	-	0	0	0	0
1995	Miami Dolphins	16	15	48	12	0.0	0	0	0	0	0	0	-	0	0	0	0
	5 NFL Seasons	78	65	183	85	7.5	1	1	1	0	0	0	-	0	0	1	6

David Klingler

Pos: QB **Rnd:** 1 (6) **College:** Houston **Ht:** 6' 3" **Wt:** 205 **Born:** 2/17/69 **Age:** 27

Year	Team	G	GS	Passing Att	Com	Pct	Yards	Yds/Att	Lg	TD	Int	Int%	Rating	Rushing Att	Yds	Avg	Lg	TD	Sckd	Yds	Fum	Recv	Yds	Pts
1992	Cincinnati Bengals	4	4	98	47	48.0	530	5.41	t83	3	2	2.0	66.3	11	53	4.8	12	0	18	146	3	0	0	0
1993	Cincinnati Bengals	14	13	343	190	55.4	1935	5.64	51	6	9	2.6	66.6	41	282	6.9	29	0	40	202	7	2	-10	0
1994	Cincinnati Bengals	10	7	231	131	56.7	1327	5.74	56	6	9	3.9	65.7	17	85	5.0	15	0	24	165	7	1	0	0
1995	Cincinnati Bengals	3	0	15	7	46.7	88	5.87	33	1	1	6.7	59.9	0	0	-	0	0	1	10	0	0	0	0
	4 NFL Seasons	31	24	687	375	54.6	3880	5.65	t83	16	21	3.1	66.1	69	420	6.1	29	0	83	523	17	3	-10	0

Other Statistics: 1994–caught 1 pass for -6 yards.

George Koonce

Pos: LB **Rnd:** FA **College:** East Carolina **Ht:** 6' 1" **Wt:** 243 **Born:** 10/15/68 **Age:** 28

Year	Team	G	GS	Tackles Tk	Ast	Sack	Misc FF	FR	TD	Blk	Int	Yds	Avg	TD	Sfty	TD	Pts
1992	Green Bay Packers	16	10	34	21	1.5	0	1	0	0	0	0	-	0	0	0	0
1993	Green Bay Packers	15	15	68	40	3.0	0	1	0	0	0	0	-	0	0	0	0
1994	Green Bay Packers	16	16	76	27	1.0	0	2	0	0	0	0	-	0	0	0	0
1995	Green Bay Packers	16	16	49	25	1.0	0	0	0	0	1	12	12.0	0	0	0	0
	4 NFL Seasons	63	57	227	113	6.5	0	4	0	0	1	12	12.0	0	0	0	0

Jeff Kopp

Pos: LB **Rnd:** 6 **College:** Southern California **Ht:** 6' 3" **Wt:** 234 **Born:** 7/8/71 **Age:** 25

			Tackles			Miscellaneous				Interceptions				Totals		
Year Team	G	GS	Tk	Ast	Sack	FF	FR	TD	Blk	Int	Yds	Avg	TD	Sfty	TD	Pts
1995 Miami Dolphins	16	0	0	0	0.0	0	0	0	0	0	0	-	0	0	0	0

Bernie Kosar

(statistical profile on page 344)

Pos: QB **Rnd:** 1(S) **College:** Miami (FL) **Ht:** 6' 5" **Wt:** 214 **Born:** 11/25/63 **Age:** 32

			Passing									Rushing					Miscellaneous			
Year Team	G	GS	Att	Com	Pct	Yards	Yds/Att	Lg	TD	Int	Int%	Rating	Att	Yds	Avg	Lg TD	Sckd	Yds	Fum Recv Yds	Pts
1985 Cleveland Browns	12	10	248	124	50.0	1578	6.36	t68	8	7	2.8	69.3	26	-12	-0.5	10 1	19	121	14 2 -25	6
1986 Cleveland Browns	16	16	531	310	58.4	3854	7.26	t72	17	10	1.9	83.8	24	19	0.8	17 0	39	274	7 3 -15	0
1987 Cleveland Browns	12	12	389	241	62.0	3033	7.80	t54	22	9	2.3	95.4	15	22	1.5	7 1	22	129	2 1 -3	6
1988 Cleveland Browns	9	9	259	156	60.2	1890	7.30	t77	10	7	2.7	84.3	12	-1	-0.1	13 1	25	172	0 2 0	6
1989 Cleveland Browns	16	16	513	303	59.1	3533	6.89	t97	18	14	2.7	80.3	30	70	2.3	23 1	34	192	2 2 -1	6
1990 Cleveland Browns	13	13	423	230	54.4	2562	6.06	50	10	15	3.5	65.7	10	13	1.3	5 0	37	220	6 1 -9	0
1991 Cleveland Browns	16	16	494	307	62.1	3487	7.06	t71	18	9	1.8	87.8	26	74	2.8	14 0	41	232	10 2 -18	0
1992 Cleveland Browns	7	7	155	103	66.5	1160	7.48	t69	8	7	4.5	87.0	5	12	2.4	8 0	21	126	1 0 0	0
1993 Cle - Dal	11	7	201	115	57.2	1217	6.05	86	8	3	1.5	82.0	23	26	1.1	10 0	23	132	6 3 -13	0
1994 Miami Dolphins	2	0	12	7	58.3	80	6.67	22	1	1	8.3	71.5	1	17	17.0	17 0	0	0	0 0 0	0
1995 Miami Dolphins	9	2	108	74	68.5	699	6.47	t31	3	5	4.6	76.1	7	19	2.7	14 1	6	28	3 1 -7	6
1993 Cleveland Browns	7	6	138	79	57.2	807	5.85	t38	5	3	2.2	77.2	14	19	1.4	10 0	21	128	4 3 -13	0
Dallas Cowboys	4	1	63	36	57.1	410	6.51	86	3	0	0.0	92.7	9	7	0.8	4 0	2	4	2 0 0	0
11 NFL Seasons	123	108	3333	1970	59.1	23093	6.93	t97	123	87	2.6	81.6	179	259	1.4	23 5	267	1626	51 17 -91	30

Other Statistics: 1986–caught 1 pass for 1 yard. 1989–caught 1 pass for -7 yards. 1991–caught 1 pass for 1 yard.

Scott Kowalkowski

Pos: LB **Rnd:** 8 **College:** Notre Dame **Ht:** 6' 2" **Wt:** 228 **Born:** 8/23/68 **Age:** 28

			Tackles			Miscellaneous				Interceptions				Totals		
Year Team	G	GS	Tk	Ast	Sack	FF	FR	TD	Blk	Int	Yds	Avg	TD	Sfty	TD	Pts
1991 Philadelphia Eagles	16	0	9	0	0.0	0	1	0	0	0	0	-	0	0	0	0
1992 Philadelphia Eagles	16	0	9	0	0.0	0	0	0	0	0	0	-	0	0	0	0
1994 Detroit Lions	16	0	0	0	0.0	0	0	0	0	0	0	-	0	0	0	0
1995 Detroit Lions	16	0	1	1	0.0	0	0	0	0	0	0	-	0	0	0	0
4 NFL Seasons	64	0	19	1	0.0	0	1	0	0	0	0	-	0	0	0	0

Bruce Kozerski

Pos: G **Rnd:** 9 **College:** Holy Cross **Ht:** 6' 4" **Wt:** 287 **Born:** 4/2/62 **Age:** 34

Year	Team	G	GS	Year	Team	G	GS	Year	Team	G	GS	Year	Team	G	GS
1984	Cincinnati Bengals	16	1	1987	Cincinnati Bengals	8	4	1990	Cincinnati Bengals	16	16	1993	Cincinnati Bengals	15	15
1985	Cincinnati Bengals	14	0	1988	Cincinnati Bengals	16	16	1991	Cincinnati Bengals	16	16	1994	Cincinnati Bengals	16	16
1986	Cincinnati Bengals	16	14	1989	Cincinnati Bengals	15	15	1992	Cincinnati Bengals	16	16	1995	Cincinnati Bengals	8	8
													12 NFL Seasons	172	137

Other Statistics: 1987–recovered 1 fumble for 0 yards. 1989–recovered 1 fumble for 0 yards. 1991–recovered 1 fumble for 0 yards. 1993–recovered 1 fumble for -14 yards; fumbled 3 times.

Brian Kozlowski

Pos: TE/RB **Rnd:** FA **College:** Connecticut **Ht:** 6' 3" **Wt:** 247 **Born:** 10/4/70 **Age:** 26

			Rushing				Receiving				Punt Returns			Kickoff Returns			Totals		
Year Team	G	GS	Att	Yds	Avg	Lg TD	Rec	Yds	Avg	Lg TD	Num	Yds	Avg TD	Num	Yds	Avg TD	Fum	TD	Pts
1994 New York Giants	16	2	0	0	-	0	1	5	5.0	5 0	0	0	- 0	2	21	10.5 0	0	0	0
1995 New York Giants	16	0	0	0	-	0	2	17	8.5	12 0	0	0	- 0	5	75	15.0 0	1	0	0
2 NFL Seasons	32	2	0	0	-	0	3	22	7.3	12 0	0	0	- 0	7	96	13.7 0	1	0	0

Other Statistics: 1995–recovered 1 fumble for 0 yards.

Greg Kragen

Pos: NT **Rnd:** FA **College:** Utah State **Ht:** 6' 3" **Wt:** 265 **Born:** 3/4/62 **Age:** 34

			Tackles			Miscellaneous				Interceptions				Totals		
Year Team	G	GS	Tk	Ast	Sack	FF	FR	TD	Blk	Int	Yds	Avg	TD	Sfty	TD	Pts
1985 Denver Broncos	16	1	11	2	2.0	0	0	0	0	0	0	-	0	0	0	0
1986 Denver Broncos	16	14	29	31	0.0	0	3	0	0	0	0	-	0	0	0	0
1987 Denver Broncos	12	9	48	30	2.0	0	1	0	0	0	0	-	0	0	0	0
1988 Denver Broncos	16	16	101	39	2.5	0	1	0	0	0	0	-	0	0	0	0
1989 Denver Broncos	14	14	43	29	2.0	0	4	1	0	0	0	-	0	0	1	6
1990 Denver Broncos	16	16	46	35	2.0	3	2	0	0	0	0	-	0	0	0	0
1991 Denver Broncos	16	16	61	31	3.5	0	0	0	0	0	0	-	0	0	0	0

Year	Team	G	GS	Tk	Ast	Sack	FF	FR	TD	Blk	Int	Yds	Avg	TD	Sfty	TD	Pts
				Tackles			**Miscellaneous**				**Interceptions**				**Totals**		
1992	Denver Broncos	16	16	66	41	5.5	2	0	0	0	0	0	-	0	0	0	0
1993	Denver Broncos	14	14	43	22	3.0	0	1	0	0	0	0	-	0	0	0	0
1994	Kansas City Chiefs	16	2	8	2	0.0	0	0	0	0	0	0	-	0	0	0	0
1995	Carolina Panthers	16	14	41	10	1.0	1	2	1	0	1	29	29.0	0	0	1	6
	11 NFL Seasons	168	132	497	272	23.5	6	14	2	0	1	29	29.0	0	0	2	12

Erik Kramer

(statistical profile on page 344)

Pos: QB **Rnd:** FA **College:** North Carolina State **Ht:** 6' 1" **Wt:** 200 **Born:** 11/6/64 **Age:** 31

Year	Team	G	GS	Att	Com	Pct	Yards	Yds/Att	Lg	TD	Int	Int%	Rating	Att	Yds	Avg	Lg	TD	Sckd	Yds	Fum	Recv	Yds	Pts
				Passing										**Rushing**					**Miscellaneous**					
1987	Atlanta Falcons	3	2	92	45	48.9	559	6.08	33	4	5	5.4	60.0	2	10	5.0	11	0	10	82	0	0	0	0
1991	Detroit Lions	13	8	265	136	51.3	1635	6.17	t73	11	8	3.0	71.8	35	26	0.7	12	1	14	74	8	4	-5	6
1992	Detroit Lions	7	3	106	58	54.7	771	7.27	t77	4	8	7.5	59.1	12	34	2.8	11	0	15	80	4	1	-1	0
1993	Detroit Lions	5	4	138	87	63.0	1002	7.26	48	8	3	2.2	95.1	10	5	0.5	4	0	5	35	1	0	0	0
1994	Chicago Bears	6	5	158	99	62.7	1129	7.15	t85	8	8	5.1	79.9	6	-2	-0.3	2	0	14	87	3	2	-5	0
1995	Chicago Bears	16	16	522	315	60.3	3838	7.35	t76	29	10	1.9	93.5	35	39	1.1	11	1	15	95	6	2	-3	6
	6 NFL Seasons	50	38	1281	740	57.8	8934	6.97	t85	64	42	3.3	82.3	100	112	1.1	12	2	73	453	22	9	-14	12

Bob Kratch

Pos: G **Rnd:** 3 **College:** Iowa **Ht:** 6' 3" **Wt:** 288 **Born:** 1/6/66 **Age:** 30

Year	Team	G	GS	Year	Team	G	GS	Year	Team	G	GS	Year	Team	G	GS
1989	New York Giants	4	1	1991	New York Giants	14	1	1993	New York Giants	16	16	1995	New England Patriots	16	16
1990	New York Giants	14	10	1992	New York Giants	16	7	1994	New England Patriots	16	16		7 NFL Seasons	96	67

Dave Krieg

(statistical profile on page 345)

Pos: QB **Rnd:** FA **College:** Milton College **Ht:** 6' 1" **Wt:** 202 **Born:** 10/20/58 **Age:** 38

Year	Team	G	GS	Att	Com	Pct	Yards	Yds/Att	Lg	TD	Int	Int%	Rating	Att	Yds	Avg	Lg	TD	Sckd	Yds	Fum	Recv	Yds	Pts
				Passing										**Rushing**					**Miscellaneous**					
1980	Seattle Seahawks	1	0	2	0	0.0	0	0.00	0	0	0	0.0	39.6	0	0	-	0	0	1	6	0	0	0	0
1981	Seattle Seahawks	7	3	112	64	57.1	843	7.53	t57	7	5	4.5	83.3	11	56	5.1	29	1	11	85	4	0	0	6
1982	Seattle Seahawks	3	2	78	49	62.8	501	6.42	44	2	2	2.6	79.1	6	-3	-0.5	4	0	16	117	5	2	-14	0
1983	Seattle Seahawks	9	8	243	147	60.5	2139	8.80	t50	18	11	4.5	95.0	16	55	3.4	t10	2	38	279	10	2	0	12
1984	Seattle Seahawks	16	16	480	276	57.5	3671	7.65	t80	32	24	5.0	83.3	46	186	4.0	t37	3	40	314	11	3	-24	18
1985	Seattle Seahawks	16	16	532	285	53.6	3602	6.77	54	27	20	3.8	76.2	35	121	3.5	17	1	52	**448**	11	3	-2	6
1986	Seattle Seahawks	15	14	375	225	60.0	2921	7.79	t72	21	11	2.9	91.0	35	122	3.5	19	1	35	281	10	1	-5	6
1987	Seattle Seahawks	12	12	294	178	60.5	2131	7.25	t75	23	15	5.1	87.6	36	155	4.3	17	2	27	247	11	5	-2	12
1988	Seattle Seahawks	9	9	228	134	58.8	1741	7.64	t75	18	8	3.5	94.6	24	64	2.7	17	0	12	92	6	0	0	0
1989	Seattle Seahawks	15	14	499	286	57.3	3309	6.63	t60	21	20	4.0	74.8	40	160	4.0	18	0	37	289	18	9	-20	0
1990	Seattle Seahawks	16	16	448	265	59.2	3194	7.13	t63	15	20	4.5	73.6	32	115	3.6	25	0	40	360	16	2	0	0
1991	Seattle Seahawks	10	9	285	187	**65.6**	2080	7.30	60	11	12	4.2	82.5	13	59	4.5	24	0	32	216	6	0	0	0
1992	Kansas City Chiefs	16	16	413	230	55.7	3115	7.54	t77	15	12	2.9	79.9	37	74	2.0	17	2	48	323	10	6	-15	12
1993	Kansas City Chiefs	12	5	189	105	55.6	1238	6.55	t66	7	3	1.6	81.4	21	24	1.1	20	0	22	138	6	1	0	0
1994	Detroit Lions	14	7	212	131	61.8	1629	7.68	t51	14	3	1.4	101.7	23	35	1.5	15	0	14	100	4	2	-1	0
1995	Arizona Cardinals	16	16	521	304	58.3	3554	6.82	48	16	21	4.0	72.6	19	29	1.5	17	0	**53**	380	16	7	-10	0
	16 NFL Seasons	187	163	4911	2866	58.4	35668	7.26	t80	247	187	3.8	81.9	394	1252	3.2	t37	12	478	3675	144	43	-93	72

Other Statistics: 1983–caught 1 pass for 11 yards. 1990–caught 1 pass for -6 yards.

Bob Kuberski

Pos: NT **Rnd:** 7 **College:** Navy **Ht:** 6' 4" **Wt:** 300 **Born:** 4/5/71 **Age:** 25

Year	Team	G	GS	Tk	Ast	Sack	FF	FR	TD	Blk	Int	Yds	Avg	TD	Sfty	TD	Pts
				Tackles			**Miscellaneous**				**Interceptions**				**Totals**		
1995	Green Bay Packers	9	0	7	4	2.0	0	0	0	0	0	0	-	0	0	0	0

Jason Kyle

Pos: LB **Rnd:** 4 **College:** Arizona State **Ht:** 6' 3" **Wt:** 240 **Born:** 5/12/72 **Age:** 24

Year	Team	G	GS	Tk	Ast	Sack	FF	FR	TD	Blk	Int	Yds	Avg	TD	Sfty	TD	Pts
				Tackles			**Miscellaneous**				**Interceptions**				**Totals**		
1995	Seattle Seahawks	16	0	0	0	0.0	0	0	0	0	0	0	-	0	0	0	0

Jeff Kysar

Pos: T **Rnd:** 5 **College:** Arizona State **Ht:** 6' 7" **Wt:** 320 **Born:** 6/14/72 **Age:** 24

Year	Team	G	GS												G	GS
1995	Oakland Raiders	2	0													
															1 NFL Season	2	0

148

Matt LaBounty

Pos: DE   **Rnd:** 12   **College:** Oregon   **Ht:** 6' 3"   **Wt:** 278   **Born:** 1/3/69   **Age:** 27

Year	Team	G	GS	Tk	Ast	Sack	FF	FR	TD	Blk	Int	Yds	Avg	TD	Sfty	TD	Pts
					Tackles			Miscellaneous				Interceptions				Totals	
1993	San Francisco 49ers	6	0	1	1	0.0	0	0	0	0	0	0	-	0	0	0	0
1995	Green Bay Packers	14	2	10	1	3.0	0	0	0	0	0	0	-	0	0	0	0
	2 NFL Seasons	20	2	11	2	3.0	0	0	0	0	0	0	-	0	0	0	0

Jim Lachey

Pos: T   **Rnd:** 1 (12)   **College:** Ohio State   **Ht:** 6' 6"   **Wt:** 294   **Born:** 6/4/63   **Age:** 33

Year	Team	G	GS	Year	Team	G	GS	Year	Team	G	GS	Year	Team	G	GS
1985	San Diego Chargers	16	16	1988	Los Angeles Raiders	1	1	1990	Washington Redskins	16	16	1994	Washington Redskins	13	13
1986	San Diego Chargers	16	15	1988	Washington Redskins	15	14	1991	Washington Redskins	15	15	1995	Washington Redskins	3	3
1987	San Diego Chargers	12	12	1989	Washington Redskins	14	14	1992	Washington Redskins	10	10		10 NFL Seasons	131	129

Other Statistics: 1988–recovered 1 fumble for 0 yards. 1989–recovered 1 fumble for 0 yards. 1990–recovered 1 fumble for 0 yards.

Corbin Lacina

Pos: G   **Rnd:** 6   **College:** Augustana (SD)   **Ht:** 6' 4"   **Wt:** 297   **Born:** 11/2/70   **Age:** 25

Year	Team	G	GS	Year	Team	G	GS			G	GS
1994	Buffalo Bills	11	10	1995	Buffalo Bills	16	3		2 NFL Seasons	27	13

Jeff Lageman

Pos: DE   **Rnd:** 1 (14)   **College:** Virginia   **Ht:** 6' 6"   **Wt:** 268   **Born:** 7/18/67   **Age:** 29

Year	Team	G	GS	Tk	Ast	Sack	FF	FR	TD	Blk	Int	Yds	Avg	TD	Sfty	TD	Pts
					Tackles			Miscellaneous				Interceptions				Totals	
1989	New York Jets	16	15	43	29	4.5	1	0	0	0	0	0	-	0	0	0	0
1990	New York Jets	16	16	37	26	4.0	1	0	0	0	0	0	-	0	0	0	0
1991	New York Jets	16	16	50	18	10.0	3	0	0	0	0	0	-	0	0	0	0
1992	New York Jets	2	2	4	2	1.0	0	0	0	0	0	0	-	0	0	0	0
1993	New York Jets	16	16	65	24	8.5	0	0	0	0	1	15	15.0	0	0	0	0
1994	New York Jets	16	16	32	19	6.5	2	3	0	0	0	0	-	0	0	0	0
1995	Jacksonville Jaguars	11	11	27	11	3.0	2	1	0	0	0	0	-	0	0	0	0
	7 NFL Seasons	93	92	258	129	37.5	9	4	0	0	1	15	15.0	0	0	0	0

Other Statistics: 1989–rushed 1 time for -5 yards.

Carnell Lake

(statistical profile on page 426)

Pos: CB/S   **Rnd:** 2   **College:** UCLA   **Ht:** 6' 1"   **Wt:** 210   **Born:** 7/15/67   **Age:** 29

Year	Team	G	GS	Tk	Ast	Sack	FF	FR	TD	Blk	Int	Yds	Avg	TD	Sfty	TD	Pts
					Tackles			Miscellaneous				Interceptions				Totals	
1989	Pittsburgh Steelers	15	15	63	7	1.0	2	6	0	0	1	0	0.0	0	0	0	0
1990	Pittsburgh Steelers	16	16	57	10	1.0	2	1	0	0	1	0	0.0	0	0	0	0
1991	Pittsburgh Steelers	16	16	70	13	1.0	0	0	0	0	0	0	-	0	0	0	0
1992	Pittsburgh Steelers	16	16	66	19	2.0	2	1	0	0	0	0	-	0	0	0	0
1993	Pittsburgh Steelers	14	14	77	14	5.0	1	2	0	0	4	31	7.8	0	0	0	0
1994	Pittsburgh Steelers	16	16	68	14	1.0	3	1	0	0	1	2	2.0	0	0	0	0
1995	Pittsburgh Steelers	16	16	63	10	1.5	1	1	0	0	1	32	32.0	1	0	1	6
	7 NFL Seasons	109	109	464	87	12.5	11	12	0	0	8	65	8.1	1	0	1	6

Dan Land

Pos: S/RB   **Rnd:** FA   **College:** Albany State   **Ht:** 6' 0"   **Wt:** 195   **Born:** 7/3/65   **Age:** 31

Year	Team	G	GS	Tk	Ast	Sack	FF	FR	TD	Blk	Int	Yds	Avg	TD	Num	Yds	Avg	TD	Num	Yds	Avg	TD	TD	Fum
					Tackles			Miscellaneous				Interceptions				Punt Returns				Kickoff Returns				Totals
1987	Tampa Bay Buccaneers	3	2	0	0	0.0	0	0	0	0	0	0	-	0	0	0	-	0	0	0	-	0	0	0
1989	Los Angeles Raiders	10	0	0	0	0.0	0	0	0	0	0	0	-	0	0	0	-	0	0	0	-	0	0	0
1990	Los Angeles Raiders	16	0	0	0	0.0	0	0	0	0	0	0	-	0	0	0	-	0	0	0	-	0	0	0
1991	Los Angeles Raiders	16	0	0	0	0.0	0	0	0	0	0	0	-	0	0	0	-	0	0	0	-	0	0	0
1992	Los Angeles Raiders	16	0	19	2	0.0	0	0	0	0	1	0	0.0	0	0	0	-	0	2	27	13.5	0	0	1
1993	Los Angeles Raiders	15	0	18	2	0.0	0	0	0	0	0	0	-	0	0	0	-	0	0	0	-	0	0	0
1994	Los Angeles Raiders	16	0	5	1	0.0	0	0	0	0	0	0	-	0	0	0	-	0	0	0	-	0	0	0
1995	Oakland Raiders	15	3	19	5	0.0	0	0	0	0	0	0	-	0	0	0	-	0	0	0	-	0	0	0
	8 NFL Seasons	107	5	61	10	0.0	0	0	0	0	1	0	0.0	0	0	0	-	0	2	27	13.5	0	0	1

Other Statistics: 1987–rushed 9 times for 20 yards.

Sean Landeta

(statistical profile on page 479)

Pos: P **Rnd:** FA **College:** Towson State **Ht:** 6' 0" **Wt:** 210 **Born:** 1/6/62 **Age:** 34

Year	Team	G	NetPunts	Yards	Avg	Long	In20	In20%	TotPunts	TB	Blocks	OppRet	RetYds	NetAvg	Att	Yards	Att	Com	Yards	Int
1985	New York Giants	16	81	3472	42.9	68	20	24.7	81	14	0	29	247	36.4	0	0	1	0	0	0
1986	New York Giants	16	79	3539	44.8	61	24	30.4	79	11	0	41	386	37.1	0	0	0	0	0	0
1987	New York Giants	12	65	2773	42.7	64	13	20.0	66	6	1	38	606	31.0	0	0	0	0	0	0
1988	New York Giants	1	6	222	37.0	53	1	16.7	6	0	0	2	7	35.8	0	0	0	0	0	0
1989	New York Giants	16	70	3019	43.1	71	19	27.1	70	7	0	29	236	37.8	0	0	0	0	0	0
1990	New York Giants	16	75	3306	44.1	67	24	32.0	75	11	0	41	291	37.3	0	0	0	0	0	0
1991	New York Giants	15	64	2768	43.3	61	16	25.0	64	8	0	35	350	35.3	0	0	0	0	0	0
1992	New York Giants	11	53	2317	43.7	71	13	24.5	55	9	2	30	406	31.5	0	0	0	0	0	0
1993	NYN - LAN	16	75	3215	42.9	66	18	24.0	76	10	1	44	444	33.8	0	0	0	0	0	0
1994	Los Angeles Rams	16	78	3494	44.8	62	23	29.5	78	9	0	47	637	34.3	0	0	0	0	0	0
1995	St. Louis Rams	16	83	3679	44.3	63	23	27.7	83	12	0	38	393	36.7	0	0	0	0	0	0
1993	New York Giants	8	33	1390	42.1	57	11	33.3	34	3	1	19	140	35.0	0	0	0	0	0	0
	Los Angeles Rams	8	42	1825	43.5	66	7	16.7	42	7	0	25	304	32.9	0	0	0	0	0	0
11 NFL Seasons		151	729	31804	43.6	71	194	26.6	733	97	4	374	4003	35.3	0	0	1	0	0	0

Max Lane

Pos: T **Rnd:** 6 **College:** Navy **Ht:** 6' 6" **Wt:** 295 **Born:** 2/22/71 **Age:** 25

Year	Team	G	GS	Year	Team	G	GS			G	GS
1994	New England Patriots	14	0	1995	New England Patriots	16	16		2 NFL Seasons	30	16

Other Statistics: 1995–recovered 1 fumble for 30 yards.

David Lang

Pos: RB **Rnd:** 12 **College:** Northern Arizona **Ht:** 5' 11" **Wt:** 210 **Born:** 3/28/68 **Age:** 28

Year	Team	G	GS	Att	Yds	Avg	Lg	TD	Rec	Yds	Avg	Lg	TD	Num	Yds	Avg	TD	Num	Yds	Avg	TD	Fum	TD	Pts
1991	Los Angeles Rams	16	0	0	0	-	-	0	0	0	-	-	0	0	0	-	0	12	194	16.2	0	1	0	0
1992	Los Angeles Rams	16	11	33	203	6.2	71	5	18	283	15.7	t67	1	0	0	-	0	13	228	17.5	0	5	6	36
1993	Los Angeles Rams	6	0	9	29	3.2	28	0	4	45	11.3	21	0	0	0	-	0	0	0	-	0	0	0	0
1994	Los Angeles Rams	13	0	6	34	5.7	17	0	8	60	7.5	12	0	0	0	-	0	27	626	23.2	0	2	0	0
1995	Dallas Cowboys	16	0	1	7	7.0	7	0	0	0	-	-	0	0	0	-	0	0	0	-	0	0	0	0
5 NFL Seasons		67	11	49	273	5.6	71	5	30	388	12.9	t67	1	0	0	-	0	52	1048	20.2	0	8	6	36

Other Statistics: 1992–recovered 2 fumbles for 0 yards.

Antonio Langham

(statistical profile on page 426)

Pos: CB **Rnd:** 1 (9) **College:** Alabama **Ht:** 6' 0" **Wt:** 180 **Born:** 7/31/72 **Age:** 24

Year	Team	G	GS	Tk	Ast	Sack	FF	FR	TD	Blk	Int	Yds	Avg	TD	Sfty	TD	Pts
1994	Cleveland Browns	16	16	55	6	0.0	1	0	0	0	2	2	1.0	0	0	0	0
1995	Cleveland Browns	16	16	66	8	0.0	0	0	0	0	2	29	14.5	0	0	0	0
2 NFL Seasons		32	32	121	14	0.0	1	0	0	0	4	31	7.8	0	0	0	0

Other Statistics: 1994–fumbled 1 time for 0 yards.

Gordon Laro

Pos: TE **Rnd:** FA **College:** Boston College **Ht:** 6' 3" **Wt:** 257 **Born:** 4/17/72 **Age:** 24

Year	Team	G	GS	Att	Yds	Avg	Lg	TD	Rec	Yds	Avg	Lg	TD	Num	Yds	Avg	TD	Num	Yds	Avg	TD	Fum	TD	Pts
1995	Jacksonville Jaguars	2	0	0	0	-	-	0	1	6	6.0	6	0	0	0	-	0	0	0	-	0	0	0	0

Kwamie Lassiter

Pos: DB **Rnd:** FA **College:** Kansas **Ht:** 5' 11" **Wt:** 180 **Born:** 12/3/69 **Age:** 26

Year	Team	G	GS	Tk	Ast	Sack	FF	FR	TD	Blk	Int	Yds	Avg	TD	Sfty	TD	Pts
1995	Arizona Cardinals	5	0	5	2	0.0	0	0	0	0	0	0	-	0	0	0	0

Other Statistics: 1995–rushed 1 time for 1 yard.

Lamar Lathon

(statistical profile on page 426)

Pos: LB **Rnd:** 1 (15) **College:** Houston **Ht:** 6' 3" **Wt:** 252 **Born:** 12/23/67 **Age:** 28

Year	Team	G	GS	Tk	Ast	Sack	FF	FR	TD	Blk	Int	Yds	Avg	TD	Sfty	TD	Pts
1990	Houston Oilers	11	1	11	2	0.0	0	1	0	0	0	0	-	0	0	0	0
1991	Houston Oilers	16	16	86	30	2.0	0	0	0	0	3	77	25.7	1	0	1	6

Year Team	G	GS	Tackles			Miscellaneous				Interceptions				Totals		
			Tk	Ast	Sack	FF	FR	TD	Blk	Int	Yds	Avg	TD	Sfty	TD	Pts
1992 Houston Oilers	11	11	40	14	1.5	0	0	0	0	0	0	-	0	0	0	0
1993 Houston Oilers	13	1	29	10	2.0	1	1	0	0	0	0	-	0	0	0	0
1994 Houston Oilers	16	15	37	16	8.5	3	1	0	0	0	0	-	0	1	0	2
1995 Carolina Panthers	15	15	54	16	8.0	1	1	0	0	0	0	-	0	0	0	0
6 NFL Seasons	82	59	257	88	22.0	5	4	0	0	3	77	25.7	1	1	1	8

Ty Law

Pos: CB **Rnd:** 1 (23) **College:** Michigan   **Ht:** 5' 11" **Wt:** 196 **Born:** 2/10/74 **Age:** 22

Year Team	G	GS	Tackles			Miscellaneous				Interceptions				Totals		
			Tk	Ast	Sack	FF	FR	TD	Blk	Int	Yds	Avg	TD	Sfty	TD	Pts
1995 New England Patriots	14	7	40	7	1.0	0	0	0	0	3	47	15.7	0	0	0	0

Harper Le Bel

Pos: LS **Rnd:** 12 **College:** Colorado State   **Ht:** 6' 4" **Wt:** 255 **Born:** 7/14/63 **Age:** 33

Year Team	G	GS	Rushing					Receiving					Punt Returns				Kickoff Returns				Totals		
			Att	Yds	Avg	Lg	TD	Rec	Yds	Avg	Lg	TD	Num	Yds	Avg	TD	Num	Yds	Avg	TD	Fum	TD	Pts
1989 Seattle Seahawks	16	0	0	0	-	0	0	0	0	-	0	0	0	0	-	0	0	0	-	0	1	0	0
1990 Philadelphia Eagles	16	0	0	0	-	0	0	1	9	9.0	9	0	0	0	-	0	0	0	-	0	1	0	0
1991 Atlanta Falcons	3	0	0	0	-	0	0	0	0	-	0	0	0	0	-	0	0	0	-	0	0	0	0
1992 Atlanta Falcons	16	2	0	0	-	0	0	0	0	-	0	0	0	0	-	0	0	0	-	0	1	0	0
1993 Atlanta Falcons	16	0	0	0	-	0	0	0	0	-	0	0	0	0	-	0	0	0	-	0	1	0	0
1994 Atlanta Falcons	16	0	0	0	-	0	0	0	0	-	0	0	0	0	-	0	0	0	-	0	1	0	0
1995 Atlanta Falcons	16	0	0	0	-	0	0	0	0	-	0	0	0	0	-	0	0	0	-	0	1	0	0
7 NFL Seasons	99	2	0	0	-	0	0	1	9	9.0	9	0	0	0	-	0	0	0	-	0	6	0	0

Wesley Leasy

Pos: LB **Rnd:** 7 **College:** Mississippi State   **Ht:** 6' 2" **Wt:** 234 **Born:** 9/7/71 **Age:** 25

Year Team	G	GS	Tackles			Miscellaneous				Interceptions				Totals		
			Tk	Ast	Sack	FF	FR	TD	Blk	Int	Yds	Avg	TD	Sfty	TD	Pts
1995 Arizona Cardinals	12	0	0	0	0.0	0	0	0	0	0	0	-	0	0	0	0

Amp Lee

(statistical profile on page 345)

Pos: RB **Rnd:** 2 **College:** Florida State   **Ht:** 5' 11" **Wt:** 198 **Born:** 10/1/71 **Age:** 25

Year Team	G	GS	Rushing					Receiving					Punt Returns				Kickoff Returns				Totals		
			Att	Yds	Avg	Lg	TD	Rec	Yds	Avg	Lg	TD	Num	Yds	Avg	TD	Num	Yds	Avg	TD	Fum	TD	Pts
1992 San Francisco 49ers	16	3	91	362	4.0	43	2	20	102	5.1	17	2	0	0	-	0	14	276	19.7	0	1	4	24
1993 San Francisco 49ers	15	3	72	230	3.2	13	1	16	115	7.2	22	2	0	0	-	0	10	160	16.0	0	1	3	18
1994 Minnesota Vikings	13	0	29	104	3.6	16	0	45	368	8.2	35	2	0	0	-	0	3	42	14.0	0	1	2	12
1995 Minnesota Vikings	16	3	69	371	5.4	t66	2	71	558	7.9	33	1	5	50	10.0	0	5	100	20.0	0	3	3	18
4 NFL Seasons	60	9	261	1067	4.1	t66	5	152	1143	7.5	35	7	5	50	10.0	0	32	578	18.1	0	6	12	72

Other Statistics: 1992–recovered 3 fumbles for 0 yards. 1994–recovered 1 fumble for 0 yards. 1995–recovered 2 fumbles for 3 yards.

Kevin Lee

Pos: WR **Rnd:** 2 **College:** Alabama   **Ht:** 6' 1" **Wt:** 194 **Born:** 1/1/71 **Age:** 25

Year Team	G	GS	Rushing					Receiving					Punt Returns				Kickoff Returns				Totals		
			Att	Yds	Avg	Lg	TD	Rec	Yds	Avg	Lg	TD	Num	Yds	Avg	TD	Num	Yds	Avg	TD	Fum	TD	Pts
1995 New England Patriots	7	2	1	4	4.0	4	0	8	107	13.4	33	0	0	0	-	0	1	14	14.0	0	0	0	0

Shawn Lee

(statistical profile on page 427)

Pos: DT **Rnd:** 6 **College:** North Alabama   **Ht:** 6' 2" **Wt:** 300 **Born:** 10/24/66 **Age:** 30

Year Team	G	GS	Tackles			Miscellaneous				Interceptions				Totals		
			Tk	Ast	Sack	FF	FR	TD	Blk	Int	Yds	Avg	TD	Sfty	TD	Pts
1988 Tampa Bay Buccaneers	15	0	10	3	2.0	0	0	0	0	0	0	-	0	0	0	0
1989 Tampa Bay Buccaneers	15	3	14	7	1.0	0	0	0	0	0	0	-	0	0	0	0
1990 Miami Dolphins	13	10	30	4	1.5	0	0	0	0	0	0	-	0	0	0	0
1991 Miami Dolphins	3	2	3	2	0.0	0	0	0	0	1	14	14.0	0	0	0	0
1992 San Diego Chargers	9	1	5	2	0.5	0	1	0	0	0	0	-	0	0	0	0
1993 San Diego Chargers	16	15	36	9	3.0	0	1	0	0	0	0	-	0	0	0	0
1994 San Diego Chargers	15	15	30	9	6.5	1	1	0	0	0	0	-	0	0	0	0
1995 San Diego Chargers	16	15	31	11	8.0	0	1	0	0	0	0	-	0	0	0	0
8 NFL Seasons	102	61	159	47	22.5	1	4	0	0	1	14	14.0	0	0	0	0

Jay Leeuwenburg

Pos: G/LS **Rnd:** 9 **College:** Colorado **Ht:** 6' 3" **Wt:** 290 **Born:** 6/18/69 **Age:** 27

Year	Team	G	GS	Year	Team	G	GS	Year	Team	G	GS	Year	Team	G	GS
1992	Chicago Bears	12	0	1993	Chicago Bears	16	16	1994	Chicago Bears	16	16	1995	Chicago Bears	16	16
													4 NFL Seasons	60	48

Other Statistics: 1992–returned 1 kickoff for 7 yards. 1995–recovered 1 fumble for 0 yards.

Tyrone Legette

Pos: CB **Rnd:** 3 **College:** Nebraska **Ht:** 5' 9" **Wt:** 177 **Born:** 2/15/70 **Age:** 26

				Tackles			Miscellaneous				Interceptions				Punt Returns				Kickoff Returns				Totals	
Year	Team	G	GS	Tk	Ast	Sack	FF	FR	TD	Blk	Int	Yds	Avg	TD	Num	Yds	Avg	TD	Num	Yds	Avg	TD	TD	Fum
1992	New Orleans Saints	8	0	2	0	0.0	0	0	0	0	0	0	-	0	0	0	-	0	0	0	-	0	0	0
1993	New Orleans Saints	14	1	9	0	0.0	0	0	0	0	0	0	-	0	0	0	-	0	0	0	-	0	0	0
1994	New Orleans Saints	15	2	30	2	1.0	0	0	0	0	0	0	-	0	1	0	0.0	0	0	0	-	0	0	1
1995	New Orleans Saints	16	1	36	5	1.0	0	0	0	0	1	43	43.0	0	1	6	6.0	0	0	0	-	0	0	0
	4 NFL Seasons	53	4	77	7	2.0	0	0	0	0	1	43	43.0	0	2	6	3.0	0	0	0	-	0	0	1

Tim Lester

Pos: RB **Rnd:** 10 **College:** Eastern Kentucky **Ht:** 5' 9" **Wt:** 215 **Born:** 6/15/68 **Age:** 28

				Rushing					Receiving					Punt Returns				Kickoff Returns				Totals		
Year	Team	G	GS	Att	Yds	Avg	Lg	TD	Rec	Yds	Avg	Lg	TD	Num	Yds	Avg	TD	Num	Yds	Avg	TD	Fum	TD	Pts
1992	Los Angeles Rams	11	0	0	0	-	-	0	0	0	-	-	0	0	0	-	0	0	0	-	0	0	0	0
1993	Los Angeles Rams	16	14	11	74	6.7	26	0	18	154	8.6	21	0	0	0	-	0	0	0	-	0	0	0	0
1994	Los Angeles Rams	14	4	7	14	2.0	8	0	1	1	1.0	1	0	0	0	-	0	1	8	8.0	0	1	0	0
1995	Pittsburgh Steelers	6	1	5	9	1.8	3	1	0	0	-	-	0	0	0	-	0	0	0	-	0	0	1	6
	4 NFL Seasons	47	19	23	97	4.2	26	1	19	155	8.2	21	0	0	0	-	0	1	8	8.0	0	1	1	6

Other Statistics: 1994–recovered 1 fumble for 0 yards.

Leon Lett

Pos: DT/DE **Rnd:** 7 **College:** Emporia State **Ht:** 6' 6" **Wt:** 288 **Born:** 10/12/68 **Age:** 28

				Tackles			Miscellaneous				Interceptions				Totals		
Year	Team	G	GS	Tk	Ast	Sack	FF	FR	TD	Blk	Int	Yds	Avg	TD	Sfty	TD	Pts
1991	Dallas Cowboys	5	0	1	1	0.0	0	0	0	0	0	0	-	0	0	0	0
1992	Dallas Cowboys	16	0	13	13	3.5	0	1	0	0	0	0	-	0	0	0	0
1993	Dallas Cowboys	11	6	18	14	0.0	0	0	0	0	0	0	-	0	0	0	0
1994	Dallas Cowboys	16	16	36	13	4.0	0	0	0	2	0	0	-	0	0	0	0
1995	Dallas Cowboys	12	12	29	8	3.0	1	2	0	1	0	0	-	0	0	0	0
	5 NFL Seasons	60	34	97	49	10.5	1	3	0	3	0	0	-	0	0	0	0

Other Statistics: 1993–fumbled 1 time for 0 yards.

Dorsey Levens

(statistical profile on page 346)

Pos: RB **Rnd:** 5 **College:** Georgia Tech **Ht:** 6' 1" **Wt:** 240 **Born:** 5/21/70 **Age:** 26

				Rushing					Receiving					Punt Returns				Kickoff Returns				Totals		
Year	Team	G	GS	Att	Yds	Avg	Lg	TD	Rec	Yds	Avg	Lg	TD	Num	Yds	Avg	TD	Num	Yds	Avg	TD	Fum	TD	Pts
1994	Green Bay Packers	14	0	5	15	3.0	5	0	1	9	9.0	9	0	0	0	-	0	2	31	15.5	0	0	0	0
1995	Green Bay Packers	15	12	36	120	3.3	22	3	48	434	9.0	27	4	0	0	-	0	0	0	-	0	0	7	42
	2 NFL Seasons	29	12	41	135	3.3	22	3	49	443	9.0	27	4	0	0	-	0	2	31	15.5	0	0	7	42

Albert Lewis

Pos: CB **Rnd:** 3 **College:** Grambling **Ht:** 6' 2" **Wt:** 195 **Born:** 10/6/60 **Age:** 36

				Tackles			Miscellaneous				Interceptions				Totals		
Year	Team	G	GS	Tk	Ast	Sack	FF	FR	TD	Blk	Int	Yds	Avg	TD	Sfty	TD	Pts
1983	Kansas City Chiefs	16	1	30	6	0.0	0	2	0	0	4	42	10.5	0	0	0	0
1984	Kansas City Chiefs	15	15	61	8	1.0	0	0	0	0	4	57	14.3	0	0	0	0
1985	Kansas City Chiefs	16	16	65	9	1.5	1	1	1	0	8	59	7.4	0	0	1	6
1986	Kansas City Chiefs	15	15	61	8	1.0	1	2	0	0	4	18	4.5	0	0	0	0
1987	Kansas City Chiefs	12	12	34	9	0.0	1	0	0	0	1	0	0.0	0	0	0	0
1988	Kansas City Chiefs	14	12	32	13	0.0	0	1	0	0	1	19	19.0	0	1	0	2
1989	Kansas City Chiefs	16	16	42	15	1.0	3	0	0	0	4	37	9.3	0	0	0	0
1990	Kansas City Chiefs	15	14	44	14	0.0	0	3	0	0	2	15	7.5	0	0	0	0
1991	Kansas City Chiefs	8	6	13	5	0.0	0	0	0	0	3	21	7.0	0	0	0	0
1992	Kansas City Chiefs	9	8	24	6	0.0	1	0	0	0	1	0	0.0	0	0	0	0
1993	Kansas City Chiefs	14	13	44	12	0.0	1	2	1	0	6	61	10.2	0	0	1	6
1994	Los Angeles Raiders	14	9	39	6	1.0	1	0	0	0	0	0	-	0	0	0	0
1995	Oakland Raiders	16	15	49	8	1.0	1	1	0	0	0	0	-	0	0	0	0
	13 NFL Seasons	180	152	538	119	6.5	9	13	2	0	38	329	8.7	0	1	2	14

Darryll Lewis

(statistical profile on page 427)

Pos: CB **Rnd:** 2 **College:** Arizona **Ht:** 5' 9" **Wt:** 184 **Born:** 12/16/68 **Age:** 27

Year Team	G	GS	Tackles Tk	Ast	Sack	Misc FF	FR	TD	Blk	Int Int	Yds	Avg	TD	Punt Returns Num	Yds	Avg	TD	Kickoff Returns Num	Yds	Avg	TD	Totals TD	Fum
1991 Houston Oilers	16	1	22	10	1.0	0	1	0	0	1	33	33.0	1	0	0	-	0	0	0	-	0	1	0
1992 Houston Oilers	13	0	30	8	1.0	0	1	0	0	0	0	-	0	0	0	-	0	8	171	21.4	0	0	0
1993 Houston Oilers	4	4	13	1	0.0	0	0	0	0	1	47	47.0	1	0	0	-	0	0	0	-	0	1	0
1994 Houston Oilers	16	15	43	12	0.0	0	0	0	0	5	57	11.4	0	0	0	-	0	0	0	-	0	0	0
1995 Houston Oilers	16	15	50	8	1.0	0	0	0	0	6	145	24.2	1	0	0	-	0	0	0	-	0	1	0
5 NFL Seasons	65	35	158	39	3.0	0	2	0	0	13	282	21.7	3	0	0	-	0	8	171	21.4	0	3	0

Mo Lewis

(statistical profile on page 427)

Pos: LB/DE **Rnd:** 3 **College:** Georgia **Ht:** 6' 3" **Wt:** 250 **Born:** 10/21/69 **Age:** 27

Year Team	G	GS	Tackles Tk	Ast	Sack	Misc FF	FR	TD	Blk	Int Int	Yds	Avg	TD	Totals Sfty	TD	Pts
1991 New York Jets	16	16	48	28	1.0	3	1	0	0	0	0	-	0	0	0	0
1992 New York Jets	16	16	105	40	2.0	3	4	0	0	1	1	1.0	0	0	0	0
1993 New York Jets	16	16	95	63	4.0	4	0	0	0	2	4	2.0	0	0	0	0
1994 New York Jets	16	16	103	27	6.0	3	1	0	1	4	106	26.5	2	0	2	12
1995 New York Jets	16	16	82	29	5.0	2	0	0	0	2	22	11.0	1	0	1	6
5 NFL Seasons	80	80	433	187	18.0	15	6	0	1	9	133	14.8	3	0	3	18

Nate Lewis

Pos: KR **Rnd:** 7 **College:** Oregon Tech **Ht:** 5' 11" **Wt:** 198 **Born:** 10/19/66 **Age:** 30

Year Team	G	GS	Rushing Att	Yds	Avg	Lg	TD	Receiving Rec	Yds	Avg	Lg	TD	Punt Returns Num	Yds	Avg	TD	Kickoff Returns Num	Yds	Avg	TD	Totals Fum	TD	Pts
1990 San Diego Chargers	12	3	4	25	6.3	t10	1	14	192	13.7	40	1	13	117	9.0	1	17	383	22.5	0	3	3	18
1991 San Diego Chargers	16	10	3	10	3.3	9	0	42	554	13.2	t49	3	5	59	11.8	0	23	578	25.1	1	0	4	24
1992 San Diego Chargers	15	7	2	7	3.5	4	0	34	580	17.1	62	4	13	127	9.8	0	19	402	21.2	0	1	4	24
1993 San Diego Chargers	15	9	3	2	0.7	7	0	38	463	12.2	47	4	3	17	5.7	0	33	684	20.7	0	2	4	24
1994 Chicago Bears	13	0	0	0	-	-	0	2	13	6.5	8	1	1	7	7.0	0	35	874	25.0	0	1	1	6
1995 Chicago Bears	11	0	0	0	-	-	0	0	0	-	-	0	0	0	-	0	42	904	21.5	0	0	0	0
6 NFL Seasons	82	29	12	44	3.7	t10	1	130	1802	13.9	62	13	35	327	9.3	1	169	3825	22.6	1	7	16	96

Other Statistics: 1990–recovered 2 fumbles for 0 yards. 1991–recovered 1 fumble for 2 yards. 1992–recovered 2 fumbles for 0 yards. 1993–recovered 2 fumbles for 0 yards.

Roderick Lewis

Pos: TE **Rnd:** 5 **College:** Arizona **Ht:** 6' 5" **Wt:** 254 **Born:** 6/9/71 **Age:** 25

Year Team	G	GS	Rushing Att	Yds	Avg	Lg	TD	Receiving Rec	Yds	Avg	Lg	TD	Punt Returns Num	Yds	Avg	TD	Kickoff Returns Num	Yds	Avg	TD	Totals Fum	TD	Pts
1994 Houston Oilers	4	1	0	0	-	-	0	4	48	12.0	19	0	0	0	-	0	0	0	-	0	0	0	0
1995 Houston Oilers	15	8	0	0	-	-	0	16	116	7.3	16	0	0	0	-	0	1	5	5.0	0	0	0	0
2 NFL Seasons	19	9	0	0	-	-	0	20	164	8.2	19	0	0	0	-	0	1	5	5.0	0	0	0	0

Ron Lewis

Pos: G **Rnd:** FA **College:** Washington State **Ht:** 6' 3" **Wt:** 299 **Born:** 11/17/72 **Age:** 23

Year Team	G	GS		G	GS
1995 Washington Redskins	4	0	1 NFL Season	4	0

Thomas Lewis

Pos: WR **Rnd:** 1 (24) **College:** Indiana **Ht:** 6' 1" **Wt:** 195 **Born:** 1/10/72 **Age:** 24

Year Team	G	GS	Rushing Att	Yds	Avg	Lg	TD	Receiving Rec	Yds	Avg	Lg	TD	Punt Returns Num	Yds	Avg	TD	Kickoff Returns Num	Yds	Avg	TD	Totals Fum	TD	Pts
1994 New York Giants	10	0	0	0	-	-	0	4	46	11.5	23	0	5	64	12.8	0	26	509	19.6	0	2	0	0
1995 New York Giants	8	2	0	0	-	-	0	12	208	17.3	t46	1	6	46	7.7	0	9	257	28.6	1	1	2	12
2 NFL Seasons	18	2	0	0	-	-	0	16	254	15.9	t46	1	11	110	10.0	0	35	766	21.9	1	3	2	12

Other Statistics: 1994–recovered 2 fumbles for 0 yards.

Vernon Lewis

Pos: CB **Rnd:** FA **College:** Pittsburgh **Ht:** 5' 10" **Wt:** 192 **Born:** 10/27/70 **Age:** 26

Year Team	G	GS	Tackles Tk	Ast	Sack	Misc FF	FR	TD	Blk	Int Int	Yds	Avg	TD	Totals Sfty	TD	Pts
1993 New England Patriots	10	0	0	0	0.0	0	0	0	0	0	0	-	0	0	0	0
1994 New England Patriots	11	0	4	0	0.0	0	0	0	0	0	0	-	0	0	0	0
1995 New England Patriots	16	2	27	9	1.5	0	1	0	0	0	0	-	0	0	0	0
3 NFL Seasons	37	2	31	9	1.5	0	1	0	0	0	0	-	0	0	0	0

Jeremy Lincoln

(statistical profile on page 428)

Pos: CB **Rnd:** 3 **College:** Tennessee **Ht:** 5' 10" **Wt:** 180 **Born:** 4/7/69 **Age:** 27

Year	Team	G	GS	Tk	Ast	Sack	FF	FR	TD	Blk	Int	Yds	Avg	TD	Sfty	TD	Pts
1993	Chicago Bears	16	7	26	11	0.0	0	0	0	0	3	109	36.3	1	0	1	6
1994	Chicago Bears	15	14	36	1	0.0	1	0	0	0	1	5	5.0	0	0	0	0
1995	Chicago Bears	16	14	65	7	1.0	0	0	0	0	1	32	32.0	0	0	0	0
	3 NFL Seasons	47	35	127	19	1.0	1	0	0	0	5	146	29.2	1	0	1	6

Everett Lindsay

Pos: G **Rnd:** 5 **College:** Mississippi **Ht:** 6' 4" **Wt:** 301 **Born:** 9/18/70 **Age:** 26

Year	Team	G	GS	Year	Team	G	GS			G	GS
1993	Minnesota Vikings	12	12	1995	Minnesota Vikings	16	0	2 NFL Seasons		28	12

Adam Lingner

Pos: LS **Rnd:** 9 **College:** Illinois **Ht:** 6' 4" **Wt:** 268 **Born:** 11/2/60 **Age:** 35

Year	Team	G	GS	Year	Team	G	GS	Year	Team	G	GS	Year	Team	G	GS
1983	Kansas City Chiefs	16	1	1987	Buffalo Bills	12	0	1991	Buffalo Bills	16	0	1995	Buffalo Bills	16	0
1984	Kansas City Chiefs	16	0	1988	Kansas City Chiefs	16	0	1992	Buffalo Bills	16	0				
1985	Kansas City Chiefs	16	0	1989	Buffalo Bills	16	0	1993	Buffalo Bills	16	0				
1986	Kansas City Chiefs	12	0	1990	Buffalo Bills	16	0	1994	Buffalo Bills	16	0		13 NFL Seasons	200	1

Other Statistics: 1987–recovered 1 fumble for 0 yards.

Greg Lloyd

(statistical profile on page 428)

Pos: LB **Rnd:** 6 **College:** Fort Valley State **Ht:** 6' 2" **Wt:** 226 **Born:** 5/26/65 **Age:** 31

Year	Team	G	GS	Tk	Ast	Sack	FF	FR	TD	Blk	Int	Yds	Avg	TD	Sfty	TD	Pts
1988	Pittsburgh Steelers	9	4	24	9	0.5	2	1	0	0	0	0	-	0	0	0	0
1989	Pittsburgh Steelers	16	16	82	10	7.0	1	3	0	0	3	49	16.3	0	0	0	0
1990	Pittsburgh Steelers	15	14	55	7	4.5	1	0	0	0	1	9	9.0	0	0	0	0
1991	Pittsburgh Steelers	16	16	64	12	8.0	6	2	0	0	1	0	0.0	0	0	0	0
1992	Pittsburgh Steelers	16	16	66	30	6.5	5	4	0	0	1	35	35.0	0	0	0	0
1993	Pittsburgh Steelers	15	15	67	44	6.0	5	1	0	0	0	0	-	0	0	0	0
1994	Pittsburgh Steelers	15	15	69	18	10.0	5	1	0	0	1	8	8.0	0	0	0	0
1995	Pittsburgh Steelers	16	16	88	28	6.5	6	0	0	0	3	85	28.3	0	0	0	0
	8 NFL Seasons	118	112	515	158	49.0	31	12	0	0	10	186	18.6	0	0	0	0

Other Statistics: 1989–fumbled 1 time. 1991–fumbled 1 time. 1992–fumbled 1 time.

Mike Lodish

Pos: DT **Rnd:** 10 **College:** UCLA **Ht:** 6' 3" **Wt:** 280 **Born:** 8/11/67 **Age:** 29

Year	Team	G	GS	Tk	Ast	Sack	FF	FR	TD	Blk	Int	Yds	Avg	TD	Sfty	TD	Pts
1990	Buffalo Bills	12	0	6	0	2.0	0	0	0	0	0	0	-	0	0	0	0
1991	Buffalo Bills	16	6	28	9	1.5	0	0	0	0	0	0	-	0	0	0	0
1992	Buffalo Bills	16	0	5	2	0.0	0	1	1	0	0	0	-	0	0	1	6
1993	Buffalo Bills	15	1	7	0	0.5	0	1	0	0	0	0	-	0	0	0	0
1994	Buffalo Bills	16	5	11	6	0.0	0	1	1	0	0	0	-	0	0	1	6
1995	Denver Broncos	16	0	7	1	0.0	0	0	0	0	0	0	-	0	0	0	0
	6 NFL Seasons	91	12	64	18	4.0	0	3	2	0	0	0	-	0	0	2	12

Steve Lofton

Pos: CB **Rnd:** FA **College:** Texas A&M **Ht:** 5' 9" **Wt:** 185 **Born:** 11/26/68 **Age:** 27

Year	Team	G	GS	Tk	Ast	Sack	FF	FR	TD	Blk	Int	Yds	Avg	TD	Num	Yds	Avg	TD	Num	Yds	Avg	TD	TD	Fum
1991	Phoenix Cardinals	11	1	3	1	0.0	0	0	0	0	0	0	-	0	0	0	-	0	0	0	-	0	0	0
1992	Phoenix Cardinals	4	0	3	0	0.0	0	0	0	0	0	0	-	0	0	0	-	0	0	0	-	0	0	0
1993	Phoenix Cardinals	13	0	5	1	0.0	0	0	0	0	0	0	-	0	0	0	-	0	1	18	18.0	0	0	0
1995	Carolina Panthers	9	2	6	1	0.0	0	0	0	0	0	0	-	0	0	0	-	0	0	0	-	0	0	0
	4 NFL Seasons	37	3	17	3	0.0	0	0	0	0	0	0	-	0	0	0	-	0	1	18	18.0	0	0	0

Ernie Logan

Pos: DE **Rnd:** 9 **College:** East Carolina **Ht:** 6' 3" **Wt:** 283 **Born:** 5/18/68 **Age:** 28

Year	Team	G	GS	Tk	Ast	Sack	FF	FR	TD	Blk	Int	Yds	Avg	TD	Sfty	TD	Pts
1991	Cleveland Browns	15	5	9	12	0.5	0	1	0	0	0	0	-	0	0	0	0
1992	Cleveland Browns	16	0	5	2	1.0	0	0	0	0	0	0	-	0	0	0	0

Year	Team	G	GS	Tackles Tk	Ast	Sack	Miscellaneous FF	FR	TD	Blk	Interceptions Int	Yds	Avg	TD	Totals Sfty	TD	Pts
1993	Atlanta Falcons	8	1	3	5	1.0	0	0	0	0	0	0	-	0	0	0	0
1995	Jacksonville Jaguars	15	1	9	4	3.0	0	0	0	0	0	0	-	0	0	0	0
	4 NFL Seasons	54	7	26	23	5.5	0	1	0	0	0	0	-	0	0	0	0

James Logan

Pos: LB **Rnd:** FA **College:** Baylor **Ht:** 6' 2" **Wt:** 210 **Born:** 12/6/72 **Age:** 23

Year	Team	G	GS	Tackles Tk	Ast	Sack	Miscellaneous FF	FR	TD	Blk	Interceptions Int	Yds	Avg	TD	Totals Sfty	TD	Pts
1995	Hou - Cin - Sea	10	0	1	0	0.0	0	0	0	0	0	0	-	0	0	0	0
1995	Houston Oilers	3	0	1	0	0.0	0	0	0	0	0	0	-	0	0	0	0
	Cincinnati Bengals	1	0	0	0	0.0	0	0	0	0	0	0	-	0	0	0	0
	Seattle Seahawks	6	0	0	0	0.0	0	0	0	0	0	0	-	0	0	0	0

Marc Logan

(statistical profile on page 346)

Pos: RB **Rnd:** 5 **College:** Kentucky **Ht:** 6' 0" **Wt:** 212 **Born:** 5/9/65 **Age:** 31

Year	Team	G	GS	Rushing Att	Yds	Avg	Lg	TD	Receiving Rec	Yds	Avg	Lg	TD	Punt Returns Num	Yds	Avg	TD	Kickoff Returns Num	Yds	Avg	TD	Totals Fum	TD	Pts
1987	Cincinnati Bengals	3	3	37	203	5.5	51	1	3	14	4.7	18	0	0	0	-	0	3	31	10.3	0	0	1	6
1988	Cincinnati Bengals	9	0	2	10	5.0	9	0	2	20	10.0	17	0	0	0	-	0	4	80	20.0	0	1	0	0
1989	Miami Dolphins	10	4	57	201	3.5	14	0	5	34	6.8	11	0	0	0	-	0	24	613	25.5	1	1	2	12
1990	Miami Dolphins	16	0	79	317	4.0	17	2	7	54	7.7	12	0	0	0	-	0	20	367	18.4	0	4	2	12
1991	Miami Dolphins	16	0	4	5	1.3	2	0	0	0	-	-	0	0	0	-	0	12	191	15.9	0	1	0	0
1992	San Francisco 49ers	16	1	8	44	5.5	26	1	2	17	8.5	13	0	0	0	-	0	22	478	21.7	0	0	1	6
1993	San Francisco 49ers	14	12	58	280	4.8	45	7	37	348	9.4	24	0	0	0	-	0	0	0	-	0	2	7	42
1994	San Francisco 49ers	10	5	33	143	4.3	22	1	16	97	6.1	15	1	0	0	-	0	0	0	-	0	0	2	12
1995	Washington Redskins	16	9	23	72	3.1	13	1	25	276	11.0	32	2	0	0	-	0	0	0	-	0	1	3	18
	9 NFL Seasons	110	34	301	1275	4.2	51	13	97	860	8.9	32	3	0	0	-	0	85	1760	20.7	1	10	18	108

Other Statistics: 1989–recovered 2 fumbles for -1 yard. 1990–recovered 1 fumble for 0 yards. 1993–recovered 1 fumble for 0 yards.

Chip Lohmiller

(statistical profile on page 479)

Pos: K **Rnd:** 2 **College:** Minnesota **Ht:** 6' 3" **Wt:** 215 **Born:** 7/16/66 **Age:** 30

Year	Team	G	1-29 Yds	Pct	30-39 Yds	Pct	40-49 Yds	Pct	50+ Yds	Pct	Overall	Pct	Long	PAT Made	Att	Tot Pts
1988	Washington Redskins	16	7-9	77.8	5-7	71.4	7-10	70.0	0-0	-	19-26	73.1	46	40	41	97
1989	Washington Redskins	16	13-13	100.0	13-15	86.7	3-11	27.3	0-1	0.0	29-40	72.5	48	41	41	128
1990	Washington Redskins	16	12-12	100.0	12-14	85.7	3-6	50.0	3-8	37.5	30-40	75.0	56	41	41	131
1991	Washington Redskins	16	8-8	100.0	11-13	84.6	10-17	58.8	2-5	40.0	31-43	72.1	53	56	56	149
1992	Washington Redskins	16	11-11	100.0	9-15	60.0	8-12	66.7	2-2	100.0	30-40	75.0	53	30	30	120
1993	Washington Redskins	16	6-6	100.0	8-12	66.7	1-4	25.0	1-6	16.7	16-28	57.1	51	24	26	72
1994	Washington Redskins	16	9-11	81.8	5-6	83.3	5-8	62.5	1-3	33.3	20-28	71.4	54	30	32	90
1995	New Orleans Saints	8	4-6	66.7	3-4	75.0	0-2	0.0	1-2	50.0	8-14	57.1	51	11	13	35
	8 NFL Seasons	120	70-76	92.1	66-86	76.7	37-70	52.9	10-27	37.0	183-259	70.7	56	273	280	822

Other Statistics: 1988–punted 6 times for 208 yards.

Antonio London

Pos: LB **Rnd:** 3 **College:** Alabama **Ht:** 6' 2" **Wt:** 234 **Born:** 4/14/71 **Age:** 25

Year	Team	G	GS	Tackles Tk	Ast	Sack	Miscellaneous FF	FR	TD	Blk	Interceptions Int	Yds	Avg	TD	Totals Sfty	TD	Pts
1993	Detroit Lions	14	0	2	0	1.0	0	0	0	0	0	0	-	0	0	0	0
1994	Detroit Lions	16	0	0	1	0.0	0	0	0	0	0	0	-	0	0	0	0
1995	Detroit Lions	15	0	12	2	7.0	4	0	0	0	0	0	-	0	0	0	0
	3 NFL Seasons	45	0	14	3	8.0	4	0	0	0	0	0	-	0	0	0	0

Keith Loneker

Pos: G **Rnd:** FA **College:** Kansas **Ht:** 6' 3" **Wt:** 330 **Born:** 6/21/71 **Age:** 25

Year	Team	G	GS	Year	Team	G	GS	Year	Team	G	GS		G	GS
1993	Los Angeles Rams	4	2	1994	Los Angeles Rams	2	2	1995	St. Louis Rams	13	1	3 NFL Seasons	19	5

Corey Louchiey

Pos: T **Rnd:** 3 **College:** South Carolina **Ht:** 6' 7" **Wt:** 305 **Born:** 10/10/71 **Age:** 25

Year	Team	G	GS						G	GS
1995	Buffalo Bills	13	3					1 NFL Season	13	3

Other Statistics: 1995–returned 1 kickoff for 13 yards.

Duval Love

Pos: G **Rnd:** 10 **College:** UCLA **Ht:** 6' 3" **Wt:** 288 **Born:** 6/24/63 **Age:** 33

Year	Team	G	GS	Year	Team	G	GS	Year	Team	G	GS	Year	Team	G	GS
1985	Los Angeles Rams	6	0	1988	Los Angeles Rams	15	15	1991	Los Angeles Rams	16	13	1994	Pittsburgh Steelers	16	16
1986	Los Angeles Rams	16	0	1989	Los Angeles Rams	15	1	1992	Pittsburgh Steelers	16	16	1995	Arizona Cardinals	16	16
1987	Los Angeles Rams	10	4	1990	Los Angeles Rams	16	16	1993	Pittsburgh Steelers	16	16		11 NFL Seasons	158	113

Other Statistics: 1986–returned 1 kickoff for -6 yards; fumbled 1 time for 0 yards. 1988–recovered 1 fumble for 0 yards. 1990–recovered 2 fumbles for 0 yards. 1991–recovered 2 fumbles for 0 yards. 1992–recovered 1 fumble for 7 yards. 1995–recovered 1 fumble for 0 yards.

Sean Love

Pos: G **Rnd:** FA **College:** Penn State **Ht:** 6' 3" **Wt:** 300 **Born:** 9/6/68 **Age:** 28

Year	Team	G	GS	Year	Team	G	GS	Year	Team	G	GS		Team	G	GS
1993	Tampa Bay Buccaneers	2	0	1994	Tampa Bay Buccaneers	6	0	1995	Carolina Panthers	11	1		3 NFL Seasons	19	1

Derek Loville

(statistical profile on page 347)

Pos: RB **Rnd:** FA **College:** Oregon **Ht:** 5' 10" **Wt:** 205 **Born:** 7/4/68 **Age:** 28

				Rushing					Receiving					Punt Returns				Kickoff Returns				Totals		
Year	Team	G	GS	Att	Yds	Avg	Lg	TD	Rec	Yds	Avg	Lg	TD	Num	Yds	Avg	TD	Num	Yds	Avg	TD	Fum	TD	Pts
1990	Seattle Seahawks	11	1	7	12	1.7	4	0	0	0	-	-	0	0	0	-	0	18	359	19.9	0	1	0	0
1991	Seattle Seahawks	16	0	22	69	3.1	22	0	0	0	-	-	0	3	16	5.3	0	18	412	22.9	0	0	0	0
1994	San Francisco 49ers	14	0	31	99	3.2	13	0	2	26	13.0	19	0	0	0	-	0	2	34	17.0	0	0	0	0
1995	San Francisco 49ers	16	16	218	723	3.3	27	10	87	662	7.6	31	3	0	0	-	0	0	0	-	0	1	13	80
	4 NFL Seasons	57	17	278	903	3.2	27	10	89	688	7.7	31	3	3	16	5.3	0	38	805	21.2	0	2	13	80

Other Statistics: 1991–recovered 1 fumble for 0 yards. 1995–scored 1 two-point conversion.

Kirk Lowdermilk

Pos: C **Rnd:** 3 **College:** Ohio State **Ht:** 6' 4" **Wt:** 284 **Born:** 4/10/63 **Age:** 33

Year	Team	G	GS	Year	Team	G	GS	Year	Team	G	GS	Year	Team	G	GS
1985	Minnesota Vikings	16	2	1988	Minnesota Vikings	12	11	1991	Minnesota Vikings	16	16	1994	Indianapolis Colts	16	16
1986	Minnesota Vikings	11	0	1989	Minnesota Vikings	16	16	1992	Minnesota Vikings	16	16	1995	Indianapolis Colts	16	16
1987	Minnesota Vikings	12	12	1990	Minnesota Vikings	15	13	1993	Indianapolis Colts	16	16		11 NFL Seasons	162	134

Other Statistics: 1989–recovered 1 fumble for 0 yards. 1990–recovered 1 fumble for 0 yards. 1991–recovered 1 fumble for -22 yards; fumbled 1 time. 1993–recovered 1 fumble for 0 yards. 1994–fumbled 1 time for -4 yards.

Nick Lowery

(statistical profile on page 479)

Pos: K **Rnd:** FA **College:** Dartmouth **Ht:** 6' 4" **Wt:** 215 **Born:** 5/27/56 **Age:** 40

			Field Goals											PAT		Tot
Year	Team	G	1-29 Yds	Pct	30-39 Yds	Pct	40-49 Yds	Pct	50+ Yds	Pct	Overall	Pct	Long	Made	Att	Pts
1978	New England Patriots	2	0-0	-	0-0	-	0-1	0.0	0-0	-	0-1	0.0	-	7	7	7
1980	Kansas City Chiefs	16	6-6	100.0	7-9	77.8	3-4	75.0	4-7	57.1	20-26	76.9	57	37	37	97
1981	Kansas City Chiefs	16	5-5	100.0	13-15	86.7	7-9	77.8	1-7	14.3	26-36	72.2	52	37	38	115
1982	Kansas City Chiefs	9	6-6	100.0	5-5	100.0	8-10	80.0	0-3	0.0	19-24	79.2	47	17	17	74
1983	Kansas City Chiefs	16	6-6	100.0	6-6	100.0	10-14	71.4	2-4	50.0	24-30	80.0	58	44	45	116
1984	Kansas City Chiefs	16	7-7	100.0	6-11	54.5	8-10	80.0	2-5	40.0	23-33	69.7	52	35	35	104
1985	Kansas City Chiefs	16	4-4	100.0	10-11	90.9	7-7	100.0	3-5	60.0	24-27	88.9	58	35	35	107
1986	Kansas City Chiefs	16	6-7	85.7	5-5	100.0	8-13	61.5	0-1	0.0	19-26	73.1	47	43	43	100
1987	Kansas City Chiefs	12	5-5	100.0	8-10	80.0	4-6	66.7	2-2	100.0	19-23	82.6	54	26	26	83
1988	Kansas City Chiefs	16	7-8	87.5	9-11	81.8	8-10	80.0	3-3	100.0	27-32	84.4	51	23	23	104
1989	Kansas City Chiefs	16	7-7	100.0	10-14	71.4	6-9	66.7	1-3	33.3	24-33	72.7	50	34	35	106
1990	Kansas City Chiefs	16	7-7	100.0	21-22	95.5	6-7	85.7	0-1	0.0	34-37	91.9	48	37	38	139
1991	Kansas City Chiefs	16	13-13	100.0	8-8	100.0	4-7	57.1	0-2	0.0	25-30	83.3	48	35	35	110
1992	Kansas City Chiefs	15	9-10	90.0	9-9	100.0	3-4	75.0	1-1	100.0	22-24	91.7	52	39	39	105
1993	Kansas City Chiefs	16	9-9	100.0	6-8	75.0	7-11	63.6	1-1	100.0	23-29	79.3	52	37	37	106
1994	New York Jets	16	8-8	100.0	6-7	85.7	6-8	75.0	0-0	-	20-23	87.0	49	26	27	86
1995	New York Jets	14	4-4	100.0	8-10	80.0	3-3	100.0	2-4	50.0	17-21	81.0	50	24	24	75
	17 NFL Seasons	244	109-112	97.3	137-161	85.1	98-133	73.7	22-49	44.9	366-455	80.4	58	536	541	1634

Other Statistics: 1981–recovered 1 fumble for 0 yards. 1992–punted 4 times for 141 yards.

Sean Lumpkin

(statistical profile on page 428)

Pos: S **Rnd:** 4 **College:** Minnesota **Ht:** 6' 0" **Wt:** 206 **Born:** 1/4/70 **Age:** 26

				Tackles			Miscellaneous				Interceptions				Totals		
Year	Team	G	GS	Tk	Ast	Sack	FF	FR	TD	Blk	Int	Yds	Avg	TD	Sfty	TD	Pts
1992	New Orleans Saints	16	0	6	0	0.0	0	1	0	0	0	0	-	0	0	0	0
1993	New Orleans Saints	12	0	3	0	0.0	1	0	0	0	0	0	-	0	0	0	0
1994	New Orleans Saints	16	15	70	29	0.0	3	1	0	0	1	1	1.0	0	0	0	0
1995	New Orleans Saints	16	16	85	25	0.0	3	0	0	0	1	47	47.0	1	0	1	6
	4 NFL Seasons	60	31	164	54	0.0	7	2	0	0	2	48	24.0	1	0	1	6

Dennis Lundy

Pos: RB **Rnd:** FA **College:** Northwestern **Ht:** 5' 9" **Wt:** 190 **Born:** 7/6/72 **Age:** 24

Year	Team	G	GS	Rushing					Receiving					Punt Returns				Kickoff Returns				Totals		
				Att	Yds	Avg	Lg	TD	Rec	Yds	Avg	Lg	TD	Num	Yds	Avg	TD	Num	Yds	Avg	TD	Fum	TD	Pts
1995	Hou - Chi	9	0	0	0	-	-	0	1	11	11.0	11	0	1	-4	-4.0	0	3	39	13.0	0	1	0	0
1995	Houston Oilers	7	0	0	0	-	-	0	1	11	11.0	11	0	0	0	-	0	2	28	14.0	0	0	0	0
	Chicago Bears	2	0	0	0	-	-	0	0	0	-	-	0	1	-4	-4.0	0	1	11	11.0	0	1	0	0

Other Statistics: 1995–recovered 1 fumble for 18 yards.

David Lutz

Pos: G **Rnd:** 2 **College:** Georgia Tech **Ht:** 6' 6" **Wt:** 305 **Born:** 12/20/59 **Age:** 36

Year	Team	G	GS	Year	Team	G	GS	Year	Team	G	GS	Year	Team	G	GS
1983	Kansas City Chiefs	16	16	1987	Kansas City Chiefs	12	7	1991	Kansas City Chiefs	16	16	1995	Detroit Lions	16	16
1984	Kansas City Chiefs	7	6	1988	Kansas City Chiefs	15	7	1992	Kansas City Chiefs	16	16				
1985	Kansas City Chiefs	16	16	1989	Kansas City Chiefs	16	16	1993	Detroit Lions	16	16				
1986	Kansas City Chiefs	9	8	1990	Kansas City Chiefs	16	15	1994	Detroit Lions	16	16		13 NFL Seasons	187	171

Other Statistics: 1985–recovered 1 fumble for 0 yards. 1989–recovered 1 fumble for 0 yards. 1991–recovered 1 fumble for 0 yards. 1992–recovered 1 fumble for 0 yards.

Todd Lyght

(statistical profile on page 429)

Pos: CB **Rnd:** 1 (5) **College:** Notre Dame **Ht:** 6' 0" **Wt:** 186 **Born:** 2/9/69 **Age:** 27

Year	Team	G	GS	Tackles			Miscellaneous				Interceptions				Punt Returns				Kickoff Returns				Totals	
				Tk	Ast	Sack	FF	FR	TD	Blk	Int	Yds	Avg	TD	Num	Yds	Avg	TD	Num	Yds	Avg	TD	TD	Fum
1991	Los Angeles Rams	12	8	37	-	0.0	0	1	0	0	1	0	0.0	0	0	0	-	0	0	0	-	0	0	1
1992	Los Angeles Rams	12	12	59	6	0.0	0	0	0	0	3	80	26.7	0	0	0	-	0	0	0	-	0	0	0
1993	Los Angeles Rams	9	9	39	5	0.0	0	1	0	0	2	0	0.0	0	0	0	-	0	0	0	-	0	0	0
1994	Los Angeles Rams	16	16	73	12	0.0	0	1	1	0	1	14	14.0	0	1	29	29.0	0	0	0	-	0	1	0
1995	St. Louis Rams	16	16	73	9	0.0	1	0	0	0	4	34	8.5	1	0	16	-	0	0	0	-	0	1	0
	5 NFL Seasons	65	61	281	32	0.0	1	3	1	0	11	128	11.6	1	1	45	45.0	0	0	0	-	0	2	1

Keith Lyle

(statistical profile on page 429)

Pos: S **Rnd:** 3 **College:** Virginia **Ht:** 6' 2" **Wt:** 204 **Born:** 4/17/72 **Age:** 24

Year	Team	G	GS	Tackles			Miscellaneous				Interceptions				Totals		
				Tk	Ast	Sack	FF	FR	TD	Blk	Int	Yds	Avg	TD	Sfty	TD	Pts
1994	Los Angeles Rams	16	0	13	2	0.0	0	0	0	0	2	1	0.5	0	0	0	0
1995	St. Louis Rams	16	16	73	18	0.0	1	0	0	0	3	42	14.0	0	0	0	0
	2 NFL Seasons	32	16	86	20	0.0	1	0	0	0	5	43	8.6	0	0	0	0

Other Statistics: 1995–rushed 1 time for 4 yards.

Eric Lynch

Pos: RB **Rnd:** FA **College:** Grand Valley State **Ht:** 5' 10" **Wt:** 224 **Born:** 5/16/70 **Age:** 26

Year	Team	G	GS	Rushing					Receiving					Punt Returns				Kickoff Returns				Totals		
				Att	Yds	Avg	Lg	TD	Rec	Yds	Avg	Lg	TD	Num	Yds	Avg	TD	Num	Yds	Avg	TD	Fum	TD	Pts
1992	Detroit Lions	1	0	0	0	-	-	0	0	0	-	-	0	0	0	-	0	0	0	-	0	0	0	0
1993	Detroit Lions	4	2	53	207	3.9	15	2	13	82	6.3	11	0	0	0	-	0	1	22	22.0	0	1	2	12
1994	Detroit Lions	12	3	1	0	0.0	0	0	2	18	9.0	12	0	0	0	-	0	9	105	11.7	0	0	0	0
1995	Detroit Lions	5	0	0	0	-	-	0	0	0	-	-	0	0	0	-	0	0	0	-	0	0	0	0
	4 NFL Seasons	22	5	54	207	3.8	15	2	15	100	6.7	12	0	0	0	-	0	10	127	12.7	0	1	2	12

John Lynch

Pos: S **Rnd:** 3 **College:** Stanford **Ht:** 6' 2" **Wt:** 216 **Born:** 9/25/71 **Age:** 25

Year	Team	G	GS	Tackles			Miscellaneous				Interceptions				Totals		
				Tk	Ast	Sack	FF	FR	TD	Blk	Int	Yds	Avg	TD	Sfty	TD	Pts
1993	Tampa Bay Buccaneers	15	4	8	5	0.0	1	0	0	0	0	0	-	0	0	0	0
1994	Tampa Bay Buccaneers	16	0	11	4	0.0	0	0	0	0	0	0	-	0	0	0	0
1995	Tampa Bay Buccaneers	9	6	27	10	0.0	0	0	0	0	3	3	1.0	0	0	0	0
	3 NFL Seasons	40	10	46	19	0.0	1	0	0	0	3	3	1.0	0	0	0	0

Lorenzo Lynch

Pos: S **Rnd:** FA **College:** Sacramento State **Ht:** 5' 11" **Wt:** 200 **Born:** 4/6/63 **Age:** 33

Year	Team	G	GS	Tackles			Miscellaneous				Interceptions				Punt Returns				Kickoff Returns				Totals	
				Tk	Ast	Sack	FF	FR	TD	Blk	Int	Yds	Avg	TD	Num	Yds	Avg	TD	Num	Yds	Avg	TD	TD	Fum
1987	Chicago Bears	2	2	5	1	0.0	0	0	0	0	0	0	-	0	0	0	-	0	3	66	22.0	0	0	0
1988	Chicago Bears	11	0	2	0	0.0	0	0	0	0	0	0	-	0	0	0	-	0	0	0	-	0	0	0
1989	Chicago Bears	16	2	21	17	0.0	0	0	0	0	3	55	18.3	0	0	0	-	0	0	0	-	0	0	0
1990	Phoenix Cardinals	16	0	14	7	0.0	0	0	0	0	0	0	-	0	0	0	-	0	0	0	-	0	0	0

Year	Team	G	GS	Tackles			Miscellaneous				Interceptions				Punt Returns				Kickoff Returns				Totals	
				Tk	Ast	Sack	FF	FR	TD	Blk	Int	Yds	Avg	TD	Num	Yds	Avg	TD	Num	Yds	Avg	TD	TD	Fum
1991	Phoenix Cardinals	16	14	62	15	0.0	0	1	0	0	3	59	19.7	1	0	0	-	0	0	0	-	0	1	0
1992	Phoenix Cardinals	16	9	47	13	0.0	0	1	0	0	0	0	-	0	0	0	-	0	0	0	-	0	0	0
1993	Phoenix Cardinals	16	15	65	22	1.0	2	3	1	0	3	13	4.3	0	0	0	-	0	0	0	-	0	1	0
1994	Arizona Cardinals	15	15	65	28	0.5	1	0	0	0	2	35	17.5	0	0	0	-	0	0	0	-	0	0	0
1995	Arizona Cardinals	12	11	52	18	1.0	4	1	0	0	1	72	72.0	1	0	0	-	0	0	0	-	0	1	0
	9 NFL Seasons	120	68	333	121	2.5	7	6	1	0	12	234	19.5	2	0	0	-	0	3	66	22.0	0	3	0

Anthony Lynn

Pos: RB **Rnd:** FA **College:** Texas Tech **Ht:** 6' 3" **Wt:** 230 **Born:** 12/21/68 **Age:** 27

Year	Team	G	GS	Rushing					Receiving					Punt Returns				Kickoff Returns				Totals		
				Att	Yds	Avg	Lg	TD	Rec	Yds	Avg	Lg	TD	Num	Yds	Avg	TD	Num	Yds	Avg	TD	Fum	TD	Pts
1993	Denver Broncos	13	0	0	0	-	-	0	0	0	-	-	0	0	0	-	0	0	0	-	0	0	0	0
1995	San Francisco 49ers	6	0	2	11	5.5	6	0	0	0	-	-	0	0	0	-	0	0	0	-	0	0	0	0
	2 NFL Seasons	19	0	2	11	5.5	6	0	0	0	-	-	0	0	0	-	0	0	0	-	0	0	0	0

Mitch Lyons

Pos: TE **Rnd:** 6 **College:** Michigan State **Ht:** 6' 4" **Wt:** 265 **Born:** 5/13/70 **Age:** 26

Year	Team	G	GS	Rushing					Receiving					Punt Returns				Kickoff Returns				Totals		
				Att	Yds	Avg	Lg	TD	Rec	Yds	Avg	Lg	TD	Num	Yds	Avg	TD	Num	Yds	Avg	TD	Fum	TD	Pts
1993	Atlanta Falcons	16	8	0	0	-	-	0	8	63	7.9	14	0	0	0	-	0	0	0	-	0	0	0	0
1994	Atlanta Falcons	7	2	0	0	-	-	0	7	54	7.7	10	0	0	0	-	0	0	0	-	0	0	0	0
1995	Atlanta Falcons	13	5	0	0	-	-	0	5	83	16.6	34	0	0	0	-	0	0	0	-	0	0	0	0
	3 NFL Seasons	36	15	0	0	-	-	0	20	200	10.0	34	0	0	0	-	0	0	0	-	0	0	0	0

Mark Maddox

Pos: LB **Rnd:** 9 **College:** Northern Michigan **Ht:** 6' 1" **Wt:** 233 **Born:** 3/23/68 **Age:** 28

Year	Team	G	GS	Tackles			Miscellaneous				Interceptions				Totals		
				Tk	Ast	Sack	FF	FR	TD	Blk	Int	Yds	Avg	TD	Sfty	TD	Pts
1992	Buffalo Bills	15	1	18	7	0.0	0	0	0	0	0	0	-	0	0	0	0
1993	Buffalo Bills	11	8	34	28	0.0	1	2	0	0	0	0	-	0	0	0	0
1994	Buffalo Bills	15	14	52	26	0.0	0	1	0	0	1	11	11.0	0	0	0	0
1995	Buffalo Bills	4	4	13	5	0.0	0	0	0	0	0	0	-	0	0	0	0
	4 NFL Seasons	45	27	117	66	0.0	1	3	0	0	1	11	11.0	0	0	0	0

Tommy Maddox

Pos: QB **Rnd:** 1 (25) **College:** UCLA **Ht:** 6' 4" **Wt:** 205 **Born:** 9/2/71 **Age:** 25

Year	Team	G	GS	Passing										Rushing					Miscellaneous				
				Att	Com	Pct	Yards	Yds/Att	Lg	TD	Int	Int%	Rating	Att	Yds	Avg	Lg	TD	Sckd	Yds	Fum	Recv	Yds	Pts
1992	Denver Broncos	13	4	121	66	54.5	757	6.26	38	5	9	7.4	56.4	9	20	2.2	11	0	10	60	4	2	0	0
1993	Denver Broncos	16	0	1	1	100.0	1	1.00	t1	1	0	0.0	118.8	2	-2	-1.0	-1	0	0	0	0	0	0	0
1994	Los Angeles Rams	5	0	19	10	52.6	141	7.42	39	0	2	10.5	37.3	1	1	1.0	1	0	0	0	0	0	0	0
1995	New York Giants	16	0	23	6	26.1	49	2.13	13	0	3	13.0	0.0	1	4	4.0	4	0	2	7	1	0	0	0
	4 NFL Seasons	50	4	164	83	50.6	948	5.78	39	6	14	8.5	45.0	13	23	1.8	11	0	12	67	5	2	0	0

Eric Mahlum

Pos: G **Rnd:** 2 **College:** California **Ht:** 6' 4" **Wt:** 290 **Born:** 12/6/70 **Age:** 25

Year	Team	G	GS	Year	Team	G	GS			G	GS
1994	Indianapolis Colts	16	2	1995	Indianapolis Colts	7	7		2 NFL Seasons	23	9

Other Statistics: 1994–returned 0 kickoffs for 4 yards. 1995–recovered 2 fumbles for 0 yards.

Don Majkowski

Pos: QB **Rnd:** 10 **College:** Virginia **Ht:** 6' 3" **Wt:** 208 **Born:** 2/25/64 **Age:** 32

Year	Team	G	GS	Passing										Rushing					Miscellaneous				
				Att	Com	Pct	Yards	Yds/Att	Lg	TD	Int	Int%	Rating	Att	Yds	Avg	Lg	TD	Sckd	Yds	Fum	Recv	Yds	Pts
1987	Green Bay Packers	7	5	127	55	43.3	875	6.89	70	5	3	2.4	70.2	15	127	8.5	33	0	10	77	5	0	0	0
1988	Green Bay Packers	13	9	336	178	53.0	2119	6.31	56	9	11	3.3	67.8	47	225	4.8	24	1	31	176	8	3	0	6
1989	Green Bay Packers	16	16	599	353	58.9	4318	7.21	t79	27	20	3.3	82.3	75	358	4.8	20	5	47	268	15	6	-13	30
1990	Green Bay Packers	9	8	264	150	56.8	1925	7.29	t76	10	12	4.5	73.5	29	186	6.4	24	1	32	178	6	3	-10	6
1991	Green Bay Packers	9	8	226	115	50.9	1362	6.03	39	3	8	3.5	59.3	25	108	4.3	15	2	30	152	10	4	-3	12
1992	Green Bay Packers	14	3	55	38	69.1	271	4.93	32	2	2	3.6	77.2	8	33	4.1	8	0	9	60	4	3	0	0
1993	Indianapolis Colts	3	0	24	13	54.2	105	4.38	17	0	1	4.2	48.1	2	4	2.0	4	0	1	5	1	1	-7	0
1994	Indianapolis Colts	9	6	152	84	55.3	1010	6.64	29	6	7	4.6	69.8	24	34	1.4	10	3	9	76	5	2	-14	18
1995	Detroit Lions	8	0	20	15	75.0	161	8.05	22	1	0	0.0	114.8	9	1	0.1	4	0	1	5	0	0	0	0
	9 NFL Seasons	88	55	1803	1001	55.5	12146	6.74	t79	63	64	3.5	73.3	234	1076	4.6	33	12	170	997	54	22	-47	72

Siupeli Malamala

Pos: T/G **Rnd:** 3   **College:** Washington   **Ht:** 6' 5" **Wt:** 315   **Born:** 1/15/69 **Age:** 27

Year	Team	G	GS	Year	Team	G	GS	Year	Team	G	GS	Year	Team	G	GS
1992	New York Jets	9	5	1993	New York Jets	15	15	1994	New York Jets	12	10	1995	New York Jets	6	4
													4 NFL Seasons	42	34

Other Statistics: 1993–recovered 1 fumble for 0 yards.

Van Malone

Pos: S **Rnd:** 2   **College:** Texas   **Ht:** 5' 11" **Wt:** 186   **Born:** 7/1/70 **Age:** 26

				Tackles			Miscellaneous				Interceptions				Punt Returns				Kickoff Returns				Totals	
Year	Team	G	GS	Tk	Ast	Sack	FF	FR	TD	Blk	Int	Yds	Avg	TD	Num	Yds	Avg	TD	Num	Yds	Avg	TD	TD	Fum
1994	Detroit Lions	16	0	0	1	0.0	0	0	0	0	0	0	-	0	0	0	-	0	3	38	12.7	0	0	1
1995	Detroit Lions	16	0	3	3	0.0	0	0	0	0	1	0	0.0	0	0	0	-	0	0	0	-	0	0	0
	2 NFL Seasons	32	0	3	4	0.0	0	0	0	0	1	0	0.0	0	0	0	-	0	3	38	12.7	0	0	1

Mike Mamula

(statistical profile on page 429)

Pos: DE **Rnd:** 1 (7)   **College:** Boston College   **Ht:** 6' 4" **Wt:** 248   **Born:** 8/14/73 **Age:** 23

				Tackles			Miscellaneous				Interceptions				Totals		
Year	Team	G	GS	Tk	Ast	Sack	FF	FR	TD	Blk	Int	Yds	Avg	TD	Sfty	TD	Pts
1995	Philadelphia Eagles	14	13	33	8	5.5	1	1	0	0	0	0	-	0	0	0	0

John Mangum

Pos: S **Rnd:** 6   **College:** Alabama   **Ht:** 5' 10" **Wt:** 186   **Born:** 3/16/67 **Age:** 29

				Tackles			Miscellaneous				Interceptions				Punt Returns				Kickoff Returns				Totals	
Year	Team	G	GS	Tk	Ast	Sack	FF	FR	TD	Blk	Int	Yds	Avg	TD	Num	Yds	Avg	TD	Num	Yds	Avg	TD	TD	Fum
1990	Chicago Bears	10	0	9	4	0.0	1	1	0	0	0	0	-	0	0	0	-	0	0	0	-	0	0	0
1991	Chicago Bears	16	1	49	19	1.0	1	2	0	0	1	5	5.0	0	0	0	-	0	0	0	-	0	0	0
1992	Chicago Bears	5	1	8	2	0.0	0	0	0	0	0	0	-	0	0	0	-	0	0	0	-	0	0	0
1993	Chicago Bears	12	1	19	19	0.0	0	0	0	0	1	0	0.0	0	0	0	-	0	1	0	0.0	0	0	0
1994	Chicago Bears	16	3	28	9	0.5	0	0	0	0	0	0	-	0	0	0	-	0	0	0	-	0	0	0
1995	Chicago Bears	11	1	28	3	1.0	0	0	0	0	1	2	2.0	0	0	0	-	0	0	0	-	0	0	0
	6 NFL Seasons	70	7	141	56	2.5	2	3	0	0	3	7	2.3	0	0	0	-	0	1	0	0.0	0	0	0

Greg Manusky

Pos: LB **Rnd:** FA   **College:** Colgate   **Ht:** 6' 1" **Wt:** 233   **Born:** 8/18/66 **Age:** 30

				Tackles			Miscellaneous				Interceptions				Totals		
Year	Team	G	GS	Tk	Ast	Sack	FF	FR	TD	Blk	Int	Yds	Avg	TD	Sfty	TD	Pts
1988	Washington Redskins	7	0	1	0	0.0	0	0	0	0	0	0	-	0	0	0	0
1989	Washington Redskins	16	7	53	19	0.0	0	1	0	0	0	0	-	0	0	0	0
1990	Washington Redskins	16	8	52	36	0.0	0	0	0	0	0	0	-	0	0	0	0
1991	Minnesota Vikings	16	0	1	0	0.0	0	0	0	0	0	0	-	0	0	0	0
1992	Minnesota Vikings	11	0	5	2	0.0	0	0	0	0	0	0	-	0	0	0	0
1993	Minnesota Vikings	16	0	0	0	0.0	0	0	0	0	0	0	-	0	0	0	0
1994	Kansas City Chiefs	16	2	6	2	0.0	0	2	0	0	0	0	-	0	0	0	0
1995	Kansas City Chiefs	16	1	5	0	0.0	0	0	0	0	0	0	-	0	0	0	0
	8 NFL Seasons	114	18	123	59	0.0	0	3	0	0	0	0	-	0	0	0	0

Dan Marino

(statistical profile on page 347)

Pos: QB **Rnd:** 1 (27)   **College:** Pittsburgh   **Ht:** 6' 4" **Wt:** 224   **Born:** 9/15/61 **Age:** 35

				Passing										Rushing					Miscellaneous			
Year	Team	G	GS	Att	Com	Pct	Yards	Yds/Att	Lg	TD	Int	Int%	Rating	Att	Yds	Avg	Lg	TD	Sckd	Yds	Fum	Recv	Yds	Pts
1983	Miami Dolphins	11	9	296	173	58.4	2210	7.47	t85	20	6	2.0	96.0	28	45	1.6	15	2	10	80	5	2	0	12
1984	Miami Dolphins	16	16	564	362	64.2	5084	9.01	t80	48	17	3.0	108.9	28	-7	-0.3	10	0	13	120	6	2	-3	0
1985	Miami Dolphins	16	16	567	336	59.3	4137	7.30	73	30	21	3.7	84.1	26	-24	-0.9	6	0	18	157	9	2	-4	0
1986	Miami Dolphins	16	16	623	378	60.7	4746	7.62	t85	44	23	3.7	92.5	12	-3	-0.3	13	0	17	119	8	4	-12	0
1987	Miami Dolphins	12	12	444	263	59.2	3245	7.31	t59	26	13	2.9	89.2	12	-5	-0.4	t5	1	9	77	5	4	-25	6
1988	Miami Dolphins	16	16	606	354	58.4	4434	7.32	t80	28	23	3.0	80.8	20	-17	0.0	6	0	6	31	10	8	-31	0
1989	Miami Dolphins	16	16	550	308	56.0	3997	7.27	t78	24	22	4.0	76.9	14	-7	-0.5	2	2	10	86	7	0	-4	12
1990	Miami Dolphins	16	16	531	306	57.6	3563	6.71	t69	21	11	2.1	82.6	16	29	1.8	15	0	15	90	3	2	0	0
1991	Miami Dolphins	16	16	549	318	57.9	3970	7.23	54	25	13	2.4	85.8	27	32	1.2	11	1	27	182	6	3	-8	6
1992	Miami Dolphins	16	16	554	330	59.6	4116	7.43	t62	24	16	2.9	85.1	20	66	3.3	12	0	28	173	5	2	-12	0
1993	Miami Dolphins	5	5	150	91	60.7	1218	8.12	t80	8	3	2.0	95.9	9	-4	-0.4	14	1	7	42	4	2	-13	6
1994	Miami Dolphins	16	16	615	385	62.6	4453	7.24	t64	30	17	2.8	89.2	23	-6	-0.3	10	1	18	113	9	3	-1	6
1995	Miami Dolphins	14	14	482	309	64.1	3668	7.61	t67	24	15	3.1	90.8	11	14	1.3	12	0	22	153	7	3	-7	0
	13 NFL Seasons	186	184	6531	3913	59.9	48841	7.48	t85	352	200	3.1	88.4	246	113	0.5	15	8	200	1423	84	37	-120	48

Other Statistics: 1995–caught 1 pass for -6 yards.

Brock Marion

(statistical profile on page 430)

Pos: S **Rnd:** 7 **College:** Nevada **Ht:** 5' 11" **Wt:** 189 **Born:** 6/11/70 **Age:** 26

Year Team	G	GS	Tackles			Miscellaneous				Interceptions				Punt Returns				Kickoff Returns				Totals	
			Tk	Ast	Sack	FF	FR	TD	Blk	Int	Yds	Avg	TD	Num	Yds	Avg	TD	Num	Yds	Avg	TD	TD	Fum
1993 Dallas Cowboys	15	0	11	5	0.0	2	1	0	0	1	2	2.0	0	0	0	-	0	0	0	-	0	0	0
1994 Dallas Cowboys	14	1	22	4	1.0	0	0	0	0	1	11	11.0	0	0	0	-	0	2	39	19.5	0	0	0
1995 Dallas Cowboys	16	16	64	16	0.0	0	0	0	0	6	40	6.7	1	0	0	-	0	1	16	16.0	0	1	0
3 NFL Seasons	45	17	97	25	1.0	2	1	0	0	8	53	6.6	1	0	0	-	0	3	55	18.3	0	1	0

Curtis Marsh

Pos: KR/WR **Rnd:** 7 **College:** Utah **Ht:** 6' 1" **Wt:** 212 **Born:** 11/24/70 **Age:** 25

Year Team	G	GS	Rushing					Receiving					Punt Returns				Kickoff Returns				Totals		
			Att	Yds	Avg	Lg	TD	Rec	Yds	Avg	Lg	TD	Num	Yds	Avg	TD	Num	Yds	Avg	TD	Fum	TD	Pts
1995 Jacksonville Jaguars	9	0	0	0	-	-	0	7	127	18.1	34	0	0	0	-	0	15	323	21.5	0	2	0	0

Other Statistics: 1995–recovered 1 fumble for 0 yards.

Anthony Marshall

Pos: S/CB **Rnd:** FA **College:** Louisiana State **Ht:** 6' 1" **Wt:** 205 **Born:** 9/16/70 **Age:** 26

Year Team	G	GS	Tackles			Miscellaneous				Interceptions				Totals		
			Tk	Ast	Sack	FF	FR	TD	Blk	Int	Yds	Avg	TD	Sfty	TD	Pts
1994 Chicago Bears	3	0	0	0	0.0	0	0	0	0	0	0	-	0	0	0	0
1995 Chicago Bears	16	2	9	7	0.0	1	0	1	2	1	0	0.0	0	0	1	6
2 NFL Seasons	19	2	9	7	0.0	1	0	1	2	1	0	0.0	0	0	1	6

Arthur Marshall

Pos: WR/PR **Rnd:** FA **College:** Georgia **Ht:** 5' 11" **Wt:** 178 **Born:** 4/29/69 **Age:** 27

Year Team	G	GS	Rushing					Receiving					Punt Returns				Kickoff Returns				Totals		
			Att	Yds	Avg	Lg	TD	Rec	Yds	Avg	Lg	TD	Num	Yds	Avg	TD	Num	Yds	Avg	TD	Fum	TD	Pts
1992 Denver Broncos	16	1	11	56	5.1	16	0	26	493	19.0	t80	1	33	349	10.6	0	8	132	16.5	0	3	1	6
1993 Denver Broncos	16	9	0	0	-	-	0	28	360	12.9	40	2	0	0	-	0	0	0	-	0	0	2	12
1994 New York Giants	16	0	2	8	4.0	6	0	16	219	13.7	34	0	1	1	1.0	0	15	249	16.6	0	1	0	0
1995 New York Giants	15	0	1	1	1.0	1	0	17	195	11.5	27	1	12	96	8.0	0	0	0	-	0	1	1	6
4 NFL Seasons	63	10	14	65	4.6	16	0	87	1267	14.6	t80	4	46	446	9.7	0	23	381	16.6	0	5	4	24

Other Statistics: 1992–recovered 1 fumble for 0 yards; attempted 1 pass with 1 completion for 81 yards and 1 touchdown. 1993–attempted 1 pass with 1 completion for 30 yards and 1 touchdown.

Wilber Marshall

Pos: LB **Rnd:** 1 (11) **College:** Florida **Ht:** 6' 1" **Wt:** 231 **Born:** 4/18/62 **Age:** 34

Year Team	G	GS	Tackles			Miscellaneous				Interceptions				Punt Returns				Kickoff Returns				Totals	
			Tk	Ast	Sack	FF	FR	TD	Blk	Int	Yds	Avg	TD	Num	Yds	Avg	TD	Num	Yds	Avg	TD	TD	Fum
1984 Chicago Bears	15	1	17	2	0.0	0	0	0	0	0	0	-	0	0	0	-	0	0	0	-	0	0	0
1985 Chicago Bears	16	15	60	18	6.0	2	1	0	0	4	23	5.8	0	0	0	-	0	0	2	-	0	0	0
1986 Chicago Bears	16	15	60	45	5.5	4	3	1	0	5	68	13.6	1	0	0	-	0	0	0	-	0	2	0
1987 Chicago Bears	12	12	53	40	5.0	2	1	0	0	0	0	-	0	0	0	-	0	0	0	-	0	0	0
1988 Washington Redskins	16	16	87	46	4.0	3	0	0	0	3	61	20.3	0	0	0	-	0	0	0	-	0	0	0
1989 Washington Redskins	16	16	60	48	4.0	1	2	0	0	1	18	18.0	0	0	0	-	0	0	0	-	0	0	0
1990 Washington Redskins	16	15	76	31	5.0	2	1	0	0	1	6	6.0	0	0	0	-	0	0	0	-	0	0	0
1991 Washington Redskins	16	16	84	51	5.5	4	1	0	0	5	75	15.0	1	0	0	-	0	0	0	-	0	1	0
1992 Washington Redskins	16	16	99	39	6.0	3	3	0	0	2	20	10.0	1	0	0	-	0	0	0	-	0	1	0
1993 Houston Oilers	10	9	28	9	2.0	1	0	0	0	0	0	-	0	0	0	-	0	0	0	-	0	0	0
1994 Arizona Cardinals	15	15	42	16	1.0	2	1	0	0	0	13	-	0	0	0	-	0	0	0	-	0	0	0
1995 New York Jets	15	6	25	7	1.0	1	2	0	0	2	20	10.0	0	0	0	-	0	0	0	-	0	0	0
12 NFL Seasons	179	152	691	352	45.0	24	16	1	0	23	304	13.2	3	0	0	-	0	0	2	-	0	4	0

Other Statistics: 1987–rushed 1 time for 1 yard.

Curtis Martin

(statistical profile on page 348)

Pos: RB **Rnd:** 3 **College:** Pittsburgh **Ht:** 5' 11" **Wt:** 203 **Born:** 5/1/73 **Age:** 23

Year Team	G	GS	Rushing					Receiving					Punt Returns				Kickoff Returns				Totals		
			Att	Yds	Avg	Lg	TD	Rec	Yds	Avg	Lg	TD	Num	Yds	Avg	TD	Num	Yds	Avg	TD	Fum	TD	Pts
1995 New England Patriots	16	15	368	1487	4.0	49	14	30	261	8.7	27	1	0	0	-	0	0	0	-	0	5	15	92

Other Statistics: 1995–recovered 3 fumbles for 0 yards; scored 1 two-point conversion.

160

Emerson Martin

Pos: G **Rnd:** FA **College:** Hampton   **Ht:** 6' 2" **Wt:** 297 **Born:** 5/6/70 **Age:** 26

Year	Team	G	GS				G	GS
1995	Carolina Panthers	2	1			1 NFL Season	2	1

Kelvin Martin

Pos: KR/WR **Rnd:** 4 **College:** Boston College   **Ht:** 5' 9" **Wt:** 162 **Born:** 5/14/65 **Age:** 31

Year	Team	G	GS	Att	Yds	Avg	Lg	TD	Rec	Yds	Avg	Lg	TD	Num	Yds	Avg	TD	Num	Yds	Avg	TD	Fum	TD	Pts
					Rushing					Receiving					Punt Returns				Kickoff Returns				Totals		
1987	Dallas Cowboys	7	0	0	0	-	-	0	5	103	20.6	33	0	22	216	9.8	0	12	237	19.8	0	1	0	0
1988	Dallas Cowboys	16	7	4	-4	-1.0	11	0	49	622	12.7	t35	3	44	360	8.2	0	12	210	17.5	0	2	3	18
1989	Dallas Cowboys	11	11	0	0	-	-	0	46	644	14.0	46	2	4	32	8.0	0	0	0	-	0	0	2	12
1990	Dallas Cowboys	16	16	4	-2	-0.5	3	0	64	732	11.4	45	0	5	46	9.2	0	0	0	-	0	2	0	0
1991	Dallas Cowboys	16	0	0	0	-	-	0	16	243	15.2	27	0	21	244	11.6	1	3	47	15.7	0	2	1	6
1992	Dallas Cowboys	16	1	2	13	6.5	8	0	32	359	11.2	27	3	42	**532**	12.7	2	24	503	21.0	0	2	5	30
1993	Seattle Seahawks	16	14	1	0	0.0	0	0	57	798	14.0	t53	5	32	270	8.4	0	3	38	12.7	0	1	5	30
1994	Seattle Seahawks	16	15	0	0	-	-	0	56	681	12.2	32	1	33	280	8.5	0	2	30	15.0	0	2	1	6
1995	Philadelphia Eagles	9	1	0	0	-	-	0	17	206	12.1	22	0	17	214	12.6	0	20	388	19.4	0	2	0	0
	9 NFL Seasons	123	65	11	7	0.6	11	0	342	4388	12.8	t53	14	220	2194	10.0	3	76	1453	19.1	0	14	17	102

Other Statistics: 1990–recovered 1 fumble for 0 yards. 1991–recovered 1 fumble for 0 yards. 1993–recovered 1 fumble for 0 yards. 1994–recovered 1 fumble for 0 yards.

Tony Martin

(statistical profile on page 348)

Pos: WR **Rnd:** 5 **College:** Mesa State   **Ht:** 6' 1" **Wt:** 181 **Born:** 9/5/65 **Age:** 31

Year	Team	G	GS	Att	Yds	Avg	Lg	TD	Rec	Yds	Avg	Lg	TD	Num	Yds	Avg	TD	Num	Yds	Avg	TD	Fum	TD	Pts
					Rushing					Receiving					Punt Returns				Kickoff Returns				Totals		
1990	Miami Dolphins	16	5	1	8	8.0	8	0	29	388	13.4	45	2	26	140	5.4	0	0	0	-	0	4	2	12
1991	Miami Dolphins	16	0	0	0	-	-	0	27	434	16.1	54	2	1	10	10.0	0	0	0	-	0	2	2	12
1992	Miami Dolphins	16	3	1	-2	-2.0	-2	0	33	553	16.8	t55	2	1	0	0.0	0	0	0	-	0	2	2	12
1993	Miami Dolphins	12	0	1	6	6.0	6	0	20	347	17.4	t80	3	0	0	-	0	0	0	-	0	1	3	18
1994	San Diego Chargers	16	1	2	-9	-4.5	4	0	50	885	17.7	**t99**	7	0	0	-	0	8	167	20.9	0	2	7	42
1995	San Diego Chargers	16	16	0	0	-	-	0	90	1224	13.6	t51	6	0	0	-	0	0	0	-	0	3	6	36
	6 NFL Seasons	92	25	5	3	0.6	8	0	249	3831	15.4	t99	22	28	150	5.4	0	8	167	20.9	0	14	22	132

Other Statistics: 1990–recovered 2 fumbles for 0 yards. 1992–recovered 1 fumble for 0 yards; attempted 1 pass with 0 completions for 0 yards. 1994–attempted 1 pass with 0 completions for 0 yards and 1 interception. 1995–attempted 1 pass with 0 completions for 0 yards.

Wayne Martin

(statistical profile on page 430)

Pos: DT **Rnd:** 1 (19) **College:** Arkansas   **Ht:** 6' 5" **Wt:** 275 **Born:** 10/26/65 **Age:** 31

Year	Team	G	GS	Tk	Ast	Sack	FF	FR	TD	Blk	Int	Yds	Avg	TD	Sfty	TD	Pts
					Tackles			Miscellaneous				Interceptions				Totals	
1989	New Orleans Saints	16	0	13	5	2.5	0	2	0	0	0	0	-	0	0	0	0
1990	New Orleans Saints	11	11	24	6	4.0	1	0	0	0	0	0	-	0	0	0	0
1991	New Orleans Saints	16	16	21	1	3.5	1	1	0	0	0	0	-	0	0	0	0
1992	New Orleans Saints	16	16	53	17	15.5	3	2	0	0	0	0	-	0	0	0	0
1993	New Orleans Saints	16	16	55	13	5.0	1	2	0	0	0	0	-	0	0	0	0
1994	New Orleans Saints	16	16	59	14	10.0	1	0	0	0	0	0	-	0	0	0	0
1995	New Orleans Saints	16	16	64	13	13.0	1	1	0	0	1	12	12.0	0	0	0	0
	7 NFL Seasons	107	91	289	69	53.5	8	8	0	0	1	12	12.0	0	0	0	0

Lonnie Marts

Pos: LB **Rnd:** FA **College:** Tulane   **Ht:** 6' 2" **Wt:** 236 **Born:** 11/10/68 **Age:** 27

Year	Team	G	GS	Tk	Ast	Sack	FF	FR	TD	Blk	Int	Yds	Avg	TD	Num	Yds	Avg	TD	Num	Yds	Avg	TD	TD	Fum
					Tackles			Miscellaneous				Interceptions				Punt Returns				Kickoff Returns				Totals	
1991	Kansas City Chiefs	16	2	15	6	1.0	0	1	0	0	0	0	-	0	0	0	-	0	0	0	-	0	0	0
1992	Kansas City Chiefs	15	3	28	13	0.0	0	1	0	0	1	36	36.0	1	0	0	-	0	0	0	-	0	1	0
1993	Kansas City Chiefs	16	15	47	26	2.0	6	1	0	0	1	20	20.0	0	0	0	-	0	1	0	0.0	0	0	0
1994	Tampa Bay Buccaneers	16	14	36	19	0.0	1	2	0	0	0	0	-	0	0	0	-	0	0	0	-	0	0	0
1995	Tampa Bay Buccaneers	15	13	48	21	0.0	0	1	0	0	1	8	8.0	0	0	0	-	0	0	0	-	0	0	0
	5 NFL Seasons	78	47	174	85	3.0	7	6	0	0	3	64	21.3	1	0	0	-	0	1	0	0.0	0	1	0

Russell Maryland

Pos: DT **Rnd:** 1 (1) **College:** Miami (FL)   **Ht:** 6' 1" **Wt:** 279 **Born:** 3/22/69 **Age:** 27

Year	Team	G	GS	Tk	Ast	Sack	FF	FR	TD	Blk	Int	Yds	Avg	TD	Sfty	TD	Pts
					Tackles			Miscellaneous				Interceptions				Totals	
1991	Dallas Cowboys	16	7	20	13	4.5	3	0	0	0	0	0	-	0	0	0	0
1992	Dallas Cowboys	14	13	26	23	2.5	1	2	1	0	0	0	-	0	0	1	6
1993	Dallas Cowboys	16	12	32	24	2.5	2	2	0	0	0	0	-	0	0	0	0

Year	Team	G	GS	Tackles			Miscellaneous				Interceptions				Totals		
				Tk	Ast	Sack	FF	FR	TD	Blk	Int	Yds	Avg	TD	Sfty	TD	Pts
1994	Dallas Cowboys	16	16	28	2	3.0	0	1	0	0	0	0	-	0	0	0	0
1995	Dallas Cowboys	13	13	25	6	2.0	1	0	0	0	0	0	-	0	0	0	0
	5 NFL Seasons	75	61	131	68	14.5	7	5	1	0	0	0	-	0	0	1	6

Eddie Mason

Pos: LB **Rnd:** 6 **College:** North Carolina **Ht:** 6' 0" **Wt:** 230 **Born:** 1/9/72 **Age:** 24

Year	Team	G	GS	Tackles			Miscellaneous				Interceptions				Totals		
				Tk	Ast	Sack	FF	FR	TD	Blk	Int	Yds	Avg	TD	Sfty	TD	Pts
1995	New York Jets	15	0	0	1	0.0	0	0	0	0	0	0	-	0	0	0	0

Robert Massey

Pos: CB/S **Rnd:** 2 **College:** North Carolina Central **Ht:** 5' 11" **Wt:** 195 **Born:** 2/17/67 **Age:** 29

Year	Team	G	GS	Tackles			Miscellaneous				Interceptions				Punt Returns				Kickoff Returns				Totals	
				Tk	Ast	Sack	FF	FR	TD	Blk	Int	Yds	Avg	TD	Num	Yds	Avg	TD	Num	Yds	Avg	TD	TD	Fum
1989	New Orleans Saints	16	16	79	8	0.0	0	0	0	0	5	26	5.2	0	0	54	-	0	0	0	-	0	0	0
1990	New Orleans Saints	16	16	67	11	0.0	0	2	0	0	0	0	-	0	0	0	-	0	0	0	-	0	0	0
1991	Phoenix Cardinals	12	5	13	9	0.0	0	1	0	0	0	0	-	0	0	0	-	0	0	0	-	0	0	0
1992	Phoenix Cardinals	15	12	32	8	0.0	0	0	0	0	5	147	29.4	3	0	0	-	0	0	0	-	0	3	0
1993	Phoenix Cardinals	10	10	41	6	0.0	1	2	0	0	0	0	-	0	0	0	-	0	0	0	-	0	0	0
1994	Detroit Lions	16	15	53	15	0.0	0	0	0	0	4	25	6.3	0	1	3	3.0	0	0	0	-	0	0	1
1995	Detroit Lions	16	16	40	10	0.0	0	0	0	0	0	0	-	0	0	0	-	0	0	0	-	0	0	0
	7 NFL Seasons	101	77	325	67	0.0	1	5	0	0	14	198	14.1	3	1	57	57.0	0	0	0	-	0	3	1

Other Statistics: 1990–credited with 1 safety.

Le'Shai Maston

Pos: RB **Rnd:** FA **College:** Baylor **Ht:** 6' 0" **Wt:** 229 **Born:** 10/7/70 **Age:** 26

Year	Team	G	GS	Rushing					Receiving					Punt Returns				Kickoff Returns				Totals		
				Att	Yds	Avg	Lg	TD	Rec	Yds	Avg	Lg	TD	Num	Yds	Avg	TD	Num	Yds	Avg	TD	Fum	TD	Pts
1993	Houston Oilers	10	0	1	10	10.0	10	0	1	14	14.0	14	0	0	0	-	0	0	0	-	0	1	0	0
1994	Houston Oilers	7	1	0	0	-	-	0	2	12	6.0	10	0	0	0	-	0	0	0	-	0	0	0	0
1995	Jacksonville Jaguars	16	10	41	186	4.5	21	0	18	131	7.3	19	0	0	0	-	0	1	5	5.0	0	3	0	0
	3 NFL Seasons	33	11	42	196	4.7	21	0	21	157	7.5	19	0	0	0	-	0	1	5	5.0	0	4	0	0

Other Statistics: 1995–recovered 1 fumble for 4 yards.

Jason Mathews

Pos: T **Rnd:** 3 **College:** Texas A&M **Ht:** 6' 5" **Wt:** 288 **Born:** 2/9/71 **Age:** 25

Year	Team	G	GS	Year	Team	G	GS			G	GS
1994	Indianapolis Colts	10	0	1995	Indianapolis Colts	16	16		2 NFL Seasons	26	16

Terance Mathis

(statistical profile on page 349)

Pos: WR **Rnd:** 6 **College:** New Mexico **Ht:** 5' 10" **Wt:** 180 **Born:** 6/7/67 **Age:** 29

Year	Team	G	GS	Rushing					Receiving					Punt Returns				Kickoff Returns				Totals		
				Att	Yds	Avg	Lg	TD	Rec	Yds	Avg	Lg	TD	Num	Yds	Avg	TD	Num	Yds	Avg	TD	Fum	TD	Pts
1990	New York Jets	16	1	2	9	4.5	10	0	19	245	12.9	23	0	11	165	15.0	1	43	787	18.3	0	1	1	6
1991	New York Jets	16	0	1	19	19.0	19	0	28	329	11.8	39	1	23	157	6.8	0	29	599	20.7	0	4	1	6
1992	New York Jets	16	0	3	25	8.3	t10	1	22	316	14.4	t55	3	2	24	12.0	0	28	492	17.6	0	2	4	24
1993	New York Jets	16	3	2	20	10.0	t17	1	24	352	14.7	46	0	14	99	7.1	0	7	102	14.6	0	5	1	6
1994	Atlanta Falcons	16	16	0	0	-	-	0	111	1342	12.1	81	11	0	0	-	0	0	0	-	0	0	11	70
1995	Atlanta Falcons	14	12	0	0	-	-	0	78	1039	13.3	t54	9	0	0	-	0	0	0	-	0	1	9	60
	6 NFL Seasons	94	32	8	73	9.1	19	2	282	3623	12.8	81	24	50	445	8.9	1	107	1980	18.5	0	13	27	172

Other Statistics: 1991–recovered 1 fumble for 0 yards. 1992–recovered 1 fumble for 0 yards. 1993–recovered 1 fumble for 0 yards. 1994–recovered 1 fumble for 0 yards; scored 2 two-point conversions. 1995–scored 3 two-point conversions.

Trevor Matich

Pos: LS/C **Rnd:** 1 (28) **College:** Brigham Young **Ht:** 6' 4" **Wt:** 297 **Born:** 10/9/61 **Age:** 35

Year	Team	G	GS	Year	Team	G	GS	Year	Team	G	GS	Year	Team	G	GS
1985	New England Patriots	1	0	1988	New England Patriots	8	6	1991	New York Jets	15	0	1994	Washington Redskins	16	0
1986	New England Patriots	11	1	1989	Detroit Lions	11	0	1992	Indianapolis Colts	16	1	1995	Washington Redskins	16	0
1987	New England Patriots	6	4	1990	New York Jets	16	0	1993	Indianapolis Colts	16	4		11 NFL Seasons	132	22

Other Statistics: 1990–recovered 1 fumble for 0 yards. 1991–caught 3 passes for 23 yards and 1 touchdown. 1995–fumbled 1 time for -2 yards.

Aubrey Matthews

Pos: WR **Rnd:** FA **College:** Delta State **Ht:** 5' 7" **Wt:** 165 **Born:** 9/15/62 **Age:** 34

			Rushing					Receiving					Punt Returns				Kickoff Returns				Totals		
Year	Team	G	GS	Att	Yds	Avg	Lg	TD	Rec	Yds	Avg	Lg	TD	Num	Yds	Avg	TD	Num	Yds	Avg	TD	Fum	TD	Pts
1986	Atlanta Falcons	4	0	1	12	12.0	12	0	1	25	25.0	25	0	0	0	-	0	3	42	14.0	0	0	0	0
1987	Atlanta Falcons	12	6	1	-4	-4.0	-4	0	32	537	16.8	57	3	0	0	-	0	0	0	-	0	2	3	18
1988	Atl - GB	11	2	3	3	1.0	4	0	20	231	11.6	25	2	6	26	4.3	0	0	0	-	0	2	2	12
1989	Green Bay Packers	13	3	0	0	-	-	0	18	200	11.1	25	0	0	0	-	0	0	0	-	0	0	0	0
1990	Detroit Lions	13	6	0	0	-	-	0	30	349	11.6	52	1	0	0	-	0	0	0	-	0	2	1	6
1991	Detroit Lions	1	1	0	0	-	-	0	3	21	7.0	11	0	0	0	-	0	0	0	-	0	0	0	0
1992	Detroit Lions	13	0	0	0	-	-	0	9	137	15.2	24	0	0	0	-	0	0	0	-	0	0	0	0
1993	Detroit Lions	15	2	2	7	3.5	9	0	11	171	15.5	40	0	0	0	-	0	0	0	-	0	0	0	0
1994	Detroit Lions	14	3	0	0	-	-	0	29	359	12.4	33	3	0	0	-	0	0	0	-	0	1	3	18
1995	Detroit Lions	12	0	0	0	-	-	0	4	41	10.3	12	0	0	0	-	0	0	0	-	0	0	0	0
1988	Atlanta Falcons	4	0	0	0	-	-	0	5	64	12.8	21	0	6	26	4.3	0	0	0	-	0	2	0	0
	Green Bay Packers	7	2	3	3	1.0	4	0	15	167	11.1	25	2	0	0	-	0	0	0	-	0	0	2	12
	10 NFL Seasons	108	23	7	18	2.6	12	0	157	2071	13.2	57	9	6	26	4.3	0	3	42	14.0	0	7	9	54

Other Statistics: 1987–recovered 1 fumble for 0 yards.

Bruce Matthews

Pos: G/LS **Rnd:** 1 (9) **College:** Southern California **Ht:** 6' 5" **Wt:** 298 **Born:** 8/8/61 **Age:** 35

Year	Team	G	GS	Year	Team	G	GS	Year	Team	G	GS	Year	Team	G	GS
1983	Houston Oilers	16	15	1987	Houston Oilers	8	5	1991	Houston Oilers	16	16	1995	Houston Oilers	16	16
1984	Houston Oilers	16	16	1988	Houston Oilers	16	16	1992	Houston Oilers	16	16				
1985	Houston Oilers	16	16	1989	Houston Oilers	16	16	1993	Houston Oilers	16	16				
1986	Houston Oilers	16	16	1990	Houston Oilers	16	16	1994	Houston Oilers	16	16		13 NFL Seasons	200	196

Other Statistics: 1985–recovered 3 fumbles for 0 yards. 1986–recovered 1 fumble for 7 yards. 1989–recovered 1 fumble for -29 yards; fumbled 2 times. 1990–recovered 1 fumble for 0 yards. 1991–recovered 1 fumble for -3 yards; fumbled 1 time. 1994–fumbled 2 times for -7 yards.

Clay Matthews

(statistical profile on page 430)

Pos: LB **Rnd:** 1 (12) **College:** Southern California **Ht:** 6' 2" **Wt:** 245 **Born:** 3/15/56 **Age:** 40

				Tackles			Miscellaneous				Interceptions				Totals		
Year	Team	G	GS	Tk	Ast	Sack	FF	FR	TD	Blk	Int	Yds	Avg	TD	Sfty	TD	Pts
1978	Cleveland Browns	15	2	34	-	1.0	0	0	0	0	1	5	5.0	0	0	0	0
1979	Cleveland Browns	16	16	103	-	2.0	0	2	0	0	1	30	30.0	0	0	0	0
1980	Cleveland Browns	14	13	83	-	5.0	0	1	0	0	1	6	6.0	0	0	0	0
1981	Cleveland Browns	16	16	128	-	5.0	0	2	0	0	2	14	7.0	0	0	0	0
1982	Cleveland Browns	2	1	11	-	0.0	0	0	0	0	0	0	-	0	0	0	0
1983	Cleveland Browns	16	16	106	-	6.0	4	0	0	0	0	0	-	0	0	0	0
1984	Cleveland Browns	16	16	126	-	12.0	3	1	0	0	0	0	-	0	0	0	0
1985	Cleveland Browns	14	14	88	-	6.0	1	1	0	0	0	0	-	0	0	0	0
1986	Cleveland Browns	16	16	89	-	1.0	2	0	0	0	2	12	6.0	0	0	0	0
1987	Cleveland Browns	12	12	72	-	2.5	0	2	0	0	3	62	20.7	1	0	1	6
1988	Cleveland Browns	16	16	101	-	6.0	0	2	0	0	0	0	-	0	0	0	0
1989	Cleveland Browns	16	16	113	-	4.0	3	2	1	0	1	25	25.0	0	0	1	6
1990	Cleveland Browns	16	16	102	-	3.5	3	0	0	0	0	0	-	0	0	0	0
1991	Cleveland Browns	15	15	80	-	6.5	3	0	0	0	1	35	35.0	0	0	0	0
1992	Cleveland Browns	16	16	111	-	9.0	3	0	0	0	1	6	6.0	0	0	0	0
1993	Cleveland Browns	16	15	39	44	5.5	2	0	0	0	1	10	10.0	0	0	0	0
1994	Atlanta Falcons	15	15	71	19	1.0	0	0	0	0	0	0	-	0	0	0	0
1995	Atlanta Falcons	16	16	49	14	0.0	0	1	0	0	2	1	0.5	0	0	0	0
	18 NFL Seasons	263	247	1506	77	63.0	24	14	1	0	16	206	12.9	1	0	2	12

Other Statistics: 1989–fumbled 1 time.

Chris Maumalanga

Pos: DT **Rnd:** 4 **College:** Kansas **Ht:** 6' 2" **Wt:** 292 **Born:** 12/15/71 **Age:** 24

				Tackles			Miscellaneous				Interceptions				Totals		
Year	Team	G	GS	Tk	Ast	Sack	FF	FR	TD	Blk	Int	Yds	Avg	TD	Sfty	TD	Pts
1994	New York Giants	7	0	6	1	0.0	1	0	0	0	0	0	-	0	0	0	0
1995	Arizona Cardinals	9	0	0	1	0.0	0	0	0	0	0	0	-	0	0	0	0
	2 NFL Seasons	16	0	6	2	0.0	1	0	0	0	0	0	-	0	0	0	0

Kevin Mawae

Pos: G **Rnd:** 2 **College:** Louisiana State **Ht:** 6' 4" **Wt:** 288 **Born:** 1/23/71 **Age:** 25

Year	Team	G	GS	Year	Team	G	GS				
1994	Seattle Seahawks	14	11	1995	Seattle Seahawks	16	16		2 NFL Seasons	30	27

Other Statistics: 1994–recovered 1 fumble for 0 yards.

163

Brett Maxie

(statistical profile on page 431)

Pos: S **Rnd:** FA **College:** Texas Southern **Ht:** 6' 2" **Wt:** 194 **Born:** 1/13/62 **Age:** 34

				Tackles			Miscellaneous				Interceptions				Punt Returns				Kickoff Returns				Totals	
Year	Team	G	GS	Tk	Ast	Sack	FF	FR	TD	Blk	Int	Yds	Avg	TD	Num	Yds	Avg	TD	Num	Yds	Avg	TD	TD	Fum
1985	New Orleans Saints	16	1	31	6	0.0	0	1	0	0	0	0	-	0	0	0	-	0	0	0	-	0	0	0
1986	New Orleans Saints	15	0	37	11	0.0	0	1	0	0	2	15	7.5	0	0	0	-	0	0	0	-	0	0	0
1987	New Orleans Saints	12	10	35	13	2.0	0	0	0	0	3	17	5.7	0	1	12	12.0	0	0	0	-	0	0	0
1988	New Orleans Saints	16	16	57	21	0.0	0	0	0	0	0	0	-	0	0	0	-	0	0	0	-	0	0	0
1989	New Orleans Saints	16	2	35	6	0.0	0	1	0	0	3	41	13.7	1	0	0	-	0	0	0	-	0	1	0
1990	New Orleans Saints	16	16	58	15	0.0	0	0	0	0	2	88	44.0	1	0	0	-	0	0	0	-	0	1	0
1991	New Orleans Saints	16	16	43	15	0.0	0	1	0	0	3	33	11.0	1	0	0	-	0	0	0	-	0	1	0
1992	New Orleans Saints	10	10	37	11	1.0	0	1	0	0	2	12	6.0	0	0	0	-	0	0	0	-	0	0	0
1993	New Orleans Saints	1	1	4	3	0.0	0	0	0	0	0	0	-	0	0	0	-	0	0	0	-	0	0	0
1994	Atlanta Falcons	4	2	3	3	0.0	0	0	0	0	0	0	-	0	0	0	-	0	0	0	-	0	0	0
1995	Carolina Panthers	16	16	71	18	0.0	1	1	0	0	6	59	9.8	0	0	0	-	0	0	0	-	0	0	0
	11 NFL Seasons	138	90	411	122	3.0	1	6	0	0	21	265	12.6	3	1	12	12.0	0	0	0	-	0	3	0

Other Statistics: 1987–credited with 1 safety.

Deems May

Pos: TE **Rnd:** 7 **College:** North Carolina **Ht:** 6' 4" **Wt:** 263 **Born:** 3/6/69 **Age:** 27

				Rushing					Receiving					Punt Returns				Kickoff Returns				Totals		
Year	Team	G	GS	Att	Yds	Avg	Lg	TD	Rec	Yds	Avg	Lg	TD	Num	Yds	Avg	TD	Num	Yds	Avg	TD	Fum	TD	Pts
1992	San Diego Chargers	16	6	0	0	-	-	0	0	0	-	-	0	0	0	-	0	0	0	-	0	0	0	0
1993	San Diego Chargers	15	1	0	0	-	-	0	0	0	-	-	0	0	0	-	0	0	0	-	0	0	0	0
1994	San Diego Chargers	5	2	0	0	-	-	0	2	22	11.0	18	0	0	0	-	0	0	0	-	0	0	0	0
1995	San Diego Chargers	5	0	0	0	-	-	0	0	-	-	-	0	0	0	-	0	0	0	-	0	0	0	0
	4 NFL Seasons	41	9	0	0	-	-	0	2	22	11.0	18	0	0	0	-	0	0	0	-	0	0	0	0

Sheriden May

Pos: RB **Rnd:** FA **College:** Idaho **Ht:** 6' 0" **Wt:** 215 **Born:** 8/10/73 **Age:** 23

				Rushing					Receiving					Punt Returns				Kickoff Returns				Totals		
Year	Team	G	GS	Att	Yds	Avg	Lg	TD	Rec	Yds	Avg	Lg	TD	Num	Yds	Avg	TD	Num	Yds	Avg	TD	Fum	TD	Pts
1995	New York Jets	5	1	2	5	2.5	3	0	0	0	-	-	0	0	0	-	0	0	0	-	0	0	0	0

Tony Mayberry

Pos: C **Rnd:** 4 **College:** Wake Forest **Ht:** 6' 4" **Wt:** 292 **Born:** 12/8/67 **Age:** 28

Year	Team	G	GS	Year	Team	G	GS	Year	Team	G	GS			G	GS
1990	Tampa Bay Buccaneers	16	16	1992	Tampa Bay Buccaneers	16	16	1994	Tampa Bay Buccaneers	16	16				
1991	Tampa Bay Buccaneers	16	16	1993	Tampa Bay Buccaneers	16	16	1995	Tampa Bay Buccaneers	16	16		6 NFL Seasons	96	81

Other Statistics: 1991–fumbled 3 times for -17 yards. 1993–recovered 1 fumble for -6 yards; fumbled 1 time. 1994–recovered 1 fumble for 0 yards.

Corey Mayfield

Pos: DT **Rnd:** 10 **College:** Oklahoma **Ht:** 6' 3" **Wt:** 302 **Born:** 2/25/70 **Age:** 26

				Tackles			Miscellaneous				Interceptions				Punt Returns				Kickoff Returns				Totals	
Year	Team	G	GS	Tk	Ast	Sack	FF	FR	TD	Blk	Int	Yds	Avg	TD	Num	Yds	Avg	TD	Num	Yds	Avg	TD	TD	Fum
1992	Tampa Bay Buccaneers	11	0	2	1	0.0	1	0	0	0	0	0	-	0	0	0	-	0	2	22	11.0	0	0	0
1995	Jacksonville Jaguars	16	4	19	6	1.5	0	1	0	0	0	0	-	0	0	0	-	0	0	0	-	0	0	0
	2 NFL Seasons	27	4	21	7	1.5	1	1	0	0	0	0	-	0	0	0	-	0	2	22	11.0	0	0	0

Martin Mayhew

(statistical profile on page 431)

Pos: CB **Rnd:** 10 **College:** Florida State **Ht:** 5' 8" **Wt:** 178 **Born:** 10/8/65 **Age:** 31

				Tackles			Miscellaneous				Interceptions				Punt Returns				Kickoff Returns				Totals	
Year	Team	G	GS	Tk	Ast	Sack	FF	FR	TD	Blk	Int	Yds	Avg	TD	Num	Yds	Avg	TD	Num	Yds	Avg	TD	TD	Fum
1989	Washington Redskins	16	7	41	6	0.0	0	0	0	0	0	0	-	0	1	0	0.0	0	0	0	-	0	0	1
1990	Washington Redskins	16	15	84	20	0.0	0	0	0	0	7	20	2.9	0	0	0	-	0	0	0	-	0	0	0
1991	Washington Redskins	16	16	78	30	0.0	0	1	0	0	3	31	10.3	1	0	0	-	0	0	0	-	0	0	0
1992	Washington Redskins	10	10	45	17	0.0	0	1	0	0	3	58	19.3	0	0	0	-	0	0	0	-	0	1	0
1993	Tampa Bay Buccaneers	15	14	48	28	0.0	2	0	0	0	0	0	-	0	0	0	-	0	0	0	-	0	0	0
1994	Tampa Bay Buccaneers	16	16	58	11	0.0	0	1	0	0	2	4	2.0	0	0	0	-	0	0	0	-	0	0	0
1995	Tampa Bay Buccaneers	13	13	58	17	0.0	1	1	1	0	5	81	16.2	0	0	0	-	0	0	0	-	0	1	0
	7 NFL Seasons	102	91	412	129	0.0	3	4	1	0	20	194	9.7	1	1	0	0.0	0	0	0	-	0	2	1

Alvoid Mays

Pos: CB **Rnd:** 8 **College:** West Virginia **Ht:** 5' 9" **Wt:** 172 **Born:** 7/10/66 **Age:** 30

Year Team	G	GS	Tk	Ast	Sack	FF	FR	TD	Blk	Int	Yds	Avg	TD	Num	Yds	Avg	TD	Num	Yds	Avg	TD	TD	Fum
			Tackles			Miscellaneous				Interceptions				Punt Returns				Kickoff Returns				Totals	
1990 Washington Redskins	15	1	9	4	0.0	0	1	0	0	0	0	-	0	0	0	-	0	0	0	-	0	0	0
1991 Washington Redskins	13	0	18	10	0.0	0	1	0	0	1	0	0.0	0	0	0	-	0	0	0	-	0	0	0
1992 Washington Redskins	16	3	34	18	1.0	0	0	0	0	2	18	9.0	0	0	0	-	0	0	0	-	0	0	0
1993 Washington Redskins	15	2	20	4	0.0	0	0	0	0	0	0	-	0	1	0	0.0	0	0	0	-	0	0	1
1994 Washington Redskins	2	0	6	1	0.0	1	0	0	0	0	0	-	0	0	0	-	0	0	0	-	0	0	0
1995 Pittsburgh Steelers	13	6	34	3	0.0	1	0	0	0	2	35	17.5	1	0	0	-	0	0	0	-	0	1	0
6 NFL Seasons	74	12	121	40	1.0	2	2	0	0	5	53	10.6	1	1	0	0.0	0	0	0	-	0	1	1

Fred McAfee

Pos: RB **Rnd:** 6 **College:** Mississippi College **Ht:** 5' 10" **Wt:** 193 **Born:** 6/20/68 **Age:** 28

Year Team	G	GS	Att	Yds	Avg	Lg	TD	Rec	Yds	Avg	Lg	TD	Num	Yds	Avg	TD	Num	Yds	Avg	TD	Fum	TD	Pts
			Rushing					Receiving					Punt Returns				Kickoff Returns				Totals		
1991 New Orleans Saints	9	0	109	494	4.5	34	2	1	8	8.0	8	0	0	0	-	0	1	14	14.0	0	2	2	12
1992 New Orleans Saints	14	1	39	114	2.9	19	1	1	16	16.0	16	0	0	0	-	0	19	393	20.7	0	0	1	6
1993 New Orleans Saints	15	4	51	160	3.1	27	1	1	3	3.0	3	0	0	0	-	0	28	580	20.7	0	3	1	6
1994 Ari - Pit	13	0	18	51	2.8	13	2	1	4	4.0	4	0	0	0	-	0	7	113	16.1	0	1	2	12
1995 Pittsburgh Steelers	16	1	39	156	4.0	t22	1	15	88	5.9	18	0	0	0	-	0	5	56	11.2	0	0	1	6
1994 Arizona Cardinals	7	0	2	-5	-2.5	t2	1	1	4	4.0	4	0	0	0	-	0	7	113	16.1	0	1	1	6
Pittsburgh Steelers	6	0	16	56	3.5	13	1	0	0	-		0	0	0	-	0	0	0	-	0	0	1	6
5 NFL Seasons	67	6	256	975	3.8	34	7	19	119	6.3	18	0	0	0	-	0	60	1156	19.3	0	6	7	42

Other Statistics: 1995–recovered 1 fumble for 0 yards.

Oscar McBride

Pos: TE **Rnd:** FA **College:** Notre Dame **Ht:** 6' 5" **Wt:** 266 **Born:** 7/23/72 **Age:** 24

Year Team	G	GS	Att	Yds	Avg	Lg	TD	Rec	Yds	Avg	Lg	TD	Num	Yds	Avg	TD	Num	Yds	Avg	TD	Fum	TD	Pts
			Rushing					Receiving					Punt Returns				Kickoff Returns				Totals		
1995 Arizona Cardinals	16	10	0	0	-	-	0	13	112	8.6	24	2	0	0	-	0	0	0	-	0	0	2	12

Gerald McBurrows

Pos: S **Rnd:** 7 **College:** Kansas **Ht:** 5' 11" **Wt:** 188 **Born:** 10/7/73 **Age:** 23

Year Team	G	GS	Tk	Ast	Sack	FF	FR	TD	Blk	Int	Yds	Avg	TD	Sfty	TD	Pts
			Tackles			Miscellaneous				Interceptions				Totals		
1995 St. Louis Rams	14	3	23	4	1.0	0	0	0	0	0	0	-	0	0	0	0

Ed McCaffrey

(statistical profile on page 349)

Pos: WR **Rnd:** 3 **College:** Stanford **Ht:** 6' 5" **Wt:** 215 **Born:** 8/17/68 **Age:** 28

Year Team	G	GS	Att	Yds	Avg	Lg	TD	Rec	Yds	Avg	Lg	TD	Num	Yds	Avg	TD	Num	Yds	Avg	TD	Fum	TD	Pts
			Rushing					Receiving					Punt Returns				Kickoff Returns				Totals		
1991 New York Giants	16	0	0	0	-	-	0	16	146	9.1	26	0	0	0	-	0	0	0	-	0	0	0	0
1992 New York Giants	16	3	0	0	-	-	0	49	610	12.4	44	5	0	0	-	0	0	0	-	0	2	5	30
1993 New York Giants	16	1	0	0	-	-	0	27	335	12.4	31	2	0	0	-	0	0	0	-	0	0	2	12
1994 San Francisco 49ers	16	0	0	0	-	-	0	11	131	11.9	32	2	0	0	-	0	0	0	-	0	0	2	12
1995 Denver Broncos	16	5	1	-1	-1.0	-1	0	39	477	12.2	35	2	0	0	-	0	0	0	-	0	1	2	14
5 NFL Seasons	80	9	1	-1	-1.0	-1	0	142	1699	12.0	44	11	0	0	-	0	0	0	-	0	3	11	68

Other Statistics: 1995–scored 1 two-point conversion.

Keith McCants

Pos: DE/DT **Rnd:** 1 (4) **College:** Alabama **Ht:** 6' 3" **Wt:** 265 **Born:** 4/19/68 **Age:** 28

Year Team	G	GS	Tk	Ast	Sack	FF	FR	TD	Blk	Int	Yds	Avg	TD	Sfty	TD	Pts
			Tackles			Miscellaneous				Interceptions				Totals		
1990 Tampa Bay Buccaneers	15	4	27	17	2.0	0	1	0	0	0	0		0	0	0	0
1991 Tampa Bay Buccaneers	16	16	42	12	5.0	0	1	0	0	0	0	-	0	0	0	0
1992 Tampa Bay Buccaneers	16	15	40	18	5.0	0	1	0	0	0	0	-	0	0	0	0
1993 Houston Oilers	13	0	4	0	0.0	0	0	0	0	0	0	-	0	0	0	0
1994 Hou - Ari	12	2	17	3	1.0	0	1	0	0	1	46	46.0	1	0	1	6
1995 Arizona Cardinals	16	2	7	5	0.5	0	2	1	0	0	0	-	0	0	1	6
1994 Houston Oilers	4	1	3	2	0.0	0	1	0	0	0	0	-	0	0	0	0
Arizona Cardinals	8	1	14	1	1.0	0	1	0	0	1	46	46.0	1	0	1	6
6 NFL Seasons	88	39	137	55	13.5	0	6	1	0	1	46	46.0	1	0	2	12

Keenan McCardell

(statistical profile on page 350)

Pos: WR/PR **Rnd:** 12   **College:** UNLV   **Ht:** 6' 1" **Wt:** 175 **Born:** 1/6/70 **Age:** 26

Year Team	G	GS	Rushing					Receiving					Punt Returns				Kickoff Returns				Totals		
			Att	Yds	Avg	Lg	TD	Rec	Yds	Avg	Lg	TD	Num	Yds	Avg	TD	Num	Yds	Avg	TD	Fum	TD	Pts
1992 Cleveland Browns	2	0	0	0	-	-	0	1	8	8.0	8	0	0	0	-	0	0	0	-	0	0	0	0
1993 Cleveland Browns	4	3	0	0	-	-	0	13	234	18.0	43	4	0	0	-	0	0	0	-	0	0	4	24
1994 Cleveland Browns	14	3	0	0	-	-	0	10	182	18.2	34	0	0	0	-	0	0	0	-	0	0	0	0
1995 Cleveland Browns	16	5	0	0	-	-	0	56	709	12.7	36	4	13	93	7.2	0	9	161	17.9	0	0	4	24
4 NFL Seasons	36	11	0	0	-	-	0	80	1133	14.2	43	8	13	93	7.2	0	9	161	17.9	0	0	8	48

J.J. McCleskey

Pos: S/CB **Rnd:** FA   **College:** Tennessee   **Ht:** 5' 7" **Wt:** 177 **Born:** 4/10/70 **Age:** 26

Year Team	G	GS	Tackles			Miscellaneous				Interceptions				Punt Returns				Kickoff Returns				Totals	
			Tk	Ast	Sack	FF	FR	TD	Blk	Int	Yds	Avg	TD	Num	Yds	Avg	TD	Num	Yds	Avg	TD	TD	Fum
1994 New Orleans Saints	13	0	0	0	0.0	0	1	0	0	0	0	-	0	0	0	-	0	0	0	-	0	0	0
1995 New Orleans Saints	14	1	1	0	0.0	0	1	0	0	1	0	0.0	0	0	0	-	0	1	0	0.0	0	0	0
2 NFL Seasons	27	1	1	0	0.0	0	2	0	0	1	0	0.0	0	0	0	-	0	1	0	0.0	0	0	0

Andy McCollum

Pos: G/C **Rnd:** FA   **College:** Toledo   **Ht:** 6' 5" **Wt:** 270 **Born:** 6/6/70 **Age:** 26

Year Team	G	GS							
1995 New Orleans Saints	11	9						G	GS
						1 NFL Season		11	9

Hurvin McCormack

Pos: DT/DE **Rnd:** FA   **College:** Indiana   **Ht:** 6' 5" **Wt:** 274 **Born:** 4/6/72 **Age:** 24

Year Team	G	GS	Tackles			Miscellaneous				Interceptions				Totals		
			Tk	Ast	Sack	FF	FR	TD	Blk	Int	Yds	Avg	TD	Sfty	TD	Pts
1994 Dallas Cowboys	3	0	0	0	0.0	0	0	0	0	0	0	-	0	0	0	0
1995 Dallas Cowboys	14	2	14	3	2.0	0	0	0	0	0	0	-	0	0	0	0
2 NFL Seasons	17	2	14	3	2.0	0	0	0	0	0	0	-	0	0	0	0

Kez McCorvey

Pos: WR **Rnd:** 5   **College:** Florida State   **Ht:** 6' 0" **Wt:** 180 **Born:** 1/23/72 **Age:** 24

Year Team	G	GS	Rushing					Receiving					Punt Returns				Kickoff Returns				Totals		
			Att	Yds	Avg	Lg	TD	Rec	Yds	Avg	Lg	TD	Num	Yds	Avg	TD	Num	Yds	Avg	TD	Fum	TD	Pts
1995 Detroit Lions	2	0	0	0	-	-	0	0	0	-	-	0	0	0	-	0	0	0	-	0	0	0	0

Tony McCoy

(statistical profile on page 431)

Pos: DT **Rnd:** 4   **College:** Florida   **Ht:** 6' 0" **Wt:** 282 **Born:** 6/10/69 **Age:** 27

Year Team	G	GS	Tackles			Miscellaneous				Interceptions				Totals		
			Tk	Ast	Sack	FF	FR	TD	Blk	Int	Yds	Avg	TD	Sfty	TD	Pts
1992 Indianapolis Colts	16	3	5	5	1.0	0	1	0	0	0	0	-	0	0	0	0
1993 Indianapolis Colts	6	0	1	0	0.0	0	0	0	0	0	0	-	0	0	0	0
1994 Indianapolis Colts	15	15	56	15	6.0	1	1	0	0	0	0	-	0	0	0	0
1995 Indianapolis Colts	16	16	50	18	2.5	2	0	0	0	0	0	-	0	0	0	0
4 NFL Seasons	53	34	112	38	9.5	3	2	0	0	0	0	-	0	0	0	0

Fred McCrary

Pos: RB **Rnd:** 6   **College:** Mississippi State   **Ht:** 6' 0" **Wt:** 210 **Born:** 9/19/72 **Age:** 24

Year Team	G	GS	Rushing					Receiving					Punt Returns				Kickoff Returns				Totals		
			Att	Yds	Avg	Lg	TD	Rec	Yds	Avg	Lg	TD	Num	Yds	Avg	TD	Num	Yds	Avg	TD	Fum	TD	Pts
1995 Philadelphia Eagles	13	5	3	1	0.3	t1	1	9	60	6.7	11	0	0	0	-	0	1	1	1.0	0	0	1	6

Michael McCrary

Pos: DE **Rnd:** 7   **College:** Wake Forest   **Ht:** 6' 4" **Wt:** 267 **Born:** 7/7/70 **Age:** 26

Year Team	G	GS	Tackles			Miscellaneous				Interceptions				Totals		
			Tk	Ast	Sack	FF	FR	TD	Blk	Int	Yds	Avg	TD	Sfty	TD	Pts
1993 Seattle Seahawks	15	0	7	1	4.0	2	0	0	0	0	0	-	0	0	0	0
1994 Seattle Seahawks	16	0	9	2	1.5	0	0	0	0	0	0	-	0	0	0	0
1995 Seattle Seahawks	11	0	7	2	1.0	0	0	0	0	0	0	-	0	0	0	0
3 NFL Seasons	42	0	23	5	6.5	2	0	0	0	0	0	-	0	0	0	0

Ed McDaniel

(statistical profile on page 432)

Pos: LB **Rnd:** 5 **College:** Clemson   **Ht:** 5' 11" **Wt:** 231 **Born:** 2/23/69 **Age:** 27

Year Team	G	GS	Tackles			Miscellaneous				Interceptions				Totals		
			Tk	Ast	Sack	FF	FR	TD	Blk	Int	Yds	Avg	TD	Sfty	TD	Pts
1992 Minnesota Vikings	8	0	8	1	0.0	0	0	0	0	0	0	-	0	0	0	0
1993 Minnesota Vikings	7	1	16	5	0.0	0	0	0	0	0	0	-	0	0	0	0
1994 Minnesota Vikings	16	16	89	30	1.5	1	0	0	0	1	0	0.0	0	0	0	0
1995 Minnesota Vikings	16	16	87	30	4.5	6	1	0	0	1	3	3.0	0	0	0	0
4 NFL Seasons	47	33	200	66	6.0	7	1	0	0	2	3	1.5	0	0	0	0

Randall McDaniel

Pos: G **Rnd:** 1 (19) **College:** Arizona State   **Ht:** 6' 3" **Wt:** 274 **Born:** 12/19/64 **Age:** 31

Year	Team	G	GS	Year	Team	G	GS	Year	Team	G	GS	Year	Team	G	GS
1988	Minnesota Vikings	16	15	1990	Minnesota Vikings	16	16	1992	Minnesota Vikings	16	16	1994	Minnesota Vikings	16	16
1989	Minnesota Vikings	14	13	1991	Minnesota Vikings	16	16	1993	Minnesota Vikings	16	16	1995	Minnesota Vikings	16	16
													8 NFL Seasons	126	124

Other Statistics: 1991–recovered 1 fumble for 0 yards. 1994–recovered 1 fumble for 0 yards.

Terry McDaniel

(statistical profile on page 432)

Pos: CB **Rnd:** 1 (9) **College:** Tennessee   **Ht:** 5' 10" **Wt:** 180 **Born:** 2/8/65 **Age:** 31

Year Team	G	GS	Tackles			Miscellaneous				Interceptions				Totals		
			Tk	Ast	Sack	FF	FR	TD	Blk	Int	Yds	Avg	TD	Sfty	TD	Pts
1988 Los Angeles Raiders	2	2	0	0	0.0	0	0	0	0	0	0	-	0	0	0	0
1989 Los Angeles Raiders	16	15	68	-	1.0	0	0	0	0	3	21	7.0	0	0	0	0
1990 Los Angeles Raiders	16	13	0	-	2.0	0	2	1	0	3	20	6.7	0	0	1	6
1991 Los Angeles Raiders	16	16	77	-	0.0	2	1	0	0	0	0	-	0	0	0	0
1992 Los Angeles Raiders	16	16	63	-	0.0	0	1	0	0	4	180	45.0	0	0	0	0
1993 Los Angeles Raiders	16	16	62	6	0.0	2	0	0	0	5	87	17.4	1	0	1	6
1994 Los Angeles Raiders	16	16	50	11	0.0	1	3	1	0	7	103	14.7	2	0	3	18
1995 Oakland Raiders	16	16	51	5	0.0	0	0	0	0	6	46	7.7	1	0	1	6
8 NFL Seasons	114	110	371	22	3.0	5	7	2	0	28	457	16.3	4	0	6	36

Pellom McDaniels

Pos: DE **Rnd:** FA **College:** Oregon State   **Ht:** 6' 3" **Wt:** 292 **Born:** 2/21/68 **Age:** 28

Year Team	G	GS	Tackles			Miscellaneous				Interceptions				Punt Returns				Kickoff Returns				Totals	
			Tk	Ast	Sack	FF	FR	TD	Blk	Int	Yds	Avg	TD	Num	Yds	Avg	TD	Num	Yds	Avg	TD	TD	Fum
1993 Kansas City Chiefs	10	0	16	-	0.0	0	0	0	0	0	0	-	0	0	0	-	0	0	0	-	0	0	0
1994 Kansas City Chiefs	12	3	11	1	2.0	1	1	0	0	0	0	-	0	0	0	-	0	0	0	-	0	0	0
1995 Kansas City Chiefs	16	2	16	1	2.0	0	0	0	0	0	0	-	0	0	0	-	0	1	0	0.0	0	0	0
3 NFL Seasons	38	5	43	2	4.0	1	1	0	0	0	0	-	0	0	0	-	0	1	0	0.0	0	0	0

Devon McDonald

Pos: LB **Rnd:** 4 **College:** Notre Dame   **Ht:** 6' 4" **Wt:** 228 **Born:** 11/8/69 **Age:** 26

Year Team	G	GS	Tackles			Miscellaneous				Interceptions				Totals		
			Tk	Ast	Sack	FF	FR	TD	Blk	Int	Yds	Avg	TD	Sfty	TD	Pts
1993 Indianapolis Colts	16	0	1	1	0.0	0	0	0	0	0	0	-	0	0	0	0
1994 Indianapolis Colts	16	4	19	12	1.0	0	1	0	0	0	0	-	0	0	0	0
1995 Indianapolis Colts	15	0	8	6	0.0	0	0	0	0	0	0	-	0	0	0	0
3 NFL Seasons	47	4	28	19	1.0	0	1	0	0	0	0	-	0	0	0	0

Ricardo McDonald

(statistical profile on page 432)

Pos: LB **Rnd:** 4 **College:** Pittsburgh   **Ht:** 6' 2" **Wt:** 235 **Born:** 11/8/69 **Age:** 26

Year Team	G	GS	Tackles			Miscellaneous				Interceptions				Totals		
			Tk	Ast	Sack	FF	FR	TD	Blk	Int	Yds	Avg	TD	Sfty	TD	Pts
1992 Cincinnati Bengals	16	13	71	24	0.0	0	1	0	0	1	0	0.0	0	0	0	0
1993 Cincinnati Bengals	14	12	87	15	1.0	1	0	0	0	0	0	-	0	0	0	0
1994 Cincinnati Bengals	13	13	30	15	1.0	1	0	0	0	0	0	-	0	0	0	0
1995 Cincinnati Bengals	16	15	46	17	5.0	1	1	0	0	0	0	-	0	0	0	0
4 NFL Seasons	59	53	234	71	7.0	3	2	0	0	1	0	0.0	0	0	0	0

Tim McDonald

(statistical profile on page 433)

Pos: S **Rnd:** 2 **College:** Southern California   **Ht:** 6' 2" **Wt:** 215 **Born:** 1/6/65 **Age:** 31

Year Team	G	GS	Tackles			Miscellaneous				Interceptions				Totals		
			Tk	Ast	Sack	FF	FR	TD	Blk	Int	Yds	Avg	TD	Sfty	TD	Pts
1987 St. Louis Cardinals	3	0	7	0	0.0	0	0	0	0	0	0	-	0	0	0	0

Year	Team	G	GS	Tackles			Miscellaneous				Interceptions				Totals		
				Tk	Ast	Sack	FF	FR	TD	Blk	Int	Yds	Avg	TD	Sfty	TD	Pts
1988	Phoenix Cardinals	16	15	101	14	2.0	4	1	0	0	2	11	5.5	0	0	0	0
1989	Phoenix Cardinals	16	16	102	53	0.0	0	1	0	0	7	170	24.3	1	0	1	6
1990	Phoenix Cardinals	16	16	101	31	0.0	1	1	0	0	4	63	15.8	0	0	0	0
1991	Phoenix Cardinals	13	13	81	15	0.0	0	1	0	0	5	36	7.2	0	0	0	0
1992	Phoenix Cardinals	16	16	89	18	0.5	1	3	0	0	2	35	17.5	0	0	0	0
1993	San Francisco 49ers	16	16	76	15	0.0	0	1	0	0	3	23	7.7	0	0	0	0
1994	San Francisco 49ers	16	16	67	5	0.0	1	1	1	0	2	79	39.5	1	0	2	12
1995	San Francisco 49ers	16	16	61	14	0.0	2	0	0	0	4	135	33.8	2	0	2	12
	9 NFL Seasons	128	124	685	165	2.5	9	9	1	1	29	552	19.0	4	0	5	30

Bubba McDowell

Pos: S **Rnd:** 3 **College:** Miami (FL) **Ht:** 6' 1" **Wt:** 198 **Born:** 11/4/66 **Age:** 29

Year	Team	G	GS	Tackles			Miscellaneous				Interceptions				Totals		
				Tk	Ast	Sack	FF	FR	TD	Blk	Int	Yds	Avg	TD	Sfty	TD	Pts
1989	Houston Oilers	16	16	72	25	1.0	4	1	0	0	4	65	16.3	0	1	0	2
1990	Houston Oilers	15	15	55	26	0.5	0	1	0	0	2	11	5.5	0	0	0	0
1991	Houston Oilers	16	16	68	27	1.0	0	2	1	0	4	31	7.8	0	0	1	6
1992	Houston Oilers	16	16	57	16	1.5	3	0	0	0	3	52	17.3	1	0	1	6
1993	Houston Oilers	14	14	56	19	1.0	2	0	0	0	3	31	10.3	0	0	0	0
1994	Houston Oilers	9	3	18	6	0.0	0	1	0	0	0	0	-	0	0	0	0
1995	Carolina Panthers	16	3	31	10	0.0	1	1	0	1	1	33	33.0	0	0	0	0
	7 NFL Seasons	102	83	357	129	5.0	10	6	1	1	17	223	13.1	1	1	2	14

Other Statistics: 1989–fumbled 1 time.

O.J. McDuffie

(statistical profile on page 350)

Pos: WR/PR **Rnd:** 1 (25) **College:** Penn State **Ht:** 5' 10" **Wt:** 188 **Born:** 12/2/69 **Age:** 26

Year	Team	G	GS	Rushing					Receiving					Punt Returns				Kickoff Returns				Totals		
				Att	Yds	Avg	Lg	TD	Rec	Yds	Avg	Lg	TD	Num	Yds	Avg	TD	Num	Yds	Avg	TD	Fum	TD	Pts
1993	Miami Dolphins	16	0	1	-4	-4.0	-4	0	19	197	10.4	18	0	28	317	11.3	2	32	755	23.6	0	4	2	12
1994	Miami Dolphins	15	3	5	32	6.4	12	0	37	488	13.2	30	3	32	228	7.1	0	36	767	21.3	0	3	3	18
1995	Miami Dolphins	16	16	3	6	2.0	11	0	62	819	13.2	48	8	24	163	6.8	0	23	564	24.5	0	4	8	50
	3 NFL Seasons	47	19	9	34	3.8	12	0	118	1504	12.7	48	11	84	708	8.4	2	91	2086	22.9	0	11	13	80

Other Statistics: 1993–recovered 1 fumble for 0 yards. 1994–recovered 1 fumble for 0 yards. 1995–recovered 2 fumbles for 0 yards; scored 1 two-point conversion.

Ray McElroy

Pos: DB/CB **Rnd:** 4 **College:** Eastern Illinois **Ht:** 5' 11" **Wt:** 195 **Born:** 7/31/72 **Age:** 24

Year	Team	G	GS	Tackles			Miscellaneous				Interceptions				Totals		
				Tk	Ast	Sack	FF	FR	TD	Blk	Int	Yds	Avg	TD	Sfty	TD	Pts
1995	Indianapolis Colts	16	0	2	1	0.0	0	0	0	0	0	0	-	0	0	0	0

Reggie McElroy

Pos: T **Rnd:** 2 **College:** West Texas State **Ht:** 6' 6" **Wt:** 290 **Born:** 3/4/60 **Age:** 36

Year	Team	G	GS	Year	Team	G	GS	Year	Team	G	GS	Year	Team	G	GS
1983	New York Jets	16	1	1986	New York Jets	8	8	1989	New York Jets	15	15	1993	Kansas City Chiefs	8	1
1984	New York Jets	16	16	1987	New York Jets	8	5	1991	Los Angeles Raiders	16	5	1994	Minnesota Vikings	10	0
1985	New York Jets	13	11	1988	New York Jets	16	16	1992	Los Angeles Raiders	16	12	1995	Denver Broncos	16	0
													12 NFL Seasons	158	90

Other Statistics: 1983–returned 1 kickoff for 7 yards. 1986–recovered 1 fumble for -2 yards. 1988–recovered 1 fumble for 0 yards.

Tony McGee

(statistical profile on page 351)

Pos: TE **Rnd:** 2 **College:** Michigan **Ht:** 6' 3" **Wt:** 246 **Born:** 4/21/71 **Age:** 25

Year	Team	G	GS	Rushing					Receiving					Punt Returns				Kickoff Returns				Totals		
				Att	Yds	Avg	Lg	TD	Rec	Yds	Avg	Lg	TD	Num	Yds	Avg	TD	Num	Yds	Avg	TD	Fum	TD	Pts
1993	Cincinnati Bengals	15	15	0	0	-	-	0	44	525	11.9	37	0	0	0	-	0	0	0	-	0	1	0	0
1994	Cincinnati Bengals	16	16	0	0	-	-	0	40	492	12.3	54	1	0	0	-	0	1	4	4.0	0	0	1	6
1995	Cincinnati Bengals	16	16	0	0	-	-	0	55	754	13.7	41	4	0	0	-	0	0	0	-	0	2	4	24
	3 NFL Seasons	47	47	0	0	-	-	0	139	1771	12.7	54	5	0	0	-	0	1	4	4.0	0	3	5	30

Kanavis McGhee

Pos: DE **Rnd:** 2 **College:** Colorado **Ht:** 6' 4" **Wt:** 257 **Born:** 10/4/68 **Age:** 28

Year	Team	G	GS	Tackles			Miscellaneous				Interceptions				Totals		
				Tk	Ast	Sack	FF	FR	TD	Blk	Int	Yds	Avg	TD	Sfty	TD	Pts
1991	New York Giants	16	0	0	0	0.0	0	0	0	0	0	0	-	0	0	0	0
1992	New York Giants	14	1	0	0	0.0	0	0	0	0	0	0	-	0	0	0	0

Year	Team	G	GS	Tackles			Miscellaneous				Interceptions				Totals		
				Tk	Ast	Sack	FF	FR	TD	Blk	Int	Yds	Avg	TD	Sfty	TD	Pts
1993	New York Giants	11	1	10	1	1.5	0	0	0	0	0	0	-	0	0	0	0
1994	Cincinnati Bengals	2	0	0	0	0.0	0	0	0	0	0	0	-	0	0	0	0
1995	Houston Oilers	9	0	4	3	1.5	0	0	0	0	0	0	-	0	0	0	0
	5 NFL Seasons	52	2	14	4	3.0	0	0	0	0	0	0	-	0	0	0	0

Lenny McGill

Pos: CB/LB **Rnd:** FA **College:** Arizona State **Ht:** 6' 1" **Wt:** 198 **Born:** 5/31/71 **Age:** 25

Year	Team	G	GS	Tackles			Miscellaneous				Interceptions				Totals		
				Tk	Ast	Sack	FF	FR	TD	Blk	Int	Yds	Avg	TD	Sfty	TD	Pts
1994	Green Bay Packers	6	0	4	2	0.0	0	0	0	0	2	16	8.0	0	0	0	0
1995	Green Bay Packers	15	1	17	10	0.0	0	1	0	0	0	0	-	0	0	0	0
	2 NFL Seasons	21	1	21	12	0.0	0	1	0	0	2	16	8.0	0	0	0	0

Willie McGinest

(statistical profile on page 433)

Pos: LB **Rnd:** 1 (4) **College:** Southern California **Ht:** 6' 5" **Wt:** 252 **Born:** 12/11/71 **Age:** 24

Year	Team	G	GS	Tackles			Miscellaneous				Interceptions				Totals		
				Tk	Ast	Sack	FF	FR	TD	Blk	Int	Yds	Avg	TD	Sfty	TD	Pts
1994	New England Patriots	16	7	29	14	4.5	2	2	0	0	0	0	-	0	0	0	0
1995	New England Patriots	16	16	70	18	11.0	4	0	0	0	0	0	-	0	0	0	0
	2 NFL Seasons	32	23	99	32	15.5	6	2	0	0	0	0	-	0	0	0	0

Chester McGlockton

(statistical profile on page 433)

Pos: DT **Rnd:** 1 (16) **College:** Clemson **Ht:** 6' 4" **Wt:** 315 **Born:** 9/16/69 **Age:** 27

Year	Team	G	GS	Tackles			Miscellaneous				Interceptions				Totals		
				Tk	Ast	Sack	FF	FR	TD	Blk	Int	Yds	Avg	TD	Sfty	TD	Pts
1992	Los Angeles Raiders	10	0	18	-	3.0	0	0	0	0	0	0	-	0	0	0	0
1993	Los Angeles Raiders	16	16	63	15	7.0	0	1	0	0	1	19	19.0	0	0	0	0
1994	Los Angeles Raiders	16	16	48	14	9.5	3	1	0	0	0	0	-	0	0	0	0
1995	Oakland Raiders	16	16	47	8	7.5	2	2	0	0	0	0	-	0	0	0	0
	4 NFL Seasons	58	48	176	37	27.0	5	4	0	0	1	19	19.0	0	0	0	0

Michael McGruder

Pos: CB **Rnd:** FA **College:** Kent State **Ht:** 5' 10" **Wt:** 182 **Born:** 5/6/64 **Age:** 32

Year	Team	G	GS	Tackles			Miscellaneous				Interceptions				Totals		
				Tk	Ast	Sack	FF	FR	TD	Blk	Int	Yds	Avg	TD	Sfty	TD	Pts
1989	Green Bay Packers	2	0	2	0	0.0	0	1	0	0	0	0	-	0	0	0	0
1990	Miami Dolphins	1	0	0	0	0.0	0	0	0	0	0	0	-	0	0	0	0
1991	Miami Dolphins	16	5	26	1	0.0	0	1	0	0	0	0	-	0	0	0	0
1992	San Francisco 49ers	9	2	18	1	0.0	0	1	0	0	0	0	-	0	0	0	0
1993	San Francisco 49ers	16	5	32	5	0.0	0	0	0	0	5	89	17.8	1	0	1	6
1994	Tampa Bay Buccaneers	15	3	25	4	0.0	1	0	0	0	1	0	0.0	0	0	0	0
1995	Tampa Bay Buccaneers	16	2	18	5	0.0	0	1	0	0	0	0	-	0	0	0	0
	7 NFL Seasons	75	17	121	16	0.0	1	4	0	0	6	89	14.8	1	0	1	6

Dan McGwire

Pos: QB **Rnd:** 1 (16) **College:** San Diego State **Ht:** 6' 8" **Wt:** 239 **Born:** 12/18/67 **Age:** 28

Year	Team	G	GS	Passing										Rushing					Miscellaneous					
				Att	Com	Pct	Yards	Yds/Att	Lg	TD	Int	Int%	Rating	Att	Yds	Avg	Lg	TD	Sckd	Yds	Fum	Recv	Yds	Pts
1991	Seattle Seahawks	1	1	7	3	42.9	27	3.86	13	0	1	14.3	14.3	0	0	-	-	0	0	0	0	0	0	0
1992	Seattle Seahawks	2	1	30	17	56.7	116	3.87	20	0	3	10.0	25.8	3	13	4.3	11	0	7	58	1	0	-1	0
1993	Seattle Seahawks	2	0	5	3	60.0	24	4.80	t17	0	0	0.0	111.7	1	-1	-1.0	-1	0	0	0	0	0	0	0
1994	Seattle Seahawks	7	3	105	51	48.6	578	5.50	36	1	2	1.9	60.7	10	-6	-0.6	2	0	13	96	9	3	-7	0
1995	Miami Dolphins	1	0	1	0	0.0	0	0.00	-	0	0	0.0	39.6	0	0	-	-	0	1	7	0	0	0	0
	5 NFL Seasons	13	5	148	74	50.0	745	5.03	36	2	6	4.1	52.3	14	6	0.4	11	0	21	161	10	3	-8	0

Tom McHale

Pos: G/T **Rnd:** FA **College:** Cornell **Ht:** 6' 4" **Wt:** 290 **Born:** 2/25/63 **Age:** 33

Year	Team	G	GS	Year	Team	G	GS	Year	Team	G	GS		G	GS
1987	Tampa Bay Buccaneers	3	0	1990	Tampa Bay Buccaneers	7	7	1993	Philadelphia Eagles	8	4			
1988	Tampa Bay Buccaneers	10	0	1991	Tampa Bay Buccaneers	15	10	1994	Philadelphia Eagles	13	2			
1989	Tampa Bay Buccaneers	15	10	1992	Tampa Bay Buccaneers	9	3	1995	Miami Dolphins	7	4	9 NFL Seasons	87	40

Other Statistics: 1987--recovered 1 fumble for 0 yards. 1988--fumbled 1 time for -4 yards.

Toddrick McIntosh

Pos: DT/DE **Rnd:** 7   **College:** Florida State   **Ht:** 6' 3" **Wt:** 267   **Born:** 1/22/72   **Age:** 24

Year	Team	G	GS	Tk	Ast	Sack	FF	FR	TD	Blk	Int	Yds	Avg	TD	Sfty	TD	Pts
1994	Tampa Bay Buccaneers	4	0	1	2	0.0	0	0	0	0	0	0	-	0	0	0	0
1995	Tampa Bay Buccaneers	11	1	7	2	2.0	1	0	0	0	0	0	-	0	0	0	0
	2 NFL Seasons	15	1	8	4	2.0	1	0	0	0	0	0	-	0	0	0	0

Guy McIntyre

Pos: G   **Rnd:** 3   **College:** Georgia   **Ht:** 6' 3" **Wt:** 276   **Born:** 2/17/61   **Age:** 35

Year	Team	G	GS	Year	Team	G	GS	Year	Team	G	GS	Year	Team	G	GS
1984	San Francisco 49ers	16	0	1987	San Francisco 49ers	3	3	1990	San Francisco 49ers	16	16	1993	San Francisco 49ers	16	16
1985	San Francisco 49ers	15	3	1988	San Francisco 49ers	16	12	1991	San Francisco 49ers	16	16	1994	Green Bay Packers	10	10
1986	San Francisco 49ers	16	2	1989	San Francisco 49ers	16	13	1992	San Francisco 49ers	16	16	1995	Philadelphia Eagles	16	16
													12 NFL Seasons	172	123

Other Statistics: 1984–returned 1 kickoff for 0 yards. 1985–recovered 1 fumble for 0 yards and 1 touchdown. 1988–caught 1 pass for 17 yards and 1 touchdown. 1991–recovered 1 fumble for 0 yards. 1992–recovered 1 fumble for 0 yards. 1993–recovered 2 fumbles for 0 yards.

Everette McIver

Pos: G/T   **Rnd:** FA   **College:** Elizabeth City State   **Ht:** 6' 6" **Wt:** 315   **Born:** 8/5/70   **Age:** 26

Year	Team	G	GS	Year	Team	G	GS			G	GS
1994	New York Jets	4	0	1995	New York Jets	14	4		2 NFL Seasons	18	4

Raleigh McKenzie

Pos: C   **Rnd:** 11   **College:** Tennessee   **Ht:** 6' 2" **Wt:** 283   **Born:** 2/8/63   **Age:** 33

Year	Team	G	GS	Year	Team	G	GS	Year	Team	G	GS	Year	Team	G	GS
1985	Washington Redskins	6	0	1988	Washington Redskins	16	14	1991	Washington Redskins	16	14	1994	Washington Redskins	16	16
1986	Washington Redskins	16	5	1989	Washington Redskins	15	8	1992	Washington Redskins	16	16	1995	Philadelphia Eagles	16	16
1987	Washington Redskins	12	12	1990	Washington Redskins	16	12	1993	Washington Redskins	16	16		11 NFL Seasons	161	129

Other Statistics: 1994–recovered 1 fumble for 0 yards. 1995–recovered 1 fumble for 0 yards.

Rich McKenzie

Pos: DE/LB **Rnd:** 6   **College:** Penn State   **Ht:** 6' 2" **Wt:** 258   **Born:** 4/15/71   **Age:** 25

Year	Team	G	GS	Tk	Ast	Sack	FF	FR	TD	Blk	Int	Yds	Avg	TD	Sfty	TD	Pts
1995	Cleveland Browns	8	0	3	2	1.5	0	1	0	0	0	0	-	0	0	0	0

James McKnight

Pos: WR   **Rnd:** FA   **College:** Liberty   **Ht:** 6' 0" **Wt:** 186   **Born:** 6/17/72   **Age:** 24

Year	Team	G	GS	Att	Yds	Avg	Lg	TD	Rec	Yds	Avg	Lg	TD	Num	Yds	Avg	TD	Num	Yds	Avg	TD	Fum	TD	Pts
1994	Seattle Seahawks	2	0	0	0	-	-	0	1	25	25.0	t25	1	0	0	-	0	0	0	-	0	0	1	6
1995	Seattle Seahawks	16	0	0	0	-	-	0	6	91	15.2	24	0	0	0	-	0	1	4	4.0	0	1	0	0
	2 NFL Seasons	18	0	0	0	-	-	0	7	116	16.6	t25	1	0	0	-	0	1	4	4.0	0	1	1	6

Other Statistics: 1995–recovered 1 fumble for 0 yards.

Tim McKyer

(statistical profile on page 434)

Pos: CB   **Rnd:** 3   **College:** Texas-Arlington   **Ht:** 6' 0" **Wt:** 178   **Born:** 9/5/63   **Age:** 33

Year	Team	G	GS	Tk	Ast	Sack	FF	FR	TD	Blk	Int	Yds	Avg	TD	Num	Yds	Avg	TD	Num	Yds	Avg	TD	TD	Fum
1986	San Francisco 49ers	16	16	45	7	0.0	0	0	0	0	6	33	5.5	1	1	5	5.0	0	1	15	15.0	0	1	0
1987	San Francisco 49ers	12	12	29	6	0.0	0	0	0	0	2	0	0.0	0	0	0	-	0	0	0	-	0	0	0
1988	San Francisco 49ers	16	16	37	2	0.0	0	0	0	0	7	11	1.6	0	0	0	-	0	0	0	-	0	0	0
1989	San Francisco 49ers	7	1	11	1	0.0	0	0	0	0	1	18	18.0	0	0	0	-	0	0	0	-	0	0	0
1990	Miami Dolphins	16	16	37	7	0.0	0	0	0	0	4	40	10.0	0	0	0	-	0	0	0	-	0	0	0
1991	Atlanta Falcons	16	16	47	14	0.0	0	0	0	0	6	24	4.0	0	0	0	-	0	0	0	-	0	0	0
1992	Atlanta Falcons	16	16	43	16	1.0	0	0	0	0	1	0	0.0	0	0	0	-	0	0	0	-	0	0	0
1993	Detroit Lions	15	3	26	1	0.0	0	1	0	0	2	10	5.0	0	0	0	-	0	0	0	-	0	0	0
1994	Pittsburgh Steelers	16	2	26	3	0.0	0	0	0	0	0	0	-	0	0	0	-	0	0	0	-	0	0	0
1995	Carolina Panthers	16	16	57	5	0.0	0	2	0	0	3	99	33.0	1	0	0	-	0	0	0	-	0	1	0
	10 NFL Seasons	146	114	358	62	1.0	0	3	0	0	32	235	7.3	2	1	5	5.0	0	1	15	15.0	0	2	0

Steve McLaughlin
(statistical profile on page 480)

Pos: K **Rnd:** 3 **College:** Arizona **Ht:** 6' 0" **Wt:** 167 **Born:** 10/2/71 **Age:** 25

| | | Field Goals | | | | | | | | | | | PAT | | Tot |
Year Team	G	1-29 Yds	Pct	30-39 Yds	Pct	40-49 Yds	Pct	50+ Yds	Pct	Overall	Pct	Long	Made	Att	Pts
1995 St. Louis Rams	8	5-6	83.3	2-6	33.3	1-3	33.3	0-1	0.0	8-16	50.0	45	17	17	41

Thomas McLemore

Pos: TE **Rnd:** 3 **College:** Southern **Ht:** 6' 5" **Wt:** 250 **Born:** 3/14/70 **Age:** 26

| | | | Rushing | | | | | Receiving | | | | | Punt Returns | | | | Kickoff Returns | | | | Totals | | |
Year Team	G	GS	Att	Yds	Avg	Lg	TD	Rec	Yds	Avg	Lg	TD	Num	Yds	Avg	TD	Num	Yds	Avg	TD	Fum	TD	Pts
1992 Detroit Lions	11	1	0	0	-	-	0	2	12	6.0	6	0	0	0	-	0	0	0	-	0	0	0	0
1993 Cleveland Browns	4	0	0	0	-	-	0	0	0	-	-	0	0	0	-	0	0	0	-	0	0	0	0
1994 Cleveland Browns	2	1	0	0	-	-	0	0	0	-	-	0	0	0	-	0	0	0	-	0	0	0	0
1995 Indianapolis Colts	1	0	0	0	-	-	0	0	0	-	-	0	0	0	-	0	0	0	-	0	0	0	0
4 NFL Seasons	18	2	0	0	-	-	0	2	12	6.0	6	0	0	0	-	0	0	0	-	0	0	0	0

Jim McMahon

Pos: QB **Rnd:** 1 (5) **College:** Brigham Young **Ht:** 6' 1" **Wt:** 195 **Born:** 8/21/59 **Age:** 37

| | | | Passing | | | | | | | | | Rushing | | | | | Miscellaneous | | | |
Year Team	G	GS	Att	Com	Pct	Yards	Yds/Att	Lg	TD	Int	Int%	Rating	Att	Yds	Avg	Lg	TD	Sckd	Yds	Fum Recv Yds	Pts
1982 Chicago Bears	8	7	210	120	57.1	1501	7.15	t50	9	7	3.3	79.9	24	105	4.4	11	1	27	196	1 0 0	6
1983 Chicago Bears	14	13	295	175	59.3	2184	7.40	t87	12	13	4.4	77.6	55	307	5.6	32	2	42	266	4 3 0	18
1984 Chicago Bears	9	9	143	85	59.4	1146	8.01	t61	8	2	1.4	97.8	39	276	7.1	30	2	10	48	1 0 0	12
1985 Chicago Bears	13	11	313	178	56.9	2392	7.64	t70	15	11	3.5	82.6	47	252	5.4	19	3	26	125	4 0 0	24
1986 Chicago Bears	6	6	150	77	51.3	995	6.63	t58	5	8	5.3	61.4	22	152	6.9	23	1	6	40	1 0 0	6
1987 Chicago Bears	7	6	210	125	59.5	1639	7.80	t59	12	8	3.8	87.4	22	88	4.0	13	2	22	136	2 0 0	12
1988 Chicago Bears	9	9	192	114	59.4	1346	7.01	t63	6	7	3.6	76.0	26	104	4.0	16	4	13	79	6 3 0	24
1989 San Diego Chargers	12	11	318	176	55.3	2132	6.70	t69	10	10	3.1	73.5	29	141	4.9	15	0	28	167	3 1 0	0
1990 Philadelphia Eagles	5	0	9	6	66.7	63	7.00	21	0	0	0.0	86.8	3	1	0.3	3	0	1	7	0 0 0	0
1991 Philadelphia Eagles	12	11	311	187	60.1	2239	7.20	t75	12	11	3.5	80.3	22	55	2.5	12	1	21	128	2 2 0	6
1992 Philadelphia Eagles	4	1	43	22	51.2	279	6.49	t42	1	2	4.7	60.1	6	23	3.8	11	0	4	25	0 0 0	0
1993 Minnesota Vikings	12	12	331	200	60.4	1968	5.95	58	9	8	2.4	76.2	33	96	2.9	16	0	23	104	4 1 -7	0
1994 Arizona Cardinals	3	1	43	23	53.5	219	5.09	33	1	3	7.0	46.6	6	32	5.3	17	0	3	23	1 0 0	0
1995 Green Bay Packers	1	0	1	1	100.0	6	6.00	6	0	0	0.0	91.7	0	0	-	-	0	0	0	0 0 0	0
14 NFL Seasons	115	97	2569	1489	58.0	18109	7.05	t87	100	90	3.5	78.1	334	1632	4.9	32	16	226	1344	29 10 -7	108

Other Statistics: 1982–punted 1 time for 59 yards. 1983–caught 1 pass for 18 yards and 1 touchdown; punted 1 time for 36 yards. 1984–caught 1 pass for 42 yards. 1985–caught 1 pass for 13 yards and 1 touchdown. 1989–caught 1 pass for 4 yards. 1991–caught 1 pass for -5 yards.

Tom McManus

Pos: LB **Rnd:** FA **College:** Boston College **Ht:** 6' 2" **Wt:** 252 **Born:** 7/30/70 **Age:** 26

| | | | Tackles | | | Miscellaneous | | | | Interceptions | | | | Totals | | |
Year Team	G	GS	Tk	Ast	Sack	FF	FR	TD	Blk	Int	Yds	Avg	TD	Sfty	TD	Pts
1995 Jacksonville Jaguars	13	2	8	10	0.0	0	0	0	0	0	0	-	0	0	0	0

Henry McMillian

Pos: DT **Rnd:** 6 **College:** Florida **Ht:** 6' 3" **Wt:** 275 **Born:** 10/17/71 **Age:** 25

| | | | Tackles | | | Miscellaneous | | | | Interceptions | | | | Totals | | |
Year Team	G	GS	Tk	Ast	Sack	FF	FR	TD	Blk	Int	Yds	Avg	TD	Sfty	TD	Pts
1995 Seattle Seahawks	1	0	0	0	0.0	0	0	0	0	0	0	-	0	0	0	0

Mark McMillian
(statistical profile on page 434)

Pos: CB **Rnd:** 10 **College:** Alabama **Ht:** 5' 7" **Wt:** 148 **Born:** 4/29/70 **Age:** 26

| | | | Tackles | | | Miscellaneous | | | | Interceptions | | | | Totals | | |
Year Team	G	GS	Tk	Ast	Sack	FF	FR	TD	Blk	Int	Yds	Avg	TD	Sfty	TD	Pts
1992 Philadelphia Eagles	16	3	18	3	0.0	0	0	0	0	1	0	0.0	0	0	0	0
1993 Philadelphia Eagles	16	12	42	7	0.0	0	1	0	0	2	25	12.5	0	0	0	0
1994 Philadelphia Eagles	16	16	44	5	0.0	0	1	0	0	2	2	1.0	0	0	0	0
1995 Philadelphia Eagles	16	16	63	0	0.0	0	2	0	0	3	27	9.0	0	0	0	0
4 NFL Seasons	64	47	167	15	0.0	0	4	0	0	8	54	6.8	0	0	0	0

Other Statistics: 1993–fumbled 1 time.

Dexter McNabb

Pos: RB **Rnd:** 5 **College:** Florida **Ht:** 6' 1" **Wt:** 245 **Born:** 7/9/69 **Age:** 27

Year	Team	G	GS	Rushing Att	Yds	Avg	Lg	TD	Receiving Rec	Yds	Avg	Lg	TD	Punt Returns Num	Yds	Avg	TD	Kickoff Returns Num	Yds	Avg	TD	Totals Fum	TD	Pts
1992	Green Bay Packers	16	0	2	11	5.5	8	0	0	0	-	-	0	0	0	-	0	1	15	15.0	0	0	0	0
1993	Green Bay Packers	16	0	0	0	-	-	0	0	0	-	-	0	0	0	-	0	0	0	-	0	0	0	0
1995	Philadelphia Eagles	1	0	0	0	-	-	0	0	0	-	-	0	0	0	-	0	0	0	-	0	0	0	0
	3 NFL Seasons	33	0	2	11	5.5	8	0	0	0	-	-	0	0	0	-	0	1	15	15.0	0	0	0	0

Steve McNair

(statistical profile on page 351)

Pos: QB **Rnd:** 1 (3) **College:** Alcorn State **Ht:** 6' 2" **Wt:** 224 **Born:** 2/14/73 **Age:** 23

Year	Team	G	GS	Passing Att	Com	Pct	Yards	Yds/Att	Lg	TD	Int	Int%	Rating	Rushing Att	Yds	Avg	Lg	TD	Miscellaneous Sckd	Yds	Fum	Recv	Yds	Pts
1995	Houston Oilers	6	2	80	41	51.3	569	7.11	53	3	1	1.3	81.7	11	38	3.5	13	0	6	63	3	2	0	0

Todd McNair

(statistical profile on page 352)

Pos: RB/WR **Rnd:** 8 **College:** Temple **Ht:** 6' 1" **Wt:** 202 **Born:** 10/7/65 **Age:** 31

Year	Team	G	GS	Rushing Att	Yds	Avg	Lg	TD	Receiving Rec	Yds	Avg	Lg	TD	Punt Returns Num	Yds	Avg	TD	Kickoff Returns Num	Yds	Avg	TD	Totals Fum	TD	Pts
1989	Kansas City Chiefs	14	0	23	121	5.3	25	0	34	372	10.9	24	1	0	0	-	0	13	257	19.8	0	1	1	6
1990	Kansas City Chiefs	15	1	14	61	4.4	13	0	40	507	12.7	65	2	0	0	-	0	14	227	16.2	0	1	2	12
1991	Kansas City Chiefs	14	0	10	51	5.1	11	0	37	342	9.2	36	1	0	0	-	0	4	66	16.5	0	2	1	6
1992	Kansas City Chiefs	16	0	21	124	5.9	30	1	44	380	8.6	36	1	0	0	-	0	2	20	10.0	0	1	2	12
1993	Kansas City Chiefs	15	0	51	278	5.5	47	2	10	74	7.4	24	0	0	0	-	0	1	28	28.0	0	2	2	12
1994	Houston Oilers	16	1	0	0	-	-	0	8	78	9.8	21	0	0	0	-	0	23	481	20.9	0	0	0	0
1995	Houston Oilers	15	7	19	136	7.2	22	0	60	501	8.4	25	1	0	0	-	0	0	0	-	0	1	1	6
	7 NFL Seasons	105	9	138	771	5.6	47	3	233	2254	9.7	65	6	0	0	-	0	57	1079	18.9	0	8	9	54

Other Statistics: 1990–recovered 1 fumble for 0 yards. 1991–recovered 2 fumbles for 0 yards. 1992–recovered 1 fumble for 0 yards. 1994–recovered 1 fumble for 0 yards.

Ryan McNeil

(statistical profile on page 434)

Pos: CB **Rnd:** 2 **College:** Miami (FL) **Ht:** 6' 2" **Wt:** 192 **Born:** 10/4/70 **Age:** 26

Year	Team	G	GS	Tackles Tk	Ast	Sack	Miscellaneous FF	FR	TD	Blk	Interceptions Int	Yds	Avg	TD	Totals Sfty	TD	Pts
1993	Detroit Lions	16	2	29	4	0.0	0	0	0	0	2	19	9.5	0	0	0	0
1994	Detroit Lions	14	13	51	7	0.0	0	0	0	0	1	14	14.0	0	0	0	0
1995	Detroit Lions	16	16	69	17	0.0	0	2	0	0	2	26	13.0	0	0	0	0
	3 NFL Seasons	46	31	149	28	0.0	0	2	0	0	5	59	11.8	0	0	0	0

Charles McRae

(statistical profile on page 434)

Pos: G/T **Rnd:** 1 (7) **College:** Tennessee **Ht:** 6' 7" **Wt:** 306 **Born:** 9/16/68 **Age:** 28

Year	Team	G	GS	Year	Team	G	GS	Year	Team	G	GS		G	GS
1991	Tampa Bay Buccaneers	16	4	1993	Tampa Bay Buccaneers	13	4	1995	Tampa Bay Buccaneers	11	4			
1992	Tampa Bay Buccaneers	16	16	1994	Tampa Bay Buccaneers	15	10					5 NFL Seasons	71	38

Natrone Means

(statistical profile on page 352)

Pos: RB **Rnd:** 2 **College:** North Carolina **Ht:** 5' 10" **Wt:** 245 **Born:** 4/26/72 **Age:** 24

Year	Team	G	GS	Rushing Att	Yds	Avg	Lg	TD	Receiving Rec	Yds	Avg	Lg	TD	Kickoff Returns Num	Yds	Avg	TD	Passing Att	Com	Yds	Int	Totals Fum	TD	Pts
1993	San Diego Chargers	16	8	160	645	4.0	t65	8	10	59	5.9	11	0	2	22	11.0	0	1	0	0	0	1	8	48
1994	San Diego Chargers	16	16	343	1350	3.9	25	12	39	235	6.0	22	0	0	0	-	0	1	0	0	0	5	12	72
1995	San Diego Chargers	10	9	186	730	3.9	36	5	7	46	6.6	14	0	0	0	-	0	0	0	0	0	2	5	30
	3 NFL Seasons	42	25	689	2725	4.0	t65	25	56	340	6.1	22	0	2	22	11.0	0	2	0	0	0	8	25	150

Other Statistics: 1993–recovered 1 fumble for 0 yards.

David Meggett

(statistical profile on page 353)

Pos: RB/PR **Rnd:** 5 **College:** Towson State **Ht:** 5' 7" **Wt:** 195 **Born:** 4/30/66 **Age:** 30

Year	Team	G	GS	Rushing Att	Yds	Avg	Lg	TD	Receiving Rec	Yds	Avg	Lg	TD	Punt Returns Num	Yds	Avg	TD	Kickoff Returns Num	Yds	Avg	TD	Totals Fum	TD	Pts
1989	New York Giants	16	2	28	117	4.2	18	0	34	531	15.6	t62	4	46	582	12.7	1	27	577	21.4	0	8	5	30
1990	New York Giants	16	1	22	164	7.5	51	0	39	410	10.5	38	1	43	467	10.9	1	21	492	23.4	0	3	2	12
1991	New York Giants	16	2	29	153	5.3	t30	1	50	412	8.2	22	3	28	287	10.3	1	25	514	20.6	0	8	5	30
1992	New York Giants	16	0	32	167	5.2	30	0	38	229	6.0	24	2	27	240	8.9	0	20	455	22.8	1	5	3	18
1993	New York Giants	16	1	69	329	4.8	23	0	38	319	8.4	50	0	32	331	10.3	1	24	403	16.8	0	1	1	6
1994	New York Giants	16	3	91	298	3.3	t26	4	32	293	9.2	34	0	26	323	12.4	2	29	548	18.9	0	6	6	36
1995	New England Patriots	16	0	60	250	4.2	25	2	52	334	6.4	19	0	45	383	8.5	0	38	964	25.4	0	5	2	16

Year Team	G	GS	Rushing					Receiving					Punt Returns				Kickoff Returns				Totals		
			Att	Yds	Avg	Lg	TD	Rec	Yds	Avg	Lg	TD	Num	Yds	Avg	TD	Num	Yds	Avg	TD	Fum	TD	Pts
7 NFL Seasons	112	9	331	1478	4.5	51	7	283	2528	8.9	t62	10	247	2613	10.6	6	184	3953	21.5	1	36	24	148

Other Statistics: 1989–recovered 3 fumbles for 0 yards. 1990–recovered 2 fumbles for 0 yards. 1991–recovered 3 fumbles for 0 yards; attempted 1 pass with 0 completions for 0 yards. 1992–recovered 3 fumbles for 0 yards. 1993–recovered 1 fumble for 0 yards; attempted 2 passes with 2 completions for 63 yards and 2 touchdowns. 1994–recovered 5 fumbles for 0 yards; attempted 2 passes with 1 completion for 16 yards and 1 touchdown. 1995–attempted 1 pass with 0 completions for 0 yards; scored 2 two-point conversions.

David Merritt

Pos: LB **Rnd:** 7 **College:** North Carolina State   **Ht:** 6' 1" **Wt:** 237 **Born:** 9/8/71 **Age:** 25

Year Team	G	GS	Tackles			Miscellaneous				Interceptions				Totals		
			Tk	Ast	Sack	FF	FR	TD	Blk	Int	Yds	Avg	TD	Sfty	TD	Pts
1993 Mia - Pho	7	0	0	0	0.0	0	0	0	0	0	0	-	0	0	0	0
1994 Arizona Cardinals	16	0	1	0	0.0	0	1	0	0	0	0	-	0	0	0	0
1995 Arizona Cardinals	15	0	0	0	0.0	0	0	0	0	0	0	-	0	0	0	0
1993 Miami Dolphins	4	0	0	0	0.0	0	0	0	0	0	0	-	0	0	0	0
Phoenix Cardinals	3	0	0	0	0.0	0	0	0	0	0	0	-	0	0	0	0
3 NFL Seasons	38	0	1	0	0.0	0	1	0	0	0	0	-	0	0	0	0

Eric Metcalf

(statistical profile on page 353)

Pos: WR/PR **Rnd:** 1 (13) **College:** Texas   **Ht:** 5' 10" **Wt:** 188 **Born:** 1/23/68 **Age:** 28

Year Team	G	GS	Rushing					Receiving					Punt Returns				Kickoff Returns				Totals		
			Att	Yds	Avg	Lg	TD	Rec	Yds	Avg	Lg	TD	Num	Yds	Avg	TD	Num	Yds	Avg	TD	Fum	TD	Pts
1989 Cleveland Browns	16	11	187	633	3.4	t43	6	54	397	7.4	t68	4	0	0	-	0	31	718	23.2	0	5	10	60
1990 Cleveland Browns	16	9	80	248	3.1	17	1	57	452	7.9	35	1	0	0	-	0	52	1052	20.2	2	8	4	24
1991 Cleveland Browns	8	3	30	107	3.6	15	0	29	294	10.1	45	0	12	100	8.3	0	23	351	15.3	0	1	0	0
1992 Cleveland Browns	16	5	73	301	4.1	31	1	47	614	13.1	t69	5	44	429	9.8	1	9	157	17.4	0	6	7	42
1993 Cleveland Browns	16	9	129	611	4.7	55	1	63	539	8.6	t49	2	36	464	12.9	2	15	318	21.2	0	4	5	30
1994 Cleveland Browns	16	8	93	329	3.5	t37	2	47	436	9.3	t57	3	35	348	9.9	2	9	210	23.3	0	6	7	42
1995 Atlanta Falcons	16	14	28	133	4.8	t23	1	104	1189	11.4	t62	8	39	383	9.8	1	12	278	23.2	0	4	10	60
7 NFL Seasons	104	59	620	2362	3.8	55	12	401	3921	9.8	t69	23	166	1724	10.4	6	151	3084	20.4	2	34	43	258

Other Statistics: 1989–attempted 2 passes with 1 completion for 32 yards and 1 touchdown. 1990–recovered 1 fumble for 0 yards. 1992–recovered 2 fumbles for 0 yards; attempted 1 pass with 0 completions for 0 yards. 1994–attempted 1 pass with 0 completions for 0 yards. 1995–recovered 2 fumbles for 0 yards; attempted 1 pass with 0 completions for 0 yards.

Pete Metzelaars

Pos: TE **Rnd:** 3 **College:** Wabash   **Ht:** 6' 7" **Wt:** 254 **Born:** 5/24/60 **Age:** 36

Year Team	G	GS	Rushing					Receiving					Punt Returns				Kickoff Returns				Totals		
			Att	Yds	Avg	Lg	TD	Rec	Yds	Avg	Lg	TD	Num	Yds	Avg	TD	Num	Yds	Avg	TD	Fum	TD	Pts
1982 Seattle Seahawks	9	2	0	0	-	-	0	15	152	10.1	26	0	0	0	-	0	0	0	-	0	2	0	0
1983 Seattle Seahawks	16	7	0	0	-	-	0	7	72	10.3	t17	1	0	0	-	0	1	0	0.0	0	1	1	6
1984 Seattle Seahawks	9	4	0	0	-	-	0	5	80	16.0	25	0	0	0	-	0	0	0	-	0	1	0	0
1985 Buffalo Bills	16	8	0	0	-	-	0	12	80	6.7	13	1	0	0	-	0	0	0	-	0	0	1	6
1986 Buffalo Bills	16	16	0	0	-	-	0	49	485	9.9	t44	3	0	0	-	0	0	0	-	0	2	4	24
1987 Buffalo Bills	12	12	0	0	-	-	0	28	290	10.4	34	0	0	0	-	0	0	0	-	0	3	0	0
1988 Buffalo Bills	16	16	0	0	-	-	0	33	438	13.3	35	1	0	0	-	0	0	0	-	0	0	1	6
1989 Buffalo Bills	16	16	0	0	-	-	0	18	179	9.9	23	2	0	0	-	0	0	0	-	0	0	2	12
1990 Buffalo Bills	16	4	0	0	-	-	0	10	60	6.0	12	1	0	0	-	0	0	0	-	0	1	1	6
1991 Buffalo Bills	16	1	0	0	-	-	0	5	54	10.8	t51	2	0	0	-	0	0	0	-	0	0	2	12
1992 Buffalo Bills	16	7	0	0	-	-	0	30	298	9.9	t53	6	0	0	-	0	0	0	-	0	0	6	36
1993 Buffalo Bills	16	16	0	0	-	-	0	68	609	9.0	51	4	0	0	-	0	0	0	-	0	1	4	24
1994 Buffalo Bills	16	16	0	0	-	-	0	49	428	8.7	t35	5	0	0	-	0	0	0	-	0	0	5	30
1995 Carolina Panthers	14	14	0	0	-	-	0	20	171	8.6	27	3	0	0	-	0	1	0	0.0	0	0	3	18
14 NFL Seasons	204	139	0	0	-	-	0	349	3396	9.7	t53	29	0	0	-	0	1	0	0.0	0	10	30	180

Other Statistics: 1982–recovered 1 fumble for 0 yards. 1985–recovered 1 fumble for 2 yards. 1986–recovered 1 fumble for 0 yards and 1 touchdown. 1987–recovered 1 fumble for 0 yards. 1988–recovered 1 fumble for 0 yards.

Rich Miano

Pos: S **Rnd:** 6 **College:** Hawaii   **Ht:** 6' 1" **Wt:** 200 **Born:** 9/3/62 **Age:** 34

Year Team	G	GS	Tackles			Miscellaneous				Interceptions				Totals		
			Tk	Ast	Sack	FF	FR	TD	Blk	Int	Yds	Avg	TD	Sfty	TD	Pts
1985 New York Jets	16	1	28	19	0.0	1	0	0	0	2	9	4.5	0	0	0	0
1986 New York Jets	14	1	10	3	0.0	0	0	0	0	0	0	-	0	0	0	0
1987 New York Jets	12	11	49	24	0.0	0	0	1	0	3	24	8.0	0	0	1	6
1988 New York Jets	16	16	80	32	0.5	1	0	0	0	2	0	0.0	0	0	0	0
1989 New York Jets	2	2	3	2	0.0	0	0	0	0	0	0	-	0	0	0	0
1991 Philadelphia Eagles	16	1	22	10	0.0	0	0	0	0	3	30	10.0	0	0	0	0
1992 Philadelphia Eagles	15	11	53	72	0.0	0	2	0	0	1	39	39.0	0	0	0	0
1993 Philadelphia Eagles	16	14	54	50	0.0	1	1	0	0	4	26	6.5	0	0	0	0
1994 Philadelphia Eagles	16	0	14	1	0.0	0	0	0	0	0	0	-	0	0	0	0

Year	Team	G	GS	Tk	Ast	Sack	FF	FR	TD	Blk	Int	Yds	Avg	TD	Sfty	TD	Pts
				Tackles			Miscellaneous				Interceptions				Totals		
1995	Atlanta Falcons	11	0	0	0	0.0	0	0	0	0	0	0	-	0	0	0	0
	10 NFL Seasons	134	57	313	213	0.5	3	3	1	0	15	128	8.5	0	0	1	6

Darren Mickell

Pos: DE **Rnd:** 2 **College:** Florida **Ht:** 6' 4" **Wt:** 284 **Born:** 8/3/70 **Age:** 26

Year	Team	G	GS	Tk	Ast	Sack	FF	FR	TD	Blk	Int	Yds	Avg	TD	Sfty	TD	Pts
				Tackles			Miscellaneous				Interceptions				Totals		
1992	Kansas City Chiefs	1	0	1	0	0.0	0	0	0	0	0	0	-	0	0	0	0
1993	Kansas City Chiefs	16	1	16	5	1.0	2	1	0	0	0	0	-	0	0	0	0
1994	Kansas City Chiefs	16	13	35	3	7.0	4	1	0	0	0	0	-	0	0	0	0
1995	Kansas City Chiefs	12	6	14	3	5.5	2	1	0	0	0	0	-	0	0	0	0
	4 NFL Seasons	45	20	66	11	13.5	8	3	0	0	0	0	-	0	0	0	0

Terry Mickens

Pos: WR **Rnd:** 5 **College:** Florida A&M **Ht:** 6' 0" **Wt:** 198 **Born:** 2/21/71 **Age:** 25

Year	Team	G	GS	Att	Yds	Avg	Lg	TD	Rec	Yds	Avg	Lg	TD	Num	Yds	Avg	TD	Num	Yds	Avg	TD	Fum	TD	Pts
				Rushing					Receiving					Punt Returns				Kickoff Returns				Totals		
1994	Green Bay Packers	12	0	0	0	-	-	0	4	31	7.8	11	0	0	0	-	0	0	0	-	0	0	0	0
1995	Green Bay Packers	16	0	0	0	-	-	0	3	50	16.7	24	0	0	0	-	0	1	0	0.0	0	0	0	0
	2 NFL Seasons	28	0	0	0	-	-	0	7	81	11.6	24	0	0	0	-	0	1	0	0.0	0	0	0	0

Ron Middleton

Pos: TE **Rnd:** FA **College:** Auburn **Ht:** 6' 2" **Wt:** 262 **Born:** 7/17/65 **Age:** 31

Year	Team	G	GS	Att	Yds	Avg	Lg	TD	Rec	Yds	Avg	Lg	TD	Num	Yds	Avg	TD	Num	Yds	Avg	TD	Fum	TD	Pts
				Rushing					Receiving					Punt Returns				Kickoff Returns				Totals		
1986	Atlanta Falcons	16	3	0	0	-	-	0	6	31	5.2	8	0	0	0	-	0	0	0	-	0	0	0	0
1987	Atlanta Falcons	12	4	0	0	-	-	0	1	1	1.0	1	0	0	0	-	0	0	0	-	0	0	0	0
1988	Washington Redskins	2	0	0	0	-	-	0	0	0	-	-	0	0	0	-	0	0	0	-	0	0	0	0
1989	Cleveland Browns	9	0	0	0	-	-	0	1	5	5.0	t5	1	0	0	-	0	0	0	-	0	0	1	6
1990	Washington Redskins	16	15	0	0	-	-	0	0	0	-	-	0	0	0	-	0	1	7	7.0	0	0	0	0
1991	Washington Redskins	12	12	0	0	-	-	0	3	25	8.3	11	0	0	0	-	0	0	0	-	0	0	0	0
1992	Washington Redskins	16	12	0	0	-	-	0	7	50	7.1	16	0	0	0	-	0	0	0	-	0	0	0	0
1993	Washington Redskins	16	16	0	0	-	-	0	24	154	6.4	18	2	0	0	-	0	0	0	-	0	0	2	12
1994	Los Angeles Rams	16	3	0	0	-	-	0	0	0	-	-	0	0	0	-	0	0	0	-	0	0	0	0
1995	San Diego Chargers	3	1	0	0	-	-	0	0	0	-	-	0	0	0	-	0	0	0	-	0	0	0	0
	10 NFL Seasons	118	66	0	0	-	-	0	42	266	6.3	18	3	0	0	-	0	1	7	7.0	0	0	3	18

Other Statistics: 1993–recovered 1 fumble for 0 yards.

Glyn Milburn

Pos: RB/KR **Rnd:** 2 **College:** Stanford **Ht:** 5' 8" **Wt:** 177 **Born:** 2/19/71 **Age:** 25

Year	Team	G	GS	Att	Yds	Avg	Lg	TD	Rec	Yds	Avg	Lg	TD	Num	Yds	Avg	TD	Num	Yds	Avg	TD	Fum	TD	Pts
				Rushing					Receiving					Punt Returns				Kickoff Returns				Totals		
1993	Denver Broncos	16	2	52	231	4.4	26	0	38	300	7.9	50	3	40	425	10.6	0	12	188	15.7	0	9	3	18
1994	Denver Broncos	16	5	58	201	3.5	20	1	77	549	7.1	33	3	41	379	9.2	0	37	793	21.4	0	4	4	24
1995	Denver Broncos	16	1	49	266	5.4	29	0	22	191	8.7	23	0	31	354	11.4	0	47	1269	27.0	0	2	0	0
	3 NFL Seasons	48	8	159	698	4.4	29	1	137	1040	7.6	50	6	112	1158	10.3	0	96	2250	23.4	0	15	7	42

Other Statistics: 1993–recovered 1 fumble for 0 yards. 1994–recovered 1 fumble for 0 yards.

Hugh Millen

Pos: QB **Rnd:** 3 **College:** Washington **Ht:** 6' 5" **Wt:** 228 **Born:** 11/22/63 **Age:** 32

Year	Team	G	GS	Att	Com	Pct	Yards	Yds/Att	Lg	TD	Int	Int%	Rating	Att	Yds	Avg	Lg	TD	Sckd	Yds	Fum	Recv	Yds	Pts
				Passing										Rushing					Miscellaneous					
1987	Los Angeles Rams	1	1	1	1	100.0	0	0.00	0	0	0	0.0	79.2	0	0	-	-	0	1	6	1	0	0	0
1988	Atlanta Falcons	3	0	31	17	54.8	215	6.94	38	0	2	6.5	49.8	1	7	7.0	7	0	4	29	1	0	0	0
1989	Atlanta Falcons	5	1	50	31	62.0	432	8.64	47	1	2	4.0	79.8	1	0	0.0	0	0	10	71	2	1	-11	0
1990	Atlanta Falcons	3	2	63	34	54.0	427	6.78	53	1	0	0.0	80.6	7	-12	-1.7	2	0	11	43	3	0	0	0
1991	New England Patriots	13	13	409	246	60.1	3073	7.51	t60	9	18	4.4	72.5	31	92	3.0	14	1	54	379	10	4	-17	6
1992	New England Patriots	8	7	203	124	61.1	1203	5.93	39	8	10	4.9	70.3	17	108	6.4	26	0	33	204	8	0	-6	0
1994	Denver Broncos	6	2	131	81	61.8	893	6.82	76	2	3	2.3	77.6	5	57	11.4	24	0	9	63	2	0	0	0
1995	Denver Broncos	3	0	40	26	65.0	197	4.93	18	1	0	0.0	85.1	3	8	2.7	7	0	4	35	1	0	0	0
	8 NFL Seasons	42	26	928	560	60.3	6440	6.94	76	22	35	3.8	73.5	65	260	4.0	26	1	126	830	28	5	-34	6

Anthony Miller

(statistical profile on page 354)

Pos: WR **Rnd:** 1 (15) **College:** Tennessee | **Ht:** 5' 11" **Wt:** 190 **Born:** 4/15/65 **Age:** 31

			Rushing					Receiving					Punt Returns				Kickoff Returns				Totals		
Year Team	G	GS	Att	Yds	Avg	Lg	TD	Rec	Yds	Avg	Lg	TD	Num	Yds	Avg	TD	Num	Yds	Avg	TD	Fum	TD	Pts
1988 San Diego Chargers	16	15	7	45	6.4	20	0	36	526	14.6	49	3	0	0	-	0	25	648	25.9	1	1	4	24
1989 San Diego Chargers	16	16	4	21	5.3	24	0	75	1252	16.7	t69	10	0	0	-	0	21	533	25.4	1	1	11	66
1990 San Diego Chargers	16	16	3	13	4.3	10	0	63	933	14.8	t31	7	0	0	-	0	1	13	13.0	0	2	7	42
1991 San Diego Chargers	13	12	0	0	-	-	0	44	649	14.8	58	3	0	0	-	0	0	0	-	0	1	3	18
1992 San Diego Chargers	16	16	1	-1	-1.0	-1	0	72	1060	14.7	t67	7	0	0	-	0	1	33	33.0	0	0	8	48
1993 San Diego Chargers	16	16	1	0	0.0	0	0	84	1162	13.8	t66	7	0	0	-	0	2	42	21.0	0	0	7	42
1994 Denver Broncos	16	14	1	3	3.0	3	0	60	1107	18.5	76	5	0	0	-	0	0	0	-	0	0	5	32
1995 Denver Broncos	14	14	1	5	5.0	5	0	59	1079	18.3	t62	14	0	0	-	0	0	0	-	0	1	14	84
8 NFL Seasons	123	119	18	86	4.8	24	0	493	7768	15.8	76	56	0	0	-	0	50	1269	25.4	2	6	59	356

Other Statistics: 1990–recovered 1 fumble for 0 yards. 1991–recovered 1 fumble for 0 yards. 1992–recovered 1 fumble for 0 yards and 1 touchdown. 1994–scored 1 two-point conversion. 1995–recovered 1 fumble for 9 yards.

Bronzell Miller

Pos: DE **Rnd:** 7 **College:** Utah | **Ht:** 6' 4" **Wt:** 245 **Born:** 10/12/71 **Age:** 25

			Tackles			Miscellaneous				Interceptions				Totals		
Year Team	G	GS	Tk	Ast	Sack	FF	FR	TD	Blk	Int	Yds	Avg	TD	Sfty	TD	Pts
1995 Jacksonville Jaguars	3	0	0	2	0.0	0	0	0	0	0	0	-	0	0	0	0

Chris Miller

(statistical profile on page 354)

Pos: QB **Rnd:** 1 (13) **College:** Oregon | **Ht:** 6' 2" **Wt:** 212 **Born:** 8/9/65 **Age:** 31

			Passing										Rushing					Miscellaneous			
Year Team	G	GS	Att	Com	Pct	Yards	Yds/Att	Lg	TD	Int	Int%	Rating	Att	Yds	Avg	Lg	TD	Sckd	Yds	Fum Recv	Yds	Pts
1987 Atlanta Falcons	3	2	92	39	42.4	552	6.00	57	1	9	9.8	26.4	4	21	5.3	11	0	5	37	0	0	0
1988 Atlanta Falcons	13	13	351	184	52.4	2133	6.08	t68	11	12	3.4	67.3	31	138	4.5	29	1	24	207	2	1	6
1989 Atlanta Falcons	15	15	526	280	53.2	3459	6.58	t72	16	10	1.9	76.1	10	20	2.0	7	0	41	318	13	5	3
1990 Atlanta Falcons	12	12	388	222	57.2	2735	7.05	t75	17	14	3.6	78.7	26	99	3.8	18	1	26	167	11	4	6
1991 Atlanta Falcons	14	14	413	220	53.3	3103	7.51	t80	26	18	4.4	80.6	32	229	7.2	20	0	23	145	5	0	0
1992 Atlanta Falcons	8	8	253	152	60.1	1739	6.87	t89	15	6	2.4	90.7	23	89	3.9	16	0	16	103	6	1	0
1993 Atlanta Falcons	3	2	66	32	48.5	345	5.23	t32	1	3	4.5	50.4	2	11	5.5	6	0	8	62	2	0	0
1994 Los Angeles Rams	13	10	317	173	54.6	2104	6.64	54	16	14	4.4	73.6	20	100	5.0	18	0	28	193	7	3	0
1995 St. Louis Rams	13	13	405	232	57.3	2623	6.48	72	18	15	3.7	76.2	22	67	3.0	13	0	31	244	4	2	0
9 NFL Seasons	95	89	2811	1534	54.6	18793	6.69	t89	121	101	3.6	74.8	170	774	4.6	29	2	202	1476	50	16	-24	15

Other Statistics: 1989–successful on 1 of 1 field goal attempt.

Corey Miller

Pos: LB **Rnd:** 6 **College:** South Carolina | **Ht:** 6' 2" **Wt:** 247 **Born:** 10/25/68 **Age:** 28

			Tackles			Miscellaneous				Interceptions				Totals		
Year Team	G	GS	Tk	Ast	Sack	FF	FR	TD	Blk	Int	Yds	Avg	TD	Sfty	TD	Pts
1991 New York Giants	16	1	5	1	2.5	0	1	0	0	0	0	-	0	0	0	0
1992 New York Giants	16	7	25	9	2.0	0	0	0	0	2	10	5.0	0	0	0	0
1993 New York Giants	16	14	45	16	6.5	4	2	0	0	2	18	9.0	0	0	0	0
1994 New York Giants	15	13	32	10	0.0	0	1	0	0	2	6	3.0	0	0	0	0
1995 New York Giants	14	9	20	5	0.0	0	0	0	0	0	0	-	0	0	0	0
5 NFL Seasons	77	44	127	41	11.0	4	4	0	0	6	34	5.7	0	0	0	0

Other Statistics: 1993–fumbled 1 time.

Jamir Miller

Pos: LB **Rnd:** 1 (6) **College:** UCLA | **Ht:** 6' 4" **Wt:** 242 **Born:** 11/19/73 **Age:** 22

			Tackles			Miscellaneous				Interceptions				Totals		
Year Team	G	GS	Tk	Ast	Sack	FF	FR	TD	Blk	Int	Yds	Avg	TD	Sfty	TD	Pts
1994 Arizona Cardinals	16	0	16	3	3.0	1	0	0	0	0	0	-	0	0	0	0
1995 Arizona Cardinals	11	8	29	23	1.0	1	2	0	0	0	0	-	0	0	0	0
2 NFL Seasons	27	8	45	26	4.0	2	2	0	0	0	0	-	0	0	0	0

Other Statistics: 1995–fumbled 1 time.

Jim Miller

(statistical profile on page 355)

Pos: QB **Rnd:** 6 **College:** Michigan State | **Ht:** 6' 2" **Wt:** 227 **Born:** 2/9/71 **Age:** 25

			Passing										Rushing					Miscellaneous			
Year Team	G	GS	Att	Com	Pct	Yards	Yds/Att	Lg	TD	Int	Int%	Rating	Att	Yds	Avg	Lg	TD	Sckd	Yds	Fum Recv	Yds	Pts
1994 Pittsburgh Steelers	1	0	0	0	-	0	-	-	0	0	-	0.0	0	0	-	-	0	0	0	0	0	0
1995 Pittsburgh Steelers	4	0	56	32	57.1	397	7.09	t42	2	5	8.9	53.9	1	2	2.0	2	0	2	8	1	0	0
2 NFL Seasons	5	0	56	32	57.1	397	7.09	t42	2	5	8.9	53.9	1	2	2.0	2	0	2	8	1	0	0

Ernie Mills

(statistical profile on page 355)

Pos: KR/WR **Rnd:** 3 **College:** Florida **Ht:** 5' 11" **Wt:** 191 **Born:** 10/28/68 **Age:** 28

Year Team	G	GS	Rushing Att	Yds	Avg	Lg	TD	Receiving Rec	Yds	Avg	Lg	TD	Punt Returns Num	Yds	Avg	TD	Kickoff Returns Num	Yds	Avg	TD	Totals Fum	TD	Pts
1991 Pittsburgh Steelers	16	2	0	0	-	-	0	3	79	26.3	t35	1	1	0	0.0	1	11	284	25.8	0	0	2	12
1992 Pittsburgh Steelers	16	4	1	20	20.0	20	0	30	383	12.8	22	3	0	0	-	0	1	11	11.0	0	2	3	18
1993 Pittsburgh Steelers	14	5	3	12	4.0	19	0	29	386	13.3	30	1	0	0	-	0	0	0	-	0	0	1	6
1994 Pittsburgh Steelers	15	6	3	18	6.0	17	0	19	384	20.2	43	1	0	0	-	0	2	6	3.0	0	1	1	6
1995 Pittsburgh Steelers	16	4	5	39	7.8	20	0	39	679	17.4	t62	8	0	0	-	0	54	1306	24.2	0	2	8	48
5 NFL Seasons	77	21	12	89	7.4	20	0	120	1911	15.9	t62	14	1	0	0.0	1	68	1607	23.6	0	5	15	90

Other Statistics: 1991–recovered 1 fumble for 0 yards. 1995–recovered 1 fumble for 0 yards.

John Henry Mills

Pos: LB/TE **Rnd:** 5 **College:** Wake Forest **Ht:** 6' 0" **Wt:** 222 **Born:** 10/31/69 **Age:** 27

Year Team	G	GS	Tackles Tk	Ast	Sack	Misc. FF	FR	TD	Blk	Int	Yds	Avg	TD	Punt Returns Num	Yds	Avg	TD	Kickoff Returns Num	Yds	Avg	TD	Totals TD	Fum
1993 Houston Oilers	16	0	0	0	0.0	0	0	0	0	0	0	-	0	0	0	-	0	11	230	20.9	0	0	0
1994 Houston Oilers	16	1	0	0	0.0	0	0	0	0	0	0	-	0	0	0	-	0	15	282	18.8	0	0	1
1995 Houston Oilers	16	0	0	0	0.0	0	0	0	0	0	0	-	0	0	0	-	0	0	0	-	0	0	0
3 NFL Seasons	48	1	0	0	0.0	0	0	0	0	0	0	-	0	0	0	-	0	26	512	19.7	0	0	1

Other Statistics: 1994–caught 1 pass for 4 yards.

Sam Mills

(statistical profile on page 435)

Pos: LB **Rnd:** FA **College:** Montclair State **Ht:** 5' 9" **Wt:** 225 **Born:** 6/3/59 **Age:** 37

Year Team	G	GS	Tackles Tk	Ast	Sack	Misc. FF	FR	TD	Blk	Int	Yds	Avg	TD	Totals Sfty	TD	Pts
1986 New Orleans Saints	16	13	69	23	0.0	1	1	0	0	0	0	-	0	0	0	0
1987 New Orleans Saints	12	12	41	17	0.0	1	3	0	0	0	0	-	0	0	0	0
1988 New Orleans Saints	16	16	77	28	0.0	0	4	0	0	0	0	-	0	0	0	0
1989 New Orleans Saints	16	15	80	15	3.0	2	1	0	0	0	0	-	0	0	0	0
1990 New Orleans Saints	16	14	101	11	0.5	2	1	0	0	0	0	-	0	0	0	0
1991 New Orleans Saints	16	16	79	23	1.0	2	2	0	0	2	13	6.5	0	0	0	0
1992 New Orleans Saints	16	16	96	34	3.0	4	3	1	0	1	10	10.0	0	0	1	6
1993 New Orleans Saints	9	7	65	20	2.0	2	1	1	0	0	0	-	0	0	1	6
1994 New Orleans Saints	16	16	115	40	1.0	2	1	0	0	1	10	10.0	0	0	1	6
1995 Carolina Panthers	16	16	86	24	4.5	5	4	0	0	5	58	11.6	0	0	1	6
10 NFL Seasons	149	141	809	235	15.0	21	21	2	0	9	91	10.1	1	0	3	18

Billy Milner

Pos: T **Rnd:** 1 (25) **College:** Houston **Ht:** 6' 5" **Wt:** 293 **Born:** 6/21/72 **Age:** 24

Year Team	G	GS		G	GS
1995 Miami Dolphins	16	9	1 NFL Season	16	9

Other Statistics: 1995–recovered 2 fumbles for 0 yards; returned 1 kickoff for 13 yards.

Rod Milstead

Pos: G **Rnd:** 5 **College:** Delaware State **Ht:** 6' 2" **Wt:** 290 **Born:** 11/10/69 **Age:** 26

Year Team	G	GS	Year Team	G	GS		G	GS
1994 San Francisco 49ers	6	0	1995 San Francisco 49ers	16	12	2 NFL Seasons	22	12

Chris Mims

Pos: DE **Rnd:** 1 (23) **College:** Tennessee **Ht:** 6' 5" **Wt:** 295 **Born:** 9/29/70 **Age:** 26

Year Team	G	GS	Tackles Tk	Ast	Sack	Misc. FF	FR	TD	Blk	Int	Yds	Avg	TD	Totals Sfty	TD	Pts
1992 San Diego Chargers	16	4	41	12	10.0	1	1	0	0	0	0	-	0	1	0	2
1993 San Diego Chargers	16	7	28	4	7.0	2	2	0	0	0	0	-	0	0	0	0
1994 San Diego Chargers	16	16	35	7	11.0	3	2	0	0	0	0	-	0	0	0	0
1995 San Diego Chargers	15	15	28	4	2.0	1	1	0	0	0	0	-	0	0	0	0
4 NFL Seasons	63	42	132	27	30.0	7	6	0	0	0	0	-	0	1	0	2

Charles Mincy

Pos: S **Rnd:** 5 **College:** Washington **Ht:** 5' 11" **Wt:** 197 **Born:** 12/16/69 **Age:** 26

Year Team	G	GS	Tackles Tk	Ast	Sack	Misc. FF	FR	TD	Blk	Int	Yds	Avg	TD	Punt Returns Num	Yds	Avg	TD	Kickoff Returns Num	Yds	Avg	TD	Totals TD	Fum
1992 Kansas City Chiefs	16	16	52	44	0.0	0	1	1	0	4	128	32.0	2	1	4	4.0	0	0	0	-	0	3	0
1993 Kansas City Chiefs	16	4	37	29	0.0	0	2	0	0	5	44	8.8	0	2	9	4.5	0	0	0	-	0	0	0
1994 Kansas City Chiefs	16	8	39	6	0.0	0	0	0	0	3	49	16.3	0	0	0	-	0	0	0	-	0	0	0

Year Team	G	GS	Tackles			Miscellaneous				Interceptions				Punt Returns				Kickoff Returns				Totals	
			Tk	Ast	Sack	FF	FR	TD	Blk	Int	Yds	Avg	TD	Num	Yds	Avg	TD	Num	Yds	Avg	TD	TD	Fum
1995 Minnesota Vikings	16	9	48	15	0.0	0	2	0	0	3	37	12.3	0	4	22	5.5	0	0	0	-	0	0	0
4 NFL Seasons	64	37	176	94	0.0	0	5	1	0	15	258	17.2	2	7	35	5.0	0	0	0	-	0	3	0

Kevin Miniefield

Pos: CB **Rnd:** 8 **College:** Arizona State **Ht:** 5' 9" **Wt:** 180 **Born:** 3/2/70 **Age:** 26

Year Team	G	GS	Tackles			Miscellaneous				Interceptions				Totals		
			Tk	Ast	Sack	FF	FR	TD	Blk	Int	Yds	Avg	TD	Sfty	TD	Pts
1993 Chicago Bears	9	0	2	0	0.0	1	0	0	0	0	0	-	0	0	0	0
1994 Chicago Bears	12	0	6	4	0.0	0	1	0	0	0	0	-	0	0	0	0
1995 Chicago Bears	15	7	48	7	0.0	0	0	0	0	3	37	12.3	0	0	0	0
3 NFL Seasons	36	7	56	11	0.0	1	1	0	0	3	37	12.3	0	0	0	0

Barry Minter

Pos: LB/DT **Rnd:** 6 **College:** Tulsa **Ht:** 6' 2" **Wt:** 240 **Born:** 1/28/70 **Age:** 26

Year Team	G	GS	Tackles			Miscellaneous				Interceptions				Totals		
			Tk	Ast	Sack	FF	FR	TD	Blk	Int	Yds	Avg	TD	Sfty	TD	Pts
1993 Chicago Bears	2	0	0	0	0.0	0	0	0	0	0	0	-	0	0	0	0
1994 Chicago Bears	13	1	23	9	0.0	0	1	0	0	0	0	-	0	0	0	0
1995 Chicago Bears	16	3	42	13	0.0	1	0	0	0	1	2	2.0	1	0	1	6
3 NFL Seasons	31	4	65	22	0.0	1	1	0	0	1	2	2.0	1	0	1	6

Rick Mirer

(statistical profile on page 356)

Pos: QB **Rnd:** 1 (2) **College:** Notre Dame **Ht:** 6' 2" **Wt:** 211 **Born:** 3/19/70 **Age:** 26

Year Team	G	GS	Passing										Rushing					Miscellaneous			
			Att	Com	Pct	Yards	Yds/Att	Lg	TD	Int	Int%	Rating	Att	Yds	Avg	Lg	TD	Sckd	Yds	Fum Rec Yds	Pts
1993 Seattle Seahawks	16	16	486	274	56.4	2833	5.83	t53	12	17	3.5	67.0	68	343	5.0	33	3	47	235	13 5 -14	18
1994 Seattle Seahawks	13	13	381	195	51.2	2151	5.65	51	11	7	1.8	70.2	34	153	4.5	14	0	27	145	2 1 -7	0
1995 Seattle Seahawks	15	13	391	209	53.5	2564	6.56	t59	13	20	5.1	63.7	43	193	4.5	24	1	42	255	5 1 -2	6
3 NFL Seasons	44	42	1258	678	53.9	7548	6.00	t59	36	44	3.5	67.0	145	689	4.8	33	4	116	635	20 7 -23	24

Brian Mitchell

(statistical profile on page 356)

Pos: KR/RB **Rnd:** 5 **College:** Southwestern Louisiana **Ht:** 5' 10" **Wt:** 221 **Born:** 8/18/68 **Age:** 28

Year Team	G	GS	Rushing					Receiving					Punt Returns				Kickoff Returns				Totals		
			Att	Yds	Avg	Lg	TD	Rec	Yds	Avg	Lg	TD	Num	Yds	Avg	TD	Num	Yds	Avg	TD	Fum	TD	Pts
1990 Washington Redskins	15	0	15	81	5.4	21	1	2	5	2.5	5	0	12	107	8.9	0	18	365	20.3	0	2	1	6
1991 Washington Redskins	16	0	3	14	4.7	8	0	0	0	-	-	0	45	600	13.3	2	29	583	20.1	0	8	2	12
1992 Washington Redskins	16	0	6	70	11.7	33	0	3	30	10.0	17	0	29	271	9.3	1	23	492	21.4	0	4	1	6
1993 Washington Redskins	16	4	63	246	3.9	t29	3	20	157	7.9	18	0	29	193	6.7	0	33	678	20.5	0	3	3	18
1994 Washington Redskins	16	7	78	311	4.0	33	0	26	236	9.1	t46	1	32	452	14.1	2	58	1478	25.5	0	4	3	20
1995 Washington Redskins	16	1	46	301	6.5	136	0	38	324	8.5	t22	1	25	315	12.6	1	55	1408	25.6	0	2	3	18
6 NFL Seasons	95	12	211	1023	4.8	t36	5	89	752	8.4	t46	2	172	1938	11.3	6	216	5004	23.2	0	23	13	80

Other Statistics: 1990–attempted 6 passes with 3 completions for 40 yards. 1991–recovered 1 fumble for 0 yards. 1992–recovered 2 fumbles for 0 yards; attempted 1 pass with 0 completions for 0 yards. 1993–recovered 1 fumble for 0 yards; attempted 2 passes with 1 completion for 50 yards and 1 interception. 1994–attempted 1 pass with 0 completions for 0 yards and 1 interception; scored 1 two-point conversion. 1995–recovered 1 fumble for 0 yards.

Johnny Mitchell

(statistical profile on page 357)

Pos: TE **Rnd:** 1 (15) **College:** Nebraska **Ht:** 6' 3" **Wt:** 241 **Born:** 1/20/71 **Age:** 25

Year Team	G	GS	Rushing					Receiving					Punt Returns				Kickoff Returns				Totals		
			Att	Yds	Avg	Lg	TD	Rec	Yds	Avg	Lg	TD	Num	Yds	Avg	TD	Num	Yds	Avg	TD	Fum	TD	Pts
1992 New York Jets	11	3	0	0	-	-	0	16	210	13.1	t37	1	0	0	-	0	0	0	-	0	0	1	6
1993 New York Jets	14	14	0	0	-	-	0	39	630	16.2	t65	6	0	0	-	0	0	0	-	0	6	6	36
1994 New York Jets	16	14	0	0	-	-	0	58	749	12.9	55	4	0	0	-	0	0	0	-	0	1	4	24
1995 New York Jets	12	11	0	0	-	-	0	45	497	11.0	t43	5	0	0	-	0	0	0	-	0	2	5	30
4 NFL Seasons	53	42	0	0	-	-	0	158	2086	13.2	t65	16	0	0	-	0	0	0	-	0	3	16	96

Other Statistics: 1994–recovered 1 fumble for 4 yards.

Kevin Mitchell

Pos: LB **Rnd:** 2 **College:** Syracuse **Ht:** 6' 1" **Wt:** 250 **Born:** 1/1/71 **Age:** 25

Year Team	G	GS	Tackles			Miscellaneous				Interceptions				Totals		
			Tk	Ast	Sack	FF	FR	TD	Blk	Int	Yds	Avg	TD	Sfty	TD	Pts
1994 San Francisco 49ers	16	0	6	0	0.0	0	0	0	0	0	0	-	0	0	0	0
1995 San Francisco 49ers	15	0	4	0	0.0	0	0	0	0	0	0	-	0	0	0	0
2 NFL Seasons	31	0	10	0	0.0	0	0	0	0	0	0	-	0	0	0	0

Pete Mitchell

Pos: TE **Rnd:** 4 **College:** Boston College   *(statistical profile on page 357)*

Ht: 6' 2" **Wt:** 243 **Born:** 10/9/71 **Age:** 25

			Rushing					Receiving					Punt Returns				Kickoff Returns				Totals		
Year Team	G	GS	Att	Yds	Avg	Lg	TD	Rec	Yds	Avg	Lg	TD	Num	Yds	Avg	TD	Num	Yds	Avg	TD	Fum	TD	Pts
1995 Jacksonville Jaguars	16	4	0	0	-	-	0	41	527	12.9	35	2	0	0	-	0	0	0	-	0	0	2	12

Scott Mitchell

Pos: QB **Rnd:** 4 **College:** Utah   *(statistical profile on page 358)*

Ht: 6' 6" **Wt:** 230 **Born:** 1/2/68 **Age:** 28

			Passing									Rushing					Miscellaneous			
Year Team	G	GS	Att	Com	Pct	Yards	Yds/Att	Lg	TD	Int	Int%	Rating	Att	Yds	Avg	Lg	TD	Sckd	Yds	Fum Recv Yds	Pts
1991 Miami Dolphins	2	0	0	0	-	0	-	-	0	0	-	0.0	0	0	-	-	0	0	0	0 0 0	0
1992 Miami Dolphins	16	0	8	2	25.0	32	4.00	18	0	1	12.5	4.2	8	10	1.3	8	0	0	0	1 0 -1	0
1993 Miami Dolphins	13	7	233	133	57.1	1773	7.61	t77	12	8	3.4	84.2	21	89	4.2	32	0	7	49	3 1 -4	6
1994 Detroit Lions	9	9	246	119	48.4	1456	5.92	34	10	11	4.5	62.0	15	24	1.6	7	1	12	63	8 2 -5	6
1995 Detroit Lions	16	16	583	346	59.3	4338	7.44	t91	32	12	2.1	92.3	36	104	2.9	18	4	31	145	8 1 0	24
5 NFL Seasons	56	32	1070	600	56.1	7599	7.10	t91	54	32	3.0	82.8	80	227	2.8	32	5	50	257	20 4 -10	30

Shannon Mitchell

Pos: TE **Rnd:** FA **College:** Georgia

Ht: 6' 2" **Wt:** 245 **Born:** 3/28/72 **Age:** 24

			Rushing					Receiving					Punt Returns				Kickoff Returns				Totals		
Year Team	G	GS	Att	Yds	Avg	Lg	TD	Rec	Yds	Avg	Lg	TD	Num	Yds	Avg	TD	Num	Yds	Avg	TD	Fum	TD	Pts
1994 San Diego Chargers	16	6	0	0	-	-	0	11	105	9.5	36	0	0	0	-	0	1	18	18.0	0	0	0	0
1995 San Diego Chargers	15	2	0	0	-	-	0	3	31	10.3	34	1	0	0	-	0	0	0	-	0	0	1	6
2 NFL Seasons	31	8	0	0	-	-	0	14	136	9.7	36	1	0	0	-	0	1	18	18.0	0	0	1	6

Chris Mohr

Pos: P **Rnd:** 6 **College:** Alabama   *(statistical profile on page 480)*

Ht: 6' 5" **Wt:** 215 **Born:** 5/11/66 **Age:** 30

			Punting										Rushing		Passing			
Year Team	G	NetPunts	Yards	Avg	Long	In20	In20%	TotPunts	TB	Blocks	OppRet	RetYds	NetAvg	Att	Yards	Att Com	Yards	Int
1989 Tampa Bay Buccaneers	16	84	3311	39.4	58	10	11.9	86	3	2	54	492	32.1	0	0	0 0	0	0
1991 Buffalo Bills	16	54	2085	38.6	58	12	22.2	54	4	0	15	53	36.1	0	0	1 1	-9	0
1992 Buffalo Bills	15	60	2531	42.2	61	12	20.0	60	7	0	22	185	36.8	1	11	0 0	0	0
1993 Buffalo Bills	16	74	2991	40.4	58	19	25.7	74	4	0	29	247	36.0	0	0	0 0	0	0
1994 Buffalo Bills	16	67	2799	41.8	71	13	19.4	67	3	0	37	324	36.0	1	-9	0 0	0	0
1995 Buffalo Bills	16	86	3473	40.4	60	23	26.7	86	7	0	23	224	36.2	0	0	0 0	0	0
6 NFL Seasons	95	425	17190	40.4	71	89	20.9	427	28	2	180	1525	35.4	2	2	1 1	-9	0

Other Statistics: 1989–scored 1 one-point conversion. 1992–recovered 1 fumble for 0 yards. 1993–recovered 1 fumble for 0 yards; fumbled 1 time.

Art Monk

Pos: WR **Rnd:** 1 (18) **College:** Syracuse

Ht: 6' 3" **Wt:** 210 **Born:** 12/5/57 **Age:** 38

			Rushing					Receiving					Kickoff Returns				Passing				Totals		
Year Team	G	GS	Att	Yds	Avg	Lg	TD	Rec	Yds	Avg	Lg	TD	Num	Yds	Avg	TD	Att	Com	Yds	Int	Fum	TD	Pts
1980 Washington Redskins	16	10	0	0	-	-	0	58	797	13.7	t54	3	1	10	10.0	0	0	0	0	0	0	3	18
1981 Washington Redskins	16	16	1	-5	-5.0	-5	0	56	894	16.0	t79	6	0	0	-	0	0	0	0	0	0	6	36
1982 Washington Redskins	9	9	7	21	3.0	14	0	35	447	12.8	43	1	0	0	-	0	0	0	0	0	3	1	6
1983 Washington Redskins	12	11	3	-19	-6.3	2	0	47	746	15.9	t43	5	0	0	-	0	1	1	46	0	0	5	30
1984 Washington Redskins	16	16	2	18	9.0	18	0	106	1372	12.9	72	7	0	0	-	0	0	0	0	0	1	7	42
1985 Washington Redskins	15	14	7	51	7.3	16	0	91	1226	13.5	53	2	0	0	-	0	0	0	0	0	2	2	12
1986 Washington Redskins	16	16	4	27	6.8	21	0	73	1068	14.6	69	4	0	0	-	0	0	0	0	0	2	4	24
1987 Washington Redskins	9	9	6	63	10.5	26	0	38	483	12.7	62	6	0	0	-	0	0	0	0	0	0	6	36
1988 Washington Redskins	16	13	7	46	6.6	23	0	72	946	13.1	t46	5	0	0	-	0	1	0	0	0	0	5	30
1989 Washington Redskins	16	12	3	8	2.7	14	0	86	1186	13.8	t60	8	0	0	-	0	0	0	0	0	2	8	48
1990 Washington Redskins	16	16	7	59	8.4	26	0	68	770	11.3	44	5	0	0	-	0	0	0	0	0	0	5	30
1991 Washington Redskins	16	16	9	19	2.1	14	0	71	1049	14.8	t64	8	0	0	-	0	0	0	0	0	2	8	48
1992 Washington Redskins	16	14	6	45	7.5	16	0	46	644	14.0	t49	3	0	0	-	0	0	0	0	0	1	3	18
1993 Washington Redskins	16	5	1	-1	-1.0	-1	0	41	398	9.7	29	2	0	0	-	0	0	0	0	0	0	2	12
1994 New York Jets	16	15	0	0	-	-	0	46	581	12.6	69	3	0	0	-	0	0	0	0	0	0	3	18
1995 Philadelphia Eagles	3	1	0	0	-	-	0	6	114	19.0	36	0	0	0	-	0	0	0	0	0	0	0	0
16 NFL Seasons	224	193	63	332	5.3	26	0	940	12721	13.5	t79	68	1	10	10.0	0	2	1	46	0	13	68	408

Other Statistics: 1986–recovered 2 fumbles for 0 yards. 1988–recovered 1 fumble for 0 yards. 1990–recovered 1 fumble for 0 yards.

Alton Montgomery

Pos: S **Rnd:** 2 **College:** Houston

Ht: 6' 0" **Wt:** 209 **Born:** 6/16/68 **Age:** 28

			Tackles			Miscellaneous				Interceptions				Punt Returns				Kickoff Returns				Totals	
Year Team	G	GS	Tk	Ast	Sack	FF	FR	TD	Blk	Int	Yds	Avg	TD	Num	Yds	Avg	TD	Num	Yds	Avg	TD	TD	Fum
1990 Denver Broncos	15	4	37	16	0.0	0	2	0	0	2	43	21.5	0	0	0	-	0	14	286	20.4	0	0	1

Year	Team	G	GS	Tackles Tk	Ast	Sack	Miscellaneous FF	FR	TD	Blk	Interceptions Int	Yds	Avg	TD	Punt Returns Num	Yds	Avg	TD	Kickoff Returns Num	Yds	Avg	TD	Totals TD	Fum
1991	Denver Broncos	16	0	3	2	0.0	0	1	0	0	0	0	-	0	0	0	-	0	26	488	18.8	0	0	1
1992	Denver Broncos	12	1	13	18	0.0	0	2	0	0	0	0	-	0	0	0	-	0	21	466	22.2	0	0	1
1993	Atlanta Falcons	8	0	4	3	0.0	0	0	0	0	0	0	-	0	0	0	-	0	2	53	26.5	0	0	0
1994	Atlanta Falcons	4	1	2	1	0.0	0	0	0	0	0	0	-	0	0	0	-	0	2	58	29.0	0	0	0
1995	Atlanta Falcons	15	0	16	3	3.0	1	0	0	0	1	71	71.0	1	0	0	-	0	0	0	-	0	1	0
	6 NFL Seasons	70	6	75	43	3.0	1	5	0	0	3	114	38.0	1	0	0	-	0	65	1351	20.8	0	1	3

Glenn Montgomery

Pos: DT   **Rnd:** 5   **College:** Houston   **Ht:** 6' 0"   **Wt:** 282   **Born:** 3/31/67   **Age:** 29

Year	Team	G	GS	Tackles Tk	Ast	Sack	Miscellaneous FF	FR	TD	Blk	Interceptions Int	Yds	Avg	TD	Punt Returns Num	Yds	Avg	TD	Kickoff Returns Num	Yds	Avg	TD	Totals TD	Fum
1989	Houston Oilers	15	0	14	9	1.5	1	0	0	0	0	0	-	0	0	0	-	0	1	0	0.0	0	0	0
1990	Houston Oilers	15	0	15	1	0.5	0	0	0	0	0	0	-	0	0	0	-	0	0	0	-	0	0	0
1991	Houston Oilers	16	0	8	4	0.0	0	1	0	0	0	0	-	0	0	0	-	0	0	0	-	0	0	0
1992	Houston Oilers	16	0	5	1	0.5	0	2	0	0	0	0	-	0	0	0	-	0	1	13	13.0	0	0	0
1993	Houston Oilers	16	11	35	10	6.0	1	3	0	0	0	0	-	0	0	0	-	0	0	0	-	0	0	0
1994	Houston Oilers	14	14	45	18	3.0	0	3	0	0	0	0	-	0	0	0	-	0	0	0	-	0	0	0
1995	Houston Oilers	15	14	26	20	2.0	0	2	0	0	0	0	-	0	0	0	-	0	0	0	-	0	0	0
	7 NFL Seasons	107	39	148	63	13.5	2	11	0	0	0	0	-	0	0	0	-	0	2	13	6.5	0	0	0

Mark Montreuil

Pos: CB   **Rnd:** 7   **College:** Concordia   **Ht:** 6' 2"   **Wt:** 200   **Born:** 12/29/71   **Age:** 24

Year	Team	G	GS	Tackles Tk	Ast	Sack	Miscellaneous FF	FR	TD	Blk	Interceptions Int	Yds	Avg	TD	Totals Sfty	TD	Pts
1995	San Diego Chargers	16	0	0	0	0.0	0	1	0	0	0	0	-	0	0	0	0

Warren Moon

(statistical profile on page 358)

Pos: QB   **Rnd:** FA   **College:** Washington   **Ht:** 6' 3"   **Wt:** 219   **Born:** 11/18/56   **Age:** 39

Year	Team	G	GS	Passing Att	Com	Pct	Yards	Yds/Att	Lg	TD	Int	Int%	Rating	Rushing Att	Yds	Avg	Lg	TD	Miscellaneous Sckd	Yds	Fum	Recv	Yds	Pts
1984	Houston Oilers	16	16	450	259	57.6	3338	7.42	76	12	14	3.1	76.9	58	211	3.6	31	1	47	371	17	7	-1	6
1985	Houston Oilers	14	14	377	200	53.1	2709	7.19	t80	15	19	5.0	68.5	39	130	3.3	17	0	46	366	12	5	-8	0
1986	Houston Oilers	15	15	488	256	52.5	3489	7.15	t81	13	26	5.3	62.3	42	157	3.7	19	2	41	332	11	3	-4	12
1987	Houston Oilers	12	12	368	184	50.0	2806	7.63	t83	21	18	4.9	74.2	34	112	3.3	20	3	25	198	8	6	-7	18
1988	Houston Oilers	11	11	294	160	54.4	2327	7.91	t57	17	8	2.7	88.4	33	88	2.7	14	5	12	120	8	4	-12	30
1989	Houston Oilers	16	16	464	280	60.3	3631	7.83	55	23	14	3.0	88.9	70	268	3.8	19	4	35	267	11	6	-13	24
1990	Houston Oilers	15	15	584	362	62.0	4689	8.03	t87	33	13	2.2	96.8	55	215	3.9	17	2	36	252	18	4	0	12
1991	Houston Oilers	16	16	655	404	61.7	4690	7.16	t61	23	21	3.2	81.7	33	68	2.1	12	2	23	174	11	4	-4	12
1992	Houston Oilers	11	10	346	224	64.7	2521	7.29	72	18	12	3.5	89.3	27	147	5.4	23	1	16	105	7	0	-6	6
1993	Houston Oilers	15	14	520	303	58.3	3485	6.70	t80	21	21	4.0	75.2	48	145	3.0	35	1	34	218	13	5	-7	6
1994	Minnesota Vikings	15	15	601	371	61.7	4264	7.09	t65	18	19	3.2	79.9	27	55	2.0	12	0	29	235	9	2	-5	0
1995	Minnesota Vikings	16	16	606	377	62.2	4228	6.98	t85	33	14	2.3	91.5	33	82	2.5	16	0	38	277	13	5	-12	0
	12 NFL Seasons	172	170	5753	3380	58.8	42177	7.33	t87	247	199	3.5	81.5	499	1678	3.4	35	21	382	2915	138	51	-79	126

Brandon Moore

Pos: T   **Rnd:** FA   **College:** Duke   **Ht:** 6' 7"   **Wt:** 295   **Born:** 6/21/70   **Age:** 26

Year	Team	G	GS	Year	Team	G	GS	Year	Team	G	GS		G	GS
1993	New England Patriots	16	0	1994	New England Patriots	4	0	1995	New England Patriots	6	0	3 NFL Seasons	26	0

Dave Moore

Pos: TE/RB   **Rnd:** 7   **College:** Pittsburgh   **Ht:** 6' 2"   **Wt:** 248   **Born:** 11/11/69   **Age:** 26

Year	Team	G	GS	Rushing Att	Yds	Avg	Lg	TD	Receiving Rec	Yds	Avg	Lg	TD	Kickoff Returns Num	Yds	Avg	TD	Passing Att	Com	Yds	Int	Totals Fum	TD	Pts
1992	Mia TD	5	2	0	0	-	-	0	1	10	10.0	10	0	0	0	-	0	0	0	0	0	0	0	0
1993	Tampa Bay Buccaneers	15	1	0	0	-	-	0	4	47	11.8	t19	1	0	0	-	0	1	0	0	0	0	1	6
1994	Tampa Bay Buccaneers	15	5	0	0	-	-	0	4	57	14.3	18	0	2	27	13.5	0	0	0	0	0	0	0	0
1995	Tampa Bay Buccaneers	16	9	1	4	4.0	4	0	13	102	7.8	21	0	0	0	-	0	0	0	0	0	0	0	0
1992	Miami Dolphins	1	0	0	0	-	-	0	0	0	-	-	0	0	0	-	0	0	0	0	0	0	0	0
	Tampa Bay Buccaneers	4	2	0	0	-	-	0	1	10	10.0	10	0	0	0	-	0	0	0	0	0	0	0	0
	4 NFL Seasons	51	17	1	4	4.0	4	0	22	216	9.8	21	1	2	27	13.5	0	1	0	0	0	0	1	6

Other Statistics: 1993–recovered 1 fumble for 0 yards.

Derrick Moore

(statistical profile on page 359)

Pos: RB **Rnd:** 8 **College:** Northeastern Oklahoma **Ht:** 6' 1" **Wt:** 227 **Born:** 10/13/67 **Age:** 29

Year Team	G	GS	Rushing Att	Yds	Avg	Lg	TD	Receiving Rec	Yds	Avg	Lg	TD	Punt Returns Num	Yds	Avg	TD	Kickoff Returns Num	Yds	Avg	TD	Totals Fum	TD	Pts
1993 Detroit Lions	13	3	88	405	4.6	48	3	21	169	8.0	20	1	0	0	-	0	1	68	68.0	0	4	4	24
1994 Detroit Lions	16	0	27	52	1.9	12	4	1	10	10.0	10	0	0	0	-	0	10	113	11.3	0	2	4	24
1995 Carolina Panthers	13	10	195	740	3.8	t53	4	4	12	3.0	5	0	0	0	-	0	0	0	-	0	4	4	24
3 NFL Seasons	42	13	310	1197	3.9	t53	11	26	191	7.3	20	1	0	0	-	0	11	181	16.5	0	10	12	72

Other Statistics: 1993–recovered 3 fumbles for 0 yards.

Eric Moore

Pos: T **Rnd:** 1 (10) **College:** Indiana **Ht:** 6' 5" **Wt:** 290 **Born:** 1/21/65 **Age:** 31

Year	Team	G	GS	Year	Team	G	GS	Year	Team	G	GS		G	GS
1988	New York Giants	11	10	1991	New York Giants	16	16	1994	Cincinnati Bengals	6	6			
1989	New York Giants	16	13	1992	New York Giants	10	10	1995	Cleveland Browns	1	0			
1990	New York Giants	15	14	1993	New York Giants	7	5	1995	Miami Dolphins	2	0			
												8 NFL Seasons	84	74

Other Statistics: 1989–recovered 3 fumbles for 0 yards.

Herman Moore

(statistical profile on page 359)

Pos: WR **Rnd:** 1 (10) **College:** Virginia **Ht:** 6' 3" **Wt:** 210 **Born:** 10/20/69 **Age:** 27

Year Team	G	GS	Rushing Att	Yds	Avg	Lg	TD	Receiving Rec	Yds	Avg	Lg	TD	Punt Returns Num	Yds	Avg	TD	Kickoff Returns Num	Yds	Avg	TD	Totals Fum	TD	Pts
1991 Detroit Lions	15	1	0	0	-	-	0	11	135	12.3	21	0	0	0	-	0	0	0	-	0	0	0	0
1992 Detroit Lions	12	11	0	0	-	-	0	51	966	18.9	t77	4	0	0	-	0	0	0	-	0	0	4	24
1993 Detroit Lions	15	15	0	0	-	-	0	61	935	15.3	t93	6	0	0	-	0	0	0	-	0	2	6	36
1994 Detroit Lions	16	16	0	0	-	-	0	72	1173	16.3	t51	11	0	0	-	0	0	0	-	0	1	11	66
1995 Detroit Lions	16	16	0	0	-	-	0	**123**	1686	13.7	t69	14	0	0	-	0	0	0	-	0	2	14	84
5 NFL Seasons	74	59	0	0	-	-	0	318	4895	15.4	t93	35	0	0	-	0	0	0	-	0	5	35	210

Marty Moore

Pos: LB **Rnd:** 7 **College:** Kentucky **Ht:** 6' 1" **Wt:** 242 **Born:** 3/19/71 **Age:** 25

Year Team	G	GS	Tackles Tk	Ast	Sack	Miscellaneous FF	FR	TD	Blk	Interceptions Int	Yds	Avg	TD	Totals Sfty	TD	Pts
1994 New England Patriots	16	4	*16*	9	0.0	2	0	0	0	0	0	-	0	0	0	0
1995 New England Patriots	16	3	*14*	1	0.0	0	0	0	0	0	0	-	0	0	0	0
2 NFL Seasons	32	7	30	10	0.0	2	0	0	0	0	0	-	0	0	0	0

Rob Moore

(statistical profile on page 360)

Pos: WR **Rnd:** 1(S) **College:** Syracuse **Ht:** 6' 3" **Wt:** 205 **Born:** 9/27/68 **Age:** 28

Year Team	G	GS	Rushing Att	Yds	Avg	Lg	TD	Receiving Rec	Yds	Avg	Lg	TD	Kickoff Returns Num	Yds	Avg	TD	Passing Att	Com	Yds	Int	Totals Fum	TD	Pts
1990 New York Jets	15	14	2	-4	-2.0	4	0	44	692	15.7	t69	6	0	0	-	0	0	0	0	0	1	6	36
1991 New York Jets	16	16	0	0	-	-	0	70	987	14.1	53	5	0	0	-	0	0	0	0	0	2	5	30
1992 New York Jets	16	16	1	21	21.0	21	0	50	726	14.5	t48	4	0	0	-	0	0	0	0	0	4	4	24
1993 New York Jets	13	13	1	-6	-6.0	-6	0	64	843	13.2	51	1	0	0	-	0	0	0	0	0	2	1	6
1994 New York Jets	16	16	1	-3	-3.0	-3	0	78	1010	12.9	t41	6	0	0	-	0	0	0	0	0	0	6	40
1995 Arizona Cardinals	15	15	0	0	-	-	0	63	907	14.4	45	5	0	0	-	0	2	1	33	1	0	5	32
6 NFL Seasons	91	90	5	8	1.6	21	0	369	5165	14.0	t69	27	0	0	-	0	2	1	33	1	5	27	168

Other Statistics: 1994–recovered 1 fumble for 0 yards; scored 2 two-point conversions. 1995–scored 1 two-point conversion.

Ronald Moore

Pos: RB **Rnd:** 4 **College:** Pittsburg State **Ht:** 5' 10" **Wt:** 225 **Born:** 1/26/70 **Age:** 26

Year Team	G	GS	Rushing Att	Yds	Avg	Lg	TD	Receiving Rec	Yds	Avg	Lg	TD	Kickoff Returns Num	Yds	Avg	TD	Passing Att	Com	Yds	Int	Totals Fum	TD	Pts
1993 Phoenix Cardinals	16	11	263	1018	3.9	20	9	3	16	5.3	6	0	1	9	9.0	0	0	0	0	0	3	9	54
1994 Arizona Cardinals	16	16	232	780	3.4	24	4	8	52	6.5	18	1	0	0	-	0	1	0	0	0	2	5	32
1995 New York Jets	15	3	43	121	2.8	14	0	8	50	6.3	13	0	8	166	20.8	0	0	0	0	0	3	0	0
3 NFL Seasons	47	30	538	1919	3.6	24	13	19	118	6.2	18	1	9	175	19.4	0	1	0	0	0	8	14	86

Other Statistics: 1993–recovered 1 fumble for 0 yards. 1994–recovered 1 fumble for 0 yards; scored 1 two-point conversion. 1995–recovered 1 fumble for 0 yards.

Stevon Moore

(statistical profile on page 435)

Pos: S **Rnd:** 7 **College:** Mississippi **Ht:** 5' 11" **Wt:** 210 **Born:** 2/9/67 **Age:** 29

Year Team	G	GS	Tackles Tk	Ast	Sack	Miscellaneous FF	FR	TD	Blk	Interceptions Int	Yds	Avg	TD	Totals Sfty	TD	Pts
1990 Miami Dolphins	7	0	1	0	0.0	0	1	0	0	0	0	-	0	0	0	0

Year Team	G	GS	Tackles			Miscellaneous				Interceptions				Totals		
			Tk	Ast	Sack	FF	FR	TD	Blk	Int	Yds	Avg	TD	Sfty	TD	Pts
1992 Cleveland Browns	13	3	29	28	2.0	1	3	1	0	0	0	-	0	0	1	6
1993 Cleveland Browns	16	16	96	59	0.0	3	1	1	0	0	0	-	0	0	1	6
1994 Cleveland Browns	16	16	65	19	0.0	0	6	0	0	0	0	-	0	0	0	0
1995 Cleveland Browns	16	16	79	13	1.0	0	0	0	0	5	55	11.0	0	0	0	0
5 NFL Seasons	68	51	270	119	3.0	4	11	2	0	5	55	11.0	0	0	2	12

Will Moore

(statistical profile on page 360)

Pos: WR **Rnd:** FA **College:** Texas Southern **Ht:** 6' 2" **Wt:** 180 **Born:** 2/21/70 **Age:** 26

Year Team	G	GS	Rushing					Receiving					Punt Returns				Kickoff Returns				Totals		
			Att	Yds	Avg	Lg	TD	Rec	Yds	Avg	Lg	TD	Num	Yds	Avg	TD	Num	Yds	Avg	TD	Fum	TD	Pts
1995 New England Patriots	14	13	0	0	-	-	0	43	502	11.7	33	1	0	0	-	0	0	0	-	0	0	1	6

Anthony Morgan

(statistical profile on page 361)

Pos: WR **Rnd:** 5 **College:** Tennessee **Ht:** 6' 1" **Wt:** 200 **Born:** 11/15/67 **Age:** 28

Year Team	G	GS	Rushing					Receiving					Punt Returns				Kickoff Returns				Totals		
			Att	Yds	Avg	Lg	TD	Rec	Yds	Avg	Lg	TD	Num	Yds	Avg	TD	Num	Yds	Avg	TD	Fum	TD	Pts
1991 Chicago Bears	14	2	3	18	6.0	13	0	13	211	16.2	t84	2	3	19	6.3	0	8	133	16.6	0	1	2	12
1992 Chicago Bears	12	4	3	68	22.7	35	0	14	323	23.1	t83	2	3	21	7.0	0	4	71	17.8	0	0	2	12
1993 Chi - GB	3	0	0	0	-	-	0	1	8	8.0	8	0	0	0	-	0	0	0	-	0	0	0	0
1994 Green Bay Packers	16	0	0	0	-	-	0	28	397	14.2	t47	4	0	0	-	0	0	0	-	0	1	4	24
1995 Green Bay Packers	16	8	0	0	-	-	0	31	344	11.1	t29	4	0	0	-	0	3	46	15.3	0	0	4	24
1993 Chicago Bears	1	0	0	0	-	-	0	0	0	-	-	0	0	0	-	0	0	0	-	0	0	0	0
Green Bay Packers	2	0	0	0	-	-	0	1	8	8.0	8	0	0	0	-	0	0	0	-	0	0	0	0
5 NFL Seasons	61	14	6	86	14.3	35	0	87	1283	14.7	t84	12	6	40	6.7	0	15	250	16.7	0	2	12	72

Bam Morris

(statistical profile on page 361)

Pos: RB **Rnd:** 3 **College:** Texas Tech **Ht:** 6' 0" **Wt:** 245 **Born:** 1/13/72 **Age:** 24

Year Team	G	GS	Rushing					Receiving					Punt Returns				Kickoff Returns				Totals		
			Att	Yds	Avg	Lg	TD	Rec	Yds	Avg	Lg	TD	Num	Yds	Avg	TD	Num	Yds	Avg	TD	Fum	TD	Pts
1994 Pittsburgh Steelers	15	6	198	836	4.2	20	7	22	204	9.3	49	0	0	0	-	0	4	114	28.5	0	3	7	42
1995 Pittsburgh Steelers	13	4	148	559	3.8	t30	9	8	36	4.5	13	0	0	0	-	0	0	0	-	0	3	9	54
2 NFL Seasons	28	10	346	1395	4.0	t30	16	30	240	8.0	49	0	0	0	-	0	4	114	28.5	0	6	16	96

Other Statistics: 1994–recovered 1 fumble for 0 yards.

Mike Morris

Pos: LS **Rnd:** FA **College:** Northeast Missouri State **Ht:** 6' 5" **Wt:** 277 **Born:** 2/22/61 **Age:** 35

Year	Team	G	GS	Year	Team	G	GS	Year	Team	G	GS	Year	Team	G	GS
1987	St. Louis Cardinals	14	0	1990	Seattle Seahawks	4	0	1992	Minnesota Vikings	16	0	1995	Minnesota Vikings	16	0
1989	Kansas City Chiefs	5	0	1990	Cleveland Browns	10	0	1993	Minnesota Vikings	16	0				
1989	New England Patriots	11	0	1991	Minnesota Vikings	16	0	1994	Minnesota Vikings	16	0		8 NFL Seasons	124	0

Other Statistics: 1990–fumbled 1 time for -23 yards.

Darryl Morrison

Pos: S **Rnd:** 6 **College:** Arizona **Ht:** 5' 11" **Wt:** 200 **Born:** 5/19/71 **Age:** 25

Year Team	G	GS	Tackles			Miscellaneous				Interceptions				Totals		
			Tk	Ast	Sack	FF	FR	TD	Blk	Int	Yds	Avg	TD	Sfty	TD	Pts
1993 Washington Redskins	4	0	0	0	0.0	0	0	0	0	0	0	-	0	0	0	0
1994 Washington Redskins	16	16	68	9	0.0	0	2	1	0	0	0	-	0	0	1	6
1995 Washington Redskins	16	0	12	2	0.0	0	1	0	0	0	0	-	0	0	0	0
3 NFL Seasons	36	16	80	11	0.0	0	3	1	0	0	0	-	0	0	1	6

Steve Morrison

Pos: LB **Rnd:** FA **College:** Michigan **Ht:** 6' 3" **Wt:** 238 **Born:** 12/28/71 **Age:** 24

Year Team	G	GS	Tackles			Miscellaneous				Interceptions				Punt Returns				Kickoff Returns				Totals	
			Tk	Ast	Sack	FF	FR	TD	Blk	Int	Yds	Avg	TD	Num	Yds	Avg	TD	Num	Yds	Avg	TD	TD	Fum
1995 Indianapolis Colts	10	0	0	0	0.0	0	0	0	0	0	0	-	0	0	0	-	0	2	6	3.0	0	0	0

Johnnie Morton

(statistical profile on page 362)

Pos: WR/KR **Rnd:** 1 (21) **College:** Southern California **Ht:** 5' 11" **Wt:** 190 **Born:** 10/7/71 **Age:** 25

Year Team	G	GS	Rushing					Receiving					Punt Returns				Kickoff Returns				Totals		
			Att	Yds	Avg	Lg	TD	Rec	Yds	Avg	Lg	TD	Num	Yds	Avg	TD	Num	Yds	Avg	TD	Fum	TD	Pts
1994 Detroit Lions	14	0	0	0	-	-	0	3	39	13.0	t18	1	0	0	-	0	4	143	35.8	1	1	2	12
1995 Detroit Lions	16	14	3	33	11.0	18	0	44	590	13.4	t32	8	7	48	6.9	0	18	390	21.7	0	1	8	48

Year Team	G	GS	Rushing					Receiving					Punt Returns				Kickoff Returns				Totals		
			Att	Yds	Avg	Lg	TD	Rec	Yds	Avg	Lg	TD	Num	Yds	Avg	TD	Num	Yds	Avg	TD	Fum	TD	Pts
2 NFL Seasons	30	14	3	33	11.0	18	0	47	629	13.4	t32	9	7	48	6.9	0	22	533	24.2	1	2	10	60

Other Statistics: 1994–recovered 1 fumble for 0 yards.

Mike Morton

Pos: LB **Rnd:** 4 **College:** North Carolina **Ht:** 6' 4" **Wt:** 235 **Born:** 3/28/72 **Age:** 24

Year Team	G	GS	Tackles			Miscellaneous				Interceptions				Totals		
			Tk	Ast	Sack	FF	FR	TD	Blk	Int	Yds	Avg	TD	Sfty	TD	Pts
1995 Oakland Raiders	12	0	3	0	0.0	0	1	0	0	0	0	-	0	0	0	0

Brent Moss

Pos: RB **Rnd:** FA **College:** Wisconsin **Ht:** 5' 8" **Wt:** 211 **Born:** 1/30/72 **Age:** 24

Year Team	G	GS	Rushing					Receiving					Punt Returns				Kickoff Returns				Totals		
			Att	Yds	Avg	Lg	TD	Rec	Yds	Avg	Lg	TD	Num	Yds	Avg	TD	Num	Yds	Avg	TD	Fum	TD	Pts
1995 St. Louis Rams	4	0	22	90	4.1	18	0	1	-3	-3.0	-3	0	0	0	-	0	0	0	-	0	0	0	0

Winston Moss

(statistical profile on page 435)

Pos: LB **Rnd:** 2 **College:** Miami (FL) **Ht:** 6' 3" **Wt:** 245 **Born:** 12/24/65 **Age:** 30

Year Team	G	GS	Tackles			Miscellaneous				Interceptions				Totals		
			Tk	Ast	Sack	FF	FR	TD	Blk	Int	Yds	Avg	TD	Sfty	TD	Pts
1987 Tampa Bay Buccaneers	12	6	0	-	1.5	0	1	1	0	0	0	-	0	0	1	6
1988 Tampa Bay Buccaneers	16	15	0	-	0.0	0	0	0	0	0	0	-	0	0	0	0
1989 Tampa Bay Buccaneers	16	16	0	-	5.5	0	0	0	0	0	0	-	0	0	0	0
1990 Tampa Bay Buccaneers	16	15	0	-	3.5	0	1	0	0	1	31	31.0	0	0	0	0
1991 Los Angeles Raiders	16	16	0	-	3.0	0	2	0	0	0	0	-	0	0	0	0
1992 Los Angeles Raiders	15	15	0	-	2.0	0	0	0	0	0	0	-	0	0	0	0
1993 Los Angeles Raiders	16	16	81	21	0.0	0	0	0	0	0	0	-	0	0	0	0
1994 Los Angeles Raiders	16	14	55	19	2.0	0	0	0	0	0	0	-	0	0	0	0
1995 Seattle Seahawks	16	16	65	23	2.0	1	2	0	0	1	0	0.0	0	0	0	0
9 NFL Seasons	139	129	201	63	19.5	1	6	1	0	2	31	15.5	0	0	1	6

Zefross Moss

Pos: T **Rnd:** FA **College:** Alabama State **Ht:** 6' 6" **Wt:** 324 **Born:** 8/17/66 **Age:** 30

Year	Team	G	GS	Year	Team	G	GS	Year	Team	G	GS	Year	Team	G	GS
1989	Indianapolis Colts	16	0	1991	Indianapolis Colts	11	10	1993	Indianapolis Colts	16	16	1995	Detroit Lions	15	14
1990	Indianapolis Colts	16	16	1992	Indianapolis Colts	13	13	1994	Indianapolis Colts	11	11		7 NFL Seasons	98	80

Eric Moten

Pos: G **Rnd:** 2 **College:** Michigan State **Ht:** 6' 3" **Wt:** 306 **Born:** 4/11/68 **Age:** 28

Year	Team	G	GS	Year	Team	G	GS	Year	Team	G	GS	Year	Team	G	GS
1991	San Diego Chargers	16	11	1992	San Diego Chargers	16	16	1993	San Diego Chargers	4	4	1995	San Diego Chargers	16	15
													4 NFL Seasons	52	46

Other Statistics: 1995–recovered 1 fumble for 0 yards.

Roderick Mullen

Pos: CB **Rnd:** 5 **College:** Grambling **Ht:** 6' 1" **Wt:** 204 **Born:** 12/5/72 **Age:** 23

Year Team	G	GS	Tackles			Miscellaneous				Interceptions				Totals		
			Tk	Ast	Sack	FF	FR	TD	Blk	Int	Yds	Avg	TD	Sfty	TD	Pts
1995 Green Bay Packers	8	0	3	1	0.0	0	0	0	0	0	0	-	0	0	0	0

Eddie Murray

(statistical profile on page 480)

Pos: K **Rnd:** 7 **College:** Tulane **Ht:** 5' 11" **Wt:** 195 **Born:** 8/29/56 **Age:** 40

Year Team	G	Field Goals													PAT		Tot
		1-29 Yds	Pct	30-39 Yds	Pct	40-49 Yds	Pct	50+ Yds	Pct	Overall	Pct	Long			Made	Att	Pts
1980 Detroit Lions	16	9-10	90.0	10-13	76.9	7-15	46.7	1-4	25.0	27-42	64.3	52			35	36	116
1981 Detroit Lions	16	6-6	100.0	9-14	64.3	7-11	63.6	3-4	75.0	25-35	71.4	53			46	46	121
1982 Detroit Lions	7	6-6	100.0	2-2	100.0	3-4	75.0	0-0	-	11-12	91.7	49			16	16	49
1983 Detroit Lions	16	6-6	100.0	13-15	86.7	3-7	42.9	3-4	75.0	25-32	78.1	54			38	38	113
1984 Detroit Lions	16	2-3	66.7	5-7	71.4	12-13	92.3	1-4	25.0	20-27	74.1	52			31	31	91
1985 Detroit Lions	16	7-10	70.0	11-11	100.0	6-7	85.7	2-3	66.7	26-31	83.9	51			31	33	109
1986 Detroit Lions	16	3-4	75.0	7-8	87.5	6-8	75.0	2-5	40.0	18-25	72.0	52			31	32	85
1987 Detroit Lions	12	7-7	100.0	7-12	58.3	5-11	45.5	1-2	50.0	20-32	62.5	53			21	21	81
1988 Detroit Lions	16	8-8	100.0	9-9	100.0	3-3	100.0	0-1	0.0	20-21	95.2	48			22	23	82
1989 Detroit Lions	16	3-3	100.0	8-9	88.9	8-8	100.0	1-1	100.0	20-21	95.2	50			36	36	96
1990 Detroit Lions	11	6-6	100.0	4-6	66.7	3-5	60.0	0-2	0.0	13-19	68.4	47			34	34	73

Year	Team	G	1-29 Yds	Pct	30-39 Yds	Pct	40-49 Yds	Pct	50+ Yds	Pct	Overall	Pct	Long	Made	Att	Pts
1991	Detroit Lions	16	4-5	80.0	8-10	80.0	5-9	55.6	2-4	50.0	19-28	67.9	50	40	40	97
1992	KC - TB	8	0-0		2-4	50.0	2-4	50.0	1-1	100.0	5-9	55.6	52	13	13	28
1993	Dallas Cowboys	14	8-8	100.0	9-12	75.0	8-8	100.0	3-5	60.0	28-33	84.8	52	38	38	122
1994	Philadelphia Eagles	16	9-9	100.0	10-10	100.0	2-6	33.3	0-0	-	21-25	84.0	42	33	33	96
1995	Washington Redskins	16	10-10	100.0	10-13	76.9	6-11	54.5	1-2	50.0	27-36	75.0	52	33	33	114
1992	Kansas City Chiefs	1	0-0	-	0-0		0-0	-	1-1	100.0	1-1	100.0	52	0	0	3
	Tampa Bay Buccaneers	7	0-0	-	2-4	50.0	2-4	50.0	0-0	-	4-8	50.0	47	13	13	25
	16 NFL Seasons	228	94-101	93.1	124-155	80.0	86-130	66.2	21-42	50.0	325-428	75.9	54	498	503	1473

Other Statistics: 1986–punted 1 time for 37 yards. 1987–punted 4 times for 155 yards.

Adrian Murrell

(statistical profile on page 362)

Pos: RB **Rnd:** 5 **College:** West Virginia **Ht:** 5' 11" **Wt:** 214 **Born:** 10/16/70 **Age:** 26

				Rushing					Receiving				Punt Returns				Kickoff Returns				Totals		
Year	Team	G	GS	Att	Yds	Avg	Lg	TD	Rec	Yds	Avg	Lg	TD	Num	Yds	Avg	TD	Num	Yds	Avg	TD	Fum	TD	Pts
1993	New York Jets	16	0	34	157	4.6	t37	1	5	12	2.4	8	0	0	0	-	0	23	342	14.9	0	4	1	6
1994	New York Jets	10	1	33	160	4.8	19	0	7	76	10.9	20	0	0	0	-	0	14	268	19.1	0	1	0	0
1995	New York Jets	15	9	192	795	4.1	30	1	71	465	6.5	43	2	0	0	-	0	1	5	5.0	0	2	3	18
	3 NFL Seasons	41	10	259	1112	4.3	t37	2	83	553	6.7	43	2	0	0	-	0	38	615	16.2	0	7	4	24

Other Statistics: 1993–recovered 2 fumbles for 0 yards. 1995–recovered 2 fumbles for 0 yards.

Bill Musgrave

Pos: QB **Rnd:** 4 **College:** Oregon **Ht:** 6' 2" **Wt:** 196 **Born:** 11/11/67 **Age:** 28

				Passing									Rushing				Miscellaneous			
Year	Team	G	GS	Att	Com	Pct	Yards	Yds/Att	Lg	TD	Int	Int%	Rating	Att	Yds	Avg	Lg	TD	Sckd	Yds	Fum Recv	Yds	Pts
1991	San Francisco 49ers	1	0	5	4	80.0	33	6.60	t15	1	0	0.0	133.8	0	0	-	-	0	0	0	0	0	0
1993	San Francisco 49ers	1	0	0	0	-	0	-	0	0	0	-	0.0	3	-3	-1.0	-1	0	-	-	0	0	0
1994	San Francisco 49ers	1	0	0	0	-	0	-	0	0	0	-	0.0	0	0	-	-	0	0	0	0	0	0
1995	Denver Broncos	4	0	12	8	66.7	93	7.75	23	0	0	0.0	89.9	4	-4	-1.0	0	0	0	0	1	0	0
	4 NFL Seasons	7	0	17	12	70.6	126	7.41	23	1	0	0.0	111.4	7	-7	-1.0	0	0	0	0	1	0	0

Najee Mustafaa

Pos: CB **Rnd:** 4 **College:** Georgia Tech **Ht:** 6' 1" **Wt:** 190 **Born:** 6/20/64 **Age:** 32

				Tackles			Miscellaneous				Interceptions				Totals		
Year	Team	G	GS	Tk	Ast	Sack	FF	FR	TD	Blk	Int	Yds	Avg	TD	Sfty	TD	Pts
1987	Minnesota Vikings	7	0	10	2	0.0	0	0	0	0	0	0	-	0	0	0	0
1988	Minnesota Vikings	16	7	28	7	0.0	0	2	0	0	3	63	21.0	0	0	0	0
1989	Minnesota Vikings	16	16	38	10	0.0	0	2	1	0	2	7	3.5	0	0	1	6
1990	Minnesota Vikings	15	15	23	7	0.0	0	0	0	0	2	21	10.5	0	0	0	0
1991	Minnesota Vikings	13	13	33	11	0.0	0	0	0	0	3	104	34.7	1	0	1	6
1993	Cleveland Browns	14	14	23	16	0.0	0	0	0	0	1	97	97.0	1	0	1	6
1995	Oakland Raiders	15	1	12	2	0.0	1	0	0	0	0	0	-	0	0	0	0
	7 NFL Seasons	96	66	167	55	0.0	1	4	1	0	11	292	26.5	2	0	3	18

Other Statistics: 1988–fumbled 1 time.

Godfrey Myles

Pos: LB **Rnd:** 3 **College:** Florida **Ht:** 6' 1" **Wt:** 242 **Born:** 9/22/68 **Age:** 28

				Tackles			Miscellaneous				Interceptions				Totals		
Year	Team	G	GS	Tk	Ast	Sack	FF	FR	TD	Blk	Int	Yds	Avg	TD	Sfty	TD	Pts
1991	Dallas Cowboys	3	0	0	0	0.0	0	0	0	0	0	0	-	0	0	0	0
1992	Dallas Cowboys	16	0	12	9	0.0	0	0	0	0	1	13	13.0	0	0	0	0
1993	Dallas Cowboys	10	0	6	11	0.0	0	0	0	0	0	0	-	0	0	0	0
1994	Dallas Cowboys	15	0	8	2	0.0	0	0	0	0	0	0	-	0	0	0	0
1995	Dallas Cowboys	16	11	55	20	0.0	1	2	0	0	1	15	15.0	0	0	0	0
	5 NFL Seasons	60	11	81	42	0.0	1	2	0	0	2	28	14.0	0	0	0	0

Tom Myslinski

Pos: G **Rnd:** 4 **College:** Tennessee **Ht:** 6' 3" **Wt:** 287 **Born:** 12/7/68 **Age:** 27

Year	Team	G	GS	Year	Team	G	GS	Year	Team	G	GS			G	GS
1992	Washington Redskins	1	0	1993	Chicago Bears	1	0	1995	Jacksonville Jaguars	9	9				
1993	Buffalo Bills	1	0	1994	Chicago Bears	4	0						4 NFL Seasons	16	9

Browning Nagle

Pos: QB **Rnd:** 2 **College:** Louisville **Ht:** 6' 3" **Wt:** 225 **Born:** 4/29/68 **Age:** 28

Year	Team	G	GS	Passing										Rushing					Miscellaneous					
				Att	Com	Pct	Yards	Yds/Att	Lg	TD	Int	Int%	Rating	Att	Yds	Avg	Lg	TD	Sckd	Yds	Fum	Recv	Yds	Pts
1991	New York Jets	1	0	2	1	50.0	10	5.00	10	0	0	0.0	64.6	1	-1	-1.0	-1	0	0	0	0	0	0	0
1992	New York Jets	14	13	387	192	49.6	2280	5.89	51	7	17	4.4	55.7	24	57	2.4	20	0	27	215	12	3	-14	0
1993	New York Jets	3	0	14	6	42.9	71	5.07	18	0	0	0.0	58.9	0	0	-	-	0	3	21	0	0	0	0
1994	Indianapolis Colts	1	1	21	8	38.1	69	3.29	23	0	1	4.8	27.7	1	12	12.0	12	0	2	18	2	0	0	0
1995	Atlanta Falcons	1	0	0	0	-	0	-	-	0	0	-	0.0	0	0	-	-	0	0	0	0	0	0	0
	5 NFL Seasons	20	14	424	207	48.8	2430	5.73	51	7	18	4.2	54.5	26	68	2.6	20	0	32	254	14	3	-14	0

Tom Nalen

Pos: C **Rnd:** 7 **College:** Boston College **Ht:** 6' 3" **Wt:** 280 **Born:** 5/13/71 **Age:** 25

Year	Team	G	GS	Year	Team	G	GS				G	GS
1994	Denver Broncos	8	1	1995	Denver Broncos	15	15		2 NFL Seasons		23	16

Joseph Nash

Pos: DT **Rnd:** FA **College:** Boston College **Ht:** 6' 3" **Wt:** 278 **Born:** 10/11/60 **Age:** 36

Year	Team	G	GS	Tackles			Miscellaneous				Interceptions				Totals		
				Tk	Ast	Sack	FF	FR	TD	Blk	Int	Yds	Avg	TD	Sfty	TD	Pts
1982	Seattle Seahawks	7	1	18	14	1.0	0	0	0	0	0	0	-	0	0	0	0
1983	Seattle Seahawks	16	8	29	14	3.0	0	0	0	0	0	0	-	0	0	0	0
1984	Seattle Seahawks	16	16	58	24	7.0	0	3	1	0	0	0	-	0	0	1	6
1985	Seattle Seahawks	16	16	67	20	9.0	0	0	0	0	0	0	-	0	0	0	0
1986	Seattle Seahawks	16	11	39	12	5.0	0	2	0	0	0	0	-	0	0	0	0
1987	Seattle Seahawks	12	12	35	9	3.5	0	0	0	0	0	0	-	0	0	0	0
1988	Seattle Seahawks	15	15	52	14	2.0	0	1	0	0	0	0	-	0	0	0	0
1989	Seattle Seahawks	16	16	65	27	8.0	0	0	0	0	0	0	-	0	0	0	0
1990	Seattle Seahawks	16	16	41	12	1.0	0	1	0	0	0	0	-	0	0	0	0
1991	Seattle Seahawks	16	0	20	4	0.0	0	0	0	0	0	0	-	0	0	0	0
1992	Seattle Seahawks	16	16	46	21	4.5	0	0	0	0	0	0	-	0	0	0	0
1993	Seattle Seahawks	16	16	33	15	0.5	0	0	0	0	1	13	13.0	1	0	1	6
1994	Seattle Seahawks	16	15	32	16	2.0	0	0	0	0	0	0	-	0	0	0	0
1995	Seattle Seahawks	16	11	18	17	1.0	0	0	0	0	0	0	-	0	0	0	0
	14 NFL Seasons	210	169	553	219	47.5	0	7	1	0	1	13	13.0	1	0	2	12

Lorenzo Neal

Pos: RB **Rnd:** 4 **College:** Fresno State **Ht:** 5' 11" **Wt:** 240 **Born:** 12/27/70 **Age:** 25

Year	Team	G	GS	Rushing					Receiving					Punt Returns				Kickoff Returns				Totals		
				Att	Yds	Avg	Lg	TD	Rec	Yds	Avg	Lg	TD	Num	Yds	Avg	TD	Num	Yds	Avg	TD	Fum	TD	Pts
1993	New Orleans Saints	2	2	21	175	8.3	t74	1	0	0	-	-	0	0	0	-	0	0	0	-	0	1	1	6
1994	New Orleans Saints	16	7	30	90	3.0	12	1	2	9	4.5	5	0	0	0	-	0	1	17	17.0	0	1	1	6
1995	New Orleans Saints	16	7	5	3	0.6	3	0	12	123	10.3	t69	1	0	0	-	0	2	28	14.0	0	2	1	6
	3 NFL Seasons	34	16	56	268	4.8	t74	2	14	132	9.4	t69	1	0	0	-	0	3	45	15.0	0	4	3	18

Randy Neal

Pos: LB **Rnd:** FA **College:** Virginia **Ht:** 6' 3" **Wt:** 236 **Born:** 12/29/72 **Age:** 23

Year	Team	G	GS	Tackles			Miscellaneous				Interceptions				Totals		
				Tk	Ast	Sack	FF	FR	TD	Blk	Int	Yds	Avg	TD	Sfty	TD	Pts
1995	Cincinnati Bengals	3	0	0	0	0.0	0	0	0	0	0	0	-	0	0	0	0

Derrick Ned

Pos: RB **Rnd:** FA **College:** Grambling **Ht:** 6' 1" **Wt:** 220 **Born:** 1/5/69 **Age:** 27

Year	Team	G	GS	Rushing					Receiving					Punt Returns				Kickoff Returns				Totals		
				Att	Yds	Avg	Lg	TD	Rec	Yds	Avg	Lg	TD	Num	Yds	Avg	TD	Num	Yds	Avg	TD	Fum	TD	Pts
1993	New Orleans Saints	14	1	9	71	7.9	t35	1	9	54	6.0	14	0	0	0	-	0	0	0	-	0	1	1	6
1994	New Orleans Saints	16	1	11	36	3.3	15	0	13	86	6.6	19	0	0	0	-	0	7	77	11.0	0	1	0	0
1995	New Orleans Saints	12	0	3	1	0.3	5	0	3	9	3.0	9	0	0	0	-	0	2	33	16.5	0	1	0	0
	3 NFL Seasons	42	2	23	108	4.7	t35	1	25	149	6.0	19	0	0	0	-	0	9	110	12.2	0	3	1	6

Tom Newberry

Pos: G **Rnd:** 2 **College:** Wisconsin-La Crosse **Ht:** 6' 2" **Wt:** 285 **Born:** 12/20/62 **Age:** 33

Year	Team	G	GS	Year	Team	G	GS	Year	Team	G	GS	Year	Team	G	GS
1986	Los Angeles Rams	16	14	1989	Los Angeles Rams	16	16	1992	Los Angeles Rams	16	16	1995	Pittsburgh Steelers	16	15
1987	Los Angeles Rams	12	12	1990	Los Angeles Rams	15	15	1993	Los Angeles Rams	9	9				
1988	Los Angeles Rams	16	16	1991	Los Angeles Rams	16	16	1994	Los Angeles Rams	15	14		10 NFL Seasons	147	143

Other Statistics: 1986–recovered 1 fumble for 0 yards and 1 touchdown. 1992–recovered 1 fumble for 0 yards. 1993–recovered 1 fumble for 0 yards. 1994–recovered 1 fumble for 0 yards. 1995–recovered 1 fumble for 0 yards.

Anthony Newman

Pos: S/CB **Rnd:** 2 **College:** Oregon **Ht:** 6' 0" **Wt:** 199 **Born:** 11/21/65 **Age:** 30

Year	Team	G	GS	Tk	Ast	Sack	FF	FR	TD	Blk	Int	Yds	Avg	TD	Sfty	TD	Pts
1988	Los Angeles Rams	16	0	13	1	0.0	0	1	0	0	2	27	13.5	0	0	0	0
1989	Los Angeles Rams	15	1	42	3	0.0	0	0	0	0	0	0	-	0	0	0	0
1990	Los Angeles Rams	16	6	38	9	0.0	0	1	0	0	2	0	0.0	0	0	0	0
1991	Los Angeles Rams	16	1	27	4	1.0	0	1	1	0	1	58	58.0	0	0	1	6
1992	Los Angeles Rams	16	16	60	11	0.0	0	3	0	0	4	33	8.3	0	0	0	0
1993	Los Angeles Rams	16	16	47	17	0.0	0	0	0	0	0	0	-	0	0	0	0
1994	Los Angeles Rams	16	14	29	9	0.0	0	1	0	0	2	46	23.0	1	0	1	6
1995	New Orleans Saints	13	1	3	2	0.0	0	0	0	0	0	0	-	0	0	0	0
	8 NFL Seasons	124	55	259	56	1.0	0	7	1	0	11	164	14.9	1	0	2	12

Other Statistics: 1995–caught 1 pass for 18 yards.

Craig Newsome

(statistical profile on page 436)

Pos: CB **Rnd:** 1 (32) **College:** Arizona State **Ht:** 5' 11" **Wt:** 188 **Born:** 8/10/71 **Age:** 25

Year	Team	G	GS	Tk	Ast	Sack	FF	FR	TD	Blk	Int	Yds	Avg	TD	Sfty	TD	Pts
1995	Green Bay Packers	16	16	54	21	0.0	0	0	0	0	1	3	3.0	0	0	0	0

Nate Newton

Pos: G **Rnd:** FA **College:** Florida A&M **Ht:** 6' 3" **Wt:** 320 **Born:** 12/20/61 **Age:** 34

Year	Team	G	GS	Year	Team	G	GS	Year	Team	G	GS	Year	Team	G	GS
1986	Dallas Cowboys	11	0	1989	Dallas Cowboys	16	16	1992	Dallas Cowboys	15	15	1995	Dallas Cowboys	16	16
1987	Dallas Cowboys	11	11	1990	Dallas Cowboys	16	16	1993	Dallas Cowboys	16	16				
1988	Dallas Cowboys	15	15	1991	Dallas Cowboys	14	14	1994	Dallas Cowboys	16	16		10 NFL Seasons	146	135

Other Statistics: 1988–caught 1 pass for 2 yards. 1990–recovered 2 fumbles for 0 yards. 1991–recovered 1 fumble for 0 yards. 1992–recovered 1 fumble for 0 yards.

Hardy Nickerson

(statistical profile on page 436)

Pos: LB **Rnd:** 5 **College:** California **Ht:** 6' 2" **Wt:** 233 **Born:** 9/1/65 **Age:** 31

Year	Team	G	GS	Tk	Ast	Sack	FF	FR	TD	Blk	Int	Yds	Avg	TD	Sfty	TD	Pts
1987	Pittsburgh Steelers	12	0	10	7	0.0	0	1	0	0	0	0	-	0	0	0	0
1988	Pittsburgh Steelers	15	10	73	26	3.5	1	1	0	0	1	0	0.0	0	0	0	0
1989	Pittsburgh Steelers	10	8	26	9	1.0	0	0	0	0	0	0	-	0	0	0	0
1990	Pittsburgh Steelers	16	14	58	9	2.0	2	0	0	0	0	0	-	0	0	0	0
1991	Pittsburgh Steelers	16	14	70	24	1.0	2	0	0	0	0	0	-	0	0	0	0
1992	Pittsburgh Steelers	15	15	68	46	2.0	0	2	0	0	0	0	-	0	0	0	0
1993	Tampa Bay Buccaneers	16	16	124	90	1.0	1	1	0	0	1	6	6.0	0	0	0	0
1994	Tampa Bay Buccaneers	14	14	86	36	1.0	1	0	0	0	2	9	4.5	0	0	0	0
1995	Tampa Bay Buccaneers	16	16	89	54	1.5	3	3	0	0	0	0	-	0	0	0	0
	9 NFL Seasons	130	107	604	301	13.0	10	8	0	0	4	15	3.8	0	0	0	0

Erik Norgard

Pos: G/C **Rnd:** FA **College:** Colorado **Ht:** 6' 1" **Wt:** 282 **Born:** 11/4/65 **Age:** 30

Year	Team	G	GS	Year	Team	G	GS	Year	Team	G	GS			G	GS
1990	Houston Oilers	16	0	1993	Houston Oilers	16	4	1995	Houston Oilers	12	0				
1992	Houston Oilers	15	0	1994	Houston Oilers	16	7						5 NFL Seasons	75	11

Other Statistics: 1990–returned 2 kickoffs for 0 yards. 1993–recovered 1 fumble for 0 yards; caught 1 pass for 13 yards.

Ken Norton

(statistical profile on page 436)

Pos: LB **Rnd:** 2 **College:** UCLA **Ht:** 6' 2" **Wt:** 241 **Born:** 9/29/66 **Age:** 30

Year	Team	G	GS	Tk	Ast	Sack	FF	FR	TD	Blk	Int	Yds	Avg	TD	Sfty	TD	Pts
1988	Dallas Cowboys	3	0	0	0	0.0	0	1	0	0	0	0	-	0	0	0	0
1989	Dallas Cowboys	13	13	56	31	2.5	1	0	0	0	0	0	-	0	0	0	0
1990	Dallas Cowboys	15	15	79	40	2.5	3	2	0	0	0	0	-	0	0	0	0
1991	Dallas Cowboys	16	16	54	40	0.0	0	0	0	0	0	0	-	0	0	0	0
1992	Dallas Cowboys	16	16	64	56	0.0	2	2	0	0	0	0	-	0	0	0	0
1993	Dallas Cowboys	16	16	93	66	2.0	0	1	0	0	1	25	25.0	0	0	0	0
1994	San Francisco 49ers	16	16	75	11	0.0	1	0	0	0	1	0	0.0	0	0	0	0
1995	San Francisco 49ers	16	16	82	14	1.0	1	0	0	0	3	102	34.0	2	0	2	12
	8 NFL Seasons	111	108	503	258	8.0	8	6	0	0	5	127	25.4	2	0	2	12

Dexter Nottage

Pos: DE/DT **Rnd:** 6 **College:** Florida A&M **Ht:** 6' 4" **Wt:** 290 **Born:** 11/14/70 **Age:** 25

Year	Team	G	GS	Tackles			Miscellaneous				Interceptions				Totals		
				Tk	Ast	Sack	FF	FR	TD	Blk	Int	Yds	Avg	TD	Sfty	TD	Pts
1994	Washington Redskins	15	1	17	4	1.0	0	0	0	0	0	0	-	0	0	0	0
1995	Washington Redskins	16	0	17	4	0.0	1	3	0	0	0	0	-	0	0	0	0
	2 NFL Seasons	31	1	34	8	1.0	1	3	0	0	0	0	-	0	0	0	0

Jay Novacek

(statistical profile on page 363)

Pos: TE **Rnd:** 6 **College:** Wyoming **Ht:** 6' 4" **Wt:** 234 **Born:** 10/24/62 **Age:** 34

Year	Team	G	GS	Rushing					Receiving					Punt Returns				Kickoff Returns				Totals		
				Att	Yds	Avg	Lg	TD	Rec	Yds	Avg	Lg	TD	Num	Yds	Avg	TD	Num	Yds	Avg	TD	Fum	TD	Pts
1985	St. Louis Cardinals	16	0	0	0	-	0	0	1	4	4.0	4	0	0	0	-	0	1	20	20.0	0	0	0	0
1986	St. Louis Cardinals	8	0	0	0	-	0	0	1	2	2.0	2	0	0	0	-	0	0	0	-	0	0	0	0
1987	St. Louis Cardinals	7	4	0	0	-	0	0	20	254	12.7	25	3	0	0	-	0	0	0	-	0	1	3	18
1988	Phoenix Cardinals	16	1	1	10	10.0	10	0	38	569	15.0	t42	4	0	0	-	0	0	0	-	0	4	4	24
1989	Phoenix Cardinals	16	1	0	0	-	0	0	23	225	9.8	30	1	0	0	-	0	0	0	-	0	1	1	6
1990	Dallas Cowboys	16	15	0	0	-	0	0	59	657	11.1	41	4	0	0	-	0	0	0	-	0	1	4	24
1991	Dallas Cowboys	16	12	0	0	-	0	0	59	664	11.3	49	4	0	0	-	0	0	0	-	0	3	4	24
1992	Dallas Cowboys	16	16	0	0	-	0	0	68	630	9.3	34	6	0	0	-	0	0	0	-	0	6	6	36
1993	Dallas Cowboys	16	16	1	2	2.0	t2	1	44	445	10.1	30	1	0	0	-	0	1	-1	-1.0	0	3	2	12
1994	Dallas Cowboys	16	14	0	0	-	0	0	47	475	10.1	27	2	0	0	-	0	0	0	-	0	2	2	12
1995	Dallas Cowboys	15	15	0	0	-	0	0	62	705	11.4	t33	5	0	0	-	0	0	0	-	0	1	5	32
	11 NFL Seasons	158	94	2	12	6.0	10	1	422	4630	11.0	49	30	0	0	-	0	2	19	9.5	0	9	31	188

Other Statistics: 1988–recovered 1 fumble for 0 yards. 1989–recovered 1 fumble for 0 yards. 1991–recovered 1 fumble for 0 yards. 1993–recovered 1 fumble for 0 yards. 1995–scored 1 two-point conversion.

Jeff Novak

Pos: G/T **Rnd:** 7 **College:** Southwest Texas State **Ht:** 6' 5" **Wt:** 296 **Born:** 7/27/67 **Age:** 29

Year	Team	G	GS	Year	Team	G	GS		G	GS
1994	Miami Dolphins	7	0	1995	Jacksonville Jaguars	16	13	2 NFL Seasons	23	13

Craig Novitsky

Pos: T/C **Rnd:** 5 **College:** UCLA **Ht:** 6' 5" **Wt:** 295 **Born:** 5/12/71 **Age:** 25

Year	Team	G	GS	Year	Team	G	GS		G	GS
1994	New Orleans Saints	9	1	1995	New Orleans Saints	16	3	2 NFL Seasons	25	4

Freddie Joe Nunn

Pos: DE **Rnd:** 1 (18) **College:** Mississippi **Ht:** 6' 5" **Wt:** 258 **Born:** 4/9/62 **Age:** 34

Year	Team	G	GS	Tackles			Miscellaneous				Interceptions				Totals		
				Tk	Ast	Sack	FF	FR	TD	Blk	Int	Yds	Avg	TD	Sfty	TD	Pts
1985	St. Louis Cardinals	16	16	67	17	3.0	0	2	0	0	0	0	-	0	0	0	0
1986	St. Louis Cardinals	16	16	38	10	7.0	0	1	0	0	0	0	-	0	0	0	0
1987	St. Louis Cardinals	12	12	45	1	11.0	0	0	0	0	0	0	-	0	0	0	0
1988	Phoenix Cardinals	16	16	44	9	14.0	0	2	0	0	0	0	-	0	0	0	0
1989	Phoenix Cardinals	12	12	22	12	5.0	0	1	0	0	0	0	-	0	0	0	0
1990	Phoenix Cardinals	16	16	21	26	9.0	0	1	0	0	0	0	-	0	0	0	0
1991	Phoenix Cardinals	16	16	44	28	7.0	0	2	0	0	0	0	-	0	0	0	0
1992	Phoenix Cardinals	11	9	19	9	4.0	0	1	0	0	0	0	-	0	0	0	0
1993	Phoenix Cardinals	16	9	18	9	6.5	2	1	0	0	0	0	-	0	0	0	0
1994	Indianapolis Colts	11	6	9	6	1.0	0	0	0	0	0	0	-	0	0	0	0
1995	Indianapolis Colts	10	1	2	2	0.0	0	0	0	0	0	0	-	0	0	0	0
	11 NFL Seasons	152	129	329	129	67.5	2	11	0	0	0	0	-	0	0	0	0

Tom Nutten

Pos: G **Rnd:** 7 **College:** Western Michigan **Ht:** 6' 4" **Wt:** 276 **Born:** 6/8/71 **Age:** 25

Year	Team	G	GS				G	GS
1995	Buffalo Bills	1	0		1 NFL Season		1	0

Neil O'Donnell

(statistical profile on page 363)

Pos: QB **Rnd:** 3 **College:** Maryland **Ht:** 6' 3" **Wt:** 226 **Born:** 7/3/66 **Age:** 30

Year	Team	G	GS	Passing										Rushing					Miscellaneous				
				Att	Com	Pct	Yards	Yds/Att	Lg	TD	Int	Int%	Rating	Att	Yds	Avg	Lg	TD	Sckd	Yds	Fum	Recv	Yds	Pts
1991	Pittsburgh Steelers	12	8	286	156	54.5	1963	6.86	t89	11	7	2.4	78.8	18	82	4.6	22	1	30	214	11	2	-3	6
1992	Pittsburgh Steelers	12	12	313	185	59.1	2283	7.29	51	13	9	2.9	83.6	27	5	0.2	9	1	27	208	6	4	-20	6
1993	Pittsburgh Steelers	16	15	486	270	55.6	3208	6.60	t71	14	7	**1.4**	79.5	26	111	4.3	27	0	41	**331**	5	0	-2	0

Year	Team	G	GS	Att	Com	Pct	Yards	Yds/Att	Lg	TD	Int	Int%	Rating	Att	Yds	Avg	Lg	TD	Sckd	Yds	Fum	Recv	Yds	Pts
								Passing								**Rushing**					**Miscellaneous**			
1994	Pittsburgh Steelers	14	14	370	212	57.3	2443	6.60	t60	13	9	2.4	78.9	31	80	2.6	18	1	35	250	4	1	0	6
1995	Pittsburgh Steelers	12	12	416	246	59.1	2970	7.14	t71	17	7	1.7	87.7	24	45	1.9	14	0	15	126	2	1	0	0
	5 NFL Seasons	66	61	1871	1069	57.1	12867	6.88	t89	68	39	2.1	81.8	126	323	2.6	27	3	148	1129	28	8	-25	18

Matt O'Dwyer

Pos: G   **Rnd:** 2   **College:** Northwestern   **Ht:** 6' 5"   **Wt:** 308   **Born:** 9/1/72   **Age:** 24

Year	Team	G	GS						G	GS
1995	New York Jets	12	2				1 NFL Season		12	2

Brian O'Neal

Pos: RB   **Rnd:** FA   **College:** Penn State   **Ht:** 6' 0"   **Wt:** 233   **Born:** 2/25/70   **Age:** 26

Year	Team	G	GS	Att	Yds	Avg	Lg	TD	Rec	Yds	Avg	Lg	TD	Num	Yds	Avg	TD	Num	Yds	Avg	TD	Fum	TD	Pts
					Rushing					**Receiving**					**Punt Returns**				**Kickoff Returns**				**Totals**		
1994	Philadelphia Eagles	14	0	0	0	-	0	0	0	0	-	0	0	1	0	0.0	0	1	0	0.0	0	1	0	0
1995	San Francisco 49ers	3	0	0	0	-	0	0	0	0	-	0	0	0	0	-	0	0	0	-	0	0	0	0
	2 NFL Seasons	17	0	0	0	-	0	0	0	0	-	0	0	1	0	0.0	0	1	0	0.0	0	1	0	0

Leslie O'Neal

(statistical profile on page 437)

Pos: DE   **Rnd:** 1 (8)   **College:** Oklahoma State   **Ht:** 6' 4"   **Wt:** 265   **Born:** 5/7/64   **Age:** 32

Year	Team	G	GS	Tk	Ast	Sack	FF	FR	TD	Blk	Int	Yds	Avg	TD	Sfty	TD	Pts
					Tackles			**Miscellaneous**				**Interceptions**				**Totals**	
1986	San Diego Chargers	13	13	61	21	12.5	3	2	0	0	2	22	11.0	1	0	1	6
1988	San Diego Chargers	9	1	22	6	4.0	1	0	0	0	0	0	-	0	0	0	0
1989	San Diego Chargers	16	16	78	18	12.5	2	2	0	0	0	0	-	0	0	0	0
1990	San Diego Chargers	16	16	64	17	13.5	2	2	0	0	0	0	-	0	0	0	0
1991	San Diego Chargers	16	16	63	5	9.0	2	0	0	0	0	0	-	0	0	0	0
1992	San Diego Chargers	15	15	68	10	17.0	1	0	0	0	0	0	-	0	0	0	0
1993	San Diego Chargers	16	16	49	7	12.0	2	1	0	0	0	0	-	0	0	0	0
1994	San Diego Chargers	16	16	47	13	12.5	2	1	0	0	0	0	-	0	0	0	0
1995	San Diego Chargers	16	16	36	12	12.5	4	0	0	0	0	0	-	0	0	0	0
	9 NFL Seasons	133	125	488	109	105.5	18	9	0	0	2	22	11.0	1	0	1	6

Other Statistics: 1990–fumbled 1 time.

Pat O'Neill

(statistical profile on page 481)

Pos: P   **Rnd:** 5   **College:** Syracuse   **Ht:** 6' 1"   **Wt:** 200   **Born:** 2/9/71   **Age:** 25

Year	Team	G	NetPunts	Yards	Avg	Long	In20	In20%	TotPunts	TB	Blocks	OppRet	RetYds	NetAvg	Att	Yards	Overall	Pct	Long
					Punting											**Rushing**	**Field Goals**		
1994	New England Patriots	16	69	2841	41.2	67	24	34.8	69	6	0	34	260	35.7	0	0	0-1	0.0	-
1995	NE - Chi	9	44	1603	36.4	57	14	31.8	44	3	0	21	183	30.9	0	0	0-0	-	-
1995	New England Patriots	8	41	1514	36.9	57	14	34.1	41	3	0	20	174	31.2	0	0	0-0	-	-
	Chicago Bears	1	3	89	29.7	39	0	0.0	3	0	0	1	9	26.7	0	0	0-0	-	-
	2 NFL Seasons	25	113	4444	39.3	67	38	33.6	113	9	0	55	443	33.8	0	0	0-1	0.0	-

Bart Oates

Pos: C/LS   **Rnd:** FA   **College:** Brigham Young   **Ht:** 6' 4"   **Wt:** 275   **Born:** 12/16/58   **Age:** 37

Year	Team	G	GS	Year	Team	G	GS	Year	Team	G	GS	Year	Team	G	GS
1985	New York Giants	16	14	1988	New York Giants	16	16	1991	New York Giants	16	16	1994	San Francisco 49ers	16	15
1986	New York Giants	16	16	1989	New York Giants	16	16	1992	New York Giants	16	15	1995	San Francisco 49ers	16	14
1987	New York Giants	12	12	1990	New York Giants	16	16	1993	New York Giants	16	15		11 NFL Seasons	172	165

Other Statistics: 1985–recovered 2 fumbles for 0 yards. 1986–fumbled 1 time for -4 yards. 1987–recovered 1 fumble for 0 yards. 1988–fumbled 1 time for -10 yards. 1989–fumbled 1 time for 0 yards. 1990–fumbled 1 time for -19 yards. 1992–fumbled 2 times for -29 yards.

Derrick Oden

Pos: LB   **Rnd:** 6   **College:** Alabama   **Ht:** 5' 11"   **Wt:** 237   **Born:** 0/20/70   **Age:** 26

Year	Team	G	GS	Tk	Ast	Sack	FF	FR	TD	Blk	Int	Yds	Avg	TD	Sfty	TD	Pts
					Tackles			**Miscellaneous**				**Interceptions**				**Totals**	
1993	Philadelphia Eagles	12	0	3	2	0.0	0	0	0	0	0	0	-	0	0	0	0
1994	Philadelphia Eagles	11	0	0	0	0.0	0	0	0	0	0	0	-	0	0	0	0
1995	Philadelphia Eagles	12	0	2	0	0.0	0	0	0	0	0	0	-	0	0	0	0
	3 NFL Seasons	35	0	5	2	0.0	0	0	0	0	0	0	-	0	0	0	0

187

Alfred Oglesby

Pos: DT **Rnd:** 3 **College:** Houston **Ht:** 6' 4" **Wt:** 290 **Born:** 1/27/67 **Age:** 29

Year Team	G	GS	Tackles			Miscellaneous				Interceptions				Totals		
			Tk	Ast	Sack	FF	FR	TD	Blk	Int	Yds	Avg	TD	Sfty	TD	Pts
1990 Miami Dolphins	13	6	20	10	2.5	1	1	0	0	0	0	-	0	0	0	0
1991 Miami Dolphins	12	12	30	5	0.0	0	0	0	0	0	0	-	0	0	0	0
1992 Mia - GB	13	0	9	4	0.0	0	0	0	0	0	0	-	0	0	0	0
1994 New York Jets	15	1	12	10	0.5	1	0	0	0	0	0	-	0	0	0	0
1995 Cincinnati Bengals	7	0	3	1	1.0	0	0	0	0	0	0	-	0	0	0	0
1992 Miami Dolphins	6	0	2	1	0.0	0	0	0	0	0	0	-	0	0	0	0
Green Bay Packers	7	0	7	3	0.0	0	0	0	0	0	0	-	0	0	0	0
5 NFL Seasons	60	19	74	30	4.0	2	1	0	0	0	0	-	0	0	0	0

Chris Oldham

Pos: CB **Rnd:** 4 **College:** Oregon **Ht:** 5' 9" **Wt:** 183 **Born:** 10/26/68 **Age:** 28

Year Team	G	GS	Tackles			Miscellaneous				Interceptions				Punt Returns				Kickoff Returns				Totals	
			Tk	Ast	Sack	FF	FR	TD	Blk	Int	Yds	Avg	TD	Num	Yds	Avg	TD	Num	Yds	Avg	TD	TD	Fum
1990 Detroit Lions	16	0	23	2	0.0	0	0	0	0	1	28	28.0	0	0	0	-	0	13	234	18.0	0	0	2
1991 Buf - Pho	4	0	0	0	0.0	0	0	0	0	0	0	-	0	0	0	-	0	0	0	-	0	0	0
1992 Phoenix Cardinals	1	0	3	0	0.0	0	0	0	0	0	0	-	0	0	0	-	0	0	0	-	0	0	0
1993 Phoenix Cardinals	16	6	42	8	1.0	3	0	0	0	1	0	0.0	0	0	0	-	0	0	0	-	0	0	0
1994 Arizona Cardinals	11	1	1	0	0.0	0	0	0	0	0	0	-	0	0	0	-	0	0	0	-	0	0	0
1995 Pittsburgh Steelers	15	0	10	5	0.0	0	1	1	0	1	12	12.0	0	0	0	-	0	0	0	-	0	1	0
1991 Buffalo Bills	2	0	0	0	0.0	0	0	0	0	0	0	-	0	0	0	-	0	0	0	-	0	0	0
Phoenix Cardinals	2	0	0	0	0.0	0	0	0	0	0	0	-	0	0	0	-	0	0	0	-	0	0	0
6 NFL Seasons	63	7	79	15	1.0	3	1	1	0	3	40	13.3	0	0	0	-	0	13	234	18.0	0	1	2

Bobby Olive

Pos: WR **Rnd:** 11 **College:** Ohio State **Ht:** 6' 0" **Wt:** 167 **Born:** 4/22/69 **Age:** 27

Year Team	G	GS	Rushing					Receiving					Punt Returns				Kickoff Returns				Totals		
			Att	Yds	Avg	Lg	TD	Rec	Yds	Avg	Lg	TD	Num	Yds	Avg	TD	Num	Yds	Avg	TD	Fum	TD	Pts
1995 Indianapolis Colts	1	0	0	0	-	-	0	0	0	-	-	0	0	0	-	0	0	0	-	0	0	0	0

Louis Oliver

Pos: S **Rnd:** 1 (25) **College:** Florida **Ht:** 6' 2" **Wt:** 224 **Born:** 3/9/66 **Age:** 30

Year Team	G	GS	Tackles			Miscellaneous				Interceptions				Totals		
			Tk	Ast	Sack	FF	FR	TD	Blk	Int	Yds	Avg	TD	Sfty	TD	Pts
1989 Miami Dolphins	15	13	51	11	0.0	1	0	0	0	4	32	8.0	0	0	0	0
1990 Miami Dolphins	16	16	54	11	1.0	0	0	0	0	5	87	17.4	0	0	0	0
1991 Miami Dolphins	16	16	73	15	0.0	0	1	0	0	5	80	16.0	0	0	0	0
1992 Miami Dolphins	16	16	66	24	0.0	0	1	0	0	5	200	40.0	1	0	1	6
1993 Miami Dolphins	11	11	45	19	0.0	2	1	0	0	2	60	30.0	1	0	1	6
1994 Cincinnati Bengals	12	12	53	10	1.0	1	0	0	0	3	36	12.0	0	0	0	0
1995 Miami Dolphins	15	5	37	10	0.0	0	0	0	0	0	0	-	0	0	0	0
7 NFL Seasons	101	89	379	100	2.0	4	3	0	0	24	495	20.6	2	0	2	12

Other Statistics: 1994–fumbled 1 time for 0 yards.

Muhammad Oliver

Pos: WR **Rnd:** 9 **College:** Oregon **Ht:** 5' 11" **Wt:** 185 **Born:** 3/12/69 **Age:** 27

Year Team	G	GS	Rushing					Receiving					Punt Returns				Kickoff Returns				Totals		
			Att	Yds	Avg	Lg	TD	Rec	Yds	Avg	Lg	TD	Num	Yds	Avg	TD	Num	Yds	Avg	TD	Fum	TD	Pts
1992 Denver Broncos	3	0	0	0	-	-	0	0	0	-	-	0	0	0	-	0	1	20	20.0	0	0	0	0
1993 KC - GB	4	0	0	0	-	-	0	0	0	-	-	0	0	0	-	0	0	0	-	0	0	0	0
1994 Miami Dolphins	13	2	0	0	-	-	0	0	0	-	-	0	0	0	-	0	0	0	-	0	0	0	0
1995 Washington Redskins	1	0	0	0	-	-	0	0	0	-	-	0	0	0	-	0	0	0	-	0	0	0	0
1993 Kansas City Chiefs	2	0	0	0	-	-	0	0	0	-	-	0	0	0	-	0	0	0	-	0	0	0	0
Green Bay Packers	2	0	0	0	-	-	0	0	0	-	-	0	0	0	-	0	0	0	-	0	0	0	0
4 NFL Seasons	21	2	0	0	-	-	0	0	0	-	-	0	0	0	-	0	1	20	20.0	0	0	0	0

Other Statistics: 1994–intercepted 1 pass for 0 yards.

Jerry Olsavsky

Pos: LB **Rnd:** 10 **College:** Pittsburgh **Ht:** 6' 1" **Wt:** 221 **Born:** 3/29/67 **Age:** 29

Year Team	G	GS	Tackles			Miscellaneous				Interceptions				Totals		
			Tk	Ast	Sack	FF	FR	TD	Blk	Int	Yds	Avg	TD	Sfty	TD	Pts
1989 Pittsburgh Steelers	16	8	37	4	1.0	0	0	0	0	0	0	-	0	0	0	0
1990 Pittsburgh Steelers	15	0	6	0	0.0	2	0	0	0	0	0	-	0	0	0	0

Year Team	G	GS	Tk	Ast	Sack	FF	FR	TD	Blk	Int	Yds	Avg	TD	Sfty	TD	Pts
			Tackles			**Miscellaneous**				**Interceptions**				**Totals**		
1991 Pittsburgh Steelers	16	4	25	7	0.0	0	0	0	0	0	0	-	0	0	0	0
1992 Pittsburgh Steelers	7	0	1	2	0.0	1	0	0	0	0	0	-	0	0	0	0
1993 Pittsburgh Steelers	7	7	24	15	0.0	0	0	0	0	0	0	-	0	0	0	0
1994 Pittsburgh Steelers	1	0	0	0	0.0	0	0	0	0	0	0	-	0	0	0	0
1995 Pittsburgh Steelers	15	5	24	10	1.0	0	0	0	0	0	0	-	0	0	0	0
7 NFL Seasons	77	24	117	38	2.0	3	0	0	0	0	0	-	0	0	0	0

Bo Orlando

(statistical profile on page 437)

Pos: S **Rnd:** 6 **College:** West Virginia **Ht:** 5' 10" **Wt:** 180 **Born:** 4/3/66 **Age:** 30

Year Team	G	GS	Tk	Ast	Sack	FF	FR	TD	Blk	Int	Yds	Avg	TD	Sfty	TD	Pts
			Tackles			**Miscellaneous**				**Interceptions**				**Totals**		
1990 Houston Oilers	16	0	11	5	0.0	0	0	0	0	0	0	-	0	0	0	0
1991 Houston Oilers	16	16	38	21	0.0	0	2	0	0	4	18	4.5	0	0	0	0
1992 Houston Oilers	6	1	3	3	0.0	0	0	0	0	0	0	-	0	0	0	0
1993 Houston Oilers	16	3	16	2	0.0	0	0	0	0	3	68	22.7	1	0	1	6
1994 Houston Oilers	16	0	5	1	0.0	0	0	0	0	0	0	-	0	0	0	0
1995 San Diego Chargers	16	16	69	16	0.0	1	0	0	0	0	37	-	0	0	0	0
6 NFL Seasons	86	36	142	48	0.0	1	2	0	0	7	123	17.6	1	0	1	6

Willie Oshodin

Pos: DE **Rnd:** FA **College:** Villanova **Ht:** 6' 4" **Wt:** 260 **Born:** 9/16/69 **Age:** 27

Year Team	G	GS	Tk	Ast	Sack	FF	FR	TD	Blk	Int	Yds	Avg	TD	Sfty	TD	Pts
			Tackles			**Miscellaneous**				**Interceptions**				**Totals**		
1993 Denver Broncos	15	5	21	15	1.0	1	0	0	0	0	0	-	0	0	0	0
1994 Denver Broncos	13	0	1	1	0.0	0	0	0	0	0	0	-	0	0	0	0
1995 Denver Broncos	2	0	0	0	0.0	0	0	0	0	0	0	-	0	0	0	0
3 NFL Seasons	30	5	22	16	1.0	1	0	0	0	0	0	-	0	0	0	0

Jerry Ostroski

Pos: G **Rnd:** 10 **College:** Tulsa **Ht:** 6' 4" **Wt:** 310 **Born:** 7/12/70 **Age:** 26

Year Team	G	GS	Year Team	G	GS		Year Team	G	GS
1994 Buffalo Bills	4	3	1995 Buffalo Bills	16	13		2 NFL Seasons	20	16

Brad Ottis

Pos: DE/DT **Rnd:** 2 **College:** Wayne State (NE) **Ht:** 6' 4" **Wt:** 272 **Born:** 8/2/72 **Age:** 24

Year Team	G	GS	Tk	Ast	Sack	FF	FR	TD	Blk	Int	Yds	Avg	TD	Sfty	TD	Pts
			Tackles			**Miscellaneous**				**Interceptions**				**Totals**		
1994 Los Angeles Rams	13	0	8	1	1.0	0	0	0	0	0	0	-	0	0	0	0
1995 St. Louis Rams	12	0	0	0	0.0	0	0	0	0	0	0	-	0	0	0	0
2 NFL Seasons	25	0	8	1	1.0	0	0	0	0	0	0	-	0	0	0	0

Dan Owens

Pos: DE/DT **Rnd:** 2 **College:** Southern California **Ht:** 6' 3" **Wt:** 280 **Born:** 3/16/67 **Age:** 29

Year Team	G	GS	Tk	Ast	Sack	FF	FR	TD	Blk	Int	Yds	Avg	TD	Num	Yds	Avg	TD	Num	Yds	Avg	TD	TD	Fum
			Tackles			**Miscellaneous**				**Interceptions**				**Punt Returns**				**Kickoff Returns**				**Totals**	
1990 Detroit Lions	16	12	32	14	3.0	0	0	0	0	0	0	-	0	0	0	-	0	0	0	-	0	0	0
1991 Detroit Lions	16	16	40	11	5.5	0	2	0	0	0	0	-	0	0	0	-	0	0	0	-	0	0	0
1992 Detroit Lions	16	4	20	5	2.0	0	1	0	0	0	0	-	0	0	0	-	0	0	0	-	0	0	0
1993 Detroit Lions	15	11	21	10	3.0	1	2	0	0	1	1	1.0	0	0	0	-	0	0	0	-	0	0	0
1994 Detroit Lions	16	8	26	15	3.0	0	0	0	0	0	0	-	0	0	0	-	0	0	0	-	0	0	0
1995 Detroit Lions	16	0	3	1	0.0	0	0	0	0	0	0	-	0	0	0	-	0	1	9	9.0	0	0	0
6 NFL Seasons	95	51	142	56	16.5	1	5	0	0	1	1	1.0	0	0	0	-	0	1	9	9.0	0	0	0

Rich Owens

Pos: DE **Rnd:** 5 **College:** Lehigh **Ht:** 6' 6" **Wt:** 263 **Born:** 5/22/72 **Age:** 24

Year Team	G	GS	Tk	Ast	Sack	FF	FR	TD	Blk	Int	Yds	Avg	TD	Sfty	TD	Pts
			Tackles			**Miscellaneous**				**Interceptions**				**Totals**		
1995 Washington Redskins	10	3	15	5	3.0	1	0	0	0	0	0	-	0	0	0	0

Jeff Pahukoa

Pos: G **Rnd:** 12 **College:** Washington **Ht:** 6' 2" **Wt:** 298 **Born:** 2/9/69 **Age:** 27

Year Team	G	GS	Year Team	G	GS	Year Team	G	GS	Year Team	G	GS
1991 Los Angeles Rams	7	0	1992 Los Angeles Rams	16	0	1993 Los Angeles Rams	16	5	1995 Atlanta Falcons	6	2
									4 NFL Seasons	45	7

Shane Pahukoa

Pos: S **Rnd:** FA **College:** Washington **Ht:** 6' 2" **Wt:** 202 **Born:** 11/25/70 **Age:** 25

Year Team	G	GS	Tackles			Miscellaneous				Interceptions				Totals		
			Tk	Ast	Sack	FF	FR	TD	Blk	Int	Yds	Avg	TD	Sfty	TD	Pts
1995 New Orleans Saints	15	2	21	5	0.0	0	0	0	0	2	12	6.0	0	0	0	0

Lonnie Palelei

Pos: G **Rnd:** 5 **College:** UNLV **Ht:** 6' 3" **Wt:** 320 **Born:** 10/15/70 **Age:** 26

Year	Team	G	GS	Year	Team	G	GS			G	GS
1993	Pittsburgh Steelers	3	0	1995	Pittsburgh Steelers	1	0		2 NFL Seasons	4	0

David Palmer

Pos: PR/KR **Rnd:** 2 **College:** Alabama **Ht:** 5' 8" **Wt:** 167 **Born:** 11/19/72 **Age:** 23

Year Team	G	GS	Rushing					Receiving					Punt Returns				Kickoff Returns				Totals		
			Att	Yds	Avg	Lg	TD	Rec	Yds	Avg	Lg	TD	Num	Yds	Avg	TD	Num	Yds	Avg	TD	Fum	TD	Pts
1994 Minnesota Vikings	13	1	1	1	1.0	1	0	6	90	15.0	39	0	30	193	6.4	0	0	0	-	0	2	0	0
1995 Minnesota Vikings	14	0	7	15	2.1	9	0	12	100	8.3	19	0	26	342	13.2	1	17	354	20.8	0	1	1	6
2 NFL Seasons	27	1	8	16	2.0	9	0	18	190	10.6	39	0	56	535	9.6	1	17	354	20.8	0	3	1	6

Sterling Palmer

(statistical profile on page 437)

Pos: DE **Rnd:** 4 **College:** Florida State **Ht:** 6' 5" **Wt:** 277 **Born:** 2/4/71 **Age:** 25

Year Team	G	GS	Tackles			Miscellaneous				Interceptions				Totals		
			Tk	Ast	Sack	FF	FR	TD	Blk	Int	Yds	Avg	TD	Sfty	TD	Pts
1993 Washington Redskins	14	10	31	26	4.5	0	0	0	0	0	0	-	0	0	0	0
1994 Washington Redskins	16	16	36	11	1.0	1	0	0	0	0	0	-	0	0	0	0
1995 Washington Redskins	13	13	30	5	4.5	2	1	0	0	0	0	-	0	0	0	0
3 NFL Seasons	43	39	97	42	10.0	3	1	0	0	0	0	-	0	0	0	0

Joe Panos

Pos: G **Rnd:** 3 **College:** Wisconsin **Ht:** 6' 2" **Wt:** 293 **Born:** 1/24/71 **Age:** 25

Year	Team	G	GS	Year	Team	G	GS			G	GS
1994	Philadelphia Eagles	16	2	1995	Philadelphia Eagles	9	9		2 NFL Seasons	25	11

Anthony Parker

(statistical profile on page 438)

Pos: CB **Rnd:** FA **College:** Arizona State **Ht:** 5' 10" **Wt:** 181 **Born:** 2/11/66 **Age:** 30

Year Team	G	GS	Tackles			Miscellaneous				Interceptions				Punt Returns				Kickoff Returns				Totals	
			Tk	Ast	Sack	FF	FR	TD	Blk	Int	Yds	Avg	TD	Num	Yds	Avg	TD	Num	Yds	Avg	TD	TD	Fum
1989 Indianapolis Colts	1	0	1	0	0.0	0	0	0	0	0	0	-	0	0	0	-	0	0	0	-	0	0	0
1991 Kansas City Chiefs	2	0	2	0	0.0	0	0	0	0	0	0	-	0	0	0	-	0	0	0	-	0	0	0
1992 Minnesota Vikings	16	3	19	10	0.0	0	2	1	0	3	23	7.7	0	33	336	10.2	0	2	30	15.0	0	1	2
1993 Minnesota Vikings	14	0	15	5	0.0	0	0	0	0	1	1	1.0	0	9	64	7.1	0	0	0	-	0	0	0
1994 Minnesota Vikings	15	15	61	15	0.0	1	1	0	0	4	99	24.8	2	4	31	7.8	0	0	0	-	0	3	1
1995 St. Louis Rams	16	16	55	4	0.0	1	4	1	0	2	-5	-2.5	0	0	0	-	0	0	0	-	0	1	0
6 NFL Seasons	64	34	153	34	0.0	1	7	3	0	10	118	11.8	2	46	431	9.4	0	2	30	15.0	0	5	3

Glenn Parker

Pos: T **Rnd:** 3 **College:** Arizona **Ht:** 6' 5" **Wt:** 310 **Born:** 4/22/66 **Age:** 30

Year	Team	G	GS	Year	Team	G	GS	Year	Team	G	GS			G	GS
1990	Buffalo Bills	16	3	1992	Buffalo Bills	13	13	1994	Buffalo Bills	16	16				
1991	Buffalo Bills	16	5	1993	Buffalo Bills	16	9	1995	Buffalo Bills	13	13		6 NFL Seasons	90	59

Other Statistics: 1992–recovered 1 fumble for 0 yards. 1995–recovered 1 fumble for 0 yards.

Vaughn Parker

Pos: T/G **Rnd:** 2 **College:** UCLA **Ht:** 6' 3" **Wt:** 296 **Born:** 6/5/71 **Age:** 25

Year	Team	G	GS	Year	Team	G	GS			G	GS
1994	San Diego Chargers	6	0	1995	San Diego Chargers	14	7		2 NFL Seasons	20	7

Other Statistics: 1994–returned 1 kickoff for 1 yard.

Bernie Parmalee

(statistical profile on page 364)

Pos: RB **Rnd:** FA **College:** Ball State **Ht:** 5' 11" **Wt:** 196 **Born:** 9/16/67 **Age:** 29

Year Team	G	GS	Rushing					Receiving					Punt Returns				Kickoff Returns				Totals		
			Att	Yds	Avg	Lg	TD	Rec	Yds	Avg	Lg	TD	Num	Yds	Avg	TD	Num	Yds	Avg	TD	Fum	TD	Pts
1992 Miami Dolphins	10	0	6	38	6.3	20	0	0	0	-	-	0	0	0	-	0	14	289	20.6	0	3	0	0
1993 Miami Dolphins	16	0	4	16	4.0	12	0	1	1	1.0	1	0	0	0	-	0	0	0	-	0	0	0	0
1994 Miami Dolphins	15	10	216	868	4.0	t47	6	34	249	7.3	22	1	0	0	-	0	2	0	0.0	0	5	7	44

190

Year Team	G	GS	Rushing					Receiving					Punt Returns				Kickoff Returns				Totals		
			Att	Yds	Avg	Lg	TD	Rec	Yds	Avg	Lg	TD	Num	Yds	Avg	TD	Num	Yds	Avg	TD	Fum	TD	Pts
1995 Miami Dolphins	16	12	236	878	3.7	40	9	39	345	8.8	35	1	0	0	-	0	0	0	-	0	5	10	60
4 NFL Seasons	57	22	462	1800	3.9	t47	15	74	595	8.0	35	2	0	0	-	0	16	289	18.1	0	13	17	104

Other Statistics: 1994–recovered 3 fumbles for 15 yards; scored 1 two-point conversion.

John Parrella

Pos: DT **Rnd:** 2 **College:** Nebraska **Ht:** 6' 3" **Wt:** 290 **Born:** 11/22/69 **Age:** 26

Year Team	G	GS	Tackles			Miscellaneous				Interceptions				Totals		
			Tk	Ast	Sack	FF	FR	TD	Blk	Int	Yds	Avg	TD	Sfty	TD	Pts
1993 Buffalo Bills	10	0	1	1	1.0	0	0	0	0	0	0	-	0	0	0	0
1994 San Diego Chargers	13	1	4	3	1.0	0	0	0	0	0	0	-	0	0	0	0
1995 San Diego Chargers	16	1	9	4	2.0	0	0	0	0	0	0	-	0	0	0	0
3 NFL Seasons	39	2	14	8	4.0	0	0	0	0	0	0	-	0	0	0	0

James Parrish

Pos: T **Rnd:** FA **College:** Temple **Ht:** 6' 6" **Wt:** 300 **Born:** 5/19/68 **Age:** 28

Year	Team	G	GS	Year	Team	G	GS			G	GS
1993	Dallas Cowboys	1	0	1995	Pittsburgh Steelers	16	1	2 NFL Seasons		17	1

Ty Parten

Pos: DE **Rnd:** 3 **College:** Arizona **Ht:** 6' 4" **Wt:** 272 **Born:** 10/13/69 **Age:** 27

Year Team	G	GS	Tackles			Miscellaneous				Interceptions				Totals		
			Tk	Ast	Sack	FF	FR	TD	Blk	Int	Yds	Avg	TD	Sfty	TD	Pts
1993 Cincinnati Bengals	11	1	5	3	0.0	0	0	0	0	0	0	-	0	0	0	0
1994 Cincinnati Bengals	14	4	16	4	0.0	0	0	0	0	0	0	-	0	0	0	0
1995 Cincinnati Bengals	1	1	1	2	0.0	0	0	0	0	0	0	-	0	0	0	0
3 NFL Seasons	26	6	22	9	0.0	0	0	0	0	0	0	-	0	0	0	0

Garin Patrick

Pos: C **Rnd:** FA **College:** Louisville **Ht:** 6' 3" **Wt:** 265 **Born:** 8/31/71 **Age:** 25

Year	Team	G	GS			G	GS
1995	Indianapolis Colts	5	0	1 NFL Season		5	0

Joe Patton

Pos: T/G **Rnd:** 3 **College:** Alabama A&M **Ht:** 6' 5" **Wt:** 288 **Born:** 1/5/72 **Age:** 24

Year	Team	G	GS	Year	Team	G	GS			G	GS
1994	Washington Redskins	4	0	1995	Washington Redskins	16	13	2 NFL Seasons		20	13

Other Statistics: 1995–recovered 1 fumble for 0 yards.

Marvcus Patton

(statistical profile on page 438)

Pos: LB **Rnd:** 8 **College:** UCLA **Ht:** 6' 2" **Wt:** 240 **Born:** 5/1/67 **Age:** 29

Year Team	G	GS	Tackles			Miscellaneous				Interceptions				Totals		
			Tk	Ast	Sack	FF	FR	TD	Blk	Int	Yds	Avg	TD	Sfty	TD	Pts
1990 Buffalo Bills	16	0	8	4	0.5	0	0	0	0	0	0	-	0	0	0	0
1991 Buffalo Bills	16	2	9	1	0.0	0	0	0	0	0	0	-	0	0	0	0
1992 Buffalo Bills	16	4	20	5	2.0	0	0	0	0	0	0	-	0	0	0	0
1993 Buffalo Bills	16	16	76	42	1.0	2	3	0	0	2	0	0.0	0	0	0	0
1994 Buffalo Bills	16	16	62	33	0.0	0	1	0	0	2	8	4.0	0	0	0	0
1995 Washington Redskins	16	16	94	19	2.0	3	1	0	0	2	7	3.5	0	0	0	0
6 NFL Seasons	96	54	269	104	5.5	5	5	0	0	6	15	2.5	0	0	0	0

Other Statistics: 1994–fumbled 1 time.

Tito Paul

Pos: DB/CB **Rnd:** 5 **College:** Ohio State **Ht:** 6' 0" **Wt:** 195 **Born:** 5/24/72 **Age:** 24

Year Team	G	GS	Tackles			Miscellaneous				Interceptions				Totals		
			Tk	Ast	Sack	FF	FR	TD	Blk	Int	Yds	Avg	TD	Sfty	TD	Pts
1995 Arizona Cardinals	15	4	19	1	0.0	0	0	0	0	1	4	4.0	0	0	0	0

Bryce Paup

(statistical profile on page 438)

Pos: LB **Rnd:** 6 **College:** Northern Iowa **Ht:** 6' 5" **Wt:** 247 **Born:** 2/29/68 **Age:** 28

Year Team	G	GS	Tackles			Miscellaneous				Interceptions				Totals		
			Tk	Ast	Sack	FF	FR	TD	Blk	Int	Yds	Avg	TD	Sfty	TD	Pts
1990 Green Bay Packers	5	0	1	0	0.0	0	0	0	0	0	0	-	0	0	0	0
1991 Green Bay Packers	12	1	24	4	7.5	3	0	0	0	0	0	-	0	1	0	2

191

Year Team	G	GS	Tackles			Miscellaneous				Interceptions				Totals		
			Tk	Ast	Sack	FF	FR	TD	Blk	Int	Yds	Avg	TD	Sfty	TD	Pts
1992 Green Bay Packers	16	10	22	21	6.5	1	2	0	0	0	0	-	0	0	0	0
1993 Green Bay Packers	15	14	51	23	11.0	2	0	0	0	1	8	8.0	0	0	0	0
1994 Green Bay Packers	16	16	47	32	7.5	2	2	0	0	3	47	15.7	1	0	1	6
1995 Buffalo Bills	15	15	70	19	17.5	3	1	0	1	2	0	0.0	0	0	0	0
6 NFL Seasons	79	56	215	99	50.0	11	5	0	1	6	55	9.2	1	1	1	8

Rodney Peete

(statistical profile on page 364)

Pos: QB **Rnd:** 6 **College:** Southern California **Ht:** 6' 0" **Wt:** 225 **Born:** 3/16/66 **Age:** 30

Year Team	G	GS	Passing										Rushing					Miscellaneous				
			Att	Com	Pct	Yards	Yds/Att	Lg	TD	Int	Int%	Rating	Att	Yds	Avg	Lg	TD	Sckd	Yds	Fum	Recv	Yds	Pts
1989 Detroit Lions	8	8	195	103	52.8	1479	7.58	69	5	9	4.6	67.0	33	148	4.5	t14	4	27	164	9	3	0	24
1990 Detroit Lions	11	11	271	142	52.4	1974	7.28	t68	13	8	3.0	79.8	47	363	7.7	37	6	27	173	9	1	0	36
1991 Detroit Lions	8	8	194	116	59.8	1339	6.90	t68	5	9	4.6	69.9	25	125	5.0	26	2	11	42	2	1	-1	12
1992 Detroit Lions	10	10	213	123	57.7	1702	7.99	t78	9	9	4.2	80.0	21	83	4.0	12	0	28	170	6	2	-7	0
1993 Detroit Lions	10	10	252	157	62.3	1670	6.63	t93	6	14	5.6	66.4	45	165	3.7	28	1	34	174	11	4	-8	6
1994 Dallas Cowboys	7	1	56	33	58.9	470	8.39	t65	4	1	1.8	102.5	9	-2	-0.2	2	0	4	21	3	2	1	0
1995 Philadelphia Eagles	15	12	375	215	57.3	2326	6.20	t37	8	14	3.7	67.3	32	147	4.6	18	1	33	166	13	5	0	6
7 NFL Seasons	69	60	1556	889	57.1	10960	7.04	t93	50	64	4.1	72.6	212	1029	4.9	37	14	164	910	53	18	-15	84

Erric Pegram

(statistical profile on page 365)

Pos: RB **Rnd:** 6 **College:** North Texas **Ht:** 5' 10" **Wt:** 188 **Born:** 1/7/69 **Age:** 27

Year Team	G	GS	Rushing					Receiving					Punt Returns				Kickoff Returns				Totals		
			Att	Yds	Avg	Lg	TD	Rec	Yds	Avg	Lg	TD	Num	Yds	Avg	TD	Num	Yds	Avg	TD	Fum	TD	Pts
1991 Atlanta Falcons	16	7	101	349	3.5	34	1	1	-1	-1.0	-1	0	0	0	-	0	16	260	16.3	0	1	1	6
1992 Atlanta Falcons	16	1	21	89	4.2	15	0	2	25	12.5	19	0	0	0	-	0	9	161	17.9	0	0	0	0
1993 Atlanta Falcons	16	14	292	1185	4.1	29	3	33	302	9.2	30	0	0	0	-	0	4	63	15.8	0	6	3	18
1994 Atlanta Falcons	13	5	103	358	3.5	25	1	16	99	6.2	28	0	0	0	-	0	9	145	16.1	0	2	1	6
1995 Pittsburgh Steelers	15	11	213	813	3.8	38	5	26	206	7.9	22	1	0	0	-	0	4	85	21.3	0	9	6	38
5 NFL Seasons	76	38	730	2794	3.8	38	10	78	631	8.1	30	1	0	0	-	0	42	714	17.0	0	18	11	68

Other Statistics: 1992–recovered 3 fumbles for 1 yard. 1993–recovered 4 fumbles for 0 yards. 1994–recovered 1 fumble for 0 yards. 1995–recovered 1 fumble for 0 yards; scored 1 two-point conversion.

Doug Pelfrey

(statistical profile on page 481)

Pos: K **Rnd:** 8 **College:** Kentucky **Ht:** 5' 11" **Wt:** 185 **Born:** 9/25/70 **Age:** 26

Year Team	G	Field Goals													PAT		Tot
		1-29 Yds	Pct	30-39 Yds	Pct	40-49 Yds	Pct	50+ Yds	Pct	Overall	Pct	Long	Made	Att	Pts
1993 Cincinnati Bengals	15	8-8	100.0	6-10	60.0	8-10	80.0	2-3	66.7	24-31	77.4	53	13	16	85
1994 Cincinnati Bengals	16	9-9	100.0	8-10	80.0	9-10	90.0	2-4	50.0	28-33	84.8	54	24	25	108
1995 Cincinnati Bengals	16	8-9	88.9	10-11	90.9	10-14	71.4	1-2	50.0	29-36	80.6	51	34	34	121
3 NFL Seasons	47	25-26	96.2	24-31	77.4	27-34	79.4	5-9	55.6	81-100	81.0	54	71	75	314

Other Statistics: 1995–punted 2 times for 52 yards.

Chris Penn

Pos: WR **Rnd:** 3 **College:** Tulsa **Ht:** 6' 0" **Wt:** 198 **Born:** 4/20/71 **Age:** 25

Year Team	G	GS	Rushing					Receiving					Punt Returns				Kickoff Returns				Totals		
			Att	Yds	Avg	Lg	TD	Rec	Yds	Avg	Lg	TD	Num	Yds	Avg	TD	Num	Yds	Avg	TD	Fum	TD	Pts
1994 Kansas City Chiefs	8	0	0	0	-	-	0	3	24	8.0	13	0	0	0	-	0	9	194	21.6	0	0	0	0
1995 Kansas City Chiefs	2	0	0	0	-	-	0	1	12	12.0	12	0	4	12	3.0	0	2	26	13.0	0	0	0	0
2 NFL Seasons	10	0	0	0	-	-	0	4	36	9.0	13	0	4	12	3.0	0	11	220	20.0	0	0	0	0

Brett Perriman

(statistical profile on page 365)

Pos: WR **Rnd:** 2 **College:** Miami (FL) **Ht:** 5' 9" **Wt:** 180 **Born:** 10/10/65 **Age:** 31

Year Team	G	GS	Rushing					Receiving					Punt Returns				Kickoff Returns				Totals		
			Att	Yds	Avg	Lg	TD	Rec	Yds	Avg	Lg	TD	Num	Yds	Avg	TD	Num	Yds	Avg	TD	Fum	TD	Pts
1988 New Orleans Saints	16	0	3	17	5.7	17	0	16	215	13.4	33	2	0	0	-	0	0	0	-	0	1	2	12
1989 New Orleans Saints	14	1	1	-10	-10.0	-10	0	20	356	17.8	47	0	1	10	10.0	0	0	0	-	0	0	0	0
1990 New Orleans Saints	16	15	0	0	-	-	0	36	382	10.6	29	2	0	0	-	0	0	0	-	0	2	2	12
1991 Detroit Lions	15	14	4	10	2.5	6	0	52	668	12.8	42	1	0	0	-	0	0	0	-	0	0	1	6
1992 Detroit Lions	16	16	0	0	-	-	0	69	810	11.7	t40	4	0	0	-	0	4	59	14.8	0	1	4	24
1993 Detroit Lions	15	15	4	16	4.0	16	0	49	496	10.1	34	2	0	0	-	0	0	0	-	0	1	2	12
1994 Detroit Lions	16	14	9	86	9.6	25	0	56	761	13.6	39	4	0	0	-	0	0	0	-	0	1	4	28
1995 Detroit Lions	16	16	5	48	9.6	16	0	108	1488	13.8	t91	9	5	50	10.0	0	5	65	13.0	0	1	9	56
8 NFL Seasons	124	91	26	167	6.4	25	0	406	5176	12.7	t91	24	6	60	10.0	0	9	124	13.8	0	7	24	150

Other Statistics: 1990–recovered 1 fumble for 0 yards. 1994–attempted 1 pass with 0 completions for 0 yards; scored 2 two-point conversions. 1995–recovered 1 fumble for 0 yards; scored 1 two-point conversion.

Darren Perry
(statistical profile on page 439)

Pos: S **Rnd:** 8 **College:** Penn State **Ht:** 5' 11" **Wt:** 195 **Born:** 12/29/68 **Age:** 27

Year Team	G	GS	Tackles Tk	Ast	Sack	Misc. FF	FR	TD	Blk	Int	Int Yds	Avg	TD	Sfty	TD	Pts
1992 Pittsburgh Steelers	16	16	43	18	0.0	0	1	0	0	6	69	11.5	0	0	0	0
1993 Pittsburgh Steelers	16	16	62	32	0.0	0	0	0	0	4	61	15.3	0	0	0	0
1994 Pittsburgh Steelers	16	16	49	16	0.0	0	2	0	0	7	112	16.0	0	0	0	0
1995 Pittsburgh Steelers	16	16	61	9	0.0	0	2	0	0	4	71	17.8	0	0	0	0
4 NFL Seasons	64	64	215	75	0.0	0	5	0	0	21	313	14.9	0	0	0	0

Other Statistics: 1995–fumbled 1 time.

Gerald Perry

Pos: T **Rnd:** 2 **College:** Southern **Ht:** 6' 6" **Wt:** 305 **Born:** 11/12/64 **Age:** 31

Year	Team	G	GS	Year	Team	G	GS	Year	Team	G	GS	Year	Team	G	GS
1988	Denver Broncos	16	6	1990	Denver Broncos	8	8	1992	Los Angeles Rams	16	16	1994	Los Angeles Raiders	12	12
1989	Denver Broncos	16	15	1991	Los Angeles Rams	11	9	1993	Los Angeles Raiders	15	15	1995	Oakland Raiders	3	3
													8 NFL Seasons	97	84

Other Statistics: 1989–recovered 1 fumble for 0 yards. 1993–recovered 1 fumble for 0 yards.

Marlo Perry

Pos: LB **Rnd:** 3 **College:** Jackson State **Ht:** 6' 4" **Wt:** 250 **Born:** 8/25/72 **Age:** 24

Year Team	G	GS	Tackles Tk	Ast	Sack	Misc. FF	FR	TD	Blk	Int	Int Yds	Avg	TD	Sfty	TD	Pts
1994 Buffalo Bills	2	0	1	0	0.0	0	0	0	0	0	0	-	0	0	0	0
1995 Buffalo Bills	16	11	44	15	0.0	0	0	0	0	0	0	-	0	0	0	0
2 NFL Seasons	18	11	45	15	0.0	0	0	0	0	0	0	-	0	0	0	0

Michael Dean Perry
(statistical profile on page 439)

Pos: DT **Rnd:** 2 **College:** Clemson **Ht:** 6' 1" **Wt:** 290 **Born:** 8/27/65 **Age:** 31

Year Team	G	GS	Tackles Tk	Ast	Sack	Misc. FF	FR	TD	Blk	Int Int	Yds	Avg	TD	Punt Returns Num	Yds	Avg	TD	Kickoff Returns Num	Yds	Avg	TD	Totals TD	Fum
1988 Cleveland Browns	16	2	20	5	6.0	2	2	1	0	0	0	-	0	0	0	-	0	1	13	13.0	0	1	0
1989 Cleveland Browns	16	16	62	30	7.0	2	2	0	0	0	0	-	0	0	0	-	0	0	0	-	0	0	0
1990 Cleveland Browns	16	16	85	22	11.5	2	1	0	0	0	0	-	0	0	0	-	0	0	0	-	0	0	0
1991 Cleveland Browns	16	15	64	17	8.5	2	0	0	0	0	0	-	0	0	0	-	0	0	0	-	0	0	0
1992 Cleveland Browns	14	14	39	12	8.5	0	0	0	0	0	0	-	0	0	0	-	0	0	0	-	0	0	0
1993 Cleveland Browns	16	13	63	18	6.0	2	2	0	0	0	0	-	0	0	0	-	0	0	0	-	0	0	0
1994 Cleveland Browns	15	14	33	10	4.0	0	0	0	0	0	0	-	0	0	0	-	0	0	0	-	0	0	0
1995 Denver Broncos	14	14	33	6	6.0	1	0	0	0	0	0	-	0	0	0	-	0	0	0	-	0	0	0
8 NFL Seasons	123	104	399	120	57.5	11	7	1	0	0	0	-	0	0	0	-	0	1	13	13.0	0	1	0

Todd Perry

Pos: G **Rnd:** 4 **College:** Kentucky **Ht:** 6' 5" **Wt:** 310 **Born:** 11/28/70 **Age:** 25

Year	Team	G	GS	Year	Team	G	GS	Year	Team	G	GS			G	GS
1993	Chicago Bears	13	3	1994	Chicago Bears	15	4	1995	Chicago Bears	15	15		3 NFL Seasons	43	22

Andrew Peterson

Pos: G **Rnd:** 5 **College:** Washington **Ht:** 6' 5" **Wt:** 310 **Born:** 6/11/72 **Age:** 24

Year	Team	G	GS			G	GS
1995	Carolina Panthers	4	2		1 NFL Season	4	2

Todd Peterson
(statistical profile on page 481)

Pos: K **Rnd:** 7 **College:** Georgia **Ht:** 5' 10" **Wt:** 180 **Born:** 2/4/70 **Age:** 26

Year Team	G	1-29 Yds	Pct	30-39 Yds	Pct	40-49 Yds	Pct	50+ Yds	Pct	Overall	Pct	Long	PAT Made	Att	Tot Pts
1994 Arizona Cardinals	2	1-1	100.0	1-1	100.0	0-2	0.0	0-0	-	2-4	50.0	35	4	4	10
1995 Seattle Seahawks	16	6-6	100.0	9-10	90.0	8-10	80.0	0-2	0.0	23-28	82.1	49	40	40	109
2 NFL Seasons	18	7-7	100.0	10-11	90.9	8-12	66.7	0-2	0.0	25-32	78.1	49	44	44	119

Tony Peterson

Pos: LB **Rnd:** 5 **College:** Notre Dame **Ht:** 6' 0" **Wt:** 223 **Born:** 1/23/72 **Age:** 24

Year Team	G	GS	Tackles Tk	Ast	Sack	Misc. FF	FR	TD	Blk	Int	Int Yds	Avg	TD	Sfty	TD	Pts
1994 San Francisco 49ers	14	0	5	1	0.0	0	0	0	0	0	0	-	0	0	0	0
1995 San Francisco 49ers	15	0	1	0	0.0	0	0	0	0	0	0	-	0	0	0	0

193

Year Team	G	GS	Tackles			Miscellaneous				Interceptions				Totals		
			Tk	Ast	Sack	FF	FR	TD	Blk	Int	Yds	Avg	TD	Sfty	TD	Pts
2 NFL Seasons	29	0	6	1	0.0	0	0	0	0	0	0	-	0	0	0	0

Roman Phifer

(statistical profile on page 439)

Pos: LB **Rnd:** 2 **College:** UCLA **Ht:** 6' 2" **Wt:** 230 **Born:** 3/5/68 **Age:** 28

Year Team	G	GS	Tackles			Miscellaneous				Interceptions				Totals		
			Tk	Ast	Sack	FF	FR	TD	Blk	Int	Yds	Avg	TD	Sfty	TD	Pts
1991 Los Angeles Rams	12	5	21	3	2.0	0	0	0	0	0	0	-	0	0	0	0
1992 Los Angeles Rams	16	14	51	15	0.0	0	2	0	0	1	3	3.0	0	0	0	0
1993 Los Angeles Rams	16	16	96	21	0.0	0	2	0	0	0	0	-	0	0	0	0
1994 Los Angeles Rams	16	16	79	17	1.5	1	0	0	0	2	7	3.5	0	0	0	0
1995 St. Louis Rams	16	16	87	28	3.0	1	0	0	0	3	52	17.3	0	0	0	0
5 NFL Seasons	76	67	334	84	6.5	2	4	0	0	6	62	10.3	0	0	0	0

Other Statistics: 1995–fumbled 1 time for 0 yards.

Ed Philion

Pos: NT/DT **Rnd:** FA **College:** Ferris State **Ht:** 6' 3" **Wt:** 281 **Born:** 3/27/70 **Age:** 26

Year Team	G	GS	Tackles			Miscellaneous				Interceptions				Totals		
			Tk	Ast	Sack	FF	FR	TD	Blk	Int	Yds	Avg	TD	Sfty	TD	Pts
1994 Buffalo Bills	4	0	2	1	0.0	0	0	0	0	0	0	-	0	0	0	0
1995 Buffalo Bills	2	0	8	1	0.0	0	0	0	0	0	0	-	0	0	0	0
2 NFL Seasons	6	0	10	2	0.0	0	0	0	0	0	0	-	0	0	0	0

Anthony Phillips

Pos: CB **Rnd:** 3 **College:** Texas A&M-Kingsville **Ht:** 6' 2" **Wt:** 207 **Born:** 10/5/70 **Age:** 26

Year Team	G	GS	Tackles			Miscellaneous				Interceptions				Totals		
			Tk	Ast	Sack	FF	FR	TD	Blk	Int	Yds	Avg	TD	Sfty	TD	Pts
1994 Atlanta Falcons	5	0	11	1	0.0	0	0	0	0	1	0	0.0	0	0	0	0
1995 Atlanta Falcons	6	4	21	2	0.0	0	0	0	0	1	43	43.0	0	0	0	0
2 NFL Seasons	11	4	32	3	0.0	0	0	0	0	2	43	21.5	0	0	0	0

Bobby Phillips

Pos: RB **Rnd:** FA **College:** Virginia Union **Ht:** 5' 9" **Wt:** 194 **Born:** 12/8/69 **Age:** 26

Year Team	G	GS	Rushing					Receiving					Punt Returns				Kickoff Returns				Totals		
			Att	Yds	Avg	Lg	TD	Rec	Yds	Avg	Lg	TD	Num	Yds	Avg	TD	Num	Yds	Avg	TD	Fum	TD	Pts
1995 Minnesota Vikings	8	0	14	26	1.9	7	0	0	0	-	-	0	0	0	-	0	4	60	15.0	0	1	0	0

Joe Phillips

(statistical profile on page 440)

Pos: DT **Rnd:** 4 **College:** Southern Methodist **Ht:** 6' 5" **Wt:** 300 **Born:** 7/15/63 **Age:** 33

Year Team	G	GS	Tackles			Miscellaneous				Interceptions				Totals		
			Tk	Ast	Sack	FF	FR	TD	Blk	Int	Yds	Avg	TD	Sfty	TD	Pts
1986 Minnesota Vikings	16	1	5	0	0.0	0	1	0	0	0	0	-	0	0	0	0
1987 San Diego Chargers	13	7	43	10	5.0	0	0	0	0	0	0	-	0	0	0	0
1988 San Diego Chargers	16	16	33	8	2.0	0	0	0	0	0	0	-	0	0	0	0
1989 San Diego Chargers	16	15	29	8	1.0	0	0	0	0	0	0	-	0	0	0	0
1990 San Diego Chargers	3	3	6	3	0.5	0	0	0	0	0	0	-	0	0	0	0
1991 San Diego Chargers	16	16	32	4	1.0	0	1	0	0	0	0	-	0	0	0	0
1992 Kansas City Chiefs	12	10	26	11	2.5	0	1	0	0	0	0	-	0	0	0	0
1993 Kansas City Chiefs	16	16	36	9	1.5	0	0	0	0	0	0	-	0	0	0	0
1994 Kansas City Chiefs	16	16	38	2	3.0	0	1	0	0	0	0	-	0	0	0	0
1995 Kansas City Chiefs	16	16	25	9	4.5	0	1	0	0	1	2	2.0	0	0	0	0
10 NFL Seasons	140	116	273	64	21.0	0	5	0	0	1	2	2.0	0	0	0	0

Dino Philyaw

Pos: RB **Rnd:** 6 **College:** Oregon **Ht:** 5' 10" **Wt:** 192 **Born:** 10/30/70 **Age:** 26

Year Team	G	GS	Rushing					Receiving					Punt Returns				Kickoff Returns				Totals		
			Att	Yds	Avg	Lg	TD	Rec	Yds	Avg	Lg	TD	Num	Yds	Avg	TD	Num	Yds	Avg	TD	Fum	TD	Pts
1995 Carolina Panthers	1	0	0	0	-	-	0	0	0	-	-	0	0	0	-	0	1	23	23.0	0	0	0	0

Bruce Pickens

Pos: CB **Rnd:** 1 (3) **College:** Nebraska **Ht:** 5' 11" **Wt:** 195 **Born:** 5/9/68 **Age:** 28

Year Team	G	GS	Tackles			Miscellaneous				Interceptions				Totals		
			Tk	Ast	Sack	FF	FR	TD	Blk	Int	Yds	Avg	TD	Sfty	TD	Pts
1991 Atlanta Falcons	7	0	5	2	0.0	0	0	0	0	0	0	-	0	0	0	0

Year Team	G	GS	Tackles			Miscellaneous				Interceptions				Totals		
			Tk	Ast	Sack	FF	FR	TD	Blk	Int	Yds	Avg	TD	Sfty	TD	Pts
1992 Atlanta Falcons	16	4	35	16	1.0	0	0	0	0	2	16	8.0	0	0	0	0
1993 Atl - GB - KC	9	3	14	4	0.0	0	0	0	0	0	0	0	0	0	0	0
1995 Oakland Raiders	16	1	12	0	0.0	0	1	0	0	0	0	-	0	0	0	0
1993 Atlanta Falcons	4	3	11	3	0.0	0	0	0	0	0	0	-	0	0	0	0
Green Bay Packers	2	0	0	1	0.0	0	0	0	0	0	0	-	0	0	0	0
Kansas City Chiefs	3	0	3	0	0.0	0	0	0	0	0	0	-	0	0	0	0
4 NFL Seasons	48	8	66	22	1.0	0	1	0	0	2	16	8.0	0	0	0	0

Carl Pickens

(statistical profile on page 366)

Pos: WR **Rnd:** 2 **College:** Tennessee **Ht:** 6' 2" **Wt:** 206 **Born:** 3/23/70 **Age:** 26

Year Team	G	GS	Rushing					Receiving					Punt Returns				Passing				Totals		
			Att	Yds	Avg	Lg	TD	Rec	Yds	Avg	Lg	TD	Num	Yds	Avg	TD	Att	Com	Yds	Int	Fum	TD	Pts
1992 Cincinnati Bengals	16	10	0	0	-	-	0	26	326	12.5	38	1	18	229	12.7	1	0	0	0	0	3	2	12
1993 Cincinnati Bengals	13	12	0	0	-	-	0	43	565	13.1	36	6	4	16	4.0	0	1	0	0	0	1	6	36
1994 Cincinnati Bengals	15	15	0	0	-	-	0	71	1127	15.9	t70	11	9	62	6.9	0	0	0	0	0	1	11	66
1995 Cincinnati Bengals	16	15	1	6	6.0	6	0	99	1234	12.5	168	**17**	5	-2	-0.4	0	0	0	0	0	1	17	102
4 NFL Seasons	60	52	1	6	6.0	6	0	239	3252	13.6	t70	35	36	305	8.5	1	1	0	0	0	6	36	216

Other Statistics: 1992–recovered 2 fumbles for 0 yards. 1994–recovered 1 fumble for 0 yards.

Aaron Pierce

(statistical profile on page 366)

Pos: TE/RB **Rnd:** 3 **College:** Washington **Ht:** 6' 5" **Wt:** 245 **Born:** 9/6/69 **Age:** 27

Year Team	G	GS	Rushing					Receiving					Punt Returns				Kickoff Returns				Totals		
			Att	Yds	Avg	Lg	TD	Rec	Yds	Avg	Lg	TD	Num	Yds	Avg	TD	Num	Yds	Avg	TD	Fum	TD	Pts
1992 New York Giants	1	0	0	0	-	-	0	0	0	-	-	0	0	0	-	0	0	0	-	0	0	0	0
1993 New York Giants	13	6	0	0	-	-	0	12	212	17.7	54	0	0	0	-	0	0	0	-	0	2	0	0
1994 New York Giants	16	11	0	0	-	-	0	20	214	10.7	29	4	0	0	-	0	0	0	-	0	0	4	24
1995 New York Giants	16	11	1	6	6.0	6	0	33	310	9.4	26	0	0	0	-	0	0	0	-	0	0	0	0
4 NFL Seasons	46	28	1	6	6.0	6	0	65	736	11.3	54	4	0	0	-	0	0	0	-	0	2	4	24

Other Statistics: 1995–recovered 1 fumble for 0 yards.

Pete Pierson

Pos: T **Rnd:** 5 **College:** Washington **Ht:** 6' 5" **Wt:** 295 **Born:** 2/4/71 **Age:** 25

Year Team	G	GS	Year Team	G	GS		G	GS
1994 Tampa Bay Buccaneers	1	0	1995 Tampa Bay Buccaneers	11	4	2 NFL Seasons	12	4

Other Statistics: 1995–recovered 1 fumble for 0 yards.

Mark Pike

Pos: DE **Rnd:** 7 **College:** Georgia Tech **Ht:** 6' 4" **Wt:** 272 **Born:** 12/27/63 **Age:** 32

Year Team	G	GS	Tackles			Miscellaneous				Interceptions				Punt Returns				Kickoff Returns				Totals	
			Tk	Ast	Sack	FF	FR	TD	Blk	Int	Yds	Avg	TD	Num	Yds	Avg	TD	Num	Yds	Avg	TD	TD	Fum
1987 Buffalo Bills	3	0	0	0	0.0	0	0	0	0	0	0	-	0	0	0	-	0	0	0	-	0	0	0
1988 Buffalo Bills	16	0	3	4	0.0	0	0	0	0	0	0	-	0	0	0	-	0	1	5	5.0	0	0	0
1989 Buffalo Bills	16	0	2	1	0.0	0	1	0	0	0	0	-	0	0	0	-	0	0	0	-	0	0	0
1990 Buffalo Bills	16	0	2	7	0.0	0	0	0	0	0	0	-	0	0	0	-	0	0	0	-	0	0	0
1991 Buffalo Bills	16	1	5	1	0.0	0	0	0	0	0	0	-	0	0	0	-	0	0	0	-	0	0	0
1992 Buffalo Bills	16	0	3	2	1.0	0	0	0	0	0	0	-	0	0	0	-	0	0	0	-	0	0	0
1993 Buffalo Bills	14	0	2	3	0.0	0	0	0	0	0	0	-	0	0	0	-	0	0	0	-	0	0	0
1994 Buffalo Bills	16	0	0	0	0.0	0	0	0	0	0	0	-	0	0	0	-	0	2	9	4.5	0	0	0
1995 Buffalo Bills	16	0	3	3	0.0	0	0	0	0	0	0	-	0	0	0	-	0	1	20	20.0	0	0	0
9 NFL Seasons	129	1	20	21	1.0	0	1	0	0	0	0	-	0	0	0	-	0	4	34	8.5	0	0	0

Lovell Pinkney

Pos: WR/TE **Rnd:** 4 **College:** Texas **Ht:** 6' 4" **Wt:** 248 **Born:** 8/18/72 **Age:** 24

Year Team	G	GS	Rushing					Receiving					Punt Returns				Kickoff Returns				Totals		
			Att	Yds	Avg	Lg	TD	Rec	Yds	Avg	Lg	TD	Num	Yds	Avg	TD	Num	Yds	Avg	TD	Fum	TD	Pts
1995 St. Louis Rams	8	0	0	0	-	-	0	1	13	13.0	13	0	0	0	-	0	1	26	26.0	0	0	0	0

Joe Planansky

Pos: TE **Rnd:** FA **College:** Chadron State **Ht:** 6' 4" **Wt:** 250 **Born:** 10/21/71 **Age:** 25

Year Team	G	GS	Rushing					Receiving					Punt Returns				Kickoff Returns				Totals		
			Att	Yds	Avg	Lg	TD	Rec	Yds	Avg	Lg	TD	Num	Yds	Avg	TD	Num	Yds	Avg	TD	Fum	TD	Pts
1995 Miami Dolphins	2	0	0	0	-	-	0	0	0	-	-	0	0	0	-	0	0	0	-	0	0	0	0

Anthony Pleasant

(statistical profile on page 440)

Pos: DE   **Rnd:** 3   **College:** Tennessee State   **Ht:** 6' 5"   **Wt:** 280   **Born:** 1/27/68   **Age:** 28

Year Team	G	GS	Tackles Tk	Ast	Sack	Misc. FF	FR	TD	Blk	Int. Int	Yds	Avg	TD	Totals Sfty	TD	Pts
1990 Cleveland Browns	16	7	38	12	3.5	1	0	0	0	0	0	-	0	0	0	0
1991 Cleveland Browns	16	7	12	9	2.5	0	1	0	0	0	0	-	0	0	0	0
1992 Cleveland Browns	16	14	35	16	4.0	1	0	0	0	0	0	-	0	0	0	0
1993 Cleveland Browns	16	13	43	23	11.0	1	0	0	0	0	0	-	0	1	0	2
1994 Cleveland Browns	14	14	44	14	4.5	0	0	0	0	0	0	-	0	0	0	0
1995 Cleveland Browns	16	16	41	10	8.0	6	0	0	0	0	0	-	0	0	0	0
6 NFL Seasons	94	71	213	84	33.5	9	1	0	0	0	0	-	0	1	0	2

Gary Plummer

(statistical profile on page 440)

Pos: LB   **Rnd:** FA   **College:** California   **Ht:** 6' 2"   **Wt:** 247   **Born:** 1/26/60   **Age:** 36

Year Team	G	GS	Tackles Tk	Ast	Sack	Misc. FF	FR	TD	Blk	Int. Int	Yds	Avg	TD	PR Num	Yds	Avg	TD	KR Num	Yds	Avg	TD	Totals TD	Fum
1986 San Diego Chargers	15	13	78	20	2.5	1	2	0	0	0	0	-	0	0	0	-	0	1	0	0.0	0	0	0
1987 San Diego Chargers	8	7	48	14	0.0	1	0	0	0	1	2	2.0	0	0	0	-	0	0	0	-	0	0	0
1988 San Diego Chargers	16	12	97	21	0.0	1	0	0	0	0	0	-	0	0	0	-	0	0	0	-	0	0	0
1989 San Diego Chargers	16	16	111	35	0.0	0	1	0	0	0	0	-	0	0	0	-	0	0	0	-	0	0	0
1990 San Diego Chargers	16	15	86	25	0.0	1	0	2	0	0	0	-	0	0	0	-	0	0	0	-	0	2	0
1991 San Diego Chargers	16	15	88	23	1.0	1	1	0	0	0	0	-	0	0	0	-	0	0	0	-	0	0	0
1992 San Diego Chargers	16	13	41	12	0.0	1	2	0	0	2	40	20.0	0	0	0	-	0	0	0	-	0	0	0
1993 San Diego Chargers	16	15	78	15	0.0	2	0	0	0	2	7	3.5	0	0	0	-	0	0	0	-	0	0	0
1994 San Francisco 49ers	16	16	56	8	0.0	0	1	0	0	1	1	1.0	0	0	0	-	0	0	0	-	0	0	0
1995 San Francisco 49ers	16	15	56	6	1.0	1	0	0	0	0	0	-	0	0	0	-	0	0	0	-	0	0	0
10 NFL Seasons	151	137	739	179	4.5	9	7	2	0	6	50	8.3	0	0	0	-	0	1	0	0.0	0	2	0

Other Statistics: 1989–rushed 1 time for 6 yards. 1990–rushed 2 times for 3 yards and 1 touchdown; caught 1 pass for 2 yards and 1 touchdown.

Frank Pollack

Pos: T   **Rnd:** 6   **College:** Northern Arizona   **Ht:** 6' 5"   **Wt:** 285   **Born:** 11/5/67   **Age:** 28

Year Team	G	GS	Year Team	G	GS	Year Team	G	GS	Year Team	G	GS
1990 San Francisco 49ers	15	0	1991 San Francisco 49ers	15	0	1994 San Francisco 49ers	12	4	1995 San Francisco 49ers	15	0
									4 NFL Seasons	57	4

Marcus Pollard

Pos: TE   **Rnd:** FA   **College:** Bradley   **Ht:** 6' 4"   **Wt:** 248   **Born:** 2/8/72   **Age:** 24

Year Team	G	GS	Rushing Att	Yds	Avg	Lg	TD	Receiving Rec	Yds	Avg	Lg	TD	PR Num	Yds	Avg	TD	KR Num	Yds	Avg	TD	Totals Fum	TD	Pts
1995 Indianapolis Colts	8	0	0	0	-	-	0	0	0	-	-	0	0	0	-	0	0	0	-	0	0	0	0

Trent Pollard

Pos: G   **Rnd:** 5   **College:** Eastern Washington   **Ht:** 6' 4"   **Wt:** 304   **Born:** 11/20/72   **Age:** 23

Year Team	G	GS	Year Team	G	GS			Year Team	G	GS
1994 Cincinnati Bengals	9	0	1995 Cincinnati Bengals	8	0			2 NFL Seasons	17	0

Tyrone Poole

(statistical profile on page 441)

Pos: CB   **Rnd:** 1 (22)   **College:** Fort Valley State   **Ht:** 5' 8"   **Wt:** 185   **Born:** 2/3/72   **Age:** 24

Year Team	G	GS	Tackles Tk	Ast	Sack	Misc. FF	FR	TD	Blk	Int. Int	Yds	Avg	TD	Totals Sfty	TD	Pts
1995 Carolina Panthers	16	13	59	9	2.0	3	0	0	0	2	8	4.0	0	0	0	0

Marquez Pope

(statistical profile on page 441)

Pos: CB   **Rnd:** 2   **College:** Fresno State   **Ht:** 5' 10"   **Wt:** 193   **Born:** 10/2/70   **Age:** 26

Year Team	G	GS	Tackles Tk	Ast	Sack	Misc. FF	FR	TD	Blk	Int. Int	Yds	Avg	TD	Totals Sfty	TD	Pts
1992 San Diego Chargers	7	0	0	0	0.0	0	0	0	0	0	0	-	0	0	0	0
1993 San Diego Chargers	16	1	32	6	0.5	2	0	0	0	2	14	7.0	0	0	0	0
1994 Los Angeles Rams	16	16	81	14	0.0	2	0	0	0	3	66	22.0	0	0	0	0
1995 San Francisco 49ers	16	16	59	5	0.0	2	0	0	0	1	-7	-7.0	0	0	0	0
4 NFL Seasons	55	33	172	25	0.5	6	0	0	0	6	73	12.2	0	0	0	0

Ted Popson

Pos: TE/LS **Rnd:** 11 **College:** Portland State **Ht:** 6' 4" **Wt:** 250 **Born:** 9/10/66 **Age:** 30

Year Team	G	GS	Rushing Att	Yds	Avg	Lg	TD	Receiving Rec	Yds	Avg	Lg	TD	Punt Returns Num	Yds	Avg	TD	Kickoff Returns Num	Yds	Avg	TD	Totals Fum	TD	Pts
1994 San Francisco 49ers	16	1	0	0	-	-	0	13	141	10.8	24	0	0	0	-	0	0	0	-	0	0	0	0
1995 San Francisco 49ers	12	0	0	0	-	-	0	16	128	8.0	16	0	0	0	-	0	0	0	-	0	1	0	0
2 NFL Seasons	28	1	0	0	-	-	0	29	269	9.3	24	0	0	0	-	0	0	0	-	0	1	0	0

Robert Porcher

(statistical profile on page 441)

Pos: DT **Rnd:** 1 (26) **College:** South Carolina State **Ht:** 6' 3" **Wt:** 283 **Born:** 7/30/69 **Age:** 27

Year Team	G	GS	Tackles Tk	Ast	Sack	Miscellaneous FF	FR	TD	Blk	Interceptions Int	Yds	Avg	TD	Totals Sfty	TD	Pts
1992 Detroit Lions	16	1	11	10	1.0	0	0	0	0	0	0	-	0	0	0	0
1993 Detroit Lions	16	4	37	10	8.5	0	0	0	0	0	0	-	0	0	0	0
1994 Detroit Lions	15	15	47	22	3.0	2	1	0	0	0	0	-	0	0	0	0
1995 Detroit Lions	16	16	29	22	5.0	1	0	0	0	0	0	-	0	0	0	0
4 NFL Seasons	63	36	124	64	17.5	3	1	0	0	0	0	-	0	0	0	0

Chris Port

Pos: G/T **Rnd:** 12 **College:** Duke **Ht:** 6' 5" **Wt:** 295 **Born:** 11/2/67 **Age:** 28

Year Team	G	GS	Year Team	G	GS	Year Team	G	GS		G	GS
1991 New Orleans Saints	14	11	1993 New Orleans Saints	15	15	1995 New Orleans Saints	8	8			
1992 New Orleans Saints	16	0	1994 New Orleans Saints	16	16				5 NFL Seasons	69	50

Other Statistics: 1993–recovered 1 fumble for 0 yards. 1995–recovered 1 fumble for 0 yards.

Rufus Porter

Pos: LB/DE **Rnd:** FA **College:** Southern **Ht:** 6' 1" **Wt:** 230 **Born:** 5/18/65 **Age:** 31

Year Team	G	GS	Tackles Tk	Ast	Sack	Miscellaneous FF	FR	TD	Blk	Interceptions Int	Yds	Avg	TD	Totals Sfty	TD	Pts
1988 Seattle Seahawks	16	0	17	-	0.0	1	1	0	0	0	0	-	0	0	0	0
1989 Seattle Seahawks	16	3	40	9	10.5	0	0	0	0	0	0	-	0	0	0	0
1990 Seattle Seahawks	12	12	42	9	5.0	0	4	0	0	0	0	-	0	0	0	0
1991 Seattle Seahawks	15	15	64	21	10.0	0	0	0	0	1	0	0.0	0	0	0	0
1992 Seattle Seahawks	16	16	68	22	9.5	0	0	0	0	0	0	-	0	0	0	0
1993 Seattle Seahawks	7	6	16	5	1.0	0	0	0	0	1	4	4.0	0	0	0	0
1994 Seattle Seahawks	15	15	61	14	1.5	0	0	0	0	1	33	33.0	0	0	0	0
1995 New Orleans Saints	14	12	48	12	3.0	1	1	0	0	0	0	-	0	0	0	0
8 NFL Seasons	111	79	356	92	40.5	2	6	0	0	3	37	12.3	0	0	0	0

Roosevelt Potts

Pos: RB **Rnd:** 2 **College:** Northeast Louisiana **Ht:** 6' 0" **Wt:** 260 **Born:** 1/8/71 **Age:** 25

Year Team	G	GS	Rushing Att	Yds	Avg	Lg	TD	Receiving Rec	Yds	Avg	Lg	TD	Punt Returns Num	Yds	Avg	TD	Kickoff Returns Num	Yds	Avg	TD	Totals Fum	TD	Pts
1993 Indianapolis Colts	16	15	179	711	4.0	34	0	26	189	7.3	24	0	0	0	-	0	0	0	-	0	8	0	0
1994 Indianapolis Colts	16	16	77	336	4.4	52	1	26	251	9.7	30	1	0	0	-	0	0	0	-	0	5	2	12
1995 Indianapolis Colts	15	15	65	309	4.8	37	0	21	228	10.9	52	1	0	0	-	0	0	0	-	0	0	1	6
3 NFL Seasons	47	46	321	1356	4.2	52	1	73	668	9.2	52	2	0	0	-	0	0	0	-	0	13	3	18

Other Statistics: 1993–recovered 2 fumbles for 0 yards. 1994–recovered 1 fumble for 0 yards.

Darryl Pounds

Pos: CB **Rnd:** 3 **College:** Nicholls State **Ht:** 5' 10" **Wt:** 177 **Born:** 7/21/72 **Age:** 24

Year Team	G	GS	Tackles Tk	Ast	Sack	Miscellaneous FF	FR	TD	Blk	Interceptions Int	Yds	Avg	TD	Totals Sfty	TD	Pts
1995 Washington Redskins	9	0	3	1	0.0	0	0	0	0	1	26	26.0	0	0	0	0

Other Statistics: 1995–fumbled 1 time for 0 yards.

Keith Powe

Pos: DE **Rnd:** FA **College:** Texas-El Paso **Ht:** 6' 3" **Wt:** 265 **Born:** 6/5/69 **Age:** 27

Year Team	G	GS	Tackles Tk	Ast	Sack	Miscellaneous FF	FR	TD	Blk	Interceptions Int	Yds	Avg	TD	Totals Sfty	TD	Pts
1994 Tampa Bay Buccaneers	5	0	3	0	0.0	0	0	0	0	0	0	-	0	0	0	0
1995 Tampa Bay Buccaneers	3	0	2	0	1.0	0	0	0	0	0	0	-	0	0	0	0
2 NFL Seasons	8	0	5	0	1.0	0	0	0	0	0	0	-	0	0	0	0

Craig Powell

Pos: LB **Rnd:** 1 (30) **College:** Ohio State **Ht:** 6' 4" **Wt:** 230 **Born:** 11/13/71 **Age:** 24

Year	Team	G	GS	Tackles			Miscellaneous				Interceptions				Totals		
				Tk	Ast	Sack	FF	FR	TD	Blk	Int	Yds	Avg	TD	Sfty	TD	Pts
1995	Cleveland Browns	3	0	0	0	0.0	0	0	0	0	0	0	-	0	0	0	0

Ricky Powers

Pos: RB **Rnd:** FA **College:** Michigan **Ht:** 6' 0" **Wt:** 213 **Born:** 11/30/71 **Age:** 24

Year	Team	G	GS	Rushing					Receiving					Punt Returns				Kickoff Returns				Totals		
				Att	Yds	Avg	Lg	TD	Rec	Yds	Avg	Lg	TD	Num	Yds	Avg	TD	Num	Yds	Avg	TD	Fum	TD	Pts
1995	Cleveland Browns	2	0	14	51	3.6	15	0	1	6	6.0	6	0	0	0	-	0	3	54	18.0	0	0	0	0

Andre President

Pos: TE **Rnd:** FA **College:** Angelo State **Ht:** 6' 3" **Wt:** 255 **Born:** 6/16/71 **Age:** 25

Year	Team	G	GS	Rushing					Receiving					Punt Returns				Kickoff Returns				Totals		
				Att	Yds	Avg	Lg	TD	Rec	Yds	Avg	Lg	TD	Num	Yds	Avg	TD	Num	Yds	Avg	TD	Fum	TD	Pts
1995	NE - Chi	3	0	0	0	-	-	0	0	0	-	-	0	0	0	-	0	0	0	-	0	0	0	0
1995	New England Patriots	1	0	0	0	-	-	0	0	0	-	-	0	0	0	-	0	0	0	-	0	0	0	0
	Chicago Bears	2	0	0	0	-	-	0	0	0	-	-	0	0	0	-	0	0	0	-	0	0	0	0

Roell Preston

Pos: KR/WR **Rnd:** 5 **College:** Mississippi **Ht:** 5' 10" **Wt:** 187 **Born:** 6/23/72 **Age:** 24

Year	Team	G	GS	Rushing					Receiving					Punt Returns				Kickoff Returns				Totals		
				Att	Yds	Avg	Lg	TD	Rec	Yds	Avg	Lg	TD	Num	Yds	Avg	TD	Num	Yds	Avg	TD	Fum	TD	Pts
1995	Atlanta Falcons	14	0	0	0	-	-	0	7	129	18.4	t61	1	0	0	-	0	30	627	20.9	0	1	1	6

Jim Price

Pos: TE/LS **Rnd:** FA **College:** Stanford **Ht:** 6' 4" **Wt:** 247 **Born:** 10/2/66 **Age:** 30

Year	Team	G	GS	Rushing					Receiving					Punt Returns				Kickoff Returns				Totals		
				Att	Yds	Avg	Lg	TD	Rec	Yds	Avg	Lg	TD	Num	Yds	Avg	TD	Num	Yds	Avg	TD	Fum	TD	Pts
1991	Los Angeles Rams	12	3	0	0	-	-	0	35	410	11.7	27	2	0	0	-	0	0	0	-	0	2	2	12
1992	Los Angeles Rams	15	2	0	0	-	-	0	34	324	9.5	25	2	0	0	-	0	0	0	-	0	2	2	12
1993	Dallas Cowboys	3	0	0	0	-	-	0	1	4	4.0	4	0	0	0	-	0	0	0	-	0	0	0	0
1995	St. Louis Rams	13	0	0	0	-	-	0	4	29	7.3	24	0	0	0	-	0	0	0	-	0	0	0	0
	4 NFL Seasons	43	5	0	0	-	-	0	74	767	10.4	27	4	0	0	-	0	0	0	-	0	4	4	24

Other Statistics: 1991–recovered 1 fumble for 0 yards. 1992–recovered 2 fumbles for 0 yards.

Shawn Price

Pos: DE **Rnd:** FA **College:** Pacific **Ht:** 6' 5" **Wt:** 260 **Born:** 3/28/70 **Age:** 26

Year	Team	G	GS	Tackles			Miscellaneous				Interceptions				Totals		
				Tk	Ast	Sack	FF	FR	TD	Blk	Int	Yds	Avg	TD	Sfty	TD	Pts
1993	Tampa Bay Buccaneers	9	6	11	14	3.0	0	0	0	0	0	0	-	0	0	0	0
1994	Tampa Bay Buccaneers	8	0	2	0	0.0	0	0	0	0	0	0	-	0	0	0	0
1995	Carolina Panthers	16	0	14	1	1.0	0	0	0	0	0	0	-	0	0	0	0
	3 NFL Seasons	33	6	27	15	4.0	0	0	0	0	0	0	-	0	0	0	0

Greg Primus

Pos: WR **Rnd:** FA **College:** Colorado State **Ht:** 5' 11" **Wt:** 190 **Born:** 10/20/70 **Age:** 26

Year	Team	G	GS	Rushing					Receiving					Punt Returns				Kickoff Returns				Totals		
				Att	Yds	Avg	Lg	TD	Rec	Yds	Avg	Lg	TD	Num	Yds	Avg	TD	Num	Yds	Avg	TD	Fum	TD	Pts
1994	Chicago Bears	3	1	0	0	-	-	0	3	25	8.3	12	0	0	0	-	0	0	0	-	0	0	0	0
1995	Chicago Bears	4	0	0	0	-	-	0	0	0	-	-	0	0	0	-	0	2	39	19.5	0	0	0	0
	2 NFL Seasons	7	1	0	0	-	-	0	3	25	8.3	12	0	0	0	-	0	2	39	19.5	0	0	0	0

Anthony Prior

Pos: CB **Rnd:** 9 **College:** Washington State **Ht:** 5' 11" **Wt:** 185 **Born:** 3/27/70 **Age:** 26

Year	Team	G	GS	Tackles			Miscellaneous				Interceptions				Punt Returns				Kickoff Returns				Totals	
				Tk	Ast	Sack	FF	FR	TD	Blk	Int	Yds	Avg	TD	Num	Yds	Avg	TD	Num	Yds	Avg	TD	TD	Fum
1993	New York Jets	16	0	3	1	0.0	0	1	0	0	0	0	-	0	0	0	-	0	9	126	14.0	0	0	0
1994	New York Jets	13	0	4	1	0.0	0	0	0	0	0	0	-	0	0	0	-	0	16	316	19.8	0	0	0
1995	New York Jets	11	0	1	0	0.0	0	0	0	0	0	0	-	0	0	0	-	0	0	0	-	0	0	0
	3 NFL Seasons	40	0	8	2	0.0	0	1	0	0	0	0	-	0	0	0	-	0	25	442	17.7	0	0	0

Mike Prior

Pos: S **Rnd:** 7 **College:** Illinois State **Ht:** 6' 0" **Wt:** 208 **Born:** 11/14/63 **Age:** 32

Year Team	G	GS	Tackles			Miscellaneous				Interceptions				Punt Returns				Kickoff Returns				Totals	
			Tk	Ast	Sack	FF	FR	TD	Blk	Int	Yds	Avg	TD	Num	Yds	Avg	TD	Num	Yds	Avg	TD	TD	Fum
1985 Tampa Bay Buccaneers	16	0	4	0	0.0	0	3	0	0	0	0	-	0	13	105	8.1	0	10	131	13.1	0	0	4
1987 Indianapolis Colts	13	7	44	24	1.0	1	3	0	0	6	57	9.5	0	0	0	-	0	3	47	15.7	0	0	0
1988 Indianapolis Colts	16	16	69	29	1.0	1	1	0	0	3	46	15.3	0	1	0	0.0	0	0	0	-	0	0	1
1989 Indianapolis Colts	16	16	74	24	0.0	1	1	0	0	6	88	14.7	1	0	0	-	0	0	0	-	0	1	0
1990 Indianapolis Colts	16	16	81	32	0.0	1	2	0	0	3	66	22.0	0	2	0	0.0	0	0	0	-	0	0	1
1991 Indianapolis Colts	9	7	36	9	0.0	0	1	0	0	3	50	16.7	0	0	0	-	0	0	0	-	0	0	0
1992 Indianapolis Colts	16	16	74	17	0.0	1	1	0	0	6	44	7.3	0	1	7	7.0	0	0	0	-	0	0	0
1993 Green Bay Packers	16	4	19	12	0.0	0	2	0	0	1	1	1.0	0	17	194	11.4	0	0	0	-	0	0	3
1994 Green Bay Packers	16	0	14	3	0.0	0	2	0	0	0	0	-	0	8	62	7.8	0	0	0	-	0	0	3
1995 Green Bay Packers	16	2	39	14	1.5	1	1	0	0	1	9	9.0	0	1	10	10.0	0	0	0	-	0	0	0
10 NFL Seasons	150	84	454	164	3.5	6	17	0	0	29	361	12.4	1	43	378	8.8	0	13	178	13.7	0	1	12

Other Statistics: 1990–caught 1 pass for 40 yards. 1992–caught 1 pass for 17 yards.

Mike Pritchard

(statistical profile on page 367)

Pos: WR **Rnd:** 1 (13) **College:** Colorado **Ht:** 5' 11" **Wt:** 186 **Born:** 10/26/69 **Age:** 27

Year Team	G	GS	Rushing					Receiving					Punt Returns				Kickoff Returns				Totals		
			Att	Yds	Avg	Lg	TD	Rec	Yds	Avg	Lg	TD	Num	Yds	Avg	TD	Num	Yds	Avg	TD	Fum	TD	Pts
1991 Atlanta Falcons	16	11	0	0	-	-	0	50	624	12.5	29	2	0	0	-	0	1	18	18.0	0	2	2	12
1992 Atlanta Falcons	16	15	5	37	7.4	22	0	77	827	10.7	t38	5	0	0	-	0	0	0	-	0	3	5	30
1993 Atlanta Falcons	15	14	2	4	2.0	4	0	74	736	9.9	34	7	0	0	-	0	0	0	-	0	1	7	42
1994 Denver Broncos	3	0	0	0	-	-	0	19	271	14.3	t50	1	0	0	-	0	0	0	-	0	1	1	6
1995 Denver Broncos	15	13	6	17	2.8	9	0	33	441	13.4	t45	3	0	0	-	0	0	0	-	0	1	3	18
5 NFL Seasons	65	53	13	58	4.5	22	0	253	2899	11.5	t50	18	0	0	-	0	1	18	18.0	0	8	18	108

Kelvin Pritchett

Pos: DT **Rnd:** 1 (20) **College:** Mississippi **Ht:** 6' 3" **Wt:** 290 **Born:** 10/24/69 **Age:** 27

Year Team	G	GS	Tackles			Miscellaneous				Interceptions				Totals		
			Tk	Ast	Sack	FF	FR	TD	Blk	Int	Yds	Avg	TD	Sfty	TD	Pts
1991 Detroit Lions	16	0	20	6	1.5	0	0	0	0	0	0	-	0	0	0	0
1992 Detroit Lions	16	15	38	21	6.5	0	0	0	0	0	0	-	0	0	0	0
1993 Detroit Lions	16	5	33	9	4.0	0	0	0	0	0	0	-	0	0	0	0
1994 Detroit Lions	16	15	41	33	5.5	0	1	0	0	0	0	-	0	0	0	0
1995 Jacksonville Jaguars	16	16	41	22	1.5	0	0	0	0	0	0	-	0	0	0	0
5 NFL Seasons	80	51	173	91	19.0	0	1	0	0	0	0	-	0	0	0	0

Bryan Proby

Pos: DE **Rnd:** 6 **College:** Arizona State **Ht:** 6' 5" **Wt:** 283 **Born:** 11/30/71 **Age:** 24

Year Team	G	GS	Tackles			Miscellaneous				Interceptions				Totals		
			Tk	Ast	Sack	FF	FR	TD	Blk	Int	Yds	Avg	TD	Sfty	TD	Pts
1995 Kansas City Chiefs	3	0	0	0	0.0	0	0	0	0	0	0	-	0	0	0	0

Ricky Proehl

Pos: WR **Rnd:** 3 **College:** Wake Forest **Ht:** 6' 0" **Wt:** 190 **Born:** 3/7/68 **Age:** 28

Year Team	G	GS	Rushing					Receiving					Punt Returns				Kickoff Returns				Totals		
			Att	Yds	Avg	Lg	TD	Rec	Yds	Avg	Lg	TD	Num	Yds	Avg	TD	Num	Yds	Avg	TD	Fum	TD	Pts
1990 Phoenix Cardinals	16	2	1	4	4.0	4	0	56	802	14.3	t45	4	1	2	2.0	0	4	53	13.3	0	0	4	24
1991 Phoenix Cardinals	16	16	3	21	7.0	17	0	55	766	13.9	t62	2	4	26	6.5	0	0	0	-	0	0	2	12
1992 Phoenix Cardinals	16	15	3	23	7.7	10	0	60	744	12.4	t63	3	0	0	-	0	0	0	-	0	5	3	18
1993 Phoenix Cardinals	16	16	8	47	5.9	17	0	65	877	13.5	t51	7	0	0	-	0	0	0	-	0	1	7	42
1994 Arizona Cardinals	16	16	0	0	-	-	0	51	651	12.8	63	5	0	0	-	0	0	0	-	0	2	5	30
1995 Seattle Seahawks	8	0	0	0	-	-	0	5	29	5.8	9	0	0	0	-	0	0	0	-	0	0	0	0
6 NFL Seasons	88	65	15	95	6.3	17	0	292	3009	10.0	t63	21	5	28	5.6	0	4	53	13.3	0	8	21	126

Other Statistics: 1991–recovered 1 fumble for 0 yards. 1992–attempted 1 pass with 0 completions for 0 yards and 1 interception. 1994–recovered 2 fumbles for 0 yards.

Alfred Pupunu

(statistical profile on page 367)

Pos: TE **Rnd:** FA **College:** Weber State **Ht:** 6' 2" **Wt:** 265 **Born:** 10/17/69 **Age:** 27

Year Team	G	GS	Rushing					Receiving					Punt Returns				Kickoff Returns				Totals		
			Att	Yds	Avg	Lg	TD	Rec	Yds	Avg	Lg	TD	Num	Yds	Avg	TD	Num	Yds	Avg	TD	Fum	TD	Pts
1992 San Diego Chargers	15	2	0	0	-	-	0	0	0	-	-	0	0	0	-	0	0	0	-	0	0	0	0
1993 San Diego Chargers	16	7	0	0	-	-	0	13	142	10.9	28	0	0	0	-	0	0	0	-	0	0	0	0
1994 San Diego Chargers	13	10	0	0	-	-	0	21	214	10.2	25	2	0	0	-	0	0	0	-	0	2	2	12
1995 San Diego Chargers	15	14	0	0	-	-	0	35	315	9.0	26	0	0	0	-	0	0	0	-	0	1	0	0

Year Team	G	GS	Rushing					Receiving					Punt Returns				Kickoff Returns				Totals		
			Att	Yds	Avg	Lg	TD	Rec	Yds	Avg	Lg	TD	Num	Yds	Avg	TD	Num	Yds	Avg	TD	Fum	TD	Pts
4 NFL Seasons	59	33	0	0	-	-	0	69	671	9.7	28	2	0	0	-	0	0	0	-	0	1	2	12

Other Statistics: 1993–recovered 1 fumble for 0 yards.

Jim Pyne

Pos: G/C **Rnd:** 7 **College:** Virginia Tech **Ht:** 6' 2" **Wt:** 282 **Born:** 11/23/71 **Age:** 24

Year	Team	G	GS
1995	Tampa Bay Buccaneers	15	13
	1 NFL Season	15	13

Other Statistics: 1995–recovered 1 fumble for 0 yards.

Jeff Query

Pos: WR **Rnd:** 5 **College:** Millikin **Ht:** 6' 0" **Wt:** 165 **Born:** 3/7/67 **Age:** 29

Year Team	G	GS	Rushing					Receiving					Punt Returns				Kickoff Returns				Totals		
			Att	Yds	Avg	Lg	TD	Rec	Yds	Avg	Lg	TD	Num	Yds	Avg	TD	Num	Yds	Avg	TD	Fum	TD	Pts
1989 Green Bay Packers	16	0	0	0	-	-	0	23	350	15.2	45	2	30	247	8.2	0	6	125	20.8	0	1	2	12
1990 Green Bay Packers	16	0	3	39	13.0	18	0	34	458	13.5	t47	2	32	308	9.6	0	0	0	-	0	3	3	18
1991 Green Bay Packers	16	0	0	0	-	-	0	7	94	13.4	26	0	14	157	11.2	0	0	0	-	0	1	0	0
1992 Cincinnati Bengals	10	2	1	1	1.0	1	0	16	265	16.6	t83	3	0	0	-	0	1	13	13.0	0	3	3	18
1993 Cincinnati Bengals	16	16	2	13	6.5	8	0	56	654	11.7	51	4	0	0	-	0	0	0	-	0	1	4	24
1994 Cincinnati Bengals	10	3	0	0	-	-	0	5	44	8.8	14	0	0	0	-	0	0	0	-	0	0	0	0
1995 Cin - Was	2	0	0	0	-	-	0	0	0	-	-	0	0	0	-	0	0	0	-	0	0	0	0
1995 Cincinnati Bengals	1	0	0	0	-	-	0	0	0	-	-	0	0	0	-	0	0	0	-	0	0	0	0
Washington Redskins	1	0	0	0	-	-	0	0	0	-	-	0	0	0	-	0	0	0	-	0	0	0	0
7 NFL Seasons	86	21	6	53	8.8	18	0	141	1865	13.2	t83	11	76	712	9.4	0	7	138	19.7	0	6	12	72

Other Statistics: 1989–recovered 1 fumble for 0 yards. 1990–recovered 3 fumbles for 0 yards and 1 touchdown. 1991–recovered 1 fumble for 0 yards.

Scott Radecic

Pos: LB **Rnd:** 2 **College:** Penn State **Ht:** 6' 3" **Wt:** 243 **Born:** 6/14/62 **Age:** 34

Year Team	G	GS	Tackles			Miscellaneous				Interceptions				Punt Returns				Kickoff Returns				Totals	
			Tk	Ast	Sack	FF	FR	TD	Blk	Int	Yds	Avg	TD	Num	Yds	Avg	TD	Num	Yds	Avg	TD	TD	Fum
1984 Kansas City Chiefs	16	2	30	19	0.0	0	0	0	0	2	54	27.0	1	0	0	-	0	0	0	-	0	1	0
1985 Kansas City Chiefs	16	16	88	-	3.0	0	1	0	0	1	21	21.0	0	0	0	-	0	0	0	-	0	0	0
1986 Kansas City Chiefs	16	13	57	-	1.0	0	1	0	0	1	20	20.0	0	0	0	-	0	0	0	-	0	0	0
1987 Buffalo Bills	12	9	81	-	0.0	0	2	0	0	2	4	2.0	0	0	0	-	0	1	14	14.0	0	0	0
1988 Buffalo Bills	16	3	57	-	1.5	0	2	0	0	0	0	-	0	0	0	-	0	0	0	-	0	0	0
1989 Buffalo Bills	16	12	77	-	1.5	0	0	0	0	0	0	-	0	0	0	-	0	0	0	-	0	0	0
1990 Indianapolis Colts	15	1	7	6	0.0	0	0	0	0	0	0	-	0	0	0	-	0	0	0	-	0	0	0
1991 Indianapolis Colts	14	9	61	57	0.0	0	0	0	0	1	26	26.0	0	0	0	-	0	0	0	-	0	0	0
1992 Indianapolis Colts	16	9	65	24	0.0	1	1	0	0	1	0	0.0	0	0	0	-	0	0	0	-	0	0	0
1993 Indianapolis Colts	16	4	19	10	0.0	0	0	0	0	0	0	-	0	0	0	-	0	1	10	10.0	0	0	0
1994 Indianapolis Colts	16	1	8	3	0.0	0	0	0	0	0	0	-	0	0	0	-	0	1	17	17.0	0	0	0
1995 Indianapolis Colts	13	0	2	3	0.0	0	0	0	0	0	0	-	0	0	0	-	0	1	-5	-5.0	0	0	0
12 NFL Seasons	182	79	552	122	7.0	1	7	0	0	8	125	15.6	1	0	0	-	0	4	36	9.0	0	1	0

John Randle

(statistical profile on page 442)

Pos: DT **Rnd:** FA **College:** Texas A&I **Ht:** 6' 1" **Wt:** 272 **Born:** 12/12/67 **Age:** 28

Year Team	G	GS	Tackles			Miscellaneous				Interceptions				Totals		
			Tk	Ast	Sack	FF	FR	TD	Blk	Int	Yds	Avg	TD	Sfty	TD	Pts
1990 Minnesota Vikings	16	0	12	9	1.0	1	0	0	0	0	0	-	0	0	0	0
1991 Minnesota Vikings	16	8	32	26	9.5	2	0	0	0	0	0	-	0	0	0	0
1992 Minnesota Vikings	16	14	45	11	11.5	0	1	0	0	0	0	-	0	0	0	0
1993 Minnesota Vikings	16	16	54	5	12.5	3	0	0	0	0	0	-	0	0	0	0
1994 Minnesota Vikings	16	16	30	12	13.5	3	2	0	0	0	0	-	0	0	0	0
1995 Minnesota Vikings	16	16	33	11	10.5	1	0	0	0	0	0	-	0	0	0	0
6 NFL Seasons	96	70	206	74	58.5	10	3	0	0	0	0	-	0	0	0	0

Thomas Randolph

(statistical profile on page 442)

Pos: CB **Rnd:** 2 **College:** Kansas State **Ht:** 5' 9" **Wt:** 176 **Born:** 10/5/70 **Age:** 26

Year Team	G	GS	Tackles			Miscellaneous				Interceptions				Totals		
			Tk	Ast	Sack	FF	FR	TD	Blk	Int	Yds	Avg	TD	Sfty	TD	Pts
1994 New York Giants	16	10	32	7	0.0	0	0	0	0	1	0	0.0	0	0	0	0
1995 New York Giants	16	16	52	6	0.0	0	1	0	0	2	15	7.5	0	0	0	0
2 NFL Seasons	32	26	84	13	0.0	0	1	0	0	3	15	5.0	0	0	0	0

Walter Rasby

Pos: TE **Rnd:** FA **College:** Wake Forest **Ht:** 6' 3" **Wt:** 247 **Born:** 9/7/72 **Age:** 24

			Rushing					Receiving					Punt Returns				Kickoff Returns				Totals		
Year Team	G	GS	Att	Yds	Avg	Lg	TD	Rec	Yds	Avg	Lg	TD	Num	Yds	Avg	TD	Num	Yds	Avg	TD	Fum	TD	Pts
1994 Pittsburgh Steelers	2	0	0	0	-	-	0	0	0	-	-	0	0	0	-	0	0	0	-	0	0	0	0
1995 Carolina Panthers	9	2	0	0	-	-	0	5	47	9.4	15	0	0	0	-	0	0	0	-	0	0	0	2
2 NFL Seasons	11	2	0	0	-	-	0	5	47	9.4	15	0	0	0	-	0	0	0	-	0	0	0	2

Other Statistics: 1995–scored 1 two-point conversion.

Kenyon Rasheed

Pos: RB **Rnd:** FA **College:** Oklahoma **Ht:** 5' 10" **Wt:** 245 **Born:** 8/23/70 **Age:** 26

			Rushing					Receiving					Punt Returns				Kickoff Returns				Totals		
Year Team	G	GS	Att	Yds	Avg	Lg	TD	Rec	Yds	Avg	Lg	TD	Num	Yds	Avg	TD	Num	Yds	Avg	TD	Fum	TD	Pts
1993 New York Giants	5	3	9	42	4.7	t23	1	1	3	3.0	3	0	0	0	-	0	0	0	-	0	0	1	6
1994 New York Giants	16	7	17	44	2.6	6	0	10	97	9.7	22	0	0	0	-	0	0	0	-	0	1	0	0
1995 New York Jets	3	0	1	3	3.0	3	0	2	15	7.5	9	0	0	0	-	0	0	0	-	0	0	0	0
3 NFL Seasons	24	10	27	89	3.3	t23	1	13	115	8.8	22	0	0	0	-	0	0	0	-	0	1	1	6

Eric Ravotti

Pos: LB **Rnd:** 6 **College:** Penn State **Ht:** 6' 3" **Wt:** 247 **Born:** 3/16/71 **Age:** 25

			Tackles			Miscellaneous				Interceptions				Totals		
Year Team	G	GS	Tk	Ast	Sack	FF	FR	TD	Blk	Int	Yds	Avg	TD	Sfty	TD	Pts
1994 Pittsburgh Steelers	2	0	0	0	0.0	0	0	0	0	0	0	-	0	0	0	0
1995 Pittsburgh Steelers	6	1	7	0	0.0	0	0	0	0	0	0	-	0	0	0	0
2 NFL Seasons	8	1	7	0	0.0	0	0	0	0	0	0	-	0	0	0	0

Terry Ray

(statistical profile on page 442)

Pos: S **Rnd:** 6 **College:** Oklahoma **Ht:** 6' 1" **Wt:** 205 **Born:** 10/12/69 **Age:** 27

			Tackles			Miscellaneous				Interceptions				Totals		
Year Team	G	GS	Tk	Ast	Sack	FF	FR	TD	Blk	Int	Yds	Avg	TD	Sfty	TD	Pts
1992 Atlanta Falcons	10	2	15	15	0.0	0	1	0	0	0	0	-	0	0	0	0
1993 New England Patriots	15	1	8	10	0.0	0	0	0	0	1	0	0.0	0	0	0	0
1994 New England Patriots	16	0	4	1	0.0	0	0	0	0	1	2	2.0	0	0	0	0
1995 New England Patriots	16	16	72	23	0.0	2	2	0	0	1	21	21.0	0	0	0	0
4 NFL Seasons	57	19	99	49	0.0	2	3	0	0	3	23	7.7	0	0	0	0

Cory Raymer

Pos: C **Rnd:** 2 **College:** Wisconsin **Ht:** 6' 2" **Wt:** 293 **Born:** 3/3/73 **Age:** 23

Year Team	G	GS				G	GS
1995 Washington Redskins	3	2		1 NFL Season		3	2

Corey Raymond

(statistical profile on page 443)

Pos: CB **Rnd:** FA **College:** Louisiana State **Ht:** 5' 11" **Wt:** 185 **Born:** 7/28/69 **Age:** 27

			Tackles			Miscellaneous				Interceptions				Totals		
Year Team	G	GS	Tk	Ast	Sack	FF	FR	TD	Blk	Int	Yds	Avg	TD	Sfty	TD	Pts
1992 New York Giants	16	0	8	0	1.0	0	0	0	0	0	0	-	0	0	0	0
1993 New York Giants	16	8	33	7	0.0	1	0	0	0	2	11	5.5	0	0	0	0
1994 New York Giants	16	12	47	6	0.0	0	0	0	0	1	0	0.0	0	0	0	0
1995 Detroit Lions	16	15	59	9	2.0	1	1	0	0	6	44	7.3	0	0	0	0
4 NFL Seasons	64	35	147	22	3.0	2	1	0	0	9	55	6.1	0	0	0	0

Anthony Redmon

Pos: G/T **Rnd:** 5 **College:** Auburn **Ht:** 6' 4" **Wt:** 308 **Born:** 4/9/71 **Age:** 25

Year Team	G	GS	Year Team	G	GS			G	GS
1994 Arizona Cardinals	6	5	1995 Arizona Cardinals	13	9		2 NFL Seasons	19	14

John Reece

Pos: CB **Rnd:** 4 **College:** Nebraska **Ht:** 6' 0" **Wt:** 203 **Born:** 1/24/71 **Age:** 25

			Tackles			Miscellaneous				Interceptions				Totals		
Year Team	G	GS	Tk	Ast	Sack	FF	FR	TD	Blk	Int	Yds	Avg	TD	Sfty	TD	Pts
1995 St. Louis Rams	5	0	0	0	0.0	0	0	0	0	0	0	-	0	0	0	0

Andre Reed

Pos: WR **Rnd:** 4 **College:** Kutztown **Ht:** 6' 2" **Wt:** 190 **Born:** 1/29/64 **Age:** 32

Year Team	G	GS	Rushing Att	Yds	Avg	Lg	TD	Receiving Rec	Yds	Avg	Lg	TD	Punt Returns Num	Yds	Avg	TD	Passing Att	Com	Yds	Int	Totals Fum	TD	Pts
1985 Buffalo Bills	16	15	3	-1	-0.3	t14	1	48	637	13.3	32	4	5	12	2.4	0	0	0	0	0	1	5	30
1986 Buffalo Bills	15	15	3	-8	-2.7	4	0	53	739	13.9	t55	7	0	0	-	0	0	0	0	0	2	7	42
1987 Buffalo Bills	12	12	1	1	1.0	1	0	57	752	13.2	40	5	0	0	-	0	0	0	0	0	0	5	30
1988 Buffalo Bills	15	14	6	64	10.7	36	0	71	968	13.6	t65	6	0	0	-	0	0	0	0	0	1	6	36
1989 Buffalo Bills	16	16	2	31	15.5	23	0	88	1312	14.9	t78	9	0	0	-	0	0	0	0	0	4	9	54
1990 Buffalo Bills	16	16	3	23	7.7	26	0	71	945	13.3	t56	8	0	0	-	0	0	0	0	0	1	8	48
1991 Buffalo Bills	16	16	12	136	11.3	46	0	81	1113	13.7	55	10	0	0	-	0	0	0	0	0	1	10	60
1992 Buffalo Bills	16	16	8	65	8.1	24	0	65	913	14.0	51	3	0	0	-	0	0	0	0	0	4	3	18
1993 Buffalo Bills	15	15	9	21	2.3	15	0	52	854	16.4	t65	6	0	0	-	0	0	0	0	0	3	6	36
1994 Buffalo Bills	16	16	10	87	8.7	20	0	90	1303	14.5	t83	8	0	0	-	0	1	1	32	0	3	8	48
1995 Buffalo Bills	6	6	7	48	6.9	14	0	24	312	13.0	t41	3	0	0	-	0	0	0	0	0	2	3	18
11 NFL Seasons	159	157	64	467	7.3	46	1	700	9848	14.1	t83	69	5	12	2.4	0	1	1	32	0	22	70	420

Other Statistics: 1985–recovered 2 fumbles for 0 yards. 1986–recovered 2 fumbles for 2 yards. 1990–recovered 1 fumble for 0 yards. 1994–recovered 2 fumbles for 0 yards.

Jake Reed

(statistical profile on page 368)

Pos: WR **Rnd:** 3 **College:** Grambling **Ht:** 6' 3" **Wt:** 217 **Born:** 9/28/67 **Age:** 29

Year Team	G	GS	Rushing Att	Yds	Avg	Lg	TD	Receiving Rec	Yds	Avg	Lg	TD	Punt Returns Num	Yds	Avg	TD	Kickoff Returns Num	Yds	Avg	TD	Totals Fum	TD	Pts
1991 Minnesota Vikings	1	0	0	0	-	-	0	0	0	-	-	0	0	0	-	0	0	0	-	0	0	0	0
1992 Minnesota Vikings	16	0	0	0	-	-	0	6	142	23.7	51	0	0	0	-	0	1	1	1.0	0	0	0	0
1993 Minnesota Vikings	10	1	0	0	-	-	0	5	65	13.0	18	0	0	0	-	0	0	0	-	0	0	0	0
1994 Minnesota Vikings	16	16	0	0	-	-	0	85	1175	13.8	59	4	0	0	-	0	0	0	-	0	3	4	24
1995 Minnesota Vikings	16	16	0	0	-	-	0	72	1167	16.2	t55	9	0	0	-	0	0	0	-	0	1	9	54
5 NFL Seasons	59	33	0	0	-	-	0	168	2549	15.2	59	13	0	0	-	0	1	1	1.0	0	4	13	78

Other Statistics: 1995–recovered 1 fumble for 0 yards.

Michael Reed

Pos: WR **Rnd:** 7 **College:** Boston College **Ht:** 5' 9" **Wt:** 177 **Born:** 8/16/72 **Age:** 24

Year Team	G	GS	Rushing Att	Yds	Avg	Lg	TD	Receiving Rec	Yds	Avg	Lg	TD	Punt Returns Num	Yds	Avg	TD	Kickoff Returns Num	Yds	Avg	TD	Totals Fum	TD	Pts
1995 Carolina Panthers	1	0	0	0	-	-	0	0	0	-	-	0	0	0	-	0	0	0	-	0	0	0	0

Bryan Reeves

Pos: WR **Rnd:** FA **College:** Nevada **Ht:** 5' 11" **Wt:** 195 **Born:** 7/10/70 **Age:** 26

Year Team	G	GS	Rushing Att	Yds	Avg	Lg	TD	Receiving Rec	Yds	Avg	Lg	TD	Punt Returns Num	Yds	Avg	TD	Kickoff Returns Num	Yds	Avg	TD	Totals Fum	TD	Pts
1994 Arizona Cardinals	14	0	1	-1	-1.0	-1	0	14	202	14.4	33	1	1	1	1.0	0	3	83	27.7	0	1	1	6
1995 Arizona Cardinals	7	0	0	0	-	-	0	6	62	10.3	22	0	4	41	10.3	0	0	0	-	0	0	0	0
2 NFL Seasons	21	0	1	-1	-1.0	-1	0	20	264	13.2	33	1	5	42	8.4	0	3	83	27.7	0	1	1	6

Other Statistics: 1994–recovered 2 fumbles for 0 yards.

Walter Reeves

Pos: TE **Rnd:** 2 **College:** Auburn **Ht:** 6' 4" **Wt:** 270 **Born:** 12/16/65 **Age:** 30

Year Team	G	GS	Rushing Att	Yds	Avg	Lg	TD	Receiving Rec	Yds	Avg	Lg	TD	Punt Returns Num	Yds	Avg	TD	Kickoff Returns Num	Yds	Avg	TD	Totals Fum	TD	Pts
1989 Phoenix Cardinals	16	3	0	0	-	-	0	1	5	5.0	5	0	0	0	-	0	1	5	5.0	0	0	0	0
1990 Phoenix Cardinals	16	16	0	0	-	-	0	18	126	7.0	16	0	0	0	-	0	0	0	-	0	1	0	0
1991 Phoenix Cardinals	15	13	0	0	-	-	0	8	45	5.6	13	0	0	0	-	0	0	0	-	0	1	0	0
1992 Phoenix Cardinals	16	16	0	0	-	-	0	6	28	4.7	12	0	0	0	-	0	0	0	-	0	0	0	0
1993 Phoenix Cardinals	16	15	0	0	-	-	0	9	67	7.4	18	1	0	0	-	0	0	0	-	0	0	1	6
1994 Cleveland Browns	5	5	0	0	-	-	0	6	61	10.2	22	1	0	0	-	0	0	0	-	0	0	1	6
1995 Cleveland Browns	5	3	0	0	-	-	0	6	12	2.0	3	1	0	0	-	0	0	0	-	0	0	1	6
7 NFL Seasons	89	71	0	0	-	-	0	54	344	6.4	22	3	0	0	-	0	1	5	5.0	0	2	3	18

Other Statistics: 1989–recovered 1 fumble for 2 yards. 1990–recovered 1 fumble for 0 yards. 1991–recovered 1 fumble for 0 yards. 1992–recovered 2 fumbles for 0 yards. 1993–recovered 1 fumble for 0 yards.

Frank Reich

(statistical profile on page 368)

Pos: QB **Rnd:** 3 **College:** Maryland **Ht:** 6' 4" **Wt:** 205 **Born:** 12/4/61 **Age:** 34

Year Team	G	GS	Passing Att	Com	Pct	Yards	Yds/Att	Lg	TD	Int	Int%	Rating	Rushing Att	Yds	Avg	Lg	TD	Miscellaneous Sckd	Yds	Fum	Recv	Yds	Pts
1985 Buffalo Bills	1	0	1	1	100.0	19	19.00	19	0	0	0.0	118.8	0	0	-	-	0	0	0	0	0	0	0
1986 Buffalo Bills	3	0	19	9	47.4	104	5.47	37	0	2	10.5	24.8	1	0	0.0	0	0	2	4	1	0	0	0

				Passing								Rushing				Miscellaneous				
Year	Team	G	GS	Att	Com	Pct	Yards	Yds/Att	Lg	TD	Int	Int%	Rating	Att	Yds	Avg	Lg TD	Sckd Yds	Fum Recv Yds	Pts
1988	Buffalo Bills	3	0	0	0	-	0	-	-	0	0	-	0.0	3	-3	-1.0	-1 0	- -	0 0 0	0
1989	Buffalo Bills	7	3	87	53	60.9	701	8.06	t63	7	2	2.3	103.7	9	30	3.3	9 0	4 24	2 0 0	0
1990	Buffalo Bills	16	2	63	36	57.1	469	7.44	43	2	0	0.0	91.3	15	24	1.6	9 0	6 41	1 0 0	0
1991	Buffalo Bills	16	1	41	27	65.9	305	7.44	29	6	2	4.9	107.2	13	6	0.5	8 0	4 42	0 0 0	0
1992	Buffalo Bills	16	0	47	24	51.1	221	4.70	21	0	2	4.3	46.5	9	-9	-1.0	0 0	9 76	3 2 -4	0
1993	Buffalo Bills	15	0	26	16	61.5	153	5.88	t30	2	0	0.0	103.5	6	-6	-1.0	-1 0	6 47	0 0 0	0
1994	Buffalo Bills	16	2	93	56	60.2	568	6.11	47	1	4	4.3	63.4	6	3	0.5	5 0	7 57	1 1 0	0
1995	Carolina Panthers	3	3	84	37	44.0	441	5.25	46	2	2	2.4	58.7	1	3	3.0	3 0	12 100	3 1 0	0
	10 NFL Seasons	96	11	461	259	56.2	2981	6.47	t63	20	14	3.0	77.7	63	48	0.8	9 0	50 391	11 4 -4	0

Jim Reid

Pos: T **Rnd:** 5 **College:** Virginia **Ht:** 6' 6" **Wt:** 306 **Born:** 2/13/71 **Age:** 25

Year	Team	G	GS				G	GS
1995	Houston Oilers	6	0		1 NFL Season		6	0

Fuad Reveiz

(statistical profile on page 482)

Pos: K **Rnd:** 7 **College:** Tennessee **Ht:** 5' 11" **Wt:** 227 **Born:** 2/24/63 **Age:** 33

			Field Goals												PAT		Tot
Year	Team	G	1-29 Yds	Pct	30-39 Yds	Pct	40-49 Yds	Pct	50+ Yds	Pct	Overall	Pct	Long	Made	Att	Pts
1985	Miami Dolphins	16	8-9	88.9	5-6	83.3	9-9	100.0	0-3	0.0	22-27	81.5	49	50	52	116
1986	Miami Dolphins	16	6-6	100.0	4-6	66.7	3-8	37.5	1-2	50.0	14-22	63.6	52	52	55	94
1987	Miami Dolphins	11	3-3	100.0	2-2	100.0	4-6	66.7	0-0	-	9-11	81.8	48	28	30	55
1988	Miami Dolphins	11	4-4	100.0	3-4	75.0	1-2	50.0	0-2	0.0	8-12	66.7	45	31	32	55
1990	SD - Min	13	6-7	85.7	3-4	75.0	4-8	50.0	0-0	-	13-19	68.4	45	26	27	65
1991	Minnesota Vikings	16	9-9	100.0	3-3	100.0	3-7	42.9	2-5	40.0	17-24	70.8	50	34	35	85
1992	Minnesota Vikings	16	4-6	66.7	7-7	100.0	5-8	62.5	3-4	75.0	19-25	76.0	52	45	45	102
1993	Minnesota Vikings	16	16-16	100.0	6-6	100.0	3-7	42.9	1-6	16.7	26-35	74.3	51	27	28	105
1994	Minnesota Vikings	16	13-13	100.0	12-13	92.3	8-10	80.0	1-3	33.3	34-39	87.2	51	30	30	132
1995	Minnesota Vikings	16	9-10	90.0	7-10	70.0	9-12	75.0	1-4	25.0	26-36	72.2	51	44	44	122
1990	San Diego Chargers	4	1-2	50.0	0-1	0.0	1-4	25.0	0-0	-	2-7	28.6	42	7	8	13
	Minnesota Vikings	9	5-5	100.0	3-3	100.0	3-4	75.0	0-0	-	11-12	91.7	45	19	19	52
	10 NFL Seasons	147	78-83	94.0	52-61	85.2	49-77	63.6	9-29	31.0	188-250	75.2	52	367	378	931

Ricky Reynolds

(statistical profile on page 443)

Pos: CB **Rnd:** 2 **College:** Washington State **Ht:** 5' 11" **Wt:** 190 **Born:** 1/19/65 **Age:** 31

				Tackles			Miscellaneous				Interceptions				Totals		
Year	Team	G	GS	Tk	Ast	Sack	FF	FR	TD	Blk	Int	Yds	Avg	TD	Sfty	TD	Pts
1987	Tampa Bay Buccaneers	12	12	58	12	0.0	2	0	0	0	0	0	-	0	0	0	0
1988	Tampa Bay Buccaneers	16	16	64	10	0.0	1	2	0	0	4	7	1.8	0	0	0	0
1989	Tampa Bay Buccaneers	16	15	66	5	0.0	2	2	1	0	5	87	17.4	1	0	2	12
1990	Tampa Bay Buccaneers	15	15	36	13	0.0	0	2	0	0	3	70	23.3	0	0	0	0
1991	Tampa Bay Buccaneers	16	16	33	12	1.0	1	0	0	0	2	7	3.5	0	0	0	0
1992	Tampa Bay Buccaneers	16	16	56	9	1.0	1	2	1	0	2	0	0.0	0	0	1	6
1993	Tampa Bay Buccaneers	14	13	50	10	1.0	1	0	0	0	1	3	3.0	0	0	0	0
1994	New England Patriots	15	10	50	7	2.0	1	3	1	0	1	11	11.0	1	0	2	12
1995	New England Patriots	16	16	68	17	2.5	2	1	0	0	3	6	2.0	0	0	0	0
	9 NFL Seasons	136	129	481	95	7.5	11	12	3	0	21	191	9.1	2	0	5	30

Steve Rhem

Pos: WR **Rnd:** FA **College:** Minnesota **Ht:** 6' 2" **Wt:** 212 **Born:** 11/9/71 **Age:** 24

				Rushing					Receiving					Punt Returns				Kickoff Returns				Totals		
Year	Team	G	GS	Att	Yds	Avg	Lg	TD	Rec	Yds	Avg	Lg	TD	Num	Yds	Avg	TD	Num	Yds	Avg	TD	Fum	TD	Pts
1994	New Orleans Saints	7	0	0	0	-	0	0	0	0	-	0	0	0	0	-	0	0	0	-	0	0	0	0
1995	New Orleans Saints	5	0	0	0	-	0	0	4	50	12.5	20	0	0	0	-	0	0	0	-	0	0	0	0
	2 NFL Seasons	12	0	0	0	-	0	0	4	50	12.5	20	0	0	0	-	0	0	0	-	0	0	0	0

Errict Rhett

(statistical profile on page 369)

Pos: RB **Rnd:** 2 **College:** Florida **Ht:** 5' 11" **Wt:** 211 **Born:** 12/11/70 **Age:** 25

				Rushing					Receiving					Punt Returns				Kickoff Returns				Totals		
Year	Team	G	GS	Att	Yds	Avg	Lg	TD	Rec	Yds	Avg	Lg	TD	Num	Yds	Avg	TD	Num	Yds	Avg	TD	Fum	TD	Pts
1994	Tampa Bay Buccaneers	16	8	284	1011	3.6	27	7	22	119	5.4	12	0	0	0	-	0	0	0	-	0	2	7	44
1995	Tampa Bay Buccaneers	16	16	332	1207	3.6	21	11	14	110	7.9	18	0	0	0	-	0	0	0	-	0	2	11	66
	2 NFL Seasons	32	24	616	2218	3.6	27	18	36	229	6.4	18	0	0	0	-	0	0	0	-	0	4	18	110

Other Statistics: 1994–recovered 1 fumble for 0 yards; scored 1 two-point conversion. 1995–recovered 1 fumble for 0 yards.

Jerry Rice

(statistical profile on page 369)

Pos: WR **Rnd:** 1 (16) **College:** Mississippi Valley State **Ht:** 6' 2" **Wt:** 200 **Born:** 10/13/62 **Age:** 34

Year	Team	G	GS	Rushing Att	Yds	Avg	Lg	TD	Receiving Rec	Yds	Avg	Lg	TD	Kickoff Returns Num	Yds	Avg	TD	Passing Att	Com	Yds	Int	Totals Fum	TD	Pts
1985	San Francisco 49ers	16	4	6	26	4.3	t15	1	49	927	18.9	t66	3	1	6	6.0	0	0	0	0	0	1	4	24
1986	San Francisco 49ers	16	15	10	72	7.2	18	1	86	1570	18.3	t66	15	0	0	-	0	2	1	16	0	2	16	96
1987	San Francisco 49ers	12	12	8	51	6.4	17	1	65	1078	16.6	t57	22	0	0	-	0	0	0	0	0	2	23	138
1988	San Francisco 49ers	16	16	13	107	8.2	29	1	64	1306	20.4	t96	9	0	0	-	0	3	1	14	1	2	10	60
1989	San Francisco 49ers	16	16	5	33	6.6	17	0	82	1483	18.1	t68	17	0	0	-	0	0	0	0	0	0	17	102
1990	San Francisco 49ers	16	16	2	0	0.0	2	0	100	1502	15.0	t64	13	0	0	-	0	0	0	0	0	1	13	78
1991	San Francisco 49ers	16	16	1	2	2.0	2	0	80	1206	15.1	t73	14	0	0	-	0	0	0	0	0	1	14	84
1992	San Francisco 49ers	16	16	9	58	6.4	t26	1	84	1201	14.3	t80	10	0	0	-	0	0	0	0	0	2	11	66
1993	San Francisco 49ers	16	16	3	69	23.0	t43	1	98	1503	15.3	t80	15	0	0	-	0	0	0	0	0	3	16	96
1994	San Francisco 49ers	16	16	7	93	13.3	t28	2	112	1499	13.4	t69	13	0	0	-	0	0	0	0	0	1	15	92
1995	San Francisco 49ers	16	16	5	36	7.2	t20	1	122	1848	15.1	t81	15	0	0	-	0	1	1	41	0	3	17	104
	11 NFL Seasons	172	159	69	547	7.9	t43	9	942	15123	16.1	t96	146	1	6	6.0	0	6	3	71	1	18	156	940

Other Statistics: 1986–recovered 3 fumbles for 0 yards. 1987–recovered 1 fumble for 0 yards. 1988–recovered 1 fumble for 0 yards. 1993–recovered 1 fumble for 0 yards. 1994–scored 1 two-point conversion. 1995–recovered 1 fumble for 0 yards and 1 touchdown; scored 1 two-point conversion; passed for 1 touchdown.

Stanley Richard

(statistical profile on page 443)

Pos: S **Rnd:** 1 (9) **College:** Texas **Ht:** 6' 2" **Wt:** 197 **Born:** 10/21/67 **Age:** 29

Year	Team	G	GS	Tackles Tk	Ast	Sack	Miscellaneous FF	FR	TD	Blk	Interceptions Int	Yds	Avg	TD	Totals Sfty	TD	Pts
1991	San Diego Chargers	15	14	50	9	0.0	1	0	0	0	2	5	2.5	0	0	0	0
1992	San Diego Chargers	14	14	59	20	0.0	0	1	0	0	3	26	8.7	0	0	0	0
1993	San Diego Chargers	16	16	69	8	2.0	1	1	0	0	1	-2	-2.0	0	0	0	0
1994	San Diego Chargers	16	16	69	10	0.0	1	0	0	0	4	224	56.0	2	0	2	12
1995	Washington Redskins	16	16	82	12	0.0	0	1	0	0	3	24	8.0	0	0	0	0
	5 NFL Seasons	77	76	329	59	2.0	3	3	0	0	13	277	21.3	2	0	2	12

Dave Richards

Pos: T/G **Rnd:** 4 **College:** UCLA **Ht:** 6' 5" **Wt:** 315 **Born:** 4/11/66 **Age:** 30

Year	Team	G	GS	Year	Team	G	GS	Year	Team	G	GS	Year	Team	G	GS
1988	San Diego Chargers	16	16	1990	San Diego Chargers	16	16	1992	San Diego Chargers	16	16	1994	Atlanta Falcons	15	14
1989	San Diego Chargers	16	16	1991	San Diego Chargers	16	16	1993	Detroit Lions	15	15	1995	Atlanta Falcons	14	12
													8 NFL Seasons	124	121

Other Statistics: 1988–recovered 1 fumble for 0 yards. 1993–recovered 1 fumble for 0 yards. 1994–recovered 1 fumble for 0 yards. 1995–recovered 1 fumble for 0 yards.

C.J. Richardson

Pos: S **Rnd:** 7 **College:** Miami (FL) **Ht:** 5' 10" **Wt:** 209 **Born:** 6/10/72 **Age:** 24

Year	Team	G	GS	Tackles Tk	Ast	Sack	Miscellaneous FF	FR	TD	Blk	Interceptions Int	Yds	Avg	TD	Totals Sfty	TD	Pts
1995	Arizona Cardinals	1	0	0	0	0.0	0	0	0	0	0	0	-	0	0	0	0

Tony Richardson

Pos: RB **Rnd:** FA **College:** Auburn **Ht:** 6' 1" **Wt:** 224 **Born:** 12/17/71 **Age:** 24

Year	Team	G	GS	Rushing Att	Yds	Avg	Lg	TD	Receiving Rec	Yds	Avg	Lg	TD	Punt Returns Num	Yds	Avg	TD	Kickoff Returns Num	Yds	Avg	TD	Totals Fum	TD	Pts
1995	Kansas City Chiefs	14	1	8	18	2.3	5	0	0	0	-	-	0	0	0	-	0	0	0	-	0	0	0	0

Louis Riddick

Pos: S **Rnd:** 9 **College:** Pittsburgh **Ht:** 6' 2" **Wt:** 215 **Born:** 3/15/69 **Age:** 27

Year	Team	G	GS	Tackles Tk	Ast	Sack	Miscellaneous FF	FR	TD	Blk	Interceptions Int	Yds	Avg	TD	Totals Sfty	TD	Pts
1992	Atlanta Falcons	16	4	33	41	1.0	0	0	0	0	0	0	-	0	0	0	0
1993	Cleveland Browns	15	0	1	0	0.0	0	0	0	0	0	0	-	0	1	0	2
1994	Cleveland Browns	16	0	10	-	0.0	0	0	0	0	0	0	-	0	0	0	0
1995	Cleveland Browns	16	0	7	0	0.0	0	0	0	0	0	0	-	0	0	0	0
	4 NFL Seasons	63	4	51	41	1.0	0	0	0	0	0	0	-	0	1	0	2

Other Statistics: 1995–caught 1 pass for 25 yards.

Doug Riesenberg

Pos: T **Rnd:** 6 **College:** California **Ht:** 6' 5" **Wt:** 280 **Born:** 7/22/65 **Age:** 31

Year	Team	G	GS	Year	Team	G	GS	Year	Team	G	GS		G	GS
1987	New York Giants	8	0	1990	New York Giants	16	16	1993	New York Giants	16	16			
1988	New York Giants	16	11	1991	New York Giants	15	15	1994	New York Giants	16	16			

Year	Team	G	GS	Year	Team	G	GS	Year	Team	G	GS			G	GS
1989	New York Giants	16	16	1992	New York Giants	16	16	1995	New York Giants	16	16		9 NFL Seasons	135	122

Other Statistics: 1988–recovered 1 fumble for 0 yards. 1989–recovered 2 fumbles for 0 yards. 1992–recovered 2 fumbles for 0 yards. 1994–recovered 1 fumble for 0 yards. 1995–recovered 1 fumble for 0 yards.

Pat Riley

Pos: DE **Rnd:** 2 **College:** Miami (FL) **Ht:** 6' 5" **Wt:** 285 **Born:** 3/8/72 **Age:** 24

				Tackles			Miscellaneous				Interceptions				Totals		
Year	Team	G	GS	Tk	Ast	Sack	FF	FR	TD	Blk	Int	Yds	Avg	TD	Sfty	TD	Pts
1995	Chicago Bears	1	0	0	0	0.0	0	0	0	0	0	0	-	0	0	0	0

Andre Rison

(statistical profile on page 370)

Pos: WR **Rnd:** 1 (22) **College:** Michigan State **Ht:** 6' 1" **Wt:** 188 **Born:** 3/18/67 **Age:** 29

				Rushing					Receiving					Punt Returns				Kickoff Returns				Totals		
Year	Team	G	GS	Att	Yds	Avg	Lg	TD	Rec	Yds	Avg	Lg	TD	Num	Yds	Avg	TD	Num	Yds	Avg	TD	Fum	TD	Pts
1989	Indianapolis Colts	16	13	3	18	6.0	18	0	52	820	15.8	61	4	2	20	10.0	0	8	150	18.8	0	1	4	24
1990	Atlanta Falcons	16	15	0	0	-	-	0	82	1208	14.7	t75	10	2	10	5.0	0	0	0	-	0	2	10	60
1991	Atlanta Falcons	16	15	1	-9	-9.0	-9	0	81	976	12.0	t39	12	0	0	-	0	0	0	-	0	1	12	72
1992	Atlanta Falcons	15	13	0	0	-	-	0	93	1119	12.0	t71	11	0	0	-	0	0	0	-	0	2	11	66
1993	Atlanta Falcons	16	16	0	0	-	-	0	86	1242	14.4	t53	15	0	0	-	0	0	0	-	0	2	15	90
1994	Atlanta Falcons	15	14	0	0	-	-	0	81	1088	13.4	t69	8	0	0	-	0	0	0	-	0	1	8	50
1995	Cleveland Browns	16	14	2	0	0.0	5	0	47	701	14.9	59	3	0	0	-	0	0	0	-	0	1	3	18
	7 NFL Seasons	110	100	6	9	1.5	18	0	522	7154	13.7	t75	63	4	30	7.5	0	8	150	18.8	0	10	63	380

Other Statistics: 1994–scored 1 two-point conversion. 1995–recovered 1 fumble for 0 yards.

Jim Ritcher

Pos: G **Rnd:** 1 (16) **College:** North Carolina State **Ht:** 6' 3" **Wt:** 273 **Born:** 5/21/58 **Age:** 38

Year	Team	G	GS	Year	Team	G	GS	Year	Team	G	GS	Year	Team	G	GS
1980	Buffalo Bills	14	0	1984	Buffalo Bills	14	14	1988	Buffalo Bills	16	16	1992	Buffalo Bills	16	16
1981	Buffalo Bills	14	3	1985	Buffalo Bills	16	16	1989	Buffalo Bills	16	16	1993	Buffalo Bills	12	10
1982	Buffalo Bills	9	0	1986	Buffalo Bills	16	16	1990	Buffalo Bills	16	16	1994	Atlanta Falcons	2	0
1983	Buffalo Bills	16	16	1987	Buffalo Bills	12	12	1991	Buffalo Bills	16	16	1995	Atlanta Falcons	12	0
													16 NFL Seasons	217	167

Other Statistics: 1986–recovered 1 fumble for 0 yards. 1990–recovered 1 fumble for 0 yards. 1992–recovered 1 fumble for 0 yards.

Reggie Rivers

Pos: RB **Rnd:** FA **College:** Southwest Texas State **Ht:** 6' 1" **Wt:** 206 **Born:** 2/22/68 **Age:** 28

				Rushing					Receiving					Kickoff Returns				Passing					Totals		
Year	Team	G	GS	Att	Yds	Avg	Lg	TD	Rec	Yds	Avg	Lg	TD	Num	Yds	Avg	TD	Att	Com	Yds	Int	Fum	TD	Pts
1991	Denver Broncos	16	0	2	5	2.5	3	0	0	0	-	-	0	0	0	-	0	0	0	0	0	0	0	0
1992	Denver Broncos	16	3	74	282	3.8	48	3	45	449	10.0	37	1	0	0	-	0	0	0	0	0	2	4	24
1993	Denver Broncos	16	2	15	50	3.3	14	1	6	59	9.8	17	1	0	0	-	0	0	0	0	0	2	2	14
1994	Denver Broncos	16	1	43	83	1.9	11	2	20	136	6.8	25	0	0	0	-	0	1	0	0	0	1	2	12
1995	Denver Broncos	16	0	2	2	1.0	1	0	3	32	10.7	23	0	0	0	-	0	0	0	0	0	0	0	0
	5 NFL Seasons	80	6	136	422	3.1	48	6	74	676	9.1	37	2	0	0	-	0	1	0	0	0	3	8	50

Other Statistics: 1992–recovered 1 fumble for 0 yards. 1993–credited with 1 safety; recovered 1 fumble for 0 yards. 1994–recovered 1 fumble for 0 yards.

Ron Rivers

Pos: KR/RB **Rnd:** FA **College:** Fresno State **Ht:** 5' 8" **Wt:** 205 **Born:** 11/13/71 **Age:** 24

				Rushing					Receiving					Punt Returns				Kickoff Returns				Totals		
Year	Team	G	GS	Att	Yds	Avg	Lg	TD	Rec	Yds	Avg	Lg	TD	Num	Yds	Avg	TD	Num	Yds	Avg	TD	Fum	TD	Pts
1995	Detroit Lions	16	0	18	73	4.1	19	1	1	5	5.0	5	0	0	0	-	0	19	420	22.1	0	2	1	6

Other Statistics: 1995–recovered 1 fumble for 0 yards.

William Roaf

Pos: T **Rnd:** 1 (8) **College:** Louisiana Tech **Ht:** 6' 5" **Wt:** 300 **Born:** 4/18/70 **Age:** 26

Year	Team	G	GS	Year	Team	G	GS	Year	Team	G	GS			G	GS
1993	New Orleans Saints	16	16	1994	New Orleans Saints	16	16	1995	New Orleans Saints	16	16		3 NFL Seasons	48	48

Other Statistics: 1994–recovered 1 fumble for 0 yards.

Michael Roan

Pos: TE **Rnd:** 4 **College:** Wisconsin **Ht:** 6' 3" **Wt:** 251 **Born:** 8/29/72 **Age:** 24

				Rushing					Receiving					Punt Returns				Kickoff Returns				Totals		
Year	Team	G	GS	Att	Yds	Avg	Lg	TD	Rec	Yds	Avg	Lg	TD	Num	Yds	Avg	TD	Num	Yds	Avg	TD	Fum	TD	Pts
1995	Houston Oilers	5	2	0	0	-	-	0	8	46	5.8	11	0	0	0	-	0	0	0	-	0	1	0	0

Other Statistics: 1995–recovered 1 fumble for 0 yards.

Austin Robbins

Pos: DT/DE **Rnd:** 4 **College:** North Carolina **Ht:** 6'6" **Wt:** 290 **Born:** 3/1/71 **Age:** 25

Year	Team	G	GS	Tk	Ast	Sack	FF	FR	TD	Blk	Int	Yds	Avg	TD	Sfty	TD	Pts
1994	Los Angeles Raiders	3	0	2	0	0.0	0	0	0	0	0	0	-	0	0	0	0
1995	Oakland Raiders	16	0	18	3	2.0	0	2	1	0	0	0	-	0	0	1	6
	2 NFL Seasons	19	0	20	3	2.0	0	2	1	0	0	0	-	0	0	1	6

Barret Robbins

Pos: C **Rnd:** 2 **College:** Texas Christian **Ht:** 6'3" **Wt:** 305 **Born:** 8/26/73 **Age:** 23

Year	Team	G	GS		Year	Team	G	GS
1995	Oakland Raiders	16	0			1 NFL Season	16	0

Ray Roberts

Pos: T **Rnd:** 1 (10) **College:** Virginia **Ht:** 6'6" **Wt:** 308 **Born:** 6/3/69 **Age:** 27

Year	Team	G	GS	Year	Team	G	GS	Year	Team	G	GS	Year	Team	G	GS
1992	Seattle Seahawks	16	16	1993	Seattle Seahawks	16	16	1994	Seattle Seahawks	14	14	1995	Seattle Seahawks	11	0
													4 NFL Seasons	57	46

Other Statistics: 1993–caught 1 pass for 4 yards.

Tim Roberts

Pos: DE **Rnd:** 5 **College:** Southern Mississippi **Ht:** 6'6" **Wt:** 318 **Born:** 4/14/69 **Age:** 27

Year	Team	G	GS	Tk	Ast	Sack	FF	FR	TD	Blk	Int	Yds	Avg	TD	Sfty	TD	Pts
1992	Houston Oilers	6	0	1	0	0.0	0	0	0	0	0	0	-	0	0	0	0
1993	Houston Oilers	6	0	0	0	0.0	0	0	0	0	0	0	-	0	0	0	0
1994	Houston Oilers	13	2	15	4	0.0	0	0	0	0	0	0	-	0	0	0	0
1995	New England Patriots	13	12	35	18	1.0	0	0	0	0	0	0	-	0	0	0	0
	4 NFL Seasons	38	14	51	22	1.0	0	0	0	0	0	0	-	0	0	0	0

William Roberts

Pos: G **Rnd:** 1 (27) **College:** Ohio State **Ht:** 6'5" **Wt:** 292 **Born:** 8/5/62 **Age:** 34

Year	Team	G	GS	Year	Team	G	GS	Year	Team	G	GS	Year	Team	G	GS
1984	New York Giants	11	8	1988	New York Giants	16	13	1991	New York Giants	16	16	1994	New York Giants	16	15
1986	New York Giants	16	0	1989	New York Giants	16	16	1992	New York Giants	16	15	1995	New England Patriots	16	11
1987	New York Giants	12	12	1990	New York Giants	16	16	1993	New York Giants	16	16		11 NFL Seasons	167	138

Other Statistics: 1984–recovered 1 fumble for 0 yards. 1988–recovered 2 fumbles for 0 yards. 1993–recovered 1 fumble for 0 yards.

Marcus Robertson

Pos: S **Rnd:** 4 **College:** Iowa State **Ht:** 5'11" **Wt:** 197 **Born:** 10/2/69 **Age:** 27

Year	Team	G	GS	Tk	Ast	Sack	FF	FR	TD	Blk	Int	Yds	Avg	TD	Num	Yds	Avg	TD	Num	Yds	Avg	TD	TD	Fum
1991	Houston Oilers	16	0	28	5	1.0	0	0	0	0	0	0	-	0	1	0	0.0	0	0	0	-	0	0	1
1992	Houston Oilers	16	14	44	35	0.0	0	0	0	0	1	27	27.0	0	0	0	-	0	0	0	-	0	0	0
1993	Houston Oilers	13	13	62	20	0.0	2	3	1	0	7	137	19.6	0	0	0	-	0	0	0	-	0	1	0
1994	Houston Oilers	16	16	80	31	0.0	2	1	0	0	3	90	30.0	0	1	0	0.0	0	0	0	-	0	0	1
1995	Houston Oilers	2	2	2	0	0.0	0	0	0	0	0	0	-	0	0	0	-	0	0	0	-	0	0	0
	5 NFL Seasons	63	45	216	91	1.0	4	4	1	0	11	254	23.1	0	2	0	0.0	0	0	0	-	0	1	2

Eddie Robinson

(statistical profile on page 444)

Pos: LB **Rnd:** 2 **College:** Alabama State **Ht:** 6'1" **Wt:** 245 **Born:** 4/13/70 **Age:** 26

Year	Team	G	GS	Tk	Ast	Sack	FF	FR	TD	Blk	Int	Yds	Avg	TD	Sfty	TD	Pts
1992	Houston Oilers	16	11	39	25	1.0	0	0	0	0	0	0	-	0	0	0	0
1993	Houston Oilers	16	15	42	15	1.0	0	0	0	0	0	0	-	0	0	0	0
1994	Houston Oilers	15	15	41	25	0.0	0	0	0	0	0	0	-	0	0	0	0
1995	Houston Oilers	16	16	48	24	3.5	1	1	0	0	1	49	49.0	1	0	1	6
	4 NFL Seasons	63	57	170	89	5.5	1	1	0	0	1	49	49.0	1	0	1	6

Eugene Robinson

(statistical profile on page 444)

Pos: S **Rnd:** FA **College:** Colgate **Ht:** 6'0" **Wt:** 195 **Born:** 5/28/63 **Age:** 33

Year	Team	G	GS	Tk	Ast	Sack	FF	FR	TD	Blk	Int	Yds	Avg	TD	Num	Yds	Avg	TD	Num	Yds	Avg	TD	TD	Fum
1985	Seattle Seahawks	16	0	18	10	0.0	0	0	0	0	2	47	23.5	0	0	0	-	0	1	10	10.0	0	0	0
1986	Seattle Seahawks	16	16	81	18	0.0	0	3	0	0	3	39	13.0	0	0	0	-	0	0	0	-	0	0	0

Year Team	G	GS	Tackles			Miscellaneous				Interceptions				Punt Returns				Kickoff Returns				Totals	
			Tk	Ast	Sack	FF	FR	TD	Blk	Int	Yds	Avg	TD	Num	Yds	Avg	TD	Num	Yds	Avg	TD	TD	Fum
1987 Seattle Seahawks	12	12	50	19	0.0	0	1	1	0	3	75	25.0	0	0	0	-	0	0	0	-	0	1	0
1988 Seattle Seahawks	16	16	86	29	1.0	1	0	0	0	1	0	0.0	0	0	0	-	0	0	0	-	0	0	0
1989 Seattle Seahawks	16	14	76	31	0.0	2	1	0	0	5	24	4.8	0	0	0	-	0	0	0	-	0	0	1
1990 Seattle Seahawks	16	16	63	19	0.0	1	4	1	0	3	89	29.7	0	0	0	-	0	0	0	-	0	1	0
1991 Seattle Seahawks	16	16	69	24	1.0	1	1	0	0	5	56	11.2	0	0	0	-	0	0	0	-	0	0	0
1992 Seattle Seahawks	16	16	64	30	0.0	2	1	0	0	7	126	18.0	0	0	0	-	0	0	0	-	0	0	0
1993 Seattle Seahawks	16	16	84	27	2.0	3	2	0	0	9	80	8.9	0	0	0	-	0	0	0	-	0	0	0
1994 Seattle Seahawks	14	14	65	15	1.0	0	1	0	0	3	18	6.0	0	0	0	-	0	0	0	-	0	0	0
1995 Seattle Seahawks	16	16	79	26	0.0	0	1	0	0	1	32	32.0	0	1	1	1.0	0	0	0	-	0	0	0
11 NFL Seasons	170	152	735	248	5.0	10	15	2	0	42	586	14.0	0	1	1	1.0	0	1	10	10.0	0	2	1

Greg Robinson

Pos: RB **Rnd:** 8 **College:** Northeast Louisiana **Ht:** 5' 10" **Wt:** 205 **Born:** 8/8/69 **Age:** 27

Year Team	G	GS	Rushing					Receiving					Punt Returns				Kickoff Returns				Totals		
			Att	Yds	Avg	Lg	TD	Rec	Yds	Avg	Lg	TD	Num	Yds	Avg	TD	Num	Yds	Avg	TD	Fum	TD	Pts
1993 Los Angeles Raiders	12	12	156	591	3.8	16	1	15	142	9.5	58	0	0	0	-	0	4	57	14.3	0	3	1	6
1995 St. Louis Rams	6	1	40	165	4.1	37	0	2	12	6.0	6	0	0	0	-	0	0	0	-	0	0	0	0
2 NFL Seasons	18	13	196	756	3.9	37	1	17	154	9.1	58	0	0	0	-	0	4	57	14.3	0	3	1	6

Other Statistics: 1993–recovered 1 fumble for 0 yards.

Jeff Robinson

Pos: DE/LS **Rnd:** 4 **College:** Idaho **Ht:** 6' 4" **Wt:** 265 **Born:** 2/20/70 **Age:** 26

Year Team	G	GS	Tackles			Miscellaneous				Interceptions				Punt Returns				Kickoff Returns				Totals	
			Tk	Ast	Sack	FF	FR	TD	Blk	Int	Yds	Avg	TD	Num	Yds	Avg	TD	Num	Yds	Avg	TD	TD	Fum
1993 Denver Broncos	16	0	7	6	3.5	1	1	0	0	0	0	-	0	0	0	-	0	0	0	-	0	0	1
1994 Denver Broncos	16	0	7	1	1.0	0	0	0	0	0	0	-	0	0	0	-	0	0	0	-	0	0	0
1995 Denver Broncos	16	0	6	1	1.0	0	1	0	0	0	0	-	0	0	0	-	0	1	14	14.0	0	0	0
3 NFL Seasons	48	0	20	8	5.5	1	2	0	0	0	0	-	0	0	0	-	0	1	14	14.0	0	0	1

Rafael Robinson

Pos: S **Rnd:** FA **College:** Wisconsin **Ht:** 5' 11" **Wt:** 200 **Born:** 6/19/69 **Age:** 27

Year Team	G	GS	Tackles			Miscellaneous				Interceptions				Totals		
			Tk	Ast	Sack	FF	FR	TD	Blk	Int	Yds	Avg	TD	Sfty	TD	Pts
1992 Seattle Seahawks	6	0	13	2	0.0	0	0	0	0	0	0	-	0	0	0	0
1993 Seattle Seahawks	16	1	35	7	1.5	2	1	0	0	0	0	-	0	0	0	0
1994 Seattle Seahawks	16	1	38	14	0.0	0	1	0	0	1	0	0.0	0	0	0	0
1995 Seattle Seahawks	13	3	30	8	0.0	1	0	0	0	0	0	-	0	0	0	0
4 NFL Seasons	51	5	116	31	1.5	3	2	0	0	1	0	0.0	0	0	0	0

Reggie Roby

(statistical profile on page 482)

Pos: P **Rnd:** 6 **College:** Iowa **Ht:** 6' 3" **Wt:** 258 **Born:** 7/30/61 **Age:** 35

Year Team	G	Punting											Rushing		Passing			
		NetPunts	Yards	Avg	Long	In20	In20%	TotPunts	TB	Blocks	OppRet	RetYds	NetAvg	Att	Yards	Att	Com	Yards	Int
1983 Miami Dolphins	16	74	3189	43.1	64	26	35.1	75	11	1	32	229	36.5	0	0	0	0	0	0
1984 Miami Dolphins	16	51	2281	44.7	69	15	29.4	51	10	0	17	138	38.1	0	0	0	0	0	0
1985 Miami Dolphins	16	59	2576	43.7	63	19	32.2	59	8	0	27	371	34.7	0	0	0	0	0	0
1986 Miami Dolphins	15	56	2476	44.2	73	13	23.2	56	9	0	23	200	37.4	2	-8	0	0	0	0
1987 Miami Dolphins	10	32	1371	42.8	77	8	25.0	32	3	0	16	87	38.3	1	0	0	0	0	0
1988 Miami Dolphins	15	64	2754	43.0	64	18	28.1	64	9	0	35	318	35.3	0	0	0	0	0	0
1989 Miami Dolphins	16	58	2458	42.4	58	18	31.0	59	6	1	26	256	35.3	2	0	0	0	0	0
1990 Miami Dolphins	16	72	3022	42.0	62	20	27.8	72	3	0	40	397	35.6	0	0	0	0	0	0
1991 Miami Dolphins	16	54	2466	45.7	64	17	31.5	55	7	1	29	324	36.4	0	0	0	0	0	0
1992 Miami Dolphins	9	35	1443	41.2	60	11	31.4	35	3	0	16	183	34.3	0	0	0	0	0	0
1993 Washington Redskins	15	78	3447	44.2	60	25	32.1	78	10	0	31	343	37.2	1	0	0	0	0	0
1994 Washington Redskins	16	82	3639	44.4	65	21	25.6	82	12	0	45	441	36.1	0	0	0	0	0	0
1995 Tampa Bay Buccaneers	16	77	3296	42.8	61	23	29.9	78	7	1	41	335	36.2	1	0	1	1	48	0
13 NFL Seasons	192	792	34418	43.5	77	234	29.5	796	98	4	378	3622	36.2	7	-8	1	1	48	0

Other Statistics: 1986–recovered 2 fumbles for -11 yards; fumbled 2 times. 1987–recovered 1 fumble for 0 yards. 1989–recovered 2 fumbles for 0 yards. 1993–recovered 1 fumble for 0 yards. 1994–recovered 1 fumble for 0 yards; fumbled 1 time.

Mark Rodenhauser

Pos: LS **Rnd:** FA **College:** Illinois State **Ht:** 6' 5" **Wt:** 280 **Born:** 6/1/61 **Age:** 35

Year	Team	G	GS	Year	Team	G	GS	Year	Team	G	GS	Year	Team	G	GS
1987	Chicago Bears	10	3	1990	San Diego Chargers	16	0	1992	Chicago Bears	13	0	1994	Detroit Lions	16	0
1989	Minnesota Vikings	16	0	1991	San Diego Chargers	10	0	1993	Detroit Lions	16	0	1995	Carolina Panthers	16	0
													8 NFL Seasons	113	3

Sam Rogers

Pos: LB **Rnd:** 2 **College:** Colorado **Ht:** 6' 3" **Wt:** 245 **Born:** 5/30/70 **Age:** 26

Year	Team	G	GS	Tackles			Miscellaneous				Interceptions				Totals		
				Tk	Ast	Sack	FF	FR	TD	Blk	Int	Yds	Avg	TD	Sfty	TD	Pts
1994	Buffalo Bills	14	0	0	0	0.0	0	0	0	0	0	0	-	0	0	0	0
1995	Buffalo Bills	16	8	32	13	2.0	1	1	0	0	0	0	-	0	0	0	0
	2 NFL Seasons	30	8	32	13	2.0	1	1	0	0	0	0	-	0	0	0	0

Tracy Rogers

Pos: LB **Rnd:** 7 **College:** Fresno State **Ht:** 6' 2" **Wt:** 241 **Born:** 8/13/67 **Age:** 29

Year	Team	G	GS	Tackles			Miscellaneous				Interceptions				Totals		
				Tk	Ast	Sack	FF	FR	TD	Blk	Int	Yds	Avg	TD	Sfty	TD	Pts
1990	Kansas City Chiefs	10	0	1	0	0.0	0	0	0	0	0	0	-	0	0	0	0
1991	Kansas City Chiefs	10	1	2	1	0.0	0	0	0	0	0	0	-	0	0	0	0
1992	Kansas City Chiefs	8	0	1	0	0.0	0	1	1	0	0	0	-	0	0	1	6
1993	Kansas City Chiefs	14	14	60	34	0.0	1	1	0	0	0	0	-	0	0	0	0
1994	Kansas City Chiefs	14	3	32	5	0.0	0	0	0	0	0	0	-	0	0	0	0
1995	Kansas City Chiefs	16	0	11	2	0.0	0	0	0	0	0	0	-	0	0	0	0
	6 NFL Seasons	72	18	107	42	0.0	1	2	1	0	0	0	-	0	0	1	6

Bill Romanowski

(statistical profile on page 444)

Pos: LB **Rnd:** 3 **College:** Boston College **Ht:** 6' 4" **Wt:** 241 **Born:** 4/2/66 **Age:** 30

Year	Team	G	GS	Tackles			Miscellaneous				Interceptions				Punt Returns				Kickoff Returns				Totals	
				Tk	Ast	Sack	FF	FR	TD	Blk	Int	Yds	Avg	TD	Num	Yds	Avg	TD	Num	Yds	Avg	TD	TD	Fum
1988	San Francisco 49ers	16	8	38	15	0.0	3	1	0	0	0	0	-	0	0	0	-	0	0	0	-	0	0	0
1989	San Francisco 49ers	16	4	47	6	1.0	1	2	0	0	1	13	13.0	0	1	0	0.0	0	0	0	-	0	0	1
1990	San Francisco 49ers	16	16	68	11	1.0	0	0	0	0	0	0	-	0	0	0	-	0	0	0	-	0	0	0
1991	San Francisco 49ers	16	16	67	9	1.0	0	2	0	0	1	7	7.0	0	0	0	-	0	0	0	-	0	0	0
1992	San Francisco 49ers	16	16	65	15	1.0	1	1	0	0	0	0	-	0	0	0	-	0	0	0	-	0	0	0
1993	San Francisco 49ers	16	16	81	23	3.0	2	1	0	0	0	0	-	0	0	0	-	0	0	0	-	0	0	0
1994	Philadelphia Eagles	16	15	49	17	2.5	0	1	0	0	2	8	4.0	0	0	0	-	0	0	0	-	0	0	0
1995	Philadelphia Eagles	16	16	50	13	1.0	0	1	0	0	2	5	2.5	0	0	0	-	0	0	0	-	0	0	0
	8 NFL Seasons	128	107	465	109	10.5	7	9	0	0	6	33	5.5	0	1	0	0.0	0	0	0	-	0	0	1

Dominique Ross

Pos: RB **Rnd:** FA **College:** Valdosta State **Ht:** 6' 0" **Wt:** 203 **Born:** 1/12/72 **Age:** 24

Year	Team	G	GS	Rushing					Receiving					Punt Returns				Kickoff Returns				Totals		
				Att	Yds	Avg	Lg	TD	Rec	Yds	Avg	Lg	TD	Num	Yds	Avg	TD	Num	Yds	Avg	TD	Fum	TD	Pts
1995	Dallas Cowboys	1	0	0	0	-	-	0	0	0	-	-	0	0	0	-	0	0	0	-	0	0	0	0

Kevin Ross

(statistical profile on page 445)

Pos: S **Rnd:** 7 **College:** Temple **Ht:** 5' 9" **Wt:** 185 **Born:** 1/16/62 **Age:** 34

Year	Team	G	GS	Tackles			Miscellaneous				Interceptions				Punt Returns				Kickoff Returns				Totals	
				Tk	Ast	Sack	FF	FR	TD	Blk	Int	Yds	Avg	TD	Num	Yds	Avg	TD	Num	Yds	Avg	TD	TD	Fum
1984	Kansas City Chiefs	16	16	77	21	0.0	0	1	0	0	6	124	20.7	0	0	0	-	0	0	0	-	0	1	0
1985	Kansas City Chiefs	16	15	81	30	0.0	0	1	0	0	3	47	15.7	0	0	0	-	0	0	0	-	0	0	0
1986	Kansas City Chiefs	16	16	76	17	2.0	0	3	1	0	4	66	16.5	0	0	0	-	0	0	0	-	0	1	0
1987	Kansas City Chiefs	12	11	46	12	1.0	0	0	1	0	3	40	13.3	0	0	0	-	0	0	0	-	0	1	0
1988	Kansas City Chiefs	15	14	61	38	0.0	0	0	0	0	1	0	-	0	0	0	-	0	0	0	-	0	0	0
1989	Kansas City Chiefs	15	13	57	18	0.0	0	0	0	0	4	29	7.3	0	2	0	0.0	0	2	0	0.0	0	0	0
1990	Kansas City Chiefs	16	15	53	11	0.0	0	0	0	0	5	97	19.4	0	0	0	-	0	0	0	-	0	1	0
1991	Kansas City Chiefs	14	13	54	14	0.0	0	1	0	0	1	0	-	0	0	0	-	0	0	0	-	0	0	0
1992	Kansas City Chiefs	16	16	44	14	0.5	1	2	0	0	1	99	99.0	1	0	0	-	0	0	0	-	0	1	0
1993	Kansas City Chiefs	15	15	70	32	0.5	1	1	0	0	2	49	24.5	0	0	0	-	0	0	0	-	0	0	0
1994	Atlanta Falcons	16	16	80	24	1.0	2	0	0	0	3	26	8.7	0	0	0	-	0	0	0	-	0	0	0
1995	Atlanta Falcons	16	15	72	18	0.0	0	2	1	0	3	70	23.3	0	0	0	-	0	0	0	-	0	1	0
	12 NFL Seasons	183	175	771	249	5.0	4	14	4	0	36	647	18.0	2	2	0	0.0	0	2	0	0.0	0	6	1

Tom Rouen

(statistical profile on page 482)

Pos: P **Rnd:** FA **College:** Colorado **Ht:** 6' 3" **Wt:** 215 **Born:** 6/9/68 **Age:** 28

Year	Team	G	Punting											Rushing		Passing			
			NetPunts	Yards	Avg	Long	In20	In20%	TotPunts	TB	Blocks	OppRet	RetYds	NetAvg	Att	Yards	Att	Com	Yards	Int
1993	Denver Broncos	16	67	3017	45.0	62	17	25.4	68	8	1	33	337	37.1	1	0	0	0	0	0
1994	Denver Broncos	16	76	3258	42.9	59	23	30.3	76	8	0	39	275	37.1	0	0	0	0	0	0
1995	Denver Broncos	16	52	2192	42.2	61	22	42.3	53	3	1	25	137	37.6	0	0	0	0	0	0
	3 NFL Seasons	48	195	8467	43.4	62	62	31.8	197	19	2	97	749	37.2	1	0	0	0	0	0

208

Wardell Rouse

Pos: LB **Rnd:** 6 **College:** Clemson **Ht:** 6' 2" **Wt:** 231 **Born:** 6/9/72 **Age:** 24

				Tackles			Miscellaneous				Interceptions				Totals		
Year	Team	G	GS	Tk	Ast	Sack	FF	FR	TD	Blk	Int	Yds	Avg	TD	Sfty	TD	Pts
1995	Tampa Bay Buccaneers	16	1	6	1	0.5	0	0	0	0	0	0	-	0	0	0	0

Andre Royal

Pos: LB **Rnd:** FA **College:** Alabama **Ht:** 6' 2" **Wt:** 220 **Born:** 12/1/72 **Age:** 23

				Tackles			Miscellaneous				Interceptions				Totals		
Year	Team	G	GS	Tk	Ast	Sack	FF	FR	TD	Blk	Int	Yds	Avg	TD	Sfty	TD	Pts
1995	Carolina Panthers	12	0	2	0	0.0	0	0	0	0	0	0	-	0	0	0	0

Mark Royals

(statistical profile on page 483)

Pos: P **Rnd:** FA **College:** Appalachian State **Ht:** 6' 5" **Wt:** 215 **Born:** 6/22/65 **Age:** 31

				Punting										Rushing		Passing			
Year	Team	G	NetPunts	Yards	Avg	Long	In20	In20%	TotPunts	TB	Blocks	OppRet	RetYds	NetAvg	Att	Yards	Att	Com	Yards	Int
1987	StL - Phi	2	11	431	39.2	48	3	27.3	11	1	0	6	155	23.3	0	0	0	0	0	0
1990	Tampa Bay Buccaneers	16	72	2902	40.3	62	8	11.1	72	5	0	39	352	34.0	0	0	0	0	0	0
1991	Tampa Bay Buccaneers	16	84	3389	40.3	56	22	26.2	84	6	0	49	559	32.3	0	0	0	0	0	0
1992	Pittsburgh Steelers	16	73	3119	42.7	58	22	30.1	74	9	1	39	308	35.6	0	0	1	1	44	0
1993	Pittsburgh Steelers	16	89	3781	42.5	61	28	31.5	89	3	0	50	678	34.2	0	0	0	0	0	0
1994	Pittsburgh Steelers	16	97	3849	39.7	64	35	36.1	97	6	0	39	263	35.7	1	-13	0	0	0	0
1995	Detroit Lions	16	57	2393	42.0	69	15	26.3	59	6	2	29	442	31.0	1	-7	0	0	0	0
1987	St. Louis Cardinals	1	6	222	37.0	48	2	33.3	6	0	0	4	119	17.2	0	0	0	0	0	0
	Philadelphia Eagles	1	5	209	41.8	48	1	20.0	5	1	0	2	36	30.6	0	0	0	0	0	0
	7 NFL Seasons	98	483	19864	41.1	69	133	27.5	486	36	3	251	2757	33.7	2	-20	1	1	44	0

T.J. Rubley

Pos: QB **Rnd:** 9 **College:** Tulsa **Ht:** 6' 3" **Wt:** 212 **Born:** 11/29/68 **Age:** 27

				Passing									Rushing				Miscellaneous			
Year	Team	G	GS	Att	Com	Pct	Yards	Yds/Att	Lg	TD	Int	Int%	Rating	Att	Yds	Avg	Lg	TD	Sckd	Yds	Fum	Recv	Yds	Pts
1993	Los Angeles Rams	9	7	189	108	57.1	1338	7.08	54	8	6	3.2	80.1	29	102	3.5	13	0	13	106	4	2	-18	0
1995	Green Bay Packers	1	0	6	4	66.7	39	6.50	17	0	1	16.7	45.1	2	6	3.0	6	0	0	0	1	0	0	0
	2 NFL Seasons	10	7	195	112	57.4	1377	7.06	54	8	7	3.6	78.1	31	108	3.5	13	0	13	106	5	2	-18	0

Todd Rucci

Pos: G **Rnd:** 2 **College:** Penn State **Ht:** 6' 5" **Wt:** 291 **Born:** 7/14/70 **Age:** 26

Year	Team	G	GS	Year	Team	G	GS	Year	Team	G	GS			G	GS
1993	New England Patriots	2	1	1994	New England Patriots	13	10	1995	New England Patriots	6	5	3 NFL Seasons		21	16

Keith Rucker

Pos: DT **Rnd:** FA **College:** Ohio Wesleyan **Ht:** 6' 4" **Wt:** 332 **Born:** 11/20/68 **Age:** 27

				Tackles			Miscellaneous				Interceptions				Totals		
Year	Team	G	GS	Tk	Ast	Sack	FF	FR	TD	Blk	Int	Yds	Avg	TD	Sfty	TD	Pts
1992	Phoenix Cardinals	14	4	24	12	2.0	0	0	0	0	0	0	-	0	0	0	0
1993	Phoenix Cardinals	16	15	29	19	0.0	1	1	0	0	0	0	-	0	0	0	0
1994	Cincinnati Bengals	16	14	52	6	2.0	1	0	0	0	0	0	-	0	0	0	0
1995	Cincinnati Bengals	15	15	32	9	2.0	1	0	0	0	0	0	-	0	0	0	0
	4 NFL Seasons	61	48	137	46	6.0	3	1	0	0	0	0	-	0	0	0	0

Tim Ruddy

Pos: C **Rnd:** 2 **College:** Notre Dame **Ht:** 6' 3" **Wt:** 290 **Born:** 4/27/72 **Age:** 24

Year	Team	G	GS	Year	Team	G	GS			G	GS
1994	Miami Dolphins	16	0	1995	Miami Dolphins	16	16	2 NFL Seasons		32	16

Other Statistics: 1995–fumbled 1 time for 0 yards.

Coleman Rudolph

Pos: DE **Rnd:** 2 **College:** Georgia Tech **Ht:** 6' 4" **Wt:** 270 **Born:** 10/22/70 **Age:** 26

				Tackles			Miscellaneous				Interceptions				Totals		
Year	Team	G	GS	Tk	Ast	Sack	FF	FR	TD	Blk	Int	Yds	Avg	TD	Sfty	TD	Pts
1993	New York Jets	4	0	4	1	0.0	0	0	0	0	0	0	-	0	0	0	0
1994	New York Giants	12	2	9	4	0.0	0	0	0	0	0	0	-	0	0	0	0
1995	New York Giants	16	0	12	1	4.0	0	0	0	0	0	0	-	0	0	0	0
	3 NFL Seasons	32	2	25	6	4.0	0	0	0	0	0	0	-	0	0	0	0

Joe Rudolph

Pos: G   **Rnd:** FA   **College:** Wisconsin   **Ht:** 6' 1"   **Wt:** 282   **Born:** 7/21/72   **Age:** 24

Year	Team	G	GS			Year	Team	G	GS
1995	Philadelphia Eagles	4	0			1 NFL Season		4	0

Ken Ruettgers

Pos: T   **Rnd:** 1 (7)   **College:** Southern California   **Ht:** 6' 6"   **Wt:** 292   **Born:** 8/20/62   **Age:** 34

Year	Team	G	GS	Year	Team	G	GS	Year	Team	G	GS	Year	Team	G	GS
1985	Green Bay Packers	16	2	1988	Green Bay Packers	15	15	1991	Green Bay Packers	4	4	1994	Green Bay Packers	16	16
1986	Green Bay Packers	16	16	1989	Green Bay Packers	16	16	1992	Green Bay Packers	16	16	1995	Green Bay Packers	15	15
1987	Green Bay Packers	12	12	1990	Green Bay Packers	11	11	1993	Green Bay Packers	16	16		11 NFL Seasons	153	139

Other Statistics: 1986–recovered 1 fumble for 0 yards. 1988–recovered 1 fumble for 0 yards. 1989–recovered 2 fumbles for 0 yards. 1990–recovered 1 fumble for 0 yards. 1991–recovered 1 fumble for 0 yards. 1993–recovered 2 fumbles for 0 yards. 1994–recovered 1 fumble for 0 yards. 1995–recovered 2 fumbles for 0 yards.

Derek Russell

Pos: WR   **Rnd:** 4   **College:** Arkansas   **Ht:** 6' 0"   **Wt:** 195   **Born:** 6/22/69   **Age:** 27

				Rushing					Receiving					Punt Returns				Kickoff Returns				Totals	
Year	Team	G	GS	Att	Yds	Avg	Lg	TD	Rec	Yds	Avg	Lg	TD	Num	Yds	Avg	TD	Num	Yds	Avg	TD	Fum	TD	Pts
1991	Denver Broncos	13	5	0	0	-	-	0	21	317	15.1	40	1	0	0	-	0	7	120	17.1	0	0	1	6
1992	Denver Broncos	12	7	0	0	-	-	0	12	140	11.7	22	0	0	0	-	0	7	154	22.0	0	0	0	0
1993	Denver Broncos	13	12	0	0	-	-	0	44	719	16.3	43	3	0	0	-	0	18	374	20.8	0	1	4	24
1994	Denver Broncos	12	12	1	6	6.0	6	0	25	342	13.7	43	1	0	0	-	0	5	105	21.0	0	0	1	6
1995	Houston Oilers	11	5	0	0	-	-	0	24	321	13.4	57	0	0	0	-	0	0	0	-	0	0	0	0
	5 NFL Seasons	61	41	1	6	6.0	6	0	126	1839	14.6	57	5	0	0	-	0	37	753	20.4	0	1	6	36

Other Statistics: 1993–recovered 1 fumble for 0 yards and 1 touchdown.

Leonard Russell

Pos: RB   **Rnd:** 1 (14)   **College:** Arizona State   **Ht:** 6' 2"   **Wt:** 240   **Born:** 11/17/69   **Age:** 26

				Rushing					Receiving					Punt Returns				Kickoff Returns				Totals	
Year	Team	G	GS	Att	Yds	Avg	Lg	TD	Rec	Yds	Avg	Lg	TD	Num	Yds	Avg	TD	Num	Yds	Avg	TD	Fum	TD	Pts
1991	New England Patriots	16	15	266	959	3.6	24	4	18	81	4.5	18	0	0	0	-	0	0	0	-	0	8	4	24
1992	New England Patriots	11	10	123	390	3.2	23	2	11	24	2.2	12	0	0	0	-	0	0	0	-	0	3	2	12
1993	New England Patriots	16	15	300	1088	3.6	21	7	26	245	9.4	69	0	0	0	-	0	0	0	-	0	4	7	42
1994	Denver Broncos	14	14	190	620	3.3	t22	9	38	227	6.0	19	0	0	0	-	0	0	0	-	0	4	9	54
1995	St. Louis Rams	13	2	66	203	3.1	18	0	16	89	5.6	17	0	0	0	-	0	0	0	-	0	2	0	0
	5 NFL Seasons	70	56	945	3260	3.4	24	22	109	666	6.1	69	0	0	0	-	0	0	0	-	0	21	22	132

Other Statistics: 1993–recovered 2 fumbles for 22 yards.

Mark Rypien

(statistical profile on page 370)

Pos: QB   **Rnd:** 6   **College:** Washington State   **Ht:** 6' 4"   **Wt:** 234   **Born:** 10/2/62   **Age:** 34

				Passing									Rushing					Miscellaneous			
Year	Team	G	GS	Att	Com	Pct	Yards	Yds/Att	Lg	TD	Int	Int%	Rating	Att	Yds	Avg	Lg	TD	Sckd	Yds	Fum	Recv	Yds	Pts
1988	Washington Redskins	9	6	208	114	54.8	1730	8.32	t60	18	13	6.3	85.2	9	31	3.4	t19	1	14	115	6	0	0	6
1989	Washington Redskins	14	14	476	280	58.8	3768	7.92	t80	22	13	2.7	88.1	26	56	2.2	15	1	16	108	14	2	0	6
1990	Washington Redskins	10	10	304	166	54.6	2070	6.81	t53	16	11	3.6	78.4	15	4	0.3	8	0	6	33	2	0	-3	0
1991	Washington Redskins	16	16	421	249	59.1	3564	8.47	t82	28	11	2.6	97.9	15	6	0.4	11	1	7	59	9	3	-5	6
1992	Washington Redskins	16	16	479	269	56.2	3282	6.85	t62	13	17	3.5	71.7	36	50	1.4	11	2	23	176	4	2	0	12
1993	Washington Redskins	12	10	319	166	52.0	1514	4.75	43	4	10	3.1	56.3	9	4	0.4	5	3	16	87	7	0	-2	18
1994	Cleveland Browns	7	3	128	59	46.1	694	5.42	43	4	3	2.3	63.7	7	4	0.6	2	0	2	11	2	0	-1	0
1995	St. Louis Rams	11	3	217	129	59.4	1448	6.67	50	9	8	3.7	77.9	9	10	1.1	5	0	11	60	1	0	0	0
	8 NFL Seasons	95	78	2552	1432	56.1	18070	7.08	t82	114	86	3.4	79.2	126	165	1.3	t19	8	95	649	45	7	-11	48

Dwayne Sabb

Pos: LB   **Rnd:** 5   **College:** New Hampshire   **Ht:** 6' 4"   **Wt:** 248   **Born:** 10/9/69   **Age:** 27

				Tackles			Miscellaneous				Interceptions				Punt Returns				Kickoff Returns				Totals	
Year	Team	G	GS	Tk	Ast	Sack	FF	FR	TD	Blk	Int	Yds	Avg	TD	Num	Yds	Avg	TD	Num	Yds	Avg	TD	TD	Fum
1992	New England Patriots	16	2	14	6	1.0	0	0	0	0	0	0	-	0	0	0	-	0	0	0	-	0	0	0
1993	New England Patriots	14	7	21	9	2.0	1	0	0	0	0	0	-	0	0	0	-	0	2	0	0.0	0	0	0
1994	New England Patriots	16	8	27	13	3.5	2	0	0	0	2	6	3.0	0	0	0	-	0	0	0	-	0	0	0
1995	New England Patriots	12	0	4	0	0.0	0	0	0	0	0	0	-	0	0	0	-	0	0	0	-	0	0	0
	4 NFL Seasons	58	17	66	28	6.5	3	0	0	0	2	6	3.0	0	0	0	-	0	2	0	0.0	0	0	0

Troy Sadowski

Pos: TE   **Rnd:** 6   **College:** Georgia   **Ht:** 6' 5"   **Wt:** 250   **Born:** 12/8/65   **Age:** 30

Year	Team	G	GS	Rushing					Receiving					Punt Returns				Kickoff Returns				Totals		
				Att	Yds	Avg	Lg	TD	Rec	Yds	Avg	Lg	TD	Num	Yds	Avg	TD	Num	Yds	Avg	TD	Fum	TD	Pts
1990	Atlanta Falcons	13	1	0	0	-	0	0	0	0	-	-	0	0	0	-	0	0	0	-	0	0	0	0
1991	Kansas City Chiefs	14	1	0	0	-	0	0	0	0	-	-	0	0	0	-	0	0	0	-	0	0	0	0
1992	New York Jets	6	2	0	0	-	0	0	1	20	20.0	20	0	0	0	-	0	0	0	-	0	0	0	0
1993	New York Jets	13	1	0	0	-	0	0	2	14	7.0	11	0	0	0	-	0	1	0	0.0	0	0	0	0
1994	Cincinnati Bengals	15	1	0	0	-	0	0	11	54	4.9	11	0	0	0	-	0	0	0	-	0	0	0	0
1995	Cincinnati Bengals	12	1	0	0	-	0	0	5	37	7.4	12	0	0	0	-	0	0	0	-	0	0	0	0
	6 NFL Seasons	73	7	0	0	-	0	0	19	125	6.6	20	0	0	0	-	0	1	0	0.0	0	0	0	0

Other Statistics: 1994–recovered 1 fumble for 0 yards. 1995–recovered 1 fumble for 0 yards.

Pio Sagapolutele

Pos: DT   **Rnd:** 4   **College:** San Diego State   **Ht:** 6' 6"   **Wt:** 297   **Born:** 11/28/69   **Age:** 26

Year	Team	G	GS	Tackles			Miscellaneous				Interceptions				Totals		
				Tk	Ast	Sack	FF	FR	TD	Blk	Int	Yds	Avg	TD	Sfty	TD	Pts
1991	Cleveland Browns	15	8	8	6	1.5	0	0	0	0	0	0	-	0	0	0	0
1992	Cleveland Browns	14	0	4	2	0.0	0	0	0	0	0	0	-	0	0	0	0
1993	Cleveland Browns	8	0	3	3	0.0	0	0	0	0	0	0	-	0	0	0	0
1994	Cleveland Browns	12	0	5	3	0.0	0	0	0	0	0	0	-	0	0	0	0
1995	Cleveland Browns	15	3	14	8	0.5	0	0	0	0	0	0	-	0	0	0	0
	5 NFL Seasons	64	11	34	22	2.0	0	0	0	0	0	0	-	0	0	0	0

Rashaan Salaam

(statistical profile on page 371)

Pos: RB   **Rnd:** 1 (21)   **College:** Colorado   **Ht:** 6' 1"   **Wt:** 226   **Born:** 10/8/74   **Age:** 22

Year	Team	G	GS	Rushing					Receiving					Punt Returns				Kickoff Returns				Totals		
				Att	Yds	Avg	Lg	TD	Rec	Yds	Avg	Lg	TD	Num	Yds	Avg	TD	Num	Yds	Avg	TD	Fum	TD	Pts
1995	Chicago Bears	16	12	296	1074	3.6	42	10	7	56	8.0	18	0	0	0	-	0	0	0	-	0	9	10	60

Other Statistics: 1995–recovered 1 fumble for 0 yards.

Dan Saleaumua

(statistical profile on page 445)

Pos: DT   **Rnd:** 7   **College:** Arizona State   **Ht:** 6' 0"   **Wt:** 300   **Born:** 11/25/64   **Age:** 31

Year	Team	G	GS	Tackles			Miscellaneous				Interceptions				Punt Returns				Kickoff Returns				Totals	
				Tk	Ast	Sack	FF	FR	TD	Blk	Int	Yds	Avg	TD	Num	Yds	Avg	TD	Num	Yds	Avg	TD	TD	Fum
1987	Detroit Lions	9	0	13	4	2.0	0	0	0	0	0	0	-	0	0	0	-	0	3	57	19.0	0	0	0
1988	Detroit Lions	16	0	10	1	2.0	0	0	0	0	0	0	-	0	0	0	-	0	1	0	0.0	0	0	1
1989	Kansas City Chiefs	16	8	56	17	2.0	0	5	0	0	1	21	21.0	0	0	0	-	0	1	8	8.0	0	0	0
1990	Kansas City Chiefs	16	16	59	29	7.0	0	6	1	0	0	0	-	0	0	0	-	0	0	0	-	0	1	0
1991	Kansas City Chiefs	16	16	50	26	1.5	0	2	0	0	0	0	-	0	0	0	-	0	0	0	-	0	0	0
1992	Kansas City Chiefs	16	16	62	19	6.0	0	1	0	0	0	0	-	0	0	0	-	0	0	0	-	0	0	0
1993	Kansas City Chiefs	16	16	47	14	3.5	1	1	1	0	1	13	13.0	0	0	0	-	0	0	0	-	0	1	0
1994	Kansas City Chiefs	14	14	23	5	1.0	0	1	0	0	0	0	-	0	0	0	-	0	0	0	-	0	0	0
1995	Kansas City Chiefs	16	16	47	8	7.0	2	1	0	0	1	0	0.0	0	0	0	-	0	0	0	-	0	0	0
	9 NFL Seasons	135	102	367	122	32.0	3	17	2	0	3	34	11.3	0	0	0	-	0	5	65	13.0	0	2	1

Other Statistics: 1991–credited with 1 safety.

Terry Samuels

Pos: RB   **Rnd:** 6   **College:** Kentucky   **Ht:** 6' 2"   **Wt:** 254   **Born:** 9/26/70   **Age:** 26

Year	Team	G	GS	Rushing					Receiving					Punt Returns				Kickoff Returns				Totals		
				Att	Yds	Avg	Lg	TD	Rec	Yds	Avg	Lg	TD	Num	Yds	Avg	TD	Num	Yds	Avg	TD	Fum	TD	Pts
1994	Arizona Cardinals	16	5	1	1	1.0	1	0	8	57	7.1	17	0	0	0	-	0	1	6	6.0	0	0	0	0
1995	Arizona Cardinals	4	1	0	0	-	-	0	2	19	9.5	12	0	0	0	-	0	0	0	-	0	0	0	0
	2 NFL Seasons	20	6	1	1	1.0	1	0	10	76	7.6	17	0	0	0	-	0	1	6	6.0	0	0	0	0

Barry Sanders

(statistical profile on page 371)

Pos: RB   **Rnd:** 1 (3)   **College:** Oklahoma State   **Ht:** 5' 8"   **Wt:** 203   **Born:** 7/16/68   **Age:** 28

Year	Team	G	GS	Rushing					Receiving					Kickoff Returns				Passing				Totals		
				Att	Yds	Avg	Lg	TD	Rec	Yds	Avg	Lg	TD	Num	Yds	Avg	TD	Att	Com	Yds	Int	Fum	TD	Pts
1989	Detroit Lions	15	13	280	1470	5.3	34	14	24	282	11.8	46	0	5	118	23.6	0	0	0	0	0	10	14	84
1990	Detroit Lions	16	16	255	1304	5.1	t45	13	36	480	13.3	t47	3	0	0	-	0	0	0	0	0	4	16	96
1991	Detroit Lions	15	15	342	1548	4.5	t69	16	41	307	7.5	34	1	0	0	-	0	0	0	0	0	5	17	102
1992	Detroit Lions	16	16	312	1352	4.3	t55	9	29	225	7.8	48	1	0	0	-	0	1	0	0	0	6	10	60
1993	Detroit Lions	11	11	243	1115	4.6	42	3	36	205	5.7	17	0	0	0	-	0	0	0	0	0	3	3	18
1994	Detroit Lions	16	16	331	1883	5.7	85	7	44	283	6.4	22	1	0	0	-	0	0	0	0	0	8	48
1995	Detroit Lions	16	16	314	1500	4.8	t75	11	48	398	8.3	40	1	0	0	-	0	2	1	11	0	3	12	72

211

(statistical profile on page 372)

Year Team	G	GS	Rushing					Receiving					Kickoff Returns				Passing				Totals		
			Att	Yds	Avg	Lg	TD	Rec	Yds	Avg	Lg	TD	Num	Yds	Avg	TD	Att	Com	Yds	Int	Fum	TD	Pts
7 NFL Seasons	105	103	2077	10172	4.9	85	73	258	2180	8.4	48	7	5	118	23.6	0	3	1	11	0	31	80	480

Other Statistics: 1990–recovered 2 fumbles for 0 yards. 1991–recovered 1 fumble for 0 yards. 1992–recovered 2 fumbles for 0 yards. 1993–recovered 3 fumbles for 0 yards. 1995–recovered 1 fumble for 0 yards.

Chris Sanders

(statistical profile on page 372)

Pos: WR **Rnd:** 3 **College:** Ohio State **Ht:** 6' 0" **Wt:** 184 **Born:** 5/8/72 **Age:** 24

Year Team	G	GS	Rushing					Receiving					Punt Returns				Kickoff Returns				Totals		
			Att	Yds	Avg	Lg	TD	Rec	Yds	Avg	Lg	TD	Num	Yds	Avg	TD	Num	Yds	Avg	TD	Fum	TD	Pts
1995 Houston Oilers	16	10	2	-19	-9.5	-6	0	35	823	23.5	t76	9	0	0	-	0	0	0	-	0	0	9	54

Deion Sanders

(statistical profile on page 445)

Pos: CB **Rnd:** 1 (5) **College:** Florida State **Ht:** 6' 1" **Wt:** 185 **Born:** 8/9/67 **Age:** 29

Year Team	G	GS	Tackles			Miscellaneous				Interceptions				Punt Returns				Kickoff Returns				Totals	
			Tk	Ast	Sack	FF	FR	TD	Blk	Int	Yds	Avg	TD	Num	Yds	Avg	TD	Num	Yds	Avg	TD	TD	Fum
1989 Atlanta Falcons	15	10	28	11	0.0	2	1	0	0	5	52	10.4	0	28	307	11.0	1	35	725	20.7	0	1	2
1990 Atlanta Falcons	16	16	31	19	0.0	0	2	0	0	3	153	51.0	2	29	250	8.6	1	39	851	21.8	0	3	4
1991 Atlanta Falcons	15	15	35	14	1.0	2	1	0	0	6	119	19.8	1	21	170	8.1	0	26	576	22.2	1	2	1
1992 Atlanta Falcons	13	12	44	22	0.0	2	2	1	0	3	105	35.0	0	13	41	3.2	0	40	1067	26.7	2	3	3
1993 Atlanta Falcons	11	10	27	7	0.0	1	0	1	0	7	91	13.0	0	2	21	10.5	0	7	169	24.1	0	1	0
1994 San Francisco 49ers	14	12	34	2	0.0	1	0	0	0	6	303	50.5	3	0	0	-	0	0	0	-	0	3	0
1995 Dallas Cowboys	9	9	25	1	0.0	0	0	0	0	2	34	17.0	0	1	54	54.0	0	1	15	15.0	0	0	0
7 NFL Seasons	93	84	224	76	1.0	7	7	2	0	32	857	26.8	6	94	843	9.0	2	148	3403	23.0	3	13	10

Other Statistics: 1989–caught 1 pass for -8 yards. 1991–caught 1 pass for 17 yards. 1992–rushed 1 time for -4 yards; caught 3 passes for 45 yards and 1 touchdown. 1993–attempted 1 pass with 0 completions for 0 yards; caught 6 passes for 106 yards and 1 touchdown. 1995–rushed 2 times for 9 yards; caught 2 passes for 25 yards.

Frank Sanders

(statistical profile on page 372)

Pos: WR **Rnd:** 2 **College:** Auburn **Ht:** 6' 1" **Wt:** 202 **Born:** 2/17/73 **Age:** 23

Year Team	G	GS	Rushing					Receiving					Punt Returns				Kickoff Returns				Totals		
			Att	Yds	Avg	Lg	TD	Rec	Yds	Avg	Lg	TD	Num	Yds	Avg	TD	Num	Yds	Avg	TD	Fum	TD	Pts
1995 Arizona Cardinals	16	15	1	1	1.0	1	0	52	883	17.0	48	2	0	0	-	0	0	0	-	0	0	2	16

Other Statistics: 1995–scored 2 two-point conversions.

Glen Sanders

Pos: LB **Rnd:** FA **College:** Louisiana Tech **Ht:** 6' 1" **Wt:** 236 **Born:** 11/4/66 **Age:** 29

Year Team	G	GS	Tackles			Miscellaneous				Interceptions				Punt Returns				Kickoff Returns				Totals	
			Tk	Ast	Sack	FF	FR	TD	Blk	Int	Yds	Avg	TD	Num	Yds	Avg	TD	Num	Yds	Avg	TD	TD	Fum
1990 Chicago Bears	2	0	0	2	0.0	0	0	0	0	0	0	-	0	0	0	-	0	0	0	-	0	0	0
1991 Los Angeles Rams	16	1	20	2	0.0	0	0	0	0	0	0	-	0	0	0	-	0	1	2	2.0	0	0	0
1994 Denver Broncos	1	0	1	1	0.0	0	0	0	0	0	0	-	0	0	0	-	0	0	0	-	0	0	0
1995 Indianapolis Colts	9	0	0	0	0.0	0	1	0	0	0	0	-	0	0	0	-	0	0	0	-	0	0	0
4 NFL Seasons	28	1	21	5	0.0	0	1	0	0	0	0	-	0	0	0	-	0	1	2	2.0	0	0	0

Ricky Sanders

Pos: WR **Rnd:** 1(S) **College:** Southwest Texas State **Ht:** 5' 11" **Wt:** 180 **Born:** 8/30/62 **Age:** 34

Year Team	G	GS	Rushing					Receiving					Punt Returns				Kickoff Returns				Totals		
			Att	Yds	Avg	Lg	TD	Rec	Yds	Avg	Lg	TD	Num	Yds	Avg	TD	Num	Yds	Avg	TD	Fum	TD	Pts
1986 Washington Redskins	10	3	0	0	-	-	0	14	286	20.4	71	2	0	0	-	0	0	0	-	0	0	2	12
1987 Washington Redskins	12	5	1	-4	-4.0	-4	0	37	630	17.0	57	3	0	0	-	0	4	118	29.5	0	0	3	18
1988 Washington Redskins	16	14	2	14	7.0	7	0	73	1148	15.7	t55	12	0	0	-	0	19	362	19.1	0	0	12	72
1989 Washington Redskins	16	12	4	19	4.8	13	0	80	1138	14.2	68	4	2	12	6.0	0	9	134	14.9	0	0	4	24
1990 Washington Redskins	16	6	4	17	4.3	12	0	56	727	13.0	38	3	0	0	-	0	1	22	22.0	0	0	3	18
1991 Washington Redskins	16	6	7	47	6.7	17	1	45	580	12.9	45	5	0	0	-	0	0	0	-	0	0	6	36
1992 Washington Redskins	15	5	4	-6	-1.5	3	0	51	707	13.9	t62	3	0	0	-	0	0	0	-	0	0	3	18
1993 Washington Redskins	16	10	1	7	7.0	7	0	58	638	11.0	50	4	0	0	-	0	0	0	-	0	1	4	24
1994 Atlanta Falcons	14	12	0	0	-	-	0	67	599	8.9	28	1	0	0	-	0	0	0	-	0	0	1	6
1995 Atlanta Falcons	3	1	0	0	-	-	0	2	24	12.0	21	0	0	0	-	0	0	0	-	0	0	0	0
10 NFL Seasons	134	64	23	94	4.1	17	1	483	6477	13.4	71	37	2	12	6.0	0	33	636	19.3	0	1	38	228

Other Statistics: 1989–attempted 1 pass with 1 completion for 32 yards. 1993–recovered 1 fumble for 0 yards. 1994–recovered 1 fumble for 0 yards.

Jesse Sapolu

Pos: G/C **Rnd:** 11 **College:** Hawaii **Ht:** 6' 4" **Wt:** 278 **Born:** 3/10/61 **Age:** 35

Year	Team	G	GS	Year	Team	G	GS	Year	Team	G	GS	Year	Team	G	GS
1983	San Francisco 49ers	16	1	1988	San Francisco 49ers	16	16	1991	San Francisco 49ers	16	16	1994	San Francisco 49ers	14	13
1984	San Francisco 49ers	1	0	1989	San Francisco 49ers	16	16	1992	San Francisco 49ers	16	16	1995	San Francisco 49ers	16	16
1987	San Francisco 49ers	12	9	1990	San Francisco 49ers	16	16	1993	San Francisco 49ers	16	16		11 NFL Seasons	155	135

Other Statistics: 1994–recovered 1 fumble for 0 yards.

Warren Sapp

Pos: DT/DE **Rnd:** 1 (12) **College:** Miami (FL)   **Ht:** 6' 2" **Wt:** 281 **Born:** 12/19/72 **Age:** 23

Year Team	G	GS	Tackles			Miscellaneous				Interceptions				Totals		
			Tk	Ast	Sack	FF	FR	TD	Blk	Int	Yds	Avg	TD	Sfty	TD	Pts
1995 Tampa Bay Buccaneers	16	8	17	10	3.0	1	0	0	0	1	5	5.0	1	0	1	6

Kevin Sargent

Pos: T   **Rnd:** FA   **College:** Eastern Washington   **Ht:** 6' 6" **Wt:** 284 **Born:** 3/31/69 **Age:** 27

Year Team	G	GS	Year Team	G	GS	Year Team	G	GS	Year Team	G	GS
1992 Cincinnati Bengals	16	8	1993 Cincinnati Bengals	1	1	1994 Cincinnati Bengals	15	15	1995 Cincinnati Bengals	15	15
									4 NFL Seasons	47	39

Other Statistics: 1992–recovered 2 fumbles for 0 yards. 1995–recovered 1 fumble for 0 yards.

Don Sasa

Pos: DT   **Rnd:** 3   **College:** Washington State   **Ht:** 6' 3" **Wt:** 286 **Born:** 9/16/72 **Age:** 24

Year Team	G	GS	Tackles			Miscellaneous				Interceptions				Totals		
			Tk	Ast	Sack	FF	FR	TD	Blk	Int	Yds	Avg	TD	Sfty	TD	Pts
1995 San Diego Chargers	5	0	0	0	0.0	0	0	0	0	0	0	-	0	0	0	0

Todd Sauerbrun

(statistical profile on page 483)

Pos: P   **Rnd:** 2   **College:** West Virginia   **Ht:** 5' 10" **Wt:** 206 **Born:** 1/20/71 **Age:** 25

Year Team	G	Punting											Rushing		Passing			
		NetPunts	Yards	Avg	Long	In20	In20%	TotPunts	TB	Blocks	OppRet	RetYds	NetAvg	Att	Yards	Att	Com	Yards	Int
1995 Chicago Bears	15	55	2080	37.8	61	16	29.1	55	6	0	27	248	31.1	0	0	0	0	0	0

Cedric Saunders

Pos: TE   **Rnd:** FA   **College:** Ohio State   **Ht:** 6' 3" **Wt:** 240 **Born:** 9/30/72 **Age:** 24

Year Team	G	GS	Rushing					Receiving					Punt Returns				Kickoff Returns				Totals		
			Att	Yds	Avg	Lg	TD	Rec	Yds	Avg	Lg	TD	Num	Yds	Avg	TD	Num	Yds	Avg	TD	Fum	TD	Pts
1995 Tampa Bay Buccaneers	3	0	0	0	-	-	0	0	0	-	-	0	0	0	-	0	0	0	-	0	0	0	0

Sebastian Savage

Pos: CB/S **Rnd:** 5   **College:** North Carolina State   **Ht:** 5' 10" **Wt:** 187 **Born:** 12/12/69 **Age:** 26

Year Team	G	GS	Tackles			Miscellaneous				Interceptions				Totals		
			Tk	Ast	Sack	FF	FR	TD	Blk	Int	Yds	Avg	TD	Sfty	TD	Pts
1994 Washington Redskins	1	0	0	0	0.0	0	0	0	0	0	0	-	0	0	0	0
1995 Washington Redskins	2	0	1	0	0.0	0	0	0	0	0	0	-	0	0	0	0
2 NFL Seasons	3	0	1	0	0.0	0	0	0	0	0	0	-	0	0	0	0

Corey Sawyer

Pos: CB   **Rnd:** 4   **College:** Florida State   **Ht:** 5' 11" **Wt:** 171 **Born:** 10/4/71 **Age:** 25

Year Team	G	GS	Tackles			Miscellaneous				Interceptions				Punt Returns				Kickoff Returns				Totals	
			Tk	Ast	Sack	FF	FR	TD	Blk	Int	Yds	Avg	TD	Num	Yds	Avg	TD	Num	Yds	Avg	TD	TD	Fum
1994 Cincinnati Bengals	15	0	26	5	0.0	0	1	0	0	2	0	0.0	0	26	307	11.8	1	1	14	14.0	0	1	2
1995 Cincinnati Bengals	12	8	49	4	2.0	2	0	0	0	2	61	30.5	0	9	58	6.4	0	2	50	25.0	0	0	1
2 NFL Seasons	27	8	75	9	2.0	2	1	0	0	4	61	15.3	0	35	365	10.4	1	3	64	21.3	0	1	3

James Saxon

Pos: RB   **Rnd:** 6   **College:** San Jose State   **Ht:** 5' 11" **Wt:** 239 **Born:** 3/23/66 **Age:** 30

Year Team	G	GS	Rushing					Receiving					Kickoff Returns				Passing				Totals		
			Att	Yds	Avg	Lg	TD	Rec	Yds	Avg	Lg	TD	Num	Yds	Avg	TD	Att	Com	Yds	Int	Fum	TD	Pts
1988 Kansas City Chiefs	16	4	60	236	3.9	14	2	19	177	9.3	22	0	2	40	20.0	0	0	0	0	0	2	2	12
1989 Kansas City Chiefs	16	2	58	233	4.0	19	3	11	86	7.8	18	0	3	16	5.3	0	1	0	0	1	2	3	18
1990 Kansas City Chiefs	6	0	3	15	5.0	8	0	1	5	5.0	5	0	5	81	16.2	0	0	0	0	0	1	0	0
1991 Kansas City Chiefs	16	0	6	13	2.2	8	0	6	55	9.2	22	0	4	56	14.0	0	0	0	0	0	1	0	0
1992 Miami Dolphins	16	0	4	7	1.8	4	0	5	41	8.2	14	0	0	0	-	0	0	0	0	0	0	0	0
1993 Miami Dolphins	16	0	5	13	2.6	9	0	1	7	7.0	-	0	1	7	7.0	0	0	0	0	0	0	0	0
1994 Miami Dolphins	16	7	8	16	2.0	7	0	27	151	5.6	25	0	1	12	12.0	0	0	0	0	0	0	0	0
1995 Philadelphia Eagles	8	3	1	0	0.0	0	0	0	0	-	-	0	1	3	3.0	0	0	0	0	0	0	0	0
8 NFL Seasons	110	16	145	533	3.7	19	5	69	515	7.5	25	0	17	215	12.6	0	1	0	0	1	4	5	30

Other Statistics: 1988–recovered 1 fumble for 0 yards.

Mike Saxon

(statistical profile on page 483)

Pos: P **Rnd:** 11 **College:** San Diego State **Ht:** 6' 3" **Wt:** 205 **Born:** 7/10/62 **Age:** 34

			Punting										Rushing		Passing			
Year	Team	G	NetPunts	Yards	Avg	Long	In20	In20%	TotPunts	TB	Blocks	OppRet	RetYds	NetAvg	Att	Yards	Att Com	Yards Int
1985	Dallas Cowboys	16	81	3396	41.9	57	20	24.7	82	10	1	44	286	35.5	0	0	0 0	0 0
1986	Dallas Cowboys	16	86	3498	40.7	58	**28**	**32.6**	87	10	1	41	301	34.4	0	0	0 0	0 0
1987	Dallas Cowboys	12	68	2685	39.5	63	20	29.4	68	5	0	36	260	34.2	0	0	0 0	0 0
1988	Dallas Cowboys	16	80	3271	40.9	55	24	30.0	80	**15**	0	37	239	34.2	0	0	0 0	0 0
1989	Dallas Cowboys	16	79	3233	40.9	56	19	24.1	81	6	**2**	37	334	34.3	1	1	1 1	4 0
1990	Dallas Cowboys	16	79	3413	43.2	62	20	25.3	79	8	0	43	438	35.6	1	20	0 0	0 0
1991	Dallas Cowboys	16	57	2426	42.6	64	16	28.1	57	5	0	28	231	36.8	0	0	0 0	0 0
1992	Dallas Cowboys	16	61	2620	43.0	58	19	31.1	61	9	0	34	397	33.5	0	0	0 0	0 0
1993	New England Patriots	16	73	3096	42.4	59	25	34.2	76	7	**3**	34	313	34.8	2	2	0 0	0 0
1994	Minnesota Vikings	16	77	3301	42.9	67	28	36.4	77	5	0	44	410	36.2	1	0	1 0	0 0
1995	Minnesota Vikings	16	72	2948	40.9	60	21	29.2	72	6	0	41	446	33.1	0	0	0 0	0 0
	11 NFL Seasons	172	813	33887	41.7	67	240	29.5	820	86	7	419	3655	34.8	5	23	2 1	4 0

Other Statistics: 1993–recovered 1 fumble for 0 yards; fumbled 1 time. 1994–fumbled 1 time for 0 yards.

Mark Schlereth

Pos: G **Rnd:** 10 **College:** Idaho **Ht:** 6' 3" **Wt:** 278 **Born:** 1/25/66 **Age:** 30

Year	Team	G	GS	Year	Team	G	GS	Year	Team	G	GS	Year	Team	G	GS
1989	Washington Redskins	6	6	1991	Washington Redskins	16	16	1993	Washington Redskins	9	8	1995	Denver Broncos	16	16
1990	Washington Redskins	12	7	1992	Washington Redskins	16	16	1994	Washington Redskins	16	7		7 NFL Seasons	91	76

Other Statistics: 1989–recovered 1 fumble for 0 yards. 1993–recovered 1 fumble for 0 yards.

Cory Schlesinger

Pos: RB **Rnd:** 6 **College:** Nebraska **Ht:** 6' 0" **Wt:** 230 **Born:** 6/23/72 **Age:** 24

				Rushing					Receiving					Punt Returns				Kickoff Returns				Totals		
Year	Team	G	GS	Att	Yds	Avg	Lg	TD	Rec	Yds	Avg	Lg	TD	Num	Yds	Avg	TD	Num	Yds	Avg	TD	Fum	TD	Pts
1995	Detroit Lions	16	1	1	1	1.0	1	0	1	2	2.0	2	0	0	0	-	0	0	0	-	0	0	0	0

Other Statistics: 1995–recovered 1 fumble for 11 yards.

Adam Schreiber

Pos: LS **Rnd:** 9 **College:** Texas **Ht:** 6' 4" **Wt:** 290 **Born:** 2/20/62 **Age:** 34

Year	Team	G	GS	Year	Team	G	GS	Year	Team	G	GS	Year	Team	G	GS
1984	Seattle Seahawks	6	0	1988	Philadelphia Eagles	6	0	1991	Minnesota Vikings	15	0	1995	New York Giants	16	0
1985	New Orleans Saints	1	0	1988	New York Jets	7	0	1992	Minnesota Vikings	16	1				
1986	Philadelphia Eagles	9	0	1989	New York Jets	15	0	1993	Minnesota Vikings	16	16				
1987	Philadelphia Eagles	12	12	1990	Minnesota Vikings	16	0	1994	New York Giants	16	2		12 NFL Seasons	151	31

Other Statistics: 1990–returned 1 kickoff for 5 yards. 1992–recovered 1 fumble for 0 yards.

William Schultz

Pos: T **Rnd:** 4 **College:** Southern California **Ht:** 6' 5" **Wt:** 305 **Born:** 5/1/67 **Age:** 29

Year	Team	G	GS	Year	Team	G	GS	Year	Team	G	GS			G	GS
1990	Indianapolis Colts	12	0	1992	Indianapolis Colts	10	2	1994	Houston Oilers	2	0				
1991	Indianapolis Colts	10	9	1993	Indianapolis Colts	14	14	1995	Denver Broncos	2	0		6 NFL Seasons	50	25

Other Statistics: 1991–recovered 2 fumbles for 0 yards. 1992–caught 1 pass for 3 yards and 1 touchdown.

Kurt Schulz

(statistical profile on page 446)

Pos: S **Rnd:** 7 **College:** Eastern Washington **Ht:** 6' 1" **Wt:** 208 **Born:** 12/12/68 **Age:** 27

				Tackles			Miscellaneous				Interceptions				Totals		
Year	Team	G	GS	Tk	Ast	Sack	FF	FR	TD	Blk	Int	Yds	Avg	TD	Sfty	TD	Pts
1992	Buffalo Bills	8	1	7	7	0.0	0	2	0	0	0	0	-	0	0	0	0
1993	Buffalo Bills	12	0	7	3	0.0	0	0	0	0	0	0	-	0	0	0	0
1994	Buffalo Bills	16	0	*13*	*10*	0.0	0	0	0	0	0	0	-	0	0	0	0
1995	Buffalo Bills	13	13	*39*	*16*	0.0	2	0	0	0	6	48	8.0	1	0	1	6
	4 NFL Seasons	49	14	66	36	0.0	2	2	0	0	6	48	8.0	1	0	1	6

Jim Schwantz

Pos: LB **Rnd:** FA **College:** Purdue **Ht:** 6' 2" **Wt:** 232 **Born:** 1/23/70 **Age:** 26

				Tackles			Miscellaneous				Interceptions				Punt Returns				Kickoff Returns				Totals	
Year	Team	G	GS	Tk	Ast	Sack	FF	FR	TD	Blk	Int	Yds	Avg	TD	Num	Yds	Avg	TD	Num	Yds	Avg	TD	TD	Fum
1992	Chicago Bears	1	0	0	0	0.0	0	0	0	0	0	0	-	0	0	0	-	0	0	0	-	0	0	0
1994	Dallas Cowboys	7	0	*3*	*1*	0.0	0	0	0	0	0	0	-	0	0	0	-	0	0	0	-	0	0	0
1995	Dallas Cowboys	16	0	*10*	*2*	0.0	0	0	0	0	0	0	-	0	0	0	-	0	1	9	9.0	0	0	0
	3 NFL Seasons	24	0	13	3	0.0	0	0	0	0	0	0	-	0	0	0	-	0	1	9	9.0	0	0	0

Bryan Schwartz

(statistical profile on page 446)

Pos: LB **Rnd:** 2 **College:** Augustana (SD) **Ht:** 6' 4" **Wt:** 256 **Born:** 12/5/71 **Age:** 24

Year Team	G	GS	Tk	Ast	Sack	FF	FR	TD	Blk	Int	Yds	Avg	TD	Sfty	TD	Pts
			Tackles			**Miscellaneous**				**Interceptions**				**Totals**		
1995 Jacksonville Jaguars	14	9	72	26	0.0	2	1	0	0	0	0	-	0	0	0	0

Darnay Scott

(statistical profile on page 373)

Pos: WR **Rnd:** 2 **College:** San Diego State **Ht:** 6' 1" **Wt:** 180 **Born:** 7/7/72 **Age:** 24

Year Team	G	GS	Att	Yds	Avg	Lg	TD	Rec	Yds	Avg	Lg	TD	Num	Yds	Avg	TD	Att	Com	Yds	Int	Fum	TD	Pts
			Rushing					**Receiving**					**Kickoff Returns**				**Passing**				**Totals**		
1994 Cincinnati Bengals	16	13	10	106	10.6	23	0	46	866	18.8	76	5	15	342	22.8	0	1	1	53	0	0	5	30
1995 Cincinnati Bengals	16	16	5	11	2.2	9	0	52	821	15.8	t88	5	0	0	-	0	0	0	0	0	0	5	30
2 NFL Seasons	32	29	15	117	7.8	23	0	98	1687	17.2	t88	10	15	342	22.8	0	1	1	53	0	0	10	60

Lance Scott

Pos: C **Rnd:** 5 **College:** Utah **Ht:** 6' 3" **Wt:** 285 **Born:** 2/15/72 **Age:** 24

Year Team	G	GS															G	GS
1995 Arizona Cardinals	1	0													1 NFL Season		1	0

Todd Scott

Pos: S **Rnd:** 6 **College:** Southwestern Louisiana **Ht:** 5' 11" **Wt:** 205 **Born:** 1/23/68 **Age:** 28

Year Team	G	GS	Tk	Ast	Sack	FF	FR	TD	Blk	Int	Yds	Avg	TD	Sfty	TD	Pts
			Tackles			**Miscellaneous**				**Interceptions**				**Totals**		
1991 Minnesota Vikings	16	1	25	8	0.0	0	0	0	0	0	0	-	0	0	0	0
1992 Minnesota Vikings	16	16	62	11	1.0	0	0	0	0	5	79	15.8	1	0	1	6
1993 Minnesota Vikings	13	12	44	17	0.0	0	1	0	0	2	26	13.0	0	0	0	0
1994 Minnesota Vikings	16	15	44	16	0.0	1	0	0	0	0	0	-	0	0	0	0
1995 NYA - TB	11	9	51	17	0.0	0	0	0	0	0	0	-	0	0	0	0
1995 New York Jets	10	9	45	16	0.0	0	0	0	0	0	0	-	0	0	0	0
Tampa Bay Buccaneers	1	0	6	1	0.0	0	0	0	0	0	0	-	0	0	0	0
5 NFL Seasons	72	53	226	69	1.0	1	1	0	0	7	105	15.0	1	0	1	6

Kirk Scrafford

Pos: T/G **Rnd:** FA **College:** Montana **Ht:** 6' 2" **Wt:** 255 **Born:** 3/13/67 **Age:** 29

Year Team	G	GS	Year Team	G	GS	Year Team	G	GS		G	GS
1990 Cincinnati Bengals	2	0	1992 Cincinnati Bengals	8	4	1994 Denver Broncos	16	8			
1991 Cincinnati Bengals	9	5	1993 Denver Broncos	16	0	1995 San Francisco 49ers	15	11	6 NFL Seasons	66	28

Other Statistics: 1994–recovered 1 fumble for 0 yards.

Tracy Scroggins

(statistical profile on page 446)

Pos: DE **Rnd:** 2 **College:** Tulsa **Ht:** 6' 2" **Wt:** 255 **Born:** 9/11/69 **Age:** 27

Year Team	G	GS	Tk	Ast	Sack	FF	FR	TD	Blk	Int	Yds	Avg	TD	Sfty	TD	Pts
			Tackles			**Miscellaneous**				**Interceptions**				**Totals**		
1992 Detroit Lions	16	7	25	3	7.5	0	0	0	0	0	0	-	0	0	0	0
1993 Detroit Lions	16	0	10	7	8.0	2	1	0	0	1	0	0.0	0	0	0	0
1994 Detroit Lions	16	9	28	8	2.5	0	1	0	0	0	0	-	0	0	0	0
1995 Detroit Lions	16	16	35	10	9.5	2	1	1	0	0	0	-	0	0	1	6
4 NFL Seasons	64	32	98	28	27.5	4	3	1	0	1	0	0.0	0	0	1	6

Mike Scurlock

Pos: DB/CB **Rnd:** 5 **College:** Arizona **Ht:** 5' 10" **Wt:** 197 **Born:** 2/26/72 **Age:** 24

Year Team	G	GS	Tk	Ast	Sack	FF	FR	TD	Blk	Int	Yds	Avg	TD	Sfty	TD	Pts
			Tackles			**Miscellaneous**				**Interceptions**				**Totals**		
1995 St. Louis Rams	14	1	7	1	0.0	0	1	0	0	1	13	13.0	0	0	0	0

Malcolm Seabron

Pos: WR **Rnd:** 3 **College:** Fresno State **Ht:** 6' 0" **Wt:** 194 **Born:** 12/29/72 **Age:** 23

Year Team	G	GS	Att	Yds	Avg	Lg	TD	Rec	Yds	Avg	Lg	TD	Num	Yds	Avg	TD	Num	Yds	Avg	TD	Fum	TD	Pts
			Rushing					**Receiving**					**Punt Returns**				**Kickoff Returns**				**Totals**		
1994 Houston Oilers	13	0	0	0	-	-	0	0	0	-	-	0	0	0	-	0	0	0	-	0	0	0	0
1995 Houston Oilers	15	1	0	0	-	-	0	12	167	13.9	34	1	0	0	-	0	0	0	-	0	0	1	6
2 NFL Seasons	28	1	0	0	-	-	0	12	167	13.9	34	1	0	0	-	0	0	0	-	0	0	1	6

Ray Seals

(statistical profile on page 447)

Pos: DE **Rnd:** FA **College:** None **Ht:** 6' 3" **Wt:** 290 **Born:** 6/17/65 **Age:** 31

Year	Team	G	GS	Tk	Ast	Sack	FF	FR	TD	Blk	Int	Yds	Avg	TD	Sfty	TD	Pts
				|Tackles			Miscellaneous				Interceptions				Totals		
1989	Tampa Bay Buccaneers	2	0	1	0	1.0	0	0	0	0	0	0	-	0	0	0	0
1990	Tampa Bay Buccaneers	8	0	3	3	0.0	0	0	0	0	0	0	-	0	0	0	0
1991	Tampa Bay Buccaneers	10	9	28	4	1.0	0	2	0	0	0	0	-	0	0	0	0
1992	Tampa Bay Buccaneers	11	8	34	3	5.0	0	0	0	0	0	0	-	0	0	0	0
1993	Tampa Bay Buccaneers	16	11	19	16	8.5	0	1	0	0	1	0	0.0	1	0	1	6
1994	Pittsburgh Steelers	13	11	28	8	7.0	0	2	0	0	0	0	-	0	0	0	0
1995	Pittsburgh Steelers	16	16	33	14	8.5	2	1	0	0	1	0	0.0	0	0	0	0
	7 NFL Seasons	76	55	146	48	31.0	2	6	0	0	2	0	0.0	1	0	1	6

Leon Searcy

Pos: T **Rnd:** 1 (11) **College:** Miami (FL) **Ht:** 6' 3" **Wt:** 304 **Born:** 12/21/69 **Age:** 26

Year	Team	G	GS	Year	Team	G	GS	Year	Team	G	GS	Year	Team	G	GS
1992	Pittsburgh Steelers	15	0	1993	Pittsburgh Steelers	16	16	1994	Pittsburgh Steelers	16	16	1995	Pittsburgh Steelers	16	16
													4 NFL Seasons	63	48

Other Statistics: 1993–recovered 1 fumble for 0 yards. 1995–recovered 1 fumble for 0 yards.

Junior Seau

(statistical profile on page 447)

Pos: LB **Rnd:** 1 (5) **College:** Southern California **Ht:** 6' 3" **Wt:** 255 **Born:** 1/19/69 **Age:** 27

Year	Team	G	GS	Tk	Ast	Sack	FF	FR	TD	Blk	Int	Yds	Avg	TD	Sfty	TD	Pts
				Tackles			Miscellaneous				Interceptions				Totals		
1990	San Diego Chargers	16	15	61	24	1.0	0	0	0	0	0	0	-	0	0	0	0
1991	San Diego Chargers	16	16	111	18	7.0	0	0	0	0	0	0	-	0	0	0	0
1992	San Diego Chargers	15	15	79	23	4.5	1	1	0	0	2	51	25.5	0	0	0	0
1993	San Diego Chargers	16	16	108	21	0.0	1	1	0	0	2	58	29.0	0	0	0	0
1994	San Diego Chargers	16	16	124	31	5.5	1	3	0	0	0	0	-	0	0	0	0
1995	San Diego Chargers	16	16	111	19	2.0	1	3	1	0	2	5	2.5	0	0	1	6
	6 NFL Seasons	95	94	594	136	20.0	4	8	1	0	6	114	19.0	0	0	1	6

Mark Seay

(statistical profile on page 373)

Pos: WR **Rnd:** FA **College:** Long Beach State **Ht:** 6' 0" **Wt:** 175 **Born:** 4/11/67 **Age:** 29

Year	Team	G	GS	Att	Yds	Avg	Lg	TD	Rec	Yds	Avg	Lg	TD	Num	Yds	Avg	TD	Num	Yds	Avg	TD	Fum	TD	Pts
				Rushing					Receiving					Punt Returns				Kickoff Returns				Totals		
1993	San Diego Chargers	1	0	0	0	-	-	0	0	0	-	-	0	0	0	-	0	0	0	-	0	0	0	0
1994	San Diego Chargers	16	14	0	0	-	-	0	58	645	11.1	t49	6	0	0	-	0	0	0	-	0	0	6	36
1995	San Diego Chargers	16	0	0	0	-	-	0	45	537	11.9	t38	3	0	0	-	0	0	0	-	0	0	3	20
	3 NFL Seasons	33	14	0	0	-	-	0	103	1182	11.5	t49	9	0	0	-	0	0	0	-	0	0	9	56

Other Statistics: 1995–scored 1 two-point conversion.

Jason Sehorn

Pos: CB/S **Rnd:** 2 **College:** Southern California **Ht:** 6' 2" **Wt:** 217 **Born:** 4/15/71 **Age:** 25

Year	Team	G	GS	Tk	Ast	Sack	FF	FR	TD	Blk	Int	Yds	Avg	TD	Sfty	TD	Pts
				Tackles			Miscellaneous				Interceptions				Totals		
1994	New York Giants	8	0	1	0	0.0	0	0	0	0	0	0	-	0	0	0	0
1995	New York Giants	14	0	4	2	0.0	1	0	0	0	0	0	-	0	0	0	0
	2 NFL Seasons	22	0	5	2	0.0	1	0	0	0	0	0	-	0	0	0	0

Rob Selby

Pos: T/G **Rnd:** 3 **College:** Auburn **Ht:** 6' 3" **Wt:** 286 **Born:** 10/11/67 **Age:** 29

Year	Team	G	GS	Year	Team	G	GS	Year	Team	G	GS			G	GS
1991	Philadelphia Eagles	12	0	1993	Philadelphia Eagles	1	0	1995	Arizona Cardinals	7	4				
1992	Philadelphia Eagles	16	1	1994	Philadelphia Eagles	2	0						5 NFL Seasons	38	5

Tony Semple

Pos: G/LS **Rnd:** 5 **College:** Memphis **Ht:** 6' 4" **Wt:** 286 **Born:** 12/20/70 **Age:** 25

Year	Team	G	GS			G	GS
1995	Detroit Lions	16	0		1 NFL Season	16	0

Sam Shade

Pos: S **Rnd:** 4 **College:** Alabama **Ht:** 6' 1" **Wt:** 191 **Born:** 6/14/73 **Age:** 23

Year Team	G	GS	Tackles			Miscellaneous				Interceptions				Totals		
			Tk	Ast	Sack	FF	FR	TD	Blk	Int	Yds	Avg	TD	Sfty	TD	Pts
1995 Cincinnati Bengals	16	2	14	2	0.0	0	0	0	0	0	0	-	0	0	0	0

Simon Shanks

Pos: LB **Rnd:** FA **College:** Coahoma Junior College **Ht:** 6' 1" **Wt:** 215 **Born:** 10/16/71 **Age:** 25

Year Team	G	GS	Tackles			Miscellaneous				Interceptions				Totals		
			Tk	Ast	Sack	FF	FR	TD	Blk	Int	Yds	Avg	TD	Sfty	TD	Pts
1995 Arizona Cardinals	15	0	1	0	0.0	0	1	0	0	0	0	-	0	0	0	0

Shannon Sharpe

(statistical profile on page 374)

Pos: TE **Rnd:** 7 **College:** Savannah State **Ht:** 6' 2" **Wt:** 230 **Born:** 6/26/68 **Age:** 28

Year Team	G	GS	Rushing					Receiving					Punt Returns				Kickoff Returns				Totals		
			Att	Yds	Avg	Lg	TD	Rec	Yds	Avg	Lg	TD	Num	Yds	Avg	TD	Num	Yds	Avg	TD	Fum	TD	Pts
1990 Denver Broncos	16	2	0	0	-	-	0	7	99	14.1	33	1	0	0	-	0	0	0	-	0	1	1	6
1991 Denver Broncos	16	9	1	15	15.0	15	0	22	322	14.6	37	1	0	0	-	0	0	0	-	0	0	1	6
1992 Denver Broncos	16	11	2	-6	-3.0	-3	0	53	640	12.1	55	2	0	0	-	0	0	0	-	0	1	2	12
1993 Denver Broncos	16	12	0	0	-	-	0	81	995	12.3	63	9	0	0	-	0	1	0	0.0	0	1	9	54
1994 Denver Broncos	15	13	0	0	-	-	0	87	1010	11.6	44	4	0	0	-	0	0	0	-	0	1	4	28
1995 Denver Broncos	13	12	0	0	-	-	0	63	756	12.0	49	4	0	0	-	0	0	0	-	0	1	4	24
6 NFL Seasons	92	59	3	9	3.0	15	0	313	3822	12.2	63	21	0	0	-	0	1	0	0.0	0	5	21	130

Other Statistics: 1991–recovered 1 fumble for 0 yards. 1994–scored 2 two-point conversions. 1995–recovered 1 fumble for 0 yards.

Terrance Shaw

(statistical profile on page 447)

Pos: CB **Rnd:** 2 **College:** Stephen F. Austin **Ht:** 5' 11" **Wt:** 190 **Born:** 11/11/73 **Age:** 22

Year Team	G	GS	Tackles			Miscellaneous				Interceptions				Totals		
			Tk	Ast	Sack	FF	FR	TD	Blk	Int	Yds	Avg	TD	Sfty	TD	Pts
1995 San Diego Chargers	16	14	53	5	0.0	0	0	0	0	1	31	31.0	0	0	0	0

Elbert Shelley

Pos: CB **Rnd:** 11 **College:** Arkansas State **Ht:** 5' 11" **Wt:** 190 **Born:** 12/24/64 **Age:** 31

Year Team	G	GS	Tackles			Miscellaneous				Interceptions				Punt Returns				Kickoff Returns				Totals	
			Tk	Ast	Sack	FF	FR	TD	Blk	Int	Yds	Avg	TD	Num	Yds	Avg	TD	Num	Yds	Avg	TD	TD	Fum
1987 Atlanta Falcons	4	0	3	0	0.0	0	0	0	0	0	0	-	0	0	0	-	0	0	0	-	0	0	0
1988 Atlanta Falcons	12	0	9	3	0.0	0	0	0	0	0	0	-	0	0	0	-	0	2	5	2.5	0	0	1
1989 Atlanta Falcons	10	0	7	7	0.0	0	0	0	0	1	31	31.0	0	0	0	-	0	0	0	-	0	0	0
1990 Atlanta Falcons	12	0	6	4	0.0	0	1	0	0	0	0	-	0	0	0	-	0	0	0	-	0	0	0
1991 Atlanta Falcons	11	0	7	2	2.0	2	0	0	0	0	0	-	0	0	0	-	0	0	0	-	0	0	0
1992 Atlanta Falcons	13	0	3	1	0.0	0	0	0	0	0	0	-	0	0	0	-	0	0	0	-	0	0	0
1993 Atlanta Falcons	16	0	1	0	0.0	0	0	0	0	0	0	-	0	0	0	-	0	0	0	-	0	0	0
1994 Atlanta Falcons	16	0	0	0	0.0	0	1	0	0	0	0	-	0	0	0	-	0	0	0	-	0	0	0
1995 Atlanta Falcons	13	0	0	0	0.0	0	0	0	0	0	0	-	0	0	0	-	0	0	0	-	0	0	0
9 NFL Seasons	107	0	36	17	2.0	2	2	0	0	1	31	31.0	0	0	0	-	0	2	5	2.5	0	0	1

Chris Shelling

Pos: CB/S **Rnd:** FA **College:** Auburn **Ht:** 5' 10" **Wt:** 180 **Born:** 11/3/72 **Age:** 23

Year Team	G	GS	Tackles			Miscellaneous				Interceptions				Totals		
			Tk	Ast	Sack	FF	FR	TD	Blk	Int	Yds	Avg	TD	Sfty	TD	Pts
1995 Cincinnati Bengals	13	0	15	0	0.0	0	0	0	0	0	0	-	0	0	0	0

Leslie Shepherd

(statistical profile on page 374)

Pos: WR **Rnd:** FA **College:** Temple **Ht:** 5' 11" **Wt:** 189 **Born:** 11/3/69 **Age:** 26

Year Team	G	GS	Rushing					Receiving					Punt Returns				Kickoff Returns				Totals		
			Att	Yds	Avg	Lg	TD	Rec	Yds	Avg	Lg	TD	Num	Yds	Avg	TD	Num	Yds	Avg	TD	Fum	TD	Pts
1994 Washington Redskins	3	0	0	0	-	-	0	1	8	8.0	8	0	0	0	-	0	0	0	-	0	0	0	0
1995 Washington Redskins	14	4	7	63	9.0	26	1	29	486	16.8	t73	2	0	0	-	0	3	85	28.3	0	0	3	18
2 NFL Seasons	17	4	7	63	9.0	26	1	30	494	16.5	t73	2	0	0	-	0	3	85	28.3	0	0	3	18

Other Statistics: 1995–recovered 1 fumble for 0 yards.

Ashley Sheppard

Pos: LB   **Rnd:** 4   **College:** Clemson   **Ht:** 6' 3" **Wt:** 240 **Born:** 1/21/69 **Age:** 27

			Tackles			Miscellaneous				Interceptions				Totals		
Year	Team	G	GS	Tk	Ast	Sack	FF	FR	TD	Blk	Int	Yds	Avg	TD	Sfty	TD	Pts
1993	Minnesota Vikings	10	0	1	0	1.0	0	0	0	0	0	0	-	0	0	0	0
1994	Minnesota Vikings	7	0	2	3	0.5	0	1	0	0	0	0	-	0	0	0	0
1995	Jac - Min - StL	5	0	3	2	0.0	0	0	0	0	0	0	-	0	0	0	0
1995	Jacksonville Jaguars	2	0	3	2	0.0	0	0	0	0	0	0	-	0	0	0	0
	Minnesota Vikings	1	0	0	0	0.0	0	0	0	0	0	0	-	0	0	0	0
	St. Louis Rams	2	0	0	0	0.0	0	0	0	0	0	0	-	0	0	0	0
	3 NFL Seasons	22	0	6	5	1.5	0	1	0	0	0	0	-	0	0	0	0

Mike Sherrard

(statistical profile on page 375)

Pos: WR   **Rnd:** 1 (18)   **College:** UCLA   **Ht:** 6' 2" **Wt:** 187 **Born:** 6/21/63 **Age:** 33

				Rushing				Receiving				Punt Returns				Kickoff Returns				Totals		
Year	Team	G	GS	Att	Yds	Avg	Lg	TD	Rec	Yds	Avg	Lg	TD	Num	Yds	Avg	TD	Num	Yds	Avg	TD	Fum	TD	Pts
1986	Dallas Cowboys	16	4	2	11	5.5	8	0	41	744	18.1	t68	5	0	0	-	0	0	0	-	0	0	5	30
1990	San Francisco 49ers	7	2	0	0	-	-	0	17	264	15.5	43	2	0	0	-	0	0	0	-	0	0	2	12
1991	San Francisco 49ers	16	0	0	0	-	-	0	24	296	12.3	31	2	0	0	-	0	0	0	-	0	0	2	12
1992	San Francisco 49ers	16	8	0	0	-	-	0	38	607	16.0	56	0	0	0	-	0	0	0	-	0	1	1	6
1993	New York Giants	6	5	0	0	-	-	0	24	433	18.0	t55	2	0	0	-	0	0	0	-	0	0	2	12
1994	New York Giants	16	14	1	-10	-10.0	-10	0	53	825	15.6	55	6	0	0	-	0	0	0	-	0	0	6	36
1995	New York Giants	13	13	0	0	-	-	0	44	577	13.1	t57	4	0	0	-	0	0	0	-	0	2	4	24
	7 NFL Seasons	90	46	3	1	0.3	8	0	241	3746	15.5	t68	21	0	0	-	0	0	0	-	0	3	22	132

Other Statistics: 1992–recovered 2 fumbles for 39 yards and 1 touchdown.

Will Shields

Pos: G   **Rnd:** 3   **College:** Nebraska   **Ht:** 6' 3" **Wt:** 300 **Born:** 9/15/71 **Age:** 25

Year	Team	G	GS	Year	Team	G	GS	Year	Team	G	GS		G	GS
1993	Kansas City Chiefs	16	15	1994	Kansas City Chiefs	16	16	1995	Kansas City Chiefs	16	16	3 NFL Seasons	48	47

Other Statistics: 1993–recovered 2 fumbles for 0 yards. 1994–recovered 1 fumble for 0 yards. 1995–recovered 1 fumble for 0 yards.

Heath Shuler

(statistical profile on page 375)

Pos: QB   **Rnd:** 1 (3)   **College:** Tennessee   **Ht:** 6' 2" **Wt:** 221 **Born:** 12/31/71 **Age:** 24

				Passing										Rushing				Miscellaneous			
Year	Team	G	GS	Att	Com	Pct	Yards	Yds/Att	Lg	TD	Int	Int%	Rating	Att	Yds	Avg	Lg	TD	Sckd	Yds	Fum Recv	Yds	Pts
1994	Washington Redskins	11	8	265	120	45.3	1658	6.26	t81	10	12	4.5	59.6	26	103	4.0	26	0	12	83	3	0	-9	0
1995	Washington Redskins	7	5	125	66	52.8	745	5.96	44	3	7	5.6	55.6	18	57	3.2	13	0	13	76	1	1	0	0
	2 NFL Seasons	18	13	390	186	47.7	2403	6.16	t81	13	19	4.9	58.3	44	160	3.6	26	0	25	159	4	1	-9	0

Ricky Siglar

Pos: T   **Rnd:** FA   **College:** San Jose State   **Ht:** 6' 7" **Wt:** 307 **Born:** 6/14/66 **Age:** 30

Year	Team	G	GS	Year	Team	G	GS	Year	Team	G	GS	Year	Team	G	GS
1990	San Francisco 49ers	16	0	1993	Kansas City Chiefs	14	14	1994	Kansas City Chiefs	16	8	1995	Kansas City Chiefs	16	12
													4 NFL Seasons	62	34

Don Silvestri

Pos: K   **Rnd:** FA   **College:** Pittsburgh   **Ht:** 6' 4" **Wt:** 205 **Born:** 12/25/68 **Age:** 27

			Field Goals											PAT		Tot
Year	Team	G	1-29 Yds	Pct	30-39 Yds	Pct	40-49 Yds	Pct	50+ Yds	Pct	Overall	Pct	Long	Made	Att	Pts
1995	New York Jets	16	0-0	-	0-0	-	0-0	-	0-0	-	0-0	-	-	0	0	0

Other Statistics: 1995–punted 5 times for 238 yards.

Tracy Simien

(statistical profile on page 448)

Pos: LB   **Rnd:** FA   **College:** Texas Christian   **Ht:** 6' 1" **Wt:** 250 **Born:** 5/21/67 **Age:** 29

				Tackles			Miscellaneous				Interceptions				Totals		
Year	Team	G	GS	Tk	Ast	Sack	FF	FR	TD	Blk	Int	Yds	Avg	TD	Sfty	TD	Pts
1991	Kansas City Chiefs	15	12	48	32	2.0	0	1	0	0	0	0	-	0	0	0	0
1992	Kansas City Chiefs	15	15	56	41	1.0	0	0	0	0	3	18	6.0	0	0	0	0
1993	Kansas City Chiefs	16	14	68	37	0.0	0	0	0	0	0	0	-	0	0	0	0
1994	Kansas City Chiefs	15	15	58	14	0.0	0	2	0	0	0	0	-	0	0	0	0
1995	Kansas City Chiefs	16	16	64	8	1.0	0	0	0	0	0	0	-	0	0	0	0
	5 NFL Seasons	77	72	294	132	4.0	0	6	0	0	3	18	6.0	0	0	0	0

Clyde Simmons

(statistical profile on page 448)

Pos: DE **Rnd:** 9 **College:** Western Carolina **Ht:** 6' 6" **Wt:** 280 **Born:** 8/4/64 **Age:** 32

Year	Team	G	GS	Tackles			Miscellaneous				Interceptions				Punt Returns				Kickoff Returns				Totals	
				Tk	Ast	Sack	FF	FR	TD	Blk	Int	Yds	Avg	TD	Num	Yds	Avg	TD	Num	Yds	Avg	TD	TD	Fum
1986	Philadelphia Eagles	16	0	3	0	2.0	0	0	0	0	0	0	-	0	0	0	-	0	1	0	0.0	0	0	0
1987	Philadelphia Eagles	12	12	59	16	6.0	1	1	0	0	0	0	-	0	0	0	-	0	0	0	-	0	0	0
1988	Philadelphia Eagles	16	16	64	25	8.0	1	3	1	0	0	0	-	0	0	0	-	0	0	0	-	0	1	0
1989	Philadelphia Eagles	16	16	85	50	15.5	3	0	0	0	1	60	60.0	1	0	0	-	0	0	0	-	0	1	0
1990	Philadelphia Eagles	16	16	69	40	7.5	1	2	1	0	0	0	-	0	0	0	-	0	0	0	-	0	1	0
1991	Philadelphia Eagles	16	16	75	40	13.0	2	3	1	0	0	0	-	0	0	0	-	0	0	0	-	0	1	0
1992	Philadelphia Eagles	16	16	69	27	**19.0**	2	1	0	0	0	0	-	0	0	0	-	0	0	0	-	0	0	0
1993	Philadelphia Eagles	16	16	64	34	5.0	2	0	0	0	1	0	0.0	0	0	0	-	0	0	0	-	0	0	0
1994	Arizona Cardinals	16	16	33	12	6.0	0	0	0	0	0	0	-	0	0	0	-	0	0	0	-	0	0	0
1995	Arizona Cardinals	16	16	40	14	11.0	6	1	0	1	1	25	25.0	1	0	0	-	0	0	0	-	0	1	0
	10 NFL Seasons	156	140	561	258	93.0	18	11	3	1	3	85	28.3	2	0	0	-	0	1	0	0.0	0	5	0

Other Statistics: 1988–credited with 1 safety.

Ed Simmons

Pos: T **Rnd:** 6 **College:** Eastern Washington **Ht:** 6' 5" **Wt:** 325 **Born:** 12/31/63 **Age:** 32

Year	Team	G	GS	Year	Team	G	GS	Year	Team	G	GS		G	GS
1987	Washington Redskins	6	3	1990	Washington Redskins	13	11	1993	Washington Redskins	13	13			
1988	Washington Redskins	16	0	1991	Washington Redskins	6	2	1994	Washington Redskins	16	16			
1989	Washington Redskins	16	8	1992	Washington Redskins	16	11	1995	Washington Redskins	16	16	9 NFL Seasons	118	80

Other Statistics: 1993–recovered 1 fumble for 0 yards. 1995–recovered 2 fumbles for 0 yards.

Wayne Simmons

(statistical profile on page 448)

Pos: LB **Rnd:** 1 (15) **College:** Clemson **Ht:** 6' 2" **Wt:** 248 **Born:** 12/15/69 **Age:** 26

Year	Team	G	GS	Tackles			Miscellaneous				Interceptions				Totals		
				Tk	Ast	Sack	FF	FR	TD	Blk	Int	Yds	Avg	TD	Sfty	TD	Pts
1993	Green Bay Packers	14	8	18	16	1.0	0	1	0	0	2	21	10.5	0	0	0	0
1994	Green Bay Packers	12	1	8	5	0.0	0	0	0	0	0	0	-	0	0	0	0
1995	Green Bay Packers	16	16	68	23	4.0	1	1	0	0	0	0	-	0	0	0	0
	3 NFL Seasons	42	25	94	44	5.0	1	2	0	0	2	21	10.5	0	0	0	0

Carl Simpson

Pos: DT/DE **Rnd:** 2 **College:** Florida State **Ht:** 6' 2" **Wt:** 298 **Born:** 4/18/70 **Age:** 26

Year	Team	G	GS	Tackles			Miscellaneous				Interceptions				Totals		
				Tk	Ast	Sack	FF	FR	TD	Blk	Int	Yds	Avg	TD	Sfty	TD	Pts
1993	Chicago Bears	11	0	2	5	0.5	0	0	0	0	0	0	-	0	0	0	0
1994	Chicago Bears	15	8	16	9	0.0	0	0	0	0	0	0	-	0	0	0	0
1995	Chicago Bears	16	8	14	6	1.0	1	2	0	0	0	0	-	0	0	0	0
	3 NFL Seasons	42	16	32	20	1.5	1	2	0	0	0	0	-	0	0	0	0

Joe Sims

Pos: T **Rnd:** 11 **College:** Nebraska **Ht:** 6' 3" **Wt:** 310 **Born:** 3/1/69 **Age:** 27

Year	Team	G	GS	Year	Team	G	GS	Year	Team	G	GS		G	GS
1991	Atlanta Falcons	6	0	1993	Green Bay Packers	13	5	1995	Green Bay Packers	4	1			
1992	Green Bay Packers	15	0	1994	Green Bay Packers	15	15					5 NFL Seasons	53	21

Other Statistics: 1992–returned 1 kickoff for 11 yards.

Keith Sims

Pos: G **Rnd:** 2 **College:** Iowa State **Ht:** 6' 3" **Wt:** 309 **Born:** 6/17/67 **Age:** 29

Year	Team	G	GS	Year	Team	G	GS	Year	Team	G	GS		G	GS
1990	Miami Dolphins	14	13	1992	Miami Dolphins	16	16	1994	Miami Dolphins	16	16			
1991	Miami Dolphins	12	12	1993	Miami Dolphins	16	16	1995	Miami Dolphins	16	16	6 NFL Seasons	90	89

Other Statistics: 1990–recovered 1 fumble for 0 yards; returned 1 kickoff for 9 yards. 1991–caught 1 pass for 9 yards. 1993–recovered 1 fumble for 0 yards. 1994–recovered 2 fumbles for 0 yards. 1995–recovered 1 fumble for 0 yards.

Michael Sinclair

(statistical profile on page 449)

Pos: DE **Rnd:** 6 **College:** Eastern New Mexico **Ht:** 6' 4" **Wt:** 271 **Born:** 1/31/68 **Age:** 28

Year	Team	G	GS	Tackles			Miscellaneous				Interceptions				Totals		
				Tk	Ast	Sack	FF	FR	TD	Blk	Int	Yds	Avg	TD	Sfty	TD	Pts
1992	Seattle Seahawks	12	1	9	1	1.0	0	0	0	0	0	0	-	0	0	0	0
1993	Seattle Seahawks	9	1	12	-	8.0	1	0	0	0	0	0	-	0	0	0	0
1994	Seattle Seahawks	12	3	10	2	4.5	0	0	0	0	0	0	-	0	0	0	0
1995	Seattle Seahawks	16	15	37	9	5.5	2	0	0	0	0	0	-	0	0	0	0

Year Team	G	GS	Tackles			Miscellaneous				Interceptions				Totals		
			Tk	Ast	Sack	FF	FR	TD	Blk	Int	Yds	Avg	TD	Sfty	TD	Pts
4 NFL Seasons	49	20	68	12	19.0	3	2	0	0	0	0	-	0	0	0	0

Chris Singleton
(statistical profile on page 449)

Pos: LB **Rnd:** 1 (8) **College:** Arizona   **Ht:** 6' 2" **Wt:** 246 **Born:** 2/20/67 **Age:** 29

Year Team	G	GS	Tackles			Miscellaneous				Interceptions				Totals		
			Tk	Ast	Sack	FF	FR	TD	Blk	Int	Yds	Avg	TD	Sfty	TD	Pts
1990 New England Patriots	13	4	20	8	3.0	0	0	0	0	0	0	-	0	0	0	0
1991 New England Patriots	12	11	41	19	1.0	0	1	0	0	0	0	-	0	0	0	0
1992 New England Patriots	8	7	27	11	0.0	0	0	0	0	1	82	82.0	1	0	1	6
1993 NE - Mia	17	4	18	8	0.0	0	0	0	0	0	0	-	0	0	0	0
1994 Miami Dolphins	11	11	42	16	2.0	0	2	0	1	0	0	-	0	0	0	0
1995 Miami Dolphins	16	15	56	26	1.0	2	2	0	0	1	3	3.0	0	0	0	0
1993 New England Patriots	8	4	18	8	0.0	0	0	0	0	0	0	-	0	0	0	0
Miami Dolphins	9	0	0	0	0.0	0	0	0	0	0	0	-	0	0	0	0
6 NFL Seasons	77	52	204	88	7.0	2	5	0	1	2	85	42.5	1	0	1	6

Nate Singleton

Pos: WR **Rnd:** 11 **College:** Grambling   **Ht:** 5' 11" **Wt:** 190 **Born:** 7/5/68 **Age:** 28

Year Team	G	GS	Rushing					Receiving					Punt Returns				Kickoff Returns				Totals		
			Att	Yds	Avg	Lg	TD	Rec	Yds	Avg	Lg	TD	Num	Yds	Avg	TD	Num	Yds	Avg	TD	Fum	TD	Pts
1993 San Francisco 49ers	16	0	0	0	-	-	0	8	126	15.8	33	1	0	0	-	0	0	0	-	0	0	1	6
1994 San Francisco 49ers	16	1	0	0	-	-	0	21	294	14.0	t43	2	2	13	6.5	0	2	23	11.5	0	0	2	12
1995 San Francisco 49ers	6	2	0	0	-	-	0	8	108	13.5	23	1	5	27	5.4	0	0	0	-	0	1	1	6
3 NFL Seasons	38	3	0	0	-	-	0	37	528	14.3	t43	4	7	40	5.7	0	2	23	11.5	0	1	4	24

Other Statistics: 1995–recovered 1 fumble for 0 yards.

Tony Siragusa

Pos: DT **Rnd:** FA **College:** Pittsburgh   **Ht:** 6' 3" **Wt:** 315 **Born:** 5/14/67 **Age:** 29

Year Team	G	GS	Tackles			Miscellaneous				Interceptions				Totals		
			Tk	Ast	Sack	FF	FR	TD	Blk	Int	Yds	Avg	TD	Sfty	TD	Pts
1990 Indianapolis Colts	13	6	24	12	1.0	0	1	0	0	0	0	-	0	0	0	0
1991 Indianapolis Colts	13	6	24	22	2.0	0	1	0	0	0	0	-	0	0	0	0
1992 Indianapolis Colts	16	12	47	18	3.0	0	1	0	0	0	0	-	0	0	0	0
1993 Indianapolis Colts	14	14	51	25	1.5	1	0	0	0	0	0	-	0	0	0	0
1994 Indianapolis Colts	16	16	62	26	5.0	2	1	0	0	0	0	-	0	0	0	0
1995 Indianapolis Colts	14	14	41	8	2.0	1	0	0	1	0	0	-	0	0	0	0
6 NFL Seasons	86	68	249	111	14.5	4	4	0	1	0	0	-	0	0	0	0

Greg Skrepenak

Pos: T **Rnd:** 2 **College:** Michigan   **Ht:** 6' 6" **Wt:** 315 **Born:** 1/31/70 **Age:** 26

Year	Team	G	GS	Year	Team	G	GS	Year	Team	G	GS			G	GS
1992	Los Angeles Raiders	10	0	1994	Los Angeles Raiders	12	10	1995	Oakland Raiders	14	14	3 NFL Seasons		36	24

Chris Slade
(statistical profile on page 449)

Pos: LB **Rnd:** 2 **College:** Virginia   **Ht:** 6' 5" **Wt:** 242 **Born:** 1/30/71 **Age:** 25

Year Team	G	GS	Tackles			Miscellaneous				Interceptions				Totals		
			Tk	Ast	Sack	FF	FR	TD	Blk	Int	Yds	Avg	TD	Sfty	TD	Pts
1993 New England Patriots	16	5	25	13	9.0	3	1	0	0	0	0	-	0	0	0	0
1994 New England Patriots	16	16	63	42	9.5	4	0	0	0	0	0	-	0	0	0	0
1995 New England Patriots	16	16	71	24	4.0	1	2	0	0	0	0	-	1	0	1	6
3 NFL Seasons	48	37	159	79	22.5	8	3	0	0	0	0	-	1	0	1	6

Jackie Slater

Pos: T **Rnd:** 3 **College:** Jackson State   **Ht:** 6' 4" **Wt:** 287 **Born:** 5/27/54 **Age:** 42

Year	Team	G	GS	Year	Team	G	GS	Year	Team	G	GS	Year	Team	G	GS
1976	Los Angeles Rams	14	0	1981	Los Angeles Rams	11	11	1986	Los Angeles Rams	16	16	1991	Los Angeles Rams	13	13
1977	Los Angeles Rams	14	1	1982	Los Angeles Rams	9	9	1987	Los Angeles Rams	12	12	1992	Los Angeles Rams	16	16
1978	Los Angeles Rams	16	0	1983	Los Angeles Rams	16	16	1988	Los Angeles Rams	16	16	1993	Los Angeles Rams	8	8
1979	Los Angeles Rams	16	16	1984	Los Angeles Rams	7	7	1989	Los Angeles Rams	16	16	1994	Los Angeles Rams	12	7
1980	Los Angeles Rams	15	15	1985	Los Angeles Rams	16	16	1990	Los Angeles Rams	15	15	1995	St. Louis Rams	1	1
													20 NFL Seasons	259	211

Other Statistics: 1978–recovered 1 fumble for 0 yards. 1980–recovered 1 fumble for 0 yards. 1983–recovered 1 fumble for 13 yards. 1985–recovered 1 fumble for 0 yards.

Webster Slaughter

(statistical profile on page 376)

Pos: WR **Rnd:** 2 **College:** San Diego State **Ht:** 6' 1" **Wt:** 175 **Born:** 10/19/64 **Age:** 32

			Rushing				Receiving				Punt Returns				Kickoff Returns				Totals		
Year Team	G	GS	Att	Yds	Avg	Lg TD	Rec	Yds	Avg	Lg TD	Num	Yds	Avg TD	Num	Yds	Avg TD	Fum	TD	Pts
1986 Cleveland Browns	16	16	1	1	1.0	1 0	40	577	14.4	t47 4	1	2	2.0 0	0	0	- 0	1	5	30
1987 Cleveland Browns	12	12	0	0	-	- 0	47	806	17.1	t54 7	0	0	- 0	0	0	- 0	1	7	42
1988 Cleveland Browns	8	8	0	0	-	- 0	30	462	15.4	41 3	0	0	- 0	0	0	- 0	1	3	18
1989 Cleveland Browns	16	16	0	0	-	- 0	65	1236	19.0	t97 6	0	0	- 0	0	0	- 0	2	6	36
1990 Cleveland Browns	16	16	5	29	5.8	17 0	59	847	14.4	50 4	0	0	- 0	0	0	- 0	2	4	24
1991 Cleveland Browns	16	16	0	0	-	- 0	64	906	14.2	t62 3	17	112	6.6 0	0	0	- 0	1	3	18
1992 Houston Oilers	12	9	3	20	6.7	10 0	39	486	12.5	t36 4	20	142	7.1 0	1	21	21.0 0	3	4	24
1993 Houston Oilers	14	14	0	0	-	- 0	77	904	11.7	41 5	0	0	- 0	0	0	- 0	4	5	30
1994 Houston Oilers	16	12	0	0	-	- 0	68	846	12.4	57 2	0	0	- 0	0	0	- 0	2	2	12
1995 Kansas City Chiefs	16	7	0	0	-	- 0	34	514	15.1	38 4	0	0	- 0	0	0	- 0	0	4	24
10 NFL Seasons	142	126	9	50	5.6	17 0	523	7584	14.5	t97 42	38	256	6.7 0	1	21	21.0 0	17	43	258

Other Statistics: 1986–recovered 1 fumble for 0 yards and 1 touchdown. 1992–recovered 2 fumbles for 0 yards. 1994–recovered 1 fumble for 0 yards.

David Sloan

Pos: TE **Rnd:** 3 **College:** New Mexico **Ht:** 6' 6" **Wt:** 254 **Born:** 6/8/72 **Age:** 24

			Rushing				Receiving				Punt Returns				Kickoff Returns				Totals		
Year Team	G	GS	Att	Yds	Avg	Lg TD	Rec	Yds	Avg	Lg TD	Num	Yds	Avg TD	Num	Yds	Avg TD	Fum	TD	Pts
1995 Detroit Lions	16	8	0	0	-	- 0	17	184	10.8	24 1	0	0	- 0	1	14	14.0 0	0	1	6

Torrance Small

(statistical profile on page 376)

Pos: WR **Rnd:** 5 **College:** Alcorn State **Ht:** 6' 3" **Wt:** 201 **Born:** 9/6/70 **Age:** 26

			Rushing				Receiving				Punt Returns				Kickoff Returns				Totals		
Year Team	G	GS	Att	Yds	Avg	Lg TD	Rec	Yds	Avg	Lg TD	Num	Yds	Avg TD	Num	Yds	Avg TD	Fum	TD	Pts
1992 New Orleans Saints	13	2	0	0	-	- 0	23	278	12.1	33 3	0	0	- 0	0	0	- 0	0	3	18
1993 New Orleans Saints	11	0	0	0	-	- 0	16	164	10.3	17 1	0	0	- 0	0	0	- 0	0	1	6
1994 New Orleans Saints	16	0	0	0	-	- 0	49	719	14.7	t75 5	0	0	- 0	0	0	- 0	0	5	32
1995 New Orleans Saints	16	1	6	75	12.5	t44 1	38	461	12.1	t32 5	0	0	- 0	0	0	- 0	0	6	36
4 NFL Seasons	56	3	6	75	12.5	t44 1	126	1622	12.9	t75 14	0	0	- 0	0	0	- 0	0	15	92

Other Statistics: 1994–recovered 1 fumble for 1 yard; scored 1 two-point conversion. 1995–recovered 1 fumble for 0 yards.

Joel Smeenge

(statistical profile on page 450)

Pos: DE/LB **Rnd:** 3 **College:** Western Michigan **Ht:** 6' 6" **Wt:** 260 **Born:** 4/1/68 **Age:** 28

			Tackles			Miscellaneous				Interceptions				Totals		
Year Team	G	GS	Tk	Ast	Sack	FF	FR	TD	Blk	Int	Yds	Avg	TD	Sfty	TD	Pts
1990 New Orleans Saints	15	0	1	0	0.0	0	0	0	0	0	0	-	0	0	0	0
1991 New Orleans Saints	14	0	2	0	0.0	0	1	0	0	0	0	-	0	0	0	0
1992 New Orleans Saints	11	0	5	2	0.5	0	1	0	0	0	0	-	0	0	0	0
1993 New Orleans Saints	16	2	13	2	1.0	0	0	0	0	0	0	-	0	0	0	0
1994 New Orleans Saints	16	2	6	2	0.0	0	0	0	0	0	0	-	0	0	0	0
1995 Jacksonville Jaguars	15	15	31	7	4.0	4	0	0	0	1	12	12.0	0	0	0	0
6 NFL Seasons	87	19	58	13	5.5	4	2	0	0	1	12	12.0	0	0	0	0

Other Statistics: 1995–fumbled 1 time for 0 yards.

Al Smith

Pos: LB **Rnd:** 6 **College:** Utah State **Ht:** 6' 1" **Wt:** 244 **Born:** 11/26/64 **Age:** 31

			Tackles			Miscellaneous				Interceptions				Totals		
Year Team	G	GS	Tk	Ast	Sack	FF	FR	TD	Blk	Int	Yds	Avg	TD	Sfty	TD	Pts
1987 Houston Oilers	12	11	44	56	0.0	0	0	0	0	0	0	-	0	0	0	0
1988 Houston Oilers	16	16	59	39	0.0	1	1	0	0	0	0	-	0	0	0	0
1989 Houston Oilers	15	15	51	25	0.0	2	1	0	0	0	0	-	0	0	0	0
1990 Houston Oilers	15	15	78	26	0.0	3	1	0	0	0	0	-	0	0	0	0
1991 Houston Oilers	16	16	101	45	1.0	2	1	1	0	1	16	16.0	0	0	1	6
1992 Houston Oilers	16	16	70	52	1.0	0	0	0	0	1	26	26.0	0	0	0	0
1993 Houston Oilers	16	16	67	28	0.0	0	0	0	0	0	0	-	0	0	0	0
1994 Houston Oilers	16	16	88	44	2.5	0	1	0	0	0	0	-	0	0	0	0
1995 Houston Oilers	2	2	4	2	0.0	0	0	0	0	0	0	-	0	0	0	0
9 NFL Seasons	124	123	562	317	5.5	8	5	1	0	2	42	21.0	0	0	1	6

Other Statistics: 1992–fumbled 1 time for 0 yards.

Anthony Smith

Pos: DE **Rnd:** 1 (11) **College:** Arizona **Ht:** 6' 3" **Wt:** 265 **Born:** 6/28/67 **Age:** 29

Year	Team	G	GS	Tk	Ast	Sack	FF	FR	TD	Blk	Int	Yds	Avg	TD	Sfty	TD	Pts
1991	Los Angeles Raiders	16	2	0	-	10.5	0	1	0	0	0	0	-	0	0	0	0
1992	Los Angeles Raiders	15	1	31	-	13.0	6	0	0	0	0	0	-	0	0	0	0
1993	Los Angeles Raiders	16	2	39	13	12.5	1	0	0	0	0	0	-	0	0	0	0
1994	Los Angeles Raiders	16	16	34	13	6.0	0	1	1	0	0	0	-	0	0	1	6
1995	Oakland Raiders	16	11	28	14	7.0	1	3	0	0	0	0	-	0	0	0	0
	5 NFL Seasons	79	32	132	40	49.0	8	5	1	0	0	0	-	0	0	1	6

Artie Smith

Pos: DE/DT **Rnd:** 5 **College:** Louisiana Tech **Ht:** 6' 4" **Wt:** 285 **Born:** 5/15/70 **Age:** 26

Year	Team	G	GS	Tk	Ast	Sack	FF	FR	TD	Blk	Int	Yds	Avg	TD	Sfty	TD	Pts
1993	San Francisco 49ers	16	6	13	2	1.5	0	0	0	0	0	0	-	0	0	0	0
1994	SF - Cin	9	0	3	0	0.0	0	0	0	0	0	0	-	0	0	0	0
1995	Cincinnati Bengals	16	16	38	6	2.0	2	0	0	0	0	0	-	0	0	0	0
1994	San Francisco 49ers	2	0	1	0	0.0	0	0	0	0	0	0	-	0	0	0	0
	Cincinnati Bengals	7	0	2	0	0.0	0	0	0	0	0	0	-	0	0	0	0
	3 NFL Seasons	41	22	54	8	3.5	2	0	0	0	0	0	-	0	0	0	0

Ben Smith

Pos: CB **Rnd:** 1 (22) **College:** Georgia **Ht:** 5' 11" **Wt:** 185 **Born:** 5/14/67 **Age:** 29

Year	Team	G	GS	Tk	Ast	Sack	FF	FR	TD	Blk	Int	Yds	Avg	TD	Sfty	TD	Pts
1990	Philadelphia Eagles	16	13	62	29	0.0	0	0	0	0	3	1	0.3	0	0	0	0
1991	Philadelphia Eagles	10	10	24	10	0.0	0	0	0	0	2	6	3.0	0	0	0	0
1993	Philadelphia Eagles	13	3	26	14	0.0	0	0	0	0	0	0	-	0	0	0	0
1994	Denver Broncos	14	14	63	9	0.0	0	0	0	0	1	0	0.0	0	0	0	0
1995	Arizona Cardinals	2	0	1	0	0.0	0	0	0	0	0	0	-	0	0	0	0
	5 NFL Seasons	55	40	176	62	0.0	0	0	0	0	6	7	1.2	0	0	0	0

Bruce Smith

(statistical profile on page 450)

Pos: DE **Rnd:** 1 (1) **College:** Virginia Tech **Ht:** 6' 4" **Wt:** 273 **Born:** 6/18/63 **Age:** 33

Year	Team	G	GS	Tk	Ast	Sack	FF	FR	TD	Blk	Int	Yds	Avg	TD	Sfty	TD	Pts
1985	Buffalo Bills	16	13	32	16	6.5	0	4	0	0	0	0	-	0	0	0	0
1986	Buffalo Bills	16	15	36	27	15.0	3	0	0	0	0	0	-	0	0	0	0
1987	Buffalo Bills	12	12	60	18	12.0	3	2	1	0	0	0	-	0	0	1	6
1988	Buffalo Bills	12	12	39	17	11.0	3	0	0	0	0	0	-	0	1	0	2
1989	Buffalo Bills	16	16	66	22	13.0	0	0	0	0	0	0	-	0	0	0	0
1990	Buffalo Bills	16	16	82	19	19.0	4	0	0	0	0	0	-	0	0	0	0
1991	Buffalo Bills	5	5	13	5	1.5	0	0	0	0	0	0	-	0	0	0	0
1992	Buffalo Bills	15	15	66	23	14.0	3	0	0	0	0	0	-	0	0	0	0
1993	Buffalo Bills	16	16	87	21	14.0	3	1	0	0	1	0	0.0	0	0	0	0
1994	Buffalo Bills	15	15	57	24	10.0	5	2	0	0	1	0	0.0	0	0	0	0
1995	Buffalo Bills	15	15	52	22	10.5	1	1	0	0	0	0	-	0	0	0	0
	11 NFL Seasons	154	150	590	214	126.5	25	10	1	0	2	0	0.0	0	1	1	8

Other Statistics: 1985–rushed 1 time for 0 yards.

Cedric Smith

Pos: RB **Rnd:** 5 **College:** Florida **Ht:** 5' 10" **Wt:** 237 **Born:** 5/27/68 **Age:** 28

Year	Team	G	GS	Att	Yds	Avg	Lg	TD	Rec	Yds	Avg	Lg	TD	Num	Yds	Avg	TD	Num	Yds	Avg	TD	Fum	TD	Pts
1990	Minnesota Vikings	15	1	9	19	2.1	7	0	0	0	-	-	0	0	0	-	0	1	16	16.0	0	0	0	0
1991	New Orleans Saints	6	0	0	0	-	-	0	0	0	-	-	0	0	0	-	0	0	0	-	0	0	0	0
1994	Washington Redskins	14	8	10	48	4.8	13	0	15	118	7.9	28	1	0	0	-	0	0	0	-	0	1	1	6
1995	Washington Redskins	6	0	3	13	4.3	5	0	0	0	-	-	0	0	0	-	0	0	0	-	0	0	0	0
	4 NFL Seasons	41	9	22	80	3.6	13	0	15	118	7.9	28	1	0	0	-	0	1	16	16.0	0	1	1	6

Chuck Smith

(statistical profile on page 450)

Pos: DE **Rnd:** 2 **College:** Tennessee **Ht:** 6' 2" **Wt:** 257 **Born:** 12/21/69 **Age:** 26

Year	Team	G	GS	Tk	Ast	Sack	FF	FR	TD	Blk	Int	Yds	Avg	TD	Sfty	TD	Pts
1992	Atlanta Falcons	16	0	13	17	2.0	0	0	0	0	0	0	-	0	0	0	0

222

			Tackles			Miscellaneous				Interceptions				Totals		
Year Team	G	GS	Tk	Ast	Sack	FF	FR	TD	Blk	Int	Yds	Avg	TD	Sfty	TD	Pts
1993 Atlanta Falcons	15	1	16	14	3.5	4	2	0	0	0	0	-	0	0	0	0
1994 Atlanta Falcons	15	10	26	5	11.0	1	2	0	0	1	36	36.0	1	0	1	6
1995 Atlanta Falcons	14	13	34	6	5.5	4	2	0	0	0	0	-	0	0	0	0
4 NFL Seasons	60	24	89	42	22.0	9	6	0	0	1	36	36.0	1	0	1	6

Darrin Smith

Pos: LB   **Rnd:** 2   **College:** Miami (FL)   **Ht:** 6' 1" **Wt:** 230 **Born:** 4/15/70 **Age:** 26

			Tackles			Miscellaneous				Interceptions				Totals		
Year Team	G	GS	Tk	Ast	Sack	FF	FR	TD	Blk	Int	Yds	Avg	TD	Sfty	TD	Pts
1993 Dallas Cowboys	16	13	49	44	1.0	0	1	0	0	0	0	-	0	0	0	0
1994 Dallas Cowboys	16	16	46	21	4.0	0	2	0	0	2	13	6.5	1	0	1	6
1995 Dallas Cowboys	9	9	40	6	3.0	0	1	0	0	0	0	-	0	0	0	0
3 NFL Seasons	41	38	135	71	8.0	0	4	0	0	2	13	6.5	1	0	1	6

Emmitt Smith

(statistical profile on page 377)

Pos: RB   **Rnd:** 1 (17)   **College:** Florida   **Ht:** 5' 9" **Wt:** 209 **Born:** 5/15/69 **Age:** 27

			Rushing					Receiving					Punt Returns				Kickoff Returns				Totals		
Year Team	G	GS	Att	Yds	Avg	Lg	TD	Rec	Yds	Avg	Lg	TD	Num	Yds	Avg	TD	Num	Yds	Avg	TD	Fum	TD	Pts
1990 Dallas Cowboys	16	15	241	937	3.9	48	11	24	228	9.5	57	0	0	0	-	0	0	0	-	0	7	11	66
1991 Dallas Cowboys	16	16	365	1563	4.3	t75	12	49	258	5.3	14	1	0	0	-	0	0	0	-	0	8	13	78
1992 Dallas Cowboys	16	16	373	1713	4.6	t68	18	59	335	5.7	t26	1	0	0	-	0	0	0	-	0	4	19	114
1993 Dallas Cowboys	14	13	283	1486	5.3	t62	9	57	414	7.3	86	1	0	0	-	0	0	0	-	0	4	10	60
1994 Dallas Cowboys	15	15	368	1484	4.0	46	21	50	341	6.8	68	1	0	0	-	0	0	0	-	0	1	22	132
1995 Dallas Cowboys	16	16	377	1773	4.7	t60	25	62	375	6.0	40	0	0	0	-	0	0	0	-	0	7	25	150
6 NFL Seasons	93	91	2007	8956	4.5	t75	96	301	1951	6.5	86	4	0	0	-	0	0	0	-	0	31	100	600

Other Statistics: 1991–recovered 1 fumble for 0 yards. 1992–recovered 1 fumble for 0 yards. 1993–recovered 3 fumbles for 0 yards.

Fernando Smith

Pos: DE   **Rnd:** 2   **College:** Jackson State   **Ht:** 6' 6" **Wt:** 276 **Born:** 8/2/71 **Age:** 25

			Tackles			Miscellaneous				Interceptions				Totals		
Year Team	G	GS	Tk	Ast	Sack	FF	FR	TD	Blk	Int	Yds	Avg	TD	Sfty	TD	Pts
1994 Minnesota Vikings	7	0	3	1	0.0	0	0	0	0	0	0	-	0	0	0	0
1995 Minnesota Vikings	12	1	5	3	2.5	1	0	0	2	0	0	-	0	0	0	0
2 NFL Seasons	19	1	8	4	2.5	1	0	0	2	0	0	-	0	0	0	0

Frankie Smith

Pos: CB   **Rnd:** 4   **College:** Baylor   **Ht:** 5' 9" **Wt:** 182 **Born:** 10/8/68 **Age:** 28

			Tackles			Miscellaneous				Interceptions				Totals		
Year Team	G	GS	Tk	Ast	Sack	FF	FR	TD	Blk	Int	Yds	Avg	TD	Sfty	TD	Pts
1993 Miami Dolphins	5	1	9	0	0.0	0	0	0	0	0	0	-	0	0	0	0
1994 Miami Dolphins	13	2	21	7	1.0	0	0	0	0	0	0	-	0	0	0	0
1995 Miami Dolphins	11	1	15	2	0.0	0	0	0	0	0	0	-	0	0	0	0
3 NFL Seasons	29	4	45	9	1.0	0	0	0	0	0	0	-	0	0	0	0

Herman Smith

Pos: DE   **Rnd:** FA   **College:** Portland State   **Ht:** 6' 5" **Wt:** 261 **Born:** 1/25/71 **Age:** 25

			Tackles			Miscellaneous				Interceptions				Totals		
Year Team	G	GS	Tk	Ast	Sack	FF	FR	TD	Blk	Int	Yds	Avg	TD	Sfty	TD	Pts
1995 Tampa Bay Buccaneers	3	0	0	1	0.0	0	0	0	0	0	0	-	0	0	0	0

Irv Smith

(statistical profile on page 377)

Pos: TE/RB   **Rnd:** 1 (20)   **College:** Notre Dame   **Ht:** 6' 3" **Wt:** 246 **Born:** 10/13/71 **Age:** 25

			Rushing					Receiving					Punt Returns				Kickoff Returns				Totals		
Year Team	G	GS	Att	Yds	Avg	Lg	TD	Rec	Yds	Avg	Lg	TD	Num	Yds	Avg	TD	Num	Yds	Avg	TD	Fum	TD	Pts
1993 New Orleans Saints	16	8	0	0	-	-	0	16	180	11.3	23	2	0	0	-	0	0	0	-	0	1	2	12
1994 New Orleans Saints	16	16	0	0	-	-	0	41	330	8.0	19	3	0	0	-	0	2	10	5.0	0	0	3	18
1995 New Orleans Saints	16	16	0	0	-	-	0	45	466	10.4	43	3	0	0	-	0	1	6	6.0	0	1	3	20
3 NFL Seasons	48	40	0	0	-	-	0	102	976	9.6	43	8	0	0	-	0	3	16	5.3	0	2	8	50

Other Statistics: 1993–recovered 1 fumble for 0 yards. 1995–scored 1 two-point conversion.

Jimmy Smith

Pos: KR/WR **Rnd:** 2   **College:** Jackson State   **Ht:** 6' 1" **Wt:** 207   **Born:** 2/9/69   **Age:** 27

Year Team	G	GS	Rushing Att	Yds	Avg	Lg	TD	Receiving Rec	Yds	Avg	Lg	TD	Punt Returns Num	Yds	Avg	TD	Kickoff Returns Num	Yds	Avg	TD	Totals Fum	TD	Pts
1992 Dallas Cowboys	7	0	0	0	-	-	0	0	0	-	-	0	0	0	-	0	0	0	-	0	0	0	0
1994 Philadelphia Eagles	1	0	0	0	-	-	0	0	0	-	-	0	0	0	-	0	0	0	-	0	0	0	0
1995 Jacksonville Jaguars	16	4	0	0	-	-	0	22	288	13.1	33	3	0	0	-	0	24	540	22.5	1	2	5	30
3 NFL Seasons	24	4	0	0	-	-	0	22	288	13.1	33	3	0	0	-	0	24	540	22.5	1	2	5	30

Other Statistics: 1995–recovered 1 fumble for 0 yards.

Kevin Smith

Pos: CB   **Rnd:** 1 (17) **College:** Texas A&M   **Ht:** 5' 11" **Wt:** 184   **Born:** 4/7/70   **Age:** 26

Year Team	G	GS	Tackles Tk	Ast	Sack	Misc FF	FR	TD	Blk	Int	Yds	Avg	TD	Punt Ret Num	Yds	Avg	TD	Kickoff Ret Num	Yds	Avg	TD	Totals TD	Fum
1992 Dallas Cowboys	16	6	22	9	0.0	1	0	0	0	2	10	5.0	0	1	17	17.0	0	1	9	9.0	0	0	0
1993 Dallas Cowboys	16	16	73	17	0.0	3	1	0	0	6	56	9.3	1	0	0	-	0	1	33	33.0	0	1	0
1994 Dallas Cowboys	16	16	53	9	0.0	0	0	0	0	2	11	5.5	0	0	0	-	0	0	0	-	0	0	0
1995 Dallas Cowboys	1	1	3	0	0.0	0	0	0	0	0	0	-	0	0	0	-	0	0	0	-	0	0	0
4 NFL Seasons	49	39	151	35	0.0	4	1	0	0	10	77	7.7	1	1	17	17.0	0	2	42	21.0	0	1	0

Lamar Smith

Pos: RB   **Rnd:** 3   **College:** Houston   **Ht:** 5' 11" **Wt:** 224   **Born:** 11/29/70 **Age:** 25

Year Team	G	GS	Rushing Att	Yds	Avg	Lg	TD	Receiving Rec	Yds	Avg	Lg	TD	Punt Returns Num	Yds	Avg	TD	Kickoff Returns Num	Yds	Avg	TD	Totals Fum	TD	Pts
1994 Seattle Seahawks	2	0	2	-1	-0.5	0	0	0	0	-	-	0	0	0	-	0	0	0	-	0	0	0	0
1995 Seattle Seahawks	13	0	36	215	6.0	68	0	1	10	10.0	10	0	0	0	-	0	1	20	20.0	0	1	0	0
2 NFL Seasons	15	0	38	214	5.6	68	0	1	10	10.0	10	0	0	0	-	0	1	20	20.0	0	1	0	0

Lance Smith

Pos: G   **Rnd:** 3   **College:** Louisiana State   **Ht:** 6' 3" **Wt:** 290   **Born:** 1/1/63   **Age:** 33

Year	Team	G	GS	Year	Team	G	GS	Year	Team	G	GS	Year	Team	G	GS
1985	St. Louis Cardinals	14	5	1988	Phoenix Cardinals	16	16	1991	Phoenix Cardinals	16	16	1994	New York Giants	13	13
1986	St. Louis Cardinals	15	13	1989	Phoenix Cardinals	16	16	1992	Phoenix Cardinals	16	16	1995	New York Giants	13	13
1987	St. Louis Cardinals	15	15	1990	Phoenix Cardinals	16	16	1993	Phoenix Cardinals	16	16	11 NFL Seasons		166	155

Other Statistics: 1985–recovered 1 fumble for 0 yards. 1989–recovered 1 fumble for 0 yards. 1991–recovered 2 fumbles for 5 yards. 1992–recovered 1 fumble for 0 yards; returned 2 kickoffs for 16 yards. 1993–recovered 2 fumbles for 0 yards; returned 1 kickoff for 11 yards.

Neil Smith

(statistical profile on page 451)

Pos: DE   **Rnd:** 1 (2)   **College:** Nebraska   **Ht:** 6' 4" **Wt:** 273   **Born:** 4/10/66   **Age:** 30

Year Team	G	GS	Tackles Tk	Ast	Sack	Misc FF	FR	TD	Blk	Int	Yds	Avg	TD	Totals Sfty	TD	Pts
1988 Kansas City Chiefs	13	7	31	22	2.5	1	0	0	0	0	0	-	0	0	0	0
1989 Kansas City Chiefs	15	15	50	17	6.5	4	2	1	0	0	0	-	0	0	1	6
1990 Kansas City Chiefs	16	15	51	17	9.5	4	1	0	0	0	0	-	0	0	0	0
1991 Kansas City Chiefs	16	16	41	24	8.0	3	2	0	0	0	0	-	0	0	0	0
1992 Kansas City Chiefs	16	16	62	15	14.5	2	2	0	0	1	22	22.0	1	0	1	6
1993 Kansas City Chiefs	16	15	43	12	15.0	4	3	0	0	1	3	3.0	0	0	0	0
1994 Kansas City Chiefs	14	13	42	4	11.5	5	1	0	0	1	41	41.0	0	0	0	0
1995 Kansas City Chiefs	16	14	42	13	12.0	4	1	0	0	0	0	-	0	0	0	0
8 NFL Seasons	122	111	362	124	79.5	27	12	1	0	3	66	22.0	1	0	2	12

Otis Smith

Pos: CB   **Rnd:** FA   **College:** Missouri   **Ht:** 5' 11" **Wt:** 190   **Born:** 10/22/65 **Age:** 31

Year Team	G	GS	Tackles Tk	Ast	Sack	Misc FF	FR	TD	Blk	Int	Yds	Avg	TD	Punt Ret Num	Yds	Avg	TD	Kickoff Ret Num	Yds	Avg	TD	Totals TD	Fum
1991 Philadelphia Eagles	15	1	7	3	0.0	1	1	0	0	2	74	37.0	1	0	0	-	0	0	0	-	0	1	0
1992 Philadelphia Eagles	16	1	16	8	0.0	1	0	0	0	1	0	0.0	0	0	0	-	0	0	0	-	0	0	0
1993 Philadelphia Eagles	15	0	3	2	0.0	0	0	0	0	1	0	0.0	0	0	9	-	0	0	24	-	0	0	0
1994 Philadelphia Eagles	16	2	19	1	1.0	0	0	0	0	0	0	-	0	0	0	-	0	1	14	14.0	0	0	0
1995 New York Jets	11	10	34	7	0.0	0	0	0	0	6	101	16.8	1	0	0	-	0	1	6	6.0	0	1	0
5 NFL Seasons	73	14	79	21	1.0	2	1	0	0	10	175	17.5	2	0	9	-	0	2	44	22.0	0	2	0

Rico Smith

Pos: WR **Rnd:** 6 **College:** Colorado **Ht:** 6' 0" **Wt:** 185 **Born:** 1/14/69 **Age:** 27

Year Team	G	GS	Rushing					Receiving					Punt Returns				Kickoff Returns				Totals		
			Att	Yds	Avg	Lg	TD	Rec	Yds	Avg	Lg	TD	Num	Yds	Avg	TD	Num	Yds	Avg	TD	Fum	TD	Pts
1992 Cleveland Browns	10	1	0	0	-	-	0	5	64	12.8	21	0	0	0	-	0	0	0	-	0	0	0	0
1993 Cleveland Browns	10	1	0	0	-	-	0	4	55	13.8	17	0	0	0	-	0	1	13	13.0	0	0	0	0
1994 Cleveland Browns	5	4	0	0	-	-	0	2	61	30.5	50	0	0	0	-	0	0	0	-	0	0	0	0
1995 Cleveland Browns	5	2	0	0	-	-	0	13	173	13.3	t29	1	0	0	-	0	0	0	-	0	1	1	6
4 NFL Seasons	30	8	0	0	-	-	0	24	353	14.7	50	1	0	0	-	0	1	13	13.0	0	1	1	6

Robert Smith

(statistical profile on page 378)

Pos: RB **Rnd:** 1 (21) **College:** Ohio State **Ht:** 6' 0" **Wt:** 206 **Born:** 3/4/72 **Age:** 24

Year Team	G	GS	Rushing					Receiving					Punt Returns				Kickoff Returns				Totals		
			Att	Yds	Avg	Lg	TD	Rec	Yds	Avg	Lg	TD	Num	Yds	Avg	TD	Num	Yds	Avg	TD	Fum	TD	Pts
1993 Minnesota Vikings	10	2	82	399	4.9	t26	2	24	111	4.6	12	0	1	4	4.0	0	3	41	13.7	0	0	2	12
1994 Minnesota Vikings	14	0	31	106	3.4	t14	1	15	105	7.0	15	0	0	0	-	0	16	419	26.2	0	0	1	6
1995 Minnesota Vikings	9	7	139	632	4.5	t58	5	7	35	5.0	11	0	0	0	-	0	0	0	-	0	1	5	32
3 NFL Seasons	33	9	252	1137	4.5	t58	8	46	251	5.5	15	0	1	4	4.0	0	19	460	24.2	0	1	8	50

Other Statistics: 1995–scored 1 two-point conversion.

Rod Smith

Pos: CB **Rnd:** 2 **College:** Notre Dame **Ht:** 5' 11" **Wt:** 187 **Born:** 3/12/70 **Age:** 26

Year Team	G	GS	Tackles			Miscellaneous				Interceptions				Punt Returns				Kickoff Returns				Totals	
			Tk	Ast	Sack	FF	FR	TD	Blk	Int	Yds	Avg	TD	Num	Yds	Avg	TD	Num	Yds	Avg	TD	TD	Fum
1992 New England Patriots	16	1	34	9	0.0	0	0	0	0	1	0	0.0	0	0	0	-	0	0	0	-	0	0	0
1993 New England Patriots	16	9	33	10	0.0	1	0	0	0	0	0	-	0	1	0	0.0	0	0	0	-	0	0	0
1994 New England Patriots	16	7	53	8	0.5	0	0	0	0	2	10	5.0	0	0	0	-	0	0	0	-	0	0	0
1995 Carolina Panthers	16	5	34	10	0.0	0	0	0	0	0	0	-	0	0	0	-	0	0	0	-	0	0	0
4 NFL Seasons	64	22	154	37	0.5	1	0	0	0	3	10	3.3	0	1	0	0.0	0	0	0	-	0	0	0

Rod Smith

Pos: WR **Rnd:** FA **College:** Missouri Southern **Ht:** 6' 0" **Wt:** 183 **Born:** 5/15/70 **Age:** 26

Year Team	G	GS	Rushing					Receiving					Punt Returns				Kickoff Returns				Totals		
			Att	Yds	Avg	Lg	TD	Rec	Yds	Avg	Lg	TD	Num	Yds	Avg	TD	Num	Yds	Avg	TD	Fum	TD	Pts
1995 Denver Broncos	16	1	0	0	-	-	0	6	152	25.3	t43	1	0	0	-	0	4	54	13.5	0	0	1	6

Steve Smith

Pos: RB **Rnd:** 3 **College:** Penn State **Ht:** 6' 1" **Wt:** 242 **Born:** 8/30/64 **Age:** 32

Year Team	G	GS	Rushing					Receiving					Punt Returns				Kickoff Returns				Totals		
			Att	Yds	Avg	Lg	TD	Rec	Yds	Avg	Lg	TD	Num	Yds	Avg	TD	Num	Yds	Avg	TD	Fum	TD	Pts
1987 Los Angeles Raiders	7	3	5	18	3.6	15	0	3	46	15.3	32	0	0	0	-	0	0	0	-	0	0	0	0
1988 Los Angeles Raiders	16	6	38	162	4.3	21	3	26	299	11.5	t45	6	0	0	-	0	3	46	15.3	0	1	9	54
1989 Los Angeles Raiders	16	16	117	471	4.0	21	1	19	140	7.4	14	0	0	0	-	0	2	19	9.5	0	2	1	6
1990 Los Angeles Raiders	16	15	81	327	4.0	17	2	4	30	7.5	17	3	0	0	-	0	0	0	-	0	3	5	30
1991 Los Angeles Raiders	16	16	62	265	4.3	19	1	15	130	8.7	t37	1	0	0	-	0	1	0	0.0	0	4	2	12
1992 Los Angeles Raiders	16	15	44	129	2.9	15	0	28	217	7.8	19	1	0	0	-	0	0	0	-	0	0	1	6
1993 Los Angeles Raiders	16	13	47	156	3.3	13	0	18	187	10.4	22	0	0	0	-	0	0	0	-	0	1	0	0
1994 Seattle Seahawks	16	0	26	80	3.1	12	2	11	142	12.9	25	1	0	0	-	0	0	0	-	0	0	3	18
1995 Seattle Seahawks	10	8	9	19	2.1	4	0	7	59	8.4	17	1	0	0	-	0	1	11	11.0	0	0	1	6
9 NFL Seasons	129	92	429	1627	3.8	21	9	131	1250	9.5	t45	13	0	0	-	0	7	76	10.9	0	11	22	132

Other Statistics: 1987–recovered 1 fumble for 0 yards. 1988–recovered 1 fumble for 0 yards. 1989–recovered 1 fumble for 0 yards. 1990–recovered 1 fumble for 0 yards. 1991–recovered 2 fumbles for 0 yards. 1993–recovered 3 fumbles for 0 yards.

Thomas Smith

Pos: CB **Rnd:** 1 (28) **College:** North Carolina **Ht:** 5' 11" **Wt:** 188 **Born:** 12/5/70 **Age:** 25

Year Team	G	GS	Tackles			Miscellaneous				Interceptions				Totals		
			Tk	Ast	Sack	FF	FR	TD	Blk	Int	Yds	Avg	TD	Sfty	TD	Pts
1993 Buffalo Bills	16	1	7	0	0.0	0	1	0	0	0	0	-	0	0	0	0
1994 Buffalo Bills	16	16	41	7	0.0	1	0	0	0	1	4	4.0	0	0	0	0
1995 Buffalo Bills	16	16	37	4	0.0	0	0	0	1	2	23	11.5	0	0	0	0
3 NFL Seasons	48	33	85	11	0.0	1	1	0	1	3	27	9.0	0	0	0	0

Vernice Smith

Pos: G/C **Rnd:** FA **College:** Florida A&M **Ht:** 6' 3" **Wt:** 298 **Born:** 10/24/65 **Age:** 31

Year	Team	G	GS	Year	Team	G	GS	Year	Team	G	GS	Year	Team	G	GS
1990	Phoenix Cardinals	15	1	1992	Phoenix Cardinals	12	2	1993	Washington Redskins	8	3	1995	Washington Redskins	9	5

Year	Team	G	GS	Year	Team	G	GS	Year	Team	G	GS	Year	Team	G	GS
1991	Phoenix Cardinals	14	7	1993	Chicago Bears	5	5	1994	Washington Redskins	4	0		6 NFL Seasons	67	23

Other Statistics: 1995–recovered 1 fumble for 0 yards.

Vinson Smith

(statistical profile on page 451)

Pos: LB **Rnd:** FA **College:** East Carolina **Ht:** 6' 2" **Wt:** 247 **Born:** 7/3/65 **Age:** 31

Year	Team	G	GS	Tackles Tk	Ast	Sack	Misc FF	FR	TD	Blk	Int	Yds	Avg	TD	Sfty	TD	Pts
1988	Atlanta Falcons	3	0	0	0	0.0	0	0	0	0	0	0	-	0	0	0	0
1990	Dallas Cowboys	16	1	15	8	0.0	1	2	0	0	0	0	-	0	0	0	0
1991	Dallas Cowboys	13	12	37	34	0.0	0	0	0	0	0	0	-	0	0	0	0
1992	Dallas Cowboys	16	13	33	36	1.0	0	2	0	0	0	0	-	0	0	0	0
1993	Chicago Bears	16	13	98	68	0.0	0	0	0	0	0	0	-	0	0	0	0
1994	Chicago Bears	12	10	18	8	1.0	1	0	0	0	0	0	-	0	0	0	0
1995	Chicago Bears	16	13	59	12	4.0	1	1	0	0	0	0	-	0	0	0	0
	7 NFL Seasons	92	62	260	166	6.0	3	5	0	0	0	0	-	0	0	0	0

Other Statistics: 1995–fumbled 1 time.

Howard Smothers

Pos: WR **Rnd:** 7 **College:** Bethune-Cookman **Ht:** 6' 3" **Wt:** 285 **Born:** 11/16/73 **Age:** 22

Year	Team	G	GS	Rushing Att	Yds	Avg	Lg	TD	Receiving Rec	Yds	Avg	Lg	TD	Punt Returns Num	Yds	Avg	TD	Kickoff Returns Num	Yds	Avg	TD	Fum	TD	Pts
1995	Philadelphia Eagles	1	0	0	0	-	-	0	0	0	-	-	0	0	0	-	0	0	0	-	0	0	0	0

Ariel Solomon

Pos: C **Rnd:** 10 **College:** Colorado **Ht:** 6' 5" **Wt:** 288 **Born:** 7/16/68 **Age:** 28

Year	Team	G	GS	Year	Team	G	GS	Year	Team	G	GS		Team	G	GS
1991	Pittsburgh Steelers	5	2	1993	Pittsburgh Steelers	16	0	1995	Pittsburgh Steelers	4	0				
1992	Pittsburgh Steelers	4	0	1994	Pittsburgh Steelers	16	0						5 NFL Seasons	45	2

Phillippi Sparks

(statistical profile on page 451)

Pos: CB **Rnd:** 2 **College:** Arizona State **Ht:** 5' 11" **Wt:** 190 **Born:** 4/15/69 **Age:** 27

Year	Team	G	GS	Tackles Tk	Ast	Sack	Misc FF	FR	TD	Blk	Int	Yds	Avg	TD	Punt Returns Num	Yds	Avg	TD	Kickoff Returns Num	Yds	Avg	TD	TD	Fum
1992	New York Giants	16	2	30	-	0.0	0	0	0	0	1	0	0.0	0	0	0	-	0	2	23	11.5	0	0	0
1993	New York Giants	5	3	10	1	0.0	0	0	0	0	0	0	-	0	0	0	-	0	0	0	-	0	0	0
1994	New York Giants	11	11	42	5	0.0	0	0	0	0	3	4	1.3	0	0	0	-	0	0	0	-	0	0	0
1995	New York Giants	16	16	71	5	0.0	0	0	0	0	5	11	2.2	0	0	0	-	0	0	0	-	0	0	0
	4 NFL Seasons	48	32	153	11	0.0	0	0	0	0	9	15	1.7	0	0	0	-	0	2	23	11.5	0	0	0

Alonzo Spellman

(statistical profile on page 452)

Pos: DE **Rnd:** 1 (22) **College:** Ohio State **Ht:** 6' 4" **Wt:** 290 **Born:** 9/27/71 **Age:** 25

Year	Team	G	GS	Tackles Tk	Ast	Sack	Misc FF	FR	TD	Blk	Int	Yds	Avg	TD	Sfty	TD	Pts
1992	Chicago Bears	15	0	15	15	4.0	0	0	0	0	0	0	-	0	0	0	0
1993	Chicago Bears	16	0	15	13	2.5	0	0	0	0	0	0	-	0	0	0	0
1994	Chicago Bears	16	16	27	12	7.0	1	0	0	1	1	31	31.0	0	0	0	0
1995	Chicago Bears	16	16	32	17	8.5	4	1	0	0	0	0	-	0	0	0	0
	4 NFL Seasons	63	32	89	57	22.0	5	1	0	1	1	31	31.0	0	0	0	0

Darryl Spencer

Pos: WR **Rnd:** FA **College:** Miami (FL) **Ht:** 5' 8" **Wt:** 172 **Born:** 3/21/70 **Age:** 26

Year	Team	G	GS	Rushing Att	Yds	Avg	Lg	TD	Receiving Rec	Yds	Avg	Lg	TD	Punt Returns Num	Yds	Avg	TD	Kickoff Returns Num	Yds	Avg	TD	Fum	TD	Pts
1994	Atlanta Falcons	8	0	0	0	-	-	0	2	51	25.5	40	0	0	0	-	0	0	0	-	0	0	0	0
1995	Atlanta Falcons	5	1	0	0	-	-	0	5	60	12.0	22	0	0	0	-	0	0	0	-	0	0	0	0
	2 NFL Seasons	13	1	0	0	-	-	0	7	111	15.9	40	0	0	0	-	0	0	0	-	0	0	0	0

Jimmy Spencer

(statistical profile on page 452)

Pos: CB **Rnd:** 8 **College:** Florida **Ht:** 5' 9" **Wt:** 180 **Born:** 3/29/69 **Age:** 27

Year	Team	G	GS	Tackles Tk	Ast	Sack	Misc FF	FR	TD	Blk	Int	Yds	Avg	TD	Sfty	TD	Pts
1992	New Orleans Saints	16	4	37	6	0.0	0	1	0	0	0	0	-	0	0	0	0
1993	New Orleans Saints	16	3	15	5	0.0	0	3	0	0	0	0	-	0	0	0	0
1994	New Orleans Saints	16	16	56	7	0.0	1	1	0	0	5	24	4.8	0	0	0	0

Year Team	G	GS	Tackles Tk	Ast	Sack	Miscellaneous FF	FR	TD	Blk	Interceptions Int	Yds	Avg	TD	Totals Sfty	TD	Pts
1995 New Orleans Saints	16	15	59	7	0.0	0	0	0	0	4	11	2.8	0	0	0	0
4 NFL Seasons	64	38	167	25	0.0	1	5	0	0	9	35	3.9	0	0	0	0

Chris Spielman

(statistical profile on page 452)

Pos: LB **Rnd:** 2 **College:** Ohio State **Ht:** 6' 0" **Wt:** 247 **Born:** 10/11/65 **Age:** 31

Year Team	G	GS	Tackles Tk	Ast	Sack	Miscellaneous FF	FR	TD	Blk	Interceptions Int	Yds	Avg	TD	Totals Sfty	TD	Pts
1988 Detroit Lions	16	16	118	35	0.0	1	1	0	0	0	0	-	0	0	0	0
1989 Detroit Lions	16	16	89	36	5.0	1	2	0	0	0	0	-	0	0	0	0
1990 Detroit Lions	12	12	79	29	2.0	1	2	0	0	1	12	12.0	0	0	0	0
1991 Detroit Lions	16	16	84	42	1.0	3	3	0	0	0	0	-	0	0	0	0
1992 Detroit Lions	16	16	94	52	1.0	0	1	0	0	0	0	-	0	0	0	0
1993 Detroit Lions	16	16	97	51	0.5	1	2	0	0	2	-2	-1.0	0	0	0	0
1994 Detroit Lions	16	16	124	71	0.0	3	3	1	0	0	0	-	0	0	1	6
1995 Detroit Lions	16	16	90	47	1.0	2	3	0	0	1	4	4.0	0	0	0	0
8 NFL Seasons	124	124	775	363	10.5	12	17	1	0	4	14	3.5	0	0	1	6

Irving Spikes

Pos: RB/KR **Rnd:** FA **College:** Northeast Louisiana **Ht:** 5' 8" **Wt:** 206 **Born:** 12/21/70 **Age:** 25

Year Team	G	GS	Rushing Att	Yds	Avg	Lg	TD	Receiving Rec	Yds	Avg	Lg	TD	Punt Returns Num	Yds	Avg	TD	Kickoff Returns Num	Yds	Avg	TD	Totals Fum	TD	Pts
1994 Miami Dolphins	12	1	70	312	4.5	40	2	4	16	4.0	9	0	0	0	-	0	19	434	22.8	0	1	2	12
1995 Miami Dolphins	9	0	32	126	3.9	t17	1	5	18	3.6	13	1	0	0	-	0	18	378	21.0	0	0	2	12
2 NFL Seasons	21	1	102	438	4.3	40	3	9	34	3.8	13	1	0	0	-	0	37	812	21.9	0	1	4	24

Marc Spindler

Pos: DT **Rnd:** 3 **College:** Pittsburgh **Ht:** 6' 5" **Wt:** 290 **Born:** 11/28/69 **Age:** 26

Year Team	G	GS	Tackles Tk	Ast	Sack	Miscellaneous FF	FR	TD	Blk	Interceptions Int	Yds	Avg	TD	Totals Sfty	TD	Pts
1990 Detroit Lions	3	2	9	2	1.0	0	0	0	0	0	0	-	0	0	0	0
1991 Detroit Lions	16	16	33	16	3.5	0	1	0	0	0	0	-	0	0	0	0
1992 Detroit Lions	13	13	25	9	2.5	0	0	0	0	0	0	-	0	0	0	0
1993 Detroit Lions	16	16	32	17	2.0	0	2	0	0	0	0	-	0	0	0	0
1994 Detroit Lions	9	8	11	4	0.0	0	0	0	0	0	0	-	0	0	0	0
1995 New York Jets	10	4	13	4	0.0	0	0	0	0	0	0	-	0	0	0	0
6 NFL Seasons	67	59	123	52	9.0	0	3	0	0	0	0	-	0	0	0	0

Brian Stablein

Pos: WR **Rnd:** 8 **College:** Ohio State **Ht:** 6' 1" **Wt:** 190 **Born:** 4/14/70 **Age:** 26

Year Team	G	GS	Rushing Att	Yds	Avg	Lg	TD	Receiving Rec	Yds	Avg	Lg	TD	Punt Returns Num	Yds	Avg	TD	Kickoff Returns Num	Yds	Avg	TD	Totals Fum	TD	Pts
1994 Indianapolis Colts	1	0	0	0	-	-	0	0	0	-	-	0	0	0	-	0	0	0	-	0	0	0	0
1995 Indianapolis Colts	15	0	0	0	-	-	0	8	95	11.9	16	0	0	0	-	0	0	0	-	0	0	0	0
2 NFL Seasons	16	0	0	0	-	-	0	8	95	11.9	16	0	0	0	-	0	0	0	-	0	0	0	0

Brenden Stai

Pos: G **Rnd:** 3 **College:** Nebraska **Ht:** 6' 4" **Wt:** 305 **Born:** 3/30/72 **Age:** 24

Year Team	G	GS
1995 Pittsburgh Steelers	15	9
1 NFL Season	15	9

Ramondo Stallings

Pos: DE/DT **Rnd:** 7 **College:** San Diego State **Ht:** 6' 7" **Wt:** 285 **Born:** 11/21/71 **Age:** 24

Year Team	G	GS	Tackles Tk	Ast	Sack	Miscellaneous FF	FR	TD	Blk	Interceptions Int	Yds	Avg	TD	Totals Sfty	TD	Pts
1994 Cincinnati Bengals	6	0	1	0	0.0	0	0	0	0	0	0	-	0	0	0	0
1995 Cincinnati Bengals	13	2	14	2	1.0	1	1	0	0	0	0	-	0	0	0	0
2 NFL Seasons	19	2	15	2	1.0	1	1	0	0	0	0	-	0	0	0	0

Other Statistics: 1995–fumbled 1 time.

Frank Stams

Pos: LB **Rnd:** 2 **College:** Notre Dame **Ht:** 6' 2" **Wt:** 230 **Born:** 7/17/65 **Age:** 31

Year Team	G	GS	Tackles Tk	Ast	Sack	Miscellaneous FF	FR	TD	Blk	Interceptions Int	Yds	Avg	TD	Totals Sfty	TD	Pts
1989 Los Angeles Rams	16	3	21	6	0.0	0	0	0	0	1	20	20.0	0	0	0	0

Year	Team	G	GS	Tk	Ast	Sack	FF	FR	TD	Blk	Int	Yds	Avg	TD	Sfty	TD	Pts
				Tackles			**Miscellaneous**				**Interceptions**				**Totals**		
1990	Los Angeles Rams	13	12	68	10	0.0	0	0	0	0	0	0	-	0	0	0	0
1991	Los Angeles Rams	5	0	7	1	0.0	0	0	0	0	0	0	-	0	0	0	0
1992	Cleveland Browns	12	0	2	1	0.0	0	0	0	0	0	0	-	0	0	0	0
1993	Cleveland Browns	14	0	1	5	0.0	0	0	0	0	0	0	-	0	0	0	0
1994	Cleveland Browns	16	15	56	13	2.0	1	0	0	0	1	7	7.0	0	0	0	0
1995	KC - Cle	5	0	0	0	0.0	0	0	0	0	0	0	-	0	0	0	0
1995	Kansas City Chiefs	1	0	0	0	0.0	0	0	0	0	0	0	-	0	0	0	0
	Cleveland Browns	4	0	0	0	0.0	0	0	0	0	0	0	-	0	0	0	0
	7 NFL Seasons	81	30	155	36	2.0	1	0	0	0	2	27	13.5	0	0	0	0

Israel Stanley

Pos: DE **Rnd:** FA **College:** Arizona State **Ht:** 6' 3" **Wt:** 260 **Born:** 4/21/70 **Age:** 26

Year	Team	G	GS	Tk	Ast	Sack	FF	FR	TD	Blk	Int	Yds	Avg	TD	Sfty	TD	Pts
				Tackles			**Miscellaneous**				**Interceptions**				**Totals**		
1995	New Orleans Saints	14	0	8	1	2.0	1	1	0	0	0	0	-	0	0	0	0

Tony Stargell

Pos: CB **Rnd:** 3 **College:** Tennessee State **Ht:** 5' 11" **Wt:** 186 **Born:** 8/7/66 **Age:** 30

Year	Team	G	GS	Tk	Ast	Sack	FF	FR	TD	Blk	Int	Yds	Avg	TD	Sfty	TD	Pts
				Tackles			**Miscellaneous**				**Interceptions**				**Totals**		
1990	New York Jets	16	16	46	43	0.0	0	1	0	0	2	-3	-1.5	0	0	0	0
1991	New York Jets	16	7	40	17	0.0	0	1	0	0	0	0	-	0	0	0	0
1992	Indianapolis Colts	13	3	20	8	0.0	0	0	0	0	2	26	13.0	0	0	0	0
1993	Indianapolis Colts	16	1	20	3	1.0	2	0	0	0	0	0	-	0	0	0	0
1994	Tampa Bay Buccaneers	10	2	13	2	0.0	0	1	0	0	1	0	0.0	0	0	0	0
1995	Tampa Bay Buccaneers	14	6	45	12	0.0	4	0	0	0	0	0	-	0	0	0	0
	6 NFL Seasons	85	35	184	85	1.0	6	3	0	0	5	23	4.6	0	0	0	0

Rohn Stark

(statistical profile on page 484)

Pos: P **Rnd:** 2 **College:** Florida State **Ht:** 6' 3" **Wt:** 203 **Born:** 5/4/59 **Age:** 37

Year	Team	G	NetPunts	Yards	Avg	Long	In20	In20%	TotPunts	TB	Blocks	OppRet	RetYds	NetAvg	Att	Yards	Att	Com	Yards	Int
				Punting											**Rushing**		**Passing**			
1982	Baltimore Colts	9	46	2044	44.4	60	8	17.4	46	12	0	26	226	34.3	1	8	1	0	0	0
1983	Baltimore Colts	16	91	4124	45.3	68	20	22.0	91	9	0	55	642	36.3	1	8	1	0	0	0
1984	Indianapolis Colts	16	98	4383	44.7	72	21	21.4	98	7	0	62	600	37.2	2	0	1	0	0	1
1985	Indianapolis Colts	16	78	3584	45.9	68	12	15.4	80	14	2	43	572	34.2	0	0	1	0	0	0
1986	Indianapolis Colts	16	76	3432	45.2	63	22	28.9	76	5	0	48	502	37.2	0	0	0	0	0	0
1987	Indianapolis Colts	12	61	2440	40.0	63	12	19.7	63	7	2	33	353	30.9	0	0	0	0	0	0
1988	Indianapolis Colts	16	64	2784	43.5	65	15	23.4	64	8	0	37	418	34.5	0	0	0	0	0	0
1989	Indianapolis Colts	16	79	3392	42.9	64	14	17.7	80	10	1	51	558	32.9	1	-11	0	0	0	0
1990	Indianapolis Colts	16	71	3084	43.4	61	24	33.8	72	3	1	42	334	37.4	0	0	1	1	40	0
1991	Indianapolis Colts	16	82	3492	42.6	65	14	17.1	82	6	0	47	516	34.8	1	-13	0	0	0	0
1992	Indianapolis Colts	16	83	3716	44.8	64	22	26.5	83	7	0	45	313	39.3	0	0	1	1	17	0
1993	Indianapolis Colts	16	83	3595	43.3	65	18	21.7	83	13	0	41	352	35.9	1	11	0	0	0	0
1994	Indianapolis Colts	16	73	3092	42.4	60	22	30.1	74	10	1	40	366	34.1	0	0	0	0	0	0
1995	Pittsburgh Steelers	16	59	2368	40.1	64	20	33.9	59	11	0	22	186	33.3	0	0	0	0	0	0
	14 NFL Seasons	213	1044	45530	43.6	72	244	23.4	1051	122	7	592	5938	35.3	7	3	6	2	57	1

Other Statistics: 1982–fumbled 1 time for 0 yards. 1984–recovered 1 fumble for 0 yards. 1985–recovered 1 fumble for 0 yards. 1986–recovered 1 fumble for 0 yards; fumbled 1 time. 1991–recovered 2 fumbles for 0 yards; fumbled 1 time.

Joe Staysniak

Pos: G **Rnd:** 7 **College:** Ohio State **Ht:** 6' 4" **Wt:** 292 **Born:** 12/8/66 **Age:** 29

Year	Team	G	GS	Year	Team	G	GS	Year	Team	G	GS		G	GS
1991	Buffalo Bills	2	0	1993	Indianapolis Colts	14	1	1995	Indianapolis Colts	16	16			
1992	Kansas City Chiefs	7	0	1994	Indianapolis Colts	16	16					5 NFL Seasons	55	33

Other Statistics: 1994–recovered 2 fumbles for -22 yards; fumbled 1 time.

Joel Steed

Pos: NT **Rnd:** 3 **College:** Colorado **Ht:** 6' 2" **Wt:** 295 **Born:** 2/17/69 **Age:** 27

Year	Team	G	GS	Tk	Ast	Sack	FF	FR	TD	Blk	Int	Yds	Avg	TD	Sfty	TD	Pts
				Tackles			**Miscellaneous**				**Interceptions**				**Totals**		
1992	Pittsburgh Steelers	11	4	6	2	0.0	0	0	0	0	0	0	-	0	0	0	0
1993	Pittsburgh Steelers	14	12	25	16	1.5	1	1	0	0	0	0	-	0	0	0	0
1994	Pittsburgh Steelers	16	16	40	12	2.0	2	0	0	0	0	0	-	0	0	0	0
1995	Pittsburgh Steelers	12	11	23	7	1.0	0	0	0	0	0	0	-	0	0	0	0

Year Team	G	GS	Tk	Ast	Sack	FF	FR	TD	Blk	Int	Yds	Avg	TD	Sfty	TD	Pts
4 NFL Seasons	53	43	94	37	4.5	3	1	0	0	0	0	-	0	0	0	0

Steve Stenstrom

Pos: QB **Rnd:** 4 **College:** Stanford **Ht:** 6' 2" **Wt:** 200 **Born:** 12/23/71 **Age:** 24

Year Team	G	GS		Passing									Rushing					Miscellaneous			
			Att	Com	Pct	Yards	Yds/Att	Lg	TD	Int	Int%	Rating	Att	Yds	Avg	Lg TD	Sckd	Yds	Fum Recv	Yds	Pts
1995 Chicago Bears	2	0	0	0	-	0	-	0	0	0	-	0.0	0	0	-	- 0	0	0	0	0	0

Darnell Stephens

Pos: LB **Rnd:** FA **College:** Clemson **Ht:** 5' 11" **Wt:** 253 **Born:** 1/29/73 **Age:** 23

Year Team	G	GS	Tk	Ast	Sack	FF	FR	TD	Blk	Int	Yds	Avg	TD	Sfty	TD	Pts
1995 Tampa Bay Buccaneers	12	0	0	0	0.0	0	0	0	0	0	0	-	0	0	0	0

Rich Stephens

Pos: T/G **Rnd:** 9 **College:** Tulsa **Ht:** 6' 7" **Wt:** 310 **Born:** 1/1/65 **Age:** 31

Year	Team	G	GS	Year	Team	G	GS				G	GS
1993	Los Angeles Raiders	16	1	1995	Oakland Raiders	13	1		2 NFL Seasons		29	2

Rod Stephens

(statistical profile on page 453)

Pos: LB **Rnd:** FA **College:** Georgia Tech **Ht:** 6' 1" **Wt:** 237 **Born:** 6/14/66 **Age:** 30

Year Team	G	GS	Tk	Ast	Sack	FF	FR	TD	Blk	Int	Yds	Avg	TD	Sfty	TD	Pts
1989 Seattle Seahawks	10	0	10	-	0.0	0	0	0	0	0	0	-	0	0	0	0
1990 Seattle Seahawks	4	0	1	1	0.0	0	0	0	0	0	0	-	0	0	0	0
1991 Seattle Seahawks	16	0	14	2	0.0	1	1	0	0	0	0	-	0	0	0	0
1992 Seattle Seahawks	16	5	49	16	0.0	2	0	0	0	0	0	-	0	0	0	0
1993 Seattle Seahawks	13	13	75	30	2.5	2	1	1	0	0	0	-	0	2	1	10
1994 Seattle Seahawks	16	16	95	33	2.5	3	2	0	0	0	0	-	0	0	0	0
1995 Washington Redskins	16	16	82	18	0.0	2	1	0	0	0	0	-	0	0	0	0
7 NFL Seasons	91	50	326	100	5.0	10	5	1	0	0	0	-	0	2	1	10

Santo Stephens

Pos: LB **Rnd:** FA **College:** Temple **Ht:** 6' 4" **Wt:** 244 **Born:** 6/16/69 **Age:** 27

Year Team	G	GS	Tk	Ast	Sack	FF	FR	TD	Blk	Int	Yds	Avg	TD	Sfty	TD	Pts
1993 Kansas City Chiefs	16	0	0	0	0.0	0	0	0	0	0	0	-	0	0	0	0
1994 Cincinnati Bengals	14	3	9	4	0.0	0	0	0	0	0	0	-	0	0	0	0
1995 Jacksonville Jaguars	13	0	2	1	0.0	0	0	0	0	0	0	-	0	0	0	0
3 NFL Seasons	43	3	11	5	0.0	0	0	0	0	0	0	-	0	0	0	0

Mark Stepnoski

Pos: C **Rnd:** 3 **College:** Pittsburgh **Ht:** 6' 2" **Wt:** 269 **Born:** 1/20/67 **Age:** 29

Year	Team	G	GS	Year	Team	G	GS	Year	Team	G	GS	Year	Team	G	GS
1989	Dallas Cowboys	16	4	1991	Dallas Cowboys	16	16	1993	Dallas Cowboys	13	13	1995	Houston Oilers	16	16
1990	Dallas Cowboys	16	16	1992	Dallas Cowboys	14	14	1994	Dallas Cowboys	16	16		7 NFL Seasons	107	95

Other Statistics: 1989–recovered 3 fumbles for 0 yards. 1990–returned 1 kickoff for 15 yards. 1992–recovered 1 fumble for 0 yards. 1993–fumbled 1 time for -1 yard. 1994–fumbled 4 times for -3 yards.

Todd Steussie

Pos: T **Rnd:** 1 (19) **College:** California **Ht:** 6' 6" **Wt:** 304 **Born:** 12/1/70 **Age:** 25

Year	Team	G	GS	Year	Team	G	GS				G	GS
1994	Minnesota Vikings	16	16	1995	Minnesota Vikings	16	16		2 NFL Seasons		32	32

Other Statistics: 1994–recovered 1 fumble for 0 yards.

James Stewart

(statistical profile on page 378)

Pos: RB **Rnd:** 1 (19) **College:** Tennessee **Ht:** 6' 1" **Wt:** 221 **Born:** 12/27/71 **Age:** 24

Year Team	G	GS		Rushing					Receiving					Punt Returns			Kickoff Returns			Totals		
			Att	Yds	Avg	Lg	TD	Rec	Yds	Avg	Lg	TD	Num	Yds	Avg TD	Num	Yds	Avg TD	Fum	TD	Pts
1995 Jacksonville Jaguars	14	7	137	525	3.8	22	2	21	190	9.0	38	1	0	0	- 0	0	0	- 0	1	3	18

James Stewart

Pos: RB **Rnd:** 5 **College:** Miami (FL) **Ht:** 6' 2" **Wt:** 245 **Born:** 12/8/71 **Age:** 24

Year Team	G	GS	Rushing Att	Yds	Avg	Lg	TD	Receiving Rec	Yds	Avg	Lg	TD	Punt Returns Num	Yds	Avg	TD	Kickoff Returns Num	Yds	Avg	TD	Totals Fum	TD	Pts
1995 Minnesota Vikings	4	0	31	144	4.6	51	0	1	3	3.0	3	0	0	0	-	0	0	0	-	0	2	0	0

Other Statistics: 1995–recovered 1 fumble for 0 yards.

Kordell Stewart

Pos: QB/WR **Rnd:** 2 **College:** Colorado **Ht:** 6' 1" **Wt:** 212 **Born:** 10/16/72 **Age:** 24

Year Team	G	GS	Passing Att	Com	Pct	Yards	Yds/Att	Lg	TD	Int	Int%	Rating	Rushing Att	Yds	Avg	Lg	TD	Miscellaneous Sckd	Yds	Fum Recv	Yds	Pts
1995 Pittsburgh Steelers	10	2	7	5	71.4	60	8.57	32	1	0	0.0	136.9	15	86	5.7	t22	1	1	0	0	0	12

Other Statistics: 1995–caught 14 passes for 235 yards and 1 touchdown.

Michael Stewart

(statistical profile on page 453)

Pos: S **Rnd:** 8 **College:** Fresno State **Ht:** 5' 11" **Wt:** 202 **Born:** 7/12/65 **Age:** 31

Year Team	G	GS	Tackles Tk	Ast	Sack	Miscellaneous FF	FR	TD	Blk	Interceptions Int	Yds	Avg	TD	Punt Returns Num	Yds	Avg	TD	Kickoff Returns Num	Yds	Avg	TD	Totals TD	Fum
1987 Los Angeles Rams	12	4	26	9	0.0	0	0	0	0	0	0	-	0	0	0	-	0	0	0	-	0	0	0
1988 Los Angeles Rams	16	10	46	14	1.0	0	2	0	0	2	61	30.5	0	0	0	-	0	1	0	0.0	0	0	0
1989 Los Angeles Rams	16	15	59	13	0.0	0	3	0	0	2	76	38.0	1	0	0	-	0	0	0	-	0	1	1
1990 Los Angeles Rams	16	11	40	12	0.0	3	2	0	0	0	0	-	0	0	0	-	0	0	0	-	0	0	0
1991 Los Angeles Rams	16	16	69	12	1.0	0	0	0	0	2	8	4.0	0	0	0	-	0	0	0	-	0	0	0
1992 Los Angeles Rams	11	6	35	7	2.0	0	1	0	0	0	0	-	0	0	0	-	0	0	0	-	0	0	0
1993 Los Angeles Rams	16	14	60	14	1.0	1	0	0	0	1	30	30.0	0	0	0	-	0	0	0	-	0	0	0
1994 Miami Dolphins	16	16	75	22	0.0	0	1	0	0	3	11	3.7	0	0	0	-	0	0	0	-	0	0	0
1995 Miami Dolphins	16	16	61	22	0.0	2	1	0	0	1	0	0.0	0	0	0	-	0	0	0	-	0	0	0
9 NFL Seasons	135	108	471	125	5.0	6	10	0	0	11	186	16.9	1	0	0	-	0	1	0	0.0	0	1	1

Other Statistics: 1987–credited with 1 safety.

Fred Stokes

Pos: DE **Rnd:** 12 **College:** Georgia Southern **Ht:** 6' 3" **Wt:** 274 **Born:** 3/14/64 **Age:** 32

Year Team	G	GS	Tackles Tk	Ast	Sack	Miscellaneous FF	FR	TD	Blk	Interceptions Int	Yds	Avg	TD	Totals Sfty	TD	Pts
1987 Los Angeles Rams	8	0	5	0	0.5	0	0	0	0	0	0	-	0	0	0	0
1988 Los Angeles Rams	5	0	3	0	1.0	0	2	0	0	0	0	-	0	0	0	0
1989 Washington Redskins	16	5	14	10	3.0	0	2	0	0	0	0	-	0	1	0	2
1990 Washington Redskins	16	3	8	11	7.5	0	4	0	0	0	0	-	0	0	0	0
1991 Washington Redskins	16	11	18	18	6.5	0	2	0	0	1	0	0.0	0	0	0	0
1992 Washington Redskins	16	11	19	29	3.5	2	1	0	0	0	0	-	0	0	0	0
1993 Los Angeles Rams	15	15	36	13	9.5	1	2	0	0	0	0	-	0	0	0	0
1994 Los Angeles Rams	16	15	17	5	2.0	1	0	0	0	0	0	-	0	0	0	0
1995 St. Louis Rams	16	2	11	5	2.5	0	0	0	0	0	0	-	0	0	0	0
9 NFL Seasons	124	62	131	91	36.0	4	13	0	0	1	0	0.0	0	1	0	2

J.J. Stokes

(statistical profile on page 379)

Pos: WR **Rnd:** 1 (10) **College:** UCLA **Ht:** 6' 4" **Wt:** 217 **Born:** 10/6/72 **Age:** 24

Year Team	G	GS	Rushing Att	Yds	Avg	Lg	TD	Receiving Rec	Yds	Avg	Lg	TD	Punt Returns Num	Yds	Avg	TD	Kickoff Returns Num	Yds	Avg	TD	Totals Fum	TD	Pts
1995 San Francisco 49ers	12	2	0	0	-	-	0	38	517	13.6	t41	4	0	0	-	0	0	0	-	0	0	4	24

Dwight Stone

Pos: KR/WR **Rnd:** FA **College:** Middle Tennessee State **Ht:** 6' 0" **Wt:** 180 **Born:** 1/28/64 **Age:** 32

Year Team	G	GS	Rushing Att	Yds	Avg	Lg	TD	Receiving Rec	Yds	Avg	Lg	TD	Punt Returns Num	Yds	Avg	TD	Kickoff Returns Num	Yds	Avg	TD	Totals Fum	TD	Pts
1987 Pittsburgh Steelers	14	0	17	135	7.9	51	0	1	22	22.0	22	0	0	0	-	0	28	568	20.3	0	0	0	0
1988 Pittsburgh Steelers	16	6	40	127	3.2	11	0	11	196	17.8	t72	1	0	0	-	0	29	610	21.0	1	5	2	12
1989 Pittsburgh Steelers	16	8	10	53	5.3	32	0	7	92	13.1	16	0	0	0	-	0	7	173	24.7	0	2	0	0
1990 Pittsburgh Steelers	16	2	2	-6	-3.0	10	0	19	332	17.5	90	1	0	0	-	0	5	91	18.2	0	1	1	6
1991 Pittsburgh Steelers	16	8	1	2	2.0	2	0	32	649	20.3	t89	5	0	0	-	0	6	75	12.5	0	5	5	30
1992 Pittsburgh Steelers	15	13	12	118	9.8	30	0	34	501	14.7	49	3	0	0	-	0	12	219	18.3	0	0	3	18
1993 Pittsburgh Steelers	16	15	12	121	10.1	t38	1	41	587	14.3	44	2	0	0	-	0	11	168	15.3	0	2	3	18
1994 Pittsburgh Steelers	15	1	2	7	3.5	4	0	7	81	11.6	25	0	0	0	-	0	11	182	16.5	0	0	0	2
1995 Carolina Panthers	16	0	1	3	3.0	3	0	0	0	-	-	0	0	0	-	0	12	269	22.4	0	0	0	0
9 NFL Seasons	140	53	97	560	5.8	51	1	152	2460	16.2	90	12	0	0	-	0	121	2355	19.5	1	10	14	86

Other Statistics: 1987–recovered 1 fumble for 0 yards. 1989–recovered 1 fumble for 0 yards. 1990–recovered 2 fumbles for 0 yards. 1993–recovered 1 fumble for 0 yards. 1994–scored 1 two-point conversion.

Ron Stone

Pos: G/T **Rnd:** 4 **College:** Boston College   **Ht:** 6' 5" **Wt:** 309 **Born:** 7/20/71 **Age:** 25

Year	Team	G	GS	Year	Team	G	GS			G	GS
1994	Dallas Cowboys	15	0	1995	Dallas Cowboys	16	1	2 NFL Seasons		31	1

Other Statistics: 1994–recovered 1 fumble for 0 yards.

Matt Stover

(statistical profile on page 484)

Pos: K **Rnd:** 12 **College:** Louisiana Tech   **Ht:** 5' 11" **Wt:** 178 **Born:** 1/27/68 **Age:** 28

			Field Goals											PAT		Tot
Year	Team	G	1-29 Yds	Pct	30-39 Yds	Pct	40-49 Yds	Pct	50+ Yds	Pct	Overall	Pct	Long	Made	Att	Pts
1991	Cleveland Browns	16	3-5	60.0	8-9	88.9	3-6	50.0	2-2	100.0	16-22	72.7	55	33	34	81
1992	Cleveland Browns	16	12-12	100.0	6-8	75.0	2-6	33.3	1-3	33.3	21-29	72.4	51	29	30	92
1993	Cleveland Browns	16	4-4	100.0	5-6	83.3	6-8	75.0	1-4	25.0	16-22	72.7	53	36	36	84
1994	Cleveland Browns	16	8-8	100.0	10-11	90.9	8-8	100.0	0-1	0.0	26-28	92.9	45	32	32	110
1995	Cleveland Browns	16	13-13	100.0	9-10	90.0	7-9	77.8	0-1	0.0	29-33	87.9	47	26	26	113
	5 NFL Seasons	80	40-42	95.2	38-44	86.4	26-37	70.3	4-11	36.4	108-134	80.6	55	156	158	480

Other Statistics: 1992–attempted 1 pass with 0 completions for 0 yards and 1 interception.

Tyronne Stowe

Pos: LB **Rnd:** FA **College:** Rutgers   **Ht:** 6' 2" **Wt:** 250 **Born:** 5/30/65 **Age:** 31

				Tackles			Miscellaneous				Interceptions				Totals		
Year	Team	G	GS	Tk	Ast	Sack	FF	FR	TD	Blk	Int	Yds	Avg	TD	Sfty	TD	Pts
1987	Pittsburgh Steelers	13	3	0	0	0.0	0	0	0	0	0	0	-	0	0	0	0
1988	Pittsburgh Steelers	10	4	0	0	0.0	0	0	0	0	0	0	-	0	0	0	0
1989	Pittsburgh Steelers	16	0	0	0	0.0	0	2	0	0	0	0	-	0	0	0	0
1990	Pittsburgh Steelers	16	0	0	-	0.0	0	1	0	0	0	0	-	0	1	0	2
1991	Phoenix Cardinals	13	4	0	0	0.0	0	1	0	0	0	0	-	0	0	0	0
1992	Phoenix Cardinals	15	15	0	0	0.0	0	0	0	0	0	0	-	0	0	0	0
1993	Phoenix Cardinals	15	15	76	43	1.5	0	0	0	0	0	0	-	0	0	0	0
1994	Washington Redskins	16	15	89	15	0.0	1	0	0	0	1	2	2.0	0	0	0	0
1995	Seattle Seahawks	6	6	40	12	0.0	0	0	0	0	0	0	-	0	0	0	0
	9 NFL Seasons	120	62	205	70	1.5	1	4	0	0	1	2	2.0	0	1	0	2

Other Statistics: 1994–fumbled 1 time for 0 yards.

Pete Stoyanovich

(statistical profile on page 484)

Pos: K **Rnd:** 8 **College:** Indiana   **Ht:** 5' 11" **Wt:** 195 **Born:** 4/28/67 **Age:** 29

			Field Goals											PAT		Tot
Year	Team	G	1-29 Yds	Pct	30-39 Yds	Pct	40-49 Yds	Pct	50+ Yds	Pct	Overall	Pct	Long	Made	Att	Pts
1989	Miami Dolphins	16	9-9	100.0	5-6	83.3	4-8	50.0	1-3	33.3	19-26	73.1	59	38	39	95
1990	Miami Dolphins	16	9-10	90.0	6-7	85.7	4-5	80.0	2-3	66.7	21-25	84.0	53	37	37	100
1991	Miami Dolphins	14	10-10	100.0	11-12	91.7	7-10	70.0	3-5	60.0	31-37	83.8	53	28	29	121
1992	Miami Dolphins	16	9-9	100.0	14-16	87.5	4-4	100.0	3-8	37.5	30-37	81.1	53	34	36	124
1993	Miami Dolphins	16	11-12	91.7	7-11	63.6	4-7	57.1	2-2	100.0	24-32	75.0	52	37	37	109
1994	Miami Dolphins	16	9-9	100.0	6-10	60.0	8-10	80.0	1-2	50.0	24-31	77.4	50	35	35	107
1995	Miami Dolphins	16	8-11	72.7	11-11	100.0	6-7	85.7	2-5	40.0	27-34	79.4	51	37	37	118
	7 NFL Seasons	110	65-70	92.9	60-73	82.2	37-51	72.5	14-28	50.0	176-222	79.3	59	246	250	774

Other Statistics: 1991–punted 2 times for 85 yards. 1992–punted 2 times for 90 yards.

Michael Strahan

(statistical profile on page 453)

Pos: DE **Rnd:** 2 **College:** Texas Southern   **Ht:** 6' 4" **Wt:** 270 **Born:** 11/21/71 **Age:** 24

				Tackles			Miscellaneous				Interceptions				Totals		
Year	Team	G	GS	Tk	Ast	Sack	FF	FR	TD	Blk	Int	Yds	Avg	TD	Sfty	TD	Pts
1993	New York Giants	9	0	1	2	1.0	0	0	0	0	0	0	-	0	0	0	0
1994	New York Giants	15	15	27	13	4.5	1	0	0	0	0	0	-	0	0	0	0
1995	New York Giants	15	15	48	10	7.5	3	0	0	1	2	56	28.0	0	0	0	0
	3 NFL Seasons	39	30	76	25	13.0	4	0	0	1	2	56	28.0	0	0	0	0

Fred Strickland

Pos: LB **Rnd:** 2 **College:** Purdue   **Ht:** 6' 2" **Wt:** 250 **Born:** 8/15/66 **Age:** 30

				Tackles			Miscellaneous				Interceptions				Totals		
Year	Team	G	GS	Tk	Ast	Sack	FF	FR	TD	Blk	Int	Yds	Avg	TD	Sfty	TD	Pts
1988	Los Angeles Rams	16	0	34	9	4.0	0	2	0	0	0	0	-	0	0	0	0
1989	Los Angeles Rams	12	12	53	10	2.0	0	1	0	0	2	56	28.0	0	0	0	0
1990	Los Angeles Rams	5	5	17	8	0.0	0	0	0	0	0	0	-	0	0	0	0
1991	Los Angeles Rams	14	10	23	6	1.0	0	0	0	0	0	0	-	0	0	0	0
1992	Los Angeles Rams	16	0	7	0	0.0	0	0	0	0	0	0	-	0	0	0	0

Year	Team	G	GS	Tk	Ast	Sack	FF	FR	TD	Blk	Int	Yds	Avg	TD	Sfty	TD	Pts
				Tackles			**Miscellaneous**				**Interceptions**				**Totals**		
1993	Minnesota Vikings	16	15	81	56	0.0	0	4	0	0	0	0	-	0	0	0	0
1994	Green Bay Packers	16	14	*40*	*33*	0.0	0	1	0	0	1	7	7.0	0	0	0	0
1995	Green Bay Packers	14	10	*34*	*17*	0.0	0	0	0	0	0	0	-	0	0	0	0
	8 NFL Seasons	109	66	289	139	7.0	0	8	0	0	3	63	21.0	0	0	0	0

Korey Stringer

Pos: T   **Rnd:** 1 (24)   **College:** Ohio State   **Ht:** 6' 4"   **Wt:** 332   **Born:** 5/8/74   **Age:** 22

Year	Team	G	GS					G	GS
1995	Minnesota Vikings	16	15				1 NFL Season	16	15

Other Statistics: 1995–recovered 2 fumbles for 0 yards; caught 1 pass for -1 yard.

Mack Strong

Pos: RB   **Rnd:** FA   **College:** Georgia   **Ht:** 6' 0"   **Wt:** 222   **Born:** 9/11/71   **Age:** 25

Year	Team	G	GS	Att	Yds	Avg	Lg	TD	Rec	Yds	Avg	Lg	TD	Num	Yds	Avg	TD	Num	Yds	Avg	TD	Fum	TD	Pts
				Rushing					**Receiving**					**Punt Returns**				**Kickoff Returns**				**Totals**		
1994	Seattle Seahawks	8	1	27	114	4.2	14	2	3	3	1.0	5	0	0	0	-	0	0	0	-	0	1	2	12
1995	Seattle Seahawks	16	1	8	23	2.9	9	1	12	117	9.8	25	3	0	0	-	0	4	65	16.3	0	2	4	24
	2 NFL Seasons	24	2	35	137	3.9	14	3	15	120	8.0	25	3	0	0	-	0	4	65	16.3	0	3	6	36

Other Statistics: 1995–recovered 1 fumble for 0 yards.

William Strong

Pos: CB   **Rnd:** 5   **College:** North Carolina State   **Ht:** 5' 10"   **Wt:** 191   **Born:** 11/3/71   **Age:** 24

Year	Team	G	GS	Tk	Ast	Sack	FF	FR	TD	Blk	Int	Yds	Avg	TD	Sfty	TD	Pts
				Tackles			**Miscellaneous**				**Interceptions**				**Totals**		
1995	New Orleans Saints	1	0	*0*	*0*	0.0	0	0	0	0	0	0	-	0	0	0	0

Dan Stryzinski

Pos: P   **Rnd:** FA   **College:** Indiana   *(statistical profile on page 485)*   **Ht:** 6' 2"   **Wt:** 200   **Born:** 5/15/65   **Age:** 31

Year	Team	G	NetPunts	Yards	Avg	Long	In20	In20%	TotPunts	TB	Blocks	OppRet	RetYds	NetAvg	Att	Yards	Att	Com	Yards	Int
									Punting						**Rushing**		**Passing**			
1990	Pittsburgh Steelers	16	65	2454	37.8	51	18	27.7	66	5	1	16	105	34.1	3	17	0	0	0	0
1991	Pittsburgh Steelers	16	74	2996	40.5	63	10	13.5	75	3	1	29	210	36.3	4	-11	0	0	0	0
1992	Tampa Bay Buccaneers	16	74	3015	40.7	57	15	20.3	74	11	0	22	117	36.2	1	7	2	2	14	0
1993	Tampa Bay Buccaneers	16	**93**	3772	40.6	57	24	25.8	**94**	3	1	**53**	394	35.3	0	0	0	0	0	0
1994	Tampa Bay Buccaneers	16	72	2800	38.9	53	20	27.8	72	6	0	18	94	35.9	0	0	1	1	21	0
1995	Atlanta Falcons	16	67	2759	41.2	64	21	31.3	67	5	0	28	236	36.2	1	0	0	0	0	0
	6 NFL Seasons	96	445	17796	40.0	64	108	24.3	448	33	3	166	1156	35.7	9	13	3	3	35	0

Other Statistics: 1990–recovered 1 fumble for 0 yards. 1991–recovered 2 fumbles for 0 yards; fumbled 1 time.

Justin Strzelczyk

Pos: G/T   **Rnd:** 11   **College:** Maine   **Ht:** 6' 6"   **Wt:** 291   **Born:** 8/18/68   **Age:** 28

Year	Team	G	GS	Year	Team	G	GS	Year	Team	G	GS		G	GS
1990	Pittsburgh Steelers	16	0	1992	Pittsburgh Steelers	16	7	1994	Pittsburgh Steelers	15	5			
1991	Pittsburgh Steelers	16	0	1993	Pittsburgh Steelers	16	12	1995	Pittsburgh Steelers	16	14	6 NFL Seasons	95	38

Other Statistics: 1993–recovered 1 fumble for 0 yards.

Dana Stubblefield

Pos: DT   **Rnd:** 1 (26)   **College:** Kansas   *(statistical profile on page 454)*   **Ht:** 6' 2"   **Wt:** 290   **Born:** 11/14/70   **Age:** 25

Year	Team	G	GS	Tk	Ast	Sack	FF	FR	TD	Blk	Int	Yds	Avg	TD	Sfty	TD	Pts
				Tackles			**Miscellaneous**				**Interceptions**				**Totals**		
1993	San Francisco 49ers	16	14	55	9	10.5	1	0	0	0	0	0	-	0	0	0	0
1994	San Francisco 49ers	14	14	*34*	4	8.5	2	0	0	0	0	0	-	0	0	0	0
1995	San Francisco 49ers	16	16	27	7	4.5	0	0	0	1	1	12	12.0	0	0	0	0
	3 NFL Seasons	46	44	116	20	23.5	3	0	0	1	1	12	12.0	0	0	0	0

Daniel Stubbs

Pos: DE   **Rnd:** 2   **College:** Miami (FL)   **Ht:** 6' 4"   **Wt:** 272   **Born:** 1/3/65   **Age:** 31

Year	Team	G	GS	Tk	Ast	Sack	FF	FR	TD	Blk	Int	Yds	Avg	TD	Sfty	TD	Pts
				Tackles			**Miscellaneous**				**Interceptions**				**Totals**		
1988	San Francisco 49ers	16	1	20	5	6.0	1	1	0	0	0	0	-	0	0	0	0
1989	San Francisco 49ers	16	0	12	1	4.5	0	0	0	0	0	0	-	0	0	0	0
1990	Dallas Cowboys	16	15	29	30	7.5	2	2	0	0	0	0	-	0	0	0	0
1991	Dal - Cin	16	0	8	3	4.0	1	0	0	0	0	0	-	0	0	0	0

Year	Team	G	GS	Tk	Ast	Sack	FF	FR	TD	Blk	Int	Yds	Avg	TD	Sfty	TD	Pts
1992	Cincinnati Bengals	16	12	24	8	9.0	2	1	0	0	0	0	-	0	0	0	0
1993	Cincinnati Bengals	16	0	20	4	5.0	0	1	0	0	0	0	-	0	0	0	0
1995	Philadelphia Eagles	16	5	19	2	5.5	1	1	0	0	0	0	-	0	0	0	0
1991	Dallas Cowboys	9	0	5	3	1.0	0	1	0	0	0	0	-	0	0	0	0
	Cincinnati Bengals	7	0	3	0	3.0	1	0	0	0	0	0	-	0	0	0	0
7 NFL Seasons		112	33	132	53	41.5	7	7	0	0	0	0	-	0	0	0	0

Darren Studstill

Pos: S **Rnd:** 6 **College:** West Virginia **Ht:** 6' 1" **Wt:** 186 **Born:** 8/9/70 **Age:** 26

Year	Team	G	GS	Tk	Ast	Sack	FF	FR	TD	Blk	Int	Yds	Avg	TD	Sfty	TD	Pts
1994	Dallas Cowboys	1	0	0	0	0.0	0	0	0	0	0	0	-	0	0	0	0
1995	Jacksonville Jaguars	8	0	0	1	0.0	0	0	0	0	0	0	-	0	0	0	0
2 NFL Seasons		9	0	0	1	0.0	0	0	0	0	0	0	-	0	0	0	0

Oscar Sturgis

Pos: DE **Rnd:** 7 **College:** North Carolina **Ht:** 6' 5" **Wt:** 280 **Born:** 1/12/71 **Age:** 25

Year	Team	G	GS	Tk	Ast	Sack	FF	FR	TD	Blk	Int	Yds	Avg	TD	Sfty	TD	Pts
1995	Dallas Cowboys	1	0	0	0	0.0	0	0	0	0	0	0	-	0	0	0	0

Lorenzo Styles

Pos: LB **Rnd:** 3 **College:** Ohio State **Ht:** 6' 1" **Wt:** 244 **Born:** 1/31/74 **Age:** 22

Year	Team	G	GS	Tk	Ast	Sack	FF	FR	TD	Blk	Int	Yds	Avg	TD	Sfty	TD	Pts
1995	Atlanta Falcons	12	0	0	0	0.0	0	0	0	0	0	0	-	0	0	0	0

Mike Sullivan

Pos: G/C **Rnd:** 6 **College:** Miami (FL) **Ht:** 6' 3" **Wt:** 292 **Born:** 12/22/67 **Age:** 28

Year	Team	G	GS	Year	Team	G	GS	Year	Team	G	GS	Year	Team	G	GS
1992	Tampa Bay Buccaneers	9	0	1993	Tampa Bay Buccaneers	11	3	1994	Tampa Bay Buccaneers	15	1	1995	Tampa Bay Buccaneers	12	0
												4 NFL Seasons		47	4

Eddie Sutter

Pos: LB **Rnd:** FA **College:** Northwestern **Ht:** 6' 3" **Wt:** 235 **Born:** 10/3/69 **Age:** 27

Year	Team	G	GS	Tk	Ast	Sack	FF	FR	TD	Blk	Int	Yds	Avg	TD	Sfty	TD	Pts
1993	Cleveland Browns	15	0	0	0	0.0	0	0	0	0	0	0	-	0	0	0	0
1994	Cleveland Browns	16	0	2	1	0.0	0	0	0	0	0	0	-	0	0	0	0
1995	Cleveland Browns	16	0	0	0	0.0	0	0	0	0	0	0	-	0	0	0	0
3 NFL Seasons		47	0	2	1	0.0	0	0	0	0	0	0	-	0	0	0	0

Eric Swann

(statistical profile on page 454)

Pos: DT/NT **Rnd:** 1 (6) **College:** Wake Technical College **Ht:** 6' 5" **Wt:** 295 **Born:** 8/16/70 **Age:** 26

Year	Team	G	GS	Tk	Ast	Sack	FF	FR	TD	Blk	Int	Yds	Avg	TD	Sfty	TD	Pts
1991	Phoenix Cardinals	12	3	19	3	4.0	0	0	0	0	0	0	-	0	0	0	0
1992	Phoenix Cardinals	16	11	51	19	2.0	0	0	0	0	0	0	-	0	1	0	2
1993	Phoenix Cardinals	9	9	35	12	3.5	1	1	0	0	0	0	-	0	1	0	2
1994	Arizona Cardinals	16	16	46	25	7.5	1	1	0	0	1	0	0.0	0	1	0	2
1995	Arizona Cardinals	13	12	45	8	8.5	1	2	0	3	0	0	-	0	0	0	0
5 NFL Seasons		66	51	196	67	25.5	3	4	0	3	1	0	0.0	0	3	0	6

Harry Swayne

Pos: T **Rnd:** 7 **College:** Rutgers **Ht:** 6' 5" **Wt:** 295 **Born:** 2/2/65 **Age:** 31

Year	Team	G	GS	Year	Team	G	GS	Year	Team	G	GS			G	GS
1987	Tampa Bay Buccaneers	8	2	1990	Tampa Bay Buccaneers	10	0	1993	San Diego Chargers	11	11				
1988	Tampa Bay Buccaneers	10	1	1991	San Diego Chargers	12	12	1994	San Diego Chargers	16	16				
1989	Tampa Bay Buccaneers	16	0	1992	San Diego Chargers	16	16	1995	San Diego Chargers	16	16	9 NFL Seasons		115	74

Jim Sweeney

Pos: C **Rnd:** 2 **College:** Pittsburgh **Ht:** 6' 4" **Wt:** 284 **Born:** 8/8/62 **Age:** 34

Year	Team	G	GS	Year	Team	G	GS	Year	Team	G	GS	Year	Team	G	GS
1984	New York Jets	10	2	1987	New York Jets	12	12	1990	New York Jets	16	16	1993	New York Jets	16	16

Year	Team	G	GS	Year	Team	G	GS	Year	Team	G	GS	Year	Team	G	GS
1985	New York Jets	16	16	1988	New York Jets	16	16	1991	New York Jets	16	16	1994	New York Jets	16	16
1986	New York Jets	16	16	1989	New York Jets	16	16	1992	New York Jets	16	16	1995	Seattle Seahawks	16	16
													12 NFL Seasons	182	174

Other Statistics: 1990–recovered 1 fumble for 0 yards. 1994–recovered 1 fumble for 0 yards.

Pat Swilling

(statistical profile on page 454)

Pos: DE **Rnd:** 3 **College:** Georgia Tech **Ht:** 6' 3" **Wt:** 245 **Born:** 10/25/64 **Age:** 32

Year	Team	G	GS	Tackles			Miscellaneous				Interceptions				Totals		
				Tk	Ast	Sack	FF	FR	TD	Blk	Int	Yds	Avg	TD	Sfty	TD	Pts
1986	New Orleans Saints	16	0	22	4	4.0	0	0	0	0	0	0	-	0	0	0	0
1987	New Orleans Saints	12	12	40	9	10.5	3	3	0	0	1	10	10.0	0	0	0	0
1988	New Orleans Saints	15	14	40	11	7.0	3	1	0	0	0	0	-	0	0	0	0
1989	New Orleans Saints	16	15	50	6	16.5	5	1	0	0	1	14	14.0	0	0	0	0
1990	New Orleans Saints	16	16	52	11	11.0	4	0	0	0	0	0	-	0	0	0	0
1991	New Orleans Saints	16	16	50	10	**17.0**	6	1	0	0	1	39	39.0	1	0	1	6
1992	New Orleans Saints	16	16	40	9	10.5	3	1	0	0	0	0	-	0	0	0	0
1993	Detroit Lions	14	14	20	9	6.5	5	1	0	0	3	16	5.3	0	0	0	0
1994	Detroit Lions	16	7	21	7	3.5	0	1	0	0	0	0	-	0	0	0	0
1995	Oakland Raiders	16	16	31	5	13.0	5	0	0	0	0	0	-	0	0	0	0
	10 NFL Seasons	153	126	366	81	99.5	34	9	0	0	6	79	13.2	1	0	1	6

Jeff Sydner

Pos: PR/KR **Rnd:** 6 **College:** Hawaii **Ht:** 5' 6" **Wt:** 170 **Born:** 11/11/69 **Age:** 26

Year	Team	G	GS	Rushing					Receiving					Punt Returns				Kickoff Returns				Totals		
				Att	Yds	Avg	Lg	TD	Rec	Yds	Avg	Lg	TD	Num	Yds	Avg	TD	Num	Yds	Avg	TD	Fum	TD	Pts
1992	Philadelphia Eagles	16	0	0	0	-	-	0	0	0	-	-	0	7	52	7.4	0	17	368	21.6	0	1	0	0
1993	Philadelphia Eagles	4	0	0	0	-	-	0	2	42	21.0	31	0	0	0	-	0	9	158	17.6	0	3	0	0
1994	Philadelphia Eagles	16	0	0	0	-	-	0	1	10	10.0	10	0	40	381	9.5	0	19	392	20.6	0	2	0	0
1995	New York Jets	6	0	0	0	-	-	0	0	0	-	-	0	17	178	10.5	0	3	45	15.0	0	0	0	0
	4 NFL Seasons	42	0	0	0	-	-	0	3	52	17.3	31	0	64	611	9.5	0	48	963	20.1	0	6	0	0

Other Statistics: 1995–recovered 1 fumble for 35 yards.

David Szott

Pos: G **Rnd:** 7 **College:** Penn State **Ht:** 6' 4" **Wt:** 290 **Born:** 12/12/67 **Age:** 28

Year	Team	G	GS	Year	Team	G	GS	Year	Team	G	GS		Team	G	GS
1990	Kansas City Chiefs	16	11	1992	Kansas City Chiefs	16	16	1994	Kansas City Chiefs	16	16				
1991	Kansas City Chiefs	16	16	1993	Kansas City Chiefs	14	13	1995	Kansas City Chiefs	16	16		6 NFL Seasons	94	88

Other Statistics: 1990–recovered 1 fumble for 0 yards. 1991–recovered 1 fumble for 0 yards.

Ben Talley

Pos: LB **Rnd:** 4 **College:** Tennessee **Ht:** 6' 3" **Wt:** 248 **Born:** 7/14/72 **Age:** 24

Year	Team	G	GS	Tackles			Miscellaneous				Interceptions				Totals		
				Tk	Ast	Sack	FF	FR	TD	Blk	Int	Yds	Avg	TD	Sfty	TD	Pts
1995	New York Giants	4	0	0	0	0.0	0	0	0	0	0	0	-	0	0	0	0

Darryl Talley

(statistical profile on page 455)

Pos: LB **Rnd:** 2 **College:** West Virginia **Ht:** 6' 4" **Wt:** 235 **Born:** 7/10/60 **Age:** 36

Year	Team	G	GS	Tackles			Miscellaneous				Interceptions				Punt Returns				Kickoff Returns				Totals	
				Tk	Ast	Sack	FF	FR	TD	Blk	Int	Yds	Avg	TD	Num	Yds	Avg	TD	Num	Yds	Avg	TD	TD	Fum
1983	Buffalo Bills	16	0	26	13	5.0	0	2	0	0	0	0	-	0	0	0	-	0	2	9	4.5	0	0	0
1984	Buffalo Bills	16	16	59	25	5.0	0	1	0	0	1	0	0.0	0	0	0	-	0	0	0	-	0	0	0
1985	Buffalo Bills	16	5	23	20	2.0	0	0	0	0	0	0	-	0	0	0	-	0	0	0	-	0	0	0
1986	Buffalo Bills	16	16	71	45	3.0	0	0	0	0	0	0	-	0	0	0	-	0	0	0	-	0	0	0
1987	Buffalo Bills	12	12	52	27	1.0	0	1	0	0	0	0	-	0	0	0	-	0	0	0	-	0	0	0
1988	Buffalo Bills	16	15	46	27	2.5	2	1	0	0	0	0	-	0	0	0	-	0	0	0	-	0	0	0
1989	Buffalo Bills	16	16	70	27	6.0	1	0	0	0	0	0	-	0	0	0	-	0	0	0	-	0	0	0
1990	Buffalo Bills	16	16	79	44	4.0	0	1	0	0	2	60	30.0	1	0	0	-	0	0	0	-	0	1	0
1991	Buffalo Bills	16	16	89	28	4.0	4	2	0	0	5	45	9.0	0	0	0	-	0	0	0	-	0	0	0
1992	Buffalo Bills	16	16	73	33	4.0	2	0	0	0	0	0	-	0	0	0	-	0	0	0	-	0	0	0
1993	Buffalo Bills	16	16	101	35	2.0	4	2	0	0	3	74	24.7	1	0	0	-	0	0	0	-	0	1	0
1994	Buffalo Bills	16	16	82	33	0.0	1	1	0	0	0	0	-	0	0	0	-	0	0	0	-	0	0	0
1995	Atlanta Falcons	16	15	54	19	0.0	2	2	0	0	0	0	-	0	0	0	-	0	0	0	-	0	0	0
	13 NFL Seasons	204	175	825	376	38.5	16	14	0	0	11	179	16.3	2	0	0	-	0	2	9	4.5	0	2	0

Ralph Tamm

Pos: G/C **Rnd:** 9 **College:** West Chester **Ht:** 6' 4" **Wt:** 280 **Born:** 3/11/66 **Age:** 30

Year	Team	G	GS	Year	Team	G	GS	Year	Team	G	GS	Year	Team	G	GS
1990	Cleveland Browns	16	12	1991	Washington Redskins	2	0	1992	San Francisco 49ers	14	1	1994	San Francisco 49ers	1	1
1991	Cleveland Browns	1	0	1991	Cincinnati Bengals	1	0	1993	San Francisco 49ers	16	16	1995	Denver Broncos	13	1
													6 NFL Seasons	64	31

Other Statistics: 1993–recovered 1 fumble for 1 yard and 1 touchdown. 1995–recovered 1 fumble for 0 yards.

Maa Tanuvasa

Pos: DT **Rnd:** 8 **College:** Hawaii **Ht:** 6' 2" **Wt:** 277 **Born:** 11/6/70 **Age:** 25

				Tackles			Miscellaneous				Interceptions				Totals		
Year Team		G	GS	Tk	Ast	Sack	FF	FR	TD	Blk	Int	Yds	Avg	TD	Sfty	TD	Pts
1995 Denver Broncos		1	0	0	0	0.0	0	0	0	0	0	0	-	0	0	0	0

Steve Tasker

Pos: WR/PR **Rnd:** 9 **College:** Northwestern **Ht:** 5' 9" **Wt:** 181 **Born:** 4/10/62 **Age:** 34

				Rushing					Receiving					Punt Returns				Kickoff Returns				Totals		
Year Team		G	GS	Att	Yds	Avg	Lg	TD	Rec	Yds	Avg	Lg	TD	Num	Yds	Avg	TD	Num	Yds	Avg	TD	Fum	TD	Pts
1985 Houston Oilers		7	0	2	16	8.0	13	0	2	19	9.5	14	0	0	0	-	0	17	447	26.3	0	0	0	0
1986 Hou - Buf		9	0	0	0	-	-	0	0	0	-	-	0	0	0	-	0	12	213	17.8	0	0	0	0
1987 Buffalo Bills		12	0	0	0	-	-	0	0	0	-	-	0	0	0	-	0	11	197	17.9	0	2	0	2
1988 Buffalo Bills		14	0	0	0	-	-	0	0	0	-	-	0	0	0	-	0	0	0	-	0	0	0	0
1989 Buffalo Bills		16	0	0	0	-	-	0	0	0	-	-	0	0	0	-	0	2	39	19.5	0	0	0	0
1990 Buffalo Bills		16	0	0	0	-	-	0	2	44	22.0	t24	2	0	0	-	0	0	0	-	0	0	2	12
1991 Buffalo Bills		16	0	0	0	-	-	0	2	39	19.5	t20	1	0	0	-	0	0	0	-	0	0	1	6
1992 Buffalo Bills		15	2	1	9	9.0	9	0	2	24	12.0	17	0	0	0	-	0	0	0	-	0	0	0	0
1993 Buffalo Bills		15	0	0	0	-	-	0	2	26	13.0	22	0	1	0	0.0	0	0	0	-	0	1	0	0
1994 Buffalo Bills		14	0	0	0	-	-	0	0	0	-	-	0	0	0	-	0	1	2	2.0	0	0	0	0
1995 Buffalo Bills		13	3	8	74	9.3	17	0	20	255	12.8	43	3	17	204	12.0	0	0	0	-	0	0	3	18
1986 Houston Oilers		2	0	0	0	-	-	0	0	0	-	-	0	0	0	-	0	3	65	21.7	0	0	0	0
Buffalo Bills		7	0	0	0	-	-	0	0	0	-	-	0	0	0	-	0	9	148	16.4	0	0	0	0
11 NFL Seasons		147	5	11	99	9.0	17	0	30	407	13.6	43	6	18	204	11.3	0	43	898	20.9	0	3	6	38

Other Statistics: 1987–credited with 1 safety. 1990–recovered 2 fumbles for 5 yards. 1992–recovered 1 fumble for 0 yards. 1993–recovered 1 fumble for 0 yards.

David Tate

(statistical profile on page 455)

Pos: S **Rnd:** 8 **College:** Colorado **Ht:** 6' 1" **Wt:** 212 **Born:** 11/22/64 **Age:** 31

				Tackles			Miscellaneous				Interceptions				Punt Returns				Kickoff Returns				Totals	
Year Team		G	GS	Tk	Ast	Sack	FF	FR	TD	Blk	Int	Yds	Avg	TD	Num	Yds	Avg	TD	Num	Yds	Avg	TD	TD	Fum
1988 Chicago Bears		16	4	20	25	0.0	0	0	0	0	4	35	8.8	0	0	0	-	0	0	0	-	0	0	0
1989 Chicago Bears		14	4	28	32	0.0	0	0	0	0	1	0	0.0	0	0	0	-	0	1	12	12.0	0	0	0
1990 Chicago Bears		16	1	30	24	0.0	0	0	0	0	0	0	-	0	0	0	-	0	0	0	-	0	0	0
1991 Chicago Bears		16	0	14	16	0.0	0	0	0	0	2	35	17.5	0	0	0	-	0	0	0	-	0	0	0
1992 Chicago Bears		16	3	22	27	0.0	1	1	0	0	0	0	-	0	0	0	-	0	0	0	-	0	0	1
1993 New York Giants		14	1	25	5	0.0	0	0	0	0	1	12	12.0	0	0	0	-	0	0	0	-	0	0	0
1994 Indianapolis Colts		16	8	29	19	0.0	0	0	0	0	3	51	17.0	0	0	0	-	0	0	0	-	0	0	0
1995 Indianapolis Colts		16	16	61	22	0.0	1	1	0	0	0	0	-	0	0	0	-	0	0	0	-	0	0	0
8 NFL Seasons		124	37	229	170	0.0	2	2	0	0	11	133	12.1	0	0	0	-	0	1	12	12.0	0	0	1

Aaron Taylor

Pos: G **Rnd:** 1 (16) **College:** Notre Dame **Ht:** 6' 4" **Wt:** 305 **Born:** 11/14/72 **Age:** 23

Year	Team	G	GS					G	GS
1995	Green Bay Packers	16	16				1 NFL Season	16	16

Other Statistics: 1995–recovered 2 fumbles for 0 yards.

Bobby Taylor

(statistical profile on page 455)

Pos: CB **Rnd:** 2 **College:** Notre Dame **Ht:** 6' 3" **Wt:** 208 **Born:** 12/28/73 **Age:** 22

				Tackles			Miscellaneous				Interceptions				Totals		
Year Team		G	GS	Tk	Ast	Sack	FF	FR	TD	Blk	Int	Yds	Avg	TD	Sfty	TD	Pts
1995 Philadelphia Eagles		16	12	47	5	0.0	0	0	0	0	2	52	26.0	0	0	0	0

John Taylor

(statistical profile on page 379)

Pos: WR/PR **Rnd:** 3 **College:** Delaware State **Ht:** 6' 1" **Wt:** 185 **Born:** 3/31/62 **Age:** 34

				Rushing					Receiving					Punt Returns				Kickoff Returns				Totals		
Year Team		G	GS	Att	Yds	Avg	Lg	TD	Rec	Yds	Avg	Lg	TD	Num	Yds	Avg	TD	Num	Yds	Avg	TD	Fum	TD	Pts
1987 San Francisco 49ers		12	2	0	0	-	-	0	9	151	16.8	34	0	1	9	9.0	0	0	0	-	0	1	0	0
1988 San Francisco 49ers		12	4	0	0	-	-	0	14	325	23.2	t73	2	44	556	12.6	2	12	225	18.8	0	6	4	24

235

Year	Team	G	GS	Rushing Att	Yds	Avg	Lg	TD	Receiving Rec	Yds	Avg	Lg	TD	Punt Returns Num	Yds	Avg	TD	Kickoff Returns Num	Yds	Avg	TD	Totals Fum	TD	Pts
1989	San Francisco 49ers	15	15	1	6	6.0	6	0	60	1077	18.0	t95	10	36	417	11.6	0	2	51	25.5	0	3	10	60
1990	San Francisco 49ers	14	14	0	0	-	-	0	49	748	15.3	t78	7	26	212	8.2	0	0	0	-	0	2	7	42
1991	San Francisco 49ers	16	16	0	0	-	-	0	64	1011	15.8	t97	9	31	267	8.6	0	0	0	-	0	1	9	54
1992	San Francisco 49ers	9	8	1	10	10.0	10	0	25	428	17.1	t54	3	0	0	-	0	0	0	-	0	0	3	18
1993	San Francisco 49ers	16	16	2	17	8.5	12	0	56	940	16.8	t76	5	0	0	-	0	0	0	-	0	1	5	30
1994	San Francisco 49ers	15	15	2	-2	-1.0	1	0	41	531	13.0	35	5	0	0	-	0	0	0	-	0	1	5	30
1995	San Francisco 49ers	12	12	0	0	-	-	0	29	387	13.3	40	2	11	56	5.1	0	0	0	-	0	2	2	12
	9 NFL Seasons	121	102	6	31	5.2	12	0	347	5598	16.1	t97	43	149	1517	10.2	2	14	276	19.7	0	16	46	276

Other Statistics: 1987–recovered 1 fumble for 26 yards and 1 touchdown. 1988–recovered 2 fumbles for 0 yards. 1993–attempted 1 pass with 1 completion for 41 yards. 1995–attempted 1 pass with 1 completion for 21 yards.

Keith Taylor

Pos: S   **Rnd:** 5   **College:** Illinois   **Ht:** 5' 11"   **Wt:** 212   **Born:** 12/21/64   **Age:** 31

Year	Team	G	GS	Tackles Tk	Ast	Sack	Miscellaneous FF	FR	TD	Blk	Interceptions Int	Yds	Avg	TD	Totals Sfty	TD	Pts
1988	Indianapolis Colts	3	0	4	0	0.0	0	0	0	0	0	0	-	0	0	0	0
1989	Indianapolis Colts	16	0	22	14	0.0	0	0	0	0	7	225	32.1	1	0	1	6
1990	Indianapolis Colts	16	16	78	32	0.0	0	1	0	0	2	51	25.5	0	0	0	0
1991	Indianapolis Colts	16	10	35	21	0.0	0	1	0	0	0	-2	-	0	0	0	0
1992	New Orleans Saints	16	4	20	3	0.0	0	0	0	0	2	20	10.0	0	0	0	0
1993	New Orleans Saints	16	14	54	28	0.0	0	1	0	0	2	32	16.0	0	0	0	0
1994	Washington Redskins	1	1	1	0	0.0	0	0	0	0	0	0	-	0	0	0	0
1995	Washington Redskins	16	4	31	9	1.0	0	1	0	0	0	0	-	0	0	0	0
	8 NFL Seasons	100	49	245	107	1.0	0	4	0	0	13	326	25.1	1	0	1	6

Terry Taylor

Pos: CB   **Rnd:** 1 (22)   **College:** Southern Illinois   **Ht:** 5' 10"   **Wt:** 185   **Born:** 7/18/61   **Age:** 35

Year	Team	G	GS	Tackles Tk	Ast	Sack	Miscellaneous FF	FR	TD	Blk	Interceptions Int	Yds	Avg	TD	Totals Sfty	TD	Pts
1984	Seattle Seahawks	16	1	32	-	0.0	0	0	0	0	3	63	21.0	0	0	0	0
1985	Seattle Seahawks	16	16	72	-	0.0	0	0	1	0	4	75	18.8	1	0	2	12
1986	Seattle Seahawks	16	15	55	-	0.0	0	0	0	0	2	0	0.0	0	0	0	0
1987	Seattle Seahawks	12	12	42	-	0.0	0	0	0	0	1	11	11.0	0	0	0	0
1988	Seattle Seahawks	14	8	41	-	0.0	0	0	0	0	5	53	10.6	1	0	1	6
1989	Detroit Lions	15	15	57	-	0.0	0	1	0	0	1	0	0.0	0	0	0	0
1990	Detroit Lions	2	2	8	2	0.0	0	0	0	0	0	0	-	0	0	0	0
1991	Detroit Lions	11	0	25	-	0.0	0	1	0	0	4	26	6.5	0	0	0	0
1992	Cleveland Browns	16	16	47	-	0.0	0	1	0	0	1	0	0.0	0	0	0	0
1993	Cleveland Browns	10	7	27	16	0.0	0	0	0	0	0	0	-	0	0	0	0
1994	Seattle Seahawks	5	3	13	4	0.0	0	0	0	0	1	0	0.0	0	0	0	0
1995	Atlanta Falcons	16	5	40	1	0.0	0	2	0	0	3	31	10.3	0	0	0	0
	12 NFL Seasons	149	100	459	23	0.0	0	5	1	0	25	259	10.4	2	0	3	18

George Teague

Pos: S   **Rnd:** 1 (29)   **College:** Alabama   **Ht:** 6' 1"   **Wt:** 195   **Born:** 2/18/71   **Age:** 25

Year	Team	G	GS	Tackles Tk	Ast	Sack	FF	FR	TD	Blk	Interceptions Int	Yds	Avg	TD	Punt Returns Num	Yds	Avg	TD	Kickoff Returns Num	Yds	Avg	TD	Totals TD	Fum
1993	Green Bay Packers	16	12	27	9	0.0	1	2	0	0	1	22	22.0	0	1	-1	-1.0	0	0	0	-	0	0	0
1994	Green Bay Packers	16	16	41	12	0.0	0	1	0	0	3	33	11.0	0	0	0	-	0	0	0	-	0	0	0
1995	Green Bay Packers	15	15	42	15	0.0	0	1	0	0	2	100	50.0	0	0	0	-	0	0	0	-	0	0	0
	3 NFL Seasons	47	43	110	36	0.0	1	3	0	0	6	155	25.8	0	1	-1	-1.0	0	0	0	-	0	0	0

Pat Terrell

(statistical profile on page 456)

Pos: S   **Rnd:** 2   **College:** Notre Dame   **Ht:** 6' 2"   **Wt:** 210   **Born:** 3/18/68   **Age:** 28

Year	Team	G	GS	Tackles Tk	Ast	Sack	Miscellaneous FF	FR	TD	Blk	Interceptions Int	Yds	Avg	TD	Totals Sfty	TD	Pts
1990	Los Angeles Rams	15	1	7	4	0.0	0	1	0	0	1	6	6.0	0	0	0	0
1991	Los Angeles Rams	16	16	64	10	0.0	0	1	0	0	1	4	4.0	0	0	0	0
1992	Los Angeles Rams	15	11	45	10	0.0	0	0	0	0	0	0	-	0	0	0	0
1993	Los Angeles Rams	13	3	24	5	0.0	0	0	0	0	2	1	0.5	0	0	0	0
1994	New York Jets	16	2	18	8	0.0	0	0	0	0	0	0	-	0	0	0	0
1995	Carolina Panthers	16	13	45	16	0.0	0	1	0	0	3	33	11.0	0	0	0	0
	6 NFL Seasons	91	46	203	53	0.0	0	3	0	0	7	44	6.3	0	0	0	0

Doug Terry

Pos: S   **Rnd:** FA   **College:** Kansas   **Ht:** 5' 11"   **Wt:** 204   **Born:** 12/12/69   **Age:** 26

			Tackles			Miscellaneous				Interceptions				Totals		
Year Team	G	GS	Tk	Ast	Sack	FF	FR	TD	Blk	Int	Yds	Avg	TD	Sfty	TD	Pts
1992 Kansas City Chiefs	16	1	20	9	0.0	0	0	0	0	1	9	9.0	0	0	0	0
1993 Kansas City Chiefs	15	8	39	15	1.0	1	0	0	0	1	21	21.0	0	0	0	0
1994 Kansas City Chiefs	10	1	8	5	0.0	0	3	0	0	0	0	-	0	0	0	0
1995 Kansas City Chiefs	16	0	7	4	0.0	1	0	0	0	0	0	-	0	0	0	0
4 NFL Seasons	57	10	74	33	1.0	2	3	0	0	2	30	15.0	0	0	0	0

Ryan Terry

Pos: KR/RB   **Rnd:** FA   **College:** Iowa   **Ht:** 5' 11"   **Wt:** 203   **Born:** 9/20/71   **Age:** 25

			Rushing					Receiving					Punt Returns				Kickoff Returns				Totals		
Year Team	G	GS	Att	Yds	Avg	Lg	TD	Rec	Yds	Avg	Lg	TD	Num	Yds	Avg	TD	Num	Yds	Avg	TD	Fum	TD	Pts
1995 Arizona Cardinals	15	0	0	0	-	-	0	0	0	-	-	0	0	0	-	0	37	808	21.8	0	1	0	0

Other Statistics: 1995–recovered 1 fumble for 0 yards.

Vinny Testaverde

(statistical profile on page 380)

Pos: QB   **Rnd:** 1 (1)   **College:** Miami (FL)   **Ht:** 6' 5"   **Wt:** 227   **Born:** 11/13/63   **Age:** 32

			Passing										Rushing					Miscellaneous			
Year Team	G	GS	Att	Com	Pct	Yards	Yds/Att	Lg	TD	Int	Int%	Rating	Att	Yds	Avg	Lg	TD	Sckd	Yds	Fum	Recv	Yds	Pts
1987 Tampa Bay Buccaneers	6	4	165	71	43.0	1081	6.55	40	5	6	3.6	60.2	13	50	3.8	17	1	18	140	7	4	-3	6
1988 Tampa Bay Buccaneers	15	15	466	222	47.6	3240	6.95	t59	13	35	7.5	48.8	28	138	4.9	24	1	33	292	8	2	0	6
1989 Tampa Bay Buccaneers	14	14	480	258	53.8	3133	6.53	t78	20	22	4.6	68.9	25	139	5.6	16	0	38	294	4	2	0	0
1990 Tampa Bay Buccaneers	14	13	365	203	55.6	2818	7.72	t89	17	18	4.9	75.6	38	280	7.4	t48	1	38	330	10	3	0	6
1991 Tampa Bay Buccaneers	13	12	326	166	50.9	1994	6.12	t87	8	15	4.6	59.0	32	101	3.2	19	0	35	234	5	3	0	0
1992 Tampa Bay Buccaneers	14	14	358	206	57.5	2554	7.13	t81	14	16	4.5	74.2	36	197	5.5	18	2	35	259	4	4	-8	12
1993 Cleveland Browns	10	6	230	130	56.5	1797	7.81	t62	14	9	3.9	85.7	18	74	4.1	14	0	17	101	4	0	0	0
1994 Cleveland Browns	14	13	376	207	55.1	2575	6.85	t81	16	18	4.8	70.7	21	37	1.8	12	2	12	83	3	2	2	12
1995 Cleveland Browns	13	12	392	241	61.5	2883	7.35	t70	17	10	2.6	87.8	18	62	3.4	14	2	17	87	4	0	-5	12
9 NFL Seasons	113	103	3158	1704	54.0	22075	6.99	t89	124	149	4.7	69.6	229	1078	4.7	t48	9	243	1820	49	20	-14	54

Other Statistics: 1990–caught 1 pass for 3 yards. 1995–caught 1 pass for 7 yards.

Larry Tharpe

Pos: T   **Rnd:** 6   **College:** Tennessee State   **Ht:** 6' 4"   **Wt:** 299   **Born:** 11/19/70   **Age:** 25

Year Team	G	GS	Year Team	G	GS	Year Team	G	GS		G	GS
1992 Detroit Lions	11	0	1993 Detroit Lions	5	3	1995 Arizona Cardinals	16	16	3 NFL Seasons	32	19

Other Statistics: 1995–recovered 1 fumble for 0 yards.

John Thierry

Pos: DE   **Rnd:** 1 (11)   **College:** Alcorn State   **Ht:** 6' 4"   **Wt:** 260   **Born:** 9/4/71   **Age:** 25

			Tackles			Miscellaneous				Interceptions				Punt Returns				Kickoff Returns				Totals	
Year Team	G	GS	Tk	Ast	Sack	FF	FR	TD	Blk	Int	Yds	Avg	TD	Num	Yds	Avg	TD	Num	Yds	Avg	TD	TD	Fum
1994 Chicago Bears	16	1	3	2	0.0	0	0	0	0	0	0	-	0	0	0	-	0	1	0	0.0	0	0	0
1995 Chicago Bears	16	7	20	5	4.0	0	4	0	0	0	0	-	0	0	0	-	0	0	0	-	0	0	0
2 NFL Seasons	32	8	23	7	4.0	0	4	0	0	0	0	-	0	0	0	-	0	1	0	0.0	0	0	0

Yancey Thigpen

(statistical profile on page 380)

Pos: WR   **Rnd:** 4   **College:** Winston-Salem State   **Ht:** 6' 1"   **Wt:** 206   **Born:** 8/15/69   **Age:** 27

			Rushing					Receiving					Punt Returns				Kickoff Returns				Totals		
Year Team	G	GS	Att	Yds	Avg	Lg	TD	Rec	Yds	Avg	Lg	TD	Num	Yds	Avg	TD	Num	Yds	Avg	TD	Fum	TD	Pts
1991 San Diego Chargers	4	1	0	0	-	-	0	0	0	-	-	0	0	0	-	0	0	0	-	0	0	0	0
1992 Pittsburgh Steelers	12	0	0	0	-	-	0	1	2	2.0	2	0	0	0	-	0	2	44	22.0	0	0	0	0
1993 Pittsburgh Steelers	12	0	0	0	-	-	0	9	154	17.1	t39	3	0	0	-	0	1	23	23.0	0	0	3	18
1994 Pittsburgh Steelers	15	6	0	0	-	-	0	36	546	15.2	t60	4	0	0	-	0	5	121	24.2	0	1	4	24
1995 Pittsburgh Steelers	16	15	1	1	1.0	1	0	85	1307	15.4	43	5	0	0	-	0	0	0	-	0	1	5	30
5 NFL Seasons	59	22	1	1	1.0	1	0	131	2009	15.3	t60	12	0	0	-	0	8	188	23.5	0	1	12	72

Blair Thomas

Pos: RB   **Rnd:** 1 (2)   **College:** Penn State   **Ht:** 5' 10"   **Wt:** 202   **Born:** 10/7/67   **Age:** 29

			Rushing					Receiving					Kickoff Returns				Passing				Totals		
Year Team	G	GS	Att	Yds	Avg	Lg	TD	Rec	Yds	Avg	Lg	TD	Num	Yds	Avg	TD	Att	Com	Yds	Int	Fum	TD	Pts
1990 New York Jets	15	13	123	620	5.0	41	1	20	204	10.2	55	1	0	0	-	0	0	0	0	0	3	2	12
1991 New York Jets	16	15	189	728	3.9	25	3	30	195	6.5	18	1	0	0	-	0	1	1	16	0	3	4	24
1992 New York Jets	9	9	97	440	4.5	19	0	7	49	7.0	10	0	0	0	-	0	0	0	0	0	2	0	0

		Rushing					Receiving					Kickoff Returns				Passing				Totals		
Year Team	G	GS	Att	Yds	Avg	Lg	TD	Rec	Yds	Avg	Lg	TD	Num	Yds	Avg	TD	Att	Com	Yds	Int	Fum	TD	Pts
1993 New York Jets	11	6	59	221	3.7	24	1	7	25	3.6	7	0	2	39	19.5	0	0	0	0	0	0	1	6
1994 NE - Dal	6	1	43	137	3.2	13	2	4	16	4.0	9	0	3	40	13.3	0	0	0	0	0	0	2	12
1995 Carolina Panthers	7	0	22	90	4.1	13	0	3	24	8.0	14	0	0	0	-	0	0	0	0	0	0	0	0
1994 New England Patriots	4	0	19	67	3.5	13	1	2	15	7.5	9	0	3	40	13.3	0	0	0	0	0	0	1	6
Dallas Cowboys	2	1	24	70	2.9	11	1	2	1	0.5	5	0	0	0	-	0	0	0	0	0	0	1	6
6 NFL Seasons	64	44	533	2236	4.2	41	7	71	513	7.2	55	2	5	79	15.8	0	1	1	16	0	8	9	54

Other Statistics: 1991–passed for 1 touchdown. 1993–recovered 1 fumble for 0 yards. 1995–recovered 0 fumbles for 8 yards.

Broderick Thomas

(statistical profile on page 456)

Pos: LB **Rnd:** 1 (6) **College:** Nebraska **Ht:** 6' 4" **Wt:** 242 **Born:** 2/20/67 **Age:** 29

			Tackles			Miscellaneous				Interceptions				Totals		
Year Team	G	GS	Tk	Ast	Sack	FF	FR	TD	Blk	Int	Yds	Avg	TD	Sfty	TD	Pts
1989 Tampa Bay Buccaneers	16	0	18	9	2.0	1	0	0	0	0	0	-	0	0	0	0
1990 Tampa Bay Buccaneers	16	15	48	24	7.5	2	2	0	0	0	0	-	0	0	0	0
1991 Tampa Bay Buccaneers	16	16	98	76	11.0	7	2	0	0	0	0	-	0	0	0	0
1992 Tampa Bay Buccaneers	16	16	62	51	5.0	1	3	0	0	2	81	40.5	1	0	1	6
1993 Tampa Bay Buccaneers	16	8	43	32	1.0	0	1	0	0	0	0	-	0	0	0	0
1994 Detroit Lions	16	16	64	24	7.0	2	2	0	0	0	0	-	0	0	0	0
1995 Minnesota Vikings	16	16	57	15	6.0	1	1	0	0	0	0	-	0	0	0	0
7 NFL Seasons	112	87	390	231	39.5	14	11	0	0	2	81	40.5	1	0	1	6

Chris Thomas

Pos: WR **Rnd:** FA **College:** Cal Poly-S.L.O. **Ht:** 6' 1" **Wt:** 180 **Born:** 7/16/71 **Age:** 25

			Rushing					Receiving					Punt Returns				Kickoff Returns				Totals		
Year Team	G	GS	Att	Yds	Avg	Lg	TD	Rec	Yds	Avg	Lg	TD	Num	Yds	Avg	TD	Num	Yds	Avg	TD	Fum	TD	Pts
1995 San Francisco 49ers	14	0	0	0	-	-	0	6	73	12.2	23	0	1	25	25.0	0	3	49	16.3	0	0	0	0

Damon Thomas

Pos: WR **Rnd:** FA **College:** Wayne State (NE) **Ht:** 6' 2" **Wt:** 215 **Born:** 12/15/70 **Age:** 25

			Rushing					Receiving					Punt Returns				Kickoff Returns				Totals		
Year Team	G	GS	Att	Yds	Avg	Lg	TD	Rec	Yds	Avg	Lg	TD	Num	Yds	Avg	TD	Num	Yds	Avg	TD	Fum	TD	Pts
1994 Buffalo Bills	3	0	0	0	-	-	0	2	31	15.5	17	0	0	0	-	0	0	0	-	0	0	0	0
1995 Buffalo Bills	14	0	0	0	-	-	0	1	18	18.0	18	0	1	0	0.0	0	0	0	-	0	1	0	0
2 NFL Seasons	17	0	0	0	-	-	0	3	49	16.3	18	0	1	0	0.0	0	0	0	-	0	1	0	0

Dave Thomas

Pos: CB **Rnd:** 8 **College:** Tennessee **Ht:** 6' 3" **Wt:** 213 **Born:** 8/25/68 **Age:** 28

			Tackles			Miscellaneous				Interceptions				Totals		
Year Team	G	GS	Tk	Ast	Sack	FF	FR	TD	Blk	Int	Yds	Avg	TD	Sfty	TD	Pts
1993 Dallas Cowboys	12	0	0	0	0.0	0	0	0	0	0	0	-	0	0	0	0
1994 Dallas Cowboys	16	0	2	0	0.0	0	0	0	0	0	0	-	0	0	0	0
1995 Jacksonville Jaguars	15	2	28	11	0.0	0	1	0	0	0	0	-	0	0	0	0
3 NFL Seasons	43	2	30	11	0.0	0	1	0	0	0	0	-	0	0	0	0

Derrick Thomas

(statistical profile on page 456)

Pos: LB **Rnd:** 1 (4) **College:** Alabama **Ht:** 6' 3" **Wt:** 247 **Born:** 1/1/67 **Age:** 29

			Tackles			Miscellaneous				Interceptions				Totals		
Year Team	G	GS	Tk	Ast	Sack	FF	FR	TD	Blk	Int	Yds	Avg	TD	Sfty	TD	Pts
1989 Kansas City Chiefs	16	16	56	19	10.0	3	1	0	0	0	0	-	0	0	0	0
1990 Kansas City Chiefs	15	15	47	16	20.0	6	2	0	0	0	0	-	0	0	0	0
1991 Kansas City Chiefs	16	15	60	19	13.5	4	4	1	0	0	0	-	0	0	1	6
1992 Kansas City Chiefs	16	16	54	13	14.5	8	3	1	0	0	0	-	0	0	1	6
1993 Kansas City Chiefs	16	15	32	11	8.0	4	1	1	0	0	0	-	0	0	1	6
1994 Kansas City Chiefs	16	15	65	6	11.0	3	3	0	0	0	0	-	0	1	0	2
1995 Kansas City Chiefs	15	15	48	5	8.0	2	1	0	0	0	0	-	0	0	0	0
7 NFL Seasons	110	107	362	89	85.0	30	15	3	0	0	0	-	0	1	3	20

Eric Thomas

Pos: CB **Rnd:** 2 **College:** Tulane **Ht:** 5' 11" **Wt:** 184 **Born:** 9/11/64 **Age:** 32

			Tackles			Miscellaneous				Interceptions				Punt Returns				Kickoff Returns				Totals	
Year Team	G	GS	Tk	Ast	Sack	FF	FR	TD	Blk	Int	Yds	Avg	TD	Num	Yds	Avg	TD	Num	Yds	Avg	TD	TD	Fum
1987 Cincinnati Bengals	12	12	15	3	1.0	0	0	0	0	1	3	3.0	0	0	0	-	0	0	0	-	0	0	0
1988 Cincinnati Bengals	16	16	46	18	0.0	0	0	0	0	7	61	8.7	0	0	0	-	0	0	0	-	0	0	0
1989 Cincinnati Bengals	16	15	40	8	2.0	0	1	0	0	4	18	4.5	1	0	0	-	0	0	0	-	0	1	0

Year Team	G	GS	Tackles			Miscellaneous				Interceptions				Punt Returns				Kickoff Returns				Totals	
			Tk	Ast	Sack	FF	FR	TD	Blk	Int	Yds	Avg	TD	Num	Yds	Avg	TD	Num	Yds	Avg	TD	TD	Fum
1990 Cincinnati Bengals	4	2	11	-	0.0	0	0	0	0	0	0	-	0	0	0	-	0	0	0	-	0	0	0
1991 Cincinnati Bengals	16	16	51	5	0.0	0	1	0	0	3	0	0.0	0	0	0	-	0	1	-1	-1.0	0	0	0
1992 Cincinnati Bengals	16	16	40	2	0.0	0	0	0	0	0	0	-	0	0	0	-	0	0	0	-	0	0	0
1993 New York Jets	16	16	46	17	0.0	2	1	0	0	2	20	10.0	0	0	0	-	0	0	0	-	0	0	0
1994 New York Jets	2	0	0	0	0.0	0	0	0	0	0	0	-	0	0	0	-	0	0	0	-	0	0	0
1995 Denver Broncos	14	0	15	5	0.0	0	0	0	0	0	0	-	0	0	0	-	0	0	0	-	0	0	0
9 NFL Seasons	112	93	264	58	3.0	2	3	0	0	17	102	6.0	1	0	0	-	0	1	-1	-1.0	0	1	0

Henry Thomas

Pos: NT/DT **Rnd:** 3 **College:** Louisiana State *(statistical profile on page 457)* **Ht:** 6' 2" **Wt:** 277 **Born:** 1/12/65 **Age:** 31

Year Team	G	GS	Tackles			Miscellaneous				Interceptions				Totals		
			Tk	Ast	Sack	FF	FR	TD	Blk	Int	Yds	Avg	TD	Sfty	TD	Pts
1987 Minnesota Vikings	12	12	56	25	2.5	0	1	0	0	1	0	0.0	0	0	0	0
1988 Minnesota Vikings	15	15	53	27	6.0	4	1	1	0	1	7	7.0	0	0	1	6
1989 Minnesota Vikings	14	14	68	26	9.0	3	3	1	0	0	0	-	0	0	1	6
1990 Minnesota Vikings	16	16	64	45	8.5	1	1	0	0	0	0	-	0	0	0	0
1991 Minnesota Vikings	16	15	61	39	8.0	0	1	0	0	0	0	-	0	0	0	0
1992 Minnesota Vikings	16	16	50	19	6.0	0	0	0	0	0	0	-	0	0	0	0
1993 Minnesota Vikings	13	13	60	6	9.0	1	0	0	0	0	0	-	0	0	1	2
1994 Minnesota Vikings	16	16	41	14	7.0	2	1	0	0	0	0	-	0	0	0	0
1995 Detroit Lions	16	16	45	23	10.5	2	2	0	2	0	0	-	0	0	0	0
9 NFL Seasons	134	133	498	224	66.5	13	10	2	2	2	7	3.5	0	1	2	14

J.T. Thomas

Pos: KR/WR **Rnd:** 7 **College:** Arizona State **Ht:** 5' 10" **Wt:** 173 **Born:** 12/15/71 **Age:** 24

Year Team	G	GS	Rushing					Receiving					Punt Returns				Kickoff Returns				Totals		
			Att	Yds	Avg	Lg	TD	Rec	Yds	Avg	Lg	TD	Num	Yds	Avg	TD	Num	Yds	Avg	TD	Fum	TD	Pts
1995 St. Louis Rams	15	1	0	0	-	-	0	5	42	8.4	12	0	0	61	-	0	32	752	23.5	0	1	0	0

Other Statistics: 1995–recovered 1 fumble for 5 yards.

Johnny Thomas

Pos: CB **Rnd:** 7 **College:** Baylor **Ht:** 5' 9" **Wt:** 191 **Born:** 8/3/64 **Age:** 32

Year Team	G	GS	Tackles			Miscellaneous				Interceptions				Punt Returns				Kickoff Returns				Totals	
			Tk	Ast	Sack	FF	FR	TD	Blk	Int	Yds	Avg	TD	Num	Yds	Avg	TD	Num	Yds	Avg	TD	TD	Fum
1988 Washington Redskins	4	0	0	0	0.0	0	0	0	0	0	0	-	0	0	0	-	0	0	0	-	0	0	0
1989 San Diego Chargers	13	0	6	1	0.0	0	0	0	0	0	0	-	0	0	0	-	0	0	0	-	0	0	0
1990 Washington Redskins	2	0	0	0	0.0	0	0	0	0	0	0	-	0	1	0	0.0	0	0	0	-	0	0	1
1992 Washington Redskins	16	0	3	1	0.0	0	1	0	0	0	0	-	0	1	0	0.0	0	0	0	-	0	0	1
1993 Washington Redskins	16	0	0	0	0.0	0	2	0	0	0	0	-	0	0	0	-	0	0	0	-	0	0	0
1994 Washington Redskins	16	0	0	0	0.0	0	0	0	0	0	0	-	0	0	0	-	0	0	0	-	0	0	0
1995 Cleveland Browns	16	0	4	1	0.0	0	1	0	0	0	0	-	0	0	0	-	0	0	0	-	0	0	0
7 NFL Seasons	83	0	13	3	0.0	0	4	0	0	0	0	-	0	2	0	0.0	0	0	0	-	0	0	2

Lamar Thomas

Pos: WR **Rnd:** 3 **College:** Miami (FL) **Ht:** 6' 2" **Wt:** 173 **Born:** 2/12/70 **Age:** 26

Year Team	G	GS	Rushing					Receiving					Punt Returns				Kickoff Returns				Totals		
			Att	Yds	Avg	Lg	TD	Rec	Yds	Avg	Lg	TD	Num	Yds	Avg	TD	Num	Yds	Avg	TD	Fum	TD	Pts
1993 Tampa Bay Buccaneers	14	2	0	0	-	-	0	8	186	23.3	t62	2	0	0	-	0	0	0	-	0	0	2	12
1994 Tampa Bay Buccaneers	10	0	0	0	-	-	0	7	94	13.4	27	0	0	0	-	0	0	0	-	0	0	0	0
1995 Tampa Bay Buccaneers	11	0	1	5	5.0	5	0	10	107	10.7	24	0	0	0	-	0	0	0	-	0	0	0	0
3 NFL Seasons	35	2	1	5	5.0	5	0	25	387	15.5	t62	2	0	0	-	0	0	0	-	0	0	2	12

Mark Thomas

Pos: DE **Rnd:** 4 **College:** North Carolina State **Ht:** 6' 5" **Wt:** 273 **Born:** 5/6/69 **Age:** 27

Year Team	G	GS	Tackles			Miscellaneous				Interceptions				Totals		
			Tk	Ast	Sack	FF	FR	TD	Blk	Int	Yds	Avg	TD	Sfty	TD	Pts
1993 San Francisco 49ers	11	1	13	2	0.5	0	1	0	0	0	0	-	0	0	0	0
1994 San Francisco 49ers	8	0	2	0	1.0	0	0	0	0	0	0	-	0	0	0	0
1995 Carolina Panthers	10	0	10	4	2.0	0	0	0	0	0	0	-	0	0	0	0
3 NFL Seasons	29	1	25	6	3.5	0	1	0	0	0	0	-	0	0	0	0

Orlanda Thomas

Pos: S **Rnd:** 2 **College:** Southwestern Louisiana **Ht:** 6' 1" **Wt:** 209 **Born:** 10/21/72 **Age:** 24

Year	Team	G	GS	Tackles Tk	Ast	Sack	Miscellaneous FF	FR	TD	Blk	Interceptions Int	Yds	Avg	TD	Totals Sfty	TD	Pts
1995	Minnesota Vikings	16	11	41	10	0.0	1	4	1	0	9	108	12.0	1	0	2	12

Other Statistics: 1995–fumbled 1 time.

Robb Thomas

Pos: WR **Rnd:** 6 **College:** Oregon State **Ht:** 5' 11" **Wt:** 175 **Born:** 3/29/66 **Age:** 30

Year	Team	G	GS	Rushing Att	Yds	Avg	Lg	TD	Receiving Rec	Yds	Avg	Lg	TD	Punt Returns Num	Yds	Avg	TD	Kickoff Returns Num	Yds	Avg	TD	Totals Fum	TD	Pts
1989	Kansas City Chiefs	8	1	0	0	-	-	0	8	58	7.3	12	2	0	0	-	0	0	0	-	0	1	2	12
1990	Kansas City Chiefs	16	12	0	0	-	-	0	41	545	13.3	t47	4	0	0	-	0	0	0	-	0	0	4	24
1991	Kansas City Chiefs	15	12	0	0	-	-	0	43	495	11.5	39	1	0	0	-	0	0	0	-	0	0	1	6
1992	Seattle Seahawks	15	0	1	-1	-1.0	-1	0	11	136	12.4	31	0	0	0	-	0	0	0	-	0	1	0	0
1993	Seattle Seahawks	16	0	0	0	-	-	0	7	67	9.6	16	0	0	0	-	0	0	0	-	0	0	0	0
1994	Seattle Seahawks	16	1	0	0	-	-	0	4	70	17.5	35	0	0	0	-	0	0	0	-	0	0	0	0
1995	Seattle Seahawks	15	2	0	0	-	-	0	12	239	19.9	t50	1	0	0	-	0	0	0	-	0	0	1	6
	7 NFL Seasons	101	28	1	-1	-1.0	-1	0	126	1610	12.8	t50	8	0	0	-	0	0	0	-	0	2	8	48

Rodney Thomas

(statistical profile on page 381)

Pos: RB **Rnd:** 3 **College:** Texas A&M **Ht:** 5' 10" **Wt:** 213 **Born:** 3/30/73 **Age:** 23

Year	Team	G	GS	Rushing Att	Yds	Avg	Lg	TD	Receiving Rec	Yds	Avg	Lg	TD	Punt Returns Num	Yds	Avg	TD	Kickoff Returns Num	Yds	Avg	TD	Totals Fum	TD	Pts
1995	Houston Oilers	16	10	251	947	3.8	t74	5	39	204	5.2	19	2	0	0	-	0	3	48	16.0	0	8	7	44

Other Statistics: 1995–scored 1 two-point conversion.

Thurman Thomas

(statistical profile on page 381)

Pos: RB **Rnd:** 2 **College:** Oklahoma State **Ht:** 5' 10" **Wt:** 198 **Born:** 5/16/66 **Age:** 30

Year	Team	G	GS	Rushing Att	Yds	Avg	Lg	TD	Receiving Rec	Yds	Avg	Lg	TD	Kickoff Returns Num	Yds	Avg	TD	Passing Att	Com	Yds	Int	Totals Fum	TD	Pts
1988	Buffalo Bills	15	15	207	881	4.3	t37	2	18	208	11.6	34	0	0	0	-	0	0	0	0	0	9	2	12
1989	Buffalo Bills	16	16	298	1244	4.2	38	6	60	669	11.2	t74	6	0	0	-	0	0	0	0	0	7	12	72
1990	Buffalo Bills	16	16	271	1297	4.8	t80	11	49	532	10.9	63	2	0	0	-	0	0	0	0	0	6	13	78
1991	Buffalo Bills	15	15	288	1407	4.9	33	7	62	631	10.2	t50	5	0	0	-	0	0	0	0	0	5	12	72
1992	Buffalo Bills	16	16	312	1487	4.8	44	9	58	626	10.8	43	3	0	0	-	0	0	0	0	0	6	12	72
1993	Buffalo Bills	16	16	355	1315	3.7	27	6	48	387	8.1	37	0	0	0	-	0	1	0	0	0	6	6	36
1994	Buffalo Bills	15	15	287	1093	3.8	29	7	50	349	7.0	28	2	0	0	-	0	0	0	0	0	1	9	54
1995	Buffalo Bills	14	14	267	1005	3.8	49	6	26	220	8.5	60	2	0	0	-	0	0	0	0	0	6	8	48
	8 NFL Seasons	123	123	2285	9729	4.3	t80	54	371	3622	9.8	t74	20	0	0	-	0	1	0	0	0	46	74	444

Other Statistics: 1988–recovered 1 fumble for 0 yards. 1989–recovered 2 fumbles for 0 yards. 1990–recovered 2 fumbles for 0 yards. 1992–recovered 1 fumble for 0 yards. 1993–recovered 1 fumble for 0 yards. 1994–recovered 2 fumbles for 0 yards.

William Thomas

(statistical profile on page 457)

Pos: LB **Rnd:** 4 **College:** Texas A&M **Ht:** 6' 2" **Wt:** 223 **Born:** 8/13/68 **Age:** 28

Year	Team	G	GS	Tackles Tk	Ast	Sack	Miscellaneous FF	FR	TD	Blk	Interceptions Int	Yds	Avg	TD	Totals Sfty	TD	Pts
1991	Philadelphia Eagles	16	7	21	19	2.0	0	1	0	0	0	0	-	0	0	0	0
1992	Philadelphia Eagles	16	15	68	26	1.5	0	2	0	0	2	4	2.0	0	0	0	0
1993	Philadelphia Eagles	16	16	67	40	6.5	4	3	0	0	2	39	19.5	0	0	0	0
1994	Philadelphia Eagles	16	16	60	27	6.0	0	0	0	0	1	7	7.0	0	0	0	0
1995	Philadelphia Eagles	16	16	62	12	2.0	1	1	0	0	7	104	14.9	1	0	1	6
	5 NFL Seasons	80	70	278	124	18.0	5	7	0	0	12	154	12.8	1	0	1	6

Jeff Thomason

Pos: TE **Rnd:** FA **College:** Oregon **Ht:** 6' 4" **Wt:** 250 **Born:** 12/30/69 **Age:** 26

Year	Team	G	GS	Rushing Att	Yds	Avg	Lg	TD	Receiving Rec	Yds	Avg	Lg	TD	Punt Returns Num	Yds	Avg	TD	Kickoff Returns Num	Yds	Avg	TD	Totals Fum	TD	Pts
1992	Cincinnati Bengals	4	1	0	0	-	-	0	2	14	7.0	10	0	0	0	-	0	0	0	-	0	0	0	0
1993	Cincinnati Bengals	3	0	0	0	-	-	0	2	8	4.0	5	0	0	0	-	0	0	0	-	0	0	0	0
1995	Green Bay Packers	16	1	0	0	-	-	0	3	32	10.7	15	0	0	0	-	0	1	16	16.0	0	0	0	0
	3 NFL Seasons	23	2	0	0	-	-	0	7	54	7.7	15	0	0	0	-	0	1	16	16.0	0	0	0	0

Other Statistics: 1995–recovered 1 fumble for 0 yards.

Bennie Thompson

Pos: S   **Rnd:** FA   **College:** Grambling   **Ht:** 6' 0"   **Wt:** 214   **Born:** 2/10/63   **Age:** 33

			Tackles			Miscellaneous				Interceptions				Totals		
Year	Team	G	GS	Tk	Ast	Sack	FF	FR	TD	Blk	Int	Yds	Avg	TD	Sfty	TD	Pts
1989	New Orleans Saints	2	0	3	0	0.0	0	0	0	0	0	0	-	0	0	0	0
1990	New Orleans Saints	16	2	29	8	0.0	0	0	0	0	2	0	0.0	0	0	0	0
1991	New Orleans Saints	16	0	7	2	0.0	0	2	0	0	1	14	14.0	0	0	0	0
1992	Kansas City Chiefs	16	0	34	10	1.5	0	0	0	0	4	26	6.5	0	0	0	0
1993	Kansas City Chiefs	16	0	16	10	0.5	0	0	0	0	0	0	-	0	0	0	0
1994	Cleveland Browns	16	0	5	1	1.0	1	1	0	0	0	0	-	0	0	0	0
1995	Cleveland Browns	13	0	3	2	0.0	0	0	0	0	0	0	-	0	0	0	0
	7 NFL Seasons	95	2	97	33	3.0	1	3	0	0	7	40	5.7	0	0	0	0

Broderick Thompson

Pos: T   **Rnd:** FA   **College:** Kansas   **Ht:** 6' 5"   **Wt:** 295   **Born:** 8/14/60   **Age:** 36

Year	Team	G	GS	Year	Team	G	GS	Year	Team	G	GS
1985	Dallas Cowboys	11	1	1989	San Diego Chargers	16	16	1992	San Diego Chargers	12	12	1995	Denver Broncos	16	16
1987	San Diego Chargers	9	4	1990	San Diego Chargers	16	16	1993	Philadelphia Eagles	10	10				
1988	San Diego Chargers	16	16	1991	San Diego Chargers	16	16	1994	Philadelphia Eagles	14	14		10 NFL Seasons	136	121

Other Statistics: 1991–recovered 1 fumble for 0 yards. 1994–recovered 1 fumble for 0 yards.

Leroy Thompson

Pos: RB   **Rnd:** 6   **College:** Penn State   **Ht:** 5' 11"   **Wt:** 216   **Born:** 2/3/68   **Age:** 28

				Rushing					Receiving					Punt Returns				Kickoff Returns				Totals		
Year	Team	G	GS	Att	Yds	Avg	Lg	TD	Rec	Yds	Avg	Lg	TD	Num	Yds	Avg	TD	Num	Yds	Avg	TD	Fum	TD	Pts
1991	Pittsburgh Steelers	13	0	20	60	3.0	14	0	14	118	8.4	32	0	0	0	-	0	1	8	8.0	0	1	0	0
1992	Pittsburgh Steelers	15	2	35	157	4.5	25	1	22	278	12.6	29	0	0	0	-	0	2	51	25.5	0	2	1	6
1993	Pittsburgh Steelers	15	6	205	763	3.7	36	3	38	259	6.8	28	0	0	0	-	0	4	77	19.3	0	7	3	18
1994	New England Patriots	16	1	102	312	3.1	13	2	65	465	7.2	t27	5	0	0	-	0	18	376	20.9	0	2	7	42
1995	Kansas City Chiefs	16	0	28	73	2.6	10	0	9	37	4.1	7	0	0	0	-	0	6	152	25.3	0	0	0	0
	5 NFL Seasons	75	9	390	1365	3.5	36	6	148	1157	7.8	32	5	0	0	-	0	31	664	21.4	0	12	11	66

Other Statistics: 1991–recovered 1 fumble for 0 yards. 1993–recovered 1 fumble for 0 yards. 1994–recovered 1 fumble for 0 yards.

Mike Thompson

Pos: DT   **Rnd:** 4   **College:** Wisconsin   **Ht:** 6' 3"   **Wt:** 276   **Born:** 12/22/72   **Age:** 23

				Tackles			Miscellaneous				Interceptions				Totals		
Year	Team	G	GS	Tk	Ast	Sack	FF	FR	TD	Blk	Int	Yds	Avg	TD	Sfty	TD	Pts
1995	Jacksonville Jaguars	1	0	0	0	0.0	0	0	0	0	0	0	-	0	0	0	0

Tommy Thompson

(statistical profile on page 485)

Pos: P   **Rnd:** FA   **College:** Oregon   **Ht:** 5' 9"   **Wt:** 192   **Born:** 4/27/72   **Age:** 24

			Punting										Rushing		Passing			
Year	Team	G	NetPunts	Yards	Avg	Long	In20	In20%	TotPunts	TB	Blocks	OppRet	RetYds	NetAvg	Att	Yards	Att	Com	Yards	Int
1995	San Francisco 49ers	16	57	2312	40.6	65	13	22.8	57	5	0	26	292	33.7	0	0	0	0	0	0

James Thornton

Pos: TE   **Rnd:** 4   **College:** California State-Fullerton   **Ht:** 6' 2"   **Wt:** 242   **Born:** 2/8/65   **Age:** 31

				Rushing					Receiving					Punt Returns				Kickoff Returns				Totals		
Year	Team	G	GS	Att	Yds	Avg	Lg	TD	Rec	Yds	Avg	Lg	TD	Num	Yds	Avg	TD	Num	Yds	Avg	TD	Fum	TD	Pts
1988	Chicago Bears	16	12	0	0	-	-	0	15	135	9.0	19	0	0	0	-	0	0	0	-	0	1	0	0
1989	Chicago Bears	16	16	1	4	4.0	4	0	24	392	16.3	t36	3	0	0	-	0	0	0	-	0	2	3	18
1990	Chicago Bears	16	16	0	0	-	-	0	19	254	13.4	32	1	0	0	-	0	0	0	-	0	1	1	6
1991	Chicago Bears	16	13	0	0	-	-	0	17	278	16.4	33	1	0	0	-	0	0	0	-	0	1	1	6
1993	New York Jets	13	6	0	0	-	-	0	12	108	9.0	22	2	0	0	-	0	0	0	-	0	0	2	12
1994	New York Jets	16	5	0	0	-	-	0	20	171	8.6	25	0	0	0	-	0	1	0	0.0	0	0	0	0
1995	Houston Oilers	4	2	0	0	-	-	0	0	0	-	-	0	0	0	-	0	0	0	-	0	0	0	0
	7 NFL Seasons	97	70	1	4	4.0	4	0	107	1338	12.5	t36	7	0	0	-	0	1	0	0.0	0	5	7	42

Other Statistics: 1994–recovered 2 fumbles for 0 yards.

Brian Thure

Pos: T   **Rnd:** 6   **College:** California   **Ht:** 6' 5"   **Wt:** 300   **Born:** 9/3/73   **Age:** 23

Year	Team	G	GS					G	GS
1995	Washington Redskins	4	0			1 NFL Season	4	0

Mike Tice

Pos: TE **Rnd:** FA **College:** Maryland **Ht:** 6' 7" **Wt:** 253 **Born:** 2/2/59 **Age:** 37

Year	Team	G	GS	Rushing Att	Yds	Avg	Lg	TD	Receiving Rec	Yds	Avg	Lg	TD	Punt Returns Num	Yds	Avg	TD	Kickoff Returns Num	Yds	Avg	TD	Totals Fum	TD	Pts
1981	Seattle Seahawks	16	3	0	0	-	-	0	5	47	9.4	14	0	0	0	-	0	0	0	-	0	0	0	0
1982	Seattle Seahawks	9	9	0	0	-	-	0	9	46	5.1	12	0	0	0	-	0	0	0	-	0	0	0	0
1983	Seattle Seahawks	15	1	0	0	-	-	0	0	0	-	-	0	0	0	-	0	2	28	14.0	0	0	0	0
1984	Seattle Seahawks	16	8	0	0	-	-	0	8	90	11.3	30	3	0	0	-	0	0	0	-	0	0	3	18
1985	Seattle Seahawks	9	2	0	0	-	-	0	2	13	6.5	7	0	0	0	-	0	1	17	17.0	0	0	0	0
1986	Seattle Seahawks	16	15	0	0	-	-	0	15	150	10.0	25	0	0	0	-	0	1	17	17.0	0	0	0	0
1987	Seattle Seahawks	12	12	0	0	-	-	0	14	106	7.6	27	2	0	0	-	0	0	0	-	0	0	2	12
1988	Seattle Seahawks	16	16	0	0	-	-	0	29	244	8.4	26	0	0	0	-	0	1	17	17.0	0	1	0	0
1989	Washington Redskins	16	5	0	0	-	-	0	1	2	2.0	2	0	0	0	-	0	0	0	-	0	0	0	0
1990	Seattle Seahawks	5	2	0	0	-	-	0	0	0	-	-	0	0	0	-	0	0	0	-	0	0	0	0
1991	Seattle Seahawks	16	15	0	0	-	-	0	10	70	7.0	16	4	0	0	-	0	3	46	15.3	0	0	4	24
1992	Minnesota Vikings	12	9	0	0	-	-	0	5	65	13.0	t34	1	0	0	-	0	0	0	-	0	1	1	6
1993	Minnesota Vikings	16	12	0	0	-	-	0	6	39	6.5	21	1	0	0	-	0	0	0	-	0	1	1	6
1995	Minnesota Vikings	2	1	0	0	-	-	0	3	22	7.3	9	0	0	0	-	0	0	0	-	0	0	0	0
	14 NFL Seasons	176	110	0	0	-	-	0	107	894	8.4	t34	11	0	0	-	0	8	125	15.6	0	2	11	66

Other Statistics: 1982–recovered 1 fumble for 0 yards. 1983–recovered 1 fumble for 0 yards. 1986–recovered 1 fumble for 0 yards. 1991–recovered 1 fumble for 0 yards. 1992–recovered 1 fumble for 4 yards.

Cedric Tillman

Pos: WR **Rnd:** 11 **College:** Alcorn State **Ht:** 6' 2" **Wt:** 219 **Born:** 7/22/70 **Age:** 26 *(statistical profile on page 382)*

Year	Team	G	GS	Rushing Att	Yds	Avg	Lg	TD	Receiving Rec	Yds	Avg	Lg	TD	Punt Returns Num	Yds	Avg	TD	Kickoff Returns Num	Yds	Avg	TD	Totals Fum	TD	Pts
1992	Denver Broncos	9	1	0	0	-	-	0	12	211	17.6	t81	1	0	0	-	0	0	0	-	0	0	1	6
1993	Denver Broncos	14	3	0	0	-	-	0	17	193	11.4	30	2	0	0	-	0	0	0	-	0	1	2	12
1994	Denver Broncos	16	3	0	0	-	-	0	28	455	16.3	63	1	0	0	-	0	0	0	-	0	1	1	6
1995	Jacksonville Jaguars	13	2	0	0	-	-	0	30	368	12.3	28	3	2	6	3.0	0	0	0	-	0	1	3	18
	4 NFL Seasons	52	9	0	0	-	-	0	87	1227	14.1	t81	7	2	6	3.0	0	0	0	-	0	3	7	42

Other Statistics: 1993–recovered 1 fumble for 0 yards.

Lawyer Tillman

Pos: TE **Rnd:** 2 **College:** Auburn **Ht:** 6' 5" **Wt:** 254 **Born:** 5/20/66 **Age:** 30

Year	Team	G	GS	Rushing Att	Yds	Avg	Lg	TD	Receiving Rec	Yds	Avg	Lg	TD	Punt Returns Num	Yds	Avg	TD	Kickoff Returns Num	Yds	Avg	TD	Totals Fum	TD	Pts
1989	Cleveland Browns	14	1	0	0	-	-	0	6	70	11.7	19	2	0	0	-	0	0	0	-	0	0	3	18
1992	Cleveland Browns	10	8	2	15	7.5	15	0	25	498	19.9	52	0	0	0	-	0	0	0	-	0	1	0	0
1993	Cleveland Browns	7	0	0	0	-	-	0	5	68	13.6	18	1	0	0	-	0	0	0	-	0	0	1	6
1995	Carolina Panthers	5	0	0	0	-	-	0	2	22	11.0	12	0	0	0	-	0	0	0	-	0	0	0	0
	4 NFL Seasons	36	9	2	15	7.5	15	0	38	658	17.3	52	3	0	0	-	0	0	0	-	0	1	4	24

Lewis Tillman

Pos: RB **Rnd:** 4 **College:** Jackson State **Ht:** 6' 0" **Wt:** 204 **Born:** 4/16/66 **Age:** 30

Year	Team	G	GS	Rushing Att	Yds	Avg	Lg	TD	Receiving Rec	Yds	Avg	Lg	TD	Punt Returns Num	Yds	Avg	TD	Kickoff Returns Num	Yds	Avg	TD	Totals Fum	TD	Pts
1989	New York Giants	16	0	79	290	3.7	19	0	1	9	9.0	9	0	0	0	-	0	0	0	-	0	1	0	0
1990	New York Giants	16	2	84	231	2.8	17	1	8	18	2.3	16	0	0	0	-	0	0	0	-	0	0	1	6
1991	New York Giants	16	1	65	287	4.4	17	1	5	30	6.0	12	0	0	0	-	0	2	29	14.5	0	2	1	6
1992	New York Giants	16	0	6	13	2.2	6	0	1	15	15.0	15	0	0	0	-	0	0	0	-	0	0	0	0
1993	New York Giants	16	7	121	585	4.8	58	3	1	21	21.0	21	0	0	0	-	0	0	0	-	0	1	3	18
1994	Chicago Bears	16	15	275	899	3.3	t25	7	27	222	8.2	39	0	0	0	-	0	0	0	-	0	1	7	42
1995	Chicago Bears	13	1	29	78	2.7	9	0	0	0	-	-	0	0	0	-	0	1	20	20.0	0	0	0	0
	7 NFL Seasons	109	26	659	2383	3.6	58	12	43	315	7.3	39	0	0	0	-	0	3	49	16.3	0	5	12	72

Other Statistics: 1995–recovered 1 fumble for 0 yards.

Adam Timmerman

Pos: G **Rnd:** 7 **College:** South Dakota State **Ht:** 6' 4" **Wt:** 289 **Born:** 8/14/71 **Age:** 25

Year	Team	G	GS			G	GS
1995	Green Bay Packers	13	0		1 NFL Season	13	0

Michael Timpson

Pos: WR/KR **Rnd:** 4 **College:** Penn State **Ht:** 5' 10" **Wt:** 180 **Born:** 6/6/67 **Age:** 29

Year	Team	G	GS	Rushing Att	Yds	Avg	Lg	TD	Receiving Rec	Yds	Avg	Lg	TD	Punt Returns Num	Yds	Avg	TD	Kickoff Returns Num	Yds	Avg	TD	Totals Fum	TD	Pts
1989	New England Patriots	2	0	0	0	-	-	0	0	0	-	-	0	0	0	-	0	2	13	6.5	0	1	0	0
1990	New England Patriots	5	0	0	0	-	-	0	5	91	18.2	42	0	0	0	-	0	3	62	20.7	0	0	0	0

Year Team	G	GS	Rushing Att	Yds	Avg	Lg	TD	Receiving Rec	Yds	Avg	Lg	TD	Punt Returns Num	Yds	Avg	TD	Kickoff Returns Num	Yds	Avg	TD	Totals Fum	TD	Pts
1991 New England Patriots	16	2	1	-4	-4.0	-4	0	25	471	18.8	t60	2	0	0	-	0	2	37	18.5	0	2	2	12
1992 New England Patriots	16	2	0	0	-	-	0	26	315	12.1	25	1	8	47	5.9	0	2	28	14.0	0	0	1	6
1993 New England Patriots	16	7	0	0	-	-	0	42	654	15.6	48	2	0	0	-	0	0	0	-	0	1	2	12
1994 New England Patriots	15	14	2	14	7.0	10	0	74	941	12.7	37	3	0	0	-	0	1	28	28.0	0	0	3	18
1995 Chicago Bears	16	0	3	28	9.3	16	1	24	289	12.0	36	2	0	0	-	0	18	420	23.3	0	1	3	18
7 NFL Seasons	86	25	6	38	6.3	16	1	196	2761	14.1	t60	10	8	47	5.9	0	28	588	21.0	0	5	11	66

Other Statistics: 1995–recovered 1 fumble for 0 yards.

Tim Tindale

Pos: RB **Rnd:** FA **College:** Western Ontario   **Ht:** 5' 10" **Wt:** 220 **Born:** 4/15/71 **Age:** 25

Year Team	G	GS	Rushing Att	Yds	Avg	Lg	TD	Receiving Rec	Yds	Avg	Lg	TD	Punt Returns Num	Yds	Avg	TD	Kickoff Returns Num	Yds	Avg	TD	Totals Fum	TD	Pts
1995 Buffalo Bills	16	0	5	16	3.2	6	0	0	0	-	-	0	0	0	-	0	6	62	10.3	0	0	0	0

Other Statistics: 1995–recovered 1 fumble for 2 yards.

Ken Tippins

Pos: LB **Rnd:** FA **College:** Middle Tennessee State   **Ht:** 6' 1" **Wt:** 235 **Born:** 7/22/66 **Age:** 30

Year Team	G	GS	Tackles Tk	Ast	Sack	Misc. FF	FR	TD	Blk	Int	Yds	Avg	TD	Punt Returns Num	Yds	Avg	TD	Kickoff Returns Num	Yds	Avg	TD	Totals TD	Fum
1989 Dallas Cowboys	6	0	3	3	0.0	0	0	0	0	0	0	-	0	0	0	-	0	0	0	-	0	0	0
1990 Atlanta Falcons	16	2	22	13	0.0	0	0	0	0	0	0	-	0	0	0	-	0	0	0	-	0	0	0
1991 Atlanta Falcons	16	7	32	40	1.0	0	1	1	0	1	35	35.0	0	0	0	-	0	0	0	-	0	1	0
1992 Atlanta Falcons	16	15	56	59	3.0	0	1	0	0	0	0	-	0	0	0	-	0	0	0	-	0	0	0
1993 Atlanta Falcons	14	1	8	13	0.0	0	1	0	0	0	0	-	0	0	0	-	0	0	0	-	0	0	0
1994 Atlanta Falcons	16	7	23	10	0.0	0	1	0	0	0	0	-	0	0	0	-	0	0	0	-	0	0	0
1995 Atlanta Falcons	16	0	2	1	0.0	0	0	0	0	1	0	0.0	0	0	0	-	0	1	15	15.0	0	0	0
7 NFL Seasons	100	32	146	139	4.0	0	4	1	0	2	35	17.5	0	0	0	-	0	1	15	15.0	0	1	0

Robbie Tobeck

Pos: G/C **Rnd:** FA **College:** Washington State   **Ht:** 6' 4" **Wt:** 292 **Born:** 3/6/70 **Age:** 26

Year Team	G	GS	Year Team	G	GS			G	GS
1994 Atlanta Falcons	6	0	1995 Atlanta Falcons	16	16	2 NFL Seasons		22	16

Tony Tolbert

(statistical profile on page 457)

Pos: DE **Rnd:** 4 **College:** Texas-El Paso   **Ht:** 6' 6" **Wt:** 263 **Born:** 12/29/67 **Age:** 28

Year Team	G	GS	Tackles Tk	Ast	Sack	Misc. FF	FR	TD	Blk	Int	Yds	Avg	TD	Totals Sfty	TD	Pts
1989 Dallas Cowboys	16	5	33	19	2.0	0	0	0	0	0	0	-	0	0	0	0
1990 Dallas Cowboys	16	4	30	25	6.0	0	0	0	0	0	0	-	0	0	0	0
1991 Dallas Cowboys	16	16	38	35	7.0	0	1	0	0	0	0	-	0	0	0	0
1992 Dallas Cowboys	16	16	46	41	8.5	0	0	0	0	0	0	-	0	0	0	0
1993 Dallas Cowboys	16	16	42	42	7.5	0	0	0	0	0	0	-	0	0	0	0
1994 Dallas Cowboys	16	15	53	10	5.5	0	1	0	0	1	54	54.0	1	0	1	6
1995 Dallas Cowboys	16	16	52	10	5.5	2	0	0	0	0	0	-	0	0	0	0
7 NFL Seasons	112	88	294	182	42.0	2	2	0	0	1	54	54.0	1	0	1	6

Mike Tomczak

(statistical profile on page 382)

Pos: QB **Rnd:** FA **College:** Ohio State   **Ht:** 6' 1" **Wt:** 202 **Born:** 10/23/62 **Age:** 34

Year Team	G	GS	Passing Att	Com	Pct	Yards	Yds/Att	Lg	TD	Int	Int%	Rating	Rushing Att	Yds	Avg	Lg	TD	Misc. Sckd	Yds	Fum	Rec	Yds	Pts
1985 Chicago Bears	6	0	6	2	33.3	33	5.50	24	0	0	0.0	52.8	2	3	1.5	3	0	0	0	1	1	-13	0
1986 Chicago Bears	13	7	151	74	49.0	1105	7.32	85	2	10	6.6	50.2	23	117	5.1	16	3	4	30	2	0	0	18
1987 Chicago Bears	12	6	178	97	54.5	1220	6.85	t56	5	10	5.6	62.0	18	54	3.0	10	1	9	59	6	1	0	6
1988 Chicago Bears	14	5	170	86	50.6	1310	7.71	t76	7	6	3.5	75.4	13	40	3.1	17	1	5	47	1	0	-3	6
1989 Chicago Bears	16	11	306	156	51.0	2058	6.73	t79	16	16	5.2	68.2	24	71	3.0	18	1	10	68	2	0	0	6
1990 Chicago Bears	16	2	104	39	37.5	521	5.01	48	3	5	4.8	43.8	12	41	3.4	14	2	11	70	2	0	-2	12
1991 Green Bay Packers	12	7	238	128	53.8	1490	6.26	t75	11	9	3.8	72.6	17	93	5.5	48	1	13	105	5	2	-1	6
1992 Cleveland Browns	12	8	211	120	56.9	1693	8.02	52	7	7	3.3	80.1	24	39	1.6	16	0	12	85	5	0	-7	0
1993 Pittsburgh Steelers	7	1	54	29	53.7	398	7.37	t39	2	5	9.3	51.3	5	-4	-0.8	2	0	7	43	2	1	0	0
1994 Pittsburgh Steelers	6	2	93	54	58.1	804	8.65	t84	4	0	0.0	100.8	4	22	5.5	13	0	4	33	2	0	-1	0
1995 Pittsburgh Steelers	7	4	113	65	57.5	666	5.89	29	1	9	8.0	44.3	11	25	2.3	11	0	6	42	2	1	0	0
11 NFL Seasons	121	53	1624	850	52.3	11298	6.96	85	58	77	4.7	66.8	153	501	3.3	48	9	81	582	30	6	-27	54

Other Statistics: 1990–caught 1 pass for 5 yards.

Steve Tovar

(statistical profile on page 458)

Pos: LB **Rnd:** 3 **College:** Ohio State **Ht:** 6' 3" **Wt:** 244 **Born:** 4/25/70 **Age:** 26

Year Team	G	GS	Tackles			Miscellaneous				Interceptions				Punt Returns				Kickoff Returns				Totals	
			Tk	Ast	Sack	FF	FR	TD	Blk	Int	Yds	Avg	TD	Num	Yds	Avg	TD	Num	Yds	Avg	TD	TD	Fum
1993 Cincinnati Bengals	16	9	72	13	0.0	0	1	0	0	1	0	0.0	0	0	0	-	0	0	0	-	0	0	0
1994 Cincinnati Bengals	16	16	95	27	3.0	3	2	0	0	1	14	14.0	0	0	0	-	0	1	8	8.0	0	0	0
1995 Cincinnati Bengals	14	13	77	22	1.0	2	0	0	0	1	13	13.0	0	0	0	-	0	0	0	-	0	0	0
3 NFL Seasons	46	38	244	62	4.0	5	3	0	0	3	27	9.0	0	0	0	-	0	1	8	8.0	0	0	0

James Trapp

Pos: CB **Rnd:** 3 **College:** Clemson **Ht:** 6' 0" **Wt:** 185 **Born:** 12/28/69 **Age:** 26

Year Team	G	GS	Tackles			Miscellaneous				Interceptions				Totals		
			Tk	Ast	Sack	FF	FR	TD	Blk	Int	Yds	Avg	TD	Sfty	TD	Pts
1993 Los Angeles Raiders	14	2	19	2	0.0	0	0	0	0	1	7	7.0	0	0	0	0
1994 Los Angeles Raiders	16	2	23	6	1.0	0	0	0	0	0	0	-	0	0	0	0
1995 Oakland Raiders	14	2	23	2	0.0	0	1	0	0	0	0	-	0	0	0	0
3 NFL Seasons	44	6	65	10	1.0	0	1	0	0	1	7	7.0	0	0	0	0

Keith Traylor

Pos: DT **Rnd:** 3 **College:** Central Oklahoma **Ht:** 6' 2" **Wt:** 290 **Born:** 9/3/69 **Age:** 27

Year Team	G	GS	Tackles			Miscellaneous				Interceptions				Punt Returns				Kickoff Returns				Totals	
			Tk	Ast	Sack	FF	FR	TD	Blk	Int	Yds	Avg	TD	Num	Yds	Avg	TD	Num	Yds	Avg	TD	TD	Fum
1991 Denver Broncos	16	2	12	15	0.0	0	0	0	0	0	0	-	0	0	0	-	0	0	0	-	0	0	0
1992 Denver Broncos	16	2	21	18	1.0	1	0	0	0	0	0	-	0	0	0	-	0	1	13	13.0	0	0	0
1993 Green Bay Packers	5	0	0	1	0.0	0	0	0	0	0	0	-	0	0	0	-	0	0	0	-	0	0	0
1995 Kansas City Chiefs	16	0	9	2	1.5	1	1	0	0	0	0	-	0	0	0	-	0	0	0	-	0	0	0
4 NFL Seasons	53	4	42	36	2.5	2	1	0	0	0	0	-	0	0	0	-	0	1	13	13.0	0	0	0

Greg Tremble

Pos: S **Rnd:** FA **College:** Georgia **Ht:** 5' 11" **Wt:** 188 **Born:** 4/16/72 **Age:** 24

Year Team	G	GS	Tackles			Miscellaneous				Interceptions				Totals		
			Tk	Ast	Sack	FF	FR	TD	Blk	Int	Yds	Avg	TD	Sfty	TD	Pts
1995 Dal - Phi	11	0	2	1	0.0	0	0	0	0	0	0	-	0	0	0	0
1995 Dallas Cowboys	7	0	2	1	0.0	0	0	0	0	0	0	-	0	0	0	0
Philadelphia Eagles	4	0	0	0	0.0	0	0	0	0	0	0	-	0	0	0	0

Jack Trudeau

Pos: QB **Rnd:** 2 **College:** Illinois **Ht:** 6' 3" **Wt:** 218 **Born:** 9/9/62 **Age:** 34

Year Team	G	GS	Passing										Rushing					Miscellaneous				
			Att	Com	Pct	Yards	Yds/Att	Lg	TD	Int	Int%	Rating	Att	Yds	Avg	Lg	TD	Sckd	Yds	Fum	Recv	Yds	Pts
1986 Indianapolis Colts	12	11	417	204	48.9	2225	5.34	t84	8	18	4.3	53.5	13	21	1.6	8	1	29	213	13	6	-15	6
1987 Indianapolis Colts	10	8	229	128	55.9	1587	6.93	55	6	6	2.6	75.4	15	7	0.5	9	0	13	100	10	2	-28	0
1988 Indianapolis Colts	2	2	34	14	41.2	158	4.65	48	0	3	8.8	19.0	0	0	-	0	0	2	13	0	0	0	0
1989 Indianapolis Colts	13	12	362	190	52.5	2317	6.40	71	15	13	3.6	71.3	35	91	2.6	17	2	20	125	10	7	-5	12
1990 Indianapolis Colts	6	4	144	84	58.3	1078	7.49	73	6	6	4.2	78.4	10	28	2.8	9	0	14	104	11	4	0	0
1991 Indianapolis Colts	2	0	7	2	28.6	19	2.71	11	0	1	14.3	14.3	0	0	-	0	0	1	6	0	0	0	0
1992 Indianapolis Colts	11	5	181	105	58.0	1271	7.02	81	4	8	4.4	68.6	13	6	0.5	5	0	11	85	3	2	-12	0
1993 Indianapolis Colts	5	5	162	85	52.5	992	6.12	68	2	7	4.3	57.4	5	3	0.6	2	0	2	11	2	1	-3	0
1994 New York Jets	5	2	91	50	54.9	496	5.45	t24	4	4	4.4	55.9	6	30	5.0	15	0	9	52	2	1	-1	0
1995 Carolina Panthers	1	0	17	11	64.7	100	5.88	19	0	3	17.6	40.9	0	0	-	0	0	2	8	1	0	0	0
10 NFL Seasons	67	49	1644	873	53.1	10243	6.23	t84	42	69	4.2	63.3	97	186	1.9	17	3	103	717	52	23	-64	18

Gregg Truitt

Pos: LS **Rnd:** FA **College:** Penn State **Ht:** 6' 0" **Wt:** 235 **Born:** 12/8/65 **Age:** 30

Year Team	G	GS	Tackles			Miscellaneous				Interceptions				Totals		
			Tk	Ast	Sack	FF	FR	TD	Blk	Int	Yds	Avg	TD	Sfty	TD	Pts
1994 Cincinnati Bengals	16	0	0	1	0.0	0	0	0	0	0	0	-	0	0	0	0
1995 Cincinnati Bengals	16	0	0	0	0.0	0	0	0	0	0	0	-	0	0	0	0
2 NFL Seasons	32	0	0	1	0.0	0	0	0	0	0	0	-	0	0	0	0

Olanda Truitt

Pos: WR **Rnd:** 5 **College:** Mississippi State **Ht:** 6' 0" **Wt:** 186 **Born:** 1/4/71 **Age:** 25

Year Team	G	GS	Rushing					Receiving					Punt Returns				Kickoff Returns				Totals		
			Att	Yds	Avg	Lg	TD	Rec	Yds	Avg	Lg	TD	Num	Yds	Avg	TD	Num	Yds	Avg	TD	Fum	TD	Pts
1993 Minnesota Vikings	8	0	0	0	-	-	0	4	40	10.0	13	0	0	0	-	0	0	0	-	0	0	0	0
1994 Washington Redskins	9	0	0	0	-	-	0	2	89	44.5	t77	1	0	0	-	0	0	0	-	0	0	1	6

Year Team	G	GS	Att	Yds	Avg	Lg	TD	Rec	Yds	Avg	Lg	TD	Num	Yds	Avg	TD	Num	Yds	Avg	TD	Fum	TD	Pts
			Rushing					Receiving					Punt Returns				Kickoff Returns				Totals		
1995 Washington Redskins	5	2	0	0	-	-	0	9	154	17.1	47	1	0	0	-	0	0	0	-	0	1	1	6
3 NFL Seasons	22	2	0	0	-	-	0	15	283	18.9	t77	2	0	0	-	0	0	0	-	0	1	2	12

Esera Tuaolo

Pos: NT   **Rnd:** 2   **College:** Oregon State   **Ht:** 6' 2" **Wt:** 263 **Born:** 7/11/68 **Age:** 28

Year Team	G	GS	Tk	Ast	Sack	FF	FR	TD	Blk	Int	Yds	Avg	TD	Sfty	TD	Pts
			Tackles			Miscellaneous				Interceptions				Totals		
1991 Green Bay Packers	16	16	30	18	3.5	0	0	0	0	1	23	23.0	0	0	0	0
1992 GB - Min	7	0	4	1	1.0	0	0	0	0	0	0	-	0	0	0	0
1993 Minnesota Vikings	11	3	15	1	0.0	0	0	0	0	0	0	-	0	0	0	0
1994 Minnesota Vikings	16	0	4	5	0.0	0	0	0	0	0	0	-	0	0	0	0
1995 Minnesota Vikings	16	16	24	21	3.0	2	2	0	0	0	0	-	0	0	0	0
1992 Green Bay Packers	4	0	4	1	1.0	0	0	0	0	0	0	-	0	0	0	0
Minnesota Vikings	3	0	0	0	0.0	0	0	0	0	0	0	-	0	0	0	0
5 NFL Seasons	66	35	77	46	7.5	2	2	0	0	1	23	23.0	0	0	0	0

Natu Tuatagaloa

Pos: DE   **Rnd:** 5   **College:** California   **Ht:** 6' 4" **Wt:** 275 **Born:** 5/25/66 **Age:** 30

Year Team	G	GS	Tk	Ast	Sack	FF	FR	TD	Blk	Int	Yds	Avg	TD	Num	Yds	Avg	TD	Num	Yds	Avg	TD	TD	Fum
			Tackles			Miscellaneous				Interceptions				Punt Returns				Kickoff Returns				Totals	
1989 Cincinnati Bengals	14	0	6	1	2.5	0	0	0	0	0	0	-	0	0	0	-	0	0	0	-	0	0	0
1990 Cincinnati Bengals	16	7	17	7	4.5	0	2	0	0	0	0	-	0	0	0	-	0	0	0	-	0	0	0
1991 Cincinnati Bengals	16	4	14	1	2.0	0	0	0	0	0	0	-	0	0	0	-	0	0	0	-	0	0	0
1992 Seattle Seahawks	14	0	12	4	3.0	0	0	0	0	1	0	0.0	0	0	0	-	0	0	0	-	0	0	0
1993 Seattle Seahawks	16	15	23	9	3.5	0	1	0	0	0	0	-	0	0	0	-	0	1	10	10.0	0	0	0
1995 Houston Oilers	2	0	0	0	0.0	0	0	0	0	0	0	-	0	0	0	-	0	0	0	-	0	0	0
6 NFL Seasons	78	26	72	22	15.5	0	3	0	0	1	0	0.0	0	0	0	-	0	1	10	10.0	0	0	0

Winfred Tubbs

Pos: LB   **Rnd:** 3   **College:** Texas   **Ht:** 6' 4" **Wt:** 250 **Born:** 9/24/70 **Age:** 26

Year Team	G	GS	Tk	Ast	Sack	FF	FR	TD	Blk	Int	Yds	Avg	TD	Sfty	TD	Pts
			Tackles			Miscellaneous				Interceptions				Totals		
1994 New Orleans Saints	13	7	41	13	1.0	0	0	0	0	1	0	0.0	0	0	0	0
1995 New Orleans Saints	7	6	44	15	1.0	1	1	0	0	1	6	6.0	0	0	0	0
2 NFL Seasons	20	13	85	28	2.0	1	1	0	0	2	6	3.0	0	0	0	0

Jessie Tuggle

(statistical profile on page 458)

Pos: LB   **Rnd:** FA   **College:** Valdosta State   **Ht:** 5' 11" **Wt:** 230 **Born:** 2/14/65 **Age:** 31

Year Team	G	GS	Tk	Ast	Sack	FF	FR	TD	Blk	Int	Yds	Avg	TD	Sfty	TD	Pts
			Tackles			Miscellaneous				Interceptions				Totals		
1987 Atlanta Falcons	12	4	18	17	1.0	0	0	0	0	0	0	-	0	0	0	0
1988 Atlanta Falcons	16	8	60	43	0.0	1	1	1	0	0	0	-	0	0	1	6
1989 Atlanta Falcons	16	16	112	71	1.0	0	1	0	0	0	0	-	0	0	0	0
1990 Atlanta Falcons	16	14	99	102	5.0	3	2	1	0	0	0	-	0	0	1	6
1991 Atlanta Falcons	16	16	106	101	1.0	1	2	1	0	1	21	21.0	0	0	1	6
1992 Atlanta Falcons	15	15	98	95	1.0	1	1	1	0	1	1	1.0	0	0	1	6
1993 Atlanta Falcons	16	16	120	65	2.0	1	1	0	0	0	0	-	0	0	0	0
1994 Atlanta Falcons	16	16	93	36	1.0	0	1	0	0	1	0	0.0	0	0	0	0
1995 Atlanta Falcons	16	16	111	41	1.0	1	0	0	0	3	84	28.0	1	0	1	6
9 NFL Seasons	139	121	817	571	12.0	8	9	4	0	6	106	17.7	1	0	5	30

Other Statistics: 1994–fumbled 1 time.

Mark Tuinei

Pos: T   **Rnd:** FA   **College:** Hawaii   **Ht:** 6' 5" **Wt:** 305 **Born:** 3/31/60 **Age:** 36

Year	Team	G	GS	Year	Team	G	GS	Year	Team	G	GS	Year	Team	G	GS
1983	Dallas Cowboys	10	0	1987	Dallas Cowboys	8	8	1991	Dallas Cowboys	12	12	1995	Dallas Cowboys	16	16
1984	Dallas Cowboys	16	0	1988	Dallas Cowboys	5	4	1992	Dallas Cowboys	15	15				
1985	Dallas Cowboys	16	0	1989	Dallas Cowboys	16	16	1993	Dallas Cowboys	16	16				
1986	Dallas Cowboys	16	11	1990	Dallas Cowboys	13	13	1994	Dallas Cowboys	15	15		13 NFL Seasons	174	126

Other Statistics: 1986–recovered 3 fumbles for 0 yards; returned 1 kickoff for 0 yards; fumbled 1 time. 1987–recovered 1 fumble for 0 yards. 1993–recovered 1 fumble for 0 yards.

Tom Tupa
(statistical profile on page 485)

Pos: P **Rnd:** 3 **College:** Ohio State **Ht:** 6' 4" **Wt:** 230 **Born:** 2/6/66 **Age:** 30

Year	Team	G	Punting												Rushing		Passing			
			NetPunts	Yards	Avg	Long	In20	In20%	TotPunts	TB	Blocks	OppRet	RetYds	NetAvg	Att	Yards	Att	Com	Yards	Int
1988	Phoenix Cardinals	2	0	0	-	-	-	-	0	0	0	0	0	-	0	0	6	4	49	0
1989	Phoenix Cardinals	14	6	280	46.7	51	2	33.3	6	0	0	4	41	39.8	15	75	134	65	973	9
1990	Phoenix Cardinals	15	0	0	-	-	-	-	0	0	0	0	0	-	1	0	0	0	0	0
1991	Phoenix Cardinals	11	0	0	-	-	-	-	0	0	0	0	0	-	28	97	315	165	2053	13
1992	Indianapolis Colts	3	0	0	-	-	-	-	0	0	0	0	0	-	3	9	33	17	156	2
1994	Cleveland Browns	16	80	3211	40.1	65	28	35.0	80	8	0	38	220	35.4	0	0	0	0	0	0
1995	Cleveland Browns	16	65	2831	43.6	64	18	27.7	65	9	0	34	296	36.2	1	9	1	1	25	0
	7 NFL Seasons	77	151	6322	41.9	65	48	31.8	151	17	0	76	557	35.9	48	190	489	252	3256	24

Other Statistics: 1989–recovered 1 fumble for -6 yards; fumbled 2 times; passed for 3 touchdowns. 1990–fumbled 1 time for -7 yards. 1991–recovered 2 fumbles for 0 yards; fumbled 8 times; passed for 6 touchdowns. 1992–recovered 1 fumble for -1 yard; fumbled 1 time; passed for 1 touchdown. 1994–scored 3 two-point conversions.

Dan Turk

Pos: C/LS **Rnd:** 4 **College:** Wisconsin **Ht:** 6' 4" **Wt:** 290 **Born:** 6/25/62 **Age:** 34

Year	Team	G	GS	Year	Team	G	GS	Year	Team	G	GS	Year	Team	G	GS
1985	Pittsburgh Steelers	1	0	1988	Tampa Bay Buccaneers	12	10	1991	Los Angeles Raiders	16	0	1994	Los Angeles Raiders	16	0
1986	Pittsburgh Steelers	16	4	1989	Los Angeles Raiders	16	4	1992	Los Angeles Raiders	16	0	1995	Oakland Raiders	16	16
1987	Tampa Bay Buccaneers	13	3	1990	Los Angeles Raiders	16	0	1993	Los Angeles Raiders	16	0		11 NFL Seasons	154	37

Other Statistics: 1988–recovered 1 fumble for -19 yards; fumbled 1 time. 1989–returned 1 kickoff for 2 yards; fumbled 1 time for -8 yards. 1990–returned 1 kickoff for 7 yards. 1991–returned 1 kickoff for 0 yards. 1992–returned 1 kickoff for 3 yards. 1993–recovered 1 fumble for 0 yards; returned 1 kickoff for 0 yards.

Matt Turk
(statistical profile on page 486)

Pos: P **Rnd:** FA **College:** Wisconsin-Whitewater **Ht:** 6' 5" **Wt:** 230 **Born:** 6/16/68 **Age:** 28

Year	Team	G	Punting												Rushing		Passing			
			NetPunts	Yards	Avg	Long	In20	In20%	TotPunts	TB	Blocks	OppRet	RetYds	NetAvg	Att	Yards	Att	Com	Yards	Int
1995	Washington Redskins	16	74	3140	42.4	60	29	39.2	74	9	0	26	173	37.7	0	0	0	0	0	0

Renaldo Turnbull
(statistical profile on page 458)

Pos: DE **Rnd:** 1 (14) **College:** West Virginia **Ht:** 6' 4" **Wt:** 250 **Born:** 1/5/66 **Age:** 30

Year	Team	G	GS	Tackles			Miscellaneous				Interceptions				Totals		
				Tk	Ast	Sack	FF	FR	TD	Blk	Int	Yds	Avg	TD	Sfty	TD	Pts
1990	New Orleans Saints	16	6	26	5	9.0	1	1	0	0	0	0	-	0	0	0	0
1991	New Orleans Saints	16	0	17	3	1.0	1	1	0	0	0	0	-	0	0	0	0
1992	New Orleans Saints	14	0	8	1	1.5	0	0	0	0	0	0	-	0	0	0	0
1993	New Orleans Saints	15	14	51	12	13.0	5	2	0	0	1	2	2.0	0	0	0	0
1994	New Orleans Saints	16	16	45	9	6.0	2	0	0	0	0	0	-	0	0	0	0
1995	New Orleans Saints	15	15	30	9	7.0	0	2	0	2	0	0	-	0	0	0	0
	6 NFL Seasons	92	51	177	39	37.5	9	6	0	2	1	2	2.0	0	0	0	0

Eric Turner

Pos: S **Rnd:** 1 (2) **College:** UCLA **Ht:** 6' 1" **Wt:** 207 **Born:** 9/20/68 **Age:** 28

Year	Team	G	GS	Tackles			Miscellaneous				Interceptions				Punt Returns				Kickoff Returns				Totals	
				Tk	Ast	Sack	FF	FR	TD	Blk	Int	Yds	Avg	TD	Num	Yds	Avg	TD	Num	Yds	Avg	TD	TD	Fum
1991	Cleveland Browns	8	7	52	32	0.0	0	1	0	0	2	42	21.0	1	0	0	-	0	0	0	-	0	1	0
1992	Cleveland Browns	15	13	67	52	1.0	0	2	0	0	1	6	6.0	0	0	0	-	0	0	0	-	0	0	0
1993	Cleveland Browns	16	16	80	79	0.0	0	0	0	0	5	25	5.0	0	0	7	-	0	0	0	-	0	0	0
1994	Cleveland Browns	16	16	82	23	1.0	1	1	0	0	9	199	22.1	1	1	0	0.0	0	0	0	-	0	1	0
1995	Cleveland Browns	8	8	40	17	0.0	0	0	0	0	0	0	-	0	0	0	-	0	0	0	-	0	0	0
	5 NFL Seasons	63	60	321	203	2.0	1	4	0	0	17	272	16.0	2	1	7	7.0	0	0	0	-	0	2	0

Floyd Turner
(statistical profile on page 383)

Pos: WR **Rnd:** 6 **College:** Northwestern Louisiana **Ht:** 5' 11" **Wt:** 199 **Born:** 5/29/66 **Age:** 30

Year	Team	G	GS	Rushing					Receiving					Punt Returns				Kickoff Returns				Totals		
				Att	Yds	Avg	Lg	TD	Rec	Yds	Avg	Lg	TD	Num	Yds	Avg	TD	Num	Yds	Avg	TD	Fum	TD	Pts
1989	New Orleans Saints	13	1	2	8	4.0	6	0	22	279	12.7	t54	1	1	7	7.0	0	0	0	-	0	1	1	6
1990	New Orleans Saints	16	0	0	0	-	-	0	21	396	18.9	t68	4	0	0	-	0	0	0	-	0	0	4	24
1991	New Orleans Saints	16	4	0	0	-	-	0	64	927	14.5	t65	8	0	0	-	0	0	0	-	0	1	8	48
1992	New Orleans Saints	2	2	0	0	-	-	0	5	43	8.6	18	0	3	10	3.3	0	0	0	-	0	2	0	0
1993	New Orleans Saints	10	2	0	0	-	-	0	12	163	13.6	52	1	0	0	-	0	0	0	-	0	0	1	6
1994	Indianapolis Colts	16	16	3	-3	-1.0	5	0	52	593	11.4	28	6	0	0	-	0	0	0	-	0	1	6	36
1995	Indianapolis Colts	14	12	0	0	-	-	0	35	431	12.3	t47	4	0	0	-	0	0	0	-	0	0	4	28
	7 NFL Seasons	87	37	5	5	1.0	6	0	211	2832	13.4	t68	24	4	17	4.3	0	0	0	-	0	5	24	148

Other Statistics: 1989–recovered 3 fumbles for 0 yards. 1994–recovered 1 fumble for 0 yards. 1995–scored 2 two-point conversions.

Kevin Turner

Pos: RB **Rnd:** 3 **College:** Alabama **Ht:** 6' 1" **Wt:** 231 **Born:** 6/12/69 **Age:** 27

			Rushing					Receiving					Kickoff Returns				Passing				Totals		
Year Team	G	GS	Att	Yds	Avg	Lg	TD	Rec	Yds	Avg	Lg	TD	Num	Yds	Avg	TD	Att	Com	Yds	Int	Fum	TD	Pts
1992 New England Patriots	16	1	10	40	4.0	11	0	7	52	7.4	t19	2	1	11	11.0	0	0	0	0	0	2	2	12
1993 New England Patriots	16	9	50	231	4.6	49	0	39	333	8.5	26	2	0	0	-	0	1	0	0	0	1	2	12
1994 New England Patriots	16	9	36	111	3.1	13	1	52	471	9.1	32	2	0	0	-	0	0	0	0	0	4	3	18
1995 Philadelphia Eagles	2	2	2	9	4.5	12	0	4	29	7.3	11	0	0	0	-	0	0	0	0	0	0	0	0
4 NFL Seasons	50	21	98	391	4.0	49	1	102	885	8.7	32	6	1	11	11.0	0	1	0	0	0	7	7	42

Other Statistics: 1992–recovered 2 fumbles for 0 yards. 1993–recovered 2 fumbles for 6 yards. 1994–recovered 2 fumbles for -3 yards.

Marcus Turner

Pos: CB **Rnd:** 11 **College:** UCLA **Ht:** 6' 0" **Wt:** 190 **Born:** 1/13/66 **Age:** 30

			Tackles			Miscellaneous				Interceptions				Totals		
Year Team	G	GS	Tk	Ast	Sack	FF	FR	TD	Blk	Int	Yds	Avg	TD	Sfty	TD	Pts
1989 Phoenix Cardinals	13	0	9	0	0.0	0	1	0	0	0	0	-	0	0	0	0
1990 Phoenix Cardinals	16	1	19	3	0.0	0	1	0	0	1	70	70.0	2	0	2	12
1991 Phoenix Cardinals	3	0	5	1	0.0	0	1	0	0	0	0	-	0	0	0	0
1992 New York Jets	16	0	9	6	0.0	0	1	0	0	2	15	7.5	0	0	0	0
1993 New York Jets	16	0	20	3	1.0	0	0	0	0	0	0	-	0	0	0	0
1994 New York Jets	16	1	26	6	0.0	1	1	0	0	5	155	31.0	1	0	1	6
1995 New York Jets	6	1	6	2	0.0	0	0	0	0	0	0	-	0	0	0	0
7 NFL Seasons	86	3	94	21	1.0	1	6	0	0	8	240	30.0	3	0	3	18

Nate Turner

Pos: RB **Rnd:** 6 **College:** Nebraska **Ht:** 6' 1" **Wt:** 255 **Born:** 5/28/69 **Age:** 27

			Rushing					Receiving					Punt Returns				Kickoff Returns				Totals		
Year Team	G	GS	Att	Yds	Avg	Lg	TD	Rec	Yds	Avg	Lg	TD	Num	Yds	Avg	TD	Num	Yds	Avg	TD	Fum	TD	Pts
1993 Buffalo Bills	13	0	11	36	3.3	10	0	0	0	-	-	0	0	0	-	0	1	10	10.0	0	0	0	0
1994 Buffalo Bills	13	0	2	4	2.0	4	0	1	26	26.0	t26	1	0	0	-	0	6	102	17.0	0	0	1	6
1995 Carolina Panthers	2	0	0	0	-	-	0	0	0	-	-	0	0	0	-	0	0	0	-	0	0	0	0
3 NFL Seasons	28	0	13	40	3.1	10	0	1	26	26.0	t26	1	0	0	-	0	7	112	16.0	0	0	1	6

Scott Turner

Pos: CB **Rnd:** 7 **College:** Illinois **Ht:** 5' 9" **Wt:** 178 **Born:** 2/26/72 **Age:** 24

			Tackles			Miscellaneous				Interceptions				Punt Returns				Kickoff Returns				Totals	
Year Team	G	GS	Tk	Ast	Sack	FF	FR	TD	Blk	Int	Yds	Avg	TD	Num	Yds	Avg	TD	Num	Yds	Avg	TD	TD	Fum
1995 Washington Redskins	16	0	27	3	1.0	1	1	0	0	1	0	0.0	0	1	0	0.0	0	0	0	-	0	0	1

Vernon Turner

Pos: KR/PR **Rnd:** FA **College:** Carson-Newman **Ht:** 5' 8" **Wt:** 185 **Born:** 1/6/67 **Age:** 29

			Rushing					Receiving					Punt Returns				Kickoff Returns				Totals		
Year Team	G	GS	Att	Yds	Avg	Lg	TD	Rec	Yds	Avg	Lg	TD	Num	Yds	Avg	TD	Num	Yds	Avg	TD	Fum	TD	Pts
1990 Buffalo Bills	1	0	0	0	-	-	0	0	0	-	-	0	0	0	-	0	0	0	-	0	0	0	0
1991 Los Angeles Rams	15	0	7	44	6.3	11	0	3	41	13.7	t19	1	23	201	8.7	0	24	457	19.0	0	4	1	6
1992 Los Angeles Rams	12	0	2	14	7.0	9	0	5	42	8.4	16	0	28	207	7.4	0	29	569	19.6	0	3	0	0
1993 Det - TB	8	0	0	0	-	-	0	1	7	7.0	7	0	17	152	8.9	0	21	391	18.6	0	1	0	0
1994 Tampa Bay Buccaneers	13	1	4	13	3.3	9	0	0	0	-	-	0	21	218	10.4	1	43	886	20.6	0	1	1	6
1995 Detroit Lions	6	0	0	0	-	-	0	0	0	-	-	0	6	39	6.5	0	17	323	19.0	0	1	0	0
1993 Detroit Lions	7	0	0	0	-	-	0	1	7	7.0	7	0	17	152	8.9	0	15	330	22.0	0	1	0	0
Tampa Bay Buccaneers	1	0	0	0	-	-	0	0	0	-	-	0	0	0	-	0	6	61	10.2	0	0	0	0
6 NFL Seasons	55	1	13	71	5.5	11	0	9	90	10.0	t19	1	95	817	8.6	1	134	2626	19.6	0	10	2	12

Other Statistics: 1991–recovered 2 fumbles for -1 yard. 1994–recovered 1 fumble for 0 yards.

Melvin Tuten

Pos: T/TE **Rnd:** 3 **College:** Syracuse **Ht:** 6' 6" **Wt:** 305 **Born:** 11/11/71 **Age:** 24

Year Team	G	GS				G	GS
1995 Cincinnati Bengals	16	2		1 NFL Season		16	2

Other Statistics: 1995–caught 2 passes for 12 yards and 1 touchdown.

Rick Tuten

(statistical profile on page 486)

Pos: P **Rnd:** FA **College:** Florida State **Ht:** 6' 2" **Wt:** 218 **Born:** 1/5/65 **Age:** 31

				Punting									Rushing		Passing			
Year Team	G	NetPunts	Yards	Avg	Long	In20	In20%	TotPunts	TB	Blocks	OppRet	RetYds	NetAvg	Att	Yards	Att	Com	Yards	Int
1989 Philadelphia Eagles	2	7	256	36.6	45	1	14.3	7	1	0	1	1	33.6	0	0	0	0	0	0
1990 Buffalo Bills	14	53	2107	39.8	55	12	22.6	53	4	0	26	214	34.2	0	0	0	0	0	0

Year	Team	G	Punting												Rushing		Passing			
			NetPunts	Yards	Avg	Long	In20	In20%	TotPunts	TB	Blocks	OppRet	RetYds	NetAvg	Att	Yards	Att	Com	Yards	Int
1991	Seattle Seahawks	10	49	2106	43.0	60	8	16.3	49	3	0	29	239	36.9	0	0	0	0	0	0
1992	Seattle Seahawks	16	108	4760	44.1	65	29	26.9	108	8	0	56	416	38.7	1	0	1	0	0	0
1993	Seattle Seahawks	16	90	4007	44.5	64	21	23.3	91	7	1	47	475	37.3	0	0	1	0	0	0
1994	Seattle Seahawks	16	91	3905	42.9	64	33	36.3	91	7	0	43	426	36.7	0	0	1	0	0	0
1995	Seattle Seahawks	16	83	3735	45.0	73	21	25.3	83	8	0	48	549	36.5	0	0	0	0	0	0
	7 NFL Seasons	90	481	20876	43.4	73	125	26.0	482	38	1	250	2320	36.9	1	0	3	0	0	0

Other Statistics: 1992–recovered 2 fumbles for -9 yards; fumbled 2 times. 1994–scored 1 two-point conversion.

Jeff Uhlenhake

Pos: C **Rnd:** 5 **College:** Ohio State **Ht:** 6' 3" **Wt:** 284 **Born:** 1/28/66 **Age:** 30

Year	Team	G	GS	Year	Team	G	GS	Year	Team	G	GS	Year	Team	G	GS
1989	Miami Dolphins	16	15	1991	Miami Dolphins	13	10	1993	Miami Dolphins	5	5	1995	New Orleans Saints	14	14
1990	Miami Dolphins	16	16	1992	Miami Dolphins	13	13	1994	New Orleans Saints	16	15		7 NFL Seasons	93	88

Other Statistics: 1989–fumbled 1 time for -19 yards. 1992–recovered 2 fumbles for -4 yards; fumbled 1 time.

Joe Valerio

Pos: T/C **Rnd:** 2 **College:** Pennsylvania **Ht:** 6' 5" **Wt:** 295 **Born:** 2/11/69 **Age:** 27

Year	Team	G	GS	Year	Team	G	GS	Year	Team	G	GS	Year	Team	G	GS
1992	Kansas City Chiefs	16	3	1993	Kansas City Chiefs	13	0	1994	Kansas City Chiefs	16	1	1995	Kansas City Chiefs	16	0
													4 NFL Seasons	61	4

Other Statistics: 1993–caught 1 pass for 1 yard and 1 touchdown. 1994–caught 2 passes for 5 yards and 2 touchdowns. 1995–caught 1 pass for 1 yard and 1 touchdown; returned 2 kickoffs for 15 yards.

Alex Van Pelt

Pos: QB **Rnd:** 8 **College:** Pittsburgh **Ht:** 6' 1" **Wt:** 219 **Born:** 5/1/70 **Age:** 26

Year	Team	G	GS	Passing										Rushing					Miscellaneous				
				Att	Com	Pct	Yards	Yds/Att	Lg	TD	Int	Int%	Rating	Att	Yds	Avg	Lg	TD	Sckd	Yds	Fum	Recv	Yds	Pts
1995	Buffalo Bills	1	0	18	10	55.6	106	5.89	t19	2	0	0.0	110.0	0	0	-	0	0	0	0	0	0	0	0

Matt Vanderbeek

Pos: LB **Rnd:** FA **College:** Michigan State **Ht:** 6' 3" **Wt:** 243 **Born:** 8/16/67 **Age:** 29

Year	Team	G	GS	Tackles			Miscellaneous				Interceptions				Punt Returns				Kickoff Returns				Totals	
				Tk	Ast	Sack	FF	FR	TD	Blk	Int	Yds	Avg	TD	Num	Yds	Avg	TD	Num	Yds	Avg	TD	TD	Fum
1990	Indianapolis Colts	16	7	30	16	0.0	1	0	0	0	0	0	-	0	0	0	-	0	0	0	-	0	0	0
1991	Indianapolis Colts	5	1	6	5	0.0	0	0	0	0	0	0	-	0	0	0	-	0	0	0	-	0	0	0
1992	Indianapolis Colts	15	0	0	0	0.0	0	0	0	0	0	0	-	0	0	0	-	0	1	6	6.0	0	0	0
1993	Dallas Cowboys	16	0	0	0	0.0	0	0	0	0	0	0	-	0	0	0	-	0	0	0	-	0	0	0
1994	Dallas Cowboys	12	0	0	0	0.0	0	0	0	0	0	0	-	0	0	0	-	0	0	0	-	0	0	0
1995	Washington Redskins	16	0	0	0	0.0	0	1	0	0	0	0	-	0	0	0	-	0	1	7	7.0	0	0	0
	6 NFL Seasons	80	8	36	21	0.0	1	1	0	0	0	0	-	0	0	0	-	0	2	13	6.5	0	0	0

Sean Vanhorse

Pos: CB **Rnd:** 6 **College:** Howard **Ht:** 5' 10" **Wt:** 180 **Born:** 7/22/68 **Age:** 28

Year	Team	G	GS	Tackles			Miscellaneous				Interceptions				Totals		
				Tk	Ast	Sack	FF	FR	TD	Blk	Int	Yds	Avg	TD	Sfty	TD	Pts
1992	San Diego Chargers	16	9	43	7	0.0	0	0	0	0	1	11	11.0	0	0	0	0
1993	San Diego Chargers	15	10	36	6	0.0	1	0	0	0	2	0	0.0	0	0	0	0
1994	San Diego Chargers	16	1	23	5	0.0	0	0	0	0	2	56	28.0	1	0	1	6
1995	Detroit Lions	14	0	16	1	0.0	0	0	0	0	1	0	0.0	0	0	0	0
	4 NFL Seasons	61	20	118	19	0.0	1	0	0	0	6	67	11.2	1	0	1	6

Tamarick Vanover

Pos: PR/KR **Rnd:** 3 **College:** Florida State **Ht:** 5' 11" **Wt:** 213 **Born:** 2/25/74 **Age:** 22

Year	Team	G	GS	Rushing					Receiving					Punt Returns				Kickoff Returns				Totals		
				Att	Yds	Avg	Lg	TD	Rec	Yds	Avg	Lg	TD	Num	Yds	Avg	TD	Num	Yds	Avg	TD	Fum	TD	Pts
1995	Kansas City Chiefs	15	0	6	31	5.2	13	0	11	231	21.0	57	2	51	540	10.6	1	43	1095	25.5	2	1	5	30

Tommy Vardell

Pos: RB **Rnd:** 1 (9) **College:** Stanford **Ht:** 6' 2" **Wt:** 230 **Born:** 2/20/69 **Age:** 27

Year	Team	G	GS	Rushing					Receiving					Punt Returns				Kickoff Returns				Totals		
				Att	Yds	Avg	Lg	TD	Rec	Yds	Avg	Lg	TD	Num	Yds	Avg	TD	Num	Yds	Avg	TD	Fum	TD	Pts
1992	Cleveland Browns	14	10	99	369	3.7	35	0	13	128	9.8	23	0	0	0	-	0	2	14	7.0	0	0	0	0
1993	Cleveland Browns	16	12	171	644	3.8	54	3	19	151	7.9	t28	1	0	0	-	0	4	58	14.5	0	3	4	24
1994	Cleveland Browns	5	5	15	48	3.2	9	0	16	137	8.6	19	1	0	0	-	0	0	0	-	0	0	1	6

Year Team	G	GS	Att	Yds	Avg	Lg	TD	Rec	Yds	Avg	Lg	TD	Num	Yds	Avg	TD	Num	Yds	Avg	TD	Fum	TD	Pts
			Rushing					**Receiving**					**Punt Returns**				**Kickoff Returns**				**Totals**		
1995 Cleveland Browns	5	0	4	9	2.3	6	0	6	18	3.0	7	0	0	0	-	0	0	0	-	0	0	0	0
4 NFL Seasons	40	27	289	1070	3.7	54	3	54	434	8.0	t28	2	0	0	-	0	6	72	12.0	0	3	5	30

Craig Veasey

Pos: DT/NT **Rnd:** 3   **College:** Houston   **Ht:** 6' 2" **Wt:** 285 **Born:** 12/25/66 **Age:** 29

Year Team	G	GS	Tk	Ast	Sack	FF	FR	TD	Blk	Int	Yds	Avg	TD	Sfty	TD	Pts
			Tackles			**Miscellaneous**				**Interceptions**				**Totals**		
1990 Pittsburgh Steelers	10	0	5	4	0.0	0	1	0	0	0	0	-	0	0	0	0
1991 Pittsburgh Steelers	13	2	13	9	2.0	0	0	0	0	0	0	-	0	0	0	0
1992 Houston Oilers	4	0	1	0	0.0	0	0	0	0	0	0	-	0	0	0	0
1993 Hou - Mia	15	0	12	8	2.0	0	0	0	0	0	0	-	0	0	0	0
1994 Miami Dolphins	12	1	9	5	2.5	1	0	0	0	1	7	7.0	0	0	0	0
1995 Houston Oilers	15	2	14	3	0.0	0	0	0	0	0	0	-	0	0	0	0
1993 Houston Oilers	1	0	0	0	0.0	0	0	0	0	0	0	-	0	0	0	0
Miami Dolphins	14	0	12	8	2.0	0	0	0	0	0	0	-	0	0	0	0
6 NFL Seasons	69	5	54	29	6.5	1	1	0	0	1	7	7.0	0	0	0	0

Kipp Vickers

Pos: T   **Rnd:** FA   **College:** Miami (FL)   **Ht:** 6' 2" **Wt:** 288 **Born:** 8/27/69 **Age:** 27

Year Team	G	GS			Year Team	G	GS
1995 Indianapolis Colts	9	0			1 NFL Season	9	0

Danny Villa

Pos: LS/G **Rnd:** 5   **College:** Arizona State   **Ht:** 6' 5" **Wt:** 308 **Born:** 9/21/64 **Age:** 32

Year Team	G	GS	Year Team	G	GS	Year Team	G	GS	Year Team	G	GS
1987 New England Patriots	11	7	1990 New England Patriots	16	16	1993 Kansas City Chiefs	14	3			
1988 New England Patriots	16	14	1991 New England Patriots	10	10	1994 Kansas City Chiefs	14	0			
1989 New England Patriots	15	15	1992 Phoenix Cardinals	16	12	1995 Kansas City Chiefs	16	0	9 NFL Seasons	128	77

Other Statistics: 1987–fumbled 1 time for -13 yards. 1988–fumbled 1 time for -39 yards. 1990–recovered 1 fumble for 0 yards. 1991–recovered 2 fumbles for 0 yards.

Troy Vincent

(statistical profile on page 459)

Pos: CB   **Rnd:** 1 (7)   **College:** Wisconsin   **Ht:** 6' 0" **Wt:** 184 **Born:** 6/8/70 **Age:** 26

Year Team	G	GS	Tk	Ast	Sack	FF	FR	TD	Blk	Int	Yds	Avg	TD	Num	Yds	Avg	TD	Num	Yds	Avg	TD	TD	Fum
			Tackles			**Miscellaneous**				**Interceptions**				**Punt Returns**				**Kickoff Returns**				**Totals**	
1992 Miami Dolphins	15	14	56	21	0.0	1	2	0	0	2	47	23.5	0	5	16	3.2	0	0	0	-	0	0	0
1993 Miami Dolphins	13	13	58	10	0.0	0	1	0	0	2	29	14.5	0	0	9	-	0	0	2	-	0	0	0
1994 Miami Dolphins	13	12	41	11	0.0	0	0	0	0	5	113	22.6	1	0	0	-	0	0	0	-	0	1	0
1995 Miami Dolphins	16	16	52	10	0.0	0	0	0	0	5	95	19.0	1	0	0	-	0	0	0	-	0	1	0
4 NFL Seasons	57	55	207	52	0.0	1	3	0	0	14	284	20.3	2	5	25	5.0	0	0	2	-	0	2	2

Kimo von Oelhoffen

Pos: DT   **Rnd:** 6   **College:** Boise State   **Ht:** 6' 4" **Wt:** 300 **Born:** 1/30/71 **Age:** 25

Year Team	G	GS	Tk	Ast	Sack	FF	FR	TD	Blk	Int	Yds	Avg	TD	Num	Yds	Avg	TD	Num	Yds	Avg	TD	TD	Fum
			Tackles			**Miscellaneous**				**Interceptions**				**Punt Returns**				**Kickoff Returns**				**Totals**	
1994 Cincinnati Bengals	7	0	2	0	0.0	0	0	0	0	0	0	-	0	0	0	-	0	0	0	-	0	0	0
1995 Cincinnati Bengals	16	0	7	1	0.0	0	0	0	0	0	0	-	0	0	0	-	0	1	10	10.0	0	0	0
2 NFL Seasons	23	0	9	1	0.0	0	0	0	0	0	0	-	0	0	0	-	0	1	10	10.0	0	0	0

Bryan Wagner

(statistical profile on page 486)

Pos: P   **Rnd:** FA   **College:** California State-Northridge   **Ht:** 6' 2" **Wt:** 200 **Born:** 3/28/62 **Age:** 34

Year Team	G	NetPunts	Yards	Avg	Long	In20	In20%	TotPunts	TB	Blocks	OppRet	RetYds	NetAvg	Att	Yards	Att	Com	Yards	Int
				Punting										**Rushing**		**Passing**			
1987 Chicago Bears	10	36	1461	40.6	71	9	25.0	37	4	1	12	195	32.1	0	0	0	0	0	0
1988 Chicago Bears	16	79	3282	41.5	70	18	22.8	79	10	0	40	447	33.4	2	0	1	1	3	0
1989 Cleveland Browns	16	97	3817	39.4	60	32	33.0	97	6	0	49	418	33.8	0	0	0	0	0	0
1990 Cleveland Browns	16	74	2879	38.9	65	13	17.6	78	2	4	41	425	30.9	0	0	0	0	0	0
1991 New England Patriots	3	14	548	39.1	54	0	0	14	0	0	11	140	29.1	0	0	0	0	0	0
1992 Green Bay Packers	7	30	1222	40.7	52	10	33.3	30	5	0	16	73	35.0	0	0	0	0	0	0
1993 Green Bay Packers	16	74	3174	42.9	60	19	25.7	74	7	0	38	350	36.3	0	0	0	0	0	0
1994 San Diego Chargers	14	65	2705	41.6	59	20	30.8	65	3	0	38	348	35.3	0	0	0	0	0	0
1995 New England Patriots	8	37	1557	42.1	57	13	35.1	37	4	0	20	168	35.4	0	0	0	0	0	0
9 NFL Seasons	106	506	20645	40.8	71	134	26.5	511	41	5	265	2564	33.8	2	0	1	1	3	0

Other Statistics: 1988–recovered 1 fumble for -9 yards; fumbled 1 time.

Frank Wainright

Pos: LS/TE **Rnd:** 8   **College:** Northern Colorado   **Ht:** 6' 3" **Wt:** 245 **Born:** 10/10/67 **Age:** 29

Year Team	G	GS	Rushing Att	Yds	Avg	Lg	TD	Receiving Rec	Yds	Avg	Lg	TD	Punt Returns Num	Yds	Avg	TD	Kickoff Returns Num	Yds	Avg	TD	Totals Fum	TD	Pts
1991 New Orleans Saints	14	2	0	0	-	-	0	1	3	3.0	3	0	0	0	-	0	0	0	-	0	0	0	0
1992 New Orleans Saints	13	4	0	0	-	-	0	9	143	15.9	29	0	0	0	-	0	0	0	-	0	0	0	0
1993 New Orleans Saints	16	2	0	0	-	-	0	0	0	-	-	0	0	0	-	0	0	0	-	0	0	0	0
1995 Phi - Mia	13	0	0	0	-	-	0	0	0	-	-	0	0	0	-	0	0	0	-	0	0	0	0
1995 Philadelphia Eagles	7	0	0	0	-	-	0	0	0	-	-	0	0	0	-	0	0	0	-	0	0	0	0
Miami Dolphins	6	0	0	0	-	-	0	0	0	-	-	0	0	0	-	0	0	0	-	0	0	0	0
4 NFL Seasons	56	8	0	0	-	-	0	10	146	14.6	29	0	0	0	-	0	0	0	-	0	0	0	0

Other Statistics: 1995–recovered 1 fumble for 0 yards.

Adam Walker

Pos: RB **Rnd:** FA   **College:** Pittsburgh   **Ht:** 6' 1" **Wt:** 210 **Born:** 6/7/68 **Age:** 28

Year Team	G	GS	Rushing Att	Yds	Avg	Lg	TD	Receiving Rec	Yds	Avg	Lg	TD	Punt Returns Num	Yds	Avg	TD	Kickoff Returns Num	Yds	Avg	TD	Totals Fum	TD	Pts
1992 San Francisco 49ers	1	0	0	0	-	-	0	0	0	-	-	0	0	0	-	0	0	0	-	0	0	0	0
1993 San Francisco 49ers	10	0	5	17	3.4	11	0	1	4	4.0	4	0	0	0	-	0	3	51	17.0	0	0	0	0
1994 San Francisco 49ers	8	0	13	54	4.2	14	1	0	0	-	-	0	0	0	-	0	6	82	13.7	0	0	1	6
1995 San Francisco 49ers	13	7	14	44	3.1	16	1	11	78	7.1	15	0	0	0	-	0	1	17	17.0	0	2	1	6
4 NFL Seasons	32	7	32	115	3.6	16	2	12	82	6.8	15	0	0	0	-	0	10	150	15.0	0	2	2	12

Other Statistics: 1994–recovered 1 fumble for 0 yards.

Bracey Walker

(statistical profile on page 459)

Pos: S **Rnd:** 4   **College:** North Carolina   **Ht:** 5' 10" **Wt:** 200 **Born:** 10/28/70 **Age:** 26

Year Team	G	GS	Tackles Tk	Ast	Sack	Miscellaneous FF	FR	TD	Blk	Interceptions Int	Yds	Avg	TD	Totals Sfty	TD	Pts
1994 KC - Cin	10	0	1	1	0.0	0	0	0	0	0	0	-	0	0	0	0
1995 Cincinnati Bengals	14	14	60	25	0.0	1	2	0	0	4	56	14.0	0	0	0	0
1994 Kansas City Chiefs	2	0	0	0	0.0	0	0	0	0	0	0	-	0	0	0	0
Cincinnati Bengals	8	0	1	1	0.0	0	0	0	0	0	0	-	0	0	0	0
2 NFL Seasons	24	14	61	26	0.0	1	2	0	0	4	56	14.0	0	0	0	0

Bruce Walker

Pos: NT/DE **Rnd:** 2   **College:** UCLA   **Ht:** 6' 4" **Wt:** 310 **Born:** 7/18/72 **Age:** 24

Year Team	G	GS	Tackles Tk	Ast	Sack	Miscellaneous FF	FR	TD	Blk	Interceptions Int	Yds	Avg	TD	Totals Sfty	TD	Pts
1995 New England Patriots	11	6	16	2	0.0	0	0	0	0	0	0	-	0	0	0	0

Darnell Walker

Pos: CB **Rnd:** 7   **College:** Oklahoma   **Ht:** 5' 8" **Wt:** 168 **Born:** 1/17/70 **Age:** 26

Year Team	G	GS	Tackles Tk	Ast	Sack	Miscellaneous FF	FR	TD	Blk	Interceptions Int	Yds	Avg	TD	Totals Sfty	TD	Pts
1993 Atlanta Falcons	15	8	36	12	0.0	0	0	0	0	3	7	2.3	0	0	0	0
1994 Atlanta Falcons	16	5	37	3	1.0	1	0	0	0	3	105	35.0	1	0	1	6
1995 Atlanta Falcons	16	7	45	5	0.0	0	0	0	0	0	0	-	0	0	0	0
3 NFL Seasons	47	20	118	20	1.0	1	0	0	0	6	112	18.7	1	0	1	6

Derrick Walker

(statistical profile on page 383)

Pos: TE **Rnd:** 6   **College:** Michigan   **Ht:** 6' 0" **Wt:** 249 **Born:** 6/23/67 **Age:** 29

Year Team	G	GS	Rushing Att	Yds	Avg	Lg	TD	Receiving Rec	Yds	Avg	Lg	TD	Punt Returns Num	Yds	Avg	TD	Kickoff Returns Num	Yds	Avg	TD	Totals Fum	TD	Pts
1990 San Diego Chargers	16	13	0	0	-	-	0	23	240	10.4	23	1	0	0	-	0	0	0	-	0	1	1	6
1991 San Diego Chargers	16	16	0	0	-	-	0	20	134	6.7	14	0	0	0	-	0	0	0	-	0	0	0	0
1992 San Diego Chargers	16	16	0	0	-	-	0	34	393	11.6	59	2	0	0	-	0	0	0	-	0	0	2	12
1993 San Diego Chargers	12	11	0	0	-	-	0	21	212	10.1	t25	1	0	0	-	0	0	0	-	0	0	1	6
1994 Kansas City Chiefs	15	11	0	0	-	-	0	36	382	10.6	t57	2	0	0	-	0	0	0	-	0	1	2	12
1995 Kansas City Chiefs	16	3	0	0	-	-	0	25	205	8.2	t18	1	0	0	-	0	0	0	-	0	0	1	6
6 NFL Seasons	91	70	0	0	-	-	0	159	1566	9.8	59	7	0	0	-	0	0	0	-	0	2	7	42

Other Statistics: 1991–recovered 1 fumble for 0 yards.

Gary Walker

Pos: DT **Rnd:** 5 **College:** Auburn **Ht:** 6' 2" **Wt:** 285 **Born:** 2/28/73 **Age:** 23

Year	Team	G	GS	Tackles			Miscellaneous				Interceptions				Totals		
				Tk	Ast	Sack	FF	FR	TD	Blk	Int	Yds	Avg	TD	Sfty	TD	Pts
1995	Houston Oilers	15	9	22	10	2.5	1	0	0	0	0	0	-	0	0	0	0

Herschel Walker

(statistical profile on page 384)

Pos: KR/RB **Rnd:** 5 **College:** Georgia **Ht:** 6' 1" **Wt:** 225 **Born:** 3/3/62 **Age:** 34

Year	Team	G	GS	Rushing					Receiving					Kickoff Returns				Passing				Totals		
				Att	Yds	Avg	Lg	TD	Rec	Yds	Avg	Lg	TD	Num	Yds	Avg	TD	Att	Com	Yds	Int	Fum	TD	Pts
1986	Dallas Cowboys	16	9	151	737	4.9	t84	12	76	837	11.0	t84	2	0	0	-	0	0	0	0	0	5	14	84
1987	Dallas Cowboys	12	11	209	891	4.3	t60	7	60	715	11.9	44	1	0	0	-	0	0	0	0	0	4	8	48
1988	Dallas Cowboys	16	16	361	1514	4.2	38	5	53	505	9.5	50	2	0	0	-	0	0	0	0	0	6	7	42
1989	Dal - Min	16	15	250	915	3.7	47	7	40	423	10.6	52	2	13	374	28.8	1	0	0	0	0	7	10	60
1990	Minnesota Vikings	16	16	184	770	4.2	t58	5	35	315	9.0	32	4	44	966	22.0	0	2	1	12	0	4	9	54
1991	Minnesota Vikings	15	15	198	825	4.2	t71	10	33	204	6.2	19	0	5	83	16.6	0	0	0	0	0	2	10	60
1992	Philadelphia Eagles	16	16	267	1070	4.0	38	8	38	278	7.3	41	2	3	69	23.0	0	1	0	0	0	6	10	60
1993	Philadelphia Eagles	16	16	174	746	4.3	35	1	75	610	8.1	55	3	11	184	16.7	0	0	0	0	0	3	4	24
1994	Philadelphia Eagles	16	14	113	528	4.7	t91	5	50	500	10.0	93	2	21	581	27.7	1	0	0	0	0	4	8	48
1995	New York Giants	16	3	31	126	4.1	36	0	31	234	7.5	34	1	41	881	21.5	0	0	0	0	0	0	1	6
1989	Dallas Cowboys	5	5	81	246	3.0	t20	2	22	261	11.9	52	1	0	0	-	0	0	0	0	0	2	3	18
	Minnesota Vikings	11	10	169	669	4.0	47	5	18	162	9.0	24	1	13	374	28.8	1	0	0	0	0	5	7	42
	10 NFL Seasons	155	131	1938	8122	4.2	t91	60	491	4621	9.4	93	19	138	3138	22.7	2	3	1	12	0	41	81	486

Other Statistics: 1986–recovered 2 fumbles for 0 yards. 1987–recovered 1 fumble for 0 yards. 1988–recovered 3 fumbles for 0 yards. 1991–recovered 1 fumble for 0 yards. 1992–recovered 2 fumbles for 0 yards. 1993–recovered 2 fumbles for 0 yards. 1994–recovered 1 fumble for 0 yards.

Aaron Wallace

Pos: DE/LB **Rnd:** 2 **College:** Texas A&M **Ht:** 6' 3" **Wt:** 245 **Born:** 4/17/67 **Age:** 29

Year	Team	G	GS	Tackles			Miscellaneous				Interceptions				Totals		
				Tk	Ast	Sack	FF	FR	TD	Blk	Int	Yds	Avg	TD	Sfty	TD	Pts
1990	Los Angeles Raiders	16	0	0	-	9.0	0	0	0	0	0	0	-	0	0	0	0
1991	Los Angeles Raiders	16	0	0	-	2.0	0	0	0	0	0	0	-	0	0	0	0
1992	Los Angeles Raiders	16	16	73	-	4.0	0	2	0	0	0	0	-	0	0	0	0
1993	Los Angeles Raiders	16	14	45	16	2.0	1	2	0	0	0	0	-	0	0	0	0
1994	Los Angeles Raiders	16	6	13	8	2.0	0	0	0	0	0	0	-	0	0	0	0
1995	Oakland Raiders	13	0	6	1	2.0	0	1	0	0	0	0	-	0	0	0	0
	6 NFL Seasons	93	36	137	25	21.0	1	5	0	0	0	0	-	0	0	0	0

Steve Wallace

Pos: T **Rnd:** 4 **College:** Auburn **Ht:** 6' 5" **Wt:** 280 **Born:** 12/27/64 **Age:** 31

Year	Team	G	GS	Year	Team	G	GS	Year	Team	G	GS	Year	Team	G	GS
1986	San Francisco 49ers	16	0	1989	San Francisco 49ers	16	1	1992	San Francisco 49ers	16	16	1995	San Francisco 49ers	13	12
1987	San Francisco 49ers	11	4	1990	San Francisco 49ers	16	16	1993	San Francisco 49ers	15	15				
1988	San Francisco 49ers	16	16	1991	San Francisco 49ers	16	16	1994	San Francisco 49ers	15	15		10 NFL Seasons	150	111

Other Statistics: 1987–recovered 1 fumble for 0 yards. 1992–recovered 1 fumble for 0 yards. 1993–recovered 1 fumble for 0 yards. 1994–recovered 2 fumbles for 0 yards.

Brett Wallerstedt

Pos: LB **Rnd:** 6 **College:** Arizona State **Ht:** 6' 1" **Wt:** 240 **Born:** 11/24/70 **Age:** 25

Year	Team	G	GS	Tackles			Miscellaneous				Interceptions				Totals		
				Tk	Ast	Sack	FF	FR	TD	Blk	Int	Yds	Avg	TD	Sfty	TD	Pts
1993	Phoenix Cardinals	7	0	9	2	0.0	0	0	0	0	0	0	-	0	0	0	0
1994	Cincinnati Bengals	10	0	3	2	0.0	0	0	0	0	0	0	-	0	0	0	0
1995	Cincinnati Bengals	11	2	20	2	0.0	0	0	0	0	0	0	-	0	0	0	0
	3 NFL Seasons	28	2	32	6	0.0	0	0	0	0	0	0	-	0	0	0	0

Wesley Walls

(statistical profile on page 384)

Pos: TE/WR **Rnd:** 2 **College:** Mississippi **Ht:** 6' 5" **Wt:** 250 **Born:** 3/26/66 **Age:** 30

Year	Team	G	GS	Rushing					Receiving					Punt Returns				Kickoff Returns				Totals		
				Att	Yds	Avg	Lg	TD	Rec	Yds	Avg	Lg	TD	Num	Yds	Avg	TD	Num	Yds	Avg	TD	Fum	TD	Pts
1989	San Francisco 49ers	16	0	0	0	-	-	0	4	16	4.0	9	1	0	0	-	0	0	0	-	0	1	1	6
1990	San Francisco 49ers	16	0	0	0	-	-	0	5	27	5.4	11	0	0	0	-	0	1	16	16.0	0	0	0	0
1991	San Francisco 49ers	15	0	0	0	-	-	0	2	24	12.0	21	0	0	0	-	0	0	0	-	0	0	0	0
1993	San Francisco 49ers	6	0	0	0	-	-	0	0	0	-	-	0	0	0	-	0	0	0	-	0	0	0	0
1994	New Orleans Saints	15	7	0	0	-	-	0	38	406	10.7	31	4	0	0	-	0	0	0	-	0	0	4	26
1995	New Orleans Saints	16	10	0	0	-	-	0	57	694	12.2	29	4	0	0	-	0	1	6	6.0	0	1	4	26

Year	Team	G	GS	Rushing					Receiving					Punt Returns				Kickoff Returns				Totals		
				Att	Yds	Avg	Lg	TD	Rec	Yds	Avg	Lg	TD	Num	Yds	Avg	TD	Num	Yds	Avg	TD	Fum	TD	Pts
	6 NFL Seasons	84	17	0	0	-	-	0	106	1167	11.0	31	9	0	0	-	0	2	22	11.0	0	2	9	58

Other Statistics: 1989–recovered 1 fumble for 0 yards. 1993–recovered 1 fumble for 0 yards. 1994–scored 1 two-point conversion. 1995–recovered 1 fumble for 0 yards; scored 1 two-point conversion.

Chris Walsh

Pos: WR   **Rnd:** 9   **College:** Stanford   **Ht:** 6' 1"   **Wt:** 193   **Born:** 12/12/68   **Age:** 27

Year	Team	G	GS	Rushing					Receiving					Punt Returns				Kickoff Returns				Totals		
				Att	Yds	Avg	Lg	TD	Rec	Yds	Avg	Lg	TD	Num	Yds	Avg	TD	Num	Yds	Avg	TD	Fum	TD	Pts
1992	Buffalo Bills	2	0	0	0	-	-	0	0	0	-	-	0	0	0	-	0	0	0	-	0	0	0	0
1993	Buffalo Bills	3	0	0	0	-	-	0	0	0	-	-	0	0	0	-	0	0	0	-	0	0	0	0
1994	Minnesota Vikings	10	0	0	0	-	-	0	0	0	-	-	0	0	0	-	0	1	6	6.0	0	0	0	0
1995	Minnesota Vikings	16	0	0	0	-	-	0	7	66	9.4	16	0	0	0	-	0	3	42	14.0	0	0	0	0
	4 NFL Seasons	31	0	0	0	-	-	0	7	66	9.4	16	0	0	0	-	0	4	48	12.0	0	0	0	0

Steve Walsh

Pos: QB   **Rnd:** 1(S)   **College:** Miami (FL)   **Ht:** 6' 3"   **Wt:** 205   **Born:** 12/1/66   **Age:** 29

Year	Team	G	GS	Passing										Rushing					Miscellaneous			
				Att	Com	Pct	Yards	Yds/Att	Lg	TD	Int	Int%	Rating	Att	Yds	Avg	Lg	TD	Sckd	Yds	Fum Recv Yds	Pts
1989	Dallas Cowboys	8	5	219	110	50.2	1371	6.26	46	5	9	4.1	60.5	6	16	2.7	14	0	11	84	3 2	-14	0
1990	Dal - NO	13	11	336	179	53.3	2010	5.98	58	12	13	3.9	67.2	20	25	1.3	18	0	10	76	6 2	0	0
1991	New Orleans Saints	8	7	255	141	55.3	1638	6.42	41	11	6	2.4	79.5	8	0	0.0	3	0	3	26	3 1	-20	0
1993	New Orleans Saints	2	1	38	20	52.6	271	7.13	t54	2	3	7.9	60.3	4	-4	-1.0	-1	0	0	0	0 0	0	0
1994	Chicago Bears	12	11	343	208	60.6	2078	6.06	50	10	8	2.3	77.9	30	4	0.1	12	1	11	52	7 3	-8	6
1995	Chicago Bears	1	0	0	0	-	0	-	-	0	0	-	0.0	0	0	-	0	0	0	0	0 0	0	0
1990	Dallas Cowboys	1	0	9	4	44.4	40	4.44	20	0	0	0.0	57.6	1	0	0.0	0	0	0	0	1 0	0	0
	New Orleans Saints	12	11	327	175	53.5	1970	6.02	58	12	13	4.0	67.5	19	25	1.3	18	0	10	76	5 2	0	0
	6 NFL Seasons	44	35	1191	658	55.2	7368	6.19	58	40	39	3.3	71.5	68	41	0.6	18	1	35	238	19 8	-42	6

Joe Walter

Pos: T   **Rnd:** 7   **College:** Texas Tech   **Ht:** 6' 7"   **Wt:** 292   **Born:** 6/18/63   **Age:** 33

Year	Team	G	GS	Year	Team	G	GS	Year	Team	G	GS	Year	Team	G	GS
1985	Cincinnati Bengals	14	0	1988	Cincinnati Bengals	16	16	1991	Cincinnati Bengals	15	14	1995	Cincinnati Bengals	16	16
1986	Cincinnati Bengals	15	8	1989	Cincinnati Bengals	10	7	1992	Cincinnati Bengals	16	16				
1987	Cincinnati Bengals	12	12	1990	Cincinnati Bengals	16	16	1993	Cincinnati Bengals	16	16		10 NFL Seasons	146	121

Other Statistics: 1987–recovered 2 fumbles for 0 yards. 1991–recovered 1 fumble for 0 yards. 1992–recovered 1 fumble for 0 yards.

Derek Ware

Pos: TE   **Rnd:** 7   **College:** Central State   **Ht:** 6' 2"   **Wt:** 255   **Born:** 9/17/67   **Age:** 29

Year	Team	G	GS	Rushing					Receiving					Punt Returns				Kickoff Returns				Totals		
				Att	Yds	Avg	Lg	TD	Rec	Yds	Avg	Lg	TD	Num	Yds	Avg	TD	Num	Yds	Avg	TD	Fum	TD	Pts
1992	Phoenix Cardinals	15	0	0	0	-	-	0	1	13	13.0	13	0	0	0	-	0	0	0	-	0	0	0	0
1993	Phoenix Cardinals	16	1	0	0	-	-	0	3	45	15.0	27	0	0	0	-	0	0	0	-	0	0	0	0
1994	Arizona Cardinals	15	12	0	0	-	-	0	17	171	10.1	33	1	0	0	-	0	0	0	-	0	1	1	6
1995	Cincinnati Bengals	7	0	0	0	-	-	0	2	36	18.0	21	0	0	0	-	0	0	0	-	0	0	0	0
	4 NFL Seasons	53	13	0	0	-	-	0	23	265	11.5	33	1	0	0	-	0	0	0	-	0	1	1	6

Other Statistics: 1994–recovered 1 fumble for 0 yards.

Chris Warren

(statistical profile on page 385)

Pos: RB   **Rnd:** 4   **College:** Ferrum   **Ht:** 6' 2"   **Wt:** 226   **Born:** 1/24/68   **Age:** 28

Year	Team	G	GS	Rushing					Receiving					Punt Returns				Kickoff Returns				Totals		
				Att	Yds	Avg	Lg	TD	Rec	Yds	Avg	Lg	TD	Num	Yds	Avg	TD	Num	Yds	Avg	TD	Fum	TD	Pts
1990	Seattle Seahawks	16	0	6	11	1.8	4	1	0	0	-	-	0	28	269	9.6	0	23	478	20.8	0	3	1	6
1991	Seattle Seahawks	16	1	11	13	1.2	7	0	2	9	4.5	12	0	32	298	9.3	1	35	792	22.6	0	3	1	6
1992	Seattle Seahawks	16	16	223	1017	4.6	52	3	16	134	8.4	33	0	34	252	7.4	0	28	524	18.7	0	2	3	18
1993	Seattle Seahawks	14	14	273	1072	3.9	t45	7	15	99	6.6	21	0	0	0	-	0	0	0	-	0	3	7	42
1994	Seattle Seahawks	16	15	333	1545	4.6	41	9	41	323	7.9	51	2	0	0	-	0	0	0	-	0	5	11	68
1995	Seattle Seahawks	16	16	310	1346	4.3	52	15	35	247	7.1	t20	1	0	0	-	0	0	0	-	0	5	16	96
	6 NFL Seasons	94	62	1156	5004	4.3	52	35	109	812	7.4	51	3	94	819	8.7	1	86	1794	20.9	0	21	39	236

Other Statistics: 1990–recovered 1 fumble for 0 yards. 1991–recovered 1 fumble for 0 yards. 1992–recovered 2 fumbles for 0 yards. 1994–recovered 2 fumbles for 0 yards; scored 1 two-point conversion. 1995–recovered 2 fumbles for 0 yards.

Lamont Warren

Pos: RB/KR **Rnd:** 6   **College:** Colorado   **Ht:** 5' 11" **Wt:** 211   **Born:** 1/4/73   **Age:** 23

Year	Team	G	GS	Rushing					Receiving					Kickoff Returns				Passing				Totals		
				Att	Yds	Avg	Lg	TD	Rec	Yds	Avg	Lg	TD	Num	Yds	Avg	TD	Att	Com	Yds	Int	Fum	TD	Pts
1994	Indianapolis Colts	11	0	18	80	4.4	34	0	3	47	15.7	29	0	2	56	28.0	0	1	0	0	0	0	0	0

Year Team	G	GS	Rushing Att	Yds	Avg	Lg	TD	Receiving Rec	Yds	Avg	Lg	TD	Kickoff Returns Num	Yds	Avg	TD	Passing Att	Com	Yds	Int	Totals Fum	TD	Pts
1995 Indianapolis Colts	12	1	47	152	3.2	42	1	17	159	9.4	18	0	15	315	21.0	0	0	0	0	0	1	1	6
2 NFL Seasons	23	1	65	232	3.6	42	1	20	206	10.3	29	0	17	371	21.8	0	1	0	0	0	1	1	6

Terrence Warren

Pos: WR **Rnd:** 5 **College:** Hampton **Ht:** 6' 1" **Wt:** 205 **Born:** 8/2/69 **Age:** 27

Year Team	G	GS	Rushing Att	Yds	Avg	Lg	TD	Receiving Rec	Yds	Avg	Lg	TD	Punt Returns Num	Yds	Avg	TD	Kickoff Returns Num	Yds	Avg	TD	Totals Fum	TD	Pts
1993 Seattle Seahawks	2	0	0	0	-	-	0	0	0	-	-	0	0	0	-	0	0	0	-	0	0	0	0
1994 Seattle Seahawks	14	0	3	15	5.0	11	0	0	0	-	-	0	0	0	-	0	14	350	25.0	0	0	0	0
1995 San Francisco 49ers	1	0	0	0	-	-	0	0	0	-	-	0	0	0	-	0	4	67	16.8	0	0	0	0
3 NFL Seasons	17	0	3	15	5.0	11	0	0	0	-	-	0	0	0	-	0	18	417	23.2	0	0	0	0

Other Statistics: 1994–recovered 1 fumble for 0 yards.

Brian Washington

(statistical profile on page 459)

Pos: S **Rnd:** 10 **College:** Nebraska **Ht:** 6' 1" **Wt:** 210 **Born:** 9/10/65 **Age:** 31

Year Team	G	GS	Tackles Tk	Ast	Sack	Misc. FF	FR	TD	Blk	Int Int	Yds	Avg	TD	Totals Sfty	TD	Pts
1988 Cleveland Browns	16	14	46	23	0.5	0	0	0	0	3	104	34.7	1	0	1	6
1990 New York Jets	14	13	46	38	1.0	0	1	0	0	3	22	7.3	0	0	0	0
1991 New York Jets	16	16	72	35	2.0	0	1	0	0	1	0	0.0	0	0	0	0
1992 New York Jets	16	16	72	36	1.0	0	2	0	0	6	59	9.8	1	0	1	6
1993 New York Jets	16	16	58	36	0.0	3	1	0	0	6	128	21.3	1	0	1	6
1994 New York Jets	15	15	67	20	0.0	3	3	0	0	2	-3	-1.5	0	0	0	0
1995 Kansas City Chiefs	16	14	53	9	0.0	2	1	0	0	3	100	33.3	1	0	1	6
7 NFL Seasons	109	104	414	197	4.5	8	9	0	0	24	410	17.1	4	0	4	24

Other Statistics: 1991–fumbled 1 time.

Dewayne Washington

(statistical profile on page 460)

Pos: CB **Rnd:** 1 (18) **College:** North Carolina State **Ht:** 5' 11" **Wt:** 189 **Born:** 12/27/72 **Age:** 23

Year Team	G	GS	Tackles Tk	Ast	Sack	Misc. FF	FR	TD	Blk	Int Int	Yds	Avg	TD	Totals Sfty	TD	Pts
1994 Minnesota Vikings	16	16	68	7	0.0	0	2	1	0	3	135	45.0	2	0	3	18
1995 Minnesota Vikings	15	15	54	8	0.0	0	0	0	0	1	25	25.0	0	0	0	0
2 NFL Seasons	31	31	122	15	0.0	0	2	1	0	4	160	40.0	2	0	3	18

James Washington

(statistical profile on page 460)

Pos: S **Rnd:** 5 **College:** UCLA **Ht:** 6' 1" **Wt:** 209 **Born:** 1/10/65 **Age:** 31

Year Team	G	GS	Tackles Tk	Ast	Sack	FF	FR	TD	Blk	Int	Yds	Avg	TD	Punt Returns Num	Yds	Avg	TD	Kickoff Returns Num	Yds	Avg	TD	Totals TD	Fum
1988 Los Angeles Rams	16	0	14	3	0.0	0	0	0	0	1	7	7.0	0	0	0	-	0	0	0	-	0	0	0
1989 Los Angeles Rams	8	0	12	2	0.0	0	1	0	0	0	0	-	0	0	0	-	0	0	0	-	0	0	0
1990 Dallas Cowboys	15	10	43	27	0.0	0	3	0	0	3	24	8.0	0	0	0	-	0	0	0	-	0	0	0
1991 Dallas Cowboys	16	16	75	38	0.0	0	0	0	0	2	9	4.5	0	0	0	-	0	0	0	-	0	0	0
1992 Dallas Cowboys	16	15	51	44	0.0	0	1	0	0	3	31	10.3	0	0	0	-	0	0	0	-	0	0	0
1993 Dallas Cowboys	14	1	28	14	0.0	1	1	0	0	1	38	38.0	0	1	0	0.0	0	0	0	-	0	0	1
1994 Dallas Cowboys	16	16	57	21	0.0	1	1	0	0	5	43	8.6	0	0	0	-	0	0	0	-	0	0	0
1995 Washington Redskins	12	12	50	6	0.0	0	0	0	0	2	35	17.5	0	0	0	-	0	0	0	-	0	0	0
8 NFL Seasons	113	70	330	155	0.0	2	7	0	0	17	187	11.0	0	1	0	0.0	0	0	0	-	0	0	1

Lionel Washington

Pos: CB **Rnd:** 4 **College:** Tulane **Ht:** 6' 0" **Wt:** 185 **Born:** 10/21/60 **Age:** 36

Year Team	G	GS	Tackles Tk	Ast	Sack	Misc. FF	FR	TD	Blk	Int Int	Yds	Avg	TD	Totals Sfty	TD	Pts
1983 St. Louis Cardinals	16	8	67	-	0.0	0	1	0	0	8	92	11.5	0	0	0	0
1984 St. Louis Cardinals	15	15	67	-	0.0	0	1	0	0	5	42	8.4	0	0	0	0
1985 St. Louis Cardinals	5	2	0	-	0.0	0	0	0	0	1	48	48.0	1	0	1	6
1986 St. Louis Cardinals	16	12	0	-	0.0	0	1	0	0	2	19	9.5	0	0	0	0
1987 Los Angeles Raiders	11	10	37	-	0.0	0	0	0	0	0	0	-	0	0	0	0
1988 Los Angeles Raiders	12	0	0	-	0.0	0	0	0	0	1	0	0.0	0	0	0	0
1989 Los Angeles Raiders	16	16	67	-	0.0	0	3	1	0	3	46	15.3	1	0	2	12
1990 Los Angeles Raiders	15	15	62	-	0.0	0	0	0	0	1	2	2.0	0	0	0	0
1991 Los Angeles Raiders	16	16	51	21	0.0	0	0	0	0	5	22	4.4	0	0	0	0
1992 Los Angeles Raiders	16	16	63	-	0.0	0	0	0	0	2	21	10.5	0	0	0	0
1993 Los Angeles Raiders	16	16	45	10	1.0	0	0	0	0	2	0	0.0	0	0	0	0
1994 Los Angeles Raiders	12	7	22	3	0.0	0	0	0	0	3	65	21.7	1	0	1	6

Year	Team	G	GS	Tackles			Miscellaneous				Interceptions				Totals		
				Tk	Ast	Sack	FF	FR	TD	Blk	Int	Yds	Avg	TD	Sfty	TD	Pts
1995	Denver Broncos	16	16	49	10	0.0	0	1	0	0	0	0	-	0	0	0	0
	13 NFL Seasons	182	149	530	44	1.0	0	7	1	0	33	357	10.8	3	0	4	24

Other Statistics: 1995–fumbled 1 time.

Marvin Washington

(statistical profile on page 460)

Pos: DE/DT **Rnd:** 6   **College:** Idaho   **Ht:** 6' 6" **Wt:** 280   **Born:** 10/22/65 **Age:** 31

Year	Team	G	GS	Tackles			Miscellaneous				Interceptions				Punt Returns				Kickoff Returns				Totals	
				Tk	Ast	Sack	FF	FR	TD	Blk	Int	Yds	Avg	TD	Num	Yds	Avg	TD	Num	Yds	Avg	TD	TD	Fum
1989	New York Jets	16	0	6	5	1.5	0	1	0	0	0	0	-	0	0	0	-	0	1	11	11.0	0	0	0
1990	New York Jets	16	0	25	23	4.5	0	0	0	0	0	0	-	0	0	0	-	0	0	0	-	0	0	0
1991	New York Jets	15	15	33	12	6.0	0	0	0	0	0	0	-	0	0	0	-	0	0	0	-	0	0	0
1992	New York Jets	16	14	39	23	8.5	0	0	0	0	0	0	-	0	0	0	-	0	0	0	-	0	0	0
1993	New York Jets	16	16	48	23	5.5	3	0	0	0	0	0	-	0	0	0	-	0	0	0	-	0	0	0
1994	New York Jets	15	15	28	16	3.0	1	1	0	0	1	7	7.0	0	0	0	-	0	0	0	-	0	0	1
1995	New York Jets	16	16	57	23	6.0	5	0	0	1	0	0	-	0	0	0	-	0	0	0	-	0	0	0
	7 NFL Seasons	110	76	236	125	35.0	9	2	0	1	1	7	7.0	0	0	0	-	0	1	11	11.0	0	0	1

Other Statistics: 1992–credited with 1 safety.

Mickey Washington

(statistical profile on page 461)

Pos: CB   **Rnd:** 8   **College:** Texas A&M   **Ht:** 5' 10" **Wt:** 191   **Born:** 7/8/68   **Age:** 28

Year	Team	G	GS	Tackles			Miscellaneous				Interceptions				Totals		
				Tk	Ast	Sack	FF	FR	TD	Blk	Int	Yds	Avg	TD	Sfty	TD	Pts
1990	New England Patriots	9	0	4	3	0.0	0	0	0	0	0	0	-	0	0	0	0
1991	New England Patriots	16	4	42	24	0.0	0	0	0	0	2	0	0.0	0	0	0	0
1992	Washington Redskins	3	0	0	0	0.0	0	0	0	0	0	0	-	0	0	0	0
1993	Buffalo Bills	16	6	34	7	0.5	0	2	0	0	1	27	27.0	1	0	1	6
1994	Buffalo Bills	16	16	65	12	0.5	0	1	0	0	3	63	21.0	0	0	0	0
1995	Jacksonville Jaguars	16	16	50	12	0.0	1	2	0	0	1	48	48.0	1	0	1	6
	6 NFL Seasons	76	42	195	58	1.0	1	5	0	0	7	138	19.7	2	0	2	12

Ted Washington

Pos: NT/DT **Rnd:** 1 (25) **College:** Louisville   **Ht:** 6' 4" **Wt:** 315   **Born:** 4/13/68 **Age:** 28

Year	Team	G	GS	Tackles			Miscellaneous				Interceptions				Totals		
				Tk	Ast	Sack	FF	FR	TD	Blk	Int	Yds	Avg	TD	Sfty	TD	Pts
1991	San Francisco 49ers	16	0	20	1	1.0	0	0	0	0	0	0	-	0	0	0	0
1992	San Francisco 49ers	16	6	27	8	2.0	0	0	0	0	0	0	-	0	0	0	0
1993	San Francisco 49ers	12	12	36	5	3.0	0	1	0	0	0	0	-	0	0	0	0
1994	Denver Broncos	16	16	44	12	2.5	2	0	0	0	1	5	5.0	0	0	0	0
1995	Buffalo Bills	16	15	42	11	2.5	0	0	0	0	0	0	-	0	0	0	0
	5 NFL Seasons	76	49	169	37	11.0	2	1	0	0	1	5	5.0	0	0	0	0

Andre Waters

Pos: S   **Rnd:** FA   **College:** Cheyney   **Ht:** 5' 11" **Wt:** 200   **Born:** 3/10/62 **Age:** 34

Year	Team	G	GS	Tackles			Miscellaneous				Interceptions				Punt Returns				Kickoff Returns				Totals	
				Tk	Ast	Sack	FF	FR	TD	Blk	Int	Yds	Avg	TD	Num	Yds	Avg	TD	Num	Yds	Avg	TD	TD	Fum
1984	Philadelphia Eagles	16	0	0	1	0.0	0	1	0	0	0	0	-	0	0	0	-	0	13	319	24.5	1	1	1
1985	Philadelphia Eagles	16	0	8	1	0.0	0	1	0	0	0	0	-	0	1	23	23.0	0	4	74	18.5	0	0	1
1986	Philadelphia Eagles	16	16	90	39	2.0	0	2	0	0	6	39	6.5	0	0	0	-	0	0	0	-	0	0	0
1987	Philadelphia Eagles	12	12	61	51	0.0	0	2	0	0	3	63	21.0	0	0	0	-	0	0	0	-	0	0	0
1988	Philadelphia Eagles	16	16	107	47	0.5	0	0	0	0	3	19	6.3	0	0	0	-	0	0	0	-	0	0	0
1989	Philadelphia Eagles	16	13	82	55	0.0	0	3	1	0	1	20	20.0	0	0	0	-	0	0	0	-	0	1	0
1990	Philadelphia Eagles	14	13	50	51	0.0	3	0	0	0	0	0	-	0	0	0	-	0	0	0	-	0	0	0
1991	Philadelphia Eagles	16	16	79	77	0.0	0	1	0	0	1	0	0.0	0	0	0	-	0	0	0	-	0	0	0
1992	Philadelphia Eagles	6	6	24	23	0.0	0	0	0	0	1	23	23.0	0	0	0	-	0	0	0	-	0	0	0
1993	Philadelphia Eagles	9	8	25	39	0.0	0	0	0	0	0	0	-	0	0	0	-	0	0	0	-	0	0	0
1994	Arizona Cardinals	12	4	14	6	0.0	1	0	0	0	0	0	-	0	0	0	-	0	0	0	-	0	0	0
1995	Arizona Cardinals	8	0	1	0	0.0	0	0	0	0	0	0	-	0	0	0	-	0	0	0	-	0	0	0
	12 NFL Seasons	157	104	541	390	3.5	4	10	1	0	15	164	10.9	0	1	23	23.0	0	17	393	23.1	1	2	2

Kendell Watkins

Pos: TE   **Rnd:** 2   **College:** Mississippi State   **Ht:** 6' 1" **Wt:** 305   **Born:** 3/8/73   **Age:** 23

Year	Team	G	GS	Rushing					Receiving					Punt Returns				Kickoff Returns				Totals		
				Att	Yds	Avg	Lg	TD	Rec	Yds	Avg	Lg	TD	Num	Yds	Avg	TD	Num	Yds	Avg	TD	Fum	TD	Pts
1995	Dallas Cowboys	15	0	0	0	-	-	0	1	8	8.0	8	0	0	0	-	0	1	-6	-6.0	0	1	0	0

Tim Watson

Pos: S **Rnd:** 6 **College:** Howard **Ht:** 6' 1" **Wt:** 215 **Born:** 8/13/70 **Age:** 26

			Tackles			Miscellaneous				Interceptions				Totals		
Year Team	G	GS	Tk	Ast	Sack	FF	FR	TD	Blk	Int	Yds	Avg	TD	Sfty	TD	Pts
1993 Kansas City Chiefs	4	0	0	0	0.0	0	0	0	0	0	0	-	0	0	0	0
1994 Kansas City Chiefs	1	0	0	0	0.0	0	0	0	0	0	0	-	0	0	0	0
1995 KC - NYN	5	0	1	2	0.0	0	0	0	0	0	0	-	0	0	0	0
1995 Kansas City Chiefs	4	0	1	2	0.0	0	0	0	0	0	0	-	0	0	0	0
New York Giants	1	0	0	0	0.0	0	0	0	0	0	0	-	0	0	0	0
3 NFL Seasons	10	0	1	2	0.0	0	0	0	0	0	0	-	0	0	0	0

Ricky Watters
(statistical profile on page 385)

Pos: RB **Rnd:** 2 **College:** Notre Dame **Ht:** 6' 1" **Wt:** 217 **Born:** 4/7/69 **Age:** 27

			Rushing					Receiving					Kickoff Returns				Passing				Totals		
Year Team	G	GS	Att	Yds	Avg	Lg	TD	Rec	Yds	Avg	Lg	TD	Num	Yds	Avg	TD	Att	Com	Yds	Int	Fum	TD	Pts
1992 San Francisco 49ers	14	13	206	1013	4.9	43	9	43	405	9.4	35	2	0	0	-	0	1	0	0	0	2	11	66
1993 San Francisco 49ers	13	13	208	950	4.6	39	10	31	326	10.5	t48	1	0	0	-	0	0	0	0	0	5	11	66
1994 San Francisco 49ers	16	16	239	877	3.7	23	6	66	719	10.9	t65	5	0	0	-	0	0	0	0	0	8	11	66
1995 Philadelphia Eagles	16	16	337	1273	3.8	57	11	62	434	7.0	24	1	0	0	-	0	0	0	0	0	6	12	72
4 NFL Seasons	59	58	990	4113	4.2	57	36	202	1884	9.3	t65	9	0	0	-	0	1	0	0	0	21	45	270

Other Statistics: 1992–recovered 1 fumble for 0 yards. 1993–recovered 1 fumble for 0 yards. 1994–recovered 2 fumbles for 0 yards.

Damon Watts

Pos: DB/CB **Rnd:** FA **College:** Indiana **Ht:** 5' 10" **Wt:** 173 **Born:** 4/8/72 **Age:** 24

			Tackles			Miscellaneous				Interceptions				Totals		
Year Team	G	GS	Tk	Ast	Sack	FF	FR	TD	Blk	Int	Yds	Avg	TD	Sfty	TD	Pts
1994 Indianapolis Colts	16	8	45	13	0.0	0	0	0	0	1	0	0.0	0	0	0	0
1995 Indianapolis Colts	13	0	10	1	0.0	0	0	0	0	1	9	9.0	0	0	0	0
2 NFL Seasons	29	8	55	14	0.0	0	0	0	0	2	9	4.5	0	0	0	0

Charles Way

Pos: RB **Rnd:** 6 **College:** Virginia **Ht:** 6' 0" **Wt:** 236 **Born:** 12/27/72 **Age:** 23

			Rushing					Receiving					Punt Returns				Kickoff Returns				Totals		
Year Team	G	GS	Att	Yds	Avg	Lg	TD	Rec	Yds	Avg	Lg	TD	Num	Yds	Avg	TD	Num	Yds	Avg	TD	Fum	TD	Pts
1995 New York Giants	16	4	2	6	3.0	6	0	7	76	10.9	34	1	0	0	-	0	1	8	8.0	0	0	1	6

Richmond Webb

Pos: T **Rnd:** 1 (9) **College:** Texas A&M **Ht:** 6' 6" **Wt:** 303 **Born:** 1/11/67 **Age:** 29

Year	Team	G	GS	Year	Team	G	GS	Year	Team	G	GS		G	GS
1990	Miami Dolphins	16	16	1992	Miami Dolphins	16	16	1994	Miami Dolphins	16	16			
1991	Miami Dolphins	14	14	1993	Miami Dolphins	16	16	1995	Miami Dolphins	16	16	6 NFL Seasons	94	94

Other Statistics: 1995–recovered 1 fumble for 0 yards.

Larry Webster

Pos: DT **Rnd:** 3 **College:** Maryland **Ht:** 6' 5" **Wt:** 288 **Born:** 1/18/69 **Age:** 27

			Tackles			Miscellaneous				Interceptions				Totals		
Year Team	G	GS	Tk	Ast	Sack	FF	FR	TD	Blk	Int	Yds	Avg	TD	Sfty	TD	Pts
1992 Miami Dolphins	16	0	7	6	1.5	0	0	0	0	0	0	-	0	0	0	0
1993 Miami Dolphins	13	9	18	12	0.0	0	1	0	0	0	0	-	0	0	0	0
1994 Miami Dolphins	15	7	15	10	0.0	0	0	0	0	0	0	-	0	0	0	0
1995 Cleveland Browns	10	0	20	1	0.0	0	0	0	0	0	0	-	0	0	0	0
4 NFL Seasons	54	16	60	29	1.5	0	1	0	0	0	0	-	0	0	0	0

Bert Weidner

Pos: G/C **Rnd:** 11 **College:** Kent State **Ht:** 6' 2" **Wt:** 295 **Born:** 1/20/66 **Age:** 30

Year	Team	G	GS	Year	Team	G	GS	Year	Team	G	GS		G	GS
1990	Miami Dolphins	8	0	1992	Miami Dolphins	16	3	1994	Miami Dolphins	15	14			
1991	Miami Dolphins	15	10	1993	Miami Dolphins	16	11	1995	Miami Dolphins	12	1	6 NFL Seasons	82	39

Other Statistics: 1993–recovered 1 fumble for 0 yards.

Casey Weldon
(statistical profile on page 386)

Pos: QB **Rnd:** 4 **College:** Florida State **Ht:** 6' 1" **Wt:** 206 **Born:** 2/3/69 **Age:** 27

			Passing										Rushing					Miscellaneous			
Year Team	G	GS	Att	Com	Pct	Yards	Yds/Att	Lg	TD	Int	Int%	Rating	Att	Yds	Avg	Lg	TD	Sckd	Yds	Fum Recv Yds	Pts
1993 Tampa Bay Buccaneers	3	0	11	6	54.5	55	5.00	20	0	1	9.1	30.5	0	0	-	-	0	1	11	0 0	0

Year Team	G	GS	Passing Att	Com	Pct	Yards	Yds/Att	Lg	TD	Int	Int%	Rating	Rushing Att	Yds	Avg	Lg	TD	Misc. Sckd	Yds	Fum	Recv	Yds	Pts
1994 Tampa Bay Buccaneers	3	0	9	7	77.8	63	7.00	27	0	0	0.0	95.8	0	0	-	-	0	0	0	0	0	0	0
1995 Tampa Bay Buccaneers	16	0	91	42	46.2	519	5.70	40	1	2	2.2	58.8	5	5	1.0	6	1	9	55	4	0	-3	6
3 NFL Seasons	22	0	111	55	49.5	637	5.74	40	1	3	2.7	59.0	5	5	1.0	6	1	10	66	4	0	-3	6

Dean Wells

Pos: LB **Rnd:** 4 **College:** Kentucky **Ht:** 6' 3" **Wt:** 242 **Born:** 7/20/70 **Age:** 26

Year Team	G	GS	Tackles Tk	Ast	Sack	Misc. FF	FR	TD	Blk	Int. Int	Yds	Avg	TD	Totals Sfty	TD	Pts
1993 Seattle Seahawks	14	1	13	2	0.0	0	0	0	0	0	0	-	0	0	0	0
1994 Seattle Seahawks	15	0	7	1	0.0	0	0	0	0	0	0	-	0	0	0	0
1995 Seattle Seahawks	14	10	38	19	0.0	0	1	0	0	0	0	-	0	0	0	0
3 NFL Seasons	43	11	58	22	0.0	0	1	0	0	0	0	-	0	0	0	0

Mike Wells

Pos: DE/DT **Rnd:** 4 **College:** Iowa **Ht:** 6' 3" **Wt:** 287 **Born:** 1/6/71 **Age:** 25

Year Team	G	GS	Tackles Tk	Ast	Sack	Misc. FF	FR	TD	Blk	Int. Int	Yds	Avg	TD	Totals Sfty	TD	Pts
1994 Detroit Lions	3	0	0	0	0.0	0	0	0	0	0	0	-	0	0	0	0
1995 Detroit Lions	15	0	3	3	0.5	0	0	0	0	0	0	-	0	0	0	0
2 NFL Seasons	18	0	3	3	0.5	0	0	0	0	0	0	-	0	0	0	0

Derek West

Pos: T **Rnd:** 5 **College:** Colorado **Ht:** 6' 8" **Wt:** 303 **Born:** 3/28/72 **Age:** 24

Year Team	G	GS			G	GS
1995 Indianapolis Colts	3	0		1 NFL Season	3	0

Ed West

Pos: TE **Rnd:** FA **College:** Auburn **Ht:** 6' 1" **Wt:** 245 **Born:** 8/2/61 **Age:** 35

Year Team	G	GS	Rushing Att	Yds	Avg	Lg	TD	Receiving Rec	Yds	Avg	Lg	TD	Punt Returns Num	Yds	Avg	TD	Kickoff Returns Num	Yds	Avg	TD	Totals Fum	TD	Pts
1984 Green Bay Packers	16	0	1	2	2.0	t2	1	6	54	9.0	t29	4	0	0	-	0	0	0	-	0	0	5	30
1985 Green Bay Packers	16	0	1	0	0.0	0	0	8	95	11.9	30	1	0	0	-	0	0	0	-	0	1	1	6
1986 Green Bay Packers	16	6	0	0	-	-	0	15	199	13.3	t46	1	0	0	-	0	0	0	-	0	1	1	6
1987 Green Bay Packers	12	11	0	0	-	-	0	19	261	13.7	40	1	0	0	-	0	0	0	-	0	1	1	6
1988 Green Bay Packers	16	16	0	0	-	-	0	30	276	9.2	35	3	0	0	-	0	0	0	-	0	1	3	18
1989 Green Bay Packers	13	12	0	0	-	-	0	22	269	12.2	31	5	0	0	-	0	0	0	-	0	0	5	30
1990 Green Bay Packers	16	16	0	0	-	-	0	27	356	13.2	50	5	0	0	-	0	1	0	0.0	0	3	5	30
1991 Green Bay Packers	16	16	0	0	-	-	0	15	151	10.1	21	3	0	0	-	0	0	0	-	0	3	3	18
1992 Green Bay Packers	16	8	0	0	-	-	0	4	30	7.5	10	0	0	0	-	0	1	0	0.0	0	0	0	0
1993 Green Bay Packers	16	7	0	0	-	-	0	25	253	10.1	24	0	0	0	-	0	0	0	-	0	0	0	0
1994 Green Bay Packers	14	12	0	0	-	-	0	31	377	12.2	26	2	0	0	-	0	0	0	-	0	1	2	14
1995 Philadelphia Eagles	16	14	0	0	-	-	0	20	190	9.5	26	1	0	0	-	0	0	0	-	0	1	1	6
12 NFL Seasons	183	118	2	2	1.0	t2	1	222	2511	11.3	50	26	0	0	-	0	2	0	0.0	0	6	27	164

Other Statistics: 1984–recovered 1 fumble for 0 yards. 1986–recovered 1 fumble for 0 yards. 1994–scored 1 two-point conversion. 1995–recovered 1 fumble for 0 yards.

Michael Westbrook

Pos: WR **Rnd:** 1 (4) **College:** Colorado *(statistical profile on page 386)* **Ht:** 6' 3" **Wt:** 215 **Born:** 7/7/72 **Age:** 24

Year Team	G	GS	Rushing Att	Yds	Avg	Lg	TD	Receiving Rec	Yds	Avg	Lg	TD	Punt Returns Num	Yds	Avg	TD	Kickoff Returns Num	Yds	Avg	TD	Totals Fum	TD	Pts
1995 Washington Redskins	11	9	6	114	19.0	t58	1	34	522	15.4	45	1	0	0	-	0	0	0	-	0	0	2	12

Ryan Wetnight

Pos: TE **Rnd:** FA **College:** Stanford **Ht:** 6' 2" **Wt:** 240 **Born:** 11/5/70 **Age:** 25

Year Team	G	GS	Rushing Att	Yds	Avg	Lg	TD	Receiving Rec	Yds	Avg	Lg	TD	Punt Returns Num	Yds	Avg	TD	Kickoff Returns Num	Yds	Avg	TD	Totals Fum	TD	Pts
1993 Chicago Bears	10	1	0	0	-	-	0	9	93	10.3	t25	1	0	0	-	0	0	0	-	0	0	1	6
1994 Chicago Bears	11	0	0	0	-	-	0	11	104	9.5	19	1	0	0	-	0	0	0	-	0	0	1	6
1995 Chicago Bears	12	2	0	0	-	-	0	24	193	8.0	22	2	0	0	-	0	0	0	-	0	0	2	12
3 NFL Seasons	33	3	0	0	-	-	0	44	390	8.9	t25	4	0	0	-	0	0	0	-	0	0	4	24

Tyrone Wheatley

(statistical profile on page 387)

Pos: RB/KR **Rnd:** 1 (17) **College:** Michigan   **Ht:** 6' 0" **Wt:** 227 **Born:** 1/19/72 **Age:** 24

Year Team	G	GS	Att	Yds	Avg	Lg	TD	Rec	Yds	Avg	Lg	TD	Num	Yds	Avg	TD	Num	Yds	Avg	TD	Fum	TD	Pts
			Rushing					Receiving					Punt Returns				Kickoff Returns				Totals		
1995 New York Giants	13	1	78	245	3.1	t19	3	5	27	5.4	16	0	0	0	-	0	10	186	18.6	0	2	3	18

Leonard Wheeler

Pos: CB/S **Rnd:** 3 **College:** Troy State   **Ht:** 5' 11" **Wt:** 189 **Born:** 1/15/69 **Age:** 27

Year Team	G	GS	Tk	Ast	Sack	FF	FR	TD	Blk	Int	Yds	Avg	TD	Sfty	TD	Pts
			Tackles			Miscellaneous				Interceptions				Totals		
1992 Cincinnati Bengals	16	2	17	4	0.0	0	0	0	0	1	12	12.0	0	0	0	0
1993 Cincinnati Bengals	16	3	22	7	0.0	0	1	0	0	0	24	-	0	0	0	0
1995 Cincinnati Bengals	16	1	21	7	0.0	0	0	0	0	0	0	-	0	0	0	0
3 NFL Seasons	48	6	60	18	0.0	0	1	0	0	1	36	36.0	0	0	0	0

Mark Wheeler

Pos: DT **Rnd:** 3 **College:** Texas A&M   **Ht:** 6' 2" **Wt:** 285 **Born:** 4/1/70 **Age:** 26

Year Team	G	GS	Tk	Ast	Sack	FF	FR	TD	Blk	Int	Yds	Avg	TD	Sfty	TD	Pts
			Tackles			Miscellaneous				Interceptions				Totals		
1992 Tampa Bay Buccaneers	16	16	42	19	5.0	0	0	0	0	0	0	-	0	0	0	0
1993 Tampa Bay Buccaneers	10	10	16	10	2.0	0	0	0	0	0	0	-	0	0	0	0
1994 Tampa Bay Buccaneers	15	8	24	6	3.0	0	0	0	0	0	0	-	0	0	0	0
1995 Tampa Bay Buccaneers	14	12	22	10	1.0	0	0	0	0	0	0	-	0	0	0	0
4 NFL Seasons	55	46	104	45	11.0	0	0	0	0	0	0	-	0	0	0	0

Larry Whigham

Pos: S **Rnd:** 4 **College:** Northeast Louisiana   **Ht:** 6' 2" **Wt:** 202 **Born:** 6/23/72 **Age:** 24

Year Team	G	GS	Tk	Ast	Sack	FF	FR	TD	Blk	Int	Yds	Avg	TD	Sfty	TD	Pts
			Tackles			Miscellaneous				Interceptions				Totals		
1994 New England Patriots	12	0	2	0	0.0	0	0	0	0	1	21	21.0	0	0	0	0
1995 New England Patriots	16	0	4	0	0.0	0	1	0	0	0	0	-	0	0	0	0
2 NFL Seasons	28	0	6	0	0.0	0	1	0	0	1	21	21.0	0	0	0	0

Other Statistics: 1994–fumbled 1 time for 0 yards.

Alberto White

Pos: DE **Rnd:** FA **College:** Texas Southern   **Ht:** 6' 3" **Wt:** 245 **Born:** 4/8/71 **Age:** 25

Year Team	G	GS	Tk	Ast	Sack	FF	FR	TD	Blk	Int	Yds	Avg	TD	Sfty	TD	Pts
			Tackles			Miscellaneous				Interceptions				Totals		
1994 Los Angeles Raiders	8	0	4	0	2.0	0	0	0	0	0	0	-	0	0	0	0
1995 St. Louis Rams	2	0	1	0	1.0	0	0	0	0	0	0	-	0	0	0	0
2 NFL Seasons	10	0	5	0	3.0	0	0	0	0	0	0	-	0	0	0	0

David White

Pos: LB **Rnd:** FA **College:** Nebraska   **Ht:** 6' 2" **Wt:** 235 **Born:** 2/27/70 **Age:** 26

Year Team	G	GS	Tk	Ast	Sack	FF	FR	TD	Blk	Int	Yds	Avg	TD	Sfty	TD	Pts
			Tackles			Miscellaneous				Interceptions				Totals		
1993 New England Patriots	6	0	0	0	0.0	0	0	0	0	0	0	-	0	0	0	0
1995 Buffalo Bills	15	1	6	1	1.0	1	1	0	0	1	9	9.0	0	0	0	0
2 NFL Seasons	21	1	6	1	1.0	1	1	0	0	1	9	9.0	0	0	0	0

Dwayne White

Pos: G **Rnd:** 7 **College:** Alcorn State   **Ht:** 6' 2" **Wt:** 315 **Born:** 2/10/67 **Age:** 29

Year Team	G	GS	Year Team	G	GS	Year Team	G	GS		G	GS
1990 New York Jets	11	5	1992 New York Jets	16	16	1994 New York Jets	16	16			
1991 New York Jets	16	16	1993 New York Jets	15	15	1995 St. Louis Rams	15	15	6 NFL Seasons	89	83

Other Statistics: 1991–recovered 1 fumble for 0 yards. 1992–recovered 1 fumble for -1 yard. 1994–recovered 1 fumble for 0 yards.

Lorenzo White

Pos: RB **Rnd:** 1 (22) **College:** Michigan State   **Ht:** 5' 11" **Wt:** 222 **Born:** 4/12/66 **Age:** 30

Year Team	G	GS	Att	Yds	Avg	Lg	TD	Rec	Yds	Avg	Lg	TD	Num	Yds	Avg	TD	Num	Yds	Avg	TD	Fum	TD	Pts
			Rushing					Receiving					Punt Returns				Kickoff Returns				Totals		
1988 Houston Oilers	11	0	31	115	3.7	16	0	0	0	-	-	0	0	0	-	0	8	196	24.5	1	0	1	6
1989 Houston Oilers	16	0	104	349	3.4	33	5	6	37	6.2	11	0	0	0	-	0	17	303	17.8	0	2	5	30
1990 Houston Oilers	16	16	168	702	4.2	22	8	39	368	9.4	29	4	0	0	-	0	0	0	-	0	7	12	72

257

Year	Team	G	GS	Rushing Att	Yds	Avg	Lg	TD	Receiving Rec	Yds	Avg	Lg	TD	Punt Returns Num	Yds	Avg	TD	Kickoff Returns Num	Yds	Avg	TD	Totals Fum	TD	Pts
1991	Houston Oilers	13	0	110	465	4.2	20	4	27	211	7.8	20	0	0	0	-	0	0	0	-	0	3	4	24
1992	Houston Oilers	16	16	265	1226	4.6	44	7	57	641	11.2	t69	1	0	0	-	0	0	0	-	0	2	8	48
1993	Houston Oilers	8	8	131	465	3.5	14	2	34	229	6.7	20	0	0	0	-	0	0	0	-	0	1	2	12
1994	Houston Oilers	16	8	191	757	4.0	33	3	21	188	9.0	41	1	0	0	-	0	8	167	20.9	0	2	4	24
1995	Cleveland Browns	13	2	62	163	2.6	11	1	8	64	8.0	28	0	0	0	-	0	0	0	-	0	0	1	6
	8 NFL Seasons	109	50	1062	4242	4.0	44	30	192	1738	9.1	t69	6	0	0	-	0	33	666	20.2	1	17	37	222

Other Statistics: 1989–recovered 1 fumble for 0 yards. 1990–recovered 3 fumbles for 0 yards. 1992–recovered 2 fumbles for 0 yards. 1994–recovered 1 fumble for 0 yards. 1995–recovered 2 fumbles for 0 yards.

Reggie White

Pos: NT **Rnd:** 6 **College:** North Carolina A&T **Ht:** 6' 4" **Wt:** 315 **Born:** 3/22/70 **Age:** 26

Year	Team	G	GS	Tackles Tk	Ast	Sack	Miscellaneous FF	FR	TD	Blk	Interceptions Int	Yds	Avg	TD	Totals Sfty	TD	Pts
1992	San Diego Chargers	3	0	1	0	1.0	0	0	0	0	0	0	-	0	0	0	0
1993	San Diego Chargers	8	0	1	0	0.0	0	0	0	0	0	0	-	0	0	0	0
1994	San Diego Chargers	11	0	6	0	2.0	1	0	0	0	0	0	-	0	0	0	0
1995	New England Patriots	16	6	12	10	1.5	0	0	0	0	0	0	-	0	0	0	0
	4 NFL Seasons	38	6	20	10	4.5	1	0	0	0	0	0	-	0	0	0	0

Reggie White

(statistical profile on page 461)

Pos: DE/DT **Rnd:** 1(S) **College:** Tennessee **Ht:** 6' 5" **Wt:** 300 **Born:** 12/19/61 **Age:** 34

Year	Team	G	GS	Tackles Tk	Ast	Sack	Miscellaneous FF	FR	TD	Blk	Interceptions Int	Yds	Avg	TD	Totals Sfty	TD	Pts
1985	Philadelphia Eagles	13	12	62	38	13.0	0	2	0	0	0	0	-	0	0	0	0
1986	Philadelphia Eagles	16	16	83	15	18.0	1	0	0	0	0	0	-	0	0	0	0
1987	Philadelphia Eagles	12	12	62	14	21.0	4	1	1	0	0	0	-	0	0	1	6
1988	Philadelphia Eagles	16	16	96	37	18.0	1	2	0	0	0	0	-	0	0	0	0
1989	Philadelphia Eagles	16	16	82	41	11.0	3	1	0	0	0	0	-	0	0	0	0
1990	Philadelphia Eagles	16	16	59	24	14.0	4	1	0	0	1	33	33.0	0	0	0	0
1991	Philadelphia Eagles	16	16	72	28	15.0	2	3	0	0	1	0	0.0	0	0	0	0
1992	Philadelphia Eagles	16	16	54	27	14.0	3	1	1	0	0	0	-	0	0	1	6
1993	Green Bay Packers	16	16	48	31	13.0	3	2	0	0	0	0	-	0	0	0	0
1994	Green Bay Packers	16	15	35	14	8.0	2	1	0	0	0	0	-	0	0	0	0
1995	Green Bay Packers	15	13	31	11	12.0	2	0	0	0	0	0	-	0	0	0	0
	11 NFL Seasons	168	164	684	280	157.0	25	14	2	0	2	33	16.5	0	0	2	12

William White

Pos: S **Rnd:** 4 **College:** Ohio State **Ht:** 5' 10" **Wt:** 205 **Born:** 2/19/66 **Age:** 30

Year	Team	G	GS	Tackles Tk	Ast	Sack	Miscellaneous FF	FR	TD	Blk	Interceptions Int	Yds	Avg	TD	Totals Sfty	TD	Pts
1988	Detroit Lions	16	0	15	1	0.0	0	1	0	0	0	0	-	0	0	0	0
1989	Detroit Lions	15	15	64	17	1.0	0	1	1	0	1	0	0.0	0	0	1	6
1990	Detroit Lions	16	16	78	28	0.0	0	0	0	0	5	120	24.0	1	0	1	6
1991	Detroit Lions	16	16	64	23	0.0	0	0	1	0	2	35	17.5	0	0	1	6
1992	Detroit Lions	16	16	57	19	0.0	0	0	0	0	4	54	13.5	0	0	0	0
1993	Detroit Lions	16	16	53	31	1.5	1	0	0	0	1	5	5.0	0	0	0	0
1994	Kansas City Chiefs	15	13	47	13	0.0	0	0	0	0	2	0	0.0	0	0	0	0
1995	Kansas City Chiefs	16	5	37	5	1.0	0	0	0	0	2	48	24.0	0	0	0	0
	8 NFL Seasons	126	97	415	137	3.5	1	2	2	0	17	262	15.4	1	0	3	18

Other Statistics: 1992–fumbled 1 time for 0 yards.

Bob Whitfield

Pos: T **Rnd:** 1 (8) **College:** Stanford **Ht:** 6' 5" **Wt:** 300 **Born:** 10/18/71 **Age:** 25

Year	Team	G	GS	Year	Team	G	GS	Year	Team	G	GS	Year	Team	G	GS
1992	Atlanta Falcons	11	0	1993	Atlanta Falcons	16	16	1994	Atlanta Falcons	16	16	1995	Atlanta Falcons	16	16
													4 NFL Seasons	59	48

Other Statistics: 1993–recovered 2 fumbles for 0 yards.

Curtis Whitley

Pos: C **Rnd:** 5 **College:** Clemson **Ht:** 6' 1" **Wt:** 288 **Born:** 5/10/69 **Age:** 27

Year	Team	G	GS	Year	Team	G	GS	Year	Team	G	GS	Year	Team	G	GS
1992	San Diego Chargers	3	0	1993	San Diego Chargers	15	0	1994	San Diego Chargers	12	2	1995	Carolina Panthers	16	16
													4 NFL Seasons	46	18

Other Statistics: 1994–recovered 1 fumble for 0 yards. 1995–recovered 1 fumble for 0 yards.

David Whitmore

Pos: S **Rnd:** 4 **College:** Stephen F. Austin **Ht:** 6' 0" **Wt:** 232 **Born:** 7/6/67 **Age:** 29

Year	Team	G	GS	Tackles			Miscellaneous				Interceptions				Punt Returns				Kickoff Returns				Totals	
				Tk	Ast	Sack	FF	FR	TD	Blk	Int	Yds	Avg	TD	Num	Yds	Avg	TD	Num	Yds	Avg	TD	TD	Fum
1990	New York Giants	16	0	18	1	0.0	0	0	0	0	0	0	-	0	0	0	-	0	1	0	0.0	0	0	1
1991	San Francisco 49ers	11	0	26	6	1.0	0	0	0	0	1	5	5.0	0	0	0	-	0	1	7	7.0	0	0	0
1992	San Francisco 49ers	16	12	50	12	0.0	0	0	0	0	1	0	0.0	0	0	0	-	0	0	0	-	0	0	0
1993	Kansas City Chiefs	6	6	24	17	0.0	1	0	0	0	0	0	-	0	0	0	-	0	0	0	-	0	0	0
1994	Kansas City Chiefs	12	10	29	12	0.0	1	1	0	0	0	0	-	0	0	0	-	0	0	0	-	0	0	0
1995	Philadelphia Eagles	3	0	0	0	0.0	0	0	0	0	0	0	-	0	0	0	-	0	0	0	-	0	0	0
	6 NFL Seasons	64	28	147	48	1.0	2	1	0	0	2	5	2.5	0	0	0	-	0	2	7	3.5	0	0	1

Bernard Whittington

Pos: DE **Rnd:** FA **College:** Indiana **Ht:** 6' 6" **Wt:** 278 **Born:** 8/20/71 **Age:** 25

Year	Team	G	GS	Tackles			Miscellaneous				Interceptions				Totals		
				Tk	Ast	Sack	FF	FR	TD	Blk	Int	Yds	Avg	TD	Sfty	TD	Pts
1994	Indianapolis Colts	13	8	22	14	0.0	1	0	0	0	0	0	-	0	0	0	0
1995	Indianapolis Colts	16	13	32	16	2.0	1	1	0	1	0	0	-	0	0	0	0
	2 NFL Seasons	29	21	54	30	2.0	2	1	0	1	0	0	-	0	0	0	0

Dave Widell

Pos: C **Rnd:** 4 **College:** Boston College **Ht:** 6' 7" **Wt:** 308 **Born:** 5/14/65 **Age:** 31

Year	Team	G	GS	Year	Team	G	GS	Year	Team	G	GS	Year	Team	G	GS
1988	Dallas Cowboys	14	9	1990	Denver Broncos	16	5	1992	Denver Broncos	16	1	1994	Denver Broncos	16	16
1989	Dallas Cowboys	15	2	1991	Denver Broncos	16	2	1993	Denver Broncos	15	15	1995	Jacksonville Jaguars	16	16
													8 NFL Seasons	124	66

Other Statistics: 1988–recovered 1 fumble for 0 yards. 1991–fumbled 1 time for -15 yards. 1994–fumbled 1 time for -1 yard.

Doug Widell

Pos: G **Rnd:** 2 **College:** Boston College **Ht:** 6' 4" **Wt:** 280 **Born:** 9/23/66 **Age:** 30

Year	Team	G	GS	Year	Team	G	GS	Year	Team	G	GS	Year	Team	G	GS
1989	Denver Broncos	16	10	1991	Denver Broncos	16	16	1993	Green Bay Packers	16	9	1995	Detroit Lions	12	10
1990	Denver Broncos	16	16	1992	Denver Broncos	16	16	1994	Detroit Lions	16	16		7 NFL Seasons	108	93

Other Statistics: 1990–recovered 1 fumble for 0 yards. 1991–recovered 1 fumble for 0 yards. 1992–recovered 2 fumbles for 0 yards; caught 1 pass for -7 yards.

Corey Widmer

Pos: LB **Rnd:** 7 **College:** Montana State **Ht:** 6' 3" **Wt:** 250 **Born:** 12/25/68 **Age:** 27

Year	Team	G	GS	Tackles			Miscellaneous				Interceptions				Punt Returns				Kickoff Returns				Totals	
				Tk	Ast	Sack	FF	FR	TD	Blk	Int	Yds	Avg	TD	Num	Yds	Avg	TD	Num	Yds	Avg	TD	TD	Fum
1992	New York Giants	8	0	5	0	0.0	0	0	0	0	0	0	-	0	0	0	-	0	0	0	-	0	0	0
1993	New York Giants	11	0	0	0	0.0	0	0	0	0	0	0	-	0	0	0	-	0	0	0	-	0	0	0
1994	New York Giants	16	5	22	10	1.0	0	0	0	0	0	0	-	0	0	0	-	0	0	0	-	0	0	0
1995	New York Giants	16	0	8	0	0.0	0	0	0	0	0	0	-	0	0	0	-	0	1	0	0.0	0	0	0
	4 NFL Seasons	51	5	35	10	1.0	0	0	0	0	0	0	-	0	0	0	-	0	1	0	0.0	0	0	0

Zach Wiegert

Pos: T/G **Rnd:** 2 **College:** Nebraska **Ht:** 6' 4" **Wt:** 311 **Born:** 8/16/72 **Age:** 24

Year	Team	G	GS			G	GS
1995	St. Louis Rams	5	2		1 NFL Season	5	2

Barry Wilburn

Pos: S **Rnd:** 8 **College:** Mississippi **Ht:** 6' 2" **Wt:** 196 **Born:** 12/9/63 **Age:** 32

Year	Team	G	GS	Tackles			Miscellaneous				Interceptions				Totals		
				Tk	Ast	Sack	FF	FR	TD	Blk	Int	Yds	Avg	TD	Sfty	TD	Pts
1985	Washington Redskins	16	1	26	13	0.0	1	1	0	0	1	10	10.0	0	0	0	0
1986	Washington Redskins	16	5	45	13	0.0	1	2	0	0	2	14	7.0	0	0	0	0
1987	Washington Redskins	12	12	43	24	0.0	0	0	0	0	9	135	15.0	1	0	1	6
1988	Washington Redskins	10	10	33	11	0.0	0	1	0	0	4	24	6.0	0	0	0	0
1989	Washington Redskins	8	1	4	4	0.0	0	0	0	0	3	13	4.3	0	0	0	0
1992	Cleveland Browns	6	3	13	1	0.0	0	1	0	0	0	0	-	0	0	0	0
1995	Philadelphia Eagles	16	0	10	1	0.0	0	1	0	0	1	0	0.0	0	0	0	0
	7 NFL Seasons	84	32	174	67	0.0	2	6	0	0	20	196	9.8	1	0	1	6

Erik Wilhelm

Pos: QB   **Rnd:** 3   **College:** Oregon State   **Ht:** 6' 3"   **Wt:** 217   **Born:** 11/16/65   **Age:** 30

Year	Team	G	GS	Rushing Att	Yds	Avg	Lg	TD	Receiving Rec	Yds	Avg	Lg	TD	Kickoff Returns Num	Yds	Avg	TD	Passing Att	Com	Yds	Int	Totals Fum	TD	Pts
1989	Cincinnati Bengals	6	0	6	30	5.0	14	0	0	0	-	-	0	0	0	-	0	56	30	425	2	2	0	0
1990	Cincinnati Bengals	7	0	6	6	1.0	4	0	0	0	-	-	0	0	0	-	0	19	12	117	0	1	0	0
1991	Cincinnati Bengals	4	1	1	9	9.0	9	0	0	0	-	-	0	0	0	-	0	42	24	217	2	1	0	0
1993	Cincinnati Bengals	1	0	0	0	-	-	0	0	0	-	-	0	0	0	-	0	6	4	63	0	0	0	0
1994	Cincinnati Bengals	2	0	0	0	-	-	0	0	0	-	-	0	0	0	-	0	0	0	0	0	0	0	0
1995	Cincinnati Bengals	1	0	0	0	-	-	0	0	0	-	-	0	0	0	-	0	0	0	0	0	0	0	0
	6 NFL Seasons	21	1	13	45	3.5	14	0	0	0	-	-	0	0	0	-	0	123	70	822	4	4	0	0

Other Statistics: 1989–recovered 1 fumble for 0 yards; passed for 4 touchdowns. 1990–recovered 1 fumble for 0 yards.

Bruce Wilkerson

Pos: T   **Rnd:** 2   **College:** Tennessee   **Ht:** 6' 5"   **Wt:** 295   **Born:** 7/28/64   **Age:** 32

Year	Team	G	GS	Year	Team	G	GS	Year	Team	G	GS		G	GS
1987	Los Angeles Raiders	11	5	1990	Los Angeles Raiders	8	1	1993	Los Angeles Raiders	14	14			
1988	Los Angeles Raiders	16	16	1991	Los Angeles Raiders	16	16	1994	Los Angeles Raiders	11	6			
1989	Los Angeles Raiders	16	16	1992	Los Angeles Raiders	15	15	1995	Jacksonville Jaguars	10	0	9 NFL Seasons	117	89

Other Statistics: 1989–recovered 2 fumbles for 0 yards. 1992–recovered 1 fumble for 0 yards. 1993–recovered 1 fumble for 0 yards. 1994–recovered 1 fumble for 0 yards.

Gabe Wilkins

Pos: DT/DE   **Rnd:** 4   **College:** Gardner-Webb   **Ht:** 6' 4"   **Wt:** 310   **Born:** 9/1/71   **Age:** 25

Year	Team	G	GS	Tackles Tk	Ast	Sack	Miscellaneous FF	FR	TD	Blk	Interceptions Int	Yds	Avg	TD	Totals Sfty	TD	Pts
1994	Green Bay Packers	15	0	3	1	1.0	0	0	0	0	0	0	-	0	0	0	0
1995	Green Bay Packers	13	8	12	3	3.0	0	0	0	0	0	0	-	0	0	0	0
	2 NFL Seasons	28	8	15	4	4.0	0	0	0	0	0	0	-	0	0	0	0

Jeff Wilkins

Pos: K   **Rnd:** FA   **College:** Youngstown State   *(statistical profile on page 487)*   **Ht:** 6' 1"   **Wt:** 190   **Born:** 4/19/72   **Age:** 24

Year	Team	G	Field Goals 1-29 Yds	Pct	30-39 Yds	Pct	40-49 Yds	Pct	50+ Yds	Pct	Overall	Pct	Long	PAT Made	Att	Tot Pts
1994	Philadelphia Eagles	6	0-0	-	0-0	-	0-0	-	0-0	-	0-0	-	-	0	0	0
1995	San Francisco 49ers	7	6-6	100.0	5-5	100.0	1-2	50.0	0-0	-	12-13	92.3	40	27	29	63
	2 NFL Seasons	13	6-6	100.0	5-5	100.0	1-2	50.0	0-0	-	12-13	92.3	40	27	29	63

Dan Wilkinson

Pos: DT/DE   **Rnd:** 1 (1)   **College:** Ohio State   *(statistical profile on page 461)*   **Ht:** 6' 5"   **Wt:** 313   **Born:** 3/13/73   **Age:** 23

Year	Team	G	GS	Tackles Tk	Ast	Sack	Miscellaneous FF	FR	TD	Blk	Interceptions Int	Yds	Avg	TD	Totals Sfty	TD	Pts
1994	Cincinnati Bengals	16	14	37	7	5.5	0	0	0	0	0	0	-	0	0	0	0
1995	Cincinnati Bengals	14	14	30	10	8.0	1	0	0	0	0	0	-	0	0	0	0
	2 NFL Seasons	30	28	67	17	13.5	1	0	0	0	0	0	-	0	0	0	0

Aeneas Williams

Pos: CB   **Rnd:** 3   **College:** Southern   *(statistical profile on page 462)*   **Ht:** 5' 10"   **Wt:** 190   **Born:** 1/29/68   **Age:** 28

Year	Team	G	GS	Tackles Tk	Ast	Sack	Miscellaneous FF	FR	TD	Blk	Interceptions Int	Yds	Avg	TD	Totals Sfty	TD	Pts
1991	Phoenix Cardinals	16	15	38	10	0.0	0	2	0	0	6	60	10.0	0	0	0	0
1992	Phoenix Cardinals	16	16	40	8	0.0	0	1	0	0	3	25	8.3	0	0	0	0
1993	Phoenix Cardinals	16	16	37	5	0.0	0	2	1	0	2	87	43.5	1	0	2	12
1994	Arizona Cardinals	16	16	40	1	0.0	0	1	0	1	9	89	9.9	0	0	0	0
1995	Arizona Cardinals	16	16	52	10	0.0	0	3	1	0	6	86	14.3	2	0	3	18
	5 NFL Seasons	80	79	207	34	0.0	0	9	2	1	26	347	13.3	3	0	5	30

Other Statistics: 1991–fumbled 1 time. 1995–fumbled 1 time.

Alfred Williams

Pos: DE   **Rnd:** 1 (18)   **College:** Colorado   **Ht:** 6' 6"   **Wt:** 265   **Born:** 11/6/68   **Age:** 27

Year	Team	G	GS	Tackles Tk	Ast	Sack	Miscellaneous FF	FR	TD	Blk	Interceptions Int	Yds	Avg	TD	Totals Sfty	TD	Pts
1991	Cincinnati Bengals	16	15	33	5	3.0	0	2	0	0	0	0	-	0	0	0	0
1992	Cincinnati Bengals	15	6	38	5	10.0	0	0	0	0	0	0	-	0	0	0	0
1993	Cincinnati Bengals	16	16	22	6	4.0	1	0	0	0	0	0	-	0	1	0	2

Year	Team	G	GS	Tk	Ast	Sack	FF	FR	TD	Blk	Int	Yds	Avg	TD	Sfty	TD	Pts
				Tackles			**Miscellaneous**				**Interceptions**				**Totals**		
1994	Cincinnati Bengals	16	16	40	8	9.5	1	1	0	0	0	0	-	0	1	0	2
1995	San Francisco 49ers	16	0	22	6	4.5	1	1	0	0	0	0	-	0	0	0	0
	5 NFL Seasons	79	53	155	30	31.0	3	4	0	0	0	0	-	0	2	0	4

Allen Williams

Pos: RB   **Rnd:** FA   **College:** Maryland   **Ht:** 5' 9"   **Wt:** 202   **Born:** 9/17/72   **Age:** 24

Year	Team	G	GS	Att	Yds	Avg	Lg	TD	Rec	Yds	Avg	Lg	TD	Num	Yds	Avg	TD	Num	Yds	Avg	TD	Fum	TD	Pts
				Rushing					**Receiving**					**Punt Returns**				**Kickoff Returns**				**Totals**		
1995	Detroit Lions	5	0	0	0	-	-	0	0	0	-	-	0	0	0	-	0	4	100	25.0	0	1	0	0

Brent Williams

Pos: DE   **Rnd:** 7   **College:** Toledo   **Ht:** 6' 4"   **Wt:** 283   **Born:** 10/23/64   **Age:** 32

Year	Team	G	GS	Tk	Ast	Sack	FF	FR	TD	Blk	Int	Yds	Avg	TD	Sfty	TD	Pts
				Tackles			**Miscellaneous**				**Interceptions**				**Totals**		
1986	New England Patriots	16	16	44	29	7.0	0	4	1	0	0	0	-	0	0	1	6
1987	New England Patriots	12	5	17	12	5.0	0	0	0	0	0	0	-	0	0	0	0
1988	New England Patriots	16	16	39	19	8.0	0	1	0	0	0	0	-	0	0	0	0
1989	New England Patriots	16	16	48	17	8.0	0	2	0	0	0	0	-	0	0	0	0
1990	New England Patriots	16	16	46	25	6.0	0	2	1	0	0	0	-	0	0	1	6
1991	New England Patriots	16	16	29	26	3.5	0	2	0	0	0	0	-	0	0	0	0
1992	New England Patriots	16	15	36	14	4.0	0	0	0	0	0	0	-	0	0	0	0
1993	New England Patriots	13	2	12	17	2.0	0	0	0	0	0	0	-	0	0	0	0
1994	Seattle Seahawks	10	9	19	12	1.0	1	0	0	0	0	0	-	0	0	0	0
1995	Seattle Seahawks	11	9	19	6	1.0	1	1	0	0	0	0	-	0	0	0	0
	10 NFL Seasons	142	120	309	177	45.5	2	12	2	0	0	0	-	0	0	2	12

Other Statistics: 1995–fumbled 1 time.

Brian Williams

Pos: C   **Rnd:** 1 (18)   **College:** Minnesota   **Ht:** 6' 5"   **Wt:** 300   **Born:** 6/8/66   **Age:** 30

Year	Team	G	GS	Year	Team	G	GS	Year	Team	G	GS	Year	Team	G	GS
1989	New York Giants	14	4	1991	New York Giants	14	1	1993	New York Giants	16	1	1995	New York Giants	16	16
1990	New York Giants	16	1	1992	New York Giants	13	1	1994	New York Giants	14	14		7 NFL Seasons	103	38

Other Statistics: 1994–recovered 1 fumble for -34 yards; fumbled 2 times.

Brian Williams

Pos: LB   **Rnd:** 3   **College:** Southern California   **Ht:** 6' 1"   **Wt:** 238   **Born:** 12/17/72   **Age:** 23

Year	Team	G	GS	Tk	Ast	Sack	FF	FR	TD	Blk	Int	Yds	Avg	TD	Sfty	TD	Pts
				Tackles			**Miscellaneous**				**Interceptions**				**Totals**		
1995	Green Bay Packers	13	0	0	0	0.0	0	0	0	0	0	0	-	0	0	0	0

Calvin Williams

(statistical profile on page 387)

Pos: WR   **Rnd:** 5   **College:** Purdue   **Ht:** 5' 11"   **Wt:** 187   **Born:** 3/3/67   **Age:** 29

Year	Team	G	GS	Att	Yds	Avg	Lg	TD	Rec	Yds	Avg	Lg	TD	Num	Yds	Avg	TD	Num	Yds	Avg	TD	Fum	TD	Pts
				Rushing					**Receiving**					**Punt Returns**				**Kickoff Returns**				**Totals**		
1990	Philadelphia Eagles	16	14	2	20	10.0	18	0	37	602	16.3	t45	9	2	-1	-0.5	0	0	0	-	0	2	9	54
1991	Philadelphia Eagles	12	11	0	0	-	-	0	33	326	9.9	30	3	0	0	-	0	0	0	-	0	1	3	18
1992	Philadelphia Eagles	16	15	0	0	-	-	0	42	598	14.2	t49	7	0	0	-	0	0	0	-	0	1	7	42
1993	Philadelphia Eagles	16	14	0	0	-	-	0	60	725	12.1	t80	10	0	0	-	0	0	0	-	0	0	10	60
1994	Philadelphia Eagles	16	14	2	11	5.5	6	0	58	813	14.0	53	3	0	0	-	0	0	0	-	0	3	3	18
1995	Philadelphia Eagles	16	15	1	-2	-2.0	-2	0	63	768	12.2	t37	2	0	0	-	0	0	0	-	0	2	2	14
	6 NFL Seasons	92	83	5	29	5.8	18	0	293	3832	13.1	t80	34	2	-1	-0.5	0	0	0	-	0	5	34	206

Other Statistics: 1990–recovered 2 fumbles for 0 yards. 1994–recovered 1 fumble for 0 yards. 1995–scored 1 two-point conversion.

Charlie Williams

Pos: S   **Rnd:** 3   **College:** Bowling Green   **Ht:** 6' 0"   **Wt:** 190   **Born:** 2/2/72   **Age:** 24

Year	Team	G	GS	Tk	Ast	Sack	FF	FR	TD	Blk	Int	Yds	Avg	TD	Sfty	TD	Pts
				Tackles			**Miscellaneous**				**Interceptions**				**Totals**		
1995	Dallas Cowboys	16	0	0	1	0.0	0	0	0	0	0	0	-	0	0	0	0

Dan Williams

Pos: DE **Rnd:** 1 (11) **College:** Toledo **Ht:** 6' 4" **Wt:** 290 **Born:** 12/15/69 **Age:** 26

Year Team	G	GS	Tackles			Miscellaneous				Interceptions				Totals		
			Tk	Ast	Sack	FF	FR	TD	Blk	Int	Yds	Avg	TD	Sfty	TD	Pts
1993 Denver Broncos	13	11	18	19	1.0	0	1	0	0	0	0	-	0	0	0	0
1994 Denver Broncos	13	8	8	3	0.0	0	0	0	0	1	-3	-3.0	0	0	0	0
1995 Denver Broncos	6	6	11	2	2.0	0	0	0	0	0	0	-	0	0	0	0
3 NFL Seasons	32	25	37	24	3.0	0	1	0	0	1	-3	-3.0	0	0	0	0

Darryl Williams

(statistical profile on page 462)

Pos: S **Rnd:** 1 (28) **College:** Miami (FL) **Ht:** 6' 0" **Wt:** 191 **Born:** 1/7/70 **Age:** 26

Year Team	G	GS	Tackles			Miscellaneous				Interceptions				Punt Returns				Kickoff Returns				Totals	
			Tk	Ast	Sack	FF	FR	TD	Blk	Int	Yds	Avg	TD	Num	Yds	Avg	TD	Num	Yds	Avg	TD	TD	Fum
1992 Cincinnati Bengals	16	12	70	8	2.0	0	1	0	0	4	65	16.3	0	0	0	-	0	0	0	-	0	0	0
1993 Cincinnati Bengals	16	16	95	28	2.0	1	2	0	0	2	126	63.0	1	0	0	-	0	0	0	-	0	1	0
1994 Cincinnati Bengals	16	16	87	15	1.0	2	2	0	0	2	45	22.5	0	1	4	4.0	0	0	0	-	0	0	0
1995 Cincinnati Bengals	16	16	78	20	1.0	0	3	0	1	1	1	1.0	0	0	0	-	0	0	0	-	0	0	0
4 NFL Seasons	64	60	330	71	6.0	3	8	0	1	9	237	26.3	1	1	4	4.0	0	0	0	-	0	1	0

David Williams

Pos: T **Rnd:** 1 (23) **College:** Florida **Ht:** 6' 5" **Wt:** 292 **Born:** 6/21/66 **Age:** 30

Year Team	G	GS	Year Team	G	GS	Year Team	G	GS	Year Team	G	GS
1989 Houston Oilers	14	0	1991 Houston Oilers	16	16	1993 Houston Oilers	15	15	1995 Houston Oilers	10	9
1990 Houston Oilers	15	9	1992 Houston Oilers	16	16	1994 Houston Oilers	16	16	7 NFL Seasons	102	81

Other Statistics: 1989–returned 2 kickoffs for 8 yards. 1990–recovered 1 fumble for 0 yards. 1991–recovered 1 fumble for 0 yards. 1992–recovered 1 fumble for 0 yards. 1993–recovered 1 fumble for 7 yards. 1994–recovered 1 fumble for 0 yards.

Erik Williams

Pos: T **Rnd:** 3 **College:** Central State **Ht:** 6' 6" **Wt:** 322 **Born:** 9/7/68 **Age:** 28

Year Team	G	GS	Year Team	G	GS	Year Team	G	GS		G	GS
1991 Dallas Cowboys	11	3	1993 Dallas Cowboys	16	16	1995 Dallas Cowboys	15	15			
1992 Dallas Cowboys	16	16	1994 Dallas Cowboys	7	7				5 NFL Seasons	65	57

Other Statistics: 1991–recovered 1 fumble for 0 yards.

Gene Williams

Pos: G **Rnd:** 5 **College:** Iowa State **Ht:** 6' 2" **Wt:** 305 **Born:** 10/14/68 **Age:** 28

Year Team	G	GS	Year Team	G	GS	Year Team	G	GS		G	GS
1991 Miami Dolphins	10	0	1993 Cleveland Browns	16	14	1995 Atlanta Falcons	12	3			
1992 Miami Dolphins	5	0	1994 Cleveland Browns	16	9				5 NFL Seasons	59	26

Gerald Williams

Pos: DE **Rnd:** 2 **College:** Auburn **Ht:** 6' 3" **Wt:** 288 **Born:** 9/8/63 **Age:** 33

Year Team	G	GS	Tackles			Miscellaneous				Interceptions				Totals		
			Tk	Ast	Sack	FF	FR	TD	Blk	Int	Yds	Avg	TD	Sfty	TD	Pts
1986 Pittsburgh Steelers	16	0	10	4	3.5	0	0	0	0	0	0	-	0	0	0	0
1987 Pittsburgh Steelers	9	1	15	2	1.0	0	1	0	0	0	0	-	0	0	0	0
1988 Pittsburgh Steelers	16	16	31	10	3.5	0	0	0	0	0	0	-	0	0	0	0
1989 Pittsburgh Steelers	16	16	46	8	3.0	1	1	0	0	0	0	-	0	0	0	0
1990 Pittsburgh Steelers	16	15	45	4	6.0	1	0	0	0	0	0	-	0	0	0	0
1991 Pittsburgh Steelers	16	15	40	10	2.0	0	0	0	0	0	0	-	0	0	0	0
1992 Pittsburgh Steelers	10	10	26	17	3.0	1	0	0	0	0	0	-	0	0	0	0
1993 Pittsburgh Steelers	10	8	19	8	1.0	0	0	0	0	0	0	-	0	0	0	0
1994 Pittsburgh Steelers	11	11	26	13	1.5	0	1	1	0	0	0	-	0	0	1	6
1995 Carolina Panthers	16	16	20	5	0.0	0	0	0	0	0	0	-	0	0	0	0
10 NFL Seasons	136	108	278	81	24.5	3	4	1	0	0	0	-	0	0	1	6

Harvey Williams

(statistical profile on page 388)

Pos: RB **Rnd:** 1 (21) **College:** Louisiana State **Ht:** 6' 2" **Wt:** 215 **Born:** 4/22/67 **Age:** 29

Year Team	G	GS	Rushing					Receiving					Kickoff Returns				Passing				Totals		
			Att	Yds	Avg	Lg	TD	Rec	Yds	Avg	Lg	TD	Num	Yds	Avg	TD	Att	Com	Yds	Int	Fum	TD	Pts
1991 Kansas City Chiefs	14	1	97	447	4.6	21	1	16	147	9.2	17	2	24	524	21.8	0	1	0	0	0	1	3	18
1992 Kansas City Chiefs	14	0	78	262	3.4	11	1	5	24	4.8	12	0	21	405	19.3	0	0	0	0	0	1	1	6
1993 Kansas City Chiefs	7	6	42	149	3.5	19	0	7	42	6.0	14	0	3	53	17.7	0	0	0	0	0	3	0	0
1994 Los Angeles Raiders	16	10	282	983	3.5	28	4	47	391	8.3	t27	3	8	153	19.1	0	0	0	0	0	4	7	44
1995 Oakland Raiders	16	16	255	1114	4.4	60	9	54	375	6.9	28	0	0	0	-	0	1	1	13	0	5	9	54
5 NFL Seasons	67	33	754	2955	3.9	60	15	129	979	7.6	28	5	56	1135	20.3	0	2	1	13	0	14	20	122

Other Statistics: 1994–recovered 2 fumbles for 0 yards; scored 1 two-point conversion. 1995–recovered 1 fumble for 0 yards; passed for 1 touchdown.

James Williams

Pos: LB **Rnd:** 6 **College:** Mississippi State **Ht:** 6' 0" **Wt:** 243 **Born:** 10/10/68 **Age:** 28

			Tackles			Miscellaneous				Interceptions				Totals		
Year Team	G	GS	Tk	Ast	Sack	FF	FR	TD	Blk	Int	Yds	Avg	TD	Sfty	TD	Pts
1990 New Orleans Saints	14	0	1	0	0.0	0	0	0	0	0	0	-	0	0	0	0
1991 New Orleans Saints	16	4	23	6	1.0	0	1	0	0	0	0	-	0	0	0	0
1992 New Orleans Saints	16	0	14	2	0.0	0	0	0	0	0	0	-	0	0	0	0
1993 New Orleans Saints	16	9	65	24	2.0	1	0	0	0	0	0	-	0	0	0	0
1994 New Orleans Saints	16	7	59	12	0.0	1	0	0	0	2	42	21.0	1	0	1	6
1995 Jacksonville Jaguars	12	6	47	15	0.0	2	0	0	0	2	19	9.5	0	0	0	0
6 NFL Seasons	90	26	209	59	3.0	4	1	0	0	4	61	15.3	1	0	1	6

James Williams

Pos: T **Rnd:** FA **College:** Cheyney **Ht:** 6' 7" **Wt:** 335 **Born:** 3/29/68 **Age:** 28

Year	Team	G	GS	Year	Team	G	GS	Year	Team	G	GS		G	GS
1991	Chicago Bears	14	0	1993	Chicago Bears	3	0	1995	Chicago Bears	16	16			
1992	Chicago Bears	5	0	1994	Chicago Bears	16	15					5 NFL Seasons	54	31

Jay Williams

Pos: DE/DT **Rnd:** FA **College:** Wake Forest **Ht:** 6' 3" **Wt:** 266 **Born:** 10/13/71 **Age:** 25

			Tackles			Miscellaneous				Interceptions				Totals		
Year Team	G	GS	Tk	Ast	Sack	FF	FR	TD	Blk	Int	Yds	Avg	TD	Sfty	TD	Pts
1995 St. Louis Rams	6	0	0	0	0.0	0	0	0	0	0	0	-	0	0	0	0

John L. Williams

Pos: RB **Rnd:** 1 (15) **College:** Florida **Ht:** 5' 11" **Wt:** 231 **Born:** 11/23/64 **Age:** 31

			Rushing					Receiving					Kickoff Returns				Passing					Totals		
Year Team	G	GS	Att	Yds	Avg	Lg	TD	Rec	Yds	Avg	Lg	TD	Num	Yds	Avg	TD	Att	Com	Yds	Int	Fum	TD	Pts
1986 Seattle Seahawks	16	16	129	538	4.2	36	0	33	219	6.6	23	0	0	0	-	0	0	0	0	0	1	0	0
1987 Seattle Seahawks	12	10	113	500	4.4	48	1	38	420	11.1	t75	3	0	0	-	0	0	0	0	0	2	4	24
1988 Seattle Seahawks	16	16	189	877	4.6	t44	4	58	651	11.2	t75	3	0	0	-	0	0	0	0	0	0	7	42
1989 Seattle Seahawks	15	15	146	499	3.4	21	1	76	657	8.6	t51	6	0	0	-	0	0	0	0	0	2	7	42
1990 Seattle Seahawks	16	16	187	714	3.8	25	3	73	699	9.6	60	0	0	0	-	0	0	0	0	0	5	3	18
1991 Seattle Seahawks	16	16	188	741	3.9	42	4	61	499	8.2	35	1	0	0	-	0	0	0	0	0	2	5	30
1992 Seattle Seahawks	16	16	114	339	3.0	14	1	74	556	7.5	27	2	0	0	-	0	0	0	0	0	4	3	18
1993 Seattle Seahawks	16	9	82	371	4.5	38	3	58	450	7.8	25	1	0	0	-	0	1	0	0	0	2	4	24
1994 Pittsburgh Steelers	15	12	68	317	4.7	23	1	51	378	7.4	23	2	0	0	-	0	0	0	0	0	0	3	18
1995 Pittsburgh Steelers	12	9	29	110	3.8	31	0	24	127	5.3	20	1	0	0	-	0	0	0	0	0	2	1	6
10 NFL Seasons	150	135	1245	5006	4.0	48	18	546	4656	8.5	t75	19	0	0	-	0	1	0	0	0	20	37	222

Other Statistics: 1987–recovered 1 fumble for 0 yards. 1988–recovered 2 fumbles for -2 yards. 1989–recovered 1 fumble for 0 yards. 1990–recovered 2 fumbles for 0 yards. 1991–recovered 1 fumble for 0 yards. 1992–recovered 1 fumble for 0 yards. 1993–recovered 1 fumble for 0 yards. 1995–recovered 1 fumble for 0 yards.

Kevin Williams

(statistical profile on page 388)

Pos: KR/WR **Rnd:** 2 **College:** Miami (FL) **Ht:** 5' 9" **Wt:** 195 **Born:** 1/25/71 **Age:** 25

			Rushing					Receiving					Punt Returns				Kickoff Returns				Totals		
Year Team	G	GS	Att	Yds	Avg	Lg	TD	Rec	Yds	Avg	Lg	TD	Num	Yds	Avg	TD	Num	Yds	Avg	TD	Fum	TD	Pts
1993 Dallas Cowboys	16	1	7	26	3.7	12	2	20	151	7.6	33	2	36	381	10.6	2	31	689	22.2	0	8	6	36
1994 Dallas Cowboys	15	2	6	20	3.3	8	0	13	181	13.9	29	0	39	349	8.9	1	43	1148	26.7	1	4	2	12
1995 Dallas Cowboys	16	16	10	53	5.3	14	0	38	613	16.1	t48	2	18	166	9.2	0	49	1108	22.6	0	3	2	12
3 NFL Seasons	47	19	23	99	4.3	14	2	71	945	13.3	t48	4	93	896	9.6	3	123	2945	23.9	1	15	10	60

Other Statistics: 1993–recovered 4 fumbles for 0 yards. 1994–recovered 3 fumbles for 0 yards.

Mark Williams

Pos: LB **Rnd:** FA **College:** Ohio State **Ht:** 6' 3" **Wt:** 243 **Born:** 5/17/71 **Age:** 25

			Tackles			Miscellaneous				Interceptions				Totals		
Year Team	G	GS	Tk	Ast	Sack	FF	FR	TD	Blk	Int	Yds	Avg	TD	Sfty	TD	Pts
1994 Green Bay Packers	16	0	1	1	0.0	0	1	0	0	0	0	-	0	0	0	0
1995 Jacksonville Jaguars	11	10	25	8	0.0	0	0	0	0	0	0	-	0	0	0	0
2 NFL Seasons	27	10	26	9	0.0	0	1	0	0	0	0	-	0	0	0	0

Michael Williams

Pos: CB **Rnd:** FA **College:** UCLA **Ht:** 5' 10" **Wt:** 185 **Born:** 5/28/70 **Age:** 26

			Tackles			Miscellaneous				Interceptions				Totals		
Year Team	G	GS	Tk	Ast	Sack	FF	FR	TD	Blk	Int	Yds	Avg	TD	Sfty	TD	Pts
1995 San Francisco 49ers	3	0	0	0	0.0	0	0	0	0	0	0	-	0	0	0	0

263

Mike Williams

Pos: WR **Rnd:** 10 **College:** Northeastern **Ht:** 6' 0" **Wt:** 183 **Born:** 10/9/66 **Age:** 30

Year Team	G	GS	Rushing					Receiving					Punt Returns				Kickoff Returns				Totals		
			Att	Yds	Avg	Lg	TD	Rec	Yds	Avg	Lg	TD	Num	Yds	Avg	TD	Num	Yds	Avg	TD	Fum	TD	Pts
1989 Detroit Lions	1	0	0	0	-	-	0	0	0	-	-	0	0	0	-	0	0	0	-	0	0	0	0
1991 Miami Dolphins	3	0	0	0	-	-	0	0	0	-	-	0	0	0	-	0	0	0	-	0	0	0	0
1992 Miami Dolphins	15	0	0	0	-	-	0	3	43	14.3	18	0	0	0	-	0	19	328	17.3	0	1	0	0
1993 Miami Dolphins	13	0	0	0	-	-	0	1	11	11.0	11	0	0	0	-	0	8	180	22.5	0	1	0	0
1994 Miami Dolphins	15	0	0	0	-	-	0	15	221	14.7	29	0	0	0	-	0	2	9	4.5	0	0	0	0
1995 Miami Dolphins	12	0	0	0	-	-	0	2	17	8.5	15	0	0	0	-	0	0	0	-	0	0	0	0
6 NFL Seasons	59	0	0	0	-	-	0	21	292	13.9	29	0	0	0	-	0	29	517	17.8	0	2	0	0

Other Statistics: 1992–recovered 1 fumble for 0 yards.

Ronnie Williams

Pos: TE/WR **Rnd:** FA **College:** Oklahoma State **Ht:** 6' 3" **Wt:** 258 **Born:** 1/19/66 **Age:** 30

Year Team	G	GS	Rushing					Receiving					Punt Returns				Kickoff Returns				Totals		
			Att	Yds	Avg	Lg	TD	Rec	Yds	Avg	Lg	TD	Num	Yds	Avg	TD	Num	Yds	Avg	TD	Fum	TD	Pts
1993 Miami Dolphins	11	0	0	0	-	-	0	0	0	-	-	0	0	0	-	0	0	0	-	0	0	0	0
1994 Miami Dolphins	14	0	0	0	-	-	0	2	26	13.0	17	0	0	0	-	0	2	25	12.5	0	0	0	0
1995 Miami Dolphins	16	2	0	0	-	-	0	3	28	9.3	13	0	0	0	-	0	2	20	10.0	0	0	0	0
3 NFL Seasons	41	2	0	0	-	-	0	5	54	10.8	17	0	0	0	-	0	4	45	11.3	0	0	0	0

Other Statistics: 1993–recovered 1 fumble for 0 yards.

Sherman Williams

Pos: RB **Rnd:** 2 **College:** Alabama **Ht:** 5' 8" **Wt:** 190 **Born:** 8/13/73 **Age:** 23

Year Team	G	GS	Rushing					Receiving					Punt Returns				Kickoff Returns				Totals		
			Att	Yds	Avg	Lg	TD	Rec	Yds	Avg	Lg	TD	Num	Yds	Avg	TD	Num	Yds	Avg	TD	Fum	TD	Pts
1995 Dallas Cowboys	12	0	48	205	4.3	t44	1	3	28	9.3	24	0	0	0	-	0	0	0	-	0	2	1	6

Wally Williams

Pos: G/C **Rnd:** FA **College:** Florida A&M **Ht:** 6' 2" **Wt:** 300 **Born:** 2/20/71 **Age:** 25

Year Team	G	GS	Year Team	G	GS	Year Team	G	GS		G	GS
1993 Cleveland Browns	2	0	1994 Cleveland Browns	12	7	1995 Cleveland Browns	16	16	3 NFL Seasons	30	23

Other Statistics: 1994–recovered 1 fumble for 0 yards.

Willie Williams

Pos: CB **Rnd:** 6 **College:** Western Carolina **Ht:** 5' 9" **Wt:** 188 **Born:** 12/26/70 **Age:** 25

(statistical profile on page 462)

Year Team	G	GS	Tackles			Miscellaneous				Interceptions				Punt Returns				Kickoff Returns				Totals	
			Tk	Ast	Sack	FF	FR	TD	Blk	Int	Yds	Avg	TD	Num	Yds	Avg	TD	Num	Yds	Avg	TD	TD	Fum
1993 Pittsburgh Steelers	16	0	7	2	0.0	1	0	0	0	0	0	-	0	0	0	-	0	1	19	19.0	0	0	0
1994 Pittsburgh Steelers	16	1	3	0	0.0	0	0	0	0	0	0	-	0	0	0	-	0	0	0	-	0	0	0
1995 Pittsburgh Steelers	16	15	69	8	0.0	1	1	0	0	7	122	17.4	1	0	0	-	0	0	0	-	0	1	0
3 NFL Seasons	48	16	79	10	0.0	2	1	0	0	7	122	17.4	1	0	0	-	0	1	19	19.0	0	1	0

Matt Willig

Pos: T **Rnd:** FA **College:** Southern California **Ht:** 6' 8" **Wt:** 317 **Born:** 1/21/69 **Age:** 27

Year Team	G	GS	Year Team	G	GS	Year Team	G	GS		G	GS
1993 New York Jets	3	0	1994 New York Jets	16	3	1995 New York Jets	15	12	3 NFL Seasons	34	15

Jamal Willis

Pos: KR/RB **Rnd:** FA **College:** Brigham Young **Ht:** 6' 2" **Wt:** 218 **Born:** 12/12/72 **Age:** 23

Year Team	G	GS	Rushing					Receiving					Punt Returns				Kickoff Returns				Totals		
			Att	Yds	Avg	Lg	TD	Rec	Yds	Avg	Lg	TD	Num	Yds	Avg	TD	Num	Yds	Avg	TD	Fum	TD	Pts
1995 San Francisco 49ers	12	1	12	35	2.9	15	0	3	8	2.7	5	0	0	0	-	0	17	427	25.1	0	0	0	0

James Willis

Pos: LB **Rnd:** 5 **College:** Auburn **Ht:** 6' 1" **Wt:** 235 **Born:** 9/2/72 **Age:** 24

Year Team	G	GS	Tackles			Miscellaneous				Interceptions				Totals		
			Tk	Ast	Sack	FF	FR	TD	Blk	Int	Yds	Avg	TD	Sfty	TD	Pts
1993 Green Bay Packers	13	0	7	6	0.0	0	1	0	0	0	0	-	0	0	0	0
1994 Green Bay Packers	12	0	23	8	0.0	0	1	0	0	2	20	10.0	0	0	0	0
1995 Philadelphia Eagles	5	0	0	0	0.0	0	0	0	0	0	0	-	0	0	0	0
3 NFL Seasons	30	0	30	14	0.0	0	2	0	0	2	20	10.0	0	0	0	0

Other Statistics: 1994–fumbled 1 time.

Trevor Wilmot

Pos: LB   **Rnd:** FA   **College:** Indiana   **Ht:** 6' 2"   **Wt:** 220   **Born:** 10/30/72   **Age:** 24

			Tackles			Miscellaneous				Interceptions				Totals		
Year Team	G	GS	Tk	Ast	Sack	FF	FR	TD	Blk	Int	Yds	Avg	TD	Sfty	TD	Pts
1995 Indianapolis Colts	7	0	0	0	0.0	0	0	0	0	0	0	-	0	0	0	0

Klaus Wilmsmeyer

(statistical profile on page 487)

Pos: P   **Rnd:** 12   **College:** Louisville   **Ht:** 6' 1"   **Wt:** 210   **Born:** 12/4/67   **Age:** 28

		Punting												Rushing		Passing			
Year Team	G	NetPunts	Yards	Avg	Long	In20	In20%	TotPunts	TB	Blocks	OppRet	RetYds	NetAvg	Att	Yards	Att	Com	Yards	Int
1992 San Francisco 49ers	15	49	1918	39.1	58	19	38.8	49	2	0	23	177	34.7	2	0	0	0	0	0
1993 San Francisco 49ers	15	42	1718	40.9	61	11	26.2	42	5	0	15	171	34.5	2	0	0	0	0	0
1994 San Francisco 49ers	16	54	2235	41.4	60	18	33.3	54	3	0	28	242	35.8	0	0	0	0	0	0
1995 New Orleans Saints	16	73	2965	40.6	53	21	28.8	74	5	1	36	233	35.6	0	0	1	1	18	0
4 NFL Seasons	62	218	8836	40.5	61	69	31.7	219	15	1	102	823	35.2	4	0	1	1	18	0

Other Statistics: 1992–recovered 1 fumble for 0 yards; fumbled 1 time. 1993–recovered 1 fumble for -10 yards; fumbled 2 times.

Jeff Wilner

Pos: TE   **Rnd:** FA   **College:** Wesleyan   **Ht:** 6' 4"   **Wt:** 245   **Born:** 12/31/71   **Age:** 24

			Rushing					Receiving					Punt Returns				Kickoff Returns				Totals		
Year Team	G	GS	Att	Yds	Avg	Lg	TD	Rec	Yds	Avg	Lg	TD	Num	Yds	Avg	TD	Num	Yds	Avg	TD	Fum	TD	Pts
1994 Green Bay Packers	11	1	0	0	-	-	0	5	31	6.2	9	0	0	0	-	0	0	0	-	0	0	0	0
1995 Green Bay Packers	2	0	0	0	-	-	0	0	0	-	-	0	0	0	-	0	0	0	-	0	0	0	0
2 NFL Seasons	13	1	0	0	-	-	0	5	31	6.2	9	0	0	0	-	0	0	0	-	0	0	0	0

Bernard Wilson

Pos: DT   **Rnd:** FA   **College:** Tennessee State   **Ht:** 6' 2"   **Wt:** 295   **Born:** 8/17/70   **Age:** 26

			Tackles			Miscellaneous				Interceptions				Totals		
Year Team	G	GS	Tk	Ast	Sack	FF	FR	TD	Blk	Int	Yds	Avg	TD	Sfty	TD	Pts
1993 Tampa Bay Buccaneers	13	2	12	10	0.0	0	0	0	0	0	0	-	0	0	0	0
1994 TB - Ari	14	12	21	12	1.0	0	0	0	0	0	0	-	0	0	0	0
1995 Arizona Cardinals	16	14	27	12	1.0	0	0	0	0	0	0	-	0	0	0	0
1994 Tampa Bay Buccaneers	1	0	0	0	0.0	0	0	0	0	0	0	-	0	0	0	0
Arizona Cardinals	13	12	21	12	1.0	0	0	0	0	0	0	-	0	0	0	0
3 NFL Seasons	43	28	60	34	2.0	0	0	0	0	0	0	-	0	0	0	0

Charles Wilson

(statistical profile on page 389)

Pos: WR   **Rnd:** 5   **College:** Memphis   **Ht:** 5' 10"   **Wt:** 185   **Born:** 7/1/68   **Age:** 28

			Rushing					Receiving					Punt Returns				Kickoff Returns				Totals		
Year Team	G	GS	Att	Yds	Avg	Lg	TD	Rec	Yds	Avg	Lg	TD	Num	Yds	Avg	TD	Num	Yds	Avg	TD	Fum	TD	Pts
1990 Green Bay Packers	15	0	0	0	-	-	0	7	84	12.0	18	0	0	0	-	0	35	798	22.8	0	0	0	0
1991 Green Bay Packers	15	2	3	3	1.0	5	0	19	305	16.1	t55	1	0	0	-	0	23	522	22.7	1	4	2	12
1992 Tampa Bay Buccaneers	2	0	0	0	-	-	0	0	0	-	-	0	0	0	-	0	1	23	23.0	0	0	0	0
1993 Tampa Bay Buccaneers	15	1	2	7	3.5	4	0	15	225	15.0	24	0	0	0	-	0	23	454	19.7	0	1	0	0
1994 Tampa Bay Buccaneers	14	8	2	15	7.5	11	0	31	652	21.0	t71	6	0	0	-	0	10	251	25.1	0	6	6	36
1995 New York Jets	15	11	0	0	-	-	0	41	484	11.8	24	4	0	0	-	0	0	0	-	0	1	4	24
6 NFL Seasons	76	22	7	25	3.6	11	0	113	1750	15.5	t75	11	0	0	-	0	92	2048	22.3	1	6	12	72

Other Statistics: 1991–recovered 1 fumble for 0 yards. 1993–recovered 2 fumbles for 0 yards.

Karl Wilson

Pos: DE   **Rnd:** 3   **College:** Louisiana State   **Ht:** 6' 5"   **Wt:** 277   **Born:** 9/10/64   **Age:** 32

			Tackles			Miscellaneous				Interceptions				Totals		
Year Team	G	GS	Tk	Ast	Sack	FF	FR	TD	Blk	Int	Yds	Avg	TD	Sfty	TD	Pts
1987 San Diego Chargers	7	0	6	2	1.0	0	0	0	0	0	0	-	0	0	0	0
1988 San Diego Chargers	13	2	11	6	0.5	0	0	0	0	0	0	-	0	0	0	0
1989 Phoenix Cardinals	16	6	26	1	1.0	0	0	0	0	0	0	-	0	1	0	2
1990 Miami Dolphins	10	2	10	0	4.0	0	0	0	0	0	0	-	0	0	0	0
1991 Los Angeles Rams	13	10	20	5	2.0	0	1	0	0	0	0	-	0	0	0	0
1992 New York Jets	2	0	3	0	0.0	0	0	0	0	0	0	-	0	0	0	0
1993 NYJ - Mia - SF	12	0	11	1	3.0	0	1	0	0	0	0	-	0	0	0	0
1994 Tampa Bay Buccaneers	14	2	11	5	2.5	0	1	0	0	0	0	-	0	0	0	0
1995 Buffalo Bills	9	1	6	3	1.0	0	0	0	0	0	0	-	0	0	0	0
1993 New York Jets	5	0	1	1	0.0	0	0	0	0	0	0	-	0	0	0	0
Miami Dolphins	2	0	0	0	0.0	0	0	0	0	0	0	-	0	0	0	0
San Francisco 49ers	5	0	10	-	3.0	0	1	0	0	0	0	-	0	0	0	0
9 NFL Seasons	102	23	112	31	15.0	0	2	0	0	0	0	-	0	1	0	2

Marcus Wilson

Pos: RB **Rnd:** 6 **College:** Virginia **Ht:** 6' 1" **Wt:** 215 **Born:** 4/16/68 **Age:** 28

				Rushing				Receiving				Punt Returns				Kickoff Returns				Totals		
Year	Team	G	GS	Att	Yds	Avg	Lg	TD	Rec	Yds	Avg	Lg	TD	Num	Yds	Avg	TD	Num	Yds	Avg	TD	Fum	TD	Pts
1991	Los Angeles Raiders	1	0	6	21	3.5	8	0	0	0	-	-	0	0	0	-	0	0	0	-	0	0	0	0
1992	Green Bay Packers	6	0	0	0	-	-	0	0	0	-	-	0	0	0	-	0	0	0	-	0	0	0	0
1993	Green Bay Packers	16	0	6	3	0.5	5	0	2	18	9.0	11	0	0	0	-	0	9	197	21.9	0	1	0	0
1994	Green Bay Packers	12	0	0	0	-	-	0	0	0	-	-	0	0	0	-	0	2	14	7.0	0	1	0	0
1995	Green Bay Packers	14	0	0	0	-	-	0	0	0	-	-	0	0	0	-	0	0	0	-	0	0	0	0
	5 NFL Seasons	49	0	12	24	2.0	8	0	2	18	9.0	11	0	0	0	-	0	11	211	19.2	0	2	0	0

Other Statistics: 1993–recovered 1 fumble for 0 yards.

Robert Wilson

Pos: RB **Rnd:** 3 **College:** Texas A&M **Ht:** 6' 0" **Wt:** 255 **Born:** 1/13/69 **Age:** 27

				Rushing				Receiving				Punt Returns				Kickoff Returns				Totals		
Year	Team	G	GS	Att	Yds	Avg	Lg	TD	Rec	Yds	Avg	Lg	TD	Num	Yds	Avg	TD	Num	Yds	Avg	TD	Fum	TD	Pts
1991	Tampa Bay Buccaneers	16	15	42	179	4.3	20	0	20	121	6.1	15	2	0	0	-	0	2	19	9.5	0	3	2	12
1994	Dal - Mia	4	0	1	-1	-1.0	-1	0	0	0	-	-	0	0	0	-	0	0	0	-	0	0	0	0
1995	Miami Dolphins	16	0	1	5	5.0	5	0	1	3	3.0	3	0	0	0	-	0	0	0	-	0	0	0	0
1994	Dallas Cowboys	2	0	1	-1	-1.0	-1	0	0	0	-	-	0	0	0	-	0	0	0	-	0	0	0	0
	Miami Dolphins	2	0	0	0	-	-	0	0	0	-	-	0	0	0	-	0	0	0	-	0	0	0	0
	3 NFL Seasons	36	15	44	183	4.2	20	0	21	124	5.9	15	2	0	0	-	0	2	19	9.5	0	3	2	12

Other Statistics: 1991–recovered 1 fumble for 0 yards. 1995–recovered 1 fumble for 0 yards.

Troy Wilson

Pos: DE **Rnd:** 7 **College:** Pittsburg State **Ht:** 6' 4" **Wt:** 250 **Born:** 11/22/70 **Age:** 25

				Tackles			Miscellaneous				Interceptions				Totals		
Year	Team	G	GS	Tk	Ast	Sack	FF	FR	TD	Blk	Int	Yds	Avg	TD	Sfty	TD	Pts
1993	San Francisco 49ers	10	0	13	2	5.5	0	0	0	0	0	0	-	0	0	0	0
1994	San Francisco 49ers	11	0	4	1	2.0	0	0	0	0	0	0	-	0	0	0	0
1995	Denver Broncos	3	0	0	1	0.5	0	0	0	0	0	0	-	0	0	0	0
	3 NFL Seasons	24	0	17	4	8.0	0	0	0	0	0	0	-	0	0	0	0

Wade Wilson

(statistical profile on page 389)

Pos: QB **Rnd:** 8 **College:** East Texas State **Ht:** 6' 3" **Wt:** 206 **Born:** 2/1/59 **Age:** 37

				Passing									Rushing				Miscellaneous			
Year	Team	G	GS	Att	Com	Pct	Yards	Yds/Att	Lg	TD	Int	Int%	Rating	Att	Yds	Avg	Lg	TD	Sckd	Yds	Fum	Rec	Yds	Pts
1981	Minnesota Vikings	3	0	13	6	46.2	48	3.69	22	0	2	15.4	16.3	0	0	-	-	0	2	19	2	1	0	0
1983	Minnesota Vikings	1	1	28	16	57.1	124	4.43	36	1	2	7.1	50.3	3	-3	-1.0	2	0	3	22	1	0	0	0
1984	Minnesota Vikings	8	5	195	102	52.3	1019	5.23	38	5	11	5.6	52.5	9	30	3.3	12	0	20	159	2	0	0	0
1985	Minnesota Vikings	4	1	60	33	55.0	404	6.73	t42	3	3	5.0	71.8	0	0	-	-	0	4	28	0	0	0	0
1986	Minnesota Vikings	9	3	143	80	55.9	1165	8.15	39	7	5	3.5	84.4	13	9	0.7	13	1	13	94	3	1	-2	6
1987	Minnesota Vikings	12	7	264	140	53.0	2106	7.98	t73	14	13	4.9	76.7	41	263	6.4	38	5	26	194	3	0	-3	30
1988	Minnesota Vikings	14	10	332	204	61.4	2746	8.27	t68	15	9	2.7	91.5	36	136	3.8	15	2	33	227	4	2	-9	12
1989	Minnesota Vikings	14	12	362	194	53.6	2543	7.02	50	9	12	3.3	70.5	32	132	4.1	23	1	27	194	5	2	-7	6
1990	Minnesota Vikings	6	4	146	82	56.2	1155	7.91	t75	9	8	5.5	79.6	12	79	6.6	24	0	15	90	3	1	-2	0
1991	Minnesota Vikings	5	5	122	72	59.0	825	6.76	146	3	10	8.2	53.5	13	33	2.5	15	0	8	42	3	1	-3	0
1992	Atlanta Falcons	9	3	163	111	68.1	1366	8.38	t60	13	4	2.5	110.1	15	62	4.1	12	0	8	58	0	0	0	0
1993	New Orleans Saints	14	14	388	221	57.0	2457	6.33	t42	12	15	3.9	70.1	31	230	7.4	44	0	37	225	9	4	-3	0
1994	New Orleans Saints	4	0	28	20	71.4	172	6.14	16	0	0	0.0	87.2	7	15	2.1	9	0	3	17	1	0	0	0
1995	Dallas Cowboys	7	0	57	38	66.7	391	6.86	38	1	3	5.3	70.1	10	12	1.2	11	0	4	29	1	1	0	0
	14 NFL Seasons	110	65	2301	1319	57.3	16521	7.18	t75	92	97	4.2	75.5	222	998	4.5	44	9	203	1398	37	15	-29	54

Other Statistics: 1986–punted 2 times for 76 yards.

Tydus Winans

Pos: WR **Rnd:** 3 **College:** Fresno State **Ht:** 5' 11" **Wt:** 180 **Born:** 7/26/72 **Age:** 24

				Rushing				Receiving				Punt Returns				Kickoff Returns				Totals		
Year	Team	G	GS	Att	Yds	Avg	Lg	TD	Rec	Yds	Avg	Lg	TD	Num	Yds	Avg	TD	Num	Yds	Avg	TD	Fum	TD	Pts
1994	Washington Redskins	15	0	1	5	5.0	5	0	19	344	18.1	51	2	0	0	-	0	0	0	-	0	0	2	14
1995	Washington Redskins	8	1	0	0	-	-	0	4	77	19.3	32	0	0	0	-	0	0	0	-	0	1	0	0
	2 NFL Seasons	23	1	1	5	5.0	5	0	23	421	18.3	51	2	0	0	-	0	0	0	-	0	1	2	14

Other Statistics: 1994–scored 1 two-point conversion.

Frank Winters

Pos: C/LS **Rnd:** 10 **College:** Western Illinois **Ht:** 6' 3" **Wt:** 295 **Born:** 1/23/64 **Age:** 32

Year	Team	G	GS	Year	Team	G	GS	Year	Team	G	GS		G	GS
1987	Cleveland Browns	12	0	1990	Kansas City Chiefs	16	6	1993	Green Bay Packers	16	16			
1988	Cleveland Browns	16	0	1991	Kansas City Chiefs	16	0	1994	Green Bay Packers	16	16			

Year	Team	G	GS	Year	Team	G	GS	Year	Team	G	GS			G	GS
1989	New York Giants	15	0	1992	Green Bay Packers	16	11	1995	Green Bay Packers	16	16	9 NFL Seasons		139	65

Other Statistics: 1987–fumbled 1 time for 0 yards. 1990–recovered 2 fumbles for 0 yards. 1992–fumbled 1 time for 0 yards. 1994–recovered 2 fumbles for -2 yards; fumbled 1 time.

Terrence Wisdom

Pos: G **Rnd:** FA **College:** Syracuse **Ht:** 6' 4" **Wt:** 300 **Born:** 12/4/71 **Age:** 24

Year	Team	G	GS							G	GS
1995	New York Jets	5	0					1 NFL Season		5	0

Steve Wisniewski

Pos: G **Rnd:** 2 **College:** Penn State **Ht:** 6' 4" **Wt:** 285 **Born:** 4/7/67 **Age:** 29

Year	Team	G	GS	Year	Team	G	GS	Year	Team	G	GS	Year	Team	G	GS
1989	Los Angeles Raiders	15	15	1991	Los Angeles Raiders	15	15	1993	Los Angeles Raiders	16	16	1995	Oakland Raiders	16	16
1990	Los Angeles Raiders	16	16	1992	Los Angeles Raiders	16	16	1994	Los Angeles Raiders	16	16	7 NFL Seasons		110	110

Other Statistics: 1989–recovered 3 fumbles for 0 yards. 1995–recovered 1 fumble for 0 yards.

Derrick Witherspoon

Pos: KR/RB **Rnd:** FA **College:** Clemson **Ht:** 5' 10" **Wt:** 197 **Born:** 2/14/71 **Age:** 25

				Rushing				Receiving				Punt Returns				Kickoff Returns				Totals		
Year	Team	G	GS	Att	Yds	Avg	Lg	TD	Rec	Yds	Avg	Lg	TD	Num	Yds	Avg	TD	Num	Yds	Avg	TD	Fum	TD	Pts
1995	Philadelphia Eagles	15	0	2	7	3.5	5	0	0	0	-	-	0	0	0	-	0	18	459	25.5	1	0	1	6

Dave Wohlabaugh

Pos: C **Rnd:** 4 **College:** Syracuse **Ht:** 6' 3" **Wt:** 304 **Born:** 4/13/72 **Age:** 24

Year	Team	G	GS							G	GS
1995	New England Patriots	11	11					1 NFL Season		11	11

Other Statistics: 1995–recovered 1 fumble for 0 yards.

Joe Wolf

Pos: T/G **Rnd:** 1 (17) **College:** Boston College **Ht:** 6' 6" **Wt:** 296 **Born:** 12/28/66 **Age:** 29

Year	Team	G	GS	Year	Team	G	GS	Year	Team	G	GS	Year	Team	G	GS
1989	Phoenix Cardinals	16	15	1991	Phoenix Cardinals	8	6	1993	Phoenix Cardinals	8	5	1995	Arizona Cardinals	7	1
1990	Phoenix Cardinals	15	0	1992	Phoenix Cardinals	3	2	1994	Arizona Cardinals	8	6	7 NFL Seasons		65	35

Ron Wolfley

Pos: RB **Rnd:** 4 **College:** West Virginia **Ht:** 6' 0" **Wt:** 230 **Born:** 10/14/62 **Age:** 34

				Rushing					Receiving					Punt Returns				Kickoff Returns				Totals		
Year	Team	G	GS	Att	Yds	Avg	Lg	TD	Rec	Yds	Avg	Lg	TD	Num	Yds	Avg	TD	Num	Yds	Avg	TD	Fum	TD	Pts
1985	St. Louis Cardinals	16	1	24	64	2.7	11	0	2	18	9.0	17	0	0	0	-	0	13	234	18.0	0	1	0	0
1986	St. Louis Cardinals	16	1	8	19	2.4	8	0	2	32	16.0	28	0	0	0	-	0	0	-6	-	0	0	0	0
1987	St. Louis Cardinals	12	4	26	87	3.3	8	1	8	68	8.5	16	0	0	0	-	0	0	0	-	0	0	1	6
1988	Phoenix Cardinals	16	0	9	43	4.8	20	0	2	11	5.5	8	0	0	0	-	0	0	0	-	0	0	0	0
1989	Phoenix Cardinals	16	1	13	36	2.8	t5	1	5	38	7.6	22	0	0	0	-	0	0	0	-	0	0	1	6
1990	Phoenix Cardinals	13	2	2	3	1.5	2	0	0	0	-	-	0	0	0	-	0	0	0	-	0	0	0	0
1991	Phoenix Cardinals	16	0	0	0	-	-	0	0	0	-	-	0	0	0	-	0	0	0	-	0	0	0	0
1992	Cleveland Browns	15	0	1	2	2.0	2	0	2	8	4.0	6	1	0	0	-	0	0	0	-	0	0	1	6
1993	Cleveland Browns	16	5	0	0	-	-	0	5	25	5.0	9	1	0	0	-	0	0	0	-	0	0	1	6
1995	St. Louis Rams	9	0	3	9	3.0	4	0	0	0	-	-	0	0	0	-	0	0	0	-	0	0	0	0
	10 NFL Seasons	145	14	86	263	3.1	20	2	26	200	7.7	28	2	0	0	-	0	13	228	17.5	0	1	4	24

Other Statistics: 1988–recovered 1 fumble for 0 yards.

Will Wolford

Pos: T **Rnd:** 1 (20) **College:** Vanderbilt **Ht:** 6' 5" **Wt:** 295 **Born:** 5/18/64 **Age:** 32

Year	Team	G	GS	Year	Team	G	GS	Year	Team	G	GS	Year	Team	G	GS
1986	Buffalo Bills	16	16	1989	Buffalo Bills	16	16	1992	Buffalo Bills	16	16	1995	Indianapolis Colts	16	16
1987	Buffalo Bills	9	9	1990	Buffalo Bills	14	14	1993	Indianapolis Colts	12	12				
1988	Buffalo Bills	16	16	1991	Buffalo Bills	15	15	1994	Indianapolis Colts	16	16	10 NFL Seasons		146	146

Other Statistics: 1988–recovered 1 fumble for 0 yards. 1994–recovered 1 fumble for 0 yards.

Lee Woodall

(statistical profile on page 463)

Pos: LB **Rnd:** 6 **College:** West Chester **Ht:** 6' 0" **Wt:** 220 **Born:** 10/31/69 **Age:** 27

				Tackles			Miscellaneous				Interceptions				Totals		
Year	Team	G	GS	Tk	Ast	Sack	FF	FR	TD	Blk	Int	Yds	Avg	TD	Sfty	TD	Pts
1994	San Francisco 49ers	15	13	45	15	1.0	1	1	0	0	0	0	-	0	0	0	0
1995	San Francisco 49ers	16	16	50	11	3.0	2	2	1	0	2	0	0.0	0	0	1	6
	2 NFL Seasons	31	29	95	26	4.0	3	3	1	0	2	0	0.0	0	0	1	6

Marc Woodard

Pos: LB **Rnd:** FA **College:** Mississippi State **Ht:** 6' 0" **Wt:** 238 **Born:** 2/21/70 **Age:** 26

Year	Team	G	GS	Tackles			Miscellaneous				Interceptions				Totals		
				Tk	Ast	Sack	FF	FR	TD	Blk	Int	Yds	Avg	TD	Sfty	TD	Pts
1994	Philadelphia Eagles	15	0	0	0	0.0	0	0	0	0	0	0	-	0	0	0	0
1995	Philadelphia Eagles	16	0	12	2	1.5	0	0	0	0	0	0	-	0	0	0	0
	2 NFL Seasons	31	0	12	2	1.5	0	0	0	0	0	0	-	0	0	0	0

Terry Wooden

(statistical profile on page 463)

Pos: LB **Rnd:** 2 **College:** Syracuse **Ht:** 6' 3" **Wt:** 239 **Born:** 1/14/67 **Age:** 29

Year	Team	G	GS	Tackles			Miscellaneous				Interceptions				Totals		
				Tk	Ast	Sack	FF	FR	TD	Blk	Int	Yds	Avg	TD	Sfty	TD	Pts
1990	Seattle Seahawks	8	8	26	13	0.0	0	0	0	0	0	0	-	0	0	0	0
1991	Seattle Seahawks	16	15	80	25	2.0	0	4	0	0	0	0	-	0	0	0	0
1992	Seattle Seahawks	8	8	38	18	0.0	0	0	0	0	1	3	3.0	0	0	0	0
1993	Seattle Seahawks	16	16	73	33	2.5	3	1	0	0	0	0	-	0	0	0	0
1994	Seattle Seahawks	16	15	94	33	1.5	1	2	0	0	3	78	26.0	1	0	1	6
1995	Seattle Seahawks	16	16	114	21	0.0	1	1	0	1	1	9	9.0	0	0	0	0
	6 NFL Seasons	80	78	425	143	6.0	5	8	0	1	5	90	18.0	1	0	1	6

Tony Woods

Pos: DE **Rnd:** 1 (18) **College:** Pittsburgh **Ht:** 6' 4" **Wt:** 282 **Born:** 9/11/65 **Age:** 31

Year	Team	G	GS	Tackles			Miscellaneous				Interceptions				Punt Returns				Kickoff Returns				Totals	
				Tk	Ast	Sack	FF	FR	TD	Blk	Int	Yds	Avg	TD	Num	Yds	Avg	TD	Num	Yds	Avg	TD	TD	Fum
1987	Seattle Seahawks	12	7	45	30	0.0	1	1	0	0	0	0	-	0	0	0	-	0	0	0	-	0	0	0
1988	Seattle Seahawks	16	16	82	59	5.0	0	1	0	0	0	0	-	0	0	0	-	0	0	0	-	0	0	0
1989	Seattle Seahawks	16	12	61	46	3.0	0	0	0	0	0	0	-	0	0	0	-	0	1	13	13.0	0	0	1
1990	Seattle Seahawks	16	15	43	42	3.0	0	0	0	0	0	0	-	0	0	0	-	0	0	0	-	0	0	0
1991	Seattle Seahawks	14	14	28	23	2.0	0	4	0	0	0	0	-	0	0	0	-	0	0	0	-	0	0	0
1992	Seattle Seahawks	15	15	47	37	3.0	0	0	0	0	0	0	-	0	0	0	-	0	0	0	-	0	0	0
1993	Los Angeles Rams	14	8	37	8	1.0	0	0	0	0	0	0	-	0	0	0	-	0	0	0	-	0	0	0
1994	Washington Redskins	15	15	46	13	4.5	0	0	0	0	0	0	-	0	0	0	-	0	0	0	-	0	0	0
1995	Washington Redskins	16	16	29	3	2.0	0	2	1	0	0	0	-	0	0	0	-	0	0	0	-	0	1	0
	9 NFL Seasons	134	118	418	261	23.5	1	8	1	0	0	0	-	0	0	0	-	0	1	13	13.0	0	1	1

Darren Woodson

(statistical profile on page 463)

Pos: S **Rnd:** 2 **College:** Arizona State **Ht:** 6' 1" **Wt:** 215 **Born:** 4/25/69 **Age:** 27

Year	Team	G	GS	Tackles			Miscellaneous				Interceptions				Totals		
				Tk	Ast	Sack	FF	FR	TD	Blk	Int	Yds	Avg	TD	Sfty	TD	Pts
1992	Dallas Cowboys	16	2	28	5	1.0	1	0	0	0	0	0	-	0	0	0	0
1993	Dallas Cowboys	16	15	89	66	0.0	1	3	0	0	0	0	-	0	0	0	0
1994	Dallas Cowboys	16	16	58	19	0.0	0	1	0	0	5	140	28.0	1	0	1	6
1995	Dallas Cowboys	16	16	84	11	0.0	1	0	0	0	2	46	23.0	1	0	1	6
	4 NFL Seasons	64	49	259	101	1.0	3	4	0	0	7	186	26.6	2	0	2	12

Rod Woodson

Pos: WR **Rnd:** 1 (10) **College:** Purdue **Ht:** 6' 0" **Wt:** 200 **Born:** 3/10/65 **Age:** 31

Year	Team	G	GS	Rushing					Receiving					Punt Returns				Kickoff Returns				Totals		
				Att	Yds	Avg	Lg	TD	Rec	Yds	Avg	Lg	TD	Num	Yds	Avg	TD	Num	Yds	Avg	TD	Fum	TD	Pts
1987	Pittsburgh Steelers	8	0	0	0	-	-	0	0	0	-	-	0	16	135	8.4	0	13	290	22.3	0	3	1	6
1988	Pittsburgh Steelers	16	16	0	0	-	-	0	0	0	-	-	0	33	281	8.5	0	37	850	23.0	1	3	1	6
1989	Pittsburgh Steelers	15	14	0	0	-	-	0	0	0	-	-	0	29	207	7.1	0	36	982	27.3	0	3	1	6
1990	Pittsburgh Steelers	16	16	0	0	-	-	0	0	0	-	-	0	38	398	10.5	1	35	764	21.8	0	3	1	6
1991	Pittsburgh Steelers	15	15	0	0	-	-	0	0	0	-	-	0	28	320	11.4	0	44	880	20.0	0	3	0	0
1992	Pittsburgh Steelers	16	16	0	0	-	-	0	0	0	-	-	0	32	364	11.4	1	25	469	18.8	0	2	1	6
1993	Pittsburgh Steelers	16	16	1	0	0.0	0	0	0	0	-	-	0	42	338	8.0	0	15	294	19.6	0	2	1	6
1994	Pittsburgh Steelers	15	15	0	0	-	-	0	0	0	-	-	0	39	319	8.2	0	15	365	24.3	0	2	2	12
1995	Pittsburgh Steelers	1	1	0	0	-	-	0	0	0	-	-	0	0	0	-	0	0	0	-	0	0	0	0
	9 NFL Seasons	118	109	1	0	0.0	0	0	0	0	-	-	0	257	2362	9.2	2	220	4894	22.2	2	21	8	48

Other Statistics: 1987–intercepted 1 pass for 45 yards and 1 touchdown; recovered 2 fumbles for 0 yards. 1988–intercepted 4 passes for 98 yards; recovered 3 fumbles for 2 yards. 1989–intercepted 3 passes for 39 yards; recovered 4 fumbles for 1 yard. 1990–intercepted 5 passes for 67 yards; recovered 3 fumbles for 0 yards. 1991–intercepted 3 passes for 72 yards; recovered 3 fumbles for 15 yards. 1992–intercepted 4 passes for 90 yards; recovered 1 fumble for 9 yards. 1993–intercepted 8 passes for 138 yards and 1 touchdown; recovered 1 fumble for 0 yards. 1994–intercepted 4 passes for 109 yards and 2 touchdowns; recovered 1 fumble for 0 yards.

Donnell Woolford

Pos: CB **Rnd:** 1 (11) **College:** Clemson   **Ht:** 5' 9" **Wt:** 188 **Born:** 1/6/66 **Age:** 30

Year Team	G	GS	Tackles Tk	Ast	Sack	Misc FF	FR	TD	Blk	Int Int	Yds	Avg	TD	Punt Returns Num	Yds	Avg	TD	Kickoff Returns Num	Yds	Avg	TD	Totals TD	Fum
1989 Chicago Bears	11	11	36	20	0.0	0	0	0	0	3	0	0.0	0	1	12	12.0	0	0	0	-	0	0	0
1990 Chicago Bears	13	13	38	32	2.0	0	0	0	0	3	18	6.0	0	0	0	-	0	0	0	-	0	0	0
1991 Chicago Bears	15	15	52	25	1.0	1	0	0	0	2	21	10.5	0	0	0	-	0	0	0	-	0	0	0
1992 Chicago Bears	16	16	69	25	0.0	2	1	0	0	7	67	9.6	0	12	127	10.6	0	0	0	-	0	0	2
1993 Chicago Bears	16	16	86	15	0.0	0	0	0	0	2	18	9.0	0	0	0	-	0	0	0	-	0	0	0
1994 Chicago Bears	16	16	52	5	0.0	1	0	0	0	5	30	6.0	0	0	0	-	0	1	28	28.0	0	0	1
1995 Chicago Bears	9	9	29	4	0.0	0	0	0	0	4	21	5.3	0	0	0	-	0	0	0	-	0	0	0
7 NFL Seasons	96	96	362	126	3.0	3	2	0	0	26	175	6.7	0	13	139	10.7	0	1	28	28.0	0	0	3

Tito Wooten

Pos: S/CB **Rnd:** 4(S) **College:** Northeast Louisiana   **Ht:** 6' 0" **Wt:** 188 **Born:** 12/12/71 **Age:** 24

Year Team	G	GS	Tackles Tk	Ast	Sack	Misc FF	FR	TD	Blk	Int Int	Yds	Avg	TD	Totals Sfty	TD	Pts
1994 New York Giants	16	2	16	4	0.0	0	0	0	0	0	0	-	0	0	0	0
1995 New York Giants	16	3	36	12	0.0	0	1	1	0	1	38	38.0	0	0	1	6
2 NFL Seasons	32	5	52	16	0.0	0	1	1	0	1	38	38.0	0	0	1	6

Vince Workman

Pos: RB **Rnd:** 5 **College:** Ohio State   **Ht:** 5' 10" **Wt:** 205 **Born:** 5/9/68 **Age:** 28

Year Team	G	GS	Rushing Att	Yds	Avg	Lg	TD	Receiving Rec	Yds	Avg	Lg	TD	Punt Returns Num	Yds	Avg	TD	Kickoff Returns Num	Yds	Avg	TD	Totals Fum	TD	Pts
1989 Green Bay Packers	15	0	4	8	2.0	3	1	0	0	-	-	0	0	0	-	0	33	547	16.6	0	1	1	6
1990 Green Bay Packers	15	0	8	51	6.4	31	0	4	30	7.5	9	1	0	0	-	0	14	210	15.0	0	0	1	6
1991 Green Bay Packers	16	0	71	237	3.3	t30	7	46	371	8.1	25	4	1	0	0.0	0	8	139	17.4	0	3	11	66
1992 Green Bay Packers	10	10	159	631	4.0	44	2	47	290	6.2	21	0	0	0	-	0	1	17	17.0	0	4	2	12
1993 Tampa Bay Buccaneers	16	11	78	284	3.6	21	2	54	411	7.6	t42	2	0	0	-	0	5	67	13.4	0	2	4	24
1994 Tampa Bay Buccaneers	15	8	79	291	3.7	18	0	11	82	7.5	23	0	0	0	-	0	0	0	-	0	2	0	0
1995 Car - Ind	10	0	44	165	3.8	14	1	13	74	5.7	14	0	0	0	-	0	0	0	-	0	0	1	6
1995 Carolina Panthers	9	0	35	139	4.0	14	1	13	74	5.7	14	0	0	0	-	0	0	0	-	0	0	1	6
Indianapolis Colts	1	0	9	26	2.9	13	0	0	0	-	-	0	0	0	-	0	0	0	-	0	0	0	0
7 NFL Seasons	97	29	443	1667	3.8	44	13	175	1258	7.2	t42	7	1	0	0.0	0	61	980	16.1	0	12	20	120

Other Statistics: 1989–recovered 1 fumble for 0 yards. 1991–recovered 4 fumbles for 9 yards. 1992–recovered 2 fumbles for 0 yards. 1993–recovered 1 fumble for 0 yards. 1994–recovered 1 fumble for 0 yards. 1995–recovered 1 fumble for 0 yards; attempted 1 pass with 0 completions for 0 yards.

Barron Wortham

Pos: LB **Rnd:** 6 **College:** Texas-El Paso   **Ht:** 5' 11" **Wt:** 244 **Born:** 11/1/69 **Age:** 27

Year Team	G	GS	Tackles Tk	Ast	Sack	Misc FF	FR	TD	Blk	Int Int	Yds	Avg	TD	Punt Returns Num	Yds	Avg	TD	Kickoff Returns Num	Yds	Avg	TD	Totals TD	Fum
1994 Houston Oilers	16	1	15	7	0.0	0	1	0	0	0	0	-	0	0	0	-	0	0	0	-	0	0	0
1995 Houston Oilers	16	5	23	15	1.0	1	0	0	0	0	0	-	0	0	0	-	0	1	-3	-3.0	0	0	0
2 NFL Seasons	32	6	38	22	1.0	1	1	0	0	0	0	-	0	0	0	-	0	1	-3	-3.0	0	0	0

Alexander Wright

Pos: WR **Rnd:** 2 **College:** Auburn   **Ht:** 6' 0" **Wt:** 195 **Born:** 7/19/67 **Age:** 29

Year Team	G	GS	Rushing Att	Yds	Avg	Lg	TD	Receiving Rec	Yds	Avg	Lg	TD	Punt Returns Num	Yds	Avg	TD	Kickoff Returns Num	Yds	Avg	TD	Totals Fum	TD	Pts
1990 Dallas Cowboys	15	1	3	26	8.7	14	0	11	104	9.5	20	0	0	0	-	0	12	276	23.0	1	1	1	6
1991 Dallas Cowboys	16	5	2	-1	-0.5	3	0	10	170	17.0	53	0	0	0	-	0	21	514	24.5	1	1	1	6
1992 Dal - LAA	14	1	0	0	-	-	0	12	175	14.6	t41	2	0	0	-	0	26	442	17.0	0	1	2	12
1993 Los Angeles Raiders	15	15	0	0	-	-	0	27	462	17.1	t68	4	0	0	-	0	10	167	16.7	0	0	4	24
1994 Los Angeles Raiders	16	15	0	0	-	-	0	16	294	18.4	t76	2	0	0	-	0	10	282	28.2	0	0	2	12
1995 St. Louis Rams	8	7	1	17	17.0	17	0	23	368	16.0	50	2	0	0	-	0	0	0	-	0	0	2	12
1992 Dallas Cowboys	4	0	0	0	-	-	0	0	0	-	-	0	0	0	-	0	0	117	14.6	0	0	0	0
Los Angeles Raiders	10	1	0	0	-	-	0	12	175	14.6	t41	2	0	0	-	0	18	325	18.1	0	1	2	12
6 NFL Seasons	84	44	6	42	7.0	17	0	99	1573	15.9	t76	10	0	0	-	0	79	1681	21.3	2	2	12	72

Other Statistics: 1990–recovered 1 fumble for 0 yards. 1994–recovered 1 fumble for 0 yards.

Sylvester Wright

Pos: LB **Rnd:** FA **College:** Kansas   **Ht:** 6' 2" **Wt:** 244 **Born:** 12/30/71 **Age:** 24

Year Team	G	GS	Tackles Tk	Ast	Sack	Misc FF	FR	TD	Blk	Int Int	Yds	Avg	TD	Totals Sfty	TD	Pts
1995 Philadelphia Eagles	6	0	0	0	0.0	0	0	0	0	0	0	-	0	0	0	0

Toby Wright

(statistical profile on page 464)

Pos: S **Rnd:** 2 **College:** Nebraska **Ht:** 5' 11" **Wt:** 203 **Born:** 11/19/70 **Age:** 25

Year	Team	G	GS	Tackles			Miscellaneous				Interceptions				Totals		
				Tk	Ast	Sack	FF	FR	TD	Blk	Int	Yds	Avg	TD	Sfty	TD	Pts
1994	Los Angeles Rams	16	2	12	5	0.0	1	1	1	1	0	0	-	0	0	1	6
1995	St. Louis Rams	16	16	98	17	1.0	1	1	1	0	6	79	13.2	0	0	1	6
	2 NFL Seasons	32	18	110	22	1.0	2	2	2	1	6	79	13.2	0	0	2	12

Other Statistics: 1995–rushed 1 time for 9 yards.

Frank Wycheck

(statistical profile on page 390)

Pos: TE/WR **Rnd:** 6 **College:** Maryland **Ht:** 6' 3" **Wt:** 247 **Born:** 10/14/71 **Age:** 25

Year	Team	G	GS	Rushing					Receiving					Punt Returns				Kickoff Returns				Totals		
				Att	Yds	Avg	Lg	TD	Rec	Yds	Avg	Lg	TD	Num	Yds	Avg	TD	Num	Yds	Avg	TD	Fum	TD	Pts
1993	Washington Redskins	9	7	0	0	-	-	0	16	113	7.1	20	0	0	0	-	0	0	0	-	0	1	0	0
1994	Washington Redskins	9	1	0	0	-	-	0	7	55	7.9	20	1	0	0	-	0	4	84	21.0	0	0	1	6
1995	Houston Oilers	16	11	1	1	1.0	t1	1	40	471	11.8	t36	1	0	0	-	0	0	0	-	0	0	2	12
	3 NFL Seasons	34	19	1	1	1.0	t1	1	63	639	10.1	t36	2	0	0	-	0	4	84	21.0	0	1	3	18

Other Statistics: 1993–recovered 1 fumble for 0 yards. 1995–recovered 1 fumble for -6 yards.

David Wyman

Pos: LB **Rnd:** 2 **College:** Stanford **Ht:** 6' 2" **Wt:** 248 **Born:** 3/31/64 **Age:** 32

Year	Team	G	GS	Tackles			Miscellaneous				Interceptions				Totals		
				Tk	Ast	Sack	FF	FR	TD	Blk	Int	Yds	Avg	TD	Sfty	TD	Pts
1987	Seattle Seahawks	4	0	3	0	0.0	0	0	0	0	0	0	-	0	0	0	0
1988	Seattle Seahawks	16	16	76	27	2.5	0	2	0	0	0	0	-	0	0	0	0
1989	Seattle Seahawks	16	16	77	27	0.0	0	0	0	0	0	0	-	0	0	0	0
1990	Seattle Seahawks	8	8	37	12	1.0	0	1	0	0	2	24	12.0	0	0	0	0
1991	Seattle Seahawks	6	5	19	3	0.0	0	0	0	0	0	0	-	0	0	0	0
1992	Seattle Seahawks	11	11	54	29	0.0	0	1	0	0	0	0	-	0	0	0	0
1993	Denver Broncos	16	16	91	42	2.0	0	2	1	0	1	9	9.0	0	0	1	6
1994	Denver Broncos	4	0	4	1	0.0	0	0	0	0	0	0	-	0	0	0	0
1995	Denver Broncos	11	11	39	12	0.0	1	0	0	0	0	0	-	0	0	0	0
	9 NFL Seasons	92	83	400	153	5.5	1	6	1	0	3	33	11.0	0	0	1	6

Other Statistics: 1993–caught 1 pass for 1 yard and 1 touchdown.

Carlos Yancy

Pos: CB **Rnd:** 7 **College:** Georgia **Ht:** 6' 1" **Wt:** 185 **Born:** 6/24/70 **Age:** 26

Year	Team	G	GS	Tackles			Miscellaneous				Interceptions				Totals		
				Tk	Ast	Sack	FF	FR	TD	Blk	Int	Yds	Avg	TD	Sfty	TD	Pts
1995	New England Patriots	4	0	0	0	0.0	0	0	0	0	0	0	-	0	0	0	0

Ryan Yarborough

Pos: WR **Rnd:** 2 **College:** Wyoming **Ht:** 6' 2" **Wt:** 195 **Born:** 4/26/71 **Age:** 25

Year	Team	G	GS	Rushing					Receiving					Punt Returns				Kickoff Returns				Totals		
				Att	Yds	Avg	Lg	TD	Rec	Yds	Avg	Lg	TD	Num	Yds	Avg	TD	Num	Yds	Avg	TD	Fum	TD	Pts
1994	New York Jets	13	0	0	0	-	-	0	6	42	7.0	12	1	0	0	-	0	0	0	-	0	0	1	6
1995	New York Jets	16	2	0	0	-	-	0	18	230	12.8	38	2	0	0	-	0	0	0	-	0	0	2	12
	2 NFL Seasons	29	2	0	0	-	-	0	24	272	11.3	38	3	0	0	-	0	0	0	-	0	0	3	18

Bryant Young

(statistical profile on page 464)

Pos: DT **Rnd:** 1 (7) **College:** Notre Dame **Ht:** 6' 2" **Wt:** 280 **Born:** 1/27/72 **Age:** 24

Year	Team	G	GS	Tackles			Miscellaneous				Interceptions				Totals		
				Tk	Ast	Sack	FF	FR	TD	Blk	Int	Yds	Avg	TD	Sfty	TD	Pts
1994	San Francisco 49ers	16	16	45	4	6.0	1	1	0	0	0	0	-	0	0	0	0
1995	San Francisco 49ers	12	12	25	3	6.0	0	2	0	0	0	0	-	0	0	0	0
	2 NFL Seasons	28	28	70	7	12.0	1	3	0	0	0	0	-	0	0	0	0

Duane Young

Pos: TE **Rnd:** 5 **College:** Michigan State **Ht:** 6' 1" **Wt:** 270 **Born:** 5/29/68 **Age:** 28

Year	Team	G	GS	Rushing					Receiving					Punt Returns				Kickoff Returns				Totals		
				Att	Yds	Avg	Lg	TD	Rec	Yds	Avg	Lg	TD	Num	Yds	Avg	TD	Num	Yds	Avg	TD	Fum	TD	Pts
1991	San Diego Chargers	7	5	0	0	-	-	0	2	12	6.0	6	0	0	0	-	0	0	0	-	0	0	0	0
1992	San Diego Chargers	16	14	0	0	-	-	0	4	45	11.3	14	0	0	0	-	0	0	0	-	0	0	0	0
1993	San Diego Chargers	16	15	0	0	-	-	0	6	41	6.8	t12	2	0	0	-	0	0	0	-	0	0	2	12
1994	San Diego Chargers	14	14	0	0	-	-	0	17	217	12.8	31	1	0	0	-	0	0	0	-	0	0	1	6

Year	Team	G	GS	Rushing Att	Yds	Avg	Lg	TD	Receiving Rec	Yds	Avg	Lg	TD	Punt Returns Num	Yds	Avg	TD	Kickoff Returns Num	Yds	Avg	TD	Totals Fum	TD	Pts
1995	San Diego Chargers	16	16	0	0	-	-	0	9	90	10.0	22	0	0	0	-	0	0	0	-	0	0	0	0
	5 NFL Seasons	69	64	0	0	-	-	0	38	405	10.7	31	3	0	0	-	0	0	0	-	0	0	3	18

Glen Young

Pos: LB **Rnd:** FA **College:** Syracuse **Ht:** 6' 3" **Wt:** 235 **Born:** 5/2/69 **Age:** 27

Year	Team	G	GS	Tackles Tk	Ast	Sack	Miscellaneous FF	FR	TD	Blk	Interceptions Int	Yds	Avg	TD	Totals Sfty	TD	Pts
1995	San Diego Chargers	16	0	23	3	1.0	0	0	0	0	0	0	-	0	0	0	0

Lonnie Young

Pos: S **Rnd:** 12 **College:** Michigan State **Ht:** 6' 1" **Wt:** 196 **Born:** 7/18/63 **Age:** 33

Year	Team	G	GS	Tackles Tk	Ast	Sack	Miscellaneous FF	FR	TD	Blk	Interceptions Int	Yds	Avg	TD	Totals Sfty	TD	Pts
1985	St. Louis Cardinals	16	10	92	-	0.0	0	1	0	0	3	0	0.0	0	0	0	0
1986	St. Louis Cardinals	13	13	72	-	1.5	0	0	0	0	0	0	-	0	0	0	0
1987	St. Louis Cardinals	12	12	87	-	0.0	0	3	0	0	1	0	0.0	0	0	0	0
1988	Phoenix Cardinals	12	12	61	-	0.0	0	2	0	0	1	2	2.0	0	0	0	0
1989	Phoenix Cardinals	10	9	47	-	0.0	0	0	0	0	1	32	32.0	0	0	0	0
1990	Phoenix Cardinals	16	16	111	-	0.0	0	2	0	0	2	8	4.0	0	0	0	0
1991	New York Jets	12	11	72	-	0.0	0	1	0	0	1	15	15.0	0	0	0	0
1992	New York Jets	13	13	68	34	0.0	0	2	0	0	0	0	-	0	0	0	0
1993	New York Jets	9	2	18	3	1.0	1	1	0	0	1	6	6.0	0	0	0	0
1994	San Diego Chargers	12	0	14	5	1.0	0	0	0	0	0	0	-	0	0	0	0
1995	New York Jets	7	0	7	5	0.0	1	2	0	0	0	0	-	0	0	0	0
	11 NFL Seasons	132	98	649	47	3.5	2	14	0	0	10	63	6.3	0	0	0	0

Robert Young

Pos: DE **Rnd:** 5 **College:** Mississippi State **Ht:** 6' 6" **Wt:** 273 **Born:** 1/29/69 **Age:** 27

Year	Team	G	GS	Tackles Tk	Ast	Sack	Miscellaneous FF	FR	TD	Blk	Interceptions Int	Yds	Avg	TD	Totals Sfty	TD	Pts
1991	Los Angeles Rams	16	13	31	11	1.0	1	0	0	0	0	0	-	0	0	0	0
1992	Los Angeles Rams	11	0	17	3	2.0	0	0	0	0	0	0	-	0	0	0	0
1993	Los Angeles Rams	6	6	13	2	7.0	1	0	0	0	0	0	-	0	0	0	0
1994	Los Angeles Rams	16	16	28	5	6.5	0	0	0	0	0	0	-	0	0	0	0
1995	St. Louis Rams	14	0	1	1	0.0	0	0	0	0	0	0	-	0	0	0	0
	5 NFL Seasons	63	35	90	22	16.5	2	0	0	0	0	0	-	0	0	0	0

Rodney Young

Pos: S **Rnd:** 3 **College:** Louisiana State **Ht:** 6' 1" **Wt:** 206 **Born:** 1/25/73 **Age:** 23

Year	Team	G	GS	Tackles Tk	Ast	Sack	Misc FF	FR	TD	Blk	Interceptions Int	Yds	Avg	TD	Punt Returns Num	Yds	Avg	TD	Kickoff Returns Num	Yds	Avg	TD	Totals TD	Fum
1995	New York Giants	10	0	0	0	0.0	0	0	0	0	1	0	0.0	0	0	0	-	0	0	0	-	0	0	1

Steve Young

(statistical profile on page 390)

Pos: QB **Rnd:** 1(S) **College:** Brigham Young **Ht:** 6' 2" **Wt:** 205 **Born:** 10/11/61 **Age:** 35

Year	Team	G	GS	Passing Att	Com	Pct	Yards	Yds/Att	Lg	TD	Int	Int%	Rating	Rushing Att	Yds	Avg	Lg	TD	Misc Sckd	Yds	Fum	Rec	Yds	Pts
1985	Tampa Bay Buccaneers	5	5	138	72	52.2	935	6.78	59	3	8	5.8	56.9	40	233	5.8	20	1	21	158	4	1	-1	6
1986	Tampa Bay Buccaneers	14	14	363	195	53.7	2282	6.29	46	8	13	3.6	65.5	74	425	5.7	31	5	47	326	11	4	-24	30
1987	San Francisco 49ers	8	3	69	37	53.6	570	8.26	t50	10	0	0.0	120.8	26	190	7.3	t29	1	3	25	0	0	0	6
1988	San Francisco 49ers	11	3	101	54	53.5	680	6.73	t73	3	3	3.0	72.2	27	184	6.8	t49	1	13	75	5	2	-10	6
1989	San Francisco 49ers	10	3	92	64	69.6	1001	10.88	t50	8	3	3.3	120.8	38	126	3.3	22	2	12	84	2	1	0	12
1990	San Francisco 49ers	6	1	62	38	61.3	427	6.89	t34	2	0	0.0	92.6	15	159	10.6	31	0	8	41	1	0	0	0
1991	San Francisco 49ers	11	10	279	180	64.5	2517	9.02	t97	17	8	2.9	101.8	66	415	6.3	21	4	13	79	3	1	-0	24
1992	San Francisco 49ers	16	16	402	268	66.7	3465	8.62	t80	25	7	1.7	107.0	76	537	7.1	t39	4	29	152	9	3	-13	24
1993	San Francisco 49ers	16	16	462	314	68.0	4023	8.71	t80	29	16	3.5	101.5	69	407	5.9	35	2	31	160	8	2	-4	12
1994	San Francisco 49ers	16	16	461	324	70.3	3969	8.61	t69	35	10	2.2	112.8	58	293	5.1	27	7	31	163	4	1	-4	42
1995	San Francisco 49ers	11	11	447	299	66.9	3200	7.16	57	20	11	2.5	92.3	50	250	5.0	29	3	25	115	3	0	0	18
	11 NFL Seasons	124	98	2876	1845	64.2	23069	8.02	t97	160	79	2.7	96.1	539	3219	6.0	t49	30	233	1378	50	15	-62	180

Other Statistics: 1993–caught 2 passes for 2 yards.

Mike Zandofsky

Pos: G **Rnd:** 3 **College:** Washington **Ht:** 6' 2" **Wt:** 305 **Born:** 11/30/65 **Age:** 30

Year	Team	G	GS	Year	Team	G	GS	Year	Team	G	GS	Year	Team	G	GS
1989	Phoenix Cardinals	15	7	1991	San Diego Chargers	10	5	1993	San Diego Chargers	16	16	1995	Atlanta Falcons	12	12
1990	San Diego Chargers	13	0	1992	San Diego Chargers	15	0	1994	Atlanta Falcons	16	16		7 NFL Seasons	97	56

Other Statistics: 1995–recovered 1 fumble for 0 yards.

Rob Zatechka

Pos: G **Rnd:** 4 **College:** Nebraska **Ht:** 6' 4" **Wt:** 307 **Born:** 12/1/71 **Age:** 24

Year	Team	G	GS									Year	Team	G	GS
1995	New York Giants	16	3										1 NFL Season	16	3

Other Statistics: 1995–returned 1 kickoff for 5 yards.

Eric Zeier

(statistical profile on page 391)

Pos: QB **Rnd:** 3 **College:** Georgia **Ht:** 6' 0" **Wt:** 205 **Born:** 9/6/72 **Age:** 24

				Passing								Rushing				Miscellaneous			
Year	Team	G	GS	Att	Com	Pct	Yards	Yds/Att	Lg	TD	Int	Int%	Rating	Att	Yds	Avg	Lg	TD	Sckd	Yds	Fum	Recv	Yds	Pts

Year	Team	G	GS	Att	Com	Pct	Yards	Yds/Att	Lg	TD	Int	Int%	Rating	Att	Yds	Avg	Lg	TD	Sckd	Yds	Fum	Recv	Yds	Pts
1995	Cleveland Browns	7	4	161	82	50.9	864	5.37	59	4	9	5.6	51.9	15	80	5.3	17	0	15	91	3	0	-5	2

Other Statistics: 1995–scored 1 two-point conversion.

Ray Zellars

Pos: RB **Rnd:** 2 **College:** Notre Dame **Ht:** 5' 11" **Wt:** 221 **Born:** 3/25/73 **Age:** 23

				Rushing					Receiving					Punt Returns				Kickoff Returns				Totals		
Year	Team	G	GS	Att	Yds	Avg	Lg	TD	Rec	Yds	Avg	Lg	TD	Num	Yds	Avg	TD	Num	Yds	Avg	TD	Fum	TD	Pts
1995	New Orleans Saints	12	0	50	162	3.2	11	2	7	33	4.7	9	0	0	0	0	- 0	0	0	0	- 0	1	2	12

Tony Zendejas

Pos: K **Rnd:** 1(S) **College:** Nevada **Ht:** 5' 8" **Wt:** 165 **Born:** 5/15/60 **Age:** 36

			Field Goals												PAT		Tot
Year	Team	G	1-29 Yds	Pct	30-39 Yds	Pct	40-49 Yds	Pct	50+ Yds	Pct	Overall	Pct	Long	Made	Att	Pts
1985	Houston Oilers	14	6-7	85.7	8-11	72.7	4-6	66.7	3-3	100.0	21-27	77.8	52	29	31	92
1986	Houston Oilers	15	8-8	100.0	7-9	77.8	6-7	85.7	1-3	33.3	22-27	81.5	51	28	29	94
1987	Houston Oilers	13	7-7	100.0	4-6	66.7	8-12	66.7	1-1	100.0	20-26	76.9	52	32	33	92
1988	Houston Oilers	16	4-6	66.7	7-8	87.5	9-16	56.3	2-4	50.0	22-34	64.7	52	48	50	114
1989	Houston Oilers	16	9-10	90.0	9-14	64.3	5-11	45.5	2-2	100.0	25-37	67.6	52	40	40	115
1990	Houston Oilers	7	2-3	66.7	3-5	60.0	2-4	50.0	0-0	-	7-12	58.3	45	20	21	41
1991	Los Angeles Rams	16	4-4	100.0	8-8	100.0	3-3	100.0	2-2	100.0	17-17	100.0	52	25	26	76
1992	Los Angeles Rams	16	5-6	83.3	7-9	77.8	3-5	60.0	0-0	-	15-20	75.0	49	38	38	83
1993	Los Angeles Rams	16	6-7	85.7	4-5	80.0	0-3	0.0	6-8	75.0	16-23	69.6	54	23	25	71
1994	Los Angeles Rams	16	11-11	100.0	6-7	85.7	1-5	20.0	0-0	-	18-23	78.3	47	28	28	82
1995	Atl - SF	4	0-0	-	1-3	33.3	2-3	66.7	0-0	-	3-6	50.0	45	5	6	14
1995	Atlanta Falcons	1	0-0	-	0-0	-	2-3	66.7	0-0	-	2-3	66.7	45	0	0	6
	San Francisco 49ers	3	0-0	-	1-3	33.3	0-0	-	0-0	-	1-3	33.3	38	5	6	8
	11 NFL Seasons	149	62-69	89.9	64-85	75.3	43-75	57.3	17-23	73.9	186-252	73.8	54	316	327	874

Other Statistics: 1985–recovered 1 fumble for 0 yards; attempted 1 pass with 1 completion for -7 yards. 1986–punted 1 time for 36 yards. 1989–recovered 1 fumble for 0 yards; attempted 1 pass with 0 completions for 0 yards and 1 interception.

Jeff Zgonina

Pos: DT **Rnd:** 7 **College:** Purdue **Ht:** 6' 1" **Wt:** 287 **Born:** 5/24/70 **Age:** 26

				Tackles			Miscellaneous				Interceptions				Punt Returns				Kickoff Returns				Totals	
Year	Team	G	GS	Tk	Ast	Sack	FF	FR	TD	Blk	Int	Yds	Avg	TD	Num	Yds	Avg	TD	Num	Yds	Avg	TD	TD	Fum
1993	Pittsburgh Steelers	5	0	11	5	0.0	0	1	0	0	0	0	-	0	0	0	-	0	0	0	-	0	0	0
1994	Pittsburgh Steelers	16	0	6	5	0.0	0	1	0	0	0	0	-	0	0	0	-	0	2	8	4.0	0	0	1
1995	Carolina Panthers	2	0	2	0	0.0	0	0	0	0	0	0	-	0	0	0	-	0	0	0	-	0	0	0
	3 NFL Seasons	23	0	19	10	0.0	0	2	0	0	0	0	-	0	0	0	-	0	2	8	4.0	0	0	1

Gary Zimmerman

Pos: T **Rnd:** 1(S) **College:** Oregon **Ht:** 6' 6" **Wt:** 294 **Born:** 12/13/61 **Age:** 34

Year	Team	G	GS	Year	Team	G	GS	Year	Team	G	GS	Year	Team	G	GS
1986	Minnesota Vikings	16	16	1989	Minnesota Vikings	16	16	1992	Minnesota Vikings	16	16	1995	Denver Broncos	16	16
1987	Minnesota Vikings	12	12	1990	Minnesota Vikings	16	16	1993	Denver Broncos	16	16				
1988	Minnesota Vikings	16	16	1991	Minnesota Vikings	16	16	1994	Denver Broncos	16	16		10 NFL Seasons	156	156

Other Statistics: 1986–recovered 2 fumbles for 0 yards. 1987–recovered 1 fumble for 4 yards. 1993–recovered 1 fumble for 0 yards.

Scott Zolak

Pos: QB **Rnd:** 4 **College:** Maryland **Ht:** 6' 5" **Wt:** 222 **Born:** 12/13/67 **Age:** 28

Year	Team	G	GS	Att	Com	Pct	Yards	Yds/Att	Lg	TD	Int	Int%	Rating	Att	Yds	Avg	Lg	TD	Sckd	Yds	Fum	Recv	Yds	Pts
							Passing								Rushing						Miscellaneous			
1992	New England Patriots	6	4	100	52	52.0	561	5.61	t65	2	4	4.0	58.8	18	71	3.9	19	0	17	137	5	3	-21	0
1993	New England Patriots	3	0	2	0	0.0	0	0.00	0	0	0	0.0	39.6	1	0	0.0	0	0	0	0	0	0	0	0
1994	New England Patriots	16	0	8	5	62.5	28	3.50	13	0	0	0.0	68.8	1	-1	-1.0	-1	0	0	0	0	0	0	0
1995	New England Patriots	16	1	49	28	57.1	282	5.76	72	1	0	0.0	80.5	4	19	4.8	12	0	4	28	4	1	-2	0
	4 NFL Seasons	41	5	159	85	53.5	871	5.48	72	3	4	2.5	65.3	24	89	3.7	19	0	21	165	9	4	-23	0

Eric Zomalt

Pos: S **Rnd:** 3 **College:** California **Ht:** 5' 11" **Wt:** 197 **Born:** 8/9/72 **Age:** 24

Year	Team	G	GS	Tk	Ast	Sack	FF	FR	TD	Blk	Int	Yds	Avg	TD	Sfty	TD	Pts
				Tackles			Miscellaneous				Interceptions				Totals		
1994	Philadelphia Eagles	12	0	1	0	0.0	0	0	0	0	0	0	-	0	0	0	0
1995	Philadelphia Eagles	16	1	13	4	0.0	0	0	0	0	0	0	-	0	0	0	0
	2 NFL Seasons	28	1	14	4	0.0	0	0	0	0	0	0	-	0	0	0	0

Michael Zordich

(statistical profile on page 464)

Pos: S **Rnd:** 9 **College:** Penn State **Ht:** 6' 1" **Wt:** 212 **Born:** 10/12/63 **Age:** 33

Year	Team	G	GS	Tk	Ast	Sack	FF	FR	TD	Blk	Int	Yds	Avg	TD	Num	Yds	Avg	TD	Num	Yds	Avg	TD	TD	Fum
				Tackles			Miscellaneous				Interceptions				Punt Returns				Kickoff Returns				Totals	
1987	New York Jets	10	0	6	2	1.0	0	0	0	0	0	0	-	0	0	0	-	0	0	0	-	0	0	0
1988	New York Jets	16	0	9	1	0.0	0	0	0	0	1	35	35.0	1	0	0	-	0	0	0	-	0	1	0
1989	Phoenix Cardinals	16	6	43	17	1.0	0	0	0	0	1	16	16.0	1	0	0	-	0	0	0	-	0	1	0
1990	Phoenix Cardinals	16	1	17	10	0.0	0	1	0	0	1	25	25.0	0	0	0	-	0	0	0	-	0	0	0
1991	Phoenix Cardinals	16	16	65	22	0.0	0	3	0	0	1	27	27.0	0	0	0	-	0	0	0	-	0	0	0
1992	Phoenix Cardinals	16	16	41	20	0.0	0	0	0	0	3	37	12.3	0	0	0	-	0	0	0	-	0	0	0
1993	Phoenix Cardinals	16	9	34	20	0.0	2	0	0	0	1	0	0.0	0	0	0	-	0	0	0	-	0	0	0
1994	Philadelphia Eagles	16	16	51	27	0.0	2	3	0	0	4	39	9.8	1	0	0	-	0	1	0	0.0	0	1	0
1995	Philadelphia Eagles	15	15	60	14	1.0	2	2	1	0	1	10	10.0	0	0	0	-	0	0	0	-	0	1	0
	9 NFL Seasons	137	79	326	133	4.0	6	9	1	0	13	189	14.5	3	0	0	-	0	1	0	0.0	0	4	0

Chris Zorich

Pos: DT **Rnd:** 2 **College:** Notre Dame **Ht:** 6' 1" **Wt:** 280 **Born:** 3/13/69 **Age:** 27

Year	Team	G	GS	Tk	Ast	Sack	FF	FR	TD	Blk	Int	Yds	Avg	TD	Sfty	TD	Pts
				Tackles			Miscellaneous				Interceptions				Totals		
1991	Chicago Bears	12	0	3	7	0.0	0	0	0	0	0	0	-	0	0	0	0
1992	Chicago Bears	16	2	26	27	2.0	0	1	1	0	0	0	-	0	0	1	6
1993	Chicago Bears	16	16	63	58	7.0	1	2	0	0	0	0	-	0	0	0	0
1994	Chicago Bears	16	16	51	21	5.5	1	1	0	0	0	0	-	0	0	0	0
1995	Chicago Bears	16	15	43	15	1.0	1	2	0	0	0	0	-	0	0	0	0
	5 NFL Seasons	76	49	186	128	15.5	3	6	1	0	0	0	-	0	0	1	6

Rushing, Returns and Overall Scoring

Team	Rush	Yds	Avg	Lg	TD	Stf	StfYds	Fum	Num	Yds	Avg	TD	Fum	Num	Yds	Avg	TD	Fum	TD	Pts
	Rushing								Punt Returns					Kickoff Returns					Scoring	
Arizona Cardinals	387	1363	3.5	38	3	54	110	22	23	172	7.5	0	1	73	1519	20.8	0	2	26	275
Atlanta Falcons	337	1393	4.1	31	8	37	66	9	39	383	9.8	1	4	70	1506	21.5	0	1	38	362
Buffalo Bills	521	1993	3.8	49	10	71	162	10	47	476	10.1	0	2	70	1302	18.6	0	3	37	350
Carolina Panthers	454	1573	3.5	t53	10	44	80	14	50	500	10.0	1	0	55	1163	21.1	0	0	30	289
Chicago Bears	492	1930	3.9	42	15	47	72	16	24	179	7.5	0	3	71	1459	20.5	0	1	46	392
Cincinnati Bengals	364	1439	4.0	30	7	49	130	9	21	103	4.9	0	1	80	1788	22.4	0	2	37	349
Cleveland Browns	398	1482	3.7	29	5	45	79	11	25	255	10.2	1	1	74	1455	19.7	0	2	29	289
Dallas Cowboys	495	2204	4.5	t60	29	57	115	17	23	255	11.1	0	1	58	1276	22.0	0	3	51	435
Denver Broncos	440	1995	4.5	t60	14	41	72	13	31	358	11.5	0	1	60	1392	23.2	0	0	42	388
Detroit Lions	387	1753	4.5	t75	16	68	142	6	24	189	7.9	0	2	67	1367	20.4	0	2	50	436
Green Bay Packers	410	1428	3.5	40	9	55	94	3	61	515	8.4	0	9	61	1282	21.0	0	1	49	404
Houston Oilers	478	1664	3.5	t74	12	68	172	15	35	339	9.7	0	3	65	1277	19.6	0	2	38	348
Indianapolis Colts	478	1855	3.9	42	14	79	156	12	29	192	6.6	0	3	63	1332	21.1	1	1	37	331
Jacksonville Jaguars	410	1705	4.2	t27	9	43	104	8	29	243	8.4	0	3	74	1532	20.7	1	4	31	275
Kansas City Chiefs	507	2222	4.4	t76	14	56	113	6	58	561	9.7	1	1	55	1306	23.7	2	0	42	358
Miami Dolphins	413	1506	3.6	40	16	54	128	10	24	163	6.8	0	2	59	1338	22.7	0	0	46	398
Minnesota Vikings	433	1733	4.0	t66	10	55	135	13	35	414	11.8	1	1	72	1612	22.4	0	3	48	412
New England Patriots	474	1866	3.9	49	16	53	94	9	45	383	8.5	0	2	75	1691	22.5	0	2	32	294
New Orleans Saints	383	1390	3.6	t66	11	50	115	6	29	268	9.2	0	2	73	1690	23.2	0	0	38	319
New York Giants	478	1833	3.8	36	17	37	91	10	31	218	7.0	0	3	70	1448	20.7	1	1	33	290
New York Jets	365	1279	3.5	30	2	54	118	15	38	323	8.5	0	3	77	1578	20.5	0	8	26	233
Oakland Raiders	463	1932	4.2	60	10	51	92	10	37	374	10.1	0	0	64	1390	21.7	1	3	41	348
Philadelphia Eagles	508	2121	4.2	57	19	62	146	11	29	293	10.1	0	2	71	1487	20.9	1	0	36	318
Pittsburgh Steelers	494	1852	3.7	38	17	57	130	12	48	474	9.9	1	1	69	1530	22.2	0	1	44	407
San Diego Chargers	479	1747	3.6	t48	14	61	128	9	31	338	10.9	1	8	70	1502	21.5	2	5	37	321
San Francisco 49ers	415	1479	3.6	29	19	44	93	6	27	272	10.1	1	3	58	1183	20.4	0	0	57	457
Seattle Seahawks	477	2178	4.6	t86	20	57	121	10	40	384	9.6	1	0	72	1620	22.5	0	6	42	363
St. Louis Rams	392	1431	3.7	41	5	53	93	8	55	587	10.7	0	4	73	1618	22.2	0	3	37	309
Tampa Bay Buccaneers	398	1587	4.0	75	19	46	116	5	29	293	10.1	0	0	76	1443	19.0	0	1	26	238
Washington Redskins	469	1956	4.2	t58	15	46	93	12	26	315	12.1	1	2	69	1646	23.9	0	1	35	326
NFL Totals	13199	51889	3.9	t86	385	1594	3360	317	1043	9819	9.4	10	68	2044	43732	21.4	9	58	1161	10314

Passing and Receiving

Team	Att	Com	Pct	Yards	Yds/Att	Lg	TD	Int	Int%	Rating	Sckd	Yds	Rec	Yds	Avg	Lg	Fum	TD
	Passing												Receiving					
Arizona Cardinals	560	327	58.4	3893	6.95	48	17	24	4.3	72.0	55	390	327	3893	11.9	48	2	17
Atlanta Falcons	603	364	60.4	4456	7.39	t62	26	12	2.0	89.3	43	270	364	4456	12.2	t62	4	26
Buffalo Bills	506	279	55.1	3348	6.62	t77	24	14	2.8	79.9	32	224	279	3348	12.0	t77	3	24
Carolina Panthers	536	263	49.1	3304	6.16	t89	16	25	4.7	59.2	38	258	263	3304	12.6	t89	5	16
Chicago Bears	523	315	60.2	3838	7.34	t76	29	10	1.9	93.4	15	95	315	3838	12.2	t76	1	29
Cincinnati Bengals	586	334	57.0	3915	6.68	t88	29	18	3.1	81.1	25	162	334	3915	11.7	t88	4	29
Cleveland Browns	555	324	58.4	3772	6.80	t70	21	20	3.6	76.6	32	178	324	3772	11.6	t70	6	21
Dallas Cowboys	494	322	65.2	3741	7.57	50	18	10	2.0	91.7	18	118	322	3741	11.6	50	2	18
Denver Broncos	594	350	58.9	4260	7.17	t62	27	14	2.4	86.4	26	215	350	4260	12.2	t62	6	27
Detroit Lions	605	362	59.8	4510	7.45	t91	33	12	2.0	92.9	32	150	362	4510	12.5	t91	4	33
Green Bay Packers	593	372	62.7	4539	7.65	t99	39	15	2.5	97.6	33	217	372	4539	12.2	t99	1	39
Houston Oilers	536	314	58.6	3512	6.55	t76	22	18	3.4	77.9	32	271	314	3512	11.2	t76	6	22
Indianapolis Colts	434	270	62.2	3373	7.77	52	20	11	2.5	91.1	49	309	270	3373	12.5	52	2	20
Jacksonville Jaguars	495	275	55.6	3144	6.35	t71	19	15	3.0	75.0	57	354	275	3144	11.4	t71	2	19
Kansas City Chiefs	531	300	56.5	3178	5.98	t60	21	10	1.9	79.4	21	158	300	3178	10.6	t60	1	21
Miami Dolphins	592	384	64.9	4398	7.43	t67	28	20	3.4	88.8	29	188	384	4398	11.5	t67	3	28
Minnesota Vikings	642	402	62.6	4500	7.01	t85	33	16	2.5	90.2	40	295	402	4500	11.2	t85	3	33
New England Patriots	686	351	51.2	3789	5.52	72	14	16	2.3	64.8	27	198	351	3789	10.8	72	6	14
New Orleans Saints	573	349	60.9	4002	6.98	t70	26	14	2.4	86.9	28	214	349	4002	11.5	t70	5	26
New York Giants	479	260	54.3	2863	5.98	t57	11	13	2.7	68.6	46	213	260	2863	11.0	t57	3	11
New York Jets	589	330	56.0	3129	5.31	t43	20	24	4.1	65.2	47	341	330	3129	9.5	t43	5	20
Oakland Raiders	543	317	58.4	3787	6.97	t80	25	21	3.9	79.0	36	214	317	3787	11.9	t80	4	25
Philadelphia Eagles	496	284	57.3	2931	5.91	t37	11	19	3.8	65.9	46	245	284	2931	10.3	t37	8	11
Pittsburgh Steelers	592	348	58.8	4093	6.91	t71	21	21	3.5	76.9	24	176	348	4093	11.8	t71	6	21
San Diego Chargers	540	318	58.9	3706	6.86	t51	17	18	3.3	76.4	32	240	318	3706	11.7	t51	5	17
San Francisco 49ers	644	432	67.1	4779	7.42	t81	29	16	2.5	93.6	33	171	432	4779	11.1	t81	9	29
Seattle Seahawks	511	273	53.4	3359	6.57	t59	19	23	4.5	67.6	45	267	273	3359	12.3	t59	4	19
St. Louis Rams	632	366	57.9	4113	6.51	72	27	23	3.6	76.5	43	308	366	4113	11.2	72	9	27
Tampa Bay Buccaneers	507	267	52.7	3341	6.59	t64	5	20	3.9	60.3	56	386	267	3341	12.5	t64	4	5
Washington Redskins	521	265	50.9	3496	6.71	t73	16	20	3.8	66.7	36	268	265	3496	13.2	t73	4	16
NFL Totals	16698	9717	58.2	113069	6.77	t99	663	512	3.1	79.3	1076	7093	9717	113069	11.6	t99	127	663

Kicking

Team	1-29 Yds	Pct	30-39 Yds	Pct	40-49 Yds	Pct	50+ Yds	Pct	Overall	Pct	Long	Made	Att	Pts
Arizona Cardinals	14-15	93.3	9-10	90.0	6-8	75.0	1-6	16.7	30-39	76.9	55	19	19	109
Atlanta Falcons	9-9	100.0	11-11	100.0	5-11	45.5	8-9	88.9	33-40	82.5	59	29	30	128
Buffalo Bills	13-14	92.9	13-15	86.7	3-6	50.0	2-5	40.0	31-40	77.5	51	33	35	126
Carolina Panthers	6-6	100.0	10-14	71.4	9-12	75.0	1-1	100.0	26-33	78.8	52	27	28	105
Chicago Bears	16-19	84.2	5-6	83.3	2-4	50.0	0-2	0.0	23-31	74.2	47	45	45	114
Cincinnati Bengals	8-9	88.9	10-11	90.9	10-14	71.4	1-2	50.0	29-36	80.6	51	34	34	121
Cleveland Browns	13-13	100.0	9-10	90.0	7-9	77.8	0-1	0.0	29-33	87.9	47	26	26	113
Dallas Cowboys	11-12	91.7	13-13	100.0	3-3	100.0	0-0	-	27-28	96.4	45	46	48	127
Denver Broncos	7-9	77.8	14-15	93.3	5-7	71.4	5-7	71.4	31-38	81.6	56	39	39	132
Detroit Lions	6-6	100.0	16-17	94.1	5-10	50.0	1-1	100.0	28-34	82.4	56	48	48	132
Green Bay Packers	6-7	85.7	2-5	40.0	9-12	75.0	3-4	75.0	20-28	71.4	51	48	48	108
Houston Oilers	6-6	100.0	8-8	100.0	10-12	83.3	3-5	60.0	27-31	87.1	53	33	33	114
Indianapolis Colts	7-7	100.0	6-12	50.0	8-12	66.7	2-2	100.0	23-33	69.7	52	34	34	103
Jacksonville Jaguars	7-9	77.8	7-8	87.5	4-7	57.1	2-3	66.7	20-27	74.1	53	27	28	87
Kansas City Chiefs	10-11	90.9	7-9	77.8	7-10	70.0	0-0	-	24-30	80.0	49	34	37	106
Miami Dolphins	8-11	72.7	11-11	100.0	6-7	85.7	2-5	40.0	27-34	79.4	51	37	37	118
Minnesota Vikings	9-10	90.0	7-10	70.0	9-12	75.0	1-4	25.0	26-36	72.2	51	44	44	122
New England Patriots	13-14	92.9	3-7	42.9	5-7	71.4	2-5	40.0	23-33	69.7	55	27	27	96
New Orleans Saints	8-10	80.0	7-10	70.0	4-8	50.0	1-3	33.3	20-31	64.5	51	27	29	87
New York Giants	7-7	100.0	9-10	90.0	2-9	22.2	2-2	100.0	20-28	71.4	51	28	28	88
New York Jets	4-4	100.0	8-10	80.0	3-3	100.0	2-4	50.0	17-21	81.0	50	24	24	75
Oakland Raiders	8-9	88.9	9-10	90.0	4-6	66.7	0-2	0.0	21-27	77.8	46	39	40	102
Philadelphia Eagles	5-5	100.0	9-10	90.0	8-12	66.7	0-3	0.0	22-30	73.3	43	32	33	98
Pittsburgh Steelers	11-11	100.0	14-16	87.5	8-13	61.5	1-1	100.0	34-41	82.9	50	39	39	141
San Diego Chargers	8-8	100.0	10-11	90.9	3-5	60.0	0-2	0.0	21-26	80.8	45	32	33	95
San Francisco 49ers	10-10	100.0	6-9	66.7	3-8	37.5	1-1	100.0	20-28	71.4	51	51	54	111
Seattle Seahawks	6-6	100.0	9-10	90.0	8-10	80.0	0-2	0.0	23-28	82.1	49	40	40	109
St. Louis Rams	9-10	90.0	5-10	50.0	2-4	50.0	1-4	25.0	17-28	60.7	51	30	31	81
Tampa Bay Buccaneers	6-7	85.7	5-7	71.4	5-9	55.6	3-3	100.0	19-26	73.1	53	25	25	82
Washington Redskins	10-10	100.0	10-13	76.9	6-11	54.5	1-2	50.0	27-36	75.0	52	33	33	114
NFL Totals	261-284	91.9	262-318	82.4	169-261	64.8	46-91	50.5	738-954	77.4	59	1030	1049	3244

Punting

Team	NetPunts	Yards	Avg	Long	In20	In20%	TotPunts	TB	TB%	Blocks	OppRet	RetYds	NetAvg
Arizona Cardinals	72	3150	43.8	60	20	27.8	72	8	11.1	0	32	242	38.2
Atlanta Falcons	67	2759	41.2	64	21	31.3	67	5	7.5	0	28	236	36.2
Buffalo Bills	86	3473	40.4	60	23	26.7	86	7	8.1	0	23	224	36.2
Carolina Panthers	96	3938	41.0	54	28	29.2	96	11	11.5	0	39	342	35.2
Chicago Bears	58	2169	37.4	61	16	27.6	58	6	10.3	0	28	257	30.9
Cincinnati Bengals	70	2913	41.6	61	26	37.1	70	4	5.7	0	27	154	38.3
Cleveland Browns	65	2831	43.6	64	18	27.7	65	9	13.8	0	34	296	36.2
Dallas Cowboys	55	2243	40.8	58	19	34.5	55	6	10.9	0	22	216	34.7
Denver Broncos	53	2209	41.7	61	23	43.4	54	3	5.7	1	25	137	37.3
Detroit Lions	58	2427	41.8	69	15	25.9	60	7	12.1	2	29	442	30.8
Green Bay Packers	65	2740	42.2	61	26	40.0	67	7	10.8	2	36	279	34.6
Houston Oilers	78	3180	40.8	60	26	33.3	79	8	10.3	1	35	288	34.6
Indianapolis Colts	63	2681	42.6	69	16	25.4	63	7	11.1	0	37	436	33.4
Jacksonville Jaguars	82	3591	43.8	63	19	23.2	82	5	6.1	0	45	323	38.6
Kansas City Chiefs	91	3990	43.8	65	29	31.9	91	12	13.2	0	42	433	36.5
Miami Dolphins	57	2433	42.7	56	15	26.3	57	5	8.8	0	35	265	36.3
Minnesota Vikings	72	2948	40.9	60	21	29.2	72	6	8.3	0	41	446	33.1
New England Patriots	79	3100	39.2	57	27	34.2	79	8	10.1	0	40	342	32.9
New Orleans Saints	73	2965	40.6	53	21	28.8	74	5	6.8	1	36	233	35.6
New York Giants	73	3078	42.2	60	15	20.5	73	8	11.0	0	34	297	35.9
New York Jets	104	4328	41.6	67	23	22.1	105	11	10.6	1	63	753	32.0
Oakland Raiders	75	3089	41.2	60	22	29.3	76	8	10.7	1	38	294	34.7
Philadelphia Eagles	85	3682	43.3	63	20	23.5	86	13	15.3	1	38	527	33.7
Pittsburgh Steelers	59	2368	40.1	64	20	33.9	59	11	18.6	0	22	186	33.3
San Diego Chargers	72	3221	44.7	66	28	38.9	72	8	11.1	0	35	429	36.6
San Francisco 49ers	57	2312	40.6	65	13	22.8	57	5	8.8	0	26	292	33.7
Seattle Seahawks	83	3735	45.0	73	21	25.3	83	8	9.6	0	48	549	36.5
St. Louis Rams	83	3679	44.3	63	23	27.7	83	12	14.5	0	38	393	36.7
Tampa Bay Buccaneers	77	3296	42.8	61	23	29.9	78	7	9.1	1	41	335	36.2
Washington Redskins	74	3140	42.4	60	29	39.2	74	9	12.2	0	26	173	37.7
NFL Totals	2182	91668	42.0	73	646	29.6	2193	229	10.5	11	1043	9819	35.2

Opponents' Rushing, Returns, and Overall Scoring

Team	Rush	Yds	Avg	Lg	TD	Stf	StfYds	Fum	Num	Yds	Avg	TD	Fum	Num	Yds	Avg	TD	Fum	TD	Pts
		Rushing								Punt Returns					Kickoff Returns				Totals	
Arizona Cardinals	503	2249	4.5	t76	14	64	143	21	32	242	7.6	0	3	65	1593	24.5	2	2	53	422
Atlanta Falcons	404	1547	3.8	41	12	46	81	10	28	236	8.4	0	0	59	1323	22.4	0	1	43	349
Buffalo Bills	453	1626	3.6	39	16	50	92	7	23	224	9.7	1	1	73	1615	22.1	0	4	33	335
Carolina Panthers	450	1576	3.5	t35	17	44	97	9	39	342	8.8	0	1	62	1159	18.7	0	4	38	325
Chicago Bears	405	1441	3.6	t29	9	51	112	5	28	257	9.2	1	4	72	1570	21.8	0	0	41	360
Cincinnati Bengals	483	2104	4.4	38	10	45	85	11	27	154	5.7	0	3	65	1475	22.7	0	2	37	374
Cleveland Browns	480	1826	3.8	t75	15	52	107	8	34	296	8.7	0	2	63	1172	18.6	0	1	40	356
Dallas Cowboys	442	1772	4.0	t48	13	33	51	7	22	216	9.8	0	1	85	1661	19.5	0	1	32	291
Denver Broncos	451	1895	4.2	t74	19	52	118	5	25	137	5.5	0	2	77	1671	21.7	2	3	44	345
Detroit Lions	409	1795	4.4	75	15	52	108	9	29	442	15.2	1	1	80	1828	22.9	0	1	36	336
Green Bay Packers	374	1515	4.1	37	12	41	84	5	36	279	7.8	0	1	74	1581	21.4	0	1	37	314
Houston Oilers	400	1526	3.8	t60	11	47	137	9	35	288	8.2	1	1	78	1467	18.8	0	5	38	324
Indianapolis Colts	418	1457	3.5	30	8	40	79	11	37	436	11.8	0	2	68	1546	22.7	1	0	34	316
Jacksonville Jaguars	504	2003	4.0	t86	17	72	140	8	45	323	7.2	0	3	55	1278	23.2	1	1	46	404
Kansas City Chiefs	404	1327	3.3	27	7	54	115	14	42	433	10.3	0	5	71	1448	20.4	0	3	28	241
Miami Dolphins	415	1675	4.0	44	7	30	60	12	35	265	7.6	0	4	85	1782	21.0	0	3	38	332
Minnesota Vikings	352	1329	3.8	53	11	65	153	14	41	446	10.9	1	3	74	1581	21.4	0	1	44	385
New England Patriots	448	1878	4.2	t66	12	51	110	8	40	342	8.6	0	2	67	1405	21.0	0	4	44	377
New Orleans Saints	469	1838	3.9	51	13	51	87	12	36	233	6.5	0	3	68	1313	19.3	0	5	38	348
New York Giants	500	2109	4.2	t60	17	46	72	12	34	297	8.7	1	4	54	1129	20.9	0	1	37	340
New York Jets	526	2016	3.8	49	15	80	162	17	63	753	12.0	0	2	42	987	23.5	0	2	42	384
Oakland Raiders	446	1794	4.0	38	15	64	155	16	38	294	7.7	0	4	68	1469	21.6	0	1	33	332
Philadelphia Eagles	466	1822	3.9	t44	14	55	100	15	38	527	13.9	2	3	61	1576	25.8	0	0	36	338
Pittsburgh Steelers	370	1321	3.6	t58	9	52	126	10	22	186	8.5	0	2	88	1544	17.5	0	2	37	327
San Diego Chargers	441	1694	3.8	60	15	72	148	9	35	429	12.3	1	1	63	1496	23.7	0	5	35	323
San Francisco 49ers	348	1061	3.0	33	5	49	100	9	26	292	11.2	0	2	82	1857	22.6	0	0	26	258
Seattle Seahawks	496	2130	4.3	46	11	56	132	6	48	549	11.4	0	0	70	1669	23.8	2	2	43	366
St. Louis Rams	410	1677	4.1	49	14	71	156	13	38	393	10.3	1	4	59	1247	21.1	0	0	51	418
Tampa Bay Buccaneers	449	1754	3.9	t66	14	64	148	14	41	335	8.2	0	3	46	856	18.6	0	0	35	335
Washington Redskins	483	2132	4.4	t55	18	45	102	11	26	173	6.7	0	1	70	1434	20.5	1	3	42	359
NFL Totals	13199	51889	3.9	t86	385	1594	3360	317	1043	9819	9.4	10	68	2044	43732	21.4	9	58	1161	10314

Opponents' Passing and Receiving

Team	Att	Com	Pct	Yards	Yds/Att	Lg	TD	Int	Int%	Rating	Sckd	Yds	Rec	Yds	Avg	Lg	Fum	TD
				Passing										Receiving				
Arizona Cardinals	461	264	57.3	3655	7.93	t73	33	19	4.1	89.5	31	200	264	3655	13.8	t73	5	33
Atlanta Falcons	650	405	62.3	4751	7.31	t89	28	18	2.8	87.3	30	210	405	4751	11.7	t89	3	28
Buffalo Bills	582	310	53.3	3864	6.64	t54	14	17	2.9	70.0	49	362	310	3864	12.5	t54	4	14
Carolina Panthers	586	310	52.9	3716	6.34	t77	15	21	3.6	66.2	36	265	310	3716	12.0	t77	10	15
Chicago Bears	595	374	62.9	4240	7.13	t99	27	16	2.7	88.1	35	239	374	4240	11.3	t99	6	27
Cincinnati Bengals	602	364	60.5	4512	7.50	t71	25	12	2.0	89.2	42	267	364	4512	12.4	t71	4	25
Cleveland Browns	573	360	62.8	4013	7.00	52	23	17	3.0	84.6	29	191	360	4013	11.1	52	3	23
Dallas Cowboys	523	293	56.0	3491	6.67	t81	17	19	3.6	72.3	36	219	293	3491	11.9	t81	1	17
Denver Broncos	529	297	56.1	3518	6.65	57	20	8	1.5	82.9	30	220	297	3518	11.8	57	3	20
Detroit Lions	580	354	61.0	4121	7.11	t85	17	22	3.8	76.5	42	317	354	4121	11.6	t85	2	17
Green Bay Packers	616	351	57.0	3915	6.36	t69	25	13	2.1	80.8	39	275	351	3915	11.2	t69	0	25
Houston Oilers	553	289	52.3	3325	6.01	t76	24	21	3.8	69.3	30	200	289	3325	11.5	t76	8	24
Indianapolis Colts	569	336	59.1	3739	6.57	t73	23	13	2.3	82.6	29	169	336	3739	11.1	t73	6	23
Jacksonville Jaguars	509	304	59.7	3584	7.04	t68	28	13	2.6	88.9	17	72	304	3584	11.8	t68	6	28
Kansas City Chiefs	596	329	55.2	3569	5.99	49	16	16	2.7	70.8	47	347	329	3569	10.8	49	4	16
Miami Dolphins	556	327	58.8	3756	6.76	t50	30	14	2.5	86.7	29	187	327	3756	11.5	t50	4	30
Minnesota Vikings	620	369	59.5	4416	7.12	t73	29	25	4.0	80.1	44	294	369	4416	12.0	t73	3	29
New England Patriots	549	342	62.3	4107	7.48	t70	29	15	2.7	91.4	37	221	342	4107	12.0	t70	5	29
New Orleans Saints	543	329	60.6	3998	7.36	t77	23	17	3.1	84.3	44	275	329	3998	12.2	t77	2	23
New York Giants	508	299	58.9	3361	6.62	47	17	16	3.1	76.7	29	177	299	3361	11.2	47	3	17
New York Jets	497	263	52.9	3055	6.15	t66	21	17	3.4	71.6	43	315	263	3055	11.6	t66	2	21
Oakland Raiders	527	301	57.1	3642	6.91	52	14	11	2.1	78.6	43	332	301	3642	12.1	52	7	14
Philadelphia Eagles	499	268	53.7	3121	6.25	t64	14	19	3.8	66.4	48	305	268	3121	11.6	t64	1	14
Pittsburgh Steelers	531	314	59.1	3512	6.61	t76	24	22	4.1	76.7	42	272	314	3512	11.2	t76	3	24
San Diego Chargers	543	321	59.1	3605	6.64	50	16	17	3.1	75.8	36	225	321	3605	11.2	50	4	16
San Francisco 49ers	611	330	54.0	3577	5.85	53	19	26	4.3	64.1	40	240	330	3577	10.8	53	5	19
Seattle Seahawks	554	310	56.0	3706	6.69	t88	26	16	2.9	80.2	28	167	310	3706	12.0	t88	5	26
St. Louis Rams	533	320	60.0	3699	6.94	52	27	22	4.1	80.7	36	258	320	3699	11.6	52	4	27
Tampa Bay Buccaneers	557	346	62.1	4098	7.36	t91	19	14	2.5	85.4	25	140	346	4098	11.8	t91	4	19
Washington Redskins	546	338	61.9	3403	6.23	t59	20	16	2.9	79.6	30	135	338	3403	10.1	t59	8	20
NFL Totals	16698	9717	58.2	113069	6.77	t99	663	512	3.1	79.3	1076	7093	9717	113069	11.6	t99	127	663

Offensive Profiles

The following section provides statistical breakdowns and game logs for most significant 1995 offensive players. To be deemed "significant," a player had to either catch 25 passes, throw 50 passes or run the ball 75 times. 227 players meet the criteria, which works out to about seven-and-a-half per team. To determine whether non-quarterbacks received the rushing or the receiving profile, we used a simple test: if a player has more receiving yards than rushing yards, he gets a receiving profile, and vice versa. That's why Arizona fullback Larry Centers, for example, has a receiving rather than a rushing profile. However, even players with rushing profiles have some receiving data, and those with receiving profiles have rushing data if applicable.

Many of the statistics here are STATS exclusives, and the abbreviations might be unfamiliar to you. Those abbreviations and what they stand for can be found below.

For ALL OFFENSIVE PLAYERS, **G** = Games; **Yds** = Yards; **Avg** = Average; **Lg** = Long; **1st** = First downs gained; Also, there might be some question about a few of the breakdown categories. **Inside 20** refers to all plays inside the opposition 20-yard line, the so-called "redzone." And on the right side of the passing splits, the 10 lines beginning with **Rec Behind Line** (Received Behind Line) refer to the location of an intended receiver. And finally, **F-L** in the game logs refers to fumbles and fumbles lost.

For QUARTERBACKS, **Att** = Attempts; **Com** = Completions; **Yds/Att** = Yards per Attempt; **Int** = Interceptions; **Int%** = Interception Percentage; **YAC** = Yards After Catch; **1st%** = First Downs Divided by (Attempts+Sacks); **Big** = Big Pass Plays; **Sck** = Times Sacked; **Rtg** = Quarterback Rating.

For RECEIVERS, **Rec** = Receptions; **Trgt** = Target; **YAC** = Yards After Catch; **Y@C** = Yards at Catch; **1st%** = First Downs Divided by Total Catches.

For RUNNERS, **Stf** = Stuffs; **YdL** = Yards Lost on Stuffs; **1st%** = First Downs Divided by Total Rushes.

For definitions of statistical categories, please consult the Glossary.

Troy Aikman

1995 Passing Splits

	G	Att	Cm	Pct	Yds	Yd/Att	TD	Int	1st	YAC	Big	Sk	Rtg
Total	16	432	280	64.8	3304	7.6	16	7	173	1317	25	14	93.6
vs. Playoff	7	173	117	67.6	1269	7.3	7	3	64	477	10	9	95.3
vs. Non-playoff	9	259	163	62.9	2035	7.9	9	4	109	840	15	5	92.4
vs. Own Division	8	218	130	59.6	1678	7.7	6	4	89	606	13	5	85.4
Home	8	232	148	63.8	1693	7.3	9	5	90	646	14	4	89.6
Away	8	200	132	66.0	1611	8.1	7	2	83	671	11	10	98.1
Games 1-8	8	208	142	68.3	1687	8.1	9	2	89	749	14	5	103.2
Games 9-16	8	224	138	61.6	1617	7.2	7	5	84	568	11	9	84.6
September	4	119	76	63.9	921	7.7	5	1	52	438	7	2	98.1
October	4	89	66	74.2	766	8.6	4	1	37	311	7	3	110.0
November	4	83	61	73.5	650	7.8	4	2	34	258	4	4	102.0
December	4	141	77	54.6	967	6.9	3	4	50	310	7	5	74.4
Grass	4	89	63	70.8	829	9.3	3	1	40	339	6	4	106.4
Turf	12	343	217	63.3	2475	7.2	13	6	133	978	17	10	90.2
Indoor	2	63	43	68.3	444	7.0	3	1	24	219	2	3	97.6
Outdoor	14	369	237	64.2	2860	7.8	13	6	149	1098	23	11	92.9
1st Half	-	225	156	69.3	1871	8.3	11	3	96	741	14	10	105.3
2nd Half/OT	-	207	124	59.9	1433	6.9	5	4	77	576	11	4	80.8
Last 2 Min. Half	-	66	37	56.1	382	5.8	2	0	22	162	2	1	83.0
4th qtr, +/-7 pts	-	48	24	50.0	229	4.8	0	2	14	112	2	2	46.3
Winning	-	242	159	65.7	1896	7.8	8	3	99	805	16	7	95.3
Tied	-	75	52	69.3	626	8.3	6	1	32	210	4	4	115.8
Trailing	-	115	69	60.0	782	6.8	2	3	42	302	5	3	75.3

	Att	Cm	Pct	Yds	Yd/Att	TD	Int	1st	YAC	Big	Sk	Rtg
Inside 20	55	31	56.4	222	4.0	10	0	18	105	0	1	105.5
Inside 10	22	12	54.5	52	2.4	6	0	8	25	0	0	99.6
1st Down	185	120	64.9	1536	8.3	7	2	64	605	16	5	98.8
2nd Down	128	88	68.8	944	7.4	4	3	51	394	6	6	90.8
3rd Down Overall	116	69	59.5	789	6.8	5	2	55	316	5	3	87.2
3rd D 0-5 to Go	47	30	63.8	276	5.9	3	2	29	150	1	0	83.3
3rd D 6+ to Go	69	39	56.5	513	7.4	2	0	26	166	4	3	89.8
4th Down	3	3	100.0	35	11.7	0	0	3	2	0	1	115.3
Rec Behind Line	70	45	64.3	265	3.8	0	0	10	439	1	0	71.4
1-10 yds	225	154	68.4	1398	6.2	9	2	85	636	6	0	94.6
11-20 yds	99	66	66.7	1102	11.1	4	3	63	168	6	0	97.3
21-30 yds	15	7	46.7	199	13.3	1	1	7	39	4	0	87.5
31+	23	8	34.8	340	14.8	3	0	8	35	8	0	122.7
Left Sideline	82	54	65.9	682	8.3	2	1	34	240	6	0	94.7
Left Side	94	60	63.8	707	7.5	4	1	35	347	6	2	96.4
Middle	78	49	62.8	617	7.9	4	2	32	218	3	12	93.8
Right Side	89	62	69.7	694	7.8	3	2	40	331	5	0	94.5
Right Sideline	89	55	61.8	604	6.8	3	1	32	181	5	0	88.4
2 Wide Receivers	226	149	65.9	1926	8.5	9	4	94	736	17	6	94.7
3+ WR	196	124	63.3	1331	6.8	4	1	75	522	7	8	87.8
Attempts 1-10	149	103	69.1	1189	8.0	7	3	63	404	6	0	100.2
Attempts 11-20	140	90	64.3	1142	8.2	5	1	56	534	12	0	98.6
Attempts 21+	143	87	60.8	973	6.8	4	3	54	379	7	0	81.7

1995 Incompletions

Type	Num	% of Inc	% of Att
Pass Dropped	22	14.5	5.1
Poor Throw	56	36.8	13.0
Pass Defensed	34	22.4	7.9
Pass Hit at Line	9	5.9	2.1
Other	31	20.4	7.2
Total	152	100.0	35.2

Game Logs (1-8)

Date	Opp	Result	Att	Cm	Pct	Yds	TD	Int	Lg	Sk	F-L
09/04	@NYN	W 35-0	20	15	75.0	228	1	0	43	1	0-0
09/10	Den	W 31-21	31	18	58.1	196	2	1	29	0	0-0
09/17	@Min	W 23-17	38	24	63.2	246	1	0	26	2	2-1
09/24	Ari	W 34-20	30	19	63.3	251	1	0	50	0	0-0
10/01	@Was	L 23-27	3	2	66.7	30	0	0	23	0	0-0
10/08	GB	W 34-24	31	24	77.4	316	2	0	48	1	0-0
10/15	@SD	W 23-9	30	21	70.0	222	0	0	30	1	0-0
10/29	@Atl	W 28-13	25	19	76.0	198	2	1	43	1	0-0

Game Logs (9-16)

Date	Opp	Result	Att	Cm	Pct	Yds	TD	Int	Lg	Sk	F-L
11/06	Phi	W 34-12	24	17	70.8	202	1	1	38	0	0-0
11/12	SF	L 20-38	6	4	66.7	29	0	1	10	1	0-0
11/19	@Oak	W 34-21	24	19	79.2	227	1	0	36	1	0-0
11/23	KC	W 24-12	29	21	72.4	192	2	0	33	2	0-0
12/03	Was	L 17-24	47	29	61.7	285	1	1	23	0	1-0
12/10	@Phi	L 17-20	28	11	39.3	117	0	0	19	3	0-0
12/17	NYN	W 21-20	34	16	47.1	222	0	1	40	0	0-0
12/25	@Ari	W 37-13	34	21	65.6	350	2	1	48	2	2-1

Marcus Allen

1995 Rushing and Receiving Splits

	G	Rush	Yds	Avg	Lg	TD	1st	Stf	YdL	Rec	Yds	Avg	TD
Total	16	207	890	4.3	38	5	51	13	29	27	210	7.8	0
vs. Playoff	4	49	181	3.7	19	1	8	4	7	7	51	7.3	0
vs. Non-playoff	12	158	709	4.5	38	4	43	9	22	20	159	8.0	0
vs. Own Division	8	119	503	4.2	38	3	29	10	26	17	157	9.2	0
Home	8	114	406	3.6	28	2	26	8	14	17	117	6.9	0
Away	8	93	484	5.2	38	3	25	5	15	10	93	9.3	0
Games 1-8	8	100	431	4.3	28	2	28	5	10	14	83	5.9	0
Games 9-16	8	107	459	4.3	38	3	23	8	19	13	127	9.8	0
September	4	41	161	3.9	17	1	11	3	6	7	47	6.7	0
October	4	59	270	4.6	28	1	17	2	4	7	36	5.1	0
November	4	44	150	3.4	16	2	11	4	5	4	43	10.8	0
December	4	63	309	4.9	38	1	12	4	14	9	84	9.3	0
Grass	14	200	867	4.3	38	5	50	12	28	25	188	7.5	0
Turf	2	7	23	3.3	10	0	1	1	1	2	22	11.0	0
Indoor	1	4	19	4.8	10	0				1	11	11.0	0
Outdoor	15	203	871	4.3	38	5	50	13	29	26	199	7.7	0
1st Half	-	100	447	4.5	38	1	19	5	15	17	141	8.3	0
2nd Half/OT	-	107	443	4.1	25	4	32	8	14	10	69	6.9	0
Last 2 Min. Half	-	8	33	4.1	11	0	1	1	4	6	41	6.8	0
4th qtr, +/-7 pts	-	31	92	3.0	15	0	9	5	8	3	9	3.0	0
Winning	-	87	371	4.3	25	3	27	6	8	9	89	9.9	0
Tied	-	52	217	4.2	28	1	9	4	9	7	60	8.6	0
Trailing	-	68	302	4.4	38	1	15	3	12	11	61	5.5	0

	Rush	Yds	Avg	Lg	TD	1st	Stf	YdL	Rec	Yds	Avg	TD
Inside 20	41	90	2.2	8	5	7	3	7	3	16	5.3	0
Inside 10	29	38	1.3	4	5	6	3	7	0	0	-	0
1st Down	108	475	4.4	25	1	12	6	9	8	43	5.4	0
2nd Down	71	329	4.6	38	2	20	5	14	13	129	9.9	0
3rd Down Overall	21	68	3.2	12	1	13	2	6	6	38	6.3	0
3rd D 0-2 to Go	16	38	2.4	12	1	12	2	6	0	0	-	0
3rd D 3-7 to Go	3	10	3.3	7	0	1	0	0	4	26	6.5	0
3rd D 8+ to Go	2	20	10.0	10	0	0	0	0	2	12	6.0	0
4th Down	7	18	2.6	7	1	6	0	0	0	0	-	0
Left Sideline	5	36	7.2	19	0	1	0	0	0	0	-	0
Left Side	40	215	5.4	23	0	11	3	12	10	74	7.4	0
Middle	112	443	4.0	38	3	31	8	12	6	72	12.0	0
Right Side	45	169	3.8	28	2	7	2	5	6	27	4.5	0
Right Sideline	5	27	5.4	10	0	1	0	0	5	37	7.4	0
Shotgun	0	0	-	0	0	0	0	0	0	0	-	0
2 Wide Receivers	142	672	4.7	38	1	32	8	10	20	172	8.6	0
3 Wide Receivers	28	146	5.2	19	0	4	2	11	2	3	1.5	0
4+ Wide Receivers	6	32	5.3	11	0	1	0	0	5	35	7.0	0
Carries 1-5	73	360	4.9	38	1	16	3	12	0	0	-	0
Carries 6-10	64	261	4.1	23	0	16	4	8	0	0	-	0
Carries 11-15	48	158	3.3	17	3	11	5	8	0	0	-	0
Carries 16-20	20	97	4.9	25	1	7	1	1	0	0	-	0
Carries 21+	2	14	7.0	10	0	1	0	0	0	0	-	0

1995 Incompletions

Type	Num	%of Inc	% Att
Pass Dropped	2	13.3	4.8
Poor Throw	5	33.3	11.9
Pass Defensed	1	6.7	2.4
Pass Hit at Line	0	0.0	0.0
Other	7	46.7	16.7
Total	15	100.0	35.7

Game Logs (1-8)

Date	Opp	Result	Rush	Yds	Rec	Yds	Trgt	F-L	TD
09/03	@Sea	W 34-10	4	19	1	11	1	0-0	0
09/10	NYN	W 20-17	19	86	2	-1	5	0-0	1
09/17	Oak	W 23-17	17	53	4	37	4	1-1	0
09/24	@Cle	L 17-35	1	3	0	0	1	0-0	0
10/01	@Ari	W 24-3	11	62	1	13	1	0-0	0
10/09	SD	W 29-23	14	26	3	14	4	0-0	1
10/15	NE	W 31-26	13	61	2	10	2	0-0	1
10/22	@Den	W 21-7	21	121	1	-1	1	0-0	1

Game Logs (9-16)

Date	Opp	Result	Rush	Yds	Rec	Yds	Trgt	F-L	TD
11/05	Was	W 24-3	9	34	1	9	2	0-0	1
11/12	@SD	W 22-7	16	63	1	19	2	0-0	1
11/19	Hou	W 20-13	16	49	1	4	4	0-0	1
11/23	@Dal	L 12-24	3	4	1	11	2	0-0	0
12/03	@Oak	W 29-23	21	124	3	33	3	0-0	1
12/11	@Mia	L 6-13	16	88	2	7	5	0-0	0
12/17	Den	W 20-17	16	54	4	44	5	0-0	0
12/24	Sea	W 26-3	10	43	0	0	1	0-0	1

Terry Allen
Washington Redskins — RB

1995 Rushing and Receiving Splits

	G	Rush	Yds	Avg	Lg	TD	1st	Stf	YdL	Rec	Yds	Avg	TD
Total	16	338	1309	3.9	28	10	66	26	55	31	232	7.5	1
vs. Playoff	6	131	542	4.1	21	6	32	9	15	14	112	8.0	1
vs. Non-playoff	10	207	767	3.7	28	4	34	17	40	17	120	7.1	0
vs. Own Division	8	181	712	3.9	28	5	37	13	31	15	115	7.7	1
Home	8	176	691	3.9	22	6	32	12	21	17	112	6.6	1
Away	8	162	618	3.8	28	4	34	14	34	14	120	8.6	0
Games 1-8	8	165	666	4.0	22	3	32	16	33	15	110	7.3	1
Games 9-16	8	173	643	3.7	28	7	34	10	22	16	122	7.6	0
September	4	78	340	4.4	22	0	14	8	11	5	24	4.8	0
October	5	102	382	3.7	21	3	20	8	22	11	89	8.1	1
November	3	51	201	3.9	14	1	9	2	6	7	47	6.7	0
December	4	107	386	3.6	28	6	23	8	16	8	72	9.0	0
Grass	12	243	962	4.0	22	6	45	17	38	22	155	7.0	1
Turf	4	95	347	3.7	28	4	21	9	17	9	77	8.6	0
Indoor	1	24	76	3.2	12	1	4	3	8	4	39	9.8	0
Outdoor	15	314	1233	3.9	28	9	62	23	47	27	193	7.1	1
1st Half	-	156	595	3.8	28	3	28	13	29	17	120	7.1	1
2nd Half/OT	-	182	714	3.9	22	7	38	13	26	14	112	8.0	0
Last 2 Min. Half	-	7	13	1.9	12	1	2	2	2	3	14	4.7	1
4th qtr, +/-7 pts	-	40	131	3.3	21	3	7	5	14	3	26	8.7	0
Winning	-	109	400	3.7	22	4	19	8	16	8	65	8.1	1
Tied	-	79	276	3.5	18	1	14	6	16	6	26	4.3	0
Trailing	-	150	633	4.2	28	5	33	12	23	17	141	8.3	0

	Rush	Yds	Avg	Lg	TD	1st	Stf	YdL	Rec	Yds	Avg	TD
Inside 20	54	128	2.4	13	10	16	6	9	2	16	8.0	1
Inside 10	29	41	1.4	7	10	12	3	5	1	5	5.0	1
1st Down	198	743	3.8	28	4	20	16	36	17	111	6.5	1
2nd Down	116	484	4.2	21	2	31	9	17	12	103	8.6	0
3rd Down Overall	17	65	3.8	14	2	10	0	0	2	18	9.0	0
3rd D 0-2 to Go	13	41	3.2	14	1	7	0	0	1	15	15.0	0
3rd D 3-7 to Go	4	24	6.0	9	1	3	0	0	1	3	3.0	0
3rd D 8+ to Go	0	0	-	0	0	0	0	0	0	0	-	0
4th Down	7	17	2.4	8	2	5	1	2	0	0	-	0
Left Sideline	14	59	4.2	16	0	2	1	1	6	45	7.5	0
Left Side	63	258	4.1	22	2	11	6	9	9	80	8.9	0
Middle	162	588	3.6	28	4	27	11	25	5	34	6.8	0
Right Side	89	317	3.6	21	4	22	8	20	8	58	7.3	0
Right Sideline	10	87	8.7	18	0	4	0	0	3	15	5.0	1
Shotgun	0	0	-	0	0	0	0	0	0	0	-	0
2 Wide Receivers	234	920	3.9	28	1	33	16	34	24	187	7.8	1
3 Wide Receivers	43	234	5.4	22	0	11	2	3	7	45	6.4	0
4+ Wide Receivers	1	1	1.0	1	0	0	0	0	1	1	1.0	0
Carries 1-5	80	223	2.8	14	1	9	8	22				
Carries 6-10	80	407	5.1	28	1	20	5	7				
Carries 11-15	79	305	3.9	22	3	18	3	5				
Carries 16-20	50	171	3.4	21	3	10	8	17				
Carries 21+	49	203	4.1	22	2	9	2	9				

1995 Incompletions

Type	Num	%of Inc	% Att
Pass Dropped	4	44.4	10.0
Poor Throw	4	44.4	10.0
Pass Defensed	0	0.0	0.0
Pass Hit at Line	0	0.0	0.0
Other	1	11.1	2.5
Total	9	100.0	22.5

Game Logs (1-8)

Date	Opp	Result	Rush	Yds	Rec	Yds	Trgt	F-L	TD
09/03	Ari	W 27-7	26	131	1	3	1	1-1	0
09/10	Oak	L 8-20	16	49	2	0	2	1-1	0
09/17	@Den	L 31-38	18	92	0	0	3	0-0	0
09/24	@TB	L 6-14	18	68	2	21	3	0-0	0
10/01	Dal	W 27-23	30	121	4	34	4	2-0	2
10/08	@Phi	L 34-37	16	53	3	18	3	0-0	0
10/15	@Ari	L 20-24	17	42	1	11	1	0-0	0
10/22	Det	W 36-30	24	110	2	23	3	0-0	2

Game Logs (9-16)

Date	Opp	Result	Rush	Yds	Rec	Yds	Trgt	F-L	TD
10/29	NYN	L 15-24	15	56	1	3	2	0-0	0
11/05	@KC	L 3-24	14	69	2	11	2	0-0	0
11/19	Sea	L 20-27	15	41	2	10	2	0-0	0
11/26	Phi	L 7-14	22	91	3	26	3	0-0	1
12/03	@Dal	W 24-17	25	98	0	0	3	0-0	2
12/10	@NYN	L 13-20	30	120	2	20	2	0-0	1
12/17	@StL	W 35-23	24	76	4	39	4	2-1	1
12/24	Car	W 20-17	28	92	2	13	2	0-0	2

Justin Armour
Buffalo Bills — WR

1995 Receiving Splits

	G	Rec	Yds	Avg	TD	Lg	Big	YAC	Trgt	Y@C	1st	1st%
Total	15	26	300	11.5	3	28	1	118	41	7.0	14	53.8
vs. Playoff	6	9	121	13.4	1	28	1	51	17	7.8	6	66.7
vs. Non-playoff	9	17	179	10.5	2	19	0	67	24	6.6	8	47.1
vs. Own Division	8	13	140	10.8	0	24	0	59	17	6.2	6	54.5
Home	8	17	200	11.8	1	24	0	85	28	6.8	10	58.8
Away	7	9	100	11.1	2	28	1	33	13	7.4	4	44.4
Games 1-8	7	10	119	11.9	1	24	0	61	14	5.8	7	70.0
Games 9-16	8	16	181	11.3	2	28	1	57	27	7.8	7	43.8
September	2	3	48	16.0	0	24	0	34	6	4.7	3	100.0
October	5	7	71	10.1	1	17	0	27	8	6.3	4	57.1
November	4	12	120	10.0	0	17	0	32	18	7.3	5	41.7
December	4	4	61	15.3	2	28	1	25	9	9.0	2	50.0
Grass	4	7	84	12.0	2	28	1	29	10	7.9	4	57.1
Turf	11	19	216	11.4	1	24	0	89	31	6.7	10	52.6
Indoor	2	1	7	7.0	0	7	0	0	1	7.0	0	-
Outdoor	13	25	293	11.7	3	28	1	118	40	7.0	14	56.0
1st Half	-	11	136	12.4	2	28	1	52	14	7.6	5	45.5
2nd Half/OT	-	15	164	10.9	1	24	0	66	27	6.5	9	60.0
Last 2 Min. Half	-	3	59	19.7	2	28	1	30	4	9.7	3	100.0
4th qtr, +/-7 pts	-	4	38	9.5	0	17	0	5	6	8.3	2	50.0
Winning	-	5	54	10.8	0	17	0	8	11	9.2	3	60.0
Tied	-	8	94	11.8	1	24	0	38	10	7.0	5	62.5
Trailing	-	13	152	11.7	2	28	1	72	20	6.2	6	46.2

	Rec	Yds	Avg	TD	Lg	Big	YAC	Trgt	Y@C	1st	1st%
Inside 20	2	33	16.5	2	19	0	17	5	8.0	2	100.0
Inside 10	0	0	-	0	0	0	0	0	-	0	-
1st Down	9	106	11.8	2	19	0	45	17	6.8	5	55.6
2nd Down	11	117	10.6	1	28	1	42	14	6.8	6	54.5
3rd Down Overall	6	77	12.8	0	24	0	31	10	7.7	3	50.0
3rd D 0-2 to Go	1	24	24.0	0	24	0	16	1	8.0	1	100.0
3rd D 3-7 to Go	1	4	4.0	0	4	0	1	2	3.0	0	0.0
3rd D 8+ to Go	4	49	12.3	0	17	0	14	7	8.8	2	50.0
4th Down	0	0	-	0	0	0	0	0	-	0	-
Rec Behind Line	0	0	-	0	0	0	0	1	-	0	-
1-10 yds	23	241	10.5	1	24	0	103	29	6.0	11	47.8
11-20 yds	3	59	19.7	2	28	1	15	7	14.7	3	100.0
21-30 yds	0	0	-	0	0	0	0	4	-	0	-
31+	0	0	-	0	0	0	0	0	-	0	-
Left Sideline	5	64	12.8	0	19	0	32	6	6.4	4	80.0
Left Side	5	41	8.2	0	13	0	8	7	6.6	1	20.0
Middle	6	64	10.7	1	15	0	25	9	6.5	2	33.3
Right Side	6	87	14.5	1	24	0	41	10	7.7	5	83.3
Right Sideline	4	44	11.0	1	28	1	12	9	8.4	2	50.0
Shotgun	6	89	14.8	1	28	1	29	10	10.0	4	66.7
2 Wide Receivers	0	0	-	0	0	0	0	0	-	0	-
3 Wide Receivers	26	300	11.5	3	28	1	118	41	7.0	14	53.8
4+ Wide Receivers	0	0	-	0	0	0	0	0	-	0	-

1995 Incompletions

Type	Num	%of Inc	%of Att
Pass Dropped	2	13.3	4.9
Poor Throw	5	33.3	12.2
Pass Defensed	5	33.3	12.2
Pass Hit at Line	0	0.0	0.0
Other	3	20.0	7.3
Total	15	100.0	36.6

Game Logs (1-8)

Date	Opp	Result	Rush	Yds	Rec	Yds	Trgt	F-L	TD
09/03	@Den	L 7-22	-	-	-	-	-	-	-
09/10	Car	W 31-9	0	0	0	0	2	0-0	0
09/17	Ind	W 20-14	0	0	3	48	4	0-0	0
10/02	@Cle	W 22-19	0	0	4	46	4	0-0	1
10/08	NYA	W 29-10	0	0	0	0	0	0-0	0
10/15	Sea	W 27-21	0	0	1	15	1	0-0	0
10/23	@NE	L 14-27	0	0	2	10	2	0-0	0
10/29	@Mia	L 6-23	0	0	0	0	1	0-0	0

Game Logs (9-16)

Date	Opp	Result	Rush	Yds	Rec	Yds	Trgt	F-L	TD
11/05	@Ind	W 16-10	0	0	1	1	1	0-0	0
11/12	Atl	W 23-17	2	-13	4	38	8	0-0	0
11/19	@NYA	W 28-26	1	6	1	9	2	1-0	0
11/26	NE	L 25-35	0	0	6	66	7	0-0	0
12/03	@SF	L 17-27	1	2	1	28	4	0-0	1
12/10	@StL	W 45-27	0	0	0	0	2	0-0	0
12/17	Mia	W 23-20	0	0	0	0	1	0-0	0
12/24	Hou	L 17-28	0	0	3	33	5	0-0	1

Johnny Bailey
St. Louis Rams — RB

1995 Receiving Splits

	G	Rec	Yds	Avg	TD	Lg	Big	YAC	Trgt	Y@C	1st	1st%
Total	12	38	265	7.0	0	25	2	240	55	0.7	13	34.2
vs. Playoff	8	25	138	5.5	0	13	0	120	37	0.7	6	24.0
vs. Non-playoff	4	13	127	9.8	0	25	2	120	18	0.5	7	53.8
vs. Own Division	4	10	52	5.2	0	16	0	51	13	0.1	2	20.0
Home	6	28	203	7.3	0	25	1	165	36	1.4	10	35.7
Away	6	10	62	6.2	0	25	1	75	19	-1.3	3	30.0
Games 1-8	6	13	54	4.2	0	12	0	75	18	-1.6	2	15.4
Games 9-16	6	25	211	8.4	0	25	2	165	37	1.8	11	44.0
September	2	4	6	1.5	0	9	0	14	6	-2.0	1	25.0
October	4	9	48	5.3	0	12	0	61	12	-1.4	1	11.1
November	2	4	20	5.0	0	16	0	16	7	1.0	1	25.0
December	4	21	191	9.1	0	25	2	149	30	2.0	10	47.6
Grass	2	4	7	1.8	0	6	0	13	8	-1.5	1	25.0
Turf	10	34	258	7.6	0	25	2	227	47	0.9	12	35.3
Indoor	5	23	189	8.2	0	25	1	155	33	1.5	10	43.5
Outdoor	7	15	76	5.1	0	25	1	85	22	-0.6	3	20.0
1st Half	-	16	97	6.1	0	25	1	84	25	0.8	5	31.3
2nd Half/OT	-	22	168	7.6	0	25	1	156	30	0.5	8	36.4
Last 2 Min. Half	-	9	68	7.6	0	16	0	43	11	2.8	3	33.3
4th qtr, +/-7 pts	-	1	4	4.0	0	4	0	7	2	-3.0	0	0.0
Winning	-	5	13	2.6	0	12	0	24	7	-2.2	1	20.0
Tied	-	6	40	6.7	0	25	1	48	9	-1.3	2	33.3
Trailing	-	27	212	7.9	0	25	1	168	39	1.6	10	37.0

	Rec	Yds	Avg	TD	Lg	Big	YAC	Trgt	Y@C	1st	1st%
Inside 20	2	4	2.0	0	2	0	15	3	-5.5	0	0.0
Inside 10	1	2	2.0	0	2	0	5	1	-3.0	0	0.0
1st Down	10	81	8.1	0	16	0	79	16	0.2	4	40.0
2nd Down	9	49	5.4	0	10	0	45	14	0.4	3	33.3
3rd Down Overall	14	79	5.6	0	25	1	71	20	0.6	3	21.4
3rd D 0-2 to Go	0	0	-	0	0	0	0	2	-	0	-
3rd D 3-7 to Go	2	8	4.0	0	6	0	14	4	-3.0	1	50.0
3rd D 8+ to Go	12	71	5.9	0	25	1	57	14	1.2	2	16.7
4th Down	5	56	11.2	0	25	1	45	5	2.2	3	60.0
Rec Behind Line	13	48	3.7	0	12	0	113	17	-5.0	4	30.8
1-10 yds	25	217	8.7	0	25	2	127	35	3.6	9	36.0
11-20 yds	0	0	-	0	0	0	0	1	-	0	-
21-30 yds	0	0	-	0	0	0	0	2	-	0	-
31+	0	0	-	0	0	0	0	0	-	0	-
Left Sideline	4	16	4.0	0	8	0	14	8	0.5	0	0.0
Left Side	12	80	6.7	0	16	0	74	16	0.5	5	41.7
Middle	12	86	7.2	0	13	0	75	15	0.9	3	25.0
Right Side	4	25	6.3	0	25	1	31	5	-1.5	1	25.0
Right Sideline	6	58	9.7	0	25	1	46	11	2.0	4	66.7
Shotgun	0	0	-	0	0	0	0	0	-	0	-
2 Wide Receivers	9	47	5.2	0	16	0	51	12	-0.4	3	33.3
3 Wide Receivers	28	213	7.6	0	25	2	186	38	1.0	10	35.7
4+ Wide Receivers	1	5	5.0	0	5	0	3	5	2.0	0	0.0

1995 Incompletions

Type	Num	%of Inc	%of Att
Pass Dropped	5	29.4	9.1
Poor Throw	8	47.1	14.5
Pass Defensed	1	5.9	1.8
Pass Hit at Line	0	0.0	0.0
Other	3	17.6	5.5
Total	17	100.0	30.9

Game Logs (1-8)

Date	Opp	Result	Rush	Yds	Rec	Yds	Trgt	F-L	TD
09/03	@GB	W 17-14	2	3	2	1	4	0-0	0
09/10	NO	W 17-13	-	-	-	-	-	-	-
09/17	@Car	W 31-10	-	-	-	-	-	-	-
09/24	Chi	W 34-28	1	9	2	5	2	0-0	0
10/01	@Ind	L 18-21	1	3	1	9	2	0-0	0
10/12	Atl	W 21-19	2	19	5	28	5	1-0	1
10/22	SF	L 10-44	1	-3	1	4	1	0-0	0
10/29	@Phi	L 9-20	3	25	2	7	4	0-0	0

Game Logs (9-16)

Date	Opp	Result	Rush	Yds	Rec	Yds	Trgt	F-L	TD
11/05	@NO	L 10-19	5	27	2	14	3	0-0	0
11/12	Car	W 28-17	-	-	-	-	-	-	-
11/19	@Atl	L 6-31	-	-	-	-	-	-	-
11/26	@SF	L 13-41	3	17	2	6	4	0-0	0
12/03	@NYA	W 23-20	1	3	1	25	2	0-0	0
12/10	Buf	L 27-45	4	15	10	69	13	0-0	0
12/17	Was	L 23-35	8	39	8	83	11	0-0	0
12/24	Mia	L 22-41	5	25	2	14	4	0-0	0

Fred Barnett
Philadelphia Eagles — WR

1995 Receiving Splits

	G	Rec	Yds	Avg	TD	Lg	Big	YAC	Trgt	Y@C	1st	1st%
Total	14	48	585	12.2	4	33	3	207	76	7.9	32	66.7
vs. Playoff	2	5	42	8.4	1	19	0	6	11	7.2	3	60.0
vs. Non-playoff	12	43	543	12.6	4	33	3	201	65	8.0	29	67.4
vs. Own Division	7	21	309	14.7	4	33	2	108	31	9.6	18	85.7
Home	7	28	303	10.8	4	26	1	95	41	7.4	19	67.9
Away	7	20	282	14.1	4	33	2	112	35	8.5	13	65.0
Games 1-8	7	26	269	10.3	3	33	1	74	41	7.5	14	53.8
Games 9-16	7	22	316	14.4	4	31	2	133	35	8.3	18	81.8
September	4	15	179	11.9	2	33	1	45	24	8.9	8	53.3
October	3	11	90	8.2	1	16	0	29	17	5.5	6	54.5
November	3	15	236	15.7	2	31	2	113	19	8.2	14	93.3
December	4	7	80	11.4	0	19	0	20	16	8.6	4	57.1
Grass	4	12	210	17.5	1	33	2	84	18	10.5	10	83.3
Turf	10	36	375	10.4	4	26	1	123	58	7.0	22	61.1
Outdoor	2	40	513	12.8	5	33	3	179	62	8.4	29	72.5
Indoor	12	8	72	9.0	0	19	0	28	14	5.5	3	37.5
1st Half	-	30	347	11.6	4	26	1	112	45	7.8	20	66.7
2nd Half/OT	-	18	238	13.2	1	33	2	95	31	7.9	12	66.7
Last 2 Min. Half	-	4	50	12.5	1	19	0	12	10	9.5	4	100.0
4th qtr, +/-7 pts	-	3	53	17.7	0	31	1	24	5	9.7	2	66.7
Winning	-	12	164	13.7	3	33	1	68	20	8.0	11	91.7
Tied	-	17	215	12.6	1	26	1	85	22	7.6	12	70.6
Trailing	-	19	206	10.8	1	31	1	54	34	8.0	9	47.4

	Rec	Yds	Avg	TD	Lg	Big	YAC	Trgt	Y@C	1st	1st%
Inside 20	7	63	9.0	5	19	0	12	12	7.3	7	100.0
Inside 10	3	7	2.3	3	4	0	0	3	2.3	3	100.0
1st Down	15	200	13.3	0	31	2	75	24	8.3	7	46.7
2nd Down	19	215	11.3	2	20	0	69	31	7.7	14	73.7
3rd Down Overall	13	166	12.8	3	33	1	63	20	7.9	11	84.6
3rd D 0-2 to Go	2	7	3.5	1	6	0	3	2	2.0	2	100.0
3rd D 3-7 to Go	5	71	14.2	1	33	1	36	7	7.0	5	100.0
3rd D 8+ to Go	6	88	14.7	1	23	0	24	11	10.7	4	66.7
4th Down	1	4	4.0	0	4	0	0	1	4.0	0	-
Rec Behind Line	0	0	-	0	0	0	0	2	-	0	-
1-10 yds	33	304	9.2	3	23	0	131	46	5.2	20	60.6
11-20 yds	14	248	17.7	0	31	2	64	21	13.1	11	78.6
21-30 yds	1	33	33.0	0	33	1	12	4	21.0	1	100.0
31+	0	0	-	0	0	0	0	3	-	0	-
Left Sideline	3	49	16.3	0	23	0	20	4	9.7	3	100.0
Left Side	8	82	10.3	1	16	0	27	15	6.9	6	75.0
Middle	10	121	12.1	4	20	0	34	13	8.7	9	90.0
Right Side	17	198	11.6	0	26	1	83	28	6.8	11	64.7
Right Sideline	10	135	13.5	0	33	2	43	16	9.2	3	30.0
Shotgun	0	0	-	0	0	0	0	0	-	0	-
2 Wide Receivers	27	340	12.6	2	33	3	122	36	8.1	15	55.6
3 Wide Receivers	16	185	11.6	1	22	0	69	31	7.3	13	81.3
4+ Wide Receivers	4	59	14.8	1	23	0	16	7	10.8	3	75.0

1995 Incompletions

Type	Num	%of Inc	%of Att
Pass Dropped	4	14.3	5.3
Poor Throw	12	42.9	15.8
Pass Defensed	10	35.7	13.2
Pass Hit at Line	2	7.1	2.6
Other	0	0.0	0.0
Total	28	100.0	36.8

Game Logs (1-8)

Date	Opp	Result	Rec	Yds	Trgt	F-L	TD
09/03	TB	L 6-21	5	47	6	0-0	0
09/10	@Ari	W 31-19	5	97	7	0-0	1
09/17	SD	L 21-27	4	23	8	0-0	0
09/24	@Oak	W 31-10	1	12	3	0-0	0
10/01	@NO	W 15-10	5	34	8	0-0	1
10/08	Was	W 37-34	6	56	6	0-0	1
10/15	@NYN	W 17-14	0	0	3	0-0	0
10/29	StL	W 20-9	-	-	-	-	-

Game Logs (9-16)

Date	Opp	Result	Rec	Yds	Trgt	F-L	TD
11/06	@Dal	L 12-34	-	-	-	-	-
11/12	Den	W 31-13	7	105	10	0-0	0
11/19	NYN	W 28-19	4	47	5	0-0	2
11/26	@Was	W 14-7	4	84	4	0-0	0
12/03	@Sea	L 14-26	3	38	6	0-0	0
12/10	Dal	W 20-17	1	19	3	0-0	0
12/17	Ari	W 21-20	1	6	3	0-0	0
12/24	@Chi	L 14-20	2	17	4	0-0	0

Mario Bates

New Orleans Saints — RB

1995 Rushing and Receiving Splits

	G	Rush	Yds	Avg	Lg	TD	1st	Stf	YdL	Rec	Yds	Avg	TD
Total	16	244	951	3.9	66	7	50	27	72	18	114	6.3	0
vs. Playoff	8	118	394	3.3	35	2	17	11	25	13	82	6.3	0
vs. Non-playoff	8	126	557	4.4	66	5	33	16	47	5	32	6.4	0
vs. Own Division	8	138	519	3.8	22	3	31	14	40	13	87	6.7	0
Home	8	120	420	3.5	35	3	22	10	31	10	71	7.1	0
Away	8	124	531	4.3	66	4	28	17	41	8	43	5.4	0
Games 1-8	8	116	456	3.9	35	3	23	13	29	12	89	7.4	0
Games 9-16	8	128	495	3.9	66	4	27	14	43	6	25	4.2	0
September	4	51	205	4.0	33	1	10	5	12	10	80	8.0	0
October	4	65	251	3.9	35	2	13	8	17	2	9	4.5	0
November	4	69	265	3.8	22	2	16	5	20	2	9	4.5	0
December	4	59	230	3.9	66	2	11	9	23	4	16	4.0	0
Grass	3	58	272	4.7	66	3	16	7	15	1	4	4.0	0
Turf	13	186	679	3.7	35	4	34	20	57	17	110	6.5	0
Indoor	10	143	508	3.6	35	3	26	12	35	13	82	6.3	0
Outdoor	6	101	443	4.4	66	4	24	15	37	5	32	6.4	0
1st Half	-	133	496	3.7	35	4	28	13	39	10	72	7.2	0
2nd Half/OT	-	111	455	4.1	66	3	22	14	33	8	42	5.3	0
Last 2 Min. Half	-	3	5	1.7	10	0	1	1	5	0	0	-	0
4th qtr. +/-7 pts	-	24	135	5.6	66	1	6	4	8	4	16	4.0	0
Winning	-	87	340	3.9	66	2	16	14	35	2	10	5.0	0
Tied	-	71	252	3.5	35	2	16	7	20	1	7	7.0	0
Trailing	-	86	359	4.2	33	3	18	6	17	15	97	6.5	0

	Rush	Yds	Avg	Lg	TD	1st	Stf	YdL	Rec	Yds	Avg	TD
Inside 20	33	61	1.8	11	6	8	4	10	0	0	-	0
Inside 10	18	32	1.8	6	5	5	1	2	0	0	-	0
1st Down	134	616	4.6	66	4	18	9	27	12	83	6.9	0
2nd Down	100	324	3.2	22	3	28	17	44	6	31	5.2	0
3rd Down Overall	9	12	1.3	4	0	4	0	0	0	0	-	0
3rd D 0-2 to Go	9	12	1.3	4	0	4	0	0	0	0	-	0
3rd D 3-7 to Go	0	0	-	0	0	0	0	0	0	0	-	0
3rd D 8+ to Go	0	0	-	0	0	0	0	0	0	0	-	0
4th Down	1	-1	-1.0	-	0	0	1	1	0	0	-	0
Left Sideline	21	160	7.6	35	1	7	3	8	6	30	5.0	0
Left Side	94	312	3.3	33	1	17	12	33	2	7	3.5	0
Middle	91	279	3.1	14	4	17	6	13	4	14	3.5	0
Right Side	33	157	4.8	66	1	5	6	18	3	41	13.7	0
Right Sideline	5	43	8.6	22	0	4	0	0	3	22	7.3	0
Shotgun	3	0	0.0	1	0	0	1	2	0	0	-	0
2 Wide Receivers	152	696	4.6	66	4	30	15	41	11	67	6.1	0
3 Wide Receivers	24	65	2.7	15	0	5	4	11	7	47	6.7	0
4+ Wide Receivers	0	0	-	0	0	0	0	0	0	0	-	0
Carries 1-5	80	341	4.3	35	4	18	5	11	0	0	-	0
Carries 6-10	78	249	3.2	22	0	14	13	32	0	0	-	0
Carries 11-15	48	238	5.0	66	2	10	3	14	0	0	-	0
Carries 16-20	27	96	3.6	14	1	6	2	6	0	0	-	0
Carries 21+	11	27	2.5	13	0	2	4	9	0	0	-	0

1995 Incompletions

Type	Num	%of Inc	% Att
Pass Dropped	1	33.3	4.8
Poor Throw	0	0.0	0.0
Pass Defensed	0	0.0	0.0
Pass Hit at Line	1	33.3	4.8
Other	1	33.3	4.8
Total	3	100.0	14.3

Game Logs (1-8)

Date	Opp	Result	Rush	Yds	Rec	Yds	Trgt	F-L	TD
09/03	SF	L 22-24	13	26	3	16	3	1-0	0
09/10	@StL	L 13-17	10	74	3	20	3	0-0	0
09/17	Atl	L 24-27	18	48	3	36	4	0-0	0
09/24	@NYN	L 29-45	10	57	1	8	2	0-0	1
10/01	Phi	L 10-15	12	61	1	5	1	0-0	0
10/15	Mia	W 33-30	10	41	0	0	0	0-0	1
10/22	@Car	L 3-20	17	43	1	4	1	0-0	0
10/29	@SF	W 11-7	26	106	0	0	0	1-0	1

Game Logs (9-16)

Date	Opp	Result	Rush	Yds	Rec	Yds	Trgt	F-L	TD
11/05	StL	W 19-10	22	106	0	0	0	0-0	0
11/12	Ind	W 17-14	18	45	2	9	2	0-0	0
11/19	@Min	L 24-43	10	43	0	0	0	0-0	0
11/26	Car	W 34-26	19	71	0	0	0	0-0	2
12/03	@NE	W 31-17	15	123	0	0	0	0-0	2
12/10	@Atl	L 14-19	13	45	3	11	3	0-0	0
12/16	GB	L 23-34	8	22	1	5	2	0-0	0
12/24	@NYA	W 12-0	23	40	0	0	0	0-0	0

Brad Baxter

New York Jets — RB

1995 Rushing and Receiving Splits

	G	Rush	Yds	Avg	Lg	TD	1st	Stf	YdL	Rec	Yds	Avg	TD
Total	15	85	296	3.5	26	1	21	8	17	26	160	6.2	0
vs. Playoff	7	39	148	3.8	26	0	10	3	7	11	70	6.4	0
vs. Non-playoff	8	46	148	3.2	17	1	11	5	10	15	90	6.0	0
vs. Own Division	4	49	179	3.7	26	1	16	4	8	17	99	5.8	0
Home	7	49	162	3.3	26	1	12	4	12	14	93	6.6	0
Away	8	36	134	3.7	17	0	9	4	5	12	67	5.6	0
Games 1-8	8	47	154	3.3	14	0	8	5	14	11	70	6.4	0
Games 9-16	7	38	142	3.7	26	1	13	3	3	15	90	6.0	0
September	4	33	121	3.7	14	0	6	3	8	6	28	4.7	0
October	5	22	58	2.6	11	0	6	3	7	8	75	9.4	0
November	3	18	64	3.6	26	1	5	1	1	8	40	5.0	0
December	3	12	53	4.4	17	0	4	1	1	4	17	4.3	0
Grass	3	10	38	3.8	17	0	3	1	1	6	30	5.0	0
Turf	12	75	258	3.4	26	1	18	7	16	20	130	6.5	0
Indoor	4	21	78	3.7	12	0	6	2	6	6	37	6.2	0
Outdoor	11	64	218	3.4	26	1	15	6	15	20	123	6.2	0
1st Half	-	45	216	4.8	26	0	13	2	6	12	73	6.1	0
2nd Half/OT	-	40	80	2.0	10	1	8	6	11	14	87	6.2	0
Last 2 Min. Half	-	1	1	1.0	1	0	0	0	1	1	7	7.0	0
4th qtr. +/-7 pts	-	6	13	2.2	6	0	1	0	2	2	23	11.5	0
Winning	-	28	77	2.8	14	0	5	4	9	1	3	3.0	0
Tied	-	25	129	5.2	26	0	7	1	1	8	67	8.4	0
Trailing	-	32	90	2.8	12	1	9	3	7	17	90	5.3	0

	Rush	Yds	Avg	Lg	TD	1st	Stf	YdL	Rec	Yds	Avg	TD
Inside 20	6	9	1.5	11	1	1	2	3	1	1	1.0	0
Inside 10	3	0	0.0	1	1	1	1	1	0	0	-	0
1st Down	46	150	3.3	17	1	6	5	8	12	70	5.8	0
2nd Down	29	112	3.9	12	0	9	1	4	8	57	7.1	0
3rd Down Overall	10	34	3.4	26	0	6	2	5	6	33	5.5	0
3rd D 0-2 to Go	9	8	0.9	4	0	5	2	5	0	0	-	0
3rd D 3-7 to Go	1	26	26.0	26	0	1	0	0	5	32	6.4	0
3rd D 8+ to Go	0	0	-	0	0	0	0	0	1	1	1.0	0
4th Down	0	0	-	0	0	0	0	0	0	0	-	0
Left Sideline	2	13	6.5	10	0	1	1	0	3	26	8.7	0
Left Side	26	85	3.3	26	0	5	1	4	9	69	7.7	0
Middle	33	116	3.5	12	0	10	4	5	1	8	8.0	0
Right Side	21	73	3.5	14	1	4	2	7	4	6	1.5	0
Right Sideline	3	9	3.0	8	0	1	1	1	9	51	5.7	0
Shotgun	0	0	-	0	0	0	0	0	0	0	-	0
2 Wide Receivers	66	230	3.5	14	0	14	6	12	23	146	6.3	0
3 Wide Receivers	2	-3	-1.5	1	0	0	1	4	1	7	7.0	0
4+ Wide Receivers	0	0	-	0	0	0	0	0	0	0	-	0
Carries 1-5	56	222	4.0	26	0	13	3	7	0	0	-	0
Carries 6-10	21	64	3.0	14	1	7	3	6	0	0	-	0
Carries 11-15	5	7	1.4	10	0	1	2	4	0	0	-	0
Carries 16-20	3	3	1.0	2	0	0	0	0	0	0	-	0
Carries 21+	0	0	-	0	0	0	0	0	0	0	-	0

1995 Incompletions

Type	Num	%of Inc	% Att
Pass Dropped	5	38.5	12.8
Poor Throw	6	46.2	15.4
Pass Defensed	0	0.0	0.0
Pass Hit at Line	1	7.7	2.6
Other	1	7.7	2.6
Total	13	100.0	33.3

Game Logs (1-8)

Date	Opp	Result	Rush	Yds	Rec	Yds	Trgt	F-L	TD
09/03	@Mia	L 14-52	0	0	2	3	3	0-0	0
09/10	Ind	L 24-27	8	18	1	3	1	0-0	0
09/17	Jac	W 27-10	18	64	1	17	1	0-0	0
09/24	@Atl	L 3-13	7	39	2	7	3	0-0	0
10/01	Oak	L 10-47	2	0	2	19	3	0-0	0
10/08	@Buf	L 10-29	5	18	0	0	0	0-0	0
10/15	@Car	L 15-26	2	0	2	15	2	0-0	0
10/22	Mia	W 17-16	5	15	1	8	3	0-0	0

Game Logs (9-16)

Date	Opp	Result	Rush	Yds	Rec	Yds	Trgt	F-L	TD
10/29	@Ind	L 10-17	8	25	3	33	4	0-0	0
11/05	NE	L 7-20	9	32	6	22	7	0-0	1
11/19	Buf	L 26-28	6	33	2	18	3	0-0	0
11/26	@Sea	W 16-10	3	-1	0	0	0	0-0	0
12/03	StL	L 20-23	1	0	1	6	1	0-0	0
12/10	@NE	L 28-31	8	38	2	12	5	0-0	0
12/17	@Hou	L 6-23	3	15	1	-1	2	0-0	0
12/24	NO	L 0-12	-	-	-	-	-	-	-

Green Bay Packers — RB

1995 Rushing and Receiving Splits

	G	Rush	Yds	Avg	Lg	TD	1st	Stf	YdL	Rec	Yds	Avg	TD
Total	16	316	1067	3.4	23	3	47	32	54	61	648	10.6	4
vs. Playoff	4	82	305	3.7	23	2	20	6	11	16	212	13.3	0
vs. Non-playoff	12	234	762	3.3	20	1	27	26	43	45	436	9.7	4
vs. Own Division	8	159	555	3.5	20	2	28	16	26	34	379	11.1	3
Home	8	144	471	3.3	23	2	22	18	30	26	289	11.1	4
Away	8	172	596	3.5	20	1	25	14	24	35	359	10.3	0
Games 1-8	8	170	589	3.5	17	1	31	18	32	27	261	9.7	1
Games 9-16	8	146	478	3.3	23	2	16	14	22	34	387	11.4	3
September	4	84	270	3.2	17	0	10	9	15	8	27	3.4	0
October	4	86	319	3.7	13	1	21	9	17	19	234	12.3	1
November	4	67	219	3.3	20	1	8	9	14	17	225	13.2	2
December	4	79	259	3.3	23	1	8	5	8	17	162	9.5	1
Grass	12	233	746	3.2	23	2	30	25	41	43	384	8.9	4
Turf	4	83	321	3.9	20	1	17	7	13	20	264	13.2	0
Indoor	3	67	271	4.0	20	1	14	6	10	16	185	11.6	0
Outdoor	13	249	796	3.2	23	2	33	26	44	45	463	10.3	4
1st Half	-	169	624	3.7	23	3	28	15	23	27	254	9.4	1
2nd Half/OT	-	147	443	3.0	15	0	19	17	31	34	394	11.6	3
Last 2 Min. Half	-	17	33	1.9	8	1	2	3	5	3	45	15.0	0
4th qtr, +/-7 pts	-	22	52	2.4	12	0	2	2	4	7	51	7.3	2
Winning	-	169	521	3.1	15	1	23	22	39	32	348	10.9	1
Tied	-	92	340	3.7	23	2	13	6	8	15	120	8.0	2
Trailing	-	55	206	3.7	13	0	11	4	7	14	180	12.9	1

	Rush	Yds	Avg	Lg	TD	1st	Stf	YdL	Rec	Yds	Avg	TD
Inside 20	53	142	2.7	13	3	7	5	7	8	77	9.6	4
Inside 10	27	49	1.8	9	2	2	4	4	2	11	5.5	1
1st Down	190	644	3.4	20	1	14	17	32	28	370	13.2	2
2nd Down	105	335	3.2	17	1	22	13	20	16	78	4.9	0
3rd Down Overall	20	89	4.5	23	1	11	1	1	17	200	11.8	2
3rd D 0-2 to Go	10	38	3.8	23	1	6	1	1	4	57	14.3	1
3rd D 3-7 to Go	8	48	6.0	13	0	5	0	0	3	51	17.0	0
3rd D 8+ to Go	2	3	1.5	3	0	0	0	0	10	92	9.2	1
4th Down	1	-1	-1.0	-1	0	0	1	1	0	0	-	0
Left Sideline	16	53	3.3	13	1	3	2	4	8	126	15.8	0
Left Side	70	270	3.9	20	1	15	6	11	19	207	10.9	2
Middle	147	449	3.1	15	0	17	13	22	8	76	9.5	0
Right Side	74	268	3.6	23	1	12	9	12	18	158	8.8	2
Right Sideline	9	27	3.0	7	0	0	2	5	8	81	10.1	0
Shotgun	0	0	-	0	0	0	0	0	0	0	-	0
2 Wide Receivers	217	711	3.3	23	2	29	22	40	32	263	8.2	2
3 Wide Receivers	57	214	3.8	17	0	9	4	6	16	236	14.8	2
4+ Wide Receivers	28	106	3.8	14	0	5	3	5	13	149	11.5	0
Carries 1-5	80	274	3.4	23	1	12	6	9	-	-	-	-
Carries 6-10	80	337	4.2	20	0	16	7	15	0	0	-	0
Carries 11-15	70	216	3.1	14	1	8	10	14	0	0	-	0
Carries 16-20	49	146	3.0	13	0	9	6	11	0	0	-	0
Carries 21+	37	94	2.5	9	0	2	3	3	0	0	-	0

1995 Incompletions

Type	Num	%of Inc	% Att
Pass Dropped	4	22.2	5.1
Poor Throw	7	38.9	8.9
Pass Defensed	0	0.0	0.0
Pass Hit at Line	1	5.6	1.3
Other	6	33.3	7.6
Total	18	100.0	22.8

Game Logs (1-8)

Date	Opp	Result	Rush	Yds	Rec	Yds	Trgt	F-L	TD
09/03	StL	L 14-17	10	21	2	2	4	0-0	0
09/11	@Chi	W 27-24	30	96	2	11	2	0-0	0
09/17	NYN	W 14-6	23	87	1	2	2	0-0	0
09/24	@Jac	W 24-14	21	66	3	12	4	1-0	0
10/08	@Dal	L 24-34	16	50	4	79	7	0-0	0
10/15	Det	W 30-21	29	77	4	71	6	0-0	1
10/22	Min	W 38-21	19	71	5	34	6	0-0	1
10/29	@Det	L 16-24	22	121	6	50	7	0-0	0

Game Logs (9-16)

Date	Opp	Result	Rush	Yds	Rec	Yds	Trgt	F-L	TD
11/05	@Min	L 24-27	19	70	7	65	8	0-0	1
11/12	Chi	W 35-28	11	18	2	33	2	0-0	2
11/19	@Cle	W 31-20	23	71	5	42	5	1-0	0
11/26	TB	W 35-13	14	60	5	85	4	0-0	0
12/03	Cin	W 24-10	23	80	7	50	8	0-0	1
12/10	@TB	L 10-13	15	42	5	30	8	0-0	0
12/16	@NO	W 34-23	26	80	3	70	3	0-0	0
12/24	Pit	W 24-19	15	57	2	12	3	0-0	1

St. Louis Rams — RB

1995 Rushing and Receiving Splits

	G	Rush	Yds	Avg	Lg	TD	1st	Stf	YdL	Rec	Yds	Avg	TD
Total	15	183	637	3.5	41	3	24	16	28	18	106	5.9	0
vs. Playoff	9	80	289	3.6	41	0	12	8	12	13	76	5.8	0
vs. Non-playoff	6	103	348	3.4	16	3	12	8	16	5	30	6.0	0
vs. Own Division	7	110	444	4.0	41	2	19	8	10	11	50	4.5	0
Home	8	113	415	3.7	16	2	17	10	17	8	71	8.9	0
Away	7	70	222	3.2	41	1	7	6	11	10	35	3.5	0
Games 1-8	8	119	408	3.4	16	1	17	11	20	9	43	4.8	0
Games 9-16	7	64	229	3.6	41	2	7	5	8	9	63	7.0	0
September	4	68	228	3.4	16	1	8	6	12	3	13	4.3	0
October	4	51	180	3.5	16	0	9	5	8	6	30	5.0	0
November	3	41	172	4.2	41	1	5	2	6	6	32	5.3	0
December	4	23	57	2.5	11	1	2	3	6	3	31	10.3	0
Grass	3	32	91	2.8	15	1	4	2	3	4	8	2.0	0
Turf	12	151	546	3.6	41	2	20	14	25	14	98	7.0	0
Indoor	6	61	228	3.7	41	2	7	3	4	9	66	7.3	0
Outdoor	9	122	409	3.4	16	1	17	13	24	9	40	4.4	0
1st Half	-	108	351	3.3	41	3	14	9	18	12	67	5.6	0
2nd Half/OT	-	75	286	3.8	16	0	10	7	10	6	39	6.5	0
Last 2 Min. Half	-	10	16	1.6	6	0	1	3	4	1	-3	-3.0	0
4th qtr, +/-7 pts	-	19	67	3.5	16	0	2	3	4	0	0	-	0
Winning	-	81	274	3.4	16	1	10	8	14	3	18	6.0	0
Tied	-	58	168	2.9	13	2	7	4	9	4	12	3.0	0
Trailing	-	44	195	4.4	41	0	7	4	5	11	76	6.9	0

	Rush	Yds	Avg	Lg	TD	1st	Stf	YdL	Rec	Yds	Avg	TD
Inside 20	28	59	2.1	13	3	4	4	5	0	0	-	0
Inside 10	15	20	1.3	6	3	3	4	5	0	0	-	0
1st Down	117	386	3.3	16	1	9	11	20	6	51	8.5	0
2nd Down	54	192	3.6	16	0	9	3	3	10	57	5.7	0
3rd Down Overall	10	50	5.0	41	1	4	2	5	2	-2	-1.0	0
3rd D 0-2 to Go	8	45	5.6	41	1	4	1	3	0	0	-	0
3rd D 3-7 to Go	1	-2	-2.0	-2	0	0	1	2	1	1	1.0	0
3rd D 8+ to Go	1	7	7.0	7	0	0	0	0	1	-3	-3.0	0
4th Down	2	9	4.5	8	1	2	0	0	0	0	-	0
Left Sideline	8	20	2.5	11	0	1	1	1	4	11	2.8	0
Left Side	39	154	3.9	41	0	8	4	6	4	45	11.3	0
Middle	81	252	3.1	16	3	9	7	11	2	14	7.0	0
Right Side	41	148	3.6	16	0	5	3	9	5	19	3.8	0
Right Sideline	14	63	4.5	13	0	1	1	1	3	17	5.7	0
Shotgun	0	0	-	0	0	0	0	0	0	0	-	0
2 Wide Receivers	117	411	3.5	16	0	13	9	14	12	83	6.9	0
3 Wide Receivers	5	22	4.4	9	0	0	0	0	4	12	3.0	0
4+ Wide Receivers	2	11	5.5	7	0	1	0	0	0	0	-	0
Carries 1-5	71	204	2.9	13	0	5	7	17	0	0	-	0
Carries 6-10	54	235	4.4	41	2	12	4	4	0	0	-	0
Carries 11-15	27	109	4.0	16	1	4	0	0	0	0	-	0
Carries 16-20	23	73	3.2	12	0	2	4	5	0	0	-	0
Carries 21+	8	16	2.0	6	0	1	1	2	0	0	-	0

1995 Incompletions

Type	Num	%of Inc	% Att
Pass Dropped	3	60.0	13.0
Poor Throw	1	20.0	4.3
Pass Defensed	0	0.0	0.0
Pass Hit at Line	0	0.0	0.0
Other	1	20.0	4.3
Total	5	100.0	21.7

Game Logs (1-8)

Date	Opp	Result	Rush	Yds	Rec	Yds	Trgt	F-L	TD
09/03	@GB	W 17-14	7	4	0	0	0	0-0	0
09/10	NO	W 17-13	20	83	0	0	0	0-0	0
09/17	@Car	W 31-10	19	67	2	1	3	1-0	1
09/24	Chi	W 34-28	22	74	1	12	2	0-0	0
10/01	@Ind	L 18-21	11	31	2	10	2	0-0	0
10/12	Atl	W 21-19	19	88	1	10	2	1-1	0
10/22	SF	L 10-44	11	34	2	7	2	0-0	0
10/29	@Phi	L 9-20	10	27	1	3	1	0-0	0

Game Logs (9-16)

Date	Opp	Result	Rush	Yds	Rec	Yds	Trgt	F-L	TD
11/05	@NO	L 10-19	-	-	-	-	-		
11/12	Car	W 28-17	26	91	1	11	1	0-0	1
11/19	@Atl	L 6-31	9	61	3	14	4	0-0	0
11/26	@SF	L 13-41	6	25	2	7	2	1-1	0
12/03	@NYA	W 23-20	8	12	0	0	0	0-0	0
12/10	Buf	L 27-45	1	3	0	0	0	0-0	0
12/17	Was	L 22-41	8	21	1	6	1	0-0	0
12/24	Mia	L 22-41	6	21	2	25	3	0-0	0

Steve Beuerlein

1995 Passing Splits

	G	Att	Cm	Pct	Yds	Yd/Att	TD	Int	1st	YAC	Big	Sk	Rtg		Att	Cm	Pct	Yds	Yd/Att	TD	Int	1st	YAC	Big	Sk	Rtg
Total	7	142	71	50.0	952	6.7	4	7	47	411	7	17	60.5	Inside 20	13	4	30.8	36	2.8	2	0	2	12	0	1	79.8
vs. Playoff	1	21	10	47.6	136	6.5	0	3	6	39	1	2	29.2	Inside 10	3	0	0.0	0	0.0	0	0	0	0	0	0	39.6
vs. Non-playoff	6	121	61	50.4	816	6.7	4	4	41	372	6	15	69.4	1st Down	50	31	62.0	417	8.3	2	2	21	155	3	2	85.2
vs. Own Division	4	81	37	45.7	514	6.3	2	2	23	274	5	10	64.5	2nd Down	48	16	33.3	202	4.2	1	4	10	63	2	7	19.6
Home	2	51	25	49.0	299	5.9	1	1	16	100	2	5	65.7	3rd Down Overall	42	22	52.4	305	7.3	1	1	14	187	2	7	74.0
Away	5	91	46	50.5	653	7.2	3	6	31	311	5	12	57.6	3rd D 0-5 to Go	13	6	46.2	136	10.5	1	0	6	96	2	0	109.8
Games 1-8	3	47	19	40.4	269	5.7	1	1	10	194	3	6	57.8	3rd D 6+ to Go	29	16	55.2	169	5.8	0	1	8	91	0	7	58.0
Games 9-16	4	95	52	54.7	683	7.2	3	6	37	217	4	11	61.9	4th Down	2	2	100.0	28	14.0	0	0	2	6	0	1	118.8
September	1	29	11	37.9	152	5.2	1	0	6	102	1	3	67.0	Rec Behind Line	16	9	56.3	102	6.4	0	0	4	129	1	0	75.5
October	1	18	8	44.4	117	6.5	0	1	4	92	2	3	43.1	1-10 yds	64	42	65.6	461	7.2	2	2	24	208	1	0	84.2
November	2	46	27	58.7	349	7.6	2	2	20	113	2	6	79.0	11-20 yds	47	17	36.2	296	6.3	1	3	16	60	2	0	39.0
December	2	49	25	51.0	334	6.8	1	4	17	104	2	5	45.8	21-30 yds	8	3	37.5	93	11.6	1	2	3	14	3	0	81.8
Grass	4	91	49	53.8	601	6.6	3	3	34	198	3	10	71.7	31+	7	0	0.0	0	0.0	0	0	0	0	0	0	39.6
Turf	3	51	22	43.1	351	6.9	1	4	13	213	4	7	40.6	Left Sideline	22	10	45.5	93	4.2	0	0	4	21	0	0	57.6
Indoor	2	39	18	46.2	253	6.5	0	4	10	131	3	5	28.0	Left Side	29	15	51.7	191	6.6	0	2	10	49	1	3	43.9
Outdoor	5	103	53	51.5	699	6.8	4	3	37	280	4	12	74.0	Middle	21	13	61.9	191	9.1	1	1	11	62	0	10	87.6
1st Half	-	89	40	44.9	601	6.8	2	3	24	272	7	9	61.1	Right Side	31	17	54.8	211	6.8	1	2	12	134	2	1	60.0
2nd Half/OT	-	53	31	58.5	351	6.6	2	4	23	139	0	8	59.6	Right Sideline	39	16	41.0	266	6.8	2	2	10	145	4	1	60.4
Last 2 Min. Half	-	19	11	57.9	116	6.1	1	4	5	32	1	4	53.7	2 Wide Receivers	40	18	45.0	275	6.9	1	2	15	82	4	2	55.7
4th qtr, +/-7 pts	-	23	14	60.9	173	7.5	1	3	12	72	0	4	59.1	3+ WR	100	53	53.0	677	6.8	3	5	32	329	3	15	63.6
Winning	-	26	10	38.5	139	5.3	0	0	6	104	2	6	56.4	Attempts 1-10	70	33	47.1	508	7.3	1	1	22	227	5	0	70.4
Tied	-	37	20	54.1	268	7.2	0	0	14	84	2	4	77.3	Attempts 11-20	49	26	53.1	292	6.0	2	4	15	121	2	0	50.7
Trailing	-	79	41	51.9	545	6.9	4	7	27	223	3	7	54.0	Attempts 21+	23	12	52.2	152	6.6	1	2	10	63	0	0	51.4

1995 Incompletions

Type	Num	% of Inc	% of Att
Pass Dropped	11	15.5	7.7
Poor Throw	25	35.2	17.6
Pass Defensed	12	16.9	8.5
Pass Hit at Line	4	5.6	2.8
Other	19	26.8	13.4
Total	71	100.0	50.0

Game Logs (1-8)

Date	Opp	Result	Att	Cm	Pct	Yds	TD	Int	Lg	Sk	F-L
09/03	Hou	L 3-10	17	7	41.2	54	0	0	13	1	0-0
09/10	@Cin	L 17-24	12	4	33.3	98	1	0	71	2	0-0
09/17	@NYA	L 10-27	-	-	-	-	-	-	-	-	-
09/24	GB	L 14-24	-	-	-	-	-	-	-	-	-
10/01	@Hou	W 17-16	18	8	44.4	117	0	1	38	3	1-1
10/08	Pit	W 20-16	-	-	-	-	-	-	-	-	-
10/15	Chi	L 27-30	-	-	-	-	-	-	-	-	-
10/22	@Cle	W 23-15	-	-	-	-	-	-	-	-	-

Game Logs (9-16)

Date	Opp	Result	Att	Cm	Pct	Yds	TD	Int	Lg	Sk	F-L
10/29	@Pit	L 7-24	-	-	-	-	-	-	-	-	-
11/12	Sea	L 30-47	-	-	-	-	-	-	-	-	-
11/19	@TB	L 16-17	12	9	75.0	104	1	1	22	2	0-0
11/26	Cin	L 13-17	34	18	52.9	245	1	1	37	4	1-0
12/03	@Den	L 23-31	28	15	53.6	198	1	1	25	3	1-1
12/10	Ind	L 31-41	-	-	-	-	-	-	-	-	-
12/17	@Det	L 0-44	21	10	47.6	136	0	3	27	2	0-0
12/24	Cle	W 24-21	-	-	-	-	-	-	-	-	-

Eric Bieniemy

1995 Receiving Splits

	G	Rec	Yds	Avg	TD	Lg	Big	YAC	Trgt	Y@C	1st	1st%		Rec	Yds	Avg	TD	Lg	Big	YAC	Trgt	Y@C	1st	1st%
Total	16	43	424	9.9	0	33	2	383	60	1.0	20	46.5	Inside 20	2	9	4.5	0	11	0	4	3	2.5	1	50.0
vs. Playoff	5	6	41	6.8	0	15	0	27	8	2.3	2	33.3	Inside 10	0	0	-	0	0	0	0	0	-	0	
vs. Non-playoff	11	37	383	10.4	0	33	2	356	52	0.7	18	48.6	1st Down	18	140	7.8	0	17	0	151	24	-0.6	5	27.8
vs. Own Division	8	26	284	10.9	0	33	2	247	34	1.4	13	50.0	2nd Down	14	185	13.2	0	33	1	153	18	2.3	10	71.4
Home	8	27	294	10.9	0	33	2	283	32	0.4	14	51.9	3rd Down Overall	11	99	9.0	0	32	1	79	18	1.8	5	45.5
Away	8	16	130	8.1	0	18	0	100	28	1.9	6	37.5	3rd D 0-2 to Go	1	32	32.0	0	32	1	28	2	4.0	1	100.0
Games 1-8	8	16	197	12.3	0	33	2	164	24	2.1	9	56.3	3rd D 3-7 to Go	5	27	5.4	0	9	0	12	6	3.0	3	60.0
Games 9-16	8	27	227	8.4	0	18	0	219	36	0.3	11	40.7	3rd D 8+ to Go	5	40	8.0	0	12	0	39	10	0.2	1	20.0
September	4	9	87	9.7	0	18	0	68	15	2.1	5	56.6	4th Down	0	-	-	0	0	0	0	0	-	0	
October	4	7	110	15.7	0	33	2	96	9	2.0	4	57.1	Rec Behind Line	16	140	8.8	0	18	0	194	25	-3.4	7	43.8
November	4	17	153	9.0	0	18	0	148	21	0.3	7	41.2	1-10 yds	26	266	10.2	0	33	2	182	33	3.2	12	46.2
December	4	10	74	7.4	0	14	0	71	15	0.3	4	40.0	11-20 yds	1	18	18.0	0	18	0	7	2	11.0	1	100.0
Grass	4	8	74	9.3	0	18	0	61	14	1.6	3	37.5	21-30 yds	0		-	0				0			
Turf	12	35	350	10.0	0	33	2	322	46	0.8	17	48.6	31+	0		-	0				0			
Indoor	3	8	56	7.0	0	12	0	39	14	2.1	3	37.5	Left Sideline	1	8	8.0	0	8	0	7	1	1.0	0	QB
Outdoor	13	35	368	10.5	0	33	2	344	46	0.7	17	48.6	Left Side	9	74	8.2	0	18	0	88	13	-1.6	4	44.4
1st Half	-	20	208	10.4	0	19	0	193	26	0.8	10	50.0	Middle	15	191	12.7	0	33	2	141	23	3.3	8	53.3
2nd Half/OT	-	23	216	9.4	0	33	2	190	34	1.1	10	43.5	Right Side	15	130	8.7	0	17	0	126	17	0.3	7	46.7
Last 2 Min. Half	-	16	152	9.5	0	18	0	148	23	0.3	7	43.8	Right Sideline	3	21	7.0	0	8	0	21	6	0.1	1	33.3
4th qtr, +/-7 pts	-	7	71	10.1	0	17	0	63	11	1.1	4	57.1	Shotgun	0		-	0				0			
Winning	-	8	82	10.3	0	17	0	80	8	0.3	5	62.5	2 Wide Receivers	28	288	10.3	0	33	2	275	38	0.5	12	42.9
Tied	-	15	121	8.1	0	19	0	97	19	1.6	6	40.0	3 Wide Receivers	15	136	9.1	0	18	0	108	22	1.9	8	53.0
Trailing	-	20	221	11.1	0	33	2	206	33	0.8	9	45.0	4+ Wide Receivers	0		-	0				0			

1995 Incompletions

Type	Num	%of Inc	%of Att
Pass Dropped	4	23.5	6.7
Poor Throw	6	35.3	10.0
Pass Defensed	1	5.9	1.7
Pass Hit at Line	2	11.8	3.3
Other	4	23.5	6.7
Total	17	100.0	28.3

Game Logs (1-8)

Date	Opp	Result	Rush	Yds	Rec	Yds	Trgt	F-L	TD
09/03	@Ind	W 24-21	0	0	0	0	0	0-0	0
09/10	Jac	W 24-17	14	65	7	79	7	0-0	0
09/17	@Sea	L 21-24	6	15	2	8	8	0-0	0
09/24	Hou	L 28-38	0	0	0	0	0	0-0	0
10/01	Mia	L 23-26	6	50	1	15	1	0-0	0
10/08	@TB	L 16-19	5	9	0	0	1	0-0	0
10/19	@Pit	W 27-9	10	27	0	0	0	0-0	0
10/29	Cle	L 26-29	4	19	6	95	7	0-0	0

Game Logs (9-16)

Date	Opp	Result	Rush	Yds	Rec	Yds	Trgt	F-L	TD
11/05	Oak	L 17-20	9	36	5	52	5	0-0	0
11/12	@Hou	L 32-25	19	55	6	48	6	0-0	1
11/19	Pit	L 31-49	1	-4	2	7	4	1-0	0
11/26	@Jac	W 17-13	2	7	4	46	6	0-0	0
12/03	@GB	L 10-24	3	1	3	19	3	0-0	0
12/10	Chi	W 16-10	6	26	3	25	3	0-0	0
12/17	@Cle	L 10-26	5	18	1	9	4	0-0	0
12/24	Min	W 27-24	8	57	3	21	5	0-0	0

J.J. Birden
Atlanta Falcons — WR

1995 Receiving Splits

	G	Rec	Yds	Avg	TD	Lg	Big	YAC	Trgt	Y@C	1st	1st%
Total	10	31	303	9.8	1	24	0	56	60	8.0	21	67.7
vs. Playoff	5	16	171	10.7	0	20	0	40	30	8.2	12	75.0
vs. Non-playoff	5	15	132	8.8	1	24	0	16	30	7.7	9	60.0
vs. Own Division	4	15	146	9.7	1	24	0	23	30	8.2	9	60.0
Home	6	20	183	9.2	1	19	0	44	46	7.0	14	70.0
Away	4	11	120	10.9	0	24	0	12	24	9.8	7	63.6
Games 1-8	7	21	203	9.7	1	24	0	25	45	8.5	14	66.7
Games 9-16	3	10	100	10.0	0	19	0	31	15	6.9	7	70.0
September	4	15	158	10.5	0	24	0	23	33	9.0	10	66.7
October	3	6	45	7.5	0	11	0	2	12	7.2	4	66.7
November	2	6	69	11.5	0	19	0	25	9	7.3	5	83.3
December	1	4	31	7.8	0	15	0	6	6	6.3	2	50.0
Grass	2	8	75	9.4	0	20	0	3	19	9.0	5	62.5
Turf	8	23	228	9.9	1	24	0	53	41	7.6	16	69.6
Outdoor	7	9	87	9.7	0	20	0	5	20	9.1	6	66.7
Indoor	3	22	216	9.8	1	24	0	51	40	7.5	15	68.2
1st Half	-	19	162	8.5	1	19	0	32	32	6.8	11	57.9
2nd Half/OT	-	12	141	11.8	0	24	0	24	28	9.8	10	83.3
Last 2 Min. Half	-	5	56	11.2	0	19	0	8	9	9.6	3	60.0
4th qtr, +/-7 pts	-	2	21	10.5	0	15	0	-1	5	11.0	2	100.0
Winning	-	10	125	12.5	0	24	0	25	19	10.0	9	90.0
Tied	-	7	50	7.1	0	12	0	6	14	6.3	3	42.9
Trailing	-	14	128	9.1	1	20	0	25	27	7.4	9	64.3

	Rec	Yds	Avg	TD	Lg	Big	YAC	Trgt	Y@C	1st	1st%
Inside 20	2	17	8.5	1	12	0	0	10	8.5	1	50.0
Inside 10	0	0	-	0	0	0	0	2	-	0	-
1st Down	14	136	9.7	1	15	0	38	24	7.0	8	57.1
2nd Down	8	50	6.3	0	17	0	1	13	6.1	4	50.0
3rd Down Overall	9	117	13.0	0	24	0	17	22	11.1	9	100.0
3rd D 0-2 to Go	2	18	9.0	0	10	0	6	3	6.0	2	100.0
3rd D 3-7 to Go	5	69	13.8	0	24	0	11	11	11.6	5	100.0
3rd D 8+ to Go	2	30	15.0	0	20	0	0	8	15.0	2	100.0
4th Down	0	0	-	0	0	0	0	1	-	0	-
Rec Behind Line	3	11	3.7	0	11	0	20	4	-3.0	1	33.3
1-10 yds	22	185	8.4	0	14	0	36	33	6.8	14	63.6
11-20 yds	4	63	15.8	1	19	0	-1	14	16.0	4	100.0
21-30 yds	2	44	22.0	0	24	0	1	6	21.5	2	100.0
31+	0	0	-	0	0	0	0	3	-	0	-
Left Sideline	13	124	9.5	0	24	0	14	31	8.5	8	61.5
Left Side	17	169	9.9	1	19	0	40	22	7.6	12	70.6
Middle	0	0	-	0	0	0	0	4	-	0	-
Right Side	1	10	10.0	0	10	0	2	3	8.0	1	100.0
Right Sideline	0	0	-	0	0	-50	0	-	-	0	-
Shotgun	10	106	10.6	0	20	0	18	21	8.8	8	80.0
2 Wide Receivers	3	27	9.0	0	12	0	6	5	7.0	2	66.7
3 Wide Receivers	4	42	10.5	0	19	0	16	7	6.5	3	75.0
4+ Wide Receivers	24	234	9.8	1	24	0	34	48	8.3	16	66.7

1995 Incompletions

Type	Num	%of Inc	%of Att
Pass Dropped	2	6.9	3.3
Poor Throw	14	48.3	23.3
Pass Defensed	7	24.1	11.7
Pass Hit at Line	0	0.0	0.0
Other	6	20.7	10.0
Total	29	100.0	48.3

Game Logs (1-8)

Date	Opp	Result	Rec	Yds	Trgt	F-L	TD
09/03	Car	W 23-20	4	22	8	0-0	0
09/10	@SF	L 10-41	5	60	12	0-0	0
09/17	@NO	W 27-24	2	33	4	0-0	0
09/24	NYA	W 13-3	4	43	9	0-0	0
10/01	NE	W 30-17	2	19	2	0-0	0
10/12	@StL	L 19-21	-	-	-	-	-
10/22	@TB	W 24-21	3	15	7	0-0	0
10/29	Dal	L 13-28	1	11	3	0-0	0

Game Logs (9-16)

Date	Opp	Result	Rec	Yds	Trgt	F-L	TD
11/05	Det	W 34-22	5	57	8	0-0	0
11/12	@Buf	L 17-23	1	12	1	0-0	0
11/19	StL	W 31-6	-	-	-	-	-
11/26	@Ari	L 37-40	-	-	-	-	-
12/03	@Mia	L 20-21	-	-	-	-	-
12/10	NO	W 19-14	-	-	-	-	-
12/17	@Car	L 17-21	-	-	-	-	-
12/24	SF	W 28-27	4	31	6	0-0	0

Brian Blades
Seattle Seahawks — WR

1995 Receiving Splits

	G	Rec	Yds	Avg	TD	Lg	Big	YAC	Trgt	Y@C	1st	1st%
Total	16	77	1001	13.0	4	49	6	362	132	8.3	49	63.6
vs. Playoff	6	20	279	14.0	2	41	1	98	44	9.1	13	65.0
vs. Non-playoff	10	57	722	12.7	2	49	5	264	88	8.0	36	63.2
vs. Own Division	8	33	461	14.0	2	49	2	152	62	9.4	23	69.7
Home	8	44	584	13.3	4	44	5	209	69	8.5	31	70.5
Away	8	33	417	12.6	0	49	1	153	63	8.0	18	54.5
Games 1-8	8	35	446	12.7	2	41	2	139	65	8.8	21	60.0
Games 9-16	8	42	555	13.2	2	49	4	223	67	7.9	28	66.7
September	3	17	209	12.3	1	29	1	44	31	9.7	12	70.6
October	5	18	237	13.2	1	41	1	95	34	7.9	9	50.0
November	4	23	294	12.8	2	44	3	110	35	8.0	15	65.2
December	4	19	261	13.7	0	49	1	113	32	7.8	13	68.4
Grass	7	30	384	12.8	0	49	1	135	57	8.3	17	56.7
Turf	9	47	616	13.1	4	44	5	227	75	8.3	32	68.1
Indoor	8	44	584	13.3	4	44	5	209	69	8.5	31	70.5
Outdoor	8	33	417	12.6	0	49	1	153	63	8.0	18	54.5
1st Half	-	34	502	14.8	3	49	6	195	49	9.0	21	61.8
2nd Half/OT	-	43	499	11.6	1	28	1	167	83	7.7	28	65.1
Last 2 Min. Half	-	11	153	13.9	0	29	1	36	19	10.6	7	63.6
4th qtr, +/-7 pts	-	9	80	8.9	0	18	0	15	22	7.2	5	55.6
Winning	-	23	268	11.7	1	44	1	107	38	7.0	15	65.2
Tied	-	20	261	13.1	2	41	3	79	28	9.1	11	55.0
Trailing	-	34	472	13.9	1	49	2	176	66	8.7	23	67.6

	Rec	Yds	Avg	TD	Lg	Big	YAC	Trgt	Y@C	1st	1st%
Inside 20	6	44	7.3	0	14	0	27	11	2.8	3	50.0
Inside 10	2	9	4.5	0	6	0	4	4	2.5	0	0.0
1st Down	27	333	12.3	0	28	1	77	48	9.5	14	51.9
2nd Down	22	223	10.1	0	29	1	50	42	7.9	13	59.1
3rd Down Overall	25	407	16.3	3	49	4	217	38	7.6	19	76.0
3rd D 0-2 to Go	1	6	6.0	0	6	0	1	1	5.0	1	100.0
3rd D 3-7 to Go	15	233	15.5	2	44	2	126	22	7.1	13	86.7
3rd D 8+ to Go	9	168	18.7	1	49	2	90	15	8.7	5	55.6
4th Down	3	38	12.7	0	21	0	18	4	6.7	3	100.0
Rec Behind Line	0	0	-	0	0	0	0	1	-	0	-
1-10 yds	58	605	10.4	3	44	2	285	80	5.5	31	53.4
11-20 yds	16	298	18.6	0	49	1	54	37	15.3	15	93.8
21-30 yds	3	98	32.7	1	41	3	23	12	25.0	3	100.0
31+	0	0	-	0	0	0	0	2	-	0	-
Left Sideline	13	210	16.2	1	41	2	31	21	13.8	9	69.2
Left Side	11	124	11.3	2	33	1	49	18	6.8	7	63.6
Middle	12	221	18.4	1	44	2	90	21	10.9	11	91.7
Right Side	26	271	10.4	0	23	0	128	44	5.5	16	61.5
Right Sideline	15	175	11.7	0	49	1	64	28	7.4	6	40.0
Shotgun	4	70	17.5	0	29	1	9	9	15.3	2	50.0
2 Wide Receivers	26	232	8.9	0	20	0	77	45	6.0	13	50.0
3 Wide Receivers	43	642	14.9	4	44	5	226	74	9.7	30	69.8
4+ Wide Receivers	8	127	15.9	0	19	1	39	13	8.5	6	75.0

1995 Incompletions

Type	Num	%of Inc	%of Att
Pass Dropped	5	9.1	3.8
Poor Throw	32	58.2	24.2
Pass Defensed	7	12.7	5.3
Pass Hit at Line	1	1.8	0.8
Other	10	18.2	7.6
Total	55	100.0	41.7

Game Logs (1-8)

Date	Opp	Result	Rush	Yds	Rec	Yds	Trgt	F-L	TD
09/03	KC	L 10-14	0	0	8	107	13	0-0	1
09/10	@SD	L 10-14	0	0	2	28	8	0-0	0
09/17	Cin	W 24-21	1	4	7	74	10	0-0	0
10/01	Den	W 27-10	0	0	4	32	7	0-0	0
10/08	@Oak	L 14-34	0	0	5	63	11	0-0	0
10/15	@Buf	L 21-27	0	0	3	32	6	0-0	0
10/22	SD	L 25-35	0	0	1	41	2	0-0	1
10/29	@Ari	L 14-20	0	0	5	69	8	0-0	0

Game Logs (9-16)

Date	Opp	Result	Rush	Yds	Rec	Yds	Trgt	F-L	TD
11/05	NYN	W 30-28	0	0	6	153	10	0-0	2
11/12	@Jac	W 47-30	0	0	5	43	9	0-0	0
11/19	@Was	W 27-20	0	0	6	55	7	0-0	0
11/26	NYA	L 10-16	0	0	6	43	9	0-0	0
12/03	Phi	W 26-14	0	0	6	71	11	0-0	0
12/10	@Den	W 31-27	0	0	7	127	10	0-0	0
12/17	Oak	W 44-10	0	0	6	63	10	0-0	0
12/24	@KC	L 3-26	1	0	0	4		0-0	0

Jeff Blake

1995 Passing Splits

	G	Att	Cm	Pct	Yds	Yd/Att	TD	Int	1st	YAC	Big	Sk	Rtg		Att	Cm	Pct	Yds	Yd/Att	TD	Int	1st	YAC	Big	Sk	Rtg
Total	16	567	326	57.5	3822	6.7	28	17	178	1789	27	24	82.1	Inside 20	78	34	43.6	221	2.8	18	2	23	61	0	1	79.8
vs. Playoff	5	152	93	61.2	1144	7.5	11	2	54	445	10	7	103.1	Inside 10	35	15	42.9	63	1.8	13	1	13	10	0	0	78.0
vs. Non-playoff	11	415	233	56.1	2678	6.5	17	15	124	1344	17	17	74.4	1st Down	214	128	59.8	1568	7.3	13	3	59	760	11	7	96.9
vs. Own Division	8	280	163	58.2	2031	7.3	16	7	94	1010	16	13	89.4	2nd Down	188	109	58.0	1195	6.4	9	7	60	546	7	10	77.3
Home	8	285	170	59.6	1913	6.7	17	6	95	927	11	17	90.9	3rd Down Overall	154	85	55.2	973	6.3	6	5	55	441	8	7	73.9
Away	8	282	156	55.3	1909	6.8	11	11	83	862	16	7	73.1	3rd D 0-5 to Go	57	32	56.1	377	6.6	3	2	27	215	5	1	72.0
Games 1-8	8	273	157	57.5	2073	7.6	17	6	90	903	17	11	93.2	3rd D 6+ to Go	97	53	54.6	596	6.1	3	2	28	226	3	6	74.9
Games 9-16	8	294	169	57.5	1749	5.9	11	11	88	886	10	13	71.7	4th Down	11	4	36.4	86	7.8	0	2	4	42	1	0	25.4
September	4	151	85	56.3	1138	7.5	8	1	47	486	9	5	95.3	Rec Behind Line	86	48	55.8	296	3.4	0	1	15	424	0	0	58.1
October	4	122	72	59.0	935	7.7	9	5	43	417	8	6	90.7	1-10 yds	335	215	64.2	1995	6.0	16	10	107	989	7	0	83.9
November	4	132	75	56.8	806	6.1	7	6	43	466	6	7	73.6	11-20 yds	90	48	53.3	931	10.3	4	2	41	278	8	0	95.2
December	4	162	94	58.0	943	5.8	4	5	45	420	4	6	70.1	21-30 yds	23	7	30.4	201	8.7	2	2	7	24	4	0	56.6
Grass	4	151	76	50.3	879	5.8	3	9	41	382	6	6	50.1	31+	33	8	24.2	399	12.1	6	2	8	74	8	0	91.8
Turf	12	416	250	60.1	2943	7.1	25	8	137	1407	21	18	93.7	Left Sideline	97	54	55.7	721	7.4	7	1	28	280	6	0	99.2
Indoor	3	109	62	56.9	755	6.9	5	2	31	364	7	1	86.0	Left Side	109	62	56.9	666	6.1	4	4	33	371	6	0	71.9
Outdoor	13	458	264	57.6	3067	6.7	23	15	147	1425	20	23	81.1	Middle	151	84	55.6	1087	7.2	9	6	49	448	9	22	81.7
1st Half	-	287	166	57.8	1877	6.5	10	8	89	900	10	11	77.5	Right Side	128	83	64.8	894	7.0	6	5	45	512	4	2	84.6
2nd Half/OT	-	280	160	57.1	1945	6.9	18	9	89	889	17	13	86.7	Right Sideline	82	43	52.4	454	5.5	2	1	23	178	2	0	71.9
Last 2 Min. Half	-	94	47	50.0	475	5.1	4	2	28	266	0	4	70.1	2 Wide Receivers	350	204	58.3	2472	7.1	17	14	108	1193	20	17	79.6
4th qtr, +/-7 pts	-	69	36	52.2	452	6.6	5	2	21	219	3	5	84.9	3+ WR	206	116	56.3	1316	6.4	7	3	65	586	7	7	80.9
Winning	-	113	77	68.1	920	8.1	8	2	41	434	9	4	109.0	Attempts 1-10	160	93	58.1	1132	7.1	6	5	49	563	8	0	79.5
Tied	-	157	89	56.7	852	5.4	4	5	44	422	2	4	67.2	Attempts 11-20	160	100	62.5	1074	6.7	6	4	57	485	5	0	84.2
Trailing	-	297	160	53.9	2050	6.9	16	10	93	933	16	16	79.7	Attempts 21+	247	133	53.8	1616	6.5	16	8	72	741	14	0	82.3

1995 Incompletions

Type	Num	% of Inc	% of Att
Pass Dropped	44	18.3	7.8
Poor Throw	107	44.4	18.9
Pass Defensed	32	13.3	5.6
Pass Hit at Line	18	7.5	3.2
Other	40	16.6	7.1
Total	241	100.0	42.5

Game Logs (1-8)

Date	Opp	Result	Att	Cm	Pct	Yds	TD	Int	Lg	Sk	F-L
09/03	@Ind	W 24-21	33	19	57.6	249	1	0	41	0	0-0
09/10	Jac	W 24-17	30	20	66.7	247	2	0	68	3	1-1
09/17	@Sea	L 21-24	42	22	52.4	286	2	1	88	1	1-0
09/24	Hou	L 28-38	46	24	52.2	356	3	0	56	1	1-0
10/01	Mia	L 23-26	34	18	52.9	201	3	0	44	1	0-0
10/08	@TB	L 16-19	31	16	51.6	210	1	3	37	1	2-2
10/19	@Pit	W 27-9	22	18	81.8	275	3	0	47	0	0-0
10/29	Cle	L 26-29	35	20	57.1	249	2	2	32	4	0-0

Game Logs (9-16)

Date	Opp	Result	Att	Cm	Pct	Yds	TD	Int	Lg	Sk	F-L
11/05	Oak	L 17-20	31	16	51.6	159	1	2	22	4	1-1
11/12	@Hou	W 32-25	34	21	61.8	220	2	1	30	0	0-0
11/19	Pit	L 31-49	28	19	67.9	217	3	0	26	3	2-1
11/26	@Jac	W 17-13	39	19	48.7	210	1	3	34	0	0-0
12/03	@GB	L 10-24	35	19	54.3	202	1	2	54	3	1-0
12/10	Chi	W 16-10	41	30	73.2	253	1	0	38	1	0-0
12/17	@Cle	L 10-26	46	22	47.8	257	0	1	47	2	1-0
12/24	Min	W 27-24	40	23	57.5	231	2	2	35	0	0-0

Drew Bledsoe

1995 Passing Splits

	G	Att	Cm	Pct	Yds	Yd/Att	TD	Int	1st	YAC	Big	Sk	Rtg		Att	Cm	Pct	Yds	Yd/Att	TD	Int	1st	YAC	Big	Sk	Rtg
Total	15	636	323	50.8	3507	5.5	13	16	192	1452	21	23	63.7	Inside 20	101	35	34.7	265	2.6	8	5	21	92	0	2	49.2
vs. Playoff	9	395	205	51.9	2181	5.5	12	13	126	867	11	18	64.8	Inside 10	42	14	33.3	74	1.8	7	4	7	18	0	1	42.4
vs. Non-playoff	6	241	118	49.0	1326	5.5	1	3	66	585	10	5	62.0	1st Down	232	117	50.4	1290	5.6	2	4	60	512	10	7	63.0
vs. Own Division	8	300	144	48.0	1718	5.7	8	9	90	693	11	10	62.3	2nd Down	200	106	53.0	1142	5.7	4	5	61	516	6	7	66.3
Home	8	344	173	50.3	1862	5.4	2	5	99	820	10	11	62.4	3rd Down Overall	188	94	50.0	1020	5.4	7	6	67	408	5	8	65.5
Away	7	292	150	51.4	1645	5.6	11	11	93	632	11	12	65.2	3rd D 0-5 to Go	63	35	55.5	384	6.1	5	1	30	200	2	2	93.6
Games 1-8	7	336	170	50.6	1785	5.3	3	6	104	789	9	10	61.9	3rd D 6+ to Go	125	59	47.2	636	5.1	2	5	37	208	3	6	51.3
Games 9-16	8	300	153	51.0	1722	5.7	10	10	88	663	12	13	65.7	4th Down	16	6	37.5	55	3.4	0	1	4	16	0	1	21.6
September	3	149	76	51.0	810	5.4	0	5	48	286	6	5	53.3	Rec Behind Line	83	30	36.1	140	1.7	0	2	9	247	0	0	34.7
October	4	187	94	50.3	975	5.2	3	1	56	503	3	5	68.8	1-10 yds	342	223	65.2	2017	5.9	9	5	116	939	3	0	83.7
November	4	136	68	50.0	825	6.1	5	3	44	330	5	7	72.1	11-20 yds	147	57	38.8	931	6.3	0	5	54	194	6	0	46.6
December	4	164	85	51.8	897	5.5	5	7	44	333	7	6	60.4	21-30 yds	45	12	26.7	372	8.3	3	2	12	61	11	0	65.2
Grass	11	467	233	49.9	2549	5.5	6	9	141	1065	16	19	62.7	31+	19	1	5.3	47	2.5	1	1	1	1	1	0	17.5
Turf	4	169	90	53.3	958	5.7	7	7	51	387	5	4	66.6	Left Sideline	100	39	39.0	503	5.0	0	3	24	224	5	0	43.0
Indoor	1	37	17	45.9	186	5.0	1	3	8	65	2	1	36.5	Left Side	121	67	55.4	672	5.6	3	2	41	257	3	2	72.7
Outdoor	14	599	306	51.1	3321	5.5	12	13	184	1387	19	22	65.4	Middle	130	66	50.8	768	5.9	6	7	42	266	4	21	62.0
1st Half	-	309	154	49.8	1775	5.7	4	6	93	790	15	11	63.0	Right Side	152	91	59.9	885	5.8	3	2	56	381	2	0	77.3
2nd Half/OT	-	327	172	52.6	1732	5.3	9	10	99	662	6	12	64.4	Right Sideline	133	60	45.1	679	5.1	1	2	29	324	7	0	57.2
Last 2 Min. Half	-	98	46	46.9	490	5.0	2	5	26	158	3	3	47.6	2 Wide Receivers	342	178	52.0	2052	6.0	7	6	110	899	11	14	70.0
4th qtr, +/-7 pts	-	67	33	49.3	332	5.0	1	3	17	139	1	2	50.1	3+ WR	270	138	51.1	1378	5.1	5	9	77	521	10	9	58.2
Winning	-	80	38	47.5	445	5.6	1	1	26	209	3	0	63.8	Attempts 1-10	150	67	44.7	785	5.2	1	3	44	328	6	0	55.0
Tied	-	169	79	46.7	921	5.4	4	2	47	415	8	4	66.7	Attempts 11-20	150	82	54.7	971	0.5	4	0	50	476	0	0	76.2
Trailing	-	387	206	53.2	2141	5.5	8	13	119	828	10	19	62.4	Attempts 21+	336	174	51.8	1751	5.5	8	13	98	648	6	0	62.5

1995 Incompletions

Type	Num	% of Inc	% of Att
Pass Dropped	39	12.5	6.1
Poor Throw	136	43.5	21.4
Pass Defensed	50	16.0	7.9
Pass Hit at Line	31	9.9	4.9
Other	57	18.2	9.0
Total	313	100.0	49.2

Game Logs (1-8)

Date	Opp	Result	Att	Cm	Pct	Yds	TD	Int	Lg	Sk	F-L
09/03	Cle	W 17-14	47	30	63.8	302	0	0	32	0	0-0
09/10	Mia	L 3-20	51	25	49.0	267	0	2	33	1	1-1
09/17	@SF	L 3-28	51	21	41.2	241	0	3	31	4	1-1
10/01	@Atl	L 17-30									
10/08	Den	L 3-37	56	24	42.9	248	0	0	33	2	2-1
10/15	@KC	L 26-31	47	25	53.2	237	2	1	22	3	1-1
10/23	Buf	W 27-14	40	23	57.5	262	1	0	35	0	0-0
10/29	Car	L 17-20	44	22	50.0	228	0	0	21	0	0-0

Game Logs (9-16)

Date	Opp	Result	Att	Cm	Pct	Yds	TD	Int	Lg	Sk	F-L
11/05	@NYA	W 20-7	27	13	48.1	173	0	0	35	0	0-0
11/12	@Mia	W 34-17	25	14	56.0	209	2	0	47	1	0-0
11/19		L 10-24	39	20	51.3	180	0	0	19	5	0-0
11/26	@Buf	W 35-25	45	21	46.7	263	3	3	22	1	0-0
12/03	NO	L 17-31	31	18	58.1	197	0	2	27	2	2-0
12/10	NYA	W 31-28	34	16	47.1	178	1	1	43	1	2-1
12/16	@Pit	L 27-41	60	39	65.0	336	1	3	31	1	1-0
12/23	@Ind	L 7-10	37	17	45.9	186	1	3	31	1	1-0

Steve Bono

1995 Passing Splits

	G	Att	Cm	Pct	Yds	Yd/Att	TD	Int	1st	YAC	Big	Sk	Rtg		Att	Cm	Pct	Yds	Yd/Att	TD	Int	1st	YAC	Big	Sk	Rtg
Total	16	520	293	56.3	3121	6.0	21	10	161	1349	20	21	79.5	Inside 20	64	38	59.4	297	4.6	16	2	25	88	0	5	97.5
vs. Playoff	4	141	79	56.0	922	6.5	4	2	49	361	9	5	79.6	Inside 10	26	15	57.7	52	2.0	9	2	10	9	0	1	70.2
vs. Non-playoff	12	379	214	56.5	2199	5.8	17	8	112	988	11	16	79.5	1st Down	176	94	53.4	992	5.6	4	3	42	393	6	6	70.5
vs. Own Division	8	227	143	63.0	1600	7.0	10	3	79	656	12	12	93.1	2nd Down	175	109	62.3	1109	6.3	11	4	61	554	7	5	91.8
Home	8	289	163	56.4	1649	5.7	11	4	90	733	9	12	79.8	3rd Down Overall	159	82	51.6	946	5.9	6	3	51	357	7	9	74.6
Away	8	231	130	56.3	1472	6.4	10	6	71	616	11	9	79.1	3rd D 0-5 to Go	56	32	57.1	287	5.1	4	1	27	125	1	2	87.4
Games 1-8	8	273	160	58.6	1677	6.1	15	4	80	810	12	10	88.7	3rd D 6+ to Go	103	50	48.5	659	6.4	2	2	24	232	6	7	67.6
Games 9-16	8	247	133	53.8	1444	5.8	6	6	81	539	8	11	69.3	4th Down	10	8	80.0	74	7.4	0	0	7	45	0	1	97.5
September	4	147	95	64.6	897	6.1	8	3	42	475	5	5	91.0	Rec Behind Line	111	75	67.6	392	3.5	1	1	23	565	0	0	72.4
October	4	126	65	51.6	780	6.2	7	1	38	335	7	5	86.1	1-10 yds	239	144	60.3	1148	4.8	9	5	67	524	1	0	76.1
November	4	130	71	54.6	736	5.7	3	3	41	317	3	7	69.3	11-20 yds	105	58	55.2	1040	9.9	8	1	55	169	5	0	110.8
December	4	117	62	53.0	708	6.1	3	3	40	222	5	4	69.3	21-30 yds	33	9	27.3	248	7.5	1	0	9	24	8	0	68.5
Grass	14	461	255	55.3	2567	5.6	17	10	135	1105	14	20	74.6	31+	30	6	20.0	269	9.0	2	3	6	67	6	0	47.1
Turf	2	59	38	64.4	554	9.4	4	0	26	244	6	1	117.5	Left Sideline	67	38	56.7	520	7.8	2	3	22	133	5	0	73.0
Indoor	1	23	18	78.3	278	12.1	3	0	11	115	3	0	156.6	Left Side	96	54	56.3	529	5.5	2	4	29	302	2	2	61.5
Outdoor	15	497	275	55.3	2843	5.7	18	10	150	1234	17	21	75.7	Middle	68	42	61.8	479	7.0	3	0	26	178	3	16	97.6
1st Half	-	254	137	53.9	1519	6.0	12	6	81	670	12	11	77.9	Right Side	155	94	60.6	966	6.2	10	2	50	525	5	2	94.7
2nd Half/OT	-	266	156	58.6	1602	6.0	9	4	80	679	8	10	81.1	Right Sideline	132	64	48.5	603	4.6	4	1	33	211	5	1	68.5
Last 2 Min. Half	-	85	49	57.6	531	6.2	3	2	30	191	4	4	78.1	2 Wide Receivers	246	132	53.7	1473	6.0	10	7	70	627	9	8	73.4
4th qtr, +/-7 pts	-	67	34	50.7	290	4.3	2	0	17	137	1	1	72.3	3+ WR	264	156	59.1	1603	6.1	9	3	87	720	11	13	83.3
Winning	-	219	118	53.9	1299	5.9	8	4	70	453	6	12	76.3	Attempts 1-10	160	78	48.8	761	4.8	5	4	45	392	4	0	62.5
Tied	-	90	52	57.8	507	5.6	4	3	27	285	2	4	74.6	Attempts 11-20	151	92	60.9	1133	7.5	9	2	55	394	10	0	98.5
Trailing	-	211	123	58.3	1315	6.2	9	3	64	611	12	5	84.9	Attempts 21+	209	123	58.9	1227	5.9	7	4	61	563	6	0	78.8

1995 Incompletions

Type	Num	% of Inc	% of Att
Pass Dropped	33	14.5	6.3
Poor Throw	108	47.6	20.8
Pass Defensed	43	18.9	8.3
Pass Hit at Line	8	3.5	1.5
Other	35	15.4	6.7
Total	227	100.0	43.7

Game Logs (1-8)

Date	Opp	Result	Att	Cm	Pct	Yds	TD	Int	Lg	Sk	F-L
09/03	@Sea	W 34-10	23	18	78.3	278	3	0	60	0	0-0
09/10	NYN	W 20-17	47	29	61.7	183	1	1	14	1	2-1
09/17	Oak	W 23-17	28	19	67.9	164	2	0	28	3	1-0
09/24	@Cle	L 17-35	49	29	59.2	272	2	2	38	1	0-0
10/01	@Ari	W 24-3	17	7	41.2	78	2	1	22	1	1-1
10/09	SD	W 29-23	41	25	65.9	329	2	0	38	1	1-1
10/15	NE	W 31-26	40	16	40.0	209	2	0	34	2	0-0
10/22	@Den	W 21-7	28	15	53.6	164	1	0	57	1	0-0

Game Logs (9-16)

Date	Opp	Result	Att	Cm	Pct	Yds	TD	Int	Lg	Sk	F-L
11/05	Was	W 24-3	37	21	56.8	201	1	1	19	2	1-1
11/12	@SD	W 22-7	27	17	63.0	137	0	1	19	3	0-0
11/19	Hou	W 20-13	30	13	43.3	122	1	1	19	1	1-1
11/23	@Dal	L 12-24	36	20	55.6	276	1	0	45	1	1-1
12/03	@Oak	W 29-23	14	9	64.3	87	0	1	26	2	1-0
12/11	@Mia	L 6-13	15	11	73.3	180	1	1	34	0	0-0
12/17	Den	W 20-17	37	23	62.2	232	1	0	23	1	1-1
12/24	Sea	W 26-3	29	15	51.7	209	1	1	27	1	0-0

Kyle Brady

1995 Receiving Splits

	G	Rec	Yds	Avg	TD	Lg	Big	YAC	Trgt	Y@C	1st	1st%		Rec	Yds	Avg	TD	Lg	Big	YAC	Trgt	Y@C	1st	1st%
Total	15	26	252	9.7	2	29	1	77	53	6.7	17	65.4	Inside 20	2	13	6.5	1	10	0	4	6	4.5	2	100.0
vs. Playoff	7	13	113	8.7	0	17	0	29	26	6.5	7	53.8	Inside 10	1	3	3.0	1	3	0	0	3	3.0	1	100.0
vs. Non-playoff	8	13	139	10.7	2	29	1	48	27	7.0	10	76.9	1st Down	13	133	10.2	2	20	0	39	22	7.2	9	69.2
vs. Own Division	8	13	113	8.7	0	17	0	35	28	6.0	6	46.2	2nd Down	6	46	7.7	0	17	0	9	18	6.2	3	50.0
Home	8	15	156	10.4	2	29	1	40	31	7.7	10	66.7	3rd Down Overall	6	70	11.7	0	29	1	29	11	6.8	4	66.7
Away	7	11	96	8.7	0	17	0	37	22	5.4	7	63.6	3rd D 0-2 to Go	0	0	-	0	0	0	0	0	-	0	-
Games 1-8	8	19	196	10.3	2	29	1	40	38	8.2	14	73.7	3rd D 3-7 to Go	3	29	9.7	0	15	0	16	6	4.3	3	100.0
Games 9-16	7	7	56	8.0	0	14	0	37	15	2.7	3	42.9	3rd D 8+ to Go	3	41	13.7	0	29	1	13	5	9.3	1	33.3
September	4	14	145	10.4	1	20	0	29	25	8.3	11	78.6	4th Down	1	3	3.0	0	3	0	0	2	3.0	1	100.0
October	5	6	56	9.3	1	29	1	18	15	6.3	3	50.0	Rec Behind Line	1	5	5.0	0	5	0	7	5	-2.0	0	0.0
November	3	6	51	8.5	0	14	0	30	12	3.5	3	50.0	1-10 yds	19	137	7.2	1	15	0	54	33	4.4	11	57.9
December	3	0	0	-	0	0	0	0	1	-	0	-	11-20 yds	6	110	18.3	1	29	1	16	14	15.7	6	100.0
Grass	3	3	39	13.0	0	17	0	6	8	11.0	3	100.0	21-30 yds	0	0	-	0	0	0	1	0	-	0	-
Turf	12	23	213	9.3	2	29	1	71	45	6.2	14	60.9	31+	0	0	-	0	0	0	0	1	-	0	-
Outdoor	3	20	201	10.1	2	29	1	47	43	7.7	13	65.0	Left Sideline	1	3	3.0	1	3	0	0	2	3.0	1	100.0
Indoor	12	6	51	8.5	0	15	0	30	10	3.5	4	66.7	Left Side	11	127	11.5	0	29	1	28	16	9.0	7	63.6
1st Half	-	12	129	10.8	0	29	1	32	27	8.1	8	66.7	Middle	4	48	12.0	0	16	0	14	11	8.5	3	75.0
2nd Half/OT	-	14	123	8.8	2	20	0	45	26	5.6	9	64.3	Right Side	6	35	5.8	0	9	0	21	18	2.3	3	50.0
Last 2 Min. Half	-	3	23	7.7	0	9	0	10	6	4.3	2	66.7	Right Sideline	4	39	9.8	1	20	0	14	6	6.3	3	75.0
4th qtr, +/-7 pts	-	2	14	7.0	0	9	0	9	2	2.5	0	0.0	Shotgun	0	0	-	0	0	0	0	0	-	0	-
Winning	-	7	72	10.3	1	20	0	19	11	7.6	6	85.7	2 Wide Receivers	19	172	9.1	0	29	1	63	43	5.7	10	52.6
Tied	-	6	54	9.0	0	16	0	12	11	7.0	3	50.0	3 Wide Receivers	5	74	14.8	1	20	0	14	7	12.0	5	100.0
Trailing	-	13	126	9.7	1	29	1	46	31	6.2	8	61.5	4+ Wide Receivers	0	0	-	0	0	0	0	0	-	0	-

1995 Incompletions

Type	Num	%of Inc	%of Att
Pass Dropped	8	29.6	15.1
Poor Throw	9	33.3	17.0
Pass Defensed	3	11.1	5.7
Pass Hit at Line	2	7.4	3.8
Other	5	18.5	9.4
Total	27	100.0	50.9

Game Logs (1-8)

Date	Opp	Result	Rec	Yds	Trgt	F-L	TD
09/03	@Mia	L 14-52	3	39	7	0-0	0
09/10	Ind	L 24-27	4	37	7	0-0	0
09/17	Jac	W 27-10	5	48	7	0-0	0
09/24	@Atl	L 3-13	2	21	4	0-0	0
10/01	Oak	L 10-47	3	45	8	0-0	0
10/08	@Buf	L 10-29	2	6	4	0-0	0
10/15	@Car	L 15-26	0	0	1	0-0	0
10/22	Mia	W 17-16	0	0	0	0-0	0

Game Logs (9-16)

Date	Opp	Result	Rec	Yds	Trgt	F-L	TD
10/29	@Ind	L 10-17	1	5	2	0-0	0
11/05	NE	L 7-20	2	21	6	0-0	0
11/26	@Sea	W 16-10	3	25	4	0-0	0
12/03	StL	L 20-23	0	0	1	0-0	0
12/10	@NE	L 28-31	0	0	0	0-0	0
12/17	@Hou	L 6-23	-	-	-	-	-
12/24	NO	L 0-12	0	0	0	0-0	0

Vincent Brisby
New England Patriots — WR

1995 Receiving Splits

	G	Rec	Yds	Avg	TD	Lg	Big	YAC	Trgt	Y@C	1st	1st%		Rec	Yds	Avg	TD	Lg	Big	YAC	Trgt	Y@C	1st	1st%
Total	16	66	974	14.8	3	72	7	251	159	11.0	54	81.8	Inside 20	4	31	7.8	1	14	0	5	23	6.5	2	50.0
vs. Playoff	10	48	720	15.0	3	72	4	189	102	11.1	41	85.4	Inside 10	2	12	6.0	1	7	0	0	9	6.0	1	50.0
vs. Non-playoff	6	18	254	14.1	0	43	3	62	57	10.7	13	72.2	1st Down	19	307	16.2	0	43	3	71	52	12.4	16	84.2
vs. Own Division	8	31	509	16.4	2	47	5	125	76	12.4	28	90.3	2nd Down	21	290	13.8	1	47	2	71	50	10.4	17	81.0
Home	8	27	323	12.0	1	43	1	79	81	9.0	20	74.1	3rd Down Overall	23	335	14.6	2	72	2	101	52	10.2	18	78.3
Away	8	39	651	16.7	2	72	6	172	78	12.3	34	87.2	3rd D 0-2 to Go	0	-	-	0	0	0	0	0	-	-	-
Games 1-8	8	39	502	12.9	2	72	1	143	91	9.2	31	79.5	3rd D 3-7 to Go	14	240	17.1	2	72	2	86	25	11.0	13	92.9
Games 9-16	8	27	472	17.5	1	47	6	108	68	13.5	23	85.2	3rd D 8+ to Go	9	95	10.6	0	17	0	15	27	8.9	5	55.6
September	3	16	172	10.8	0	20	0	31	38	8.8	13	81.3	4th Down	3	42	14.0	0	16	0	8	5	11.3	3	100.0
October	5	23	330	14.3	2	72	1	112	53	9.5	18	78.3	Rec Behind Line	2	-1	-0.5	0	0	0	3	4	-2.0	0	0.0
November	4	16	300	18.8	1	47	4	69	33	14.4	15	93.8	1-10 yds	31	369	11.9	1	72	1	140	54	7.4	21	67.7
December	4	11	172	15.6	0	43	2	39	35	12.1	8	72.7	11-20 yds	28	431	15.4	0	26	2	70	72	12.9	28	100.0
Grass	11	40	526	13.2	3	47	3	104	110	10.6	32	80.0	21-30 yds	4	128	32.0	1	43	3	27	16	25.3	4	100.0
Turf	5	26	448	17.2	0	72	4	147	49	11.6	22	84.6	31+	1	47	47.0	1	47	1	11	13	36.0	1	100.0
Outdoor	2	56	800	14.3	3	47	6	168	136	11.3	46	82.1	Left Sideline	23	308	13.4	0	43	2	55	70	11.0	19	82.6
Indoor	14	10	174	17.4	0	72	1	83	23	9.1	8	80.0	Left Side	19	249	13.1	1	25	1	37	41	11.2	16	84.2
1st Half	-	29	442	15.2	1	72	4	144	71	10.3	21	72.4	Middle	3	81	27.0	1	47	1	25	9	18.7	3	100.0
2nd Half/OT	-	37	532	14.4	2	47	3	107	88	11.5	33	89.2	Right Side	16	260	16.3	1	72	2	118	25	8.9	13	81.3
Last 2 Min. Half	-	13	153	11.8	0	16	0	29	35	9.5	10	76.9	Right Sideline	5	76	15.2	0	28	1	16	14	12.0	3	60.0
4th qtr, +/-7 pts	-	7	109	15.6	0	20	0	30	22	11.3	7	100.0	Shotgun	0	-	-	0	0	0	0	0	-	-	-
Winning	-	10	151	15.1	1	35	2	28	21	12.3	9	90.0	2 Wide Receivers	38	583	15.3	2	47	5	136	93	11.8	33	86.8
Tied	-	20	291	14.6	1	47	3	69	44	11.1	15	75.0	3 Wide Receivers	26	370	14.2	1	72	2	114	60	9.8	19	73.1
Trailing	-	36	532	14.8	2	72	2	154	94	11.5	30	83.3	4+ Wide Receivers	1	9	9.0	0	9	0	4	7	4.0	1	100.0

1995 Incompletions

Type	Num	%of Inc	%of Att
Pass Dropped	12	12.9	7.5
Poor Throw	55	59.1	34.6
Pass Defensed	9	9.7	5.7
Pass Hit at Line	4	4.3	2.5
Other	13	14.0	8.2
Total	93	100.0	58.5

Game Logs (1-8)

Date	Opp	Result	Rec	Yds	Trgt	F-L	TD
09/03	Cle	W 17-14	7	58	15	0-0	0
09/10	Mia	L 3-20	5	77	12	0-0	0
09/17	@SF	L 3-28	4	37	11	0-0	0
10/01	@Atl	L 17-30	9	161	14	0-0	0
10/08	Den	L 3-37	0	0	11	0-0	0
10/15	@KC	L 26-31	3	48	8	0-0	1
10/23	Buf	W 27-14	6	59	10	0-0	0
10/29	Car	L 17-20	5	62	10	0-0	0

Game Logs (9-16)

Date	Opp	Result	Rec	Yds	Trgt	F-L	TD
11/05	@NYA	W 20-7	3	74	5	0-0	0
11/12	@Mia	W 34-17	6	118	10	0-0	1
11/19	Ind	L 10-24	1	7	7	0-0	0
11/26	@Buf	L 35-25	6	101	11	0-0	0
12/03	NO	L 17-31	0	0	4	0-0	0
12/10	NYA	W 31-28	3	60	12	0-0	0
12/16	@Pit	L 27-41	7	99	10	0-0	0
12/23	@Ind	L 7-10	1	13	9	0-0	0

Bubby Brister
New York Jets — QB

1995 Passing Splits

	G	Att	Cm	Pct	Yds	Yd/Att	TD	Int	1st	YAC	Big	Sk	Rtg		Att	Cm	Pct	Yds	Yd/Att	TD	Int	1st	YAC	Big	Sk	Rtg
Total	9	170	93	54.7	726	4.3	4	8	35	396	2	16	53.7	Inside 20	18	10	55.6	71	3.9	4	1	5	24	0	1	81.3
vs. Playoff	5	88	52	59.1	455	5.2	4	4	25	214	1	9	69.1	Inside 10	7	3	42.9	7	1.0	1	1	1	1	0	0	50.3
vs. Non-playoff	4	82	41	50.0	271	3.3	0	4	10	182	1	7	37.2	1st Down	65	36	55.4	263	4.0	1	4	10	182	0	9	44.6
vs. Own Division	6	96	55	57.3	473	4.9	4	4	26	234	1	10	66.9	2nd Down	52	26	50.0	238	4.6	1	4	12	106	1	4	37.2
Home	5	67	39	58.2	280	4.2	2	2	13	165	0	7	65.5	3rd Down Overall	43	24	55.8	200	4.7	2	0	9	83	1	3	83.5
Away	4	103	54	52.4	446	4.3	2	6	22	231	2	9	46.0	3rd D 0-5 to Go	13	10	76.9	58	4.5	1	0	6	25	0	0	110.4
Games 1-8	6	102	51	50.0	444	4.4	3	6	22	222	2	10	47.2	3rd D 6+ to Go	30	14	46.7	142	4.7	1	0	3	58	1	3	71.8
Games 9-16	3	68	42	61.8	282	4.1	1	2	13	174	0	6	63.5	4th Down	10	7	70.0	25	2.5	0	0	4	25	0	0	72.9
September	2	8	5	62.5	37	4.6	0	1	3	29	0	1	33.9	Rec Behind Line	29	22	75.9	91	3.1	0	3	5	165	0	0	38.8
October	5	125	65	52.0	561	4.5	4	6	27	267	2	11	54.8	1-10 yds	102	63	61.8	486	4.8	2	3	22	196	0	0	67.7
November	1	8	3	37.5	18	2.3	0	1	1	20	0	1	45.8	11-20 yds	25	7	28.0	119	4.8	1	1	7	30	1	0	56.9
December	1	29	20	69.0	110	3.8	0	0	4	80	0	3	61.0	21-30 yds	9	1	11.1	30	3.3	0	1	1	5	1	0	41.0
Grass	2	49	22	44.9	180	3.7	0	4	8	105	1	4	20.8	31+	5	0	0.0	0	0.0	0	1	0	0	0	0	0.0
Turf	7	121	71	58.7	546	4.5	4	4	27	291	1	12	67.0	Left Sideline	32	14	43.8	117	3.7	1	2	5	46	1	0	38.2
Indoor	1	31	19	61.3	154	5.0	1	1	8	74	0	2	71.2	Left Side	25	13	52.0	80	3.2	0	3	5	62	0	0	19.2
Outdoor	8	139	74	53.2	572	4.1	3	7	27	322	2	14	49.8	Middle	33	20	60.6	172	5.2	1	1	11	91	0	15	71.8
1st Half	-	62	32	51.6	246	4.0	0	3	8	142	1	4	41.5	Right Side	41	28	68.3	224	5.5	0	1	9	128	1	0	71.8
2nd Half/OT	-	108	61	56.5	480	4.4	4	5	27	254	1	12	60.7	Right Sideline	39	18	46.2	133	3.4	2	1	5	69	0	1	61.2
Last 2 Min. Half	-	25	13	52.0	93	3.7	0	5	5	46	0	1	21.3	2 Wide Receivers	146	81	55.5	664	4.5	2	6	30	350	2	14	54.7
4th qtr, +/-7 pts	-	22	11	50.0	84	3.8	1	1	6	47	0	0	55.9	3+ WR	18	6	33.3	33	1.8	0	2	2	30	0	2	2.8
Winning	-	11	4	36.4	45	4.1	0	2	2	10	0	0	9.8	Attempts 1-10	70	40	57.1	278	4.0	0	2	12	177	1	0	54.3
Tied	-	14	10	71.4	70	5.0	0	0	3	24	0	0	82.4	Attempts 11-20	50	31	62.0	273	5.5	2	2	11	140	1	0	70.2
Trailing	-	145	79	54.5	611	4.2	4	6	30	362	2	16	57.0	Attempts 21+	50	22	44.0	175	3.5	2	4	12	76	0	0	33.3

1995 Incompletions

Type	Num	% of Inc	% of Att
Pass Dropped	16	20.8	9.4
Poor Throw	32	41.6	18.8
Pass Defensed	16	20.8	9.4
Pass Hit at Line	2	2.6	1.2
Other	11	14.3	6.5
Total	77	100.0	45.3

Game Logs (1-8)

Date	Opp	Result	Att	Cm	Pct	Yds	TD	Int	Lg	Sk	F-L
09/03	@Mia	L 14-52	8	5	62.5	37	0	1	12	1	0-0
09/10	Ind	L 24-27	0	0	-	0	0	0	0	0	0-0
09/17	Jac	W 27-10	-	-	-	-	-	-	-	-	-
09/24	@Atl	L 3-13	-	-	-	-	-	-	-	-	-
10/01	Oak	L 10-47	4	1	25.0	0	0	0	0	0	0-0
10/08	@Buf	L 10-29	23	13	56.5	112	1	1	30	3	1-1
10/15	@Car	L 15-26	41	17	41.5	143	0	3	32	3	1-0
10/22	Mia	W 17-16	26	15	57.7	152	2	1	18	2	0-1

Game Logs (9-16)

Date	Opp	Result	Att	Cm	Pct	Yds	TD	Int	Lg	Sk	F-L
10/29	@Ind	L 10-17	31	19	61.3	154	1	1	20	2	0-0
11/05	NE	L 7-20	8	3	37.5	18	0	0	11	1	0-0
11/19	Buf	L 26-28	-	-	-	-	-	-	-	-	-
11/26	@Sea	W 16-10	-	-	-	-	-	-	-	-	-
12/03	StL	L 20-23	-	-	-	-	-	-	-	-	-
12/10	@NE	L 28-31	-	-	-	-	-	-	-	-	-
12/17	@Hou	L 6-23	-	-	-	-	-	-	-	-	-
12/24	NO	L 0-12	29	20	69.0	110	0	1	16	3	0-0

Bill Brooks
Buffalo Bills — WR

1995 Receiving Splits

	G	Rec	Yds	Avg	TD	Lg	Big	YAC	Trgt	Y@C	1st	1st%		Rec	Yds	Avg	TD	Lg	Big	YAC	Trgt	Y@C	1st	1st%
Total	15	53	763	14.4	11	51	8	156	88	11.5	32	60.4	Inside 20	4	56	14.0	3	18	0	5	9	12.8	4	100.0
vs. Playoff	6	24	294	12.3	3	51	3	65	39	9.5	13	54.2	Inside 10	0	0	-	0	0	0	0	4	-	0	-
vs. Non-playoff	9	29	469	16.2	8	45	5	91	49	13.0	19	65.5	1st Down	26	366	14.1	5	45	4	65	38	11.6	14	53.8
vs. Own Division	8	26	410	15.8	6	51	5	104	43	11.8	16	61.5	2nd Down	16	216	13.5	2	51	1	58	24	9.9	10	62.5
Home	7	22	347	15.8	6	32	5	51	36	13.5	16	72.7	3rd Down Overall	10	165	16.5	4	45	3	33	25	13.2	8	80.0
Away	8	31	416	13.4	5	51	3	105	52	10.0	16	51.6	3rd D 0-2 to Go	1	8	8.0	0	8	0	1	2	7.0	1	100.0
Games 1-8	8	15	231	15.4	4	45	3	48	28	12.2	9	60.0	3rd D 3-7 to Go	4	22	5.5	0	10	0	-1	8	5.8	2	50.0
Games 9-16	7	38	532	14.0	7	51	5	108	60	11.2	23	60.5	3rd D 8+ to Go	5	135	27.0	4	45	3	33	15	20.4	5	100.0
September	3	2	23	11.5	0	16	0	1	7	11.0	0	0.0	4th Down	1	16	16.0	0	16	0	0	1	16.0	0	0.0
October	5	13	208	16.0	4	45	3	47	21	12.4	9	69.2	Rec Behind Line	0	0	-	0	0	0	0	5	-	0	-
November	4	23	378	16.4	6	51	4	92	36	12.4	17	73.9	1-10 yds	29	205	7.1	0	16	0	51	44	5.3	9	31.0
December	3	15	154	10.3	1	25	1	16	24	9.2	6	40.0	11-20 yds	17	322	18.9	5	45	2	52	26	15.9	16	94.1
Grass	5	13	146	11.2	1	45	1	37	27	8.4	5	38.5	21-30 yds	7	236	33.7	6	51	6	53	12	26.1	7	100.0
Turf	10	40	617	15.4	10	51	7	119	61	12.5	27	67.5	31+	0	0	-	0	0	0	0	0	-	0	-
Indoor	2	11	163	14.8	2	51	1	43	13	10.9	6	54.5	Left Sideline	12	228	19.0	4	51	4	62	22	13.8	9	75.0
Outdoor	13	42	600	14.3	9	45	7	113	75	11.6	26	61.9	Left Side	6	47	7.8	0	14	0	6	11	6.8	2	33.3
1st Half	-	31	503	16.2	10	51	6	115	46	12.5	22	71.0	Middle	10	151	15.1	2	32	1	24	15	12.7	7	70.0
2nd Half/OT	-	22	260	11.8	1	30	2	41	42	10.0	10	45.5	Right Side	12	194	16.2	3	45	2	52	18	11.8	9	75.0
Last 2 Min. Half	-	6	101	16.8	3	45	1	26	9	12.5	3	50.0	Right Sideline	13	143	11.0	2	30	1	12	22	10.1	5	38.5
4th qtr, +/-7 pts	-	4	36	9.0	0	24	0	9	7	6.8	1	25.0	Shotgun	14	202	14.4	3	45	2	33	29	12.1	7	50.0
Winning	-	23	280	12.2	3	30	1	41	37	10.4	14	60.9	2 Wide Receivers	3	45	15.0	1	28	1	9	4	12.0	2	66.7
Tied	-	8	153	19.1	3	51	2	37	14	14.5	6	75.0	3 Wide Receivers	47	696	14.8	10	51	7	143	79	11.8	29	61.7
Trailing	-	22	330	15.0	5	45	5	78	37	11.5	12	54.5	4+ Wide Receivers	3	22	7.3	0	12	0	4	5	6.0	1	33.3

1995 Incompletions

Type	Num	%of Inc	%of Att
Pass Dropped	2	5.7	2.3
Poor Throw	17	48.6	19.3
Pass Defensed	7	20.0	8.0
Pass Hit at Line	4	11.4	4.5
Other	5	14.3	5.7
Total	35	100.0	39.8

Game Logs (1-8)

Date	Opp	Result	Rush	Yds	Rec	Yds	Trgt	F-L	TD
09/03	@Den	L 7-22	0	0	2	23	6	0-0	0
09/10	Car	W 31-9	0	0	0	0	1	0-0	0
09/17	Ind	W 20-14	0	0	0	0	5	0-0	0
10/02	@Cle	W 22-19	0	0	1	8	1	0-0	0
10/08	NYN	W 29-10	0	0	1	15	1	0-0	1
10/15	Sea	W 27-21	1	-3	6	109	9	0-0	2
10/23	@NE	L 14-27	0	0	2	54	5	0-0	0
10/29	@Mia	L 6-23	0	0	3	22	5	0-0	0

Game Logs (9-16)

Date	Opp	Result	Rush	Yds	Rec	Yds	Trgt	F-L	TD
11/05	@Ind	W 16-10	1	9	5	90	6	0-0	1
11/12	Atl	W 23-17	0	0	7	101	11	0-0	2
11/19	@NYA	W 28-26	0	0	7	107	12	0-0	2
11/26	NE	L 25-35	1	1	4	80	7	0-0	1
12/03	@SF	L 17-27	0	0	5	39	10	0-0	0
12/10	@StL	W 45-27	0	0	6	73	7	0-0	1
12/17	@Mia	W 23-20	0	0	4	42	7	0-0	0
12/24	Hou	L 17-28	-	-	-	-	-	-	-

Robert Brooks
Green Bay Packers — WR

1995 Receiving Splits

	G	Rec	Yds	Avg	TD	Lg	Big	YAC	Trgt	Y@C	1st	1st%		Rec	Yds	Avg	TD	Lg	Big	YAC	Trgt	Y@C	1st	1st%
Total	16	102	1497	14.7	13	99	14	496	167	9.8	70	68.6	Inside 20	9	97	10.8	7	19	0	5	16	10.2	7	77.8
vs. Playoff	4	31	454	14.6	3	77	4	177	46	8.9	20	64.5	Inside 10	3	13	4.3	3	6	0	1	6	4.0	3	100.0
vs. Non-playoff	12	71	1043	14.7	10	99	10	319	121	10.2	50	70.4	1st Down	37	601	16.2	4	54	9	171	64	11.6	20	54.1
vs. Own Division	8	50	889	17.8	8	99	10	315	84	11.5	38	76.0	2nd Down	35	494	14.1	4	77	4	185	59	8.8	24	68.6
Home	8	46	647	14.1	7	54	7	192	80	9.9	29	63.0	3rd Down Overall	29	389	13.4	5	99	1	138	42	8.7	25	86.2
Away	8	56	850	15.2	6	99	7	304	87	9.8	41	73.2	3rd D 0-2 to Go	4	18	4.5	1	7	0	5	5	3.3	4	100.0
Games 1-8	8	47	666	14.2	6	99	5	248	86	8.9	31	66.0	3rd D 3-7 to Go	13	145	11.2	3	17	0	41	18	8.0	12	92.3
Games 9-16	8	55	831	15.1	7	54	9	248	81	10.6	39	70.9	3rd D 8+ to Go	12	226	18.8	1	99	1	92	19	11.2	9	75.0
September	4	25	308	12.3	4	99	1	111	42	7.9	16	64.0	4th Down	1	13	13.0	0	13	0	2	2	11.0	1	100.0
October	4	22	358	16.3	2	77	4	137	44	10.0	15	68.2	Rec Behind Line	0	0	-	0	0	0	0	2	-	0	-
November	4	26	420	16.2	4	54	4	127	39	11.3	19	73.1	1-10 yds	69	685	9.9	4	77	0	308	96	5.5	38	55.1
December	4	29	411	14.2	3	40	5	121	42	10.0	20	69.0	11-20 yds	22	365	16.6	5	32	2	45	35	14.5	21	95.5
Grass	12	72	1008	14.0	10	99	9	327	117	9.5	47	65.3	21-30 yds	8	318	39.8	2	99	8	114	24	25.5	8	100.0
Turf	4	30	489	16.3	3	77	4	169	50	10.7	23	76.7	31+	3	129	43.0	2	54	3	29	10	33.3	3	100.0
Indoor	3	20	365	18.3	3	77	3	128	34	11.9	16	80.0	Left Sideline	14	261	18.6	4	54	4	86	20	12.5	11	78.6
Outdoor	13	82	1132	13.8	10	99	11	368	133	9.3	54	65.9	Left Side	19	214	11.3	1	32	1	79	31	7.1	12	63.2
1st Half	-	64	1000	15.6	10	99	9	358	99	10.0	44	68.8	Middle	13	190	14.6	2	35	2	45	21	11.2	8	61.5
2nd Half/OT	-	38	497	13.1	3	44	5	138	68	9.4	26	68.4	Right Side	28	391	14.0	4	77	4	148	43	8.7	21	75.0
Last 2 Min. Half	-	12	166	13.8	2	35	2	23	16	11.9	8	66.7	Right Sideline	28	441	15.8	2	99	3	138	52	10.8	18	64.3
4th qtr, +/-7 pts	-	11	167	15.2	0	35	2	39	16	11.6	9	81.8	Shotgun	0	0	-	0	0	0	0	0	-	0	-
Winning	-	39	575	14.7	7	99	5	187	60	9.9	24	61.5	2 Wide Receivers	50	766	15.3	7	99	8	252	86	10.3	33	66.0
Tied	-	38	498	13.1	3	35	5	127	60	9.8	26	68.4	3 Wide Receivers	34	518	15.2	3	77	5	185	53	9.8	23	67.6
Trailing	-	25	424	17.0	3	77	4	182	47	9.2	20	80.0	4+ Wide Receivers	15	195	13.0	3	29	1	53	25	9.5	11	73.3

1995 Incompletions

Type	Num	%of Inc	%of Att
Pass Dropped	12	18.5	7.2
Poor Throw	35	53.8	21.0
Pass Defensed	9	13.8	5.4
Pass Hit at Line	1	1.5	0.6
Other	8	12.3	4.8
Total	65	100.0	38.9

Game Logs (1-8)

Date	Opp	Result	Rush	Yds	Rec	Yds	Trgt	F-L	TD
09/03	StL	L 14-17	1	-5	8	70	15	0-0	0
09/11	@Chi	W 27-24	0	0	8	161	12	0-0	2
09/17	NYN	W 14-6	0	0	5	47	9	0-0	1
09/24	@Jac	W 24-14	0	0	4	30	6	0-0	1
10/08	@Dal	L 24-34	0	0	10	124	16	0-0	0
10/15	Det	W 30-21	1	21	4	66	5	0-0	1
10/22	Min	W 38-21	0	0	2	41	12	0-0	0
10/29	@Det	L 16-24	1	0	6	127	11	0-0	1

Game Logs (9-16)

Date	Opp	Result	Rush	Yds	Rec	Yds	Trgt	F-L	TD
11/05	@Min	L 24-27	0	0	9	120	15	0-0	0
11/12	Chi	W 35-28	1	0	6	138	10	0-0	2
11/19	@Cle	W 31-20	0	0	5	48	7	0-0	0
11/26	TB	W 35-13	0	0	6	114	7	0-0	2
12/03	Cin	W 24-10	0	0	4	34	8	0-0	0
12/10	@TB	L 10-13	0	0	9	122	12	0-0	0
12/16	@NO	W 34-23	0	0	5	118	8	0-0	0
12/24	Pit	W 24-19	0	0	11	137	14	0-0	1

Dave Brown
New York Giants — QB

1995 Passing Splits

	G	Att	Cm	Pct	Yds	Yd/Att	TD	Int	1st	YAC	Big	Sk	Rtg		Att	Cm	Pct	Yds	Yd/Att	TD	Int	1st	YAC	Big	Sk	Rtg
Total	16	456	254	55.7	2814	6.2	11	10	147	1258	20	44	73.1	Inside 20	39	15	38.5	122	3.1	5	2	9	45	0	3	65.4
vs. Playoff	8	240	128	53.3	1285	5.4	2	7	69	614	6	25	59.5	Inside 10	14	5	35.7	23	1.6	4	0	4	2	0	1	83.9
vs. Non-playoff	8	216	126	58.3	1529	7.1	9	3	78	644	14	19	88.3	1st Down	152	85	55.9	922	6.1	1	2	37	458	7	12	70.7
vs. Own Division	8	181	104	57.5	1048	5.8	6	6	56	513	5	27	71.3	2nd Down	170	107	62.9	1218	7.2	8	3	60	506	11	12	92.7
Home	8	214	128	59.8	1393	6.5	5	5	73	665	10	19	77.1	3rd Down Overall	127	60	47.2	658	5.2	2	5	48	290	2	20	51.9
Away	8	242	126	52.1	1421	5.9	6	5	74	593	10	25	69.6	3rd D 0-5 to Go	49	30	61.2	305	6.2	1	1	28	165	1	7	77.3
Games 1-8	8	231	128	55.4	1368	5.9	5	6	73	624	9	20	69.3	3rd D 6+ to Go	78	30	38.5	353	4.5	1	4	20	125	1	13	35.9
Games 9-16	8	225	126	56.0	1446	6.4	6	4	74	634	11	24	77.0	4th Down	7	2	28.6	16	2.3	0	0	2	4	0	0	39.6
September	4	125	72	57.6	763	6.1	2	3	38	340	5	9	70.8	Rec Behind Line	79	54	68.4	288	3.6	1	2	14	445	0	0	67.9
October	4	106	56	52.8	605	5.7	3	3	35	284	4	11	67.5	1-10 yds	239	143	59.8	1299	5.4	3	5	79	630	4	0	70.1
November	5	157	85	54.1	1035	6.6	5	2	52	367	9	17	80.0	11-20 yds	90	42	46.7	699	7.8	2	3	39	117	2	0	66.9
December	3	68	41	60.3	411	6.0	1	2	22	267	2	7	70.2	21-30 yds	25	9	36.0	279	11.2	3	0	9	41	8	0	118.2
Grass	5	156	83	53.2	851	5.5	3	2	45	382	5	13	70.2	31+	23	6	26.1	249	10.8	2	0	6	25	6	0	101.2
Turf	11	300	171	57.0	1963	6.5	8	8	102	876	15	31	74.6	Left Sideline	66	30	45.5	402	6.1	3	1	20	117	4	0	74.2
Indoor	1	41	20	48.8	299	7.3	2	0	16	81	4	3	89.4	Left Side	97	61	62.9	579	6.0	1	3	39	294	2	4	69.9
Outdoor	15	415	234	56.4	2515	6.1	9	10	131	1177	16	41	71.5	Middle	102	56	54.9	576	5.6	1	2	26	229	4	31	66.5
1st Half	-	230	137	59.6	1551	6.7	8	6	78	764	13	21	80.5	Right Side	105	58	55.2	706	6.7	5	3	34	383	5	9	80.1
2nd Half/OT	-	226	117	51.8	1263	5.6	3	4	69	494	7	23	65.6	Right Sideline	86	49	57.0	551	6.4	1	1	28	235	5	0	75.3
Last 2 Min. Half	-	78	39	50.0	460	5.9	2	2	23	157	5	8	66.2	2 Wide Receivers	249	149	59.8	1606	6.4	4	7	82	803	11	18	72.5
4th qtr, +/-7 pts	-	53	25	47.2	382	7.2	1	1	18	99	5	7	69.9	3+ WR	184	91	49.5	1078	5.9	4	3	56	411	9	22	68.2
Winning	-	92	52	56.5	543	5.9	1	1	26	260	2	11	72.9	Attempts 1-10	160	101	63.1	1145	7.2	5	5	55	581	10	0	81.9
Tied	-	74	40	54.1	488	6.6	3	4	25	263	5	4	65.9	Attempts 11-20	144	81	56.3	804	5.6	5	2	46	303	9	0	78.0
Trailing	-	290	162	55.9	1783	6.1	7	5	96	735	13	29	75.1	Attempts 21+	152	72	47.4	865	5.7	1	3	46	298	8	0	59.2

1995 Incompletions

Type	Num	% of Inc	% of Att
Pass Dropped	28	13.9	6.1
Poor Throw	89	44.1	19.5
Pass Defensed	37	18.3	8.1
Pass Hit at Line	9	4.5	2.0
Other	39	19.3	8.6
Total	202	100.0	44.3

Game Logs (1-8)

Date	Opp	Result	Att	Cm	Pct	Yds	TD	Int	Lg	Sk	F-L
09/04	Dal	L 0-35	34	20	58.8	155	0	1	18	2	1-0
09/10	@KC	L 17-20	14	10	71.4	151	1	0	37	1	1-1
09/17	@GB	L 6-14	50	23	46.0	199	0	1	30	2	0-0
09/24	NO	W 45-29	29	19	70.4	258	1	1	38	1	0-0
10/01	@SF	L 6-20	43	22	51.2	218	0	1	25	2	1-0
10/08	Ari	W 27-21	23	14	60.9	166	2	2	49	2	1-1
10/15	Phi	L 14-17	18	9	50.0	82	0	0	16	1	1-0
10/29	@Was	W 24-15	22	11	50.0	139	1	0	57	2	0-0

Game Logs (9-16)

Date	Opp	Result	Att	Cm	Pct	Yds	TD	Int	Lg	Sk	F-L
11/05	@Sea	L 28-30	41	20	48.8	299	2	0	30	3	0-0
11/12	Oak	L 13-17	31	18	58.1	215	0	0	42	4	1-1
11/19	@Phi	L 19-28	25	13	52.0	160	1	2	46	7	2-0
11/26	Chi	L 24-27	33	17	51.5	217	1	0	38	0	0-0
11/30	@Ari	W 10-6	27	17	63.0	144	1	0	22	0	0-0
12/10	Was	W 20-13	12	10	83.3	91	1	0	40	4	0-0
12/17	@Dal	L 20-21	20	10	50.0	111	0	1	19	2	0-0
12/23	SD	L 17-27	36	21	58.3	209	1	0	34	1	2-1

Derek Brown
New Orleans Saints — RB

1995 Receiving Splits

	G	Rec	Yds	Avg	TD	Lg	Big	YAC	Trgt	Y@C	1st	1st%		Rec	Yds	Avg	TD	Lg	Big	YAC	Trgt	Y@C	1st	1st%
Total	16	35	266	7.6	1	19	0	264	49	0.1	12	34.3	Inside 20	5	24	4.8	1	7	0	14	6	2.0	2	40.0
vs. Playoff	8	17	129	7.6	0	17	0	134	27	-0.3	6	35.3	Inside 10	2	10	5.0	1	6	0	5	3	2.5	1	50.0
vs. Non-playoff	8	18	137	7.6	1	19	0	130	22	0.4	6	33.3	1st Down	13	92	7.1	0	17	0	98	16	-0.5	3	23.1
vs. Own Division	8	16	119	7.4	0	15	0	133	21	-0.9	5	31.3	2nd Down	5	37	7.4	0	11	0	45	9	-1.6	2	40.0
Home	8	13	99	7.6	0	17	0	97	23	0.2	4	30.8	3rd Down Overall	15	114	7.6	0	17	0	113	22	0.1	5	33.3
Away	8	22	167	7.6	1	19	0	167	26	0	8	36.4	3rd D 0-2 to Go	0	0	-	0	0	0	0	0	-	0	
Games 1-8	8	18	135	7.5	1	17	0	139	25	-0.2	4	38.9	3rd D 3-7 to Go	6	36	6.0	0	14	0	37	9	-0.2	3	50.0
Games 9-16	8	17	131	7.7	0	19	0	125	24	0.4	5	29.4	3rd D 8+ to Go	9	78	8.7	0	17	0	76	13	0.2	2	22.2
September	4	10	86	8.6	1	17	0	93	13	-0.7	4	40.0	4th Down	2	23	11.5	1	19	0	8	2	7.5	2	100.0
October	4	8	49	6.1	0	17	0	46	12	0.4	3	37.5	Rec Behind Line	16	126	7.9	0	17	0	176	22	-3.1	5	31.3
November	4	7	52	7.4	0	11	0	50	10	0.3	2	28.6	1-10 yds	18	121	6.7	1	17	0	81	25	2.2	6	33.3
December	4	10	79	7.9	0	19	0	75	14	0.4	3	30.0	11-20 yds	1	19	19.0	0	19	0	7	2	12.0	1	100.0
Grass	3	6	38	6.3	0	11	0	41	7	-0.5	2	33.3	21-30 yds	0	0	-	0	0	0	0	0	-	0	
Turf	13	29	228	7.9	1	19	0	223	42	0.2	10	34.5	31+	0	0	-	0	0	0	0	0	-	0	
Indoor	10	22	164	7.5	0	17	0	167	34	-0.1	7	31.8	Left Sideline	6	41	6.8	0	9	0	39	9	0.3	2	33.3
Outdoor	6	13	102	7.8	1	19	0	97	15	0.4	5	38.5	Left Side	5	36	7.2	1	14	0	39	5	-0.6	2	40.0
1st Half	-	19	137	7.2	0	17	0	140	23	-0.2	4	21.1	Middle	7	65	9.3	0	19	0	53	13	1.7	2	28.6
2nd Half/OT	-	16	129	8.1	1	19	0	124	26	0.3	8	50.0	Right Side	10	76	7.6	0	17	0	99	12	-2.3	3	30.0
Last 2 Min. Half	-	14	91	6.5	1	15	0	97	17	-0.4	4	28.6	Right Sideline	7	48	6.9	0	17	0	34	10	2.0	3	42.9
4th qtr, +/-7 pts	-	3	17	5.7	0	8	0	14	6	1.0	1	33.3	Shotgun	28	224	8.0	1	19	0	219	37	0.2	11	39.3
Winning	-	6	55	9.2	0	19	0	36	7	3.2	2	33.3	2 Wide Receivers	3	18	6.0	0	9	0	21	4	-1.0	0	0.0
Tied	-	5	39	7.8	0	10	0	36	9	0.6	1	20.0	3 Wide Receivers	32	248	7.8	1	19	0	243	44	0.2	12	37.5
Trailing	-	24	172	7.2	1	17	0	192	33	-0.2	9	37.5	4+ Wide Receivers	0	0	-	0	0	0	0	0	-	0	

1995 Incompletions

Type	Num	%of Inc	%of Att
Pass Dropped	2	14.3	4.1
Poor Throw	7	50.0	14.3
Pass Defensed	0	0.0	0.0
Pass Hit at Line	3	21.4	6.1
Other	2	14.3	4.1
Total	14	100.0	28.6

Game Logs (1-8)

Date	Opp	Result	Rush	Yds	Rec	Yds	Trgt	F-L	TD
09/03	SF	L 22-24	0	0	1	15	2	0-0	0
09/10	@StL	L 13-17	2	16	2	12	2	0-0	0
09/17	Atl	L 24-27	3	4	4	32	5	0-0	0
09/24	@NYN	L 29-45	5	7	3	27	4	0-1	0
10/01	Phi	L 10-15	2	8	1	2	3	0-0	0
10/15	Mia	W 33-30	18	41	2	20	3	0-0	0
10/22	@Car	L 3-20	5	15	3	10	4	0-0	0
10/29	@SF	W 11-7	3	5	2	17	2	0-0	0

Game Logs (9-16)

Date	Opp	Result	Rush	Yds	Rec	Yds	Trgt	F-L	TD
11/05	StL	W 19-10	0	0	1	10	2	0-0	0
11/12	@Atl	W 17-14	0	0	1	0	1	0-0	0
11/19	@Min	L 24-43	2	17	6	42	7	0-0	0
11/26	Car	W 34-26	3	34	0	0	0	0-0	1
12/03	@NE	W 31-17	0	0	1	11	1	0-0	0
12/10	@Atl	L 14-19	1	2	3	23	4	0-0	0
12/16	GB	L 23-34	3	10	4	20	4	0-0	0
12/24	@NYA	W 12-0	2	0	2	25	2	0-0	0

Gary Brown
Houston Oilers — RB

1995 Rushing and Receiving Splits

	G	Rush	Yds	Avg	Lg	TD	1st	Stf	YdL	Rec	Yds	Avg	TD		Rush	Yds	Avg	Lg	TD	1st	Stf	YdL	Rec	Yds	Avg	TD
Total	9	86	293	3.4	21	0	16	4	5	6	16	2.7	0	Inside 20	11	18	1.6	6	0	1	0	0	0	0	-	0
vs. Playoff	3	19	42	2.2	5	0	3	1	1	3	9	3.0	0	Inside 10	6	7	1.2	4	0	0	0	0	0	0	-	0
vs. Non-playoff	6	67	251	3.7	21	0	13	3	4	3	7	2.3	0	1st Down	44	151	3.4	12	0	1	3	4	4	12	3.0	0
vs. Own Division	5	63	199	3.2	21	0	11	4	5	3	9	3.0	0	2nd Down	34	126	3.7	21	0	12	1	1	2	4	2.0	0
Home	5	44	125	2.8	12	0	7	2	2	6	16	2.7	0	3rd Down Overall	8	16	2.0	5	0	3	0	0	0	0	-	0
Away	4	42	168	4.0	21	0	9	2	3	0	0	-	0	3rd D 0-2 to Go	6	9	1.5	5	0	3	0	0	0	0	-	0
Games 1-8	4	61	194	3.2	21	0	11	4	5	3	9	3.0	0	3rd D 3-7 to Go	0	0	-	0	0	0	0	0	0	0	-	0
Games 9-16	5	25	99	4.0	12	0	5	0	0	3	7	2.3	0	3rd D 8+ to Go	2	7	3.5	4	0	0	0	0	0	0	-	0
September	4	61	194	3.2	21	0	11	4	5	3	9	3.0	0	4th Down	0	0	-	0	0	0	0	0	0	0	-	0
October	0	0	0	-	0	0	0	0	0	0	0	-	0	Left Sideline	3	19	6.3	10	0	1	0	0	1	0	0.0	0
November	2	8	39	4.9	12	0	1	0	0	2	8	4.0	0	Left Side	22	97	4.4	13	0	5	0	0	0	0	-	0
December	3	17	60	3.5	8	0	4	0	0	1	-1	-1.0	0	Middle	33	90	2.7	9	0	7	1	1	0	0	-	0
Grass	2	31	106	3.4	21	0	6	2	3	0	0	-	0	Right Side	24	50	2.1	9	0	1	3	4	3	12	4.0	0
Turf	7	55	187	3.4	13	0	10	2	2	6	16	2.7	0	Right Sideline	4	37	9.3	21	0	2	0	0	2	4	2.0	0
Indoor	5	44	125	2.8	12	0	7	2	2	6	16	2.7	0	Shotgun	0	0	-	0	0	0	0	0	0	0	-	0
Outdoor	4	42	168	4.0	21	0	9	2	3	0	0	-	0	2 Wide Receivers	56	220	3.9	21	0	12	3	4	3	12	4.0	0
1st Half	-	49	186	3.8	21	0	11	3	3	6	16	2.7	0	3 Wide Receivers	14	46	3.3	12	0	1	1	1	3	4	1.3	0
2nd Half/OT	-	37	107	2.9	8	0	5	1	2	0	0	-	0	4+ Wide Receivers	0	0	-	0	0	0	0	0	0	0	-	0
Last 2 Min. Half	-	3	8	2.7	4	0	0	0	0	0	0	-	0	Carries 1-5	37	173	4.7	21	0	9	1	1	0	0	-	0
4th qtr, +/-7 pts	-	11	23	2.1	5	0	1	1	2	0	0	-	0	Carries 6-10	22	60	2.7	9	0	5	1	1	0	0	-	0
Winning	-	43	150	3.5	12	0	6	2	3	2	8	4.0	0	Carries 11-15	13	18	1.4	4	0	0	1	1	0	0	-	0
Tied	-	21	99	4.7	21	0	6	1	1	1	-1	-1.0	0	Carries 16-20	5	19	3.8	8	0	1	0	0	0	0	-	0
Trailing	-	22	44	2.0	10	0	4	1	1	3	9	3.0	0	Carries 21+	9	23	2.6	5	0	1	1	2	0	0	-	0

1995 Incompletions

Type	Num	%of Inc	% Att
Pass Dropped	2	100.0	25.0
Poor Throw	0	0.0	0.0
Pass Defensed	0	0.0	0.0
Pass Hit at Line	0	0.0	0.0
Other	0	0.0	0.0
Total	2	100.0	25.0

Game Logs (1-8)

Date	Opp	Result	Rush	Yds	Rec	Yds	Trgt	F-L TD
09/03	@Jac	W 10-3	29	101	0	0	1	0-0 0
09/10	Pit	L 17-34	14	22	3	9	4	0-0 0
09/17	Cle	L 7-14	12	29	0	0	0	0-0 0
09/24	@Cin	W 38-28	6	42	0	0	0	1-1 0
10/01	Jac	L 16-17	-	-	-	-	-	-
10/08	@Min	L 17-23	-	-	-	-	-	-
10/22	@Chi	L 32-35	-	-	-	-	-	-
10/29	TB	W 19-7	-	-	-	-	-	-

Game Logs (9-16)

Date	Opp	Result	Rush	Yds	Rec	Yds	Trgt	F-L TD
11/05	@Cle	W 37-10	2	5	0	0	0	0-0 0
11/12	Cin	L 25-32	-	-	-	-	-	-
11/19	@KC	L 13-20	-	-	-	-	-	-
11/26	Den	W 42-33	6	34	2	8	2	1-1 0
12/03	@Pit	L 7-21	-	-	-	-	-	-
12/10	Det	L 17-24	0	0	0	0	0	0-0 0
12/17	NYA	W 23-6	12	40	1	-1	1	0-0 0
12/24	@Buf	W 28-17	5	20	0	0	0	0-0 0

Tim Brown
Oakland Raiders — WR

1995 Receiving Splits

	G	Rec	Yds	Avg	TD	Lg	Big	YAC	Trgt	Y@C	1st	1st%		Rec	Yds	Avg	TD	Lg	Big	YAC	Trgt	Y@C	1st	1st%
Total	16	89	1342	15.1	10	80	9	534	148	9.1	66	74.2	Inside 20	7	54	7.7	4	17	0	11	15	6.1	6	85.7
vs. Playoff	8	51	645	12.6	3	30	3	215	77	8.4	35	68.6	Inside 10	3	10	3.3	3	5	0	0	6	3.3	3	100.0
vs. Non-playoff	8	38	697	18.3	7	80	6	319	71	9.9	31	81.6	1st Down	38	539	14.2	3	80	3	162	65	9.9	26	68.4
vs. Own Division	8	41	662	16.1	6	80	6	309	74	8.6	31	75.6	2nd Down	27	343	12.7	3	34	3	126	42	8.0	18	66.7
Home	8	54	816	15.1	6	80	6	291	83	9.7	39	72.2	3rd Down Overall	23	436	19.0	3	80	3	237	38	8.7	21	91.3
Away	8	35	526	15.0	4	80	3	243	65	8.1	27	77.1	3rd D 0-2 to Go	1	5	5.0	1	5	0	0	2	5.0	1	100.0
Games 1-8	8	41	605	14.8	4	80	3	242	64	8.9	30	73.2	3rd D 3-7 to Go	11	185	16.8	1	80	1	133	13	4.7	10	90.9
Games 9-16	8	48	737	15.4	6	80	6	292	84	9.3	36	75.0	3rd D 8+ to Go	11	246	22.4	1	66	2	104	23	12.9	10	90.9
September	4	18	192	10.7	1	24	0	54	25	7.7	12	66.7	4th Down	1	24	24.0	1	24	0	9	3	15.0	1	100.0
October	4	23	413	18.0	3	80	3	188	39	9.8	18	78.3	Rec Behind Line	2	5	2.5	0	3	0	9	4	-2.0	1	50.0
November	4	22	302	13.7	2	34	2	115	38	8.5	15	68.2	1-10 yds	46	465	10.1	4	80	2	253	70	4.6	24	52.2
December	4	26	435	16.7	4	80	4	177	46	9.9	21	80.8	11-20 yds	40	824	20.6	5	80	6	262	64	14.1	40	100.0
Grass	12	71	970	13.7	6	80	6	348	115	8.8	49	69.0	21-30 yds	0	0	-	0	0	0	0	6	-	0	-
Turf	4	18	372	20.7	4	80	3	186	33	10.3	17	94.4	31+	1	48	48.0	1	48	1	10	4	38.0	1	100.0
Outdoor	1	86	1240	14.4	9	80	8	453	140	9.2	63	73.3	Left Sideline	24	339	14.1	3	48	2	91	40	10.3	17	70.8
Indoor	15	3	102	34.0	1	80	1	81	8	7.0	3	100.0	Left Side	13	198	15.2	2	80	1	93	19	8.1	10	76.9
1st Half	-	41	602	14.7	4	80	2	235	74	9.9	31	75.6	Middle	16	343	21.4	2	80	4	163	25	11.3	13	81.3
2nd Half/OT	-	48	740	15.4	6	80	7	299	74	9.2	35	72.9	Right Side	22	254	11.5	1	30	1	89	34	7.5	15	68.2
Last 2 Min. Half	-	13	185	14.2	2	80	1	92	29	7.2	9	69.2	Right Sideline	14	208	14.9	2	66	1	98	30	7.9	11	78.6
4th qtr, +/-7 pts	-	5	45	9.0	0	14	0	12	9	6.6	4	80.0	Shotgun	0	0	-	0	0	0	0	0	-	0	-
Winning	-	31	538	17.4	5	80	5	235	48	9.8	23	74.2	2 Wide Receivers	35	500	14.3	3	48	2	99	59	11.5	26	74.3
Tied	-	20	230	11.5	1	21	0	72	26	7.9	13	65.0	3 Wide Receivers	41	546	13.3	3	80	4	253	68	7.1	29	70.7
Trailing	-	38	574	15.1	4	80	4	227	74	9.1	30	78.9	4+ Wide Receivers	12	290	24.2	4	80	3	177	18	9.4	11	91.7

1995 Incompletions

Type	Num	%of Inc	%of Att
Pass Dropped	8	13.6	5.4
Poor Throw	23	39.0	15.5
Pass Defensed	15	25.4	10.1
Pass Hit at Line	2	3.4	1.4
Other	11	18.6	7.4
Total	59	100.0	39.9

Game Logs (1-8)

Date	Opp	Result	Rec	Yds	Trgt	F-L	TD
09/03	SD	W 17-7	2	16	3	0-0	1
09/10	@Was	W 20-8	4	30	5	0-0	0
09/17	@KC	L 17-23	7	72	9	0-0	0
09/24	Phi	W 48-17	5	74	9	0-0	0
10/01	@NYA	W 47-10	8	156	9	0-0	2
10/08	Sea	W 34-14	5	143	9	0-0	0
10/16	@Den	L 0-27	3	25	11	0-0	0
10/22	Ind	W 30-17	7	89	10	0-0	0

Game Logs (9-16)

Date	Opp	Result	Rec	Yds	Trgt	F-L	TD
11/05	@Cin	W 20-17	4	67	10	0-0	1
11/12	@NYN	W 17-13	3	47	6	0-0	0
11/19	Dal	L 21-34	12	161	15	0-0	1
11/27	@SD	L 6-12	3	27	7	0-0	0
12/03	KC	L 23-29	10	150	14	0-0	0
12/10	Pit	L 29-49	5	56	11	0-0	0
12/17	@Sea	L 10-44	3	102	8	0-0	0
12/24	Den	L 28-31	8	127	13	0-0	0

Isaac Bruce
St. Louis Rams — WR

1995 Receiving Splits

	G	Rec	Yds	Avg	TD	Lg	Big	YAC	Trgt	Y@C	1st	1st%
Total	16	119	1781	15.0	13	72	18	556	199	10.3	82	68.9
vs. Playoff	9	73	1166	16.0	8	72	12	351	120	11.2	51	69.9
vs. Non-playoff	7	46	615	13.4	5	55	6	205	79	8.9	31	67.4
vs. Own Division	8	53	874	16.5	6	59	9	275	86	11.3	43	81.1
Home	8	70	1021	14.6	5	59	11	313	110	10.1	48	68.6
Away	8	49	760	15.5	8	72	7	243	89	10.6	34	69.4
Games 1-8	8	54	938	17.4	7	72	9	295	83	11.9	42	77.8
Games 9-16	8	65	843	13.0	6	55	9	261	116	9.0	40	61.5
September	4	18	288	16.0	2	37	2	106	29	10.1	14	77.8
October	4	36	650	18.1	5	72	7	189	54	12.8	28	77.8
November	4	26	360	13.8	3	55	3	100	44	10.0	18	69.2
December	4	39	483	12.4	3	38	6	161	72	8.3	22	56.4
Grass	3	11	179	16.3	2	37	1	54	22	11.4	8	72.7
Turf	13	108	1602	14.8	11	72	17	502	177	10.2	74	68.5
Indoor	7	65	931	14.3	5	72	10	277	100	10.1	40	61.5
Outdoor	9	54	850	15.7	8	59	8	279	99	10.6	42	77.8
1st Half	-	54	959	17.8	7	72	12	311	93	12.0	38	70.4
2nd Half/OT	-	65	822	12.6	6	38	6	245	106	8.9	44	67.7
Last 2 Min. Half	-	11	162	14.7	2	34	2	41	22	11.0	7	63.6
4th qtr, +/-7 pts	-	11	178	16.2	2	26	2	37	16	12.8	10	90.9
Winning	-	27	358	13.3	3	26	3	93	51	9.8	20	74.1
Tied	-	22	454	20.6	4	72	5	144	36	14.1	17	77.3
Trailing	-	70	969	13.8	6	53	10	319	112	9.3	45	64.3

	Rec	Yds	Avg	TD	Lg	Big	YAC	Trgt	Y@C	1st	1st%
Inside 20	10	73	7.3	7	12	0	11	19	6.2	8	80.0
Inside 10	5	23	4.6	4	9	0	6	9	3.4	4	80.0
1st Down	51	897	17.6	3	72	10	238	78	12.9	31	60.8
2nd Down	42	522	12.4	6	37	5	177	64	8.2	26	61.9
3rd Down Overall	25	349	14.0	4	55	3	140	53	8.4	24	96.0
3rd D 0-2 to Go	1	1	1.0	1	1	0	0	2	1.0	1	100.0
3rd D 3-7 to Go	17	224	13.2	0	34	2	102	22	7.2	17	100.0
3rd D 8+ to Go	7	124	17.7	3	55	1	38	29	12.3	6	85.7
4th Down	1	13	13.0	0	13	0	1	4	12.0	1	100.0
Rec Behind Line	4	28	7.0	0	13	0	33	6	-1.3	2	50.0
1-10 yds	63	542	8.6	4	34	2	216	82	5.2	31	49.2
11-20 yds	44	868	19.7	4	38	10	210	71	15.0	41	93.2
21-30 yds	5	184	36.8	4	59	3	57	13	25.4	5	100.0
31+	3	159	53.0	1	72	3	40	27	39.7	3	100.0
Left Sideline	25	361	14.4	3	37	3	89	45	10.9	18	72.0
Left Side	16	299	18.7	3	59	4	120	27	11.2	12	75.0
Middle	13	302	23.2	1	72	5	96	22	15.8	9	69.2
Right Side	26	302	11.6	1	34	3	121	47	7.0	13	50.0
Right Sideline	39	517	13.3	5	55	3	130	58	9.9	30	76.9
Shotgun	0	0	-	0	0	0	0	2	-	0	-
2 Wide Receivers	63	1022	16.2	9	72	11	322	100	11.1	45	71.4
3 Wide Receivers	39	522	13.4	3	55	7	193	75	8.4	25	64.1
4+ Wide Receivers	5	78	15.6	1	24	0	7	6	14.2	4	80.0

1995 Incompletions

Type	Num	%of Inc	%of Att
Pass Dropped	6	7.5	3.0
Poor Throw	48	60.0	24.1
Pass Defensed	14	17.5	7.0
Pass Hit at Line	1	1.3	0.5
Other	11	13.8	5.5
Total	80	100.0	40.2

Game Logs (1-8)

Date	Opp	Result	Rush	Yds	Rec	Yds	Trgt	F-L	TD
09/03	@GB	W 17-14	0	0	4	55	8	0-0	1
09/10	NO	W 17-13	0	0	3	50	8	0-0	1
09/17	@Car	W 31-10	1	-1	5	100	6	0-0	0
09/24	Chi	W 34-28	0	0	6	83	7	0-0	0
10/01	@Ind	L 18-21	0	0	8	181	11	0-0	2
10/12	Atl	W 21-19	0	0	10	191	13	0-0	2
10/22	SF	L 10-44	0	0	9	173	15	1-0	0
10/29	@Phi	L 9-20	0	0	9	105	15	0-0	1

Game Logs (9-16)

Date	Opp	Result	Rush	Yds	Rec	Yds	Trgt	F-L	TD
11/05	@NO	L 10-19	0	0	8	135	11	0-0	1
11/12	Car	W 28-17	0	0	9	110	14	0-0	1
11/19	@Atl	L 6-31	0	0	7	91	11	0-0	0
11/26	@SF	L 13-41	1	6	2	24	8	0-0	1
12/03	@NYA	W 23-20	0	0	6	69	19	0-0	2
12/10	Buf	L 27-45	0	0	9	136	20	1-1	0
12/17	Was	L 23-35	0	0	8	68	14	0-0	0
12/24	Mia	L 22-41	1	12	15	210	19	0-0	1

Mark Bruener
Pittsburgh Steelers — TE

1995 Receiving Splits

	G	Rec	Yds	Avg	TD	Lg	Big	YAC	Trgt	Y@C	1st	1st%
Total	16	26	238	9.2	3	29	1	94	48	5.5	12	46.2
vs. Playoff	4	6	49	8.2	0	14	0	29	10	3.3	5	50.0
vs. Non-playoff	12	20	189	9.5	3	29	1	65	38	6.2	9	45.0
vs. Own Division	8	16	137	8.6	3	21	0	41	29	6.0	7	43.8
Home	8	9	109	12.1	1	29	1	52	21	6.3	6	66.7
Away	8	17	129	7.6	2	15	0	42	27	5.1	6	35.3
Games 1-8	8	11	126	11.5	1	29	1	53	16	6.6	6	54.5
Games 9-16	8	15	112	7.5	2	14	0	41	32	4.7	6	40.0
September	4	4	57	14.3	1	29	1	22	6	8.8	3	75.0
October	4	7	69	9.9	0	21	0	31	10	5.4	3	42.9
November	4	10	71	7.1	1	14	0	29	17	4.2	3	30.0
December	4	5	41	8.2	1	14	0	12	15	5.8	3	60.0
Grass	6	11	73	6.6	1	12	0	32	20	3.7	3	27.3
Turf	10	15	165	11.0	2	29	1	62	28	6.9	9	60.0
Outdoor	1	24	214	8.9	2	29	1	92	46	5.1	10	41.7
Indoor	15	2	24	12.0	1	15	0	2	2	11.0	2	100.0
1st Half	-	16	171	10.7	3	29	1	51	25	7.5	10	62.5
2nd Half/OT	-	10	67	6.7	0	14	0	43	23	2.4	2	20.0
Last 2 Min. Half	-	1	7	7.0	1	7	0	2	1	5.0	1	100.0
4th qtr, +/-7 pts	-	2	19	9.5	0	11	0	3	5	8.0	1	50.0
Winning	-	7	73	10.4	2	15	0	28	15	6.4	5	71.4
Tied	-	7	46	6.6	1	14	0	22	12	3.4	3	42.9
Trailing	-	12	119	9.9	0	29	1	44	21	6.3	4	33.3

	Rec	Yds	Avg	TD	Lg	Big	YAC	Trgt	Y@C	1st	1st%
Inside 20	5	45	9.0	3	15	0	5	11	8.0	3	60.0
Inside 10	2	11	5.5	1	7	0	4	6	3.5	1	50.0
1st Down	14	135	9.6	2	29	1	59	24	5.4	5	35.7
2nd Down	12	103	8.6	1	21	0	35	19	5.7	7	58.3
3rd Down Overall	0	0	-	0	0	0	0	5	-	0	-
3rd D 0-2 to Go	0	0	-	0	0	0	0	0	-	0	-
3rd D 3-7 to Go	0	0	-	0	0	0	0	1	-	0	-
3rd D 8+ to Go	0	0	-	0	0	0	0	2	-	0	-
4th Down	0	0	-	0	0	0	0	0	-	0	-
Rec Behind Line	2	12	6.0	0	9	0	20	2	-4.0	1	50.0
1-10 yds	19	135	7.1	1	14	0	50	29	4.5	6	31.6
11-20 yds	5	91	18.2	2	29	1	24	14	13.4	5	100.0
21-30 yds	0	0	-	0	0	0	0	0	-	0	-
31+	0	0	-	0	0	0	0	0	-	0	-
Left Sideline	2	14	7.0	0	8	0	10	4	2.0	1	50.0
Left Side	9	74	8.2	2	15	0	34	10	4.4	3	33.3
Middle	7	79	11.3	0	21	0	18	15	8.7	4	57.1
Right Side	8	71	8.9	1	29	1	32	15	4.9	4	50.0
Right Sideline	0	0	-	0	0	0	0	4	-	0	-
Shotgun	0	0	-	0	0	0	0	0	-	0	-
2 Wide Receivers	10	181	0.5	3	20	1	70	04	5.4	10	52.6
3 Wide Receivers	7	57	8.1	0	21	0	16	12	5.9	2	28.6
4+ Wide Receivers	0	0	-	0	0	0	0	0	-	0	-

1995 Incompletions

Type	Num	%of Inc	%of Att
Pass Dropped	2	9.1	4.2
Poor Throw	13	59.1	27.1
Pass Defensed	4	18.2	8.3
Pass Hit at Line	0	0.0	0.0
Other	3	13.6	6.3
Total	22	100.0	45.8

Game Logs (1-8)

Date	Opp	Result	Rec	Yds	Trgt	F-L	TD
09/03	Det	W 23-20	0	0	1	0-0	0
09/10	@Hou	W 34-17	2	24	2	0-0	0
09/18	@Mia	L 10-23	0	0	1	0-0	0
09/24	Min	L 24-44	2	33	2	0-0	0
10/01	SD	W 31-16	3	29	3	0-0	0
10/08	@Jac	L 16-20	2	14	2	0-0	0
10/19	Cin	L 9-27	2	26	4	0-0	0
10/29	Jac	W 24-7	0	0	2	0-0	0

Game Logs (9-16)

Date	Opp	Result	Rec	Yds	Trgt	F-L	TD
11/05	@Chi	W 37-34	1	5	3	0-0	0
11/13	Cle	W 20-3	0	0	2	0-0	0
11/19	@Cin	W 49-31	4	32	5	0-0	0
11/26	@Cle	W 20-17	5	34	7	0-0	1
12/03	Hou	W 21-7	1	7	6	0-0	1
12/10	@Oak	W 29-10	0	0	3	0-0	0
12/16	NE	W 41-27	1	14	2	0-0	0
12/24	@GB	L 19-24	3	20	5	0-0	0

Mark Brunell

Jacksonville Jaguars — QB

1995 Passing Splits

	G	Att	Cm	Pct	Yds	Yd/Att	TD	Int	1st	YAC	Big	Sk	Rtg		Att	Cm	Pct	Yds	Yd/Att	TD	Int	1st	YAC	Big	Sk	Rtg
Total	13	346	201	58.1	2168	6.3	15	7	107	761	12	39	82.6	Inside 20	38	21	55.3	175	4.6	13	1	17	50	0	6	95.9
vs. Playoff	4	131	77	58.8	846	6.5	7	1	45	314	4	18	92.6	Inside 10	13	8	61.5	44	3.4	7	1	7	10	0	3	75.0
vs. Non-playoff	9	215	124	57.7	1322	6.1	8	6	62	447	8	21	76.5	1st Down	124	73	58.9	829	6.7	6	2	34	284	8	15	88.4
vs. Own Division	7	156	86	55.1	970	6.2	5	3	48	359	6	21	76.6	2nd Down	127	74	58.3	808	6.4	4	3	39	295	3	12	77.8
Home	7	204	122	59.8	1370	6.7	11	4	70	463	9	19	89.7	3rd Down Overall	90	51	56.7	499	5.5	4	2	31	175	1	9	78.0
Away	6	142	79	55.6	798	5.6	4	3	37	298	3	20	72.4	3rd D 0-5 to Go	22	13	59.1	143	6.5	1	0	12	38	0	1	93.6
Games 1-8	8	204	112	54.9	1102	5.4	9	5	60	412	2	25	74.8	3rd D 6+ to Go	68	38	55.9	356	5.2	3	2	19	137	1	8	72.9
Games 9-16	5	142	89	62.7	1066	7.5	6	2	47	349	10	14	93.8	4th Down	5	3	60.0	32	6.4	1	0	3	7	0	3	118.3
September	4	89	42	47.2	390	4.4	3	3	22	154	0	19	56.9	Rec Behind Line	40	26	65.0	130	3.3	2	0	5	203	0	0	86.5
October	5	148	88	59.5	901	6.1	7	2	47	342	2	13	87.1	1-10 yds	184	128	69.6	1098	6.0	7	4	57	406	0	0	88.5
November	2	41	28	68.3	290	7.1	1	1	11	96	3	4	86.4	11-20 yds	81	37	45.7	620	7.7	4	2	35	108	4	0	78.2
December	2	68	43	63.2	587	8.6	4	1	27	169	7	3	104.2	21-30 yds	27	7	25.9	208	7.7	1	0	7	36	5	0	71.5
Grass	9	253	153	60.5	1703	6.7	12	5	84	582	12	21	88.1	31+	14	3	21.4	112	8.0	1	1	3	8	3	0	54.5
Turf	4	93	48	51.6	465	5.0	3	2	23	179	0	18	67.7	Left Sideline	90	41	45.6	503	5.6	1	2	25	146	4	3	57.8
Indoor	1	9	7	77.8	57	6.3	1	0	3	23	0	0	130.1	Left Side	82	53	64.6	537	6.3	7	2	27	231	3	5	100.5
Outdoor	12	337	194	57.6	2111	6.3	14	7	104	738	12	39	81.3	Middle	49	25	51.0	322	6.6	4	0	17	121	1	28	99.2
1st Half	-	135	78	57.8	829	6.1	5	2	38	306	6	14	82.0	Right Side	74	53	71.6	549	7.4	3	3	27	217	3	2	89.3
2nd Half/OT	-	211	123	58.3	1339	6.3	10	5	69	455	6	25	83.0	Right Sideline	51	29	56.9	277	5.4	0	1	11	46	1	1	72.1
Last 2 Min. Half	-	65	41	63.1	384	5.9	5	1	21	112	0	8	98.5	2 Wide Receivers	87	56	64.4	632	7.3	3	2	30	204	6	7	87.9
4th qtr, +/-7 pts	-	42	25	59.5	245	5.8	1	3	12	88	1	6	54.2	3+ WR	254	143	56.3	1531	6.0	12	5	77	557	6	30	81.7
Winning	-	72	39	54.2	431	6.0	1	2	20	156	3	4	65.2	Attempts 1-10	128	67	52.3	709	5.5	5	3	35	262	5	0	72.0
Tied	-	38	23	60.5	268	7.1	2	0	13	93	2	3	78.3	Attempts 11-20	108	63	58.3	676	6.3	3	2	29	221	5	0	78.3
Trailing	-	236	139	58.9	1469	6.2	12	5	74	512	7	32	85.2	Attempts 21+	110	71	64.5	783	7.1	7	2	43	278	2	0	99.2

1995 Incompletions

Type	Num	% of Inc	% of Att
Pass Dropped	24	16.6	6.9
Poor Throw	68	46.9	19.7
Pass Defensed	18	12.4	5.2
Pass Hit at Line	9	6.2	2.6
Other	26	17.9	7.5
Total	145	100.0	41.9

Game Logs (1-8)

Date	Opp	Result	Att	Cm	Pct	Yds	TD	Int	Lg	Sk	F-L
09/03	Hou	L 3-10	9	3	33.3	15	0	1	8	3	0-0
09/10	@Cin	L 17-24	18	8	44.4	81	0	1	22	5	1-1
09/17	@NYA	L 10-27	33	15	45.5	138	1	1	18	6	2-1
09/24	GB	L 14-24	29	16	55.2	156	2	0	19	5	0-0
10/01	@Hou	W 17-16	9	7	77.8	57	1	0	15	0	0-0
10/08	Pit	W 20-16	30	17	56.7	189	1	0	39	4	1-0
10/15	Chi	L 27-30	48	30	62.5	302	3	1	23	1	0-0
10/22	@Cle	W 23-15	28	16	57.1	164	1	1	28	1	0-0

Game Logs (9-16)

Date	Opp	Result	Att	Cm	Pct	Yds	TD	Int	Lg	Sk	F-L
10/29	@Pit	L 7-24	33	18	54.5	189	1	0	24	7	0-0
11/12	Sea	L 30-47	20	13	65.0	121	1	1	28	3	0-0
11/19	@TB	L 16-17	21	15	71.4	169	0	0	35	1	1-0
11/26	Cin	L 13-17	-	-	-	-	-	-	-	-	-
12/03	@Den	L 23-31	-	-	-	-	-	-	-	-	-
12/10	Ind	L 31-41	39	26	66.7	312	3	1	45	2	0-0
12/17	@Det	L 0-44	-	-	-	-	-	-	-	-	-
12/24	Cle	W 24-21	29	17	58.6	275	1	0	34	1	0-0

Keith Byars

Miami Dolphins — RB

1995 Receiving Splits

	G	Rec	Yds	Avg	TD	Lg	Big	YAC	Trgt	Y/C	1st	1st%		Rec	Yds	Avg	TD	Lg	Big	YAC	Trgt	Y@C	1st	1st%
Total	16	51	362	7.1	2	26	1	265	70	1.9	18	35.3	Inside 20	6	39	6.5	2	13	0	31	11	1.3	3	50.0
vs. Playoff	9	29	198	6.8	1	26	1	150	43	1.7	10	34.5	Inside 10	2	7	3.5	2	6	0	6	3	0.5	2	100.0
vs. Non-playoff	7	22	164	7.5	1	24	0	115	27	2.2	8	36.4	1st Down	20	126	6.3	0	13	0	106	31	1.0	3	15.0
vs. Own Division	8	25	213	8.5	2	26	1	140	34	2.9	10	40.0	2nd Down	28	195	7.0	2	24	0	136	33	2.1	13	46.4
Home	8	25	168	6.7	1	24	0	121	36	1.9	8	36.0	3rd Down Overall	3	41	13.7	0	26	1	23	6	6.0	2	66.7
Away	8	26	194	7.5	1	26	1	144	34	1.9	9	34.6	3rd D 0-2 to Go	0	0	-	0	0	0	0	0	-	0	-
Games 1-8	8	24	162	6.8	1	24	0	123	33	1.6	7	29.2	3rd D 3-7 to Go	2	15	7.5	0	11	0	9	5	3.0	1	50.0
Games 9-16	8	27	200	7.4	1	26	1	142	37	2.1	11	40.7	3rd D 8+ to Go	1	26	26.0	0	26	1	14	1	12.0	1	100.0
September	3	7	62	8.9	1	24	0	42	10	2.9	4	57.1	4th Down	0	0	-	0	0	0	0	0	-	0	-
October	5	17	100	5.9	0	13	0	81	23	1.1	3	17.6	Rec Behind Line	16	52	3.3	1	11	0	78	24	-1.6	2	18.8
November	4	14	125	8.9	1	14	0	83	20	3.0	8	57.1	1-10 yds	33	260	7.9	1	14	0	163	41	2.9	13	39.4
December	4	13	75	5.8	0	26	1	59	17	1.2	3	23.1	11-20 yds	2	50	25.0	0	26	1	24	5	13.0	2	100.0
Grass	10	33	245	7.4	1	24	0	176	45	1.9	13	39.4	21-30 yds	0	0	-	0	0	0	0	0	-	0	-
Turf	6	18	117	6.5	1	26	1	89	25	1.6	5	27.8	31+	0	0	-	0	0	0	0	0	-	0	-
Indoor	3	9	46	5.1	1	10	0	40	14	0.7	3	33.3	Left Sideline	15	152	10.1	0	26	1	108	19	2.9	6	40.0
Outdoor	13	42	316	7.5	1	26	1	225	56	2.2	15	35.7	Middle	3	18	6.0	1	10	0	14	7	1.3	2	66.7
1st Half	-	36	238	6.6	2	14	0	193	49	1.3	12	33.3	Right Side	9	45	5.0	0	13	0	32	15	1.4	3	33.3
2nd Half/OT	-	15	124	8.3	0	26	1	72	21	3.5	6	40.0	Right Sideline	15	79	5.3	0	11	0	64	18	1.0	3	20.0
Last 2 Min. Half	-	5	22	4.4	0	9	0	24	6	-0.4	3	60.0	Shotgun	9	68	7.6	1	24	0	47	11	2.3	4	44.4
4th qtr, +/-7 pts	-	3	44	14.7	0	26	1	19	4	8.3	2	66.7	2 Wide Receivers	28	188	6.7	2	24	0	141	38	1.7	11	39.3
Winning	-	21	166	7.9	0	24	0	115	24	2.4	9	42.9	3 Wide Receivers	23	174	7.6	0	26	1	124	31	2.2	7	30.4
Tied	-	7	34	4.9	1	13	0	25	15	1.3	1	14.3	4+ Wide Receivers	0	0	-	0	0	0	0	0	-	0	-
Trailing	-	23	162	7.0	1	26	1	125	31	1.6	8	34.8												

1995 Incompletions

Type	Num	%of Inc	%of Att
Pass Dropped	9	47.4	12.9
Poor Throw	5	26.3	7.1
Pass Defensed	2	10.5	2.9
Pass Hit at Line	3	15.8	4.3
Other	0	0.0	0.0
Total	19	100.0	27.1

Game Logs (1-8)

Date	Opp	Result	Rush	Yds	Rec	Yds	Trgt	F-L	TD
09/03	NYA	W 52-14	1	1	2	25	3	0-0	1
09/10	@NE	W 20-3	0	0	2	22	2	0-0	0
09/18	Pit	W 23-10	0	0	3	15	5	0-0	0
10/01	@Cin	W 26-23	0	0	2	12	3	0-0	0
10/08	Ind	L 24-27	3	5	5	32	5	0-0	0
10/15	@NO	L 30-33	1	2	4	26	6	0-0	0
10/22	@NYA	L 16-17	0	0	4	23	4	0-0	0
10/29	Buf	W 23-6	2	5	2	7	5	0-0	0

Game Logs (9-16)

Date	Opp	Result	Rush	Yds	Rec	Yds	Trgt	F-L	TD
11/05	@SD	W 24-14	2	3	6	55	7	0-0	1
11/12	NE	L 17-34	1	3	5	52	6	0-0	0
11/20	SF	L 20-44	0	0	1	2	2	0-0	0
11/26	@Ind	L 28-36	1	4	2	16	5	0-0	0
12/03	Atl	W 21-20	1	5	5	23	8	0-0	0
12/11	KC	W 13-6	0	0	5	23	8	0-0	0
12/17	@Buf	L 20-23	2	17	3	36	4	0-0	0
12/24	@StL	W 41-22	1	0	3	4	3	0-0	0

Earnest Byner
Cleveland Browns — RB

1995 Receiving Splits

	G	Rec	Yds	Avg	TD	Lg	Big	YAC	Trgt	Y@C	1st	1st%		Rec	Yds	Avg	TD	Lg	Big	YAC	Trgt	Y@C	1st	1st%
Total	16	61	494	8.1	2	29	1	510	84	-0.3	31	50.8	Inside 20	5	18	3.6	1	6	0	25	8	-1.4	1	20.0
vs. Playoff	7	27	202	7.5	1	20	0	241	40	-1.4	14	51.9	Inside 10	1	3	3.0	1	3	0	7	2	-4.0	1	100.0
vs. Non-playoff	9	34	292	8.6	1	29	1	269	44	0.7	17	50.0	1st Down	14	121	8.6	0	20	0	95	19	1.9	7	50.0
vs. Own Division	8	32	266	8.3	0	22	0	292	47	-0.8	16	50.0	2nd Down	24	135	5.6	1	14	0	198	30	-2.6	8	33.3
Home	8	34	262	7.7	1	20	0	236	47	0.8	19	55.9	3rd Down Overall	23	238	10.3	1	29	1	217	35	0.9	16	69.6
Away	8	27	232	8.6	1	29	1	274	37	-1.6	12	44.4	3rd D 0-2 to Go	4	59	14.8	1	29	1	47	4	3.0	4	100.0
Games 1-8	8	26	231	8.9	1	22	0	212	34	0.7	18	69.2	3rd D 3-7 to Go	12	109	9.1	0	22	0	96	15	1.1	9	75.0
Games 9-16	8	35	263	7.5	1	29	1	298	50	-1.0	13	37.1	3rd D 8+ to Go	7	70	10.0	0	15	0	74	16	-0.6	3	42.9
September	4	14	124	8.9	1	15	0	126	15	-0.1	11	78.6	4th Down	0	0	-	0	0	0	0	0	-	0	-
October	4	12	107	8.9	0	22	0	86	19	1.8	7	58.3	Rec Behind Line	30	215	7.2	2	29	1	365	38	-5.0	12	40.0
November	4	14	113	8.1	0	20	0	133	24	-1.4	6	42.9	1-10 yds	29	251	8.7	0	20	0	141	42	3.8	17	58.6
December	4	21	150	7.1	1	29	1	165	26	-0.7	7	33.3	11-20 yds	2	28	14.0	0	14	0	4	4	12.0	2	100.0
Grass	11	47	351	7.5	1	20	0	327	62	0.5	25	53.2	21-30 yds	0	0	-	0	0	0	0	0	-	0	-
Turf	5	14	143	10.2	1	29	1	183	22	-2.9	6	42.9	31+	0	0	-	0	0	0	0	0	-	0	-
Indoor	3	8	86	10.8	1	29	1	66	12	2.5	3	37.5	Left Sideline	11	80	7.3	0	14	0	64	18	1.5	6	54.5
Outdoor	13	53	408	7.7	1	22	0	444	72	-0.7	28	52.8	Left Side	19	154	8.1	0	22	0	167	27	-0.7	8	42.1
1st Half	-	38	294	7.7	0	22	0	319	48	-0.7	20	52.6	Middle	17	161	9.5	1	29	1	185	19	-1.4	9	52.9
2nd Half/OT	-	23	200	8.7	2	29	1	191	36	0.4	11	47.8	Right Side	5	31	6.2	0	13	0	30	9	0.2	2	40.0
Last 2 Min. Half	-	11	86	7.8	0	20	0	123	11	-3.4	6	54.5	Right Sideline	9	68	7.6	1	14	0	64	11	0.4	6	66.7
4th qtr, +/-7 pts	-	3	22	7.3	0	17	0	25	4	-1.0	1	33.3	Shotgun	0	0	-	0	0	0	0	0	-	0	-
Winning	-	16	125	7.8	1	15	0	124	18	0.1	9	56.3	2 Wide Receivers	4	33	8.3	0	16	0	40	7	-1.8	2	50.0
Tied	-	11	70	6.4	0	17	0	88	17	-1.6	5	45.5	3 Wide Receivers	51	430	8.4	1	29	1	385	68	0.9	26	51.0
Trailing	-	34	299	8.8	1	29	1	298	49	0.0	17	50.0	4+ Wide Receivers	5	34	6.8	1	17	0	84	7	-10.0	3	60.0

1995 Incompletions

Type	Num	%of Inc	%of Att
Pass Dropped	4	17.4	4.8
Poor Throw	12	52.2	14.3
Pass Defensed	2	8.7	2.4
Pass Hit at Line	1	4.3	1.2
Other	4	17.4	4.8
Total	23	100.0	27.4

Game Logs (1-8)

Date	Opp	Result	Rush	Yds	Rec	Yds	Trgt	F-L	TD
09/03	@NE	L 14-17	3	15	2	15	2	0-0	0
09/10	TB	W 22-6	0	0	3	30	3	0-0	0
09/17	@Hou	W 14-7	2	8	2	20	3	0-0	0
09/24	KC	W 35-17	9	38	7	59	7	0-0	2
10/02	Buf	L 19-22	7	24	2	8	6	0-0	0
10/08	@Det	L 20-38	1	0	3	26	5	0-0	0
10/22	Jac	L 15-23	1	0	3	30	3	0-0	0
10/29	@Cin	W 29-26	17	74	4	43	5	0-0	1

Game Logs (9-16)

Date	Opp	Result	Rush	Yds	Rec	Yds	Trgt	F-L	TD
11/05	Hou	L 10-37	4	23	4	36	7	0-0	0
11/13	@Pit	L 3-20	5	20	2	14	5	0-0	0
11/19	GB	L 20-31	6	10	4	18	5	0-0	0
11/26	Pit	L 17-20	8	27	4	45	7	1-0	0
12/03	@SD	L 13-31	5	9	5	32	5	0-0	0
12/09	@Min	L 11-27	3	11	3	40	4	0-0	1
12/17	Cin	W 26-10	31	121	7	36	9	0-0	0
12/24	@Jac	L 21-24	13	52	6	42	8	0-0	0

Chris Calloway
New York Giants — WR

1995 Receiving Splits

	G	Rec	Yds	Avg	TD	Lg	Big	YAC	Trgt	Y@C	1st	1st%		Rec	Yds	Avg	TD	Lg	Big	YAC	Trgt	Y@C	1st	1st%
Total	16	56	796	14.2	3	49	5	249	104	9.8	43	76.8	Inside 20	1	12	12.0	0	12	0	9	6	3.0	1	100.0
vs. Playoff	8	26	340	13.1	2	37	2	93	51	9.5	20	76.9	Inside 10	0	0	-	0	0	0	0	1	-	0	-
vs. Non-playoff	8	30	456	15.2	1	49	3	156	53	10.0	23	76.7	1st Down	14	183	13.1	0	23	0	60	28	8.8	10	71.4
vs. Own Division	8	25	356	14.2	1	49	2	91	44	10.6	20	80.0	2nd Down	22	351	16.0	3	49	4	104	42	11.2	15	68.2
Home	8	27	416	15.4	2	49	3	116	44	11.1	21	77.8	3rd Down Overall	20	262	13.1	0	37	1	85	34	8.9	18	90.0
Away	8	29	380	13.1	1	37	2	133	60	8.5	22	75.9	3rd D 0-2 to Go	2	15	7.5	0	9	0	6	3	4.5	2	100.0
Games 1-8	8	29	453	15.6	2	49	4	139	51	10.8	23	79.3	3rd D 3-7 to Go	9	114	12.7	0	37	1	62	16	5.8	8	88.9
Games 9-16	8	27	343	12.7	1	40	1	110	53	8.6	20	74.1	3rd D 8+ to Go	9	133	14.8	0	22	0	17	15	12.9	8	88.9
September	4	16	265	16.6	2	38	3	106	31	9.9	13	81.3	4th Down	0	0	-	0	0	0	0	0	-	0	-
October	4	13	188	14.5	0	49	1	33	20	11.9	10	76.9	Rec Behind Line	0	0	-	0	0	0	0	1	-	0	-
November	5	20	234	11.7	0	22	0	79	39	7.8	14	70.0	1-10 yds	34	344	10.1	0	37	1	161	65	5.4	23	67.6
December	3	7	109	15.6	1	40	1	31	14	11.1	6	85.7	11-20 yds	19	337	17.7	1	38	1	64	29	14.4	17	89.5
Grass	5	21	269	12.8	1	37	2	86	42	8.7	15	71.4	21-30 yds	1	26	26.0	0	26	1	0	4	26.0	1	100.0
Turf	11	35	527	15.1	2	49	3	163	62	10.4	28	80.0	31+	2	89	44.5	1	49	2	24	5	32.5	2	100.0
Indoor	1	4	59	14.8	0	21	0	20	9	9.8	3	75.0	Left Sideline	3	43	14.3	0	23	0	11	12	10.7	2	66.7
Outdoor	15	52	737	14.2	3	49	5	229	95	9.8	40	76.9	Left Side	11	122	11.1	0	20	0	44	20	7.1	10	90.9
1st Half	-	28	401	14.3	2	38	3	177	52	8.0	20	71.4	Middle	11	115	10.5	0	22	0	23	15	8.4	7	63.6
2nd Half/OT	-	28	395	14.1	1	49	2	72	52	11.5	23	82.1	Right Side	12	259	21.6	2	40	3	92	23	13.9	11	91.7
Last 2 Min. Half	-	10	140	14.0	1	40	1	37	21	10.3	6	60.0	Right Sideline	19	257	13.5	1	49	2	79	34	9.4	13	68.4
4th qtr, +/-7 pts	-	8	176	22.0	1	49	2	32	13	18.0	7	87.5	Shotgun	13	201	15.5	0	49	1	41	24	12.3	10	76.9
Winning	-	11	102	9.3	0	23	0	20	23	7.5	7	63.6	2 Wide Receivers	33	444	13.5	2	38	3	165	60	8.5	25	75.8
Tied	-	5	131	26.2	2	40	3	55	13	15.2	5	100.0	3 Wide Receivers	17	279	16.4	1	49	2	67	24	12.5	14	82.4
Trailing	-	40	563	14.1	1	49	2	174	68	9.7	31	77.5	4+ Wide Receivers	6	73	12.2	0	23	0	17	18	9.3	4	66.7

1995 Incompletions

Type	Num	%of Inc	%of Att
Pass Dropped	8	16.7	7.7
Poor Throw	23	47.9	22.1
Pass Defensed	10	20.8	9.6
Pass Hit at Line	1	2.1	1.0
Other	6	12.5	5.8
Total	48	100.0	46.2

Game Logs (1-8)

Date	Opp	Result	Rush	Yds	Rec	Yds	Trgt	F-L	TD
09/04	Dal	L 0-35	0	0	3	35	6	0-0	0
09/10	@KC	L 17-20	0	0	5	100	6	0-0	1
09/17	@GB	L 6-14	0	0	3	35	11	0-0	0
09/24	NO	W 45-29	1	-3	5	95	8	0-0	1
10/01	@SF	L 6-20	0	0	4	46	7	0-0	0
10/08	Ari	W 27-21	1	-6	3	78	4	0-0	1
10/15	Phi	L 14-17	0	0	4	47	5	0-0	0
10/29	@Was	W 24-15	0	0	2	17	4	0-0	0

Game Logs (9-16)

Date	Opp	Result	Rush	Yds	Rec	Yds	Trgt	F-L	TD
11/05	@Sea	L 28-30	0	0	4	59	9	0-0	0
11/12	Oak	L 13-17	0	0	5	60	9	0-0	0
11/19	@Phi	L 19-28	0	0	2	14	4	0-0	0
11/26	Chi	L 24-27	0	0	2	20	3	0-0	0
11/30	@Ari	W 10-6	0	0	7	71	14	0-0	0
12/10	Was	W 20-13	0	0	2	56	2	0-0	1
12/17	@Dal	L 20-21	0	0	2	28	5	0-0	0
12/23	SD	L 17-27	0	0	3	25	7	0-0	0

Rob Carpenter
Philadelphia Eagles — WR

1995 Receiving Splits

	G	Rec	Yds	Avg	TD	Lg	Big	YAC	Trgt	Y@C	1st	1st%
Total	16	29	318	11.0	0	29	2	82	58	8.1	19	65.5
vs. Playoff	3	5	66	13.2	0	20	0	17	11	9.8	5	100.0
vs. Non-playoff	13	24	252	10.5	0	29	2	65	47	7.8	14	58.3
vs. Own Division	8	8	90	11.3	0	20	0	19	20	8.9	6	75.0
Home	8	16	168	10.5	0	29	1	50	27	7.4	9	56.3
Away	8	13	150	11.5	0	29	1	32	31	9.1	10	76.9
Games 1-8	8	9	72	8.0	0	11	0	19	18	5.9	5	55.6
Games 9-16	8	20	246	12.3	0	29	2	63	40	9.2	14	70.0
September	4	3	28	9.3	0	10	0	6	7	7.3	3	100.0
October	4	6	44	7.3	0	11	0	13	11	5.2	2	33.3
November	4	7	75	10.7	0	29	1	21	17	7.7	4	57.1
December	4	13	171	13.2	0	29	1	42	23	9.9	10	76.9
Grass	4	8	90	11.3	0	15	0	18	17	9.0	6	75.0
Turf	12	21	228	10.9	0	29	2	64	41	7.8	13	61.9
Outdoor	2	25	261	10.4	0	29	1	69	51	7.7	16	64.0
Indoor	14	4	57	14.3	0	29	1	13	7	11.0	3	75.0
1st Half	-	17	220	12.9	0	29	2	60	30	9.4	12	70.6
2nd Half/OT	-	12	98	8.2	0	15	0	22	28	6.3	7	58.3
Last 2 Min. Half	-	7	78	11.1	0	16	0	12	12	9.4	4	57.1
4th qtr, +/-7 pts	-	4	39	9.8	0	15	0	7	10	8.0	2	50.0
Winning	-	8	53	6.6	0	14	0	13	15	5.0	3	37.5
Tied	-	6	74	12.3	0	29	1	24	11	8.3	4	66.7
Trailing	-	15	191	12.7	0	29	1	45	32	9.7	12	80.0

	Rec	Yds	Avg	TD	Lg	Big	YAC	Trgt	Y@C	1st	1st%
Inside 20	1	7	7.0	0	7	0	1	3	6.0	0	0.0
Inside 10	0	0	0	0	0	0	0	0	-	0	-
1st Down	6	58	9.7	0	14	0	14	13	7.3	4	66.7
2nd Down	9	90	10.0	0	16	0	29	21	6.8	5	55.6
3rd Down Overall	13	155	11.9	0	29	2	39	22	8.9	9	69.2
3rd D 0-2 to Go	0	0	0	0	0	0	0	1	-	0	-
3rd D 3-7 to Go	6	68	11.3	0	29	1	16	9	8.7	6	100.0
3rd D 8+ to Go	7	87	12.4	0	29	1	23	12	9.1	3	42.9
4th Down	1	15	15.0	0	15	0	0	2	15.0	1	100.0
Rec Behind Line	0	0	0	0	0	0	0	2	-	0	-
1-10 yds	22	183	8.3	0	14	0	59	37	5.6	12	54.5
11-20 yds	6	106	17.7	0	29	1	19	14	14.5	6	100.0
21-30 yds	1	29	29.0	0	29	1	4	4	25.0	1	100.0
31+	0	0	0	0	0	0	0	2	-	0	-
Left Sideline	3	36	12.0	0	20	0	4	4	10.7	2	66.7
Left Side	7	59	8.4	0	14	0	22	16	5.3	2	28.6
Middle	7	100	14.3	0	29	1	27	15	10.4	6	85.7
Right Side	9	102	11.3	0	29	1	21	17	9.0	7	77.8
Right Sideline	3	21	7.0	0	10	0	8	6	4.3	2	66.7
Shotgun	0	0	-	0	0	0	0	0	-	0	-
2 Wide Receivers	9	70	7.8	0	14	0	21	17	5.4	5	55.6
3 Wide Receivers	13	160	12.3	0	29	2	40	28	9.2	8	61.5
4+ Wide Receivers	7	88	12.6	0	20	0	21	13	9.6	5	85.7

1995 Incompletions

Type	Num	%of Inc	%of Att
Pass Dropped	4	13.8	6.9
Poor Throw	13	44.8	22.4
Pass Defensed	5	17.2	8.6
Pass Hit at Line	1	3.4	1.7
Other	6	20.7	10.3
Total	29	100.0	50.0

Game Logs (1-8)

Date	Opp	Result	Rec	Yds	Trgt	F-L	TD
09/03	TB	L 6-21	0	0	0	0-0	0
09/10	@Ari	W 31-19	0	0	0	0-0	0
09/17	SD	L 21-27	2	18	3	0-0	0
09/24	@Oak	L 17-48	1	10	4	0-0	0
10/01	@NO	W 15-10	0	0	0	0-0	0
10/08	Was	W 37-34	0	0	1	0-0	0
10/15	@NYN	W 17-14	1	3	2	0-0	0
10/29	StL	W 20-9	5	41	8	0-0	0

Game Logs (9-16)

Date	Opp	Result	Rec	Yds	Trgt	F-L	TD
11/06	@Dal	L 12-34	0	0	5	0-0	0
11/12	Den	W 31-13	3	36	5	0-0	0
11/19	NYN	W 28-19	3	25	5	1-0	0
11/26	@Was	W 14-7	1	14	2	0-0	0
12/03	@Sea	L 14-26	4	57	7	0-0	0
12/10	Dal	W 20-17	3	48	3	0-0	0
12/17	Ari	W 21-20	0	0	2	0-0	0
12/24	@Chi	L 14-20	6	66	11	1-0	0

Mark Carrier
Carolina Panthers — WR

1995 Receiving Splits

	G	Rec	Yds	Avg	TD	Lg	Big	YAC	Trgt	Y@C	1st	1st%
Total	16	66	1002	15.2	3	66	11	385	141	9.3	45	68.2
vs. Playoff	6	24	295	12.3	0	46	2	99	56	8.2	14	58.3
vs. Non-playoff	10	42	707	16.8	3	66	9	286	85	10.0	31	73.8
vs. Own Division	8	33	438	13.3	2	60	4	169	71	8.2	19	57.6
Home	8	29	386	13.3	0	41	4	122	63	9.1	16	55.2
Away	8	37	616	16.6	3	66	7	263	78	9.5	29	78.4
Games 1-8	8	28	469	16.8	1	66	5	174	64	10.5	19	67.9
Games 9-16	8	38	533	14.0	2	60	6	211	77	8.5	26	68.4
September	3	11	156	14.2	0	46	1	50	29	9.6	6	54.5
October	5	17	313	18.4	1	66	4	124	35	11.1	13	76.5
November	4	20	319	16.0	2	60	4	123	40	9.8	15	75.0
December	4	18	214	11.9	0	30	2	88	37	7.0	11	61.1
Grass	12	50	709	14.2	1	66	7	259	103	9.0	33	66.0
Turf	4	16	293	18.3	2	60	4	126	38	10.4	12	75.0
Indoor	3	14	266	19.0	2	60	4	109	31	11.2	10	71.4
Outdoor	13	52	736	14.2	1	66	7	276	110	8.8	35	67.3
1st Half	-	35	518	14.8	1	66	5	202	66	9.0	21	60.0
2nd Half/OT	-	31	484	15.6	2	60	6	183	75	9.7	24	77.4
Last 2 Min. Half	-	3	102	34.0	1	60	1	64	11	12.7	3	100.0
4th qtr, +/-7 pts	-	5	57	11.4	0	17	0	2	17	11.0	3	60.0
Winning	-	12	231	19.3	0	46	3	55	25	14.7	9	75.0
Tied	-	21	222	10.6	0	26	1	45	40	6.5	13	61.9
Trailing	-	33	549	16.6	3	66	7	245	76	9.2	23	69.7

	Rec	Yds	Avg	TD	Lg	Big	YAC	Trgt	Y@C	1st	1st%
Inside 20	5	44	8.8	1	17	0	22	10	4.4	2	40.0
Inside 10	1	3	3.0	1	3	0	0	2	3.0	1	100.0
1st Down	27	558	20.7	3	66	10	231	60	12.1	19	59.3
2nd Down	19	198	10.4	0	30	1	74	46	6.5	10	52.6
3rd Down Overall	19	236	12.4	0	22	0	74	33	8.5	18	94.7
3rd D 0-2 to Go	2	28	14.0	0	21	0	15	4	6.5	2	100.0
3rd D 3-7 to Go	10	100	10.0	0	22	0	39	11	6.1	10	100.0
3rd D 8+ to Go	7	108	15.4	0	22	0	20	18	12.6	6	85.7
4th Down	1	10	10.0	0	10	0	6	2	4.0	1	100.0
Rec Behind Line	0	0	-	0	0	0	0	1	-	0	-
1-10 yds	46	432	9.4	1	22	0	81	25	5.4	25	54.3
11-20 yds	17	449	26.4	2	66	8	185	37	15.5	17	100.0
21-30 yds	0	0	-	0	0	0	0	9	-	0	-
31+	3	121	40.3	0	46	3	15	13	35.3	3	100.0
Left Sideline	6	126	21.0	0	36	2	38	13	14.7	6	100.0
Left Side	9	203	22.6	1	66	3	90	15	12.6	8	88.9
Middle	12	216	18.0	0	46	4	92	24	10.3	10	83.3
Right Side	21	264	12.6	2	60	1	98	46	7.9	11	52.4
Right Sideline	18	193	10.7	0	41	1	67	43	10.5	10	55.6
Shotgun	0	0	-	0	0	0	0	0	-	0	-
2 Wide Receivers	34	530	15.6	2	66	7	195	82	9.9	21	61.8
3 Wide Receivers	30	383	12.8	0	28	2	133	52	8.3	22	73.3
4+ Wide Receivers	2	89	44.5	1	60	2	57	7	16.0	2	100.0

1995 Incompletions

Type	Num	%of Inc	%of Att
Pass Dropped	13	17.3	9.2
Poor Throw	43	57.3	30.5
Pass Defensed	14	18.7	9.9
Pass Hit at Line	2	2.7	1.4
Other	3	4.0	2.1
Total	75	100.0	53.2

Game Logs (1-8)

Date	Opp	Result	Rush	Yds	Rec	Yds	Trgt	F-L	TD
09/03	@Atl	L 20-23	0	0	5	96	12	0-0	0
09/10	@Buf	L 9-31	0	0	2	27	7	0-0	0
09/17	StL	L 10-31	1	-1	4	33	10	0-0	0
10/01	TB	L 13-20	0	0	5	90	9	0-0	0
10/08	@Chi	L 27-31	1	-7	5	114	8	0-0	0
10/15	NYA	W 26-15	0	0	2	42	4	0-0	0
10/22	NO	W 20-3	0	0	2	18	5	0-0	0
10/29	@NE	W 20-17	0	0	3	49	10	0-0	0

Game Logs (9-16)

Date	Opp	Result	Rush	Yds	Rec	Yds	Trgt	F-L	TD
11/05	@SF	W 13-7	0	0	5	59	11	0-0	0
11/12	@StL	L 17-28	0	0	3	38	7	0-0	0
11/19	Ari	W 27-7	0	0	5	90	10	0-0	0
11/26	@NO	L 26-34	0	0	6	132	12	0-0	0
12/03	Ind	W 13-10	0	0	4	51	11	0-0	0
12/10	SF	L 10-31	0	0	0	0	4	0-0	0
12/17	Atl	W 21-17	1	4	7	62	11	0-0	0
12/24	@Was	L 17-20	0	0	7	101	11	0-0	0

Cris Carter
Minnesota Vikings — WR

1995 Receiving Splits

	G	Rec	Yds	Avg	TD	Lg	Big	YAC	Trgt	Y@C	1st	1st%		Rec	Yds	Avg	TD	Lg	Big	YAC	Trgt	Y@C	1st	1st%
Total	16	122	1371	11.2	17	60	9	438	197	7.6	80	65.6	Inside 20	20	165	8.3	13	18	0	27	32	6.9	17	85.0
vs. Playoff	7	48	451	9.4	8	37	3	142	84	6.4	28	58.3	Inside 10	8	39	4.9	8	8	0	0	15	4.9	8	100.0
vs. Non-playoff	9	74	920	12.4	9	60	6	296	113	8.4	52	70.3	1st Down	38	513	13.5	7	60	3	161	62	9.3	22	57.9
vs. Own Division	8	48	565	11.8	5	60	6	186	88	7.9	27	56.3	2nd Down	52	604	11.6	7	37	5	185	72	8.1	30	57.7
Home	8	66	767	11.6	8	60	5	246	98	7.9	41	62.1	3rd Down Overall	32	254	7.9	3	28	1	92	62	5.1	28	87.5
Away	8	56	604	10.8	9	37	4	192	99	7.4	39	69.6	3rd D 0-2 to Go	12	55	4.6	1	12	0	32	14	1.9	12	100.0
Games 1-8	8	51	508	10.0	5	37	3	171	93	6.6	29	56.9	3rd D 3-7 to Go	13	130	10.0	1	28	1	42	25	6.8	11	84.6
Games 9-16	8	71	863	12.2	12	60	6	267	104	8.4	51	71.8	3rd D 8+ to Go	7	69	9.9	1	14	0	18	23	7.3	5	71.4
September	4	22	246	11.2	3	34	2	104	39	6.5	15	68.2	4th Down	0	0	-	0	0	0	0	1	-	0	-
October	4	29	262	9.0	2	37	1	67	54	6.7	14	48.3	Rec Behind Line	8	30	3.8	0	11	0	34	10	-0.5	3	37.5
November	4	38	436	11.5	7	29	3	113	55	8.5	27	71.1	1-10 yds	75	530	7.1	10	22	0	234	112	3.9	40	53.3
December	4	33	427	12.9	5	60	3	154	49	8.3	24	72.7	11-20 yds	34	639	18.8	5	52	4	137	55	14.8	32	94.1
Grass	5	38	407	10.7	4	37	4	125	66	7.4	25	65.8	21-30 yds	4	112	28.0	1	29	4	9	13	25.8	4	100.0
Turf	11	84	964	11.5	13	60	5	313	131	7.8	55	65.5	31+	1	60	60.0	1	60	1	0	1	36.0	1	100.0
Indoor	9	71	818	11.5	10	60	5	249	110	8.0	44	62.0	Left Sideline	31	304	9.8	4	27	1	106	46	6.4	19	61.3
Outdoor	7	51	553	10.8	7	37	4	189	87	7.1	36	70.6	Left Side	14	128	9.1	2	22	0	43	26	6.1	5	35.7
1st Half	-	70	799	11.4	10	60	5	245	105	7.9	45	64.3	Middle	10	172	17.2	2	52	2	47	26	12.5	8	80.0
2nd Half/OT	-	52	572	11.0	7	37	4	193	92	7.3	35	67.3	Right Side	19	193	10.2	2	37	1	68	28	6.6	14	73.7
Last 2 Min. Half	-	14	157	11.2	4	21	0	15	27	10.1	10	71.4	Right Sideline	48	574	12.0	7	60	5	174	71	8.3	34	70.8
4th qtr, +/-7 pts	-	12	91	7.6	2	16	0	25	22	5.5	7	58.3	Shotgun	3	27	9.0	0	12	0	5	11	7.3	1	33.3
Winning	-	44	611	13.9	9	60	4	192	70	9.5	34	77.3	2 Wide Receivers	35	438	12.5	5	28	3	97	58	9.7	25	71.4
Tied	-	32	344	10.8	1	29	2	109	51	7.3	24	75.0	3 Wide Receivers	73	826	11.3	8	60	6	320	113	6.9	47	64.4
Trailing	-	46	416	9.0	7	37	3	137	76	6.1	22	47.8	4+ Wide Receivers	9	74	8.2	0	18	0	21	16	5.9	4	44.4

1995 Incompletions

Type	Num	%of Inc	%of Att
Pass Dropped	6	8.0	3.0
Poor Throw	41	54.7	20.8
Pass Defensed	18	24.0	9.1
Pass Hit at Line	1	1.3	0.5
Other	9	12.0	4.6
Total	75	100.0	38.1

Game Logs (1-8)

Date	Opp	Result	Rush	Yds	Rec	Yds	Trgt	F-L	TD
09/03	@Chi	L 14-31	0	0	5	83	10	0-0	0
09/10	Det	W 20-10	0	0	6	57	10	0-0	0
09/17	Dal	L 17-23	0	0	5	39	10	0-0	1
09/24	@Pit	W 44-24	0	0	6	67	9	0-0	2
10/08	Hou	W 23-17	0	0	12	115	20	0-0	2
10/15	@TB	L 17-20	0	0	4	21	9	0-0	0
10/22	@GB	L 21-38	0	0	5	58	14	0-0	0
10/30	Chi	L 6-14	0	0	8	68	11	0-0	0

Game Logs (9-16)

Date	Opp	Result	Rush	Yds	Rec	Yds	Trgt	F-L	TD
11/05	GB	W 27-24	0	0	9	91	13	0-0	1
11/12	@Ari	W 30-24	0	0	12	157	17	0-0	2
11/19	NO	W 43-24	0	0	12	137	13	0-0	2
11/23	@Det	L 38-44	0	0	5	51	12	0-0	2
12/03	TB	W 31-17	0	0	6	136	9	0-0	2
12/09	Cle	W 27-11	0	0	8	124	12	0-0	0
12/18	@SF	L 30-37	1	0	12	88	16	0-0	2
12/24	@Cin	L 24-27	0	0	7	79	12	0-0	1

Tony Carter
Chicago Bears — RB

1995 Receiving Splits

	G	Rec	Yds	Avg	TD	Lg	Big	YAC	Trgt	Y@C	1st	1st%		Rec	Yds	Avg	TD	Lg	Big	YAC	Trgt	Y@C	1st	1st%
Total	16	40	329	8.2	1	27	1	297	57	0.8	18	45.0	Inside 20	6	50	8.3	1	13	0	36	8	2.3	3	50.0
vs. Playoff	6	11	104	9.5	1	27	1	86	15	1.6	7	63.6	Inside 10	1	7	7.0	0	7	0	5	2	2.0	0	0.0
vs. Non-playoff	10	29	225	7.8	0	17	0	211	42	0.5	11	37.9	1st Down	16	140	8.8	1	17	0	117	21	1.4	7	43.8
vs. Own Division	8	18	150	8.3	0	17	0	127	24	1.3	10	55.6	2nd Down	16	126	7.9	0	17	0	128	24	-0.1	8	50.0
Home	8	16	165	10.3	1	27	1	138	22	1.7	9	56.3	3rd Down Overall	8	63	7.9	0	27	1	52	12	1.4	3	37.5
Away	8	24	164	6.8	0	15	0	159	35	0.2	9	37.5	3rd D 0-2 to Go	2	18	9.0	0	13	0	15	4	1.5	2	100.0
Games 1-8	8	19	149	7.8	0	17	0	127	26	1.2	8	42.1	3rd D 3-7 to Go	3	29	9.7	0	27	1	26	4	1.0	1	33.3
Games 9-16	8	21	180	8.6	1	27	1	170	31	0.5	10	47.6	3rd D 8+ to Go	3	16	5.3	0	7	0	11	4	1.7	0	0.0
September	4	6	34	5.7	0	15	0	29	9	0.8	1	16.7	4th Down	0	0	-	0	0	0	0	0	-	0	-
October	4	13	115	8.8	0	17	0	98	17	1.3	7	53.8	Rec Behind Line	12	67	5.6	0	9	0	90	17	-1.9	4	33.3
November	4	5	45	9.0	1	15	0	32	11	2.6	3	60.0	1-10 yds	28	262	9.4	1	27	1	207	39	2.0	14	50.0
December	4	16	135	8.4	0	27	1	138	20	-0.2	7	43.8	11-20 yds	0	0	-	0	0	0	0	1	-	0	-
Grass	11	21	215	10.2	1	27	1	179	30	1.7	12	57.1	21-30 yds	0	0	-	0	0	0	0	0	-	0	-
Turf	5	19	114	6.0	0	13	0	118	27	-0.2	6	31.6	31+	0	0	-	0	0	0	0	0	-	0	-
Indoor	2	8	58	7.3	0	13	0	54	9	0.5	5	62.5	Left Sideline	5	46	9.2	0	15	0	44	8	0.4	3	60.0
Outdoor	14	32	271	8.5	1	27	1	243	48	0.9	13	40.6	Left Side	7	57	8.1	0	17	0	52	8	0.7	3	42.9
1st Half	-	19	155	8.2	0	17	0	143	24	0.6	9	47.4	Middle	10	87	8.7	0	27	1	73	15	1.4	3	30.0
2nd Half/OT	-	21	174	8.3	1	27	1	154	33	1.0	9	42.9	Right Side	14	109	7.8	0	17	0	102	17	0.5	7	50.0
Last 2 Min. Half	-	3	18	6.0	0	7	0	18	3	0.0	0	0.0	Right Sideline	4	30	7.5	1	15	0	26	9	1.0	2	50.0
4th qtr, +/-7 pts	-	7	67	9.6	0	27	1	55	14	1.7	3	42.9	Shotgun	0	0	-	0	0	0	0	0	-	0	-
Winning	-	8	89	11.1	0	27	1	79	12	1.3	4	50.0	2 Wide Receivers	27	219	8.1	1	17	0	191	37	1.0	13	48.1
Tied	-	9	92	10.2	0	15	0	83	14	1.0	7	77.8	3 Wide Receivers	7	80	11.4	0	27	1	73	8	1.0	2	28.6
Trailing	-	23	148	6.4	1	13	0	135	31	0.6	7	30.4	4+ Wide Receivers	4	13	3.3	0	7	0	17	6	-1.0	1	25.0

1995 Incompletions

Type	Num	%of Inc	%of Att
Pass Dropped	5	29.4	8.8
Poor Throw	6	35.3	10.5
Pass Defensed	1	5.9	1.8
Pass Hit at Line	2	11.8	3.5
Other	3	17.6	5.3
Total	17	100.0	29.8

Game Logs (1-8)

Date	Opp	Result	Rush	Yds	Rec	Yds	Trgt	F-L	TD
09/03	Min	W 31-14	1	1	1	15	2	0-0	1
09/11	GB	L 24-27	0	0	2	8	2	0-0	0
09/17	@TB	W 25-6	0	0	0	0	0	0-0	0
09/24	@StL	L 28-34	0	0	3	11	5	0-0	0
10/08	Car	W 31-27	0	0	4	35	6	0-0	0
10/15	@Jac	W 30-27	3	13	3	27	4	0-0	0
10/22	Hou	W 35-32	0	0	2	22	2	0-0	0
10/30	@Min	W 14-6	1	2	4	31	5	1-0	0

Game Logs (9-16)

Date	Opp	Result	Rush	Yds	Rec	Yds	Trgt	F-L	TD
11/05	Pit	L 34-37	0	0	1	12	2	0-0	1
11/12	@GB	L 28-35	0	0	2	23	4	0-0	0
11/19	Det	L 17-24	1	3	1	7	2	0-0	0
11/26	@NYN	W 27-24	0	0	1	3	3	0-0	0
12/04	@Det	L 7-27	0	0	4	27	4	0-0	0
12/10	@Cin	L 10-16	2	10	7	42	10	0-0	0
12/17	TB	W 31-10	0	0	4	39	5	0-0	0
12/24	Phi	W 20-14	0	0	2	5	1	0-0	0

Keith Cash
Kansas City Chiefs — TE

1995 Receiving Splits

	G	Rec	Yds	Avg	TD	Lg	Big	YAC	Trgt	Y@C	1st	1st%
Total	14	42	419	10.0	1	38	1	218	61	4.8	23	54.8
vs. Playoff	3	9	90	10.0	0	18	0	39	11	5.7	4	44.4
vs. Non-playoff	11	33	329	10.0	1	38	1	179	50	4.5	19	57.6
vs. Own Division	7	15	132	8.8	0	22	0	65	21	4.5	8	53.3
Home	7	23	205	8.9	0	22	0	124	31	3.5	13	56.5
Away	7	19	214	11.3	1	38	1	94	30	6.3	10	52.6
Games 1-8	6	18	200	11.1	1	38	1	106	32	5.2	11	61.1
Games 9-16	8	24	219	9.1	0	22	0	112	29	4.5	12	50.0
September	4	17	190	11.2	1	38	1	104	25	5.1	11	64.7
October	2	1	10	10.0	0	10	0	2	7	8.0	0	0.0
November	4	12	112	9.3	0	18	0	63	14	4.1	7	58.3
December	4	12	107	8.9	0	22	0	49	15	4.8	5	41.7
Grass	12	38	375	9.9	1	38	1	199	55	4.6	20	52.6
Turf	2	4	44	11.0	0	18	0	19	6	6.3	3	75.0
Outdoor	1	41	406	9.9	1	38	1	217	58	4.6	22	53.7
Indoor	13	1	13	13.0	0	13	0	1	3	12.0	1	100.0
1st Half	-	17	134	7.9	0	16	0	81	26	3.1	8	47.1
2nd Half/OT	-	25	285	11.4	1	38	1	137	35	5.9	15	60.0
Last 2 Min. Half	-	8	66	8.3	0	16	0	26	11	5.0	4	50.0
4th qtr. +/-7 pts	-	5	41	8.2	0	14	0	23	8	3.6	3	60.0
Winning	-	14	136	9.7	0	22	0	68	21	4.9	8	57.1
Tied	-	5	45	9.0	0	16	0	16	10	5.8	3	60.0
Trailing	-	23	238	10.3	1	38	1	134	30	4.5	12	52.2

	Rec	Yds	Avg	TD	Lg	Big	YAC	Trgt	Y@C	1st	1st%
Inside 20	3	15	5.0	0	8	0	4	6	3.7	1	33.3
Inside 10	1	0	0.0	0	0	0	0	2	0.0	0	0.0
1st Down	11	120	10.9	0	22	0	60	20	5.5	7	63.6
2nd Down	18	133	7.4	0	16	0	85	22	2.7	7	38.9
3rd Down Overall	12	158	13.2	1	38	1	72	18	7.2	8	66.7
3rd D 0-2 to Go	0	0	-	0	0	0	0	2	-	0	-
3rd D 3-7 to Go	7	108	15.4	1	38	1	54	10	7.7	7	100.0
3rd D 8+ to Go	5	50	10.0	0	24	0	18	6	6.4	1	20.0
4th Down	1	8	8.0	0	8	0	1	1	7.0	1	100.0
Rec Behind Line	10	49	4.9	0	12	0	58	12	-0.9	4	40.0
1-10 yds	23	199	8.7	0	18	0	120	36	3.4	10	43.5
11-20 yds	8	147	18.4	1	38	1	40	11	13.4	8	100.0
21-30 yds	0	0	0.0	0	0	0	0	1	-	0	-
31+	0	0	-	0	0	0	0	0	-	0	-
Left Sideline	1	9	9.0	0	9	0	7	3	2.0	1	100.0
Left Side	4	49	12.3	0	18	0	28	6	5.3	3	75.0
Middle	7	61	8.7	0	16	0	22	11	5.6	4	57.1
Right Side	18	210	11.7	1	38	1	129	23	4.5	11	61.1
Right Sideline	11	66	6.0	0	15	0	32	17	3.1	3	27.3
Shotgun	0	0	-	0	0	0	0	0	-	0	-
2 Wide Receivers	19	216	11.4	1	38	1	104	27	5.9	13	68.4
3 Wide Receivers	20	166	8.3	0	16	0	110	28	2.8	8	40.0
4+ Wide Receivers	2	13	6.5	0	10	0	4	4	4.5	1	50.0

1995 Incompletions

Type	Num	%of Inc	%of Att
Pass Dropped	5	26.3	8.2
Poor Throw	8	42.1	13.1
Pass Defensed	5	26.3	8.2
Pass Hit at Line	0	0.0	0.0
Other	1	5.3	1.6
Total	19	100.0	31.1

Game Logs (1-8)

Date	Opp	Result	Rec	Yds	Trgt	F-L	TD
09/03	@Sea	W 34-10	1	13	3	0-0	0
09/10	NYN	W 20-17	4	31	6	0-0	0
09/17	Oak	W 23-17	4	35	4	0-0	0
09/24	@Cle	L 17-35	8	111	12	0-0	1
10/01	@Ari	W 24-3	-	-	-		
10/09	SD	W 29-23	-	-	-		
10/15	NE	W 31-26	1	10	4	0-0	0
10/22	@Den	W 21-7	0	0	3	0-0	0

Game Logs (9-16)

Date	Opp	Result	Rec	Yds	Trgt	F-L	TD
11/05	Was	W 24-3	5	48	6	0-0	0
11/12	@SD	W 22-7	2	18	2	0-0	0
11/19	Hou	W 20-13	2	15	3	0-0	0
11/23	@Dal	L 12-24	3	31	3	0-0	0
12/03	@Oak	W 29-23	1	0	1	0-0	0
12/11	@Mia	L 6-13	4	41	6	0-0	0
12/17	Den	W 20-17	4	21	5	0-0	0
12/24	Sea	W 26-3	3	45	3	0-0	0

Kerry Cash
Oakland Raiders — TE

1995 Receiving Splits

	G	Rec	Yds	Avg	TD	Lg	Big	YAC	Trgt	Y@C	1st	1st%
Total	16	25	254	10.2	2	23	0	121	40	5.3	15	60.0
vs. Playoff	8	14	153	10.9	1	23	0	69	23	6.9	9	64.3
vs. Non-playoff	8	11	101	9.2	1	21	0	52	17	4.5	6	54.5
vs. Own Division	8	14	147	10.5	1	23	0	48	22	7.1	7	50.0
Home	8	14	144	10.3	2	23	0	62	22	5.9	8	57.1
Away	8	11	110	10.0	0	22	0	59	18	4.6	7	63.6
Games 1-8	8	11	124	11.3	1	22	0	56	19	6.2	10	90.9
Games 9-16	8	14	130	9.3	1	23	0	65	21	4.6	5	35.7
September	4	9	96	10.7	0	22	0	51	13	5.0	8	88.9
October	4	2	28	14.0	1	16	0	5	6	11.5	2	100.0
November	4	5	65	13.0	1	21	0	41	9	4.8	4	80.0
December	4	9	65	7.2	0	23	0	24	12	4.6	1	11.1
Grass	12	20	213	10.7	2	23	0	88	32	6.3	13	65.0
Turf	4	5	41	8.2	0	21	0	33	8	1.6	2	40.0
Outdoor	1	22	244	11.1	2	23	0	118	36	5.7	15	68.2
Indoor	15	3	10	3.3	0	6	0	3	4	2.3	0	0.0
1st Half	-	9	75	8.3	0	15	0	39	13	4.0	6	66.7
2nd Half/OT	-	16	179	11.2	2	23	0	82	27	6.1	9	56.3
Last 2 Min. Half	-	4	42	10.5	0	15	0	20	9	5.5	2	50.0
4th qtr. +/-7 pts	-	2	25	12.5	0	13	0	16	4	4.5	2	100.0
Winning	-	6	77	12.8	1	22	0	39	11	6.3	4	66.7
Tied	-	7	63	9.0	0	12	0	39	8	3.4	6	85.7
Trailing	-	12	114	9.5	1	23	0	43	21	5.9	5	41.7

	Rec	Yds	Avg	TD	Lg	Big	YAC	Trgt	Y@C	1st	1st%
Inside 20	2	32	16.0	2	16	0	2	3	15.0	2	100.0
Inside 10	0	0	0.0	0	0	0	0	0	-	0	-
1st Down	13	145	11.2	0	22	0	53	17	7.1	10	76.9
2nd Down	6	53	8.8	0	23	0	23	12	5.0	2	33.3
3rd Down Overall	6	56	9.3	0	21	0	45	11	1.8	3	50.0
3rd D 0-2 to Go	1	12	12.0	0	12	0	11	1	1.0	1	100.0
3rd D 3-7 to Go	4	39	9.8	0	21	0	30	6	2.3	2	50.0
3rd D 8+ to Go	1	5	5.0	0	5	0	4	4	1.0	0	0.0
4th Down	0	0	-	0	0	0	0	0	-	0	-
Rec Behind Line	5	25	5.0	0	10	0	28	8	-0.6	2	40.0
1-10 yds	16	152	9.5	0	21	0	81	23	4.4	10	62.5
11-20 yds	4	77	19.3	2	23	0	12	5	16.3	3	75.0
21-30 yds	0	0	-	0	0	0	0	4	-	0	-
31+	0	0	-	0	0	0	0	0	-	0	-
Left Sideline	0	0	-	0	0	0	0	2	-	0	-
Left Side	3	48	16.0	0	23	0	27	7	7.0	1	33.3
Middle	3	27	9.0	0	15	0	6	5	7.0	2	66.7
Right Side	7	84	12.0	1	22	0	30	9	7.7	5	71.4
Right Sideline	12	95	7.9	1	16	0	58	17	3.1	7	58.3
Shotgun	0	0	-	0	0	0	0	0	-	0	-
2 Wide Receivers	11	112	10.2	1	23	0	33	13	7.2	6	54.5
3 Wide Receivers	11	122	11.1	1	21	0	74	24	4.4	8	72.7
4+ Wide Receivers	1	2	2.0	0	2	0	-4	1	6.0	0	0.0

1995 Incompletions

Type	Num	%of Inc	%of Att
Pass Dropped	2	13.3	5.0
Poor Throw	7	46.7	17.5
Pass Defensed	2	13.3	5.0
Pass Hit at Line	0	0.0	0.0
Other	4	26.7	10.0
Total	15	100.0	37.5

Game Logs (1-8)

Date	Opp	Result	Rec	Yds	Trgt	F-L	TD
09/03	SD	W 17-7	1	10	3	0-0	0
09/10	@Was	W 20-8	3	20	4	1-1	0
09/17	@KC	L 17-23	3	49	4	0-0	0
09/24	Phi	W 48-17	2	17	2	0-0	0
10/01	@NYA	W 47-10	0	0	1	0-0	0
10/08	Sea	W 34-14	2	28	3	0-0	1
10/16	@Den	L 0-27	0	0	1	0-0	0
10/22	Ind	W 30-17	0	0	1	0-0	0

Game Logs (9-16)

Date	Opp	Result	Rec	Yds	Trgt	F-L	TD
11/05	@Cin	W 20-17	2	31	3	0-0	0
11/12	@NYN	W 17-13	0	0	0	0-0	0
11/19	Dal	L 21-34	3	34	5	0-0	1
11/27	@SD	L 6-12	0	0	1	0-0	0
12/03	KC	L 23-29	4	38	5	0-0	0
12/10	Pit	L 10-29	1	5	2	0-0	0
12/17	@Sea	L 10-44	3	10	4	1-1	0
12/24	Den	L 28-31	1	12	1	0-0	0

Larry Centers

Arizona Cardinals — RB

1995 Receiving Splits

	G	Rec	Yds	Avg	TD	Lg	Big	YAC	Trgt	Y@C	1st	1st%
Total	16	101	962	9.5	2	32	4	855	119	1.1	45	44.6
vs. Playoff	8	58	644	11.1	2	32	4	554	66	1.6	28	48.3
vs. Non-playoff	8	43	318	7.4	0	23	0	301	53	0.4	17	39.5
vs. Own Division	8	50	516	10.3	1	30	3	472	60	0.9	25	50.0
Home	8	61	636	10.4	0	32	3	557	71	1.3	33	54.1
Away	8	40	326	8.2	2	30	1	298	48	0.7	12	30.0
Games 1-8	8	53	446	8.4	1	30	1	423	63	0.4	21	39.6
Games 9-16	8	48	516	10.8	1	32	3	432	56	1.8	24	50.0
September	4	23	204	8.9	1	30	1	188	28	0.7	8	34.8
October	4	30	242	8.1	0	24	0	235	35	0.2	13	43.3
November	5	24	231	9.6	0	32	1	184	30	2.0	13	54.2
December	3	24	285	11.9	1	29	2	248	26	1.5	11	45.8
Grass	12	80	768	9.6	1	32	3	677	92	1.1	37	46.3
Turf	4	21	194	9.2	1	30	1	178	27	0.8	8	38.1
Indoor	1	6	37	6.2	0	11	0	29	9	1.3	2	33.3
Outdoor	15	95	925	9.7	2	32	4	826	110	1.0	43	45.3
1st Half	-	44	421	9.6	2	32	2	356	52	1.5	18	40.9
2nd Half/OT	-	57	541	9.5	0	30	2	499	67	0.7	27	47.4
Last 2 Min. Half	-	23	184	8.0	0	17	0	199	25	-0.7	10	43.5
4th qtr, +/-7 pts	-	11	73	6.6	0	19	0	74	15	-0.1	4	36.4
Winning	-	10	73	7.3	0	21	0	75	13	-0.2	3	30.0
Tied	-	15	149	9.9	0	32	1	107	18	2.8	6	30.0
Trailing	-	76	740	9.7	2	30	3	673	88	0.9	36	47.4

	Rec	Yds	Avg	TD	Lg	Big	YAC	Trgt	Y@C	1st	1st%
Inside 20	7	45	6.4	1	13	0	20	9	3.6	2	28.6
Inside 10	1	3	3.0	0	3	0	2	2	1.0	0	0.0
1st Down	33	316	9.6	1	32	2	285	38	0.9	14	42.4
2nd Down	35	374	10.7	1	28	1	294	40	2.3	18	51.4
3rd Down Overall	33	272	8.2	0	29	1	276	41	-0.1	13	39.4
3rd D 0-2 to Go	2	24	12.0	0	20	0	3	3	10.5	2	100.0
3rd D 3-7 to Go	10	107	10.7	0	29	1	103	13	0.4	8	80.0
3rd D 8+ to Go	21	141	6.7	0	20	0	170	25	-1.4	3	14.3
4th Down	0	0		0	0	0	0	0		0	
Rec Behind Line	47	348	7.4	0	30	1	501	49	-3.3	16	34.0
1-10 yds	49	514	10.5	1	29	2	331	62	3.7	24	49.0
11-20 yds	5	100	20.0	0	32	1	23	6	15.4	5	100.0
21-30 yds	0	0		0	0	0	0	2		0	
31+	0	0		0	0	0	0	0		0	
Left Sideline	10	110	11.0	0	24	0	105	17	0.5	6	60.0
Left Side	18	164	9.1	0	30	1	190	20	-1.4	8	44.4
Middle	33	340	10.3	1	32	1	243	33	2.9	19	57.6
Right Side	24	210	8.8	0	28	1	225	27	-0.6	7	29.2
Right Sideline	16	138	8.6	1	29	1	92	22	2.9	5	31.3
Shotgun	51	477	9.4	0	30	1	540	58	-1.2	22	43.1
2 Wide Receivers	32	308	9.6	2	32	1	201	37	3.3	14	43.8
3 Wide Receivers	46	408	8.9	0	30	1	402	56	0.1	20	43.5
4+ Wide Receivers	22	226	10.3	0	29	2	251	23	-1.1	10	45.5

1995 Incompletions

Type	Num	%of Inc	%of Att
Pass Dropped	3	16.7	2.5
Poor Throw	10	55.6	8.4
Pass Defensed	2	11.1	1.7
Pass Hit at Line	0	0.0	0.0
Other	3	16.7	2.5
Total	18	100.0	15.1

Game Logs (1-8)

Date	Opp	Result	Rush	Yds	Rec	Yds	Trgt	F-L	TD
09/03	@Was	L 7-27	6	13	5	23	6	0-0	0
09/10	Phi	L 19-31	4	8	5	61	6	0-0	0
09/17	@Det	W 20-17	1	2	6	37	9	0-0	0
09/24	@Dal	L 20-34	4	29	7	83	7	0-0	1
10/01	KC	L 3-24	5	2	9	77	10	0-0	0
10/08	@NYN	L 21-27	7	18	5	40	7	0-0	0
10/15	Was	W 24-20	4	33	7	52	8	0-0	1
10/29	Sea	W 20-14	8	28	9	73	10	1-1	0

Game Logs (9-16)

Date	Opp	Result	Rush	Yds	Rec	Yds	Trgt	F-L	TD
11/05	@Den	L 6-38	9	24	2	19	3	0-0	0
11/12	Min	L 24-30	5	15	6	49	7	0-0	0
11/19	@Car	L 7-27	2	2	3	11	3	0-0	0
11/26	Atl	W 40-37	13	62	7	101	8	0-0	0
11/30	NYN	L 6-10	0	0	6	51	9	0-0	0
12/09	@SD	L 25-28	3	15	9	79	9	1-0	1
12/17	@Phi	L 20-21	5	3	3	34	4	0-0	0
12/25	Dal	L 13-37	2	0	12	172	13	0-0	0

Chris Chandler

Houston Oilers — QB

1995 Passing Splits

	G	Att	Cm	Pct	Yds	Yd/Att	TD	Int	1st	YAC	Big	Sk	Rtg
Total	13	356	225	63.2	2460	6.9	17	10	111	860	18	21	87.8
vs. Playoff	4	100	57	57.0	619	6.2	4	7	24	210	6	9	59.5
vs. Non-playoff	9	256	168	65.6	1841	7.2	13	3	87	650	12	12	98.8
vs. Own Division	7	174	110	63.2	1229	7.1	9	4	54	407	9	13	91.9
Home	6	179	106	59.2	1146	6.4	5	6	54	418	9	11	73.5
Away	7	177	119	67.2	1314	7.4	12	4	57	442	9	10	102.2
Games 1-8	7	214	137	64.0	1433	6.7	8	4	65	540	10	14	88.0
Games 9-16	6	142	88	62.0	1027	7.2	9	6	46	320	8	7	87.4
September	3	70	47	67.1	589	8.4	5	2	26	226	7	5	105.0
October	4	144	90	62.5	844	5.9	3	2	39	314	9	9	79.7
November	4	110	65	59.1	773	7.0	7	4	36	223	6	2	86.7
December	2	32	23	71.9	254	7.9	2	2	10	97	2	5	89.8
Grass	4	110	68	61.8	695	6.3	7	3	32	194	4	2	86.9
Turf	9	246	157	63.8	1765	7.2	10	7	79	666	14	19	86.9
Indoor	7	209	126	60.3	1302	6.2	5	7	62	493	9	14	72.3
Outdoor	6	147	99	67.3	1158	7.9	12	3	49	367	9	7	109.7
1st Half	-	218	134	61.5	1490	6.8	12	6	62	507	11	14	86.3
2nd Half/OT	-	138	91	65.9	970	7.0	5	4	49	353	7	7	86.3
Last 2 Min. Half	-	56	31	55.4	397	7.1	5	1	19	113	4	5	100.0
4th qtr, +/-7 pts	-	33	20	60.6	190	5.8	1	1	9	41	1	2	74.1
Winning	-	91	66	72.5	752	8.3	7	0	38	320	6	3	122.6
Tied	-	60	39	65.0	354	5.9	2	3	14	143	1	5	71.1
Trailing	-	205	120	58.5	1354	6.6	8	7	59	397	11	13	77.2

	Att	Cm	Pct	Yds	Yd/Att	TD	Int	1st	YAC	Big	Sk	Rtg
Inside 20	39	20	51.3	145	3.7	8	2	11	50	0	3	78.5
Inside 10	12	7	58.3	42	3.5	5	0	6	12	0	0	104.9
1st Down	141	88	62.4	946	6.7	3	4	28	389	7	7	77.3
2nd Down	118	76	64.4	746	6.3	4	3	36	272	3	6	82.8
3rd Down Overall	95	59	62.1	707	7.6	9	3	45	195	7	8	103.9
3rd D 0-5 to Go	39	26	66.7	217	5.6	4	0	22	93	2	0	115.0
3rd D 6+ to Go	56	33	58.9	504	9.0	5	3	23	102	5	8	96.1
4th Down	2	2	100.0	47	23.5	1	0	2	4	1	0	158.3
Rec Behind Line	62	42	67.7	166	2.7	0	2	5	257	0	0	57.6
1-10 yds	174	126	72.4	959	5.5	6	3	51	399	1	0	89.7
11-20 yds	70	41	58.6	708	10.1	2	3	39	97	4	0	84.7
21-30 yds	20	7	35.0	203	10.2	3	1	7	35	4	0	92.3
31+	30	9	30.0	424	14.1	6	1	9	72	9	0	104.9
Left Sideline	78	53	67.9	510	6.5	5	1	25	166	3	1	102.0
Left Side	50	28	56.0	364	7.3	1	1	18	106	4	0	77.4
Middle	88	54	61.4	635	7.2	4	4	23	274	6	20	79.5
Right Side	59	34	57.6	376	6.4	2	3	17	141	2	0	66.8
Right Sideline	81	56	69.1	575	7.1	5	1	28	173	3	0	104.7
2 Wide Receivers	81	53	65.4	596	7.4	2	2	23	211	3	7	85.2
3+ WR	271	169	62.4	1840	6.8	14	8	85	637	15	13	87.3
Attempts 1-10	130	79	60.8	912	7.0	7	4	36	308	7	0	97.1
Attempts 11-20	115	72	62.6	767	6.7	7	2	37	288	5	0	95.1
Attempts 21+	111	74	66.7	781	7.0	3	4	38	249	6	0	80.9

1995 Incompletions

Type	Num	% of Inc	% of Att
Pass Dropped	21	16.0	5.9
Poor Throw	54	41.2	15.2
Pass Defensed	26	19.8	7.3
Pass Hit at Line	8	6.1	2.2
Other	22	16.8	6.2
Total	131	100.0	36.8

Game Logs (1-8)

Date	Opp	Result	Att	Cm	Pct	Yds	TD	Int	Lg	Sk	F-L
09/03	@Jac	W 10-3	14	9	64.3	61	1	0	14	0	2-0
09/10	Pit	L 17-34	30	15	50.0	176	0	2	35	4	2-1
09/17	Cle	L 7-14									
09/24	@Cin	W 38-28	26	23	88.5	352	4	0	58	1	0-0
10/01	Jac	L 16-17	47	27	57.4	225	1	1	21	2	0-0
10/08	@Min	L 17-23	26	15	57.7	156	0	1	18	3	0-0
10/22	@Chi	L 32-35	38	24	63.2	296	2	0	42	2	2-1
10/29	TB	W 19-7	29	19	65.5	167	0	0	18	2	1-1

Game Logs (9-16)

Date	Opp	Result	Att	Cm	Pct	Yds	TD	Int	Lg	Sk	F-L
11/05	@Cle	W 37-10	20	16	80.0	149	2	0	23	0	0-0
11/12	Cin	L 25-32	26	12	46.2	155	0	1	33	2	2-1
11/19	@KC	L 13-20	38	19	50.0	189	2	3	40	1	1-0
11/26	Den	W 42-33	26	18	69.2	280	3	0	36	0	0-0
12/03	@Pit	L 7-21	11	8	72.7	111	1	0	76	4	1-0
12/10	Det	L 17-24	21	15	71.4	143	1	2	30	1	1-1
12/17	NYA	W 23-6									
12/24	@Buf	W 28-17									

Mark Chmura

1995 Receiving Splits

	G	Rec	Yds	Avg	TD	Lg	Big	YAC	Trgt	Y@C	1st	1st%
Total	16	54	679	12.6	7	33	3	264	75	7.7	44	81.5
vs. Playoff	4	13	153	11.8	2	33	1	64	19	6.8	10	76.9
vs. Non-playoff	12	41	526	12.8	5	29	2	200	56	8.0	34	82.9
vs. Own Division	8	23	284	12.3	2	33	1	100	37	8.0	18	78.3
Home	8	33	471	14.3	4	33	3	158	43	9.5	27	81.8
Away	8	21	208	9.9	3	21	0	106	32	4.9	17	81.0
Games 1-8	8	28	384	13.7	3	33	2	130	40	9.1	23	82.1
Games 9-16	8	26	295	11.3	4	29	1	134	35	6.2	21	80.8
September	4	14	178	12.7	1	27	1	61	19	8.4	11	78.6
October	4	14	206	14.7	2	33	1	69	21	9.8	12	85.7
November	4	9	79	8.8	2	18	0	29	16	5.6	7	77.8
December	4	17	216	12.7	2	29	1	105	19	6.5	14	82.4
Grass	12	41	558	13.6	5	33	3	207	54	8.6	34	82.9
Turf	4	13	121	9.3	2	21	0	57	21	4.9	10	76.9
Outdoor	3	43	590	13.7	6	33	3	218	58	8.7	36	83.7
Indoor	13	11	89	8.1	1	18	0	46	17	3.9	8	72.7
1st Half	-	24	301	12.5	2	29	2	120	36	7.5	17	70.8
2nd Half/OT	-	30	378	12.6	5	33	1	144	39	7.8	27	90.0
Last 2 Min. Half	-	0	0	-	0	0	0	0	2	-	0	-
4th qtr, +/-7 pts	-	7	74	10.6	1	20	0	38	8	5.1	6	85.7
Winning	-	24	310	12.9	3	33	1	148	29	6.8	21	87.5
Tied	-	17	233	13.7	1	29	2	79	24	9.1	13	76.5
Trailing	-	13	136	10.5	3	22	0	37	22	7.6	10	76.9

	Rec	Yds	Avg	TD	Lg	Big	YAC	Trgt	Y@C	1st	1st%
Inside 20	10	67	6.7	7	12	0	13	14	5.4	9	90.0
Inside 10	5	21	4.2	5	8	0	4	7	3.4	5	100.0
1st Down	17	196	11.5	3	29	1	65	26	7.7	11	64.7
2nd Down	24	253	10.5	3	23	0	114	31	5.8	20	83.3
3rd Down Overall	12	207	17.3	1	33	2	78	17	10.8	12	100.0
3rd D 0-2 to Go	5	86	17.2	1	33	1	34	6	10.4	5	100.0
3rd D 3-7 to Go	6	100	16.7	0	27	1	44	8	9.3	6	100.0
3rd D 8+ to Go	1	21	21.0	0	21	0	0	3	21.0	1	100.0
4th Down	1	23	23.0	0	23	0	7	1	16.0	1	100.0
Rec Behind Line	2	19	9.5	0	13	0	22	2	-1.5	1	50.0
1-10 yds	41	416	10.1	6	23	0	194	56	5.4	32	78.0
11-20 yds	8	167	20.9	1	33	1	39	12	16.0	8	100.0
21-30 yds	3	77	25.7	0	29	2	9	5	22.7	3	100.0
31+	0	0	-	0	0	0	0	0	-	0	-
Left Sideline	2	16	8.0	1	13	0	11	2	2.5	2	100.0
Left Side	11	138	12.5	1	23	0	69	13	6.3	10	90.9
Middle	11	139	12.6	2	22	0	59	18	7.3	9	81.8
Right Side	18	202	11.2	3	29	1	76	26	7.0	14	77.8
Right Sideline	12	184	15.3	0	33	2	49	16	11.3	9	75.0
Shotgun	0	0	-	0	0	0	0	0	-	0	-
2 Wide Receivers	30	389	13.0	4	33	2	151	43	7.9	23	76.7
3 Wide Receivers	19	248	13.1	0	27	1	98	26	7.9	16	84.2
4+ Wide Receivers	0	0	-	0	0	0	0	1	-	0	-

1995 Incompletions

Type	Num	%of Inc	%of Att
Pass Dropped	3	14.3	4.0
Poor Throw	8	38.1	10.7
Pass Defensed	8	38.1	10.7
Pass Hit at Line	0	0.0	0.0
Other	2	9.5	2.7
Total	21	100.0	28.0

Game Logs (1-8)

Date	Opp	Result	Rec	Yds	Trgt	F-L	TD
09/03	StL	L 14-17	7	97	10	0-0	1
09/11	@Chi	W 27-24	3	35	3	0-0	0
09/17	NYN	W 14-6	2	22	3	0-0	0
09/24	@Jac	W 24-14	2	24	3	0-0	0
10/08	@Dal	L 24-34	2	32	4	0-0	0
10/15	Det	W 30-21	5	61	7	0-0	0
10/22	Min	W 38-21	5	101	6	0-0	1
10/29	@Det	L 16-24	2	12	4	0-0	0

Game Logs (9-16)

Date	Opp	Result	Rec	Yds	Trgt	F-L	TD
11/05	@Min	L 24-27	4	30	8	0-0	1
11/12	Chi	W 35-28	3	33	5	0-0	0
11/19	@Cle	W 31-20	2	16	2	0-0	1
11/26	TB	W 35-13	0	0	1	0-0	0
12/03	Cin	W 24-10	7	109	7	0-0	1
12/10	@TB	L 10-13	1	12	3	0-0	0
12/16	@NO	W 34-23	5	47	5	0-0	0
12/24	Pit	W 24-19	4	48	4	0-0	0

Wayne Chrebet

1995 Receiving Splits

	G	Rec	Yds	Avg	TD	Lg	Big	YAC	Trgt	Y@C	1st	1st%
Total	16	66	726	11.0	4	32	5	240	123	7.4	37	56.1
vs. Playoff	7	25	287	11.5	3	32	2	110	46	7.1	14	56.0
vs. Non-playoff	9	41	439	10.7	1	32	3	130	77	7.5	23	56.1
vs. Own Division	8	29	342	11.8	3	32	2	82	52	9.0	16	55.2
Home	8	37	405	10.9	3	32	2	102	63	8.2	23	62.2
Away	8	29	321	11.1	1	32	3	138	60	6.3	14	48.3
Games 1-8	8	34	388	11.4	4	32	2	132	63	7.5	21	61.8
Games 9-16	8	32	338	10.6	0	32	2	108	60	7.2	16	50.0
September	4	16	171	10.7	2	32	2	64	26	6.7	9	56.3
October	5	21	234	11.1	2	32	1	74	42	7.6	12	57.1
November	3	8	114	14.3	0	32	1	21	18	11.6	6	62.5
December	4	21	207	9.9	0	26	1	81	37	6.0	11	52.4
Grass	3	11	144	13.1	0	32	2	37	21	9.7	6	54.5
Turf	13	55	582	10.6	4	32	3	203	102	6.9	31	56.4
Indoor	4	11	103	9.4	0	32	1	68	26	3.2	4	36.4
Outdoor	12	55	623	11.3	4	32	4	172	97	8.2	33	60.0
1st Half	-	27	273	10.1	1	32	2	101	57	6.4	14	51.9
2nd Half/OT	-	39	453	11.6	3	32	3	139	66	8.1	23	59.0
Last 2 Min. Half	-	7	72	10.3	0	22	0	10	13	8.9	3	42.9
4th qtr, +/-7 pts	-	5	67	13.4	0	18	0	14	9	10.6	4	80.0
Winning	-	11	89	8.1	1	13	0	22	18	6.1	7	63.6
Tied	-	9	85	9.4	1	21	0	23	17	6.9	3	33.3
Trailing	-	46	552	12.0	2	32	5	195	88	7.8	27	58.7

	Rec	Yds	Avg	TD	Lg	Big	YAC	Trgt	Y@C	1st	1st%
Inside 20	4	44	11.0	4	16	0	12	10	8.0	4	100.0
Inside 10	1	5	5.0	1	5	0	3	5	5.0	1	100.0
1st Down	32	322	10.1	1	26	1	94	53	7.1	15	46.9
2nd Down	21	226	10.8	2	32	2	75	36	7.2	13	61.9
3rd Down Overall	13	178	13.7	1	32	2	71	33	8.2	9	69.2
3rd D 0-2 to Go	0	0	-	0	0	0	0	0	-	0	-
3rd D 3-7 to Go	5	40	8.0	1	11	0	19	15	4.2	4	80.0
3rd D 8+ to Go	8	138	17.3	1	32	2	52	18	10.8	5	62.5
4th Down	0	0	-	0	0	0	0	0	-	0	-
Rec Behind Line	1	7	7.0	0	7	0	9	5	-2.0	1	100.0
1-10 yds	50	427	8.5	2	32	1	188	71	4.8	23	46.0
11-20 yds	12	215	17.9	2	32	2	43	28	14.3	11	91.7
21-30 yds	3	77	25.7	0	32	0	2	15	25.7	2	66.7
31+	0	0	-	0	0	0	0	4	-	0	-
Left Sideline	7	108	15.4	0	32	3	20	17	12.6	3	42.9
Left Side	12	140	11.7	0	18	0	60	21	6.7	11	91.7
Middle	11	95	8.6	2	16	0	44	22	4.6	6	54.5
Right Side	20	231	11.6	1	32	2	81	31	7.5	11	55.0
Right Sideline	16	152	9.5	1	26	1	35	32	7.3	6	37.5
Shotgun	0	0	-	0	0	0	0	0	-	0	-
2 Wide Receivers	55	609	11.1	3	32	4	165	102	8.1	30	54.5
3 Wide Receivers	9	94	10.4	1	32	1	59	19	3.9	5	55.6
4+ Wide Receivers	0	0	-	0	0	0	0	0	-	0	-

1995 Incompletions

Type	Num	%of Inc	%of Att
Pass Dropped	6	10.5	4.9
Poor Throw	34	59.6	27.6
Pass Defensed	11	19.3	8.9
Pass Hit at Line	1	1.8	0.8
Other	5	8.8	4.1
Total	57	100.0	46.3

Game Logs (1-8)

Date	Opp	Result	Rush	Yds	Rec	Yds	Trgt	F-L	TD
09/03	@Mia	L 14-52	0	0	3	43	6	0-0	0
09/10	Ind	L 24-27	0	0	2	14	3	0-0	1
09/17	Jac	W 27-10	0	0	7	58	10	0-0	1
09/24	@Atl	L 3-13	0	0	4	56	7	0-0	0
10/01	Oak	L 10-47	0	0	4	46	9	1-1	0
10/08	@Buf	L 10-29	0	0	7	74	13	0-0	1
10/15	@Car	L 15-26	0	0	4	56	9	0-0	0
10/22	Mia	W 17-16	1	1	3	41	6	0-0	1

Game Logs (9-16)

Date	Opp	Result	Rush	Yds	Rec	Yds	Trgt	F-L	TD
10/29	@Ind	L 10-17	0	0	3	17	5	0-0	0
11/05	NE	L 7-20	0	0	4	66	7	0-0	0
11/19	Buf	L 26-28	0	0	3	42	6	0-0	0
11/26	@Sea	W 16-10	0	0	1	6	5	0-0	0
12/03	StL	L 20-23	0	0	7	98	12	0-0	0
12/10	@NE	L 28-31	0	0	4	45	6	0-0	0
12/17	@Hou	L 6-23	0	0	3	24	9	0-0	0
12/24	NO	L 0-12	0	0	6	40	10	0-0	0

Bob Christian — Carolina Panthers — RB

1995 Receiving Splits

	G	Rec	Yds	Avg	TD	Lg	Big	YAC	Trgt	Y@C	1st	1st%
Total	14	29	255	8.8	1	23	0	200	35	1.9	13	44.8
vs. Playoff	5	11	110	10.0	0	23	0	91	12	1.7	6	54.5
vs. Non-playoff	9	18	145	8.1	1	19	0	109	23	2.0	7	38.9
vs. Own Division	7	18	178	9.9	0	23	0	135	21	2.4	8	44.4
Home	8	17	119	7.0	1	16	0	94	20	1.5	7	41.2
Away	6	12	136	11.3	0	23	0	106	15	2.5	6	50.0
Games 1-8	7	14	116	8.3	0	23	0	83	18	2.4	4	28.6
Games 9-16	7	15	139	9.3	1	19	0	117	17	1.5	9	60.0
September	3	9	82	9.1	0	23	0	56	11	2.9	3	33.3
October	4	5	34	6.8	0	13	0	27	7	1.4	1	20.0
November	3	6	61	10.2	1	19	0	49	7	2.0	4	66.7
December	4	9	78	8.7	0	16	0	68	10	1.1	5	55.6
Grass	10	20	143	7.2	0	16	0	112	24	1.6	8	40.0
Turf	4	9	112	12.4	0	23	0	88	11	2.7	5	55.6
Indoor	3	8	109	13.6	0	23	0	87	10	2.8	5	62.5
Outdoor	11	21	146	7.0	1	16	0	113	25	1.6	8	38.1
1st Half	-	13	99	7.6	1	14	0	86	15	1.0	7	53.8
2nd Half/OT	-	16	156	9.8	0	23	0	114	20	2.6	6	37.5
Last 2 Min. Half	-	3	53	17.7	0	23	0	40	5	4.3	3	100.0
4th qtr, +/-7 pts	-	2	39	19.5	0	23	0	32	4	3.5	2	100.0
Winning	-	4	21	5.3	1	13	0	14	5	1.8	2	50.0
Tied	-	6	57	9.5	0	16	0	43	7	2.3	2	33.3
Trailing	-	19	177	9.3	0	23	0	143	23	1.8	9	47.4

	Rec	Yds	Avg	TD	Lg	Big	YAC	Trgt	Y@C	1st	1st%
Inside 20	3	10	3.3	1	5	0	3	4	2.3	1	33.3
Inside 10	1	2	2.0	1	2	0	0	1	2.0	1	100.0
1st Down	12	96	8.0	0	23	0	75	17	1.8	3	25.0
2nd Down	12	103	8.6	1	18	0	80	13	1.9	7	58.3
3rd Down Overall	5	56	11.2	0	19	0	45	5	2.2	3	60.0
3rd D 0-2 to Go	1	7	7.0	0	7	0	9	1	-2.0	1	100.0
3rd D 3-7 to Go	2	32	16.0	0	19	0	28	2	2.0	2	100.0
3rd D 8+ to Go	2	17	8.5	0	12	0	8	2	4.5	0	0.0
4th Down	0	0	-	0	0	0	0	0	-	0	-
Rec Behind Line	6	37	6.2	0	8	0	40	9	-0.5	2	33.3
1-10 yds	23	218	9.5	1	23	0	160	26	2.5	11	47.8
11-20 yds	0	0	-	0	0	0	0	0	-	0	-
21-30 yds	0	0	-	0	0	0	0	0	-	0	-
31+	0	0	-	0	0	0	0	0	-	0	-
Left Sideline	1	16	16.0	0	16	0	15	2	1.0	1	100.0
Left Side	4	39	9.8	0	13	0	34	5	1.3	2	50.0
Middle	5	38	7.6	0	19	0	26	6	2.4	1	20.0
Right Side	8	78	9.8	0	18	0	62	10	2.0	4	50.0
Right Sideline	11	84	7.6	1	23	0	63	12	1.9	5	45.5
Shotgun	0	0	-	0	0	0	0	0	-	0	-
2 Wide Receivers	16	120	7.5	0	16	0	106	20	0.9	7	43.8
3 Wide Receivers	7	78	11.1	0	23	0	52	8	3.7	3	42.9
4+ Wide Receivers	4	46	11.5	0	19	0	36	4	2.5	2	50.0

1995 Incompletions

Type	Num	%of Inc	%of Att
Pass Dropped	3	50.0	8.6
Poor Throw	0	0.0	0.0
Pass Defensed	1	16.7	2.9
Pass Hit at Line	2	33.3	5.7
Other	0	0.0	0.0
Total	6	100.0	17.1

Game Logs (1-8)

Date	Opp	Result	Rush	Yds	Rec	Yds	Trgt	F-L	TD
09/03	@Atl	L 20-23	1	1	4	53	5	0-0	0
09/10	@Buf	L 9-31	4	12	1	3	1	0-0	0
09/17	StL	L 10-31	4	13	4	26	5	0-0	0
10/01	TB	L 13-20	5	19	2	9	3	1-1	0
10/08	@Chi	L 27-31	1	4	0	0	0	0-0	0
10/15	NYA	W 26-15	2	7	1	13	2	0-0	0
10/22	NO	W 20-3	3	9	2	12	2	0-0	0
10/29	@NE	W 20-17	-						

Game Logs (9-16)

Date	Opp	Result	Rush	Yds	Rec	Yds	Trgt	F-L	TD
11/05	@SF	W 13-7	-						
11/12	@StL	L 17-28	0	0	1	13	2	0-0	0
11/19	Ari	W 27-7	0	0	2	5	2	0-0	1
11/26	@NO	L 26-34	6	39	3	43	3	0-0	0
12/03	Ind	W 13-10	6	24	2	23	2	0-0	0
12/10	SF	L 10-31	4	16	2	12	2	0-0	0
12/17	Atl	W 21-17	3	4	2	19	2	0-0	0
12/24	@Was	L 17-20	2	10	3	24	4	0-0	0

Gary Clark — Miami Dolphins — WR

1995 Receiving Splits

	G	Rec	Yds	Avg	TD	Lg	Big	YAC	Trgt	Y@C	1st	1st%
Total	16	37	525	14.2	2	42	2	92	64	11.7	27	73.0
vs. Playoff	9	16	207	12.9	2	42	1	24	34	11.4	13	81.3
vs. Non-playoff	7	21	318	15.1	0	30	1	68	30	11.9	14	66.7
vs. Own Division	8	12	168	14.0	0	24	0	26	23	11.8	10	83.3
Home	8	14	209	14.9	2	42	1	29	29	12.9	12	85.7
Away	8	23	316	13.7	0	30	1	63	35	11.0	15	65.2
Games 1-8	8	18	249	13.8	0	24	0	49	33	11.1	12	66.7
Games 9-16	8	19	276	14.5	2	42	2	43	31	12.3	15	78.9
September	3	3	56	18.7	0	24	0	8	7	16.0	3	100.0
October	5	15	193	12.9	0	24	0	41	26	10.1	9	60.0
November	4	11	170	15.5	1	42	1	26	16	13.1	10	90.9
December	4	8	106	13.3	1	30	1	17	15	11.1	5	62.5
Grass	10	19	277	14.6	2	42	1	38	35	12.6	16	84.2
Turf	6	18	248	13.8	0	30	1	54	29	10.9	11	61.1
Outdoor	3	28	392	14.0	2	42	1	66	49	11.6	22	78.6
Indoor	13	9	133	14.8	0	30	1	26	15	11.9	5	62.5
1st Half	-	21	314	15.0	2	42	2	48	36	12.7	15	71.4
2nd Half/OT	-	16	211	13.2	0	24	0	44	28	10.4	12	75.0
Last 2 Min. Half	-	4	49	12.3	1	19	0	9	9	10.0	3	75.0
4th qtr, +/-7 pts	-	3	40	13.3	0	17	0	5	5	11.7	3	100.0
Winning	-	12	189	15.8	0	30	1	35	25	12.8	10	83.3
Tied	-	8	105	13.1	0	19	0	18	13	10.9	5	62.5
Trailing	-	17	231	13.6	2	42	1	39	26	11.3	12	75.0

	Rec	Yds	Avg	TD	Lg	Big	YAC	Trgt	Y@C	1st	1st%
Inside 20	2	11	5.5	1	6	0	1	8	5.0	1	50.0
Inside 10	1	6	6.0	1	6	0	0	4	6.0	1	100.0
1st Down	12	165	13.8	0	24	0	39	19	10.5	9	75.0
2nd Down	6	63	10.5	0	17	0	11	17	8.7	3	50.0
3rd Down Overall	19	297	15.6	2	42	2	42	28	13.4	15	78.9
3rd D 0-2 to Go	1	13	13.0	0	13	0	2	1	11.0	1	100.0
3rd D 3-7 to Go	7	109	15.6	0	42	1	12	10	13.9	7	100.0
3rd D 8+ to Go	11	175	15.9	0	30	1	28	17	13.4	7	63.6
4th Down	0	0	-	0	0	0	0	0	-	0	-
Rec Behind Line	0	0	-	0	0	0	0	1	-	0	-
1-10 yds	18	159	8.8	1	19	0	33	30	7.0	9	50.0
11-20 yds	17	294	17.3	0	24	0	52	28	14.2	16	94.1
21-30 yds	1	30	30.0	0	30	1	6	3	24.0	1	100.0
31+	1	42	42.0	1	42	1	1	2	41.0	1	100.0
Left Sideline	9	153	17.0	1	42	1	36	11	13.0	7	77.8
Left Side	7	96	13.7	0	30	1	17	11	11.3	3	42.9
Middle	6	96	16.0	0	24	0	15	14	13.5	6	100.0
Right Side	8	81	10.1	1	17	0	12	11	8.6	5	62.5
Right Sideline	7	99	14.1	0	19	0	12	17	12.4	6	85.7
Shotgun	28	425	15.2	2	42	2	73	44	12.6	22	78.6
2 Wide Receivers	7	70	11.1	0	24	0	15	15	9.0	4	57.1
3 Wide Receivers	9	125	13.9	0	24	0	25	18	11.1	7	77.8
4+ Wide Receivers	21	322	15.3	2	42	2	52	31	12.9	16	76.2

1995 Incompletions

Type	Num	%of Inc	%of Att
Pass Dropped	2	7.4	3.1
Poor Throw	12	44.4	18.8
Pass Defensed	8	29.6	12.5
Pass Hit at Line	1	3.7	1.6
Other	4	14.8	6.3
Total	27	100.0	42.2

Game Logs (1-8)

Date	Opp	Result	Rec	Yds	Trgt	F-L	TD
09/03	NYA	W 52-14	0	0	0	0-0	0
09/10	@NE	W 20-3	2	42	3	0-0	0
09/18	Pit	W 23-10	1	14	4	0-0	0
10/01	@Cin	W 26-23	6	79	7	0-0	0
10/08	Ind	L 24-27	2	16	5	0-0	1
10/15	@NO	L 30-33	4	60	7	0-0	0
10/22	@NYA	L 16-17	2	19	5	0-0	0
10/29	Buf	W 23-6	1	19	2	0-0	0

Game Logs (9-16)

Date	Opp	Result	Rec	Yds	Trgt	F-L	TD
11/05	@SD	W 24-14	3	26	3	0-0	0
11/12	NE	L 17-34	3	50	3	0-0	0
11/20	SF	L 20-44	4	89	7	0-0	0
11/26	@Ind	L 28-36	1	5	3	0-0	0
12/03	Atl	W 21-20	3	21	4	0-0	1
12/11	KC	W 13-6	0	0	4	0-0	0
12/17	@Buf	L 20-23	1	17	2	0-0	0
12/24	@StL	W 41-22	4	68	5	0-0	0

Ben Coates

New England Patriots — TE

1995 Receiving Splits

	G	Rec	Yds	Avg	TD	Lg	Big	YAC	Trgt	Y@C	1st	1st%		Rec	Yds	Avg	TD	Lg	Big	YAC	Trgt	Y@C	1st	1st%
Total	16	84	915	10.9	6	35	5	362	137	6.6	51	60.7	Inside 20	14	122	8.7	6	15	0	43	30	5.6	12	85.7
vs. Playoff	10	50	517	10.3	6	35	3	194	84	6.5	31	62.0	Inside 10	6	36	6.0	5	8	0	12	16	4.0	5	83.3
vs. Non-playoff	6	34	398	11.7	0	27	2	168	53	6.8	20	58.8	1st Down	26	265	10.2	0	28	1	106	44	6.1	12	46.2
vs. Own Division	8	36	398	11.1	4	35	2	167	65	6.4	21	58.3	2nd Down	25	288	11.5	2	27	2	96	40	7.7	14	56.0
Home	8	47	550	11.7	0	35	3	221	71	7.0	27	57.4	3rd Down Overall	30	340	11.3	4	35	2	151	47	6.3	23	76.7
Away	8	37	365	9.9	6	31	2	141	66	6.1	24	64.9	3rd D 0-2 to Go	2	29	14.5	0	18	0	21	7	4.0	2	100.0
Games 1-8	8	38	442	11.6	0	35	3	193	60	6.6	23	60.5	3rd D 3-7 to Go	15	155	10.3	3	35	1	65	19	6.0	14	93.3
Games 9-16	8	46	473	10.3	6	28	2	169	77	6.6	28	60.9	3rd D 8+ to Go	13	156	12.0	1	31	1	65	21	7.0	7	53.8
September	3	17	201	11.8	0	31	1	75	32	7.4	11	64.7	4th Down	3	22	7.3	0	11	0	9	6	4.3	2	66.7
October	5	21	241	11.5	0	35	2	118	28	5.9	12	57.1	Rec Behind Line	2	10	5.0	0	6	0	10	13	0.0	0	-
November	4	21	202	9.6	4	19	0	71	38	6.2	11	52.4	1-10 yds	70	654	9.3	6	35	1	280	99	5.3	41	58.6
December	4	25	271	10.8	2	28	2	98	39	6.9	17	68.0	11-20 yds	10	193	19.3	0	28	2	59	19	13.4	8	80.0
Grass	11	57	674	11.8	1	35	4	274	93	7.0	35	61.4	21-30 yds	2	58	29.0	0	31	2	13	5	22.5	2	100.0
Turf	5	27	241	8.9	5	28	1	88	44	5.7	16	59.3	31+	0	0	-	0	0	0	0	1	-	0	-
Outdoor	2	78	852	10.9	6	35	4	339	128	6.6	48	61.5	Left Sideline	3	49	16.3	0	28	1	34	4	5.0	2	66.7
Indoor	14	6	63	10.5	0	28	1	23	9	6.7	3	50.0	Left Side	14	172	12.3	1	35	1	73	21	7.1	10	71.4
1st Half	-	38	466	12.3	1	35	4	204	68	6.9	24	63.2	Middle	32	372	11.6	4	25	1	128	48	7.6	21	65.6
2nd Half/OT	-	46	449	9.8	5	27	1	158	69	6.3	27	58.7	Right Side	26	206	7.9	1	17	0	92	43	4.4	12	46.2
Last 2 Min. Half	-	16	150	9.4	1	24	0	33	19	7.3	7	43.8	Right Sideline	9	116	12.9	0	31	2	35	21	6	4	66.7
4th qtr, +/-7 pts	-	12	106	8.8	1	16	0	35	16	5.9	5	41.7	Shotgun	0	0	-	0	0	0	0	0	-	0	-
Winning	-	11	134	12.2	0	35	1	82	17	4.7	8	72.7	2 Wide Receivers	41	478	11.7	2	35	3	199	62	6.8	25	61.0
Tied	-	19	214	11.3	2	31	2	76	36	7.3	12	63.2	3 Wide Receivers	40	415	10.4	3	31	2	157	65	6.5	24	60.0
Trailing	-	54	567	10.5	4	27	2	204	84	6.7	31	57.4	4+ Wide Receivers	2	16	8.0	0	12	0	6	2	5.0	1	50.0

1995 Incompletions

Type	Num	%of Inc	%of Att
Pass Dropped	4	7.5	2.9
Poor Throw	25	47.2	18.2
Pass Defensed	13	24.5	9.5
Pass Hit at Line	7	13.2	5.1
Other	4	7.5	2.9
Total	53	100.0	38.7

Game Logs (1-8)

Date	Opp	Result	Rec	Yds	Trgt	F-L	TD
09/03	Cle	W 17-14	9	106	11	0-0	0
09/10	Mia	L 3-20	3	23	9	0-0	0
09/17	@SF	L 3-28	5	72	12	0-0	0
10/01	@Atl	L 17-30	2	7	2	0-0	0
10/08	Den	L 3-37	7	84	9	0-0	0
10/15	@KC	L 26-31	3	34	5	0-0	0
10/23	Buf	W 27-14	5	75	5	0-0	0
10/29	Car	L 17-20	4	41	7	1-1	0

Game Logs (9-16)

Date	Opp	Result	Rec	Yds	Trgt	F-L	TD
11/05	@NYA	W 20-7	4	35	9	0-0	0
11/12	@Mia	W 34-17	2	18	5	0-0	1
11/19	Ind	L 10-24	9	89	13	2-2	0
11/26	@Buf	W 35-25	6	60	11	0-0	3
12/03	NO	L 17-31	7	90	11	0-0	0
12/10	NYA	W 31-28	3	42	6	0-0	0
12/16	@Pit	L 27-41	11	83	15	1-1	2
12/23	@Ind	L 7-10	4	56	7	0-0	0

Kerry Collins

Carolina Panthers — QB

1995 Passing Splits

	G	Att	Cm	Pct	Yds	Yd/Att	TD	Int	1st	YAC	Big	Sk	Rtg		Att	Cm	Pct	Yds	Yd/Att	TD	Int	1st	YAC	Big	Sk	Rtg
Total	15	432	214	49.5	2717	6.3	14	19	130	1270	25	24	62.0	Inside 20	38	18	47.4	126	3.3	7	2	12	45	0	1	73.0
vs. Playoff	5	123	61	49.6	730	5.9	1	3	35	381	6	4	60.7	Inside 10	18	6	33.3	20	1.1	6	2	6	0	0	0	42.4
vs. Non-playoff	10	309	153	49.5	1987	6.4	13	16	95	889	19	20	62.6	1st Down	159	70	44.0	884	5.5	8	8	28	417	11	7	51.5
vs. Own Division	7	199	95	47.7	1216	6.1	7	12	55	622	11	13	53.9	2nd Down	123	64	52.0	717	5.8	5	4	35	388	6	7	69.7
Home	8	204	106	52.0	1266	6.2	5	6	62	637	12	12	67.2	3rd Down Overall	144	78	54.2	1105	7.7	4	7	65	459	8	10	68.2
Away	7	228	108	47.4	1451	6.4	9	13	68	633	13	12	57.5	3rd D 0-5 to Go	53	33	62.3	370	7.0	2	2	31	211	1	2	79.9
Games 1-8	7	165	86	52.1	1022	6.2	5	6	49	432	8	10	66.3	3rd D 6+ to Go	91	45	49.5	735	8.1	2	5	34	248	7	8	61.4
Games 9-16	8	267	128	47.9	1695	6.3	9	13	81	838	17	14	59.4	4th Down	6	2	33.3	11	1.8	0	0	2	6	0	0	42.4
September	2	13	7	53.8	45	3.5	0	1	2	26	0	1	29.3	Rec Behind Line	55	26	47.3	149	2.7	0	0	8	198	1	0	54.0
October	5	152	79	52.0	977	6.4	5	7	47	406	9	10	69.4	1-10 yds	241	143	59.3	1330	5.5	7	10	78	642	5	0	66.9
November	4	133	65	48.9	914	6.9	7	9	44	402	10	11	60.8	11-20 yds	80	36	45.0	863	10.8	5	2	35	316	11	0	94.9
December	4	134	63	47.0	781	5.8	2	4	37	436	7	3	58.1	21-30 yds	29	5	17.2	214	7.4	2	4	5	87	4	0	41.2
Grass	12	350	181	51.7	2154	6.2	9	11	108	990	18	19	66.3	31+	26	4	15.4	161	6.2	0	3	4	27	4	0	33.5
Turf	3	82	33	40.2	563	6.9	4	8	22	280	7	5	45.0	Left Sideline	60	34	56.7	553	9.2	3	3	27	252	6	2	83.5
Indoor	2	80	33	41.3	563	7.0	4	8	22	280	7	5	47.0	Left Side	75	41	54.7	560	7.5	3	3	26	286	5	2	75.4
Outdoor	13	352	181	51.4	2154	6.1	9	11	108	990	18	19	65.9	Middle	61	23	37.7	364	6.0	2	3	18	165	5	17	48.8
1st Half	-	194	100	51.5	1206	6.2	5	9	62	532	10	12	60.2	Right Side	133	70	52.6	809	6.1	4	2	35	408	8	3	75.0
2nd Half/OT	-	238	114	47.9	1511	6.3	9	10	68	738	15	12	63.6	Right Sideline	103	46	44.7	431	4.2	2	8	24	159	1	0	30.8
Last 2 Min. Half	-	51	22	43.1	377	7.4	3	3	18	122	3	0	63.9	2 Wide Receivers	184	91	49.5	973	5.3	3	3	45	506	8	10	64.0
4th qtr, +/-7 pts	-	55	20	36.4	340	6.2	1	2	14	155	3	3	49.1	3+ WR	235	116	49.4	1693	7.2	8	13	80	738	16	12	61.5
Winning	-	78	46	59.0	485	6.2	3	2	29	195	4	10	79.3	Attempts 1-10	142	78	54.9	851	6.0	3	5	44	413	7	0	65.2
Tied	-	104	44	42.3	489	4.7	2	1	25	195	3	6	59.3	Attempts 11-20	131	72	55.0	882	6.7	4	5	42	394	8	0	70.2
Trailing	-	250	124	49.6	1743	7.0	9	16	76	880	18	8	57.8	Attempts 21+	159	64	40.3	984	6.2	7	9	44	463	10	0	52.5

1995 Incompletions

Type	Num	% of Inc	% of Att
Pass Dropped	36	16.5	8.3
Poor Throw	101	46.3	23.4
Pass Defensed	32	14.7	7.4
Pass Hit at Line	18	8.3	4.2
Other	31	14.2	7.2
Total	218	100.0	50.5

Game Logs (1-8)

Date	Opp	Result	Att	Cm	Pct	Yds	TD	Int	Lg	Sk	F-L
09/03	@Atl	L 20-23	-	-	-	-	-	-	-	-	-
09/10	@Buf	L 9-31	2	0	0.0	0	0	0	0	0	0-0
09/17	StL	L 10-31	11	7	63.6	45	0	1	14	0	0-0
10/01	TB	L 13-20	32	18	56.3	234	1	1	41	0	0-0
10/08	@Chi	L 28-14	28	14	50.0	228	1	1	66	0	1-0
10/15	NYA	W 26-15	26	14	53.8	158	0	2	36	4	0-0
10/22	NO	W 20-3	21	8	38.1	48	1	0	12	4	2-0
10/29	@NE	W 20-17	45	25	55.6	309	2	1	33	2	1-1

Game Logs (9-16)

Date	Opp	Result	Att	Cm	Pct	Yds	TD	Int	Lg	Sk	F-L
11/05	@SF	W 13-7	30	17	56.7	150	0	1	17	3	1-1
11/12	@StL	L 17-28	34	16	47.1	228	2	4	39	3	2-2
11/19	Ari	W 27-7	35	21	65.2	201	2	0	39	3	2-1
11/26	@NO	L 26-34	46	17	37.0	335	3	4	60	2	3-1
12/03	Ind	W 13-10	34	14	41.2	170	0	0	33	0	0-0
12/10	SF	L 10-31	23	8	34.8	127	0	1	28	1	0-0
12/17	Atl	W 21-17	28	18	64.3	283	1	1	89	0	0-0
12/24	@Was	L 17-20	43	19	44.2	201	1	2	28	2	0-0

Curtis Conway
St. Louis...

1995 Receiving Splits

	G	Rec	Yds	Avg	TD	Lg	Big	YAC	Trgt	Y@C	1st	1st%		Rec	Yds	Avg	TD	Lg	Big	YAC	Trgt	Y@C	1st	1st%
Total	16	62	1037	16.7	12	76	8	320	117	11.6	47	75.8	Inside 20	5	30	6.0	4	10	0	2	13	5.6	4	80.0
vs. Playoff	6	16	267	16.7	3	46	3	69	39	12.4	12	75.0	Inside 10	4	20	5.0	3	6	0	2	10	4.5	3	75.0
vs. Non-playoff	10	46	770	16.7	9	76	5	251	78	11.3	35	76.1	1st Down	28	573	20.5	5	73	6	180	49	14.0	24	85.7
vs. Own Division	8	29	503	17.3	5	73	5	164	55	11.7	19	65.5	2nd Down	14	205	14.6	4	46	1	45	28	11.4	10	71.4
Home	8	28	515	18.4	5	76	4	185	57	11.8	22	78.6	3rd Down Overall	17	245	14.4	3	76	1	93	37	8.9	12	70.6
Away	8	34	522	15.4	7	48	4	135	60	11.4	25	73.5	3rd D 0-2 to Go	1	13	13.0	0	13	0	11	2	2.0	1	100.0
Games 1-8	8	30	602	20.1	9	76	6	198	58	13.5	25	83.3	3rd D 3-7 to Go	7	140	20.0	2	76	1	62	19	11.1	7	100.0
Games 9-16	8	32	435	13.6	3	46	2	122	59	9.8	22	68.8	3rd D 8+ to Go	9	92	10.2	1	20	0	20	16	8.0	4	44.4
September	4	18	292	16.2	3	73	2	97	33	10.8	13	72.2	4th Down	3	14	4.7	0	6	0	2	3	4.0	1	33.3
October	4	12	310	25.8	6	76	4	101	25	17.4	12	100.0	Rec Behind Line	0	0	-	0	0	0	0	1	-	0	-
November	4	16	270	16.9	3	46	2	62	29	13.0	15	93.8	1-10 yds	35	317	9.1	4	22	0	115	55	5.8	20	57.1
December	4	16	165	10.3	0	22	0	60	30	6.6	7	43.8	11-20 yds	21	415	19.8	2	46	3	115	36	14.3	21	100.0
Grass	11	42	771	18.4	10	76	7	260	83	12.2	34	81.0	21-30 yds	1	21	21.0	1	21	0	0	1	21.0	1	100.0
Turf	5	20	266	13.3	2	48	1	60	34	10.3	13	65.0	31+	5	284	56.8	5	76	5	90	20	38.8	5	100.0
Indoor	2	3	60	20.0	1	48	1	6	10	18.0	1	33.3	Left Sideline	9	163	18.1	2	46	1	61	17	11.3	8	88.9
Outdoor	14	59	977	16.6	11	76	7	314	107	11.2	46	78.0	Left Side	13	167	12.8	1	31	1	58	18	8.4	10	76.9
1st Half	-	37	719	19.4	10	76	7	213	70	13.7	30	81.1	Middle	5	97	19.4	2	76	1	40	15	11.4	2	40.0
2nd Half/OT	-	25	318	12.7	2	46	1	107	47	8.4	17	68.0	Right Side	22	353	16.0	5	48	3	78	39	12.5	15	68.2
Last 2 Min. Half	-	12	193	16.1	4	48	2	33	20	13.3	10	83.3	Right Sideline	13	257	19.8	2	73	2	83	28	13.4	12	92.3
4th qtr, +/-7 pts	-	10	148	14.8	1	46	1	54	17	9.4	7	70.0	Shotgun	0	0	-	0	0	0	0	0	-	0	-
Winning	-	19	367	19.3	3	76	3	145	41	11.7	14	73.7	2 Wide Receivers	32	538	16.8	8	73	4	172	57	11.4	24	75.0
Tied	-	14	211	15.1	3	41	1	28	31	13.1	12	85.7	3 Wide Receivers	19	353	18.6	2	76	3	122	37	12.2	17	89.5
Trailing	-	29	459	15.8	6	73	4	147	45	10.8	21	72.4	4+ Wide Receivers	11	146	13.3	2	46	1	26	23	10.9	6	54.5

1995 Incompletions

Type	Num	%of Inc	%of Att
Pass Dropped	12	21.8	10.3
Poor Throw	25	45.5	21.4
Pass Defensed	11	20.0	9.4
Pass Hit at Line	0	0.0	0.0
Other	7	12.7	6.0
Total	55	100.0	47.0

Game Logs (1-8)

Date	Opp	Result	Rush	Yds	Rec	Yds	Trgt	F-L	TD
09/03	Min	W 31-14	0	0	5	110	7	0-0	2
09/11	GB	L 24-27	0	0	3	63	6	0-0	0
09/17	@TB	W 25-6	0	0	4	56	11	0-0	0
09/24	@StL	L 28-34	0	0	6	63	9	0-0	1
10/08	Car	W 31-27	1	11	4	77	8	0-0	1
10/15	@Jac	W 30-27	0	0	4	74	7	0-0	3
10/22	Hou	W 35-32	1	19	3	111	7	0-0	0
10/30	@Min	W 14-6	0	0	1	48	3	0-0	0

Game Logs (9-16)

Date	Opp	Result	Rush	Yds	Rec	Yds	Trgt	F-L	TD
11/05	Pit	L 34-37	1	18	4	55	11	0-0	1
11/12	@GB	L 28-35	0	0	6	126	8	0-0	2
11/19	Det	L 17-24	0	0	0	0	2	0-0	0
11/26	@NYN	W 27-24	0	0	6	89	8	0-0	0
12/04	@Det	L 7-27	0	0	2	12	7	0-0	0
12/10	@Cin	L 10-16	0	0	5	54	7	0-0	0
12/17	TB	W 31-10	1	20	8	88	11	0-0	0
12/24	Phi	W 20-14	1	9	1	11	5	0-0	0

Marv Cook

1995 Receiving Splits

	G	Rec	Yds	Avg	TD	Lg	Big	YAC	Trgt	Y@C	1st	1st%		Rec	Yds	Avg	TD	Lg	Big	YAC	Trgt	Y@C	1st	1st%
Total	16	26	135	5.2	1	16	0	89	32	1.8	5	19.2	Inside 20	6	16	2.7	1	12	0	11	7	0.8	3	50.0
vs. Playoff	9	17	102	6.0	0	16	0	63	21	2.3	3	17.6	Inside 10	2	2	1.0	1	1	0	1	2	0.5	1	50.0
vs. Non-playoff	7	9	33	3.7	1	9	0	26	11	0.8	2	22.2	1st Down	8	52	6.5	0	11	0	37	10	1.9	1	12.5
vs. Own Division	8	10	65	6.5	0	16	0	45	12	2.0	2	20.0	2nd Down	14	80	5.7	0	16	0	45	18	2.5	2	14.3
Home	8	9	60	6.7	1	16	0	35	13	2.8	4	44.4	3rd Down Overall	3	2	0.7	0	3	0	7	3	-1.7	1	33.3
Away	8	17	75	4.4	0	9	0	54	19	1.2	1	5.9	3rd D 0-2 to Go	1	3	3.0	0	3	0	3	1	0.0	1	100.0
Games 1-8	8	14	74	5.3	1	16	0	47	18	1.9	2	14.3	3rd D 3-7 to Go	1	-3	-3.0	0	-3	0	1	1	-3.0	0	0.0
Games 9-16	8	12	61	5.1	0	12	0	42	14	1.6	3	25.0	3rd D 8+ to Go	1	2	2.0	0	2	0	4	1	-2.0	0	0.0
September	4	6	24	4.0	1	9	0	24	7	0.0	1	16.7	4th Down	1	1	1.0	1	1	0	0	1	1.0	1	100.0
October	4	8	50	6.3	0	16	0	23	11	3.4	1	12.5	Rec Behind Line	9	23	2.6	0	9	0	35	10	-1.3	1	11.1
November	4	6	24	4.0	0	9	0	22	6	0.3	1	16.7	1-10 yds	16	96	6.0	1	12	0	50	19	2.9	3	18.8
December	4	6	37	6.2	0	12	0	20	8	2.8	2	33.3	11-20 yds	1	16	16.0	0	16	0	4	3	12.0	1	100.0
Grass	3	6	29	4.8	0	9	0	24	6	0.8	0	0.0	21-30 yds	0	0	-	0	0	0	0	0	-	0	-
Turf	13	20	106	5.3	1	16	0	65	26	2.1	5	25.0	31+	0	0	-	0	0	0	0	0	-	0	-
Outdoor	7	14	72	5.1	1	16	0	47	17	1.8	2	14.3	Left Sideline	4	25	6.3	0	9	0	21	6	1.0	0	0.0
Indoor	9	12	63	5.3	0	12	0	42	15	1.8	3	25.0	Left Side	3	7	2.3	0	5	0	10	3	-1.0	0	0.0
1st Half	-	12	49	4.1	0	9	0	41	16	0.7	1	8.3	Middle	3	34	11.3	0	16	0	8	3	8.7	2	66.7
2nd Half/OT	-	14	86	6.1	1	16	0	48	16	2.7	4	28.6	Right Side	8	20	2.5	1	8	0	15	10	0.6	1	12.5
Last 2 Min. Half	-	3	14	4.7	0	6	0	8	3	2.0	1	33.3	Right Sideline	8	49	6.1	0	11	0	35	10	1.8	2	25.0
4th qtr, +/-7 pts	-	1	6	6.0	0	6	0	4	2	2.0	0	0.0	Shotgun	0	0	-	0	0	0	0	0	-	0	-
Winning	-	5	20	4.0	0	9	0	22	8	-0.4	0	0.0	2 Wide Receivers	17	70	4.1	0	9	0	56	21	0.8	0	0.0
Tied	-	5	20	4.0	0	7	0	13	5	1.4	0	0.0	3 Wide Receivers	5	54	10.8	0	16	0	26	5	5.6	3	60.0
Trailing	-	16	95	5.9	1	16	0	54	19	2.6	5	31.3	4+ Wide Receivers	0	0	-	0	0	0	0	0	-	0	-

1995 Incompletions

Type	Num	%of Inc	%of Att
Pass Dropped	2	33.3	6.3
Poor Throw	4	66.7	12.5
Pass Defensed	0	0.0	0.0
Pass Hit at Line	0	0.0	0.0
Other	0	0.0	0.0
Total	6	100.0	18.8

Game Logs (1-8)

Date	Opp	Result	Rec	Yds	Trgt	F-L	TD
09/03	@GB	W 17-14	2	8	2	0-0	0
09/10	NO	W 17-13	1	9	2	0-0	0
09/17	@Car	W 31-10	1	9	1	0-0	0
09/24	Chi	W 34-28	2	-2	2	0-0	1
10/01	@Ind	L 18-21	5	21	6	1-1	0
10/12	Atl	W 21-19	1	7	2	0-0	0
10/22	SF	L 10-44	1	16	1	0-0	0
10/29	@Phi	L 9-20	1	6	2	0-0	0

Game Logs (9-16)

Date	Opp	Result	Rec	Yds	Trgt	F-L	TD
11/05	@NO	L 10-19	1	3	1	0-0	0
11/12	Car	W 28-17	0	0	0	0-0	0
11/19	@Atl	L 6-31	2	9	2	0-0	0
11/26	@SF	L 13-41	3	12	3	0-0	0
12/03	@NYA	W 23-20	2	7	2	0-0	0
12/10	Buf	L 27-45	2	23	2	0-0	0
12/17	Was	L 23-35	2	7	3	0-0	0
12/24	Mia	L 22-41	0	0	1	0-0	0

Horace Copeland

1995 Receiving Splits

	G	Rec	Yds	Avg	TD	Lg	Big	YAC	Trgt	Y@C	1st	1st%		Rec	Yds	Avg	TD	Lg	Big	YAC	Trgt	Y@C	1st	1st%
Total	15	35	605	17.3	2	64	4	94	63	14.6	30	85.7	Inside 20	1	4	4.0	0	4	0	0	2	4.0	1	100.0
vs. Playoff	5	15	310	20.7	1	64	2	69	25	16.1	13	86.7	Inside 10	0	0	-	0	0	0	0	1	-	0	-
vs. Non-playoff	10	20	295	14.8	1	40	2	25	38	13.5	17	85.0	1st Down	12	232	19.3	1	64	1	51	22	15.1	9	75.0
vs. Own Division	7	23	329	14.3	1	31	1	61	40	11.7	18	78.3	2nd Down	11	165	15.0	1	40	2	18	20	13.4	11	100.0
Home	8	16	236	14.8	0	23	0	49	29	11.7	14	87.5	3rd Down Overall	12	208	17.3	0	44	1	25	20	15.3	10	83.3
Away	7	19	369	19.4	2	64	4	45	34	17.1	16	84.2	3rd D 0-2 to Go	0	0	-	0	0	0	0	0	-	0	-
Games 1-8	8	14	310	22.1	1	64	3	32	26	19.9	14	100.0	3rd D 3-7 to Go	4	42	10.5	0	13	0	1	4	10.3	3	75.0
Games 9-16	7	21	295	14.0	1	31	1	62	37	11.1	16	76.2	3rd D 8+ to Go	8	166	20.8	0	44	1	24	16	17.8	7	87.5
September	4	10	223	22.3	1	64	2	26	18	19.7	10	100.0	4th Down	0	0	-	0	0	0	0	1	-	0	-
October	5	4	87	21.8	0	40	1	6	9	20.3	4	100.0	Rec Behind Line	0	0	-	0	0	0	0	0	-	0	-
November	2	1	11	11.0	0	11	0	3	3	8.0	1	100.0	1-10 yds	14	137	9.8	0	23	0	50	19	6.2	9	64.3
December	4	20	284	14.2	1	31	1	59	33	11.3	15	75.0	11-20 yds	14	220	15.7	1	24	0	8	23	15.1	14	100.0
Grass	11	25	390	15.6	2	40	2	64	46	13.0	21	84.0	21-30 yds	4	100	25.0	0	31	1	9	10	22.8	4	100.0
Turf	4	10	215	21.5	1	64	2	30	17	18.5	9	90.0	31+	3	148	49.3	1	64	3	27	11	40.3	3	100.0
Outdoor	3	30	545	18.2	2	64	4	88	53	15.2	26	86.7	Left Sideline	14	229	16.4	0	40	2	45	26	13.1	13	92.9
Indoor	12	5	60	12.0	0	24	0	6	10	10.8	4	80.0	Left Side	5	77	15.4	0	23	0	9	12	13.6	3	60.0
1st Half	-	15	294	19.6	2	64	3	58	26	15.7	14	93.3	Middle	5	149	29.8	1	64	2	22	9	25.4	4	80.0
2nd Half/OT	-	20	311	15.6	0	44	1	36	37	13.8	16	80.0	Right Side	2	35	17.5	0	24	0	11	5	12.0	2	100.0
Last 2 Min. Half	-	4	79	19.8	0	40	1	13	7	16.5	3	75.0	Right Sideline	9	115	12.8	1	20	0	7	11	12.0	8	88.9
4th qtr, +/-7 pts	-	2	36	18.0	0	23	0	2	4	17.0	2	100.0	Shotgun	3	39	13.0	0	16	0	1	5	12.7	2	66.7
Winning	-	8	167	20.9	0	44	2	7	11	20.0	7	87.5	2 Wide Receivers	16	362	22.6	2	64	3	79	32	17.7	16	100.0
Tied	-	5	71	14.2	0	23	0	24	10	9.4	5	100.0	3 Wide Receivers	15	191	12.7	0	40	1	9	24	12.1	11	73.3
Trailing	-	22	367	16.7	2	64	2	63	42	13.8	18	81.8	4+ Wide Receivers	3	29	9.7	0	16	0	4	6	8.3	2	66.7

1995 Incompletions

Type	Num	%of Inc	%of Att
Pass Dropped	8	28.6	12.7
Poor Throw	10	35.7	15.9
Pass Defensed	8	28.6	12.7
Pass Hit at Line	1	3.6	1.6
Other	1	3.6	1.6
Total	28	100.0	44.4

Game Logs (1-8)

Date	Opp	Result		Rec	Yds	Trgt	F-L	TD
09/03	@Phi	W	21-6	5	155	7	0-0	1
09/10	@Cle	L	6-22	2	22	4	0-0	0
09/17	Chi	L	6-25	2	29	5	0-0	0
09/24	Was	W	14-6	1	17	2	0-0	0
10/01	@Car	W	20-13	1	40	2	0-0	0
10/08	Cin	W	19-16	1	8	2	0-0	0
10/15	Min	W	20-17	1	16	1	0-0	0
10/22	Atl	L	21-24	1	23	3	0-0	0

Game Logs (9-16)

Date	Opp	Result		Rec	Yds	Trgt	F-L	TD
10/29	@Hou	L	7-19	0	0	1	0-0	0
11/12	@Det	L	24-27	0	0	0	-	-
11/19	Jac	W	17-16	1	11	2	0-0	0
11/26	@GB	L	13-35	-	-	-	-	-
12/03	@Min	L	17-31	5	60	8	0-0	0
12/10	GB	W	13-10	8	122	9	0-0	0
12/17	@Chi	L	10-31	6	92	11	0-0	1
12/23	Det	L	10-37	1	10	5	0-0	0

Russell Copeland

1995 Receiving Splits

	G	Rec	Yds	Avg	TD	Lg	Big	YAC	Trgt	Y@C	1st	1st%		Rec	Yds	Avg	TD	Lg	Big	YAC	Trgt	Y@C	1st	1st%
Total	16	42	646	15.4	1	77	4	180	95	11.1	30	71.4	Inside 20	0	0	-	0	0	0	0	7	-	0	-
vs. Playoff	6	16	226	14.1	0	65	1	46	43	11.3	12	75.0	Inside 10	0	0	-	0	0	0	0	2	-	0	-
vs. Non-playoff	10	26	420	16.2	1	77	3	134	52	11.0	18	69.2	1st Down	17	259	15.2	0	65	2	46	37	12.5	11	64.7
vs. Own Division	8	19	278	14.6	0	65	1	53	52	11.8	13	68.4	2nd Down	14	196	14.0	0	35	1	61	31	9.6	12	85.7
Home	8	21	325	15.5	1	77	3	107	53	10.4	13	61.9	3rd Down Overall	9	173	19.2	1	77	1	72	25	11.2	5	55.6
Away	8	21	321	15.3	0	65	1	73	42	11.8	17	81.0	3rd D 0-2 to Go	1	12	12.0	0	12	0	0	1	12.0	1	100.0
Games 1-8	8	28	441	15.8	1	77	3	153	55	10.3	20	71.4	3rd D 3-7 to Go	2	90	45.0	0	77	1	66	6	12.0	2	100.0
Games 9-16	8	14	205	14.6	0	65	1	27	40	12.7	10	71.4	3rd D 8+ to Go	6	71	11.8	0	23	0	6	18	10.8	2	33.3
September	3	9	200	22.2	1	77	2	95	17	11.7	8	88.9	4th Down	2	18	9.0	0	10	0	1	2	8.5	2	100.0
October	5	19	241	12.7	0	25	1	58	38	9.6	12	63.2	Rec Behind Line	1	0	0.0	0	0	0	0	2	0.0	0	0.0
November	4	9	146	16.2	0	65	1	20	23	14.0	6	66.7	1-10 yds	22	212	9.6	0	20	0	70	48	6.5	13	59.1
December	4	5	59	11.8	0	23	0	7	17	10.4	4	80.0	11-20 yds	16	311	19.4	1	77	2	84	37	14.2	14	87.5
Grass	5	16	189	11.8	0	20	0	52	31	8.6	12	75.0	21-30 yds	2	58	29.0	0	35	1	11	2	23.5	2	100.0
Turf	11	26	457	17.6	1	77	4	128	64	12.7	18	69.2	31+	1	65	65.0	0	65	1	15	6	50.0	1	100.0
Indoor	2	5	132	26.4	0	65	1	21	10	22.2	5	100.0	Left Sideline	12	137	11.4	0	18	0	16	27	10.1	9	75.0
Outdoor	14	37	514	13.9	1	77	3	159	85	9.6	25	67.6	Left Side	7	142	20.3	0	65	1	27	14	16.4	5	71.4
1st Half	-	18	258	14.3	0	65	1	43	44	11.9	11	61.1	Middle	6	155	25.8	0	77	2	91	13	10.7	5	83.3
2nd Half/OT	-	24	388	16.2	1	77	3	137	51	10.5	19	79.2	Right Side	9	102	11.3	0	20	0	33	17	7.7	6	66.7
Last 2 Min. Half	-	7	79	11.3	0	23	0	11	10	9.7	5	71.4	Right Sideline	8	110	13.8	0	35	1	13	24	12.1	5	62.5
4th qtr, +/-7 pts	-	3	45	15.0	0	20	0	14	7	10.3	3	100.0	Shotgun	18	307	17.1	1	77	2	113	36	10.8	13	72.2
Winning	-	13	265	20.4	0	65	3	48	31	16.7	11	84.6	2 Wide Receivers	6	103	17.2	0	25	1	28	16	12.5	6	100.0
Tied	-	11	121	11.0	0	20	0	16	25	9.5	5	45.5	3 Wide Receivers	35	536	15.3	1	77	3	152	76	11.0	24	68.6
Trailing	-	18	260	14.4	1	77	1	116	39	8.0	14	77.8	4+ Wide Receivers	1	7	7.0	0	7	0	0	3	7.0	0	0.0

1995 Incompletions

Type	Num	%of Inc	%of Att
Pass Dropped	4	7.5	4.2
Poor Throw	31	58.5	32.6
Pass Defensed	13	24.5	13.7
Pass Hit at Line	1	1.9	1.1
Other	4	7.5	4.2
Total	53	100.0	55.8

Game Logs (1-8)

Date	Opp	Result		Rush	Yds	Rec	Yds	Trgt	F-L	TD
09/03	@Den	L	7-22	0	0	6	75	7	0-0	1
09/10	Car	W	31-9	0	0	2	112	4	0-0	1
09/17	Ind	W	20-14	0	0	1	13	1	0-0	0
09/24	@Cle	W	22-19	0	0	2	34	3	0-0	0
10/08	NYA	W	29-10	0	0	5	67	11	0-0	0
10/15	Sea	W	27-21	0	0	5	67	7	0-0	0
10/23	@NE	L	14-27	1	-1	3	25	6	0-0	0
10/29	@Mia	L	6-23	0	0	4	48	11	0-0	0

Game Logs (9-16)

Date	Opp	Result		Rush	Yds	Rec	Yds	Trgt	F-L	TD
11/05	@Ind	W	16-10	0	0	3	99	7	0-0	0
11/12	Atl	W	23-17	0	0	5	40	10	0-0	0
11/19	@NYA	W	28-26	0	0	0	0	1	0-0	0
11/26	NE	L	25-35	0	0	1	7	5	0-0	0
12/03	@SF	L	17-27	0	0	1	4	4	0-0	0
12/10	@StL	W	45-27	0	0	2	33	3	0-0	0
12/17	Mia	W	23-20	0	0	2	19	5	0-0	0
12/24	Hou	L	17-28	0	0	0	0	5	1-0	0

Aaron Craver
Denver Broncos — RB

1995 Receiving Splits

	G	Rec	Yds	Avg	TD	Lg	Big	YAC	Trgt	Y@C	1st	1st%		Rec	Yds	Avg	TD	Lg	Big	YAC	Trgt	Y@C	1st	1st%
Total	16	43	369	8.6	1	32	1	331	57	0.9	21	48.8	Inside 20	2	8	4.0	1	7	0	12	4	-2.0	1	50.0
vs. Playoff	7	16	118	7.4	0	15	0	87	20	1.9	7	43.8	Inside 10	1	1	1.0	1	1	0	1	3	0.0	1	100.0
vs. Non-playoff	9	27	251	9.3	1	32	1	244	37	0.3	14	51.9	1st Down	15	129	8.6	0	19	0	146	21	-1.1	7	46.7
vs. Own Division	8	26	202	7.8	0	23	0	173	34	1.1	10	38.5	2nd Down	21	197	9.4	1	32	1	157	28	1.9	12	57.1
Home	8	18	148	8.2	1	32	1	139	24	0.5	8	44.4	3rd Down Overall	6	39	6.5	0	15	0	27	6	2.0	2	33.3
Away	8	25	221	8.8	0	23	0	192	33	1.2	13	52.0	3rd D 0-2 to Go	0	0	-	0	0	0	0	0	-	0	-
Games 1-8	8	21	159	7.6	0	15	0	121	30	1.8	8	38.1	3rd D 3-7 to Go	2	14	7.0	0	9	0	4	2	5.0	2	100.0
Games 9-16	8	22	210	9.5	1	32	1	210	27	0.0	13	59.1	3rd D 8+ to Go	4	25	6.3	0	15	0	23	4	0.5	0	0.0
September	4	5	45	9.0	0	12	0	24	8	4.2	3	60.0	4th Down	1	4	4.0	0	4	0	1	2	3.0	0	0.0
October	4	16	114	7.1	0	15	0	97	22	1.1	5	31.3	Rec Behind Line	19	122	6.4	1	19	0	155	25	-1.7	9	47.4
November	4	5	66	13.2	1	32	1	57	6	1.8	4	80.0	1-10 yds	24	247	10.3	0	32	1	176	31	3.0	12	50.0
December	4	17	144	8.5	0	23	0	153	21	-0.5	9	52.9	11-20 yds	0	0	-	0	0	0	0	1	-	0	-
Grass	12	37	325	8.8	1	32	1	304	48	0.6	19	51.4	21-30 yds	0	0	-	0	0	0	0	0	-	0	-
Turf	4	6	44	7.3	0	12	0	27	9	2.8	2	33.3	31+	0	0	-	0	0	0	0	0	-	0	-
Indoor	2	6	44	7.3	0	12	0	27	9	2.8	2	33.3	Left Sideline	4	34	8.5	0	15	0	34	5	0.0	2	50.0
Outdoor	14	37	325	8.8	1	32	1	304	48	0.6	19	51.4	Left Side	8	43	5.4	1	13	0	59	12	-2.0	3	37.5
1st Half	-	21	178	8.5	1	32	1	166	29	0.6	11	52.4	Middle	10	72	7.2	0	15	0	38	11	3.4	4	40.0
2nd Half/OT	-	22	191	8.7	0	23	0	165	28	1.2	10	45.5	Right Side	16	156	9.8	0	23	0	152	18	0.3	9	56.3
Last 2 Min. Half	-	8	62	7.8	0	13	0	60	9	0.3	4	50.0	Right Sideline	5	64	12.8	0	32	1	48	11	3.2	3	60.0
4th qtr, +/-7 pts	-	3	16	5.3	0	9	0	11	4	1.7	0	0.0	Shotgun	20	171	8.6	0	23	0	167	27	0.2	8	40.0
Winning	-	14	144	10.3	1	32	1	140	18	0.3	10	71.4	2 Wide Receivers	19	172	9.1	0	32	1	174	26	-0.1	12	63.2
Tied	-	9	63	7.0	0	15	0	54	14	1.0	3	33.3	3 Wide Receivers	16	129	8.1	0	15	0	93	21	2.3	8	37.5
Trailing	-	20	162	8.1	0	23	0	137	25	1.3	8	40.0	4+ Wide Receivers	6	48	8.0	0	23	0	42	7	1.0	1	16.7

1995 Incompletions

Type	Num	%of Inc	%of Att
Pass Dropped	3	21.4	5.3
Poor Throw	4	28.6	7.0
Pass Defensed	1	7.1	1.8
Pass Hit at Line	3	21.4	5.3
Other	3	21.4	5.3
Total	14	100.0	24.6

Game Logs (1-8)

Date	Opp	Result	Rush	Yds	Rec	Yds	Trgt	F-L	TD
09/03	Buf	W 22-7	1	3	1	9	1	0-0	0
09/10	@Dal	L 21-31	1	-1	0	0	0	0-0	0
09/17	Was	W 38-31	6	48	0	0	2	0-0	0
09/24	@SD	L 6-17	4	9	4	36	5	0-0	0
10/01	@Sea	L 10-27	1	3	5	32	7	0-0	0
10/08	@NE	W 37-3	2	1	6	57	8	0-0	1
10/16	Oak	W 27-0	7	40	0	0	0	0-0	0
10/22	KC	L 7-21	5	11	5	25	7	0-0	0

Game Logs (9-16)

Date	Opp	Result	Rush	Yds	Rec	Yds	Trgt	F-L	TD
11/05	Ari	W 38-6	1	3	3	52	3	0-0	2
11/12	@Phi	L 13-31	1	11	0	0	0	0-0	0
11/19	SD	W 30-27	0	0	1	2	1	0-0	0
11/26	@Hou	L 33-42	4	25	1	12	2	0-0	1
12/03	Jac	W 31-23	5	-4	6	37	7	0-0	0
12/10	Sea	L 27-31	12	61	2	23	3	0-0	1
12/17	@KC	L 17-20	3	17	5	46	6	0-0	0
12/24	@Oak	W 31-28	20	108	4	38	5	1-1	1

Randall Cunningham
Philadelphia Eagles — QB

1995 Passing Splits

	G	Att	Cm	Pct	Yds	Yd/Att	TD	Int	1st	YAC	Big	Sk	Rtg		Att	Cm	Pct	Yds	Yd/Att	TD	Int	1st	YAC	Big	Sk	Rtg
Total	7	121	69	57.0	605	5.0	3	5	34	295	2	13	61.5	Inside 20	6	5	83.3	21	3.5	3	0	4	21	0	1	120.8
vs. Playoff	1	39	23	59.0	196	5.0	3	1	11	114	2	1	87.1	Inside 10	3	3	100.0	8	2.7	3	0	3	4	0	0	118.8
vs. Non-playoff	6	82	46	56.1	409	5.0	0	4	23	181	0	12	49.3	1st Down	40	20	50.0	165	4.1	0	1	6	90	1	3	50.5
vs. Own Division	4	27	10	37.0	116	4.3	0	2	8	45	0	2	20.0	2nd Down	42	27	64.3	246	5.9	2	2	14	123	1	5	76.1
Home	3	82	52	63.4	448	5.5	3	2	23	234	2	7	79.7	3rd Down Overall	37	20	54.1	176	4.8	1	2	13	74	0	5	53.4
Away	4	39	17	43.6	157	4.0	0	3	11	61	0	6	23.1	3rd D 0-5 to Go	14	9	64.3	67	4.8	1	1	9	31	0	1	69.6
Games 1-8	5	111	65	58.6	544	4.9	3	5	30	273	2	12	61.5	3rd D 6+ to Go	23	11	47.8	109	4.7	0	1	4	43	0	4	43.6
Games 9-16	2	10	4	40.0	61	6.1	0	0	4	22	0	1	104.2	4th Down	2	2	100.0	18	9.0	0	0	1	8	0	0	104.2
September	4	102	62	60.8	518	5.1	3	4	27	262	2	12	67.4	Rec Behind Line	23	16	69.6	78	3.4	1	0	4	122	0	0	88.7
October	1	9	3	33.3	26	2.9	0	1	3	11	0	0	2.8	1-10 yds	64	41	64.1	317	5.0	2	2	21	128	1	0	73.5
November	2	10	4	40.0	61	6.1	0	0	4	22	0	1	60.8	11-20 yds	25	12	48.0	210		0	2	9	45	1	0	43.7
December	0	0	0	-	0	-	0	0	0	0	0	0	-	21-30 yds	3	0	0.0	0	0.0	0	0	0	0	0	0	0.0
Grass	3	30	14	46.7	131	4.4	0	2	8	50	0	6	31.4	31+	6	0	0.0	0	0.0	0	0	0	0	0	0	0.0
Turf	4	91	55	60.4	474	5.2	3	3	26	245	2	7	71.4	Left Sideline	13	7	53.8	71	5.5	0	0	3	69	0	0	69.7
Indoor	0	0	0	-	0	-	0	0	0	0	0	0	-	Left Side	22	11	50.0	93	4.2	0	2	5	56	1	1	23.5
Outdoor	7	121	69	57.0	605	5.0	3	5	34	295	2	13	61.5	Middle	27	13	48.1	170	6.3	1	1	10	45	1	9	65.4
1st Half	-	61	41	67.2	349	5.7	2	1	19	170	1	9	86.0	Right Side	32	20	62.5	146	4.6	1	2	10	89	0	3	57.6
2nd Half/OT	-	60	28	46.7	256	4.3	1	4	15	125	1	4	36.5	Right Sideline	27	18	66.7	125	4.6	1	0	6	36	0	0	89.3
Last 2 Min. Half	-	22	11	50.0	91	4.1	0	1	5	21	0	1	42.0	2 Wide Receivers	59	35	55.9	322		1	3	17	176	2	5	55.9
4th qtr, +/-7 pts	-	16	6	37.5	47	2.9	0	1	2	21	0	0	19.8	3+ WR	61	35	57.4	282	4.6	1	2	16	119	0	8	61.0
Winning	-	33	19	57.6	173	5.2	1	1	11	81	1	4	69.4	Attempts 1-10	57	33	57.9	328	5.8	2	2	22	156	1	0	71.4
Tied	-	29	16	55.2	158	5.4	1	1	10	78	0	2	67.9	Attempts 11-20	29	18	62.1	122	4.2	0	1	5	53	0	0	57.0
Trailing	-	59	34	57.6	274	4.6	1	3	13	136	1	7	49.1	Attempts 21+	35	18	51.4	155	4.4	1	2	7	86	1	0	49.1

1995 Incompletions

Type	Num	% of Inc	% of Att
Pass Dropped	9	17.3	7.4
Poor Throw	21	40.4	17.4
Pass Defensed	13	25.0	10.7
Pass Hit at Line	3	5.8	2.5
Other	6	11.5	5.0
Total	52	100.0	43.0

Game Logs (1-8)

Date	Opp	Result	Att	Cm	Pct	Yds	TD	Int	Lg	Sk	F-L
09/03	TB	L 6-21	36	25	69.4	191	0	1	16	5	0-0
09/10	@Ari	W 31-19	8	3	37.5	29	0	1	14	1	0-0
09/17	SD	L 21-27	39	23	59.0	196	3	1	33	1	0-0
09/24	@Oak	L 17-48	19	11	57.9	102	0	1	24	5	2-1
10/01	@NO	W 15-10	-	-	-	-	-	-	-	-	-
10/08	Was	W 37-34	-	-	-	-	-	-	-	-	-
10/15	@NYN	W 17-14	9	3	33.3	26	0	1	16	0	1-1
10/29	StL	W 20-9	-	-	-	-	-	-	-	-	-

Game Logs (9-16)

Date	Opp	Result	Att	Cm	Pct	Yds	TD	Int	Lg	Sk	F-L
11/06	@Dal	L 12-34	-	-	-	-	-	-	-	-	-
11/12	Den	W 31-13	-	-	-	-	-	-	-	-	-
11/19	NYN	W 28-19	7	4	57.1	61	0	0	20	1	0-0
11/26	@Was	W 14-7	3	0	0.0	0	0	0	0	0	0-0
12/03	@Sea	L 14-26	-	-	-	-	-	-	-	-	-
12/10	Dal	W 20-17	-	-	-	-	-	-	-	-	-
12/17	Ari	W 21-20	-	-	-	-	-	-	-	-	-
12/24	@Chi	L 14-20	-	-	-	-	-	-	-	-	-

Terrell Davis

Denver Broncos — RB

1995 Rushing and Receiving Splits

	G	Rush	Yds	Avg	Lg	TD	1st	Stf	YdL	Rec	Yds	Avg	TD
Total	14	237	1117	4.7	60	7	58	12	23	49	367	7.5	1
vs. Playoff	6	100	488	4.9	36	2	27	4	5	18	136	7.6	0
vs. Non-playoff	8	137	629	4.6	60	5	31	8	18	31	231	7.5	1
vs. Own Division	6	93	407	4.4	31	1	21	9	17	19	144	7.6	0
Home	8	147	676	4.6	34	5	36	10	19	25	191	7.6	1
Away	6	90	441	4.9	60	2	22	2	4	24	176	7.3	0
Games 1-8	8	126	487	3.9	32	4	28	9	17	34	274	8.1	1
Games 9-16	6	111	630	5.7	60	3	30	3	6	15	93	6.2	0
September	4	51	226	4.4	21	3	14	0	0	16	132	8.3	1
October	4	75	261	3.5	32	1	14	9	17	18	142	7.9	0
November	4	85	506	6.0	60	3	24	3	6	14	81	5.8	0
December	2	26	124	4.8	28	0	6	0	0	1	12	12.0	0
Grass	10	178	800	4.5	34	6	42	11	20	34	281	8.3	1
Turf	4	59	317	5.4	60	1	16	1	3	15	86	5.7	0
Indoor	2	34	171	5.0	60	1	7	1	3	10	54	5.4	0
Outdoor	12	203	946	4.7	36	6	51	11	20	39	313	8.0	1
1st Half	-	140	758	5.4	60	5	33	4	7	21	155	7.4	1
2nd Half/OT	-	97	359	3.7	19	2	25	8	16	28	212	7.6	0
Last 2 Min. Half	-	15	67	4.5	13	1	5	1	3	14	90	6.4	1
4th qtr, +/-7 pts	-	12	74	6.2	19	1	6	1	1	3	16	5.3	0
Winning	-	108	412	3.8	19	3	21	7	15	20	177	8.9	1
Tied	-	73	395	5.4	34	3	22	3	4	9	72	8.0	0
Trailing	-	56	310	5.5	60	1	15	2	4	20	118	5.9	0

	Rush	Yds	Avg	Lg	TD	1st	Stf	YdL	Rec	Yds	Avg	TD
Inside 20	49	160	3.3	9	6	13	2	2	3	26	8.7	1
Inside 10	24	70	2.9	6	6	8	2	2	2	15	7.5	1
1st Down	139	700	5.0	60	3	17	9	20	28	205	7.3	0
2nd Down	74	286	3.9	34	2	25	2	2	13	127	9.8	1
3rd Down Overall	21	117	5.6	36	2	13	1	1	8	35	4.4	0
3rd D 0-2 to Go	13	42	3.2	13	1	8	1	1	0	0	-	0
3rd D 3-7 to Go	5	52	10.4	36	1	4	0	0	4	14	3.5	0
3rd D 8+ to Go	3	23	7.7	17	0	1	0	0	4	21	5.3	0
4th Down	3	14	4.7	7	0	3	0	0	0	0	-	0
Left Sideline	6	47	7.8	13	0	2	0	0	13	84	6.5	0
Left Side	49	284	5.8	60	4	11	2	7	7	57	8.1	0
Middle	130	544	4.2	36	3	33	5	9	8	52	6.5	1
Right Side	49	238	4.9	34	0	12	5	7	15	124	8.3	0
Right Sideline	3	4	1.3	2	0	0	0	0	6	50	8.3	0
Shotgun	20	68	3.4	12	0	4	3	3	19	113	5.9	0
2 Wide Receivers	171	837	4.9	60	4	44	8	16	30	225	7.5	0
3 Wide Receivers	51	207	4.1	36	1	8	4	7	15	106	7.1	1
4+ Wide Receivers	1	17	17.0	17	0	1	0	0	2	21	10.5	0
Carries 1-5	70	423	6.0	36	1	18	0	0	0	0	-	0
Carries 6-10	62	305	4.9	60	4	17	2	3	0	0	-	0
Carries 11-15	53	200	3.8	17	1	10	4	6	0	0	-	0
Carries 16-20	35	104	3.0	19	1	8	5	13	0	0	-	0
Carries 21+	17	85	5.0	19	0	5	1	1	0	0	-	0

1995 Incompletions

Type	Num	%of Inc	% Att
Pass Dropped	12	36.4	14.6
Poor Throw	13	39.4	15.9
Pass Defensed	1	3.0	1.2
Pass Hit at Line	0	0.0	0.0
Other	7	21.2	8.5
Total	33	100.0	40.2

Game Logs (1-8)

Date	Opp	Result	Rush	Yds	Rec	Yds	Trgt	F-L	TD
09/03	Buf	W 22-7	20	70	2	9	6	0-0	1
09/10	@Dal	L 21-31	11	61	3	26	5	0-0	0
09/17	Was	W 38-31	13	68	7	61	8	0-0	3
09/24	@SD	L 6-17	7	27	4	36	5	0-0	0
10/01	@Sea	L 10-27	15	61	3	24	6	1-0	0
10/08	@NE	W 37-3	24	97	5	54	6	0-0	1
10/16	Oak	W 27-0	18	34	5	25	11	1-1	0
10/22	KC	L 7-21	18	69	5	39	9	1-0	0

Game Logs (9-16)

Date	Opp	Result	Rush	Yds	Rec	Yds	Trgt	F-L	TD
11/05	Ari	W 38-6	22	135	3	25	4	0-0	1
11/12	@Phi	L 13-31	14	85	2	6	3	0-0	0
11/19	SD	W 30-27	30	176	2	20	5	0-0	1
11/26	@Hou	L 33-42	19	110	7	30	9	1-0	1
12/03	Jac	W 31-23	21	84	1	12	5	1-1	0
12/10	Sea	L 27-31	5	40	0	0	0	0-0	0
12/17	@KC	L 17-20	-	-	-	-	-	-	-
12/24	@Oak	W 31-28	-	-	-	-	-	-	-

Willie Davis

Kansas City Chiefs — WR

1995 Receiving Splits

	G	Rec	Yds	Avg	TD	Lg	Big	YAC	Trgt	Y@C	1st	1st%
Total	16	33	527	16.0	5	60	5	126	76	12.2	22	66.7
vs. Playoff	4	7	109	15.6	0	28	1	9	22	14.3	4	57.1
vs. Non-playoff	12	26	418	16.1	5	60	4	117	54	11.6	18	69.2
vs. Own Division	8	17	288	16.9	3	60	3	67	33	13.0	10	58.8
Home	8	14	194	13.9	3	34	1	30	39	11.7	10	71.4
Away	8	19	333	17.5	2	60	4	96	37	12.5	12	63.2
Games 1-8	8	22	351	16.0	4	60	4	98	43	11.5	12	54.5
Games 9-16	8	11	176	16.0	1	28	1	28	33	13.5	10	90.9
September	4	15	248	16.5	3	60	3	80	23	11.2	9	60.0
October	4	7	103	14.7	1	34	1	18	20	12.1	3	42.9
November	4	5	85	17.0	1	19	0	10	19	15.0	4	80.0
December	4	6	91	15.2	0	28	1	18	14	12.2	6	100.0
Grass	14	24	318	13.3	3	34	2	69	63	10.4	16	66.7
Turf	2	9	209	23.2	2	60	3	57	13	16.9	6	66.7
Outdoor	1	27	372	13.8	3	34	2	78	70	10.9	19	70.4
Indoor	15	6	155	25.8	2	60	3	48	6	17.8	3	50.0
1st Half	-	17	298	17.5	4	60	3	83	41	12.6	11	64.7
2nd Half/OT	-	16	229	14.3	1	29	2	43	35	11.6	11	68.8
Last 2 Min. Half	-	9	93	10.3	0	20	0	29	14	7.1	5	55.6
4th qtr, +/-7 pts	-	2	9	4.5	0	7	0	1	4	4.0	1	50.0
Winning	-	11	176	16.0	2	40	2	28	30	13.5	8	72.7
Tied	-	5	85	17.0	1	34	1	18	13	14.2	4	40.0
Trailing	-	17	266	15.6	2	60	2	80	33	10.9	12	70.6

	Rec	Yds	Avg	TD	Lg	Big	YAC	Trgt	Y@C	1st	1st%
Inside 20	5	69	13.8	3	19	0	1	6	13.6	4	80.0
Inside 10	1	5	5.0	0	5	0	1	1	4.0	1	100.0
1st Down	13	187	14.4	2	40	1	37	26	11.5	6	46.2
2nd Down	12	190	15.8	2	60	2	46	27	12.0	10	83.3
3rd Down Overall	7	130	18.6	1	34	2	30	22	14.3	5	71.4
3rd D 0-2 to Go	0	0	-	0	0	0	0	1	-	0	-
3rd D 3-7 to Go	2	47	23.5	1	29	1	3	9	22.0	2	100.0
3rd D 8+ to Go	5	83	16.6	0	34	1	27	12	11.2	3	60.0
4th Down	1	20	20.0	0	20	0	0	1	7.0	1	100.0
Rec Behind Line	1	8	8.0	0	8	0	8	2	0.0	0	0.0
1-10 yds	16	146	9.1	0	20	0	52	23	5.9	8	50.0
11-20 yds	12	216	18.0	3	34	1	33	27	15.3	10	83.3
21-30 yds	2	57	28.5	0	29	2	3	8	27.0	2	100.0
31+	2	100	50.0	2	60	2	30	16	35.0	2	100.0
Left Sideline	5	39	7.8	0	18	0	12	12	5.4	3	60.0
Left Side	3	47	15.7	0	19	0	11	10	12.0	2	66.7
Middle	3	32	10.7	1	19	0	7	6	8.3	1	33.3
Right Side	13	249	19.2	3	60	2	67	22	14.0	11	84.6
Right Sideline	9	160	17.8	1	40	3	29	26	14.6	5	55.6
Shotgun	0	0	-	0	0	0	0	0	-	0	-
2 Wide Receivers	13	284	21.8	5	60	3	52	45	17.8	10	76.9
3 Wide Receivers	15	190	12.7	0	34	2	58	25	8.8	9	60.0
4+ Wide Receivers	5	53	10.6	0	20	0	16	8	7.4	3	60.0

1995 Incompletions

Type	Num	%of Inc	%of Att
Pass Dropped	4	9.3	5.3
Poor Throw	16	37.2	21.1
Pass Defensed	16	37.2	21.1
Pass Hit at Line	1	2.3	1.3
Other	6	14.0	7.9
Total	43	100.0	56.6

Game Logs (1-8)

Date	Opp	Result	Rec	Yds	Trgt	F-L	TD
09/03	@Sea	W 34-10	6	155	6	0-0	2
09/10	NYN	W 20-17	3	21	8	0-0	0
09/17	Oak	W 23-17	1	19	2	0-0	0
09/24	@Cle	L 17-35	5	53	7	0-0	0
10/01	@Ari	W 24-3	0	0	3	0-0	0
10/09	SD	W 29-23	3	27	7	0-0	0
10/15	NE	W 31-26	2	52	6	0-0	0
10/22	@Den	W 21-7	2	24	4	0-0	0

Game Logs (9-16)

Date	Opp	Result	Rec	Yds	Trgt	F-L	TD
11/05	Was	W 24-3	1	19	5	0-0	1
11/12	@SD	W 22-7	0	0	4	0-0	0
11/19	Hou	W 20-13	1	12	3	0-0	0
11/23	@Dal	L 12-24	3	54	7	0-0	0
12/03	@Oak	W 29-23	2	19	2	0-0	0
12/11	@Mia	L 6-13	1	28	4	0-0	0
12/17	Den	W 20-17	1	18	4	0-0	0
12/24	Sea	W 26-3	2	26	6	0-0	0

Sean Dawkins
Indianapolis Colts — WR

1995 Receiving Splits

	G	Rec	Yds	Avg	TD	Lg	Big	YAC	Trgt	Y@C	1st	1st%
Total	16	52	784	15.1	3	52	7	184	84	11.5	37	71.2
vs. Playoff	6	22	327	14.9	1	36	2	98	38	10.4	17	77.3
vs. Non-playoff	10	30	457	15.2	2	52	5	86	46	12.4	20	66.7
vs. Own Division	8	28	407	14.5	2	40	2	112	45	10.5	22	78.6
Home	8	19	264	13.9	1	36	2	67	38	10.4	15	78.9
Away	8	33	520	15.8	2	52	5	117	46	12.2	22	66.7
Games 1-8	8	26	335	12.9	1	52	1	64	35	10.4	18	69.2
Games 9-16	8	26	449	17.3	2	40	6	120	49	12.7	19	73.1
September	3	12	152	12.7	1	24	0	36	15	9.0	10	83.3
October	5	14	183	13.1	0	52	1	28	20	11.1	8	57.1
November	4	10	186	18.6	1	40	2	73	18	11.3	9	90.0
December	4	16	263	16.4	1	36	4	47	31	13.5	10	62.5
Grass	5	22	357	16.2	1	52	5	70	32	13.0	12	54.5
Turf	11	30	427	14.2	2	36	2	114	52	10.4	25	83.3
Outdoor	9	31	485	15.6	2	52	5	105	43	12.3	20	64.5
Indoor	7	21	299	14.2	1	36	2	79	41	10.5	17	81.0
1st Half	-	24	377	15.7	2	52	4	78	37	12.5	17	70.8
2nd Half/OT	-	28	407	14.5	1	40	3	106	47	10.8	20	71.4
Last 2 Min. Half	-	3	37	12.3	0	15	0	13	5	8.0	1	100.0
4th qtr, +/-7 pts	-	12	200	16.7	0	40	1	61	22	11.6	9	91.7
Winning	-	7	147	21.0	0	40	3	30	15	16.7	5	71.4
Tied	-	19	238	12.5	2	31	1	43	28	10.3	13	68.4
Trailing	-	26	399	15.3	1	52	3	111	41	11.1	19	73.1

	Rec	Yds	Avg	TD	Lg	Big	YAC	Trgt	Y@C	1st	1st%
Inside 20	2	20	10.0	2	15	0	6	8	7.0	2	100.0
Inside 10	1	5	5.0	1	5	0	2	3	3.0	1	100.0
1st Down	18	258	14.3	1	52	2	70	28	10.4	13	72.2
2nd Down	18	226	12.6	1	31	1	58	30	9.3	10	55.6
3rd Down Overall	14	274	19.6	1	40	4	46	23	16.3	12	85.7
3rd D 0-2 to Go	2	47	23.5	0	40	1	14	2	16.5	2	100.0
3rd D 3-7 to Go	6	89	14.8	1	40	1	17	10	12.0	5	83.3
3rd D 8+ to Go	6	138	23.0	0	36	2	15	11	20.5	5	83.3
4th Down	2	26	13.0	0	14	0	10	3	8.0	2	100.0
Rec Behind Line	0	0	-	0	0	0	0	1	-		
1-10 yds	29	268	9.2	1	20	0	107	42	5.6	16	55.2
11-20 yds	16	266	16.6	1	28	1	39	24	14.2	14	87.5
21-30 yds	4	122	30.5	0	31	3	21	11	25.3	4	100.0
31+	3	128	42.7	0	52	3	17	6	37.0	3	100.0
Left Sideline	19	287	15.1	0	52	3	70	31	11.4	10	52.6
Left Side	20	310	15.5	2	40	3	95	34	10.8	17	85.0
Middle	5	78	15.6	0	19	0	12	6	13.2	5	100.0
Right Side	5	50	10.0	0	16	0	2	7	9.6	3	60.0
Right Sideline	3	59	19.7	1	31	1	5	6	18.0	2	66.7
Shotgun	17	269	15.8	0	40	3	57	28	12.5	13	76.5
2 Wide Receivers	24	365	15.2	1	52	3	109	35	10.7	17	70.8
3 Wide Receivers	17	309	18.2	2	40	4	39	31	15.9	13	76.5
4+ Wide Receivers	11	110	10.0	0	16	0	36	18	6.7	7	63.6

1995 Incompletions

Type	Num	%of Inc	%of Att
Pass Dropped	3	9.4	3.6
Poor Throw	19	59.4	22.6
Pass Defensed	4	12.5	4.8
Pass Hit at Line	0	0.0	0.0
Other	6	18.8	7.1
Total	32	100.0	38.1

Game Logs (1-8)

Date	Opp	Result	Rec	Yds	Trgt	F-L	TD
09/03	Cin	L 21-24	3	24	4	0-0	0
09/10	@NYA	W 27-24	5	60	6	0-0	1
09/17	@Buf	L 14-20	4	68	5	1-0	0
10/01	StL	W 21-18	1	7	2	0-0	0
10/08	@Mia	W 27-24	7	77	10	0-0	0
10/15	SF	W 18-17	1	9	1	0-0	0
10/22	@Oak	L 17-30	4	71	6	0-0	0
10/29	NYA	W 17-10	1	19	1	0-0	0

Game Logs (9-16)

Date	Opp	Result	Rec	Yds	Trgt	F-L	TD
11/05	Buf	L 10-16	2	30	6	0-0	0
11/12	@NO		2	35	3	0-0	0
11/19	@NE	W 24-10	4	101	5	0-0	0
11/26	Mia	W 36-28	2	20	4	0-0	1
12/03	@Car	L 10-13	6	81	7	0-0	1
12/10	@Jac	W 41-31	1	27	4	0-0	0
12/17	SD	L 24-27	6	123	12	0-0	0
12/23	NE	W 10-7	3	32	8	0-0	0

Lawrence Dawsey
Tampa Bay Buccaneers — WR

1995 Receiving Splits

	G	Rec	Yds	Avg	TD	Lg	Big	YAC	Trgt	Y@C	1st	1st%
Total	12	30	372	12.4	0	26	1	91	61	9.4	21	70.0
vs. Playoff	4	8	114	14.3	0	23	0	15	19	12.4	6	75.0
vs. Non-playoff	8	22	258	11.7	0	26	1	76	42	8.3	15	68.2
vs. Own Division	4	16	202	12.6	0	23	0	34	31	10.5	12	75.0
Home	6	15	186	12.4	0	20	0	42	27	9.6	12	80.0
Away	6	15	186	12.4	0	26	1	49	34	9.1	9	60.0
Games 1-8	8	17	218	12.8	0	26	1	54	40	9.6	13	76.5
Games 9-16	4	13	154	11.8	0	23	0	37	21	9.0	8	61.5
September	4	7	114	16.3	0	26	1	27	20	12.4	6	85.7
October	5	14	136	9.7	0	15	0	40	25	6.9	6	64.3
November	3	9	122	13.6	0	23	0	24	16	10.9	6	66.7
December	0	0	0	-	0	0	0	0	0	-		
Grass	9	21	275	13.1	0	26	1	73	45	9.6	15	71.4
Turf	3	9	97	10.8	0	22	0	18	16	8.8	6	66.7
Outdoor	2	22	291	13.2	0	26	1	73	50	9.9	16	72.7
Indoor	10	8	81	10.1	0	22	0	18	11	7.9	5	62.5
1st Half	-	14	159	11.4	0	23	0	42	30	8.4	17	78.6
2nd Half/OT	-	16	213	13.3	0	26	1	49	31	10.3	10	62.5
Last 2 Min. Half	-	4	40	10.0	0	14	0	14	9	6.5	3	75.0
4th qtr, +/-7 pts	-	2	30	15.0	0	16	0	16	8		2	100.0
Winning	-	8	101	12.6	0	20	0	27	17	9.3	7	87.5
Tied	-	7	77	11.0	0	22	0	19	16	8.3	3	42.9
Trailing	-	15	194	12.9	0	26	1	45	28	9.9	11	73.1

	Rec	Yds	Avg	TD	Lg	Big	YAC	Trgt	Y@C	1st	1st%
Inside 20	0	0	-	0	0	0	0	6	-		
Inside 10	0	0	-	0	0	0	0	1	-		
1st Down	9	103	11.4	0	20	0	22	18	9.0	6	66.7
2nd Down	10	125	12.5	0	26	1	32	20	9.3	6	60.0
3rd Down Overall	11	144	13.1	0	23	0	37	22	9.7	9	81.8
3rd D 0-2 to Go	0	0	-	0	0	0	0	2	-		
3rd D 3-7 to Go	6	57	9.5	0	13	0	12	11	7.5	5	83.3
3rd D 8+ to Go	5	87	17.4	0	23	0	25	9	12.4	4	80.0
4th Down	0	0	-	0	0	0	0	1	-		
Rec Behind Line	2	12	6.0	0	8	0	19	4	-3.5	0	0.0
1-10 yds	17	177	10.4	0	26	1	54	29	7.2	10	58.8
11-20 yds	11	183	16.6	0	23	0	18	22	15.0	11	100.0
21-30 yds	0	0	-	0	0	0	0	3	-		
31+	0	0	-	0	0	0	0	3	-		
Left Sideline	8	102	12.8	0	26	1	22	19	10.0	4	50.0
Left Side	6	73	14.6	0	23	0	15	10	11.6	5	100.0
Middle	5	65	13.0	0	22	0	13	10	10.4	5	100.0
Right Side	8	89	11.1	0	18	0	30	11	7.4	5	62.5
Right Sideline	4	43	10.8	0	16	0	11	11	8.0	2	50.0
Shotgun	2	12	6.0	0	8	0	19	5	-3.5	0	0.0
2 Wide Receivers	14	215	15.4	0	26	1	53	30	11.6	12	85.7
3 Wide Receivers	15	153	10.2	0	16	0	33	25	8.0	9	60.0
4+ Wide Receivers	1	4	4.0	0	4	0		5	-1.0	0	0.0

1995 Incompletions

Type	Num	%of Inc	%of Att
Pass Dropped	3	9.7	4.9
Poor Throw	18	58.1	29.5
Pass Defensed	5	16.1	8.2
Pass Hit at Line	2	6.5	3.3
Other	3	9.7	4.9
Total	31	100.0	50.8

Game Logs (1-8)

Date	Opp	Result	Rec	Yds	Trgt	F-L	TD
09/03	@Phi	W 21-6	1	16	5	0-0	0
09/10	@Cle	L 6-22	2	36	5	0-0	0
09/17	Chi	L 6-25	2	29	8	0-0	0
09/24	Was	W 14-6	2	33	2	0-0	0
10/01	@Car	W 20-13	1	4	2	0-0	0
10/08	Cin	W 19-16	2	25	6	0-0	0
10/15	Min	W 20-17	7	75	9	0-0	0
10/22	Atl	L 21-24	0	0	0	0-0	0

Game Logs (9-16)

Date	Opp	Result	Rec	Yds	Trgt	F-L	TD
10/29	@Hou	L 7-19	4	32	5	0-0	0
11/12	@Det	L 24-27	4	49	6	0-0	0
11/19	Jac	W 17-16	2	24	2	0-0	0
11/26	@GB	L 13-35	3	49	8	0-0	0
12/03	@Min	L 17-31	-	-	-	-	-
12/10	GB	W 13-10	-	-	-	-	-
12/17	@Chi	L 10-31	-	-	-	-	-
12/23	Det	L 10-37	-	-	-	-	-

Lake Dawson
Kansas City Chiefs — WR

1995 Receiving Splits

	G	Rec	Yds	Avg	TD	Lg	Big	YAC	Trgt	Y@C	1st	1st%		Rec	Yds	Avg	TD	Lg	Big	YAC	Trgt	Y@C	1st	1st%
Total	16	40	513	12.8	5	45	2	120	75	9.8	30	75.0	Inside 20	10	119	11.9	4	18	0	34	13	8.5	9	90.0
vs. Playoff	4	10	177	17.7	1	45	2	63	17	11.4	8	80.0	Inside 10	1	4	4.0	1	4	0	0	1	4.0	1	100.0
vs. Non-playoff	12	30	336	11.2	4	20	0	57	58	9.3	22	73.3	1st Down	10	146	14.6	0	23	0	24	23	12.2	7	70.0
vs. Own Division	8	24	285	11.9	3	27	1	66	37	9.1	17	70.8	2nd Down	14	203	14.5	2	45	2	57	24	10.4	10	71.4
Home	8	22	278	12.6	1	27	1	57	42	10.0	17	77.3	3rd Down Overall	13	131	10.1	3	19	0	25	24	8.2	10	76.9
Away	8	18	235	13.1	4	45	1	63	33	9.6	13	72.2	3rd D 0-2 to Go	1	16	16.0	1	16	0	10	1	6.0	1	100.0
Games 1-8	8	20	279	14.0	4	27	1	48	42	11.6	17	85.0	3rd D 3-7 to Go	7	52	7.4	2	15	0	16	12	5.1	5	71.4
Games 9-16	8	20	234	11.7	1	45	1	72	33	8.1	13	65.0	3rd D 8+ to Go	5	63	12.6	0	19	0	-1	11	12.8	4	80.0
September	4	10	101	10.1	2	20	0	14	20	8.7	7	70.0	4th Down	3	33	11.0	0	15	0	14	4	6.3	3	100.0
October	4	10	178	17.8	2	27	1	34	22	14.4	10	100.0	Rec Behind Line	0	0	-	0	0	0	0	2	-	0	-
November	4	10	132	13.2	1	45	1	53	20	7.9	7	70.0	1-10 yds	22	186	8.5	2	20	0	70	35	5.3	13	59.1
December	4	10	102	10.2	0	19	0	19	13	8.3	6	60.0	11-20 yds	17	300	17.6	3	45	1	45	30	15.0	16	94.1
Grass	14	34	423	12.4	3	27	1	76	64	10.2	26	76.5	21-30 yds	1	27	27.0	0	27	1	5	4	22.0	1	100.0
Turf	2	6	90	15.0	2	45	1	44	11	7.7	4	66.7	31+	0	0	-	0	0	0	0	3	-	0	-
Indoor	1	3	29	9.7	1	16	0	10	4	6.3	2	66.7	Left Sideline	7	86	12.3	1	20	0	5	11	11.6	4	57.1
Outdoor	15	37	484	13.1	4	45	2	110	71	10.1	28	75.7	Left Side	6	99	16.5	0	23	0	23	8	12.7	6	100.0
1st Half	-	21	223	10.6	2	20	0	53	39	8.1	16	76.2	Middle	9	168	18.7	2	45	2	54	12	12.7	9	100.0
2nd Half/OT	-	19	290	15.3	3	45	2	67	36	11.7	14	73.7	Right Side	8	84	10.5	1	18	0	23	21	7.6	5	62.5
Last 2 Min. Half	-	5	64	12.8	0	27	1	12	9	10.4	3	60.0	Right Sideline	10	76	7.6	1	16	0	15	22	6.1	6	60.0
4th qtr, +/-7 pts	-	5	81	16.2	0	27	1	14	10	13.4	4	80.0	Shotgun	0	0	-	0	0	0	0	0	-	0	-
Winning	-	21	238	11.3	2	19	0	42	35	9.3	15	71.4	2 Wide Receivers	17	223	13.1	2	23	0	35	33	11.1	12	70.6
Tied	-	7	70	10.0	2	23	0	13	16	8.1	5	71.4	3 Wide Receivers	15	209	13.9	3	45	1	53	29	10.4	13	86.7
Trailing	-	12	205	17.1	1	45	2	65	24	11.7	10	83.3	4+ Wide Receivers	8	81	10.1	0	27	1	32	11	6.1	5	62.5

1995 Incompletions

Type	Num	%of Inc	%of Att
Pass Dropped	4	11.4	5.3
Poor Throw	22	62.9	29.3
Pass Defensed	6	17.1	8.0
Pass Hit at Line	1	2.9	1.3
Other	2	5.7	2.7
Total	35	100.0	46.7

Game Logs (1-8)

Date	Opp	Result	Rush	Yds	Rec	Yds	Trgt	F-L	TD
09/03	@Sea	W 34-10	1	-9	3	29	4	0-0	1
09/10	NYN	W 20-17	0	0	1	11	4	0-0	0
09/17	Oak	W 23-17	0	0	2	9	5	0-0	0
09/24	@Cle	L 17-35	0	0	4	52	7	0-0	0
10/01	@Ari	W 24-3	0	0	2	29	4	0-0	1
10/09	SD	W 29-23	0	0	4	86	6	0-0	0
10/15	NE	W 31-26	0	0	2	34	7	0-0	0
10/22	@Den	W 21-7	0	0	2	29	5	0-0	1

Game Logs (9-16)

Date	Opp	Result	Rush	Yds	Rec	Yds	Trgt	F-L	TD
11/05	Was	W 24-3	0	0	3	29	5	0-0	0
11/12	@SD	W 22-7	0	0	3	30	4	0-0	0
11/19	Hou	W 20-13	0	0	1	12	4	0-0	0
11/23	@Dal	L 12-24	0	0	3	61	7	0-0	1
12/03	@Oak	W 29-23	0	0	1	5	2	0-0	0
12/11	@Mia	L 6-13	0	0	0	0	0	0-0	0
12/17	Den	W 20-17	0	0	5	58	5	0-0	0
12/24	Sea	W 26-3	0	0	4	39	6	0-0	0

Trent Dilfer
Tampa Bay Buccaneers — QB

1995 Passing Splits

	G	Att	Cm	Pct	Yds	Yd/Att	TD	Int	1st	YAC	Big	Sk	Rtg		Att	Cm	Pct	Yds	Yd/Att	TD	Int	1st	YAC	Big	Sk	Rtg
Total	16	415	224	54.0	2774	6.7	4	18	133	1082	16	47	60.1	Inside 20	35	14	40.0	90	2.6	2	2	6	51	0	4	43.2
vs. Playoff	6	161	91	56.5	1186	7.4	2	5	53	536	8	15	71.1	Inside 10	15	5	33.3	31	2.1	1	2	1	15	0	2	25.0
vs. Non-playoff	10	254	133	52.4	1588	6.3	2	13	80	546	8	32	53.1	1st Down	163	90	55.2	1207	7.4	1	10	47	554	9	17	55.4
vs. Own Division	8	233	132	56.7	1566	6.7	1	12	73	701	7	26	57.3	2nd Down	133	76	57.1	857	6.4	2	4	47	351	5	13	69.0
Home	8	209	114	54.5	1339	6.4	1	7	67	466	5	20	61.9	3rd Down Overall	116	58	50.0	710	6.1	1	3	39	177	2	16	61.4
Away	8	206	110	53.4	1435	7.0	3	11	66	616	11	27	58.2	3rd D 0-5 to Go	30	16	53.3	161	5.4	0	0	15	38	0	3	68.9
Games 1-8	8	203	108	53.2	1421	7.0	3	7	72	432	8	22	66.1	3rd D 6+ to Go	86	42	48.8	549	6.4	1	3	24	139	2	13	58.7
Games 9-16	8	212	116	54.7	1353	6.4	1	11	61	650	8	25	54.2	4th Down	3	0	0.0	0	0.0	0	1	0	0	0	1	0.0
September	4	100	55	55.0	755	7.6	3	7	39	230	4	12	60.2	Rec Behind Line	54	31	57.4	307	5.7	0	0	12	448	4	0	73.6
October	5	126	63	50.0	748	5.9	0	3	38	220	4	13	58.6	1-10 yds	202	116	57.4	1121	5.5	2	6	57	432	3	0	67.7
November	3	81	44	54.3	557	6.9	0	1	28	242	4	10	70.9	11-20 yds	98	58	59.2	1003	10.2	1	5	54	161	4	0	76.2
December	4	108	62	57.4	714	6.6	1	7	28	390	4	14	53.5	21-30 yds	34	6	17.6	148	4.4	0	2	6	12	1	0	20.7
Grass	12	342	186	54.4	2187	6.4	2	12	108	856	11	34	61.4	31+	27	4	14.8	195	7.2	1	5	4	29	4	0	29.9
Turf	4	73	38	52.1	587	8.0	2	6	25	226	5	13	53.9	Left Sideline	89	50	56.2	629	7.1	1	1	33	271	4	0	77.4
Indoor	3	54	27	50.0	372	6.9	0	5	17	173	3	12	33.9	Left Side	76	39	51.3	463	6.1	0	3	18	192	2	11	53.8
Outdoor	13	361	197	54.6	2402	6.7	4	13	116	909	13	35	62.7	Middle	78	40	51.3	547	7.0	2	5	27	164	4	35	55.9
1st Half	-	211	110	52.1	1416	6.7	2	7	67	667	11	23	62.8	Right Side	90	50	55.6	601	6.7	0	3	28	311	4	1	62.3
2nd Half/OT	-	204	114	55.9	1358	6.7	2	11	66	415	5	24	57.2	Right Sideline	82	45	54.9	534	6.5	1	6	27	144	2	0	48.5
Last 2 Min. Half	-	33	13	39.4	157	4.8	0	2	8	44	1	5	29.5	2 Wide Receivers	205	113	55.1	1651	8.1	3	9	79	487	12	29	68.2
4th qtr, +/-7 pts	-	37	17	45.9	176	4.8	2	1	9	36	0	2	66.9	3+ WR	193	105	54.4	1073	5.6	1	8	51	566	4	18	55.0
Winning	-	84	43	51.2	544	6.5	2	1	28	145	3	9	74.7	Attempts 1-10	160	88	55.0	1191	7.4	2	6	57	542	10	0	67.5
Tied	-	111	54	48.6	655	5.9	0	5	28	318	4	9	48.4	Attempts 11-20	131	74	56.5	921	7.0	2	7	46	356	5	0	61.3
Trailing	-	220	127	57.7	1575	7.2	2	12	77	619	9	29	60.3	Attempts 21+	124	62	50.0	662	5.3	0	5	30	184	1	0	49.2

1995 Incompletions

Type	Num	% of Inc	% of Att
Pass Dropped	28	14.7	6.7
Poor Throw	84	44.0	20.2
Pass Defensed	39	20.4	9.4
Pass Hit at Line	10	5.2	2.4
Other	30	15.7	7.2
Total	191	100.0	46.0

Game Logs (1-8)

Date	Opp	Result	Att	Cm	Pct	Yds	TD	Int	Lg	Sk	F-L
09/03	@Phi	W 21-6	19	11	57.9	215	2	1	64	1	0-0
09/10	@Cle	L 6-22	36	20	55.6	255	0	2	38	7	1-1
09/17	Chi	L 6-25	27	11	40.7	149	0	4	20	2	0-0
09/24	Was	W 14-6	18	13	72.2	136	1	0	20	2	1-0
10/01	@Car	W 20-13	12	3	25.0	55	0	1	31	1	0-0
10/08	Cin	W 19-16	26	14	46.2	185	0	0	45	5	0-0
10/15	Min	W 20-17	37	24	64.9	249	0	0	16	3	1-0
10/22	Atl	L 21-24	28	14	50.0	177	0	2	28	1	0-0

Game Logs (9-16)

Date	Opp	Result	Att	Cm	Pct	Yds	TD	Int	Lg	Sk	F-L
10/29	@Hou	L 7-19	23	10	43.5	82	0	3	22	3	0-0
11/12	@Det	L 24-27	13	8	61.5	142	0	1	37	3	2-1
11/19	Jac	W 17-16	20	9	45.0	103	0	0	26	1	0-0
11/26	@GB	L 13-35	48	27	56.3	312	0	0	26	4	1-0
12/03	@Min	L 17-31	18	9	50.0	148	1	1	29	6	3-1
12/10	GB	W 13-10	22	23	54.8	240	0	2	23	3	0-0
12/17	@Chi	L 10-31	28	22	59.5	226	1	3	47	2	2-1
12/23	Det	L 10-37	11	8	72.7	100	0	1	36	3	2-2

Ken Dilger
St. Louis...

Ken Dilger — Indianapolis Colts — TE

1995 Receiving Splits

	G	Rec	Yds	Avg	TD	Lg	Big	YAC	Trgt	Y@C	1st	1st%
Total	16	42	635	15.1	4	42	9	281	55	8.4	25	59.5
vs. Playoff	6	18	362	20.1	2	42	7	147	24	11.9	14	77.8
vs. Non-playoff	10	24	273	11.4	2	36	2	134	31	5.8	11	45.8
vs. Own Division	8	23	382	16.6	1	39	6	172	26	9.1	14	60.9
Home	8	24	386	16.1	2	42	5	181	33	8.5	15	62.5
Away	8	18	249	13.8	2	38	4	100	22	8.3	10	55.6
Games 1-8	8	22	351	16.0	1	42	5	163	28	8.5	14	63.6
Games 9-16	8	20	284	14.2	3	39	4	118	27	8.3	11	55.0
September	3	4	56	14.0	0	32	1	20	8	9.0	2	50.0
October	5	18	295	16.4	1	42	4	143	20	8.4	12	66.7
November	4	10	135	13.5	1	39	2	54	12	8.1	4	40.0
December	4	10	149	14.9	2	36	2	64	15	8.5	7	70.0
Grass	5	12	171	14.3	2	38	3	79	16	7.7	8	58.3
Turf	11	30	464	15.5	2	42	6	202	39	8.7	18	60.0
Outdoor	9	15	223	14.9	2	38	4	98	19	8.3	9	60.0
Indoor	7	27	412	15.3	2	42	5	183	36	8.5	16	59.3
1st Half	-	19	247	13.0	2	39	3	123	28	6.5	11	57.9
2nd Half/OT	-	23	388	16.9	2	42	6	158	27	10.0	14	60.9
Last 2 Min. Half	-	1	13	13.0	1	13	0	0	1	13.0	1	100.0
4th qtr, +/-7 pts	-	5	82	16.4	0	36	2	27	5	11.0	2	40.0
Winning	-	8	122	15.3	1	39	2	67	11	6.9	4	50.0
Tied	-	11	161	14.6	0	36	2	69	12	8.4	7	63.6
Trailing	-	23	352	15.3	2	42	5	145	32	9.0	14	60.9

	Rec	Yds	Avg	TD	Lg	Big	YAC	Trgt	Y@C	1st	1st%
Inside 20	6	60	10.0	4	16	0	20	11	6.7	4	66.7
Inside 10	1	3	3.0	1	3	0	0	4	3.0	1	100.0
1st Down	20	299	15.0	1	42	4	128	26	8.6	10	50.0
2nd Down	20	315	15.8	2	36	5	145	26	8.5	13	65.0
3rd Down Overall	2	21	10.5	1	16	0	8	3	6.5	2	100.0
3rd D 0-2 to Go	1	5	5.0	0	5	0	6	1	-1.0	1	100.0
3rd D 3-7 to Go	1	16	16.0	1	16	0	2	2	14.0	1	100.0
3rd D 8+ to Go	0	0	-	0	0	0	0	0	-	0	-
4th Down	0	0	-	0	0	0	0	0	-	0	-
Rec Behind Line	2	27	13.5	0	22	0	34	2	-3.5	2	100.0
1-10 yds	26	221	8.5	2	26	1	139	32	3.2	9	34.6
11-20 yds	5	83	16.6	2	19	0	13	11	14.0	5	100.0
21-30 yds	8	266	33.3	0	42	7	88	9	22.3	8	100.0
31+	1	38	38.0	0	38	1	7	1	31.0	1	100.0
Left Sideline	7	124	17.7	0	39	2	57	8	9.6	5	71.4
Left Side	6	54	9.0	1	15	0	35	9	3.2	3	50.0
Middle	12	237	19.8	0	42	4	85	15	12.7	8	66.7
Right Side	11	102	9.3	2	26	1	42	12	5.5	4	36.4
Right Sideline	6	118	19.7	1	39	2	62	11	9.3	5	83.3
Shotgun	0	0	-	0	0	0	0	0	-	0	-
2 Wide Receivers	29	436	15.0	1	42	7	175	35	9.0	15	51.7
3 Wide Receivers	8	153	19.1	0	39	2	82	12	8.9	6	75.0
4+ Wide Receivers	0	0	-	0	0	0	0	0	-	0	-

1995 Incompletions

Type	Num	%of Inc	%of Att
Pass Dropped	4	30.8	7.3
Poor Throw	4	30.8	7.3
Pass Defensed	2	15.4	3.6
Pass Hit at Line	0	0.0	0.0
Other	3	23.1	5.5
Total	13	100.0	23.6

Game Logs (1-8)

Date	Opp	Result	Rec	Yds	Trgt	F-L	TD
09/03	Cin	L 21-24	1	4	5	0-0	0
09/10	@NYA	W 27-24	1	18	1	0-0	0
09/17	@Buf	L 14-20	2	34	2	0-0	0
10/01	StL	W 21-18	2	17	2	0-0	0
10/08	@Mia	W 27-24	4	92	5	0-0	0
10/15	SF	W 18-17	7	125	7	0-0	1
10/22	@Oak	L 17-30	1	6	2	0-0	0
10/29	NYA	W 17-10	4	55	4	0-0	0

Game Logs (9-16)

Date	Opp	Result	Rec	Yds	Trgt	F-L	TD
11/05	Buf	L 10-16	1	39	3	0-0	0
11/12	@NO	L 14-17	3	26	3	0-0	0
11/19	@NE	W 24-10	5	31	5	0-0	1
11/26	Mia	W 36-28	1	39	1	0-0	0
12/03	@Car	L 10-13	0	0	0	0-0	0
12/10	@Jac	W 41-31	2	42	4	0-0	1
12/17	SD	L 24-27	3	33	6	0-0	1
12/23	NE	W 10-7	5	74	5	0-0	0

Troy Drayton — St. Louis Rams — TE

1995 Receiving Splits

	G	Rec	Yds	Avg	TD	Lg	Big	YAC	Trgt	Y@C	1st	1st%
Total	16	47	458	9.7	4	31	3	218	68	5.1	29	61.7
vs. Playoff	9	25	157	6.3	1	17	0	57	41	4.0	12	48.0
vs. Non-playoff	7	22	301	13.7	3	31	3	161	27	6.4	17	77.3
vs. Own Division	8	25	246	9.8	2	31	2	114	34	5.3	16	64.0
Home	8	26	283	10.9	2	31	2	109	35	6.7	18	69.2
Away	8	21	175	8.3	2	28	1	109	33	3.1	11	52.4
Games 1-8	8	24	285	11.9	1	31	2	99	39	7.8	17	70.8
Games 9-16	8	23	173	7.5	3	28	1	119	29	2.3	12	52.2
September	4	16	215	13.4	1	31	2	80	21	8.4	11	68.8
October	4	8	70	8.8	0	17	0	19	18	6.4	6	75.0
November	4	16	114	7.1	2	17	0	65	19	3.1	9	56.3
December	4	7	59	8.4	1	28	1	54	10	0.7	3	42.9
Grass	3	7	63	9.0	0	17	0	27	12	5.1	2	28.6
Turf	13	40	395	9.9	4	31	3	191	56	5.1	27	67.5
Outdoor	7	25	323	12.9	2	31	3	131	39	7.7	18	72.0
Indoor	9	22	135	6.1	2	16	0	87	29	2.2	11	50.0
1st Half	-	24	237	9.9	2	31	2	114	30	5.1	16	66.7
2nd Half/OT	-	23	221	9.6	2	27	1	104	38	5.1	13	56.5
Last 2 Min. Half	-	5	30	6.0	1	10	0	5	7	5.0	3	60.0
4th qtr, +/-7 pts	-	5	53	10.6	1	27	1	22	7	6.2	4	80.0
Winning	-	18	224	12.4	2	31	2	83	23	7.8	13	72.2
Tied	-	6	57	9.5	1	28	1	51	9	1.0	2	33.3
Trailing	-	23	177	7.7	1	23	0	84	36	4.0	14	60.9

	Rec	Yds	Avg	TD	Lg	Big	YAC	Trgt	Y@C	1st	1st%
Inside 20	6	19	3.2	3	12	0	2	10	2.8	4	66.7
Inside 10	2	4	2.0	2	2	0	0	6	2.0	2	100.0
1st Down	12	80	6.7	1	16	0	37	20	3.6	2	16.7
2nd Down	19	222	11.7	2	31	2	123	21	5.2	15	78.9
3rd Down Overall	15	147	9.8	1	27	1	58	20	5.9	11	73.3
3rd D 0-2 to Go	5	60	12.0	1	27	1	12	6	9.6	5	100.0
3rd D 3-7 to Go	6	38	6.3	0	9	0	16	8	3.7	4	66.7
3rd D 8+ to Go	4	49	12.3	0	23	0	30	6	4.8	2	50.0
4th Down	1	9	9.0	0	9	0	0	1	9.0	1	100.0
Rec Behind Line	6	41	6.8	1	28	1	64	8	-3.8	2	33.3
1-10 yds	31	233	7.5	2	16	0	112	48	3.9	18	58.1
11-20 yds	10	184	18.4	1	31	2	42	12	14.2	9	90.0
21-30 yds	0	0	-	0	0	0	0	0	-	0	-
31+	0	0	-	0	0	0	0	0	-	0	-
Left Sideline	6	31	5.2	0	10	0	13	9	3.0	1	16.7
Left Side	5	42	8.4	1	28	1	41	11	0.2	2	40.0
Middle	12	148	12.3	0	27	1	39	15	9.1	9	75.0
Right Side	12	96	8.0	2	23	0	55	15	3.4	7	58.3
Right Sideline	12	141	11.8	1	31	1	70	15	5.9	10	83.3
Shotgun	0	0	-	0	0	0	0	0	-	0	-
2 Wide Receivers	17	233	13.7	1	31	2	90	28	8.4	12	70.6
3 Wide Receivers	23	174	7.6	0	17	0	85	30	3.9	12	52.2
4+ Wide Receivers	3	15	5.0	1	9	0	4	5	5.0	2	66.7

1995 Incompletions

Type	Num	%of Inc	%of Att
Pass Dropped	8	38.1	11.8
Poor Throw	6	28.6	8.8
Pass Defensed	4	19.0	5.9
Pass Hit at Line	1	4.8	1.5
Other	2	9.5	2.9
Total	21	100.0	30.9

Game Logs (1-8)

Date	Opp	Result	Rec	Yds	Trgt	F-L	TD
09/03	@GB	W 17-14	3	13	6	0-0	0
09/10	NO	W 17-13	4	80	4	0-0	0
09/17	@Car	W 31-10	1	16	2	0-0	0
09/24	Chi	W 34-28	8	106	9	0-0	1
10/01	@Ind	L 18-21	3	24	6	0-0	0
10/15	Atl	W 21-19	3	27	5	0-0	0
10/22	SF	L 10-44	1	9	4	0-0	0
10/29	@Phi	L 9-20	1	10	3	0-0	0

Game Logs (9-16)

Date	Opp	Result	Rec	Yds	Trgt	F-L	TD
11/05	@NO	L 10-19	1	12	1	0-0	0
11/12	Car	L 28-17	4	30	5	1-1	1
11/19	@Atl	L 6-31	8	38	9	0-0	0
11/26	@SF	L 13-41	3	34	4	0-0	0
12/03	@NYA	W 23-20	1	28	2	0-0	1
12/10	Buf	L 27-45	2	8	3	0-0	0
12/17	Was	L 23-35	3	29	4	1-0	0
12/24	Mia	L 22-41	1	-6	1	0-0	0

Vaughn Dunbar

New Orleans Saints / Jacksonville Jaguars — RB

1995 Rushing and Receiving Splits

	G	Rush	Yds	Avg	Lg	TD	1st	Stf	YdL	Rec	Yds	Avg	TD		Rush	Yds	Avg	Lg	TD	1st	Stf	YdL	Rec	Yds	Avg	TD
Total	15	110	361	3.3	26	2	23	14	28	2	11	5.5	0	Inside 20	13	11	0.8	4	2	2	3	6	0	0	-	0
vs. Playoff	6	20	103	5.2	26	0	5	1	1	1	8	8.0	0	Inside 10	7	0	0.0	2	2	2	3	6	0	0	-	0
vs. Non-playoff	9	90	258	2.9	18	2	18	13	27	1	3	3.0	0	1st Down	63	236	3.7	26	0	6	6	13	2	11	5.5	0
vs. Own Division	8	67	195	2.9	13	1	12	8	13	0	0	-	0	2nd Down	34	106	3.1	18	1	12	5	11	0	0	-	0
Home	8	44	131	3.0	18	1	8	5	12	2	11	5.5	0	3rd Down Overall	13	19	1.5	9	1	5	3	4	0	0	-	0
Away	7	66	230	3.5	26	1	15	9	16	0	0	-	0	3rd D 0-2 to Go	10	20	2.0	9	1	5	2	2	0	0	-	0
Games 1-8	7	30	100	3.3	13	1	8	4	6	2	11	5.5	0	3rd D 3-7 to Go	3	-1	-0.3	1	0	0	1	2	0	0	-	0
Games 9-16	8	80	261	3.3	26	1	15	10	22	0	0	-	0	3rd D 8+ to Go	0	0	-	0	0	0	0	0	0	0	-	0
September	3	4	10	2.5	5	0	1	1	1	1	8	8.0	0	4th Down	0	0	-	0	0	0	0	0	0	0	-	0
October	5	36	117	3.3	13	1	7	4	6	1	3	3.0	0	Left Sideline	8	43	5.4	9	0	3	0	0	0	0	-	0
November	3	34	115	3.4	18	1	8	4	11	0	0	-	0	Left Side	33	128	3.9	26	1	8	1	1	0	0	-	0
December	4	36	119	3.3	26	0	7	5	10	0	0	-	0	Middle	36	95	2.6	18	1	6	9	17	0	0	-	0
Grass	10	88	258	2.9	18	2	17	12	26	2	11	5.5	0	Right Side	28	80	2.9	13	0	6	4	10	2	11	5.5	0
Turf	5	22	103	4.7	26	0	6	2	2	0	0	-	0	Right Sideline	5	15	3.0	4	0	0	0	0	0	0	-	0
Indoor	3	9	71	7.9	26	0	5	0	0	0	0	-	0	Shotgun	0	0	-	0	0	0	0	0	0	0	-	0
Outdoor	12	101	290	2.9	18	2	18	14	28	2	11	5.5	0	2 Wide Receivers	64	211	3.3	18	0	11	10	22	0	0	-	0
1st Half	-	49	160	3.3	18	2	12	7	16	1	3	3.0	0	3 Wide Receivers	18	89	4.9	26	0	4	1	2	1	8	8.0	0
2nd Half/OT	-	61	201	3.3	26	0	11	7	12	1	8	8.0	0	4+ Wide Receivers	0	0	-	0	0	0	0	0	0	0	-	0
Last 2 Min. Half	-	5	3	0.6	3	1	1	1	2	0	0	-	0	Carries 1-5	44	123	2.8	16	1	12	6	14	0	0	-	0
4th qtr, +/-7 pts	-	21	68	3.2	13	0	4	2	5	0	0	-	0	Carries 6-10	36	153	4.3	26	1	6	5	7	0	0	-	0
Winning	-	37	109	2.9	13	1	6	5	8	1	3	3.0	0	Carries 11-15	18	40	2.2	9	0	1	2	5	0	0	-	0
Tied	-	25	66	2.6	14	0	5	5	13	0	0	-	0	Carries 16-20	6	17	2.8	8	0	2	1	2	0	0	-	0
Trailing	-	48	186	3.9	26	1	12	4	7	1	8	8.0	0	Carries 21+	6	28	4.7	13	0	2	0	0	0	0	-	0

1995 Incompletions

Type	Num	%of Inc	% Att
Pass Dropped	1	50.0	25.0
Poor Throw	0	0.0	0.0
Pass Defensed	0	0.0	0.0
Pass Hit at Line	1	50.0	25.0
Other	0	0.0	0.0
Total	2	100.0	50.0

Game Logs (1-8)

Date	Opp	Result	Rush	Yds	Rec	Yds	Trgt	F-L	TD
09/03	SF	L 22-24	0	0	0	0	0	0-0	0
09/10	@Cin	L 17-24	3	5	0	0	0	0-0	0
09/17	@NYA	L 10-27	-	-	-	-	-	-	-
09/24	GB	L 14-24	1	5	1	8	1	0-0	0
10/01	@Hou	W 17-16	0	0	0	0	0	0-0	0
10/08	Pit	W 20-16	0	0	0	0	0	0-0	0
10/15	Chi	L 27-30	0	0	1	3	1	0-0	0
10/22	@Cle	W 23-15	26	90	0	0	0	0-0	1

Game Logs (9-16)

Date	Opp	Result	Rush	Yds	Rec	Yds	Trgt	F-L	TD
10/29	@Pit	L 7-24	10	27	0	0	0	0-0	0
11/12	Sea	L 30-47	15	53	0	0	0	0-0	1
11/19	@TB	L 16-17	7	25	0	0	0	0-0	0
11/26	Cin	L 13-17	12	37	0	0	1	0-0	0
12/03	@Den	L 23-31	11	12	0	0	0	0-0	0
12/10	Ind	L 31-41	0	0	0	0	0	0-0	0
12/17	@Det	L 0-44	9	71	0	0	0	0-0	0
12/24	Cle	W 24-21	16	36	0	0	0	0-0	0

Quinn Early

New Orleans Saints — WR

1995 Receiving Splits

	G	Rec	Yds	Avg	TD	Lg	Big	YAC	Trgt	Y@C	1st	1st%		Rec	Yds	Avg	TD	Lg	Big	YAC	Trgt	Y@C	1st	1st%
Total	16	81	1087	13.4	8	70	10	267	134	10.1	54	66.7	Inside 20	6	60	10.0	2	18	0	5	10	9.2	6	100.0
vs. Playoff	8	41	521	12.7	4	70	5	143	63	9.2	25	61.0	Inside 10	2	9	4.5	1	7	0	0	5	4.5	2	100.0
vs. Non-playoff	8	40	566	14.2	4	50	5	124	71	11.1	29	72.5	1st Down	34	447	13.1	3	50	4	96	53	10.3	17	50.0
vs. Own Division	8	39	508	13.0	3	70	4	123	71	9.9	27	69.2	2nd Down	15	216	14.4	3	28	3	20	35	13.1	13	86.7
Home	8	37	509	13.8	5	70	7	152	60	9.6	23	62.2	3rd Down Overall	31	414	13.4	2	70	3	146	45	8.6	23	74.2
Away	8	44	578	13.1	3	50	3	115	74	10.5	31	70.5	3rd D 0-2 to Go	4	85	21.3	2	70	1	49	6	9.0	4	100.0
Games 1-8	8	39	495	12.7	3	70	3	100	62	10.1	23	59.0	3rd D 3-7 to Go	13	132	10.2	0	22	0	36	19	7.4	11	84.6
Games 9-16	8	42	592	14.1	5	50	7	167	72	10.1	31	73.8	3rd D 8+ to Go	14	197	14.1	0	41	2	61	20	9.7	8	57.1
September	4	20	297	14.9	2	70	2	82	31	10.8	15	75.0	4th Down	1	10	10.0	0	10	0	5	1	5.0	1	100.0
October	4	19	198	10.4	1	25	1	18	31	9.5	8	42.1	Rec Behind Line	0	0	-	0	0	0	0	3	-	0	-
November	4	19	279	14.7	4	47	3	79	35	10.5	18	94.7	1-10 yds	54	471	8.7	1	41	1	151	71	5.9	28	51.9
December	4	23	313	13.6	1	50	4	88	37	9.8	13	56.5	11-20 yds	18	288	16.0	1	25	1	34	27	14.1	17	94.4
Grass	3	16	192	12.0	1	50	2	18	27	10.9	7	43.8	21-30 yds	7	244	34.9	5	70	6	78	19	23.7	7	100.0
Turf	13	65	895	13.8	7	70	8	249	107	9.9	47	72.3	31+	2	84	42.0	1	50	2	4	14	40.0	2	100.0
Indoor	10	52	725	13.9	7	70	8	210	84	9.9	37	71.2	Left Sideline	22	275	12.5	2	47	3	82	43	8.8	13	59.1
Outdoor	6	29	362	12.5	1	50	2	57	50	10.5	17	58.6	Left Side	19	244	12.8	1	50	2	53	23	10.1	12	63.2
1st Half	-	44	583	13.3	4	70	5	166	76	9.5	27	61.4	Middle	14	177	12.6	1	25	1	56	23	8.6	13	92.9
2nd Half/OT	-	37	504	13.6	4	47	5	101	58	10.9	27	73.0	Right Side	11	185	16.8	2	34	2	30	16	14.1	10	90.9
Last 2 Min. Half	-	11	139	12.6	1	47	2	37	18	9.3	8	72.7	Right Sideline	15	206	13.7	2	70	2	46	29	10.7	6	40.0
4th qtr, +/-7 pts	-	7	89	12.7	0	23	0	16	12	10.4	5	71.4	Shotgun	32	432	13.5	3	47	4	142	49	9.1	24	75.0
Winning	-	18	219	12.2	2	27	3	26	34	10.7	9	50.0	2 Wide Receivers	37	473	12.8	4	50	5	79	68	10.6	22	59.5
Tied	-	17	189	11.1	2	50	2	29	28	9.4	8	47.1	3 Wide Receivers	44	614	14.0	4	70	5	188	63	9.7	32	72.7
Trailing	-	46	679	14.8	4	70	5	212	72	10.2	37	80.4	4+ Wide Receivers	0	0	-	0	0	0	0	1	-	0	-

1995 Incompletions

Type	Num	%of Inc	%of Att
Pass Dropped	5	9.4	3.7
Poor Throw	27	50.9	20.1
Pass Defensed	6	11.3	4.5
Pass Hit at Line	3	5.7	2.2
Other	12	22.6	9.0
Total	53	100.0	39.6

Game Logs (1-8)

Date	Opp	Result	Rush	Yds	Rec	Yds	Trgt	F-L	TD
09/03	SF	L 22-24	0	0	6	66	7	0-0	1
09/10	@StL	L 13-17	0	0	5	73	9	0-0	0
09/17	Atl	L 24-27	0	0	5	99	9	0-0	1
09/24	@NYN	L 29-45	0	0	4	59	6	0-0	0
10/01	Phi	L 15-17	0	0	2	14	4	0-0	0
10/15	Mia	W 33-30	0	0	6	84	7	0-0	1
10/22	@Car	L 3-20	0	0	7	50	11	0-0	0
10/29	@SF	W 11-7	0	0	4	50	9	0-0	0

Game Logs (9-16)

Date	Opp	Result	Rush	Yds	Rec	Yds	Trgt	F-L	TD
11/05	StL	W 19-10	0	0	3	44	7	0-0	0
11/12	Ind	W 17-14	0	0	4	25	5	0-0	1
11/19	@Min	L 24-43	0	0	9	150	14	0-0	2
11/26	Car	W 34-26	1	9	3	60	9	0-0	1
12/03	@NE	W 31-17	1	-12	5	92	7	1-0	1
12/10	@Atl	L 23-34	0	0	6	66	10	0-0	0
12/16	GB	L 23-34	0	0	8	117	12	0-0	0
12/24	@NYA	W 12-0	0	0	4	38	8	0-0	0

Anthony Edwards

Arizona Cardinals — WR

1995 Receiving Splits

	G	Rec	Yds	Avg	TD	Lg	Big	YAC	Trgt	Y@C	1st	1st%		Rec	Yds	Avg	TD	Lg	Big	YAC	Trgt	Y@C	1st	1st%
Total	15	29	417	14.4	2	28	3	81	48	11.6	20	69.0	Inside 20	1	11	11.0	0	11	0	5	3	6.0	0	0.0
vs. Playoff	7	12	184	15.3	2	28	2	36	17	12.3	8	66.7	Inside 10	0	-	-	0	0	0	0	1	-	0	-
vs. Non-playoff	8	17	233	13.7	0	27	1	45	31	11.1	12	70.6	1st Down	6	83	13.8	0	27	1	13	9	11.7	3	50.0
vs. Own Division	8	17	221	13.0	0	27	2	53	27	9.9	10	58.8	2nd Down	10	138	13.8	1	28	2	22	17	11.6	8	80.0
Home	7	10	156	15.6	1	28	1	29	20	12.7	8	80.0	3rd Down Overall	12	172	14.3	0	22	0	46	21	10.5	8	66.7
Away	8	19	261	13.7	1	27	2	52	28	11.0	12	63.2	3rd D 0-2 to Go	1	11	11.0	0	11	0	1	1	10.0	1	100.0
Games 1-8	7	11	161	14.6	1	27	1	35	21	11.5	7	63.6	3rd D 3-7 to Go	3	23	7.7	0	13	0	11	12	4.0	1	33.3
Games 9-16	8	18	256	14.2	1	28	2	46	27	11.7	13	72.2	3rd D 8+ to Go	8	138	17.3	0	22	0	34	8	13.0	6	75.0
September	4	2	33	16.5	1	24	0	1	3	16.0	1	50.0	4th Down	1	24	24.0	0	24	0	1	1	24.0	1	100.0
October	3	9	128	14.2	0	27	1	34	18	10.4	6	66.7	Rec Behind Line	0	0	-	0	0	0	0	0	-	0	-
November	5	9	147	16.3	1	28	1	22	15	13.9	8	88.9	1-10 yds	14	135	9.6	0	22	0	44	25	6.5	6	42.9
December	3	9	109	12.1	0	25	1	24	12	9.4	5	55.6	11-20 yds	13	235	18.1	1	28	3	35	20	15.4	12	92.3
Grass	11	18	253	14.1	1	28	1	43	31	11.7	13	72.2	21-30 yds	2	47	23.5	0	24	0	2	3	22.5	2	100.0
Turf	4	11	164	14.9	1	27	2	38	17	11.5	7	63.6	31+	0	0	-	0	0	0	0	0	-	0	-
Outdoor	1	28	393	14.0	1	28	3	81	47	11.1	19	67.9	Left Sideline	6	108	18.0	0	27	2	33	13	12.5	4	66.7
Indoor	14	1	24	24.0	1	24	0	1	1	24.0	1	100.0	Left Side	7	68	9.7	0	14	0	6	9	8.9	4	57.1
1st Half	-	12	166	13.8	1	28	1	38	18	10.7	9	75.0	Middle	6	103	17.2	0	23	0	17	10	14.3	6	100.0
2nd Half/OT	-	17	251	14.8	1	27	2	43	30	12.2	11	64.7	Right Side	2	20	10.0	0	14	0	2	4	9.0	0	0.0
Last 2 Min. Half	-	5	82	16.4	1	28	1	13	9	13.8	4	80.0	Right Sideline	8	118	14.8	2	28	1	23	12	11.9	6	75.0
4th qtr, +/-7 pts	-	5	85	17.0	1	25	1	12	8	14.6	4	80.0	Shotgun	13	223	17.2	2	28	1	36	22	14.4	11	84.6
Winning	-	5	44	8.8	0	14	0	2	8	8.4	2	40.0	2 Wide Receivers	7	103	14.7	0	27	2	14	10	12.7	5	71.4
Tied	-	1	14	14.0	0	14	0	1	8	13.0	1	100.0	3 Wide Receivers	15	189	12.6	1	24	0	23	27	11.1	10	66.7
Trailing	-	23	359	15.6	2	28	3	78	32	12.2	17	73.9	4+ Wide Receivers	7	125	17.9	1	28	1	44	11	11.6	5	71.4

1995 Incompletions

Type	Num	%of Inc	%of Att
Pass Dropped	2	10.5	4.2
Poor Throw	9	47.4	18.8
Pass Defensed	6	31.6	12.5
Pass Hit at Line	0	0.0	0.0
Other	2	10.5	4.2
Total	19	100.0	39.6

Game Logs (1-8)

Date	Opp	Result		Rec	Yds	Trgt	F-L	TD
09/03	@Was	L	7-27	1	9	1	0-0	0
09/10	Phi	L	19-31	0	0	0	0-0	0
09/17	@Det	W	20-17	1	24	1	0-0	0
09/24	@Dal	L	20-34	0	0	1	0-0	0
10/01	KC	L	3-24	-	-	-	-	-
10/08	@NYN	L	21-27	5	81	10	0-0	0
10/15	Was	W	24-20	4	47	6	0-0	0
10/29	Sea	W	20-14	0	0	2	0-0	0

Game Logs (9-16)

Date	Opp	Result		Rec	Yds	Trgt	F-L	TD
11/05	@Den	L	6-38	3	44	3	0-0	0
11/12	Min	L	24-30	2	33	5	0-0	0
11/19	@Car	L	7-27	1	5	2	0-0	0
11/26	Atl	W	40-37	2	51	3	0-0	1
11/30	NYN	L	6-10	1	14	2	0-0	0
12/09	@SD	L	25-28	3	39	5	0-0	0
12/17	@Phi	L	20-21	5	59	5	0-0	0
12/25	Dal	L	13-37	1	11	2	0-0	0

Henry Ellard

Washington Redskins — WR

1995 Receiving Splits

	G	Rec	Yds	Avg	TD	Lg	Big	YAC	Trgt	Y@C	1st	1st%		Rec	Yds	Avg	TD	Lg	Big	YAC	Trgt	Y@C	1st	1st%
Total	15	56	1005	17.9	5	59	8	132	113	15.6	50	89.3	Inside 20	5	54	10.8	3	14	0	6	13	9.6	4	80.0
vs. Playoff	5	17	312	18.4	4	40	3	49	40	15.5	16	94.1	Inside 10	0	0	-	0	0	0	0	3	-	0	-
vs. Non-playoff	10	39	693	17.8	1	59	5	83	73	15.6	34	87.2	1st Down	25	505	20.2	1	59	6	74	44	17.2	23	92.0
vs. Own Division	8	25	474	19.0	4	46	5	97	59	15.1	24	96.0	2nd Down	12	169	14.1	0	24	0	12	33	13.1	10	83.3
Home	8	32	589	18.4	1	59	3	52	63	16.8	30	93.8	3rd Down Overall	19	331	17.4	3	40	2	46	35	15.0	17	89.5
Away	7	24	416	17.3	4	46	5	80	50	14.0	20	83.3	3rd D 0-2 to Go	1	18	18.0	0	18	0	0	1	18.0	1	100.0
Games 1-8	8	34	610	17.9	4	46	5	81	68	15.6	31	91.2	3rd D 3-7 to Go	6	88	14.7	0	21	0	7	12	13.5	5	83.3
Games 9-16	7	22	395	18.0	1	59	3	51	45	15.6	19	86.4	3rd D 8+ to Go	12	225	18.8	3	40	2	39	22	15.5	11	91.7
September	4	19	294	15.5	0	29	2	19	31	14.5	16	84.2	4th Down	0	0	-	0	0	0	0	1	-	0	-
October	5	21	427	20.3	4	46	4	79	46	16.6	21	100.0	Rec Behind Line	0	0	-	0	0	0	0	0	-	0	-
November	2	5	92	18.4	0	28	1	5	13	17.4	5	100.0	1-10 yds	11	89	8.1	1	11	0	14	24	6.8	6	54.5
December	4	11	192	17.5	1	59	1	29	23	14.8	8	72.7	11-20 yds	38	688	18.1	3	40	4	66	69	16.4	37	97.4
Grass	11	43	801	18.6	2	59	6	88	83	16.6	40	93.0	21-30 yds	6	169	28.2	1	46	3	37	16	22.0	6	100.0
Turf	4	13	204	15.7	3	40	2	44	30	12.3	10	76.9	31+	1	59	59.0	0	59	1	15	3	44.0	1	100.0
Outdoor	1	53	977	18.4	5	59	8	132	108	15.9	49	92.5	Left Sideline	19	301	15.8	1	27	1	18	37	14.9	17	89.5
Indoor	14	3	28	9.3	0	21	0	0	5	9.3	1	33.3	Left Side	5	101	20.2	0	28	2	9	12	18.4	4	80.0
1st Half	-	23	436	19.0	2	59	4	75	49	15.7	21	91.3	Middle	6	131	21.8	2	40	1	25	16	17.7	6	100.0
2nd Half/OT	-	33	569	17.2	3	59	4	57	64	15.5	29	87.9	Right Side	13	251	19.3	2	59	3	66	23	14.2	11	84.6
Last 2 Min. Half	-	11	163	14.8	0	28	1	11	20	13.8	10	90.9	Right Sideline	13	221	17.0	0	29	1	14	25	15.9	12	92.3
4th qtr, +/-7 pts	-	8	127	15.9	1	28	1	6	18	15.1	7	87.5	Shotgun	0	0	-	0	0	0	0	0	-	0	-
Winning	-	13	215	16.5	0	29	1	18	28	15.2	11	84.6	2 Wide Receivers	25	504	20.2	1	59	4	63	51	17.6	24	96.0
Tied	-	15	326	21.7	2	59	4	71	32	17.0	13	86.7	3 Wide Receivers	24	402	16.8	4	40	3	67	52	14.0	21	87.5
Trailing	-	28	464	16.6	3	28	3	43	50	15.0	26	92.9	4+ Wide Receivers	5	66	13.2	0	28	2	7	7	12.8	3	60.0

1995 Incompletions

Type	Num	%of Inc	%of Att
Pass Dropped	6	10.5	5.3
Poor Throw	36	63.2	31.9
Pass Defensed	9	15.8	8.0
Pass Hit at Line	0	0.0	0.0
Other	6	10.5	5.3
Total	57	100.0	50.4

Game Logs (1-8)

Date	Opp	Result		Rec	Yds	Trgt	F-L	TD
09/03	Ari	W	27-7	4	65	10	0-0	0
09/10	Oak	L	8-20	6	81	8	1-1	0
09/17	@Den	L	31-38	4	58	6	0-0	0
09/24	@TB	L	6-14	5	90	7	0-0	0
10/01	Dal	W	27-23	2	30	4	0-0	0
10/08	@Phi	L	34-37	5	110	14	0-0	2
10/15	@Ari	L	20-24	2	64	7	0-0	0
10/22	Det	L	36-30	6	112	12	0-0	1

Game Logs (9-16)

Date	Opp	Result		Rec	Yds	Trgt	F-L	TD
10/29	NYN	L	15-24	6	111	9	0-0	0
11/05	@KC	L	3-24	-	-	-	-	-
11/19	Sea	L	20-27	4	64	9	0-0	0
11/26	Phi	L	7-14	1	28	4	0-0	0
12/03	@Dal	W	24-17	3	32	6	0-0	1
12/10	@NYN	L	20-27	2	34	5	0-0	0
12/17	@StL	W	35-23	3	28	5	0-0	0
12/24	Car	W	20-17	3	98	7	0-0	0

John Elway
Denver Broncos — QB

1995 Passing Splits

	G	Att	Cm	Pct	Yds	Yd/Att	TD	Int	1st	YAC	Big	Sk	Rtg
Total	16	542	316	58.3	3970	7.3	26	14	190	1762	29	22	86.4
vs. Playoff	7	212	118	55.7	1455	6.9	7	6	67	611	9	11	76.3
vs. Non-playoff	9	330	198	60.0	2515	7.6	19	8	123	1151	20	11	92.9
vs. Own Division	8	297	165	55.6	1959	6.6	10	8	98	845	12	15	75.9
Home	8	292	169	57.9	2188	7.5	15	9	103	972	16	13	85.8
Away	8	250	147	58.8	1782	7.1	11	5	87	790	13	9	87.1
Games 1-8	8	303	166	54.8	2016	6.7	10	5	94	799	12	12	79.6
Games 9-16	8	239	150	62.8	1954	8.2	16	9	96	963	17	10	95.1
September	4	146	82	56.2	982	6.7	4	2	44	359	6	6	80.3
October	4	157	84	53.5	1034	6.6	4	3	50	440	6	6	78.9
November	4	99	64	64.6	932	9.4	8	4	42	406	11	1	105.3
December	4	140	86	61.4	1022	7.3	8	5	54	557	6	9	87.9
Grass	12	437	257	58.8	3223	7.4	20	11	156	1539	22	20	86.6
Turf	4	105	59	56.2	747	7.1	6	3	34	223	7	2	85.7
Indoor	2	78	46	59.0	541	6.9	3	2	26	174	5	0	82.3
Outdoor	14	464	270	58.2	3429	7.4	23	12	164	1588	24	22	87.1
1st Half	-	293	170	58.0	2084	7.1	14	7	105	973	15	8	86.0
2nd Half/OT	-	249	146	58.6	1886	7.6	12	7	85	789	14	14	86.9
Last 2 Min. Half	-	95	56	58.9	658	6.9	4	2	36	232	5	3	85.3
4th qtr, +/-7 pts	-	45	27	60.0	328	7.2	1	0	11	100	3	3	89.7
Winning	-	216	127	58.8	1716	7.9	14	8	84	811	13	8	90.4
Tied	-	117	65	55.6	703	6.0	2	2	33	323	5	2	72.0
Trailing	-	209	124	59.3	1551	7.4	10	4	73	628	11	12	90.4

	Att	Cm	Pct	Yds	Yd/Att	TD	Int	1st	YAC	Big	Sk	Rtg
Inside 20	58	25	43.1	169	2.9	12	1	18	89	0	2	82.9
Inside 10	28	13	46.4	55	2.0	9	0	9	19	0	2	92.9
1st Down	199	120	60.3	1302	6.5	5	2	57	707	8	6	83.8
2nd Down	201	119	59.2	1655	8.2	15	7	79	719	15	7	96.1
3rd Down Overall	135	74	54.8	960	7.1	5	4	53	335	5	9	77.4
3rd D 0-5 to Go	41	23	56.1	212	5.2	3	1	18	83	1	4	84.6
3rd D 6+ to Go	94	51	54.3	748	8.0	2	3	35	252	4	5	74.2
4th Down	7	3	42.9	53	7.6	1	1	1	1	1	0	69.3
Rec Behind Line	94	55	58.5	358	3.8	1	1	19	473	1	0	65.8
1-10 yds	274	179	65.3	1714	6.3	12	4	94	935	4	0	91.1
11-20 yds	114	60	52.6	1105	9.7	5	5	55	233	5	0	76.8
21-30 yds	35	10	28.6	286	8.2	1	3	10	56	7	0	34.9
31+	25	12	48.0	507	20.3	9	1	12	65	12	0	117.1
Left Sideline	89	46	51.7	575	6.5	4	3	28	218	4	0	73.0
Left Side	102	66	64.7	948	9.3	8	1	46	441	6	6	116.8
Middle	119	72	60.5	859	7.2	6	4	41	335	6	15	85.4
Right Side	118	80	67.8	846	7.2	2	1	38	486	4	1	90.6
Right Sideline	114	52	45.6	742	6.5	6	5	37	282	9	0	66.5
2 Wide Receivers	200	116	58.0	1457	7.3	10	6	69	738	12	8	84.9
3+ WR	330	190	57.6	2389	7.2	13	8	114	962	16	14	83.3
Attempts 1-10	153	94	61.4	1222	8.0	10	2	62	636	9	0	102.9
Attempts 11-20	150	84	56.0	1021	6.8	5	5	46	435	8	0	74.3
Attempts 21+	239	138	57.7	1727	7.2	11	9	82	691	12	0	83.4

1995 Incompletions

Type	Num	% of Inc	% of Att
Pass Dropped	33	14.6	6.1
Poor Throw	96	42.5	17.7
Pass Defensed	28	12.4	5.2
Pass Hit at Line	15	6.6	2.8
Other	54	23.9	10.0
Total	226	100.0	41.7

Game Logs (1-8)

Date	Opp	Result	Att	Cm	Pct	Yds	TD	Int	Lg	Sk	F-L
09/03	Buf	W 22-7	41	22	53.7	317	0	1	49	2	2-0
09/10	@Dal	L 21-31	24	11	45.8	152	2	1	59	2	1-1
09/17	Was	W 38-31	47	30	63.8	327	2	0	43	1	0-0
09/24	@SD	L 6-17	34	19	55.9	186	0	0	22	1	0-0
10/01	Sea	L 10-27	37	23	62.2	209	1	0	26	0	1-1
10/08	@NE	W 37-3	34	21	61.8	287	2	1	60	1	0-0
10/16	Oak	W 27-0	46	23	50.0	324	2	0	36	2	1-1
10/22	KC	L 7-21	40	21	52.5	214	1	2	22	3	2-1

Game Logs (9-16)

Date	Opp	Result	Att	Cm	Pct	Yds	TD	Int	Lg	Sk	F-L
11/05	Ari	W 38-6	21	16	76.2	256	3	0	47	1	0-0
11/12	@Phi	L 3-31	3	2	66.7	54	1	0	46	0	0-0
11/19	SD	W 30-27	34	19	55.9	290	2	2	40	0	0-0
11/26	@Hou	L 33-42	41	27	65.9	332	2	2	50	0	0-0
12/03	Jac	W 31-23	34	22	64.7	286	4	1	62	0	0-0
12/10	Sea	L 27-31	29	16	55.2	174	1	3	21	4	1-1
12/17	@KC	L 17-20	36	24	66.7	242	1	0	24	3	1-1
12/24	@Oak	W 31-28	41	24	58.5	320	2	1	30	2	0-0

Bert Emanuel
Atlanta Falcons — WR

1995 Receiving Splits

	G	Rec	Yds	Avg	TD	Lg	Big	YAC	Trgt	Y@C	1st	1st%
Total	16	74	1039	14.0	5	52	12	399	137	8.6	47	63.5
vs. Playoff	6	29	414	14.3	1	37	4	241	54	6.0	22	75.9
vs. Non-playoff	10	45	625	13.9	4	52	8	158	83	10.4	25	55.6
vs. Own Division	8	32	423	13.2	1	49	4	129	67	9.2	19	59.4
Home	8	42	569	13.5	2	52	7	260	71	7.4	24	57.1
Away	8	32	470	14.7	3	49	5	139	66	10.3	23	71.9
Games 1-8	8	37	544	14.7	4	52	7	111	66	11.7	24	64.9
Games 9-16	8	37	495	13.4	1	37	5	288	71	5.6	23	62.2
September	4	19	284	14.9	2	49	3	56	32	12.0	13	68.4
October	4	18	260	14.4	2	52	4	55	34	11.4	11	61.1
November	4	18	250	13.9	0	37	2	167	33	4.6	10	55.6
December	4	19	245	12.9	1	32	3	121	38	6.5	13	68.4
Grass	5	19	245	12.9	1	32	3	66	37	9.4	13	68.4
Turf	11	55	794	14.4	4	52	9	333	100	8.4	34	61.8
Indoor	9	48	673	14.0	2	52	8	266	81	8.5	28	58.3
Outdoor	7	26	366	14.1	3	34	4	133	56	9.0	19	73.1
1st Half	-	43	618	14.4	3	52	8	249	75	8.6	26	60.5
2nd Half/OT	-	31	421	13.6	2	37	4	150	62	8.7	21	67.7
Last 2 Min. Half	-	11	157	14.3	0	34	1	102	25	5.0	7	63.6
4th qtr, +/-7 pts	-	12	174	14.5	0	27	1	49	25	10.4	9	75.0
Winning	-	24	318	13.3	0	37	4	165	48	6.4	15	62.5
Tied	-	25	296	11.8	4	44	3	92	37	8.2	15	60.0
Trailing	-	25	425	17.0	1	52	5	142	52	11.3	17	68.0

	Rec	Yds	Avg	TD	Lg	Big	YAC	Trgt	Y@C	1st	1st%
Inside 20	8	41	5.1	3	10	0	14	19	3.4	4	50.0
Inside 10	3	10	3.3	3	5	0	0	8	3.3	3	100.0
1st Down	35	482	13.8	0	52	5	197	58	8.1	16	45.7
2nd Down	21	289	13.8	3	44	3	143	42	7.0	16	76.2
3rd Down Overall	18	268	14.9	2	49	4	59	36	11.6	15	83.3
3rd D 0-2 to Go	3	15	5.0	1	7	0	1	9	4.7	3	100.0
3rd D 3-7 to Go	7	85	12.1	1	30	1	18	13	9.6	6	85.7
3rd D 8+ to Go	8	168	21.0	0	49	3	40	14	16.0	6	75.0
4th Down	0	0	-	0	0	0	0	1	-	0	-
Rec Behind Line	13	163	12.5	0	37	2	185	18	-1.7	8	61.5
1-10 yds	42	397	9.5	3	44	3	164	66	5.5	20	47.6
11-20 yds	10	173	17.3	0	24	0	33	29	14.0	10	100.0
21-30 yds	5	127	25.4	1	30	3		11	24.8	5	100.0
31+	4	179	44.8	1	52	4		14	41.3	4	100.0
Left Sideline	0	0	-	0	0	0	0	2	-	0	-
Left Side	1	10	10.0	0	10	0	7	1	3.0	1	100.0
Middle	7	178	25.7	1	32	1	11	9	22.0	3	100.0
Right Side	35	500	14.3	2	52	6	279	47	6.3	24	68.6
Right Sideline	35	452	12.9	2	49	5	102	78	10.0	19	54.3
Shotgun	13	225	17.3	0	52	3	53	23	13.2	8	61.5
2 Wide Receivers	2	27	13.5	0	21	0	6	3	10.5	1	50.0
3 Wide Receivers	9	97	10.8	1	15	0	44	19	5.9	8	88.9
4+ Wide Receivers	63	915	14.5	4	52	12	349	115	9.0	38	60.3

1995 Incompletions

Type	Num	%of Inc	%of Att
Pass Dropped	11	17.5	8.0
Poor Throw	30	47.6	21.9
Pass Defensed	12	19.0	8.8
Pass Hit at Line	2	3.2	1.5
Other	8	12.7	5.8
Total	63	100.0	46.0

Game Logs (1-8)

Date	Opp	Result	Rush	Yds	Rec	Yds	Trgt	F-L	TD
09/03	Car	W 23-20	0	0	6	90	10	0-0	1
09/10	@SF	L 10-41	0	0	2	16	6	0-0	0
09/17	@NO	W 27-24	0	0	6	104	10	0-0	1
09/24	NYA	W 13-3	0	0	5	74	6	0-0	1
10/01	NE	W 30-17	0	0	6	95	10	1-1	0
10/12	@StL	L 19-21	0	0	1	21	6	0-0	0
10/22	@TB	W 24-21	0	0	9	121	10	0-0	2
10/29	@Dal	L 13-28	0	0	2	23	8	0-0	0

Game Logs (9-16)

Date	Opp	Result	Rush	Yds	Rec	Yds	Trgt	F-L	TD
11/05	Det	W 34-22	0	0	7	104	9	0-0	0
11/12	@Buf	L 17-23	0	0	6	100	13	1-1	0
11/19	StL	W 31-6	0	0	3	32	4	0-0	0
11/26	@Ari	L 37-40	1	0	2	14	7	0-0	0
12/03	@Mia	L 20-21	0	0	5	85	7	0-0	0
12/10	NO	W 19-14	0	0	6	65	13	0-0	0
12/17	@Car	L 17-21	0	0	1	9	7	0-0	0
12/24	SF	W 28-27	0	0	7	86	11	0-0	0

Craig Erickson
Indianapolis Colts — QB

1995 Passing Splits

	G	Att	Cm	Pct	Yds	Yd/Att	TD	Int	1st	YAC	Big	Sk	Rtg
Total	6	83	50	60.2	586	7.1	3	4	23	279	6	10	73.7
vs. Playoff	1	15	9	60.0	122	8.1	0	0	3	74	2	1	86.0
vs. Non-playoff	5	68	41	60.3	464	6.8	3	4	20	205	4	9	71.0
vs. Own Division	3	35	21	60.0	263	7.5	0	1	7	137	4	7	71.5
Home	3	48	28	58.3	318	6.6	1	3	13	151	2	6	59.2
Away	3	35	22	62.9	268	7.7	2	1	10	128	4	4	93.5
Games 1-8	4	52	32	61.5	335	6.4	1	4	14	140	2	8	54.6
Games 9-16	2	31	18	58.1	251	8.1	2	0	9	139	4	2	105.7
September	2	49	31	63.3	337	6.9	1	4	14	140	2	5	56.3
October	2	3	1	33.3	-2	-0.7	0	0	0	0	0	3	42.4
November	1	15	9	60.0	122	8.1	0	0	3	74	2	1	86.0
December	1	16	9	56.3	129	8.1	2	0	6	65	2	1	122.1
Grass	2	17	10	58.8	127	7.5	2	0	6	65	2	1	121.4
Turf	4	66	40	60.6	459	7.0	1	4	17	214	4	9	61.4
Indoor	3	48	28	58.3	318	6.6	1	3	13	151	2	6	59.2
Outdoor	3	35	22	62.9	268	7.7	2	1	10	128	4	4	93.5
1st Half	-	57	34	59.6	347	6.1	2	3	14	171	2	4	66.9
2nd Half/OT	-	26	16	61.5	239	9.2	1	1	9	108	4	6	88.5
Last 2 Min. Half	-	14	9	64.3	91	6.5	0	0	3	55	1	2	82.7
4th qtr, +/-7 pts	-	8	4	50.0	52	6.5	0	0	1	40	1	2	70.8
Winning	-	23	11	47.8	165	7.2	2	2	8	87	2	4	64.6
Tied	-	6	5	83.3	53	8.8	1	0	3	8	0	1	143.1
Trailing	-	54	34	63.0	368	6.8	0	2	12	184	4	5	67.5

	Att	Cm	Pct	Yds	Yd/Att	TD	Int	1st	YAC	Big	Sk	Rtg
Inside 20	12	6	50.0	58	4.8	3	0	3	4	0	1	103.5
Inside 10	3	2	66.7	6	2.0	0	0	0	1	0	1	70.1
1st Down	31	17	54.8	218	7.0	0	2	8	107	3	2	50.2
2nd Down	26	17	65.4	157	6.0	1	1	4	100	1	3	78.5
3rd Down Overall	23	14	60.9	191	8.3	2	1	9	65	2	5	98.3
3rd D 0-5 to Go	9	5	55.6	72	8.0	1	1	4	23	1	2	79.2
3rd D 6+ to Go	14	9	64.3	119	8.5	1	0	5	42	1	3	114.9
4th Down	3	2	66.7	20	6.7	0	0	2	7	0	0	85.4
Rec Behind Line	19	11	57.9	73	3.8	0	0	2	106	0	0	66.3
1-10 yds	35	26	74.3	231	6.6	0	1	9	101	1	0	79.6
11-20 yds	21	10	47.6	188	9.0	3	3	9	48	2	0	79.1
21-30 yds	7	3	42.9	94	13.4	0	0	3	24	3	0	89.9
31+	1	0	0.0	0	0.0	0	0	0	0	0	0	39.6
Left Sideline	17	9	52.9	101	5.9	1	0	3	48	1	0	90.6
Left Side	20	12	60.0	134	6.7	0	2	5	54	2	4	40.4
Middle	13	7	53.8	92	7.1	1	0	5	38	0	5	102.1
Right Side	18	13	72.2	140	7.8	1	1	7	86	1	0	90.0
Right Sideline	15	9	60.0	119	7.9	0	1	3	53	2	1	57.4
2 Wide Receivers	29	18	62.1	219	7.6	0	3	7	102	4	3	45.7
3+ WR	49	30	61.2	343	7.0	2	1	15	167	2	6	87.4
Attempts 1-10	43	24	55.8	313	7.3	2	3	12	170	4	0	65.4
Attempts 11-20	29	20	69.0	211	7.3	1	0	8	76	2	0	101.4
Attempts 21+	11	6	54.5	62	5.6	0	1	3	33	0	0	33.1

1995 Incompletions

Type	Num	% of Inc	% of Att
Pass Dropped	3	9.1	3.6
Poor Throw	14	42.4	16.9
Pass Defensed	4	12.1	4.8
Pass Hit at Line	2	6.1	2.4
Other	10	30.3	12.0
Total	33	100.0	39.8

Game Logs (1-8)

Date	Opp	Result	Att	Cm	Pct	Yds	TD	Int	Lg	Sk	F-L
09/03	Cin	L 21-24	31	19	61.3	196	1	3	19	2	1-0
09/10	@NYA	W 27-24	18	12	66.7	141	0	1	29	3	1-1
09/17	@Buf	L 14-20	-								
10/01	StL	W 21-18	-								
10/08	@Mia	W 27-24	-								
10/15	SF	W 18-17	-								
10/22	@Oak	L 17-30	1	1	100.0	-2	0	0	-2	0	0-0
10/29	NYA	W 17-10	2	0	0.0	0	0	0	0	3	0-0

Game Logs (9-16)

Date	Opp	Result	Att	Cm	Pct	Yds	TD	Int	Lg	Sk	F-L
11/05	Buf	L 10-16	15	9	60.0	122	0	0	39	1	0-0
11/12	@NO	L 14-17	-								
11/19	@NE	W 24-10	-								
11/26	Mia	W 36-28	-								
12/03	@Car	L 10-13	-								
12/10	@Jac	W 41-31	16	9	56.3	129	2	0	27	1	0-0
12/17	SD	L 24-27	-								
12/23	NE	W 10-7	-								

Boomer Esiason
New York Jets — QB

1995 Passing Splits

	G	Att	Cm	Pct	Yds	Yd/Att	TD	Int	1st	YAC	Big	Sk	Rtg
Total	12	389	221	56.8	2275	5.8	16	15	118	1093	13	27	71.4
vs. Playoff	5	154	86	55.8	919	6.0	6	9	44	457	5	8	62.1
vs. Non-playoff	7	235	135	57.4	1356	5.8	10	6	74	636	8	19	77.5
vs. Own Division	5	178	93	58.5	1025	6.4	10	7	50	493	7	10	80.3
Home	6	198	113	57.1	1260	6.4	10	6	68	526	8	15	80.4
Away	6	191	108	56.5	1015	5.3	6	9	50	567	5	12	62.2
Games 1-8	6	184	104	56.5	1074	5.8	7	8	59	510	6	8	68.1
Games 9-16	6	205	117	57.1	1201	5.9	9	7	59	583	7	19	74.5
September	4	145	85	58.6	857	5.9	6	7	46	429	5	3	69.2
October	2	39	19	48.7	217	5.6	1	1	13	81	1	5	63.7
November	2	77	43	55.8	461	6.0	3	3	21	239	2	5	70.3
December	4	128	74	57.8	740	5.8	6	4	38	344	5	14	77.0
Grass	2	77	46	59.7	469	6.1	5	4	23	261	4	5	77.2
Turf	10	312	175	56.1	1806	5.8	11	11	95	832	9	22	70.0
Indoor	3	105	58	55.2	500	4.8	1	4	24	298	1	6	55.3
Outdoor	9	284	163	57.4	1775	6.3	15	11	94	795	12	21	77.4
1st Half	-	200	106	53.0	1007	5.0	4	7	56	532	5	19	59.3
2nd Half/OT	-	189	115	60.8	1268	6.7	12	8	62	561	8	8	84.3
Last 2 Min. Half	-	44	20	45.5	236	5.4	3	1	12	58	1	5	75.6
4th qtr, +/-7 pts	-	28	20	71.4	146	5.2	1	1	5	77	0	0	80.4
Winning	-	87	50	57.5	519	6.0	3	2	28	249	3	2	76.7
Tied	-	85	53	62.4	558	6.6	4	1	29	319	4	9	92.2
Trailing	-	217	118	54.4	1198	5.5	9	12	61	525	6	16	61.2

	Att	Cm	Pct	Yds	Yd/Att	TD	Int	1st	YAC	Big	Sk	Rtg
Inside 20	39	16	41.0	122	3.1	11	2	14	52	0	2	67.5
Inside 10	15	8	53.3	34	2.3	8	1	8	1	0	2	70.8
1st Down	156	99	63.5	981	6.3	6	10	47	436	4	4	67.3
2nd Down	116	65	56.0	600	5.2	5	3	33	316	3	11	73.9
3rd Down Overall	111	55	49.5	670	6.0	5	2	36	338	6	12	76.0
3rd D 0-5 to Go	36	19	52.8	240	6.7	2	0	17	128	2	1	92.4
3rd D 6+ to Go	75	36	48.0	430	5.7	3	2	19	210	4	11	68.2
4th Down	6	2	33.3	24	4.0	0	0	2	3	0	0	46.5
Rec Behind Line	73	42	57.5	200	2.7	0	1	8	389	0	0	56.8
1-10 yds	197	133	67.5	1136	5.8	10	6	65	527	4	0	86.6
11-20 yds	79	40	50.6	744	9.4	3	2	40	144	5	0	85.6
21-30 yds	26	4	15.4	111	4.3	2	4	3	19	2	0	30.9
31+	13	2	15.4	84	6.5	1	2	2	14	2	0	40.1
Left Sideline	52	25	48.1	345	6.6	5	1	15	120	4	0	93.8
Left Side	91	57	62.6	606	6.7	1	5	35	338	3	3	62.8
Middle	68	32	47.1	330	4.9	4	2	20	125	1	22	68.9
Right Side	106	67	63.2	559	5.3	3	2	27	330	2	2	78.3
Right Sideline	71	40	56.3	435	6.1	3	5	21	180	3	0	59.3
2 Wide Receivers	306	172	56.2	1776	5.8	8	11	86	864	10	21	66.8
3+ WR	48	27	56.3	312	6.5	4	2	18	139	2	2	86.5
Attempts 1-10	119	71	59.7	703	5.9	2	4	41	348	4	0	68.0
Attempts 11-20	107	51	47.7	567	5.3	4	4	27	325	4	0	60.8
Attempts 21+	163	99	60.7	1005	6.2	10	7	50	420	5	0	80.9

1995 Incompletions

Type	Num	% of Inc	% of Att
Pass Dropped	32	19.0	8.2
Poor Throw	79	47.0	20.3
Pass Defensed	22	13.1	5.7
Pass Hit at Line	12	7.1	3.1
Other	23	13.7	5.9
Total	168	100.0	43.2

Game Logs (1-8)

Date	Opp	Result	Att	Cm	Pct	Yds	TD	Int	Lg	Sk	F-L
09/03	@Mia	L 14-52	35	19	54.3	173	1	3	27	1	1-0
09/10	Ind	L 24-27	30	19	63.3	198	2	0	43	0	2-1
09/17	Jac	W 27-10	43	27	62.8	296	3	1	30	0	0-1
09/24	@Atl	L 3-13	37	20	54.1	190	0	2	32	2	1-0
10/01	Oak	L 10-47	30	15	50.0	171	1	0	29	4	2-1
10/08	@Buf	L 10-29	9	4	44.4	46	0	1	17	1	0-0
10/15	@Car	L 15-26	-								
10/22	Mia	W 17-16	-								

Game Logs (9-16)

Date	Opp	Result	Att	Cm	Pct	Yds	TD	Int	Lg	Sk	F-L
10/29	@Ind	L 10-17	-								
11/05	NE	L 7-20	-								
11/19	Buf	L 26-28	43	24	55.8	312	3	2	43	4	0-0
11/26	@Sea	W 16-10	34	19	55.9	149	0	1	20	1	0-0
12/03	StL	L 20-23	35	20	57.1	218	1	1	32	6	0-0
12/10	NE	L 28-31	42	27	64.3	296	4	1	38	4	3-1
12/17	@Hou	L 6-23	34	19	55.9	161	1	0	24	3	2-0
12/24	NO	L 0-12	17	8	47.1	65	0	2	17	1	1-0

Vince Evans

1995 Passing Splits

	G	Att	Cm	Pct	Yds	Yd/Att	TD	Int	1st	YAC	Big	Sk	Rtg
Total	9	175	100	57.1	1236	7.1	6	8	56	633	7	11	71.5
vs. Playoff	5	149	86	57.7	1065	7.1	5	7	49	531	6	10	71.6
vs. Non-playoff	4	26	14	53.8	171	6.6	1	1	7	102	1	1	71.2
vs. Own Division	4	94	54	57.4	590	6.3	1	6	29	350	3	8	53.1
Home	5	128	78	60.9	980	7.7	6	4	44	428	5	7	87.4
Away	4	47	22	46.8	256	5.4	0	4	12	205	2	4	28.3
Games 1-8	4	53	31	58.5	478	9.0	3	2	17	235	4	4	91.5
Games 9-16	5	122	69	56.6	758	6.2	3	6	39	398	3	7	62.8
September	1	4	3	75.0	79	19.8	1	0	3	38	1	0	156.3
October	3	49	28	57.1	399	8.1	2	2	14	197	3	4	80.2
November	3	74	37	50.0	424	5.7	2	4	22	253	2	3	54.1
December	2	48	32	66.7	334	7.0	1	2	17	145	1	4	76.2
Grass	7	174	100	57.5	1236	7.1	6	8	56	633	7	11	71.9
Turf	2	1	0	0.0	0	0.0	0	0	0	0	0	0	39.6
Indoor	0	0	0	-	0	-	0	0	0	0	0	0	-
Outdoor	9	175	100	57.1	1236	7.1	6	8	56	633	7	11	71.5
1st Half	-	60	38	63.3	387	6.5	1	1	20	235	0	4	80.3
2nd Half/OT	-	115	62	53.9	849	7.4	5	7	36	398	7	7	66.9
Last 2 Min. Half	-	36	20	55.6	201	5.6	1	1	8	138	0	2	69.3
4th qtr, +/-7 pts	-	17	8	47.1	109	6.4	0	1	4	60	1	1	43.5
Winning	-	37	24	64.9	304	8.2	2	0	10	164	2	2	108.4
Tied	-	12	9	75.0	148	12.3	1	0	8	58	1	2	143.8
Trailing	-	126	67	53.2	784	6.2	3	8	38	411	4	7	53.8

	Att	Cm	Pct	Yds	Yd/Att	TD	Int	1st	YAC	Big	Sk	Rtg
Inside 20	13	2	15.4	25	1.9	2	1	2	8	0	1	47.1
Inside 10	4	1	25.0	9	2.3	1	0	1	8	0	1	79.2
1st Down	69	40	58.0	503	7.3	4	1	20	230	4	2	94.1
2nd Down	58	34	58.6	360	6.2	0	4	17	202	1	5	48.1
3rd Down Overall	44	25	56.8	349	7.9	1	3	18	192	2	4	61.6
3rd D 0-5 to Go	14	11	78.6	144	10.3	1	0	9	84	1	1	133.3
3rd D 6+ to Go	30	14	46.7	205	6.8	0	3	9	108	1	3	29.9
4th Down	4	1	25.0	24	6.0	0	1	1	9	0	0	91.7
Rec Behind Line	32	24	75.0	143	4.5	0	0	6	224	0	0	83.2
1-10 yds	80	49	61.3	445	5.6	1	3	25	231	0	0	64.8
11-20 yds	39	24	61.5	499	12.8	3	4	22	142	4	0	91.5
21-30 yds	11	1	9.1	30	2.7	0	0	1	4	1	0	39.6
31+	13	2	15.4	119	9.2	2	1	2	32	2	0	72.8
Left Sideline	36	19	52.8	295	8.2	0	1	12	139	2	0	77.9
Left Side	30	21	70.0	239	8.0	0	1	13	143	1	1	79.7
Middle	26	15	57.7	241	9.3	2	2	11	119	2	10	82.4
Right Side	31	21	67.7	234	7.5	1	1	8	77	2	0	87.3
Right Sideline	52	24	46.2	227	4.4	2	3	12	155	0	0	47.5
2 Wide Receivers	40	31	77.5	352	8.8	2	1	16	169	1	2	109.6
3+ WR	130	66	50.8	850	6.5	4	7	38	447	6	8	55.9
Attempts 1-10	65	38	58.5	490	7.5	2	2	24	284	3	0	79.6
Attempts 11-20	45	23	51.1	266	5.9	1	2	11	137	0	0	58.2
Attempts 21+	65	39	60.0	480	7.4	3	4	21	212	4	0	72.6

1995 Incompletions

Type	Num	% of Inc	% of Att
Pass Dropped	9	12.0	5.1
Poor Throw	33	44.0	18.9
Pass Defensed	15	20.0	8.6
Pass Hit at Line	3	4.0	1.7
Other	15	20.0	8.6
Total	75	100.0	42.9

Game Logs (1-8)

Date	Opp	Result	Att	Cm	Pct	Yds	TD	Int	Lg	Sk	F-L
09/03	SD	W 17-7	-	-	-	-	-	-	-	-	-
09/10	@Was	W 20-8	-	-	-	-	-	-	-	-	-
09/17	@KC	L 17-23	-	-	-	-	-	-	-	-	-
09/24	Phi	W 48-17	4	3	75.0	79	1	0	54	0	0-0
10/01	@NYA	W 47-10	0	0	-	0	0	0	0	0	0-0
10/08	Sea	W 34-14	-	-	-	-	-	-	-	-	-
10/16	@Den	L 0-27	14	5	35.7	64	0	1	43	1	0-0
10/22	Ind	W 30-17	35	23	65.7	335	2	1	73	3	0-0

Game Logs (9-16)

Date	Opp	Result	Att	Cm	Pct	Yds	TD	Int	Lg	Sk	F-L
11/05	@Cin	W 20-17	1	0	0.0	0	0	0	0	0	0-0
11/12	@NYN	W 17-13	-	-	-	-	-	-	-	-	-
11/19	Dal	L 21-34	41	20	48.8	232	2	1	25	0	0-0
11/27	@SD	L 6-12	32	17	53.1	192	0	3	30	3	1-1
12/03	KC	L 23-29	37	23	62.2	227	0	2	30	4	3-2
12/10	Pit	L 10-29	-	-	-	-	-	-	-	-	-
12/17	@Sea	L 10-44	-	-	-	-	-	-	-	-	-
12/24	Den	L 28-31	11	9	81.8	107	1	0	20	0	1-1

Jim Everett

1995 Passing Splits

	G	Att	Cm	Pct	Yds	Yd/Att	TD	Int	1st	YAC	Big	Sk	Rtg
Total	16	567	345	60.8	3970	7.0	26	14	201	1628	28	27	87.0
vs. Playoff	8	292	181	62.0	2015	6.9	15	5	105	747	17	12	92.5
vs. Non-playoff	8	275	164	59.6	1955	7.1	11	9	96	881	11	15	81.1
vs. Own Division	8	296	178	60.1	1951	6.6	8		100	809	13	16	78.5
Home	8	273	170	62.3	1956	7.2	14	5	101	710	18	16	93.3
Away	8	294	175	59.5	2014	6.9	12	9	100	918	10	11	81.1
Games 1-8	8	283	164	58.0	1880	6.6	13	9	92	664	12	17	80.1
Games 9-16	8	284	181	63.7	2090	7.4	13	5	109	964	16	10	93.8
September	4	153	95	62.1	1139	7.4	9	4	57	428	9	11	93.6
October	4	130	69	53.1	741	5.7	4	5	35	236	3	6	64.3
November	4	128	84	65.6	947	7.4	6	2	53	409	7	8	96.7
December	4	156	97	62.2	1143	7.3	7	3	56	555	9	2	91.4
Grass	3	100	56	56.0	690	6.9	2	5	27	318	5	2	63.3
Turf	13	467	289	61.9	3280	7.0	24	9	174	1310	23	25	92.0
Indoor	10	357	226	63.3	2578	7.2	19	6	135	1024	22	18	95.7
Outdoor	6	210	119	56.7	1392	6.6	7	8	66	604	6	9	72.2
1st Half	-	289	167	57.8	1877	6.5	8	6	89	827	14	10	77.9
2nd Half/OT	-	278	178	64.0	2093	7.5	18	8	112	801	14	17	96.4
Last 2 Min. Half	-	88	51	58.0	596	6.8	5	4	29	233	6	4	78.6
4th qtr, +/-7 pts	-	67	40	59.7	503	7.5	3	2	22	228	3	4	85.6
Winning	-	131	77	58.8	833	6.4	7	2	44	281	5	5	89.0
Tied	-	142	83	58.5	933	6.6	4	3	44	432	4	5	78.8
Trailing	-	294	185	62.9	2204	7.5	15	9	113	915	19	17	90.0

	Att	Cm	Pct	Yds	Yd/Att	TD	Int	1st	YAC	Big	Sk	Rtg
Inside 20	70	35	50.0	201	2.9	14	2	21	44	0	5	83.9
Inside 10	37	19	51.4	72	1.9	12	1	13	9	0	2	85.7
1st Down	220	146	66.4	1676	7.6	8	3	66	690	10	10	95.6
2nd Down	164	90	54.9	1034	6.3	9	5	52	482	9	8	79.7
3rd Down Overall	175	104	59.4	1222	7.0	7	6	79	443	9	8	79.7
3rd D 0-5 to Go	67	43	64.2	456	6.8	4	4	41	193	1	1	78.9
3rd D 6+ to Go	108	61	56.5	766	7.1	3	2	38	250	8	7	80.2
4th Down	8	5	62.5	38	4.8	2	0	4	13	0	1	113.5
Rec Behind Line	84	58	69.0	427	5.1	1	0	14	545	2	0	84.8
1-10 yds	283	197	69.6	1667	5.9	12	6	100	729	4	0	89.9
11-20 yds	121	69	57.0	1198	9.9	2	3	66	228	5	0	86.0
21-30 yds	47	17	36.2	525	11.2	2	2	17	119	13	0	100.6
31+	32	4	12.5	153	4.8	2	3	4	7	4	0	28.8
Left Sideline	130	72	55.4	788	6.1	3	3	37	296	6	0	69.0
Left Side	79	61	77.2	746	9.4	6	0	36	316	6	3	131.1
Middle	115	67	58.3	736	6.4	6	4	47	248	2	22	80.2
Right Side	110	66	60.0	759	6.9	7	4	40	382	7	1	86.9
Right Sideline	133	79	59.4	941	7.1	5	3	41	386	7	1	84.2
2 Wide Receivers	223	142	63.7	1645	7.4	10	5	71	704	13	7	91.5
3+ WR	310	181	58.4	2125	6.9	13	9	113	855	15	20	81.2
Attempts 1-10	160	97	60.6	1122	7.0	4	2	54	522	6	0	84.9
Attempts 11-20	160	85	53.1	1003	6.3	4	5	45	368	9	0	65.2
Attempts 21+	247	163	66.0	1845	7.5	18	6	102	738	13	0	102.4

1995 Incompletions

Type	Num	% of Inc	% of Att
Pass Dropped	26	11.7	4.6
Poor Throw	105	47.3	18.5
Pass Defensed	39	17.6	6.9
Pass Hit at Line	14	6.3	2.5
Other	38	17.1	6.7
Total	222	100.0	39.2

Game Logs (1-8)

Date	Opp	Result	Att	Cm	Pct	Yds	TD	Int	Lg	Sk	F-L
09/03	SF	L 22-24	38	23	60.5	266	2	1	37	1	1-1
09/10	@StL	L 13-17	40	24	60.0	247	1	1	24	5	1-0
09/17	Atl	L 43-29	43	29	67.4	370	3	0	70	3	0-0
09/24	@NYN	L 29-45	32	19	59.4	256	1	2	30	2	0-0
10/01	Phi	L 10-15	24	10	41.7	102	0	1	29	3	0-0
10/15	Mia	W 33-30	32	20	62.5	242	4	0	25	1	0-0
10/22	@Car	L 3-20	48	27	56.3	241	0	4	32	1	0-0
10/29	@SF	W 11-7	26	12	46.2	156	0	0	26	1	0-0

Game Logs (9-16)

Date	Opp	Result	Att	Cm	Pct	Yds	TD	Int	Lg	Sk	F-L
11/05	StL	W 19-10	25	17	68.0	189	0	0	20	3	1-1
11/12	Ind	W 17-14	37	27	73.0	228	2	1	32	1	0-0
11/19	@Min	L 24-43	27	16	67.6	335	3	0	48	2	0-0
11/26	Car	W 34-26	29	15	51.7	195	1	1	27	2	2-2
12/03	@NE	W 31-17	26	17	65.4	293	2	1	69	0	0-0
12/10	@Atl	L 14-19	47	31	66.0	287	2	1	39	0	0-0
12/16	GB	L 23-34	45	29	64.4	364	2	1	41	2	1-0
12/24	@NYA	W 12-0	38	20	52.6	199	1	0	22	0	0-0

Marshall Faulk
Indianapolis Colts — RB

1995 Rushing and Receiving Splits

	G	Rush	Yds	Avg	Lg	TD	1st	Stf	YdL	Rec	Yds	Avg	TD		Rush	Yds	Avg	Lg	TD	1st	Stf	YdL	Rec	Yds	Avg	TD
Total	16	289	1078	3.7	40	11	68	43	94	56	475	8.5	3	Inside 20	50	92	1.8	13	9	13	13	27	6	54	9.0	3
vs. Playoff	6	113	380	3.4	40	2	24	14	25	18	151	8.4	2	Inside 10	28	40	1.4	9	7	10	8	15	3	8	2.7	1
vs. Non-playoff	10	176	698	4.0	33	8	44	29	69	38	324	8.5	1	1st Down	154	545	3.5	33	3	13	26	53	26	226	8.7	3
vs. Own Division	8	143	497	3.5	40	3	32	18	33	33	257	7.8	3	2nd Down	93	393	4.2	40	5	32	11	31	21	127	6.0	0
Home	8	140	566	4.0	40	5	33	17	37	25	211	8.4	1	3rd Down Overall	38	138	3.6	32	3	21	5	8	8	88	11.0	0
Away	8	149	512	3.4	30	6	35	26	57	31	264	8.5	2	3rd D 0-2 to Go	27	89	3.3	32	3	18	3	3	1	1	1.0	0
Games 1-8	8	139	528	3.8	33	6	31	24	52	27	249	9.2	2	3rd D 3-7 to Go	6	17	2.8	11	0	3	2	5	2	24	12.0	0
Games 9-16	8	150	550	3.7	40	5	37	19	42	29	226	7.8	1	3rd D 8+ to Go	5	32	6.4	19	0	0	0	0	5	63	12.6	0
September	3	55	177	3.2	18	1	14	8	14	13	122	9.4	2	4th Down	4	2	0.5	3	0	2	1	2	1	34	34.0	0
October	5	84	351	4.2	33	5	17	16	38	14	127	9.1	0	Left Sideline	10	48	4.8	30	1	3	2	4	12	153	12.8	1
November	4	88	376	4.3	40	3	22	7	13	21	166	7.9	1	Left Side	78	313	4.0	40	2	22	13	27	11	71	6.5	0
December	4	62	174	2.8	19	2	15	12	29	8	60	7.5	0	Middle	120	394	3.3	33	4	20	18	38	9	64	7.1	1
Grass	5	96	286	3.0	19	4	23	19	46	18	162	9.0	0	Right Side	57	193	3.4	17	3	17	10	25	12	101	8.4	1
Turf	11	193	792	4.1	40	7	45	24	48	38	313	8.2	3	Right Sideline	24	130	5.4	33	1	6	0	0	12	86	7.2	0
Indoor	9	157	664	4.2	40	6	37	17	37	28	232	8.3	1	Shotgun	14	66	4.7	14	0	4	1	1	16	165	10.3	0
Outdoor	7	132	414	3.1	19	5	31	26	57	28	243	8.7	2	2 Wide Receivers	158	521	3.3	33	2	26	22	53	25	200	8.0	2
1st Half	-	160	606	3.8	33	8	43	22	49	28	237	8.5	2	3 Wide Receivers	29	132	4.6	18	0	7	5	11	17	125	7.4	1
2nd Half/OT	-	129	472	3.7	40	3	25	21	45	28	238	8.5	1	4+ Wide Receivers	11	43	3.9	19	0	2	3	3	14	150	10.7	0
Last 2 Min. Half	-	14	75	5.4	14	1	5	1	2	7	77	11.0	0	Carries 1-5	80	303	3.8	33	2	18	10	26	0	0	-	0
4th qtr. +/-7 pts	-	23	87	3.8	8	0	3	0	0	12	88	7.3	1	Carries 6-10	75	266	3.5	33	4	19	11	22	0	0	-	0
Winning	-	93	329	3.5	40	3	21	17	34	13	84	6.5	1	Carries 11-15	74	273	3.7	30	5	20	15	33	0	0	-	0
Tied	-	77	269	3.5	33	2	14	8	19	12	111	9.3	1	Carries 16-20	46	186	4.0	40	0	8	5	10	0	0	-	0
Trailing	-	119	480	4.0	33	6	33	18	41	31	280	9.0	1	Carries 21+	14	50	3.6	7	0	3	2	3	0	0	-	0

1995 Incompletions

Type	Num	%of Inc	% Att
Pass Dropped	4	22.2	5.4
Poor Throw	6	33.3	8.1
Pass Defensed	0	0.0	0.0
Pass Hit at Line	0	0.0	0.0
Other	8	44.4	10.8
Total	18	100.0	24.3

Game Logs (1-8)

Date	Opp	Result	Rush	Yds	Rec	Yds	Trgt	F-L	TD
09/03	Cin	L 21-24	19	49	3	41	3	1-0	0
09/10	@NYA	W 27-24	21	81	8	58	11	1-1	1
09/17	@Buf	L 14-20	15	47	2	23	4	0-0	2
10/01	StL	W 21-18	19	117	5	45	7	1-0	3
10/08	@Mia	W 27-24	16	42	2	17	2	1-1	0
10/15	SF	W 18-17	20	61	1	6	3	0-1	1
10/22	@Oak	L 17-30	14	41	5	58	7	2-1	2
10/29	NYA	W 17-10	15	30	1	1	2	0-0	1

Game Logs (9-16)

Date	Opp	Result	Rush	Yds	Rec	Yds	Trgt	F-L	TD
11/05	Buf	L 10-16	25	87	5	36	7	1-1	1
11/12	@NO	L 14-17	17	98	3	21	4	1-1	1
11/19	@NE	W 24-10	24	96	8	71	9	0-0	1
11/26	Mia	W 36-28	22	95	5	38	5	0-0	1
12/03	@Car	L 10-13	20	53	2	12	4	0-0	1
12/10	@Jac	W 41-31	22	54	1	4	1	0-0	1
12/17	SD	L 24-27	15	48	3	31	3	0-0	1
12/23	NE	W 10-7	5	19	2	13	2	0-0	0

Brett Favre
Green Bay Packers — QB

1995 Passing Splits

	G	Att	Cm	Pct	Yds	Yd/Att	TD	Int	1st	YAC	Big	Sk	Rtg		Att	Cm	Pct	Yds	Yd/Att	TD	Int	1st	YAC	Big	Sk	Rtg
Total	16	570	359	63.0	4413	7.7	38	13	227	2134	36	33	99.5	Inside 20	68	45	66.2	400	5.9	31	3	35	143	0	3	102.9
vs. Playoff	4	150	93	62.0	1242	8.3	6	4	62	670	12	5	90.5	Inside 10	28	16	57.1	84	3.0	15	2	15	24	0	2	72.0
vs. Non-playoff	12	420	266	63.3	3171	7.6	32	9	165	1464	24	28	102.8	1st Down	213	137	64.3	1708	8.0	19	3	77	874	19	10	113.0
vs. Own Division	8	290	177	61.0	2318	8.0	19	7	116	1142	18	16	98.0	2nd Down	200	126	63.0	1377	6.9	8	7	73	673	6	12	82.0
Home	8	285	183	64.2	2320	8.1	23	4	120	1042	21	20	110.6	3rd Down Overall	155	95	61.3	1305	8.4	11	3	76	580	11	11	103.8
Away	8	285	176	61.8	2093	7.3	15	9	107	1092	15	13	88.5	3rd D 0-5 to Go	59	40	67.8	526	8.9	7	0	40	241	5	6	135.3
Games 1-8	8	304	176	57.9	2190	7.2	17	9	113	1050	16	18	86.7	3rd D 6+ to Go	96	55	57.3	779	8.1	4	3	36	339	6	5	84.5
Games 9-16	8	266	183	68.8	2223	8.4	21	4	114	1084	20	15	114.3	4th Down	2	1	50.0	3	11.5	0	0	1	7	0	0	91.7
September	4	143	84	58.7	954	6.7	9	5	51	396	5	12	85.2	Rec Behind Line	84	57	67.9	430	5.1	4	1	24	578	2	1	90.9
October	4	161	92	57.1	1236	7.7	8	4	62	654	11	6	87.9	1-10 yds	319	224	70.2	2209	6.9	17	6	126	1135	6	0	99.4
November	4	115	81	70.4	990	8.6	11	2	50	420	9	10	121.3	11-20 yds	103	58	56.3	1068	10.4	12	3	57	246	9	0	118.9
December	4	151	102	67.5	1233	8.2	10	2	64	664	11	5	109.0	21-30 yds	50	17	34.0	577	11.5	3	2	17	146	16	0	81.8
Grass	12	426	274	64.3	3329	7.8	32	7	172	1556	27	26	106.4	31+	14	3	21.4	129	9.2	2	1	3	29	3	0	75.3
Turf	4	144	85	59.0	1084	7.5	6	6	55	578	9	7	79.2	Left Sideline	86	46	53.5	662	7.7	6	1	33	272	9	1	97.1
Indoor	3	103	64	62.1	789	7.7	5	5	41	439	5	7	90.3	Left Side	101	66	65.3	826	8.2	6	3	44	530	6	4	98.0
Outdoor	13	467	295	63.2	3624	7.8	33	8	186	1695	31	26	103.5	Middle	97	54	55.7	631	6.5	5	3	31	281	4	23	79.9
1st Half	-	318	206	64.8	2593	8.2	24	8	131	1223	19	21	104.7	Right Side	149	110	73.8	1304	8.8	14	5	73	692	10	2	117.4
2nd Half/OT	-	252	153	60.7	1820	7.2	14	5	96	911	17	12	93.0	Right Sideline	137	83	60.6	990	7.2	7	1	46	359	8	3	96.7
Last 2 Min. Half	-	55	28	50.9	376	6.8	4	0	17	134	4	2	97.2	2 Wide Receivers	299	190	63.5	2240	7.5	20	9	112	1189	15	13	96.0
4th qtr. +/-7 pts	-	49	34	69.4	377	7.7	4	1	21	201	3	2	110.7	3+ WR	262	161	61.5	2114	8.1	13	4	107	923	21	18	97.1
Winning	-	221	145	65.6	1884	8.5	16	2	94	954	18	17	112.6	Attempts 1-10	160	109	68.1	1273	8.0	11	6	69	605	9	0	99.3
Tied	-	187	120	64.2	1353	7.2	12	6	71	563	8	9	81.7	Attempts 11-20	160	97	60.6	1345	8.4	11	2	63	670	11	0	105.3
Trailing	-	162	94	58.0	1176	7.3	10	5	62	617	10	3	88.4	Attempts 21+	250	153	61.2	1795	7.2	16	5	95	859	16	0	96.0

1995 Incompletions

Type	Num	% of Inc	% of Att
Pass Dropped	34	16.1	6.0
Poor Throw	97	46.0	17.0
Pass Defensed	31	14.7	5.4
Pass Hit at Line	8	3.8	1.4
Other	41	19.4	7.2
Total	211	100.0	37.0

Game Logs (1-8)

Date	Opp	Result	Att	Cm	Pct	Yds	TD	Int	Lg	Sk	F-L
09/03	StL	L 14-17	51	29	56.9	299	2	3	29	4	0-0
09/11	@Chi	W 27-24	37	21	56.8	312	3	1	99	2	0-0
09/17	NYN	W 14-6	25	14	56.0	141	2	0	19	4	1-0
09/24	@Jac	W 24-14	30	20	66.7	202	2	1	29	2	0-0
10/08	@Dal	L 24-34	41	21	51.2	295	1	1	30	0	0-0
10/15	Det	W 30-21	34	23	67.6	342	2	0	35	2	0-0
10/22	Min	W 38-21	43	22	51.2	295	4	0	32	3	1-0
10/29	@Det	L 16-24	43	26	60.5	304	1	3	77	1	1-1

Game Logs (9-16)

Date	Opp	Result	Att	Cm	Pct	Yds	TD	Int	Lg	Sk	F-L
11/05	@Min	L 24-27	30	17	56.7	177	0	2	21	4	1-1
11/12	Chi	W 35-28	33	25	75.8	336	5	0	44	3	1-0
11/19	@Cle	W 31-20	28	23	82.1	210	3	0	27	2	1-1
11/26	TB	W 35-13	24	16	66.7	267	3	0	54	1	1-0
12/03	Cin	W 24-10	43	31	72.1	339	1	3	29	1	0-0
12/10	@TB	L 10-13	46	27	58.7	285	1	1	35	0	0-0
12/16	@NO	W 34-23	30	21	70.0	308	4	0	40	2	0-0
12/24	Pit	W 24-19	32	23	71.9	301	2	0	28	2	1-1

Derrick Fenner

1995 Receiving Splits

	G	Rec	Yds	Avg	TD	Lg	Big	YAC	Trgt	Y@C	1st	1st%		Rec	Yds	Avg	TD	Lg	Big	YAC	Trgt	Y@C	1st	1st%
Total	16	35	252	7.2	3	23	0	196	45	1.6	16	45.7	Inside 20	6	45	7.5	3	12	0	22	7	3.8	4	66.7
vs. Playoff	8	15	135	9.0	1	23	0	78	21	3.8	9	60.0	Inside 10	3	24	8.0	3	9	0	8	3	5.3	3	100.0
vs. Non-playoff	8	20	117	5.9	2	16	0	118	24	-0.1	7	35.0	1st Down	13	108	8.3	1	23	0	94	19	1.1	6	46.2
vs. Own Division	8	18	118	6.6	1	15	0	79	23	2.2	9	50.0	2nd Down	10	72	7.2	1	16	0	44	13	2.8	3	30.0
Home	8	19	136	7.2	2	23	0	90	24	2.4	8	42.1	3rd Down Overall	12	72	6.0	1	18	0	58	13	1.2	7	58.3
Away	8	16	116	7.3	1	16	0	106	21	0.6	8	50.0	3rd D 0-2 to Go	3	32	10.7	0	18	0	12	3	6.7	3	100.0
Games 1-8	8	18	157	8.7	2	23	0	95	25	3.4	10	55.6	3rd D 3-7 to Go	7	36	5.1	1	10	0	29	8	1.0	4	57.1
Games 9-16	8	17	95	5.6	1	15	0	101	20	-0.4	6	35.3	3rd D 8+ to Go	2	4	2.0	0	4	0	17	2	-6.5	0	0.0
September	4	7	49	7.0	2	12	0	28	9	3.0	4	57.1	4th Down	0	0	-	0	0	0	0	0	-	0	-
October	4	11	108	9.8	0	23	0	67	16	3.7	6	54.5	Rec Behind Line	13	58	4.5	0	15	0	109	15	-3.9	3	23.1
November	4	5	26	5.2	0	15	0	46	7	-4.0	1	20.0	1-10 yds	22	194	8.8	3	23	0	87	29	4.9	13	59.1
December	4	12	69	5.8	1	12	0	55	13	1.2	5	41.7	11-20 yds	0	0	-	0	0	0	0	1	-	0	-
Grass	12	30	225	7.5	3	23	0	159	39	2.2	15	50.0	21-30 yds	0	0	-	0	0	0	0	0	-	0	-
Turf	4	5	27	5.4	0	16	0	37	6	-2.0	1	20.0	31+	0	0	-	0	0	0	0	0	-	0	-
Indoor	1	0	0	-	0	0	0	0	0	-	0	-	Left Sideline	2	14	7.0	0	12	0	14	3	0.0	1	50.0
Outdoor	15	35	252	7.2	3	23	0	196	45	1.6	16	45.7	Left Side	3	25	8.3	1	10	0	14	3	3.7	2	66.7
1st Half	-	22	181	8.2	1	23	0	140	29	1.9	11	50.0	Middle	2	20	10.0	1	12	0	4	3	8.0	2	100.0
2nd Half/OT	-	13	71	5.5	2	18	0	56	16	1.2	5	38.5	Right Side	12	78	6.5	0	23	0	72	12	0.5	4	33.3
Last 2 Min. Half	-	2	14	7.0	1	9	0	8	2	3.0	1	50.0	Right Sideline	16	115	7.2	1	18	0	92	24	1.4	7	43.8
4th qtr. +/-7 pts	-	1	8	8.0	1	8	0	0	2	8.0	1	100.0	Shotgun	0	0	-	0	0	0	0	0	-	0	-
Winning	-	12	64	5.3	2	18	0	53	17	0.9	4	33.3	2 Wide Receivers	12	93	7.8	2	23	0	81	16	1.0	6	50.0
Tied	-	10	78	7.8	0	16	0	63	13	1.5	4	40.0	3 Wide Receivers	20	115	5.8	1	12	0	97	25	0.9	7	35.0
Trailing	-	13	110	8.5	1	23	0	80	15	2.3	8	61.5	4+ Wide Receivers	1	16	16.0	0	16	0	6	1	10.0	1	100.0

1995 Incompletions

Type	Num	%of Inc	%of Att
Pass Dropped	4	40.0	8.9
Poor Throw	3	30.0	6.7
Pass Defensed	1	10.0	2.2
Pass Hit at Line	1	10.0	2.2
Other	1	10.0	2.2
Total	10	100.0	22.2

Game Logs (1-8)

Date	Opp	Result	Rush	Yds	Rec	Yds	Trgt	F-L	TD
09/03	SD	W 17-7	8	13	1	5	1	1-0	0
09/10	@Was	W 20-8	5	11	4	29	5	0-0	1
09/17	@KC	L 17-23	2	8	1	8	2	0-0	0
09/24	Phi	W 48-17	0	0	1	7	1	0-0	0
10/01	@NYA	W 47-10	3	10	1	16	2	0-0	0
10/08	Sea	W 34-14	2	7	1	4	3	0-0	0
10/16	@Den	L 0-27	2	3	5	37	5	0-0	0
10/22	Ind	W 30-17	2	7	5	16	5	0-0	0

Game Logs (9-16)

Date	Opp	Result	Rush	Yds	Rec	Yds	Trgt	F-L	TD
11/05	@Cin	W 20-17	1	3	3	7	3	1-0	0
11/12	@NYN	W 17-13	3	12	1	4	1	0-0	0
11/19	Dal	L 21-34	2	8	0	0	0	0-0	0
11/27	@SD	L 6-12	0	0	1	15	3	0-0	0
12/03	KC	L 23-29	2	4	4	29	4	0-0	0
12/10	Pit	L 10-29	1	1	3	20	4	0-0	0
12/17	@Sea	L 10-44	5	22	0	0	0	0-0	0
12/24	Den	L 28-31	1	1	5	20	5	0-0	0

William Floyd

1995 Receiving Splits

	G	Rec	Yds	Avg	TD	Lg	Big	YAC	Trgt	Y@C	1st	1st%		Rec	Yds	Avg	TD	Lg	Big	YAC	Trgt	Y@C	1st	1st%
Total	8	47	348	7.4	1	23	0	329	62	0.4	19	40.4	Inside 20	4	20	5.0	1	8	0	15	9	1.3	2	50.0
vs. Playoff	3	18	133	7.4	0	17	0	141	29	-0.4	8	44.4	Inside 10	1	4	4.0	1	4	0	2	6	2.0	1	100.0
vs. Non-playoff	5	29	215	7.4	1	23	0	188	33	0.9	11	37.9	1st Down	22	160	7.3	1	21	0	155	29	0.2	7	31.8
vs. Own Division	4	22	203	9.2	1	23	0	177	27	1.2	11	50.0	2nd Down	18	131	7.3	0	23	0	127	24	0.2	8	44.4
Home	4	23	154	6.7	0	16	0	153	31	0.0	10	43.5	3rd Down Overall	7	57	8.1	0	16	0	47	8	1.4	4	57.1
Away	4	24	194	8.1	1	23	0	176	31	0.8	9	37.5	3rd D 0-2 to Go	1	16	16.0	0	16	0	6	2	10.0	1	100.0
Games 1-8	8	47	348	7.4	1	23	0	329	62	0.4	19	40.4	3rd D 3-7 to Go	2	14	7.0	0	10	0	20	2	-3.0	2	100.0
Games 9-16	0	0	0	-	0	0	0	0	0	-	0	-	3rd D 8+ to Go	4	27	6.8	0	11	0	21	4	1.5	1	25.0
September	4	24	205	8.5	1	23	0	194	35	0.5	12	50.0	4th Down	0	0	-	0	0	0	0	1	-	0	-
October	4	23	143	6.2	0	21	0	135	27	0.3	7	30.4	Rec Behind Line	24	146	6.1	0	17	0	210	29	-2.7	9	29.2
November	0	0	0	-	0	0	0	0	0	-	0	-	1-10 yds	21	158	7.5	1	16	0	100	31	2.8	10	47.6
December	0	0	0	-	0	0	0	0	0	-	0	-	11-20 yds	2	44	22.0	0	23	0	19	2	12.5	2	100.0
Grass	4	23	154	6.7	0	16	0	153	31	0.0	10	43.5	21-30 yds	0	0	-	0	0	0	0	0	-	0	-
Turf	4	24	194	8.1	1	23	0	176	31	0.8	9	37.5	31+	0	0	-	0	0	0	0	0	-	0	-
Indoor	3	19	147	7.7	1	23	0	148	26	-0.1	7	36.8	Left Sideline	8	34	4.3	0	11	0	49	12	-1.9	2	25.0
Outdoor	5	28	201	7.2	0	21	0	181	36	0.7	12	42.9	Left Side	13	134	10.3	0	23	0	128	19	0.5	6	46.2
1st Half	-	26	173	6.7	0	17	0	167	37	0.9	9	34.6	Middle	12	77	6.4	0	16	0	50	15	2.3	5	25.0
2nd Half/OT	-	21	175	8.3	1	23	0	162	25	0.6	10	47.6	Right Side	9	60	6.7	1	13	0	60	10	0.0	6	66.7
Last 2 Min. Half	-	13	90	6.9	0	13	0	88	15	0.2	5	38.5	Right Sideline	5	43	8.6	0	16	0	42	6	0.2	2	40.0
4th qtr. +/-7 pts	-	4	23	5.8	0	9	0	31	5	-2.0	1	25.0	Shotgun	0	0	-	0	0	0	0	0	-	0	-
Winning	-	29	221	7.6	1	23	0	185	35	1.2	13	44.8	2 Wide Receivers	31	243	7.8	1	23	0	202	40	1.3	13	41.9
Tied	-	7	48	6.9	0	16	0	55	11	-1.0	2	28.6	3 Wide Receivers	12	67	5.6	0	12	0	85	15	-1.5	4	33.3
Trailing	-	11	79	7.2	0	17	0	89	16	-0.9	4	36.4	4+ Wide Receivers	3	32	10.7	0	17	0	35	5	-1.0	2	66.7

1995 Incompletions

Type	Num	%of Inc	%of Att
Pass Dropped	6	40.0	9.7
Poor Throw	3	20.0	4.8
Pass Defensed	1	6.7	1.6
Pass Hit at Line	2	13.3	3.2
Other	3	20.0	4.8
Total	15	100.0	24.2

Game Logs (1-8)

Date	Opp	Result	Rush	Yds	Rec	Yds	Trgt	F-L	TD
09/03	@NO	W 24-22	10	48	6	66	6	1-1	0
09/10	Atl	W 41-10	9	38	5	52	9	0-0	0
09/17	NE	W 28-3	3	6	8	49	11	0-0	0
09/25	@Det	L 24-27	8	49	5	38	5	0-0	0
10/01	NYN	W 20-6	12	29	4	15	4	0-0	1
10/15	@Ind	L 17-18	5	8	8	43	11	0-0	0
10/22	@StL	W 44-10	9	49	5	47	5	0-0	1
10/29	NO	L 7-11	8	10	6	38	7	0-0	0

Game Logs (9-16)

Date	Opp	Result	Rush	Yds	Rec	Yds	Trgt	F-L	TD

Washington Redskins — QB

1995 Passing Splits

	G	Att	Cm	Pct	Yds	Yd/Att	TD	Int	1st	YAC	Big	Sk	Rtg		Att	Cm	Pct	Yds	Yd/Att	TD	Int	1st	YAC	Big	Sk	Rtg
Total	16	396	199	50.3	2751	6.9	13	13	129	1031	23	23	70.2	Inside 20	48	23	47.9	167	3.5	9	3	11	62	0	4	70.1
vs. Playoff	6	142	67	47.2	829	5.8	5	2	41	376	5	7	71.6	Inside 10	20	10	50.0	45	2.3	6	1	6	28	0	1	75.0
vs. Non-playoff	10	254	132	52.0	1922	7.6	8	11	88	655	18	16	69.4	1st Down	141	76	53.9	1144	8.1	5	4	47	411	13	5	80.8
vs. Own Division	8	157	81	51.6	1188	7.6	8	7	52	501	12	10	75.0	2nd Down	125	55	44.0	646	5.2	1	6	31	267	2	9	42.9
Home	8	212	109	51.4	1596	7.5	6	8	72	544	12	11	70.0	3rd Down Overall	127	66	52.0	952	7.5	7	3	49	350	8	8	85.2
Away	8	184	90	48.9	1155	6.3	7	5	57	487	11	12	70.4	3rd D 0-5 to Go	42	24	57.1	227	5.4	3	2	17	89	2	2	76.2
Games 1-8	8	252	137	54.4	1823	7.2	12	6	88	749	16	13	83.5	3rd D 6+ to Go	85	42	49.4	725	8.5	4	1	32	261	6	6	89.6
Games 9-16	8	144	62	43.1	928	6.4	1	7	41	282	7	10	46.9	4th Down	3	2	66.7	9	3.0	0	0	2	3	0	1	70.1
September	4	115	66	57.4	892	7.8	5	3	43	331	8	6	85.9	Rec Behind Line	60	33	55.0	266	4.4	1	2	11	362	0	0	58.1
October	5	181	93	51.4	1276	7.0	7	7	60	524	11	11	71.1	1-10 yds	170	93	54.7	811	4.8	5	5	48	381	1	0	65.1
November	3	66	25	37.9	340	5.2	1	2	17	112	2	3	47.5	11-20 yds	110	56	50.9	1028	9.3	5	3	53	132	8	0	87.2
December	4	34	15	44.1	243	7.1	0	1	9	64	2	3	56.4	21-30 yds	31	11	35.5	336	10.8	1	1	11	78	8	0	74.1
Grass	12	341	172	50.4	2441	7.2	11	11	114	891	21	19	71.3	31+	25	6	24.0	310	12.4	1	2	6	78	6	0	58.7
Turf	4	55	27	49.1	310	5.6	2	2	15	140	2	4	63.4	Left Sideline	78	40	51.3	652	8.4	2	1	29	160	6	0	82.9
Indoor	1	10	5	50.0	58	5.8	0	1	3	20	0	1	28.3	Left Side	76	34	44.7	418	5.5	1	3	15	229	3	2	50.2
Outdoor	15	386	194	50.3	2693	7.0	13	12	126	1011	23	22	71.3	Middle	86	47	54.7	614	7.1	3	4	29	218	5	16	69.6
1st Half	-	186	97	52.2	1367	7.3	6	7	65	504	12	10	71.2	Right Side	82	44	53.7	580	7.1	5	2	30	267	5	4	86.4
2nd Half/OT	-	210	102	48.6	1384	6.6	7	6	64	527	11	13	69.2	Right Sideline	74	34	45.9	487	6.6	2	3	26	157	4	1	59.9
Last 2 Min. Half	-	74	38	51.4	445	6.0	3	3	24	102	3	3	66.6	2 Wide Receivers	189	97	51.3	1326	7.0	5	3	62	575	10	10	76.3
4th qtr, +/-7 pts	-	44	23	52.3	257	5.8	2	0	14	97	1	3	85.1	3+ WR	193	97	50.3	1380	7.2	5	9	62	450	13	12	63.0
Winning	-	71	38	53.5	550	7.7	3	2	25	215	4	6	81.3	Attempts 1-10	130	68	52.3	886	6.8	3	7	42	367	7	0	59.3
Tied	-	107	47	43.9	675	6.3	2	4	30	218	7	4	55.6	Attempts 11-20	115	59	51.3	954	8.3	6	2	42	360	9	0	89.5
Trailing	-	218	114	52.3	1526	7.0	8	7	74	598	12	13	73.7	Attempts 21+	151	72	47.7	911	6.0	4	4	45	304	7	0	64.7

1995 Incompletions

Type	Num	% of Inc	% of Att
Pass Dropped	30	15.2	7.6
Poor Throw	94	47.7	23.7
Pass Defensed	32	16.2	8.1
Pass Hit at Line	10	5.1	2.5
Other	31	15.7	7.8
Total	197	100.0	49.7

Game Logs (1-8)

Date	Opp	Result	Att	Cm	Pct	Yds	TD	Int	Lg	Sk	F-L
09/03	Ari	W 27-7	15	9	60.0	157	2	0	73	0	1-0
09/10	Oak	L 8-20	34	20	58.8	272	0	1	42	2	2-0
09/17	@Den	L 31-38	26	16	61.5	233	3	1	45	1	0-0
09/24	@TB	L 6-14	40	21	52.5	230	1	1	29	3	0-0
10/01	Dal	W 27-23	24	13	54.2	192	2	1	41	1	0-0
10/08	@Phi	L 34-37	45	22	48.9	252	2	1	40	3	1-1
10/15	@Ari	L 20-24	29	15	51.7	242	2	1	46	2	2-0
10/22	Det	W 36-30	39	21	53.8	245	1	0	24	1	0-0

Game Logs (9-16)

Date	Opp	Result	Att	Cm	Pct	Yds	TD	Int	Lg	Sk	F-L
10/29	NYN	L 15-24	44	22	50.0	345	0	4	45	4	0-0
11/05	@KC	L 3-24	31	14	32.4	140	0	0	30	2	0-0
11/19	Sea	L 20-27	32	14	43.8	200	1	2	47	1	0-0
11/26	Phi	L 7-14	0	0	-	0	0	0	0	0	0-0
12/03	Dal	W 24-17	0	0	-	0	0	0	0	0	0-0
12/10	@NYN	L 13-20	0	0	-	0	0	0	0	0	0-0
12/17	@StL	W 35-23	10	5	50.0	58	0	1	21	1	1-0
12/24	Car	W 20-17	24	10	41.7	185	0	0	59	2	0-0

John Friesz

Seattle Seahawks — QB

1995 Passing Splits

	G	Att	Cm	Pct	Yds	Yd/Att	TD	Int	1st	YAC	Big	Sk	Rtg		Att	Cm	Pct	Yds	Yd/Att	TD	Int	1st	YAC	Big	Sk	Rtg
Total	6	120	64	53.3	795	6.6	6	3	44	347	2	3	80.4	Inside 20	8	4	50.0	38	4.8	3	0	4	25	0	1	103.1
vs. Playoff	3	40	19	47.5	213	5.3	1	0	11	103	0	2	72.2	Inside 10	4	2	50.0	7	1.8	2	0	2	0	0	0	95.8
vs. Non-playoff	3	80	45	56.3	582	7.3	5	3	33	244	2	1	84.5	1st Down	53	32	60.4	404	7.6	2	1	20	175	2	0	88.9
vs. Own Division	5	88	47	53.4	590	6.7	4	1	33	240	2	2	84.9	2nd Down	31	16	51.6	166	5.4	2	1	10	57	0	1	75.5
Home	3	39	25	64.1	353	9.1	2	0	19	127	0	0	110.3	3rd Down Overall	34	14	41.2	197	5.8	1	1	12	101	0	2	58.1
Away	3	81	39	48.1	442	5.5	4	3	25	220	2	3	66.0	3rd D 0-5 to Go	10	5	50.0	68	6.8	1	0	5	37	0	2	105.4
Games 1-8	3	46	26	56.5	338	7.3	3	2	18	161	0	1	83.4	3rd D 6+ to Go	24	9	37.5	129	5.4	0	1	7	64	0	0	38.4
Games 9-16	3	74	38	51.4	457	6.2	3	1	26	186	2	2	78.5	4th Down	2	2	100.0	28	14.0	1	0	2	14	0	0	158.3
September	1	9	5	55.6	77	8.6	1	0	4	32	0	0	121.1	Rec Behind Line	13	6	46.2	57	4.4	1	0	3	75	0	0	84.5
October	2	37	21	56.8	261	7.1	2	2	14	129	0	1	74.3	1-10 yds	70	45	64.3	492	7.0	4	1	30	234	0	0	99.2
November	0	0	0	-	0	-	0	0	0	0	0	0	-	11-20 yds	25	11	44.0	203	8.1	0	0	10	36	1	0	72.6
December	3	74	38	51.4	457	6.2	3	1	26	186	2	2	78.5	21-30 yds	7	0	0.0	0	0.0	0	1	0	0	0	0	0.0
Grass	3	81	39	48.1	442	5.5	4	3	25	220	0	3	66.0	31+	5	1	20.0	43	8.6	1	1	1	2	1	0	62.9
Turf	3	39	25	64.1	353	9.1	2	0	19	127	2	0	110.3	Left Sideline	21	8	38.1	103	4.9	0	0	6	16	0	0	54.3
Indoor	3	39	25	64.1	353	9.1	2	0	19	127	2	0	110.3	Left Side	24	14	58.3	175	7.3	2	1	9	89	0	0	91.5
Outdoor	3	81	39	48.1	442	5.5	4	3	25	220	0	3	66.0	Middle	23	13	56.5	143	6.2	1	0	10	71	0	3	89.6
1st Half	-	46	21	45.7	297	6.5	1	1	16	117	2	2	56.2	Right Side	24	13	54.2	150	6.3	1	2	9	96	0	0	52.4
2nd Half/OT	-	74	43	58.1	498	6.7	5	1	28	230	0	1	95.4	Right Sideline	28	16	57.1	224	8.0	2	0	10	75	2	0	106.8
Last 2 Min. Half	-	22	8	36.4	94	4.3	1	2	6	55	0	0	27.5	2 Wide Receivers	37	21	56.8	289	7.8	1	1	13	118	2	0	79.7
4th qtr, +/-7 pts	-	16	10	62.5	97	6.1	2	0	7	47	0	0	119.0	3+ WR	81	41	50.6	487	6.0	3	2	29	215	0	2	71.4
Winning	-	24	15	62.5	203	8.5	1	0	11	72	2	0	103.3	Attempts 1-10	54	27	50.0	410	7.6	2	1	22	146	2	0	80.0
Tied	-	12	7	58.3	81	6.8	0	1	4	27	0	0	44.1	Attempts 11-20	40	22	55.0	243	0.1	2	1	14	120	0	0	70.5
Trailing	-	84	42	50.0	511	6.1	5	2	29	248	0	3	79.0	Attempts 21+	26	15	57.7	142	5.5	2	1	8	81	0	0	82.5

1995 Incompletions

Type	Num	% of Inc	% of Att
Pass Dropped	8	14.3	6.7
Poor Throw	33	58.9	27.5
Pass Defensed	3	5.4	2.5
Pass Hit at Line	4	7.1	3.3
Other	8	14.3	6.7
Total	56	100.0	46.7

Game Logs (1-8)

Date	Opp	Result	Att	Cm	Pct	Yds	TD	Int	Lg	Sk	F-L
09/03	KC	L 10-34	9	5	55.6	77	1	0	23	0	0-0
09/10	@SD	L 10-14	-	-	-	-	-	-	-	-	-
09/17	Cin	W 24-21	-	-	-	-	-	-	-	-	-
10/01	Den	W 27-10	-	-	-	-	-	-	-	-	-
10/08	@Oak	L 14-34	-	-	-	-	-	-	-	-	-
10/15	@Buf	L 21-27	-	-	-	-	-	-	-	-	-
10/22	SD	L 25-35	5	4	80.0	56	0	0	20	0	0-0
10/29	@Ari	L 14-20	32	17	53.1	205	2	2	23	1	2-1

Game Logs (9-16)

Date	Opp	Result	Att	Cm	Pct	Yds	TD	Int	Lg	Sk	F-L
11/05	NYN	W 30-28	-	-	-	-	-	-	-	-	-
11/12	@Jac	W 47-30	-	-	-	-	-	-	-	-	-
11/19	@Was	W 24-21	-	-	-	-	-	-	-	-	-
11/26	NYA	L 10-16	-	-	-	-	-	-	-	-	-
12/03	Phi	W 26-14	-	-	-	-	-	-	-	-	-
12/10	@Den	W 31-27	23	12	52.2	157	2	1	20	0	0-0
12/17	Oak	W 44-10	25	16	64.0	220	1	0	43	0	0-0
12/24	@KC	L 3-26	26	10	38.5	80	0	0	15	2	0-0

Irving Fryar
Miami Dolphins — WR

1995 Receiving Splits

	G	Rec	Yds	Avg	TD	Lg	Big	YAC	Trgt	Y@C	1st	1st%
Total	16	62	910	14.7	8	67	3	240	109	10.8	46	74.2
vs. Playoff	9	34	431	12.7	3	24	0	84	59	10.2	23	67.6
vs. Non-playoff	7	28	479	17.1	5	67	3	156	50	11.5	23	82.1
vs. Own Division	8	28	472	16.9	5	67	3	158	53	11.2	20	71.4
Home	8	32	453	14.2	3	50	1	83	52	11.6	25	78.1
Away	8	30	457	15.2	5	67	2	157	57	10.0	21	70.0
Games 1-8	8	30	517	17.2	4	67	3	166	55	11.7	22	73.3
Games 9-16	8	32	393	12.3	4	24	0	74	54	10.0	24	75.0
September	3	12	258	21.5	4	67	3	104	22	12.8	10	83.3
October	5	18	259	14.4	0	22	0	62	33	10.9	12	66.7
November	4	12	139	11.6	2	23	0	36	20	8.6	9	75.0
December	4	20	254	12.7	2	24	0	38	34	10.8	15	75.0
Grass	10	39	623	16.0	6	67	3	172	67	11.6	31	79.5
Turf	6	23	287	12.5	2	22	0	68	42	9.5	15	65.2
Outdoor	3	48	742	15.5	6	67	3	191	89	11.5	35	72.9
Indoor	13	14	168	12.0	2	22	0	49	20	8.5	11	78.6
1st Half	-	39	551	14.1	5	67	2	169	70	9.8	27	69.2
2nd Half/OT	-	23	359	15.6	3	50	1	71	39	12.5	19	82.6
Last 2 Min. Half	-	10	132	13.2	1	23	0	33	19	9.9	6	60.0
4th qtr, +/-7 pts	-	9	145	16.1	1	21	0	30	13	12.8	9	100.0
Winning	-	23	394	17.1	5	67	3	128	39	11.6	18	78.3
Tied	-	12	157	13.1	0	23	0	33	30	10.3	8	66.7
Trailing	-	27	359	13.3	3	23	0	79	40	10.4	20	74.1

	Rec	Yds	Avg	TD	Lg	Big	YAC	Trgt	Y@C	1st	1st%
Inside 20	6	52	8.7	3	17	0	10	10	7.0	5	83.3
Inside 10	3	15	5.0	3	6	0	0	7	5.0	3	100.0
1st Down	24	418	17.4	4	67	2	122	43	12.3	18	75.0
2nd Down	16	215	13.4	1	24	0	52	36	10.2	13	81.3
3rd Down Overall	22	277	12.6	3	50	1	66	30	9.6	15	68.2
3rd D 0-2 to Go	1	11	11.0	0	11	0	3	1	8.0	1	100.0
3rd D 3-7 to Go	13	173	13.3	3	50	1	49	19	9.4	9	92.3
3rd D 8+ to Go	8	95	11.9	0	19	0	14	10	10.1	2	25.0
4th Down	0	0	-	0	0	0	0	0	-	0	-
Rec Behind Line	0	0	-	0	0	0	0	0	-	0	-
1-10 yds	33	325	9.8	4	23	0	126	47	6.0	21	63.6
11-20 yds	25	423	16.9	1	31	1	47	39	15.0	21	84.0
21-30 yds	4	162	40.5	3	67	2	67	14	23.8	4	100.0
31+	0	0	-	0	0	0	0	9	-	0	-
Left Sideline	16	287	17.9	5	67	2	104	31	11.4	13	81.3
Left Side	15	188	12.5	0	20	0	47	21	9.4	10	66.7
Middle	10	145	14.5	1	22	0	30	14	11.5	8	80.0
Right Side	9	124	13.8	1	21	0	24	12	11.1	6	66.7
Right Sideline	12	166	13.8	1	31	1	35	31	10.9	9	75.0
Shotgun	32	448	14.0	3	50	1	102	52	10.8	20	62.5
2 Wide Receivers	23	371	16.1	4	67	2	107	44	11.5	21	91.3
3 Wide Receivers	15	232	15.5	3	50	1	61	27	11.4	11	73.3
4+ Wide Receivers	24	307	12.8	1	23	0	72	38	9.8	14	58.3

1995 Incompletions

Type	Num	%of Inc	%of Att
Pass Dropped	8	17.0	7.3
Poor Throw	21	44.7	19.3
Pass Defensed	12	25.5	11.0
Pass Hit at Line	0	0.0	0.0
Other	6	12.8	5.5
Total	47	100.0	43.1

Game Logs (1-8)

Date	Opp	Result	Rec	Yds	Trgt	F-L	TD
09/03	NYA	W 52-14	5	110	10	0-0	2
09/10	@NE	W 20-3	3	113	7	0-0	2
09/18	Pit	W 23-10	4	35	5	0-0	0
10/01	@Cin	W 26-23	4	54	9	0-0	0
10/08	Ind	L 24-27	3	54	5	0-0	0
10/15	@NO	L 30-33	5	83	7	0-0	0
10/22	@NYA	L 16-17	2	20	5	0-0	0
10/29	Buf	W 23-6	4	48	7	0-0	0

Game Logs (9-16)

Date	Opp	Result	Rec	Yds	Trgt	F-L	TD
11/05	@SD	W 24-14	4	57	8	0-0	1
11/12	NE	L 17-34	4	48	5	0-0	0
11/20	SF	L 20-44	0	0	1	0-0	0
11/26	@Ind	L 28-36	4	34	6	0-0	0
12/03	Atl	W 21-20	6	78	10	0-0	1
12/11	KC	W 13-6	6	80	9	0-0	0
12/17	@Buf	L 20-23	3	45	8	0-0	0
12/24	@StL	W 41-22	5	51	7	0-0	1

Will Furrer
Houston Oilers — QB

1995 Passing Splits

	G	Att	Cm	Pct	Yds	Yd/Att	TD	Int	1st	YAC	Big	Sk	Rtg
Total	7	99	48	48.5	483	4.9	2	7	23	247	3	5	40.1
vs. Playoff	2	27	13	48.1	136	5.0	0	1	6	70	1	2	47.8
vs. Non-playoff	5	72	35	48.6	347	4.8	2	6	17	177	2	3	37.2
vs. Own Division	6	97	48	49.5	483	5.0	2	6	23	247	3	5	45.2
Home	3	64	34	53.1	364	5.7	2	4	17	187	2	1	54.4
Away	4	35	14	40.0	119	3.4	0	3	6	60	1	2	13.9
Games 1-8	4	57	30	52.6	327	5.7	1	5	14	168	2	1	39.1
Games 9-16	3	42	18	42.9	156	3.7	1	2	9	79	1	4	41.4
September	3	55	30	54.5	327	5.9	1	4	14	168	2	1	48.1
October	1	2	0	0.0	0	0.0	0	1	0	0	0	0	0.0
November	2	20	9	45.0	60	3.0	1	4	4	34	0	2	10.4
December	1	22	9	40.9	96	4.4	0	1	5	45	1	2	35.4
Grass	2	11	5	45.5	23	2.1	0	1	1	15	0	1	14.6
Turf	5	88	43	48.9	460	5.2	2	6	22	232	3	5	43.5
Indoor	4	66	34	51.5	364	5.5	2	5	17	187	2	4	46.5
Outdoor	3	33	14	42.4	119	3.6	0	2	6	60	1	2	27.2
1st Half	-	25	12	48.0	163	6.5	0	4	9	101	1	1	29.7
2nd Half/OT	-	74	36	48.6	320	4.3	2	3	14	146	2	4	52.8
Last 2 Min. Half	-	9	3	33.3	32	3.6	0	2	2	14	0	1	5.1
4th qtr, +/-7 pts	-	20	7	35.0	47	2.4	1	0	3	20	0	0	60.4
Winning	-	11	5	45.5	23	2.1	0	1	1	15	0	1	29.1
Tied	-	9	3	33.3	68	7.6	0	3	3	33	1	1	21.8
Trailing	-	79	40	50.6	392	5.0	2	3	19	199	2	4	57.6

	Att	Cm	Pct	Yds	Yd/Att	TD	Int	1st	YAC	Big	Sk	Rtg
Inside 20	11	6	54.5	27	2.5	2	1	3	20	0	0	61.7
Inside 10	6	4	66.7	15	2.5	2	0	2	9	0	0	109.7
1st Down	34	15	44.1	168	4.9	0	1	6	101	1	1	47.2
2nd Down	33	17	51.5	193	5.8	0	4	6	73	2	3	29.8
3rd Down Overall	29	14	48.3	109	3.8	2	2	10	67	0	1	52.2
3rd D 0-5 to Go	11	7	63.6	46	4.2	2	1	7	15	0	0	74.2
3rd D 6+ to Go	18	7	38.9	63	3.5	0	1	3	52	0	1	25.9
4th Down	3	2	66.7	13	4.3	0	0	1	6	0	0	75.7
Rec Behind Line	16	11	68.8	79	4.9	0	0	3	108	0	0	79.9
1-10 yds	55	30	54.5	230	4.2	2	0	13	110	0	0	77.1
11-20 yds	16	5	31.3	84	5.3	0	2	5	16	1	0	10.4
21-30 yds	5	0	0.0	0	0.0	0	3	0	0	0	0	0.0
31+	7	2	28.6	90	12.9	0	2	2	13	2	0	39.6
Left Sideline	20	10	50.0	99	5.0	1	2	5	28	1	3	41.5
Left Side	24	11	45.8	85	3.5	0	2	6	29	0	0	20.3
Middle	24	11	45.8	118	4.9	1	2	5	100	1	2	39.9
Right Side	14	6	42.9	84	6.0	0	0	3	22	1	0	62.8
Right Sideline	17	10	58.8	97	5.7	0	1	4	68	0	0	50.4
2 Wide Receivers	16	10	62.5	94	5.9	0	2	4	70	0	1	39.1
3+ WR	81	37	45.7	381	4.7	2	5	18	173	3	4	42.3
Attempts 1-10	48	24	50.0	231	4.8	0	4	11	113	1	0	29.1
Attempts 11-20	28	11	39.3	115	4.1	1	1	7	90	1	0	49.0
Attempts 21+	23	13	56.5	137	6.0	1	2	5	44	1	0	52.3

1995 Incompletions

Type	Num	% of Inc	% of Att
Pass Dropped	12	23.5	12.1
Poor Throw	20	39.2	20.2
Pass Defensed	9	17.6	9.1
Pass Hit at Line	4	7.8	4.0
Other	6	11.8	6.1
Total	51	100.0	51.5

Game Logs (1-8)

Date	Opp	Result	Att	Cm	Pct	Yds	TD	Int	Lg	Sk	F-L
09/03	@Jac	W 10-3	9	4	44.4	19	0	0	10	0	0-0
09/10	Pit	L 17-34	5	4	80.0	40	0	0	24	0	0-0
09/17	Cle	L 7-14	41	22	53.7	268	1	4	48	1	2-0
09/24	@Cin	W 38-28	-	-	-	-	-	-	-	-	-
10/01	Jac	L 16-17	-	-	-	-	-	-	-	-	-
10/08	@Min	L 17-23	2	0	0.0	0	0	1	0	0	0-0
10/22	@Chi	L 32-35	-	-	-	-	-	-	-	-	-
10/29	TB	W 19-7	-	-	-	-	-	-	-	-	-

Game Logs (9-16)

Date	Opp	Result	Att	Cm	Pct	Yds	TD	Int	Lg	Sk	F-L
11/05	@Cle	W 37-10	2	1	50.0	4	0	1	4	0	0-0
11/12	Cin	L 25-32	18	8	44.4	56	1	0	11	2	1-0
11/19	@KC	L 13-20	-	-	-	-	-	-	-	-	-
11/26	Den	W 42-33	-	-	-	-	-	-	-	-	-
12/03	@Pit	L 7-21	22	9	40.9	96	0	1	29	2	0-0
12/10	Det	L 17-24	-	-	-	-	-	-	-	-	-
12/17	NYA	W 23-6	-	-	-	-	-	-	-	-	-
12/24	@Buf	L 28-17	-	-	-	-	-	-	-	-	-

1995 Receiving Splits

	G	Rec	Yds	Avg	TD	Lg	Big	YAC	Trgt	Y@C	1st	1st%		Rec	Yds	Avg	TD	Lg	Big	YAC	Trgt	Y@C	1st	1st%
Total	16	67	1039	15.5	7	59	11	246	133	11.8	46	68.7	Inside 20	3	17	5.7	1	7	0	-2	7	6.3	2	66.7
vs. Playoff	6	26	330	12.7	1	54	2	97	57	9.0	14	53.8	Inside 10	1	5	5.0	1	5	0	0	2	5.0	1	100.0
vs. Non-playoff	10	41	709	17.3	6	59	9	149	76	13.7	32	78.0	1st Down	28	510	18.2	4	59	6	124	55	13.8	16	57.1
vs. Own Division	8	31	493	15.9	3	51	6	92	60	12.9	23	74.2	2nd Down	25	340	13.6	2	35	4	75	42	10.6	17	68.0
Home	8	35	486	13.9	1	51	5	92	62	11.3	24	68.6	3rd Down Overall	12	153	12.8	1	38	1	40	33	9.4	11	91.7
Away	8	32	553	17.3	6	59	6	154	71	12.5	22	68.8	3rd D 0-2 to Go	1	8	8.0	0	8	0	0	1	8.0	1	100.0
Games 1-8	8	30	501	16.7	2	54	6	99	62	13.4	23	76.7	3rd D 3-7 to Go	7	108	15.4	1	38	1	35	11	10.4	7	100.0
Games 9-16	8	37	538	14.5	5	59	5	147	71	10.6	23	62.2	3rd D 8+ to Go	4	37	9.3	0	11	0	5	21	8.0	3	75.0
September	3	13	173	13.3	0	31	2	23	26	11.5	9	69.2	4th Down	2	36	18.0	0	18	0	7	3	14.5	2	100.0
October	5	17	328	19.3	2	54	4	76	36	14.8	14	82.4	Rec Behind Line	0	0	-	0	0	0	0	2	-	0	-
November	4	16	263	16.4	3	59	3	75	38	11.8	11	68.8	1-10 yds	44	409	9.3	1	21	0	102	55	7.0	25	56.8
December	4	21	275	13.1	2	43	2	72	33	9.7	12	57.1	11-20 yds	14	295	21.1	1	54	3	85	35	15.0	13	92.9
Grass	7	27	451	16.7	5	59	5	112	59	12.6	18	66.7	21-30 yds	6	182	30.3	0	38	5	34	20	24.7	5	83.3
Turf	9	40	588	14.7	2	54	6	134	74	11.4	28	70.0	31+	3	153	51.0	2	59	3	25	21	42.7	3	100.0
Indoor	8	35	486	13.9	1	51	5	92	62	11.3	24	68.6	Left Sideline	12	182	15.2	1	35	2	34	23	12.3	9	75.0
Outdoor	8	32	553	17.3	6	59	6	154	71	12.5	22	68.8	Left Side	9	135	15.0	0	27	1	42	24	10.3	8	88.9
1st Half	-	38	633	16.7	3	59	8	153	78	12.6	30	68.4	Middle	5	94	18.8	2	54	1	42	14	10.4	4	80.0
2nd Half/OT	-	29	406	14.0	4	54	3	93	55	10.8	20	69.0	Right Side	9	108	12.0	0	18	0	25	20	9.2	5	55.6
Last 2 Min. Half	-	9	136	15.1	0	27	2	35	20	11.2	6	66.7	Right Sideline	32	520	16.3	4	59	7	103	52	13.0	20	62.5
4th qtr, +/-7 pts	-	6	78	13.0	0	28	1	9	13	11.5	5	83.3	Shotgun	3	62	20.7	0	27	2	18	7	14.7	3	100.0
Winning	-	14	208	14.9	1	43	3	48	28	11.4	11	78.6	2 Wide Receivers	23	317	13.8	1	43	3	57	43	11.3	14	60.9
Tied	-	20	335	16.8	2	59	3	83	35	12.6	12	60.0	3 Wide Receivers	32	507	15.8	4	54	5	126	66	11.9	27	84.4
Trailing	-	33	496	15.0	4	54	5	115	70	11.5	23	69.7	4+ Wide Receivers	12	215	17.9	2	59	3	63	23	12.7	5	41.7

1995 Incompletions

Type	Num	%of Inc	%of Att
Pass Dropped	4	6.1	3.0
Poor Throw	46	69.7	34.6
Pass Defensed	10	15.2	7.5
Pass Hit at Line	1	1.5	0.8
Other	5	7.6	3.8
Total	66	100.0	49.6

Game Logs (1-8)

Date	Opp	Result	Rush	Yds	Rec	Yds	Trgt	F-L	TD
09/03	KC	L 10-34	0	0	4	69	10	1-1	0
09/10	@SD	L 10-14	0	0	3	26	8	0-0	0
09/17	Cin	W 24-21	0	0	6	78	8	0-0	0
10/01	Den	W 27-10	3	54	4	89	6	0-0	0
10/08	@Oak	L 14-34	0	0	4	87	8	0-0	1
10/15	@Buf	L 21-27	2	9	5	102	12	0-0	1
10/22	SD	L 25-35	0	0	2	15	5	0-0	0
10/29	@Ari	L 14-20	0	0	2	35	5	0-0	0

Game Logs (9-16)

Date	Opp	Result	Rush	Yds	Rec	Yds	Trgt	F-L	TD
11/05	NYN	W 30-28	1	8	4	35	9	0-0	1
11/12	@Jac	W 47-30	1	86	5	114	10	0-0	3
11/19	@Was	W 27-20	1	-16	4	90	11	0-0	1
11/26	NYA	L 10-16	2	8	3	24	8	0-0	0
12/03	Phi	W 26-14	1	5	7	68	10	0-0	0
12/10	@Den	W 31-27	0	0	4	49	5	0-0	0
12/17	Oak	W 44-10	0	0	5	108	6	0-0	1
12/24	@KC	L 3-26	0	0	5	50	12	0-0	0

Charlie Garner   Philadelphia Eagles — RB

1995 Rushing and Receiving Splits

	G	Rush	Yds	Avg	Lg	TD	1st	Stf	YdL	Rec	Yds	Avg	TD		Rush	Yds	Avg	Lg	TD	1st	Stf	YdL	Rec	Yds	Avg	TD
Total	15	108	588	5.4	55	6	25	10	26	10	61	6.1	0	Inside 20	21	84	4.0	17	5	7	4	10	0	0	-	0
vs. Playoff	3	17	66	3.9	13	0	2	0	0	2	8	4.0	0	Inside 10	9	26	2.9	8	4	4	2	3	0	0	-	0
vs. Non-playoff	12	91	522	5.7	55	6	23	10	26	8	53	6.6	0	1st Down	71	426	6.0	36	4	15	4	8	2	2	1.0	0
vs. Own Division	8	54	323	6.0	55	4	10	4	11	6	40	6.7	0	2nd Down	33	147	4.5	55	1	7	6	18	5	43	8.6	0
Home	8	55	362	6.6	55	3	13	2	8	5	23	4.6	0	3rd Down Overall	3	14	4.7	8	0	2	0	3	3	16	5.3	0
Away	7	53	226	4.3	28	3	12	8	18	5	38	7.6	0	3rd D 0-2 to Go	2	6	3.0	3	0	2	0	1	1	5	5.0	0
Games 1-8	8	64	389	6.1	55	5	19	7	20	3	35	11.7	0	3rd D 3-7 to Go	0	0	-	0	0	0	0	0	1	9	9.0	0
Games 9-16	7	44	199	4.5	16	1	6	3	6	7	26	3.7	0	3rd D 8+ to Go	1	8	8.0	8	0	0	0	0	1	2	2.0	0
September	4	30	156	5.2	28	2	10	3	7	1	4	4.0	0	4th Down	1	1	1.0	1	1	1	0	0	0	0	-	0
October	4	34	233	6.9	55	3	9	4	13	2	31	15.5	0	Left Sideline	7	111	15.9	55	1	3	0	0	2	4	2.0	0
November	4	38	177	4.7	16	0	4	2	4	7	26	3.7	0	Left Side	24	121	5.0	17	1	7	2	7	2	33	16.5	0
December	3	6	22	3.7	11	1	2	1	2	0	0	-	0	Middle	67	289	4.3	36	3	12	8	19	1	2	2.0	0
Grass	4	30	156	5.2	28	3	9	5	12	3	5	1.7	0	Right Side	8	54	6.8	28	1	3	0	0	2	13	6.5	0
Turf	11	78	432	5.5	55	3	16	5	14	7	56	8.0	0	Right Sideline	2	13	6.5	8	0	0	0	0	3	9	3.0	0
Indoor	1	14	48	3.4	8	0	3	2	3	0	0	-	0	Shotgun	0	0	-	0	0	0	0	0	0	0	-	0
Outdoor	14	94	540	5.7	55	6	22	8	23	10	61	6.1	0	2 Wide Receivers	77	475	6.2	55	4	18	7	16	6	50	8.3	0
1st Half	-	49	244	5.0	55	4	9	5	14	8	54	6.8	0	4+ Wide Receivers	2	9	4.5	7	0	0	0	0	0	0	-	0
2nd Half/OT	-	59	344	5.8	36	2	16	5	12	2	7	3.5	0	Carries 1-5	65	370	5.7	55	5	18	7	18	0	0	-	0
Last 2 Min. Half	-	1	7	7.0	7	0	0	0	0	0	0	-	0	Carries 6-10	35	182	5.2	36	1	7	3	8	0	0	-	0
4th qtr, +/-7 pts	-	13	100	7.7	36	0	4	0	0	1	5	5.0	0	Carries 11-15	8	36	4.5	8	0	2	0	0	0	0	-	0
Winning	-	54	276	5.1	36	1	10	5	18	5	11	2.2	0	Carries 16-20	0	0	-	0	0	0	0	0	0	0	-	0
Tied	-	23	163	7.1	55	3	6	2	4	1	16	11.5	0	Carries 21+	0	0	-	0	0	0	0	0	0	0	-	0
Trailing	-	31	149	4.8	28	2	9	3	4	4	34	8.5	0													

1995 Incompletions

Type	Num	%of Inc	% Att
Pass Dropped	1	20.0	6.7
Poor Throw	1	20.0	6.7
Pass Defensed	0	0.0	0.0
Pass Hit at Line	1	20.0	6.7
Other	2	40.0	13.3
Total	5	100.0	33.3

Game Logs (1-8)

Date	Opp	Result	Rush	Yds	Rec	Yds	Trgt	F-L	TD
09/03	TB	L 6-21	5	23	0	0	0	0-0	0
09/10	@Ari	W 31-19	10	71	0	0	0	0-0	1
09/17	SD	L 21-27	10	47	1	4	2	0-0	0
09/24	@Oak	L 17-48	5	15	0	0	0	0-0	0
10/01	@NO	W 15-10	14	48	0	0	0	0-0	0
10/08	Was	W 37-34	9	120	1	2	1	1-1	3
10/15	@NYN	W 17-14	4	5	1	29	1	0-0	0
10/29	StL	W 20-9	7	60	0	0	0	1-0	0

Game Logs (9-16)

Date	Opp	Result	Rush	Yds	Rec	Yds	Trgt	F-L	TD
11/06	@Dal	L 12-34	5	17	1	4	2	0-0	0
11/12	Den	W 31-13	9	52	3	17	4	0-0	0
11/19	NYN	W 28-19	13	58	0	0	1	0-0	0
11/26	@Was	W 14-7	11	50	3	5	3	0-0	0
12/03	@Sea	L 14-26	-	-	-	-	-	-	-
12/10	Dal	W 20-17	2	2	0	0	0	0-0	0
12/17	Ari	W 21-20	0	0	0	0	0	0-0	0
12/24	@Chi	L 14-20	4	20	0	0	0	0-0	0

1995 Receiving Splits

	G	Rec	Yds	Avg	TD	Lg	Big	YAC	Trgt	Y@C	1st	1st%
Total	15	26	242	9.3	1	30	1	176	43	2.5	15	57.7
vs. Playoff	10	20	169	8.5	1	18	0	117	33	2.6	11	55.0
vs. Non-playoff	5	6	73	12.2	0	30	1	59	10	2.3	4	66.7
vs. Own Division	8	16	150	9.4	0	18	0	106	27	2.8	8	50.0
Home	7	11	120	10.9	0	30	1	90	16	2.7	6	54.5
Away	8	15	122	8.1	1	14	0	86	27	2.4	9	60.0
Games 1-8	7	9	96	10.7	1	30	1	73	14	2.6	7	77.8
Games 9-16	8	17	146	8.6	0	14	0	103	29	2.5	8	47.1
September	3	4	55	13.8	0	30	1	40	5	3.8	2	50.0
October	4	5	41	8.2	1	18	0	33	9	1.6	5	100.0
November	4	9	83	9.2	0	14	0	65	14	2.0	5	55.6
December	4	8	63	7.9	0	12	0	38	15	3.1	3	37.5
Grass	10	12	125	10.4	0	30	1	94	19	2.6	6	50.0
Turf	5	14	117	8.4	1	14	0	82	24	2.5	9	64.3
Indoor	2	5	30	6.0	0	12	0	15	7	3.0	4	80.0
Outdoor	13	21	212	10.1	0	30	1	161	36	2.4	11	52.4
1st Half	-	13	123	9.5	1	18	0	96	18	2.1	10	76.9
2nd Half/OT	-	13	119	9.2	0	30	1	80	25	3.1	5	38.5
Last 2 Min. Half	-	2	6	3.0	0	4	0	1	2	2.5	1	50.0
4th qtr, +/-7 pts	-	3	43	14.3	0	30	1	35	6	2.7	1	33.3
Winning	-	6	52	8.7	0	14	0	33	9	3.2	4	66.7
Tied	-	6	65	10.8	0	18	0	51	12	2.3	4	66.7
Trailing	-	14	125	8.9	1	30	1	92	22	2.4	7	50.0

	Rec	Yds	Avg	TD	Lg	Big	YAC	Trgt	Y@C	1st	1st%
Inside 20	4	29	7.3	1	12	0	17	8	3.0	2	50.0
Inside 10	2	8	4.0	1	6	0	2	5	3.0	1	50.0
1st Down	12	112	9.3	1	30	1	72	23	3.3	4	33.3
2nd Down	8	78	9.8	0	14	0	61	12	2.1	6	75.0
3rd Down Overall	5	48	9.6	0	18	0	40	7	1.6	4	80.0
3rd D 0-2 to Go	1	18	18.0	0	18	0	16	2	2.0	1	100.0
3rd D 3-7 to Go	3	19	6.3	0	8	0	17	3	0.7	2	66.7
3rd D 8+ to Go	1	11	11.0	0	11	0	7	2	4.0	1	100.0
4th Down	1	4	4.0	0	4	0	3	1	1.0	1	100.0
Rec Behind Line	2	19	9.5	0	11	0	21	8	-1.0	2	100.0
1-10 yds	24	223	9.3	1	30	1	155	35	2.8	13	54.2
11-20 yds	0	0	-	0	0	0	0	0	-	0	-
21-30 yds	0	0	-	0	0	0	0	0	-	0	-
31+	0	0	-	0	0	0	0	0	-	0	-
Left Sideline	2	13	6.5	0	9	0	8	4	2.5	1	50.0
Left Side	3	37	12.3	0	14	0	33	6	1.3	3	100.0
Middle	3	23	7.7	0	11	0	11	5	4.0	1	33.3
Right Side	9	74	8.2	1	13	0	52	14	2.4	6	66.7
Right Sideline	9	95	10.6	0	30	1	72	14	2.6	4	44.4
Shotgun	0	0	-	0	0	0	0	0	-	0	-
2 Wide Receivers	22	201	9.1	1	30	1	152	36	2.2	12	54.5
3 Wide Receivers	1	12	12.0	0	12	0	2	1	10.0	1	100.0
4+ Wide Receivers	0	0	-	0	0	0	0	0	-	0	-

1995 Incompletions

Type	Num	%of Inc	%of Att
Pass Dropped	4	23.5	9.3
Poor Throw	5	29.4	11.6
Pass Defensed	1	5.9	2.3
Pass Hit at Line	3	17.6	7.0
Other	4	23.5	9.3
Total	17	100.0	39.5

Game Logs (1-8)

Date	Opp	Result	Rush	Yds	Rec	Yds	Trgt	F-L	TD
09/03	Cle	W 17-14	0	0	2	37	2	0-0	0
09/10	Mia	L 3-20	0	0	2	18	3	0-0	0
09/17	@SF	L 3-28	0	0	0	0	0	0-0	0
10/01	@Atl	L 17-30	0	0	3	13	4	0-0	1
10/08	Den	L 3-37	-	-	-	-	-	-	-
10/15	@KC	L 26-31	0	0	0	0	2	0-0	0
10/23	Buf	W 27-14	2	4	2	28	0	0-0	0
10/29	Car	L 17-20	2	4	0	0	0	0-0	0

Game Logs (9-16)

Date	Opp	Result	Rush	Yds	Rec	Yds	Trgt	F-L	TD
11/05	@NYA	W 20-7	0	0	1	14	2	0-0	0
11/12	@Mia	W 34-17	0	0	1	5	1	0-0	0
11/19	Ind	L 10-24	0	0	2	15	2	0-0	0
11/26	@Buf	W 35-25	1	9	5	49	9	0-0	0
12/03	NO	L 17-31	2	4	2	18	2	0-0	0
12/10	NYA	W 31-28	0	0	1	4	4	0-0	0
12/16	@Pit	L 27-41	0	0	2	24	6	0-0	0
12/23	@Ind	L 7-10	1	3	2	17	3	0-0	0

1995 Passing Splits

	G	Att	Cm	Pct	Yds	Yd/Att	TD	Int	1st	YAC	Big	Sk	Rtg
Total	16	557	336	60.3	4143	7.4	24	11	201	2017	35	43	89.5
vs. Playoff	6	173	110	63.6	1300	7.5	6	3	73	615	8	15	90.7
vs. Non-playoff	10	384	226	58.9	2843	7.4	18	8	128	1402	27	28	88.9
vs. Own Division	8	286	166	58.0	2023	7.1	12	6	100	864	15	19	85.2
Home	8	274	173	63.1	2061	7.5	12	3	103	1029	17	19	96.1
Away	8	283	163	57.6	2082	7.4	12	8	98	988	18	24	83.1
Games 1-8	8	287	178	62.0	1987	6.9	10	7	95	938	16	26	84.1
Games 9-16	8	270	158	58.5	2156	8.0	14	4	106	1079	19	17	95.2
September	4	152	94	61.8	1062	7.0	5	5	54	424	7	15	80.0
October	4	135	84	62.2	925	6.9	5	2	41	514	9	11	88.7
November	4	142	83	58.5	1273	9.0	8	2	55	649	13	14	101.1
December	4	128	75	58.6	883	6.9	6	2	51	430	6	3	88.8
Grass	5	180	103	57.2	1257	7.0	11	6	62	625	10	10	85.3
Turf	11	377	233	61.8	2886	7.7	13	5	139	1392	25	33	91.5
Indoor	9	313	200	63.9	2447	7.8	13	4	119	1172	21	26	96.4
Outdoor	7	244	136	55.7	1696	7.0	11	7	82	845	14	17	80.6
1st Half	-	319	196	61.4	2382	7.5	13	3	113	1201	19	18	96.2
2nd Half/OT	-	238	140	58.8	1761	7.4	9	8	88	816	16	25	80.5
Last 2 Min. Half	-	61	28	45.9	422	6.9	1	2	18	228	4	4	61.0
4th qtr, +/-7 pts	-	79	42	53.2	552	7.0	2	5	28	251	5	4	57.6
Winning	-	215	126	58.6	1588	7.4	9	5	80	854	13	17	86.0
Tied	-	157	102	65.0	1205	7.7	8	3	58	601	10	10	110.2
Trailing	-	185	108	58.4	1350	7.3	7	3	63	562	12	16	87.0

	Att	Cm	Pct	Yds	Yd/Att	TD	Int	1st	YAC	Big	Sk	Rtg
Inside 20	71	32	45.1	249	3.5	13	1	20	88	0	3	88.0
Inside 10	22	8	36.4	36	1.6	7	1	7	13	0	0	65.5
1st Down	237	153	64.6	1967	8.3	10	5	76	919	18	16	95.7
2nd Down	172	104	60.5	1082	6.3	7	3	62	594	7	12	85.0
3rd Down Overall	144	77	53.5	1074	7.5	7	3	61	495	10	14	85.2
3rd D 0-5 to Go	68	42	61.8	541	8.0	5	1	41	247	6	2	105.1
3rd D 6+ to Go	76	35	46.1	533	7.0	2	2	20	248	4	12	67.5
4th Down	4	2	50.0	20	5.0	0	0	2	9	0	1	64.6
Rec Behind Line	114	80	70.2	768	6.7	2	2	42	1002	4	0	87.2
1-10 yds	264	186	70.5	1658	6.3	7	5	90	680	6	0	87.9
11-20 yds	96	45	46.9	906	9.4	8	1	44	254	5	0	103.9
21-30 yds	50	16	32.0	431	8.6	3	2	16	41	11	0	68.0
31+	33	9	27.3	380	11.5	4	1	9	40	9	0	102.0
Left Sideline	99	53	53.5	650	6.6	3	2	33	269	4	0	75.7
Left Side	113	74	65.5	909	8.0	6	3	45	540	6	5	96.8
Middle	61	28	45.9	395	6.5	2	2	20	195	3	33	81.0
Right Side	147	103	70.1	1218	8.3	5	2	63	691	11	3	100.7
Right Sideline	137	78	56.9	971	7.1	5	2	42	322	11	2	85.1
2 Wide Receivers	20	13	65.0	116	5.8	1	0	8	49	0	1	97.1
3+ WR	536	322	60.1	4013	7.5	23	11	192	1951	35	41	89.1
Attempts 1-10	160	102	63.8	1154	7.2	5	2	55	596	10	0	90.5
Attempts 11-20	153	97	63.4	1249	8.2	11	1	61	616	8	0	110.2
Attempts 21+	244	137	56.1	1740	7.1	8	8	85	805	17	0	75.9

1995 Incompletions

Type	Num	% of Inc	% of Att
Pass Dropped	33	14.9	5.9
Poor Throw	104	47.1	18.7
Pass Defensed	40	18.1	7.2
Pass Hit at Line	10	4.5	1.8
Other	34	15.4	6.1
Total	221	100.0	39.7

Game Logs (1-8)

Date	Opp	Result	Att	Cm	Pct	Yds	TD	Int	Lg	Sk	F-L
09/03	Car	W 23-20	45	27	60.0	290	2	1	46	3	0-0
09/10	@SF	L 10-41	33	18	54.5	162	1	2	23	2	1-0
09/17	@NO	W 27-24	39	27	69.2	386	1	1	54	7	0-0
09/24	NYA	W 13-3	35	22	62.9	224	1	1	44	3	0-0
10/01	NE	W 30-17	38	26	68.4	295	1	1	52	2	0-0
10/12	@StL	L 19-21	30	16	53.3	160	0	0	21	2	0-0
10/22	@TB	W 24-21	37	24	64.9	295	3	1	62	4	0-0
10/29	Dal	L 13-28	30	18	60.0	175	1	2	42	3	0-0

Game Logs (9-16)

Date	Opp	Result	Att	Cm	Pct	Yds	TD	Int	Lg	Sk	F-L
11/05	Det	W 34-22	40	31	77.5	362	1	0	37	3	1-1
11/12	@Buf	L 17-23	34	17	50.0	279	0	1	34	5	2-0
11/19	StL	W 31-16	34	20	58.8	352	4	0	41	3	0-0
11/26	@Ari	L 37-40	34	15	44.1	280	3	1	61	3	2-1
12/03	@Mia	L 20-21	23	17	73.9	210	2	0	25	1	0-0
12/10	NO	W 19-14	39	20	51.3	251	1	0	25	1	0-0
12/17	@Car	L 17-21	53	29	54.7	310	2	2	38	0	0-0
12/24	SF	W 28-27	13	9	69.2	112	1	0	41	1	0-0

Gale Gilbert
San Diego Chargers — QB

1995 Passing Splits

	G	Att	Cm	Pct	Yds	Yd/Att	TD	Int	1st	YAC	Big	Sk	Rtg		Att	Cm	Pct	Yds	Yd/Att	TD	Int	1st	YAC	Big	Sk	Rtg
Total	16	61	36	59.0	325	5.3	0	4	15	149	1	9	46.1	Inside 20	3	1	33.3	4	1.3	0	1	0	-1	0	0	2.8
vs. Playoff	7	40	24	60.0	228	5.7	0	4	12	122	1	8	36.3	Inside 10	1	0	0.0	0	0.0	0	1	0	0	0	0	0.0
vs. Non-playoff	9	21	12	57.1	97	4.6	0	0	3	27	0	1	68.9	1st Down	18	9	50.0	81	4.5	0	2	3	59	0	3	22.9
vs. Own Division	8	8	4	50.0	22	2.8	0	1	1	22	0	2	16.7	2nd Down	26	18	69.2	135	5.2	0	2	8	66	0	2	49.4
Home	8	32	20	62.5	206	6.4	0	3	11	100	1	6	41.9	3rd Down Overall	14	7	50.0	90	6.4	0	0	3	17	1	4	70.5
Away	8	29	16	55.2	119	4.1	0	1	4	49	0	3	50.8	3rd D 0-5 to Go	2	2	100.0	11	5.5	0	0	1	1	0	0	89.6
Games 1-8	8	40	24	60.0	228	5.7	0	4	12	122	1	8	36.3	3rd D 6+ to Go	12	5	41.7	79	6.6	0	0	2	16	1	4	64.2
Games 9-16	8	21	12	57.1	97	4.6	0	0	3	27	0	1	68.9	4th Down	3	2	66.7	19	6.3	0	0	1	7	0	0	84.0
September	4	0	0	-	0	-	0	0	0	0	0	0	-	Rec Behind Line	10	8	80.0	32	3.2	0	0	1	65	0	0	80.0
October	4	40	24	60.0	228	5.7	0	4	12	122	1	8	36.3	1-10 yds	33	24	72.7	208	6.3	0	1	10	82	0	0	76.3
November	4	0	0	-	0	-	0	0	0	0	0	0	-	11-20 yds	10	3	30.0	44	4.4	0	0	3	1	0	0	45.4
December	4	21	12	57.1	97	4.6	0	0	3	27	0	1	68.9	21-30 yds	3	0	0.0	0	0.0	0	1	0	0	0	0	0.0
Grass	11	40	24	60.0	228	5.7	0	4	12	122	1	8	36.3	31+	5	1	20.0	41	8.2	0	2	1	1	1	0	21.7
Turf	5	21	12	57.1	97	4.6	0	0	3	27	0	1	68.9	Left Sideline	12	3	25.0	23	1.9	0	1	2	7	0	0	4.9
Indoor	2	0	0	-	0	-	0	0	0	0	0	0	-	Left Side	13	10	76.9	67	5.2	0	0	3	45	0	1	87.7
Outdoor	14	61	36	59.0	325	5.3	0	4	15	149	1	9	46.1	Middle	6	2	33.3	18	3.0	0	2	1	5	0	7	2.8
1st Half	-	23	14	60.9	154	6.7	0	3	7	69	1	3	41.1	Right Side	11	8	72.7	71	6.5	0	0	4	61	0	1	89.6
2nd Half/OT	-	38	22	57.9	171	4.5	0	1	8	80	0	6	58.1	Right Sideline	19	13	68.4	146	7.7	0	1	5	31	1	0	69.2
Last 2 Min. Half	-	4	2	50.0	19	4.8	0	1	1	29	0	1	24.0	2 Wide Receivers	30	18	60.0	161	5.4	0	2	8	80	0	1	46.7
4th qtr, +/-7 pts	-	8	3	37.5	26	3.3	0	1	1	6	0	1	7.3	3+ WR	31	18	58.1	164	5.3	0	2	7	69	1	7	45.6
Winning	-	2	1	50.0	3	1.5	0	0	0	1	0	1	56.3	Attempts 1-10	28	18	64.3	173	6.2	0	2	7	71	1	0	51.6
Tied	-	13	6	46.2	52	4.0	0	2	3	41	0	2	17.6	Attempts 11-20	20	12	60.0	102	5.1	0	2	6	47	0	0	33.8
Trailing	-	46	29	63.0	270	5.9	0	2	12	107	1	6	61.0	Attempts 21+	13	6	46.2	50	3.8	0	0	2	31	0	0	56.6

1995 Incompletions

Type	Num	% of Inc	% of Att
Pass Dropped	2	8.0	3.3
Poor Throw	11	44.0	18.0
Pass Defensed	5	20.0	8.2
Pass Hit at Line	2	8.0	3.3
Other	5	20.0	8.2
Total	25	100.0	41.0

Game Logs (1-8)

Date	Opp	Result	Att	Cm	Pct	Yds	TD	Int	Lg	Sk	F-L
09/03	@Oak	L 7-17	0	0	-	0	0	0	0	0	0-0
09/10	Sea	W 14-10	0	0	-	0	0	0	0	0	0-0
09/17	@Phi	W 27-21	0	0	-	0	0	0	0	0	0-0
09/24	Den	W 17-6	0	0	-	0	0	0	0	0	0-0
10/01	@Pit	L 16-31	0	0	-	0	0	0	0	0	0-0
10/09	@KC	L 23-29	8	4	50.0	22	0	1	9	2	0-0
10/15	Dal	L 9-23	32	20	62.5	206	0	3	41	6	1-1
10/22	@Sea	W 35-25	0	0	-	0	0	0	0	0	0-0

Game Logs (9-16)

Date	Opp	Result	Att	Cm	Pct	Yds	TD	Int	Lg	Sk	F-L
11/05	Mia	L 14-24	0	0	-	0	0	0	0	0	0-0
11/12	KC	L 7-22	0	0	-	0	0	0	0	0	0-0
11/19	@Den	L 27-30	0	0	-	0	0	0	0	0	0-0
11/27	Oak	W 12-6	0	0	-	0	0	0	0	0	0-0
12/03	Cle	W 31-13	0	0	-	0	0	0	0	0	0-0
12/09	@Ari	W 28-25	0	0	-	0	0	0	0	0	0-1
12/17	@Ind	W 27-24	0	0	-	0	0	0	0	0	0-0
12/23	@NYN	W 27-17	21	12	57.1	97	0	0	22	1	0-0

Ernest Givins
Jacksonville Jaguars — WR

1995 Receiving Splits

	G	Rec	Yds	Avg	TD	Lg	Big	YAC	Trgt	Y@C	1st	1st%		Rec	Yds	Avg	TD	Lg	Big	YAC	Trgt	Y@C	1st	1st%
Total	9	29	280	9.7	3	18	0	42	56	8.2	17	58.6	Inside 20	3	34	11.3	3	15	0	0	5	11.3	3	100.0
vs. Playoff	1	1	3	3.0	0	3	0	1	2	2.0	0	0.0	Inside 10	1	7	7.0	1	7	0	0	1	7.0	1	100.0
vs. Non-playoff	8	28	277	9.9	3	18	0	41	54	8.4	17	60.7	1st Down	12	126	10.5	2	15	0	16	20	9.2	7	58.3
vs. Own Division	4	8	74	9.3	0	11	0	11	20	7.9	4	50.0	2nd Down	11	110	10.0	1	18	0	20	21	8.2	6	54.5
Home	4	18	179	9.9	2	17	0	18	33	8.9	12	66.7	3rd Down Overall	5	37	7.4	0	13	0	5	13	6.4	3	60.0
Away	5	11	101	9.2	1	18	0	24	23	7.0	5	45.5	3rd D 0-2 to Go	0	0	-	0	0	0	0	2	-	0	-
Games 1-8	4	14	133	9.5	2	17	0	22	28	7.9	8	57.1	3rd D 3-7 to Go	2	17	8.5	0	10	0	-1	4	9.0	2	100.0
Games 9-16	5	15	147	9.8	1	18	0	20	28	8.5	9	60.0	3rd D 8+ to Go	3	20	6.7	0	13	0	6	7	4.7	1	33.3
September	3	7	60	8.6	1	11	0	13	17	6.7	3	42.9	4th Down	1	7	7.0	0	7	0	1	2	6.0	1	100.0
October	2	8	76	9.5	1	17	0	10	13	8.3	5	62.5	Rec Behind Line	0	0	-	0	0	0	0	0	-	0	-
November	3	13	126	9.7	1	15	0	15	19	8.5	8	61.5	1-10 yds	22	181	8.2	1	14	0	32	31	6.8	10	45.5
December	1	1	18	18.0	0	18	0	4	7	14.0	1	100.0	11-20 yds	7	99	14.1	2	18	0	10	20	12.7	7	100.0
Grass	6	23	236	10.3	3	18	0	31	45	8.9	15	65.2	21-30 yds	0	0	-	0	0	0	0	1	-	0	-
Turf	3	6	44	7.3	1	11	0	11	11	5.5	2	33.3	31+	0	0	-	0	0	0	0	0	-	0	-
Outdoor	0	29	280	9.7	3	18	0	42	56	8.2	17	58.6	Left Sideline	9	84	9.3	1	12	0	9	19	8.3	5	55.6
Indoor	9	0	0	-	0	0	0	0	0	-	0	-	Left Side	9	85	9.4	1	17	0	15	15	7.8	4	44.4
1st Half	-	10	99	9.9	1	18	0	12	23	8.7	7	70.0	Middle	3	38	12.7	1	15	0	8	5	10.0	3	100.0
2nd Half/OT	-	19	181	9.5	2	17	0	30	33	7.9	10	52.6	Right Side	4	47	11.8	0	18	0	6	5	10.3	4	75.0
Last 2 Min. Half	-	5	41	8.2	1	13	0	9	10	6.4	6	60.0	Right Sideline	4	26	6.5	0	10	0	4	12	5.5	2	50.0
4th qtr, +/-7 pts	-	4	42	10.5	0	14	0	14	9	7.0	3	75.0	Shotgun	9	71	7.9	0	14	0	17	18	6.0	4	44.4
Winning	-	0	0	-	0	0	0	0	1	-	0	-	2 Wide Receivers	5	39	7.8	0	10	0	2	12	7.4	3	60.0
Tied	-	6	65	10.0	0	10	0	12	12	0.0	4	66.7	3 Wide Receivers	22	219	10.0	3	10	0	35	42	8.4	13	59.1
Trailing	-	23	215	9.3	3	17	0	30	43	8.0	13	56.5	4+ Wide Receivers	2	22	11.0	0	13	0	5	2	8.5	1	50.0

1995 Incompletions

Type	Num	%of Inc	%of Att
Pass Dropped	5	18.5	8.9
Poor Throw	11	40.7	19.6
Pass Defensed	3	11.1	5.4
Pass Hit at Line	0	0.0	0.0
Other	8	29.6	14.3
Total	27	100.0	48.2

Game Logs (1-8)

Date	Opp	Result	Rec	Yds	Trgt	F-L	TD
09/03	Hou	L 3-10	2	19	8	0-0	0
09/10	@Cin	L 17-24	1	11	2	0-0	0
09/17	@NYA	L 10-27	4	30	7	0-0	1
09/24	GB	L 14-24	-	-	-	-	-
10/01	@Hou	W 17-16	-	-	-	-	-
10/08	Pit	W 20-16	-	-	-	-	-
10/15	Chi	L 27-30	7	73	11	0-0	1
10/22	@Cle	W 23-15	-	-	-	-	-

Game Logs (9-16)

Date	Opp	Result	Rec	Yds	Trgt	F-L	TD
10/29	@Pit	L 7-24	1	3	2	1-1	0
11/12	Sea	L 30-47	5	46	6	0-0	1
11/19	@TB	L 16-17	4	39	5	0-0	0
11/26	Cin	L 13-17	4	41	8	0-0	0
12/03	@Den	L 23-31	1	18	7	0-0	0

Andrew Glover
Oakland Raiders — TE

1995 Receiving Splits

	G	Rec	Yds	Avg	TD	Lg	Big	YAC	Trgt	Y@C	1st	1st%
Total	16	26	220	8.5	3	25	1	80	40	5.4	12	46.2
vs. Playoff	8	12	107	8.9	0	25	1	31	21	6.3	4	33.3
vs. Non-playoff	8	14	113	8.1	3	24	0	49	19	4.6	8	57.1
vs. Own Division	8	16	137	8.6	1	24	0	46	25	5.7	7	43.8
Home	8	15	142	9.5	1	25	1	35	23	7.1	5	33.3
Away	8	11	78	7.1	2	12	0	45	17	3.0	7	63.6
Games 1-8	8	12	120	10.0	3	25	1	29	16	7.6	7	58.3
Games 9-16	8	14	100	7.1	0	12	0	51	24	3.5	5	35.7
September	4	4	50	12.5	1	25	1	8	6	10.5	3	75.0
October	4	8	70	8.8	2	24	0	21	10	6.1	4	50.0
November	4	5	45	9.0	0	11	0	28	9	3.4	6	60.0
December	4	9	55	6.1	0	12	0	23	15	3.6	2	22.2
Grass	12	19	167	8.8	2	25	1	45	30	6.4	8	42.1
Turf	4	7	53	7.6	1	12	0	35	10	2.6	4	57.1
Outdoor	1	23	193	8.4	3	25	1	64	34	5.6	10	43.5
Indoor	15	3	27	9.0	0	12	0	16	6	3.7	2	66.7
1st Half	-	15	114	7.6	1	15	0	45	22	4.6	6	40.0
2nd Half/OT	-	11	106	9.6	2	25	1	35	18	6.5	6	54.5
Last 2 Min. Half	-	4	24	6.0	0	12	0	10	5	3.5	1	25.0
4th qtr, +/-7 pts	-	0	0	-	0	0	0	0	1	-	0	-
Winning	-	7	82	11.7	1	25	1	25	9	8.1	3	42.9
Tied	-	4	27	6.8	2	15	0	5	6	5.5	3	75.0
Trailing	-	15	111	7.4	0	12	0	50	25	4.4	6	40.0

	Rec	Yds	Avg	TD	Lg	Big	YAC	Trgt	Y@C	1st	1st%
Inside 20	3	16	5.3	3	13	0		7	5.3	3	100.0
Inside 10	2	3	1.5	2	2	0	0	5	1.5	2	100.0
1st Down	12	127	10.6	0	25	1	50	17	6.4	4	33.3
2nd Down	8	46	5.8	1	11	0	16	14	3.8	3	37.5
3rd Down Overall	6	47	7.8	2	13	0	14	9	5.5	5	83.3
3rd D 0-2 to Go	3	23	7.7	2	13	0	8	3	5.0	3	100.0
3rd D 3-7 to Go	3	24	8.0	0	12	0	6	5	6.0	2	66.7
3rd D 8+ to Go	0	0	-	0	0	0	0	1	-	0	-
4th Down	0	0	0	-	0	0	0	0	-	0	-
Rec Behind Line	2	19	9.5	0	11	0	20	2	-0.5	2	100.0
1-10 yds	19	113	5.9	2	12	0	42	31	3.7	5	26.3
11-20 yds	5	88	17.6	1	25	1	18	6	14.0	5	100.0
21-30 yds	0	0	-	0	0	0	0	1	-	0	-
31+	0	0	-	0	0	0	0	0	-	0	-
Left Sideline	1	1	1.0	1	1	0		2	1.0	1	100.0
Left Side	6	64	10.7	1	24	0	25	9	6.5	3	50.0
Middle	5	57	11.4	1	25	1	9	7	9.6	4	80.0
Right Side	11	82	7.5	0	12	0	42	13	3.6	3	27.3
Right Sideline	3	16	5.3	0	8	0	4	9	4.0	1	33.3
Shotgun	0	0	-	0	0	0	0	0	-	0	-
2 Wide Receivers	10	106	10.6	0	25	1	42	15	6.4	4	40.0
3 Wide Receivers	10	74	7.4	0	15	0	16	17	5.8	3	30.0
4+ Wide Receivers	1	5	5.0	0	5	0	2	1	3.0	0	0.0

1995 Incompletions

Type	Num	%of Inc	%of Att
Pass Dropped	3	21.4	7.5
Poor Throw	5	35.7	12.5
Pass Defensed	2	14.3	5.0
Pass Hit at Line	0	0.0	0.0
Other	4	28.6	10.0
Total	14	100.0	35.0

Game Logs (1-8)

Date	Opp	Result	Rec	Yds	Trgt	F-L	TD
09/03	SD	W 17-7	1	15	1	0-0	0
09/10	@Was	W 20-8	1	1	1	0-0	1
09/17	@KC	L 17-23	0	0	1	0-0	0
09/24	Phi	W 48-17	2	34	3	0-0	0
10/01	@NYA	W 47-10	1	2	1	0-0	1
10/08	Sea	W 34-14	4	45	5	0-0	1
10/16	@Den	L 0-27	2	14	2	0-0	0
10/22	Ind	W 30-17	1	9	2	0-0	0

Game Logs (9-16)

Date	Opp	Result	Rec	Yds	Trgt	F-L	TD
11/05	@Cin	W 20-17	2	13	2	0-0	0
11/12	@NYN	W 17-13	1	11	1	0-0	0
11/19	Dal	L 21-34	1	11	3	0-0	0
11/27	@SD	L 6-12	1	10	3	0-0	0
12/03	KC	L 23-29	5	26	6	0-0	0
12/10	Pit	L 10-29	1	2	2	0-0	0
12/17	@Sea	L 10-44	3	27	6	0-0	0
12/24	Den	L 28-31	0	0	1	0-0	0

Jeff Graham
Chicago Bears — WR

1995 Receiving Splits

	G	Rec	Yds	Avg	TD	Lg	Big	YAC	Trgt	Y@C	1st	1st%
Total	16	82	1301	15.9	4	51	14	346	138	11.6	67	81.7
vs. Playoff	6	30	469	15.6	0	51	4	82	52	12.9	26	86.7
vs. Non-playoff	10	52	832	16.0	4	49	10	264	86	10.9	41	78.8
vs. Own Division	8	40	618	15.5	1	51	8	141	62	11.9	29	72.5
Home	8	44	706	16.0	2	51	8	177	76	12.0	36	81.8
Away	8	38	595	15.7	2	49	6	169	62	11.2	31	81.6
Games 1-8	8	40	632	15.8	2	49	7	230	67	10.1	33	82.5
Games 9-16	8	42	669	15.9	2	51	7	116	71	13.2	34	81.0
September	4	20	326	16.3	1	49	4	118	32	10.4	15	75.0
October	4	20	306	15.3	1	32	3	112	35	9.7	18	90.0
November	4	23	384	16.7	1	51	4	64	37	13.9	19	82.6
December	4	19	285	15.0	1	47	3	52	34	12.3	15	78.9
Grass	11	58	919	15.8	2	51	10	225	98	12.0	48	82.8
Turf	5	24	382	15.9	2	49	4	121	40	10.9	19	79.2
Outdoor	2	73	1183	16.2	4	51	13	307	125	12.0	60	82.2
Indoor	14	9	118	13.1	0	29	1	39	13	8.8	7	77.8
1st Half	-	44	701	15.9	1	51	8	191	75	11.6	36	81.8
2nd Half/OT	-	38	600	15.8	3	47	6	155	63	11.7	31	81.6
Last 2 Min. Half	-	8	91	11.4	1	23	0	42	13	6.1	6	75.0
4th qtr, +/-7 pts	-	11	130	11.8	1	23	0	26	19	9.5	8	72.7
Winning	-	30	478	15.9	2	47	5	126	46	11.7	27	90.0
Tied	-	24	381	15.9	0	51	6	115	41	11.1	17	70.8
Trailing	-	28	442	15.8	2	47	3	105	51	12.0	23	82.1

	Rec	Yds	Avg	TD	Lg	Big	YAC	Trgt	Y@C	1st	1st%
Inside 20	7	53	7.6	2	18	0	15	21	5.4	4	57.1
Inside 10	2	8	4.0	1	6	0	0	10	4.0	1	50.0
1st Down	31	506	16.3	2	51	6	100	53	13.1	22	71.0
2nd Down	29	527	18.2	2	47	7	162	47	12.6	25	86.2
3rd Down Overall	19	243	12.8	0	32	1	75	35	8.3	17	89.5
3rd D 0-2 to Go	0	0	-	0	0	0	0	2	-	0	-
3rd D 3-7 to Go	14	160	11.4	0	32	1	60	24	7.1	12	85.7
3rd D 8+ to Go	5	83	16.6	0	22	0	15	9	13.6	5	100.0
4th Down	3	25	8.3	0	9	0	9	3	5.3	3	100.0
Rec Behind Line	0	0	-	0	0	0	0	7	-	0	-
1-10 yds	44	401	9.1	1	29	2	148	69	5.8	29	65.9
11-20 yds	27	481	17.8	1	32	3	112	44	13.7	27	100.0
21-30 yds	5	145	29.0	0	49	3	33	7	22.4	5	100.0
31+	6	274	45.7	2	51	6	53	11	36.8	6	100.0
Left Sideline	24	391	16.3	0	51	6	90	35	12.5	18	75.0
Left Side	20	254	12.7	0	24	0	55	31	10.0	17	85.0
Middle	8	151	18.9	3	47	1	46	17	13.1	7	87.5
Right Side	15	258	17.2	0	49	4	89	29	11.3	13	86.7
Right Sideline	15	247	16.5	0	46	3	66	26	12.1	12	80.0
Shotgun	0	0	-	0	0	0	0	0	-	0	-
2 Wide Receivers	43	772	18.0	2	49	10	188	77	13.6	34	79.1
3 Wide Receivers	20	329	16.5	1	51	4	96	29	11.7	18	90.0
4+ Wide Receivers	19	200	10.5	1	23	0	62	30	7.3	15	78.9

1995 Incompletions

Type	Num	%of Inc	%of Att
Pass Dropped	9	16.1	6.5
Poor Throw	23	41.1	16.7
Pass Defensed	8	14.3	5.8
Pass Hit at Line	6	10.7	4.3
Other	10	17.9	7.2
Total	56	100.0	40.6

Game Logs (1-8)

Date	Opp	Result	Rec	Yds	Trgt	F-L	TD
09/03	Min	W 31-14	8	107	12	1-0	0
09/11	GB	L 24-27	2	21	7	0-0	0
09/17	@TB	W 4	53	6	0-0	0	
09/24	@StL	L 28-34	6	145	7	1-0	0
10/08	Car	W 31-27	3	44	6	0-0	0
10/15	@Jac	W 30-27	3	52	6	0-0	0
10/22	Hou	W 35-32	9	137	16	0-0	0
10/30	@Min	W 14-6	5	73	7	0-0	0

Game Logs (9-16)

Date	Opp	Result	Rec	Yds	Trgt	F-L	TD
11/05	Pit	L 34-37	5	111	8	0-0	0
11/12	@GB	L 28-35	7	108	10	0-0	0
11/19	Det	L	5	88	8	0-0	0
11/26	@NYN	W 27-24	6	56	11	0-1	1
12/04	@Det	L 7-27	4	45	6	0-0	1
12/10	@Cin	L 10-16	3	63	9	0-0	0
12/17	TB	W 31-10	5	102	6	0-1	1
12/24	Phi	W 20-14	7	75	13	1-0	1

Scottie Graham
Minnesota Vikings — RB

1995 Rushing and Receiving Splits

	G	Rush	Yds	Avg	Lg	TD	1st	Stf	YdL	Rec	Yds	Avg	TD
Total	16	110	406	3.7	26	2	21	11	23	4	30	7.5	0
vs. Playoff	7	23	48	2.1	15	0	1	4	7	1	6	6.0	0
vs. Non-playoff	9	87	358	4.1	26	2	20	7	16	3	24	8.0	0
vs. Own Division	8	46	163	3.5	26	1	9	4	11	2	17	8.5	0
Home	8	54	214	4.0	26	2	12	6	15	3	24	8.0	0
Away	8	56	192	3.4	15	0	9	5	8	1	6	6.0	0
Games 1-8	8	28	48	1.7	7	0	2	3	10	0	0	-	0
Games 9-16	8	82	358	4.4	26	2	19	8	13	4	30	7.5	0
September	4	14	26	1.9	7	0	1	1	4	0	0	-	0
October	4	14	22	1.6	6	0	1	2	6	0	0	-	0
November	4	21	70	3.3	15	1	4	2	2	1	6	6.0	0
December	4	61	288	4.7	26	1	15	6	11	3	24	8.0	0
Grass	5	20	46	2.3	7	0	1	2	2	0	0	-	0
Turf	11	90	360	4.0	26	2	20	9	21	4	30	7.5	0
Indoor	9	60	236	3.9	26	2	13	7	16	4	30	7.5	0
Outdoor	7	50	170	3.4	14	0	8	4	7	0	0	-	0
1st Half	-	55	215	3.9	26	1	11	6	12	0	0	-	0
2nd Half/OT	-	55	191	3.5	26	1	10	5	11	4	30	7.5	0
Last 2 Min. Half	-	4	4	1.0	4	0	0	1	4	0	0	-	0
4th qtr, +/-7 pts	-	13	46	3.5	11	0	2	1	1	0	0	-	0
Winning	-	58	263	4.5	26	2	14	5	12	4	30	7.5	0
Tied	-	43	137	3.2	11	0	7	4	9	0	0	-	0
Trailing	-	9	6	0.7	3	0	2	2	0	0	0	-	0

	Rush	Yds	Avg	Lg	TD	1st	Stf	YdL	Rec	Yds	Avg	TD
Inside 20	24	68	2.8	7	1	3	2	3	0	0	-	0
Inside 10	15	35	2.3	7	1	3	2	3	0	0	-	0
1st Down	64	233	3.6	26	0	5	9	18	1	4	4.0	0
2nd Down	44	169	3.8	26	2	14	2	5	2	17	8.5	0
3rd Down Overall	2	4	2.0	3	0	2	0	0	1	9	9.0	0
3rd D 0-2 to Go	2	4	2.0	3	0	2	0	0	0	0	-	0
3rd D 3-7 to Go	0	0	-	0	0	0	0	0	0	0	-	0
3rd D 8+ to Go	0	0	-	0	0	0	0	0	1	9	9.0	0
4th Down	0	0	-	0	0	0	0	0	0	0	-	0
Left Sideline	0	0	-	0	0	0	0	0	0	0	-	0
Left Side	34	105	3.1	26	0	5	3	7	0	0	-	0
Middle	55	157	2.9	15	1	9	7	12	2	10	5.0	0
Right Side	21	144	6.9	26	1	7	1	4	2	20	10.0	0
Right Sideline	0	0	-	0	0	0	0	0	0	0	-	0
Shotgun	0	0	-	0	0	0	0	0	0	0	-	0
2 Wide Receivers	73	234	3.2	23	1	10	8	18	2	17	8.5	0
3 Wide Receivers	19	129	6.8	26	0	8	2	4	2	13	6.5	0
4+ Wide Receivers	0	0	-	0	0	0	0	0	0	0	-	0
Carries 1-5	56	198	3.5	26	0	8	6	11	0	0	-	0
Carries 6-10	25	81	3.2	23	2	6	2	5	0	0	-	0
Carries 11-15	15	55	3.7	14	0	3	2	6	0	0	-	0
Carries 16-20	9	46	5.1	26	0	2	1	1	0	0	-	0
Carries 21+	5	26	5.2	11	0	2	0	0	0	0	-	0

1995 Incompletions

Type	Num	%of Inc	% Att
Pass Dropped	1	100.0	20.0
Poor Throw	0	0.0	0.0
Pass Defensed	0	0.0	0.0
Pass Hit at Line	0	0.0	0.0
Other	0	0.0	0.0
Total	1	100.0	20.0

Game Logs (1-8)

Date	Opp	Result	Rush	Yds	Rec	Yds	Trgt	F-L	TD
09/03	@Chi	L 14-31	7	17	0	0	0	0-0	0
09/10	Det	W 20-10	1	0	0	0	0	0-0	0
09/17	Dal	L 17-23	1	0	0	0	0	0-0	0
09/24	@Pit	W 44-24	5	9	0	0	0	0-0	0
10/08	Hou	W 23-17	0	0	0	0	0	0-0	0
10/15	@TB	L 17-20	0	0	0	0	0	0-0	0
10/22	@GB	L 21-38	6	15	0	0	0	0-0	0
10/30	Chi	L 6-14	8	7	0	0	1	0-0	0

Game Logs (9-16)

Date	Opp	Result	Rush	Yds	Rec	Yds	Trgt	F-L	TD
11/05	GB	W 27-24	2	4	0	0	0	0-0	0
11/12	@Ari	W 30-24	5	16	0	0	0	0-0	0
11/19	NO	W 43-24	8	28	0	0	0	0-0	1
11/23	@Det	L 38-44	6	22	1	6	1	0-0	1
12/03	TB	W 31-17	16	98	1	11	1	0-0	1
12/09	Cle	W 27-11	18	77	2	13	2	0-0	0
12/18	@SF	L 30-37	2	-2	0	0	0	0-0	0
12/24	@Cin	L 24-27	25	115	0	0	0	0-0	0

Elvis Grbac
San Francisco 49ers — QB

1995 Passing Splits

	G	Att	Cm	Pct	Yds	Yd/Att	TD	Int	1st	YAC	Big	Sk	Rtg
Total	16	183	127	69.4	1469	8.0	8	6	68	844	11	6	96.6
vs. Playoff	7	72	51	70.8	687	9.5	6	0	30	402	5	3	128.6
vs. Non-playoff	9	111	76	68.5	782	7.0	2	5	38	442	6	3	75.7
vs. Own Division	8	111	76	68.5	782	7.0	2	5	38	442	6	3	75.7
Home	8	87	60	69.0	614	7.1	0	4	30	336	5	3	69.8
Away	8	96	67	69.8	855	8.9	8	1	38	508	6	3	120.8
Games 1-8	8	65	45	69.2	411	6.3	2	3	22	237	1	1	77.1
Games 9-16	8	118	82	69.5	1058	9.0	6	2	46	607	10	5	107.2
September	4	8	5	62.5	49	6.1	0	1	3	49	0	0	40.1
October	4	57	40	70.2	362	6.4	2	2	19	188	1	1	84.1
November	4	116	82	70.7	1058	9.1	6	2	46	607	10	5	109.1
December	4	0	0	0	0	0.0	0	0	0	0	0	0	39.6
Grass	10	130	91	70.0	996	7.7	4	4	49	542	7	4	89.8
Turf	6	53	36	67.9	473	8.9	4	2	19	302	4	2	113.2
Indoor	4	9	5	55.6	49	5.4	0	1	3	49	0	0	31.5
Outdoor	12	174	122	70.1	1420	8.2	8	4	65	795	11	6	100.3
1st Half	-	106	75	70.8	875	8.3	6	3	39	488	7	3	102.5
2nd Half/OT	-	77	52	67.5	594	7.7	2	2	29	356	4	3	88.3
Last 2 Min. Half	-	18	11	61.1	146	8.1	2	1	8	102	1	0	100.7
4th qtr, +/-7 pts	-	21	12	57.1	115	5.5	1	1	7	73	1	1	52.7
Winning	-	99	65	65.7	706	7.1	5	2	34	412	3	3	113.2
Tied	-	32	29	90.6	364	11.4	3	0	15	213	3	1	145.3
Trailing	-	52	33	63.5	399	7.7	0	3	10	210	5	2	62.9

	Att	Cm	Pct	Yds	Yd/Att	TD	Int	1st	YAC	Big	Sk	Rtg
Inside 20	26	14	53.8	94	3.6	3	1	4	84	0	0	84.5
Inside 10	11	4	36.4	13	1.2	2	1	2	11	0	0	46.6
1st Down	75	55	73.3	659	8.8	4	0	27	358	5	3	117.6
2nd Down	62	48	77.4	578	9.3	4	1	25	301	4	1	120.2
3rd Down Overall	46	24	52.2	232	5.0	4	4	16	185	2	1	30.3
3rd D 0-5 to Go	18	12	66.7	94	5.2	0	0	10	91	0	1	79.4
3rd D 6+ to Go	28	12	42.9	138	4.9	0	4	6	94	2	0	18.7
4th Down	0	0	-	0	-	0	0	0	0	0	1	-
Rec Behind Line	41	32	78.0	248	6.0	0	0	13	319	0	0	91.9
1-10 yds	93	73	78.5	726	7.8	4	1	36	428	3	0	109.1
11-20 yds	33	16	48.5	295	8.9	0	3	13	65	4	0	41.9
21-30 yds	8	4	50.0	119	14.9	2	1	4	25	2	0	95.8
31+	8	2	25.0	81	10.1	2	0	2	7	2	0	108.9
Left Sideline	16	12	75.0	129	8.1	0	0	7	69	1	0	98.2
Left Side	21	20	95.2	233	11.1	2	1	11	103	1	1	124.8
Middle	39	23	59.0	322	8.3	4	1	11	183	3	4	109.1
Right Side	42	30	71.4	289	6.9	0	1	14	201	1	1	80.4
Right Sideline	65	42	64.6	496	7.6	2	2	25	288	5	0	85.2
2 Wide Receivers	108	79	73.1	792	7.3	2	2	38	443	5	4	92.1
3+ WR	73	47	64.4	675	9.2	5	3	29	401	6	2	100.0
Attempts 1-10	69	45	65.2	536	7.8	3	1	24	294	5	0	97.3
Attempts 11-20	44	33	75.0	364	8.3	2	1	10	230	2	0	104.7
Attempts 21+	70	49	70.0	569	8.1	3	3	28	320	4	0	90.7

1995 Incompletions

Type	Num	% of Inc	% of Att
Pass Dropped	5	8.9	2.7
Poor Throw	20	35.7	10.9
Pass Defensed	10	17.9	5.5
Pass Hit at Line	2	3.6	1.1
Other	19	33.9	10.4
Total	56	100.0	30.6

Game Logs (1-8)

Date	Opp	Result	Att	Cm	Pct	Yds	TD	Int	Lg	Sk	F-L
09/03	@NO	W 24-22	8	5	62.5	49	0	1	17	0	0-0
09/10	Atl	W 41-10	0	0	-	0	0	0	0	0	0-0
09/17	NE	W 28-3	0	0	-	0	0	0	0	1	0-0
09/25	@Det	L 24-27	0	0	-	0	0	0	0	0	0-0
10/01	NYN	W 20-6	0	0	-	0	0	0	0	0	0-0
10/15	@Ind	L 17-18	1	0	0.0	0	0	0	0	0	0-0
10/22	@StL	W 44-10	14	11	78.6	119	2	0	35	0	0-0
10/29	NO	L 7-11	42	29	69.0	243	0	2	17	1	0-0

Game Logs (9-16)

Date	Opp	Result	Att	Cm	Pct	Yds	TD	Int	Lg	Sk	F-L
11/05	Car	L 7-13	37	26	70.3	327	0	2	40	1	0-0
11/12	@Dal	W 38-20	30	20	66.7	305	2	0	81	2	0-0
11/20	@Mia	W 44-20	41	31	75.6	382	4	0	47	1	0-0
11/26	StL	W 41-13	8	5	62.5	44	0	0	16	1	1-0
12/03	Buf	W 27-17	0	0	-	0	0	0	0	0	0-0
12/10	@Car	W 31-10	2	0	0.0	0	0	0	0	0	0-0
12/18	Min	W 37-30	0	0	-	0	0	0	0	0	0-0
12/24	@Atl	L 27-28	0	0	-	0	0	0	0	0	0-0

Eric Green
Miami Dolphins — TE

1995 Receiving Splits

	G	Rec	Yds	Avg	TD	Lg	Big	YAC	Trgt	Y@C	1st	1st%
Total	14	43	499	11.6	3	31	4	183	64	7.3	26	60.5
vs. Playoff	8	22	211	9.6	1	25	1	70	37	6.4	11	50.0
vs. Non-playoff	6	21	288	13.7	2	31	3	113	27	8.3	15	71.4
vs. Own Division	6	15	153	10.2	1	25	2	69	21	5.6	8	53.3
Home	7	19	199	10.5	0	25	1	67	28	6.9	11	57.9
Away	7	24	300	12.5	3	31	3	116	36	7.7	15	62.5
Games 1-8	6	17	209	12.3	2	31	1	62	26	8.6	12	70.6
Games 9-16	8	26	290	11.2	1	30	3	121	38	6.5	14	53.8
September	3	7	75	10.7	0	18	0	30	10	6.4	4	57.1
October	3	10	134	13.4	2	31	1	32	16	10.2	8	80.0
November	4	12	151	12.6	0	25	1	55	19	8.0	8	66.7
December	4	14	139	9.9	1	30	2	66	19	5.2	6	42.9
Grass	9	24	253	10.5	0	25	1	98	38	6.5	14	58.3
Turf	5	19	246	12.9	3	31	3	85	26	8.5	12	63.2
Outdoor	3	35	382	10.9	2	25	2	139	51	6.9	20	57.1
Indoor	11	8	117	14.6	1	31	2	44	13	9.1	6	75.0
1st Half	-	18	244	13.6	2	31	2	81	27	9.1	15	83.3
2nd Half/OT	-	25	255	10.2	1	25	2	102	37	6.1	11	44.0
Last 2 Min. Half	-	1	5	5.0	0	5	0	1	2	4.0	1	100.0
4th qtr, +/-7 pts	-	3	38	12.7	0	20	0	11	6	9.0	1	33.3
Winning	-	14	149	10.6	0	30	1	73	24	5.4	8	57.1
Tied	-	7	81	11.6	0	21	0	32	12	7.0	4	57.1
Trailing	-	22	269	12.2	3	31	3	78	28	8.7	14	63.6

	Rec	Yds	Avg	TD	Lg	Big	YAC	Trgt	Y@C	1st	1st%
Inside 20	4	23	5.8	1	8	0	6	9	4.3	1	25.0
Inside 10	2	10	5.0	1	8	0	1	6	4.5	1	50.0
1st Down	21	281	13.4	3	31	3	86	28	9.3	13	61.9
2nd Down	20	197	9.9	0	30	1	84	30	5.7	11	55.0
3rd Down Overall	2	21	10.5	0	13	0	13	6	4.0	2	100.0
3rd D 0-2 to Go	0	-	-	0	0	0	0	1	-	-	0
3rd D 3-7 to Go	2	21	10.5	0	13	0	13	4	4.0	2	100.0
3rd D 8+ to Go	0	0	-	0	0	0	0	1	-	-	0
4th Down	0	-	-	0	0	0	0	0	-	-	0
Rec Behind Line	1	2	2.0	0	2	0	2	1	0.0	0	0.0
1-10 yds	30	244	8.1	1	18	0	115	47	4.3	14	46.7
11-20 yds	11	222	20.2	1	30	3	64	14	14.4	11	100.0
21-30 yds	1	31	31.0	0	31	1	2	2	29.0	1	100.0
31+	0	0	-	0	0	0	0	0	-	-	0
Left Sideline	2	21	10.5	0	15	0	15	5	3.0	1	50.0
Left Side	15	139	9.3	0	22	0	70	21	4.6	8	53.3
Middle	14	175	12.5	1	25	1	42	19	9.5	10	71.4
Right Side	11	146	13.3	2	31	3	53	17	8.5	6	54.5
Right Sideline	1	18	18.0	0	18	0	1	2	15.0	1	100.0
Shotgun	8	81	10.1	0	17	0	15	11	8.3	5	62.5
2 Wide Receivers	27	304	11.3	2	31	1	117	41	6.9	16	59.3
3 Wide Receivers	15	180	12.0	1	30	3	66	20	7.6	9	60.0
4+ Wide Receivers	1	15	15.0	0	15	0	2	2	15.0	1	100.0

1995 Incompletions

Type	Num	%of Inc	%of Att
Pass Dropped	9	42.9	14.1
Poor Throw	4	19.0	6.3
Pass Defensed	5	23.8	7.8
Pass Hit at Line	0	0.0	0.0
Other	3	14.3	4.7
Total	21	100.0	32.8

Game Logs (1-8)

Date	Opp	Result	Rec	Yds	Trgt	F-L	TD
09/03	NYA	W 52-14	4	36	4	0-0	0
09/10	@NE	W 20-3	1	13	2	0-0	0
09/18	Pit	W 23-10	2	26	4	0-0	0
10/01	@Cin	W 26-23	7	91	9	0-0	1
10/08	Ind	L 24-27	1	5	4	0-0	0
10/15	@NO	L 30-33	2	38	3	0-0	1
10/22	@NYA	L 16-17	-	-	-	-	-
10/29	Buf	W 23-6	-	-	-	-	-

Game Logs (9-16)

Date	Opp	Result	Rec	Yds	Trgt	F-L	TD
11/05	@SD	W 24-14	4	41	8	0-0	0
11/12	NE	L 17-34	3	46	3	0-0	0
11/20	SF	L 20-44	3	49	4	0-0	0
11/26	@Ind	L 28-36	2	15	4	0-0	0
12/03	Atl	W 21-20	5	35	8	0-0	0
12/11	KC	L 13-6	1	2	1	0-0	0
12/17	@Buf	L 20-23	4	38	4	0-0	1
12/24	@StL	W 41-22	4	64	6	0-0	0

Harold Green
Cincinnati Bengals — RB

1995 Rushing and Receiving Splits

	G	Rush	Yds	Avg	Lg	TD	1st	Stf	YdL	Rec	Yds	Avg	TD
Total	15	171	661	3.9	23	2	35	20	51	27	182	6.7	1
vs. Playoff	5	62	235	3.8	14	0	15	7	21	8	59	7.4	0
vs. Non-playoff	10	109	426	3.9	23	2	20	13	30	19	123	6.5	1
vs. Own Division	7	83	308	3.7	23	2	13	10	27	12	76	6.3	1
Home	8	90	355	3.9	23	2	17	14	34	15	46	3.1	1
Away	7	81	306	3.8	20	0	18	6	17	12	136	11.3	0
Games 1-8	8	101	410	4.1	23	2	25	9	25	16	133	8.3	1
Games 9-16	7	70	251	3.6	15	0	10	11	26	11	49	4.5	0
September	4	49	176	3.6	23	2	12	7	17	5	38	7.6	0
October	4	52	234	4.5	20	0	13	2	8	11	95	8.6	1
November	3	40	145	3.6	14	0	4	5	13	2	8	4.0	0
December	4	30	106	3.5	15	0	6	6	13	9	41	4.6	0
Grass	4	43	171	4.0	20	0	9	4	11	7	82	11.7	0
Turf	11	128	490	3.8	23	2	26	16	40	20	100	5.0	1
Indoor	2	27	101	3.7	11	0	8	2	6	3	32	10.7	0
Outdoor	13	144	560	3.9	23	2	27	18	45	24	150	6.3	1
1st Half	-	104	426	4.1	23	1	24	11	26	13	63	4.8	1
2nd Half/OT	-	67	235	3.5	15	1	11	9	25	14	119	8.5	0
Last 2 Min. Half	-	4	27	6.8	15	0	2	0	0	1	6	6.0	0
4th qtr, +/-7 pts	-	13	65	5.0	15	0	4	2	5	2	9	4.5	0
Winning	-	43	157	3.7	15	0	7	6	17	10	62	6.2	0
Tied	-	55	207	3.8	20	1	12	6	19	9	58	6.4	1
Trailing	-	73	297	4.1	23	1	16	8	15	8	62	7.8	0

	Rush	Yds	Avg	Lg	TD	1st	Stf	YdL	Rec	Yds	Avg	TD
Inside 20	14	45	3.2	10	1	2	1	5	1	1	1.0	1
Inside 10	4	12	3.0	6	0	1	0	1	1	1	1.0	1
1st Down	96	383	4.0	23	1	8	5	12	9	100	11.1	0
2nd Down	64	243	3.8	20	1	21	13	36	12	57	4.8	1
3rd Down Overall	10	30	3.0	9	0	5	2	3	6	25	4.2	0
3rd D 0-2 to Go	3	9	3.0	9	0	1	2		0	-		0
3rd D 3-7 to Go	7	21	3.0	9	0	3	1	1	3	9	3.0	0
3rd D 8+ to Go	0	0	-	0	0	0	0		3	16	5.3	0
4th Down	1	5	5.0	5	0	1	0	0	0	-		0
Left Sideline	6	18	3.0	10	0	3	1	4	3	34	11.3	0
Left Side	29	81	2.8	15	0	7	4	6	9	32	3.2	0
Middle	81	331	4.1	20	1	13	6	12	6	61	10.2	0
Right Side	44	170	3.9	23	1	9	7	19	12	68	5.7	1
Right Sideline	11	61	5.5	16	0	3	2	10	0	0	-	0
Shotgun	0	0	-	0	0	0	0	0	0	-		0
2 Wide Receivers	126	454	3.6	23	1	24	16	41	20	137	6.9	0
3 Wide Receivers	29	138	4.8	14	0	7	4	10	6	44	7.3	0
4+ Wide Receivers	1	5	5.0	5	0	0	0	0	0	-		0
Carries 1-5	75	295	3.9	23	1	19	7	17	0	0	-	0
Carries 6-10	65	263	4.0	20	0	10	8	18	0	0	-	0
Carries 11-15	27	99	3.7	10	1	6	4	15	0	0	-	0
Carries 16-20	4	4	1.0	2	0	0	1	1	0	0	-	0
Carries 21+	0	0	-	0	0	0	0	0	0	0	-	0

1995 Incompletions

Type	Num	%of Inc	% Att
Pass Dropped	8	57.1	19.5
Poor Throw	4	28.6	9.8
Pass Defensed	1	7.1	2.4
Pass Hit at Line	0	0.0	0.0
Other	1	7.1	2.4
Total	14	100.0	34.1

Game Logs (1-8)

Date	Opp	Result	Rush	Yds	Rec	Yds	Trgt	F-L	TD
09/03	@Ind	W 24-21	17	65	2	22	2	0-0	0
09/10	Jac	W 24-17	12	36	1	3	2	0-0	1
09/17	@Sea	L 21-24	10	36	1	10	2	0-0	0
09/24	Hou	L 28-38	10	39	1	3	2	0-0	0
10/01	Mia	L 23-26	15	71	2	22	3	0-0	0
10/08	@TB	L 16-19	12	63	3	48	5	0-0	0
10/19	@Pit	W 27-9	11	34	2	22	3	1-0	0
10/29	Cle	L 26-29	14	66	4	23	6	1-1	1

Game Logs (9-16)

Date	Opp	Result	Rush	Yds	Rec	Yds	Trgt	F-L	TD
11/05	Oak	L 17-20	11	45	0	0	0	0-0	0
11/12	@Hou	W 32-25	-	-	-	-	-	-	-
11/19	Pit	L 31-49	12	45	1	2	1	0-0	0
11/26	@Jac	W 17-13	17	55	1	6	2	0-0	0
12/03	@GB	L 10-24	7	20	1	11	3	0-0	0
12/10	Chi	W 16-10	9	42	6	13	7	0-0	0
12/17	@Cle	L	7	33	2	17	3	0-0	0
12/24	Min	W 27-24	3	11	0	0	0	0-0	0

Robert Green
Chicago Bears — RB

1995 Rushing and Receiving Splits

	G	Rush	Yds	Avg	Lg	TD	1st	Stf	YdL	Rec	Yds	Avg	TD
Total	12	107	570	5.3	38	3	26	4	6	28	246	8.8	0
vs. Playoff	5	51	272	5.3	18	1	10	1	1	13	107	8.2	0
vs. Non-playoff	7	56	298	5.3	38	2	16	3	5	15	139	9.3	0
vs. Own Division	7	75	426	5.7	38	2	18	2	3	17	136	8.0	0
Home	6	40	229	5.7	38	1	10	1	1	17	153	9.0	0
Away	6	67	341	5.1	25	2	16	3	5	11	93	8.5	0
Games 1-8	7	54	302	5.6	38	2	16	2	4	16	148	9.3	0
Games 9-16	5	53	268	5.1	18	1	10	2	2	12	98	8.2	0
September	3	27	199	7.4	38	1	9	1	2	8	82	10.3	0
October	4	27	103	3.8	16	1	7	1	2	8	66	8.3	0
November	4	45	205	4.6	15	0	7	2	2	10	90	9.0	0
December	1	8	63	7.9	18	1	3	0	0	2	8	4.0	0
Grass	9	76	410	5.4	38	2	18	3	5	21	190	9.0	0
Turf	3	31	160	5.2	18	1	8	1	1	7	56	8.0	0
Indoor	2	19	101	5.3	18	1	5	0	0	3	10	3.3	0
Outdoor	10	88	469	5.3	38	2	21	4	6	25	236	9.4	0
1st Half	-	42	216	5.1	25	0	9	1	1	16	136	8.5	0
2nd Half/OT	-	65	354	5.4	38	3	17	3	5	12	110	9.2	0
Last 2 Min. Half	-	9	66	7.3	18	1	4	0	0	4	25	6.3	0
4th qtr, +/-7 pts	-	27	131	4.9	16	1	6	1	1	6	57	9.5	0
Winning	-	30	173	5.8	38	1	7	2	4	6	42	7.0	0
Tied	-	43	189	4.4	15	0	9	2	2	8	59	7.4	0
Trailing	-	34	208	6.1	18	2	10	0	0	14	145	10.4	0

	Rush	Yds	Avg	Lg	TD	1st	Stf	YdL	Rec	Yds	Avg	TD
Inside 20	18	63	3.5	11	3	4	3	4	4	23	5.8	0
Inside 10	8	24	3.0	7	2	2	2	3	1	-2	-2.0	0
1st Down	54	278	5.1	38	1	8	3	4	8	59	7.4	0
2nd Down	34	215	6.3	25	1	10	1	2	8	70	8.8	0
3rd Down Overall	19	77	4.1	16	1	8	0	0	12	117	9.8	0
3rd D 0-2 to Go	8	30	3.8	16	1	5	0	0	0	0	-	0
3rd D 3-7 to Go	9	29	3.2	5	0	2	0	0	6	70	11.7	0
3rd D 8+ to Go	2	18	9.0	14	0	1	0	0	6	47	7.8	0
4th Down	0	0	-	0	0	0	0	0	0	0	-	0
Left Sideline	3	3	1.0	3	0	0	1	2	5	48	9.6	0
Left Side	21	116	5.5	38	0	2	2	3	4	51	12.8	0
Middle	54	278	5.1	18	2	16	0	0	4	24	6.0	0
Right Side	26	136	5.2	25	1	6	1	1	11	99	9.0	0
Right Sideline	3	37	12.3	15	0	0	0	0	4	24	6.0	0
Shotgun	0	0	-	0	0	0	0	0	0	0	-	0
2 Wide Receivers	73	343	4.7	25	2	14	4	6	8	66	8.3	0
3 Wide Receivers	13	108	8.3	38	0	5	0	0	12	116	9.7	0
4+ Wide Receivers	18	104	5.8	16	0	5	0	0	8	64	8.0	0
Carries 1-5	56	287	5.1	38	0	11	2	3	0	0	-	0
Carries 6-10	36	226	6.3	25	2	12	1	1	0	0	-	0
Carries 11-15	14	54	3.9	8	1	3	1	2	0	0	-	0
Carries 16-20	1	3	3.0	3	0	1	0	0	0	0	-	0
Carries 21+	0	0	-	0	0	0	0	0	0	0	-	0

1995 Incompletions

Type	Num	%of Inc	% Att
Pass Dropped	1	10.0	2.6
Poor Throw	7	70.0	18.4
Pass Defensed	0	0.0	0.0
Pass Hit at Line	0	0.0	0.0
Other	2	20.0	5.3
Total	10	100.0	26.3

Game Logs (1-8)

Date	Opp	Result	Rush	Yds	Rec	Yds	Trgt	F-L	TD
09/03	Min	W 31-14	4	64	1	9	1	0-0	0
09/11	GB	L 24-27	10	63	5	55	6	0-0	0
09/17	@TB	W 25-6	13	72	2	18	3	0-0	1
09/24	@StL	L 28-34	-	-	-	-	-	-	-
10/08	Car	W 31-27	6	19	4	48	5	1-0	1
10/15	@Jac	W 30-27	7	41	0	0	1	0-0	0
10/22	Hou	W 35-32	3	5	3	16	4	0-0	0
10/30	@Min	W 14-6	11	38	1	2	1	0-0	0

Game Logs (9-16)

Date	Opp	Result	Rush	Yds	Rec	Yds	Trgt	F-L	TD
11/05	Pit	L 34-37	4	20	0	0	0	1-1	0
11/12	@GB	L 28-35	16	68	2	19	3	0-0	0
11/19	Det	L 17-24	13	58	4	25	5	0-0	0
11/26	@NYN	W 27-24	12	59	4	46	5	0-0	0
12/04	@Det	L 7-27	8	63	2	8	4	0-0	1

Willie Green
Carolina Panthers — WR

1995 Receiving Splits

	G	Rec	Yds	Avg	TD	Lg	Big	YAC	Trgt	Y@C	1st	1st%
Total	16	47	882	18.8	6	89	10	304	93	12.3	38	80.9
vs. Playoff	6	20	405	20.3	2	89	4	150	39	12.8	17	85.0
vs. Non-playoff	10	27	477	17.7	4	60	6	154	54	12.0	21	77.8
vs. Own Division	8	33	671	20.3	4	89	7	246	57	12.9	28	84.8
Home	8	19	333	17.5	1	89	3	137	36	10.3	14	73.7
Away	8	28	549	19.6	5	60	7	167	57	13.6	24	85.7
Games 1-8	8	22	315	14.3	2	44	3	71	38	11.1	15	68.2
Games 9-16	8	25	567	22.7	4	89	7	233	55	13.4	23	92.0
September	3	11	158	14.4	1	44	1	33	19	11.4	8	72.7
October	5	11	157	14.3	1	33	2	38	19	10.8	7	63.6
November	4	15	320	21.3	2	60	4	108	28	14.1	14	93.3
December	4	10	247	24.7	2	89	3	125	27	12.2	9	81.8
Grass	12	30	499	16.6	3	89	5	186	60	10.4	24	80.0
Turf	4	17	383	22.5	3	60	5	118	33	15.6	14	82.4
Outdoor	3	30	499	16.6	3	89	5	186	60	10.4	24	80.0
Indoor	13	17	383	22.5	3	60	5	118	29	15.6	14	82.4
1st Half	-	26	483	18.6	1	60	5	145	49	13.0	22	84.6
2nd Half/OT	-	21	399	19.0	5	89	5	159	44	11.4	16	76.2
Last 2 Min. Half	-	9	172	19.1	2	44	3	21	12	16.8	8	88.9
4th qtr, +/-7 pts	-	6	203	33.8	2	89	3	72	13	21.8	6	100.0
Winning	-	10	120	12.0	1	00	1	38	18	8.8	7	70.0
Tied	-	11	204	18.5	0	46	2	41	26	14.8	9	81.8
Trailing	-	26	552	21.2	5	89	7	225	49	12.6	22	84.6

	Rec	Yds	Avg	TD	Lg	Big	YAC	Trgt	Y@C	1st	1st%
Inside 20	5	42	8.4	2	17	0	13	5	5.8	5	100.0
Inside 10	1	2	2.0	1	2	0	0	1	2.0	1	100.0
1st Down	12	202	16.8	2	46	2	32	28	14.2	9	75.0
2nd Down	10	232	23.2	2	89	3	97	19	13.5	8	80.0
3rd Down Overall	25	448	17.9	2	60	5	175	44	10.9	21	84.0
3rd D 0-2 to Go	0	0	-	0	0	0	0	1	-	0	-
3rd D 3-7 to Go	13	207	15.9	1	60	1	84	21	9.5	13	100.0
3rd D 8+ to Go	12	241	20.1	1	47	4	91	22	12.5	8	66.7
4th Down	0	0	-	0	0	0	0	2	-	0	-
Rec Behind Line	2	3	1.5	0	7	0	5	6	-1.0	1	50.0
1-10 yds	28	349	12.5	2	33	2	148	49	7.2	21	75.0
11-20 yds	10	201	20.1	2	60	1	58	18	14.3	9	90.0
21-30 yds	3	153	51.0	1	89	3	69	8	28.0	3	100.0
31+	4	176	44.0	1	47	4	24	12	38.0	4	100.0
Left Sideline	16	390	24.4	4	89	5	137	26	15.8	15	93.8
Left Side	11	139	12.6	1	33	1	56	27	7.5	7	63.6
Middle	2	61	30.5	0	47	1	14	6	23.5	2	100.0
Right Side	11	163	14.8	0	33	2	83	18	7.3	8	72.7
Right Sideline	7	129	18.4	1	46	1	14	16	16.4	6	85.7
Shotgun	0	0	-	0	0	0	0	0	-	0	-
2 Wide Receivers	11	188	17.1	0	47	2	47	18	12.8	8	72.7
3 Wide Receivers	31	602	19.4	6	89	6	223	66	12.2	26	83.9
4+ Wide Receivers	5	92	18.4	0	32	2	34	8	11.6	4	80.0

1995 Incompletions

Type	Num	%of Inc	%of Att
Pass Dropped	7	15.2	7.5
Poor Throw	20	43.5	21.5
Pass Defensed	9	19.6	9.7
Pass Hit at Line	3	6.5	3.2
Other	7	15.2	7.5
Total	46	100.0	49.5

Game Logs (1-8)

Date	Opp	Result	Rec	Yds	Trgt	F-L	TD
09/03	@Atl	L 20-23	7	121	10	0-0	1
09/10	@Buf	L 9-31	0	0	4	0-0	0
09/17	StL	L 10-31	4	37	5	1-1	0
10/01	TB	L 13-20	3	33	7	0-0	0
10/08	@Chi	L 27-31	0	0	1	0-0	0
10/15	NYA	W 26-15	4	37	5	0-0	0
10/22	NO	W 20-3	0	0	1	0-0	0
10/29	@NE	W 20-17	4	87	5	0-0	1

Game Logs (9-16)

Date	Opp	Result	Rec	Yds	Trgt	F-L	TD
11/05	@SF	W 13-7	5	58	8	0-0	0
11/12	@StL	L 17-28	6	157	8	0-0	1
11/19	Ari	W 27-7	0	0	1	0-0	0
11/26	@NO	L 26-34	4	105	11	0-0	1
12/03	Ind	W 13-10	1	33	3	0-0	0
12/10	SF	L 10-31	3	46	9	0-0	0
12/17	Atl	W 21-17	4	147	5	0-0	0
12/24	@Was	L 17-20	2	21	10	0-0	0

Eric Guliford
Carolina Panthers — PR

1995 Receiving Splits

	G	Rec	Yds	Avg	TD	Lg	Big	YAC	Trgt	Y@C	1st	1st%
Total	14	29	444	15.3	1	49	5	187	70	8.9	22	75.9
vs. Playoff	5	6	57	9.5	0	28	1	21	18	6.0	3	50.0
vs. Non-playoff	9	23	387	16.8	1	49	4	166	52	9.6	19	82.6
vs. Own Division	7	12	151	12.6	0	36	2	58	38	7.8	8	66.7
Home	7	13	219	16.8	0	40	3	101	26	9.1	12	92.3
Away	7	16	225	14.1	1	49	2	86	44	8.7	10	62.5
Games 1-8	8	17	284	16.7	1	49	2	110	38	10.2	14	82.4
Games 9-16	6	12	160	13.3	0	36	3	77	32	6.9	8	66.7
September	3	4	53	13.3	0	19	0	17	12	9.0	4	100.0
October	5	13	231	17.8	1	49	2	93	26	10.6	10	76.9
November	4	10	130	13.0	0	36	2	59	25	7.1	7	70.0
December	2	2	30	15.0	0	28	1	18	7	6.0	1	50.0
Grass	10	27	403	14.9	1	49	4	167	52	8.7	21	77.8
Turf	4	2	41	20.5	0	36	1	20	18	10.5	1	50.0
Indoor	3	2	41	20.5	0	36	1	20	18	10.5	1	50.0
Outdoor	11	27	403	14.9	1	49	4	167	52	8.7	21	77.8
1st Half	-	15	182	12.1	0	30	2	77	34	7.0	12	80.0
2nd Half/OT	-	14	262	18.7	1	49	3	110	36	10.9	10	71.4
Last 2 Min. Half	-	5	71	14.2	0	20	0	22	15	9.8	5	100.0
4th qtr, +/-7 pts	-	2	45	22.5	0	40	1	18	8	13.5	1	50.0
Winning	-	9	91	10.1	0	20	0	28	14	7.0	6	66.7
Tied	-	5	94	18.8	1	30	1	44	14	10.0	5	100.0
Trailing	-	15	259	17.3	0	49	4	115	42	9.6	11	73.3

	Rec	Yds	Avg	TD	Lg	Big	YAC	Trgt	Y@C	1st	1st%
Inside 20	1	8	8.0	0	8	0	1	7	7.0	1	100.0
Inside 10	0	0	-	0	0	0	0	4	-	0	-
1st Down	7	113	16.1	0	36	1	34	23	11.3	4	57.1
2nd Down	9	91	10.1	0	28	1	39	17	5.8	6	66.7
3rd Down Overall	13	240	18.5	1	49	3	114	30	9.7	12	92.3
3rd D 0-2 to Go	2	12	6.0	0	8	0	3	2	4.5	2	100.0
3rd D 3-7 to Go	6	84	14.0	0	30	1	49	17	5.8	5	83.3
3rd D 8+ to Go	5	144	28.8	1	49	2	62	11	16.4	5	100.0
4th Down	0	0	-	0	0	0	0	0	-	0	-
Rec Behind Line	0	0	-	0	0	0	0	4	-	0	-
1-10 yds	21	214	10.2	0	30	2	91	37	5.9	14	66.7
11-20 yds	7	190	27.1	1	49	2	78	19	16.0	7	100.0
21-30 yds	1	40	40.0	0	40	1	18	7	22.0	1	100.0
31+	0	0	-	0	0	0	0	3	-	0	-
Left Sideline	5	41	8.2	0	11	0	13	13	5.6	1	100.0
Left Side	11	170	15.5	0	40	1	65	20	9.5	10	90.9
Middle	3	82	27.3	1	36	1	37	8	15.0	3	100.0
Right Side	7	128	18.3	0	49	3	72	16	8.0	3	42.9
Right Sideline	3	23	7.7	0	8	0	0	13	7.7	1	33.3
Shotgun	0	0	-	0	0	0	0	1	-	0	-
2 Wide Receivers	7	111	15.9	0	49	1	45	20	9.4	5	71.4
3 Wide Receivers	16	205	12.8	1	30	2	84	34	7.6	11	68.8
4+ Wide Receivers	6	128	21.3	0	40	2	58	16	11.7	6	100.0

1995 Incompletions

Type	Num	%of Inc	%of Att
Pass Dropped	5	12.2	7.1
Poor Throw	22	53.7	31.4
Pass Defensed	4	9.8	5.7
Pass Hit at Line	4	9.8	5.7
Other	6	14.6	8.6
Total	41	100.0	58.6

Game Logs (1-8)

Date	Opp	Result	Rush	Yds	Rec	Yds	Trgt	F-L	TD
09/03	@Atl	L 20-23	0	0	0	0	4	0-0	0
09/10	@Buf	L 9-31	1	1	0	0	0	0-0	0
09/17	StL	L 10-31	0	0	4	53	8	0-0	0
10/01	TB	L 13-20	0	0	1	40	1	0-0	0
10/08	@Chi	L 27-31	0	0	3	63	7	0-0	1
10/15	NYA	W 26-15	0	0	2	34	4	0-0	0
10/22	NO	W 20-3	0	0	0	0	2	0-0	0
10/29	@NE	W 20-17	0	0	7	94	12	0-0	1

Game Logs (9-16)

Date	Opp	Result	Rush	Yds	Rec	Yds	Trgt	F-L	TD
11/05	@SF	W 13-7	1	1	4	27	7	1-0	0
11/12	@StL	L 17-28	0	0	1	5	6	0-0	0
11/19	Ari	W 27-7	0	0	4	62	4	0-0	0
11/26	@NO	L 26-34	0	0	1	36	8	0-0	0
12/03	Ind	W 13-10	0	0	0	0	4	0-0	0
12/10	SF	L 10-31	0	0	2	30	3	0-0	0

Rodney Hampton
New York Giants — RB

1995 Rushing and Receiving Splits

	G	Rush	Yds	Avg	Lg	TD	1st	Stf	YdL	Rec	Yds	Avg	TD
Total	16	306	1182	3.9	32	10	74	24	50	24	142	5.9	0
vs. Playoff	8	157	615	3.9	28	2	36	11	31	13	67	5.2	0
vs. Non-playoff	8	149	567	3.8	32	8	38	12	19	11	75	6.8	0
vs. Own Division	8	145	628	4.3	28	1	35	9	12	11	49	4.5	0
Home	8	144	553	3.8	32	7	38	12	21	16	86	5.4	0
Away	8	162	629	3.9	28	3	36	11	29	8	56	7.0	0
Games 1-8	8	141	563	4.0	32	4	34	10	27	9	41	4.6	0
Games 9-16	8	165	619	3.8	28	6	40	13	23	15	101	6.7	0
September	4	89	362	4.1	32	4	23	7	11	6	31	5.2	0
October	4	52	201	3.9	16	0	11	3	16	3	10	3.3	0
November	5	93	294	3.2	12	5	21	6	11	6	53	8.8	0
December	3	72	325	4.5	28	1	19	7	12	9	48	5.3	0
Grass	5	89	304	3.4	20	0	16	9	27	4	14	3.5	0
Turf	11	217	878	4.0	32	10	58	14	23	20	128	6.4	0
Indoor	1	18	54	3.0	10	2	5	1	1	1	14	14.0	0
Outdoor	15	288	1128	3.9	32	8	69	22	49	23	128	5.6	0
1st Half	-	169	650	3.8	32	5	41	12	21	16	124	7.8	0
2nd Half/OT	-	137	532	3.9	28	5	33	11	29	8	18	2.3	0
Last 2 Min. Half	-	17	55	3.2	9	2	6	1	1	2	10	5.0	0
4th qtr, +/-7 pts	-	47	226	4.8	16	2	16	2	4	1	1	1.0	0
Winning	-	103	409	4.0	28	3	24	6	11	7	41	5.9	0
Tied	-	76	294	3.9	32	2	18	8	12	4	23	5.8	0
Trailing	-	127	479	3.8	20	5	32	9	27	13	78	6.0	0

	Rush	Yds	Avg	Lg	TD	1st	Stf	YdL	Rec	Yds	Avg	TD
Inside 20	62	150	2.4	10	10	20	6	22	0	0	-	0
Inside 10	38	55	1.4	6	10	16	4	19	0	0	-	0
1st Down	172	693	4.0	28	3	16	17	37	10	52	5.2	0
2nd Down	108	395	3.7	32	5	36	6	13	11	73	6.6	0
3rd Down Overall	24	91	3.8	14	1	20	0	0	3	17	5.7	0
3rd D 0-2 to Go	24	91	3.8	14	1	20	0	0	3	17	5.7	0
3rd D 3-7 to Go	0	0	-	0	0	0	0	0	0	0	-	0
3rd D 8+ to Go	0	0	-	0	0	0	0	0	0	0	-	0
4th Down	2	3	1.5	2	1	2	0	0	0	0	-	0
Left Sideline	7	52	7.4	20	0	2	0	0	0	0	-	0
Left Side	53	168	3.2	16	4	14	8	23	10	58	5.8	0
Middle	186	704	3.8	28	5	46	10	18	6	20	3.3	0
Right Side	58	249	4.3	32	1	12	5	9	8	64	8.0	0
Right Sideline	2	9	4.5	5	0	0	0	0	0	0	-	0
Shotgun	1	2	2.0	2	0	0	0	0	0	0	-	0
2 Wide Receivers	248	1017	4.1	32	4	55	19	32	18	98	5.4	0
3 Wide Receivers	11	54	4.9	9	0	1	0	0	5	43	8.6	0
4+ Wide Receivers	0	0	-	0	0	0	0	0	0	0	-	0
Carries 1-5	80	354	4.4	32	1	14	4	6	0	0	-	0
Carries 6-10	79	301	3.8	16	0	21	7	11	0	0	-	0
Carries 11-15	69	186	2.7	20	4	14	10	29	0	0	-	0
Carries 16-20	42	184	4.4	28	1	13	1	3	0	0	-	0
Carries 21+	36	157	4.4	16	4	12	1	1	0	0	-	0

1995 Incompletions

Type	Num	%of Inc	% Att
Pass Dropped	3	75.0	10.7
Poor Throw	0	0.0	0.0
Pass Defensed	0	0.0	0.0
Pass Hit at Line	1	25.0	3.6
Other	0	0.0	0.0
Total	4	100.0	14.3

Game Logs (1-8)

Date	Opp	Result	Rush	Yds	Rec	Yds	Trgt	F-L	TD
09/04	Dal	L 0-35	14	48	2	7	2	0-0	0
09/10	@KC	L 17-20	26	79	1	8	1	1-1	0
09/17	@GB	L 6-14	16	86	1	1	2	0-0	0
09/24	NO	W 45-29	33	149	2	15	2	0-0	4
10/01	@SF	L 6-20	12	13	0	0	1	1-0	0
10/08	Ari	W 27-21	9	47	0	0	0	0-0	0
10/15	Phi	L 14-17	14	58	2	6	5	1-1	0
10/29	@Was	W 24-15	17	83	1	1	1	1-1	0

Game Logs (9-16)

Date	Opp	Result	Rush	Yds	Rec	Yds	Trgt	F-L	TD
11/05	@Sea	L 28-30	18	54	1	14	1	0-0	2
11/12	Oak	L 13-17	14	44	3	25	3	0-0	0
11/19	@Phi	L 19-28	21	84	0	0	0	0-0	1
11/26	Chi	L 24-27	22	69	1	13	1	0-0	2
11/30	@Ari	W 10-6	18	43	1	1	1	0-0	0
12/10	Was	W 20-13	18	78	2	3	2	0-0	0
12/17	@Dal	L 20-21	34	187	3	28	3	0-0	0
12/23	SD	L 17-27	20	60	4	17	4	0-0	1

Jim Harbaugh

1995 Passing Splits

	G	Att	Cm	Pct	Yds	Yd/Att	TD	Int	1st	YAC	Big	Sk	Rtg
Total	15	314	200	63.7	2575	8.2	17	5	115	1151	22	36	100.7
vs. Playoff	6	152	92	60.5	1275	8.4	9	2	60	520	11	16	101.7
vs. Non-playoff	9	162	108	66.7	1300	8.0	8	3	55	631	11	20	99.8
vs. Own Division	8	177	120	67.8	1482	8.4	12	1	69	649	11	20	113.7
Home	8	162	97	59.9	1259	7.8	7	3	60	635	10	18	91.0
Away	7	152	103	67.8	1316	8.7	10	2	55	516	12	18	111.1
Games 1-8	8	171	112	65.5	1379	8.1	8	2	63	554	10	16	101.0
Games 9-16	7	143	88	61.5	1196	8.4	9	3	52	597	12	20	100.5
September	3	62	39	62.9	450	7.3	4	0	22	165	2	8	106.3
October	5	109	73	67.0	929	8.5	4	2	41	389	8	8	98.0
November	4	58	41	70.7	584	10.1	6	1	24	318	7	5	130.2
December	3	85	47	55.3	612	7.2	3	2	28	279	5	15	80.1
Grass	4	96	68	70.8	855	8.9	6	2	33	329	10	12	110.4
Turf	11	218	132	60.6	1720	7.9	11	3	82	822	12	24	96.5
Indoor	9	169	102	60.4	1356	8.0	8	3	64	687	11	18	94.2
Outdoor	6	145	98	67.6	1219	8.4	9	2	51	464	11	18	108.4
1st Half	-	139	88	63.3	1190	8.6	7	3	52	548	13	18	98.3
2nd Half/OT	-	175	112	64.0	1385	7.9	10	2	63	603	9	18	102.7
Last 2 Min. Half	-	35	18	51.4	229	6.5	3	1	13	104	1	6	88.9
4th qtr. +/-7 pts	-	69	42	60.9	578	8.4	4	1	27	249	4	7	101.0
Winning	-	64	35	54.7	433	6.8	3	4	18	204	5	8	65.4
Tied	-	83	51	61.4	632	7.6	3	1	32	239	4	11	92.0
Trailing	-	167	114	68.3	1510	9.0	11	0	65	708	13	17	118.6

	Att	Cm	Pct	Yds	Yd/Att	TD	Int	1st	YAC	Big	Sk	Rtg
Inside 20	44	23	52.3	186	4.2	12	1	14	67	0	5	93.4
Inside 10	17	9	52.9	29	1.7	5	0	5	17	0	2	98.3
1st Down	116	87	75.0	1111	9.6	7	2	42	551	11	10	117.4
2nd Down	102	61	59.8	723	7.1	6	2	35	325	5	17	92.9
3rd Down Overall	89	46	51.7	659	7.4	2	1	33	263	5	9	78.8
3rd D 0-5 to Go	27	14	51.9	173	6.4	0	0	12	64	2	2	72.0
3rd D 6+ to Go	62	32	51.6	486	7.8	2	1	21	199	3	7	81.8
4th Down	7	6	85.7	82	11.7	2	0	5	12	1	0	155.1
Rec Behind Line	57	38	66.7	242	4.2	0	2	11	363	0	0	60.7
1-10 yds	157	107	68.2	1016	6.5	8	2	55	510	2	0	97.5
11-20 yds	54	35	64.8	618	11.4	5	0	29	126	3	0	134.6
21-30 yds	28	13	46.4	407	14.5	3	1	13	103	10	0	113.7
31+	18	7	38.9	292	16.2	1	0	7	49	7	0	105.1
Left Sideline	71	48	67.6	717	10.1	2	0	32	234	8	0	109.9
Left Side	70	44	62.9	585	8.4	6	1	33	281	4	8	111.9
Middle	47	32	68.1	427	9.1	1	0	21	161	4	25	103.8
Right Side	59	39	66.1	326	5.5	2	3	10	190	1	1	70.3
Right Sideline	67	37	55.2	520	7.8	6	1	19	285	5	2	104.1
2 Wide Receivers	117	90	76.9	1103	9.4	6	3	44	541	11	12	111.9
3+ WR	184	103	56.0	1416	7.7	8	2	67	577	11	22	90.8
Attempts 1-10	144	98	68.1	1301	9.0	8	2	60	585	13	0	109.2
Attempts 11-20	100	60	60.0	765	7.7	6	1	33	336	6	0	99.8
Attempts 21+	70	42	60.0	509	7.3	3	2	22	230	3	0	84.8

1995 Incompletions

Type	Num	% of Inc	% of Att
Pass Dropped	19	16.7	6.1
Poor Throw	53	46.5	16.9
Pass Defensed	15	13.2	4.8
Pass Hit at Line	1	0.9	0.3
Other	26	22.8	8.3
Total	114	100.0	36.3

Game Logs (1-8)

Date	Opp	Result	Att	Cm	Pct	Yds	TD	Int	Lg	Sk	F-L
09/03	Cin	L 21-24	13	9	69.2	86	1	0	34	2	1-0
09/10	@NYA	W 27-24	16	11	68.8	123	2	0	24	1	0-0
09/17	@Buf	L 14-20	13	9	57.6	241	1	0	32	5	2-1
10/01	StL	W 21-18	19	11	57.9	146	0	1	52	1	1-1
10/08	@Mia	W 27-24	33	25	75.8	319	3	0	47	2	0-0
10/15	SF	W 18-17	18	12	66.7	175	1	1	42	1	0-0
10/22	@Oak	L 17-30	25	16	64.0	202	0	0	52	4	0-0
10/29	NYA	W 17-10	14	9	64.3	87	0	0	22	1	0-0

Game Logs (9-16)

Date	Opp	Result	Att	Cm	Pct	Yds	TD	Int	Lg	Sk	F-L
11/05	Buf	L 10-16	7	4	57.1	75	0	0	45	2	0-0
11/12	@NO	L 14-17	7	5	71.4	97	1	0	40	0	0-0
11/19	@NE	W 24-10	26	20	76.9	232	2	1	40	0	0-0
11/26	Mia	W 36-28	18	12	66.7	180	3	0	39	3	0-0
12/03	@Car	L 10-13	12	7	58.3	102	1	1	33	6	0-0
12/10	@Jac	W 41-31	-	-	-	-	-	-	-	-	-
12/17	SD	L 24-27	43	20	46.5	285	1	1	36	3	0-0
12/23	NE	W 10-7	30	20	66.7	225	1	0	36	6	0-0

Ronnie Harmon

1995 Receiving Splits

	G	Rec	Yds	Avg	TD	Lg	Big	YAC	Trgt	Y@C	1st	1st%
Total	16	62	662	10.7	5	44	2	399	88	4.2	33	53.2
vs. Playoff	7	30	330	11.0	0	44	2	219	44	3.7	14	46.7
vs. Non-playoff	9	32	332	10.4	5	23	0	180	44	4.8	19	59.4
vs. Own Division	8	35	434	12.4	4	44	2	239	46	5.6	20	57.1
Home	8	37	387	10.5	2	31	1	229	52	4.3	20	54.1
Away	8	25	275	11.0	3	44	1	170	36	4.2	13	52.0
Games 1-8	8	29	289	10.0	3	44	1	197	35	3.2	12	41.4
Games 9-16	8	33	373	11.3	2	31	1	202	53	5.2	21	63.6
September	4	10	107	10.7	1	19	0	59	16	4.8	5	50.0
October	4	19	182	9.6	2	44	1	138	19	2.3	7	36.8
November	4	22	276	12.5	1	31	1	134	31	6.5	15	68.2
December	4	11	97	8.8	1	17	0	68	22	2.6	6	54.5
Grass	11	50	555	11.1	3	44	2	352	67	4.1	28	56.0
Turf	5	12	107	8.9	2	23	0	47	21	5.0	5	41.7
Indoor	2	7	78	11.1	2	23	0	13	13	6.4	4	57.1
Outdoor	14	55	584	10.6	3	44	2	366	75	4.0	29	52.7
1st Half	-	26	246	9.5	2	31	1	147	39	3.8	13	50.0
2nd Half/OT	-	36	416	11.6	3	44	1	252	49	4.6	20	55.6
Last 2 Min. Half	-	13	127	9.8	1	22	0	99	21	2.2	7	53.8
4th qtr. +/-7 pts	-	6	100	16.7	1	44	1	62	10	6.3	4	66.7
Winning	-	13	169	13.0	1	44	1	120	20	3.8	7	53.8
Tied	-	8	99	12.4	0	17	0	53	14	5.8	4	50.0
Trailing	-	41	394	9.6	4	31	1	226	54	4.1	22	53.7

	Rec	Yds	Avg	TD	Lg	Big	YAC	Trgt	Y@C	1st	1st%
Inside 20	8	82	10.3	4	15	0	23	9	7.4	7	87.5
Inside 10	1	3	3.0	1	3	0	1	1	2.0	1	100.0
1st Down	17	164	9.6	1	22	0	100	20	3.8	8	47.1
2nd Down	20	168	8.4	2	19	0	121	27	2.4	9	45.0
3rd Down Overall	24	325	13.5	2	44	2	179	38	6.1	16	66.7
3rd D 0-2 to Go	2	6	3.0	0	5	0	7	2	-0.5	1	50.0
3rd D 3-7 to Go	9	113	12.6	0	31	1	51	18	6.9	7	77.8
3rd D 8+ to Go	13	206	15.8	2	44	1	121	18	6.5	8	61.5
4th Down	1	5	5.0	0	5	0	-1	3	6.0	0	0.0
Rec Behind Line	11	49	4.5	0	14	0	99	12	-4.5	2	18.2
1-10 yds	45	490	10.9	2	44	1	271	61	4.9	25	55.6
11-20 yds	5	92	18.4	3	23	0	22	9	14.0	5	100.0
21-30 yds	1	31	31.0	0	31	1	7	5	24.0	1	100.0
31+	0	0	-	0	0	0	0	1	-	0	-
Left Sideline	13	148	11.4	1	31	1	75	15	5.6	6	46.2
Left Side	12	117	9.8	0	20	0	92	14	2.1	7	58.3
Middle	14	166	11.9	2	22	0	82	25	6.0	9	64.3
Right Side	12	99	8.3	1	18	0	66	14	2.8	4	33.3
Right Sideline	11	132	12.0	1	44	1	84	20	4.4	7	63.6
Shotgun	0	0	-	0	0	0	0	0	-	0	-
2 Wide Receivers	11	120	10.9	1	44	1	90	13	2.7	5	45.5
3 Wide Receivers	40	402	10.1	3	31	1	238	56	4.1	19	47.5
4+ Wide Receivers	11	140	12.7	1	20	0	71	19	6.3	9	81.8

1995 Incompletions

Type	Num	%of Inc	%of Att
Pass Dropped	5	19.2	5.7
Poor Throw	16	61.5	18.2
Pass Defensed	4	15.4	4.5
Pass Hit at Line	0	0.0	0.0
Other	1	3.8	1.1
Total	26	100.0	29.5

Game Logs (1-8)

Date	Opp	Result	Rush	Yds	Rec	Yds	Trgt	F-L	TD
09/03	@Oak	L 7-17	2	12	4	53	5	0-0	0
09/10	Sea	W 14-10	1	-3	1	15	3	0-0	0
09/17	@Phi	W 27-21	5	11	0	0	3	0-0	0
09/24	Den	W 17-6	10	29	5	39	5	0-0	0
10/01	@Pit	L 16-31	1	3	4	25	4	0-0	0
10/09	@KC	L 23-29	4	-3	4	65	4	0-0	1
10/15	Dal	L 9-23	3	54	8	52	8	0-0	1
10/22	@Sea	W 35-25	2	7	3	40	3	0-0	2

Game Logs (9-16)

Date	Opp	Result	Rush	Yds	Rec	Yds	Trgt	F-L	TD
11/05	Mia	L 14-24	14	52	4	54	5	0-0	0
11/12	KC	L 7-22	4	8	6	96	10	0-0	0
11/19	@Den	L 27-30	4	5	5	50	6	1-1	1
11/27	Oak	W 12-6	2	-3	7	76	10	0-0	0
12/03	Cle	W 31-13	1	10	2	20	3	0-0	0
12/09	Ari	W 28-25	0	0	4	35	8	0-0	1
12/17	@Ind	W 27-24	1	9	4	38	10	0-0	0
12/23	@NYN	W 27-17	1	1	1	4	1	0-0	0

Alvin Harper
Tampa Bay Buccaneers — WR

1995 Receiving Splits

	G	Rec	Yds	Avg	TD	Lg	Big	YAC	Trgt	Y@C	1st	1st%
Total	13	46	633	13.8	2	49	6	132	103	10.9	32	69.6
vs. Playoff	5	22	287	13.0	0	31	3	93	48	10.8	16	72.7
vs. Non-playoff	8	24	346	14.4	2	49	3	39	55	12.8	16	66.7
vs. Own Division	7	24	333	13.9	1	38	3	71	60	10.9	17	70.8
Home	7	28	381	13.6	1	49	3	67	54	11.2	19	67.9
Away	6	18	252	14.0	1	38	3	65	49	10.4	13	72.2
Games 1-8	5	21	290	13.8	1	49	2	47	39	11.6	16	76.2
Games 9-16	8	25	343	13.7	1	38	4	85	64	10.3	16	64.0
September	1	3	27	9.0	1	13	0	2	3	8.3	3	100.0
October	5	19	266	14.0	0	49	2	45	40	11.6	13	68.4
November	3	15	217	14.5	0	31	3	76	28	9.4	11	73.3
December	4	9	123	13.7	1	38	1	9	32	12.7	5	55.6
Grass	10	39	501	12.8	1	49	4	96	84	10.4	26	66.7
Turf	3	7	132	18.9	1	38	2	36	19	13.7	6	85.7
Outdoor	3	39	501	12.8	1	49	4	96	84	10.4	26	66.7
Indoor	10	7	132	18.9	1	38	2	36	19	13.7	6	85.7
1st Half	-	25	387	15.5	0	49	4	90	54	11.9	18	72.0
2nd Half/OT	-	21	246	11.7	2	38	2	42	49	9.7	14	66.7
Last 2 Min. Half	-	4	76	19.0	0	26	1	17	12	14.8	4	100.0
4th qtr, +/-7 pts	-	4	30	7.5	1	10	0	4	12	6.5	3	75.0
Winning	-	6	85	14.2	1	26	1	19	18	11.0	5	83.3
Tied	-	17	266	15.6	0	49	2	54	34	12.5	11	64.7
Trailing	-	23	282	12.3	1	38	3	59	51	9.7	16	69.6

	Rec	Yds	Avg	TD	Lg	Big	YAC	Trgt	Y@C	1st	1st%
Inside 20	5	32	6.4	1	7	0	6	11	5.2	2	40.0
Inside 10	3	19	6.3	1	7	0	3	5	5.3	1	33.3
1st Down	22	367	16.7	1	49	4	65	48	13.7	16	72.7
2nd Down	17	208	12.2	0	28	2	63	28	8.5	12	70.6
3rd Down Overall	7	58	8.3	1	13	0	4	26	7.7	4	57.1
3rd D 0-2 to Go	0	0	-	0	0	0	0	0	-	0	-
3rd D 3-7 to Go	4	36	9.0	1	13	0	3	10	8.3	4	100.0
3rd D 8+ to Go	3	22	7.3	0	12	0	1	16	7.0	0	0.0
4th Down	0	0	-	0	0	0	0	0	-	0	-
Rec Behind Line	0	0	-	0	0	0	0	1	-	0	-
1-10 yds	26	216	8.3	1	28	1	59	47	6.0	14	53.8
11-20 yds	16	282	17.6	0	31	3	65	28	13.6	14	87.5
21-30 yds	2	48	24.0	0	24	0	3	17	22.5	2	100.0
31+	2	87	43.5	1	49	2	5	10	41.0	2	100.0
Left Sideline	6	65	10.8	1	24	0	7	16	9.7	3	50.0
Left Side	6	43	7.2	0	12	0	5	11	6.3	1	16.7
Middle	2	35	17.5	0	28	1	25	9	5.0	1	50.0
Right Side	17	249	14.6	0	31	3	73	34	10.4	15	88.2
Right Sideline	15	241	16.1	1	49	2	22	33	14.6	12	80.0
Shotgun	0	0	-	0	0	0	0	8	-	0	-
2 Wide Receivers	31	414	13.4	0	49	4	90	56	10.5	22	71.0
3 Wide Receivers	14	193	13.8	2	38	1	28	41	11.8	9	64.3
4+ Wide Receivers	1	26	26.0	0	26	1	14	5	12.0	1	100.0

1995 Incompletions

Type	Num	%of Inc	%of Att
Pass Dropped	4	7.0	3.9
Poor Throw	31	54.4	30.1
Pass Defensed	15	26.3	14.6
Pass Hit at Line	0	0.0	0.0
Other	7	12.3	6.8
Total	57	100.0	55.3

Game Logs (1-8)

Date	Opp	Result	Rec	Yds	Trgt	F-L	TD
09/03	@Phi	W 21-6	-	-	-	-	-
09/10	@Cle	L 6-22	-	-	-	-	-
09/17	Chi	L 6-25	-	-	-	-	-
09/24	Was	W 14-6	3	27	3	0-0	1
10/01	@Car	W 20-13	2	23	9	0-0	0
10/08	Cin	W 19-16	6	117	10	0-0	0
10/15	Min	W 20-17	4	51	7	0-0	0
10/22	Atl	L 21-24	6	72	10	0-0	0

Game Logs (9-16)

Date	Opp	Result	Rec	Yds	Trgt	F-L	TD
10/29	@Hou	L 7-19	1	3	4	0-0	0
11/12	@Det	L 24-27	5	91	7	0-0	0
11/19	Jac	W 17-16	4	58	7	0-0	0
11/26	@GB	L 13-35	6	68	14	0-0	0
12/03	@Min	L 17-31	1	38	8	0-0	1
12/10	GB	W 13-10	1	7	8	0-0	0
12/17	@Chi	L 10-31	3	29	7	0-0	0
12/23	Det	L 10-37	4	49	9	0-0	0

Jackie Harris
Tampa Bay Buccaneers — TE

1995 Receiving Splits

	G	Rec	Yds	Avg	TD	Lg	Big	YAC	Trgt	Y@C	1st	1st%
Total	16	62	751	12.1	1	33	4	290	99	7.4	34	54.8
vs. Playoff	6	27	308	11.4	0	27	1	110	39	7.3	14	51.9
vs. Non-playoff	10	35	443	12.7	0	33	3	180	60	7.5	20	57.1
vs. Own Division	8	38	406	10.7	0	23	0	138	59	7.1	18	47.4
Home	8	23	265	11.5	0	27	1	109	43	6.8	12	52.2
Away	8	39	486	12.5	0	33	3	181	56	7.8	22	56.4
Games 1-8	8	31	407	13.1	0	33	4	173	48	7.5	19	61.3
Games 9-16	8	31	344	11.1	0	23	0	117	51	7.3	15	48.4
September	4	13	145	11.2	0	24	0	58	23	6.7	8	61.5
October	5	20	298	14.9	0	33	4	119	29	9.0	13	65.0
November	3	14	158	11.3	0	23	0	50	22	7.7	8	57.1
December	4	15	150	10.0	0	21	0	63	25	5.8	5	33.3
Grass	12	50	614	12.3	0	33	4	249	82	7.3	29	58.0
Turf	4	12	137	11.4	1	22	0	41	17	8.0	5	41.7
Outdoor	3	52	632	12.2	1	33	4	251	84	7.3	30	57.7
Indoor	13	10	119	11.9	0	22	0	39	15	8.0	4	40.0
1st Half	-	21	241	11.5	0	31	1	117	40	5.9	11	52.4
2nd Half/OT	-	41	510	12.4	1	33	3	173	59	8.2	23	56.1
Last 2 Min. Half	-	2	26	13.0	0	14	0	16	4	5.0	2	100.0
4th qtr, +/-7 pts	-	7	85	12.1	1	25	1	17	7	9.7	4	57.1
Winning	-	14	176	12.6	1	31	2	70	21	7.6	8	57.1
Tied	-	13	151	11.6	0	33	2	76	23	5.8	5	38.5
Trailing	-	35	424	12.1	0	24	0	144	55	8.0	21	60.0

	Rec	Yds	Avg	TD	Lg	Big	YAC	Trgt	Y@C	1st	1st%
Inside 20	2	16	8.0	1	10	0	5	9	5.5	1	50.0
Inside 10	1	6	6.0	1	6	0	5	4	1.0	0	0.0
1st Down	25	309	12.4	0	31	3	160	43	6.0	14	56.0
2nd Down	22	252	11.5	1	24	0	71	32	8.2	12	54.5
3rd Down Overall	15	190	12.7	0	33	1	59	23	8.7	8	53.3
3rd D 0-2 to Go	0	0	-	0	0	0	0	1	-	0	-
3rd D 3-7 to Go	5	45	9.0	0	15	0	12	7	6.6	3	60.0
3rd D 8+ to Go	10	145	14.5	0	33	1	47	15	9.8	5	50.0
4th Down	0	0	-	0	0	0	0	1	-	0	-
Rec Behind Line	4	10	2.5	0	8	0	32	7	-5.5	0	0.0
1-10 yds	40	395	9.9	1	27	1	177	58	5.5	19	47.5
11-20 yds	17	313	18.4	0	31	2	76	24	13.9	14	82.4
21-30 yds	1	33	33.0	0	33	1	5	6	28.0	1	100.0
31+	0	0	-	0	0	0	0	4	-	0	-
Left Sideline	3	34	11.3	0	15	0	13	6	7.0	2	66.7
Left Side	12	151	12.6	0	25	1	47	19	8.7	6	50.0
Middle	23	305	13.3	1	33	2	101	30	8.9	17	73.9
Right Side	13	158	12.2	0	31	1	88	22	5.4	5	38.5
Right Sideline	11	103	9.4	0	23	0	41	22	5.6	4	36.4
Shotgun	1	21	21.0	0	21	0	10	2	11.0	0	0.0
2 Wide Receivers	39	525	13.5	1	33	4	175	63	9.0	25	64.1
3 Wide Receivers	22	212	9.6	0	19	0	104	30	4.9	8	36.4
4+ Wide Receivers	1	14	14.0	0	14	0	11	1	3.0	1	100.0

1995 Incompletions

Type	Num	%of Inc	%of Att
Pass Dropped	6	16.2	6.1
Poor Throw	17	45.9	17.2
Pass Defensed	8	21.6	8.1
Pass Hit at Line	0	0.0	0.0
Other	6	16.2	6.1
Total	37	100.0	37.4

Game Logs (1-8)

Date	Opp	Result	Rec	Yds	Trgt	F-L	TD
09/03	@Phi	W 21-6	2	18	2	0-0	1
09/10	@Cle	L 6-22	8	95	11	0-0	0
09/17	Chi	L 6-25	2	28	6	0-0	0
09/24	Was	W 14-6	1	4	4	0-0	0
10/01	@Car	W 20-13	5	108	9	0-0	0
10/08	Cin	W 19-16	2	31	3	0-0	0
10/15	Min	W 20-17	7	70	9	2-2	0
10/22	Atl	L 21-24	4	53	4	0-0	0

Game Logs (9-16)

Date	Opp	Result	Rec	Yds	Trgt	F-L	TD
10/29	@Hou	L 7-19	2	36	4	0-0	0
11/12	@Det	L 24-27	4	36	5	0-0	0
11/19	Jac	W 17-16	0	0	3	0-0	0
11/26	@GB	L 13-35	10	122	14	0-0	0
12/03	@Min	L 17-31	4	47	6	0-0	0
12/10	GB	W 13-10	3	23	5	0-0	0
12/17	@Chi	L 10-31	4	24	6	0-0	0
12/23	Det	L 10-37	4	56	8	0-0	0

Andre Hastings

1995 Receiving Splits

	G	Rec	Yds	Avg	TD	Lg	Big	YAC	Trgt	Y@C	1st	1st%
Total	16	48	502	10.5	1	36	3	267	67	4.9	26	54.2
vs. Playoff	4	19	205	10.8	0	36	2	116	22	4.7	11	57.9
vs. Non-playoff	12	29	297	10.2	1	26	1	151	45	5.0	15	51.7
vs. Own Division	8	14	167	11.9	0	24	0	72	23	6.8	10	71.4
Home	8	20	198	9.9	0	24	0	113	27	4.3	9	45.0
Away	8	28	304	10.9	1	36	3	154	40	5.4	17	60.7
Games 1-8	8	26	237	9.1	0	26	1	125	35	4.3	12	46.2
Games 9-16	8	22	265	12.0	1	36	2	142	32	5.6	14	63.6
September	4	18	142	7.9	0	26	1	78	23	3.6	7	38.9
October	4	8	95	11.9	0	24	0	47	12	6.0	5	62.5
November	4	6	56	9.3	1	17	0	6	13	8.3	4	66.7
December	4	16	209	13.1	0	36	2	136	19	4.6	10	62.5
Grass	6	25	275	11.0	0	36	3	152	36	4.9	15	60.0
Turf	10	23	227	9.9	1	24	0	115	31	4.9	11	47.8
Indoor	1	2	14	7.0	0	8	0	2	2	6.0	1	50.0
Outdoor	15	46	488	10.6	1	36	3	265	65	4.8	25	54.3
1st Half	-	19	158	8.3	0	18	0	94	24	3.4	11	57.9
2nd Half/OT	-	29	344	11.9	1	36	3	173	43	5.9	15	51.7
Last 2 Min. Half	-	11	96	8.7	0	17	0	40	16	5.1	4	36.4
4th qtr, +/-7 pts	-	7	82	11.7	0	24	0	45	12	5.3	3	42.9
Winning	-	11	136	12.4	0	26	1	123	16	1.2	6	54.5
Tied	-	8	43	5.4	0	9	0	24	9	2.4	3	37.5
Trailing	-	29	323	11.1	1	36	2	120	42	7.0	17	58.6

	Rec	Yds	Avg	TD	Lg	Big	YAC	Trgt	Y@C	1st	1st%
Inside 20	4	30	7.5	1	15	0	3	7	6.8	2	50.0
Inside 10	1	6	6.0	0	6	0	1	1	5.0	0	0.0
1st Down	9	81	9.0	0	16	0	42	16	4.3	3	33.3
2nd Down	8	71	8.9	0	26	1	38	9	4.1	3	37.5
3rd Down Overall	31	350	11.3	1	36	2	187	41	5.3	20	64.5
3rd D 0-2 to Go	2	21	10.5	0	15	0	12	4	4.5	2	100.0
3rd D 3-7 to Go	18	171	9.5	1	26	1	65	21	5.9	14	77.8
3rd D 8+ to Go	11	158	14.4	0	36	1	110	16	4.4	4	36.4
4th Down	0	0	-	0	0	0	0	1	-	0	-
Rec Behind Line	7	48	6.9	0	18	0	77	7	-4.1	1	14.3
1-10 yds	36	344	9.6	0	26	2	177	48	4.6	21	58.3
11-20 yds	3	50	16.7	1	18	0	1	6	16.3	2	66.7
21-30 yds	2	60	30.0	0	36	1	12	4	24.0	2	100.0
31+	0	0	-	0	0	0	0	2	-	0	-
Left Sideline	3	31	10.3	0	18	0	4	4	9.0	2	66.7
Left Side	15	138	9.2	0	24	0	66	18	4.8	7	46.7
Middle	11	131	11.9	1	26	2	63	16	6.2	7	63.6
Right Side	14	141	10.1	0	24	0	94	17	3.4	7	50.0
Right Sideline	5	61	12.2	0	36	1	40	12	4.2	3	60.0
Shotgun	46	485	10.5	1	36	3	260	65	4.9	24	52.2
2 Wide Receivers	0	0	-	0	1	0	0	0	-	0	-
3 Wide Receivers	7	49	7.0	0	17	0	53	8	-0.6	2	28.6
4+ Wide Receivers	41	453	11.0	1	36	3	214	59	5.8	24	58.5

1995 Incompletions

Type	Num	%of Inc	%of Att
Pass Dropped	5	26.3	7.5
Poor Throw	6	31.6	9.0
Pass Defensed	5	26.3	7.5
Pass Hit at Line	0	0.0	0.0
Other	3	15.8	4.5
Total	19	100.0	28.4

Game Logs (1-8)

Date	Opp	Result	Rush	Yds	Rec	Yds	Trgt	F-L	TD
09/03	Det	W 23-20	0	0	1	10	1	0-0	0
09/10	@Hou	W 34-17	0	0	2	14	2	0-0	1
09/18	@Mia	L 10-23	0	0	10	86	13	0-0	0
09/24	Min	L 24-44	0	0	5	32	7	0-0	0
10/01	SD	W 31-16	0	0	1	12	1	0-0	0
10/08	@Jac	L 16-20	0	0	1	10	4	1-1	0
10/19	Cin	L 9-27	0	0	5	69	6	0-0	0
10/29	Jac	W 24-7	0	0	1	4	1	0-0	0

Game Logs (9-16)

Date	Opp	Result	Rush	Yds	Rec	Yds	Trgt	F-L	TD
11/05	@Chi	W 37-34	0	0	3	32	7	0-0	0
11/13	Cle	W 20-3	0	0	2	9	4	0-0	0
11/19	@Cle	W 49-31	0	0	1	15	2	0-0	1
11/26	@Cle	W 20-17	0	0	0	0	0	0-0	0
12/03	Hou	W 21-7	1	14	2	46	4	0-0	0
12/10	@Oak	L 20-29	0	0	4	50	5	0-0	0
12/16	NE	W 41-27	0	0	3	16	3	0-0	0
12/24	@GB	L 19-24	0	0	7	97	7	0-0	0

Courtney Hawkins

1995 Receiving Splits

	G	Rec	Yds	Avg	TD	Lg	Big	YAC	Trgt	Y@C	1st	1st%
Total	16	41	493	12.0	0	47	4	334	64	3.9	23	56.1
vs. Playoff	6	20	227	11.4	0	37	2	216	30	0.6	9	45.0
vs. Non-playoff	10	21	266	12.7	0	47	2	118	34	7.0	14	66.7
vs. Own Division	8	28	341	12.2	0	47	3	307	40	1.2	14	50.0
Home	8	25	276	11.0	0	36	1	193	39	3.3	12	48.0
Away	8	16	217	13.6	0	47	3	141	25	4.8	11	68.8
Games 1-8	8	20	236	11.8	0	38	1	65	32	8.6	12	60.0
Games 9-16	8	21	257	12.2	0	47	3	269	32	-0.6	11	52.4
September	4	13	169	13.0	0	38	1	44	19	9.6	8	61.5
October	5	8	72	9.0	0	13	0	21	14	6.4	5	62.5
November	3	6	69	11.5	0	37	1	73	11	-0.7	3	50.0
December	4	14	183	13.1	0	47	2	196	20	-0.9	7	50.0
Grass	12	36	428	11.9	0	47	3	267	56	4.5	20	55.6
Turf	4	5	65	13.0	0	37	1	67	8	-0.4	3	60.0
Indoor	3	4	61	15.3	0	37	1	66	6	-1.3	3	75.0
Outdoor	13	37	432	11.7	0	47	3	268	58	4.4	20	54.1
1st Half	-	19	260	13.7	0	47	3	240	29	1.1	9	47.4
2nd Half/OT	-	22	233	10.6	0	38	1	94	35	6.3	14	63.6
Last 2 Min. Half	-	1	4	4.0	0	4	0	2	4	2.0	0	0.0
4th qtr, +/-7 pts	-	2	9	4.5	0	5	0	2	4	3.5	0	0.0
Winning	-	2	19	9.5	0	10	0	5	7	5.0	1	50.0
Tied	-	11	143	13.0	0	47	1	106	16	3.4	6	54.5
Trailing	-	28	301	11.0	0	38	3	223	43	3.9	16	57.1

	Rec	Yds	Avg	TD	Lg	Big	YAC	Trgt	Y@C	1st	1st%
Inside 20	2	20	10.0	0	12	0	10	5	5.0	1	50.0
Inside 10	0	0	-	0	0	0	0	1	-	0	-
1st Down	15	194	12.9	0	47	2	154	20	2.7	6	40.0
2nd Down	15	161	10.7	0	36	1	139	22	1.5	10	66.7
3rd Down Overall	10	124	12.4	0	38	1	21	21	10.3	6	60.0
3rd D 0-2 to Go	1	8	8.0	0	0	0	2	3	5.0	1	100.0
3rd D 3-7 to Go	2	23	11.5	0	18	0	3	6	10.0	2	100.0
3rd D 8+ to Go	7	93	13.3	0	38	1	16	12	11.0	3	42.9
4th Down	1	14	14.0	0	14	0	20	1	-6.0	1	100.0
Rec Behind Line	12	197	16.4	0	47	3	254	14	-4.8	8	66.7
1-10 yds	24	190	7.9	0	17	0	71	37	5.0	10	41.7
11-20 yds	4	68	17.0	0	19	0	9	9	14.8	4	100.0
21-30 yds	0	0	-	0	0	0	0	1	-	0	-
31+	1	38	38.0	0	38	1	0	2	38.0	1	100.0
Left Sideline	16	213	13.3	0	37	2	155	24	3.6	11	68.8
Left Side	7	127	18.1	0	47	2	95	11	4.6	5	71.4
Middle	7	71	10.1	0	18	0	18	12	7.6	4	57.1
Right Side	6	53	8.8	0	19	0	47	8	1.0	2	33.3
Right Sideline	5	29	5.8	0	7	0	19	9	2.0	1	20.0
Shotgun	7	84	12.0	0	18	0	52	8	4.6	5	71.4
2 Wide Receivers	11	150	13.6	0	38	1	41	21	9.9	8	72.7
3 Wide Receivers	26	310	11.9	0	47	3	287	37	0.9	13	50.0
4+ Wide Receivers	4	33	8.3	0	18	0	6	5	6.8	2	50.0

1995 Incompletions

Type	Num	%of Inc	%of Att
Pass Dropped	2	8.7	3.1
Poor Throw	11	47.8	17.2
Pass Defensed	7	30.4	10.9
Pass Hit at Line	1	4.3	1.6
Other	2	8.7	3.1
Total	23	100.0	35.9

Game Logs (1-8)

Date	Opp	Result	Rush	Yds	Rec	Yds	Trgt	F-L	TD
09/03	@Phi	W 21-6	0	0	1	4	2	0-0	0
09/10	@Cle	L 6-22	0	0	3	67	6	0-0	0
09/17	Chi	L 6-25	0	0	6	74	8	1-1	0
09/24	Was	W 14-6	0	0	3	24	3	0-0	0
10/01	@Car	W 20-13	0	0	2	23	3	0-0	0
10/08	Cin	W 19-16	0	0	1	9	4	0-0	0
10/15	Min	W 20-17	1	2	2	15	3	0-0	0
10/22	Atl	L 21-24	0	0	2	20	3	0-0	0

Game Logs (9-16)

Date	Opp	Result	Rush	Yds	Rec	Yds	Trgt	F-L	TD
10/29	@Hou	L 7-19	1	11	1	5	1	0-0	0
11/12	@Det	L 24-27	1	-1	3	56	4	0-0	0
11/19	Jac	W 17-16	1	-7	0	0	2	0-0	0
11/26	@GB	L 13-35	0	0	3	13	5	0-0	0
12/03	@Min	L 17-31	0	0	0	0	1	0-0	0
12/10	GB	W 13-10	0	0	6	65	8	0-0	0
12/17	@Chi	L 10-31	0	0	3	49	3	0-0	0
12/23	Det	L 10-37	0	0	5	69	8	0-0	0

1995 Rushing and Receiving Splits

	G	Rush	Yds	Avg	Lg	TD	1st	Stf	YdL	Rec	Yds	Avg	TD
Total	7	128	470	3.7	20	3	22	8	10	5	53	10.6	0
vs. Playoff	2	26	96	3.7	11	0	6	2	3	0	0	-	0
vs. Non-playoff	5	102	374	3.7	20	3	16	6	7	5	53	10.6	0
vs. Own Division	3	24	83	3.5	15	0	4	3	3	3	32	10.7	0
Home	4	72	270	3.8	20	2	10	4	5	3	25	8.3	0
Away	3	56	200	3.6	15	1	12	4	5	2	28	14.0	0
Games 1-8	0	0	0	-	0	0	0	0	0	0	0	-	0
Games 9-16	7	128	470	3.7	20	3	22	8	10	5	53	10.6	0
September	0	0	0	-	0	0	0	0	0	0	0	-	0
October	0	0	0	-	0	0	0	0	0	0	0	-	0
November	3	24	83	3.5	15	0	4	3	3	3	32	10.7	0
December	4	104	387	3.7	20	3	18	5	7	2	21	10.5	0
Grass	5	80	294	3.7	20	2	12	5	6	5	53	10.6	0
Turf	2	48	176	3.7	15	1	10	3	4	0	0	-	0
Indoor	1	26	96	3.7	11	0	6	2	3	0	0	-	0
Outdoor	6	102	374	3.7	20	3	16	6	7	5	53	10.6	0
1st Half	-	52	175	3.4	15	2	9	2	2	1	11	11.0	0
2nd Half/OT	-	76	295	3.9	20	1	13	6	8	4	42	10.5	0
Last 2 Min. Half	-	8	38	4.8	12	1	3	0	0	0	0	-	0
4th qtr, +/-7 pts	-	31	131	4.2	15	0	7	2	2	1	16	16.0	0
Winning	-	65	235	3.6	20	1	11	3	4	2	14	7.0	0
Tied	-	27	103	3.8	15	1	3	1	1	1	11	11.0	0
Trailing	-	36	132	3.7	15	1	8	4	5	2	28	14.0	0

	Rush	Yds	Avg	Lg	TD	1st	Stf	YdL	Rec	Yds	Avg	TD
Inside 20	27	80	3.0	8	3	5	2	2	0	0	-	0
Inside 10	7	20	2.9	8	3	3	1	1	0	0	-	0
1st Down	79	305	3.9	20	1	9	5	7	3	32	10.7	0
2nd Down	45	161	3.6	15	2	12	2	2	1	11	11.0	0
3rd Down Overall	4	4	1.0	3	0	1	1	1	1	10	10.0	0
3rd D 0-2 to Go	2	2	1.0	3	0	1	1	1	0	0	-	0
3rd D 3-7 to Go	2	2	1.0	2	0	0	0	0	1	10	10.0	0
3rd D 8+ to Go	0	0	-	0	0	0	0	0	0	0	-	0
4th Down	0	0	-	0	0	0	0	0	0	0	-	0
Left Sideline	10	58	5.8	20	1	5	2	2	1	4	4.0	0
Left Side	46	178	3.9	15	0	10	3	5	2	23	11.5	0
Middle	42	121	2.9	13	2	5	2	2	1	16	16.0	0
Right Side	26	98	3.8	15	0	2	1	1	0	0	-	0
Right Sideline	4	15	3.8	7	0	0	0	0	1	10	10.0	0
Shotgun	0	0	-	0	0	0	0	0	0	0	-	0
2 Wide Receivers	98	359	3.7	20	2	17	7	9	5	53	10.6	0
3 Wide Receivers	16	74	4.6	15	0	3	1	1	0	0	-	0
4+ Wide Receivers	0	0	-	0	0	0	0	0	0	0	-	0
Carries 1-5	30	103	3.4	13	1	6	2	2	0	0	-	0
Carries 6-10	28	117	4.2	15	1	5	1	1	0	0	-	0
Carries 11-15	25	67	2.7	11	0	4	3	4	0	0	-	0
Carries 16-20	21	107	5.1	20	1	5	1	1	0	0	-	0
Carries 21+	24	76	3.2	15	0	2	1	2	0	0	-	0

1995 Incompletions

Type	Num	%of Inc	% Att
Pass Dropped	0	-	0.0
Poor Throw	0	-	0.0
Pass Defensed	0	-	0.0
Pass Hit at Line	0	-	0.0
Other	0	-	0.0
Total	0	-	0.0

Game Logs (1-8)

Date	Opp	Result	Rush	Yds	Rec	Yds	Trgt	F-L	TD
11/12	KC	L 7-22	0	0	0	0	0	0-0	0
11/19	@Den	L 27-30	8	24	2	28	2	0-0	0
11/27	Oak	W 12-6	16	59	1	4	1	0-0	0
12/03	Cle	W 31-13	32	127	0	0	0	0-0	2
12/09	Ari	W 28-25	24	84	2	21	2	0-0	0
12/17	@Ind	W 27-24	26	96	0	0	0	0-0	0
12/23	@NYN	W 27-17	22	80	0	0	0	0-0	1

Game Logs (9-16)

Date	Opp	Result	Rush	Yds	Rec	Yds	Trgt	F-L	TD

1995 Receiving Splits

	G	Rec	Yds	Avg	TD	Lg	Big	YAC	Trgt	Y@C	1st	1st%
Total	16	41	597	14.6	4	48	4	153	95	10.8	28	68.3
vs. Playoff	8	21	327	15.6	4	39	3	50	51	13.2	15	71.4
vs. Non-playoff	8	20	270	13.5	0	48	1	103	44	8.4	13	65.0
vs. Own Division	8	31	411	13.3	2	39	3	83	61	10.6	21	67.7
Home	8	15	233	15.5	4	37	2	25	44	13.9	13	86.7
Away	8	26	364	14.0	0	48	2	128	51	9.1	15	57.7
Games 1-8	8	28	415	14.8	4	37	2	68	56	12.4	21	75.0
Games 9-16	8	13	182	14.0	0	48	2	85	39	7.5	7	53.8
September	4	18	273	15.2	2	37	2	53	32	12.2	13	72.2
October	4	10	142	14.2	2	23	0	15	24	12.7	8	80.0
November	4	5	87	17.4	0	48	1	47	16	8.0	4	80.0
December	4	8	95	11.9	0	39	1	38	23	7.1	3	37.5
Grass	3	8	97	12.1	0	20	0	15	21	10.3	6	75.0
Turf	13	33	500	15.2	4	48	4	138	74	11.0	22	66.7
Outdoor	10	18	232	12.9	0	24	0	59	38	9.6	12	66.7
Indoor	6	23	365	15.9	4	48	4	94	57	11.8	16	69.6
1st Half	-	21	263	12.5	1	48	1	92	49	8.1	12	57.1
2nd Half/OT	-	20	334	16.7	3	39	3	61	46	13.7	16	80.0
Last 2 Min. Half	-	5	85	17.0	0	48	1	45	18	8.0	2	40.0
4th qtr, +/-7 pts	-	1	17	17.0	0	17	0	3	12	14.0	1	100.0
Winning	-	6	92	15.3	2	23	0	6	19	14.3	5	83.3
Tied	-	11	110	10.0	0	20	0	43	28	6.1	4	54.5
Trailing	-	24	395	16.5	2	48	4	104	48	12.1	17	70.8

	Rec	Yds	Avg	TD	Lg	Big	YAC	Trgt	Y@C	1st	1st%
Inside 20	3	17	5.7	1	9	0	1	9	5.3	1	33.3
Inside 10	2	13	6.5	1	9	0	0	5	6.5	1	50.0
1st Down	18	298	16.6	2	39	2	60	40	13.2	12	66.7
2nd Down	13	196	15.1	2	48	2	77	27	9.2	9	69.2
3rd Down Overall	9	99	11.0	0	17	0	16	27	9.2	7	77.8
3rd D 0-2 to Go	0	0	-	0	0	0	0	0	0	-	0
3rd D 3-7 to Go	5	57	11.4	0	17	0	7	12	10.0	4	80.0
3rd D 8+ to Go	4	42	10.5	0	17	0	9	15	8.3	3	75.0
4th Down	1	4	4.0	0	4	0	0	1	4.0	0	0.0
Rec Behind Line	0	0	-	0	0	0	0	1	-	0	-
1-10 yds	25	260	10.4	1	48	1	108	39	6.1	12	48.0
11-20 yds	10	163	16.3	0	24	0	24	26	13.9	10	100.0
21-30 yds	5	137	27.4	3	39	2	18	15	23.8	5	100.0
31+	1	37	37.0	0	37	1	3	14	34.0	1	100.0
Left Sideline	13	166	12.8	0	37	1	39	32	9.8	8	61.5
Left Side	7	140	20.0	0	48	1	61	10	11.3	5	71.4
Middle	3	43	14.3	1	22	0	10	8	11.0	2	66.7
Right Side	2	39	19.5	1	29	1	3	12	18.0	2	100.0
Right Sideline	16	209	13.1	2	39	1	40	33	10.6	11	68.8
Shotgun	10	119	11.9	0	17	0	25	35	9.4	8	80.0
2 Wide Receivers	19	344	18.1	2	48	3	105	42	12.6	14	73.7
3 Wide Receivers	21	243	11.6	2	39	1	48	52	9.3	13	61.9
4+ Wide Receivers	1	10	10.0	0	10	0	0	1	10.0	1	100.0

1995 Incompletions

Type	Num	%of Inc	%of Att
Pass Dropped	3	5.6	3.2
Poor Throw	31	57.4	32.6
Pass Defensed	12	22.2	12.6
Pass Hit at Line	1	1.9	1.1
Other	7	13.0	7.4
Total	54	100.0	56.8

Game Logs (1-8)

Date	Opp	Result	Rec	Yds	Trgt	F-L	TD
09/03	SF	L 22-24	5	97	11	0-0	1
09/10	@StL	L 13-17	4	49	4	0-0	0
09/17	Atl	L 24-27	5	59	11	0-0	1
09/24	@NYN	L 29-45	4	68	6	0-0	0
10/01	Phi	L 10-15	0	0	4	0-0	0
10/15	Mia	W 33-30	2	45	3	0-0	2
10/22	@Car	L 3-20	5	48	10	0-0	0
10/29	@SF	W 11-7	3	49	7	0-0	0

Game Logs (9-16)

Date	Opp	Result	Rec	Yds	Trgt	F-L	TD
11/05	StL	W 19-10	2	19	5	0-0	0
11/12	Ind	W 17-14	0	0	3	0-0	0
11/19	@Min	L 24-43	2	55	4	0-0	0
11/26	Car	W 34-26	1	13	4	0-0	0
12/03	@NE	W 31-17	0	0	4	0-0	0
12/10	@Atl	L 14-19	6	77	9	0-0	0
12/16	GB	L 23-34	0	0	3	0-0	0
12/24	@NYA	W 12-0	2	18	7	0-0	0

Garrison Hearst

1995 Rushing and Receiving Splits

	G	Rush	Yds	Avg	Lg	TD	1st	Stf	YdL	Rec	Yds	Avg	TD		Rush	Yds	Avg	Lg	TD	1st	Stf	YdL	Rec	Yds	Avg	TD
Total	16	284	1070	3.8	38	1	52	38	83	29	243	8.4	1	Inside 20	38	58	1.5	8	1	9	7	15	3	-1	-0.3	1
vs. Playoff	8	139	448	3.2	29	1	22	24	55	12	76	6.3	0	Inside 10	18	12	0.7	6	1	5	5	10	2	-4	-2.0	1
vs. Non-playoff	8	145	622	4.3	38	0	30	14	28	17	167	9.8	1	1st Down	174	619	3.6	38	1	13	25	52	13	69	5.3	0
vs. Own Division	8	155	579	3.7	38	1	27	21	39	15	130	8.7	1	2nd Down	92	388	4.2	32	0	28	11	25	10	119	11.9	1
Home	8	151	512	3.4	32	1	26	19	41	16	79	4.9	1	3rd Down Overall	18	63	3.5	17	0	11	2	6	6	55	9.2	0
Away	8	133	558	4.2	38	0	26	19	42	13	164	12.6	0	3rd D 0-2 to Go	11	38	3.5	14	0	9	1	3	0	0	-	0
Games 1-8	8	152	571	3.8	38	1	30	20	41	14	106	7.6	1	3rd D 3-7 to Go	6	25	4.2	17	0	2	1	3	4	32	8.0	0
Games 9-16	8	132	499	3.8	32	0	22	18	42	15	137	9.1	0	3rd D 8+ to Go	1	0	0.0	0	0	0	0	0	2	23	11.5	0
September	4	69	262	3.8	38	1	14	12	25	6	46	7.7	0	4th Down	0	0	-	0	0	0	0	0	0	0	-	0
October	4	83	309	3.7	20	0	16	8	16	8	60	7.5	1	Left Sideline	17	134	7.9	27	0	4	0	0	3	21	7.0	0
November	5	81	329	4.1	32	0	16	9	19	11	102	9.3	0	Left Side	84	238	2.8	29	0	13	21	48	13	117	9.0	1
December	3	51	170	3.3	29	0	6	9	23	4	35	8.8	0	Middle	111	427	3.8	38	0	22	8	17	2	12	6.0	0
Grass	12	200	709	3.5	38	1	34	25	59	23	157	6.8	1	Right Side	61	208	3.4	14	1	11	9	18	9	93	10.3	0
Turf	4	84	361	4.3	29	0	18	13	24	6	86	14.3	0	Right Sideline	11	63	5.7	20	0	2	0	0	2	0	0.0	0
Indoor	1	22	121	5.5	27	0	6	3	6	2	26	13.0	0	Shotgun	5	9	1.8	7	0	0	1	3	4	38	9.5	0
Outdoor	15	262	949	3.6	38	1	46	35	77	27	217	8.0	1	2 Wide Receivers	215	753	3.5	27	0	36	27	59	17	150	8.8	0
1st Half	-	156	588	3.8	38	0	28	22	48	20	213	10.7	0	3 Wide Receivers	45	279	6.2	38	0	11	4	13	11	92	8.4	0
2nd Half/OT	-	128	482	3.8	32	1	24	16	35	9	30	3.3	1	4+ Wide Receivers	2	9	4.5	7	0	0	0	0	0	0	-	0
Last 2 Min. Half	-	8	19	2.4	7	0	0	1	1	1	1	1.0	1	Carries 1-5	80	308	3.9	38	0	14	10	22	0	0	-	0
4th qtr. +/-7 pts	-	37	131	3.5	15	0	8	5	9	3	9	3.0	1	Carries 6-10	79	272	3.4	20	0	12	14	34	0	0	-	0
Winning	-	45	161	3.6	29	0	7	5	13	5	44	8.8	0	Carries 11-15	65	270	4.2	32	0	11	7	14	0	0	-	0
Tied	-	75	268	3.6	38	0	13	12	26	7	51	7.3	0	Carries 16-20	42	184	4.4	15	1	12	4	9	0	0	-	0
Trailing	-	164	641	3.9	32	1	32	21	44	17	148	8.7	1	Carries 21+	18	36	2.0	8	0	2	3	4	0	0	-	0

1995 Incompletions

Type	Num	%of Inc	% Att
Pass Dropped	3	16.7	6.4
Poor Throw	6	33.3	12.8
Pass Defensed	2	11.1	4.3
Pass Hit at Line	3	16.7	6.4
Other	4	22.2	8.5
Total	18	100.0	38.3

Game Logs (1-8)

Date	Opp	Result	Rush	Yds	Rec	Yds	Trgt	F-L	TD
09/03	@Was	L 7-27	17	97	1	6	2	0-0	0
09/10	Phi	L 19-31	17	21	2	12	4	0-0	1
09/17	@Det	W 20-17	22	121	2	26	2	0-0	0
09/24	@Dal	L 20-34	13	23	1	2	1	1-0	0
10/01	KC	L 3-24	15	54	1	-5	2	1-1	0
10/08	@NYN	L 21-27	23	122	2	40	4	1-0	0
10/15	Was	W 24-20	24	79	3	13	5	1-0	1
10/29	Sea	W 20-14	21	54	2	12	7	1-1	0

Game Logs (9-16)

Date	Opp	Result	Rush	Yds	Rec	Yds	Trgt	F-L	TD
11/05	@Den	L 6-38	12	50	2	52	3	0-0	0
11/12	Min	L 24-30	18	103	1	2	1	0-0	0
11/19	@Car	L 7-27	9	32	2	10	2	1-1	0
11/26	Atl	W 40-37	21	59	2	6	2	1-1	0
11/30	NYN	L 6-10	21	85	4	32	5	0-0	0
12/09	@SD	L 25-28	11	18	2	10	3	2-1	0
12/17	@Phi	L 20-21	26	95	1	18	1	3-3	0
12/25	Dal	L 13-37	14	57	1	7	3	0-0	0

Jessie Hester

1995 Receiving Splits

	G	Rec	Yds	Avg	TD	Lg	Big	YAC	Trgt	Y@C	1st	1st%		Rec	Yds	Avg	TD	Lg	Big	YAC	Trgt	Y@C	1st	1st%
Total	12	30	399	13.3	3	38	2	97	54	10.1	19	63.3	Inside 20	2	17	8.5	1	12	0	8	8	4.5	2	100.0
vs. Playoff	7	25	314	12.6	2	38	2	88	42	9.0	15	60.0	Inside 10	1	5	5.0	1	5	0	1	4	4.0	1	100.0
vs. Non-playoff	5	5	85	17.0	1	23	0	9	12	15.2	4	80.0	1st Down	14	178	12.7	0	27	1	43	26	9.6	7	50.0
vs. Own Division	7	15	237	15.8	2	38	2	73	31	10.9	11	73.3	2nd Down	7	65	9.3	1	15	0	9	13	8.0	4	57.1
Home	6	11	160	14.5	2	38	1	51	26	9.9	8	72.7	3rd Down Overall	8	118	14.8	1	23	0	14	14	13.0	7	87.5
Away	6	19	239	12.6	1	27	1	46	28	10.2	11	57.9	3rd D 0-2 to Go	0	0	-	0	0	0	0	0	-	0	-
Games 1-8	8	22	298	13.5	2	38	1	74	39	10.2	13	59.1	3rd D 3-7 to Go	5	82	16.4	1	23	0	8	9	14.8	5	100.0
Games 9-16	4	8	101	12.6	1	27	1	23	15	9.8	6	75.0	3rd D 8+ to Go	3	36	12.0	0	16	0	6	5	10.0	2	66.7
September	4	8	111	13.9	1	23	0	17	11	11.8	5	62.5	4th Down	1	38	38.0	0	38	1	31	1	7.0	1	100.0
October	4	14	187	13.4	1	38	1	57	28	9.3	8	57.1	Rec Behind Line	0	0	-	0	0	0	0	1	-	0	-
November	3	5	70	14.0	0	27	1	17	11	10.6	4	80.0	1-10 yds	16	161	10.1	2	38	1	69	25	5.8	5	31.3
December	1	3	31	10.3	1	18	0	6	4	8.3	2	66.7	11-20 yds	13	215	16.5	0	27	1	28	21	14.4	13	100.0
Grass	2	6	80	13.3	1	23	0	18	7	10.3	3	50.0	21-30 yds	1	23	23.0	1	23	0	0	4	23.0	1	100.0
Turf	10	24	319	13.3	2	38	2	79	47	10.0	16	66.7	31+	0	0	-	0	0	0	0	3	-	0	0.0
Outdoor	5	21	278	13.2	2	38	1	71	33	9.9	12	57.1	Left Sideline	11	143	13.0	0	27	1	22	18	11.0	6	54.5
Indoor	7	9	121	13.4	1	27	1	26	21	10.6	7	77.8	Left Side	6	109	18.2	1	38	1	40	10	11.5	6	100.0
1st Half	-	11	143	13.0	1	23	0	25	26	10.7	7	63.6	Middle	6	63	10.5	1	20	0	14	8	8.2	3	50.0
2nd Half/OT	-	19	256	13.5	2	38	2	72	28	9.7	12	63.2	Right Side	2	36	18.0	0	19	0	13	5	11.5	2	100.0
Last 2 Min. Half	-	5	43	8.6	0	18	0	12	9	6.2	2	40.0	Right Sideline	5	48	9.6	0	16	0	8	13	8.0	2	40.0
4th qtr. +/-7 pts	-	4	47	11.8	0	17	0	4	6	10.8	3	75.0	Shotgun	1	11	11.0	0	11	0	6	1	5.0	0	0.0
Winning	-	9	130	14.0	1	23	0	23	9	12.2	7	77.8	2 Wide Receivers	14	210	15.0	2	38	1	67	28	10.2	9	64.3
Tied	-	6	63	10.5	0	20	0	12	11	8.5	2	33.3	3 Wide Receivers	15	186	12.4	1	27	1	30	23	10.4	10	66.7
Trailing	-	15	203	13.5	2	38	2	62	27	9.4	10	66.7	4+ Wide Receivers	1	3	3.0	0	3	0	0	3	3.0	0	0.0

1995 Incompletions

Type	Num	%of Inc	%of Att
Pass Dropped	4	16.7	7.4
Poor Throw	15	62.5	27.8
Pass Defensed	0	0.0	0.0
Pass Hit at Line	1	4.2	1.9
Other	4	16.7	7.4
Total	24	100.0	44.4

Game Logs (1-8)

Date	Opp	Result	Rec	Yds	Trgt	F-L	TD
09/03	@GB	W 17-14	3	26	3	0-0	0
09/10	NO	W 17-13	1	15	1	0-0	0
09/17	@Car	W 31-10	3	54	4	0-0	1
09/24	Chi	W 34-28	1	16	3	0-0	0
10/01	@Ind	L 18-21	1	20	6	0-0	0
10/12	Atl	W 21-19	3	39	5	0-0	0
10/22	SF	L 10-44	3	59	10	0-0	0
10/29	@Phi	L 9-20	7	69	7	0-0	0

Game Logs (9-16)

Date	Opp	Result	Rec	Yds	Trgt	F-L	TD
11/05	@NO	L 10-19	0	0	1	0-0	0
11/12	Car	W 28-17	0	0	3	0-0	0
11/19	@Atl	L 6-31	5	70	7	0-0	0
11/26	@SF	L 13-41	-	-	-	-	-
12/03	@NYA	W 23-20	-	-	-	-	-
12/10	Buf	L 27-45	3	31	4	0-0	1
12/17	Was	L 23-35	-	-	-	-	-
12/24	Mia	L 22-41	-	-	-	-	-

Craig Heyward

Atlanta Falcons — RB

1995 Rushing and Receiving Splits

	G	Rush	Yds	Avg	Lg	TD	1st	Stf	YdL	Rec	Yds	Avg	TD		Rush	Yds	Avg	Lg	TD	1st	Stf	YdL	Rec	Yds	Avg	TD
Total	16	236	1083	4.6	31	6	64	15	30	37	350	9.5	2	Inside 20	33	122	3.7	15	6	12	1	1	4	32	8.0	2
vs. Playoff	6	64	299	4.7	31	4	18	2	8	9	99	11.0	0	Inside 10	18	42	2.3	9	6	7	1	1	2	10	5.0	2
vs. Non-playoff	10	172	784	4.6	22	2	46	13	22	28	251	9.0	2	1st Down	132	574	4.3	31	3	19	7	16	13	109	8.4	0
vs. Own Division	8	124	536	4.3	19	1	26	9	15	16	168	10.5	2	2nd Down	83	426	5.1	22	2	33	6	9	14	115	8.2	1
Home	8	125	645	5.2	31	3	35	5	5	20	191	9.6	1	3rd Down Overall	18	75	4.2	13	1	10	2	5	10	126	12.6	1
Away	8	111	438	3.9	16	3	29	10	25	17	159	9.4	1	3rd D 0-2 to Go	9	38	4.2	10	1	7	1	1	2	28	14.0	0
Games 1-8	8	129	550	4.3	22	2	30	10	17	23	186	8.1	0	3rd D 3-7 to Go	4	20	5.0	13	0	2	0	0	3	14	4.7	1
Games 9-16	8	107	533	5.0	31	4	34	5	13	14	164	11.7	2	3rd D 8+ to Go	5	17	3.4	12	0	1	1	4	5	84	16.8	0
September	4	70	306	4.4	22	1	15	5	7	5	19	3.8	0	4th Down	3	8	2.7	5	0	2	0	0	0	0	-	0
October	4	59	244	4.1	22	1	15	5	10	18	167	9.3	0	Left Sideline	6	42	7.0	13	0	3	2	0	2	16	8.0	0
November	4	52	283	5.4	31	4	22	3	5	4	57	14.3	0	Left Side	46	222	4.8	19	1	14	2	2	12	121	10.1	1
December	4	55	250	4.5	19	0	12	2	8	10	107	10.7	2	Middle	128	473	3.7	22	5	29	11	26	6	45	7.5	1
Grass	5	61	247	4.0	16	0	16	5	14	10	76	7.6	1	Right Side	53	322	6.1	31	0	17	2	2	12	149	12.4	0
Turf	11	175	836	4.8	31	6	48	10	16	27	274	10.1	1	Right Sideline	3	24	8.0	12	0	1	0	0	5	19	3.8	0
Indoor	9	150	747	5.0	31	4	41	7	9	21	192	9.1	1	Shotgun	7	34	4.9	22	0	1	2	8	3	17	5.7	0
Outdoor	7	86	336	3.9	16	2	23	8	21	16	158	9.9	1	2 Wide Receivers	11	49	4.5	15	3	6	1	1	0	0	-	0
1st Half	-	108	503	4.7	22	3	29	8	20	21	222	10.6	1	3 Wide Receivers	59	263	4.5	13	1	19	2	3	7	67	9.6	0
2nd Half/OT	-	128	580	4.5	31	3	35	7	10	16	128	8.0	1	4+ Wide Receivers	166	771	4.6	31	2	39	12	26	30	283	9.4	2
Last 2 Min. Half	-	19	105	5.5	22	1	8	1	7	3	44	14.7	0	Carries 1-5	80	356	4.5	19	3	18	7	13	0	0	-	0
4th qtr, +/-7 pts	-	47	199	4.2	13	0	11	1	1	5	34	6.8	0	Carries 6-10	72	348	4.8	31	1	21	4	11	0	0	-	0
Winning	-	115	582	5.1	31	2	32	3	9	13	124	9.5	2	Carries 11-15	52	264	5.1	22	1	17	1	1	0	0	-	0
Tied	-	58	244	4.2	22	1	15	6	12	12	119	9.9	0	Carries 16-20	27	101	3.7	13	1	7	2	2	0	0	-	0
Trailing	-	63	257	4.1	22	3	17	6	9	12	107	8.9	0	Carries 21+	5	14	2.8	13	0	1	1	4	0	0	-	0

1995 Incompletions

Type	Num	%of Inc	% Att
Pass Dropped	1	11.1	2.2
Poor Throw	3	33.3	6.5
Pass Defensed	2	22.2	4.3
Pass Hit at Line	0	0.0	0.0
Other	3	33.3	6.5
Total	9	100.0	19.6

Game Logs (1-8)

Date	Opp	Result	Rush	Yds	Rec	Yds	Trgt	F-L	TD
09/03	Car	W 23-20	19	61	0	0	1	1-1	0
09/10	@SF	L 10-41	7	23	1	4	1	0-0	0
09/17	@NO	W 27-24	25	102	1	1	1	0-0	1
09/24	NYA	W 13-3	19	120	3	14	3	0-0	0
10/01	NE	W 30-17	18	84	8	66	9	0-1	1
10/08	@StL	L 19-21	11	24	4	56	6	0-0	0
10/22	@TB	W 24-21	16	69	4	24	5	0-0	0
10/29	Dal	L 13-28	14	67	2	21	2	0-0	0

Game Logs (9-16)

Date	Opp	Result	Rush	Yds	Rec	Yds	Trgt	F-L	TD
11/05	Det	W 34-22	9	68	2	31	2	0-0	2
11/12	@Buf	L 17-23	14	65	2	26	3	0-0	2
11/19	StL	W 31-6	20	117	0	0	0	0-0	0
11/26	@Ari	L 37-40	9	33	0	0	0	1-0	0
12/03	@Mia	L 20-21	13	41	0	0	0	1-0	0
12/10	NO	W 19-14	19	93	3	42	3	0-0	1
12/17	@Car	L 17-21	16	81	5	48	8	0-0	0
12/24	SF	W 28-27	7	35	2	17	2	0-0	0

Greg Hill

Kansas City Chiefs — RB

1995 Rushing and Receiving Splits

	G	Rush	Yds	Avg	Lg	TD	1st	Stf	YdL	Rec	Yds	Avg	TD		Rush	Yds	Avg	Lg	TD	1st	Stf	YdL	Rec	Yds	Avg	TD
Total	16	155	667	4.3	27	1	27	19	37	7	45	6.4	0	Inside 20	13	38	2.9	9	1	1	1	2	0	0	-	0
vs. Playoff	4	30	133	4.4	17	0	6	4	4	3	19	6.3	0	Inside 10	5	14	2.8	9	1	1	1	2	0	0	-	0
vs. Non-playoff	12	125	534	4.3	27	1	21	15	33	4	26	6.5	0	1st Down	95	427	4.5	23	0	11	8	10	3	17	5.7	0
vs. Own Division	8	83	398	4.8	27	0	16	8	9	3	22	7.3	0	2nd Down	53	231	4.4	27	1	14	9	24	4	28	7.0	0
Home	8	81	342	4.2	23	1	15	10	28	6	43	7.2	0	3rd Down Overall	6	9	1.5	5	0	2	2	3	0	0	-	0
Away	8	74	325	4.4	27	0	12	9	9	1	2	2.0	0	3rd D 0-2 to Go	1	5	5.0	5	0	0	0	0	0	0	-	0
Games 1-8	8	74	338	4.6	27	1	14	5	6	4	35	8.8	0	3rd D 3-7 to Go	5	4	0.8	4	0	1	2	3	0	0	-	0
Games 9-16	8	81	329	4.1	23	0	13	14	31	3	10	3.3	0	3rd D 8+ to Go	0	0	-	0	0	0	0	0	0	0	-	0
September	4	35	171	4.9	27	0	6	1	1	1	13	13.0	0	4th Down	1	0	0.0	0	0	0	0	0	0	0	-	0
October	4	39	167	4.3	18	1	8	4	5	3	22	7.3	0	Left Sideline	5	25	5.0	16	0	1	0	2	3	17	5.7	0
November	4	47	176	3.7	23	0	8	11	27	2	5	2.5	0	Left Side	46	206	4.5	23	0	8	5	11	3	23	7.7	0
December	4	34	153	4.5	16	0	5	3	4	1	5	5.0	0	Middle	71	290	4.1	27	1	11	7	14	0	0	-	0
Grass	14	132	517	3.9	23	1	22	19	37	6	43	7.2	0	Right Side	29	110	3.8	19	0	5	6	10	1	5	5.0	0
Turf	2	23	150	6.5	27	0	5	0	0	1	2	2.0	0	Right Sideline	4	36	9.0	17	0	1	0	0	0	0	-	0
Indoor	1	15	109	7.3	27	0	4	0	0	0	0	-	0	Shotgun	0	0	-	0	0	0	0	0	0	0	-	0
Outdoor	15	140	558	4.0	23	1	23	19	37	7	45	6.4	0	2 Wide Receivers	127	522	4.1	23	1	22	17	34	5	27	5.4	0
1st Half	-	60	243	4.1	15	0	12	7	14	2	12	6.0	0	3 Wide Receivers	19	99	5.2	16	0	4	0	1	1	13	13.0	0
2nd Half/OT	-	95	424	4.5	27	1	15	12	23	5	33	6.6	0	4+ Wide Receivers	0	0	-	0	0	0	0	0	1	5	5.0	0
Last 2 Min. Half	-	8	50	6.3	27	0	2	1	1	0	0	-	0	Carries 1-5	73	264	3.6	15	0	12	9	18	0	0	-	0
4th qtr, +/-7 pts	-	12	60	5.0	10	1	3	2	3	0	0	-	0	Carries 6-10	46	224	4.9	19	0	9	4	7	0	0	-	0
Winning	-	113	503	4.5	27	1	20	17	35	2	8	4.0	0	Carries 11-15	26	143	5.5	27	1	5	4	9	0	0	-	0
Tied	-	13	50	3.8	8	0	3	1	1	2	15	7.5	0	Carries 16-20	9	27	3.0	16	0	1	2	3	0	0	-	0
Trailing	-	29	114	3.9	13	0	4	1	1	3	22	7.3	0	Carries 21+	1	9	9.0	9	0	0	0	0	0	0	-	0

1995 Incompletions

Type	Num	%of Inc	% Att
Pass Dropped	1	14.3	7.1
Poor Throw	5	71.4	35.7
Pass Defensed	1	14.3	7.1
Pass Hit at Line	0	0.0	0.0
Other	0	0.0	0.0
Total	7	100.0	50.0

Game Logs (1-8)

Date	Opp	Result	Rush	Yds	Rec	Yds	Trgt	F-L	TD
09/03	@Sea	W 34-10	15	109	0	0	1	0-0	0
09/10	NYN	W 20-17	6	22	1	13	2	1-0	0
09/17	Oak	W 23-17	6	23	0	0	1	0-0	0
09/24	@Cle	L 17-35	8	17	0	0	1	0-0	0
10/01	@Ari	W 24-3	11	46	0	0	1	0-0	0
10/09	SD	W 29-23	3	11	2	17	2	0-0	0
10/15	NE	W 31-26	15	83	1	5	2	0-0	0
10/22	@Den	W 21-7	10	27	0	0	0	0-0	0

Game Logs (9-16)

Date	Opp	Result	Rush	Yds	Rec	Yds	Trgt	F-L	TD
11/05	Was	W 24-3	17	51	1	3	1	0-0	0
11/12	@SD	W 22-7	17	78	0	0	0	0-0	0
11/19	Hou	W 20-13	5	6	0	0	0	0-0	0
11/23	@Dal	L 12-24	8	41	1	2	2	0-0	0
12/03	@Oak	W 29-23	3	4	0	0	0	0-0	0
12/11	@Mia	L 6-13	2	3	0	0	0	1-1	0
12/17	Den	W 20-17	8	33	1	5	1	0-0	0
12/24	Sea	W 26-3	21	113	0	0	0	0-0	0

Leroy Hoard
Cleveland Browns — RB

1995 Rushing and Receiving Splits

	G	Rush	Yds	Avg	Lg	TD	1st	Stf	YdL	Rec	Yds	Avg	TD
Total	12	136	547	4.0	25	0	28	10	15	13	103	7.9	0
vs. Playoff	7	67	254	3.8	17	0	14	6	7	8	57	7.1	0
vs. Non-playoff	5	69	293	4.2	25	0	14	4	8	5	46	9.2	0
vs. Own Division	5	68	302	4.4	25	0	15	4	8	6	48	8.0	0
Home	6	77	287	3.7	25	0	14	4	8	7	66	9.4	0
Away	6	59	260	4.4	24	0	14	6	7	6	37	6.2	0
Games 1-8	8	96	378	3.9	25	0	20	7	12	7	66	9.4	0
Games 9-16	4	40	169	4.2	17	0	8	3	3	6	37	6.2	0
September	4	55	221	4.0	24	0	11	3	5	2	23	11.5	0
October	4	41	157	3.8	25	0	9	4	7	5	43	8.6	0
November	3	32	149	4.7	17	0	6	1	1	3	14	4.7	0
December	1	8	20	2.5	12	0	2	2	2	3	23	7.7	0
Grass	8	94	346	3.7	25	0	17	7	11	10	89	8.9	0
Turf	4	42	201	4.8	24	0	11	3	4	3	14	4.7	0
Indoor	2	27	110	4.1	24	0	7	2	3	1	9	9.0	0
Outdoor	10	109	437	4.0	25	0	21	8	12	12	94	7.8	0
1st Half	-	80	319	4.0	25	0	17	7	11	8	64	8.0	0
2nd Half/OT	-	56	228	4.1	24	0	11	3	4	5	39	7.8	0
Last 2 Min. Half	-	2	27	13.5	24	0	1	0	0	0	0	-	0
4th qtr, +/-7 pts	-	17	73	4.3	24	0	2	2	2	1	24	24.0	0
Winning	-	27	117	4.3	24	0	6	2	3	1	12	12.0	0
Tied	-	38	179	4.7	25	0	8	2	5	3	16	5.3	0
Trailing	-	71	251	3.5	14	0	14	6	7	9	75	8.3	0

	Rush	Yds	Avg	Lg	TD	1st	Stf	YdL	Rec	Yds	Avg	TD
Inside 20	17	48	2.8	10	0	4	1	2	0	0	-	0
Inside 10	7	7	1.0	4	0	1	1	2	0	0	-	0
1st Down	88	351	4.0	25	0	7	5	8	8	75	9.4	0
2nd Down	43	182	4.2	24	0	17	4	5	4	29	7.3	0
3rd Down Overall	5	14	2.8	6	0	4	1	2	0	0	-	0
3rd D 0-2 to Go	4	8	2.0	6	0	3	1	2	0	0	-	0
3rd D 3-7 to Go	1	6	6.0	6	0	1	0	0	0	0	-	0
3rd D 8+ to Go	0	0	-	0	0	0	0	0	0	0	-	0
4th Down	0	0	-	0	0	0	0	0	1	-1	-1.0	0
Left Sideline	8	43	5.4	24	0	3	0	0	1	9	9.0	0
Left Side	14	69	4.9	10	0	2	1	2	4	47	11.8	0
Middle	53	186	3.5	17	0	11	5	7	3	20	6.7	0
Right Side	47	194	4.1	25	0	9	2	3	1	-1	-1.0	0
Right Sideline	14	55	3.9	12	0	3	2	3	4	28	7.0	0
Shotgun	0	0	-	0	0	0	0	0	0	0	-	0
2 Wide Receivers	103	420	4.1	25	0	21	7	10	11	95	8.6	0
3 Wide Receivers	28	106	3.8	12	0	6	1	1	2	8	4.0	0
4+ Wide Receivers	0	0	-	0	0	0	0	0	0	0	-	0
Carries 1-5	60	250	4.2	25	0	13	4	6	0	0	-	0
Carries 6-10	46	183	4.0	15	0	10	5	7	0	0	-	0
Carries 11-15	21	58	2.8	10	0	3	1	2	0	0	-	0
Carries 16-20	9	56	6.2	24	0	2	0	0	0	0	-	0
Carries 21+	0	0	-	0	0	0	0	0	0	0	-	0

1995 Incompletions

Type	Num	%of Inc	% Att
Pass Dropped	1	33.3	6.3
Poor Throw	0	0.0	0.0
Pass Defensed	0	0.0	0.0
Pass Hit at Line	1	33.3	6.3
Other	1	33.3	6.3
Total	3	100.0	18.8

Game Logs (1-8)

Date	Opp	Result	Rush	Yds	Rec	Yds	Trgt	F-L	TD
09/03	@NE	L 14-17	9	39	0	0	0	0-0	0
09/10	TB	W 22-6	13	44	1	12	2	1-1	0
09/17	@Hou	W 14-7	20	88	0	0	0	0-0	0
09/24	KC	W 35-17	13	50	1	11	2	1-0	0
10/02	Buf	L 19-22	7	13	0	0	0	0-0	0
10/08	@Det	L 20-38	7	22	1	9	1	0-0	0
10/22	Jac	L 15-23	19	74	2	29	2	1-1	0
10/29	@Cin	W 29-26	8	48	2	5	2	1-0	0

Game Logs (9-16)

Date	Opp	Result	Rush	Yds	Rec	Yds	Trgt	F-L	TD
11/05	Hou	L 10-37	-	-	-	-	-	-	-
11/13	@Pit	L 3-20	7	43	0	0	0	0-0	0
11/19	GB	L 20-31	11	57	1	0	1	0-0	0
11/26	Pit	L 17-20	14	49	2	14	2	1-1	0
12/03	@SD	L 13-31	8	20	3	23	4	0-0	0
12/09	@Min	L 11-27	-	-	-	-	-	-	-

Daryl Hobbs
Oakland Raiders — WR

1995 Receiving Splits

	G	Rec	Yds	Avg	TD	Lg	Big	YAC	Trgt	Y@C	1st	1st%
Total	16	38	612	16.1	3	54	5	196	80	10.9	33	86.8
vs. Playoff	8	24	403	16.8	1	54	3	120	50	11.8	21	87.5
vs. Non-playoff	8	14	209	14.9	2	43	2	76	30	9.5	12	85.7
vs. Own Division	8	18	324	18.0	1	49	4	111	39	11.8	16	88.9
Home	8	26	435	16.7	2	54	3	133	50	11.6	24	92.3
Away	8	12	177	14.8	1	43	2	63	30	9.5	9	75.0
Games 1-8	8	20	342	17.1	2	54	3	130	37	10.6	17	85.0
Games 9-16	8	18	270	15.0	1	49	2	66	43	11.3	16	88.9
September	4	12	201	16.8	1	54	1	63	18	11.5	10	83.3
October	4	8	141	17.6	1	43	2	67	19	9.3	7	87.5
November	4	10	126	12.6	0	30	1	35	25	9.1	8	80.0
December	4	8	144	18.0	1	49	1	31	18	14.1	8	100.0
Grass	12	33	569	17.2	2	54	5	190	66	11.5	30	90.9
Turf	4	5	43	8.6	1	17	0	6	14	7.4	3	60.0
Outdoor	1	37	606	16.4	3	54	5	195	77	11.1	32	86.5
Indoor	15	1	6	6.0	0	6	0	1	3	5.0	1	100.0
1st Half	-	18	253	14.1	2	29	1	54	36	11.1	17	94.4
2nd Half/OT	-	20	359	18.0	1	54	4	142	44	10.9	16	80.0
Last 2 Min. Half	-	4	51	12.8	1	16	0	7	11	11.0	4	100.0
4th qtr, +/-7 pts	-	4	70	17.5	0	30	1	15	6	13.8	3	75.0
Winning	-	11	170	15.5	2	54	1	79	21	8.3	7	63.6
Tied	-	11	140	12.7	1	29	1	41	23	9.0	10	90.9
Trailing	-	16	302	18.9	0	49	3	76	36	14.1	16	100.0

	Rec	Yds	Avg	TD	Lg	Big	YAC	Trgt	Y@C	1st	1st%
Inside 20	3	27	9.0	2	11	0	10	12	5.7	3	100.0
Inside 10	1	6	6.0	1	6	0	5	5	6.0	1	100.0
1st Down	8	112	14.0	0	30	1	19	17	11.6	8	100.0
2nd Down	14	193	13.8	2	49	1	58	23	9.6	12	85.7
3rd Down Overall	16	307	19.2	1	54	3	119	38	11.8	13	81.3
3rd D 0-2 to Go	1	14	14.0	0	14	0	7	2	7.0	1	100.0
3rd D 3-7 to Go	7	144	20.6	1	54	2	60	11	12.0	7	100.0
3rd D 8+ to Go	8	149	18.6	0	43	1	52	25	12.1	5	62.5
4th Down	0	0	-	0	0	0	0	2	-	0	-
Rec Behind Line	0	0	-	0	0	0	0	0	-	0	-
1-10 yds	20	205	10.3	2	17	0	84	35	6.1	17	85.0
11-20 yds	15	299	19.9	1	54	2	95	28	13.6	13	86.7
21-30 yds	2	59	29.5	0	30	2	9	9	25.0	2	100.0
31+	1	49	49.0	0	49	1	8	8	44.0	1	100.0
Left Sideline	14	192	13.7	2	30	2	48	34	10.3	12	85.7
Left Side	15	247	16.5	1	49	2	77	27	11.3	13	86.7
Middle	5	112	22.4	1	54	1	56	8	11.2	4	80.0
Right Side	4	61	15.3	0	20	0	15	7	11.5	4	80.0
Right Sideline	0	0	-	0	0	0	0	4	-	0	-
Shotgun	0	0	-	0	0	0	0	0	-	0	-
2 Wide Receivers	2	26	13.0	0	16	0	2	3	12.0	2	100.0
3 Wide Receivers	29	486	16.8	3	54	4	162	65	11.2	25	86.2
4+ Wide Receivers	7	100	14.3	0	29	1	32	11	9.7	6	85.7

1995 Incompletions

Type	Num	%of Inc	%of Att
Pass Dropped	7	16.7	8.8
Poor Throw	19	45.2	23.8
Pass Defensed	10	23.8	12.5
Pass Hit at Line	0	0.0	0.0
Other	6	14.3	7.5
Total	42	100.0	52.5

Game Logs (1-8)

Date	Opp	Result	Rec	Yds	Trgt	F-L	TD
09/03	SD	W 17-7	2	27	4	0-0	0
09/10	@Was	W 20-8	1	14	4	0-0	0
09/17	@KC	L 17-23	2	25	4	0-0	0
09/24	Phi	W 48-17	9	135	9	0-0	1
10/01	@NYA	W 47-10	1	6	4	0-0	0
10/08	Sea	W 34-14	4	68	6	0-0	0
10/16	@Den	L 0-27	1	43	5	0-0	0
10/22	Ind	W 30-17	2	24	4	0-0	0

Game Logs (9-16)

Date	Opp	Result	Rec	Yds	Trgt	F-L	TD
11/05	@Cin	W 20-17	2	14	3	0-0	0
11/12	@NYN	W 17-13	1	17	4	0-0	0
11/19	Dal	L 21-34	4	43	12	0-0	0
11/27	@SD	L 6-12	3	52	6	0-0	0
12/03	KC	L 23-29	2	62	7	0-0	0
12/10	Pit	L 10-29	2	35	4	0-0	0
12/17	@Sea	L 10-44	1	6	3	0-0	0
12/24	Den	L 28-31	3	41	4	0-0	0

Billy Joe Hobert

Oakland Raiders — QB

1995 Passing Splits

	G	Att	Cm	Pct	Yds	Yd/Att	TD	Int	1st	YAC	Big	Sk	Rtg		Att	Cm	Pct	Yds	Yd/Att	TD	Int	1st	YAC	Big	Sk	Rtg
Total	4	80	44	55.0	540	6.8	6	4	23	225	5	3	80.2	Inside 20	9	5	55.6	27	3.0	3	1	4	8	0	0	60.9
vs. Playoff	2	48	25	52.1	280	5.8	2	4	13	79	3	0	49.0	Inside 10	7	3	42.9	12	1.7	2	1	3	4	0	0	50.3
vs. Non-playoff	2	32	19	59.4	260	8.1	4	0	10	146	2	3	125.0	1st Down	29	15	51.7	146	5.0	3	1	6	31	2	2	86.3
vs. Own Division	3	43	24	55.8	378	8.8	6	0	15	177	5	3	124.8	2nd Down	24	13	54.2	137	5.7	2	2	6	43	1	0	64.1
Home	3	67	36	53.7	413	6.2	5	4	19	132	4	1	72.5	3rd Down Overall	26	15	57.7	238	9.2	1	1	10	150	2	1	85.1
Away	1	13	8	61.5	127	9.8	1	0	4	93	1	2	119.7	3rd D 0-5 to Go	7	5	71.4	101	14.4	1	0	3	87	1	1	153.3
Games 1-8	0	0	0	-	0	-	0	0	0	0	0	0	-	3rd D 6+ to Go	19	10	52.6	137	7.2	0	1	7	63	1	0	54.1
Games 9-16	4	80	44	55.0	540	6.8	6	4	23	225	5	3	80.2	4th Down	1	1	100.0	19	19.0	0	0	1	1	0	0	118.8
September	0	0	0	-	0	-	0	0	0	0	0	0	-	Rec Behind Line	9	7	77.8	11	1.2	0	0	0	33	0	0	79.2
October	0	0	0	-	0	-	0	0	0	0	0	0	-	1-10 yds	44	26	59.1	271	6.2	4	2	12	155	2	0	88.4
November	0	0	0	-	0	-	0	0	0	0	0	0	-	11-20 yds	16	8	50.0	135	8.4	0	1	8	18	0	0	52.9
December	4	80	44	55.0	540	6.8	6	4	23	225	5	3	80.2	21-30 yds	6	1	16.7	26	4.3	1	1	1	1	0	0	45.1
Grass	3	67	36	53.7	413	6.2	5	4	19	132	4	1	72.5	31+	5	2	40.0	97	19.4	1	0	2	18	2	0	127.1
Turf	1	13	8	61.5	127	9.8	1	0	4	93	1	2	119.7	Left Sideline	10	5	50.0	87	8.7	1	0	4	21	1	0	113.3
Indoor	1	13	8	61.5	127	9.8	1	0	4	93	1	2	119.7	Left Side	17	8	47.1	172	10.1	3	2	6	97	2	1	83.5
Outdoor	3	67	36	53.7	413	6.2	5	4	19	132	4	1	72.5	Middle	8	5	62.5	57	7.1	0	0	3	25	1	2	83.9
1st Half	-	29	17	58.6	147	5.1	1	1	7	55	0	1	69.2	Right Side	18	12	66.7	104	5.8	1	1	5	48	0	0	77.1
2nd Half/OT	-	51	27	52.9	393	7.7	5	3	16	170	5	2	86.5	Right Sideline	27	14	51.9	120	4.4	1	1	5	34	1	0	60.7
Last 2 Min. Half	-	9	3	33.3	17	1.9	1	1	2	0	0	0	39.8	2 Wide Receivers	22	14	63.6	138	6.3	1	1	6	42	1	0	77.5
4th qtr, +/-7 pts	-	0	0	-	0	-	0	0	0	0	0	0	-	3+ WR	55	29	52.7	396	7.2	5	2	17	176	4	3	91.2
Winning	-	12	6	50.0	90	7.5	1	0	3	38	1	1	102.8	Attempts 1-10	40	22	55.0	343	8.6	3	0	12	160	4	0	108.6
Tied	-	10	7	70.0	65	6.5	1	0	3	19	0	0	120.8	Attempts 11-20	23	14	60.9	127	5.5	3	1	7	51	1	0	97.3
Trailing	-	58	31	53.4	385	6.6	4	4	17	168	4	2	68.5	Attempts 21+	17	8	47.1	70	4.1	0	3	4	14	0	1	18.9

1995 Incompletions

Type	Num	% of Inc	% of Att
Pass Dropped	5	13.9	6.3
Poor Throw	14	38.9	17.5
Pass Defensed	8	22.2	10.0
Pass Hit at Line	1	2.8	1.3
Other	8	22.2	10.0
Total	36	100.0	45.0

Game Logs (1-8)

Date	Opp	Result	Att	Cm	Pct	Yds	TD	Int	Lg	Sk	F-L
09/03	SD	W 17-7	-	-	-	-	-	-	-	-	-
09/10	@Was	W 20-8	-	-	-	-	-	-	-	-	-
09/17	@KC	L 17-23	-	-	-	-	-	-	-	-	-
09/24	Phi	W 48-17	-	-	-	-	-	-	-	-	-
10/01	@NYA	W 47-10	-	-	-	-	-	-	-	-	-
10/08	Sea	W 34-14	-	-	-	-	-	-	-	-	-
10/16	@Den	L 0-27	-	-	-	-	-	-	-	-	-
10/22	Ind	W 30-17	-	-	-	-	-	-	-	-	-

Game Logs (9-16)

Date	Opp	Result	Att	Cm	Pct	Yds	TD	Int	Lg	Sk	F-L
11/05	@Cin	W 20-17	-	-	-	-	-	-	-	-	-
11/12	@NYN	W 17-13	-	-	-	-	-	-	-	-	-
11/19	Dal	L 21-34	-	-	-	-	-	-	-	-	-
11/27	@SD	L 6-12	-	-	-	-	-	-	-	-	-
12/03	KC	L 23-29	11	5	45.5	118	2	0	49	0	0-0
12/10	Pit	L 10-29	37	20	54.1	162	0	4	20	0	0-0
12/17	@Sea	L 10-44	13	8	61.5	127	1	0	80	2	0-0
12/24	Den	L 28-31	19	11	57.9	133	3	0	48	1	0-0

Darick Holmes

Buffalo Bills — RB

1995 Rushing and Receiving Splits

	G	Rush	Yds	Avg	Lg	TD	1st	Stf	YdL	Rec	Yds	Avg	TD		Rush	Yds	Avg	Lg	TD	1st	Stf	YdL	Rec	Yds	Avg	TD
Total	16	172	698	4.1	38	4	41	18	47	24	214	8.9	0	Inside 20	34	107	3.1	19	3	5	2	4	0	0	-	0
vs. Playoff	6	77	276	3.6	17	0	16	8	19	11	65	5.9	0	Inside 10	11	20	1.8	6	3	3	1	3	0	0	-	0
vs. Non-playoff	10	95	422	4.4	38	4	25	10	28	13	149	11.5	0	1st Down	80	341	4.3	38	2	8	5	18	13	132	10.2	0
vs. Own Division	8	85	303	3.6	24	1	17	8	26	19	186	9.8	0	2nd Down	67	247	3.7	17	1	22	11	26	7	47	6.7	0
Home	8	82	352	4.3	24	1	20	7	14	2	9	4.5	0	3rd Down Overall	24	112	4.7	24	1	11	1	1	4	35	8.8	0
Away	8	90	346	3.8	38	3	21	11	33	22	205	9.3	0	3rd D 0-2 to Go	12	38	3.2	9	0	6	0	0	0	0	-	0
Games 1-8	8	75	298	4.0	16	1	18	6	19	15	112	7.5	0	3rd D 3-7 to Go	7	47	6.7	24	1	4	0	0	0	0	-	0
Games 9-16	8	97	400	4.1	38	3	23	12	28	9	102	11.3	0	3rd D 8+ to Go	5	27	5.4	12	0	1	1	1	4	35	8.8	0
September	3	18	62	3.4	8	1	4	1	1	0	0	-	0	4th Down	1	-2	-2.0	-2	0	0	1	2	0	0	-	0
October	5	57	236	4.1	16	0	14	5	18	15	112	7.5	0	Left Sideline	4	18	4.5	6	1	1	0	0	4	26	6.5	0
November	4	62	235	3.8	24	1	14	6	15	7	80	11.4	0	Left Side	46	163	3.5	15	1	14	5	14	4	31	7.8	0
December	4	35	165	4.7	38	2	9	6	13	2	22	11.0	0	Middle	83	300	3.6	24	1	17	10	29	5	47	9.4	0
Grass	5	45	167	3.7	16	0	10	6	18	17	134	7.9	0	Right Side	35	178	5.1	38	1	7	3	4	9	99	11.0	0
Turf	11	127	531	4.2	38	4	31	12	29	7	80	11.4	0	Right Sideline	4	39	9.8	17	0	2	0	0	2	11	5.5	0
Indoor	2	33	157	4.8	38	2	8	2	3	3	19	6.3	0	Shotgun	14	103	7.4	24	0	6	2	4	8	79	9.9	0
Outdoor	14	139	541	3.9	24	2	33	16	44	21	195	9.3	0	2 Wide Receivers	29	78	2.7	12	0	5	4	12	3	9	3.0	0
1st Half	-	64	255	4.0	24	1	15	6	17	7	47	4.5	0	3 Wide Receivers	115	542	4.7	38	3	29	11	28	21	205	9.8	0
2nd Half/OT	-	108	443	4.1	38	3	26	12	30	18	187	10.4	0	4+ Wide Receivers	0	0	-	0	0	0	0	0	0	0	-	0
Last 2 Min. Half	-	6	4	0.7	7	0	1	2	6	5	53	10.6	0	Carries 1-5	73	316	4.3	24	3	19	8	17	0	0	-	0
4th qtr, +/-7 pts	-	21	101	4.8	11	0	5	0		3	11	3.7	0	Carries 6-10	61	242	4.0	38	1	14	7	25	0	0	-	0
Winning	-	82	331	4.0	38	4	22	7	22	4	62	15.5	0	Carries 11-15	24	82	3.4	11	0	5	3	5	0	0	-	0
Tied	-	40	136	3.4	16	0	7	6	13	5	30	6.0	0	Carries 16-20	10	47	4.7	11	0	3	0	0	0	0	-	0
Trailing	-	50	231	4.6	24	0	12	5	12	15	122	8.1	0	Carries 21+	4	11	2.8	4	0	0	0	0	0	0	-	0

1995 Incompletions

Type	Num	%of Inc	% Att
Pass Dropped	2	20.0	5.9
Poor Throw	2	20.0	5.9
Pass Defensed	1	10.0	2.9
Pass Hit at Line	0	0.0	0.0
Other	5	50.0	14.7
Total	10	100.0	29.4

Game Logs (1-8)

Date	Opp	Result	Rush	Yds	Rec	Yds	Trgt	F-L	TD
09/03	@Den	L 7-22	0	0	0	0	0	0-0	0
09/10	Car	W 31-9	11	30	0	0	0	1-0	1
09/17	Ind	W 20-14	7	32	0	0	0	0-0	0
10/02	@Cle	W 22-19	9	62	2	7	3	0-0	0
10/08	NYA	W 29-10	11	60	0	0	0	0-0	0
10/15	Sea	W 27-21	12	50	0	0	0	0-0	0
10/22	@NE	L 14-27	13	40	8	80	8	2-2	0
10/29	@Mia	L 6-23	12	24	5	25	5	0-0	0

Game Logs (9-16)

Date	Opp	Result	Rush	Yds	Rec	Yds	Trgt	F-L	TD
11/05	@Ind	W 16-10	21	67	3	19	4	0-0	0
11/12	Atl	W 23-17	23	100	1	-1	2	0-0	0
11/19	@NYA	W 28-26	12	22	2	52	4	0-0	0
11/26	NE	L 25-35	6	46	1	10	2	0-0	0
12/03	@SF	L 17-27	11	41	2	22	3	1-1	0
12/10	@StL	W 45-27	12	90	0	0	0	0-0	2
12/17	Mia	W 23-20	3	12	0	0	0	0-0	0
12/24	Hou	L 17-28	9	22	0	0	0	0-0	0

Jeff Hostetler — Oakland Raiders — QB

1995 Passing Splits

	G	Att	Cm	Pct	Yds	Yd/Att	TD	Int	1st	YAC	Big	Sk	Rtg
Total	11	286	172	60.1	1998	7.0	12	9	109	876	10	22	82.2
vs. Playoff	4	102	62	60.8	688	6.7	2	6	38	288	2	9	62.9
vs. Non-playoff	7	184	110	59.8	1310	7.1	10	3	71	588	8	13	92.9
vs. Own Division	5	140	77	55.0	853	6.1	3	3	44	370	3	13	71.5
Home	4	105	63	60.0	818	7.8	4	4	44	366	5	10	81.4
Away	7	181	109	60.2	1180	6.5	8	5	65	510	5	12	82.7
Games 1-8	7	204	125	61.3	1521	7.5	10	5	86	639	8	18	90.3
Games 9-16	4	82	47	57.3	477	5.8	2	4	23	237	2	4	61.9
September	4	117	77	65.8	816	7.0	4	4	50	337	3	9	83.1
October	3	87	48	55.2	705	8.1	6	1	36	302	5	9	100.0
November	3	62	37	59.7	407	6.6	2	4	19	207	2	3	63.0
December	1	20	10	50.0	70	3.5	0	0	4	30	0	1	58.3
Grass	7	195	118	60.5	1337	6.9	6	7	76	597	6	14	76.4
Turf	4	91	54	59.3	661	7.3	6	2	33	279	4	8	94.6
Indoor	1	20	10	50.0	70	3.5	0	0	4	30	0	1	58.3
Outdoor	10	266	162	60.9	1928	7.2	12	9	105	846	10	21	84.0
1st Half	-	176	103	58.5	1204	6.8	7	5	66	544	5	12	80.8
2nd Half/OT	-	110	69	62.7	794	7.2	5	4	43	332	5	10	84.4
Last 2 Min. Half	-	38	19	50.0	259	6.8	2	0	13	153	1	4	89.7
4th qtr, +/-7 pts	-	17	12	70.6	116	6.8	1	2	8	40	1	0	79.7
Winning	-	109	66	60.6	931	8.5	9	1	43	384	7	10	111.8
Tied	-	89	56	62.9	570	6.4	3	3	37	268	2	8	78.4
Trailing	-	88	50	56.8	497	5.6	0	5	29	224	1	4	49.3

	Att	Cm	Pct	Yds	Yd/Att	TD	Int	1st	YAC	Big	Sk	Rtg
Inside 20	32	17	53.1	138	4.3	8	1	14	43	0	4	90.9
Inside 10	13	6	46.2	29	2.2	6	0	6	0	0	3	92.6
1st Down	121	77	63.6	955	7.9	2	5	45	438	5	5	76.3
2nd Down	83	50	60.2	522	6.3	6	3	31	186	3	5	87.5
3rd Down Overall	81	45	55.6	521	6.4	4	1	33	252	2	12	86.5
3rd D 0-5 to Go	32	24	75.0	205	6.4	2	0	21	129	1	5	112.1
3rd D 6+ to Go	49	21	42.9	316	6.4	2	1	12	123	1	7	69.8
4th Down	1	0	0.0	0	0.0	0	0	0	0	0	0	39.6
Rec Behind Line	41	32	78.0	225	5.5	0	2	12	325	1	0	69.2
1-10 yds	136	89	65.4	724	5.3	6	3	49	279	0	0	84.3
11-20 yds	80	48	60.0	932	11.7	5	3	45	262	6	0	105.8
21-30 yds	10	1	10.0	29	2.9	0	1	0	5	1	0	39.6
31+	19	2	10.5	88	4.6	1	1	2	5	2	0	42.0
Left Sideline	59	32	54.2	366	6.2	4	1	24	121	2	0	88.7
Left Side	54	36	66.7	355	6.6	1	0	19	186	0	3	91.2
Middle	43	22	51.2	411	9.6	4	4	16	148	5	15	76.8
Right Side	66	45	68.2	471	7.1	1	3	25	196	1	2	74.7
Right Sideline	64	37	57.8	395	6.2	2	1	25	225	2	2	79.9
2 Wide Receivers	103	64	62.1	852	8.3	5	2	44	270	6	5	96.4
3+ WR	172	102	59.3	1102	6.4	5	6	59	562	4	16	73.4
Attempts 1-10	110	72	65.5	794	7.2	4	3	48	358	3	0	87.5
Attempts 11-20	103	56	54.4	718	7.0	3	3	33	312	4	0	74.0
Attempts 21+	73	44	60.3	486	6.7	5	3	28	206	3	0	85.8

1995 Incompletions

Type	Num	% of Inc	% of Att
Pass Dropped	20	17.5	7.0
Poor Throw	45	39.5	15.7
Pass Defensed	23	20.2	8.0
Pass Hit at Line	3	2.6	1.0
Other	23	20.2	8.0
Total	114	100.0	39.9

Game Logs (1-8)

Date	Opp	Result	Att	Cm	Pct	Yds	TD	Int	Lg	Sk	F-L
09/03	SD	W 17-7	26	14	53.8	136	1	0	18	5	1-0
09/10	@Was	W 20-8	29	22	75.9	205	2	0	28	0	0-0
09/17	@KC	L 17-23	30	19	63.3	203	0	2	22	2	0-0
09/24	Phi	W 48-17	32	22	68.8	272	1	2	28	2	1-1
10/01	@NYA	W 47-10	23	14	60.9	261	4	0	66	4	0-0
10/08	Sea	W 34-14	33	20	60.6	333	2	0	80	3	0-0
10/16	@Den	L 0-27	31	14	45.2	111	0	1	21	2	2-1
10/22	Ind	W 30-17	-	-	-	-	-	-	-	-	-

Game Logs (9-16)

Date	Opp	Result	Att	Cm	Pct	Yds	TD	Int	Lg	Sk	F-L
11/05	@Cin	W 20-17	29	17	58.6	178	1	1	34	2	0-0
11/12	@NYN	W 17-13	19	13	68.4	152	1	1	40	1	0-0
11/19	Dal	L 21-34	14	7	50.0	77	0	2	21	0	1-0
11/27	@SD	L 6-12	-	-	-	-	-	-	-	-	-
12/03	KC	L 23-29	-	-	-	-	-	-	-	-	-
12/10	Pit	L 10-29	-	-	-	-	-	-	-	-	-
12/17	@Sea	L 10-44	20	10	50.0	70	0	0	14	1	0-0

Desmond Howard — Jacksonville Jaguars — WR

1995 Receiving Splits

	G	Rec	Yds	Avg	TD	Lg	Big	YAC	Trgt	Y@C	1st	1st%
Total	13	26	276	10.6	1	24	0	106	56	6.5	15	57.7
vs. Playoff	4	6	50	8.3	0	12	0	7	12	7.2	2	33.3
vs. Non-playoff	9	20	226	11.3	1	24	0	99	44	6.4	13	65.0
vs. Own Division	6	13	154	11.8	1	24	0	76	30	6.0	9	69.2
Home	7	9	99	11.0	0	24	0	42	21	6.3	6	66.7
Away	6	17	177	10.4	1	22	0	64	35	6.6	9	52.9
Games 1-8	6	14	163	11.6	1	22	0	57	36	7.6	11	78.6
Games 9-16	7	12	113	9.4	0	24	0	49	20	5.3	4	33.3
September	4	11	131	11.9	0	22	0	28	29	9.4	10	90.9
October	2	3	32	10.7	1	15	0	29	7	1.0	1	33.3
November	3	4	28	7.0	0	10	0	12	8	4.0	1	25.0
December	4	8	85	10.6	0	24	0	37	12	6.0	3	37.5
Grass	9	13	144	11.1	0	24	0	55	27	6.8	9	69.2
Turf	4	13	132	10.2	1	22	0	51	29	6.2	6	46.2
Indoor	2	7	58	8.3	1	15	0	35	14	3.3	1	33.3
Outdoor	11	19	218	11.5	0	24	0	71	42	7.7	14	73.7
1st Half	-	10	111	11.1	0	24	0	53	26	5.8	3	30.0
2nd Half/OT	-	16	165	10.3	1	24	0	53	30	7.0	12	75.0
Last 2 Min. Half	-	8	92	11.5	1	22	0	34	13	7.3	5	62.5
4th qtr, +/-7 pts	-	6	75	12.5	1	22	0	24	9	8.5	5	83.3
Winning	-	2	32	16.0	0	24	0	32	7	0.0	1	50.0
Tied	-	4	29	7.3	0	11	0	11	6	4.5	0	0.0
Trailing	-	20	215	10.8	1	22	0	63	41	7.6	14	70.0

	Rec	Yds	Avg	TD	Lg	Big	YAC	Trgt	Y@C	1st	1st%
Inside 20	4	39	9.8	1	15	0	24	9	3.8	2	50.0
Inside 10	0	0	-	0	0	0	0	3	-	0	-
1st Down	10	106	10.6	1	15	0	31	20	7.5	5	50.0
2nd Down	6	76	12.7	0	24	0	36	17	6.7	3	50.0
3rd Down Overall	8	75	9.4	0	22	0	31	17	5.5	5	62.5
3rd D 0-2 to Go	0	0	-	0	0	0	0	1	-	0	-
3rd D 3-7 to Go	2	6	3.0	0	7	0	2	8	2.0	1	50.0
3rd D 8+ to Go	6	69	11.5	0	22	0	29	8	6.7	4	66.7
4th Down	2	19	9.5	0	10	0	8	2	5.5	2	100.0
Rec Behind Line	4	25	6.3	1	15	0	34	5	-2.3	1	25.0
1-10 yds	15	153	10.2	0	24	0	61	25	6.1	8	53.3
11-20 yds	7	98	14.0	0	22	0	11	21	12.4	6	85.7
21-30 yds	0	0	-	0	0	0	0	2	-	0	-
31+	0	0	-	0	0	0	0	3	-	0	-
Left Sideline	4	44	11.0	0	12	0	10	16	8.5	1	25.0
Left Side	6	73	12.2	1	16	0	31	11	7.0	4	66.7
Middle	6	70	11.7	0	24	0	34	8	6.0	5	83.3
Right Side	6	68	8.5	0	22	0	29	10	4.9	4	50.0
Right Sideline	2	21	10.5	0	12	0	11	9	9.5	1	50.0
Shotgun	6	63	10.5	0	16	0	30	13	5.5	4	66.7
2 Wide Receivers	7	72	10.3	0	13	0	22	18	7.1	5	71.4
3 Wide Receivers	19	204	10.7	1	24	0	84	36	6.3	10	52.6
4+ Wide Receivers	0	0	-	0	0	0	0	1	-	0	-

1995 Incompletions

Type	Num	%of Inc	%of Att
Pass Dropped	3	10.0	5.4
Poor Throw	13	43.3	23.2
Pass Defensed	6	20.0	10.7
Pass Hit at Line	1	3.3	1.8
Other	7	23.3	12.5
Total	30	100.0	53.6

Game Logs (1-8)

Date	Opp	Result	Rush	Yds	Rec	Yds	Trgt	F-L	TD
09/03	Hou	L 3-10	0	0	3	33	9	0-0	0
09/10	@Cin	L 17-24	1	8	4	50	4	0-0	0
09/17	@NYA	L 10-27	0	0	2	24	7	0-0	0
09/24	GB	L 14-24	0	0	2	24	5	0-0	0
10/01	@Hou	W 17-16	0	0	3	32	7	0-0	1
10/08	Pit	W 20-16	0	0	0	0	0	0-0	0
10/15	Chi	L 27-30	-	-	-	-	-	-	-
10/22	@Cle	W 23-15	-	-	-	-	-	-	-

Game Logs (9-16)

Date	Opp	Result	Rush	Yds	Rec	Yds	Trgt	F-L	TD
10/29	@Pit	L 7-24	-	-	-	-	-	-	-
11/12	Sea	L 30-47	0	0	1	3	1	0-0	0
11/19	@TB	L 16-17	0	0	1	10	3	0-0	0
11/26	Cin	L 13-17	0	0	2	15	4	0-0	0
12/03	@Den	L 23-31	0	0	3	35	3	0-0	0
12/10	Ind	L 31-41	0	0	0	0	0	0-0	0
12/17	@Det	L 0-44	0	0	4	26	7	0-0	0
12/24	Cle	W 24-21	0	0	1	24	2	0-0	0

Stan Humphries

San Diego Chargers — QB

1995 Passing Splits

	G	Att	Cm	Pct	Yds	Yd/Att	TD	Int	1st	YAC	Big	Sk	Rtg		Att	Cm	Pct	Yds	Yd/Att	TD	Int	1st	YAC	Big	Sk	Rtg
Total	15	478	282	59.0	3381	7.1	17	14	170	1241	20	23	80.4	Inside 20	36	20	55.6	184	5.1	9	1	17	59	0	6	97.7
vs. Playoff	6	207	117	56.5	1489	7.2	6	6	67	507	11	13	76.7	Inside 10	7	4	57.1	14	2.0	4	0	4	4	0	3	101.8
vs. Non-playoff	9	271	165	60.9	1892	7.0	11	8	103	734	9	10	83.1	1st Down	170	105	61.8	1283	7.5	6	5	50	424	11	7	84.5
vs. Own Division	8	278	164	59.0	1921	6.9	8	4	99	758	9	15	83.6	2nd Down	151	94	62.3	1023	6.8	4	4	53	414	2	8	80.0
Home	7	237	149	62.9	1705	7.2	7	7	88	656	9	13	82.0	3rd Down Overall	149	79	53.0	1038	7.0	7	5	64	392	7	8	77.0
Away	8	241	133	55.2	1676	7.0	10	7	82	585	11	10	78.8	3rd D 0-5 to Go	49	31	63.3	332	6.8	2	2	30	140	3	2	79.6
Games 1-8	7	237	134	56.5	1635	6.9	9	8	79	562	9	11	76.5	3rd D 6+ to Go	100	48	48.0	706	7.1	5	3	34	252	4	6	75.7
Games 9-16	8	241	148	61.4	1746	7.2	8	6	91	679	11	12	84.1	4th Down	8	4	50.0	37	4.6	0	0	3	11	0	0	63.0
September	4	137	74	54.0	897	6.5	4	3	43	276	5	5	75.0	Rec Behind Line	39	24	61.5	162	4.2	0	2	7	267	1	0	49.3
October	3	100	60	60.0	738	7.4	5	5	36	286	4	6	78.7	1-10 yds	245	182	74.3	1725	7.0	7	6	97	801	2	0	92.6
November	4	132	81	61.4	944	7.2	2	1	48	364	4	11	84.9	11-20 yds	116	60	51.7	931	8.0	4	3	50	116	3	0	79.3
December	4	109	67	61.5	802	7.4	6	5	43	315	7	1	83.2	21-30 yds	41	8	19.5	230	5.6	1	2	8	36	6	0	38.3
Grass	10	346	213	61.6	2531	7.3	10	8	128	1036	14	16	83.9	31+	37	8	21.6	333	9.0	5	1	8	21	8	0	92.9
Turf	5	132	69	52.3	850	6.4	7	6	42	205	6	7	71.2	Left Sideline	125	69	55.2	809	6.5	3	2	42	242	6	0	76.4
Indoor	2	66	35	53.0	438	6.6	5	2	23	115	4	3	86.6	Left Side	80	50	62.5	578	7.2	0	4	33	293	2	3	63.4
Outdoor	13	412	247	60.0	2943	7.1	12	12	147	1126	16	20	79.4	Middle	78	44	56.4	594	7.6	8	2	29	217	5	18	104.3
1st Half	-	239	129	54.0	1478	6.2	8	8	75	537	9	13	70.0	Right Side	84	56	66.7	589	7.0	3	5	28	228	1	2	74.0
2nd Half/OT	-	239	153	64.0	1903	8.0	9	6	95	704	11	10	90.7	Right Sideline	111	63	56.8	811	7.3	3	1	38	261	6	0	85.1
Last 2 Min. Half	-	66	34	51.5	440	6.7	2	0	23	194	3	6	82.9	2 Wide Receivers	177	108	61.0	1232	7.0	5	4	54	426	9	7	81.9
4th qtr, +/-7 pts	-	56	36	64.3	550	9.8	4	2	24	195	5	1	105.5	3+ WR	290	170	58.6	2095	7.2	11	9	113	808	11	15	80.7
Winning	-	135	82	60.7	941	7.0	4	3	49	354	6	4	82.4	Attempts 1-10	143	82	57.3	924	6.5	4	6	49	324	6	0	68.6
Tied	-	98	57	58.2	623	6.4	2	6	35	269	2	5	58.3	Attempts 11-20	140	76	54.3	811	5.8	4	2	40	276	2	0	75.0
Trailing	-	245	143	58.4	1817	7.4	11	5	86	618	12	14	88.1	Attempts 21+	195	124	63.6	1646	8.4	9	6	81	641	12	0	92.8

1995 Incompletions

Type	Num	% of Inc	% of Att
Pass Dropped	35	17.9	7.3
Poor Throw	97	49.5	20.3
Pass Defensed	26	13.3	5.4
Pass Hit at Line	10	5.1	2.1
Other	28	14.3	5.9
Total	196	100.0	41.0

Game Logs (1-8)

Date	Opp	Result		Att	Cm	Pct	Yds	TD	Int	Lg	Sk	F-L
09/03	@Oak	L	7-17	47	23	48.9	305	1	1	39	1	1-0
09/10	Sea	W	14-10	35	23	65.7	260	2	1	24	1	0-0
09/17	@Phi	W	27-21	23	10	43.5	143	1	0	39	1	1-0
09/24	Den	W	17-6	32	18	56.3	189	1	4	25	2	0-0
10/01	@Pit	L	16-31	40	22	55.0	257	1	4	23	3	1-0
10/09	@KC	L	23-29	34	24	70.6	315	1	0	45	1	0-0
10/15	Dal	L	9-23									
10/22	@Sea	W	35-25	26	14	53.8	166	3	1	37	2	0-0

Game Logs (9-16)

Date	Opp	Result		Att	Cm	Pct	Yds	TD	Int	Lg	Sk	F-L
11/05	Mia	L	14-24	28	19	67.9	258	1	1	50	2	0-0
11/12	KC	L	7-22	42	21	50.0	244	0	0	31	4	2-0
11/19	@Den	L	27-30	28	17	60.7	206	1	0	24	1	0-0
11/27	Oak	W	12-6	34	24	70.6	236	0	0	35	3	0-0
12/03	Cle	W	31-13	25	18	72.0	230	1	0	29	0	1-0
12/09	Ari	W	28-25	41	26	63.4	288	3	4	38	0	0-0
12/17	@Ind	W	27-24	40	25	52.5	272	2	1	51	1	1-0
12/23	@NYN	W	27-17	3	2	66.7	12	0	0	8	0	0-0

Mark Ingram

Green Bay Packers — WR

1995 Receiving Splits

	G	Rec	Yds	Avg	TD	Lg	Big	YAC	Trgt	Y@C	1st	1st%		Rec	Yds	Avg	TD	Lg	Big	YAC	Trgt	Y@C	1st	1st%
Total	16	39	469	12.0	3	29	3	131	77	8.7	27	69.2	Inside 20	3	33	11.0	3	13	0	0	7	11.0	3	100.0
vs. Playoff	4	12	166	13.8	0	28	1	55	21	9.3	11	91.7	Inside 10	1	9	9.0	1	9	0	0	3	9.0	1	100.0
vs. Non-playoff	12	27	303	11.2	3	29	2	76	56	8.4	16	59.3	1st Down	13	148	11.4	2	29	1	47	27	7.8	7	53.8
vs. Own Division	8	24	292	12.2	1	28	1	97	49	9.0	15	65.5	2nd Down	13	179	13.8	0	28	1	52	24	9.8	11	84.6
Home	8	24	331	13.8	3	29	3	82	37	10.4	18	75.0	3rd Down Overall	13	142	10.9	1	28	1	32	26	8.5	9	69.2
Away	8	15	138	9.2	0	16	0	49	40	5.9	9	60.0	3rd D 0-2 to Go	0	0	-	0	0	0	0	1	-	0	-
Games 1-8	8	22	260	11.8	1	29	1	66	43	8.8	16	72.7	3rd D 3-7 to Go	7	71	10.1	1	15	0	15	13	8.0	7	100.0
Games 9-16	8	17	209	12.3	2	28	2	65	34	8.5	11	64.7	3rd D 8+ to Go	6	71	11.8	0	28	1	17	12	9.0	2	33.3
September	4	12	124	10.3	1	29	1	18	23	8.8	6	50.0	4th Down	0	0	-	0	0	0	0	0	-	0	-
October	4	10	136	13.6	0	21	0	48	20	8.8	10	100.0	Rec Behind Line	0	0	-	0	0	0	0	2	-	0	-
November	4	10	119	11.9	1	28	1	39	18	8.0	6	60.0	1-10 yds	27	244	9.0	1	16	0	83	45	6.0	15	55.6
December	4	7	90	12.9	1	28	1	26	16	9.1	5	71.4	11-20 yds	11	196	17.8	2	28	2	44	23	13.8	11	100.0
Grass	12	32	395	12.3	3	29	3	97	58	9.3	21	65.6	21-30 yds	1	29	29.0	0	29	1	4	6	25.0	1	100.0
Turf	4	7	74	10.6	0	15	0	34	19	5.7	6	85.7	31+	0	0	-	0	0	0	0	1	-	0	-
Indoor	3	7	74	10.6	0	15	0	34	17	5.7	6	85.7	Left Sideline	12	177	14.8	2	28	2	69	29	9.0	10	83.3
Outdoor	13	32	395	12.3	3	29	3	97	60	9.3	21	65.6	Left Side	3	41	13.7	1	21	0	8	8	11.0	3	100.0
1st Half	-	24	307	12.8	3	28	2	86	44	9.2	19	79.2	Middle	6	46	7.7	1	13	0	3	11	7.2	3	50.0
2nd Half/OT	-	15	162	10.8	0	29	1	45	33	7.8	8	53.3	Right Side	7	109	15.6	0	29	1	25	11	12.0	6	85.7
Last 2 Min. Half	-	6	72	12.0	1	17	0	13	12	9.8	4	66.7	Right Sideline	11	96	8.7	0	16	0	26	20	6.4	5	45.5
4th qtr, +/-7 pts	-	3	16	5.3	0	8	0	8	8	2.7	0	0.0	Shotgun	0	0	-	0	0	0	0	0	-	0	-
Winning	-	11	143	13.0	0	28	1	36	30	9.7	7	63.6	2 Wide Receivers	14	165	11.8	0	21	0	63	32	7.3	9	64.3
Tied	-	15	152	10.1	2	17	0	39	26	7.5	10	66.7	3 Wide Receivers	19	230	12.1	2	29	3	49	31	9.5	14	73.7
Trailing	-	13	174	13.4	1	29	2	56	21	9.1	10	76.9	4+ Wide Receivers	6	74	12.3	1	17	0	19	14	9.2	4	66.7

1995 Incompletions

Type	Num	%of Inc	%of Att
Pass Dropped	5	13.2	6.5
Poor Throw	19	50.0	24.7
Pass Defensed	7	18.4	9.1
Pass Hit at Line	2	5.3	2.6
Other	5	13.2	6.5
Total	38	100.0	49.4

Game Logs (1-8)

Date	Opp	Result		Rush	Yds	Rec	Yds	Trgt	F-L	TD
09/03	StL	L	14-17	0	0	6	77	7	0-0	0
09/11	@Chi	W	27-24	0	0	3	27	10	1-0	0
09/17	NYN	W	14-6	0	0	1	2	2	0-0	0
09/24	@Jac	W	24-14	0	0	2	9	4	0-0	0
10/08	@Dal	L	24-34	0	0	1	8	2	0-0	1
10/15	Det	W	30-21	0	0	4	61	7	0-0	0
10/22	Min	W	38-21	0	0	1	17	3	0-0	0
10/29	@Det	L	16-24	0	0	5	58	8	0-0	0

Game Logs (9-16)

Date	Opp	Result		Rush	Yds	Rec	Yds	Trgt	F-L	TD
11/05	@Min	L	24-27	0	0	2	16	6	0-0	0
11/12	Chi	W	35-28	1	-3	3	47	4	0-0	0
11/19	@Cle	W	31-20	0	0	1	9	2	0-0	0
11/26	TB	W	35-13	0	0	4	47	6	0-0	1
12/03	Cin	W	24-10	0	0	2	24	4	0-0	0
12/10	@TB	L	10-13	0	0	2	19	5	0-0	0
12/16	@NO	W	34-23	0	0	0	0	4	0-0	0
12/24	Pit	W	24-19	0	0	3	47	3	0-0	1

Michael Irvin
Dallas Cowboys — WR

1995 Receiving Splits

	G	Rec	Yds	Avg	TD	Lg	Big	YAC	Trgt	Y@C	1st	1st%		Rec	Yds	Avg	TD	Lg	Big	YAC	Trgt	Y@C	1st	1st%
Total	16	111	1603	14.4	10	50	15	302	165	11.7	88	79.3	Inside 20	12	110	9.2	6	19	0	21	18	7.4	9	75.0
vs. Playoff	7	51	701	13.7	5	48	7	146	75	10.9	36	70.6	Inside 10	4	23	5.8	3	8	0	6	8	4.3	3	75.0
vs. Non-playoff	9	60	902	15.0	5	50	8	156	90	12.4	52	86.7	1st Down	55	898	16.3	7	48	11	146	83	13.7	40	72.7
vs. Own Division	8	50	747	14.9	4	50	7	132	74	12.3	43	86.0	2nd Down	28	318	11.4	0	38	1	72	39	8.8	21	75.0
Home	8	57	813	14.3	5	50	8	179	83	11.1	44	77.2	3rd Down Overall	26	368	14.2	3	50	3	83	40	11.0	25	96.2
Away	8	54	790	14.6	5	47	7	123	82	12.4	44	81.5	3rd D 0-2 to Go	0	0	-	0	0	0	0	1	-	0	-
Games 1-8	8	58	908	15.7	5	50	10	201	89	12.2	50	86.2	3rd D 3-7 to Go	18	167	9.3	2	22	0	58	24	6.1	17	94.4
Games 9-16	8	53	695	13.1	5	47	5	101	76	11.2	38	71.7	3rd D 8+ to Go	8	201	25.1	1	50	3	25	15	22.0	8	100.0
September	4	26	415	16.0	2	50	4	97	44	12.2	24	92.3	4th Down	2	19	9.5	0	16	0	1	3	9.0	2	100.0
October	4	32	493	15.4	3	48	6	104	45	12.2	26	81.3	Rec Behind Line	0	0	-	0	0	0	0	2	-	0	-
November	4	30	382	12.7	4	38	3	67	39	10.5	21	70.0	1-10 yds	56	464	8.3	3	29	1	159	80	5.4	34	60.7
December	4	23	313	13.6	1	47	2	34	37	12.1	17	73.9	11-20 yds	43	703	16.3	3	38	4	102	57	14.0	42	97.7
Grass	4	26	399	15.3	2	47	5	64	33	12.9	22	84.6	21-30 yds	4	96	24.0	1	28	2	6	7	22.5	4	100.0
Turf	12	85	1204	14.2	8	50	10	238	132	11.4	66	77.6	31+	8	340	42.5	3	50	8	35	19	38.1	8	100.0
Outdoor	2	93	1361	14.6	8	50	14	270	134	11.7	75	80.6	Left Sideline	33	526	15.9	2	50	5	112	45	12.5	31	93.9
Indoor	14	18	242	13.4	2	43	1	32	31	11.7	13	72.2	Left Side	18	273	15.2	2	40	3	36	27	13.2	12	66.7
1st Half	-	65	973	15.0	5	50	9	200	91	11.9	55	84.6	Middle	11	139	12.6	2	48	1	20	18	10.8	7	63.6
2nd Half/OT	-	46	630	13.7	5	48	6	102	74	11.5	33	71.7	Right Side	24	295	12.3	2	29	2	80	34	9.0	18	75.0
Last 2 Min. Half	-	11	160	14.5	1	29	2	49	19	10.1	10	90.9	Right Sideline	25	370	14.8	2	47	4	54	41	12.6	20	80.0
4th qtr, +/-7 pts	-	6	65	10.8	0	16	0	6	15	9.8	5	83.3	Shotgun	0	0	-	0	0	0	0	0	-	0	-
Winning	-	58	856	14.8	5	48	10	167	82	11.9	46	79.3	2 Wide Receivers	64	1016	15.9	5	48	10	163	96	13.3	53	82.8
Tied	-	20	317	15.9	2	50	2	66	30	12.6	16	80.0	3 Wide Receivers	41	534	13.0	4	50	5	124	59	10.0	30	73.2
Trailing	-	33	430	13.0	3	40	3	69	53	10.9	26	78.8	4+ Wide Receivers	5	49	9.8	1	16	0	14	7	7.0	4	80.0

1995 Incompletions

Type	Num	%of Inc	%of Att
Pass Dropped	4	7.4	2.4
Poor Throw	24	44.4	14.5
Pass Defensed	20	37.0	12.1
Pass Hit at Line	2	3.7	1.2
Other	4	7.4	2.4
Total	54	100.0	32.7

Game Logs (1-8)

Date	Opp	Result		Rec	Yds	Trgt	F-L	TD
09/04	@NYN	L	35-0	7	109	11	0-0	1
09/10	Den	W	31-21	6	94	10	0-0	0
09/17	@Min	W	23-17	8	107	16	0-0	1
09/24	Ari	W	34-20	5	105	7	0-0	0
10/01	@Was	L	23-27	7	105	8	0-0	1
10/08	GB	W	34-24	8	150	13	0-0	1
10/15	@SD	W	23-9	7	103	9	0-0	0
10/29	@Atl	W	28-13	10	135	15	0-0	1

Game Logs (9-16)

Date	Opp	Result		Rec	Yds	Trgt	F-L	TD
11/06	Phi	W	34-12	8	115	11	0-0	1
11/12	SF	L	20-38	4	37	7	1-1	1
11/19	@Oak	W	34-21	7	109	8	0-0	1
11/23	KC	W	24-12	11	121	13	0-0	0
12/03	Was	L	17-24	10	101	15	0-0	1
12/10	@Phi	L	17-20	3	40	7	0-0	0
12/17	NYN	W	21-20	5	90	7	0-0	0
12/25	@Ari	W	37-13	5	82	8	0-0	0

Qadry Ismail
Minnesota Vikings — KR

1995 Receiving Splits

	G	Rec	Yds	Avg	TD	Lg	Big	YAC	Trgt	Y@C	1st	1st%		Rec	Yds	Avg	TD	Lg	Big	YAC	Trgt	Y@C	1st	1st%
Total	16	32	597	18.7	3	85	7	203	54	12.3	19	59.4	Inside 20	0	0	-	0	0	0	0	2	-	0	-
vs. Playoff	7	5	180	36.0	1	85	3	63	15	23.4	5	100.0	Inside 10	0	0	-	0	0	0	0	0	-	0	-
vs. Non-playoff	9	27	417	15.4	2	77	4	140	39	10.3	14	51.9	1st Down	12	165	13.8	0	49	1	43	18	10.2	7	58.3
vs. Own Division	8	17	246	14.5	1	85	2	89	24	9.2	8	47.1	2nd Down	5	55	11.0	0	28	1	7	11	9.6	2	40.0
Home	8	24	438	18.3	2	85	5	136	33	12.6	12	50.0	3rd Down Overall	15	377	25.1	3	85	5	153	25	14.9	10	66.7
Away	8	8	159	19.9	1	50	2	67	21	11.5	7	87.5	3rd D 0-2 to Go	0	0	-	0	0	0	0	0	-	0	-
Games 1-8	8	15	265	17.7	1	85	3	83	21	12.1	7	46.7	3rd D 3-7 to Go	6	103	17.2	1	50	1	53	9	8.3	5	83.3
Games 9-16	8	17	332	19.5	2	77	4	120	33	12.5	12	70.6	3rd D 8+ to Go	9	274	30.4	2	85	4	100	16	19.3	5	55.6
September	4	4	139	34.8	1	85	2	61	7	19.5	4	100.0	4th Down	0	0	-	0	0	0	0	0	-	0	-
October	4	11	126	11.5	0	49	1	22	14	9.5	3	27.3	Rec Behind Line	0	0	-	0	0	0	0	0	-	0	-
November	4	9	251	27.9	2	77	4	97	16	17.1	8	88.9	1-10 yds	23	226	9.8	1	50	1	100	31	5.5	10	43.5
December	4	8	81	10.1	0	24	0	23	17	7.3	4	50.0	11-20 yds	2	33	16.5	0	21	0	4	8	14.5	2	100.0
Grass	5	5	92	18.4	1	50	1	60	15	6.4	4	80.0	21-30 yds	3	137	45.7	1	85	2	59	7	26.0	3	100.0
Turf	11	27	505	18.7	2	85	6	143	39	13.4	15	55.6	31+	4	201	50.3	1	77	4	40	8	40.3	4	100.0
Indoor	9	26	469	18.0	2	85	5	141	35	12.6	14	53.8	Left Sideline	5	35	7.0	0	10	0	10	6.8	2	40.0
Outdoor	7	6	128	21.3	1	50	2	62	19	11.0	5	83.3	Left Side	2	15	7.5	0	11	0	6	3	4.5	1	50.0
1st Half	-	14	188	13.4	1	77	1	71	22	8.4	7	50.0	Middle	5	135	27.0	0	39	3	12	7	24.6	4	80.0
2nd Half/OT	-	18	409	22.7	2	85	6	132	32	15.4	12	66.7	Right Side	6	173	28.8	2	77	2	91	12	13.7	4	66.7
Last 2 Min. Half	-	12	228	19.0	1	77	2	67	16	13.4	7	58.3	Right Sideline	14	239	17.1	1	85	2	93	22	10.4	8	57.1
4th qtr, +/-7 pts	-	5	193	38.6	1	85	3	62	6	26.2	5	100.0	Shotgun	11	192	17.5	1	77	3	58	14	12.2	5	45.5
Winning	-	15	343	22.9	2	85	4	126	27	14.5	10	66.7	2 Wide Receivers	2	63	31.5	1	50	1	63	0	5.0	2	100.0
Tied	-	7	162	23.1	1	50	3	51	9	15.0	5	71.4	3 Wide Receivers	22	436	19.8	2	85	5	133	40	13.8	15	68.2
Trailing	-	10	92	9.2	0	21	0	26	18	6.6	4	40.0	4+ Wide Receivers	8	98	12.3	0	49	1	17	11	10.1	2	25.0

1995 Incompletions

Type	Num	%of Inc	%of Att
Pass Dropped	3	13.6	5.6
Poor Throw	13	59.1	24.1
Pass Defensed	2	9.1	3.7
Pass Hit at Line	0	0.0	0.0
Other	4	18.2	7.4
Total	22	100.0	40.7

Game Logs (1-8)

Date	Opp	Result		Rush	Yds	Rec	Yds	Trgt	F-L	TD
09/03	@Chi	L	14-31	0	0	2	18	3	0-0	0
09/10	Det	W	20-10	0	0	1	85	2	1-1	1
09/17	Dal	L	17-23	0	0	0	0	0	0-0	0
09/24	@Pit	W	44-24	0	0	1	36	2	0-0	0
10/08	Hou	W	23-17	0	0	2	53	2	0-0	0
10/15	@TB	L	17-20	0	0	2	24	2	0-0	0
10/22	@GB	L	21-38	1	7	0	0	2	0-0	0
10/30	Chi	L	6-14	0	0	7	49	8	1-1	0

Game Logs (9-16)

Date	Opp	Result		Rush	Yds	Rec	Yds	Trgt	F-L	TD
11/05	GB	W	27-24	0	0	1	28	3	0-0	0
11/12	@Ari	W	30-24	0	0	1	50	4	0-0	1
11/19	NO	W	43-24	0	0	5	142	7	1-0	1
11/23	@Det	L	38-44	0	0	2	31	2	0-0	0
12/03	TB	W	31-17	0	0	2	11	2	0-0	0
12/09	Cle	W	27-11	0	0	6	70	9	0-0	0
12/18	@SF	L	30-37	0	0	0	0	0	0-0	0
12/24	@Cin	L	24-27	0	0	0	0	2	0-0	0

Raghib Ismail

Oakland Raiders — KR

1995 Receiving Splits

	G	Rec	Yds	Avg	TD	Lg	Big	YAC	Trgt	Y@C	1st	1st%		Rec	Yds	Avg	TD	Lg	Big	YAC	Trgt	Y@C	1st	1st%
Total	16	28	491	17.5	3	73	5	86	57	14.5	18	64.3	Inside 20	0	0	0	-	0	0	0	0	0	-	0	-
vs. Playoff	8	10	206	20.6	2	73	2	48	25	15.8	6	60.0	Inside 10	0	0	0	-	0	0	0	0	0	-	0	-
vs. Non-playoff	8	18	285	15.8	1	48	3	38	32	13.7	12	66.7	1st Down	13	286	22.0	2	73	4	61	26	17.3	8	61.5
vs. Own Division	8	10	101	10.1	0	21	0	29	25	7.2	3	30.0	2nd Down	6	85	14.2	1	40	1	6	12	13.2	3	50.0
Home	8	9	190	21.1	1	73	2	43	24	16.3	6	66.7	3rd Down Overall	8	101	12.6	0	21	0	18	18	10.4	6	75.0
Away	8	19	301	15.8	1	48	3	43	33	13.6	12	63.2	3rd D 0-2 to Go	1	4	4.0	0	4	0	0	3	4.0	1	100.0
Games 1-8	8	19	348	18.3	2	73	4	65	28	14.9	13	68.4	3rd D 3-7 to Go	3	34	11.3	0	21	0	5	6	9.7	3	100.0
Games 9-16	8	9	143	15.9	1	40	1	21	29	13.6	5	55.6	3rd D 8+ to Go	4	63	15.8	0	20	0	13	9	12.5	2	50.0
September	4	9	96	10.7	0	28	1	12	15	9.3	5	55.6	4th Down	1	19	19.0	0	19	0	1	1	18.0	1	100.0
October	4	10	252	25.2	2	73	3	53	13	19.9	8	80.0	Rec Behind Line	1	6	6.0	0	6	0	6	1	0.0	0	0.0
November	4	6	109	18.2	1	40	1	17	15	15.3	4	66.7	1-10 yds	12	89	7.4	0	20	0	20	19	5.8	4	33.3
December	4	3	34	11.3	0	19	0	4	14	10.0	1	33.3	11-20 yds	11	189	17.2	0	28	1	23	21	15.1	10	90.9
Grass	12	19	323	17.0	2	73	3	74	39	13.1	13	68.4	21-30 yds	0	0	0	-	0	0	0	2	-	0	-
Turf	4	9	168	18.7	1	48	2	12	18	17.3	5	55.6	31+	4	207	51.8	3	73	4	37	14	42.5	4	100.0
Indoor	1	2	15	7.5	0	8	0	3	7	6.0	0	0.0	Left Sideline	4	100	25.0	1	73	1	33	5	16.8	3	75.0
Outdoor	15	26	476	18.3	3	73	5	83	50	15.1	18	69.2	Left Side	3	25	8.3	0	13	0	4	4	7.0	1	33.3
1st Half	-	15	223	14.9	1	48	2	19	29	13.6	10	66.7	Middle	3	108	36.0	1	48	2	19	8	29.7	3	100.0
2nd Half/OT	-	13	268	20.6	2	73	3	67	28	15.5	8	61.5	Right Side	9	169	18.8	1	46	2	20	18	16.6	6	66.7
Last 2 Min. Half	-	1	18	18.0	0	18	0	-1	4	19.0	0	0.0	Right Sideline	9	89	9.9	0	19	0	10	22	8.8	5	55.6
4th qtr, +/-7 pts	-	1	8	8.0	0	8	0	-1	3	9.0	0	0.0	Shotgun	0	0	0	-	0	0	0	0	-	0	-
Winning	-	9	238	26.4	2	73	3	41	18	21.9	6	66.7	2 Wide Receivers	11	245	22.3	2	48	4	21	20	20.4	9	81.8
Tied	-	8	110	13.8	1	46	1	6	12	13.0	6	75.0	3 Wide Receivers	14	216	15.4	1	73	1	55	33	11.5	8	57.1
Trailing	-	11	143	13.0	0	28	1	39	27	9.5	6	54.5	4+ Wide Receivers	3	30	10.0	0	16	0	10	4	6.7	1	33.3

1995 Incompletions

Type	Num	%of Inc	%of Att
Pass Dropped	2	6.9	3.5
Poor Throw	11	37.9	19.3
Pass Defensed	13	44.8	22.8
Pass Hit at Line	0	0.0	0.0
Other	3	10.3	5.3
Total	29	100.0	50.9

Game Logs (1-8)

Date	Opp	Result	Rush	Yds	Rec	Yds	Trgt	F-L	TD
09/03	SD	W 17-7	0	0	1	4	4	0-0	0
09/10	@Was	W 20-8	1	8	5	71	7	0-0	0
09/17	@KC	L 17-23	0	0	2	16	2	0-0	0
09/24	Phi	W 48-17	1	2	1	5	2	1-1	0
10/01	@NYA	W 47-10	0	0	3	81	4	0-0	0
10/08	Sea	W 34-14	1	2	2	20	2	0-0	0
10/16	@Den	L 0-27	0	0	2	26	4	0-0	0
10/22	Ind	W 30-17	0	0	3	125	5	0-0	2

Game Logs (9-16)

Date	Opp	Result	Rush	Yds	Rec	Yds	Trgt	F-L	TD
11/05	@Cin	W 20-17	1	4	1	18	4	0-0	0
11/12	@NYN	W 17-13	0	0	3	54	3	0-0	1
11/19	Dal	L 21-34	1	13	1	17	6	0-0	0
11/27	@SD	L 6-12	1	0	1	20	2	1-0	0
12/03	KC	L 23-29	0	0	0	0	0	0-0	0
12/10	Pit	L 10-29	0	0	1	19	3	0-0	0
12/17	@Sea	L 10-44	0	0	2	15	7	1-0	0
12/24	Den	L 28-31	0	0	1	1	1	1-0	0

Michael Jackson

Cleveland Browns — WR

1995 Receiving Splits

	G	Rec	Yds	Avg	TD	Lg	Big	YAC	Trgt	Y@C	1st	1st%		Rec	Yds	Avg	TD	Lg	Big	YAC	Trgt	Y@C	1st	1st%
Total	13	44	714	16.2	9	70	10	156	81	12.7	32	72.7	Inside 20	5	52	10.4	3	17	0	11	12	8.2	5	100.0
vs. Playoff	7	21	273	13.0	5	37	3	41	42	11.0	15	71.4	Inside 10	1	8	8.0	1	8	0	0	5	8.0	1	100.0
vs. Non-playoff	6	23	441	19.2	4	70	7	115	39	14.2	17	73.9	1st Down	19	307	16.2	4	70	4	96	32	11.1	9	47.4
vs. Own Division	6	21	307	14.6	3	39	4	51	33	12.2	15	71.4	2nd Down	6	88	14.7	2	32	2	6	18	13.7	5	83.3
Home	6	17	206	12.1	3	37	2	38	32	9.9	10	58.8	3rd Down Overall	16	243	15.2	2	36	3	33	28	13.1	15	93.8
Away	7	27	508	18.8	6	70	8	118	49	14.4	22	81.5	3rd D 0-2 to Go	2	41	20.5	0	36	1	6	6	17.5	2	100.0
Games 1-8	5	14	273	19.5	4	70	4	81	29	13.7	9	64.3	3rd D 3-7 to Go	6	71	11.8	0	22	0	13	8	9.7	6	100.0
Games 9-16	8	30	441	14.7	5	39	6	75	52	12.2	23	76.7	3rd D 8+ to Go	8	131	16.4	2	35	2	14	14	14.6	7	87.5
September	3	10	210	21.0	3	70	3	75	20	13.5	7	70.0	4th Down	3	76	25.3	0	39	1	21	3	18.3	3	100.0
October	2	4	63	15.8	1	32	1	6	9	14.3	2	50.0	Rec Behind Line	0	0	0	-	0	0	0	1	-	0	-
November	4	14	154	11.0	3	37	1	24	24	9.3	10	71.4	1-10 yds	25	191	7.6	2	13	0	57	39	5.4	13	52.0
December	4	16	287	17.9	2	39	5	51	28	14.8	13	81.3	11-20 yds	9	162	18.0	1	30	1	26	20	15.1	9	100.0
Grass	9	34	544	16.0	7	70	7	132	57	12.1	23	67.6	21-30 yds	6	214	35.7	3	70	5	55	11	26.5	6	100.0
Turf	4	10	170	17.0	2	35	3	24	24	14.6	9	90.0	31+	4	147	36.8	3	39	4	18	10	32.3	4	100.0
Outdoor	3	36	570	15.8	7	70	7	134	61	12.1	25	69.4	Left Sideline	31	549	17.7	8	70	9	127	49	13.6	21	67.7
Indoor	10	8	144	18.0	2	35	3	22	20	15.3	7	80.0	Left Side	6	98	16.3	1	32	1	13	15	14.2	5	83.3
1st Half	-	24	422	17.6	4	70	7	114	43	12.8	16	66.7	Middle	2	20	10.0	0	15	0	5	4	7.5	2	100.0
2nd Half/OT	-	20	292	14.6	5	37	3	42	38	12.5	16	80.0	Right Side	2	24	12.0	0	17	0	1	6	11.5	2	100.0
Last 2 Min. Half	-	5	93	18.6	2	32	2	12	11	16.2	5	100.0	Right Sideline	3	23	7.7	0	13	0	10	7	4.3	2	66.7
4th qtr, +/-7 pts	-	5	81	16.2	1	35	1	8	8	14.6	3	60.0	Shotgun	0	0	0	-	0	0	0	0	-	0	-
Winning	-	10	148	14.8	1	32	2	28	20	12.0	7	70.0	2 Wide Receivers	10	126	12.6	0	32	2	24	21	10.2	5	50.0
Tied	-	5	102	20.4	1	35	2	25	7	15.4	3	60.0	3 Wide Receivers	28	485	17.3	8	70	7	109	51	13.4	21	75.0
Trailing	-	29	464	16.0	7	70	6	103	54	12.4	22	75.9	4+ Wide Receivers	5	79	15.8	1	36	1	17	8	12.4	5	100.0

1995 Incompletions

Type	Num	%of Inc	%of Att
Pass Dropped	5	13.5	6.2
Poor Throw	20	54.1	24.7
Pass Defensed	7	18.9	8.6
Pass Hit at Line	1	2.7	1.2
Other	4	10.8	4.9
Total	37	100.0	45.7

Game Logs (1-8)

Date	Opp	Result	Rec	Yds	Trgt	F-L	TD
09/03	@NE	L 14-17	7	157	9	0-0	2
09/10	TB	W 22-6	-	-	-	-	-
09/17	@Hou	W 14-7	2	45	5	0-0	1
09/24	KC	W 35-17	1	8	6	0-0	0
10/02	Buf	L 19-22	1	9	2	0-0	0
10/08	@Det	L 20-38	3	54	7	0-0	1
10/22	Jac	L 15-23	-	-	-	-	-
10/29	@Cin	W 29-26	-	-	-	-	-

Game Logs (9-16)

Date	Opp	Result	Rec	Yds	Trgt	F-L	TD
11/05	Hou	L 10-37	1	3	4	1-1	0
11/13	@Pit	L 3-20	2	26	4	0-0	0
11/19	GB	L 20-31	5	83	9	0-0	2
11/26	Pit	L 17-20	6	42	7	0-0	1
12/03	@SD	L 13-31	3	51	7	0-0	0
12/09	@Min	L 11-27	3	45	8	0-0	0
12/17	Cin	W 26-10	3	61	6	0-0	0
12/24	@Jac	L 21-24	7	130	9	0-0	1

Willie Jackson
Jacksonville Jaguars — WR

1995 Receiving Splits

	G	Rec	Yds	Avg	TD	Lg	Big	YAC	Trgt	Y@C	1st	1st%		Rec	Yds	Avg	TD	Lg	Big	YAC	Trgt	Y@C	1st	1st%
Total	14	53	589	11.1	2	45	3	133	91	8.6	29	54.7	Inside 20	7	48	6.9	4	15	0	8	10	5.7	5	71.4
vs. Playoff	5	22	298	13.5	4	45	2	79	38	10.0	16	72.7	Inside 10	3	18	6.0	3	8	0	0	3	6.0	3	100.0
vs. Non-playoff	9	31	291	9.4	1	33	1	54	53	7.6	13	41.9	1st Down	21	221	10.5	2	31	1	37	33	8.8	11	52.4
vs. Own Division	7	25	288	11.5	1	33	1	64	47	9.0	14	56.0	2nd Down	21	251	12.0	2	45	1	56	36	9.3	13	61.9
Home	7	33	428	13.0	5	45	3	107	47	9.7	22	66.7	3rd Down Overall	11	117	10.6	1	33	1	40	22	7.0	5	45.5
Away	7	20	161	8.1	0	18	0	26	44	6.8	7	35.0	3rd D 0-2 to Go	0	0	-	0	0	0	0	1	-	0	-
Games 1-8	8	34	321	9.4	2	22	0	90	58	6.8	17	50.0	3rd D 3-7 to Go	4	70	17.5	1	33	1	12	5	14.5	4	100.0
Games 9-16	6	19	268	14.1	3	45	3	43	33	11.8	12	63.2	3rd D 8+ to Go	7	47	6.7	0	19	0	28	16	2.7	1	14.3
September	4	9	69	7.7	2	19	0	31	20	4.2	5	55.6	4th Down	0	0	-	0	0	0	0	0	-	0	-
October	5	26	263	10.1	0	22	0	66	44	7.6	13	50.0	Rec Behind Line	2	2	1.0	0	1	0	5	4	-1.5	0	0.0
November	2	6	49	8.2	0	18	0	8	7	6.8	2	33.3	1-10 yds	37	309	8.4	3	19	0	106	47	5.5	16	43.2
December	3	12	208	17.3	3	45	3	28	20	15.0	9	75.0	11-20 yds	10	147	14.7	1	22	0	15	20	13.2	9	90.0
Grass	9	43	514	12.0	5	45	3	115	63	9.3	25	58.1	21-30 yds	2	53	26.5	0	31	1	1	14	26.0	2	100.0
Turf	5	10	75	7.5	0	15	0	18	28	5.7	4	40.0	31+	2	78	39.0	1	45	2	6	6	36.0	2	100.0
Outdoor	2	45	527	11.7	5	45	3	121	79	9.0	26	57.8	Left Sideline	18	201	11.2	0	45	1	34	31	9.3	10	55.6
Indoor	12	8	62	7.8	0	15	0	12	13	6.3	3	37.5	Left Side	10	114	11.4	2	33	1	37	17	7.7	7	70.0
1st Half	-	24	288	12.0	1	45	2	60	41	9.5	13	54.2	Middle	5	76	15.2	2	31	1	10	12	13.2	4	80.0
2nd Half/OT	-	29	301	10.4	1	31	1	73	50	7.9	16	55.2	Right Side	12	121	10.1	1	22	0	47	18	6.2	6	50.0
Last 2 Min. Half	-	13	124	9.5	2	22	0	36	21	6.8	7	53.8	Right Sideline	8	77	9.6	0	22	0	5	13	9.0	2	25.0
4th qtr, +/-7 pts	-	6	73	12.2	0	22	0	12	11	10.2	3	50.0	Shotgun	21	193	9.2	3	33	1	34	37	7.6	8	38.1
Winning	-	17	208	12.2	1	33	1	46	30	9.5	10	58.8	2 Wide Receivers	16	228	14.3	1	45	2	35	23	12.1	11	68.8
Tied	-	9	103	11.4	0	22	0	24	12	8.8	5	55.6	3 Wide Receivers	34	325	9.6	4	33	1	89	64	6.9	16	47.1
Trailing	-	27	278	10.3	4	45	2	63	49	8.0	14	51.9	4+ Wide Receivers	3	36	12.0	0	22	0	9	4	9.0	2	66.7

1995 Incompletions

Type	Num	%of Inc	%of Att
Pass Dropped	4	10.5	4.4
Poor Throw	22	57.9	24.2
Pass Defensed	7	18.4	7.7
Pass Hit at Line	2	5.3	2.2
Other	3	7.9	3.3
Total	38	100.0	41.8

Game Logs (1-8)

Date	Opp	Result	Rec	Yds	Trgt	F-L	TD
09/03	Hou	L 3-10	1	1	1	0-0	0
09/10	@Cin	L 17-24	0	0	5	0-0	0
09/17	@NYA	L 10-27	1	2	4	0-0	0
09/24	GB	L 14-24	7	66	10	0-0	2
10/01	@Hou	W 17-16	6	48	7	0-0	0
10/08	Pit	W 20-16	6	94	9	0-0	0
10/15	Chi	L 27-30	6	57	10	0-0	0
10/22	@Cle	W 23-15	7	53	12	1-0	0

Game Logs (9-16)

Date	Opp	Result	Rec	Yds	Trgt	F-L	TD
10/29	@Pit	L 7-24	1	11	6	0-0	0
11/12	Sea	L 30-47	3	16	3	1-1	0
11/19	@TB	L 16-17	3	33	4	0-0	0
11/26	Cin	L 13-17	-	-	-	-	-
12/03	@Den	L 23-31	-	-	-	-	-
12/10	Ind	L 31-41	6	113	7	0-0	2
12/17	@Det	L 0-44	2	14	6	0-0	0
12/24	Cle	W 24-21	4	81	7	0-0	1

Shawn Jefferson
San Diego Chargers — WR

1995 Receiving Splits

	G	Rec	Yds	Avg	TD	Lg	Big	YAC	Trgt	Y@C	1st	1st%		Rec	Yds	Avg	TD	Lg	Big	YAC	Trgt	Y@C	1st	1st%
Total	16	48	621	12.9	2	45	5	125	101	10.3	30	62.5	Inside 20	2	11	5.5	0	9	0	0	8	5.5	1	50.0
vs. Playoff	7	20	270	13.5	1	45	2	56	49	10.7	13	65.0	Inside 10	0	0	-	0	0	0	0	0	-	0	-
vs. Non-playoff	9	28	351	12.5	1	39	3	69	52	10.1	17	60.7	1st Down	23	323	14.0	2	45	4	63	41	11.3	12	52.2
vs. Own Division	8	27	380	14.1	1	45	4	75	52	11.3	19	70.4	2nd Down	16	176	11.0	0	21	0	38	31	8.6	10	62.5
Home	8	21	200	9.5	0	35	1	20	45	8.6	13	61.9	3rd Down Overall	9	122	13.6	0	35	1	24	29	10.9	8	88.9
Away	8	27	421	15.6	2	45	4	105	56	11.7	17	63.0	3rd D 0-2 to Go	0	0	-	0	0	0	0	0	-	0	-
Games 1-8	8	30	442	14.7	2	45	4	93	59	11.6	21	70.0	3rd D 3-7 to Go	7	90	12.9	0	35	1	15	15	10.7	6	85.7
Games 9-16	8	18	179	9.9	0	35	1	32	42	8.2	9	50.0	3rd D 8+ to Go	2	32	16.0	0	16	0	9	14	11.5	2	100.0
September	4	17	254	14.9	2	39	3	53	28	11.8	11	64.7	4th Down	0	0	-	0	0	0	0	4	-	0	-
October	4	13	188	14.5	0	45	1	40	31	11.4	10	76.9	Rec Behind Line	0	0	-	0	0	0	0	4	-	0	-
November	4	12	124	10.3	0	35	1	19	23	8.8	7	58.3	1-10 yds	31	267	8.6	0	21	0	93	43	5.6	14	45.2
December	4	6	55	9.2	0	12	0	13	19	7.0	2	33.3	11-20 yds	12	164	13.7	0	19	0	11	28	12.8	11	91.7
Grass	11	35	434	12.4	1	45	4	85	70	10.0	23	65.7	21-30 yds	1	33	33.0	0	33	1	7	11	26.0	1	100.0
Turf	5	13	187	14.4	1	38	1	40	31	11.3	7	53.8	31+	4	157	39.3	2	45	4	14	15	35.8	4	100.0
Indoor	2	2	22	11.0	0	13	0	4	10		1	50.0	Left Sideline	10	138	13.8	0	35	2	27	28	11.1	7	70.0
Outdoor	14	46	599	13.0	2	45	5	121	91	10.4	29	63.0	Left Side	6	62	10.3	0	16	0	10	14	8.7	4	66.7
1st Half	-	20	277	13.9	2	39	3	54	50	11.2	13	65.0	Middle	6	113	18.8	2	39	2	16	11	16.2	4	66.7
2nd Half/OT	-	28	344	12.3	0	45	2	71	51	9.8	17	60.7	Right Side	9	86	9.6	0	16	0	23	18	7.0	7	77.8
Last 2 Min. Half	-	1	39	39.0	0	39	1	0	7	39.0	1	100.0	Right Sideline	17	222	13.1	0	45	1	49	30	10.2	8	47.1
4th qtr, +/-7 pts	-	5	82	16.4	0	45	1	15	10	13.4	3	60.0	Shotgun	0	0	-	0	0	0	0	0	-	0	-
Winning	-	13	115	8.8	0	16	0	15	27	7.7	7	53.8	2 Wide Receivers	30	364	12.1	2	45	3	59	51	10.2	14	46.7
Tied	-	6	48	8.0	0	12	0	13	20	5.8	4	66.7	3 Wide Receivers	15	195	13.0	0	35	1	47	38	9.9	14	93.3
Trailing	-	29	458	15.8	2	45	5	97	54	12.4	19	65.5	4+ Wide Receivers	3	62	20.7	0	33	1	19	12	14.3	2	66.7

1995 Incompletions

Type	Num	%of Inc	%of Att
Pass Dropped	5	9.4	5.0
Poor Throw	26	49.1	25.7
Pass Defensed	11	20.8	10.9
Pass Hit at Line	4	7.5	4.0
Other	7	13.2	6.9
Total	53	100.0	52.5

Game Logs (1-8)

Date	Opp	Result	Rush	Yds	Rec	Yds	Trgt	F-L	TD
09/03	@Oak	L 7-17	0	0	6	120	9	0-0	1
09/10	Sea	W 14-10	0	0	3	31	4	0-0	0
09/17	@Phi	W 27-21	0	0	4	67	4	0-0	1
09/24	@Hou	W 17-6	1	11	4	36	7	0-0	0
10/01	@Pit	L 16-31	0	0	5	81	9	0-0	0
10/09	@KC	L 23-29	0	0	3	64	8	0-0	0
10/15	Dal	L 9-23	0	0	4	30	9	0-0	0
10/22	@Sea	W 35-25	0	0	1	13	5	0-0	0

Game Logs (9-16)

Date	Opp	Result	Rush	Yds	Rec	Yds	Trgt	F-L	TD
11/05	Mia	L 14-24	0	0	2	8	4	0-0	0
11/12	KC	L 7-22	0	0	1	11	6	0-0	0
11/19	@Den	L 27-30	1	-10	5	50	8	0-0	0
11/27	Oak	L 17-6	0	0	4	55	5	0-0	0
12/03	Cle	W 31-13	0	0	2	23	4	0-0	0
12/09	Ari	W 28-25	0	0	1	6	6	0-0	0
12/17	@Ind	W 27-24	0	0	1	9	5	0-0	0
12/23	@NYN	W 27-17	0	0	2	17	4	0-0	0

Haywood Jeffires

Houston Oilers — WR

1995 Receiving Splits

	G	Rec	Yds	Avg	TD	Lg	Big	YAC	Trgt	Y@C	1st	1st%		Rec	Yds	Avg	TD	Lg	Big	YAC	Trgt	Y@C	1st	1st%
Total	16	61	684	11.2	8	35	2	101	96	9.6	37	60.7	Inside 20	6	39	6.5	5	12	0	7	11	5.3	6	100.0
vs. Playoff	5	21	205	9.8	1	27	1	35	30	8.1	9	42.9	Inside 10	4	23	5.8	4	9	0	0	6	5.8	4	100.0
vs. Non-playoff	11	40	479	12.0	7	35	1	66	66	10.3	28	70.0	1st Down	21	230	11.0	0	21	0	42	35	9.0	9	42.9
vs. Own Division	8	31	341	11.0	4	23	0	43	51	9.6	20	64.5	2nd Down	25	288	11.5	3	35	1	55	36	9.3	15	60.0
Home	8	31	336	10.8	4	35	1	55	52	9.1	18	58.1	3rd Down Overall	15	166	11.1	5	27	1	4	25	10.8	13	86.7
Away	8	30	348	11.6	4	27	1	46	44	10.1	19	63.3	3rd D 0-2 to Go	2	5	2.5	0	4	0	-1	3	3.0	1	50.0
Games 1-8	8	29	323	11.1	4	23	0	36	49	9.9	19	65.5	3rd D 3-7 to Go	9	104	11.6	5	27	1	2	11	11.3	9	100.0
Games 9-16	8	32	361	11.3	4	35	2	65	47	9.3	18	56.3	3rd D 8+ to Go	4	57	14.3	0	19	0	3	11	13.5	3	75.0
September	4	12	124	10.3	3	23	0	18	22	8.8	8	66.7	4th Down	0	0	-	0	0	0	0	0	-	0	-
October	4	17	199	11.7	1	21	0	18	27	10.6	11	64.7	Rec Behind Line	1	11	11.0	0	11	0	11	2	0.0	1	100.0
November	4	17	190	11.2	2	23	0	32	27	9.3	10	58.8	1-10 yds	37	265	7.2	5	14	0	49	46	5.8	13	35.1
December	4	15	171	11.4	2	35	2	33	20	9.2	8	53.3	11-20 yds	19	300	15.8	0	21	0	29	34	14.3	19	100.0
Grass	4	16	182	11.4	2	23	0	23	22	9.9	10	62.5	21-30 yds	4	108	27.0	3	35	2	12	8	24.0	4	100.0
Turf	12	45	502	11.2	5	35	2	78	74	9.4	27	60.0	31+	0	0	-	0	0	0	0	0	-	0	-
Outdoor	9	26	307	11.8	4	27	1	40	37	10.3	17	65.4	Left Sideline	21	215	10.2	4	35	2	20	29	9.3	10	47.6
Indoor	7	35	377	10.8	4	35	1	61	59	9.0	20	57.1	Left Side	6	55	9.2	0	18	0	6	12	8.2	3	50.0
1st Half	-	32	395	12.3	5	35	2	56	54	10.6	18	56.3	Middle	3	43	14.3	1	19	0	13	6	10.0	3	100.0
2nd Half/OT	-	29	289	10.0	3	19	0	45	42	8.4	19	65.5	Right Side	8	118	14.8	0	19	0	19	15	12.4	7	87.5
Last 2 Min. Half	-	7	105	15.0	1	23	0	10	10	13.6	5	71.4	Right Sideline	23	253	11.0	3	23	0	43	34	9.1	14	60.9
4th qtr, +/-7 pts	-	10	105	10.5	1	19	0	14	12	9.1	6	60.0	Shotgun	0	0	-	0	0	0	0	0	-	0	-
Winning	-	12	201	16.8	4	35	2	30	24	14.3	11	91.7	2 Wide Receivers	16	155	9.7	1	21	0	35	26	7.5	8	50.0
Tied	-	10	82	8.2	1	19	0	11	16	7.1	3	30.0	3 Wide Receivers	42	506	12.0	6	35	2	64	67	10.5	27	64.3
Trailing	-	39	401	10.3	3	21	0	60	56	8.7	23	59.0	4+ Wide Receivers	2	19	9.5	0	14	0	2	2	8.5	1	50.0

1995 Incompletions

Type	Num	%of Inc	%of Att
Pass Dropped	4	11.4	4.2
Poor Throw	17	48.6	17.7
Pass Defensed	13	37.1	13.5
Pass Hit at Line	1	2.9	1.0
Other	0	0.0	0.0
Total	35	100.0	36.5

Game Logs (1-8)

Date	Opp	Result	Rec	Yds	Trgt	F-L	TD
09/03	@Jac	W 10-3	1	4	4	0-0	1
09/10	Pit	L 17-34	2	15	6	0-0	0
09/17	Cle	L 7-14	5	44	7	0-0	1
09/24	@Cin	W 38-28	4	61	5	0-0	0
10/01	Jac	L 16-17	5	66	8	0-0	0
10/08	@Min	L 17-23	4	41	7	0-0	0
10/22	@Chi	L 32-35	6	67	7	0-0	1
10/29	TB	W 19-7	2	25	5	0-0	0

Game Logs (9-16)

Date	Opp	Result	Rec	Yds	Trgt	F-L	TD
11/05	@Cle	W 37-10	4	57	5	0-0	1
11/12	Cin	L 25-32	6	62	10	0-0	0
11/19	@KC	L 13-20	5	54	6	0-0	0
11/26	Den	W 42-33	2	17	6	0-0	0
12/03	@Pit	L 7-21	4	32	6	0-0	0
12/10	Det	L 17-24	8	72	8	0-0	1
12/17	NYA	W 23-6	1	35	2	0-0	0
12/24	@Buf	W 28-17	2	32	4	0-0	0

Keith Jennings

Chicago Bears — TE

1995 Receiving Splits

	G	Rec	Yds	Avg	TD	Lg	Big	YAC	Trgt	Y@C	1st	1st%		Rec	Yds	Avg	TD	Lg	Big	YAC	Trgt	Y@C	1st	1st%
Total	16	25	217	8.7	6	20	0	113	39	4.2	14	56.0	Inside 20	7	50	7.1	6	15	0	19	10	4.4	7	100.0
vs. Playoff	6	8	61	7.6	3	14	0	39	12	2.8	4	50.0	Inside 10	4	9	2.3	4	5	0	0	5	2.3	4	100.0
vs. Non-playoff	10	17	156	9.2	3	20	0	74	27	4.8	10	58.8	1st Down	14	127	9.1	2	20	0	75	22	3.7	8	57.1
vs. Own Division	8	8	62	7.8	2	14	0	33	13	3.6	5	62.5	2nd Down	10	89	8.9	3	15	0	38	15	5.1	5	50.0
Home	8	13	98	7.5	5	15	0	56	21	3.2	8	61.5	3rd Down Overall	1	1	1.0	1	1	0	0	2	1.0	1	100.0
Away	8	12	119	9.9	1	20	0	57	18	5.2	6	50.0	3rd D 0-2 to Go	1	1	1.0	1	1	0	0	1	1.0	1	100.0
Games 1-8	8	16	148	9.3	3	20	0	67	24	5.1	10	62.5	3rd D 3-7 to Go	0	0	-	0	0	0	0	1	-	0	-
Games 9-16	8	9	69	7.7	3	14	0	46	15	2.6	4	44.4	3rd D 8+ to Go	0	0	-	0	0	0	0	0	-	0	-
September	4	7	61	8.7	2	15	0	18	10	6.1	4	57.1	4th Down	0	0	-	0	0	0	0	0	-	0	-
October	4	9	87	9.7	1	20	0	49	14	4.2	6	66.7	Rec Behind Line	0	0	-	0	0	0	0	1	-	0	-
November	4	5	42	8.4	1	14	0	28	7	2.8	2	40.0	1-10 yds	24	202	8.4	5	20	0	113	34	3.7	13	54.2
December	4	4	27	6.8	2	13	0	18	8	2.2	2	50.0	11-20 yds	1	15	15.0	1	15	0	0	3	15.0	1	100.0
Grass	11	17	145	8.5	5	20	0	78	27	3.9	11	64.7	21-30 yds	0	0	-	0	0	0	0	1	-	0	-
Turf	5	8	72	9.0	1	15	0	35	12	4.6	3	37.5	31+	0	0	-	0	0	0	0	0	-	0	-
Outdoor	2	22	194	8.8	6	20	0	97	34	4.4	13	59.1	Left Sideline	3	30	10.0	0	14	0	23	6	2.3	1	33.3
Indoor	14	3	23	7.7	0	10	0	16	5	2.3	1	33.3	Left Side	8	59	7.4	2	13	0	34	11	3.1	4	50.0
1st Half	-	13	105	8.1	5	15	0	57	21	3.7	8	61.5	Middle	1	8	8.0	0	8	0	3	5	5.0	0	0.0
2nd Half/OT	-	12	112	9.3	1	20	0	56	18	4.7	6	50.0	Right Side	10	110	11.0	2	20	0	53	14	5.7	7	70.0
Last 2 Min. Half	-	3	25	8.3	1	13	0	14	3	3.7	3	100.0	Right Sideline	3	10	3.3	2	7	0	0	3	3.3	2	66.7
4th qtr, +/-7 pts	-	2	12	6.0	0	7	0	6	4	3.0	0	0.0	Shotgun	0	0	-	0	0	0	0	0	-	0	-
Winning	-	5	40	8.0	1	15	0	22	11	3.6	3	60.0	2 Wide Receivers	18	171	9.5	3	20	0	95	27	4.2	9	50.0
Tied	-	7	58	8.3	3	20	0	32	12	3.7	4	57.1	3 Wide Receivers	2	15	7.5	0	8	0	5	5	5.0	0	0.0
Trailing	-	13	119	9.2	2	15	0	59	16	4.6	7	53.8	4+ Wide Receivers	0	0	-	0	0	0	0	0	-	0	-

1995 Incompletions

Type	Num	%of Inc	%of Att
Pass Dropped	2	14.3	5.1
Poor Throw	9	64.3	23.1
Pass Defensed	2	14.3	5.1
Pass Hit at Line	0	0.0	0.0
Other	1	7.1	2.6
Total	14	100.0	35.9

Game Logs (1-8)

Date	Opp	Result	Rec	Yds	Trgt	F-L	TD
09/03	Min	W 31-14	2	9	4	0-0	1
09/11	GB	L 24-27	0	0	0	0-0	0
09/17	@TB	W 25-6	1	11	2	0-0	0
09/24	@StL	L 28-34	4	41	4	0-0	0
10/08	Car	W 31-27	4	26	5	0-0	0
10/15	@Jac	W 30-27	3	36	4	0-0	1
10/22	Hou	W 35-32	1	15	3	0-0	0
10/30	@Min	W 14-6	1	10	2	0-0	0

Game Logs (9-16)

Date	Opp	Result	Rec	Yds	Trgt	F-L	TD
11/05	Pit	L 34-37	2	15	3	0-0	0
11/12	@GB	L 28-35	0	0	0	0-0	0
11/19	Det	L 17-24	2	19	2	0-0	1
11/26	@NYN	W 27-24	1	8	2	0-0	0
12/04	@Det	L 7-27	2	13	3	0-0	0
12/10	@Cin	L 10-16	0	0	1	0-0	0
12/17	TB	W 31-10	0	0	1	0-0	0
12/24	Phi	W 20-14	2	14	4	0-0	0

Anthony Johnson
Chicago Bears / Carolina Panthers — RB

1995 Receiving Splits

	G	Rec	Yds	Avg	TD	Lg	Big	YAC	Trgt	Y@C	1st	1st%		Rec	Yds	Avg	TD	Lg	Big	YAC	Trgt	Y@C	1st	1st%
Total	15	29	207	7.1	0	37	1	165	34	1.4	10	34.5	Inside 20	2	19	9.5	0	14	0	11	3	4.0	1	50.0
vs. Playoff	5	13	112	8.6	0	37	1	100	16	0.9	6	46.2	Inside 10	0	0	-	0	0	0	0	0	-	0	-
vs. Non-playoff	10	16	95	5.9	0	18	0	65	18	1.9	4	25.0	1st Down	8	43	5.4	0	14	0	43	10	0.0	1	12.5
vs. Own Division	7	15	120	8.0	0	37	1	105	20	1.0	6	40.0	2nd Down	9	83	9.2	0	37	1	79	10	0.4	4	44.4
Home	8	15	122	8.1	0	37	1	103	18	1.3	6	40.0	3rd Down Overall	12	81	6.8	0	18	0	43	13	3.2	5	41.7
Away	7	14	85	6.1	0	18	0	62	16	1.6	4	28.6	3rd D 0-2 to Go	1	15	15.0	0	15	0	16	1	-1.0	1	100.0
Games 1-8	7	13	86	6.6	0	18	0	56	14	2.3	5	38.5	3rd D 3-7 to Go	6	25	4.2	0	7	0	15	6	1.7	3	50.0
Games 9-16	8	16	121	7.6	0	37	1	109	20	0.8	5	31.3	3rd D 8+ to Go	5	41	8.2	0	18	0	12	6	5.8	1	20.0
September	3	8	47	5.9	0	14	0	45	9	0.3	4	50.0	4th Down	0	0	-	0	0	0	0	1	-	0	-
October	4	5	39	7.8	0	18	0	11	5	5.6	1	20.0	Rec Behind Line	10	73	7.3	0	37	1	98	11	-2.5	3	30.0
November	4	1	2	2.0	0	2	0	5	2	-3.0	0	0.0	1-10 yds	18	116	6.4	0	14	0	63	20	2.9	6	33.3
December	4	15	119	7.9	0	37	1	104	18	1.0	5	33.3	11-20 yds	1	18	18.0	0	18	0	4	3	14.0	1	100.0
Grass	11	22	176	8.0	0	37	1	133	26	2.0	9	40.9	21-30 yds	0	0	-	0	0	0	0	0	-	0	-
Turf	4	7	31	4.4	0	14	0	32	8	-0.1	1	14.3	31+	0	0	-	0	0	0	0	0	-	0	-
Indoor	3	3	13	4.3	0	6	0	9	4	1.3	0	0.0	Left Sideline	3	25	8.3	0	15	0	21	3	1.3	1	33.3
Outdoor	12	26	194	7.5	0	37	1	156	30	1.5	10	38.5	Left Side	7	42	6.0	0	14	0	49	8	-1.0	2	28.6
1st Half	-	17	108	6.4	0	18	0	80	17	1.6	5	29.4	Middle	3	29	9.7	0	18	0	6	4	7.7	1	33.3
2nd Half/OT	-	12	99	8.3	0	37	1	85	17	1.2	5	41.7	Right Side	14	91	6.5	0	37	1	73	16	1.3	4	28.6
Last 2 Min. Half	-	4	32	8.0	0	14	0	24	4	2.0	1	25.0	Right Sideline	2	20	10.0	0	14	0	16	3	2.0	2	100.0
4th qtr, +/-7 pts	-	2	5	2.5	0	6	0	6	2	-0.5	1	50.0	Shotgun	0	0	-	0	0	0	0	0	-	0	-
Winning	-	6	33	5.5	0	14	0	23	7	1.7	1	16.7	2 Wide Receivers	10	55	5.5	0	15	0	54	10	0.1	2	20.0
Tied	-	3	15	5.0	0	6	0	5	3	3.3	0	0.0	3 Wide Receivers	15	128	8.5	0	37	1	98	20	2.0	6	40.0
Trailing	-	20	159	8.0	0	37	1	137	24	1.1	9	45.0	4+ Wide Receivers	4	24	6.0	0	8	0	13	4	2.8	2	50.0

1995 Incompletions

Type	Num	%of Inc	%of Att
Pass Dropped	1	20.0	2.9
Poor Throw	2	40.0	5.9
Pass Defensed	1	20.0	2.9
Pass Hit at Line	1	20.0	2.9
Other	0	0.0	0.0
Total	5	100.0	14.7

Game Logs (1-8)

Date	Opp	Result	Rush	Yds	Rec	Yds	Trgt	F-L	TD
09/03	Min	W 31-14	-	-	-	-	-	-	-
09/11	GB	L 24-27	1	2	2	13	2	0-0	0
09/17	@TB	W 25-6	1	2	2	16	3	1-1	0
09/24	@StL	L 28-34	1	1	4	18	4	0-0	0
10/08	Car	W 31-27	0	0	0	0	0	0-0	0
10/15	@Jac	W 30-27	0	0	1	18	1	0-0	0
10/22	Hou	W 35-32	0	0	2	10	2	0-0	0
10/30	@Min	W 14-6	1	7	2	11	2	0-0	0

Game Logs (9-16)

Date	Opp	Result	Rush	Yds	Rec	Yds	Trgt	F-L	TD
11/05	Pit	L 34-37	2	18	0	0	0	1-1	0
11/12	@StL	L 17-28	4	7	0	0	1	0-0	0
11/19	Ari	W 27-7	4	33	0	0	0	0-0	0
11/26	@NO	L 26-34	4	30	1	2	1	0-0	0
12/03	Ind	W 13-10	1	1	3	21	3	0-0	0
12/10	SF	L 10-31	7	22	5	39	7	0-0	0
12/17	Atl	W 21-17	1	4	3	39	4	0-0	0
12/24	@Was	L 17-20	3	13	4	20	4	0-0	0

Charles Johnson
Pittsburgh Steelers — WR

1995 Receiving Splits

	G	Rec	Yds	Avg	TD	Lg	Big	YAC	Trgt	Y@C	1st	1st%		Rec	Yds	Avg	TD	Lg	Big	YAC	Trgt	Y@C	1st	1st%
Total	14	38	432	11.4	0	33	1	61	76	9.8	24	63.2	Inside 20	3	30	10.0	0	11	0	10	4	6.7	2	66.7
vs. Playoff	3	10	83	8.3	0	12	0	9	17	7.4	4	40.0	Inside 10	0	0	-	0	0	0	0	1	-	0	-
vs. Non-playoff	11	28	349	12.5	0	33	1	52	59	10.6	20	71.4	1st Down	13	140	10.8	0	24	0	17	25	9.5	5	38.5
vs. Own Division	8	18	222	12.3	0	33	1	38	45	10.2	12	66.7	2nd Down	12	114	9.5	0	13	0	30	23	7.0	8	66.7
Home	8	24	255	10.6	0	24	0	38	50	9.0	15	62.5	3rd Down Overall	13	178	13.7	0	33	1	14	28	12.6	11	84.6
Away	6	14	177	12.6	0	33	1	23	26	11.0	9	64.3	3rd D 0-2 to Go	0	0	-	0	0	0	0	4	-	0	-
Games 1-8	8	27	267	9.9	0	22	0	34	52	8.6	15	55.6	3rd D 3-7 to Go	5	44	8.8	0	12	0	3	7	8.2	5	100.0
Games 9-16	6	11	165	15.0	0	33	1	27	24	12.5	9	81.8	3rd D 8+ to Go	8	134	16.8	0	33	1	11	17	15.4	6	75.0
September	4	17	163	9.6	0	22	0	18	26	8.5	11	64.7	4th Down	0	0	-	0	0	0	0	0	-	0	-
October	4	10	104	10.4	0	22	0	16	26	8.8	4	40.0	Rec Behind Line	0	0	-	0	0	0	0	0	-	0	-
November	4	10	150	15.0	0	33	1	28	19	12.2	8	80.0	1-10 yds	25	212	8.5	0	15	0	50	36	6.5	11	44.0
December	2	1	15	15.0	0	15	0	-1	5	16.0	1	100.0	11-20 yds	11	163	14.8	0	22	0	3	25	14.5	11	100.0
Grass	4	11	130	11.8	0	22	0	13	21	10.6	6	54.5	21-30 yds	2	57	28.5	0	33	1	8	10	24.5	2	100.0
Turf	10	27	302	11.2	0	33	1	48	55	9.4	18	66.7	31+	0	0	-	0	0	0	0	5	-	0	-
Indoor	1	2	14	7.0	0	9	0	3	4	5.5	2	100.0	Left Sideline	3	40	13.3	0	22	0	2	7	12.7	2	66.7
Outdoor	13	36	418	11.6	0	33	1	58	72	10.0	22	61.1	Left Side	5	50	10.0	0	13	0	16	9	6.8	3	60.0
1st Half	-	20	203	10.2	0	33	1	26	41	8.9	10	50.0	Middle	6	104	17.3	0	33	1	16	6	14.7	6	100.0
2nd Half/OT	-	18	229	12.7	0	22	0	35	35	10.8	14	77.8	Right Side	11	133	12.1	0	24	0	18	22	10.5	8	72.7
Last 2 Min. Half	-	5	50	10.0	0	12	0	3	8	9.4	3	60.0	Right Sideline	13	105	8.1	0	11	0	9	32	7.4	5	38.5
4th qtr, +/-7 pts	-	5	51	10.2	0	13	0	2	10	9.8	6	60.0	Shotgun	17	216	12.7	0	33	1	18	34	11.6	13	76.5
Winning	-	6	53	8.8	0	11	0	5	22	8.0	4	66.7	2 Wide Receivers	16	170	10.6	0	24	0	29	35	8.8	10	62.5
Tied	-	16	159	9.9	0	24	0	22	25	8.6	10	62.5	3 Wide Receivers	7	98	14.0	0	33	1	19	13	11.3	3	42.9
Trailing	-	16	220	13.8	0	33	1	34	29	11.6	10	62.5	4+ Wide Receivers	15	164	10.9	0	22	0	13	28	10.1	11	73.3

1995 Incompletions

Type	Num	%of Inc	%of Att
Pass Dropped	7	18.4	9.2
Poor Throw	23	60.5	30.3
Pass Defensed	4	10.5	5.3
Pass Hit at Line	0	0.0	0.0
Other	4	10.5	5.3
Total	38	100.0	50.0

Game Logs (1-8)

Date	Opp	Result	Rush	Yds	Rec	Yds	Trgt	F-L	TD
09/03	Det	W 23-20	0	0	6	51	10	0-0	0
09/10	@Hou	W 34-17	1	-10	2	14	4	0-0	0
09/18	@Mia	L 10-23	0	0	3	23	4	0-0	0
09/24	Min	L 24-44	0	0	6	75	8	0-0	0
10/01	SD	W 31-16	0	0	1	9	3	0-0	0
10/08	@Jac	L 16-20	0	0	3	40	7	0-0	0
10/19	Cin	L 9-27	0	0	4	34	11	0-0	0
10/29	Jac	W 24-7	0	0	2	21	5	0-0	0

Game Logs (9-16)

Date	Opp	Result	Rush	Yds	Rec	Yds	Trgt	F-L	TD
11/05	@Chi	W 37-34	0	0	4	52	6	0-0	0
11/13	Cle	W 20-3	0	0	4	50	8	0-0	0
11/19	@Cin	W 49-31	0	0	1	33	1	0-0	0
11/26	@Cle	W 20-17	0	0	1	15	4	0-0	0
12/03	Hou	W 21-7	0	0	1	15	5	0-0	0
12/10	@Oak	W 29-10	-	-	-	-	-	-	-
12/16	NE	W 41-27	0	0	0	0	0	0-0	0

Lonnie Johnson
Buffalo Bills — TE

1995 Receiving Splits

	G	Rec	Yds	Avg	TD	Lg	Big	YAC	Trgt	Y@C	1st	1st%		Rec	Yds	Avg	TD	Lg	Big	YAC	Trgt	Y@C	1st	1st%
Total	16	49	504	10.3	1	52	5	259	81	5.0	21	42.9	Inside 20	8	42	5.3	1	8	0	33	9	1.1	3	37.5
vs. Playoff	6	25	289	11.6	0	52	3	154	34	5.4	11	44.0	Inside 10	2	8	4.0	1	6	0	5	2	1.5	1	50.0
vs. Non-playoff	10	24	215	9.0	1	31	2	105	47	4.6	10	41.7	1st Down	21	200	9.5	0	27	1	88	32	5.3	8	38.1
vs. Own Division	8	28	223	8.0	0	27	1	103	39	4.3	10	35.7	2nd Down	15	143	9.5	1	43	2	61	23	5.5	6	40.0
Home	8	30	308	10.3	1	43	2	164	45	4.8	15	50.0	3rd Down Overall	13	161	12.4	0	52	2	110	26	3.9	7	53.8
Away	8	19	196	10.3	0	52	3	95	36	5.3	6	31.6	3rd D 0-2 to Go	0	0	-	0	0	0	0	2	-	0	-
Games 1-8	8	23	171	7.4	1	31	1	95	45	3.3	8	34.8	3rd D 3-7 to Go	9	89	9.9	0	31	1	70	15	2.1	6	66.7
Games 9-16	8	26	333	12.8	0	52	4	164	36	6.5	13	50.0	3rd D 8+ to Go	4	72	18.0	0	52	1	40	9	8.0	1	25.0
September	3	7	38	5.4	0	15	0	30	16	1.1	2	28.6	4th Down	0	0	-	0	0	0	0	0	-	0	-
October	5	16	133	8.3	1	31	1	65	29	4.3	6	37.5	Rec Behind Line	8	36	4.5	0	10	0	62	9	-3.3	3	37.5
November	4	14	188	13.4	0	43	2	97	18	6.5	9	64.3	1-10 yds	35	308	8.8	1	31	3	142	58	4.7	12	34.3
December	4	12	145	12.1	0	52	2	67	18	6.5	4	33.3	11-20 yds	5	108	21.6	0	43	1	29	11	15.8	5	100.0
Grass	5	12	119	9.9	0	52	1	51	28	5.7	3	25.0	21-30 yds	1	52	52.0	0	52	1	26	3	26.0	1	100.0
Turf	11	37	385	10.4	1	43	4	208	53	4.8	18	48.6	31+	0	0	-	0	-50	0	0	0	-	0	-
Outdoor	2	45	444	9.9	1	52	3	214	77	5.1	19	42.2	Left Sideline	4	43	10.8	0	19	0	8	10	8.8	2	50.0
Indoor	14	4	60	15.0	0	27	2	45	4	3.8	2	50.0	Left Side	17	183	10.8	1	43	2	105	22	4.6	8	47.1
1st Half	-	24	178	7.4	0	19	0	70	40	4.5	8	33.3	Middle	8	73	9.1	0	25	1	28	16	5.6	2	25.0
2nd Half/OT	-	25	326	13.0	1	52	5	189	41	5.5	13	52.0	Right Side	15	138	9.2	0	31	1	82	26	3.7	8	53.3
Last 2 Min. Half	-	3	39	13.0	0	19	0	3	5	12.0	2	66.7	Right Sideline	5	67	13.4	0	52	1	36	7	6.2	1	20.0
4th qtr, +/-7 pts	-	5	58	11.6	0	16	0	40	6	3.6	3	60.0	Shotgun	14	191	13.6	0	52	3	99	26	6.6	7	50.0
Winning	-	15	209	13.9	1	43	4	135	20	4.9	10	66.7	2 Wide Receivers	4	28	7.0	0	13	0	20	6	2.0	1	25.0
Tied	-	18	128	7.1	0	18	0	32	29	5.3	4	22.2	3 Wide Receivers	42	458	10.9	0	52	5	239	71	5.2	19	45.2
Trailing	-	16	167	10.4	0	52	1	92	32	4.7	7	43.8	4+ Wide Receivers	1	8	8.0	0	8	0	1	2	7.0	0	0.0

1995 Incompletions

Type	Num	%of Inc	%of Att
Pass Dropped	8	25.0	9.9
Poor Throw	9	28.1	11.1
Pass Defensed	9	28.1	11.1
Pass Hit at Line	1	3.1	1.2
Other	5	15.6	6.2
Total	32	100.0	39.5

Game Logs (1-8)

Date	Opp	Result	Rec	Yds	Trgt	F-L	TD
09/03	@Den	L	7-22	0	0	4	0-0	0
09/10	Car	W	31-9	0	0	4	0-0	0
09/17	Ind	W	20-14	7	38	8	0-0	0
10/02	@Cle	W	22-19	4	24	6	0-0	0
10/08	NYA	W	29-10	0	0	0	0-0	0
10/15	Sea	W	27-21	7	74	12	0-0	1
10/23	@NE	L	14-27	2	9	6	0-0	0
10/29	@Mia	L	6-23	3	26	5	0-0	0

Game Logs (9-16)

Date	Opp	Result	Rec	Yds	Trgt	F-L	TD
11/05	@Ind	W	16-10	2	31	2	0-0	0
11/12	Atl	W	23-17	4	86	5	0-0	0
11/19	@NYA	W	28-26	3	17	4	0-0	0
11/26	NE	L	25-35	5	54	7	0-0	0
12/03	@SF	L	17-27	3	60	7	0-0	0
12/10	@StL	W	45-27	2	29	2	0-0	0
12/17	Mia	W	23-20	6	48	7	0-0	0
12/24	Hou	L	17-28	1	8	2	0-0	0

Daryl Johnston
Dallas Cowboys — RB

1995 Receiving Splits

	G	Rec	Yds	Avg	TD	Lg	Big	YAC	Trgt	Y@C	1st	1st%		Rec	Yds	Avg	TD	Lg	Big	YAC	Trgt	Y@C	1st	1st%
Total	16	30	248	8.3	1	24	0	193	46	1.8	11	36.7	Inside 20	5	33	6.6	1	12	0	23	12	2.0	4	80.0
vs. Playoff	7	12	93	7.8	0	23	0	70	16	1.9	4	33.3	Inside 10	4	21	5.3	1	7	0	16	6	1.3	3	75.0
vs. Non-playoff	9	18	155	8.6	1	24	0	123	30	1.8	7	38.9	1st Down	11	66	6.0	0	14	0	65	18	0.1	1	9.1
vs. Own Division	8	12	89	7.4	0	16	0	71	21	1.5	5	41.7	2nd Down	16	156	9.8	1	24	0	108	20	3.0	7	43.8
Home	8	15	111	7.4	1	23	0	85	19	1.7	5	33.3	3rd Down Overall	3	26	8.7	0	16	0	20	8	2.0	3	100.0
Away	8	15	137	9.1	0	24	0	108	27	1.9	6	40.0	3rd D 0-2 to Go	0	0	-	0	0	0	0	1	-	0	-
Games 1-8	8	14	125	8.9	1	24	0	99	21	1.9	5	35.7	3rd D 3-7 to Go	3	26	8.7	0	16	0	20	7	2.0	3	100.0
Games 9-16	8	16	123	7.7	0	16	0	94	25	1.8	6	37.5	3rd D 8+ to Go	0	0	-	0	0	0	0	0	-	0	-
September	4	8	64	8.0	0	24	0	56	11	1.0	3	37.5	4th Down	0	0	-	0	0	0	0	0	-	0	-
October	4	6	61	10.2	0	23	0	43	10	3.0	2	33.3	Rec Behind Line	8	65	8.1	0	24	0	88	11	-2.9	1	12.5
November	4	8	58	7.3	0	14	0	43	11	1.9	2	25.0	1-10 yds	22	183	8.3	1	23	0	105	35	3.5	10	45.5
December	4	8	65	8.1	0	16	0	51	14	1.8	4	50.0	11-20 yds	0	0	-	0	0	0	0	0	-	0	-
Grass	4	9	84	9.3	0	16	0	55	18	3.2	3	33.3	21-30 yds	0	0	-	0	0	0	0	0	-	0	-
Turf	12	21	164	7.8	1	24	0	138	28	1.2	8	38.1	31+	0	0	-	0	0	0	0	0	-	0	-
Indoor	2	4	43	10.8	0	24	0	47	6	-1.0	2	25.0	Left Sideline	5	40	8.0	0	12	0	33	7	1.4	1	20.0
Outdoor	14	26	205	7.9	1	23	0	146	40	2.3	10	38.5	Left Side	6	59	9.8	0	24	0	64	9	-0.8	1	16.7
1st Half	-	15	114	7.6	1	19	0	89	25	1.7	4	26.7	Middle	8	89	11.1	0	23	0	48	11	5.1	5	62.5
2nd Half/OT	-	15	134	8.9	0	24	0	104	21	2.0	7	46.7	Right Side	5	19	3.8	0	7	0	18	5	0.2	2	40.0
Last 2 Min. Half	-	5	56	11.2	0	23	0	43	10	2.6	2	40.0	Right Sideline	6	41	6.8	1	16	0	30	10	1.8	2	33.3
4th qtr, +/-7 pts	-	4	44	11.0	0	24	0	41	4	0.8	3	75.0	Shotgun	0	0	-	0	0	0	0	0	-	0	-
Winning	-	19	157	8.3	0	23	0	110	28	2.5	7	36.8	2 Wide Receivers	19	144	7.6	0	24	0	130	33	0.7	6	31.6
Tied	-	3	17	5.7	1	7	0	10	7	2.3	1	33.3	3 Wide Receivers	9	89	9.9	0	23	0	48	11	4.6	4	44.4
Trailing	-	8	74	9.3	0	24	0	73	11	0.1	3	37.5	4+ Wide Receivers	0	0	-	0	0	0	0	0	-	0	-

1995 Incompletions

Type	Num	%of Inc	%of Att
Pass Dropped	2	12.5	4.3
Poor Throw	8	50.0	17.4
Pass Defensed	1	6.3	2.2
Pass Hit at Line	2	12.5	4.3
Other	3	18.8	6.5
Total	16	100.0	34.8

Game Logs (1-8)

Date	Opp	Result	Rush	Yds	Rec	Yds	Trgt	F-L	TD
09/04	@NYN	W	35-0	1	4	1	7	2	0-0	0
09/10	Den	W	31-21	3	22	1	5	1	1-0	1
09/17	@Min	W	23-17	1	4	4	43	6	0-0	0
09/24	Ari	W	34-20	1	4	2	9	2	0-0	0
10/01	@Was	L	23-27	1	0	0	0	2	0-0	0
10/08	GB	W	34-24	2	20	3	43	3	0-0	0
10/15	@SD	W	23-9	4	16	3	18	5	0-0	1
10/29	@Atl	W	28-13	4	23	0	0	0	0-0	1

Game Logs (9-16)

Date	Opp	Result	Rush	Yds	Rec	Yds	Trgt	F-L	TD
11/06	Phi	W	34-12	0	0	1	8	1	0-0	0
11/12	SF	L	20-38	0	0	2	17	2	0-0	0
11/19	@Oak	W	34-21	1	3	3	29	4	0-0	0
11/23	KC	W	24-12	5	11	2	4	4	0-0	0
12/03	Was	L	17-24	1	4	2	7	2	0-0	0
12/10	@Phi	L	17-20	0	0	1	3	1	0-0	0
12/17	NYN	W	21-20	0	0	2	18	4	0-0	0
12/25	@Ari	W	37-13	0	0	3	37	7	0-0	0

Brent Jones

San Francisco 49ers — TE

1995 Receiving Splits

	G	Rec	Yds	Avg	TD	Lg	Big	YAC	Trgt	Y@C	1st	1st%		Rec	Yds	Avg	TD	Lg	Big	YAC	Trgt	Y@C	1st	1st%
Total	16	60	595	9.9	3	39	2	294	101	5.0	38	63.3	Inside 20	8	58	7.3	2	15	0	24	15	4.3	6	75.0
vs. Playoff	7	24	225	9.4	3	23	0	94	46	5.5	14	58.3	Inside 10	3	10	3.3	2	6	0	8	3.3	2	66.7
vs. Non-playoff	9	36	370	10.3	0	39	2	200	55	4.7	24	66.7	1st Down	23	194	8.4	2	39	1	114	36	3.5	9	39.1
vs. Own Division	8	27	291	10.8	1	39	1	171	40	4.4	19	70.4	2nd Down	26	276	10.6	1	23	0	123	42	5.9	19	73.1
Home	8	31	323	10.4	1	39	2	160	52	5.3	18	58.1	3rd Down Overall	10	118	11.8	0	28	1	53	21	6.5	9	90.0
Away	8	29	272	9.4	2	23	0	134	49	4.8	20	69.0	3rd D 0-2 to Go	4	21	5.3	0	10	0	13	4	2.0	4	100.0
Games 1-8	8	25	250	10.0	1	23	0	110	49	5.6	18	72.0	3rd D 3-7 to Go	3	53	17.7	0	21	0	20	8	11.0	3	100.0
Games 9-16	8	35	345	9.9	2	39	2	184	52	4.6	20	57.1	3rd D 8+ to Go	3	44	14.7	0	28	1	20	9	8.0	2	66.7
September	4	13	161	12.4	1	23	0	68	28	7.2	10	76.9	4th Down	1	7	7.0	0	7	0	4	2	3.0	1	100.0
October	4	12	89	7.4	0	13	0	42	21	3.9	8	66.7	Rec Behind Line	9	46	5.1	0	13	0	52	11	-0.7	3	33.3
November	4	16	169	10.6	2	39	1	81	24	5.5	9	56.3	1-10 yds	42	372	8.9	2	39	1	192	62	4.3	26	61.9
December	4	19	176	9.3	0	28	1	103	28	3.8	11	57.9	11-20 yds	8	154	19.3	0	28	1	48	25	13.3	8	100.0
Grass	10	42	416	9.9	3	39	2	206	65	5.0	26	61.9	21-30 yds	1	23	23.0	1	23	0	2	2	21.0	1	100.0
Turf	6	18	179	9.9	0	21	0	88	36	5.1	12	66.7	31+	0	0	-	0	0	0	0	1	-	0	-
Outdoor	4	47	453	9.6	3	39	2	222	71	4.9	28	59.6	Left Sideline	11	49	4.5	1	13	0	33	16	1.5	4	36.4
Indoor	12	13	142	10.9	0	21	0	72	30	5.4	10	76.9	Left Side	20	183	9.2	2	23	0	75	27	5.4	13	65.0
1st Half	-	31	312	10.1	2	28	1	141	54	5.5	16	51.6	Middle	12	161	13.4	0	28	1	63	31	8.2	10	83.3
2nd Half/OT	-	29	283	9.8	1	39	1	153	47	4.5	22	75.9	Right Side	12	122	10.2	0	21	0	57	16	5.4	7	58.3
Last 2 Min. Half	-	10	97	9.7	1	23	0	39	19	5.8	5	50.0	Right Sideline	5	80	16.0	0	39	1	66	11	2.8	4	80.0
4th qtr, +/-7 pts	-	7	88	12.6	0	39	1	57	14	4.4	7	100.0	Shotgun	0	0	-	0	0	0	0	0	-	0	-
Winning	-	33	301	9.1	3	23	0	157	56	4.4	23	69.7	2 Wide Receivers	35	366	10.5	0	39	2	194	57	4.9	21	60.0
Tied	-	10	107	10.7	0	28	1	45	16	6.2	4	40.0	3 Wide Receivers	17	170	10.0	1	23	0	72	32	5.8	10	58.8
Trailing	-	17	187	11.0	0	39	1	92	29	5.6	11	64.7	4+ Wide Receivers	5	52	10.4	0	16	0	28	8	6.0	4	80.0

1995 Incompletions

Type	Num	%of Inc	%of Att
Pass Dropped	2	4.9	2.0
Poor Throw	18	43.9	17.8
Pass Defensed	8	19.5	7.9
Pass Hit at Line	1	2.4	1.0
Other	12	29.3	11.9
Total	41	100.0	40.6

Game Logs (1-8)

Date	Opp	Result		Rec	Yds	Trgt	F-L	TD
09/03	@NO	W	24-22	4	66	8	0-0	0
09/10	Atl	W	41-10	2	25	4	0-0	1
09/17	NE	W	28-3	6	67	9	0-0	2
09/25	@Det	L	24-27	1	3	7	0-0	0
10/01	NYN	W	20-6	4	27	6	0-0	0
10/15	@Ind	L	17-18	5	44	11	0-0	0
10/22	@StL	W	44-10	1	12	1	0-0	0
10/29	NO	L	7-11	2	6	3	0-0	0

Game Logs (9-16)

Date	Opp	Result		Rec	Yds	Trgt	F-L	TD
11/05	Car	L	7-13	4	64	6	1-1	0
11/12	@Dal	W	38-20	4	25	5	1-0	0
11/20	@Mia	W	44-20	4	42	6	0-0	0
11/26	StL	W	41-13	4	38	7	0-0	0
12/03	Buf	W	27-17	5	57	9	0-0	0
12/10	Car	W	31-10	7	51	7	1-0	0
12/18	Min	W	37-30	4	39	8	0-0	0
12/24	@Atl	L	27-28	3	29	4	0-0	0

Andrew Jordan

Minnesota Vikings — TE

1995 Receiving Splits

	G	Rec	Yds	Avg	TD	Lg	Big	YAC	Trgt	Y@C	1st	1st%		Rec	Yds	Avg	TD	Lg	Big	YAC	Trgt	Y@C	1st	1st%
Total	13	27	185	6.9	2	17	0	86	33	3.7	10	37.0	Inside 20	5	31	6.2	2	11	0	16	7	3.0	3	60.0
vs. Playoff	6	15	111	7.4	1	17	0	48	17	4.2	7	46.7	Inside 10	2	7	3.5	1	4	0	0	4	3.5	1	50.0
vs. Non-playoff	7	12	74	6.2	1	12	0	38	16	3.0	3	25.0	1st Down	16	113	7.1	0	14	0	54	17	3.7	4	25.0
vs. Own Division	8	17	119	7.0	2	17	0	48	20	4.2	8	47.1	2nd Down	10	65	6.5	2	17	0	29	13	3.6	5	50.0
Home	7	15	99	6.6	1	12	0	53	17	3.1	4	46.7	3rd Down Overall	1	7	7.0	0	7	0	3	3	4.0	1	100.0
Away	6	12	86	7.2	1	17	0	33	16	4.4	3	25.0	3rd D 0-2 to Go	0	0	-	0	0	0	0	1	-	0	-
Games 1-8	8	20	144	7.2	1	17	0	65	24	4.0	7	35.0	3rd D 3-7 to Go	1	7	7.0	0	7	0	3	2	4.0	1	100.0
Games 9-16	5	7	41	5.9	1	12	0	21	9	2.9	3	42.9	3rd D 8+ to Go	0	0	-	0	0	0	0	0	-	0	-
September	4	11	79	7.2	1	12	0	46	13	3.0	5	45.5	4th Down	0	0	-	0	0	0	0	0	-	0	-
October	4	9	65	7.2	0	17	0	19	11	5.1	2	22.2	Rec Behind Line	1	0	0.0	0	0	0	2	1	-2.0	0	0.0
November	4	4	27	6.8	1	12	0	14	6	3.3	2	50.0	1-10 yds	24	154	6.4	2	12	0	80	29	3.1	8	33.3
December	1	3	14	4.7	0	7	0	7	3	2.3	1	33.3	11-20 yds	2	31	15.5	0	17	0	4	3	13.5	2	100.0
Grass	4	9	68	7.6	1	17	0	26	12	4.7	3	33.3	21-30 yds	0	0	-	0	-50	0	0	0	-	0	-
Turf	9	18	117	6.5	1	12	0	60	21	3.2	7	38.9	31+	0	0	-	0	0	0	0	0	-	0	-
Outdoor	8	11	79	7.2	1	17	0	30	15	4.5	4	27.3	Left Sideline	5	36	7.2	1	10	0	23	6	2.6	2	40.0
Indoor	5	16	106	6.6	1	12	0	56	18	3.1	7	43.8	Left Side	4	30	7.5	0	10	0	7	4	5.8	2	50.0
1st Half	-	20	152	7.6	2	17	0	72	25	4.0	10	50.0	Middle	4	33	8.3	0	17	0	6	4	6.8	1	25.0
2nd Half/OT	-	7	33	4.7	0	14	0	14	8	2.7	0	0.0	Right Side	6	33	5.5	1	10	0	20	10	2.2	3	33.3
Last 2 Min. Half	-	4	23	5.8	0	12	0	7	5	4.0	1	25.0	Right Sideline	8	53	6.6	0	12	0	30	9	2.9	3	37.5
4th qtr, +/-7 pts	-	2	9	4.5	0	5	0	2	2	3.5	0	0.0	Shotgun	0	0	-	0	0	0	0	0	-	0	-
Winning	-	7	43	6.1	0	12	0	21	10	3.1	2	28.6	2 Wide Receivers	12	92	7.7	1	17	0	46	14	3.8	5	41.7
Tied	-	11	69	6.3	1	12	0	41	13	2.5	4	36.4	3 Wide Receivers	12	81	6.8	0	12	0	39	15	3.5	4	33.3
Trailing	-	9	73	8.1	1	17	0	24	10	5.4	4	44.4	4+ Wide Receivers	1	5	5.0	0	5	0	1	1	4.0	0	0.0

1995 Incompletions

Type	Num	%of Inc	%of Att
Pass Dropped	1	16.7	3.0
Poor Throw	3	50.0	9.1
Pass Defensed	2	33.3	6.1
Pass Hit at Line	0	0.0	0.0
Other	0	0.0	0.0
Total	6	100.0	18.2

Game Logs (1-8)

Date	Opp	Result		Rec	Yds	Trgt	F-L	TD
09/03	@Chi	L	14-31	2	16	3	0-0	1
09/10	Det	W	20-10	3	24	3	0-0	0
09/17	Dal	L	17-23	4	28	4	0-0	0
09/24	@Pit	W	44-24	2	11	3	0-0	0
10/08	Hou	W	23-17	2	10	2	1-1	0
10/15	@TB	L	17-20	2	9	3	0-0	0
10/22	@GB	L	21-38	4	38	5	0-0	0
10/30	Chi	L	6-14	1	8	1	0-0	0

Game Logs (9-16)

Date	Opp	Result		Rec	Yds	Trgt	F-L	TD
11/05	GB	W	27-24	1	3	1	0-0	0
11/12	@Ari	W	30-24	1	5	1	0-0	0
11/19	NO	W	43-24	1	12	3	0-0	0
11/23	@Det	L	38-44	1	7	1	0-0	0
12/03	TB	W	31-17	3	14	3	0-0	0
12/09	Cle	W	27-11					
12/18	@SF	L	30-37					
12/24	@Cin	L	24-27					

Napoleon Kaufman
Oakland Raiders — RB

1995 Rushing and Receiving Splits

	G	Rush	Yds	Avg	Lg	TD	1st	Stf	YdL	Rec	Yds	Avg	TD		Rush	Yds	Avg	Lg	TD	1st	Stf	YdL	Rec	Yds	Avg	TD
Total	16	108	490	4.5	28	1	28	10	24	9	62	6.9	0	Inside 20	8	31	3.9	16	1	1	1	1	0	0	-	0
vs. Playoff	8	49	200	4.1	16	1	15	6	14	7	53	7.6	0	Inside 10	3	4	1.3	4	0	0	1	1	0	0	-	0
vs. Non-playoff	8	59	290	4.9	28	0	13	4	10	2	9	4.5	0	1st Down	60	265	4.4	28	1	10	6	13	6	36	6.0	0
vs. Own Division	8	47	164	3.5	16	1	12	6	19	5	51	10.2	0	2nd Down	38	183	4.8	22	0	12	4	11	1	12	12.0	0
Home	8	42	152	3.6	16	1	9	5	11	4	23	5.8	0	3rd Down Overall	9	42	4.7	16	0	6	0	0	2	14	7.0	0
Away	8	66	338	5.1	28	0	19	5	13	5	39	7.8	0	3rd D 0-2 to Go	7	21	3.0	8	0	4	0	0	0	0	-	0
Games 1-8	8	65	301	4.6	28	1	17	5	9	6	38	6.3	0	3rd D 3-7 to Go	2	21	10.5	16	0	2	0	0	1	5	5.0	0
Games 9-16	8	43	189	4.4	22	0	11	5	15	3	24	8.0	0	3rd D 8+ to Go	0	0	-	0	0	0	0	0	1	9	9.0	0
September	4	35	162	4.6	19	1	11	3	4	4	38	9.5	0	4th Down	1	0	0.0	0	0	0	0	0	0	0	-	0
October	4	30	139	4.6	28	0	6	2	5	2	0	0.0	0	Left Sideline	6	35	5.8	14	0	3	1	7	1	7	7.0	0
November	4	26	149	5.7	22	0	8	3	10	2	21	10.5	0	Left Side	35	191	5.5	28	1	10	3	4	3	33	11.0	0
December	4	17	40	2.4	8	0	3	2	5	1	3	3.0	0	Middle	42	99	2.4	11	0	5	4	8	1	-7	-7.0	0
Grass	12	68	270	4.0	19	1	17	9	22	8	59	7.4	0	Right Side	17	101	5.9	15	0	7	0	0	1	3	3.0	0
Turf	4	40	220	5.5	28	0	11	1	2	1	3	3.0	0	Right Sideline	8	64	8.0	22	0	3	2	5	3	26	8.7	0
Indoor	1	14	45	3.2	8	0	3	0	0	1	3	3.0	0	Shotgun	0	0	-	0	0	0	0	0	0	0	-	0
Outdoor	15	94	445	4.7	28	1	25	10	24	8	59	7.4	0	2 Wide Receivers	68	289	4.3	24	1	20	7	20	2	19	9.5	0
1st Half	-	49	209	4.3	16	0	13	3	4	6	56	9.3	0	3 Wide Receivers	20	91	4.6	12	0	3	1	1	6	38	6.3	0
2nd Half/OT	-	59	281	4.8	28	1	15	7	20	3	6	2.0	0	4+ Wide Receivers	2	11	5.5	7	0	0	0	0	1	5	5.0	0
Last 2 Min. Half	-	7	34	4.9	10	0	3	0	0	2	21	10.5	0	Carries 1-5	67	301	4.5	24	1	18	7	19	0	0	-	0
4th qtr, +/-7 pts	-	6	27	4.5	19	0	2	3	10	1	6	6.0	0	Carries 6-10	31	129	4.2	19	0	7	3	5	0	0	-	0
Winning	-	50	257	5.1	28	1	13	6	13	4	15	3.8	0	Carries 11-15	10	60	6.0	28	0	3	0	0	0	0	-	0
Tied	-	14	52	3.7	12	0	4	1	1	2	30	15.0	0	Carries 16-20	0	0	-	0	0	0	0	0	0	0	-	0
Trailing	-	44	181	4.1	22	0	11	3	10	3	17	5.7	0	Carries 21+	0	0	-	0	0	0	0	0	0	0	-	0

1995 Incompletions

Type	Num	%of Inc	% Att
Pass Dropped	3	42.9	18.8
Poor Throw	3	42.9	18.8
Pass Defensed	0	0.0	0.0
Pass Hit at Line	0	0.0	0.0
Other	1	14.3	6.3
Total	7	100.0	43.8

Game Logs (1-8)

Date	Opp	Result	Rush	Yds	Rec	Yds	Trgt	F-L	TD
09/03	SD	W 17-7	5	32	1	18	2	0-0	1
09/10	@Was	W 20-8	7	44	1	6	1	0-0	0
09/17	@KC	L 17-23	10	44	1	9	1	0-0	0
09/24	Phi	W 48-17	13	42	1	5	3	0-0	0
10/01	@NYA	W 47-10	13	95	0	0	1	0-0	0
10/08	Sea	W 34-14	6	18	0	0	0	0-0	0
10/16	@Den	L 0-27	4	11	0	0	1	0-0	0
10/22	Ind	W 30-17	7	15	2	0	3	0-1	0

Game Logs (9-16)

Date	Opp	Result	Rush	Yds	Rec	Yds	Trgt	F-L	TD
11/05	@Cin	W 20-17	6	38	0	0	0	0-0	0
11/12	@NYN	W 17-13	7	42	0	0	0	0-0	0
11/19	Dal	L 21-34	8	50	0	0	0	0-0	0
11/27	@SD	L 6-12	5	19	2	21	3	0-0	0
12/03	KC	L 23-29	1	-2	0	0	0	0-0	0
12/10	Pit	L 10-29	0	0	0	0	0	0-0	0
12/17	@Sea	L 10-44	14	45	1	3	1	0-0	0
12/24	Den	L 28-31	2	-3	0	0	0	0-0	0

Jim Kelly
Buffalo Bills — QB

1995 Passing Splits

	G	Att	Cm	Pct	Yds	Yd/Att	TD	Int	1st	YAC	Big	Sk	Rtg		Att	Cm	Pct	Yds	Yd/Att	TD	Int	1st	YAC	Big	Sk	Rtg
Total	15	458	255	55.7	3130	6.8	22	13	129	1282	28	26	81.1	Inside 20	48	18	37.5	153	3.2	9	1	12	56	0	3	77.5
vs. Playoff	6	196	107	54.6	1223	6.2	6	5	53	478	10	10	73.2	Inside 10	16	4	25.0	15	0.9	3	0	3	5	0	1	79.2
vs. Non-playoff	9	262	148	56.5	1907	7.3	16	8	76	804	18	16	87.1	1st Down	178	111	62.4	1282	7.2	7	4	47	559	10	6	87.8
vs. Own Division	8	237	132	55.7	1546	6.5	7	4	59	673	12	15	78.5	2nd Down	146	83	56.8	1002	6.9	7	3	46	352	9	5	85.5
Home	7	206	105	51.0	1345	6.5	9	8	59	514	13	9	70.1	3rd Down Overall	129	56	43.4	801	6.2	6	8	33	368	9	14	65.4
Away	8	252	150	59.5	1785	7.1	13	5	70	768	15	17	90.1	3rd D 0-5 to Go	36	11	30.6	98	2.7	0	3	8	46	0	2	5.3
Games 1-8	8	239	129	54.0	1521	6.4	9	5	60	708	13	17	77.4	3rd D 6+ to Go	93	45	48.4	703	7.6	8	3	25	322	9	12	89.1
Games 9-16	7	219	126	57.5	1609	7.3	13	8	69	574	15	13	85.2	4th Down	5	5	100.0	45	9.0	0	0	3	0	0	1	104.2
September	3	84	35	41.7	531	6.3	2	3	18	297	6	3	56.2	Rec Behind Line	65	35	53.8	265	4.1	0	1	9	391	2	1	57.5
October	5	155	94	60.6	990	6.4	7	2	42	411	7	10	88.9	1-10 yds	257	155	60.3	1341	5.2	4	5	59	552	5	0	71.2
November	4	125	73	58.4	1019	8.2	6	3	41	408	10	8	90.7	11-20 yds	98	49	50.0	930	9.5	9	4	45	207	7	0	96.9
December	3	94	53	56.4	590	6.3	7	5	28	166	5	5	77.9	21-30 yds	26	13	50.0	454	17.5	7	2	13	114	11	0	103.4
Grass	5	166	94	56.6	982	5.9	6	4	39	428	6	12	75.9	31+	12	3	25.0	140	11.7	2	1	3	18	3	0	80.6
Turf	10	292	161	55.1	2148	7.4	16	9	90	854	22	14	84.1	Left Sideline	97	56	57.7	679	7.0	5	1	31	199	6	0	92.2
Indoor	2	49	34	69.4	487	9.9	5	1	20	170	5	2	126.8	Left Side	80	47	58.8	504	6.3	1	4	20	225	4	0	60.6
Outdoor	13	409	221	54.0	2643	6.5	17	12	109	1112	23	24	75.7	Middle	86	43	50.0	622	7.2	7	3	25	226	5	19	86.5
1st Half	-	232	131	56.5	1480	6.4	14	8	61	528	12	15	81.5	Right Side	106	62	58.5	793	7.5	3	2	33	504	7	2	83.6
2nd Half/OT	-	226	124	54.9	1650	7.3	8	5	68	754	16	11	80.8	Right Sideline	89	47	52.8	532	6.0	6	3	20	128	6	2	79.4
Last 2 Min. Half	-	29	18	62.1	255	8.8	4	0	12	85	2	5	130.0	2 Wide Receivers	49	26	53.1	293	6.0	3	1	13	137	4	3	83.1
4th qtr, +/-7 pts	-	46	24	52.2	259	5.6	1	1	12	88	1	1	67.2	3+ WR	402	226	56.2	2827	7.0	17	11	113	1144	24	22	80.9
Winning	-	161	86	53.4	1175	7.3	6	5	50	466	13	7	76.5	Attempts 1-10	150	85	56.7	872	5.8	6	6	32	334	6	0	70.2
Tied	-	119	67	56.3	663	5.6	5	4	28	254	3	6	72.2	Attempts 11-20	150	85	56.7	1206	8.0	5	5	41	545	14	0	86.7
Trailing	-	178	102	57.3	1292	7.3	11	4	51	562	12	13	91.3	Attempts 21+	158	85	53.8	1052	6.7	8	2	46	403	8	0	86.3

1995 Incompletions

Type	Num	% of Inc	% of Att
Pass Dropped	26	12.8	5.7
Poor Throw	85	41.9	18.6
Pass Defensed	43	21.2	9.4
Pass Hit at Line	15	7.4	3.3
Other	34	16.7	7.4
Total	203	100.0	44.3

Game Logs (1-8)

Date	Opp	Result	Att	Cm	Pct	Yds	TD	Int	Lg	Sk	F-L
09/03	@Den	L 7-22	28	12	42.9	154	1	0	34	2	0-0
09/10	Car	W 31-9	21	4	19.0	176	1	3	77	2	0-0
09/17	Ind	W 20-14	35	19	54.3	201	0	0	37	1	0-0
10/02	@Cle	W 22-19	34	27	79.4	256	2	1	41	1	1-1
10/08	NYA	W 29-10	22	9	40.9	101	1	1	18	1	0-0
10/15	Sea	W 27-21	36	21	58.3	275	3	0	31	2	1-0
10/23	@NE	L 14-27	31	20	64.5	211	1	0	45	4	0-0
10/29	@Mia	L 6-23	32	17	53.1	147	0	0	17	2	0-0

Game Logs (9-16)

Date	Opp	Result	Att	Cm	Pct	Yds	TD	Int	Lg	Sk	F-L
11/05	@Ind	W 16-10	24	15	62.5	250	1	0	65	1	0-0
11/12	Atl	W 23-17	36	22	61.1	272	1	1	43	2	2-1
11/19	@NYA	W 28-26	37	22	59.5	316	2	0	47	3	0-0
11/26	NE	L 25-35	28	14	50.0	181	1	2	32	2	1-1
12/03	@SF	L 17-27	41	18	43.9	214	2	3	52	3	2-1
12/10	@StL	W 45-27	25	19	76.0	237	4	1	28	1	0-0
12/17	Mia	W 23-20	28	16	57.1	139	1	1	25	1	0-0
12/24	Hou	L 17-28	-	-	-	-	-	-	-	-	-

Todd Kinchen

1995 Receiving Splits

	G	Rec	Yds	Avg	TD	Lg	Big	YAC	Trgt	Y@C	1st	1st%
Total	16	36	419	11.6	4	35	4	156	55	7.3	24	66.7
vs. Playoff	9	24	265	11.0	3	35	2	102	39	6.8	15	62.5
vs. Non-playoff	7	12	154	12.8	1	31	2	54	16	8.3	9	75.0
vs. Own Division	8	15	198	13.2	1	31	3	61	25	9.1	10	66.7
Home	8	17	188	11.1	3	31	1	70	27	6.9	10	58.8
Away	8	19	231	12.2	1	35	3	86	28	7.6	14	73.7
Games 1-8	8	15	179	11.9	1	35	2	88	21	6.1	9	60.0
Games 9-16	8	21	240	11.4	3	31	2	68	34	8.2	15	71.4
September	4	7	80	11.4	1	28	1	30	9	7.1	5	71.4
October	4	8	99	12.4	0	35	1	58	12	5.1	4	50.0
November	4	11	140	12.7	1	31	2	40	18	9.1	8	72.7
December	4	10	100	10.0	2	14	0	28	16	7.2	7	70.0
Grass	3	7	88	12.6	1	31	2	19	9	9.9	5	71.4
Turf	13	29	331	11.4	3	35	2	137	46	6.7	19	65.5
Indoor	7	18	203	11.3	2	31	1	67	32	7.6	12	66.7
Outdoor	9	18	216	12.0	2	35	3	89	23	7.1	12	66.7
1st Half	-	17	158	9.3	4	28	1	53	24	6.2	12	70.6
2nd Half/OT	-	19	261	13.7	0	35	3	103	31	8.3	12	63.2
Last 2 Min. Half	-	9	134	14.9	1	35	2	54	10	8.9	7	77.8
4th qtr, +/-7 pts	-	2	13	6.5	0	9	0	9	2	2.0	0	0.0
Winning	-	10	138	13.8	1	31	2	53	15	8.5	6	60.0
Tied	-	7	47	6.7	1	15	0	12	8	5.0	5	71.4
Trailing	-	19	234	12.3	2	35	2	91	32	7.5	13	68.4

	Rec	Yds	Avg	TD	Lg	Big	YAC	Trgt	Y@C	1st	1st%
Inside 20	5	28	5.6	4	7	0	1	8	5.4	5	100.0
Inside 10	4	21	5.3	4	7	0	0	6	5.3	4	100.0
1st Down	11	144	13.1	1	28	1	56	17	8.0	7	63.6
2nd Down	8	73	9.1	0	14	0	25	10	6.0	4	50.0
3rd Down Overall	16	167	10.4	3	31	2	56	26	6.9	12	75.0
3rd D 0-2 to Go	2	7	3.5	1	5	0	0	2	3.5	2	100.0
3rd D 3-7 to Go	10	121	12.1	2	31	2	27	16	9.4	8	80.0
3rd D 8+ to Go	4	39	9.8	0	14	0	29	8	2.5	2	50.0
4th Down	1	35	35.0	0	35	1	19	2	16.0	1	100.0
Rec Behind Line	3	10	3.3	0	9	0	18	5	-2.7	0	0.0
1-10 yds	26	234	9.0	4	14	0	89	36	5.6	18	69.2
11-20 yds	4	85	21.3	0	35	1	29	8	14.0	3	75.0
21-30 yds	3	90	30.0	0	31	3	20	6	23.3	3	100.0
31+	0	0	-	0	0	0	0	0	-	0	-
Left Sideline	7	104	14.9	0	31	2	34	7	10.0	4	57.1
Left Side	4	25	6.3	1	10	0	8	7	4.3	3	75.0
Middle	9	77	8.6	2	14	0	36	15	4.6	7	77.8
Right Side	9	117	13.0	1	35	1	53	14	7.1	5	55.6
Right Sideline	7	96	13.7	0	28	1	25	12	10.1	5	71.4
Shotgun	0	0	-	0	0	0	0	0	-	0	-
2 Wide Receivers	10	94	9.4	1	24	0	30	12	6.4	4	40.0
3 Wide Receivers	23	300	13.0	3	35	4	120	37	7.8	17	73.9
4+ Wide Receivers	3	25	8.3	0	13	0	6	6	6.3	3	100.0

1995 Incompletions

Type	Num	%of Inc	%of Att
Pass Dropped	5	26.3	9.1
Poor Throw	7	36.8	12.7
Pass Defensed	4	21.1	7.3
Pass Hit at Line	2	10.5	3.6
Other	1	5.3	1.8
Total	19	100.0	34.5

Game Logs (1-8)

Date	Opp	Result	Rush	Yds	Rec	Yds	Trgt	F-L	TD
09/03	@GB	W 17-14	1	5	2	11	2	0-0	0
09/10	NO	W 17-13	0	0	1	12	2	0-0	0
09/17	@Car	W 31-10	0	0	1	28	2	0-0	0
09/24	Chi	W 34-28	0	0	3	29	3	1-0	1
10/01	@Ind	L 18-21	0	0	3	31	5	0-0	0
10/12	Atl	W 21-19	0	0	2	18	3	0-0	0
10/22	SF	L 10-44	0	0	0	0	2	2-0	0
10/29	@Phi	L 9-20	1	15	3	50	4	0-0	0

Game Logs (9-16)

Date	Opp	Result	Rush	Yds	Rec	Yds	Trgt	F-L	TD
11/05	@NO	L 10-19	1	-5	0	0	0	1-1	0
11/12	Car	W 28-17	0	0	3	48	5	0-0	0
11/19	@Atl	L 6-31	1	1	4	43	8	0-0	0
11/26	@SF	L 13-41	0	0	4	49	5	0-0	1
12/03	@NYA	W 23-20	0	0	2	19	2	1-0	0
12/10	Buf	L 27-45	0	0	3	32	7	0-0	1
12/17	Was	L 23-35	0	0	2	18	2	1-1	0
12/24	Mia	L 22-41	0	0	3	31	5	2-2	1

Terry Kirby

1995 Receiving Splits

	G	Rec	Yds	Avg	TD	Lg	Big	YAC	Trgt	Y@C	1st	1st%
Total	16	66	618	9.4	3	46	5	522	83	1.5	30	45.5
vs. Playoff	9	37	347	9.4	2	31	3	273	44	2.0	17	45.9
vs. Non-playoff	7	29	271	9.3	1	46	2	249	39	0.8	13	44.8
vs. Own Division	8	30	315	10.5	0	32	3	285	37	1.0	15	50.0
Home	8	37	292	7.9	1	32	3	231	47	1.6	15	27.0
Away	8	29	326	11.2	2	46	2	291	36	1.2	20	69.0
Games 1-8	8	32	355	11.1	2	46	4	286	40	2.2	17	53.1
Games 9-16	8	34	263	7.7	1	28	1	236	43	0.8	13	38.2
September	3	10	101	10.1	1	32	2	89	11	1.2	2	20.0
October	5	22	254	11.5	1	46	2	197	29	2.6	15	68.2
November	4	24	193	8.0	1	28	1	158	32	1.5	10	41.7
December	4	10	70	7.0	0	16	0	78	11	-0.8	3	30.0
Grass	10	43	338	7.9	2	32	3	274	54	1.5	14	32.6
Turf	6	23	280	12.2	1	46	2	248	29	1.4	16	69.5
Indoor	3	9	111	12.3	1	28	1	90	12	2.3	7	77.8
Outdoor	13	57	507	8.9	2	46	4	432	71	1.3	23	40.4
1st Half	-	28	293	10.5	1	46	2	262	35	1.1	13	46.4
2nd Half/OT	-	38	325	8.6	2	31	2	260	48	1.7	17	44.7
Last 2 Min. Half	-	28	289	10.3	1	32	2	233	31	2.0	15	53.6
4th qtr, +/-7 pts	-	7	70	10.0	0	19	0	66	9	0.6	3	42.9
Winning	-	21	142	6.8	2	28	1	120	25	1.0	7	33.3
Tied	-	11	144	13.1	0	32	2	104	15	3.6	7	63.6
Trailing	-	34	332	9.8	1	46	2	298	43	1.0	16	47.1

	Rec	Yds	Avg	TD	Lg	Big	YAC	Trgt	Y@C	1st	1st%
Inside 20	8	52	6.5	2	16	0	32	9	2.5	4	50.0
Inside 10	1	5	5.0	1	5	0	1	1	4.0	1	100.0
1st Down	20	194	9.7	0	46	2	185	26	0.5	6	30.0
2nd Down	22	211	9.6	0	28	1	174	27	1.7	12	54.5
3rd Down Overall	24	213	8.9	3	31	2	163	30	2.1	12	50.0
3rd D 0-2 to Go	1	3	3.0	0	3	0	4	1	-1.0	1	100.0
3rd D 3-7 to Go	10	68	6.8	1	19	0	67	11	0.1	7	70.0
3rd D 8+ to Go	13	142	10.9	2	31	2	92	18	3.8	4	30.8
4th Down	0	0	-	0	0	0	0	0	-	0	-
Rec Behind Line	26	177	6.8	0	32	1	257	27	-3.1	9	34.6
1-10 yds	36	320	8.9	1	28	1	202	47	3.3	17	47.2
11-20 yds	4	121	30.3	2	46	3	60	7	14.5	4	100.0
21-30 yds	0	0	-	0	0	0	0	1	-	0	-
31+	0	0	-	0	0	0	0	0	-	0	-
Left Sideline	10	107	10.7	0	28	1	98	12	0.9	6	60.0
Left Side	14	132	9.4	1	32	1	118	17	1.0	7	50.0
Middle	20	163	8.2	1	31	2	136	27	1.4	8	40.0
Right Side	13	139	10.7	0	46	1	118	14	1.6	6	46.2
Right Sideline	9	77	8.6	1	16	0	52	13	2.8	3	33.3
Shotgun	59	531	9.0	3	32	4	458	72	1.2	26	44.1
2 Wide Receivers	7	87	12.4	0	46	1	64	10	3.3	4	57.1
3 Wide Receivers	11	68	6.2	0	12	0	80	15	-1.1	3	27.3
4+ Wide Receivers	48	463	9.6	3	32	4	378	58	1.8	23	47.9

1995 Incompletions

Type	Num	%of Inc	%of Att
Pass Dropped	4	23.5	4.8
Poor Throw	7	41.2	8.4
Pass Defensed	1	5.9	1.2
Pass Hit at Line	1	5.9	1.2
Other	4	23.5	4.8
Total	17	100.0	20.5

Game Logs (1-8)

Date	Opp	Result	Rush	Yds	Rec	Yds	Trgt	F-L	TD
09/03	NYA	W 52-14	3	5	2	37	3	0-0	0
09/10	@NE	W 20-3	13	82	2	9	2	0-0	0
09/18	Pit	W 23-10	12	33	6	55	6	0-0	0
10/01	@Cin	W 26-23	9	28	7	89	8	0-0	0
10/08	Ind	L 24-27	19	77	2	20	2	0-0	2
10/15	@NO	L 30-33	4	15	3	37	6	1-1	1
10/22	@NYA	L 16-17	2	12	5	51	7	0-0	0
10/29	Buf	W 23-6	12	60	5	55	6	0-0	0

Game Logs (9-16)

Date	Opp	Result	Rush	Yds	Rec	Yds	Trgt	F-L	TD
11/05	@SD	W 24-14	7	21	4	37	5	0-0	1
11/12	NE	L 17-34	6	14	4	43	11	0-0	0
11/20	SF	L 20-44	4	18	4	44	12	0-0	0
12/03	Atl	W 21-20	1	1	4	30	4	0-0	0
12/11	KC	W 13-6	8	21	2	3	3	0-0	0
12/17	@Buf	L 20-23	2	8	2	3	2	1-0	0
12/24	@StL	W 41-22	4	29	2	5	2	0-0	0

Bernie Kosar
Miami Dolphins — QB

1995 Passing Splits

	G	Att	Cm	Pct	Yds	Yd/Att	TD	Int	1st	YAC	Big	Sk	Rtg
Total	9	108	74	68.5	699	6.5	3	5	35	344	1	6	76.1
vs. Playoff	5	12	10	83.3	76	6.3	0	0	4	47	0	2	93.1
vs. Non-playoff	4	96	64	66.7	623	6.5	3	5	31	297	1	4	73.4
vs. Own Division	6	56	37	66.1	266	4.8	0	3	12	162	0	3	54.6
Home	5	23	17	73.9	130	5.7	0	0	7	97	0	2	87.2
Away	4	85	57	67.1	569	6.7	3	5	28	247	1	4	73.1
Games 1-8	5	94	63	67.0	610	6.5	3	5	31	282	1	5	73.4
Games 9-16	4	14	11	78.6	89	6.4	0	0	4	62	0	1	93.2
September	2	9	6	66.7	50	5.6	0	0	3	29	0	1	80.8
October	3	85	57	67.1	560	6.6	3	5	28	253	1	4	72.7
November	3	13	10	76.9	79	6.1	0	0	4	64	0	1	91.5
December	1	1	1	100.0	10	10.0	0	0	0	-2	0	0	108.3
Grass	5	23	17	73.9	130	5.7	0	0	7	97	0	2	87.2
Turf	4	85	57	67.1	569	6.7	3	5	28	247	1	4	73.1
Indoor	2	42	29	69.0	368	8.8	3	2	19	137	1	1	100.1
Outdoor	7	66	45	68.2	331	5.0	0	3	16	207	0	5	60.9
1st Half	-	43	31	72.1	306	7.1	1	1	14	124	1	2	89.9
2nd Half/OT	-	65	43	66.2	393	6.0	2	4	21	220	0	4	67.0
Last 2 Min. Half	-	25	18	72.0	164	6.6	1	1	8	116	0	1	86.1
4th qtr, +/-7 pts	-	14	8	57.1	69	4.9	0	2	4	41	0	1	30.7
Winning	-	24	14	58.3	85	3.5	0	1	4	52	0	2	48.1
Tied	-	11	9	81.8	83	7.5	0	0	4	32	0	1	98.1
Trailing	-	73	51	69.9	531	7.3	3	4	27	260	1	3	81.5

	Att	Cm	Pct	Yds	Yd/Att	TD	Int	1st	YAC	Big	Sk	Rtg
Inside 20	10	5	50.0	55	5.5	2	0	3	32	0	1	106.3
Inside 10	2	0	0.0	0	0.0	0	0	0	0	0	0	39.6
1st Down	47	35	74.5	320	6.8	1	2	13	158	1	4	81.9
2nd Down	36	21	58.3	185	5.1	0	2	11	122	0	1	49.0
3rd Down Overall	24	17	70.8	175	7.3	2	1	10	60	0	1	101.9
3rd D 0-5 to Go	9	6	66.7	48	5.3	0	0	4	18	0	0	79.9
3rd D 6+ to Go	15	11	73.3	127	8.5	2	1	6	42	0	1	110.3
4th Down	1	1	100.0	19	19.0	0	0	1	4	0	0	118.8
Rec Behind Line	22	18	81.8	71	3.2	0	1	4	139	0	0	61.2
1-10 yds	56	42	75.0	373	6.7	1	2	19	179	0	0	83.4
11-20 yds	22	12	54.5	204	9.3	1	1	10	25	0	0	82.4
21-30 yds	5	2	40.0	51	10.2	1	1	2	1	1	0	77.9
31+	3	0	0.0	0	0.0	0	0	0	0	0	0	39.6
Left Sideline	19	15	78.9	129	6.8	0	1	6	77	0	0	76.4
Left Side	23	18	78.3	174	7.6	0	2	10	102	0	1	76.4
Middle	27	14	51.9	137	5.1	0	1	7	43	0	4	51.0
Right Side	18	14	77.8	123	6.8	1	0	5	68	1	1	113.7
Right Sideline	21	13	61.9	136	6.5	1	1	7	54	0	1	76.7
2 Wide Receivers	32	23	71.9	207	6.5	2	2	12	72	1	3	73.3
3+ WR	74	51	68.9	492	6.6	2	3	23	272	0	3	79.3
Attempts 1-10	44	35	79.5	344	7.8	1	0	17	167	1	0	106.8
Attempts 11-20	20	11	55.0	72	3.6	0	1	3	34	0	0	42.1
Attempts 21+	44	28	63.6	283	6.4	2	4	15	143	0	0	59.2

1995 Incompletions

Type	Num	% of Inc	% of Att
Pass Dropped	4	11.8	3.7
Poor Throw	16	47.1	14.8
Pass Defensed	7	20.6	6.5
Pass Hit at Line	0	0.0	0.0
Other	7	20.6	6.5
Total	34	100.0	31.5

Game Logs (1-8)

Date	Opp	Result	Att	Cm	Pct	Yds	TD	Int	Lg	Sk	F-L
09/03	NYA	W 52-14	3	1	33.3	8	0	0	8	0	1-0
09/10	@NE	W 20-3	-	-	-	-	-	-	-	-	-
09/18	Pit	W 23-10	6	5	83.3	42	0	0	12	1	0-0
10/01	@Cin	W 26-23	-	-	-	-	-	-	-	-	-
10/08	Ind	L 24-27	1	1	100.0	4	0	0	1	0	0-0
10/15	@NO	L 30-33	42	29	69.0	368	3	2	31	1	1-1
10/22	@NYA	L 16-17	42	27	64.3	191	0	3	20	3	1-1
10/29	Buf	W 23-6	-	-	-	-	-	-	-	-	-

Game Logs (9-16)

Date	Opp	Result	Att	Cm	Pct	Yds	TD	Int	Lg	Sk	F-L
11/05	@SD	W 24-14	-	-	-	-	-	-	-	-	-
11/12	NE	L 17-34	9	7	77.8	56	0	0	19	0	0-0
11/20	SF	L 20-44	3	3	75.0	23	0	0	14	1	0-0
11/26	@Ind	L 28-36	0	0	-	-	-	-	-	-	-
12/03	Ind	W 21-20	-	-	-	-	-	-	-	-	-
12/11	KC	W 13-6	-	-	-	-	-	-	-	-	-
12/17	@Buf	L 20-23	1	1	100.0	10	0	0	10	0	0-0
12/24	@StL	W 41-22	-	-	-	-	-	-	-	-	-

Erik Kramer
Chicago Bears — QB

1995 Passing Splits

	G	Att	Cm	Pct	Yds	Yd/Att	TD	Int	1st	YAC	Big	Sk	Rtg
Total	16	522	315	60.3	3838	7.4	29	10	201	1607	25	15	93.5
vs. Playoff	6	180	106	58.9	1248	6.9	9	7	69	476	8	9	80.5
vs. Non-playoff	10	342	209	61.1	2590	7.6	20	3	132	1131	17	6	100.4
vs. Own Division	8	241	151	62.7	1807	7.5	10	4	90	735	14	9	92.5
Home	8	247	148	59.9	1916	7.8	16	9	104	805	13	5	90.7
Away	8	275	167	60.7	1922	7.0	13	1	97	802	12	10	96.1
Games 1-8	8	265	161	60.8	2032	7.7	18	4	106	907	14	4	101.0
Games 9-16	8	257	154	59.9	1806	7.0	11	6	95	700	11	11	85.8
September	4	129	79	61.2	948	7.3	8	2	47	385	6	3	97.9
October	4	136	82	60.3	1084	8.0	10	2	59	522	8	1	103.9
November	4	130	80	61.5	1045	8.0	8	5	55	352	7	4	91.3
December	4	127	74	58.3	761	6.0	3	1	40	348	4	7	80.2
Grass	11	352	206	58.5	2686	7.6	21	10	145	1095	18	7	90.7
Turf	5	170	109	64.1	1152	6.8	8	0	56	512	7	8	99.4
Indoor	2	58	39	67.2	371	6.4	2	0	19	192	0	4	96.3
Outdoor	14	464	276	59.5	3467	7.5	27	10	182	1415	22	11	93.2
1st Half	-	278	166	59.7	2223	8.0	18	7	112	897	17	6	96.3
2nd Half/OT	-	244	149	61.1	1615	6.6	11	3	89	710	8	9	90.5
Last 2 Min. Half	-	76	49	64.5	544	7.2	7	3	31	196	2	1	99.9
4th qtr, +/-7 pts	-	96	58	60.4	581	6.1	4	2	30	278	2	3	82.9
Winning	-	164	95	57.9	1265	7.7	6	3	87	506	9	2	87.1
Tied	-	137	78	56.9	928	6.8	8	5	50	361	4	3	82.0
Trailing	-	221	142	64.3	1645	7.4	15	2	84	740	8	11	105.5

	Att	Cm	Pct	Yds	Yd/Att	TD	Int	1st	YAC	Big	Sk	Rtg
Inside 20	83	39	47.0	282	3.4	19	2	26	126	0	0	84.9
Inside 10	40	16	40.0	58	1.5	12	1	12	11	0	0	77.1
1st Down	192	125	65.1	1663	8.7	11	4	75	617	12	8	102.8
2nd Down	172	100	58.1	1211	7.0	11	4	65	557	8	5	91.5
3rd Down Overall	148	83	56.1	922	6.2	7	1	56	421	5	1	87.7
3rd D 0-5 to Go	55	31	56.4	272	4.9	5	0	25	153	1	1	100.0
3rd D 6+ to Go	93	52	55.9	650	7.0	2	1	31	268	4	0	80.5
4th Down	10	7	70.0	42	4.2	0	1	5	12	0	1	38.3
Rec Behind Line	58	34	58.6	194	3.3	0	1	12	275	0	0	57.7
1-10 yds	302	203	67.2	1799	6.0	17	3	111	888	4	0	97.5
11-20 yds	113	61	54.0	1121	9.9	4	1	61	268	7	0	96.5
21-30 yds	16	6	37.5	166	10.4	1	1	6	33	3	0	71.4
31+	33	11	33.3	558	16.9	7	4	11	143	11	0	81.9
Left Sideline	103	60	58.3	818	7.9	4	1	43	299	7	0	92.6
Left Side	102	72	70.6	779	7.6	4	2	48	372	2	3	97.6
Middle	74	35	47.3	438	5.9	5	0	15	215	3	11	88.7
Right Side	149	95	63.8	1143	7.7	9	4	58	485	8	1	96.1
Right Sideline	94	53	56.4	660	7.0	7	3	37	236	5	0	89.8
2 Wide Receivers	258	156	60.5	2029	7.9	15	4	98	865	14	12	98.2
3+ WR	241	147	61.0	1740	7.2	8	5	91	704	11	3	85.4
Attempts 1-10	160	94	58.8	1304	8.2	6	5	62	567	13	0	84.5
Attempts 11-20	160	103	64.4	1224	7.7	15	2	67	489	6	0	113.6
Attempts 21+	202	118	58.4	1310	6.5	8	3	72	551	6	0	84.8

1995 Incompletions

Type	Num	% of Inc	% of Att
Pass Dropped	33	15.9	6.3
Poor Throw	93	44.9	17.8
Pass Defensed	33	15.9	6.3
Pass Hit at Line	13	6.3	2.5
Other	35	16.9	6.7
Total	207	100.0	39.7

Game Logs (1-8)

Date	Opp	Result	Att	Cm	Pct	Yds	TD	Int	Lg	Sk	F-L
09/03	Min	W 31-14	28	19	67.9	262	3	1	73	1	0-0
09/11	GB	L 24-27	25	15	60.0	162	1	1	42	2	2-1
09/17	@TB	W 25-6	38	18	47.4	207	0	0	23	0	0-0
09/24	@StL	L 28-34	38	27	71.1	317	4	0	49	1	1-1
10/08	Car	W 31-27	41	23	56.1	259	3	0	41	1	1-1
10/15	@Jac	W 30-27	29	17	58.6	245	3	0	46	1	0-0
10/22	Hou	W 35-32	41	24	58.5	349	2	1	76	0	0-0
10/30	@Min	L 14-6	25	18	72.0	231	2	0	48	0	0-0

Game Logs (9-16)

Date	Opp	Result	Att	Cm	Pct	Yds	TD	Int	Lg	Sk	F-L
11/05	Pit	L 34-37	28	15	53.6	228	3	3	46	1	0-0
11/12	@GB	L 28-35	38	23	60.5	318	2	1	46	2	0-0
11/26	@NYN	W 27-24	38	25	65.8	268	2	0	28	1	1-1
12/04	@Det	L 7-27	33	21	63.6	140	0	0	19	4	1-0
12/10	@Cin	L 10-16	36	18	50.0	196	0	0	47	3	0-0
12/17	TB	W 31-10	28	20	71.4	256	1	0	47	0	0-0
12/24	Phi	W 20-14	30	15	50.0	169	2	1	27	0	0-0

Dave Krieg
Arizona Cardinals — QB

1995 Passing Splits

	G	Att	Cm	Pct	Yds	Yd/Att	TD	Int	1st	YAC	Big	Sk	Rtg
Total	16	521	304	58.3	3554	6.8	16	21	168	1691	28	53	72.6
vs. Playoff	8	256	154	60.2	1945	7.6	9	12	89	925	17	32	76.1
vs. Non-playoff	8	265	150	56.6	1609	6.1	7	9	79	766	11	21	69.2
vs. Own Division	8	238	140	58.8	1622	6.8	6	15	80	803	13	17	61.6
Home	8	272	156	57.4	1800	6.6	8	12	90	867	12	22	68.9
Away	8	249	148	59.4	1754	7.0	8	9	78	824	16	31	76.6
Games 1-8	8	245	148	60.4	1648	6.7	8	13	79	835	11	24	69.2
Games 9-16	8	276	156	56.5	1906	6.9	8	8	89	856	17	29	75.5
September	4	88	55	62.5	628	7.1	4	8	29	310	5	12	61.2
October	4	157	93	59.2	1020	6.5	4	5	50	525	6	12	73.7
November	5	170	99	58.2	1218	7.2	6	4	59	494	11	18	82.4
December	3	106	57	53.8	688	6.5	2	4	30	362	6	11	64.5
Grass	12	388	221	57.0	2514	6.5	11	15	120	1208	18	38	69.9
Turf	4	133	83	62.4	1040	7.8	5	6	48	483	10	15	80.4
Indoor	1	24	15	62.5	158	6.6	1	0	8	97	0	7	95.5
Outdoor	15	497	289	58.1	3396	6.8	15	21	160	1594	28	46	71.5
1st Half	-	254	149	58.7	1736	6.8	8	12	82	908	14	20	70.3
2nd Half/OT	-	267	155	58.1	1818	6.8	8	9	86	783	14	33	74.8
Last 2 Min. Half	-	77	46	59.7	532	6.9	5	3	27	216	4	5	86.1
4th qtr, +/-7 pts	-	70	41	58.6	461	6.6	3	2	24	158	3	6	80.7
Winning	-	80	44	55.0	476	6.0	0	3	20	239	3	3	57.1
Tied	-	94	50	53.2	545	5.8	1	6	26	233	4	9	47.5
Trailing	-	347	210	60.5	2533	7.3	15	12	122	1219	21	41	82.9

	Att	Cm	Pct	Yds	Yd/Att	TD	Int	1st	YAC	Big	Sk	Rtg
Inside 20	61	26	42.6	164	2.7	11	3	13	47	0	3	69.2
Inside 10	28	11	39.3	38	1.4	7	1	7	5	0	0	72.0
1st Down	183	110	60.1	1412	7.7	6	7	55	626	14	19	79.3
2nd Down	183	107	58.5	1194	6.5	6	7	59	595	8	14	73.0
3rd Down Overall	149	85	57.0	912	6.1	2	7	52	470	6	19	60.0
3rd D 0-5 to Go	53	25	47.2	233	4.4	2	4	24	153	2	3	40.8
3rd D 6+ to Go	96	60	62.5	679	7.1	0	3	28	317	4	16	70.6
4th Down	6	2	33.3	36	6.0	2	0	2	0	0	1	94.4
Rec Behind Line	103	70	68.0	548	5.3	0	0	23	798	3	0	80.9
1-10 yds	246	158	64.2	1351	5.5	9	9	75	604	1	0	75.4
11-20 yds	110	55	50.0	986	9.0	5	8	49	172	7	0	65.9
21-30 yds	47	18	38.3	541	11.5	2	1	18	101	14	0	87.3
31+	15	3	20.0	128	8.5	0	3	3	16	3	0	23.1
Left Sideline	109	51	46.8	683	6.3	1	4	32	279	7	0	55.0
Left Side	111	72	64.9	715	6.4	5	3	41	435	3	8	86.7
Middle	90	58	64.4	769	8.5	3	6	39	349	4	42	74.7
Right Side	107	67	62.6	672	6.3	1	5	28	443	4	3	64.1
Right Sideline	104	56	53.8	715	6.9	4	6	28	185	10	0	82.8
2 Wide Receivers	222	124	55.9	1511	6.8	6	10	67	637	14	22	67.2
3+ WR	286	174	60.8	2001	7.0	5	11	95	1050	14	30	71.7
Attempts 1-10	159	94	59.1	1092	6.9	5	9	53	597	8	0	66.9
Attempts 11-20	150	92	61.3	1139	7.6	3	4	49	535	10	0	80.4
Attempts 21+	212	118	55.7	1323	6.2	8	6	66	559	10	0	71.3

1995 Incompletions

Type	Num	% of Inc	% of Att
Pass Dropped	25	11.5	4.8
Poor Throw	84	38.7	16.1
Pass Defensed	50	23.0	9.6
Pass Hit at Line	16	7.4	3.1
Other	42	19.4	8.1
Total	217	100.0	41.7

Game Logs (1-8)

Date	Opp	Result	Att	Cm	Pct	Yds	TD	Int	Lg	Sk	F-L
09/03	@Was	L 7-27	22	10	45.5	92	1	3	36	1	1-0
09/10	Phi	L 19-31	9	6	66.7	54	0	2	13	1	1-0
09/17	@Det	W 20-17	24	15	62.5	158	1	0	24	7	2-0
09/24	@Dal	L 20-34	33	24	72.7	324	2	3	45	3	0-0
10/01	KC	L 3-24	41	25	61.0	308	0	1	35	7	1-0
10/08	@NYN	L 21-27	38	23	60.5	305	2	1	47	2	2-2
10/15	Was	W 24-20	33	22	66.7	207	1	1	24	1	1-1
10/29	Sea	W 20-14	45	23	51.1	200	1	2	23	1	0-0

Game Logs (9-16)

Date	Opp	Result	Att	Cm	Pct	Yds	TD	Int	Lg	Sk	F-L
11/05	@Den	L 6-38	29	17	58.6	233	0	0	44	4	0-0
11/12	Min	L 24-30	36	19	52.8	231	2	1	36	3	3-1
11/19	@Car	L 7-27	25	14	56.0	106	0	0	22	6	1-0
11/26	Atl	W 40-37	43	27	62.8	413	4	2	48	3	0-0
11/30	NYN	L 6-10	37	22	59.5	235	0	1	35	2	2-1
12/09	@SD	L 25-28	40	24	60.0	283	2	0	36	5	1-0
12/17	@Phi	L 20-21	38	21	55.3	253	0	2	27	5	0-0
12/25	Dal	L 13-37	28	12	42.9	152	0	2	29	3	1-1

Amp Lee
Minnesota Vikings — RB

1995 Receiving Splits

	G	Rec	Yds	Avg	TD	Lg	Big	YAC	Trgt	Y@C	1st	1st%
Total	16	71	558	7.9	1	33	1	516	95	0.6	29	40.8
vs. Playoff	7	23	187	8.1	0	20	0	177	34	0.4	9	39.1
vs. Non-playoff	9	48	371	7.7	1	33	1	339	61	0.7	20	41.7
vs. Own Division	8	45	363	8.1	0	33	1	333	63	0.7	20	44.4
Home	8	27	220	8.1	1	33	1	188	38	1.2	13	48.1
Away	8	44	338	7.7	0	20	0	328	57	0.2	16	36.4
Games 1-8	8	35	220	6.3	0	18	0	195	47	0.7	15	42.9
Games 9-16	8	36	338	9.4	1	33	1	321	48	0.5	14	38.9
September	4	11	40	3.6	0	11	0	42	15	-0.2	1	9.1
October	4	24	180	7.5	0	18	0	153	32	1.1	14	58.3
November	4	23	226	9.8	1	21	0	220	28	0.3	10	43.5
December	4	13	112	8.6	0	33	1	101	20	0.8	4	30.8
Grass	5	28	197	7.0	0	20	0	194	37	0.1	10	35.7
Turf	11	43	361	8.4	1	33	1	322	58	0.9	19	44.2
Indoor	9	36	312	8.7	1	33	1	280	49	0.9	17	47.2
Outdoor	7	35	246	7.0	0	20	0	236	46	0.3	12	34.3
1st Half	-	38	311	8.2	1	33	1	279	44	0.8	18	47.4
2nd Half/OT	-	33	247	7.5	0	20	0	237	51	0.3	11	33.3
Last 2 Min. Half	-	12	68	5.7	0	13	0	39	17	2.4	5	41.7
4th qtr, +/-7 pts	-	4	24	6.0	0	9	0	32	8	-2.0	0	0.0
Winning	-	20	196	9.8	1	33	1	184	27	0.6	10	50.0
Tied	-	15	111	7.4	0	18	0	95	18	1.1	4	26.7
Trailing	-	36	251	7.0	0	20	0	237	50	0.4	15	41.7

	Rec	Yds	Avg	TD	Lg	Big	YAC	Trgt	Y@C	1st	1st%
Inside 20	6	9	1.5	1	12	0	21	9	-2.0	2	33.3
Inside 10	2	0	0.0	1	2	0	2	4	-1.0	1	50.0
1st Down	25	180	7.2	1	19	0	166	31	0.6	5	20.0
2nd Down	22	180	8.2	0	33	1	184	31	-0.2	6	27.3
3rd Down Overall	24	198	8.3	0	20	0	166	32	1.3	18	75.0
3rd D 0-2 to Go	3	32	10.7	0	20	0	28	4	1.3	3	100.0
3rd D 3-7 to Go	16	134	8.4	0	20	0	96	18	2.4	13	81.3
3rd D 8+ to Go	5	32	6.4	0	13	0	42	10	-2.0	2	40.0
4th Down	0	0	-	0	0	0	0	1	-	0	-
Rec Behind Line	25	166	6.6	0	33	1	276	28	-4.4	7	28.0
1-10 yds	46	392	8.5	1	21	0	240	64	3.3	22	47.8
11-20 yds	0	0	-	0	0	0	0	2	-	0	-
21-30 yds	0	0	-	0	0	0	0	1	-	0	-
31+	0	0	-	0	0	0	0	0	-	0	-
Left Sideline	19	157	8.3	0	19	0	163	25	-0.3	11	57.9
Left Side	15	116	7.7	0	20	0	126	18	-0.7	6	40.0
Middle	8	54	6.8	0	13	0	25	11	3.6	1	12.5
Right Side	18	132	7.3	1	33	1	117	23	0.8	6	33.3
Right Sideline	11	99	9.0	0	21	0	85	18	1.3	5	45.5
Shotgun	11	117	10.6	0	21	0	75	15	3.8	7	63.6
2 Wide Receivers	15	138	9.2	1	20	0	128	18	0.7	8	53.3
3 Wide Receivers	44	338	7.7	0	33	1	308	61	0.7	15	34.1
4+ Wide Receivers	12	82	6.8	0	13	0	80	16	0.2	6	50.0

1995 Incompletions

Type	Num	%of Inc	%of Att
Pass Dropped	4	16.7	4.2
Poor Throw	12	50.0	12.6
Pass Defensed	1	4.2	1.1
Pass Hit at Line	1	4.2	1.1
Other	6	25.0	6.3
Total	24	100.0	25.3

Game Logs (1-8)

Date	Opp	Result	Rush	Yds	Rec	Yds	Trgt	F-L	TD
09/03	@Chi	L 14-31	4	22	8	36	11	0-0	0
09/10	Det	W 20-10	8	44	0	0	0	0-0	0
09/17	@Pit	L 17-23	6	12	3	4	4	0-0	0
09/24	@Dal	W 44-24	1	0	0	0	0	0-0	0
10/08	Hou	W 23-17	5	32	4	30	4	0-0	1
10/15	@TB	L 17-20	3	7	10	71	10	1-1	0
10/22	@GB	L 21-38	2	9	6	52	10	0-0	1
10/30	Chi	L 6-14	7	33	4	27	8	0-0	0

Game Logs (9-16)

Date	Opp	Result	Rush	Yds	Rec	Yds	Trgt	F-L	TD
11/05	GB	W 27-24	6	30	4	35	6	0-0	0
11/12	@Ari	W 30-24	0	0	3	34	3	0-0	0
11/19	NO	W 43-24	6	10	7	65	8	1-0	1
11/23	@Det	L 38-44	4	2	9	92	11	0-0	0
12/03	TB	W 31-17	8	90	4	50	7	0-0	1
12/09	Cle	W 27-11	0	0	1	9	1	0-0	0
12/18	@SF	L 30-37	5	44	1	4	3	0-0	0
12/24	@Cin	L 24-27	4	36	7	49	9	1-1	0

Dorsey Levens
Green Bay Packers — RB

1995 Receiving Splits

	G	Rec	Yds	Avg	TD	Lg	Big	YAC	Trgt	Y@C	1st	1st%		Rec	Yds	Avg	TD	Lg	Big	YAC	Trgt	Y@C	1st	1st%
Total	15	48	434	9.0	4	27	1	375	57	1.2	24	50.0	Inside 20	5	23	4.6	4	7	0	15	5	1.6	4	80.0
vs. Playoff	3	14	149	10.6	1	23	0	130	17	1.4	8	57.1	Inside 10	4	19	4.8	4	7	0	13	4	1.5	4	100.0
vs. Non-playoff	12	34	285	8.4	3	27	1	245	40	1.2	16	47.1	1st Down	28	277	9.9	4	27	1	253	32	0.9	17	60.7
vs. Own Division	8	26	201	7.7	3	20	0	193	30	0.3	10	38.5	2nd Down	18	140	7.8	0	23	0	112	21	1.6	6	33.3
Home	8	26	228	8.8	3	23	0	208	31	0.8	15	57.7	3rd Down Overall	2	17	8.5	0	13	0	10	4	3.5	1	50.0
Away	7	22	206	9.4	1	27	1	167	26	1.8	9	40.9	3rd D 0-2 to Go	0	0	-	0	0	-0	0	1	-	0	-
Games 1-8	7	24	246	10.3	2	27	1	214	30	1.3	14	58.3	3rd D 3-7 to Go	2	17	8.5	0	13	0	10	3	3.5	1	50.0
Games 9-16	8	24	188	7.8	2	23	0	161	27	1.1	10	41.7	3rd D 8+ to Go	0	0	-	0	0	0	0	0	-	0	-
September	4	11	123	11.2	0	27	1	99	15	2.2	7	63.6	4th Down	0	0	-	0	0	0	0	0	-	0	-
October	3	13	123	9.5	2	20	0	115	15	0.6	7	53.8	Rec Behind Line	13	103	7.9	1	20	0	134	18	-2.4	8	61.5
November	4	11	60	5.5	2	20	0	45	12	1.4	4	36.4	1-10 yds	34	304	8.9	3	23	0	229	38	2.2	15	44.1
December	4	13	128	9.8	0	23	0	116	15	0.9	6	46.2	11-20 yds	1	27	27.0	0	27	1	12	1	15.0	1	100.0
Grass	12	40	371	9.3	4	27	1	318	47	1.3	22	55.0	21-30 yds	0	0	-	0	0	0	0	0	-	0	-
Turf	3	8	63	7.9	0	11	0	57	10	0.8	2	25.0	31+	0	0	-	0	0	0	0	0	-	0	-
Indoor	3	8	63	7.9	0	11	0	57	10	0.8	2	25.0	Left Sideline	4	17	4.3	0	9	0	23	5	-1.5	0	0.0
Outdoor	12	40	371	9.3	4	27	1	318	47	1.3	22	55.0	Left Side	7	77	11.0	0	17	0	73	8	0.6	5	71.4
1st Half	-	31	270	8.7	3	27	1	229	36	1.3	16	51.6	Middle	10	110	11.0	0	20	0	83	13	2.7	6	60.0
2nd Half/OT	-	17	164	9.6	1	23	0	146	21	1.1	8	47.1	Right Side	17	173	10.2	2	27	1	154	19	1.1	10	58.8
Last 2 Min. Half	-	5	51	10.2	0	18	0	46	6	1.0	3	60.0	Right Sideline	10	57	5.7	2	12	0	42	12	1.5	3	30.0
4th qtr, +/-7 pts	-	6	51	8.5	0	12	0	56	7	-0.8	3	50.0	Shotgun	0	0	-	0	0	0	0	0	-	0	-
Winning	-	17	209	12.3	1	27	1	169	22	2.4	13	76.5	2 Wide Receivers	36	335	9.3	2	27	1	287	41	1.3	18	50.0
Tied	-	16	100	6.3	2	20	0	84	17	1.0	4	25.0	3 Wide Receivers	11	98	8.9	1	23	0	87	15	1.0	5	45.5
Trailing	-	15	125	8.3	1	20	0	122	18	0.2	7	46.7	4+ Wide Receivers	0	0	-	0	0	0	0	0	-	0	-

1995 Incompletions

Type	Num	%of Inc	%of Att
Pass Dropped	3	33.3	5.3
Poor Throw	4	44.4	7.0
Pass Defensed	0	0.0	0.0
Pass Hit at Line	0	0.0	0.0
Other	2	22.2	3.5
Total	9	100.0	15.8

Game Logs (1-8)

Date	Opp	Result	Rush	Yds	Rec	Yds	Trgt	F-L	TD
09/03	StL	L 14-17	3	10	2	23	3	0-0	0
09/11	@Chi	W 27-24	2	22	2	24	3	0-0	0
09/17	NYN	W 14-6	1	0	3	27	4	0-0	0
09/24	@Jac	W 24-14	3	9	4	49	5	0-0	1
10/08	@Dal	L 24-34	-	-	-	-	-	-	-
10/15	Det	W 30-21	1	-2	4	36	5	0-0	1
10/22	Min	W 38-21	2	-4	3	37	3	0-0	1
10/29	@Det	L 16-24	1	4	6	50	7	0-0	0

Game Logs (9-16)

Date	Opp	Result	Rush	Yds	Rec	Yds	Trgt	F-L	TD
11/05	@Min	L 24-27	0	0	1	4	2	0-0	0
11/12	Chi	W 35-28	3	26	5	16	5	0-0	1
11/19	@Cle	W 31-20	4	12	4	38	4	0-0	0
11/26	TB	W 35-13	7	18	1	2	1	0-0	2
12/03	Cin	W 24-10	1	0	4	24	5	0-0	0
12/10	@TB	L 10-13	5	19	4	32	4	0-0	0
12/16	@NO	W 34-23	2	5	1	9	1	0-0	0
12/24	Pit	W 24-19	1	1	4	63	5	0-0	0

Marc Logan
Washington Redskins — RB

1995 Receiving Splits

	G	Rec	Yds	Avg	TD	Lg	Big	YAC	Trgt	Y@C	1st	1st%		Rec	Yds	Avg	TD	Lg	Big	YAC	Trgt	Y@C	1st	1st%
Total	16	25	276	11.0	2	32	1	272	39	0.2	13	52.0	Inside 20	5	39	7.8	2	11	0	31	5	1.6	2	40.0
vs. Playoff	6	13	132	10.2	1	32	1	127	20	0.4	6	46.2	Inside 10	3	22	7.3	2	9	0	14	3	2.7	2	66.7
vs. Non-playoff	10	12	144	12.0	1	22	0	145	19	-0.1	7	58.3	1st Down	11	106	9.6	2	22	0	103	17	0.3	6	54.5
vs. Own Division	8	14	192	13.7	1	32	1	183	22	0.6	9	64.3	2nd Down	13	150	11.5	0	32	1	152	21	-0.2	6	46.2
Home	8	15	189	12.6	1	32	1	192	21	-0.2	9	60.0	3rd Down Overall	1	20	20.0	0	20	0	17	1	3.0	1	100.0
Away	8	10	87	8.7	1	18	0	80	18	0.7	4	40.0	3rd D 0-2 to Go	0	0	-	0	0	0	0	0	-	0	-
Games 1-8	8	19	187	9.8	2	20	0	186	23	0.1	10	52.6	3rd D 3-7 to Go	0	0	-	0	0	0	0	0	-	0	-
Games 9-16	8	6	89	14.8	0	32	1	86	16	0.5	3	50.0	3rd D 8+ to Go	1	20	20.0	0	20	0	17	1	3.0	1	100.0
September	4	8	81	10.1	1	20	0	84		-0.4	4	50.0	4th Down	0	0	-	0	0	0	0	0	-	0	-
October	5	13	149	11.5	1	22	0	148	20	0.1	8	61.5	Rec Behind Line	10	144	14.4	0	32	1	180	15	-3.6	6	60.0
November	3	3	43	14.3	0	32	1	39	6	1.1	3	33.3	1-10 yds	15	132	8.8	2	20	0	92	24	2.7	7	46.7
December	4	1	3	3.0	0	3	0	1	5	2.0	0	0.0	11-20 yds	0	0	-	0	0	0	0	0	-	0	-
Grass	12	24	248	11.8	2	32	1	245	31	0.1	12	57.1	21-30 yds	0	0	-	0	0	0	0	0	-	0	-
Turf	4	4	28	7.0	0	14	0	27	8	0.3	1	25.0	31+	0	0	-	0	0	0	0	0	-	0	-
Indoor	1	1	3	3.0	0	3	0	1	2	2.0	0	0.0	Left Sideline	1	3	3.0	0	3	0	1	2	2.0	0	0.0
Outdoor	15	24	273	11.4	2	32	1	271	37	0.1	13	54.2	Left Side	5	66	13.2	0	21	0	70	8	-0.8	3	60.0
1st Half	-	11	129	11.7	2	32	1	129	15	0.0	7	63.6	Middle	6	53	8.8	1	18	0	45	9	1.3	2	33.3
2nd Half/OT	-	14	147	10.5	0	22	0	143	24	0.2	6	42.9	Right Side	11	120	10.9	1	32	1	127	15	-0.6	4	54.5
Last 2 Min. Half	-	3	24	8.0	1	11	0	26	3	-0.7	2	66.7	Right Sideline	2	34	17.0	0	20	0	29	4	2.5	2	100.0
4th qtr, +/-7 pts	-	2	14	7.0	0	8	0	20	3	-3.0	0	0.0	Shotgun	0	0	-	0	0	0	0	0	-	0	-
Winning	-	7	69	9.9	0	20	0	60	8	1.3	3	42.9	2 Wide Receivers	24	267	11.1	1	32	1	266	35	0.0	12	50.0
Tied	-	5	74	14.8	0	32	1	72	9	0.4	3	60.0	3 Wide Receivers	0	0	-	0	0	0	0	3	-	0	-
Trailing	-	13	133	10.2	2	22	0	140	24	-0.5	7	53.8	4+ Wide Receivers	0	0	-	0	0	0	0	0	-	0	-

1995 Incompletions

Type	Num	%of Inc	%of Att
Pass Dropped	7	50.0	17.9
Poor Throw	5	35.7	12.8
Pass Defensed	0	0.0	0.0
Pass Hit at Line	0	0.0	0.0
Other	2	14.3	5.1
Total	14	100.0	35.9

Game Logs (1-8)

Date	Opp	Result	Rush	Yds	Rec	Yds	Trgt	F-L	TD
09/03	Ari	W 27-7	2	8	4	44	4	1-0	0
09/10	Oak	L 8-20	0	0	1	6	1	0-0	0
09/17	@Den	L 31-38	1	1	3	31	3	0-0	1
09/24	@TB	L 6-14	2	8	0	0	4	0-0	0
10/01	Dal	W 27-23	1	4	3	31	4	0-0	1
10/08	@Phi	L 34-37	0	3	3	25	3	0-0	0
10/15	@Ari	L 20-24	1	0	1	17	2	0-0	0
10/22	Det	W 36-30	3	14	4	33	6	0-0	0

Game Logs (9-16)

Date	Opp	Result	Rush	Yds	Rec	Yds	Trgt	F-L	TD
10/29	NYN	L 15-24	3	8	2	43	4	0-0	1
11/05	@KC	L 3-24	1	0	2	11	5	0-0	0
11/12	Sea	L 20-27	2	15	0	0	0	0-0	0
11/26	Phi	L 7-14	2	5	1	32	1	0-0	0
12/03	@Dal	W 24-17	2	4	0	0	1	0-0	0
12/10	@NYN	L 13-20	1	2	0	0	0	0-0	0
12/17	@StL	W 35-23	1	1	1	3	2	0-0	0
12/24	Car	W 20-17	2	2	0	0	0	0-0	0

Derek Loville

San Francisco 49ers — RB

1995 Rushing and Receiving Splits

	G	Rush	Yds	Avg	Lg	TD	1st	Stf	YdL	Rec	Yds	Avg	TD
Total	16	218	723	3.3	27	10	47	18	37	87	662	7.6	3
vs. Playoff	7	112	387	3.5	16	7	31	9	19	46	372	8.1	1
vs. Non-playoff	9	106	336	3.2	27	3	16	9	18	41	290	7.1	2
vs. Own Division	8	102	338	3.3	16	5	20	8	9	44	304	6.9	1
Home	8	104	371	3.6	27	4	21	8	17	43	335	7.8	2
Away	8	114	352	3.1	16	6	26	10	20	44	327	7.4	2
Games 1-8	8	90	332	3.7	27	3	25	8	21	39	285	7.3	1
Games 9-16	8	128	391	3.1	16	7	22	10	16	48	377	7.9	2
September	4	48	186	3.9	27	2	17	4	13	23	170	7.4	1
October	4	42	146	3.5	12	1	8	4	8	16	115	7.2	0
November	4	61	186	3.0	13	4	14	4	8	20	191	9.6	1
December	4	67	205	3.1	16	3	8	6	8	28	186	6.6	1
Grass	10	135	456	3.4	27	6	27	9	22	58	455	7.8	2
Turf	6	83	267	3.2	16	4	20	9	15	29	207	7.1	1
Indoor	4	50	175	3.5	16	3	13	7	13	26	168	6.5	0
Outdoor	12	168	548	3.3	27	7	34	11	24	61	494	8.1	3
1st Half	-	113	333	2.9	12	6	23	14	33	52	435	8.4	2
2nd Half/OT	-	105	390	3.7	27	4	24	4	4	35	227	6.5	1
Last 2 Min. Half	-	9	19	2.1	6	0	1	2	3	12	95	7.9	1
4th qtr. +/-7 pts	-	24	97	4.0	16	1	4	1	1	9	48	5.3	0
Winning	-	131	475	3.6	27	6	31	7	13	42	306	7.3	2
Tied	-	42	102	2.4	10	1	5	6	15	22	191	8.7	1
Trailing	-	45	146	3.2	12	3	11	5	9	23	165	7.2	0

	Rush	Yds	Avg	Lg	TD	1st	Stf	YdL	Rec	Yds	Avg	TD
Inside 20	52	151	2.9	11	10	17	3	6	8	47	5.9	3
Inside 10	30	57	1.9	8	10	14	2	3	3	9	3.0	2
1st Down	124	396	3.2	13	4	9	11	24	38	277	7.3	1
2nd Down	74	246	3.3	27	3	23	6	11	26	205	7.9	0
3rd Down Overall	18	81	4.5	16	3	15	0	0	23	180	7.8	2
3rd D 0-2 to Go	15	63	4.2	16	3	10	0	0	5	26	5.2	0
3rd D 3-7 to Go	3	18	6.0	7	0	2	0	0	14	111	7.9	2
3rd D 8+ to Go	0	0	-	0	0	0	0	0	4	43	10.8	0
4th Down	2	0	0.0	2	0	0	1	2	0	0	-	0
Left Sideline	9	46	5.1	13	0	2	1	2	28	180	6.4	2
Left Side	37	106	2.9	12	4	11	4	13	15	78	5.2	0
Middle	100	351	3.5	27	2	18	7	13	12	104	8.7	1
Right Side	64	178	2.8	11	4	14	6	9	11	118	10.7	0
Right Sideline	8	42	5.3	16	0	2	0	0	21	182	8.7	0
Shotgun	0	0	-	0	0	0	0	0	0	0	-	0
2 Wide Receivers	170	598	3.5	27	3	30	14	26	60	435	7.3	2
3 Wide Receivers	27	78	2.9	13	1	6	2	8	22	172	7.8	1
4+ Wide Receivers	2	10	5.0	9	0	1	0	0	5	55	11.0	0
Carries 1-5	80	240	3.0	12	3	15	12	27	0	0	-	0
Carries 6-10	77	262	3.4	27	5	19	4	8	0	0	-	0
Carries 11-15	43	175	4.1	16	1	9	0	0	0	0	-	0
Carries 16-20	11	34	3.1	8	1	3	0	0	0	0	-	0
Carries 21+	7	12	1.7	4	0	1	2	2	0	0	-	0

1995 Incompletions

Type	Num	%of Inc	% Att
Pass Dropped	3	13.0	2.7
Poor Throw	10	43.5	9.1
Pass Defensed	2	8.7	1.8
Pass Hit at Line	2	8.7	1.8
Other	6	26.1	5.5
Total	23	100.0	20.9

Game Logs (1-8)

Date	Opp	Result	Rush	Yds	Rec	Yds	Trgt	F-L	TD
09/03	@NO	W 24-22	14	49	6	37	6	0-0	0
09/10	Atl	W 41-10	14	61	6	50	7	0-0	1
09/17	NE	W 28-3	12	58	6	42	9	0-0	1
09/25	@Det	L 24-27	8	18	5	41	8	0-0	1
10/01	NYN	W 20-6	9	42	4	30	4	1-1	0
10/15	@Ind	L 17-18	13	46	6	43	7	0-0	1
10/22	@StL	W 44-10	10	31	1	12	1	0-0	0
10/29	NO	L 7-11	10	24	5	30	7	0-0	0

Game Logs (9-16)

Date	Opp	Result	Rush	Yds	Rec	Yds	Trgt	F-L	TD
11/05	Car	L 7-13	12	40	6	55	7	0-0	1
11/12	@Dal	W 38-20	23	61	2	27	3	0-0	2
11/20	@Mia	W 44-20	15	51	8	78	9	0-0	1
11/26	StL	W 41-13	11	34	4	31	6	0-0	1
12/03	Buf	W 27-17	24	88	10	86	12	0-0	1
12/10	@Car	W 31-10	16	34	7	42	9	0-0	0
12/18	Min	W 37-30	13	21	2	11	4	0-0	0
12/24	@Atl	L 27-28	15	62	9	47	11	0-0	1

Dan Marino

Miami Dolphins — QB

1995 Passing Splits

	G	Att	Cm	Pct	Yds	Yd/Att	TD	Int	1st	YAC	Big	Sk	Rtg
Total	14	482	309	64.1	3668	7.6	24	15	189	1596	25	22	90.8
vs. Playoff	9	316	196	62.0	2152	6.8	14	7	115	884	14	16	87.7
vs. Non-playoff	5	166	113	68.1	1516	9.1	10	8	74	712	11	6	96.9
vs. Own Division	7	211	136	64.5	1700	8.1	12	7	85	833	13	12	94.5
Home	8	277	174	62.8	1946	7.0	12	8	104	768	13	12	86.1
Away	6	205	135	65.9	1722	8.4	12	7	85	828	12	10	97.2
Games 1-8	8	186	118	63.4	1502	8.1	8	4	74	664	11	6	94.0
Games 9-16	8	296	191	64.5	2166	7.3	16	11	115	932	14	16	88.9
September	3	73	46	63.0	626	8.6	5	3	29	333	5	3	96.0
October	3	113	72	63.7	876	7.8	3	1	45	331	6	3	92.6
November	4	150	98	65.3	1133	7.6	10	5	64	509	5	10	96.3
December	4	146	93	63.7	1033	7.1	6	6	51	423	9	6	81.2
Grass	10	336	213	63.4	2430	7.2	15	10	128	1039	15	12	87.5
Turf	4	146	96	65.8	1238	8.5	9	5	61	557	10	10	98.5
Indoor	2	71	46	64.8	544	7.7	6	3	29	270	5	6	98.6
Outdoor	12	411	263	64.0	3124	7.6	18	12	160	1326	20	16	89.5
1st Half	-	270	166	61.5	1973	7.3	14	11	99	912	15	13	84.1
2nd Half/OT	-	212	143	67.5	1695	8.0	10	4	90	684	10	9	99.5
Last 2 Min. Half	-	79	46	58.2	538	6.8	7	1	28	247	3	2	103.2
4th qtr. +/-7 pts	-	56	35	62.5	426	7.6	2	2	25	149	1	1	82.9
Winning	-	178	113	63.5	1331	7.5	9	6	71	584	9	5	89.0
Tied	-	115	60	52.2	801	7.0	1	4	36	363	7	10	63.0
Trailing	-	189	136	72.0	1536	8.1	14	5	82	659	9	7	109.6

	Att	Cm	Pct	Yds	Yd/Att	TD	Int	1st	YAC	Big	Sk	Rtg
Inside 20	64	35	54.7	241	3.8	15	6	23	88	0	1	63.9
Inside 10	29	15	51.7	69	2.4	13	2	13	12	0	0	68.5
1st Down	185	116	62.7	1486	8.0	9	3	68	648	10	5	97.3
2nd Down	167	102	61.1	1105	6.6	4	6	59	550	6	9	73.6
3rd Down Overall	126	88	69.8	1056	8.4	11	6	60	380	9	8	104.5
3rd D 0-5 to Go	49	32	65.3	232	4.7	7	4	27	103	0	0	81.8
3rd D 6+ to Go	77	56	72.7	824	10.7	4	2	33	277	9	8	113.8
4th Down	4	3	75.0	21	5.3	0	0	2	18	0	0	86.5
Rec Behind Line	63	44	69.8	241	3.8	1	1	11	364	1	0	74.9
1-10 yds	260	181	69.6	1559	6.0	13	10	98	749	1	0	85.7
11-20 yds	111	71	64.0	1368	12.3	6	4	67	345	12	0	109.7
21-30 yds	30	11	36.7	408	13.6	3	0	11	131	9	0	118.1
31+	18	2	11.1	92	5.1	1	0	2	7	2	0	66.9
Left Sideline	102	65	63.7	885	8.7	9	1	42	378	7	0	116.7
Left Side	103	65	65.0	724	7.0	3	4	36	326	4	1	86.4
Middle	102	71	69.6	834	8.2	5	2	44	371	7	18	104.3
Right Side	90	64	71.1	643	7.1	3	7	37	343	3	1	69.8
Right Sideline	85	44	49.4	582	6.8	3	2	30	178	4	0	73.8
2 Wide Receivers	194	119	61.3	1308	6.7	10	9	73	654	7	9	79.1
3+ WR	285	188	66.0	2347	8.2	14	6	115	932	18	13	99.0
Attempts 1-10	140	85	60.7	1049	7.5	5	6	51	462	6	0	77.9
Attempts 11-20	140	93	66.4	1103	7.0	8	6	55	534	10	0	94.4
Attempts 21+	202	131	64.9	1516	7.5	11	3	83	600	9	0	97.3

1995 Incompletions

Type	Num	% of Inc	% of Att
Pass Dropped	37	21.4	7.7
Poor Throw	68	39.3	14.1
Pass Defensed	25	14.5	5.2
Pass Hit at Line	11	6.4	2.3
Other	32	18.5	6.6
Total	173	100.0	35.9

Game Logs (1-8)

Date	Opp	Result	Att	Cm	Pct	Yds	TD	Int	Lg	Sk	F-L
09/03	NYA	W 52-14	26	16	61.5	250	3	2	50	1	0-0
09/10	@NE	W 20-3	21	11			1	1	67	0	0-0
09/18	Pit	W 23-10	27	16	59.3	183	1	0	35	1	2-0
10/01	@Cin	W 26-23	48	33	68.8	450	2	1	58	1	0-0
10/08	Ind	L 24-27	30	19	63.3	194	1	0	35	0	0-0
10/15	@NO	-	-	-	-	-	-	-	-	-	-
10/22	@NYA	L 16-17	-	-	-	-	-	-	-	-	-
10/29	Buf	W 23-6	35	20	57.1	232	0	0	31	2	0-0

Game Logs (9-16)

Date	Opp	Result	Att	Cm	Pct	Yds	TD	Int	Lg	Sk	F-L
11/05	@SD	W 24-14	39	25	64.1	291	2	1	50	0	0-0
11/12	@Dal	L 17-34	37	27	73.0	333	2	2	31	2	1-1
11/20	SF	L 20-44	38	23	60.5	255	2	1	42	4	0-0
11/26	@Ind	L 28-36	36	23	63.9	254	4	1	28	4	2-1
12/03	Atl	W 21-20	50	35	70.0	343	2	2	32	0	0-0
12/11	KC	L 13-23	34	18	52.9	156	1	1	24	1	1-0
12/17	@Buf	L 20-23	27	17	63.0	244	1	1	32	3	0-0
12/24	@StL	W 41-22	35	23	65.7	290	2	2	48	2	2-0

1995 Rushing and Receiving Splits

	G	Rush	Yds	Avg	Lg	TD	1st	Stf	YdL	Rec	Yds	Avg	TD		Rush	Yds	Avg	Lg	TD	1st	Stf	YdL	Rec	Yds	Avg	TD
Total	16	368	1487	4.0	49	14	80	36	68	30	261	8.7	1	Inside 20	83	166	2.0	15	13	18	10	24	1	6	6.0	0
vs. Playoff	10	222	866	3.9	39	5	45	22	35	23	200	8.7	1	Inside 10	46	70	1.5	9	13	15	7	11	0	0	-	0
vs. Non-playoff	6	146	621	4.3	49	9	35	14	33	7	61	8.7	0	1st Down	213	914	4.3	49	5	24	23	49	16	122	7.6	0
vs. Own Division	8	217	922	4.2	49	8	48	21	43	13	139	10.7	0	2nd Down	117	490	4.2	23	4	35	11	16	13	117	9.0	0
Home	8	181	670	3.7	32	9	37	13	31	9	51	5.7	0	3rd Down Overall	24	61	2.5	15	3	12	1	1	1	22	22.0	0
Away	8	187	817	4.4	49	5	43	23	37	21	210	10.0	1	3rd D 0-2 to Go	20	53	2.7	15	2	11	1	1	0	0	-	0
Games 1-8	8	154	500	3.2	50	5	26	10	18	11	67	6.1	0	3rd D 3-7 to Go	3	8	2.7	5	1	1	0	0	1	22	22.0	0
Games 9-16	8	214	987	4.6	49	9	54	26	50	19	194	10.2	1	3rd D 8+ to Go	1	0	0.0	0	0	0	0	0	0	0	-	0
September	3	61	205	3.4	30	1	12	4	5	1	9	9.0	0	4th Down	14	22	1.6	5	2	9	1	2	0	0	-	0
October	5	93	295	3.2	20	4	14	6	13	10	58	5.8	0	Left Sideline	17	109	6.4	19	0	4	0	0	7	60	8.6	0
November	4	108	504	4.7	49	5	27	14	24	7	102	14.6	0	Left Side	113	429	3.8	49	4	18	16	34	3	17	5.7	0
December	4	106	483	4.6	32	4	27	12	26	12	92	7.7	1	Middle	155	503	3.2	32	7	30	9	13	3	13	4.3	0
Grass	11	248	906	3.7	32	11	47	19	39	15	124	8.3	0	Right Side	59	282	4.8	39	3	17	8	14	4	58	14.5	1
Turf	5	120	581	4.8	49	3	33	17	29	15	137	9.1	1	Right Sideline	24	164	6.8	23	0	11	3	7	13	113	8.7	0
Indoor	2	38	147	3.9	22	1	9	3	4	4	23	5.8	0	Shotgun	0	0	-	0	0	0	0	0	0	0	-	0
Outdoor	14	330	1340	4.1	49	13	71	33	64	26	238	9.2	1	2 Wide Receivers	312	1345	4.3	49	7	58	33	63	26	224	8.6	1
1st Half	-	199	852	4.3	49	6	45	19	42	18	151	8.4	0	3 Wide Receivers	7	34	4.9	18	0	1	0	0	4	37	9.3	0
2nd Half/OT	-	169	635	3.8	32	8	35	17	26	12	110	9.2	1	4+ Wide Receivers	0	0	-	0	0	0	0	0	0	0	-	0
Last 2 Min. Half	-	4	1	0.3	2	2	3	1	4	1	4	4.0	0	Carries 1-5	80	395	4.9	39	1	19	7	15	0	0	-	0
4th qtr, +/-7 pts	-	34	176	5.2	23	4	11	0	0	2	12	6.0	0	Carries 6-10	76	300	3.9	23	3	19	6	10	0	0	-	0
Winning	-	93	386	4.2	49	4	17	9	16	2	8	4.0	0	Carries 11-15	72	273	3.8	49	2	15	11	26	0	0	-	0
Tied	-	135	584	4.3	32	2	29	12	29	16	148	9.3	0	Carries 16-20	58	191	3.3	19	4	11	9	13	0	0	-	0
Trailing	-	140	517	3.7	39	8	34	15	23	12	105	8.8	1	Carries 21+	82	328	4.0	23	4	16	3	4	0	0	-	0

1995 Incompletions

Type	Num	%of Inc	% Att
Pass Dropped	2	10.0	4.0
Poor Throw	7	35.0	14.0
Pass Defensed	3	15.0	6.0
Pass Hit at Line	2	10.0	4.0
Other	6	30.0	12.0
Total	20	100.0	40.0

Game Logs (1-8)

Date	Opp	Result	Rush	Yds	Rec	Yds	Trgt	F-L	TD
09/03	Cle	W 17-14	19	102	0	0	1	0-0	1
09/10	Mia	L 3-20	18	40	1	9	2	0-0	0
09/17	@SF	L 3-28	24	63	0	0	2	0-0	0
10/01	@Atl	L 17-30	14	44	1	-1	2	0-0	1
10/08	Den	L 3-37	6	8	1	3	1	0-0	0
10/15	@KC	L 26-31	13	31	3	28	6	0-0	0
10/23	Buf	W 27-14	36	127	1	-2	2	1-1	1
10/29	Car	L 17-20	24	85	4	30	8	0-0	2

Game Logs (9-16)

Date	Opp	Result	Rush	Yds	Rec	Yds	Trgt	F-L	TD
11/05	@NYA	W 20-7	35	166	1	22	1	1-1	2
11/12	@Mia	W 34-17	30	142	3	45	3	1-0	1
11/19	Ind	L 10-24	16	48	1	5	2	1-0	1
11/26	@Buf	W 35-25	27	148	2	30	4	0-0	0
12/03	NO	L 17-31	31	112	0	0	1	0-0	2
12/10	NYA	W 31-28	31	148	1	6	2	1-1	2
12/16	@Pit	L 27-41	20	120	8	62	9	0-0	1
12/23	@Ind	L 7-10	24	103	3	24	4	0-0	0

1995 Receiving Splits

	G	Rec	Yds	Avg	TD	Lg	Big	YAC	Trgt	Y@C	1st	1st%		Rec	Yds	Avg	TD	Lg	Big	YAC	Trgt	Y@C	1st	1st%
Total	16	90	1224	13.6	6	51	9	256	165	10.8	60	66.7	Inside 20	4	44	11.0	2	19	0	2	9	10.5	4	100.0
vs. Playoff	7	40	581	14.5	4	51	5	103	76	12.0	25	62.5	Inside 10	1	5	5.0	1	5	0	1	2	4.0	1	100.0
vs. Non-playoff	9	50	643	12.9	2	37	4	153	89	9.8	35	70.0	1st Down	32	458	14.3	1	39	5	91	62	11.5	16	50.0
vs. Own Division	8	40	549	13.7	1	37	3	151	79	10.0	27	67.5	2nd Down	35	424	12.1	2	25	1	86	54	9.7	23	65.7
Home	8	47	636	13.5	3	50	4	160	75	10.1	33	70.2	3rd Down Overall	22	329	15.0	3	51	3	72	47	11.7	20	90.9
Away	8	43	588	13.7	3	51	5	96	90	11.4	27	62.8	3rd D 0-2 to Go	1	6	6.0	0	6	0	3	1	3.0	1	100.0
Games 1-8	8	45	597	13.3	2	39	4	161	93	9.7	27	60.0	3rd D 3-7 to Go	16	176	11.0	1	25	1	55	26	7.6	15	93.8
Games 9-16	8	45	627	13.9	4	51	5	95	72	11.8	33	73.3	3rd D 8+ to Go	5	147	29.4	2	51	2	14	20	26.6	4	80.0
September	4	29	377	13.0	1	39	2	112	54	9.1	19	65.5	4th Down	1	13	13.0	0	13	0	7	2	6.0	1	100.0
October	4	16	220	13.8	1	37	2	49	39	10.7	8	50.0	Rec Behind Line	2	11	5.5	0	6	0	13	3	-1.0	1	100.0
November	4	15	233	15.5	1	50	1	39	27	12.9	11	73.3	1-10 yds	53	486	9.2	1	24	0	182	67	5.7	27	50.9
December	4	30	394	13.1	3	51	4	56	45	11.3	22	73.3	11-20 yds	26	418	16.1	1	30	2	38	55	14.6	23	88.5
Grass	11	64	845	13.2	3	50	5	210	110	9.9	41	64.1	21-30 yds	5	133	26.6	1	39	3	16	19	23.4	5	100.0
Turf	5	26	379	14.6	3	51	4	46	55	12.8	19	73.1	31+	4	176	44.0	3	51	4	7	21	42.3	4	100.0
Outdoor	2	79	1019	12.9	4	50	6	242	145	9.8	50	63.3	Left Sideline	27	347	12.9	2	29	3	33	57	11.6	18	66.7
Indoor	14	11	205	18.6	2	51	3	14	20	17.4	10	90.9	Left Side	17	220	12.9	0	30	1	86	27	7.9	9	52.9
1st Half	-	40	524	13.1	2	51	4	130	86	9.9	23	57.5	Middle	6	91	15.2	2	38	1	11	15	13.3	6	100.0
2nd Half/OT	-	50	700	14.0	4	50	5	126	79	11.5	37	74.0	Right Side	18	239	13.3	1	51	1	78	27	8.9	12	66.7
Last 2 Min. Half	-	4	64	16.0	0	22	0	20	16	11.0	3	75.0	Right Sideline	22	327	14.9	1	50	3	48	39	12.7	15	68.2
4th qtr, +/-7 pts	-	16	241	15.1	2	38	2	50	22	11.9	12	75.0	Shotgun	0	0	-	0	0	0	0	0	-	0	0
Winning	-	26	365	14.0	2	38	4	81	40	10.9	20	76.9	2 Wide Receivers	46	579	12.6	2	39	5	133	75	9.7	25	54.3
Tied	-	22	273	12.4	1	30	1	81	37	8.7	14	63.6	3 Wide Receivers	38	553	14.6	3	51	3	118	71	11.4	29	76.3
Trailing	-	42	586	14.0	3	51	4	94	88	11.7	26	61.9	4+ Wide Receivers	4	54	13.5	1	25	1	3	14	12.8	4	100.0

1995 Incompletions

Type	Num	%of Inc	%of Att
Pass Dropped	11	14.7	6.7
Poor Throw	41	54.7	24.8
Pass Defensed	8	10.7	4.8
Pass Hit at Line	0	0.0	0.0
Other	15	20.0	9.1
Total	75	100.0	45.5

Game Logs (1-8)

Date	Opp	Result	Rec	Yds	Trgt	F-L	TD
09/03	@Oak	L 7-17	6	67	17	0-0	0
09/10	Sea	W 14-10	13	163	16	1-1	1
09/17	@Phi	W 27-21	5	65	8	0-0	0
09/24	Den	W 17-6	5	82	13	0-0	0
10/01	@Pit	L 16-31	6	72	17	0-0	1
10/09	@KC	L 23-29	7	88	12	1-1	0
10/15	Dal	L 9-23	2	23	5	0-0	0
10/22	@Sea	W 35-25	1	37	5	0-0	0

Game Logs (9-16)

Date	Opp	Result	Rec	Yds	Trgt	F-L	TD
11/05	Mia	L 14-24	7	121	11	0-0	1
11/12	KC	L 7-22	3	44	8	0-0	0
11/19	@Den	L 27-30	4	54	6	0-0	0
11/27	Oak	W 12-6	1	14	2	0-0	0
12/03	Cle	W 31-13	9	132	11	0-0	1
12/09	Ari	W 28-25	7	57	9	1-1	0
12/17	@Ind	W 27-24	10	168	15	0-0	2
12/23	@NYN	W 27-17	4	37	10	0-0	0

Terance Mathis
Atlanta Falcons — WR

1995 Receiving Splits

	G	Rec	Yds	Avg	TD	Lg	Big	YAC	Trgt	Y@C	1st	1st%		Rec	Yds	Avg	TD	Lg	Big	YAC	Trgt	Y@C	1st	1st%
Total	14	78	1039	13.3	9	54	9	381	118	8.4	50	64.1	Inside 20	7	77	11.0	4	18	0	5	14	10.3	5	71.4
vs. Playoff	6	35	388	11.1	4	37	2	101	44	8.2	21	60.0	Inside 10	1	7	7.0	1	7	0	1	7	7.0	1	100.0
vs. Non-playoff	8	43	651	15.1	5	54	7	280	74	8.6	29	67.4	1st Down	37	549	14.8	5	54	6	207	50	9.2	21	56.8
vs. Own Division	7	53	678	12.8	7	39	6	218	79	8.7	32	60.4	2nd Down	22	307	14.0	3	38	3	130	38	8.0	15	68.2
Home	8	48	621	12.9	5	39	5	223	73	8.3	31	64.6	3rd Down Overall	18	174	9.7	1	23	0	41	28	7.4	13	72.2
Away	6	30	418	13.9	4	54	4	158	45	8.7	19	63.3	3rd D 0-2 to Go	6	51	8.5	0	23	0	17	7	5.7	6	100.0
Games 1-8	6	33	355	10.8	2	31	2	131	49	6.8	18	54.5	3rd D 3-7 to Go	5	41	8.2	0	14	0	9	8	6.4	4	80.0
Games 9-16	8	45	684	15.2	7	54	7	250	69	9.6	32	71.1	3rd D 8+ to Go	7	82	11.7	1	19	0	15	13	9.6	3	42.9
September	4	24	255	10.6	2	31	1	72	35	7.6	14	58.3	4th Down	1	9	9.0	0	9	0	3	2	6.0	1	100.0
October	2	9	100	11.1	0	30	1	59	14	4.6	4	44.4	Rec Behind Line	5	86	17.2	0	30	1	107	6	-4.2	3	60.0
November	4	21	384	18.3	4	54	4	155	31	10.9	18	85.7	1-10 yds	51	487	9.5	2	54	2	195	61	5.7	26	51.0
December	4	24	300	12.5	3	38	3	95	38	8.5	14	58.3	11-20 yds	16	270	16.9	3	25	1	44	27	14.1	15	93.8
Grass	4	20	266	13.3	3	54	2	121	29	7.3	11	55.0	21-30 yds	5	157	31.4	3	37	4	35	18	24.4	5	100.0
Turf	10	58	773	13.3	6	39	7	260	89	8.8	39	67.2	31+	1	39	39.0	1	39	1	0	4	39.0	1	100.0
Outdoor	9	24	337	14.0	3	54	3	138	35	8.3	14	58.3	Left Sideline	18	301	16.7	3	39	4	90	29	11.7	13	72.2
Indoor	5	54	702	13.0	6	39	6	243	83	8.5	36	66.7	Left Side	29	411	14.2	4	54	4	213	46	6.8	19	65.5
1st Half	-	44	536	12.2	3	34	4	198	65	7.7	25	56.8	Middle	11	121	11.0	1	17	0	22	16	9.0	7	63.6
2nd Half/OT	-	34	503	14.8	6	54	5	183	53	9.4	25	73.5	Right Side	12	132	11.0	1	23	0	36	14	8.0	8	66.7
Last 2 Min. Half	-	5	96	19.2	1	37	2	28	9	13.6	3	60.0	Right Sideline	8	74	9.3	0	25	1	20	13	6.8	3	37.5
4th qtr, +/-7 pts	-	8	112	14.0	2	37	1	20	12	11.5	6	70.0	Shotgun	16	163	10.2	0	23	0	73	27	5.6	10	62.5
Winning	-	30	420	14.0	3	39	3	157	52	8.8	22	73.3	2 Wide Receivers	2	22	11.0	0	12	0	12	2	5.0	2	100.0
Tied	-	22	344	15.6	2	54	3	173	28	7.8	16	72.7	3 Wide Receivers	10	134	13.4	1	39	1	21	14	11.3	8	80.0
Trailing	-	26	275	10.6	4	37	3	51	38	8.6	12	46.2	4+ Wide Receivers	66	883	13.4	8	54	8	348	102	8.1	40	60.6

1995 Incompletions

Type	Num	%of Inc	%of Att
Pass Dropped	7	17.5	5.9
Poor Throw	24	60.0	20.3
Pass Defensed	6	15.0	5.1
Pass Hit at Line	1	2.5	0.8
Other	2	5.0	1.7
Total	40	100.0	33.9

Game Logs (1-8)

Date	Opp	Result	Rec	Yds	Trgt	F-L	TD
09/03	Car	W 23-20	8	83	12	0-0	0
09/10	@SF	L 10-41	8	70	9	0-0	1
09/17	@NO	W 27-24	6	81	10	0-0	1
09/24	NYA	W 13-3	2	21	4	0-0	0
10/01	NE	W 30-17	3	52	7	1-0	0
10/12	@StL	L 19-21	-	-	-	-	-
10/22	@TB	W 24-21	-	-	-	-	-
10/29	Dal	L 13-28	6	48	7	0-0	0

Game Logs (9-16)

Date	Opp	Result	Rec	Yds	Trgt	F-L	TD
11/05	Det	W 34-22	6	75	7	0-0	0
11/12	@Buf	L 21-23	4	71	6	0-0	0
11/19	StL	W 31-6	10	184	14	0-0	3
11/26	@Ari	L 37-40	1	54	4	0-0	1
12/03	@Mia	L 20-21	3	40	4	0-0	1
12/10	NO	W 19-14	5	74	11	0-0	0
12/17	@Car	L 17-21	8	102	12	0-0	0
12/24	SF	W 28-27	8	84	11	0-0	2

Ed McCaffrey
Denver Broncos — WR

1995 Receiving Splits

	G	Rec	Yds	Avg	TD	Lg	Big	YAC	Trgt	Y@C	1st	1st%		Rec	Yds	Avg	TD	Lg	Big	YAC	Trgt	Y@C	1st	1st%
Total	16	39	477	12.2	2	35	2	157	63	8.2	25	64.1	Inside 20	5	38	7.6	1	13	0	23	11	3.0	3	60.0
vs. Playoff	7	13	130	10.0	0	35	1	42	26	6.8	5	38.5	Inside 10	2	7	3.5	1	4	0	1	5	3.0	1	50.0
vs. Non-playoff	9	26	347	13.3	2	27	1	115	37	8.9	20	76.9	1st Down	8	78	9.8	0	27	1	20	14	7.3	3	37.5
vs. Own Division	8	22	227	10.3	1	27	1	80	38	6.7	13	59.1	2nd Down	16	210	13.1	1	35	1	45	21	10.3	10	62.5
Home	8	18	255	14.2	1	35	1	86	28	9.4	13	72.2	3rd Down Overall	15	189	12.6	1	24	0	92	26	6.5	12	80.0
Away	8	21	222	10.6	1	27	1	71	35	7.2	12	57.1	3rd D 0-2 to Go	2	22	11.0	0	11	0	10	2	6.0	2	100.0
Games 1-8	8	18	213	11.8	0	35	1	72	33	7.8	11	61.1	3rd D 3-7 to Go	7	90	12.9	1	24	0	42	12	6.9	6	85.7
Games 9-16	8	21	264	12.6	2	27	1	85	30	8.5	14	66.7	3rd D 8+ to Go	6	77	12.8	0	19	0	40	12	6.2	4	66.7
September	4	11	131	11.9	0	35	1	41	18	8.2	6	54.5	4th Down	0	0	-	0	0	0	0	2	-	0	-
October	4	7	82	11.7	0	19	0	31	15	7.3	5	71.4	Rec Behind Line	0	0	-	0	0	0	0	2	-	0	-
November	4	4	70	17.5	1	23	0	8	10		4	100.0	1-10 yds	29	264	9.1	1	19	0	123	43	4.9	15	51.7
December	4	17	194	11.4	1	27	1	55	22	8.2	10	58.8	11-20 yds	8	151	18.9	1	24	0	28	14	15.4	8	100.0
Grass	12	35	425	12.1	2	35	2	136	52	8.3	21	60.0	21-30 yds	1	27	27.0	0	27	1	2	3	25.0	1	100.0
Turf	4	4	52	13.0	0	17	0	21	11	7.8	4	100.0	31+	1	35	35.0	0	35	1	4	1	31.0	1	100.0
Indoor	2	4	52	13.0	0	17	0	21	7	7.8	4	100.0	Left Sideline	2	22	11.0	0	19	0	12	4	5.0	1	50.0
Outdoor	14	35	425	12.1	2	35	2	136	56	8.3	21	60.0	Left Side	4	62	15.5	0	24	0	19	6	10.8	3	75.0
1st Half	-	18	219	12.2	0	27	1	99	27	6.7	12	66.7	Middle	16	181	11.3	1	23	0	60	19	7.6	8	50.0
2nd Half/OT	-	21	258	12.3	2	35	1	58	36	9.5	13	61.9	Right Side	10	142	14.2	0	35	2	33	18	10.9	7	70.0
Last 2 Min. Half	-	5	78	15.6	0	27	1	17	10	12.2	4	80.0	Right Sideline	7	70	10.0	1	13	0	33	16	5.3	6	85.7
4th qtr, +/-7 pts	-	3	49	16.3	0	19	0	7	5	14.0	3	100.0	Shotgun	24	296	12.3	0	27	1	88	35	8.7	15	62.5
Winning	-	13	198	15.2	1	35	1	55	20	11.0	9	69.2	2 Wide Receivers	5	91	18.2	1	35	1	14	11	15.4	4	80.0
Tied	-	9	117	13.0	0	27	1	45	13	8.0	6	66.7	3 Wide Receivers	19	236	12.4	0	27	1	86	30	7.9	12	63.2
Trailing	-	17	162	9.5	1	19	0	57	30	6.2	10	58.8	4+ Wide Receivers	14	132	9.4	1	18	0	44	21	6.3	8	57.1

1995 Incompletions

Type	Num	%of Inc	%of Att
Pass Dropped	1	4.2	1.6
Poor Throw	13	54.2	20.6
Pass Defensed	6	25.0	9.5
Pass Hit at Line	1	4.2	1.6
Other	3	12.5	4.8
Total	24	100.0	38.1

Game Logs (1-8)

Date	Opp	Result	Rush	Yds	Rec	Yds	Trgt	F-L	TD
09/03	Buf	W 22-7	0	0	4	52	5	0-0	0
09/10	@Dal	L 21-31	0	0	2	0	2	0-0	0
09/17	Was	W 38-31	0	0	5	70	6	0-0	0
09/24	@SD	L 6-17	0	0	2	9	5	0-0	0
10/01	@Sea	L 10-27	0	0	2	23	5	0-0	0
10/08	@NE	W 37-3	0	0	2	28	2	0-0	0
10/16	Oak	W 27-0	0	0	1	14	3	0-0	0
10/22	KC	L 7-21	0	0	2	17	5	0-0	0

Game Logs (9-16)

Date	Opp	Result	Rush	Yds	Rec	Yds	Trgt	F-L	TD
11/05	Ari	W 38-6	0	0	1	23	2	0-0	1
11/12	@Phi	L 13-31	0	0	2	0	2	0-0	0
11/19	SD	W 30-27	0	0	1	18	2	0-0	0
11/26	@Hou	L 33-42	0	0	2	29	2	0-0	0
12/03	Jac	W 31-23	1	-1	3	48	4	0-0	0
12/10	Sea	L 27-31	0	0	1	13	1	0-0	0
12/17	@KC	L 17-20	0	0	4	34	5	0-0	0
12/24	@Oak	W 31-28	0	0	9	99	12	1-1	2

Keenan McCardell
Cleveland Browns — WR

1995 Receiving Splits

	G	Rec	Yds	Avg	TD	Lg	Big	YAC	Trgt	Y@C	1st	1st%		Rec	Yds	Avg	TD	Lg	Big	YAC	Trgt	Y@C	1st	1st%
Total	16	56	709	12.7	4	36	7	239	89	8.4	32	57.1	Inside 20	4	47	11.8	3	16	0	6	10	10.3	4	100.0
vs. Playoff	7	28	381	13.6	0	36	4	159	40	7.9	15	53.6	Inside 10	1	6	6.0	1	6	0	0	4	6.0	1	100.0
vs. Non-playoff	9	28	328	11.7	4	32	3	80	49	8.9	17	60.7	1st Down	23	327	14.2	3	36	4	128	29	8.7	12	52.2
vs. Own Division	8	20	235	11.8	2	31	2	64	42	8.6	12	60.0	2nd Down	16	188	11.8	1	30	2	44	23	9.0	8	50.0
Home	8	31	433	14.0	3	36	5	152	46	9.1	19	61.3	3rd Down Overall	16	190	11.9	0	26	1	67	34	7.7	11	68.8
Away	8	25	276	11.0	1	31	2	87	43	7.6	13	52.0	3rd D 0-2 to Go	1	12	12.0	0	12	0	9	3	3.0	1	100.0
Games 1-8	8	24	317	13.2	3	32	3	93	36	9.3	13	54.2	3rd D 3-7 to Go	7	57	8.1	0	14	0	19	14	5.4	5	71.4
Games 9-16	8	32	392	12.3	1	36	4	146	53	7.7	19	59.4	3rd D 8+ to Go	8	121	15.1	0	26	1	39	17	10.3	5	62.5
September	4	16	231	14.4	3	32	3	60	24	10.7	9	56.3	4th Down	1	4	4.0	0	4	0	0	3	4.0	1	100.0
October	4	8	86	10.8	0	22	0	33	12	6.6	4	50.0	Rec Behind Line	1	0	0.0	0	0	0	0	1	0.0	0	0.0
November	4	10	164	16.4	0	36	3	62	22	10.2	7	70.0	1-10 yds	40	388	9.7	1	36	2	182	57	5.2	18	45.0
December	4	22	228	10.4	1	31	1	84	31	6.5	12	54.5	11-20 yds	11	199	18.1	2	26	1	43	19	14.2	10	90.9
Grass	11	48	619	12.9	3	36	6	222	70	8.3	29	60.4	21-30 yds	3	90	30.0	0	31	3	14	8	25.3	3	100.0
Turf	5	8	90	11.3	1	29	1	17	19	9.1	3	37.5	31+	1	32	32.0	1	32	1	0	4	32.0	1	100.0
Outdoor	3	48	619	12.9	3	36	6	222	72	8.3	29	60.4	Left Sideline	20	187	9.4	2	32	1	50	28	6.9	10	50.0
Indoor	13	8	90	11.3	1	29	1	17	17	9.1	3	37.5	Left Side	10	162	16.2	0	36	2	63	16	9.9	9	90.0
1st Half	-	22	269	12.2	4	32	1	68	33	9.1	12	54.5	Middle	10	148	14.8	2	22	0	30	16	11.8	6	60.0
2nd Half/OT	-	34	440	12.9	0	36	6	171	56	7.9	20	58.8	Right Side	12	156	13.0	0	31	3	84	16	6.0	5	41.7
Last 2 Min. Half	-	9	133	14.8	3	32	2	26	14	11.9	7	77.8	Right Sideline	4	56	14.0	0	29	1	12	13	11.0	2	50.0
4th qtr, +/-7 pts	-	9	131	14.6	0	31	2	39	12	10.2	6	66.7	Shotgun	0	0	-	0	0	0	0	0	0	-	0	-
Winning	-	16	209	13.1	3	32	2	72	26	8.6	9	56.3	2 Wide Receivers	5	71	14.2	1	29	1	14	11	11.4	3	60.0
Tied	-	7	106	15.1	1	29	1	25	9	11.6	5	71.4	3 Wide Receivers	48	606	12.6	3	36	6	226	68	7.9	29	60.4
Trailing	-	33	394	11.9	0	36	4	142	54	7.6	18	54.5	4+ Wide Receivers	3	32	10.7	0	16	0	-1	10	11.0	0	0.0

1995 Incompletions

Type	Num	%of Inc	%of Att
Pass Dropped	3	9.1	3.4
Poor Throw	13	39.4	14.6
Pass Defensed	5	15.2	5.6
Pass Hit at Line	0	0.0	0.0
Other	12	36.4	13.5
Total	33	100.0	37.1

Game Logs (1-8)

Date	Opp	Result	Rec	Yds	Trgt	F-L	TD
09/03	@NE	L 14-17	1	14	3	0-0	0
09/10	TB	W 22-6	6	79	6	0-0	2
09/17	@Hou	W 14-7	3	53	7	0-0	1
09/24	KC	W 35-17	6	85	8	0-0	0
10/02	Buf	L 19-22	5	60	5	0-0	0
10/08	@Det	L 20-38	2	14	6	0-0	0
10/22	Jac	L 15-23	1	12	1	0-0	0
10/29	@Cin	W 29-26	0	0	0	0-0	0

Game Logs (9-16)

Date	Opp	Result	Rec	Yds	Trgt	F-L	TD
11/05	Hou	L 10-37	4	39	10	0-0	0
11/13	@Pit	L 3-20	0	0	2	0-0	0
11/19	GB	L 20-31	4	102	6	0-0	0
11/26	Pit	L 17-20	2	23	4	0-0	0
12/03	@SD	L 13-31	9	97	9	0-0	0
12/09	@Min	L 11-27	3	23	4	0-0	0
12/17	Cin	W 26-10	3	33	6	0-0	1
12/24	@Jac	L 21-24	7	75	12	0-0	0

O.J. McDuffie
Miami Dolphins — WR

1995 Receiving Splits

	G	Rec	Yds	Avg	TD	Lg	Big	YAC	Trgt	Y@C	1st	1st%		Rec	Yds	Avg	TD	Lg	Big	YAC	Trgt	Y@C	1st	1st%
Total	16	62	819	13.2	8	48	6	266	92	8.9	50	80.6	Inside 20	11	102	9.3	7	19	0	34	15	6.2	10	90.9
vs. Playoff	9	36	477	13.3	4	35	4	176	55	8.4	30	83.3	Inside 10	4	19	4.8	4	7	0	2	5	4.3	4	100.0
vs. Non-playoff	7	26	342	13.2	4	48	1	90	37	9.7	20	76.9	1st Down	28	394	14.1	2	35	2	127	41	9.5	22	78.6
vs. Own Division	8	26	350	13.5	3	32	2	102	37	9.5	20	76.9	2nd Down	9	138	15.3	1	32	1	42	20	10.7	6	66.7
Home	8	31	396	12.8	3	35	3	140	48	8.3	26	83.9	3rd Down Overall	24	273	11.4	5	48	2	89	30	7.7	21	87.5
Away	8	31	423	13.6	5	48	2	126	44	9.6	24	77.4	3rd D 0-2 to Go	3	18	6.0	0	7	0	4	3	4.7	3	100.0
Games 1-8	8	29	354	12.2	2	35	2	96	39	8.9	23	79.3	3rd D 3-7 to Go	12	78	6.5	4	16	0	19	15	4.9	9	75.0
Games 9-16	8	33	465	14.1	6	48	3	170	53	8.9	27	81.8	3rd D 8+ to Go	9	177	19.7	1	48	2	66	12	12.3	9	100.0
September	3	7	100	14.3	0	35	1	48	9	7.4	6	85.7	4th Down	1	14	14.0	0	14	0	8	1	6.0	1	100.0
October	5	22	254	11.5	2	26	1	48	30	9.4	17	77.3	Rec Behind Line	1	5	5.0	0	5	0	6	1	-1.0	0	0.0
November	4	16	195	12.2	4	22	0	54	26	8.8	12	75.0	1-10 yds	40	369	9.2	5	22	0	141	57	5.7	29	72.5
December	4	17	270	15.9	2	48	3	116	27	9.1	15	88.2	11-20 yds	18	369	20.5	3	48	3	106	24	14.6	18	100.0
Grass	10	32	403	12.6	3	35	3	140	51	8.2	27	84.4	21-30 yds	3	76	25.3	0	30	2	13	7	21.0	3	100.0
Turf	6	30	416	13.9	5	48	2	126	41	9.7	23	76.7	31+	0	0	-	0	0	0	0	3	-	0	-
Indoor	3	16	223	13.9	4	48	1	70	24	9.6	11	68.8	Left Sideline	12	146	12.2	0	19	0	26	16	10.0	10	83.3
Outdoor	13	46	596	13.0	4	35	4	196	68	8.7	39	84.8	Left Side	15	188	12.5	3	35	1	66	23	8.1	11	73.3
1st Half	-	25	320	12.8	2	35	3	112	37	8.3	18	72.0	Middle	16	259	16.2	1	48	3	106	20	9.6	11	68.8
2nd Half/OT	-	37	499	13.5	6	48	2	154	55	9.3	32	86.5	Right Side	11	108	9.8	0	17	0	33	16	6.8	10	90.9
Last 2 Min. Half	-	10	122	12.2	2	19	0	25	17	9.7	5	50.0	Right Sideline	8	118	14.8	2	32	1	35	17	10.4	8	100.0
4th qtr, +/-7 pts	-	10	124	12.4	1	19	0	29	14	9.5	10	100.0	Shotgun	40	521	13.0	5	48	2	147	58	9.4	30	75.0
Winning	-	16	190	11.9	2	48	1	85	26	6.6	14	87.5	2 Wide Receivers	17	254	14.9	3	35	3	108	28	8.6	17	100.0
Tied	-	11	180	16.4	0	35	3	59	18	11.0	9	81.8	3 Wide Receivers	13	142	10.9	1	20	0	25	18	9.0	10	76.9
Trailing	-	35	449	12.8	6	30	1	122	48	9.3	27	77.1	4+ Wide Receivers	32	423	13.2	4	48	2	133	46	9.1	23	71.9

1995 Incompletions

Type	Num	%of Inc	%of Att
Pass Dropped	6	20.0	6.5
Poor Throw	16	53.3	17.4
Pass Defensed	2	6.7	2.2
Pass Hit at Line	0	0.0	0.0
Other	6	20.0	6.5
Total	30	100.0	32.6

Game Logs (1-8)

Date	Opp	Result	Rush	Yds	Rec	Yds	Trgt	F-L	TD
09/03	NYA	W 52-14	0	0	3	35	4	0-0	0
09/10	@NE	W 20-3	0	0	0	0	0	1-1	0
09/18	Pit	W 23-10	0	0	4	65	5	0-0	0
10/01	@Cin	W 26-23	0	0	5	54	5	0-0	0
10/08	Ind	L 24-27	0	0	2	15	2	0-0	0
10/15	@NO	L 30-33	0	0	7	86	10	1-1	1
10/22	@NYA	L 16-17	0	0	5	60	7	0-0	0
10/29	Buf	W 23-6	0	0	3	39	6	0-0	0

Game Logs (9-16)

Date	Opp	Result	Rush	Yds	Rec	Yds	Trgt	F-L	TD
11/05	@SD	W 24-14	0	0	1	7	3	0-0	0
11/12	NE	L 17-34	1	11	3	46	5	0-0	1
11/20	SF	L 20-44	0	0	6	66	10	2-1	1
11/26	@Ind	L 28-36	0	0	6	76	8	0-0	2
12/03	Atl	W 21-20	0	0	6	96	8	0-0	0
12/11	KC	W 13-6	0	0	4	34	8	0-0	1
12/17	@Buf	L 20-23	1	0	4	79	5	0-0	0
12/24	@StL	W 41-22	1	-5	3	61	6	0-0	0

Tony McGee — Cincinnati Bengals — TE

1995 Receiving Splits

	G	Rec	Yds	Avg	TD	Lg	Big	YAC	Trgt	Y@C	1st	1st%		Rec	Yds	Avg	TD	Lg	Big	YAC	Trgt	Y@C	1st	1st%
Total	16	55	754	13.7	4	41	6	282	92	8.6	31	56.4	Inside 20	4	23	5.8	3	12	0	10	8	3.3	3	75.0
vs. Playoff	5	17	263	15.5	2	41	2	135	26	7.5	9	52.9	Inside 10	2	6	3.0	2	5	0	0	2	3.0	2	100.0
vs. Non-playoff	11	38	491	12.9	2	35	4	147	66	9.1	22	57.9	1st Down	23	315	13.7	2	34	2	124	34	8.3	13	56.5
vs. Own Division	8	26	371	14.3	3	35	3	121	41	9.6	16	61.5	2nd Down	21	265	12.6	1	41	2	105	33	7.6	12	57.1
Home	8	28	336	12.0	3	35	1	132	46	7.3	14	50.0	3rd Down Overall	10	147	14.7	1	35	1	45	23	10.2	5	50.0
Away	8	27	418	15.5	1	41	5	150	46	9.9	17	63.0	3rd D 0-2 to Go	0	0	-	0	0	0	0	2	-	0	-
Games 1-8	8	32	474	14.8	2	41	4	187	49	9.0	19	59.4	3rd D 3-7 to Go	2	10	5.0	1	5	0	1	8	4.5	2	100.0
Games 9-16	8	23	280	12.2	2	34	2	95	43	8.0	12	52.2	3rd D 8+ to Go	8	137	17.1	0	35	1	44	13	11.6	3	37.5
September	4	20	314	15.7	1	41	4	122	31	9.6	10	50.0	4th Down	1	27	27.0	0	27	1	8	2	19.0	1	100.0
October	4	12	160	13.3	1	24	0	65	18	7.9	9	75.0	Rec Behind Line	2	8	4.0	0	7	0	8	4	0.0	0	0.0
November	4	13	154	11.8	1	34	2	59	23	7.3	6	46.2	1-10 yds	33	302	9.2	3	29	1	161	53	4.3	15	45.5
December	4	10	126	12.6	1	24	0	36	20	9.0	6	60.0	11-20 yds	17	362	21.3	1	41	4	102	29	15.3	13	76.5
Grass	4	11	177	16.1	0	34	2	41	22	12.4	8	72.7	21-30 yds	3	82	27.3	0	34	1	11	6	23.7	3	100.0
Turf	12	44	577	13.1	4	41	4	241	70	7.6	23	52.3	31+	0	0	-	0	0	0	0	0	-	0	-
Outdoor	3	42	542	12.9	4	35	3	192	71	8.3	24	57.1	Left Sideline	7	91	13.0	1	29	1	55	11	5.1	4	57.1
Indoor	13	13	212	16.3	0	41	3	90	21	9.4	7	53.8	Left Side	4	28	7.0	0	8	0	8	10	5.0	1	25.0
1st Half	-	26	361	13.9	0	41	2	121	42	9.2	14	53.8	Middle	26	407	15.7	2	35	4	131	45	10.6	16	61.5
2nd Half/OT	-	29	393	13.6	4	35	4	161	50	8.0	17	58.6	Right Side	12	117	9.8	0	19	0	41	16	6.3	5	41.7
Last 2 Min. Half	-	9	126	14.0	0	21	0	33	16	10.3	7	77.8	Right Sideline	6	111	18.5	1	41	1	47	10	10.7	5	83.3
4th qtr, +/-7 pts	-	4	57	14.3	1	24	0	15	12	10.5	3	75.0	Shotgun	0	0	-	0	0	0	0	0	-	0	-
Winning	-	9	105	11.7	2	29	1	66	16	4.3	4	44.4	2 Wide Receivers	39	630	16.2	3	41	6	229	64	10.3	26	66.7
Tied	-	13	168	12.9	0	30	1	45	23	9.5	4	69.2	3 Wide Receivers	11	79	7.2	0	13	0	36	18	3.9	2	18.2
Trailing	-	33	481	14.6	2	41	4	171	53	9.4	18	54.5	4+ Wide Receivers	4	44	11.0	0	15	0	17	9	6.8	2	50.0

1995 Incompletions

Type	Num	%of Inc	%of Att
Pass Dropped	11	29.7	12.0
Poor Throw	15	40.5	16.3
Pass Defensed	5	13.5	5.4
Pass Hit at Line	2	5.4	2.2
Other	4	10.8	4.3
Total	37	100.0	40.2

Game Logs (1-8)

Date	Opp	Result	Rec	Yds	Trgt	F-L	TD
09/03	@Ind	W 24-21	6	118	8	1-1	0
09/10	Jac	W 24-17	0	0	1	0-0	0
09/17	@Sea	L 21-24	6	87	11	0-0	0
09/24	Hou	L 28-38	8	109	11	1-1	1
10/01	Mia	L 23-26	2	43	5	0-0	0
10/08	@TB	L 16-19	3	25	5	0-0	0
10/19	@Pit	W 27-9	3	29	3	0-0	1
10/29	Cle	L 26-29	4	63	5	0-0	0

Game Logs (9-16)

Date	Opp	Result	Rec	Yds	Trgt	F-L	TD
11/05	Oak	L 17-20	4	27	6	0-0	0
11/12	@Hou	W 32-25	1	7	2	0-0	0
11/19	Pit	L 31-49	4	42	6	0-0	1
11/26	@Jac	W 17-13	4	78	9	0-0	0
12/03	@GB	L 10-24	2	31	4	0-0	0
12/10	Chi	W 16-10	2	13	5	0-0	0
12/17	@Cle	L 10-26	2	43	4	0-0	0
12/24	Min	L 27-24	4	39	7	0-0	0

Steve McNair — Houston Oilers — QB

1995 Passing Splits

	G	Att	Cm	Pct	Yds	Yd/Att	TD	Int	1st	YAC	Big	Sk	Rtg		Att	Cm	Pct	Yds	Yd/Att	TD	Int	1st	YAC	Big	Sk	Rtg
Total	6	80	41	51.3	569	7.1	3	1	23	254	6	6	81.7	Inside 20	6	1	16.7	12	2.0	0	1	1	0	0	1	0.0
vs. Playoff	2	53	28	52.8	371	7.0	2	1	13	149	4	3	80.0	Inside 10	1	0	0.0	0	0.0	0	0	0	0	0	1	0.0
vs. Non-playoff	4	27	13	48.1	198	7.3	1	0	10	105	2	3	85.1	1st Down	26	16	61.5	185	7.1	0	1	6	84	1	2	67.0
vs. Own Division	2	0	0	-	0	-	0	0	0	0	0	1	-	2nd Down	28	14	50.0	218	7.8	2	0	9	103	3	0	100.0
Home	4	54	29	53.7	401	7.4	2	1	18	173	3	4	82.4	3rd Down Overall	25	11	44.0	166	6.6	1	0	8	67	2	4	79.7
Away	2	26	12	46.2	168	6.5	1	0	5	81	3	2	80.3	3rd D 0-5 to Go	7	4	57.1	68	9.7	1	0	4	46	1	1	129.8
Games 1-8	2	0	0	-	0	-	0	0	0	0	0	0	-	3rd D 6+ to Go	18	7	38.9	98	5.4	0	0	4	21	1	3	57.2
Games 9-16	4	80	41	51.3	569	7.1	3	1	23	254	6	6	81.7	4th Down	1	0	0.0	0	0.0	0	0	0	0	0	0	39.6
September	0	0	0	-	0	-	0	0	0	0	0	0	-	Rec Behind Line	13	9	69.2	55	4.2	0	0	3	80	0	0	77.4
October	2	0	0	-	0	-	0	0	0	0	0	0	-	1-10 yds	37	19	51.4	183	4.9	1	1	8	107	1	0	63.2
November	1	0	0	-	0	-	0	0	0	0	0	0	-	11-20 yds	21	8	38.1	133	6.3	0	0	7	21	0	0	60.2
December	3	80	41	51.3	569	7.1	3	1	23	254	6	5	81.7	21-30 yds	5	3	60.0	115	23.0	1	0	3	39	3	0	143.8
Grass	1	0	0	-	0	-	0	0	0	0	0	1	-	31+	4	2	50.0	83	20.8	1	0	2	7	2	0	135.4
Turf	5	80	41	51.3	569	7.1	3	1	23	254	6	5	81.7	Left Sideline	19	8	42.1	178	9.4	1	0	3	93	3	0	93.8
Indoor	4	54	29	53.7	401	7.4	2	1	18	173	3	4	82.4	Left Side	20	9	45.0	83	4.2	0	0	5	52	0	2	56.9
Outdoor	2	26	12	46.2	168	6.5	1	0	5	81	3	2	80.3	Middle	10	3	30.0	45	4.5	0	1	1	40	1	2	79.2
1st Half	-	29	12	41.4	130	4.5	1	0	6	78	2	3	66.7	Right Side	15	12	80.0	106	7.1	0	1	5	83	0	1	68.3
2nd Half/OT	-	51	29	56.9	439	8.6	2	1	17	176	4	3	90.2	Right Sideline	16	9	56.3	157	9.8	1	0	6	157	2	1	110.7
Last 2 Min. Half	-	11	4	36.4	64	5.8	0	0	2	28	0	2	56.6	2 Wide Receivers	26	18	69.2	176	6.8	0	0	7	97	1	1	94.0
4th qtr, +/-7 pts	-	14	7	50.0	93	6.6	0	1	4	33	0	1	41.7	3+ WR	54	23	42.6	393	7.3	1	1	16	157	5	5	78.7
Winning	-	39	20	51.3	327	8.4	2	0	12	150	5	4	96.8	Attempts 1-10	30	14	46.7	157	5.2	1	0	7	75	2	0	73.9
Tied	-	14	5	35.7	39	2.8	0	0	3	36	0	4	44.3	Attempts 11-20	30	18	60.0	233	7.8	1	0	9	86	2	0	81.7
Trailing	-	27	16	59.3	203	7.5	1	1	8	68	1	2	79.7	Attempts 21+	20	9	45.0	179	9.0	1	0	7	93	2	0	93.5

1995 Incompletions

Type	Num	% of Inc	% of Att
Pass Dropped	4	10.3	5.0
Poor Throw	17	43.6	21.3
Pass Defensed	7	17.9	8.8
Pass Hit at Line	2	5.1	2.5
Other	9	23.1	11.3
Total	39	100.0	48.8

Game Logs (1-8)

Date	Opp	Result	Att	Cm	Pct	Yds	TD	Int	Lg	Sk	F-L
09/03	@Jac	W 10-3	-	-	-	-	-	-	-	-	-
09/10	Pit	L 17-34	-	-	-	-	-	-	-	-	-
09/17	Cle	L 7-14	-	-	-	-	-	-	-	-	-
09/24	@Cin	W 38-28	-	-	-	-	-	-	-	-	-
10/01	Jac	L 16-17	0	0	-	0	0	0	0	0	0-0
10/08	@Min	L 17-23	-	-	-	-	-	-	-	-	-
10/22	@Chi	L 32-35	-	-	-	-	-	-	-	-	-
10/29	TB	W 19-7	0	0	-	0	0	0	0	0	0-0

Game Logs (9-16)

Date	Opp	Result	Att	Cm	Pct	Yds	TD	Int	Lg	Sk	F-L
11/05	@Cle	W 37-10	0	0	-	0	0	0	0	1	0-0
11/12	Cin	L 25-32	-	-	-	-	-	-	-	-	-
11/19	@KC	L 13-20	-	-	-	-	-	-	-	-	-
11/26	Den	W 42-33	-	-	-	-	-	-	-	-	-
12/03	@Pit	L 7-21	-	-	-	-	-	-	-	-	-
12/10	Det	L 17-24	27	16	59.3	203	1	1	39	2	1-0
12/17	NYA	W 23-6	27	13	48.1	198	1	0	53	2	2-0
12/24	@Buf	W 28-17	26	12	46.2	168	1	0	44	1	0-0

Todd McNair
Houston Oilers — RB

1995 Receiving Splits

	G	Rec	Yds	Avg	TD	Lg	Big	YAC	Trgt	Y@C	1st	1st%		Rec	Yds	Avg	TD	Lg	Big	YAC	Trgt	Y@C	1st	1st%
Total	15	60	501	8.4	1	25	1	357	84	2.4	19	31.7	Inside 20	3	21	7.0	0	9	0	21	5	0.0	0	0.0
vs. Playoff	5	17	143	8.4	0	24	0	102	26	2.4	5	29.4	Inside 10	1	4	4.0	0	4	0	6	1	-2.0	0	0.0
vs. Non-playoff	10	43	358	8.3	1	25	1	255	58	2.4	14	32.6	1st Down	24	187	7.8	0	25	1	145	34	1.8	5	20.8
vs. Own Division	8	38	296	7.8	0	25	1	224	52	1.9	9	23.7	2nd Down	18	134	7.4	1	24	0	91	25	2.4	3	16.7
Home	8	38	324	8.5	0	24	0	228	54	2.5	13	34.2	3rd Down Overall	16	168	10.5	0	24	0	115	22	3.3	10	62.5
Away	7	22	177	8.0	1	25	1	129	30	2.2	6	27.3	3rd D 0-2 to Go	1	15	15.0	0	15	0	12	1	3.0	1	100.0
Games 1-8	7	40	349	8.7	1	25	1	235	52	2.9	14	35.0	3rd D 3-7 to Go	7	80	11.4	0	18	0	53	10	3.9	7	100.0
Games 9-16	8	20	152	7.6	0	20	0	122	32	1.5	5	25.0	3rd D 8+ to Go	8	73	9.1	0	24	0	50	11	2.9	2	25.0
September	4	25	208	8.3	0	25	1	148	31	2.4	9	36.0	4th Down	2	12	6.0	0	7	0	6	3	3.0	1	50.0
October	3	15	141	9.4	1	24	0	87	21	3.6	5	33.3	Rec Behind Line	20	100	5.0	0	18	0	135	23	-1.8	3	15.0
November	4	12	95	7.9	0	20	0	73	18	1.8	3	25.0	1-10 yds	36	323	9.0	0	25	1	207	53	3.2	12	33.3
December	4	8	57	7.1	0	15	0	49	14	1.0	2	25.0	11-20 yds	3	54	18.0	0	20	0	15	5	13.0	3	100.0
Grass	4	15	98	6.5	1	24	0	53	19	3.0	3	20.0	21-30 yds	1	24	24.0	1	24	0	0	3	24.0	1	100.0
Turf	11	45	403	9.0	0	25	1	304	65	2.2	16	35.6	31+	0	0	-	0	0	0	0	0	-	0	0.0
Indoor	8	38	324	8.5	0	24	0	228	54	2.5	13	34.2	Left Sideline	9	93	10.3	0	25	1	45	12	5.3	4	44.4
Outdoor	7	22	177	8.0	1	25	1	129	30	2.2	6	27.3	Left Side	10	68	6.8	0	14	0	43	13	2.5	1	10.0
1st Half	-	27	221	8.2	1	25	1	135	38	3.2	10	37.0	Middle	19	163	8.6	0	24	0	155	26	0.4	6	31.6
2nd Half/OT	-	33	280	8.5	0	24	0	222	46	1.8	9	27.3	Right Side	11	89	8.1	0	20	0	62	16	2.5	3	27.3
Last 2 Min. Half	-	11	105	9.5	0	25	1	90	13	1.4	5	45.5	Right Sideline	11	88	8.0	0	16	0	52	17	3.3	5	45.5
4th qtr, +/-7 pts	-	6	29	4.8	0	15	0	23	11	1.0	1	16.7	Shotgun	0	0	-	0	0	0	0	0	-	0	-
Winning	-	15	144	9.6	0	25	1	118	20	1.7	7	46.7	2 Wide Receivers	14	93	6.6	0	18	0	55	15	2.7	3	21.4
Tied	-	6	42	7.0	0	18	0	24	9	3.0	2	33.3	3 Wide Receivers	45	399	8.9	1	25	1	299	67	2.2	16	35.6
Trailing	-	39	315	8.1	1	24	0	215	55	2.6	10	41.8	4+ Wide Receivers	1	9	9.0	0	9	0	3	2	6.0	0	0.0

1995 Incompletions

Type	Num	%of Inc	%of Att
Pass Dropped	10	41.7	11.9
Poor Throw	6	25.0	7.1
Pass Defensed	4	16.7	4.8
Pass Hit at Line	2	8.3	2.4
Other	2	8.3	2.4
Total	24	100.0	28.6

Game Logs (1-8)

Date	Opp	Result	Rush	Yds	Rec	Yds	Trgt	F-L	TD
09/03	@Jac	W 10-3	1	3	4	10	4	0-0	0
09/10	Pit	L 17-34	0	0	7	66	9	0-0	0
09/17	Cle	L 7-14	0	0	9	70	13	0-0	0
09/24	@Cin	W 38-28	0	0	5	62	5	0-0	0
10/01	Jac	L 16-17	1	4	3	24	6	0-0	0
10/08	@Min	L 17-23	-	-	-	-	-	-	-
10/22	@Chi	L 32-35	1	7	6	52	7	0-1	0
10/29	TB	W 19-7	1	8	6	65	8	0-0	0

Game Logs (9-16)

Date	Opp	Result	Rush	Yds	Rec	Yds	Trgt	F-L	TD
11/05	@Cle	W 37-10	1	5	3	16	3	0-0	0
11/12	Cin	L 25-32	4	37	5	31	7	0-0	0
11/19	@KC	L 13-20	4	44	2	20	5	1-1	0
11/26	Den	W 42-33	1	-7	2	28	3	0-0	0
12/03	@Pit	L 7-21	4	18	2	17	5	0-0	0
12/10	Det	L 24-27	0	0	6	40	6	0-0	0
12/17	NYA	W 23-6	0	0	0	0	0	0-0	0
12/24	@Buf	W 28-17	1	17	0	0	1	0-0	0

Natrone Means
San Diego Chargers — RB

1995 Rushing and Receiving Splits

	G	Rush	Yds	Avg	Lg	TD	1st	Stf	YdL	Rec	Yds	Avg	TD		Rush	Yds	Avg	Lg	TD	1st	Stf	YdL	Rec	Yds	Avg	TD
Total	10	186	730	3.9	36	5	39	19	44	7	46	6.6	0	Inside 20	30	76	2.5	13	5	8	4	8	0	0	-	0
vs. Playoff	6	92	349	3.8	21	2	17	10	24	6	38	6.3	0	Inside 10	16	19	1.2	7	4	4	4	8	0	0	-	0
vs. Non-playoff	4	94	381	4.1	36	3	22	9	20	1	8	8.0	0	1st Down	110	468	4.3	35	1	11	10	20	2	7	3.5	0
vs. Own Division	5	118	414	3.5	36	4	25	16	38	6	41	6.8	0	2nd Down	62	186	3.0	21	2	20	7	21	5	39	7.8	0
Home	4	77	326	4.2	26	2	20	6	16	1	5	5.0	0	3rd Down Overall	14	76	5.4	36	2	8	2	3	0	0	-	0
Away	6	109	404	3.7	36	3	19	13	28	6	41	6.8	0	3rd D 0-2 to Go	12	71	5.9	36	2	8	2	3	0	0	-	0
Games 1-8	8	181	718	4.0	36	5	39	19	44	6	41	6.8	0	3rd D 3-7 to Go	1	2	2.0	2	0	0	0	0	0	0	-	0
Games 9-16	2	5	12	2.4	9	0	0	0	0	1	5	5.0	0	3rd D 8+ to Go	1	3	3.0	3	0	0	0	0	0	0	-	0
September	4	91	412	4.5	35	2	24	6	17	0	0	-	0	4th Down	0	0	-	0	0	0	0	0	0	0	-	0
October	4	90	306	3.4	36	3	15	13	27	6	41	6.8	0	Left Sideline	5	59	11.8	35	0	3	0	0	2	16	8.0	0
November	1	2	6	3.0	3	0	0	0	0	1	5	5.0	0	Left Side	41	172	4.2	26	2	10	3	9	1	5	5.0	0
December	1	3	6	2.0	3	0	0	0	0	0	0	-	0	Middle	72	236	3.3	21	2	13	6	10	1	5	5.0	0
Grass	6	116	419	3.6	35	3	26	14	37	6	38	6.3	0	Right Side	59	169	2.9	16	0	8	10	25	1	-1	-1.0	0
Turf	4	70	311	4.4	36	2	13	5	7	1	8	8.0	0	Right Sideline	9	94	10.4	36	1	5	0	0	2	21	10.5	0
Indoor	2	29	97	3.3	36	1	3	4	5	1	8	8.0	0	Shotgun	0	0	-	0	0	0	0	0	0	0	-	0
Outdoor	8	157	633	4.0	35	4	36	15	39	6	38	6.3	0	2 Wide Receivers	125	523	4.2	35	2	23	12	33	7	46	6.6	0
1st Half	-	94	418	4.4	36	2	22	6	12	4	32	8.0	0	3 Wide Receivers	7	12	1.7	8	0	2	2	5	0	0	-	0
2nd Half/OT	-	92	312	3.4	21	1	17	13	32	3	14	4.7	0	4+ Wide Receivers	0	0	-	0	0	0	0	0	0	0	-	0
Last 2 Min. Half	-	6	21	3.5	7	1	2	1	2	0	0	-	0	Carries 1-5	45	216	4.8	35	0	9	2	3	0	0	-	0
4th qtr, +/-7 pts	-	28	89	3.2	19	1	6	5	11	1	8	8.0	0	Carries 6-10	40	110	2.8	13	2	8	5	12	0	0	-	0
Winning	-	65	282	4.3	36	2	15	8	18	0	0	-	0	Carries 11-15	40	199	5.0	36	2	9	3	7	0	0	-	0
Tied	-	48	155	3.2	26	1	9	6	14	6	38	6.3	0	Carries 16-20	33	147	4.5	19	0	8	2	3	0	0	-	0
Trailing	-	73	293	4.0	35	2	15	5	12	1	8	8.0	0	Carries 21+	28	58	2.1	10	1	5	7	19	0	0	-	0

1995 Incompletions

Type	Num	%of Inc	% Att
Pass Dropped	0	0.0	0.0
Poor Throw	0	0.0	0.0
Pass Defensed	1	50.0	11.1
Pass Hit at Line	1	50.0	11.1
Other	0	0.0	0.0
Total	2	100.0	22.2

Game Logs (1-8)

Date	Opp	Result	Rush	Yds	Rec	Yds	Trgt	F-L	TD
09/03	@Oak	L 7-17	15	60	0	0	0	1-1	0
09/10	Sea	W 14-10	26	115	0	0	0	0-0	0
09/17	@Phi	W 27-21	23	122	0	0	0	1-1	0
09/24	Den	W 17-6	27	115	0	0	0	0-0	2
10/01	@Pit	L 16-31	18	92	0	0	1	0-0	0
10/09	@KC	L 23-29	24	33	5	33	5	0-0	0
10/15	Dal	W 9-23	22	90	0	0	0	0-0	0
10/22	@Sea	W 35-25	26	91	1	8	1	0-0	1

Game Logs (9-16)

Date	Opp	Result	Rush	Yds	Rec	Yds	Trgt	F-L	TD
11/05	Mia	L 14-24	2	6	1	5	1	0-0	0
11/12	KC	L 7-22	-	-	-	-	-	-	-
11/19	@Den	L 27-30	-	-	-	-	-	-	-
11/27	Oak	W 12-6	-	-	-	-	-	-	-
12/03	Cle	W 31-13	-	-	-	-	-	-	-
12/09	Ari	W 28-25	-	-	-	-	-	-	-
12/17	@Ind	W 27-24	3	6	0	0	0	0-0	0
12/23	@NYN	W 27-17	-	-	-	-	-	-	-

David Meggett

1995 Receiving Splits

	G	Rec	Yds	Avg	TD	Lg	Big	YAC	Trgt	Y@C	1st	1st%
Total	16	52	334	6.4	0	19	0	266	86	1.3	17	32.7
vs. Playoff	10	30	188	6.3	0	19	0	154	55	1.1	10	33.3
vs. Non-playoff	6	22	146	6.6	0	18	0	112	31	1.5	7	31.8
vs. Own Division	8	19	126	6.6	0	18	0	107	33	1.0	8	42.1
Home	8	33	209	6.3	0	18	0	184	47	0.8	11	33.3
Away	8	19	125	6.6	0	19	0	82	39	2.3	6	31.6
Games 1-8	8	37	217	5.9	0	19	0	184	60	0.9	12	32.4
Games 9-16	8	15	117	7.8	0	15	0	82	26	2.3	5	33.3
September	3	12	55	4.6	0	12	0	45	23	0.8	2	16.7
October	5	25	162	6.5	0	19	0	139	37	0.9	10	40.0
November	4	7	60	8.6	0	14	0	45	13	2.1	4	57.1
December	4	8	57	7.1	0	15	0	37	13	2.5	1	12.5
Grass	11	42	269	6.4	0	18	0	222	63	1.1	14	33.3
Turf	5	10	65	6.5	0	19	0	44	23	2.1	3	30.0
Indoor	2	6	26	4.3	0	19	0	18	11	1.3	1	16.7
Outdoor	14	46	308	6.7	0	18	0	248	75	1.3	16	34.8
1st Half	-	24	167	7.0	0	19	0	140	39	1.1	11	45.8
2nd Half/OT	-	28	167	6.0	0	18	0	126	47	1.5	6	21.4
Last 2 Min. Half	-	9	64	7.1	0	18	0	74	20	-1.1	4	44.4
4th qtr, +/-7 pts	-	7	30	4.3	0	18	0	21	11	1.3	1	14.3
Winning	-	7	48	6.9	0	18	0	46	11	0.3	3	42.9
Tied	-	10	95	9.5	0	19	0	62	15	3.3	6	60.0
Trailing	-	35	191	5.5	0	18	0	158	60	0.9	8	22.9

	Rec	Yds	Avg	TD	Lg	Big	YAC	Trgt	Y@C	1st	1st%
Inside 20	5	25	5.0	0	10	0	8	14	3.4	1	20.0
Inside 10	3	9	3.0	0	4	0	3	8	2.0	0	0.0
1st Down	19	115	6.1	0	18	0	79	29	1.9	4	21.1
2nd Down	19	130	6.8	0	18	0	102	24	1.5	7	36.8
3rd Down Overall	14	89	6.4	0	15	0	85	31	0.3	6	42.9
3rd D 0-2 to Go	1	10	10.0	0	10	0	5	1	5.0	1	100.0
3rd D 3-7 to Go	7	38	5.4	0	15	0	42	16	-0.6	3	42.9
3rd D 8+ to Go	6	41	6.8	0	13	0	38	14	0.5	2	33.3
4th Down	0	0	-	0	0	0	0	2	-	0	-
Rec Behind Line	14	48	3.4	0	18	0	104	26	-4.0	4	28.6
1-10 yds	38	286	7.5	0	19	0	162	60	3.3	13	34.2
11-20 yds	0	0	-	0	0	0	0	0	-	0	-
21-30 yds	0	0	-	0	0	0	0	0	-	0	-
31+	0	0	-	0	0	0	0	0	-	0	-
Left Sideline	4	52	13.0	0	19	0	47	7	1.3	3	75.0
Left Side	15	48	3.2	0	14	0	54	24	-0.4	2	13.3
Middle	8	74	9.3	0	18	0	46	19	3.5	4	50.0
Right Side	19	122	6.4	0	15	0	89	24	1.7	6	31.6
Right Sideline	6	38	6.3	0	15	0	30	12	1.3	2	33.3
Shotgun	0	0	-	0	0	0	0	0	-	0	-
2 Wide Receivers	20	149	7.5	0	18	0	105	32	2.2	9	45.0
3 Wide Receivers	31	167	5.4	0	19	0	142	51	0.8	7	22.6
4+ Wide Receivers	1	18	18.0	0	18	0	19	1	-1.0	1	100.0

1995 Incompletions

Type	Num	%of Inc	%of Att
Pass Dropped	6	17.6	7.0
Poor Throw	11	32.4	12.8
Pass Defensed	3	8.8	3.5
Pass Hit at Line	4	11.8	4.7
Other	10	29.4	11.6
Total	34	100.0	39.5

Game Logs (1-8)

Date	Opp	Result	Rush	Yds	Rec	Yds	Trgt	F-L	TD
09/03	Cle	W 17-14	7	23	4	16	6	0-0	0
09/10	Mia	L 3-20	2	0	5	15	10	0-0	0
09/17	@SF	L 3-28	2	12	3	24	7	0-0	0
10/01	@Atl	L 17-30	10	52	4	18	8	0-0	0
10/08	Den	L 3-37	3	15	7	51	9	1-1	0
10/15	@KC	L 26-31	7	63	4	13	7	1-0	1
10/23	Buf	W 27-14	9	26	5	43	7	0-0	1
10/29	Car	L 17-20	3	-1	5	37	6	1-1	0

Game Logs (9-16)

Date	Opp	Result	Rush	Yds	Rec	Yds	Trgt	F-L	TD
11/05	@NYA	W 20-7	1	7	2	16	4	1-1	0
11/12	@Mia	W 34-17	3	3	2	23	2	0-0	0
11/19	Ind	L 10-24	1	2	3	21	3	0-0	0
11/26	@Buf	W 35-25	3	17	0	0	4	0-0	0
12/03	NO	L 17-31	4	16	4	26	6	0-0	0
12/10	NYA	W 31-28	2	13	0	0	0	1-0	0
12/16	@Pit	L 27-41	2	-2	2	23	4	0-0	0
12/23	@Ind	L 7-10	1	4	2	8	3	0-0	0

Eric Metcalf

1995 Receiving Splits

	G	Rec	Yds	Avg	TD	Lg	Big	YAC	Trgt	Y@C	1st	1st%
Total	16	104	1189	11.4	8	62	13	582	153	5.8	53	51.0
vs. Playoff	6	38	400	10.5	3	42	4	180	57	5.8	21	55.3
vs. Non-playoff	10	66	789	12.0	5	62	9	402	96	5.9	32	48.5
vs. Own Division	8	57	682	12.0	3	54	7	318	86	6.4	32	56.1
Home	8	47	519	11.0	5	42	6	244	70	5.9	22	46.8
Away	8	57	670	11.8	3	62	7	338	83	5.8	31	54.4
Games 1-8	8	57	613	10.8	3	62	8	378	73	4.1	23	40.4
Games 9-16	8	47	576	12.3	5	41	5	204	80	7.9	30	63.8
September	4	36	380	10.6	0	54	4	249	45	3.6	17	47.2
October	4	21	233	11.1	3	62	4	129	28	5.0	6	28.6
November	4	24	302	12.6	3	41	4	123	41	7.5	12	50.0
December	4	23	274	11.9	2	41	1	81	39	8.4	18	78.3
Grass	5	37	437	11.8	3	62	4	218	56	5.9	24	64.9
Turf	11	67	752	11.2	5	54	9	364	97	5.8	29	43.3
Indoor	9	58	674	11.6	5	54	8	339	82	5.8	27	46.6
Outdoor	7	46	515	11.2	3	62	5	243	71	5.9	26	56.5
1st Half	-	58	657	11.3	6	62	6	337	88	5.5	30	51.7
2nd Half/OT	-	46	532	11.6	2	41	7	245	65	6.2	23	50.0
Last 2 Min. Half	-	9	144	16.0	1	35	3	78	12	7.3	6	66.7
4th qtr, +/-7 pts	-	11	191	17.4	1	33	3	90	18	9.2	9	81.8
Winning	-	33	336	10.2	3	41	3	166	47	5.2	16	48.5
Tied	-	29	332	11.4	2	54	4	144	40	6.5	12	41.4
Trailing	-	42	521	12.4	3	62	6	272	58	5.9	25	59.5

	Rec	Yds	Avg	TD	Lg	Big	YAC	Trgt	Y@C	1st	1st%
Inside 20	12	84	7.0	4	15	0	25	21	4.9	8	66.7
Inside 10	3	16	5.3	2	7	0	1	7	5.0	2	66.7
1st Down	40	469	11.7	4	42	6	198	61	6.8	16	40.0
2nd Down	39	307	7.9	1	30	2	134	54	4.4	19	48.7
3rd Down Overall	23	379	16.5	3	54	5	228	36	6.6	16	69.6
3rd D 0-2 to Go	8	164	20.5	1	54	3	95	9	8.6	7	87.5
3rd D 3-7 to Go	7	152	21.7	1	62	2	101	13	7.3	7	100.0
3rd D 8+ to Go	8	63	7.9	1	20	0	32	14	3.9	2	25.0
4th Down	2	34	17.0	0	23	0	22	2	6.0	2	100.0
Rec Behind Line	18	87	4.8	0	21	0	172	22	-4.7	6	33.3
1-10 yds	69	597	8.7	3	36	3	269	92	4.8	30	43.5
11-20 yds	9	229	25.4	0	62	2	104	17	13.9	9	100.0
21-30 yds	4	114	28.5	0	30	4	11	12	25.8	4	100.0
31+	4	162	40.5	2	42	4	26	10	34.0	4	100.0
Left Sideline	10	95	9.5	0	20	0	68	18	2.7	4	40.0
Left Side	13	119	9.2	0	27	1	54	20	5.0	4	30.8
Middle	8	142	17.8	2	62	2	104	19	4.8	5	62.5
Right Side	44	449	10.2	3	42	5	218	57	5.3	23	52.3
Right Sideline	29	384	13.2	3	54	5	138	39	8.5	17	58.6
Shotgun	23	276	12.0	1	42	3	162	35	5.0	12	52.2
2 Wide Receivers	7	41	5.9	1	19	0	13	10	4.0	3	42.9
3 Wide Receivers	18	203	11.3	4	42	4	115	26	4.9	6	33.3
4+ Wide Receivers	78	931	11.9	3	62	9	437	116	6.3	43	55.1

1995 Incompletions

Type	Num	%of Inc	%of Att
Pass Dropped	4	8.2	2.6
Poor Throw	30	61.2	19.6
Pass Defensed	9	18.4	5.9
Pass Hit at Line	0	0.0	0.0
Other	6	12.2	3.9
Total	49	100.0	32.0

Game Logs (1-8)

Date	Opp	Result	Rush	Yds	Rec	Yds	Trgt	F-L	TD
09/03	Car	W 23-20	7	56	9	95	10	0-0	0
09/10	@SF	L 10-41	3	2	10	89	14	0-0	0
09/17	@NO	W 27-24	3	16	11	155	12	0-0	0
09/24	NYA	W 13-3	2	10	6	41	6	0-0	1
10/01	NE	W 30-17	0	0	6	41	7	0-0	1
10/12	@StL	L 19-21	3	20	6	34	7	0-0	0
10/22	@TB	W 24-21	1	-2	4	106	7	0-0	0
10/29	Dal	L 13-28	1	-1	5	52	7	0-0	0

Game Logs (9-16)

Date	Opp	Result	Rush	Yds	Rec	Yds	Trgt	F-L	TD
11/05	Det	W 34-22	2	-7	9	65	12	1-0	1
11/12	@Buf	L 17-23	0	0	3	44	8	0-0	0
11/19	StL	W 31-6	0	0	4	94	7	0-0	1
11/26	@Ari	W 37-40	0	0	8	99	14	1-1	1
12/03	@Mia	L 20-21	2	27	6	59	6	1-0	1
12/10	NO	W 19-14	0	0	3	40	8	1-0	0
12/17	@Car	L 17-21	0	0	9	84	15	0-0	1
12/24	SF	W 28-27	4	12	5	91	10	0-0	1

353

Anthony Miller

Denver Broncos — WR

1995 Receiving Splits

	G	Rec	Yds	Avg	TD	Lg	Big	YAC	Trgt	Y@C	1st	1st%		Rec	Yds	Avg	TD	Lg	Big	YAC	Trgt	Y@C	1st	1st%
Total	14	59	1079	18.3	14	62	11	320	108	12.9	44	74.6	Inside 20	6	48	8.0	4	15	0	17	14	5.2	5	83.3
vs. Playoff	6	28	424	15.1	5	59	3	108	53	11.3	19	67.9	Inside 10	3	8	2.7	2	3	0	0	8	2.7	2	66.7
vs. Non-playoff	8	31	655	21.1	9	62	8	212	55	14.3	25	80.6	1st Down	19	237	12.5	3	34	2	76	32	8.5	12	63.2
vs. Own Division	7	31	469	15.1	5	36	3	118	63	11.3	22	71.0	2nd Down	20	499	25.0	7	62	6	175	38	16.2	16	80.0
Home	7	30	553	18.4	6	62	5	188	53	12.2	23	76.7	3rd Down Overall	19	340	17.9	3	59	3	69	37	14.3	15	78.9
Away	7	29	526	18.1	8	60	6	132	55	13.6	21	72.4	3rd D 0-2 to Go	1	35	35.0	1	35	1	0	2	35.0	1	100.0
Games 1-8	6	28	484	17.3	6	60	4	136	52	12.4	21	75.0	3rd D 3-7 to Go	6	53	8.8	0	23	0	10	11	7.2	5	83.3
Games 9-16	8	31	595	19.2	8	62	7	184	56	13.3	23	74.2	3rd D 8+ to Go	12	252	21.0	2	59	2	59	24	16.1	9	75.0
September	3	13	175	13.5	3	59	1	47	24	9.8	9	69.2	4th Down	1	3	3.0	1	3	0	0	1	3.0	1	100.0
October	3	15	309	20.6	3	60	3	89	28	14.7	12	80.0	Rec Behind Line	0	0	-	0	0	0	0	3	-	0	-
November	4	17	368	21.6	5	50	6	79	28	17.0	13	76.5	1-10 yds	28	313	11.2	5	62	2	162	43	5.4	16	57.1
December	4	14	227	16.2	3	62	1	105	28	8.7	10	71.4	11-20 yds	23	436	19.0	2	60	2	109	37	14.2	20	87.0
Grass	11	43	747	17.4	8	62	6	263	83	11.3	32	74.4	21-30 yds	1	24	24.0	0	24	0	1	11	23.0	1	100.0
Turf	3	16	332	20.8	6	59	5	57	25	17.2	12	75.0	31+	7	306	43.7	7	59	7	48	14	36.9	7	100.0
Indoor	1	6	152	25.3	2	50	3	22	7	21.7	5	83.3	Left Sideline	16	273	17.1	3	36	3	36	36	14.8	12	75.0
Outdoor	13	53	927	17.5	12	62	8	298	101	11.9	39	73.6	Left Side	16	307	19.2	4	59	3	117	26	11.9	13	81.3
1st Half	-	33	586	17.8	8	62	6	206	60	11.5	24	72.7	Middle	11	244	22.2	3	62	3	97	17	13.4	9	81.8
2nd Half/OT	-	26	493	19.0	6	60	5	114	48	14.6	20	76.9	Right Side	8	90	11.3	1	18	0	14	13	9.5	4	50.0
Last 2 Min. Half	-	10	126	12.6	2	24	0	16	20	11.0	8	80.0	Right Sideline	8	165	20.6	3	60	2	56	16	13.6	6	75.0
4th qtr, +/-7 pts	-	4	41	10.3	0	18	0	14	9	6.8	1	25.0	Shotgun	26	488	18.8	4	60	4	110	52	14.5	21	80.8
Winning	-	23	464	20.2	6	60	5	154	41	13.5	18	78.3	2 Wide Receivers	18	397	22.1	5	60	4	117	37	15.6	15	83.3
Tied	-	9	104	11.6	0	23	0	27	17	8.6	6	66.7	3 Wide Receivers	31	527	17.0	5	62	5	178	53	11.3	21	67.7
Trailing	-	27	511	18.9	8	62	6	139	50	11.4	20	74.1	4+ Wide Receivers	8	106	13.3	2	33	1	15	14	11.4	6	75.0

1995 Incompletions

Type	Num	%of Inc	%of Att
Pass Dropped	3	6.1	2.8
Poor Throw	30	61.2	27.8
Pass Defensed	8	16.3	7.4
Pass Hit at Line	3	6.1	2.8
Other	5	10.2	4.6
Total	49	100.0	45.4

Game Logs (1-8)

Date	Opp	Result	Rush	Yds	Rec	Yds	Trgt	F-L	TD
09/03	Buf	W 22-7	-	-	-	-	-	-	-
09/10	@Dal	L 21-31	0	0	6	108	11	0-0	3
09/17	Was	W 38-31	0	0	4	39	6	0-0	0
09/24	@SD	L 6-17	0	0	3	28	7	0-0	0
10/01	@Sea	L 10-27	-	-	-	-	-	-	-
10/08	@NE	W 37-3	0	0	3	87	7	0-0	1
10/16	Oak	W 27-0	0	0	7	149	12	1-1	2
10/22	KC	L 7-21	0	0	5	73	9	0-0	0

Game Logs (9-16)

Date	Opp	Result	Rush	Yds	Rec	Yds	Trgt	F-L	TD
11/05	Ari	W 38-6	0	0	2	61	4	0-0	1
11/12	@Phi	L 13-31	1	5	4	72	7	0-0	1
11/19	SD	W 30-27	0	0	5	83	10	0-0	1
11/26	@Hou	L 33-42	0	0	6	152	7	0-0	2
12/03	Jac	W 31-23	0	0	3	91	3	0-0	1
12/10	Sea	L 27-31	0	0	4	57	9	0-0	1
12/17	@KC	L 17-20	0	0	5	60	9	0-0	0
12/24	@Oak	W 31-28	0	0	2	19	7	0-0	1

Chris Miller

St. Louis Rams — QB

1995 Passing Splits

	G	Att	Cm	Pct	Yds	Yd/Att	TD	Int	1st	YAC	Big	Sk	Rtg		Att	Cm	Pct	Yds	Yd/Att	TD	Int	1st	YAC	Big	Sk	Rtg
Total	13	405	232	57.3	2623	6.5	18	15	129	1124	20	31	76.2	Inside 20	44	20	45.5	103	2.3	10	1	15	34	0	3	82.6
vs. Playoff	7	246	148	60.2	1529	6.2	9	12	71	644	9	18	70.0	Inside 10	17	7	41.2	26	1.5	7	0	7	0	0	1	88.5
vs. Non-playoff	6	159	84	52.8	1094	6.9	9	3	58	480	11	13	85.8	1st Down	136	76	55.9	1023	7.5	3	5	37	363	7	8	72.0
vs. Own Division	8	241	135	56.0	1568	6.5	9	10	78	685	15	11	71.0	2nd Down	141	84	59.6	816	5.8	8	4	40	427	6	11	82.9
Home	5	154	87	56.5	1104	7.2	8	6	59	449	9	10	80.1	3rd Down Overall	123	68	55.3	730	5.9	6	6	49	299	6	11	68.8
Away	8	251	145	57.8	1519	6.1	10	9	70	675	11	21	73.8	3rd D 0-5 to Go	40	30	75.0	249	6.2	2	1	25	73	2	2	96.8
Games 1-8	8	266	154	57.9	1867	7.0	12	9	88	772	14	22	80.5	3rd D 6+ to Go	83	38	45.8	481	5.8	4	5	24	226	4	9	55.3
Games 9-16	5	139	78	56.1	756	5.4	6	6	41	352	6	9	67.9	4th Down	5	4	80.0	54	10.8	1	0	3	35	1	1	151.3
September	4	118	67	56.8	810	6.9	7	0	42	319	6	11	97.8	Rec Behind Line	75	46	61.3	214	2.9	1	2	10	374	1	0	59.0
October	4	148	87	58.8	1057	7.1	5	9	46	453	8	11	66.8	1-10 yds	187	122	65.2	1015	5.4	7	5	59	451	3	0	80.4
November	4	124	73	58.9	686	5.5	5	5	38	293	4	7	70.8	11-20 yds	95	53	55.8	960	10.1	4	5	49	187	7	0	82.8
December	1	15	5	33.3	70	4.7	1	1	3	59	2	2	43.8	21-30 yds	21	8	38.1	275	13.1	5	1	8	72	6	0	105.7
Grass	3	80	46	57.5	461	5.8	4	2	20	191	3	8	80.3	31+	27	3	11.1	159	5.9	1	2	3	40	3	0	33.1
Turf	10	325	186	57.2	2162	6.7	14	13	109	933	17	23	75.2	Left Sideline	85	47	55.3	499	5.9	2	2	24	204	2	1	70.7
Indoor	4	145	87	60.0	942	6.5	6	6	47	400	6	13	78.6	Left Side	60	33	55.0	403	6.7	5	2	21	212	3	2	89.8
Outdoor	9	260	145	55.8	1681	6.5	12	10	82	724	14	23	74.9	Middle	66	40	60.6	555	8.4	2	4	21	191	6	24	72.5
1st Half	-	241	130	53.9	1491	6.2	12	10	70	674	13	18	72.1	Right Side	95	55	57.9	534	5.6	5	5	27	283	5	4	69.4
2nd Half/OT	-	164	102	62.2	1132	6.9	6	5	59	450	7	13	82.2	Right Sideline	99	57	57.6	632	6.4	4	2	36	234	4	0	81.7
Last 2 Min. Half	-	53	26	49.1	275	5.2	3	3	15	107	4	3	59.9	2 Wide Receivers	208	115	55.3	1411	6.8	9	7	59	602	10	14	76.8
4th qtr, +/-7 pts	-	37	23	62.2	281	7.6	2	1	17	82	2	3	92.3	3+ WR	166	97	58.4	1016	6.1	6	8	59	420	9	15	68.2
Winning	-	138	75	54.3	884	6.4	6	3	48	332	6	12	79.5	Attempts 1-10	130	75	57.7	911	7.0	6	5	38	433	9	0	87.6
Tied	-	88	56	63.6	697	7.9	7	3	27	312	7	9	100.4	Attempts 11-20	125	67	53.6	737	5.9	5	4	38	308	4	0	71.3
Trailing	-	179	101	56.4	1042	5.8	5	9	54	480	7	10	61.7	Attempts 21+	150	90	60.0	975	6.5	7	6	53	383	7	0	78.1

1995 Incompletions

Type	Num	% of Inc	% of Att
Pass Dropped	32	18.5	7.9
Poor Throw	77	44.5	19.0
Pass Defensed	27	15.6	6.7
Pass Hit at Line	11	6.4	2.7
Other	26	15.0	6.4
Total	173	100.0	42.7

Game Logs (1-8)

Date	Opp	Result	Att	Cm	Pct	Yds	TD	Int	Lg	Sk	F-L
09/03	@GB	W 17-14	30	19	63.3	166	2	0	30	5	0-0
09/10	NO	W 17-13	31	12	38.7	188	1	0	33	3	0-0
09/17	@Car	W 31-10	26	19	73.1	225	1	0	37	2	1-0
09/24	Chi	W 34-28	31	21	67.7	231	3	0	23	1	0-0
10/01	@Ind	L 18-21	45	26	57.8	326	2	2	72	2	0-0
10/12	Atl	W 21-19	38	27	71.1	328	2	1	59	1	0-0
10/22	SF	L 10-44	22	8	36.4	141	0	4	53	2	0-0
10/29	@Phi	L 9-20	43	26	60.5	262	1	2	35	6	1-1

Game Logs (9-16)

Date	Opp	Result	Att	Cm	Pct	Yds	TD	Int	Lg	Sk	F-L
11/05	@NO	L 10-19	24	12	50.0	164	1	1	55	2	0-0
11/12	Car	W 28-17	32	19	59.4	216	2	1	31	3	0-0
11/19	@Atl	L 6-31	44	30	68.2	236	1	1	24	1	1-1
11/26	@SF	L 13-41	24	10	50.0	70	1	2	17	1	0-0
12/03	@NYA	W 23-20	15	5	33.3	70	1	1	28	2	1-0
12/10	Buf	L 27-45	-	-	-	-	-	-	-	-	-

Jim Miller

1995 Passing Splits

	G	Att	Cm	Pct	Yds	Yd/Att	TD	Int	1st	YAC	Big	Sk	Rtg		Att	Cm	Pct	Yds	Yd/Att	TD	Int	1st	YAC	Big	Sk	Rtg
Total	4	56	32	57.1	397	7.1	2	5	17	157	5	2	53.9	Inside 20	7	3	42.9	14	2.0	0	1	0	4	0	0	10.7
vs. Playoff	2	29	17	58.6	202	7.0	1	2	9	86	3	1	62.7	Inside 10	5	2	40.0	10	2.0	0	1	0	3	0	0	8.3
vs. Non-playoff	2	27	15	55.6	195	7.2	1	3	8	71	2	1	51.2	1st Down	21	9	42.9	67	3.2	0	0	2	32	0	1	51.1
vs. Own Division	0	0	0	-	0	-	0	0	0	0	0	0	-	2nd Down	19	14	73.7	190	10.0	1	1	7	86	3	1	100.8
Home	2	28	15	53.6	195	7.0	1	4	8	71	2	1	48.1	3rd Down Overall	12	6	50.0	66	5.5	0	3	5	15	0	0	27.1
Away	2	28	17	60.7	202	7.2	1	1	9	86	3	1	79.8	3rd D 0-5 to Go	5	2	40.0	11	2.2	0	2	2	2	0	0	47.9
Games 1-8	4	56	32	57.1	397	7.1	2	5	17	157	5	2	53.9	3rd D 6+ to Go	4	3	57.1	55	7.9	0	3	13	0	0	42.9
Games 9-16	0	0	0	-	0	-	0	0	0	0	0	0	-	4th Down	4	3	75.0	74	18.5	1	1	3	24	2	0	116.7
September	4	56	32	57.1	397	7.1	2	5	17	157	5	2	53.9	Rec Behind Line	10	5	50.0	35	3.5	0	0	0	47	0	0	58.3
October	0	0	0	-	0	-	0	0	0	0	0	0	-	1-10 yds	31	17	54.8	139	4.5	0	2	7	49	1	0	39.6
November	0	0	0	-	0	-	0	0	0	0	0	0	-	11-20 yds	11	8	72.7	171	15.5	1	1	8	57	2	0	107.2
December	0	0	0	-	0	-	0	0	0	0	0	0	-	21-30 yds	3	2	66.7	52	17.3	1	1	2	4	2	0	109.7
Grass	1	28	17	60.7	202	7.2	1	1	9	86	3	1	79.8	31+	1	0	0.0	0	0.0	0	1	0	0	0	0	0.0
Turf	3	28	15	53.6	195	7.0	1	4	8	71	2	1	48.1	Left Sideline	9	6	66.7	64	7.1	1	1	3	17	1	0	84.7
Indoor	1	0	0	-	0	-	0	0	0	0	0	0	-	Left Side	9	4	44.4	46	5.1	0	1	2	30	0	1	20.8
Outdoor	3	56	32	57.1	397	7.1	2	5	17	157	5	2	53.9	Middle	14	8	57.1	137	9.8	1	0	6	57	2	1	114.3
1st Half	-	0	0	-	0	-	0	0	0	0	0	0	-	Right Side	13	9	69.2	91	7.0	0	1	3	43	1	0	56.9
2nd Half/OT	-	56	32	57.1	397	7.1	2	5	17	157	5	2	53.9	Right Sideline	11	5	45.5	59	5.4	0	2	3	10	1	0	22.7
Last 2 Min. Half	-	11	5	45.5	52	4.7	0	1	3	25	0	1	21.8	2 Wide Receivers	10	6	60.0	46	4.6	0	1	2	11	0	1	31.7
4th qtr, +/-7 pts	-	1	0	0.0	0	0.0	0	0	0	0	0	0	0.0	3+ WR	46	26	56.5	351	7.6	2	4	15	146	5	1	59.2
Winning	-	1	0	0.0	0	0.0	0	0	0	0	0	0	0.0	Attempts 1-10	21	13	61.9	127	6.0	0	3	7	48	1	0	39.3
Tied	-	0	0	-	0	-	0	0	0	0	0	0	-	Attempts 11-20	20	12	60.0	173	8.7	2	1	6	59	3	0	100.6
Trailing	-	55	32	58.2	397	7.2	2	4	11	157	5	2	62.5	Attempts 21+	15	7	46.7	97	6.5	0	1	4	50	1	0	40.1

1995 Incompletions

Type	Num	% of Inc	% of Att
Pass Dropped	5	20.8	8.9
Poor Throw	10	41.7	17.9
Pass Defensed	7	29.2	12.5
Pass Hit at Line	0	0.0	0.0
Other	2	8.3	3.6
Total	24	100.0	42.9

Game Logs (1-8)

Date	Opp	Result	Att	Cm	Pct	Yds	TD	Int	Lg	Sk	F-L
09/03	Det	W 23-20	1	0	0.0	0	0	1	0	0	0-0
09/10	@Hou	W 34-17	0	0	-	0	0	0	0	0	0-0
09/18	@Mia	L 10-23	28	17	60.7	202	1	1	27	1	0-0
09/24	Min	L 24-44	27	15	55.6	195	1	3	42	1	1-0
10/01	SD	W 31-16									
10/08	@Jac	L 16-20									
10/19	Cin	L 9-27									
10/29	Jac	W 24-7									

Game Logs (9-16)

Date	Opp	Result	Att	Cm	Pct	Yds	TD	Int	Lg	Sk	F-L
11/05	@Chi	W 37-34	-	-	-	-	-	-	-	-	-
11/13	Cle	W 20-3	-	-	-	-	-	-	-	-	-
11/19	@Cin	W 49-31	-	-	-	-	-	-	-	-	-
11/26	@Cle	W 20-17	-	-	-	-	-	-	-	-	-
12/03	Hou	W 21-7	-	-	-	-	-	-	-	-	-
12/10	@Oak	W 29-10	-	-	-	-	-	-	-	-	-
12/16	NE	W 41-27	-	-	-	-	-	-	-	-	-
12/24	@GB	L 19-24	-	-	-	-	-	-	-	-	-

Ernie Mills

1995 Receiving Splits

	G	Rec	Yds	Avg	TD	Lg	Big	YAC	Trgt	Y@C	1st	1st%		Rec	Yds	Avg	TD	Lg	Big	YAC	Trgt	Y@C	1st	1st%
Total	16	39	679	17.4	8	62	11	215	69	11.9	29	74.4	Inside 20	4	34	8.5	4	14	0	0	10	8.5	4	100.0
vs. Playoff	4	10	118	11.8	2	27	1	23	21	9.5	6	60.0	Inside 10	2	10	5.0	2	8	0	0	5	5.0	2	100.0
vs. Non-playoff	12	29	561	19.3	6	62	10	192	48	12.7	23	79.3	1st Down	11	180	16.4	2	42	3	39	25	12.8	5	45.5
vs. Own Division	8	17	281	16.5	2	42	5	77	25	12.0	13	76.5	2nd Down	9	180	20.0	2	62	2	83	15	10.8	7	77.8
Home	8	16	317	19.8	2	62	6	137	30	11.3	12	75.0	3rd Down Overall	16	243	15.2	2	37	4	69	26	10.9	14	87.5
Away	8	23	362	15.7	6	42	5	78	39	12.3	17	73.9	3rd D 0-2 to Go	5	53	10.6	1	27	1	14	7	7.8	4	80.0
Games 1-8	8	11	190	17.3	1	39	4	50	17	12.7	8	72.7	3rd D 3-7 to Go	6	82	13.7	0	20	0	30	10	8.7	6	100.0
Games 9-16	8	28	489	17.5	7	62	7	165	52	11.6	21	75.0	3rd D 8+ to Go	5	108	21.6	1	37	3	25	9	16.6	4	80.0
September	4	5	99	19.8	0	39	2	32	7	13.4	5	100.0	4th Down	3	76	25.3	2	39	2	24	3	17.3	3	100.0
October	4	6	91	15.2	0	27	2	18	10	12.2	3	50.0	Rec Behind Line	0	0	-	0	0	0	0	2	-	0	-
November	4	12	192	16.0	3	42	3	48	14	12.0	11	91.7	1-10 yds	23	270	11.7	0	62	1	116	36	6.7	14	60.9
December	4	16	297	18.6	4	62	4	117	38	11.3	10	62.5	11-20 yds	8	167	20.9	1	39	3	52	17	14.4	7	87.5
Grass	6	18	282	15.7	5	37	4	62	33	12.2	13	72.2	21-30 yds	7	200	28.6	2	37	6	40	11	22.9	7	100.0
Turf	10	21	397	18.9	3	62	7	153	36	11.6	16	76.2	31+	1	42	42.0	1	42	1	7	3	35.0	1	100.0
Indoor	1	0	0	-	0	0	0	0	0	-	0	-	Left Sideline	2	29	14.5	2	27	1	0	5	14.5	2	100.0
Outdoor	15	39	679	17.4	8	62	11	215	69	11.9	29	74.4	Left Side	5	58	11.6	1	18	0	11	6	9.4	3	60.0
1st Half	-	23	346	15.0	5	42	5	95	41	10.9	17	73.9	Middle	10	115	11.5	2	20	0	34	16	8.1	8	80.0
2nd Half/OT	-	16	333	20.8	3	62	6	120	28	13.3	12	75.0	Right Side	14	369	26.4	3	62	8	146	24	15.9	12	85.7
Last 2 Min. Half	-	10	232	23.2	4	62	5	91	17	14.1	9	90.0	Right Sideline	8	108	13.5	0	28	2	24	18	10.5	4	50.0
4th qtr, +/-7 pts	-	6	142	23.7	2	62	3	74	8	11.3	5	83.3	Shotgun	25	485	19.4	5	62	9	178	39	12.3	21	84.0
Winning	-	6	86	14.3	1	26	1	12	14	12.3	4	66.7	2 Wide Receivers	6	74	12.3	1	22	0	6	14	11.3	3	50.0
Tied	-	16	289	18.1	3	42	4	127	25	10.1	13	81.3	3 Wide Receivers	9	126	14.0	2	42	1	37	19	9.9	5	55.6
Trailing	-	17	304	17.9	4	42	6	76	30	13.4	12	70.6	4+ Wide Receivers	24	479	20.0	5	62	10	172	36	12.8	21	87.5

1995 Incompletions

Type	Num	%of Inc	%of Att
Pass Dropped	7	23.3	10.1
Poor Throw	14	46.7	20.3
Pass Defensed	2	6.7	2.9
Pass Hit at Line	2	6.7	2.9
Other	5	16.7	7.2
Total	30	100.0	43.5

Game Logs (1-8)

Date	Opp	Result	Rush	Yds	Rec	Yds	Trgt	F-L	TD
09/03	Det	W 23-20	0	0	2	19	3	0-0	0
09/10	@Hou	W 34-17	0	0	0	0	0	0-0	0
09/18	@Mia	L 10-23	0	0	2	41	2	0-0	0
09/24	Min	L 24-44	0	0	1	39	2	0-0	0
10/01	SD	W 31-16	0	0	0	0	1	0-0	0
10/08	@Jac	L 16-20	0	0	0	0	0	1-0	0
10/19	Cin	L 9-27	1	17	6	91	8	0-0	1
10/29	Jac	W 24-7	0	0	0	0	1	0-0	0

Game Logs (9-16)

Date	Opp	Result	Rush	Yds	Rec	Yds	Trgt	F-L	TD
11/05	@Chi	W 37-34	1	6	3	49	4	0-0	1
11/13	Cle	W 20-3	0	0	2	22	2	0-0	0
11/19	@Cin	W 49-31	1	20	5	80	6	1-1	0
11/26	@Cle	W 20-17	0	0	2	41	2	0-0	0
12/03	Hou	W 21-7	0	0	2	47	6	0-0	0
12/10	@Oak	W 29-10	1	-12	5	93	10	0-0	2
12/16	NE	W 41-27	1	8	3	99	7	0-0	1
12/24	@GB	L 19-24	0	0	6	58	15	0-0	1

Rick Mirer
Seattle Seahawks — QB

1995 Passing Splits

	G	Att	Cm	Pct	Yds	Yd/Att	TD	Int	1st	YAC	Big	Sk	Rtg
Total	15	391	209	53.5	2564	6.6	13	20	127	1080	19	42	63.7
vs. Playoff	6	163	83	50.9	951	5.8	3	9	47	423	3	22	52.0
vs. Non-playoff	9	228	126	55.3	1613	7.1	10	11	80	657	16	20	72.1
vs. Own Division	7	167	86	51.5	1078	6.5	3	9	52	415	7	21	55.4
Home	7	212	124	58.5	1486	7.0	6	7	76	609	11	26	75.7
Away	8	179	85	47.5	1078	6.0	7	13	51	471	8	16	49.5
Games 1-8	8	215	116	54.0	1507	7.0	6	14	72	529	11	24	58.4
Games 9-16	7	176	93	52.8	1057	6.0	7	6	55	551	8	18	70.2
September	3	96	53	55.2	615	6.4	3	4	31	192	5	6	67.8
October	5	119	63	52.9	892	7.5	3	10	41	337	6	18	50.8
November	4	128	70	54.7	820	6.4	7	5	45	410	7	9	76.3
December	3	48	23	47.9	237	4.9	0	1	10	141	1	9	53.9
Grass	7	145	70	48.3	860	5.9	6	10	41	383	7	12	52.1
Turf	8	246	139	56.5	1704	6.9	7	10	86	697	12	30	70.6
Indoor	7	212	124	58.5	1486	7.0	6	7	76	609	11	26	75.7
Outdoor	8	179	85	47.5	1078	6.0	7	13	51	471	8	16	49.5
1st Half	-	195	106	54.4	1359	7.0	8	11	59	584	14	27	66.6
2nd Half/OT	-	196	103	52.6	1205	6.1	5	9	68	496	5	15	60.9
Last 2 Min. Half	-	57	27	47.4	461	8.1	1	5	21	162	5	4	44.6
4th qtr, +/-7 pts	-	49	24	49.0	230	4.7	0	2	15	71	1	2	45.5
Winning	-	96	52	54.2	549	5.7	1	4	31	296	5	10	57.2
Tied	-	98	62	63.3	798	8.1	7	3	35	328	9	10	99.8
Trailing	-	197	95	48.2	1217	6.2	5	13	61	456	7	22	49.0

	Att	Cm	Pct	Yds	Yd/Att	TD	Int	1st	YAC	Big	Sk	Rtg
Inside 20	26	14	53.8	92	3.5	3	2	7	37	0	6	68.1
Inside 10	9	5	55.6	25	2.8	2	1	2	9	0	1	60.9
1st Down	144	74	51.4	949	6.6	5	6	39	291	6	14	66.6
2nd Down	133	81	60.9	866	6.5	3	4	46	385	5	15	75.0
3rd Down Overall	106	49	46.2	674	6.4	5	9	37	379	8	12	47.4
3rd D 0-5 to Go	31	17	54.8	184	5.9	2	1	16	94	2	2	80.6
3rd D 6+ to Go	75	32	42.7	490	6.5	3	8	21	285	6	10	38.6
4th Down	8	5	62.5	75	9.4	0	1	5	25	0	1	53.6
Rec Behind Line	55	36	65.5	245	4.5	0	1	15	397	1	0	67.6
1-10 yds	173	120	69.4	1105	6.4	5	4	62	444	3	0	86.5
11-20 yds	93	40	43.0	747	8.0	2	8	38	155	3	0	42.7
21-30 yds	39	10	25.6	307	7.9	4	1	9	61	9	0	83.4
31+	29	3	10.3	160	5.5	2	6	3	23	3	0	33.5
Left Sideline	47	27	57.4	368	7.8	2	1	16	82	4	2	87.9
Left Side	74	38	51.4	446	6.0	2	6	25	218	4	3	45.2
Middle	54	27	50.0	421	7.8	3	5	21	217	3	31	56.2
Right Side	108	62	57.4	581	5.4	2	6	33	358	1	5	55.4
Right Sideline	105	54	51.4	736	7.0	4	2	31	205	7	0	78.9
2 Wide Receivers	117	66	56.4	604	5.2	4	6	33	267	2	14	60.6
3+ WR	268	142	53.0	1948	7.3	9	13	93	813	17	27	67.5
Attempts 1-10	139	75	54.0	876	6.3	7	7	40	428	7	0	69.1
Attempts 11-20	121	68	56.2	989	8.2	3	6	44	391	10	0	70.6
Attempts 21+	131	66	50.4	699	5.3	3	7	43	261	2	0	51.7

1995 Incompletions

Type	Num	% of Inc	% of Att
Pass Dropped	15	8.2	3.8
Poor Throw	98	53.8	25.1
Pass Defensed	28	15.4	7.2
Pass Hit at Line	9	4.9	2.3
Other	32	17.6	8.2
Total	182	100.0	46.5

Game Logs (1-8)

Date	Opp	Result	Att	Cm	Pct	Yds	TD	Int	Lg	Sk	F-L
09/03	KC	L 10-34	37	19	51.4	209	0	1	31	3	0-0
09/10	@SD	L 10-14	29	13	44.8	127	1	2	20	1	0-0
09/17	Cin	W 24-21	30	21	70.0	279	2	1	50	2	0-0
10/01	Den	W 27-10	24	16	66.7	222	0	0	51	4	0-0
10/08	@Oak	L 14-34	33	15	45.5	236	1	2	35	2	1-0
10/15	@Buf	L 21-27	34	15	44.1	218	1	3	54	4	0-0
10/22	SD	L 25-35	26	17	65.4	216	1	3	41	7	1-1
10/29	@Ari	L 14-20	2	0	0.0	0	0	2	0	1	0-0

Game Logs (9-16)

Date	Opp	Result	Att	Cm	Pct	Yds	TD	Int	Lg	Sk	F-L
11/05	NYN	W 30-28	31	17	54.8	253	2	1	44	2	0-0
11/12	@Jac	W 47-30	31	18	58.1	244	2	1	38	2	1-0
11/19	@Was	W 27-20	32	18	56.3	185	2	2	59	2	0-0
11/26	NYA	L 10-16	34	17	50.0	138	1	1	20	3	1-1
12/03	Phi	W 26-14	30	17	56.7	169	0	0	21	5	1-0
12/10	@Den	W 31-27	11	4	36.4	56	0	1	49	2	0-0
12/17	Oak	W 44-10									
12/24	@KC	L 3-26	7	2	28.6	12	0	0	9	2	0-0

Brian Mitchell
Washington Redskins — KR

1995 Receiving Splits

	G	Rec	Yds	Avg	TD	Lg	Big	YAC	Trgt	Y@C	1st	1st%
Total	16	38	324	8.5	1	22	0	292	50	0.8	13	34.2
vs. Playoff	6	14	116	8.3	0	20	0	118	20	-0.1	4	28.6
vs. Non-playoff	10	24	208	8.7	1	22	0	174	30	1.4	9	37.5
vs. Own Division	8	12	97	8.1	0	20	0	114	19	-1.4	4	33.3
Home	8	17	145	8.5	0	21	0	98	25	2.8	6	35.3
Away	8	21	179	8.5	1	22	0	194	25	-0.7	7	33.3
Games 1-8	8	19	162	8.5	0	21	0	150	22	0.6	6	31.6
Games 9-16	8	19	162	8.5	1	22	0	142	28	1.1	7	36.8
September	4	10	84	8.4	0	21	0	75	11	0.9	3	30.0
October	5	9	78	8.7	0	15	0	75	12	0.3	3	33.3
November	3	10	84	8.4	0	21	0	55	14	2.9	4	40.0
December	4	9	78	8.7	1	22	0	87	13	-1.0	3	33.3
Grass	12	27	220	8.1	0	21	0	169	36	1.9	8	29.6
Turf	4	11	104	9.5	1	22	0	123	14	-1.7	5	45.5
Indoor	1	2	25	12.5	1	22	0	26	2	-0.5	1	50.0
Outdoor	15	36	299	8.3	0	21	0	266	48	0.9	12	33.3
1st Half	-	17	144	8.5	1	22	0	133	22	0.6	5	29.4
2nd Half/OT	-	21	180	8.6	0	21	0	159	28	1.0	8	38.1
Last 2 Min. Half	-	11	64	5.8	0	12	0	46	13	1.6	2	18.2
4th qtr, +/-7 pts	-	5	54	10.8	0	14	0	55	8	-0.2	1	20.0
Winning	-	3	17	5.7	0	9	0	19	4	-0.7	0	0.0
Tied	-	7	54	7.7	0	14	0	35	12	2.7	3	42.9
Trailing	-	28	253	9.0	1	22	0	238	34	0.5	10	35.7

	Rec	Yds	Avg	TD	Lg	Big	YAC	Trgt	Y@C	1st	1st%
Inside 20	5	25	5.0	0	9	0	12	6	2.6	1	20.0
Inside 10	2	7	3.5	0	4	0	1	2	3.0	0	0.0
1st Down	10	70	7.0	0	12	0	64	11	0.6	2	20.0
2nd Down	9	48	5.4	0	14	0	33	11	1.8	2	22.2
3rd Down Overall	19	205	10.8	1	22	0	195	28	0.5	9	47.4
3rd D 0-2 to Go	0	0	-	0	0	0	0	1	-	0	-
3rd D 3-7 to Go	4	42	10.5	0	22	0	35	6	1.8	3	75.0
3rd D 8+ to Go	15	163	10.9	0	21	0	160	21	0.2	6	40.0
4th Down	0	0	-	0	0	0	0	0	-	0	-
Rec Behind Line	16	159	9.9	1	22	0	197	19	-2.4	6	37.5
1-10 yds	22	165	7.5	0	21	0	95	31	3.2	7	31.8
11-20 yds	0	0	-	0	0	0	0	0	-	0	-
21-30 yds	0	0	-	0	0	0	0	0	-	0	-
31+	0	0	-	0	0	0	0	0	-	0	-
Left Sideline	6	50	8.3	0	15	0	43	7	0.7	2	33.3
Left Side	7	49	7.0	0	12	0	43	12	0.9	1	14.3
Middle	12	89	7.4	0	20	0	80	13	0.4	4	33.3
Right Side	9	96	10.7	1	22	0	100	13	-0.4	4	44.4
Right Sideline	4	40	10.0	0	21	0	23	6	4.3	2	50.0
Shotgun	0	0	-	0	0	0	0	0	-	0	-
2 Wide Receivers	4	27	6.8	0	14	0	16	5	2.8	1	25.0
3 Wide Receivers	31	266	8.6	1	22	0	239	42	0.9	11	35.5
4+ Wide Receivers	3	31	10.3	0	20	0	37	3	-2.0	1	33.3

1995 Incompletions

Type	Num	%of Inc	%of Att
Pass Dropped	3	25.0	6.0
Poor Throw	5	41.7	10.0
Pass Defensed	0	0.0	0.0
Pass Hit at Line	2	16.7	4.0
Other	2	16.7	4.0
Total	12	100.0	24.0

Game Logs (1-8)

Date	Opp	Result	Rush	Yds	Rec	Yds	Trgt	F-L	TD
09/03	Ari	W 27-7	5	32	0	0	0	0-0	0
09/10	Oak	L 8-20	3	33	2	25	3	0-0	0
09/17	@Den	L 31-38	1	36	1	14	1	0-0	0
09/24	@TB	L 6-14	1	4	7	45	7	0-0	0
10/01	Dal	W 27-23	2	13	0	0	0	1-0	0
10/08	@Phi	L 34-37	3	7	3	34	4	1-0	0
10/15	@Ari	L 20-24	0	0	1	9	1	0-0	0
10/22	Det	W 36-30	4	33	5	35	6	0-0	0

Game Logs (9-16)

Date	Opp	Result	Rush	Yds	Rec	Yds	Trgt	F-L	TD
10/29	NYN	L 15-24	6	20	0	0	1	0-0	0
11/05	@KC	L 3-24	2	5	1	7	2	0-0	0
11/19	Sea	L 20-27	3	10	7	68	8	0-0	0
11/26	Phi	L 14-31	3	34	2	9	4	0-0	0
12/03	@Dal	W 24-17	3	17	3	31	4	0-0	0
12/10	@NYN	L 13-20	4	16	3	14	4	0-0	0
12/17	@StL	W 35-23	3	21	2	25	2	0-0	1
12/24	Car	W 20-17	3	20	1	8	3	0-0	0

Johnny Mitchell New York Jets — TE

1995 Receiving Splits

	G	Rec	Yds	Avg	TD	Lg	Big	YAC	Trgt	Y@C	1st	1st%		Rec	Yds	Avg	TD	Lg	Big	YAC	Trgt	Y@C	1st	1st%
Total	12	45	497	11.0	5	43	2	201	80	6.6	25	55.6	Inside 20	5	41	8.2	4	17	0	12	8	5.8	4	80.0
vs. Playoff	5	14	183	13.1	3	43	1	68	23	8.2	9	64.3	Inside 10	2	6	3.0	2	3	0	0	3	3.0	2	100.0
vs. Non-playoff	7	31	314	10.1	2	26	1	133	57	5.8	16	51.6	1st Down	18	173	9.6	2	17	0	67	33	5.9	9	50.0
vs. Own Division	7	25	305	12.2	4	43	2	122	42	7.3	16	64.0	2nd Down	13	179	13.8	2	43	2	85	22	7.2	10	76.9
Home	5	16	182	11.4	2	43	1	68	32	7.1	7	43.8	3rd Down Overall	13	124	9.5	1	20	0	46	24	6.0	5	38.5
Away	7	29	315	10.9	3	26	1	133	48	6.3	18	62.1	3rd D 0-2 to Go	2	33	16.5	1	20	0	7	2	13.0	2	100.0
Games 1-8	4	7	61	8.7	1	19	0	26	13	5.0	3	42.9	3rd D 3-7 to Go	3	26	8.7	0	14	0	14	6	4.0	3	100.0
Games 9-16	8	38	436	11.5	4	43	2	175	67	6.9	22	57.9	3rd D 8+ to Go	8	65	8.1	0	15	0	25	16	5.0	0	0.0
September	1	2	23	11.5	0	19	0	14	3	4.5	1	50.0	4th Down	1	21	21.0	0	21	0	3	1	18.0	1	100.0
October	4	8	80	10.0	2	17	0	24	14	7.0	5	62.5	Rec Behind Line	1	5	5.0	0	5	0	6	2	-1.0	1	100.0
November	3	12	151	12.6	1	43	1	72	21	6.6	8	58.3	1-10 yds	36	329	9.1	3	26	1	151	52	4.9	16	44.4
December	4	23	243	10.6	2	26	1	91	42	6.6	12	52.2	11-20 yds	7	120	17.1	1	21	0	22	14	14.0	7	100.0
Grass	3	12	138	11.5	1	26	1	61	22	6.4	7	58.3	21-30 yds	1	43	43.0	0	43	1	22	8	21.0	1	100.0
Turf	9	33	359	10.9	4	43	1	140	58	6.6	18	54.5	31+	0	0	-	0	0	0	0	3	-	0	-
Outdoor	3	30	333	11.1	3	43	2	133	57	6.7	15	50.0	Left Sideline	5	69	13.8	3	43	1	39	11	6.0	4	80.0
Indoor	9	15	164	10.9	2	21	0	68	23	6.4	10	66.7	Left Side	11	125	11.4	0	19	0	54	12	6.5	7	63.6
1st Half	-	20	191	9.6	0	19	0	87	41	5.2	9	45.0	Middle	11	122	11.1	1	21	0	45	23	7.0	7	63.6
2nd Half/OT	-	25	306	12.2	5	43	2	114	39	7.7	16	64.0	Right Side	12	112	9.3	0	26	1	53	20	4.9	3	25.0
Last 2 Min. Half	-	4	49	12.3	0	17	0	9	11	10.0	3	75.0	Right Sideline	6	69	11.5	0	20	0	10	13	9.8	4	66.7
4th qtr, +/-7 pts	-	3	17	5.7	1	8	0	8	6	3.0	1	33.3	Shotgun	0	0	-	0	0	0	0	0	-	0	-
Winning	-	7	71	10.1	0	15	0	35	11	5.1	3	42.9	2 Wide Receivers	34	385	11.3	2	43	2	161	63	6.6	17	50.0
Tied	-	8	108	13.5	1	26	1	47	16	7.6	6	75.0	3 Wide Receivers	4	42	10.5	0	19	0	21	7	5.3	3	75.0
Trailing	-	30	318	10.6	4	43	1	119	53	6.6	16	53.3	4+ Wide Receivers	0	0	-	0	0	0	0	0	-	0	-

1995 Incompletions

Type	Num	%of Inc	%of Att
Pass Dropped	7	20.0	8.8
Poor Throw	25	71.4	31.3
Pass Defensed	1	2.9	1.3
Pass Hit at Line	1	2.9	1.3
Other	1	2.9	1.3
Total	35	100.0	43.8

Game Logs (1-8)

Date	Opp	Result		Rec	Yds	Trgt	F-L	TD
09/03	@Mia	L	14-52	2	23	3	0-0	0
09/10	Ind	L	24-27	-	-	-	-	-
09/17	Jac	W	27-10	-	-	-	-	-
09/24	@Atl	L	3-13	-	-	-	-	-
10/01	Oak	L	10-47	-	-	-	-	-
10/08	@Buf	L	10-29	2	13	3	0-0	0
10/15	@Car	L	15-26	1	7	4	0-0	0
10/22	Mia	W	17-16	2	18	3	1-1	1

Game Logs (9-16)

Date	Opp	Result		Rec	Yds	Trgt	F-L	TD
10/29	@Ind	L	10-17	3	42	4	0-0	1
11/05	NE	L	7-20	2	14	4	0-0	0
11/19	Buf	L	26-28	5	87	10	0-0	1
11/26	@Sea	W	16-10	5	50	7	0-0	0
12/03	StL	L	20-23	2	19	4	0-0	0
12/10	@NE	L	28-31	8	108	15	1-1	1
12/17	@Hou	L	6-23	7	72	12	0-0	1
12/24	NO	L	0-12	5	44	11	0-0	0

Pete Mitchell Jacksonville Jaguars — TE

1995 Receiving Splits

	G	Rec	Yds	Avg	TD	Lg	Big	YAC	Trgt	Y@C	1st	1st%		Rec	Yds	Avg	TD	Lg	Big	YAC	Trgt	Y@C	1st	1st%
Total	16	41	527	12.9	2	35	4	163	64	8.9	29	70.7	Inside 20	3	30	10.0	2	16	0	0	5	10.0	2	66.7
vs. Playoff	5	14	145	10.4	1	23	0	34	9	7.9	9	64.3	Inside 10	1	2	2.0	0	2	0	0	2	2.0	0	0.0
vs. Non-playoff	11	27	382	14.1	1	35	4	129	40	9.4	20	74.1	1st Down	16	206	12.9	1	35	3	54	23	9.5	9	56.3
vs. Own Division	8	20	245	12.3	1	29	2	80	32	8.3	15	75.0	2nd Down	8	104	13.0	0	29	1	40	17	8.0	6	75.0
Home	8	15	168	11.2	0	27	1	49	28	7.9	11	73.3	3rd Down Overall	15	183	12.2	0	23	0	65	22	7.9	12	80.0
Away	8	26	359	13.8	2	35	3	114	36	9.4	18	69.2	3rd D 0-2 to Go	0	0	-	0	0	0	0	1	-	0	-
Games 1-8	8	11	120	10.9	0	29	1	43	20	7.0	7	63.6	3rd D 3-7 to Go	7	77	11.0	0	22	0	39	11	5.4	6	85.7
Games 9-16	8	30	407	13.6	2	35	3	120	44	9.4	22	73.3	3rd D 8+ to Go	8	106	13.3	0	23	0	26	10	10.0	6	75.0
September	4	4	39	9.8	0	15	0	8	8	7.8	2	50.0	4th Down	2	34	17.0	1	18	0	4	2	15.0	2	100.0
October	5	11	129	11.7	1	29	1	43	17	7.8	8	72.7	Rec Behind Line	0	0	-	0	0	0	0	0	-	0	-
November	3	16	245	15.3	1	35	2	80	19	10.3	13	81.3	1-10 yds	27	255	9.4	0	22	0	98	39	5.8	15	55.6
December	4	10	114	11.4	0	27	1	32	20	8.2	6	60.0	11-20 yds	13	237	18.2	2	29	3	56	23	13.9	13	100.0
Grass	11	28	377	13.5	1	35	3	125	44	9.0	21	75.0	21-30 yds	1	35	35.0	0	35	1	9	2	26.0	1	100.0
Turf	5	13	150	11.5	1	29	1	38	20	8.6	8	61.5	31+	0	0	-	0	0	0	0	0	-	0	-
Outdoor	2	35	449	12.8	2	35	3	136	55	8.9	25	71.4	Left Sideline	3	45	15.0	0	35	1	12	8	11.0	2	66.7
Indoor	14	6	78	13.0	0	29	1	27	9	8.5	4	66.7	Left Side	9	116	12.9	0	27	1	31	15	9.4	6	66.7
1st Half	-	18	208	11.6	0	29	2	65	32	7.9	12	66.7	Middle	9	120	13.3	1	23	0	24	12	10.7	7	77.8
2nd Half/OT	-	23	319	13.9	2	35	2	98	32	9.7	17	73.9	Right Side	14	162	11.6	1	22	0	59	19	7.4	10	71.4
Last 2 Min. Half	-	8	62	7.8	1	12	0	8	10	6.8	3	37.5	Right Sideline	6	84	14.0	0	29	2	37	10	7.8	4	66.7
4th qtr, +/-7 pts	-	8	91	11.4	1	22	0	30	10	7.6	6	75.0	Shotgun	24	273	11.4	2	23	0	73	31	8.3	17	70.8
Winning	-	8	94	11.8	0	29	1	36	12	7.3	5	62.5	2 Wide Receivers	9	154	17.1	0	35	3	56	14	10.9	8	88.9
Tied	-	6	96	16.0	0	27	1	35	12	10.2	6	100.0	3 Wide Receivers	29	357	12.3	1	27	1	107	45	8.6	20	69.0
Trailing	-	27	337	12.5	2	35	2	92	40	9.1	18	66.7	4+ Wide Receivers	2	14	7.0	0	12	0	0	2	7.0	1	50.0

1995 Incompletions

Type	Num	%of Inc	%of Att
Pass Dropped	5	21.7	7.8
Poor Throw	12	52.2	18.8
Pass Defensed	3	13.0	4.7
Pass Hit at Line	0	0.0	0.0
Other	3	13.0	4.7
Total	23	100.0	35.9

Game Logs (1-8)

Date	Opp	Result		Rec	Yds	Trgt	F-L	TD
09/03	Hou	L	3-10	0	0	0	0-0	0
09/10	@Cin	L	17-24	2	18	4	0-0	0
09/17	@NYA	L	10-27	1	6	2	0-0	0
09/24	GB	L	14-24	1	15	2	0-0	0
10/01	@Hou	W	17-16	3	36	4	0-0	0
10/08	Pit	W	20-16	2	15	4	0-0	0
10/15	Chi	L	27-30	0	0	0	0-0	0
10/22	@Cle	W	23-15	2	30	3	0-0	0

Game Logs (9-16)

Date	Opp	Result		Rec	Yds	Trgt	F-L	TD
10/29	@Pit	L	7-24	4	48	5	0-0	1
11/12	Sea	L	30-47	1	15	1	0-0	0
11/19	@TB	L	16-17	10	161	11	0-0	0
11/26	Cin	L	13-17	5	69	7	0-0	0
12/03	@Den	L	23-31	1	18	2	0-0	0
12/10	Ind	L	31-41	4	25	8	0-0	0
12/17	@Det	L	0-44	3	42	5	0-0	0
12/24	Cle	W	24-21	2	29	5	0-0	0

Scott Mitchell

Detroit Lions — QB

1995 Passing Splits

	G	Att	Cm	Pct	Yds	Yd/Att	TD	Int	1st	YAC	Big	Sk	Rtg		Att	Cm	Pct	Yds	Yd/Att	TD	Int	1st	YAC	Big	Sk	Rtg
Total	16	583	346	59.3	4338	7.4	32	12	221	1628	30	31	92.3	Inside 20	78	34	43.6	324	4.2	18	3	25	60	0	7	79.3
vs. Playoff	5	188	101	53.7	1261	6.7	11	4	61	432	10	8	85.4	Inside 10	24	8	33.3	47	2.0	7	1	7	7	0	0	64.6
vs. Non-playoff	11	395	245	62.0	3077	7.8	21	8	160	1196	20	23	95.5	1st Down	222	130	58.6	1724	7.8	12	4	70	698	13	10	93.8
vs. Own Division	8	281	171	60.9	2198	7.8	17	5	110	886	14	13	98.1	2nd Down	196	122	62.2	1413	7.2	9	3	70	546	8	12	92.9
Home	8	274	180	65.7	2253	8.2	17	2	120	865	13	17	108.7	3rd Down Overall	158	88	55.7	1081	6.8	10	5	75	351	7	9	84.9
Away	8	309	166	53.7	2085	6.7	15	10	101	763	17	14	77.7	3rd D 0-5 to Go	62	46	74.2	459	7.4	6	1	45	151	3	4	120.3
Games 1-8	8	299	176	58.9	2036	6.8	16	5	108	740	12	18	90.4	3rd D 6+ to Go	96	42	43.8	622	6.5	4	4	30	200	4	5	62.1
Games 9-16	8	284	170	59.9	2302	8.1	16	7	113	888	18	13	94.2	4th Down	7	6	85.7	120	17.1	1	0	6	33	2	0	158.3
September	4	147	90	61.2	982	6.7	5	2	57	318	6	11	86.6	Rec Behind Line	41	28	68.3	230	5.6	0	0	8	308	1	0	82.4
October	4	152	86	56.6	1054	6.9	11	3	51	422	6	7	94.0	1-10 yds	327	231	70.6	2175	6.7	12	6	130	931	4	0	93.3
November	4	141	83	58.9	1114	7.9	7	4	53	367	9	5	88.8	11-20 yds	141	68	48.2	1285	9.1	12	2	64	268	9	0	102.7
December	4	143	87	60.8	1188	8.3	9	3	60	521	9	8	99.6	21-30 yds	59	14	23.7	390	6.6	6	3	14	55	11	0	67.3
Grass	4	144	82	56.9	1007	7.0	8	4	52	393	5	4	85.6	31+	15	5	33.3	258	17.2	2	1	5	66	6	0	93.8
Turf	12	439	264	60.1	3331	7.6	24	8	169	1235	25	27	94.4	Left Sideline	157	85	54.1	1006	6.4	7	2	56	377	7	1	83.5
Indoor	11	407	246	60.4	3136	7.7	22	7	159	1183	23	25	95.4	Left Side	109	69	63.3	692	6.3	4	5	38	254	1	3	74.4
Outdoor	5	176	100	56.8	1202	6.8	10	5	62	445	7	6	85.0	Middle	83	44	53.0	803	9.7	8	3	36	284	8	25	103.6
1st Half	-	301	178	59.1	2213	7.4	19	6	111	844	15	16	94.7	Right Side	113	71	62.8	858	7.6	3	2	46	367	5	0	87.6
2nd Half/OT	-	282	168	59.6	2125	7.5	13	6	110	784	15	15	89.6	Right Sideline	121	77	63.6	979	8.1	10	0	45	346	9	0	116.4
Last 2 Min. Half	-	66	28	42.4	355	5.4	5	2	15	119	4	4	72.5	2 Wide Receivers	109	63	57.8	829	7.6	5	3	39	289	8	5	85.8
4th qtr, +/-7 pts	-	72	48	66.7	623	8.7	3	0	29	189	5	1	107.6	3+ WR	468	282	60.3	3480	7.4	27	8	181	1335	21	26	95.4
Winning	-	243	147	60.5	1904	7.8	13	5	96	767	13	18	94.4	Attempts 1-10	160	97	60.6	1233	7.7	10	5	65	504	8	0	92.5
Tied	-	144	93	64.6	1102	7.7	7	3	61	429	7	5	95.3	Attempts 11-20	152	87	57.2	1121	7.4	8	1	51	422	8	0	95.3
Trailing	-	196	106	54.1	1332	6.8	12	4	64	432	10	8	87.4	Attempts 21+	271	162	59.8	1984	7.3	14	6	105	702	14	0	90.4

1995 Incompletions

Type	Num	% of Inc	% of Att
Pass Dropped	27	11.4	4.6
Poor Throw	114	48.1	19.6
Pass Defensed	37	15.6	6.3
Pass Hit at Line	8	3.4	1.4
Other	51	21.5	8.7
Total	237	100.0	40.7

Game Logs (1-8)

Date	Opp	Result	Att	Cm	Pct	Yds	TD	Int	Lg	Sk	F-L
09/03	@Pit	L 20-23	32	18	56.3	195	2	1	30	2	0-0
09/10	@Min	L 27-37	47	27	57.4	279	1	1	47	4	1-0
09/17	Ari	L 17-20	26	17	65.4	217	1	0	39	2	0-0
09/25	SF	W 27-24	42	28	66.7	291	1	0	25	3	0-0
10/08	Cle	W 38-20	38	24	63.2	273	2	1	40	3	2-0
10/15	@GB	L 21-30	41	17	41.5	205	3	1	31	0	0-0
10/22	@Was	L 30-36	50	30	60.0	327	3	1	51	2	2-2
10/29	GB	W 24-16	23	15	65.2	249	3	0	69	2	0-0

Game Logs (9-16)

Date	Opp	Result	Att	Cm	Pct	Yds	TD	Int	Lg	Sk	F-L
11/05	@Atl	L 22-34	50	23	46.0	321	2	2	42	1	0-0
11/12	TB	W 27-24	34	21	61.8	260	1	0	37	1	0-0
11/19	@Chi	W 24-17	12	9	75.0	123	0	1	29	0	0-0
11/23	Min	W 44-38	45	30	66.7	410	4	1	29	3	0-0
12/04	Chi	W 27-7	38	26	68.4	320	3	0	46	1	0-0
12/10	@Hou	W 24-17	36	16	44.4	283	2	4	42	3	1-0
12/17	Jac	W 44-0	28	19	67.9	233	2	0	27	2	1-0
12/23	@TB	W 37-10	41	26	63.4	352	2	1	91	2	1-0

Warren Moon

Minnesota Vikings — QB

1995 Passing Splits

	G	Att	Cm	Pct	Yds	Yd/Att	TD	Int	1st	YAC	Big	Sk	Rtg		Att	Cm	Pct	Yds	Yd/Att	TD	Int	1st	YAC	Big	Sk	Rtg
Total	16	606	377	62.2	4228	7.0	33	14	213	1820	30	38	91.5	Inside 20	67	40	59.7	239	3.6	22	1	28	78	0	4	100.1
vs. Playoff	7	257	147	57.2	1595	6.2	15	6	80	705	11	20	85.3	Inside 10	32	19	59.4	77	2.4	16	0	16	14	0	1	103.6
vs. Non-playoff	9	349	230	65.9	2633	7.5	18	8	133	1115	19	18	96.1	1st Down	224	146	65.2	1643	7.3	8	5	62	711	11	14	89.6
vs. Own Division	8	309	193	62.5	2076	6.7	12	9	104	920	16	19	82.9	2nd Down	199	128	64.3	1338	6.7	10	3	68	566	9	13	94.2
Home	8	284	183	64.4	2073	7.3	16	5	104	899	13	16	97.6	3rd Down Overall	179	102	57.0	1238	6.9	15	5	82	542	10	11	94.7
Away	8	322	194	60.2	2155	6.7	17	9	109	921	17	22	86.1	3rd D 0-5 to Go	74	52	70.3	432	5.8	7	3	49	230	3	2	99.6
Games 1-8	8	302	189	62.6	1870	6.2	10	9	97	813	11	17	78.7	3rd D 6+ to Go	105	50	47.6	806	7.7	8	2	33	312	7	9	91.2
Games 9-16	8	304	188	61.8	2358	7.8	23	5	116	1007	19	21	104.3	4th Down	4	1	25.0	9	2.3	0	1	1	0	0	0	0.0
September	4	134	84	62.7	878	6.6	6	3	45	428	6	9	87.2	Rec Behind Line	55	39	70.9	206	3.7	1	1	11	342	1	0	75.3
October	4	168	105	62.5	992	5.9	4	6	52	385	5	9	71.8	1-10 yds	364	257	70.6	2038	5.6	19	8	123	985	2	0	92.5
November	4	161	100	62.1	1301	8.1	14	2	65	561	10	13	111.3	11-20 yds	112	62	55.4	1182	10.6	5	2	60	278	8	0	99.6
December	4	143	88	61.5	1057	7.4	9	3	51	446	9	8	96.4	21-30 yds	38	11	28.9	380	10.0	3	1	11	102	11	0	84.1
Grass	5	202	121	59.9	1264	6.3	10	5	60	560	12	16	84.3	31+	37	8	21.6	422	11.4	5	2	8	113	8	0	91.7
Turf	11	404	256	63.4	2964	7.3	23	9	148	1260	18	22	95.2	Left Sideline	156	98	62.8	1107	7.1	6	1	58	490	5	0	94.2
Indoor	9	331	213	64.4	2457	7.4	19	7	122	1059	16	16	97.0	Left Side	90	58	64.4	667	7.4	5	3	31	310	6	3	91.3
Outdoor	7	275	164	59.6	1771	6.4	14	7	91	761	14	18	85.0	Middle	61	34	55.7	370	6.1	2	3	14	103	4	33	64.2
1st Half	-	315	208	66.0	2347	7.5	20	6	118	1014	17	20	101.4	Right Side	127	81	63.8	819	6.4	10	3	44	423	4	0	98.5
2nd Half/OT	-	291	169	58.1	1881	6.5	13	8	95	806	13	18	80.8	Right Sideline	172	106	61.6	1265	7.4	10	4	66	494	9	2	93.8
Last 2 Min. Half	-	93	62	66.7	775	8.3	6	1	38	215	4	6	109.4	2 Wide Receivers	184	111	60.3	1197	6.5	13	2	62	526	8	13	94.9
4th qtr, +/-7 pts	-	80	45	56.3	569	7.1	3	1	27	206	3	8	85.9	3+ WR	406	257	63.3	2938	7.2	17	11	144	1262	21	24	87.7
Winning	-	213	126	59.2	1590	7.5	16	7	77	712	11	12	93.8	Attempts 1-10	160	104	65.0	1071	6.7	8	2	58	509	7	0	95.6
Tied	-	155	95	61.3	1084	7.0	4	3	58	426	8	9	82.8	Attempts 11-20	160	104	65.0	1166	7.3	9	4	54	484	10	0	94.9
Trailing	-	238	156	65.5	1554	6.5	13	4	78	682	11	17	95.1	Attempts 21+	286	169	59.1	1991	7.0	16	8	101	827	13	0	87.3

1995 Incompletions

Type	Num	% of Inc	% of Att
Pass Dropped	35	15.3	5.8
Poor Throw	113	49.3	18.6
Pass Defensed	39	17.0	6.4
Pass Hit at Line	3	1.3	0.5
Other	39	17.0	6.4
Total	229	100.0	37.8

Game Logs (1-8)

Date	Opp	Result	Att	Cm	Pct	Yds	TD	Int	Lg	Sk	F-L
09/03	@Chi	L 14-31	37	26	70.3	247	1	1	34	3	0-0
09/10	Det	W 20-10	29	19	65.5	233	1	0	85	2	0-0
09/17	Dal	L 17-23	38	20	52.6	185	2	0	29	3	2-1
09/24	@Pit	W 44-24	30	17	56.7	213	2	2	41	1	1-0
10/08	Hou	W 23-17	43	28	65.1	289	2	2	49	1	1-0
10/15	@TB	L 17-20	48	33	68.8	332	1	2	33	0	0-0
10/22	@GB	L 21-38	35	16	45.7	119	1	2	18	3	1-1
10/30	Chi	L 6-14	42	28	66.7	252	0	0	14	4	1-0

Game Logs (9-16)

Date	Opp	Result	Att	Cm	Pct	Yds	TD	Int	Lg	Sk	F-L
11/05	GB	W 27-24	39	21	53.8	237	3	0	28	2	1-0
11/12	@Ari	W 30-24	43	24	55.8	342	4	0	50	5	1-1
11/19	NO	W 43-24	32	25	78.1	338	4	0	77	2	0-0
11/26	@Det	L 38-44	45	30	63.8	384	3	2	55	4	1-1
12/03	TB	W 31-17	32	20	62.5	272	2	2	60	1	1-0
12/09	Cle	W 27-11	29	20	69.0	267	2	1	52	1	1-0
12/18	@SF	L 30-37	39	22	56.4	224	3	0	53	5	3-0
12/24	@Cin	L 24-27	43	26	60.5	294	2	0	51	1	0-0

358

Derrick Moore
Carolina Panthers — RB

1995 Rushing and Receiving Splits

	G	Rush	Yds	Avg	Lg	TD	1st	Stf	YdL	Rec	Yds	Avg	TD		Rush	Yds	Avg	Lg	TD	1st	Stf	YdL	Rec	Yds	Avg	TD
Total	13	195	740	3.8	53	4	35	17	28	4	12	3.0	0	Inside 20	23	48	2.1	9	3	4	3	7	0	0	-	0
vs. Playoff	6	70	212	3.0	14	2	10	4	7	0	0	-	0	Inside 10	15	30	2.0	8	3	4	2	2	0	0	-	0
vs. Non-playoff	7	125	528	4.2	53	2	25	13	21	4	12	3.0	0	1st Down	96	361	3.8	33	0	7	7	10	1	5	5.0	0
vs. Own Division	6	63	200	3.2	33	2	10	5	8	1	4	4.0	0	2nd Down	82	347	4.2	53	2	22	7	15	2	3	1.5	0
Home	7	106	432	4.1	53	3	19	5	7	1	4	4.0	0	3rd Down Overall	16	31	1.9	9	1	5	3	3	1	4	4.0	0
Away	6	89	308	3.5	18	1	16	12	21	3	8	2.7	0	3rd D 0-2 to Go	10	20	2.0	9	1	5	3	3	1	4	4.0	0
Games 1-8	8	125	534	4.3	53	1	23	13	22	4	12	3.0	0	3rd D 3-7 to Go	4	7	1.8	5	0	0	0	0	0	0	-	0
Games 9-16	5	70	206	2.9	12	3	12	4	6	0	0	-	0	3rd D 8+ to Go	2	4	2.0	3	0	0	0	0	0	0	-	0
September	3	19	64	3.4	14	0	4	1	2	0	0	-	0	4th Down	1	1	1.0	1	1	1	0	0	0	0	-	0
October	5	106	470	4.4	53	1	19	12	20	4	12	3.0	0	Left Sideline	6	73	12.2	33	0	3	1	2	3	7	2.3	0
November	1	18	42	2.3	6	0	2	3	5	0	0	-	0	Left Side	26	113	4.3	53	2	6	4	5	1	5	5.0	0
December	4	52	164	3.2	12	3	10	1	1	0	0	-	0	Middle	101	323	3.2	14	1	16	6	9	0	0	-	0
Grass	11	181	687	3.8	53	4	33	16	26	4	12	3.0	0	Right Side	53	176	3.3	15	1	8	5	7	0	0	-	0
Turf	2	14	53	3.8	14	0	2	1	2	0	0	-	0	Right Sideline	9	55	6.1	18	0	2	1	5	0	0	-	0
Indoor	1	0	0	-	0	0	0	0	0	0	0	-	0	Shotgun	0	0	-	0	0	0	0	0	0	0	-	0
Outdoor	12	195	740	3.8	53	4	35	17	28	4	12	3.0	0	2 Wide Receivers	158	670	4.2	53	2	27	9	17	4	12	3.0	0
1st Half	-	98	409	4.2	53	2	19	7	12	1	5	5.0	0	3 Wide Receivers	3	-1	-0.3	2	0	0	2	3	0	0	-	0
2nd Half/OT	-	97	331	3.4	33	2	16	10	16	3	7	2.3	0	4+ Wide Receivers	0	0	-	0	0	0	0	0	0	0	-	0
Last 2 Min. Half	-	16	46	2.9	12	1	2	2	3	0	0	-	0	Carries 1-5	60	241	4.0	18	0	15	3	4	0	0	-	0
4th qtr, +/-7 pts	-	23	77	3.3	15	0	3	5	8	2	3	1.5	0	Carries 6-10	54	234	4.3	53	4	9	4	8	0	0	-	0
Winning	-	64	250	3.9	33	0	10	6	10	3	7	2.3	0	Carries 11-15	43	141	3.3	33	0	5	5	8	0	0	-	0
Tied	-	59	195	3.3	18	0	11	4	9	1	5	5.0	0	Carries 16-20	27	85	3.1	15	0	4	4	6	0	0	-	0
Trailing	-	72	295	4.1	53	4	14	7	9	0	0	-	0	Carries 21+	11	39	3.5	8	0	2	1	2	0	0	-	0

1995 Incompletions

Type	Num	%of Inc	% Att
Pass Dropped	2	50.0	25.0
Poor Throw	1	25.0	12.5
Pass Defensed	0	0.0	0.0
Pass Hit at Line	0	0.0	0.0
Other	1	25.0	12.5
Total	4	100.0	50.0

Game Logs (1-8)

Date	Opp	Result	Rush	Yds	Rec	Yds	Trgt	F-L	TD
09/03	@Atl	L 20-23	0	0	0	0	0	0-0	0
09/10	@Buf	L 9-31	14	53	0	0	0	0-0	0
09/17	StL	L 10-31	5	11	0	0	0	0-0	0
10/01	TB	L 13-20	21	123	0	0	0	2-2	1
10/08	@Chi	L 27-31	15	47	0	0	1	0-0	0
10/15	NYA	W 26-15	21	93	0	0	0	0-0	0
10/22	NO	W 20-3	21	88	1	4	1	0-0	0
10/29	@NE	W 20-17	28	119	3	8	4	0-0	0

Game Logs (9-16)

Date	Opp	Result	Rush	Yds	Rec	Yds	Trgt	F-L	TD
11/05	@SF	W 13-7	18	42	0	0	1	0-0	0
11/12	@StL	L 17-28	-	-	-	-	-	-	-
11/19	Ari	W 27-7	-	-	-	-	-	-	-
11/26	@NO	L 26-34	-	-	-	-	-	-	-
12/03	Ind	W 13-10	19	58	0	0	0	1-0	0
12/10	SF	L 10-31	9	28	0	0	1	0-0	1
12/17	Atl	W 21-17	10	31	0	0	0	1-1	0
12/24	@Was	L 17-20	14	47	0	0	0	0-0	0

Herman Moore
Detroit Lions — WR

1995 Receiving Splits

	G	Rec	Yds	Avg	TD	Lg	Big	YAC	Trgt	Y@C	1st	1st%		Rec	Yds	Avg	TD	Lg	Big	YAC	Trgt	Y@C	1st	1st%
Total	16	123	1686	13.7	14	69	13	560	206	9.2	90	73.2	Inside 20	13	134	10.3	7	17	0	26	31	8.3	10	76.9
vs. Playoff	5	35	568	16.2	7	69	7	181	66	11.1	27	77.1	Inside 10	2	15	7.5	1	8	0	0	10	7.5	1	50.0
vs. Non-playoff	11	88	1118	12.7	7	47	6	379	140	8.4	63	71.6	1st Down	47	708	15.1	5	69	6	277	79	9.2	29	61.7
vs. Own Division	8	61	848	13.9	9	69	6	320	100	8.7	43	70.5	2nd Down	46	579	12.6	6	42	3	162	71	9.1	33	71.7
Home	8	63	885	14.0	6	69	6	328	93	8.8	47	74.6	3rd Down Overall	25	299	12.0	2	40	2	93	51	8.2	23	92.0
Away	8	60	801	13.4	8	47	7	232	113	9.5	43	71.7	3rd D 0-2 to Go	6	52	8.7	0	13	0	22	8	5.0	6	100.0
Games 1-8	8	55	759	13.8	9	69	6	219	98	9.8	42	76.4	3rd D 3-7 to Go	12	145	12.1	1	40	1	49	22	8.0	12	100.0
Games 9-16	8	68	927	13.6	5	46	7	341	108	8.6	48	70.6	3rd D 8+ to Go	7	102	14.6	1	29	1	22	21	11.4	5	71.4
September	4	26	344	13.2	3	47	3	59	45	11.0	19	73.1	4th Down	5	100	20.0	1	42	2	28	5	14.4	5	100.0
October	4	29	415	14.3	6	69	3	160	53	8.8	23	79.3	Rec Behind Line	0	0	-	0	0	0	0	2	-	0	-
November	4	32	475	14.8	2	42	5	164	51	9.7	22	68.8	1-10 yds	95	1029	10.8	6	69	6	432	122	6.3	63	66.3
December	4	36	452	12.6	3	46	2	177	57	7.6	26	72.2	11-20 yds	20	384	19.2	4	40	3	80	45	15.2	19	95.0
Grass	4	30	316	10.5	4	22	1	101	56	7.2	20	66.7	21-30 yds	6	184	30.7	3	42	6	37	30	24.5	6	100.0
Turf	12	93	1370	14.7	10	69	13	459	150	9.8	70	75.3	31+	2	89	44.5	1	47	2	11	7	39.0	2	100.0
Outdoor	11	40	447	11.2	5	30	2	127	73	8.0	26	65.0	Left Sideline	4	41	10.3	1	13	0	17	12	6.0	3	75.0
Indoor	5	83	1239	14.9	9	69	11	433	133	9.7	64	77.1	Left Side	6	85	14.2	1	20	0	17	7	11.3	4	66.7
1st Half	-	63	895	14.2	7	69	8	342	107	8.8	45	71.4	Middle	11	151	13.7	0	42	2	51	22	9.1	8	72.7
2nd Half/OT	-	60	791	13.2	7	42	5	218	99	9.6	45	75.0	Right Side	49	648	13.2	4	69	3	225	78	8.6	37	75.5
Last 2 Min. Half	-	8	151	18.9	2	35	3	34	15	14.6	6	75.0	Right Sideline	53	761	14.4	8	47	8	250	87	9.6	38	71.7
4th qtr, +/-7 pts	-	17	249	14.6	3	29	1	77	24	10.1	13	76.5	Shotgun	1	16	16.0	0	16	0	1	1	15.0	1	100.0
Winning	-	49	637	13.0	3	69	3	215	79	8.6	36	73.5	2 Wide Receivers	25	428	17.1	4	47	6	101	41	13.1	19	76.0
Tied	-	34	430	12.6	4	46	3	203	51	6.7	24	70.6	3 Wide Receivers	96	1220	12.7	10	69	8	455	161	8.0	69	71.9
Trailing	-	40	619	15.5	7	47	7	142	76	11.9	30	75.0	4+ Wide Receivers	1	9	9.0	0	9	0	1	1	9.0	1	100.0

1995 Incompletions

Type	Num	%of Inc	%of Att
Pass Dropped	7	8.4	3.4
Poor Throw	46	55.4	22.3
Pass Defensed	12	14.5	5.8
Pass Hit at Line	3	3.6	1.5
Other	15	18.1	7.3
Total	83	100.0	40.3

Game Logs (1-8)

Date	Opp	Result	Rec	Yds	Trgt	F-L	TD
09/03	@Pit	L 20-23	10	131	17	0-0	1
09/10	@Min	L 10-20	4	73	10	0-0	0
09/17	Ari	L 17-20	6	67	8	0-0	0
09/25	SF	W 27-24	6	73	10	0-0	0
10/08	Cle	W 38-20	9	125	12	0-0	1
10/15	@GB	L 21-30	4	41	14	0-0	2
10/22	@Was	L 30-36	10	102	19	0-0	1
10/29	GB	W 24-16	6	147	8	0-0	3

Game Logs (9-16)

Date	Opp	Result	Rec	Yds	Trgt	F-L	TD
11/05	@Atl	L 22-34	9	176	17	0-0	0
11/12	TB	W 10-4	4	104	13	1-1	0
11/19	@Chi	W 24-17	6	68	8	0-0	1
11/23	Min	W 44-38	8	127	13	0-0	1
12/04	Chi	W 27-7	14	183	19	0-0	1
12/10	@Hou	W 24-17	7	105	11	1-1	2
12/17	Jac	W 44-0	5	59	10	0-0	0
12/23	@TB	W 37-10	10	105	15	0-0	0

Rob Moore
Arizona Cardinals — WR

1995 Receiving Splits

	G	Rec	Yds	Avg	TD	Lg	Big	YAC	Trgt	Y@C	1st	1st%
Total	15	63	907	14.4	5	45	8	125	116	12.4	46	73.0
vs. Playoff	8	36	561	15.6	3	45	6	84	69	13.3	28	77.8
vs. Non-playoff	7	27	346	12.8	2	44	2	41	47	11.3	18	66.7
vs. Own Division	7	24	341	14.2	2	45	3	30	51	13.0	17	70.8
Home	7	36	470	13.1	4	31	2	50	67	11.7	25	69.4
Away	8	27	437	16.2	1	45	6	75	49	13.4	21	77.8
Games 1-8	7	29	400	13.8	3	45	2	49	52	12.1	22	75.9
Games 9-16	8	34	507	14.9	2	44	6	76	64	12.7	24	70.6
September	4	17	252	14.8	2	45	2	21	30	13.6	14	82.4
October	3	12	148	12.3	1	21	0	28	22	10.0	8	66.7
November	5	27	370	13.7	2	44	3	43	43	12.1	19	70.4
December	3	7	137	19.6	0	36	3	33	21	14.9	5	71.4
Grass	11	51	704	13.8	4	44	5	103	93	11.8	37	72.5
Turf	4	12	203	16.9	1	45	3	22	23	15.1	9	75.0
Outdoor	1	62	890	14.4	5	45	8	127	113	12.3	45	72.6
Indoor	14	1	17	17.0	0	17	0	-2	3	19.0	1	100.0
1st Half	-	33	440	13.3	3	45	4	53	53	11.7	24	72.7
2nd Half/OT	-	30	467	15.6	2	36	4	72	63	13.2	22	73.3
Last 2 Min. Half	-	9	130	14.4	1	27	2	16	12	12.7	6	66.7
4th qtr, +/-7 pts	-	11	160	14.5	0	27	1	17	18	13.0	7	63.6
Winning	-	3	62	20.7	0	27	1	6	11	18.7	3	100.0
Tied	-	16	187	11.7	1	27	1	10	22	11.1	10	62.5
Trailing	-	44	658	15.0	4	45	6	109	83	12.5	33	75.0

	Rec	Yds	Avg	TD	Lg	Big	YAC	Trgt	Y@C	1st	1st%
Inside 20	5	46	9.2	4	18	0	2	15	8.8	4	80.0
Inside 10	4	28	7.0	3	9	0	0	10	7.0	3	75.0
1st Down	30	483	16.1	3	45	5	75	48	13.6	22	73.3
2nd Down	19	263	13.8	2	44	2	31	38	12.2	14	73.7
3rd Down Overall	14	161	11.5	0	31	1	19	28	10.1	10	71.4
3rd D 0-2 to Go	2	17	8.5	0	15	0	2	3	7.5	2	100.0
3rd D 3-7 to Go	6	69	11.5	0	31	1	9	12	10.0	5	83.3
3rd D 8+ to Go	6	75	12.5	0	21	0	8	13	11.2	3	50.0
4th Down	0	0	-	0	0	0	0	2	-	0	-
Rec Behind Line	0	0	-	0	0	0	0	0	-	0	-
1-10 yds	31	255	8.2	3	16	0	47	53	6.7	18	58.1
11-20 yds	24	395	16.5	1	35	1	40	39	14.8	20	83.3
21-30 yds	7	212	30.3	1	44	6	33	19	25.6	7	100.0
31+	1	45	45.0	0	45	1	5	5	40.0	1	100.0
Left Sideline	14	226	16.1	0	44	4	28	36	14.1	11	78.6
Left Side	17	205	12.1	2	31	1	22	28	10.8	11	64.7
Middle	8	129	16.1	1	35	1	33	12	12.0	6	75.0
Right Side	10	125	12.5	0	22	0	23	16	10.2	8	80.0
Right Sideline	14	222	15.9	2	45	2	19	24	14.5	10	71.4
Shotgun	8	140	17.5	1	27	2	12	16	16.0	5	62.5
2 Wide Receivers	29	492	17.0	3	45	5	63	59	14.8	24	82.8
3 Wide Receivers	31	390	12.6	2	44	3	61	44	10.6	20	64.5
4+ Wide Receivers	2	13	6.5	0	7	0	0	6	6.5	1	50.0

1995 Incompletions

Type	Num	%of Inc	%of Att
Pass Dropped	7	13.2	6.0
Poor Throw	22	41.5	19.0
Pass Defensed	19	35.8	16.4
Pass Hit at Line	1	1.9	0.9
Other	4	7.5	3.4
Total	53	100.0	45.7

Game Logs (1-8)

Date	Opp	Result		Rec	Yds	Trgt	F-L	TD
09/03	@Was	L	7-27	1	15	5	0-0	0
09/10	Phi	L	19-31	6	66	9	0-0	1
09/17	@Det	W	20-17	1	17	3	0-0	0
09/24	@Dal	L	20-34	9	154	13	0-0	1
10/01	KC	L	3-24	5	66	10	0-0	0
10/09	@NYN	L	21-27	1	5	1	0-0	0
10/15	Was	W	24-20	-	-	-		
10/29	Sea	W	20-14	6	77	11	0-0	1

Game Logs (9-16)

Date	Opp	Result		Rec	Yds	Trgt	F-L	TD
11/05	@Den	L	6-38	6	84	9	0-0	0
11/12	Min	L	24-30	5	66	7	0-0	1
11/19	@Car	L	7-27	3	31	5	0-0	0
11/26	Atl	W	40-37	8	121	13	0-0	1
11/30	NYN	L	6-10	5	68	9	0-0	0
12/09	@SD	L	25-28	5	104	7	0-0	0
12/17	@Phi	L	20-21	1	27	6	0-0	0
12/25	Dal	L	13-37	1	6	8	0-0	0

Will Moore
New England Patriots — WR

1995 Receiving Splits

	G	Rec	Yds	Avg	TD	Lg	Big	YAC	Trgt	Y@C	1st	1st%
Total	14	43	502	11.7	1	33	3	117	79	9.0	33	76.7
vs. Playoff	8	26	283	10.9	1	33	1	61	45	8.5	19	73.1
vs. Non-playoff	6	17	219	12.9	0	32	2	56	34	9.6	14	82.4
vs. Own Division	6	14	165	11.8	0	33	1	32	30	9.5	9	64.3
Home	7	25	337	13.5	0	33	3	80	48	10.3	21	84.0
Away	7	18	165	9.2	1	17	0	37	31	7.1	12	66.7
Games 1-8	7	30	367	12.2	1	33	2	99	52	8.9	24	80.0
Games 9-16	7	13	135	10.4	0	25	1	18	27	9.0	9	69.2
September	3	17	220	12.9	0	33	2	52	28	9.9	14	82.4
October	4	13	147	11.3	1	17	0	47	24	7.7	10	76.9
November	4	6	53	8.8	0	13	0	13	15	6.7	3	50.0
December	3	7	82	11.7	0	25	1	5	12	11.0	6	85.7
Grass	10	35	433	12.4	1	33	3	104	66	9.4	29	82.9
Turf	4	8	69	8.6	0	13	0	13	13	7.0	4	50.0
Outdoor	1	42	492	11.7	1	33	3	113	77	9.0	33	78.6
Indoor	13	1	10	10.0	0	10	0	4	2	6.0	0	0.0
1st Half	-	23	294	12.8	0	33	3	70	44	9.7	18	78.3
2nd Half/OT	-	20	208	10.4	1	17	0	47	35	8.1	15	75.0
Last 2 Min. Half	-	8	88	11.0	0	25	1	12	11	9.5	5	62.5
4th qtr, +/-7 pts	-	2	24	12.0	0	14	0	8	3	8.0	2	100.0
Winning	-	2	12	6.0	0	7	0	2	5	5.0	0	0.0
Tied	-	3	31	10.3	0	11	0	4	12	9.0	2	66.7
Trailing	-	38	459	12.1	1	33	3	111	61	9.2	31	81.6

	Rec	Yds	Avg	TD	Lg	Big	YAC	Trgt	Y@C	1st	1st%
Inside 20	6	46	7.7	1	12	0	3	11	7.2	4	66.7
Inside 10	1	6	6.0	1	6	0	0	2	6.0	1	100.0
1st Down	16	210	13.1	1	33	2	33	30	11.1	13	81.3
2nd Down	13	152	11.7	0	32	1	50	25	7.8	11	84.6
3rd Down Overall	14	140	10.0	0	19	0	34	23	7.6	9	64.3
3rd D 0-2 to Go	0	0	-	0	0	0	0	1	-	0	-
3rd D 3-7 to Go	7	60	8.6	0	14	0	13	12	6.7	5	71.4
3rd D 8+ to Go	7	80	11.4	0	19	0	21	10	8.4	4	57.1
4th Down	0	0	-	0	0	0	0	0	-	0	-
Rec Behind Line	0	0	-	0	0	0	0	1	-	0	-
1-10 yds	29	283	9.8	1	32	1	96	44	6.4	20	69.0
11-20 yds	12	161	13.4	0	19	0	16	25	12.1	11	91.7
21-30 yds	2	58	29.0	0	33	2	5	8	26.5	2	100.0
31+	0	0	-	0	0	0	0	0	-	0	-
Left Sideline	4	92	23.0	0	33	2	36	6	14.0	4	100.0
Left Side	3	29	9.7	0	10	0	6	8	7.7	3	100.0
Middle	11	111	10.1	1	17	0	25	18	7.8	7	63.6
Right Side	16	184	11.5	0	25	1	28	22	9.8	14	87.5
Right Sideline	9	86	9.6	0	14	0	22	24	7.1	5	55.6
Shotgun	0	0	-	0	0	0	0	0	-	0	-
2 Wide Receivers	17	207	12.2	1	33	1	28	38	10.5	16	94.1
3 Wide Receivers	25	270	10.8	0	32	1	87	40	7.3	16	64.0
4+ Wide Receivers	1	25	25.0	0	25	1	2	1	23.0	1	100.0

1995 Incompletions

Type	Num	%of Inc	%of Att
Pass Dropped	4	11.1	5.1
Poor Throw	14	38.9	17.7
Pass Defensed	11	30.6	13.9
Pass Hit at Line	1	2.8	1.3
Other	6	16.7	7.6
Total	36	100.0	45.6

Game Logs (1-8)

Date	Opp	Result		Rec	Yds	Trgt	F-L	TD
09/03	Cle	W	17-14	6	77	9	0-0	0
09/10	Mia	L	3-20	8	112	12	0-0	0
09/17	@SF	L	3-28	3	31	7	0-0	0
10/01	@Atl	L	17-30	1	10	2	0-0	0
10/08	Den	L	3-37	2	31	7	0-0	0
10/15	@KC	L	26-31	7	65	9	0-0	1
10/23	Buf	W	27-14	-	-	-		
10/29	Car	L	17-20	3	41	6	0-0	0

Game Logs (9-16)

Date	Opp	Result		Rec	Yds	Trgt	F-L	TD
11/05	@NYA	L	20-7	2	12	4	0-0	0
11/12	@Mia	W	34-17	0	0	2	0-0	0
11/19	Ind	L	10-24	2	18	6	0-0	0
11/26	@Buf	W	35-25	2	23	3	0-0	0
12/03	NO	L	17-31	4	58	5	0-0	0
12/10	NYA	W	31-28	0	0	0	0-0	0
12/16	@Pit	L	27-41	3	24	4	0-0	0
12/23	@Ind	L	7-10	1	6	8	0-0	0

Anthony Morgan
Green Bay Packers — WR

1995 Receiving Splits

	G	Rec	Yds	Avg	TD	Lg	Big	YAC	Trgt	Y@C	1st	1st%
Total	16	31	344	11.1	4	29	2	117	53	7.3	17	54.8
vs. Playoff	4	3	21	7.0	0	13	0	4	5	5.7	1	33.3
vs. Non-playoff	12	28	323	11.5	4	29	2	113	48	7.5	16	57.1
vs. Own Division	8	13	150	11.5	1	22	0	59	23	7.0	9	69.2
Home	8	12	132	11.0	0	25	1	54	21	6.5	6	50.0
Away	8	19	212	11.2	4	29	1	63	32	7.8	11	57.9
Games 1-8	8	12	135	11.3	2	29	1	38	24	8.1	6	50.0
Games 9-16	8	19	209	11.0	2	25	1	79	29	6.8	11	57.9
September	4	6	78	13.0	2	29	1	19	15	9.8	3	50.0
October	4	6	57	9.5	0	22	0	19	9	6.3	3	50.0
November	4	9	108	12.0	1	21	0	22	15	9.6	7	77.8
December	4	10	101	10.1	1	25	1	57	14	4.4	1	40.0
Grass	12	20	239	12.0	3	29	2	84	37	7.8	12	60.0
Turf	4	11	105	9.5	1	19	0	33	16	6.5	5	45.5
Outdoor	3	23	260	11.3	3	29	2	88	42	7.5	13	56.5
Indoor	13	8	84	10.5	1	19	0	29	11	6.9	4	50.0
1st Half	-	20	261	13.1	3	25	1	91	29	8.5	14	70.0
2nd Half/OT	-	11	83	7.5	1	29	1	26	24	5.2	3	27.3
Last 2 Min. Half	-	2	31	15.5	0	25	1	20	5	5.5	1	50.0
4th qtr, +/-7 pts	-	2	9	4.5	0	6	0	6	2	1.5	0	0.0
Winning	-	9	111	12.3	3	29	1	22	14	9.9	6	66.7
Tied	-	15	166	11.1	1	22	0	65	20	6.7	8	53.3
Trailing	-	7	67	9.6	0	25	1	30	19	5.3	3	42.9

	Rec	Yds	Avg	TD	Lg	Big	YAC	Trgt	Y@C	1st	1st%
Inside 20	4	53	13.3	3	19	0	14	4	9.8	3	75.0
Inside 10	0	0	-	0	0	0	0	0	-	0	-
1st Down	10	99	9.9	2	19	0	36	19	6.3	6	60.0
2nd Down	8	69	8.6	0	22	0	20	17	6.1	2	25.0
3rd Down Overall	13	176	13.5	2	29	2	61	17	8.8	9	69.2
3rd D 0-2 to Go	0	0	-	0	0	0	0	0	-	0	-
3rd D 3-7 to Go	5	75	15.0	1	25	1	33	6	8.4	5	100.0
3rd D 8+ to Go	8	101	12.6	1	29	1	28	11	9.1	4	50.0
4th Down	0	0	-	0	0	0	0	0	-	0	-
Rec Behind Line	3	17	5.7	0	15	0	23	3	-2.0	1	33.3
1-10 yds	19	166	8.7	1	25	1	69	26	5.1	7	36.8
11-20 yds	8	132	16.5	2	22	0	25	16	13.4	8	100.0
21-30 yds	1	29	29.0	0	29	1	0	1	29.0	1	100.0
31+	0	0	-	0	0	0	0	1	-	0	-
Left Sideline	7	90	12.9	1	22	0	27	17	9.0	6	85.7
Left Side	5	77	15.4	2	29	2	25	7	10.4	3	60.0
Middle	4	23	5.8	0	7	0	5	9	4.5	0	0.0
Right Side	7	85	12.1	1	21	0	37	8	6.9	5	71.4
Right Sideline	8	69	8.6	0	16	0	23	12	5.8	3	37.5
Shotgun	0	0	-	0	0	0	0	0	-	0	-
2 Wide Receivers	16	165	10.3	3	29	1	37	28	8.0	8	50.0
3 Wide Receivers	7	72	10.3	1	21	0	17	17	7.9	3	42.9
4+ Wide Receivers	8	107	13.4	0	25	1	63	8	5.5	6	75.0

1995 Incompletions

Type	Num	%of Inc	%of Att
Pass Dropped	2	9.1	3.8
Poor Throw	14	63.6	26.4
Pass Defensed	1	4.5	1.9
Pass Hit at Line	0	0.0	0.0
Other	5	22.7	9.4
Total	22	100.0	41.5

Game Logs (1-8)

Date	Opp	Result	Rec	Yds	Trgt	F-L	TD
09/03	StL	L 14-17	2	12	7	0-0	0
09/11	@Chi	W 27-24	1	15	4	0-0	1
09/17	NYN	W 14-6	0	0	0	0-0	0
09/24	@Jac	W 24-14	3	51	4	0-0	0
10/08	@Dal	L 24-34	3	21	5	0-0	0
10/15	Det	W 30-21	0	0	0	0-0	0
10/22	Min	W 38-21	3	36	4	0-0	0
10/29	@Det	L 16-24	0	0	0	0-0	0

Game Logs (9-16)

Date	Opp	Result	Rec	Yds	Trgt	F-L	TD
11/05	@Min	L 24-27	5	51	8	0-0	0
11/12	Chi	W 35-28	1	21	1	0-0	0
11/19	@Cle	W 31-20	2	25	4	0-0	1
11/26	TB	W 35-13	1	11	2	0-0	0
12/03	Cin	W 24-10	5	52	7	0-0	0
12/10	@TB	L 10-13	2	16	4	0-0	0
12/16	@NO	W 34-23	3	33	3	0-0	0
12/24	Pit	W 24-19	0	0	0	0-0	0

Bam Morris
Pittsburgh Steelers — RB

1995 Rushing and Receiving Splits

	G	Rush	Yds	Avg	Lg	TD	1st	Stf	YdL	Rec	Yds	Avg	TD
Total	13	148	559	3.8	30	7	37	4	8	9	36	4.5	0
vs. Playoff	3	44	127	2.9	13	4	13	2	4	2	13	6.5	0
vs. Non-playoff	10	104	432	4.2	30	5	24	2	4	6	23	3.8	0
vs. Own Division	8	93	397	4.3	30	5	22	2	4	5	19	3.8	0
Home	7	70	245	3.5	30	5	16	4	8	5	12	2.4	0
Away	6	78	314	4.0	22	4	21	0	0	3	24	8.0	0
Games 1-8	8	88	275	3.1	14	4	21	3	7	5	30	6.0	0
Games 9-16	5	60	284	4.7	30	5	16	1	1	3	6	2.0	0
September	4	62	201	3.2	14	2	13	1	3	4	30	7.5	0
October	4	26	74	2.8	11	2	8	2	4	1	0	0.0	0
November	3	39	166	4.3	22	4	12	1	1	2	11	5.5	0
December	2	21	118	5.6	30	1	4	0	0	1	-5	-5.0	0
Grass	4	39	129	3.3	11	1	10	0	0	1	5	5.0	0
Turf	9	109	430	3.9	30	8	27	4	8	7	31	4.4	0
Indoor	1	23	84	3.7	14	0	4	0	0	1	13	13.0	0
Outdoor	12	125	475	3.8	30	9	33	4	8	7	23	3.3	0
1st Half	-	69	228	3.3	22	3	17	2	4	2	20	6.7	0
2nd Half/OT	-	79	331	4.2	30	6	20	2	4	5	16	3.2	0
Last 2 Min. Half	-	7	12	1.7	3	1	2	0	0	0	0	-	0
4th qtr, +/-7 pts	-	25	123	4.9	30	3	9	1	3	2	0	0.0	0
Winning	-	97	363	3.7	30	6	22	2	4	5	23	4.6	0
Tied	-	27	75	2.8	11	1	6	2	4	1	4	4.0	0
Trailing	-	24	121	5.0	22	2	9	0	0	2	9	4.5	0

	Rush	Yds	Avg	Lg	TD	1st	Stf	YdL	Rec	Yds	Avg	TD
Inside 20	28	81	2.9	11	8	13	0	0	1	3	3.0	0
Inside 10	17	26	1.5	8	8	8	0	0	1	3	3.0	0
1st Down	80	336	4.2	30	4	11	2	2	4	13	3.3	0
2nd Down	58	204	3.5	18	5	21	2	6	4	23	5.8	0
3rd Down Overall	7	16	2.3	4	0	4	0	0	-	0	-	0
3rd D 0-2 to Go	5	12	2.4	4	0	4	0	0	0	0	-	0
3rd D 3-7 to Go	1	3	3.0	3	0	0	0	0	0	0	-	0
3rd D 8+ to Go	1	1	1.0	1	0	0	0	0	0	0	-	0
4th Down	3	3	1.0	3	0	1	0	0	0	0	-	0
Left Sideline	2	28	14.0	14	0	2	0	0	1	13	13.0	0
Left Side	34	103	3.0	12	0	5	3	7	4	12	3.0	0
Middle	64	237	3.7	30	6	22	0	0	0	0	-	0
Right Side	41	140	3.4	11	3	6	1	1	3	11	3.7	0
Right Sideline	7	51	7.3	18	0	2	0	0	0	0	-	0
Shotgun	0	0	-	0	0	0	0	0	0	0	-	0
2 Wide Receivers	94	351	3.7	30	2	17	3	7	7	32	4.6	0
3 Wide Receivers	14	93	6.6	22	0	4	1	1	1	4	4.0	0
4+ Wide Receivers	0	0	-	0	0	0	0	0	0	0	-	0
Carries 1-5	61	228	3.7	22	3	17	2	4	0	0	-	0
Carries 6-10	39	160	4.1	14	2	9	0	0	0	0	-	0
Carries 11-15	32	96	3.0	13	3	7	1	1	0	0	-	0
Carries 16-20	13	69	5.3	30	1	4	1	3	0	0	-	0
Carries 21+	3	6	2.0	3	0	0	0	0	0	0	-	0

1995 Incompletions

Type	Num	%of Inc	%Att
Pass Dropped	1	50.0	10.0
Poor Throw	0	0.0	0.0
Pass Defensed	0	0.0	0.0
Pass Hit at Line	0	0.0	0.0
Other	1	50.0	10.0
Total	2	100.0	20.0

Game Logs (1-8)

Date	Opp	Result	Rush	Yds	Rec	Yds	Trgt	F-L	TD
09/03	Det	W 23-20	17	50	2	13	2	1-0	2
09/10	@Hou	W 34-17	23	84	1	13	2	0-0	0
09/18	@Mia	L 10-23	14	48	0	0	0	0-0	0
09/24	Min	L 24-44	8	19	1	4	1	1-1	0
10/01	SD	W 31-16	13	29	0	0	0	0-0	2
10/08	@Jac	L 16-20	5	10	0	0	0	0-0	0
10/19	Cin	L 9-27	5	16	0	0	1	1-0	0
10/29	Jac	W 24-7	3	19	1	0	1	0-0	0

Game Logs (9-16)

Date	Opp	Result	Rush	Yds	Rec	Yds	Trgt	F-L	TD
11/05	@Chi	W 37-34	-	-	-	-	-	-	-
11/13	Cle	W 20-3	6	10	0	0	0	0-0	0
11/19	@Cin	W 49-31	16	101	1	6	1	0-0	3
11/26	@Cle	W 20-17	17	55	1	5	1	0-0	1
12/03	Hou	W 21-7	18	102	1	-5	1	0-0	1
12/10	@Oak	W 29-10	3	16	0	0	0	0-0	0
12/16	NE	W 41-27	-	-	-	-	-	-	-
12/24	@GB	L 19-24	-	-	-	-	-	-	-

Johnnie Morton

1995 Receiving Splits

	G	Rec	Yds	Avg	TD	Lg	Big	YAC	Trgt	Y@C	1st	1st%		Rec	Yds	Avg	TD	Lg	Big	YAC	Trgt	Y@C	1st	1st%
Total	16	44	590	13.4	8	32	4	191	80	9.1	29	65.9	Inside 20	6	65	10.8	6	17	0	7	15	9.7	6	100.0
vs. Playoff	5	10	138	13.8	2	32	1	44	24	9.4	6	60.0	Inside 10	3	16	5.3	3	7	0	1	3		3	100.0
vs. Non-playoff	11	34	452	13.3	6	27	3	147	56	9.0	23	67.6	1st Down	21	317	15.1	4	32	4	106	39	10.0	14	66.7
vs. Own Division	8	22	316	14.4	4	27	2	111	40	9.3	16	72.7	2nd Down	14	155	11.1	2	21	0	45	21	7.9	8	57.1
Home	8	18	247	13.7	4	27	1	68	31	9.9	12	66.7	3rd Down Overall	8	98	12.3	2	22	0	35	19	7.9	6	75.0
Away	8	26	343	13.2	4	32	3	123	49	8.5	17	65.4	3rd D 0-2 to Go	2	24	12.0	2	17	0	6	2	9.0	2	100.0
Games 1-8	8	22	237	10.8	2	27	1	59	37	8.1	11	50.0	3rd D 3-7 to Go	1	7	7.0	0	7	0	1	5	6.0	1	100.0
Games 9-16	8	22	353	16.0	6	32	3	132	43	10.0	18	81.8	3rd D 8+ to Go	5	67	13.4	0	22	0	28	12	7.8	3	60.0
September	4	3	38	12.7	0	27	1	12	9	8.7	1	33.3	4th Down	1	20	20.0	0	20	0	5	1	15.0	1	100.0
October	4	19	199	10.5	2	20	0	47	28	8.0	10	52.6	Rec Behind Line	2	12	6.0	0	11	0	19	5	-3.5	1	50.0
November	4	12	188	15.7	2	32	1	76	23	9.3	8	66.7	1-10 yds	24	193	8.0	3	18	0	88	34	4.4	10	41.7
December	4	10	165	16.5	4	27	2	56	20	10.9	10	100.0	11-20 yds	15	303	20.2	3	27	2	70	32	15.5	15	100.0
Grass	4	19	234	12.3	3	25	1	81	29	8.1	13	68.4	21-30 yds	3	82	27.3	2	32	2	14	8	22.7	3	100.0
Turf	12	25	356	14.2	5	32	3	110	51	9.8	16	64.0	31+	0	0	-	0	0	0	0	1		0	
Indoor	11	24	352	14.7	5	32	3	109	48	10.1	16	66.7	Left Sideline	7	82	11.7	1	22	0	44	12	5.4	5	71.4
Outdoor	5	20	238	11.9	3	25	1	82	32	7.8	13	65.0	Left Side	11	144	13.1	2	27	1	45	19	9.0	8	72.7
1st Half	-	26	380	14.6	5	32	3	105	47	10.6	19	73.1	Middle	13	214	16.5	4	32	2	45	28	13.0	10	76.9
2nd Half/OT	-	18	210	11.7	3	25	1	86	33	6.9	10	55.6	Right Side	4	58	14.5	0	25	1	35	8	5.8	2	50.0
Last 2 Min. Half	-	5	82	16.4	1	32	1	22	10	12.0	3	60.0	Right Sideline	9	92	10.2	1	22	0	22	13	7.8	4	44.4
4th qtr, +/-7 pts	-	7	67	9.6	0	22	0	20	10	6.7	2	28.6	Shotgun	0	0	-	0	0	0	0	0		0	
Winning	-	19	266	14.0	4	27	2	86	36	9.5	13	68.4	2 Wide Receivers	0	0	-	0	0	0	0	3		0	
Tied	-	12	159	13.3	2	27	1	50	19	9.1	9	75.0	3 Wide Receivers	42	574	13.7	8	32	4	184	74	9.3	29	69.0
Trailing	-	13	165	12.7	2	32	1	55	25	8.5	7	53.8	4+ Wide Receivers	2	16	8.0	0	9	0	7	2	4.5	0	0.0

1995 Incompletions

Type	Num	%of Inc	%of Att
Pass Dropped	6	16.7	7.5
Poor Throw	14	38.9	17.5
Pass Defensed	8	22.2	10.0
Pass Hit at Line	1	2.8	1.3
Other	7	19.4	8.8
Total	36	100.0	45.0

Game Logs (1-8)

Date	Opp	Result	Rush	Yds	Rec	Yds	Trgt	F-L	TD
09/03	@Pit	L 20-23	0	0	1	4	3	0-0	0
09/10	@Min	L 10-20	0	0	2	34	5	1-0	0
09/17	Ari	L 17-20	0	0	0	0	0	0-0	0
09/25	SF	W 27-24	0	0	0	1	0	0-0	0
10/08	Cle	W 38-20	0	0	5	43	7	0-0	0
10/15	@GB	L 21-30	0	0	5	62	8	0-0	1
10/22	@Was	L 30-36	0	0	8	76	10	0-0	1
10/29	GB	W 24-16	0	0	1	18	3	0-0	0

Game Logs (9-16)

Date	Opp	Result	Rush	Yds	Rec	Yds	Trgt	F-L	TD
11/05	@Atl	L 22-34	0	0	3	54	9	0-0	1
11/12	TB	W 27-24	0	0	0	0	0	0-0	0
11/19	@Chi	W 24-17	0	0	2	32	4	0-0	0
11/23	Min	W 44-38	0	0	7	102	10	0-0	0
12/04	Chi	W 27-7	1	18	1	4	3	0-0	1
12/10	@Hou	W 24-17	1	8	1	17	3	0-0	0
12/17	Jac	W 44-0	1	7	4	80	7	0-0	2
12/23	@TB	W 37-10	0	0	4	64	7	0-0	1

Adrian Murrell

1995 Rushing and Receiving Splits

	G	Rush	Yds	Avg	Lg	TD	1st	Stf	YdL	Rec	Yds	Avg	TD		Rush	Yds	Avg	Lg	TD	1st	Stf	YdL	Rec	Yds	Avg	TD
Total	15	192	795	4.1	30	1	44	28	77	71	465	6.5	2	Inside 20	21	37	1.8	11	1	5	4	12	5	29	5.8	1
vs. Playoff	7	85	333	3.9	30	1	20	9	21	31	299	9.6	1	Inside 10	8	6	0.8	5	1	3	2	7	2	3	1.5	1
vs. Non-playoff	8	107	462	4.3	24	1	24	19	56	40	166	4.2	1	1st Down	99	385	3.9	24	1	10	16	43	31	190	6.1	1
vs. Own Division	8	104	407	3.9	30	0	25	12	35	33	310	8.9	2	2nd Down	76	303	4.0	30	0	25	11	29	17	64	3.8	0
Home	8	89	399	4.5	30	0	19	13	30	33	215	6.5	1	3rd Down Overall	16	100	6.3	22	0	8	1	5	18	195	10.8	1
Away	7	103	396	3.8	22	1	25	15	47	38	250	6.6	1	3rd D 0-2 to Go	9	43	4.8	22	0	7	1	5	1	1	1.0	0
Games 1-8	8	82	350	4.3	30	0	20	13	32	33	279	8.5	0	3rd D 3-7 to Go	0	0	-	0	0	0	0	0	8	78	9.8	0
Games 9-16	7	110	445	4.0	22	1	24	15	45	38	186	4.9	2	3rd D 8+ to Go	7	57	8.1	21	0	1	0	0	9	116	12.9	1
September	4	31	150	4.8	30	0	9	3	6	16	152	9.5	0	4th Down	1	7	7.0	7	0	1	0	0	5	16	3.2	0
October	5	70	268	3.8	24	0	15	11	28	22	149	6.8	0	Left Sideline	11	86	7.8	20	0	3	1	4	9	96	10.7	1
November	3	45	222	4.9	21	1	14	4	12	14	110	7.9	1	Left Side	44	192	4.4	21	0	9	7	16	12	34	2.8	0
December	3	46	155	3.4	22	0	6	10	31	19	54	2.8	1	Middle	64	211	3.3	10	0	14	8	21	14	113	8.1	0
Grass	3	36	128	3.6	22	0	8	7	24	19	119	6.3	1	Right Side	50	194	3.9	24	1	10	10	27	24	106	4.4	0
Turf	12	156	667	4.3	30	1	36	21	53	52	346	6.7	1	Right Sideline	23	112	4.9	30	0	9	2	9	12	116	9.7	1
Indoor	3	53	235	4.4	21	0	14	4	12	16	91	5.7	0	Shotgun	0	0	-	0	0	0	0	0	0	0	-	0
Outdoor	12	139	560	4.0	30	0	30	24	65	55	374	6.8	2	2 Wide Receivers	156	665	4.3	30	0	32	22	57	57	361	6.3	0
1st Half	-	98	412	4.2	24	1	23	14	41	28	198	7.1	0	3 Wide Receivers	8	54	6.8	20	0	4	0	0	8	87	10.9	1
2nd Half/OT	-	94	383	4.1	30	0	21	14	36	43	267	6.2	2	4+ Wide Receivers	1	-1	-1.0	1	0	0	1	1	1	2	2.0	0
Last 2 Min. Half	-	12	74	6.2	21	0	5	11	92	8.4	1		Carries 1-5	70	267	3.8	20	1	13	11	31	0	0	-	0
4th qtr, +/-7 pts	-	29	158	5.4	30	0	10	1	2	11	37	3.4	1	Carries 6-10	68	297	4.4	30	0	17	8	27	0	0	-	0
Winning	-	32	153	4.8	30	0	8	4	15	10	96	9.6	0	Carries 11-15	34	145	4.3	21	0	8	5	12	0	0	-	0
Tied	-	46	124	2.7	13	1	9	8	28	11	48	4.4	0	Carries 16-20	16	62	3.9	22	0	4	4	7	0	0	-	0
Trailing	-	114	518	4.5	24	0	27	16	34	50	321	6.4	2	Carries 21+	4	24	6.0	9	0	2	0	0	0	0	-	0

1995 Incompletions

Type	Num	%of Inc	% Att
Pass Dropped	13	44.8	13.0
Poor Throw	9	31.0	9.0
Pass Defensed	0	0.0	0.0
Pass Hit at Line	1	3.4	1.0
Other	6	20.7	6.0
Total	29	100.0	29.0

Game Logs (1-8)

Date	Opp	Result	Rush	Yds	Rec	Yds	Trgt	F-L	TD
09/03	@Mia	L 14-52	10	47	7	52	9	0-0	0
09/10	Ind	L 24-27	11	52	4	68	6	0-0	0
09/17	Jac	W 27-10	0	0	1	0	3	0-0	0
09/24	Atl	L 3-13	10	51	4	32	5	0-0	0
10/01	Oak	L 10-47	16	95	3	9	3	0-0	0
10/08	@Buf	L 10-29	14	33	3	40	5	0-0	0
10/15	@Car	L 15-26	9	26	7	45	11	0-0	0
10/22	Mia	W 17-16	12	46	4	33	6	0-0	0

Game Logs (9-16)

Date	Opp	Result	Rush	Yds	Rec	Yds	Trgt	F-L	TD
10/29	@Ind	L 10-17	19	68	5	22	9	0-0	0
11/05	NE	L 7-20	12	70	3	21	6	0-0	0
11/19	Buf	L 26-28	9	36	4	52	6	1-1	1
11/26	@Sea	W 16-10	24	116	7	37	7	0-0	0
12/03	StL	L 20-23	19	57	5	20	8	0-0	0
12/10	@NE	L 28-31	17	55	5	22	6	0-0	1
12/17	@Hou	L 6-23	-	-	-	-	-	-	-
12/24	NO	L 0-12	10	43	9	12	10	1-0	0

Jay Novacek

1995 Receiving Splits

	G	Rec	Yds	Avg	TD	Lg	Big	YAC	Trgt	Y@C	1st	1st%
Total	15	62	705	11.4	5	33	3	270	90	7.0	40	64.5
vs. Playoff	7	27	290	10.7	3	33	2	97	44	7.1	15	55.6
vs. Non-playoff	8	35	415	11.9	2	26	1	173	46	6.9	25	71.4
vs. Own Division	7	23	276	12.0	1	22	0	78	37	8.6	16	69.6
Home	8	36	371	10.3	4	33	2	115	57	7.1	22	61.1
Away	7	26	334	12.8	1	26	1	155	33	6.9	18	69.2
Games 1-8	8	34	410	12.1	4	29	2	149	43	7.7	24	70.6
Games 9-16	7	28	295	10.5	1	33	1	121	47	6.2	16	57.1
September	4	18	234	13.0	2	26	1	102	25	7.3	15	83.3
October	4	16	176	11.0	2	29	1	47	18	8.1	9	56.3
November	4	20	211	10.6	1	33	1	98	31	5.7	11	55.0
December	3	8	84	10.5	0	19	0	23	16	7.6	5	62.5
Grass	3	14	159	11.4	0	19	0	70	15	6.4	8	57.1
Turf	12	48	546	11.4	5	33	3	200	75	7.2	32	66.7
Outdoor	2	56	636	11.4	4	33	2	224	82	7.4	35	62.5
Indoor	13	6	69	11.5	1	26	1	46	8	3.8	5	83.3
1st Half	-	29	307	10.6	3	22	0	103	38	7.0	18	62.1
2nd Half/OT	-	33	398	12.1	2	33	3	167	52	7.0	22	66.7
Last 2 Min. Half	-	7	40	5.7	1	10	0	13	12	3.9	4	28.6
4th qtr, +/-7 pts	-	6	73	12.2	0	26	1	33	10	6.7	3	50.0
Winning	-	30	368	12.3	2	33	2	163	44	6.8	20	66.7
Tied	-	9	106	11.8	2	18	0	28	11	8.7	8	88.9
Trailing	-	23	231	10.0	1	26	1	79	35	6.6	12	52.2

	Rec	Yds	Avg	TD	Lg	Big	YAC	Trgt	Y@C	1st	1st%
Inside 20	11	61	5.5	4	10	0	29	14	2.9	4	36.4
Inside 10	4	15	3.8	3	7	0	3	7	3.0	3	75.0
1st Down	23	265	11.5	0	26	1	121	35	6.3	12	52.2
2nd Down	23	272	11.8	3	33	2	84	31	8.2	14	60.9
3rd Down Overall	16	168	10.5	2	20	0	65	24	6.4	14	87.5
3rd D 0-2 to Go	2	10	5.0	1	9	0	5	3	2.5	2	100.0
3rd D 3-7 to Go	10	104	10.4	1	20	0	42	15	6.2	8	80.0
3rd D 8+ to Go	4	54	13.5	0	17	0	18	6	9.0	4	100.0
4th Down	0	0	-	0	0	0	0	0	-	0	-
Rec Behind Line	3	41	13.7	0	26	1	54	5	-4.3	2	66.7
1-10 yds	42	370	8.8	5	33	1	167	61	4.8	22	52.4
11-20 yds	17	294	17.3	0	29	1	49	22	14.4	16	94.1
21-30 yds	0	0	-	0	0	0	0	2	-	0	-
31+	0	0	-	0	0	0	0	0	-	0	-
Left Sideline	8	60	7.5	0	14	0	26	11	4.3	2	25.0
Left Side	19	219	11.5	2	33	2	120	21	5.2	13	68.4
Middle	13	173	13.3	2	22	0	32	26	10.8	12	92.3
Right Side	13	193	14.8	1	29	1	75	16	9.1	10	76.9
Right Sideline	9	60	6.7	0	15	0	17	16	4.8	3	33.3
Shotgun	0	0	-	0	0	0	0	0	-	0	-
2 Wide Receivers	29	387	13.3	3	33	2	126	45	9.0	19	65.5
3 Wide Receivers	27	256	9.5	0	19	0	106	36	5.6	16	59.3
4+ Wide Receivers	2	30	15.0	0	17	0	0	4	15.0	2	100.0

1995 Incompletions

Type	Num	%of Inc	%of Att
Pass Dropped	5	17.9	5.6
Poor Throw	8	28.6	8.9
Pass Defensed	6	21.4	6.7
Pass Hit at Line	2	7.1	2.2
Other	7	25.0	7.8
Total	28	100.0	31.1

Game Logs (1-8)

Date	Opp	Result	Rec	Yds	Trgt	F-L	TD
09/04	@NYN	W 35-0	5	91	5	1-1	0
09/10	Den	W 31-21	5	56	7	0-0	1
09/17	@Min	W 23-17	5	68	7	0-0	0
09/24	Ari	W 34-20	3	19	6	0-0	1
10/01	@Was	L 23-27	4	45	4	0-0	0
10/08	GB	W 34-24	7	83	8	0-0	1
10/15	@SD	W 23-9	4	47	5	0-0	0
10/29	@Atl	W 28-13	4	9	1	0-0	1

Game Logs (9-16)

Date	Opp	Result	Rec	Yds	Trgt	F-L	TD
11/06	Phi	W 34-12	3	37	6	0-0	0
11/12	SF	L 20-38	7	55	13	0-0	0
11/19	@Oak	W 34-21	6	67	6	0-0	0
11/23	KC	W 24-12	4	52	6	0-0	0
12/03	Was	L 17-24	5	46	7	0-0	0
12/10	@Phi	L 17-20	1	15	5	0-0	0
12/17	NYN	W 21-20	3	23	4	0-0	0
12/25	@Ari	W 37-13	-	-	-	-	-

Neil O'Donnell

1995 Passing Splits

	G	Att	Cm	Pct	Yds	Yd/Att	TD	Int	1st	YAC	Big	Sk	Rtg
Total	12	416	246	59.1	2970	7.1	17	7	137	1230	26	15	87.7
vs. Playoff	2	65	40	61.5	381	5.9	1	0	22	164	1	1	82.9
vs. Non-playoff	10	351	206	58.7	2589	7.4	16	7	115	1066	25	14	88.6
vs. Own Division	7	243	143	58.8	1823	7.5	10	3	80	760	17	6	91.0
Home	6	182	100	54.9	1171	6.4	7	4	59	544	8	5	78.3
Away	6	234	146	62.4	1799	7.7	10	3	78	686	18	10	95.0
Games 1-8	4	122	73	59.8	882	7.2	3	1	41	361	6	1	86.9
Games 9-16	8	294	173	58.8	2088	7.1	14	6	96	869	20	14	88.1
September	1	10	7	70.0	63	6.3	0	0	5	24	0	0	86.7
October	3	112	66	58.9	819	7.3	3	1	36	337	6	1	86.9
November	4	144	96	66.7	1136	7.9	7	2	52	433	11	8	100.9
December	4	150	77	51.3	952	6.3	7	4	44	436	9	6	75.8
Grass	5	203	122	60.1	1422	7.0	7	3	64	557	14	9	86.7
Turf	7	213	124	58.2	1548	7.3	10	4	73	673	12	6	88.7
Indoor	0	0	0	-	0	-	0	0	0	0	0	0	-
Outdoor	12	416	246	59.1	2970	7.1	17	7	137	1230	26	15	87.7
1st Half	-	213	137	64.3	1606	7.5	12	2	76	658	15	7	102.0
2nd Half/OT	-	203	109	53.7	1364	6.7	5	5	61	572	11	8	72.8
Last 2 Min. Half	-	59	34	57.6	440	7.5	8	1	21	171	5	0	113.7
4th qtr, +/-7 pts	-	72	41	56.9	547	7.6	3	2	23	231	5	1	83.5
Winning	-	105	51	48.6	626	6.0	5	3	32	305	7	4	71.4
Tied	-	116	74	63.8	862	7.4	5	2	42	380	7	4	93.4
Trailing	-	195	121	62.1	1482	7.6	7	2	63	545	12	7	93.2

	Att	Cm	Pct	Yds	Yd/Att	TD	Int	1st	YAC	Big	Sk	Rtg
Inside 20	66	32	48.5	233	3.5	12	1	17	85	0	3	90.5
Inside 10	25	8	32.0	51	2.0	5	1	7	15	0	2	64.2
1st Down	153	94	61.4	1189	7.8	7	1	44	487	10	7	98.2
2nd Down	136	82	60.3	917	6.7	4	2	43	436	8	6	84.1
3rd Down Overall	122	69	56.6	854	7.0	5	4	49	307	8	2	78.4
3rd D 0-5 to Go	44	21	47.7	235	5.3	0	1	20	101	1	0	54.6
3rd D 6+ to Go	78	48	61.5	619	7.9	5	3	29	206	7	2	91.8
4th Down	5	1	20.0	10	2.0	1	0	1	0	0	0	79.2
Rec Behind Line	55	40	72.7	173	3.1	0	2	7	316	0	0	60.6
1-10 yds	214	142	66.4	1339	6.3	10	3	68	612	3	0	93.2
11-20 yds	92	44	47.8	805	8.8	4	1	42	126	6	0	88.4
21-30 yds	42	19	45.2	611	14.5	2	1	19	169	16	0	97.8
31+	13	1	7.7	42	3.2	1	0	1	7	1	0	66.2
Left Sideline	72	34	47.2	367	5.1	2	2	24	163	2	1	60.4
Left Side	71	50	71.4	426	6.1	2	0	16	217	1	0	96.5
Middle	95	62	65.3	854	9.0	6	2	40	285	7	13	106.2
Right Side	98	60	61.2	821	8.4	6	3	36	389	9	1	95.7
Right Sideline	81	40	49.4	502	6.2	1	0	21	176	7	0	73.2
2 Wide Receivers	170	97	57.1	1173	6.9	9	2	52	496	10	13	91.1
3+ WR	237	145	61.2	1748	7.4	8	5	83	699	15	2	86.3
Attempts 1-10	120	72	60.0	830	6.0	5	0	37	316	0	0	84.8
Attempts 11-20	110	73	66.4	870	7.9	4	2	40	401	7	0	94.9
Attempts 21+	186	101	54.3	1270	6.8	8	5	60	513	10	0	78.9

1995 Incompletions

Type	Num	% of Inc	% of Att
Pass Dropped	26	15.3	6.3
Poor Throw	86	50.6	20.7
Pass Defensed	23	13.5	5.5
Pass Hit at Line	6	3.5	1.4
Other	29	17.1	7.0
Total	170	100.0	40.9

Game Logs (1-8)

Date	Opp	Result	Att	Cm	Pct	Yds	TD	Int	Lg	Sk	F-L
09/03	Det	W 23-20	10	7	70.0	63	0	0	17	0	1-0
09/10	@Hou	W 34-17	-	-	-	-	-	-	-	-	-
09/18	@Mia	L 10-23	-	-	-	-	-	-	-	-	-
09/24	Min	L 24-44	-	-	-	-	-	-	-	-	-
10/01	SD	L 31-16	-	-	-	-	-	-	-	-	-
10/08	@Jac	L 16-20	35	19	54.3	282	1	0	43	0	0-0
10/19	Cin	L 9-27	52	30	57.7	359	0	1	27	1	0-0
10/29	Jac	W 24-7	25	17	68.0	178	2	0	32	0	0-0

Game Logs (9-16)

Date	Opp	Result	Att	Cm	Pct	Yds	TD	Int	Lg	Sk	F-L
11/05	@Chi	W 37-34	52	34	65.4	341	2	2	27	5	1-0
11/13	Cle	W 20-3	31	17	54.8	167	1	0	24	1	0-0
11/19	@Cin	W 49-31	31	24	77.4	377	3	0	71	1	0-0
11/26	@Cle	W 20-17	30	21	70.0	251	1	0	37	1	0-0
12/03	Hou	W 21-7	39	15	38.5	209	2	2	34	2	0-0
12/10	@Oak	W 29-10	31	15	48.4	230	2	1	37	2	0-0
12/16	NE	W 41-27	25	14	56.0	195	2	1	62	1	0-0
12/24	@GB	L 19-24	55	33	60.0	318	1	0	36	1	0-0

Bernie Parmalee

Miami Dolphins — RB

1995 Rushing and Receiving Splits

	G	Rush	Yds	Avg	Lg	TD	1st	Stf	YdL	Rec	Yds	Avg	TD
Total	16	236	878	3.7	40	9	55	31	78	39	345	8.8	1
vs. Playoff	9	139	532	3.8	40	5	33	17	38	19	178	9.4	0
vs. Non-playoff	7	97	346	3.6	25	4	22	14	40	20	167	8.4	1
vs. Own Division	8	129	516	4.0	25	4	33	16	40	26	268	10.3	1
Home	8	118	402	3.4	27	6	26	14	40	21	236	11.2	1
Away	8	118	476	4.0	40	3	29	17	38	18	109	6.1	0
Games 1-8	8	105	395	3.8	25	4	26	16	40	19	163	8.6	0
Games 9-16	8	131	483	3.7	40	5	29	15	35	20	182	9.1	1
September	3	39	137	3.5	24	3	9	5	13	4	37	9.3	0
October	5	66	258	3.9	25	1	17	11	30	15	126	8.4	0
November	4	62	282	4.5	40	1	13	4	13	13	152	11.7	1
December	4	69	201	2.9	27	4	16	11	30	7	30	4.3	0
Grass	10	152	577	3.8	40	6	33	17	44	25	267	10.7	1
Turf	6	84	301	3.6	25	3	22	14	34	14	78	5.6	0
Indoor	3	42	139	3.3	15	2	11	8	20	8	66	8.3	0
Outdoor	13	194	739	3.8	40	7	44	23	58	31	279	9.0	1
1st Half	-	133	478	3.6	27	3	30	16	45	19	170	8.9	1
2nd Half/OT	-	103	400	3.9	40	6	25	15	33	20	175	8.8	0
Last 2 Min. Half	-	5	0	0.0	1	0	1	2	2	3	28	9.3	0
4th qtr, +/-7 pts	-	19	67	3.5	12	2	5	1	2	4	9	2.3	0
Winning	-	95	346	3.6	40	3	18	11	33	10	84	8.4	0
Tied	-	63	252	4.0	27	3	15	9	25	9	101	11.2	0
Trailing	-	78	280	3.6	25	3	22	11	20	20	160	8.0	1

	Rush	Yds	Avg	Lg	TD	1st	Stf	YdL	Rec	Yds	Avg	TD
Inside 20	40	87	2.2	7	7	10	7	19	2	12	6.0	0
Inside 10	26	44	1.7	7	7	8	6	14	1	2	2.0	0
1st Down	142	538	3.8	25	8	18	16	50	19	176	9.3	1
2nd Down	67	211	3.1	17	1	19	13	25	16	157	9.8	0
3rd Down Overall	24	119	5.0	40	0	15	2	3	4	12	3.0	0
3rd D 0-2 to Go	21	79	3.8	27	0	14	1	2	2	1	0.5	0
3rd D 3-7 to Go	1	40	40.0	40	0	1	0	1	2	2	2.0	0
3rd D 8+ to Go	2	0	0.0	1	0	0	1	1	1	9	9.0	0
4th Down	3	10	3.3	6	0	3	0	0	0	0	-	0
Left Sideline	21	99	4.7	14	0	5	2	3	11	76	6.9	0
Left Side	56	266	4.8	40	2	16	5	13	11	78	7.1	0
Middle	88	213	2.4	24	5	17	13	31	7	72	10.3	1
Right Side	46	193	4.2	27	2	11	8	23	7	61	8.7	0
Right Sideline	25	107	4.3	25	0	6	3	8	3	58	19.3	0
Shotgun	1	3	3.0	3	0	0	0	0	6	63	10.5	0
2 Wide Receivers	202	742	3.7	40	8	37	28	74	28	231	8.3	1
3 Wide Receivers	7	47	6.7	13	0	3	0	0	10	114	11.4	0
4+ Wide Receivers	0	0	-	0	0	0	0	0	0	0	-	0
Carries 1-5	80	276	3.5	27	2	17	8	26	0	0	-	0
Carries 6-10	69	238	3.4	24	2	14	12	27	0	0	-	0
Carries 11-15	50	190	3.8	20	3	14	7	14	0	0	-	0
Carries 16-20	29	150	5.2	40	2	9	4	11	0	0	-	0
Carries 21+	8	24	3.0	5	0	1	0	0	0	0	-	0

1995 Incompletions

Type	Num	%of Inc	% Att
Pass Dropped	1	14.3	2.2
Poor Throw	5	71.4	10.9
Pass Defensed	0	0.0	0.0
Pass Hit at Line	0	0.0	0.0
Other	1	14.3	2.2
Total	7	100.0	15.2

Game Logs (1-8)

Date	Opp	Result	Rush	Yds	Rec	Yds	Trgt	F-L	TD
09/03	NYA	W 52-14	16	52	1	15	1	2-2	2
09/10	@NE	W 20-3	15	72	3	22	3	1-1	0
09/18	Pit	W 23-10	8	13	0	0	0	0-0	1
10/01	@Cin	W 26-23	6	22	0	0	2	0-0	0
10/08	Ind	L 24-27	8	24	3	41	3	0-0	0
10/15	@NO	L 30-33	8	9	3	25	3	0-0	0
10/22	@NYA	L 16-17	24	120	6	12	6	0-0	0
10/29	Buf	W 23-6	20	83	3	48	3	0-0	1

Game Logs (9-16)

Date	Opp	Result	Rush	Yds	Rec	Yds	Trgt	F-L	TD
11/05	@SD	W 24-14	19	103	1	9	1	0-0	0
11/12	NE	L 17-34	14	43	6	91	6	0-0	1
11/20	SF	L 20-44	9	34	2	13	2	0-0	1
11/26	@Ind	L 28-36	20	102	4	39	6	0-0	0
12/03	Atl	W 21-20	19	70	4	19	5	0-0	1
12/11	KC	W 13-6	24	83	2	9	4	2-1	0
12/17	@Buf	L 20-23	12	20	0	0	0	0-0	0
12/24	@StL	W 41-22	14	28	1	2	1	0-0	2

Rodney Peete

Philadelphia Eagles — QB

1995 Passing Splits

	G	Att	Cm	Pct	Yds	Yd/Att	TD	Int	1st	YAC	Big	Sk	Rtg
Total	15	375	215	57.3	2326	6.2	8	14	111	1053	13	33	67.3
vs. Playoff	3	55	31	56.4	320	5.8	0	3	12	139	1	7	50.6
vs. Non-playoff	12	320	184	57.5	2006	6.3	8	11	99	914	12	26	70.1
vs. Own Division	7	194	117	60.3	1264	6.5	6	6	60	614	6	13	78.7
Home	7	196	118	60.2	1219	6.2	7	7	62	584	5	12	75.2
Away	8	179	97	54.2	1107	6.2	1	7	49	469	8	21	58.6
Games 1-8	7	142	81	57.0	857	6.0	3	4	42	356	3	13	73.0
Games 9-16	8	233	134	57.5	1469	6.3	5	11	69	697	10	20	63.8
September	3	28	14	50.0	215	7.7	1	1	11	91	1	3	72.8
October	4	114	67	58.8	642	5.6	2	2	31	265	2	10	73.1
November	4	106	66	62.3	680	6.4	3	4	36	364	4	10	74.4
December	4	127	68	53.5	789	6.2	2	7	33	333	6	10	54.9
Grass	4	82	45	54.9	554	6.8	1	4	26	252	4	10	59.7
Turf	11	293	170	58.0	1772	6.0	7	10	85	801	9	23	69.4
Indoor	2	64	37	57.8	373	5.8	0	1	17	159	2	6	68.0
Outdoor	13	311	178	57.2	1953	6.3	8	13	94	894	11	27	67.1
1st Half	-	222	131	59.0	1428	6.4	5	6	70	660	7	17	74.3
2nd Half/OT	-	153	84	54.9	898	5.9	3	8	41	393	6	16	57.0
Last 2 Min. Half	-	72	40	55.6	393	5.5	1	4	20	146	0	4	52.6
4th qtr, +/-7 pts	-	38	21	55.3	235	6.2	1	3	18	138	2	5	49.8
Winning	-	106	60	56.6	558	5.3	2	2	29	284	1	11	69.6
Tied	-	89	57	64.0	597	6.7	3	2	32	268	4	6	85.3
Trailing	-	180	98	54.4	1171	6.5	3	10	50	501	8	16	57.0

	Att	Cm	Pct	Yds	Yd/Att	TD	Int	1st	YAC	Big	Sk	Rtg
Inside 20	27	9	33.3	82	3.0	5	1	8	21	0	3	66.7
Inside 10	9	3	33.3	7	0.8	3	1	3	0	0	2	42.4
1st Down	123	77	62.6	750	6.1	1	3	25	361	5	7	72.2
2nd Down	138	76	55.1	816	5.9	5	4	41	394	4	9	72.6
3rd Down Overall	107	59	55.1	713	6.7	2	6	42	294	4	17	58.7
3rd D 0-5 to Go	37	20	54.1	245	6.6	1	1	17	103	3	4	72.5
3rd D 6+ to Go	70	39	55.7	468	6.7	1	5	25	191	1	13	51.4
4th Down	7	3	42.9	47	6.7	0	1	3	4	0	0	26.2
Rec Behind Line	65	34	52.3	163	2.5	0	3	8	258	0	1	38.9
1-10 yds	211	136	64.5	1265	6.0	4	4	60	615	1	9	79.2
11-20 yds	72	36	50.0	629	8.7	2	2	34	134	4	0	77.8
21-30 yds	19	9	47.4	269	14.2	2	3	9	46	8	0	89.1
31+	8	0	0.0	0	0.0	0	2	0	0	0	0	0.0
Left Sideline	42	25	59.5	275	6.5	1	2	15	102	1	0	67.1
Left Side	72	45	62.5	544	7.6	2	2	24	270	3	3	89.1
Middle	74	39	52.7	478	6.5	3	5	23	145	3	26	58.3
Right Side	117	69	59.0	724	6.2	2	3	37	353	3	4	75.6
Right Sideline	70	37	52.9	305	4.4	0	4	12	183	3	0	40.5
2 Wide Receivers	144	93	64.6	942	6.5	3	2	42	483	6	6	84.3
3+ WR	226	119	52.7	1365	6.0	4	12	66	558	7	26	54.9
Attempts 1-10	137	79	57.7	902	6.6	3	3	41	429	4	0	75.7
Attempts 11-20	118	73	61.9	790	6.7	2	5	37	319	6	0	69.5
Attempts 21+	120	63	52.5	634	5.3	3	6	33	305	3	0	55.3

1995 Incompletions

Type	Num	% of Inc	% of Att
Pass Dropped	25	15.6	6.7
Poor Throw	67	41.9	17.9
Pass Defensed	25	15.6	6.7
Pass Hit at Line	19	11.9	5.1
Other	24	15.0	6.4
Total	160	100.0	42.7

Game Logs (1-8)

Date	Opp	Result	Att	Cm	Pct	Yds	TD	Int	Lg	Sk	F-L
09/03	TB	L 6-21									
09/10	@Ari	W 31-19	13	8	61.5	145	1	0	33	0	0-0
09/17	SD	L 21-27									
09/24	@Oak	L 17-48	15	6	40.0	70	0	1	21	2	1-1
10/01	@NO	W 15-10	28	18	64.3	173	0	0	23	5	1-1
10/08	Was	W 37-34	45	30	66.7	256	1	1	17	2	2-1
10/15	@NYN	W 17-14	7	4	57.1	47	0	0	29	2	1-0
10/29	StL	W 20-9	34	15	44.1	166	1	1	33	1	1-0

Game Logs (9-16)

Date	Opp	Result	Att	Cm	Pct	Yds	TD	Int	Lg	Sk	F-L
11/06	@Dal	L 12-34	26	11	42.3	133	0	2	25	3	0-0
11/12	Den	W 31-13	37	25	67.6	264	1	0	29	5	0-0
11/19	NYN	W 28-19	20	14	70.0	133	2	1	21	2	1-1
11/26	@Was	W 14-7	23	16	69.6	150	0	1	31	4	1-0
12/03	@Sea	L 14-26	36	19	52.8	200	1	2	29	1	1-0
12/10	Dal	W 20-17	29	20	69.0	187	0	1	20	3	1-1
12/17	Ari	W 21-20	31	14	45.2	213	2	3	37	2	1-0
12/24	@Chi	L 14-20	31	15	48.4	189	0	2	36	4	2-1

Erric Pegram

1995 Rushing and Receiving Splits

	G	Rush	Yds	Avg	Lg	TD	1st	Stf	YdL	Rec	Yds	Avg	TD
Total	15	213	813	3.8	38	5	34	28	69	26	206	7.9	1
vs. Playoff	3	30	147	4.9	17	0	6	6	11	5	45	9.0	0
vs. Non-playoff	12	183	666	3.6	38	5	28	22	58	21	161	7.7	1
vs. Own Division	8	107	398	3.7	38	1	15	11	33	15	124	8.3	0
Home	8	119	506	4.3	38	3	20	11	23	16	144	9.0	0
Away	7	94	307	3.3	22	2	14	17	46	10	62	6.2	1
Games 1-8	8	100	414	4.1	38	3	17	15	37	13	134	10.3	0
Games 9-16	7	113	399	3.5	22	2	17	13	32	13	72	5.5	1
September	4	31	119	3.8	17	2	6	7	20	3	25	8.3	0
October	4	69	295	4.3	38	1	11	8	17	10	109	10.9	0
November	4	69	217	3.1	15	2	10	10	26	13	72	5.5	1
December	3	44	182	4.1	22	0	7	3	6	0	0	-	0
Grass	5	75	251	3.3	22	2	12	13	34	8	48	6.0	1
Turf	10	138	562	4.1	38	3	22	15	35	18	158	8.8	0
Indoor	1	8	18	2.3	10	0	1	3	10	1	12	12.0	0
Outdoor	14	205	795	3.9	38	5	33	25	59	25	194	7.8	1
1st Half	-	114	402	3.5	22	2	15	14	30	16	130	8.1	1
2nd Half/OT	-	99	411	4.2	38	3	19	14	39	10	76	7.6	0
Last 2 Min. Half	-	4	14	3.5	8	0	0	1	3	1	7	7.0	1
4th qtr, +/-7 pts	-	11	55	5.0	17	1	3	3	6	0	0	-	0
Winning	-	91	400	4.4	22	0	16	11	26	7	54	7.7	0
Tied	-	58	158	2.7	17	1	7	8	21	11	106	9.6	1
Trailing	-	64	255	4.0	38	4	11	9	22	8	46	5.8	0

	Rush	Yds	Avg	Lg	TD	1st	Stf	YdL	Rec	Yds	Avg	TD
Inside 20	32	74	2.3	12	5	8	7	20	7	27	3.9	1
Inside 10	18	29	1.6	6	5	5	4	6	1	7	7.0	1
1st Down	139	512	3.7	18	3	18	15	14	32	14	110	7.9	0
2nd Down	68	289	4.3	38	1	14	14	37	8	84	10.5	0
3rd Down Overall	5	11	2.2	5	0	4	0	0	4	12	3.0	1
3rd D 0-2 to Go	5	11	2.2	5	0	4	0	0	0	0	-	0
3rd D 3-7 to Go	0	0	-	0	0	0	0	0	1	7	7.0	1
3rd D 8+ to Go	0	0	-	0	0	0	0	0	3	5	1.7	0
4th Down	1	1	1.0	1	1	1	0	0	0	0	-	0
Left Sideline	21	93	4.4	14	1	4	4	6	6	41	6.8	1
Left Side	42	156	3.7	38	0	4	8	24	6	30	5.0	0
Middle	79	277	3.5	22	1	9	6	13	2	15	7.5	0
Right Side	59	225	3.8	17	3	14	9	23	9	99	11.0	0
Right Sideline	12	62	5.2	18	0	3	1	3	3	21	7.0	0
Shotgun	3	14	4.7	7	0	1	0	0	1	-3	-3.0	0
2 Wide Receivers	155	573	3.7	22	3	21	22	51	19	182	9.6	1
3 Wide Receivers	24	122	5.1	38	0	4	2	6	5	23	4.6	0
4+ Wide Receivers	2	9	4.5	7	0	0	0	0	1	-3	-3.0	0
Carries 1-5	71	252	3.5	22	1	10	10	22	-	-	-	-
Carries 6-10	60	253	4.2	38	1	10	7	20	-	-	-	-
Carries 11-15	37	147	4.0	13	1	4	3	13	-	-	-	-
Carries 16-20	26	78	3.0	14	2	6	8	14	-	-	-	-
Carries 21+	19	83	4.4	15	0	4	0	0	-	-	-	-

1995 Incompletions

Type	Num	%of Inc	% Att
Pass Dropped	3	33.3	8.6
Poor Throw	3	33.3	8.6
Pass Defensed	0	0.0	0.0
Pass Hit at Line	0	0.0	0.0
Other	3	33.3	8.6
Total	9	100.0	25.7

Game Logs (1-8)

Date	Opp	Result	Rush	Yds	Rec	Yds	Trgt	F-L	TD
09/03	Det	W 23-20	6	46	2	13	2	0-0	0
09/10	@Hou	W 34-17	8	18	1	12	2	1-1	0
09/18	@Mia	L 10-23	1	6	0	0	0	0-0	0
09/24	Min	L 24-44	16	49	0	0	0	0-0	0
10/01	SD	W 31-16	23	95	3	32	4	1-0	0
10/08	@Jac	L 16-20	16	56	0	0	1	1-0	0
10/19	Cin	L 9-27	11	60	3	39	5	0-0	0
10/29	Jac	W 24-7	19	84	4	38	4	1-0	1

Game Logs (9-16)

Date	Opp	Result	Rush	Yds	Rec	Yds	Trgt	F-L	TD
11/05	@Chi	W 37-34	24	61	6	37	7	2-2	3
11/13	Cle	W 20-3	26	112	4	22	4	0-0	0
11/19	@Cin	W 49-31	11	38	1	2	1	1-1	0
11/26	@Cle	W 20-17	8	6	2	11	2	0-0	0
12/03	Hou	W 21-7	8	24	0	0	0	1-1	0
12/10	@Oak	W 29-10	26	122	0	0	2	1-1	0
12/16	NE	W 41-27	10	36	0	0	1	0-0	0
12/24	@GB	L 19-24							

Brett Perriman

1995 Receiving Splits

	G	Rec	Yds	Avg	TD	Lg	Big	YAC	Trgt	Y@C	1st	1st%
Total	16	108	1488	13.8	9	91	12	384	179	10.2	74	68.5
vs. Playoff	5	25	323	12.9	2	31	2	68	50	10.2	18	72.0
vs. Non-playoff	11	83	1165	14.0	7	91	10	316	129	10.2	56	67.5
vs. Own Division	8	59	791	13.4	3	91	5	207	96	9.9	38	64.4
Home	8	56	694	12.4	5	39	5	159	85	9.6	38	67.9
Away	8	52	794	15.3	4	91	7	225	94	10.9	36	69.2
Games 1-8	8	48	669	13.9	5	51	5	186	82	10.1	37	77.1
Games 9-16	8	60	819	13.7	4	91	7	198	97	10.4	37	61.7
September	4	29	366	12.6	2	39	2	72	43	10.1	23	79.3
October	4	19	303	15.9	3	51	3	114	39	9.9	14	73.7
November	4	39	473	12.1	3	37	3	104	63	9.5	23	59.0
December	4	21	346	16.5	1	91	4	94	34	12.0	14	66.7
Grass	4	28	476	17.0	2	91	4	191	48	10.2	22	78.6
Turf	12	80	1012	12.7	7	41	8	193	131	10.2	52	65.0
Indoor	11	76	967	12.7	6	41	8	189	124	10.2	49	64.5
Outdoor	5	32	521	16.3	3	91	4	195	55	10.2	25	78.1
1st Half	-	49	623	12.7	5	41	4	144	85	9.8	33	67.3
2nd Half/OT	-	59	865	14.7	4	91	8	240	94	10.6	41	69.5
Last 2 Min. Half	-	5	55	11.0	1	20	0	6	22	9.8	4	80.0
4th qtr, +/-7 pts	-	19	309	16.3	1	51	4	91	27	11.5	14	73.7
Winning	-	41	614	15.0	5	91	7	160	66	11.1	28	68.3
Tied	-	41	516	12.6	1	41	3	116	57	9.8	28	68.3
Trailing	-	26	358	13.8	3	51	2	108	56	9.6	18	69.2

	Rec	Yds	Avg	TD	Lg	Big	YAC	Trgt	Y@C	1st	1st%
Inside 20	10	104	10.4	4	17	0	17	25	8.7	8	80.0
Inside 10	2	7	3.5	2	5	0	0	10	3.5	2	100.0
1st Down	40	499	12.5	3	39	2	115	65	9.6	20	50.0
2nd Down	36	476	13.2	1	51	5	160	61	8.8	22	61.1
3rd Down Overall	32	513	16.0	5	91	5	109	52	12.6	32	100.0
3rd D 0-2 to Go	7	53	7.6	2	16	0	9	9	6.3	7	100.0
3rd D 3-7 to Go	15	207	13.8	2	37	3	46	21	10.7	15	100.0
3rd D 8+ to Go	10	253	25.3	1	91	2	54	22	19.9	10	100.0
4th Down	0	0	-	0	0	0	0	1	-	0	-
Rec Behind Line	1	4	4.0	0	4	0	4	2	0.0	0	0.0
1-10 yds	66	600	9.1	3	51	2	209	93	5.9	37	56.1
11-20 yds	33	591	17.9	4	39	4	112	57	14.5	29	87.9
21-30 yds	5	124	24.8	1	28	3	4	20	24.0	5	100.0
31+	3	169	56.3	1	91	3	55	7	38.0	3	100.0
Left Sideline	58	740	12.8	3	41	6	164	101	9.9	39	67.2
Left Side	35	339	9.7	1	17	0	47	55	8.3	21	60.0
Middle	9	308	34.2	4	91	4	133	15	19.4	9	100.0
Right Side	3	43	14.3	0	25	1	30	5	4.3	2	66.7
Right Sideline	3	58	19.3	1	26	1	10	3	16.0	3	100.0
Shotgun	3	39	13.0	0	20	0	0	3	13.0	3	100.0
2 Wide Receivers	20	268	13.4	1	39	2	53	32	10.8	14	70.0
3 Wide Receivers	86	1202	14.0	8	91	10	327	142	10.2	60	69.8
4+ Wide Receivers	2	18	9.0	0	9	0	4	4	7.0	0	0.0

1995 Incompletions

Type	Num	%of Inc	%of Att
Pass Dropped	8	11.3	4.5
Poor Throw	37	52.1	20.7
Pass Defensed	14	19.7	7.8
Pass Hit at Line	1	1.4	0.6
Other	11	15.5	6.1
Total	71	100.0	39.7

Game Logs (1-8)

Date	Opp	Result	Rush	Yds	Rec	Yds	Trgt	F-L	TD
09/03	@Pit	L 20-23	1	14	4	45	7	0-0	1
09/10	@Min	L 10-20	0	0	9	92	13	0-0	0
09/17	Ari	L 17-20	1	3	7	114	11	0-0	1
09/25	SF	W 27-24	0	0	9	115	12	0-0	0
10/08	Cle	W 38-20	0	0	6	78	10	0-0	2
10/15	@GB	L 21-30	0	0	5	84	14	0-0	0
10/22	@Was	L 30-36	1	16	6	115	11	1-1	0
10/29	GB	W 24-16	0	0	2	26	4	0-0	0

Game Logs (9-16)

Date	Opp	Result	Rush	Yds	Rec	Yds	Trgt	F-L	TD
11/05	@Atl	L 22-34	0	0	5	53	13	0-0	1
11/12	TB	W 27-24	0	0	10	125	17	0-0	0
11/19	@Chi	W 24-17	1	9	12	142	15	0-0	0
11/23	Min	W 44-38	0	0	12	153	18	0-0	2
12/04	Chi	W 27-7	0	0	4	34	7	0-0	0
12/10	@Hou	W 24-17	0	0	6	128	13	0-0	0
12/17	Jac	W 44-0	0	0	6	49	6	0-0	0
12/23	@TB	W 37-10	1	9	5	135	8	0-0	0

Carl Pickens

1995 Receiving Splits

	G	Rec	Yds	Avg	TD	Lg	Big	YAC	Trgt	Y@C	1st	1st%		Rec	Yds	Avg	TD	Lg	Big	YAC	Trgt	Y@C	1st	1st%
Total	16	99	1234	12.5	17	68	9	386	168	8.6	65	65.7	Inside 20	16	103	6.4	12	14	0	14	34	5.6	14	87.5
vs. Playoff	5	37	483	13.1	7	54	5	125	54	9.7	25	67.6	Inside 10	10	42	4.2	9	8	0	5	22	3.7	9	90.0
vs. Non-playoff	11	62	751	12.1	10	68	4	261	114	7.9	40	64.5	1st Down	36	428	11.9	9	54	4	98	61	9.2	20	55.6
vs. Own Division	8	45	649	14.4	9	68	7	272	76	8.4	33	73.3	2nd Down	30	348	11.6	3	68	1	111	57	7.9	19	63.3
Home	8	53	667	12.6	10	68	4	208	88	8.7	39	73.6	3rd Down Overall	30	399	13.3	5	47	4	143	43	8.5	23	76.7
Away	8	46	567	12.3	7	54	5	178	80	8.5	26	56.5	3rd D 0-2 to Go	3	67	22.3	1	30	2	33	4	11.3	3	100.0
Games 1-8	8	49	572	11.7	10	68	3	127	85	9.1	32	65.3	3rd D 3-7 to Go	13	158	12.2	1	47	1	72	18	6.6	12	92.3
Games 9-16	8	50	662	13.2	7	54	6	259	83	8.1	33	66.0	3rd D 8+ to Go	14	174	12.4	3	41	1	38	21	9.7	8	57.1
September	4	25	306	12.2	4	68	1	74	44	9.3	17	68.0	4th Down	3	59	19.7	0	22	0	34	7	8.3	3	100.0
October	4	24	266	11.1	6	44	2	53	41	8.9	15	62.5	Rec Behind Line	3	17	5.7	0	8	0	19	9	-0.7	0	0.0
November	4	21	310	14.8	5	30	4	152	36	7.5	18	85.7	1-10 yds	71	659	9.3	10	27	2	265	107	5.5	42	59.2
December	4	29	352	12.1	2	54	2	107	47	8.4	15	51.7	11-20 yds	19	299	15.7	2	47	2	56	33	12.8	17	89.5
Grass	4	18	224	12.4	2	54	2	90	38	7.4	9	50.0	21-30 yds	2	52	26.0	2	30	1	4	6	24.0	2	100.0
Turf	12	81	1010	12.5	15	68	7	296	130	8.8	56	69.1	31+	4	207	51.8	3	68	4	42	13	41.3	4	100.0
Indoor	3	20	235	11.8	4	30	2	60	34	8.8	13	65.0	Left Sideline	23	309	13.4	4	68	2	82	46	9.9	14	60.9
Outdoor	13	79	999	12.6	13	68	7	326	134	8.5	52	65.8	Left Side	27	412	15.3	4	54	5	181	40	8.6	21	77.8
1st Half	-	47	510	10.9	5	54	4	159	76	7.5	27	57.4	Middle	11	117	10.6	5	22	0	22	19	8.6	7	63.6
2nd Half/OT	-	52	724	13.9	12	68	5	227	92	9.6	38	73.1	Right Side	21	244	11.6	3	44	2	62	35	8.7	14	66.7
Last 2 Min. Half	-	10	89	8.9	4	18	0	36	25	5.3	8	80.0	Right Sideline	17	152	8.9	1	15	0	39	28	6.6	9	52.9
4th qtr, +/-7 pts	-	13	181	13.9	4	68	1	66	25	8.8	9	69.2	Shotgun	0	0	-	0	0	0	0	0	-	0	-
Winning	-	27	390	14.4	5	68	5	106	38	10.5	17	63.0	2 Wide Receivers	62	757	12.2	8	54	7	241	102	8.3	40	64.5
Tied	-	23	222	9.7	1	23	0	94	38	5.6	11	47.8	3 Wide Receivers	25	350	14.0	7	68	2	91	44	10.4	17	68.0
Trailing	-	49	622	12.7	11	54	4	186	92	8.9	37	75.5	4+ Wide Receivers	10	125	12.5	0	23	0	54	18	7.1	6	60.0

1995 Incompletions

Type	Num	%of Inc	%of Att
Pass Dropped	6	8.7	3.6
Poor Throw	38	55.1	22.6
Pass Defensed	12	17.4	7.1
Pass Hit at Line	4	5.8	2.4
Other	9	13.0	5.4
Total	69	100.0	41.1

Game Logs (1-8)

Date	Opp	Result	Rush	Yds	Rec	Yds	Trgt	F-L	TD
09/03	@Ind	W 24-21	0	0	5	39	11	0-0	1
09/10	Jac	W 24-17	0	0	5	102	10	0-0	1
09/17	@Sea	L 21-24	0	0	8	88	12	0-0	1
09/24	Hou	L 28-38	0	0	7	77	11	0-0	1
10/01	Mia	L 23-26	0	0	9	117	13	0-0	3
10/08	@TB	L 16-19	1	6	4	25	9	0-0	0
10/19	@Pit	W 27-9	0	0	8	108	8	0-0	1
10/29	Cle	L 26-29	0	0	3	16	11	0-0	2

Game Logs (9-16)

Date	Opp	Result	Rush	Yds	Rec	Yds	Trgt	F-L	TD
11/05	Oak	L 17-20	0	0	4	54	9	0-0	1
11/12	@Hou	W 32-25	0	0	7	108	11	0-0	2
11/19	Pit	L 31-49	0	0	8	129	9	0-0	1
11/26	@Jac	W 17-13	0	0	2	19	7	0-0	1
12/03	@GB	L 10-24	0	0	7	90	13	0-0	1
12/10	Chi	L 16-10	0	0	11	99	14	0-0	0
12/17	Cle	L 10-26	0	0	5	90	9	1-0	0
12/24	Min	W 27-24	0	0	6	73	11	0-0	0

Aaron Pierce

1995 Receiving Splits

	G	Rec	Yds	Avg	TD	Lg	Big	YAC	Trgt	Y@C	1st	1st%		Rec	Yds	Avg	TD	Lg	Big	YAC	Trgt	Y@C	1st	1st%
Total	16	33	310	9.4	0	26	1	161	54	4.5	15	45.5	Inside 20	1	2	2.0	0	2	0	6	5	-4.0	0	0.0
vs. Playoff	8	17	170	10.0	0	24	0	69	32	5.9	9	52.9	Inside 10	0	0	-	0	0	0	0	1	-	0	-
vs. Non-playoff	8	16	140	8.8	0	26	1	92	22	3.0	6	37.5	1st Down	6	51	8.5	0	11	0	30	12	3.5	2	33.3
vs. Own Division	8	12	97	8.1	0	16	0	88	19	0.8	4	33.3	2nd Down	17	160	9.4	0	26	1	81	23	4.6	6	35.3
Home	8	16	148	9.3	0	26	1	61	25	5.4	7	43.8	3rd Down Overall	10	99	9.9	0	16	0	50	18	4.9	7	70.0
Away	8	17	162	9.5	0	16	0	100	29	3.6	8	47.1	3rd D 0-2 to Go	3	22	7.3	0	9	0	7	3	5.0	3	100.0
Games 1-8	8	19	189	9.9	0	26	1	97	32	4.8	7	36.8	3rd D 3-7 to Go	3	32	10.7	0	16	0	12	6	6.7	3	100.0
Games 9-16	8	14	121	8.6	0	24	0	64	22	4.1	8	57.1	3rd D 8+ to Go	4	45	11.3	0	16	0	31	9	3.5	1	25.0
September	4	11	100	9.1	0	26	1	27	15	6.6	3	27.3	4th Down	0	0	-	0	0	0	0	1	-	0	-
October	4	8	89	11.1	0	16	0	70	17	2.4	4	50.0	Rec Behind Line	6	31	5.2	0	10	0	56	7	-4.2	0	0.0
November	5	7	58	8.3	0	11	0	26	11	4.6	5	71.4	1-10 yds	21	170	8.1	0	16	0	91	32	3.8	10	47.6
December	3	7	63	9.0	0	24	0	38	11	3.6	3	42.9	11-20 yds	4	59	14.8	0	16	0	9	11	12.5	3	75.0
Grass	5	13	125	9.6	0	16	0	78	23	3.6	5	38.5	21-30 yds	2	50	25.0	0	26	1	5	3	22.5	2	100.0
Turf	11	20	185	9.3	0	26	1	83	31	5.1	10	50.0	31+	0	0	-	0	0	0	0	1	-	0	-
Indoor	1	3	26	8.7	0	9	0	13	4	4.3	2	66.7	Left Sideline	2	25	12.5	0	16	0	4	9	4.5	0	0.0
Outdoor	15	30	284	9.5	0	26	1	148	50	4.5	13	43.3	Left Side	7	55	7.9	0	16	0	26	10	4.1	4	57.1
1st Half	-	15	135	9.0	0	16	0	81	23	3.6	6	40.0	Middle	6	69	11.5	0	16	0	23	12	7.7	4	66.7
2nd Half/OT	-	18	175	9.7	0	26	1	80	31	5.3	9	50.0	Right Side	9	89	9.9	0	24	0	70	16	2.1	4	44.4
Last 2 Min. Half	-	1	3	3.0	0	3	0	1	4	2.0	0	0.0	Right Sideline	9	72	8.0	0	26	1	36	12	4.0	3	33.3
4th qtr, +/-7 pts	-	3	18	6.0	0	11	0	10	4	2.7	2	66.7	Shotgun	5	38	7.6	0	16	0	21	9	3.4	3	60.0
Winning	-	11	129	11.7	0	26	1	66	14	5.7	4	36.4	2 Wide Receivers	17	161	9.5	0	24	0	79	26	4.8	6	35.3
Tied	-	8	65	8.1	0	16	0	36	11	3.6	2	25.0	3 Wide Receivers	8	95	11.9	0	26	1	58	6	5.3	6	75.0
Trailing	-	14	116	8.3	0	16	0	59	29	4.1	9	64.3	4+ Wide Receivers	7	43	6.1	0	11	0	27	17	2.3	2	28.6

1995 Incompletions

Type	Num	%of Inc	%of Att
Pass Dropped	2	9.5	3.7
Poor Throw	13	61.9	24.1
Pass Defensed	2	9.5	3.7
Pass Hit at Line	0	0.0	0.0
Other	4	19.0	7.4
Total	21	100.0	38.9

Game Logs (1-8)

Date	Opp	Result	Rush	Yds	Rec	Yds	Trgt	F-L	TD
09/04	Dal	L 0-35	0	0	3	18	3	0-0	0
09/10	@KC	L 17-20	0	0	3	34	3	0-0	0
09/17	@GB	L 6-14	0	0	2	8	5	0-0	0
09/24	NO	W 45-29	0	0	3	40	4	0-0	0
10/01	@SF	L 6-20	0	0	4	45	8	0-0	0
10/08	Ari	W 27-21	0	0	1	24	3	0-0	0
10/15	Phi	L 14-17	0	0	1	16	4	0-0	0
10/29	@Was	W 24-15	0	0	3	28	5	0-0	0

Game Logs (9-16)

Date	Opp	Result	Rush	Yds	Rec	Yds	Trgt	F-L	TD
11/05	@Sea	L 28-30	0	0	3	26	4	0-0	0
11/12	Oak	L 13-17	0	0	1	5	2	0-0	0
11/19	@Phi	L 19-28	0	0	0	0	1	0-0	0
11/26	Chi	L 24-27	0	0	2	17	2	0-0	0
11/30	@Ari	W 10-6	1	6	1	10	2	0-0	0
12/10	Was	W 20-13	0	0	3	14	3	0-0	0
12/17	@Dal	L 20-21	0	0	1	11	1	0-0	0
12/23	SD	L 17-27	0	0	3	38	7	0-0	0

Mike Pritchard
Denver Broncos — WR

1995 Receiving Splits

	G	Rec	Yds	Avg	TD	Lg	Big	YAC	Trgt	Y@C	1st	1st%
Total	15	33	441	13.4	3	45	3	81	69	10.9	23	69.7
vs. Playoff	6	14	177	12.6	1	23	0	44	29	9.5	9	64.3
vs. Non-playoff	9	19	264	13.9	2	45	3	37	40	11.9	14	73.7
vs. Own Division	7	15	224	14.9	2	26	2	45	30	11.9	13	86.7
Home	7	18	241	13.4	1	45	1	47	35	10.8	10	55.6
Away	8	15	200	13.3	2	26	2	34	34	11.1	13	86.7
Games 1-8	7	15	216	14.4	1	26	1	25	36	12.7	10	66.7
Games 9-16	8	18	225	12.5	2	45	2	56	33	9.4	13	72.2
September	4	12	146	12.2	0	20	0	23	28	10.3	7	58.3
October	3	3	70	23.3	1	26	1	2	8	22.7	3	100.0
November	4	7	74	10.6	0	23	0	22	11	7.4	3	42.9
December	4	11	151	13.7	2	45	2	34	22	10.6	10	90.9
Grass	11	27	359	13.3	2	45	2	76	56	10.5	19	70.4
Turf	4	6	82	13.7	1	26	1	5	13	12.8	4	66.7
Indoor	2	2	40	20.0	1	26	1	0	6	20.0	2	100.0
Outdoor	13	31	401	12.9	2	45	2	81	63	10.3	21	67.7
1st Half	-	19	245	12.9	0	24	0	56	39	9.9	15	78.9
2nd Half/OT	-	14	196	14.0	3	45	3	25	30	12.2	8	57.1
Last 2 Min. Half	-	5	53	10.6	1	24	0	6	12	9.4	4	80.0
4th qtr, +/-7 pts	-	5	58	11.6	0	25	1	4	7	10.8	2	40.0
Winning	-	10	167	16.7	1	45	1	26	24	14.1	7	70.0
Tied	-	9	99	11.0	0	25	1	13	19	9.6	6	66.7
Trailing	-	14	175	12.5	2	26	1	42	26	9.5	10	71.4

	Rec	Yds	Avg	TD	Lg	Big	YAC	Trgt	Y@C	1st	1st%
Inside 20	3	7	2.3	1	6	0	5	5	0.7	2	66.7
Inside 10	1	3	3.0	1	3	0	0	2	3.0	1	100.0
1st Down	13	176	13.5	1	26	2	25	26	11.6	8	61.5
2nd Down	10	126	12.6	2	45	1	22	22	10.4	7	70.0
3rd Down Overall	9	133	14.8	0	24	0	35	19	10.9	8	88.9
3rd D 0-2 to Go	0	0	-	0	0	0	0	1	-	0	-
3rd D 3-7 to Go	4	54	13.5	0	24	0	28	6	6.5	4	100.0
3rd D 8+ to Go	5	79	15.8	0	20	0	7	12	14.4	4	80.0
4th Down	1	6	6.0	0	6	0	-1	2	7.0	0	-
Rec Behind Line	3	22	7.3	0	17	0	26	5	-1.3	1	33.3
1-10 yds	17	149	8.8	1	16	0	43	30	6.2	11	64.7
11-20 yds	9	150	16.7	0	23	0	6	21	16.0	7	77.8
21-30 yds	3	75	25.0	1	26	2	6	11	23.0	3	100.0
31+	1	45	45.0	1	45	1	0	2	45.0	1	100.0
Left Sideline	2	51	25.5	1	45	1	-1	7	26.0	1	50.0
Left Side	8	109	13.6	0	24	0	24	11	10.6	8	100.0
Middle	2	14	7.0	1	11	0	1	6	6.5	2	100.0
Right Side	12	134	11.2	0	23	0	33	20	8.4	5	41.7
Right Sideline	9	133	14.8	0	26	2	24	25	12.1	7	77.8
Shotgun	12	200	16.7	1	26	2	29	29	14.3	9	75.0
2 Wide Receivers	7	96	13.7	1	45	1	1	16	13.6	4	57.1
3 Wide Receivers	16	209	13.1	1	26	1	51	31	9.9	11	68.8
4+ Wide Receivers	10	136	13.6	1	25	1	29	22	10.7	8	80.0

1995 Incompletions

Type	Num	%of Inc	%of Att
Pass Dropped	5	13.9	7.2
Poor Throw	12	33.3	17.4
Pass Defensed	6	16.7	8.7
Pass Hit at Line	2	5.6	2.9
Other	11	30.6	15.9
Total	36	100.0	52.2

Game Logs (1-8)

Date	Opp	Result	Rush	Yds	Rec	Yds	Trgt	F-L	TD
09/03	Buf	W 22-7	0	0	4	61	10	0-0	0
09/10	@Dal	L 21-31	1	0	1	15	4	0-0	0
09/17	Was	W 38-31	1	-4	5	39	9	0-0	0
09/24	@SD	L 6-17	0	0	2	31	5	0-0	0
10/01	@Sea	L 10-27	0	0	1	26	3	0-0	1
10/08	@NE	W 37-3	1	-2	0	0	2	0-0	0
10/16	Oak	W 27-0	0	0	2	44	3	0-0	0
10/22	KC	L 7-21	-	-	-	-	-	-	-

Game Logs (9-16)

Date	Opp	Result	Rush	Yds	Rec	Yds	Trgt	F-L	TD
11/05	Ari	W 38-6	0	0	1	3	1	0-0	0
11/12	@Phi	L 13-31	0	0	3	27	3	0-0	0
11/19	SD	W 30-27	0	0	2	30	4	0-0	0
11/26	@Hou	L 33-42	0	0	1	14	3	0-0	0
12/03	Jac	W 31-23	1	7	3	58	7	0-0	1
12/10	Sea	L 27-31	1	7	1	6	1	1-1	0
12/17	@KC	L 17-20	1	9	2	13	3	0-0	1
12/24	@Oak	W 31-28	0	0	5	74	11	0-0	0

Alfred Pupunu
San Diego Chargers — TE

1995 Receiving Splits

	G	Rec	Yds	Avg	TD	Lg	Big	YAC	Trgt	Y@C	1st	1st%
Total	15	35	315	9.0	0	26	2	184	50	3.7	16	45.7
vs. Playoff	6	18	182	10.1	0	26	1	102	27	4.4	9	50.0
vs. Non-playoff	9	17	133	7.8	0	26	1	82	23	3.0	7	41.2
vs. Own Division	8	14	115	8.2	0	21	0	67	23	3.4	8	57.1
Home	8	13	148	11.4	0	26	1	98	23	3.8	6	46.2
Away	7	22	167	7.6	0	26	1	86	27	3.7	10	45.5
Games 1-8	7	16	132	8.3	0	21	0	81	24	3.2	9	56.3
Games 9-16	8	19	183	9.6	0	26	2	103	26	4.2	7	36.8
September	3	7	48	6.9	0	13	0	30	9	2.6	3	42.9
October	4	9	84	9.3	0	21	0	51	15	3.7	6	66.7
November	4	5	53	10.6	0	17	0	27	11	5.2	2	40.0
December	4	14	130	9.3	0	26	2	76	15	3.9	5	35.7
Grass	11	21	218	10.4	0	26	1	147	33	3.4	11	52.4
Turf	4	14	97	6.9	0	26	1	37	17	4.3	5	35.7
Outdoor	2	29	264	9.1	0	26	1	160	43	3.6	13	44.8
Indoor	13	6	51	8.5	0	26	1	24	7	4.5	3	50.0
1st Half	-	14	107	7.6	0	26	1	73	24	2.4	6	42.9
2nd Half/OT	-	21	208	9.9	0	26	1	111	26	4.6	10	47.6
Last 2 Min. Half	-	9	127	14.1	0	26	2	85	12	4.7	6	66.7
4th qtr, +/-7 pts	-	4	53	13.3	0	26	1	19	6	8.5	2	50.0
Winning	-	6	42	7.0	0	19	0	17	9	4.2	3	50.0
Tied	-	7	80	11.4	0	26	1	49	9	4.4	5	71.4
Trailing	-	22	193	8.8	0	26	1	118	32	3.4	8	36.4

	Rec	Yds	Avg	TD	Lg	Big	YAC	Trgt	Y@C	1st	1st%
Inside 20	0	0	-	0	0	0	0	1	-	0	-
Inside 10	0	0	-	0	0	0	0	0	-	0	-
1st Down	18	167	9.3	0	26	1	94	22	4.1	6	33.3
2nd Down	11	99	9.0	0	21	0	56	17	3.9	6	54.5
3rd Down Overall	4	40	10.0	0	26	1	34	8	1.5	2	50.0
3rd D 0-2 to Go	0	0	-	0	0	0	0	-	-	0	-
3rd D 3-7 to Go	3	34	11.3	0	26	1	33	6	0.3	2	66.7
3rd D 8+ to Go	1	6	6.0	0	6	0	1	2	5.0	0	0.0
4th Down	2	9	4.5	0	6	0	0	3	4.5	2	100.0
Rec Behind Line	4	51	12.8	0	26	1	57	4	-1.5	2	50.0
1-10 yds	28	202	7.2	0	21	0	103	37	3.5	11	39.3
11-20 yds	3	62	20.7	0	26	1	24	7	12.7	3	100.0
21-30 yds	0	0	-	0	0	0	0	2	-	0	-
31+	0	0	-	0	0	0	0	0	-	0	-
Left Sideline	6	48	8.0	0	13	0	38	9	1.7	5	83.3
Left Side	6	72	12.0	0	26	1	52	10	3.3	4	66.7
Middle	5	50	10.0	0	19	0	15	6	7.0	2	40.0
Right Side	10	87	8.7	0	21	0	55	13	3.3	3	30.0
Right Sideline	8	58	7.3	0	26	1	24	12	4.3	2	25.0
Shotgun	0	0	-	0	0	0	0	0	-	0	-
2 Wide Receivers	14	96	6.9	0	21	0	50	23	3.3	5	35.7
3 Wide Receivers	21	219	10.4	0	26	2	134	25	4.0	11	52.4
4+ Wide Receivers	0	0	-	0	0	0	0	1	-	0	-

1995 Incompletions

Type	Num	%of Inc	%of Att
Pass Dropped	5	33.3	10.0
Poor Throw	7	46.7	14.0
Pass Defensed	3	20.0	6.0
Pass Hit at Line	0	0.0	0.0
Other	0	0.0	0.0
Total	15	100.0	30.0

Game Logs (1-8)

Date	Opp	Result	Rec	Yds	Trgt	F-L	TD
09/03	@Oak	L 7-17	5	40	5	0-0	0
09/10	Sea	W 14-10	2	8	4	0-0	0
09/17	@Phi	W 27-21	-	-	-	-	-
09/24	Den	W 17-6	0	0	0	0-0	0
10/01	@Pit	L 16-31	4	31	6	0-0	0
10/09	@KC	L 23-29	3	30	4	0-0	0
10/15	Dal	L 9-23	1	20	3	0-0	0
10/22	@Sea	W 35-25	1	3	2	0-0	0

Game Logs (9-16)

Date	Opp	Result	Rec	Yds	Trgt	F-L	TD
11/05	Mia	L 14-24	2	19	3	1-1	0
11/12	KC	L 7-22	3	34	6	0-0	0
11/19	@Den	L 27-30	0	0	1	0-0	0
11/27	Oak	W 12-6	0	0	1	0-0	0
12/03	Cle	W 31-13	2	23	2	0-0	0
12/09	Ari	W 28-25	3	44	4	0-0	0
12/17	@Ind	W 27-24	5	48	5	0-0	0
12/23	@NYN	W 27-17	4	15	4	0-0	0

Jake Reed
Minnesota Vikings — WR

1995 Receiving Splits

	G	Rec	Yds	Avg	TD	Lg	Big	YAC	Trgt	Y@C	1st	1st%		Rec	Yds	Avg	TD	Lg	Big	YAC	Trgt	Y@C	1st	1st%
Total	16	72	1167	16.2	9	55	13	331	142	11.6	55	76.4	Inside 20	5	29	5.8	5	9	0	1	15	5.6	5	100.0
vs. Playoff	7	29	502	17.3	5	55	6	154	67	12.0	23	79.3	Inside 10	5	29	5.8	5	9	0	1	10	5.6	5	100.0
vs. Non-playoff	9	43	665	15.5	4	51	7	177	75	11.3	32	74.4	1st Down	21	352	16.8	0	53	4	100	47	12.0	14	66.7
vs. Own Division	8	34	529	15.6	4	55	6	126	69	11.9	27	79.4	2nd Down	24	329	13.7	1	45	3	96	42	9.7	16	66.7
Home	8	33	477	14.5	3	44	3	167	67	9.4	26	78.8	3rd Down Overall	27	486	18.0	8	55	6	135	52	13.0	25	92.6
Away	8	39	690	17.7	6	55	10	164	75	13.5	29	74.4	3rd D 0-2 to Go	3	35	11.7	2	26	1	4	5	10.3	3	100.0
Games 1-8	8	38	498	13.1	3	33	4	146	72	9.3	28	73.7	3rd D 3-7 to Go	12	160	13.3	2	32	1	59	18	8.4	12	100.0
Games 9-16	8	34	669	19.7	6	55	9	185	70	14.2	27	79.4	3rd D 8+ to Go	12	291	24.3	4	55	4	72	29	18.3	10	83.3
September	4	20	254	12.7	1	29	2	79	36	8.8	14	70.0	4th Down	0	0	-	0	0	0	0	1	-	0	
October	4	18	244	13.6	2	33	2	67	36	9.8	14	77.8	Rec Behind Line	1	0	0.0	0	0	0	0	2	0.0	0	
November	4	19	330	17.4	3	55	4	84	40	12.9	14	73.7	1-10 yds	40	365	9.1	5	22	0	131	62	5.9	24	60.0
December	4	15	339	22.6	3	53	5	101	30	15.9	13	86.7	11-20 yds	21	411	19.6	0	33	3	107	41	14.5	21	100.0
Grass	5	23	362	15.7	4	53	6	90	44	11.8	17	73.9	21-30 yds	5	155	31.0	1	44	5	37	15	23.6	5	100.0
Turf	11	49	805	16.4	5	55	7	241	98	11.5	38	77.6	31+	5	236	47.2	3	55	5	56	22	36.0	5	100.0
Outdoor	9	33	541	16.4	5	53	7	128	63	12.5	24	72.7	Left Sideline	32	524	16.4	1	55	4	172	60	11.0	23	71.9
Indoor	7	39	626	16.1	4	55	6	203	79	10.8	31	79.5	Left Side	17	324	19.1	3	33	6	95	29	13.5	14	82.4
1st Half	-	34	629	18.5	5	55	9	188	66	13.0	24	70.6	Middle	1	9	9.0	0	9	0	2	4	7.0	0	
2nd Half/OT	-	38	538	14.2	4	33	4	143	76	10.4	31	81.6	Right Side	11	150	13.6	3	31	1	35	19	10.5	10	90.9
Last 2 Min. Half	-	11	197	17.9	1	45	2	51	19	13.3	9	81.8	Right Sideline	11	160	14.5	2	51	2	27	30	12.1	8	72.7
4th qtr, +/-7 pts	-	10	169	16.9	0	23	0	55	25	11.4	10	100.0	Shotgun	6	136	22.7	0	33	1	46	19	15.0	6	100.0
Winning	-	24	331	13.8	3	32	3	98	51	9.7	16	66.7	2 Wide Receivers	19	258	13.6	2	32	3	70	44	9.9	11	57.9
Tied	-	20	313	15.7	1	51	2	89	40	11.2	15	75.0	3 Wide Receivers	46	796	17.3	5	55	8	241	84	12.1	38	82.6
Trailing	-	28	523	18.7	5	55	8	144	51	13.5	24	85.7	4+ Wide Receivers	6	101	16.8	2	31	2	17	13	14.0	5	83.3

1995 Incompletions

Type	Num	%of Inc	%of Att
Pass Dropped	7	10.0	4.9
Poor Throw	39	55.7	27.5
Pass Defensed	12	17.1	8.5
Pass Hit at Line	1	1.4	0.7
Other	11	15.7	7.7
Total	70	100.0	49.3

Game Logs (1-8)

Date	Opp	Result	Rec	Yds	Trgt	F-L	TD
09/03	@Chi	L 14-31	6	68	6	0-0	0
09/10	Det	W 20-10	2	11	5	0-0	0
09/17	Dal	L 17-23	7	107	15	0-0	1
09/24	@Pit	W 44-24	5	68	10	1-1	0
10/08	Hou	W 23-17	5	58	9	0-0	0
10/15	@TB	L 17-20	5	99	11	0-0	1
10/22	@GB	L 21-38	2	9	7	0-0	0
10/30	Chi	L 6-14	6	78	9	0-0	0

Game Logs (9-16)

Date	Opp	Result	Rec	Yds	Trgt	F-L	TD
11/05	GB	W 27-24	4	68	11	0-0	1
11/12	@Ari	W 30-24	7	96	13	0-0	1
11/19	NO	W 43-24	2	17	4	0-0	0
11/23	@Det	L 38-44	6	149	12	0-0	1
12/03	TB	W 31-17	3	47	8	0-0	0
12/09	Cle	W 27-11	4	91	6	0-0	0
12/18	@SF	L 30-37	3	90	7	0-0	0
12/24	@Cin	L 24-27	5	111	9	0-0	1

Frank Reich
Carolina Panthers — QB

1995 Passing Splits

	G	Att	Cm	Pct	Yds	Yd/Att	TD	Int	1st	YAC	Big	Sk	Rtg		Att	Cm	Pct	Yds	Yd/Att	TD	Int	1st	YAC	Big	Sk	Rtg
Total	3	84	37	44.0	441	5.3	2	2	19	152	2	12	58.7	Inside 20	6	2	33.3	8	1.3	1	0	1	0	0	0	81.9
vs. Playoff	2	65	29	44.6	373	5.7	2	1	16	124	2	12	67.0	Inside 10	1	1	100.0	8	8.0	1	0	1	0	0	0	139.6
vs. Non-playoff	1	19	8	42.1	68	3.6	0	1	3	28	0	0	30.2	1st Down	28	13	46.4	198	7.1	2	0	7	66	2	3	94.0
vs. Own Division	2	63	31	49.2	397	6.3	2	1	17	129	2	9	73.3	2nd Down	24	12	50.0	110	4.6	0	0	4	27	0	2	62.8
Home	1	19	8	42.1	68	3.6	0	1	3	28	0	0	30.2	3rd Down Overall	32	12	37.5	133	4.2	0	2	8	59	0	6	24.6
Away	2	65	29	44.6	373	5.7	2	1	16	124	2	12	67.0	3rd D 0-5 to Go	11	5	45.5	59	5.4	0	0	5	33	0	3	62.3
Games 1-8	3	84	37	44.0	441	5.3	2	2	19	152	2	12	58.7	3rd D 6+ to Go	21	7	33.3	74	3.5	0	2	3	26	0	3	5.0
Games 9-16	0	0	0	-	0	-	0	0	0	0	0	0	-	4th Down	0	0	-	0	-	0	0	0	0	0	1	-
September	3	84	37	44.0	441	5.3	2	2	19	152	2	12	58.7	Rec Behind Line	9	2	22.2	6	0.7	0	0	0	8	0	0	39.6
October	0	0	0	-	0	-	0	0	0	0	0	0	-	1-10 yds	54	30	55.6	296	5.5	1	0	14	130	0	0	69.7
November	0	0	0	-	0	-	0	0	0	0	0	0	-	11-20 yds	16	3	18.8	49	3.1	0	1	3	7	0	0	13.8
December	0	0	0	-	0	-	0	0	0	0	0	0	-	21-30 yds	1	0	0.0	0	-	0	0	0	0	0	0	39.6
Grass	1	19	8	42.1	68	3.6	0	1	3	28	0	0	30.2	31+	4	2	50.0	90	22.5	1	0	2	7	2	0	135.4
Turf	2	65	29	44.6	373	5.7	2	1	16	124	2	12	67.0	Left Sideline	14	6	42.9	92	6.6	2	0	5	15	1	0	104.8
Indoor	1	44	23	52.3	329	7.5	2	0	14	101	2	9	92.0	Left Side	18	8	44.4	82	4.6	0	0	4	31	0	0	58.1
Outdoor	2	40	14	35.0	112	2.8	0	2	5	51	0	3	22.9	Middle	13	8	61.5	106	8.2	0	0	3	23	1	11	87.3
1st Half	-	50	24	48.0	277	5.5	1	1	13	106	1	5	63.5	Right Side	17	8	47.1	66	3.9	0	2	2	33	0	1	17.9
2nd Half/OT	-	34	13	38.2	164	4.8	1	1	6	46	1	7	51.6	Right Sideline	22	7	31.8	95	4.3	0	0	5	50	0	0	46.6
Last 2 Min. Half	-	11	6	54.5	114	10.4	1	0	5	37	1	0	121.0	2 Wide Receivers	35	16	45.7	179	5.1	1	0	7	49	1	3	71.0
4th qtr, +/-7 pts	-	14	6	42.9	106	7.6	1	0	5	23	1	2	93.2	3+ WR	48	20	41.7	248	5.2	1	2	11	91	1	9	47.9
Winning	-	14	7	50.0	110	7.9	0	0	4	41	1	3	76.5	Attempts 1-10	30	14	46.7	183	6.1	1	0	9	61	1	0	77.5
Tied	-	34	18	52.9	178	5.2	1	0	9	68	0	4	77.8	Attempts 11-20	29	12	41.4	103	3.6	0	2	4	50	0	0	22.6
Trailing	-	36	12	33.3	153	4.3	1	2	6	43	1	5	33.7	Attempts 21+	25	11	44.0	155	6.2	1	0	6	41	1	0	77.9

1995 Incompletions

Type	Num	% of Inc	% of Att
Pass Dropped	4	8.5	4.8
Poor Throw	25	53.2	29.8
Pass Defensed	8	17.0	9.5
Pass Hit at Line	4	8.5	4.8
Other	6	12.8	7.1
Total	47	100.0	56.0

Game Logs (1-8)

Date	Opp	Result	Att	Cm	Pct	Yds	TD	Int	Lg	Sk	F-L
09/03	@Atl	L 20-23	44	23	52.3	329	2	0	46	9	1-1
09/10	@Buf	L 9-31	21	6	28.6	44	0	1	21	3	2-0
09/17	StL	L 10-31	19	8	42.1	68	0	1	12	0	0-0
10/01	TB	L 13-20	-	-	-	-	-	-	-	-	-
10/08	@Chi	L 27-31	-	-	-	-	-	-	-	-	-
10/15	NYA	W 26-15	-	-	-	-	-	-	-	-	-
10/22	NO	W 20-3	-	-	-	-	-	-	-	-	-
10/29	@NE	W 20-17	-	-	-	-	-	-	-	-	-

Game Logs (9-16)

Date	Opp	Result	Att	Cm	Pct	Yds	TD	Int	Lg	Sk	F-L
11/05	@SF	W 13-7	-	-	-	-	-	-	-	-	-
11/12	@StL	L 17-28	-	-	-	-	-	-	-	-	-
11/19	Ari	W 27-7	-	-	-	-	-	-	-	-	-
11/26	@NO	L 26-34	-	-	-	-	-	-	-	-	-
12/03	Ind	W 13-10	-	-	-	-	-	-	-	-	-
12/10	SF	L 10-31	-	-	-	-	-	-	-	-	-
12/17	Atl	W 21-17	-	-	-	-	-	-	-	-	-
12/24	@Was	L 17-20	-	-	-	-	-	-	-	-	-

Errict Rhett

1995 Rushing and Receiving Splits

	G	Rush	Yds	Avg	Lg	TD	1st	Stf	YdL	Rec	Yds	Avg	TD		Rush	Yds	Avg	Lg	TD	1st	Stf	YdL	Rec	Yds	Avg	TD
Total	16	332	1207	3.6	21	11	76	35	89	14	110	7.9	0	Inside 20	57	163	2.9	19	11	16	4	4	2	18	9.0	0
vs. Playoff	6	122	499	4.1	21	4	31	12	33	5	53	10.6	0	Inside 10	27	41	1.5	6	9	12	3	3	0	0	-	0
vs. Non-playoff	10	210	708	3.4	19	7	45	23	56	9	57	6.3	0	1st Down	189	621	3.3	20	7	18	21	54	4	32	8.0	0
vs. Own Division	8	145	563	3.9	21	2	36	21	54	5	30	6.0	0	2nd Down	118	465	3.9	14	2	41	12	32	5	31	6.2	0
Home	8	178	662	3.7	21	7	43	22	57	6	51	8.5	0	3rd Down Overall	22	116	5.3	21	2	14	2	3	5	47	9.4	0
Away	8	154	545	3.5	20	4	33	13	32	8	59	7.4	0	3rd D 0-2 to Go	16	87	5.4	21	2	13	1	1	0	0	-	0
Games 1-8	8	191	615	3.2	19	8	39	21	55	10	87	8.7	0	3rd D 3-7 to Go	3	14	4.7	12	0	1	0	0	3	21	7.0	0
Games 9-16	8	141	592	4.2	21	3	37	14	34	4	23	5.8	0	3rd D 8+ to Go	3	15	5.0	9	0	0	1	2	2	26	13.0	0
September	4	95	344	3.6	19	3	19	7	20	4	28	7.0	0	4th Down	3	5	1.7	2	0	3	0	0	0	0	-	0
October	5	109	308	2.8	11	5	21	16	41	6	59	9.8	0	Left Sideline	24	148	6.2	18	1	9	2	7	2	31	15.5	0
November	3	63	255	4.0	20	3	18	8	18	1	17	17.0	0	Left Side	86	302	3.5	17	5	18	7	12	3	6	2.0	0
December	4	65	300	4.6	21	0	18	4	10	3	6	2.0	0	Middle	143	484	3.4	21	5	36	15	42	4	30	7.5	0
Grass	12	248	845	3.4	21	10	56	30	77	11	91	8.3	0	Right Side	74	251	3.4	19	0	12	11	28	2	16	8.0	0
Turf	4	84	362	4.3	20	1	20	5	12	3	19	6.3	0	Right Sideline	5	22	4.4	12	0	1	0	0	3	27	9.0	0
Indoor	3	58	277	4.8	20	0	16	4	9	1	-3	-3.0	0	Shotgun	0	0	-	0	0	0	0	0	0	0	-	0
Outdoor	13	274	930	3.4	21	11	60	31	80	13	113	8.7	0	2 Wide Receivers	195	675	3.5	21	3	45	19	56	6	54	9.0	0
1st Half	-	184	657	3.6	14	6	43	15	49	7	52	7.4	0	3 Wide Receivers	59	251	4.3	19	1	9	9	21	7	38	5.4	0
2nd Half/OT	-	148	550	3.7	21	5	33	20	40	7	58	8.3	0	4+ Wide Receivers	9	76	8.4	19	0	4	0	0	0	0	-	0
Last 2 Min. Half	-	27	144	5.3	19	1	9	2	6	1	5	5.0	0	Carries 1-5	80	288	3.6	14	2	17	5	16	0	0	-	0
4th qtr, +/-7 pts	-	38	146	3.8	20	1	10	6	13	3	34	11.3	0	Carries 6-10	80	267	3.3	11	3	18	8	26	0	0	-	0
Winning	-	94	286	3.0	19	2	18	11	27	4	34	8.5	0	Carries 11-15	70	231	3.3	21	1	15	11	26	0	0	-	0
Tied	-	81	290	3.6	18	3	20	7	18	3	37	12.3	0	Carries 16-20	59	260	4.4	19	2	18	4	5	0	0	-	0
Trailing	-	157	631	4.0	21	6	38	17	44	7	39	5.6	0	Carries 21+	43	161	3.7	20	3	8	7	16	0	0	-	0

1995 Incompletions

Type	Num	%of Inc	% Att
Pass Dropped	5	33.3	17.2
Poor Throw	4	26.7	13.8
Pass Defensed	1	6.7	3.4
Pass Hit at Line	2	13.3	6.9
Other	3	20.0	10.3
Total	15	100.0	51.7

Game Logs (1-8)

Date	Opp	Result	Rush	Yds	Rec	Yds	Trgt	F-L	TD
09/03	@Phi	W 21-6	26	85	2	22	2	0-0	1
09/10	@Cle	L 6-22	23	89	2	6	2	0-0	1
09/17	Chi	L 6-25	19	66	0	0	2	0-0	1
09/24	Was	W 14-6	27	104	0	0	1	1-1	1
10/01	@Car	W 20-13	22	50	1	13	1	0-0	1
10/08	Cin	W 19-16	29	91	3	30	6	1-0	1
10/15	Min	W 20-17	22	42	1	7	1	0-0	1
10/22	Atl	L 21-24	23	88	1	9	5	0-0	2

Game Logs (9-16)

Date	Opp	Result	Rush	Yds	Rec	Yds	Trgt	F-L	TD
10/29	@Hou	L 7-19	13	37	0	0	2	0-0	0
11/12	@Det	L 24-27	25	144	0	0	0	0-0	0
11/19	Jac	W 17-16	24	100	0	0	0	0-0	2
11/26	@GB	L 13-35	14	11	1	17	1	0-0	1
12/03	@Min	L 17-31	20	96	1	-3	3	0-0	0
12/10	GB	W 13-10	22	118	0	0	1	0-0	0
12/17	@Chi	L 10-31	11	33	1	4	1	0-0	0
12/23	Det	L 10-37	12	53	1	5	2	0-0	0

Jerry Rice

1995 Receiving Splits

	G	Rec	Yds	Avg	TD	Lg	Big	YAC	Trgt	Y@C	1st	1st%		Rec	Yds	Avg	TD	Lg	Big	YAC	Trgt	Y@C	1st	1st%
Total	16	122	1848	15.1	15	81	21	692	176	9.5	76	62.3	Inside 20	16	127	7.9	7	18	0	66	27	3.8	9	56.3
vs. Playoff	7	58	886	15.3	6	81	12	377	78	8.8	33	56.9	Inside 10	8	35	4.4	4	8	0	30	14	0.6	5	62.5
vs. Non-playoff	9	64	962	15.0	9	52	9	315	98	10.1	43	67.2	1st Down	53	845	15.9	4	57	11	264	79	11.0	29	54.7
vs. Own Division	8	60	835	13.9	5	57	9	316	91	8.7	36	60.0	2nd Down	34	543	16.0	6	81	5	244	46	8.8	20	58.8
Home	8	66	932	14.1	9	54	8	309	96	9.4	41	62.1	3rd Down Overall	31	381	12.3	4	41	3	140	47	7.8	23	74.2
Away	8	56	916	16.4	6	81	13	383	80	9.5	35	62.5	3rd D 0-2 to Go	6	50	8.3	0	14	0	23	9	4.5	5	83.3
Games 1-8	8	57	765	13.4	8	54	6	242	84	9.2	37	64.9	3rd D 3-7 to Go	12	121	10.1	2	18	0	45	16	6.3	10	83.3
Games 9-16	8	65	1083	16.7	7	81	15	450	92	9.7	39	60.0	3rd D 8+ to Go	13	210	16.2	2	41	3	72	22	10.6	8	61.5
September	4	34	522	15.4	5	54	6	174	45	10.2	19	55.9	4th Down	4	79	19.8	1	29	2	44	4	8.8	4	100.0
October	4	23	243	10.6	3	17	0	68	39	7.6	18	78.3	Rec Behind Line	14	97	6.9	2	29	1	114	16	-1.2	5	35.7
November	4	28	488	17.4	4	81	7	227	43	9.3	18	64.3	1-10 yds	69	748	10.8	6	81	3	372	90	5.4	34	49.3
December	4	37	595	16.1	3	57	8	223	49	10.1	21	56.8	11-20 yds	24	405	16.9	4	41	3	68	32	14.0	22	91.7
Grass	10	80	1202	15.0	11	54	12	381	115	10.3	50	62.5	21-30 yds	8	279	34.9	3	57	7	66	17	26.6	8	100.0
Turf	6	42	646	15.4	4	81	9	311	61	8.0	26	61.9	31+	7	319	45.6	2	54	7	72	21	35.3	7	100.0
Indoor	4	35	464	13.3	2	57	6	177	47	8.2	20	57.1	Left Sideline	35	621	17.7	1	57	9	173	43	12.8	24	68.6
Outdoor	12	87	1384	15.9	13	81	15	515	129	10.0	56	64.4	Left Side	40	501	12.5	3	50	2	204	43	6.2	20	62.5
1st Half	-	67	1162	17.3	11	81	13	473	96	10.3	45	67.2	Middle	20	377	18.9	8	81	5	177	26	10.0	12	60.0
2nd Half/OT	-	55	686	12.5	4	52	8	219	80	8.5	31	56.4	Right Side	16	154	9.6	2	33	2	63	25	5.7	5	31.3
Last 2 Min. Half	-	14	198	14.1	2	28	2	57	23	10.1	9	64.3	Right Sideline	19	295	15.5	1	46	3	75	39	11.6	15	78.9
4th qtr, +/-7 pts	-	21	237	11.3	0	33	3	53	32	8.8	12	57.1	Shotgun	0	0	-	0	0	0	0	0	-	0	-
Winning	-	62	867	14.0	8	57	10	299	90	9.2	54	64.8	2 Wide Receivers	52	799	15.4	5	57	9	215	88	11.2	33	63.5
Tied	-	26	485	18.7	5	81	5	261	37	8.6	19	73.1	3 Wide Receivers	46	717	15.6	6	81	7	294	59	9.2	28	60.9
Trailing	-	34	496	14.6	2	39	6	132	51	10.7	23	67.6	4+ Wide Receivers	22	301	13.7	2	54	4	154	27	6.7	13	59.1

1995 Incompletions

Type	Num	%of Inc	%of Att
Pass Dropped	6	11.1	3.4
Poor Throw	19	35.2	10.8
Pass Defensed	15	27.8	8.5
Pass Hit at Line	1	1.9	0.6
Other	13	24.1	7.4
Total	54	100.0	30.7

Game Logs (1-8)

Date	Opp	Result	Rush	Yds	Rec	Yds	Trgt	F-L	TD
09/03	@NO	W 24-22	1	5	6	87	9	0-0	1
09/10	Atl	W 41-10	0	0	11	167	14	0-0	1
09/17	NE	W 28-3	0	0	6	87	9	0-0	2
09/25	@Det	L 24-27	0	0	11	181	13	0-0	1
10/01	NYN	W 20-6	0	0	7	71	13	0-0	1
10/15	@Ind	L 17-18	0	0	6	43	8	0-0	1
10/22	@StL	W 44-10	1	20	2	21	5	0-0	2
10/29	NO	L 7-11	1	0	8	108	13	0-0	0

Game Logs (9-16)

Date	Opp	Result	Rush	Yds	Rec	Yds	Trgt	F-L	TD
11/05	Car	L 7-13	1	1	8	111	13	1-0	1
11/12	@Dal	W 38-20	0	0	5	161	9	0-0	1
11/20	@Mia	W 44-20	0	0	8	149	10	0-0	2
11/26	StL	W 41-13	0	0	7	67	11	1-1	1
12/03	Buf	W 27-17	0	0	5	32	7	0-0	0
12/10	@Car	W 31-10	0	0	6	121	9	0-0	0
12/18	Min	W 37-30	1	10	14	289	16	1-1	3
12/24	@Atl	L 27-28	0	0	12	153	17	0-0	1

Andre Rison
Cleveland Browns — WR

1995 Receiving Splits

	G	Rec	Yds	Avg	TD	Lg	Big	YAC	Trgt	Y@C	1st	1st%		Rec	Yds	Avg	TD	Lg	Big	YAC	Trgt	Y@C	1st	1st%
Total	16	47	701	14.9	3	59	6	106	103	12.7	38	80.9	Inside 20	3	25	8.3	0	17	0	1	10	8.0	3	100.0
vs. Playoff	7	22	264	12.0	1	43	2	35	48	10.4	17	77.3	Inside 10	2	8	4.0	2	4	0	1	3	3.5	2	100.0
vs. Non-playoff	9	25	437	17.5	2	59	4	71	55	14.6	21	84.0	1st Down	23	392	17.0	1	59	4	46	39	15.0	14	60.9
vs. Own Division	8	27	416	15.4	2	59	3	60	54	13.2	23	85.2	2nd Down	12	124	10.3	1	21	0	9	33	9.6	12	100.0
Home	8	31	394	12.7	2	43	3	58	70	10.8	25	80.6	3rd Down Overall	11	180	16.4	1	43	2	51	29	11.7	11	100.0
Away	8	16	307	19.2	1	59	3	48	33	16.2	13	81.3	3rd D 0-2 to Go	0	0	-	0	0	0	0	1	-	0	-
Games 1-8	8	24	408	17.0	2	59	4	74	58	13.9	19	79.2	3rd D 3-7 to Go	7	70	10.0	1	16	0	19	15	7.3	7	100.0
Games 9-16	8	23	293	12.7	1	49	2	32	45	11.3	19	82.6	3rd D 8+ to Go	4	110	27.5	0	43	2	32	13	19.5	4	100.0
September	4	9	82	9.1	1	15	0	24	21	6.4	6	66.7	4th Down	1	5	5.0	0	5	0	0	2	5.0	1	100.0
October	4	15	326	21.7	1	59	4	50	37	18.4	13	86.7	Rec Behind Line	0	0	-	0	0	0	0	2	-	0	-
November	4	13	137	10.5	1	40	1	16	27	9.3	10	76.9	1-10 yds	27	220	8.1	2	16	0	53	38	6.2	18	66.7
December	4	10	156	15.6	0	49	1	16	18	14.0	9	90.0	11-20 yds	14	219	15.6	1	23	0	11	33	14.9	14	100.0
Grass	11	36	442	12.3	2	43	3	69	82	10.4	28	77.8	21-30 yds	3	108	36.0	0	43	3	23	13	28.3	3	100.0
Turf	5	11	259	23.5	1	59	3	37	21	20.2	10	90.9	31+	3	154	51.3	0	59	3	19	17	45.0	3	100.0
Indoor	3	2	64	32.0	1	49	1	9	6	27.5	2	100.0	Left Sideline	6	60	10.0	1	19	0	11	10	6.2	4	66.7
Outdoor	13	45	637	14.2	3	59	5	97	97	12.0	36	80.0	Left Side	3	33	11.0	1	23	0	8	5	8.3	3	100.0
1st Half	-	24	352	14.7	1	49	3	38	54	13.1	20	83.3	Middle	2	99	49.5	0	59	2	21	5	39.0	2	100.0
2nd Half/OT	-	23	349	15.2	2	59	3	68	49	12.2	18	78.3	Right Side	10	154	15.4	1	49	1	7	22	14.7	9	90.0
Last 2 Min. Half	-	11	137	12.5	0	46	1	12	19	11.4	8	72.7	Right Sideline	26	355	13.7	0	46	3	59	61	11.4	20	76.9
4th qtr, +/-7 pts	-	4	75	18.8	1	43	1	18	12	14.3	3	75.0	Shotgun	0	0	-	0	0	0	0	0	-	0	-
Winning	-	12	125	10.4	1	21	0	21	27	8.7	10	83.3	2 Wide Receivers	16	333	20.8	2	59	4	42	36	18.2	13	81.3
Tied	-	9	106	11.8	1	23	0	20	17	9.6	8	88.9	3 Wide Receivers	27	322	11.9	1	43	2	69	58	9.4	21	77.8
Trailing	-	26	470	18.1	1	59	6	65	59	15.6	20	76.9	4+ Wide Receivers	4	46	11.5	0	15	0	-5	9	12.8	4	100.0

1995 Incompletions

Type	Num	%of Inc	%of Att
Pass Dropped	3	5.4	2.9
Poor Throw	32	57.1	31.1
Pass Defensed	11	19.6	10.7
Pass Hit at Line	0	0.0	0.0
Other	10	17.9	9.7
Total	56	100.0	54.4

Game Logs (1-8)

Date	Opp	Result	Rush	Yds	Rec	Yds	Trgt	F-L	TD
09/03	@NE	L 14-17	0	0	2	14	5	0-0	0
09/10	TB	W 22-6	0	0	2	18	6	0-0	0
09/17	@Hou	W 14-7	0	0	1	15	2	0-0	0
09/24	KC	W 35-17	0	0	4	35	8	0-0	1
10/02	Buf	L 19-22	0	0	6	126	15	0-0	0
10/08	@Det	L 20-38	0	0	0	0	2	0-0	0
10/22	Jac	L 15-23	0	0	2	27	8	0-0	0
10/29	@Cin	W 29-26	0	0	7	173	12	0-0	1

Game Logs (9-16)

Date	Opp	Result	Rush	Yds	Rec	Yds	Trgt	F-L	TD
11/05	Hou	L 10-37	0	0	1	5	3	0-0	1
11/13	@Pit	L 3-20	0	0	2	22	3	0-0	0
11/19	GB	L 20-31	0	0	3	20	7	0-0	0
11/26	Pit	L 17-20	0	0	5	38	9	1-0	0
12/03	@SD	L 13-31	1	-5	2	23	4	0-0	0
12/09	@Min	L 11-27	0	0	1	49	2	0-0	0
12/17	Cin	W 26-10	0	0	6	73	9	0-0	0
12/24	@Jac	L 21-24	0	0	1	11	3	0-0	0

Mark Rypien
St. Louis Rams — QB

1995 Passing Splits

	G	Att	Cm	Pct	Yds	Yd/Att	TD	Int	1st	YAC	Big	Sk	Rtg		Att	Cm	Pct	Yds	Yd/Att	TD	Int	1st	YAC	Big	Sk	Rtg
Total	11	217	129	59.4	1448	6.7	9	8	69	609	13	11	77.9	Inside 20	26	15	57.7	67	2.6	6	0	7	44	0	1	102.2
vs. Playoff	6	141	80	56.7	985	7.0	6	4	48	388	10	6	80.8	Inside 10	15	9	60.0	33	2.2	5	0	5	15	0	0	104.2
vs. Non-playoff	5	76	49	64.5	463	6.1	3	4	21	221	3	5	72.4	1st Down	85	51	60.0	653	7.7	2	4	26	268	6	2	72.3
vs. Own Division	5	45	23	51.1	290	6.4	2	3	12	111	3	0	58.6	2nd Down	68	45	66.2	404	5.9	3	1	22	171	2	5	90.6
Home	6	171	107	62.6	1215	7.1	6	2	57	527	10	9	90.7	3rd Down Overall	53	26	49.1	268	5.1	3	3	15	97	2	4	59.3
Away	5	46	22	47.8	233	5.1	3	6	12	82	3	2	45.2	3rd D 0-5 to Go	17	8	47.1	115	6.8	1	1	7	42	2	3	64.6
Games 1-8	5	25	16	64.0	173	6.9	1	0	7	94	1	1	97.6	3rd D 6+ to Go	36	18	50.0	153	4.3	2	2	8	55	0	1	56.8
Games 9-16	6	192	113	58.9	1275	6.6	8	8	62	515	12	10	75.3	4th Down	11	7	63.6	123	11.2	1	0	6	73	3	0	132.0
September	4	3	3	100.0	15	5.0	0	0	0	19	0	1	87.5	Rec Behind Line	28	18	64.3	67	2.4	0	0	3	147	0	0	68.2
October	1	22	13	59.1	158	7.2	1	0	7	75	1	0	96.4	1-10 yds	111	77	69.4	648	5.8	6	3	35	284	0	1	91.0
November	2	22	9	40.9	135	6.1	1	3	5	33	2	0	37.3	11-20 yds	52	29	55.8	560	10.8	1	4	26	148	8	0	67.8
December	4	170	104	61.2	1140	6.7	7	5	57	482	10	10	82.5	21-30 yds	9	3	33.3	73	8.1	2	0	1	3	1	0	103.2
Grass	3	17	7	41.2	77	4.5	1	2	3	20	1	0	35.3	31+	17	2	11.8	100	5.9	0	1	2	25	2	0	27.1
Turf	8	200	122	61.0	1371	6.9	8	6	66	589	12	11	82.3	Left Sideline	58	33	56.9	409	7.1	3	3	15	125	5	0	74.6
Indoor	4	153	95	62.1	1094	7.2	5	3	52	452	10	8	86.3	Left Side	37	22	59.5	280	7.6	1	1	11	171	4	1	80.9
Outdoor	7	64	34	53.1	354	5.5	4	5	17	157	3	3	57.7	Middle	30	21	70.0	246	8.2	3	1	15	107	2	7	114.0
1st Half	-	66	41	62.1	481	7.3	2	4	21	160	5	3	69.1	Right Side	40	18	45.0	132	3.3	0	2	6	73	0	2	32.5
2nd Half/OT	-	151	88	58.3	967	6.4	7	4	48	449	8	8	81.7	Right Sideline	52	35	67.3	381	7.3	2	1	22	133	2	0	93.5
Last 2 Min. Half	-	28	19	67.9	187	6.7	1	2	11	55	0	1	68.6	2 Wide Receivers	84	52	61.9	650	7.7	5	4	28	283	7	3	85.9
4th qtr, +/-7 pts	-	10	7	70.0	73	7.3	1	1	2	33	1	1	84.6	3+ WR	129	74	57.4	778	6.0	4	4	39	323	6	8	72.4
Winning	-	29	17	58.6	142	4.9	1	3	5	52	1	2	43.2	Attempts 1-10	69	36	52.2	453	6.6	2	4	18	173	6	0	58.4
Tied	-	17	8	47.1	127	7.5	0	1	5	48	2	1	47.9	Attempts 11-20	56	37	66.1	364	6.5	4	1	19	135	2	0	78.3
Trailing	-	171	104	60.8	1179	6.9	8	4	59	509	10	8	87.3	Attempts 21+	92	56	60.9	631	6.9	3	0	32	301	5	0	92.3

1995 Incompletions

Type	Num	% of Inc	% of Att
Pass Dropped	16	18.2	7.4
Poor Throw	51	58.0	23.5
Pass Defensed	10	11.4	4.6
Pass Hit at Line	2	2.3	0.9
Other	9	10.2	4.1
Total	88	100.0	40.6

Game Logs (1-8)

Date	Opp	Result	Att	Cm	Pct	Yds	TD	Int	Lg	Sk	F-L
09/03	@GB	W 17-14	0	0	-	0	0	0	0	0	0-0
09/10	NO	W 17-13	0	0	-	0	0	0	0	0	0-0
09/17	@Car	W 31-10	1	1	100.0	-3	0	0	-3	0	0-0
09/24	Chi	W 34-28	2	2	100.0	18	0	0	9	0	0-0
10/01	@Ind	L 18-21	-	-	-	-	-	-	-	-	-
10/12	Atl	W 21-19	-	-	-	-	-	-	-	-	-
10/22	SF	L 10-44	22	13	59.1	158	1	0	38	0	0-0
10/29	@Phi	L 9-20	-	-	-	-	-	-	-	-	-

Game Logs (9-16)

Date	Opp	Result	Att	Cm	Pct	Yds	TD	Int	Lg	Sk	F-L
11/05	@NO	L 10-19	-	-	-	-	-	-	-	-	-
11/12	Car	W 28-17	-	-	-	-	-	-	-	-	-
11/19	@Atl	L 6-31	6	3	50.0	55	0	1	27	0	0-0
11/26	@SF	L 13-41	16	6	37.5	80	1	2	31	0	0-0
12/03	@NYA	W 23-20	23	12	52.2	101	2	3	26	2	0-0
12/10	Buf	L 27-45	55	31	56.4	372	2	0	50	4	0-0
12/17	Was	L 23-35	50	34	68.0	347	1	1	50	2	1-1
12/24	Mia	L 22-41	42	27	64.3	320	2	1	31	2	0-0

Rashaan Salaam

Chicago Bears — RB

1995 Rushing and Receiving Splits

	G	Rush	Yds	Avg	Lg	TD	1st	Stf	YdL	Rec	Yds	Avg	TD
Total	16	296	1074	3.6	42	10	59	28	50	7	56	8.0	0
vs. Playoff	6	94	288	3.1	21	4	18	11	21	1	6	6.0	0
vs. Non-playoff	10	202	786	3.9	42	6	41	17	29	6	50	8.3	0
vs. Own Division	8	114	375	3.3	42	8	25	14	23	3	17	5.7	0
Home	8	168	626	3.7	42	7	33	14	24	1	7	7.0	0
Away	8	128	448	3.5	19	3	26	14	26	6	49	8.2	0
Games 1-8	8	148	500	3.4	16	4	29	14	22	3	29	9.7	0
Games 9-16	8	148	574	3.9	42	6	30	14	28	4	27	6.8	0
September	4	57	171	3.0	11	3	12	5	11	0	0	-	0
October	4	91	329	3.6	16	1	17	9	11	3	29	9.7	0
November	4	62	210	3.4	18	2	13	4	7	2	14	7.0	0
December	4	86	364	4.2	42	4	17	10	21	2	13	6.5	0
Grass	11	221	814	3.7	42	9	45	19	33	3	32	10.7	0
Turf	5	75	260	3.5	19	1	14	9	17	4	24	6.0	0
Indoor	2	21	39	1.9	14	0	2	6	9	2	10	5.0	0
Outdoor	14	275	1035	3.8	42	10	57	22	41	5	46	9.2	0
1st Half	-	146	543	3.7	42	5	29	14	25	3	34	11.3	0
2nd Half/OT	-	150	531	3.5	19	5	30	14	25	4	22	5.5	0
Last 2 Min. Half	-	7	11	1.6	6	0	1	1	3	0	0	-	0
4th qtr. +/-7 pts	-	35	100	2.9	18	0	6	6	10	2	12	6.0	0
Winning	-	128	387	3.0	16	3	20	15	28	2	11	5.5	0
Tied	-	79	387	4.9	42	3	19	4	5	3	21	7.0	0
Trailing	-	89	300	3.4	19	4	20	9	17	2	24	12.0	0

	Rush	Yds	Avg	Lg	TD	1st	Stf	YdL	Rec	Yds	Avg	TD
Inside 20	58	144	2.5	15	10	16	6	12	0	0	-	0
Inside 10	33	36	1.1	8	9	10	6	12	0	0	-	0
1st Down	177	609	3.4	19	4	17	19	35	4	38	9.5	0
2nd Down	101	437	4.3	42	6	31	7	11	2	14	7.0	0
3rd Down Overall	17	27	1.6	4	0	10	2	4	1	4	4.0	0
3rd D 0-2 to Go	15	22	1.5	4	0	10	2	4	1	4	4.0	0
3rd D 3-7 to Go	2	5	2.5	3	0	0	0	0	0	0	-	0
3rd D 8+ to Go	0	0	-	0	0	0	0	0	0	0	-	0
4th Down	1	1	1.0	1	0	1	0	0	0	0	-	0
Left Sideline	10	37	3.7	9	0	0	1	3	0	0	-	0
Left Side	45	241	5.4	42	2	11	2	4	1	6	6.0	0
Middle	174	564	3.2	21	6	32	16	27	2	16	8.0	0
Right Side	61	200	3.3	12	2	14	9	16	4	34	8.5	0
Right Sideline	6	32	5.3	18	0	2	0	0	0	0	-	0
Shotgun	0	0	-	0	0	0	0	0	0	0	-	0
2 Wide Receivers	255	994	3.9	42	3	44	26	47	5	45	9.0	0
3 Wide Receivers	5	11	2.2	4	0	0	0	0	1	7	7.0	0
4+ Wide Receivers	0	0	-	0	0	0	0	0	0	0	-	0
Carries 1-5	80	344	4.3	42	2	15	8	16	0	0	-	0
Carries 6-10	77	251	3.3	15	5	17	4	4	0	0	-	0
Carries 11-15	60	246	4.1	18	1	13	3	4	0	0	-	0
Carries 16-20	42	145	3.5	19	0	8	6	15	0	0	-	0
Carries 21+	37	88	2.4	10	2	7	0	0	0	0	-	0

1995 Incompletions

Type	Num	%of Inc	% Att
Pass Dropped	2	33.3	15.4
Poor Throw	2	33.3	15.4
Pass Defensed	0	0.0	0.0
Pass Hit at Line	1	16.7	7.7
Other	1	16.7	7.7
Total	6	100.0	46.2

Game Logs (1-8)

Date	Opp	Result	Rush	Yds	Rec	Yds	Trgt	F-L	TD
09/03	Min	W 31-14	10	47	0	0	0	0-0	1
09/11	GB	L 24-27	11	29	0	0	0	0-0	2
09/17	@TB	W 25-6	20	55	0	0	1	1-0	1
09/24	@StL	L 28-34	16	40	0	0	1	1-1	0
10/08	Car	W 31-27	28	105	0	0	1	0-0	0
10/15	@Jac	W 30-27	20	79	2	25	3	0-0	0
10/22	Hou	W 35-32	29	109	0	0	0	1-1	1
10/30	@Min	W 14-6	14	36	1	4	1	1-1	0

Game Logs (9-16)

Date	Opp	Result	Rush	Yds	Rec	Yds	Trgt	F-L	TD
11/05	Pit	L 34-37	21	63	0	0	0	0-0	0
11/12	@GB	L 28-35	13	54	0	0	0	0-0	2
11/19	Det	L 17-24	12	17	0	0	0	0-0	0
11/26	@NYN	W 27-24	16	76	2	14	3	0-0	0
12/04	@Det	L 7-27	7	3	1	6	1	0-0	0
12/10	@Cin	L 10-16	22	105	0	0	0	1-1	1
12/17	TB	W 31-10	27	134	1	7	3	1-1	3
12/24	Phi	W 20-14	30	122	0	0	0	3-2	0

Barry Sanders

Detroit Lions — RB

1995 Rushing and Receiving Splits

	G	Rush	Yds	Avg	Lg	TD	1st	Stf	YdL	Rec	Yds	Avg	TD
Total	16	314	1500	4.8	75	11	70	54	113	48	398	8.3	1
vs. Playoff	5	90	467	5.2	44	0	23	15	26	12	78	6.5	0
vs. Non-playoff	11	224	1033	4.6	75	11	47	39	87	36	320	8.9	1
vs. Own Division	8	161	814	5.1	55	4	39	27	58	26	243	9.3	1
Home	8	169	891	5.3	75	8	36	27	56	22	227	10.3	1
Away	8	145	609	4.2	44	3	34	27	57	26	171	6.6	0
Games 1-8	8	153	838	5.5	75	4	36	18	34	27	182	6.7	0
Games 9-16	8	161	662	4.1	55	7	34	36	79	21	216	10.3	1
September	4	75	314	4.2	47	1	9	12	19	18	120	6.7	0
October	4	78	524	6.7	75	3	27	6	15	9	62	6.9	0
November	4	79	394	5.0	55	4	18	21	47	7	43	6.1	0
December	4	82	268	3.3	23	3	16	15	32	14	173	12.4	1
Grass	4	80	368	4.6	30	2	23	11	26	9	49	5.4	0
Turf	12	234	1132	4.8	75	9	47	43	87	39	349	8.9	1
Indoor	11	213	1024	4.8	75	9	43	40	82	37	343	9.3	1
Outdoor	5	101	476	4.7	44	2	27	14	31	11	55	5.0	0
1st Half	-	165	770	4.7	75	7	40	32	67	24	164	6.8	1
2nd Half/OT	-	149	730	4.9	53	4	30	22	46	24	234	9.8	0
Last 2 Min. Half	-	28	87	3.1	13	2	8	6	14	8	48	6.0	1
4th qtr. +/-7 pts	-	44	217	4.9	53	1	8	7	13	5	17	3.4	0
Winning	-	145	789	5.4	75	7	32	20	44	25	262	10.5	1
Tied	-	87	264	3.0	29	2	12	21	44	11	76	6.9	0
Trailing	-	82	447	5.5	55	2	26	13	25	12	60	5.0	0

	Rush	Yds	Avg	Lg	TD	1st	Stf	YdL	Rec	Yds	Avg	TD
Inside 20	52	73	1.4	13	6	9	13	29	3	19	6.3	1
Inside 10	22	18	0.8	9	5	5	6	17	1	9	9.0	1
1st Down	195	919	4.7	55	5	27	37	84	13	128	9.8	0
2nd Down	98	520	5.3	75	6	35	14	21	21	171	8.1	0
3rd Down Overall	19	61	3.2	13	0	8	3	8	14	99	7.1	1
3rd D 0-2 to Go	11	43	3.9	13	0	7	2	5	2	13	6.5	0
3rd D 3-7 to Go	4	9	2.3	6	0	1	0	0	4	31	7.8	0
3rd D 8+ to Go	4	9	2.3	7	0	0	1	3	8	55	6.9	1
4th Down	2	0	0.0	0	0	0	0	0	0	0	-	0
Left Sideline	39	393	10.1	55	5	16	3	8	15	141	9.4	1
Left Side	56	146	2.6	44	1	8	16	28	12	70	5.8	0
Middle	127	533	4.2	75	3	28	17	34	7	68	9.7	0
Right Side	62	225	3.6	53	0	8	17	40	4	40	10.0	0
Right Sideline	30	203	6.8	50	2	10	1	3	10	79	7.9	0
Shotgun	0	0	-	0	0	0	0	0	1	6	6.0	0
2 Wide Receivers	81	381	4.7	47	1	13	9	13	15	109	7.3	0
3 Wide Receivers	213	1068	5.0	75	9	50	41	91	28	220	7.9	1
4+ Wide Receivers	4	31	7.8	12	0	2	0	0	5	69	13.8	0
Carries 1-5	80	333	4.2	75	2	14	19	33	0	0	-	0
Carries 6-10	80	442	5.5	55	4	23	11	29	0	0	-	0
Carries 11-15	75	281	3.7	20	0	15	10	19	0	0	-	0
Carries 16-20	59	401	6.8	53	3	16	10	19	0	0	-	0
Carries 21+	20	43	2.2	11	0	2	4	7	0	0	-	0

1995 Incompletions

Type	Num	%of Inc	% Att
Pass Dropped	6	27.3	8.6
Poor Throw	7	31.8	10.0
Pass Defensed	2	9.1	2.9
Pass Hit at Line	1	4.5	1.4
Other	6	27.3	8.6
Total	22	100.0	31.4

Game Logs (1-8)

Date	Opp	Result	Rush	Yds	Rec	Yds	Trgt	F-L	TD
09/03	@Pit	L 20-23	21	108	2	6	4	0-0	0
09/10	@Min	L 10-20	13	35	9	60	13	0-0	0
09/17	Ari	L 17-20	24	147	4	36	5	2-2	1
09/25	SF	W 27-24	17	24	3	18	7	0-0	0
10/08	Cle	W 38-20	18	157	4	27	4	0-0	3
10/15	@GB	L 21-30	18	124	0	0	0	0-0	0
10/22	@Was	L 30-36	20	76	2	4	2	0-0	0
10/29	GB	W 24-16	22	167	3	31	5	0-0	0

Game Logs (9-16)

Date	Opp	Result	Rush	Yds	Rec	Yds	Trgt	F-L	TD
11/05	@Atl	L 22-34	12	44	4	23	6	0-0	0
11/12	TB	W 27-24	19	92	1	14	2	0-0	1
11/19	@Chi	W 24-17	24	120	2	6	2	0-0	2
11/23	Min	W 44-38	24	138	0	0	1	1-1	0
12/04	Chi	W 27-7	23	90	6	93	8	0-0	0
12/10	@Hou	W 24-17	19	54	2	33	4	0-0	0
12/17	Jac	W 44-0	22	76	1	8	2	0-0	0
12/23	@TB	W 37-10	18	48	5	39	6	0-0	0

Chris Sanders — Houston Oilers — WR

1995 Receiving Splits

	G	Rec	Yds	Avg	TD	Lg	Big	YAC	Trgt	Y@C	1st	1st%
Total	16	35	823	23.5	9	76	14	159	87	19.0	27	77.1
vs. Playoff	5	13	298	22.9	4	76	5	46	31	19.4	9	69.2
vs. Non-playoff	11	22	525	23.9	5	58	9	113	56	18.7	18	81.8
vs. Own Division	8	14	388	27.7	4	76	6	87	38	21.5	11	78.6
Home	8	22	499	22.7	4	53	9	95	48	18.4	17	77.3
Away	8	13	324	24.9	5	76	5	64	39	20.0	10	76.9
Games 1-8	8	12	301	25.1	2	58	5	56	35	20.4	10	83.3
Games 9-16	8	23	522	22.7	7	76	9	103	52	18.2	17	73.9
September	4	7	251	35.9	2	58	5	55	17	28.0	7	100.0
October	4	5	50	10.0	0	13	0	1	18	9.8	3	60.0
November	4	13	254	19.5	5	40	5	34	29	16.9	10	76.9
December	4	10	268	26.8	2	76	4	69	23	19.9	7	70.0
Grass	4	6	70	11.7	2	40	1	3	23	11.2	4	66.7
Turf	12	29	753	26.0	7	76	13	156	64	20.6	23	79.3
Indoor	9	24	524	21.8	4	53	9	96	52	17.8	19	79.2
Outdoor	7	11	299	27.2	5	76	5	63	35	21.5	8	72.7
1st Half	-	20	441	22.1	6	76	7	89	51	17.6	13	65.0
2nd Half/OT	-	15	382	25.5	3	53	7	70	36	20.8	14	93.3
Last 2 Min. Half	-	7	141	20.1	4	46	3	17	12	17.7	5	71.4
4th qtr, +/-7 pts	-	3	63	21.0	1	40	1	-1	6	21.3	3	100.0
Winning	-	11	293	26.6	2	53	6	77	22	19.6	9	81.8
Tied	-	5	141	28.2	1	58	2	30	12	22.2	4	80.0
Trailing	-	19	389	20.5	6	76	6	52	53	17.7	14	73.7

	Rec	Yds	Avg	TD	Lg	Big	YAC	Trgt	Y@C	1st	1st%
Inside 20	3	8	2.7	2	4	0	0	11	2.7	2	66.7
Inside 10	2	4	2.0	2	3	0	0	6	2.0	2	100.0
1st Down	12	300	25.0	3	76	5	71	26	19.1	7	58.3
2nd Down	12	305	25.4	1	53	5	58	31	20.6	10	83.3
3rd Down Overall	10	178	17.8	4	58	3	30	29	14.8	9	90.0
3rd D 0-2 to Go	1	1	1.0	1	1	0	0	2	1.0	1	100.0
3rd D 3-7 to Go	6	66	11.0	1	34	1	10	12	9.3	5	83.3
3rd D 8+ to Go	3	111	37.0	2	58	2	20	15	30.3	3	100.0
4th Down	1	40	40.0	1	40	1	0	1	40.0	1	100.0
Rec Behind Line	0	0	-	0	0	0	0	1	-	0	-
1-10 yds	14	95	6.8	2	12	0	15	26	5.7	7	50.0
11-20 yds	8	142	17.8	0	34	1	22	27	15.0	7	87.5
21-30 yds	3	122	40.7	0	53	3	42	8	26.7	3	100.0
31+	10	464	46.4	7	76	10	80	25	38.4	10	100.0
Left Sideline	12	235	19.6	1	44	4	30	31	17.1	9	75.0
Left Side	3	65	21.7	1	36	1	5	15	20.0	3	100.0
Middle	6	124	20.7	3	76	1	32	12	15.3	5	83.3
Right Side	5	161	32.2	2	58	3	22	14	27.8	4	80.0
Right Sideline	9	238	26.4	2	53	5	70	15	18.7	6	66.7
Shotgun	0	0	-	0	0	0	0	0	-	0	-
2 Wide Receivers	4	151	37.8	0	76	2	32	20	29.8	3	75.0
3 Wide Receivers	29	633	21.8	8	58	11	111	63	18.0	23	79.3
4+ Wide Receivers	2	39	19.5	0	34	1	16	4	11.5	1	50.0

1995 Incompletions

Type	Num	%of Inc	%of Att
Pass Dropped	2	3.8	2.3
Poor Throw	30	57.7	34.5
Pass Defensed	14	26.9	16.1
Pass Hit at Line	0	0.0	0.0
Other	6	11.5	6.9
Total	52	100.0	59.8

Game Logs (1-8)

Date	Opp	Result	Rush	Yds	Rec	Yds	Trgt	F-L	TD
09/03	@Jac	W 10-3	0	0	1	5	2	0-0	0
09/10	Pit	L 17-34	1	-6	2	52	5	0-0	0
09/17	Cle	L 7-14	0	0	2	90	7	0-0	0
09/24	@Cin	W 38-28	0	0	2	104	3	0-0	2
10/01	Jac	L 16-17	0	0	1	9	2	0-0	0
10/08	@Min	L 17-23	0	0	2	25	4	0-0	0
10/22	@Chi	L 32-35	0	0	0	0	7	0-0	0
10/29	TB	W 19-7	1	-13	2	16	5	0-0	0

Game Logs (9-16)

Date	Opp	Result	Rush	Yds	Rec	Yds	Trgt	F-L	TD
11/05	@Cle	W 37-10	0	0	1	5	4	0-0	0
11/12	Cin	L 25-32	0	0	3	42	9	0-0	1
11/19	@KC	L 13-20	0	0	4	60	10	0-0	2
11/26	Den	W 42-33	0	0	5	147	6	0-0	0
12/03	@Pit	L 7-21	0	0	2	81	6	0-0	1
12/10	Det	L 24-34	0	0	4	61	7	0-0	1
12/17	NYA	W 23-6	0	0	3	82	7	0-0	0
12/24	@Buf	W 28-17	0	0	1	44	3	0-0	0

Frank Sanders — Arizona Cardinals — WR

1995 Receiving Splits

	G	Rec	Yds	Avg	TD	Lg	Big	YAC	Trgt	Y@C	1st	1st%
Total	16	52	883	17.0	2	48	15	218	110	12.8	36	69.2
vs. Playoff	8	26	474	18.2	0	48	9	107	52	14.1	19	73.1
vs. Non-playoff	8	26	409	15.7	2	47	6	111	58	11.5	17	65.4
vs. Own Division	8	33	522	15.8	2	47	8	128	58	11.9	22	66.7
Home	8	27	504	18.7	0	48	9	116	51	14.4	20	74.1
Away	8	25	379	15.2	2	47	6	102	59	11.1	16	64.0
Games 1-8	8	26	486	18.7	2	47	9	117	47	14.2	21	80.8
Games 9-16	8	26	397	15.3	0	48	6	101	63	11.4	15	57.7
September	4	11	224	20.4	0	36	5	56	18	15.3	8	72.7
October	4	15	262	17.5	2	47	4	61	29	13.4	13	86.7
November	5	18	302	16.8	0	48	5	79	41	12.4	10	55.6
December	3	8	95	11.9	0	25	1	22	22	9.1	5	62.5
Grass	12	34	619	18.2	0	48	11	158	75	13.6	24	70.6
Turf	4	18	264	14.7	2	47	4	60	35	11.3	12	66.7
Indoor	1	1	12	12.0	0	12	0	8	3	4.0	1	100.0
Outdoor	15	51	871	17.1	2	48	15	210	107	13.0	35	68.6
1st Half	-	19	353	18.6	1	48	7	90	47	13.8	12	63.2
2nd Half/OT	-	33	530	16.1	1	47	8	128	63	12.2	24	72.7
Last 2 Min. Half	-	4	96	24.0	0	47	1	15	15	20.3	3	75.0
4th qtr, +/-7 pts	-	9	131	14.6	0	47	1	30	20	11.2	7	77.8
Winning	-	12	180	15.0	0	48	2	60	23	10.0	6	50.0
Tied	-	4	104	26.0	0	47	2	10	15	23.5	4	100.0
Trailing	-	36	599	16.6	2	36	11	148	72	12.5	26	72.2

	Rec	Yds	Avg	TD	Lg	Big	YAC	Trgt	Y@C	1st	1st%
Inside 20	6	33	5.5	2	11	0	14	16	3.2	3	50.0
Inside 10	2	9	4.5	1	6	0	2	6	3.5	1	50.0
1st Down	21	422	20.1	1	48	7	94	43	15.6	14	66.7
2nd Down	19	242	12.7	1	35	3	79	39	8.6	12	63.2
3rd Down Overall	12	219	18.3	0	36	5	45	28	14.5	10	83.3
3rd D 0-2 to Go	1	36	36.0	0	36	1	24	1	12.0	1	100.0
3rd D 3-7 to Go	4	50	12.5	0	28	1	9	11	10.3	4	100.0
3rd D 8+ to Go	7	133	19.0	0	30	3	12	16	17.3	5	71.4
4th Down	0	0	-	0	0	0	0	0	-	0	-
Rec Behind Line	0	0	-	0	0	0	0	1	-	0	-
1-10 yds	27	213	7.9	2	16	0	73	52	5.2	12	44.4
11-20 yds	12	242	20.2	0	36	2	64	28	14.8	11	91.7
21-30 yds	10	312	31.2	0	48	10	68	19	24.4	10	100.0
31+	3	116	38.7	0	47	3	13	10	34.3	3	100.0
Left Sideline	9	139	15.4	0	35	1	28	23	12.3	5	55.6
Left Side	6	67	11.2	0	20	0	16	8	8.5	3	50.0
Middle	10	170	17.0	1	48	3	71	20	9.9	7	70.0
Right Side	8	155	19.4	0	47	3	55	25	12.5	5	50.0
Right Sideline	19	352	18.5	1	36	8	48	34	16.0	13	68.4
Shotgun	13	246	18.9	0	30	5	38	33	16.0	11	84.6
2 Wide Receivers	25	403	16.1	1	48	6	108	50	11.8	18	72.0
3 Wide Receivers	25	438	17.5	1	47	8	108	47	13.2	16	64.0
4+ Wide Receivers	2	42	21.0	0	28	1	2	13	20.0	2	100.0

1995 Incompletions

Type	Num	%of Inc	%of Att
Pass Dropped	5	8.6	4.5
Poor Throw	27	46.6	24.5
Pass Defensed	16	27.6	14.5
Pass Hit at Line	1	1.7	0.9
Other	9	15.5	8.2
Total	58	100.0	52.7

Game Logs (1-8)

Date	Opp	Result	Rush	Yds	Rec	Yds	Trgt	F-L	TD
09/03	@Was	L 7-27	0	0	1	36	3	0-0	0
09/10	Phi	L 19-31	0	0	5	102	5	0-0	0
09/17	@Det	W 20-17	0	0	1	12	3	0-0	0
09/24	@Dal	L 20-34	0	0	4	74	7	0-0	0
10/01	KC	L 3-24	0	0	4	97	6	0-0	0
10/08	@NYN	L 21-27	0	0	6	108	10	0-0	2
10/15	Was	W 24-20	1	1	4	48	7	0-0	0
10/29	Sea	W 20-14	0	0	1	19	5	0-0	0

Game Logs (9-16)

Date	Opp	Result	Rush	Yds	Rec	Yds	Trgt	F-L	TD
11/05	@Den	L 6-38	0	0	2	17	7	0-0	0
11/12	Min	L 24-30	0	0	3	70	7	0-0	0
11/19	@Car	L 7-27	0	0	3	37	8	0-0	0
11/30	Atl	W 40-37	0	0	4	94	9	0-0	0
12/09	@SD	L 25-28	0	0	1	25	6	0-0	0
12/17	@Phi	L 20-21	0	0	7	70	15	0-0	0
12/25	Dal	L 13-37	0	0	1	1		0-0	0

Darnay Scott — Cincinnati Bengals — WR

1995 Receiving Splits

	G	Rec	Yds	Avg	TD	Lg	Big	YAC	Trgt	Y@C	1st	1st%		Rec	Yds	Avg	TD	Lg	Big	YAC	Trgt	Y@C	1st	1st%
Total	16	52	821	15.8	5	88	9	311	109	9.8	33	63.5	Inside 20	6	48	8.0	1	15	0	14	18	5.7	2	33.3
vs. Playoff	5	19	237	12.5	2	47	2	51	40	9.8	13	68.4	Inside 10	1	4	4.0	1	4	0	0	5	4.0	1	100.0
vs. Non-playoff	11	33	584	17.7	3	88	7	260	69	9.8	20	60.6	1st Down	21	438	20.9	3	88	5	187	45	12.0	11	52.4
vs. Own Division	8	25	399	16.0	3	56	4	134	55	10.6	15	60.0	2nd Down	17	233	13.7	2	47	3	72	37	9.5	12	70.6
Home	8	26	415	16.0	3	56	5	156	53	10.0	17	65.4	3rd Down Overall	14	150	10.7	0	30	1	52	26	7.0	10	71.4
Away	8	26	406	15.6	2	88	4	155	56	9.7	16	61.5	3rd D 0-2 to Go	3	21	7.0	0	9	0	10	6	3.7	3	100.0
Games 1-8	8	25	522	20.9	3	88	7	210	53	12.5	15	60.0	3rd D 3-7 to Go	6	87	14.5	0	30	1	25	10	10.5	5	83.3
Games 9-16	8	27	299	11.1	2	38	2	101	56	7.3	18	66.7	3rd D 8+ to Go	5	42	8.4	0	18	0	17	10	5.0	2	40.0
September	4	15	322	21.5	2	88	4	142	30	12.0	8	53.3	4th Down	0	0	-	0	0	0	0	1	-	0	-
October	4	10	200	20.0	1	47	3	68	23	13.2	7	70.0	Rec Behind Line	3	3	1.0	0	5	0	7	6	-1.3	1	33.3
November	4	10	92	9.2	1	23	0	30	26	6.2	7	70.0	1-10 yds	36	385	10.7	1	35	2	165	56	6.1	19	52.8
December	4	17	207	12.2	1	38	2	71	30	8.0	11	64.7	11-20 yds	8	211	26.4	1	88	2	105	19	13.3	8	100.0
Grass	4	13	150	11.5	0	30	1	28	31	9.4	9	69.2	21-30 yds	1	30	30.0	0	30	1	2	7	28.0	1	100.0
Turf	12	39	671	17.2	5	88	8	283	78	9.9	24	61.5	31+	4	192	48.0	3	56	4	32	21	40.0	4	100.0
Indoor	3	10	183	18.3	1	88	2	111	19	7.2	5	50.0	Left Sideline	9	153	17.0	2	51	2	45	14	12.0	3	33.3
Outdoor	13	42	638	15.2	4	56	7	200	90	10.4	28	66.7	Left Side	9	60	6.7	1	12	0	6	21	6.0	4	44.4
1st Half	-	31	468	15.1	3	88	3	205	60	8.5	19	61.3	Middle	13	251	19.3	1	56	4	67	24	14.2	10	76.9
2nd Half/OT	-	21	353	16.8	2	56	6	106	49	11.8	14	66.7	Right Side	14	259	18.5	1	88	2	159	32	7.1	11	78.6
Last 2 Min. Half	-	4	58	14.5	0	22	0	20	12	9.5	3	75.0	Right Sideline	7	98	14.0	0	26	1	34	14	9.1	5	71.4
4th qtr, +/-7 pts	-	2	41	20.5	0	35	1	26	8	7.5	1	50.0	Shotgun	0	0	-	0	0	0	0	0	-	0	-
Winning	-	14	184	13.1	1	38	2	52	26	9.4	8	57.1	2 Wide Receivers	29	487	16.8	5	88	5	174	71	10.8	17	58.6
Tied	-	11	156	14.2	2	47	1	59	27	8.8	7	63.6	3 Wide Receivers	20	320	16.0	0	35	4	140	33	9.0	15	75.0
Trailing	-	27	481	17.8	2	88	6	200	56	10.4	18	64.3	4+ Wide Receivers	2	7	3.5	0	14	0	-3	2	5.0	1	50.0

1995 Incompletions

Type	Num	%of Inc	%of Att
Pass Dropped	9	15.8	8.3
Poor Throw	31	54.4	28.4
Pass Defensed	6	10.5	5.5
Pass Hit at Line	3	5.3	2.8
Other	8	14.0	7.3
Total	57	100.0	52.3

Game Logs (1-8)

Date	Opp	Result	Rush	Yds	Rec	Yds	Trgt	F-L	TD
09/03	@Ind	W 24-21	0	0	5	68	8	0-0	0
09/10	Jac	W 24-17	0	0	3	31	6	0-0	0
09/17	@Sea	L 21-24	0	0	3	98	5	0-0	1
09/24	Hou	L 28-38	1	5	4	125	11	0-0	1
10/01	Mia	L 23-26	0	0	1	8	6	0-0	0
10/08	@TB	L 16-19	1	9	3	57	6	0-0	0
10/19	@Pit	W 27-9	1	-10	3	73	6	0-0	0
10/29	Cle	L 26-29	0	0	3	62	5	0-0	0

Game Logs (9-16)

Date	Opp	Result	Rush	Yds	Rec	Yds	Trgt	F-L	TD
11/05	Oak	L 17-20	0	0	2	20	7	0-0	0
11/12	@Hou	W 32-25	0	0	2	17	6	0-0	0
11/19	Pit	L 31-49	0	0	5	43	8	0-0	0
11/26	@Jac	W 17-13	0	0	1	12	5	0-0	0
12/03	@GB	L 10-24	0	0	5	45	12	0-0	0
12/10	Chi	W 16-10	1	4	5	75	6	0-0	1
12/17	@Cle	L 10-26	0	0	4	36	8	0-0	0
12/24	Min	W 27-24	1	3	3	51	4	0-0	0

Mark Seay — San Diego Chargers — WR

1995 Receiving Splits

	G	Rec	Yds	Avg	TD	Lg	Big	YAC	Trgt	Y@C	1st	1st%		Rec	Yds	Avg	TD	Lg	Big	YAC	Trgt	Y@C	1st	1st%
Total	16	45	537	11.9	3	38	2	155	70	8.5	29	64.4	Inside 20	4	37	9.3	2	15	0	21	7	4.0	3	75.0
vs. Playoff	7	16	183	11.4	0	33	1	30	23	9.6	10	62.5	Inside 10	1	2	2.0	1	2	0	1	2	1.0	1	100.0
vs. Non-playoff	9	29	354	12.2	3	38	1	125	47	7.9	19	65.5	1st Down	9	127	14.1	1	38	1	36	17	10.1	5	55.6
vs. Own Division	8	27	283	10.5	1	18	0	65	45	8.1	17	63.0	2nd Down	11	146	13.3	0	33	1	29	16	10.6	4	36.4
Home	8	31	386	12.5	2	38	2	114	40	8.8	18	58.1	3rd Down Overall	23	235	10.2	2	18	0	78	34	6.8	19	82.6
Away	8	14	151	10.8	1	19	0	41	30	7.9	11	78.6	3rd D 0-2 to Go	2	10	5.0	1	8	0	4	3	3.0	2	100.0
Games 1-8	8	21	227	10.8	1	19	0	43	32	8.8	14	66.7	3rd D 3-7 to Go	12	117	9.8	0	18	0	35	16	6.8	11	91.7
Games 9-16	8	24	310	12.9	2	38	2	112	38	8.3	15	62.5	3rd D 8+ to Go	9	108	12.0	1	18	0	39	15	7.7	6	66.7
September	4	10	115	11.5	0	18	0	18	18	9.7	5	50.0	4th Down	2	29	14.5	0	23	0	12	3	8.5	1	50.0
October	4	11	112	10.2	1	19	0	25	14	7.9	9	81.8	Rec Behind Line	1	8	8.0	0	8	0	10	1	-2.0	0	0.0
November	4	13	155	11.9	0	33	1	34	22	9.3	7	53.8	1-10 yds	28	285	10.2	3	38	1	119	39	5.9	19	67.9
December	4	11	155	14.1	2	38	1	78	16	7.0	8	72.7	11-20 yds	15	211	14.1	0	23	0	20	22	12.7	9	60.0
Grass	11	37	452	12.2	2	38	2	134	57	8.6	23	62.2	21-30 yds	1	33	33.0	0	33	1	6	6	27.0	1	100.0
Turf	5	8	85	10.6	1	19	0	21	13	8.0	6	75.0	31+	0	0	-	0	0	0	0	2	-	0	-
Outdoor	2	40	494	12.4	2	38	2	139	62	8.9	25	62.5	Left Sideline	7	79	11.3	0	17	0	7	16	10.3	5	71.4
Indoor	14	5	43	8.6	1	17	0	16	8	5.4	4	80.0	Left Side	8	66	8.3	0	11	0	16	11	6.3	5	62.5
1st Half	-	23	248	10.8	2	23	0	56	31	8.3	16	69.6	Middle	11	170	15.5	2	38	2	76	13	8.5	8	72.7
2nd Half/OT	-	22	289	13.1	1	38	2	99	39	8.6	13	59.1	Right Side	10	121	12.1	0	23	0	42	13	7.9	5	50.0
Last 2 Min. Half	-	8	96	12.0	0	23	0	16	9	10.0	6	75.0	Right Sideline	9	101	11.2	1	18	0	14	17	9.7	6	66.7
4th qtr, +/-7 pts	-	3	36	12.0	0	13	0	6	6	10.0	1	33.3	Shotgun	0	0	-	0	0	0	0	0	-	0	-
Winning	-	16	212	13.3	1	38	1	80	24	8.3	10	62.5	2 Wide Receivers	2	28	14.0	0	19	0	-2	12	15.0	1	50.0
Tied	-	10	108	10.8	1	15	0	28	14	8.0	8	80.0	3 Wide Receivers	34	423	12.4	2	38	2	117	48	9.0	23	67.6
Trailing	-	19	217	11.4	1	33	1	47	32	8.9	11	57.9	4+ Wide Receivers	9	86	9.6	1	15	0	40	10	5.1	5	55.6

1995 Incompletions

Type	Num	%of Inc	%of Att
Pass Dropped	7	28.0	10.0
Poor Throw	13	52.0	18.6
Pass Defensed	5	20.0	7.1
Pass Hit at Line	0	0.0	0.0
Other	0	0.0	0.0
Total	25	100.0	35.7

Game Logs (1-8)

Date	Opp	Result	Rec	Yds	Trgt	F-L	TD
09/03	@Oak	L 7-17	2	25	7	0-0	0
09/10	Sea	W 14-10	4	43	5	0-0	0
09/17	@Phi	W 27-21	1	11	2	0-0	0
09/24	Den	W 17-6	3	36	4	0-0	0
10/01	@Pit	L 16-31	2	31	2	0-0	0
10/09	@KC	L 23-29	4	41	6	0-0	0
10/15	Dal	L 9-23	1	6	1	0-0	0
10/22	@Sea	W 35-25	4	34	5	0-0	1

Game Logs (9-16)

Date	Opp	Result	Rec	Yds	Trgt	F-L	TD
11/05	Mia	L 14-24	3	51	4	0-0	0
11/12	KC	L 7-22	4	34	5	0-0	0
11/19	@Den	L 27-30	0	0	4	0-0	0
11/27	Oak	W 12-6	6	70	9	0-0	0
12/03	Cle	W 31-13	3	32	4	0-0	0
12/09	Ari	W 28-25	7	114	8	0-0	0
12/17	@Ind	W 27-24	1	9	3	0-0	0
12/23	@NYN	W 27-17	0	0	1	0-0	0

Shannon Sharpe
Denver Broncos — TE

1995 Receiving Splits

	G	Rec	Yds	Avg	TD	Lg	Big	YAC	Trgt	Y@C	1st	1st%
Total	13	63	756	12.0	4	49	7	355	94	6.4	39	61.9
vs. Playoff	6	32	447	14.0	2	49	5	190	46	8.0	22	68.8
vs. Non-playoff	7	31	309	10.0	2	29	2	165	48	4.6	17	54.8
vs. Own Division	5	23	294	12.8	3	40	4	128	38	7.2	14	60.9
Home	7	31	444	14.3	3	49	6	209	43	7.6	21	67.7
Away	6	32	312	9.8	1	25	1	146	51	5.2	18	56.3
Games 1-8	8	35	449	12.8	2	49	3	206	57	6.9	22	62.9
Games 9-16	5	28	307	11.0	2	40	4	149	37	5.6	17	60.7
September	4	16	249	15.6	0	49	2	108	23	8.8	11	68.8
October	4	19	200	10.5	2	25	1	98	34	5.4	11	57.9
November	4	26	295	11.3	1	40	4	142	35	5.9	16	61.5
December	1	2	12	6.0	1	6	0	7	2	2.5	1	50.0
Grass	9	35	487	13.9	4	49	6	234	51	7.2	24	68.6
Turf	4	28	269	9.6	0	25	1	121	43	5.3	15	53.6
Outdoor	2	47	597	12.7	4	49	6	290	68	6.5	31	66.0
Indoor	11	16	159	9.9	0	25	1	65	26	5.9	8	50.0
1st Half	-	35	448	12.8	3	49	6	220	53	6.5	20	57.1
2nd Half/OT	-	28	308	11.0	1	29	1	135	41	6.2	19	67.9
Last 2 Min. Half	-	10	147	14.7	0	31	3	37	15	11.0	7	70.0
4th qtr, +/-7 pts	-	5	78	15.6	0	29	1	32	5	9.2	3	60.0
Winning	-	27	353	13.1	3	40	4	166	37	6.9	18	66.7
Tied	-	11	146	13.3	1	49	2	86	16	5.5	4	45.5
Trailing	-	25	257	10.3	0	25	1	103	41	6.2	16	64.0

	Rec	Yds	Avg	TD	Lg	Big	YAC	Trgt	Y@C	1st	1st%
Inside 20	5	29	5.8	4	10	0	9	10	4.0	4	80.0
Inside 10	4	19	4.8	3	8	0	4	6	3.8	3	75.0
1st Down	24	282	11.8	1	49	2	163	35	5.0	10	41.7
2nd Down	28	334	11.9	2	40	4	133	38	7.2	20	71.4
3rd Down Overall	11	140	12.7	1	29	1	59	21	7.4	9	81.8
3rd D 0-2 to Go	1	4	4.0	1	4	0	2	4	4.0	1	100.0
3rd D 3-7 to Go	7	73	10.4	0	18	0	28	9	6.4	6	85.7
3rd D 8+ to Go	3	63	21.0	0	29	1	31	10	10.7	2	66.7
4th Down	0	0	-	0	0	0	0	0	-	0	-
Rec Behind Line	6	28	4.7	0	8	0	30	6	-0.3	1	16.7
1-10 yds	43	388	9.0	4	29	1	215	59	4.4	25	55.8
11-20 yds	10	190	19.0	0	29	2	60	20	13.0	10	100.0
21-30 yds	3	110	36.7	0	49	3	42	8	22.7	3	100.0
31+	1	40	40.0	0	40	1	8	1	32.0	1	100.0
Left Sideline	1	8	8.0	0	8	0	6	3	2.0	0	0.0
Left Side	16	222	13.9	2	29	2	120	22	6.4	14	87.5
Middle	16	209	13.1	0	30	2	75	25	8.4	11	68.8
Right Side	17	145	8.5	1	16	0	83	20	3.6	8	47.1
Right Sideline	13	172	13.2	1	49	3	71	24	7.8	6	46.2
Shotgun	20	278	13.9	1	31	4	100	33	8.9	14	70.0
2 Wide Receivers	27	340	12.6	3	31	4	158	41	6.7	18	66.7
3 Wide Receivers	28	363	13.0	1	49	3	166	39	7.0	18	64.3
4+ Wide Receivers	6	43	7.2	0	14	0	21	12	3.7	3	50.0

1995 Incompletions

Type	Num	%of Inc	%of Att
Pass Dropped	6	19.4	6.4
Poor Throw	15	48.4	16.0
Pass Defensed	7	22.6	7.4
Pass Hit at Line	0	0.0	0.0
Other	3	9.7	3.2
Total	31	100.0	33.0

Game Logs (1-8)

Date	Opp	Result	Rec	Yds	Trgt	F-L	TD
09/03	Buf	W 22-7	10	180	14	0-0	0
09/10	@Dal	L 21-31	5	67	7	0-0	0
09/17	Was	W 38-31	1	2	1	0-0	0
09/24	@SD	L 6-17	0	0	1	0-0	0
10/01	@Sea	L 10-27	8	94	14	0-0	0
10/08	@NE	W 37-3	4	43	7	1-0	1
10/16	Oak	W 27-0	5	43	9	0-0	0
10/22	KC	L 7-21	2	20	4	0-0	1

Game Logs (9-16)

Date	Opp	Result	Rec	Yds	Trgt	F-L	TD
11/05	Ari	W 38-6	3	50	3	0-0	0
11/12	@Phi	L 13-31	7	43	10	0-0	0
11/19	SD	W 30-27	8	137	10	0-0	1
11/26	@Hou	L 33-42	8	65	12	0-0	0
12/03	Jac	W 31-23	2	12	2	0-0	1
12/10	Sea	L 27-31	-	-	-	-	-
12/17	@KC	L 17-20	-	-	-	-	-
12/24	@Oak	W 31-28	-	-	-	-	-

Leslie Shepherd
Washington Redskins — WR

1995 Receiving Splits

	G	Rec	Yds	Avg	TD	Lg	Big	YAC	Trgt	Y@C	1st	1st%
Total	14	29	486	16.8	2	73	7	136	61	12.1	20	69.0
vs. Playoff	5	12	168	14.0	0	44	2	41	32	10.6	7	58.3
vs. Non-playoff	9	17	318	18.7	2	73	5	95	29	13.1	13	76.5
vs. Own Division	7	19	351	18.5	1	73	5	90	31	13.7	12	63.2
Home	6	14	341	24.4	1	73	6	91	26	17.9	12	85.7
Away	8	15	145	9.7	1	44	1	45	35	6.7	8	53.3
Games 1-8	8	16	270	16.9	2	73	4	90	26	11.3	11	68.8
Games 9-16	6	13	216	16.6	0	45	3	46	35	13.1	9	69.2
September	4	7	165	23.6	2	73	3	72	9	13.3	6	85.7
October	5	16	240	15.0	0	45	3	36	29	12.8	11	68.8
November	1	2	19	9.5	0	14	0	13	14	3.0	1	50.0
December	4	4	62	15.5	0	44	1	15	9	11.8	2	50.0
Grass	10	21	399	19.0	2	73	6	117	47	13.4	17	81.0
Turf	4	8	87	10.9	0	44	1	19	14	8.5	3	37.5
Indoor	1	0	0	0	0	0	0	0	0	-	0	-
Outdoor	13	29	486	16.8	2	73	7	136	61	12.1	20	69.0
1st Half	-	16	194	12.1	0	41	2	48	31	9.1	10	62.5
2nd Half/OT	-	13	292	22.5	2	73	5	88	30	15.7	10	76.9
Last 2 Min. Half	-	9	100	11.1	0	25	1	13	19	9.7	6	66.7
4th qtr, +/-7 pts	-	2	11	5.5	0	8	0	2	6	4.5	1	50.0
Winning	-	5	168	33.6	1	73	3	55	8	22.6	4	80.0
Tied	-	8	67	8.4	0	12	0	16	14	6.4	4	50.0
Trailing	-	16	251	15.7	1	45	4	65	39	11.6	12	75.0

	Rec	Yds	Avg	TD	Lg	Big	YAC	Trgt	Y@C	1st	1st%
Inside 20	4	17	4.3	1	7	0	10	6	1.8	1	25.0
Inside 10	2	8	4.0	1	7	0	5	3	1.5	1	50.0
1st Down	7	138	19.7	0	45	2	38	17	14.3	5	71.4
2nd Down	5	46	9.2	0	14	0	15	19	6.2	2	40.0
3rd Down Overall	16	299	18.7	2	73	5	84	23	13.4	12	75.0
3rd D 0-2 to Go	2	14	7.0	1	7	0	5	2	4.5	2	100.0
3rd D 3-7 to Go	9	189	21.0	1	73	3	73	12	12.9	6	66.7
3rd D 8+ to Go	5	96	19.2	0	44	2	6	9	18.0	4	80.0
4th Down	1	3	3.0	0	3	0	-1	2	4.0	1	100.0
Rec Behind Line	2	7	3.5	0	6	0	8	3	-0.5	0	0.0
1-10 yds	17	134	7.9	1	14	0	37	32	5.7	10	58.8
11-20 yds	3	37	12.3	0	13	0	-4	7	13.7	3	100.0
21-30 yds	3	105	35.0	0	42	3	35	9	23.3	3	100.0
31+	4	203	50.8	1	73	4	60	10	35.8	4	100.0
Left Sideline	7	185	26.4	1	73	3	61	12	17.7	5	71.4
Left Side	2	56	28.0	0	42	1	30	6	13.0	2	100.0
Middle	11	127	11.5	0	45	2	26	20	9.2	6	54.5
Right Side	5	46	9.2	1	13	0	15	12	6.2	3	60.0
Right Sideline	4	72	18.0	0	41	1	4	11	17.0	4	100.0
Shotgun	0	0	-	0	0	0	0	0	-	0	-
2 Wide Receivers	5	81	16.2	1	45	1	25	20	11.2	4	80.0
3 Wide Receivers	20	377	18.9	0	73	6	107	34	13.5	13	65.0
4+ Wide Receivers	4	28	7.0	0	13	0	4	4	6.0	3	75.0

1995 Incompletions

Type	Num	%of Inc	%of Att
Pass Dropped	5	15.6	8.2
Poor Throw	19	59.4	31.1
Pass Defensed	4	12.5	6.6
Pass Hit at Line	1	3.1	1.6
Other	3	9.4	4.9
Total	32	100.0	52.5

Game Logs (1-8)

Date	Opp	Result	Rush	Yds	Rec	Yds	Trgt	F-L	TD
09/03	Ari	W 27-7	1	26	1	73	1	0-0	1
09/10	Oak	L 8-20	1	3	3	68	4	0-0	0
09/17	@Den	L 31-38	0	0	1	7	1	0-0	1
09/24	@TB	W 6-14	0	0	2	17	3	0-0	0
10/01	Dal	W 27-23	0	0	1	41	1	0-0	0
10/08	@Phi	L 34-37	1	3	4	25	6	0-0	0
10/15	@Ari	L 20-24	0	0	2	15	3	0-0	0
10/22	Det	W 36-30	0	0	2	24	7	0-0	0

Game Logs (9-16)

Date	Opp	Result	Rush	Yds	Rec	Yds	Trgt	F-L	TD
10/29	NYN	L 15-24	2	6	7	135	19	0-0	0
11/05	@KC	L 3-24	0	0	2	19	14	0-0	0
11/19	Sea	L 20-27	-	-	-	-	-	-	-
11/26	Phi	L 7-14	-	-	-	-	-	-	-
12/03	@Dal	W 24-17	0	0	3	59	4	0-0	0
12/10	@NYN	L 13-20	0	0	1	3	4	0-0	0
12/17	@StL	W 35-23	1	8	0	0	1	0-0	0
12/24	Car	W 20-17	1	17	0	0	1	0-0	0

Mike Sherrard
New York Giants — WR

1995 Receiving Splits

	G	Rec	Yds	Avg	TD	Lg	Big	YAC	Trgt	Y@C	1st	1st%		Rec	Yds	Avg	TD	Lg	Big	YAC	Trgt	Y@C	1st	1st%
Total	13	44	577	13.1	4	57	6	104	86	10.8	30	68.2	Inside 20	2	18	9.0	2	12	0	1	8	8.5	2	100.0
vs. Playoff	6	22	224	10.2	0	30	1	33	47	8.7	13	59.1	Inside 10	1	6	6.0	1	6	0	0	3	6.0	1	100.0
vs. Non-playoff	7	22	353	16.0	4	57	5	71	39	12.8	17	77.3	1st Down	14	204	14.6	1	42	2	11	31	13.8	8	57.1
vs. Own Division	7	20	238	11.9	3	57	1	75	43	8.2	14	70.0	2nd Down	17	250	14.7	2	57	3	64	29	10.9	11	64.7
Home	7	19	188	9.9	1	42	1	14	44	9.2	12	63.2	3rd Down Overall	11	114	10.4	1	25	1	28	23	7.8	9	81.8
Away	6	25	389	15.6	3	57	5	90	42	12.0	18	72.0	3rd D 0-2 to Go	1	0	0.0	0	0	0	-3	1	3.0	0	0.0
Games 1-8	7	27	307	11.4	2	57	2	54	54	9.4	16	59.3	3rd D 3-7 to Go	6	54	9.0	1	18	0	20	11	5.7	6	100.0
Games 9-16	6	17	270	15.9	2	42	4	50	32	12.9	14	82.4	3rd D 8+ to Go	4	60	15.0	0	25	1	11	11	12.3	3	75.0
September	3	13	127	9.8	0	30	1	12	22	8.8	5	38.5	4th Down	2	9	4.5	0	5	0	1	3	4.0	2	100.0
October	4	14	180	12.9	2	57	1	42	32	9.9	11	78.6	Rec Behind Line	0	0	-	0	0	0	-	1	-	0	-
November	3	12	213	17.8	2	42	4	33	23	15.0	10	83.3	1-10 yds	25	183	7.3	1	18	0	53	40	5.2	12	48.0
December	3	5	57	11.4	0	18	0	17	9	8.0	4	80.0	11-20 yds	14	207	14.8	1	25	1	22	26	13.2	13	92.9
Grass	4	17	226	13.3	2	57	2	55	26	10.1	10	58.8	21-30 yds	3	145	36.3	2	57	4	33	12	28.0	4	100.0
Turf	9	27	351	13.0	2	42	4	49	60	11.2	20	74.1	31+	1	42	42.0	0	42	1	-4	7	46.0	1	100.0
Outdoor	1	38	449	11.8	3	57	3	83	74	9.6	24	63.2	Left Sideline	14	242	17.3	1	42	4	20	28	15.9	10	71.4
Indoor	12	6	128	21.3	1	30	3	21	12	17.8	6	100.0	Left Side	8	72	9.0	1	16	0	4	14	8.5	4	50.0
1st Half	-	23	354	15.4	3	57	5	60	46	12.8	16	69.6	Middle	6	46	7.7	0	25	1	9	13	6.2	3	50.0
2nd Half/OT	-	21	223	10.6	1	42	1	44	40	8.5	14	66.7	Right Side	10	149	14.9	2	57	1	50	17	9.9	8	80.0
Last 2 Min. Half	-	7	138	19.7	1	42	3	4	15	19.1	6	85.7	Right Sideline	6	68	11.3	0	18	0	21	14	7.8	5	83.3
4th qtr. +/-7 pts	-	6	92	15.3	0	42	1	9	9	13.8	6	100.0	Shotgun	3	61	20.3	1	42	1	-5	11	22.0	3	100.0
Winning	-	9	140	15.6	1	57	1	54	14	9.6	6	66.7	2 Wide Receivers	24	300	12.5	1	57	2	68	46	9.7	15	62.5
Tied	-	7	74	10.6	0	14	0	7	10	9.6	6	85.7	3 Wide Receivers	12	192	16.0	2	42	4	14	24	14.8	10	83.3
Trailing	-	28	363	13.0	3	42	5	43	62	11.4	18	64.3	4+ Wide Receivers	5	54	10.8	0	16	0	12	7	7.8	3	60.0

1995 Incompletions

Type	Num	%of Inc	%of Att
Pass Dropped	0	0.0	0.0
Poor Throw	27	64.3	31.4
Pass Defensed	8	19.0	9.3
Pass Hit at Line	1	2.4	1.2
Other	6	14.3	7.0
Total	42	100.0	48.8

Game Logs (1-8)

Date	Opp	Result	Rec	Yds	Trgt	F-L	TD
09/04	Dal	L 0-35	4	32	11	0-0	0
09/10	@KC	L 17-20	-	-	-	-	-
09/17	@GB	L 6-14	7	74	9	0-0	0
09/24	NO	W 45-29	2	21	2	0-0	0
10/01	@SF	L 6-20	4	45	9	0-0	0
10/08	Ari	W 27-21	4	32	9	0-0	1
10/15	Phi	L 14-17	3	24	10	0-0	0
10/29	@Was	W 24-15	3	79	4	0-0	1

Game Logs (9-16)

Date	Opp	Result	Rec	Yds	Trgt	F-L	TD
11/05	@Sea	L 28-30	6	128	12	0-0	1
11/12	Oak	L 13-17	3	57	7	1-0	0
11/19	@Phi	L 19-28	-	-	-	-	-
11/26	Chi	L 24-27	-	-	-	-	-
11/30	@Ari	W 10-6	3	28	4	0-0	1
12/10	Was	W 20-13	1	8	1	0-0	0
12/17	@Dal	L 20-21	2	35	4	0-0	0
12/23	SD	L 17-27	2	14	4	1-1	0

Heath Shuler
Washington Redskins — QB

1995 Passing Splits

	G	Att	Cm	Pct	Yds	Yd/Att	TD	Int	1st	YAC	Big	Sk	Rtg		Att	Cm	Pct	Yds	Yd/Att	TD	Int	1st	YAC	Big	Sk	Rtg
Total	7	125	66	52.8	745	6.0	3	7	40	396	4	13	55.6	Inside 20	10	6	60.0	50	5.0	2	0	4	37	0	3	112.5
vs. Playoff	3	56	24	42.9	322	5.8	1	3	15	179	3	5	45.4	Inside 10	1	1	100.0	5	5.0	1	0	1	2	0	2	127.1
vs. Non-playoff	4	69	42	60.9	423	6.1	2	4	25	217	1	8	63.9	1st Down	42	24	57.1	267	6.4	1	1	13	109	2	2	74.2
vs. Own Division	4	95	45	47.4	540	5.7	1	3	29	300	3	10	50.0	2nd Down	43	21	48.8	217	5.0	1	3	12	132	1	6	42.5
Home	3	51	27	52.9	309	6.1	1	4	17	151	2	6	45.3	3rd Down Overall	38	21	55.3	261	6.9	1	3	15	155	1	5	52.6
Away	4	74	39	52.7	436	5.9	2	3	23	245	2	7	62.7	3rd D 0-5 to Go	3	3	100.0	26	8.7	0	0	3	12	0	1	102.8
Games 1-8	1	12	5	41.7	47	3.9	0	1	3	23	0	2	18.4	3rd D 6+ to Go	35	18	51.4	235	6.7	1	3	12	143	1	4	46.7
Games 9-16	6	113	61	54.0	698	6.2	3	6	37	373	4	11	59.3	4th Down	2	0	0.0	0	0.0	0	0	0	0	0	0	39.6
September	1	12	5	41.7	47	3.9	0	1	3	23	0	2	18.4	Rec Behind Line	17	13	76.5	157	9.2	1	0	8	196	1	0	123.9
October	0	0	0	0	-	0	0	0	0	0	0	0	-	1-10 yds	61	37	60.7	268	4.4	2	2	16	156	0	0	68.2
November	3	44	23	52.3	266	6.0	1	5	14	131	2	5	38.8	11-20 yds	33	13	39.4	223	6.8	0	4	13	29	0	3	23.5
December	3	69	38	55.1	432	6.3	2	1	23	242	2	6	77.7	21-30 yds	7	2	28.6	53	7.6	0	1	2	9	2	0	19.0
Grass	4	56	28	50.0	313	5.6	1	6	17	154	2	7	33.4	31+	7	1	14.3	44	6.3	0	0	1	6	1	0	53.3
Turf	3	69	38	55.1	432	6.3	2	1	23	242	2	6	77.7	Left Sideline	24	10	41.7	105	4.4	0	0	4	50	1	0	55.0
Indoor	1	13	10	76.9	103	7.9	1	0	5	49	1	1	124.8	Left Side	21	13	61.9	167	8.0	0	2	9	74	1	1	47.2
Outdoor	6	112	56	50.0	642	5.7	2	7	35	347	3	12	47.5	Middle	25	12	48.0	130	5.2	0	1	8	66	0	8	24.2
1st Half	-	64	34	53.1	351	5.5	1	2	18	217	2	10	61.4	Right Side	32	18	56.3	213	6.7	3	2	11	179	2	7	81.9
2nd Half/OT	-	61	32	52.5	394	6.5	2	5	22	179	2	3	49.5	Right Sideline	23	13	56.5	130	5.7	0	0	8	27	0	2	72.7
Last 2 Min. Half	-	28	13	46.4	145	5.2	1	2	8	52	2	2	44.5	2 Wide Receivers	48	22	45.8	280	5.8	0	4	15	136	1	3	29.9
4th qtr. +/-7 pts	-	21	7	33.3	96	4.6	0	2	6	41	1	1	9.3	3+ WR	77	44	57.1	465	6.0	3	3	25	260	3	8	71.6
Winning	-	18	11	61.1	148	8.1	0	1	7	50	2	3	63.7	Attempts 1-10	65	37	56.9	362	5.6	1	5	19	225	1	0	45.8
Tied	-	17	7	41.2	77	4.5	0	0	3	54	1	5	66.0	Attempts 11-20	37	19	51.4	228	6.2	2	2	13	117	1	0	66.0
Trailing	-	90	48	53.3	522	5.8	3	6	30	292	1	5	54.0	Attempts 21+	23	10	43.5	155	6.7	0	0	8	54	2	0	66.4

1995 Incompletions

Type	Num	% of Inc	% of Att
Pass Dropped	11	18.6	8.8
Poor Throw	30	50.8	24.0
Pass Defensed	11	18.6	8.8
Pass Hit at Line	1	1.7	0.8
Other	6	10.2	4.8
Total	59	100.0	47.2

Game Logs (1-8)

Date	Opp	Result	Att	Cm	Pct	Yds	TD	Int	Lg	Sk	F-L
09/03	Ari	W 27-7	12	5	41.7	47	0	1	20	2	0-0
09/10	Oak	L 8-20	-	-	-	-	-	-	-	-	-
09/17	@Den	L 31-38	-	-	-	-	-	-	-	-	-
09/24	@TB	L 6-14	-	-	-	-	-	-	-	-	-
10/01	Dal	W 27-23	-	-	-	-	-	-	-	-	-
10/08	@Phi	L 34-37	-	-	-	-	-	-	-	-	-
10/15	@Ari	L 20-24	-	-	-	-	-	-	-	-	-
10/22	Det	W 36-30	-	-	-	-	-	-	-	-	-

Game Logs (9-16)

Date	Opp	Result	Att	Cm	Pct	Yds	TD	Int	Lg	Sk	F-L
10/29	NYN	L 15-24	-	-	-	-	-	-	-	-	-
11/05	@KC	L 3-24	5	1	20.0	4	0	2	4	1	0-0
11/19	Sea	L 20-27	12	10	83.3	98	1	2	21	1	0-0
11/26	Phi	L 14-26	27	12	44.4	164	0	1	32	3	0-0
12/03	@Dal	W 24-17	24	11	45.8	154	1	0	44	1	0-0
12/10	@NYN	L 13-20	32	17	53.1	175	0	1	20	4	0-0
12/17	@StL	W 35-23	13	10	76.9	103	1	0	25	1	1-1
12/24	Car	W 20-17	-	-	-	-	-	-	-	-	-

Webster Slaughter

Kansas City Chiefs — WR

1995 Receiving Splits

Split	G	Rec	Yds	Avg	TD	Lg	Big	YAC	Trgt	Y@C	1st	1st%
Total	16	34	514	15.1	4	38	6	65	75	13.2	28	82.4
vs. Playoff	4	10	175	17.5	1	38	3	19	20	15.6	9	90.0
vs. Non-playoff	12	24	339	14.1	3	28	3	46	55	12.2	19	79.2
vs. Own Division	8	18	342	19.0	1	38	5	44	34	16.6	16	88.9
Home	8	20	349	17.5	2	38	5	42	40	15.4	18	90.0
Away	8	14	165	11.8	2	34	1	23	35	10.1	10	71.4
Games 1-8	8	11	197	17.9	1	38	3	35	25	14.7	9	81.8
Games 9-16	8	23	317	13.8	3	34	3	30	50	12.5	19	82.6
September	4	6	78	13.0	1	28	1	13	13	10.8	4	66.7
October	4	5	119	23.8	0	38	2	22	12	19.4	5	100.0
November	4	9	103	11.4	1	19	0	3	19	11.1	8	88.9
December	4	14	214	15.3	2	34	3	27	31	13.4	11	78.6
Grass	14	31	467	15.1	4	38	6	56	70	13.3	25	80.6
Turf	2	3	47	15.7	0	17	0	9	5	12.7	3	100.0
Outdoor	1	32	480	15.0	4	38	6	56	73	13.3	26	81.3
Indoor	15	2	34	17.0	0	17	0	9	2	12.5	2	100.0
1st Half	-	17	315	18.5	2	38	4	40	35	16.2	16	94.1
2nd Half/OT	-	17	199	11.7	2	34	2	25	40	12.0	12	70.6
Last 2 Min. Half	-	10	173	17.3	1	36	2	21	18	15.2	8	80.0
4th qtr, +/-7 pts	-	3	33	11.0	0	16	0	5	12	9.3	2	66.7
Winning	-	19	302	15.9	1	36	3	41	39	13.7	16	84.2
Tied	-	4	53	13.3	1	19	0	9	7	11.0	4	100.0
Trailing	-	11	159	14.5	2	38	3	15	29	13.1	8	72.7

Category	Rec	Yds	Avg	TD	Lg	Big	YAC	Trgt	Y@C	1st	1st%
Inside 20	4	15	3.8	4	5	0	0	10	3.8	4	100.0
Inside 10	4	15	3.8	4	5	0	0	7	3.8	4	100.0
1st Down	13	195	15.0	1	36	3	21	28	13.4	8	61.5
2nd Down	7	106	15.1	2	28	1	11	21	13.6	7	100.0
3rd Down Overall	14	213	15.2	1	38	2	33	25	12.9	13	92.9
3rd D 0-2 to Go	1	7	7.0	0	7	0	1	2	6.0	1	100.0
3rd D 3-7 to Go	7	97	13.9	1	38	1	16	11	11.6	7	100.0
3rd D 8+ to Go	6	109	18.2	0	25	1	16	12	15.5	5	83.3
4th Down	0	0	-	0	0	0	0	1	-	0	-
Rec Behind Line	1	2	2.0	0	2	0	2	1	0.0	0	0.0
1-10 yds	16	124	7.8	4	17	0	28	32	6.0	11	68.8
11-20 yds	10	178	17.8	0	23	0	11	22	16.7	10	100.0
21-30 yds	5	138	27.6	0	36	4	16	13	24.4	5	100.0
31+	2	72	36.0	0	38	2	8	7	32.0	2	100.0
Left Sideline	12	238	19.8	0	36	4	31	19	17.3	9	75.0
Left Side	9	113	12.6	0	38	1	23	25	10.0	6	66.7
Middle	0	0	-	0	0	0	0	4	-	0	-
Right Side	5	69	13.8	1	19	0	6	11	12.6	5	100.0
Right Sideline	8	94	11.8	2	25	1	5	16	11.1	8	100.0
Shotgun	0	0	-	0	0	0	0	0	-	0	-
2 Wide Receivers	11	160	14.5	1	28	2	18	27	12.9	9	81.8
3 Wide Receivers	16	248	15.5	3	38	4	30	37	13.6	13	81.3
4+ Wide Receivers	7	106	15.1	0	23	0	17	11	12.7	6	85.7

1995 Incompletions

Type	Num	%of Inc	%of Att
Pass Dropped	4	9.8	5.3
Poor Throw	22	53.7	29.3
Pass Defensed	7	17.1	9.3
Pass Hit at Line	0	0.0	0.0
Other	8	19.5	10.7
Total	41	100.0	54.7

Game Logs (1-8)

Date	Opp	Result	Rec	Yds	Trgt	F-L	TD
09/03	@Sea	W 34-10	2	34	2	0-0	0
09/10	NYN	W 20-17	1	9	1	0-0	0
09/17	Oak	W 23-17	1	28	3	0-0	0
09/24	@Cle	L 17-35	2	7	7	0-0	1
10/01	@Ari	W 24-3	0	0	2	0-0	0
10/09	SD	W 29-23	3	90	4	0-0	0
10/15	NE	W 31-26	2	29	5	0-0	0
10/22	@Den	W 21-7	0	0	1	0-0	0

Game Logs (9-16)

Date	Opp	Result	Rec	Yds	Trgt	F-L	TD
11/05	Was	W 24-3	3	36	8	0-0	0
11/12	@SD	W 22-7	2	24	3	0-0	0
11/19	Hou	W 20-13	3	30	5	0-0	1
11/23	@Dal	L 12-24	1	13	3	0-0	0
12/03	@Oak	W 29-23	3	39	7	0-0	0
12/11	@Mia	L 6-13	4	48	10	0-0	1
12/17	Den	W 20-17	4	54	8	0-0	0
12/24	Sea	W 26-3	3	73	6	0-0	0

Torrance Small

New Orleans Saints — WR

1995 Receiving Splits

Split	G	Rec	Yds	Avg	TD	Lg	Big	YAC	Trgt	Y@C	1st	1st%
Total	16	38	461	12.1	5	32	4	139	69	8.5	28	73.7
vs. Playoff	8	22	311	14.1	3	32	4	88	43	10.1	17	77.3
vs. Non-playoff	8	16	150	9.4	2	20	0	51	26	6.2	11	68.8
vs. Own Division	8	17	214	12.6	1	31	2	76	31	8.1	11	64.7
Home	8	24	338	14.1	3	32	4	83	41	10.6	17	70.8
Away	8	14	123	8.8	2	20	0	56	28	4.8	11	78.6
Games 1-8	8	17	183	10.8	2	31	2	42	36	8.3	11	64.7
Games 9-16	8	21	278	13.2	3	32	2	97	33	8.6	17	81.0
September	4	12	132	11.0	2	31	2	33	19	8.3	8	66.7
October	4	5	51	10.2	0	20	0	9	17	8.4	3	60.0
November	4	13	103	14.7	1	32	1	26	9	11.4	6	57.1
December	4	14	175	12.5	2	28	1	71	24	7.4	13	92.9
Grass	3	2	25	12.5	0	15	0	4	7	10.5	2	100.0
Turf	13	36	436	12.1	5	32	4	135	62	8.4	26	72.2
Indoor	10	26	366	14.1	3	32	4	107	47	10.0	19	73.1
Outdoor	6	12	95	7.9	2	15	0	32	22	5.3	9	75.0
1st Half	-	19	246	12.9	2	32	3	70	36	9.3	13	68.4
2nd Half/OT	-	19	215	11.3	3	31	1	69	33	7.7	15	78.9
Last 2 Min. Half	-	9	118	13.1	3	32	2	24	15	10.4	6	66.7
4th qtr, +/-7 pts	-	5	48	9.6	0	20	0	22	10	5.2	3	60.0
Winning	-	8	101	12.6	0	20	0	28	16	9.1	6	75.0
Tied	-	8	90	11.3	0	20	0	29	15	7.6	6	75.0
Trailing	-	22	270	12.3	5	32	4	82	38	8.5	16	72.7

Category	Rec	Yds	Avg	TD	Lg	Big	YAC	Trgt	Y@C	1st	1st%
Inside 20	5	26	5.2	4	14	0	3	10	4.6	4	80.0
Inside 10	4	12	3.0	4	6	0	0	6	3.0	4	100.0
1st Down	12	159	13.3	2	28	1	58	19	8.4	10	83.3
2nd Down	7	50	7.1	1	18	0	14	14	5.1	2	28.6
3rd Down Overall	18	251	13.9	1	32	3	67	33	10.2	15	83.3
3rd D 0-2 to Go	1	12	12.0	0	12	0	8	2	4.0	1	100.0
3rd D 3-7 to Go	10	123	12.3	1	32	1	24	17	9.9	9	90.0
3rd D 8+ to Go	7	116	16.6	0	31	2	35	14	11.6	5	71.4
4th Down	1	1	1.0	1	1	0	0	1	1.0	1	100.0
Rec Behind Line	1	8	8.0	0	8	0	9	2	-1.0	1	100.0
1-10 yds	26	227	8.7	4	20	0	92	39	5.2	18	69.2
11-20 yds	9	163	18.1	0	28	2	31	19	14.7	7	77.8
21-30 yds	1	31	31.0	0	31	1	7	6	24.0	1	100.0
31+	1	32	32.0	1	32	1	0	3	32.0	1	100.0
Left Sideline	6	73	12.2	0	20	0	28	9	7.5	4	66.7
Left Side	9	116	12.9	1	28	1	52	12	7.1	8	88.9
Middle	11	90	8.2	0	14	0	30	20	5.5	6	54.5
Right Side	7	104	14.9	4	32	2	17	16	12.4	7	100.0
Right Sideline	5	78	15.6	0	25	1	12	12	13.2	6	60.0
Shotgun	27	349	12.9	3	32	4	111	49	8.8	20	74.1
2 Wide Receivers	3	26	8.7	1	20	0	6	4	6.7	2	66.7
3 Wide Receivers	30	389	13.0	3	32	4	128	56	8.7	22	73.3
4+ Wide Receivers	1	12	12.0	0	12	0	7	2	5.0	1	100.0

1995 Incompletions

Type	Num	%of Inc	%of Att
Pass Dropped	6	19.4	8.7
Poor Throw	16	51.6	23.2
Pass Defensed	4	12.9	5.8
Pass Hit at Line	2	6.5	2.9
Other	3	9.7	4.3
Total	31	100.0	44.9

Game Logs (1-8)

Date	Opp	Result	Rush	Yds	Rec	Yds	Trgt	F-L	TD
09/03	SF	L 22-24	0	0	2	28	5	0-0	0
09/10	@StL	L 13-17	0	0	5	29	7	0-0	1
09/17	Atl	L 24-27	0	0	4	74	5	0-0	0
09/24	@NYN	L 29-45	0	0	1	1	2	0-0	0
10/01	Phi	L 10-15	1	44	4	36	7	0-0	1
10/15	Mia	W 33-30	0	0	1	15	6	0-0	0
10/22	@Car	L 3-20	1	0	0	0	2	0-0	0
10/29	@SF	W 11-7	0	0	0	0	2	0-0	0

Game Logs (9-16)

Date	Opp	Result	Rush	Yds	Rec	Yds	Trgt	F-L	TD
11/05	StL	W 19-10	0	0	2	34	2	0-0	0
11/12	Ind	W 17-14	1	11	3	48	3	0-0	1
11/19	@Min	L 24-43	1	6	0	1	4	0-0	0
11/26	Car	W 34-26	0	0	2	21	3	0-0	0
12/03	@NE	W 31-17	1	13	2	25	3	0-0	0
12/10	@Atl	L 14-19	0	0	2	28	5	0-0	0
12/16	GB	L 23-34	1	1	6	82	10	0-0	2
12/24	@NYA	W 12-0	0	0	2	40	6	0-0	0

Emmitt Smith Dallas Cowboys — RB

1995 Rushing and Receiving Splits

	G	Rush	Yds	Avg	Lg	TD	1st	Stf	YdL	Rec	Yds	Avg	TD		Rush	Yds	Avg	Lg	TD	1st	Stf	YdL	Rec	Yds	Avg	TD
Total	16	377	1773	4.7	60	25	107	34	72	62	375	6.0	0	Inside 20	81	227	2.8	16	22	30	9	19	7	39	5.6	0
vs. Playoff	7	169	763	4.5	41	10	50	19	36	28	155	5.5	0	Inside 10	49	83	1.7	7	18	21	8	17	2	1	0.5	0
vs. Non-playoff	9	208	1010	4.9	60	15	57	15	36	34	220	6.5	0	1st Down	206	930	4.5	39	14	35	19	36	26	150	5.8	0
vs. Own Division	8	187	902	4.8	60	12	49	16	27	27	181	6.7	0	2nd Down	131	684	5.2	60	9	50	11	31	21	120	5.7	0
Home	8	186	844	4.5	39	11	53	17	31	28	212	7.6	0	3rd Down Overall	34	150	4.4	45	2	18	3	4	15	105	7.0	0
Away	8	191	929	4.9	60	14	54	17	41	34	163	4.8	0	3rd D 0-2 to Go	23	99	4.3	45	2	14	2	2	3	19	6.3	0
Games 1-8	8	189	979	5.2	60	14	57	14	35	35	202	5.8	0	3rd D 3-7 to Go	9	46	5.1	13	0	4	1	2	3	31	10.3	0
Games 9-16	8	188	794	4.2	39	11	50	20	37	27	173	6.4	0	3rd D 8+ to Go	2	5	2.5	4	0	0	0	0	9	55	6.1	0
September	4	88	543	6.2	60	9	27	5	14	14	100	7.1	0	4th Down	6	9	1.5	3	0	4	1	1	0	0	-	0
October	4	101	436	4.3	41	5	30	9	21	21	102	4.9	0	Left Sideline	26	137	5.3	41	5	10	3	4	7	25	3.6	0
November	4	92	424	4.6	39	7	29	10	20	15	105	7.0	0	Left Side	95	459	4.8	33	5	25	10	18	15	65	4.3	0
December	4	96	370	3.9	23	4	21	10	17	12	68	5.7	0	Middle	180	891	5.0	60	11	53	9	20	12	113	9.4	0
Grass	4	97	341	3.5	15	6	26	10	28	19	113	5.9	0	Right Side	64	223	3.5	39	3	13	10	24	19	136	7.2	0
Turf	12	280	1432	5.1	60	19	81	24	44	43	262	6.1	0	Right Sideline	12	63	5.3	14	1	6	2	6	9	36	4.0	0
Indoor	2	46	317	6.9	45	3	15	3	9	11	42	3.8	0	Shotgun	0	0	-	0	0	0	0	0	0	0	-	0
Outdoor	14	331	1456	4.4	60	22	92	31	63	51	333	6.5	0	2 Wide Receivers	240	1213	5.1	45	6	65	21	47	31	202	6.5	0
1st Half	-	189	874	4.6	60	14	54	18	38	39	282	7.2	0	3 Wide Receivers	32	201	6.3	60	2	5	3	6	25	143	5.7	0
2nd Half/OT	-	188	899	4.8	45	11	53	16	34	23	93	4.0	0	4+ Wide Receivers	9	46	5.1	12	0	0	0	0	3	12	4.0	0
Last 2 Min. Half	-	15	91	6.1	41	1	5	1	1	10	59	5.9	0	Carries 1-5	80	418	5.2	60	3	17	5	14	0	0	-	0
4th qtr, +/-7 pts	-	33	134	4.1	15	3	10	1	1	8	18	2.3	0	Carries 6-10	80	367	4.6	33	9	29	8	17	0	0	-	0
Winning	-	224	979	4.4	41	14	65	22	44	27	181	6.7	0	Carries 11-15	80	459	5.7	45	3	26	9	17	0	0	-	0
Tied	-	65	293	4.5	60	4	14	7	19	12	62	5.2	0	Carries 16-20	76	310	4.1	31	5	20	5	6	0	0	-	0
Trailing	-	88	501	5.7	45	7	28	5	9	23	132	5.7	0	Carries 21+	61	219	3.6	41	5	15	7	18	0	0	-	0

1995 Incompletions

Type	Num	%of Inc	% Att
Pass Dropped	3	18.8	3.8
Poor Throw	3	18.8	3.8
Pass Defensed	0	0.0	0.0
Pass Hit at Line	2	12.5	2.6
Other	8	50.0	10.3
Total	16	100.0	20.5

Game Logs (1-8)

Date	Opp	Result	Rush	Yds	Rec	Yds	Trgt	F-L	TD
09/04	@NYN	W 35-0	21	163	1	0	1	0-0	1
09/10	Den	W 31-21	26	114	4	35	6	0-0	1
09/17	@Min	W 23-17	20	150	6	12	6	1-1	2
09/24	Ari	W 34-20	21	116	3	53	3	0-0	2
10/01	@Was	L 23-27	22	95	8	38	8	1-1	0
10/08	GB	W 34-24	31	106	3	19	3	0-0	2
10/15	@SD	W 23-9	22	68	5	15	7	0-0	2
10/29	@Atl	W 28-13	26	167	5	30	5	0-0	1

Game Logs (9-16)

Date	Opp	Result	Rush	Yds	Rec	Yds	Trgt	F-L	TD
11/06	Phi	W 34-12	27	158	3	22	3	1-1	2
11/12	SF	L 20-38	18	100	6	50	7	0-0	1
11/19	@Oak	W 34-21	29	110	3	22	5	1-1	3
11/23	KC	W 24-12	18	56	3	11	4	0-0	1
12/03	Was	L 17-20	21	91	4	16	8	2-1	1
12/10	@Phi	L 17-20	27	108	3	8	5	1-1	1
12/17	NYN	W 21-20	24	103	2	6	4	0-0	1
12/25	@Ari	W 37-13	24	68	3	38	3	0-0	1

Irv Smith New Orleans Saints — TE

1995 Receiving Splits

	G	Rec	Yds	Avg	TD	Lg	Big	YAC	Trgt	Y@C	1st	1st%		Rec	Yds	Avg	TD	Lg	Big	YAC	Trgt	Y@C	1st	1st%
Total	16	45	466	10.4	3	43	4	254	55	4.7	24	53.3	Inside 20	8	35	4.4	3	8	0	16	12	2.4	4	50.0
vs. Playoff	8	26	208	8.0	3	26	1	106	31	3.9	15	57.7	Inside 10	4	12	3.0	3	5	0	2	7	2.5	3	75.0
vs. Non-playoff	8	19	258	13.6	0	43	3	148	24	5.8	9	47.4	1st Down	22	255	11.6	1	43	2	143	25	5.1	10	45.5
vs. Own Division	8	17	141	8.3	2	26	1	75	20	3.9	9	52.9	2nd Down	17	168	9.9	0	30	2	94	22	4.4	8	47.1
Home	8	24	191	8.0	1	22	0	105	29	3.6	12	50.0	3rd Down Overall	6	43	7.2	2	16	0	17	8	4.3	6	100.0
Away	8	21	275	13.1	2	43	4	149	26	6.0	12	57.1	3rd D 0-2 to Go	5	32	6.4	2	16	0	11	7	4.2	5	100.0
Games 1-8	8	10	99	9.9	1	30	2	62	13	3.7	5	50.0	3rd D 3-7 to Go	0	0	-	0	0	0	0	0	-	0	-
Games 9-16	8	35	367	10.5	2	43	2	192	42	5.0	19	54.3	3rd D 8+ to Go	1	11	11.0	0	11	0	6	1	5.0	1	100.0
September	4	4	46	11.5	0	30	1	22	5	6.0	3	75.0	4th Down	0	0	-	0	0	0	0	0	-	0	-
October	4	6	53	8.8	1	26	1	40	8	2.2	3	33.3	Rec Behind Line	9	50	5.6	0	13	0	66	10	-1.8	0	0.0
November	4	19	202	10.6	0	30	1	90	24	5.9	10	52.6	1-10 yds	29	255	8.8	3	43	1	137	38	4.1	17	58.6
December	4	16	165	10.3	2	43	1	102	18	3.9	9	56.3	11-20 yds	6	131	21.8	0	30	2	45	6	14.3	6	100.0
Grass	3	6	93	15.5	0	43	2	66	9	4.5	2	33.3	21-30 yds	1	30	30.0	0	30	1	6	1	24.0	1	100.0
Turf	13	39	373	9.6	3	30	2	188	46	4.7	22	56.4	31+	0	0	-	0	0	0	0	0	-	0	-
Outdoor	10	10	165	16.5	0	43	3	106	14	5.9	6	60.0	Left Sideline	4	46	11.5	0	30	1	17	4	7.3	1	25.0
Indoor	6	35	301	8.6	3	30	1	148	41	4.4	18	51.4	Left Side	9	85	9.4	0	30	1	64	11	2.3	3	33.3
1st Half	-	23	269	11.7	0	43	4	137	31	5.7	12	52.2	Middle	9	82	9.1	3	16	0	16	10	7.3	9	100.0
2nd Half/OT	-	22	197	9.0	3	22	0	117	24	3.6	12	54.5	Right Side	14	154	11.0	0	43	1	107	18	3.4	7	50.0
Last 2 Min. Half	-	1	6	6.0	0	6	0	2	2	4.0	0	0.0	Right Sideline	9	99	11.0	0	26	1	50	12	5.4	4	44.4
4th qtr, +/-7 pts	-	4	46	11.5	0	22	0	35	4	2.8	2	50.0	Shotgun	3	35	11.7	0	22	0	9	3	8.7	1	33.3
Winning	-	13	120	9.2	1	22	0	84	14	2.8	7	53.8	2 Wide Receivers	35	354	10.1	2	43	3	201	41	4.4	16	45.7
Tied	-	14	142	10.1	0	43	1	85	18	4.1	6	42.9	3 Wide Receivers	3	58	19.3	0	30	1	23	4	11.7	2	66.7
Trailing	-	18	204	11.3	2	30	3	85	23	6.6	11	61.1	4+ Wide Receivers	0	0	-	0	0	0	0	0	-	0	-

1995 Incompletions

Type	Num	%of Inc	%of Att
Pass Dropped	1	10.0	1.8
Poor Throw	1	10.0	1.8
Pass Defensed	2	20.0	3.6
Pass Hit at Line	1	10.0	1.8
Other	5	50.0	9.1
Total	10	100.0	18.2

Game Logs (1-8)

Date	Opp	Result	Rec	Yds	Trgt	F-L	TD
09/03	SF	L 22-24	1	4	1	0-0	0
09/10	@StL	L 13-17	0	0	0	0-0	0
09/17	Atl	L 24-27	2	12	2	0-0	0
09/24	@NYN	L 29-45	1	30	2	0-0	0
10/01	Phi	L 10-15	1	2	1	0-0	0
10/15	Mia	W 33-30	4	25	4	1-1	0
10/22	@Car	L 3-20	0	0	1	0-0	0
10/29	@SF	W 11-7	1	26	2	0-0	0

Game Logs (9-16)

Date	Opp	Result	Rec	Yds	Trgt	F-L	TD
11/05	StL	W 19-10	3	26	3	0-0	0
11/12	Ind	W 17-14	9	83	12	0-0	0
11/19	@Min	L 24-43	4	65	5	0-0	0
11/26	Car	W 34-26	3	28	4	0-0	0
12/03	@NE	W 31-17	5	67	6	0-0	0
12/10	@Atl	L 14-19	7	45	7	0-0	2
12/16	GB	L 23-34	1	11	2	0-0	0
12/24	@NYA	W 12-0	3	42	3	0-0	0

Robert Smith

1995 Rushing and Receiving Splits

	G	Rush	Yds	Avg	Lg	TD	1st	Stf	YdL	Rec	Yds	Avg	TD
Total	9	139	632	4.5	58	5	28	16	40	7	35	5.0	0
vs. Playoff	5	72	388	5.4	58	3	15	8	21	4	13	3.3	0
vs. Non-playoff	4	67	244	3.6	20	2	13	8	19	3	22	7.3	0
vs. Own Division	4	63	286	4.5	28	3	14	6	10	4	21	5.3	0
Home	3	57	247	4.3	44	2	11	7	16	4	14	3.5	0
Away	6	82	385	4.7	58	3	17	9	24	3	21	7.0	0
Games 1-8	7	115	537	4.7	58	5	24	13	29	7	35	5.0	0
Games 9-16	2	24	95	4.0	26	0	4	3	11	0	0	-	0
September	4	64	365	5.7	58	3	13	7	17	4	13	3.3	0
October	3	51	172	3.4	28	2	11	6	12	3	22	7.3	0
November	1	15	62	4.1	19	0	3	2	7	0	0	-	0
December	1	9	33	3.7	26	0	1	1	4	0	0	-	0
Grass	5	67	270	4.0	28	2	13	8	19	2	15	7.5	0
Turf	4	72	362	5.0	58	3	15	8	21	5	20	4.0	0
Indoor	3	57	247	4.3	44	2	11	7	16	4	14	3.5	0
Outdoor	6	82	385	4.7	58	3	17	9	24	3	21	7.0	0
1st Half	-	79	435	5.5	58	4	21	7	20	4	13	3.3	0
2nd Half/OT	-	60	197	3.3	26	1	7	9	20	3	22	7.3	0
Last 2 Min. Half	-	8	27	3.4	12	0	1	0	0	1	11	11.0	0
4th qtr, +/-7 pts	-	16	47	2.9	12	0	3	1	6	2	15	7.5	0
Winning	-	34	140	4.1	19	0	7	5	10	1	6	6.0	0
Tied	-	46	167	3.6	20	3	9	4	14	2	7	3.5	0
Trailing	-	59	325	5.5	58	2	12	7	16	4	22	5.5	0

	Rush	Yds	Avg	Lg	TD	1st	Stf	YdL	Rec	Yds	Avg	TD
Inside 20	20	39	2.0	9	3	5	2	7	1	1	1.0	0
Inside 10	12	14	1.2	5	3	4	1	2	1	1	1.0	0
1st Down	90	381	4.2	58	1	7	10	20	6	34	5.7	0
2nd Down	41	207	5.0	44	1	15	5	18	1	1	1.0	0
3rd Down Overall	7	38	5.4	20	3	5	1	2	0	0	-	0
3rd D 0-2 to Go	6	29	4.8	20	3	5	1	2	0	0	-	0
3rd D 3-7 to Go	0	0	-	0	0	0	0	0	0	0	-	0
3rd D 8+ to Go	1	9	9.0	9	0	0	0	0	0	0	-	0
4th Down	1	6	6.0	6	0	1	0	0	0	0	-	0
Left Sideline	14	126	9.0	58	1	4	2	6	2	7	3.5	0
Left Side	34	179	5.3	44	1	9	4	9	0	0	-	0
Middle	52	146	2.8	19	1	6	8	17	2	10	5.0	0
Right Side	29	111	3.8	12	1	6	1	2	2	17	8.5	0
Right Sideline	10	70	7.0	28	1	3	1	6	1	1	1.0	0
Shotgun	0	0	-	0	0	0	0	0	1	7	7.0	0
2 Wide Receivers	92	412	4.5	44	0	16	9	20	4	25	6.3	0
3 Wide Receivers	22	95	4.3	26	0	4	4	7	3	10	3.3	0
4+ Wide Receivers	1	5	5.0	5	0	0	0	0	0	0	-	0
Carries 1-5	45	219	4.9	44	2	12	5	16	0	0	-	0
Carries 6-10	44	248	5.6	58	2	8	3	8	0	0	-	0
Carries 11-15	33	91	2.8	13	0	4	6	11	0	0	-	0
Carries 16-20	17	74	4.4	20	1	4	2	5	0	0	-	0
Carries 21+	0	0	-	0	0	0	0	0	0	0	-	0

1995 Incompletions

Type	Num	%of Inc	% Att
Pass Dropped	4	100.0	36.4
Poor Throw	0	0.0	0.0
Pass Defensed	0	0.0	0.0
Pass Hit at Line	0	0.0	0.0
Other	0	0.0	0.0
Total	4	100.0	36.4

Game Logs (1-8)

Date	Opp	Result	Rush	Yds	Rec	Yds	Trgt	F-L	TD
09/03	@Chi	L 14-31	12	66	0	0	0	0-0	1
09/10	Det	W 20-10	20	111	2	6	3	0-0	1
09/17	Dal	L 17-23	17	73	1	1	3	0-0	1
09/24	@Pit	W 44-24	15	115	1	6	1	1-1	1
10/08	Hou	W 23-17	20	63	1	7	2	0-0	1
10/15	@TB	L 17-20	20	53	2	15	2	0-0	1
10/22	@GB	L 21-38	11	56	0	0	0	0-0	1
10/30	Chi	L 6-14	-	-	-	-	-	-	-

Game Logs (9-16)

Date	Opp	Result	Rush	Yds	Rec	Yds	Trgt	F-L	TD
11/05	GB	W 27-24	-	-	-	-	-	-	-
11/12	@Ari	W 30-24	15	62	0	0	0	0-0	0
11/19	NO	W 43-24	-	-	-	-	-	-	-
11/23	@Det	L 38-44	-	-	-	-	-	-	-
12/03	TB		-	-	-	-	-	-	-
12/09	Cle	W 27-11	-	-	-	-	-	-	-
12/18	@SF	L 30-37	9	33	0	0	0	0-0	0
12/24	@Cin	L 24-27	-	-	-	-	-	-	-

James Stewart

1995 Rushing and Receiving Splits

	G	Rush	Yds	Avg	Lg	TD	1st	Stf	YdL	Rec	Yds	Avg	TD
Total	14	137	525	3.8	22	2	27	12	25	21	190	9.0	1
vs. Playoff	4	52	179	3.4	16	2	11	4	7	7	33	4.7	0
vs. Non-playoff	10	85	346	4.1	22	0	16	8	18	14	157	11.2	1
vs. Own Division	7	52	150	2.9	13	1	9	5	9	10	109	10.9	0
Home	8	84	357	4.3	22	2	20	5	9	10	60	6.0	1
Away	6	53	168	3.2	18	0	7	7	16	11	130	11.8	0
Games 1-8	7	94	292	3.1	22	1	14	9	18	10	98	9.8	1
Games 9-16	7	43	233	5.4	18	1	13	3	7	11	92	8.4	0
September	3	39	117	3.0	18	0	3	3	7	1	18	18.0	0
October	5	56	180	3.2	22	1	12	6	11	11	94	8.5	1
November	3	14	85	6.1	13	0	4	0	0	4	38	9.5	0
December	3	28	143	5.1	18	1	8	3	7	5	40	8.0	0
Grass	11	105	443	4.2	22	2	23	7	16	16	111	6.9	1
Turf	3	32	82	2.6	18	0	4	5	9	5	79	15.8	0
Indoor	1	11	23	2.1	10	0	1	2	2	2	47	23.5	0
Outdoor	13	126	502	4.0	22	2	26	10	23	19	143	7.5	1
1st Half	-	77	279	3.6	18	2	16	8	19	10	106	10.6	1
2nd Half/OT	-	60	246	4.1	22	0	11	4	6	11	84	7.6	0
Last 2 Min. Half	-	9	33	3.7	18	0	2	2	2	2	6	3.0	0
4th qtr, +/-7 pts	-	7	19	2.7	6	0	1	0	0	4	35	8.8	0
Winning	-	33	83	2.5	10	1	7	5	6	6	67	11.2	0
Tied	-	20	83	4.2	13	0	4	1	5	3	28	9.3	0
Trailing	-	84	359	4.3	22	1	16	6	14	12	95	7.9	1

	Rush	Yds	Avg	Lg	TD	1st	Stf	YdL	Rec	Yds	Avg	TD
Inside 20	17	67	3.9	11	2	4	1	1	2	10	5.0	1
Inside 10	6	22	3.7	6	2	2	0	0	1	7	7.0	1
1st Down	88	346	3.9	22	1	10	10	23	9	96	10.7	0
2nd Down	42	164	3.9	18	1	13	2	9	9	62	6.9	0
3rd Down Overall	7	15	2.1	4	0	4	0	0	3	32	10.7	0
3rd D 0-2 to Go	5	11	2.2	4	0	4	0	0	0	0	-	0
3rd D 3-7 to Go	1	2	2.0	2	0	0	0	0	1	7	7.0	0
3rd D 8+ to Go	1	2	2.0	2	0	0	0	0	2	25	12.5	0
4th Down	0	0	-	0	0	0	0	0	0	0	-	0
Left Sideline	8	45	5.6	22	0	2	2	6	0	0	-	0
Left Side	41	157	3.8	18	0	5	4	6	9	63	7.0	1
Middle	41	145	3.5	16	2	13	1	1	1	22	22.0	0
Right Side	44	156	3.5	11	0	6	5	12	7	72	10.3	0
Right Sideline	3	22	7.3	18	0	1	0	0	4	33	8.3	0
Shotgun	4	7	1.8	2	0	0	0	0	3	19	6.3	0
2 Wide Receivers	86	320	3.7	18	2	13	8	15	7	42	6.0	0
3 Wide Receivers	38	162	4.3	22	0	11	3	9	13	142	10.9	1
4+ Wide Receivers	1	2	2.0	2	0	0	0	0	1	6	6.0	0
Carries 1-5	61	239	3.9	18	0	12	5	14	0	0	-	0
Carries 6-10	37	110	3.0	7	2	6	4	7	0	0	-	0
Carries 11-15	24	137	5.7	22	0	6	1	1	0	0	-	0
Carries 16-20	15	39	2.6	16	0	3	2	4	0	0	-	0
Carries 21+	0	0	-	0	0	0	0	0	0	0	-	0

1995 Incompletions

Type	Num	%of Inc	% Att
Pass Dropped	3	50.0	11.1
Poor Throw	1	16.7	3.7
Pass Defensed	0	0.0	0.0
Pass Hit at Line	1	16.7	3.7
Other	1	16.7	3.7
Total	6	100.0	22.2

Game Logs (1-8)

Date	Opp	Result	Rush	Yds	Rec	Yds	Trgt	F-L	TD
09/03	Hou	L 3-10	6	25	0	0	0	0-0	0
09/10	@Cin	L 17-24	-	-	-	-	-	-	-
09/17	@NYA	L 10-27	20	54	1	18	2	0-0	0
09/24	GB	L 14-24	13	38	0	0	0	0-0	0
10/01	@Hou	W 17-16	11	23	2	47	4	1-1	0
10/08	Pit	W 20-16	19	44	3	10	3	0-0	1
10/15	Chi	L 27-30	17	97	3	13	4	0-0	1
10/22	@Cle	W 23-15	8	11	1	10	1	0-0	0

Game Logs (9-16)

Date	Opp	Result	Rush	Yds	Rec	Yds	Trgt	F-L	TD
10/29	@Pit	L 7-24	1	5	2	14	3	0-0	0
11/12	@Den	L 30-47	3	19	0	0	0	0-0	0
11/19	@TB	L 16-17	6	36	2	10	2	0-0	0
11/26	Cin	L 13-17	5	30	2	28	2	0-0	0
12/03	@Den	L 23-31	7	39	3	31	3	0-0	1
12/10	Ind	L 31-41	19	92	2	9	2	0-0	1
12/17	@Det	L 0-44	-	-	-	-	-	-	-
12/24	Cle	W 24-21	2	12	0	0	1	0-0	0

J.J. Stokes
San Francisco 49ers — WR

1995 Receiving Splits

	G	Rec	Yds	Avg	TD	Lg	Big	YAC	Trgt	Y@C	1st	1st%		Rec	Yds	Avg	TD	Lg	Big	YAC	Trgt	Y@C	1st	1st%
Total	12	38	517	13.6	4	41	3	123	52	10.4	25	65.8	Inside 20	4	50	12.5	2	18	0	23	4	6.8	3	75.0
vs. Playoff	5	17	265	15.6	1	41	2	63	23	11.9	12	70.6	Inside 10	1	6	6.0	0	6	0	3	1	3.0	0	0.0
vs. Non-playoff	7	21	252	12.0	3	26	1	60	29	9.1	13	61.9	1st Down	17	243	14.3	3	41	1	64	21	10.5	10	58.8
vs. Own Division	6	17	271	15.9	4	41	3	54	23	12.8	13	76.5	2nd Down	14	175	12.5	1	30	1	26	19	10.6	10	71.4
Home	6	21	242	11.5	2	26	1	70	27	8.2	12	57.1	3rd Down Overall	7	99	14.1	0	26	1	33	12	9.4	5	71.4
Away	6	17	275	16.2	2	41	2	53	25	13.1	13	76.5	3rd D 0-2 to Go	0	0	-	0	0	0	0	0	-	0	-
Games 1-8	4	3	36	12.0	0	20	0	10	6	8.7	1	33.3	3rd D 3-7 to Go	4	49	12.3	0	24	0	12	6	9.3	3	75.0
Games 9-16	8	35	481	13.7	4	41	3	113	46	10.5	24	68.6	3rd D 8+ to Go	3	50	16.7	0	26	1	21	6	9.7	2	66.7
September	0	0	0	-	0	0	0	0	0	-	0	-	4th Down	0	0	-	0	0	0	0	0	-	0	-
October	4	3	36	12.0	0	20	0	10	6	8.7	1	33.3	Rec Behind Line	1	5	5.0	0	5	0	6	1	-1.0	0	0.0
November	4	15	206	13.7	2	26	1	59	19	9.8	11	73.3	1-10 yds	21	174	8.3	1	16	0	62	27	5.3	11	52.4
December	4	20	275	13.8	2	41	2	54	27	11.1	13	65.0	11-20 yds	12	222	18.5	2	26	1	50	15	14.3	10	83.3
Grass	8	29	369	12.7	3	26	1	92	36	9.6	19	65.5	21-30 yds	3	75	25.0	0	30	1	4	4	23.7	3	100.0
Turf	4	9	148	16.4	1	41	2	31	16	13.0	6	66.7	31+	1	41	41.0	1	41	1	1	5	40.0	1	100.0
Outdoor	2	32	391	12.2	3	26	1	100	45	9.1	20	62.5	Left Sideline	7	79	11.3	0	26	1	36	9	6.1	5	71.4
Indoor	10	6	126	21.0	1	41	2	23	7	17.2	5	83.3	Left Side	11	139	12.6	0	23	0	28	15	10.1	5	45.5
1st Half	-	21	313	14.9	4	41	3	62	24	12.0	16	76.2	Middle	2	24	12.0	1	18	0	3	3	10.5	1	50.0
2nd Half/OT	-	17	204	12.0	0	24	0	61	28	8.4	9	52.9	Right Side	11	165	15.0	2	30	1	43	13	11.1	9	81.8
Last 2 Min. Half	-	2	30	15.0	1	20	0	3	3	13.5	2	100.0	Right Sideline	7	110	15.7	1	41	1	13	12	13.9	5	71.4
4th qtr, +/-7 pts	-	3	41	13.7	0	22	0	12	6	9.7	2	66.7	Shotgun	0	0	-	0	0	0	0	0	-	0	-
Winning	-	24	311	13.0	2	41	1	65	35	10.3	15	62.5	2 Wide Receivers	27	402	14.9	3	41	2	71	36	12.3	18	66.7
Tied	-	10	132	13.2	1	30	1	25	12	10.7	6	60.0	3 Wide Receivers	8	77	9.6	0	26	1	25	12	6.5	4	50.0
Trailing	-	4	74	18.5	1	26	1	33	5	10.3	4	100.0	4+ Wide Receivers	3	38	12.7	1	16	0	27	4	3.7	3	100.0

1995 Incompletions

Type	Num	%of Inc	%of Att
Pass Dropped	1	7.1	1.9
Poor Throw	9	64.3	17.3
Pass Defensed	1	7.1	1.9
Pass Hit at Line	0	0.0	0.0
Other	3	21.4	5.8
Total	14	100.0	26.9

Game Logs (1-8)

Date	Opp	Result		Rec	Yds	Trgt	F-L	TD
09/03	@NO	W	24-22	-	-	-	-	-
09/10	Atl	W	41-10	-	-	-	-	-
09/17	NE	W	28-3	-	-	-	-	-
09/25	@Det	L	24-27	-	-	-	-	-
10/01	NYN	W	20-6	1	14	1	0-0	0
10/15	@Ind	L	17-18	1	20	1	0-0	0
10/22	@StL	W	44-10	1	2	4	0-0	0
10/29	NO	L	7-11	0	0	0	0-0	0

Game Logs (9-16)

Date	Opp	Result		Rec	Yds	Trgt	F-L	TD
11/05	Car	L	7-13	3	46	4	0-0	0
11/12	@Dal	W	38-20	2	20	5	0-0	0
11/20	@Mia	W	44-20	5	75	5	0-0	0
11/26	StL	W	41-13	5	65	5	0-0	2
12/03	Buf	W	27-17	4	44	6	0-0	0
12/10	@Car	W	31-10	3	52	4	0-0	0
12/18	Min	W	37-30	8	73	11	0-0	0
12/24	@Atl	L	27-28	5	106	6	0-0	1

John Taylor
San Francisco 49ers — WR

1995 Receiving Splits

	G	Rec	Yds	Avg	TD	Lg	Big	YAC	Trgt	Y@C	1st	1st%		Rec	Yds	Avg	TD	Lg	Big	YAC	Trgt	Y@C	1st	1st%
Total	12	29	387	13.3	2	40	5	102	49	9.8	17	58.6	Inside 20	1	13	13.0	0	13	0	12	1	1.0	1	100.0
vs. Playoff	4	8	133	16.6	1	29	2	19	10	14.3	8	100.0	Inside 10	0	0	-	0	0	0	0	0	-	0	-
vs. Non-playoff	8	21	254	12.1	1	40	3	83	39	8.1	9	42.9	1st Down	9	120	13.3	1	35	1	19	22	11.2	5	55.6
vs. Own Division	6	19	248	13.1	1	40	3	84	33	8.6	9	47.4	2nd Down	15	216	14.4	1	40	3	62	15	10.3	8	53.3
Home	5	9	101	11.2	0	40	1	43	21	6.4	3	33.3	3rd Down Overall	5	51	10.2	0	29	1	21	12	6.0	4	80.0
Away	7	20	286	14.3	2	36	4	59	28	11.4	14	70.0	3rd D 0-2 to Go	2	10	5.0	0	6	0	6	2	2.0	2	100.0
Games 1-8	6	16	237	14.8	2	36	4	50	25	11.7	10	62.5	3rd D 3-7 to Go	1	29	29.0	0	29	1	4	2	25.0	1	100.0
Games 9-16	6	13	150	11.5	0	40	1	52	24	7.5	7	53.8	3rd D 8+ to Go	2	12	6.0	0	9	0	11	8	0.5	1	50.0
September	2	8	130	16.3	1	36	3	32	10	12.3	6	75.0	4th Down	0	0	-	0	0	0	0	0	-	0	-
October	4	8	107	13.4	1	35	1	18	15	11.1	4	50.0	Rec Behind Line	2	18	9.0	0	9	0	20	3	-1.0	1	50.0
November	4	7	98	14.0	0	40	1	42	12	8.0	4	57.1	1-10 yds	16	110	6.9	0	14	0	41	24	4.3	6	37.5
December	2	6	52	8.7	0	13	0	10	12	7.0	3	50.0	11-20 yds	6	112	18.7	0	40	1	22	12	15.0	5	83.3
Grass	7	16	173	10.8	0	40	1	65	33	6.8	8	50.0	21-30 yds	4	112	28.0	1	36	3	19	8	23.3	4	100.0
Turf	5	13	214	16.5	2	36	4	37	16	13.6	9	69.2	31+	1	35	35.0	1	35	1	0	2	35.0	1	100.0
Outdoor	3	19	221	11.6	0	40	2	67	36	8.1	9	47.4	Left Sideline	7	89	12.7	1	26	1	3	12	12.3	5	71.4
Indoor	9	10	166	16.6	1	36	3	35	13	13.1	8	80.0	Left Side	4	46	11.5	0	15	0	9	7	9.3	2	50.0
1st Half	-	18	222	12.3	1	36	3	42	27	10.0	10	55.6	Middle	5	71	14.2	0	29	1	38	8	6.6	3	60.0
2nd Half/OT	-	11	165	15.0	1	40	2	60	22	9.5	7	63.6	Right Side	9	97	10.8	0	40	1	32	10	7.2	3	33.3
Last 2 Min. Half	-	3	47	15.7	0	21	0	1	7	15.3	2	66.7	Right Sideline	4	84	21.0	1	36	2	20	12	16.0	4	100.0
4th qtr, +/-7 pts	-	4	68	17.0	1	26	1	15	7	13.3	4	100.0	Shotgun	0	0	-	0	0	0	0	0	-	0	-
Winning	-	12	118	9.8	0	21	0	32	23	7.2	6	50.0	2 Wide Receivers	17	247	14.5	1	40	3	73	29	10.2	10	58.8
Tied	-	9	107	11.9	1	36	2	29	12	8.7	4	44.4	3 Wide Receivers	9	124	13.8	1	35	2	22	10	11.0	6	66.7
Trailing	-	8	162	20.3	1	40	3	41	14	15.1	7	87.5	4+ Wide Receivers	3	16	5.3	0	10	0	7	4	3.0	1	33.3

1995 Incompletions

Type	Num	%of Inc	%of Att
Pass Dropped	2	10.0	4.1
Poor Throw	8	40.0	16.3
Pass Defensed	4	20.0	8.2
Pass Hit at Line	1	5.0	2.0
Other	5	25.0	10.2
Total	20	100.0	40.8

Game Logs (1-8)

Date	Opp	Result		Rec	Yds	Trgt	F-L	TD
09/03	@NO	W	24-22	4	53	5	0-0	0
09/10	Atl	W	41-10	-	-	-	-	-
09/17	NE	W	28-3	-	-	-	-	-
09/25	@Det	L	24-27	4	77	5	0-0	1
10/01	NYN	W	20-6	1	6	4	1-0	0
10/15	@Ind	L	17-18	2	36	3	0-0	0
10/22	@StL	W	44-10	3	48	3	0-0	1
10/29	NO	L	7-11	2	17	5	0-0	0

Game Logs (9-16)

Date	Opp	Result		Rec	Yds	Trgt	F-L	TD
11/05	Car	L	7-13	4	69	7	1-1	0
11/12	@Dal	W	38-20	0	0	0	0-0	0
11/20	@Mia	W	44-20	2	20	2	0-0	0
11/26	StL	W	41-13	1	9	3	0-0	0
12/03	Buf	W	27-17	-	-	-	-	-
12/10	@Car	W	31-10	5	52	10	0-0	0
12/18	Min	W	37-30	1	0	2	0-0	0
12/24	@Atl	L	27-28	-	-	-	-	-

Vinny Testaverde
Cleveland Browns — QB

1995 Passing Splits

	G	Att	Cm	Pct	Yds	Yd/Att	TD	Int	1st	YAC	Big	Sk	Rtg		Att	Cm	Pct	Yds	Yd/Att	TD	Int	1st	YAC	Big	Sk	Rtg
Total	13	392	241	61.5	2883	7.4	17	10	146	1191	24	17	87.8	Inside 20	40	15	37.5	123	3.1	9	1	12	36	0	1	75.3
vs. Playoff	6	196	119	60.7	1307	6.7	7	4	67	580	9	7	83.9	Inside 10	15	5	33.3	22	1.5	5	0	5	8	0	0	81.9
vs. Non-playoff	7	196	122	62.2	1576	8.0	10	6	79	611	15	10	91.7	1st Down	137	98	71.5	1182	8.6	7	4	44	520	10	2	102.5
vs. Own Division	5	167	100	59.9	1190	7.1	7	7	65	447	8	5	78.2	2nd Down	127	74	58.3	796	6.3	6	3	45	341	8	8	82.7
Home	7	218	134	61.5	1646	7.6	10	5	89	640	14	6	90.5	3rd Down Overall	121	63	52.1	803	6.6	3	2	51	297	5	7	74.5
Away	6	174	107	61.5	1237	7.1	7	5	57	551	10	11	84.4	3rd D 0-5 to Go	42	21	50.0	240	5.7	1	1	21	98	1	4	65.6
Games 1-8	7	213	122	57.3	1538	7.2	10	3	74	630	14	11	89.7	3rd D 6+ to Go	79	42	53.2	563	7.1	2	1	30	199	4	3	79.2
Games 9-16	6	179	119	66.5	1345	7.5	7	7	72	561	10	6	85.5	4th Down	7	6	85.7	102	14.6	1	1	6	33	1	0	118.8
September	4	115	68	59.1	861	7.5	8	1	43	398	9	6	102.1	Rec Behind Line	61	42	68.9	231	3.8	1	0	14	351	0	0	80.7
October	3	98	54	55.1	677	6.9	2	2	31	232	5	5	75.1	1-10 yds	204	139	68.1	1240	6.1	5	2	73	583	2	0	88.3
November	2	55	36	65.5	422	7.7	3	3	24	147	4	0	84.1	11-20 yds	75	40	53.3	724	9.7	3	4	39	132	3	0	77.9
December	4	124	83	66.9	923	7.4	4	4	48	414	6	6	86.2	21-30 yds	30	14	46.7	469	15.6	4	1	14	104	13	0	118.8
Grass	10	333	210	63.1	2528	7.6	14	10	131	1061	20	14	87.8	31+	22	6	27.3	219	10.0	4	3	6	21	6	0	68.6
Turf	3	59	31	52.5	355	6.0	3	0	15	130	4	3	87.9	Left Sideline	102	69	67.6	910	8.9	11	2	41	291	0	0	123.4
Indoor	3	59	31	52.5	355	6.0	3	0	15	130	4	3	87.9	Left Side	75	51	68.0	626	8.3	3	2	32	299	7	0	95.8
Outdoor	10	333	210	63.1	2528	7.6	14	10	131	1061	20	14	87.8	Middle	48	32	66.7	354	7.4	2	0	17	162	0	9	102.3
1st Half	-	191	120	62.8	1440	7.5	10	5	72	581	13	5	92.4	Right Side	63	33	52.4	381	6.0	0	2	21	188	3	2	57.7
2nd Half/OT	-	201	121	60.2	1443	7.2	7	5	74	610	11	12	82.4	Right Sideline	104	56	53.8	612	5.9	1	4	35	251	4	6	58.7
Last 2 Min. Half	-	57	37	64.9	503	8.8	6	3	26	126	7	3	106.1	2 Wide Receivers	106	63	59.4	679	6.4	1	5	33	320	4	6	61.8
4th qtr, +/-7 pts	-	48	27	56.3	369	7.7	1	3	15	133	4	7	61.9	3+ WR	275	172	62.5	2148	7.8	15	5	109	838	20	11	97.4
Winning	-	122	72	59.0	799	6.5	6	3	43	344	6	7	84.7	Attempts 1-10	126	77	61.1	881	7.0	4	2	47	412	7	0	86.1
Tied	-	50	29	58.0	372	7.4	3	1	21	148	4	0	93.1	Attempts 11-20	120	80	66.7	1063	8.9	8	4	47	375	12	0	102.9
Trailing	-	220	140	63.6	1712	7.8	8	6	82	699	14	10	88.3	Attempts 21+	146	84	57.5	939	6.4	5	4	52	404	5	0	76.8

1995 Incompletions / Game Logs

Type	Num	% of Inc	% of Att		Date	Opp	Result	Att	Cm	Pct	Yds	TD	Int	Lg	Sk	F-L		Date	Opp	Result	Att	Cm	Pct	Yds	TD	Int	Lg	Sk	F-L
Pass Dropped	22	14.6	5.6		09/03	@NE	L 14-17	29	20	69.0	254	2	1	70	3	0-0		11/05	Hou	L 10-37									
Poor Throw	67	44.4	17.1		09/10	TB	W 22-6	27	17	63.0	256	2	0	40	1	0-0		11/13	@Pit	L 3-20									
Pass Defensed	23	15.2	5.9		09/17	@Hou	W 14-7	23	10	43.5	147	2	0	35	1	0-0		11/19	GB	L 20-31	22	16	72.7	244	2	1	37	0	0-0
Pass Hit at Line	3	2.0	0.8		09/24	KC	W 35-17	36	21	58.3	204	2	0	28	1	0-0		11/26	Pit	L 17-20	33	20	60.6	178	1	2	20	0	0-0
Other	36	23.8	9.2		10/02	Buf	L 19-22	34	18	52.9	224	0	0	43	3	1-0		12/03	@SD	L 13-31	41	28	68.3	303	1	1	28	2	0-0
Total	151	100.0	38.5		10/08	@Det	L 20-38	30	16	53.3	154	1	0	32	1	0-0		12/09	@Min	L 17-27									2-0
					10/22	Jac	L 15-23	34	20	58.8	299	1	2	41	1	1-1		12/17	Cin	W 26-10	32	22	68.8	241	2	0	32	0	0-0
					10/29	@Cin	W 29-26											12/24	@Jac	L 21-24	45	28	62.2	325	1	3	39	3	0-0

Yancey Thigpen
Pittsburgh Steelers — WR

1995 Receiving Splits

	G	Rec	Yds	Avg	TD	Lg	Big	YAC	Trgt	Y@C	1st	1st%		Rec	Yds	Avg	TD	Lg	Big	YAC	Trgt	Y@C	1st	1st%
Total	16	85	1307	15.4	5	43	13	375	151	11.0	64	75.3	Inside 20	8	77	9.6	3	15	0	14	19	7.9	5	62.5
vs. Playoff	4	21	292	13.9	0	25	1	87	41	9.8	18	85.7	Inside 10	1	9	9.0	1	9	0	6	6	9.0	1	100.0
vs. Non-playoff	12	64	1015	15.9	5	43	12	288	110	11.4	46	71.9	1st Down	35	593	16.9	1	43	6	145	54	12.8	25	71.4
vs. Own Division	8	35	614	17.5	3	43	8	177	66	12.5	26	74.3	2nd Down	32	503	15.7	2	42	6	158	57	10.8	24	75.0
Home	8	41	626	15.3	5	42	6	185	79	10.8	31	75.6	3rd Down Overall	17	203	11.9	2	25	1	72	36	7.7	14	82.4
Away	8	44	681	15.5	0	43	7	190	72	11.2	33	75.0	3rd D 0-2 to Go	0	0	-	0	0	0	0	2	-	0	-
Games 1-8	8	42	672	16.0	2	43	6	199	79	11.3	33	78.6	3rd D 3-7 to Go	8	88	11.0	0	19	0	50	16	4.8	6	75.0
Games 9-16	8	43	635	14.8	3	37	7	176	72	10.7	31	72.1	3rd D 8+ to Go	9	115	12.8	2	25	1	22	18	10.3	8	88.9
September	4	24	312	13.0	1	42	1	96	46	9.0	17	70.8	4th Down	1	8	8.0	0	8	0	0	1	8.0	1	100.0
October	4	18	360	20.0	1	43	5	103	33	14.3	16	88.9	Rec Behind Line	0	0	-	0	0	0	0	0	-	0	-
November	4	22	309	14.0	1	37	3	57	35	11.5	14	63.6	1-10 yds	48	500	10.4	3	33	1	208	72	6.1	27	56.3
December	4	21	326	15.5	2	33	4	119	37	9.9	17	81.0	11-20 yds	26	485	18.7	2	42	3	93	48	15.1	26	100.0
Grass	6	36	578	16.1	0	43	7	180	58	11.1	28	77.8	21-30 yds	11	322	29.3	0	43	9	74	23	22.5	11	100.0
Turf	10	49	729	14.9	5	42	6	195	93	10.9	36	73.5	31+	0	0	-	0	0	0	0	8	-	0	-
Indoor	1	2	17	8.5	0	12	0	2	5	7.5	1	50.0	Left Sideline	20	284	14.2	0	37	2	50	51	11.7	17	85.0
Outdoor	15	83	1290	15.5	5	43	13	373	146	11.0	63	75.9	Left Side	19	240	12.6	0	25	1	70	28	8.9	11	57.9
1st Half	-	47	740	15.7	3	43	9	225	69	11.0	36	76.6	Middle	18	316	17.6	2	42	3	119	23	10.9	13	72.2
2nd Half/OT	-	38	567	14.9	2	42	4	150	82	11.0	28	73.7	Right Side	9	122	13.6	2	33	1	45	19	8.6	7	77.8
Last 2 Min. Half	-	11	143	13.0	0	25	1	27	21	10.5	9	81.8	Right Sideline	19	345	18.2	1	43	6	91	30	13.4	16	84.2
4th qtr, +/-7 pts	-	14	177	12.6	0	28	1	30	24	10.5	9	64.3	Shotgun	23	300	13.0	2	42	2	105	50	8.5	18	78.3
Winning	-	22	381	17.3	2	37	6	118	46	12.0	18	81.8	2 Wide Receivers	46	814	17.7	3	43	11	240	74	12.5	35	76.1
Tied	-	21	289	13.8	1	33	2	87	32	9.6	16	76.2	3 Wide Receivers	19	228	12.0	0	33	0	50	32	9.4	13	68.4
Trailing	-	42	637	15.2	2	43	5	170	73	11.1	30	71.4	4+ Wide Receivers	20	265	13.3	2	42	2	85	45	9.0	16	80.0

1995 Incompletions / Game Logs

Type	Num	%of Inc	%of Att		Date	Opp	Result	Rush	Yds	Rec	Yds	Trgt	F-L	TD		Date	Opp	Result	Rush	Yds	Rec	Yds	Trgt	F-L	TD
Pass Dropped	8	12.1	5.3		09/03	Det	W 23-20	0	0	7	91	13	0-0	0		11/05	@Chi	W 37-34	1	1	10	108	13	0-0	1
Poor Throw	36	54.5	23.8		09/10	@Hou	W 34-17	0	0	2	17	5	0-0	0		11/13	Cle	W 20-3	0	0	1	9	5	0-0	0
Pass Defensed	14	21.2	9.3		09/18	@Mia	L 10-23	0	0	5	63	11	0-0	0		11/19	@Cin	W 49-31	0	0	6	86	9	0-0	0
Pass Hit at Line	0	0.0	0.0		09/24	Min	L 24-44	0	0	10	141	17	1-1	2		11/26	@Cle	W 20-17	0	0	5	58	8	0-0	0
Other	8	12.1	5.3		10/01	SD	W 31-16	0	0	3	58	6	0-0	0		12/03	Hou	W 21-7	0	0	6	94	12	1-1	1
Total	66	100.0	43.7		10/08	@Jac	L 16-20	0	0	6	160	9	0-0	0		12/10	@Oak	W 29-10	0	0	4	61	6	0-0	0
					10/19	Cin	L 9-27	0	0	4	55	11	0-0	0		12/16	NE	W 41-27	0	0	5	91	8	0-0	0
					10/29	Jac	W 24-7	0	0	5	87	7	0-0	1		12/24	@GB	L 19-24	0	0	6	80	11	0-0	0

Rodney Thomas
Houston Oilers — RB

1995 Rushing and Receiving Splits

	G	Rush	Yds	Avg	Lg	TD	1st	Stf	YdL	Rec	Yds	Avg	TD
Total	16	251	947	3.8	74	5	49	45	105	39	204	5.2	2
vs. Playoff	5	95	291	3.1	20	3	19	20	46	11	41	3.7	0
vs. Non-playoff	11	156	656	4.2	74	2	30	25	59	28	163	5.8	2
vs. Own Division	8	120	460	3.8	43	2	24	17	44	23	125	5.4	2
Home	8	121	466	3.9	74	2	27	21	46	19	146	7.7	1
Away	8	130	481	3.7	43	3	22	24	59	20	58	2.9	1
Games 1-8	8	103	376	3.7	32	2	22	15	38	23	132	5.7	2
Games 9-16	8	148	571	3.9	74	3	27	30	67	16	72	4.5	0
September	4	50	172	3.4	32	2	12	5	15	8	51	6.4	1
October	4	53	204	3.8	27	0	10	10	23	15	81	5.4	1
November	4	71	335	4.7	74	1	13	10	28	8	30	3.8	0
December	4	77	236	3.1	20	2	14	20	39	8	42	5.3	0
Grass	4	52	224	4.3	43	0	10	7	20	7	16	2.3	0
Turf	12	199	723	3.6	74	5	39	38	85	32	188	5.9	2
Indoor	9	130	511	3.9	74	2	28	24	53	24	166	6.9	1
Outdoor	7	121	436	3.6	43	3	21	21	52	15	38	2.5	1
1st Half	-	111	450	4.1	74	1	23	16	31	22	118	5.4	1
2nd Half/OT	-	140	497	3.6	43	4	26	29	74	17	86	5.1	1
Last 2 Min. Half	-	15	37	2.5	9	0	1	3	6	5	21	4.2	0
4th qtr, +/-7 pts	-	17	41	2.4	8	0	1	5	10	4	16	4.0	0
Winning	-	103	375	3.6	43	3	19	18	37	11	55	5.0	1
Tied	-	39	148	3.8	27	0	5	8	17	8	50	6.3	0
Trailing	-	109	424	3.9	74	2	25	19	51	20	99	5.0	1

	Rush	Yds	Avg	Lg	TD	1st	Stf	YdL	Rec	Yds	Avg	TD
Inside 20	23	41	1.8	8	4	6	6	15	4	28	7.0	2
Inside 10	13	24	1.8	7	4	4	3	6	2	14	7.0	1
1st Down	129	397	3.1	16	3	11	25	53	14	83	5.9	0
2nd Down	104	466	4.5	74	2	30	17	39	13	34	2.6	0
3rd Down Overall	17	84	4.9	32	0	8	3	13	12	87	7.3	2
3rd D 0-2 to Go	7	19	2.7	12	0	4	0	0	0	0	-	0
3rd D 3-7 to Go	6	30	5.0	32	0	3	3	13	8	47	5.9	1
3rd D 8+ to Go	4	35	8.8	27	0	1	0	0	4	40	10.0	1
4th Down	1	0	0.0	0	0	0	0	0	0	0	-	0
Left Sideline	9	83	9.2	32	0	4	1	3	6	19	3.2	0
Left Side	51	171	3.4	14	1	7	8	10	6	42	7.0	0
Middle	130	442	3.4	43	1	26	23	64	17	90	5.3	1
Right Side	56	155	2.8	15	2	10	13	28	5	11	2.2	0
Right Sideline	5	96	19.2	74	1	2	0	0	5	42	8.4	1
Shotgun	0	0	-	0	0	0	0	0	0	0	-	0
2 Wide Receivers	136	478	3.5	74	3	24	29	63	7	54	7.7	0
3 Wide Receivers	100	420	4.2	43	0	20	16	42	24	98	4.1	0
4+ Wide Receivers	4	25	6.3	14	1	3	0	0	8	52	6.5	2
Carries 1-5	79	357	4.5	74	2	16	13	27	0	0	-	0
Carries 6-10	65	291	4.5	43	1	16	11	22	0	0	-	0
Carries 11-15	54	155	2.9	15	2	11	9	28	0	0	-	0
Carries 16-20	35	108	3.1	10	0	5	7	15	0	0	-	0
Carries 21+	18	36	2.0	7	0	1	5	13	0	0	-	0

1995 Incompletions

Type	Num	%of Inc	% Att
Pass Dropped	9	45.0	15.3
Poor Throw	4	20.0	6.8
Pass Defensed	1	5.0	1.7
Pass Hit at Line	0	0.0	0.0
Other	6	30.0	10.2
Total	20	100.0	33.9

Game Logs (1-8)

Date	Opp	Result	Rush	Yds	Rec	Yds	Trgt	F-L	TD
09/03	@Jac	W 10-3	6	47	1	0	4	1-1	0
09/10	Pit	L 17-34	5	23	1	3	1	0-0	1
09/17	Cle	L 7-14	14	26	2	32	2	0-0	0
09/24	@Cin	W 38-28	25	76	4	16	4	0-0	2
10/01	Jac	L 16-17	17	59	8	53	13	2-2	1
10/08	@Min	L 17-23	9	45	5	20	5	1-1	0
10/22	@Chi	L 32-35	4	11	1	4	2	1-1	0
10/29	TB	W 19-7	23	89	1	4	1	0-0	0

Game Logs (9-16)

Date	Opp	Result	Rush	Yds	Rec	Yds	Trgt	F-L	TD
11/05	@Cle	W 37-10	17	108	2	1	2	0-0	1
11/12	Cin	L 25-32	16	65	2	14	6	0-0	0
11/19	@KC	L 13-20	25	58	3	11	6	0-0	0
11/26	Den	W 42-33	13	104	1	4	1	0-0	1
12/03	@Pit	L 7-21	20	56	3	6	3	1-1	0
12/10	Det	L 17-24	21	74	3	21	3	2-2	0
12/17	NYA	W 23-6	12	26	1	15	1	0-0	0
12/24	@Buf	W 28-17	24	80	1	0	2	0-0	0

Thurman Thomas
Buffalo Bills — RB

1995 Rushing and Receiving Splits

	G	Rush	Yds	Avg	Lg	TD	1st	Stf	YdL	Rec	Yds	Avg	TD
Total	14	267	1005	3.8	49	6	63	30	71	26	220	8.5	2
vs. Playoff	4	81	279	3.4	22	2	19	8	23	5	29	5.8	1
vs. Non-playoff	10	186	726	3.9	49	4	44	22	48	21	191	9.1	1
vs. Own Division	6	127	476	3.7	26	5	32	16	31	10	72	7.2	1
Home	8	171	619	3.6	26	5	43	17	43	8	96	12.0	1
Away	6	96	386	4.0	49	1	20	13	28	18	124	6.9	1
Games 1-8	7	136	474	3.5	26	3	31	15	40	16	149	9.3	0
Games 9-16	7	131	531	4.1	49	3	32	15	31	10	71	7.1	2
September	3	58	162	2.8	13	2	9	8	20	6	78	13.0	0
October	4	78	312	4.0	26	1	22	7	20	10	71	7.1	0
November	3	59	194	3.3	13	2	10	9	15	4	33	8.3	0
December	4	72	337	4.7	49	1	22	6	16	6	38	6.3	2
Grass	4	54	214	4.0	22	0	13	6	12	11	75	6.8	0
Turf	10	213	791	3.7	49	6	50	24	59	15	145	9.7	2
Indoor	1	24	129	5.4	49	0	6	3	8	3	16	5.3	1
Outdoor	13	243	876	3.6	26	6	57	27	63	23	204	8.9	1
1st Half	-	151	650	4.3	49	3	39	14	42	20	105	5.3	1
2nd Half/OT	-	116	355	3.1	18	3	24	16	29	6	115	19.2	1
Last 2 Min. Half	-	17	70	4.1	18	1	5	3	10	2	7	3.5	0
4th qtr, +/-7 pts	-	26	90	3.5	18	0	4	4	5	0	0	-	0
Winning	-	111	373	3.4	49	4	22	15	24	10	103	10.3	1
Tied	-	86	381	4.4	26	0	27	3	18	8	81	10.1	1
Trailing	-	70	251	3.6	22	2	14	12	29	8	36	4.5	1

	Rush	Yds	Avg	Lg	TD	1st	Stf	YdL	Rec	Yds	Avg	TD
Inside 20	51	108	2.1	12	6	10	7	20	2	12	6.0	2
Inside 10	26	41	1.6	7	5	5	3	8	1	1	1.0	1
1st Down	138	538	3.9	49	0	11	15	35	15	117	7.8	0
2nd Down	98	369	3.8	26	3	33	12	26	7	45	6.4	1
3rd Down Overall	29	96	3.3	13	2	17	3	10	4	58	14.5	1
3rd D 0-2 to Go	15	55	3.7	13	1	12	0	0	0	0	-	0
3rd D 3-7 to Go	10	38	3.8	10	1	5	2	2	1	4	4.0	0
3rd D 8+ to Go	4	3	0.8	5	0	0	1	8	3	54	18.0	1
4th Down	2	2	1.0	1	1	2	0	0	0	0	-	0
Left Sideline	6	47	7.8	15	0	3	1	3	8	34	4.3	0
Left Side	81	266	3.3	14	0	21	11	23	6	41	6.8	0
Middle	116	438	3.8	49	6	28	9	27	2	18	9.0	1
Right Side	55	195	3.5	20	0	8	9	18	7	122	17.4	0
Right Sideline	9	59	6.6	26	0	3	0	0	3	5	1.7	1
Shotgun	24	108	4.5	49	0	3	5	17	8	87	10.9	1
2 Wide Receivers	41	136	3.3	11	0	4	2	5	5	20	4.0	0
3 Wide Receivers	205	827	4.0	49	4	50	25	60	18	183	10.2	1
4+ Wide Receivers	0	0	-	0	0	0	0	0	2	16	8.0	1
Carries 1-5	67	313	4.7	26	0	20	4	8	0	0	-	0
Carries 6-10	60	268	4.5	49	2	13	6	16	0	0	-	0
Carries 11-15	55	183	3.3	14	0	10	7	25	0	0	-	0
Carries 16-20	46	86	1.9	15	3	5	12	21	0	0	-	0
Carries 21+	39	155	4.0	18	1	5	1	1	0	0	-	0

1995 Incompletions

Type	Num	%of Inc	% Att
Pass Dropped	4	26.7	9.8
Poor Throw	7	46.7	17.1
Pass Defensed	1	6.7	2.4
Pass Hit at Line	2	13.3	4.9
Other	1	6.7	2.4
Total	15	100.0	36.6

Game Logs (1-8)

Date	Opp	Result	Rush	Yds	Rec	Yds	Trgt	F-L	TD
09/03	@Den	L 7-22	17	46	2	7	4	0-0	0
09/10	Car	W 31-9	22	91	2	64	4	1-0	1
09/17	Ind	W 20-14	19	25	2	7	3	1-0	1
10/02	@Cle	W 22-19	23	86	5	40	5	0-0	0
10/08	NYA	W 29-10	27	133	1	4	4	0-0	0
10/15	Sea	W 27-21	24	51	2	10	4	0-0	0
10/23	@NE	L 14-27	4	42	2	17	2	1-1	0
10/29	@Mia	L 6-23	-	-	-	-	-	-	-

Game Logs (9-16)

Date	Opp	Result	Rush	Yds	Rec	Yds	Trgt	F-L	TD
11/05	@Ind	W 16-10	-	-	-	-	-	-	-
11/12	Atl	W 23-17	17	66	0	0	0	1-0	0
11/19	@NYA	W 28-26	18	43	4	33	5	1-0	1
11/26	NE	L 25-35	24	85	0	0	3	0-0	1
12/03	@SF	L 17-27	10	40	2	11	3	0-0	1
12/10	@StL	W 45-27	24	129	3	16	3	0-0	1
12/17	Mia	W 23-20	35	148	1	11	1	1-0	2
12/24	Hou	L 17-28	3	20	1	0	2	0-0	0

Cedric Tillman — Jacksonville Jaguars — WR

1995 Receiving Splits

	G	Rec	Yds	Avg	TD	Lg	Big	YAC	Trgt	Y@C	1st	1st%
Total	13	30	368	12.3	3	28	2	71	49	9.9	19	63.3
vs. Playoff	5	9	102	11.3	1	27	1	28	18	8.2	5	55.6
vs. Non-playoff	8	21	266	12.7	2	28	1	43	31	10.6	14	66.7
vs. Own Division	7	10	125	12.5	2	28	1	22	23	10.3	7	70.0
Home	6	13	138	10.6	2	23	0	30	21	8.3	8	61.5
Away	7	17	230	13.5	1	28	2	41	28	11.1	11	64.7
Games 1-8	8	22	252	11.5	3	28	1	53	37	9.0	13	59.1
Games 9-16	5	8	116	14.5	0	27	1	18	12	12.3	6	75.0
September	4	11	100	9.1	0	17	0	24	18	6.9	3	27.3
October	5	12	168	14.0	3	28	1	29	23	11.6	10	83.3
November	0	0	0	-	0	0	0	0	0	-	0	-
December	4	7	100	14.3	0	27	1	18	8	11.7	6	85.7
Grass	8	21	254	12.1	3	28	1	44	32	10.0	15	71.4
Turf	5	9	114	12.7	0	27	1	27	17	9.7	4	44.4
Outdoor	2	29	341	11.8	3	28	1	59	47	9.7	18	62.1
Indoor	11	1	27	27.0	0	27	1	12	2	15.0	1	100.0
1st Half	-	13	156	12.0	2	27	1	41	21	8.8	8	61.5
2nd Half/OT	-	17	212	12.5	1	28	1	30	28	10.7	11	64.7
Last 2 Min. Half	-	9	111	12.3	1	27	1	25	12	9.6	5	55.6
4th qtr, +/-7 pts	-	3	22	7.3	0	11	0	5	6	5.7	1	33.3
Winning	-	3	53	17.7	0	28	1	11	10	14.0	3	100.0
Tied	-	5	58	11.6	2	19	0	15	7	8.6	5	100.0
Trailing	-	22	257	11.7	1	27	1	45	32	9.6	11	50.0

	Rec	Yds	Avg	TD	Lg	Big	YAC	Trgt	Y@C	1st	1st%
Inside 20	3	24	8.0	2	10	0	4	7	6.7	3	100.0
Inside 10	1	6	6.0	1	6	0	0	3	6.0	1	100.0
1st Down	7	90	12.9	0	20	0	15	11	10.7	5	71.4
2nd Down	8	102	12.8	1	28	1	16	16	10.9	4	50.0
3rd Down Overall	15	176	11.7	2	27	1	41	22	9.0	10	66.7
3rd D 0-2 to Go	3	46	15.3	1	23	0	4	3	14.0	3	100.0
3rd D 3-7 to Go	3	47	15.7	0	27	1	18	6	9.7	3	100.0
3rd D 8+ to Go	9	83	9.2	1	15	0	19	13	7.1	4	44.4
4th Down	0	0	-	0	0	0	0	0	-	0	-
Rec Behind Line	0	0	-	0	0	0	0	1	-	0	-
1-10 yds	20	173	8.7	2	10	0	41	24	6.6	10	50.0
11-20 yds	8	144	18.0	0	27	1	23	17	15.1	7	87.5
21-30 yds	2	51	25.5	1	28	1	7	6	22.0	2	100.0
31+	0	0	-	0	0	0	0	1	-	0	-
Left Sideline	4	73	18.3	0	28	1	21	9	13.0	4	100.0
Left Side	5	55	11.0	1	20	0	11	6	8.8	4	80.0
Middle	5	52	10.4	1	15	0	12	10	8.0	3	60.0
Right Side	6	81	13.5	1	27	1	20	11	10.2	5	50.0
Right Sideline	10	107	10.7	0	17	0	7	13	10.0	5	50.0
Shotgun	14	135	9.6	2	23	0	23	23	8.0	7	50.0
2 Wide Receivers	3	31	10.3	1	16	0	-1	6	10.7	1	33.3
3 Wide Receivers	24	302	12.6	2	28	2	68	40	9.8	16	66.7
4+ Wide Receivers	3	35	11.7	0	15	0	4	4	10.3	2	66.7

1995 Incompletions

Type	Num	%of Inc	%of Att
Pass Dropped	1	5.3	2.0
Poor Throw	9	47.4	18.4
Pass Defensed	5	26.3	10.2
Pass Hit at Line	1	5.3	2.0
Other	3	15.8	6.1
Total	19	100.0	38.8

Game Logs (1-8)

Date	Opp	Result	Rec	Yds	Trgt	F-L	TD
09/03	Hou	L 3-10	1	8	2	0-0	0
09/10	@Cin	L 17-24	2	20	4	0-0	0
09/17	@NYA	L 10-27	5	51	7	0-0	0
09/24	GB	L 14-24	3	21	5	0-0	0
10/01	@Hou	W 17-16	0	0	1	0-0	0
10/08	Pit	W 20-16	2	20	5	0-0	1
10/15	Chi	L 27-30	5	71	6	0-0	1
10/22	@Cle	W 23-15	4	61	7	0-0	1

Game Logs (9-16)

Date	Opp	Result	Rec	Yds	Trgt	F-L	TD
10/29	@Pit	L 7-24	1	16	4	0-0	0
11/12	Sea	L 30-47	-	-	-	-	-
11/19	@TB	L 16-17	-	-	-	-	-
11/26	Cin	L 13-17	-	-	-	-	-
12/03	@Den	L 23-31	4	55	4	0-0	0
12/10	Ind	L 31-41	2	18	3	1-1	0
12/17	@Det	L 0-44	1	27	1	0-0	0
12/24	Cle	W 24-21	0	0	0	0-0	0

Mike Tomczak — Pittsburgh Steelers — QB

1995 Passing Splits

	G	Att	Cm	Pct	Yds	Yd/Att	TD	Int	1st	YAC	Big	Sk	Rtg
Total	7	113	65	57.5	666	5.9	1	9	36	321	2	6	44.3
vs. Playoff	3	69	38	55.1	400	5.8	0	6	22	184	1	5	35.9
vs. Non-playoff	4	44	27	61.4	266	6.0	1	3	14	137	1	1	57.6
vs. Own Division	2	22	13	59.1	123	5.6	1	0	8	69	0	2	89.8
Home	3	67	41	61.2	439	6.6	0	7	21	218	2	3	40.8
Away	4	46	24	52.2	227	4.9	1	2	15	103	0	3	55.3
Games 1-8	5	113	65	57.5	666	5.9	1	9	36	321	2	6	44.3
Games 9-16	2	0	0	-	0	-	0	0	0	0	0	0	-
September	4	92	53	57.6	519	5.6	1	8	29	238	1	5	41.0
October	1	21	12	57.1	147	7.0	0	1	7	83	1	1	59.0
November	0	0	0	-	0	-	0	0	0	0	0	0	-
December	1	0	0	-	0	-	0	0	0	0	0	0	-
Grass	2	24	11	45.8	104	4.3	0	2	7	34	0	3	23.6
Turf	5	89	54	60.7	562	6.3	1	7	29	287	2	3	49.9
Indoor	1	22	13	59.1	123	5.6	1	0	8	69	0	0	89.8
Outdoor	6	91	52	57.1	543	6.0	0	9	28	252	2	6	35.0
1st Half	-	77	42	54.5	428	5.6	1	6	23	168	2	3	42.6
2nd Half/OT	-	36	23	63.9	238	6.6	0	3	13	153	0	3	48.1
Last 2 Min. Half	-	21	11	52.4	136	6.5	0	2	6	43	1	0	33.1
4th qtr, +/-7 pts	-	9	7	77.8	62	6.9	0	1	3	10	1	0	55.8
Winning	-	51	29	56.9	310	6.1	1	2	17	176	1	2	65.0
Tied	-	27	20	74.1	183	6.8	0	1	10	73	0	1	76.6
Trailing	-	35	16	45.7	173	4.9	0	6	9	72	1	3	21.2

	Att	Cm	Pct	Yds	Yd/Att	TD	Int	1st	YAC	Big	Sk	Rtg
Inside 20	12	8	66.7	57	4.8	1	0	4	21	0	1	105.2
Inside 10	2	1	50.0	3	1.5	0	0	0	2	0	0	56.3
1st Down	43	23	53.5	267	6.2	0	4	8	135	1	2	33.8
2nd Down	36	22	61.1	215	6.0	1	3	17	96	0	2	52.4
3rd Down Overall	34	20	58.8	184	5.4	0	2	11	90	1	2	49.1
3rd D 0-5 to Go	12	8	66.7	70	5.8	0	1	7	30	0	2	47.2
3rd D 6+ to Go	22	12	54.5	114	5.2	0	1	4	60	1	0	50.2
4th Down	0	0	-	0	-	0	0	0	0	0	0	-
Rec Behind Line	17	11	64.7	103	6.1	0	1	5	153	0	0	56.7
1-10 yds	61	43	70.5	360	5.9	0	4	20	137	0	0	58.1
11-20 yds	21	8	38.1	132	6.3	1	1	8	26	1	0	56.1
21-30 yds	9	3	33.3	71	7.9	0	1	3	5	1	0	23.1
31+	5	0	0.0	0	-	0	2	0	0	0	0	0.0
Left Sideline	26	13	50.0	144	5.5	0	3	8	90	0	0	27.2
Left Side	26	20	76.9	186	7.2	1	0	10	88	0	1	108.8
Middle	13	7	53.8	51	3.9	0		3	17	0	5	23.7
Right Side	21	12	57.1	142	6.8	0	1	8	109	1	0	58.0
Right Sideline	27	13	48.1	143	5.3	0	3	7	53	1	2	24.7
2 Wide Receivers	58	34	58.6	354	6.1	1	5	20	190	1	4	46.2
3+ WR	54	31	57.4	312	5.8	0	4	16	131	1	2	43.1
Attempts 1-10	50	25	50.0	223	4.5	1	5	15	105	0	0	29.4
Attempts 11-20	50	33	66.0	377	7.5	0	2	18	184	2	0	71.8
Attempts 21+	13	7	53.8	66	5.1	0	2	3	32	0	0	28.5

1995 Incompletions

Type	Num	% of Inc	% of Att
Pass Dropped	9	18.8	8.0
Poor Throw	18	37.5	15.9
Pass Defensed	8	16.7	7.1
Pass Hit at Line	1	2.1	0.9
Other	12	25.0	10.6
Total	48	100.0	42.5

Game Logs (1-8)

Date	Opp	Result	Att	Cm	Pct	Yds	TD	Int	Lg	Sk	F-L
09/03	Det	W 23-20	24	15	62.5	149	0	3	23	1	0-0
09/10	@Hou	W 34-17	22	13	59.1	123	0	1	18	1	0-0
09/18	@Mia	L 10-23	24	11	45.8	104	0	2	19	3	1-1
09/24	Min	L 24-44	22	14	63.6	143	0	3	19	1	0-0
10/01	SD	W 31-16	21	12	57.1	147	0	1	25	1	0-0
10/08	@Jac	L 16-20	-	-	-	-	-	-	-	-	-
10/19	Cin	L 9-27	-	-	-	-	-	-	-	-	-
10/29	Jac	W 24-7	-	-	-	-	-	-	-	-	-

Game Logs (9-16)

Date	Opp	Result	Att	Cm	Pct	Yds	TD	Int	Lg	Sk	F-L
11/05	@Chi	W 37-34	-	-	-	-	-	-	-	-	-
11/13	Cle	W 20-3	-	-	-	-	-	-	-	-	-
11/19	@Cin	W 49-31	0	0	-	0	0	0	-	0	0-0
11/26	@Cle	W 20-17	-	-	-	-	-	-	-	-	-
12/03	Hou	W 21-7	-	-	-	-	-	-	-	-	-
12/10	@Oak	W 29-10	-	-	-	-	-	-	-	-	-
12/16	NE	W 41-27	-	-	-	-	-	-	-	-	-
12/24	@GB	L 19-24	0	0	-	0	0	0	-	0	1-0

Floyd Turner
Indianapolis Colts — WR

1995 Receiving Splits

	G	Rec	Yds	Avg	TD	Lg	Big	YAC	Trgt	Y@C	1st	1st%
Total	14	35	431	12.3	4	47	1	97	64	9.5	24	68.6
vs. Playoff	6	14	202	14.4	2	47	1	53	28	10.6	12	85.7
vs. Non-playoff	8	21	229	10.9	2	19	0	44	36	8.8	12	57.1
vs. Own Division	7	19	240	12.6	4	47	1	52	33	9.9	14	73.7
Home	7	15	177	11.8	1	22	0	57	29	8.0	9	60.0
Away	7	20	254	12.7	3	47	1	40	35	10.7	15	75.0
Games 1-8	6	18	216	12.0	2	47	1	47	31	9.4	12	66.7
Games 9-16	8	17	215	12.6	2	22	0	50	33	9.7	12	70.6
September	3	10	105	10.5	0	20	0	26	19	7.9	5	50.0
October	3	8	111	13.9	2	47	1	21	12	11.3	7	87.5
November	4	7	95	13.6	0	22	0	28	10	9.6	5	71.4
December	4	10	120	12.0	1	17	0	22	23	9.8	7	70.0
Grass	4	13	162	12.5	3	47	1	22	21	10.8	9	69.2
Turf	10	22	269	12.2	1	22	0	75	43	8.8	15	68.2
Outdoor	8	18	223	12.4	3	47	1	31	33	10.7	13	72.2
Indoor	6	17	208	12.2	1	22	0	66	31	8.4	11	64.7
1st Half	-	14	161	11.5	0	22	0	51	33	7.9	8	57.1
2nd Half/OT	-	21	270	12.9	4	47	1	46	31	10.7	16	76.2
Last 2 Min. Half	-	3	28	9.3	0	17	0	11	9	5.7	2	66.7
4th qtr, +/-7 pts	-	8	98	12.3	1	16	0	14	15	10.5	6	75.0
Winning	-	5	53	10.6	1	14	0	4	12	9.8	3	60.0
Tied	-	11	143	13.0	0	22	0	39	20	9.5	7	63.6
Trailing	-	19	235	12.4	3	47	1	54	32	9.5	14	73.7

	Rec	Yds	Avg	TD	Lg	Big	YAC	Trgt	Y@C	1st	1st%
Inside 20	7	52	7.4	3	14	0	4	12	6.9	4	57.1
Inside 10	2	5	2.5	1	3	0	1	2	2.0	1	50.0
1st Down	11	148	13.5	1	47	1	35	21	10.3	5	45.5
2nd Down	8	96	12.0	0	19	0	18	17	9.8	6	75.0
3rd Down Overall	14	171	12.2	0	22	0	38	24	9.5	11	78.6
3rd D 0-2 to Go	2	21	10.5	0	12	0	8	3	6.5	2	100.0
3rd D 3-7 to Go	4	32	8.0	0	13	0	3	6	7.3	3	75.0
3rd D 8+ to Go	8	118	14.8	0	22	0	27	15	11.4	6	75.0
4th Down	2	16	8.0	1	13	0	6	2	5.0	2	100.0
Rec Behind Line	0	0	-	0	0	0	0	2	-	0	-
1-10 yds	21	201	9.6	1	22	0	70	32	6.2	11	52.4
11-20 yds	13	183	14.1	2	20	0	17	19	12.8	12	92.3
21-30 yds	0	0	-	0	0	0	0	6	-	0	-
31+	1	47	47.0	1	47	1	10	5	37.0	1	100.0
Left Sideline	6	93	15.5	1	47	1	18	12	12.5	4	66.7
Left Side	7	77	11.0	1	22	0	18	12	8.4	6	85.7
Middle	7	100	14.3	0	20	0	23	13	11.0	6	85.7
Right Side	7	81	11.6	0	19	0	18	16	9.0	3	42.9
Right Sideline	8	80	10.0	2	14	0	20	11	7.5	5	62.5
Shotgun	14	213	15.2	2	47	1	50	29	11.6	13	92.9
2 Wide Receivers	11	108	9.8	1	19	0	30	19	7.1	5	45.5
3 Wide Receivers	12	143	11.9	0	20	0	16	24	10.6	8	66.7
4+ Wide Receivers	11	167	15.2	4	47	1	51	19	10.5	10	90.9

1995 Incompletions

Type	Num	%of Inc	%of Att
Pass Dropped	3	10.3	4.7
Poor Throw	13	44.8	20.3
Pass Defensed	7	24.1	10.9
Pass Hit at Line	1	3.4	1.6
Other	5	17.2	7.8
Total	29	100.0	45.3

Game Logs (1-8)

Date	Opp	Result	Rec	Yds	Trgt	F-L	TD
09/03	Cin	L 21-24	5	44	7	0-0	0
09/10	@NYA	W 27-24	4	41	6	0-0	0
09/17	@Buf	W 14-20	1	20	6	0-0	0
10/01	StL	W 21-18	0	0	1	0-0	0
10/08	@Mia	W 27-24	6	82	7	0-0	2
10/15	SF	W 18-17	2	29	4	0-0	0
10/22	@Oak	L 17-30	-	-	-	-	-
10/29	NYA	W 17-10	-	-	-	-	-

Game Logs (9-16)

Date	Opp	Result	Rec	Yds	Trgt	F-L	TD
11/05	Buf	L 10-16	2	20	2	0-0	0
11/12	@NO	L 14-17	2	31	2	0-0	0
11/19	@NE	W 24-10	2	22	4	0-0	0
11/26	Mia	W 36-28	1	22	2	0-0	0
12/03	@Car	L 10-13	3	36	8	0-0	0
12/10	@Jac	W 41-31	2	22	2	0-0	0
12/17	SD	L 24-27	2	29	7	0-0	0
12/23	NE	W 10-7	3	33	6	0-0	1

Derrick Walker
Kansas City Chiefs — TE

1995 Receiving Splits

	G	Rec	Yds	Avg	TD	Lg	Big	YAC	Trgt	Y@C	1st	1st%
Total	16	25	205	8.2	1	18	0	95	35	4.4	11	44.0
vs. Playoff	4	11	106	9.6	1	18	0	39	12	6.1	7	63.6
vs. Non-playoff	12	14	99	7.1	0	17	0	56	23	3.1	4	28.6
vs. Own Division	8	14	93	6.6	1	18	0	58	19	2.5	5	35.7
Home	8	12	88	7.3	1	18	0	41	19	3.9	3	25.0
Away	8	13	117	9.0	0	17	0	54	16	4.8	8	61.5
Games 1-8	8	17	124	7.3	1	18	0	75	23	5.9	5	29.4
Games 9-16	8	8	81	10.1	0	17	0	20	12	7.6	6	75.0
September	4	7	39	5.6	0	9	0	27	8	1.7	1	14.3
October	4	10	85	8.5	1	18	0	48	15	3.7	4	40.0
November	4	3	27	9.0	0	15	0	3	4	8.0	2	66.7
December	4	5	54	10.8	0	17	0	17	8	7.4	4	80.0
Grass	14	23	194	8.4	1	18	0	88	32	4.6	10	43.5
Turf	2	2	11	5.5	0	7	0	7	3	2.0	1	50.0
Outdoor	1	23	194	8.4	1	18	0	88	33	4.6	10	43.5
Indoor	15	2	11	5.5	0	7	0	7	2	2.0	1	50.0
1st Half	-	10	83	8.3	0	17	0	53	15	3.0	6	60.0
2nd Half/OT	-	15	122	8.1	1	18	0	42	20	5.3	5	33.3
Last 2 Min. Half	-	2	26	13.0	1	18	0	5	3	10.5	2	100.0
4th qtr, +/-7 pts	-	5	49	9.8	1	18	0	19	7	6.0	2	40.0
Winning	-	8	59	7.4	0	15	0	23	15	4.5	4	50.0
Tied	-	6	45	7.5	0	17	0	33	7	2.0	3	50.0
Trailing	-	11	101	9.2	1	18	0	39	13	5.6	4	36.4

	Rec	Yds	Avg	TD	Lg	Big	YAC	Trgt	Y@C	1st	1st%
Inside 20	2	18	9.0	1	18	0	3	4	7.5	1	50.0
Inside 10	0	0	-	0	0	0	0	2	-	0	-
1st Down	9	74	8.2	0	17	0	28	15	5.1	3	33.3
2nd Down	15	114	7.6	1	18	0	67	17	3.1	7	46.7
3rd Down Overall	1	17	17.0	0	17	0	0	3	17.0	1	100.0
3rd D 0-2 to Go	1	17	17.0	0	17	0	0	2	17.0	1	100.0
3rd D 3-7 to Go	0	0	-	0	0	0	0	1	-	0	-
3rd D 8+ to Go	0	0	-	0	0	0	0	0	-	0	-
4th Down	0	0	-	0	0	0	0	0	-	0	-
Rec Behind Line	5	11	2.2	0	7	0	19	6	-1.6	1	20.0
1-10 yds	16	127	7.9	0	17	0	70	23	3.6	6	37.5
11-20 yds	4	67	16.8	1	18	0	6	5	15.3	4	100.0
21-30 yds	0	0	-	0	0	0	0	1	-	0	-
31+	0	0	-	0	0	0	0	0	-	0	-
Left Sideline	1	17	17.0	0	17	0	13	1	4.0	1	100.0
Left Side	2	15	7.5	0	10	0	3	0	7.5	2	100.0
Middle	5	28	5.6	0	10	0	8	5	4.0	2	40.0
Right Side	13	101	7.8	1	18	0	51	18	3.8	4	30.8
Right Sideline	4	44	11.0	0	17	0	23	8	5.3	2	50.0
Shotgun	0	0	-	0	0	0	0	0	-	0	-
2 Wide Receivers	11	71	6.5	0	17	0	42	17	2.6	3	27.3
3 Wide Receivers	13	117	9.0	1	18	0	53	16	4.9	7	53.8
4+ Wide Receivers	0	0	-	0	0	0	0	0	-	0	-

1995 Incompletions

Type	Num	%of Inc	%of Att
Pass Dropped	1	10.0	2.9
Poor Throw	8	80.0	22.9
Pass Defensed	1	10.0	2.9
Pass Hit at Line	0	0.0	0.0
Other	0	0.0	0.0
Total	10	100.0	28.6

Game Logs (1-8)

Date	Opp	Result	Rec	Yds	Trgt	F-L	TD
09/03	@Sea	W 34-10	2	11	2	0-0	0
09/10	NYN	W 20-17	3	17	3	0-0	0
09/17	Oak	W 23-17	1	4	2	0-0	0
09/24	@Cle	L 17-35	1	7	1	0-0	0
10/01	@Ari	W 24-3	1	10	2	0-0	0
10/09	SD	W 29-23	6	45	6	0-0	1
10/15	NE	W 31-26	0	0	3	0-0	0
10/22	@Den	W 21-7	3	30	4	0-0	0

Game Logs (9-16)

Date	Opp	Result	Rec	Yds	Trgt	F-L	TD
11/05	Was	W 24-3	1	7	1	0-0	0
11/12	@SD	W 22-7	1	5	1	0-0	0
11/19	Hou	W 20-13	1	15	1	0-0	0
11/23	@Dal	L 12-24	0	0	1	0-0	0
12/03	@Oak	W 29-23	1	-2	1	0-0	0
12/11	@Mia	L 6-13	4	56	4	0-0	0
12/17	Den	W 20-17	0	0	1	0-0	0
12/24	Sea	W 26-3	0	0	1	0-0	0

Herschel Walker
New York Giants — KR

1995 Receiving Splits

	G	Rec	Yds	Avg	TD	Lg	Big	YAC	Trgt	Y@C	1st	1st%		Rec	Yds	Avg	TD	Lg	Big	YAC	Trgt	Y@C	1st	1st%
Total	16	31	234	7.5	1	34	1	174	44	1.9	13	41.9	Inside 20	2	10	5.0	1	8	0	0	4	5.0	1	50.0
vs. Playoff	8	20	121	6.1	0	12	0	127	26	-0.3	6	30.0	Inside 10	2	10	5.0	1	8	0	0	3	5.0	1	50.0
vs. Non-playoff	8	11	113	10.3	1	34	1	47	18	6.0	7	63.6	1st Down	11	74	6.7	0	11	0	82	16	-0.7	2	18.2
vs. Own Division	8	10	61	6.1	0	10	0	64	15	-0.3	3	30.0	2nd Down	13	104	8.0	1	34	1	52	18	4.0	8	61.5
Home	8	17	152	8.9	0	34	1	99	22	3.1	7	41.2	3rd Down Overall	7	56	8.0	0	22	0	40	10	2.3	3	42.9
Away	8	14	82	5.9	1	12	0	75	22	0.5	6	42.9	3rd D 0-2 to Go	1	22	22.0	0	22	0	4	1	18.0	1	100.0
Games 1-8	8	26	175	6.7	0	22	0	154	36	0.8	10	38.5	3rd D 3-7 to Go	2	15	7.5	0	9	0	16	4	-0.5	2	100.0
Games 9-16	8	5	59	11.8	1	34	1	20	8	7.8	3	60.0	3rd D 8+ to Go	4	19	4.8	0	10	0	20	5	-0.3	0	0.0
September	4	15	116	7.7	0	22	0	99	17	1.1	6	40.0	4th Down	0	0	-	0	0	0	0	0	-	0	-
October	4	11	59	5.4	0	12	0	55	19	0.4	4	36.4	Rec Behind Line	14	66	4.7	0	11	0	105	17	-2.8	3	21.4
November	5	5	59	11.8	1	34	1	20	8	7.8	3	60.0	1-10 yds	15	112	7.5	1	12	0	64	21	3.2	8	53.3
December	3	0	0	-	0	0	0	0	0	-	0	-	11-20 yds	1	22	22.0	0	22	0	4	2	18.0	1	100.0
Grass	5	12	67	5.6	0	12	0	69	19	-0.2	4	33.3	21-30 yds	0	0	-	0	0	0	0	0	-	0	-
Turf	11	19	167	8.8	1	34	1	105	25	3.3	9	47.4	31+	1	34	34.0	0	34	1	1	4	33.0	1	100.0
Indoor	1	2	15	7.5	1	8	0	6	3	4.5	2	100.0	Left Sideline	5	40	8.0	1	11	0	27	6	2.6	4	80.0
Outdoor	15	29	219	7.6	0	34	1	168	41	1.8	11	37.9	Left Side	8	59	7.4	0	12	0	42	10	2.1	3	37.5
1st Half	-	19	138	7.3	1	34	1	98	26	2.1	8	42.1	Middle	8	59	7.4	0	22	0	43	11	2.0	2	25.0
2nd Half/OT	-	12	96	8.0	0	22	0	76	18	1.7	5	41.7	Right Side	5	53	10.6	0	34	1	25	8	5.6	3	60.0
Last 2 Min. Half	-	9	57	6.3	0	9	0	50	10	0.8	4	44.4	Right Sideline	5	24	4.6	0	9	0	37	9	-2.8	1	20.0
4th qtr, +/-7 pts	-	1	7	7.0	0	7	0	2	3	5.0	0	0.0	Shotgun	8	47	5.9	0	10	0	49	9	-0.3	0	0.0
Winning	-	4	45	11.3	0	22	0	18	8	6.8	2	50.0	2 Wide Receivers	16	107	6.7	0	12	0	107	23	0.0	8	50.0
Tied	-	2	12	6.0	0	6	0	7	3	2.5	1	50.0	3 Wide Receivers	11	89	8.1	0	34	1	60	17	2.6	3	27.3
Trailing	-	25	177	7.1	1	34	1	149	33	1.1	10	40.0	4+ Wide Receivers	1	7	7.0	0	7	0	2	1	5.0	0	0.0

1995 Incompletions

Type	Num	%of Inc	%of Att
Pass Dropped	3	23.1	6.8
Poor Throw	5	38.5	11.4
Pass Defensed	2	15.4	4.5
Pass Hit at Line	1	7.7	2.3
Other	2	15.4	4.5
Total	13	100.0	29.5

Game Logs (1-8)

Date	Opp	Result	Rush	Yds	Rec	Yds	Trgt	F-L	TD
09/04	Dal	L 0-35	2	2	4	28	4	0-0	0
09/10	@KC	L 17-20	3	6	1	9	2	0-0	0
09/17	@GB	L 6-14	3	14	6	32	7	0-0	0
09/24	NO	W 45-29	3	11	4	47	4	0-0	0
10/01	@SF	L 6-20	1	4	5	26	8	0-0	0
10/08	Ari	W 27-21	2	42	2	7	4	0-0	0
10/15	Phi	L 14-17	5	12	4	26	5	0-0	0
10/29	@Was	W 24-15	2	-2	0	0	2	0-0	0

Game Logs (9-16)

Date	Opp	Result	Rush	Yds	Rec	Yds	Trgt	F-L	TD
11/05	@Sea	L 28-30	3	12	2	15	3	0-0	1
11/12	Oak	L 13-17	6	7	3	44	5	0-0	0
11/19	@Phi	L 19-28	0	0	0	0	0	0-0	0
11/26	Chi	L 24-27	1	18	0	0	0	0-0	0
11/30	@Ari	W 10-6	0	0	0	0	0	0-0	0
12/10	Was	L 20-13	0	0	0	0	0	0-0	0
12/17	@Dal	L 20-21	0	0	0	0	0	0-0	0
12/23	SD	L 17-27	0	0	0	0	0	0-0	0

Wesley Walls
New Orleans Saints — TE

1995 Receiving Splits

	G	Rec	Yds	Avg	TD	Lg	Big	YAC	Trgt	Y@C	1st	1st%		Rec	Yds	Avg	TD	Lg	Big	YAC	Trgt	Y@C	1st	1st%
Total	16	57	694	12.2	4	29	3	211	92	8.5	40	70.2	Inside 20	4	24	6.0	3	12	0	-2	13	6.5	3	75.0
vs. Playoff	8	32	367	11.5	1	29	2	95	48	8.5	22	68.8	Inside 10	2	11	5.5	2	9	0	0	6	5.5	2	100.0
vs. Non-playoff	8	25	327	13.1	3	26	1	116	44	8.4	18	72.0	1st Down	21	247	11.8	0	24	0	80	32	8.0	12	57.1
vs. Own Division	8	31	357	11.5	1	28	2	129	51	7.4	20	64.5	2nd Down	16	165	10.3	2	20	0	59	27	6.6	9	56.3
Home	8	33	409	12.4	1	29	3	109	46	9.1	24	72.7	3rd Down Overall	20	282	14.1	2	29	3	72	32	10.5	19	95.0
Away	8	24	285	11.9	3	24	0	102	46	7.6	16	66.7	3rd D 0-2 to Go	4	38	9.5	0	22	0	15	4	5.8	4	100.0
Games 1-8	8	30	394	13.1	2	29	2	113	51	9.4	21	70.0	3rd D 3-7 to Go	9	117	13.0	1	28	1	35	14	9.1	9	100.0
Games 9-16	8	27	300	11.1	2	26	1	98	41	7.5	19	70.4	3rd D 8+ to Go	7	127	18.1	1	29	2	22	14	15.0	6	85.7
September	4	18	217	12.1	2	28	1	63	27	8.6	13	72.2	4th Down	0	0	-	0	0	0	0	1	-	0	-
October	4	12	177	14.8	0	29	1	50	24	10.6	6	66.7	Rec Behind Line	8	44	5.5	0	15	0	49	11	-0.6	2	25.0
November	4	13	137	10.5	1	26	1	49	18	6.8	9	69.2	1-10 yds	23	165	7.2	0	14	0	70	40	4.1	12	52.2
December	4	14	163	11.6	1	20	0	49	23	8.1	10	71.4	11-20 yds	23	402	17.5	1	24	0	82	36	13.9	23	100.0
Grass	3	8	90	11.3	0	22	0	37	16	6.6	3	37.5	21-30 yds	3	83	27.7	3	29	3	10	5	24.3	3	100.0
Turf	13	49	604	12.3	4	29	3	174	76	8.8	37	75.5	31+	0	0	-	0	0	0	0	0	-	0	-
Outdoor	10	18	239	13.3	2	24	0	84	35	8.6	11	61.1	Left Sideline	7	90	12.9	0	22	0	16	18	10.6	6	85.7
Indoor	6	39	455	11.7	2	29	3	127	57	8.4	29	74.4	Left Side	7	89	12.7	3	28	1	20	9	9.9	4	57.1
1st Half	-	25	286	11.4	1	24	0	112	42	7.0	18	72.0	Middle	15	212	14.1	1	26	1	46	25	11.1	12	80.0
2nd Half/OT	-	32	408	12.8	3	29	3	99	50	9.7	22	68.8	Right Side	12	139	11.6	0	24	0	50	18	7.4	9	75.0
Last 2 Min. Half	-	11	154	14.0	0	29	1	37	16	10.6	8	72.7	Right Sideline	16	164	10.3	0	29	1	79	22	5.3	9	56.3
4th qtr, +/-7 pts	-	12	179	14.9	2	29	2	33	14	12.2	8	66.7	Shotgun	23	306	13.3	3	29	3	76	34	10.0	20	87.0
Winning	-	16	198	12.4	2	28	2	54	26	9.0	11	68.8	2 Wide Receivers	22	241	11.0	0	24	0	89	33	6.9	12	54.5
Tied	-	17	235	13.8	1	24	0	87	26	8.7	13	76.5	3 Wide Receivers	29	358	12.3	3	29	3	104	49	8.8	22	75.9
Trailing	-	24	261	10.9	1	29	1	70	40	8.0	16	66.7	4+ Wide Receivers	1	21	21.0	0	21	0	6	2	15.0	1	100.0

1995 Incompletions

Type	Num	%of Inc	%of Att
Pass Dropped	5	14.3	5.4
Poor Throw	13	37.1	14.1
Pass Defensed	12	34.3	13.0
Pass Hit at Line	1	2.9	1.1
Other	4	11.4	4.3
Total	35	100.0	38.0

Game Logs (1-8)

Date	Opp	Result	Rec	Yds	Trgt	F-L	TD
09/03	SF	L 22-24	5	40	8	0-0	0
09/10	@StL	L 13-17	3	56	5	0-0	0
09/17	Atl	L 24-27	6	61	7	1-1	1
09/24	@NYN	L 29-45	4	60	7	0-0	0
10/01	Phi	L 10-15	2	48	5	0-0	0
10/15	Mia	W 33-30	4	59	6	0-0	0
10/22	@Car	L 3-20	4	56	9	0-0	0
10/29	@SF	W 11-7	2	14	4	0-0	0

Game Logs (9-16)

Date	Opp	Result	Rec	Yds	Trgt	F-L	TD
11/05	StL	W 19-10	3	34	3	0-0	0
11/12	Ind	W 17-14	4	35	5	0-0	0
11/19	@Min	L 24-43	2	9	3	0-0	1
11/26	Car	W 34-26	4	59	7	0-0	0
12/03	@NE	W 31-17	2	20	5	0-0	0
12/10	@Atl	L 14-19	4	37	8	0-0	0
12/16	GB	L 23-34	5	73	5	0-0	0
12/24	@NYA	W 12-0	3	33	7	0-0	1

Chris Warren
Seattle Seahawks — RB

1995 Rushing and Receiving Splits

	G	Rush	Yds	Avg	Lg	TD	1st	Stf	YdL	Rec	Yds	Avg	TD
Total	16	310	1346	4.3	52	15	77	34	75	35	247	7.1	1
vs. Playoff	6	109	388	3.6	18	5	25	13	26	15	122	8.1	0
vs. Non-playoff	10	201	958	4.8	52	10	52	21	49	20	125	6.3	1
vs. Own Division	8	134	609	4.5	35	9	35	16	38	17	140	8.2	1
Home	8	147	677	4.6	35	10	41	15	33	19	132	6.9	0
Away	8	163	669	4.1	52	5	36	19	42	16	115	7.2	1
Games 1-8	8	158	696	4.4	52	8	38	17	38	17	134	7.9	0
Games 9-16	8	152	650	4.3	35	7	39	17	37	18	113	6.3	1
September	3	54	221	4.1	30	1	11	7	16	9	59	6.6	0
October	5	104	475	4.6	52	7	27	10	22	8	75	9.4	0
November	4	79	344	4.4	29	2	8		17	11	53	4.8	0
December	4	73	306	4.2	35	5	17	9	20	7	60	8.6	1
Grass	7	140	605	4.3	52	3	31	16	35	14	102	7.3	1
Turf	9	170	741	4.4	35	12	46	18	40	21	145	6.9	0
Indoor	8	147	677	4.6	35	10	41	15	33	19	132	6.9	0
Outdoor	8	163	669	4.1	52	5	36	19	42	16	115	7.2	1
1st Half	-	162	630	3.9	30	6	38	16	32	18	94	5.2	0
2nd Half/OT	-	148	716	4.8	52	9	39	18	43	17	153	9.0	1
Last 2 Min. Half	-	8	31	3.9	15	1	4	1	2	3	46	15.3	1
4th qtr, +/-7 pts	-	30	190	6.3	52	2	9	2	5	5	41	8.2	1
Winning	-	97	386	4.0	35	6	20	11	28	14	74	5.3	0
Tied	-	104	507	4.9	52	5	31	9	15	6	13	2.2	0
Trailing	-	109	453	4.2	24	4	26	14	32	15	160	10.7	1

	Rush	Yds	Avg	Lg	TD	1st	Stf	YdL	Rec	Yds	Avg	TD
Inside 20	40	149	3.7	15	12	17	3	6	0	0	-	0
Inside 10	21	52	2.5	6	9	11	2	4	0	0	-	0
1st Down	174	692	4.0	35	6	24	17	42	14	77	5.5	0
2nd Down	109	502	4.6	30	5	37	12	22	15	115	7.7	1
3rd Down Overall	27	152	5.6	52	4	16	5	11	6	55	9.2	0
3rd D 0-2 to Go	13	34	2.6	7	2	10	1	2	0	0	-	0
3rd D 3-7 to Go	9	66	7.3	24	2	6	2	5	0	0	-	0
3rd D 8+ to Go	5	52	10.4	52	0	0	2	4	6	55	9.2	0
4th Down	0	0	-	0	0	0	0	0	0	0	-	0
Left Sideline	10	50	5.0	15	1	3	0	0	3	20	6.7	0
Left Side	54	250	4.6	52	3	12	11	28	7	72	10.3	0
Middle	155	636	4.1	30	5	37	12	24	6	42	7.0	0
Right Side	70	336	4.8	29	5	20	8	16	15	80	5.3	1
Right Sideline	21	74	3.5	15	1	5	3	7	4	33	8.3	0
Shotgun	0	0	-	0	0	0	0	0	1	15	15.0	0
2 Wide Receivers	208	892	4.3	52	7	47	18	39	10	39	3.9	0
3 Wide Receivers	55	201	3.7	17	3	14	14	33	21	210	10.0	1
4+ Wide Receivers	17	94	5.5	29	1	5	1	1	4	-2	-0.5	0
Carries 1-5	80	319	4.0	29	3	16	7	12	0	0	-	0
Carries 6-10	77	334	4.3	30	1	22	7	15	0	0	-	0
Carries 11-15	70	257	3.7	22	3	12	11	24	0	0	-	0
Carries 16-20	46	268	5.8	52	4	14	8	21	0	0	-	0
Carries 21+	37	168	4.5	18	4	13			0	0	-	0

1995 Incompletions

Type	Num	%of Inc	% Att
Pass Dropped	3	20.0	6.0
Poor Throw	6	40.0	12.0
Pass Defensed	3	20.0	6.0
Pass Hit at Line	2	13.3	4.0
Other	1	6.7	2.0
Total	15	100.0	30.0

Game Logs (1-8)

Date	Opp	Result	Rush	Yds	Rec	Yds	Trgt	F-L	TD
09/03	KC	L 10-34	14	56	4	16	6	0-0	0
09/10	@SD	L 10-14	16	56	2	21	4	0-0	0
09/17	Cin	W 24-21	24	109	3	22	3	0-1	1
10/01	Den	W 27-10	24	115	1	3	2	0-0	3
10/08	@Oak	L 14-34	16	57	1	14	3	0-0	0
10/15	@Buf	L 21-27	23	64	2	13	2	0-0	2
10/22	SD	L 25-35	18	112	4	45	5	1-0	2
10/29	@Ari	L 14-20	23	127	0	0	1	2-2	0

Game Logs (9-16)

Date	Opp	Result	Rush	Yds	Rec	Yds	Trgt	F-L	TD
11/05	NYN	W 30-28	7	24	2	13	2	0-0	0
11/12	@Jac	W 47-30	27	121	4	52	5	0-0	1
11/19	@Was	W 27-20	29	136	3	-24	4	1-0	1
11/26	NYA	L 10-16	16	63	2	12	3	1-1	0
12/03	Phi	W 26-14	27	93	2	19	2	0-0	1
12/10	@Den	W 31-27	18	101	3	31	6	0-0	2
12/17	Oak	W 44-10	17	105	1	2	1	0-0	3
12/24	@KC	L 3-26	11	7	1	8	1	0-0	0

Ricky Watters
Philadelphia Eagles — RB

1995 Rushing and Receiving Splits

	G	Rush	Yds	Avg	Lg	TD	1st	Stf	YdL	Rec	Yds	Avg	TD
Total	16	337	1273	3.8	57	11	76	44	104	62	434	7.0	1
vs. Playoff	3	70	268	3.8	18	2	18	6	8	12	55	4.6	1
vs. Non-playoff	13	267	1005	3.8	57	9	58	38	96	50	379	7.6	0
vs. Own Division	8	196	829	4.2	57	7	47	20	39	30	235	7.8	0
Home	8	168	617	3.7	57	5	35	29	66	40	283	7.1	1
Away	8	169	656	3.9	28	6	41	15	38	22	151	6.9	0
Games 1-8	8	167	660	4.0	28	1	33	22	47	34	264	7.8	1
Games 9-16	8	170	613	3.6	57	10	43	22	57	28	170	6.1	0
September	4	73	282	3.9	28	1	13	11	22	18	120	6.7	1
October	4	94	378	4.0	26	1	20	11	25	16	144	9.0	0
November	4	81	345	4.3	57	7	25	9	18	13	83	6.4	0
December	4	89	268	3.0	36	3	18	13	39	15	87	5.8	0
Grass	4	74	306	4.1	28	2	17	8	23	14	93	6.6	0
Turf	12	263	967	3.7	57	9	59	36	81	48	341	7.1	1
Indoor	2	47	148	3.1	16	2	12	6	14	8	58	7.3	0
Outdoor	14	290	1125	3.9	57	9	64	38	90	54	376	7.0	1
1st Half	-	142	641	4.5	57	5	39	12	34	38	286	7.5	1
2nd Half/OT	-	195	632	3.2	28	6	37	32	70	24	148	6.2	0
Last 2 Min. Half	-	22	53	2.4	19	1	3	5	11	12	51	4.3	0
4th qtr, +/-7 pts	-	53	138	2.6	16	1	8	9	18	9	51	5.7	0
Winning	-	123	371	3.0	28	2	18	20	40	22	124	5.6	0
Tied	-	74	356	4.8	28	4	25	5	12	15	136	9.1	1
Trailing	-	140	546	3.9	57	5	33	19	52	25	174	7.0	0

	Rush	Yds	Avg	Lg	TD	1st	Stf	YdL	Rec	Yds	Avg	TD
Inside 20	44	123	2.8	12	11	15	4	8	3	17	5.7	1
Inside 10	31	68	2.2	9	11	12	3	6	1	4	4.0	1
1st Down	186	771	4.1	57	3	19	24	57	25	121	4.8	0
2nd Down	113	436	3.9	28	5	37	10	25	19	130	6.8	1
3rd Down Overall	36	63	1.8	17	3	19	10	22	18	183	10.2	0
3rd D 0-2 to Go	24	55	2.3	17	3	17	4	5	1	7	7.0	0
3rd D 3-7 to Go	7	7	1.0	11	0	2	4	13	8	84	10.5	0
3rd D 8+ to Go	5	1	0.2	3	0	0	2	4	9	92	10.2	0
4th Down	2	3	1.5	2	0	1	0	0	0	0	-	0
Left Sideline	22	155	7.0	25	0	9	2	4	6	56	9.3	0
Left Side	59	184	3.1	36	2	15	15	42	13	85	6.5	0
Middle	161	565	3.5	57	5	38	20	36	5	39	7.8	0
Right Side	79	316	4.0	28	3	17	4	7	21	170	8.1	0
Right Sideline	16	53	3.3	10	1	5	3	15	17	84	4.9	1
Shotgun	0	0	-	0	0	0	0	0	0	0	-	0
2 Wide Receivers	214	797	3.7	57	4	39	29	83	28	190	6.8	0
3 Wide Receivers	66	324	4.9	25	1	19	5	8	26	164	6.3	1
4+ Wide Receivers	4	11	2.8	7	0	0	0	0	8	80	10.0	0
Carries 1-5	80	377	4.7	57	2	22	8	20	0	0	-	0
Carries 6-10	80	309	3.9	28	1	19	10	33	0	0	-	0
Carries 11-15	75	294	3.9	19	5	18	9	20	0	0	-	0
Carries 16-20	57	165	2.9	24	3	11	12	23	0	0	-	0
Carries 21+	45	128	2.8	15	0	6	5	8	0	0	-	0

1995 Incompletions

Type	Num	%of Inc	% Att
Pass Dropped	9	29.0	9.7
Poor Throw	13	41.9	14.0
Pass Defensed	2	6.5	2.2
Pass Hit at Line	4	12.9	4.3
Other	3	9.7	3.2
Total	31	100.0	33.3

Game Logs (1-8)

Date	Opp	Result	Rush	Yds	Rec	Yds	Trgt	F-L	TD
09/03	TB	L 6-21	17	37	5	34	9	2-1	0
09/10	@Ari	W 31-19	22	94	3	34	5	0-0	0
09/17	SD	L 21-27	19	76	6	19	7	1-0	1
	@Oak	L 17-48			3	75		1-1	0
10/01	@NO	W 15-10	26	79	3	37	3	0-0	1
10/08	Was	W 37-34	25	139	11	90	17	0-0	0
10/15	@NYN	W 17-14	30	122	0	0	1	0-0	1
10/29	StL	W 20-9	13	38	2	17	7	0-0	0

Game Logs (9-16)

Date	Opp	Result	Rush	Yds	Rec	Yds	Trgt	F-L	TD
11/06	@Dal	L 12-34	18	80	0	0	2	0-0	1
11/12	Den	W 31-13	18	57	4	26	4	0-0	2
11/19	NYN	W 28-19	20	84	5	43	6	2-1	2
11/26	@Was	W 14-7	25	124	4	14	4	0-0	2
12/03	@Sea	L 14-26	21	69	5	21	8	0-0	2
12/10	Dal	W 20-17	33	112	6	36	6	0-1	0
12/17	Ari	W 21-20	23	74	1	18	4	0-0	2
12/24	@Chi	L 14-20	12	13	3	12	5	0-0	2

Casey Weldon
Tampa Bay Buccaneers — QB

1995 Passing Splits

	G	Att	Cm	Pct	Yds	Yd/Att	TD	Int	1st	YAC	Big	Sk	Rtg		Att	Cm	Pct	Yds	Yd/Att	TD	Int	1st	YAC	Big	Sk	Rtg
Total	16	91	42	46.2	519	5.7	1	2	25	203	4	9	58.8	Inside 20	10	3	30.0	26	2.6	0	1	1	29	0	1	0.0
vs. Playoff	6	44	20	45.5	214	4.9	0	2	10	113	0	3	41.3	Inside 10	1	0	0.0	0	-	0	0	0	0	0	0	39.6
vs. Non-playoff	10	47	22	46.8	305	6.5	1	0	15	90	4	6	75.2	1st Down	36	18	50.0	208	5.8	1	0	9	75	2	3	77.1
vs. Own Division	8	64	30	46.9	328	5.1	1	2	15	143	1	7	54.7	2nd Down	29	15	51.7	169	5.8	0	0	9	71	1	4	69.5
Home	8	42	18	42.9	180	4.3	0	1	9	99	0	6	45.7	3rd Down Overall	24	8	33.3	128	5.3	0	2	6	37	1	2	17.4
Away	8	49	24	49.0	339	6.9	1	1	16	104	4	3	70.0	3rd D 0-5 to Go	8	1	12.5	12	1.5	0	1	1	4	0	0	0.0
Games 1-8	8	34	16	47.1	230	6.8	0	0	12	79	3	4	69.5	3rd D 6+ to Go	16	7	43.8	116	7.3	0	1	5	33	1	2	42.7
Games 9-16	8	57	26	45.6	289	5.1	1	2	13	124	1	5	52.4	4th Down	2	1	50.0	14	7.0	0	0	1	20	0	1	72.9
September	4	7	4	57.1	39	5.6	0	0	2	19	0	2	72.9	Rec Behind Line	11	6	54.5	36	3.3	0	0	1	61	0	0	61.2
October	5	27	12	44.4	191	7.1	0	0	10	60	3	2	68.6	1-10 yds	51	27	52.9	266	5.2	0	2	16	115	0	0	51.6
November	3	16	9	56.3	108	6.8	0	1	6	49	0	1	51.0	11-20 yds	15	6	40.0	106	7.1	0	0	5	19	1	0	64.9
December	4	41	17	41.5	181	4.4	1	1	7	75	1	4	53.0	21-30 yds	7	1	14.3	33	4.7	0	0	1	5	1	0	46.7
Grass	12	62	27	43.5	336	5.4	0	1	16	143	3	6	54.2	31+	7	2	28.6	78	11.1	1	0	2	3	2	0	113.1
Turf	4	29	15	51.7	183	6.3	1	1	9	60	1	3	68.6	Left Sideline	20	8	40.0	114	5.7	0	0	6	31	1	0	59.2
Indoor	3	29	15	51.7	183	6.3	1	1	9	60	1	3	68.6	Left Side	15	9	60.0	83	5.5	0	2	4	59	1	2	35.6
Outdoor	13	62	27	43.5	336	5.4	0	1	16	143	3	6	54.2	Middle	16	8	50.0	122	7.6	0	0	6	32	1	6	75.5
1st Half	-	16	5	31.3	83	5.2	0	0	4	24	1	1	49.7	Right Side	14	7	50.0	65	4.6	0	0	4	20	0	1	63.1
2nd Half/OT	-	75	37	49.3	436	5.8	1	2	21	179	3	8	60.8	Right Sideline	26	10	38.5	135	5.2	1	0	5	61	1	0	68.6
Last 2 Min. Half	-	19	8	42.1	103	5.4	0	1	4	51	1	1	37.8	2 Wide Receivers	45	21	46.7	257	5.7	0	0	14	107	2	2	64.8
4th qtr, +/-7 pts	-	14	6	42.9	83	5.9	0	0	5	42	1	2	62.5	3+ WR	43	20	46.5	256	6.0	1	2	11	96	2	7	54.0
Winning	-	10	4	40.0	84	8.4	0	0	3	25	2	1	70.4	Attempts 1-10	54	24	44.4	317	5.9	1	0	17	101	2	0	69.8
Tied	-	13	7	53.8	99	7.6	0	0	5	21	1	0	78.7	Attempts 11-20	29	14	48.3	169	5.8	0	1	7	74	2	0	52.2
Trailing	-	68	31	45.6	336	4.9	1	2	17	157	1	8	53.3	Attempts 21+	8	4	50.0	33	4.1	0	1	1	28	0	0	21.4

1995 Incompletions

Type	Num	% of Inc	% of Att
Pass Dropped	5	10.2	5.5
Poor Throw	24	49.0	26.4
Pass Defensed	9	18.4	9.9
Pass Hit at Line	0	0.0	0.0
Other	11	22.4	12.1
Total	49	100.0	53.8

Game Logs (1-8)

Date	Opp	Result	Att	Cm	Pct	Yds	TD	Int	Lg	Sk	F-L
09/03	@Phi	W 21-6	0	0	-	0	0	0	0	0	0-0
09/10	@Cle	L 6-22	0	0	-	0	0	0	0	0	0-0
09/17	Chi	L 6-25	7	4	57.1	39	0	0	16	2	2-2
09/24	Was	W 14-6	0	0	-	0	0	0	0	0	0-0
10/01	@Car	W 20-13	20	9	45.0	156	0	0	40	1	0-0
10/08	Cin	W 19-16	7	3	42.9	35	0	0	13	2	0-0
10/15	Min	W 20-17	0	0	-	0	0	0	0	0	0-0
10/22	Atl	L 21-24	0	0	-	0	0	0	0	0	0-0

Game Logs (9-16)

Date	Opp	Result	Att	Cm	Pct	Yds	TD	Int	Lg	Sk	F-L
10/29	@Hou	L 7-19	0	0	-	0	0	0	0	0	0-0
11/12	@Det	L 24-27	16	9	56.3	108	0	1	22	1	2-1
11/19	Jac	W 17-16	0	0	-	0	0	0	0	0	0-0
11/26	@GB	L 13-35	0	0	-	0	0	0	0	0	0-0
12/03	@Min	L 17-31	13	6	46.2	75	1	0	38	2	0-0
12/10	GB	W 13-10	0	0	-	0	0	0	0	0	0-0
12/17	@Chi	L 10-31	0	0	-	0	0	0	0	0	0-0
12/23	Det	L 10-37	28	11	39.3	106	0	1	18	2	0-0

Michael Westbrook
Washington Redskins — WR

1995 Receiving Splits

	G	Rec	Yds	Avg	TD	Lg	Big	YAC	Trgt	Y@C	1st	1st%		Rec	Yds	Avg	TD	Lg	Big	YAC	Trgt	Y@C	1st	1st%
Total	11	34	522	15.4	1	45	6	121	88	11.8	25	73.5	Inside 20	2	9	4.5	1	5	0	3	8	3.0	1	50.0
vs. Playoff	2	5	85	17.0	0	34	1	31	12	10.8	4	80.0	Inside 10	1	5	5.0	1	5	0	2	3	3.0	1	100.0
vs. Non-playoff	9	29	437	15.1	1	45	5	90	76	12.0	21	72.4	1st Down	14	242	17.3	1	45	4	41	32	14.4	10	71.4
vs. Own Division	5	13	153	11.8	0	34	1	60	35	7.2	8	61.5	2nd Down	10	122	12.2	0	21	0	12	27	11.0	6	60.0
Home	5	17	264	15.5	1	34	3	86	40	10.5	12	70.6	3rd Down Overall	10	158	15.8	0	33	2	68	29	9.0	9	90.0
Away	6	17	258	15.2	0	45	3	35	48	13.1	13	76.5	3rd D 0-2 to Go	0	0	-	0	0	0	0	3	-	0	-
Games 1-8	7	19	315	16.6	0	45	4	78	58	12.5	13	68.4	3rd D 3-7 to Go	5	67	13.4	0	33	1	37	9	6.0	4	80.0
Games 9-16	4	15	207	13.8	1	32	2	43	30	10.9	12	80.0	3rd D 8+ to Go	5	91	18.2	0	32	1	31	17	12.0	5	100.0
September	4	13	218	16.8	0	45	3	42	40	13.5	9	69.2	4th Down	0	0	-	0	0	0	0	0	-	0	-
October	3	6	97	16.2	0	34	1	36	18	10.2	4	66.7	Rec Behind Line	0	0	-	0	0	0	0	0	-	0	-
November	1	3	45	15.0	0	21	0	10	6	11.7	3	100.0	1-10 yds	17	155	9.1	1	33	1	77	39	4.6	8	47.1
December	3	12	162	13.5	0	32	2	33	24	10.8	9	75.0	11-20 yds	13	239	18.4	0	34	1	34	32	15.8	13	100.0
Grass	8	23	388	16.9	1	45	5	95	64	12.7	16	69.6	21-30 yds	3	83	27.7	0	32	3	8	8	25.0	3	100.0
Turf	3	11	134	12.2	0	25	1	26	24	9.8	9	81.8	31+	1	45	45.0	0	45	1	2	9	43.0	1	100.0
Indoor	1	5	66	13.2	0	25	1	6	10	12.0	4	80.0	Left Sideline	7	130	18.6	0	45	2	10	20	17.1	4	57.1
Outdoor	10	29	456	15.7	1	45	5	115	78	11.8	21	72.4	Left Side	11	140	12.7	0	21	0	42	25	8.9	9	81.8
1st Half	-	23	365	15.9	0	45	5	95	54	11.7	16	69.6	Middle	3	58	19.3	0	20	0	2	6	18.7	3	100.0
2nd Half/OT	-	11	157	14.3	1	32	1	26	34	11.9	9	81.8	Right Side	6	90	15.0	1	34	2	28	15	10.3	4	66.7
Last 2 Min. Half	-	9	154	17.1	0	45	2	31	17	13.7	7	77.8	Right Sideline	7	104	14.9	0	33	2	39	22	9.3	5	71.4
4th qtr, +/-7 pts	-	3	44	14.7	0	20	0	2	7	14.0	3	100.0	Shotgun	0	0	-	0	0	0	0	0	-	0	-
Winning	-	10	133	13.3	0	32	2	25	24	10.8	7	70.0	2 Wide Receivers	14	218	15.6	0	34	2	35	41	13.1	10	71.4
Tied	-	7	105	15.0	0	34	2	25	23	11.4	3	42.9	3 Wide Receivers	18	255	14.2	1	33	3	83	44	9.6	14	77.8
Trailing	-	17	284	16.7	1	45	2	71	41	12.5	15	88.2	4+ Wide Receivers	2	49	24.5	0	45	1	3	3	23.0	1	50.0

1995 Incompletions

Type	Num	%of Inc	%of Att
Pass Dropped	8	14.8	9.1
Poor Throw	30	55.6	34.1
Pass Defensed	11	20.4	12.5
Pass Hit at Line	0	0.0	0.0
Other	5	9.3	5.7
Total	54	100.0	61.4

Game Logs (1-8)

Date	Opp	Result	Rush	Yds	Rec	Yds	Trgt	F-L	TD
09/03	Ari	W 27-7	1	58	3	17	9	0-0	1
09/10	Oak	L 8-20	1	7	5	89	13	0-0	0
09/17	@Den	L 31-38	0	0	3	91	7	0-0	0
09/24	@TB	L 6-14	1	13	2	21	11	0-0	0
10/01	Dal	W 27-23	0	0	3	56	6	0-0	0
10/08	@Phi	L 34-37	0	0	2	29	6	0-0	0
10/15	@Ari	L 20-24	0	0	1	12	6	0-0	0
10/22	Det	W 36-30							

Game Logs (9-16)

Date	Opp	Result	Rush	Yds	Rec	Yds	Trgt	F-L	TD
10/29	NYN	L 15-24	-	-	-	-	-	-	-
11/05	@KC	L 3-24	-	-	-	-	-	-	-
11/19	Sea	L 20-27	0	0	3	45	6	0-0	1
11/26	Phi	L 7-14	-	-	-	-	-	-	-
12/03	@Dal	W 24-17	-	-	-	-	-	-	-
12/10	@NYN	L 13-20	0	0	4	39	8	0-0	0
12/17	@StL	W 35-23	0	1	10	66	10	0-0	0
12/24	Car	W 20-17	0	2	3	57	6	0-0	0

Tyrone Wheatley

1995 Rushing and Receiving Splits

	G	Rush	Yds	Avg	Lg	TD	1st	Stf	YdL	Rec	Yds	Avg	TD
Total	13	78	245	3.1	19	3	14	8	26	5	27	5.4	0
vs. Playoff	6	23	60	2.6	12	1	3	3	9	2	14	7.0	0
vs. Non-playoff	7	55	185	3.4	19	2	11	5	17	3	13	4.3	0
vs. Own Division	6	41	124	3.0	16	2	7	2	8	3	13	4.3	0
Home	6	43	139	3.2	19	1	8	6	16	1	-1	-1.0	0
Away	7	35	106	3.0	12	2	6	2	10	4	28	7.0	0
Games 1-8	6	45	172	3.8	19	2	11	4	14	3	13	4.3	0
Games 9-16	7	33	73	2.2	9	1	3	4	12	2	14	7.0	0
September	2	11	61	5.5	19	1	4	1	1	0	0	-	0
October	4	34	111	3.3	16	1	7	3	13	3	13	4.3	0
November	5	21	51	2.4	7	0	1	2	8	2	14	7.0	0
December	2	12	22	1.8	9	1	2	2	4	0	0	-	0
Grass	4	20	66	3.3	12	1	4	1	5	4	28	7.0	0
Turf	9	58	179	3.1	19	2	10	7	21	1	-1	-1.0	0
Indoor	1	7	23	3.3	7	0	1	1	5	0	0	-	0
Outdoor	12	71	222	3.1	19	3	13	7	21	5	27	5.4	0
1st Half	-	35	77	2.2	10	2	4	3	8	3	13	4.3	0
2nd Half/OT	-	43	168	3.9	19	1	10	5	18	2	14	7.0	0
Last 2 Min. Half	-	10	27	2.7	7	0	2	1	1	1	16	16.0	0
4th qtr, +/-7 pts	-	11	44	4.0	9	0	3	1	5	0	0	-	0
Winning	-	32	95	3.0	19	2	7	4	10	0	0	-	0
Tied	-	10	24	2.4	9	0	2	2	8	0	0	-	0
Trailing	-	36	126	3.5	16	1	5	2	8	5	27	5.4	0

	Rush	Yds	Avg	Lg	TD	1st	Stf	YdL	Rec	Yds	Avg	TD
Inside 20	14	46	3.3	19	3	4	0	0	0	0	-	0
Inside 10	8	14	1.8	5	2	2	0	0	0	0	-	0
1st Down	48	130	2.7	12	0	1	6	19	1	6	6.0	0
2nd Down	23	71	3.1	16	2	8	2	7	3	5	1.7	0
3rd Down Overall	5	40	8.0	19	1	4	0	0	1	16	16.0	0
3rd D 0-2 to Go	2	9	4.5	5	0	2	0	0	0	0	-	0
3rd D 3-7 to Go	2	21	10.5	19	1	1	0	0	0	0	-	0
3rd D 8+ to Go	1	10	10.0	10	0	1	0	0	1	16	16.0	0
4th Down	2	4	2.0	2	0	1	0	0	0	0	-	0
Left Sideline	4	8	2.0	5	0	0	1	2	0	0	-	0
Left Side	25	65	2.6	9	1	5	3	10	1	-2	-2.0	0
Middle	32	110	3.4	16	1	6	2	6	2	14	7.0	0
Right Side	13	47	3.6	19	1	2	1	5	2	15	7.5	0
Right Sideline	4	15	3.8	9	0	1	1	3	0	0	-	0
Shotgun	1	10	10.0	10	0	1	0	0	0	0	-	0
2 Wide Receivers	57	181	3.2	19	1	8	7	21	4	21	5.3	0
3 Wide Receivers	3	8	2.7	10	0	1	1	5	0	0	-	0
4+ Wide Receivers	0	0	-	0	0	0	0	0	0	0	-	0
Carries 1-5	50	147	2.9	12	2	7	3	10				
Carries 6-10	20	75	3.8	19	1	5	4	11				
Carries 11-15	5	14	2.8	5	0	1	0	0				
Carries 16-20	3	9	3.0	9	0	1	1	5				
Carries 21+	0	0	-	0	0	0	0	0				

1995 Incompletions

Type	Num	%of Inc	% Att
Pass Dropped	0	-	0.0
Poor Throw	0	-	0.0
Pass Defensed	0	-	0.0
Pass Hit at Line	0	-	0.0
Other	0	-	0.0
Total	0	-	0.0

Game Logs (1-8)

Date	Opp	Result	Rush	Yds	Rec	Yds	Trgt	F-L	TD
09/04	Dal	L 0-35	-	-	-	-	-	-	-
09/10	@KC	L 17-20	-	-	-	-	-	-	-
09/17	@GB	L 6-14	1	7	0	0	0	0-0	0
09/24	NO	W 45-29	10	54	0	0	0	0-0	1
10/01	@SF	L 6-20	5	16	2	14	2	0-0	0
10/08	Ari	W 27-21	18	61	1	-1	1	1-0	0
10/15	Phi	L 14-17	1	3	0	0	0	0-0	0
10/29	@Was	W 24-15	10	31	0	0	0	0-0	1

Game Logs (9-16)

Date	Opp	Result	Rush	Yds	Rec	Yds	Trgt	F-L	TD
11/05	@Sea	L 28-30	7	23	0	0	0	0-0	0
11/12	Oak	L 13-17	1	0	0	0	0	0-0	0
11/19	@Phi	L 19-28	4	12	0	0	0	1-1	0
11/26	Chi	L 24-27	5	4	0	0	0	0-0	0
11/30	@Ari	W 10-6	4	12	2	14	2	0-0	0
12/10	Was	W 20-13	-	-	-	-	-	-	-
12/17	@Dal	L 20-21	4	5	0	0	0	0-0	1
12/23	SD	L 17-27	8	17	0	0	0	0-0	0

Calvin Williams

1995 Receiving Splits

	G	Rec	Yds	Avg	TD	Lg	Big	YAC	Trgt	Y@C	1st	1st%
Total	16	63	768	12.2	2	37	5	268	111	7.9	36	57.1
vs. Playoff	3	14	167	11.9	0	33	2	82	23	6.1	6	42.9
vs. Non-playoff	13	49	601	12.3	2	37	3	186	88	8.5	30	61.2
vs. Own Division	8	30	362	12.1	1	37	2	147	48	7.2	18	60.0
Home	8	38	456	12.0	2	37	3	187	58	7.1	20	52.6
Away	8	25	312	12.5	0	27	2	81	53	9.2	16	64.0
Games 1-8	8	28	339	12.1	1	33	2	92	56	8.8	17	60.7
Games 9-16	8	35	429	12.3	1	37	3	176	55	7.2	19	54.3
September	4	15	185	12.3	0	33	1	64	32	8.1	9	60.0
October	4	13	154	11.8	1	33	1	28	24	9.7	8	61.5
November	4	18	222	12.3	0	25	1	67	26	8.6	12	66.7
December	4	17	207	12.2	1	37	2	109	29	5.8	7	41.2
Grass	4	10	123	12.3	0	21	0	26	23	9.7	7	70.0
Turf	12	53	645	12.2	2	37	5	242	88	7.6	29	54.7
Indoor	2	8	98	12.3	0	27	1	24	20	9.3	4	50.0
Outdoor	14	55	670	12.2	2	37	4	244	93	7.7	32	58.2
1st Half	-	35	417	11.9	1	33	2	132	60	8.1	19	54.3
2nd Half/OT	-	28	351	12.5	1	37	3	136	51	7.7	17	60.7
Last 2 Min. Half	-	11	133	12.1	0	20	0	24	20	9.9	8	72.7
4th qtr, +/-7 pts	-	4	69	17.3	1	37	1	42	9	6.8	3	75.0
Winning	-	19	217	11.4	0	21	0	52	31	8.7	13	68.4
Tied	-	15	167	11.1	1	33	1	26	30	9.4	7	46.7
Trailing	-	29	384	13.2	1	37	4	190	50	6.7	16	55.2

	Rec	Yds	Avg	TD	Lg	Big	YAC	Trgt	Y@C	1st	1st%
Inside 20	1	12	12.0	0	12	0	8	6	4.0	1	100.0
Inside 10	0	0	-	0	0	0	0	2	-	0	-
1st Down	26	333	12.8	1	33	4	119	42	8.2	11	42.3
2nd Down	21	267	12.7	1	37	1	110	37	7.5	13	61.9
3rd Down Overall	14	136	9.7	0	21	0	35	30	7.2	10	71.4
3rd D 0-2 to Go	2	23	11.5	0	21	0	12	4	5.5	2	100.0
3rd D 3-7 to Go	3	27	9.0	0	13	0	6	10	7.0	3	100.0
3rd D 8+ to Go	9	86	9.6	0	20	0	17	16	7.7	5	55.6
4th Down	2	32	16.0	0	18	0	4	2	14.0	2	100.0
Rec Behind Line	1	-1	-1.0	0	0	0	4	4	-5.0	0	-
1-10 yds	44	427	9.7	1	37	1	202	62	5.1	18	40.9
11-20 yds	16	284	17.8	0	33	2	57	36	14.2	16	100.0
21-30 yds	2	58	29.0	1	33	2	5	5	26.5	2	100.0
31+	0	0	-	0	0	0	0	4	-	0	-
Left Sideline	11	137	12.5	1	33	1	26	17	10.1	7	63.6
Left Side	17	243	14.3	1	37	2	106	22	8.1	10	58.8
Middle	8	116	14.5	0	27	1	36	14	10.0	6	75.0
Right Side	19	178	9.4	0	21	0	72	39	5.6	9	47.4
Right Sideline	8	94	11.8	0	25	1	28	19	8.3	4	50.0
Shotgun	0	0	-	0	0	0	0	0	-	0	-
2 Wide Receivers	29	366	12.6	1	33	3	131	52	8.1	15	51.7
3 Wide Receivers	25	308	12.3	1	37	2	109	40	8.0	15	60.0
4+ Wide Receivers	9	94	10.4	0	16	0	28	19	7.3	6	66.7

1995 Incompletions

Type	Num	%of Inc	%of Att
Pass Dropped	8	16.7	7.2
Poor Throw	23	47.9	20.7
Pass Defensed	13	27.1	11.7
Pass Hit at Line	2	4.2	1.8
Other	2	4.2	1.8
Total	48	100.0	43.2

Game Logs (1-8)

Date	Opp	Result	Rush	Yds	Rec	Yds	Trgt	F-L	TD
09/03	TB	L 6-21	0	0	4	28	7	0-0	0
09/10	@Ari	W 31-19	0	0	2	26	6	0-0	0
09/17	SD	L 21-27	0	0	3	49	8	1-1	0
09/24	@Oak	L 17-48	0	0	6	82	11	0-0	0
10/01	@NO	W 15-10	0	0	4	43	7	0-0	0
10/08	Was	W 37-34	0	0	2	21	4	0-0	0
10/15	@NYN	W 17-14	0	0	2	20	5	0-0	0
10/29	StL	W 20-9	1	-2	5	70	8	0-0	0

Game Logs (9-16)

Date	Opp	Result	Rush	Yds	Rec	Yds	Trgt	F-L	TD
11/06	@Dal	L 12-34	0	0	5	71	7	0-0	0
11/12	Den	W 31-13	0	0	7	79	10	0-0	0
11/19	NYN	W 28-19	0	0	4	57	4	0-0	0
11/26	@Was	W 14-7	0	0	2	15	5	0-0	0
12/03	@Sea	L 14-26	0	0	4	55	11	0-0	0
12/10	Dal	W 20-17	0	0	6	47	8	0-0	0
12/17	Ari	W 21-20	0	0	7	105	9	1-1	1
12/24	@Chi	L 14-20	0	0	1	1	1	0-0	0

Harvey Williams
Oakland Raiders — RB

1995 Rushing and Receiving Splits

	G	Rush	Yds	Avg	Lg	TD	1st	Stf	YdL	Rec	Yds	Avg	TD		Rush	Yds	Avg	Lg	TD	1st	Stf	YdL	Rec	Yds	Avg	TD
Total	16	255	1114	4.4	60	9	59	22	47	54	375	6.9	0	Inside 20	50	129	2.6	9	8	15	2	4	2	12	6.0	0
vs. Playoff	8	113	392	3.5	60	5	23	15	32	33	240	7.3	0	Inside 10	28	77	2.8	8	8	10	0	0	0	0	-	0
vs. Non-playoff	8	142	722	5.1	37	4	36	7	15	21	135	6.4	0	1st Down	143	559	3.9	37	3	16	13	29	24	168	7.0	0
vs. Own Division	8	122	550	4.5	60	3	26	17	39	26	165	6.3	0	2nd Down	87	465	5.3	60	4	26	9	18	18	133	7.4	0
Home	8	114	464	4.1	37	4	26	10	20	29	214	7.4	0	3rd Down Overall	21	84	4.0	29	2	13	0	0	12	74	6.2	0
Away	8	141	650	4.6	60	5	33	12	27	25	161	6.4	0	3rd D 0-2 to Go	16	34	2.1	7	2	11	0	0	2	5	2.5	0
Games 1-8	8	122	548	4.5	37	6	27	10	17	21	166	7.9	0	3rd D 3-7 to Go	1	6	6.0	6	0	1	0	0	7	42	6.0	0
Games 9-16	8	133	566	4.3	60	3	32	12	30	33	209	6.3	0	3rd D 8+ to Go	4	44	11.0	29	0	1	0	0	3	27	9.0	0
September	4	69	267	3.9	23	4	16	4	7	12	111	9.3	0	4th Down	4	6	1.5	2	0	4	0	0	0	0	-	0
October	4	53	281	5.3	37	2	11	6	10	9	55	6.1	0	Left Sideline	16	118	7.4	30	0	6	1	1	8	73	9.1	0
November	4	80	379	4.7	60	3	22	6	16	19	137	7.2	0	Left Side	37	181	4.9	29	3	9	8	17	19	125	6.6	0
December	4	53	187	3.5	15	0	10	6	14	14	72	5.1	0	Middle	127	477	3.8	60	4	30	10	20	7	49	7.0	0
Grass	12	178	731	4.1	60	6	37	19	42	43	308	7.2	0	Right Side	57	259	4.5	23	2	11	2	4	10	47	4.7	0
Turf	4	77	383	5.0	29	3	22	3	5	11	67	6.1	0	Right Sideline	18	79	4.4	10	0	3	1	5	10	81	8.1	0
Indoor	1	12	67	5.6	14	0	4	0	0	4	20	5.0	0	Shotgun	0	0	-	0	0	0	0	0	0	0	-	0
Outdoor	15	243	1047	4.3	60	9	55	22	47	50	355	7.1	0	2 Wide Receivers	138	552	4.0	30	2	20	14	33	19	140	7.4	0
1st Half	-	146	543	3.7	37	6	31	12	29	29	204	7.0	0	3 Wide Receivers	52	277	5.3	37	1	12	4	4	31	186	6.0	0
2nd Half/OT	-	109	571	5.2	60	3	28	10	18	25	171	6.8	0	4+ Wide Receivers	1	2	2.0	2	0	0	0	0	3	39	13.0	0
Last 2 Min. Half	-	9	32	3.6	9	2	4	0	0	12	122	10.2	0	Carries 1-5	80	275	3.4	16	0	10	9	18	0	0	-	0
4th qtr. +/-7 pts	-	18	120	6.7	60	1	5	0	0	4	32	8.0	0	Carries 6-10	71	313	4.4	37	5	22	4	9	0	0	-	0
Winning	-	91	461	5.1	37	3	23	11	22	11	72	6.5	0	Carries 11-15	59	322	5.5	60	3	16	3	9	0	0	-	0
Tied	-	79	280	3.5	15	2	13	5	13	9	85	9.4	0	Carries 16-20	38	163	4.3	21	0	9	5	10	0	0	-	0
Trailing	-	85	373	4.4	60	4	23	6	12	34	218	6.4	0	Carries 21+	7	41	5.9	21	1	1	0	0	0	0	-	0

1995 Incompletions

Type	Num	%of Inc	% Att
Pass Dropped	1	16.7	1.7
Poor Throw	3	50.0	5.0
Pass Defensed	0	0.0	0.0
Pass Hit at Line	1	16.7	1.7
Other	1	16.7	1.7
Total	6	100.0	10.0

Game Logs (1-8)

Date	Opp	Result	Rush	Yds	Rec	Yds	Trgt	F-L	TD
09/03	SD	W 17-7	16	48	4	24	5	0-0	0
09/10	@Was	W 20-8	18	84	2	23	3	0-0	0
09/17	@KC	L 17-23	20	74	2	15	2	1-1	0
09/24	Phi	W 48-17	15	61	4	49	4	0-0	2
10/01	@NYA	W 47-10	20	97	0	0	0	0-0	1
10/08	Sea	W 34-14	19	160	2	16	2	0-0	1
10/16	@Den	L 0-27	6	8	4	9	6	2-1	0
10/22	Ind	W 30-17	8	16	3	30	3	2-1	0

Game Logs (9-16)

Date	Opp	Result	Rush	Yds	Rec	Yds	Trgt	F-L	TD
11/05	@Cin	W 20-17	24	134	3	28	3	0-0	1
11/12	@NYN	W 17-13	21	85	4	19	4	0-0	1
11/19	Dal	L 21-34	15	59	6	43	7	0-0	1
11/27	@SD	L 6-12	20	101	6	47	6	0-0	0
12/03	KC	L 23-29	7	5	2	14	2	0-0	0
12/10	Pit	L 10-29	12	28	6	18	7	0-0	0
12/17	@Sea	L 10-44	12	67	4	20	4	0-0	0
12/24	Den	L 28-31	22	87	2	20	2	0-0	0

Kevin Williams
Dallas Cowboys — KR

1995 Receiving Splits

	G	Rec	Yds	Avg	TD	Lg	Big	YAC	Trgt	Y@C	1st	1st%		Rec	Yds	Avg	TD	Lg	Big	YAC	Trgt	Y@C	1st	1st%
Total	16	38	613	16.1	2	48	9	166	67	11.8	32	84.2	Inside 20	0	0	-	0	0	0	0	3	-	0	
vs. Playoff	7	9	115	12.8	0	30	1	21	17	10.4	7	77.8	Inside 10	0	0	-	0	0	0	0	2	-	0	
vs. Non-playoff	9	29	498	17.2	2	48	8	145	50	12.2	25	86.2	1st Down	14	285	20.4	2	48	5	93	24	13.7	14	100.0
vs. Own Division	8	30	517	17.2	2	48	8	151	51	12.2	26	86.7	2nd Down	12	158	13.2	0	30	1	18	21	11.7	9	75.0
Home	8	20	258	12.9	0	26	3	70	34	9.4	15	75.0	3rd Down Overall	12	170	14.2	0	32	3	55	22	9.6	9	75.0
Away	8	18	355	19.7	2	48	6	96	33	14.4	17	94.4	3rd D 0-2 to Go	0	0	-	0	0	0	0	0	-	0	
Games 1-8	8	16	220	13.8	0	38	3	63	28	9.8	12	75.0	3rd D 3-7 to Go	8	109	13.6	0	32	2	42	15	8.4	6	75.0
Games 9-16	8	22	393	17.9	2	48	6	103	39	13.2	20	90.9	3rd D 8+ to Go	4	61	15.3	0	30	1	13	7	12.0	3	75.0
September	4	6	71	11.8	0	25	1	33	11	6.3	4	66.7	4th Down	0	0	-	0	0	0	0	0	-	0	
October	4	10	149	14.9	0	38	2	30	17	11.9	8	80.0	Rec Behind Line	0	0	-	0	0	0	0	0	-	0	
November	4	3	32	10.7	0	12	0	4	7	9.3	2	66.7	1-10 yds	24	280	11.7	1	25	3	100	39	7.5	18	75.0
December	4	19	361	19.0	2	48	6	99	32	13.8	18	94.7	11-20 yds	8	132	16.5	0	26	1	18	16	14.3	8	100.0
Grass	4	15	308	20.5	2	48	6	70	25	15.9	14	93.3	21-30 yds	6	201	33.5	1	48	5	48	8	25.5	6	100.0
Turf	12	23	305	13.3	0	26	3	96	42	9.1	18	78.3	31+	0	0	-	0	0	0	0	0	-	0	
Indoor	2	2	26	13.0	0	16	0	12	4	7.0	2	100.0	Left Sideline	4	84	21.0	1	38	2	24	7	15.0	4	100.0
Outdoor	14	36	587	16.3	2	48	9	154	63	12.0	30	83.3	Left Side	7	142	20.3	1	48	2	45	17	13.9	6	85.7
1st Half	-	15	243	16.2	2	48	4	73	30	11.3	11	73.3	Middle	8	130	16.3	0	30	1	34	13	12.0	6	75.0
2nd Half/OT	-	23	370	16.1	0	38	5	93	37	12.0	21	91.3	Right Side	11	144	13.1	0	25	2	53	17	8.3	10	90.9
Last 2 Min. Half	-	4	51	12.8	0	23	0	5	12	11.5	3	75.0	Right Sideline	8	113	14.1	0	32	2	10	13	12.9	6	75.0
4th qtr. +/-7 pts	-	4	60	15.0	0	26	1	18	11	10.5	4	100.0	Shotgun	0	0	-	0	0	0	0	0	-	0	
Winning	-	17	291	17.1	1	48	4	81	28	12.4	15	88.2	2 Wide Receivers	19	358	18.8	2	48	7	101	24	13.5	18	94.7
Tied	-	9	124	13.8	1	30	2	24	12	11.1	6	66.7	3 Wide Receivers	17	235	13.8	0	30	2	63	39	10.1	13	76.5
Trailing	-	12	198	16.5	0	38	3	61	27	11.7	11	91.7	4+ Wide Receivers	2	20	10.0	0	15	0	2	4	9.0	1	50.0

1995 Incompletions

Type	Num	%of Inc	%of Att
Pass Dropped	4	13.8	6.0
Poor Throw	15	51.7	22.4
Pass Defensed	6	20.7	9.0
Pass Hit at Line	0	0.0	0.0
Other	4	13.8	6.0
Total	29	100.0	43.3

Game Logs (1-8)

Date	Opp	Result	Rush	Yds	Rec	Yds	Trgt	F-L	TD
09/04	@NYN	W 35-0	1	12	1	21	1	0-0	0
09/10	Den	W 31-21	2	9	1	1	2	0-0	0
09/17	@Min	W 34-21	0	0	0	0	2	0-0	0
09/24	Ari	W 34-20	1	-7	4	49	6	0-0	0
10/01	@Was	L 23-27	1	12	4	66	9	0-0	0
10/08	GB	W 34-24	0	0	2	21	2	1-0	0
10/15	@SD	W 23-9	0	0	2	39	4	0-0	0
10/29	@Atl	W 28-13	0	0	2	26	2	0-0	0

Game Logs (9-16)

Date	Opp	Result	Rush	Yds	Rec	Yds	Trgt	F-L	TD
11/06	Phi	W 34-12	1	-1	2	20	3	1-0	0
11/12	SF	L 20-38	0	0	1	12	3	0-0	0
11/19	@Oak	W 34-21	0	0	0	0	1	0-0	0
11/23	KC	W 24-12	1	7	0	0	0	0-0	0
12/03	Was	L 17-24	0	0	5	73	7	0-0	0
12/10	@Phi	L 17-20	0	0	0	3	0	0-0	0
12/17	NYN	W 21-20	0	0	5	85	11	0-0	0
12/25	@Ari	W 37-13	3	21	9	203	11	1-1	2

Charles Wilson

1995 Receiving Splits

	G	Rec	Yds	Avg	TD	Lg	Big	YAC	Trgt	Y@C	1st	1st%
Total	15	41	484	11.8	4	24	0	83	91	9.8	31	75.6
vs. Playoff	7	22	257	11.7	2	24	0	58	39	9.0	16	72.7
vs. Non-playoff	8	19	227	11.9	2	23	0	25	52	10.6	15	78.9
vs. Own Division	7	21	252	12.0	2	24	0	61	36	9.1	16	76.2
Home	8	27	353	13.1	3	24	0	71	52	10.4	22	81.5
Away	7	14	131	9.4	1	17	0	12	39	8.5	9	64.3
Games 1-8	8	25	282	11.3	3	21	0	45	52	9.5	20	80.0
Games 9-16	7	16	202	12.6	1	24	0	38	39	10.3	11	68.8
September	4	14	148	10.6	3	19	0	26	26	8.7	11	78.6
October	5	14	167	11.9	0	21	0	26	31	10.1	12	85.7
November	3	8	111	13.9	0	24	0	30	19	10.1	5	62.5
December	3	5	58	11.6	0	23	0	1	15	11.4	3	60.0
Grass	2	4	27	6.8	1	12	0	0	13	6.8	3	75.0
Turf	13	37	457	12.4	3	24	0	83	78	10.1	28	75.7
Outdoor	4	32	397	12.4	3	24	0	72	69	10.2	26	81.3
Indoor	11	9	87	9.7	0	16	0	11	22	8.4	5	55.6
1st Half	-	17	185	10.9	2	24	0	36	43	8.8	14	82.4
2nd Half/OT	-	24	299	12.5	2	23	0	47	48	10.5	17	70.8
Last 2 Min. Half	-	3	42	14.0	1	20	0	7	9	11.7	3	100.0
4th qtr. +/-7 pts	-	6	63	10.5	0	19	0	21	9	7.0	3	50.0
Winning	-	10	122	12.2	1	19	0	26	21	9.6	7	70.0
Tied	-	9	94	10.4	1	17	0	12	12	9.1	8	88.9
Trailing	-	22	268	12.2	2	24	0	45	58	10.1	16	72.7

	Rec	Yds	Avg	TD	Lg	Big	YAC	Trgt	Y@C	1st	1st%
Inside 20	3	26	8.7	3	15	0	0	8	8.7	3	100.0
Inside 10	2	11	5.5	2	6	0	0	3	5.5	2	100.0
1st Down	15	184	12.3	1	24	0	29	32	10.3	9	60.0
2nd Down	13	145	11.2	0	20	0	21	25	9.5	9	69.2
3rd Down Overall	12	150	12.5	3	21	0	33	31	9.8	12	100.0
3rd D 0-2 to Go	1	16	16.0	0	16	0	5	4	11.0	1	100.0
3rd D 3-7 to Go	6	58	9.7	3	19	0	16	15	7.0	6	100.0
3rd D 8+ to Go	5	76	15.2	0	21	0	12	12	12.8	5	100.0
4th Down	1	5	5.0	0	5	0	0	3	5.0	1	100.0
Rec Behind Line	0	0	-	0	0	0	0	3	-	0	-
1-10 yds	27	248	9.2	2	19	0	48	43	7.4	17	63.0
11-20 yds	13	213	16.4	1	24	0	35	31	13.7	13	100.0
21-30 yds	1	23	23.0	0	23	0	0	8	23.0	1	100.0
31+	0	0	-	0	0	0	0	6	-	0	-
Left Sideline	9	106	11.8	1	23	0	3	20	11.4	5	55.6
Left Side	6	62	10.3	0	16	0	6	21	9.3	5	83.3
Middle	5	48	9.6	1	17	0	8	10	8.0	4	80.0
Right Side	13	161	12.4	1	24	0	47	22	8.8	10	76.9
Right Sideline	8	107	13.4	1	21	0	19	18	11.0	7	87.5
Shotgun	0	0	-	0	0	0	0	0	-	0	-
2 Wide Receivers	38	452	11.9	3	24	0	81	83	9.8	28	73.7
3 Wide Receivers	3	32	10.7	1	17	0	2	8	10.0	3	100.0
4+ Wide Receivers	0	0	-	0	0	0	0	0	-	0	-

1995 Incompletions

Type	Num	%of Inc	%of Att
Pass Dropped	8	16.0	8.8
Poor Throw	20	40.0	22.0
Pass Defensed	12	24.0	13.2
Pass Hit at Line	3	6.0	3.3
Other	7	14.0	7.7
Total	50	100.0	54.9

Game Logs (1-8)

Date	Opp	Result	Rec	Yds	Trgt	F-L	TD
09/03	@Mia	L 14-52	2	10	4	0-0	1
09/10	Ind	L 24-27	5	60	5	0-0	1
09/17	Jac	W 27-10	5	62	10	0-0	1
09/24	@Atl	L 3-13	2	16	7	0-0	0
10/01	Oak	L 10-47	3	48	6	0-0	0
10/08	@Buf	L 10-29	1	17	4	0-0	0
10/15	@Car	L 15-26	2	17	9	0-0	0
10/22	Mia	W 17-16	5	52	7	0-0	0

Game Logs (9-16)

Date	Opp	Result	Rec	Yds	Trgt	F-L	TD
10/29	@Ind	L 10-17	3	33	5	0-0	0
11/05	NE	L 7-20	1	11	4	0-0	0
11/19	Buf	L 26-28	4	69	7	0-0	0
11/26	@Sea	W 16-10	3	31	8	0-0	0
12/03	StL	L 20-23	3	43	8	0-0	1
12/10	@NE	L 28-31	-	-	-	-	-
12/17	@Hou	L 6-23	1	7	2	0-0	0
12/24	NO	L 0-12	1	8	5	1-0	0

Wade Wilson

1995 Passing Splits

	G	Att	Cm	Pct	Yds	Yd/Att	TD	Int	1st	YAC	Big	Sk	Rtg
Total	7	57	38	66.7	391	6.9	1	3	19	190	3	4	70.1
vs. Playoff	2	26	15	57.7	134	5.2	0	2	6	87	0	2	39.6
vs. Non-playoff	5	31	23	74.2	257	8.3	1	1	13	103	3	2	95.8
vs. Own Division	5	31	23	74.2	257	8.3	1	1	13	103	3	2	95.8
Home	4	26	15	57.7	134	5.2	0	2	6	87	0	2	39.6
Away	3	31	23	74.2	257	8.3	1	1	13	103	3	2	95.8
Games 1-8	4	30	22	73.3	225	7.5	1	1	12	97	2	2	91.7
Games 9-16	3	27	16	59.3	166	6.1	0	2	7	93	1	2	46.2
September	3	1	1	100.0	1	1.0	0	0	0	7	0	0	79.2
October	1	29	21	72.4	224	7.7	1	1	12	90	2	2	91.7
November	2	26	15	57.7	134	5.2	0	2	6	87	0	2	39.6
December	1	1	1	100.0	32	32.0	0	0	1	6	1	0	118.8
Grass	2	30	22	73.3	256	8.5	1	1	13	96	3	2	96.0
Turf	5	27	16	59.3	135	5.0	0	2	6	94	0	2	41.4
Indoor	0	0	0	-	0	-	0	0	0	0	0	0	-
Outdoor	7	57	38	66.7	391	6.9	1	3	19	190	3	4	70.1
1st Half	-	22	13	59.1	121	5.5	1	1	6	89	0	3	55.3
2nd Half/OT	-	35	25	71.4	270	7.7	1	2	13	101	3	1	79.5
Last 2 Min. Half	-	10	4	40.0	38	3.8	0	2	2	22	0	1	11.7
4th qtr. +/-7 pts	-	9	6	66.7	56	6.2	0	1	3	32	0	0	44.0
Winning	-	2	2	100.0	33	16.5	0	0	1	10	1	0	118.8
Tied	-	7	4	57.1	41	5.9	0	0	2	30	0	1	74.1
Trailing	-	48	32	66.7	317	6.6	1	3	16	147	2	3	66.1

	Att	Cm	Pct	Yds	Yd/Att	TD	Int	1st	YAC	Big	Sk	Rtg
Inside 20	5	2	40.0	4	0.8	0	0	0	6	0	0	47.9
Inside 10	3	1	33.3	0	0.0	0	0	0	4	0	0	42.4
1st Down	23	14	60.9	177	7.7	1	1	7	66	2	2	81.3
2nd Down	18	17	94.4	136	7.6	0	0	9	90	0	1	98.1
3rd Down Overall	15	7	46.7	78	5.2	0	1	3	34	1	1	34.9
3rd D 0-5 to Go	4	1	25.0	1	0.3	0	1	0	7	0	0	0.0
3rd D 6+ to Go	11	6	54.5	77	7.0	0	0	3	27	1	1	76.7
4th Down	1	0	0.0	0	0.0	0	1	0	0	0	0	0.0
Rec Behind Line	15	12	80.0	70	4.7	0	0	3	119	0	0	86.1
1-10 yds	26	17	65.4	130	5.0	0	1	7	47	0	0	61.4
11-20 yds	8	6	75.0	93	11.6	0	0	6	9	0	0	113.0
21-30 yds	4	3	75.0	98	24.5	1	0	3	15	3	0	156.3
31+	4	0	0.0	0	0.0	0	2	0	0	0	0	0.0
Left Sideline	9	6	66.7	81	9.0	0	0	4	13	1	0	95.1
Left Side	9	6	66.7	56	6.2	1	0	1	24	1	0	120.6
Middle	13	5	38.5	59	4.5	0	0	3	27	0	4	53.0
Right Side	15	13	86.7	133	8.9	0	2	8	94	0	0	64.0
Right Sideline	11	8	72.7	62	5.6	0	1	3	32	1	0	48.3
2 Wide Receivers	26	21	80.8	265	10.2	1	1	13	108	3	3	105.9
3+ WR	28	14	50.0	104	3.7	0	2	4	52	0	1	29.5
Attempts 1-10	22	15	68.2	152	6.9	0	0	8	100	1	0	87.7
Attempts 11-20	20	13	65.0	155	7.8	1	1	7	31	2	0	84.4
Attempts 21+	15	10	66.7	84	5.6	0	2	4	59	0	0	41.4

1995 Incompletions

Type	Num	% of Inc	% of Att
Pass Dropped	1	5.3	1.8
Poor Throw	7	36.8	12.3
Pass Defensed	3	15.8	5.3
Pass Hit at Line	3	15.8	5.3
Other	5	26.3	8.8
Total	19	100.0	33.3

Game Logs (1-8)

Date	Opp	Result	Att	Cm	Pct	Yds	TD	Int	Lg	Sk	F-L
09/04	@NYN	W 35-0	1	1	100.0	1	0	0	1	0	1-0
09/10	Den	W 31-21	0	0	-	0	0	0	0	0	0-0
09/17	@Min	W 23-17	-	-	-	-	-	-	-	-	-
09/24	Ari	W 34-20	0	0	-	0	0	0	0	0	0-0
10/01	@Was	L 23-27	29	21	72.4	224	1	1	38	2	0-0
10/08	GB	W 34-24	-	-	-	-	-	-	-	-	-
10/15	@SD	W 23-9	-	-	-	-	-	-	-	-	-
10/29	@Atl	W 28-13	-	-	-	-	-	-	-	-	-

Game Logs (9-16)

Date	Opp	Result	Att	Cm	Pct	Yds	TD	Int	Lg	Sk	F-L
11/06	Phi	W 34-12	0	0	-	0	0	0	0	0	0-0
11/12	SF	L 20-38	26	15	57.7	134	0	2	20	2	0-0
11/19	@Oak	W 34-21	-	-	-	-	-	-	-	-	-
11/23	KC	W 24-12	-	-	-	-	-	-	-	-	-
12/03	Was	L 17-24	-	-	-	-	-	-	-	-	-
12/10	@Phi	L 17-20	-	-	-	-	-	-	-	-	-
12/17	NYN	W 21-20	-	-	-	-	-	-	-	-	-
12/25	@Ari	W 37-13	1	1	100.0	32	0	0	32	0	0-0

Frank Wycheck

1995 Receiving Splits

	G	Rec	Yds	Avg	TD	Lg	Big	YAC	Trgt	Y@C	1st	1st%
Total	16	40	471	11.8	1	36	4	266	51	5.1	21	52.5
vs. Playoff	5	18	237	13.2	1	36	3	127	24	6.1	7	38.9
vs. Non-playoff	11	22	234	10.6	0	33	1	139	27	4.3	14	63.6
vs. Own Division	8	12	155	12.9	0	33	2	70	17	7.1	6	50.0
Home	8	22	262	11.9	0	33	2	147	27	5.2	14	63.6
Away	8	18	209	11.6	1	36	2	119	24	5.0	7	38.9
Games 1-8	8	11	91	8.3	0	16	0	74	12	1.5	4	36.4
Games 9-16	8	29	380	13.1	1	36	4	192	39	6.5	17	58.6
September	4	3	31	10.3	0	13	0	30	4	0.3	1	33.3
October	4	8	60	7.5	0	16	0	44	8	2.0	3	37.5
November	4	13	152	11.7	0	33	1	57	16	7.3	8	61.5
December	4	16	228	14.3	1	36	3	135	23	5.8	9	56.3
Grass	4	8	71	8.9	0	18	0	22	9	6.1	2	25.0
Turf	12	32	400	12.5	1	36	4	244	42	4.9	19	59.4
Indoor	9	24	278	11.6	0	33	2	161	29	4.9	15	62.5
Outdoor	7	16	193	12.1	1	36	2	105	22	5.5	6	37.5
1st Half	-	18	202	11.2	0	30	1	139	22	3.5	10	55.6
2nd Half/OT	-	22	269	12.2	1	36	3	127	29	6.5	11	50.0
Last 2 Min. Half	-	4	61	15.3	0	18	0	17	4	11.0	3	75.0
4th qtr, +/-7 pts	-	4	44	11.0	0	18	0	14	6	7.5	1	25.0
Winning	-	13	137	10.5	1	36	1	101	18	2.8	7	53.8
Tied	-	7	58	8.3	0	14	0	53	11	0.7	3	42.9
Trailing	-	20	276	13.8	0	33	3	112	22	8.2	11	55.0

	Rec	Yds	Avg	TD	Lg	Big	YAC	Trgt	Y@C	1st	1st%
Inside 20	2	20	10.0	0	18	0		18	2	1.0	1	50.0
Inside 10	0	0	-	0	0	0		0	0	-	0	
1st Down	21	223	10.6	0	29	1	127	27	4.6	8	38.1
2nd Down	10	93	9.3	0	18	0	58	10	3.5	7	70.0
3rd Down Overall	9	155	17.2	0	36	3	81	14	8.2	6	66.7
3rd D 0-2 to Go	1	3	3.0	0	4	0			1	1.0	1	100.0
3rd D 3-7 to Go	3	49	16.3	0	36	1	43	7	2.0	2	66.7
3rd D 8+ to Go	5	103	20.6	0	33	2	36	6	13.4	3	60.0
4th Down	0	0	-	0	0	0		0	0	-	0	
Rec Behind Line	9	47	5.2	0	12	0	67	10	-2.2	1	11.1
1-10 yds	21	219	10.4	0	36	1	154	27	3.1	12	57.1
11-20 yds	9	172	19.1	0	30	2	35	12	15.2	7	77.8
21-30 yds	1	33	33.0	0	33	1	10	2	23.0	1	100.0
31+	0	0	-	0	0	0		0	0	-	0	
Left Sideline	9	112	12.4	0	18	0	63	12	5.4	5	55.6
Left Side	8	78	9.8	0	16	0	52	11	3.3	5	62.5
Middle	5	146	29.2	1	36	4	65	6	16.2	4	80.0
Right Side	10	79	7.9	0	20	0	53	13	2.6	5	50.0
Right Sideline	8	56	7.0	0	16	0	33	9	2.9	2	25.0
Shotgun	0	0	-	0	0	0		0	0	-	0	
2 Wide Receivers	17	154	9.1	0	14	0	115	20	2.3	7	41.2
3 Wide Receivers	23	317	13.8	1	36	4	151	30	7.2	14	60.9
4+ Wide Receivers	0	0	-	0	0	0		0	0	-	0	

1995 Incompletions

Type	Num	%of Inc	%of Att
Pass Dropped	2	18.2	3.9
Poor Throw	5	45.5	9.8
Pass Defensed	1	9.1	2.0
Pass Hit at Line	1	9.1	2.0
Other	2	18.2	3.9
Total	11	100.0	21.6

Game Logs (1-8)

Date	Opp	Result	Rush	Yds	Rec	Yds	Trgt	F-L	TD
09/03	@Jac	W 10-3	0	0	1	9	1	0-0	0
09/10	Pit	L 17-34	0	0	0	0	0	0-0	0
09/17	Cle	L 7-14	0	0	2	22	3	0-0	0
09/24	@Cin	W 38-28	0	0	0	0	0	0-0	0
10/01	Jac	L 16-17	0	0	2	17	2	0-0	0
10/08	@Min	L 17-23	0	0	2	16	2	0-0	0
10/22	@Chi	L 32-35	1	1	0	0	0	0-0	1
10/29	TB	W 19-7	0	0	4	27	4	0-0	0

Game Logs (9-16)

Date	Opp	Result	Rush	Yds	Rec	Yds	Trgt	F-L	TD
11/05	@Cle	W 37-10	0	0	2	18	3	0-0	0
11/12	Cin	L 25-32	0	0	2	39	3	0-0	0
11/19	@KC	L 13-20	0	0	5	44	5	0-0	0
11/26	Den	W 42-33	0	0	4	51	5	0-0	0
12/03	@Pit	L 7-21	0	0	3	50	5	0-0	0
12/10	Det	L 17-24	0	0	5	71	6	0-0	0
12/17	NYA	W 23-6	0	0	3	35	4	0-0	0
12/24	@Buf	W 28-17	0	0	5	72	8	0-0	1

Steve Young

1995 Passing Splits

	G	Att	Cm	Pct	Yds	Yd/Att	TD	Int	1st	YAC	Big	Sk	Rtg
Total	11	447	299	66.9	3200	7.2	20	11	159	1597	20	25	92.3
vs. Playoff	5	212	141	66.5	1467	6.9	6	5	73	800	11	13	85.9
vs. Non-playoff	6	235	158	67.2	1733	7.4	14	6	86	797	9	12	98.1
vs. Own Division	5	188	131	69.7	1469	7.8	10	5	74	801	9	10	99.4
Home	6	247	161	65.2	1711	6.9	13	7	83	868	8	8	91.0
Away	5	200	138	69.0	1489	7.4	7	4	76	729	12	17	93.9
Games 1-8	6	233	158	67.8	1654	7.1	12	4	84	840	9	15	98.2
Games 9-16	5	214	141	65.9	1546	7.2	8	7	75	757	11	10	85.9
September	4	153	104	68.0	1223	8.0	10	3	57	645	9	9	105.7
October	2	80	54	67.5	431	5.4	2	1	27	195	0	6	83.9
November	1	32	21	65.6	226	7.1	2	2	12	114	0	9	91.4
December	4	182	120	65.9	1320	7.3	5	5	63	643	11	10	85.0
Grass	7	292	192	65.8	2047	7.0	15	8	103	1002	10	11	91.8
Turf	4	155	107	69.0	1153	7.4	5	3	56	595	10	14	93.3
Indoor	4	155	107	69.0	1153	7.4	5	3	56	595	10	14	93.3
Outdoor	7	292	192	65.8	2047	7.0	15	8	103	1002	10	11	91.8
1st Half	-	243	161	66.3	1876	7.7	14	7	90	942	13	16	96.7
2nd Half/OT	-	204	138	67.6	1324	6.5	4	4	69	655	7	10	87.1
Last 2 Min. Half	-	72	47	65.3	425	5.9	4	1	23	198	0	2	93.8
4th qtr, +/-7 pts	-	62	41	66.1	407	6.6	1	1	23	156	3	3	83.2
Winning	-	246	163	66.3	1628	6.6	10	6	82	816	7	14	88.3
Tied	-	100	64	64.0	777	7.8	5	3	37	440	7	9	92.0
Trailing	-	101	72	71.3	795	7.9	5	2	40	341	6	5	102.5

	Att	Cm	Pct	Yds	Yd/Att	TD	Int	1st	YAC	Big	Sk	Rtg
Inside 20	57	31	54.4	246	4.3	13	2	22		0	4	90.4
Inside 10	33	15	45.5	67	2.0	8	1	9	49	0	4	79.4
1st Down	186	117	62.9	1236	6.6	7	3	40	613	8	6	88.0
2nd Down	150	100	70.7	1132	7.5	5	4	60	567	6	8	92.4
3rd Down Overall	104	71	68.3	761	7.3	7	3	54	366	5	11	99.9
3rd D 0-5 to Go	46	31	67.4	235	5.1	4	1	29	114	0	5	99.5
3rd D 6+ to Go	58	40	69.0	526	9.1	3	2	25	252	5	6	100.2
4th Down	7	5	71.4	71	10.1	1	1	5	51	1	0	103.9
Rec Behind Line	112	77	68.8	448	4.0	4	1	23	604	0	0	84.2
1-10 yds	233	167	71.7	1449	6.2	8	5	83	707	2	0	90.2
11-20 yds	62	38	61.3	688	11.1	4	5	36	155	3	0	87.3
21-30 yds	23	11	47.8	342	14.9	3	0	11	66	8	0	133.6
31+	17	6	35.3	273	16.1	1	0	6	65	6	0	103.2
Left Sideline	126	90	71.4	947	7.5	5	2	46	478	7	0	99.5
Left Side	127	85	66.9	810	6.4	3	4	43	473	1	1	79.2
Middle	88	55	62.5	635	7.2	7	4	28	276	4	17	91.8
Right Side	59	44	74.6	482	8.2	5	0	24	215	4	5	126.5
Right Sideline	47	25	53.2	326	6.9	0	1	18	155	2	0	66.4
2 Wide Receivers	263	170	64.6	1842	7.0	9	9	92	867	11	11	82.3
3+ WR	176	124	70.5	1316	7.5	8	2	63	688	8	13	102.4
Attempts 1-10	110	74	67.3	819	7.4	6	3	43	494	6	0	96.0
Attempts 11-20	110	72	65.5	915	8.3	4	4	38	405	7	0	88.3
Attempts 21+	227	153	67.4	1466	6.5	10	4	78	698	7	0	92.5

1995 Incompletions

Type	Num	% of Inc	% of Att
Pass Dropped	24	16.2	5.4
Poor Throw	52	35.1	11.6
Pass Defensed	23	15.5	5.1
Pass Hit at Line	11	7.4	2.5
Other	38	25.7	8.5
Total	148	100.0	33.1

Game Logs (1-8)

Date	Opp	Result	Att	Cm	Pct	Yds	TD	Int	Lg	Sk	F-L
09/03	@NO	W 24-22	27	21	77.8	260	2	0	50	5	1-1
09/10	Atl	W 41-10	40	27	67.5	331	3	1	54	0	0-0
09/17	NE	W 28-3	24	17	70.8	284	3	1	23	3	0-0
09/25	@Det	L 24-27	44	29	61.4	348	2	1	39	1	0-0
10/01	NYN	W 20-6	40	26	65.0	202	1	0	21	0	0-0
10/15	@Ind	L 17-18	40	28	70.0	229	1	1	21	6	1-1
10/22	StL	W 44-10	-								
10/29	NO	L 7-11	-								

Game Logs (9-16)

Date	Opp	Result	Att	Cm	Pct	Yds	TD	Int	Lg	Sk	F-L
11/05	Car	L 7-13	-								
11/12	@Dal	W 38-20	-								
11/20	@Mia	W 44-20	-								
11/26	StL	W 41-13	32	21	65.6	226	3	2	23	0	0-0
12/03	Buf	W 27-17	44	28	63.6	243	0	1	31	4	0-0
12/10	@Car	W 31-10	45	31	68.9	336	2	1	46	3	1-1
12/18	Min	W 37-30	49	30	61.2	425	3	2	52	1	0-0
12/24	@Atl	L 27-28	44	31	70.5	316	0	1	57	2	0-0

Eric Zeier

1995 Passing Splits

	G	Att	Cm	Pct	Yds	Yd/Att	TD	Int	1st	YAC	Big	Sk	Rtg		Att	Cm	Pct	Yds	Yd/Att	TD	Int	1st	YAC	Big	Sk	Rtg
Total	7	161	82	50.9	864	5.4	4	9	42	404	6	15	51.9	Inside 20	18	6	33.3	47	2.6	3	1	5	25	0	1	58.8
vs. Playoff	4	39	18	46.2	127	3.3	1	1	9	112	0	6	52.0	Inside 10	10	2	20.0	5	0.5	2	0	2	1	0	1	79.2
vs. Non-playoff	3	122	64	52.5	737	6.0	3	8	33	292	6	9	51.8	1st Down	53	31	58.5	423	8.0	1	4	16	128	3	5	58.9
vs. Own Division	3	119	61	51.3	650	5.5	2	5	32	288	4	9	55.7	2nd Down	56	28	50.0	201	3.6	1	0	12	150	1	5	64.7
Home	3	64	33	51.6	287	4.5	1	3	15	118	2	5	49.4	3rd Down Overall	45	19	42.2	227	5.0	1	4	12	125	2	3	28.7
Away	4	97	49	50.5	577	5.9	3	6	27	286	4	10	53.5	3rd D 0-5 to Go	14	7	50.0	71	5.1	1	1	5	50	1	0	58.9
Games 1-8	3	56	32	57.1	356	6.4	2	1	16	146	2	2	80.7	3rd D 6+ to Go	31	12	38.7	156	5.0	0	3	7	75	1	3	15.7
Games 9-16	4	105	50	47.6	508	4.8	2	8	26	258	4	13	36.5	4th Down	7	4	57.1	13	1.9	1	1	2	1	0	2	62.2
September	1	0	0	-	0	-	0	0	0	0	0	0	-	Rec Behind Line	26	18	69.2	122	4.7	2	2	5	227	1	0	72.9
October	2	56	32	57.1	356	6.4	1	1	16	146	2	2	80.7	1-10 yds	78	46	59.0	325	4.2	1	2	20	114	0	0	62.2
November	3	83	40	48.2	354	4.3	1	4	20	186	2	9	44.0	11-20 yds	34	14	41.2	223	6.6	1	1	13	33	1	0	61.3
December	1	22	10	45.5	154	7.0	1	4	6	72	4	4	44.7	21-30 yds	9	1	11.1	40	4.4	0	1	1	11	1	0	6.0
Grass	3	64	33	51.6	287	4.5	1	3	15	118	2	5	49.4	31+	14	3	21.4	154	11.0	0	3	3	19	3	0	33.3
Turf	4	97	49	50.5	577	5.9	3	6	27	286	4	10	53.5	Left Sideline	37	15	40.5	105	2.8	0	2	6	33	0	1	25.8
Indoor	2	32	16	50.0	200	6.3	2	4	9	101	2	4	51.0	Left Side	27	16	59.3	172	6.4	1	2	10	124	0	1	59.5
Outdoor	5	129	66	51.2	664	5.1	2	5	33	303	4	11	55.2	Middle	29	14	48.3	232	8.0	1	1	8	152	4	10	72.8
1st Half	-	70	41	58.6	420	6.0	1	1	23	213	3	5	74.7	Right Side	28	20	71.4	172	6.1	2	0	8	47	1	2	111.0
2nd Half/OT	-	91	41	45.1	444	4.9	3	8	19	191	3	10	34.3	Right Sideline	40	17	42.5	183	4.6	0	4	10	48	1	1	17.0
Last 2 Min. Half	-	40	22	55.0	232	5.8	1	2	14	127	1	2	59.6	2 Wide Receivers	34	17	50.0	278	8.2	2	2	11	76	3	3	72.9
4th qtr. +/-7 pts	-	9	4	44.4	40	4.4	1	0	2	11	0	0	94.7	3+ WR	127	65	51.2	586	4.6	2	7	31	328	3	11	46.2
Winning	-	7	2	28.6	17	2.4	0	0	1	4	0	0	39.6	Attempts 1-10	60	32	53.3	303	5.1	2	1	19	207	2	0	71.7
Tied	-	26	16	61.5	147	5.7	1	0	7	78	1	3	89.7	Attempts 11-20	39	21	53.8	226	5.8	1	3	9	75	2	0	47.6
Trailing	-	128	64	50.0	700	5.5	3	9	34	322	5	12	45.1	Attempts 21+	62	29	46.8	335	5.4	1	5	14	122	2	0	35.3

1995 Incompletions

Type	Num	% of Inc	% of Att
Pass Dropped	8	10.1	5.0
Poor Throw	38	48.1	23.6
Pass Defensed	11	13.9	6.8
Pass Hit at Line	5	6.3	3.1
Other	17	21.5	10.6
Total	79	100.0	49.1

Game Logs (1-8)

Date	Opp	Result	Att	Cm	Pct	Yds	TD	Int	Lg	Sk	F-L
09/03	@NE	L 14-17	-	-	-	-	-	-	-	-	-
09/10	TB	W 22-6	-	-	-	-	-	-	-	-	-
09/17	@Hou	W 14-7	-	-	-	-	-	-	-	-	-
09/24	KC	W 35-17	0	0	-	0	0	0	0	0	0-0
10/02	Buf	L 19-22	-	-	-	-	-	-	-	-	-
10/08	@Det	L 20-38	10	6	60.0	46	1	0	17	0	0-0
10/22	Jac	L 15-23	-	-	-	-	-	-	-	-	-
10/29	@Cin	W 29-26	46	26	56.5	310	1	1	59	2	0-0

Game Logs (9-16)

Date	Opp	Result	Att	Cm	Pct	Yds	TD	Int	Lg	Sk	F-L
11/05	Hou	L 10-37	54	28	51.9	273	1	3	40	3	0-0
11/13	@Pit	L 3-20	19	7	36.8	67	0	1	17	4	2-0
11/19	GB	L 20-31	10	5	50.0	14	0	0	5	2	0-0
11/26	Pit	L 17-20	-	-	-	-	-	-	-	-	-
12/03	@SD	L 13-31	-	-	-	-	-	-	-	-	-
12/09	@Min	L 11-27	22	10	45.5	154	1	4	49	4	1-0
12/17	Cin	W 26-10	-	-	-	-	-	-	-	-	-
12/24	@Jac	L 21-24	-	-	-	-	-	-	-	-	-

Defensive Profiles

The following section provides statistical breakdowns and game logs for nearly every significant defensive player in 1995. To be included in this section a defender had to meet two criteria: (1) he had to start 12 games, and (2) he had to register at least 50 tackles (special teams included) OR 4 sacks OR 3 interceptions. In addition, we added the following defenders, three of them Pro Bowlers: Eric Allen, Corey Fuller, Charles Haley, Deion Sanders, Brian Schwartz. That worked out to 216, or about seven defensive players per team.

Many of the statistics used here are STATS exclusives, and the abbreviations might be unfamiliar. Those abbreviations and what they stand for:

G = Games; **Tk** = Tackles; **Ast** = Tackles Assisted; **Yds** = Yards, which refer to stuff yards when appearing after "Stuff," and interception-return yards when appearing after "Int"; **PD** = Passes Defensed; **FF** = Fumbles Forced; **FR** = Fumbles Recovered; **TD** = Touchdowns, and includes all touchdowns scored by the player, including on special teams.

For definitions of statistical categories, please see the Glossary.

Allen Aldridge

Denver Broncos – LB

1995 Defensive Splits

	G	Tk	Ast	Sack	Yds	Stuff	Yds	Int	Yds	PD	TD
Total	16	73	24	1.5	10.5	3.5	6.5	0	0	3	0
vs. Playoff	7	33	8	0.0	0.0	1.5	1.5	0	0	1	0
vs. Non-Playoff	9	40	16	1.5	10.5	2.0	5.0	0	0	2	0
vs. Own Division	8	49	10	1.5	10.5	1.5	1.5	0	0	1	0
Home	8	31	15	0.5	4.5	2.5	2.5	0	0	2	0
Away	8	42	9	1.0	6.0	1.0	4.0	0	0	1	0
Games 1-8	8	31	9	1.5	10.5	1.0	1.0	0	0	1	0
Games 9-16	8	42	15	0.0	0.0	2.5	5.5	0	0	2	0
September	4	7	1	0.0	0.0	0.0	0.0	0	0	0	0
October	4	24	8	1.5	10.5	1.0	1.0	0	0	1	0
November	4	15	10	0.0	0.0	1.5	4.5	0	0	2	0
December	4	27	5	0.0	0.0	1.0	1.0	0	0	0	0
Grass	12	56	17	0.5	4.5	3.0	3.0	0	0	3	0
Turf	4	17	7	1.0	6.0	0.5	3.5	0	0	0	0
Indoor	2	11	4	1.0	6.0	0.5	3.5	0	0	0	0
Outdoor	14	62	20	0.5	4.5	3.0	3.0	0	0	3	0

Game Logs

Date	Opp	Result	Tk	Ast	Sack	Yds	Stuff	Yds	Int	Yds	PD	FF	FR	TD
09/03	Buf	W 22-7	2	0	0.0	0.0	0.0	0.0	0	0	0	0	0	0
09/10	@Dal	L 21-31	1	1	0.0	0.0	0.0	0.0	0	0	0	0	0	0
09/17	Was	W 38-31	1	0	0.0	0.0	0.0	0.0	0	0	0	0	0	0
09/24	@SD	L 6-17	3	0	0.0	0.0	0.0	0.0	0	0	0	0	0	0
10/01	@Sea	L 10-27	6	2	1.0	6.0	0.0	0.0	0	0	0	0	0	0
10/08	@NE	W 37-3	5	1	0.0	0.0	0.0	0.0	0	0	1	0	0	0
10/16	Oak	W 27-0	4	2	0.5	4.5	0.0	0.0	0	0	0	0	0	0
10/22	KC	L 7-21	9	3	0.0	0.0	1.0	1.0	0	0	0	0	0	0
11/05	Ari	W 38-6	2	5	0.0	0.0	1.0	1.0	0	0	1	0	1	0
11/12	@Phi	L 13-31	5	2	0.0	0.0	0.0	0.0	0	0	0	0	0	0
11/19	SD	W 30-27	3	1	0.0	0.0	0.0	0.0	0	0	1	0	0	0
11/26	@Hou	L 33-42	5	2	0.0	0.0	0.5	3.5	0	0	1	0	0	0
12/03	Jac	W 31-23	3	3	0.0	0.0	0.5	0.5	0	0	0	0	0	0
12/10	Sea	L 27-31	7	1	0.0	0.0	0.0	0.0	0	0	0	0	0	0
12/17	@KC	L 17-20	10	1	0.0	0.0	0.5	0.5	0	0	0	0	0	0
12/24	@Oak	W 31-28	7	0	0.0	0.0	0.0	0.0	0	0	0	0	0	0

Brent Alexander

Arizona Cardinals – S

1995 Defensive Splits

	G	Tk	Ast	Sack	Yds	Stuff	Yds	Int	Yds	PD	TD
Total	16	51	18	0.5	4.5	3.0	4.0	2	14	3	0
vs. Playoff	8	28	14	0.5	4.5	2.0	3.0	2	14	3	0
vs. Non-Playoff	8	23	4	0.0	0.0	1.0	1.0	0	0	0	0
vs. Own Division	8	33	8	0.0	0.0	2.0	2.0	1	14	1	0
Home	8	24	15	0.0	0.0	1.5	2.0	0	0	1	0
Away	8	27	3	0.5	4.5	1.5	2.0	2	14	2	0
Games 1-8	8	35	13	0.5	4.5	0.5	1.0	0	0	0	0
Games 9-16	8	16	5	0.0	0.0	2.5	3.0	2	14	3	0
September	4	18	7	0.5	4.5	0.5	1.0	0	0	0	0
October	4	17	6	0.0	0.0	0.0	0.0	0	0	0	0
November	5	6	4	0.0	0.0	1.5	2.0	0	0	1	0
December	3	10	1	0.0	0.0	1.0	1.0	2	14	2	0
Grass	12	32	15	0.0	0.0	1.5	2.0	1	0	2	0
Turf	4	19	3	0.5	4.5	1.5	2.0	1	14	1	0
Indoor	1	5	2	0.5	4.5	0.5	1.0	0	0	0	0
Outdoor	15	46	16	0.0	0.0	2.5	3.0	2	14	3	0

Game Logs

Date	Opp	Result	Tk	Ast	Sack	Yds	Stuff	Yds	Int	Yds	PD	FF	FR	TD
09/03	@Was	L 7-27	6	0	0.0	0.0	0.0	0.0	0	0	0	0	0	0
09/10	Phi	L 19-31	4	5	0.0	0.0	0.0	0.0	0	0	0	0	0	0
09/17	@Det	W 20-17	5	2	0.5	4.5	0.5	1.0	0	0	0	0	0	0
09/24	@Dal	L 20-34	3	0	0.0	0.0	0.0	0.0	0	0	0	0	0	0
10/01	KC	L 3-24	4	3	0.0	0.0	0.0	0.0	0	0	0	0	0	0
10/08	@NYN	L 21-27	6	1	0.0	0.0	0.0	0.0	0	0	0	1	0	0
10/15	Was	W 24-20	2	1	0.0	0.0	0.0	0.0	0	0	0	0	0	0
10/29	Sea	W 20-14	5	1	0.0	0.0	0.0	0.0	0	0	1	0	0	0
11/05	@Den	L 6-38	0	0	0.0	0.0	0.0	0.0	0	0	0	0	0	0
11/12	Min	L 24-30	0	1	0.0	0.0	0.0	0.0	0	0	0	0	0	0
11/19	@Car	L 7-27	0	0	0.0	0.0	0.0	0.0	0	0	0	0	0	0
11/26	Atl	W 40-37	2	3	0.0	0.0	0.5	1.0	0	0	1	0	0	0
11/30	NYN	L 6-10	4	0	0.0	0.0	1.0	1.0	0	0	0	0	0	0
12/09	@SD	L 25-28	2	0	0.0	0.0	0.0	0.0	1	0	1	0	0	0
12/17	@Phi	L 20-21	5	0	0.0	0.0	1.0	1.0	1	14	1	1	0	0
12/25	Dal	L 13-37	3	1	0.0	0.0	0.0	0.0	0	0	0	0	0	0

Eric Allen

New Orleans Saints – CB

1995 Defensive Splits

	G	Tk	Ast	Sack	Yds	Stuff	Yds	Int	Yds	PD	TD
Total	16	44	15	0.0	0.0	0.0	0.0	2	28	6	0
vs. Playoff	8	20	9	0.0	0.0	0.0	0.0	0	0	1	0
vs. Non-Playoff	8	24	6	0.0	0.0	0.0	0.0	2	28	5	0
vs. Own Division	8	26	7	0.0	0.0	0.0	0.0	2	28	3	0
Home	8	19	10	0.0	0.0	0.0	0.0	2	28	4	0
Away	8	25	5	0.0	0.0	0.0	0.0	0	0	2	0
Games 1-8	8	26	9	0.0	0.0	0.0	0.0	0	0	1	0
Games 9-16	8	18	6	0.0	0.0	0.0	0.0	2	28	5	0
September	4	14	7	0.0	0.0	0.0	0.0	0	0	0	0
October	4	12	2	0.0	0.0	0.0	0.0	0	0	1	0
November	4	16	2	0.0	0.0	0.0	0.0	2	28	3	0
December	4	2	4	0.0	0.0	0.0	0.0	0	0	2	0
Grass	3	8	2	0.0	0.0	0.0	0.0	0	0	1	0
Turf	13	36	13	0.0	0.0	0.0	0.0	2	28	5	0
Indoor	10	29	10	0.0	0.0	0.0	0.0	2	28	4	0
Outdoor	6	15	5	0.0	0.0	0.0	0.0	0	0	2	0

Game Logs

Date	Opp	Result	Tk	Ast	Sack	Yds	Stuff	Yds	Int	Yds	PD	FF	FR	TD
09/03	SF	L 22-24	3	2	0.0	0.0	0.0	0.0	0	0	0	0	0	0
09/10	@StL	L 13-17	4	1	0.0	0.0	0.0	0.0	0	0	0	0	0	0
09/17	Atl	L 24-27	4	3	0.0	0.0	0.0	0.0	0	0	0	0	0	0
09/24	@NYN	L 29-45	3	1	0.0	0.0	0.0	0.0	0	0	0	0	0	0
10/01	Phi	L 10-15	2	1	0.0	0.0	0.0	0.0	0	0	0	0	0	0
10/15	Mia	W 33-30	2	1	0.0	0.0	0.0	0.0	0	0	1	0	0	0
10/22	@Car	L 3-20	2	1	0.0	0.0	0.0	0.0	0	0	0	0	0	0
10/29	@SF	W 11-7	4	0	0.0	0.0	0.0	0.0	0	0	0	0	0	0
11/05	StL	W 19-10	4	0	0.0	0.0	0.0	0.0	1	28	1	0	0	0
11/12	Ind	W 17-14	3	1	0.0	0.0	0.0	0.0	0	0	0	0	0	0
11/19	@Min	L 24-43	8	0	0.0	0.0	0.0	0.0	0	0	0	0	0	0
11/26	Car	W 34-26	1	1	0.0	0.0	0.0	0.0	1	0	2	0	0	0
12/03	@NE	W 31-17	0	2	0.0	0.0	0.0	0.0	0	0	1	0	0	0
12/10	@Atl	L 14-19	2	0	0.0	0.0	0.0	0.0	0	0	0	0	0	0
12/16	GB	L 23-34	0	1	0.0	0.0	0.0	0.0	0	0	0	0	0	0
12/24	@NYA	W 12-0	0	1	0.0	0.0	0.0	0.0	0	0	1	0	0	0

Eddie Anderson
Oakland Raiders – S

1995 Defensive Splits

	G	Tk	Ast	Sack	Yds	Stuff	Yds	Int	Yds	PD	TD
Total	14	60	17	0.0	0.0	1.0	4.0	1	0	3	0
vs. Playoff	8	36	6	0.0	0.0	1.0	4.0	1	0	2	0
vs. Non-Playoff	6	24	11	0.0	0.0	0.0	0.0	0	0	1	0
vs. Own Division	8	29	10	0.0	0.0	0.0	0.0	1	0	3	0
Home	8	38	10	0.0	0.0	1.0	4.0	1	0	1	0
Away	6	22	7	0.0	0.0	0.0	0.0	0	0	2	0
Games 1-8	8	31	14	0.0	0.0	1.0	4.0	1	0	3	0
Games 9-16	6	29	3	0.0	0.0	0.0	0.0	0	0	0	0
September	4	16	4	0.0	0.0	1.0	4.0	1	0	2	0
October	4	15	10	0.0	0.0	0.0	0.0	0	0	1	0
November	2	6	2	0.0	0.0	0.0	0.0	0	0	0	0
December	4	23	1	0.0	0.0	0.0	0.0	0	0	0	0
Grass	12	52	15	0.0	0.0	1.0	4.0	1	0	3	0
Turf	2	8	2	0.0	0.0	0.0	0.0	0	0	0	0
Indoor	1	3	1	0.0	0.0	0.0	0.0	0	0	0	0
Outdoor	13	57	16	0.0	0.0	1.0	4.0	1	0	3	0

Game Logs

Date	Opp	Result	Tk	Ast	Sack	Yds	Stuff	Yds	Int	Yds	PD	FF	FR	TD
09/03	SD	W 17-7	4	1	0.0	0.0	0.0	0.0	1	0	1	0	0	0
09/10	@Was	W 20-8	4	1	0.0	0.0	0.0	0.0	0	0	0	0	1	0
09/17	@KC	L 17-23	3	0	0.0	0.0	0.0	0.0	0	0	1	0	0	0
09/24	Phi	W 48-17	5	2	0.0	0.0	1.0	4.0	0	0	0	1	0	0
10/01	@NYA	W 47-10	5	1	0.0	0.0	0.0	0.0	0	0	0	0	0	0
10/08	Sea	W 34-14	4	4	0.0	0.0	0.0	0.0	0	0	0	0	0	0
10/16	@Den	L 0-27	4	4	0.0	0.0	0.0	0.0	0	0	1	1	0	0
10/22	Ind	W 30-17	2	1	0.0	0.0	0.0	0.0	0	0	0	1	0	0
11/05	@Cin	W 20-17	-	-	-	-	-	-	-	-	-	-	-	-
11/12	@NYN	W 17-13	-	-	-	-	-	-	-	-	-	-	-	-
11/19	Dal	L 21-34	3	2	0.0	0.0	0.0	0.0	0	0	0	0	0	0
11/27	@SD	L 6-12	3	0	0.0	0.0	0.0	0.0	0	0	0	0	0	0
12/03	KC	L 23-29	4	0	0.0	0.0	0.0	0.0	0	0	0	0	0	0
12/10	Pit	L 10-29	12	0	0.0	0.0	0.0	0.0	0	0	0	0	0	0
12/17	@Sea	L 10-44	3	1	0.0	0.0	0.0	0.0	0	0	0	0	0	0
12/24	Den	L 28-31	4	0	0.0	0.0	0.0	0.0	0	0	0	1	0	0

Steve Atwater
Denver Broncos – S

1995 Defensive Splits

	G	Tk	Ast	Sack	Yds	Stuff	Yds	Int	Yds	PD	TD
Total	16	82	21	0.0	0.0	4.0	9.5	3	54	12	0
vs. Playoff	7	36	9	0.0	0.0	1.5	2.0	1	11	2	0
vs. Non-Playoff	9	46	12	0.0	0.0	2.5	7.5	2	43	10	0
vs. Own Division	8	32	11	0.0	0.0	2.5	4.0	2	43	8	0
Home	8	26	11	0.0	0.0	2.0	3.5	2	43	8	0
Away	8	56	10	0.0	0.0	2.0	6.0	1	11	4	0
Games 1-8	8	41	10	0.0	0.0	2.0	3.5	2	29	6	0
Games 9-16	8	41	11	0.0	0.0	2.0	6.0	1	25	6	0
September	4	22	5	0.0	0.0	0.5	0.5	1	11	3	0
October	4	19	5	0.0	0.0	1.5	3.0	1	18	3	0
November	4	23	6	0.0	0.0	1.0	5.0	0	0	1	0
December	4	18	5	0.0	0.0	1.0	1.0	1	25	5	0
Grass	12	53	14	0.0	0.0	3.0	4.5	2	43	10	0
Turf	4	29	7	0.0	0.0	1.0	5.0	1	11	2	0
Indoor	2	16	5	0.0	0.0	1.0	5.0	0	0	0	0
Outdoor	14	66	16	0.0	0.0	3.0	4.5	3	54	12	0

Game Logs

Date	Opp	Result	Tk	Ast	Sack	Yds	Stuff	Yds	Int	Yds	PD	FF	FR	TD
09/03	Buf	W 22-7	8	1	0.0	0.0	0.0	0.0	0	0	0	0	0	0
09/10	@Dal	L 21-31	3	1	0.0	0.0	0.0	0.0	1	11	2	0	0	0
09/17	Was	W 38-31	6	2	0.0	0.0	0.5	0.5	0	0	1	0	0	0
09/24	@SD	L 6-17	5	1	0.0	0.0	0.0	0.0	0	0	0	0	0	0
10/01	@Sea	L 10-27	7	3	0.0	0.0	0.0	0.0	0	0	0	0	0	0
10/08	@NE	W 37-3	9	0	0.0	0.0	0.0	0.0	0	0	0	1	0	0
10/16	Oak	W 27-0	2	0	0.0	0.0	1.0	2.0	1	18	3	0	0	0
10/22	KC	L 7-21	1	2	0.0	0.0	0.5	1.0	0	0	0	0	0	0
11/05	Ari	W 38-6	1	2	0.0	0.0	0.0	0.0	0	0	1	1	0	0
11/12	@Phi	L 13-31	10	1	0.0	0.0	0.0	0.0	0	0	0	0	0	0
11/19	SD	W 30-27	3	1	0.0	0.0	0.0	0.0	0	0	0	0	0	0
11/26	@Hou	L 33-42	9	2	0.0	0.0	1.0	5.0	0	0	0	0	0	0
12/03	Jac	W 31-23	4	1	0.0	0.0	0.0	0.0	0	0	0	0	0	0
12/10	Sea	L 27-31	1	2	0.0	0.0	0.0	0.0	1	25	3	0	0	0
12/17	@KC	L 17-20	6	2	0.0	0.0	1.0	1.0	0	0	0	0	0	0
12/24	@Oak	W 31-28	7	0	0.0	0.0	0.0	0.0	0	0	2	0	0	0

Carlton Bailey
Carolina Panthers – LB

1995 Defensive Splits

	G	Tk	Ast	Sack	Yds	Stuff	Yds	Int	Yds	PD	TD
Total	16	76	25	3.0	23.5	4.5	11.5	0	0	5	0
vs. Playoff	6	24	8	0.5	2.0	0.5	0.5	0	0	4	0
vs. Non-Playoff	10	52	17	2.5	21.5	4.0	11.0	0	0	1	0
vs. Own Division	8	38	8	1.0	9.0	1.5	1.5	0	0	1	0
Home	8	29	6	2.0	14.5	2.5	3.5	0	0	4	0
Away	8	47	19	1.0	9.0	2.0	8.0	0	0	1	0
Games 1-8	8	36	16	1.5	12.5	2.0	2.0	0	0	1	0
Games 9-16	8	40	9	1.5	11.0	2.5	9.5	0	0	4	0
September	3	11	4	0.0	0.0	1.0	1.0	0	0	0	0
October	5	25	12	1.5	12.5	1.0	1.0	0	0	1	0
November	4	22	5	1.0	9.0	1.0	2.0	0	0	0	0
December	4	18	4	0.5	2.0	1.5	7.5	0	0	4	0
Grass	12	62	16	2.0	14.5	4.5	11.5	0	0	5	0
Turf	4	14	9	1.0	9.0	0.0	0.0	0	0	0	0
Indoor	3	11	6	1.0	9.0	0.0	0.0	0	0	0	0
Outdoor	13	65	19	2.0	14.5	4.5	11.5	0	0	5	0

Game Logs

Date	Opp	Result	Tk	Ast	Sack	Yds	Stuff	Yds	Int	Yds	PD	FF	FR	TD
09/03	@Atl	L 20-23	1	1	0.0	0.0	0.0	0.0	0	0	0	0	0	0
09/10	@Buf	L 9-31	3	3	0.0	0.0	0.0	0.0	0	0	0	0	0	0
09/17	StL	L 10-31	7	0	0.0	0.0	1.0	1.0	0	0	0	0	0	0
10/01	TB	L 13-20	3	2	0.5	3.5	0.0	0.0	0	0	0	0	0	0
10/08	@Chi	L 27-31	9	5	0.0	0.0	1.0	1.0	0	0	1	0	0	0
10/15	NYA	W 26-15	2	0	1.0	9.0	0.0	0.0	0	0	0	0	0	0
10/22	NO	W 20-3	5	0	0.0	0.0	0.0	0.0	0	0	0	0	0	0
10/29	@NE	W 20-17	6	5	0.0	0.0	0.0	0.0	0	0	0	0	0	0
11/05	@SF	W 13-7	10	0	0.0	0.0	0.0	0.0	0	0	0	0	0	0
11/12	@StL	L 17-28	5	1	0.0	0.0	0.0	0.0	0	0	0	0	0	0
11/19	Ari	W 27-7	2	0	0.0	0.0	1.0	2.0	0	0	0	0	0	0
11/26	@NO	L 26-34	5	1	1.0	9.0	0.0	0.0	0	0	0	0	0	0
12/03	Ind	W 13-10	5	2	0.5	2.0	0.0	0.0	0	0	3	0	0	0
12/10	SF	L 10-31	5	2	0.0	0.0	0.5	0.5	0	0	1	1	0	0
12/17	Atl	W 21-17	0	0	0.0	0.0	0.0	0.0	0	0	0	0	0	0
12/24	@Was	L 17-20	8	0	0.0	0.0	1.0	7.0	0	0	0	0	0	0

Michael Bankston
Arizona Cardinals – DE

1995 Defensive Splits

	G	Tk	Ast	Sack	Yds	Stuff	Yds	Int	Yds	PD	TD
Total	16	56	24	2.0	5.0	4.5	8.0	1	28	1	0
vs. Playoff	8	28	11	0.0	0.0	2.0	3.0	0	0	0	0
vs. Non-Playoff	8	28	13	2.0	5.0	2.5	5.0	1	28	1	0
vs. Own Division	8	34	10	1.0	3.0	1.5	3.5	0	0	0	0
Home	8	32	16	2.0	5.0	0.5	0.5	1	28	1	0
Away	8	24	8	0.0	0.0	4.0	7.5	0	0	0	0
Games 1-8	8	31	13	1.0	2.0	1.0	2.0	1	28	1	0
Games 9-16	8	25	11	1.0	3.0	3.5	6.0	0	0	0	0
September	4	20	5	0.0	0.0	0.0	0.0	0	0	0	0
October	4	11	8	1.0	2.0	1.0	2.0	1	28	1	0
November	5	15	9	1.0	3.0	1.5	3.0	0	0	0	0
December	3	10	2	0.0	0.0	2.0	3.0	0	0	0	0
Grass	12	47	18	2.0	5.0	3.0	4.5	1	28	1	0
Turf	4	9	6	0.0	0.0	1.5	3.5	0	0	0	0
Indoor	1	2	3	0.0	0.0	0.0	0.0	0	0	0	0
Outdoor	15	54	21	2.0	5.0	4.5	8.0	1	28	1	0

Game Logs

Date	Opp	Result	Tk	Ast	Sack	Yds	Stuff	Yds	Int	Yds	PD	FF	FR	TD
09/03	@Was	L 7-27	4	0	0.0	0.0	0.0	0.0	0	0	0	0	0	0
09/10	Phi	L 19-31	11	1	0.0	0.0	0.0	0.0	0	0	0	0	0	0
09/17	@Det	W 20-17	2	3	0.0	0.0	0.0	0.0	0	0	0	0	0	0
09/24	@Dal	L 20-34	3	1	0.0	0.0	0.0	0.0	0	0	0	0	0	0
10/01	KC	L 3-24	1	2	0.0	0.0	0.0	0.0	0	0	0	0	0	0
10/08	@NYN	L 21-27	3	1	0.0	0.0	0.5	1.5	0	0	0	0	0	0
10/15	Was	W 24-20	1	1	0.0	0.0	0.0	0.0	0	0	0	0	0	0
10/29	Sea	W 20-14	6	4	1.0	2.0	0.5	0.5	1	28	1	0	0	0
11/05	@Den	L 6-38	3	2	0.0	0.0	1.0	2.0	0	0	0	0	0	0
11/12	Min	L 24-30	1	1	0.0	0.0	0.0	0.0	0	0	0	0	0	0
11/19	@Car	L 7-27	5	0	0.0	0.0	0.5	1.0	0	0	0	0	0	0
11/26	Atl	W 40-37	1	2	0.0	0.0	0.0	0.0	0	0	0	0	0	0
11/30	NYN	L 6-10	5	4	1.0	3.0	0.0	0.0	0	0	0	0	0	0
12/09	@SD	L 25-28	3	0	0.0	0.0	1.0	1.0	0	0	0	0	0	0
12/17	@Phi	L 20-21	1	1	0.0	0.0	1.0	2.0	0	0	0	0	0	0
12/25	Dal	L 13-37	6	1	0.0	0.0	0.0	0.0	0	0	0	0	0	0

Micheal Barrow
Houston Oilers – LB

1995 Defensive Splits

	G	Tk	Ast	Sack	Yds	Stuff	Yds	Int	Yds	PD	TD
Total	13	55	32	3.0	29.5	7.5	25.5	0	0	1	0
vs. Playoff	5	21	15	2.0	22.0	4.0	16.0	0	0	0	0
vs. Non-Playoff	8	34	17	1.0	7.5	3.5	9.5	0	0	1	0
vs. Own Division	5	19	22	0.5	4.0	2.5	9.0	0	0	1	0
Home	6	24	23	1.5	8.5	6.0	19.5	0	0	0	0
Away	7	31	9	1.5	21.0	1.5	6.0	0	0	1	0
Games 1-8	5	15	16	0.5	4.0	3.0	13.5	0	0	0	0
Games 9-16	8	40	16	2.5	25.5	4.5	12.0	0	0	1	0
September	2	4	12	0.5	4.0	1.5	8.0	0	0	0	0
October	3	11	4	0.0	0.0	1.5	5.5	0	0	0	0
November	4	23	8	0.0	0.0	1.0	1.0	0	0	1	0
December	4	17	8	2.5	25.5	3.5	11.0	0	0	0	0
Grass	4	22	3	0.5	4.0	1.0	3.0	0	0	1	0
Turf	9	33	29	2.5	25.5	6.5	22.5	0	0	0	0
Indoor	7	25	25	1.5	8.5	6.0	19.5	0	0	0	0
Outdoor	6	30	7	1.5	21.0	1.5	6.0	0	0	1	0

Game Logs

Date	Opp	Result	Tk	Ast	Sack	Yds	Stuff	Yds	Int	Yds	PD	FF	FR	TD
09/03	@Jac	W 10-3	3	2	0.5	4.0	1.0	3.0	0	0	0	1	0	0
09/10	Pit	L 17-34	1	10	0.0	0.0	0.5	5.0	0	0	0	0	0	0
09/17	Cle	L 7-14	-	-	-	-	-	-	-	-	-	-	-	-
09/24	@Cin	W 38-28	-	-	-	-	-	-	-	-	-	-	-	-
10/01	Jac	L 16-17	-	-	-	-	-	-	-	-	-	-	-	-
10/08	@Min	L 17-23	1	2	0.0	0.0	0.0	0.0	0	0	0	0	0	0
10/22	@Chi	L 32-35	5	0	0.0	0.0	0.0	0.0	0	0	0	0	0	0
10/29	TB	W 19-7	5	2	0.0	0.0	1.5	5.5	0	0	0	0	0	0
11/05	@Cle	W 37-10	8	1	0.0	0.0	0.0	0.0	0	0	1	0	0	0
11/12	Cin	L 25-32	4	5	0.0	0.0	1.0	1.0	0	0	0	0	0	0
11/19	@KC	L 13-20	6	0	0.0	0.0	0.0	0.0	0	0	0	0	0	0
11/26	Den	W 42-33	5	2	0.0	0.0	0.0	0.0	0	0	0	0	0	0
12/03	@Pit	L 7-21	3	4	0.0	0.0	0.0	0.0	0	0	0	0	1	0
12/10	Det	L 17-24	6	1	1.0	5.0	3.0	8.0	0	0	0	1	0	0
12/17	NYA	W 23-6	3	3	0.5	3.5	0.0	0.0	0	0	0	0	0	0
12/24	@Buf	W 28-17	5	0	1.0	17.0	0.5	3.0	0	0	0	0	0	0

Jason Belser
Indianapolis Colts – S

1995 Defensive Splits

	G	Tk	Ast	Sack	Yds	Stuff	Yds	Int	Yds	PD	TD
Total	16	64	13	0.0	0.0	1.0	2.0	1	0	6	0
vs. Playoff	6	31	3	0.0	0.0	1.0	2.0	0	0	1	0
vs. Non-Playoff	10	33	10	0.0	0.0	0.0	0.0	1	0	5	0
vs. Own Division	8	40	6	0.0	0.0	0.0	0.0	1	0	2	0
Home	8	34	8	0.0	0.0	1.0	2.0	1	0	3	0
Away	8	30	5	0.0	0.0	0.0	0.0	0	0	3	0
Games 1-8	8	35	6	0.0	0.0	1.0	2.0	0	0	1	0
Games 9-16	8	29	7	0.0	0.0	0.0	0.0	1	0	5	0
September	3	14	2	0.0	0.0	0.0	0.0	0	0	0	0
October	5	21	4	0.0	0.0	1.0	2.0	0	0	1	0
November	4	14	3	0.0	0.0	0.0	0.0	0	0	0	0
December	4	15	4	0.0	0.0	0.0	0.0	1	0	5	0
Grass	5	18	5	0.0	0.0	0.0	0.0	0	0	3	0
Turf	11	46	8	0.0	0.0	1.0	2.0	1	0	3	0
Indoor	9	34	8	0.0	0.0	1.0	2.0	1	0	3	0
Outdoor	7	30	5	0.0	0.0	0.0	0.0	0	0	3	0

Game Logs

Date	Opp	Result	Tk	Ast	Sack	Yds	Stuff	Yds	Int	Yds	PD	FF	FR	TD
09/03	Cin	L 21-24	2	2	0.0	0.0	0.0	0.0	0	0	0	0	0	0
09/10	@NYA	W 27-24	7	0	0.0	0.0	0.0	0.0	0	0	0	0	0	0
09/17	@Buf	L 14-20	5	0	0.0	0.0	0.0	0.0	0	0	0	0	0	0
10/01	StL	W 21-18	4	0	0.0	0.0	0.0	0.0	0	0	0	0	0	0
10/08	@Mia	W 27-24	6	0	0.0	0.0	0.0	0.0	0	0	0	0	0	0
10/15	SF	W 18-17	8	1	0.0	0.0	1.0	2.0	0	0	1	0	0	0
10/22	@Oak	L 17-30	2	1	0.0	0.0	0.0	0.0	0	0	0	0	1	0
10/29	NYA	W 17-10	1	2	0.0	0.0	0.0	0.0	0	0	0	0	0	0
11/05	Buf	L 10-16	6	2	0.0	0.0	0.0	0.0	0	0	0	0	0	0
11/12	@NO	L 14-17	0	0	0.0	0.0	0.0	0.0	0	0	0	0	0	0
11/19	@NE	W 24-10	2	1	0.0	0.0	0.0	0.0	0	0	0	0	1	0
11/26	Mia	W 36-28	6	0	0.0	0.0	0.0	0.0	0	0	0	0	0	0
12/03	@Car	L 10-13	2	1	0.0	0.0	0.0	0.0	0	0	0	1	0	0
12/10	@Jac	W 41-31	6	2	0.0	0.0	0.0	0.0	0	0	3	0	0	0
12/17	SD	L 24-27	0	0	0.0	0.0	0.0	0.0	0	0	0	0	0	0
12/23	NE	W 10-7	7	1	0.0	0.0	0.0	0.0	1	0	2	0	0	0

Cornelius Bennett

1995 Defensive Splits

	G	Tk	Ast	Sack	Yds	Stuff	Yds	Int	Yds	PD	TD
Total	14	81	23	2.0	16.0	3.0	5.5	1	69	10	1
vs. Playoff	5	30	5	1.0	7.0	0.0	0.0	0	0	1	0
vs. Non-Playoff	9	51	18	1.0	9.0	3.0	5.5	1	69	9	1
vs. Own Division	8	42	17	1.0	7.0	1.0	2.0	1	69	6	1
Home	6	29	13	1.0	9.0	2.0	4.0	1	69	5	1
Away	8	52	10	1.0	7.0	1.0	1.5	0	0	5	0
Games 1-8	8	47	9	1.0	9.0	2.5	4.5	0	0	6	0
Games 9-16	6	34	14	1.0	7.0	0.5	1.0	1	69	4	1
September	3	10	2	1.0	9.0	0.0	0.0	0	0	1	0
October	5	37	7	0.0	0.0	2.5	4.5	0	0	5	0
November	3	11	10	1.0	7.0	0.5	1.0	1	69	2	1
December	3	23	4	0.0	0.0	0.0	0.0	0	0	2	0
Grass	5	39	6	0.0	0.0	0.5	0.5	0	0	4	0
Turf	9	42	17	2.0	16.0	2.5	5.0	1	69	6	1
Indoor	2	8	0	1.0	7.0	0.0	0.0	0	0	1	0
Outdoor	12	73	23	1.0	9.0	3.0	5.5	1	69	9	1

Game Logs

Date	Opp	Result	Tk	Ast	Sack	Yds	Stuff	Yds	Int	Yds	PD	FF	FR	TD
09/03	@Den	L 7-22	2	1	0.0	0.0	0.0	0.0	0	0	0	0	0	0
09/10	Car	W 31-9	3	0	1.0	9.0	0.0	0.0	0	0	1	0	0	0
09/17	Ind	W 20-14	5	1	0.0	0.0	0.0	0.0	0	0	0	0	0	0
10/02	@Cle	W 22-19	8	1	0.0	0.0	0.5	0.5	0	0	2	0	0	0
10/08	NYA	W 29-10	3	2	0.0	0.0	0.5	1.0	0	0	1	0	0	0
10/15	Sea	W 27-21	8	2	0.0	0.0	1.5	3.0	0	0	0	0	0	0
10/23	@NE	L 14-27	10	2	0.0	0.0	0.0	0.0	0	0	2	0	0	0
10/29	@Mia	L 6-23	8	0	0.0	0.0	0.0	0.0	0	0	0	0	0	0
11/05	@Ind	W 16-10	1	0	1.0	7.0	0.0	0.0	0	0	0	0	0	0
11/12	Atl	W 23-17	-	-	-	-	-	-	-	-	-	-	-	-
11/19	@NYA	W 28-26	5	4	0.0	0.0	0.5	1.0	0	0	0	0	1	0
11/26	NE	L 25-35	5	6	0.0	0.0	0.0	0.0	1	69	2	0	0	1
12/03	@SF	L 17-27	11	2	0.0	0.0	0.0	0.0	0	0	0	0	0	0
12/10	@StL	W 45-27	7	0	0.0	0.0	0.0	0.0	0	0	1	0	1	0
12/17	Mia	W 23-20	5	2	0.0	0.0	0.0	0.0	0	0	1	1	0	0
12/24	Hou	L 17-28	-	-	-	-	-	-	-	-	-	-	-	-

Tony Bennett

1995 Defensive Splits

	G	Tk	Ast	Sack	Yds	Stuff	Yds	Int	Yds	PD	TD
Total	16	47	10	10.5	67.5	6.0	20.0	0	0	4	1
vs. Playoff	6	21	4	4.0	13.0	4.5	15.0	0	0	1	0
vs. Non-Playoff	10	26	6	6.5	54.5	1.5	5.0	0	0	3	1
vs. Own Division	8	27	7	5.5	40.5	3.5	15.0	0	0	1	1
Home	8	24	4	8.0	59.0	3.0	6.0	0	0	1	0
Away	8	23	6	2.5	8.5	3.0	14.0	0	0	3	1
Games 1-8	8	25	5	6.0	35.0	3.5	16.0	0	0	2	1
Games 9-16	8	22	5	4.5	32.5	2.5	4.0	0	0	2	0
September	3	9	1	0.0	0.0	3.0	14.0	0	0	2	1
October	5	16	4	6.0	35.0	0.5	2.0	0	0	0	0
November	4	12	3	3.5	15.5	0.0	0.0	0	0	0	0
December	4	10	2	1.0	17.0	2.5	4.0	0	0	2	0
Grass	5	14	5	2.5	8.5	0.0	0.0	0	0	2	0
Turf	11	33	5	8.0	59.0	6.0	20.0	0	0	2	1
Indoor	9	25	4	8.0	59.0	3.0	6.0	0	0	1	0
Outdoor	7	22	6	2.5	8.5	3.0	14.0	0	0	3	1

Game Logs

Date	Opp	Result	Tk	Ast	Sack	Yds	Stuff	Yds	Int	Yds	PD	FF	FR	TD
09/03	Cin	L 21-24	1	0	0.0	0.0	0.0	0.0	0	0	1	0	0	0
09/10	@NYA	W 27-24	5	0	0.0	0.0	1.0	4.0	0	0	0	0	1	1
09/17	@Buf	L 14-20	3	1	0.0	0.0	2.0	10.0	0	0	1	0	0	0
10/01	StL	W 21-18	3	0	2.0	21.0	0.0	0.0	0	0	0	0	0	0
10/08	@Mia	W 27-24	3	1	0.0	0.0	0.0	0.0	0	0	0	0	0	0
10/15	SF	W 18-17	2	1	1.0	0.0	0.5	2.0	0	0	1	0	0	0
10/22	@Oak	L 17-30	5	0	2.0	6.0	0.0	0.0	0	0	0	0	0	0
10/29	NYA	W 17-10	3	2	1.0	8.0	0.0	0.0	0	0	0	0	0	0
11/05	Buf	L 10-16	4	1	0.0	0.0	0.0	0.0	0	0	0	0	0	0
11/12	@NO	L 14-17	1	0	0.0	0.0	0.0	0.0	0	0	0	0	0	0
11/19	@NE	W 24-10	2	2	0.5	2.5	0.0	0.0	0	0	0	0	0	0
11/26	Mia	W 36-28	5	0	3.0	13.0	0.0	0.0	0	0	0	1	0	0
12/03	@Car	L 10-13	2	0	0.0	0.0	0.0	0.0	0	0	1	0	0	0
12/10	@Jac	W 41-31	2	2	0.0	0.0	0.0	0.0	0	0	1	0	0	0
12/17	SD	L 24-27	4	0	0.0	0.0	2.0	3.0	0	0	0	0	0	0
12/23	NE	W 10-7	2	0	1.0	17.0	0.5	1.0	0	0	0	0	1	0

Greg Biekert

1995 Defensive Splits

	G	Tk	Ast	Sack	Yds	Stuff	Yds	Int	Yds	PD	TD
Total	16	71	16	1.0	9.0	3.5	4.5	0	0	4	0
vs. Playoff	8	49	9	0.0	0.0	3.0	4.0	0	0	2	0
vs. Non-Playoff	8	22	7	1.0	9.0	0.5	0.5	0	0	2	0
vs. Own Division	8	34	9	0.0	0.0	2.0	2.0	0	0	3	0
Home	8	42	10	0.0	0.0	1.0	2.0	0	0	1	0
Away	8	29	6	1.0	9.0	2.5	2.5	0	0	3	0
Games 1-8	8	25	7	1.0	9.0	0.5	0.5	0	0	2	0
Games 9-16	8	46	9	0.0	0.0	3.0	4.0	0	0	2	0
September	4	17	4	1.0	9.0	0.5	0.5	0	0	0	0
October	4	8	3	0.0	0.0	0.0	0.0	0	0	2	0
November	4	26	4	0.0	0.0	2.0	2.0	0	0	1	0
December	4	20	5	0.0	0.0	1.0	2.0	0	0	1	0
Grass	12	56	14	1.0	9.0	3.5	4.5	0	0	4	0
Turf	4	15	2	0.0	0.0	0.0	0.0	0	0	0	0
Indoor	1	6	0	0.0	0.0	0.0	0.0	0	0	0	0
Outdoor	15	65	16	1.0	9.0	3.5	4.5	0	0	4	0

Game Logs

Date	Opp	Result	Tk	Ast	Sack	Yds	Stuff	Yds	Int	Yds	PD	FF	FR	TD
09/03	SD	W 17-7	8	2	0.0	0.0	0.0	0.0	0	0	0	0	0	0
09/10	@Was	W 20-8	2	1	1.0	9.0	0.5	0.5	0	0	0	1	0	0
09/17	@KC	L 17-23	3	0	0.0	0.0	0.0	0.0	0	0	0	0	0	0
09/24	Phi	W 48-17	4	1	0.0	0.0	0.0	0.0	0	0	0	0	0	0
10/01	@NYA	W 47-10	2	0	0.0	0.0	0.0	0.0	0	0	0	0	0	0
10/08	Sea	W 34-14	0	1	0.0	0.0	0.0	0.0	0	0	0	0	0	0
10/16	@Den	L 0-27	2	2	0.0	0.0	0.0	0.0	0	0	2	0	0	0
10/22	Ind	W 30-17	4	0	0.0	0.0	0.0	0.0	0	0	1	0	0	0
11/05	@Cin	W 20-17	5	0	0.0	0.0	0.0	0.0	0	0	0	0	0	0
11/12	@NYN	W 17-13	2	2	0.0	0.0	0.0	0.0	0	0	0	0	0	0
11/19	Dal	L 21-34	12	1	0.0	0.0	0.0	0.0	0	0	0	0	0	0
11/27	@SD	L 6-12	7	1	0.0	0.0	2.0	2.0	0	0	1	0	0	0
12/03	KC	L 23-29	5	2	0.0	0.0	0.0	0.0	0	0	0	0	0	0
12/10	Pit	L 10-29	6	2	0.0	0.0	1.0	2.0	0	0	1	0	0	0
12/17	@Sea	L 10-44	6	0	0.0	0.0	0.0	0.0	0	0	0	0	0	0
12/24	Den	L 28-31	3	1	0.0	0.0	0.0	0.0	0	0	0	0	0	0

Blaine Bishop

1995 Defensive Splits

	G	Tk	Ast	Sack	Yds	Stuff	Yds	Int	Yds	PD	TD
Total	16	76	23	1.5	10.5	4.0	10.0	1	62	11	1
vs. Playoff	5	24	5	1.0	7.0	3.0	9.0	0	0	3	0
vs. Non-Playoff	11	52	18	0.5	3.5	1.0	1.0	1	62	8	1
vs. Own Division	8	26	12	0.0	0.0	1.0	1.0	1	62	8	1
Home	8	32	19	0.5	3.5	3.0	9.0	0	0	4	0
Away	8	44	4	1.0	7.0	1.0	1.0	1	62	7	1
Games 1-8	8	41	12	0.5	3.5	1.5	1.5	0	0	4	0
Games 9-16	8	35	11	1.0	7.0	2.5	8.5	1	62	7	1
September	4	16	5	0.0	0.0	1.0	1.0	0	0	4	0
October	4	25	7	0.5	3.5	0.5	0.5	0	0	0	0
November	4	14	7	1.0	7.0	1.0	1.0	1	62	6	1
December	4	21	4	0.0	0.0	1.5	7.5	0	0	1	0
Grass	4	24	0	1.0	7.0	1.0	1.0	1	62	4	1
Turf	12	52	23	0.5	3.5	3.0	9.0	0	0	7	0
Indoor	9	40	22	0.5	3.5	3.0	9.0	0	0	4	0
Outdoor	7	36	1	1.0	7.0	1.0	1.0	1	62	7	1

Game Logs

Date	Opp	Result	Tk	Ast	Sack	Yds	Stuff	Yds	Int	Yds	PD	FF	FR	TD
09/03	@Jac	W 10-3	6	0	0.0	0.0	0.0	0.0	0	0	1	0	1	0
09/10	Pit	L 17-34	2	4	0.0	0.0	1.0	1.0	0	0	1	0	0	0
09/17	Cle	L 7-14	5	1	0.0	0.0	0.0	0.0	0	0	0	0	0	0
09/24	@Cin	W 38-28	3	0	0.0	0.0	0.0	0.0	0	0	2	0	0	0
10/01	Jac	L 16-17	3	2	0.0	0.0	0.0	0.0	0	0	0	0	0	0
10/08	@Min	L 17-23	8	3	0.0	0.0	0.0	0.0	0	0	1	1	0	0
10/22	@Chi	L 32-35	0	0	0.0	0.0	0.0	0.0	0	0	0	0	0	0
10/29	TB	W 19-7	6	2	0.5	3.5	0.5	0.5	0	0	0	0	0	0
11/05	@Cle	W 37-10	3	0	0.0	0.0	0.0	0.0	1	62	2	1	1	1
11/12	Cin	L 25-32	1	4	0.0	0.0	0.0	0.0	0	0	2	0	0	0
11/19	@KC	L 13-20	7	0	1.0	7.0	1.0	1.0	0	0	1	1	1	0
11/26	Den	W 42-33	3	3	0.0	0.0	0.0	0.0	0	0	1	0	0	0
12/03	@Pit	L 7-21	3	1	0.0	0.0	0.0	0.0	0	0	0	0	0	0
12/10	Det	L 17-24	6	0	0.0	0.0	1.0	7.0	0	0	0	0	0	0
12/17	NYA	W 23-6	6	3	0.0	0.0	0.5	0.5	0	0	0	0	0	0
12/24	@Buf	W 28-17	6	0	0.0	0.0	0.0	0.0	0	0	1	0	0	0

Robert Blackmon

1995 Defensive Splits

	G	Tk	Ast	Sack	Yds	Stuff	Yds	Int	Yds	PD	TD
Total	13	49	11	1.0	12.0	0.5	0.5	5	46	12	0
vs. Playoff	5	20	4	0.0	0.0	0.0	0.0	1	21	5	0
vs. Non-Playoff	8	29	7	1.0	12.0	0.5	0.5	4	25	7	0
vs. Own Division	6	30	4	1.0	12.0	0.0	0.0	1	13	6	0
Home	7	22	8	0.0	0.0	0.5	0.5	2	21	5	0
Away	6	27	3	1.0	12.0	0.0	0.0	3	25	7	0
Games 1-8	5	13	4	0.0	0.0	0.0	0.0	1	0	3	0
Games 9-16	8	36	7	1.0	12.0	0.5	0.5	4	46	9	0
September	3	11	3	0.0	0.0	0.0	0.0	1	0	3	0
October	2	2	1	0.0	0.0	0.0	0.0	0	0	0	0
November	4	14	2	0.0	0.0	0.5	0.5	2	12	4	0
December	4	22	5	1.0	12.0	0.0	0.0	2	34	5	0
Grass	5	25	2	1.0	12.0	0.0	0.0	3	25	7	0
Turf	8	24	9	0.0	0.0	0.5	0.5	2	21	5	0
Indoor	7	22	8	0.0	0.0	0.5	0.5	2	21	5	0
Outdoor	6	27	3	1.0	12.0	0.0	0.0	3	25	7	0

Game Logs

Date	Opp	Result	Tk	Ast	Sack	Yds	Stuff	Yds	Int	Yds	PD	FF	FR	TD
09/03	KC	L 10-34	6	0	0.0	0.0	0.0	0.0	0	0	1	0	0	0
09/10	@SD	L 10-14	4	1	0.0	0.0	0.0	0.0	0	0	1	0	0	0
09/17	Cin	W 24-21	1	2	0.0	0.0	0.0	0.0	1	0	1	0	0	0
10/01	Den	W 27-10	0	0	0.0	0.0	0.0	0.0	0	0	0	0	0	0
10/08	@Oak	L 14-34	-	-	-	-	-	-	-	-	-	-	-	-
10/15	@Buf	L 21-27	2	1	0.0	0.0	0.0	0.0	0	0	0	0	0	0
10/22	SD	L 25-35	-	-	-	-	-	-	-	-	-	-	-	-
10/29	@Ari	L 14-20	-	-	-	-	-	-	-	-	-	-	-	-
11/05	NYN	W 30-28	2	2	0.0	0.0	0.0	0.0	0	0	1	0	0	0
11/12	@Jac	W 47-30	3	0	0.0	0.0	0.0	0.0	0	0	0	0	0	0
11/19	@Was	W 27-20	4	0	0.0	0.0	0.0	0.0	2	12	3	0	0	0
11/26	NYA	L 10-16	5	0	0.0	0.0	0.5	0.5	0	0	0	0	0	0
12/03	Phi	W 26-14	2	0	0.0	0.0	0.0	0.0	1	21	1	0	0	0
12/10	@Den	W 31-27	8	1	1.0	12.0	0.0	0.0	1	13	1	1	0	0
12/17	Oak	W 44-10	6	2	0.0	0.0	0.0	0.0	0	0	1	0	0	0
12/24	@KC	L 3-26	6	0	0.0	0.0	0.0	0.0	0	0	2	0	0	0

Bennie Blades

1995 Defensive Splits

	G	Tk	Ast	Sack	Yds	Stuff	Yds	Int	Yds	PD	TD
Total	16	72	29	1.0	4.0	0.5	0.5	1	0	7	0
vs. Playoff	5	27	10	1.0	4.0	0.0	0.0	1	0	5	0
vs. Non-Playoff	11	45	19	0.0	0.0	0.5	0.5	0	0	2	0
vs. Own Division	8	38	15	0.0	0.0	0.5	0.5	0	0	3	0
Home	8	28	21	0.0	0.0	0.5	0.5	0	0	3	0
Away	8	44	8	1.0	4.0	0.0	0.0	1	0	4	0
Games 1-8	8	38	14	0.0	0.0	0.0	0.0	1	0	5	0
Games 9-16	8	34	15	1.0	4.0	0.5	0.5	0	0	2	0
September	4	15	7	0.0	0.0	0.0	0.0	1	0	2	0
October	4	23	7	0.0	0.0	0.0	0.0	0	0	3	0
November	4	18	4	1.0	4.0	0.0	0.0	0	0	1	0
December	4	16	11	0.0	0.0	0.5	0.5	0	0	1	0
Grass	4	23	3	0.0	0.0	0.0	0.0	0	0	2	0
Turf	12	49	26	1.0	4.0	0.5	0.5	1	0	5	0
Indoor	11	45	26	1.0	4.0	0.5	0.5	0	0	4	0
Outdoor	5	27	3	0.0	0.0	0.0	0.0	1	0	3	0

Game Logs

Date	Opp	Result	Tk	Ast	Sack	Yds	Stuff	Yds	Int	Yds	PD	FF	FR	TD
09/03	@Pit	L 20-23	4	0	0.0	0.0	0.0	0.0	1	0	1	0	0	0
09/10	@Min	L 10-20	5	1	0.0	0.0	0.0	0.0	0	0	0	0	0	0
09/17	Ari	L 17-20	4	2	0.0	0.0	0.0	0.0	0	0	0	0	0	0
09/25	SF	W 27-24	2	4	0.0	0.0	0.0	0.0	0	0	1	0	0	0
10/08	Cle	W 38-20	5	1	0.0	0.0	0.0	0.0	0	0	0	0	0	0
10/15	@GB	L 21-30	7	1	0.0	0.0	0.0	0.0	0	0	0	0	0	0
10/22	@Was	L 30-36	4	0	0.0	0.0	0.0	0.0	0	0	1	0	0	0
10/29	GB	W 24-16	7	5	0.0	0.0	0.0	0.0	0	0	0	0	0	0
11/05	@Atl	L 22-34	7	0	1.0	4.0	0.0	0.0	0	0	1	0	0	0
11/12	TB	W 27-24	4	3	0.0	0.0	0.0	0.0	0	0	0	0	0	0
11/19	@Chi	W 24-17	2	0	0.0	0.0	0.0	0.0	0	0	0	0	0	0
11/23	Min	W 44-38	1	1	0.0	0.0	0.0	0.0	0	0	0	0	0	0
12/04	Chi	W 27-7	2	2	0.0	0.0	0.5	0.5	0	0	0	0	0	0
12/10	@Hou	W 24-17	5	4	0.0	0.0	0.0	0.0	0	0	0	0	0	0
12/17	Jac	W 44-0	3	3	0.0	0.0	0.0	0.0	0	0	0	0	0	0
12/23	@TB	W 37-10	6	2	0.0	0.0	0.0	0.0	0	0	1	0	0	0

Tyrone Braxton
Denver Broncos – S

1995 Defensive Splits	G	Tk	Ast	Sack	Yds	Stuff	Yds	Int	Yds	PD	TD
Total	16	70	23	0.0	0.0	1.0	4.0	2	36	8	0
vs. Playoff	7	31	10	0.0	0.0	1.0	4.0	0	0	4	0
vs. Non-Playoff	9	39	13	0.0	0.0	0.0	0.0	2	36	4	0
vs. Own Division	8	39	10	0.0	0.0	0.0	0.0	1	36	6	0
Home	8	30	6	0.0	0.0	0.0	0.0	2	36	7	0
Away	8	40	17	0.0	0.0	1.0	4.0	0	0	1	0
Games 1-8	8	33	10	0.0	0.0	0.0	0.0	0	0	4	0
Games 9-16	8	37	13	0.0	0.0	1.0	4.0	2	36	4	0
September	4	14	4	0.0	0.0	0.0	0.0	0	0	0	0
October	4	19	6	0.0	0.0	0.0	0.0	0	0	4	0
November	4	19	7	0.0	0.0	1.0	4.0	0	0	1	0
December	4	18	6	0.0	0.0	0.0	0.0	2	36	3	0
Grass	12	53	11	0.0	0.0	0.0	0.0	2	36	8	0
Turf	4	17	12	0.0	0.0	1.0	4.0	0	0	0	0
Indoor	2	6	8	0.0	0.0	0.0	0.0	0	0	0	0
Outdoor	14	64	15	0.0	0.0	1.0	4.0	2	36	8	0

Date	Opp	Result	Tk	Ast	Sack	Yds	Stuff	Yds	Int	Yds	PD	FF	FR	TD
09/03	Buf	W 22-7	0	2	0.0	0.0	0.0	0.0	0	0	0	0	0	0
09/10	@Dal	L 21-31	6	2	0.0	0.0	0.0	0.0	0	0	0	0	0	0
09/17	Was	W 38-31	3	0	0.0	0.0	0.0	0.0	0	0	0	0	0	0
09/24	@SD	L 6-17	5	0	0.0	0.0	0.0	0.0	0	0	0	0	0	0
10/01	@Sea	L 10-27	3	3	0.0	0.0	0.0	0.0	0	0	0	0	0	0
10/08	@NE	W 37-3	6	1	0.0	0.0	0.0	0.0	0	0	0	0	0	0
10/16	Oak	W 27-0	5	0	0.0	0.0	0.0	0.0	0	0	1	1	0	0
10/22	KC	L 7-21	5	2	0.0	0.0	0.0	0.0	0	0	3	0	0	0
11/05	Ari	W 38-6	6	0	0.0	0.0	0.0	0.0	0	0	1	0	0	0
11/12	@Phi	L 13-31	5	2	0.0	0.0	1.0	4.0	0	0	0	0	0	0
11/19	SD	W 30-27	5	0	0.0	0.0	0.0	0.0	0	0	0	0	0	0
11/26	@Hou	L 33-42	3	5	0.0	0.0	0.0	0.0	0	0	0	0	0	0
12/03	Jac	W 31-23	2	1	0.0	0.0	0.0	0.0	1	0	1	0	0	0
12/10	Sea	L 27-31	4	1	0.0	0.0	0.0	0.0	1	36	0	0	0	0
12/17	@KC	L 17-20	5	2	0.0	0.0	0.0	0.0	0	0	1	0	0	0
12/24	@Oak	W 31-28	7	2	0.0	0.0	0.0	0.0	0	0	0	0	0	0

Matt Brock
New York Jets – DT

1995 Defensive Splits	G	Tk	Ast	Sack	Yds	Stuff	Yds	Int	Yds	PD	TD
Total	16	46	20	5.0	33.0	10.0	26.0	1	9	8	1
vs. Playoff	7	18	8	1.0	7.0	5.0	17.0	0	0	3	1
vs. Non-Playoff	9	28	12	4.0	26.0	5.0	9.0	1	9	5	0
vs. Own Division	8	22	11	2.0	18.0	5.0	17.5	1	9	5	1
Home	8	19	12	1.0	5.0	5.5	16.0	0	0	4	0
Away	8	27	8	4.0	28.0	4.5	10.0	1	9	4	1
Games 1-8	8	25	8	4.0	22.0	4.5	13.5	0	0	3	1
Games 9-16	8	21	12	1.0	11.0	5.5	12.5	1	9	5	0
September	4	14	1	1.0	7.0	3.0	8.0	0	0	3	1
October	5	13	7	3.0	15.0	2.5	8.5	0	0	0	0
November	3	10	6	0.0	0.0	1.5	5.0	0	0	3	0
December	4	9	6	1.0	11.0	3.0	4.5	1	9	2	0
Grass	3	14	4	4.0	28.0	1.5	5.0	1	9	2	1
Turf	13	32	16	1.0	5.0	8.5	21.0	0	0	6	0
Indoor	4	12	3	0.0	0.0	3.0	5.0	0	0	2	0
Outdoor	12	34	17	5.0	33.0	7.0	21.0	1	9	6	1

Date	Opp	Result	Tk	Ast	Sack	Yds	Stuff	Yds	Int	Yds	PD	FF	FR	TD
09/03	@Mia	L 14-52	8	0	1.0	7.0	1.0	4.0	0	0	0	0	1	1
09/10	Ind	L 24-27	3	0	0.0	0.0	0.0	0.0	0	0	1	0	0	0
09/17	Jac	W 27-10	2	0	0.0	0.0	1.0	3.0	0	0	1	0	0	0
09/24	@Atl	L 3-13	1	1	0.0	0.0	1.0	1.0	0	0	1	0	0	0
10/01	Oak	L 10-47	6	3	1.0	5.0	0.5	1.0	0	0	0	0	0	0
10/08	@Buf	L 10-29	1	1	0.0	0.0	0.0	0.0	0	0	0	0	0	0
10/15	@Car	L 15-26	4	1	2.0	10.0	0.0	0.0	0	0	1	0	0	0
10/22	Mia	W 17-16	0	2	0.0	0.0	1.0	4.5	0	0	0	0	0	0
10/29	@Ind	L 10-17	2	0	0.0	0.0	1.0	3.0	0	0	0	0	0	0
11/05	NE	L 7-20	3	1	0.0	0.0	0.5	0.5	0	0	1	0	0	0
11/19	Buf	L 26-28	3	4	0.0	0.0	1.0	4.5	0	0	1	0	0	0
11/26	@Sea	W 16-10	4	1	0.0	0.0	0.0	0.0	0	0	1	0	0	0
12/03	StL	L 20-23	1	0	0.0	0.0	0.5	0.5	0	0	0	0	0	0
12/10	@NE	L 28-31	2	3	1.0	11.0	0.5	1.0	1	9	2	1	1	0
12/17	@Hou	L 6-23	5	1	0.0	0.0	1.0	1.0	0	0	0	0	0	0
12/24	NO	L 0-12	1	1	0.0	0.0	1.0	2.0	0	0	0	0	0	0

Derrick Brooks
Tampa Bay Buccaneers – LB

1995 Defensive Splits	G	Tk	Ast	Sack	Yds	Stuff	Yds	Int	Yds	PD	TD
Total	16	63	19	1.0	10.0	8.0	27.5	0	0	4	0
vs. Playoff	6	22	9	0.0	0.0	1.5	4.5	0	0	3	0
vs. Non-Playoff	10	41	10	1.0	10.0	6.5	23.0	0	0	1	0
vs. Own Division	8	35	8	1.0	10.0	4.5	15.0	0	0	2	0
Home	8	24	13	0.0	0.0	2.0	3.5	0	0	2	0
Away	8	39	6	1.0	10.0	6.0	24.0	0	0	2	0
Games 1-8	8	27	14	0.0	0.0	3.0	7.5	0	0	1	0
Games 9-16	8	36	5	1.0	10.0	5.0	20.0	0	0	3	0
September	4	18	10	0.0	0.0	2.5	7.0	0	0	1	0
October	5	14	4	0.0	0.0	2.5	8.5	0	0	0	0
November	3	10	4	0.0	0.0	0.0	0.0	0	0	2	0
December	4	21	1	1.0	10.0	3.0	12.0	0	0	1	0
Grass	12	40	15	0.0	0.0	3.0	6.5	0	0	2	0
Turf	4	23	4	1.0	10.0	5.0	21.0	0	0	2	0
Indoor	3	18	2	1.0	10.0	4.0	17.0	0	0	1	0
Outdoor	13	45	17	0.0	0.0	4.0	10.5	0	0	3	0

Date	Opp	Result	Tk	Ast	Sack	Yds	Stuff	Yds	Int	Yds	PD	FF	FR	TD
09/03	@Phi	W 21-6	5	2	0.0	0.0	1.0	4.0	0	0	1	0	0	0
09/10	@Cle	L 6-22	3	1	0.0	0.0	0.0	0.0	0	0	0	0	0	0
09/17	Chi	L 6-25	5	3	0.0	0.0	1.5	3.0	0	0	0	0	0	0
09/24	Was	W 14-6	5	4	0.0	0.0	0.0	0.0	0	0	0	0	0	0
10/01	@Car	W 20-13	6	0	0.0	0.0	0.0	0.0	0	0	0	0	0	0
10/08	Cin	W 19-16	2	0	0.0	0.0	0.0	0.0	0	0	1	0	0	0
10/15	Min	W 20-17	1	0	0:0	0.0	0.0	0.0	0	0	0	0	0	0
10/22	Atl	L 21-24	0	3	0.0	0.0	0.5	0.5	0	0	0	0	0	0
10/29	@Hou	L 7-19	5	0	0.0	0.0	2.0	8.0	0	0	0	0	0	0
11/12	@Det	L 24-27	5	2	0.0	0.0	0.0	0.0	0	0	1	0	0	0
11/19	Jac	W 17-16	2	1	0.0	0.0	0.0	0.0	0	0	1	0	0	0
11/26	@GB	L 13-35	3	1	0.0	0.0	0.0	0.0	0	0	0	0	0	0
12/03	@Min	L 17-31	8	0	1.0	10.0	2.0	9.0	0	0	0	0	0	0
12/10	GB	W 13-10	7	1	0.0	0.0	0.0	0.0	0	0	1	0	0	0
12/17	@Chi	L 10-31	4	0	0.0	0.0	1.0	3.0	0	0	0	0	0	0
12/23	Det	L 10-37	2	0	0.0	0.0	0.0	0.0	0	0	0	0	0	0

Michael Brooks

New York Giants – LB

1995 Defensive Splits

	G	Tk	Ast	Sack	Yds	Stuff	Yds	Int	Yds	PD	TD
Total	16	95	21	1.0	10.0	1.5	1.5	0	0	1	0
vs. Playoff	8	59	5	1.0	10.0	0.5	0.5	0	0	1	0
vs. Non-Playoff	8	36	16	0.0	0.0	1.0	1.0	0	0	0	0
vs. Own Division	8	49	9	1.0	10.0	1.5	1.5	0	0	0	0
Home	8	47	12	0.0	0.0	1.0	1.0	0	0	0	0
Away	8	48	9	1.0	10.0	0.5	0.5	0	0	1	0
Games 1-8	8	40	8	0.0	0.0	1.0	1.0	0	0	1	0
Games 9-16	8	55	13	1.0	10.0	0.5	0.5	0	0	0	0
September	4	18	3	0.0	0.0	0.0	0.0	0	0	1	0
October	4	22	5	0.0	0.0	1.0	1.0	0	0	0	0
November	5	31	11	1.0	10.0	0.0	0.0	0	0	0	0
December	3	24	2	0.0	0.0	0.5	0.5	0	0	0	0
Grass	5	25	5	0.0	0.0	0.0	0.0	0	0	1	0
Turf	11	70	16	1.0	10.0	1.5	1.5	0	0	0	0
Indoor	1	4	4	0.0	0.0	0.0	0.0	0	0	0	0
Outdoor	15	91	17	1.0	10.0	1.5	1.5	0	0	1	0

Game Logs

Date	Opp	Result	Tk	Ast	Sack	Yds	Stuff	Yds	Int	Yds	PD	FF	FR	TD
09/04	Dal	L 0-35	4	0	0.0	0.0	0.0	0.0	0	0	0	0	0	0
09/10	@KC	L 17-20	8	0	0.0	0.0	0.0	0.0	0	0	0	0	0	0
09/17	@GB	L 6-14	5	3	0.0	0.0	0.0	0.0	0	0	1	0	0	0
09/24	NO	W 45-29	1	0	0.0	0.0	0.0	0.0	0	0	0	0	0	0
10/01	@SF	L 6-20	8	0	0.0	0.0	0.0	0.0	0	0	0	0	0	0
10/08	Ari	W 27-21	5	3	0.0	0.0	1.0	1.0	0	0	0	0	0	0
10/15	Phi	L 14-17	8	2	0.0	0.0	0.0	0.0	0	0	0	0	0	0
10/29	@Was	W 24-15	1	0	0.0	0.0	0.0	0.0	0	0	0	0	0	0
11/05	@Sea	L 28-30	4	4	0.0	0.0	0.0	0.0	0	0	0	0	0	0
11/12	Oak	L 13-17	4	3	0.0	0.0	0.0	0.0	0	0	0	0	0	0
11/19	@Phi	L 19-28	11	0	1.0	10.0	0.0	0.0	0	0	0	0	0	0
11/26	Chi	L 24-27	9	2	0.0	0.0	0.0	0.0	0	0	0	0	0	0
11/30	@Ari	W 10-6	3	2	0.0	0.0	0.0	0.0	0	0	0	0	0	0
12/10	Was	W 20-13	9	2	0.0	0.0	0.0	0.0	0	0	0	0	0	0
12/17	@Dal	L 20-21	8	0	0.0	0.0	0.5	0.5	0	0	0	0	0	0
12/23	SD	L 17-27	7	0	0.0	0.0	0.0	0.0	0	0	0	0	0	0

Larry Brown

Dallas Cowboys – CB

1995 Defensive Splits

	G	Tk	Ast	Sack	Yds	Stuff	Yds	Int	Yds	PD	TD
Total	16	43	4	0.0	0.0	1.0	3.0	6	124	12	2
vs. Playoff	7	20	3	0.0	0.0	0.0	0.0	3	88	5	2
vs. Non-Playoff	9	23	1	0.0	0.0	1.0	3.0	3	36	7	0
vs. Own Division	8	17	2	0.0	0.0	0.0	0.0	4	103	7	2
Home	8	18	3	0.0	0.0	0.0	0.0	3	38	6	1
Away	8	25	1	0.0	0.0	1.0	3.0	3	86	6	1
Games 1-8	8	21	0	0.0	0.0	1.0	3.0	3	21	8	0
Games 9-16	8	22	4	0.0	0.0	0.0	0.0	3	103	4	2
September	4	11	0	0.0	0.0	1.0	3.0	2	18	6	0
October	4	10	0	0.0	0.0	0.0	0.0	1	3	2	0
November	4	13	3	0.0	0.0	0.0	0.0	1	20	2	1
December	4	9	1	0.0	0.0	0.0	0.0	2	83	2	1
Grass	4	11	1	0.0	0.0	0.0	0.0	2	21	2	0
Turf	12	32	3	0.0	0.0	1.0	3.0	4	103	10	2
Indoor	2	6	0	0.0	0.0	1.0	3.0	0	0	1	0
Outdoor	14	37	4	0.0	0.0	0.0	0.0	6	124	11	2

Game Logs

Date	Opp	Result	Tk	Ast	Sack	Yds	Stuff	Yds	Int	Yds	PD	FF	FR	TD
09/04	@NYN	W 35-0	4	0	0.0	0.0	0.0	0.0	0	0	2	0	0	0
09/10	Den	W 31-21	2	0	0.0	0.0	0.0	0.0	1	18	1	0	0	0
09/17	@Min	W 23-17	4	0	0.0	0.0	1.0	3.0	0	0	1	0	0	0
09/24	Ari	W 34-20	1	0	0.0	0.0	0.0	0.0	1	0	2	0	0	0
10/01	@Was	L 23-27	2	0	0.0	0.0	0.0	0.0	0	0	0	0	0	0
10/08	GB	W 34-24	2	0	0.0	0.0	0.0	0.0	0	0	1	0	0	0
10/15	@SD	W 23-9	4	0	0.0	0.0	0.0	0.0	1	3	1	0	0	0
10/29	@Atl	W 28-13	2	0	0.0	0.0	0.0	0.0	0	0	0	0	0	0
11/06	Phi	W 34-12	1	1	0.0	0.0	0.0	0.0	1	20	1	0	0	1
11/12	SF	L 20-38	3	1	0.0	0.0	0.0	0.0	0	0	1	0	0	0
11/19	@Oak	W 34-21	5	0	0.0	0.0	0.0	0.0	0	0	0	0	0	0
11/23	KC	W 24-12	4	1	0.0	0.0	0.0	0.0	0	0	0	0	0	0
12/03	Was	L 17-24	3	0	0.0	0.0	0.0	0.0	0	0	0	0	0	0
12/10	@Phi	L 17-20	4	0	0.0	0.0	0.0	0.0	1	65	1	0	0	1
12/17	NYN	W 21-20	2	0	0.0	0.0	0.0	0.0	0	0	0	0	0	0
12/25	@Ari	W 37-13	0	1	0.0	0.0	0.0	0.0	1	18	1	0	0	0

Vincent Brown

New England Patriots – LB

1995 Defensive Splits

	G	Tk	Ast	Sack	Yds	Stuff	Yds	Int	Yds	PD	TD
Total	16	77	38	4.0	19.0	0.0	0.0	4	1	5	0
vs. Playoff	10	50	20	2.0	1.0	0.0	0.0	3	1	3	0
vs. Non-Playoff	6	27	18	2.0	18.0	0.0	0.0	1	0	2	0
vs. Own Division	8	48	24	1.0	10.0	0.0	0.0	2	0	2	0
Home	8	40	25	1.0	8.0	0.0	0.0	0	0	1	0
Away	8	37	13	3.0	11.0	0.0	0.0	4	1	4	0
Games 1-8	8	33	19	3.0	9.0	0.0	0.0	1	1	2	0
Games 9-16	8	44	19	1.0	10.0	0.0	0.0	3	0	3	0
September	3	13	8	1.0	8.0	0.0	0.0	1	1	1	0
October	5	20	11	2.0	1.0	0.0	0.0	0	0	1	0
November	4	26	13	1.0	10.0	0.0	0.0	2	0	2	0
December	4	18	6	0.0	0.0	0.0	0.0	1	0	1	0
Grass	11	55	30	2.0	9.0	0.0	0.0	2	1	3	0
Turf	5	22	8	2.0	10.0	0.0	0.0	2	0	2	0
Indoor	2	9	3	1.0	0.0	0.0	0.0	0	0	0	0
Outdoor	14	68	35	3.0	19.0	0.0	0.0	4	1	5	0

Game Logs

Date	Opp	Result	Tk	Ast	Sack	Yds	Stuff	Yds	Int	Yds	PD	FF	FR	TD
09/03	Cle	W 17-14	4	2	1.0	8.0	0.0	0.0	0	0	0	0	0	0
09/10	Mia	L 3-20	6	5	0.0	0.0	0.0	0.0	0	0	0	0	0	0
09/17	@SF	L 3-28	3	1	0.0	0.0	0.0	0.0	1	1	1	0	0	0
10/01	@Atl	L 17-30	1	1	1.0	0.0	0.0	0.0	0	0	0	0	0	0
10/08	Den	L 3-37	4	7	0.0	0.0	0.0	0.0	0	0	0	0	0	0
10/15	@KC	L 26-31	6	0	1.0	1.0	0.0	0.0	0	0	0	0	0	0
10/23	Buf	W 27-14	3	2	0.0	0.0	0.0	0.0	0	0	0	0	1	0
10/29	Car	L 17-20	6	1	0.0	0.0	0.0	0.0	0	0	1	0	0	0
11/05	@NYA	W 20-7	5	4	1.0	10.0	0.0	0.0	1	0	1	0	0	0
11/12	@Mia	W 34-17	6	4	0.0	0.0	0.0	0.0	1	0	1	0	0	0
11/19	Ind	L 10-24	9	4	0.0	0.0	0.0	0.0	0	0	0	0	0	0
11/26	@Buf	W 35-25	6	1	0.0	0.0	0.0	0.0	0	0	0	0	0	0
12/03	NO	L 17-31	3	2	0.0	0.0	0.0	0.0	0	0	0	0	0	0
12/10	NYA	W 31-28	5	2	0.0	0.0	0.0	0.0	0	0	0	0	1	0
12/16	@Pit	L 27-41	2	0	0.0	0.0	0.0	0.0	1	0	1	0	0	0
12/23	@Ind	L 7-10	8	2	0.0	0.0	0.0	0.0	0	0	0	0	0	0

Ray Buchanan
Indianapolis Colts – CB

1995 Defensive Splits

	G	Tk	Ast	Sack	Yds	Stuff	Yds	Int	Yds	PD	TD
Total	16	68	15	1.0	8.0	1.0	4.0	2	60	16	0
vs. Playoff	6	30	7	0.0	0.0	0.0	0.0	0	0	6	0
vs. Non-Playoff	10	38	8	1.0	8.0	1.0	4.0	2	60	10	0
vs. Own Division	8	28	8	1.0	8.0	0.0	0.0	0	0	6	0
Home	8	35	10	0.0	0.0	0.0	0.0	0	0	8	0
Away	8	33	5	1.0	8.0	1.0	4.0	2	60	8	0
Games 1-8	8	41	10	0.0	0.0	0.0	0.0	0	0	5	0
Games 9-16	8	27	5	1.0	8.0	1.0	4.0	2	60	11	0
September	3	14	5	0.0	0.0	0.0	0.0	0	0	0	0
October	5	27	5	0.0	0.0	0.0	0.0	0	0	5	0
November	4	11	5	1.0	8.0	0.0	0.0	1	60	4	0
December	4	16	0	0.0	0.0	1.0	4.0	1	0	7	0
Grass	5	19	2	1.0	8.0	1.0	4.0	1	0	7	0
Turf	11	49	13	0.0	0.0	0.0	0.0	1	60	9	0
Indoor	9	40	10	0.0	0.0	0.0	0.0	1	60	9	0
Outdoor	7	28	5	1.0	8.0	1.0	4.0	1	0	7	0

Game Logs

Date	Opp	Result	Tk	Ast	Sack	Yds	Stuff	Yds	Int	Yds	PD	FF	FR	TD
09/03	Cin	L 21-24	5	2	0.0	0.0	0.0	0.0	0	0	0	0	1	0
09/10	@NYA	W 27-24	2	2	0.0	0.0	0.0	0.0	0	0	0	0	0	0
09/17	@Buf	L 14-20	7	1	0.0	0.0	0.0	0.0	0	0	0	0	0	0
10/01	StL	W 21-18	4	2	0.0	0.0	0.0	0.0	0	0	1	0	0	0
10/08	@Mia	W 27-24	5	0	0.0	0.0	0.0	0.0	0	0	1	0	0	0
10/15	SF	W 18-17	5	2	0.0	0.0	0.0	0.0	0	0	2	0	0	0
10/22	@Oak	L 17-30	7	1	0.0	0.0	0.0	0.0	0	0	1	0	0	0
10/29	NYA	W 17-10	6	0	0.0	0.0	0.0	0.0	0	0	0	0	0	0
11/05	Buf	L 10-16	1	2	0.0	0.0	0.0	0.0	0	0	2	0	0	0
11/12	@NO	L 14-17	5	0	0.0	0.0	0.0	0.0	1	60	1	0	0	0
11/19	@NE	W 24-10	2	1	1.0	8.0	0.0	0.0	0	0	1	0	1	0
11/26	Mia	W 36-28	3	2	0.0	0.0	0.0	0.0	0	0	1	0	0	0
12/03	@Car	L 10-13	2	0	0.0	0.0	0.0	0.0	1	0	3	0	0	0
12/10	@Jac	W 41-31	3	0	0.0	0.0	1.0	4.0	0	0	1	0	0	0
12/17	SD	L 24-27	9	0	0.0	0.0	0.0	0.0	0	0	1	0	0	0
12/23	NE	W 10-7	2	0	0.0	0.0	0.0	0.0	0	0	2	0	0	0

Vince Buck
New Orleans Saints – S

1995 Defensive Splits

	G	Tk	Ast	Sack	Yds	Stuff	Yds	Int	Yds	PD	TD
Total	13	53	15	0.0	0.0	0.0	0.0	0	0	4	0
vs. Playoff	6	30	11	0.0	0.0	0.0	0.0	0	0	3	0
vs. Non-Playoff	7	23	4	0.0	0.0	0.0	0.0	0	0	1	0
vs. Own Division	7	27	10	0.0	0.0	0.0	0.0	0	0	3	0
Home	7	31	13	0.0	0.0	0.0	0.0	0	0	3	0
Away	6	22	2	0.0	0.0	0.0	0.0	0	0	1	0
Games 1-8	8	40	12	0.0	0.0	0.0	0.0	0	0	4	0
Games 9-16	5	13	3	0.0	0.0	0.0	0.0	0	0	0	0
September	4	20	9	0.0	0.0	0.0	0.0	0	0	2	0
October	4	20	3	0.0	0.0	0.0	0.0	0	0	2	0
November	4	13	2	0.0	0.0	0.0	0.0	0	0	0	0
December	1	0	1	0.0	0.0	0.0	0.0	0	0	0	0
Grass	3	9	1	0.0	0.0	0.0	0.0	0	0	1	0
Turf	10	44	14	0.0	0.0	0.0	0.0	0	0	3	0
Indoor	8	35	13	0.0	0.0	0.0	0.0	0	0	3	0
Outdoor	5	18	2	0.0	0.0	0.0	0.0	0	0	1	0

Game Logs

Date	Opp	Result	Tk	Ast	Sack	Yds	Stuff	Yds	Int	Yds	PD	FF	FR	TD
09/03	SF	L 22-24	6	6	0.0	0.0	0.0	0.0	0	0	2	0	1	0
09/10	@StL	L 13-17	3	0	0.0	0.0	0.0	0.0	0	0	0	0	0	0
09/17	Atl	L 24-27	5	2	0.0	0.0	0.0	0.0	0	0	0	0	0	0
09/24	@NYN	L 29-45	6	1	0.0	0.0	0.0	0.0	0	0	0	0	0	0
10/01	Phi	L 10-15	7	2	0.0	0.0	0.0	0.0	0	0	0	0	0	0
10/15	Mia	W 33-30	4	1	0.0	0.0	0.0	0.0	0	0	1	0	1	0
10/22	@Car	L 3-20	6	0	0.0	0.0	0.0	0.0	0	0	1	0	0	0
10/29	@SF	W 11-7	3	0	0.0	0.0	0.0	0.0	0	0	0	0	0	0
11/05	StL	W 19-10	2	0	0.0	0.0	0.0	0.0	0	0	0	0	0	0
11/12	Ind	W 17-14	5	0	0.0	0.0	0.0	0.0	0	0	0	0	1	0
11/19	@Min	L 24-43	4	0	0.0	0.0	0.0	0.0	0	0	0	0	0	0
11/26	Car	W 34-26	2	2	0.0	0.0	0.0	0.0	0	0	0	0	1	0
12/03	@NE	W 31-17	0	1	0.0	0.0	0.0	0.0	0	0	0	0	0	0

Rob Burnett
Cleveland Browns – DE

1995 Defensive Splits

	G	Tk	Ast	Sack	Yds	Stuff	Yds	Int	Yds	PD	TD
Total	16	40	15	7.5	50.5	5.0	11.0	0	0	2	0
vs. Playoff	7	15	7	1.5	10.5	2.5	8.0	0	0	0	0
vs. Non-Playoff	9	25	8	6.0	40.0	2.5	3.0	0	0	2	0
vs. Own Division	8	26	6	5.5	40.0	4.5	9.0	0	0	1	0
Home	8	17	3	2.5	22.0	2.0	4.5	0	0	1	0
Away	8	23	12	5.0	28.5	3.0	6.5	0	0	1	0
Games 1-8	8	14	12	5.5	34.5	1.0	3.0	0	0	1	0
Games 9-16	8	26	3	2.0	16.0	4.0	8.0	0	0	1	0
September	4	4	7	0.5	4.0	0.5	1.0	0	0	1	0
October	4	10	5	5.0	30.5	0.5	2.0	0	0	0	0
November	4	13	2	1.0	10.0	2.0	6.0	0	0	0	0
December	4	13	1	1.0	6.0	2.0	2.0	0	0	1	0
Grass	11	22	7	2.5	22.0	3.0	5.5	0	0	2	0
Turf	5	18	8	5.0	28.5	2.0	5.5	0	0	0	0
Indoor	3	10	5	1.5	6.5	1.0	3.0	0	0	0	0
Outdoor	13	30	10	6.0	44.0	4.0	8.0	0	0	2	0

Game Logs

Date	Opp	Result	Tk	Ast	Sack	Yds	Stuff	Yds	Int	Yds	PD	FF	FR	TD
09/03	@NE	L 14-17	1	3	0.0	0.0	0.0	0.0	0	0	1	0	0	0
09/10	TB	W 22-6	1	1	0.5	4.0	0.0	0.0	0	0	0	0	1	0
09/17	@Hou	W 14-7	2	3	0.0	0.0	0.5	1.0	0	0	0	0	0	0
09/24	KC	W 35-17	0	0	0.0	0.0	0.0	0.0	0	0	0	0	0	0
10/02	Buf	L 19-22	2	2	0.0	0.0	0.0	0.0	0	0	0	0	0	0
10/08	@Det	L 20-38	2	2	0.5	0.5	0.5	2.0	0	0	0	0	0	0
10/22	Jac	L 15-23	2	0	1.0	8.0	0.0	0.0	0	0	0	0	0	0
10/29	@Cin	W 29-26	4	1	3.5	22.0	0.0	0.0	0	0	0	0	0	0
11/05	Hou	L 10-37	3	0	0.0	0.0	0.0	0.0	0	0	0	0	0	0
11/13	@Pit	L 3-20	4	2	0.0	0.0	1.0	2.5	0	0	0	0	0	0
11/19	GB	L 20-31	1	0	0.0	0.0	0.0	0.0	0	0	0	0	0	0
11/26	Pit	L 17-20	5	0	1.0	10.0	1.0	3.5	0	0	0	0	0	0
12/03	@SD	L 13-31	1	1	0.0	0.0	0.0	0.0	0	0	0	0	0	0
12/09	@Min	L 11-27	6	0	1.0	6.0	0.0	0.0	0	0	0	0	0	0
12/17	Cin	W 26-10	3	0	0.0	0.0	1.0	1.0	0	0	1	0	0	0
12/24	@Jac	L 21-24	3	0	0.0	0.0	1.0	1.0	0	0	0	0	0	0

Leroy Butler
Green Bay Packers – S

1995 Defensive Splits

	G	Tk	Ast	Sack	Yds	Stuff	Yds	Int	Yds	PD	TD
Total	16	82	20	1.0	11.0	1.0	1.0	5	105	13	0
vs. Playoff	4	23	7	0.0	0.0	1.0	1.0	0	0	1	0
vs. Non-Playoff	12	59	13	1.0	11.0	0.0	0.0	5	105	12	0
vs. Own Division	8	40	12	1.0	11.0	0.0	0.0	3	29	6	0
Home	8	34	12	1.0	11.0	1.0	1.0	2	0	7	0
Away	8	48	8	0.0	0.0	0.0	0.0	3	105	6	0
Games 1-8	8	41	13	0.0	0.0	0.0	0.0	1	0	4	0
Games 9-16	8	41	7	1.0	11.0	1.0	1.0	4	105	9	0
September	4	19	6	0.0	0.0	0.0	0.0	1	0	4	0
October	4	22	7	0.0	0.0	0.0	0.0	0	0	0	0
November	4	22	4	1.0	11.0	0.0	0.0	2	76	3	0
December	4	19	3	0.0	0.0	1.0	1.0	2	29	6	0
Grass	12	56	14	1.0	11.0	1.0	1.0	5	105	12	0
Turf	4	26	6	0.0	0.0	0.0	0.0	0	0	1	0
Indoor	3	14	5	0.0	0.0	0.0	0.0	0	0	1	0
Outdoor	13	68	15	1.0	11.0	1.0	1.0	5	105	12	0

Game Logs

Date	Opp	Result	Tk	Ast	Sack	Yds	Stuff	Yds	Int	Yds	PD	FF	FR	TD
09/03	StL	L 14-17	2	3	0.0	0.0	0.0	0.0	0	0	0	0	0	0
09/11	@Chi	W 27-24	5	0	0.0	0.0	0.0	0.0	1	0	1	0	0	0
09/17	NYN	W 14-6	6	3	0.0	0.0	0.0	0.0	0	0	3	0	0	0
09/24	@Jac	W 24-14	6	0	0.0	0.0	0.0	0.0	0	0	0	0	0	0
10/08	@Dal	L 24-34	12	1	0.0	0.0	0.0	0.0	0	0	0	0	0	0
10/15	Det	W 30-21	4	1	0.0	0.0	0.0	0.0	0	0	0	0	0	0
10/22	Min	W 38-21	5	1	0.0	0.0	0.0	0.0	0	0	0	0	0	0
10/29	@Det	L 16-24	1	4	0.0	0.0	0.0	0.0	0	0	0	0	0	0
11/05	@Min	L 24-27	9	1	0.0	0.0	0.0	0.0	0	0	1	0	0	0
11/12	Chi	W 35-28	5	2	1.0	11.0	0.0	0.0	1	0	1	0	0	0
11/19	@Cle	W 31-20	4	0	0.0	0.0	0.0	0.0	1	76	1	0	0	0
11/26	TB	W 35-13	4	1	0.0	0.0	0.0	0.0	0	0	0	0	0	0
12/03	Cin	W 24-10	2	0	0.0	0.0	0.0	0.0	1	0	1	0	0	0
12/10	@TB	L 10-13	7	2	0.0	0.0	0.0	0.0	1	29	3	0	0	0
12/16	@NO	W 34-23	4	0	0.0	0.0	0.0	0.0	0	0	1	0	0	0
12/24	Pit	W 24-19	6	1	0.0	0.0	1.0	1.0	0	0	1	0	0	0

Joe Cain
Chicago Bears – LB

1995 Defensive Splits

	G	Tk	Ast	Sack	Yds	Stuff	Yds	Int	Yds	PD	TD
Total	16	60	19	0.0	0.0	5.0	5.0	0	0	4	0
vs. Playoff	6	22	13	0.0	0.0	2.0	2.0	0	0	1	0
vs. Non-Playoff	10	38	6	0.0	0.0	3.0	3.0	0	0	3	0
vs. Own Division	8	24	13	0.0	0.0	1.0	1.0	0	0	1	0
Home	8	26	8	0.0	0.0	3.0	3.0	0	0	1	0
Away	8	34	11	0.0	0.0	2.0	2.0	0	0	3	0
Games 1-8	8	26	5	0.0	0.0	2.0	2.0	0	0	1	0
Games 9-16	8	34	14	0.0	0.0	3.0	3.0	0	0	3	0
September	4	16	4	0.0	0.0	1.0	1.0	0	0	0	0
October	4	10	1	0.0	0.0	1.0	1.0	0	0	1	0
November	4	20	10	0.0	0.0	2.0	2.0	0	0	2	0
December	4	14	4	0.0	0.0	1.0	1.0	0	0	1	0
Grass	11	38	11	0.0	0.0	3.0	3.0	0	0	2	0
Turf	5	22	8	0.0	0.0	2.0	2.0	0	0	2	0
Indoor	2	2	4	0.0	0.0	0.0	0.0	0	0	0	0
Outdoor	14	58	15	0.0	0.0	5.0	5.0	0	0	4	0

Game Logs

Date	Opp	Result	Tk	Ast	Sack	Yds	Stuff	Yds	Int	Yds	PD	FF	FR	TD
09/03	Min	W 31-14	2	1	0.0	0.0	0.0	0.0	0	0	0	0	0	0
09/11	GB	L 24-27	3	3	0.0	0.0	0.0	0.0	0	0	0	0	0	0
09/17	@TB	W 25-6	3	0	0.0	0.0	0.0	0.0	0	0	0	0	0	0
09/24	@StL	L 28-34	8	0	0.0	0.0	1.0	1.0	0	0	0	0	0	0
10/08	Car	W 31-27	3	1	0.0	0.0	1.0	1.0	0	0	1	0	0	0
10/15	@Jac	W 30-27	4	0	0.0	0.0	0.0	0.0	0	0	0	0	0	0
10/22	Hou	W 35-32	3	0	0.0	0.0	0.0	0.0	0	0	0	0	0	0
10/30	@Min	W 14-6	0	0	0.0	0.0	0.0	0.0	0	0	0	0	0	0
11/05	Pit	L 34-37	4	1	0.0	0.0	1.0	1.0	0	0	0	0	0	0
11/12	@GB	L 28-35	5	3	0.0	0.0	0.0	0.0	0	0	1	0	0	0
11/19	Det	L 17-24	6	2	0.0	0.0	1.0	1.0	0	0	0	0	0	0
11/26	@NYN	W 27-24	5	4	0.0	0.0	0.0	0.0	0	0	1	0	0	0
12/04	@Det	L 7-27	2	4	0.0	0.0	0.0	0.0	0	0	0	0	0	0
12/10	@Cin	L 10-16	7	0	0.0	0.0	1.0	1.0	0	0	1	0	0	0
12/17	TB	W 31-10	3	0	0.0	0.0	0.0	0.0	0	0	0	0	0	0
12/24	Phi	W 20-14	2	0	0.0	0.0	0.0	0.0	0	0	0	0	0	0

Jesse Campbell
New York Giants – S

1995 Defensive Splits

	G	Tk	Ast	Sack	Yds	Stuff	Yds	Int	Yds	PD	TD
Total	16	74	28	0.0	0.0	0.5	1.5	0	0	9	0
vs. Playoff	8	33	14	0.0	0.0	0.5	1.5	0	0	5	0
vs. Non-Playoff	8	41	14	0.0	0.0	0.0	0.0	0	0	4	0
vs. Own Division	8	38	18	0.0	0.0	0.5	1.5	0	0	4	0
Home	8	36	17	0.0	0.0	0.5	1.5	0	0	3	0
Away	8	38	11	0.0	0.0	0.0	0.0	0	0	6	0
Games 1-8	8	39	13	0.0	0.0	0.5	1.5	0	0	3	0
Games 9-16	8	35	15	0.0	0.0	0.0	0.0	0	0	6	0
September	4	18	5	0.0	0.0	0.0	0.0	0	0	2	0
October	4	21	8	0.0	0.0	0.5	1.5	0	0	1	0
November	5	24	8	0.0	0.0	0.0	0.0	0	0	5	0
December	3	11	7	0.0	0.0	0.0	0.0	0	0	1	0
Grass	5	26	5	0.0	0.0	0.0	0.0	0	0	3	0
Turf	11	48	23	0.0	0.0	0.5	1.5	0	0	6	0
Indoor	1	4	3	0.0	0.0	0.0	0.0	0	0	1	0
Outdoor	15	70	25	0.0	0.0	0.5	1.5	0	0	8	0

Game Logs

Date	Opp	Result	Tk	Ast	Sack	Yds	Stuff	Yds	Int	Yds	PD	FF	FR	TD
09/04	Dal	L 0-35	5	2	0.0	0.0	0.0	0.0	0	0	0	1	0	0
09/10	@KC	L 17-20	10	0	0.0	0.0	0.0	0.0	0	0	1	0	0	0
09/17	@GB	L 6-14	0	3	0.0	0.0	0.0	0.0	0	0	1	0	0	0
09/24	NO	W 45-29	3	0	0.0	0.0	0.0	0.0	0	0	0	0	0	0
10/01	@SF	L 6-20	5	0	0.0	0.0	0.0	0.0	0	0	0	0	0	0
10/08	Ari	W 27-21	6	4	0.0	0.0	0.0	0.0	0	0	1	0	0	0
10/15	Phi	L 14-17	3	4	0.0	0.0	0.5	1.5	0	0	0	0	0	0
10/22	@Was	W 24-15	7	0	0.0	0.0	0.0	0.0	0	0	0	0	0	0
11/05	@Sea	L 28-30	4	3	0.0	0.0	0.0	0.0	0	0	1	0	0	0
11/12	Oak	L 13-17	5	2	0.0	0.0	0.0	0.0	0	0	0	0	0	0
11/19	@Phi	L 19-28	4	1	0.0	0.0	0.0	0.0	0	0	2	0	0	0
11/26	Chi	L 24-27	7	0	0.0	0.0	0.0	0.0	0	0	1	0	0	0
11/30	@Ari	W 10-6	4	2	0.0	0.0	0.0	0.0	0	0	1	0	0	0
12/10	Was	W 20-13	5	3	0.0	0.0	0.0	0.0	0	0	0	0	0	0
12/17	@Dal	L 20-21	4	2	0.0	0.0	0.0	0.0	0	0	0	0	0	0
12/23	SD	L 17-27	2	2	0.0	0.0	0.0	0.0	0	0	1	0	0	0

Mark Carrier

Chicago Bears – S

1995 Defensive Splits

	G	Tk	Ast	Sack	Yds	Stuff	Yds	Int	Yds	PD	TD
Total	16	64	8	0.0	0.0	1.0	2.0	0	0	10	0
vs. Playoff	6	23	2	0.0	0.0	0.0	0.0	0	0	5	0
vs. Non-Playoff	10	41	6	0.0	0.0	1.0	2.0	0	0	5	0
vs. Own Division	8	38	4	0.0	0.0	0.0	0.0	0	0	6	0
Home	8	38	5	0.0	0.0	1.0	2.0	0	0	5	0
Away	8	26	3	0.0	0.0	0.0	0.0	0	0	5	0
Games 1-8	8	42	7	0.0	0.0	1.0	2.0	0	0	5	0
Games 9-16	8	22	1	0.0	0.0	0.0	0.0	0	0	5	0
September	4	25	2	0.0	0.0	0.0	0.0	0	0	2	0
October	4	17	5	0.0	0.0	1.0	2.0	0	0	3	0
November	4	10	1	0.0	0.0	0.0	0.0	0	0	3	0
December	4	12	0	0.0	0.0	0.0	0.0	0	0	2	0
Grass	11	41	7	0.0	0.0	1.0	2.0	0	0	7	0
Turf	5	23	1	0.0	0.0	0.0	0.0	0	0	3	0
Indoor	2	13	1	0.0	0.0	0.0	0.0	0	0	2	0
Outdoor	14	51	7	0.0	0.0	1.0	2.0	0	0	8	0

Game Logs

Date	Opp	Result	Tk	Ast	Sack	Yds	Stuff	Yds	Int	Yds	PD	FF	FR	TD
09/03	Min	W 31-14	9	0	0.0	0.0	0.0	0.0	0	0	0	0	0	0
09/11	GB	L 24-27	9	1	0.0	0.0	0.0	0.0	0	0	1	0	0	0
09/17	@TB	W 25-6	2	1	0.0	0.0	0.0	0.0	0	0	1	0	0	0
09/24	@StL	L 28-34	5	0	0.0	0.0	0.0	0.0	0	0	0	0	0	0
10/08	Car	W 31-27	3	3	0.0	0.0	0.0	0.0	0	0	0	0	0	0
10/15	@Jac	W 30-27	1	1	0.0	0.0	0.0	0.0	0	0	1	0	0	0
10/22	Hou	W 35-32	5	0	0.0	0.0	1.0	2.0	0	0	0	0	0	0
10/30	@Min	W 14-6	8	1	0.0	0.0	0.0	0.0	0	0	2	0	0	0
11/05	Pit	L 34-37	5	0	0.0	0.0	0.0	0.0	0	0	1	0	0	0
11/12	@GB	L 28-35	0	0	0.0	0.0	0.0	0.0	0	0	0	0	0	0
11/19	Det	L 17-24	2	1	0.0	0.0	0.0	0.0	0	0	2	0	0	0
11/26	@NYN	W 27-24	3	0	0.0	0.0	0.0	0.0	0	0	0	0	0	0
12/04	@Det	L 7-27	5	0	0.0	0.0	0.0	0.0	0	0	0	0	0	0
12/10	@Cin	L 10-16	2	0	0.0	0.0	0.0	0.0	0	0	1	0	0	0
12/17	TB	W 31-10	3	0	0.0	0.0	0.0	0.0	0	0	0	0	0	0
12/24	Phi	W 20-14	2	0	0.0	0.0	0.0	0.0	0	0	1	0	1	0

Dale Carter

Kansas City Chiefs – CB

1995 Defensive Splits

	G	Tk	Ast	Sack	Yds	Stuff	Yds	Int	Yds	PD	TD
Total	16	53	5	0.0	0.0	0.0	0.0	4	45	13	0
vs. Playoff	4	16	2	0.0	0.0	0.0	0.0	0	0	4	0
vs. Non-Playoff	12	37	3	0.0	0.0	0.0	0.0	4	45	9	0
vs. Own Division	8	24	0	0.0	0.0	0.0	0.0	2	29	5	0
Home	8	22	0	0.0	0.0	0.0	0.0	2	16	6	0
Away	8	31	5	0.0	0.0	0.0	0.0	2	29	7	0
Games 1-8	8	28	3	0.0	0.0	0.0	0.0	3	45	9	0
Games 9-16	8	25	2	0.0	0.0	0.0	0.0	1	0	4	0
September	4	15	0	0.0	0.0	0.0	0.0	0	0	1	0
October	4	13	3	0.0	0.0	0.0	0.0	3	45	8	0
November	4	14	0	0.0	0.0	0.0	0.0	1	0	3	0
December	4	11	2	0.0	0.0	0.0	0.0	0	0	1	0
Grass	14	42	5	0.0	0.0	0.0	0.0	4	45	12	0
Turf	2	11	0	0.0	0.0	0.0	0.0	0	0	1	0
Indoor	1	5	0	0.0	0.0	0.0	0.0	0	0	0	0
Outdoor	15	48	5	0.0	0.0	0.0	0.0	4	45	13	0

Game Logs

Date	Opp	Result	Tk	Ast	Sack	Yds	Stuff	Yds	Int	Yds	PD	FF	FR	TD
09/03	@Sea	W 34-10	5	0	0.0	0.0	0.0	0.0	0	0	0	0	0	0
09/10	NYN	W 20-17	2	0	0.0	0.0	0.0	0.0	0	0	0	0	0	0
09/17	Oak	W 23-17	3	0	0.0	0.0	0.0	0.0	0	0	0	0	1	0
09/24	@Cle	L 17-35	5	0	0.0	0.0	0.0	0.0	0	0	1	0	0	0
10/01	@Ari	W 24-3	3	3	0.0	0.0	0.0	0.0	0	0	1	0	1	0
10/09	SD	W 29-23	3	0	0.0	0.0	0.0	0.0	0	0	2	0	0	0
10/15	NE	W 31-26	4	0	0.0	0.0	0.0	0.0	1	16	2	0	0	0
10/22	@Den	W 21-7	3	0	0.0	0.0	0.0	0.0	2	29	3	0	0	0
11/05	Was	W 24-3	3	0	0.0	0.0	0.0	0.0	1	0	0	0	0	0
11/12	@SD	W 22-7	3	0	0.0	0.0	0.0	0.0	0	0	0	0	0	0
11/19	Hou	W 20-13	2	0	0.0	0.0	0.0	0.0	0	0	0	0	0	0
11/23	@Dal	L 12-24	6	0	0.0	0.0	0.0	0.0	0	0	1	0	0	0
12/03	@Oak	W 29-23	2	0	0.0	0.0	0.0	0.0	0	0	0	0	0	0
12/11	@Mia	L 6-13	4	2	0.0	0.0	0.0	0.0	0	0	1	0	0	0
12/17	Den	W 20-17	1	0	0.0	0.0	0.0	0.0	0	0	0	0	0	0
12/24	Sea	W 26-3	4	0	0.0	0.0	0.0	0.0	0	0	0	0	0	0

Kevin Carter

St. Louis Rams – DE

1995 Defensive Splits

	G	Tk	Ast	Sack	Yds	Stuff	Yds	Int	Yds	PD	TD
Total	16	33	4	6.0	35.0	4.5	10.5	0	0	0	0
vs. Playoff	9	16	1	2.0	15.0	2.0	6.0	0	0	0	0
vs. Non-Playoff	7	17	3	4.0	20.0	2.5	4.5	0	0	0	0
vs. Own Division	8	17	3	3.0	19.0	1.0	1.0	0	0	0	0
Home	8	11	2	2.0	17.0	2.0	6.0	0	0	0	0
Away	8	22	2	4.0	18.0	2.5	4.5	0	0	0	0
Games 1-8	8	10	0	2.0	16.0	0.0	0.0	0	0	0	0
Games 9-16	8	23	4	4.0	19.0	4.5	10.5	0	0	0	0
September	4	5	0	2.0	16.0	0.0	0.0	0	0	0	0
October	4	5	0	0.0	0.0	0.0	0.0	0	0	0	0
November	4	13	3	2.0	13.0	1.0	1.0	0	0	0	0
December	4	10	1	2.0	6.0	3.5	9.5	0	0	0	0
Grass	3	7	0	2.0	16.0	0.0	0.0	0	0	0	0
Turf	13	26	4	4.0	19.0	4.5	10.5	0	0	0	0
Indoor	7	17	4	3.0	18.0	3.0	7.0	0	0	0	0
Outdoor	9	16	0	3.0	17.0	1.5	3.5	0	0	0	0

Game Logs

Date	Opp	Result	Tk	Ast	Sack	Yds	Stuff	Yds	Int	Yds	PD	FF	FR	TD
09/03	@GB	W 17-14	2	0	1.0	10.0	0.0	0.0	0	0	0	0	0	0
09/10	NO	W 17-13	0	0	1.0	6.0	0.0	0.0	0	0	0	0	0	0
09/17	@Car	W 31-10	2	0	1.0	6.0	0.0	0.0	0	0	0	0	1	0
09/24	Chi	W 34-28	1	0	0.0	0.0	0.0	0.0	0	0	0	0	0	0
10/01	@Ind	L 18-21	1	0	0.0	0.0	0.0	0.0	0	0	0	0	0	0
10/12	Atl	W 21-19	1	0	0.0	0.0	0.0	0.0	0	0	0	0	0	0
10/22	SF	L 10-44	1	0	0.0	0.0	0.0	0.0	0	0	0	0	0	0
10/29	@Phi	L 9-20	2	0	0.0	0.0	0.0	0.0	0	0	0	0	0	0
11/05	@NO	L 10-19	6	2	1.0	1.0	0.0	0.0	0	0	0	0	1	0
11/12	Car	W 28-17	2	1	1.0	12.0	0.0	0.0	0	0	0	0	0	0
11/19	@Atl	L 6-31	2	0	0.0	0.0	1.0	1.0	0	0	0	0	0	0
11/26	@SF	L 13-41	3	0	0.0	0.0	0.0	0.0	0	0	0	0	0	0
12/03	@NYA	W 23-20	4	0	1.0	1.0	1.5	3.5	0	0	0	0	0	0
12/10	Buf	L 27-45	3	1	1.0	5.0	0.0	0.0	0	0	0	0	0	0
12/17	Was	L 23-35	2	0	0.0	0.0	1.0	1.0	0	0	0	0	0	0
12/24	Mia	L 22-41	1	0	0.0	0.0	1.0	5.0	0	0	0	0	0	0

Marty Carter
Chicago Bears – S

1995 Defensive Splits

	G	Tk	Ast	Sack	Yds	Stuff	Yds	Int	Yds	PD	TD
Total	16	80	15	0.0	0.0	1.0	3.0	2	20	5	0
vs. Playoff	6	31	7	0.0	0.0	1.0	3.0	1	5	1	0
vs. Non-Playoff	10	49	8	0.0	0.0	0.0	0.0	1	15	4	0
vs. Own Division	8	36	11	0.0	0.0	0.0	0.0	1	15	3	0
Home	8	43	5	0.0	0.0	1.0	3.0	1	5	2	0
Away	8	37	10	0.0	0.0	0.0	0.0	1	15	3	0
Games 1-8	8	44	5	0.0	0.0	0.0	0.0	1	15	3	0
Games 9-16	8	36	10	0.0	0.0	1.0	3.0	1	5	2	0
September	4	22	4	0.0	0.0	0.0	0.0	1	15	2	0
October	4	22	1	0.0	0.0	0.0	0.0	0	0	1	0
November	4	18	5	0.0	0.0	1.0	3.0	0	0	1	0
December	4	18	5	0.0	0.0	0.0	0.0	1	5	1	0
Grass	11	54	8	0.0	0.0	1.0	3.0	2	20	3	0
Turf	5	26	7	0.0	0.0	0.0	0.0	0	0	2	0
Indoor	2	10	4	0.0	0.0	0.0	0.0	0	0	1	0
Outdoor	14	70	11	0.0	0.0	1.0	3.0	2	20	4	0

Game Logs

Date	Opp	Result	Tk	Ast	Sack	Yds	Stuff	Yds	Int	Yds	PD	FF	FR	TD
09/03	Min	W 31-14	3	2	0.0	0.0	0.0	0.0	0	0	1	0	0	0
09/11	GB	L 24-27	8	1	0.0	0.0	0.0	0.0	0	0	0	0	0	0
09/17	@TB	W 25-6	4	1	0.0	0.0	0.0	0.0	1	15	1	0	0	0
09/24	@StL	L 28-34	7	0	0.0	0.0	0.0	0.0	0	0	0	0	0	0
10/08	Car	W 31-27	6	0	0.0	0.0	0.0	0.0	0	0	0	0	0	0
10/15	@Jac	W 30-27	4	1	0.0	0.0	0.0	0.0	0	0	0	0	0	0
10/22	Hou	W 35-32	5	0	0.0	0.0	0.0	0.0	0	0	0	2	0	0
10/30	@Min	W 14-6	7	0	0.0	0.0	0.0	0.0	0	0	1	0	0	0
11/05	Pit	L 34-37	8	0	0.0	0.0	1.0	3.0	0	0	0	0	0	0
11/12	@GB	L 28-35	3	1	0.0	0.0	0.0	0.0	0	0	0	0	0	0
11/19	Det	L 17-24	4	1	0.0	0.0	0.0	0.0	0	0	0	1	0	0
11/26	@NYN	W 27-24	3	3	0.0	0.0	0.0	0.0	0	0	1	0	0	0
12/04	@Det	L 7-27	3	4	0.0	0.0	0.0	0.0	0	0	0	0	0	0
12/10	@Cin	L 10-16	6	0	0.0	0.0	0.0	0.0	0	0	0	0	0	0
12/17	TB	W 31-10	4	1	0.0	0.0	0.0	0.0	0	0	0	0	0	0
12/24	Phi	W 20-14	5	0	0.0	0.0	0.0	0.0	1	5	1	0	0	0

Tom Carter
Washington Redskins – CB

1995 Defensive Splits

	G	Tk	Ast	Sack	Yds	Stuff	Yds	Int	Yds	PD	TD
Total	16	74	4	0.0	0.0	0.0	0.0	4	116	19	1
vs. Playoff	6	33	1	0.0	0.0	0.0	0.0	1	34	8	0
vs. Non-Playoff	10	41	3	0.0	0.0	0.0	0.0	3	82	11	1
vs. Own Division	8	31	3	0.0	0.0	0.0	0.0	2	65	7	0
Home	8	34	1	0.0	0.0	0.0	0.0	3	65	15	0
Away	8	40	3	0.0	0.0	0.0	0.0	1	51	4	1
Games 1-8	8	45	3	0.0	0.0	0.0	0.0	2	65	11	0
Games 9-16	8	29	1	0.0	0.0	0.0	0.0	2	51	8	1
September	4	18	2	0.0	0.0	0.0	0.0	1	31	4	0
October	5	29	1	0.0	0.0	0.0	0.0	1	34	8	0
November	3	9	0	0.0	0.0	0.0	0.0	1	0	4	0
December	4	18	1	0.0	0.0	0.0	0.0	1	51	3	1
Grass	12	52	2	0.0	0.0	0.0	0.0	3	65	15	0
Turf	4	22	2	0.0	0.0	0.0	0.0	1	51	4	1
Indoor	1	6	0	0.0	0.0	0.0	0.0	1	51	1	1
Outdoor	15	68	4	0.0	0.0	0.0	0.0	3	65	18	0

Game Logs

Date	Opp	Result	Tk	Ast	Sack	Yds	Stuff	Yds	Int	Yds	PD	FF	FR	TD
09/03	Ari	W 27-7	2	1	0.0	0.0	0.0	0.0	1	31	2	0	0	0
09/10	Oak	L 8-20	6	0	0.0	0.0	0.0	0.0	0	0	2	0	0	0
09/17	@Den	L 31-38	6	0	0.0	0.0	0.0	0.0	0	0	0	0	0	0
09/24	@TB	L 6-14	4	1	0.0	0.0	0.0	0.0	0	0	0	0	0	0
10/01	Dal	W 27-23	3	0	0.0	0.0	0.0	0.0	1	34	1	0	0	0
10/08	@Phi	L 34-37	9	1	0.0	0.0	0.0	0.0	0	0	2	1	0	0
10/15	@Ari	L 20-24	5	0	0.0	0.0	0.0	0.0	0	0	0	0	0	0
10/22	Det	W 36-30	10	0	0.0	0.0	0.0	0.0	0	0	4	0	0	0
10/29	NYN	L 15-24	2	0	0.0	0.0	0.0	0.0	0	0	1	0	0	0
11/05	@KC	L 3-24	3	0	0.0	0.0	0.0	0.0	0	0	0	0	0	0
11/19	Sea	L 20-27	3	0	0.0	0.0	0.0	0.0	1	0	4	0	0	0
11/26	Phi	L 7-14	3	0	0.0	0.0	0.0	0.0	0	0	0	0	0	0
12/03	@Dal	W 24-17	5	0	0.0	0.0	0.0	0.0	0	0	1	0	0	0
12/10	@NYN	L 13-20	2	1	0.0	0.0	0.0	0.0	0	0	0	0	0	0
12/17	@StL	W 35-23	6	0	0.0	0.0	0.0	0.0	1	51	1	0	0	1
12/24	Car	W 20-17	5	0	0.0	0.0	0.0	0.0	0	0	1	0	0	0

Chuck Cecil
Houston Oilers – S

1995 Defensive Splits

	G	Tk	Ast	Sack	Yds	Stuff	Yds	Int	Yds	PD	TD
Total	14	45	16	0.0	0.0	1.5	2.0	3	35	4	1
vs. Playoff	4	12	3	0.0	0.0	0.0	0.0	2	15	3	0
vs. Non-Playoff	10	33	13	0.0	0.0	1.5	2.0	1	20	1	1
vs. Own Division	6	13	10	0.0	0.0	1.5	2.0	1	13	1	0
Home	7	12	9	0.0	0.0	0.5	1.0	1	2	2	0
Away	7	33	7	0.0	0.0	1.0	1.0	2	33	2	1
Games 1-8	6	22	4	0.0	0.0	1.0	1.0	1	20	1	1
Games 9-16	8	23	12	0.0	0.0	1.0	1.0	2	15	3	0
September	2	5	2	0.0	0.0	0.5	1.0	0	0	0	0
October	4	17	2	0.0	0.0	0.0	0.0	1	20	1	1
November	4	14	7	0.0	0.0	1.0	1.0	0	0	0	0
December	4	9	5	0.0	0.0	0.0	0.0	2	15	3	0
Grass	3	19	2	0.0	0.0	1.0	1.0	0	0	0	0
Turf	11	26	14	0.0	0.0	0.5	1.0	3	35	4	1
Indoor	8	18	11	0.0	0.0	0.5	1.0	2	22	3	1
Outdoor	6	27	5	0.0	0.0	1.0	1.0	1	13	1	0

Game Logs

Date	Opp	Result	Tk	Ast	Sack	Yds	Stuff	Yds	Int	Yds	PD	FF	FR	TD
09/03	@Jac	W 10-3	-	-	-	-	-	-	-	-	-	-	-	-
09/10	Pit	L 17-34	-	-	-	-	-	-	-	-	-	-	-	-
09/17	Cle	L 7-14	3	2	0.0	0.0	0.5	1.0	0	0	0	0	0	0
09/24	@Cin	W 38-28	2	0	0.0	0.0	0.0	0.0	0	0	0	0	0	0
10/01	Jac	L 16-17	0	0	0.0	0.0	0.0	0.0	0	0	0	0	0	0
10/08	@Min	L 17-23	6	2	0.0	0.0	0.0	0.0	1	20	1	0	0	1
10/22	@Chi	L 32-35	9	0	0.0	0.0	0.0	0.0	0	0	0	0	0	0
10/29	TB	W 19-7	2	0	0.0	0.0	0.0	0.0	0	0	0	0	0	0
11/05	@Cle	W 37-10	5	2	0.0	0.0	1.0	1.0	0	0	0	0	0	0
11/12	Cin	L 25-32	1	3	0.0	0.0	0.0	0.0	0	0	0	0	0	0
11/19	@KC	L 13-20	5	0	0.0	0.0	0.0	0.0	0	0	0	0	0	0
11/26	Den	W 42-33	3	2	0.0	0.0	0.0	0.0	0	0	0	0	0	0
12/03	@Pit	L 7-21	2	3	0.0	0.0	0.0	0.0	1	13	1	0	0	0
12/10	Det	L 17-24	1	0	0.0	0.0	0.0	0.0	1	2	2	0	0	0
12/17	NYA	W 23-6	2	2	0.0	0.0	0.0	0.0	0	0	0	0	0	0
12/24	@Buf	W 28-17	4	0	0.0	0.0	0.0	0.0	0	0	0	0	0	0

Vinnie Clark
Jacksonville Jaguars – CB

1995 Defensive Splits

	G	Tk	Ast	Sack	Yds	Stuff	Yds	Int	Yds	PD	TD
Total	16	56	10	0.0	0.0	1.0	1.0	1	0	9	0
vs. Playoff	5	16	3	0.0	0.0	0.0	0.0	0	0	1	0
vs. Non-Playoff	11	40	7	0.0	0.0	1.0	1.0	1	0	8	0
vs. Own Division	8	31	4	0.0	0.0	0.0	0.0	1	0	6	0
Home	8	23	6	0.0	0.0	0.0	0.0	1	0	5	0
Away	8	33	4	0.0	0.0	1.0	1.0	0	0	4	0
Games 1-8	8	30	9	0.0	0.0	1.0	1.0	0	0	6	0
Games 9-16	8	26	1	0.0	0.0	0.0	0.0	1	0	3	0
September	4	18	5	0.0	0.0	1.0	1.0	0	0	2	0
October	5	17	4	0.0	0.0	0.0	0.0	0	0	4	0
November	3	10	1	0.0	0.0	0.0	0.0	0	0	2	0
December	4	11	0	0.0	0.0	0.0	0.0	1	0	1	0
Grass	11	29	6	0.0	0.0	0.0	0.0	1	0	7	0
Turf	5	27	4	0.0	0.0	1.0	1.0	0	0	2	0
Indoor	2	9	1	0.0	0.0	0.0	0.0	0	0	1	0
Outdoor	14	47	9	0.0	0.0	1.0	1.0	1	0	8	0

Game Logs

Date	Opp	Result	Tk	Ast	Sack	Yds	Stuff	Yds	Int	Yds	PD	FF	FR	TD
09/03	Hou	L 3-10	3	1	0.0	0.0	0.0	0.0	0	0	1	0	0	0
09/10	@Cin	L 17-24	6	0	0.0	0.0	0.0	0.0	0	0	1	0	0	0
09/17	@NYA	L 10-27	7	3	0.0	0.0	1.0	1.0	0	0	0	0	0	0
09/24	GB	L 14-24	2	1	0.0	0.0	0.0	0.0	0	0	0	0	0	0
10/01	@Hou	W 17-16	4	1	0.0	0.0	0.0	0.0	0	0	1	0	0	0
10/08	Pit	W 20-16	3	2	0.0	0.0	0.0	0.0	0	0	1	0	0	0
10/15	Chi	L 27-30	3	1	0.0	0.0	0.0	0.0	0	0	0	0	0	0
10/22	@Cle	W 23-15	2	0	0.0	0.0	0.0	0.0	0	0	1	0	0	0
10/29	@Pit	L 7-24	5	0	0.0	0.0	0.0	0.0	0	0	0	0	0	0
11/12	Sea	L 30-47	3	1	0.0	0.0	0.0	0.0	0	0	1	0	0	0
11/19	@TB	L 16-17	3	0	0.0	0.0	0.0	0.0	0	0	1	0	0	0
11/26	Cin	L 13-17	4	0	0.0	0.0	0.0	0.0	0	0	0	0	0	0
12/03	@Den	L 23-31	1	0	0.0	0.0	0.0	0.0	0	0	0	0	0	0
12/10	Ind	L 31-41	1	0	0.0	0.0	0.0	0.0	0	0	0	0	0	0
12/17	@Det	L 0-44	5	0	0.0	0.0	0.0	0.0	0	0	0	0	0	0
12/24	Cle	W 24-21	4	0	0.0	0.0	0.0	0.0	1	0	1	0	0	0

Willie Clay
Detroit Lions – S

1995 Defensive Splits

	G	Tk	Ast	Sack	Yds	Stuff	Yds	Int	Yds	PD	TD
Total	16	50	17	0.0	0.0	0.0	0.0	8	173	13	0
vs. Playoff	5	12	3	0.0	0.0	0.0	0.0	3	63	5	0
vs. Non-Playoff	11	38	14	0.0	0.0	0.0	0.0	5	110	8	0
vs. Own Division	8	26	9	0.0	0.0	0.0	0.0	5	107	7	0
Home	8	24	6	0.0	0.0	0.0	0.0	5	135	7	0
Away	8	26	11	0.0	0.0	0.0	0.0	3	38	6	0
Games 1-8	8	26	7	0.0	0.0	0.0	0.0	3	63	3	0
Games 9-16	8	24	10	0.0	0.0	0.0	0.0	5	110	10	0
September	4	17	6	0.0	0.0	0.0	0.0	1	10	1	0
October	4	9	1	0.0	0.0	0.0	0.0	2	53	2	0
November	4	12	2	0.0	0.0	0.0	0.0	2	43	5	0
December	4	12	8	0.0	0.0	0.0	0.0	3	67	5	0
Grass	4	11	2	0.0	0.0	0.0	0.0	1	11	1	0
Turf	12	39	15	0.0	0.0	0.0	0.0	7	162	12	0
Indoor	11	37	12	0.0	0.0	0.0	0.0	6	152	11	0
Outdoor	5	13	5	0.0	0.0	0.0	0.0	2	21	2	0

Game Logs

Date	Opp	Result	Tk	Ast	Sack	Yds	Stuff	Yds	Int	Yds	PD	FF	FR	TD
09/03	@Pit	L 20-23	2	3	0.0	0.0	0.0	0.0	1	10	1	0	0	0
09/10	@Min	L 10-20	8	3	0.0	0.0	0.0	0.0	0	0	0	0	0	0
09/17	Ari	L 17-20	4	0	0.0	0.0	0.0	0.0	0	0	0	0	0	0
09/25	SF	W 27-24	3	0	0.0	0.0	0.0	0.0	0	0	0	0	0	0
10/08	Cle	W 38-20	1	1	0.0	0.0	0.0	0.0	0	0	0	0	0	0
10/15	@GB	L 21-30	2	0	0.0	0.0	0.0	0.0	0	0	0	0	0	0
10/22	@Was	L 30-36	4	0	0.0	0.0	0.0	0.0	0	0	0	0	0	0
10/29	GB	W 24-16	2	0	0.0	0.0	0.0	0.0	2	53	2	0	0	0
11/05	@Atl	L 22-34	3	0	0.0	0.0	0.0	0.0	0	0	2	0	0	0
11/12	TB	W 27-24	3	2	0.0	0.0	0.0	0.0	2	43	3	0	0	0
11/19	@Chi	W 24-17	2	0	0.0	0.0	0.0	0.0	0	0	0	0	0	0
11/23	Min	W 44-38	4	0	0.0	0.0	0.0	0.0	0	0	0	0	0	0
12/04	Chi	W 27-7	2	2	0.0	0.0	0.0	0.0	0	0	1	0	0	0
12/10	@Hou	W 24-17	2	3	0.0	0.0	0.0	0.0	1	17	2	0	0	0
12/17	Jac	W 44-0	5	1	0.0	0.0	0.0	0.0	1	39	1	0	0	0
12/23	@TB	W 37-10	3	2	0.0	0.0	0.0	0.0	1	11	1	0	0	0

Marco Coleman
Miami Dolphins – DE

1995 Defensive Splits

	G	Tk	Ast	Sack	Yds	Stuff	Yds	Int	Yds	PD	TD
Total	16	33	12	6.5	49.0	2.0	6.0	0	0	4	0
vs. Playoff	9	22	8	2.5	22.0	2.0	6.0	0	0	2	0
vs. Non-Playoff	7	11	4	4.0	27.0	0.0	0.0	0	0	2	0
vs. Own Division	8	18	6	3.0	17.0	2.0	6.0	0	0	2	0
Home	8	17	7	2.5	20.0	1.0	3.0	0	0	3	0
Away	8	16	5	4.0	29.0	1.0	3.0	0	0	1	0
Games 1-8	8	19	6	4.5	26.0	1.0	3.0	0	0	3	0
Games 9-16	8	14	6	2.0	23.0	1.0	3.0	0	0	1	0
September	3	5	5	1.5	14.0	0.0	0.0	0	0	1	0
October	5	14	1	3.0	12.0	1.0	3.0	0	0	2	0
November	4	7	2	1.0	12.0	0.0	0.0	0	0	1	0
December	4	7	4	1.0	11.0	1.0	3.0	0	0	0	0
Grass	10	18	9	3.5	32.0	1.0	3.0	0	0	3	0
Turf	6	15	3	3.0	17.0	1.0	3.0	0	0	1	0
Indoor	3	11	2	2.0	16.0	0.0	0.0	0	0	0	0
Outdoor	13	22	10	4.5	33.0	2.0	6.0	0	0	4	0

Game Logs

Date	Opp	Result	Tk	Ast	Sack	Yds	Stuff	Yds	Int	Yds	PD	FF	FR	TD
09/03	NYA	W 52-14	2	1	1.0	10.0	0.0	0.0	0	0	1	0	0	0
09/10	@NE	W 20-3	0	2	0.0	0.0	0.0	0.0	0	0	0	0	0	0
09/18	Pit	W 23-10	3	2	0.5	4.0	0.0	0.0	0	0	0	0	0	0
10/01	@Cin	W 26-23	0	0	0.0	0.0	0.0	0.0	0	0	1	0	0	0
10/08	Ind	L 24-27	4	0	0.0	0.0	0.0	0.0	0	0	0	0	0	0
10/15	@NO	L 30-33	4	0	1.0	5.0	0.0	0.0	0	0	0	0	0	0
10/22	@NYA	L 16-17	2	1	1.0	1.0	0.0	0.0	0	0	0	0	0	0
10/29	Buf	W 23-6	4	0	1.0	6.0	1.0	3.0	0	0	1	0	0	0
11/05	@SD	W 24-14	1	0	1.0	12.0	0.0	0.0	0	0	0	0	0	0
11/12	NE	L 17-34	0	0	0.0	0.0	0.0	0.0	0	0	0	0	0	0
11/20	SF	L 20-44	2	0	0.0	0.0	0.0	0.0	0	0	1	0	0	0
11/26	@Ind	L 28-36	4	2	0.0	0.0	0.0	0.0	0	0	0	0	0	0
12/03	Atl	W 21-20	1	3	0.0	0.0	0.0	0.0	0	0	0	0	0	0
12/11	KC	W 13-6	1	1	0.0	0.0	0.0	0.0	0	0	0	0	0	0
12/17	@Buf	L 20-23	2	0	0.0	0.0	1.0	3.0	0	0	0	0	0	0
12/24	@StL	W 41-22	3	0	1.0	11.0	0.0	0.0	0	0	0	0	0	0

Mark Collins
Kansas City Chiefs – S

1995 Defensive Splits

	G	Tk	Ast	Sack	Yds	Stuff	Yds	Int	Yds	PD	TD
Total	16	66	8	0.0	0.0	1.5	3.0	1	8	9	1
vs. Playoff	4	22	1	0.0	0.0	0.0	0.0	0	0	2	0
vs. Non-Playoff	12	44	7	0.0	0.0	1.5	3.0	1	8	7	1
vs. Own Division	8	34	2	0.0	0.0	0.5	1.0	0	0	5	0
Home	8	34	3	0.0	0.0	0.5	1.0	1	8	2	1
Away	8	32	5	0.0	0.0	1.0	2.0	0	0	7	0
Games 1-8	8	38	4	0.0	0.0	1.5	3.0	0	0	5	0
Games 9-16	8	28	4	0.0	0.0	0.0	0.0	1	8	4	1
September	4	15	2	0.0	0.0	1.5	3.0	0	0	3	0
October	4	23	2	0.0	0.0	0.0	0.0	0	0	2	0
November	4	20	1	0.0	0.0	0.0	0.0	1	8	3	1
December	4	8	3	0.0	0.0	0.0	0.0	0	0	1	0
Grass	14	58	8	0.0	0.0	1.5	3.0	1	8	6	1
Turf	2	8	0	0.0	0.0	0.0	0.0	0	0	3	0
Indoor	1	3	0	0.0	0.0	0.0	0.0	0	0	3	0
Outdoor	15	63	8	0.0	0.0	1.5	3.0	1	8	6	1

Game Logs

Date	Opp	Result	Tk	Ast	Sack	Yds	Stuff	Yds	Int	Yds	PD	FF	FR	TD
09/03	@Sea	W 34-10	3	0	0.0	0.0	0.0	0.0	0	0	3	0	0	0
09/10	NYN	W 20-17	4	0	0.0	0.0	0.0	0.0	0	0	0	0	0	0
09/17	Oak	W 23-17	5	0	0.0	0.0	0.5	1.0	0	0	1	0	0	0
09/24	@Cle	L 17-35	3	2	0.0	0.0	1.0	2.0	0	0	0	0	0	0
10/01	@Ari	W 24-3	6	1	0.0	0.0	0.0	0.0	0	0	1	0	0	0
10/09	SD	W 29-23	8	0	0.0	0.0	0.0	0.0	0	0	1	0	0	0
10/15	NE	W 31-26	6	1	0.0	0.0	0.0	0.0	0	0	1	0	0	0
10/22	@Den	W 21-7	3	0	0.0	0.0	0.0	0.0	0	0	1	0	0	0
11/05	Was	W 24-3	3	1	0.0	0.0	0.0	0.0	1	8	1	0	0	0
11/12	@SD	W 22-7	8	0	0.0	0.0	0.0	0.0	0	0	1	0	0	0
11/19	Hou	W 20-13	4	0	0.0	0.0	0.0	0.0	0	0	1	0	1	1
11/23	@Dal	L 12-24	5	0	0.0	0.0	0.0	0.0	0	0	0	0	0	0
12/03	@Oak	W 29-23	3	1	0.0	0.0	0.0	0.0	0	0	0	0	0	0
12/11	@Mia	L 6-13	1	1	0.0	0.0	0.0	0.0	0	0	1	0	0	0
12/17	Den	W 20-17	4	0	0.0	0.0	0.0	0.0	0	0	0	0	0	0
12/24	Sea	W 26-3	0	1	0.0	0.0	0.0	0.0	0	0	0	0	0	0

Harry Colon
Jacksonville Jaguars – S

1995 Defensive Splits

	G	Tk	Ast	Sack	Yds	Stuff	Yds	Int	Yds	PD	TD
Total	16	55	24	0.0	0.0	2.0	4.0	3	46	7	0
vs. Playoff	5	17	7	0.0	0.0	0.0	0.0	0	0	1	0
vs. Non-Playoff	11	38	17	0.0	0.0	2.0	4.0	3	46	6	0
vs. Own Division	8	30	9	0.0	0.0	1.0	2.0	1	0	5	0
Home	8	22	12	0.0	0.0	1.0	2.0	2	41	4	0
Away	8	33	12	0.0	0.0	1.0	2.0	1	5	3	0
Games 1-8	8	36	13	0.0	0.0	2.0	4.0	1	5	4	0
Games 9-16	8	19	11	0.0	0.0	0.0	0.0	2	41	3	0
September	4	20	4	0.0	0.0	0.0	0.0	1	5	1	0
October	5	21	9	0.0	0.0	2.0	4.0	0	0	3	0
November	3	6	5	0.0	0.0	0.0	0.0	1	41	2	0
December	4	8	6	0.0	0.0	0.0	0.0	1	0	1	0
Grass	11	31	15	0.0	0.0	2.0	4.0	2	41	6	0
Turf	5	24	9	0.0	0.0	0.0	0.0	1	5	1	0
Indoor	2	6	6	0.0	0.0	0.0	0.0	0	0	0	0
Outdoor	14	49	18	0.0	0.0	2.0	4.0	3	46	7	0

Game Logs

Date	Opp	Result	Tk	Ast	Sack	Yds	Stuff	Yds	Int	Yds	PD	FF	FR	TD
09/03	Hou	L 3-10	4	0	0.0	0.0	0.0	0.0	0	0	0	0	0	0
09/10	@Cin	L 17-24	7	0	0.0	0.0	0.0	0.0	0	0	1	0	0	0
09/17	@NYA	L 10-27	6	3	0.0	0.0	0.0	0.0	1	5	1	0	0	0
09/24	GB	L 14-24	3	1	0.0	0.0	0.0	0.0	0	0	0	0	0	0
10/01	@Hou	W 17-16	4	3	0.0	0.0	0.0	0.0	0	0	0	0	0	0
10/08	Pit	W 20-16	3	2	0.0	0.0	0.0	0.0	0	0	1	0	0	0
10/15	Chi	L 27-30	4	3	0.0	0.0	1.0	2.0	0	0	0	0	0	0
10/22	@Cle	W 23-15	5	1	0.0	0.0	1.0	2.0	0	0	2	1	0	0
10/29	@Pit	L 7-24	5	0	0.0	0.0	0.0	0.0	0	0	1	0	0	0
11/12	Sea	L 30-47	2	2	0.0	0.0	0.0	0.0	1	41	1	0	0	0
11/19	@TB	L 16-17	2	1	0.0	0.0	0.0	0.0	0	0	0	0	0	0
11/26	Cin	L 13-17	2	2	0.0	0.0	0.0	0.0	0	0	1	0	0	0
12/03	@Den	L 23-31	2	1	0.0	0.0	0.0	0.0	0	0	0	0	0	0
12/10	Ind	L 31-41	2	0	0.0	0.0	0.0	0.0	0	0	0	0	0	0
12/17	@Det	L 0-44	2	3	0.0	0.0	0.0	0.0	0	0	0	0	0	0
12/24	Cle	W 24-21	0	1	0.0	0.0	0.0	0.0	1	0	1	0	0	0

Darion Conner
Carolina Panthers – LB

1995 Defensive Splits

	G	Tk	Ast	Sack	Yds	Stuff	Yds	Int	Yds	PD	TD
Total	16	41	11	7.0	39.0	5.0	12.0	0	0	2	0
vs. Playoff	6	9	3	3.0	13.0	1.0	1.0	0	0	1	0
vs. Non-Playoff	10	32	8	4.0	26.0	4.0	11.0	0	0	1	0
vs. Own Division	8	19	3	2.0	8.0	3.0	4.0	0	0	2	0
Home	8	19	4	5.0	24.0	2.0	5.0	0	0	0	0
Away	8	22	7	2.0	15.0	3.0	7.0	0	0	2	0
Games 1-8	8	16	9	1.0	3.0	4.0	11.0	0	0	1	0
Games 9-16	8	25	2	6.0	36.0	1.0	1.0	0	0	1	0
September	3	6	2	0.0	0.0	2.0	3.0	0	0	1	0
October	5	10	7	1.0	3.0	2.0	8.0	0	0	0	0
November	4	12	1	2.0	13.0	1.0	1.0	0	0	1	0
December	4	13	1	4.0	23.0	0.0	0.0	0	0	0	0
Grass	12	30	8	6.0	34.0	3.0	10.0	0	0	0	0
Turf	4	11	3	1.0	5.0	2.0	2.0	0	0	2	0
Indoor	3	10	1	1.0	5.0	2.0	2.0	0	0	2	0
Outdoor	13	31	10	6.0	34.0	3.0	10.0	0	0	0	0

Game Logs

Date	Opp	Result	Tk	Ast	Sack	Yds	Stuff	Yds	Int	Yds	PD	FF	FR	TD
09/03	@Atl	L 20-23	1	0	0.0	0.0	1.0	1.0	0	0	1	0	0	0
09/10	@Buf	L 9-31	1	2	0.0	0.0	0.0	0.0	0	0	0	1	0	0
09/17	StL	L 10-31	4	0	0.0	0.0	1.0	2.0	0	0	0	0	0	0
10/01	TB	L 13-20	0	1	0.0	0.0	0.0	0.0	0	0	0	0	0	0
10/08	@Chi	L 27-31	2	0	0.0	0.0	0.0	0.0	0	0	0	0	0	0
10/15	NYA	W 26-15	3	1	0.0	0.0	1.0	3.0	0	0	0	0	0	0
10/22	NO	W 20-3	2	1	1.0	3.0	0.0	0.0	0	0	0	0	0	0
10/29	@NE	W 20-17	3	4	0.0	0.0	1.0	5.0	0	0	0	0	0	0
11/05	@SF	W 13-7	0	0	0.0	0.0	0.0	0.0	0	0	0	0	0	0
11/12	@StL	L 17-28	5	1	1.0	5.0	0.0	0.0	0	0	1	0	0	0
11/19	Ari	W 27-7	3	0	1.0	8.0	0.0	0.0	0	0	0	0	0	0
11/26	@NO	L 26-34	4	0	0.0	0.0	1.0	1.0	0	0	0	0	0	0
12/03	Ind	W 13-10	4	0	3.0	13.0	0.0	0.0	0	0	0	0	0	0
12/10	SF	L 10-31	2	1	0.0	0.0	0.0	0.0	0	0	0	0	0	0
12/17	Atl	W 21-17	1	0	0.0	0.0	0.0	0.0	0	0	0	0	0	0
12/24	@Was	L 17-20	6	0	1.0	10.0	0.0	0.0	0	0	0	0	0	0

John Copeland
Cincinnati Bengals – DE

1995 Defensive Splits

	G	Tk	Ast	Sack	Yds	Stuff	Yds	Int	Yds	PD	TD
Total	16	55	8	9.0	61.0	6.5	13.5	0	0	4	0
vs. Playoff	5	17	1	3.0	14.0	2.0	3.0	0	0	2	0
vs. Non-Playoff	11	38	7	6.0	47.0	4.5	10.5	0	0	2	0
vs. Own Division	8	27	5	3.0	20.0	5.0	11.0	0	0	2	0
Home	8	30	1	3.0	24.0	5.0	9.0	0	0	2	0
Away	8	25	7	6.0	37.0	1.5	4.5	0	0	2	0
Games 1-8	8	28	4	7.0	57.0	2.5	6.5	0	0	1	0
Games 9-16	8	27	4	2.0	4.0	4.0	7.0	0	0	3	0
September	4	17	4	4.0	30.0	1.5	4.5	0	0	1	0
October	4	11	0	3.0	27.0	1.0	2.0	0	0	0	0
November	4	12	3	1.0	4.0	4.0	7.0	0	0	1	0
December	4	15	1	1.0	0.0	0.0	0.0	0	0	1	0
Grass	4	12	2	2.0	11.0	1.0	3.0	0	0	0	0
Turf	12	43	6	7.0	50.0	5.5	10.5	0	0	4	0
Indoor	3	12	5	4.0	26.0	0.5	1.5	0	0	2	0
Outdoor	13	43	3	5.0	35.0	6.0	12.0	0	0	2	0

Game Logs

Date	Opp	Result	Tk	Ast	Sack	Yds	Stuff	Yds	Int	Yds	PD	FF	FR	TD
09/03	@Ind	W 24-21	5	1	1.0	6.0	0.0	0.0	0	0	1	0	0	
09/10	Jac	W 24-17	3	1	1.0	8.0	0.5	1.5	0	0	0	0	0	
09/17	@Sea	L 21-24	5	2	2.0	16.0	0.5	1.5	0	0	0	0	0	
09/24	Hou	L 28-38	4	0	0.0	0.0	0.5	1.5	0	0	0	0	0	
10/01	Mia	L 23-26	2	0	1.0	8.0	0.0	0.0	0	0	0	0	0	
10/08	@TB	L 16-19	3	0	1.0	11.0	0.0	0.0	0	0	0	0	0	
10/19	@Pit	W 27-9	1	0	0.0	0.0	0.0	0.0	0	0	0	0	0	
10/29	Cle	L 26-29	5	0	1.0	8.0	1.0	2.0	0	0	1	0	0	
11/05	Oak	L 17-20	3	0	0.0	0.0	1.0	1.0	0	0	0	0	0	
11/12	@Hou	W 32-25	2	2	1.0	4.0	0.0	0.0	0	0	1	0	0	
11/19	Pit	L 31-49	6	0	0.0	0.0	2.0	3.0	0	0	1	1	0	
11/26	@Jac	W 17-13	1	1	0.0	0.0	1.0	3.0	0	0	0	0	0	
12/03	@GB	L 10-24	3	0	1.0	0.0	0.0	0.0	0	0	0	0	0	
12/10	Chi	W 16-10	6	0	0.0	0.0	0.0	0.0	0	0	1	0	0	
12/17	@Cle	L 10-26	5	1	0.0	0.0	0.0	0.0	0	0	0	0	0	
12/24	Min	W 27-24	1	0	0.0	0.0	0.0	0.0	0	0	0	0	0	

Quentin Coryatt
Indianapolis Colts – LB

1995 Defensive Splits

	G	Tk	Ast	Sack	Yds	Stuff	Yds	Int	Yds	PD	TD
Total	16	93	22	2.5	5.0	4.0	5.0	1	6	8	0
vs. Playoff	6	44	9	1.5	0.0	2.0	2.0	1	6	7	0
vs. Non-Playoff	10	49	13	1.0	5.0	2.0	3.0	0	0	1	0
vs. Own Division	8	48	13	1.5	5.0	3.5	4.0	0	0	3	0
Home	8	51	14	1.0	0.0	3.0	4.0	1	6	8	0
Away	8	42	8	1.5	5.0	1.0	1.0	0	0	0	0
Games 1-8	8	47	11	1.5	0.0	2.5	3.0	0	0	2	0
Games 9-16	8	46	11	1.0	5.0	1.5	2.0	1	6	6	0
September	3	10	5	0.5	0.0	1.0	1.0	0	0	0	0
October	5	37	6	1.0	0.0	1.5	2.0	0	0	2	0
November	4	27	5	1.0	5.0	1.0	1.0	0	0	2	0
December	4	19	6	1.0	0.0	0.5	1.0	1	6	4	0
Grass	5	28	4	1.0	5.0	0.0	0.0	0	0	0	0
Turf	11	65	18	1.5	0.0	4.0	5.0	1	6	8	0
Indoor	9	57	15	1.0	0.0	3.0	4.0	1	6	8	0
Outdoor	7	36	7	1.5	5.0	1.0	1.0	0	0	0	0

Game Logs

Date	Opp	Result	Tk	Ast	Sack	Yds	Stuff	Yds	Int	Yds	PD	FF	FR	TD
09/03	Cin	L 21-24	2	2	0.0	0.0	0.0	0.0	0	0	0	0	0	
09/10	@NYA	W 27-24	2	0	0.0	0.0	0.0	0.0	0	0	0	0	0	
09/17	@Buf	L 14-20	6	3	0.5	0.0	1.0	1.0	0	0	0	0	0	
10/01	StL	W 21-18	6	2	0.0	0.0	0.5	1.0	0	0	0	1	0	
10/08	@Mia	W 27-24	7	1	0.0	0.0	0.0	0.0	0	0	0	0	0	
10/15	SF	W 18-17	12	0	1.0	0.0	0.0	0.0	0	0	2	0	0	
10/22	@Oak	L 17-30	3	1	0.0	0.0	0.0	0.0	0	0	0	1	0	
10/29	NYA	W 17-10	9	2	0.0	0.0	1.0	1.0	0	0	0	0	0	
11/05	Buf	L 10-16	8	4	0.0	0.0	0.0	0.0	0	0	1	0	0	
11/12	@NO	L 14-17	6	1	0.0	0.0	0.0	0.0	0	0	0	0	0	
11/19	@NE	W 24-10	9	0	1.0	5.0	0.0	0.0	0	0	0	1	0	
11/26	Mia	W 36-28	4	0	0.0	0.0	1.0	1.0	0	0	1	1	0	
12/03	@Car	L 10-13	6	0	0.0	0.0	0.0	0.0	0	0	1	0	0	
12/10	@Jac	W 41-31	3	2	0.0	0.0	0.0	0.0	0	0	1	0	0	
12/17	SD	L 24-27	7	1	0.0	0.0	0.0	0.0	1	6	3	0	0	
12/23	NE	W 10-7	3	3	0.0	0.0	0.5	1.0	0	0	1	0	0	

Bryan Cox
Miami Dolphins – LB

1995 Defensive Splits

	G	Tk	Ast	Sack	Yds	Stuff	Yds	Int	Yds	PD	TD
Total	16	96	24	7.5	46.0	3.5	9.0	1	12	3	0
vs. Playoff	9	58	13	4.5	27.0	2.5	7.5	0	0	2	0
vs. Non-Playoff	7	38	11	3.0	19.0	1.0	1.5	1	12	1	0
vs. Own Division	8	53	14	7.0	41.0	2.0	7.5	1	12	2	0
Home	8	41	12	3.5	20.0	1.5	6.5	0	0	1	0
Away	8	55	12	4.0	26.0	2.0	2.5	1	12	2	0
Games 1-8	8	41	16	5.5	34.0	2.0	7.5	1	12	2	0
Games 9-16	8	55	8	2.0	12.0	1.5	1.5	0	0	1	0
September	3	14	9	2.5	24.0	0.5	1.0	1	12	1	0
October	5	27	7	3.0	10.0	1.5	6.5	0	0	1	0
November	4	32	4	2.0	12.0	1.0	1.0	0	0	0	0
December	4	23	4	0.0	0.0	0.5	0.5	0	0	1	0
Grass	10	56	18	4.5	34.0	3.0	8.5	1	12	2	0
Turf	6	40	6	3.0	12.0	0.5	0.5	0	0	1	0
Indoor	3	20	2	2.0	12.0	0.5	0.5	0	0	0	0
Outdoor	13	76	22	5.5	34.0	3.0	8.5	1	12	3	0

Game Logs

Date	Opp	Result	Tk	Ast	Sack	Yds	Stuff	Yds	Int	Yds	PD	FF	FR	TD
09/03	NYA	W 52-14	4	1	1.0	5.0	0.0	0.0	0	0	0	1	1	0
09/10	@NE	W 20-3	7	6	1.0	14.0	0.5	1.0	1	12	1	1	0	0
09/18	Pit	W 23-10	3	2	0.5	5.0	0.0	0.0	0	0	0	0	0	0
10/01	@Cin	W 26-23	4	1	0.0	0.0	0.0	0.0	0	0	0	0	0	0
10/08	Ind	L 24-27	8	1	0.0	5.0	0.5	0.5	0	0	0	0	0	0
10/15	@NO	L 30-33	4	1	0.0	0.0	0.0	0.0	0	0	0	0	0	0
10/22	@NYA	L 16-17	8	2	1.0	0.0	0.0	0.0	0	0	1	0	0	0
10/29	Buf	W 23-6	3	2	1.0	5.0	1.0	6.0	0	0	0	0	0	0
11/05	@SD	W 24-14	8	0	0.0	0.0	1.0	1.0	0	0	0	0	0	0
11/12	NE	L 17-34	5	0	0.0	0.0	0.0	0.0	0	0	0	0	0	0
11/20	SF	L 20-44	9	3	0.0	0.0	0.0	0.0	0	0	0	0	0	0
11/26	@Ind	L 28-36	10	1	2.0	12.0	0.0	0.0	0	0	0	0	0	0
12/03	Atl	W 21-20	4	2	0.0	0.0	0.0	0.0	0	0	0	0	0	0
12/11	KC	W 13-6	5	1	0.0	0.0	0.0	0.0	0	0	1	0	0	0
12/17	@Buf	L 20-23	8	1	0.0	0.0	0.0	0.0	0	0	1	0	0	0
12/24	@StL	W 41-22	6	0	0.0	0.0	0.5	0.5	0	0	0	0	0	0

Ray Crockett

Denver Broncos – CB

1995 Defensive Splits

	G	Tk	Ast	Sack	Yds	Stuff	Yds	Int	Yds	PD	TD
Total	16	62	12	3.0	32.0	0.0	0.0	0	0	18	1
vs. Playoff	7	37	5	2.0	21.0	0.0	0.0	0	0	7	1
vs. Non-Playoff	9	25	7	1.0	11.0	0.0	0.0	0	0	11	0
vs. Own Division	8	29	7	1.0	13.0	0.0	0.0	0	0	7	1
Home	8	32	7	1.0	11.0	0.0	0.0	0	0	10	0
Away	8	30	5	2.0	21.0	0.0	0.0	0	0	8	1
Games 1-8	8	28	6	0.0	0.0	0.0	0.0	0	0	9	0
Games 9-16	8	34	6	3.0	32.0	0.0	0.0	0	0	9	1
September	4	14	3	0.0	0.0	0.0	0.0	0	0	5	0
October	4	14	3	0.0	0.0	0.0	0.0	0	0	4	0
November	4	19	2	2.0	19.0	0.0	0.0	0	0	4	0
December	4	15	4	1.0	13.0	0.0	0.0	0	0	5	1
Grass	12	48	9	2.0	24.0	0.0	0.0	0	0	15	1
Turf	4	14	3	1.0	8.0	0.0	0.0	0	0	3	0
Indoor	2	5	0	0.0	0.0	0.0	0.0	0	0	1	0
Outdoor	14	57	12	3.0	32.0	0.0	0.0	0	0	17	1

Game Logs

Date	Opp	Result	Tk	Ast	Sack	Yds	Stuff	Yds	Int	Yds	PD	FF	FR	TD
09/03	Buf	W 22-7	5	0	0.0	0.0	0.0	0.0	0	0	2	0	0	0
09/10	@Dal	L 21-31	2	2	0.0	0.0	0.0	0.0	0	0	1	0	0	0
09/17	Was	W 38-31	1	1	0.0	0.0	0.0	0.0	0	0	2	0	0	0
09/24	@SD	L 6-17	6	0	0.0	0.0	0.0	0.0	0	0	0	0	0	0
10/01	@Sea	L 10-27	1	0	0.0	0.0	0.0	0.0	0	0	0	0	0	0
10/08	@NE	W 37-3	4	0	0.0	0.0	0.0	0.0	0	0	2	0	0	0
10/16	Oak	W 27-0	2	2	0.0	0.0	0.0	0.0	0	0	1	0	0	0
10/22	KC	L 7-21	7	1	0.0	0.0	0.0	0.0	0	0	1	0	0	0
11/05	Ari	W 38-6	4	1	1.0	11.0	0.0	0.0	0	0	1	0	0	0
11/12	@Phi	L 13-31	7	1	1.0	8.0	0.0	0.0	0	0	1	0	0	0
11/19	SD	W 30-27	4	0	0.0	0.0	0.0	0.0	0	0	1	0	0	0
11/26	@Hou	L 33-42	4	0	0.0	0.0	0.0	0.0	0	0	1	0	0	0
12/03	Jac	W 31-23	6	0	0.0	0.0	0.0	0.0	0	0	1	0	0	0
12/10	Sea	L 27-31	3	2	0.0	0.0	0.0	0.0	0	0	1	0	0	0
12/17	@KC	L 17-20	6	1	1.0	13.0	0.0	0.0	0	0	1	1	1	1
12/24	@Oak	W 31-28	0	1	0.0	0.0	0.0	0.0	0	0	2	0	0	0

Jeff Cross

Miami Dolphins – DE

1995 Defensive Splits

	G	Tk	Ast	Sack	Yds	Stuff	Yds	Int	Yds	PD	TD
Total	16	31	7	6.0	37.0	1.5	3.0	0	0	5	0
vs. Playoff	9	17	3	4.0	29.0	0.0	0.0	0	0	2	0
vs. Non-Playoff	7	14	4	2.0	8.0	1.5	3.0	0	0	3	0
vs. Own Division	8	15	1	3.0	18.0	0.5	1.0	0	0	4	0
Home	8	13	3	2.0	10.0	0.0	0.0	0	0	2	0
Away	8	18	4	4.0	27.0	1.5	3.0	0	0	3	0
Games 1-8	8	12	3	0.0	0.0	1.5	3.0	0	0	3	0
Games 9-16	8	19	4	6.0	37.0	0.0	0.0	0	0	2	0
September	3	6	0	0.0	0.0	0.5	1.0	0	0	1	0
October	5	6	3	0.0	0.0	1.0	2.0	0	0	2	0
November	4	7	0	3.0	22.0	0.0	0.0	0	0	2	0
December	4	12	4	3.0	15.0	0.0	0.0	0	0	0	0
Grass	10	16	3	3.0	19.0	0.5	1.0	0	0	3	0
Turf	6	15	4	3.0	18.0	1.0	2.0	0	0	2	0
Indoor	3	8	4	2.0	13.0	1.0	2.0	0	0	2	0
Outdoor	13	23	3	4.0	24.0	0.5	1.0	0	0	3	0

Game Logs

Date	Opp	Result	Tk	Ast	Sack	Yds	Stuff	Yds	Int	Yds	PD	FF	FR	TD
09/03	NYA	W 52-14	2	0	0.0	0.0	0.0	0.0	0	0	0	0	0	0
09/10	@NE	W 20-3	2	0	0.0	0.0	0.5	1.0	0	0	1	0	1	0
09/18	Pit	W 23-10	2	0	0.0	0.0	0.0	0.0	0	0	0	0	1	0
10/01	@Cin	W 26-23	3	0	0.0	0.0	0.0	0.0	0	0	0	0	0	0
10/08	Ind	L 24-27	1	0	0.0	0.0	0.0	0.0	0	0	0	0	0	0
10/15	@NO	L 30-33	1	2	0.0	0.0	1.0	2.0	0	0	1	0	0	0
10/22	@NYA	L 16-17	1	0	0.0	0.0	0.0	0.0	0	0	0	0	0	0
10/29	Buf	W 23-6	0	1	0.0	0.0	0.0	0.0	0	0	1	0	0	0
11/05	@SD	W 24-14	1	0	1.0	9.0	0.0	0.0	0	0	1	0	0	0
11/12	NE	L 17-34	2	0	1.0	4.0	0.0	0.0	0	0	1	0	0	0
11/20	SF	L 20-44	0	0	0.0	0.0	0.0	0.0	0	0	0	0	0	0
11/26	@Ind	L 28-36	4	0	1.0	9.0	0.0	0.0	0	0	0	0	0	0
12/03	Atl	W 21-20	4	2	1.0	6.0	0.0	0.0	0	0	0	0	0	0
12/11	KC	W 13-6	2	0	0.0	0.0	0.0	0.0	0	0	0	0	0	0
12/17	@Buf	L 20-23	3	0	1.0	5.0	0.0	0.0	0	0	0	0	0	0
12/24	@StL	W 41-22	3	2	1.0	4.0	0.0	0.0	0	0	0	0	0	0

Eugene Daniel

Indianapolis Colts – CB

1995 Defensive Splits

	G	Tk	Ast	Sack	Yds	Stuff	Yds	Int	Yds	PD	TD
Total	16	28	7	0.0	0.0	0.0	0.0	3	142	12	1
vs. Playoff	6	11	4	0.0	0.0	0.0	0.0	1	0	3	0
vs. Non-Playoff	10	17	3	0.0	0.0	0.0	0.0	2	142	9	1
vs. Own Division	8	12	2	0.0	0.0	0.0	0.0	2	97	7	1
Home	8	16	4	0.0	0.0	0.0	0.0	2	97	10	1
Away	8	12	3	0.0	0.0	0.0	0.0	1	45	2	0
Games 1-8	8	10	5	0.0	0.0	0.0	0.0	1	97	6	1
Games 9-16	8	18	2	0.0	0.0	0.0	0.0	2	45	6	0
September	3	5	1	0.0	0.0	0.0	0.0	0	0	3	0
October	5	5	4	0.0	0.0	0.0	0.0	1	97	3	1
November	4	7	1	0.0	0.0	0.0	0.0	1	0	3	0
December	4	11	1	0.0	0.0	0.0	0.0	1	45	3	0
Grass	5	8	2	0.0	0.0	0.0	0.0	1	45	1	0
Turf	11	20	5	0.0	0.0	0.0	0.0	2	97	11	1
Indoor	9	18	4	0.0	0.0	0.0	0.0	2	97	10	1
Outdoor	7	10	3	0.0	0.0	0.0	0.0	1	45	2	0

Game Logs

Date	Opp	Result	Tk	Ast	Sack	Yds	Stuff	Yds	Int	Yds	PD	FF	FR	TD
09/03	Cin	L 21-24	3	0	0.0	0.0	0.0	0.0	0	0	2	0	0	0
09/10	@NYA	W 27-24	1	0	0.0	0.0	0.0	0.0	0	0	1	0	0	0
09/17	@Buf	L 14-20	1	1	0.0	0.0	0.0	0.0	0	0	0	0	0	0
10/01	StL	L 21-18	1	0	0.0	0.0	0.0	0.0	0	0	2	0	0	0
10/08	@Mia	W 27-24	1	0	0.0	0.0	0.0	0.0	0	0	0	0	0	0
10/15	SF	W 18-17	1	2	0.0	0.0	0.0	0.0	0	0	0	0	0	0
10/22	@Oak	L 17-30	2	1	0.0	0.0	0.0	0.0	0	0	0	0	0	0
10/29	NYA	W 17-10	1	0	0.0	0.0	0.0	0.0	1	97	1	0	0	1
11/05	Buf	L 10-16	0	0	0.0	0.0	0.0	0.0	0	0	3	0	0	0
11/12	@NO	L 14-17	2	0	0.0	0.0	0.0	0.0	0	0	0	0	0	0
11/19	@NE	W 24-10	1	1	0.0	0.0	0.0	0.0	0	0	0	0	0	0
11/26	Mia	W 36-28	4	0	0.0	0.0	0.0	0.0	1	0	2	0	0	0
12/03	@Car	L 10-13	1	0	0.0	0.0	0.0	0.0	0	0	0	0	0	0
12/10	@Jac	W 41-31	4	0	0.0	0.0	0.0	0.0	1	45	1	0	0	0
12/17	SD	L 24-27	4	1	0.0	0.0	0.0	0.0	0	0	0	0	0	0
12/23	NE	W 10-7	3	0	0.0	0.0	0.0	0.0	0	0	2	0	0	0

Eric Davis
San Francisco 49ers – CB

1995 Defensive Splits											Game Logs												
	G	Tk	Ast	Sack	Yds	Stuff	Yds	Int	Yds	PD	TD	Date	Opp	Result	Tk	Ast	Sack	Yds	Stuff	Yds	Int	Yds	PD	FF	FR	TD
Total	15	43	8	1.0	8.0	0.0	0.0	3	84	22	1	09/03	@NO	W 24-22	4	0	0.0	0.0	0.0	0.0	0	0	1	0	0	0
vs. Playoff	7	14	4	0.0	0.0	0.0	0.0	2	-2	7	0	09/10	Atl	W 41-10	2	0	0.0	0.0	0.0	0.0	0	0	0	0	0	0
vs. Non-Playoff	8	29	4	1.0	8.0	0.0	0.0	1	86	15	1	09/17	NE	W 28-3	6	1	1.0	8.0	0.0	0.0	0	0	1	0	0	0
vs. Own Division	8	25	2	0.0	0.0	0.0	0.0	1	86	13	1	09/25	@Det	L 24-27	3	1	0.0	0.0	0.0	0.0	0	0	1	0	0	0
Home	7	24	3	1.0	8.0	0.0	0.0	3	84	12	1	10/01	NYN	W 20-6	-	-	-	-	-	-	-	-	-	-	-	-
Away	8	19	5	0.0	0.0	0.0	0.0	0	0	10	0	10/15	@Ind	L 17-18	3	1	0.0	0.0	0.0	0.0	0	0	0	0	0	0
Games 1-8	7	23	4	1.0	8.0	0.0	0.0	0	0	6	0	10/22	@StL	W 44-10	3	1	0.0	0.0	0.0	0.0	0	0	2	1	0	0
Games 9-16	8	20	4	0.0	0.0	0.0	0.0	3	84	16	1	10/29	NO	L 7-11	2	0	0.0	0.0	0.0	0.0	0	0	1	0	0	0
September	4	15	2	1.0	8.0	0.0	0.0	0	0	3	0	11/05	Car	L 7-13	10	0	0.0	0.0	0.0	0.0	0	0	3	1	0	0
October	3	8	2	0.0	0.0	0.0	0.0	0	0	3	0	11/12	@Dal	W 38-20	2	1	0.0	0.0	0.0	0.0	0	0	0	0	0	0
November	4	14	1	0.0	0.0	0.0	0.0	1	86	5	1	11/20	@Mia	W 44-20	1	0	0.0	0.0	0.0	0.0	0	0	1	0	0	0
December	4	6	3	0.0	0.0	0.0	0.0	2	-2	11	0	11/26	StL	W 41-13	1	0	0.0	0.0	0.0	0.0	1	86	1	0	0	1
Grass	9	25	4	1.0	8.0	0.0	0.0	3	84	17	1	12/03	Buf	W 27-17	0	1	0.0	0.0	0.0	0.0	2	-2	4	0	0	0
Turf	6	18	4	0.0	0.0	0.0	0.0	0	0	5	0	12/10	@Car	W 31-10	0	0	0.0	0.0	0.0	0.0	0	0	4	0	0	0
Indoor	4	13	2	0.0	0.0	0.0	0.0	0	0	3	0	12/18	Min	W 37-30	3	1	0.0	0.0	0.0	0.0	0	0	2	0	0	0
Outdoor	11	30	6	1.0	8.0	0.0	0.0	3	84	19	1	12/24	@Atl	L 27-28	3	0	0.0	0.0	0.0	0.0	0	0	1	0	0	0

Charles Dimry
Tampa Bay Buccaneers – CB

1995 Defensive Splits											Game Logs												
	G	Tk	Ast	Sack	Yds	Stuff	Yds	Int	Yds	PD	TD	Date	Opp	Result	Tk	Ast	Sack	Yds	Stuff	Yds	Int	Yds	PD	FF	FR	TD
Total	16	64	14	0.0	0.0	2.5	6.0	1	0	17	0	09/03	@Phi	W 21-6	5	1	0.0	0.0	0.0	0.0	0	0	0	0	0	0
vs. Playoff	6	31	7	0.0	0.0	0.0	0.0	0	0	6	0	09/10	@Cle	L 6-22	5	0	0.0	0.0	0.0	0.0	0	0	0	0	0	0
vs. Non-Playoff	10	33	7	0.0	0.0	2.5	6.0	1	0	11	0	09/17	Chi	L 6-25	4	1	0.0	0.0	0.5	1.0	0	0	1	0	0	0
vs. Own Division	8	39	9	0.0	0.0	1.5	2.0	0	0	9	0	09/24	Was	W 14-6	2	1	0.0	0.0	0.0	0.0	0	0	2	0	0	0
Home	8	34	8	0.0	0.0	1.5	2.0	1	0	12	0	10/01	@Car	W 20-13	5	0	0.0	0.0	1.0	4.0	0	0	0	0	0	0
Away	8	30	6	0.0	0.0	1.0	4.0	0	0	5	0	10/08	Cin	W 19-16	2	1	0.0	0.0	0.0	0.0	1	0	2	2	0	0
Games 1-8	8	27	5	0.0	0.0	2.5	6.0	1	0	10	0	10/15	Min	W 20-17	5	1	0.0	0.0	1.0	1.0	0	0	3	0	0	0
Games 9-16	8	37	9	0.0	0.0	0.0	0.0	0	0	7	0	10/22	Atl	L 21-24	4	0	0.0	0.0	0.0	0.0	0	0	2	0	0	0
September	4	11	3	0.0	0.0	0.5	1.0	0	0	3	0	10/29	@Hou	L 7-19	5	0	0.0	0.0	0.0	0.0	0	0	1	0	0	0
October	5	21	2	0.0	0.0	2.0	5.0	1	0	8	0	11/12	@Det	L 24-27	5	2	0.0	0.0	0.0	0.0	0	0	3	0	0	0
November	3	9	6	0.0	0.0	0.0	0.0	0	0	4	0	11/19	Jac	W 17-16	2	1	0.0	0.0	0.0	0.0	0	0	1	0	0	0
December	4	23	3	0.0	0.0	0.0	0.0	0	0	2	0	11/26	@GB	L 13-35	2	2	0.0	0.0	0.0	0.0	0	0	0	0	0	0
Grass	12	47	10	0.0	0.0	2.5	6.0	1	0	13	0	12/03	@Min	L 17-31	2	1	0.0	0.0	0.0	0.0	0	0	0	0	0	0
Turf	4	17	4	0.0	0.0	0.0	0.0	0	0	4	0	12/10	GB	W 13-10	7	2	0.0	0.0	0.0	0.0	0	0	0	0	0	0
Indoor	3	12	3	0.0	0.0	0.0	0.0	0	0	4	0	12/17	@Chi	L 10-31	6	0	0.0	0.0	0.0	0.0	0	0	1	0	0	0
Outdoor	13	52	11	0.0	0.0	2.5	6.0	1	0	13	0	12/23	Det	L 10-37	8	0	0.0	0.0	0.0	0.0	0	0	1	0	0	0

Cris Dishman
Houston Oilers – CB

1995 Defensive Splits											Game Logs												
	G	Tk	Ast	Sack	Yds	Stuff	Yds	Int	Yds	PD	TD	Date	Opp	Result	Tk	Ast	Sack	Yds	Stuff	Yds	Int	Yds	PD	FF	FR	TD
Total	15	48	10	0.0	0.0	1.0	1.0	3	17	11	0	09/03	@Jac	W 10-3	2	0	0.0	0.0	0.0	0.0	0	0	1	0	0	0
vs. Playoff	4	16	2	0.0	0.0	0.0	0.0	1	0	3	0	09/10	Pit	L 17-34	4	2	0.0	0.0	0.0	0.0	0	0	0	0	0	0
vs. Non-Playoff	11	32	8	0.0	0.0	1.0	1.0	2	17	8	0	09/17	Cle	L 7-14	1	1	0.0	0.0	0.0	0.0	0	0	0	0	0	0
vs. Own Division	8	25	6	0.0	0.0	1.0	1.0	0	0	5	0	09/24	@Cin	W 38-28	3	0	0.0	0.0	0.0	0.0	0	0	0	0	0	0
Home	8	22	6	0.0	0.0	1.0	1.0	2	17	4	0	10/01	Jac	L 16-17	1	1	0.0	0.0	1.0	1.0	0	0	1	0	0	0
Away	7	26	4	0.0	0.0	0.0	0.0	1	0	7	0	10/08	@Min	L 17-23	5	2	0.0	0.0	0.0	0.0	0	0	0	0	0	0
Games 1-8	8	22	7	0.0	0.0	1.0	1.0	2	17	6	0	10/22	@Chi	L 32-35	5	1	0.0	0.0	0.0	0.0	0	0	2	0	1	0
Games 9-16	7	26	3	0.0	0.0	0.0	0.0	1	0	5	0	10/29	TB	W 19-7	1	0	0.0	0.0	0.0	0.0	2	17	2	0	0	0
September	4	10	3	0.0	0.0	0.0	0.0	0	0	1	0	11/05	@Cle	W 37-10	5	1	0.0	0.0	0.0	0.0	0	0	1	0	1	0
October	4	12	4	0.0	0.0	1.0	1.0	2	17	5	0	11/12	Cin	L 25-32	4	1	0.0	0.0	0.0	0.0	0	0	1	0	0	0
November	4	14	3	0.0	0.0	0.0	0.0	1	0	4	0	11/19	@KC	L 13-20	1	0	0.0	0.0	0.0	0.0	1	0	2	0	0	0
December	3	12	0	0.0	0.0	0.0	0.0	0	0	1	0	11/26	Den	W 42-33	4	1	0.0	0.0	0.0	0.0	0	0	0	0	0	0
Grass	4	13	2	0.0	0.0	0.0	0.0	1	0	6	0	12/03	@Pit	L 7-21	5	0	0.0	0.0	0.0	0.0	0	0	1	0	0	0
Turf	11	35	8	0.0	0.0	1.0	1.0	2	17	5	0	12/10	Det	L 17-24	6	0	0.0	0.0	0.0	0.0	0	0	1	0	0	0
Indoor	9	27	8	0.0	0.0	1.0	1.0	2	17	4	0	12/17	NYA	W 23-6	1	0	0.0	0.0	0.0	0.0	0	0	0	0	0	0
Outdoor	6	21	2	0.0	0.0	0.0	0.0	1	0	7	0	12/24	@Buf	W 28-17	-	-	-	-	-	-	-	-	-	-	-	-

Chris Doleman
Atlanta Falcons – DE

1995 Defensive Splits

	G	Tk	Ast	Sack	Yds	Stuff	Yds	Int	Yds	PD	TD
Total	16	36	15	9.0	62.5	4.0	7.0	0	0	5	0
vs. Playoff	6	11	2	0.5	2.0	1.0	2.0	0	0	1	0
vs. Non-Playoff	10	25	13	8.5	60.5	3.0	5.0	0	0	4	0
vs. Own Division	8	22	6	6.5	44.5	2.5	4.5	0	0	2	0
Home	8	21	9	6.0	44.5	2.0	3.0	0	0	1	0
Away	8	15	6	3.0	18.0	2.0	4.0	0	0	4	0
Games 1-8	8	15	10	7.0	42.5	1.5	3.5	0	0	4	0
Games 9-16	8	21	5	2.0	20.0	2.5	3.5	0	0	1	0
September	4	10	5	5.5	33.5	1.0	2.0	0	0	1	0
October	4	5	5	1.5	9.0	0.5	1.5	0	0	3	0
November	4	11	4	2.0	20.0	2.5	3.5	0	0	0	0
December	4	10	1	0.0	0.0	0.0	0.0	0	0	1	0
Grass	5	6	4	1.0	9.0	0.5	0.5	0	0	3	0
Turf	11	30	11	8.0	53.5	3.5	6.5	0	0	2	0
Indoor	9	25	11	8.0	53.5	3.0	5.0	0	0	1	0
Outdoor	7	11	4	1.0	9.0	1.0	2.0	0	0	4	0

Game Logs

Date	Opp	Result	Tk	Ast	Sack	Yds	Stuff	Yds	Int	Yds	PD	FF	FR	TD
09/03	Car	W 23-20	3	3	3.5	24.5	0.0	0.0	0	0	1	0	0	0
09/10	@SF	L 10-41	0	0	0.0	0.0	0.0	0.0	0	0	0	0	0	0
09/17	@NO	W 27-24	4	2	2.0	9.0	1.0	2.0	0	0	1	0	0	0
09/24	NYA	W 13-3	3	0	0.0	0.0	0.0	0.0	0	0	0	0	0	0
10/01	NE	W 30-17	1	4	1.0	7.0	0.0	0.0	0	0	0	0	2	0
10/12	@StL	L 19-21	2	0	0.0	0.0	0.5	1.5	0	0	1	0	0	0
10/22	@TB	W 24-21	1	0	0.0	0.0	0.0	0.0	0	0	2	0	0	0
10/29	Dal	L 13-28	1	1	0.5	2.0	0.0	0.0	0	0	0	0	0	0
11/05	Det	W 34-22	2	0	0.0	0.0	1.0	2.0	0	0	0	0	0	0
11/12	@Buf	L 17-23	3	0	0.0	0.0	0.0	0.0	0	0	0	0	0	0
11/19	StL	W 31-6	4	1	1.0	11.0	1.0	1.0	0	0	0	0	0	0
11/26	@Ari	L 37-40	2	3	1.0	9.0	0.5	0.5	0	0	0	0	0	0
12/03	@Mia	L 20-21	1	1	0.0	0.0	0.0	0.0	0	0	1	0	0	0
12/10	NO	W 19-14	3	0	0.0	0.0	0.0	0.0	0	0	0	0	0	0
12/17	@Car	L 17-21	2	0	0.0	0.0	0.0	0.0	0	0	0	0	0	0
12/24	SF	W 28-27	4	0	0.0	0.0	0.0	0.0	0	0	0	0	0	0

Doug Evans
Green Bay Packers – CB

1995 Defensive Splits

	G	Tk	Ast	Sack	Yds	Stuff	Yds	Int	Yds	PD	TD
Total	16	75	15	1.0	9.0	1.0	2.0	2	24	27	0
vs. Playoff	4	22	7	0.0	0.0	0.5	0.5	0	0	6	0
vs. Non-Playoff	12	53	8	1.0	9.0	0.5	1.5	2	24	21	0
vs. Own Division	8	29	8	1.0	9.0	0.5	1.5	2	24	18	0
Home	8	41	7	0.0	0.0	0.5	1.5	2	24	16	0
Away	8	34	8	1.0	9.0	0.5	0.5	0	0	11	0
Games 1-8	8	37	13	1.0	9.0	0.5	0.5	2	24	16	0
Games 9-16	8	38	2	0.0	0.0	0.5	1.5	0	0	11	0
September	4	15	4	1.0	9.0	0.0	0.0	0	0	5	0
October	4	22	9	0.0	0.0	0.5	0.5	2	24	11	0
November	4	18	1	0.0	0.0	0.5	1.5	0	0	7	0
December	4	20	1	0.0	0.0	0.0	0.0	0	0	4	0
Grass	12	55	9	1.0	9.0	0.5	1.5	2	24	22	0
Turf	4	20	6	0.0	0.0	0.5	0.5	0	0	5	0
Indoor	3	9	4	0.0	0.0	0.0	0.0	0	0	4	0
Outdoor	13	66	11	1.0	9.0	1.0	2.0	2	24	23	0

Game Logs

Date	Opp	Result	Tk	Ast	Sack	Yds	Stuff	Yds	Int	Yds	PD	FF	FR	TD
09/03	StL	L 14-17	5	1	0.0	0.0	0.0	0.0	0	0	1	0	0	0
09/11	@Chi	W 27-24	2	0	1.0	9.0	0.0	0.0	0	0	1	0	0	0
09/17	NYN	W 14-6	6	1	0.0	0.0	0.0	0.0	0	0	2	0	0	0
09/24	@Jac	W 24-14	2	2	0.0	0.0	0.0	0.0	0	0	1	0	0	0
10/08	@Dal	L 24-34	11	2	0.0	0.0	0.5	0.5	0	0	1	0	0	0
10/15	Det	W 30-21	3	3	0.0	0.0	0.0	0.0	0	0	3	0	0	0
10/22	Min	W 38-21	7	2	0.0	0.0	0.0	0.0	2	24	7	0	0	0
10/29	@Det	L 16-24	1	2	0.0	0.0	0.0	0.0	0	0	0	0	0	0
11/05	@Min	L 24-27	3	1	0.0	0.0	0.0	0.0	0	0	4	0	0	0
11/12	Chi	W 35-28	5	0	0.0	0.0	0.0	0.0	0	0	1	0	0	0
11/19	@Cle	W 31-20	6	0	0.0	0.0	0.0	0.0	0	0	2	0	0	0
11/26	TB	W 35-13	4	0	0.0	0.0	0.5	1.5	0	0	0	0	0	0
12/03	Cin	W 24-10	4	0	0.0	0.0	0.0	0.0	0	0	0	0	0	0
12/10	@TB	L 10-13	4	0	0.0	0.0	0.0	0.0	0	0	2	0	0	0
12/16	@NO	W 34-23	5	1	0.0	0.0	0.0	0.0	0	0	0	0	0	0
12/24	Pit	W 24-19	7	0	0.0	0.0	0.0	0.0	0	0	2	0	0	0

D'Marco Farr
St. Louis Rams – DT

1995 Defensive Splits

	G	Tk	Ast	Sack	Yds	Stuff	Yds	Int	Yds	PD	TD
Total	16	48	2	11.5	79.0	10.0	20.0	1	5	3	0
vs. Playoff	9	30	0	4.0	39.0	7.5	12.5	0	0	2	0
vs. Non-Playoff	7	18	2	7.5	40.0	2.5	7.5	1	5	1	0
vs. Own Division	8	23	1	7.0	51.0	3.5	3.5	0	0	1	0
Home	8	21	0	5.0	34.0	3.5	9.5	0	0	0	0
Away	8	27	2	6.5	45.0	6.5	10.5	1	5	3	0
Games 1-8	8	21	1	5.0	37.0	4.5	8.5	0	0	1	0
Games 9-16	8	27	1	6.5	42.0	5.5	11.5	1	5	2	0
September	4	8	1	3.0	15.0	1.5	1.5	0	0	0	0
October	4	13	0	2.0	22.0	3.0	7.0	0	0	1	0
November	4	12	0	3.0	23.0	2.0	2.0	0	0	1	0
December	4	15	1	3.5	19.0	3.5	9.5	1	5	1	0
Grass	3	9	1	1.0	9.0	3.5	3.5	0	0	1	0
Turf	13	39	1	10.5	70.0	6.5	16.5	1	5	2	0
Indoor	7	22	0	3.0	23.0	2.5	8.5	0	0	0	0
Outdoor	9	26	2	8.5	56.0	7.5	11.5	1	5	3	0

Game Logs

Date	Opp	Result	Tk	Ast	Sack	Yds	Stuff	Yds	Int	Yds	PD	FF	FR	TD
09/03	@GB	W 17-14	3	0	1.0	9.0	1.0	1.0	0	0	0	0	0	0
09/10	NO	W 17-13	2	0	2.0	6.0	0.0	0.0	0	0	0	1	0	0
09/17	@Car	W 31-10	3	1	0.0	0.0	0.5	0.5	0	0	0	1	0	0
09/24	Chi	W 34-28	0	0	0.0	0.0	0.0	0.0	0	0	0	0	0	0
10/01	@Ind	L 18-21	3	0	0.0	0.0	0.0	0.0	0	0	0	0	0	0
10/12	Atl	W 21-19	2	0	1.0	6.0	0.0	0.0	0	0	0	0	0	0
10/22	SF	L 10-44	4	0	1.0	16.0	1.0	1.0	0	0	0	0	0	0
10/29	@Phi	L 9-20	4	0	0.0	0.0	2.0	6.0	0	0	1	0	0	0
11/05	@NO	L 10-19	4	0	1.0	6.0	0.0	0.0	0	0	0	0	0	0
11/12	Car	W 28-17	3	0	1.0	6.0	0.0	0.0	0	0	1	0	0	0
11/19	@Atl	L 6-31	2	0	1.0	8.0	0.0	0.0	0	0	0	0	0	0
11/26	@SF	L 13-41	3	0	0.0	0.0	2.0	2.0	0	0	1	0	0	0
12/03	@NYA	W 23-20	5	1	3.5	19.0	1.0	1.0	1	5	1	1	0	0
12/10	Buf	L 27-45	5	0	0.0	0.0	1.0	2.0	0	0	0	0	0	0
12/17	Was	L 23-35	1	0	0.0	0.0	1.0	6.0	0	0	1	0	0	0
12/24	Mia	L 22-41	4	0	0.0	0.0	0.5	0.5	0	0	0	0	0	0

Jim Flanigan
Chicago Bears – DT

1995 Defensive Splits

	G	Tk	Ast	Sack	Yds	Stuff	Yds	Int	Yds	PD	TD
Total	16	39	10	11.0	74.5	6.5	15.5	0	0	1	0
vs. Playoff	6	13	6	4.5	25.5	1.0	2.0	0	0	0	0
vs. Non-Playoff	10	26	4	6.5	49.0	5.5	13.5	0	0	1	0
vs. Own Division	8	18	8	6.0	32.5	3.0	9.0	0	0	0	0
Home	8	22	3	5.5	25.5	4.5	10.5	0	0	0	0
Away	8	17	7	5.5	49.0	2.0	5.0	0	0	1	0
Games 1-8	8	23	3	6.5	43.0	5.5	13.5	0	0	1	0
Games 9-16	8	16	7	4.5	31.5	1.0	2.0	0	0	0	0
September	4	11	1	4.5	22.0	2.0	4.0	0	0	0	0
October	4	12	2	2.0	21.0	3.5	9.5	0	0	1	0
November	4	6	3	1.5	8.5	1.0	2.0	0	0	0	0
December	4	10	4	3.0	23.0	0.0	0.0	0	0	0	0
Grass	11	25	5	7.0	41.5	4.5	10.5	0	0	1	0
Turf	5	14	4	4.0	33.0	2.0	5.0	0	0	0	0
Indoor	2	6	4	2.0	17.0	1.0	4.0	0	0	0	0
Outdoor	14	33	6	9.0	57.5	5.5	11.5	0	0	1	0

Game Logs

Date	Opp	Result	Tk	Ast	Sack	Yds	Stuff	Yds	Int	Yds	PD	FF	FR	TD
09/03	Min	W 31-14	4	0	2.0	10.0	1.0	3.0	0	0	0	0	0	0
09/11	GB	L 24-27	3	0	1.0	1.0	0.0	0.0	0	0	0	0	1	0
09/17	@TB	W 25-6	1	1	0.5	2.0	0.0	0.0	0	0	0	0	0	0
09/24	@StL	L 28-34	3	0	1.0	9.0	1.0	1.0	0	0	0	0	0	0
10/08	Car	W 31-27	3	1	0.0	0.0	1.5	1.5	0	0	0	0	0	0
10/15	@Jac	W 30-27	2	0	1.0	14.0	0.0	0.0	0	0	1	0	0	0
10/22	Hou	W 35-32	3	0	0.0	0.0	1.0	4.0	0	0	0	0	0	0
10/30	@Min	W 14-6	4	1	1.0	7.0	1.0	4.0	0	0	0	0	0	0
11/05	Pit	L 34-37	3	0	1.0	6.0	0.0	0.0	0	0	0	0	0	0
11/12	@GB	L 28-35	0	1	0.0	0.0	0.0	0.0	0	0	0	0	0	0
11/19	Det	L 17-24	3	2	0.5	2.5	1.0	2.0	0	0	0	0	0	0
11/26	@NYN	W 27-24	0	0	0.0	0.0	0.0	0.0	0	0	0	0	0	0
12/04	@Det	L 7-27	2	3	1.0	10.0	0.0	0.0	0	0	0	0	0	0
12/10	@Cin	L 10-16	5	1	1.0	7.0	0.0	0.0	0	0	0	0	0	0
12/17	TB	W 31-10	1	0	0.0	0.0	0.0	0.0	0	0	0	0	0	0
12/24	Phi	W 20-14	2	0	1.0	6.0	0.0	0.0	0	0	0	0	0	0

Simon Fletcher
Denver Broncos – DE

1995 Defensive Splits

	G	Tk	Ast	Sack	Yds	Stuff	Yds	Int	Yds	PD	TD
Total	16	36	8	5.0	42.0	4.0	4.5	0	0	3	0
vs. Playoff	7	17	3	0.0	0.0	3.5	4.0	0	0	1	0
vs. Non-Playoff	9	19	5	5.0	42.0	0.5	0.5	0	0	2	0
vs. Own Division	8	20	5	4.0	38.0	4.0	4.5	0	0	3	0
Home	8	13	4	4.0	38.0	2.5	3.0	0	0	3	0
Away	8	23	4	1.0	4.0	1.5	1.5	0	0	0	0
Games 1-8	8	22	4	3.0	22.0	2.0	2.5	0	0	1	0
Games 9-16	8	14	4	2.0	20.0	2.0	2.0	0	0	2	0
September	4	12	0	0.0	0.0	0.0	0.0	0	0	0	0
October	4	10	4	3.0	22.0	2.0	2.5	0	0	1	0
November	4	5	4	0.0	0.0	1.0	1.0	0	0	1	0
December	4	9	0	2.0	20.0	1.0	1.0	0	0	1	0
Grass	12	21	4	4.0	38.0	3.5	4.0	0	0	3	0
Turf	4	15	4	1.0	4.0	0.5	0.5	0	0	0	0
Indoor	2	8	4	1.0	4.0	0.5	0.5	0	0	0	0
Outdoor	14	28	4	4.0	38.0	3.5	4.0	0	0	3	0

Game Logs

Date	Opp	Result	Tk	Ast	Sack	Yds	Stuff	Yds	Int	Yds	PD	FF	FR	TD
09/03	Buf	W 22-7	2	0	0.0	0.0	0.0	0.0	0	0	0	0	0	0
09/10	@Dal	L 21-31	7	0	0.0	0.0	0.0	0.0	0	0	0	0	0	0
09/17	Was	W 38-31	1	0	0.0	0.0	0.0	0.0	0	0	0	0	0	0
09/24	@SD	L 6-17	2	0	0.0	0.0	0.0	0.0	0	0	0	0	0	0
10/01	@Sea	L 10-27	5	2	1.0	4.0	0.5	0.5	0	0	0	0	0	0
10/08	@NE	W 37-3	1	0	0.0	0.0	0.0	0.0	0	0	0	0	0	0
10/16	Oak	W 27-0	2	0	2.0	18.0	0.0	0.0	0	0	1	1	0	0
10/22	KC	L 7-21	2	2	0.0	0.0	1.5	2.0	0	0	0	0	0	0
11/05	Ari	W 38-6	0	1	0.0	0.0	0.0	0.0	0	0	0	0	0	0
11/12	@Phi	L 13-31	0	0	0.0	0.0	0.0	0.0	0	0	0	0	0	0
11/19	SD	W 30-27	2	1	0.0	0.0	1.0	1.0	0	0	1	0	0	0
11/26	@Hou	L 33-42	3	2	0.0	0.0	0.0	0.0	0	0	0	0	0	0
12/03	Jac	W 31-23	2	0	1.0	4.0	0.0	0.0	0	0	1	0	0	0
12/10	Sea	L 27-31	2	0	1.0	16.0	0.0	0.0	0	0	1	0	0	0
12/17	@KC	L 17-20	2	0	0.0	0.0	1.0	1.0	0	0	0	0	0	0
12/24	@Oak	W 31-28	3	0	0.0	0.0	0.0	0.0	0	0	0	0	0	0

Dan Footman
Cleveland Browns – DT

1995 Defensive Splits

	G	Tk	Ast	Sack	Yds	Stuff	Yds	Int	Yds	PD	TD
Total	16	33	6	5.0	27.0	1.5	4.0	0	0	3	0
vs. Playoff	7	17	4	2.0	14.0	0.0	0.0	0	0	0	0
vs. Non-Playoff	9	16	2	3.0	13.0	1.5	4.0	0	0	3	0
vs. Own Division	8	14	2	4.0	25.0	1.5	4.0	0	0	0	0
Home	8	19	2	3.0	12.0	0.5	1.0	0	0	1	0
Away	8	14	4	2.0	15.0	1.0	3.0	0	0	2	0
Games 1-8	8	13	4	1.0	3.0	1.5	4.0	0	0	3	0
Games 9-16	8	20	2	4.0	24.0	0.0	0.0	0	0	0	0
September	4	11	2	0.0	0.0	1.0	3.0	0	0	3	0
October	4	10	2	1.0	3.0	0.5	1.0	0	0	0	0
November	4	13	2	2.0	14.0	0.0	0.0	0	0	0	0
December	4	7	0	2.0	10.0	0.0	0.0	0	0	0	0
Grass	11	20	2	3.0	12.0	0.5	1.0	0	0	3	0
Turf	5	13	4	2.0	15.0	1.0	3.0	0	0	0	0
Indoor	3	7	3	0.0	0.0	1.0	3.0	0	0	0	0
Outdoor	13	26	3	5.0	27.0	0.5	1.0	0	0	3	0

Game Logs

Date	Opp	Result	Tk	Ast	Sack	Yds	Stuff	Yds	Int	Yds	PD	FF	FR	TD
09/03	@NE	L 14-17	0	0	0.0	0.0	0.0	0.0	0	0	2	0	0	0
09/10	TB	W 22-6	2	1	0.0	0.0	0.0	0.0	0	0	1	0	0	0
09/17	@Hou	W 14-7	1	1	0.0	0.0	1.0	3.0	0	0	0	0	0	0
09/24	KC	W 35-17	0	0	0.0	0.0	0.0	0.0	0	0	0	0	0	0
10/02	Buf	L 19-22	3	0	0.0	0.0	0.0	0.0	0	0	0	0	0	0
10/08	@Det	L 20-38	2	2	0.0	0.0	0.0	0.0	0	0	0	0	0	0
10/22	Jac	L 15-23	3	0	0.0	0.0	0.5	1.0	0	0	0	0	1	0
10/29	@Cin	W 29-26	2	0	1.0	3.0	0.0	0.0	0	0	0	0	0	0
11/05	Hou	L 10-37	2	0	0.0	0.0	0.0	0.0	0	0	0	0	0	0
11/13	@Pit	L 3-20	4	1	1.0	12.0	0.0	0.0	0	0	0	0	0	0
11/19	GB	L 20-31	7	1	1.0	2.0	0.0	0.0	0	0	0	0	0	0
11/26	Pit	L 17-20	0	0	0.0	0.0	0.0	0.0	0	0	0	0	0	0
12/03	@SD	L 13-31	1	0	0.0	0.0	0.0	0.0	0	0	0	0	0	0
12/09	@Min	L 11-27	4	0	0.0	0.0	0.0	0.0	0	0	0	0	0	0
12/17	Cin	W 26-10	2	0	2.0	10.0	0.0	0.0	0	0	0	0	0	0
12/24	@Jac	L 21-24	0	0	0.0	0.0	0.0	0.0	0	0	0	0	0	0

Henry Ford

Houston Oilers – DE

1995 Defensive Splits

	G	Tk	Ast	Sack	Yds	Stuff	Yds	Int	Yds	PD	TD
Total	16	27	16	4.5	39.0	2.5	3.0	0	0	3	0
vs. Playoff	5	9	6	1.5	9.0	0.5	1.0	0	0	0	0
vs. Non-Playoff	11	18	10	3.0	30.0	2.0	2.0	0	0	3	0
vs. Own Division	8	17	9	3.0	22.0	0.5	1.0	0	0	2	0
Home	8	9	12	2.0	21.0	1.5	2.0	0	0	1	0
Away	8	18	4	2.5	18.0	1.0	1.0	0	0	2	0
Games 1-8	8	12	9	2.0	18.0	1.5	2.0	0	0	2	0
Games 9-16	8	15	7	2.5	21.0	1.0	1.0	0	0	1	0
September	4	9	5	2.0	18.0	0.5	1.0	0	0	1	0
October	4	3	4	0.0	0.0	1.0	1.0	0	0	1	0
November	4	6	4	0.0	0.0	0.0	0.0	0	0	1	0
December	4	9	3	2.5	21.0	1.0	1.0	0	0	0	0
Grass	4	10	0	0.0	0.0	1.0	1.0	0	0	1	0
Turf	12	17	16	4.5	39.0	1.5	2.0	0	0	2	0
Indoor	9	10	13	2.0	21.0	1.5	2.0	0	0	1	0
Outdoor	7	17	3	2.5	18.0	1.0	1.0	0	0	2	0

Game Logs

Date	Opp	Result	Tk	Ast	Sack	Yds	Stuff	Yds	Int	Yds	PD	FF	FR	TD
09/03	@Jac	W 10-3	4	0	0.0	0.0	0.0	0.0	0	0	0	0	0	0
09/10	Pit	L 17-34	0	3	0.0	0.0	0.5	1.0	0	0	0	0	0	0
09/17	Cle	L 7-14	3	2	1.0	9.0	0.0	0.0	0	0	0	0	0	0
09/24	@Cin	W 38-28	2	0	1.0	9.0	0.0	0.0	0	0	1	0	0	0
10/01	Jac	L 16-17	0	1	0.0	0.0	0.0	0.0	0	0	0	0	0	0
10/08	@Min	L 17-23	1	1	0.0	0.0	0.0	0.0	0	0	0	0	0	0
10/22	@Chi	L 32-35	2	0	0.0	0.0	1.0	1.0	0	0	0	0	0	0
10/29	TB	W 19-7	2	0	0.0	0.0	0.0	0.0	0	0	1	0	0	0
11/05	@Cle	W 37-10	2	0	0.0	0.0	0.0	0.0	0	0	1	0	0	0
11/12	Cin	L 25-32	1	2	0.0	0.0	0.0	0.0	0	0	0	0	0	0
11/19	@KC	L 13-20	2	0	0.0	0.0	0.0	0.0	0	0	0	0	0	0
11/26	Den	W 42-33	1	2	0.0	0.0	0.0	0.0	0	0	0	0	0	0
12/03	@Pit	L 7-21	5	1	1.0	4.0	0.0	0.0	0	0	0	0	0	0
12/10	Det	L 17-24	2	0	0.0	0.0	0.0	0.0	0	0	0	0	0	0
12/17	NYA	W 23-6	2	0	1.0	12.0	1.0	1.0	0	0	0	0	0	0
12/24	@Buf	W 28-17	0	2	0.5	5.0	0.0	0.0	0	0	0	0	0	0

Mike Fox

Carolina Panthers – DE

1995 Defensive Splits

	G	Tk	Ast	Sack	Yds	Stuff	Yds	Int	Yds	PD	TD
Total	16	42	11	4.5	27.5	3.0	5.0	0	0	7	0
vs. Playoff	6	23	2	4.0	24.0	1.0	1.0	0	0	4	0
vs. Non-Playoff	10	19	9	0.5	3.5	2.0	4.0	0	0	3	0
vs. Own Division	8	23	6	2.0	6.0	2.0	2.0	0	0	5	0
Home	8	24	6	2.5	21.5	2.0	4.0	0	0	4	0
Away	8	18	5	2.0	6.0	1.0	1.0	0	0	3	0
Games 1-8	8	22	6	1.5	5.5	3.0	5.0	0	0	2	0
Games 9-16	8	20	5	3.0	22.0	0.0	0.0	0	0	5	0
September	3	9	0	1.0	2.0	1.0	1.0	0	0	2	0
October	5	13	6	0.5	3.5	2.0	4.0	0	0	0	0
November	4	7	3	1.0	4.0	0.0	0.0	0	0	2	0
December	4	13	2	2.0	18.0	0.0	0.0	0	0	3	0
Grass	12	33	9	3.5	25.5	2.0	4.0	0	0	4	0
Turf	4	9	2	1.0	2.0	1.0	1.0	0	0	3	0
Indoor	3	6	2	1.0	2.0	1.0	1.0	0	0	3	0
Outdoor	13	36	9	3.5	25.5	2.0	4.0	0	0	4	0

Game Logs

Date	Opp	Result	Tk	Ast	Sack	Yds	Stuff	Yds	Int	Yds	PD	FF	FR	TD
09/03	@Atl	L 20-23	4	0	1.0	2.0	1.0	1.0	0	0	1	0	0	0
09/10	@Buf	L 9-31	3	0	0.0	0.0	0.0	0.0	0	0	0	0	0	0
09/17	StL	L 10-31	2	0	0.0	0.0	0.0	0.0	0	0	1	0	0	0
10/01	TB	L 13-20	2	1	0.5	3.5	1.0	3.0	0	0	0	0	0	0
10/08	@Chi	L 27-31	4	1	0.0	0.0	0.0	0.0	0	0	0	0	0	0
10/15	NYA	W 26-15	2	0	0.0	0.0	0.0	0.0	0	0	0	0	0	0
10/22	NO	W 20-3	3	2	0.0	0.0	1.0	1.0	0	0	0	0	0	0
10/29	@NE	W 20-17	2	0	0.0	0.0	0.0	0.0	0	0	0	0	0	0
11/05	@SF	W 13-7	3	0	1.0	4.0	0.0	0.0	0	0	0	0	0	0
11/12	@StL	L 17-28	1	1	0.0	0.0	0.0	0.0	0	0	1	0	0	0
11/19	Ari	W 27-7	2	1	0.0	0.0	0.0	0.0	0	0	0	0	0	0
11/26	@NO	L 26-34	1	1	0.0	0.0	0.0	0.0	0	0	1	0	0	0
12/03	Ind	W 13-10	4	0	2.0	18.0	0.0	0.0	0	0	2	0	0	0
12/10	SF	L 10-31	7	2	0.0	0.0	0.0	0.0	0	0	1	0	0	0
12/17	Atl	W 21-17	2	0	0.0	0.0	0.0	0.0	0	0	0	0	0	0
12/24	@Was	L 17-20	0	0	0.0	0.0	0.0	0.0	0	0	0	0	0	0

Rob Fredrickson

Oakland Raiders – LB

1995 Defensive Splits

	G	Tk	Ast	Sack	Yds	Stuff	Yds	Int	Yds	PD	TD
Total	16	71	14	0.0	0.0	2.0	6.0	1	14	2	1
vs. Playoff	8	39	8	0.0	0.0	1.0	5.0	1	14	2	1
vs. Non-Playoff	8	32	6	0.0	0.0	1.0	1.0	0	0	0	0
vs. Own Division	8	34	4	0.0	0.0	1.0	1.0	0	0	0	0
Home	8	36	11	0.0	0.0	1.0	5.0	1	14	2	1
Away	8	35	3	0.0	0.0	1.0	1.0	0	0	0	0
Games 1-8	8	34	5	0.0	0.0	1.0	1.0	1	14	1	0
Games 9-16	8	37	9	0.0	0.0	1.0	5.0	0	0	1	1
September	4	17	3	0.0	0.0	0.0	0.0	1	14	1	0
October	4	17	2	0.0	0.0	1.0	1.0	0	0	0	0
November	4	25	4	0.0	0.0	1.0	5.0	0	0	0	0
December	4	12	5	0.0	0.0	0.0	0.0	0	0	0	1
Grass	12	55	11	0.0	0.0	2.0	6.0	1	14	2	1
Turf	4	16	3	0.0	0.0	0.0	0.0	0	0	0	0
Indoor	1	1	0	0.0	0.0	0.0	0.0	0	0	0	0
Outdoor	15	70	14	0.0	0.0	2.0	6.0	1	14	2	1

Game Logs

Date	Opp	Result	Tk	Ast	Sack	Yds	Stuff	Yds	Int	Yds	PD	FF	FR	TD
09/03	SD	W 17-7	5	1	0.0	0.0	0.0	0.0	0	0	0	0	0	0
09/10	@Was	W 20-8	5	0	0.0	0.0	0.0	0.0	0	0	0	0	0	0
09/17	@KC	W 17-23	3	0	0.0	0.0	0.0	0.0	0	0	0	0	0	0
09/24	Phi	W 48-17	4	2	0.0	0.0	0.0	0.0	1	14	1	0	1	1
10/01	@NYA	W 47-10	3	0	0.0	0.0	0.0	0.0	0	0	0	0	1	0
10/08	Sea	W 34-14	4	1	0.0	0.0	0.0	0.0	0	0	0	0	0	0
10/16	@Den	L 0-27	5	0	0.0	0.0	1.0	1.0	0	0	0	0	0	0
10/22	Ind	W 30-17	5	1	0.0	0.0	0.0	0.0	0	0	0	0	0	0
11/05	@Cin	W 20-17	7	1	0.0	0.0	0.0	0.0	0	0	0	0	0	0
11/12	@NYN	W 17-13	5	2	0.0	0.0	0.0	0.0	0	0	0	0	0	0
11/19	Dal	L 21-34	7	1	0.0	0.0	1.0	5.0	0	0	0	0	0	0
11/27	@SD	L 6-12	6	0	0.0	0.0	0.0	0.0	0	0	0	0	0	0
12/03	KC	L 23-29	8	0	0.0	0.0	0.0	0.0	0	0	0	0	0	0
12/10	Pit	L 10-29	1	3	0.0	0.0	0.0	0.0	0	0	1	0	1	0
12/17	@Sea	L 10-44	1	0	0.0	0.0	0.0	0.0	0	0	0	0	0	0
12/24	Den	L 28-31	2	2	0.0	0.0	0.0	0.0	0	0	0	0	1	0

Corey Fuller

Minnesota Vikings – CB

1995 Defensive Splits

	G	Tk	Ast	Sack	Yds	Stuff	Yds	Int	Yds	PD	TD
Total	16	64	9	0.5	7.5	1.0	2.0	1	0	6	1
vs. Playoff	7	32	4	0.5	7.5	1.0	2.0	1	0	6	1
vs. Non-Playoff	9	32	5	0.0	0.0	0.0	0.0	0	0	0	0
vs. Own Division	8	33	5	0.5	7.5	1.0	2.0	0	0	3	0
Home	8	32	8	0.5	7.5	0.0	0.0	0	0	5	0
Away	8	32	1	0.0	0.0	1.0	2.0	1	0	1	1
Games 1-8	8	36	5	0.0	0.0	1.0	2.0	1	0	4	1
Games 9-16	8	28	4	0.5	7.5	0.0	0.0	0	0	2	0
September	4	18	1	0.0	0.0	0.0	0.0	1	0	4	1
October	4	18	4	0.0	0.0	1.0	2.0	0	0	0	0
November	4	20	3	0.5	7.5	0.0	0.0	0	0	2	0
December	4	8	1	0.0	0.0	0.0	0.0	0	0	0	0
Grass	5	20	0	0.0	0.0	1.0	2.0	0	0	0	0
Turf	11	44	9	0.5	7.5	0.0	0.0	1	0	6	1
Indoor	9	39	8	0.5	7.5	0.0	0.0	0	0	5	0
Outdoor	7	25	1	0.0	0.0	1.0	2.0	1	0	1	1

Game Logs

Date	Opp	Result	Tk	Ast	Sack	Yds	Stuff	Yds	Int	Yds	PD	FF	FR	TD
09/03	@Chi	L 14-31	3	0	0.0	0.0	0.0	0.0	0	0	0	0	0	0
09/10	Det	W 20-10	3	0	0.0	0.0	0.0	0.0	0	0	1	0	0	0
09/17	Dal	L 17-23	7	0	0.0	0.0	0.0	0.0	0	0	2	1	0	0
09/24	@Pit	W 44-24	5	1	0.0	0.0	0.0	0.0	1	0	1	0	1	1
10/08	Hou	W 23-17	5	3	0.0	0.0	0.0	0.0	0	0	0	0	0	0
10/15	@TB	L 17-20	6	0	0.0	0.0	0.0	0.0	0	0	0	0	0	0
10/22	@GB	L 21-38	3	0	0.0	0.0	1.0	2.0	0	0	0	0	0	0
10/30	Chi	L 6-14	4	1	0.0	0.0	0.0	0.0	0	0	0	0	0	0
11/05	GB	W 27-24	4	3	0.5	7.5	0.0	0.0	0	0	2	0	0	0
11/12	@Ari	W 30-24	5	0	0.0	0.0	0.0	0.0	0	0	0	0	0	0
11/19	NO	W 43-24	4	0	0.0	0.0	0.0	0.0	0	0	0	0	0	0
11/23	@Det	L 38-44	7	0	0.0	0.0	0.0	0.0	0	0	0	2	0	0
12/03	TB	W 31-17	3	1	0.0	0.0	0.0	0.0	0	0	0	0	0	0
12/09	Cle	W 27-11	2	0	0.0	0.0	0.0	0.0	0	0	0	0	0	0
12/18	@SF	L 30-37	3	0	0.0	0.0	0.0	0.0	0	0	0	0	0	0
12/24	@Cin	L 24-27	0	0	0.0	0.0	0.0	0.0	0	0	0	0	0	0

William Fuller

Philadelphia Eagles – DE

1995 Defensive Splits

	G	Tk	Ast	Sack	Yds	Stuff	Yds	Int	Yds	PD	TD
Total	14	35	11	13.0	106.0	4.5	8.0	0	0	4	0
vs. Playoff	3	6	4	2.0	12.0	2.0	2.0	0	0	1	0
vs. Non-Playoff	11	29	7	11.0	94.0	2.5	6.0	0	0	3	0
vs. Own Division	6	15	7	6.5	46.0	2.5	3.0	0	0	0	0
Home	7	20	4	8.0	65.0	4.0	7.0	0	0	3	0
Away	7	15	7	5.0	41.0	0.5	1.0	0	0	1	0
Games 1-8	6	11	6	5.5	50.0	2.5	6.0	0	0	1	0
Games 9-16	8	24	5	7.5	56.0	2.0	2.0	0	0	3	0
September	4	7	6	3.5	36.0	1.5	4.0	0	0	1	0
October	2	4	0	2.0	14.0	1.0	2.0	0	0	0	0
November	4	8	3	2.0	13.0	0.0	0.0	0	0	2	0
December	4	16	2	5.5	43.0	2.0	2.0	0	0	1	0
Grass	4	6	4	3.0	23.0	0.5	1.0	0	0	1	0
Turf	10	29	7	10.0	83.0	4.0	7.0	0	0	3	0
Indoor	2	8	1	2.0	18.0	0.0	0.0	0	0	0	0
Outdoor	12	27	10	11.0	88.0	4.5	8.0	0	0	4	0

Game Logs

Date	Opp	Result	Tk	Ast	Sack	Yds	Stuff	Yds	Int	Yds	PD	FF	FR	TD
09/03	TB	L 6-21	4	2	1.0	13.0	1.0	3.0	0	0	0	0	0	0
09/10	@Ari	W 31-19	1	3	1.0	8.0	0.5	1.0	0	0	0	0	0	0
09/17	SD	L 21-27	1	1	0.5	2.0	0.0	0.0	0	0	1	1	0	0
09/24	@Oak	L 17-48	1	0	1.0	13.0	0.0	0.0	0	0	0	0	0	0
10/01	@NO	W 15-10	0	0	0.0	0.0	0.0	0.0	0	0	0	0	0	0
10/08	Was	W 37-34	-	-	-	-	-	-	-	-	-	-	-	-
10/15	@NYN	W 17-14	-	-	-	-	-	-	-	-	-	-	-	-
10/29	StL	W 20-9	4	0	2.0	14.0	1.0	2.0	0	0	2	0	0	0
11/06	@Dal	L 12-34	1	2	0.0	0.0	0.0	0.0	0	0	0	0	0	0
11/12	Den	W 31-13	1	0	0.0	0.0	0.0	0.0	0	0	2	0	0	0
11/19	NYN	W 28-19	3	0	1.0	11.0	0.0	0.0	0	0	1	1	0	0
11/26	@Was	W 14-7	3	1	1.0	2.0	0.0	0.0	0	0	0	0	0	0
12/03	@Sea	L 14-26	8	1	2.0	18.0	0.0	0.0	0	0	1	0	0	0
12/10	Dal	W 20-17	4	1	1.5	10.0	2.0	2.0	0	0	0	0	0	0
12/17	Ari	W 21-20	3	0	2.0	15.0	0.0	0.0	0	0	0	0	0	0
12/24	@Chi	W 14-20	1	0	0.0	0.0	0.0	0.0	0	0	1	0	0	0

Shaun Gayle

San Diego Chargers – S

1995 Defensive Splits

	G	Tk	Ast	Sack	Yds	Stuff	Yds	Int	Yds	PD	TD
Total	16	73	12	0.0	0.0	4.5	13.5	2	99	4	2
vs. Playoff	7	43	5	0.0	0.0	3.0	8.0	0	0	1	0
vs. Non-Playoff	9	30	7	0.0	0.0	1.5	5.5	2	99	3	2
vs. Own Division	8	30	6	0.0	0.0	0.0	0.0	1	0	2	0
Home	8	35	3	0.0	0.0	1.5	5.5	0	0	0	0
Away	8	38	9	0.0	0.0	3.0	8.0	2	99	4	2
Games 1-8	8	41	8	0.0	0.0	2.0	4.0	1	0	2	1
Games 9-16	8	32	4	0.0	0.0	2.5	9.5	1	99	2	1
September	4	18	2	0.0	0.0	0.0	0.0	0	0	0	0
October	4	23	6	0.0	0.0	2.0	4.0	1	0	2	0
November	4	20	0	0.0	0.0	0.0	0.0	0	0	0	0
December	4	12	4	0.0	0.0	2.5	9.5	1	99	2	1
Grass	11	45	4	0.0	0.0	1.5	5.5	0	0	1	0
Turf	5	28	8	0.0	0.0	3.0	8.0	2	99	3	2
Indoor	2	8	7	0.0	0.0	1.0	4.0	1	0	1	1
Outdoor	14	65	5	0.0	0.0	3.5	9.5	1	99	3	1

Game Logs

Date	Opp	Result	Tk	Ast	Sack	Yds	Stuff	Yds	Int	Yds	PD	FF	FR	TD
09/03	@Oak	L 7-17	5	1	0.0	0.0	0.0	0.0	0	0	0	0	0	0
09/10	Sea	W 14-10	4	0	0.0	0.0	0.0	0.0	0	0	0	0	0	0
09/17	@Phi	W 27-21	6	0	0.0	0.0	0.0	0.0	0	0	0	0	0	0
09/24	Den	W 17-6	3	1	0.0	0.0	0.0	0.0	0	0	0	0	0	0
10/01	@Pit	L 16-31	11	1	0.0	0.0	2.0	4.0	0	0	0	0	0	0
10/09	@KC	L 23-29	1	0	0.0	0.0	0.0	0.0	0	0	1	0	0	0
10/15	Dal	L 9-23	7	1	0.0	0.0	0.0	0.0	0	0	0	0	0	0
10/22	@Sea	W 35-25	4	4	0.0	0.0	0.0	0.0	1	0	1	0	1	1
11/05	Mia	L 14-24	7	0	0.0	0.0	0.0	0.0	0	0	0	0	0	0
11/12	KC	L 7-22	7	0	0.0	0.0	0.0	0.0	0	0	0	0	0	0
11/19	@Den	L 27-30	4	0	0.0	0.0	0.0	0.0	0	0	0	0	0	0
11/27	Oak	W 12-6	2	0	0.0	0.0	0.0	0.0	0	0	0	0	0	0
12/03	Cle	W 31-13	2	1	0.0	0.0	0.5	0.5	0	0	0	0	0	0
12/09	Ari	W 28-25	3	0	0.0	0.0	1.0	5.0	0	0	0	0	0	0
12/17	@Ind	W 27-24	4	3	0.0	0.0	1.0	4.0	0	0	0	0	0	0
12/23	@NYN	W 27-17	3	0	0.0	0.0	0.0	0.0	1	99	2	0	0	1

Dennis Gibson

San Diego Chargers – LB

1995 Defensive Splits

	G	Tk	Ast	Sack	Yds	Stuff	Yds	Int	Yds	PD	TD
Total	13	59	14	0.0	0.0	2.0	2.0	0	0	0	0
vs. Playoff	6	32	4	0.0	0.0	1.5	1.5	0	0	0	0
vs. Non-Playoff	7	27	10	0.0	0.0	0.5	0.5	0	0	0	0
vs. Own Division	8	38	9	0.0	0.0	0.5	0.5	0	0	0	0
Home	6	27	4	0.0	0.0	1.0	1.0	0	0	0	0
Away	7	32	10	0.0	0.0	1.0	1.0	0	0	0	0
Games 1-8	8	32	12	0.0	0.0	2.0	2.0	0	0	0	0
Games 9-16	5	27	2	0.0	0.0	0.0	0.0	0	0	0	0
September	4	13	6	0.0	0.0	0.5	0.5	0	0	0	0
October	4	19	6	0.0	0.0	1.5	1.5	0	0	0	0
November	4	20	1	0.0	0.0	0.0	0.0	0	0	0	0
December	1	7	1	0.0	0.0	0.0	0.0	0	0	0	0
Grass	9	43	9	0.0	0.0	1.5	1.5	0	0	0	0
Turf	4	16	5	0.0	0.0	0.5	0.5	0	0	0	0
Indoor	1	5	2	0.0	0.0	0.0	0.0	0	0	0	0
Outdoor	12	54	12	0.0	0.0	2.0	2.0	0	0	0	0

Game Logs

Date	Opp	Result	Tk	Ast	Sack	Yds	Stuff	Yds	Int	Yds	PD	FF	FR	TD
09/03	@Oak	L 7-17	6	4	0.0	0.0	0.5	0.5	0	0	0	0	0	0
09/10	Sea	W 14-10	3	1	0.0	0.0	0.0	0.0	0	0	0	0	0	0
09/17	@Phi	W 27-21	2	0	0.0	0.0	0.0	0.0	0	0	0	0	0	0
09/24	Den	W 17-6	2	1	0.0	0.0	0.0	0.0	0	0	0	0	0	0
10/01	@Pit	L 16-31	2	2	0.0	0.0	0.5	0.5	0	0	0	0	0	0
10/09	@KC	L 23-29	7	0	0.0	0.0	0.0	0.0	0	0	0	0	0	0
10/15	Dal	L 9-23	5	2	0.0	0.0	1.0	1.0	0	0	0	0	0	0
10/22	@Sea	W 35-25	5	2	0.0	0.0	0.0	0.0	0	0	0	0	0	0
11/05	Mia	L 14-24	5	0	0.0	0.0	0.0	0.0	0	0	0	0	0	0
11/12	KC	L 7-22	11	0	0.0	0.0	0.0	0.0	0	0	0	0	0	0
11/19	@Den	L 27-30	3	1	0.0	0.0	0.0	0.0	0	0	0	0	0	0
11/27	Oak	W 12-6	1	0	0.0	0.0	0.0	0.0	0	0	0	0	0	0
12/03	Cle	W 31-13	-	-	-	-	-	-	-	-	-	-	-	-
12/09	Ari	W 28-25	-	-	-	-	-	-	-	-	-	-	-	-
12/17	@Ind	W 27-24	-	-	-	-	-	-	-	-	-	-	-	-
12/23	@NYN	W 27-17	7	1	0.0	0.0	0.0	0.0	0	0	0	0	0	0

Sean Gilbert

St. Louis Rams – DE

1995 Defensive Splits

	G	Tk	Ast	Sack	Yds	Stuff	Yds	Int	Yds	PD	TD
Total	14	25	9	6.5	55.0	5.0	16.0	0	0	0	1
vs. Playoff	8	18	5	4.5	36.5	5.0	16.0	0	0	0	1
vs. Non-Playoff	6	7	4	2.0	18.5	0.0	0.0	0	0	0	0
vs. Own Division	8	10	4	3.5	33.5	1.0	1.0	0	0	0	0
Home	7	16	3	2.5	18.5	4.0	9.0	0	0	0	1
Away	7	9	6	4.0	36.5	1.0	7.0	0	0	0	0
Games 1-8	6	7	6	2.0	18.0	2.0	8.0	0	0	0	0
Games 9-16	8	18	3	4.5	37.0	3.0	8.0	0	0	0	1
September	3	4	5	2.0	18.0	0.0	0.0	0	0	0	0
October	3	3	1	0.0	0.0	2.0	8.0	0	0	0	0
November	4	6	1	3.0	29.0	0.0	0.0	0	0	0	0
December	4	12	2	1.5	8.0	3.0	8.0	0	0	0	1
Grass	3	3	4	1.5	13.5	0.0	0.0	0	0	0	0
Turf	11	22	5	5.0	41.5	5.0	16.0	0	0	0	1
Indoor	6	16	2	4.0	33.0	3.0	8.0	0	0	0	1
Outdoor	8	9	7	2.5	22.0	2.0	8.0	0	0	0	0

Game Logs

Date	Opp	Result	Tk	Ast	Sack	Yds	Stuff	Yds	Int	Yds	PD	FF	FR	TD
09/03	@GB	W 17-14	2	3	1.5	13.5	0.0	0.0	0	0	0	0	0	0
09/10	NO	W 17-13	2	1	0.5	4.5	0.0	0.0	0	0	0	0	0	0
09/17	@Car	W 31-10	0	1	0.0	0.0	0.0	0.0	0	0	0	0	0	0
09/24	Chi	W 34-28	-	-	-	-	-	-	-	-	-	-	-	-
10/01	@Ind	L 18-21	-	-	-	-	-	-	-	-	-	-	-	-
10/12	Atl	W 21-19	2	0	0.0	0.0	1.0	1.0	0	0	0	0	0	0
10/22	SF	L 10-44	0	1	0.0	0.0	1.0	7.0	0	0	0	0	0	0
10/29	@Phi	L 9-20	1	0	0.0	0.0	1.0	7.0	0	0	0	1	0	0
11/05	@NO	L 10-19	1	1	0.0	0.0	0.0	0.0	0	0	0	0	0	0
11/12	Car	W 28-17	1	0	1.0	10.0	0.0	0.0	0	0	0	0	0	0
11/19	@Atl	L 6-31	3	0	2.0	19.0	0.0	0.0	0	0	0	0	0	0
11/26	@SF	L 13-41	1	0	0.0	0.0	0.0	0.0	0	0	0	0	0	0
12/03	@NYA	W 23-20	1	1	0.5	4.0	0.0	0.0	0	0	0	0	0	0
12/10	Buf	L 27-45	7	0	0.0	0.0	3.0	8.0	0	0	0	1	0	0
12/17	Was	L 23-35	2	0	0.0	0.0	0.0	0.0	0	0	0	0	1	0
12/24	Mia	L 22-41	2	1	1.0	4.0	0.0	0.0	0	0	0	1	0	0

Vencie Glenn

New York Giants – S

1995 Defensive Splits

	G	Tk	Ast	Sack	Yds	Stuff	Yds	Int	Yds	PD	TD
Total	15	67	18	0.0	0.0	1.0	4.0	5	91	7	1
vs. Playoff	8	33	9	0.0	0.0	1.0	4.0	1	10	1	0
vs. Non-Playoff	7	34	9	0.0	0.0	0.0	0.0	4	81	6	1
vs. Own Division	8	38	8	0.0	0.0	0.0	0.0	3	88	4	1
Home	7	34	11	0.0	0.0	0.0	0.0	2	3	2	0
Away	8	33	7	0.0	0.0	1.0	4.0	3	88	5	1
Games 1-8	8	34	8	0.0	0.0	1.0	4.0	3	78	4	1
Games 9-16	7	33	10	0.0	0.0	0.0	0.0	2	13	3	0
September	4	17	5	0.0	0.0	0.0	0.0	2	3	2	0
October	4	17	3	0.0	0.0	1.0	4.0	1	75	2	1
November	4	20	4	0.0	0.0	0.0	0.0	2	13	3	0
December	3	13	6	0.0	0.0	0.0	0.0	0	0	0	0
Grass	5	20	5	0.0	0.0	1.0	4.0	2	78	3	1
Turf	10	47	13	0.0	0.0	0.0	0.0	3	13	4	0
Indoor	1	3	1	0.0	0.0	0.0	0.0	0	0	1	0
Outdoor	14	64	17	0.0	0.0	1.0	4.0	5	91	6	1

Game Logs

Date	Opp	Result	Tk	Ast	Sack	Yds	Stuff	Yds	Int	Yds	PD	FF	FR	TD
09/04	Dal	L 0-35	2	1	0.0	0.0	0.0	0.0	0	0	0	0	0	0
09/10	@KC	L 17-20	5	0	0.0	0.0	0.0	0.0	0	0	0	0	0	0
09/17	@GB	L 6-14	2	2	0.0	0.0	0.0	0.0	0	0	0	0	0	0
09/24	NO	W 45-29	8	2	0.0	0.0	0.0	0.0	2	3	2	0	0	0
10/01	@SF	L 6-20	5	1	0.0	0.0	1.0	4.0	0	0	0	1	0	0
10/08	Ari	W 27-21	4	1	0.0	0.0	0.0	0.0	0	0	0	0	0	0
10/15	Phi	L 14-17	5	1	0.0	0.0	0.0	0.0	0	0	1	0	0	0
10/29	@Was	W 24-15	3	0	0.0	0.0	0.0	0.0	1	75	2	1	1	1
11/05	@Sea	L 28-30	3	1	0.0	0.0	0.0	0.0	0	0	1	0	0	0
11/12	Oak	L 13-17	-	-	-	-	-	-	-	-	-	-	-	-
11/19	@Phi	L 19-28	5	0	0.0	0.0	0.0	0.0	1	10	1	0	1	0
11/26	Chi	L 24-27	7	1	0.0	0.0	0.0	0.0	0	0	0	0	0	0
11/30	@Ari	W 10-6	5	2	0.0	0.0	0.0	0.0	1	3	1	0	0	0
12/10	Was	W 20-13	4	2	0.0	0.0	0.0	0.0	0	0	0	0	0	0
12/17	@Dal	L 20-21	5	1	0.0	0.0	0.0	0.0	0	0	0	0	0	0
12/23	SD	L 17-27	4	3	0.0	0.0	0.0	0.0	0	0	0	0	0	0

Keith Goganious
Jacksonville Jaguars – LB

1995 Defensive Splits												Game Logs												
	G	Tk	Ast	Sack	Yds	Stuff	Yds	Int	Yds	PD	TD	Date	Opp	Result	Tk	Ast	Sack	Yds	Stuff	Yds	Int	Yds	PD	FF	FR	TD
Total	16	56	27	0.0	0.0	5.5	11.5	2	11	4	0	09/03	Hou	L 3-10	2	0	0.0	0.0	0.5	0.5	0	0	0	0	0	0
vs. Playoff	5	19	10	0.0	0.0	4.0	10.0	0	0	1	0	09/10	@Cin	L 17-24	0	0	0.0	0.0	0.0	0.0	0	0	0	0	0	0
vs. Non-Playoff	11	37	17	0.0	0.0	1.5	1.5	2	11	3	0	09/17	@NYA	L 10-27	4	2	0.0	0.0	0.0	0.0	0	0	0	0	0	0
vs. Own Division	8	27	14	0.0	0.0	0.5	0.5	2	11	3	0	09/24	GB	L 14-24	5	0	0.0	0.0	2.0	3.0	0	0	1	0	0	0
Home	8	29	11	0.0	0.0	3.5	4.5	2	11	4	0	10/01	@Hou	W 17-16	7	6	0.0	0.0	0.0	0.0	0	0	0	0	0	0
Away	8	27	16	0.0	0.0	2.0	7.0	0	0	0	0	10/08	Pit	W 20-16	5	1	0.0	0.0	0.0	0.0	0	0	0	0	0	0
Games 1-8	8	26	11	0.0	0.0	2.5	3.5	0	0	1	0	10/15	Chi	L 27-30	2	2	0.0	0.0	0.0	0.0	0	0	0	0	0	0
Games 9-16	8	30	16	0.0	0.0	3.0	8.0	2	11	3	0	10/22	@Cle	W 23-15	1	0	0.0	0.0	0.0	0.0	0	0	0	0	0	0
September	4	11	2	0.0	0.0	2.5	3.5	0	0	1	0	10/29	@Pit	L 7-24	3	1	0.0	0.0	0.0	0.0	0	0	0	0	0	0
October	5	18	10	0.0	0.0	0.0	0.0	0	0	0	0	11/12	Sea	L 30-47	4	0	0.0	0.0	0.0	0.0	0	0	0	0	0	0
November	3	16	2	0.0	0.0	0.0	0.0	1	6	2	0	11/19	@TB	L 16-17	5	0	0.0	0.0	0.0	0.0	0	0	0	0	0	0
December	4	11	13	0.0	0.0	3.0	8.0	1	5	1	0	11/26	Cin	L 13-17	7	2	0.0	0.0	0.0	0.0	1	6	2	0	0	0
Grass	11	38	12	0.0	0.0	4.5	5.5	2	11	4	0	12/03	@Den	L 23-31	3	1	0.0	0.0	1.0	1.0	0	0	0	0	0	0
Turf	5	18	15	0.0	0.0	1.0	6.0	0	0	0	0	12/10	Ind	L 31-41	2	2	0.0	0.0	1.0	1.0	0	0	0	0	0	0
Indoor	2	11	12	0.0	0.0	1.0	6.0	0	0	0	0	12/17	@Det	L 0-44	4	6	0.0	0.0	1.0	6.0	0	0	0	0	0	0
Outdoor	14	45	15	0.0	0.0	4.5	5.5	2	11	4	0	12/24	Cle	W 24-21	2	4	0.0	0.0	0.0	0.0	1	5	1	0	0	0

Kurt Gouveia
Philadelphia Eagles – LB

1995 Defensive Splits												Game Logs												
	G	Tk	Ast	Sack	Yds	Stuff	Yds	Int	Yds	PD	TD	Date	Opp	Result	Tk	Ast	Sack	Yds	Stuff	Yds	Int	Yds	PD	FF	FR	TD
Total	16	88	18	0.0	0.0	8.0	13.5	1	20	4	0	09/03	TB	L 6-21	5	1	0.0	0.0	0.0	0.0	0	0	1	0	0	0
vs. Playoff	3	16	4	0.0	0.0	1.5	3.0	0	0	0	0	09/10	@Ari	W 31-19	10	0	0.0	0.0	0.0	0.0	0	0	0	0	0	0
vs. Non-Playoff	13	72	14	0.0	0.0	6.5	10.5	1	20	4	0	09/17	SD	L 21-27	9	1	0.0	0.0	1.0	2.0	0	0	0	0	0	0
vs. Own Division	8	49	6	0.0	0.0	3.0	5.5	0	0	0	0	09/24	@Oak	L 17-48	2	2	0.0	0.0	0.0	0.0	1	20	1	0	0	0
Home	8	51	3	0.0	0.0	3.5	6.5	0	0	3	0	10/01	@NO	W 15-10	3	3	0.0	0.0	1.0	2.0	0	0	0	0	0	0
Away	8	37	15	0.0	0.0	4.5	7.0	1	20	1	0	10/08	Was	W 37-34	7	1	0.0	0.0	1.5	1.5	0	0	0	0	0	0
Games 1-8	8	48	8	0.0	0.0	3.5	5.5	1	20	4	0	10/15	@NYN	W 17-14	6	0	0.0	0.0	0.0	0.0	0	0	0	1	0	0
Games 9-16	8	40	10	0.0	0.0	4.5	8.0	0	0	0	0	10/29	StL	W 20-9	6	0	0.0	0.0	0.0	0.0	0	0	2	0	0	0
September	4	26	4	0.0	0.0	1.0	2.0	1	20	2	0	11/06	@Dal	L 12-34	2	3	0.0	0.0	0.5	1.0	0	0	0	0	0	0
October	4	22	4	0.0	0.0	2.5	3.5	0	0	2	0	11/12	Den	W 31-13	3	0	0.0	0.0	0.0	0.0	0	0	0	0	0	0
November	4	16	5	0.0	0.0	0.5	1.0	0	0	0	0	11/19	NYN	W 28-19	8	0	0.0	0.0	0.0	0.0	0	0	0	0	1	0
December	4	24	5	0.0	0.0	4.0	7.0	0	0	0	0	11/26	@Was	W 14-7	3	2	0.0	0.0	0.0	0.0	0	0	0	0	0	0
Grass	4	25	6	0.0	0.0	2.0	3.0	1	20	1	0	12/03	@Sea	L 14-26	1	3	0.0	0.0	1.0	1.0	0	0	0	0	0	0
Turf	12	63	12	0.0	0.0	6.0	10.5	0	0	3	0	12/10	Dal	W 20-17	5	0	0.0	0.0	0.0	0.0	0	0	0	0	0	0
Indoor	2	4	6	0.0	0.0	2.0	3.0	0	0	0	0	12/17	Ari	W 21-20	8	0	0.0	0.0	1.0	3.0	0	0	0	0	0	0
Outdoor	14	84	12	0.0	0.0	6.0	10.5	1	20	4	0	12/24	@Chi	L 14-20	10	2	0.0	0.0	2.0	3.0	0	0	0	0	0	0

Stephen Grant
Indianapolis Colts – LB

1995 Defensive Splits												Game Logs												
	G	Tk	Ast	Sack	Yds	Stuff	Yds	Int	Yds	PD	TD	Date	Opp	Result	Tk	Ast	Sack	Yds	Stuff	Yds	Int	Yds	PD	FF	FR	TD
Total	15	76	32	2.0	13.0	2.0	4.0	1	9	5	0	09/03	Cin	L 21-24	10	1	0.0	0.0	0.5	2.5	0	0	0	0	0	0
vs. Playoff	5	20	13	1.0	10.0	0.5	0.5	0	0	3	0	09/10	@NYA	W 27-24	3	0	0.0	0.0	0.0	0.0	0	0	0	0	1	0
vs. Non-Playoff	10	56	19	1.0	3.0	1.5	3.5	1	9	2	0	09/17	@Buf	L 14-20	5	4	0.0	0.0	0.5	0.5	0	0	2	0	1	0
vs. Own Division	8	38	17	0.0	0.0	0.5	0.5	0	0	4	0	10/01	StL	W 21-18	6	3	0.0	0.0	0.0	0.0	0	0	0	0	0	0
Home	7	41	17	1.0	10.0	0.5	2.5	0	0	1	0	10/08	@Mia	W 27-24	3	0	0.0	0.0	0.0	0.0	0	0	0	0	0	0
Away	8	35	15	1.0	3.0	1.5	1.5	1	9	4	0	10/15	SF	W 18-17	4	2	0.0	0.0	0.0	0.0	0	0	0	0	0	0
Games 1-8	8	44	15	0.0	0.0	2.0	4.0	1	9	3	0	10/22	@Oak	L 17-30	7	1	0.0	0.0	1.0	1.0	1	9	1	0	0	0
Games 9-16	7	32	17	2.0	13.0	0.0	0.0	0	0	2	0	10/29	NYA	W 17-10	6	4	0.0	0.0	0.0	0.0	0	0	0	0	0	0
September	3	18	5	0.0	0.0	1.0	3.0	0	0	2	0	11/05	Buf	L 10-16	2	2	0.0	0.0	0.0	0.0	0	0	1	0	0	0
October	5	26	10	0.0	0.0	1.0	1.0	1	9	1	0	11/12	@NO	L 14-17	7	5	1.0	3.0	0.0	0.0	0	0	0	0	0	0
November	4	21	14	2.0	13.0	0.0	0.0	0	0	2	0	11/19	@NE	W 24-10	6	2	0.0	0.0	0.0	0.0	0	0	1	0	0	0
December	3	11	3	0.0	0.0	0.0	0.0	0	0	0	0	11/26	Mia	W 36-28	6	5	1.0	10.0	0.0	0.0	0	0	0	0	0	0
Grass	5	20	6	0.0	0.0	1.0	1.0	1	9	2	0	12/03	@Car	L 10-13	4	2	0.0	0.0	0.0	0.0	0	0	0	0	1	0
Turf	10	56	26	2.0	13.0	1.0	3.0	0	0	3	0	12/10	@Jac	W 41-31	0	1	0.0	0.0	0.0	0.0	0	0	0	0	0	0
Indoor	8	48	22	2.0	13.0	0.5	2.5	0	0	1	0	12/17	SD	L 24-27	-	-	-	-	-	-	-	-	-	-	-	-
Outdoor	7	28	10	0.0	0.0	1.5	1.5	1	9	4	0	12/23	NE	W 10-7	7	0	0.0	0.0	0.0	0.0	0	0	0	0	0	0

Carlton Gray
Seattle Seahawks – CB

1995 Defensive Splits	G	Tk	Ast	Sack	Yds	Stuff	Yds	Int	Yds	PD	TD
Total	16	68	5	0.0	0.0	0.5	0.5	4	45	19	0
vs. Playoff	6	22	4	0.0	0.0	0.5	0.5	1	14	9	0
vs. Non-Playoff	10	46	1	0.0	0.0	0.0	0.0	3	31	10	0
vs. Own Division	8	32	2	0.0	0.0	0.5	0.5	1	3	8	0
Home	8	36	0	0.0	0.0	0.5	0.5	2	40	11	0
Away	8	32	5	0.0	0.0	0.0	0.0	2	5	8	0
Games 1-8	8	37	4	0.0	0.0	0.5	0.5	3	8	12	0
Games 9-16	8	31	1	0.0	0.0	0.0	0.0	1	37	7	0
September	3	17	1	0.0	0.0	0.0	0.0	0	0	3	0
October	5	20	3	0.0	0.0	0.5	0.5	3	8	9	0
November	4	16	0	0.0	0.0	0.0	0.0	1	26	2	0
December	4	15	1	0.0	0.0	0.0	0.0	0	11	5	0
Grass	7	30	4	0.0	0.0	0.0	0.0	2	5	6	0
Turf	9	38	2	0.0	0.0	0.5	0.5	2	40	13	0
Indoor	8	36	0	0.0	0.0	0.5	0.5	2	40	11	0
Outdoor	8	32	5	0.0	0.0	0.0	0.0	2	5	8	0

Game Logs Date	Opp	Result	Tk	Ast	Sack	Yds	Stuff	Yds	Int	Yds	PD	FF	FR	TD
09/03	KC	L 10-34	3	0	0.0	0.0	0.0	0.0	0	0	1	0	0	0
09/10	@SD	L 10-14	7	1	0.0	0.0	0.0	0.0	0	0	1	0	0	0
09/17	Cin	W 24-21	7	0	0.0	0.0	0.0	0.0	0	0	1	0	0	0
10/01	Den	W 27-10	6	0	0.0	0.0	0.0	0.0	0	0	1	0	0	0
10/08	@Oak	L 14-34	3	0	0.0	0.0	0.0	0.0	0	0	1	0	0	0
10/15	@Buf	L 21-27	2	2	0.0	0.0	0.0	0.0	0	0	2	0	0	0
10/22	SD	L 25-35	3	0	0.0	0.0	0.5	0.5	1	3	2	0	0	0
10/29	@Ari	L 14-20	6	1	0.0	0.0	0.0	0.0	2	5	3	0	0	0
11/05	NYN	W 30-28	4	0	0.0	0.0	0.0	0.0	0	0	1	0	0	0
11/12	@Jac	W 47-30	4	0	0.0	0.0	0.0	0.0	0	0	0	0	0	0
11/19	@Was	W 27-20	3	0	0.0	0.0	0.0	0.0	0	0	0	0	0	0
11/26	NYA	L 10-16	5	0	0.0	0.0	0.0	0.0	1	26	1	0	0	0
12/03	Phi	W 26-14	5	0	0.0	0.0	0.0	0.0	0	11	3	0	0	0
12/10	@Den	W 31-27	5	0	0.0	0.0	0.0	0.0	0	0	1	0	0	0
12/17	Oak	W 44-10	3	0	0.0	0.0	0.0	0.0	0	0	1	0	0	0
12/24	@KC	L 3-26	2	1	0.0	0.0	0.0	0.0	0	0	0	0	0	0

Darrell Green
Washington Redskins – CB

1995 Defensive Splits	G	Tk	Ast	Sack	Yds	Stuff	Yds	Int	Yds	PD	TD
Total	16	48	5	0.0	0.0	3.5	9.5	3	42	14	1
vs. Playoff	6	25	1	0.0	0.0	1.5	5.5	2	29	8	1
vs. Non-Playoff	10	23	4	0.0	0.0	2.0	4.0	1	13	6	0
vs. Own Division	8	21	2	0.0	0.0	1.0	2.0	1	13	8	0
Home	8	20	0	0.0	0.0	3.5	9.5	2	20	7	1
Away	8	28	5	0.0	0.0	0.0	0.0	1	22	7	0
Games 1-8	8	27	3	0.0	0.0	2.5	7.5	2	20	7	1
Games 9-16	8	21	2	0.0	0.0	1.0	2.0	1	22	7	0
September	4	9	2	0.0	0.0	1.0	2.0	1	13	3	0
October	5	21	1	0.0	0.0	1.5	5.5	1	7	5	1
November	3	6	0	0.0	0.0	1.0	2.0	1	22	3	0
December	4	12	2	0.0	0.0	0.0	0.0	0	0	3	0
Grass	12	30	3	0.0	0.0	3.5	9.5	3	42	10	1
Turf	4	18	2	0.0	0.0	0.0	0.0	0	0	4	0
Indoor	1	5	1	0.0	0.0	0.0	0.0	0	0	2	0
Outdoor	15	43	4	0.0	0.0	3.5	9.5	3	42	12	1

Game Logs Date	Opp	Result	Tk	Ast	Sack	Yds	Stuff	Yds	Int	Yds	PD	FF	FR	TD
09/03	Ari	W 27-7	1	0	0.0	0.0	1.0	2.0	1	13	2	0	0	0
09/10	Oak	L 8-20	2	0	0.0	0.0	0.0	0.0	0	0	0	0	0	0
09/17	@Den	L 31-38	2	1	0.0	0.0	0.0	0.0	0	0	1	0	0	0
09/24	@TB	L 6-14	4	1	0.0	0.0	0.0	0.0	0	0	0	0	0	0
10/01	Dal	W 27-23	1	0	0.0	0.0	0.0	0.0	0	0	2	0	0	0
10/08	@Phi	L 34-37	7	0	0.0	0.0	0.0	0.0	0	0	1	0	0	0
10/15	@Ari	L 20-24	2	1	0.0	0.0	0.0	0.0	0	0	0	0	0	0
10/22	Det	W 36-30	8	0	0.0	0.0	1.5	5.5	1	7	1	0	0	1
10/29	NYN	L 15-24	3	0	0.0	0.0	0.0	0.0	0	0	1	0	0	0
11/05	@KC	L 3-24	2	0	0.0	0.0	0.0	0.0	1	22	2	0	0	0
11/19	Sea	L 20-27	3	0	0.0	0.0	1.0	2.0	0	0	0	0	0	0
11/26	Phi	L 7-14	1	0	0.0	0.0	0.0	0.0	0	0	1	0	0	0
12/03	@Dal	W 24-17	6	1	0.0	0.0	0.0	0.0	0	0	1	0	0	0
12/10	@NYN	L 13-20	1	0	0.0	0.0	0.0	0.0	0	0	0	0	0	0
12/17	@StL	W 35-23	5	1	0.0	0.0	0.0	0.0	0	0	2	0	0	0
12/24	Car	W 20-17	1	0	0.0	0.0	0.0	0.0	0	0	0	0	0	0

Victor Green
New York Jets – S

1995 Defensive Splits	G	Tk	Ast	Sack	Yds	Stuff	Yds	Int	Yds	PD	TD
Total	16	109	34	2.0	19.0	1.5	2.5	1	2	7	0
vs. Playoff	7	45	13	1.0	7.0	0.5	0.5	1	2	4	0
vs. Non-Playoff	9	64	21	1.0	12.0	1.0	2.0	0	0	3	0
vs. Own Division	8	45	21	0.0	0.0	0.5	0.5	1	2	3	0
Home	8	52	12	1.0	12.0	0.0	0.0	1	2	3	0
Away	8	57	22	1.0	7.0	1.5	2.5	0	0	4	0
Games 1-8	8	50	12	1.0	7.0	0.5	0.5	1	2	4	0
Games 9-16	8	59	22	1.0	12.0	1.0	2.0	0	0	3	0
September	4	28	2	1.0	7.0	0.5	0.5	0	0	2	0
October	5	27	13	0.0	0.0	0.0	0.0	1	2	3	0
November	3	19	8	0.0	0.0	0.5	1.0	0	0	1	0
December	4	35	11	1.0	12.0	0.5	1.0	0	0	1	0
Grass	3	18	8	0.0	0.0	0.5	0.5	0	0	0	0
Turf	13	91	26	2.0	10.0	1.0	2.0	1	2	7	0
Indoor	4	33	9	1.0	7.0	1.0	2.0	0	0	4	0
Outdoor	12	76	25	1.0	12.0	0.5	0.5	1	2	3	0

Game Logs Date	Opp	Result	Tk	Ast	Sack	Yds	Stuff	Yds	Int	Yds	PD	FF	FR	TD
09/03	@Mia	L 14-52	4	1	0.0	0.0	0.5	0.5	0	0	0	0	0	0
09/10	Ind	L 24-27	3	0	0.0	0.0	0.0	0.0	0	0	0	0	0	0
09/17	Jac	W 27-10	6	1	0.0	0.0	0.0	0.0	0	0	1	0	0	0
09/24	@Atl	L 3-13	15	0	1.0	7.0	0.0	0.0	0	0	1	0	0	0
10/01	Oak	L 10-47	4	0	0.0	0.0	0.0	0.0	0	0	0	0	0	0
10/08	@Buf	L 10-29	6	5	0.0	0.0	0.0	0.0	0	0	1	0	0	0
10/15	@Car	L 15-26	6	3	0.0	0.0	0.0	0.0	0	0	0	0	0	0
10/22	Mia	W 17-16	6	2	0.0	0.0	0.0	0.0	1	2	2	0	0	0
10/29	@Ind	L 10-17	5	3	0.0	0.0	0.0	0.0	0	0	1	0	0	0
11/05	NE	L 7-20	7	4	0.0	0.0	0.0	0.0	0	0	0	0	0	0
11/19	Buf	L 26-28	6	2	0.0	0.0	0.0	0.0	0	0	0	0	0	0
11/26	@Sea	W 16-10	6	2	0.0	0.0	0.5	1.0	0	0	1	0	0	0
12/03	StL	L 20-23	8	2	1.0	12.0	0.0	0.0	0	0	0	0	0	0
12/10	@NE	L 28-31	8	4	0.0	0.0	0.0	0.0	0	0	0	0	1	0
12/17	@Hou	L 6-23	7	4	0.0	0.0	0.5	1.0	0	0	1	0	0	0
12/24	NO	L 0-12	12	1	0.0	0.0	0.0	0.0	0	0	0	0	0	0

Kevin Greene
Pittsburgh Steelers – LB

1995 Defensive Splits

	G	Tk	Ast	Sack	Yds	Stuff	Yds	Int	Yds	PD	TD
Total	16	34	14	9.0	64.0	2.5	12.5	1	0	4	0
vs. Playoff	4	8	2	2.0	9.0	0.0	0.0	0	0	1	0
vs. Non-Playoff	12	26	12	7.0	55.0	2.5	12.5	1	0	3	0
vs. Own Division	8	22	9	6.0	49.0	2.5	12.5	0	0	1	0
Home	8	14	9	2.5	17.5	0.5	1.5	1	0	3	0
Away	8	20	5	6.5	46.5	2.0	11.0	0	0	1	0
Games 1-8	8	17	5	5.0	38.0	1.0	6.0	1	0	4	0
Games 9-16	8	17	9	4.0	26.0	1.5	6.5	0	0	0	0
September	4	8	0	2.0	23.0	1.0	6.0	1	0	3	0
October	4	9	5	3.0	15.0	0.0	0.0	0	0	1	0
November	4	7	4	1.0	8.0	1.0	5.0	0	0	0	0
December	4	10	5	3.0	18.0	0.5	1.5	0	0	0	0
Grass	6	13	5	4.5	20.5	0.0	0.0	0	0	0	0
Turf	10	21	9	4.5	43.5	2.5	12.5	1	0	4	0
Indoor	1	5	0	1.0	18.0	1.0	6.0	0	0	1	0
Outdoor	15	29	14	8.0	46.0	1.5	6.5	1	0	3	0

Game Logs

Date	Opp	Result	Tk	Ast	Sack	Yds	Stuff	Yds	Int	Yds	PD	FF	FR	TD
09/03	Det	W 23-20	1	0	0.0	0.0	0.0	0.0	0	0	0	0	0	0
09/10	@Hou	W 34-17	5	0	1.0	18.0	1.0	6.0	0	0	1	1	0	0
09/18	@Mia	L 10-23	1	0	1.0	5.0	0.0	0.0	0	0	0	1	0	0
09/24	Min	L 24-44	1	0	0.0	0.0	0.0	0.0	1	0	2	0	0	0
10/01	SD	W 31-16	1	1	0.0	0.0	0.0	0.0	0	0	1	0	0	0
10/08	@Jac	L 16-20	4	1	2.5	11.5	0.0	0.0	0	0	0	0	0	0
10/19	Cin	L 9-27	3	1	0.0	0.0	0.0	0.0	0	0	0	0	0	0
10/29	Jac	W 24-7	1	2	0.5	3.5	0.0	0.0	0	0	0	0	0	0
11/05	@Chi	W 37-34	0	1	0.0	0.0	0.0	0.0	0	0	0	0	0	0
11/13	Cle	W 20-3	2	2	0.0	0.0	0.0	0.0	0	0	0	0	0	0
11/19	@Cin	W 49-31	2	0	1.0	8.0	1.0	5.0	0	0	0	0	0	0
11/26	@Cle	W 20-17	3	1	0.0	0.0	0.0	0.0	0	0	0	0	0	0
12/03	Hou	W 21-7	2	2	1.0	8.0	0.5	1.5	0	0	0	0	0	0
12/10	@Oak	W 29-10	0	1	0.0	0.0	0.0	0.0	0	0	0	0	0	0
12/16	NE	W 41-27	3	1	1.0	6.0	0.0	0.0	0	0	0	0	0	0
12/24	@GB	L 19-24	5	1	1.0	4.0	0.0	0.0	0	0	0	0	0	0

Myron Guyton
New England Patriots – S

1995 Defensive Splits

	G	Tk	Ast	Sack	Yds	Stuff	Yds	Int	Yds	PD	TD
Total	14	60	14	0.0	0.0	1.0	2.0	3	68	5	0
vs. Playoff	8	27	12	0.0	0.0	1.0	2.0	3	68	4	0
vs. Non-Playoff	6	33	2	0.0	0.0	0.0	0.0	0	0	1	0
vs. Own Division	7	31	10	0.0	0.0	1.0	2.0	3	68	5	0
Home	7	36	6	0.0	0.0	1.0	2.0	1	0	2	0
Away	7	24	8	0.0	0.0	0.0	0.0	2	68	3	0
Games 1-8	6	20	6	0.0	0.0	1.0	2.0	0	0	0	0
Games 9-16	8	40	8	0.0	0.0	0.0	0.0	3	68	5	0
September	3	5	4	0.0	0.0	1.0	2.0	0	0	0	0
October	3	15	2	0.0	0.0	0.0	0.0	0	0	0	0
November	4	14	6	0.0	0.0	0.0	0.0	3	68	3	0
December	4	26	2	0.0	0.0	0.0	0.0	0	0	2	0
Grass	9	41	8	0.0	0.0	1.0	2.0	2	45	3	0
Turf	5	19	6	0.0	0.0	0.0	0.0	1	23	2	0
Indoor	2	9	3	0.0	0.0	0.0	0.0	0	0	1	0
Outdoor	12	51	11	0.0	0.0	1.0	2.0	3	68	4	0

Game Logs

Date	Opp	Result	Tk	Ast	Sack	Yds	Stuff	Yds	Int	Yds	PD	FF	FR	TD
09/03	Cle	W 17-14	1	0	0.0	0.0	0.0	0.0	0	0	0	0	0	0
09/10	Mia	L 3-20	3	2	0.0	0.0	1.0	2.0	0	0	0	0	0	0
09/17	@SF	L 3-28	1	2	0.0	0.0	0.0	0.0	0	0	0	0	0	0
10/01	@Atl	L 17-30	3	2	0.0	0.0	0.0	0.0	0	0	0	1	0	0
10/08	Den	L 3-37	4	0	0.0	0.0	0.0	0.0	0	0	0	0	0	0
10/15	@KC	L 26-31	-	-	-	-	-	-	-	-	-	-	-	-
10/23	Buf	W 27-14	-	-	-	-	-	-	-	-	-	-	-	-
10/29	Car	L 17-20	8	0	0.0	0.0	0.0	0.0	0	0	0	0	0	0
11/05	@NYA	W 20-7	3	1	0.0	0.0	0.0	0.0	0	0	0	0	0	0
11/12	@Mia	W 34-17	4	0	0.0	0.0	0.0	0.0	1	45	1	0	0	0
11/19	Ind	L 10-24	3	3	0.0	0.0	0.0	0.0	1	0	1	0	0	0
11/26	@Buf	W 35-25	4	2	0.0	0.0	0.0	0.0	1	23	1	0	0	0
12/03	NO	L 17-31	9	0	0.0	0.0	0.0	0.0	0	0	0	0	0	0
12/10	NYA	W 31-28	8	1	0.0	0.0	0.0	0.0	0	0	1	0	0	0
12/16	@Pit	L 27-41	3	0	0.0	0.0	0.0	0.0	0	0	0	0	0	0
12/23	@Ind	L 7-10	6	1	0.0	0.0	0.0	0.0	0	0	1	0	1	0

Charles Haley
Dallas Cowboys – DE

1995 Defensive Splits

	G	Tk	Ast	Sack	Yds	Stuff	Yds	Int	Yds	PD	TD
Total	13	31	3	10.5	76.5	1.0	3.0	0	0	0	0
vs. Playoff	6	15	2	6.5	35.5	0.0	0.0	0	0	0	0
vs. Non-Playoff	7	16	1	4.0	41.0	1.0	3.0	0	0	0	0
vs. Own Division	5	7	0	1.0	4.0	0.0	0.0	0	0	0	0
Home	7	14	0	4.0	27.0	0.0	0.0	0	0	0	0
Away	6	17	3	6.5	49.5	1.0	3.0	0	0	0	0
Games 1-8	8	26	3	8.5	71.5	1.0	3.0	0	0	0	0
Games 9-16	5	5	0	2.0	5.0	0.0	0.0	0	0	0	0
September	4	14	1	4.0	41.0	1.0	3.0	0	0	0	0
October	4	12	2	4.5	30.5	0.0	0.0	0	0	0	0
November	4	4	0	2.0	5.0	0.0	0.0	0	0	0	0
December	1	1	0	0.0	0.0	0.0	0.0	0	0	0	0
Grass	3	4	1	2.5	15.5	0.0	0.0	0	0	0	0
Turf	10	27	2	8.0	61.0	1.0	3.0	0	0	0	0
Indoor	2	12	2	4.0	34.0	1.0	3.0	0	0	0	0
Outdoor	11	19	1	6.5	42.5	0.0	0.0	0	0	0	0

Game Logs

Date	Opp	Result	Tk	Ast	Sack	Yds	Stuff	Yds	Int	Yds	PD	FF	FR	TD
09/04	@NYN	W 35-0	1	0	0.0	0.0	0.0	0.0	0	0	0	0	0	0
09/10	Den	W 31-21	5	0	2.0	22.0	0.0	0.0	0	0	0	1	0	0
09/17	@Min	W 23-17	6	1	2.0	19.0	1.0	3.0	0	0	0	1	0	0
09/24	Ari	W 34-20	2	0	0.0	0.0	0.0	0.0	0	0	0	0	0	0
10/01	@Was	L 23-27	1	0	0.0	0.0	0.0	0.0	0	0	0	0	0	0
10/08	GB	W 34-24	2	0	0.0	0.0	0.0	0.0	0	0	0	0	0	0
10/15	@SD	W 23-9	3	1	2.5	15.5	0.0	0.0	0	0	0	0	0	0
10/29	@Atl	W 28-13	6	1	2.0	15.0	0.0	0.0	0	0	0	0	0	0
11/06	Phi	W 34-12	2	0	1.0	4.0	0.0	0.0	0	0	0	0	0	0
11/12	SF	L 20-38	1	0	1.0	1.0	0.0	0.0	0	0	0	0	0	0
11/19	@Oak	W 34-21	0	0	0.0	0.0	0.0	0.0	0	0	0	1	0	0
11/23	KC	W 24-12	1	0	0.0	0.0	0.0	0.0	0	0	0	0	0	0
12/03	Was	L 17-24	1	0	0.0	0.0	0.0	0.0	0	0	0	0	0	0
12/10	@Phi	L 17-20	-	-	-	-	-	-	-	-	-	-	-	-
12/17	NYN	W 21-20	-	-	-	-	-	-	-	-	-	-	-	-
12/25	@Ari	W 37-13	-	-	-	-	-	-	-	-	-	-	-	-

Merton Hanks

1995 Defensive Splits

	G	Tk	Ast	Sack	Yds	Stuff	Yds	Int	Yds	PD	TD
Total	16	54	9	0.0	0.0	0.0	0.0	5	31	13	1
vs. Playoff	7	23	8	0.0	0.0	0.0	0.0	3	23	6	1
vs. Non-Playoff	9	31	1	0.0	0.0	0.0	0.0	2	8	7	0
vs. Own Division	8	28	2	0.0	0.0	0.0	0.0	0	0	5	0
Home	8	37	1	0.0	0.0	0.0	0.0	2	8	7	1
Away	8	17	8	0.0	0.0	0.0	0.0	3	23	6	1
Games 1-8	8	23	6	0.0	0.0	0.0	0.0	3	31	6	0
Games 9-16	8	31	3	0.0	0.0	0.0	0.0	2	0	7	1
September	4	11	4	0.0	0.0	0.0	0.0	2	8	2	0
October	4	12	2	0.0	0.0	0.0	0.0	1	23	4	0
November	4	12	3	0.0	0.0	0.0	0.0	2	0	3	1
December	4	19	0	0.0	0.0	0.0	0.0	0	0	4	0
Grass	10	42	2	0.0	0.0	0.0	0.0	3	8	9	0
Turf	6	12	7	0.0	0.0	0.0	0.0	2	23	4	1
Indoor	4	10	5	0.0	0.0	0.0	0.0	1	23	3	0
Outdoor	12	44	4	0.0	0.0	0.0	0.0	4	8	10	1

Game Logs

Date	Opp	Result	Tk	Ast	Sack	Yds	Stuff	Yds	Int	Yds	PD	FF	FR	TD
09/03	@NO	W 24-22	1	1	0.0	0.0	0.0	0.0	0	0	0	0	0	0
09/10	Atl	W 41-10	5	1	0.0	0.0	0.0	0.0	0	0	0	0	0	0
09/17	NE	W 28-3	4	0	0.0	0.0	0.0	0.0	2	8	2	0	0	0
09/25	@Det	L 24-27	1	2	0.0	0.0	0.0	0.0	0	0	0	0	0	0
10/01	NYN	W 20-6	5	0	0.0	0.0	0.0	0.0	0	0	2	0	0	0
10/15	@Ind	L 17-18	1	2	0.0	0.0	0.0	0.0	1	23	1	0	0	0
10/22	@StL	W 44-10	2	0	0.0	0.0	0.0	0.0	0	0	0	0	0	0
10/29	NO	L 7-11	4	0	0.0	0.0	0.0	0.0	0	0	1	0	0	0
11/05	Car	L 7-13	3	0	0.0	0.0	0.0	0.0	0	0	0	0	0	0
11/12	@Dal	W 38-20	0	2	0.0	0.0	0.0	0.0	1	0	1	0	1	1
11/20	@Mia	W 44-20	4	1	0.0	0.0	0.0	0.0	1	0	1	0	1	0
11/26	StL	W 41-13	5	0	0.0	0.0	0.0	0.0	0	0	1	0	0	0
12/03	Buf	W 27-17	5	0	0.0	0.0	0.0	0.0	0	0	1	0	0	0
12/10	@Car	W 31-10	1	0	0.0	0.0	0.0	0.0	0	0	1	0	0	0
12/18	Min	W 37-30	6	0	0.0	0.0	0.0	0.0	0	0	0	0	0	0
12/24	@Atl	L 27-28	7	0	0.0	0.0	0.0	0.0	0	0	2	0	0	0

Phil Hansen

1995 Defensive Splits

	G	Tk	Ast	Sack	Yds	Stuff	Yds	Int	Yds	PD	TD
Total	16	53	23	10.0	83.5	4.0	7.5	0	0	0	0
vs. Playoff	6	21	7	3.5	31.5	1.5	1.5	0	0	0	0
vs. Non-Playoff	10	32	16	6.5	52.0	2.5	6.0	0	0	0	0
vs. Own Division	8	28	15	5.5	47.5	3.0	4.5	0	0	0	0
Home	8	22	12	6.0	53.5	2.5	4.0	0	0	0	0
Away	8	31	11	4.0	30.0	1.5	3.5	0	0	0	0
Games 1-8	8	31	17	4.5	45.0	4.0	7.5	0	0	0	0
Games 9-16	8	22	6	5.5	38.5	0.0	0.0	0	0	0	0
September	3	13	5	2.5	28.0	2.5	4.5	0	0	0	0
October	5	18	12	2.0	17.0	1.5	3.0	0	0	0	0
November	4	11	2	2.0	16.0	0.0	0.0	0	0	0	0
December	4	11	4	3.5	22.5	0.0	0.0	0	0	0	0
Grass	5	19	9	1.0	8.0	1.5	3.5	0	0	0	0
Turf	11	34	14	9.0	75.5	2.5	4.0	0	0	0	0
Indoor	2	9	2	1.0	6.0	0.0	0.0	0	0	0	0
Outdoor	14	44	21	9.0	77.5	4.0	7.5	0	0	0	0

Game Logs

Date	Opp	Result	Tk	Ast	Sack	Yds	Stuff	Yds	Int	Yds	PD	FF	FR	TD
09/03	@Den	L 7-22	4	0	0.0	0.0	1.0	3.0	0	0	0	0	0	0
09/10	Car	W 31-9	4	2	0.5	9.0	0.0	0.0	0	0	0	0	0	0
09/17	Ind	W 20-14	5	3	2.0	19.0	1.5	1.5	0	0	0	0	0	0
10/02	@Cle	W 22-19	4	1	1.0	8.0	0.0	0.0	0	0	0	0	0	0
10/08	NYA	W 29-10	2	1	0.0	0.0	1.0	2.5	0	0	0	0	1	0
10/15	Sea	W 27-21	4	2	1.0	9.0	0.0	0.0	0	0	0	0	0	0
10/23	@NE	L 14-27	5	7	0.0	0.0	0.5	0.5	0	0	0	0	0	0
10/29	@Mia	L 6-23	3	1	0.0	0.0	0.0	0.0	0	0	0	0	0	0
11/05	@Ind	W 16-10	6	0	0.0	0.0	0.0	0.0	0	0	0	0	0	0
11/12	Atl	W 23-17	1	1	0.0	0.0	0.0	0.0	0	0	0	0	0	0
11/19	@NYA	W 28-26	3	0	2.0	16.0	0.0	0.0	0	0	0	0	0	0
11/26	NE	L 25-35	1	1	0.0	0.0	0.0	0.0	0	0	0	0	0	0
12/03	@SF	L 17-27	3	0	0.0	0.0	0.0	0.0	0	0	0	0	0	0
12/10	@StL	W 45-27	3	2	1.0	6.0	0.0	0.0	0	0	0	0	0	0
12/17	Mia	W 23-20	3	2	1.5	12.5	0.0	0.0	0	0	0	0	0	0
12/24	Hou	L 17-28	2	0	1.0	4.0	0.0	0.0	0	0	0	0	0	0

Andy Harmon

1995 Defensive Splits

	G	Tk	Ast	Sack	Yds	Stuff	Yds	Int	Yds	PD	TD
Total	15	56	7	11.0	71.0	2.0	4.5	0	0	1	0
vs. Playoff	3	8	3	1.0	4.0	1.0	2.0	0	0	0	0
vs. Non-Playoff	12	48	4	10.0	67.0	1.0	2.5	0	0	1	0
vs. Own Division	8	33	4	7.5	49.0	2.0	4.5	0	0	1	0
Home	8	28	3	8.0	55.0	0.0	0.0	0	0	1	0
Away	7	28	4	3.0	16.0	2.0	4.5	0	0	0	0
Games 1-8	7	27	4	8.5	57.0	1.0	2.5	0	0	0	0
Games 9-16	8	29	3	2.5	14.0	1.0	2.0	0	0	1	0
September	4	13	3	1.5	9.0	1.0	2.5	0	0	0	0
October	3	14	1	7.0	48.0	0.0	0.0	0	0	0	0
November	4	16	1	2.0	12.0	1.0	2.0	0	0	0	0
December	4	13	2	0.5	2.0	0.0	0.0	0	0	1	0
Grass	4	14	2	1.0	7.0	1.0	2.5	0	0	0	1
Turf	11	42	5	10.0	64.0	1.0	2.0	0	0	1	0
Indoor	1	7	0	0.0	0.0	0.0	0.0	0	0	0	0
Outdoor	14	49	7	11.0	71.0	2.0	4.5	0	0	1	0

Game Logs

Date	Opp	Result	Tk	Ast	Sack	Yds	Stuff	Yds	Int	Yds	PD	FF	FR	TD
09/03	TB	L 6-21	2	1	0.0	0.0	0.0	0.0	0	0	0	0	0	0
09/10	@Ari	W 31-19	4	1	0.0	0.0	1.0	2.5	0	0	0	0	0	0
09/17	SD	L 21-27	2	1	0.5	2.0	0.0	0.0	0	0	0	0	0	0
09/24	@Oak	L 17-48	5	0	1.0	7.0	0.0	0.0	0	0	0	1	1	0
10/01	@NO	W 15-10	-	-	-	-	-	-	-	-	-	-	-	-
10/08	Was	W 37-34	4	0	3.0	26.0	0.0	0.0	0	0	0	1	0	0
10/15	@NYN	W 17-14	5	1	2.0	9.0	0.0	0.0	0	0	0	0	0	0
10/29	StL	W 20-9	5	0	2.0	13.0	0.0	0.0	0	0	0	0	0	0
11/06	@Dal	L 12-34	2	1	0.0	0.0	1.0	2.0	0	0	0	0	0	0
11/12	Den	W 31-13	1	0	0.0	0.0	0.0	0.0	0	0	0	0	0	0
11/19	NYN	W 28-19	9	0	2.0	12.0	0.0	0.0	0	0	0	0	0	0
11/26	@Was	W 14-7	4	0	0.0	0.0	0.0	0.0	0	0	0	0	0	0
12/03	@Sea	L 14-26	7	0	0.0	0.0	0.0	0.0	0	0	0	0	0	0
12/10	Dal	W 20-17	4	1	0.5	2.0	0.0	0.0	0	0	0	0	0	0
12/17	Ari	W 21-20	1	0	0.0	0.0	0.0	0.0	0	0	1	1	0	0
12/24	@Chi	L 14-20	1	1	0.0	0.0	0.0	0.0	0	0	0	0	0	0

Dwayne Harper

San Diego Chargers – CB

1995 Defensive Splits

	G	Tk	Ast	Sack	Yds	Stuff	Yds	Int	Yds	PD	TD
Total	16	61	15	0.0	0.0	3.0	9.0	4	12	14	0
vs. Playoff	7	29	8	0.0	0.0	2.0	8.0	0	0	4	0
vs. Non-Playoff	9	32	7	0.0	0.0	1.0	1.0	4	12	10	0
vs. Own Division	8	30	6	0.0	0.0	0.0	0.0	4	12	5	0
Home	8	41	4	0.0	0.0	3.0	9.0	3	13	7	0
Away	8	20	11	0.0	0.0	0.0	0.0	1	-1	7	0
Games 1-8	8	26	8	0.0	0.0	1.0	7.0	1	-1	5	0
Games 9-16	8	35	7	0.0	0.0	2.0	2.0	3	13	9	0
September	4	14	4	0.0	0.0	0.0	0.0	0	0	3	0
October	4	12	4	0.0	0.0	1.0	7.0	1	-1	2	0
November	4	22	4	0.0	0.0	1.0	1.0	3	13	3	0
December	4	13	3	0.0	0.0	1.0	1.0	0	0	6	0
Grass	11	49	8	0.0	0.0	3.0	9.0	3	13	8	0
Turf	5	12	7	0.0	0.0	0.0	0.0	1	-1	6	0
Indoor	2	7	1	0.0	0.0	0.0	0.0	1	-1	1	0
Outdoor	14	54	14	0.0	0.0	3.0	9.0	3	13	13	0

Game Logs

Date	Opp	Result	Tk	Ast	Sack	Yds	Stuff	Yds	Int	Yds	PD	FF	FR	TD
09/03	@Oak	L 7-17	4	1	0.0	0.0	0.0	0.0	0	0	0	0	0	0
09/10	Sea	W 14-10	5	0	0.0	0.0	0.0	0.0	0	0	0	0	0	0
09/17	@Phi	W 27-21	2	3	0.0	0.0	0.0	0.0	0	0	3	0	0	0
09/24	Den	W 17-6	3	0	0.0	0.0	0.0	0.0	0	0	0	0	0	0
10/01	@Pit	L 16-31	2	1	0.0	0.0	0.0	0.0	0	0	0	0	0	0
10/09	@KC	L 23-29	3	2	0.0	0.0	0.0	0.0	0	0	1	0	0	0
10/15	Dal	L 9-23	6	0	0.0	0.0	1.0	7.0	0	0	0	0	0	0
10/22	@Sea	W 35-25	1	1	0.0	0.0	0.0	0.0	1	-1	1	0	0	0
11/05	Mia	L 14-24	8	2	0.0	0.0	1.0	1.0	0	0	0	0	0	0
11/12	KC	L 7-22	2	0	0.0	0.0	0.0	0.0	0	0	0	0	0	0
11/19	@Den	L 27-30	1	0	0.0	0.0	0.0	0.0	0	0	0	0	0	0
11/27	Oak	W 12-6	11	1	0.0	0.0	0.0	0.0	3	13	3	0	0	0
12/03	Cle	W 31-13	4	0	0.0	0.0	1.0	1.0	0	0	1	0	0	0
12/09	Ari	W 28-25	2	1	0.0	0.0	0.0	0.0	0	0	3	0	1	0
12/17	@Ind	W 27-24	6	0	0.0	0.0	0.0	0.0	0	0	0	0	0	0
12/23	@NYN	W 27-17	1	2	0.0	0.0	0.0	0.0	0	0	2	0	0	0

Corey Harris

Seattle Seahawks – CB

1995 Defensive Splits

	G	Tk	Ast	Sack	Yds	Stuff	Yds	Int	Yds	PD	TD
Total	16	76	9	0.0	0.0	0.0	0.0	3	-5	12	1
vs. Playoff	6	29	2	0.0	0.0	0.0	0.0	0	0	0	0
vs. Non-Playoff	10	47	7	0.0	0.0	0.0	0.0	3	-5	12	1
vs. Own Division	8	37	4	0.0	0.0	0.0	0.0	1	0	4	1
Home	8	38	4	0.0	0.0	0.0	0.0	0	0	4	1
Away	8	38	5	0.0	0.0	0.0	0.0	3	-5	8	0
Games 1-8	8	40	5	0.0	0.0	0.0	0.0	0	0	5	0
Games 9-16	8	36	4	0.0	0.0	0.0	0.0	3	-5	7	1
September	3	13	0	0.0	0.0	0.0	0.0	0	0	1	0
October	5	27	5	0.0	0.0	0.0	0.0	0	0	4	0
November	4	20	2	0.0	0.0	0.0	0.0	2	-5	6	0
December	4	16	2	0.0	0.0	0.0	0.0	1	0	1	1
Grass	7	33	3	0.0	0.0	0.0	0.0	3	-5	8	0
Turf	9	43	6	0.0	0.0	0.0	0.0	0	0	4	1
Indoor	8	38	4	0.0	0.0	0.0	0.0	0	0	4	1
Outdoor	8	38	5	0.0	0.0	0.0	0.0	3	-5	8	0

Game Logs

Date	Opp	Result	Tk	Ast	Sack	Yds	Stuff	Yds	Int	Yds	PD	FF	FR	TD
09/03	KC	L 10-34	6	0	0.0	0.0	0.0	0.0	0	0	0	0	0	0
09/10	@SD	L 10-14	3	0	0.0	0.0	0.0	0.0	0	0	0	0	0	0
09/17	Cin	W 24-21	4	0	0.0	0.0	0.0	0.0	0	0	1	0	0	0
10/01	Den	W 27-10	6	1	0.0	0.0	0.0	0.0	0	0	1	0	0	0
10/08	@Oak	L 14-34	5	1	0.0	0.0	0.0	0.0	0	0	2	0	0	0
10/15	@Buf	L 21-27	5	2	0.0	0.0	0.0	0.0	0	0	0	0	0	0
10/22	SD	L 25-35	5	0	0.0	0.0	0.0	0.0	0	0	0	0	0	0
10/29	@Ari	L 14-20	6	1	0.0	0.0	0.0	0.0	0	0	1	1	0	0
11/05	NYN	W 30-28	3	1	0.0	0.0	0.0	0.0	0	0	0	0	0	0
11/12	@Jac	W 47-30	2	0	0.0	0.0	0.0	0.0	1	0	3	0	0	0
11/19	@Was	W 27-20	8	0	0.0	0.0	0.0	0.0	1	-5	0	0	0	0
11/26	NYA	L 10-16	7	1	0.0	0.0	0.0	0.0	0	0	1	0	0	0
12/03	Phi	W 26-14	4	0	0.0	0.0	0.0	0.0	0	0	0	0	0	0
12/10	@Den	W 31-27	3	1	0.0	0.0	0.0	0.0	1	0	1	0	0	0
12/17	Oak	W 44-10	3	1	0.0	0.0	0.0	0.0	0	0	0	0	1	1
12/24	@KC	L 3-26	6	0	0.0	0.0	0.0	0.0	0	0	0	0	0	0

Robert Harris

New York Giants – DE

1995 Defensive Splits

	G	Tk	Ast	Sack	Yds	Stuff	Yds	Int	Yds	PD	TD
Total	15	34	7	5.0	28.0	1.0	1.0	0	0	1	0
vs. Playoff	7	11	5	2.0	16.0	0.0	0.0	0	0	0	0
vs. Non-Playoff	8	23	2	3.0	12.0	1.0	1.0	0	0	1	0
vs. Own Division	8	20	5	2.0	10.0	1.0	1.0	0	0	0	0
Home	7	17	5	1.0	1.0	1.0	1.0	0	0	1	0
Away	8	17	2	4.0	27.0	0.0	0.0	0	0	0	0
Games 1-8	8	15	5	3.0	25.0	1.0	1.0	0	0	1	0
Games 9-16	7	19	2	2.0	3.0	0.0	0.0	0	0	0	0
September	4	6	3	2.0	16.0	0.0	0.0	0	0	1	0
October	4	9	2	1.0	9.0	1.0	1.0	0	0	0	0
November	5	14	1	1.0	2.0	0.0	0.0	0	0	0	0
December	2	5	1	1.0	1.0	0.0	0.0	0	0	0	0
Grass	5	9	1	3.0	25.0	0.0	0.0	0	0	0	0
Turf	10	25	6	2.0	3.0	1.0	1.0	0	0	1	0
Indoor	1	3	0	1.0	2.0	0.0	0.0	0	0	0	0
Outdoor	14	31	7	4.0	26.0	1.0	1.0	0	0	1	0

Game Logs

Date	Opp	Result	Tk	Ast	Sack	Yds	Stuff	Yds	Int	Yds	PD	FF	FR	TD
09/04	Dal	L 0-35	0	2	0.0	0.0	0.0	0.0	0	0	0	0	0	0
09/10	@KC	L 17-20	3	0	1.0	5.0	0.0	0.0	0	0	0	1	0	0
09/17	@GB	L 6-14	1	1	1.0	11.0	0.0	0.0	0	0	1	0	0	0
09/24	NO	W 45-29	2	0	0.0	0.0	0.0	0.0	0	0	1	0	0	0
10/01	@SF	L 6-20	0	0	0.0	0.0	0.0	0.0	0	0	0	0	0	0
10/08	Ari	W 27-21	4	1	0.0	0.0	1.0	1.0	0	0	0	0	0	0
10/15	Phi	L 14-17	2	1	0.0	0.0	0.0	0.0	0	0	0	0	0	0
10/29	@Was	W 24-15	3	0	1.0	9.0	0.0	0.0	0	0	0	0	0	0
11/05	@Sea	L 28-30	3	1	1.0	2.0	0.0	0.0	0	0	0	0	0	0
11/12	Oak	L 13-17	2	1	0.0	0.0	0.0	0.0	0	0	0	0	0	0
11/19	@Phi	L 19-28	4	0	0.0	0.0	0.0	0.0	0	0	0	0	1	0
11/26	Chi	L 24-27	3	0	0.0	0.0	0.0	0.0	0	0	0	0	0	0
11/30	@Ari	W 10-6	2	0	0.0	0.0	0.0	0.0	0	0	0	0	1	0
12/10	Was	W 20-13	4	0	1.0	1.0	0.0	0.0	0	0	0	0	0	0
12/17	@Dal	L 20-21	1	1	0.0	0.0	0.0	0.0	0	0	0	0	0	0
12/23	SD	L 17-27	-	-	-	-	-	-	-	-	-	-	-	-

Ken Harvey

1995 Defensive Splits

	G	Tk	Ast	Sack	Yds	Stuff	Yds	Int	Yds	PD	TD
Total	16	78	6	7.5	37.0	7.0	29.0	0	0	4	0
vs. Playoff	6	32	2	5.5	28.0	4.5	8.5	0	0	1	0
vs. Non-Playoff	10	46	4	2.0	9.0	2.5	20.5	0	0	3	0
vs. Own Division	8	47	5	4.5	22.0	2.5	2.5	0	0	2	0
Home	8	35	2	4.5	22.0	2.5	17.5	0	0	2	0
Away	8	43	4	3.0	15.0	4.5	11.5	0	0	2	0
Games 1-8	8	46	5	3.5	18.0	3.0	6.0	0	0	3	0
Games 9-16	8	32	1	4.0	19.0	4.0	23.0	0	0	1	0
September	4	17	0	1.0	4.0	1.0	4.0	0	0	2	0
October	5	31	5	2.5	14.0	2.0	2.0	0	0	1	0
November	3	18	0	4.0	19.0	4.0	23.0	0	0	0	0
December	4	12	1	0.0	0.0	0.0	0.0	0	0	1	0
Grass	12	62	5	7.5	37.0	6.0	28.0	0	0	3	0
Turf	4	16	1	0.0	0.0	1.0	1.0	0	0	1	0
Indoor	1	4	0	0.0	0.0	0.0	0.0	0	0	0	0
Outdoor	15	74	6	7.5	37.0	7.0	29.0	0	0	4	0

Game Logs

Date	Opp	Result	Tk	Ast	Sack	Yds	Stuff	Yds	Int	Yds	PD	FF	FR	TD
09/03	Ari	W 27-7	6	0	0.0	0.0	0.0	0.0	0	0	1	0	0	
09/10	Oak	L 8-20	3	0	0.0	0.0	0.0	0.0	0	0	1	0	0	
09/17	@Den	L 31-38	4	0	0.0	0.0	1.0	4.0	0	0	0	0	0	
09/24	@TB	L 6-14	4	0	1.0	4.0	0.0	0.0	0	0	1	0	0	
10/01	Dal	W 27-23	9	1	0.5	4.0	0.0	0.0	0	0	1	0	0	
10/08	@Phi	L 34-37	7	0	0.0	0.0	1.0	1.0	0	0	1	0	0	
10/15	@Ari	L 20-24	12	3	1.0	5.0	0.5	0.5	0	0	1	0	0	
10/22	Det	W 36-30	1	1	1.0	5.0	0.5	0.5	0	0	0	1	0	
10/29	NYN	L 15-24	2	0	0.0	0.0	0.0	0.0	0	0	0	0	0	
11/05	@KC	L 3-24	7	0	1.0	6.0	2.0	6.0	0	0	0	0	0	
11/19	Sea	L 20-27	5	0	0.0	0.0	1.0	16.0	0	0	0	0	0	
11/26	Phi	L 7-14	6	0	3.0	13.0	1.0	1.0	0	0	0	0	0	
12/03	@Dal	W 24-17	2	0	0.0	0.0	0.0	0.0	0	0	0	0	0	
12/10	@NYN	L 13-20	3	1	0.0	0.0	0.0	0.0	0	0	0	0	0	
12/17	@StL	W 35-23	4	0	0.0	0.0	0.0	0.0	0	0	0	1	0	
12/24	Car	W 20-17	3	0	0.0	0.0	0.0	0.0	0	0	1	0	0	

Richard Harvey

1995 Defensive Splits

	G	Tk	Ast	Sack	Yds	Stuff	Yds	Int	Yds	PD	TD
Total	16	88	27	2.0	9.0	4.0	6.0	0	0	7	0
vs. Playoff	8	50	10	1.0	8.0	0.5	0.5	0	0	1	0
vs. Non-Playoff	8	38	17	1.0	1.0	3.5	5.5	0	0	6	0
vs. Own Division	8	34	12	0.0	0.0	1.0	1.0	0	0	3	0
Home	8	46	15	1.0	8.0	0.5	0.5	0	0	1	0
Away	8	42	12	1.0	1.0	3.5	5.5	0	0	6	0
Games 1-8	8	56	14	1.0	8.0	3.0	5.0	0	0	5	0
Games 9-16	8	32	13	1.0	1.0	1.0	1.0	0	0	2	0
September	4	29	7	0.0	0.0	2.5	4.5	0	0	1	0
October	4	27	7	1.0	8.0	0.5	0.5	0	0	4	0
November	4	12	7	1.0	1.0	1.0	1.0	0	0	0	0
December	4	20	6	0.0	0.0	0.0	0.0	0	0	2	0
Grass	3	16	5	0.0	0.0	0.0	0.0	0	0	4	0
Turf	13	72	22	2.0	9.0	4.0	6.0	0	0	3	0
Indoor	10	52	16	2.0	9.0	1.5	1.5	0	0	1	0
Outdoor	6	36	11	0.0	0.0	2.5	4.5	0	0	6	0

Game Logs

Date	Opp	Result	Tk	Ast	Sack	Yds	Stuff	Yds	Int	Yds	PD	FF	FR	TD
09/03	SF	L 22-24	5	0	0.0	0.0	0.0	0.0	0	0	1	0	0	
09/10	@StL	L 13-17	5	0	0.0	0.0	1.0	1.0	0	0	0	0	0	
09/17	Atl	L 24-27	9	3	0.0	0.0	0.0	0.0	0	0	0	0	0	
09/24	@NYN	L 29-45	10	4	0.0	0.0	1.5	3.5	0	0	1	0	0	
10/01	Phi	L 10-15	8	2	0.0	0.0	0.5	0.5	0	0	0	0	0	
10/15	Mia	W 33-30	10	2	1.0	8.0	0.0	0.0	0	0	1	0	0	
10/22	@Car	L 3-20	3	2	0.0	0.0	0.0	0.0	0	0	3	0	0	
10/29	@SF	W 11-7	6	1	0.0	0.0	0.0	0.0	0	0	0	0	0	
11/05	StL	W 19-10	2	3	0.0	0.0	0.0	0.0	0	0	0	0	0	
11/12	Ind	W 17-14	4	0	0.0	0.0	0.0	0.0	0	0	0	0	0	
11/19	@Min	L 24-43	4	1	1.0	1.0	1.0	1.0	0	0	0	0	0	
11/26	Car	W 34-26	2	3	0.0	0.0	0.0	0.0	0	0	0	0	0	
12/03	@NE	W 31-17	7	2	0.0	0.0	0.0	0.0	0	0	1	0	0	
12/10	@Atl	L 14-19	2	0	0.0	0.0	0.0	0.0	0	0	0	0	0	
12/16	GB	L 23-34	6	2	0.0	0.0	0.0	0.0	0	0	0	0	0	
12/24	@NYA	W 12-0	5	2	0.0	0.0	0.0	0.0	0	0	1	0	0	

James Hasty

1995 Defensive Splits

	G	Tk	Ast	Sack	Yds	Stuff	Yds	Int	Yds	PD	TD
Total	16	72	1	0.0	0.0	2.0	2.0	3	89	12	0
vs. Playoff	4	19	1	0.0	0.0	0.0	0.0	0	0	3	0
vs. Non-Playoff	12	53	2	0.0	0.0	2.0	2.0	3	89	9	1
vs. Own Division	8	40	1	0.0	0.0	2.0	2.0	3	89	8	1
Home	8	35	1	0.0	0.0	2.0	2.0	1	64	2	1
Away	8	37	2	0.0	0.0	0.0	0.0	2	25	10	0
Games 1-8	8	38	1	0.0	0.0	0.0	0.0	2	89	7	1
Games 9-16	8	34	2	0.0	0.0	2.0	2.0	1	0	5	0
September	4	21	1	0.0	0.0	0.0	0.0	2	89	4	1
October	4	17	0	0.0	0.0	0.0	0.0	0	0	3	0
November	4	14	1	0.0	0.0	0.0	0.0	0	0	2	0
December	4	20	0	0.0	0.0	2.0	2.0	1	0	3	0
Grass	14	59	2	0.0	0.0	2.0	2.0	2	64	10	1
Turf	2	13	1	0.0	0.0	0.0	0.0	1	25	2	0
Indoor	1	8	0	0.0	0.0	0.0	0.0	1	25	2	0
Outdoor	15	64	3	0.0	0.0	2.0	2.0	2	64	10	1

Game Logs

Date	Opp	Result	Tk	Ast	Sack	Yds	Stuff	Yds	Int	Yds	PD	FF	FR	TD
09/03	@Sea	W 34-10	8	0	0.0	0.0	0.0	0.0	1	25	2	1	0	
09/10	NYN	W 20-17	3	0	0.0	0.0	0.0	0.0	0	0	0	0	0	
09/17	Oak	W 23-17	5	0	0.0	0.0	0.0	0.0	1	64	1	0	1	
09/24	@Cle	L 17-35	5	1	0.0	0.0	0.0	0.0	0	0	1	0	0	
10/01	@Ari	W 24-3	3	0	0.0	0.0	0.0	0.0	0	0	2	0	0	
10/09	SD	W 29-23	6	0	0.0	0.0	0.0	0.0	0	0	0	0	0	
10/15	NE	W 31-26	5	0	0.0	0.0	0.0	0.0	0	0	0	0	0	
10/22	@Den	W 21-7	2	0	0.0	0.0	0.0	0.0	0	0	0	0	0	
11/05	Was	W 24-3	2	0	0.0	0.0	0.0	0.0	0	0	0	0	0	
11/12	@SD	W 22-7	3	0	0.0	0.0	0.0	0.0	0	0	2	0	0	
11/19	Hou	W 20-13	4	0	0.0	0.0	0.0	0.0	0	0	0	0	0	
11/23	@Dal	L 12-24	5	1	0.0	0.0	0.0	0.0	0	0	0	0	0	
12/03	@Oak	W 29-23	5	0	0.0	0.0	0.0	0.0	1	0	1	0	0	
12/11	@Mia	L 0-13	5	0	0.0	0.0	0.0	0.0	0	0	1	0	0	
12/17	Den	W 20-17	6	1	0.0	0.0	2.0	2.0	0	0	1	0	0	
12/24	Sea	W 26-3	4	0	0.0	0.0	0.0	0.0	0	0	0	0	0	

Jeff Herrod
Indianapolis Colts – LB

1995 Defensive Splits

	G	Tk	Ast	Sack	Yds	Stuff	Yds	Int	Yds	PD	TD
Total	16	82	42	0.0	0.0	3.0	6.0	0	0	3	0
vs. Playoff	6	29	13	0.0	0.0	0.0	0.0	0	0	2	0
vs. Non-Playoff	10	53	29	0.0	0.0	3.0	6.0	0	0	1	0
vs. Own Division	8	35	26	0.0	0.0	1.0	2.0	0	0	2	0
Home	8	41	20	0.0	0.0	1.0	3.0	0	0	2	0
Away	8	41	22	0.0	0.0	2.0	3.0	0	0	1	0
Games 1-8	8	39	24	0.0	0.0	1.0	3.0	0	0	0	0
Games 9-16	8	43	18	0.0	0.0	2.0	3.0	0	0	3	0
September	3	15	9	0.0	0.0	1.0	3.0	0	0	0	0
October	5	24	15	0.0	0.0	0.0	0.0	0	0	0	0
November	4	19	10	0.0	0.0	1.0	2.0	0	0	2	0
December	4	24	8	0.0	0.0	1.0	1.0	0	0	1	0
Grass	5	25	12	0.0	0.0	2.0	3.0	0	0	1	0
Turf	11	57	30	0.0	0.0	1.0	3.0	0	0	2	0
Indoor	9	48	24	0.0	0.0	1.0	3.0	0	0	2	0
Outdoor	7	34	18	0.0	0.0	2.0	3.0	0	0	1	0

Game Logs

Date	Opp	Result	Tk	Ast	Sack	Yds	Stuff	Yds	Int	Yds	PD	FF	FR	TD
09/03	Cin	L 21-24	6	3	0.0	0.0	1.0	3.0	0	0	0	1	0	0
09/10	@NYA	W 27-24	4	4	0.0	0.0	0.0	0.0	0	0	0	0	0	0
09/17	@Buf	L 14-20	5	2	0.0	0.0	0.0	0.0	0	0	0	1	0	0
10/01	StL	W 21-18	5	0	0.0	0.0	0.0	0.0	0	0	0	0	0	0
10/08	@Mia	W 27-24	4	4	0.0	0.0	0.0	0.0	0	0	0	0	0	0
10/15	SF	W 18-17	3	3	0.0	0.0	0.0	0.0	0	0	0	0	0	0
10/22	@Oak	L 17-30	5	0	0.0	0.0	0.0	0.0	0	0	0	0	0	0
10/29	NYA	W 17-10	7	8	0.0	0.0	0.0	0.0	0	0	0	0	0	0
11/05	Buf	L 10-16	3	1	0.0	0.0	0.0	0.0	0	0	0	0	0	0
11/12	@NO	L 14-17	7	4	0.0	0.0	0.0	0.0	0	0	0	0	0	0
11/19	@NE	W 24-10	3	4	0.0	0.0	1.0	2.0	0	0	0	0	0	0
11/26	Mia	W 36-28	6	1	0.0	0.0	0.0	0.0	0	0	2	0	0	0
12/03	@Car	L 10-13	5	0	0.0	0.0	0.0	0.0	0	0	1	0	0	0
12/10	@Jac	W 41-31	8	4	0.0	0.0	1.0	1.0	0	0	0	0	0	0
12/17	SD	L 24-27	8	2	0.0	0.0	0.0	0.0	0	0	0	0	0	0
12/23	NE	W 10-7	3	2	0.0	0.0	0.0	0.0	0	0	0	0	0	0

Eric Hill
Arizona Cardinals – LB

1995 Defensive Splits

	G	Tk	Ast	Sack	Yds	Stuff	Yds	Int	Yds	PD	TD
Total	15	89	29	2.0	13.0	2.5	3.0	0	0	0	0
vs. Playoff	7	40	9	2.0	13.0	1.0	1.5	0	0	0	0
vs. Non-Playoff	8	49	20	0.0	0.0	1.5	1.5	0	0	0	0
vs. Own Division	7	37	12	0.0	0.0	1.0	1.0	0	0	0	0
Home	8	41	22	2.0	13.0	1.5	2.0	0	0	0	0
Away	7	48	7	0.0	0.0	1.0	1.0	0	0	0	0
Games 1-8	7	31	13	0.0	0.0	2.0	2.5	0	0	0	0
Games 9-16	8	58	16	2.0	13.0	0.5	0.5	0	0	0	0
September	3	3	2	0.0	0.0	0.0	0.0	0	0	0	0
October	4	28	11	0.0	0.0	2.0	2.5	0	0	0	0
November	5	35	14	2.0	13.0	0.5	0.5	0	0	0	0
December	3	23	2	0.0	0.0	0.0	0.0	0	0	0	0
Grass	12	75	27	2.0	13.0	1.5	2.0	0	0	0	0
Turf	3	14	2	0.0	0.0	1.0	1.0	0	0	0	0
Indoor	1	0	0	0.0	0.0	0.0	0.0	0	0	0	0
Outdoor	14	89	29	2.0	13.0	2.5	3.0	0	0	0	0

Game Logs

Date	Opp	Result	Tk	Ast	Sack	Yds	Stuff	Yds	Int	Yds	PD	FF	FR	TD
09/03	@Was	L 7-27	3	1	0.0	0.0	0.0	0.0	0	0	0	0	0	0
09/10	Phi	L 19-31	0	1	0.0	0.0	0.0	0.0	0	0	0	0	0	0
09/17	@Det	W 20-17	0	0	0.0	0.0	0.0	0.0	0	0	0	0	0	0
09/24	@Dal	L 20-34	-	-	-	-	-	-	-	-	-	-	-	-
10/01	KC	L 3-24	10	5	0.0	0.0	1.0	1.5	0	0	0	0	0	0
10/08	@NYN	L 21-27	8	1	0.0	0.0	1.0	1.0	0	0	0	1	0	0
10/15	Was	W 24-20	8	2	0.0	0.0	0.0	0.0	0	0	0	0	0	0
10/29	Sea	W 20-14	2	3	0.0	0.0	0.0	0.0	0	0	0	0	0	0
11/05	@Den	L 6-38	2	4	0.0	0.0	0.0	0.0	0	0	0	0	0	0
11/12	Min	L 24-30	2	4	0.0	0.0	0.5	0.5	0	0	0	0	0	0
11/19	@Car	L 7-27	19	0	0.0	0.0	0.0	0.0	0	0	0	0	0	0
11/26	Atl	W 40-37	7	1	2.0	13.0	0.0	0.0	0	0	0	1	0	0
11/30	NYN	L 6-10	5	5	0.0	0.0	0.0	0.0	0	0	0	0	0	0
12/09	@SD	L 25-28	10	0	0.0	0.0	0.0	0.0	0	0	0	0	0	0
12/17	@Phi	L 20-21	6	1	0.0	0.0	0.0	0.0	0	0	0	0	0	0
12/25	Dal	L 13-37	7	1	0.0	0.0	0.0	0.0	0	0	0	0	0	0

Derrick Hoskins
Oakland Raiders – S

1995 Defensive Splits

	G	Tk	Ast	Sack	Yds	Stuff	Yds	Int	Yds	PD	TD
Total	13	54	12	0.0	0.0	1.0	2.0	1	26	5	0
vs. Playoff	7	27	7	0.0	0.0	0.0	0.0	0	0	0	0
vs. Non-Playoff	6	27	5	0.0	0.0	1.0	2.0	1	26	5	0
vs. Own Division	6	27	6	0.0	0.0	0.0	0.0	0	0	1	0
Home	6	18	8	0.0	0.0	0.0	0.0	0	0	1	0
Away	7	36	4	0.0	0.0	1.0	2.0	1	26	4	0
Games 1-8	8	33	8	0.0	0.0	1.0	2.0	1	26	2	0
Games 9-16	5	21	4	0.0	0.0	0.0	0.0	0	0	3	0
September	4	19	4	0.0	0.0	1.0	2.0	1	26	1	0
October	4	14	4	0.0	0.0	0.0	0.0	0	0	1	0
November	4	21	2	0.0	0.0	0.0	0.0	0	0	3	0
December	1	0	2	0.0	0.0	0.0	0.0	0	0	0	0
Grass	10	40	9	0.0	0.0	1.0	2.0	1	26	2	0
Turf	3	14	3	0.0	0.0	0.0	0.0	0	0	3	0
Indoor	0	0	0	0.0	0.0	0	0	0	0	0	0
Outdoor	13	54	12	0.0	0.0	1.0	2.0	1	26	5	0

Game Logs

Date	Opp	Result	Tk	Ast	Sack	Yds	Stuff	Yds	Int	Yds	PD	FF	FR	TD
09/03	SD	W 17-7	4	2	0.0	0.0	0.0	0.0	0	0	0	0	0	0
09/10	@Was	W 20-8	4	0	0.0	0.0	1.0	2.0	1	26	1	0	0	0
09/17	@KC	L 17-23	8	0	0.0	0.0	0.0	0.0	0	0	0	0	0	0
09/24	Phi	W 48-17	3	2	0.0	0.0	0.0	0.0	0	0	0	0	0	0
10/01	@NYA	W 47-10	4	2	0.0	0.0	0.0	0.0	0	0	0	0	0	0
10/08	Sea	W 34-14	5	1	0.0	0.0	0.0	0.0	0	0	1	0	0	0
10/16	@Den	L 0-27	4	1	0.0	0.0	0.0	0.0	0	0	0	0	0	0
10/22	Ind	W 30-17	1	0	0.0	0.0	0.0	0.0	0	0	0	0	0	0
11/05	@Cin	W 20-17	5	0	0.0	0.0	0.0	0.0	0	0	2	0	0	0
11/12	@NYN	W 17-13	5	1	0.0	0.0	0.0	0.0	0	0	1	0	0	0
11/19	Dal	L 21-34	5	1	0.0	0.0	0.0	0.0	0	0	0	1	0	0
11/27	@SD	L 6-12	6	0	0.0	0.0	0.0	0.0	0	0	0	0	0	0
12/03	KC	L 23-29	0	2	0.0	0.0	0.0	0.0	0	0	0	0	0	0

Greg Jackson

1995 Defensive Splits

	G	Tk	Ast	Sack	Yds	Stuff	Yds	Int	Yds	PD	TD
Total	16	56	14	0.0	0.0	1.5	2.5	1	18	7	1
vs. Playoff	3	8	1	0.0	0.0	0.0	0.0	0	0	3	0
vs. Non-Playoff	13	48	13	0.0	0.0	1.5	2.5	1	18	4	1
vs. Own Division	8	26	8	0.0	0.0	1.5	2.5	1	18	5	0
Home	8	32	3	0.0	0.0	1.5	2.5	1	18	4	0
Away	8	24	11	0.0	0.0	0.0	0.0	0	0	3	1
Games 1-8	8	26	8	0.0	0.0	0.0	0.0	1	18	3	1
Games 9-16	8	30	6	0.0	0.0	1.5	2.5	0	0	4	0
September	4	13	5	0.0	0.0	0.0	0.0	0	0	1	1
October	4	13	3	0.0	0.0	0.0	0.0	1	18	2	0
November	4	12	1	0.0	0.0	0.0	0.0	0	0	2	0
December	4	18	5	0.0	0.0	1.5	2.5	0	0	2	0
Grass	4	13	6	0.0	0.0	0.0	0.0	0	0	2	1
Turf	12	43	8	0.0	0.0	1.5	2.5	1	18	5	0
Indoor	2	7	2	0.0	0.0	0.0	0.0	0	0	1	0
Outdoor	14	49	12	0.0	0.0	1.5	2.5	1	18	6	0

Game Logs

Date	Opp	Result	Tk	Ast	Sack	Yds	Stuff	Yds	Int	Yds	PD	FF	FR	TD
09/03	TB	L 6-21	5	1	0.0	0.0	0.0	0.0	0	0	0	0	0	0
09/10	@Ari	W 31-19	3	3	0.0	0.0	0.0	0.0	0	0	0	0	0	0
09/17	SD	L 21-27	2	1	0.0	0.0	0.0	0.0	0	0	1	1	0	0
09/24	@Oak	L 17-48	3	0	0.0	0.0	0.0	0.0	0	0	0	0	1	1
10/01	@NO	W 15-10	5	0	0.0	0.0	0.0	0.0	0	0	1	0	0	0
10/08	Was	W 37-34	2	0	0.0	0.0	0.0	0.0	1	18	1	0	0	0
10/15	@NYN	W 17-14	2	3	0.0	0.0	0.0	0.0	0	0	0	0	0	0
10/29	StL	W 20-9	4	0	0.0	0.0	0.0	0.0	0	0	0	0	0	0
11/06	@Dal	L 12-34	2	0	0.0	0.0	0.0	0.0	0	0	0	0	0	0
11/12	Den	W 31-13	5	0	0.0	0.0	0.0	0.0	0	0	0	0	0	0
11/19	NYN	W 28-19	2	0	0.0	0.0	0.0	0.0	0	0	0	0	0	0
11/26	@Was	W 14-7	3	1	0.0	0.0	0.0	0.0	0	0	2	0	0	0
12/03	@Sea	L 14-26	2	2	0.0	0.0	0.0	0.0	0	0	2	0	0	0
12/10	Dal	W 20-17	4	0	0.0	0.0	0.0	0.0	0	0	2	0	0	0
12/17	Ari	W 21-20	8	1	0.0	0.0	1.5	2.5	0	0	0	0	1	0
12/24	@Chi	L 14-20	4	2	0.0	0.0	0.0	0.0	0	0	2	0	0	0

Rickey Jackson

1995 Defensive Splits

	G	Tk	Ast	Sack	Yds	Stuff	Yds	Int	Yds	PD	TD
Total	16	32	4	9.5	49.0	5.0	10.0	1	1	3	0
vs. Playoff	7	8	2	3.0	10.0	0.0	0.0	1	1	3	0
vs. Non-Playoff	9	24	2	6.5	39.0	5.0	10.0	0	0	0	0
vs. Own Division	8	20	1	5.5	33.0	3.0	5.0	0	0	0	0
Home	8	18	2	5.5	32.0	3.0	6.0	0	0	0	0
Away	8	14	2	4.0	17.0	2.0	4.0	1	1	3	0
Games 1-8	8	12	3	3.0	20.0	2.0	4.0	0	0	0	0
Games 9-16	8	20	1	6.5	29.0	3.0	6.0	1	1	1	0
September	4	4	3	1.0	5.0	0.0	0.0	0	0	0	0
October	4	8	0	2.0	15.0	2.0	4.0	0	0	0	0
November	4	10	1	4.5	24.0	0.0	0.0	1	1	3	0
December	4	10	0	2.0	5.0	3.0	6.0	0	0	0	0
Grass	10	23	2	6.5	34.0	4.0	7.0	0	0	1	0
Turf	6	9	2	3.0	15.0	1.0	3.0	1	1	2	0
Indoor	4	4	2	1.0	2.0	0.0	0.0	0	0	0	0
Outdoor	12	28	2	8.5	47.0	5.0	10.0	1	1	3	0

Game Logs

Date	Opp	Result	Tk	Ast	Sack	Yds	Stuff	Yds	Int	Yds	PD	FF	FR	TD
09/03	@NO	W 24-22	2	0	0.0	0.0	0.0	0.0	0	0	0	0	0	0
09/10	Atl	W 41-10	0	0	0.0	0.0	0.0	0.0	0	0	0	0	0	0
09/17	NE	W 28-3	2	1	1.0	5.0	0.0	0.0	0	0	0	0	0	0
09/25	@Det	L 24-27	0	2	0.0	0.0	0.0	0.0	0	0	0	0	0	0
10/01	NYN	W 20-6	0	0	0.0	0.0	0.0	0.0	0	0	0	0	0	0
10/15	@Ind	L 17-18	0	0	0.0	0.0	0.0	0.0	0	0	0	0	0	0
10/22	@StL	W 44-10	2	0	1.0	7.0	1.0	3.0	0	0	0	0	0	0
10/29	NO	L 7-11	6	0	1.0	8.0	1.0	1.0	0	0	0	0	0	0
11/05	Car	L 7-13	4	1	2.5	16.0	0.0	0.0	0	0	0	0	0	0
11/12	@Dal	W 38-20	3	0	1.0	6.0	0.0	0.0	1	1	2	0	0	0
11/20	@Mia	W 44-20	2	0	1.0	2.0	0.0	0.0	0	0	1	0	0	0
11/26	StL	W 41-13	1	0	0.0	0.0	0.0	0.0	0	0	0	0	0	0
12/03	Buf	W 27-17	1	0	0.0	0.0	0.0	0.0	0	0	0	0	0	0
12/10	@Car	W 31-10	3	0	0.0	0.0	1.0	1.0	0	0	0	0	0	0
12/18	Min	W 37-30	4	0	1.0	3.0	2.0	5.0	0	0	0	0	0	0
12/24	@Atl	L 27-28	2	0	1.0	2.0	0.0	0.0	0	0	0	0	0	0

Carlos Jenkins

1995 Defensive Splits

	G	Tk	Ast	Sack	Yds	Stuff	Yds	Int	Yds	PD	TD
Total	16	52	8	1.5	6.5	1.5	3.5	0	0	1	0
vs. Playoff	9	27	5	0.0	0.0	1.5	3.5	0	0	0	0
vs. Non-Playoff	7	25	3	1.5	6.5	0.0	0.0	0	0	1	0
vs. Own Division	8	19	3	1.5	6.5	0.5	0.5	0	0	0	0
Home	8	25	3	0.5	4.5	0.5	0.5	0	0	0	1
Away	8	27	5	1.0	2.0	1.0	3.0	0	0	0	0
Games 1-8	8	27	6	1.5	6.5	1.5	3.5	0	0	1	0
Games 9-16	8	25	2	0.0	0.0	0.0	0.0	0	0	0	0
September	4	22	6	1.5	6.5	0.0	0.0	0	0	1	0
October	4	5	0	0.0	0.0	1.5	3.5	0	0	0	0
November	4	10	1	0.0	0.0	0.0	0.0	0	0	0	0
December	4	15	1	0.0	0.0	0.0	0.0	0	0	0	0
Grass	3	13	5	1.0	2.0	0.0	0.0	0	0	0	0
Turf	13	39	3	0.5	4.5	1.5	3.5	0	0	1	0
Indoor	7	18	2	0.0	0.0	0.0	0.0	0	0	0	0
Outdoor	9	34	6	1.5	6.5	1.5	3.5	0	0	1	0

Game Logs

Date	Opp	Result	Tk	Ast	Sack	Yds	Stuff	Yds	Int	Yds	PD	FF	FR	TD
09/03	@GB	W 17-14	8	4	0.0	0.0	0.0	0.0	0	0	0	0	0	0
09/10	NO	W 17-13	5	1	0.5	4.5	0.0	0.0	0	0	0	0	0	0
09/17	@Car	W 31-10	2	1	1.0	2.0	0.0	0.0	0	0	1	0	0	0
09/24	Chi	W 34-28	7	0	0.0	0.0	0.0	0.0	0	0	1	0	0	0
10/01	@Ind	L 18-21	1	0	0.0	0.0	0.0	0.0	0	0	0	0	0	0
10/12	Atl	W 21-19	0	0	0.0	0.0	0.0	0.0	0	0	0	0	0	0
10/22	SF	L 10-44	2	0	0.0	0.0	0.5	0.5	0	0	0	0	0	0
10/29	@Phi	L 9-20	2	0	0.0	0.0	1.0	3.0	0	0	0	0	0	0
11/05	@NO	L 10-19	3	0	0.0	0.0	0.0	0.0	0	0	0	0	0	0
11/12	Car	W 28-17	1	1	0.0	0.0	0.0	0.0	0	0	0	0	1	0
11/19	@Atl	L 6-31	3	0	0.0	0.0	0.0	0.0	0	0	0	0	0	0
11/26	@SF	L 13-41	3	0	0.0	0.0	0.0	0.0	0	0	0	0	0	0
12/03	@NYA	W 23-20	5	0	0.0	0.0	0.0	0.0	0	0	0	0	0	0
12/10	Buf	L 27-45	5	1	0.0	0.0	0.0	0.0	0	0	0	0	1	0
12/17	Was	L 23-35	2	0	0.0	0.0	0.0	0.0	0	0	0	0	0	0
12/24	Mia	L 22-41	3	0	0.0	0.0	0.0	0.0	0	0	0	0	0	0

D.J. Johnson

1995 Defensive Splits

	G	Tk	Ast	Sack	Yds	Stuff	Yds	Int	Yds	PD	TD
Total	13	60	9	0.0	0.0	1.0	1.0	2	4	12	0
vs. Playoff	6	34	2	0.0	0.0	1.0	1.0	1	2	6	0
vs. Non-Playoff	7	26	7	0.0	0.0	0.0	0.0	1	2	6	0
vs. Own Division	7	24	5	0.0	0.0	0.0	0.0	0	0	7	0
Home	7	29	5	0.0	0.0	1.0	1.0	1	2	7	0
Away	6	31	4	0.0	0.0	0.0	0.0	1	2	5	0
Games 1-8	5	14	2	0.0	0.0	0.0	0.0	1	2	6	0
Games 9-16	8	46	7	0.0	0.0	1.0	1.0	1	2	6	0
September	3	9	2	0.0	0.0	0.0	0.0	0	0	4	0
October	2	5	0	0.0	0.0	0.0	0.0	1	2	2	0
November	4	28	3	0.0	0.0	1.0	1.0	1	2	4	0
December	4	18	4	0.0	0.0	0.0	0.0	0	0	2	0
Grass	4	21	4	0.0	0.0	0.0	0.0	1	2	4	0
Turf	9	39	5	0.0	0.0	1.0	1.0	1	2	8	0
Indoor	8	30	5	0.0	0.0	1.0	1.0	1	2	8	0
Outdoor	5	30	4	0.0	0.0	0.0	0.0	1	2	4	0

Game Logs

Date	Opp	Result	Tk	Ast	Sack	Yds	Stuff	Yds	Int	Yds	PD	FF	FR	TD
09/03	Car	W 23-20	4	2	0.0	0.0	0.0	0.0	0	0	1	0	0	0
09/10	@SF	L 10-41	4	0	0.0	0.0	0.0	0.0	0	0	2	0	0	0
09/17	@NO	W 27-24	1	0	0.0	0.0	0.0	0.0	0	0	1	0	0	0
09/24	NYA	W 13-3	-	-	-	-	-	-	-	-	-	-	-	-
10/01	NE	W 30-17	1	0	0.0	0.0	0.0	0.0	0	0	0	0	0	0
10/12	@StL	L 19-21	-	-	-	-	-	-	-	-	-	-	-	-
10/22	@TB	W 24-21	-	-	-	-	-	-	-	-	-	-	-	-
10/29	Dal	L 13-28	4	0	0.0	0.0	0.0	0.0	1	2	2	0	0	0
11/05	Det	W 34-22	6	0	0.0	0.0	1.0	1.0	0	0	2	0	0	0
11/12	@Buf	L 17-23	9	0	0.0	0.0	0.0	0.0	0	0	0	0	0	0
11/19	StL	W 31-6	3	1	0.0	0.0	0.0	0.0	0	0	1	0	0	0
11/26	@Ari	L 37-40	10	2	0.0	0.0	0.0	0.0	1	2	1	0	0	0
12/03	@Mia	L 20-21	6	2	0.0	0.0	0.0	0.0	0	0	0	0	0	0
12/10	NO	W 19-14	6	2	0.0	0.0	0.0	0.0	0	0	1	0	0	0
12/17	@Car	L 17-21	1	0	0.0	0.0	0.0	0.0	0	0	1	0	0	0
12/24	SF	W 28-27	5	0	0.0	0.0	0.0	0.0	0	0	0	0	0	0

Joe Johnson

1995 Defensive Splits

	G	Tk	Ast	Sack	Yds	Stuff	Yds	Int	Yds	PD	TD
Total	14	36	14	5.5	32.5	1.0	3.5	0	0	0	0
vs. Playoff	7	17	8	1.5	12.5	1.0	1.0	0	0	0	0
vs. Non-Playoff	7	19	6	4.0	20.0	0.5	2.5	0	0	0	0
vs. Own Division	6	19	5	3.5	17.5	1.0	1.0	0	0	0	0
Home	8	17	8	2.5	12.5	1.0	1.0	0	0	0	0
Away	6	19	6	3.0	20.0	0.5	2.5	0	0	0	0
Games 1-8	6	16	9	2.5	17.5	1.0	1.0	0	0	0	0
Games 9-16	8	20	5	3.0	15.0	0.5	2.5	0	0	0	0
September	4	14	5	2.5	17.5	1.0	1.0	0	0	0	0
October	2	2	4	0.0	0.0	0.0	0.0	0	0	0	0
November	4	8	0	1.0	0.0	0.0	0.0	0	0	0	0
December	4	12	5	2.0	15.0	0.5	2.5	0	0	0	0
Grass	1	2	1	0.0	0.0	0.0	0.0	0	0	0	0
Turf	13	34	13	5.5	32.5	1.5	3.5	0	0	0	0
Indoor	10	23	8	2.5	12.5	1.0	1.0	0	0	0	0
Outdoor	4	13	6	3.0	20.0	0.5	2.5	0	0	0	0

Game Logs

Date	Opp	Result	Tk	Ast	Sack	Yds	Stuff	Yds	Int	Yds	PD	FF	FR	TD
09/03	SF	L 22-24	3	1	0.5	3.5	0.0	0.0	0	0	0	0	0	0
09/10	@StL	L 13-17	3	2	1.0	5.0	0.0	0.0	0	0	0	0	0	0
09/17	Atl	L 24-27	7	2	1.0	9.0	1.0	1.0	0	0	0	0	0	0
09/24	@NYN	L 29-45	1	0	0.0	0.0	0.0	0.0	0	0	0	0	0	0
10/01	Phi	L 10-15	1	4	0.0	0.0	0.0	0.0	0	0	0	0	0	0
10/15	Mia	W 33-30	1	0	0.0	0.0	0.0	0.0	0	0	0	0	0	0
10/22	@Car	L 3-20	-	-	-	-	-	-	-	-	-	-	-	-
10/29	@SF	W 11-7	-	-	-	-	-	-	-	-	-	-	-	-
11/05	StL	W 19-10	1	0	0.0	0.0	0.0	0.0	0	0	0	0	0	0
11/12	Ind	W 17-14	2	0	0.0	0.0	0.0	0.0	0	0	0	0	0	0
11/19	@Min	L 24-43	3	0	0.0	0.0	0.0	0.0	0	0	0	0	0	0
11/26	Car	W 34-26	2	0	1.0	0.0	0.0	0.0	0	0	0	1	0	0
12/03	@NE	W 31-17	2	1	0.0	0.0	0.0	0.0	0	0	0	0	0	0
12/10	@Atl	L 14-19	3	0	0.0	0.0	0.0	0.0	0	0	0	0	0	0
12/16	GB	L 23-34	0	1	0.0	0.0	0.0	0.0	0	0	0	0	0	0
12/24	@NYA	W 12-0	7	3	2.0	15.0	0.5	2.5	0	0	0	0	0	0

Mike Johnson

1995 Defensive Splits

	G	Tk	Ast	Sack	Yds	Stuff	Yds	Int	Yds	PD	TD
Total	16	81	36	2.0	14.0	6.0	12.0	2	23	6	0
vs. Playoff	5	23	20	0.0	0.0	0.0	0.0	0	0	1	0
vs. Non-Playoff	11	58	16	2.0	14.0	6.0	12.0	2	23	5	0
vs. Own Division	8	38	22	1.0	12.0	0.5	2.5	0	0	2	0
Home	8	40	25	1.0	12.0	3.0	9.0	0	0	2	0
Away	8	41	11	1.0	2.0	3.0	3.0	2	23	4	0
Games 1-8	8	50	22	2.0	14.0	3.5	7.5	0	0	3	0
Games 9-16	8	31	14	0.0	0.0	2.5	4.5	2	23	3	0
September	4	28	10	2.0	14.0	1.5	2.5	0	0	2	0
October	4	22	12	0.0	0.0	2.0	5.0	0	0	1	0
November	4	13	6	0.0	0.0	0.5	2.5	0	0	0	0
December	4	18	8	0.0	0.0	2.0	2.0	2	23	3	0
Grass	4	18	7	0.0	0.0	1.0	1.0	0	0	0	0
Turf	12	63	29	2.0	14.0	5.0	11.0	2	23	6	0
Indoor	11	55	26	2.0	14.0	5.0	11.0	2	23	5	0
Outdoor	5	26	10	0.0	0.0	1.0	1.0	0	0	1	0

Game Logs

Date	Opp	Result	Tk	Ast	Sack	Yds	Stuff	Yds	Int	Yds	PD	FF	FR	TD
09/03	@Pit	L 20-23	8	3	0.0	0.0	0.0	0.0	0	0	1	1	0	0
09/10	@Min	L 10-20	8	0	1.0	2.0	0.0	0.0	0	0	1	0	0	0
09/17	Ari	L 17-20	9	1	1.0	12.0	1.5	2.5	0	0	0	0	0	0
09/25	SF	W 27-24	3	6	0.0	0.0	0.0	0.0	0	0	0	0	0	0
10/08	Cle	W 38-20	5	1	0.0	0.0	1.0	4.0	0	0	1	1	1	0
10/15	@GB	L 21-30	4	4	0.0	0.0	0.0	0.0	0	0	0	0	0	0
10/22	@Was	L 30-36	7	0	0.0	0.0	1.0	1.0	0	0	0	0	0	0
10/29	GB	W 24-16	6	7	0.0	0.0	0.0	0.0	0	0	0	0	0	0
11/05	@Atl	L 22-34	2	0	0.0	0.0	0.0	0.0	0	0	0	0	1	0
11/12	TB	W 27-24	3	2	0.0	0.0	0.0	0.0	0	0	0	0	1	0
11/19	@Chi	W 24-17	6	1	0.0	0.0	0.0	0.0	0	0	0	0	0	0
11/23	Min	W 44-38	2	0	0.0	0.0	0.5	2.5	0	0	0	0	0	0
12/04	Chi	W 27-7	8	3	0.0	0.0	1.0	1.0	0	0	1	0	0	0
12/10	@Hou	W 24-17	5	1	0.0	0.0	2.0	2.0	2	23	2	0	0	0
12/17	Jac	W 44-0	4	2	0.0	0.0	0.0	0.0	0	0	0	0	1	0
12/23	@TB	W 37-10	1	2	0.0	0.0	0.0	0.0	0	0	0	0	0	0

Pepper Johnson
Cleveland Browns – LB

1995 Defensive Splits

	G	Tk	Ast	Sack	Yds	Stuff	Yds	Int	Yds	PD	TD
Total	16	100	30	2.0	19.0	6.5	14.0	2	22	5	0
vs. Playoff	7	37	12	0.0	0.0	1.0	2.0	1	0	2	0
vs. Non-Playoff	9	63	18	2.0	19.0	5.5	12.0	1	22	3	0
vs. Own Division	8	52	13	2.0	19.0	2.5	4.0	1	22	3	0
Home	8	47	13	1.0	12.0	2.0	4.0	2	22	3	0
Away	8	53	17	1.0	7.0	4.5	10.0	0	0	2	0
Games 1-8	8	43	16	0.0	0.0	1.5	3.0	1	0	3	0
Games 9-16	8	57	14	2.0	19.0	5.0	11.0	1	22	2	0
September	4	18	10	0.0	0.0	0.5	1.0	0	0	1	0
October	4	25	6	0.0	0.0	1.0	2.0	1	0	2	0
November	4	27	8	1.0	12.0	1.0	2.0	0	0	0	0
December	4	30	6	1.0	7.0	4.0	9.0	1	22	2	0
Grass	11	70	20	2.0	19.0	3.0	5.0	2	22	4	0
Turf	5	30	10	0.0	0.0	3.5	9.0	0	0	1	0
Indoor	3	19	6	0.0	0.0	3.5	9.0	0	0	1	0
Outdoor	13	81	24	2.0	19.0	3.0	5.0	2	22	4	0

Game Logs

Date	Opp	Result	Tk	Ast	Sack	Yds	Stuff	Yds	Int	Yds	PD	FF	FR	TD
09/03	@NE	L 14-17	11	6	0.0	0.0	0.0	0.0	0	0	0	0	0	0
09/10	TB	W 22-6	3	1	0.0	0.0	0.0	0.0	0	0	0	0	0	0
09/17	@Hou	W 14-7	4	2	0.0	0.0	0.5	1.0	0	0	1	0	0	0
09/24	KC	W 35-17	0	1	0.0	0.0	0.0	0.0	0	0	0	0	0	0
10/02	Buf	L 19-22	5	3	0.0	0.0	0.0	0.0	1	0	2	0	0	0
10/08	@Det	L 20-38	4	1	0.0	0.0	0.0	0.0	0	0	0	0	0	0
10/22	Jac	L 15-23	10	0	0.0	0.0	1.0	2.0	0	0	1	0	0	0
10/29	@Cin	W 29-26	6	2	0.0	0.0	0.0	0.0	0	0	0	0	0	0
11/05	Hou	L 10-37	5	1	1.0	12.0	0.0	0.0	0	0	0	0	0	0
11/13	@Pit	L 3-20	5	2	0.0	0.0	0.0	0.0	0	0	0	0	0	0
11/19	GB	L 20-31	8	2	0.0	0.0	1.0	2.0	0	0	0	0	0	0
11/26	Pit	L 17-20	9	3	0.0	0.0	0.0	0.0	0	0	0	0	0	0
12/03	@SD	L 13-31	6	0	0.0	0.0	0.0	0.0	0	0	0	0	0	0
12/09	@Min	L 11-27	11	3	0.0	0.0	3.0	8.0	0	0	1	0	0	0
12/17	Cin	W 26-10	7	2	0.0	0.0	0.0	0.0	1	22	1	0	0	0
12/24	@Jac	L 21-24	6	1	1.0	7.0	1.0	1.0	0	0	1	0	0	0

Henry Jones
Buffalo Bills – S

1995 Defensive Splits

	G	Tk	Ast	Sack	Yds	Stuff	Yds	Int	Yds	PD	TD
Total	13	57	21	0.0	0.0	3.5	7.5	1	10	6	0
vs. Playoff	5	21	4	0.0	0.0	0.0	0.0	0	0	1	0
vs. Non-Playoff	8	36	17	0.0	0.0	3.5	7.5	1	10	5	0
vs. Own Division	7	35	12	0.0	0.0	2.5	6.0	0	0	2	0
Home	6	30	10	0.0	0.0	3.0	7.0	0	0	2	0
Away	7	27	11	0.0	0.0	0.5	0.5	1	10	4	0
Games 1-8	8	32	18	0.0	0.0	1.5	4.0	1	10	5	0
Games 9-16	5	25	3	0.0	0.0	2.0	3.5	0	0	1	0
September	3	11	6	0.0	0.0	0.0	0.0	1	10	3	0
October	5	21	12	0.0	0.0	1.5	4.0	0	0	2	0
November	4	18	2	0.0	0.0	2.0	3.5	0	0	0	0
December	1	7	1	0.0	0.0	0.0	0.0	0	0	1	0
Grass	5	20	10	0.0	0.0	0.5	0.5	1	10	4	0
Turf	8	37	11	0.0	0.0	3.0	7.0	0	0	2	0
Indoor	1	3	1	0.0	0.0	0.0	0.0	0	0	0	0
Outdoor	12	54	20	0.0	0.0	3.5	7.5	1	10	6	0

Game Logs

Date	Opp	Result	Tk	Ast	Sack	Yds	Stuff	Yds	Int	Yds	PD	FF	FR	TD
09/03	@Den	L 7-22	2	1	0.0	0.0	0.0	0.0	1	10	2	0	0	0
09/10	Car	W 31-9	4	4	0.0	0.0	0.0	0.0	0	0	1	0	0	0
09/17	Ind	W 20-14	5	1	0.0	0.0	0.0	0.0	0	0	0	0	0	0
10/02	@Cle	W 22-19	2	1	0.0	0.0	0.5	0.5	0	0	0	0	0	0
10/08	NYA	W 29-10	6	2	0.0	0.0	0.5	2.5	0	0	1	0	0	0
10/15	Sea	W 27-21	4	2	0.0	0.0	0.5	1.0	0	0	0	0	0	0
10/23	@NE	L 14-27	6	6	0.0	0.0	0.0	0.0	0	0	1	0	0	0
10/29	@Mia	L 6-23	3	1	0.0	0.0	0.0	0.0	0	0	0	0	0	0
11/05	@Ind	W 16-10	3	1	0.0	0.0	0.0	0.0	0	0	0	0	1	0
11/12	Atl	W 23-17	3	0	0.0	0.0	0.0	0.0	0	0	0	0	0	0
11/19	@NYA	W 28-26	4	0	0.0	0.0	0.0	0.0	0	0	0	0	0	0
11/26	NE	L 25-35	8	1	0.0	0.0	2.0	3.5	0	0	0	0	0	0
12/03	@SF	L 17-27	7	1	0.0	0.0	0.0	0.0	0	0	1	0	0	0
12/10	@StL	W 45-27	-	-	-	-	-	-	-	-	-	-	-	-
12/17	Mia	W 23-20	-	-	-	-	-	-	-	-	-	-	-	-
12/24	Hou	L 17-28	-	-	-	-	-	-	-	-	-	-	-	-

Mike Jones
Oakland Raiders – LB

1995 Defensive Splits

	G	Tk	Ast	Sack	Yds	Stuff	Yds	Int	Yds	PD	TD
Total	16	85	17	0.0	0.0	7.0	9.0	1	23	2	1
vs. Playoff	8	43	11	0.0	0.0	4.0	5.0	0	0	0	0
vs. Non-Playoff	8	42	6	0.0	0.0	3.0	4.0	1	23	2	0
vs. Own Division	8	52	7	0.0	0.0	5.0	6.0	1	23	2	0
Home	8	42	11	0.0	0.0	5.0	7.0	1	23	2	0
Away	8	43	6	0.0	0.0	2.0	2.0	0	0	0	1
Games 1-8	8	38	8	0.0	0.0	2.0	3.0	1	23	2	0
Games 9-16	8	47	9	0.0	0.0	5.0	6.0	0	0	0	0
September	4	20	3	0.0	0.0	0.0	0.0	0	0	0	0
October	4	18	5	0.0	0.0	2.0	3.0	1	23	2	0
November	4	25	4	0.0	0.0	2.0	2.0	0	0	0	0
December	4	22	5	0.0	0.0	3.0	4.0	0	0	0	0
Grass	12	71	13	0.0	0.0	7.0	9.0	1	23	2	0
Turf	4	14	4	0.0	0.0	0.0	0.0	0	0	0	0
Indoor	1	2	0	0.0	0.0	0.0	0.0	0	0	0	0
Outdoor	15	83	17	0.0	0.0	7.0	9.0	1	23	2	1

Game Logs

Date	Opp	Result	Tk	Ast	Sack	Yds	Stuff	Yds	Int	Yds	PD	FF	FR	TD
09/03	SD	W 17-7	2	1	0.0	0.0	0.0	0.0	0	0	0	0	0	0
09/10	@Was	W 20-8	5	0	0.0	0.0	0.0	0.0	0	0	0	0	0	0
09/17	@KC	L 17-23	10	1	0.0	0.0	0.0	0.0	0	0	1	0	0	0
09/24	Phi	W 48-17	3	1	0.0	0.0	0.0	0.0	0	0	0	0	0	0
10/01	@NYA	W 47-10	2	3	0.0	0.0	0.0	0.0	0	0	0	0	1	1
10/08	Sea	W 34-14	8	1	0.0	0.0	1.0	2.0	1	23	2	0	0	0
10/16	@Den	L 0-27	5	1	0.0	0.0	1.0	1.0	0	0	0	0	1	0
10/22	Ind	W 30-17	3	0	0.0	0.0	1.0	1.0	0	0	0	0	0	0
11/05	@Cin	W 20-17	4	0	0.0	0.0	0.0	0.0	0	0	0	0	0	0
11/12	@NYN	W 17-13	6	1	0.0	0.0	0.0	0.0	0	0	0	0	0	0
11/19	Dal	L 21-34	6	3	0.0	0.0	1.0	1.0	0	0	0	0	0	0
11/27	@SD	L 6-12	9	0	0.0	0.0	1.0	1.0	0	0	0	0	0	0
12/03	KC	L 23-29	6	3	0.0	0.0	1.0	1.0	0	0	0	0	0	0
12/10	Pit	L 10-29	4	2	0.0	0.0	1.0	2.0	0	0	0	0	0	0
12/17	@Sea	L 10-44	2	0	0.0	0.0	0.0	0.0	0	0	0	0	0	0
12/24	Den	L 28-31	10	0	0.0	0.0	1.0	1.0	0	0	0	0	0	0

Robert Jones

Dallas Cowboys – LB

1995 Defensive Splits

	G	Tk	Ast	Sack	Yds	Stuff	Yds	Int	Yds	PD	TD
Total	12	55	18	1.0	2.0	6.0	9.0	0	0	2	0
vs. Playoff	5	25	12	0.0	0.0	2.0	2.0	0	0	0	0
vs. Non-Playoff	7	30	6	1.0	2.0	4.0	7.0	0	0	2	0
vs. Own Division	5	24	5	1.0	2.0	3.0	6.0	0	0	1	0
Home	6	32	12	1.0	2.0	3.0	6.0	0	0	1	0
Away	6	23	6	0.0	0.0	3.0	3.0	0	0	1	0
Games 1-8	8	35	13	0.0	0.0	5.0	8.0	0	0	2	0
Games 9-16	4	20	5	1.0	2.0	1.0	1.0	0	0	0	0
September	4	19	6	0.0	0.0	4.0	7.0	0	0	2	0
October	4	16	7	0.0	0.0	1.0	1.0	0	0	0	0
November	3	13	5	0.0	0.0	1.0	1.0	0	0	0	0
December	1	7	0	1.0	2.0	0.0	0.0	0	0	0	0
Grass	3	11	1	0.0	0.0	0.0	0.0	0	0	0	0
Turf	9	44	17	1.0	2.0	6.0	9.0	0	0	2	0
Indoor	2	8	4	0.0	0.0	2.0	2.0	0	0	1	0
Outdoor	10	47	14	1.0	2.0	4.0	7.0	0	0	1	0

Game Logs

Date	Opp	Result	Tk	Ast	Sack	Yds	Stuff	Yds	Int	Yds	PD	FF	FR	TD
09/04	@NYN	W 35-0	4	1	0.0	0.0	1.0	1.0	0	0	0	0	0	0
09/10	Den	W 31-21	4	2	0.0	0.0	0.0	0.0	0	0	0	0	0	0
09/17	@Min	W 23-17	4	2	0.0	0.0	1.0	1.0	0	0	1	0	0	0
09/24	Ari	W 34-20	7	1	0.0	0.0	2.0	5.0	0	0	1	0	0	0
10/01	@Was	L 23-27	4	0	0.0	0.0	0.0	0.0	0	0	0	0	0	0
10/08	GB	W 34-24	1	4	0.0	0.0	0.0	0.0	0	0	0	0	0	0
10/15	@SD	W 23-9	7	1	0.0	0.0	0.0	0.0	0	0	0	0	0	0
10/29	@Atl	W 28-13	4	2	0.0	0.0	1.0	1.0	0	0	0	0	0	0
11/06	Phi	W 34-12	2	3	0.0	0.0	0.0	0.0	0	0	0	0	0	0
11/12	SF	L 20-38	11	2	0.0	0.0	1.0	1.0	0	0	0	0	0	0
11/19	@Oak	W 34-21	0	0	0.0	0.0	0.0	0.0	0	0	0	0	0	0
11/23	KC	W 24-12	-	-	-	-	-	-	-	-	-	-	-	-
12/03	Was	L 17-24	7	0	1.0	2.0	0.0	0.0	0	0	0	0	0	0
12/10	@Phi	L 17-20	-	-	-	-	-	-	-	-	-	-	-	-
12/17	NYN	W 21-20	-	-	-	-	-	-	-	-	-	-	-	-
12/25	@Ari	W 37-13	-	-	-	-	-	-	-	-	-	-	-	-

Roger Jones

Cincinnati Bengals – CB

1995 Defensive Splits

	G	Tk	Ast	Sack	Yds	Stuff	Yds	Int	Yds	PD	TD
Total	16	82	11	2.0	8.0	4.0	10.0	1	17	11	1
vs. Playoff	5	32	3	1.0	0.0	1.0	1.0	0	0	2	0
vs. Non-Playoff	11	50	8	2.0	8.0	3.0	9.0	1	17	9	1
vs. Own Division	8	34	6	2.0	8.0	1.0	3.0	0	0	5	0
Home	8	43	3	1.0	0.0	0.0	0.0	0	0	6	0
Away	8	39	8	1.0	8.0	4.0	10.0	1	17	5	1
Games 1-8	8	41	4	1.0	0.0	2.0	6.0	1	17	8	1
Games 9-16	8	41	7	1.0	8.0	2.0	4.0	0	0	3	0
September	4	24	2	1.0	0.0	1.0	2.0	1	17	4	1
October	4	17	2	0.0	0.0	1.0	4.0	0	0	4	0
November	4	22	7	1.0	8.0	1.0	3.0	0	0	2	0
December	4	19	0	0.0	0.0	1.0	1.0	0	0	1	0
Grass	4	18	2	0.0	0.0	2.0	5.0	0	0	3	0
Turf	12	64	9	2.0	8.0	2.0	5.0	1	17	8	1
Indoor	3	17	5	1.0	8.0	2.0	5.0	1	17	2	1
Outdoor	13	65	6	1.0	0.0	2.0	5.0	0	0	9	0

Game Logs

Date	Opp	Result	Tk	Ast	Sack	Yds	Stuff	Yds	Int	Yds	PD	FF	FR	TD
09/03	@Ind	W 24-17	8	1	0.0	0.0	0.0	0.0	0	0	0	0	0	0
09/10	Jac	W 24-17	3	0	1.0	0.0	0.0	0.0	0	0	0	0	0	0
09/17	@Sea	L 21-24	8	1	0.0	0.0	1.0	2.0	1	17	2	0	0	1
09/24	Hou	L 28-38	5	0	0.0	0.0	0.0	0.0	0	0	2	0	0	0
10/01	Mia	L 23-26	5	0	0.0	0.0	0.0	0.0	0	0	2	0	0	0
10/08	@TB	L 16-19	5	1	0.0	0.0	1.0	4.0	0	0	1	0	0	0
10/19	@Pit	W 27-9	4	1	0.0	0.0	0.0	0.0	0	0	0	0	0	0
10/29	Cle	L 26-29	3	0	0.0	0.0	0.0	0.0	0	0	1	0	0	0
11/05	Oak	L 17-20	8	2	0.0	0.0	0.0	0.0	0	0	1	0	0	0
11/12	@Hou	W 32-25	1	3	1.0	8.0	1.0	3.0	0	0	1	0	0	0
11/19	Pit	L 31-49	10	1	0.0	0.0	0.0	0.0	0	0	1	0	0	0
11/26	@Jac	L 17-13	3	1	0.0	0.0	0.0	0.0	0	0	1	0	0	0
12/03	@GB	L 10-24	5	0	0.0	0.0	1.0	1.0	0	0	0	0	0	0
12/10	Chi	W 16-10	4	0	0.0	0.0	0.0	0.0	0	0	0	0	0	0
12/17	@Cle	L 10-26	5	3	0.0	0.0	0.0	0.0	0	0	1	0	0	0
12/24	Min	W 27-24	5	0	0.0	0.0	0.0	0.0	0	0	0	0	0	0

Sean Jones

Green Bay Packers – DE

1995 Defensive Splits

	G	Tk	Ast	Sack	Yds	Stuff	Yds	Int	Yds	PD	TD
Total	16	33	18	9.0	56.5	7.0	22.0	0	0	0	1
vs. Playoff	4	2	3	0.0	0.0	1.0	2.0	0	0	0	0
vs. Non-Playoff	12	31	15	9.0	56.5	6.0	20.0	0	0	0	1
vs. Own Division	8	16	6	6.0	41.5	5.0	18.5	0	0	0	1
Home	8	13	11	5.0	26.5	1.5	6.0	0	0	0	1
Away	8	20	7	4.0	30.0	5.5	16.0	0	0	0	0
Games 1-8	8	14	4	2.0	16.0	1.5	3.5	0	0	0	0
Games 9-16	8	19	14	7.0	40.5	5.5	18.5	0	0	0	1
September	4	11	3	1.0	8.0	0.5	1.5	0	0	0	0
October	4	3	1	1.0	8.0	2.0	2.0	0	0	0	0
November	4	9	10	3.0	18.5	3.0	9.5	0	0	0	0
December	4	10	4	4.0	22.0	2.5	9.0	0	0	0	1
Grass	12	22	15	7.0	41.5	3.0	14.5	0	0	0	1
Turf	4	11	3	2.0	15.0	4.0	7.5	0	0	0	0
Indoor	3	10	2	2.0	15.0	4.0	7.5	0	0	0	0
Outdoor	13	23	16	7.0	41.5	3.0	14.5	0	0	0	1

Game Logs

Date	Opp	Result	Tk	Ast	Sack	Yds	Stuff	Yds	Int	Yds	PD	FF	FR	TD
09/03	StL	L 14-17	6	2	1.0	8.0	0.0	0.0	0	0	0	0	0	0
09/11	@Chi	W 27-24	2	0	0.0	0.0	0.0	0.0	0	0	0	0	0	0
09/17	NYN	W 14-6	1	1	0.0	0.0	0.0	0.0	0	0	0	0	0	0
09/24	@Jac	W 24-14	2	0	0.0	0.0	0.5	1.5	0	0	0	0	0	0
10/08	@Dal	L 24-34	1	1	0.0	0.0	0.0	0.0	0	0	0	0	0	0
10/15	Det	W 30-21	0	0	0.0	0.0	0.0	0.0	0	0	0	0	0	0
10/22	Min	W 38-21	1	0	1.0	8.0	0.0	0.0	0	0	0	1	0	1
10/29	@Det	L 16-24	1	0	0.0	0.0	1.0	2.0	0	0	0	0	0	0
11/05	@Min	L 24-27	4	2	1.0	9.0	2.0	4.5	0	0	0	1	0	0
11/12	Chi	W 35-28	1	2	0.5	1.5	0.0	0.0	0	0	0	0	0	0
11/19	@Cle	W 31-20	1	4	0.0	0.0	0.0	0.0	0	0	0	0	0	0
11/26	TB	W 35-13	3	2	1.5	8.0	1.0	5.0	0	0	0	1	0	0
12/03	Cin	W 24-10	1	2	1.0	1.0	0.5	1.0	0	0	0	0	0	0
12/10	@TB	L 10-13	4	0	2.0	15.0	1.0	7.0	0	0	0	0	0	0
12/16	@NO	W 34-23	5	0	1.0	6.0	1.0	1.0	0	0	0	0	0	0
12/24	Pit	W 24-19	0	2	0.0	0.0	0.0	0.0	0	0	0	0	0	0

Seth Joyner

1995 Defensive Splits

	G	Tk	Ast	Sack	Yds	Stuff	Yds	Int	Yds	PD	TD
Total	16	50	20	1.0	5.0	1.5	6.5	3	9	13	0
vs. Playoff	8	25	13	0.0	0.0	0.5	0.5	2	11	8	0
vs. Non-Playoff	8	25	7	1.0	5.0	1.0	6.0	1	-2	5	0
vs. Own Division	8	24	9	1.0	5.0	0.5	0.5	2	9	4	0
Home	8	18	16	0.0	0.0	1.0	6.0	1	0	8	0
Away	8	32	4	1.0	5.0	0.5	0.5	2	9	5	0
Games 1-8	8	26	14	1.0	5.0	0.5	0.5	1	-2	5	0
Games 9-16	8	24	6	0.0	0.0	1.0	6.0	2	11	8	0
September	4	11	7	0.0	0.0	0.5	0.5	0	0	2	0
October	4	15	7	1.0	5.0	0.0	0.0	1	-2	3	0
November	5	12	3	0.0	0.0	1.0	6.0	1	0	6	0
December	3	12	3	0.0	0.0	0.0	0.0	1	11	2	0
Grass	12	32	16	0.0	0.0	1.0	6.0	1	0	10	0
Turf	4	18	4	1.0	5.0	0.5	0.5	2	9	3	0
Indoor	1	2	3	0.0	0.0	0.0	0.0	0	0	1	0
Outdoor	15	48	17	1.0	5.0	1.5	6.5	3	9	12	0

Game Logs

Date	Opp	Result	Tk	Ast	Sack	Yds	Stuff	Yds	Int	Yds	PD	FF	FR	TD
09/03	@Was	L 7-27	1	0	0.0	0.0	0.0	0.0	0	0	0	0	1	0
09/10	Phi	L 19-31	2	4	0.0	0.0	0.0	0.0	0	0	1	0	0	0
09/17	@Det	W 20-17	2	3	0.0	0.0	0.0	0.0	0	0	1	0	0	0
09/24	@Dal	L 20-34	6	0	0.0	0.0	0.5	0.5	0	0	1	0	0	0
10/01	KC	L 3-24	3	3	0.0	0.0	0.0	0.0	0	0	1	0	0	0
10/08	@NYN	L 21-27	7	0	1.0	5.0	0.0	0.0	1	-2	1	0	0	0
10/15	Was	W 24-20	1	1	0.0	0.0	0.0	0.0	0	0	0	0	0	0
10/29	Sea	W 20-14	4	3	0.0	0.0	0.0	0.0	0	0	1	0	1	0
11/05	@Den	L 6-38	2	0	0.0	0.0	0.0	0.0	0	0	0	0	0	0
11/12	Min	L 24-30	4	2	0.0	0.0	1.0	6.0	0	0	1	0	0	0
11/19	@Car	L 7-27	4	0	0.0	0.0	0.0	0.0	0	0	2	0	1	0
11/26	Atl	W 40-37	0	0	0.0	0.0	0.0	0.0	1	0	3	0	0	0
11/30	NYN	L 6-10	2	1	0.0	0.0	0.0	0.0	0	0	0	0	0	0
12/09	@SD	L 25-28	7	0	0.0	0.0	0.0	0.0	0	0	0	1	0	0
12/17	@Phi	L 20-21	3	1	0.0	0.0	0.0	0.0	1	11	1	0	0	0
12/25	Dal	L 13-37	2	2	0.0	0.0	0.0	0.0	0	0	1	0	0	0

Cortez Kennedy

1995 Defensive Splits

	G	Tk	Ast	Sack	Yds	Stuff	Yds	Int	Yds	PD	TD
Total	16	40	14	6.5	38.5	2.5	9.5	0	0	3	0
vs. Playoff	6	15	4	3.5	23.5	0.5	4.5	0	0	2	0
vs. Non-Playoff	10	25	10	3.0	15.0	2.0	5.0	0	0	1	0
vs. Own Division	8	23	9	4.0	30.5	0.5	4.5	0	0	0	0
Home	8	22	7	2.5	14.5	1.0	5.0	0	0	2	0
Away	8	18	7	4.0	24.0	1.5	4.5	0	0	1	0
Games 1-8	8	20	6	3.5	27.5	1.0	6.0	0	0	1	0
Games 9-16	8	20	8	3.0	11.0	1.5	3.5	0	0	2	0
September	3	9	2	1.0	9.0	0.5	4.5	0	0	0	0
October	5	11	4	2.5	18.5	0.5	1.5	0	0	1	0
November	4	10	4	1.5	8.0	1.5	3.5	0	0	1	0
December	4	10	4	1.5	3.0	0.0	0.0	0	0	1	0
Grass	7	16	7	4.0	24.0	1.5	4.5	0	0	0	0
Turf	9	24	7	2.5	14.5	1.0	5.0	0	0	3	0
Indoor	8	22	7	2.5	14.5	1.0	5.0	0	0	2	0
Outdoor	8	18	7	4.0	24.0	1.5	4.5	0	0	1	0

Game Logs

Date	Opp	Result	Tk	Ast	Sack	Yds	Stuff	Yds	Int	Yds	PD	FF	FR	TD
09/03	KC	L 10-34	3	1	0.0	0.0	0.5	4.5	0	0	0	0	0	0
09/10	@SD	L 10-14	3	1	1.0	9.0	0.0	0.0	0	0	0	0	0	0
09/17	Cin	W 24-21	3	0	0.0	0.0	0.0	0.0	0	0	0	0	0	0
10/01	Den	W 27-10	2	1	0.0	0.0	0.0	0.0	0	0	0	0	0	0
10/08	@Oak	L 14-34	3	1	1.0	4.0	0.0	0.0	0	0	0	0	0	0
10/15	@Buf	L 21-27	2	0	0.0	0.0	0.0	0.0	0	0	1	0	0	0
10/22	SD	L 25-35	4	1	1.5	14.5	0.0	0.0	0	0	0	0	0	0
10/29	@Ari	L 14-20	0	1	0.0	0.0	0.5	1.5	0	0	0	0	0	0
11/05	NYN	W 30-28	1	1	0.0	0.0	0.0	0.0	0	0	1	0	0	0
11/12	@Jac	W 47-30	3	1	0.5	1.0	0.0	0.0	0	0	0	0	0	0
11/19	@Was	W 27-20	4	0	1.0	7.0	1.0	3.0	0	0	0	0	0	0
11/26	NYA	L 10-16	2	2	0.0	0.0	0.5	0.5	0	0	0	0	0	0
12/03	Phi	W 26-14	2	0	1.0	0.0	0.0	0.0	0	0	1	1	0	0
12/10	@Den	W 31-27	2	2	0.5	3.0	0.0	0.0	0	0	0	0	0	0
12/17	Oak	W 44-10	5	1	0.0	0.0	0.0	0.0	0	0	0	0	0	0
12/24	@KC	L 3-26	1	1	0.0	0.0	0.0	0.0	0	0	0	0	0	0

Levon Kirkland

1995 Defensive Splits

	G	Tk	Ast	Sack	Yds	Stuff	Yds	Int	Yds	PD	TD
Total	16	58	30	1.0	7.0	5.0	10.0	0	0	1	0
vs. Playoff	4	10	6	0.0	0.0	0.5	1.0	0	0	1	0
vs. Non-Playoff	12	48	24	1.0	7.0	4.5	9.0	0	0	0	0
vs. Own Division	8	27	16	1.0	7.0	0.5	0.5	0	0	0	0
Home	8	28	17	1.0	7.0	4.0	7.0	0	0	1	0
Away	8	30	13	0.0	0.0	1.0	3.0	0	0	0	0
Games 1-8	8	24	16	0.0	0.0	1.0	2.5	0	1	0	0
Games 9-16	8	34	14	1.0	7.0	4.0	7.5	0	0	1	0
September	4	12	10	0.0	0.0	1.0	2.5	0	0	1	0
October	4	12	6	0.0	0.0	0.0	0.0	0	0	0	0
November	4	20	5	1.0	7.0	1.0	3.0	0	0	0	0
December	4	14	9	0.0	0.0	3.0	4.5	0	0	0	0
Grass	6	24	7	0.0	0.0	1.0	3.0	0	0	0	0
Turf	10	34	23	1.0	7.0	4.0	7.0	0	0	1	0
Indoor	1	3	5	0.0	0.0	0.0	0.0	0	0	0	0
Outdoor	15	55	25	1.0	7.0	5.0	10.0	0	0	1	0

Game Logs

Date	Opp	Result	Tk	Ast	Sack	Yds	Stuff	Yds	Int	Yds	PD	FF	FR	TD
09/03	Det	W 23-20	4	2	0.0	0.0	0.5	1.0	0	0	1	0	0	0
09/10	@Hou	W 34-17	3	5	0.0	0.0	0.0	0.0	0	0	0	0	0	0
09/18	@Mia	L 10-23	3	0	0.0	0.0	0.0	0.0	0	0	0	0	0	0
09/24	Min	L 24-44	2	3	0.0	0.0	0.5	1.5	0	0	0	0	2	0
10/01	SD	W 31-16	2	2	0.0	0.0	0.0	0.0	0	0	0	0	0	0
10/08	@Jac	L 16-20	3	2	0.0	0.0	0.0	0.0	0	0	0	0	0	0
10/19	Cin	L 9-27	5	2	0.0	0.0	0.0	0.0	0	0	0	0	0	0
10/29	Jac	W 24-7	2	0	0.0	0.0	0.0	0.0	0	0	0	0	0	0
11/05	@Chi	W 37-34	10	1	0.0	0.0	1.0	3.0	0	0	0	0	0	0
11/13	Cle	W 20-3	3	1	1.0	7.0	0.0	0.0	0	0	0	0	0	0
11/19	@Cin	W 49-31	3	1	0.0	0.0	0.0	0.0	0	0	0	0	0	0
11/26	@Cle	W 20-17	4	2	0.0	0.0	0.0	0.0	0	0	0	0	0	0
12/03	Hou	W 21-7	4	3	0.0	0.0	0.5	0.5	0	0	0	0	0	0
12/10	@Oak	W 29-10	3	0	0.0	0.0	0.0	0.0	0	0	0	0	0	0
12/16	NE	W 41-27	6	4	0.0	0.0	2.5	4.0	0	0	0	0	0	0
12/24	@GB	L 19-24	1	2	0.0	0.0	0.0	0.0	0	0	0	0	0	0

Carnell Lake
Pittsburgh Steelers – CB

1995 Defensive Splits

	G	Tk	Ast	Sack	Yds	Stuff	Yds	Int	Yds	PD	TD
Total	16	63	10	1.5	4.5	1.5	3.0	1	32	11	1
vs. Playoff	4	19	4	0.5	4.5	0.5	1.0	0	0	2	0
vs. Non-Playoff	12	44	6	1.0	0.0	1.0	2.0	1	32	9	1
vs. Own Division	8	31	3	1.0	0.0	1.0	2.0	1	32	6	1
Home	8	31	6	1.0	0.0	0.5	1.0	0	0	3	0
Away	8	32	4	0.5	4.5	1.0	2.0	1	32	8	1
Games 1-8	8	35	8	1.5	4.5	0.5	1.0	1	32	5	1
Games 9-16	8	28	2	0.0	0.0	1.0	2.0	0	0	6	0
September	4	15	5	0.5	4.5	0.5	1.0	1	32	2	1
October	4	20	3	1.0	0.0	0.0	0.0	0	0	3	0
November	4	13	2	0.0	0.0	1.0	2.0	0	0	3	0
December	4	15	0	0.0	0.0	0.0	0.0	0	0	3	0
Grass	6	28	4	0.5	4.5	1.0	2.0	0	0	7	0
Turf	10	35	6	1.0	0.0	0.5	1.0	1	32	4	1
Indoor	1	1	0	0.0	0.0	0.0	0.0	1	32	1	1
Outdoor	15	62	10	1.5	4.5	1.5	3.0	0	0	10	0

Game Logs

Date	Opp	Result	Tk	Ast	Sack	Yds	Stuff	Yds	Int	Yds	PD	FF	FR	TD
09/03	Det	W 23-20	5	1	0.0	0.0	0.5	1.0	0	0	0	0	0	0
09/10	@Hou	W 34-17	1	0	0.0	0.0	0.0	0.0	1	32	1	0	0	1
09/18	@Mia	L 10-23	6	2	0.5	4.5	0.0	0.0	0	0	1	0	0	0
09/24	Min	L 24-44	3	2	0.0	0.0	0.0	0.0	0	0	0	1	0	0
10/01	SD	W 31-16	4	1	0.0	0.0	0.0	0.0	0	0	1	0	0	0
10/08	@Jac	L 16-20	8	0	0.0	0.0	0.0	0.0	0	0	1	0	0	0
10/19	Cin	L 9-27	4	2	0.0	0.0	0.0	0.0	0	0	0	0	0	0
10/29	Jac	W 24-7	4	0	1.0	0.0	0.0	0.0	0	0	0	0	0	0
11/05	@Chi	W 37-34	3	1	0.0	0.0	0.0	0.0	0	0	1	0	0	0
11/13	Cle	W 20-3	1	0	0.0	0.0	0.0	0.0	0	0	0	0	0	0
11/19	@Cin	W 49-31	3	0	0.0	0.0	0.0	0.0	0	0	0	0	0	0
11/26	@Cle	W 20-17	6	1	0.0	0.0	1.0	2.0	0	0	2	0	0	0
12/03	Hou	W 21-7	4	0	0.0	0.0	0.0	0.0	0	0	1	0	0	0
12/10	@Oak	W 29-10	1	0	0.0	0.0	0.0	0.0	0	0	2	0	0	0
12/16	NE	W 41-27	6	0	0.0	0.0	0.0	0.0	0	0	0	0	0	0
12/24	@GB	L 19-24	4	0	0.0	0.0	0.0	0.0	0	0	0	0	1	0

Antonio Langham
Cleveland Browns – CB

1995 Defensive Splits

	G	Tk	Ast	Sack	Yds	Stuff	Yds	Int	Yds	PD	TD
Total	16	68	8	0.0	0.0	0.0	0.0	2	29	10	0
vs. Playoff	7	33	2	0.0	0.0	0.0	0.0	0	0	7	0
vs. Non-Playoff	9	35	6	0.0	0.0	0.0	0.0	2	29	3	0
vs. Own Division	8	26	5	0.0	0.0	0.0	0.0	2	29	5	0
Home	8	39	1	0.0	0.0	0.0	0.0	2	29	7	0
Away	8	29	7	0.0	0.0	0.0	0.0	0	0	3	0
Games 1-8	8	44	3	0.0	0.0	0.0	0.0	1	0	3	0
Games 9-16	8	24	5	0.0	0.0	0.0	0.0	1	29	7	0
September	4	25	1	0.0	0.0	0.0	0.0	0	0	1	0
October	4	19	2	0.0	0.0	0.0	0.0	1	0	2	0
November	4	14	1	0.0	0.0	0.0	0.0	1	29	6	0
December	4	10	4	0.0	0.0	0.0	0.0	0	0	1	0
Grass	11	49	5	0.0	0.0	0.0	0.0	2	29	8	0
Turf	5	19	3	0.0	0.0	0.0	0.0	0	0	2	0
Indoor	3	14	2	0.0	0.0	0.0	0.0	0	0	0	0
Outdoor	13	54	6	0.0	0.0	0.0	0.0	2	29	10	0

Game Logs

Date	Opp	Result	Tk	Ast	Sack	Yds	Stuff	Yds	Int	Yds	PD	FF	FR	TD
09/03	@NE	L 14-17	6	1	0.0	0.0	0.0	0.0	0	0	0	0	0	0
09/10	TB	W 22-6	6	0	0.0	0.0	0.0	0.0	0	0	0	0	0	0
09/17	@Hou	W 14-7	5	0	0.0	0.0	0.0	0.0	0	0	0	0	0	0
09/24	KC	W 35-17	8	0	0.0	0.0	0.0	0.0	0	0	1	0	0	0
10/02	Buf	L 19-22	5	0	0.0	0.0	0.0	0.0	0	0	1	0	0	0
10/08	@Det	L 20-38	7	1	0.0	0.0	0.0	0.0	0	0	0	0	0	0
10/22	Jac	L 15-23	4	1	0.0	0.0	0.0	0.0	1	0	1	0	0	0
10/29	@Cin	W 29-26	3	0	0.0	0.0	0.0	0.0	0	0	0	0	0	0
11/05	@NE	L 10-37	4	0	0.0	0.0	0.0	0.0	1	29	2	0	0	0
11/13	@Pit	L 3-20	2	1	0.0	0.0	0.0	0.0	0	0	2	0	0	0
11/19	GB	L 20-31	5	0	0.0	0.0	0.0	0.0	0	0	2	0	0	0
11/26	Pit	L 17-20	3	0	0.0	0.0	0.0	0.0	0	0	0	0	0	0
12/03	@SD	L 13-31	3	0	0.0	0.0	0.0	0.0	0	0	1	0	0	0
12/09	@Min	L 11-27	2	1	0.0	0.0	0.0	0.0	0	0	0	0	0	0
12/17	Cin	W 26-10	4	0	0.0	0.0	0.0	0.0	0	0	0	0	0	0
12/24	@Jac	L 21-24	1	3	0.0	0.0	0.0	0.0	0	0	0	0	0	0

Lamar Lathon
Carolina Panthers – LB

1995 Defensive Splits

	G	Tk	Ast	Sack	Yds	Stuff	Yds	Int	Yds	PD	TD
Total	15	54	16	8.0	76.0	5.5	18.5	0	0	3	0
vs. Playoff	6	19	10	3.0	26.0	1.5	2.5	0	0	2	0
vs. Non-Playoff	9	35	6	5.0	50.0	4.0	16.0	0	0	1	0
vs. Own Division	7	28	10	5.0	49.0	1.0	6.0	0	0	2	0
Home	7	24	11	4.0	32.0	2.0	5.0	0	0	1	0
Away	8	30	5	4.0	44.0	3.5	13.5	0	0	1	0
Games 1-8	7	28	10	2.0	18.0	3.5	7.5	0	0	1	0
Games 9-16	8	26	6	6.0	58.0	2.0	11.0	0	0	2	0
September	3	12	5	2.0	18.0	1.5	2.5	0	0	1	0
October	4	16	5	0.0	0.0	2.0	5.0	0	0	0	0
November	4	13	1	4.0	44.0	1.0	6.0	0	0	1	0
December	4	13	5	2.0	14.0	1.0	5.0	0	0	1	0
Grass	11	40	12	6.0	53.0	3.0	10.0	0	0	3	0
Turf	4	14	4	2.0	23.0	2.5	8.5	0	0	0	0
Indoor	3	12	3	2.0	23.0	1.0	6.0	0	0	0	0
Outdoor	12	42	13	6.0	53.0	4.5	12.5	0	0	3	0

Game Logs

Date	Opp	Result	Tk	Ast	Sack	Yds	Stuff	Yds	Int	Yds	PD	FF	FR	TD
09/03	@Atl	L 20-23	5	3	1.0	9.0	0.0	0.0	0	0	0	1	0	0
09/10	@Buf	L 9-31	2	1	0.0	0.0	1.5	2.5	0	0	0	0	0	0
09/17	StL	L 10-31	5	1	1.0	9.0	0.0	0.0	0	0	1	0	0	0
10/01	TB	L 13-20	2	5	0.0	0.0	1.0	2.0	0	0	0	0	0	0
10/08	@Chi	L 27-31	6	0	0.0	0.0	0.0	0.0	0	0	0	0	0	0
10/15	NYA	W 26-15	5	0	0.0	0.0	1.0	3.0	0	0	0	0	0	0
10/22	NO	W 20-3	-	-	-	-	-	-	-	-	-	-	-	-
10/29	@NE	W 20-17	3	0	0.0	0.0	0.0	0.0	0	0	0	0	1	0
11/05	@SF	W 13-7	3	1	1.0	12.0	0.0	0.0	0	0	1	0	0	0
11/12	@StL	L 17-28	2	0	0.0	0.0	0.0	0.0	0	0	0	0	0	0
11/19	Ari	W 27-7	3	0	2.0	18.0	0.0	0.0	0	0	0	0	0	0
11/26	@NO	L 26-34	5	0	1.0	14.0	1.0	6.0	0	0	0	0	0	0
12/03	Ind	W 13-10	1	0	0.0	0.0	0.0	0.0	0	0	1	0	0	0
12/10	SF	L 10-31	4	4	1.0	5.0	0.0	0.0	0	0	0	0	0	0
12/17	Atl	W 21-17	4	1	0.0	0.0	0.0	0.0	0	0	0	0	0	0
12/24	@Was	L 17-20	4	0	1.0	9.0	1.0	5.0	0	0	0	0	0	0

Shawn Lee

San Diego Chargers – DT

1995 Defensive Splits

	G	Tk	Ast	Sack	Yds	Stuff	Yds	Int	Yds	PD	TD
Total	16	31	11	8.0	56.0	8.0	14.0	0	0	1	0
vs. Playoff	7	11	5	2.0	15.0	5.0	7.0	0	0	1	0
vs. Non-Playoff	9	20	6	6.0	41.0	3.0	7.0	0	0	0	0
vs. Own Division	8	17	3	3.0	18.0	5.0	10.0	0	0	0	0
Home	8	14	3	3.5	25.5	6.0	10.0	0	0	0	0
Away	8	17	8	4.5	30.5	2.0	4.0	0	0	1	0
Games 1-8	8	17	4	5.0	33.0	3.0	7.0	0	0	1	0
Games 9-16	8	14	7	3.0	23.0	5.0	7.0	0	0	0	0
September	4	15	2	4.5	30.5	3.0	7.0	0	0	0	0
October	4	2	2	0.5	2.5	0.0	0.0	0	0	1	0
November	4	8	2	0.0	0.0	4.0	6.0	0	0	0	0
December	4	6	5	3.0	23.0	1.0	1.0	0	0	0	0
Grass	11	23	3	5.5	38.5	7.0	13.0	0	0	0	0
Turf	5	8	8	2.5	17.5	1.0	1.0	0	0	1	0
Indoor	2	2	3	0.5	2.5	0.0	0.0	0	0	0	0
Outdoor	14	29	8	7.5	53.5	8.0	14.0	0	0	1	0

Game Logs

Date	Opp	Result	Tk	Ast	Sack	Yds	Stuff	Yds	Int	Yds	PD	FF	FR	TD
09/03	@Oak	L 7-17	7	0	2.0	13.0	1.0	3.0	0	0	0	0	0	0
09/10	Sea	W 14-10	1	0	0.0	0.0	0.0	0.0	0	0	0	0	0	0
09/17	@Phi	W 27-21	6	1	2.0	15.0	1.0	1.0	0	0	0	0	0	0
09/24	Den	W 17-6	1	1	0.5	2.5	1.0	3.0	0	0	0	0	0	0
10/01	@Pit	L 16-31	0	1	0.0	0.0	0.0	0.0	0	0	1	0	0	0
10/09	@KC	L 23-29	0	0	0.0	0.0	0.0	0.0	0	0	0	0	0	0
10/15	Dal	L 9-23	0	0	0.0	0.0	0.0	0.0	0	0	0	0	0	0
10/22	@Sea	W 35-25	2	1	0.5	2.5	0.0	0.0	0	0	0	0	0	0
11/05	Mia	L 14-24	2	1	0.0	0.0	1.0	2.0	0	0	0	0	0	0
11/12	KC	L 7-22	3	0	0.0	0.0	3.0	4.0	0	0	0	0	0	0
11/19	@Den	L 27-30	2	0	0.0	0.0	0.0	0.0	0	0	0	0	0	0
11/27	Oak	W 12-6	1	1	0.0	0.0	0.0	0.0	0	0	0	0	0	0
12/03	Cle	W 31-13	3	0	1.0	8.0	1.0	1.0	0	0	0	0	0	0
12/09	Ari	W 28-25	3	0	2.0	15.0	0.0	0.0	0	0	0	0	0	0
12/17	@Ind	W 27-24	0	2	0.0	0.0	0.0	0.0	0	0	0	0	0	0
12/23	@NYN	W 27-17	0	3	0.0	0.0	0.0	0.0	0	0	0	0	0	0

Darryll Lewis

Houston Oilers – CB

1995 Defensive Splits

	G	Tk	Ast	Sack	Yds	Stuff	Yds	Int	Yds	PD	TD
Total	16	53	9	1.0	9.0	0.5	1.0	6	145	21	1
vs. Playoff	5	12	3	1.0	9.0	0.5	1.0	0	0	4	0
vs. Non-Playoff	11	41	6	0.0	0.0	0.0	0.0	6	145	17	1
vs. Own Division	8	27	6	0.0	0.0	0.5	1.0	3	47	12	0
Home	8	20	7	1.0	9.0	0.5	1.0	1	12	6	0
Away	8	33	2	0.0	0.0	0.0	0.0	5	133	15	1
Games 1-8	8	33	4	0.0	0.0	0.5	1.0	5	120	14	1
Games 9-16	8	20	5	1.0	9.0	0.0	0.0	1	25	7	0
September	4	15	2	0.0	0.0	0.5	1.0	1	10	6	0
October	4	18	2	0.0	0.0	0.0	0.0	4	110	8	1
November	4	13	5	0.0	0.0	0.0	0.0	1	25	3	0
December	4	7	0	1.0	9.0	0.0	0.0	0	0	4	0
Grass	4	16	1	0.0	0.0	0.0	0.0	4	131	10	1
Turf	12	37	8	1.0	9.0	0.5	1.0	2	14	11	0
Indoor	9	26	8	1.0	9.0	0.5	1.0	2	14	8	0
Outdoor	7	27	1	0.0	0.0	0.0	0.0	4	131	13	1

Game Logs

Date	Opp	Result	Tk	Ast	Sack	Yds	Stuff	Yds	Int	Yds	PD	FF	FR	TD
09/03	@Jac	W 10-3	3	0	0.0	0.0	0.0	0.0	1	10	5	0	0	0
09/10	Pit	L 17-34	4	2	0.0	0.0	0.5	1.0	0	0	0	0	0	0
09/17	Cle	L 7-14	2	0	0.0	0.0	0.0	0.0	0	0	0	0	0	0
09/24	@Cin	W 38-28	6	0	0.0	0.0	0.0	0.0	0	0	1	0	0	0
10/01	Jac	L 16-17	2	0	0.0	0.0	0.0	0.0	1	12	3	0	0	0
10/08	@Min	L 17-23	6	1	0.0	0.0	0.0	0.0	1	2	2	0	0	0
10/22	@Chi	L 32-35	7	0	0.0	0.0	0.0	0.0	2	96	3	0	0	1
10/29	TB	W 19-7	3	1	0.0	0.0	0.0	0.0	0	0	0	0	0	0
11/05	@Cle	W 37-10	5	0	0.0	0.0	0.0	0.0	1	25	2	0	0	0
11/12	Cin	L 25-32	2	4	0.0	0.0	0.0	0.0	0	0	1	0	0	0
11/19	@KC	L 13-20	1	1	0.0	0.0	0.0	0.0	0	0	0	0	0	0
11/26	Den	W 42-33	5	0	0.0	0.0	0.0	0.0	0	0	0	0	0	0
12/03	@Pit	L 7-21	3	0	0.0	0.0	0.0	0.0	0	0	0	0	0	0
12/10	Det	L 17-24	2	0	1.0	9.0	0.0	0.0	0	0	2	0	0	0
12/17	NYA	W 23-6	0	0	0.0	0.0	0.0	0.0	0	0	0	0	0	0
12/24	@Buf	W 28-17	2	0	0.0	0.0	0.0	0.0	0	0	2	0	0	0

Mo Lewis

New York Jets – LB

1995 Defensive Splits

	G	Tk	Ast	Sack	Yds	Stuff	Yds	Int	Yds	PD	TD
Total	16	82	29	5.0	44.0	9.0	26.5	2	22	11	1
vs. Playoff	7	42	15	2.0	14.0	1.5	2.0	1	7	4	0
vs. Non-Playoff	9	40	14	3.0	30.0	7.5	24.5	1	15	7	1
vs. Own Division	8	48	14	2.0	14.0	6.0	17.0	1	7	5	0
Home	8	49	22	2.0	20.0	7.0	17.5	1	7	5	0
Away	8	33	7	3.0	24.0	2.0	9.0	1	15	6	1
Games 1-8	8	49	19	1.0	9.0	1.0	1.0	2	22	5	1
Games 9-16	8	33	10	4.0	35.0	8.0	25.5	0	0	6	0
September	4	24	7	0.0	0.0	1.0	1.0	0	0	3	0
October	5	29	12	3.0	23.0	0.0	0.0	2	22	2	1
November	3	14	7	0.0	0.0	4.0	8.0	0	0	1	0
December	4	15	3	2.0	21.0	4.0	17.5	0	0	5	0
Grass	3	10	3	0.0	0.0	1.5	8.5	1	15	3	1
Turf	13	72	26	5.0	44.0	7.5	18.0	1	7	8	0
Indoor	4	12	4	3.0	24.0	0.5	0.5	0	0	3	0
Outdoor	12	70	25	2.0	20.0	8.5	26.0	2	22	8	1

Game Logs

Date	Opp	Result	Tk	Ast	Sack	Yds	Stuff	Yds	Int	Yds	PD	FF	FR	TD
09/03	@Mia	L 14-52	5	1	0.0	0.0	0.0	0.0	0	0	0	0	0	0
09/10	Ind	L 24-27	8	2	0.0	0.0	1.0	1.0	0	0	1	0	0	0
09/17	Jac	W 27-10	8	2	0.0	0.0	0.0	0.0	0	0	0	0	0	0
09/24	@Atl	L 3-13	3	2	0.0	0.0	0.0	0.0	0	0	2	0	0	0
10/01	Oak	L 10-47	4	6	1.0	9.0	0.0	0.0	0	0	0	0	0	0
10/08	@Buf	L 10-29	11	0	0.0	0.0	0.0	0.0	0	0	0	0	0	0
10/15	@Car	L 15-26	3	1	0.0	0.0	0.0	0.0	1	15	1	0	0	1
10/22	Mia	W 17-16	7	5	0.0	0.0	0.0	0.0	1	7	1	0	0	0
10/29	@Ind	L 10-17	4	0	2.0	14.0	0.0	0.0	0	0	0	0	0	0
11/05	NE	L 7-20	7	0	0.0	0.0	3.0	6.5	0	0	1	0	0	0
11/19	Buf	L 26-28	4	5	0.0	0.0	0.5	1.0	0	0	1	0	1	0
11/26	@Sea	W 16-10	3	2	0.0	0.0	0.5	0.5	0	0	0	0	0	0
12/03	StL	L 20-23	8	0	1.0	11.0	1.0	1.0	0	0	0	0	0	0
12/10	@NE	L 28-31	2	1	0.0	0.0	1.5	8.5	0	0	2	0	0	0
12/17	@Hou	L 6-23	2	0	1.0	10.0	0.0	0.0	0	0	1	1	0	0
12/24	NO	L 0-12	3	2	0.0	0.0	1.5	8.0	0	0	2	0	0	0

Jeremy Lincoln

Chicago Bears – CB

1995 Defensive Splits

	G	Tk	Ast	Sack	Yds	Stuff	Yds	Int	Yds	PD	TD
Total	16	65	7	1.0	8.0	1.0	2.0	1	32	5	0
vs. Playoff	6	26	3	1.0	8.0	1.0	2.0	0	0	2	0
vs. Non-Playoff	10	39	4	0.0	0.0	0.0	0.0	1	32	3	0
vs. Own Division	8	28	4	0.0	0.0	0.0	0.0	1	32	2	0
Home	8	33	2	1.0	8.0	1.0	2.0	0	0	3	0
Away	8	32	5	0.0	0.0	0.0	0.0	1	32	2	0
Games 1-8	8	32	1	0.0	0.0	0.0	0.0	1	32	4	0
Games 9-16	8	33	6	1.0	8.0	1.0	2.0	0	0	1	0
September	4	14	0	0.0	0.0	0.0	0.0	1	32	2	0
October	4	18	1	0.0	0.0	0.0	0.0	0	0	2	0
November	4	15	3	1.0	8.0	0.0	0.0	0	0	1	0
December	4	18	3	0.0	0.0	1.0	2.0	0	0	0	0
Grass	11	46	3	1.0	8.0	1.0	2.0	1	32	5	0
Turf	5	19	4	0.0	0.0	0.0	0.0	0	0	0	0
Indoor	2	9	2	0.0	0.0	0.0	0.0	0	0	0	0
Outdoor	14	56	5	1.0	8.0	1.0	2.0	1	32	5	0

Game Logs

Date	Opp	Result	Tk	Ast	Sack	Yds	Stuff	Yds	Int	Yds	PD	FF	FR	TD
09/03	Min	W 31-14	3	0	0.0	0.0	0.0	0.0	0	0	0	0	0	0
09/11	GB	L 24-27	3	0	0.0	0.0	0.0	0.0	0	0	1	0	0	0
09/17	@TB	W 25-6	5	0	0.0	0.0	0.0	0.0	1	32	1	0	0	0
09/24	@StL	L 28-34	3	0	0.0	0.0	0.0	0.0	0	0	0	0	0	0
10/08	Car	W 31-27	3	1	0.0	0.0	0.0	0.0	0	0	0	0	0	0
10/15	@Jac	W 30-27	6	0	0.0	0.0	0.0	0.0	0	0	1	0	0	0
10/22	Hou	W 35-32	4	0	0.0	0.0	0.0	0.0	0	0	1	0	0	0
10/30	@Min	W 14-6	5	0	0.0	0.0	0.0	0.0	0	0	0	0	0	0
11/05	Pit	L 34-37	7	0	1.0	8.0	0.0	0.0	0	0	1	0	0	0
11/12	@GB	L 28-35	2	1	0.0	0.0	0.0	0.0	0	0	0	0	0	0
11/19	Det	L 17-24	3	0	0.0	0.0	0.0	0.0	0	0	0	0	0	0
11/26	@NYN	W 27-24	3	2	0.0	0.0	0.0	0.0	0	0	0	0	0	0
12/04	@Det	L 7-27	4	2	0.0	0.0	0.0	0.0	0	0	0	0	0	0
12/10	@Cin	L 10-16	4	0	0.0	0.0	0.0	0.0	0	0	0	0	0	0
12/17	TB	W 31-10	3	1	0.0	0.0	0.0	0.0	0	0	0	0	0	0
12/24	Phi	W 20-14	7	0	0.0	0.0	1.0	2.0	0	0	0	0	0	0

Greg Lloyd

Pittsburgh Steelers – LB

1995 Defensive Splits

	G	Tk	Ast	Sack	Yds	Stuff	Yds	Int	Yds	PD	TD
Total	16	88	28	6.5	38.0	8.0	35.5	3	85	5	0
vs. Playoff	4	13	4	1.5	11.0	2.5	11.5	0	0	1	0
vs. Non-Playoff	12	75	24	5.0	27.0	5.5	24.0	3	85	4	0
vs. Own Division	8	51	16	4.0	22.0	5.0	22.5	1	9	2	0
Home	8	47	21	4.5	31.0	4.0	18.5	1	9	3	0
Away	8	41	7	2.0	7.0	4.0	17.0	2	76	2	0
Games 1-8	8	49	10	3.5	20.0	5.5	27.5	0	0	1	0
Games 9-16	8	39	18	3.0	18.0	2.5	8.0	3	85	4	0
September	4	18	6	1.5	9.0	3.5	16.5	0	0	1	0
October	4	31	4	2.0	11.0	2.0	11.0	0	0	0	0
November	4	17	4	3.0	18.0	0.0	0.0	2	61	2	0
December	4	22	14	0.0	0.0	2.5	8.0	1	24	2	0
Grass	6	29	4	1.0	4.0	3.0	12.0	2	76	2	0
Turf	10	59	24	5.5	34.0	5.0	23.5	1	9	3	0
Indoor	1	6	3	0.0	0.0	1.0	5.0	0	0	0	0
Outdoor	15	82	25	6.5	38.0	7.0	30.5	3	85	5	0

Game Logs

Date	Opp	Result	Tk	Ast	Sack	Yds	Stuff	Yds	Int	Yds	PD	FF	FR	TD
09/03	Det	W 23-20	1	2	0.5	4.0	0.5	0.5	0	0	1	0	0	0
09/10	@Hou	W 34-17	6	3	0.0	0.0	1.0	5.0	0	0	0	0	0	0
09/18	@Mia	L 10-23	4	0	0.0	0.0	2.0	11.0	0	0	0	0	0	0
09/24	Min	L 24-44	7	1	1.0	5.0	0.0	0.0	0	0	0	1	0	0
10/01	SD	W 31-16	5	1	1.0	7.0	0.0	0.0	0	0	0	1	0	0
10/08	@Jac	L 16-20	6	0	1.0	4.0	1.0	1.0	0	0	0	1	0	0
10/19	Cin	L 9-27	8	1	0.0	0.0	1.0	10.0	0	0	0	1	0	0
10/29	Jac	W 24-7	10	2	0.0	0.0	0.0	0.0	0	0	0	0	0	0
11/05	@Chi	W 37-34	4	1	0.0	0.0	0.0	0.0	1	52	1	0	0	0
11/13	Cle	W 20-3	3	1	2.0	15.0	0.0	0.0	1	9	1	1	0	0
11/19	@Cin	W 49-31	6	0	1.0	3.0	0.0	0.0	0	0	0	0	0	0
11/26	@Cle	W 20-17	4	2	0.0	0.0	0.0	0.0	0	0	0	0	0	0
12/03	Hou	W 21-7	6	7	0.0	0.0	2.0	6.5	0	0	1	0	0	0
12/10	@Oak	W 29-10	6	0	0.0	0.0	0.0	0.0	1	24	1	0	0	0
12/16	NE	W 41-27	7	6	0.0	0.0	0.5	1.5	0	0	1	0	0	0
12/24	@GB	L 19-24	3	1	0.0	0.0	0.0	0.0	0	0	0	0	0	0

Sean Lumpkin

New Orleans Saints – S

1995 Defensive Splits

	G	Tk	Ast	Sack	Yds	Stuff	Yds	Int	Yds	PD	TD
Total	16	86	26	0.0	0.0	5.0	10.5	1	47	3	1
vs. Playoff	8	47	10	0.0	0.0	3.0	7.5	1	47	1	1
vs. Non-Playoff	8	39	16	0.0	0.0	2.0	3.0	0	0	2	0
vs. Own Division	8	40	10	0.0	0.0	3.5	6.5	1	47	2	1
Home	8	44	13	0.0	0.0	4.0	8.5	1	47	2	1
Away	8	42	13	0.0	0.0	1.0	2.0	0	0	1	0
Games 1-8	8	48	9	0.0	0.0	4.0	9.5	1	47	1	1
Games 9-16	8	38	17	0.0	0.0	1.0	1.0	0	0	2	0
September	4	28	6	0.0	0.0	1.5	3.5	1	47	1	1
October	4	20	3	0.0	0.0	2.5	6.0	0	0	0	0
November	4	14	10	0.0	0.0	1.0	1.0	0	0	2	0
December	4	24	7	0.0	0.0	0.0	0.0	0	0	0	0
Grass	3	13	6	0.0	0.0	1.0	2.0	0	0	0	0
Turf	13	73	20	0.0	0.0	4.0	8.5	1	47	3	1
Indoor	10	54	16	0.0	0.0	4.0	8.5	1	47	3	1
Outdoor	6	32	10	0.0	0.0	1.0	2.0	0	0	1	0

Game Logs

Date	Opp	Result	Tk	Ast	Sack	Yds	Stuff	Yds	Int	Yds	PD	FF	FR	TD
09/03	SF	L 22-24	6	0	0.0	0.0	0.0	0.0	1	47	1	0	0	1
09/10	@StL	L 13-17	5	1	0.0	0.0	0.0	0.0	0	0	0	0	0	0
09/17	Atl	L 24-27	8	2	0.0	0.0	1.5	3.5	0	0	0	0	0	0
09/24	@NYN	L 29-45	9	3	0.0	0.0	0.0	0.0	0	0	0	0	0	0
10/01	Phi	L 10-15	9	1	0.0	0.0	1.5	4.0	0	0	0	0	0	0
10/15	Mia	W 33-30	2	0	0.0	0.0	0.0	0.0	0	0	0	0	0	0
10/22	@Car	L 3-20	6	2	0.0	0.0	1.0	2.0	0	0	0	0	0	0
10/29	@SF	W 11-7	3	0	0.0	0.0	0.0	0.0	0	0	0	1	0	0
11/05	StL	W 19-10	2	1	0.0	0.0	1.0	1.0	0	0	0	0	0	0
11/12	Ind	W 17-14	4	4	0.0	0.0	0.0	0.0	0	0	0	1	0	0
11/19	@Min	L 24-43	4	2	0.0	0.0	0.0	0.0	0	0	1	0	0	0
11/26	Car	W 34-26	4	3	0.0	0.0	0.0	0.0	0	0	1	0	0	0
12/03	@NE	W 31-17	4	4	0.0	0.0	0.0	0.0	0	0	1	0	0	0
12/10	@Atl	L 14-19	6	1	0.0	0.0	0.0	0.0	0	0	0	0	0	0
12/16	GB	L 23-34	9	2	0.0	0.0	0.0	0.0	0	0	0	0	0	0
12/24	@NYA	W 12-0	5	0	0.0	0.0	0.0	0.0	0	0	0	1	0	0

Todd Lyght
St. Louis Rams – CB

1995 Defensive Splits

	G	Tk	Ast	Sack	Yds	Stuff	Yds	Int	Yds	PD	TD
Total	16	76	10	0.0	0.0	4.5	14.0	4	34	11	1
vs. Playoff	9	46	5	0.0	0.0	3.0	6.5	1	5	6	0
vs. Non-Playoff	7	30	5	0.0	0.0	1.5	7.5	3	29	5	1
vs. Own Division	8	30	5	0.0	0.0	2.0	7.0	3	29	8	1
Home	8	35	5	0.0	0.0	1.5	2.5	2	29	4	1
Away	8	41	5	0.0	0.0	3.0	11.5	2	5	7	0
Games 1-8	8	38	7	0.0	0.0	3.0	6.5	3	34	6	1
Games 9-16	8	38	3	0.0	0.0	1.5	7.5	1	0	5	0
September	4	20	4	0.0	0.0	0.5	2.0	2	29	4	1
October	4	18	3	0.0	0.0	2.5	4.5	1	5	2	0
November	4	16	1	0.0	0.0	1.0	6.0	1	0	5	0
December	4	22	2	0.0	0.0	0.5	1.5	0	0	0	0
Grass	3	13	2	0.0	0.0	0.5	2.0	1	0	5	0
Turf	13	63	8	0.0	0.0	4.0	12.0	3	34	6	1
Indoor	7	33	5	0.0	0.0	2.0	9.0	1	0	3	0
Outdoor	9	43	5	0.0	0.0	2.5	5.0	3	34	8	1

Game Logs

Date	Opp	Result	Tk	Ast	Sack	Yds	Stuff	Yds	Int	Yds	PD	FF	FR	TD
09/03	@GB	W 17-14	8	1	0.0	0.0	0.5	2.0	0	0	2	0	0	0
09/10	NO	W 17-13	5	2	0.0	0.0	0.0	0.0	1	29	1	0	0	1
09/17	@Car	W 31-10	2	1	0.0	0.0	0.0	0.0	1	0	1	0	0	0
09/24	Chi	W 34-28	5	0	0.0	0.0	0.0	0.0	0	0	0	0	0	0
10/01	@Ind	L 18-21	5	2	0.0	0.0	0.5	1.5	0	0	0	1	0	0
10/12	Atl	W 21-19	5	1	0.0	0.0	1.0	1.0	0	0	1	0	0	0
10/22	SF	L 10-44	2	0	0.0	0.0	0.0	0.0	0	0	0	0	0	0
10/29	@Phi	L 9-20	6	0	0.0	0.0	1.0	2.0	1	5	1	0	0	0
11/05	@NO	L 10-19	4	1	0.0	0.0	1.0	6.0	0	0	1	0	0	0
11/12	Car	W 28-17	3	0	0.0	0.0	0.0	0.0	1	0	2	0	0	0
11/19	@Atl	L 6-31	6	0	0.0	0.0	0.0	0.0	0	0	0	0	0	0
11/26	@SF	L 13-41	3	0	0.0	0.0	0.0	0.0	0	0	2	0	0	0
12/03	@NYA	W 23-20	7	0	0.0	0.0	0.0	0.0	0	0	0	0	0	0
12/10	Buf	L 27-45	6	0	0.0	0.0	0.0	0.0	0	0	0	0	0	0
12/17	Was	L 23-35	4	1	0.0	0.0	0.5	1.5	0	0	0	0	0	0
12/24	Mia	L 22-41	5	1	0.0	0.0	0.0	0.0	0	0	0	0	0	0

Keith Lyle
St. Louis Rams – S

1995 Defensive Splits

	G	Tk	Ast	Sack	Yds	Stuff	Yds	Int	Yds	PD	TD
Total	16	73	18	0.0	0.0	1.5	5.5	3	42	6	0
vs. Playoff	9	38	5	0.0	0.0	0.5	1.5	1	31	3	0
vs. Non-Playoff	7	35	13	0.0	0.0	1.0	4.0	2	11	3	0
vs. Own Division	8	34	12	0.0	0.0	1.0	4.0	1	11	2	0
Home	8	31	4	0.0	0.0	0.0	0.0	1	0	3	0
Away	8	42	14	0.0	0.0	1.5	5.5	2	42	3	0
Games 1-8	8	28	6	0.0	0.0	0.5	1.5	2	42	3	0
Games 9-16	8	45	12	0.0	0.0	1.0	4.0	1	0	3	0
September	4	14	4	0.0	0.0	0.0	0.0	2	42	3	0
October	4	14	2	0.0	0.0	0.5	1.5	0	0	0	0
November	4	22	8	0.0	0.0	1.0	4.0	0	0	1	0
December	4	23	4	0.0	0.0	0.0	0.0	1	0	2	0
Grass	3	13	1	0.0	0.0	0.0	0.0	2	42	3	0
Turf	13	60	17	0.0	0.0	1.5	5.5	1	0	3	0
Indoor	7	41	10	0.0	0.0	1.5	5.5	1	0	2	0
Outdoor	9	32	8	0.0	0.0	0.0	0.0	2	42	4	0

Game Logs

Date	Opp	Result	Tk	Ast	Sack	Yds	Stuff	Yds	Int	Yds	PD	FF	FR	TD
09/03	@GB	W 17-14	4	0	0.0	0.0	0.0	0.0	1	31	1	0	0	0
09/10	NO	W 17-13	4	3	0.0	0.0	0.0	0.0	0	0	0	0	0	0
09/17	@Car	W 31-10	4	1	0.0	0.0	0.0	0.0	1	11	1	0	0	0
09/24	Chi	W 34-28	2	0	0.0	0.0	0.0	0.0	0	0	1	0	0	0
10/01	@Ind	L 18-21	6	1	0.0	0.0	0.5	1.5	0	0	0	0	0	0
10/12	Atl	W 21-19	2	0	0.0	0.0	0.0	0.0	0	0	0	0	0	0
10/22	SF	L 10-44	2	0	0.0	0.0	0.0	0.0	0	0	0	0	0	0
10/29	@Phi	L 9-20												
11/05	@NO	L 10-19	10	6	0.0	0.0	1.0	4.0	0	0	0	0	0	0
11/12	Car	W 28-17	4	2	0.0	0.0	0.0	0.0	0	0	0	0	0	0
11/19	@Atl	L 6-31	4	2	0.0	0.0	1.0	4.0	0	0	0	0	0	0
11/26	@SF	L 13-41	5	0	0.0	0.0	0.0	0.0	0	0	1	1	0	0
12/03	@NYA	W 23-20	5	3	0.0	0.0	0.0	0.0	0	0	0	0	0	0
12/10	Buf	L 27-45	6	0	0.0	0.0	0.0	0.0	0	0	1	0	0	0
12/17	Was	L 23-35	7	0	0.0	0.0	0.0	0.0	1	0	1	0	0	0
12/24	Mia	L 22-41	5	1	0.0	0.0	0.0	0.0	0	0	0	0	0	0

Mike Mamula
Philadelphia Eagles – DE

1995 Defensive Splits

	G	Tk	Ast	Sack	Yds	Stuff	Yds	Int	Yds	PD	TD
Total	14	33	8	5.5	30.0	2.0	3.5	0	0	1	0
vs. Playoff	3	3	1	0.0	0.0	0.5	1.0	0	0	0	0
vs. Non-Playoff	11	30	7	5.5	30.0	1.5	2.5	0	0	1	0
vs. Own Division	7	16	6	3.5	13.0	2.0	3.5	0	0	0	0
Home	8	16	2	3.0	12.0	1.0	1.0	0	0	0	0
Away	6	17	6	2.5	18.0	1.0	2.5	0	0	1	0
Games 1-8	8	21	7	2.5	18.0	0.5	1.5	0	0	0	0
Games 9-16	6	12	1	3.0	12.0	1.5	2.0	0	0	0	0
September	4	10	1	0.0	0.0	0.5	1.5	0	0	0	0
October	4	11	6	2.5	18.0	0.0	0.0	0	0	1	0
November	3	7	1	3.0	12.0	0.5	1.0	0	0	0	0
December	3	5	0	0.0	0.0	1.0	1.0	0	0	0	0
Grass	3	10	1	0.0	0.0	0.5	1.5	0	0	0	0
Turf	11	23	7	5.5	30.0	1.5	2.0	0	0	1	0
Indoor	1	3	1	2.0	17.0	0.0	0.0	0	0	1	0
Outdoor	13	30	7	3.5	13.0	2.0	3.5	0	0	0	0

Game Logs

Date	Opp	Result	Tk	Ast	Sack	Yds	Stuff	Yds	Int	Yds	PD	FF	FR	TD
09/03	TB	L 6-21	1	0	0.0	0.0	0.0	0.0	0	0	0	0	0	0
09/10	@Ari	W 31-19	3	1	0.0	0.0	0.5	1.5	0	0	0	0	0	0
09/17	SD	L 21-27	2	0	0.0	0.0	0.0	0.0	0	0	0	0	0	0
09/24	@Oak	L 17-48	4	0	0.0	0.0	0.0	0.0	0	0	0	0	0	0
10/01	@NO	W 15-10	3	1	2.0	17.0	0.0	0.0	0	0	1	0	0	0
10/08	Was	W 37-34	2	1	0.0	0.0	0.0	0.0	0	0	0	0	0	0
10/15	@NYN	W 17-14	4	3	0.5	1.0	0.0	0.0	0	0	0	0	0	0
10/29	StL	W 20-9	2	1	0.0	0.0	0.0	0.0	0	0	0	0	0	0
11/06	@Dal	L 12-34	0	1	0.0	0.0	0.5	1.0	0	0	0	0	0	0
11/12	Den	W 31-13	2	0	0.0	0.0	0.0	0.0	0	0	0	0	1	0
11/19	NYN	W 28-19	5	0	3.0	12.0	0.0	0.0	0	0	0	0	0	0
11/26	@Was	W 14-7												
12/03	@Sea	L 14-26	-	-	-	-	-	-	-	-	-	-	-	-
12/10	Dal	W 20-17	1	0	0.0	0.0	0.0	0.0	0	0	0	0	0	0
12/17	Ari	W 21-20	1	0	0.0	0.0	1.0	1.0	0	0	0	0	0	0
12/24	@Chi	L 14-20	3	0	0.0	0.0	0.0	0.0	0	0	1	0	0	0

Brock Marion
Dallas Cowboys – S

1995 Defensive Splits

	G	Tk	Ast	Sack	Yds	Stuff	Yds	Int	Yds	PD	TD
Total	16	72	18	0.0	0.0	0.0	0.0	6	40	10	1
vs. Playoff	7	25	7	0.0	0.0	0.0	0.0	1	0	3	0
vs. Non-Playoff	9	47	11	0.0	0.0	0.0	0.0	5	40	7	1
vs. Own Division	8	40	6	0.0	0.0	0.0	0.0	4	32	4	1
Home	8	36	14	0.0	0.0	0.0	0.0	2	0	4	0
Away	8	36	4	0.0	0.0	0.0	0.0	4	40	6	1
Games 1-8	8	25	8	0.0	0.0	0.0	0.0	3	0	7	0
Games 9-16	8	47	10	0.0	0.0	0.0	0.0	3	40	3	1
September	4	16	6	0.0	0.0	0.0	0.0	2	0	4	0
October	4	9	2	0.0	0.0	0.0	0.0	1	0	3	0
November	4	21	5	0.0	0.0	0.0	0.0	1	8	1	0
December	4	26	5	0.0	0.0	0.0	0.0	2	32	2	1
Grass	4	21	0	0.0	0.0	0.0	0.0	3	40	3	1
Turf	12	51	18	0.0	0.0	0.0	0.0	3	0	7	0
Indoor	2	5	4	0.0	0.0	0.0	0.0	0	0	2	0
Outdoor	14	67	14	0.0	0.0	0.0	0.0	6	40	8	1

Game Logs

Date	Opp	Result	Tk	Ast	Sack	Yds	Stuff	Yds	Int	Yds	PD	FF	FR	TD
09/04	@NYN	W 35-0	5	0	0.0	0.0	0.0	0.0	1	0	1	0	0	0
09/10	Den	W 31-21	7	3	0.0	0.0	0.0	0.0	0	0	1	0	0	0
09/17	@Min	W 23-17	1	3	0.0	0.0	0.0	0.0	0	0	1	0	0	0
09/24	Ari	W 34-20	3	0	0.0	0.0	0.0	0.0	1	0	1	0	0	0
10/01	@Was	L 23-27	3	0	0.0	0.0	0.0	0.0	0	0	0	0	0	0
10/08	GB	W 34-24	2	1	0.0	0.0	0.0	0.0	0	0	0	0	0	0
10/15	@SD	W 23-9	0	0	0.0	0.0	0.0	0.0	1	0	1	0	0	0
10/29	@Atl	W 28-13	4	1	0.0	0.0	0.0	0.0	0	0	1	0	0	0
11/06	Phi	W 34-12	3	1	0.0	0.0	0.0	0.0	0	0	0	0	0	0
11/12	SF	L 20-38	7	2	0.0	0.0	0.0	0.0	0	0	0	0	0	0
11/19	@Oak	W 34-21	7	0	0.0	0.0	0.0	0.0	1	8	1	0	0	0
11/23	KC	W 24-12	4	2	0.0	0.0	0.0	0.0	0	0	0	0	0	0
12/03	Was	L 17-24	4	2	0.0	0.0	0.0	0.0	0	0	0	0	0	0
12/10	@Phi	L 17-20	5	0	0.0	0.0	0.0	0.0	0	0	0	0	0	0
12/17	NYN	W 21-20	6	3	0.0	0.0	0.0	0.0	1	0	1	0	0	0
12/25	@Ari	W 37-13	11	0	0.0	0.0	0.0	0.0	1	32	1	0	0	1

Wayne Martin
New Orleans Saints – DT

1995 Defensive Splits

	G	Tk	Ast	Sack	Yds	Stuff	Yds	Int	Yds	PD	TD
Total	16	64	14	13.0	89.0	4.0	11.0	1	12	10	0
vs. Playoff	8	36	5	8.0	50.0	3.0	9.0	0	0	5	0
vs. Non-Playoff	8	28	8	5.0	39.0	1.0	2.0	1	12	5	0
vs. Own Division	8	39	4	10.0	72.0	1.0	4.0	0	0	5	0
Home	8	41	5	10.0	67.0	3.0	9.0	0	0	4	0
Away	8	23	8	3.0	22.0	1.0	2.0	1	12	6	0
Games 1-8	8	34	6	7.0	40.0	3.0	9.0	1	12	7	0
Games 9-16	8	30	7	6.0	49.0	1.0	2.0	0	0	3	0
September	4	17	6	4.0	24.0	1.0	4.0	1	12	5	0
October	4	17	0	3.0	16.0	2.0	5.0	0	0	2	0
November	4	16	4	3.0	26.0	1.0	2.0	0	0	1	0
December	4	14	3	3.0	23.0	0.0	0.0	0	0	2	0
Grass	3	12	1	2.0	13.0	0.0	0.0	0	0	1	0
Turf	13	52	12	11.0	76.0	4.0	11.0	1	12	9	0
Indoor	10	48	8	11.0	76.0	4.0	11.0	0	0	4	0
Outdoor	6	16	5	2.0	13.0	0.0	0.0	1	12	6	0

Game Logs

Date	Opp	Result	Tk	Ast	Sack	Yds	Stuff	Yds	Int	Yds	PD	FF	FR	TD
09/03	SF	L 22-24	5	1	2.0	9.0	1.0	4.0	0	0	1	0	0	0
09/10	@StL	L 13-17	2	0	0.0	0.0	0.0	0.0	0	0	3	0	0	0
09/17	Atl	L 24-27	8	1	2.0	15.0	0.0	0.0	0	0	0	0	0	0
09/24	@NYN	L 29-45	2	4	0.0	0.0	0.0	0.0	1	12	1	0	0	0
10/01	Phi	L 10-15	4	0	1.0	3.0	1.0	2.0	0	0	1	0	1	0
10/15	Mia	W 33-30	4	0	0.0	0.0	1.0	3.0	0	0	0	0	0	0
10/22	@Car	L 3-20	7	0	2.0	13.0	0.0	0.0	0	0	0	0	0	0
10/29	@SF	W 11-7	2	0	0.0	0.0	0.0	0.0	0	0	0	0	0	0
11/05	StL	W 19-10	6	1	2.0	20.0	0.0	0.0	0	0	0	0	0	0
11/12	Ind	W 17-14	2	1	0.0	0.0	0.0	0.0	0	0	1	0	0	0
11/19	@Min	L 24-43	3	2	0.0	0.0	1.0	2.0	0	0	0	0	0	0
11/26	Car	W 34-26	5	0	1.0	6.0	0.0	0.0	0	0	0	1	0	0
12/03	@NE	W 31-17	3	1	0.0	0.0	0.0	0.0	0	0	0	0	0	0
12/10	@Atl	L 14-19	4	1	1.0	9.0	0.0	0.0	0	0	0	0	0	0
12/16	GB	L 23-34	7	1	2.0	14.0	0.0	0.0	0	0	1	0	0	0
12/24	@NYA	W 12-0	0	0	0.0	0.0	0.0	0.0	0	0	1	0	0	0

Clay Matthews
Atlanta Falcons – LB

1995 Defensive Splits

	G	Tk	Ast	Sack	Yds	Stuff	Yds	Int	Yds	PD	TD
Total	16	51	14	0.0	0.0	4.0	14.0	2	1	4	0
vs. Playoff	6	18	4	0.0	0.0	2.5	12.5	1	1	1	0
vs. Non-Playoff	10	33	10	0.0	0.0	1.5	1.5	1	0	3	0
vs. Own Division	8	30	3	0.0	0.0	1.5	1.5	1	0	2	0
Home	8	25	4	0.0	0.0	2.0	2.0	0	0	2	0
Away	8	26	10	0.0	0.0	2.0	12.0	2	1	2	0
Games 1-8	8	29	5	0.0	0.0	0.5	0.5	1	0	2	0
Games 9-16	8	22	9	0.0	0.0	3.5	13.5	1	1	2	0
September	4	15	2	0.0	0.0	0.0	0.0	0	0	1	0
October	4	14	3	0.0	0.0	0.0	0.0	1	0	1	0
November	4	8	5	0.0	0.0	1.5	10.5	0	0	1	0
December	4	14	4	0.0	0.0	2.0	3.0	1	1	1	0
Grass	5	17	9	0.0	0.0	1.0	2.0	1	1	1	0
Turf	11	34	5	0.0	0.0	3.0	12.0	1	0	3	0
Indoor	9	29	5	0.0	0.0	2.0	2.0	0	0	2	0
Outdoor	7	22	9	0.0	0.0	2.0	12.0	2	1	2	0

Game Logs

Date	Opp	Result	Tk	Ast	Sack	Yds	Stuff	Yds	Int	Yds	PD	FF	FR	TD
09/03	Car	W 23-20	5	0	0.0	0.0	0.0	0.0	0	0	0	0	0	0
09/10	@SF	L 10-41	4	0	0.0	0.0	0.0	0.0	0	0	0	0	0	0
09/17	@NO	W 27-24	4	1	0.0	0.0	0.0	0.0	0	0	0	0	0	0
09/24	NYA	W 13-3	2	1	0.0	0.0	0.0	0.0	0	0	1	0	0	0
10/01	NE	W 30-17	3	0	0.0	0.0	0.5	0.5	0	0	0	0	0	0
10/12	@StL	L 19-21	3	0	0.0	0.0	0.0	0.0	1	0	1	0	0	0
10/22	@TB	W 24-21	4	1	0.0	0.0	0.0	0.0	0	0	0	0	0	0
10/29	Dal	L 13-28	4	2	0.0	0.0	0.0	0.0	0	0	0	0	0	0
11/05	Det	W 34-22	1	0	0.0	0.0	0.0	0.0	0	0	0	0	0	0
11/12	@Buf	L 17-23	2	0	0.0	0.0	1.0	10.0	0	0	0	0	0	0
11/19	StL	W 31-6	2	0	0.0	0.0	0.0	0.0	0	0	1	0	0	0
11/26	@Ari	L 37-40	3	5	0.0	0.0	0.5	0.5	0	0	0	0	0	0
12/03	@Mia	L 20-21	2	2	0.0	0.0	0.5	1.5	1	1	1	0	0	0
12/10	NO	W 19-14	3	1	0.0	0.0	0.5	0.5	0	0	0	0	0	0
12/17	@Car	L 17-21	4	1	0.0	0.0	1.0	1.0	0	0	0	0	1	0
12/24	SF	W 28-27	5	0	0.0	0.0	1.0	1.0	0	0	0	0	0	0

Brett Maxie
Carolina Panthers – S

1995 Defensive Splits

	G	Tk	Ast	Sack	Yds	Stuff	Yds	Int	Yds	PD	TD
Total	16	71	18	0.0	0.0	0.0	2.0	6	59	20	0
vs. Playoff	6	25	9	0.0	0.0	0.0	0.0	2	49	8	0
vs. Non-Playoff	10	46	9	0.0	0.0	1.0	2.0	4	10	12	0
vs. Own Division	8	43	14	0.0	0.0	1.0	2.0	4	9	11	0
Home	8	34	4	0.0	0.0	1.0	2.0	3	10	12	0
Away	8	37	14	0.0	0.0	0.0	0.0	3	49	8	0
Games 1-8	8	33	12	0.0	0.0	1.0	2.0	5	59	13	0
Games 9-16	8	38	6	0.0	0.0	0.0	0.0	1	0	7	0
September	3	8	10	0.0	0.0	0.0	0.0	2	49	4	0
October	5	25	2	0.0	0.0	1.0	2.0	3	10	9	0
November	4	18	5	0.0	0.0	0.0	0.0	1	0	4	0
December	4	20	1	0.0	0.0	0.0	0.0	0	0	3	0
Grass	12	54	7	0.0	0.0	1.0	2.0	3	10	14	0
Turf	4	17	11	0.0	0.0	0.0	0.0	3	49	6	0
Indoor	3	16	9	0.0	0.0	0.0	0.0	2	0	3	0
Outdoor	13	55	9	0.0	0.0	1.0	2.0	4	59	17	0

Game Logs

Date	Opp	Result	Tk	Ast	Sack	Yds	Stuff	Yds	Int	Yds	PD	FF	FR	TD
09/03	@Atl	L 20-23	5	5	0.0	0.0	0.0	0.0	1	0	1	0	1	0
09/10	@Buf	L 9-31	1	2	0.0	0.0	0.0	0.0	1	49	3	0	0	0
09/17	StL	L 10-31	2	3	0.0	0.0	0.0	0.0	0	0	0	0	0	0
10/01	TB	L 13-20	1	0	0.0	0.0	0.0	0.0	0	0	1	0	0	0
10/08	@Chi	L 27-31	7	0	0.0	0.0	0.0	0.0	0	0	0	0	0	0
10/15	NYA	W 26-15	2	0	0.0	0.0	0.0	0.0	1	1	3	0	0	0
10/22	NO	W 20-3	9	0	0.0	0.0	1.0	2.0	2	9	4	1	0	0
10/29	@NE	W 20-17	6	2	0.0	0.0	0.0	0.0	0	0	1	0	0	0
11/05	@SF	W 13-7	3	1	0.0	0.0	0.0	0.0	0	0	1	0	0	0
11/12	@StL	L 17-28	4	0	0.0	0.0	0.0	0.0	0	0	0	0	0	0
11/19	Ari	W 27-7	4	0	0.0	0.0	0.0	0.0	0	0	1	0	0	0
11/26	@NO	L 26-34	7	4	0.0	0.0	0.0	0.0	1	0	2	0	0	0
12/03	Ind	W 13-10	3	0	0.0	0.0	0.0	0.0	0	0	0	0	0	0
12/10	SF	L 10-31	4	0	0.0	0.0	0.0	0.0	0	0	0	0	0	0
12/17	Atl	W 21-17	9	1	0.0	0.0	0.0	0.0	0	0	3	0	0	0
12/24	@Was	L 17-20	4	0	0.0	0.0	0.0	0.0	0	0	0	0	0	0

Martin Mayhew
Tampa Bay Buccaneers – CB

1995 Defensive Splits

	G	Tk	Ast	Sack	Yds	Stuff	Yds	Int	Yds	PD	TD
Total	13	58	17	0.0	0.0	1.0	3.0	5	81	15	1
vs. Playoff	6	28	9	0.0	0.0	1.0	3.0	0	0	5	0
vs. Non-Playoff	7	30	8	0.0	0.0	1.0	3.0	5	81	10	1
vs. Own Division	6	32	8	0.0	0.0	1.0	3.0	2	26	6	1
Home	7	40	12	0.0	0.0	1.0	3.0	3	55	8	1
Away	6	18	5	0.0	0.0	0.0	0.0	2	26	7	0
Games 1-8	6	24	10	0.0	0.0	1.0	3.0	2	40	6	0
Games 9-16	7	34	7	0.0	0.0	1.0	3.0	3	41	9	0
September	2	4	3	0.0	0.0	0.0	0.0	1	0	1	0
October	5	24	7	0.0	0.0	0.0	0.0	1	40	7	0
November	3	14	4	0.0	0.0	0.0	0.0	1	15	3	0
December	3	16	3	0.0	0.0	1.0	3.0	2	26	4	0
Grass	9	48	13	0.0	0.0	1.0	3.0	3	55	9	1
Turf	4	10	4	0.0	0.0	0.0	0.0	2	26	6	0
Indoor	3	10	3	0.0	0.0	0.0	0.0	2	26	6	0
Outdoor	10	48	14	0.0	0.0	1.0	3.0	3	55	9	1

Game Logs

Date	Opp	Result	Tk	Ast	Sack	Yds	Stuff	Yds	Int	Yds	PD	FF	FR	TD
09/03	@Phi	W 21-6	0	1	0.0	0.0	0.0	0.0	0	0	0	0	0	0
09/10	@Cle	L 6-22	-	-	-	-	-	-	-	-	-	-	-	-
09/17	Chi	L 6-25	-	-	-	-	-	-	-	-	-	-	-	-
09/24	Was	W 14-6	4	2	0.0	0.0	0.0	0.0	1	0	1	1	0	0
10/01	@Car	W 20-13	2	0	0.0	0.0	0.0	0.0	0	0	0	0	0	0
10/08	Cin	W 19-16	5	2	0.0	0.0	0.0	0.0	1	40	3	0	0	0
10/15	Min	W 20-17	7	2	0.0	0.0	0.0	0.0	0	0	0	0	1	1
10/22	Atl	L 21-24	6	3	0.0	0.0	0.0	0.0	0	0	2	0	0	0
10/29	@Hou	L 7-19	4	0	0.0	0.0	0.0	0.0	0	0	0	0	0	0
11/12	@Det	L 24-27	3	2	0.0	0.0	0.0	0.0	0	0	1	0	0	0
11/19	Jac	W 17-16	5	1	0.0	0.0	0.0	0.0	1	15	1	0	0	0
11/26	@GB	L 13-35	6	1	0.0	0.0	0.0	0.0	0	0	1	0	0	0
12/03	@Min	L 17-31	3	1	0.0	0.0	0.0	0.0	2	26	3	0	0	0
12/10	GB	W 13-10	4	0	0.0	0.0	0.0	0.0	0	0	0	0	0	0
12/17	@Chi	L 10-31	-	-	-	-	-	-	-	-	-	-	-	-
12/23	Det	L 10-37	9	2	0.0	0.0	1.0	3.0	0	0	1	0	0	0

Tony McCoy
Indianapolis Colts – DT

1995 Defensive Splits

	G	Tk	Ast	Sack	Yds	Stuff	Yds	Int	Yds	PD	TD
Total	16	50	18	2.5	15.5	6.5	11.5	0	0	1	0
vs. Playoff	6	11	10	0.0	0.0	3.0	7.0	0	0	0	0
vs. Non-Playoff	10	39	8	2.5	15.5	3.5	4.5	0	0	1	0
vs. Own Division	8	28	10	2.5	15.5	5.5	9.0	0	0	0	0
Home	8	26	12	1.0	6.0	4.0	6.5	0	0	0	0
Away	8	24	6	1.5	9.5	2.5	5.0	0	0	1	0
Games 1-8	8	27	8	1.0	6.0	3.5	8.5	0	0	0	0
Games 9-16	8	23	10	1.5	9.5	3.0	3.0	0	0	1	0
September	3	9	2	0.0	0.0	0.5	0.5	0	0	0	0
October	5	18	6	1.0	6.0	3.0	8.0	0	0	0	0
November	4	13	7	1.5	9.5	2.0	2.0	0	0	1	0
December	4	10	3	0.0	0.0	1.0	1.0	0	0	0	0
Grass	5	16	3	1.5	9.5	2.5	5.0	0	0	0	0
Turf	11	34	15	1.0	6.0	4.0	6.5	0	0	1	0
Indoor	9	30	13	1.0	6.0	4.0	6.5	0	0	1	0
Outdoor	7	20	5	1.5	9.5	2.5	5.0	0	0	0	0

Game Logs

Date	Opp	Result	Tk	Ast	Sack	Yds	Stuff	Yds	Int	Yds	PD	FF	FR	TD
09/03	Cin	L 21-24	5	0	0.0	0.0	0.5	0.5	0	0	0	0	0	0
09/10	@NYA	W 27-24	4	0	0.0	0.0	0.0	0.0	0	0	0	1	0	0
09/17	@Buf	L 14-20	0	2	0.0	0.0	0.0	0.0	0	0	0	0	0	0
10/01	StL	W 21-18	1	2	0.0	0.0	0.0	0.0	0	0	0	0	0	0
10/08	@Mia	W 27-24	3	0	0.0	0.0	1.5	4.0	0	0	0	0	0	0
10/15	SF	W 18-17	2	3	0.0	0.0	0.5	2.0	0	0	0	0	0	0
10/22	@Oak	L 17-30	5	0	0.0	0.0	0.0	0.0	0	0	0	1	0	0
10/29	NYA	W 17-10	7	1	1.0	6.0	1.0	2.0	0	0	0	0	0	0
11/05	Buf	L 10-16	3	2	0.0	0.0	1.0	1.0	0	0	0	0	0	0
11/12	@NO	L 14-17	4	1	0.0	0.0	0.0	0.0	0	0	1	0	0	0
11/19	@NE	W 24-10	4	2	1.5	9.5	1.0	1.0	0	0	0	0	0	0
11/26	Mia	W 36-28	2	2	0.0	0.0	0.0	0.0	0	0	0	0	0	0
12/03	@Car	L 10-13	3	0	0.0	0.0	0.0	0.0	0	0	0	0	0	0
12/10	@Jac	W 41-31	1	1	0.0	0.0	0.0	0.0	0	0	0	0	0	0
12/17	SD	L 24-27	1	1	0.0	0.0	0.0	0.0	0	0	0	0	0	0
12/23	NE	W 10-7	5	1	0.0	0.0	1.0	1.0	0	0	0	0	0	0

Ed McDaniel

Minnesota Vikings – LB

1995 Defensive Splits

	G	Tk	Ast	Sack	Yds	Stuff	Yds	Int	Yds	PD	TD
Total	16	89	30	4.5	36.5	18.5	39.5	1	3	4	0
vs. Playoff	7	42	12	2.0	12.0	8.5	24.0	1	3	2	0
vs. Non-Playoff	9	47	18	2.5	24.5	10.0	15.5	0	0	2	0
vs. Own Division	8	49	21	2.5	15.5	12.0	20.5	1	3	3	0
Home	8	43	20	2.5	24.5	9.0	18.0	1	3	1	0
Away	8	46	10	2.0	12.0	9.5	21.5	0	0	3	0
Games 1-8	8	53	19	3.0	23.0	11.5	26.5	1	3	4	0
Games 9-16	8	36	11	1.5	13.5	7.0	13.0	0	0	0	0
September	4	24	7	0.0	0.0	5.0	12.5	1	3	3	0
October	4	29	12	3.0	23.0	6.5	14.0	0	0	1	0
November	4	18	8	0.0	0.0	4.0	8.0	0	0	0	0
December	4	18	3	1.5	13.5	3.0	5.0	0	0	0	0
Grass	5	26	7	2.0	12.0	4.5	8.5	0	0	2	0
Turf	11	63	23	2.5	24.5	14.0	31.0	1	3	2	0
Indoor	9	48	22	2.5	24.5	11.0	23.0	1	3	1	0
Outdoor	7	41	8	2.0	12.0	7.5	16.5	0	0	3	0

Game Logs

Date	Opp	Result	Tk	Ast	Sack	Yds	Stuff	Yds	Int	Yds	PD	FF	FR	TD
09/03	@Chi	L 14-31	8	2	0.0	0.0	1.5	1.5	0	0	1	0	0	0
09/10	Det	W 20-10	3	2	0.0	0.0	1.0	1.0	1	3	1	0	0	0
09/17	Dal	L 17-23	8	2	0.0	0.0	1.5	6.0	0	0	0	0	1	0
09/24	@Pit	W 44-24	5	1	0.0	0.0	1.0	4.0	0	0	1	0	0	0
10/08	Hou	W 23-17	7	4	1.0	11.0	1.0	4.0	0	0	0	1	0	0
10/15	@TB	L 17-20	4	4	0.0	0.0	2.0	2.0	0	0	1	1	0	0
10/22	@GB	L 21-38	7	1	2.0	12.0	1.0	5.0	0	0	1	0	0	0
10/30	Chi	L 6-14	11	3	0.0	0.0	2.5	3.0	0	0	0	2	0	0
11/05	GB	W 27-24	10	4	0.0	0.0	2.0	3.0	0	0	0	0	0	0
11/12	@Ari	W 30-24	3	0	0.0	0.0	0.0	0.0	0	0	0	0	0	0
11/19	NO	L 43-24	0	2	0.0	0.0	0.0	0.0	0	0	0	0	0	0
11/23	@Det	L 38-44	5	2	0.0	0.0	2.0	5.0	0	0	0	0	0	0
12/03	TB	W 31-17	1	3	0.5	3.5	0.0	0.0	0	0	0	0	0	0
12/09	Cle	W 27-11	3	0	1.0	10.0	1.0	1.0	0	0	1	0	0	0
12/18	@SF	L 30-37	4	0	0.0	0.0	0.0	0.0	0	0	0	0	0	0
12/24	@Cin	L 24-27	10	0	0.0	0.0	2.0	4.0	0	0	0	0	0	0

Terry McDaniel

Oakland Raiders – CB

1995 Defensive Splits

	G	Tk	Ast	Sack	Yds	Stuff	Yds	Int	Yds	PD	TD
Total	16	51	5	0.0	0.0	0.5	1.5	6	46	13	1
vs. Playoff	8	29	2	0.0	0.0	0.5	1.5	2	42	4	1
vs. Non-Playoff	8	22	3	0.0	0.0	0.0	0.0	4	4	9	0
vs. Own Division	8	26	3	0.0	0.0	0.5	1.5	3	42	5	1
Home	8	30	3	0.0	0.0	0.5	1.5	4	42	7	1
Away	8	21	2	0.0	0.0	0.0	0.0	2	4	6	0
Games 1-8	8	26	5	0.0	0.0	0.5	1.5	2	0	4	0
Games 9-16	8	25	0	0.0	0.0	0.0	0.0	4	46	9	1
September	4	13	2	0.0	0.0	0.5	1.5	1	0	2	0
October	4	13	3	0.0	0.0	0.0	0.0	1	0	2	0
November	4	11	0	0.0	0.0	0.0	0.0	2	4	6	0
December	4	14	0	0.0	0.0	0.0	0.0	2	42	3	1
Grass	12	41	5	0.0	0.0	0.5	1.5	4	42	8	1
Turf	4	10	0	0.0	0.0	0.0	0.0	2	4	5	0
Indoor	1	3	0	0.0	0.0	0.0	0.0	0	0	0	0
Outdoor	15	48	5	0.0	0.0	0.5	1.5	6	46	13	1

Game Logs

Date	Opp	Result	Tk	Ast	Sack	Yds	Stuff	Yds	Int	Yds	PD	FF	FR	TD
09/03	SD	W 17-7	4	1	0.0	0.0	1.5	1.5	0	0	0	0	0	0
09/10	@Was	W 20-8	2	1	0.0	0.0	0.0	0.0	0	0	1	0	0	0
09/17	@KC	L 17-23	3	0	0.0	0.0	0.0	0.0	0	0	0	0	0	0
09/24	Phi	W 48-17	4	0	0.0	0.0	0.0	0.0	1	0	1	0	0	0
10/01	@NYA	W 47-10	3	0	0.0	0.0	0.0	0.0	0	0	0	0	0	0
10/08	Sea	W 34-14	4	1	0.0	0.0	0.0	0.0	1	0	2	0	0	0
10/16	@Den	L 0-27	2	1	0.0	0.0	0.0	0.0	0	0	0	0	0	0
10/22	Ind	W 30-17	4	1	0.0	0.0	0.0	0.0	0	0	0	0	0	0
11/05	@Cin	W 20-17	1	0	0.0	0.0	0.0	0.0	2	4	3	0	0	0
11/12	@NYN	W 17-13	0	0	0.0	0.0	0.0	0.0	0	0	2	0	0	0
11/19	Dal	L 21-34	3	0	0.0	0.0	0.0	0.0	0	0	1	0	0	0
11/27	@SD	L 6-12	4	0	0.0	0.0	0.0	0.0	0	0	0	0	0	0
12/03	KC	L 23-29	2	0	0.0	0.0	0.0	0.0	1	42	2	0	0	1
12/10	Pit	L 10-29	5	0	0.0	0.0	0.0	0.0	0	0	0	0	0	0
12/17	@Sea	L 10-44	3	0	0.0	0.0	0.0	0.0	0	0	0	0	0	0
12/24	Den	L 28-31	4	0	0.0	0.0	0.0	0.0	1	0	1	0	0	0

Ricardo McDonald

Cincinnati Bengals – LB

1995 Defensive Splits

	G	Tk	Ast	Sack	Yds	Stuff	Yds	Int	Yds	PD	TD
Total	16	46	17	5.0	17.0	1.5	2.5	0	0	1	0
vs. Playoff	5	16	8	1.0	0.0	0.0	0.0	0	0	0	0
vs. Non-Playoff	11	30	9	4.0	17.0	1.5	2.5	0	0	1	0
vs. Own Division	8	22	10	2.0	6.0	1.5	2.5	0	0	0	0
Home	8	21	5	2.0	6.0	0.5	1.5	0	0	0	0
Away	8	25	12	3.0	11.0	1.0	1.0	0	0	1	0
Games 1-8	8	23	7	4.0	17.0	0.5	1.5	0	0	0	0
Games 9-16	8	23	10	1.0	0.0	1.0	1.0	0	0	1	0
September	4	11	3	1.0	6.0	0.5	1.5	0	0	0	0
October	4	12	4	3.0	11.0	0.0	0.0	0	0	0	0
November	4	12	5	1.0	0.0	1.0	1.0	0	0	1	0
December	4	11	5	0.0	0.0	0.0	0.0	0	0	0	0
Grass	4	14	6	3.0	11.0	0.0	0.0	0	0	0	0
Turf	12	32	11	2.0	6.0	1.5	2.5	0	0	1	0
Indoor	3	8	4	0.0	0.0	1.0	1.0	0	0	1	0
Outdoor	13	38	13	5.0	17.0	0.5	1.5	0	0	0	0

Game Logs

Date	Opp	Result	Tk	Ast	Sack	Yds	Stuff	Yds	Int	Yds	PD	FF	FR	TD
09/03	@Ind	W 24-21	6	1	0.0	0.0	0.0	0.0	0	0	0	0	0	0
09/10	Jac	W 24-17	3	0	1.0	6.0	0.0	0.0	0	0	0	0	1	0
09/17	@Sea	L 21-24	1	0	0.0	0.0	0.0	0.0	0	0	0	0	0	0
09/24	Hou	L 28-38	1	2	0.0	0.0	0.5	1.5	0	0	0	0	0	0
10/01	Mia	L 23-26	2	1	0.0	0.0	0.0	0.0	0	0	0	0	0	0
10/08	@TB	L 16-19	3	1	3.0	11.0	0.0	0.0	0	0	0	1	0	0
10/19	@Pit	W 27-9	3	2	0.0	0.0	0.0	0.0	0	0	0	0	0	0
10/29	Cle	L 26-29	4	0	0.0	0.0	0.0	0.0	0	0	0	0	0	0
11/05	Oak	L 17-20	6	0	0.0	0.0	0.0	0.0	0	0	0	0	0	0
11/12	@Hou	W 32-25	1	3	0.0	0.0	1.0	1.0	0	0	1	0	0	0
11/19	Pit	L 31-49	2	1	1.0	0.0	0.0	0.0	0	0	0	0	0	0
11/26	@Jac	W 17-13	3	1	0.0	0.0	0.0	0.0	0	0	0	0	0	0
12/03	@GB	L 10-24	3	3	0.0	0.0	0.0	0.0	0	0	0	0	0	0
12/10	Chi	W 16-10	3	0	0.0	0.0	0.0	0.0	0	0	0	0	0	0
12/17	@Cle	L 10-26	5	1	0.0	0.0	0.0	0.0	0	0	0	0	0	0
12/24	Min	W 27-24	0	1	0.0	0.0	0.0	0.0	0	0	0	0	0	0

Tim McDonald
San Francisco 49ers – S

1995 Defensive Splits

	G	Tk	Ast	Sack	Yds	Stuff	Yds	Int	Yds	PD	TD
Total	16	61	14	0.0	0.0	3.5	4.5	4	135	17	2
vs. Playoff	7	37	7	0.0	0.0	1.5	1.5	1	13	7	1
vs. Non-Playoff	9	24	7	0.0	0.0	2.0	3.0	3	122	10	1
vs. Own Division	8	20	4	0.0	0.0	1.0	2.0	4	135	7	2
Home	8	24	5	0.0	0.0	1.0	1.0	2	48	10	1
Away	8	37	9	0.0	0.0	2.5	3.5	2	87	7	1
Games 1-8	8	32	7	0.0	0.0	3.5	4.5	2	65	10	2
Games 9-16	8	29	7	0.0	0.0	0.0	0.0	2	70	7	0
September	4	19	5	0.0	0.0	3.0	4.0	2	65	8	2
October	4	13	2	0.0	0.0	0.5	0.5	0	0	2	0
November	4	18	3	0.0	0.0	0.0	0.0	1	35	3	0
December	4	11	4	0.0	0.0	0.0	0.0	1	35	4	0
Grass	10	31	7	0.0	0.0	1.0	1.0	3	83	11	1
Turf	6	30	7	0.0	0.0	2.5	3.5	1	52	6	1
Indoor	4	20	5	0.0	0.0	2.5	3.5	1	52	4	1
Outdoor	12	41	9	0.0	0.0	1.0	1.0	3	83	13	1

Game Logs

Date	Opp	Result	Tk	Ast	Sack	Yds	Stuff	Yds	Int	Yds	PD	FF	FR	TD
09/03	@NO	W 24-22	2	1	0.0	0.0	1.0	2.0	1	52	2	1	0	1
09/10	Atl	W 41-10	3	0	0.0	0.0	1.0	1.0	1	13	1	0	0	1
09/17	NE	W 28-3	5	2	0.0	0.0	1.0	1.0	0	0	4	0	0	0
09/25	@Det	L 24-27	9	2	0.0	0.0	1.0	1.0	0	0	1	0	0	0
10/01	NYN	W 20-6	4	0	0.0	0.0	0.0	0.0	0	0	1	0	0	0
10/15	@Ind	L 17-18	5	2	0.0	0.0	0.5	0.5	0	0	0	0	0	0
10/22	@StL	W 44-10	2	0	0.0	0.0	0.0	0.0	0	0	0	0	0	0
10/29	NO	L 7-11	2	0	0.0	0.0	0.0	0.0	0	0	1	0	0	0
11/05	Car	L 7-13	1	0	0.0	0.0	0.0	0.0	0	0	0	0	0	0
11/12	@Dal	W 38-20	8	2	0.0	0.0	0.0	0.0	0	0	2	0	0	0
11/20	@Mia	W 44-20	5	0	0.0	0.0	0.0	0.0	0	0	0	0	0	0
11/26	StL	W 41-13	4	1	0.0	0.0	0.0	0.0	1	35	1	0	0	0
12/03	Buf	W 27-17	3	1	0.0	0.0	0.0	0.0	0	0	2	0	0	0
12/10	@Car	W 31-10	2	2	0.0	0.0	0.0	0.0	1	35	1	0	0	0
12/18	Min	W 37-30	2	1	0.0	0.0	0.0	0.0	0	0	0	0	0	0
12/24	@Atl	L 27-28	4	0	0.0	0.0	1.0	1.0	0	0	1	0	0	0

Willie McGinest
New England Patriots – LB

1995 Defensive Splits

	G	Tk	Ast	Sack	Yds	Stuff	Yds	Int	Yds	PD	TD
Total	16	70	18	11.0	96.0	9.0	20.0	0	0	6	0
vs. Playoff	10	45	5	8.0	65.0	5.5	9.5	0	0	3	0
vs. Non-Playoff	6	25	13	3.0	31.0	3.5	10.5	0	0	3	0
vs. Own Division	8	42	6	9.0	81.0	4.5	7.5	0	0	0	0
Home	8	36	14	5.0	46.0	6.5	16.5	0	0	3	0
Away	8	34	4	6.0	50.0	2.5	3.5	0	0	3	0
Games 1-8	8	32	11	3.0	20.0	2.5	4.0	0	0	4	0
Games 9-16	8	38	7	8.0	76.0	6.5	16.0	0	0	2	0
September	3	9	4	0.0	0.0	0.5	0.5	0	0	1	0
October	5	23	7	3.0	20.0	2.0	3.5	0	0	3	0
November	4	20	5	3.0	24.0	3.0	5.0	0	0	0	0
December	4	18	2	5.0	52.0	3.5	11.0	0	0	2	0
Grass	11	46	15	7.0	62.0	6.5	16.5	0	0	3	0
Turf	5	24	3	4.0	34.0	2.5	3.5	0	0	3	0
Indoor	2	9	0	2.0	16.0	0.5	0.5	0	0	1	0
Outdoor	14	61	18	9.0	80.0	8.5	19.5	0	0	5	0

Game Logs

Date	Opp	Result	Tk	Ast	Sack	Yds	Stuff	Yds	Int	Yds	PD	FF	FR	TD
09/03	Cle	W 17-14	1	3	0.0	0.0	0.5	0.5	0	0	1	0	0	0
09/10	Mia	L 3-20	4	1	0.0	0.0	0.0	0.0	0	0	0	0	0	0
09/17	@SF	L 3-28	4	0	0.0	0.0	0.0	0.0	0	0	0	0	0	0
10/01	@Atl	L 17-30	4	0	0.0	0.0	0.0	0.0	0	0	1	1	0	0
10/08	Den	L 3-37	5	1	1.0	5.0	0.0	0.0	0	0	1	0	0	0
10/15	@KC	L 26-31	1	0	0.0	0.0	0.0	0.0	0	0	0	0	0	0
10/23	Buf	W 27-14	8	0	2.0	15.0	1.0	2.0	0	0	0	0	0	0
10/29	Car	L 17-20	5	6	0.0	0.0	1.0	1.5	0	0	1	0	0	0
11/05	@NYA	W 20-7	6	1	0.0	0.0	0.0	0.0	0	0	0	0	0	0
11/12	@Mia	W 34-17	5	1	2.0	16.0	0.0	0.0	0	0	1	0	0	0
11/19	Ind	L 10-24	5	1	0.0	0.0	2.0	4.0	0	0	0	0	0	0
11/26	@Buf	W 35-25	4	2	1.0	8.0	1.0	1.0	0	0	1	0	0	0
12/03	NO	L 17-31	3	2	0.0	0.0	2.0	8.5	0	0	0	0	0	0
12/10	NYA	W 31-28	5	0	2.0	26.0	0.0	0.0	0	0	1	0	0	0
12/16	@Pit	L 27-41	5	0	1.0	10.0	1.0	2.0	0	0	2	0	0	0
12/23	@Ind	L 7-10	5	0	2.0	16.0	0.5	0.5	0	0	0	0	0	0

Chester McGlockton
Oakland Raiders – DT

1995 Defensive Splits

	G	Tk	Ast	Sack	Yds	Stuff	Yds	Int	Yds	PD	TD
Total	16	47	8	7.5	51.0	11.0	20.0	0	0	4	0
vs. Playoff	8	22	3	4.5	38.0	7.0	14.0	0	0	1	0
vs. Non-Playoff	8	25	5	3.0	13.0	4.0	6.0	0	0	3	0
vs. Own Division	8	22	5	4.0	31.0	3.0	3.0	0	0	1	0
Home	8	20	6	1.5	14.0	6.0	13.0	0	0	2	0
Away	8	27	2	6.0	37.0	5.0	7.0	0	0	2	0
Games 1-8	8	20	0	5.5	39.0	5.0	12.0	0	0	1	0
Games 9-16	8	27	8	2.0	12.0	6.0	8.0	0	0	3	0
September	4	10	0	3.0	18.0	2.0	3.0	0	0	0	0
October	4	10	0	2.5	21.0	3.0	9.0	0	0	1	0
November	4	13	1	2.0	12.0	3.0	4.0	0	0	1	0
December	4	14	7	0.0	0.0	3.0	4.0	0	0	2	0
Grass	12	36	6	6.5	48.0	9.0	17.0	0	0	2	0
Turf	4	11	2	1.0	3.0	2.0	3.0	0	0	2	0
Indoor	1	3	1	0.0	0.0	0.0	0.0	0	0	0	0
Outdoor	15	44	7	7.5	51.0	11.0	20.0	0	0	4	0

Game Logs

Date	Opp	Result	Tk	Ast	Sack	Yds	Stuff	Yds	Int	Yds	PD	FF	FR	TD
09/03	SD	W 17-7	0	0	0.0	0.0	0.0	0.0	0	0	0	0	0	0
09/10	@Was	W 20-8	5	0	1.0	3.0	1.0	2.0	0	0	0	0	0	0
09/17	@KC	L 17-23	4	0	2.0	15.0	1.0	1.0	0	0	0	1	0	0
09/24	Phi	W 48-17	1	0	0.0	0.0	0.0	0.0	0	0	0	1	1	0
10/01	@NYA	W 47-10	0	0	0.0	0.0	0.0	0.0	0	0	1	0	0	0
10/08	Sea	W 34-14	1	0	0.0	0.0	0.0	0.0	0	0	0	0	0	0
10/16	@Den	L 0-27	4	0	1.0	7.0	0.0	0.0	0	0	0	0	0	0
10/22	Ind	W 30-17	5	0	1.5	14.0	3.0	9.0	0	0	0	0	0	0
11/05	@Cin	W 20-17	5	1	0.0	0.0	1.0	1.0	0	0	0	0	1	0
11/12	@NYN	W 17-13	3	1	0.0	0.0	1.0	2.0	0	0	1	0	0	0
11/19	Dal	L 21-34	2	0	0.0	0.0	0.0	0.0	0	0	0	0	0	0
11/27	@SD	L 6-12	3	0	1.0	9.0	1.0	1.0	0	0	0	0	0	0
12/03	KC	L 23-29	3	1	0.0	0.0	0.0	0.0	0	0	0	0	0	0
12/10	Pit	L 10-29	4	2	0.0	0.0	2.0	3.0	0	0	1	0	0	0
12/17	@Sea	L 10-44	3	1	0.0	0.0	0.0	0.0	0	0	0	0	0	0
12/24	Den	L 28-31	4	3	0.0	0.0	1.0	1.0	0	0	1	0	0	0

Tim McKyer
Carolina Panthers – CB

	G	Tk	Ast	Sack	Yds	Stuff	Yds	Int	Yds	PD	TD
1995 Defensive Splits											
Total	16	57	5	0.0	0.0	0.0	0.0	3	99	19	1
vs. Playoff	6	22	0	0.0	0.0	0.0	0.0	2	99	10	1
vs. Non-Playoff	10	35	5	0.0	0.0	0.0	0.0	1	0	9	0
vs. Own Division	8	34	3	0.0	0.0	0.0	0.0	2	96	11	1
Home	8	34	1	0.0	0.0	0.0	0.0	0	0	11	0
Away	8	23	4	0.0	0.0	0.0	0.0	3	99	8	1
Games 1-8	8	28	2	0.0	0.0	0.0	0.0	1	3	5	0
Games 9-16	8	29	3	0.0	0.0	0.0	0.0	2	96	14	1
September	3	10	0	0.0	0.0	0.0	0.0	1	3	3	0
October	5	18	2	0.0	0.0	0.0	0.0	0	0	2	0
November	4	11	3	0.0	0.0	0.0	0.0	2	96	8	1
December	4	18	0	0.0	0.0	0.0	0.0	0	0	6	0
Grass	12	48	2	0.0	0.0	0.0	0.0	1	96	14	1
Turf	4	9	3	0.0	0.0	0.0	0.0	2	3	5	0
Indoor	3	9	3	0.0	0.0	0.0	0.0	1	0	3	0
Outdoor	13	48	2	0.0	0.0	0.0	0.0	2	99	16	1

Date	Opp	Result	Tk	Ast	Sack	Yds	Stuff	Yds	Int	Yds	PD	FF	FR	TD
09/03	@Atl	L 20-23	4	0	0.0	0.0	0.0	0.0	0	0	1	0	0	0
09/10	@Buf	L 9-31	0	0	0.0	0.0	0.0	0.0	1	3	2	0	0	0
09/17	StL	L 10-31	6	0	0.0	0.0	0.0	0.0	0	0	0	0	0	0
10/01	TB	L 13-20	3	1	0.0	0.0	0.0	0.0	0	0	0	0	0	0
10/08	@Chi	L 27-31	4	0	0.0	0.0	0.0	0.0	0	0	0	0	0	0
10/15	NYA	W 26-15	2	0	0.0	0.0	0.0	0.0	0	0	1	0	0	0
10/22	NO	W 20-3	5	0	0.0	0.0	0.0	0.0	0	0	1	0	1	0
10/29	@NE	W 20-17	4	1	0.0	0.0	0.0	0.0	0	0	0	0	1	0
11/05	@SF	W 13-7	3	0	0.0	0.0	0.0	0.0	1	96	2	0	0	1
11/12	@StL	L 17-28	3	0	0.0	0.0	0.0	0.0	1	0	1	0	0	0
11/19	Ari	W 27-7	3	0	0.0	0.0	0.0	0.0	0	0	4	0	0	0
11/26	@NO	L 26-34	2	3	0.0	0.0	0.0	0.0	0	0	1	0	0	0
12/03	Ind	W 13-10	4	0	0.0	0.0	0.0	0.0	0	0	0	0	0	0
12/10	SF	L 10-31	8	0	0.0	0.0	0.0	0.0	0	0	3	0	0	0
12/17	Atl	W 21-17	3	0	0.0	0.0	0.0	0.0	0	0	2	0	0	0
12/24	@Was	L 17-20	3	0	0.0	0.0	0.0	0.0	0	0	1	0	0	0

Mark McMillian
Philadelphia Eagles – CB

	G	Tk	Ast	Sack	Yds	Stuff	Yds	Int	Yds	PD	TD
1995 Defensive Splits											
Total	16	63	0	0.0	0.0	0.0	0.0	3	27	21	0
vs. Playoff	3	10	0	0.0	0.0	0.0	0.0	0	0	2	0
vs. Non-Playoff	13	53	0	0.0	0.0	0.0	0.0	3	27	19	0
vs. Own Division	8	25	0	0.0	0.0	0.0	0.0	1	7	12	0
Home	8	22	0	0.0	0.0	0.0	0.0	2	26	12	0
Away	8	41	0	0.0	0.0	0.0	0.0	1	1	9	0
Games 1-8	8	31	0	0.0	0.0	0.0	0.0	2	20	10	0
Games 9-16	8	32	0	0.0	0.0	0.0	0.0	1	7	11	0
September	4	15	0	0.0	0.0	0.0	0.0	1	1	3	0
October	4	16	0	0.0	0.0	0.0	0.0	1	19	7	0
November	4	12	0	0.0	0.0	0.0	0.0	1	7	4	0
December	4	20	0	0.0	0.0	0.0	0.0	0	0	7	0
Grass	4	16	0	0.0	0.0	0.0	0.0	1	1	4	0
Turf	12	47	0	0.0	0.0	0.0	0.0	2	26	17	0
Indoor	2	14	0	0.0	0.0	0.0	0.0	0	0	4	0
Outdoor	14	49	0	0.0	0.0	0.0	0.0	3	27	17	0

Date	Opp	Result	Tk	Ast	Sack	Yds	Stuff	Yds	Int	Yds	PD	FF	FR	TD
09/03	TB	L 6-21	4	0	0.0	0.0	0.0	0.0	0	0	1	0	0	0
09/10	@Ari	W 31-19	3	0	0.0	0.0	0.0	0.0	0	0	1	0	0	0
09/17	SD	L 21-27	2	0	0.0	0.0	0.0	0.0	0	0	0	0	0	0
09/24	@Oak	L 17-48	6	0	0.0	0.0	0.0	0.0	1	1	1	0	0	0
10/01	@NO	W 15-10	3	0	0.0	0.0	0.0	0.0	0	0	2	0	0	0
10/08	Was	W 37-34	3	0	0.0	0.0	0.0	0.0	0	0	2	0	0	0
10/15	@NYN	W 17-14	4	0	0.0	0.0	0.0	0.0	0	0	0	0	0	0
10/29	StL	W 20-9	6	0	0.0	0.0	0.0	0.0	1	19	2	0	0	0
11/06	@Dal	L 12-34	7	0	0.0	0.0	0.0	0.0	0	0	0	0	1	0
11/12	Den	W 31-13	2	0	0.0	0.0	0.0	0.0	0	0	0	0	0	0
11/19	NYN	W 28-19	0	0	0.0	0.0	0.0	0.0	1	7	3	0	0	0
11/26	@Was	W 14-7	3	0	0.0	0.0	0.0	0.0	0	0	1	0	0	0
12/03	@Sea	L 14-26	11	0	0.0	0.0	0.0	0.0	0	0	2	0	0	0
12/10	Dal	W 20-17	1	0	0.0	0.0	0.0	0.0	0	0	2	0	0	0
12/17	Ari	W 21-20	4	0	0.0	0.0	0.0	0.0	0	0	2	0	0	0
12/24	@Chi	L 14-20	4	0	0.0	0.0	0.0	0.0	0	0	1	0	1	0

Ryan McNeil
Detroit Lions – CB

	G	Tk	Ast	Sack	Yds	Stuff	Yds	Int	Yds	PD	TD
1995 Defensive Splits											
Total	16	69	17	0.0	0.0	1.0	1.0	2	26	13	0
vs. Playoff	5	27	9	0.0	0.0	1.0	1.0	1	21	5	0
vs. Non-Playoff	11	42	8	0.0	0.0	0.0	0.0	1	5	8	0
vs. Own Division	8	34	7	0.0	0.0	1.0	1.0	0	0	4	0
Home	8	36	14	0.0	0.0	0.0	0.0	1	5	8	0
Away	8	33	3	0.0	0.0	1.0	1.0	1	21	5	0
Games 1-8	8	37	13	0.0	0.0	0.0	0.0	1	21	7	0
Games 9-16	8	32	4	0.0	0.0	0.0	0.0	1	5	6	0
September	4	19	5	0.0	0.0	0.0	0.0	1	21	4	0
October	4	18	8	0.0	0.0	1.0	1.0	0	0	3	0
November	4	19	1	0.0	0.0	0.0	0.0	0	0	2	0
December	4	13	3	0.0	0.0	0.0	0.0	1	5	4	0
Grass	4	15	1	0.0	0.0	1.0	1.0	0	0	1	0
Turf	12	54	16	0.0	0.0	0.0	0.0	2	26	12	0
Indoor	11	46	15	0.0	0.0	0.0	0.0	1	5	10	0
Outdoor	5	23	2	0.0	0.0	1.0	1.0	1	21	3	0

Date	Opp	Result	Tk	Ast	Sack	Yds	Stuff	Yds	Int	Yds	PD	FF	FR	TD
09/03	@Pit	L 20-23	8	1	0.0	0.0	0.0	0.0	1	21	2	0	0	0
09/10	@Min	L 10-20	2	0	0.0	0.0	0.0	0.0	0	0	1	0	1	0
09/17	Ari	L 17-20	4	1	0.0	0.0	0.0	0.0	0	0	1	0	0	0
09/25	SF	W 27-24	5	3	0.0	0.0	0.0	0.0	0	0	1	0	0	0
10/08	Cle	W 38-20	5	3	0.0	0.0	0.0	0.0	0	0	0	0	0	0
10/15	@GB	L 21-30	6	1	0.0	0.0	1.0	1.0	0	0	0	0	0	0
10/22	@Was	L 30-36	4	0	0.0	0.0	0.0	0.0	0	0	1	0	0	0
10/29	GB	W 24-16	3	4	0.0	0.0	0.0	0.0	0	0	1	0	0	0
11/05	@Atl	L 23-34	5	0	0.0	0.0	0.0	0.0	0	0	1	0	0	0
11/12	TB	W 27-24	9	1	0.0	0.0	0.0	0.0	0	0	0	0	0	0
11/19	@Chi	W 24-17	0	0	0.0	0.0	0.0	0.0	0	0	1	0	0	0
11/23	Min	W 44-38	5	0	0.0	0.0	0.0	0.0	0	0	1	0	0	0
12/04	Chi	W 27-7	4	1	0.0	0.0	0.0	0.0	0	0	1	0	0	0
12/10	@Hou	W 24-17	3	1	0.0	0.0	0.0	0.0	0	0	0	0	1	0
12/17	Jac	W 44-0	1	1	0.0	0.0	0.0	0.0	1	5	3	0	0	0
12/23	@TB	W 37-10	5	0	0.0	0.0	0.0	0.0	0	0	0	0	0	0

Sam Mills
Carolina Panthers – LB

1995 Defensive Splits

	G	Tk	Ast	Sack	Yds	Stuff	Yds	Int	Yds	PD	TD
Total	16	87	24	4.5	39.0	2.5	6.0	5	58	8	1
vs. Playoff	6	35	10	1.5	10.0	0.5	1.5	3	22	6	0
vs. Non-Playoff	10	52	14	3.0	29.0	2.0	4.5	2	36	2	1
vs. Own Division	8	45	12	3.0	28.0	0.5	0.5	3	9	5	0
Home	8	35	12	3.5	30.0	0	0	4	45	5	1
Away	8	52	12	1.0	9.0	2.5	6.0	1	13	3	0
Games 1-8	8	43	12	2.0	20.0	2.0	5.5	3	49	4	1
Games 9-16	8	44	12	2.5	19.0	0.5	0.5	2	9	4	0
September	3	14	3	1.0	11.0	0.5	1.5	1	13	2	0
October	5	29	9	1.0	9.0	1.5	4.0	2	36	2	1
November	4	22	5	1.0	9.0	0.5	0.5	0	0	1	0
December	4	22	7	1.5	10.0	0	0	2	9	3	0
Grass	12	61	16	3.5	30.0	1.5	4.0	4	45	6	1
Turf	4	26	8	1.0	9.0	1.0	2.0	1	13	2	0
Indoor	3	20	5	1.0	9.0	0.5	0.5	0	0	0	0
Outdoor	13	67	19	3.5	30.0	2.0	5.5	5	58	8	1

Game Logs

Date	Opp	Result	Tk	Ast	Sack	Yds	Stuff	Yds	Int	Yds	PD	FF	FR	TD
09/03	@Atl	L 20-23	6	0	0.0	0.0	0.0	0.0	0	0	0	0	0	0
09/10	@Buf	L 9-31	6	3	0.0	0.0	0.5	1.5	1	13	2	0	0	0
09/17	StL	L 10-31	2	0	1.0	11.0	0.0	0.0	0	0	0	0	0	0
10/01	TB	L 13-20	4	3	0.0	0.0	0.0	0.0	0	0	0	0	0	0
10/08	@Chi	L 27-31	9	0	0.0	0.0	1.0	1.0	0	0	0	0	0	0
10/15	NYA	W 26-15	3	1	1.0	9.0	0.0	0.0	1	36	1	0	0	1
10/22	NO	W 20-3	7	1	0.0	0.0	0.0	0.0	1	0	1	0	0	0
10/29	@NE	W 20-17	6	4	0.0	0.0	0.5	3.0	0	0	0	2	0	0
11/05	@SF	W 13-7	6	0	0.0	0.0	0.0	0.0	0	0	1	1	2	0
11/12	@StL	L 17-28	5	2	1.0	9.0	0.5	0.5	0	0	0	0	0	0
11/19	Ari	W 27-7	2	0	0.0	0.0	0.0	0.0	0	0	0	0	0	0
11/26	@NO	L 26-34	9	3	0.0	0.0	0.0	0.0	0	0	0	1	0	0
12/03	Ind	W 13-10	7	1	0.5	2.0	0.0	0.0	0	0	0	0	0	0
12/10	SF	L 10-31	5	3	1.0	8.0	0.0	0.0	1	3	1	1	1	0
12/17	Atl	W 21-17	5	3	0.0	0.0	0.0	0.0	1	6	2	1	0	0
12/24	@Was	L 17-20	5	0	0.0	0.0	0.0	0.0	0	0	0	0	0	0

Stevon Moore
Cleveland Browns – S

1995 Defensive Splits

	G	Tk	Ast	Sack	Yds	Stuff	Yds	Int	Yds	PD	TD
Total	16	79	13	1.0	8.0	2.5	5.0	5	55	12	0
vs. Playoff	7	37	7	0.0	0.0	2.0	4.5	0	0	3	0
vs. Non-Playoff	9	42	6	1.0	8.0	0.5	0.5	5	55	9	0
vs. Own Division	8	26	6	0.0	0.0	1.5	4.0	3	36	7	0
Home	8	45	5	1.0	8.0	1.5	4.0	1	19	7	0
Away	8	34	8	0.0	0.0	1.0	1.0	4	36	5	0
Games 1-8	8	42	7	1.0	8.0	1.5	1.5	4	55	7	0
Games 9-16	8	37	6	0.0	0.0	1.0	3.5	1	0	5	0
September	4	19	5	1.0	8.0	1.5	1.5	4	55	6	0
October	4	23	2	0.0	0.0	0.0	0.0	0	0	1	0
November	4	19	4	0.0	0.0	1.0	3.5	0	0	2	0
December	4	18	2	0.0	0.0	0.0	0.0	1	0	3	0
Grass	11	56	6	1.0	8.0	1.5	4.0	1	19	7	0
Turf	5	23	7	0.0	0.0	1.0	1.0	4	36	5	0
Indoor	3	19	5	0.0	0.0	0.5	0.5	4	36	3	0
Outdoor	13	60	8	1.0	8.0	2.0	4.5	1	19	9	0

Game Logs

Date	Opp	Result	Tk	Ast	Sack	Yds	Stuff	Yds	Int	Yds	PD	FF	FR	TD
09/03	@NE	L 14-17	3	1	0.0	0.0	0.0	0.0	0	0	0	0	0	0
09/10	TB	W 22-6	8	1	1.0	8.0	0.0	0.0	1	19	2	0	0	0
09/17	@Hou	W 14-7	5	2	0.0	0.0	0.5	0.5	3	36	2	0	0	0
09/24	KC	W 35-17	3	1	0.0	0.0	1.0	1.0	0	0	2	0	0	0
10/02	Buf	L 19-22	9	1	0.0	0.0	0.0	0.0	0	0	0	0	0	0
10/08	@Det	L 20-38	5	1	0.0	0.0	0.0	0.0	0	0	0	0	0	0
10/22	Jac	L 15-23	7	0	0.0	0.0	0.0	0.0	0	0	0	0	0	0
10/29	@Cin	W 29-26	2	0	0.0	0.0	0.0	0.0	0	0	1	0	0	0
11/05	Hou	L 10-37	6	0	0.0	0.0	0.0	0.0	0	0	1	0	0	0
11/13	@Pit	L 3-20	2	2	0.0	0.0	0.5	0.5	0	0	0	0	0	0
11/19	GB	L 20-31	9	0	0.0	0.0	0.0	0.0	0	0	0	0	0	0
11/26	Pit	L 17-20	2	0	0.0	0.0	0.5	3.0	0	0	0	0	0	0
12/03	@SD	L 13-31	7	0	0.0	0.0	0.0	0.0	0	0	0	0	0	0
12/09	@Min	L 11-27	9	2	0.0	0.0	0.0	0.0	1	0	1	0	0	0
12/17	Cin	W 26-10	1	0	0.0	0.0	0.0	0.0	0	0	2	0	0	0
12/24	@Jac	L 21-24	1	0	0.0	0.0	0.0	0.0	0	0	0	0	0	0

Winston Moss
Seattle Seahawks – LB

1995 Defensive Splits

	G	Tk	Ast	Sack	Yds	Stuff	Yds	Int	Yds	PD	TD
Total	16	65	23	2.0	8.0	3.5	9.5	1	0	5	0
vs. Playoff	6	30	7	0.0	0.0	2.0	7.0	0	0	0	0
vs. Non-Playoff	10	35	16	2.0	8.0	1.5	2.5	1	0	5	0
vs. Own Division	8	34	11	1.0	6.0	2.0	7.0	0	0	1	0
Home	8	23	17	1.0	2.0	0.0	0.0	0	0	3	0
Away	8	42	6	1.0	6.0	3.5	9.5	1	0	2	0
Games 1-8	8	35	13	0.0	0.0	0.5	0.5	0	0	1	0
Games 9-16	8	30	10	2.0	8.0	3.0	9.0	1	0	4	0
September	3	11	5	0.0	0.0	0.0	0.0	0	0	0	0
October	5	24	8	0.0	0.0	0.5	0.5	0	0	1	0
November	4	11	7	1.0	2.0	1.0	2.0	1	0	3	0
December	4	19	3	1.0	6.0	2.0	7.0	0	0	1	0
Grass	7	37	4	1.0	6.0	3.5	9.5	1	0	2	0
Turf	0	28	19	1.0	2.0	0.0	0.0	0	0	3	0
Indoor	8	23	17	1.0	2.0	0.0	0.0	0	0	3	0
Outdoor	8	42	6	1.0	6.0	3.5	9.5	1	0	2	0

Game Logs

Date	Opp	Result	Tk	Ast	Sack	Yds	Stuff	Yds	Int	Yds	PD	FF	FR	TD
09/03	KC	L 10-34	2	3	0.0	0.0	0.0	0.0	0	0	0	0	0	0
09/10	@SD	L 10-14	7	0	0.0	0.0	0.0	0.0	0	0	0	0	0	0
09/17	Cin	W 24-21	2	2	0.0	0.0	0.0	0.0	0	0	0	0	0	0
10/01	Den	W 27-10	2	3	0.0	0.0	0.0	0.0	0	0	0	0	0	0
10/08	@Oak	L 14-34	5	2	0.0	0.0	0.0	0.0	0	0	0	0	0	0
10/15	@Buf	L 21-27	5	2	0.0	0.0	0.0	0.0	0	0	0	0	0	0
10/22	SD	L 25-35	4	1	0.0	0.0	0.0	0.0	0	0	0	0	0	0
10/29	@Ari	L 14-20	8	0	0.0	0.0	0.5	0.5	0	0	1	0	1	0
11/05	NYN	W 30-28	4	3	1.0	2.0	0.0	0.0	0	0	0	0	0	0
11/12	@Jac	W 47-30	2	2	0.0	0.0	1.0	2.0	0	0	0	0	0	0
11/19	@Was	W 27-20	4	0	0.0	0.0	0.0	0.0	1	0	1	0	0	0
11/26	NYA	L 10-16	1	2	0.0	0.0	0.0	0.0	0	0	2	0	0	0
12/03	Phi	W 26-14	5	1	0.0	0.0	0.0	0.0	0	0	0	0	0	0
12/10	@Den	W 31-27	4	0	1.0	6.0	0.0	0.0	0	0	0	0	1	0
12/17	Oak	W 44-10	3	2	0.0	0.0	0.0	0.0	0	0	1	1	0	0
12/24	@KC	L 3-26	7	0	0.0	0.0	2.0	7.0	0	0	0	0	0	0

Craig Newsome
Green Bay Packers – CB

1995 Defensive Splits

	G	Tk	Ast	Sack	Yds	Stuff	Yds	Int	Yds	PD	TD
Total	16	54	21	0.0	0.0	0.0	0.0	1	3	19	0
vs. Playoff	4	13	9	0.0	0.0	0.0	0.0	0	3	7	0
vs. Non-Playoff	12	41	12	0.0	0.0	0.0	0.0	1	0	12	0
vs. Own Division	8	21	11	0.0	0.0	0.0	0.0	0	3	8	0
Home	8	35	13	0.0	0.0	0.0	0.0	0	3	16	0
Away	8	19	8	0.0	0.0	0.0	0.0	1	0	3	0
Games 1-8	8	20	12	0.0	0.0	0.0	0.0	0	3	6	0
Games 9-16	8	34	9	0.0	0.0	0.0	0.0	1	0	13	0
September	4	10	4	0.0	0.0	0.0	0.0	0	0	4	0
October	4	10	8	0.0	0.0	0.0	0.0	0	3	2	0
November	4	18	3	0.0	0.0	0.0	0.0	0	0	4	0
December	4	16	6	0.0	0.0	0.0	0.0	1	0	9	0
Grass	12	47	16	0.0	0.0	0.0	0.0	0	3	18	0
Turf	4	7	5	0.0	0.0	0.0	0.0	1	0	1	0
Indoor	3	7	3	0.0	0.0	0.0	0.0	1	0	1	0
Outdoor	13	47	18	0.0	0.0	0.0	0.0	0	3	18	0

Game Logs

Date	Opp	Result	Tk	Ast	Sack	Yds	Stuff	Yds	Int	Yds	PD	FF	FR	TD
09/03	StL	L 14-17	4	1	0.0	0.0	0.0	0.0	0	0	2	0	0	0
09/11	@Chi	W 27-24	1	0	0.0	0.0	0.0	0.0	0	0	0	0	0	0
09/17	NYN	W 14-6	2	2	0.0	0.0	0.0	0.0	0	0	2	0	0	0
09/24	@Jac	W 24-14	3	1	0.0	0.0	0.0	0.0	0	0	0	0	0	0
10/08	@Dal	L 24-34	0	2	0.0	0.0	0.0	0.0	0	0	0	0	0	0
10/15	Det	W 30-21	5	0	0.0	0.0	0.0	0.0	0	3	2	0	0	0
10/22	Min	W 38-21	4	3	0.0	0.0	0.0	0.0	0	0	0	0	0	0
10/29	@Det	L 16-24	1	3	0.0	0.0	0.0	0.0	0	0	0	0	0	0
11/05	@Min	L 24-27	3	0	0.0	0.0	0.0	0.0	0	0	0	0	0	0
11/12	Chi	W 35-28	4	1	0.0	0.0	0.0	0.0	0	0	2	0	0	0
11/19	@Cle	W 31-20	8	0	0.0	0.0	0.0	0.0	0	0	0	0	0	0
11/26	TB	W 35-13	3	2	0.0	0.0	0.0	0.0	0	0	2	0	0	0
12/03	Cin	W 24-10	6	0	0.0	0.0	0.0	0.0	0	0	1	0	0	0
12/10	@TB	L 10-13	0	2	0.0	0.0	0.0	0.0	0	0	2	0	0	0
12/16	@NO	W 34-23	3	0	0.0	0.0	0.0	0.0	1	0	1	0	0	0
12/24	Pit	W 24-19	7	4	0.0	0.0	0.0	0.0	0	0	5	0	0	0

Hardy Nickerson
Tampa Bay Buccaneers – LB

1995 Defensive Splits

	G	Tk	Ast	Sack	Yds	Stuff	Yds	Int	Yds	PD	TD
Total	16	90	54	1.5	12.5	5.0	7.5	0	0	5	0
vs. Playoff	6	21	22	1.5	12.5	0.5	0.5	0	0	2	0
vs. Non-Playoff	10	69	32	0.0	0.0	4.5	7.0	0	0	3	0
vs. Own Division	8	39	30	0.0	0.0	2.0	2.5	0	0	2	0
Home	8	45	36	0.5	4.5	3.5	5.5	0	0	2	0
Away	8	45	18	1.0	8.0	1.5	2.0	0	0	3	0
Games 1-8	8	53	28	1.5	12.5	3.0	5.0	0	0	1	0
Games 9-16	8	37	26	0.0	0.0	2.0	2.5	0	0	4	0
September	4	30	13	1.0	8.0	0.0	0.0	0	0	1	0
October	5	29	18	0.5	4.5	4.0	6.0	0	0	1	0
November	3	12	9	0.0	0.0	0.0	0.0	0	0	1	0
December	4	19	14	0.0	0.0	1.0	1.5	0	0	2	0
Grass	12	66	41	0.5	4.5	3.5	5.5	0	0	3	0
Turf	4	24	13	1.0	8.0	1.5	2.0	0	0	2	0
Indoor	3	18	13	0.0	0.0	1.5	2.0	0	0	1	0
Outdoor	13	72	41	1.5	12.5	3.5	5.5	0	0	4	0

Game Logs

Date	Opp	Result	Tk	Ast	Sack	Yds	Stuff	Yds	Int	Yds	PD	FF	FR	TD
09/03	@Phi	W 21-6	6	0	1.0	8.0	0.0	0.0	0	0	1	0	0	0
09/10	@Cle	L 6-22	10	2	0.0	0.0	0.0	0.0	0	0	1	0	0	0
09/17	Chi	L 6-25	7	5	0.0	0.0	0.0	0.0	0	0	1	0	0	0
09/24	Was	W 14-6	7	6	0.0	0.0	0.0	0.0	0	0	0	0	0	0
10/01	@Car	W 20-13	4	1	0.0	0.0	0.0	0.0	0	0	0	0	1	0
10/08	Cin	W 19-16	6	4	0.0	0.0	2.0	4.0	0	0	0	0	0	0
10/15	Min	W 20-17	8	4	0.0	0.0	1.0	1.0	0	0	1	0	0	0
10/22	Atl	L 21-24	5	6	0.5	4.5	0.0	0.0	0	0	0	0	0	0
10/29	@Hou	L 7-19	6	3	0.0	0.0	1.0	1.0	0	0	1	0	0	0
11/12	@Det	L 24-27	4	5	0.0	0.0	0.0	0.0	0	0	0	0	1	0
11/19	Jac	W 17-16	7	2	0.0	0.0	0.0	0.0	0	0	1	0	0	0
11/26	@GB	L 13-35	1	2	0.0	0.0	0.0	0.0	0	0	0	0	0	0
12/03	@Min	L 17-31	8	5	0.0	0.0	0.5	1.0	0	0	0	0	0	0
12/10	GB	W 13-10	4	9	0.0	0.0	0.5	0.5	0	0	0	0	0	0
12/17	@Chi	L 10-31	6	0	0.0	0.0	0.0	0.0	0	0	1	0	1	0
12/23	Det	L 10-37	1	0	0.0	0.0	0.0	0.0	0	0	1	0	0	0

Ken Norton
San Francisco 49ers – LB

1995 Defensive Splits

	G	Tk	Ast	Sack	Yds	Stuff	Yds	Int	Yds	PD	TD
Total	16	82	14	1.0	4.0	7.5	15.0	3	102	5	2
vs. Playoff	7	35	8	0.0	0.0	5.0	12.0	0	0	2	0
vs. Non-Playoff	9	47	6	1.0	4.0	2.5	3.0	3	102	3	2
vs. Own Division	8	38	7	1.0	4.0	1.5	2.0	2	56	2	2
Home	8	38	4	1.0	4.0	3.0	4.0	1	46	1	0
Away	8	44	10	0.0	0.0	4.5	11.0	2	56	4	2
Games 1-8	8	42	10	1.0	4.0	5.5	12.0	3	102	4	2
Games 9-16	8	40	4	0.0	0.0	2.0	3.0	0	0	1	0
September	4	17	5	0.0	0.0	2.0	4.0	0	0	1	0
October	4	25	5	1.0	4.0	3.5	8.0	3	102	3	2
November	4	20	2	0.0	0.0	0.0	0.0	0	0	1	0
December	4	20	2	0.0	0.0	2.0	3.0	0	0	0	0
Grass	10	50	5	1.0	4.0	3.0	4.0	1	46	1	0
Turf	6	32	9	0.0	0.0	4.5	11.0	2	56	4	2
Indoor	4	20	5	0.0	0.0	3.0	9.0	0	0	1	0
Outdoor	12	62	9	1.0	4.0	4.5	6.0	3	102	4	2

Game Logs

Date	Opp	Result	Tk	Ast	Sack	Yds	Stuff	Yds	Int	Yds	PD	FF	FR	TD
09/03	@NO	W 24-22	3	0	0.0	0.0	0.0	0.0	0	0	0	0	0	0
09/10	Atl	W 41-10	1	1	0.0	0.0	0.0	0.0	0	0	0	0	0	0
09/17	NE	W 28-3	6	0	0.0	0.0	0.0	0.0	0	0	0	0	0	0
09/25	@Det	L 24-27	7	4	0.0	0.0	2.0	4.0	0	0	1	0	0	0
10/01	NYN	W 20-6	4	1	0.0	0.0	1.0	1.0	1	46	1	0	0	0
10/15	@Ind	L 17-18	7	0	0.0	0.0	1.0	5.0	0	0	0	0	0	0
10/22	@StL	W 44-10	7	2	0.0	0.0	1.5	2.0	2	56	2	0	0	2
10/29	NO	L 7-11	7	2	1.0	4.0	0.0	0.0	0	0	0	0	0	0
11/05	Car	L 7-13	6	0	0.0	0.0	0.0	0.0	0	0	1	0	0	0
11/12	@Dal	W 38-20	5	2	0.0	0.0	0.0	0.0	0	0	1	0	0	0
11/20	@Mia	W 44-20	5	0	0.0	0.0	0.0	0.0	0	0	0	0	0	0
11/26	StL	W 41-13	4	0	0.0	0.0	0.0	0.0	0	0	0	0	0	0
12/03	Buf	W 27-17	7	0	0.0	0.0	2.0	3.0	0	0	0	0	0	0
12/10	@Car	W 31-10	7	1	0.0	0.0	0.0	0.0	0	0	0	0	0	0
12/18	Min	W 37-30	3	0	0.0	0.0	0.0	0.0	0	0	0	0	0	0
12/24	@Atl	L 27-28	3	1	0.0	0.0	0.0	0.0	0	0	0	0	0	0

Leslie O'Neal
San Diego Chargers – DE

1995 Defensive Splits	G	Tk	Ast	Sack	Yds	Stuff	Yds	Int	Yds	PD	TD		Game Logs	Date	Opp	Result	Tk	Ast	Sack	Yds	Stuff	Yds	Int	Yds	PD	FF	FR	TD
Total	16	36	12	12.5	78.5	7.0	22.5	0	0	6	0			09/03	@Oak	L 7-17	3	1	1.0	12.0	0.0	0.0	0	0	0	2	0	0
vs. Playoff	7	13	5	3.0	13.0	3.0	4.0	0	0	4	0			09/10	Sea	W 14-10	3	0	0.0	0.0	0.5	1.0	0	0	0	0	0	0
vs. Non-Playoff	9	23	7	9.5	65.5	4.0	18.5	0	0	2	0			09/17	@Phi	W 27-21	2	3	0.0	0.0	1.0	2.0	0	0	1	0	0	0
vs. Own Division	8	21	5	7.5	51.5	4.5	17.0	0	0	1	0			09/24	Den	W 17-6	1	1	0.5	2.5	0.0	0.0	0	0	0	0	0	0
Home	8	15	4	5.5	31.5	5.0	17.5	0	0	4	0			10/01	@Pit	L 16-31	2	1	1.0	6.0	0.0	0.0	0	0	0	0	0	0
Away	8	21	8	7.0	47.0	2.0	5.0	0	0	2	0			10/09	@KC	L 23-29	1	0	0.0	0.0	0.0	0.0	0	0	0	0	0	0
Games 1-8	8	17	8	6.5	46.5	1.5	3.0	0	0	4	0			10/15	Dal	L 9-23	0	0	0.0	0.0	0.0	0.0	0	0	3	0	0	0
Games 9-16	8	19	4	6.0	32.0	5.5	19.5	0	0	2	0			10/22	@Sea	W 35-25	5	2	4.0	26.0	0.0	0.0	0	0	0	0	0	0
September	4	9	5	1.5	14.5	1.5	3.0	0	0	1	0			11/05	Mia	L 14-24	2	1	0.0	0.0	1.0	1.0	0	0	0	0	0	0
October	4	8	3	5.0	32.0	0.0	0.0	0	0	3	0			11/12	KC	L 7-22	3	0	1.0	4.0	1.0	1.0	0	0	0	0	0	0
November	4	10	2	2.0	11.0	5.0	17.0	0	0	1	0			11/19	@Den	L 27-30	2	0	0.0	0.0	1.0	3.0	0	0	1	0	0	0
December	4	9	2	4.0	21.0	0.5	2.5	0	0	1	0			11/27	Oak	W 12-6	3	1	1.0	7.0	2.0	12.0	0	0	0	0	0	0
Grass	11	21	5	6.5	43.5	6.0	20.5	0	0	5	0			12/03	Cle	W 31-13	0	1	0.0	0.0	0.5	2.5	0	0	0	0	0	0
Turf	5	15	7	6.0	35.0	1.0	2.0	0	0	1	0			12/09	Ari	W 28-25	3	0	3.0	18.0	0.0	0.0	0	0	1	1	0	0
Indoor	2	8	2	5.0	29.0	0.0	0.0	0	0	0	0			12/17	@Ind	W 27-24	3	0	1.0	3.0	0.0	0.0	0	0	0	0	0	0
Outdoor	14	28	10	7.5	49.5	7.0	22.5	0	0	6	0			12/23	@NYN	W 27-17	3	1	0.0	0.0	0.0	0.0	0	0	0	1	0	0

Bo Orlando
San Diego Chargers – S

1995 Defensive Splits	G	Tk	Ast	Sack	Yds	Stuff	Yds	Int	Yds	PD	TD		Game Logs	Date	Opp	Result	Tk	Ast	Sack	Yds	Stuff	Yds	Int	Yds	PD	FF	FR	TD
Total	16	84	17	0.0	0.0	0.0	0.0	0	37	6	0			09/03	@Oak	L 7-17	1	2	0.0	0.0	0.0	0.0	0	0	0	0	0	0
vs. Playoff	7	37	9	0.0	0.0	0.0	0.0	0	0	4	0			09/10	Sea	W 14-10	5	1	0.0	0.0	0.0	0.0	0	0	0	0	0	0
vs. Non-Playoff	9	47	8	0.0	0.0	0.0	0.0	0	37	2	0			09/17	@Phi	W 27-21	5	3	0.0	0.0	0.0	0.0	0	0	0	0	0	0
vs. Own Division	8	34	10	0.0	0.0	0.0	0.0	0	37	3	0			09/24	Den	W 17-6	3	2	0.0	0.0	0.0	0.0	0	0	0	0	0	0
Home	8	43	6	0.0	0.0	0.0	0.0	0	0	4	0			10/01	@Pit	L 16-31	8	2	0.0	0.0	0.0	0.0	0	0	0	0	0	0
Away	8	41	11	0.0	0.0	0.0	0.0	0	37	2	0			10/09	@KC	L 23-29	3	1	0.0	0.0	0.0	0.0	0	0	0	0	0	0
Games 1-8	8	41	15	0.0	0.0	0.0	0.0	0	37	1	0			10/15	Dal	L 9-23	9	1	0.0	0.0	0.0	0.0	0	0	1	0	0	0
Games 9-16	8	43	2	0.0	0.0	0.0	0.0	0	0	5	0			10/22	@Sea	W 35-25	7	3	0.0	0.0	0.0	0.0	0	37	0	0	0	0
September	4	14	8	0.0	0.0	0.0	0.0	0	0	0	0			11/05	Mia	L 14-24	5	1	0.0	0.0	0.0	0.0	0	0	0	0	0	0
October	4	27	7	0.0	0.0	0.0	0.0	0	37	1	0			11/12	KC	L 7-22	4	1	0.0	0.0	0.0	0.0	0	0	0	0	0	0
November	4	20	2	0.0	0.0	0.0	0.0	0	0	3	0			11/19	@Den	L 27-30	6	0	0.0	0.0	0.0	0.0	0	0	0	0	0	0
December	4	23	0	0.0	0.0	0.0	0.0	0	0	4	0			11/27	Oak	W 12-6	5	0	0.0	0.0	0.0	0.0	0	0	2	0	0	0
Grass	11	53	9	0.0	0.0	0.0	0.0	0	0	4	0			12/03	Cle	W 31-13	7	0	0.0	0.0	0.0	0.0	0	0	0	0	0	0
Turf	5	31	8	0.0	0.0	0.0	0.0	0	37	2	0			12/09	Ari	W 28-25	5	0	0.0	0.0	0.0	0.0	0	0	1	0	0	0
Indoor	2	10	3	0.0	0.0	0.0	0.0	0	37	2	0			12/17	@Ind	W 27-24	3	0	0.0	0.0	0.0	0.0	0	0	2	0	0	0
Outdoor	14	74	14	0.0	0.0	0.0	0.0	0	0	4	0			12/23	@NYN	W 27-17	8	0	0.0	0.0	0.0	0.0	0	0	0	0	0	0

Sterling Palmer
Washington Redskins – DE

1995 Defensive Splits	G	Tk	Ast	Sack	Yds	Stuff	Yds	Int	Yds	PD	TD		Game Logs	Date	Opp	Result	Tk	Ast	Sack	Yds	Stuff	Yds	Int	Yds	PD	FF	FR	TD
Total	13	30	5	4.5	32.0	2.0	6.0	0	0	2	0			09/03	Ari	W 27-7	2	1	0.0	0.0	0.0	0.0	0	0	0	0	0	0
vs. Playoff	6	8	1	0.5	4.0	1.0	4.0	0	0	0	0			09/10	Oak	L 8-20	3	1	0.0	0.0	1.0	2.0	0	0	0	0	0	0
vs. Non-Playoff	7	22	4	4.0	28.0	1.0	2.0	0	0	2	0			09/17	@Den	L 31-38	8	0	1.0	9.0	0.0	0.0	0	0	0	0	0	0
vs. Own Division	7	13	2	1.5	8.0	0.0	0.0	0	0	1	0			09/24	@TB	L 6-14	5	0	1.0	9.0	0.0	0.0	0	0	1	0	0	0
Home	7	15	5	2.5	14.0	2.0	6.0	0	0	1	0			10/01	Dal	W 27-23	2	1	0.5	4.0	0.0	0.0	0	0	0	0	0	0
Away	6	15	0	2.0	18.0	0.0	0.0	0	0	1	0			10/08	@Phi	L 34-37	0	0	0.0	0.0	0.0	0.0	0	0	0	1	0	0
Games 1-8	8	20	3	2.5	22.0	2.0	6.0	0	0	1	0			10/15	@Ari	L 20-24	1	0	0.0	0.0	0.0	0.0	0	0	1	0	1	0
Games 9-16	5	10	2	2.0	10.0	0.0	0.0	0	0	1	0			10/22	Det	W 36-30	1	0	0.0	0.0	1.0	4.0	0	0	0	0	0	0
September	4	16	2	2.0	18.0	1.0	2.0	0	0	0	0			10/29	NYN	L 15-24	4	0	1.0	4.0	0.0	0.0	0	0	0	0	0	0
October	5	8	1	1.5	8.0	1.0	4.0	0	0	1	0			11/05	@KC	L 3-24	1	0	0.0	0.0	0.0	0.0	0	0	0	0	0	0
November	3	4	2	1.0	6.0	0.0	0.0	0	0	1	0			11/19	Sea	L 20-27	1	2	1.0	6.0	0.0	0.0	0	0	1	0	0	0
December	1	2	0	0.0	0.0	0.0	0.0	0	0	0	0			11/26	Phi	L 7-14	2	0	0.0	0.0	0.0	0.0	0	0	0	0	0	0
Grass	11	28	5	4.5	32.0	2.0	6.0	0	0	2	0			12/03	@Dal	W 24-17	2	0	0.0	0.0	0.0	0.0	0	0	0	0	0	0
Turf	2	2	0	0.0	0.0	0.0	0.0	0	0	0	0																	
Indoor	0	0	0	0	0	0	0	0	0	0	0																	
Outdoor	13	30	5	4.5	32.0	2.0	6.0	0	0	2	0																	

Anthony Parker
St. Louis Rams – CB

1995 Defensive Splits

	G	Tk	Ast	Sack	Yds	Stuff	Yds	Int	Yds	PD	TD
Total	16	55	4	0.0	0.0	0.0	0.0	2	-5	13	1
vs. Playoff	9	25	2	0.0	0.0	0.0	0.0	1	3	6	0
vs. Non-Playoff	7	30	2	0.0	0.0	0.0	0.0	1	-8	7	1
vs. Own Division	8	26	4	0.0	0.0	0.0	0.0	2	-5	7	1
Home	8	24	2	0.0	0.0	0.0	0.0	1	-8	2	0
Away	8	31	2	0.0	0.0	0.0	0.0	1	3	11	1
Games 1-8	8	24	1	0.0	0.0	0.0	0.0	0	0	6	1
Games 9-16	8	31	3	0.0	0.0	0.0	0.0	2	-5	7	0
September	4	13	0	0.0	0.0	0.0	0.0	0	0	3	0
October	4	11	1	0.0	0.0	0.0	0.0	0	0	3	0
November	4	19	3	0.0	0.0	0.0	0.0	2	-5	5	0
December	4	12	0	0.0	0.0	0.0	0.0	0	0	2	1
Grass	3	12	0	0.0	0.0	0.0	0.0	1	3	5	1
Turf	13	43	4	0.0	0.0	0.0	0.0	1	-8	8	0
Indoor	7	25	3	0.0	0.0	0.0	0.0	1	-8	4	0
Outdoor	9	30	1	0.0	0.0	0.0	0.0	1	3	9	1

Game Logs

Date	Opp	Result	Tk	Ast	Sack	Yds	Stuff	Yds	Int	Yds	PD	FF	FR	TD
09/03	@GB	W 17-14	1	0	0.0	0.0	0.0	0.0	0	0	1	0	0	0
09/10	NO	W 17-13	2	0	0.0	0.0	0.0	0.0	0	0	0	0	0	0
09/17	@Car	W 31-10	3	0	0.0	0.0	0.0	0.0	0	0	2	0	1	1
09/24	Chi	W 34-28	7	0	0.0	0.0	0.0	0.0	0	0	0	1	1	0
10/01	@Ind	L 18-21	5	0	0.0	0.0	0.0	0.0	0	0	1	0	1	0
10/12	Atl	W 21-19	1	0	0.0	0.0	0.0	0.0	0	0	0	0	0	0
10/22	SF	L 10-44	1	1	0.0	0.0	0.0	0.0	0	0	0	0	0	0
10/29	@Phi	L 9-20	4	0	0.0	0.0	0.0	0.0	0	0	2	0	0	0
11/05	@NO	L 10-19	7	1	0.0	0.0	0.0	0.0	0	0	1	0	0	0
11/12	Car	W 28-17	4	1	0.0	0.0	0.0	0.0	1	-8	2	0	0	0
11/19	@Atl	L 6-31	0	1	0.0	0.0	0.0	0.0	0	0	0	0	0	0
11/26	@SF	L 13-41	8	0	0.0	0.0	0.0	0.0	1	3	2	0	0	0
12/03	@NYA	W 23-20	3	0	0.0	0.0	0.0	0.0	0	0	2	0	1	0
12/10	Buf	L 27-45	2	0	0.0	0.0	0.0	0.0	0	0	0	0	0	0
12/17	Was	L 23-35	4	0	0.0	0.0	0.0	0.0	0	0	0	0	0	0
12/24	Mia	L 22-41	3	0	0.0	0.0	0.0	0.0	0	0	0	0	0	0

Marvcus Patton
Washington Redskins – LB

1995 Defensive Splits

	G	Tk	Ast	Sack	Yds	Stuff	Yds	Int	Yds	PD	TD
Total	16	94	19	2.0	9.0	1.0	1.0	2	7	4	0
vs. Playoff	6	33	3	0.0	0.0	0.0	0.0	0	0	0	0
vs. Non-Playoff	10	61	16	2.0	9.0	1.0	1.0	2	7	4	0
vs. Own Division	8	42	5	1.0	3.0	0.0	0.0	1	1	2	0
Home	8	44	3	1.0	6.0	1.0	1.0	2	7	4	0
Away	8	50	16	1.0	3.0	0.0	0.0	0	0	0	0
Games 1-8	8	40	14	0.0	0.0	0.0	0.0	1	1	3	0
Games 9-16	8	54	5	2.0	9.0	1.0	1.0	1	6	1	0
September	4	16	12	0.0	0.0	0.0	0.0	1	1	3	0
October	5	30	2	0.0	0.0	0.0	0.0	0	0	0	0
November	3	15	2	0.0	0.0	0.0	0.0	1	6	1	0
December	4	33	3	2.0	9.0	1.0	1.0	0	0	0	0
Grass	12	63	17	1.0	6.0	1.0	1.0	2	7	4	0
Turf	4	31	2	1.0	3.0	0.0	0.0	0	0	0	0
Indoor	1	15	0	0.0	0.0	0.0	0.0	0	0	0	0
Outdoor	15	79	19	2.0	9.0	1.0	1.0	2	7	4	0

Game Logs

Date	Opp	Result	Tk	Ast	Sack	Yds	Stuff	Yds	Int	Yds	PD	FF	FR	TD
09/03	Ari	W 27-7	4	1	0.0	0.0	0.0	0.0	1	1	2	0	0	0
09/10	Oak	L 8-20	4	1	0.0	0.0	0.0	0.0	0	0	1	0	0	0
09/17	@Den	L 31-38	5	6	0.0	0.0	0.0	0.0	0	0	0	0	0	0
09/24	@TB	L 6-14	3	4	0.0	0.0	0.0	0.0	0	0	0	0	0	0
10/01	Dal	W 27-23	5	0	0.0	0.0	0.0	0.0	0	0	0	0	0	0
10/08	@Phi	L 34-37	7	0	0.0	0.0	0.0	0.0	0	0	0	0	0	0
10/15	@Ari	L 20-24	6	2	0.0	0.0	0.0	0.0	0	0	0	0	0	0
10/22	Det	W 36-30	6	0	0.0	0.0	0.0	0.0	0	0	0	0	0	0
10/29	NYN	L 15-24	6	0	0.0	0.0	0.0	0.0	0	0	0	0	1	0
11/05	@KC	L 3-24	5	2	0.0	0.0	0.0	0.0	0	0	0	0	0	0
11/19	Sea	L 20-27	5	0	0.0	0.0	0.0	0.0	1	6	1	1	0	0
11/26	Phi	L 7-14	5	0	0.0	0.0	0.0	0.0	0	0	0	0	0	0
12/03	@Dal	W 24-17	5	1	0.0	0.0	0.0	0.0	0	0	0	0	0	0
12/10	@NYN	L 13-20	4	1	1.0	3.0	0.0	0.0	0	0	0	0	0	0
12/17	@StL	W 35-23	15	0	0.0	0.0	0.0	0.0	0	0	0	2	0	0
12/24	Car	W 20-17	9	1	1.0	6.0	1.0	1.0	0	0	0	0	0	0

Bryce Paup
Buffalo Bills – LB

1995 Defensive Splits

	G	Tk	Ast	Sack	Yds	Stuff	Yds	Int	Yds	PD	TD
Total	15	70	19	17.5	132.5	3.5	10.5	2	0	6	0
vs. Playoff	6	36	8	11.5	74.5	2.0	8.0	1	0	3	0
vs. Non-Playoff	9	34	11	6.0	58.0	1.5	2.5	1	0	3	0
vs. Own Division	8	45	11	10.5	79.5	3.5	10.5	1	0	3	0
Home	7	29	10	8.5	58.5	1.0	1.5	1	0	2	0
Away	8	41	9	9.0	74.0	2.5	9.0	1	0	4	0
Games 1-8	8	39	11	8.0	63.0	2.0	8.0	0	0	1	0
Games 9-16	7	31	8	9.5	69.5	1.5	2.5	2	0	5	0
September	3	14	7	4.0	31.0	0.0	0.0	0	0	0	0
October	5	25	4	4.0	32.0	2.0	8.0	0	0	1	0
November	4	21	5	7.0	49.0	1.5	2.5	1	0	2	0
December	3	10	3	2.5	20.5	0.0	0.0	1	0	3	0
Grass	5	24	5	4.0	33.0	2.0	8.0	1	0	3	0
Turf	10	46	14	13.5	99.5	1.5	2.5	1	0	3	0
Indoor	2	11	3	3.0	22.0	0.0	0.0	0	0	1	0
Outdoor	13	59	16	14.5	110.5	3.5	10.5	2	0	5	0

Game Logs

Date	Opp	Result	Tk	Ast	Sack	Yds	Stuff	Yds	Int	Yds	PD	FF	FR	TD
09/03	@Den	L 7-22	4	1	1.0	14.0	0.0	0.0	0	0	0	0	0	0
09/10	Car	W 31-9	3	3	0.0	0.0	0.0	0.0	0	0	0	0	0	0
09/17	Ind	W 20-14	7	3	3.0	17.0	0.0	0.0	0	0	2	0	0	0
10/02	@Cle	W 22-19	3	1	1.0	6.0	0.0	0.0	0	0	1	0	0	0
10/08	NYA	W 29-10	3	0	0.0	0.0	0.0	0.0	0	0	0	0	0	0
10/15	Sea	W 27-21	5	1	2.0	19.0	0.0	0.0	0	0	0	0	0	0
10/23	@NE	L 14-27	1	0	0.0	0.0	0.0	0.0	0	0	0	0	1	0
10/29	@Mia	L 6-23	7	1	1.0	7.0	2.0	8.0	0	0	1	0	0	0
11/05	@Ind	W 16-10	9	2	3.0	22.0	0.0	0.0	0	0	0	0	0	0
11/12	Atl	W 23-17	5	0	2.0	8.0	0.0	0.0	0	0	0	0	0	0
11/19	@NYA	W 28-26	6	1	2.0	19.0	0.5	1.0	0	0	0	0	0	0
11/26	NE	L 25-35	1	2	0.0	0.0	1.0	1.5	1	0	2	0	0	0
12/03	@SF	L 17-27	3	1	1.0	6.0	0.0	0.0	1	0	2	0	0	0
12/10	@StL	W 45-27	2	1	0.0	0.0	0.0	0.0	0	0	1	0	0	0
12/17	Mia	W 23-20	5	1	1.5	14.5	0.0	0.0	0	0	0	0	0	0
12/24	Hou	L 17-28	-	-	-	-	-	-	-	-	-	-	-	-

Darren Perry
Pittsburgh Steelers – S

1995 Defensive Splits

	G	Tk	Ast	Sack	Yds	Stuff	Yds	Int	Yds	PD	TD
Total	16	67	11	0.0	0.0	1.0	2.0	4	71	9	0
vs. Playoff	4	15	2	0.0	0.0	0.0	0.0	1	26	4	0
vs. Non-Playoff	12	52	9	0.0	0.0	1.0	2.0	3	45	5	0
vs. Own Division	8	24	5	0.0	0.0	1.0	2.0	1	23	3	0
Home	8	32	7	0.0	0.0	0.0	0.0	3	55	8	0
Away	8	35	4	0.0	0.0	1.0	2.0	1	16	1	0
Games 1-8	8	28	7	0.0	0.0	0.0	0.0	2	32	7	0
Games 9-16	8	39	4	0.0	0.0	1.0	2.0	2	39	2	0
September	4	18	4	0.0	0.0	0.0	0.0	2	32	3	0
October	4	10	3	0.0	0.0	0.0	0.0	0	0	4	0
November	4	19	2	0.0	0.0	1.0	2.0	1	16	1	0
December	4	20	2	0.0	0.0	0.0	0.0	1	23	1	0
Grass	6	27	3	0.0	0.0	0.0	0.0	1	16	1	0
Turf	10	40	8	0.0	0.0	1.0	2.0	3	55	8	0
Indoor	1	4	1	0.0	0.0	0.0	0.0	0	0	0	0
Outdoor	15	63	10	0.0	0.0	1.0	2.0	4	71	9	0

Game Logs

Date	Opp	Result	Tk	Ast	Sack	Yds	Stuff	Yds	Int	Yds	PD	FF	FR	TD
09/03	Det	W 23-20	3	0	0.0	0.0	0.0	0.0	1	26	2	0	0	0
09/10	@Hou	W 34-17	4	1	0.0	0.0	0.0	0.0	0	0	0	0	0	0
09/18	@Mia	L 10-23	2	0	0.0	0.0	0.0	0.0	0	0	0	0	0	0
09/24	Min	L 24-44	9	3	0.0	0.0	0.0	0.0	1	6	1	0	0	0
10/01	SD	W 31-16	5	1	0.0	0.0	0.0	0.0	0	0	2	0	0	0
10/08	@Jac	L 16-20	4	1	0.0	0.0	0.0	0.0	0	0	0	0	0	0
10/19	Cin	L 9-27	1	0	0.0	0.0	0.0	0.0	0	0	1	0	0	0
10/29	Jac	W 24-7	0	1	0.0	0.0	0.0	0.0	0	0	0	0	0	0
11/05	@Chi	W 37-34	7	1	0.0	0.0	0.0	0.0	1	16	1	0	2	0
11/13	Cle	W 20-3	2	1	0.0	0.0	0.0	0.0	0	0	0	0	0	0
11/19	@Cin	W 49-31	4	0	0.0	0.0	1.0	2.0	0	0	0	0	0	0
11/26	@Cle	W 20-17	6	0	0.0	0.0	0.0	0.0	0	0	0	0	0	0
12/03	Hou	W 21-7	3	1	0.0	0.0	0.0	0.0	1	23	1	0	0	0
12/10	@Oak	W 29-10	3	0	0.0	0.0	0.0	0.0	0	0	0	0	0	0
12/16	NE	W 41-27	9	0	0.0	0.0	0.0	0.0	0	0	0	0	0	0
12/24	@GB	L 19-24	5	1	0.0	0.0	0.0	0.0	0	0	0	0	0	0

Michael Dean Perry
Denver Broncos – DT

1995 Defensive Splits

	G	Tk	Ast	Sack	Yds	Stuff	Yds	Int	Yds	PD	TD
Total	14	33	6	6.0	52.0	8.5	22.5	0	0	5	0
vs. Playoff	6	19	1	1.0	6.0	3.5	8.5	0	0	2	0
vs. Non-Playoff	8	14	5	5.0	46.0	5.0	14.0	0	0	3	0
vs. Own Division	8	21	2	2.0	14.0	5.0	16.0	0	0	0	0
Home	7	14	3	2.0	15.0	4.5	7.5	0	0	4	0
Away	7	19	3	4.0	37.0	4.0	15.0	0	0	1	0
Games 1-8	6	18	3	4.0	41.0	2.5	7.5	0	0	2	0
Games 9-16	8	15	3	2.0	11.0	6.0	15.0	0	0	3	0
September	2	5	1	1.0	6.0	1.5	5.5	0	0	2	0
October	4	13	2	3.0	35.0	1.0	2.0	0	0	0	0
November	4	8	2	1.0	9.0	2.5	3.5	0	0	2	0
December	4	7	1	1.0	2.0	3.5	11.5	0	0	1	0
Grass	11	25	3	5.0	40.0	8.5	22.5	0	0	4	0
Turf	3	8	3	1.0	12.0	0.0	0.0	0	0	1	0
Indoor	2	5	3	1.0	12.0	0.0	0.0	0	0	1	0
Outdoor	12	28	3	5.0	40.0	8.5	22.5	0	0	4	0

Game Logs

Date	Opp	Result	Tk	Ast	Sack	Yds	Stuff	Yds	Int	Yds	PD	FF	FR	TD
09/03	Buf	W 22-7	2	1	1.0	6.0	0.5	0.5	0	0	2	0	0	0
09/10	@Dal	L 21-31	-	-	-	-	-	-	-	-	-	-	-	-
09/17	Was	W 38-31	-	-	-	-	-	-	-	-	-	-	-	-
09/24	@SD	L 6-17	3	0	0.0	0.0	1.0	5.0	0	0	0	0	0	0
10/01	@Sea	L 10-27	4	2	1.0	12.0	0.0	0.0	0	0	0	0	0	0
10/08	@NE	W 37-3	3	0	2.0	23.0	1.0	2.0	0	0	1	0	0	0
10/16	Oak	W 27-0	0	0	0.0	0.0	0.0	0.0	0	0	0	0	0	0
10/22	KC	L 7-21	6	0	0.0	0.0	0.0	0.0	0	0	0	0	0	0
11/05	Ari	W 38-6	1	1	1.0	9.0	0.5	0.5	0	0	1	0	0	0
11/12	@Phi	L 13-31	3	0	0.0	0.0	0.0	0.0	0	0	0	0	0	0
11/19	SD	W 30-27	3	0	0.0	0.0	2.0	3.0	0	0	0	0	0	0
11/26	@Hou	L 33-42	1	1	0.0	0.0	0.0	0.0	0	0	1	0	0	0
12/03	Jac	L 31-23	2	1	0.0	0.0	1.5	3.5	0	0	1	0	0	0
12/10	Sea	L 27-31	0	0	0.0	0.0	0.0	0.0	0	0	1	0	0	0
12/17	@KC	L 17-20	2	0	0.0	0.0	0.0	0.0	0	0	0	0	0	0
12/24	@Oak	W 31-28	3	0	1.0	2.0	2.0	8.0	0	0	0	0	0	0

Roman Phifer
St. Louis Rams – LB

1995 Defensive Splits

	G	Tk	Ast	Sack	Yds	Stuff	Yds	Int	Yds	PD	TD
Total	16	88	28	3.0	23.0	8.0	14.5	3	52	13	0
vs. Playoff	9	49	8	2.0	12.0	4.0	5.5	2	32	8	0
vs. Non-Playoff	7	39	20	1.0	11.0	4.0	9.0	1	20	5	0
vs. Own Division	8	46	17	2.0	17.0	2.0	2.0	1	20	7	0
Home	8	49	11	3.0	23.0	4.0	8.0	1	7	7	0
Away	8	39	17	0.0	0.0	4.0	6.5	2	45	6	0
Games 1-8	8	51	12	2.0	17.0	6.5	11.0	2	45	7	0
Games 9-16	8	37	16	1.0	6.0	1.5	3.5	1	7	6	0
September	4	28	9	1.0	11.0	2.5	5.5	2	45	4	0
October	4	23	3	1.0	6.0	4.0	5.5	0	0	3	0
November	4	16	10	0.0	0.0	0.0	0.0	0	0	4	0
December	4	21	6	1.0	6.0	1.5	3.5	1	7	2	0
Grass	3	18	5	0.0	0.0	0.5	0.5	2	45	3	0
Turf	13	70	23	3.0	23.0	7.5	14.0	1	7	10	0
Indoor	7	35	15	1.0	6.0	3.0	5.5	1	7	6	0
Outdoor	9	53	13	2.0	17.0	5.0	9.0	2	45	7	0

Game Logs

Date	Opp	Result	Tk	Ast	Sack	Yds	Stuff	Yds	Int	Yds	PD	FF	FR	TD
09/03	@GB	W 17-14	6	2	0.0	0.0	0.0	0.0	1	25	1	0	0	0
09/10	NO	W 17-13	7	3	1.0	11.0	0.0	0.0	0	0	1	0	0	0
09/17	@Car	W 31-10	8	3	0.0	0.0	0.5	0.5	1	20	1	0	0	0
09/24	Chi	W 34-28	7	1	0.0	0.0	2.0	5.0	0	0	1	0	0	0
10/01	@Ind	L 18-21	6	1	0.0	0.0	2.5	4.0	0	0	1	0	0	0
10/12	Atl	W 21-19	2	0	1.0	6.0	0.0	0.0	0	0	1	0	0	0
10/22	SF	L 10-44	13	1	0.0	0.0	1.5	1.5	0	0	0	0	0	0
10/29	@Phi	L 9-20	2	1	0.0	0.0	0.0	0.0	0	0	1	0	0	0
11/05	@NO	L 10-19	5	7	0.0	0.0	0.0	0.0	0	0	0	0	0	0
11/12	Car	W 28-17	3	2	0.0	0.0	0.0	0.0	0	0	2	0	0	0
11/19	@Atl	L 6-31	4	1	0.0	0.0	0.0	0.0	0	0	1	0	0	0
11/26	@SF	L 13-41	4	0	0.0	0.0	0.0	0.0	0	0	1	0	0	0
12/03	@NYA	W 23-20	4	2	0.0	0.0	1.0	2.0	0	0	1	0	0	0
12/10	Buf	L 27-45	4	2	0.0	0.0	0.0	0.0	0	0	0	0	0	0
12/17	Was	L 23-35	5	2	0.0	0.0	0.5	1.5	0	0	1	0	0	0
12/24	Mia	L 22-41	8	0	1.0	6.0	0.0	0.0	1	7	2	0	0	0

Joe Phillips
Kansas City Chiefs – DT

1995 Defensive Splits

	G	Tk	Ast	Sack	Yds	Stuff	Yds	Int	Yds	PD	TD
Total	16	25	9	4.5	20.5	2.5	4.0	1	2	3	0
vs. Playoff	4	8	3	1.0	6.0	0.5	1.0	0	0	0	0
vs. Non-Playoff	12	17	6	3.5	14.5	2.0	3.0	1	2	3	0
vs. Own Division	8	13	3	3.5	13.5	1.0	2.0	0	0	2	0
Home	8	12	2	2.0	4.0	1.0	1.0	1	2	3	0
Away	8	13	7	2.5	16.5	1.5	3.0	0	0	0	0
Games 1-8	8	16	4	2.5	12.5	1.0	1.0	0	0	0	0
Games 9-16	8	9	5	2.0	8.0	1.5	3.0	1	2	3	0
September	4	9	1	1.5	5.5	1.0	1.0	0	0	0	0
October	4	7	3	1.0	7.0	0.0	0.0	0	0	0	0
November	4	3	4	1.0	6.0	0.5	1.0	1	2	1	0
December	4	6	1	1.0	2.0	1.0	2.0	0	0	2	0
Grass	14	23	6	4.0	17.0	2.0	3.0	1	2	3	0
Turf	2	2	3	0.5	3.5	0.5	1.0	0	0	0	0
Indoor	1	1	1	0.5	3.5	0.0	0.0	0	0	0	0
Outdoor	15	24	8	4.0	17.0	2.5	4.0	1	2	3	0

Game Logs

Date	Opp	Result	Tk	Ast	Sack	Yds	Stuff	Yds	Int	Yds	PD	FF	FR	TD
09/03	@Sea	W 34-10	1	1	0.5	3.5	0.0	0.0	0	0	0	0	0	0
09/10	NYN	W 20-17	3	0	0.0	0.0	1.0	1.0	0	0	0	0	0	0
09/17	Oak	W 23-17	4	0	1.0	2.0	0.0	0.0	0	0	0	0	0	0
09/24	@Cle	L 17-35	1	0	0.0	0.0	0.0	0.0	0	0	0	0	0	0
10/01	@Ari	W 24-3	3	1	1.0	7.0	0.0	0.0	0	0	0	0	0	0
10/09	SD	W 29-23	2	0	0.0	0.0	0.0	0.0	0	0	0	0	0	0
10/15	NE	W 31-26	1	0	0.0	0.0	0.0	0.0	0	0	0	1	0	0
10/22	@Den	W 21-7	1	2	0.0	0.0	0.0	0.0	0	0	0	0	0	0
11/05	Was	W 24-3	0	1	0.0	0.0	0.0	0.0	0	0	0	0	0	0
11/12	@SD	W 22-7	2	0	1.0	6.0	0.0	0.0	0	0	0	0	0	0
11/19	Hou	W 20-13	0	1	0.0	0.0	0.0	0.0	1	2	1	0	0	0
11/23	@Dal	L 12-24	1	2	0.0	0.0	0.5	1.0	0	0	0	0	0	0
12/03	@Oak	W 29-23	1	0	0.0	0.0	1.0	2.0	0	0	0	0	0	0
12/11	@Mia	L 6-13	3	1	0.0	0.0	0.0	0.0	0	0	0	0	0	0
12/17	Den	W 20-17	1	0	0.0	0.0	0.0	0.0	0	0	0	0	0	0
12/24	Sea	W 26-3	1	0	1.0	2.0	0.0	0.0	0	0	2	0	0	0

Anthony Pleasant
Cleveland Browns – DE

1995 Defensive Splits

	G	Tk	Ast	Sack	Yds	Stuff	Yds	Int	Yds	PD	TD
Total	16	41	10	8.0	53.0	1.5	1.5	0	0	2	0
vs. Playoff	7	21	4	4.5	26.0	1.0	1.0	0	0	0	0
vs. Non-Playoff	9	20	6	3.5	27.0	0.5	0.5	0	0	1	0
vs. Own Division	8	15	4	1.5	17.0	1.0	1.0	0	0	1	0
Home	8	20	1	5.0	34.0	1.0	1.0	0	0	2	0
Away	8	21	9	3.0	19.0	0.5	0.5	0	0	0	0
Games 1-8	8	29	7	7.0	48.0	0.5	0.5	0	0	0	0
Games 9-16	8	12	3	1.0	5.0	1.0	1.0	0	0	2	0
September	4	16	4	4.0	31.0	0.5	0.5	0	0	0	0
October	4	13	3	3.0	17.0	0.0	0.0	0	0	0	0
November	4	8	2	1.0	5.0	1.0	1.0	0	0	2	0
December	4	4	1	0.0	0.0	0.0	0.0	0	0	0	0
Grass	11	25	4	5.0	34.0	1.5	1.5	0	0	2	0
Turf	5	16	6	3.0	19.0	0.0	0.0	0	0	0	0
Indoor	3	11	3	2.5	14.0	0.0	0.0	0	0	0	0
Outdoor	13	30	7	5.5	39.0	1.5	1.5	0	0	2	0

Game Logs

Date	Opp	Result	Tk	Ast	Sack	Yds	Stuff	Yds	Int	Yds	PD	FF	FR	TD
09/03	@NE	L 14-17	3	3	0.0	0.0	0.5	0.5	0	0	0	0	0	0
09/10	TB	W 22-6	4	0	2.0	10.0	0.0	0.0	0	0	0	1	0	0
09/17	@Hou	W 14-7	6	1	1.0	12.0	0.0	0.0	0	0	0	1	0	0
09/24	KC	W 35-17	3	0	1.0	9.0	0.0	0.0	0	0	0	0	0	0
10/02	Buf	L 19-22	6	1	1.0	10.0	0.0	0.0	0	0	0	0	0	0
10/08	@Det	L 20-38	3	1	1.5	2.0	0.0	0.0	0	0	0	2	0	0
10/22	Jac	L 15-23	2	0	0.0	0.0	0.0	0.0	0	0	0	0	0	0
10/29	@Cin	W 29-26	2	1	0.5	5.0	0.0	0.0	0	0	0	0	0	0
11/05	Hou	L 10-37	1	0	0.0	0.0	0.0	0.0	0	0	1	0	0	0
11/13	@Pit	L 3-20	3	2	0.0	0.0	0.0	0.0	0	0	0	0	0	0
11/19	GB	L 20-31	3	0	1.0	5.0	0.0	0.0	0	0	1	1	0	0
11/26	Pit	L 17-20	1	0	0.0	0.0	1.0	1.0	0	0	0	0	0	0
12/03	@SD	L 13-31	2	0	0.0	0.0	0.0	0.0	0	0	0	0	0	0
12/09	@Min	L 11-27	2	1	0.0	0.0	0.0	0.0	0	0	0	0	0	0
12/17	Cin	W 26-10	0	0	0.0	0.0	0.0	0.0	0	0	0	0	0	0
12/24	@Jac	L 21-24	0	0	0.0	0.0	0.0	0.0	0	0	0	0	0	0

Gary Plummer
San Francisco 49ers – LB

1995 Defensive Splits

	G	Tk	Ast	Sack	Yds	Stuff	Yds	Int	Yds	PD	TD
Total	16	58	6	1.0	8.0	4.5	8.5	0	0	1	0
vs. Playoff	7	22	4	1.0	8.0	2.0	4.0	0	0	0	0
vs. Non-Playoff	9	36	2	0.0	0.0	2.5	4.5	0	0	1	0
vs. Own Division	8	26	1	0.0	0.0	2.5	4.5	0	0	0	0
Home	8	28	2	1.0	8.0	3.0	7.0	0	0	1	0
Away	8	30	4	0.0	0.0	1.5	1.5	0	0	0	0
Games 1-8	8	27	3	0.0	0.0	2.5	2.5	0	0	1	0
Games 9-16	8	31	3	1.0	8.0	2.0	6.0	0	0	0	0
September	4	9	2	0.0	0.0	0.0	0.0	0	0	0	0
October	4	18	1	0.0	0.0	2.5	2.5	0	0	1	0
November	4	18	2	0.0	0.0	1.0	3.0	0	0	0	0
December	4	13	1	1.0	8.0	1.0	3.0	0	0	0	0
Grass	10	36	4	1.0	8.0	3.0	7.0	0	0	1	0
Turf	6	22	2	0.0	0.0	1.5	1.5	0	0	0	0
Indoor	4	13	2	0.0	0.0	1.0	1.0	0	0	0	0
Outdoor	12	45	4	1.0	8.0	3.5	7.5	0	0	1	0

Game Logs

Date	Opp	Result	Tk	Ast	Sack	Yds	Stuff	Yds	Int	Yds	PD	FF	FR	TD
09/03	@NO	W 24-22	3	0	0.0	0.0	0.0	0.0	0	0	0	0	0	0
09/10	Atl	W 41-10	0	0	0.0	0.0	0.0	0.0	0	0	0	0	0	0
09/17	NE	W 28-3	4	0	0.0	0.0	0.0	0.0	0	0	0	0	0	0
09/25	@Det	L 24-27	2	2	0.0	0.0	0.0	0.0	0	0	0	0	0	0
10/01	NYN	W 20-6	4	0	0.0	0.0	0.0	0.0	0	0	1	0	0	0
10/15	@Ind	L 17-18	8	0	0.0	0.0	1.0	1.0	0	0	1	0	0	0
10/22	@StL	W 44-10	2	0	0.0	0.0	0.5	0.5	0	0	0	0	0	0
10/29	NO	L 7-11	4	1	0.0	0.0	0.0	0.0	0	0	0	0	0	0
11/05	Car	L 7-13	7	0	0.0	0.0	1.0	3.0	0	0	0	0	0	0
11/12	@Dal	W 38-20	7	0	0.0	0.0	0.0	0.0	0	0	0	0	0	0
11/20	@Mia	W 44-20	1	2	0.0	0.0	0.0	0.0	0	0	0	0	0	0
11/26	StL	W 41-13	3	0	0.0	0.0	0.0	0.0	0	0	0	0	0	0
12/03	Buf	W 27-17	4	0	1.0	8.0	1.0	3.0	0	0	0	1	0	0
12/10	@Car	W 31-10	7	0	0.0	0.0	0.0	0.0	0	0	0	0	0	0
12/18	Min	W 37-30	2	1	0.0	0.0	0.0	0.0	0	0	0	0	0	0
12/24	@Atl	L 27-28	0	0	0.0	0.0	0.0	0.0	0	0	0	0	0	0

Tyrone Poole

Carolina Panthers – CB

1995 Defensive Splits

	G	Tk	Ast	Sack	Yds	Stuff	Yds	Int	Yds	PD	TD
Total	16	65	9	2.0	16.0	0.0	0.0	2	8	19	0
vs. Playoff	6	30	3	0.0	0.0	0.0	0.0	0	0	10	0
vs. Non-Playoff	10	35	6	2.0	16.0	0.0	0.0	2	8	9	0
vs. Own Division	8	39	7	1.0	11.0	0.0	0.0	0	0	7	0
Home	8	30	4	1.0	5.0	0.0	0.0	2	8	16	0
Away	8	35	5	1.0	11.0	0.0	0.0	0	0	3	0
Games 1-8	8	24	6	0.0	0.0	0.0	0.0	1	4	7	0
Games 9-16	8	41	3	2.0	16.0	0.0	0.0	1	4	12	0
September	3	6	2	0.0	0.0	0.0	0.0	0	0	1	0
October	5	18	4	0.0	0.0	0.0	0.0	1	4	6	0
November	4	22	2	2.0	16.0	0.0	0.0	1	4	2	0
December	4	19	1	0.0	0.0	0.0	0.0	0	0	10	0
Grass	12	52	5	1.0	5.0	0.0	0.0	2	8	18	0
Turf	4	13	4	1.0	11.0	0.0	0.0	0	0	1	0
Indoor	3	13	4	1.0	11.0	0.0	0.0	0	0	1	0
Outdoor	13	52	5	1.0	5.0	0.0	0.0	2	8	18	0

Game Logs

Date	Opp	Result	Tk	Ast	Sack	Yds	Stuff	Yds	Int	Yds	PD	FF	FR	TD
09/03	@Atl	L 20-23	4	2	0.0	0.0	0.0	0.0	0	0	1	0	0	0
09/10	@Buf	L 9-31	0	0	0.0	0.0	0.0	0.0	0	0	0	0	0	0
09/17	StL	L 10-31	2	0	0.0	0.0	0.0	0.0	0	0	0	0	0	0
10/01	TB	L 13-20	2	1	0.0	0.0	0.0	0.0	0	0	1	0	0	0
10/08	@Chi	L 27-31	4	0	0.0	0.0	0.0	0.0	0	0	1	0	0	0
10/15	NYA	W 26-15	4	0	0.0	0.0	0.0	0.0	1	4	3	0	0	0
10/22	NO	W 20-3	5	2	0.0	0.0	0.0	0.0	0	0	1	0	0	0
10/29	@NE	W 20-17	3	1	0.0	0.0	0.0	0.0	0	0	0	0	0	0
11/05	@SF	W 13-7	11	0	0.0	0.0	0.0	0.0	0	0	2	0	0	0
11/12	@StL	L 17-28	4	1	1.0	11.0	0.0	0.0	0	0	0	0	0	0
11/19	Ari	W 27-7	2	0	1.0	5.0	0.0	0.0	1	4	2	1	0	0
11/26	@NO	L 26-34	5	1	0.0	0.0	0.0	0.0	0	0	0	0	0	0
12/03	Ind	W 13-10	7	0	0.0	0.0	0.0	0.0	0	0	4	0	0	0
12/10	SF	L 10-31	5	0	0.0	0.0	0.0	0.0	0	0	4	0	0	0
12/17	Atl	W 21-17	3	1	0.0	0.0	0.0	0.0	0	0	1	0	0	0
12/24	@Was	L 17-20	4	0	0.0	0.0	0.0	0.0	0	0	1	0	0	0

Marquez Pope

San Francisco 49ers – CB

1995 Defensive Splits

	G	Tk	Ast	Sack	Yds	Stuff	Yds	Int	Yds	PD	TD
Total	16	59	5	0.0	0.0	3.0	20.0	1	-7	13	0
vs. Playoff	7	28	1	0.0	0.0	0.0	0.0	1	-7	3	0
vs. Non-Playoff	9	31	4	0.0	0.0	3.0	20.0	0	0	10	0
vs. Own Division	8	25	4	0.0	0.0	2.0	6.0	0	0	7	0
Home	8	25	2	0.0	0.0	1.0	14.0	1	-7	9	0
Away	8	34	3	0.0	0.0	2.0	6.0	0	0	4	0
Games 1-8	8	38	4	0.0	0.0	3.0	20.0	0	0	7	0
Games 9-16	8	21	1	0.0	0.0	0.0	0.0	1	-7	6	0
September	4	22	2	0.0	0.0	1.0	5.0	0	0	2	0
October	4	16	2	0.0	0.0	2.0	15.0	0	0	5	0
November	4	8	1	0.0	0.0	0.0	0.0	0	0	3	0
December	4	13	0	0.0	0.0	0.0	0.0	1	-7	3	0
Grass	10	31	3	0.0	0.0	1.0	14.0	1	-7	10	0
Turf	6	28	2	0.0	0.0	2.0	6.0	0	0	3	0
Indoor	4	19	2	0.0	0.0	1.0	5.0	0	0	3	0
Outdoor	12	40	3	0.0	0.0	2.0	15.0	1	-7	10	0

Game Logs

Date	Opp	Result	Tk	Ast	Sack	Yds	Stuff	Yds	Int	Yds	PD	FF	FR	TD
09/03	@NO	W 24-22	4	2	0.0	0.0	1.0	5.0	0	0	1	0	0	0
09/10	Atl	W 41-10	3	0	0.0	0.0	0.0	0.0	0	0	0	0	0	0
09/17	NE	W 28-3	6	0	0.0	0.0	0.0	0.0	0	0	0	0	0	0
09/25	@Det	L 24-27	9	0	0.0	0.0	0.0	0.0	0	0	1	0	0	0
10/01	NYN	W 20-6	3	0	0.0	0.0	1.0	14.0	0	2	0	0	0	0
10/15	@Ind	L 17-18	3	0	0.0	0.0	0.0	0.0	0	0	1	0	0	0
10/22	@StL	W 44-10	6	0	0.0	0.0	1.0	1.0	0	0	1	0	0	0
10/29	NO	L 7-11	4	2	0.0	0.0	0.0	0.0	0	0	2	0	0	0
11/05	Car	L 7-13	2	0	0.0	0.0	0.0	0.0	0	0	0	0	0	0
11/12	@Dal	W 38-20	3	0	0.0	0.0	0.0	0.0	0	0	1	0	0	0
11/20	@Mia	W 44-20	3	1	0.0	0.0	0.0	0.0	0	0	0	0	0	0
11/26	StL	W 41-13	0	0	0.0	0.0	0.0	0.0	0	0	3	0	0	0
12/03	Buf	W 27-17	4	0	0.0	0.0	0.0	0.0	1	-7	1	0	0	0
12/10	@Car	W 31-10	3	0	0.0	0.0	0.0	0.0	0	0	1	0	0	0
12/18	Min	W 37-30	3	0	0.0	0.0	0.0	0.0	0	0	1	0	0	0
12/24	@Atl	L 27-28	3	0	0.0	0.0	0.0	0.0	0	0	0	0	0	0

Robert Porcher

Detroit Lions – DT

1995 Defensive Splits

	G	Tk	Ast	Sack	Yds	Stuff	Yds	Int	Yds	PD	TD
Total	16	29	22	5.0	38.0	7.5	14.0	0	0	2	0
vs. Playoff	5	5	11	1.0	10.0	1.5	2.5	0	0	0	0
vs. Non-Playoff	11	24	11	4.0	28.0	6.0	11.5	0	0	2	0
vs. Own Division	8	16	12	2.0	17.0	2.5	4.5	0	0	1	0
Home	8	21	13	5.0	38.0	5.0	11.5	0	0	1	0
Away	8	8	9	0.0	0.0	2.5	2.5	0	0	1	0
Games 1-8	8	13	14	3.0	21.0	4.5	7.5	0	0	0	0
Games 9-16	8	16	8	2.0	17.0	3.0	6.5	0	0	2	0
September	4	6	6	3.0	21.0	0.5	1.5	0	0	0	0
October	4	7	8	0.0	0.0	4.0	6.0	0	0	0	0
November	4	12	3	1.0	8.0	1.0	3.0	0	0	0	0
December	4	4	5	1.0	9.0	2.0	3.5	0	0	2	0
Grass	4	5	3	0.0	0.0	2.5	2.5	0	0	0	0
Turf	12	24	19	5.0	38.0	5.0	11.5	0	0	2	0
Indoor	11	24	16	5.0	38.0	5.0	11.5	0	0	2	0
Outdoor	5	5	6	0.0	0.0	2.5	2.5	0	0	0	0

Game Logs

Date	Opp	Result	Tk	Ast	Sack	Yds	Stuff	Yds	Int	Yds	PD	FF	FR	TD
09/03	@Pit	L 20-23	0	3	0.0	0.0	0.0	0.0	0	0	0	0	0	0
09/10	@Min	L 10-20	1	1	0.0	0.0	0.0	0.0	0	0	0	0	0	0
09/17	Ari	L 17-20	3	1	2.0	11.0	0.0	0.0	0	0	0	0	0	0
09/25	SF	W 27-24	2	1	1.0	10.0	0.5	1.5	0	0	0	0	0	0
10/08	Cle	W 38-20	4	2	0.0	0.0	2.0	4.0	0	0	0	0	0	0
10/15	@GB	L 21-30	2	2	0.0	0.0	1.0	1.0	0	0	0	0	0	0
10/22	@Was	L 30-36	1	0	0.0	0.0	1.0	1.0	0	0	0	0	0	0
10/29	GB	W 24-16	0	4	0.0	0.0	0.0	0.0	0	0	0	0	0	0
11/05	@Atl	L 22-34	1	1	0.0	0.0	0.0	0.0	0	0	0	0	0	0
11/12	TB	W 27-24	4	1	1.0	8.0	0.5	0.5	0	0	1	0	0	0
11/19	@Chi	W 24-17	2	0	0.0	0.0	0.0	0.0	0	0	0	0	0	0
11/23	Min	W 44-38	5	1	0.0	0.0	0.5	2.5	0	0	0	0	0	0
12/04	Chi	W 27-7	2	2	1.0	9.0	0.0	0.0	0	0	1	0	0	0
12/10	@Hou	W 24-17	1	1	0.0	0.0	0.0	0.0	0	0	1	0	0	0
12/17	Jac	W 44-0	1	1	0.0	0.0	1.5	3.0	0	0	0	0	0	0
12/23	@TB	W 37-10	0	1	0.0	0.0	0.5	0.5	0	0	0	0	0	0

John Randle

New England... Minnesota Vikings – DT

1995 Defensive Splits

	G	Tk	Ast	Sack	Yds	Stuff	Yds	Int	Yds	PD	TD
Total	16	33	11	10.5	79.0	5.5	10.5	0	0	2	0
vs. Playoff	7	18	4	5.0	31.0	4.0	7.0	0	0	1	0
vs. Non-Playoff	9	15	7	5.5	48.0	1.5	3.5	0	0	1	0
vs. Own Division	8	19	9	6.5	44.0	3.0	6.0	0	0	1	0
Home	8	13	4	5.0	37.0	0.5	0.5	0	0	0	0
Away	8	20	7	5.5	42.0	5.0	10.0	0	0	2	0
Games 1-8	8	15	5	3.5	23.0	2.0	2.0	0	0	2	0
Games 9-16	8	18	6	7.0	56.0	3.5	8.5	0	0	0	0
September	4	8	3	3.0	17.0	1.5	1.5	0	0	2	0
October	4	7	2	0.5	6.0	0.5	0.5	0	0	0	0
November	4	13	5	5.0	41.0	3.5	8.5	0	0	0	0
December	4	5	1	2.0	15.0	0.0	0.0	0	0	0	0
Grass	5	11	5	3.5	33.0	2.0	4.0	0	0	1	0
Turf	11	22	6	7.0	46.0	3.5	6.5	0	0	1	0
Indoor	9	19	6	7.0	46.0	2.5	5.5	0	0	0	0
Outdoor	7	14	5	3.5	33.0	3.0	5.0	0	0	2	0

Game Logs

Date	Opp	Result	Tk	Ast	Sack	Yds	Stuff	Yds	Int	Yds	PD	FF	FR	TD
09/03	@Chi	L 14-31	2	2	1.0	8.0	0.0	0.0	0	0	1	0	0	0
09/10	Det	W 20-10	3	1	1.0	1.0	0.5	0.5	0	0	0	0	0	0
09/17	Dal	L 17-23	2	0	1.0	8.0	0.0	0.0	0	0	0	0	0	0
09/24	@Pit	W 44-24	1	0	0.0	0.0	1.0	1.0	0	0	1	0	0	0
10/08	Hou	W 23-17	2	0	0.0	0.0	0.0	0.0	0	0	0	0	0	0
10/15	@TB	L 17-20	1	1	0.5	6.0	0.0	0.0	0	0	0	0	0	0
10/22	@GB	L 21-38	4	0	0.0	0.0	0.5	0.5	0	0	0	0	0	0
10/30	Chi	L 6-14	0	1	0.0	0.0	0.0	0.0	0	0	0	0	0	0
11/05	GB	W 27-24	2	1	1.0	13.0	0.0	0.0	0	0	0	0	0	0
11/12	@Ari	W 30-24	4	2	2.0	19.0	1.5	3.5	0	0	1	0	0	0
11/19	NO	W 43-24	1	0	0.0	0.0	0.0	0.0	0	0	0	0	0	0
11/23	@Det	L 38-44	6	2	2.0	9.0	2.0	5.0	0	0	0	0	0	0
12/03	TB	W 31-17	1	1	1.0	7.0	0.0	0.0	0	0	0	0	0	0
12/09	Cle	W 27-11	2	0	1.0	8.0	0.0	0.0	0	0	0	0	0	0
12/18	@SF	L 30-37	0	0	0.0	0.0	0.0	0.0	0	0	0	0	0	0
12/24	@Cin	L 24-27	2	0	0.0	0.0	0.0	0.0	0	0	0	0	0	0

Thomas Randolph

New York Giants – CB

1995 Defensive Splits

	G	Tk	Ast	Sack	Yds	Stuff	Yds	Int	Yds	PD	TD
Total	16	52	6	0.0	0.0	0.5	1.5	2	15	9	0
vs. Playoff	8	27	2	0.0	0.0	0.5	1.5	0	0	3	0
vs. Non-Playoff	8	25	4	0.0	0.0	0.0	0.0	2	15	6	0
vs. Own Division	8	30	2	0.0	0.0	0.5	1.5	2	15	7	0
Home	8	27	4	0.0	0.0	0.5	1.5	0	0	4	0
Away	8	25	2	0.0	0.0	0.0	0.0	2	15	5	0
Games 1-8	8	21	3	0.0	0.0	0.5	1.5	1	0	5	0
Games 9-16	8	31	3	0.0	0.0	0.0	0.0	1	15	4	0
September	4	10	1	0.0	0.0	0.0	0.0	0	0	2	0
October	4	11	2	0.0	0.0	0.5	1.5	1	0	3	0
November	5	20	2	0.0	0.0	0.0	0.0	1	15	2	0
December	3	11	1	0.0	0.0	0.0	0.0	0	0	2	0
Grass	5	14	1	0.0	0.0	0.0	0.0	2	15	5	0
Turf	11	38	5	0.0	0.0	0.5	1.5	0	0	4	0
Indoor	1	1	1	0.0	0.0	0.0	0.0	0	0	0	0
Outdoor	15	51	5	0.0	0.0	0.5	1.5	2	15	9	0

Game Logs

Date	Opp	Result	Tk	Ast	Sack	Yds	Stuff	Yds	Int	Yds	PD	FF	FR	TD
09/04	Dal	L 0-35	5	0	0.0	0.0	0.0	0.0	0	0	1	0	0	0
09/10	@KC	L 17-20	4	0	0.0	0.0	0.0	0.0	0	0	0	0	0	0
09/17	@GB	L 6-14	0	1	0.0	0.0	0.0	0.0	0	0	1	0	0	0
09/24	NO	W 45-29	1	0	0.0	0.0	0.0	0.0	0	0	0	0	0	0
10/01	@SF	L 6-20	3	0	0.0	0.0	0.0	0.0	0	0	0	0	0	0
10/08	Ari	W 27-21	3	2	0.0	0.0	0.0	0.0	0	0	1	0	0	0
10/15	Phi	L 14-17	2	0	0.0	0.0	0.5	1.5	0	0	0	0	0	0
10/29	@Was	W 24-15	3	0	0.0	0.0	0.0	0.0	1	0	2	0	0	0
11/05	@Sea	L 28-30	1	1	0.0	0.0	0.0	0.0	0	0	0	0	1	0
11/12	Oak	L 13-17	4	0	0.0	0.0	0.0	0.0	0	0	0	0	0	0
11/19	@Phi	L 19-28	5	0	0.0	0.0	0.0	0.0	0	0	0	0	0	0
11/26	Chi	L 24-27	6	1	0.0	0.0	0.0	0.0	0	0	0	0	0	0
11/30	@Ari	W 10-6	4	0	0.0	0.0	0.0	0.0	1	15	2	0	0	0
12/10	Was	W 20-13	3	0	0.0	0.0	0.0	0.0	0	0	1	0	0	0
12/17	@Dal	L 20-21	5	0	0.0	0.0	0.0	0.0	0	0	0	0	0	0
12/23	SD	L 17-27	3	1	0.0	0.0	0.0	0.0	0	0	1	0	0	0

Terry Ray

New England Patriots – S

1995 Defensive Splits

	G	Tk	Ast	Sack	Yds	Stuff	Yds	Int	Yds	PD	TD
Total	16	82	23	0.0	0.0	3.0	8.0	1	21	8	0
vs. Playoff	10	51	16	0.0	0.0	2.0	3.0	1	21	5	0
vs. Non-Playoff	6	31	7	0.0	0.0	1.0	5.0	0	0	3	0
vs. Own Division	8	46	14	0.0	0.0	2.0	3.0	0	0	4	0
Home	8	43	14	0.0	0.0	2.0	7.0	0	0	2	0
Away	8	39	9	0.0	0.0	1.0	1.0	1	21	6	0
Games 1-8	8	40	12	0.0	0.0	2.0	7.0	1	21	5	0
Games 9-16	8	42	11	0.0	0.0	1.0	1.0	0	0	3	0
September	3	20	6	0.0	0.0	1.0	2.0	0	0	2	0
October	5	20	6	0.0	0.0	1.0	5.0	1	21	3	0
November	4	23	9	0.0	0.0	1.0	1.0	0	0	3	0
December	4	19	2	0.0	0.0	0.0	0.0	0	0	0	0
Grass	11	53	18	0.0	0.0	2.0	7.0	0	0	4	0
Turf	5	29	5	0.0	0.0	1.0	1.0	1	21	4	0
Indoor	2	14	2	0.0	0.0	0.0	0.0	1	21	1	0
Outdoor	14	68	21	0.0	0.0	3.0	8.0	0	0	7	0

Game Logs

Date	Opp	Result	Tk	Ast	Sack	Yds	Stuff	Yds	Int	Yds	PD	FF	FR	TD
09/03	Cle	W 17-14	8	2	0.0	0.0	0.0	0.0	0	0	0	0	0	0
09/10	Mia	L 3-20	9	3	0.0	0.0	1.0	2.0	0	0	1	0	0	0
09/17	@SF	L 3-28	3	1	0.0	0.0	0.0	0.0	0	0	2	0	0	0
10/01	@Atl	L 17-30	9	1	0.0	0.0	0.0	0.0	1	21	1	0	1	0
10/08	Den	L 3-37	3	2	0.0	0.0	0.0	0.0	0	0	1	0	0	0
10/15	@KC	L 26-31	2	0	0.0	0.0	0.0	0.0	0	0	0	0	0	0
10/23	Buf	W 27-14	3	1	0.0	0.0	0.0	0.0	0	0	1	0	1	0
10/29	Car	L 17-20	3	2	0.0	0.0	1.0	5.0	0	0	0	0	0	0
11/05	@NYA	W 20-7	7	1	0.0	0.0	1.0	1.0	0	0	2	1	0	0
11/12	@Mia	W 34-17	5	3	0.0	0.0	0.0	0.0	0	0	0	0	0	0
11/19	Ind	L 10-24	7	4	0.0	0.0	0.0	0.0	0	0	0	0	0	0
11/26	@Buf	W 35-25	4	1	0.0	0.0	1.0	1.0	0	0	1	0	0	0
12/03	NO	L 17-31	4	0	0.0	0.0	0.0	0.0	0	0	1	0	0	0
12/10	NYA	W 31-28	6	0	0.0	0.0	0.0	0.0	0	0	0	0	0	0
12/16	@Pit	L 27-41	4	1	0.0	0.0	0.0	0.0	0	0	0	0	0	0
12/23	@Ind	L 7-10	5	1	0.0	0.0	0.0	0.0	0	0	0	0	0	0

Corey Raymond

Detroit Lions – CB

1995 Defensive Splits

	G	Tk	Ast	Sack	Yds	Stuff	Yds	Int	Yds	PD	TD
Total	16	59	9	2.0	13.0	2.0	2.0	6	44	24	0
vs. Playoff	5	20	4	1.0	1.0	0.0	0.0	2	0	7	0
vs. Non-Playoff	11	39	5	1.0	12.0	2.0	2.0	4	44	17	0
vs. Own Division	8	32	2	0.0	0.0	1.5	1.5	4	26	12	0
Home	8	29	6	1.0	12.0	1.5	1.5	3	33	15	0
Away	8	30	3	1.0	1.0	0.5	0.5	3	11	9	0
Games 1-8	8	29	5	0.0	0.0	0.5	0.5	2	0	11	0
Games 9-16	8	30	4	2.0	13.0	1.5	1.5	4	44	13	0
September	4	15	3	0.0	0.0	0.0	0.0	1	0	6	0
October	4	14	2	0.0	0.0	0.5	0.5	1	0	5	0
November	4	17	0	1.0	1.0	0.0	0.0	2	15	6	0
December	4	13	4	1.0	12.0	1.5	1.5	2	29	7	0
Grass	4	12	1	0.0	0.0	0.5	0.5	2	11	5	0
Turf	12	47	8	2.0	13.0	1.5	1.5	4	33	19	0
Indoor	11	42	8	2.0	13.0	1.5	1.5	3	33	18	0
Outdoor	5	17	1	0.0	0.0	0.5	0.5	3	11	6	0

Game Logs

Date	Opp	Result	Tk	Ast	Sack	Yds	Stuff	Yds	Int	Yds	PD	FF	FR	TD
09/03	@Pit	L 20-23	5	0	0.0	0.0	0.0	0.0	1	0	1	0	0	0
09/10	@Min	L 10-20	5	0	0.0	0.0	0.0	0.0	0	0	1	0	1	0
09/17	Ari	L 17-20	0	0	0.0	0.0	0.0	0.0	0	0	0	0	0	0
09/25	SF	W 27-24	5	3	0.0	0.0	0.0	0.0	0	0	4	0	0	0
10/08	Cle	W 38-20	4	1	0.0	0.0	0.5	0.5	0	0	2	0	0	0
10/15	@GB	L 21-30	2	0	0.0	0.0	0.0	0.0	0	0	0	0	0	0
10/22	@Was	L 30-36	3	0	0.0	0.0	0.0	0.0	0	0	1	0	0	0
10/29	GB	W 24-16	5	1	0.0	0.0	0.0	0.0	1	0	2	0	0	0
11/05	@Atl	L 22-34	3	0	1.0	1.0	0.0	0.0	0	0	0	1	0	0
11/12	TB	W 27-24	7	0	0.0	0.0	0.0	0.0	0	0	2	0	0	0
11/19	@Chi	W 24-17	3	0	0.0	0.0	0.0	0.0	1	0	1	0	0	0
11/23	Min	W 44-38	4	0	0.0	0.0	0.0	0.0	1	15	3	0	0	0
12/04	Chi	W 27-7	2	0	0.0	0.0	1.0	1.0	0	0	0	0	0	0
12/10	@Hou	W 24-17	5	2	0.0	0.0	0.0	0.0	0	0	2	0	0	0
12/17	Jac	W 44-0	2	1	1.0	12.0	0.0	0.0	1	18	2	0	0	0
12/23	@TB	W 37-10	4	1	0.0	0.0	0.5	0.5	1	11	3	0	0	0

Ricky Reynolds

New England Patriots – CB

1995 Defensive Splits

	G	Tk	Ast	Sack	Yds	Stuff	Yds	Int	Yds	PD	TD
Total	16	69	19	2.5	21.0	3.5	11.5	3	6	9	0
vs. Playoff	10	39	10	1.0	7.0	2.5	4.5	1	2	6	0
vs. Non-Playoff	6	30	9	1.5	14.0	1.0	7.0	2	4	3	0
vs. Own Division	8	32	8	0.0	0.0	3.5	11.5	1	2	3	0
Home	8	32	14	1.5	14.0	2.0	10.0	3	6	4	0
Away	8	37	5	1.0	7.0	1.5	1.5	0	0	5	0
Games 1-8	8	33	12	2.5	21.0	0.0	0.0	3	4	6	0
Games 9-16	8	36	7	0.0	0.0	3.5	11.5	0	2	3	0
September	3	9	5	0.0	0.0	0.0	0.0	2	0	2	0
October	5	24	7	2.5	21.0	0.0	0.0	1	4	4	0
November	4	19	3	0.0	0.0	2.5	4.5	0	2	0	0
December	4	17	4	0.0	0.0	1.0	7.0	0	0	3	0
Grass	11	44	16	1.5	14.0	2.0	10.0	3	6	6	0
Turf	5	25	3	1.0	7.0	1.5	1.5	0	0	3	0
Indoor	2	8	2	1.0	7.0	0.0	0.0	0	0	2	0
Outdoor	14	61	17	1.5	14.0	3.5	11.5	3	6	7	0

Game Logs

Date	Opp	Result	Tk	Ast	Sack	Yds	Stuff	Yds	Int	Yds	PD	FF	FR	TD
09/03	Cle	W 17-14	3	2	0.0	0.0	0.0	0.0	1	0	1	0	0	0
09/10	Mia	L 3-20	1	2	0.0	0.0	0.0	0.0	1	0	1	0	1	0
09/17	@SF	L 3-28	5	1	0.0	0.0	0.0	0.0	0	0	0	0	0	0
10/01	@Atl	L 17-30	7	1	1.0	7.0	0.0	0.0	0	0	0	0	0	0
10/08	Den	L 3-37	3	3	0.0	0.0	0.0	0.0	0	0	1	0	0	0
10/15	@KC	L 26-31	3	0	0.0	0.0	0.0	0.0	0	0	2	0	0	0
10/23	Buf	W 27-14	4	1	0.0	0.0	0.0	0.0	0	0	0	1	0	0
10/29	Car	L 17-20	7	2	1.5	14.0	0.0	0.0	1	4	1	1	0	0
11/05	@NYA	W 20-7	7	0	0.0	0.0	0.0	0.0	0	0	0	0	0	0
11/12	@Mia	W 34-17	4	1	0.0	0.0	0.0	0.0	0	0	0	0	0	0
11/19	Ind	L 10-24	4	2	0.0	0.0	1.0	3.0	0	2	0	0	0	0
11/26	@Buf	W 35-25	4	0	0.0	0.0	1.5	1.5	0	0	0	0	0	0
12/03	NO	L 17-31	3	1	0.0	0.0	0.0	0.0	0	0	0	0	0	0
12/10	NYA	W 31-28	7	1	0.0	0.0	1.0	7.0	0	0	0	0	0	0
12/16	@Pit	L 27-41	6	1	0.0	0.0	0.0	0.0	0	0	1	0	0	0
12/23	@Ind	L 7-10	1	1	0.0	0.0	0.0	0.0	0	0	2	0	0	0

Stanley Richard

Washington Redskins – S

1995 Defensive Splits

	G	Tk	Ast	Sack	Yds	Stuff	Yds	Int	Yds	PD	TD
Total	16	85	12	0.0	0.0	1.5	2.0	3	24	11	0
vs. Playoff	6	43	5	0.0	0.0	1.0	1.0	2	24	5	0
vs. Non-Playoff	10	42	7	0.0	0.0	0.5	1.0	1	0	6	0
vs. Own Division	8	44	8	0.0	0.0	1.5	2.0	3	24	7	0
Home	8	45	4	0.0	0.0	1.0	1.0	0	0	4	0
Away	8	40	8	0.0	0.0	0.5	1.0	3	24	7	0
Games 1-8	8	37	7	0.0	0.0	0.0	0.0	2	0	4	0
Games 9-16	8	48	5	0.0	0.0	1.5	2.0	1	24	7	0
September	4	17	3	0.0	0.0	0.0	0.0	0	0	1	0
October	5	23	4	0.0	0.0	0.0	0.0	2	0	3	0
November	3	26	1	0.0	0.0	1.0	1.0	0	0	2	0
December	4	19	4	0.0	0.0	0.5	1.0	1	24	5	0
Grass	12	67	8	0.0	0.0	1.0	1.0	1	0	6	0
Turf	4	10	4	0.0	0.0	0.5	1.0	2	24	5	0
Indoor	1	5	0	0.0	0.0	0.0	0.0	0	0	1	0
Outdoor	15	80	12	0.0	0.0	1.5	2.0	3	24	10	0

Game Logs

Date	Opp	Result	Tk	Ast	Sack	Yds	Stuff	Yds	Int	Yds	PD	FF	FR	TD
09/03	Ari	W 27-7	4	0	0.0	0.0	0.0	0.0	0	0	1	0	0	0
09/10	Oak	L 8-20	6	1	0.0	0.0	0.0	0.0	0	0	0	0	0	0
09/17	@Den	L 31-38	4	0	0.0	0.0	0.0	0.0	0	0	0	0	0	0
09/24	@TB	L 6-14	3	2	0.0	0.0	0.0	0.0	0	0	0	0	0	0
10/01	Dal	W 27-23	4	1	0.0	0.0	0.0	0.0	0	0	0	0	0	0
10/08	@Phi	L 34-37	3	1	0.0	0.0	0.0	0.0	1	0	1	0	0	0
10/15	@Ari	L 20-24	7	2	0.0	0.0	0.0	0.0	1	0	1	0	0	0
10/22	Det	W 36-30	6	0	0.0	0.0	0.0	0.0	0	0	0	0	0	0
10/29	NYN	L 15-24	3	0	0.0	0.0	0.0	0.0	0	0	0	0	1	0
11/05	@KC	L 3-24	8	0	0.0	0.0	0.0	0.0	0	0	1	0	0	0
11/19	Sea	L 20-27	5	0	0.0	0.0	0.0	0.0	0	0	0	0	0	0
11/26	Phi	L 7-14	13	1	0.0	0.0	1.0	1.0	0	0	1	0	0	0
12/03	@Dal	W 24-17	9	2	0.0	0.0	0.0	0.0	1	24	1	0	0	0
12/10	@NYN	L 13-20	1	0	0.0	0.0	0.5	1.0	0	0	2	0	0	0
12/17	@StL	W 35-23	5	0	0.0	0.0	0.0	0.0	0	0	1	0	0	0
12/24	Car	W 20-17	4	1	0.0	0.0	0.0	0.0	0	0	1	0	0	0

Eddie Robinson
Houston Oilers – LB

1995 Defensive Splits

	G	Tk	Ast	Sack	Yds	Stuff	Yds	Int	Yds	PD	TD
Total	16	50	24	3.5	14.5	2.5	19.0	1	49	6	1
vs. Playoff	5	13	6	1.0	6.0	0.5	5.0	0	0	1	0
vs. Non-Playoff	11	37	18	2.5	8.5	2.0	14.0	1	49	5	1
vs. Own Division	8	22	15	2.0	5.0	1.5	18.0	1	49	3	1
Home	8	27	15	1.5	9.5	1.5	18.0	1	49	4	1
Away	8	23	9	2.0	5.0	1.0	1.0	0	0	2	0
Games 1-8	8	19	14	0.5	3.5	1.5	6.0	0	0	1	0
Games 9-16	8	31	10	3.0	11.0	1.0	13.0	1	49	5	1
September	4	7	6	0.0	0.0	0.5	5.0	0	0	1	0
October	4	12	8	0.5	3.5	1.0	1.0	0	0	0	0
November	4	22	6	2.0	5.0	1.0	13.0	1	49	3	1
December	4	9	4	1.0	6.0	0.0	0.0	0	0	2	0
Grass	4	14	3	2.0	5.0	1.0	1.0	0	0	1	0
Turf	12	36	21	1.5	9.5	1.5	18.0	1	49	5	1
Indoor	9	30	17	1.5	9.5	1.0	18.0	1	49	4	1
Outdoor	7	20	7	2.0	5.0	1.0	1.0	0	0	2	0

Game Logs

Date	Opp	Result	Tk	Ast	Sack	Yds	Stuff	Yds	Int	Yds	PD	FF	FR	TD
09/03	@Jac	W 10-3	2	1	0.0	0.0	0.0	0.0	0	0	1	0	0	0
09/10	Pit	L 17-34	2	2	0.0	0.0	0.5	5.0	0	0	0	0	0	0
09/17	Cle	L 7-14	1	3	0.0	0.0	0.0	0.0	0	0	0	0	0	0
09/24	@Cin	W 38-28	2	0	0.0	0.0	0.0	0.0	0	0	0	0	1	0
10/01	Jac	L 16-17	2	3	0.0	0.0	0.0	0.0	0	0	0	0	0	0
10/08	@Min	L 17-23	3	2	0.0	0.0	0.0	0.0	0	0	0	0	0	0
10/22	@Chi	L 32-35	4	0	0.0	0.0	1.0	1.0	0	0	0	0	0	0
10/29	TB	W 19-7	3	3	0.5	3.5	0.0	0.0	0	0	0	0	0	0
11/05	@Cle	W 37-10	5	2	2.0	5.0	0.0	0.0	0	0	0	0	0	0
11/12	Cin	L 25-32	5	3	0.0	0.0	1.0	13.0	1	49	2	0	0	1
11/19	@KC	L 13-20	3	0	0.0	0.0	0.0	0.0	0	0	0	0	0	0
11/26	Den	W 42-33	9	1	0.0	0.0	0.0	0.0	0	0	1	0	0	0
12/03	@Pit	L 7-21	3	1	0.0	0.0	0.0	0.0	0	0	1	0	0	0
12/10	Det	L 17-24	4	0	1.0	6.0	0.0	0.0	0	0	0	0	0	0
12/17	NYA	W 23-6	1	0	0.0	0.0	0.0	0.0	0	0	1	0	0	0
12/24	@Buf	W 28-17	1	3	0.0	0.0	0.0	0.0	0	0	1	0	0	0

Eugene Robinson
Seattle Seahawks – S

1995 Defensive Splits

	G	Tk	Ast	Sack	Yds	Stuff	Yds	Int	Yds	PD	TD
Total	16	80	26	0.0	0.0	1.0	2.0	1	32	4	0
vs. Playoff	6	26	13	0.0	0.0	1.0	2.0	0	0	1	0
vs. Non-Playoff	10	54	13	0.0	0.0	0.0	0.0	1	32	3	0
vs. Own Division	8	41	18	0.0	0.0	1.0	2.0	1	11	3	0
Home	8	34	16	0.0	0.0	0.0	0.0	0	0	1	0
Away	8	46	10	0.0	0.0	1.0	2.0	1	32	3	0
Games 1-8	8	37	18	0.0	0.0	0.0	0.0	0	0	0	0
Games 9-16	8	43	8	0.0	0.0	1.0	2.0	1	32	4	0
September	3	17	5	0.0	0.0	0.0	0.0	0	0	0	0
October	5	20	13	0.0	0.0	0.0	0.0	0	0	0	0
November	4	21	2	0.0	0.0	0.0	0.0	0	21	1	0
December	4	22	6	0.0	0.0	1.0	2.0	1	11	3	0
Grass	7	42	8	0.0	0.0	1.0	2.0	1	32	3	0
Turf	9	38	18	0.0	0.0	0.0	0.0	0	0	1	0
Indoor	8	34	16	0.0	0.0	0.0	0.0	0	0	1	0
Outdoor	8	46	10	0.0	0.0	1.0	2.0	1	32	3	0

Game Logs

Date	Opp	Result	Tk	Ast	Sack	Yds	Stuff	Yds	Int	Yds	PD	FF	FR	TD
09/03	KC	L 10-34	4	2	0.0	0.0	0.0	0.0	0	0	0	0	0	0
09/10	@SD	L 10-14	9	2	0.0	0.0	0.0	0.0	0	0	0	0	0	0
09/17	Cin	W 24-21	4	1	0.0	0.0	0.0	0.0	0	0	0	0	0	0
10/01	Den	W 27-10	3	2	0.0	0.0	0.0	0.0	0	0	0	0	0	0
10/08	@Oak	L 14-34	6	0	0.0	0.0	0.0	0.0	0	0	0	0	0	0
10/15	@Buf	L 21-27	4	2	0.0	0.0	0.0	0.0	0	0	0	0	0	0
10/22	SD	L 25-35	1	6	0.0	0.0	0.0	0.0	0	0	0	0	0	0
10/29	@Ari	L 14-20	6	3	0.0	0.0	0.0	0.0	0	0	0	0	1	0
11/05	NYN	W 30-28	9	0	0.0	0.0	0.0	0.0	0	0	1	0	0	0
11/12	@Jac	W 47-30	2	0	0.0	0.0	0.0	0.0	0	0	0	0	0	0
11/19	@Was	W 27-20	3	0	0.0	0.0	0.0	0.0	0	21	0	0	0	0
11/26	NYA	L 10-16	7	2	0.0	0.0	0.0	0.0	0	0	0	0	0	0
12/03	Phi	W 26-14	4	0	0.0	0.0	0.0	0.0	0	0	0	0	0	0
12/10	@Den	W 31-27	12	2	0.0	0.0	0.0	0.0	1	11	2	0	0	0
12/17	Oak	W 44-10	2	3	0.0	0.0	0.0	0.0	0	0	0	0	0	0
12/24	@KC	L 3-26	4	1	0.0	0.0	1.0	2.0	0	0	1	0	0	0

Bill Romanowski
Philadelphia Eagles – LB

1995 Defensive Splits

	G	Tk	Ast	Sack	Yds	Stuff	Yds	Int	Yds	PD	TD
Total	16	50	13	1.0	1.0	2.5	6.5	2	5	7	0
vs. Playoff	3	9	1	0.0	0.0	0.0	0.0	0	0	1	0
vs. Non-Playoff	13	41	12	1.0	1.0	2.5	6.5	2	5	6	0
vs. Own Division	8	27	7	0.0	0.0	1.5	3.5	1	7	3	0
Home	8	15	2	0.0	0.0	0.0	0.0	0	0	3	0
Away	8	35	11	1.0	1.0	2.5	6.5	2	5	4	0
Games 1-8	8	15	9	0.0	0.0	0.5	0.5	1	7	3	0
Games 9-16	8	35	4	1.0	1.0	2.0	6.0	1	-2	4	0
September	4	9	6	0.0	0.0	0.5	0.5	1	7	2	0
October	4	6	3	0.0	0.0	0.0	0.0	0	0	1	0
November	4	12	1	0.0	0.0	1.0	3.0	0	0	1	0
December	4	23	3	1.0	1.0	1.0	3.0	1	-2	3	0
Grass	4	24	6	0.0	0.0	2.5	6.5	2	5	3	0
Turf	12	26	7	1.0	1.0	0.0	0.0	0	0	4	0
Indoor	2	3	3	1.0	1.0	0.0	0.0	0	0	1	0
Outdoor	14	47	10	0.0	0.0	2.5	6.5	2	5	6	0

Game Logs

Date	Opp	Result	Tk	Ast	Sack	Yds	Stuff	Yds	Int	Yds	PD	FF	FR	TD
09/03	TB	L 6-21	0	0	0.0	0.0	0.0	0.0	0	0	0	0	0	0
09/10	@Ari	W 31-19	2	4	0.0	0.0	0.5	0.5	1	7	2	0	0	0
09/17	SD	L 21-27	2	1	0.0	0.0	0.0	0.0	0	0	0	0	0	0
09/24	@Oak	L 17-48	5	1	0.0	0.0	0.0	0.0	0	0	0	0	0	0
10/01	@NO	W 15-10	1	0	0.0	0.0	0.0	0.0	0	0	0	0	0	0
10/08	Was	W 37-34	1	0	0.0	0.0	0.0	0.0	0	0	0	0	0	0
10/15	@NYN	W 17-14	4	2	0.0	0.0	0.0	0.0	0	0	0	0	0	0
10/29	StL	W 20-9	0	1	0.0	0.0	0.0	0.0	0	0	1	0	0	0
11/06	@Dal	L 12-34	4	0	0.0	0.0	0.0	0.0	0	0	0	0	0	0
11/12	Den	W 31-13	1	0	0.0	0.0	0.0	0.0	0	0	1	0	0	0
11/19	NYN	W 28-19	2	0	0.0	0.0	0.0	0.0	0	0	0	0	0	0
11/26	@Was	W 14-7	5	1	0.0	0.0	1.0	3.0	0	0	0	0	0	0
12/03	@Sea	L 14-26	2	3	1.0	1.0	0.0	0.0	0	0	1	0	0	0
12/10	Dal	W 20-17	3	0	0.0	0.0	0.0	0.0	0	0	1	0	0	0
12/17	Ari	W 21-20	6	0	0.0	0.0	0.0	0.0	0	0	0	0	0	0
12/24	@Chi	L 14-20	12	0	0.0	0.0	1.0	3.0	1	-2	1	0	1	0

Kevin Ross

1995 Defensive Splits

	G	Tk	Ast	Sack	Yds	Stuff	Yds	Int	Yds	PD	TD
Total	16	76	18	0.0	0.0	4.5	5.5	3	70	13	1
vs. Playoff	6	29	8	0.0	0.0	3.0	3.0	2	50	4	0
vs. Non-Playoff	10	47	10	0.0	0.0	1.5	2.5	1	20	9	1
vs. Own Division	8	42	2	0.0	0.0	1.5	2.5	1	17	5	1
Home	8	33	6	0.0	0.0	0.5	0.5	2	37	8	0
Away	8	43	12	0.0	0.0	4.0	5.0	1	33	5	1
Games 1-8	8	44	8	0.0	0.0	1.5	2.5	1	20	7	1
Games 9-16	8	32	10	0.0	0.0	3.0	3.0	2	50	6	0
September	4	22	2	0.0	0.0	0.0	0.0	1	20	5	0
October	4	22	6	0.0	0.0	1.5	2.5	0	0	2	1
November	4	16	6	0.0	0.0	2.5	2.5	0	0	3	0
December	4	16	4	0.0	0.0	0.5	0.5	2	50	3	0
Grass	5	22	10	0.0	0.0	0.5	0.5	1	33	4	0
Turf	11	54	8	0.0	0.0	4.0	5.0	2	37	9	1
Indoor	9	37	7	0.0	0.0	0.5	0.5	2	37	9	0
Outdoor	7	39	11	0.0	0.0	4.0	5.0	1	33	4	1

Game Logs

Date	Opp	Result	Tk	Ast	Sack	Yds	Stuff	Yds	Int	Yds	PD	FF	FR	TD
09/03	Car	W 23-20	4	1	0.0	0.0	0.0	0.0	0	0	2	0	0	0
09/10	@SF	L 10-41	8	0	0.0	0.0	0.0	0.0	0	0	0	0	0	0
09/17	@NO	W 27-24	4	1	0.0	0.0	0.0	0.0	0	0	1	0	0	0
09/24	NYA	W 13-3	6	0	0.0	0.0	0.0	0.0	1	20	2	0	1	0
10/01	NE	W 30-17	5	2	0.0	0.0	0.0	0.0	0	0	0	0	0	0
10/12	@StL	L 19-21	9	0	0.0	0.0	1.5	2.5	0	0	0	0	1	1
10/22	@TB	W 24-21	4	2	0.0	0.0	0.0	0.0	0	0	2	0	0	0
10/29	Dal	L 13-28	4	2	0.0	0.0	0.0	0.0	0	0	0	0	0	0
11/05	Det	W 34-22	1	1	0.0	0.0	0.5	0.5	0	0	2	0	0	0
11/12	@Buf	L 17-23	8	1	0.0	0.0	2.0	2.0	0	0	0	0	0	0
11/19	StL	W 31-6	3	0	0.0	0.0	0.0	0.0	0	0	0	0	0	0
11/26	@Ari	L 37-40	4	4	0.0	0.0	0.0	0.0	0	0	1	0	0	0
12/03	@Mia	L 20-21	2	4	0.0	0.0	0.5	0.5	1	33	1	0	0	0
12/10	NO	W 19-14	4	0	0.0	0.0	0.0	0.0	0	0	1	0	0	0
12/17	@Car	L 17-21	4	0	0.0	0.0	0.0	0.0	0	0	1	0	0	0
12/24	SF	W 28-27	6	0	0.0	0.0	0.0	0.0	1	17	1	0	0	0

Dan Saleaumua

1995 Defensive Splits

	G	Tk	Ast	Sack	Yds	Stuff	Yds	Int	Yds	PD	TD
Total	16	47	8	7.0	50.0	6.5	14.5	1	0	4	0
vs. Playoff	4	9	2	0.0	0.0	2.0	3.0	0	0	0	0
vs. Non-Playoff	12	38	6	7.0	50.0	4.5	11.5	1	0	4	0
vs. Own Division	8	21	2	3.0	24.0	3.0	5.0	1	0	3	0
Home	8	31	2	4.0	28.0	4.5	11.5	1	0	3	0
Away	8	16	6	3.0	22.0	2.0	3.0	0	0	1	0
Games 1-8	8	32	7	4.0	30.0	5.0	8.0	1	0	3	0
Games 9-16	8	15	1	3.0	20.0	1.5	6.5	0	0	1	0
September	4	22	3	3.0	18.0	1.5	2.5	1	0	2	0
October	4	10	4	1.0	12.0	3.5	5.5	0	0	1	0
November	4	9	0	1.0	4.0	1.0	5.0	0	0	0	0
December	4	6	1	2.0	16.0	0.5	1.5	0	0	1	0
Grass	14	43	8	6.0	42.0	6.5	14.5	1	0	3	0
Turf	2	4	0	1.0	8.0	0.0	0.0	0	0	1	0
Indoor	1	3	0	1.0	8.0	0.0	0.0	0	0	1	0
Outdoor	15	44	8	6.0	42.0	6.5	14.5	1	0	3	0

Game Logs

Date	Opp	Result	Tk	Ast	Sack	Yds	Stuff	Yds	Int	Yds	PD	FF	FR	TD
09/03	@Sea	W 34-10	3	0	1.0	8.0	0.0	0.0	0	0	1	0	0	0
09/10	NYN	W 20-17	8	1	1.0	2.0	0.0	0.0	0	0	0	0	0	0
09/17	Oak	W 23-17	7	0	0.0	0.0	0.0	0.0	1	0	1	0	0	0
09/24	@Cle	L 17-35	4	2	1.0	8.0	1.5	2.5	0	0	0	0	0	0
10/01	@Ari	W 24-3	1	2	0.0	0.0	0.0	0.0	0	0	1	1	0	0
10/09	SD	W 29-23	3	1	0.0	0.0	2.0	3.0	0	0	0	0	0	0
10/15	NE	W 31-26	5	0	1.0	12.0	1.0	2.0	0	0	1	0	0	0
10/22	@Den	W 21-7	1	1	0.0	0.0	0.5	0.5	0	0	0	0	0	0
11/05	Was	W 24-3	2	0	1.0	4.0	0.0	0.0	0	0	0	0	0	0
11/12	@SD	W 22-7	3	0	0.0	0.0	0.0	0.0	0	0	0	0	0	0
11/19	Hou	W 20-13	3	0	0.0	0.0	1.0	5.0	0	0	0	0	0	0
11/23	@Dal	L 12-24	1	0	0.0	0.0	0.0	0.0	0	0	0	0	0	0
12/03	@Oak	W 29-23	1	0	1.0	6.0	0.0	0.0	0	0	1	0	0	0
12/11	@Mia	L 6-13	2	1	0.0	0.0	0.0	0.0	0	0	0	0	0	0
12/17	Den	W 20-17	2	0	0.0	0.0	0.5	1.5	0	0	1	0	0	0
12/24	Sea	W 26-3	1	0	1.0	10.0	0.0	0.0	0	0	0	0	0	0

Deion Sanders

1995 Defensive Splits

	G	Tk	Ast	Sack	Yds	Stuff	Yds	Int	Yds	PD	TD
Total	9	25	1	0.0	0.0	1.0	2.0	2	34	8	0
vs. Playoff	5	12	0	0.0	0.0	1.0	2.0	1	0	4	0
vs. Non-Playoff	4	13	1	0.0	0.0	0.0	0.0	1	34	4	0
vs. Own Division	5	14	1	0.0	0.0	1.0	2.0	1	0	5	0
Home	5	11	1	0.0	0.0	0.0	0.0	1	0	3	0
Away	4	14	0	0.0	0.0	1.0	2.0	1	34	5	0
Games 1-8	1	0	0	0.0	0.0	0.0	0.0	0	0	1	0
Games 9-16	8	25	1	0.0	0.0	1.0	2.0	2	34	7	0
September	0	0	0	0	0	0	0	0	0	0	0
October	1	0	0	0.0	0.0	0.0	0.0	0	0	1	0
November	4	13	0	0.0	0.0	0.0	0.0	2	34	3	0
December	4	12	1	0.0	0.0	1.0	2.0	0	0	4	0
Grass	2	9	0	0.0	0.0	0.0	0.0	1	34	3	0
Turf	7	16	1	0.0	0.0	1.0	2.0	1	0	5	0
Indoor	1	0	0	0.0	0.0	0.0	0.0	0	0	1	0
Outdoor	8	25	1	0.0	0.0	1.0	2.0	2	34	7	0

Game Logs

Date	Opp	Result	Tk	Ast	Sack	Yds	Stuff	Yds	Int	Yds	PD	FF	FR	TD
09/24	Ari	W 34-20	-	-	-	-	-	-	-	-	-	-	-	-
10/01	@Was	L 23-27	-	-	-	-	-	-	-	-	-	-	-	-
10/08	GB	W 34-24	-	-	-	-	-	-	-	-	-	-	-	-
10/15	@SD	W 23-9	-	-	-	-	-	-	-	-	-	-	-	-
10/29	@Atl	W 28-13	0	0	0.0	0.0	0.0	0.0	0	0	1	0	0	0
11/06	Phi	W 34-12	2	0	0.0	0.0	0.0	0.0	1	0	1	0	0	0
11/12	SF	L 20-38	2	0	0.0	0.0	0.0	0.0	0	0	0	0	0	0
11/19	@Oak	W 34-21	6	0	0.0	0.0	0.0	0.0	1	34	1	0	0	0
11/23	KC	W 24-12	3	0	0.0	0.0	0.0	0.0	0	0	1	0	0	0
12/03	Was	L 17-24	2	0	0.0	0.0	1.0	2.0	0	0	1	0	0	0
12/10	@Phi	L 17-20	5	0	0.0	0.0	0.0	0.0	0	0	1	0	0	0
12/17	NYN	W 21-20	2	1	0.0	0.0	0.0	0.0	0	0	1	0	0	0
12/25	@Ari	W 37-13	3	0	0.0	0.0	0.0	0.0	0	0	2	0	0	0

Kurt Schulz
Buffalo Bills – S

1995 Defensive Splits

	G	Tk	Ast	Sack	Yds	Stuff	Yds	Int	Yds	PD	TD
Total	13	39	16	0.0	0.0	2.5	6.5	6	48	12	1
vs. Playoff	6	19	7	0.0	0.0	0.5	0.5	2	0	4	0
vs. Non-Playoff	7	20	9	0.0	0.0	2.0	6.0	4	48	8	1
vs. Own Division	6	18	9	0.0	0.0	1.5	3.5	2	16	4	0
Home	6	12	7	0.0	0.0	2.0	6.0	4	48	8	1
Away	7	27	9	0.0	0.0	0.5	0.5	2	0	4	0
Games 1-8	8	27	11	0.0	0.0	2.5	6.5	4	48	9	1
Games 9-16	5	12	5	0.0	0.0	0.0	0.0	2	0	3	0
September	3	12	4	0.0	0.0	0.5	0.5	1	32	4	1
October	5	15	7	0.0	0.0	2.0	6.0	3	16	5	0
November	2	5	3	0.0	0.0	0.0	0.0	2	0	3	0
December	3	7	2	0.0	0.0	0.0	0.0	0	0	0	0
Grass	5	21	6	0.0	0.0	0.5	0.5	1	0	3	0
Turf	8	18	10	0.0	0.0	2.0	6.0	5	48	9	1
Indoor	2	6	3	0.0	0.0	0.0	0.0	1	0	1	0
Outdoor	11	33	13	0.0	0.0	2.5	6.5	5	48	11	1

Game Logs

Date	Opp	Result	Tk	Ast	Sack	Yds	Stuff	Yds	Int	Yds	PD	FF	FR	TD
09/03	@Den	L 7-22	7	0	0.0	0.0	0.0	0.0	0	0	2	1	0	0
09/10	Car	W 31-9	1	2	0.0	0.0	0.0	0.0	1	32	1	0	0	1
09/17	Ind	W 20-14	4	2	0.0	0.0	0.5	0.5	0	0	1	1	0	0
10/02	@Cle	W 22-19	3	1	0.0	0.0	0.0	0.0	1	0	1	0	0	0
10/08	NYA	W 29-10	2	1	0.0	0.0	0.5	2.5	1	16	2	0	0	0
10/15	Sea	W 27-21	2	1	0.0	0.0	1.0	3.0	1	0	2	0	0	0
10/23	@NE	L 14-27	2	3	0.0	0.0	0.5	0.5	0	0	0	0	0	0
10/29	@Mia	L 6-23	6	1	0.0	0.0	0.0	0.0	0	0	0	0	0	0
11/05	@Ind	W 16-10	3	2	0.0	0.0	0.0	0.0	1	0	1	0	0	0
11/12	Atl	W 23-17	2	1	0.0	0.0	0.0	0.0	1	0	2	0	0	0
11/19	@NYA	W 28-26	-											
11/26	NE	L 25-35	-											
12/03	@SF	L 17-27	3	1	0.0	0.0	0.0	0.0	0	0	0	0	0	0
12/10	@StL	W 45-27	3	1	0.0	0.0	0.0	0.0	0	0	0	0	0	0
12/17	Mia	W 23-20	1	0	0.0	0.0	0.0	0.0	0	0	0	0	0	0
12/24	Hou	L 17-28	-											

Bryan Schwartz
Jacksonville Jaguars – LB

1995 Defensive Splits

	G	Tk	Ast	Sack	Yds	Stuff	Yds	Int	Yds	PD	TD
Total	14	75	26	0.0	0.0	6.5	13.5	0	0	2	0
vs. Playoff	4	16	14	0.0	0.0	3.5	6.5	0	0	1	0
vs. Non-Playoff	10	59	12	0.0	0.0	3.0	7.0	0	0	1	0
vs. Own Division	7	33	14	0.0	0.0	1.0	1.0	0	0	0	0
Home	7	28	12	0.0	0.0	1.0	3.0	0	0	1	0
Away	7	47	14	0.0	0.0	5.5	10.5	0	0	1	0
Games 1-8	6	28	6	0.0	0.0	2.0	4.0	0	0	1	0
Games 9-16	8	47	20	0.0	0.0	4.5	9.5	0	0	1	0
September	3	15	2	0.0	0.0	2.0	4.0	0	0	0	0
October	4	19	7	0.0	0.0	0.0	0.0	0	0	1	0
November	3	12	5	0.0	0.0	0.0	0.0	0	0	0	0
December	4	29	12	0.0	0.0	4.5	9.5	0	0	1	0
Grass	10	48	15	0.0	0.0	2.0	6.0	0	0	2	0
Turf	4	27	11	0.0	0.0	4.5	7.5	0	0	0	0
Indoor	1	7	7	0.0	0.0	2.5	3.5	0	0	0	0
Outdoor	13	68	19	0.0	0.0	4.0	10.0	0	0	2	0

Game Logs

Date	Opp	Result	Tk	Ast	Sack	Yds	Stuff	Yds	Int	Yds	PD	FF	FR	TD
09/03	Hou	L 3-10	1	1	0.0	0.0	0.0	0.0	0	0	0	0	0	0
09/10	@Cin	L 17-24	6	0	0.0	0.0	1.0	1.0	0	0	0	0	0	0
09/17	@NYA	L 10-27	8	1	0.0	0.0	1.0	3.0	0	0	0	0	0	0
09/24	GB	L 14-24	-											
10/01	@Hou	W 17-16	-											
10/08	Pit	W 20-16	0	2	0.0	0.0	0.0	0.0	0	0	1	0	0	0
10/15	Chi	L 27-30	6	0	0.0	0.0	0.0	0.0	0	0	0	0	0	0
10/22	@Cle	W 23-15	7	2	0.0	0.0	0.0	0.0	0	0	0	0	1	0
10/29	@Pit	L 7-24	6	3	0.0	0.0	0.0	0.0	0	0	1	0	0	0
11/12	Sea	L 30-47	5	1	0.0	0.0	0.0	0.0	0	0	0	0	0	0
11/19	@TB	L 16-17	4	1	0.0	0.0	0.0	0.0	0	0	0	0	0	0
11/26	Cin	L 13-17	3	3	0.0	0.0	0.0	0.0	0	0	0	0	0	0
12/03	@Den	L 23-31	9	0	0.0	0.0	1.0	3.0	0	0	1	0	0	0
12/10	Ind	L 31-41	3	2	0.0	0.0	1.0	3.0	0	0	0	0	0	0
12/17	@Det	L 0-44	7	7	0.0	0.0	2.5	3.5	0	0	0	0	0	0
12/24	Cle	W 24-21	10	3	0.0	0.0	0.0	0.0	0	0	0	1	0	0

Tracy Scroggins
Detroit Lions – DE

1995 Defensive Splits

	G	Tk	Ast	Sack	Yds	Stuff	Yds	Int	Yds	PD	TD
Total	16	35	10	9.5	56.0	5.5	20.0	0	0	6	1
vs. Playoff	5	9	5	3.0	14.0	4.0	17.5	0	0	4	0
vs. Non-Playoff	11	26	5	6.5	42.0	1.5	2.5	0	0	2	1
vs. Own Division	8	24	7	4.0	20.0	2.5	4.0	0	0	3	1
Home	8	11	4	5.0	30.0	2.0	4.0	0	0	5	0
Away	8	24	6	4.5	26.0	3.5	16.0	0	0	1	1
Games 1-8	8	15	7	6.0	31.0	3.5	9.0	0	0	5	0
Games 9-16	8	20	3	3.5	25.0	2.0	11.0	0	0	1	1
September	4	8	3	4.0	25.0	2.0	6.0	0	0	3	0
October	4	7	4	2.0	6.0	1.5	3.0	0	0	2	0
November	4	10	0	0.0	0.0	2.0	11.0	0	0	1	0
December	4	10	3	3.5	25.0	0.0	0.0	0	0	0	1
Grass	4	15	4	2.0	7.0	1.5	3.0	0	0	1	0
Turf	12	20	6	7.5	49.0	4.0	17.0	0	0	5	1
Indoor	11	18	6	6.5	41.0	3.0	14.0	0	0	5	1
Outdoor	5	17	4	3.0	15.0	2.5	6.0	0	0	1	1

Game Logs

Date	Opp	Result	Tk	Ast	Sack	Yds	Stuff	Yds	Int	Yds	PD	FF	FR	TD
09/03	@Pit	L 20-23	2	0	1.0	8.0	1.0	3.0	0	0	0	0	0	0
09/10	@Min	L 10-20	3	1	0.0	0.0	0.0	0.0	0	0	0	0	0	0
09/17	Ari	L 17-20	3	1	3.0	17.0	0.5	1.5	0	0	1	0	0	0
09/25	SF	W 27-24	0	1	0.0	0.0	0.5	1.5	0	0	2	0	0	0
10/08	Cle	W 38-20	0	0	0.0	0.0	0.0	0.0	0	0	0	0	0	0
10/15	@GB	L 21-30	5	2	1.0	0.0	1.5	3.0	0	0	1	0	0	0
10/22	@Was	L 30-36	1	0	0.0	0.0	0.0	0.0	0	0	0	0	0	0
10/29	GB	W 24-16	1	2	1.0	6.0	0.0	0.0	0	0	1	1	0	0
11/05	@Atl	L 22-34	1	0	0.0	0.0	1.0	10.0	0	0	0	0	0	0
11/12	TB	W 27-24	3	0	0.0	0.0	1.0	1.0	0	0	1	0	0	0
11/19	@Chi	W 24-17	5	0	0.0	0.0	0.0	0.0	0	0	0	0	0	0
11/23	Min	W 44-38	1	0	0.0	0.0	0.0	0.0	0	0	0	0	0	0
12/04	Chi	W 27-7	2	0	1.0	7.0	0.0	0.0	0	0	0	0	0	0
12/10	@Hou	W 24-17	3	1	1.5	11.0	0.0	0.0	0	0	0	1	0	0
12/17	Jac	W 44-0	1	0	0.0	0.0	0.0	0.0	0	0	0	0	0	1
12/23	@TB	W 37-10	4	2	1.0	7.0	0.0	0.0	0	0	0	1	1	1

Ray Seals
San Diego... Pittsburgh Steelers – DE

1995 Defensive Splits

	G	Tk	Ast	Sack	Yds	Stuff	Yds	Int	Yds	PD	TD
Total	16	33	15	8.5	56.0	7.0	11.0	1	0	8	0
vs. Playoff	4	14	3	2.5	15.0	3.0	5.0	0	0	1	0
vs. Non-Playoff	12	19	12	6.0	41.0	4.0	6.0	1	0	7	0
vs. Own Division	8	14	8	4.0	28.0	2.5	3.0	1	0	4	0
Home	8	19	8	6.5	50.0	3.0	4.0	0	0	4	0
Away	8	14	7	2.0	6.0	4.0	7.0	1	0	4	0
Games 1-8	8	19	11	4.5	35.0	4.0	6.0	0	0	1	0
Games 9-16	8	14	4	4.0	21.0	3.0	5.0	1	0	7	0
September	4	12	8	1.5	5.0	3.0	5.0	0	0	1	0
October	4	7	3	3.0	30.0	1.0	1.0	0	0	0	0
November	4	6	1	2.0	7.0	0.0	0.0	1	0	4	0
December	4	8	3	2.0	14.0	3.0	5.0	0	0	3	0
Grass	6	12	3	2.0	6.0	4.0	7.0	0	0	2	0
Turf	10	21	12	6.5	50.0	3.0	4.0	1	0	6	0
Indoor	1	0	3	0.0	0.0	0.0	0.0	0	0	0	0
Outdoor	15	33	12	8.5	56.0	7.0	11.0	1	0	8	0

Game Logs

Date	Opp	Result	Tk	Ast	Sack	Yds	Stuff	Yds	Int	Yds	PD	FF	FR	TD
09/03	Det	W 23-20	4	2	0.5	4.0	0.0	0.0	0	0	0	0	0	0
09/10	@Hou	W 34-17	0	3	0.0	0.0	0.0	0.0	0	0	0	0	1	0
09/18	@Mia	L 10-23	7	0	1.0	1.0	3.0	5.0	0	0	1	0	0	0
09/24	Min	L 24-44	1	3	0.0	0.0	0.0	0.0	0	0	0	0	0	0
10/01	SD	W 31-16	2	0	1.0	10.0	0.0	0.0	0	0	0	0	0	0
10/08	@Jac	L 16-20	0	2	0.0	0.0	0.0	0.0	0	0	0	0	0	0
10/19	Cin	L 9-27	1	0	0.0	0.0	0.0	0.0	0	0	0	0	0	0
10/29	Jac	W 24-7	4	1	2.0	20.0	1.0	1.0	0	0	0	0	0	0
11/05	@Chi	W 37-34	2	0	1.0	5.0	0.0	0.0	0	0	0	0	0	0
11/13	Cle	W 20-3	1	0	1.0	2.0	0.0	0.0	0	0	2	0	0	0
11/19	@Cin	W 49-31	2	1	0.0	0.0	0.0	0.0	1	0	2	0	0	0
11/26	@Cle	W 20-17	1	0	0.0	0.0	0.0	0.0	0	0	0	0	0	0
12/03	Hou	W 21-7	5	1	1.0	6.0	1.5	2.0	0	0	1	0	0	0
12/10	@Oak	W 29-10	1	0	0.0	0.0	1.0	2.0	0	0	1	0	0	0
12/16	NE	W 41-27	1	1	1.0	8.0	0.5	1.0	0	0	2	1	0	0
12/24	@GB	L 19-24	1	1	0.0	0.0	0.0	0.0	0	0	0	0	0	0

Junior Seau
San Diego Chargers – LB

1995 Defensive Splits

	G	Tk	Ast	Sack	Yds	Stuff	Yds	Int	Yds	PD	TD
Total	16	111	19	2.0	10.0	10.5	21.0	2	5	8	1
vs. Playoff	7	51	7	1.0	3.0	5.0	9.5	1	3	2	1
vs. Non-Playoff	9	60	12	1.0	7.0	5.5	11.5	1	2	6	0
vs. Own Division	8	51	11	2.0	10.0	3.0	7.0	1	2	5	0
Home	8	52	10	1.0	3.0	2.0	5.0	1	3	5	0
Away	8	59	9	1.0	7.0	8.5	16.0	1	2	3	1
Games 1-8	8	47	11	1.0	7.0	4.0	5.5	0	0	3	0
Games 9-16	8	64	8	1.0	3.0	6.5	15.5	2	5	5	0
September	4	26	5	0.0	0.0	1.0	1.0	0	0	2	0
October	4	21	6	1.0	7.0	3.0	4.5	0	0	1	0
November	4	32	4	1.0	3.0	2.0	5.0	2	5	3	0
December	4	32	4	0.0	0.0	4.5	10.5	0	0	2	0
Grass	11	72	15	1.0	3.0	3.0	6.0	2	5	7	0
Turf	5	39	4	1.0	7.0	7.5	15.0	0	0	1	1
Indoor	2	12	1	1.0	7.0	3.0	8.0	0	0	0	0
Outdoor	14	99	18	1.0	3.0	7.5	13.0	2	5	8	1

Game Logs

Date	Opp	Result	Tk	Ast	Sack	Yds	Stuff	Yds	Int	Yds	PD	FF	FR	TD
09/03	@Oak	L 7-17	2	2	0.0	0.0	0.0	0.0	0	0	0	0	0	0
09/10	Sea	W 14-10	2	2	0.0	0.0	0.0	0.0	0	0	1	0	0	0
09/17	@Phi	W 27-21	12	0	0.0	0.0	1.0	1.0	0	0	0	1	1	1
09/24	Den	W 17-6	10	1	0.0	0.0	0.0	0.0	0	0	1	0	0	0
10/01	@Pit	L 16-31	4	1	0.0	0.0	1.5	2.0	0	0	1	0	0	0
10/09	@KC	L 23-29	8	1	0.0	0.0	0.0	0.0	0	0	1	0	0	0
10/15	Dal	L 9-23	5	3	0.0	0.0	0.5	0.5	0	0	0	1	0	0
10/22	@Sea	W 35-25	4	1	1.0	7.0	1.0	2.0	0	0	0	0	0	0
11/05	Mia	L 14-24	7	0	0.0	0.0	0.0	0.0	1	3	1	0	0	0
11/12	KC	L 7-22	7	2	1.0	3.0	0.0	0.0	0	0	0	0	0	0
11/19	@Den	L 27-30	10	2	0.0	0.0	1.0	1.0	1	2	1	0	0	0
11/27	Oak	W 12-6	8	0	0.0	0.0	1.0	4.0	0	0	1	0	0	0
12/03	Cle	W 31-13	8	2	0.0	0.0	0.5	0.5	0	0	0	0	0	0
12/09	Ari	W 28-25	5	0	0.0	0.0	0.0	0.0	0	0	0	0	0	0
12/17	@Ind	W 27-24	8	1	0.0	0.0	2.0	6.0	0	0	0	0	0	0
12/23	@NYN	W 27-17	11	2	0.0	0.0	2.0	4.0	0	0	1	0	1	0

Terrance Shaw
San Diego Chargers – CB

1995 Defensive Splits

	G	Tk	Ast	Sack	Yds	Stuff	Yds	Int	Yds	PD	TD
Total	16	57	5	0.0	0.0	1.5	6.5	1	31	9	0
vs. Playoff	7	21	3	0.0	0.0	0.0	0.0	0	0	4	0
vs. Non-Playoff	9	36	2	0.0	0.0	1.5	6.5	1	31	5	0
vs. Own Division	8	26	1	0.0	0.0	0.0	0.0	1	31	4	0
Home	8	26	2	0.0	0.0	1.5	6.5	0	0	3	0
Away	8	31	3	0.0	0.0	0.0	0.0	1	31	6	0
Games 1-8	8	26	3	0.0	0.0	0.0	0.0	0	0	3	0
Games 9-16	8	31	2	0.0	0.0	1.5	6.5	0	0	6	0
September	4	14	2	0.0	0.0	0.0	0.0	0	0	2	0
October	4	12	1	0.0	0.0	0.0	0.0	1	31	1	0
November	4	16	0	0.0	0.0	0.0	0.0	0	0	5	0
December	4	15	2	0.0	0.0	1.5	6.5	0	0	1	0
Grass	11	39	2	0.0	0.0	1.5	6.5	0	0	6	0
Turf	5	18	3	0.0	0.0	0.0	0.0	1	31	3	0
Indoor	2	7	1	0.0	0.0	0.0	0.0	1	31	1	0
Outdoor	14	50	4	0.0	0.0	1.5	6.5	0	0	8	0

Game Logs

Date	Opp	Result	Tk	Ast	Sack	Yds	Stuff	Yds	Int	Yds	PD	FF	FR	TD
09/03	@Oak	L 7-17	4	0	0.0	0.0	0.0	0.0	0	0	0	0	0	0
09/10	Sea	W 14-10	2	0	0.0	0.0	0.0	0.0	0	0	0	0	0	0
09/17	@Phi	W 27-21	5	1	0.0	0.0	0.0	0.0	0	0	2	0	0	0
09/24	Den	W 17-6	3	1	0.0	0.0	0.0	0.0	0	0	0	0	0	0
10/01	@Pit	L 16-31	2	1	0.0	0.0	0.0	0.0	0	0	0	0	0	0
10/09	@KC	L 23-29	2	0	0.0	0.0	0.0	0.0	0	0	0	0	0	0
10/15	Dal	L 9-23	3	0	0.0	0.0	0.0	0.0	0	0	0	0	0	0
10/22	@Sea	W 35-25	5	0	0.0	0.0	0.0	0.0	1	31	1	0	0	0
11/05	Mia	L 14-24	6	0	0.0	0.0	0.0	0.0	0	0	2	0	0	0
11/12	KC	L 7-22	1	0	0.0	0.0	0.0	0.0	0	0	0	0	0	0
11/19	@Den	L 27-30	7	0	0.0	0.0	0.0	0.0	0	0	3	0	0	0
11/27	Oak	W 12-6	2	0	0.0	0.0	0.0	0.0	0	0	0	0	0	0
12/03	Cle	W 31-13	6	1	0.0	0.0	0.5	2.5	0	0	1	0	0	0
12/09	Ari	W 28-25	3	0	0.0	0.0	1.0	4.0	0	0	0	0	0	0
12/17	@Ind	W 27-24	2	1	0.0	0.0	0.0	0.0	0	0	0	0	0	0
12/23	@NYN	W 27-17	4	0	0.0	0.0	0.0	0.0	0	0	0	0	0	0

Tracy Simien
Kansas City Chiefs – LB

1995 Defensive Splits

	G	Tk	Ast	Sack	Yds	Stuff	Yds	Int	Yds	PD	TD
Total	16	64	8	1.0	10.0	3.5	3.5	0	0	0	0
vs. Playoff	4	23	3	0.0	0.0	0.0	0.0	0	0	0	0
vs. Non-Playoff	12	41	5	1.0	10.0	3.5	3.5	0	0	0	0
vs. Own Division	8	28	4	0.0	0.0	3.5	3.5	0	0	0	0
Home	8	36	4	1.0	10.0	1.0	1.0	0	0	0	0
Away	8	28	4	0.0	0.0	2.5	2.5	0	0	0	0
Games 1-8	8	41	4	0.0	0.0	2.5	2.5	0	0	0	0
Games 9-16	8	23	4	1.0	10.0	1.0	1.0	0	0	0	0
September	4	17	2	0.0	0.0	1.0	1.0	0	0	0	0
October	4	24	2	0.0	0.0	1.5	1.5	0	0	0	0
November	4	12	2	1.0	10.0	0.0	0.0	0	0	0	0
December	4	11	2	0.0	0.0	1.0	1.0	0	0	0	0
Grass	14	58	6	1.0	10.0	3.5	3.5	0	0	0	0
Turf	2	6	2	0.0	0.0	0.0	0.0	0	0	0	0
Indoor	1	1	1	0.0	0.0	0.0	0.0	0	0	0	0
Outdoor	15	63	7	1.0	10.0	3.5	3.5	0	0	0	0

Game Logs

Date	Opp	Result	Tk	Ast	Sack	Yds	Stuff	Yds	Int	Yds	PD	FF	FR	TD
09/03	@Sea	W 34-10	1	1	0.0	0.0	0.0	0.0	0	0	0	0	0	0
09/10	NYN	W 20-17	6	1	0.0	0.0	0.0	0.0	0	0	0	0	1	0
09/17	Oak	W 23-17	4	0	0.0	0.0	1.0	1.0	0	0	0	0	0	0
09/24	@Cle	L 17-35	6	0	0.0	0.0	0.0	0.0	0	0	0	0	0	0
10/01	@Ari	W 24-3	4	0	0.0	0.0	0.0	0.0	0	0	0	0	0	0
10/09	SD	W 29-23	11	1	0.0	0.0	0.0	0.0	0	0	0	0	1	0
10/15	NE	W 31-26	5	0	0.0	0.0	0.0	0.0	0	0	0	0	0	0
10/22	@Den	W 21-7	4	1	0.0	0.0	1.5	1.5	0	0	0	0	1	0
11/05	Was	W 24-3	3	0	1.0	10.0	0.0	0.0	0	0	0	0	0	0
11/12	@SD	W 22-7	2	0	0.0	0.0	0.0	0.0	0	0	0	0	0	0
11/19	Hou	W 20-13	2	1	0.0	0.0	0.0	0.0	0	0	0	0	0	0
11/23	@Dal	L 12-24	5	1	0.0	0.0	0.0	0.0	0	0	0	0	0	0
12/03	@Oak	W 29-23	1	0	0.0	0.0	1.0	1.0	0	0	0	0	0	0
12/11	@Mia	L 6-13	5	1	0.0	0.0	0.0	0.0	0	0	0	0	0	0
12/17	Den	W 20-17	4	0	0.0	0.0	0.0	0.0	0	0	0	0	0	0
12/24	Sea	W 26-3	1	1	0.0	0.0	0.0	0.0	0	0	0	0	0	0

Clyde Simmons
Arizona Cardinals – DE

1995 Defensive Splits

	G	Tk	Ast	Sack	Yds	Stuff	Yds	Int	Yds	PD	TD
Total	16	40	14	11.0	87.0	5.5	12.5	1	25	4	1
vs. Playoff	8	18	8	5.0	30.0	3.0	4.5	1	25	2	1
vs. Non-Playoff	8	22	6	6.0	57.0	2.5	8.0	0	0	2	0
vs. Own Division	8	26	7	6.0	45.0	4.5	11.0	0	0	0	0
Home	8	24	5	6.0	52.0	3.5	5.0	0	0	2	0
Away	8	16	9	5.0	35.0	2.0	7.5	1	25	2	1
Games 1-8	8	24	10	3.0	27.0	4.0	9.5	0	0	1	0
Games 9-16	8	16	4	8.0	60.0	1.5	3.0	1	25	3	1
September	4	12	5	1.0	3.0	2.0	2.5	0	0	0	0
October	4	12	5	2.0	24.0	2.0	7.0	0	0	1	0
November	5	9	2	4.0	36.0	0.5	1.0	0	0	2	0
December	3	7	2	4.0	24.0	1.0	2.0	1	25	1	1
Grass	12	32	6	9.0	72.0	3.5	5.0	1	25	4	1
Turf	4	8	8	2.0	15.0	2.0	7.5	0	0	0	0
Indoor	1	1	4	0.0	0.0	0.5	1.0	0	0	0	0
Outdoor	15	39	10	11.0	87.0	5.0	11.5	1	25	4	1

Game Logs

Date	Opp	Result	Tk	Ast	Sack	Yds	Stuff	Yds	Int	Yds	PD	FF	FR	TD
09/03	@Was	L 7-27	5	0	1.0	3.0	0.0	0.0	0	0	0	0	0	0
09/10	Phi	L 19-31	4	1	0.0	0.0	1.5	1.5	0	0	0	0	0	0
09/17	@Det	W 20-17	1	4	0.0	0.0	0.5	1.0	0	0	0	0	1	0
09/24	@Dal	L 20-34	2	0	0.0	0.0	0.0	0.0	0	0	0	0	0	0
10/01	KC	L 3-24	4	1	1.0	6.0	0.0	0.0	0	0	0	1	0	0
10/08	@NYN	L 21-29	2	4	0.0	0.0	1.5	6.5	0	0	0	0	0	0
10/15	Was	W 24-20	3	0	1.0	18.0	0.0	0.0	0	0	0	1	0	0
10/29	Sea	W 20-14	3	0	0.0	0.0	0.5	0.5	0	0	1	1	0	0
11/05	@Den	L 6-38	2	1	1.0	10.0	0.0	0.0	0	0	0	0	0	0
11/12	Min	L 24-30	3	1	2.0	19.0	0.0	0.0	0	0	0	0	0	0
11/19	@Car	L 7-27	1	0	1.0	7.0	0.0	0.0	0	0	1	0	0	0
11/26	Atl	W 40-37	0	0	0.0	0.0	0.0	0.0	0	0	1	0	1	0
11/30	NYN	L 6-10	3	0	0.0	0.0	0.5	1.0	0	0	0	0	0	0
12/09	@SD	L 25-28	0	0	0.0	0.0	0.0	0.0	1	25	1	0	0	1
12/17	@Phi	L 20-21	3	0	2.0	15.0	0.0	0.0	0	0	0	1	0	0
12/25	Dal	L 13-37	4	2	2.0	9.0	1.0	2.0	0	0	1	0	0	0

Wayne Simmons
Green Bay Packers – LB

1995 Defensive Splits

	G	Tk	Ast	Sack	Yds	Stuff	Yds	Int	Yds	PD	TD
Total	16	68	23	4.0	31.0	2.0	6.0	0	0	4	0
vs. Playoff	4	12	7	0.0	0.0	0.0	0.0	0	0	0	0
vs. Non-Playoff	12	56	16	4.0	31.0	2.0	6.0	0	0	4	0
vs. Own Division	8	35	11	0.0	0.0	1.0	2.0	0	0	3	0
Home	8	34	11	1.0	8.0	1.5	5.5	0	0	3	0
Away	8	34	12	3.0	23.0	0.5	0.5	0	0	1	0
Games 1-8	8	38	8	3.0	22.0	0.0	0.0	0	0	1	0
Games 9-16	8	30	15	1.0	9.0	2.0	6.0	0	0	3	0
September	4	22	4	3.0	22.0	0.0	0.0	0	0	1	0
October	4	16	4	0.0	0.0	0.0	0.0	0	0	0	0
November	4	17	5	0.0	0.0	0.5	1.5	0	0	3	0
December	4	13	10	1.0	9.0	1.5	4.5	0	0	0	0
Grass	12	57	15	3.0	22.0	2.0	6.0	0	0	4	0
Turf	4	11	8	1.0	9.0	0.0	0.0	0	0	0	0
Indoor	3	8	6	1.0	9.0	0.0	0.0	0	0	1	0
Outdoor	13	60	17	3.0	22.0	2.0	6.0	0	0	4	0

Game Logs

Date	Opp	Result	Tk	Ast	Sack	Yds	Stuff	Yds	Int	Yds	PD	FF	FR	TD
09/03	StL	L 14-17	3	3	0.0	0.0	0.0	0.0	0	0	0	0	0	0
09/11	@Chi	W 27-24	6	0	0.0	0.0	0.0	0.0	0	0	0	0	1	0
09/17	NYN	W 14-6	5	1	1.0	8.0	0.0	0.0	0	0	0	0	0	0
09/24	@Jac	W 24-14	8	0	2.0	14.0	0.0	0.0	0	0	1	0	0	0
10/08	@Dal	L 24-34	3	2	0.0	0.0	0.0	0.0	0	0	0	0	0	0
10/15	Det	W 30-21	4	0	0.0	0.0	0.0	0.0	0	0	0	0	0	0
10/22	Min	W 38-21	5	0	0.0	0.0	0.0	0.0	0	0	0	0	0	0
10/29	@Det	L 16-24	4	2	0.0	0.0	0.0	0.0	0	0	0	0	0	0
11/05	@Min	L 24-27	1	2	0.0	0.0	0.0	0.0	0	0	0	0	0	0
11/12	Chi	W 35-28	5	1	0.0	0.0	0.0	0.0	0	0	0	0	0	0
11/19	@Cle	W 31-20	5	0	0.0	0.0	0.0	0.0	0	0	0	0	0	0
11/26	TB	W 35-13	6	2	0.0	0.0	0.5	1.5	0	0	3	0	0	0
12/03	Cin	W 24-10	5	1	0.0	0.0	1.0	4.0	0	0	0	0	0	0
12/10	@TB	L 10-13	4	4	0.0	0.0	0.5	0.5	0	0	0	0	0	0
12/16	@NO	W 34-23	3	2	1.0	9.0	0.0	0.0	0	0	0	0	1	0
12/24	Pit	W 24-19	1	3	0.0	0.0	0.0	0.0	0	0	0	0	0	0

Michael Sinclair

1995 Defensive Splits

	G	Tk	Ast	Sack	Yds	Stuff	Yds	Int	Yds	PD	TD
Total	16	37	9	5.5	25.0	5.0	10.5	0	0	2	0
vs. Playoff	6	13	2	0.0	0.0	2.5	3.5	0	0	0	0
vs. Non-Playoff	10	24	7	5.5	25.0	2.5	7.0	0	0	2	0
vs. Own Division	8	21	3	3.0	14.0	3.5	6.5	0	0	0	0
Home	8	15	5	3.0	15.0	2.0	6.5	0	0	1	0
Away	8	22	4	2.5	10.0	3.0	4.0	0	0	1	0
Games 1-8	8	15	3	1.0	5.0	3.5	6.5	0	0	1	0
Games 9-16	8	22	6	4.5	20.0	1.5	4.0	0	0	1	0
September	3	3	0	0.0	0.0	1.0	2.0	0	0	0	0
October	5	12	3	1.0	5.0	2.5	4.5	0	0	1	0
November	4	9	5	2.0	11.0	0.5	3.0	0	0	1	0
December	4	13	1	2.0	9.0	1.0	1.0	0	0	0	0
Grass	7	20	3	2.5	10.0	3.0	4.0	0	0	1	0
Turf	9	17	6	3.0	15.0	2.0	6.5	0	0	1	0
Indoor	8	15	5	3.0	15.0	2.0	6.5	0	0	1	0
Outdoor	8	22	4	2.5	10.0	3.0	4.0	0	0	1	0

Game Logs

Date	Opp	Result	Tk	Ast	Sack	Yds	Stuff	Yds	Int	Yds	PD	FF	FR	TD
09/03	KC	L 10-34	0	0	0.0	0.0	0.0	0.0	0	0	0	0	0	0
09/10	@SD	L 10-14	3	0	0.0	0.0	1.0	2.0	0	0	0	1	0	0
09/17	Cin	W 24-21	0	0	0.0	0.0	0.0	0.0	0	0	0	0	0	0
10/01	Den	W 27-10	3	0	0.0	0.0	1.0	3.0	0	0	2	0	0	0
10/08	@Oak	L 14-34	3	1	1.0	5.0	0.0	0.0	0	0	0	0	0	0
10/15	@Buf	L 21-27	2	1	0.0	0.0	0.0	0.0	0	0	0	0	0	0
10/22	SD	L 25-35	1	1	0.0	0.0	0.5	0.5	0	0	0	0	0	0
10/29	@Ari	L 14-20	3	0	0.0	0.0	1.0	1.0	0	0	0	0	0	0
11/05	NYN	W 30-28	1	2	0.0	0.0	0.0	0.0	0	0	1	0	0	0
11/12	@Jac	W 47-30	3	2	1.5	5.0	0.0	0.0	0	0	0	1	0	0
11/19	@Was	W 27-20	3	0	0.0	0.0	0.0	0.0	0	0	0	0	0	0
11/26	NYA	L 10-16	2	1	1.0	6.0	0.5	3.0	0	0	0	0	0	0
12/03	Phi	W 26-14	2	0	0.0	0.0	0.0	0.0	0	0	0	0	0	0
12/10	@Den	W 31-27	0	0	0.0	0.0	0.0	0.0	0	0	0	0	0	0
12/17	Oak	W 44-10	6	1	2.0	9.0	0.0	0.0	0	0	0	0	0	0
12/24	@KC	L 3-26	5	0	0.0	0.0	1.0	1.0	0	0	0	0	0	0

Chris Singleton

1995 Defensive Splits

	G	Tk	Ast	Sack	Yds	Stuff	Yds	Int	Yds	PD	TD
Total	16	56	26	1.0	7.0	1.5	2.5	1	3	1	0
vs. Playoff	9	32	14	1.0	7.0	0.5	0.5	1	3	1	0
vs. Non-Playoff	7	24	12	0.0	0.0	1.0	2.0	0	0	0	0
vs. Own Division	8	39	16	0.0	0.0	1.5	2.5	0	0	0	0
Home	8	23	13	1.0	7.0	1.5	2.5	0	0	0	0
Away	8	33	13	0.0	0.0	0.0	0.0	1	3	1	0
Games 1-8	8	29	13	1.0	7.0	0.5	0.5	0	0	0	0
Games 9-16	8	27	13	0.0	0.0	1.0	2.0	1	3	1	0
September	3	18	6	1.0	7.0	0.0	0.0	0	0	0	0
October	5	11	7	0.0	0.0	0.5	0.5	0	0	0	0
November	4	13	7	0.0	0.0	1.0	2.0	1	3	1	0
December	4	14	6	0.0	0.0	0.0	0.0	0	0	0	0
Grass	10	34	16	1.0	7.0	1.5	2.5	1	3	1	0
Turf	6	22	10	0.0	0.0	0.0	0.0	0	0	0	0
Indoor	3	10	2	0.0	0.0	0.0	0.0	0	0	0	0
Outdoor	13	46	24	1.0	7.0	1.5	2.5	1	3	1	0

Game Logs

Date	Opp	Result	Tk	Ast	Sack	Yds	Stuff	Yds	Int	Yds	PD	FF	FR	TD
09/03	NYA	W 52-14	3	1	0.0	0.0	0.0	0.0	0	0	0	0	0	0
09/10	@NE	W 20-3	10	3	0.0	0.0	0.0	0.0	0	0	0	0	0	0
09/18	Pit	W 23-10	5	2	1.0	7.0	0.0	0.0	0	0	0	1	0	0
10/01	@Cin	W 26-23	1	2	0.0	0.0	0.0	0.0	0	0	0	0	0	0
10/08	Ind	L 24-27	2	1	0.0	0.0	0.5	0.5	0	0	0	1	0	0
10/15	@NO	L 30-33	3	1	0.0	0.0	0.0	0.0	0	0	0	0	0	0
10/22	@NYA	L 16-17	1	2	0.0	0.0	0.0	0.0	0	0	0	0	0	0
10/29	Buf	W 23-6	4	1	0.0	0.0	0.0	0.0	0	0	0	0	0	0
11/05	@SD	W 24-14	1	0	0.0	0.0	0.0	0.0	1	3	1	0	0	0
11/12	NE	L 17-34	4	3	0.0	0.0	1.0	2.0	0	0	1	0	0	0
11/20	SF	L 20-44	3	3	0.0	0.0	0.0	0.0	0	0	0	0	0	0
11/26	@Ind	L 28-36	5	1	0.0	0.0	0.0	0.0	0	0	0	0	0	0
12/03	Atl	W 21-20	0	0	0.0	0.0	0.0	0.0	0	0	0	0	0	0
12/11	KC	W 13-6	2	2	0.0	0.0	0.0	0.0	0	0	0	1	0	0
12/17	@Buf	L 20-23	10	4	0.0	0.0	0.0	0.0	0	0	0	0	0	0
12/24	@StL	W 41-22	2	0	0.0	0.0	0.0	0.0	0	0	0	0	0	0

Chris Slade

1995 Defensive Splits

	G	Tk	Ast	Sack	Yds	Stuff	Yds	Int	Yds	PD	TD
Total	16	72	24	4.0	16.0	11.5	25.0	0	0	4	1
vs. Playoff	10	42	12	1.0	4.0	7.0	16.5	0	0	3	1
vs. Non-Playoff	6	30	12	3.0	12.0	4.5	8.5	0	0	1	0
vs. Own Division	8	37	13	3.0	15.0	8.0	14.5	0	0	2	1
Home	8	42	18	3.0	14.0	7.0	12.5	0	0	1	0
Away	8	30	6	1.0	2.0	4.5	12.5	0	0	3	1
Games 1-8	8	40	13	2.0	5.0	5.5	13.5	0	0	1	0
Games 9-16	8	32	11	2.0	11.0	6.0	11.5	0	0	3	1
September	3	17	3	1.0	1.0	2.5	8.5	0	0	0	0
October	5	23	10	1.0	4.0	3.0	5.0	0	0	1	0
November	4	19	8	1.0	2.0	3.0	3.5	0	0	1	0
December	4	13	3	1.0	9.0	3.0	8.0	0	0	2	0
Grass	11	55	20	3.0	14.0	9.0	20.5	0	0	1	0
Turf	5	17	4	1.0	2.0	2.5	4.5	0	0	3	1
Indoor	2	4	0	0.0	0.0	1.0	3.0	0	0	0	0
Outdoor	14	68	24	4.0	16.0	10.5	22.0	0	0	4	1

Game Logs

Date	Opp	Result	Tk	Ast	Sack	Yds	Stuff	Yds	Int	Yds	PD	FF	FR	TD
09/03	Cle	W 17-14	9	3	1.0	1.0	0.5	0.5	0	0	0	0	0	0
09/10	Mia	L 3-20	6	0	0.0	0.0	1.0	2.0	0	0	0	0	0	0
09/17	@SF	L 3-28	2	0	0.0	0.0	1.0	6.0	0	0	0	0	0	0
10/01	@Atl	L 17-30	1	0	0.0	0.0	0.0	0.0	0	0	0	0	0	0
10/08	Den	L 3-37	5	2	0.0	0.0	1.0	2.0	0	0	0	0	0	0
10/15	@KC	L 26-31	7	1	0.0	0.0	1.0	2.0	0	0	0	0	0	0
10/22	@NYA	W 27-14	5	3	1.0	4.0	1.0	1.0	0	0	1	1	1	0
10/29	Car	L 17-20	5	4	0.0	0.0	0.0	0.0	0	0	0	0	0	0
11/05	@NYA	W 20-7	4	1	1.0	2.0	1.0	1.0	0	0	1	0	0	0
11/12	@Mia	W 34-17	4	1	0.0	0.0	0.0	0.0	0	0	0	0	0	0
11/19	Ind	L 10-24	5	4	0.0	0.0	1.5	2.0	0	0	0	0	0	0
11/26	@Buf	W 35-25	6	2	0.0	0.0	0.5	0.5	0	0	0	1	1	1
12/03	NO	L 17-31	3	0	0.0	0.0	0.0	0.0	0	0	0	0	0	0
12/10	NYA	W 31-28	4	2	1.0	9.0	2.0	5.0	0	0	0	0	0	0
12/16	@Pit	L 27-41	3	1	0.0	0.0	1.0	3.0	0	0	2	0	0	0
12/23	@Ind	L 7-10	3	0	0.0	0.0	1.0	3.0	0	0	0	0	0	0

Joel Smeenge

Jacksonville Jaguars – DE

1995 Defensive Splits

	G	Tk	Ast	Sack	Yds	Stuff	Yds	Int	Yds	PD	TD
Total	15	32	7	4.0	19.5	9.0	21.0	1	12	5	0
vs. Playoff	5	11	0	1.0	0.0	6.0	14.0	0	0	2	0
vs. Non-Playoff	10	21	7	3.0	19.5	3.0	7.0	1	12	3	0
vs. Own Division	7	12	3	2.0	13.5	3.0	12.0	1	12	3	0
Home	8	15	3	1.5	7.5	5.0	14.0	1	12	1	0
Away	7	17	4	2.5	12.0	4.0	7.0	0	0	4	0
Games 1-8	7	14	3	1.5	12.0	4.0	14.0	0	0	1	0
Games 9-16	8	18	4	2.5	7.5	5.0	7.0	1	12	4	0
September	4	7	3	1.5	12.0	1.0	4.0	0	0	0	0
October	4	7	0	0.0	0.0	3.0	10.0	0	0	2	0
November	3	9	1	1.0	6.0	1.0	1.0	1	12	1	0
December	4	9	3	1.5	1.5	4.0	6.0	0	0	2	0
Grass	11	21	4	1.5	7.5	6.0	15.0	1	12	3	0
Turf	4	11	3	2.5	12.0	3.0	6.0	0	0	2	0
Indoor	1	4	0	1.0	0.0	2.0	2.0	0	0	1	0
Outdoor	14	28	7	3.0	19.5	7.0	19.0	1	12	4	0

Game Logs

Date	Opp	Result	Tk	Ast	Sack	Yds	Stuff	Yds	Int	Yds	PD	FF	FR	TD
09/03	Hou	L 3-10	0	0	0.0	0.0	0.0	0.0	0	0	0	0	0	0
09/10	@Cin	L 17-24	4	1	1.5	12.0	1.0	4.0	0	0	0	1	0	0
09/17	@NYA	L 10-27	3	2	0.0	0.0	0.0	0.0	0	0	0	0	0	0
09/24	GB	L 14-24	0	0	0.0	0.0	0.0	0.0	0	0	0	0	0	0
10/01	@Hou	W 17-16	-	-	-	-	-	-	-	-	-	-	-	-
10/08	Pit	W 20-16	4	0	0.0	0.0	2.0	8.0	0	0	0	1	0	0
10/15	Chi	L 27-30	2	0	0.0	0.0	1.0	2.0	0	0	0	0	0	0
10/22	@Cle	W 23-15	1	0	0.0	0.0	0.0	0.0	0	0	1	0	0	0
10/29	@Pit	L 7-24	0	0	0.0	0.0	0.0	0.0	0	0	1	0	0	0
11/12	Sea	L 30-47	3	1	1.0	6.0	0.0	0.0	0	0	1	0	0	0
11/19	@TB	L 16-17	4	0	0.0	0.0	1.0	1.0	0	0	0	0	0	0
11/26	Cin	L 13-17	2	0	0.0	0.0	0.0	0.0	1	12	1	0	0	0
12/03	@Den	L 23-31	1	1	0.0	0.0	0.0	0.0	0	0	0	0	0	0
12/10	Ind	L 31-41	3	0	0.0	0.0	2.0	4.0	0	0	0	0	0	0
12/17	@Det	L 0-44	4	0	1.0	0.0	2.0	2.0	0	0	1	1	0	0
12/24	Cle	W 24-21	1	2	0.5	1.5	0.0	0.0	0	0	0	0	0	0

Bruce Smith

Buffalo Bills – DE

1995 Defensive Splits

	G	Tk	Ast	Sack	Yds	Stuff	Yds	Int	Yds	PD	TD
Total	15	52	22	10.5	66.0	6.0	11.5	0	0	3	0
vs. Playoff	6	22	3	5.0	24.0	2.0	2.0	0	0	3	0
vs. Non-Playoff	9	30	19	5.5	42.0	4.0	9.5	0	0	0	0
vs. Own Division	8	31	14	2.5	20.0	4.0	7.5	0	0	2	0
Home	7	28	10	4.5	28.0	5.5	9.5	0	0	1	0
Away	8	24	12	6.0	38.0	0.5	2.0	0	0	2	0
Games 1-8	8	28	15	3.0	23.0	4.0	8.0	0	0	1	0
Games 9-16	7	24	7	7.5	43.0	2.0	3.5	0	0	2	0
September	3	9	4	0.0	0.0	1.5	1.5	0	0	0	0
October	5	19	11	3.0	23.0	2.5	6.5	0	0	1	0
November	4	12	6	2.5	11.0	0.5	2.0	0	0	0	0
December	3	12	1	5.0	32.0	1.5	1.5	0	0	2	0
Grass	5	17	9	4.0	22.0	0.0	0.0	0	0	2	0
Turf	10	35	13	6.5	44.0	6.0	11.5	0	0	1	0
Indoor	2	4	0	2.0	16.0	0.0	0.0	0	0	0	0
Outdoor	13	48	22	8.5	50.0	6.0	11.5	0	0	3	0

Game Logs

Date	Opp	Result	Tk	Ast	Sack	Yds	Stuff	Yds	Int	Yds	PD	FF	FR	TD
09/03	@Den	L 7-22	2	2	0.0	0.0	0.0	0.0	0	0	0	0	0	0
09/10	Car	W 31-9	2	2	0.0	0.0	1.0	1.0	0	0	0	0	0	0
09/17	Ind	W 20-14	5	0	0.0	0.0	0.5	0.5	0	0	0	0	1	0
10/02	@Cle	W 22-19	3	1	1.0	6.0	0.0	0.0	0	0	0	0	0	0
10/08	NYA	W 29-10	5	2	2.0	17.0	1.5	3.5	0	0	0	0	0	0
10/15	Sea	W 27-21	4	2	0.0	0.0	1.0	3.0	0	0	0	0	0	0
10/23	@NE	L 14-27	5	5	0.0	0.0	0.0	0.0	0	0	0	0	0	0
10/29	@Mia	L 6-23	2	1	0.0	0.0	0.0	0.0	0	0	0	1	0	0
11/05	@Ind	W 16-10	2	0	0.0	0.0	0.0	0.0	0	0	0	0	0	0
11/12	Atl	W 23-17	3	1	2.0	8.0	0.0	0.0	0	0	0	0	0	0
11/19	@NYA	W 28-26	3	3	0.0	0.0	0.5	2.0	0	0	0	0	0	0
11/26	NE	L 25-35	4	2	0.5	3.0	0.0	0.0	0	0	0	0	0	0
12/03	@SF	L 17-27	5	0	3.0	16.0	0.0	0.0	0	0	1	0	0	0
12/10	@StL	W 45-27	2	0	2.0	16.0	0.0	0.0	0	0	0	0	0	0
12/17	Mia	W 23-20	5	1	0.0	0.0	1.5	1.5	0	0	1	0	0	0
12/24	Hou	L 17-28	-	-	-	-	-	-	-	-	-	-	-	-

Chuck Smith

Atlanta Falcons – DE

1995 Defensive Splits

	G	Tk	Ast	Sack	Yds	Stuff	Yds	Int	Yds	PD	TD
Total	14	34	6	5.5	31.5	3.0	4.0	0	0	2	0
vs. Playoff	4	5	1	0.0	0.0	0.0	0.0	0	0	0	0
vs. Non-Playoff	10	29	5	5.5	31.5	3.0	4.0	0	0	2	0
vs. Own Division	8	16	3	1.5	7.5	2.0	3.0	0	0	2	0
Home	6	18	2	4.5	28.5	2.0	2.0	0	0	1	0
Away	8	16	4	1.0	3.0	1.0	2.0	0	0	1	0
Games 1-8	7	21	2	4.5	28.5	2.0	3.0	0	0	2	0
Games 9-16	7	13	4	1.0	3.0	1.0	1.0	0	0	0	0
September	4	7	2	3.5	21.5	2.0	3.0	0	0	2	0
October	3	14	0	1.0	7.0	0.0	0.0	0	0	0	0
November	3	7	2	1.0	3.0	1.0	1.0	0	0	0	0
December	4	6	2	0.0	0.0	0.0	0.0	0	0	0	0
Grass	5	8	3	1.0	3.0	0.0	0.0	0	0	0	0
Turf	9	26	3	4.5	28.5	3.0	4.0	0	0	2	0
Indoor	7	20	3	4.5	28.5	3.0	4.0	0	0	2	0
Outdoor	7	14	3	1.0	3.0	0.0	0.0	0	0	0	0

Game Logs

Date	Opp	Result	Tk	Ast	Sack	Yds	Stuff	Yds	Int	Yds	PD	FF	FR	TD
09/03	Car	W 23-20	1	1	1.5	7.5	0.0	0.0	0	0	1	0	0	0
09/10	@SF	L 10-41	1	0	0.0	0.0	0.0	0.0	0	0	0	0	0	0
09/17	@NO	W 27-24	2	1	0.0	0.0	1.0	2.0	0	0	1	0	0	0
09/24	NYA	W 13-3	3	0	2.0	14.0	1.0	1.0	0	0	0	0	0	0
10/01	NE	W 30-17	7	0	1.0	7.0	0.0	0.0	0	0	1	0	0	0
10/12	@StL	L 19-21	4	0	0.0	0.0	0.0	0.0	0	0	1	0	0	0
10/22	@TB	W 24-21	3	0	0.0	0.0	0.0	0.0	0	0	0	0	0	0
10/29	Dal	L 13-28	-	-	-	-	-	-	-	-	-	-	-	-
11/05	Det	W 34-22	-	-	-	-	-	-	-	-	-	-	-	-
11/12	@Buf	L 17-23	2	0	0.0	0.0	0.0	0.0	0	0	0	1	0	0
11/19	StL	W 31-6	2	0	0.0	0.0	1.0	1.0	0	0	0	0	0	0
11/26	@Ari	L 37-40	3	2	1.0	3.0	0.0	0.0	0	0	1	1	0	0
12/03	@Mia	L 20-21	0	1	0.0	0.0	0.0	0.0	0	0	0	0	0	0
12/10	NO	W 19-14	3	1	0.0	0.0	0.0	0.0	0	0	0	0	0	0
12/17	@Car	L 17-21	1	0	0.0	0.0	0.0	0.0	0	0	0	1	0	0
12/24	SF	W 28-27	2	0	0.0	0.0	0.0	0.0	0	0	0	0	0	0

Neil Smith

1995 Defensive Splits

	G	Tk	Ast	Sack	Yds	Stuff	Yds	Int	Yds	PD	TD
Total	16	42	13	12.0	84.0	6.0	13.5	0	0	1	0
vs. Playoff	4	14	6	4.5	33.0	4.0	10.0	0	0	0	0
vs. Non-Playoff	12	28	7	7.5	51.0	2.0	3.5	0	0	1	0
vs. Own Division	8	23	7	9.0	57.0	4.0	10.5	0	0	1	0
Home	8	16	4	5.0	32.0	3.0	8.5	0	0	0	0
Away	8	26	9	7.0	52.0	3.0	5.0	0	0	1	0
Games 1-8	8	24	8	6.5	41.0	3.5	8.0	0	0	1	0
Games 9-16	8	18	5	5.5	43.0	2.5	5.5	0	0	0	0
September	4	12	2	1.0	8.0	1.5	2.0	0	0	1	0
October	4	12	6	5.5	33.0	2.0	6.0	0	0	0	0
November	4	4	2	1.5	13.0	1.0	2.0	0	0	0	0
December	4	14	3	4.0	30.0	1.5	3.5	0	0	0	0
Grass	14	38	11	11.0	76.0	6.0	13.5	0	0	0	0
Turf	2	4	2	1.0	8.0	0.0	0.0	0	0	1	0
Indoor	1	2	1	0.0	0.0	0.0	0.0	0	0	1	0
Outdoor	15	40	12	12.0	84.0	6.0	13.5	0	0	0	0

Game Logs

Date	Opp	Result	Tk	Ast	Sack	Yds	Stuff	Yds	Int	Yds	PD	FF	FR	TD
09/03	@Sea	W 34-10	2	1	0.0	0.0	0.0	0.0	0	0	1	0	0	0
09/10	NYN	W 20-17	5	0	0.0	0.0	0.0	0.0	0	0	0	0	0	0
09/17	Oak	W 23-17	2	1	1.0	8.0	0.5	1.0	0	0	0	0	0	0
09/24	@Cle	L 17-35	3	0	0.0	0.0	1.0	1.0	0	0	0	0	0	0
10/01	@Ari	W 24-3	2	3	1.0	9.0	0.0	0.0	0	0	0	0	0	0
10/09	SD	W 29-23	4	2	2.0	10.0	2.0	6.0	0	0	0	0	0	0
10/15	NE	W 31-26	1	0	0.0	0.0	0.0	0.0	0	0	0	0	0	0
10/22	@Den	W 21-7	5	1	2.5	14.0	0.0	0.0	0	0	0	0	0	0
11/05	Was	W 24-3	0	0	0.0	0.0	0.0	0.0	0	0	0	0	0	0
11/12	@SD	W 22-7	2	1	0.5	5.0	1.0	2.0	0	0	0	0	0	0
11/19	Hou	W 20-13	0	0	0.0	0.0	0.0	0.0	0	0	0	0	0	0
11/23	@Dal	L 12-24	2	1	1.0	8.0	0.0	0.0	0	0	0	0	0	0
12/03	@Oak	W 29-23	4	0	1.0	6.0	0.0	0.0	0	0	0	1	0	0
12/11	@Mia	L 6-13	6	2	1.0	10.0	1.0	2.0	0	0	0	2	0	0
12/17	Den	W 20-17	2	1	1.0	5.0	0.5	1.5	0	0	0	1	1	0
12/24	Sea	W 26-3	2	0	1.0	9.0	0.0	0.0	0	0	0	0	0	0

Vinson Smith

1995 Defensive Splits

	G	Tk	Ast	Sack	Yds	Stuff	Yds	Int	Yds	PD	TD
Total	16	60	12	4.0	30.0	4.5	13.0	0	0	0	0
vs. Playoff	6	16	7	2.0	16.0	0.0	0.0	0	0	0	0
vs. Non-Playoff	10	44	5	2.0	14.0	4.5	13.0	0	0	0	0
vs. Own Division	8	24	5	4.0	30.0	2.0	10.0	0	0	0	0
Home	8	23	3	1.0	8.0	2.0	10.0	0	0	0	0
Away	8	37	9	3.0	22.0	2.5	3.0	0	0	0	0
Games 1-8	8	30	4	1.0	6.0	2.5	3.0	0	0	0	0
Games 9-16	8	30	8	3.0	24.0	2.0	10.0	0	0	0	0
September	4	14	2	0.0	0.0	1.0	1.0	0	0	0	0
October	4	16	2	1.0	6.0	1.5	2.0	0	0	0	0
November	4	16	7	2.0	16.0	0.0	0.0	0	0	0	0
December	4	14	1	1.0	8.0	2.0	10.0	0	0	0	0
Grass	11	40	8	3.0	24.0	3.5	12.0	0	0	0	0
Turf	5	20	4	1.0	6.0	1.0	1.0	0	0	0	0
Indoor	2	2	1	1.0	6.0	0.0	0.0	0	0	0	0
Outdoor	14	58	11	3.0	24.0	4.5	13.0	0	0	0	0

Game Logs

Date	Opp	Result	Tk	Ast	Sack	Yds	Stuff	Yds	Int	Yds	PD	FF	FR	TD
09/03	Min	W 31-14	0	0	0.0	0.0	0.0	0.0	0	0	0	0	0	0
09/11	GB	L 24-27	7	1	0.0	0.0	0.0	0.0	0	0	0	0	0	0
09/17	@TB	W 25-6	3	0	0.0	0.0	1.0	1.0	0	0	0	0	0	0
09/24	@StL	L 28-34	4	1	0.0	0.0	0.0	0.0	0	0	0	0	0	0
10/08	Car	W 31-27	5	0	0.0	0.0	1.0	1.0	0	0	0	0	0	0
10/15	@Jac	W 30-27	9	2	0.0	0.0	0.5	1.0	0	0	0	0	0	0
10/22	Hou	W 35-32	0	0	0.0	0.0	0.0	0.0	0	0	0	0	0	0
10/30	@Min	W 14-6	2	0	1.0	6.0	0.0	0.0	0	0	0	0	0	0
11/05	Pit	L 34-37	4	2	0.0	0.0	0.0	0.0	0	0	0	0	1	0
11/12	@GB	L 28-35	5	3	2.0	16.0	0.0	0.0	0	0	0	0	0	0
11/19	Det	L 17-24	0	0	0.0	0.0	0.0	0.0	0	0	0	0	0	0
11/26	@NYN	W 27-24	7	2	0.0	0.0	0.0	0.0	0	0	0	0	0	0
12/04	@Det	L 7-27	0	1	0.0	0.0	0.0	0.0	0	0	0	0	0	0
12/10	@Cin	L 10-16	7	0	0.0	0.0	1.0	1.0	0	0	0	0	0	0
12/17	TB	W 31-10	7	0	1.0	8.0	1.0	9.0	0	0	0	1	0	0
12/24	Phi	W 20-14	0	0	0.0	0.0	0.0	0.0	0	0	0	0	0	0

Phillippi Sparks

1995 Defensive Splits

	G	Tk	Ast	Sack	Yds	Stuff	Yds	Int	Yds	PD	TD
Total	16	71	5	0.0	0.0	1.0	1.0	5	11	16	0
vs. Playoff	8	34	2	0.0	0.0	1.0	1.0	2	2	7	0
vs. Non-Playoff	8	37	3	0.0	0.0	0.0	0.0	3	9	9	0
vs. Own Division	8	30	1	0.0	0.0	1.0	1.0	3	8	8	0
Home	8	23	3	0.0	0.0	0.0	0.0	2	2	6	0
Away	8	48	2	0.0	0.0	1.0	1.0	3	9	10	0
Games 1-8	8	38	3	0.0	0.0	0.0	0.0	2	8	8	0
Games 9-16	8	33	2	0.0	0.0	1.0	1.0	3	3	8	0
September	4	21	2	0.0	0.0	0.0	0.0	0	0	3	0
October	4	17	1	0.0	0.0	0.0	0.0	2	8	5	0
November	5	22	2	0.0	0.0	1.0	1.0	2	3	4	0
December	3	11	0	0.0	0.0	1.0	1.0	1	0	4	0
Grass	5	34	1	0.0	0.0	0.0	0.0	1	6	8	0
Turf	11	07	4	0.0	0.0	1.0	1.0	4	5	8	0
Indoor	1	5	1	0.0	0.0	0.0	0.0	1	3	1	0
Outdoor	15	66	4	0.0	0.0	1.0	1.0	4	8	15	0

Game Logs

Date	Opp	Result	Tk	Ast	Sack	Yds	Stuff	Yds	Int	Yds	PD	FF	FR	TD
09/04	Dal	L 0-35	1	1	0.0	0.0	0.0	0.0	0	0	0	0	0	0
09/10	@KC	L 17-20	10	0	0.0	0.0	0.0	0.0	0	0	2	0	0	0
09/17	@GB	L 6-14	6	0	0.0	0.0	0.0	0.0	0	0	1	0	0	0
09/24	NO	W 45-29	4	1	0.0	0.0	0.0	0.0	0	0	0	0	0	0
10/01	@SF	L 6-20	6	1	0.0	0.0	0.0	0.0	0	0	2	0	0	0
10/08	Ari	W 27-21	2	0	0.0	0.0	0.0	0.0	0	0	0	0	0	0
10/15	Phi	L 14-17	1	0	0.0	0.0	0.0	0.0	1	2	1	0	0	0
10/29	@Was	W 24-15	8	0	0.0	0.0	0.0	0.0	1	6	2	0	0	0
11/05	@Sea	L 28-30	5	1	0.0	0.0	0.0	0.0	1	3	1	0	0	0
11/12	Oak	L 13-17	7	0	0.0	0.0	0.0	0.0	1	0	1	0	0	0
11/19	@Phi	L 19-28	4	0	0.0	0.0	0.0	0.0	0	0	0	0	0	0
11/26	Chi	L 24-27	2	1	0.0	0.0	0.0	0.0	0	0	1	0	0	0
11/30	@Ari	W 10-6	4	0	0.0	0.0	0.0	0.0	0	0	1	0	0	0
12/10	Was	W 20-13	5	0	0.0	0.0	0.0	0.0	0	0	3	0	0	0
12/17	@Dal	L 20-21	5	0	0.0	0.0	1.0	1.0	1	0	1	0	0	0
12/23	SD	L 17-27	1	0	0.0	0.0	0.0	0.0	0	0	0	0	0	0

Alonzo Spellman
Chicago Bears – DE

1995 Defensive Splits

	G	Tk	Ast	Sack	Yds	Stuff	Yds	Int	Yds	PD	TD
Total	16	32	17	8.5	53.0	7.0	17.0	0	0	5	0
vs. Playoff	6	11	7	4.0	21.0	2.0	2.0	0	0	1	0
vs. Non-Playoff	10	21	10	4.5	32.0	5.0	15.0	0	0	4	0
vs. Own Division	8	15	10	4.5	27.0	3.0	6.0	0	0	0	0
Home	8	16	6	7.0	43.0	2.5	8.5	0	0	3	0
Away	8	16	11	1.5	10.0	4.5	8.5	0	0	2	0
Games 1-8	8	16	10	4.5	32.0	5.0	15.0	0	0	3	0
Games 9-16	8	16	7	4.0	21.0	2.0	2.0	0	0	2	0
September	4	9	5	3.5	22.0	2.5	5.5	0	0	0	0
October	4	7	5	1.0	10.0	2.5	9.5	0	0	3	0
November	4	8	5	0.0	0.0	2.0	2.0	0	0	1	0
December	4	8	2	4.0	21.0	0.0	0.0	0	0	1	0
Grass	11	21	10	8.5	53.0	4.5	12.5	0	0	4	0
Turf	5	11	7	0.0	0.0	2.5	4.5	0	0	1	0
Indoor	2	3	4	0.0	0.0	1.0	2.0	0	0	0	0
Outdoor	14	29	13	8.5	53.0	6.0	15.0	0	0	5	0

Game Logs

Date	Opp	Result	Tk	Ast	Sack	Yds	Stuff	Yds	Int	Yds	PD	FF	FR	TD
09/03	Min	W 31-14	2	1	1.0	7.0	0.0	0.0	0	0	0	0	0	0
09/11	GB	L 24-27	2	2	1.0	5.0	0.0	0.0	0	0	0	0	0	0
09/17	@TB	W 25-6	2	1	1.5	10.0	1.0	3.0	0	0	0	1	0	0
09/24	@StL	L 28-34	3	1	0.0	0.0	1.5	2.5	0	0	0	0	0	0
10/08	Car	W 31-27	1	1	0.0	0.0	1.5	7.5	0	0	1	0	0	0
10/15	@Jac	W 30-27	1	0	0.0	0.0	0.0	0.0	0	0	1	0	0	0
10/22	Hou	W 35-32	2	1	1.0	10.0	0.0	0.0	0	0	1	1	0	0
10/30	@Min	W 14-6	3	2	0.0	0.0	1.0	2.0	0	0	0	0	0	0
11/05	Pit	L 34-37	1	1	0.0	0.0	1.0	1.0	0	0	1	0	0	0
11/12	@GB	L 28-35	2	2	0.0	0.0	1.0	1.0	0	0	0	0	0	0
11/19	Det	L 17-24	2	0	0.0	0.0	0.0	0.0	0	0	0	0	0	0
11/26	@NYN	W 27-24	3	2	0.0	0.0	0.0	0.0	0	0	0	0	0	0
12/04	@Det	L 7-27	0	2	0.0	0.0	0.0	0.0	0	0	0	0	0	0
12/10	@Cin	L 10-16	2	0	0.0	0.0	0.0	0.0	0	0	1	0	0	0
12/17	TB	W 31-10	2	0	1.0	5.0	0.0	0.0	0	0	0	1	0	0
12/24	Phi	W 20-14	4	0	3.0	16.0	0.0	0.0	0	0	2	0	0	0

Jimmy Spencer
New Orleans Saints – CB

1995 Defensive Splits

	G	Tk	Ast	Sack	Yds	Stuff	Yds	Int	Yds	PD	TD
Total	16	64	7	0.0	0.0	0.0	0.0	4	11	16	0
vs. Playoff	8	34	3	0.0	0.0	0.0	0.0	1	1	7	0
vs. Non-Playoff	8	30	4	0.0	0.0	0.0	0.0	3	10	9	0
vs. Own Division	8	35	2	0.0	0.0	0.0	0.0	3	10	12	0
Home	8	29	5	0.0	0.0	0.0	0.0	2	9	6	0
Away	8	35	2	0.0	0.0	0.0	0.0	2	2	10	0
Games 1-8	8	34	1	0.0	0.0	0.0	0.0	1	1	8	0
Games 9-16	8	30	6	0.0	0.0	0.0	0.0	3	10	8	0
September	4	18	0	0.0	0.0	0.0	0.0	0	0	2	0
October	4	16	1	0.0	0.0	0.0	0.0	1	1	6	0
November	4	13	3	0.0	0.0	0.0	0.0	2	9	4	0
December	4	17	3	0.0	0.0	0.0	0.0	1	1	4	0
Grass	3	12	0	0.0	0.0	0.0	0.0	1	1	5	0
Turf	13	52	7	0.0	0.0	0.0	0.0	3	10	11	0
Indoor	10	40	5	0.0	0.0	0.0	0.0	2	9	8	0
Outdoor	6	24	2	0.0	0.0	0.0	0.0	2	2	8	0

Game Logs

Date	Opp	Result	Tk	Ast	Sack	Yds	Stuff	Yds	Int	Yds	PD	FF	FR	TD
09/03	SF	L 22-24	6	0	0.0	0.0	0.0	0.0	0	0	0	0	0	0
09/10	@StL	L 13-17	2	0	0.0	0.0	0.0	0.0	0	0	0	0	0	0
09/17	Atl	L 24-27	7	0	0.0	0.0	0.0	0.0	0	0	1	0	0	0
09/24	@NYN	L 29-45	3	0	0.0	0.0	0.0	0.0	0	0	1	0	0	0
10/01	Phi	L 10-15	6	0	0.0	0.0	0.0	0.0	0	0	1	0	0	0
10/15	Mia	W 33-30	2	1	0.0	0.0	0.0	0.0	0	0	0	0	0	0
10/22	@Car	L 3-20	1	0	0.0	0.0	0.0	0.0	0	0	2	0	0	0
10/29	@SF	W 11-7	7	0	0.0	0.0	0.0	0.0	1	1	3	0	0	0
11/05	StL	W 19-10	2	1	0.0	0.0	0.0	0.0	0	0	0	0	0	0
11/12	Ind	W 17-14	0	1	0.0	0.0	0.0	0.0	0	0	0	0	0	0
11/19	@Min	L 24-43	6	0	0.0	0.0	0.0	0.0	0	0	0	0	0	0
11/26	Car	W 34-26	5	1	0.0	0.0	0.0	0.0	2	9	4	0	0	0
12/03	@NE	W 31-17	4	0	0.0	0.0	0.0	0.0	0	0	0	0	0	0
12/10	@Atl	L 14-19	5	0	0.0	0.0	0.0	0.0	0	0	2	0	0	0
12/16	GB	L 23-34	1	1	0.0	0.0	0.0	0.0	0	0	0	0	0	0
12/24	@NYA	W 12-0	7	2	0.0	0.0	0.0	0.0	1	1	2	0	0	0

Chris Spielman
Detroit Lions – LB

1995 Defensive Splits

	G	Tk	Ast	Sack	Yds	Stuff	Yds	Int	Yds	PD	TD
Total	16	90	47	1.0	10.0	6.5	14.5	1	4	3	0
vs. Playoff	5	36	25	0.0	0.0	1.5	2.5	1	4	2	0
vs. Non-Playoff	11	54	22	1.0	10.0	5.0	12.0	0	0	1	0
vs. Own Division	8	40	32	1.0	10.0	4.0	6.0	0	0	2	0
Home	8	40	27	0.0	0.0	5.5	13.5	1	4	2	0
Away	8	50	20	1.0	10.0	1.0	1.0	0	0	1	0
Games 1-8	8	54	30	0.0	0.0	2.5	4.5	1	4	2	0
Games 9-16	8	36	17	1.0	10.0	4.0	10.0	0	0	1	0
September	4	31	11	0.0	0.0	1.5	3.5	1	4	1	0
October	4	23	19	0.0	0.0	1.0	1.0	0	0	1	0
November	4	19	10	0.0	0.0	2.0	2.0	0	0	0	0
December	4	17	7	1.0	10.0	2.0	8.0	0	0	1	0
Grass	4	21	11	1.0	10.0	1.0	1.0	0	0	1	0
Turf	12	69	36	0.0	0.0	5.5	13.5	1	4	2	0
Indoor	11	57	35	0.0	0.0	5.5	13.5	1	4	2	0
Outdoor	5	33	12	1.0	10.0	1.0	1.0	0	0	1	0

Game Logs

Date	Opp	Result	Tk	Ast	Sack	Yds	Stuff	Yds	Int	Yds	PD	FF	FR	TD
09/03	@Pit	L 20-23	12	1	0.0	0.0	0.0	0.0	0	0	0	0	0	0
09/10	@Min	L 10-20	6	3	0.0	0.0	0.0	0.0	0	0	0	0	0	0
09/17	Ari	L 17-20	7	2	0.0	0.0	1.0	2.0	0	0	0	0	0	0
09/25	SF	W 27-24	6	5	0.0	0.0	0.5	1.5	1	4	1	0	0	0
10/08	Cle	W 38-20	5	2	0.0	0.0	0.0	0.0	0	0	0	0	0	0
10/15	@GB	L 21-30	9	7	0.0	0.0	1.0	1.0	0	0	0	0	0	0
10/22	@Was	L 30-36	5	0	0.0	0.0	0.0	0.0	0	0	1	0	0	0
10/29	GB	W 24-16	4	10	0.0	0.0	0.0	0.0	0	0	1	0	1	0
11/05	@Atl	L 22-34	5	2	0.0	0.0	0.0	0.0	0	0	0	0	0	0
11/12	TB	W 27-24	4	3	0.0	0.0	0.5	0.5	0	0	0	1	0	0
11/19	@Chi	W 24-17	3	3	0.0	0.0	0.0	0.0	0	0	0	0	0	0
11/23	Min	W 44-38	7	2	0.0	0.0	1.5	1.5	0	0	0	0	0	0
12/04	Chi	W 27-7	3	3	0.0	0.0	1.0	3.0	0	0	0	0	0	0
12/10	@Hou	W 24-17	6	3	0.0	0.0	0.0	0.0	0	0	0	0	1	0
12/17	Jac	W 44-0	4	0	0.0	0.0	1.0	5.0	0	0	1	0	0	0
12/23	@TB	W 37-10	4	1	1.0	10.0	0.0	0.0	0	0	1	1	0	0

Rod Stephens
Washington Redskins – LB

1995 Defensive Splits

	G	Tk	Ast	Sack	Yds	Stuff	Yds	Int	Yds	PD	TD
Total	16	82	18	0.0	0.0	3.5	4.5	0	0	4	0
vs. Playoff	6	34	5	0.0	0.0	1.0	1.0	0	0	1	0
vs. Non-Playoff	10	48	13	0.0	0.0	2.5	3.5	0	0	3	0
vs. Own Division	8	42	10	0.0	0.0	1.5	1.5	0	0	1	0
Home	8	48	1	0.0	0.0	2.0	3.0	0	0	3	0
Away	8	34	17	0.0	0.0	1.5	1.5	0	0	1	0
Games 1-8	8	42	9	0.0	0.0	1.5	1.5	0	0	1	0
Games 9-16	8	40	9	0.0	0.0	2.0	3.0	0	0	3	0
September	4	16	4	0.0	0.0	1.0	1.0	0	0	1	0
October	5	34	5	0.0	0.0	0.5	0.5	0	0	0	0
November	3	17	1	0.0	0.0	2.0	3.0	0	0	1	0
December	4	15	8	0.0	0.0	0.0	0.0	0	0	2	0
Grass	12	65	9	0.0	0.0	3.5	4.5	0	0	4	0
Turf	4	17	9	0.0	0.0	0.0	0.0	0	0	0	0
Indoor	1	2	2	0.0	0.0	0.0	0.0	0	0	0	0
Outdoor	15	80	16	0.0	0.0	3.5	4.5	0	0	4	0

Game Logs

Date	Opp	Result	Tk	Ast	Sack	Yds	Stuff	Yds	Int	Yds	PD	FF	FR	TD
09/03	Ari	W 27-7	2	0	0.0	0.0	1.0	1.0	0	0	0	0	0	0
09/10	Oak	L 8-20	8	0	0.0	0.0	0.0	0.0	0	0	0	0	1	0
09/17	@Den	L 31-38	4	1	0.0	0.0	0.0	0.0	0	0	1	0	0	0
09/24	@TB	L 6-14	2	3	0.0	0.0	0.0	0.0	0	0	0	0	0	0
10/01	Dal	W 27-23	7	0	0.0	0.0	0.0	0.0	0	0	0	0	0	0
10/08	@Phi	L 34-37	7	1	0.0	0.0	0.0	0.0	0	0	0	0	0	0
10/15	@Ari	L 20-24	5	3	0.0	0.0	0.5	0.5	0	0	0	0	0	0
10/22	Det	W 36-30	7	1	0.0	0.0	0.0	0.0	0	0	0	0	1	0
10/29	NYN	L 15-24	8	0	0.0	0.0	0.0	0.0	0	0	0	0	1	0
11/05	@KC	L 3-24	6	1	0.0	0.0	1.0	1.0	0	0	0	0	0	0
11/19	Sea	L 20-27	6	0	0.0	0.0	1.0	2.0	0	0	0	0	0	0
11/26	Phi	L 7-14	5	0	0.0	0.0	0.0	0.0	0	0	1	0	0	0
12/03	@Dal	W 24-17	2	2	0.0	0.0	0.0	0.0	0	0	0	0	0	0
12/10	@NYN	L 13-20	6	4	0.0	0.0	0.0	0.0	0	0	0	0	0	0
12/17	@StL	W 35-23	2	2	0.0	0.0	0.0	0.0	0	0	0	0	0	0
12/24	Car	W 20-17	5	0	0.0	0.0	0.0	0.0	0	0	2	0	0	0

Michael Stewart
Miami Dolphins – S

1995 Defensive Splits

	G	Tk	Ast	Sack	Yds	Stuff	Yds	Int	Yds	PD	TD
Total	16	64	22	0.0	0.0	2.5	3.0	1	0	6	0
vs. Playoff	9	35	7	0.0	0.0	0.0	0.0	0	0	4	0
vs. Non-Playoff	7	29	15	0.0	0.0	2.5	3.0	1	0	2	0
vs. Own Division	8	41	12	0.0	0.0	1.5	2.0	1	0	3	0
Home	8	33	10	0.0	0.0	1.0	1.0	0	0	3	0
Away	8	31	12	0.0	0.0	1.5	2.0	1	0	3	0
Games 1-8	8	28	14	0.0	0.0	1.5	2.0	1	0	3	0
Games 9-16	8	36	8	0.0	0.0	1.0	1.0	0	0	3	0
September	3	11	8	0.0	0.0	0.5	1.0	1	0	3	0
October	5	17	6	0.0	0.0	1.0	1.0	0	0	0	0
November	4	22	2	0.0	0.0	1.0	1.0	0	0	0	0
December	4	14	6	0.0	0.0	0.0	0.0	0	0	3	0
Grass	10	41	16	0.0	0.0	1.5	2.0	1	0	5	0
Turf	6	23	6	0.0	0.0	1.0	1.0	0	0	1	0
Indoor	3	12	4	0.0	0.0	1.0	1.0	0	0	0	0
Outdoor	13	52	18	0.0	0.0	1.5	2.0	1	0	6	0

Game Logs

Date	Opp	Result	Tk	Ast	Sack	Yds	Stuff	Yds	Int	Yds	PD	FF	FR	TD
09/03	NYA	W 52-14	2	1	0.0	0.0	0.0	0.0	0	0	0	0	0	0
09/10	@NE	W 20-3	5	6	0.0	0.0	0.5	1.0	1	0	2	0	1	0
09/18	Pit	W 23-10	4	1	0.0	0.0	0.0	0.0	0	0	1	0	0	0
10/01	@Cin	W 26-23	0	0	0.0	0.0	0.0	0.0	0	0	0	0	0	0
10/08	Ind	L 24-27	6	0	0.0	0.0	0.0	0.0	0	0	0	0	0	0
10/15	@NO	L 30-33	4	3	0.0	0.0	1.0	1.0	0	0	0	0	0	0
10/22	@NYA	L 16-17	4	2	0.0	0.0	0.0	0.0	0	0	1	0	0	0
10/29	Buf	W 23-6	3	1	0.0	0.0	0.0	0.0	0	0	0	0	0	0
11/05	@SD	W 24-14	3	0	0.0	0.0	0.0	0.0	0	0	0	0	0	0
11/12	NE	L 17-34	10	2	0.0	0.0	1.0	1.0	0	0	0	0	0	0
11/20	SF	L 20-44	5	0	0.0	0.0	0.0	0.0	0	0	0	0	0	0
11/26	@Ind	L 28-36	4	0	0.0	0.0	0.0	0.0	0	0	0	0	0	0
12/03	Atl	W 21-20	1	5	0.0	0.0	0.0	0.0	0	0	0	0	0	0
12/11	KC	W 13-6	2	0	0.0	0.0	0.0	0.0	0	0	2	0	0	0
12/17	@Buf	L 20-23	7	0	0.0	0.0	0.0	0.0	0	0	1	0	1	0
12/24	@StL	W 41-22	4	1	0.0	0.0	0.0	0.0	0	0	0	0	0	0

Michael Strahan
New York Giants – DE

1995 Defensive Splits

	G	Tk	Ast	Sack	Yds	Stuff	Yds	Int	Yds	PD	TD
Total	15	49	10	7.5	38.5	4.5	7.5	2	56	5	0
vs. Playoff	7	27	5	3.0	17.0	2.5	3.5	1	0	2	0
vs. Non-Playoff	8	22	5	4.5	21.5	2.0	4.0	1	56	3	0
vs. Own Division	7	22	7	4.5	21.5	1.5	1.5	1	56	3	0
Home	8	24	6	2.0	14.0	2.5	4.5	0	0	2	0
Away	7	25	4	5.5	24.5	2.0	3.0	2	56	3	0
Games 1-8	8	25	6	4.5	28.5	0.5	0.5	2	56	5	0
Games 9-16	7	24	4	3.0	10.0	4.0	7.0	0	0	0	0
September	4	12	3	3.0	17.0	0.0	0.0	1	0	1	0
October	4	13	3	1.5	11.5	0.5	0.5	1	56	4	0
November	5	19	3	2.0	4.0	3.0	5.0	0	0	0	0
December	2	5	1	1.0	6.0	1.0	2.0	0	0	0	0
Grass	5	18	3	5.5	24.5	0.0	0.0	2	56	3	0
Turf	10	31	7	2.0	14.0	4.5	7.5	0	0	2	0
Indoor	1	3	1	0.0	0.0	1.0	2.0	0	0	0	0
Outdoor	14	46	9	7.5	38.5	3.5	5.5	2	56	5	0

Game Logs

Date	Opp	Result	Tk	Ast	Sack	Yds	Stuff	Yds	Int	Yds	PD	FF	FR	TD
09/04	Dal	L 0-35	1	2	0.0	0.0	0.0	0.0	0	0	0	0	0	0
09/10	@KC	L 17-20	3	0	0.0	0.0	0.0	0.0	1	0	1	0	0	0
09/17	@GB	L 6-14	6	1	3.0	17.0	0.0	0.0	0	0	0	0	0	0
09/24	NO	W 45-29	2	0	0.0	0.0	0.0	0.0	0	0	0	0	0	0
10/01	@SF	L 6-20	3	0	0.0	0.0	0.0	0.0	0	0	1	0	0	0
10/08	Ari	W 27-21	4	0	1.0	8.0	0.0	0.0	0	0	2	1	0	0
10/15	Phi	L 14-17	6	2	0.0	0.0	0.5	0.5	0	0	0	0	0	0
10/29	@Was	W 24-15	0	1	0.5	3.5	0.0	0.0	1	56	1	0	0	0
11/05	@Sea	L 28-30	3	1	0.0	0.0	1.0	2.0	0	0	0	0	0	0
11/12	Oak	L 13-17	4	0	0.0	0.0	1.0	2.0	0	0	0	0	0	0
11/19	@Phi	L 19-28	4	0	0.0	0.0	1.0	1.0	0	0	0	0	0	0
11/26	Chi	L 24-27	2	1	0.0	0.0	0.0	0.0	0	0	0	0	0	0
11/30	@Ari	W 10-6	6	1	2.0	4.0	0.0	0.0	0	0	0	2	0	0
12/10	Was	W 20-13	1	1	1.0	6.0	0.0	0.0	0	0	0	0	0	0
12/17	@Dal	L 20-21	-	-	-	-	-	-	-	-	-	-	-	-
12/23	SD	L 17-27	4	0	0.0	0.0	1.0	2.0	0	0	0	0	0	0

Dana Stubblefield
San Francisco 49ers – DT

1995 Defensive Splits

	G	Tk	Ast	Sack	Yds	Stuff	Yds	Int	Yds	PD	TD
Total	16	27	7	4.5	25.0	2.0	2.0	1	12	4	0
vs. Playoff	7	13	3	3.0	16.0	0.5	0.5	0	0	1	0
vs. Non-Playoff	9	14	4	1.5	9.0	1.5	1.5	1	12	3	0
vs. Own Division	8	12	3	0.5	2.0	0.5	0.5	1	12	2	0
Home	8	13	2	1.5	9.0	1.0	1.0	0	0	3	0
Away	8	14	5	3.0	16.0	1.0	1.0	1	12	1	0
Games 1-8	8	11	6	2.0	8.0	1.0	1.0	1	12	2	0
Games 9-16	8	16	1	2.5	17.0	1.0	1.0	0	0	2	0
September	4	4	2	1.0	1.0	0.0	0.0	0	0	0	0
October	4	7	4	1.0	7.0	1.0	1.0	1	12	2	0
November	4	12	1	2.5	17.0	0.0	0.0	0	0	1	0
December	4	4	0	0.0	0.0	1.0	1.0	0	0	1	0
Grass	10	16	2	2.5	16.0	1.0	1.0	0	0	3	0
Turf	6	11	5	2.0	9.0	1.0	1.0	1	12	1	0
Indoor	4	6	4	1.0	1.0	0.5	0.5	0	0	0	0
Outdoor	12	21	3	3.5	24.0	1.5	1.5	1	12	4	0

Game Logs

Date	Opp	Result	Tk	Ast	Sack	Yds	Stuff	Yds	Int	Yds	PD	FF	FR	TD
09/03	@NO	W 24-22	1	1	0.0	0.0	0.0	0.0	0	0	0	0	0	0
09/10	Atl	W 41-10	2	0	0.0	0.0	0.0	0.0	0	0	0	0	0	0
09/17	NE	W 28-3	0	0	0.0	0.0	0.0	0.0	0	0	0	0	0	0
09/25	@Det	L 24-27	1	1	1.0	1.0	0.0	0.0	0	0	0	0	0	0
10/01	NYN	W 20-6	2	1	1.0	7.0	0.0	0.0	0	0	1	0	0	0
10/15	@Ind	L 17-18	3	2	0.0	0.0	0.5	0.5	0	0	0	0	0	0
10/22	@StL	W 44-10	2	1	0.0	0.0	0.5	0.5	1	12	1	0	0	0
10/29	NO	L 7-11	0	0	0.0	0.0	0.0	0.0	0	0	0	0	0	0
11/05	Car	L 7-13	2	1	0.5	2.0	0.0	0.0	0	0	0	0	0	0
11/12	@Dal	W 38-20	3	0	1.0	8.0	0.0	0.0	0	0	0	0	0	0
11/20	@Mia	W 44-20	1	0	1.0	7.0	0.0	0.0	0	0	0	0	0	0
11/26	StL	W 41-13	4	0	0.0	0.0	0.0	0.0	0	0	1	0	0	0
12/03	Buf	W 27-17	0	0	0.0	0.0	0.0	0.0	0	0	1	0	0	0
12/10	@Car	W 31-10	0	0	0.0	0.0	0.0	0.0	0	0	0	0	0	0
12/18	Min	W 37-30	3	0	0.0	0.0	1.0	1.0	0	0	0	0	0	0
12/24	@Atl	L 27-28	1	0	0.0	0.0	0.0	0.0	0	0	0	0	0	0

Eric Swann
Arizona Cardinals – DT

1995 Defensive Splits

	G	Tk	Ast	Sack	Yds	Stuff	Yds	Int	Yds	PD	TD
Total	13	45	8	8.5	50.5	8.0	29.0	0	0	2	0
vs. Playoff	6	15	2	2.0	11.0	3.0	11.5	0	0	1	0
vs. Non-Playoff	7	30	6	6.5	39.5	5.0	17.5	0	0	1	0
vs. Own Division	6	16	6	2.5	14.0	2.0	14.0	0	0	2	0
Home	7	30	7	6.5	38.5	3.5	12.0	0	0	1	0
Away	6	15	1	2.0	12.0	4.5	17.0	0	0	1	0
Games 1-8	5	15	3	2.5	12.5	1.0	7.0	0	0	1	0
Games 9-16	8	30	5	6.0	38.0	7.0	22.0	0	0	1	0
September	3	5	0	1.0	4.0	0.0	0.0	0	0	0	0
October	2	10	3	1.5	8.5	1.0	7.0	0	0	1	0
November	5	23	6	6.0	38.0	6.0	15.0	0	0	0	0
December	3	7	2	0.0	0.0	1.0	7.0	0	0	1	0
Grass	11	43	8	8.5	50.5	7.0	22.0	0	0	1	0
Turf	2	2	0	0.0	0.0	1.0	7.0	0	0	1	0
Indoor	1	0	0	0.0	0.0	0.0	0.0	0	0	0	0
Outdoor	12	45	8	8.5	50.5	8.0	29.0	0	0	2	0

Game Logs

Date	Opp	Result	Tk	Ast	Sack	Yds	Stuff	Yds	Int	Yds	PD	FF	FR	TD
09/03	@Was	L 7-27	4	0	0.0	0.0	0.0	0.0	0	0	0	0	0	0
09/10	Phi	L 19-31	1	0	1.0	4.0	0.0	0.0	0	0	0	0	0	0
09/17	@Det	W 20-17	0	0	0.0	0.0	0.0	0.0	0	0	0	0	0	0
09/24	@Dal	L 20-34	-	-	-	-	-	-	-	-	-	-	-	-
10/01	KC	L 3-24	-	-	-	-	-	-	-	-	-	-	-	-
10/08	@NYN	L 21-27	-	-	-	-	-	-	-	-	-	-	-	-
10/15	Was	W 24-20	3	3	0.5	3.5	1.0	7.0	0	0	1	0	0	0
10/29	Sea	W 20-14	7	0	1.0	5.0	0.0	0.0	0	0	0	0	0	0
11/05	@Den	L 6-38	2	0	0.0	0.0	1.0	3.0	0	0	0	0	0	0
11/12	Min	L 24-30	6	1	2.0	18.0	0.5	0.5	0	0	0	0	0	0
11/19	@Car	L 7-27	5	1	2.0	12.0	2.5	7.0	0	0	0	0	0	0
11/26	Atl	W 40-37	7	0	1.0	7.0	2.0	4.5	0	0	0	0	0	0
11/30	NYN	L 6-10	3	1	1.0	1.0	0.0	0.0	0	0	0	0	0	0
12/09	@SD	L 25-28	2	0	0.0	0.0	0.0	0.0	0	0	0	0	0	0
12/17	@Phi	L 20-21	2	0	0.0	0.0	1.0	7.0	0	0	1	0	1	0
12/25	Dal	L 13-37	3	0	0.0	0.0	0.0	0.0	0	0	0	0	1	0

Pat Swilling
Oakland Raiders – DE

1995 Defensive Splits

	G	Tk	Ast	Sack	Yds	Stuff	Yds	Int	Yds	PD	TD
Total	16	31	5	13.0	119.0	5.5	26.5	0	0	3	0
vs. Playoff	8	18	2	8.0	69.0	2.0	18.0	0	0	2	0
vs. Non-Playoff	8	13	3	5.0	50.0	3.5	8.5	0	0	1	0
vs. Own Division	8	11	4	3.0	34.0	2.0	5.0	0	0	1	0
Home	8	16	3	7.0	62.0	3.0	21.0	0	0	2	0
Away	8	15	2	6.0	57.0	2.5	5.5	0	0	1	0
Games 1-8	8	14	0	5.0	40.0	3.5	12.5	0	0	2	0
Games 9-16	8	17	5	8.0	79.0	2.0	14.0	0	0	1	0
September	4	9	0	4.0	27.0	0.5	0.5	0	0	1	0
October	4	5	0	1.0	13.0	3.0	12.0	0	0	1	0
November	4	8	0	5.0	44.0	0.0	0.0	0	0	0	0
December	4	9	5	3.0	35.0	2.0	14.0	0	0	1	0
Grass	12	23	3	8.0	69.0	3.5	21.5	0	0	2	0
Turf	4	8	2	5.0	50.0	2.0	5.0	0	0	1	0
Indoor	1	1	0	0.0	0.0	1.0	2.0	0	0	0	0
Outdoor	15	30	3	13.0	119.0	4.5	24.5	0	0	3	0

Game Logs

Date	Opp	Result	Tk	Ast	Sack	Yds	Stuff	Yds	Int	Yds	PD	FF	FR	TD
09/03	SD	W 17-7	1	0	1.0	11.0	0.0	0.0	0	0	1	1	0	0
09/10	@Was	W 20-8	2	0	0.0	0.0	0.5	0.5	0	0	0	0	0	0
09/17	@KC	L 17-23	2	0	0.0	0.0	0.0	0.0	0	0	0	0	0	0
09/24	Phi	W 48-17	4	0	3.0	16.0	0.0	0.0	0	0	0	0	0	0
10/01	@NYA	W 47-10	2	0	1.0	13.0	1.0	3.0	0	0	1	0	0	0
10/08	Sea	W 34-14	1	0	0.0	0.0	1.0	1.0	0	0	0	0	0	0
10/16	@Den	L 0-27	1	0	0.0	0.0	0.0	0.0	0	0	0	0	0	0
10/22	Ind	W 30-17	1	0	0.0	0.0	1.0	6.0	0	0	0	1	0	0
11/05	@Cin	W 20-17	4	0	3.0	35.0	0.0	0.0	0	0	1	0	0	0
11/12	@NYN	W 17-13	1	0	1.0	2.0	0.0	0.0	0	0	0	0	0	0
11/19	Dal	L 21-34	1	0	0.0	0.0	0.0	0.0	0	0	0	0	0	0
11/27	@SD	L 6-12	2	0	1.0	7.0	0.0	0.0	0	0	0	0	0	0
12/03	KC	L 23-29	2	1	1.0	16.0	0.0	0.0	0	0	1	0	0	0
12/10	Pit	L 10-29	5	1	2.0	19.0	1.0	12.0	0	0	1	0	0	0
12/17	@Sea	L 10-44	1	2	0.0	0.0	1.0	2.0	0	0	0	0	0	0
12/24	Den	L 28-31	1	1	0.0	0.0	0.0	0.0	0	0	0	0	0	0

Darryl Talley

1995 Defensive Splits

	G	Tk	Ast	Sack	Yds	Stuff	Yds	Int	Yds	PD	TD
Total	16	54	19	0.0	0.0	6.5	15.5	0	0	1	0
vs. Playoff	6	22	4	0.0	0.0	2.0	6.0	0	0	0	0
vs. Non-Playoff	10	32	15	0.0	0.0	4.5	9.5	0	0	1	0
vs. Own Division	8	22	9	0.0	0.0	3.0	5.0	0	0	0	0
Home	8	18	9	0.0	0.0	2.0	4.0	0	0	1	0
Away	8	36	10	0.0	0.0	4.5	11.5	0	0	0	0
Games 1-8	8	27	14	0.0	0.0	4.0	9.0	0	0	1	0
Games 9-16	8	27	5	0.0	0.0	2.5	6.5	0	0	0	0
September	4	15	5	0.0	0.0	0.0	0.0	0	0	0	0
October	4	12	9	0.0	0.0	4.0	9.0	0	0	1	0
November	4	16	2	0.0	0.0	2.5	6.5	0	0	0	0
December	4	11	3	0.0	0.0	0.0	0.0	0	0	0	0
Grass	5	23	8	0.0	0.0	1.0	4.0	0	0	0	0
Turf	11	31	11	0.0	0.0	5.5	11.5	0	0	1	0
Indoor	9	22	9	0.0	0.0	2.0	4.0	0	0	1	0
Outdoor	7	32	10	0.0	0.0	4.5	11.5	0	0	0	0

Game Logs

Date	Opp	Result	Tk	Ast	Sack	Yds	Stuff	Yds	Int	Yds	PD	FF	FR	TD
09/03	Car	W 23-20	1	3	0.0	0.0	0.0	0.0	0	0	0	1	0	0
09/10	@SF	L 10-41	5	1	0.0	0.0	0.0	0.0	0	0	0	0	0	0
09/17	@NO	W 27-24	4	0	0.0	0.0	0.0	0.0	0	0	0	0	0	0
09/24	NYA	W 13-3	5	1	0.0	0.0	0.0	0.0	0	0	0	0	0	0
10/01	NE	W 30-17	1	2	0.0	0.0	0.5	0.5	0	0	1	0	1	0
10/12	@StL	L 19-21	5	2	0.0	0.0	2.5	4.5	0	0	0	0	0	0
10/22	@TB	W 24-21	2	3	0.0	0.0	1.0	4.0	0	0	0	0	0	0
10/29	Dal	L 13-28	4	2	0.0	0.0	0.0	0.0	0	0	0	0	0	0
11/05	Det	W 34-22	1	0	0.0	0.0	1.0	3.0	0	0	0	0	0	0
11/12	@Buf	L 17-23	4	0	0.0	0.0	1.0	3.0	0	0	0	0	0	0
11/19	StL	W 31-6	3	1	0.0	0.0	0.5	0.5	0	0	0	0	1	0
11/26	@Ari	L 37-40	8	1	0.0	0.0	0.0	0.0	0	0	0	0	0	0
12/03	@Mia	L 20-21	7	1	0.0	0.0	0.0	0.0	0	0	0	0	0	0
12/10	NO	W 19-14	2	0	0.0	0.0	0.0	0.0	0	0	0	0	0	0
12/17	@Car	L 17-21	1	2	0.0	0.0	0.0	0.0	0	0	0	0	0	0
12/24	SF	W 28-27	1	0	0.0	0.0	0.0	0.0	0	0	0	1	0	0

David Tate

1995 Defensive Splits

	G	Tk	Ast	Sack	Yds	Stuff	Yds	Int	Yds	PD	TD
Total	16	61	22	0.0	0.0	0.0	0.0	0	0	5	0
vs. Playoff	6	22	12	0.0	0.0	0.0	0.0	0	0	0	0
vs. Non-Playoff	10	39	10	0.0	0.0	0.0	0.0	0	0	5	0
vs. Own Division	8	32	11	0.0	0.0	0.0	0.0	0	0	0	0
Home	8	29	10	0.0	0.0	0.0	0.0	0	0	1	0
Away	8	32	12	0.0	0.0	0.0	0.0	0	0	4	0
Games 1-8	8	31	9	0.0	0.0	0.0	0.0	0	0	1	0
Games 9-16	8	30	13	0.0	0.0	0.0	0.0	0	0	4	0
September	3	12	3	0.0	0.0	0.0	0.0	0	0	0	0
October	5	19	6	0.0	0.0	0.0	0.0	0	0	1	0
November	4	15	4	0.0	0.0	0.0	0.0	0	0	0	0
December	4	15	9	0.0	0.0	0.0	0.0	0	0	4	0
Grass	5	18	8	0.0	0.0	0.0	0.0	0	0	4	0
Turf	11	43	14	0.0	0.0	0.0	0.0	0	0	1	0
Indoor	9	35	11	0.0	0.0	0.0	0.0	0	0	1	0
Outdoor	7	26	11	0.0	0.0	0.0	0.0	0	0	4	0

Game Logs

Date	Opp	Result	Tk	Ast	Sack	Yds	Stuff	Yds	Int	Yds	PD	FF	FR	TD
09/03	Cin	L 21-24	4	0	0.0	0.0	0.0	0.0	0	0	0	0	0	0
09/10	@NYA	W 27-24	5	2	0.0	0.0	0.0	0.0	0	0	0	0	1	0
09/17	@Buf	L 14-20	3	1	0.0	0.0	0.0	0.0	0	0	0	0	0	0
10/01	StL	W 21-18	3	0	0.0	0.0	0.0	0.0	0	0	1	0	0	0
10/08	@Mia	W 27-24	6	3	0.0	0.0	0.0	0.0	0	0	0	0	0	0
10/15	SF	W 18-17	3	1	0.0	0.0	0.0	0.0	0	0	0	0	0	0
10/22	@Oak	L 17-30	2	1	0.0	0.0	0.0	0.0	0	0	0	0	0	0
10/29	NYA	W 17-10	5	1	0.0	0.0	0.0	0.0	0	0	0	0	0	0
11/05	Buf	L 10-16	3	0	0.0	0.0	0.0	0.0	0	0	0	0	0	0
11/12	@NO	L 14-17	6	1	0.0	0.0	0.0	0.0	0	0	0	0	0	0
11/19	@NE	W 24-10	2	2	0.0	0.0	0.0	0.0	0	0	0	0	1	0
11/26	Mia	W 36-28	4	1	0.0	0.0	0.0	0.0	0	0	0	0	0	0
12/03	@Car	L 10-13	4	0	0.0	0.0	0.0	0.0	0	0	4	0	0	0
12/10	@Jac	W 41-31	4	2	0.0	0.0	0.0	0.0	0	0	0	0	0	0
12/17	SD	L 24-27	3	6	0.0	0.0	0.0	0.0	0	0	0	0	0	0
12/23	NE	W 10-7	4	1	0.0	0.0	0.0	0.0	0	0	0	0	0	0

Bobby Taylor

1995 Defensive Splits

	G	Tk	Ast	Sack	Yds	Stuff	Yds	Int	Yds	PD	TD
Total	16	53	5	0.0	0.0	0.0	0.0	2	52	17	0
vs. Playoff	3	9	1	0.0	0.0	0.0	0.0	1	35	5	0
vs. Non-Playoff	13	44	4	0.0	0.0	0.0	0.0	1	17	12	0
vs. Own Division	8	31	2	0.0	0.0	0.0	0.0	2	52	15	0
Home	8	25	1	0.0	0.0	0.0	0.0	0	0	12	0
Away	8	28	4	0.0	0.0	0.0	0.0	2	52	5	0
Games 1-8	8	21	3	0.0	0.0	0.0	0.0	0	0	7	0
Games 9-16	8	32	2	0.0	0.0	0.0	0.0	2	52	10	0
September	4	4	1	0.0	0.0	0.0	0.0	0	0	0	0
October	4	17	2	0.0	0.0	0.0	0.0	0	0	7	0
November	4	17	1	0.0	0.0	0.0	0.0	2	52	3	0
December	4	15	1	0.0	0.0	0.0	0.0	0	0	7	0
Grass	4	9	1	0.0	0.0	0.0	0.0	1	17	1	0
Turf	12	44	4	0.0	0.0	0.0	0.0	1	35	16	0
Indoor	2	8	1	0.0	0.0	0.0	0.0	0	0	1	0
Outdoor	14	45	4	0.0	0.0	0.0	0.0	2	52	16	0

Game Logs

Date	Opp	Result	Tk	Ast	Sack	Yds	Stuff	Yds	Int	Yds	PD	FF	FR	TD
09/03	TB	L 6-21	1	0	0.0	0.0	0.0	0.0	0	0	0	0	0	0
09/10	@Ari	W 31-19	2	0	0.0	0.0	0.0	0.0	0	0	0	0	0	0
09/17	SD	L 21-27	0	0	0.0	0.0	0.0	0.0	0	0	0	0	0	0
09/24	@Oak	L 17-48	1	1	0.0	0.0	0.0	0.0	0	0	0	0	0	0
10/01	@NO	W 15-10	3	0	0.0	0.0	0.0	0.0	0	0	1	0	0	0
10/08	Was	W 37-34	4	0	0.0	0.0	0.0	0.0	0	0	4	0	0	0
10/15	@NYN	W 17-14	5	1	0.0	0.0	0.0	0.0	0	0	2	0	0	0
10/29	StL	W 20-9	5	1	0.0	0.0	0.0	0.0	0	0	0	0	0	0
11/06	@Dal	L 12-34	6	1	0.0	0.0	0.0	0.0	1	35	1	0	0	0
11/12	Den	W 31-13	4	0	0.0	0.0	0.0	0.0	0	0	1	0	0	0
11/19	NYN	W 28-19	4	0	0.0	0.0	0.0	0.0	0	0	0	0	0	0
11/26	@Was	W 14-7	3	0	0.0	0.0	0.0	0.0	1	17	1	0	0	0
12/03	@Sea	L 14-26	5	1	0.0	0.0	0.0	0.0	0	0	0	0	0	0
12/10	Dal	W 20-17	3	0	0.0	0.0	0.0	0.0	0	0	4	0	0	0
12/17	Ari	W 21-20	4	0	0.0	0.0	0.0	0.0	0	0	3	0	0	0
12/24	@Chi	L 14-20	3	0	0.0	0.0	0.0	0.0	0	0	0	0	0	0

Pat Terrell
Carolina Panthers – S

1995 Defensive Splits

	G	Tk	Ast	Sack	Yds	Stuff	Yds	Int	Yds	PD	TD
Total	16	45	17	0.0	0.0	1.5	3.5	3	33	12	0
vs. Playoff	6	12	3	0.0	0.0	0.0	0.0	3	33	8	0
vs. Non-Playoff	10	33	14	0.0	0.0	1.5	3.5	0	0	4	0
vs. Own Division	8	24	5	0.0	0.0	0.0	0.0	2	21	7	0
Home	8	21	11	0.0	0.0	1.5	3.5	2	12	9	0
Away	8	24	6	0.0	0.0	0.0	0.0	1	21	3	0
Games 1-8	8	16	12	0.0	0.0	1.5	3.5	0	0	3	0
Games 9-16	8	29	5	0.0	0.0	0.0	0.0	3	33	9	0
September	3	0	1	0.0	0.0	0.0	0.0	0	0	0	0
October	5	16	11	0.0	0.0	1.5	3.5	0	0	3	0
November	4	19	1	0.0	0.0	0.0	0.0	1	21	2	0
December	4	10	4	0.0	0.0	0.0	0.0	2	12	7	0
Grass	12	34	15	0.0	0.0	1.5	3.5	3	33	12	0
Turf	4	11	2	0.0	0.0	0.0	0.0	0	0	0	0
Indoor	3	11	1	0.0	0.0	0.0	0.0	0	0	0	0
Outdoor	13	34	16	0.0	0.0	1.5	3.5	3	33	12	0

Game Logs

Date	Opp	Result	Tk	Ast	Sack	Yds	Stuff	Yds	Int	Yds	PD	FF	FR	TD
09/03	@Atl	L 20-23	0	0	0.0	0.0	0.0	0.0	0	0	0	0	0	0
09/10	@Buf	L 9-31	0	1	0.0	0.0	0.0	0.0	0	0	0	0	0	0
09/17	StL	L 10-31	0	0	0.0	0.0	0.0	0.0	0	0	0	0	0	0
10/01	TB	L 13-20	6	7	0.0	0.0	0.5	0.5	0	0	1	0	0	0
10/08	@Chi	L 27-31	2	2	0.0	0.0	0.0	0.0	0	0	0	0	0	0
10/15	NYA	W 26-15	2	0	0.0	0.0	1.0	3.0	0	0	1	0	0	0
10/22	NO	W 20-3	3	2	0.0	0.0	0.0	0.0	0	0	1	0	0	0
10/29	@NE	W 20-17	3	0	0.0	0.0	0.0	0.0	0	0	0	0	0	0
11/05	@SF	W 13-7	5	0	0.0	0.0	0.0	0.0	1	21	2	0	0	0
11/12	@StL	L 17-28	7	0	0.0	0.0	0.0	0.0	0	0	0	0	0	0
11/19	Ari	W 27-7	3	0	0.0	0.0	0.0	0.0	0	0	0	0	1	0
11/26	@NO	L 26-34	4	1	0.0	0.0	0.0	0.0	0	0	0	0	0	0
12/03	Ind	W 13-10	2	0	0.0	0.0	0.0	0.0	1	12	2	0	0	0
12/10	SF	L 10-31	3	0	0.0	0.0	0.0	0.0	0	0	2	0	0	0
12/17	Atl	W 21-17	2	2	0.0	0.0	0.0	0.0	1	0	2	0	0	0
12/24	@Was	L 17-20	3	2	0.0	0.0	0.0	0.0	0	0	1	0	0	0

Broderick Thomas
Minnesota Vikings – LB

1995 Defensive Splits

	G	Tk	Ast	Sack	Yds	Stuff	Yds	Int	Yds	PD	TD
Total	16	57	15	6.0	35.5	4.5	12.5	0	0	7	0
vs. Playoff	7	27	6	1.5	1.0	3.5	8.5	0	0	3	0
vs. Non-Playoff	9	30	9	4.5	34.5	1.0	4.0	0	0	4	0
vs. Own Division	8	27	9	4.0	26.5	3.5	10.5	0	0	2	0
Home	8	27	7	4.0	25.5	0.0	0.0	0	0	2	0
Away	8	30	8	2.0	10.0	4.5	12.5	0	0	5	0
Games 1-8	8	29	7	2.5	20.0	3.5	10.5	0	0	4	0
Games 9-16	8	28	8	3.5	15.5	1.0	2.0	0	0	3	0
September	4	14	1	0.5	1.0	1.0	2.0	0	0	3	0
October	4	15	6	2.0	19.0	2.5	8.5	0	0	1	0
November	4	13	5	0.0	0.0	1.0	2.0	0	0	2	0
December	4	15	3	3.5	15.5	0.0	0.0	0	0	1	0
Grass	5	21	5	2.0	10.0	2.5	8.5	0	0	3	0
Turf	11	36	10	4.0	25.5	2.0	4.0	0	0	4	0
Indoor	9	29	9	4.0	25.5	1.0	2.0	0	0	2	0
Outdoor	7	28	6	2.0	10.0	3.5	10.5	0	0	5	0

Game Logs

Date	Opp	Result	Tk	Ast	Sack	Yds	Stuff	Yds	Int	Yds	PD	FF	FR	TD
09/03	@Chi	L 14-31	4	0	0.0	0.0	0.0	0.0	0	0	0	0	0	0
09/10	Det	W 20-10	1	1	0.5	1.0	0.0	0.0	0	0	0	0	0	0
09/17	Dal	L 17-23	6	0	0.0	0.0	0.0	0.0	0	0	1	0	0	0
09/24	@Pit	W 44-24	3	0	0.0	0.0	1.0	2.0	0	0	2	0	0	0
10/08	Hou	W 23-17	5	2	1.0	9.0	0.0	0.0	0	0	0	0	0	0
10/15	@TB	L 17-20	5	1	1.0	10.0	1.0	4.0	0	0	1	0	0	0
10/22	@GB	L 21-38	4	2	0.0	0.0	1.5	4.5	0	0	0	0	0	0
10/30	Chi	L 6-14	1	1	0.0	0.0	0.0	0.0	0	0	0	0	1	0
11/05	GB	W 27-24	6	1	0.0	0.0	0.0	0.0	0	0	0	0	0	0
11/12	@Ari	W 30-24	3	2	0.0	0.0	0.0	0.0	0	0	2	0	0	0
11/19	NO	W 43-24	2	0	0.0	0.0	0.0	0.0	0	0	0	0	0	0
11/23	@Det	L 38-44	2	0	0.0	0.0	1.0	2.0	0	0	0	0	0	0
12/03	TB	W 31-17	4	1	2.5	15.5	0.0	0.0	0	0	1	0	0	0
12/09	Cle	W 27-11	2	1	0.0	0.0	0.0	0.0	0	0	0	0	0	0
12/18	@SF	L 30-37	5	0	1.0	0.0	0.0	0.0	0	0	0	0	0	0
12/24	@Cin	L 24-27	4	1	0.0	0.0	0.0	0.0	0	0	0	0	0	0

Derrick Thomas
Kansas City Chiefs – LB

1995 Defensive Splits

	G	Tk	Ast	Sack	Yds	Stuff	Yds	Int	Yds	PD	TD
Total	15	48	5	8.0	57.5	6.5	15.5	0	0	3	0
vs. Playoff	3	8	1	0.5	5.0	1.0	1.0	0	0	0	0
vs. Non-Playoff	12	40	4	7.5	52.5	5.5	14.5	0	0	3	0
vs. Own Division	8	26	4	2.0	15.5	3.5	8.5	0	0	1	0
Home	8	25	1	4.0	19.0	5.0	13.0	0	0	2	0
Away	7	23	4	4.0	38.5	1.5	2.5	0	0	1	0
Games 1-8	8	25	3	5.5	37.5	2.5	7.5	0	0	2	0
Games 9-16	7	23	2	2.5	20.0	4.0	8.0	0	0	1	0
September	4	18	3	2.5	9.5	2.5	7.5	0	0	1	0
October	4	7	0	3.0	28.0	0.0	0.0	0	0	1	0
November	4	15	1	1.5	13.0	2.0	3.0	0	0	1	0
December	3	8	1	1.0	7.0	2.0	5.0	0	0	0	0
Grass	13	39	3	7.5	54.0	5.0	13.0	0	0	2	0
Turf	2	9	2	0.5	3.5	1.5	2.5	0	0	1	0
Indoor	1	7	2	0.5	3.5	0.5	1.5	0	0	1	0
Outdoor	14	41	3	7.5	54.0	6.0	14.0	0	0	2	0

Game Logs

Date	Opp	Result	Tk	Ast	Sack	Yds	Stuff	Yds	Int	Yds	PD	FF	FR	TD
09/03	@Sea	W 34-10	7	2	0.5	3.5	0.5	1.5	0	0	1	0	0	0
09/10	NYN	W 20-17	6	0	2.0	6.0	1.0	4.0	0	0	0	1	0	0
09/17	Oak	W 23-17	3	0	0.0	0.0	1.0	2.0	0	0	0	0	0	0
09/24	@Cle	L 17-35	2	1	0.0	0.0	0.0	0.0	0	0	0	0	1	0
10/01	@Ari	W 24-3	2	0	2.0	23.0	0.0	0.0	0	0	0	0	0	0
10/09	SD	W 29-23	1	0	0.0	0.0	0.0	0.0	0	0	0	0	0	0
10/15	NE	W 31-26	2	0	1.0	5.0	0.0	0.0	0	0	1	0	0	0
10/22	@Den	W 21-7	2	0	0.0	0.0	0.0	0.0	0	0	0	0	0	0
11/05	Was	W 24-3	3	0	1.0	8.0	0.0	0.0	0	0	0	0	0	0
11/12	@SD	W 22-7	5	1	0.5	5.0	0.0	0.0	0	0	0	0	0	0
11/19	Hou	W 20-13	5	0	0.0	0.0	1.0	2.0	0	0	1	0	0	0
11/23	@Dal	L 12-24	2	0	0.0	0.0	1.0	1.0	0	0	0	0	0	0
12/03	@Oak	W 29-23	3	0	1.0	7.0	0.0	0.0	0	0	0	0	1	0
12/11	@Mia	L 6-13	-	-	-	-	-	-	-	-	-	-	-	-
12/17	Den	W 20-17	3	0	0.0	0.0	0.0	0.0	0	0	0	0	0	0
12/24	Sea	W 26-3	2	1	0.0	0.0	2.0	5.0	0	0	0	0	0	0

Henry Thomas

1995 Defensive Splits

	G	Tk	Ast	Sack	Yds	Stuff	Yds	Int	Yds	PD	TD
Total	16	45	23	10.5	82.0	10.5	21.0	0	0	0	0
vs. Playoff	5	14	7	2.0	23.0	3.0	7.5	0	0	0	0
vs. Non-Playoff	11	31	16	8.5	59.0	7.5	13.5	0	0	0	0
vs. Own Division	8	23	14	5.5	46.0	6.0	9.5	0	0	0	0
Home	8	13	19	6.5	49.0	1.0	2.0	0	0	0	0
Away	8	32	4	4.0	33.0	9.5	19.0	0	0	0	0
Games 1-8	8	23	14	4.0	34.0	5.0	11.5	0	0	0	0
Games 9-16	8	22	9	6.5	48.0	5.5	9.5	0	0	0	0
September	4	8	5	1.0	9.0	2.5	6.5	0	0	0	0
October	4	15	9	3.0	25.0	2.5	5.0	0	0	0	0
November	4	12	6	3.5	26.0	2.5	3.5	0	0	0	0
December	4	10	3	3.0	22.0	3.0	6.0	0	0	0	0
Grass	4	20	1	3.0	25.0	5.5	9.0	0	0	0	0
Turf	12	25	22	7.5	57.0	5.0	12.0	0	0	0	0
Indoor	11	23	22	7.5	57.0	4.0	9.0	0	0	0	0
Outdoor	5	22	1	3.0	25.0	6.5	12.0	0	0	0	0

Game Logs

Date	Opp	Result	Tk	Ast	Sack	Yds	Stuff	Yds	Int	Yds	PD	FF	FR	TD
09/03	@Pit	L 20-23	2	0	0.0	0.0	1.0	3.0	0	0	0	0	0	0
09/10	@Min	L 10-20	2	2	0.0	0.0	1.0	2.0	0	0	0	0	0	0
09/17	Ari	L 17-20	3	0	1.0	9.0	0.0	0.0	0	0	0	0	0	0
09/25	SF	W 27-24	1	3	0.0	0.0	0.5	1.5	0	0	0	0	0	0
10/08	Cle	W 38-20	3	5	1.0	4.0	0.0	0.0	0	0	0	0	0	0
10/15	@GB	L 21-30	6	1	1.0	15.0	1.5	3.0	0	0	0	0	0	0
10/22	@Was	L 30-36	4	0	1.0	6.0	1.0	2.0	0	0	0	0	0	0
10/29	GB	W 24-16	2	3	0.0	0.0	0.0	0.0	0	0	0	0	0	0
11/05	@Atl	L 22-34	3	0	1.0	8.0	0.0	0.0	0	0	0	0	0	0
11/12	TB	W 27-24	1	4	1.5	11.0	0.0	0.0	0	0	0	1	0	0
11/19	@Chi	W 24-17	7	0	0.0	0.0	2.0	3.0	0	0	0	0	0	0
11/23	Min	W 44-38	1	2	1.0	7.0	0.5	0.5	0	0	0	0	1	0
12/04	Chi	W 27-7	1	2	1.0	9.0	0.0	0.0	0	0	0	0	0	0
12/10	@Hou	W 24-17	5	1	0.0	0.0	2.0	5.0	0	0	0	1	1	0
12/17	Jac	W 44-0	1	0	1.0	9.0	0.0	0.0	0	0	0	0	0	0
12/23	@TB	W 37-10	3	0	1.0	4.0	1.0	1.0	0	0	0	0	0	0

William Thomas

1995 Defensive Splits

	G	Tk	Ast	Sack	Yds	Stuff	Yds	Int	Yds	PD	TD
Total	16	62	12	2.0	10.0	8.5	12.5	7	104	17	1
vs. Playoff	3	10	2	0.0	0.0	4.0	5.0	0	0	1	0
vs. Non-Playoff	13	52	10	2.0	10.0	4.5	7.5	7	104	16	1
vs. Own Division	8	32	6	1.0	4.0	7.5	11.5	6	100	14	1
Home	8	29	7	1.0	6.0	4.5	7.5	4	36	9	0
Away	8	33	5	1.0	4.0	4.0	5.0	3	68	8	1
Games 1-8	8	25	9	0.0	0.0	2.0	2.0	4	72	11	1
Games 9-16	8	37	3	2.0	10.0	6.5	10.5	3	32	6	0
September	4	7	4	0.0	0.0	0.0	0.0	1	37	2	1
October	4	18	5	0.0	0.0	2.0	2.0	3	35	9	0
November	4	22	1	2.0	10.0	3.0	4.0	1	29	2	0
December	4	15	2	0.0	0.0	3.5	6.5	2	3	4	0
Grass	4	16	2	1.0	4.0	1.0	1.0	1	37	3	1
Turf	12	46	10	1.0	6.0	7.5	11.5	6	67	14	0
Indoor	2	7	1	0.0	0.0	0.0	0.0	0	0	1	0
Outdoor	14	55	11	2.0	10.0	8.5	12.5	7	104	16	1

Game Logs

Date	Opp	Result	Tk	Ast	Sack	Yds	Stuff	Yds	Int	Yds	PD	FF	FR	TD
09/03	TB	L 6-21	0	2	0.0	0.0	0.0	0.0	0	0	0	0	0	0
09/10	@Ari	W 31-19	1	1	0.0	0.0	0.0	0.0	1	37	2	0	0	1
09/17	SD	L 21-27	1	1	0.0	0.0	0.0	0.0	0	0	0	0	0	0
09/24	@Oak	L 17-48	5	0	0.0	0.0	0.0	0.0	0	0	0	0	0	0
10/01	@NO	W 15-10	3	1	0.0	0.0	0.0	0.0	0	0	1	0	0	0
10/08	Was	W 37-34	6	2	0.0	0.0	2.0	2.0	0	0	2	0	0	0
10/15	@NYN	W 17-14	3	1	0.0	0.0	0.0	0.0	2	31	4	0	0	0
10/29	StL	W 20-9	6	1	0.0	0.0	0.0	0.0	1	4	2	0	1	0
11/06	@Dal	L 12-34	7	1	0.0	0.0	3.0	4.0	0	0	0	0	0	0
11/12	Den	W 31-13	6	0	1.0	6.0	0.0	0.0	0	0	0	0	0	0
11/19	NYN	W 28-19	4	0	0.0	0.0	0.0	0.0	1	29	1	0	0	0
11/26	@Was	W 14-7	5	0	1.0	4.0	0.0	0.0	0	0	1	0	0	0
12/03	@Sea	L 14-26	4	0	0.0	0.0	0.0	0.0	0	0	0	0	0	0
12/10	Dal	W 20-17	2	0	0.0	0.0	1.0	1.0	0	0	1	1	0	0
12/17	Ari	W 21-20	4	1	0.0	0.0	1.5	4.5	2	3	3	0	0	0
12/24	@Chi	L 14-20	5	1	0.0	0.0	1.0	1.0	0	0	0	0	0	0

Tony Tolbert

1995 Defensive Splits

	G	Tk	Ast	Sack	Yds	Stuff	Yds	Int	Yds	PD	TD
Total	16	52	10	5.5	46.0	1.0	1.0	0	0	0	0
vs. Playoff	7	23	4	1.5	16.0	0.0	0.0	0	0	0	0
vs. Non-Playoff	9	29	6	4.0	30.0	1.0	1.0	0	0	0	0
vs. Own Division	8	26	2	3.0	28.0	1.0	1.0	0	0	0	0
Home	8	25	3	4.0	36.0	0.0	0.0	0	0	0	0
Away	8	27	7	1.5	10.0	1.0	1.0	0	0	0	0
Games 1-8	8	31	7	4.5	31.0	1.0	1.0	0	0	0	0
Games 9-16	8	21	3	1.0	15.0	0.0	0.0	0	0	0	0
September	4	17	3	4.0	30.0	0.0	0.0	0	0	0	0
October	4	14	4	0.5	1.0	1.0	1.0	0	0	0	0
November	4	10	1	1.0	15.0	0.0	0.0	0	0	0	0
December	4	11	2	0.0	0.0	0.0	0.0	0	0	0	0
Grass	4	13	2	0.0	0.0	1.0	1.0	0	0	0	0
Turf	12	39	8	5.5	46.0	0.0	0.0	0	0	0	0
Indoor	2	8	5	0.5	1.0	0.0	0.0	0	0	0	0
Outdoor	14	44	5	5.0	45.0	1.0	1.0	0	0	0	0

Game Logs

Date	Opp	Result	Tk	Ast	Sack	Yds	Stuff	Yds	Int	Yds	PD	FF	FR	TD
09/04	@NYN	W 35-0	3	0	1.0	9.0	0.0	0.0	0	0	0	1	0	0
09/10	Den	W 31-21	3	0	1.0	2.0	0.0	0.0	0	0	0	0	0	0
09/17	@Min	W 23-17	5	3	0.0	0.0	0.0	0.0	0	0	0	0	0	0
09/24	Ari	W 34-20	6	0	2.0	19.0	0.0	0.0	0	0	0	0	0	0
10/01	@Was	L 23-27	2	0	0.0	0.0	1.0	1.0	0	0	0	0	0	0
10/08	GB	W 34-24	3	2	0.0	0.0	0.0	0.0	0	0	0	0	0	0
10/15	@SD	W 23-9	6	0	0.0	0.0	0.0	0.0	0	0	0	0	0	0
10/29	@Atl	W 28-13	3	2	0.5	1.0	0.0	0.0	0	0	0	0	0	0
11/06	Phi	W 34-12	4	0	0.0	0.0	0.0	0.0	0	0	0	0	0	0
11/12	SF	L 20-38	1	0	0.0	0.0	0.0	0.0	0	0	0	0	0	0
11/19	@Oak	W 34-21	2	1	0.0	0.0	0.0	0.0	0	0	0	0	0	0
11/23	KC	W 24-12	3	0	1.0	15.0	0.0	0.0	0	0	0	1	0	0
12/03	Was	L 17-24	2	0	0.0	0.0	0.0	0.0	0	0	0	0	0	0
12/10	@Phi	L 17-20	3	0	0.0	0.0	0.0	0.0	0	0	0	0	0	0
12/17	NYN	W 21-20	3	1	0.0	0.0	0.0	0.0	0	0	0	0	0	0
12/25	@Ari	W 37-13	3	1	0.0	0.0	0.0	0.0	0	0	0	0	0	0

Steve Tovar
Cincinnati Bengals – LB

1995 Defensive Splits

	G	Tk	Ast	Sack	Yds	Stuff	Yds	Int	Yds	PD	TD
Total	14	77	22	1.0	1.0	2.5	8.5	1	13	5	0
vs. Playoff	5	32	9	0.0	0.0	0.0	0.0	0	0	2	0
vs. Non-Playoff	9	45	13	1.0	1.0	2.5	8.5	1	13	3	0
vs. Own Division	8	36	9	1.0	1.0	2.0	7.0	1	13	4	0
Home	6	23	6	1.0	1.0	0.0	0.0	1	13	1	0
Away	8	54	16	0.0	0.0	2.5	8.5	0	0	4	0
Games 1-8	8	52	11	1.0	1.0	0.5	1.5	1	13	4	0
Games 9-16	6	25	11	0.0	0.0	2.0	7.0	0	0	1	0
September	4	31	5	1.0	1.0	0.5	1.5	0	0	0	0
October	4	21	6	0.0	0.0	0.0	0.0	1	13	4	0
November	3	13	5	0.0	0.0	2.0	7.0	0	0	1	0
December	3	12	6	0.0	0.0	0.0	0.0	0	0	0	0
Grass	4	22	9	0.0	0.0	1.0	6.0	0	0	2	0
Turf	10	55	13	1.0	1.0	1.5	2.5	1	13	3	0
Indoor	3	26	6	0.0	0.0	1.5	2.5	0	0	0	0
Outdoor	11	51	16	1.0	1.0	1.0	6.0	1	13	5	0

Game Logs

Date	Opp	Result	Tk	Ast	Sack	Yds	Stuff	Yds	Int	Yds	PD	FF	FR	TD
09/03	nd	W 24-21	8	3	0.0	0.0	0.0	0.0	0	0	0	0	0	0
09/10	Jac	W 24-17	4	1	1.0	1.0	0.0	0.0	0	0	0	1	0	0
09/17	@Sea	L 21-24	13	1	0.0	0.0	0.5	1.5	0	0	0	0	0	0
09/24	Hou	L 28-38	6	0	0.0	0.0	0.0	0.0	0	0	0	0	0	0
10/01	Mia	L 23-26	5	1	0.0	0.0	0.0	0.0	0	0	0	0	0	0
10/08	@TB	L 16-19	6	3	0.0	0.0	0.0	0.0	0	0	1	0	0	0
10/19	@Pit	W 27-9	6	1	0.0	0.0	0.0	0.0	0	0	2	0	0	0
10/29	Cle	L 26-29	4	1	0.0	0.0	0.0	0.0	1	13	1	0	0	0
11/05	Oak	L 17-20	-	-	-	-	-	-	-	-	-	-	-	-
11/12	@Hou	W 32-25	5	2	0.0	0.0	1.0	1.0	0	0	0	0	0	0
11/19	Pit	L 31-49	4	1	0.0	0.0	0.0	0.0	0	0	0	0	0	0
11/26	@Jac	W 17-13	4	2	0.0	0.0	1.0	6.0	0	0	1	1	0	0
12/03	@GB	L 10-24	9	3	0.0	0.0	0.0	0.0	0	0	0	0	0	0
12/10	Chi	W 16-10	0	2	0.0	0.0	0.0	0.0	0	0	0	0	0	0
12/17	@Cle	L 10-26	3	1	0.0	0.0	0.0	0.0	0	0	0	0	0	0
12/24	Min	W 27-24	-	-	-	-	-	-	-	-	-	-	-	-

Jessie Tuggle
Atlanta Falcons – LB

1995 Defensive Splits

	G	Tk	Ast	Sack	Yds	Stuff	Yds	Int	Yds	PD	TD
Total	16	112	42	1.0	5.0	3.5	4.5	3	84	10	1
vs. Playoff	6	36	13	1.0	5.0	2.5	3.5	1	8	3	0
vs. Non-Playoff	10	76	29	0.0	0.0	1.0	1.0	2	76	7	1
vs. Own Division	8	57	18	1.0	5.0	1.5	1.5	1	49	5	0
Home	8	56	15	1.0	5.0	2.5	3.5	2	57	5	0
Away	8	56	27	0.0	0.0	1.0	1.0	1	27	5	1
Games 1-8	8	57	22	0.0	0.0	1.0	2.0	0	0	5	0
Games 9-16	8	55	20	1.0	5.0	2.5	2.5	3	84	5	1
September	4	27	14	0.0	0.0	0.0	0.0	0	0	2	0
October	4	30	8	0.0	0.0	1.0	2.0	0	0	3	0
November	4	29	10	0.0	0.0	1.0	1.0	2	35	4	0
December	4	26	10	1.0	5.0	1.5	1.5	1	49	1	0
Grass	5	26	19	0.0	0.0	1.0	1.0	1	27	5	1
Turf	11	86	23	1.0	5.0	2.5	3.5	2	57	5	0
Indoor	9	68	19	1.0	5.0	2.5	3.5	2	57	5	0
Outdoor	7	44	23	0.0	0.0	1.0	1.0	1	27	5	1

Game Logs

Date	Opp	Result	Tk	Ast	Sack	Yds	Stuff	Yds	Int	Yds	PD	FF	FR	TD
09/03	Car	W 23-20	10	4	0.0	0.0	0.0	0.0	0	0	0	0	0	0
09/10	@SF	L 10-41	2	2	0.0	0.0	0.0	0.0	0	0	2	0	0	0
09/17	@NO	W 27-24	12	4	0.0	0.0	0.0	0.0	0	0	0	0	0	0
09/24	NYA	W 13-3	3	4	0.0	0.0	0.0	0.0	0	0	0	0	0	0
10/01	NE	W 30-17	13	1	0.0	0.0	0.0	0.0	0	0	1	0	0	0
10/12	@StL	L 19-21	6	1	0.0	0.0	0.0	0.0	0	0	0	0	0	0
10/22	@TB	W 24-21	4	2	0.0	0.0	0.0	0.0	0	0	2	0	0	0
10/29	Dal	L 13-28	7	4	0.0	0.0	1.0	2.0	0	0	0	0	0	0
11/05	Det	W 34-22	3	1	0.0	0.0	0.0	0.0	1	8	1	0	0	0
11/12	@Buf	L 17-23	12	3	0.0	0.0	0.0	0.0	0	0	1	0	0	0
11/19	StL	W 31-6	6	0	0.0	0.0	0.5	0.5	0	0	2	0	0	0
11/26	@Ari	L 37-40	8	6	0.0	0.0	0.5	0.5	1	27	1	0	0	1
12/03	@Mia	L 20-21	5	3	0.0	0.0	0.5	0.5	0	0	0	0	0	0
12/10	NO	W 19-14	7	1	0.0	0.0	0.0	0.0	1	49	1	0	0	0
12/17	@Car	L 17-21	7	6	0.0	0.0	0.0	0.0	0	0	0	0	0	0
12/24	SF	W 28-27	7	0	1.0	5.0	1.0	1.0	0	0	0	0	0	0

Renaldo Turnbull
New Orleans Saints – DE

1995 Defensive Splits

	G	Tk	Ast	Sack	Yds	Stuff	Yds	Int	Yds	PD	TD
Total	15	30	9	7.0	37.0	4.0	4.0	0	0	1	0
vs. Playoff	8	20	4	6.0	35.0	3.0	3.0	0	0	0	0
vs. Non-Playoff	7	10	5	1.0	2.0	1.0	1.0	0	0	0	0
vs. Own Division	7	17	3	3.0	15.0	3.0	3.0	0	0	1	0
Home	8	19	6	6.0	35.0	1.0	1.0	0	0	0	0
Away	7	11	3	1.0	2.0	3.0	3.0	0	0	1	0
Games 1-8	7	20	2	6.0	30.0	3.0	3.0	0	0	0	0
Games 9-16	8	10	7	1.0	7.0	1.0	1.0	0	0	1	0
September	4	14	1	4.0	17.0	1.0	1.0	0	0	0	0
October	3	6	1	2.0	13.0	2.0	2.0	0	0	0	0
November	4	6	4	1.0	7.0	0.0	0.0	0	0	0	0
December	4	4	3	0.0	0.0	1.0	1.0	0	0	1	0
Grass	2	5	2	0.0	0.0	3.0	3.0	0	0	0	0
Turf	13	25	7	7.0	37.0	1.0	1.0	0	0	1	0
Indoor	10	20	7	6.0	35.0	1.0	1.0	0	0	1	0
Outdoor	5	10	2	1.0	2.0	3.0	3.0	0	0	0	0

Game Logs

Date	Opp	Result	Tk	Ast	Sack	Yds	Stuff	Yds	Int	Yds	PD	FF	FR	TD
09/03	SF	L 22-24	6	0	1.0	5.0	1.0	1.0	0	0	0	0	0	0
09/10	@StL	L 13-17	1	0	0.0	0.0	0.0	0.0	0	0	0	0	0	0
09/17	Atl	L 24-27	4	1	2.0	10.0	0.0	0.0	0	0	0	0	0	0
09/24	@NYN	L 29-45	4	0	1.0	2.0	0.0	0.0	0	0	0	0	0	0
10/01	Phi	L 10-15	2	0	1.0	6.0	0.0	0.0	0	0	0	0	0	0
10/15	Mia	W 33-30	1	1	1.0	7.0	0.0	0.0	0	0	0	0	1	0
10/22	@Car	L 3-20	-	-	-	-	-	-	-	-	-	-	-	-
10/29	@SF	W 11-7	3	0	0.0	0.0	2.0	2.0	0	0	0	0	0	0
11/05	StL	W 19-10	2	2	0.0	0.0	0.0	0.0	0	0	0	0	0	0
11/12	Ind	W 17-14	3	1	1.0	7.0	0.0	0.0	0	0	0	0	0	0
11/19	@Min	L 24-43	0	1	0.0	0.0	0.0	0.0	0	0	0	0	0	0
11/26	Car	W 34-26	1	0	0.0	0.0	0.0	0.0	0	0	0	0	1	0
12/03	@NE	W 31-17	2	2	0.0	0.0	1.0	1.0	0	0	0	0	0	0
12/10	@Atl	L 14-19	1	0	0.0	0.0	0.0	0.0	0	0	0	1	0	0
12/16	GB	L 23-34	0	1	0.0	0.0	0.0	0.0	0	0	0	0	0	0
12/24	@NYA	W 12-0	1	0	0.0	0.0	0.0	0.0	0	0	0	0	0	0

Troy Vincent

1995 Defensive Splits

	G	Tk	Ast	Sack	Yds	Stuff	Yds	Int	Yds	PD	TD
Total	16	52	10	0.0	0.0	0.0	0.0	5	95	12	1
vs. Playoff	9	28	5	0.0	0.0	0.0	0.0	2	21	6	0
vs. Non-Playoff	7	24	5	0.0	0.0	0.0	0.0	3	74	6	1
vs. Own Division	8	19	8	0.0	0.0	0.0	0.0	3	74	10	1
Home	8	24	5	0.0	0.0	0.0	0.0	4	90	9	1
Away	8	28	5	0.0	0.0	0.0	0.0	1	5	3	0
Games 1-8	8	24	4	0.0	0.0	0.0	0.0	4	78	9	1
Games 9-16	8	28	6	0.0	0.0	0.0	0.0	1	17	3	0
September	3	8	1	0.0	0.0	0.0	0.0	3	73	5	1
October	5	16	3	0.0	0.0	0.0	0.0	1	5	4	0
November	4	12	5	0.0	0.0	0.0	0.0	0	0	2	0
December	4	16	1	0.0	0.0	0.0	0.0	1	17	1	0
Grass	10	31	6	0.0	0.0	0.0	0.0	4	90	10	1
Turf	6	21	4	0.0	0.0	0.0	0.0	1	5	2	0
Indoor	3	8	2	0.0	0.0	0.0	0.0	0	0	1	0
Outdoor	13	44	8	0.0	0.0	0.0	0.0	5	95	11	1

Game Logs

Date	Opp	Result	Tk	Ast	Sack	Yds	Stuff	Yds	Int	Yds	PD	FF	FR	TD
09/03	NYA	W 52-14	1	0	0.0	0.0	0.0	0.0	2	69	3	0	0	1
09/10	@NE	W 20-3	3	1	0.0	0.0	0.0	0.0	0	0	1	0	0	0
09/18	Pit	W 23-10	4	0	0.0	0.0	0.0	0.0	1	4	1	0	0	0
10/01	@Cin	W 26-23	7	0	0.0	0.0	0.0	0.0	0	0	0	0	0	0
10/08	Ind	L 24-27	2	1	0.0	0.0	0.0	0.0	0	0	1	0	0	0
10/15	@NO	L 30-33	1	0	0.0	0.0	0.0	0.0	0	0	0	0	0	0
10/22	@NYA	L 16-17	3	2	0.0	0.0	0.0	0.0	1	5	1	0	0	0
10/29	Buf	W 23-6	3	0	0.0	0.0	0.0	0.0	0	0	2	0	0	0
11/05	@SD	W 24-14	4	0	0.0	0.0	0.0	0.0	0	0	0	0	0	0
11/12	NE	L 17-34	3	2	0.0	0.0	0.0	0.0	0	0	0	0	0	0
11/20	SF	L 20-44	4	1	0.0	0.0	0.0	0.0	0	0	0	0	0	0
11/26	@Ind	L 28-36	1	2	0.0	0.0	0.0	0.0	0	0	1	0	0	0
12/03	Atl	W 21-20	0	1	0.0	0.0	0.0	0.0	0	0	0	0	0	0
12/11	KC	W 13-6	7	0	0.0	0.0	0.0	0.0	1	17	1	0	0	0
12/17	@Buf	L 20-23	3	0	0.0	0.0	0.0	0.0	0	0	0	0	0	0
12/24	@StL	W 41-22	6	0	0.0	0.0	0.0	0.0	0	0	0	0	0	0

Bracey Walker

1995 Defensive Splits

	G	Tk	Ast	Sack	Yds	Stuff	Yds	Int	Yds	PD	TD
Total	14	61	25	0.0	0.0	1.5	3.0	4	56	13	0
vs. Playoff	4	23	7	0.0	0.0	0.5	2.0	2	28	5	0
vs. Non-Playoff	10	38	18	0.0	0.0	1.0	1.0	2	28	8	0
vs. Own Division	7	32	10	0.0	0.0	1.0	1.0	1	5	4	0
Home	7	35	8	0.0	0.0	0.5	2.0	1	23	7	0
Away	7	26	17	0.0	0.0	1.0	1.0	3	33	6	0
Games 1-8	7	29	14	0.0	0.0	0.5	2.0	2	28	5	0
Games 9-16	7	32	11	0.0	0.0	1.0	1.0	2	28	8	0
September	4	18	7	0.0	0.0	0.0	0.0	2	28	2	0
October	3	11	7	0.0	0.0	0.5	2.0	0	0	3	0
November	4	15	9	0.0	0.0	0.0	0.0	2	28	6	0
December	3	17	2	0.0	0.0	1.0	1.0	0	0	2	0
Grass	4	18	7	0.0	0.0	1.0	1.0	1	5	2	0
Turf	10	43	18	0.0	0.0	0.5	2.0	3	51	11	0
Indoor	3	8	10	0.0	0.0	0.0	0.0	2	28	4	0
Outdoor	11	53	15	0.0	0.0	1.5	3.0	2	28	9	0

Game Logs

Date	Opp	Result	Tk	Ast	Sack	Yds	Stuff	Yds	Int	Yds	PD	FF	FR	TD
09/03	@Ind	W 24-21	2	2	0.0	0.0	0.0	0.0	2	28	2	0	0	0
09/10	Jac	W 24-17	7	0	0.0	0.0	0.0	0.0	0	0	0	0	0	0
09/17	@Sea	L 21-24	4	4	0.0	0.0	0.0	0.0	0	0	0	0	0	0
09/24	Hou	L 28-38	5	1	0.0	0.0	0.0	0.0	0	0	0	1	0	0
10/01	Mia	L 23-26	7	2	0.0	0.0	0.5	2.0	0	0	2	0	0	0
10/08	@TB	L 16-19	2	3	0.0	0.0	0.0	0.0	0	0	1	0	0	0
10/19	@Pit	W 27-9	-	-	-	-	-	-	-	-	-	-	-	-
10/29	Cle	L 26-29	2	2	0.0	0.0	0.0	0.0	0	0	0	0	0	0
11/05	Oak	L 17-20	3	2	0.0	0.0	0.0	0.0	1	23	2	0	0	0
11/12	@Hou	W 32-25	2	4	0.0	0.0	0.0	0.0	0	0	2	0	0	0
11/19	Pit	L 31-49	7	1	0.0	0.0	0.0	0.0	0	0	1	0	1	0
11/26	@Jac	W 17-13	3	2	0.0	0.0	0.0	0.0	1	5	1	0	0	0
12/03	@GB	L 10-24	7	2	0.0	0.0	0.0	0.0	0	0	0	0	0	0
12/10	Chi	W 16-10	4	0	0.0	0.0	0.0	0.0	0	0	2	0	1	0
12/17	@Cle	L 10-26	6	0	0.0	0.0	1.0	1.0	0	0	0	0	0	0
12/24	Min	W 27-24	-	-	-	-	-	-	-	-	-	-	-	-

Brian Washington

1995 Defensive Splits

	G	Tk	Ast	Sack	Yds	Stuff	Yds	Int	Yds	PD	TD
Total	16	53	9	0.0	0.0	1.0	4.0	3	100	8	1
vs. Playoff	4	10	3	0.0	0.0	0.0	0.0	1	1	1	0
vs. Non-Playoff	12	43	6	0.0	0.0	1.0	4.0	2	99	7	1
vs. Own Division	8	27	5	0.0	0.0	1.0	4.0	2	75	4	1
Home	8	26	3	0.0	0.0	0.0	0.0	1	1	3	0
Away	8	27	6	0.0	0.0	1.0	4.0	2	99	5	1
Games 1-8	8	23	5	0.0	0.0	0.0	0.0	2	26	5	0
Games 9-16	8	30	4	0.0	0.0	1.0	4.0	1	74	3	1
September	4	12	3	0.0	0.0	0.0	0.0	0	0	2	0
October	4	11	2	0.0	0.0	0.0	0.0	2	26	3	0
November	4	13	1	0.0	0.0	0.0	0.0	0	0	1	0
December	4	17	3	0.0	0.0	1.0	4.0	1	74	2	1
Grass	14	49	6	0.0	0.0	1.0	4.0	3	100	7	1
Turf	2	4	3	0.0	0.0	0.0	0.0	0	0	1	0
Indoor	1	4	2	0.0	0.0	0.0	0.0	0	0	1	0
Outdoor	15	49	7	0.0	0.0	1.0	4.0	3	100	7	1

Game Logs

Date	Opp	Result	Tk	Ast	Sack	Yds	Stuff	Yds	Int	Yds	PD	FF	FR	TD
09/03	@Sea	W 34-10	4	2	0.0	0.0	0.0	0.0	0	0	1	0	1	0
09/10	NYN	W 20-17	1	0	0.0	0.0	0.0	0.0	0	0	1	0	0	0
09/17	Oak	W 23-17	4	0	0.0	0.0	0.0	0.0	0	0	0	0	0	0
09/24	@Cle	L 17-35	3	1	0.0	0.0	0.0	0.0	0	0	0	1	0	0
10/01	@Ari	W 24-3	4	1	0.0	0.0	0.0	0.0	1	25	2	0	0	0
10/09	SD	W 29-23	2	1	0.0	0.0	0.0	0.0	1	1	1	0	0	0
10/15	NE	W 31-26	3	0	0.0	0.0	0.0	0.0	0	0	0	0	0	0
10/22	@Den	W 21-7	2	0	0.0	0.0	0.0	0.0	0	0	1	0	0	0
11/05	Was	W 24-3	3	0	0.0	0.0	0.0	0.0	0	0	0	0	0	0
11/12	@SD	W 22-7	3	0	0.0	0.0	0.0	0.0	0	0	0	0	0	0
11/19	Hou	W 20-13	7	0	0.0	0.0	0.0	0.0	0	0	0	0	0	0
11/23	@Dal	L 12-24	0	1	0.0	0.0	0.0	0.0	0	0	1	0	0	0
12/03	@Oak	W 29-23	6	0	0.0	0.0	1.0	4.0	1	74	2	0	0	1
12/11	@Mia	L 6-13	5	0	0.0	0.0	0.0	0.0	0	0	0	1	0	0
12/17	Den	W 20-17	3	1	0.0	0.0	0.0	0.0	0	0	0	0	0	0
12/24	Sea	W 26-3	3	1	0.0	0.0	0.0	0.0	0	0	0	0	0	0

Dewayne Washington

Minnesota Vikings – CB

1995 Defensive Splits

	G	Tk	Ast	Sack	Yds	Stuff	Yds	Int	Yds	PD	TD
Total	15	54	8	0.0	0.0	0.0	0.0	1	25	10	0
vs. Playoff	6	20	6	0.0	0.0	0.0	0.0	0	0	5	0
vs. Non-Playoff	9	34	2	0.0	0.0	0.0	0.0	1	25	5	0
vs. Own Division	8	34	6	0.0	0.0	0.0	0.0	0	0	7	0
Home	8	31	7	0.0	0.0	0.0	0.0	1	25	7	0
Away	7	23	1	0.0	0.0	0.0	0.0	0	0	3	0
Games 1-8	7	27	5	0.0	0.0	0.0	0.0	1	25	4	0
Games 9-16	8	27	3	0.0	0.0	0.0	0.0	0	0	6	0
September	3	11	4	0.0	0.0	0.0	0.0	0	0	2	0
October	4	16	1	0.0	0.0	0.0	0.0	1	25	2	0
November	4	18	3	0.0	0.0	0.0	0.0	0	0	4	0
December	4	9	0	0.0	0.0	0.0	0.0	0	0	2	0
Grass	5	16	1	0.0	0.0	0.0	0.0	0	0	2	0
Turf	10	38	7	0.0	0.0	0.0	0.0	1	25	8	0
Indoor	9	38	7	0.0	0.0	0.0	0.0	1	25	7	0
Outdoor	6	16	1	0.0	0.0	0.0	0.0	0	0	3	0

Game Logs

Date	Opp	Result	Tk	Ast	Sack	Yds	Stuff	Yds	Int	Yds	PD	FF	FR	TD
09/03	@Chi	L 14-31	4	1	0.0	0.0	0.0	0.0	0	0	0	0	0	0
09/10	Det	W 20-10	5	2	0.0	0.0	0.0	0.0	0	0	2	0	0	0
09/17	Dal	L 17-23	2	1	0.0	0.0	0.0	0.0	0	0	0	0	0	0
09/24	@Pit	W 44-24	-	-	-	-	-	-	-	-	-	-	-	-
10/08	Hou	W 23-17	5	1	0.0	0.0	0.0	0.0	1	25	1	0	0	0
10/15	@TB	L 17-20	7	0	0.0	0.0	0.0	0.0	0	0	1	0	0	0
10/22	@GB	L 21-38	1	0	0.0	0.0	0.0	0.0	0	0	0	0	0	0
10/30	Chi	L 6-14	3	0	0.0	0.0	0.0	0.0	0	0	0	0	0	0
11/05	GB	W 27-24	3	3	0.0	0.0	0.0	0.0	0	0	3	0	0	0
11/12	@Ari	W 30-24	2	0	0.0	0.0	0.0	0.0	0	0	1	0	0	0
11/19	NO	W 43-24	6	0	0.0	0.0	0.0	0.0	0	0	0	0	0	0
11/23	@Det	L 38-44	7	0	0.0	0.0	0.0	0.0	0	0	0	0	0	0
12/03	TB	W 31-17	4	0	0.0	0.0	0.0	0.0	0	0	1	0	0	0
12/09	Cle	W 27-11	3	0	0.0	0.0	0.0	0.0	0	0	0	0	0	0
12/18	@SF	L 30-37	2	0	0.0	0.0	0.0	0.0	0	0	0	0	0	0
12/24	@Cin	L 24-27	0	0	0.0	0.0	0.0	0.0	0	0	1	0	0	0

James Washington

Washington Redskins – S

1995 Defensive Splits

	G	Tk	Ast	Sack	Yds	Stuff	Yds	Int	Yds	PD	TD
Total	12	51	6	0.0	0.0	1.0	1.0	2	35	3	0
vs. Playoff	3	13	1	0.0	0.0	0.0	0.0	0	0	0	0
vs. Non-Playoff	9	38	5	0.0	0.0	1.0	1.0	2	35	3	0
vs. Own Division	5	20	2	0.0	0.0	0.0	0.0	1	21	2	0
Home	6	24	3	0.0	0.0	1.0	1.0	2	35	3	0
Away	6	27	3	0.0	0.0	0.0	0.0	0	0	0	0
Games 1-8	4	17	3	0.0	0.0	0.0	0.0	1	21	1	0
Games 9-16	8	34	3	0.0	0.0	1.0	1.0	1	14	2	0
September	4	17	3	0.0	0.0	0.0	0.0	1	21	1	0
October	1	2	1	0.0	0.0	0.0	0.0	0	0	1	0
November	3	15	0	0.0	0.0	0.0	0.0	0	0	0	0
December	4	17	2	0.0	0.0	1.0	1.0	1	14	1	0
Grass	9	39	5	0.0	0.0	1.0	1.0	2	35	3	0
Turf	3	12	1	0.0	0.0	0.0	0.0	0	0	0	0
Indoor	1	4	0	0.0	0.0	0.0	0.0	0	0	0	0
Outdoor	11	47	6	0.0	0.0	1.0	1.0	2	35	3	0

Game Logs

Date	Opp	Result	Tk	Ast	Sack	Yds	Stuff	Yds	Int	Yds	PD	FF	FR	TD
09/03	Ari	W 27-7	4	0	0.0	0.0	0.0	0.0	1	21	1	0	0	0
09/10	Oak	L 8-20	2	1	0.0	0.0	0.0	0.0	0	0	0	0	0	0
09/17	@Den	L 31-38	8	2	0.0	0.0	0.0	0.0	0	0	0	0	0	0
09/24	@TB	L 6-14	3	0	0.0	0.0	0.0	0.0	0	0	0	0	0	0
10/01	Dal	W 27-23	-	-	-	-	-	-	-	-	-	-	-	-
10/08	@Phi	L 34-37	-	-	-	-	-	-	-	-	-	-	-	-
10/15	@Ari	L 20-24	-	-	-	-	-	-	-	-	-	-	-	-
10/22	Det	W 36-30	-	-	-	-	-	-	-	-	-	-	-	-
10/29	NYN	L 15-24	2	1	0.0	0.0	0.0	0.0	0	0	1	0	0	0
11/05	@KC	L 3-24	4	0	0.0	0.0	0.0	0.0	0	0	0	0	0	0
11/19	Sea	L 20-27	5	0	0.0	0.0	0.0	0.0	0	0	0	0	0	0
11/26	Phi	L 7-14	6	0	0.0	0.0	0.0	0.0	0	0	0	0	0	0
12/03	@Dal	W 24-17	3	1	0.0	0.0	0.0	0.0	0	0	0	0	0	0
12/10	@NYN	L 13-20	5	0	0.0	0.0	0.0	0.0	0	0	0	0	0	0
12/17	@StL	W 35-23	4	0	0.0	0.0	0.0	0.0	0	0	0	0	0	0
12/24	Car	W 20-17	5	1	0.0	0.0	1.0	1.0	1	14	1	0	0	0

Marvin Washington

New York Jets – DE

1995 Defensive Splits

	G	Tk	Ast	Sack	Yds	Stuff	Yds	Int	Yds	PD	TD
Total	16	57	23	6.0	49.0	9.5	24.0	0	0	2	0
vs. Playoff	7	31	10	4.0	30.0	8.0	19.0	0	0	0	0
vs. Non-Playoff	9	26	13	2.0	19.0	1.5	5.0	0	0	2	0
vs. Own Division	8	30	10	3.0	25.0	8.0	19.0	0	0	0	0
Home	8	26	11	4.0	38.0	5.5	17.0	0	0	1	0
Away	8	31	12	2.0	11.0	4.0	7.0	0	0	1	0
Games 1-8	8	33	13	4.0	32.0	7.5	18.0	0	0	1	0
Games 9-16	8	24	10	2.0	17.0	2.0	6.0	0	0	1	0
September	4	20	7	3.0	25.0	5.5	13.5	0	0	1	0
October	5	14	6	1.0	7.0	2.0	4.5	0	0	0	0
November	3	12	6	2.0	17.0	1.5	4.0	0	0	0	0
December	4	11	4	0.0	0.0	0.5	2.0	0	0	1	0
Grass	3	16	2	0.0	0.0	2.5	4.5	0	0	0	0
Turf	13	41	21	6.0	49.0	7.0	19.5	0	0	2	0
Indoor	4	13	6	2.0	11.0	0.0	0.0	0	0	1	0
Outdoor	12	44	17	4.0	38.0	9.5	24.0	0	0	1	0

Game Logs

Date	Opp	Result	Tk	Ast	Sack	Yds	Stuff	Yds	Int	Yds	PD	FF	FR	TD
09/03	@Mia	L 14-52	4	1	0.0	0.0	2.5	4.5	0	0	0	2	0	0
09/10	Ind	L 24-27	6	2	1.0	7.0	2.0	6.0	0	0	0	0	0	0
09/17	Jac	W 27-10	4	4	1.0	13.0	1.0	3.0	0	0	1	1	0	0
09/24	@Atl	L 3-13	6	0	1.0	5.0	0.0	0.0	0	0	0	0	0	0
10/01	Oak	L 10-47	1	0	0.0	0.0	0.0	0.0	0	0	0	0	0	0
10/08	@Buf	L 10-29	2	4	0.0	0.0	1.5	2.5	0	0	0	0	0	0
10/15	@Car	L 15-26	7	1	0.0	0.0	0.0	0.0	0	0	0	0	0	0
10/22	Mia	W 17-16	4	0	1.0	7.0	0.5	2.0	0	0	0	1	0	0
10/29	@Ind	L 10-17	1	0	0.0	0.0	0.0	0.0	0	0	0	0	0	0
11/05	NE	L 7-20	0	0	0.0	0.0	0.0	0.0	0	0	0	0	0	0
11/19	Buf	L 26-28	8	3	1.0	11.0	1.5	4.0	0	0	0	0	0	0
11/26	@Sea	W 16-10	4	3	1.0	6.0	0.0	0.0	0	0	0	0	0	0
12/03	StL	L 20-23	0	0	0.0	0.0	0.0	0.0	0	0	0	0	0	0
12/10	@NE	L 28-31	5	0	0.0	0.0	0.0	0.0	0	0	0	1	0	0
12/17	@Hou	L 6-23	2	3	0.0	0.0	0.0	0.0	0	0	1	0	0	0
12/24	NO	L 0-12	4	1	0.0	0.0	0.5	2.0	0	0	0	0	0	0

Mickey Washington

1995 Defensive Splits

	G	Tk	Ast	Sack	Yds	Stuff	Yds	Int	Yds	PD	TD
Total	16	50	12	0.0	0.0	4.0	18.0	1	48	15	1
vs. Playoff	5	15	6	0.0	0.0	2.0	7.0	0	0	2	0
vs. Non-Playoff	11	35	6	0.0	0.0	2.0	11.0	1	48	13	1
vs. Own Division	8	28	4	0.0	0.0	0.0	0.0	1	48	11	1
Home	8	25	8	0.0	0.0	1.0	4.0	0	0	7	0
Away	8	25	4	0.0	0.0	3.0	14.0	1	48	8	1
Games 1-8	8	28	5	0.0	0.0	0.0	0.0	1	48	7	1
Games 9-16	8	22	7	0.0	0.0	4.0	18.0	0	0	8	0
September	4	14	2	0.0	0.0	0.0	0.0	0	0	3	0
October	5	15	3	0.0	0.0	0.0	0.0	1	48	4	1
November	3	11	2	0.0	0.0	2.0	11.0	0	0	2	0
December	4	10	5	0.0	0.0	2.0	7.0	0	0	6	0
Grass	11	34	8	0.0	0.0	2.0	11.0	1	48	9	1
Turf	5	16	4	0.0	0.0	2.0	7.0	0	0	6	0
Indoor	2	8	4	0.0	0.0	2.0	7.0	0	0	3	0
Outdoor	14	42	8	0.0	0.0	2.0	11.0	1	48	12	1

Game Logs

Date	Opp	Result	Tk	Ast	Sack	Yds	Stuff	Yds	Int	Yds	PD	FF	FR	TD
09/03	Hou	L 3-10	3	1	0.0	0.0	0.0	0.0	0	0	0	0	0	0
09/10	@Cin	L 17-24	6	0	0.0	0.0	0.0	0.0	0	0	2	0	1	0
09/17	@NYA	L 10-27	1	0	0.0	0.0	0.0	0.0	0	0	1	0	0	0
09/24	GB	L 14-24	4	1	0.0	0.0	0.0	0.0	0	0	0	0	0	0
10/01	@Hou	W 17-16	5	1	0.0	0.0	0.0	0.0	0	0	2	0	0	0
10/08	Pit	W 20-16	3	1	0.0	0.0	0.0	0.0	0	0	0	0	0	0
10/15	Chi	L 27-30	1	1	0.0	0.0	0.0	0.0	0	0	0	0	0	0
10/22	@Cle	W 23-15	5	0	0.0	0.0	0.0	0.0	1	48	2	0	0	1
10/29	@Pit	L 7-24	1	0	0.0	0.0	0.0	0.0	0	0	0	0	0	0
11/12	Sea	L 30-47	5	2	0.0	0.0	1.0	4.0	0	0	1	0	0	0
11/19	@TB	L 16-17	3	0	0.0	0.0	1.0	7.0	0	0	1	0	0	0
11/26	Cin	L 13-17	3	0	0.0	0.0	0.0	0.0	0	0	0	0	0	0
12/03	@Den	L 23-31	1	0	0.0	0.0	0.0	0.0	0	0	0	1	1	0
12/10	Ind	L 31-41	4	1	0.0	0.0	0.0	0.0	0	0	1	0	0	0
12/17	@Det	L 0-44	3	3	0.0	0.0	2.0	7.0	0	0	1	0	0	0
12/24	Cle	W 24-21	2	1	0.0	0.0	0.0	0.0	0	0	4	0	0	0

Reggie White

1995 Defensive Splits

	G	Tk	Ast	Sack	Yds	Stuff	Yds	Int	Yds	PD	TD
Total	15	31	11	12.0	96.5	2.0	3.0	0	0	4	0
vs. Playoff	4	7	3	1.0	4.0	1.0	1.0	0	0	0	0
vs. Non-Playoff	11	24	8	11.0	92.5	1.0	2.0	0	0	4	0
vs. Own Division	7	14	5	5.5	51.5	0.0	0.0	0	0	2	0
Home	8	14	9	7.0	69.5	1.0	2.0	0	0	4	0
Away	7	17	2	5.0	27.0	1.0	1.0	0	0	0	0
Games 1-8	8	18	8	7.5	65.0	2.0	3.0	0	0	1	0
Games 9-16	7	13	3	4.5	31.5	0.0	0.0	0	0	3	0
September	4	9	4	4.5	26.0	1.0	2.0	0	0	1	0
October	4	9	4	3.0	39.0	1.0	1.0	0	0	0	0
November	4	10	2	3.5	25.5	0.0	0.0	0	0	2	0
December	3	3	1	1.0	6.0	0.0	0.0	0	0	1	0
Grass	11	22	9	10.0	89.5	1.0	2.0	0	0	4	0
Turf	4	9	2	2.0	7.0	1.0	1.0	0	0	0	0
Indoor	3	5	1	1.0	3.0	0.0	0.0	0	0	0	0
Outdoor	12	26	10	11.0	93.5	2.0	3.0	0	0	4	0

Game Logs

Date	Opp	Result	Tk	Ast	Sack	Yds	Stuff	Yds	Int	Yds	PD	FF	FR	TD
09/03	StL	L 14-17	2	1	2.5	17.0	0.0	0.0	0	0	0	0	0	0
09/11	@Chi	W 27-24	2	0	1.0	2.0	0.0	0.0	0	0	0	1	0	0
09/17	NYN	W 14-6	2	3	0.0	0.0	1.0	2.0	0	0	1	0	0	0
09/24	@Jac	W 24-14	3	0	1.0	7.0	0.0	0.0	0	0	0	0	0	0
10/08	@Dal	L 24-34	4	1	1.0	4.0	1.0	1.0	0	0	0	0	0	0
10/15	Det	W 30-21	1	0	0.0	0.0	0.0	0.0	0	0	0	0	0	0
10/22	Min	W 38-21	3	1	2.0	35.0	0.0	0.0	0	0	0	1	0	0
10/29	@Det	L 16-24	2	1	0.0	0.0	0.0	0.0	0	0	0	0	0	0
11/05	@Min	L 24-27	2	0	1.0	3.0	0.0	0.0	0	0	0	0	0	0
11/12	Chi	W 35-28	2	2	0.5	1.5	0.0	0.0	0	0	1	0	0	0
11/19	@Cle	W 31-20	3	0	1.0	11.0	0.0	0.0	0	0	1	0	0	0
11/26	TB	W 35-13	3	0	1.0	10.0	0.0	0.0	0	0	1	0	0	0
12/03	Cin	W 24-10	1	1	1.0	6.0	0.0	0.0	0	0	1	0	0	0
12/10	@TB	L 10-13	-	-	-	-	-	-	-	-	-	-	-	-
12/16	@NO	W 34-23	1	0	0.0	0.0	0.0	0.0	0	0	0	0	0	0
12/24	Pit	W 24-19	1	0	0.0	0.0	0.0	0.0	0	0	0	0	0	0

Dan Wilkinson

1995 Defensive Splits

	G	Tk	Ast	Sack	Yds	Stuff	Yds	Int	Yds	PD	TD
Total	14	30	10	8.0	48.0	2.0	4.0	0	0	0	0
vs. Playoff	5	6	1	0.0	0.0	0.0	0.0	0	0	0	0
vs. Non-Playoff	9	24	9	8.0	48.0	2.0	4.0	0	0	0	1
vs. Own Division	7	12	5	5.0	30.0	0.5	1.5	0	0	0	0
Home	7	16	4	4.0	21.0	0.5	1.5	0	0	0	1
Away	7	14	6	4.0	27.0	1.5	2.5	0	0	0	0
Games 1-8	8	16	7	5.0	29.0	2.0	4.0	0	0	0	0
Games 9-16	6	14	3	3.0	19.0	0.0	0.0	0	0	0	1
September	4	10	4	3.0	16.0	1.0	3.0	0	0	0	0
October	4	6	3	2.0	13.0	1.0	1.0	0	0	0	0
November	4	10	3	3.0	19.0	0.0	0.0	0	0	0	0
December	2	4	0	0.0	0.0	0.0	0.0	0	0	0	1
Grass	3	9	1	4.0	27.0	1.0	1.0	0	0	0	0
Turf	11	21	9	4.0	21.0	1.0	3.0	0	0	0	1
Indoor	3	5	5	0.0	0.0	0.5	1.5	0	0	0	0
Outdoor	11	25	5	8.0	48.0	1.5	2.5	0	0	0	1

Game Logs

Date	Opp	Result	Tk	Ast	Sack	Yds	Stuff	Yds	Int	Yds	PD	FF	FR	TD
09/03	@Ind	W 24-21	0	1	0.0	0.0	0.0	0.0	0	0	0	0	0	0
09/10	Jac	W 24-17	5	0	2.0	14.0	0.5	1.5	0	0	0	0	0	0
09/17	@Sea	L 21-24	4	3	0.0	0.0	0.5	1.5	0	0	0	0	0	0
09/24	Hou	L 28-38	1	0	1.0	2.0	0.0	0.0	0	0	0	0	0	0
10/01	Mia	L 23-26	1	0	0.0	0.0	0.0	0.0	0	0	0	0	0	0
10/08	@TB	L 16-19	4	0	2.0	13.0	1.0	1.0	0	0	0	0	0	0
10/19	@Pit	W 27-9	0	0	0.0	0.0	0.0	0.0	0	0	0	0	0	0
10/29	Cle	L 26-29	1	3	0.0	0.0	0.0	0.0	0	0	0	0	0	0
11/05	Oak	L 17-20	5	1	1.0	5.0	0.0	0.0	0	0	0	0	0	0
11/12	@Hou	W 32-25	1	1	0.0	0.0	0.0	0.0	0	0	0	0	0	0
11/19	Pit	L 31-49	2	0	0.0	0.0	0.0	0.0	0	0	0	0	0	0
11/26	@Jac	W 17-13	2	1	2.0	14.0	0.0	0.0	0	0	0	1	0	0
12/03	@GB	L 10-24	3	0	0.0	0.0	0.0	0.0	0	0	0	0	0	0
12/10	Chi	W 16-10	1	0	0.0	0.0	0.0	0.0	0	0	0	1	0	0
12/17	@Cle	L 10-26	-	-	-	-	-	-	-	-	-	-	-	-
12/24	Min	W 27-24												

Aeneas Williams

Arizona Cardinals – CB

1995 Defensive Splits

	G	Tk	Ast	Sack	Yds	Stuff	Yds	Int	Yds	PD	TD
Total	16	52	10	0.0	0.0	0.5	1.0	6	86	22	3
vs. Playoff	8	25	6	0.0	0.0	0.5	1.0	4	51	5	1
vs. Non-Playoff	8	27	4	0.0	0.0	0.0	0.0	2	35	17	2
vs. Own Division	8	28	7	0.0	0.0	0.5	1.0	3	77	11	2
Home	8	27	8	0.0	0.0	0.5	1.0	3	83	13	2
Away	8	25	2	0.0	0.0	0.0	0.0	3	3	9	1
Games 1-8	8	25	4	0.0	0.0	0.0	0.0	2	35	8	1
Games 9-16	8	27	6	0.0	0.0	0.5	1.0	4	51	14	2
September	4	14	2	0.0	0.0	0.0	0.0	0	0	2	0
October	4	11	2	0.0	0.0	0.0	0.0	2	35	6	1
November	5	14	3	0.0	0.0	0.0	0.0	0	0	10	1
December	3	13	3	0.0	0.0	0.5	1.0	4	51	4	1
Grass	12	42	8	0.0	0.0	0.5	1.0	5	85	20	3
Turf	4	10	2	0.0	0.0	0.0	0.0	1	1	2	0
Indoor	1	5	0	0.0	0.0	0.0	0.0	0	0	0	0
Outdoor	15	47	10	0.0	0.0	0.5	1.0	6	86	22	3

Game Logs

Date	Opp	Result	Tk	Ast	Sack	Yds	Stuff	Yds	Int	Yds	PD	FF	FR	TD
09/03	@Was	L 7-27	5	0	0.0	0.0	0.0	0.0	0	0	2	0	0	0
09/10	Phi	L 19-31	3	1	0.0	0.0	0.0	0.0	0	0	0	0	0	0
09/17	@Det	W 20-17	5	0	0.0	0.0	0.0	0.0	0	0	0	0	0	0
09/24	@Dal	L 20-34	1	1	0.0	0.0	0.0	0.0	0	0	0	0	0	0
10/01	KC	L 3-24	2	0	0.0	0.0	0.0	0.0	0	0	0	0	0	0
10/08	@NYN	L 21-27	3	1	0.0	0.0	0.0	0.0	0	0	1	0	0	0
10/15	Was	W 24-20	3	0	0.0	0.0	0.0	0.0	1	28	4	0	0	1
10/29	Sea	W 20-14	3	1	0.0	0.0	0.0	0.0	1	7	1	0	1	0
11/05	@Den	L 6-38	1	0	0.0	0.0	0.0	0.0	0	0	1	0	0	0
11/12	Min	L 24-30	3	1	0.0	0.0	0.0	0.0	0	0	4	0	0	0
11/19	@Car	L 7-27	3	0	0.0	0.0	0.0	0.0	0	0	2	0	0	1
11/26	Atl	W 40-37	1	0	0.0	0.0	0.0	0.0	0	0	1	0	0	0
11/30	NYN	L 6-10	6	1	0.0	0.0	0.0	0.0	0	0	2	0	0	0
12/09	@SD	L 25-28	6	0	0.0	0.0	0.0	0.0	2	2	2	0	2	0
12/17	@Phi	L 20-21	1	0	0.0	0.0	0.0	0.0	1	1	1	0	0	0
12/25	Dal	L 13-37	6	3	0.0	0.0	0.5	1.0	1	48	1	0	0	1

Darryl Williams

Cincinnati Bengals – S

1995 Defensive Splits

	G	Tk	Ast	Sack	Yds	Stuff	Yds	Int	Yds	PD	TD
Total	16	88	24	1.0	9.0	1.0	1.0	1	1	10	0
vs. Playoff	5	26	12	0.0	0.0	0.0	0.0	0	0	3	0
vs. Non-Playoff	11	62	12	1.0	9.0	1.0	1.0	1	1	7	0
vs. Own Division	8	43	13	0.0	0.0	1.0	1.0	1	1	4	0
Home	8	45	3	0.0	0.0	1.0	1.0	0	0	7	0
Away	8	43	21	1.0	9.0	1.0	1.0	1	1	3	0
Games 1-8	8	57	9	0.0	0.0	1.0	1.0	0	0	5	0
Games 9-16	8	31	15	1.0	9.0	1.0	1.0	1	1	5	0
September	4	34	9	0.0	0.0	1.0	1.0	0	0	3	0
October	4	23	6	0.0	0.0	1.0	1.0	0	0	2	0
November	4	13	7	0.0	0.0	0.0	0.0	1	1	2	0
December	4	18	8	1.0	9.0	0.0	0.0	0	0	3	0
Grass	4	18	10	0.0	0.0	0.0	0.0	0	0	0	0
Turf	12	70	14	1.0	9.0	1.0	1.0	1	1	10	0
Indoor	3	19	7	0.0	0.0	0.0	0.0	1	1	3	0
Outdoor	13	69	17	1.0	9.0	1.0	1.0	0	0	7	0

Game Logs

Date	Opp	Result	Tk	Ast	Sack	Yds	Stuff	Yds	Int	Yds	PD	FF	FR	TD
09/03	@Ind	W 24-21	11	1	0.0	0.0	0.0	0.0	0	0	1	0	0	0
09/10	Jac	W 24-17	6	0	0.0	0.0	0.0	0.0	0	0	1	0	0	0
09/17	@Sea	L 21-24	7	2	0.0	0.0	0.0	0.0	0	0	1	0	0	0
09/24	Hou	L 28-38	11	0	0.0	0.0	0.0	0.0	0	0	0	0	1	0
10/01	Mia	L 23-26	6	0	0.0	0.0	0.0	0.0	0	0	1	0	0	0
10/08	@TB	L 16-19	5	2	0.0	0.0	0.0	0.0	0	0	0	0	0	0
10/19	@Pit	W 27-9	6	4	0.0	0.0	0.0	0.0	0	0	0	0	0	0
10/29	Cle	L 26-29	6	0	0.0	0.0	1.0	1.0	0	0	1	0	1	0
11/05	Oak	L 17-20	4	0	0.0	0.0	0.0	0.0	0	0	0	0	0	0
11/12	@Hou	W 32-25	1	4	0.0	0.0	0.0	0.0	1	1	1	0	0	0
11/19	Pit	L 31-49	2	2	0.0	0.0	0.0	0.0	0	0	1	0	0	0
11/26	@Jac	W 17-13	6	1	0.0	0.0	0.0	0.0	0	0	0	0	0	0
12/03	@GB	L 10-24	1	5	0.0	0.0	0.0	0.0	0	0	0	0	0	0
12/10	Chi	W 16-10	5	1	0.0	0.0	0.0	0.0	0	0	2	0	0	0
12/17	@Cle	L 10-26	6	2	0.0	0.0	0.0	0.0	0	0	0	0	0	0
12/24	Min	W 27-24	6	0	1.0	9.0	0.0	0.0	0	0	1	0	0	0

Willie Williams

Pittsburgh Steelers – CB

1995 Defensive Splits

	G	Tk	Ast	Sack	Yds	Stuff	Yds	Int	Yds	PD	TD
Total	16	70	8	0.0	0.0	0.5	1.5	7	122	20	1
vs. Playoff	4	20	0	0.0	0.0	0.0	0.0	2	73	5	1
vs. Non-Playoff	12	50	8	0.0	0.0	0.5	1.5	5	49	15	0
vs. Own Division	8	26	3	0.0	0.0	0.0	0.0	1	10	9	0
Home	8	30	4	0.0	0.0	0.5	1.5	3	73	10	1
Away	8	40	4	0.0	0.0	0.0	0.0	4	49	10	0
Games 1-8	8	26	5	0.0	0.0	0.5	1.5	2	73	10	1
Games 9-16	8	44	3	0.0	0.0	0.0	0.0	5	49	10	0
September	4	15	3	0.0	0.0	0.5	1.5	0	0	3	0
October	4	11	2	0.0	0.0	0.0	0.0	2	73	7	1
November	4	20	0	0.0	0.0	0.0	0.0	2	21	5	0
December	4	24	3	0.0	0.0	0.0	0.0	3	28	5	0
Grass	6	32	3	0.0	0.0	0.0	0.0	4	49	6	0
Turf	10	38	5	0.0	0.0	0.5	1.5	3	73	14	1
Indoor	1	2	1	0.0	0.0	0.0	0.0	0	0	2	0
Outdoor	15	68	7	0.0	0.0	0.5	1.5	7	122	18	1

Game Logs

Date	Opp	Result	Tk	Ast	Sack	Yds	Stuff	Yds	Int	Yds	PD	FF	FR	TD
09/03	Det	W 23-20	4	0	0.0	0.0	0.0	0.0	0	0	0	0	0	0
09/10	@Hou	W 34-17	2	1	0.0	0.0	0.0	0.0	0	0	2	0	0	0
09/18	@Mia	L 10-23	3	0	0.0	0.0	0.0	0.0	0	0	1	0	0	0
09/24	Min	L 24-44	6	2	0.0	0.0	0.5	1.5	0	0	0	0	0	0
10/01	SD	W 31-16	6	0	0.0	0.0	0.0	0.0	2	73	4	0	0	1
10/08	@Jac	L 16-20	3	0	0.0	0.0	0.0	0.0	0	0	0	0	0	0
10/19	Cin	L 9-27	2	1	0.0	0.0	0.0	0.0	0	0	0	0	0	0
10/29	Jac	W 24-7	0	1	0.0	0.0	0.0	0.0	0	0	3	0	0	0
11/05	@Chi	W 37-34	4	0	0.0	0.0	0.0	0.0	1	11	2	0	0	0
11/13	Cle	W 20-3	2	0	0.0	0.0	0.0	0.0	0	0	0	0	0	0
11/19	@Cin	W 49-31	6	0	0.0	0.0	0.0	0.0	0	0	2	0	0	0
11/26	@Cle	W 20-17	8	0	0.0	0.0	0.0	0.0	1	10	1	1	1	0
12/03	Hou	W 21-7	3	0	0.0	0.0	0.0	0.0	0	0	1	0	0	0
12/10	@Oak	W 29-10	7	3	0.0	0.0	0.0	0.0	2	28	2	0	0	0
12/16	NE	W 41-27	7	0	0.0	0.0	0.0	0.0	1	0	2	0	0	0
12/24	@GB	L 19-24	7	0	0.0	0.0	0.0	0.0	0	0	0	0	0	0

Lee Woodall
San Francisco 49ers – LB

1995 Defensive Splits

	G	Tk	Ast	Sack	Yds	Stuff	Yds	Int	Yds	PD	TD
Total	16	50	11	3.0	14.0	3.5	7.5	2	0	5	1
vs. Playoff	7	22	8	2.0	11.0	0.5	0.5	1	0	2	1
vs. Non-Playoff	9	28	3	1.0	3.0	3.0	7.0	1	0	3	0
vs. Own Division	8	20	3	0.0	0.0	2.0	6.0	0	0	0	0
Home	8	28	2	2.0	10.0	3.0	7.0	1	0	4	1
Away	8	22	9	1.0	4.0	0.5	0.5	1	0	1	0
Games 1-8	8	27	6	2.0	7.0	2.5	6.5	1	0	3	0
Games 9-16	8	23	5	1.0	7.0	1.0	1.0	1	0	2	1
September	4	15	3	2.0	7.0	1.0	1.0	1	0	1	0
October	4	12	3	0.0	0.0	1.5	5.5	0	0	2	0
November	4	11	3	0.0	0.0	1.0	1.0	1	0	1	0
December	4	12	2	1.0	7.0	0.0	0.0	0	0	1	1
Grass	10	32	3	2.0	10.0	3.0	7.0	1	0	4	1
Turf	6	18	8	1.0	4.0	0.5	0.5	1	0	1	0
Indoor	4	14	5	1.0	4.0	0.5	0.5	0	0	0	0
Outdoor	12	36	6	2.0	10.0	3.0	7.0	2	0	5	1

Game Logs

Date	Opp	Result	Tk	Ast	Sack	Yds	Stuff	Yds	Int	Yds	PD	FF	FR	TD
09/03	@NO	W 24-22	7	1	0.0	0.0	0.0	0.0	0	0	0	0	0	0
09/10	Atl	W 41-10	1	0	0.0	0.0	0.0	0.0	0	0	0	0	0	0
09/17	NE	W 28-3	3	0	1.0	3.0	1.0	1.0	1	0	1	1	0	0
09/25	@Det	L 24-27	4	2	1.0	4.0	0.0	0.0	0	0	0	0	0	0
10/01	NYN	W 20-6	5	0	0.0	0.0	0.0	0.0	0	0	2	0	0	0
10/15	@Ind	L 17-18	2	2	0.0	0.0	0.5	0.5	0	0	0	0	0	0
10/22	@StL	W 44-10	1	0	0.0	0.0	0.0	0.0	0	0	0	0	0	0
10/29	NO	L 7-11	4	1	0.0	0.0	1.0	5.0	0	0	0	0	0	0
11/05	Car	L 7-13	4	0	0.0	0.0	1.0	1.0	0	0	0	0	0	0
11/12	@Dal	W 38-20	3	3	0.0	0.0	0.0	0.0	1	0	1	0	0	0
11/20	@Mia	W 44-20	3	0	0.0	0.0	0.0	0.0	0	0	0	0	0	0
11/26	StL	W 41-13	1	0	0.0	0.0	0.0	0.0	0	0	0	0	0	0
12/03	Buf	W 27-17	8	1	1.0	7.0	0.0	0.0	0	0	1	1	2	1
12/10	@Car	W 31-10	1	0	0.0	0.0	0.0	0.0	0	0	0	0	0	0
12/18	Min	W 37-30	2	0	0.0	0.0	0.0	0.0	0	0	0	0	0	0
12/24	@Atl	L 27-28	1	0	0.0	0.0	0.0	0.0	0	0	0	0	0	0

Terry Wooden
Seattle Seahawks – LB

1995 Defensive Splits

	G	Tk	Ast	Sack	Yds	Stuff	Yds	Int	Yds	PD	TD
Total	16	114	21	0.0	0.0	10.5	29.0	1	9	8	0
vs. Playoff	6	46	9	0.0	0.0	6.0	14.5	1	9	4	0
vs. Non-Playoff	10	68	12	0.0	0.0	4.5	14.5	0	0	4	0
vs. Own Division	8	52	9	0.0	0.0	3.0	5.5	1	9	5	0
Home	8	57	11	0.0	0.0	4.0	8.5	0	0	3	0
Away	8	57	10	0.0	0.0	6.5	20.5	1	9	5	0
Games 1-8	8	51	13	0.0	0.0	5.5	16.0	1	9	4	0
Games 9-16	8	63	8	0.0	0.0	5.0	13.0	0	0	4	0
September	3	20	5	0.0	0.0	0.5	1.0	1	9	1	0
October	5	31	8	0.0	0.0	5.0	15.0	0	0	3	0
November	4	29	6	0.0	0.0	3.0	9.0	0	0	1	0
December	4	34	2	0.0	0.0	2.0	4.0	0	0	3	0
Grass	7	49	10	0.0	0.0	4.5	13.5	1	9	3	0
Turf	9	65	11	0.0	0.0	6.0	15.5	0	0	5	0
Indoor	8	57	11	0.0	0.0	4.0	8.5	0	0	3	0
Outdoor	8	57	10	0.0	0.0	6.5	20.5	1	9	5	0

Game Logs

Date	Opp	Result	Tk	Ast	Sack	Yds	Stuff	Yds	Int	Yds	PD	FF	FR	TD
09/03	KC	L 10-34	8	3	0.0	0.0	0.5	1.0	0	0	0	0	0	0
09/10	@SD	L 10-14	6	2	0.0	0.0	0.0	0.0	1	9	1	0	0	0
09/17	Cin	W 24-21	6	0	0.0	0.0	0.0	0.0	0	0	0	0	0	0
10/01	Den	W 27-10	4	1	0.0	0.0	0.0	0.0	0	0	0	0	0	0
10/08	@Oak	L 14-34	4	1	0.0	0.0	0.0	0.0	0	0	0	0	0	0
10/15	@Buf	L 21-27	8	0	0.0	0.0	2.0	7.0	0	0	2	0	0	0
10/22	SD	L 25-35	5	2	0.0	0.0	1.5	2.5	0	0	1	0	0	0
10/29	@Ari	L 14-20	10	4	0.0	0.0	1.5	5.5	0	0	0	0	1	0
11/05	NYN	W 30-28	9	2	0.0	0.0	0.0	0.0	0	0	0	0	0	0
11/12	@Jac	W 47-30	4	3	0.0	0.0	2.0	6.0	0	0	0	0	0	0
11/19	@Was	W 27-20	10	0	0.0	0.0	0.0	0.0	0	0	1	1	0	0
11/26	NYA	L 10-16	6	1	0.0	0.0	1.0	3.0	0	0	0	0	0	0
12/03	Phi	W 26-14	9	2	0.0	0.0	1.0	2.0	0	0	0	0	0	0
12/10	@Den	W 31-27	5	0	0.0	0.0	0.0	0.0	0	0	1	0	0	0
12/17	Oak	W 44-10	10	0	0.0	0.0	0.0	0.0	0	0	2	0	0	0
12/24	@KC	L 3-26	10	0	0.0	0.0	1.0	2.0	0	0	0	0	0	0

Darren Woodson
Dallas Cowboys – S

1995 Defensive Splits

	G	Tk	Ast	Sack	Yds	Stuff	Yds	Int	Yds	PD	TD
Total	16	91	12	0.0	0.0	2.0	3.5	2	46	6	1
vs. Playoff	7	38	1	0.0	0.0	0.0	0.0	0	0	2	0
vs. Non-Playoff	9	53	11	0.0	0.0	2.0	3.5	2	46	4	1
vs. Own Division	8	44	11	0.0	0.0	2.0	3.5	1	37	4	1
Home	8	37	7	0.0	0.0	0.5	0.5	0	0	2	0
Away	8	54	5	0.0	0.0	1.5	3.0	2	46	4	1
Games 1-8	8	42	5	0.0	0.0	1.0	2.0	1	37	3	0
Games 9-16	8	49	7	0.0	0.0	1.0	1.5	1	9	3	0
September	4	17	5	0.0	0.0	0.0	0.0	0	0	2	0
October	4	25	0	0.0	0.0	1.0	2.0	1	37	1	1
November	4	26	1	0.0	0.0	0.0	0.0	1	9	2	0
December	4	23	6	0.0	0.0	1.0	1.5	0	0	1	0
Grass	4	32	2	0.0	0.0	1.5	3.0	2	46	2	1
Turf	12	59	10	0.0	0.0	0.5	0.5	0	0	4	0
Indoor	2	13	1	0.0	0.0	0.0	0.0	0	0	1	0
Outdoor	14	70	11	0.0	0.0	2.0	3.5	2	46	5	1

Game Logs

Date	Opp	Result	Tk	Ast	Sack	Yds	Stuff	Yds	Int	Yds	PD	FF	FR	TD
09/04	@NYN	W 35-0	1	2	0.0	0.0	0.0	0.0	0	0	0	0	0	0
09/10	Den	W 31-21	3	0	0.0	0.0	0.0	0.0	0	0	0	0	0	0
09/17	@Min	W 23-17	8	1	0.0	0.0	0.0	0.0	0	0	1	0	0	0
09/24	Ari	W 34-20	5	2	0.0	0.0	0.0	0.0	0	0	1	0	0	0
10/01	@Was	L 23-27	11	0	0.0	0.0	1.0	2.0	1	37	1	1	0	1
10/08	GB	W 34-24	3	0	0.0	0.0	0.0	0.0	0	0	0	0	0	0
10/15	@SD	W 23-9	6	0	0.0	0.0	0.0	0.0	0	0	0	0	0	0
10/29	@Atl	W 28-13	5	0	0.0	0.0	0.0	0.0	0	0	0	0	0	0
11/06	Phi	W 34-12	4	1	0.0	0.0	0.0	0.0	0	0	1	0	0	0
11/12	SF	L 20-38	8	0	0.0	0.0	0.0	0.0	0	0	0	0	0	0
11/19	@Oak	W 34-21	10	0	0.0	0.0	0.0	0.0	1	9	1	0	0	0
11/23	KC	W 24-12	4	0	0.0	0.0	0.0	0.0	0	0	0	0	0	0
12/03	Was	L 17-24	4	0	0.0	0.0	0.5	0.5	0	0	0	0	0	0
12/10	@Phi	L 17-20	8	0	0.0	0.0	0.0	0.0	0	0	1	0	0	0
12/17	NYN	W 21-20	6	4	0.0	0.0	0.0	0.0	0	0	0	0	0	0
12/25	@Ari	W 37-13	5	2	0.0	0.0	0.5	1.0	0	0	0	0	0	0

Toby Wright
St. Louis Rams – S

1995 Defensive Splits

	G	Tk	Ast	Sack	Yds	Stuff	Yds	Int	Yds	PD	TD
Total	16	103	17	1.0	1.0	4.0	10.0	6	79	12	1
vs. Playoff	9	59	7	1.0	1.0	2.0	6.0	4	47	8	0
vs. Non-Playoff	7	44	10	0.0	0.0	2.0	4.0	2	32	4	1
vs. Own Division	8	52	9	1.0	1.0	0.0	0.0	3	34	6	0
Home	8	52	10	0.0	0.0	1.0	1.0	3	50	5	1
Away	8	51	7	1.0	1.0	3.0	9.0	3	29	7	0
Games 1-8	8	52	6	0.0	0.0	1.0	5.0	2	27	6	1
Games 9-16	8	51	11	1.0	1.0	3.0	5.0	4	52	6	0
September	4	29	5	0.0	0.0	1.0	5.0	1	27	3	1
October	4	23	1	0.0	0.0	0.0	0.0	1	0	3	0
November	4	25	6	1.0	1.0	0.0	0.0	3	34	5	0
December	4	26	5	0.0	0.0	3.0	5.0	1	18	1	0
Grass	3	22	3	1.0	1.0	1.0	5.0	2	29	3	0
Turf	13	81	14	0.0	0.0	3.0	5.0	4	50	9	1
Indoor	7	46	11	0.0	0.0	1.0	1.0	4	50	7	0
Outdoor	9	57	6	1.0	1.0	3.0	9.0	2	29	5	1

Game Logs

Date	Opp	Result	Tk	Ast	Sack	Yds	Stuff	Yds	Int	Yds	PD	FF	FR	TD
09/03	@GB	W 17-14	6	3	0.0	0.0	1.0	5.0	1	27	2	0	0	0
09/10	NO	W 17-13	6	2	0.0	0.0	0.0	0.0	0	0	1	0	0	0
09/17	@Car	W 31-10	9	0	0.0	0.0	0.0	0.0	0	0	0	0	0	0
09/24	Chi	W 34-28	8	0	0.0	0.0	0.0	0.0	0	0	0	0	1	1
10/01	@Ind	L 18-21	7	0	0.0	0.0	0.0	0.0	1	0	2	0	0	0
10/12	Atl	W 21-19	7	0	0.0	0.0	0.0	0.0	0	0	0	0	0	0
10/22	SF	L 10-44	5	1	0.0	0.0	0.0	0.0	0	0	0	0	0	0
10/29	@Phi	L 9-20	4	0	0.0	0.0	0.0	0.0	0	0	1	0	0	0
11/05	@NO	L 10-19	6	3	0.0	0.0	0.0	0.0	0	0	0	0	0	0
11/12	Car	W 28-17	5	2	0.0	0.0	0.0	0.0	2	32	3	0	0	0
11/19	@Atl	L 6-31	7	1	0.0	0.0	0.0	0.0	0	0	1	0	0	0
11/26	@SF	L 13-41	7	0	1.0	1.0	0.0	0.0	1	2	1	0	0	0
12/03	@NYA	W 23-20	5	0	0.0	0.0	2.0	4.0	0	0	0	0	0	0
12/10	Buf	L 27-45	9	0	0.0	0.0	0.0	0.0	0	0	0	0	0	0
12/17	Was	L 23-35	5	3	0.0	0.0	0.0	0.0	0	0	1	0	0	0
12/24	Mia	L 22-41	7	2	0.0	0.0	1.0	1.0	1	18	1	0	0	0

Bryant Young
San Francisco 49ers – DT

1995 Defensive Splits

	G	Tk	Ast	Sack	Yds	Stuff	Yds	Int	Yds	PD	TD
Total	12	25	3	6.0	33.0	2.0	3.0	0	0	2	0
vs. Playoff	6	8	3	3.0	11.0	1.0	1.0	0	0	1	0
vs. Non-Playoff	6	17	0	3.0	22.0	1.0	2.0	0	0	1	0
vs. Own Division	6	11	0	0.0	0.0	2.0	3.0	0	0	1	0
Home	6	14	1	3.0	22.0	0.0	0.0	0	0	1	0
Away	6	11	2	3.0	11.0	2.0	3.0	0	0	1	0
Games 1-8	4	8	2	2.0	6.0	0.0	0.0	0	0	0	0
Games 9-16	8	17	1	4.0	27.0	2.0	3.0	0	0	2	0
September	4	8	2	2.0	6.0	0.0	0.0	0	0	0	0
October	0	0	0	0	0	0	0	0	0	0	0
November	4	7	0	2.0	11.0	0.0	0.0	0	0	0	0
December	4	10	1	2.0	16.0	2.0	3.0	0	0	2	0
Grass	8	21	1	5.0	33.0	1.0	2.0	0	0	2	0
Turf	4	4	2	1.0	0.0	1.0	1.0	0	0	0	0
Indoor	3	4	2	1.0	0.0	1.0	1.0	0	0	0	0
Outdoor	9	21	1	5.0	33.0	1.0	2.0	0	0	2	0

Game Logs

Date	Opp	Result	Tk	Ast	Sack	Yds	Stuff	Yds	Int	Yds	PD	FF	FR	TD
09/03	@NO	W 24-22	1	0	0.0	0.0	0.0	0.0	0	0	0	0	1	0
09/10	Atl	W 41-10	0	0	0.0	0.0	0.0	0.0	0	0	0	0	0	0
09/17	NE	W 28-3	4	0	1.0	6.0	0.0	0.0	0	0	0	0	0	0
09/25	@Det	L 24-27	2	2	1.0	0.0	0.0	0.0	0	0	0	0	0	0
10/01	NYN	W 20-6	-	-	-	-	-	-	-	-	-	-	-	-
10/15	@Ind	L 17-18	-	-	-	-	-	-	-	-	-	-	-	-
10/22	@StL	W 44-10	-	-	-	-	-	-	-	-	-	-	-	-
10/29	NO	L 7-11	-	-	-	-	-	-	-	-	-	-	-	-
11/05	Car	L 7-13	2	0	0.0	0.0	0.0	0.0	0	0	0	0	0	0
11/12	@Dal	W 38-20	0	0	0.0	0.0	0.0	0.0	0	0	0	0	0	0
11/20	@Mia	W 44-20	3	0	2.0	11.0	0.0	0.0	0	0	0	0	0	0
11/26	StL	W 41-13	2	0	0.0	0.0	0.0	0.0	0	0	0	0	1	0
12/03	Buf	W 27-17	1	1	0.0	0.0	0.0	0.0	0	0	1	0	0	0
12/10	@Car	W 31-10	4	0	0.0	0.0	1.0	2.0	0	0	1	0	0	0
12/18	Min	W 37-30	4	0	2.0	16.0	0.0	0.0	0	0	0	0	0	0
12/24	@Atl	L 27-28	1	0	0.0	0.0	1.0	1.0	0	0	0	0	0	0

Michael Zordich
Philadelphia Eagles – S

1995 Defensive Splits

	G	Tk	Ast	Sack	Yds	Stuff	Yds	Int	Yds	PD	TD
Total	15	62	14	1.0	12.0	3.0	4.0	1	10	6	1
vs. Playoff	3	10	2	0.0	0.0	1.0	1.0	0	0	1	0
vs. Non-Playoff	12	52	12	1.0	12.0	2.0	3.0	1	10	5	1
vs. Own Division	8	36	8	0.0	0.0	2.0	3.0	1	10	5	0
Home	8	25	5	1.0	12.0	1.0	1.0	0	0	4	0
Away	7	37	9	0.0	0.0	2.0	3.0	1	10	2	1
Games 1-8	7	19	10	0.0	0.0	2.0	3.0	1	10	5	1
Games 9-16	8	43	4	1.0	12.0	1.0	1.0	0	0	1	0
September	3	5	5	0.0	0.0	1.0	2.0	0	0	1	0
October	4	14	5	0.0	0.0	1.0	1.0	1	10	4	1
November	4	27	3	1.0	12.0	1.0	1.0	0	0	0	0
December	4	16	1	0.0	0.0	0.0	0.0	0	0	1	0
Grass	3	23	4	0.0	0.0	1.0	2.0	0	0	1	0
Turf	12	39	10	1.0	12.0	2.0	2.0	1	10	5	1
Indoor	2	3	1	0.0	0.0	0.0	0.0	0	0	0	0
Outdoor	13	59	13	1.0	12.0	3.0	4.0	1	10	6	1

Game Logs

Date	Opp	Result	Tk	Ast	Sack	Yds	Stuff	Yds	Int	Yds	PD	FF	FR	TD
09/03	TB	L 6-21	2	3	0.0	0.0	0.0	0.0	0	0	0	0	0	0
09/10	@Ari	W 31-19	3	2	0.0	0.0	1.0	2.0	0	0	1	0	0	0
09/17	SD	L 21-27	0	0	0.0	0.0	0.0	0.0	0	0	0	0	0	0
09/24	@Oak	L 17-48	-	-	-	-	-	-	-	-	-	-	-	-
10/01	@NO	W 15-10	1	1	0.0	0.0	0.0	0.0	0	0	0	0	0	0
10/08	Was	W 37-34	6	1	0.0	0.0	0.0	0.0	0	0	2	0	0	1
10/15	@NYN	W 17-14	3	2	0.0	0.0	0.0	0.0	1	10	1	0	1	1
10/29	StL	W 20-9	4	1	0.0	0.0	1.0	1.0	0	0	1	0	0	0
11/06	@Dal	L 12-34	8	2	0.0	0.0	1.0	1.0	0	0	0	0	0	0
11/12	Den	W 31-13	7	0	1.0	12.0	0.0	0.0	0	0	0	1	0	0
11/19	NYN	W 28-19	2	0	0.0	0.0	0.0	0.0	0	0	0	0	0	0
11/26	@Was	W 14-7	10	1	0.0	0.0	0.0	0.0	0	0	0	0	0	0
12/03	@Sea	L 14-26	2	0	0.0	0.0	0.0	0.0	0	0	0	0	0	0
12/10	Dal	W 20-17	2	0	0.0	0.0	0.0	0.0	0	0	1	0	1	0
12/17	Ari	W 21-20	2	0	0.0	0.0	0.0	0.0	0	0	0	0	0	0
12/24	@Chi	L 14-20	10	1	0.0	0.0	0.0	0.0	0	0	1	0	0	0

Kicking & Punting Profiles

The following section provides statistical breakdowns and game logs for nearly every player who attempted a field goal or punted in 1995. The only players of note not included are (1) New York Jets punter Don Silvestri, who booted the ball five times for an impressive 238 yards, and (2) veteran kicker Tony Zendejas, who tried three field goals for the Falcons, then three more for the 49ers. That leaves us with 34 kickers and 31 punters.

Some of the statistics used here aren't seen too often, and the abbreviations might be unfamiliar. Those abbreviations and what they stand for:

For KICKERS, **1-29 Yd**, for example, refers to the number of field-goal attempts and field goals made at that distance. The **Pct** appearing after a distance, and after "Overall," gives the percentage of field goals made at that distance. **Lg** = Longest Field Goal Made. For the kickoff splits, **Num** = Number of Kickoffs; **Avg** = Average Length of Kickoff; **TB** = Touchbacks; **TD** = Kickoffs Returned for Touchdowns; **NetAvg** = Kickoff Net Average.

For PUNTERS, **NPunts** = Net Punts; **Lg** = Longest Punt; **In20** = Punts Inside 20; **FC** = Fair Catches; **TPunts** = Total Punts; **TB** = Touchbacks; **BLK** = Punts Blocked; **Ret** = Punts Returned; **Yds** = Return Yards; **NetAvg** = Net Punting Average.

For definitions of statistical categories, please consult the Glossary.

Louis Aguiar

1995 Punter Splits

	G	NPunts	Avg	Lg	In20	FC	TPunts	TB	Blk	Ret	Yds	NetAvg
Total	16	91	43.8	65	28	18	91	12	0	42	433	36.5
vs. Playoff	4	16	43.8	61	6	4	16	1	0	7	29	40.8
vs. Non-playoff	12	75	43.9	65	22	14	75	11	0	35	404	35.5
vs. Own Division	8	43	43.0	65	13	9	43	6	0	20	212	35.2
Home	8	51	42.8	59	17	12	51	5	0	22	244	36.1
Away	8	40	45.2	65	11	6	40	7	0	20	189	36.9
September	4	26	45.5	56	8	6	26	1	0	15	160	38.6
October	4	23	46.7	65	6	4	23	4	0	11	135	37.4
November	4	22	41.1	56	9	5	22	2	0	10	80	35.7
December	4	20	41.4	61	5	3	20	5	0	6	58	33.5
Grass	14	83	44.4	65	24	14	83	12	0	39	420	36.4
Turf	2	8	38.5	51	4	4	8	0	0	3	13	36.9
Indoor	1	5	38.8	51	2	2	5	0	0	2	10	36.8
Outdoor	15	86	44.1	65	26	16	86	12	0	40	423	36.4
Outdoors, Temp < 40	3	15	40.4	56	4	3	15	4	0	4	62	30.9
Outdoors, Temp 40-80	11	66	44.1	61	22	13	66	7	0	32	324	37.1
Outdoors, Temp > 80	1	5	55.6	65	0	0	5	1	0	4	37	44.2
Winning	-	45	42.9	65	15	7	45	6	0	20	201	35.7
Tied	-	18	44.7	56	5	5	18	2	0	9	133	35.1
Trailing	-	28	44.9	61	8	6	28	4	0	13	99	38.5

Game Logs

Date	Opp	Result	NPunts	Avg	In20	TPunts	TB	Blk	Ret	Yds	NetAvg
09/03	@Sea	W 34-10	5	38.8	2	5	0	0	2	10	36.8
09/10	NYN	W 20-17	6	50.2	1	6	0	0	4	40	43.5
09/17	Oak	W 23-17	8	47.1	3	8	0	0	6	85	36.5
09/24	@Cle	L 17-35	7	44.4	2	7	1	0	3	25	38.0
10/01	@Ari	W 24-3	5	55.6	1	5	0	0	4	37	44.2
10/09	SD	W 29-23	4	46.0	1	4	0	0	1	1	45.8
10/15	NE	W 31-26	9	41.9	4	9	1	0	4	46	34.6
10/22	@Den	W 21-7	5	47.2	1	5	2	0	2	51	29.0
11/05	Was	W 24-3	7	37.6	3	7	1	0	1	8	33.6
11/12	@SD	W 22-7	5	43.2	2	5	0	0	4	16	40.0
11/19	Hou	W 20-13	7	44.6	2	7	1	0	4	53	34.1
11/23	@Dal	L 12-24	3	38.0	2	3	0	0	1	3	37.0
12/03	@Oak	W 29-23	6	45.0	1	6	2	0	3	38	32.0
12/11	@Mia	L 6-13	4	46.8	1	4	1	0	1	9	39.5
12/17	Den	W 20-17	6	37.7	2	6	2	0	1	5	30.2
12/24	Sea	W 26-3	4	36.0	1	4	0	0	1	6	34.5

Morten Andersen

1995 Field Goal Splits / 1995 Kickoff Splits

	G	1-29 Yd	30-39 Yd	40-49 Yd	50+ Yd	Overall	Pct	Lg	Num	Avg	TB	TD	NetAvg
Total	16	9-9	11-11	3-8	8-9	31-37	83.8	59	82	68.6	27	0	46.7
vs. Playoff	6	3-3	1-1	2-6	3-3	9-13	69.2	59	29	69.6	10	0	49.3
vs. Non-playoff	10	6-6	10-10	1-2	5-6	22-24	91.7	55	53	68.0	17	0	45.2
vs. Own Division	8	7-7	3-3	1-2	6-7	17-19	89.5	59	39	69.4	12	0	47.5
Home	8	5-5	8-8	2-5	7-8	22-26	84.6	59	48	70.7	18	0	49.1
Away	8	4-4	3-3	1-3	1-1	9-11	81.8	50	34	65.6	9	0	43.2
Games 1-8	8	5-5	9-9	2-2	2-3	18-19	94.7	54	37	68.1	10	0	44.4
Games 9-16	8	4-4	2-2	1-6	6-6	13-18	72.2	59	45	69.0	17	0	48.6
September	4	4-4	4-4	1-1	1-2	10-11	90.9	51	20	70.7	7	0	46.2
October	4	1-1	5-5	1-1	1-1	8-8	100.0	54	17	65.3	3	0	42.2
November	4	2-2	1-1	1-6	1-1	5-10	50.0	50	24	68.9	10	0	48.5
December	4	2-2	1-1	0-0	5-5	8-8	100.0	59	21	69.1	7	0	48.6
Grass	5	2-2	2-2	0-0	0-0	4-4	100.0	34	23	63.2	6	0	42.3
Turf	11	7-7	9-9	3-8	8-9	27-33	81.8	59	59	70.7	21	0	48.4
Indoor	9	7-7	9-9	3-6	7-8	26-30	86.7	59	55	71.0	18	0	48.5
Outdoor	7	2-2	2-2	0-2	1-1	5-7	71.4	50	27	63.7	9	0	43.0
4th qtr, +/-3 pts	-	0-0	3-3	0-0	1-2	4-5	80.0	55	4	72.0	0	0	39.5
Winning	-	3-3	4-4	2-5	3-3	12-15	80.0	55	52	68.3	14	0	45.9
Tied	-	3-3	7-7	0-1	0-1	10-12	83.3	37	18	69.9	10	0	50.5
Trailing	-	3-3	0-0	1-2	5-5	9-10	90.0	59	12	67.8	3	0	44.3

Game Logs

Date	Opp	Result	1-39 Yd	40-49 Yd	50+ Yd	Lg
09/03	Car	W 23-20	2-2	0-0	1-2	51
09/10	@SF	L 10-41	1-1	0-0	0-0	26
09/17	@NO	W 27-24	3-3	1-1	0-0	46
09/24	NYA	W 13-3	2-2	0-0	0-0	37
10/01	NE	W 30-17	4-4	0-0	1-1	54
10/12	@StL	L 19-21	0-0	0-0	0-0	0
10/22	@TB	L 24-21	1-1	0-0	0-0	30
10/29	Dal	L 13-28	1-1	1-1	0-0	40
11/05	Det	W 34-22	1-1	1-3	0-0	47
11/12	@Buf	L 17-23	0-0	0-0	1-1	50
11/19	StL	W 31-6	1-1	0-1	0-0	23
11/26	@Ari	L 37-40	1-1	0-0	0-0	21
12/03	@Mia	L 20-21	0-0	0-0	0-0	0
12/10	NO	L 19-14	1-1	1-1	0-0	34
12/17	@Car	L 17-21	1-1	0-0	0-0	34
12/24	SF	W 28-27	1-1	0-0	2-2	59

Gary Anderson

1995 Field Goal Splits / 1995 Kickoff Splits

	G	1-29 Yd	30-39 Yd	40-49 Yd	50+ Yd	Overall	Pct	Lg	Num	Avg	TB	TD	NetAvg
Total	16	5-5	9-10	8-12	0-3	22-30	73.3	43	72	62.1	10	0	36.5
vs. Playoff	3	1-1	3-3	2-3	0-0	6-7	85.7	42	14	62.2	3	0	40.4
vs. Non-playoff	13	4-4	6-7	6-9	0-3	16-23	69.6	43	58	62.1	7	0	35.5
vs. Own Division	8	1-1	4-4	6-9	0-1	11-15	73.3	43	39	62.3	7	0	36.0
Home	8	4-4	4-4	4-6	0-1	12-15	80.0	43	41	61.3	8	0	37.2
Away	8	1-1	5-6	4-6	0-2	10-15	66.7	43	31	63.1	2	0	35.5
Games 1-8	8	4-4	5-5	6-8	0-2	15-19	78.9	43	38	62.7	6	0	36.9
Games 9-16	8	1-1	4-5	2-4	0-1	7-11	63.6	42	34	61.5	4	0	36.0
September	4	2-2	1-1	1-2	0-2	4-7	57.1	43	16	61.9	0	0	35.4
October	4	2-2	4-4	5-6	0-0	11-12	91.7	43	22	63.2	6	0	38.0
November	4	0-0	3-3	0-1	0-1	3-5	60.0	39	18	62.1	2	0	38.3
December	4	1-1	1-2	2-3	0-0	4-6	66.7	42	16	60.8	2	0	33.4
Grass	4	0-0	1-1	1-2	0-2	2-5	40.0	43	15	60.0	0	0	34.1
Turf	12	5-5	8-9	7-10	0-1	20-25	80.0	43	57	62.7	10	0	37.1
Indoor	2	1-1	2-3	2-2	0-0	5-6	83.3	43	8	67.3	0	0	35.9
Outdoor	14	4-4	7-7	6-10	0-3	17-24	70.8	43	64	61.5	10	0	36.5
4th qtr, +/-3 pts	-	0-0	2-2	2-2	0-0	4-4	100.0	42	4	63.5	2	0	42.8
Winning	-	1-1	4-4	4-7	0-1	9-13	69.2	43	42	61.8	6	0	36.7
Tied	-	1-1	2-2	3-3	0-2	6-8	75.0	43	18	64.9	4	0	38.6
Trailing	-	3-3	3-4	1-2	0-0	7-9	77.8	40	12	58.9	0	0	32.4

Game Logs

Date	Opp	Result	1-39 Yd	40-49 Yd	50+ Yd	Lg
09/03	TB	L 6-21	2-2	0-0	0-0	28
09/10	@Ari	W 31-19	0-0	1-1	0-1	43
09/17	SD	L 21-27	0-0	0-1	0-0	0
09/24	@Oak	L 17-48	1-1	0-0	0-1	30
10/01	@NO	W 15-10	3-3	2-2	0-0	43
10/08	Was	W 37-34	1-1	2-2	0-0	43
10/15	@NYN	W 17-14	0-0	1-2	0-0	40
10/29	StL	W 20-9	2-2	0-0	0-0	36
11/06	@Dal	L 12-34	2-2	0-0	0-0	37
11/12	Den	W 31-13	1-1	0-0	0-1	39
11/19	NYN	W 28-19	0-0	0-1	0-0	29
11/26	@Was	W 14-7	0-0	0-0	0-1	0
12/03	@Sea	L 14-26	0-1	0-0	0-0	0
12/10	Dal	W 20-17	2-2	2-2	0-0	42
12/17	Ari	W 21-20	0-0	0-1	0-0	0
12/24	@Chi	L 14-20	0-0	0-0	0-0	0

Matt Bahr
New England Patriots — K

		1995 Field Goal Splits							1995 Kickoff Splits							Game Logs				
	G	1-29 Yd	30-39 Yd	40-49 Yd	50+ Yd	Overall	Pct	Lg	Num	Avg	TB	TD	NetAvg	Date	Opp	Result	1-39 Yd	40-49 Yd	50+ Yd	Lg
Total	16	13-14	3-7	5-7	2-5	23-33	69.7	55	2	67.0	0	0	43.5	09/03	Cle	W 17-14	3-3	0-0	0-0	28
vs. Playoff	10	8-9	1-2	4-5	1-4	14-20	70.0	55	2	67.0	0	0	43.5	09/10	Mia	L 3-20	1-1	0-0	0-0	29
vs. Non-playoff	6	5-5	2-5	1-2	1-1	9-13	69.2	51	0	-	0	0	-	09/17	@SF	L 3-28	0-1	1-1	0-0	43
vs. Own Division	8	4-5	2-5	4-5	1-4	11-19	57.9	55	0	-	0	0	-	10/01	@Atl	L 17-30	1-1	0-0	0-0	27
Home	8	6-6	3-6	1-3	1-1	11-16	68.8	51	0	-	0	0	-	10/08	Den	L 3-37	0-0	0-0	1-1	51
Away	8	7-8	0-1	4-4	1-4	12-17	70.6	55	2	67.0	0	0	43.5	10/15	@KC	L 26-31	2-2	0-0	0-0	29
Games 1-8	8	9-9	1-2	1-2	1-1	12-14	85.7	51	2	67.0	0	0	43.5	10/23	Buf	W 27-14	2-2	0-1	0-0	39
Games 9-16	8	4-5	2-5	4-5	1-4	11-19	57.9	55	0	-	0	0	-	10/29	Car	L 17-20	1-1	0-0	0-0	19
September	3	4-4	0-1	1-1	0-0	5-6	83.3	43	2	67.0	0	0	43.5	11/05	@NYA	W 20-7	1-1	1-1	0-0	41
October	5	5-5	1-1	0-1	1-1	7-8	87.5	51	0	-	0	0	-	11/12	@Mia	W 34-17	0-1	1-1	1-1	55
November	4	2-3	0-0	4-4	1-1	7-8	87.5	55	0	-	0	0	-	11/19	Ind	L 10-24	0-0	1-1	0-0	41
December	4	2-2	2-5	0-1	0-3	4-11	36.4	39	0	-	0	0	-	11/26	@Buf	W 35-25	1-1	1-1	0-0	43
Grass	11	8-9	3-7	3-5	2-2	16-23	69.6	55	2	67.0	0	0	43.5	12/03	NO	L 17-31	1-1	0-1	0-0	39
Turf	5	5-5	0-0	2-2	0-3	7-10	70.0	43	0	-	0	0	-	12/10	NYA	W 31-28	1-4	0-0	0-0	31
Indoor	2	1-1	0-0	0-0	0-3	1-4	25.0	27	0	-	0	0	-	12/16	@Pit	L 27-41	2-2	0-0	0-0	23
Outdoor	14	12-13	3-7	5-7	2-2	22-29	75.9	55	2	67.0	0	0	43.5	12/23	@Ind	L 7-10	0-0	0-0	0-3	0
4th qtr, +/-3 pts	-	0-0	2-2	0-0	0-1	2-3	66.7	39	0	-	0	0	-							
Winning	-	2-2	1-1	1-2	0-1	4-6	66.7	47	1	66.0	0	0	47.0							
Tied	-	4-5	1-5	3-3	0-1	8-14	57.1	43	0	-	0	0	-							
Trailing	-	7-7	1-1	1-2	2-3	11-13	84.6	55	1	68.0	0	0	40.0							

Bryan Barker
Jacksonville Jaguars — P

			1995 Punter Splits										Game Logs										
	G	NPunts	Avg	Lg	In20	FC	TPunts	TB	Blk	Ret	Yds	NetAvg	Date	Opp	Result	NPunts	Avg	In20	TPunts	TB	Blk	Ret	Yds	NetAvg
Total	16	82	43.8	63	19	11	82	5	0	45	323	38.6	09/03	Hou	L 3-10	8	43.1	1	8	1	0	4	27	37.3
vs. Playoff	5	30	44.7	61	5	0	30	2	0	18	149	38.4	09/10	@Cin	L 17-24	6	41.5	1	6	1	0	1	-3	38.7
vs. Non-playoff	11	52	43.3	63	14	11	52	3	0	27	174	38.8	09/17	@NYA	L 10-27	6	46.5	0	6	1	0	4	24	39.2
vs. Own Division	8	48	43.1	61	11	8	48	3	0	21	122	39.3	09/24	GB	L 14-24	8	45.4	2	8	1	0	5	64	34.9
Home	8	39	44.8	61	8	4	39	2	0	23	172	39.4	10/01	@Hou	W 17-16	5	46.2	2	5	0	0	3	14	43.4
Away	8	43	42.8	63	11	7	43	3	0	22	151	37.9	10/08	Pit	W 20-16	8	48.5	1	8	0	0	4	32	44.5
September	4	28	44.1	63	4	4	28	4	0	14	112	37.3	10/15	Chi	L 27-30	1	55.0	0	1	0	0	1	1	54.0
October	5	26	44.4	61	6	3	26	1	0	13	68	41.0	10/22	@Cle	W 23-15	3	37.0	2	3	0	0	0	0	37.0
November	3	13	44.2	59	3	1	13	0	0	9	68	38.9	10/29	@Pit	L 7-24	9	41.0	1	9	1	0	5	21	36.4
December	4	15	41.8	61	6	3	15	0	0	9	75	36.8	11/12	Sea	L 30-47	3	46.3	0	3	0	0	3	7	44.0
Grass	11	53	43.9	61	15	8	53	2	0	30	245	38.5	11/19	@TB	L 16-17	6	41.8	2	6	0	0	4	48	33.8
Turf	5	29	43.6	63	4	3	29	3	0	15	78	38.8	11/26	Cin	L 13-17	4	46.0	1	4	0	0	2	13	42.8
Indoor	2	8	45.9	53	2	1	8	0	0	5	36	41.4	12/03	@Den	L 23-31	5	43.2	3	5	0	0	3	25	38.2
Outdoor	14	74	43.6	63	17	10	74	5	0	40	287	38.3	12/10	Ind	L 31-41	2	42.5	1	2	0	0	2	10	37.5
Outdoors, Temp < 40	0	0	-	0	0	0	0	0	0	0	0	-	12/17	@Det	L 0-44	3	45.3	0	3	0	0	2	22	38.0
Outdoors, Temp 40-80	13	66	43.0	63	16	10	66	5	0	36	255	37.6	12/24	Cle	W 24-21	5	38.0	2	5	0	0	2	18	34.4
Outdoors, Temp > 80	1	8	48.5	61	1	0	8	0	0	4	32	44.5												
Winning	-	21	43.0	61	4	4	21	1	0	8	55	39.4												
Tied	-	11	45.5	59	4	1	11	0	0	7	54	40.6												
Trailing	-	50	43.8	63	11	6	50	4	0	30	214	37.9												

Tommy Barnhardt
Carolina Panthers — P

			1995 Punter Splits										Game Logs										
	G	NPunts	Avg	Lg	In20	FC	TPunts	TB	Blk	Ret	Yds	NetAvg	Date	Opp	Result	NPunts	Avg	In20	TPunts	TB	Blk	Ret	Yds	NetAvg
Total	16	95	41.1	54	27	23	95	11	0	39	342	35.2	09/03	@Atl	L 20-23	10	40.6	5	10	1	0	2	7	37.9
vs. Playoff	6	40	40.1	53	12	11	40	6	0	12	82	35.1	09/10	@Buf	L 9-31	9	44.0	2	9	1	0	4	26	38.9
vs. Non-playoff	10	55	41.9	54	15	12	55	5	0	27	260	35.3	09/17	StL	L 10-31	6	39.0	0	6	0	0	5	48	31.0
vs. Own Division	8	47	40.9	54	11	12	47	6	0	19	146	35.2	10/01	TB	L 13-20	3	42.3	0	3	0	0	2	54	24.3
Home	8	42	40.8	54	8	8	42	4	0	19	197	34.2	10/08	@Chi	L 27-31	8	42.6	2	8	1	0	3	24	37.1
Away	8	53	41.4	54	19	15	53	7	0	20	145	36.0	10/15	NYA	W 26-15	4	44.3	1	4	2	0	1	14	30.8
September	3	25	41.4	53	7	6	25	2	0	11	81	36.6	10/22	NO	W 20-3	10	44.6	1	10	1	0	6	36	39.0
October	5	31	42.4	54	5	6	31	5	0	16	151	34.3	10/29	@NE	W 20-17	6	37.0	1	6	1	0	4	23	29.8
November	4	17	42.4	54	5	5	17	3	0	6	52	35.8	11/05	@SF	W 13-7	6	41.7	1	6	3	0	2	9	30.2
December	4	22	38.0	40	10	6	22	1	0	6	50	34.5	11/12	@Atl	L 17-20	2	42.0	1	2	0	0	1	0	30.0
Grass	12	69	40.7	54	17	14	69	9	0	30	271	34.2	11/19	Ari	W 27-7	4	44.3	2	4	0	0	1	5	43.0
Turf	4	26	42.1	53	10	9	26	2	0	9	71	37.8	11/26	@NO	L 26-34	5	41.8	2	5	0	0	2	30	35.8
Indoor	3	17	41.1	51	8	7	17	1	0	5	45	37.3	12/03	Ind	W 13-10	7	37.0	3	7	0	0	3	32	32.4
Outdoor	13	78	41.1	54	19	16	78	10	0	34	297	34.7	12/10	SF	L 10-31	5	37.2	0	5	1	0	0	0	33.2
Outdoors, Temp < 40	2	12	39.3	49	6	3	12	1	0	2	18	36.1	12/17	Atl	W 21-17	3	35.7	0	3	0	0	1	8	33.0
Outdoors, Temp 40-80	11	66	41.5	54	13	13	66	9	0	32	279	34.5	12/24	@Was	L 17-20	7	40.7	5	7	2	0	2	18	38.1
Outdoors, Temp > 80	0	0	-	0	0	0	0	0	0	0	0	-												
Winning	-	22	42.6	54	3	1	22	6	0	8	57	34.6												
Tied	-	33	40.5	54	9	6	33	1	0	19	174	34.7												
Trailing	-	40	40.8	52	15	16	40	4	0	12	111	36.0												

Darren Bennett
San Diego Chargers — P

1995 Punter Splits

	G	NPunts	Avg	Lg	In20	FC	TPunts	TB	Blk	Ret	Yds	NetAvg
Total	16	72	44.7	66	28	13	72	8	0	35	429	36.6
vs. Playoff	7	32	46.7	66	13	6	32	4	0	16	278	35.5
vs. Non-playoff	9	40	43.2	62	15	7	40	4	0	19	151	37.4
vs. Own Division	8	40	43.8	66	14	7	40	2	0	20	292	35.5
Home	8	33	43.1	62	10	6	33	3	0	17	180	35.8
Away	8	39	46.1	66	18	7	39	5	0	18	249	37.2
September	4	21	41.0	62	6	4	21	2	0	8	82	35.2
October	4	16	52.5	66	7	3	16	2	0	10	169	39.4
November	4	20	43.4	59	7	4	20	1	0	10	133	35.7
December	4	15	43.5	61	8	2	15	3	0	7	45	36.5
Grass	11	46	44.5	66	16	8	46	5	0	22	307	35.6
Turf	5	26	45.2	66	12	5	26	3	0	13	122	38.2
Indoor	2	8	46.0	55	5	1	8	0	0	4	29	42.4
Outdoor	14	64	44.6	66	23	12	64	8	0	31	400	35.8
Outdoors, Temp < 40	1	6	39.3	55	4	1	6	0	0	4	23	35.5
Outdoors, Temp 40-80	13	58	45.1	66	19	11	58	8	0	27	377	35.9
Outdoors, Temp > 80	0	0	-	0	0	0	0	0	0	0	0	-
Winning	-	25	43.3	62	10	3	25	5	0	11	90	35.7
Tied	-	16	45.9	66	4	3	16	0	0	11	222	32.0
Trailing	-	31	45.3	66	14	7	31	3	0	13	117	39.6

Game Logs

Date	Opp	Result	NPunts	Avg	In20	TPunts	TB	Blk	Ret	Yds	NetAvg
09/03	@Oak	L 7-17	4	44.5	3	4	0	0	1	11	41.8
09/10	Sea	W 14-10	4	39.3	1	4	0	0	2	8	37.3
09/17	@Phi	W 27-21	8	41.8	2	8	2	0	3	42	31.5
09/24	Den	W 17-6	5	38.6	0	5	0	0	2	21	34.4
10/01	@Pit	L 16-31	4	59.5	1	4	1	0	2	28	47.5
10/09	@KC	L 23-29	4	50.8	2	4	1	0	2	96	21.8
10/15	Dal	L 9-23	3	54.3	2	3	0	0	3	22	47.0
10/22	@Sea	W 35-25	5	47.2	2	5	0	0	3	23	42.6
11/05	Mia	L 14-24	2	40.5	1	2	0	0	0	0	40.5
11/12	KC	L 7-22	8	43.0	2	8	0	0	5	84	32.5
11/19	@Den	L 27-30	5	48.4	1	5	1	0	2	20	40.4
11/27	Oak	W 12-6	5	40.0	3	5	0	0	3	29	34.2
12/03	Cle	W 31-13	4	44.3	1	4	2	0	1	12	31.3
12/09	Ari	W 28-25	2	53.5	0	2	1	0	1	4	41.5
12/17	@Ind	W 27-24	3	44.0	3	3	0	0	1	6	42.0
12/23	@NYN	W 27-17	6	39.3	4	6	0	0	4	23	35.5

Dean Biasucci
St. Louis Rams — K

1995 Field Goal Splits / 1995 Kickoff Splits

	G	1-29 Yd	30-39 Yd	40-49 Yd	50+ Yd	Overall	Pct	Lg	Num	Avg	TB	TD	NetAvg
Total	8	4-4	3-4	1-1	1-3	9-12	75.0	51	32	60.6	0	0	37.8
vs. Playoff	4	3-3	2-3	1-1	1-1	7-8	87.5	51	15	62.9	0	0	38.9
vs. Non-playoff	4	1-1	1-1	0-0	0-2	2-4	50.0	32	17	58.5	0	0	36.8
vs. Own Division	4	0-0	1-1	0-0	0-1	1-2	50.0	32	13	60.5	0	0	42.9
Home	4	4-4	2-3	1-1	1-2	8-10	80.0	51	20	59.7	0	0	36.0
Away	4	0-0	1-1	0-0	0-1	1-2	50.0	32	12	62.0	0	0	40.8
Games 1-8	0	0-0	0-0	0-0	0-0	0-0	-	0	0	-	0	0	-
Games 9-16	8	4-4	3-4	1-1	1-3	9-12	75.0	51	32	60.6	0	0	37.8
September	0	0-0	0-0	0-0	0-0	0-0	-	0	0	-	0	0	-
October	0	0-0	0-0	0-0	0-0	0-0	-	0	0	-	0	0	-
November	4	0-0	1-1	0-0	0-1	1-2	50.0	32	13	60.5	0	0	42.9
December	4	4-4	2-3	1-1	1-2	8-10	80.0	51	19	60.6	0	0	34.3
Grass	1	0-0	0-0	0-0	0-0	0-0	-	0	3	61.7	0	0	43.7
Turf	7	4-4	3-4	1-1	1-3	9-12	75.0	51	29	60.4	0	0	37.2
Indoor	6	4-4	3-4	1-1	1-3	9-12	75.0	51	25	60.3	0	0	37.9
Outdoor	2	0-0	0-0	0-0	0-0	0-0	-	0	7	61.6	0	0	37.4
4th qtr, +/-3 pts	-	0-0	0-0	0-0	0-0	0-0	-	0	0	-	0	0	-
Winning	-	0-0	0-0	0-0	0-0	0-0	-	0	14	61.4	0	0	37.0
Tied	-	2-2	0-0	1-1	0-0	3-3	100.0	42	5	64.8	0	0	45.4
Trailing	-	2-2	3-4	0-0	1-1	6-9	66.7	51	13	58.1	0	0	35.7

Game Logs

Date	Opp	Result	1-39 Yd	40-49 Yd	50+ Yd	Lg
11/05	@NO	L 10-19	1-1	0-0	0-1	32
11/12	Car	W 28-17	0-0	0-0	0-0	0
11/19	@Atl	L 6-31	0-0	0-0	0-0	0
11/26	@SF	L 13-41	0-0	0-0	0-0	0
12/03	@NYA	W 23-20	0-0	0-0	0-0	0
12/10	Buf	L 27-45	3-3	0-0	1-1	51
12/17	Was	L 23-35	1-1	0-0	0-1	25
12/24	Mia	L 22-41	2-3	1-1	0-0	42

Cary Blanchard
Indianapolis Colts — K

1995 Field Goal Splits / 1995 Kickoff Splits

	G	1-29 Yd	30-39 Yd	40-49 Yd	50+ Yd	Overall	Pct	Lg	Num	Avg	TB	TD	NetAvg
Total	12	5-5	6-8	7-10	1-1	19-24	79.2	50	1	54.0	0	0	36.0
vs. Playoff	5	3-3	4-5	4-4	1-1	12-13	92.3	50	0	-	0	0	-
vs. Non-playoff	7	2-2	2-3	3-6	0-0	7-11	63.6	47	1	54.0	0	0	36.0
vs. Own Division	6	3-3	4-5	1-2	0-0	8-10	80.0	46	0	-	0	0	-
Home	6	1-1	5-7	5-6	1-1	12-15	80.0	50	0	-	0	0	-
Away	6	4-4	1-1	2-4	0-0	7-9	77.8	47	1	54.0	0	0	36.0
Games 1-8	4	3-3	1-1	4-4	0-0	8-8	100.0	46	0	-	0	0	-
Games 9-16	8	2-2	5-7	3-6	1-1	11-16	68.8	50	1	54.0	0	0	36.0
September	0	0-0	0-0	0-0	0-0	0-0	-	0	0	-	0	0	-
October	4	3-3	1-1	4-4	0-0	8-8	100.0	46	0	-	0	0	-
November	4	1-1	3-3	0-2	0-0	4-6	66.7	37	0	-	0	0	-
December	4	1-1	2-4	3-4	1-1	7-10	70.0	50	1	54.0	0	0	36.0
Grass	5	4-4	1-1	2-2	0-0	7-7	100.0	47	1	54.0	0	0	36.0
Turf	7	1-1	5-7	5-8	1-1	12-17	70.6	50	0	-	0	0	-
Indoor	7	1-1	5-7	5-8	1-1	12-17	70.6	50	0	-	0	0	-
Outdoor	5	4-4	1-1	2-2	0-0	7-7	100.0	47	1	54.0	0	0	36.0
4th qtr, +/-3 pts	-	0-0	1-2	1-2	1-1	3-5	60.0	50	0	-	0	0	-
Winning	-	2-2	2-2	2-2	0-0	6-6	100.0	47	1	54.0	0	0	36.0
Tied	-	2-2	3-4	0-2	0-0	5-8	62.5	36	0	-	0	0	-
Trailing	-	1-1	1-2	5-6	1-1	8-10	80.0	50	0	-	0	0	-

Game Logs

Date	Opp	Result	1-39 Yd	40-49 Yd	50+ Yd	Lg
10/08	@Mia	W 27-24	2-2	0-0	0-0	27
10/15	SF	W 18-17	1-1	3-3	0-0	46
10/22	@Oak	L 17-30	1-1	0-0	0-0	25
10/29	NYA	W 17-10	0-0	1-1	0-0	46
11/05	Buf	L 16-13	1-1	0-0	0-0	37
11/12	@NO	L 14-17	0-0	0-2	0-0	0
11/19	@NE	W 24-10	1-1	0-0	0-0	36
11/26	Mia	W 36-28	2-2	0-0	0-0	31
12/03	@Car	L 10-13	0-0	1-1	0-0	47
12/10	@Jac	W 41-31	1-1	1-1	0-0	44
12/17	SD	L 24-27	1-2	1-1	1-1	50
12/23	NE	W 10-7	1-2	0-1	0-0	30

Chris Boniol
Dallas Cowboys — K

	G	|| 1995 Field Goal Splits							|| 1995 Kickoff Splits					|| Game Logs						
	G	1-29 Yd	30-39 Yd	40-49 Yd	50+ Yd	Overall	Pct	Lg	Num	Avg	TB	TD	NetAvg	Date	Opp	Result	1-39 Yd	40-49 Yd	50+ Yd	Lg
Total	16	11-12	13-13	3-3	0-0	27-28	96.4	45	73	62.5	3	0	42.9	09/04	@NYN	W 35-0	0-0	0-0	0-0	0
vs. Playoff	7	4-4	4-4	1-1	0-0	9-9	100.0	42	37	62.2	1	0	43.3	09/10	Den	W 31-21	0-0	1-1	0-0	45
vs. Non-playoff	9	7-8	9-9	2-2	0-0	18-19	94.7	45	36	62.7	2	0	42.4	09/17	@Min	W 23-17	1-2	0-0	0-0	39
vs. Own Division	8	7-7	8-8	2-2	0-0	17-17	100.0	45	40	62.8	1	0	41.7	09/24	Ari	W 34-20	2-2	0-0	0-0	30
Home	8	6-6	7-7	3-3	0-0	16-16	100.0	45	38	63.7	2	0	44.1	10/01	@Was	L 23-27	3-3	0-0	0-0	34
Away	8	5-6	6-6	0-0	0-0	11-12	91.7	39	35	61.2	1	0	41.5	10/08	GB	W 34-24	2-2	0-0	0-0	35
Games 1-8	8	3-4	6-6	1-1	0-0	10-11	90.9	45	30	62.9	1	0	42.8	10/15	@SD	W 23-9	1-1	0-0	0-0	30
Games 9-16	8	8-8	7-7	2-2	0-0	17-17	100.0	45	43	62.1	2	0	42.9	10/29	@Atl	W 28-13	0-0	0-0	0-0	0
September	4	1-2	2-2	1-1	0-0	4-5	80.0	45	7	66.4	0	0	45.1	11/06	Phi	W 34-12	1-1	1-1	0-0	42
October	4	2-2	4-4	0-0	0-0	6-6	100.0	35	23	61.9	1	0	42.1	11/12	SF	L 20-38	2-2	0-0	0-0	37
November	4	3-3	3-3	1-1	0-0	7-7	100.0	45	23	62.7	1	0	44.7	11/19	@Oak	W 34-21	2-2	0-0	0-0	38
December	4	5-5	4-4	1-1	0-0	10-10	100.0	45	20	61.5	1	0	40.8	11/23	KC	W 24-12	1-1	0-0	0-0	20
Grass	4	4-4	5-5	0-0	0-0	9-9	100.0	39	26	61.6	1	0	43.2	12/03	Was	L 17-24	1-1	0-0	0-0	37
Turf	12	7-8	8-8	3-3	0-0	18-19	94.7	45	47	62.9	2	0	42.7	12/10	@Phi	L 17-20	1-1	0-0	0-0	21
Indoor	2	0-1	1-1	0-0	0-0	1-2	50.0	39	5	59.4	0	0	38.2	12/17	NYN	W 21-20	4-4	1-1	0-0	45
Outdoor	14	11-11	12-12	3-3	0-0	26-26	100.0	45	68	62.7	3	0	43.2	12/25	@Ari	W 37-13	3-3	0-0	0-0	39
4th qtr, +/-3 pts	-	0-0	1-1	0-0	0-0	1-1	100.0	35	1	64.0	0	0	42.0							
Winning	-	7-7	6-6	2-2	0-0	15-15	100.0	45	56	62.0	1	0	42.3							
Tied	-	1-1	2-2	0-0	0-0	3-3	100.0	37	7	67.6	2	0	47.9							
Trailing	-	3-4	5-5	1-1	0-0	9-10	90.0	45	10	61.7	0	0	42.5							

Doug Brien
San Francisco 49ers / New Orleans Saints — K

	G	1-29 Yd	30-39 Yd	40-49 Yd	50+ Yd	Overall	Pct	Lg	Num	Avg	TB	TD	NetAvg	Date	Opp	Result	1-39 Yd	40-49 Yd	50+ Yd	Lg
Total	14	8-8	4-7	6-12	1-2	19-29	65.5	51	70	60.8	3	0	40.3	09/03	@NO	W 24-22	1-2	0-0	0-0	28
vs. Playoff	6	3-3	0-0	2-7	1-1	6-11	54.5	51	28	60.8	1	0	40.2	09/10	Atl	W 41-10	1-1	1-2	0-0	45
vs. Non-playoff	8	5-5	4-7	4-5	0-1	13-18	72.2	47	42	60.7	2	0	40.4	09/17	NE	W 28-3	0-0	0-0	0-0	0
vs. Own Division	5	3-3	2-4	4-5	0-0	9-12	75.0	47	29	62.3	0	0	42.6	09/25	@Det	L 24-27	1-1	0-2	0-0	23
Home	7	4-4	2-3	6-8	0-0	12-15	80.0	47	39	60.3	1	0	40.8	10/01	NYN	W 20-6	1-1	1-1	0-0	46
Away	7	4-4	2-4	0-4	1-2	7-14	50.0	51	31	61.4	2	0	39.7	10/15	@Ind	L 17-18	0-0	0-1	1-1	51
Games 1-8	6	4-4	0-1	2-6	1-1	7-12	58.3	51	32	62.8	2	0	42.3	11/05	StL	W 19-10	2-2	2-2	0-0	47
Games 9-16	8	4-4	4-6	4-6	0-1	12-17	70.6	47	38	59.1	1	0	38.7	11/12	Ind	W 17-14	1-1	0-0	0-0	25
September	4	3-3	0-1	1-4	0-0	4-8	50.0	45	23	62.7	1	0	41.3	11/19	@Min	L 24-43	1-1	0-1	0-0	30
October	2	1-1	0-0	1-2	1-1	3-4	75.0	51	9	62.8	1	0	44.8	11/26	Car	W 34-26	1-2	0-0	0-0	45
November	4	2-2	3-4	3-4	0-0	8-10	80.0	47	20	62.1	0	0	43.2	12/03	@NE	W 31-17	1-1	0-0	0-0	24
December	4	2-2	1-2	1-2	0-1	4-7	57.1	43	18	55.7	1	0	33.7	12/10	@Atl	L 14-19	0-0	0-0	0-0	0
Grass	4	3-3	0-0	2-3	0-0	5-6	83.3	46	24	59.5	1	0	38.0	12/16	GB	L 23-34	0-0	1-2	0-0	43
Turf	10	5-5	4-7	4-9	1-2	14-23	60.9	51	46	61.4	2	0	41.6	12/24	@NYA	W 12-0	2-3	0-0	0-1	32
Indoor	9	4-4	3-5	4-9	1-1	12-19	63.2	51	41	61.9	1	0	41.3							
Outdoor	5	4-4	1-2	2-3	0-1	7-10	70.0	46	29	59.1	2	0	38.9							
4th qtr, +/-3 pts	-	1-1	0-0	1-3	1-1	3-5	60.0	51	4	64.3	0	0	36.3							
Winning	-	4-4	1-3	5-6	0-1	10-14	71.4	47	46	60.5	2	0	40.3							
Tied	-	2-2	2-3	0-1	0-0	4-6	66.7	35	15	64.9	1	0	44.5							
Trailing	-	2-2	1-1	1-5	1-1	5-9	55.6	51	9	55.4	0	0	33.4							

Kevin Butler
Chicago Bears — K

	G	1-29 Yd	30-39 Yd	40-49 Yd	50+ Yd	Overall	Pct	Lg	Num	Avg	TB	TD	NetAvg	Date	Opp	Result	1-39 Yd	40-49 Yd	50+ Yd	Lg
Total	16	16-19	5-6	2-4	0-2	23-31	74.2	47	17	57.6	1	0	35.2	09/03	Min	W 31-14	1-1	0-0	0-0	21
vs. Playoff	6	4-5	1-2	1-3	0-2	6-12	50.0	40	8	57.6	0	0	32.6	09/11	GB	L 24-27	1-1	0-0	0-0	20
vs. Non-playoff	10	12-14	4-4	1-1	0-0	17-19	89.5	47	9	57.7	1	0	37.6	09/17	@TB	W 25-6	4-4	0-0	0-0	37
vs. Own Division	8	6-8	2-2	0-0	0-0	8-12	66.7	39	5	57.8	0	0	28.6	09/24	@StL	L 28-34	0-0	0-0	0-0	0
Home	8	9-11	2-3	2-4	0-1	13-19	68.4	47	11	58.3	1	0	38.2	10/08	Car	W 31-27	1-1	0-0	0-0	23
Away	8	7-8	3-3	0-0	0-1	10-12	83.3	37	6	56.5	0	0	29.8	10/15	@Jac	W 30-27	3-3	0-0	0-0	25
Games 1-8	8	11-11	2-2	1-1	0-0	14-14	100.0	47	8	58.6	1	0	37.8	10/22	Hou	W 35-32	3-3	1-1	0-0	47
Games 9-16	8	5-8	3-4	1-3	0-2	9-17	52.9	40	9	56.8	0	0	33.0	10/30	@Min	W 14-6	0-0	0-0	0-0	0
September	4	5-5	1-1	0-0	0-0	6-6	100.0	37	0		0	0		11/05	Pit	L 34-37	1-1	1-2	0-0	40
October	4	6-6	1-1	1-1	0-0	8-8	100.0	47	8	58.6	1	0	37.8	11/12	@GB	L 28-35	0-0	0-0	0-0	0
November	4	1-3	3-3	1-2	0-1	5-9	55.6	40	9	56.8	0	0	33.0	11/19	Det	L 17-24	1-2	0-0	0-1	39
December	4	4-5	0-1	0-1	0-1	4-8	50.0	28	0		0	0		11/26	@NYN	W 27-24	2-3	0-0	0-0	37
Grass	11	15-17	3-4	2-4	0-1	20-26	76.9	47	14	59.1	1	0	36.5	12/04	@Det	L 7-27	0-0	0-0	0-1	0
Turf	5	1-2	2-2	0-0	0-1	3-5	60.0	37	3	50.7	0	0	29.3	12/10	@Cin	L 10-16	1-1	0-0	0-0	27
Indoor	2	0-0	0-0	0-0	0-1	0-1	0.0	0	2	51.0	0	0	26.0	12/17	TB	W 31-10	1-2	0-0	0-0	23
Outdoor	14	16-19	5-6	2-4	0-1	23-30	76.7	47	15	58.5	1	0	36.5	12/24	Phi	W 20-14	2-3	0-1	0-0	28
4th qtr, +/-3 pts	-	1-1	1-1	0-0	0-1	2-3	66.7	37	1	50.0	0	0	36.0							
Winning	-	10-11	1-2	1-3	0-0	12-16	75.0	47	13	57.5	1	0	34.0							
Tied	-	4-6	2-2	1-1	0-1	7-10	70.0	40	3	59.0	0	0	39.7							
Trailing	-	2-2	2-2	0-0	0-1	4-5	80.0	39	1	56.0	0	0	38.0							

Rich Camarillo
Houston Oilers — P

1995 Punter Splits

	G	NPunts	Avg	Lg	In20	FC	TPunts	TB	Blk	Ret	Yds	NetAvg
Total	16	77	41.1	60	26	16	78	8	1	35	288	34.8
vs. Playoff	5	33	40.3	60	9	4	33	2	0	17	172	33.9
vs. Non-playoff	11	44	41.7	58	17	12	45	6	1	18	116	35.5
vs. Own Division	8	43	40.0	58	14	6	44	7	1	19	176	31.9
Home	8	30	41.7	56	10	9	31	2	1	12	185	33.1
Away	8	47	40.7	60	16	7	47	6	0	23	103	36.0
September	4	22	40.5	58	6	4	22	5	0	7	97	31.6
October	4	14	42.6	55	6	5	14	0	0	8	60	38.4
November	4	14	41.1	49	6	2	15	0	1	7	9	37.7
December	4	27	40.8	60	8	5	27	3	0	13	122	34.0
Grass	4	20	43.7	58	8	3	20	2	0	10	46	39.4
Turf	12	57	40.2	60	18	13	58	6	1	25	242	33.3
Indoor	9	35	41.4	56	13	12	36	2	1	14	189	33.9
Outdoor	7	42	40.8	60	13	4	42	6	0	21	99	35.6
Outdoors, Temp < 40	2	9	42.4	60	2	0	9	0	0	5	11	41.2
Outdoors, Temp 40-80	5	33	40.4	58	11	4	33	6	0	16	88	34.1
Outdoors, Temp > 80	0	0	-	0	0	0	0	0	0	0	0	-
Winning	-	27	42.7	58	9	5	27	4	0	11	67	37.3
Tied	-	16	40.5	60	5	2	16	1	0	7	86	33.9
Trailing	-	34	40.1	55	12	9	35	3	1	17	135	33.4

Game Logs

Date	Opp	Result	NPunts	Avg	In20	TPunts	TB	Blk	Ret	Yds	NetAvg
09/03	@Jac	W 10-3	9	44.4	5	9	2	0	2	16	38.2
09/10	Pit	L 17-34	5	42.6	0	5	0	0	3	83	26.0
09/17	Cle	L 7-14	4	36.0	1	4	1	0	0	0	31.0
09/24	@Cin	W 38-28	4	33.8	0	4	2	0	2	-2	24.3
10/01	Jac	L 16-17	4	44.8	2	4	0	0	3	29	37.5
10/08	@Min	L 17-23	5	39.8	3	5	0	0	2	4	39.0
10/22	@Chi	L 32-35	3	45.0	1	3	0	0	2	21	38.0
10/29	TB	W 19-7	2	42.0	0	2	0	0	1	6	39.0
11/05	@Cle	W 37-10	2	42.5	0	2	0	0	2	3	41.0
11/12	Cin	L 25-32	4	38.8	3	5	0	1	1	0	31.0
11/19	@KC	L 13-20	6	42.3	2	6	0	0	4	6	41.3
11/26	Den	W 42-33	2	40.5	1	2	0	0	0	0	40.5
12/03	@Pit	L 7-21	11	37.2	3	11	2	0	6	47	29.3
12/10	Det	L 17-24	4	39.3	2	4	0	0	1	28	32.3
12/17	NYA	W 23-6	5	47.6	1	5	1	0	3	39	35.8
12/24	@Buf	W 28-17	7	42.4	2	7	0	0	3	8	41.3

John Carney
San Diego Chargers — K

1995 Field Goal Splits / 1995 Kickoff Splits

	G	1-29 Yd	30-39 Yd	40-49 Yd	50+ Yd	Overall	Pct	Lg	Num	Avg	TB	TD	NetAvg
Total	16	8-8	10-11	3-5	0-2	21-26	80.8	45	74	65.3	9	0	41.9
vs. Playoff	7	4-4	5-6	1-2	0-1	10-13	76.9	45	30	66.0	5	0	43.4
vs. Non-playoff	9	4-4	5-5	2-3	0-1	11-13	84.6	45	44	64.9	4	0	40.9
vs. Own Division	8	6-6	4-4	1-3	0-1	11-14	78.6	45	35	65.7	4	0	41.7
Home	8	2-2	5-5	1-2	0-1	8-10	80.0	45	31	64.7	4	0	43.4
Away	8	6-6	5-6	2-3	0-1	13-16	81.3	45	43	65.8	5	0	40.9
Games 1-8	8	5-5	2-2	1-2	0-0	8-9	88.9	45	34	65.7	3	0	43.4
Games 9-16	8	3-3	8-9	2-3	0-1	13-17	76.5	45	40	65.1	6	0	40.7
September	4	1-1	1-1	1-2	0-0	3-4	75.0	45	15	65.9	2	0	44.7
October	4	4-4	1-1	0-0	0-0	5-5	100.0	36	19	65.5	1	0	42.3
November	4	3-3	5-5	0-1	0-1	8-10	80.0	39	17	67.4	5	0	39.2
December	4	0-0	3-4	2-2	0-1	5-7	71.4	45	23	63.3	1	0	41.7
Grass	11	5-5	7-7	1-3	0-1	13-16	81.3	45	45	65.3	6	0	42.3
Turf	5	3-3	3-4	2-2	0-1	8-10	80.0	45	29	65.4	3	0	41.2
Indoor	2	1-1	1-2	1-1	0-1	3-5	60.0	43	13	66.5	1	0	42.1
Outdoor	14	7-7	9-9	2-4	0-1	18-21	85.7	45	61	65.1	8	0	41.9
4th qtr, +/-3 pts	-	0-0	2-2	1-1	0-0	3-3	100.0	43	4	62.3	1	0	38.8
Winning	-	4-4	2-2	2-2	0-2	8-10	80.0	45	40	65.4	4	0	43.2
Tied	-	2-2	2-2	1-1	0-0	5-5	100.0	43	16	62.4	1	0	36.8
Trailing	-	2-2	6-7	0-2	0-0	8-11	72.7	39	18	67.9	4	0	43.5

Game Logs

Date	Opp	Result	1-39 Yd	40-49 Yd	50+ Yd	Lg
09/03	@Oak	L 7-17	0-0	0-1	0-0	0
09/10	Sea	W 14-10	0-0	0-0	0-0	0
09/17	@Phi	W 27-21	2-2	0-0	0-0	35
09/24	Den	W 17-6	0-0	1-1	0-0	45
10/01	@Pit	L 16-31	1-1	0-0	0-0	28
10/09	@KC	L 23-29	3-3	0-0	0-0	36
10/15	Dal	L 9-23	0-0	0-0	0-0	0
10/22	@Sea	W 35-25	1-1	0-0	0-0	25
11/05	Mia	L 14-24	2-2	0-0	0-0	39
11/12	KC	L 7-22	0-0	0-0	0-0	0
11/19	@Den	L 27-30	2-2	0-0	0-0	32
11/27	Oak	W 12-6	4-4	0-0	0-1	39
12/03	Cle	W 31-13	1-1	0-0	0-0	31
12/09	Ari	W 28-25	0-0	0-0	0-0	0
12/17	@Ind	W 27-24	1-2	1-1	0-1	43
12/23	@NYN	W 27-17	1-1	1-1	0-0	45

Steve Christie
Buffalo Bills — K

1995 Field Goal Splits / 1995 Kickoff Splits

	G	1-29 Yd	30-39 Yd	40-49 Yd	50+ Yd	Overall	Pct	Lg	Num	Avg	TB	TD	NetAvg
Total	16	13-14	13-15	3-6	2-5	31-40	77.5	51	82	63.2	9	0	41.0
vs. Playoff	6	7-7	7-8	0-0	0-1	14-16	87.5	39	29	63.6	3	0	39.7
vs. Non-playoff	10	6-7	6-7	3-6	2-4	17-24	70.8	51	53	63.0	6	0	41.8
vs. Own Division	8	8-8	8-10	1-4	2-3	19-25	76.0	51	42	63.9	4	0	43.3
Home	8	8-8	6-6	3-4	2-3	19-21	90.5	51	45	61.3	4	0	40.9
Away	8	5-6	7-9	0-2	0-2	12-19	63.2	39	37	65.6	5	0	41.2
Games 1-8	8	5-6	10-10	1-3	1-2	17-21	81.0	51	40	63.6	9	0	43.9
Games 9-16	8	8-8	3-5	2-3	1-3	14-19	73.7	51	42	62.9	0	0	38.3
September	3	0-0	3-3	0-0	0-0	3-3	100.0	39	13	66.8	1	0	44.6
October	5	5-6	7-7	1-3	1-2	14-18	77.8	51	27	62.0	4	0	43.5
November	4	3-3	3-5	1-2	1-2	8-12	66.7	51	22	62.4	0	0	38.6
December	4	5-5	0-0	1-1	0-1	6-7	85.7	44	20	61.1	4	0	38.1
Grass	5	3-4	5-5	0-1	0-0	8-10	80.0	38	19	65.1	5	0	42.2
Turf	11	10-10	8-10	3-5	2-5	23-30	76.7	51	63	62.7	4	0	40.7
Indoor	2	2-2	2-3	0-0	0-2	4-5	80.0	42	13	68.8	0	0	42.0
Outdoor	14	11-12	11-12	3-6	2-3	27-33	81.8	51	69	62.2	9	0	40.8
4th qtr, +/-3 pts	-	2-3	2-2	0-0	0-0	4-5	80.0	38	4	57.3	1	0	37.3
Winning	-	7-7	4-6	0-2	1-3	12-18	66.7	51	56	62.6	4	0	40.7
Tied	-	3-3	7-7	1-1	1-2	12-13	92.3	51	16	66.0	3	0	42.9
Trailing	-	3-4	2-2	2-3	0-0	7-9	77.8	48	10	62.1	2	0	40.0

Game Logs

Date	Opp	Result	1-39 Yd	40-49 Yd	50+ Yd	Lg
09/03	@Den	L 7-22	0-0	0-0	0-0	0
09/10	Car	W 31-9	1-1	0-0	0-0	39
09/17	Ind	W 20-14	2-2	0-0	0-0	38
10/02	@Cle	W 22-19	3-4	0-0	0-0	38
10/08	NYA	W 29-10	4-4	0-1	1-1	51
10/15	Sea	W 27-21	1-1	1-1	0-1	43
10/23	@NE	L 14-27	2-2	0-1	0-0	23
10/29	@Mia	L 6-23	2-2	0-0	0-0	32
11/05	@Ind	W 16-10	3-4	0-0	0-1	39
11/12	Atl	W 23-17	3-3	0-0	0-0	38
11/19	@NYA	W 28-26	0-1	0-1	0-0	15
11/26	NE	L 25-35	1-1	0-0	0-0	0
12/03	@SF	L 17-27	1-1	0-0	0-0	23
12/10	@StL	W 45-27	1-1	0-0	0-1	28
12/17	Mia	W 23-20	3-3	0-0	0-0	25
12/24	Hou	L 17-28	0-0	1-1	0-0	44

Mike Cofer
Indianapolis Colts — K

	G	1-29 Yd	30-39 Yd	40-49 Yd	50+ Yd	Overall	Pct	Lg	Num	Avg	TB	TD	NetAvg	Date	Opp	Result	1-39 Yd	40-49 Yd	50+ Yd	Lg
				1995 Field Goal Splits						1995 Kickoff Splits						Game Logs				
Total	4	2-2	0-4	1-2	1-1	4-9	44.4	52	0	-	0	0	-	09/03	Cin	L 21-24	1-1	1-2	0-0	40
vs. Playoff	1	0-0	0-1	0-0	0-0	0-1	0.0	0	0	-	0	0	-	09/10	@NYA	W 27-24	1-3	0-0	1-1	52
vs. Non-playoff	3	2-2	0-3	1-2	1-1	4-8	50.0	52	0	-	0	0	-	09/17	@Buf	L 14-20	0-1	0-0	0-0	0
vs. Own Division	2	1-1	0-3	0-0	1-1	2-5	40.0	52	0	-	0	0	-	10/01	StL	W 21-18	0-1	0-0	0-0	0
Home	2	1-1	0-1	1-2	0-0	2-4	50.0	40	0	-	0	0	-							
Away	2	1-1	0-3	0-0	1-1	2-5	40.0	52	0	-	0	0	-							
Games 1-8	4	2-2	0-4	1-2	1-1	4-9	44.4	52	0	-	0	0	-							
Games 9-16	0	0-0	0-0	0-0	0-0	0-0		0	0	-	0	0	-							
September	3	2-2	0-3	1-2	1-1	4-8	50.0	52	0	-	0	0	-							
October	1	0-0	0-1	0-0	0-0	0-1	0.0	0	0	-	0	0	-							
November	0	0-0	0-0	0-0	0-0	0-0		0	0	-	0	0	-							
December	0	0-0	0-0	0-0	0-0	0-0	-	0	0	-	0	0	-							
Grass	0	0-0	0-0	0-0	0-0	0-0		0	0	-	0	0	-							
Turf	4	2-2	0-4	1-2	1-1	4-9	44.4	52	0	-	0	0	-							
Indoor	2	1-1	0-1	1-2	0-0	2-4	50.0	40	0	-	0	0	-							
Outdoor	2	1-1	0-3	0-0	1-1	2-5	40.0	52	0	-	0	0	-							
4th qtr. +/-3 pts	-	0-0	0-0	0-0	0-0	0-0	-	0	0	-	0	0	-							
Winning	-	0-0	0-0	0-0	0-0	0-0	-	0	0	-	0	0	-							
Tied	-	0-0	0-1	0-0	1-1	1-2	50.0	52	0	-	0	0	-							
Trailing	-	2-2	0-3	1-2	0-0	3-7	42.9	40	0	-	0	0	-							

Brad Daluiso
New York Giants — K

	G	1-29 Yd	30-39 Yd	40-49 Yd	50+ Yd	Overall	Pct	Lg	Num	Avg	TB	TD	NetAvg	Date	Opp	Result	1-39 Yd	40-49 Yd	50+ Yd	Lg
				1995 Field Goal Splits						1995 Kickoff Splits						Game Logs				
Total	16	7-7	9-10	2-9	2-2	20-28	71.4	51	68	64.4	13	0	43.9	09/04	Dal	L 0-35	0-0	0-1	0-0	0
vs. Playoff	8	5-5	5-6	1-5	0-0	11-16	68.8	44	28	63.0	4	0	42.6	09/10	@KC	L 17-20	1-1	0-0	0-0	23
vs. Non-playoff	8	2-2	4-4	1-4	2-2	9-12	75.0	51	40	65.4	9	0	44.7	09/17	@GB	L 6-14	2-2	0-0	0-0	37
vs. Own Division	8	4-4	2-3	2-6	1-1	9-14	64.3	51	33	64.0	6	0	43.7	09/24	NO	W 45-29	0-0	0-0	1-1	51
Home	8	3-3	4-4	1-3	1-1	9-11	81.8	51	35	63.5	9	0	44.9	10/01	@SF	L 6-20	2-2	0-1	0-0	37
Away	8	4-4	5-6	1-6	1-1	11-17	64.7	51	33	65.5	4	0	42.7	10/08	Ari	W 27-21	0-0	0-0	0-0	0
Games 1-8	8	3-3	5-5	0-2	1-1	9-11	81.8	51	33	63.9	7	0	42.7	10/15	Phi	L 14-17	2-2	0-0	0-0	21
Games 9-16	8	4-4	4-5	2-7	1-1	11-17	64.7	51	35	64.9	6	0	44.9	10/29	@Was	W 24-15	1-1	0-0	0-0	31
September	4	1-1	2-2	0-1	1-1	4-5	80.0	51	15	66.6	3	0	41.6	11/05	@Sea	L 28-30	1-1	0-1	0-0	23
October	4	2-2	3-3	0-1	0-0	5-6	83.3	37	18	61.6	4	0	43.6	11/12	Oak	L 13-17	2-2	0-0	0-0	32
November	5	2-2	2-3	1-4	1-1	6-10	60.0	51	21	66.6	5	0	46.7	11/19	@Phi	L 19-28	0-1	1-1	0-0	44
December	3	2-2	2-2	1-3	0-0	5-7	71.4	42	14	62.4	1	0	42.3	11/26	Chi	L 24-27	1-1	0-0	0-0	22
Grass	5	1-1	5-5	0-3	1-1	7-10	70.0	51	18	65.0	2	0	42.2	11/30	@Ari	W 10-6	0-0	0-2	1-1	51
Turf	11	6-6	4-5	2-6	1-1	13-18	72.2	51	50	64.2	11	0	44.4	12/10	Was	W 20-13	1-1	1-1	0-0	42
Indoor	1	1-1	0-0	0-1	0-0	1-2	50.0	23	6	63.3	1	0	42.3	12/17	@Dal	L 20-21	2-2	0-1	0-0	27
Outdoor	15	6-6	9-10	2-8	2-2	19-26	73.1	51	62	64.5	12	0	44.0	12/23	SD	L 17-27	1-1	0-1	0-0	30
4th qtr. +/-3 pts	-	2-2	0-0	0-1	0-0	2-3	66.7	27	5	60.6	1	0	42.4							
Winning	-	2-2	1-1	1-3	1-1	5-7	71.4	51	37	63.7	6	0	43.1							
Tied	-	1-1	3-3	0-1	0-0	4-5	80.0	37	16	68.4	4	0	45.8							
Trailing	-	4-4	5-6	1-5	1-1	11-16	68.8	51	15	62.1	3	0	43.7							

Greg Davis
Arizona Cardinals — K

	G	1-29 Yd	30-39 Yd	40-49 Yd	50+ Yd	Overall	Pct	Lg	Num	Avg	TB	TD	NetAvg	Date	Opp	Result	1-39 Yd	40-49 Yd	50+ Yd	Lg
				1995 Field Goal Splits						1995 Kickoff Splits						Game Logs				
Total	16	14-15	9-10	6-8	1-6	30-39	76.9	55	67	61.8	1	2	37.7	09/03	@Was	L 7-27	0-0	0-0	0-1	0
vs. Playoff	8	10-10	6-7	3-5	1-2	20-24	83.3	55	39	62.5	1	2	37.4	09/10	Phi	L 19-31	2-2	0-0	0-0	29
vs. Non-playoff	8	4-5	3-3	3-3	0-4	10-15	66.7	44	28	60.9	0	0	38.2	09/17	@Det	W 20-17	2-2	1-1	1-1	55
vs. Own Division	8	8-8	6-6	1-2	0-4	15-20	75.0	44	32	62.0	0	1	36.9	09/24	@Dal	L 20-34	2-2	0-0	0-1	31
Home	8	9-10	1-1	5-6	0-0	15-17	88.2	48	37	62.2	1	0	39.7	10/01	KC	L 3-24	0-0	1-1	0-0	48
Away	8	5-5	8-9	1-2	1-6	15-22	68.2	55	30	61.3	0	2	35.3	10/08	@NYN	L 21-27	2-2	0-0	0-2	36
Games 1-8	8	7-8	2-2	2-2	1-5	12-17	70.6	55	30	63.3	0	0	40.7	10/15	Was	W 24-20	1-1	0-0	0-0	24
Games 9-16	8	7-7	7-8	4-6	0-1	18-22	81.8	44	37	60.6	1	2	35.3	10/29	Sea	W 20-14	0-1	0-0	0-0	0
September	4	5-5	1-1	1-1	1-3	8-10	80.0	55	16	64.2	0	0	40.7	11/05	@Den	L 6-38	2-2	0-0	0-1	31
October	4	2-3	1-1	1-1	0-2	4-7	57.1	48	14	62.4	0	0	40.7	11/12	Min	L 24-30	1-1	2-2	0-0	44
November	5	5-5	2-2	4-5	0-1	11-13	84.6	44	23	60.6	1	0	38.5	11/19	@Car	L 7-27	0-0	0-0	0-0	0
December	3	2-2	5-6	0-1	0-0	7-9	77.8	37	14	60.5	0	2	30.1	11/26	Atl	W 40-37	3-3	1-2	0-0	44
Grass	12	10-11	3-4	5-6	0-2	18-23	78.3	48	47	62.4	1	0	38.7	11/30	NYN	L 6-10	1-1	1-1	0-0	44
Turf	4	4-4	6-6	1-2	1-4	12-16	75.0	55	20	60.5	0	1	35.4	12/09	@SD	L 25-28	1-2	0-0	0-0	36
Indoor	1	2-2	0-0	1-1	1-1	4-4	100.0	55	6	62.0	0	0	39.3	12/17	@Phi	L 20-21	4-4	0-1	0-0	37
Outdoor	15	12-13	9-10	5-7	0-5	26-35	74.3	48	61	61.8	1	2	37.6	12/25	Dal	L 13-37	2-2	0-0	0-0	23
4th qtr. +/-3 pts	-	1-1	0-0	0-2	0-1	1-4	25.0	23	4	61.0	0	0	36.5							
Winning	-	2-2	4-4	0-0	0-1	6-7	85.7	37	23	60.4	0	1	36.4							
Tied	-	3-4	1-2	2-3	0-1	6-10	60.0	44	16	63.6	1	1	37.7							
Trailing	-	9-9	4-4	4-5	1-4	18-22	81.8	55	28	61.9	0	0	38.9							

Al Del Greco
Houston Oilers — K

1995 Field Goal Splits / 1995 Kickoff Splits

	G	1-29 Yd	30-39 Yd	40-49 Yd	50+ Yd	Overall	Pct	Lg	Num	Avg	TB	TD	NetAvg
Total	16	6-6	8-8	10-12	3-5	27-31	87.1	53	76	58.6	0	0	39.8
vs. Playoff	5	0-0	2-2	2-2	0-0	4-4	100.0	47	18	58.8	0	0	39.5
vs. Non-playoff	11	6-6	6-6	8-10	3-5	23-27	85.2	53	58	58.6	0	0	39.9
vs. Own Division	8	3-3	4-4	5-6	1-2	13-15	86.7	53	33	59.1	0	0	39.9
Home	8	4-4	4-4	6-7	2-4	16-19	84.2	53	36	59.8	0	0	38.9
Away	8	2-2	4-4	4-5	1-1	11-12	91.7	50	40	57.6	0	0	40.7
Games 1-8	8	4-4	3-3	5-7	2-4	14-18	77.8	53	36	59.3	0	0	42.2
Games 9-16	8	2-2	5-5	5-5	1-1	13-13	100.0	53	40	58.0	0	0	37.7
September	4	1-1	0-0	2-3	0-0	3-4	75.0	43	15	60.9	0	0	42.1
October	4	3-3	3-3	3-4	2-4	11-14	78.6	53	21	58.1	0	0	37.9
November	4	1-1	3-3	3-3	0-0	7-7	100.0	45	22	56.5	0	0	36.1
December	4	1-1	2-2	2-2	1-1	6-6	100.0	53	18	59.9	0	0	39.6
Grass	4	1-1	2-2	2-3	0-0	5-6	83.3	45	19	53.8	0	0	38.8
Turf	12	5-5	6-6	8-9	3-5	22-25	88.0	53	57	60.2	0	0	40.2
Indoor	9	5-5	4-4	7-8	3-5	19-22	86.4	53	42	59.8	0	0	39.1
Outdoor	7	1-1	4-4	3-4	0-0	8-9	88.9	45	34	57.2	0	0	40.7
4th qtr, +/-3 pts	-	0-0	1-1	1-1	0-1	2-3	66.7	44	3	57.0	0	0	42.0
Winning	-	2-2	5-5	3-3	1-2	11-12	91.7	53	45	59.7	0	0	40.8
Tied	-	2-2	0-0	1-1	1-1	4-4	100.0	50	11	57.5	0	0	37.6
Trailing	-	2-2	3-3	6-8	1-2	12-15	80.0	53	20	56.9	0	0	38.9

Game Logs

Date	Opp	Result	1-39 Yd	40-49 Yd	50+ Yd	Lg
09/03	@Jac	W 10-3	1-1	0-0	0-0	19
09/10	Pit	L 17-34	0-0	1-1	0-0	43
09/17	Cle	L 7-14	0-0	0-1	0-0	0
09/24	@Cin	W 38-28	0-0	1-1	0-0	41
10/01	Jac	L 16-17	2-2	0-0	1-2	53
10/08	@Min	L 17-23	1-1	1-1	1-1	50
10/22	@Chi	L 32-35	1-1	0-1	0-0	39
10/29	TB	W 19-7	2-2	2-2	0-1	45
11/05	@Cle	W 37-10	1-1	2-2	0-0	45
11/12	Cin	L 25-32	3-3	1-1	0-0	40
11/19	@KC	L 13-20	0-0	0-0	0-0	0
11/26	Den	W 42-33	0-0	0-0	0-0	0
12/03	@Pit	L 7-21	0-0	0-0	0-0	0
12/10	Det	L 17-24	0-0	0-1	0-0	47
12/17	NYA	W 23-6	1-1	1-1	1-1	53
12/24	@Buf	W 28-17	2-2	0-0	0-0	39

Jason Elam
Denver Broncos — K

1995 Field Goal Splits / 1995 Kickoff Splits

	G	1-29 Yd	30-39 Yd	40-49 Yd	50+ Yd	Overall	Pct	Lg	Num	Avg	TB	TD	NetAvg
Total	16	7-9	14-15	5-7	5-7	31-38	81.6	56	85	62.9	8	2	41.3
vs. Playoff	7	4-4	4-5	3-4	2-2	13-15	86.7	52	29	59.4	0	1	37.9
vs. Non-playoff	9	3-5	10-10	2-3	3-5	18-23	78.3	56	56	64.6	8	1	43.1
vs. Own Division	8	4-6	8-8	3-4	1-3	16-21	76.2	52	37	62.5	6	1	41.6
Home	8	5-5	9-10	1-2	2-3	17-20	85.0	53	48	65.8	8	2	41.1
Away	8	2-4	5-5	4-5	3-4	14-18	77.8	56	37	59.0	0	0	41.5
Games 1-8	8	4-5	9-10	0-0	3-4	16-19	84.2	52	39	62.8	5	0	40.6
Games 9-16	8	3-4	5-5	5-7	2-3	15-19	78.9	56	46	62.9	3	2	41.9
September	4	4-4	2-3	0-0	2-2	8-9	88.9	52	19	63.5	1	0	40.3
October	4	0-1	7-7	0-0	1-2	8-10	80.0	51	20	62.2	4	0	41.0
November	4	1-1	3-3	2-4	2-2	8-10	80.0	56	25	63.2	1	1	42.2
December	4	2-3	2-2	3-3	0-1	7-9	77.8	49	21	62.6	2	1	41.5
Grass	12	7-8	12-13	3-4	4-5	26-30	86.7	53	68	63.5	8	2	41.1
Turf	4	0-1	2-2	2-3	1-2	5-8	62.5	56	17	60.5	0	0	42.3
Indoor	2	0-1	2-2	0-1	1-2	3-6	50.0	56	10	62.5	0	0	43.7
Outdoor	14	7-8	12-13	5-6	4-5	28-32	87.5	53	75	62.9	8	2	41.0
4th qtr, +/-3 pts	-	0-0	2-2	0-0	0-0	2-2	100.0	37	3	53.3	0	0	40.7
Winning	-	2-2	9-10	1-2	2-3	14-17	82.4	53	56	64.4	8	2	41.1
Tied	-	3-4	3-3	1-1	1-1	8-9	88.9	56	10	59.8	0	0	42.7
Trailing	-	2-3	2-2	3-4	2-3	9-12	75.0	52	19	59.9	0	0	41.2

Game Logs

Date	Opp	Result	1-39 Yd	40-49 Yd	50+ Yd	Lg
09/03	Buf	W 22-7	4-5	0-0	1-1	52
09/10	@Dal	L 21-31	0-0	0-0	0-0	0
09/17	Was	W 38-31	1-1	0-0	0-0	20
09/24	@SD	L 6-17	1-1	0-0	1-1	52
10/01	@Sea	L 10-27	1-2	0-0	0-1	30
10/08	@NE	W 37-3	2-2	0-0	1-1	51
10/16	Oak	W 27-0	4-4	0-0	0-0	37
10/22	KC	L 7-21	0-0	0-0	0-0	0
11/05	Ari	W 38-6	0-0	0-0	1-1	53
11/12	@Phi	L 13-31	0-0	2-2	0-0	48
11/19	SD	W 30-27	3-3	0-1	0-0	35
11/26	@Hou	L 33-42	1-1	0-1	1-1	56
12/03	Jac	W 31-23	1-1	0-0	0-0	38
12/10	Sea	L 27-31	1-1	0-0	0-1	46
12/17	@KC	L 17-20	0-0	1-1	0-0	49
12/24	@Oak	W 31-28	2-3	1-1	0-0	45

Lin Elliott
Kansas City Chiefs — K

1995 Field Goal Splits / 1995 Kickoff Splits

	G	1-29 Yd	30-39 Yd	40-49 Yd	50+ Yd	Overall	Pct	Lg	Num	Avg	TB	TD	NetAvg
Total	16	10-11	7-9	7-10	0-0	24-30	80.0	49	78	62.4	6	0	41.9
vs. Playoff	4	2-2	3-3	3-4	0-0	8-9	88.9	49	19	61.8	2	0	39.7
vs. Non-playoff	12	8-9	4-6	4-6	0-0	16-21	76.2	49	59	62.5	4	0	42.7
vs. Own Division	8	5-6	4-6	5-6	0-0	14-18	77.8	49	44	62.5	4	0	41.4
Home	8	8-9	3-4	3-3	0-0	14-16	87.5	49	42	62.2	2	0	41.4
Away	8	2-2	4-5	4-7	0-0	10-14	71.4	49	36	62.5	4	0	42.6
Games 1-8	8	6-7	1-2	4-5	0-0	11-14	78.6	49	39	64.1	3	0	42.1
Games 9-16	8	4-4	6-7	3-5	0-0	13-16	81.3	48	39	60.6	3	0	41.8
September	4	2-3	1-1	3-4	0-0	6-8	75.0	49	17	65.5	1	0	43.5
October	4	4-4	0-1	1-1	0-0	5-6	83.3	49	22	63.0	2	0	41.0
November	4	1-1	4-4	3-3	0-0	8-8	100.0	48	20	61.0	3	0	42.7
December	4	3-3	2-3	0-2	0-0	5-8	62.5	37	19	60.3	0	0	40.9
Grass	14	10-11	5-7	5-8	0-0	20-26	76.9	49	68	62.2	5	0	42.4
Turf	2	0-0	2-2	2-2	0-0	4-4	100.0	49	10	63.3	1	0	39.2
Indoor	1	0-0	0-0	2-2	0-0	2-2	100.0	49	6	66.3	1	0	44.0
Outdoor	15	10-11	7-9	5-8	0-0	22-28	78.6	49	72	62.0	5	0	41.8
4th qtr, +/-3 pts	-	0-1	1-1	1-1	0-0	2-3	66.7	49	5	63.8	0	0	39.6
Winning	-	5-5	4-5	3-4	0-0	12-14	85.7	49	49	61.5	5	0	42.4
Tied	-	2-3	0-1	3-3	0-0	5-7	71.4	49	16	64.9	1	0	40.1
Trailing	-	3-3	3-3	1-3	0-0	7-9	77.8	42	13	62.6	0	0	42.5

Game Logs

Date	Opp	Result	1-39 Yd	40-49 Yd	50+ Yd	Lg
09/03	@Sea	W 34-10	0-0	2-2	0-0	49
09/10	NYN	W 20-17	1-1	1-1	0-0	42
09/17	Oak	W 23-17	1-2	0-0	0-0	35
09/24	@Cle	L 17-35	1-1	0-1	0-0	25
10/01	Ari	W 24-3	1-1	0-0	0-0	28
10/09	SD	W 29-23	2-2	0-1	0-0	49
10/15	NE	W 31-26	1-1	0-0	0-0	27
10/22	@Den	W 21-7	0-1	0-0	0-0	0
11/05	Was	W 24-3	1-1	0-0	0-0	38
11/12	@SD	W 22-7	1-1	2-2	0-0	48
11/19	Hou	W 20-13	1-1	1-1	0-0	47
11/23	@Dal	L 12-24	2-2	0-0	0-0	37
12/03	@Oak	W 29-23	1-1	0-1	0-0	35
12/11	@Mia	L 6-13	0-0	0-1	0-0	0
12/17	Den	W 20-17	0-1	0-0	0-0	0
12/24	Sea	W 26-3	4-4	0-0	0-0	37

Jeff Feagles
Arizona Cardinals — P

	G	NPunts	Avg	Lg	In20	FC	TPunts	TB	Blk	Ret	Yds	NetAvg
Total	16	72	43.8	60	20	14	72	8	0	32	242	38.2
vs. Playoff	8	36	43.3	59	9	10	36	2	0	18	111	39.1
vs. Non-playoff	8	36	44.3	60	11	4	36	6	0	14	131	37.3
vs. Own Division	8	27	42.9	60	8	7	27	4	0	8	50	38.0
Home	8	33	43.0	60	9	4	33	4	0	15	105	37.4
Away	8	39	44.4	60	11	10	39	4	0	17	137	38.8
September	4	16	44.9	59	1	5	16	1	0	7	67	39.4
October	4	18	42.4	60	8	2	18	4	0	5	24	36.6
November	5	22	45.2	58	5	0	22	2	0	15	119	38.0
December	3	16	42.1	55	6	7	16	1	0	5	32	38.0
Grass	12	57	43.5	60	15	9	57	7	0	26	206	37.5
Turf	4	15	44.6	60	5	5	15	1	0	6	36	40.9
Indoor	1	5	47.8	57	0	2	5	0	0	2	19	44.0
Outdoor	15	67	43.4	60	20	12	67	8	0	30	223	37.7
Outdoors, Temp < 40	1	5	39.4	47	4	2	5	0	0	2	2	39.0
Outdoors, Temp 40-80	9	38	44.9	60	8	6	38	4	0	20	164	38.4
Outdoors, Temp > 80	5	24	42.0	60	8	4	24	4	0	8	57	36.3
Winning	-	13	43.0	52	7	4	13	0	0	5	21	41.4
Tied	-	15	43.5	60	3	2	15	4	0	6	32	36.0
Trailing	-	44	44.1	58	10	8	44	4	0	21	189	38.0

1995 Punter Splits (above) — **Game Logs** (below)

Date	Opp	Result	NPunts	Avg	In20	TPunts	TB	Blk	Ret	Yds	NetAvg
09/03	@Was	L 7-27	5	39.2	1	5	0	0	1	15	36.2
09/10	Phi	L 19-31	3	51.0	0	3	1	0	2	18	38.3
09/17	@Det	W 20-17	5	47.8	0	5	0	0	2	19	44.0
09/24	@Dal	L 20-34	3	43.3	0	3	0	0	2	15	38.3
10/01	KC	L 3-24	5	33.6	2	5	0	0	3	17	30.2
10/08	@NYN	L 21-27	2	51.5	1	2	1	0	0	0	41.5
10/15	Was	W 24-20	3	44.7	1	3	2	0	0	0	31.3
10/29	Sea	W 20-14	8	44.8	4	8	1	0	2	7	41.4
11/05	@Den	L 6-38	4	50.8	1	4	2	0	2	17	36.5
11/12	Min	L 24-30	4	42.5	0	4	0	0	3	53	29.3
11/19	@Car	L 7-27	8	44.0	3	8	0	0	5	39	39.1
11/26	Atl	W 40-37	4	48.3	1	4	0	0	4	10	45.8
11/30	NYN	L 6-10	2	38.5	0	2	0	0	1	0	38.5
12/09	@SD	L 25-28	7	44.3	1	7	1	0	3	30	37.1
12/17	@Phi	L 20-21	5	39.4	4	5	0	0	2	2	39.0
12/25	Dal	L 13-37	4	41.8	1	4	0	0	0	0	41.8

Cole Ford
Oakland Raiders — K

1995 Field Goal Splits — **1995 Kickoff Splits**

	G	1-29 Yd	30-39 Yd	40-49 Yd	50+ Yd	Overall	Pct	Lg	Num	Avg	TB	TD	NetAvg
Total	5	4-4	3-3	1-1	0-1	8-9	88.9	46	32	64.2	3	0	41.7
vs. Playoff	3	1-1	2-2	1-1	0-0	4-4	100.0	46	18	63.2	2	0	43.9
vs. Non-playoff	2	3-3	1-1	0-0	0-1	4-5	80.0	34	14	65.4	1	0	38.9
vs. Own Division	2	0-0	1-1	1-1	0-0	2-2	100.0	46	9	65.1	1	0	42.8
Home	2	1-1	1-1	1-1	0-0	3-3	100.0	46	13	62.6	1	0	44.9
Away	3	3-3	2-2	0-0	0-1	5-6	83.3	34	19	65.2	2	0	39.5
Games 1-8	5	4-4	3-3	1-1	0-1	8-9	88.9	46	32	64.2	3	0	41.7
Games 9-16	0	0-0	0-0	0-0	0-0	0-0	-	0	0	-	0	0	-
September	4	2-2	3-3	1-1	0-1	6-7	85.7	46	23	64.1	2	0	42.5
October	1	2-2	0-0	0-0	0-0	2-2	100.0	29	9	64.2	1	0	39.6
November	0	0-0	0-0	0-0	0-0	0-0	-	0	0	-	0	0	-
December	0	0-0	0-0	0-0	0-0	0-0	-	0	0	-	0	0	-
Grass	4	2-2	3-3	1-1	0-1	6-7	85.7	46	23	64.1	2	0	42.5
Turf	1	2-2	0-0	0-0	0-0	2-2	100.0	29	9	64.2	1	0	39.6
Indoor	0	0-0	0-0	0-0	0-0	0-0	-	0	0	-	0	0	-
Outdoor	5	4-4	3-3	1-1	0-1	8-9	88.9	46	32	64.2	3	0	41.7
4th qtr, +/-3 pts	-	0-0	0-0	0-0	0-0	0-0	-	0	0	-	0	0	-
Winning	-	2-2	1-1	0-0	0-0	3-3	100.0	33	22	65.2	2	0	42.0
Tied	-	2-2	0-0	1-1	0-1	3-4	75.0	46	8	62.3	1	0	41.1
Trailing	-	0-0	2-2	0-0	0-0	2-2	100.0	35	2	60.0	0	0	40.0

Game Logs

Date	Opp	Result	1-39 Yd	40-49 Yd	50+ Yd	Lg
09/03	SD	W 17-7	0-0	1-1	0-0	46
09/10	@Was	W 20-8	2-2	0-0	0-1	34
09/17	@KC	L 17-23	1-1	0-0	0-0	33
09/24	Phi	W 48-17	2-2	0-0	0-0	35
10/01	@NYA	W 47-10	2-2	0-0	0-0	29
10/08	Sea	W 34-14	-	-	-	-
10/16	@Den	L 0-27	-	-	-	-
10/22	Ind	W 30-17	-	-	-	-
11/05	@Cin	W 20-17	-	-	-	-
11/12	@NYN	W 17-13	-	-	-	-
11/19	Dal	L 21-34	-	-	-	-
11/27	@SD	L 6-12	-	-	-	-
12/03	KC	L 23-29	-	-	-	-
12/10	Pit	L 10-29	-	-	-	-
12/17	@Sea	L 10-44	-	-	-	-
12/24	Den	L 28-31	-	-	-	-

Chris Gardocki
Indianapolis Colts — P

	G	NPunts	Avg	Lg	In20	FC	TPunts	TB	Blk	Ret	Yds	NetAvg
Total	16	63	42.6	69	16	5	63	7	0	37	436	33.4
vs. Playoff	6	22	45.3	69	7	3	22	4	0	10	144	35.1
vs. Non-playoff	10	41	41.1	56	9	2	41	3	0	27	292	32.5
vs. Own Division	8	32	43.2	69	9	1	32	5	0	19	182	34.4
Home	8	30	42.8	55	8	3	30	4	0	16	235	32.3
Away	8	33	42.4	69	8	2	33	3	0	21	201	34.5
September	3	9	45.6	69	4	1	9	2	0	3	15	39.4
October	5	21	42.8	55	4	1	21	1	0	14	165	34.0
November	4	14	42.7	53	6	1	14	2	0	8	102	32.5
December	4	10	40.7	56	2	2	10	2	0	12	154	30.5
Grass	5	22	41.6	56	3	0	22	0	0	17	183	33.3
Turf	11	41	43.1	69	13	5	41	7	0	20	253	33.5
Indoor	9	33	42.8	55	10	4	33	5	0	17	238	32.5
Outdoor	7	30	42.3	69	6	1	30	2	0	20	198	34.4
Outdoors, Temp < 40	0	0	-	0	0	0	0	0	0	0	0	-
Outdoors, Temp 40-80	6	28	41.7	69	6	1	28	2	0	18	181	33.8
Outdoors, Temp > 80	1	2	51.0	51	0	0	2	0	0	2	17	42.5
Winning	-	21	42.0	56	5	1	21	3	0	11	148	32.1
Tied	-	21	44.5	69	6	2	21	4	0	12	169	32.7
Trailing	-	21	41.1	53	5	2	21	0	0	14	119	35.4

1995 Punter Splits (above) — **Game Logs** (below)

Date	Opp	Result	NPunts	Avg	In20	TPunts	TB	Blk	Ret	Yds	NetAvg
09/03	Cin	L 21-24	1	55.0	1	1	0	0	0	0	55.0
09/10	@NYA	W 27-24	1	48.0	0	1	0	0	1	1	47.0
09/17	@Buf	L 14-20	7	43.9	3	7	2	0	2	14	36.1
10/01	StL	W 21-18	5	37.2	1	5	0	0	3	71	23.0
10/08	@Mia	W 27-24	2	51.0	0	2	0	0	2	17	42.5
10/15	SF	W 18-17	3	48.7	1	3	1	0	1	11	38.3
10/22	@Oak	L 17-30	6	37.7	1	6	0	0	4	36	31.7
10/29	NYA	W 17-10	5	47.8	1	5	0	0	4	30	41.8
11/05	Buf	L 10-16	5	48.0	2	5	0	0	4	73	33.4
11/12	@NO	L 14-17	3	42.7	2	3	1	0	1	3	35.0
11/19	@NE	W 24-10	4	41.0	1	4	0	0	3	26	34.5
11/26	Mia	W 36-28	2	33.0	1	2	1	0	0	0	23.0
12/03	@Car	L 10-13	8	42.1	0	8	0	0	7	107	28.8
12/10	@Jac	W 41-31	2	43.0	1	2	0	0	1	-3	44.5
12/17	SD	L 24-27	3	45.0	0	3	0	0	1	29	35.3
12/23	NE	W 10-7	1	36.0	1	6	2	0	3	21	25.8

Jeff Gossett
Oakland Raiders — P

1995 Punter Splits

	G	NPunts	Avg	Lg	In20	FC	TPunts	TB	Blk	Ret	Yds	NetAvg
Total	16	75	41.2	60	22	8	76	8	1	38	294	34.7
vs. Playoff	8	35	40.7	58	11	3	35	4	0	17	93	35.7
vs. Non-playoff	8	40	41.6	60	11	5	41	4	0	21	201	33.8
vs. Own Division	8	49	41.9	60	14	5	49	6	0	23	188	35.6
Home	8	34	41.0	58	11	2	34	5	0	16	110	34.3
Away	8	41	41.3	60	11	6	42	3	1	22	184	34.5
September	4	17	41.6	58	6	1	18	3	1	6	32	34.2
October	4	20	43.5	60	6	2	20	5	0	10	52	35.9
November	4	14	35.7	48	4	2	14	0	0	7	50	32.1
December	4	24	42.2	53	6	3	24	0	0	15	160	35.5
Grass	12	53	41.7	60	17	4	54	7	1	26	167	35.2
Turf	4	22	40.0	58	5	4	22	1	0	12	127	34.3
Indoor	1	8	43.1	53	1	2	8	0	0	5	75	33.8
Outdoor	15	67	41.0	60	21	6	68	8	1	33	219	34.8
Outdoors, Temp < 40	1	6	38.7	47	3	1	6	0	0	3	27	34.2
Outdoors, Temp 40-80	14	61	41.2	60	18	5	62	8	1	30	192	34.8
Outdoors, Temp > 80	0	0	-	0	0	0	0	0	0	0	0	-
Winning	-	36	41.5	58	8	1	37	5	1	19	143	33.8
Tied	-	15	39.9	48	6	2	15	2	0	7	48	34.1
Trailing	-	24	41.5	60	8	5	24	1	0	12	103	36.3

Game Logs

Date	Opp	Result	NPunts	Avg	In20	TPunts	TB	Blk	Ret	Yds	NetAvg
09/03	SD	W 17-7	9	42.4	4	9	2	0	2	4	37.6
09/10	@Was	W 20-8	1	49.0	0	2	0	1	1	19	15.0
09/17	@KC	L 17-23	7	39.4	2	7	1	0	3	9	35.3
09/24	Phi	W 48-17	0	0	0	0	0	0	0	0	0
10/01	@NYA	W 47-10	5	42.2	1	5	1	0	3	19	34.4
10/08	Sea	W 34-14	4	38.8	1	4	2	0	1	10	26.3
10/16	@Den	L 0-27	8	47.0	3	8	1	0	4	17	42.4
10/22	Ind	W 30-17	3	42.3	1	3	1	0	2	6	33.7
11/05	@Cin	W 20-17	6	38.7	3	6	0	0	3	27	34.2
11/12	@NYN	W 17-13	3	31.0	0	3	0	0	1	6	29.0
11/19	Dal	L 21-34	2	31.5	0	2	0	0	1	5	29.0
11/27	@SD	L 6-12	3	37.3	1	3	0	0	2	12	33.3
12/03	KC	L 23-29	5	40.8	0	5	0	0	3	33	33.8
12/10	Pit	L 10-29	6	43.3	3	6	0	0	4	24	39.3
12/17	@Sea	L 10-44	8	43.1	1	8	0	0	5	75	33.8
12/24	Den	L 28-31	5	40.8	2	5	0	0	3	28	35.2

Brian Hansen
New York Jets — P

1995 Punter Splits

	G	NPunts	Avg	Lg	In20	FC	TPunts	TB	Blk	Ret	Yds	NetAvg
Total	16	99	41.3	67	23	13	100	10	1	59	703	31.9
vs. Playoff	7	37	41.6	54	6	2	37	7	0	20	237	31.5
vs. Non-playoff	9	62	41.1	67	17	11	63	3	1	39	466	32.1
vs. Own Division	8	49	39.9	58	8	3	49	7	0	29	364	29.6
Home	8	47	41.1	67	10	6	47	6	0	27	324	31.6
Away	8	52	41.5	56	13	7	53	4	1	32	379	32.1
September	4	21	42.5	54	5	3	21	3	0	10	146	32.7
October	5	29	42.7	67	7	3	30	5	1	15	147	33.0
November	3	20	41.1	56	4	1	20	0	0	16	185	31.8
December	4	29	39.3	56	7	6	29	2	0	18	225	30.2
Grass	3	23	39.6	56	5	3	24	2	1	14	169	29.3
Turf	13	76	41.8	67	18	10	76	8	0	45	534	32.7
Indoor	4	24	43.0	56	7	4	24	2	0	14	168	34.3
Outdoor	12	75	40.8	67	16	9	76	8	1	45	535	31.1
Outdoors, Temp < 40	2	11	35.5	51	1	2	11	1	0	8	101	24.5
Outdoors, Temp 40-80	9	57	41.8	67	14	6	58	6	1	34	396	32.2
Outdoors, Temp > 80	1	7	40.6	51	1	1	7	1	0	3	38	32.3
Winning	-	17	43.6	56	4	2	17	3	0	11	139	31.9
Tied	-	23	40.7	54	3	2	24	4	1	14	190	27.8
Trailing	-	59	40.9	67	16	9	59	3	0	34	374	33.5

Game Logs

Date	Opp	Result	NPunts	Avg	In20	TPunts	TB	Blk	Ret	Yds	NetAvg
09/03	@Mia	L 14-52	7	40.6	1	7	1	0	3	38	32.3
09/10	Ind	L 24-27	4	45.0	1	4	1	0	1	32	32.0
09/17	Jac	W 27-10	5	39.0	3	5	0	0	2	24	34.2
09/24	@Atl	L 3-13	5	46.6	0	5	1	0	4	52	32.2
10/01	Oak	L 10-47	7	48.3	2	7	1	0	3	35	40.4
10/08	@Buf	L 10-29	5	43.4	1	5	0	0	4	42	35.0
10/15	@Car	L 15-26	7	40.0	3	8	0	1	4	36	30.5
10/22	Mia	W 17-16	6	41.2	0	6	3	0	3	23	27.3
10/29	@Ind	L 10-17	4	38.8	1	4	1	0	1	11	31.0
11/05	NE	L 7-20	8	37.4	1	8	0	0	6	84	26.9
11/19	Buf	L 26-28	6	37.5	2	6	0	0	4	39	31.0
11/26	@Sea	W 16-10	6	49.5	1	6	0	0	6	62	39.2
12/03	StL	L 20-23	9	44.9	1	9	1	0	7	81	33.7
12/10	@NE	L 28-31	9	38.6	1	9	1	0	4	95	25.8
12/17	@Hou	L 6-23	9	38.4	5	9	0	0	3	43	33.7
12/24	NO	L 0-12	2	21.5	0	2	0	0	1	6	18.5

Jason Hanson
Detroit Lions — K

1995 Field Goal Splits / 1995 Kickoff Splits

	G	1-29 Yd	30-39 Yd	40-49 Yd	50+ Yd	Overall	Pct	Lg	Num	Avg	TB	TD	NetAvg
Total	16	6-6	16-17	5-10	1-1	28-34	82.4	56	93	66.9	13	0	44.5
vs. Playoff	5	1-1	5-5	1-1	0-0	7-7	100.0	43	25	68.4	8	0	46.6
vs. Non-playoff	11	5-5	11-12	4-9	1-1	21-27	77.8	56	68	66.3	5	0	43.6
vs. Own Division	8	3-3	7-8	3-7	0-0	13-18	72.2	45	45	66.0	3	0	43.3
Home	8	4-4	10-11	2-3	1-1	17-19	89.5	56	52	68.4	8	0	45.5
Away	8	2-2	6-6	3-7	0-0	11-15	73.3	45	41	65.0	5	0	43.1
Games 1-8	8	3-3	7-7	2-4	1-1	13-15	86.7	56	42	67.3	8	0	45.8
Games 9-16	8	3-3	9-10	3-6	0-0	15-19	78.9	45	51	66.6	5	0	43.4
September	4	2-2	5-5	1-3	0-0	8-10	80.0	43	19	68.9	7	0	48.3
October	4	1-1	2-2	1-1	1-1	5-5	100.0	56	23	66.0	1	0	43.7
November	4	3-3	2-3	1-3	0-0	6-9	66.7	40	23	67.3	4	0	44.9
December	4	0-0	7-7	2-3	0-0	9-10	90.0	45	28	66.0	1	0	42.1
Grass	4	2-2	3-3	2-3	0-0	7-8	87.5	45	24	63.3	1	0	41.8
Turf	12	4-4	13-14	3-7	1-1	21-26	80.8	56	69	68.2	12	0	45.4
Indoor	11	4-4	12-13	2-6	1-1	19-24	79.2	56	64	68.2	10	0	45.3
Outdoor	5	2-2	4-4	3-4	0-0	9-10	90.0	45	29	64.0	3	0	42.7
4th qtr, +/-3 pts	-	1-1	4-4	0-1	0-0	5-6	83.3	39	6	71.5	3	0	51.2
Winning	-	1-1	8-8	3-5	1-1	13-15	86.7	56	64	66.5	8	0	44.0
Tied	-	3-3	7-7	0-2	0-0	10-12	83.3	39	18	66.7	2	0	44.1
Trailing	-	2-2	1-2	2-3	0-0	5-7	71.4	42	11	69.4	3	0	47.6

Game Logs

Date	Opp	Result	1-39 Yd	40-49 Yd	50+ Yd	Lg
09/03	@Pit	L 20-23	1-1	1-1	0-0	43
09/10	@Min	L 10-20	1-1	0-2	0-0	33
09/17	Ari	L 17-20	1-1	0-0	0-0	21
09/25	SF	W 27-24	4-4	0-0	0-0	38
10/08	Cle	W 38-20	0-0	0-0	1-1	56
10/15	@GB	L 21-30	0-0	0-0	0-0	0
10/22	@Was	L 30-36	2-2	1-1	0-0	42
10/29	GB	W 24-16	1-1	0-0	0-0	38
11/05	@Atl	L 22-34	0-0	0-0	0-0	0
11/12	TB	W 27-24	2-3	0-0	0-0	29
11/19	@Chi	W 24-17	1-1	0-1	0-0	25
11/23	Min	W 44-38	2-2	1-2	0-0	40
12/04	Chi	W 27-7	1-1	1-1	0-0	42
12/10	@Hou	W 24-17	1-1	0-1	0-0	36
12/17	Jac	W 44-0	3-3	0-0	0-0	39
12/23	@TB	W 37-10	2-2	1-1	0-0	45

Craig Hentrich
Green Bay Packers — P

1995 Punter Splits

	G	NPunts	Avg	Lg	In20	FC	TPunts	TB	Blk	Ret	Yds	NetAvg
Total	16	65	42.2	61	26	11	67	7	2	36	279	34.6
vs. Playoff	4	13	43.4	57	8	1	13	1	0	6	42	38.6
vs. Non-playoff	12	52	41.8	61	18	10	54	6	2	30	237	33.7
vs. Own Division	8	29	39.9	57	12	5	30	1	1	17	106	34.4
Home	8	42	41.5	61	17	7	43	7	1	21	111	34.7
Away	8	23	43.4	55	9	4	24	0	1	15	168	34.6
September	4	21	44.7	61	7	2	23	3	2	13	125	32.8
October	4	16	44.2	57	8	1	16	0	0	12	89	38.6
November	4	14	38.1	50	5	4	14	1	0	6	29	34.6
December	4	14	40.0	54	6	4	14	3	0	5	36	33.1
Grass	12	54	41.7	61	20	8	56	7	2	31	231	33.6
Turf	4	11	44.5	55	6	3	11	0	0	5	48	40.2
Indoor	3	6	46.3	55	3	2	6	0	0	2	20	43.0
Outdoor	13	59	41.7	61	23	9	61	7	2	34	259	33.8
Outdoors, Temp < 40	5	18	36.8	47	7	5	18	4	0	5	18	31.3
Outdoors, Temp 40-80	8	41	43.9	61	16	4	43	3	2	29	241	34.9
Outdoors, Temp > 80	0	0	-	0	0	0	0	0	0	0	0	-
Winning	-	32	41.5	61	12	8	33	2	1	18	157	34.3
Tied	-	21	40.5	57	10	2	22	4	1	10	41	33.1
Trailing	-	12	46.8	60	4	1	12	1	0	8	81	38.4

Game Logs

Date	Opp	Result	NPunts	Avg	In20	TPunts	TB	Blk	Ret	Yds	NetAvg
09/03	StL	L 14-17	7	48.9	2	8	2	1	4	32	33.8
09/11	@Chi	W 27-24	1	11.0	0	2	0	1	0	0	5.5
09/17	NYN	W 14-6	9	43.3	4	9	1	0	5	11	39.9
09/24	@Jac	W 24-14	4	49.0	1	4	0	0	4	82	28.5
10/08	@Dal	L 24-34	5	42.4	3	5	0	0	3	28	36.8
10/15	Det	W 30-21	4	43.3	2	4	0	0	3	14	39.8
10/22	Min	W 38-21	6	44.5	2	6	0	0	6	47	36.7
10/29	@Det	L 16-24	1	55.0	1	1	0	0	0	0	55.0
11/05	@Min	L 24-27	3	44.3	1	3	0	0	1	11	40.7
11/12	Chi	W 35-28	5	32.6	2	5	1	0	2	7	27.2
11/19	@Cle	W 31-20	2	46.0	0	2	0	0	2	11	40.5
11/26	TB	W 35-13	4	36.5	2	4	0	0	1	0	36.5
12/03	Cin	W 24-10	4	33.4	1	4	2	0	0	0	24.3
12/10	@TB	L 10-13	5	41.8	2	5	0	0	4	27	36.4
12/16	@NO	W 34-23	2	45.0	1	2	0	0	1	9	40.5
12/24	Pit	W 24-19	3	41.3	2	3	1	0	0	0	34.7

Mike Hollis
Jacksonville Jaguars — K

1995 Field Goal Splits / 1995 Kickoff Splits

	G	1-29 Yd	30-39 Yd	40-49 Yd	50+ Yd	Overall	Pct	Lg	Num	Avg	TB	TD	NetAvg
Total	16	7-9	7-8	4-7	2-3	20-27	74.1	53	57	61.6	3	1	38.1
vs. Playoff	5	0-2	2-2	0-0	1-1	3-5	60.0	53	12	61.2	0	1	30.6
vs. Non-playoff	11	7-7	5-6	4-7	1-2	17-22	77.3	50	45	61.7	3	0	40.1
vs. Own Division	8	4-4	5-6	1-3	1-1	11-14	78.6	53	31	62.9	2	0	40.4
Home	8	4-5	5-6	3-6	2-3	14-20	70.0	53	31	62.8	2	1	38.4
Away	8	3-4	2-2	1-1	0-0	6-7	85.7	47	26	60.1	1	0	37.7
Games 1-8	8	3-3	3-4	2-3	1-2	9-12	75.0	53	28	63.9	3	0	39.7
Games 9-16	8	4-6	4-4	2-4	1-1	11-15	73.3	50	29	59.3	0	1	36.6
September	4	2-2	1-2	0-0	0-0	3-4	75.0	34	9	63.1	1	0	37.8
October	5	1-1	2-2	2-3	1-2	6-8	75.0	53	21	64.5	2	0	39.7
November	3	3-3	2-2	0-2	1-1	6-8	75.0	50	13	61.8	0	0	40.6
December	4	1-3	2-2	2-2	0-0	5-7	71.4	47	14	55.9	0	1	33.6
Grass	11	5-6	6-7	4-7	2-3	17-23	73.9	53	44	60.9	3	1	38.8
Turf	5	2-3	1-1	0-0	0-0	3-4	75.0	34	13	63.7	0	0	35.8
Indoor	2	1-2	0-0	0-0	0-0	1-2	50.0	22	5	64.4	0	0	38.4
Outdoor	14	6-7	7-8	4-7	2-3	19-25	76.0	53	52	61.3	3	1	38.1
4th qtr, +/-3 pts		0-0	2-2	0-0	0-1	2-3	66.7	39	4	60.0	0	0	38.0
Winning	-	2-2	2-2	1-1	2-2	7-7	100.0	53	24	61.4	0	0	40.5
Tied	-	1-1	3-3	2-5	0-0	6-9	66.7	47	18	62.1	2	1	35.3
Trailing	-	4-6	2-3	1-1	0-1	7-11	63.6	40	15	61.3	1	0	37.7

Game Logs

Date	Opp	Result	1-39 Yd	40-49 Yd	50+ Yd	Lg
09/03	Hou	L 3-10	1-2	0-0	0-0	26
09/10	@Cin	L 17-24	1-1	0-0	0-0	29
09/17	@NYA	L 10-27	1-1	0-0	0-0	34
09/24	GB	L 14-24	0-0	0-0	0-0	0
10/01	@Hou	W 17-16	1-1	0-0	0-0	22
10/08	Pit	W 20-16	1-1	0-0	1-1	53
10/15	Chi	L 27-30	0-0	2-3	0-1	49
10/22	@Cle	W 23-15	1-1	0-0	0-0	31
10/29	@Pit	L 7-24	0-0	0-0	0-0	0
11/12	Sea	L 30-47	2-2	0-0	1-1	50
11/19	@TB	L 16-17	1-1	0-0	0-0	22
11/26	Cin	L 13-17	2-2	0-2	0-0	39
12/03	@Den	L 23-31	0-0	1-1	0-0	47
12/10	Ind	L 31-41	1-2	0-0	0-0	37
12/17	@Det	L 0-44	0-1	0-0	0-0	0
12/24	Cle	W 24-21	2-2	1-1	0-0	42

Mike Horan
New York Giants — P

1995 Punter Splits

	G	NPunts	Avg	Lg	In20	FC	TPunts	TB	Blk	Ret	Yds	NetAvg
Total	16	72	42.5	60	15	11	72	8	0	34	297	36.2
vs. Playoff	8	41	42.6	55	9	4	41	4	0	21	155	36.9
vs. Non-playoff	8	31	42.5	60	6	7	31	4	0	13	142	35.3
vs. Own Division	8	37	42.5	54	10	10	37	4	0	12	70	38.4
Home	8	31	41.6	60	2	5	31	4	0	12	98	35.9
Away	8	41	43.2	55	13	6	41	4	0	22	199	36.4
September	4	21	42.9	55	2	2	21	1	0	13	89	37.7
October	4	18	40.1	50	4	4	18	1	0	7	53	36.1
November	5	23	43.8	60	7	4	23	5	0	10	137	33.5
December	3	10	43.2	54	2	1	10	1	0	4	18	39.4
Grass	5	28	42.3	55	8	5	28	2	0	16	78	38.1
Turf	11	44	42.7	60	7	6	44	6	0	18	219	35.0
Indoor	1	5	47.6	54	1	0	5	0	0	4	105	26.6
Outdoor	15	67	42.2	60	14	11	67	8	0	30	192	36.9
Outdoors, Temp < 40	2	7	42.9	54	1	1	7	0	0	3	7	41.9
Outdoors, Temp 40-80	13	60	42.1	60	13	10	60	8	0	27	185	36.3
Outdoors, Temp > 80	0	0	-	0	0	0	0	0	0	0	0	-
Winning	-	25	41.0	54	5	4	25	2	0	13	44	37.6
Tied	-	13	41.5	52	2	2	13	3	0	6	33	34.4
Trailing	-	34	44.1	60	8	5	34	3	0	15	220	35.8

Game Logs

Date	Opp	Result	NPunts	Avg	In20	TPunts	TB	Blk	Ret	Yds	NetAvg
09/04	Dal	L 0-35	5	43.8	0	5	0	0	1	6	42.6
09/10	@KC	L 17-20	6	39.3	1	6	0	0	5	25	35.2
09/17	@GB	L 6-14	8	47.1	1	8	1	0	6	51	38.3
09/24	NO	W 45-29	2	34.5	0	2	0	0	1	7	31.0
10/01	@SF	L 6-20	3	36.3	2	3	0	0	1	0	36.3
10/08	Ari	W 27-21	1	40.0	0	1	0	0	0	0	40.0
10/15	Phi	L 14-17	8	40.9	1	8	1	0	4	48	32.4
10/29	@Was	W 24-15	6	41.0	1	6	0	0	2	5	40.2
11/05	@Sea	L 28-30	5	47.6	1	5	0	0	4	105	26.6
11/12	Oak	L 13-17	4	40.0	0	4	1	0	3	30	36.3
11/19	@Phi	L 19-28	5	43.8	3	5	1	0	1	5	38.8
11/26	Chi	L 24-27	4	35.0	0	4	2	0	0	0	25.0
11/30	@Ari	W 10-6	5	43.2	3	5	1	0	2	-3	39.8
12/10	Was	W 20-13	4	43.3	1	4	0	0	1	-2	43.8
12/17	@Dal	L 20-21	3	44.0	1	3	1	0	1	11	33.7
12/23	SD	L 17-27	3	42.3	0	3	0	0	2	9	39.3

Michael Husted
Tampa Bay Buccaneers — K

	G	1995 Field Goal Splits							1995 Kickoff Splits					Game Logs					
		1-29 Yd	30-39 Yd	40-49 Yd	50+ Yd	Overall	Pct	Lg	Num	Avg	TB	TD	NetAvg	Date	Opp	Result	1-39 Yd	40-49 Yd	50+ Yd	Lg
Total	16	6-7	5-7	5-9	3-3	19-26	73.1	53	57	65.2	8	0	45.7	09/03	@Phi	W 21-6	0-0	0-0	0-0	0
vs. Playoff	6	2-2	2-3	2-3	0-0	6-8	75.0	48	22	66.6	2	0	47.2	09/10	@Cle	L 6-22	0-1	0-0	0-0	0
vs. Non-playoff	10	4-5	3-4	3-6	3-3	13-18	72.2	53	35	64.3	6	0	44.8	09/17	Chi	L 6-25	0-0	2-2	0-0	43
vs. Own Division	8	2-2	3-3	5-6	2-2	12-13	92.3	53	28	64.1	3	0	44.1	09/24	Was	W 14-6	0-0	0-0	0-0	0
Home	8	3-3	4-5	3-5	2-2	12-15	80.0	53	30	65.3	6	0	45.0	10/01	@Car	W 20-13	2-2	0-1	0-0	27
Away	8	3-4	1-2	2-4	1-1	7-11	63.6	50	27	65.1	2	0	46.6	10/08	Cin	W 19-16	3-3	0-2	1-1	53
Games 1-8	8	4-5	2-3	2-5	2-2	10-15	66.7	53	30	65.5	5	0	45.0	10/15	Min	W 20-17	1-1	0-0	1-1	51
Games 9-16	8	2-2	3-4	3-4	1-1	9-11	81.8	50	27	64.9	3	0	46.6	10/22	Atl	L 21-24	0-1	0-0	0-0	0
September	4	0-1	0-0	2-2	0-0	2-3	66.7	43	12	66.0	2	0	47.3	10/29	@Hou	L 7-19	0-1	0-0	0-0	0
October	5	4-4	2-4	0-3	2-2	8-13	61.5	53	20	64.7	3	0	43.4	11/12	@Det	L 24-27	1-1	0-1	0-0	34
November	3	1-1	2-2	1-2	0-0	4-5	80.0	48	12	67.5	1	0	48.8	11/19	Jac	W 17-16	1-1	0-0	0-0	33
December	4	1-1	1-1	2-2	1-1	5-5	100.0	50	13	63.2	2	0	45.0	11/26	@GB	L 13-35	1-1	1-1	0-0	48
Grass	12	6-7	4-5	4-7	3-3	17-22	77.3	53	43	64.4	7	0	44.8	12/03	@Min	L 17-31	0-0	1-1	0-0	47
Turf	4	0-0	1-2	1-2	0-0	2-4	50.0	47	14	67.6	1	0	48.6	12/10	GB	W 13-10	1-1	1-1	0-0	47
Indoor	3	0-0	1-2	1-2	0-0	2-4	50.0	47	10	67.1	1	0	47.6	12/17	@Chi	L 10-31	0-0	0-1	1-1	50
Outdoor	13	6-7	4-5	4-7	3-3	17-22	77.3	53	47	64.8	7	0	45.3	12/23	Det	L 10-37	1-1	0-0	0-0	27
4th qtr, +/-3 pts	-	0-0	2-3	0-1	1-1	3-5	60.0	53	3	68.3	1	0	45.7							
Winning	-	2-2	1-1	0-2	0-0	3-5	60.0	36	25	65.5	2	0	46.5							
Tied	-	2-2	2-3	1-2	2-2	7-9	77.8	53	21	66.7	6	0	45.9							
Trailing	-	2-3	2-3	4-5	1-1	9-12	75.0	50	11	61.7	0	0	43.7							

Tom Hutton
Philadelphia Eagles — P

	G	1995 Punter Splits										Game Logs									
		NPunts	Avg	Lg	In20	FC	TPunts	TB	Blk	Ret	Yds	NetAvg	Date	Opp	Result	NPunts	Avg	In20	TPunts	TB	Blk	Ret	Yds	NetAvg
Total	16	85	43.3	63	20	17	86	13	1	38	527	33.7	09/03	TB	L 6-21	6	44.7	1	6	2	0	3	17	35.2
vs. Playoff	3	17	46.0	63	3	4	17	2	0	7	221	30.6	09/10	@Ari	W 31-19	4	44.0	0	4	1	0	2	27	32.3
vs. Non-playoff	13	68	42.6	62	17	13	69	11	1	51	306	34.4	09/17	SD	L 21-27	7	51.1	1	7	2	0	4	133	26.4
vs. Own Division	8	44	42.0	62	7	11	45	5	1	19	285	32.5	09/24	@Oak	L 17-48	2	46.5	0	2	0	0	2	9	42.0
Home	8	45	43.7	63	8	9	46	8	1	19	345	31.7	10/01	@NO	W 15-10	4	44.3	4	4	0	0	1	0	44.3
Away	8	40	42.9	62	8	8	40	5	0	19	182	35.9	10/08	Was	W 37-34	4	37.0	1	4	0	0	2	63	21.3
September	4	19	47.1	63	2	3	19	5	0	11	186	32.1	10/15	@NYN	W 20-17	6	40.3	0	6	3	0	2	8	29.0
October	4	21	42.5	56	6	3	21	4	0	9	130	32.5	10/29	StL	W 20-9	7	46.6	1	7	1	0	4	59	35.3
November	4	22	43.0	58	4	5	23	2	1	10	154	32.7	11/06	@Dal	L 12-34	6	46.3	0	6	0	0	3	88	31.7
December	4	23	41.3	62	8	6	23	2	0	8	57	37.0	11/12	Den	W 31-13	4	38.0	1	4	2	0	0	0	28.0
Grass	4	19	41.8	53	6	4	19	2	0	9	58	36.7	11/19	NYN	W 28-19	5	44.8	0	6	0	1	3	40	30.7
Turf	12	66	43.7	63	14	13	67	11	1	29	469	32.8	11/26	@Was	W 14-7	7	41.6	3	7	0	0	4	26	37.9
Indoor	2	9	44.7	62	6	2	9	0	0	5	58	41.6	12/03	@Sea	L 14-26	5	45.0	2	5	0	0	4	28	39.4
Outdoor	14	76	43.2	63	14	15	77	13	1	33	499	32.7	12/10	Dal	L 14-20	4	36.5	2	4	0	0	0	0	36.5
Outdoors, Temp < 40	4	22	39.8	62	7	5	22	4	0	4	29	34.9	12/17	Ari	W 21-20	8	42.9	1	8	1	0	3	33	36.3
Outdoors, Temp 40-80	9	50	44.6	63	7	9	51	8	1	27	443	31.9	12/24	@Chi	L 14-20	6	39.2	3	6	1	0	1	-4	36.5
Outdoors, Temp > 80	1	4	44.0	51	0	1	4	1	0	2	27	32.3												
Winning	-	39	43.5	63	7	6	40	8	1	18	224	32.8												
Tied	-	10	42.7	57	5	3	10	1	0	5	42	36.5												
Trailing	-	36	43.3	62	8	8	36	4	0	15	261	33.9												

Chris Jacke
Green Bay Packers — K

	G	1995 Field Goal Splits							1995 Kickoff Splits					Game Logs					
		1-29 Yd	30-39 Yd	40-49 Yd	50+ Yd	Overall	Pct	Lg	Num	Avg	TB	TD	NetAvg	Date	Opp	Result	1-39 Yd	40-49 Yd	50+ Yd	Lg
Total	14	6-7	0-2	8-10	3-4	17-23	73.9	51	13	64.1	0	0	45.2	09/03	StL	L 14-17	0-0	0-0	0-0	0
vs. Playoff	4	3-4	0-1	4-4	1-1	8-10	80.0	50	0	-	0	0	-	09/11	@Chi	W 27-24	0-0	0-0	0-0	0
vs. Non-playoff	10	3-3	0-1	4-6	2-3	9-13	69.2	51	13	64.1	0	0	45.2	09/17	NYN	W 14-6	-	-	-	-
vs. Own Division	8	4-5	0-2	4-6	3-4	11-17	64.7	51	13	64.1	0	0	45.2	09/24	@Jac	W 24-14	-	-	-	-
Home	7	2-3	0-2	4-4	0-1	6-10	60.0	47	3	67.3	0	0	48.0	10/08	@Dal	L 24-34	0-0	1-1	0-0	42
Away	7	4-4	0-0	4-6	3-3	11-13	84.6	51	10	63.1	0	0	44.3	10/15	Det	W 30-21	1-3	2-2	0-0	43
Games 1-8	6	4-5	0-2	3-3	1-2	8-12	66.7	50	2	62.0	0	0	48.5	10/22	Min	W 38-21	1-2	0-0	0-1	26
Games 9-16	8	2-2	0-0	5-7	2-2	9-11	81.8	51	11	64.5	0	0	44.5	10/29	@Det	L 16-24	2-2	0-0	1-1	50
September	2	0-0	0-0	0-0	0-0	0-0	-	0	2	62.0	0	0	48.5	11/05	@Min	L 24-27	0-0	2-2	1-1	50
October	4	4-5	0-2	3-3	1-2	8-12	66.7	50	0	-	0	0	-	11/12	Chi	W 35-28	0-0	0-0	0-0	0
November	4	1-1	0-0	2-2	1-1	4-4	100.0	50	9	64.7	0	0	44.6	11/19	@Cle	W 31-20	1-1	0-0	0-0	28
December	4	1-1	0-0	3-5	1-1	5-7	71.4	51	2	63.5	0	0	44.5	11/26	TB	W 35-13	0-0	0-0	0-0	0
Grass	10	3-4	0-2	4-6	1-2	8-14	57.1	51	7	64.7	0	0	47.1	12/03	Cin	W 24-10	0-0	1-1	0-0	41
Turf	4	3-3	0-0	4-4	2-2	9-9	100.0	50	6	63.3	0	0	42.8	12/10	@TB	L 10-13	0-0	0-2	1-1	51
Indoor	3	3-3	0-0	3-3	2-2	8-8	100.0	50	6	63.3	0	0	42.8	12/16	@NO	W 34-23	1-1	1-1	0-0	47
Outdoor	11	3-4	0-2	5-7	1-2	9-15	60.0	51	7	64.7	0	0	47.1	12/24	Pit	W 24-19	0-0	1-1	0-0	47
4th qtr, +/-3 pts	-	0-0	0-0	0-1	0-0	0-1	0.0	0	1	63.0	0	0	46.0							
Winning	-	4-5	0-1	4-4	0-1	8-11	72.7	47	11	63.7	0	0	44.4							
Tied	-	0-0	0-1	2-4	2-2	4-7	57.1	51	2	66.0	0	0	49.5							
Trailing	-	2-2	0-0	2-2	1-1	5-5	100.0	50	0	-	0	0	-							

Jeff Jaeger

	G	1995 Field Goal Splits							1995 Kickoff Splits				
		1-29 Yd	30-39 Yd	40-49 Yd	50+ Yd	Overall	Pct	Lg	Num	Avg	TB	TD	NetAvg
Total	11	4-5	6-7	3-5	0-1	13-18	72.2	46	45	58.8	4	0	37.5
vs. Playoff	5	3-3	3-4	1-3	0-0	7-10	70.0	46	21	58.0	1	0	39.5
vs. Non-playoff	6	1-2	3-3	2-2	0-1	6-8	75.0	46	24	59.5	3	0	35.8
vs. Own Division	6	2-3	2-2	2-3	0-0	6-8	75.0	46	22	59.8	1	0	37.0
Home	6	3-4	3-4	1-3	0-0	7-11	63.6	46	30	56.7	1	0	37.1
Away	5	1-1	3-3	2-2	0-1	6-7	85.7	46	15	63.1	3	0	38.4
Games 1-8	3	3-4	2-2	0-1	0-0	5-7	71.4	37	15	59.2	1	0	41.1
Games 9-16	8	1-1	4-5	3-4	0-1	8-11	72.7	46	30	58.6	3	0	35.8
September	0	0-0	0-0	0-0	0-0	0-0	-	0	0	-	0	0	-
October	3	3-4	2-2	0-1	0-0	5-7	71.4	37	15	59.2	1	0	41.1
November	4	1-1	3-4	1-1	0-1	5-7	71.4	46	16	60.9	3	0	39.7
December	4	0-0	1-1	2-3	0-0	3-4	75.0	46	14	56.1	0	0	31.3
Grass	8	4-5	4-5	1-3	0-0	9-13	69.2	46	34	58.2	2	0	38.7
Turf	3	0-0	2-2	2-2	0-1	4-5	80.0	46	11	60.6	2	0	33.9
Indoor	1	0-0	0-0	1-1	0-0	1-1	100.0	42	2	64.5	0	0	14.5
Outdoor	10	4-5	6-7	2-4	0-1	12-17	70.6	46	43	58.6	4	0	38.6
4th qtr, +/-3 pts	-	0-0	0-0	0-0	0-0	0-0	-	0	1	67.0	0	0	52.0
Winning	-	2-3	2-2	2-3	0-1	6-9	66.7	46	26	57.9	1	0	38.3
Tied	-	0-0	3-4	0-0	0-0	3-4	75.0	37	7	62.9	1	0	38.6
Trailing	-	2-2	1-1	1-2	0-0	4-5	80.0	42	12	58.5	2	0	35.3

Game Logs

Date	Opp	Result	1-39 Yd	40-49 Yd	50+ Yd	Lg
09/03	SD	W 17-7	-	-	-	-
09/10	@Was	W 20-8	-	-	-	-
09/17	@KC	L 17-23	-	-	-	-
09/24	Phi	W 48-17	-	-	-	-
10/01	@NYA	W 47-10	-	-	-	-
10/08	Sea	W 34-14	2-3	0-0	0-0	37
10/16	@Den	L 0-27	0-0	0-0	0-0	0
10/22	Ind	W 30-17	3-3	0-1	0-0	35
11/05	@Cin	W 20-17	1-1	1-1	0-1	46
11/12	@NYN	W 17-13	1-1	0-0	0-0	30
11/19	Dal	L 21-34	0-1	0-0	0-0	30
11/27	@SD	L 6-12	2-2	0-0	0-0	30
12/03	KC	L 23-29	0-0	1-2	0-0	46
12/10	Pit	L 10-29	1-1	0-0	0-0	39
12/17	@Sea	L 10-44	0-0	1-1	0-0	42
12/24	Den	L 28-31	0-0	0-0	0-0	0

John Jett

	G	NPunts	Avg	Lg	In20	FC	TPunts	TB	Blk	Ret	Yds	NetAvg
Total	16	53	40.9	58	17	10	53	6	0	22	216	34.5
vs. Playoff	7	23	41.5	57	6	4	23	2	0	12	124	34.4
vs. Non-playoff	9	30	40.4	58	11	6	30	4	0	10	92	34.6
vs. Own Division	8	28	38.9	58	9	6	28	4	0	9	76	33.3
Home	8	25	40.5	55	7	6	25	2	0	13	123	34.0
Away	8	28	41.2	58	10	4	28	4	0	9	93	35.0
September	4	14	38.1	51	6	5	14	2	0	3	29	36.5
October	4	13	46.0	58	3	0	13	3	0	6	64	36.5
November	4	10	40.0	53	4	3	10	1	0	5	64	31.6
December	4	16	39.7	53	4	2	16	0	0	8	59	36.0
Grass	4	13	41.0	58	5	0	13	2	0	4	49	34.2
Turf	12	40	40.8	55	12	10	40	4	0	18	167	34.7
Indoor	2	6	43.3	51	3	2	6	1	0	1	6	39.0
Outdoor	14	47	40.6	58	14	8	47	5	0	21	210	34.0
Outdoors, Temp < 40		6	39.3	51	1	1	6	0	0	3	21	35.8
Outdoors, Temp 40-80	12	38	41.2	58	12	5	38	5	0	17	183	33.8
Outdoors, Temp > 80	1	3	34.3	50	1	2	3	0	0	1	6	32.3
Winning	-	31	38.0	57	10	8	31	2	0	11	121	32.8
Tied	-	14	43.5	58	3	1	14	2	0	8	62	36.2
Trailing	-	8	47.5	53	4	1	8	2	0	3	33	38.4

Game Logs

Date	Opp	Result	NPunts	Avg	In20	TPunts	TB	Blk	Ret	Yds	NetAvg
09/04	@NYN	W 35-0	3	41.3	1	3	1	0	1	17	29.0
09/10	Den	W 31-21	3	34.3	1	3	0	0	1	6	32.3
09/17	@Min	W 23-17	5	42.8	3	5	0	0	1	6	41.6
09/24	Ari	W 34-20	3	30.7	1	3	1	0	0	0	24.0
10/01	@Was	L 23-27	3	49.7	1	3	2	0	0	0	36.3
10/08	GB	W 34-24	4	51.5	0	4	0	0	4	40	41.5
10/15	@SD	W 23-9	5	39.4	2	5	0	0	2	24	34.6
10/29	@Atl	W 28-13	1	46.0	0	1	1	0	0	0	26.0
11/06	Phi	W 34-12	3	29.3	2	3	0	0	0	0	29.3
11/12	SF	L 20-38	3	47.3	1	3	1	0	2	27	31.7
11/19	@Oak	W 34-21	3	43.3	1	3	0	0	2	25	35.0
11/23	KC	W 24-12	1	40.0	0	1	0	0	1	12	28.0
12/03	Was	L 17-24	6	40.3	2	6	0	0	3	11	38.5
12/10	@Phi	L 17-20	6	39.3	1	6	0	0	3	21	35.8
12/17	NYN	W 21-20	2	50.0	0	2	0	0	2	27	36.5
12/25	@Ari	W 37-13	2	28.5	1	2	0	0	0	0	28.5

Lee Johnson

	G	NPunts	Avg	Lg	In20	FC	TPunts	TB	Blk	Ret	Yds	NetAvg
Total	16	68	42.1	61	26	19	68	4	0	27	154	38.6
vs. Playoff	5	19	44.0	61	6	4	19	1	0	8	35	41.1
vs. Non-playoff	11	49	41.3	60	20	15	49	3	0	19	119	37.7
vs. Own Division	8	33	42.8	61	13	7	33	2	0	14	79	39.2
Home	8	36	39.2	61	15	13	36	2	0	12	50	36.7
Away	8	32	45.3	60	11	6	32	2	0	15	104	40.8
September	4	16	45.9	60	7	3	16	2	0	6	27	41.7
October	4	16	44.1	53	6	3	16	1	0	7	43	40.1
November	4	18	41.4	61	8	3	18	1	0	8	61	36.9
December	4	18	37.6	56	5	10	16	0	0	6	23	36.3
Grass	4	16	43.3	54	4	4	16	0	0	10	56	39.8
Turf	12	52	41.7	61	22	15	52	4	0	17	98	38.3
Indoor	3	13	47.8	60	5	2	13	2	0	4	48	41.0
Outdoor	13	55	40.7	61	21	17	55	2	0	23	106	38.1
Outdoors, Temp < 40	5	23	37.3	56	8	11	23	0	0	8	30	36.0
Outdoors, Temp 40-80	7	29	42.7	61	12	6	29	2	0	13	65	39.1
Outdoors, Temp > 80	1	3	48.0	53	1	0	3	0	0	2	11	44.3
Winning	-	18	39.8	61	9	6	18	2	0	3	25	36.2
Tied	-	25	44.6	56	9	7	25	2	0	10	60	40.6
Trailing	-	25	41.2	60	8	6	25	0	0	14	69	38.4

Game Logs

Date	Opp	Result	NPunts	Avg	In20	TPunts	TB	Blk	Ret	Yds	NetAvg
09/03	@Ind	W 24-21	2	52.0	1	2	0	0	0	0	52.0
09/10	Jac	W 24-17	4	40.3	3	4	0	0	2	8	38.3
09/17	@Sea	L 21-24	6	47.3	2	6	1	0	2	18	41.0
09/24	Hou	L 28-38	4	46.3	1	4	1	0	2	1	41.0
10/01	Mia	L 23-26	5	45.4	1	5	1	0	3	17	38.0
10/08	@TB	L 16-19	3	48.0	1	3	0	0	2	11	44.3
10/19	@Pit	W 27-9	3	45.0	2	3	0	0	1	0	45.0
10/29	Cle	L 26-29	5	39.8	2	5	0	0	1	15	36.8
11/05	Oak	L 17-20	5	36.2	3	5	0	0	2	7	34.8
11/12	@Hou	L 32-25	5	46.6	2	5	1	0	2	30	36.6
11/19	Pit	L 31-49	4	40.0	1	4	0	0	1	-1	40.3
11/26	@Jac	W 17-13	4	42.8	2	4	0	0	3	25	36.5
12/03	@GB	L 10-24	5	42.0	1	5	0	0	3	19	38.2
12/10	Chi	W 16-10	4	28.0	0	4	0	0	0	0	28.0
12/17	@Cle	L 10-26	4	42.0	0	4	0	0	2	1	41.8
12/24	Min	W 27-24	5	37.4	1	5	0	0	1	3	36.8

Norm Johnson

	G	1-29 Yd	30-39 Yd	40-49 Yd	50+ Yd	Overall	Pct	Lg	Num	Avg	TB	TD	NetAvg
		1995 Field Goal Splits							1995 Kickoff Splits				
Total	16	11-11	14-16	8-13	1-1	34-41	82.9	50	93	58.6	3	0	40.6
vs. Playoff	4	2-2	3-3	2-3	0-0	7-8	87.5	47	19	60.1	1	0	43.6
vs. Non-playoff	12	9-9	11-13	6-10	1-1	27-33	81.8	50	74	58.2	2	0	39.8
vs. Own Division	8	6-6	5-7	3-4	1-1	15-18	83.3	50	44	58.6	1	0	41.3
Home	8	3-3	10-12	1-6	0-0	14-21	66.7	47	43	58.6	1	0	41.4
Away	8	8-8	4-4	7-7	1-1	20-20	100.0	50	50	58.5	2	0	39.9
Games 1-8	8	5-5	6-8	5-8	0-0	16-21	76.2	47	41	59.2	2	0	43.0
Games 9-16	8	6-6	8-8	3-5	1-1	18-20	90.0	50	52	58.0	1	0	38.6
September	4	0-0	4-4	4-7	0-0	8-11	72.7	47	21	58.1	0	0	41.8
October	4	5-5	2-4	1-1	0-0	8-10	80.0	41	20	60.4	2	0	44.3
November	4	3-3	3-3	2-3	1-1	9-10	90.0	50	27	57.5	0	0	37.3
December	4	3-3	5-5	1-2	0-0	9-10	90.0	41	25	58.6	0	0	40.1
Grass	6	7-7	4-4	5-5	0-0	16-16	100.0	46	34	58.6	2	0	39.5
Turf	10	4-4	10-12	3-8	1-1	18-25	72.0	50	59	58.5	1	0	41.2
Indoor	1	0-0	0-0	2-2	0-0	2-2	100.0	42	7	54.7	0	0	42.4
Outdoor	15	11-11	14-16	6-11	1-1	32-39	82.1	50	86	58.9	3	0	40.4
4th qtr, +/-3 pts	-	1-1	1-1	0-0	0-0	2-2	100.0	31	3	48.3	0	0	36.7
Winning	-	3-3	6-6	4-6	0-0	13-15	86.7	47	54	58.0	2	0	41.0
Tied	-	2-2	4-6	0-3	0-0	6-11	54.5	39	12	58.3	0	0	37.3
Trailing	-	6-6	4-4	4-4	1-1	15-15	100.0	50	27	59.9	1	0	41.1

Game Logs

Date	Opp	Result	1-39 Yd	40-49 Yd	50+ Yd	Lg
09/03	Det	W 23-20	2-2	1-2	0-0	47
09/10	@Hou	W 34-17	0-0	2-2	0-0	42
09/18	@Mia	L 10-23	0-0	1-1	0-0	40
09/24	Min	L 24-44	2-2	0-2	0-0	35
10/01	SD	W 31-16	1-1	0-0	0-0	25
10/08	@Jac	L 16-20	2-2	1-1	0-0	41
10/19	Cin	W 9-27	3-5	0-0	0-0	38
10/29	Jac	W 24-7	1-1	0-0	0-0	36
11/05	@Chi	W 37-34	1-1	2-2	0-0	46
11/13	Cle	W 20-3	2-2	0-1	0-0	38
11/19	@Cin	W 49-31	1-1	0-0	1-1	50
11/26	@Cle	W 20-17	2-2	0-0	0-0	33
12/03	Hou	W 21-7	0-0	0-0	0-0	0
12/10	@Oak	W 29-10	4-4	1-1	0-0	41
12/16	NE	W 41-27	2-2	0-1	0-0	32
12/24	@GB	L 19-24	2-2	0-0	0-0	33

John Kasay

	G	1-29 Yd	30-39 Yd	40-49 Yd	50+ Yd	Overall	Pct	Lg	Num	Avg	TB	TD	NetAvg
		1995 Field Goal Splits							1995 Kickoff Splits				
Total	16	6-6	10-14	9-12	1-1	26-33	78.8	52	66	59.6	3	0	40.9
vs. Playoff	6	0-0	6-7	3-4	1-1	10-12	83.3	52	24	61.0	0	0	45.7
vs. Non-playoff	10	6-6	4-7	6-8	0-0	16-21	76.2	47	42	58.7	3	0	38.2
vs. Own Division	8	2-2	3-3	5-6	0-0	10-11	90.9	47	29	62.4	1	0	40.4
Home	8	1-1	6-7	5-7	0-0	12-15	80.0	45	33	60.1	3	0	43.2
Away	8	5-5	4-7	4-5	1-1	14-18	77.8	52	33	59.1	0	0	38.7
Games 1-8	8	4-4	6-9	5-6	1-1	16-20	80.0	52	35	59.5	3	0	41.5
Games 9-16	8	2-2	4-5	4-6	0-0	10-13	76.9	47	31	59.6	0	0	40.3
September	3	0-0	3-4	2-2	1-1	6-7	85.7	52	10	62.9	1	0	46.3
October	5	4-4	3-5	3-4	0-0	10-13	76.9	49	25	58.2	2	0	39.6
November	4	2-2	2-3	2-3	0-0	6-8	75.0	47	17	58.9	0	0	38.4
December	4	0-0	2-2	2-3	0-0	4-5	80.0	43	14	60.4	0	0	42.6
Grass	12	4-4	7-10	8-10	0-0	19-24	79.2	49	50	58.9	3	0	41.4
Turf	4	2-2	3-4	1-2	1-1	7-9	77.8	52	16	61.5	0	0	39.4
Indoor	3	2-2	1-1	1-2	0-0	4-5	80.0	41	12	62.3	0	0	35.4
Outdoor	13	4-4	9-13	8-10	1-1	22-28	78.6	52	54	59.0	3	0	42.1
4th qtr, +/-3 pts	-	0-0	1-2	0-0	0-0	1-2	50.0	38	4	47.8	0	0	33.8
Winning	-	0-0	5-6	4-5	1-1	10-12	83.3	52	33	56.9	1	0	40.3
Tied	-	3-3	3-6	1-3	0-0	7-12	58.3	42	18	62.9	2	0	43.9
Trailing	-	3-3	2-2	4-4	0-0	9-9	100.0	49	15	61.4	0	0	38.7

Game Logs

Date	Opp	Result	1-39 Yd	40-49 Yd	50+ Yd	Lg
09/03	@Atl	L 20-23	1-1	1-1	0-0	41
09/10	@Buf	L 9-31	2-3	0-0	1-1	52
09/17	StL	L 10-31	0-0	1-1	0-0	45
10/01	TB	L 13-20	0-0	0-0	0-0	45
10/08	@Chi	L 27-31	1-1	1-1	0-0	49
10/15	NYA	W 26-15	3-3	1-1	0-0	40
10/22	NO	W 20-3	1-1	1-1	0-0	45
10/29	@NE	W 20-17	2-4	0-0	0-0	29
11/05	@SF	W 13-7	1-1	1-1	0-0	47
11/12	@StL	L 17-28	1-1	0-1	0-0	23
11/19	Ari	W 27-7	1-2	1-1	0-0	42
11/26	@NO	L 26-34	1-1	0-0	0-0	22
12/03	Ind	W 13-10	2-2	0-1	0-0	38
12/10	SF	L 10-31	0-0	1-1	0-0	43
12/17	Atl	W 21-17	0-0	0-0	0-0	0
12/24	@Was	L 17-20	0-0	1-1	0-0	42

John Kidd

	G	NPunts	Avg	Lg	In20	FC	TPunts	TB	Blk	Ret	Yds	NetAvg
		1995 Punter Splits										
Total	16	57	42.7	56	15	10	57	5	0	35	265	36.3
vs. Playoff	9	34	42.1	53	11	7	34	1	0	22	156	36.9
vs. Non-playoff	7	23	43.5	56	4	3	23	4	0	13	109	35.3
vs. Own Division	8	26	42.9	56	6	4	26	3	0	16	139	35.2
Home	8	31	42.7	53	7	6	31	3	0	20	150	36.0
Away	8	26	42.6	56	8	4	26	2	0	15	115	36.7
September	3	13	42.4	56	1	3	13	2	0	7	54	35.2
October	5	16	44.1	53	6	3	16	2	0	9	85	36.3
November	4	10	38.9	51	4	1	10	0	0	6	22	36.7
December	4	18	43.7	54	4	3	18	1	0	13	104	36.8
Grass	10	35	42.5	56	9	6	35	3	0	22	160	36.3
Turf	6	22	42.9	54	6	4	22	2	0	13	105	36.3
Indoor	3	11	43.9	54	2	2	11	1	0	7	56	37.0
Outdoor	13	46	42.4	56	13	8	46	4	0	28	209	36.1
Outdoors, Temp < 40	1	5	41.8	46	1	2	5	0	0	3	25	36.8
Outdoors, Temp 40-80	8	23	41.2	56	9	2	23	1	0	14	81	36.8
Outdoors, Temp > 80	4	18	44.1	53	3	4	18	3	0	11	103	35.1
Winning	-	31	43.1	56	9	5	31	2	0	21	172	36.2
Tied	-	11	44.4	54	2	0	11	2	0	7	68	34.5
Trailing	-	15	40.7	51	4	5	15	1	0	7	25	37.7

Game Logs

Date	Opp	Result	NPunts	Avg	In20	TPunts	TB	Blk	Ret	Yds	NetAvg
09/03	NYA	W 52-14	5	44.4	0	5	2	0	2	16	33.2
09/10	@NE	W 20-3	2	40.0	0	2	0	0	1	10	35.0
09/18	Pit	W 23-10	6	41.5	1	6	0	0	4	28	36.8
10/01	@Cin	W 26-23	2	48.5	1	2	1	0	0	0	38.5
10/08	Ind	L 24-27	2	36.0	2	2	0	0	1	5	33.5
10/15	@NO	L 30-33	3	43.7	1	3	0	0	1	2	43.0
10/22	@NYA	L 16-17	4	38.8	2	4	0	0	3	24	32.8
10/29	Buf	W 23-6	5	50.2	0	5	1	0	4	54	35.4
11/05	@SD	W 24-14	2	42.0	2	2	0	0	1	0	36.7
11/12	NE	L 17-34	1	45.0	0	1	0	0	1	4	41.0
11/20	SF	L 20-44	5	35.8	1	5	0	0	3	17	32.4
12/03	Atl	W 21-20	1	38.0	0	1	0	0	1	0	
12/11	KC	W 13-6	6	44.8	3	6	0	0	4	26	40.5
12/17	@Buf	L 20-23	5	41.8	1	5	0	0	3	25	36.8
12/24	@StL	W 41-22	6	45.2	0	6	1	0	5	53	33.0

Sean Landeta

1995 Punter Splits

	G	NPunts	Avg	Lg	In20	FC	TPunts	TB	Blk	Ret	Yds	NetAvg
Total	16	83	44.3	63	23	16	83	12	0	38	393	36.7
vs. Playoff	9	43	44.6	63	10	8	43	5	0	20	256	36.3
vs. Non-playoff	7	40	44.0	57	13	8	40	7	0	18	137	37.1
vs. Own Division	8	39	43.8	57	12	10	39	6	0	17	186	35.9
Home	8	35	43.5	57	14	9	35	7	0	14	185	34.2
Away	8	48	44.9	63	9	7	48	5	0	24	208	38.5
September	4	26	43.6	57	6	5	26	5	0	13	101	35.8
October	4	18	43.1	63	5	3	18	2	0	9	130	33.7
November	4	17	44.2	57	6	5	17	1	0	7	51	40.0
December	4	22	46.3	57	6	3	22	4	0	9	111	37.6
Grass	3	21	44.8	53	3	4	21	2	0	11	93	38.4
Turf	13	62	44.2	63	20	12	62	10	0	27	300	36.1
Indoor	7	28	43.4	57	10	5	28	2	0	13	121	37.7
Outdoor	9	55	44.8	63	13	11	55	10	0	25	272	36.2
Outdoors, Temp < 40	0	0	-	0	0	0	0	0	0	0	0	-
Outdoors, Temp 40-80	9	55	44.8	63	13	11	55	10	0	25	272	36.2
Outdoors, Temp > 80	0	0	-	0	0	0	0	0	0	0	0	-
Winning	-	32	43.7	57	11	8	32	6	0	13	174	34.5
Tied	-	25	44.4	53	5	4	25	2	0	14	105	38.6
Trailing	-	26	45.1	63	7	4	26	4	0	11	114	37.7

Game Logs

Date	Opp	Result	NPunts	Avg	In20	TPunts	TB	Blk	Ret	Yds	NetAvg
09/03	@GB	W 17-14	9	45.2	1	9	0	0	6	61	38.4
09/10	NO	W 17-13	6	44.0	2	6	3	0	1	0	34.0
09/17	@Car	W 31-10	7	42.4	1	7	1	0	4	30	35.3
09/24	Chi	W 34-28	4	41.3	2	4	1	0	2	10	33.8
10/01	@Ind	L 18-21	4	41.5	1	4	0	0	3	18	37.0
10/12	Atl	W 21-19	4	40.5	2	4	1	0	2	68	18.5
10/22	SF	L 10-44	5	46.6	1	5	0	0	3	37	39.2
10/29	@Phi	L 9-20	5	43.0	1	5	1	0	1	7	37.6
11/05	@NO	L 10-19	5	44.0	1	5	0	0	3	20	40.0
11/12	Car	W 28-17	4	40.8	3	4	0	0	2	16	36.8
11/19	@Atl	L 6-31	3	44.0	1	3	0	0	1	13	39.7
11/26	@SF	L 13-41	5	47.2	1	5	1	0	1	2	42.8
12/03	@NYA	W 23-20	10	48.4	2	10	2	0	5	57	38.7
12/10	Buf	L 27-45	5	47.2	1	5	1	0	3	50	33.2
12/17	Was	L 23-35	4	42.0	2	4	0	0	1	4	41.0
12/24	Mia	L 22-41	3	43.7	1	3	1	0	0	0	37.0

Chip Lohmiller

1995 Field Goal Splits / 1995 Kickoff Splits

	G	1-29 Yd	30-39 Yd	40-49 Yd	50+ Yd	Overall	Pct	Lg	Num	Avg	TB	TD	NetAvg
Total	8	4-6	3-4	0-2	1-2	8-14	57.1	51	32	64.0	1	0	46.0
vs. Playoff	5	2-4	1-1	0-2	1-2	4-9	44.4	51	21	63.8	0	0	45.7
vs. Non-playoff	3	2-2	2-3	0-0	0-0	4-5	80.0	34	11	64.5	1	0	46.5
vs. Own Division	5	3-4	2-3	0-1	1-1	6-9	66.7	51	18	62.7	0	0	46.4
Home	4	1-2	1-1	0-1	1-2	3-6	50.0	51	18	64.9	0	0	45.7
Away	4	3-4	2-3	0-1	0-0	5-8	62.5	34	14	62.9	1	0	46.4
Games 1-8	8	4-6	3-4	0-2	1-2	8-14	57.1	51	32	64.0	1	0	46.0
Games 9-16	0	0-0	0-0	0-0	0-0	0-0	-	0	0	-	0	0	-
September	4	2-2	2-3	0-0	1-1	5-6	83.3	51	18	63.5	1	0	44.9
October	4	2-4	1-1	0-2	0-1	3-8	37.5	34	14	64.7	0	0	47.4
November	0	0-0	0-0	0-0	0-0	0-0	-	0	0	-	0	0	-
December	0	0-0	0-0	0-0	0-0	0-0	-	0	0	-	0	0	-
Grass	2	2-3	0-0	0-1	0-0	2-4	50.0	29	5	61.8	0	0	48.4
Turf	6	2-3	3-4	0-1	1-2	6-10	60.0	51	27	64.4	1	0	45.6
Indoor	4	1-2	1-1	0-1	1-2	3-6	50.0	51	18	64.9	0	0	45.7
Outdoor	4	3-4	2-3	0-1	0-0	5-8	62.5	34	14	62.9	1	0	46.4
4th qtr, +/-3 pts	-	0-0	0-0	0-0	0-0	0-0	-	0	0	60.0	0	0	43.0
Winning	-	1-3	0-0	0-1	0-0	1-5	20.0	21	16	64.6	0	0	46.6
Tied	-	2-2	2-2	0-0	0-0	4-4	100.0	34	7	64.3	1	0	45.9
Trailing	-	1-1	1-2	0-1	1-1	3-5	60.0	51	9	62.9	0	0	45.0

Game Logs

Date	Opp	Result	1-39 Yd	40-49 Yd	50+ Yd	Lg
09/03	SF	L 22-24	0-0	0-0	1-1	51
09/10	@StL	L 13-17	2-3	0-0	0-0	34
09/17	Atl	L 24-27	1-1	0-0	0-0	21
09/24	@NYN	L 29-45	1-1	0-0	0-0	20
10/01	Phi	L 10-15	1-1	0-0	0-0	34
10/15	Mia	W 33-30	0-0	0-1	0-1	0
10/22	@Car	L 3-20	1-1	0-0	0-0	29
10/29	@SF	W 11-7	1-2	0-1	0-0	20

Nick Lowery

1995 Field Goal Splits / 1995 Kickoff Splits

	G	1-29 Yd	30-39 Yd	40-49 Yd	50+ Yd	Overall	Pct	Lg	Num	Avg	TB	TD	NetAvg
Total	14	4-4	8-10	3-3	2-4	17-21	81.0	50	0	-	0	0	-
vs. Playoff	7	2-2	3-4	1-1	1-2	7-9	77.8	50	0	-	0	0	-
vs. Non-playoff	7	2-2	5-6	2-2	1-2	10-12	83.3	50	0	-	0	0	-
vs. Own Division	8	2-2	2-4	1-1	1-2	6-9	66.7	50	0	-	0	0	-
Home	7	3-3	4-4	1-1	1-1	9-9	100.0	50	0	-	0	0	-
Away	7	1-1	4-6	2-2	1-3	8-12	66.7	50	0	-	0	0	-
Games 1-8	8	3-3	3-4	1-1	2-3	9-11	81.8	50	0	-	0	0	-
Games 9-16	6	1-1	5-6	2-2	0-1	8-10	80.0	42	0	-	0	0	-
September	4	2-2	1-1	1-1	0-1	4-5	80.0	48	0	-	0	0	-
October	5	2-2	2-3	1-1	2-2	6-7	85.7	50	0	-	0	0	-
November	3	0-0	4-4	1-1	0-1	5-6	83.3	41	0	-	0	0	-
December	2	1-1	1-2	0-0	0-0	2-3	66.7	34	0	-	0	0	-
Grass	3	0-0	1-2	0-0	1-2	2-4	50.0	50	0	-	0	0	-
Turf	11	4-4	7-8	3-3	1-2	15-17	88.2	50	0	-	0	0	-
Indoor	3	0-0	3-3	2-2	0-1	5-6	83.3	42	0	-	0	0	-
Outdoor	11	4-4	5-7	1-1	2-3	12-15	80.0	50	0	-	0	0	-
4th qtr, +/-3 pts	-	0-0	0-0	0-0	1-1	1-1	100.0	41	0	-	0	0	-
Winning	-	2-2	2-2	2-2	0-1	6-7	85.7	48	0	-	0	0	-
Tied	-	0-0	2-3	1-1	0-1	3-5	60.0	42	0	-	0	0	-
Trailing	-	2-2	4-5	0-0	2-2	8-9	88.9	50	0	-	0	0	-

Game Logs

Date	Opp	Result	1-39 Yd	40-49 Yd	50+ Yd	Lg
09/03	@Mia	L 14-52	0-0	0-0	0-1	0
09/10	Ind	L 24-27	1-1	0-0	0-0	28
09/17	Jac	W 27-10	1-1	1-1	0-0	48
09/24	@Atl	L 3-13	1-1	0-0	0-0	37
10/01	Oak	L 10-47	1-1	0-0	0-0	33
10/08	@Buf	L 10-29	1-2	0-0	0-0	26
10/15	@Car	L 15-26	1-1	0-0	1-1	50
10/22	Mia	W 17-16	0-0	0-0	1-1	50
10/29	@Ind	L 10-17	0-0	1-1	0-0	42
11/05	NE	L 7-20	0-0	0-0	0-0	0
11/19	Buf	L 26-28	2-2	0-0	0-0	35
11/26	@Sea	W 16-10	2-2	1-1	0-1	41
12/03	StL	L 20-23	0-1	0-0	0-0	34
12/10	@NE	L 28-31	0-1	0-0	0-0	0
12/17	@Hou	L 6-23	-	-	-	-
12/24	NO	L 0-12	-	-	-	-

Steve McLaughlin
St. Louis Rams — K

	G	1995 Field Goal Splits							1995 Kickoff Splits					Game Logs						
		1-29 Yd	30-39 Yd	40-49 Yd	50+ Yd	Overall	Pct	Lg	Num	Avg	TB	TD	NetAvg	Date	Opp	Result	1-39 Yd	40-49 Yd	50+ Yd	Lg
Total	8	5-6	2-6	1-3	0-1	8-16	50.0	45	34	60.5	2	0	41.3	09/03	@GB	W 17-14	1-1	0-0	0-0	19
vs. Playoff	5	4-5	0-2	0-0	0-1	4-8	50.0	29	17	59.1	0	0	41.5	09/10	NO	W 17-13	1-1	0-1	0-0	31
vs. Non-playoff	3	1-1	2-4	1-3	0-0	4-8	50.0	45	17	62.0	2	0	41.0	09/17	@Car	W 31-10	1-3	0-1	0-0	34
vs. Own Division	4	1-2	2-5	0-2	0-0	3-9	33.3	34	17	62.1	2	0	41.9	09/24	Chi	W 34-28	1-1	1-1	0-0	45
Home	4	2-3	1-2	1-2	0-0	4-7	57.1	45	18	57.7	0	0	39.5	10/01	@Ind	L 18-21	1-1	0-0	0-0	29
Away	4	3-3	1-4	0-1	0-1	4-9	44.4	34	16	63.7	2	0	43.3	10/12	Atl	W 21-19	0-1	0-0	0-0	0
Games 1-8	8	5-6	2-6	1-3	0-1	8-16	50.0	45	34	60.5	2	0	41.3	10/22	SF	L 10-44	1-2	0-0	0-0	25
Games 9-16	0	0-0	0-0	0-0	0-0	0-0	-	0	0	-	0	0	-	10/29	@Phi	L 9-20	1-2	0-0	0-1	29
September	4	2-2	2-4	1-3	0-0	5-9	55.6	45	21	61.7	2	0	40.9							
October	4	3-4	0-2	0-0	0-1	3-7	42.9	29	13	58.7	0	0	41.9							
November	0	0-0	0-0	0-0	0-0	0-0	-	0	0	-	0	0	-							
December	0	0-0	0-0	0-0	0-0	0-0	-	0	0	-	0	0	-							
Grass	2	1-1	1-3	0-1	0-0	2-5	40.0	34	10	65.8	2	0	42.4							
Turf	6	4-5	1-3	1-2	0-1	6-11	54.5	45	24	58.3	0	0	40.8							
Indoor	1	1-1	0-0	0-0	0-0	1-1	100.0	29	3	66.0	0	0	48.0							
Outdoor	7	4-5	2-6	1-3	0-1	7-15	46.7	45	31	60.0	2	0	40.6							
4th qtr, +/-3 pts	-	1-1	0-0	0-0	0-0	1-1	100.0	25	1	35.0	0	0	32.0							
Winning	-	2-3	2-4	1-3	0-0	5-10	50.0	45	25	62.3	2	0	42.0							
Tied	-	1-1	0-0	0-0	0-0	1-1	100.0	29	2	55.5	0	0	35.0							
Trailing	-	2-2	0-2	0-0	0-1	2-5	40.0	29	7	55.6	0	0	40.6							

Chris Mohr
Buffalo Bills — P

	G	NPunts	Avg	1995 Punter Splits			TPunts	TB	Blk	Ret	Yds	NetAvg	Date	Opp	Result	NPunts	Avg	In20	TPunts	TB	Blk	Ret	Yds	NetAvg
				Lg	In20	FC																		
Total	16	86	40.4	60	23	30	86	7	0	23	224	36.2	09/03	@Den	L 7-22	8	41.5	1	8	0	0	2	34	37.3
vs. Playoff	6	31	40.1	60	6	11	31	2	0	9	33	37.7	09/10	Car	W 31-9	6	41.0	0	6	0	0	1	4	40.3
vs. Non-playoff	10	55	40.6	56	17	19	55	5	0	14	191	35.3	09/17	Ind	W 20-14	6	37.3	0	6	0	0	1	4	36.7
vs. Own Division	8	41	38.7	54	11	17	41	3	0	12	68	35.6	10/02	@Cle	W 22-19	2	47.5	1	2	0	0	1	69	13.0
Home	8	43	39.9	60	12	15	43	4	0	8	59	36.7	10/08	NYA	W 29-10	2	36.0	1	2	0	0	0	0	36.0
Away	8	43	40.9	56	11	15	43	3	0	15	165	35.7	10/15	Sea	W 27-21	7	39.6	1	7	1	0	1	11	35.1
September	3	20	40.1	56	1	12	20	0	0	4	42	38.0	10/23	@NE	L 14-27	6	35.5	2	6	0	0	1	13	33.3
October	5	23	40.5	55	6	8	23	1	0	7	115	34.6	10/29	@Mia	L 6-23	6	45.7	1	6	0	0	4	22	42.0
November	4	21	39.2	60	7	4	21	3	0	7	34	34.8	11/05	@Ind	W 16-10	5	43.4	0	5	1	0	3	3	38.8
December	4	22	41.6	55	9	6	22	3	0	5	34	37.4	11/12	Atl	W 23-17	4	40.3	2	4	0	0	1	4	39.3
Grass	5	28	40.6	56	6	13	28	1	0	8	138	35.0	11/19	@NYA	W 28-26	7	36.3	3	7	1	0	2	11	31.9
Turf	11	58	40.3	60	17	17	58	6	0	15	86	36.7	11/26	NE	L 25-35	5	38.4	2	5	1	0	1	15	31.4
Indoor	2	8	45.8	55	2	1	8	1	0	5	16	41.3	12/03	@SF	L 17-27	6	37.3	1	6	1	0	0	0	34.0
Outdoor	14	78	39.8	60	21	29	78	6	0	18	208	35.6	12/10	@StL	W 45-27	3	49.7	2	3	0	0	2	13	45.3
Outdoors, Temp < 40	4	22	40.7	60	10	6	22	3	0	5	40	36.2	12/17	Mia	W 23-20	4	35.5	2	4	0	0	0	0	35.5
Outdoors, Temp 40-80	8	42	38.2	55	9	16	42	3	0	7	112	34.1	12/24	Hou	L 17-28	9	44.6	4	9	2	0	3	21	37.8
Outdoors, Temp > 80	2	14	43.3	56	2	7	14	0	0	6	56	39.3												
Winning	-	31	39.9	56	9	10	31	2	0	10	137	34.2												
Tied	-	24	38.5	60	8	9	24	3	0	2	8	35.7												
Trailing	-	31	42.3	56	6	11	31	2	0	11	79	38.5												

Eddie Murray
Washington Redskins — K

	G	1995 Field Goal Splits							1995 Kickoff Splits					Game Logs						
		1-29 Yd	30-39 Yd	40-49 Yd	50+ Yd	Overall	Pct	Lg	Num	Avg	TB	TD	NetAvg	Date	Opp	Result	1-39 Yd	40-49 Yd	50+ Yd	Lg
Total	16	10-10	10-13	6-11	1-2	27-36	75.0	52	76	59.8	2	1	38.8	09/03	Ari	W 27-7	2-2	0-0	0-0	36
vs. Playoff	6	2-2	4-4	3-6	0-1	9-13	69.2	47	29	59.5	1	0	39.7	09/10	Oak	L 8-20	1-2	1-1	0-0	43
vs. Non-playoff	10	8-8	6-9	3-5	1-1	18-23	78.3	52	47	60.0	1	1	38.2	09/17	@Den	L 31-38	1-2	0-0	0-0	21
vs. Own Division	8	3-3	6-7	4-7	1-2	14-19	73.7	52	40	59.2	1	1	37.9	09/24	@TB	L 6-14	2-2	0-1	0-0	37
Home	8	6-6	5-6	4-6	1-2	16-20	80.0	52	38	59.0	0	0	37.5	10/01	Dal	W 27-23	1-1	1-1	0-0	46
Away	8	4-4	5-7	2-5	0-0	11-16	68.8	47	38	60.6	2	1	40.1	10/08	@Phi	L 34-37	1-1	1-2	0-0	46
Games 1-8	8	6-6	7-9	3-6	0-0	16-21	76.2	46	43	61.5	2	0	39.9	10/15	@Ari	L 20-24	2-2	0-0	0-0	38
Games 9-16	8	4-4	3-4	3-5	1-2	11-15	73.3	52	33	57.6	0	1	37.3	10/22	Det	W 36-30	3-3	0-1	0-0	39
September	4	4-4	2-4	1-2	0-0	7-10	70.0	43	18	64.0	1	0	39.9	10/29	NYN	L 15-24	1-1	1-1	1-1	52
October	5	3-3	5-5	3-5	1-1	12-14	85.7	52	30	59.0	1	0	39.4	11/05	@KC	L 3-24	1-1	0-0	0-0	29
November	3	2-2	0-0	1-2	0-1	3-5	60.0	48	8	60.4	0	0	37.5	11/19	Sea	L 20-27	1-1	0-0	0-0	48
December	4	1-1	3-4	1-2	0-0	5-7	71.4	47	20	57.0	0	0	37.4	11/26	Phi	L 7-14	0-0	0-1	0-1	0
Grass	12	10-10	7-9	4-7	1-2	22-28	78.6	52	54	59.8	1	0	38.2	12/03	@Dal	W 24-17	0-0	0-0	0-0	47
Turf	4	0-0	3-4	2-4	0-0	5-8	62.5	47	22	59.8	1	1	40.1	12/10	@NYN	L 13-20	2-3	0-0	0-0	34
Indoor	1	0-0	0-0	0-0	0-0	0-0	-	0	6	61.3	0	0	45.5	12/17	@StL	W 35-23	0-0	0-0	0-0	0
Outdoor	15	10-10	10-13	6-11	1-2	27-36	75.0	52	70	59.7	2	1	38.2	12/24	Car	W 20-17	2-2	0-0	0-0	32
4th qtr, +/-3 pts	-	0-0	1-1	1-1	0-0	2-2	100.0	46	6	59.7	1	0	42.0							
Winning	-	3-3	1-1	1-2	0-0	5-6	83.3	47	36	59.1	1	0	39.6							
Tied	-	2-2	3-6	2-4	0-0	7-12	58.3	46	23	62.1	1	1	37.2							
Trailing	-	5-5	6-6	3-5	1-2	15-18	83.3	52	17	58.1	0	0	39.2							

Pat O'Neill

	G	NPunts	Avg	Lg	In20	FC	TPunts	TB	Blk	Ret	Yds	NetAvg
Total	9	44	36.4	57	14	6	44	3	0	21	183	30.9
vs. Playoff	6	26	36.8	57	9	3	26	1	0	12	85	32.8
vs. Non-playoff	3	18	35.9	52	5	3	18	2	0	9	98	28.2
vs. Own Division	3	11	29.9	42	1	0	11	1	0	4	13	26.9
Home	6	29	33.6	52	6	3	29	3	0	13	111	27.7
Away	3	15	41.9	57	8	3	15	0	0	8	72	37.1
September	3	11	37.2	52	5	3	11	2	0	3	21	31.6
October	5	30	36.8	57	9	3	30	1	0	17	153	31.1
November	1	3	29.7	39	0	0	3	0	0	1	9	26.7
December	0	0	-	0	0	0	0	0	0	0	0	-
Grass	8	39	36.2	57	10	4	39	3	0	18	166	30.4
Turf	1	5	38.4	46	4	2	5	0	0	3	17	35.0
Indoor	1	5	38.4	46	4	2	5	0	0	3	17	35.0
Outdoor	8	39	36.2	57	10	4	39	3	0	18	166	30.4
Outdoors, Temp < 40	1	5	37.8	52	3	2	5	1	0	2	21	29.6
Outdoors, Temp 40-80	7	34	35.9	57	7	2	34	2	0	16	145	30.5
Outdoors, Temp > 80	0	0	-	0	0	0	0	0	0	0	0	
Winning	-	8	32.9	42	3	1	8	0	0	4	45	27.3
Tied	-	17	34.3	46	6	3	17	0	0	7	42	31.8
Trailing	-	19	39.8	57	5	2	19	3	0	10	96	31.6

Game Logs

Date	Opp	Result	NPunts	Avg	In20	TPunts	TB	Blk	Ret	Yds	NetAvg
09/03	Cle	W 17-14	5	37.8	3	5	1	0	2	21	29.6
09/10	Mia	L 3-20	3	33.0	0	3	1	0	1	0	26.3
09/17	@SF	L 3-28	3	40.3	2	3	0	0	3	0	40.3
10/01	@Atl	L 17-30	5	38.4	4	5	0	0	3	17	35.0
10/08	Den	L 3-37	5	39.6	0	5	1	0	2	12	33.2
10/15	@KC	L 26-31	7	45.0	2	7	0	0	5	55	37.1
10/23	Buf	W 27-14	5	28.2	1	5	0	0	2	4	27.4
10/29	Car	L 17-20	8	32.4	2	8	0	0	5	65	24.3
11/19	Det	L 17-24	3	29.7	0	3	0	0	1	9	26.7
11/26	@NYN	W 27-24	-								
12/04	@Det	L 7-27	-								
12/10	@Cin	L 10-16	-								
12/17	@Hou	L 6-23	-								
12/24	NO	L 0-12	-								

Doug Pelfrey

1995 Field Goal Splits / 1995 Kickoff Splits

	G	1-29 Yd	30-39 Yd	40-49 Yd	50+ Yd	Overall	Pct	Lg	Num	Avg	TB	TD	NetAvg
Total	16	8-9	10-11	10-14	1-2	29-36	80.6	51	15	62.9	0	0	37.5
vs. Playoff	5	5-5	3-3	2-3	0-0	10-11	90.9	47	6	60.5	0	0	36.5
vs. Non-playoff	11	3-4	7-8	8-11	1-2	19-25	76.0	51	9	64.6	0	0	38.2
vs. Own Division	8	3-4	5-5	3-4	0-1	11-14	78.6	49	11	61.9	0	0	37.0
Home	8	4-4	3-3	5-8	1-2	13-17	76.5	51	11	61.9	0	0	37.0
Away	8	4-5	7-8	5-6	0-0	16-19	84.2	49	4	65.8	0	0	39.0
Games 1-8	8	3-3	5-6	6-9	0-1	14-19	73.7	47	9	64.6	0	0	38.2
Games 9-16	8	5-6	5-5	4-5	1-1	15-17	88.2	51	6	60.5	0	0	36.5
September	4	1-1	2-3	3-5	0-0	6-9	66.7	47	9	64.6	0	0	38.2
October	4	2-2	3-3	3-4	0-1	8-10	80.0	45	0	-	0	0	-
November	4	3-3	2-2	3-3	0-0	8-8	100.0	49	6	60.5	0	0	36.5
December	4	2-3	3-3	1-2	1-1	7-9	77.8	51	0	-	0	0	-
Grass	4	1-2	3-3	2-2	0-0	6-7	85.7	45	0	-	0	0	-
Turf	12	7-7	7-8	8-12	1-2	23-29	79.3	51	15	62.9	0	0	37.5
Indoor	3	2-2	3-4	3-4	0-0	8-10	80.0	49	4	65.8	0	0	39.0
Outdoor	13	6-7	7-7	7-10	1-2	21-26	80.8	51	11	61.9	0	0	37.0
4th qtr, +/-3 pts	-	0-0	1-1	0-2	1-1	2-4	50.0	51	2	68.0	0	0	40.5
Winning	-	3-3	5-5	0-2	0-0	8-10	80.0	39	11	61.9	0	0	37.0
Tied	-	1-1	2-3	4-4	0-0	8-10	80.0	51	1	62.0	0	0	34.0
Trailing	-	4-5	3-3	6-8	0-0	13-16	81.3	48	3	67.0	0	0	40.7

Game Logs

Date	Opp	Result	1-39 Yd	40-49 Yd	50+ Yd	Lg
09/03	@Ind	W 24-21	3-3	2-2	0-0	47
09/10	Jac	W 24-17	0-0	1-2	0-0	42
09/17	@Sea	L 21-24	0-1	0-1	0-0	0
09/24	Hou	L 28-38	0-0	0-0	0-0	0
10/01	Mia	L 23-26	1-1	0-1	0-0	28
10/08	@TB	L 16-19	1-1	2-2	0-0	45
10/19	@Pit	W 27-9	2-2	0-0	0-0	31
10/29	Cle	L 26-29	1-1	1-1	0-1	41
11/05	Oak	L 17-20	1-1	2-2	0-0	48
11/12	@Hou	W 32-25	2-2	1-1	0-0	49
11/19	Pit	L 31-49	1-1	0-0	0-0	27
11/26	@Jac	W 17-13	1-1	0-0	0-0	31
12/03	@GB	L 10-24	1-1	0-0	0-0	28
12/10	Chi	W 16-10	3-3	0-1	0-0	39
12/17	@Cle	L 10-26	1-2	0-0	0-0	30
12/24	Min	W 27-24	0-0	1-1	1-1	51

Todd Peterson

1995 Field Goal Splits / 1995 Kickoff Splits

	G	1-29 Yd	30-39 Yd	40-49 Yd	50+ Yd	Overall	Pct	Lg	Num	Avg	TB	TD	NetAvg
Total	16	6-6	9-10	8-10	0-2	23-28	82.1	49	79	64.2	8	2	40.6
vs. Playoff	6	2-2	3-3	4-4	0-0	9-9	100.0	49	23	62.4	2	2	35.3
vs. Non-playoff	10	4-4	6-7	4-6	0-2	14-19	73.7	47	56	64.9	6	0	42.7
vs. Own Division	8	4-4	4-5	3-4	0-0	11-13	84.6	49	37	65.0	5	2	38.4
Home	8	4-4	6-6	7-8	0-1	17-19	89.5	49	43	65.3	6	1	41.7
Away	8	2-2	3-4	1-2	0-1	6-9	66.7	47	36	62.8	2	1	39.2
Games 1-8	8	3-3	1-2	3-5	0-1	7-11	63.6	49	32	64.5	5	1	40.9
Games 9-16	8	3-3	8-8	5-5	0-1	16-17	94.1	47	47	63.9	3	1	40.4
September	3	1-1	1-1	1-1	0-1	3-4	75.0	49	10	66.8	1	1	39.7
October	5	2-2	0-1	2-4	0-0	4-7	57.1	48	22	63.4	4	0	41.5
November	4	2-2	2-2	3-3	0-1	7-8	87.5	47	24	63.0	1	0	40.8
December	4	1-1	6-6	2-2	0-0	9-9	100.0	49	23	64.9	2	1	40.0
Grass	7	2-2	3-4	1-2	0-1	6-9	66.7	47	32	63.7	1	1	39.0
Turf	9	4-4	6-6	7-8	0-1	17-19	89.5	49	47	64.5	7	1	41.6
Indoor	8	4-4	6-6	7-8	0-1	17-19	89.5	49	43	65.3	6	1	41.7
Outdoor	8	2-2	3-4	1-2	0-1	6-9	66.7	47	36	62.8	2	1	39.2
4th qtr, +/-3 pts	-	0-0	1-1	1-1	0-0	2-2	100.0	41	4	66.3	0	0	40.8
Winning	-	3-3	5-5	5-5	0-1	13-14	92.9	47	45	63.5	4	0	42.8
Tied	-	1-1	1-1	1-3	0-1	3-6	50.0	47	12	66.3	3	1	37.8
Trailing	-	2-2	3-4	2-2	0-0	7-8	87.5	48	22	64.3	1	1	37.7

Game Logs

Date	Opp	Result	1-39 Yd	40-49 Yd	50+ Yd	Lg
09/03	KC	L 10-34	0-0	1-1	0-0	49
09/10	@SD	L 10-14	1-1	0-0	0-0	23
09/17	Cin	W 24-21	1-1	0-0	0-1	38
10/01	Den	W 27-10	1-1	1-2	0-0	45
10/08	@Oak	L 14-34	0-1	0-0	0-0	0
10/15	@Buf	L 21-27	0-0	0-0	0-0	0
10/22	SD	L 25-35	1-1	1-1	0-0	48
10/29	@Ari	L 14-20	0-0	0-1	0-0	0
11/05	NYN	W 30-28	2-2	1-1	0-0	41
11/12	@Jac	W 47-30	1-1	0-0	0-0	25
11/19	@Was	W 27-20	1-1	1-1	0-1	47
11/26	NYA	L 10-16	0-0	1-1	0-0	42
12/03	Phi	W 26-14	2-2	2-2	0-0	47
12/10	@Den	W 31-27	1-1	0-0	0-0	36
12/17	Oak	W 44-10	3-3	0-0	0-0	39
12/24	@KC	L 3-26	1-1	0-0	0-0	34

Fuad Reveiz

1995 Field Goal Splits / 1995 Kickoff Splits

	G	1-29 Yd	30-39 Yd	40-49 Yd	50+ Yd	Overall	Pct	Lg	Num	Avg	TB	TD	NetAvg
Total	16	9-10	7-10	9-12	1-4	26-36	72.2	51	83	63.0	8	0	41.6
vs. Playoff	7	2-2	5-6	5-7	0-0	12-15	80.0	49	38	63.7	6	0	41.6
vs. Non-playoff	9	7-8	2-4	4-5	1-4	14-21	66.7	51	45	62.4	2	0	41.5
vs. Own Division	8	3-3	3-4	4-6	1-3	11-16	68.8	51	36	63.7	2	0	42.7
Home	8	6-6	5-5	3-6	0-2	14-19	73.7	43	42	64.1	3	0	42.5
Away	8	3-4	2-5	6-6	1-2	12-17	70.6	51	41	61.9	5	0	40.7
Games 1-8	8	3-3	3-3	5-6	1-2	12-14	85.7	51	36	64.9	5	0	42.7
Games 9-16	8	6-7	4-7	4-6	0-2	14-22	63.6	49	47	61.6	3	0	40.7
September	4	1-1	2-2	3-4	0-0	6-7	85.7	43	21	65.8	5	0	43.5
October	4	2-2	1-1	2-2	1-2	6-7	85.7	51	15	63.6	0	0	41.5
November	4	2-2	3-5	2-3	0-0	7-10	70.0	49	24	64.0	3	0	44.1
December	4	4-5	1-2	2-3	0-2	7-12	58.3	43	23	59.2	0	0	37.2
Grass	5	2-2	1-2	3-3	1-2	7-9	77.8	51	22	62.1	2	0	41.5
Turf	11	7-8	6-8	6-9	0-2	19-27	70.4	49	61	63.4	6	0	41.6
Indoor	9	6-6	5-6	4-7	0-2	15-21	71.4	49	48	64.1	4	0	42.9
Outdoor	7	3-4	2-4	5-5	1-2	11-15	73.3	51	35	61.6	4	0	39.8
4th qtr, +/-3 pts	-	1-2	1-1	0-1	0-0	2-4	50.0	39	2	65.7	1	0	46.3
Winning	-	3-3	2-4	4-6	0-1	9-14	64.3	49	51	62.8	5	0	41.0
Tied	-	4-5	2-2	1-2	1-3	8-12	66.7	51	21	64.7	3	0	42.7
Trailing	-	2-2	3-4	4-4	0-0	9-10	90.0	43	11	60.9	0	0	42.3

Game Logs

Date	Opp	Result	1-39 Yd	40-49 Yd	50+ Yd	Lg
09/03	@Chi	L 14-31	0-0	0-0	0-0	0
09/10	Det	W 20-10	2-2	0-0	0-0	32
09/17	Dal	L 17-23	0-0	1-2	0-0	42
09/24	@Pit	W 44-24	1-1	2-2	0-0	43
10/08	Hou	W 23-17	1-1	0-0	0-0	38
10/15	@TB	L 17-20	1-1	1-1	1-2	51
10/22	@GB	L 21-38	0-0	0-0	0-0	
10/30	Chi	L 6-14	1-1	1-1	0-0	43
11/05	GB	W 27-24	2-2	0-1	0-0	39
11/12	@Ari	W 30-24	0-1	1-1	0-0	43
11/19	NO	W 43-24	3-3	0-0	0-0	37
11/23	@Det	L 38-44	0-1	1-1	0-0	49
12/03	TB	W 31-17	0-0	1-2	0-1	42
12/09	Cle	W 27-11	2-2	0-0	0-1	28
12/18	@SF	L 30-37	2-2	1-1	0-0	43
12/24	@Cin	L 24-27	1-3	0-0	0-0	20

Reggie Roby

1995 Punter Splits

	G	NPunts	Avg	Lg	In20	FC	TPunts	TB	Blk	Ret	Yds	NetAvg
Total	16	77	42.8	61	23	11	78	7	1	41	335	36.2
vs. Playoff	6	30	41.3	58	11	7	30	2	0	14	100	36.6
vs. Non-playoff	10	47	43.8	61	12	4	48	5	1	27	235	35.9
vs. Own Division	8	37	41.2	61	10	6	38	3	1	19	103	35.8
Home	8	44	44.0	58	11	6	45	7	1	23	150	36.6
Away	8	33	41.2	61	12	5	33	0	0	18	185	35.5
September	4	15	44.1	57	5	1	16	1	1	9	105	33.6
October	5	28	44.8	58	7	4	28	4	0	17	143	36.8
November	3	13	40.6	56	5	0	13	1	0	6	55	34.8
December	4	21	40.6	61	6	6	21	1	0	9	32	38.1
Grass	12	60	42.9	58	16	7	61	7	1	32	227	36.2
Turf	4	17	42.5	61	7	4	17	0	0	9	108	36.1
Indoor	3	12	44.2	61	4	3	12	0	0	7	66	38.7
Outdoor	13	65	42.6	58	19	8	66	7	1	34	269	35.7
Outdoors, Temp < 40	2	9	31.8	43	3	1	9	0	0	4	23	29.2
Outdoors, Temp 40-80	8	42	44.5	58	13	7	42	5	0	20	164	38.2
Outdoors, Temp > 80	3	14	43.8	57	3	0	15	2	1	10	82	32.7
Winning	-	26	43.3	58	9	2	26	4	0	13	113	35.9
Tied	-	22	46.3	61	6	2	22	3	0	14	125	37.9
Trailing	-	29	39.7	60	8	7	30	0	1	14	97	35.1

Game Logs

Date	Opp	Result	NPunts	Avg	In20	TPunts	TB	Blk	Ret	Yds	NetAvg
09/03	@Phi	W 21-6	5	38.4	3	5	0	0	2	42	30.0
09/10	@Cle	L 6-22	2	49.0	1	2	0	0	1	9	44.5
09/17	Chi	L 6-25	3	51.3	0	4	0	1	3	14	35.0
09/24	Was	W 14-6	5	43.6	1	5	1	0	3	40	31.6
10/01	@Car	W 20-13	5	50.4	1	5	0	0	4	45	41.4
10/08	Cin	W 19-16	6	40.2	2	6	1	0	4	28	32.2
10/15	Min	W 20-17	6	43.5	1	6	2	0	3	23	33.0
10/22	Atl	L 21-24	6	47.7	2	6	1	0	4	25	40.2
10/29	@Hou	L 7-19	5	42.6	1	5	0	0	2	38	38.2
11/12	@Det	L 24-27	2	41.0	1	2	0	0	1	16	33.0
11/19	Jac	W 17-16	6	45.5	2	6	1	0	2	21	38.7
11/26	@GB	L 13-35	5	34.6	2	5	0	0	3	18	31.0
12/03	@Min	L 17-31	5	47.0	2	5	0	0	4	28	41.4
12/10	GB	W 13-10	6	42.7	3	6	1	0	3	-1	39.5
12/17	@Chi	L 10-31	4	28.3	1	4	0	0	1	5	27.0
12/23	Det	L 10-37	6	41.5	0	6	0	0	1	0	41.5

Tom Rouen

1995 Punter Splits

	G	NPunts	Avg	Lg	In20	FC	TPunts	TB	Blk	Ret	Yds	NetAvg
Total	16	52	42.2	61	22	12	53	3	1	25	137	37.6
vs. Playoff	7	31	42.8	57	11	5	31	3	0	15	59	38.9
vs. Non-playoff	9	21	41.2	61	11	7	22	0	1	10	78	35.8
vs. Own Division	8	28	41.5	61	11	7	28	1	0	13	54	38.9
Home	8	20	46.5	61	9	4	21	0	1	10	95	39.8
Away	8	32	39.4	58	13	8	32	3	0	15	42	36.3
September	4	16	45.4	59	8	3	16	1	0	9	89	38.6
October	4	15	41.3	61	10	5	15	0	0	7	24	39.7
November	4	8	43.1	58	2	1	8	1	0	3	10	39.4
December	4	13	38.5	50	2	3	14	1	1	6	14	33.4
Grass	12	39	41.9	61	17	10	40	1	1	20	121	37.3
Turf	4	13	43.0	58	5	2	13	2	0	5	16	38.7
Indoor	2	4	44.5	58	2	2	4	0	0	2	7	42.8
Outdoor	14	48	42.0	61	20	10	49	3	1	23	130	37.2
Outdoors, Temp < 40	3	15	40.5	51	3	3	15	0	0	6	22	36.4
Outdoors, Temp 40-80	9	24	41.0	61	13	7	25	0	1	12	87	35.8
Outdoors, Temp > 80	2	9	47.0	57	4	0	9	1	0	5	21	42.4
Winning	-	15	45.1	61	7	3	16	0	1	9	77	37.4
Tied	-	13	38.5	51	9	4	13	1	0	3	1	36.8
Trailing	-	24	42.3	58	6	5	24	2	0	13	59	38.2

Game Logs

Date	Opp	Result	NPunts	Avg	In20	TPunts	TB	Blk	Ret	Yds	NetAvg
09/03	Buf	W 22-7	4	47.8	1	4	0	0	3	15	44.0
09/10	@Dal	L 21-31	5	46.4	3	5	1	0	2	6	41.2
09/17	Was	W 38-31	2	52.5	1	2	0	0	1	52	26.5
09/24	@SD	L 10-27	5	39.8	3	5	0	0	3	16	36.6
10/01	@Sea	L 10-27	3	40.0	2	3	0	0	1	0	40.0
10/08	@NE	W 37-3	5	33.2	4	5	0	0	3	-2	33.6
10/16	Oak	W 27-0	3	56.0	2	3	0	0	2	19	49.7
10/22	KC	L 7-21	4	41.3	2	4	0	0	1	7	39.5
11/05	Ari	W 38-6	1	42.0	1	1	0	0	0	0	42.0
11/12	@Phi	L 13-31	4	37.3	0	4	1	0	1	3	31.5
11/19	SD	W 30-27	2	48.0	1	2	0	0	1	0	48.0
11/26	@Hou	L 33-42	1	58.0	0	1	0	0	1	7	51.0
12/03	Jac	W 31-23	2	43.5	1	3	0	1	1	2	28.3
12/10	@Sea	L 27-31	2	38.0	0	2	0	0	1	0	38.0
12/17	@KC	L 17-20	7	42.0	1	7	1	0	4	12	37.4
12/24	@Oak	W 31-28	2	22.0	0	2	0	0	0	0	22.0

Mark Royals

Detroit Lions — P

1995 Punter Splits

	G	NPunts	Avg	Lg	In20	FC	TPunts	TB	Blk	Ret	Yds	NetAvg
Total	16	57	42.0	69	15	6	59	6	2	29	442	31.0
vs. Playoff	5	24	42.5	57	4	2	24	1	0	17	207	33.1
vs. Non-playoff	11	33	41.6	69	11	4	35	5	2	12	235	29.6
vs. Own Division	8	30	41.0	69	5	2	32	3	2	16	280	27.8
Home	8	23	40.0	51	6	1	24	3	1	12	208	27.2
Away	8	34	43.3	69	9	5	35	3	1	17	234	33.7
September	4	15	41.3	69	7	2	15	1	0	5	55	36.3
October	4	18	41.8	60	2	1	18	2	0	12	135	32.1
November	4	13	43.8	51	2	0	14	1	1	9	193	25.5
December	4	11	41.0	64	3	3	12	2	1	3	59	29.3
Grass	4	13	43.4	60	0	0	14	3	1	7	100	28.9
Turf	12	44	41.6	69	15	6	45	3	1	22	342	31.7
Indoor	11	40	41.6	69	13	5	41	3	1	20	326	31.1
Outdoor	5	17	42.9	60	2	1	18	3	1	9	116	30.8
Outdoors, Temp < 40	0	0	-	0	0	0	0	0	0	0	0	-
Outdoors, Temp 40-80	5	17	42.9	60	2	1	18	3	1	9	116	30.8
Outdoors, Temp > 80	0	0	-	0	0	0	0	0	0	0	0	-
Winning	-	26	42.0	60	6	3	28	4	2	14	199	29.0
Tied	-	14	40.1	49	3	1	14	1	0	6	111	30.7
Trailing	-	17	43.5	69	6	2	17	1	0	9	132	34.6

Game Logs

Date	Opp	Result	NPunts	Avg	In20	TPunts	TB	Blk	Ret	Yds	NetAvg
09/03	@Pit	L 20-23	4	41.5	2	4	0	0	2	16	37.5
09/10	@Min	L 10-20	6	42.8	3	6	0	0	2	28	38.2
09/17	Ari	L 17-20	3	33.7	2	3	0	0	0	0	33.7
09/25	SF	W 27-24	2	48.0	0	2	1	0	1	11	32.5
10/08	Cle	W 38-20	4	44.5	1	4	1	0	3	28	32.5
10/15	@GB	L 21-30	7	40.4	0	7	0	0	5	75	29.7
10/22	@Was	L 30-36	2	54.0	0	2	1	0	1	17	35.5
10/29	GB	W 24-16	5	36.6	1	5	0	0	3	15	33.6
11/05	@Atl	L 22-31	6	48.8	1	6	0	0	6	90	33.8
11/12	TB	W 27-24	3	36.0	1	4	0	1	1	13	28.0
11/19	@Chi	W 24-17	2	45.0	0	2	1	0	0	0	35.0
11/23	Min	W 44-38	2	39.5	0	2	0	0	2	90	-5.5
12/04	Chi	W 27-7	3	49.0	0	3	1	0	2	51	25.3
12/10	@Hou	W 24-17	5	38.6	3	5	0	0	0	0	38.6
12/17	Jac	W 44-0	1	28.0	1	1	0	0	0	0	28.0
12/23	@TB	W 37-10	2	41.5	0	3	1	1	1	8	18.3

Todd Sauerbrun

Chicago Bears — P

1995 Punter Splits

	G	NPunts	Avg	Lg	In20	FC	TPunts	TB	Blk	Ret	Yds	NetAvg
Total	15	55	37.8	61	16	13	55	6	0	27	248	31.1
vs. Playoff	5	16	38.2	48	7	4	16	1	0	8	39	34.5
vs. Non-playoff	10	39	37.7	61	9	9	39	5	0	19	209	29.7
vs. Own Division	7	29	39.0	61	10	7	29	2	0	15	118	33.5
Home	7	24	38.0	52	9	5	24	1	0	13	157	30.6
Away	8	31	37.7	61	7	8	31	5	0	14	91	34.5
September	4	16	38.7	61	5	4	16	1	0	9	77	32.6
October	4	14	38.1	51	7	3	14	2	0	6	103	27.9
November	3	10	40.0	50	1	2	10	1	0	5	28	35.2
December	4	15	35.1	48	3	4	15	2	0	7	40	29.8
Grass	10	34	39.0	61	11	7	34	1	0	19	202	32.4
Turf	5	21	36.0	50	5	6	21	5	0	8	46	29.0
Indoor	2	9	37.8	48	5	3	9	2	0	3	16	31.6
Outdoor	13	46	37.8	61	11	10	46	4	0	24	232	31.0
Outdoors, Temp < 40	5	17	35.9	45	2	3	17	1	0	9	60	31.2
Outdoors, Temp 40-80	7	24	38.0	52	8	5	24	3	0	12	153	29.1
Outdoors, Temp > 80	1	5	43.6	61	1	2	5	0	0	3	19	39.8
Winning	-	21	38.4	61	7	5	21	1	0	12	151	30.2
Tied	-	15	40.3	52	4	4	15	1	0	8	57	35.1
Trailing	-	19	35.3	50	5	4	19	4	0	7	40	28.9

Game Logs

Date	Opp	Result	NPunts	Avg	In20	TPunts	TB	Blk	Ret	Yds	NetAvg
09/03	Min	W 31-14	5	38.4	1	5	0	0	3	35	31.4
09/11	GB	L 24-27	3	34.3	3	3	0	0	1	0	34.3
09/17	@TB	W 25-6	5	43.6	1	5	0	0	3	19	39.8
09/24	@StL	L 28-34	3	35.3	0	3	1	0	2	23	21.0
10/08	Car	W 31-27	7	39.6	2	7	0	0	5	95	26.0
10/15	@Jac	W 30-27	1	29.0	1	1	0	0	0	0	29.0
10/22	Hou	W 35-32	2	39.5	1	2	1	0	0	0	29.5
10/30	@Min	W 14-6	4	37.3	3	4	1	0	1	8	30.3
11/05	Pit	L 34-37	3	35.7	1	3	0	0	1	2	35.0
11/12	@GB	L 28-35	4	41.8	0	4	0	0	3	26	35.3
11/19	Det	L 17-24	-	-	-	-	-	-	-	-	-
11/26	@NYN	W 27-24	3	42.0	0	3	1	0	1	0	35.3
12/04	@Det	L 7-27	5	38.2	2	5	1	0	2	8	32.6
12/10	@Cin	L 10-16	6	30.5	0	6	1	0	2	7	26.0
12/17	TB	W 31-10	3	36.7	0	3	0	0	2	22	29.3
12/24	Phi	W 20-14	1	43.0	1	1	0	0	1	3	40.0

Mike Saxon

Minnesota Vikings — P

1995 Punter Splits

	G	NPunts	Avg	Lg	In20	FC	TPunts	TB	Blk	Ret	Yds	NetAvg
Total	16	72	40.9	60	21	10	72	6	0	41	446	33.1
vs. Playoff	7	43	42.3	60	10	5	43	3	0	28	326	33.3
vs. Non-playoff	9	29	39.0	56	11	5	29	3	0	13	120	32.8
vs. Own Division	8	38	42.4	60	12	4	38	2	0	25	219	35.6
Home	8	31	42.6	56	9	2	31	3	0	19	174	35.1
Away	8	41	39.7	60	12	8	41	3	0	22	272	31.6
September	4	21	42.4	57	9	2	21	1	0	12	91	37.1
October	4	18	40.4	56	6	2	18	0	0	11	92	35.3
November	4	17	42.4	60	3	3	17	2	0	10	98	34.3
December	4	16	38.1	51	3	3	16	3	0	8	165	24.0
Grass	5	29	39.6	55	10	6	29	2	0	16	215	30.8
Turf	11	43	41.8	60	11	4	43	4	0	25	231	34.6
Indoor	9	36	43.0	60	10	3	36	3	0	22	206	35.6
Outdoor	7	36	38.9	57	11	7	36	3	0	19	240	30.6
Outdoors, Temp < 40	1	5	32.4	47	1	1	5	1	0	1	21	24.2
Outdoors, Temp 40-80	6	31	40.0	57	10	6	31	2	0	18	219	31.6
Outdoors, Temp > 80	0	0	-	0	0	0	0	0	0	0	0	-
Winning	-	22	41.0	57	5	2	22	4	0	10	61	34.5
Tied	-	20	41.4	55	8	4	20	1	0	10	111	34.8
Trailing	-	30	40.7	60	8	4	30	1	0	21	274	30.9

Game Logs

Date	Opp	Result	NPunts	Avg	In20	TPunts	TB	Blk	Ret	Yds	NetAvg
09/03	@Chi	L 14-31	6	39.5	4	6	0	0	3	17	36.7
09/10	Det	W 20-10	6	44.8	3	6	0	0	3	23	41.0
09/17	Dal	L 17-23	7	42.1	2	7	1	0	4	47	32.6
09/24	@Pit	W 44-24	2	45.0	0	2	0	0	2	4	43.0
10/08	Hou	W 23-17	5	38.8	2	5	0	0	1	7	37.4
10/15	@TB	L 17-20	2	43.0	0	2	0	0	2	36	25.0
10/22	@GB	L 21-38	8	40.3	2	8	0	0	5	32	36.3
10/30	Chi	L 6-14	3	41.7	2	3	0	0	3	17	36.0
11/05	GB	W 27-24	7	43.3	0	7	1	0	6	62	31.6
11/12	@Ari	W 30-24	5	38.4	2	5	0	1	4		33.6
11/19	NO	W 43-24	0	0	0	0	0	0	0	0	0
11/23	@Det	L 38-44	5	45.2	1	5	0	0	3	32	38.8
12/03	TB	W 31-17	1	42.0	0	1	1	0	0	0	22.0
12/09	Cle	W 27-11	2	46.5	0	2	0	0	2	18	37.5
12/18	@SF	L 30-37	8	39.0	2	8	1	0	5	126	20.8
12/24	@Cin	L 24-27	5	32.4	1	5	1	0	1	21	24.2

Rohn Stark

1995 Punter Splits / Game Logs

	G	NPunts	Avg	Lg	In20	FC	TPunts	TB	Blk	Ret	Yds	NetAvg	Date	Opp	Result	NPunts	Avg	In20	TPunts	TB	Blk	Ret	Yds	NetAvg
Total	16	59	40.1	64	20	9	59	11	0	22	186	33.3	09/03	Det	W 23-20	1	45.0	1	1	0	0	0	0	45.0
vs. Playoff	4	13	41.5	51	4	2	13	4	0	5	44	32.0	09/10	@Hou	W 34-17	4	39.3	1	4	0	0	2	30	31.8
vs. Non-playoff	12	46	39.7	64	16	7	46	7	0	17	142	33.6	09/18	@Mia	L 10-23	4	37.8	1	4	0	0	2	19	33.0
vs. Own Division	8	34	39.7	55	12	4	34	6	0	14	111	32.9	09/24	Min	L 24-44	1	42.0	1	1	0	0	0	0	42.0
Home	8	33	40.8	64	9	2	33	9	0	11	61	33.5	10/01	SD	W 31-16	5	42.0	1	5	4	0	0	0	26.0
Away	8	26	39.3	55	11	7	26	2	0	11	125	34.0	10/08	@Jac	L 16-20	5	42.0	3	5	1	0	2	20	34.0
September	4	10	39.5	53	4	2	10	0	0	4	49	34.6	10/19	Cin	L 9-27	1	46.0	1	1	0	0	0	0	46.0
October	4	17	40.5	55	8	1	17	5	0	5	22	33.4	10/29	Jac	W 24-7	6	37.2	3	6	0	0	3	2	36.8
November	4	12	37.8	54	4	3	12	3	0	4	41	29.4	11/05	@Chi	W 37-34	3	29.3	1	3	0	0	1	16	24.0
December	4	20	41.5	64	3	0	20	3	0	9	74	34.8	11/13	Cle	W 20-3	5	42.8	0	5	2	0	3	25	29.8
Grass	6	21	39.5	55	9	6	21	2	0	9	95	33.1	11/19	@Cin	W 49-31	1	34.0	1	1	0	0	0	0	34.0
Turf	10	38	40.5	64	11	3	38	9	0	13	91	33.3	11/26	@Cle	W 20-17	3	39.3	2	3	1	0	0	0	32.7
Indoor	1	4	39.3	53	1	1	4	0	0	2	30	31.8	12/03		W 21-7	9	38.8	1	9	2	0	4	34	30.6
Outdoor	15	55	40.2	64	19	8	55	11	0	20	156	33.4	12/10	@Oak	W 29-10	3	43.0	1	3	0	0	1	15	38.0
Outdoors, Temp < 40	4	16	40.9	64	3	1	16	3	0	8	66	33.0	12/16	NE	W 41-27	5	43.6	1	5	1	0	1	0	39.6
Outdoors, Temp 40-80	9	30	39.9	54	12	6	30	7	0	8	51	33.5	12/24	@GB	L 19-24	3	44.7	1	3	0	0	3	25	36.3
Outdoors, Temp > 80	2	9	40.1	54	4	1	9	1	0	4	39	33.6												
Winning	-	29	39.9	54	9	6	29	6	0	11	75	33.1												
Tied	-	16	41.6	64	5	1	16	4	0	4	31	34.6												
Trailing	-	14	39.1	55	6	2	14	1	0	7	80	31.9												

Matt Stover

1995 Field Goal Splits / 1995 Kickoff Splits / Game Logs

	G	1-29 Yd	30-39 Yd	40-49 Yd	50+ Yd	Overall	Pct	Lg	Num	Avg	TB	TD	NetAvg	Date	Opp	Result	1-39 Yd	40-49 Yd	50+ Yd	Lg
Total	16	13-13	9-10	7-9	0-1	29-33	87.9	47	71	62.7	7	0	43.6	09/03	@NE	L 14-17	0-0	0-0	0-0	0
vs. Playoff	7	4-4	4-5	4-5	0-0	12-14	85.7	47	30	61.0	3	0	41.8	09/10	TB	W 22-6	2-2	1-1	0-0	43
vs. Non-playoff	9	9-9	5-5	3-4	0-1	17-19	89.5	44	41	63.9	4	0	45.0	09/17	@Hou	W 14-7	0-0	0-0	0-0	0
vs. Own Division	8	7-7	5-5	3-4	0-1	15-17	88.2	44	34	61.6	2	0	41.4	09/24	KC	W 35-17	0-1	0-0	0-0	0
Home	8	8-8	5-6	5-6	0-1	18-21	85.7	47	42	61.7	4	0	42.6	10/02	Buf	L 19-22	3-3	1-2	0-0	47
Away	8	5-5	4-4	2-3	0-0	11-12	91.7	44	29	64.0	3	0	45.1	10/08	@Det	L 20-38	2-2	0-0	0-0	38
Games 1-8	8	8-8	6-7	3-4	0-0	17-19	89.5	47	41	63.5	4	0	43.7	10/22	Jac	L 15-23	3-3	0-0	0-0	36
Games 9-16	8	5-5	3-3	4-5	0-1	12-14	85.7	46	30	61.5	3	0	43.5	10/29	@Cin	W 29-26	4-4	1-1	0-0	44
September	4	2-2	0-1	1-1	0-0	3-4	75.0	43	18	64.4	2	0	44.8	11/05	Hou	L 10-37	1-1	0-0	0-1	29
October	4	6-6	6-6	2-3	0-0	14-15	93.3	47	23	62.7	2	0	42.9	11/13	@Pit	L 3-20	1-1	0-0	0-0	29
November	4	3-3	0-0	2-2	0-1	5-6	83.3	46	13	57.5	1	0	41.2	11/19	GB	L 20-31	1-1	1-1	0-0	46
December	4	2-2	3-3	2-3	0-0	7-8	87.5	42	17	64.6	2	0	45.2	11/26	Pit	L 17-20	0-0	1-1	0-0	44
Grass	11	8-8	6-7	6-8	0-1	20-24	83.3	47	52	62.0	5	0	43.2	12/03	@SD	L 13-31	1-1	0-0	0-0	40
Turf	5	5-5	3-3	1-1	0-0	9-9	100.0	44	19	64.4	2	0	44.7	12/09	@Min	L 11-27	1-1	0-0	0-0	26
Indoor	3	2-2	1-1	0-0	0-0	3-3	100.0	38	11	64.0	1	0	46.3	12/17	Cin	W 26-10	3-3	1-1	0-0	42
Outdoor	13	11-11	8-9	7-9	0-1	26-30	86.7	47	60	62.4	6	0	43.1	12/24	@Jac	L 21-24	0-0	0-1	0-0	0
4th qtr, +/-3 pts	-	0-0	1-1	0-0	0-0	1-1	100.0	38	3	64.0	0	0	43.3							
Winning	-	3-3	2-2	1-1	0-1	6-7	85.7	42	30	63.9	3	0	44.1							
Tied	-	2-2	1-2	2-2	0-0	5-6	83.3	46	17	60.5	0	0	40.9							
Trailing	-	8-8	6-6	4-6	0-1	18-20	90.0	47	24	62.6	4	0	44.9							

Pete Stoyanovich

1995 Field Goal Splits / 1995 Kickoff Splits / Game Logs

	G	1-29 Yd	30-39 Yd	40-49 Yd	50+ Yd	Overall	Pct	Lg	Num	Avg	TB	TD	NetAvg	Date	Opp	Result	1-39 Yd	40-49 Yd	50+ Yd	Lg
Total	16	8-11	11-11	6-7	2-5	27-34	79.4	51	88	62.4	3	0	41.2	09/03	NYA	W 52-14	1-1	0-0	0-0	25
vs. Playoff	9	3-5	7-7	1-2	2-3	13-17	76.5	51	45	62.3	1	0	43.4	09/10	@NE	W 20-3	2-2	0-0	0-1	22
vs. Non-playoff	7	5-6	4-4	5-5	0-2	14-17	82.4	49	43	62.5	2	0	39.0	09/18	Pit	W 23-10	3-3	0-0	0-0	39
vs. Own Division	8	5-7	3-3	3-4	2-3	13-17	76.5	51	44	61.6	0	0	40.9	10/01	@Cin	W 26-23	3-3	1-1	0-0	46
Home	8	4-7	6-6	1-2	1-2	12-17	70.6	51	44	62.6	1	0	42.0	10/08	Ind	L 24-27	0-1	0-1	1-1	51
Away	8	4-4	5-5	5-5	1-3	15-17	88.2	50	44	62.2	2	0	40.5	10/15	@NO	L 30-33	1-1	0-0	0-1	20
Games 1-8	8	8-9	5-5	4-5	1-4	18-23	78.3	51	50	61.9	2	0	42.3	10/22	@NYA	L 16-17	0-0	3-3	0-0	49
Games 9-16	8	0-2	6-6	2-2	1-1	9-11	81.8	50	38	62.9	1	0	39.8	10/29	Buf	W 23-6	3-3	0-0	0-0	33
September	3	4-4	2-2	0-0	0-2	6-8	75.0	39	20	60.9	0	0	41.2	11/05	@SD	W 24-14	1-1	0-0	0-0	36
October	5	4-5	3-3	4-5	1-2	12-15	80.0	51	30	62.7	2	0	43.1	11/12	NE	L 17-34	1-2	0-0	0-0	36
November	4	0-1	2-2	0-0	0-0	2-3	66.7	36	17	65.2	0	0	39.8	11/20	SF	L 20-44	0-0	0-0	0-0	0
December	4	0-1	4-4	2-2	1-1	7-8	87.5	50	21	61.0	1	0	39.8	11/26	@Ind	L 28-36	0-0	0-0	0-0	0
Grass	10	6-9	7-7	1-2	1-3	15-21	71.4	50	54	62.7	1	0	41.4	12/03	Atl	W 21-20	0-1	1-1	0-0	42
Turf	6	2-2	4-4	5-5	1-2	12-13	92.3	50	34	61.8	2	0	40.9	12/11	KC	W 13-6	2-2	0-0	0-0	33
Indoor	3	1-1	1-1	1-1	0-1	3-4	75.0	48	17	62.6	1	0	41.9	12/17	@Buf	L 20-23	1-1	0-0	1-1	50
Outdoor	13	7-10	10-10	5-6	2-4	24-30	80.0	51	71	62.3	2	0	41.1	12/24	@StL	W 41-22	1-1	1-1	0-0	48
4th qtr, +/-3 pts	-	0-0	2-2	0-1	0-0	2-3	66.7	36	6	62.2	1	0	43.7							
Winning	-	4-5	3-3	3-3	1-3	11-14	78.6	51	56	61.9	1	0	40.6							
Tied	-	3-4	5-5	3-4	0-0	11-13	84.6	49	14	63.4	0	0	40.2							
Trailing	-	1-2	3-3	0-0	1-2	5-7	71.4	50	18	63.1	2	0	43.9							

Dan Stryzinski
Atlanta Falcons — P

1995 Punter Splits

	G	NPunts	Avg	Lg	In20	FC	TPunts	TB	Blk	Ret	Yds	NetAvg
Total	16	67	41.2	64	21	21	67	5	0	28	236	36.2
vs. Playoff	6	20	41.7	64	4	3	20	3	0	8	35	36.9
vs. Non-playoff	10	47	41.0	54	17	18	47	2	0	20	201	35.9
vs. Own Division	8	37	42.0	54	13	14	37	1	0	19	177	36.7
Home	8	29	40.4	53	12	12	29	0	0	11	76	37.8
Away	8	38	41.8	64	9	9	38	5	0	17	160	34.9
September	4	21	40.1	54	5	10	21	1	0	9	63	36.2
October	4	16	43.2	54	4	5	16	2	0	8	102	34.3
November	4	17	42.1	64	6	2	17	1	0	6	42	38.5
December	4	13	39.2	53	6	4	13	1	0	5	29	35.4
Grass	5	22	42.3	54	4	3	22	4	0	9	79	35.0
Turf	11	45	40.6	64	17	18	45	1	0	19	157	36.7
Indoor	9	34	39.9	53	13	15	34	0	0	13	83	37.5
Outdoor	7	33	42.5	64	8	6	33	5	0	15	153	34.8
Outdoors, Temp < 40	1	5	39.2	64	1	1	5	1	0	2	0	35.2
Outdoors, Temp 40-80	6	28	43.0	54	7	5	28	4	0	13	153	34.7
Outdoors, Temp > 80	0	0	-	0	0	0	0	0	0	0	0	
Winning	-	32	40.2	53	13	9	32	1	0	12	99	36.5
Tied	-	13	38.2	51	4	5	13	2	0	5	22	33.4
Trailing	-	22	44.4	64	4	7	22	2	0	11	115	37.3

Game Logs

Date	Opp	Result	NPunts	Avg	In20	TPunts	TB	Blk	Ret	Yds	NetAvg
09/03	Car	W 23-20	7	40.7	1	7	0	0	2	20	37.9
09/10	@SF	L 10-41	5	46.4	0	5	1	0	4	27	37.0
09/17	@NO	W 27-24	5	37.4	1	5	0	0	2	7	36.0
09/24	NYA	W 13-3	4	34.8	3	4	0	0	1	9	32.5
10/01	NE	W 30-17	3	42.3	0	3	0	0	3	13	38.0
10/12	@StL	L 19-21	6	45.8	3	6	0	0	4	74	33.5
10/22	@TB	W 24-21	5	40.4	1	5	2	0	1	15	29.4
10/29	Dal	L 13-28	2	43.5	0	2	0	0	0	0	43.5
11/05	Det	W 34-22	2	37.5	1	2	0	0	0	0	37.5
11/12	@Buf	L 17-23	5	39.2	1	5	1	0	2	0	35.2
11/19	StL	W 31-6	4	42.8	2	4	0	0	3	28	35.8
11/26	@Ari	L 37-40	6	45.7	2	6	0	0	1	14	43.3
12/03	@Mia	L 20-21	3	35.0	0	3	1	0	1	8	25.7
12/10	NO	W 19-14	4	37.3	3	4	0	0	1	6	35.8
12/17	@Car	L 17-21	3	39.0	1	3	0	0	2	15	34.0
12/24	SF	W 28-27	3	46.0	2	3	0	0	1	0	46.0

Tommy Thompson
San Francisco 49ers — P

1995 Punter Splits

	G	NPunts	Avg	Lg	In20	FC	TPunts	TB	Blk	Ret	Yds	NetAvg
Total	16	57	40.6	65	13	20	57	5	0	26	292	33.7
vs. Playoff	7	23	40.3	54	3	9	23	1	0	11	108	34.7
vs. Non-playoff	9	34	40.8	65	10	11	34	4	0	15	184	33.0
vs. Own Division	8	25	42.4	65	7	7	25	2	0	15	142	35.1
Home	8	31	39.6	53	7	10	31	4	0	14	211	30.3
Away	8	26	41.7	65	6	10	26	1	0	12	81	37.8
September	4	12	37.2	48	1	7	12	2	0	3	7	33.3
October	4	16	43.4	65	5	5	16	1	0	8	121	34.6
November	4	13	39.0	53	4	3	13	0	0	8	48	35.3
December	4	16	41.6	52	3	5	16	2	0	7	116	31.8
Grass	10	37	39.8	53	7	10	37	5	0	17	221	31.1
Turf	6	20	42.0	65	6	10	20	0	0	9	71	38.4
Indoor	4	10	40.5	50	2	7	10	0	0	3	4	40.1
Outdoor	12	47	40.6	65	11	13	47	5	0	23	288	32.3
Outdoors, Temp < 40	1	3	40.0	52	0	0	3	1	0	1	2	32.7
Outdoors, Temp 40-80	11	44	40.6	65	11	13	44	4	0	22	286	32.3
Outdoors, Temp > 80	0	0	-	0	0	0	0	0	0	0	0	
Winning	-	39	41.2	65	10	14	39	3	0	17	217	34.1
Tied	-	10	37.9	48	1	3	10	1	0	5	64	29.5
Trailing	-	8	40.6	53	2	3	8	1	0	4	11	36.8

Game Logs

Date	Opp	Result	NPunts	Avg	In20	TPunts	TB	Blk	Ret	Yds	NetAvg
09/03	@NO	W 24-22	2	39.5	1	2	0	0	0	0	39.5
09/10	Atl	W 41-10	1	41.0	0	1	0	0	1	2	39.0
09/17	NE	W 28-3	7	37.7	0	7	2	0	1	31	31.7
09/25	@Det	L 24-27	2	31.0	0	2	0	0	1	3	29.5
10/01	NYN	W 20-6	3	34.3	2	3	0	0	0	0	34.3
10/15	@Ind	L 17-18	3	46.0	0	3	0	0	1	0	46.0
10/22	@StL	W 44-10	6	48.5	2	6	0	0	5	43	41.3
10/29	NO	L 7-11	4	40.5	1	4	1	0	2	78	16.0
11/05	Car	L 7-13	3	39.0	1	3	0	0	2	10	35.7
11/12	@Dal	W 38-20	4	35.8	2	4	0	0	1	24	29.8
11/20	@Mia	W 44-20	3	41.0	0	3	0	0	2	8	38.7
11/26	StL	W 41-13	3	41.0	1	3	0	0	3	6	39.0
12/03	Buf	W 27-17	7	41.7	0	7	1	0	4	70	28.9
12/10	@Car	W 31-10	3	40.0	0	3	1	0	1	2	32.7
12/18	Min	W 37-30	3	42.3	0	3	0	0	1	43	28.0
12/24	@Atl	L 27-28	3	42.0	1	3	0	0	1	1	41.7

Tom Tupa
Cleveland Browns — P

1995 Punter Splits

	G	NPunts	Avg	Lg	In20	FC	TPunts	TB	Blk	Ret	Yds	NetAvg
Total	16	65	43.6	64	18	9	65	9	0	34	296	36.2
vs. Playoff	7	33	43.4	59	7	4	33	1	0	21	202	36.7
vs. Non-playoff	9	32	43.7	64	11	5	32	8	0	13	94	35.8
vs. Own Division	8	30	45.7	64	8	4	30	4	0	18	195	36.6
Home	8	21	40.6	52	4	1	21	5	0	9	52	33.4
Away	8	44	45.0	64	14	8	44	4	0	25	244	37.6
September	4	23	40.9	56	6	2	23	4	0	10	77	34.0
October	4	15	44.1	64	5	3	15	2	0	9	48	38.3
November	4	13	47.2	59	1	0	13	0	0	12	147	35.9
December	4	14	43.9	56	6	4	14	3	0	3	24	37.9
Grass	11	34	40.9	52	9	5	34	7	0	13	69	34.7
Turf	5	31	46.5	64	9	4	31	2	0	21	227	37.9
Indoor	3	18	46.1	57	7	3	18	2	0	9	87	39.1
Outdoor	13	47	42.6	64	11	6	47	7	0	25	209	35.1
Outdoors, Temp < 40	5	20	44.8	59	3	2	20	2	0	14	155	35.1
Outdoors, Temp 40-80	8	27	40.9	64	8	4	27	5	0	11	54	35.2
Outdoors, Temp > 80	0	0	-	0	0	0	0	0	0	0	0	
Winning	-	23	42.3	64	6	2	23	4	0	11	77	35.4
Tied	-	14	42.6	49	2	2	14	4	0	6	59	32.7
Trailing	-	28	45.1	59	10	5	28	1	0	17	160	38.6

Game Logs

Date	Opp	Result	NPunts	Avg	In20	TPunts	TB	Blk	Ret	Yds	NetAvg
09/03	@NE	L 14-17	6	41.2	2	6	1	0	3	15	35.3
09/10	TB	W 22-6	3	38.7	0	3	2	0	0	0	25.3
09/17	@Hou	W 14-7	8	43.6	3	8	1	0	4	50	34.9
09/24	KC	W 35-17	6	38.0	1	6	0	0	3	12	36.0
10/02	Buf	L 19-22	3	38.7	0	3	1	0	2	26	23.3
10/08	@Det	L 20-38	6	47.8	2	6	0	0	3	15	45.3
10/22	Jac	L 15-23	2	40.5	1	2	1	0	1	-2	31.5
10/29	@Cin	W 29-26	4	44.5	2	4	0	0	3	9	42.3
11/05	Hou	L 10-37	0	0	0	0	0	0	0	0	0
11/13	@Pit	L 3-20	9	48.2	0	9	0	0	9	131	33.7
11/19	GB	L 20-31	2	41.5	0	2	0	0	2	9	37.0
11/26	Pit	L 17-20	2	48.5	1	2	0	0	1	7	45.0
12/03	@SD	L 13-31	5	37.6	3	5	0	0	1	2	37.2
12/09	@Min	L 11-27	4	48.5	2	4	1	0	2	22	38.0
12/17	Cin	W 26-10	3	44.0	1	3	1	0	0	0	37.3
12/24	@Jac	L 21-24	2	50.5	0	2	1	0	0	0	40.5

Matt Turk
Washington Redskins — P

1995 Punter Splits	G	NPunts	Avg	Lg	In20	FC	TPunts	TB	Blk	Ret	Yds	NetAvg
Total	16	74	42.4	60	29	13	74	9	0	26	173	37.7
vs. Playoff	6	35	41.7	58	13	7	35	5	0	8	64	37.1
vs. Non-playoff	10	39	43.1	60	16	6	39	4	0	18	109	38.2
vs. Own Division	8	33	43.5	60	16	7	33	1	0	12	57	41.1
Home	8	35	41.7	60	17	6	35	5	0	12	50	37.4
Away	8	39	43.1	58	12	7	39	4	0	14	123	37.9
September	4	12	43.2	60	4	2	12	2	0	5	36	36.8
October	5	21	43.3	56	9	4	21	3	0	7	38	38.7
November	3	20	39.2	58	7	3	20	3	0	6	60	33.2
December	4	21	44.2	56	9	4	21	1	0	8	39	41.4
Grass	12	55	41.6	60	20	9	55	8	0	19	124	36.4
Turf	4	19	44.8	56	9	4	19	1	0	7	49	41.2
Indoor	1	5	46.2	56	2	0	5	0	0	3	31	44.0
Outdoor	15	69	42.2	60	27	13	69	9	0	23	142	37.5
Outdoors, Temp < 40	2	10	42.5	56	4	2	10	1	0	4	8	39.7
Outdoors, Temp 40-80	10	47	41.9	58	19	10	47	8	0	12	87	36.7
Outdoors, Temp > 80	3	12	42.8	60	4	1	12	0	0	7	47	38.9
Winning	-	20	42.9	60	8	1	20	3	0	8	60	36.9
Tied	-	25	42.5	56	13	4	25	2	0	8	66	38.2
Trailing	-	29	42.1	58	8	8	29	4	0	10	47	37.7

Game Logs Date	Opp	Result	NPunts	Avg	In20	TPunts	TB	Blk	Ret	Yds	NetAvg
09/03	Ari	W 27-7	4	44.8	2	4	0	0	3	19	40.0
09/10	Oak	L 8-20	2	38.5	1	2	1	0	0	0	28.5
09/17	@Den	L 31-38	2	49.0	0	2	1	0	0	0	39.0
09/24	@TB	L 6-14	4	41.0	1	4	0	0	2	17	36.8
10/01	Dal	W 27-23	3	40.3	1	3	0	0	0	0	40.3
10/08	@Phi	L 34-37	5	40.8	2	5	1	0	2	18	33.2
10/15	@Ari	L 20-24	4	42.8	1	4	0	0	2	11	40.0
10/22	Det	W 36-30	6	44.8	3	6	2	0	1	0	38.2
10/29	NYN	L 15-24	3	48.3	2	3	0	0	2	9	45.3
11/05	@KC	L 3-24	10	39.7	1	10	2	0	3	46	31.1
11/19	Sea	L 20-27	5	37.8	3	5	1	0	2	14	31.0
11/26	Phi	L 7-14	5	39.4	3	5	0	0	1	0	39.4
12/03	@Dal	W 24-17	6	45.5	3	6	0	0	1	0	45.5
12/10	@NYN	L 13-20	3	48.0	2	3	0	0	1	0	48.0
12/17	@StL	W 35-23	5	46.2	2	5	0	0	3	31	40.0
12/24	Car	W 20-17	7	40.1	2	7	1	0	3	8	36.1

Rick Tuten
Seattle Seahawks — P

1995 Punter Splits	G	NPunts	Avg	Lg	In20	FC	TPunts	TB	Blk	Ret	Yds	NetAvg
Total	16	83	45.0	73	21	7	83	8	0	48	549	36.5
vs. Playoff	6	35	47.3	73	8	0	35	4	0	20	238	38.2
vs. Non-playoff	10	48	43.3	60	13	7	48	4	0	28	311	35.2
vs. Own Division	8	44	45.0	65	10	2	44	4	0	28	340	35.5
Home	8	37	43.1	59	9	6	37	2	0	20	251	35.2
Away	8	46	46.5	73	12	1	46	6	0	28	298	37.5
September	3	17	44.1	59	5	2	17	2	0	11	89	36.5
October	5	25	45.6	73	6	2	25	4	0	11	122	37.6
November	4	18	42.4	57	3	3	18	0	0	11	130	35.2
December	4	23	47.0	65	7	0	23	2	0	15	208	36.2
Grass	7	40	45.6	65	11	1	40	4	0	27	288	36.4
Turf	9	43	44.4	73	10	6	43	4	0	21	261	36.5
Indoor	8	37	43.1	59	9	6	37	2	0	20	251	35.2
Outdoor	8	46	46.5	73	12	1	46	6	0	28	298	37.5
Outdoors, Temp < 40	1	10	46.4	65	2	0	10	1	0	6	58	38.6
Outdoors, Temp 40-80	6	31	46.1	73	8	1	31	4	0	19	219	36.4
Outdoors, Temp > 80	1	5	49.8	60	2	0	5	1	0	3	21	41.6
Winning	-	19	43.8	59	7	3	19	2	0	11	119	35.4
Tied	-	16	44.0	55	5	1	16	1	0	10	85	37.4
Trailing	-	48	45.8	73	9	3	48	5	0	27	345	36.5

Game Logs Date	Opp	Result	NPunts	Avg	In20	TPunts	TB	Blk	Ret	Yds	NetAvg
09/03	KC	L 10-34	7	45.0	1	7	0	0	6	63	36.0
09/10	@SD	L 10-14	4	49.8	1	4	1	0	3	23	39.0
09/17	Cin	W 24-21	6	39.2	3	6	1	0	2	3	35.3
10/01	Den	W 27-10	3	39.7	0	3	0	0	2	23	32.0
10/08	@Oak	L 14-34	7	40.7	2	7	1	0	4	29	33.7
10/15	@Buf	L 21-27	6	52.8	1	6	2	0	1	10	44.5
10/22	SD	L 25-35	4	42.8	1	4	0	0	1	39	33.0
10/29	@Ari	L 14-20	5	49.8	2	5	1	0	3	21	41.6
11/05	NYN	W 30-28	3	46.0	0	3	0	0	2	29	36.3
11/12	@Jac	W 47-30	3	48.0	1	3	0	0	3	19	41.7
11/19	@Was	W 27-20	5	41.8	2	5	0	0	3	39	34.0
11/26	NYA	L 10-16	7	39.0	0	7	0	0	3	43	32.9
12/03	Phi	W 26-14	4	47.5	2	4	0	0	3	45	36.3
12/10	@Den	W 31-27	6	45.7	1	6	0	0	5	99	29.2
12/17	Oak	W 44-10	3	51.0	0	3	1	0	1	6	42.3
12/24	@KC	L 3-26	10	46.4	2	10	1	0	6	58	38.6

Bryan Wagner
New England Patriots — P

1995 Punter Splits	G	NPunts	Avg	Lg	In20	FC	TPunts	TB	Blk	Ret	Yds	NetAvg
Total	8	37	42.1	57	13	5	37	4	0	20	168	35.4
vs. Playoff	5	21	42.8	57	3	3	21	1	0	12	126	35.9
vs. Non-playoff	3	16	41.1	49	10	2	16	3	0	8	42	34.8
vs. Own Division	6	28	42.3	57	9	3	28	4	0	14	102	35.8
Home	3	17	41.9	56	9	1	17	2	0	10	50	36.6
Away	5	20	42.3	57	4	4	20	2	0	10	118	34.4
September	0	0	-	0	0	0	0	0	0	0	0	-
October	0	0	-	0	0	0	0	0	0	0	0	-
November	4	17	42.2	56	6	2	17	2	0	8	44	37.3
December	4	20	42.0	57	7	3	20	2	0	12	124	33.8
Grass	4	19	42.1	56	10	1	19	3	0	10	50	36.3
Turf	4	18	42.1	57	3	4	18	1	0	10	118	34.4
Indoor	1	4	44.8	57	0	1	4	0	0	3	38	35.3
Outdoor	7	33	41.8	56	13	4	33	4	0	17	130	35.4
Outdoors, Temp < 40	4	20	41.1	49	7	3	20	2	0	11	106	33.8
Outdoors, Temp 40-80	3	13	42.8	56	6	1	13	2	0	6	24	37.8
Outdoors, Temp > 80	0	0	-	0	0	0	0	0	0	0	0	-
Winning	-	10	42.2	48	3	1	10	1	0	6	44	35.8
Tied	-	15	42.1	57	5	2	15	3	0	6	95	31.8
Trailing	-	12	41.9	56	5	2	12	0	0	8	29	39.5

Game Logs Date	Opp	Result	NPunts	Avg	In20	TPunts	TB	Blk	Ret	Yds	NetAvg
11/05	@NYA	W 20-7	5	41.4	3	5	1	0	2	8	35.8
11/12	@Mia	W 34-17	2	44.0	1	2	1	0	0	0	34.0
11/19	Ind	L 10-24	6	43.5	2	6	0	0	4	16	40.8
11/26	@Buf	W 35-25	4	40.5	0	4	0	0	2	20	35.5
12/03	NO	L 17-31	4	41.0	4	4	0	0	3	14	37.5
12/10	NYA	W 31-28	7	41.0	3	7	2	0	3	20	32.4
12/16	@Pit	L 27-41	5	41.8	0	5	0	0	3	52	31.4
12/23	@Ind	L 7-10	4	44.8	0	4	0	0	3	38	35.3

Jeff Wilkins
San Francisco 49ers — K

	G	1995 Field Goal Splits							1995 Kickoff Splits					Game Logs						
		1-29 Yd	30-39 Yd	40-49 Yd	50+ Yd	Overall	Pct	Lg	Num	Avg	TB	TD	NetAvg	Date	Opp	Result	1-39 Yd	40-49 Yd	50+ Yd	Lg
Total	7	6-6	5-5	1-2	0-0	12-13	92.3	40	49	65.6	6	0	41.2	11/12	@Dal	W 38-20	1-1	0-0	0-0	26
vs. Playoff	4	3-3	4-4	1-2	0-0	8-9	88.9	40	28	67.0	6	0	42.7	11/20	@Mia	W 44-20	3-3	0-0	0-0	33
vs. Non-playoff	3	3-3	1-1	0-0	0-0	4-4	100.0	35	21	63.9	0	0	39.2	11/26	StL	W 41-13	2-2	0-0	0-0	35
vs. Own Division	3	2-2	3-3	0-0	0-0	5-5	100.0	39	20	66.2	0	0	41.2	12/03	Buf	W 27-17	1-1	1-2	0-0	40
Home	3	3-3	1-1	1-2	0-0	5-6	83.3	40	21	63.7	1	0	39.6	12/10	@Car	W 31-10	1-1	0-0	0-0	20
Away	4	3-3	4-4	0-0	0-0	7-7	100.0	39	28	67.1	5	0	42.4	12/18	Min	W 37-30	1-1	0-0	0-0	20
Games 1-8	0	0-0	0-0	0-0	0-0	0-0	-	0	0	-	0	0	-	12/24	@Atl	L 27-28	2-2	0-0	0-0	39
Games 9-16	7	6-6	5-5	1-2	0-0	12-13	92.3	40	49	65.6	6	0	41.2							
September	0	0-0	0-0	0-0	0-0	0-0	-	0	0	-	0	0	-							
October	0	0-0	0-0	0-0	0-0	0-0	-	0	0	-	0	0	-							
November	3	3-3	3-3	0-0	0-0	6-6	100.0	35	24	66.8	5	0	43.3							
December	4	3-3	2-2	1-2	0-0	6-7	85.7	40	25	64.5	1	0	39.2							
Grass	5	5-5	3-3	1-2	0-0	9-10	90.0	40	36	65.1	5	0	41.6							
Turf	2	1-1	2-2	0-0	0-0	3-3	100.0	39	13	67.1	1	0	40.1							
Indoor	1	0-0	2-2	0-0	0-0	2-2	100.0	39	6	68.0	0	0	39.7							
Outdoor	6	6-6	3-3	1-2	0-0	10-11	90.9	40	43	65.3	6	0	41.4							
4th qtr. +/-3 pts	-	0-0	2-2	0-0	0-0	2-2	100.0	39	1	73.0	0	0	45.0							
Winning	-	4-4	4-4	1-2	0-0	9-10	90.0	40	42	65.6	5	0	40.6							
Tied	-	1-1	0-0	0-0	0-0	1-1	100.0	20	7	65.7	1	0	44.9							
Trailing	-	1-1	1-1	0-0	0-0	2-2	100.0	39	0	-	0	0								

Klaus Wilmsmeyer
New Orleans Saints — P

	1995 Punter Splits												Game Logs										
	G	NPunts	Avg	Lg	In20	FC	TPunts	TB	Blk	Ret	Yds	NetAvg	Date	Opp	Result	NPunts	Avg	In20	TPunts	TB	Blk	Ret	Yds	NetAvg
Total	16	73	40.6	53	21	22	74	5	1	36	233	35.6	09/03	SF	L 22-24	5	38.2	2	5	0	0	2	0	38.2
vs. Playoff	8	40	41.9	53	9	11	40	2	0	21	161	36.9	09/10	@StL	L 13-17	4	39.5	2	4	0	0	3	11	36.8
vs. Non-playoff	8	33	39.1	53	12	11	34	3	1	15	72	34.0	09/17	Atl	L 24-27	8	44.3	3	8	0	0	5	64	36.3
vs. Own Division	8	38	41.7	53	13	14	38	4	0	17	116	36.5	09/24	@NYN	L 29-45	3	38.0	1	3	0	0	2	8	35.3
Home	8	37	42.1	53	11	9	37	2	0	19	148	37.0	10/01	Phi	L 10-15	7	44.4	0	7	0	0	3	39	38.9
Away	8	36	39.1	53	10	13	37	3	1	17	85	34.2	10/15	Mia	W 33-30	3	37.3	0	3	0	0	2	2	36.7
September	4	20	40.9	53	8	5	20	0	0	12	83	36.7	10/22	@Car	L 3-20	6	38.8	0	6	2	0	1	0	32.2
October	4	19	41.0	52	1	8	19	2	0	7	46	36.5	10/29	@SF	W 11-7	3	41.0	1	3	0	0	1	5	39.3
November	4	14	40.9	53	7	2	14	1	0	7	37	36.9	11/05	StL	W 19-10	2	42.0	1	2	1	0	1	6	29.0
December	4	20	39.8	53	5	7	21	2	1	10	67	32.8	11/12	Ind	W 17-14	4	37.0	2	4	0	0	2	10	34.5
Grass	3	13	39.8	53	6	2	13	2	0	5	23	35.0	11/19	@Min	L 24-43	4	40.3	1	4	0	0	3	13	37.0
Turf	13	60	40.8	53	19	16	61	3	1	31	210	35.7	11/26	Car	W 34-26	4	45.0	3	4	0	0	1	8	43.0
Indoor	10	47	42.1	53	13	11	47	3	0	25	183	36.9	12/03	@NE	W 31-17	4	40.5	1	4	0	0	3	18	36.0
Outdoor	6	26	38.0	51	8	11	27	2	1	11	50	32.2	12/10	@Atl	L 14-19	6	43.5	1	6	1	0	3	22	36.5
Outdoors, Temp < 40	2	10	35.9	50	4	5	11	0	1	4	26	30.3	12/16	GB	L 23-34	4	44.0	0	4	1	0	3	19	34.3
Outdoors, Temp 40-80	4	16	39.3	51	4	6	16	2	0	7	24	35.3	12/24	@NYA	W 12-0	6	32.8	3	7	0	1	1	8	27.0
Outdoors, Temp > 80	0	0	-	0	0	0	0	0	0	0	0	-												
Winning	-	20	38.1	53	6	8	21	2	1	8	40	32.5												
Tied	-	21	39.7	51	5	7	21	1	0	8	97	34.1												
Trailing	-	32	42.8	53	10	7	32	2	0	20	96	38.6												

League Profiles

1995 NFL Passing Splits

	Att	Cm	Pct	Yds	Yd/Att	TD	Int	Int%	Rtg		Att	Cm	Pct	Yds	Yd/Att	TD	Int	Int%	Rtg
Total	16698	9717	58.2	113069	6.77	663	512	3.1	79.3	Inside 20	1895	906	47.8	6681	3.53	404	72	3.8	80.4
vs. Playoff	6856	3938	57.4	45021	6.57	243	216	3.2	76.0	Inside 10	774	343	44.3	1472	1.90	248	34	4.4	72.8
vs. Non-playoff	9842	5779	58.7	68048	6.91	420	296	3.0	81.5	1st Down	6252	3756	60.1	44766	7.16	227	166	2.7	83.0
vs. Own Division	8225	4763	57.9	56026	6.81	309	259	3.1	78.1	2nd Down	5482	3253	59.3	35406	6.46	215	165	3.0	79.0
Home	8429	4973	59.0	57635	6.84	335	243	2.9	81.0	3rd Down Overall	4697	2557	54.4	31002	6.60	201	167	3.6	74.4
Away	8269	4744	57.4	55434	6.70	328	269	3.3	77.5	3rd D 0-5 to Go	1652	986	59.7	10165	6.15	102	53	3.2	84.7
Games 1-8	8354	4846	58.0	55850	6.69	320	245	2.9	78.8	3rd D 6+ to Go	3045	1571	51.6	20837	6.84	99	114	3.7	68.8
Games 9-16	8344	4871	58.4	57219	6.86	343	267	3.2	79.7	4th Down	267	151	56.6	1895	7.10	20	14	5.2	81.9
September	3919	2295	58.6	26466	6.75	159	124	3.2	79.4	Rec Behind Line	2559	1632	63.8	10264	4.01	26	43	1.7	68.3
October	4566	2620	57.4	30154	6.60	163	129	2.8	77.5	1-10 yds	8674	5755	66.3	51227	5.91	308	200	2.3	84.2
November	3997	2372	59.3	28412	7.11	183	127	3.2	83.2	11-20 yds	3501	1798	51.4	32590	9.31	153	136	3.9	82.0
December	4216	2430	57.6	28037	6.65	158	132	3.1	77.3	21-30 yds	1118	351	31.4	10826	9.68	92	60	5.4	73.7
Grass	8489	4892	57.6	56670	6.68	316	269	3.2	77.1	31+	840	180	21.4	8138	9.69	84	73	8.7	64.6
Turf	8209	4825	58.8	56399	6.87	347	243	3.0	81.4	Left Sideline	3241	1790	55.2	22151	6.83	124	72	2.2	80.1
Indoor	4226	2544	60.2	29990	7.10	183	117	2.8	84.7	Left Side	3172	1961	61.8	21697	6.84	117	108	3.4	80.2
Outdoor	12472	7173	57.5	83079	6.66	480	395	3.2	77.4	Middle	2931	1644	56.1	20855	7.12	148	113	3.9	79.2
1st Half	8291	4852	58.5	56919	6.87	343	244	2.9	81.0	Right Side	3729	2346	62.9	25331	6.79	144	117	3.1	82.6
2nd Half/OT	8407	4865	57.9	56150	6.68	320	268	3.2	77.5	Right Sideline	3619	1974	54.5	22999	6.36	130	102	2.8	74.2
Last 2 Min. Half	2496	1356	54.3	15743	6.31	126	93	3.7	74.9	2 Wide Receivers	6730	3969	59.0	45989	6.83	237	208	3.1	78.6
4th qtr, +/-7 pts	1996	1107	55.5	12849	6.44	71	71	3.6	72.2	3+ WR	9511	5496	57.8	64844	6.82	349	288	3.0	78.3
Winning	4710	2776	58.9	33137	7.04	206	112	2.4	85.2	Attempts 1-10	5639	3301	58.5	38338	6.80	193	177	3.1	77.5
Tied	3670	2148	58.5	24493	6.67	134	104	2.8	79.0	Attempts 11-20	4841	2858	59.0	34006	7.02	210	138	2.9	83.1
Trailing	8318	4793	57.6	55439	6.66	323	296	3.6	76.0	Attempts 21+	6218	3558	57.2	40725	6.55	260	197	3.2	77.8

1995 NFL Incompletions

Type	Num	% of Inc	% of Att
Pass Dropped	1036	14.8	6.2
Poor Throw	3144	45.0	18.8
Pass Defensed	1155	16.5	6.9
Pass Hit at Line	388	5.6	2.3
Other	1258	18.0	7.5
Total	6981	100.0	41.8

1995 NFL Receiving Splits

	Rec	Yds	Avg	TD	Trgt	Y@C	1st	1st%		Rec	Yds	Avg	TD	Trgt	Y@C	1st	1st%
Total	9717	113069	11.6	663	16129	6.6	5567	57.3	Inside 20	906	6681	7.4	404	1812	4.6	588	64.9
vs. Playoff	3938	45021	11.4	243	6650	6.5	2221	56.3	Inside 10	343	1472	4.3	248	736	3.1	257	74.9
vs. Non-playoff	5779	68048	11.8	420	9479	6.6	3346	57.9	1st Down	3756	44766	11.9	227	6011	6.8	1789	47.6
vs. Own Division	4763	56026	11.8	309	7958	6.5	2737	57.5	2nd Down	3253	35406	10.9	215	5299	5.9	1817	55.8
Home	4973	57635	11.6	335	8152	6.6	2914	58.6	3rd Down Overall	2557	31002	12.1	201	4556	7.1	1833	71.7
Away	4744	55434	11.7	328	7977	6.6	2653	55.9	3rd D 0-2 to Go	288	2811	9.8	43	462	5.2	273	94.8
Games 1-8	4846	55850	11.5	320	8063	6.6	2755	56.8	3rd D 3-7 to Go	1142	12780	11.2	93	1909	6.2	953	83.5
Games 9-16	4871	57219	11.7	343	8066	6.6	2812	57.7	3rd D 8+ to Go	1127	15411	13.7	65	2185	8.4	607	53.9
September	2295	26466	11.5	159	3757	6.6	1320	57.5	4th Down	151	1895	12.5	20	263	7.9	128	84.8
October	2620	30154	11.5	163	4430	6.5	1472	56.2	Rec Behind Line	1632	10264	6.3	26	2254	-3.0	488	29.9
November	2372	28412	12.0	183	3870	6.8	1413	59.6	1-10 yds	5755	51227	8.9	308	8509	4.8	2867	49.8
December	2430	28037	11.5	158	4072	6.4	1362	56.0	11-20 yds	1798	32590	18.1	153	3439	14.4	1682	93.5
Grass	4892	56670	11.6	316	8167	6.5	2826	57.8	21-30 yds	351	10826	30.8	92	1100	24.5	349	99.4
Turf	4825	56399	11.7	347	7962	6.6	2741	56.8	31+	180	8138	45.2	84	822	37.8	180	100.0
Indoor	2544	29990	11.8	183	4114	6.7	1458	57.3	Left Sideline	1790	22151	12.4	124	3188	7.8	1076	60.1
Outdoor	7173	83079	11.6	480	12015	6.5	4109	57.3	Left Side	1961	21697	11.1	117	3070	5.5	1119	57.1
1st Half	4852	56919	11.7	343	8002	6.5	2763	56.9	Middle	1644	20855	12.7	148	2703	7.6	997	60.6
2nd Half/OT	4865	56150	11.5	320	8127	6.6	2804	57.6	Right Side	2346	25331	10.8	144	3631	5.2	1271	54.2
Last 2 Min. Half	1356	15743	11.6	126	2332	7.0	805	59.3	Right Sideline	1974	22999	11.7	130	3531	7.3	1102	55.8
4th qtr, +/-7 pts	1107	12849	11.6	71	1911	7.0	636	57.5	Shotgun	1175	14472	12.3	68	1965	7.3	714	60.8
Winning	2776	33137	11.9	206	4571	6.6	1652	59.5	2 Wide Receivers	3969	45989	11.6	237	6520	6.4	2190	55.2
Tied	2148	24493	11.4	134	3538	6.4	1215	56.6	3 Wide Rec	4165	48866	11.7	264	6954	6.8	2394	57.5
Trailing	4793	55439	11.6	323	8020	6.6	2700	56.3	4+ Wide Rec	1331	15978	12.0	85	2217	6.7	799	60.0

1995 NFL Rushing Splits

	Rush	Yds	Avg	Lg	TD	1st	Stf	YdL		Rush	Yds	Avg	Lg	TD	1st	Stf	YdL
Total	13199	51886	3.9	86	385	3019	1594	3360	Inside 20	2173	5220	2.4	19	336	580	274	600
vs. Playoff	4944	18609	3.8	75	133	1116	574	1144	Inside 10	1154	1876	1.6	9	305	377	161	308
vs. Non-playoff	8255	33277	4.0	86	252	1903	1020	2216	1st Down	7031	26964	3.8	75	135	741	883	1796
vs. Own Division	6635	26427	4.0	75	187	1537	790	1620	2nd Down	4484	18394	4.1	75	142	1347	527	1171
Home	6870	27237	4.0	75	213	1578	808	1695	3rd Down Overall	1474	6069	4.1	86	91	792	161	320
Away	6329	24649	3.9	86	172	1441	786	1665	3rd D 0-2 to Go	790	2561	3.2	76	58	558	58	109
Games 1-8	6661	26467	4.0	76	173	1510	797	1651	3rd D 3-7 to Go	398	2099	5.3	86	28	195	42	101
Games 9-16	6538	25419	3.9	86	212	1509	797	1709	3rd D 8+ to Go	286	1409	4.9	52	5	39	61	110
September	3115	12469	4.0	60	76	695	341	704	4th Down	210	459	2.2	46	17	139	23	73
October	3644	14380	3.9	76	99	837	464	962	Left Sideline	728	4889	6.7	58	33	257	63	165
November	3272	13007	4.0	86	111	766	379	800	Left Side	2878	11748	4.1	75	83	614	356	874
December	3168	12030	3.8	75	99	721	410	894	Middle	6201	20418	3.3	75	174	1348	801	1452
Grass	6583	25210	3.8	86	187	1462	768	1628	Right Side	2732	10950	4.0	86	73	593	322	722
Turf	6616	26676	4.0	75	198	1557	826	1732	Right Sideline	659	3881	5.9	76	22	207	52	147
Indoor	3139	12619	4.0	75	93	728	399	873	Shotgun	281	1490	5.3	49	3	87	30	88
Outdoor	10060	39267	3.9	86	292	2291	1195	2487	2 Wide Receivers	7538	30218	4.0	86	117	1467	756	1743
1st Half	6429	26066	4.1	86	186	1509	666	1464	3 Wide Rec	2796	13140	4.7	75	55	703	308	759
2nd Half/OT	6770	25820	3.8	75	199	1510	928	1896	4+ Wide Rec	602	3110	5.2	40	16	183	32	60
Last 2 Min. Half	1159	2918	2.5	42	35	234	396	572	Carries 1-5	6357	25361	4.0	86	169	1520	833	1713
4th qtr, +/-7 pts	1593	5876	3.7	68	46	358	243	435	Carries 6-10	2964	11702	3.9	60	88	665	324	727
Winning	5337	19635	3.7	75	156	1119	789	1567	Carries 11-15	1950	7544	3.9	66	60	411	212	482
Tied	3139	12536	4.0	86	76	714	300	701	Carries 16-20	1195	4718	3.9	53	41	268	153	296
Trailing	4723	19715	4.2	75	153	1186	505	1092	Carries 21+	733	2561	3.5	41	27	148	72	142

1995 NFL Field Goal Splits

	1-29 Yd	Pct	30-39 Yd	Pct	40-49 Yd	Pct	50+ Yd	Pct	Overall	Pct	Lg
Total	261-284	91.9	262-318	82.4	169-261	64.8	46-91	50.5	738-954	77.4	59
vs. Playoff	102-112	91.1	105-124	84.7	65-103	63.1	17-30	56.7	289-369	78.3	59
vs. Non-playoff	159-172	92.4	157-194	80.9	104-158	65.8	29-61	47.5	449-585	76.8	56
vs. Own Division	126-139	90.6	126-157	80.3	83-128	64.8	26-51	51.0	361-475	76.0	50
Home	141-153	92.2	141-167	84.4	93-142	65.5	27-46	58.7	402-508	79.1	59
Away	120-131	91.6	121-151	80.1	76-119	63.9	19-45	42.2	336-446	75.3	56
Games 1-8	148-160	92.5	123-153	80.4	80-124	64.5	24-47	51.1	375-484	77.5	56
Games 9-16	113-124	91.1	139-165	84.2	89-137	65.0	22-44	50.0	363-470	77.2	59
September	60-63	95.2	50-66	75.8	35-56	62.5	8-18	44.4	153-203	75.4	55
October	89-98	90.8	73-88	83.0	47-70	67.1	17-30	56.7	226-286	79.0	56
November	56-60	93.3	69-79	87.3	45-72	62.5	9-20	45.0	179-231	77.5	56
December	56-63	88.9	70-85	82.4	42-63	66.7	12-23	52.2	180-234	76.9	59
Grass	143-159	89.9	119-147	81.0	74-116	63.8	17-34	50.0	353-456	77.4	55
Turf	118-125	94.4	143-171	83.6	95-145	65.5	29-57	50.9	385-498	77.3	59
Indoor	57-61	93.4	68-81	84.0	54-81	66.7	19-38	50.0	198-261	75.9	59
Outdoor	204-223	91.5	194-237	81.9	115-180	63.9	27-53	50.9	540-693	77.9	55

1995 NFL Kickoff Splits

	Num	Avg	TB	Pct	TD	Pct	NetAvg
Total	2307	62.7	213	9.2	9	0.4	41.3
vs. Playoff	864	62.9	81	9.4	6	0.7	41.7
vs. Non-playoff	1443	62.6	132	9.1	3	0.2	41.1
vs. Own Division	1123	62.6	93	8.3	5	0.4	41.4
Home	1205	62.8	122	10.1	4	0.3	41.6
Away	1102	62.6	91	8.3	5	0.5	41.0
Games 1-8	1139	63.4	128	11.2	2	0.2	42.6
Games 9-16	1168	62.0	85	7.3	7	0.6	41.2
September	512	64.4	59	11.5	1	0.2	42.7
October	639	62.6	70	11.0	1	0.2	41.7
November	591	62.4	53	9.0	1	0.2	41.4
December	565	61.6	31	5.5	6	1.1	39.5
Grass	1125	62.0	93	8.3	6	0.5	40.9
Turf	1182	63.4	120	10.2	3	0.3	41.7
Indoor	588	64.9	51	8.7	1	0.2	42.5
Outdoor	1719	62.0	162	9.4	8	0.5	40.9

1995 NFL Punting Splits

	NPunts	Avg	Lg	In20	In20%	FC	FC%	TPunts	TB	Blk	Ret	Yds	NetAvg
Total	2182	42.0	73	645	29.6	411	18.8	2193	229	11	1042	9819	35.2
vs. Playoff	900	42.3	73	244	27.1	152	16.9	900	84	0	440	4111	35.9
vs. Non-playoff	1282	41.8	69	401	31.3	259	20.2	1293	145	11	602	5708	34.8
vs. Own Division	1099	41.8	69	320	29.1	209	19.0	1105	113	6	523	4768	35.2
Home	1048	41.6	67	304	29.0	192	18.3	1054	120	6	485	4717	34.6
Away	1134	42.4	73	341	30.1	219	19.3	1139	109	5	557	5102	35.8
September	548	42.3	69	152	27.7	115	21.0	552	62	4	252	2287	35.6
October	593	42.8	73	179	30.2	100	16.9	594	70	1	293	2829	35.6
November	482	41.5	64	148	30.7	75	15.6	485	40	3	243	2291	34.9
December	559	41.3	65	166	29.7	121	21.6	562	57	3	254	2412	34.7
Grass	1097	42.0	66	318	29.0	182	16.6	1104	118	7	546	4857	35.2
Turf	1085	42.1	73	327	30.1	229	21.1	1089	111	4	496	4962	35.3
Indoor	498	42.6	69	165	33.1	115	23.1	500	32	2	244	2554	36.1
Outdoor	1684	41.8	73	480	28.5	296	17.6	1693	197	9	798	7265	35.0
Outdoors, Temp < 40	318	39.6	65	96	30.2	67	21.1	319	34	1	134	1032	34.1
Outdoors, Temp 40-80	1224	42.1	73	349	28.5	206	16.8	1231	148	7	589	5620	34.9
Outdoors, Temp > 80	142	44.1	65	35	24.6	23	16.2	143	15	1	75	613	37.4
Winning	782	41.8	65	238	30.4	144	18.4	789	95	7	357	3352	34.6
Tied	544	41.8	69	167	30.7	96	17.6	546	62	2	254	2493	34.8
Trailing	856	42.5	73	240	28.0	171	20.0	858	72	2	431	3974	36.1

Offensive Lines

It may not be glamorous, but it's practically impossible to run an effective offense without quality play from your offensive line. The problem is, until this book was first released a year ago, there was virtually no objective way to evaluate offensive linemen. But taking a page from the groundbreaking material in *The Hidden Game of Football* (Warner Books, 1988), we compared linemen in the context of their *teams*. We were more than pleased with the results, so we're presenting the data again this year.

STATS reporters track the *direction* of each running play (actually, we're missing direction for a tiny number of rushes). So we not only can compare teams in terms of average yards per rushing attempt, but average yards per rushing attempt to the left side, the middle, and the right. Obviously, it makes little sense to consider the results of left sweeps when you're evaluating a right tackle.

Also, this is the second year we have attributed responsibility for sacks to offensive linemen when appropriate. Subjective? Sure, but our reporters are given quite specific instructions, and we're confident in their judgment. They don't "assign" a sack to an offensive lineman unless he was obviously beaten by a defender.

We've done a couple of things to help you compare the various lines to each other. First, before the teams themselves, you'll find a chart showing the NFL averages when running left, up the middle, and right, along with the NFL sack percentage. Also, with each of those categories for the individual teams, we list (in parentheses) where that team ranked in the NFL, 1 through 30.

We should explain how individual linemen are listed. A lineman is listed at each position at which he started, and the "sacks allowed" include only those in games the lineman started at that position. Confused? Wait, there's more. If a lineman allowed a sack in a game he did not start, he and the number of sacks allowed are listed as "Non-start sacks allowed." It's not perfect, but one of the few things STATS *doesn't* record is the position of every lineman on every play.

We would like to see more work done on the subject of offensive lines, but until then we hope this holds you.

— Rob Neyer

National Football League

	Rushing	Sacks Allowed
	51886 Yards/13199 Attempts	1076 Sks/17774 Pass Plays
	3.9 Average	16.5 Pass Plays/Sack

Running Left	**Running Middle**	**Running Right**
16637 Yards/3606 Carries	20418 Yards/6201 Carries	14831 Yards/3391 Carries
4.6 Average	3.3 Average	4.4 Average

Arizona Cardinals

	Rushing	Sacks Allowed
	1363 Yards/387 Attempts	55 Sacks/615 Pass Plays
	3.5 Average (26)	11.2 Pass Plays/Sack (27)

Running Left	**Running Middle**	**Running Right**
423 Yards/119 Carries	609 Yards/178 Carries	331 Yards/90 Carries
3.6 Average (29)	3.4 Average (9)	3.7 Average (27)

		Sacks			Sacks			Sacks			Sacks			Sacks
Left Tackle	GS	Allowed	Left Guard	GS	Allowed	Center	GS	Allowed	Right Guard	GS	Allowed	Right Tackle	GS	Allowed
Larry Tharpe	10	6.5	Duval Love	16	8.0	Jamie Dukes	8	0.0	Bernard Dafney	8	5.0	Larry Tharpe	6	3.0
Ernest Dye	6	5.0				Ed Cunningham	8	3.0	Anthony Redmon	8	2.0	Rob Selby	4	3.5
												Cecil Gray	4	2.5
												Joe Wolf	1	0.0
												Anthony Redmon	1	0.0

Non-Start Sacks Allowed: Rob Selby 1.0

Atlanta Falcons

	Rushing	Sacks Allowed
	1393 Yards/337 Attempts	43 Sacks/646 Pass Plays
	4.1 Average (10)	15.0 Pass Plays/Sack (22)

Running Left	**Running Middle**	**Running Right**
419 Yards/82 Carries	538 Yards/184 Carries	436 Yards/71 Carries
5.1 Average (8)	2.9 Average (24)	6.1 Average (1)

		Sacks			Sacks			Sacks			Sacks			Sacks
Left Tackle	GS	Allowed	Left Guard	GS	Allowed	Center	GS	Allowed	Right Guard	GS	Allowed	Right Tackle	GS	Allowed
Bob Whitfield	16	4.0	Robbie Tobeck	15	5.0	Roman Fortin	15	2.5	Mike Zandofsky	12	4.0	Dave Richards	12	7.0
			Gene Williams	1	0.0	Robbie Tobeck	1	0.0	Gene Williams	2	0.0	Lincoln Kennedy	4	3.0
									Jeff Pahukoa	2	2.0			

Non-Start Sacks Allowed: Dave Richards .5

Buffalo Bills

	Rushing	Sacks Allowed
	1993 Yards/521 Attempts	32 Sacks/538 Pass Plays
	3.8 Average (18)	16.8 Pass Plays/Sack (17)

Running Left	**Running Middle**	**Running Right**
604 Yards/162 Carries	820 Yards/239 Carries	569 Yards/120 Carries
3.7 Average (28)	3.4 Average (8)	4.7 Average (8)

		Sacks			Sacks			Sacks			Sacks			Sacks
Left Tackle	GS	Allowed	Left Guard	GS	Allowed	Center	GS	Allowed	Right Guard	GS	Allowed	Right Tackle	GS	Allowed
John Fina	16	6.5	Ruben Brown	16	1.5	Kent Hull	16	3.5	Jerry Ostroski	13	1.0	Glenn Parker	13	2.0
									Corbin Lacina	3	0.0	Corey Louchiey	3	0.0

Non-Start Sacks Allowed: Corbin Lacina 2.0, Corey Louchiey 1.0

Carolina Panthers

Rushing
1573 Yards/454 Attempts
3.5 Average (30)

Sacks Allowed
38 Sacks/574 Pass Plays
15.1 Pass Plays/Sack (21)

Running Left
437 Yards/101 Carries
4.3 Average (17)

Running Middle
703 Yards/236 Carries
3.0 Average (23)

Running Right
433 Yards/117 Carries
3.7 Average (25)

Left Tackle	GS	Sacks Allowed	Left Guard	GS	Sacks Allowed	Center	GS	Sacks Allowed	Right Guard	GS	Sacks Allowed	Right Tackle	GS	Sacks Allowed
Bl. Brockermeyer	16	7.0	Frank Garcia	14	4.0	Curtis Whitley	16	1.5	Matt Elliott	14	7.0	Mark Dennis	9	3.0
			Andrew Peterson	2	1.0				Sean Love	1	0.0	Derrick Graham	7	3.0
									Emerson Martin	1	0.0			

Chicago Bears

Rushing
1930 Yards/492 Attempts
3.9 Average (15)

Sacks Allowed
15 Sacks/538 Pass Plays
35.9 Pass Plays/Sack (1)

Running Left
517 Yards/100 Carries
5.2 Average (7)

Running Middle
912 Yards/279 Carries
3.3 Average (15)

Running Right
501 Yards/113 Carries
4.4 Average (14)

Left Tackle	GS	Sacks Allowed	Left Guard	GS	Sacks Allowed	Center	GS	Sacks Allowed	Right Guard	GS	Sacks Allowed	Right Tackle	GS	Sacks Allowed
Andy Heck	16	0.5	Todd Perry	15	0.5	Jerry Fontenot	16	1.0	Jay Leeuwenburg	16	1.5	James Williams	16	2.0
			Todd Burger	1	0.0									

Non-Start Sacks Allowed: Troy Auzenne 1.0

Cincinnati Bengals

Rushing
1439 Yards/364 Attempts
4.0 Average (13)

Sacks Allowed
25 Sacks/611 Pass Plays
24.4 Pass Plays/Sack (6)

Running Left
233 Yards/70 Carries
3.3 Average (30)

Running Middle
671 Yards/179 Carries
3.7 Average (4)

Running Right
535 Yards/115 Carries
4.7 Average (11)

Left Tackle	GS	Sacks Allowed	Left Guard	GS	Sacks Allowed	Center	GS	Sacks Allowed	Right Guard	GS	Sacks Allowed	Right Tackle	GS	Sacks Allowed
Kevin Sargent	15	6.5	Scott Brumfield	11	1.5	Darrick Brilz	16	2.0	Todd Kalis	8	2.0	Joe Walter	16	6.5
Melvin Tuten	1	0.0	Todd Kalis	3	0.0				Bruce Kozerski	8	1.0			
			Anthony Brown	2	0.0									

Non-Start Sacks Allowed: Todd Kalis 1.0, Trent Pollard 1.0, Melvin Tuten 1.0

Cleveland Browns

Rushing
1482 Yards/398 Attempts
3.7 Average (20)

Sacks Allowed
32 Sacks/587 Pass Plays
18.3 Pass Plays/Sack (13)

Running Left
261 Yards/61 Carries
4.3 Average (20)

Running Middle
641 Yards/193 Carries
3.3 Average (11)

Running Right
580 Yards/144 Carries
4.0 Average (22)

Left Tackle	GS	Sacks Allowed	Left Guard	GS	Sacks Allowed	Center	GS	Sacks Allowed	Right Guard	GS	Sacks Allowed	Right Tackle	GS	Sacks Allowed
Tony Jones	16	4.0	Wally Williams	14	4.5	Steve Everitt	14	1.0	Bob Dahl	16	5.0	Orlando Brown	16	4.0
			Herman Arvie	2	0.0	Wally Williams	2	0.5						

Non-Start Sacks Allowed: Herman Arvie .5

492

Dallas Cowboys

	Rushing	Sacks Allowed
	2201 Yards/495 Attempts	18 Sacks/512 Pass Plays
	4.4 Average (4)	28.4 Pass Plays/Sack (2)

Running Left
764 Yards/150 Carries
5.1 Average (9)

Running Middle
1109 Yards/250 Carries
4.4 Average (1)

Running Right
328 Yards/95 Carries
3.5 Average (30)

Left Tackle	GS	Sacks Allowed	Left Guard	GS	Sacks Allowed	Center	GS	Sacks Allowed	Right Guard	GS	Sacks Allowed	Right Tackle	GS	Sacks Allowed
Mark Tuinei	16	3.5	Nate Newton	16	3.5	Ray Donaldson	12	0.5	Larry Allen	16	0.5	Erik Williams	15	7.5
						Derek Kennard	4	0.0				Ron Stone	1	0.0

Denver Broncos

	Rushing	Sacks Allowed
	1995 Yards/440 Attempts	26 Sacks/620 Pass Plays
	4.5 Average (2)	23.8 Pass Plays/Sack (7)

Running Left
663 Yards/120 Carries
5.5 Average (5)

Running Middle
940 Yards/232 Carries
4.1 Average (2)

Running Right
392 Yards/88 Carries
4.5 Average (13)

Left Tackle	GS	Sacks Allowed	Left Guard	GS	Sacks Allowed	Center	GS	Sacks Allowed	Right Guard	GS	Sacks Allowed	Right Tackle	GS	Sacks Allowed
Gary Zimmerman	16	4.5	Mark Schlereth	16	1.5	Tom Nalen	15	0.0	Brian Habib	16	3.5	Br. Thompson	16	8.5
						Ralph Tamm	1	0.0						

Non-Start Sacks Allowed: Reggie McElroy 1.0

Detroit Lions

	Rushing	Sacks Allowed
	1753 Yards/387 Attempts	32 Sacks/637 Pass Plays
	4.5 Average (3)	19.9 Pass Plays/Sack (11)

Running Left
614 Yards/110 Carries
5.6 Average (3)

Running Middle
612 Yards/168 Carries
3.6 Average (7)

Running Right
527 Yards/109 Carries
4.8 Average (6)

Left Tackle	GS	Sacks Allowed	Left Guard	GS	Sacks Allowed	Center	GS	Sacks Allowed	Right Guard	GS	Sacks Allowed	Right Tackle	GS	Sacks Allowed
Lomas Brown	14	2.5	Doug Widell	10	4.0	Kevin Glover	16	2.5	David Lutz	16	3.0	Zefross Moss	14	1.0
Mike Compton	2	0.5	Mike Compton	6	2.0							Scott Conover	2	1.0

Non-Start Sacks Allowed: Lomas Brown .5, Scott Conover 1.5

Green Bay Packers

	Rushing	Sacks Allowed
	1428 Yards/410 Attempts	33 Sacks/626 Pass Plays
	3.5 Average (28)	19.0 Pass Plays/Sack (12)

Running Left
474 Yards/108 Carries
4.4 Average (16)

Running Middle
559 Yards/195 Carries
2.9 Average (26)

Running Right
395 Yards/107 Carries
3.7 Average (26)

Left Tackle	GS	Sacks Allowed	Left Guard	GS	Sacks Allowed	Center	GS	Sacks Allowed	Right Guard	GS	Sacks Allowed	Right Tackle	GS	Sacks Allowed
Ken Ruettgers	15	5.0	Aaron Taylor	16	4.5	Frank Winters	16	0.5	Harry Galbreath	16	3.0	Earl Dotson	16	4.0
Joe Sims	1	1.5												

Houston Oilers

	Rushing	Sacks Allowed
	1664 Yards/478 Attempts	32 Sacks/568 Pass Plays
	3.5 Average (29)	17.8 Pass Plays/Sack (15)

Running Left
476 Yards/115 Carries
4.1 Average (22)

Running Middle
770 Yards/243 Carries
3.2 Average (19)

Running Right
418 Yards/120 Carries
3.5 Average (29)

Left Tackle	GS	Sacks Allowed	Left Guard	GS	Sacks Allowed	Center	GS	Sacks Allowed	Right Guard	GS	Sacks Allowed	Right Tackle	GS	Sacks Allowed
Brad Hopkins	16	7.0	Bruce Matthews	16	1.5	Mark Stepnoski	16	2.0	Kevin Donnalley	16	4.5	David Williams	9	4.5
												Irv Eatman	7	1.0

Non-Start Sacks Allowed: Erik Norgard .5

Indianapolis Colts

	Rushing	Sacks Allowed
	1855 Yards/478 Attempts	49 Sacks/483 Pass Plays
	3.9 Average (16)	9.9 Pass Plays/Sack (29)

Running Left
581 Yards/144 Carries
4.0 Average (24)

Running Middle
662 Yards/204 Carries
3.2 Average (16)

Running Right
612 Yards/130 Carries
4.7 Average (9)

Left Tackle	GS	Sacks Allowed	Left Guard	GS	Sacks Allowed	Center	GS	Sacks Allowed	Right Guard	GS	Sacks Allowed	Right Tackle	GS	Sacks Allowed
Will Wolford	16	7.5	Randy Dixon	9	2.0	Kirk Lowdermilk	16	2.5	Joe Staysniak	9	0.0	Jason Mathews	16	13.5
			Joe Staysniak	7	1.0				Eric Mahlum	7	0.0			

Non-Start Sacks Allowed: Randy Dixon .5

Jacksonville Jaguars

	Rushing	Sacks Allowed
	1705 Yards/410 Attempts	57 Sacks/552 Pass Plays
	4.2 Average (9)	9.7 Pass Plays/Sack (30)

Running Left
697 Yards/149 Carries
4.7 Average (14)

Running Middle
425 Yards/128 Carries
3.3 Average (12)

Running Right
583 Yards/133 Carries
4.4 Average (15)

Left Tackle	GS	Sacks Allowed	Left Guard	GS	Sacks Allowed	Center	GS	Sacks Allowed	Right Guard	GS	Sacks Allowed	Right Tackle	GS	Sacks Allowed
Tony Boselli	12	4.0	Shawn Bouwens	9	3.0	Dave Widell	16	5.0	Tom Myslinski	9	4.5	Brian DeMarco	16	12.0
Jeff Novak	4	3.0	Jeff Novak	7	2.5				Ben Coleman	5	1.0			
									Jeff Novak	2	0.0			

Non-Start Sacks Allowed: Ben Coleman 1.0, Frank Cornish 1.0, Bruce Wilkerson 1.0

Kansas City Chiefs

	Rushing	Sacks Allowed
	2222 Yards/507 Attempts	21 Sacks/552 Pass Plays
	4.4 Average (5)	26.3 Pass Plays/Sack (4)

Running Left
769 Yards/139 Carries
5.5 Average (4)

Running Middle
868 Yards/255 Carries
3.4 Average (10)

Running Right
585 Yards/113 Carries
5.2 Average (3)

Left Tackle	GS	Sacks Allowed	Left Guard	GS	Sacks Allowed	Center	GS	Sacks Allowed	Right Guard	GS	Sacks Allowed	Right Tackle	GS	Sacks Allowed
John Alt	16	4.0	David Szott	16	2.5	Tim Grunhard	16	4.5	Will Shields	16	0.0	Ricky Siglar	12	2.0
												Jeff Criswell	4	0.0

Non-Start Sacks Allowed: Ricky Siglar 1.0

Miami Dolphins

	Rushing	Sacks Allowed
	1506 Yards/413 Attempts	29 Sacks/621 Pass Plays
	3.6 Average (23)	21.4 Pass Plays/Sack (9)

Running Left
613 Yards/122 Carries
5.0 Average (11)

Running Middle
387 Yards/166 Carries
2.3 Average (30)

Running Right
506 Yards/124 Carries
4.1 Average (21)

Left Tackle	GS	Sacks Allowed	Left Guard	GS	Sacks Allowed	Center	GS	Sacks Allowed	Right Guard	GS	Sacks Allowed	Right Tackle	GS	Sacks Allowed
Richmond Webb	16	4.0	Keith Sims	16	3.5	Tim Ruddy	16	1.5	Chris Gray	10	1.0	Billy Milner	9	6.5
									Tom McHale	4	0.0	Ron Heller	7	6.0
									Bert Weidner	1	1.0			
									Andrew Greene	1	0.0			

Minnesota Vikings

	Rushing	Sacks Allowed
	1733 Yards/433 Attempts	40 Sacks/682 Pass Plays
	4.0 Average (11)	17.1 Pass Plays/Sack (16)

Running Left
734 Yards/139 Carries
5.3 Average (6)

Running Middle
553 Yards/199 Carries
2.8 Average (27)

Running Right
446 Yards/95 Carries
4.7 Average (10)

Left Tackle	GS	Sacks Allowed	Left Guard	GS	Sacks Allowed	Center	GS	Sacks Allowed	Right Guard	GS	Sacks Allowed	Right Tackle	GS	Sacks Allowed
Todd Steussie	16	6.5	Randall McDaniel	16	1.5	Jeff Christy	16	2.5	John Gerak	6	3.5	Korey Stringer	15	7.0
									David Dixon	6	2.0	Rick Cunningham	1	1.0
									Chris Hinton	4	1.5			

Non-Start Sacks Allowed: Rick Cunningham 1.0, John Gerak 1.0

New England Patriots

	Rushing	Sacks Allowed
	1866 Yards/474 Attempts	27 Sacks/713 Pass Plays
	3.9 Average (14)	26.4 Pass Plays/Sack (3)

Running Left
651 Yards/153 Carries
4.3 Average (21)

Running Middle
658 Yards/215 Carries
3.1 Average (20)

Running Right
557 Yards/106 Carries
5.3 Average (2)

Left Tackle	GS	Sacks Allowed	Left Guard	GS	Sacks Allowed	Center	GS	Sacks Allowed	Right Guard	GS	Sacks Allowed	Right Tackle	GS	Sacks Allowed
Bruce Armstrong	16	5.5	William Roberts	11	0.0	Dave Wohlabaugh	11	2.0	Bob Kratch	11	0.5	Max Lane	16	6.0
			Bob Kratch	5	1.0	Jeff Dellenbach	5	2.0	Todd Rucci	5	2.5			

Non-Start Sacks Allowed: William Roberts 1.0

New Orleans Saints

	Rushing	Sacks Allowed
	1390 Yards/383 Attempts	28 Sacks/601 Pass Plays
	3.6 Average (24)	21.5 Pass Plays/Sack (8)

Running Left
681 Yards/166 Carries
4.1 Average (23)

Running Middle
454 Yards/158 Carries
2.9 Average (25)

Running Right
255 Yards/59 Carries
4.3 Average (16)

Left Tackle	GS	Sacks Allowed	Left Guard	GS	Sacks Allowed	Center	GS	Sacks Allowed	Right Guard	GS	Sacks Allowed	Right Tackle	GS	Sacks Allowed
William Roaf	16	7.5	Jim Dombrowski	16	4.5	Jeff Uhlenhake	14	0.5	Andy McCollum	9	2.0	Richard Cooper	14	2.0
						Craig Novitsky	2	0.0	Chris Port	7	4.0	Chris Port	1	1.0
												Craig Novitsky	1	0.0

New York Giants

Rushing
1833 Yards/478 Attempts
3.8 Average (17)

Sacks Allowed
46 Sacks/525 Pass Plays
11.4 Pass Plays/Sack (26)

Running Left
420 Yards/108 Carries
3.9 Average (26)

Running Middle
991 Yards/272 Carries
3.6 Average (6)

Running Right
422 Yards/98 Carries
4.3 Average (17)

Left Tackle	GS	Sacks Allowed	Left Guard	GS	Sacks Allowed	Center	GS	Sacks Allowed	Right Guard	GS	Sacks Allowed	Right Tackle	GS	Sacks Allowed
John Elliott	16	7.0	Greg Bishop	16	7.0	Brian Williams	16	0.5	Lance Smith	13	4.5	Doug Riesenberg	16	7.5
									Rob Zatechka	3	1.0			

Non-Start Sacks Allowed: Rob Zatechka 1.0

New York Jets

Rushing
1279 Yards/365 Attempts
3.5 Average (27)

Sacks Allowed
47 Sacks/636 Pass Plays
13.5 Pass Plays/Sack (23)

Running Left
467 Yards/109 Carries
4.3 Average (19)

Running Middle
355 Yards/138 Carries
2.6 Average (29)

Running Right
457 Yards/118 Carries
3.9 Average (24)

Left Tackle	GS	Sacks Allowed	Left Guard	GS	Sacks Allowed	Center	GS	Sacks Allowed	Right Guard	GS	Sacks Allowed	Right Tackle	GS	Sacks Allowed
Matt Willig	12	5.5	Roger Duffy	16	3.5	Cal Dixon	11	2.0	Carlton Haselrig	11	2.0	James Brown	12	7.5
Everette McIver	4	4.5				John Bock	5	2.0	Matt O'Dwyer	2	0.0	Siupeli Malamala	4	3.0
									John Bock	2	2.0			
									Cal Dixon	1	0.0			

Non-Start Sacks Allowed: Terrence Wisdom 1.0

Oakland Raiders

Rushing
1932 Yards/463 Attempts
4.2 Average (7)

Sacks Allowed
36 Sacks/579 Pass Plays
16.1 Pass Plays/Sack (18)

Running Left
664 Yards/118 Carries
5.6 Average (2)

Running Middle
682 Yards/223 Carries
3.1 Average (21)

Running Right
586 Yards/122 Carries
4.8 Average (7)

Left Tackle	GS	Sacks Allowed	Left Guard	GS	Sacks Allowed	Center	GS	Sacks Allowed	Right Guard	GS	Sacks Allowed	Right Tackle	GS	Sacks Allowed
Robert Jenkins	12	4.0	Steve Wisniewski	16	7.0	Dan Turk	16	3.0	Kevin Gogan	16	2.5	Greg Skrepenak	14	5.5
Gerald Perry	3	1.0										Robert Jenkins	1	1.0
Rich Stephens	1	0.0										Russell Freeman	1	1.0

Non-Start Sacks Allowed: Russell Freeman 3.0, Rich Stephens .5

Philadelphia Eagles

Rushing
2121 Yards/508 Attempts
4.2 Average (6)

Sacks Allowed
46 Sacks/542 Pass Plays
11.8 Pass Plays/Sack (25)

Running Left
616 Yards/125 Carries
4.9 Average (13)

Running Middle
947 Yards/258 Carries
3.7 Average (5)

Running Right
558 Yards/125 Carries
4.5 Average (12)

Left Tackle	GS	Sacks Allowed	Left Guard	GS	Sacks Allowed	Center	GS	Sacks Allowed	Right Guard	GS	Sacks Allowed	Right Tackle	GS	Sacks Allowed
Barrett Brooks	16	13.5	Guy McIntyre	16	3.5	Raleigh McKenzie	16	3.0	Joe Panos	9	7.0	Antone Davis	14	7.0
									Harry Boatswain	7	1.0	Lester Holmes	2	1.5

Non-Start Sacks Allowed: Mo Elewonibi 1.0

496

Pittsburgh Steelers

Rushing
1852 Yards/494 Attempts
3.7 Average (19)

Sacks Allowed
24 Sacks/616 Pass Plays
25.7 Pass Plays/Sack (5)

Running Left
594 Yards/138 Carries
4.3 Average (18)

Running Middle
645 Yards/212 Carries
3.0 Average (22)

Running Right
613 Yards/144 Carries
4.3 Average (18)

Left Tackle	GS	Sacks Allowed	Left Guard	GS	Sacks Allowed	Center	GS	Sacks Allowed	Right Guard	GS	Sacks Allowed	Right Tackle	GS	Sacks Allowed
John Jackson	9	5.0	Tom Newberry	15	2.0	Dermontti Dawson	16	3.5	Brenden Stai	9	3.0	Leon Searcy	16	1.5
Justin Strzelczyk	6	2.5	Justin Strzelczyk	1	0.0				Justin Strzelczyk	7	0.5			
James Parrish	1	0.0												

San Diego Chargers

Rushing
1747 Yards/479 Attempts
3.6 Average (22)

Sacks Allowed
32 Sacks/572 Pass Plays
17.9 Pass Plays/Sack (14)

Running Left
686 Yards/151 Carries
4.5 Average (15)

Running Middle
489 Yards/189 Carries
2.6 Average (28)

Running Right
572 Yards/139 Carries
4.1 Average (20)

Left Tackle	GS	Sacks Allowed	Left Guard	GS	Sacks Allowed	Center	GS	Sacks Allowed	Right Guard	GS	Sacks Allowed	Right Tackle	GS	Sacks Allowed
Harry Swayne	16	9.5	Eric Moten	15	4.5	Courtney Hall	16	1.0	Isaac Davis	9	3.0	Stan Brock	9	4.5
			Isaac Davis	1	0.0				Joe Cocozzo	7	2.5	Vaughn Parker	7	0.5

Non-Start Sacks Allowed: Joe Cocozzo 1.0, Vaughn Parker 1.0

San Francisco 49ers

Rushing
1479 Yards/415 Attempts
3.6 Average (25)

Sacks Allowed
33 Sacks/677 Pass Plays
20.5 Pass Plays/Sack (10)

Running Left
413 Yards/108 Carries
3.8 Average (27)

Running Middle
572 Yards/180 Carries
3.2 Average (18)

Running Right
494 Yards/127 Carries
3.9 Average (23)

Left Tackle	GS	Sacks Allowed	Left Guard	GS	Sacks Allowed	Center	GS	Sacks Allowed	Right Guard	GS	Sacks Allowed	Right Tackle	GS	Sacks Allowed
Steve Wallace	12	2.0	Jesse Sapolu	14	3.5	Bart Oates	14	1.5	Rod Milstead	12	5.5	Harris Barton	12	2.5
Kirk Scrafford	4	2.0	Kirk Scrafford	2	0.0	Jesse Sapolu	2	0.0	Derrick Deese	2	2.0	Kirk Scrafford	4	1.0
									Kirk Scrafford	1	2.0			
									Chris Dalman	1	0.0			

Seattle Seahawks

Rushing
2178 Yards/477 Attempts
4.6 Average (1)

Sacks Allowed
45 Sacks/556 Pass Plays
12.4 Pass Plays/Sack (24)

Running Left
534 Yards/94 Carries
5.7 Average (1)

Running Middle
978 Yards/254 Carries
3.9 Average (3)

Running Right
666 Yards/129 Carries
5.2 Average (4)

Left Tackle	GS	Sacks Allowed	Left Guard	GS	Sacks Allowed	Center	GS	Sacks Allowed	Right Guard	GS	Sacks Allowed	Right Tackle	GS	Sacks Allowed
James Atkins	16	6.5	Matt Joyce	13	3.0	Jim Sweeney	16	4.0	Kevin Mawae	16	5.0	Howard Ballard	16	11.0
			Jeff Blackshear	3	0.0									

Non-Start Sacks Allowed: Ray Roberts 2.0

St. Louis Rams

Rushing
1431 Yards/392 Attempts
3.7 Average (21)

Sacks Allowed
43 Sacks/675 Pass Plays
15.7 Pass Plays/Sack (19)

Running Left
408 Yards/103 Carries
4.0 Average (25)

Running Middle
605 Yards/188 Carries
3.2 Average (17)

Running Right
418 Yards/101 Carries
4.1 Average (19)

Left Tackle	GS	Sacks Allowed	Left Guard	GS	Sacks Allowed	Center	GS	Sacks Allowed	Right Guard	GS	Sacks Allowed	Right Tackle	GS	Sacks Allowed
Wayne Gandy	16	10.0	Leo Goeas	14	4.0	Bern Brostek	16	3.5	Dwayne White	15	6.5	Darryl Ashmore	15	2.0
			Keith Loneker	1	1.0				Zach Wiegert	1	0.0	Jackie Slater	1	0.0
			Zach Wiegert	1	0.0									

Non-Start Sacks Allowed: Chuck Belin 1.0, Clarence Jones 1.5, Keith Loneker .5

Tampa Bay Buccaneers

Rushing
1587 Yards/398 Attempts
4.0 Average (12)

Sacks Allowed
56 Sacks/563 Pass Plays
10.1 Pass Plays/Sack (28)

Running Left
702 Yards/138 Carries
5.1 Average (10)

Running Middle
543 Yards/166 Carries
3.3 Average (14)

Running Right
342 Yards/94 Carries
3.6 Average (28)

Left Tackle	GS	Sacks Allowed	Left Guard	GS	Sacks Allowed	Center	GS	Sacks Allowed	Right Guard	GS	Sacks Allowed	Right Tackle	GS	Sacks Allowed
Paul Gruber	16	10.0	Jim Pyne	12	6.0	Tony Mayberry	16	1.5	Ian Beckles	15	2.5	Scott Dill	12	8.0
			Charles McRae	4	2.5				Jim Pyne	1	0.0	Pete Pierson	4	2.5

Non-Start Sacks Allowed: Mike Sullivan 1.0

Washington Redskins

Rushing
1956 Yards/469 Attempts
4.2 Average (8)

Sacks Allowed
36 Sacks/557 Pass Plays
15.5 Pass Plays/Sack (20)

Running Left
522 Yards/104 Carries
5.0 Average (12)

Running Middle
720 Yards/220 Carries
3.3 Average (13)

Running Right
714 Yards/145 Carries
4.9 Average (5)

Left Tackle	GS	Sacks Allowed	Left Guard	GS	Sacks Allowed	Center	GS	Sacks Allowed	Right Guard	GS	Sacks Allowed	Right Tackle	GS	Sacks Allowed
Joe Patton	13	4.0	Ray Brown	16	2.0	John Gesek	12	1.0	Tre Johnson	9	5.0	Ed Simmons	16	4.0
Jim Lachey	3	0.5				Vernice Smith	2	2.0	John Gesek	4	0.0			
						Cory Raymer	2	1.0	Vernice Smith	3	3.5			

Non-Start Sacks Allowed: Vernice Smith 1.0

Leader Boards

The following pages feature leader boards in a number of categories, most of which you'll not find in any other book. We should probably offer a few words of explanation on how the boards are arranged. You'll notice that all the passing leaders aren't on one page; that's because we wanted to show you more than would fit on one page. Our solution was to group most of the "official leaders"—those categories which are ranked in the NFL's own record book—on the following page, "1995 NFL Primary Statistics." After that, you'll find other boards for passing, rushing, receiving, defense and special teams.

New this year are *career* leader boards, which list the active leaders in a number of categories.

We should also mention qualifications. For all "percentage" categories, like yards/rush, interception-return average, etc., a player must meet a certain minimum standard for inclusion among the leaders. When applicable, the minimum qualification is listed with the leaders. Most of the categories in question are official, and we've used the NFL's standard when determining minimums.

However, some of the statistics here are not official, and for those we had to decide on our own minimums. The unofficial categories are:

Passing: 4th Quarter QB Rating.

Rushing: Yards/Carry, Grass; Yards/Carry, Turf; Yards/Carry, Attempts 21+; Touchdown Percentage Inside 3-Yard Line; Stuffs/Carry; 4th Quarter Rushing Yards.

Receiving: Average Throw; Percent Passes Caught per Target.

Defense: Yards/Interception Return.

Special Teams: Field-Goal Percentage; 1-39 Field-Goal Pct.; 40-49 Yard Field-Goal Pct.; 50+ Yard Field-Goal Pct.; Net Kickoff Average; Net Punt Average; Inside 20 Percentage; Touchback Percentage.

For questions on the definitions of particular categories, please consult the Glossary.

1995 NFL Primary Statistics

Points

Player, Team	TD	FG	PAT	Pts
E Smith, Dal	25	0	0	**150**
N Johnson, Pit	0	34	39	141
J Hanson, Det	0	28	48	132
J Elam, Den	0	31	39	132
C Boniol, Dal	0	27	46	127
S Christie, Buf	0	31	33	126
M Andersen, Atl	0	31	29	122
F Reveiz, Min	0	26	44	122
D Pelfrey, Cin	0	29	34	121
P Stoyanovich, Mia	0	27	37	118

Touchdowns

Player, Team	Rush	Rec	Misc	Tot
E Smith, Dal	25	0	0	**25**
J Rice, SF	1	15	1	17
C Pickens, Cin	0	17	0	17
C Carter, Min	0	17	0	17
C Warren, Sea	15	1	0	16
C Martin, NE	14	1	0	15
M Faulk, Ind	11	3	0	14
H Moore, Det	0	14	0	14
A Miller, Den	0	14	0	14
3 tied with				13

Rushing Yards

Player, Team	Carries	Y/C	Yds
E Smith, Dal	377	4.7	**1773**
B Sanders, Det	314	4.8	1500
C Martin, NE	368	4.0	1487
C Warren, Sea	310	4.3	1346
T Allen, Was	338	3.9	1309
R Watters, Phi	337	3.8	1273
E Rhett, TB	332	3.6	1207
R Hampton, NYN	306	3.9	1182
T Davis, Den	237	4.7	1117
H Williams, Oak	255	4.4	1114

Quarterback Rating
(Minimum 224 Attempts)

Player, Team	Att	Rating
J Harbaugh, Ind	314	**100.7**
B Favre, GB	570	99.5
T Aikman, Dal	432	93.6
E Kramer, Chi	522	93.5
S Young, SF	447	92.3
S Mitchell, Det	583	92.3
W Moon, Min	606	91.5
D Marino, Mia	482	90.8
J George, Atl	557	89.5
V Testaverde, Cle	392	87.8

Passing Yards

Player, Team	Att	Y/A	Yds
B Favre, GB	570	7.7	**4413**
S Mitchell, Det	583	7.4	4338
W Moon, Min	606	7.0	4228
J George, Atl	557	7.4	4143
J Elway, Den	542	7.3	3970
J Everett, NO	567	7.0	3970
E Kramer, Chi	522	7.4	3838
J Blake, Cin	567	6.7	3822
D Marino, Mia	482	7.6	3668
D Krieg, Ari	521	6.8	3554

Receptions

Player, Team	Rec
H Moore, Det	**123**
J Rice, SF	122
C Carter, Min	122
I Bruce, StL	119
M Irvin, Dal	111
B Perriman, Det	108
E Metcalf, Atl	104
R Brooks, GB	102
L Centers, Ari	101
C Pickens, Cin	99

Receiving Yards

Player, Team	Rec	Y/R	Yds
J Rice, SF	122	15.1	**1848**
I Bruce, StL	119	15.0	1781
H Moore, Det	123	13.7	1686
M Irvin, Dal	111	14.4	1603
R Brooks, GB	102	14.7	1497
B Perriman, Det	108	13.8	1488
C Carter, Min	122	11.2	1371
T Brown, Oak	89	15.1	1342
Y Thigpen, Pit	85	15.4	1307
J Graham, Chi	82	15.9	1301

Fumbles

Player, Team	Lost	Fum
D Krieg, Ari	6	**16**
R Peete, Phi	6	13
K Collins, Car	7	13
T Dilfer, TB	6	13
W Moon, Min	4	13
B Esiason, NYA	3	12
G Hearst, Ari	8	12
C Chandler, Hou	5	12
D Bledsoe, NE	6	11
4 tied with		10

Interceptions

Player, Team	Ret Yd	Int
O Thomas, Min	108	**9**
W Clay, Det	173	8
W Thomas, Phi	104	7
W Williams, Pit	122	7
10 tied with		6

Sacks

Player, Team	Sacks
B Paup, Buf	**17.5**
P Swilling, Oak	13.0
W Fuller, Phi	13.0
W Martin, NO	13.0
L O'Neal, SD	12.5
N Smith, KC	12.0
R White, GB	12.0
D Farr, StL	11.5
4 tied with	11.0

KO Return Average
(Minimum 20 Returns)

Player, Team	Ret	Yds	Avg
G Milburn, Den	47	1269	**27.0**
R Carpenter, NYA	21	553	26.3
N Kaufman, Oak	22	572	26.0
B Mitchell, Was	55	1408	25.6
T Vanover, KC	43	1095	25.5
D Meggett, NE	38	964	25.4
S Broussard, Sea	43	1064	24.7
Q Ismail, Min	42	1037	24.7
O McDuffie, Mia	23	564	24.5
T Hughes, NO	66	1617	24.5

Punt Return Average
(Minimum 20 Returns)

Player, Team	Ret	Yds	Avg
D Palmer, Min	26	342	**13.2**
B Mitchell, Was	25	315	12.6
A Coleman, SD	28	326	11.6
J Burris, Buf	20	229	11.4
G Milburn, Den	31	354	11.4
E Guliford, Car	43	475	11.0
T Vanover, KC	51	540	10.6
D Carter, NYA-SF	30	309	10.3
D Howard, Jac	24	246	10.3
C Jordan, GB	21	213	10.1

1995 NFL Passing Statistics

Touchdowns

Player, Team	TDs
B Favre, GB	**38**
W Moon, Min	33
S Mitchell, Det	32
E Kramer, Chi	29
J Blake, Cin	28
J Elway, Den	26
J Everett, NO	26
J George, Atl	24
D Marino, Mia	24
J Kelly, Buf	22

Yards/Attempt
(Minimum 224 Attempts)

Player, Team	Att	Yds	Y/A
J Harbaugh, Ind	314	2575	**8.20**
B Favre, GB	570	4413	7.74
T Aikman, Dal	432	3304	7.65
D Marino, Mia	482	3668	7.61
S Mitchell, Det	583	4338	7.44
J George, Atl	557	4143	7.44
V Testaverde, Cle	392	2883	7.35
E Kramer, Chi	522	3838	7.35
J Elway, Den	542	3970	7.32
S Young, SF	447	3200	7.16

Attempts

Player, Team	Att
D Bledsoe, NE	**636**
W Moon, Min	606
S Mitchell, Det	583
B Favre, GB	570
J Blake, Cin	567
J Everett, NO	567
J George, Atl	557
J Elway, Den	542
E Kramer, Chi	522
D Krieg, Ari	521

Completions

Player, Team	Att	Comp
W Moon, Min	606	**377**
B Favre, GB	570	359
S Mitchell, Det	583	346
J Everett, NO	567	345
J George, Atl	557	336
J Blake, Cin	567	326
D Bledsoe, NE	636	323
J Elway, Den	542	316
E Kramer, Chi	522	315
D Marino, Mia	482	309

Completion Pct
(Minimum 224 Attempts)

Player, Team	Att	Comp	Pct
S Young, SF	447	299	**66.9**
T Aikman, Dal	432	280	64.8
D Marino, Mia	482	309	64.1
J Harbaugh, Ind	314	200	63.7
C Chandler, Hou	356	225	63.2
B Favre, GB	570	359	63.0
W Moon, Min	606	377	62.2
V Testaverde, Cle	392	241	61.5
J Everett, NO	567	345	60.9
E Kramer, Chi	522	315	60.4

Interceptions

Player, Team	Passes	Int
D Krieg, Ari	521	**21**
R Mirer, Sea	391	20
K Collins, Car	432	19
T Dilfer, TB	415	18
J Blake, Cin	567	17
D Bledsoe, NE	636	16
B Esiason, NYA	389	15
D Marino, Mia	482	15
C Miller, StL	405	15
5 tied with		14

Interception Pct
(Minimum 224 Attempts)

Player, Team	Att	Int	Pct
J Harbaugh, Ind	314	5	**1.6**
T Aikman, Dal	432	7	1.6
N O'Donnell, Pit	416	7	1.7
E Kramer, Chi	522	10	1.9
S Bono, KC	520	10	1.9
J George, Atl	557	11	2.0
M Brunell, Jac	346	7	2.0
S Mitchell, Det	583	12	2.1
D Brown, NYN	456	10	2.2
B Favre, GB	570	13	2.3

Passing Yards/Game

Player, Team	Yds	G	Y/G
S Young, SF	3200	11	**290.9**
B Favre, GB	4413	16	275.8
S Mitchell, Det	4338	16	271.1
W Moon, Min	4228	16	264.3
D Marino, Mia	3668	14	262.0
J George, Atl	4143	16	258.9
J Elway, Den	3970	16	248.1
J Everett, NO	3970	16	248.1
N O'Donnell, Pit	2970	12	247.5
E Kramer, Chi	3838	16	239.9

Big Play Passes

Player, Team	Passes
B Favre, GB	**36**
J George, Atl	35
W Moon, Min	30
S Mitchell, Det	30
J Elway, Den	29
J Kelly, Buf	28
D Krieg, Ari	28
J Everett, NO	28
J Blake, Cin	27
N O'Donnell, Pit	26

Longest Completion

Player, Team	Yards
B Favre, GB	**99**
S Mitchell, Det	91
K Collins, Car	89
J Blake, Cin	88
W Moon, Min	85
E Grbac, SF	81
B Hobert, Oak	80
J Hostetler, Oak	80
3 tied with	77

Times Sacked

Player, Team	Sacks
D Krieg, Ari	**53**
T Dilfer, TB	47
D Brown, NYN	44
J George, Atl	43
R Mirer, Sea	42
M Brunell, Jac	39
W Moon, Min	38
J Harbaugh, Ind	36
B Favre, GB	33
R Peete, Phi	33

Sack Pct
(Minimum 224 Attempts)

Player, Team	Plays	Sacks	Pct
E Kramer, Chi	537	15	**2.8**
T Aikman, Dal	446	14	3.1
N O'Donnell, Pit	431	15	3.5
D Bledsoe, NE	659	23	3.5
S Bono, KC	541	21	3.9
J Elway, Den	564	22	3.9
J Blake, Cin	591	24	4.1
V Testaverde, Cle	409	17	4.2
D Marino, Mia	504	22	4.4
J Everett, NO	594	27	4.5

1995 NFL Rushing Statistics

Carries

Player, Team	Carries
E Smith, Dal	**377**
C Martin, NE	368
T Allen, Was	338
R Watters, Phi	337
E Rhett, TB	332
E Bennett, GB	316
B Sanders, Det	314
C Warren, Sea	310
R Hampton, NYN	306
R Salaam, Chi	296

Yards/Carry
(Minimum 100 Carries)

Player, Team	Yds	Carries	Y/C
C Garner, Phi	588	108	**5.4**
R Green, Chi	570	107	5.3
B Sanders, Det	1500	314	4.8
T Davis, Den	1117	237	4.7
E Smith, Dal	1773	377	4.7
C Heyward, Atl	1083	236	4.6
R Smith, Min	632	139	4.5
N Kaufman, Oak	490	108	4.5
H Williams, Oak	1114	255	4.4
C Warren, Sea	1346	310	4.3

Touchdowns

Player, Team	TDs
E Smith, Dal	**25**
C Warren, Sea	15
C Martin, NE	14
M Faulk, Ind	11
B Sanders, Det	11
R Watters, Phi	11
E Rhett, TB	11
4 tied with	10

Big Runs

Player, Team	Big Runs
E Smith, Dal	**49**
C Warren, Sea	44
B Sanders, Det	41
C Martin, NE	34
C Heyward, Atl	32
E Rhett, TB	30
T Allen, Was	30
R Watters, Phi	28
M Bates, NO	25
H Williams, Oak	25

Longest Run

Player, Team	Yds
J Galloway, Sea	**86**
S Bono, KC	76
B Sanders, Det	75
J Ellison, TB	75
R Thomas, Hou	74
L Smith, Sea	68
M Bates, NO	66
A Lee, Min	66
3 tied with	60

Yards/Carry, Grass
(Minimum 40 Carries)

Player, Team	Yds	Carries	Y/C
K Anders, KC	372	48	**7.8**
M Brunell, Jac	338	46	7.3
R Green, Chi	410	76	5.4
G Milburn, Den	232	45	5.2
M Bates, NO	272	58	4.7
B Sanders, Det	368	80	4.6
T Davis, Den	800	178	4.5
A Craver, Den	295	66	4.5
M Allen, KC	867	200	4.3
C Warren, Sea	605	140	4.3

Yards/Carry, Turf
(Minimum 60 Carries)

Player, Team	Yds	Carries	Y/C
C Garner, Phi	432	78	**5.5**
E Smith, Dal	1432	280	5.1
R Smith, Min	362	72	5.0
H Williams, Oak	383	77	5.0
C Martin, NE	581	120	4.8
B Sanders, Det	1132	234	4.8
C Heyward, Atl	836	175	4.8
N Means, SD	311	70	4.4
C Warren, Sea	741	170	4.4
E Rhett, TB	362	84	4.3

Yards/Carry, Att 21+
(Minimum 20 Carries)

Player, Team	Yds	Carries	Y/C
C Warren, Sea	168	37	**4.5**
R Hampton, NYN	157	36	4.4
T Allen, Was	203	49	4.1
C Martin, NE	328	82	4.0
T Thomas, Buf	155	39	4.0
E Rhett, TB	161	43	3.7
E Smith, Dal	219	61	3.6
A Hayden, SD	76	24	3.2
R Watters, Phi	128	45	2.8
E Bennett, GB	94	37	2.5

%TD, Inside 3
(Minimum 5 Attempts)

Player, Team	Tds	Att	TD%
A Craver, Den	5	6	**83.3**
E Smith, Dal	10	13	76.9
T Allen, Was	9	13	69.2
H Williams, Oak	4	6	66.7
D Loville, SF	7	11	63.6
R Salaam, Chi	5	8	62.5
R Hampton, NYN	8	13	61.5
R Watters, Phi	6	10	60.0
S Mitchell, Det	3	5	60.0
J Bettis, StL	3	5	60.0

Stuffs

Player, Team	Stuffs
B Sanders, Det	**54**
R Thomas, Hou	45
R Watters, Phi	44
M Faulk, Ind	43
G Hearst, Ari	38
C Martin, NE	36
E Rhett, TB	35
E Smith, Dal	34
C Warren, Sea	34
E Bennett, GB	32

Stuffs/Carry
(Minimum 100 Carries)

Player, Team	Stf	Carries	S/C
B Morris, Pit	4	148	**.027**
R Green, Chi	4	107	.037
T Davis, Den	12	237	.051
A Hayden, SD	8	128	.063
M Allen, KC	13	207	.063
C Heyward, Atl	15	236	.064
L Hoard, Cle	10	136	.074
R Hampton, NYN	23	306	.075
T Allen, Was	26	338	.077
D Loville, SF	18	218	.083

4th+ Qtr Rushing Yards

Player, Team	Rush	Yds
C Warren, Sea	69	**405**
B Sanders, Det	76	385
E Smith, Dal	84	371
T Allen, Was	79	327
C Heyward, Atl	75	297
E Rhett, TB	70	288
C Martin, NE	70	279
H Williams, Oak	48	276
G Hill, KC	55	270
R Watters, Phi	103	268

1995 NFL Receiving Statistics

Yards/Catch
(Minimum 32 Catches)

Player, Team	Yards	Catch	Y/C
C Sanders, Hou	823	35	**23.5**
W Green, Car	882	47	18.8
Q Ismail, Min	597	32	18.7
A Miller, Den	1079	59	18.3
H Ellard, Was	1005	56	18.0
E Mills, Pit	679	39	17.4
H Copeland, TB	605	35	17.3
F Sanders, Ari	883	52	17.0
C Conway, Chi	1037	62	16.7
M Jackson, Cle	714	44	16.2

Touchdowns

Player, Team	TDs
C Pickens, Cin	**17**
C Carter, Min	**17**
J Rice, SF	15
A Miller, Den	14
H Moore, Det	14
I Bruce, StL	13
R Brooks, GB	13
C Conway, Chi	12
B Brooks, Buf	11
2 tied with	10

Target

Player, Team	Target
H Moore, Det	**206**
I Bruce, StL	199
C Carter, Min	197
B Perriman, Det	179
J Rice, SF	176
C Pickens, Cin	168
R Brooks, GB	167
M Irvin, Dal	165
T Martin, SD	165
V Brisby, NE	159

Yards After Catch

Player, Team	Catches	Yds
L Centers, Ari	101	**855**
J Rice, SF	122	692
D Loville, SF	87	662
E Bennett, GB	61	590
E Metcalf, Atl	104	582
H Moore, Det	123	560
I Bruce, StL	119	556
T Brown, Oak	89	534
T Kirby, Mia	66	522
A Lee, Min	71	516

Average Throw
(Minimum 32 Targets)

Player, Team	Tgt	Yds	Avg
C Sanders, Hou	87	1726	**19.8**
J Jett, Oak	37	705	19.1
H Copeland, TB	63	1162	18.4
R Ismail, Oak	57	1028	18.0
W Davis, KC	76	1367	18.0
J Galloway, Sea	133	2311	17.4
A Rison, Cle	103	1738	16.9
A Wright, StL	51	844	16.5
H Ellard, Was	113	1827	16.2
D Scott, Cin	109	1707	15.7

% Passes Caught/Target
(Minimum 50 Targets)

Player, Team	Tgt	Catches	%
H Williams, Oak	60	54	**90.0**
L Centers, Ari	119	101	84.9
D Levens, GB	57	48	84.2
I Smith, NO	55	45	81.8
T Kirby, Mia	83	66	79.5
E Smith, Dal	78	62	79.5
D Loville, SF	110	87	79.1
F Wycheck, Hou	51	40	78.4
E Bennett, GB	79	61	77.2
K Dilger, Ind	55	42	76.4

1st Down Catches

Player, Team	Catches
H Moore, Det	**90**
M Irvin, Dal	88
I Bruce, StL	82
C Carter, Min	80
J Rice, SF	75
B Perriman, Det	74
R Brooks, GB	70
J Graham, Chi	67
T Brown, Oak	66
C Pickens, Cin	65

Longest Reception

Player, Team	Yds
R Brooks, GB	**99**
B Perriman, Det	91
W Green, Car	89
D Scott, Cin	88
Q Ismail, Min	85
J Rice, SF	81
T Brown, Oak	80
T Brown, Oak	80
3 tied with	77

Big Catches

Player, Team	Catches
J Rice, SF	**21**
I Bruce, StL	18
F Sanders, Ari	15
M Irvin, Dal	15
C Sanders, Hou	14
J Graham, Chi	14
R Brooks, GB	14
4 tied with	13

4th Qtr TD Catches

Player, Team	TDs
C Pickens, Cin	**7**
H Moore, Det	5
W Green, Car	4
C Carter, Min	4
W Jackson, Jac	4
12 tied with	3

Rec Lost/Penalty

Player, Team	Rec
B Coates, NE	**6**
A Hastings, Pit	5
Y Thigpen, Pit	5
B Blades, Sea	5
J Reed, Min	5
8 tied with	4

Passes Dropped

Player, Team	Drops
A Murrell, NYA	**13**
M Carrier, Car	**13**
T Davis, Den	12
C Conway, Chi	12
V Brisby, NE	12
R Brooks, GB	12
T McGee, Cin	11
B Emanuel, Atl	11
T Martin, SD	11
T McNair, Hou	10

1995 NFL Defensive Statistics

Tackles

Player, Team	Tackles
T Wooden, Sea	**114**
J Seau, SD	111
J Tuggle, Atl	111
V Green, NYA	103
P Johnson, Cle	100
T Wright, StL	98
B Cox, Mia	95
M Brooks, NYN	95
M Patton, Was	94
C Spielman, Det	90

Assists

Player, Team	Assists
H Nickerson, TB	**54**
C Spielman, Det	47
J Herrod, Ind	42
J Tuggle, Atl	41
V Brown, NE	38
M Johnson, Det	36
V Green, NYA	34
M Jones, NYA	33
M Barrow, Hou	32
S Grant, Ind	31

Sack Yards

Player, Team	Sacks	Yards
B Paup, Buf	17.5	**132.5**
P Swilling, Oak	13.0	119.0
W Fuller, Phi	13.0	106.0
R White, GB	12.0	96.5
W McGinest, NE	11.0	96.0
W Martin, NO	13.0	89.0
C Simmons, Ari	11.0	87.0
N Smith, KC	12.0	84.0
P Hansen, Buf	10.0	83.5
H Thomas, Det	10.5	82.0

Interception Return Yards

Player, Team	Int	Ret Yds
W Clay, Det	8	**173**
D Lewis, Hou	6	145
E Daniel, Ind	3	142
T McDonald, SF	4	135
L Brown, Dal	6	124
W Williams, Pit	7	122
T Carter, Was	4	116
O Thomas, Min	9	108
L Butler, GB	5	105
W Thomas, Phi	7	104

Yards/Int Return
(Minimum 4 Ints)

Player, Team	Int	Yds	Y/R
T McDonald, SF	4	135	**33.8**
T Carter, Was	4	116	29.0
D Lewis, Hou	6	145	24.2
W Clay, Det	8	173	21.6
L Butler, GB	5	105	21.0
L Brown, Dal	6	124	20.7
T Vincent, Mia	5	95	19.0
V Glenn, NYN	5	91	18.2
D Perry, Pit	4	71	17.8
W Williams, Pit	7	122	17.4

Passes Defensed

Player, Team	PD
D Evans, GB	**27**
C Raymond, Det	24
E Davis, SF	22
A Williams, Ari	22
D Lewis, Hou	21
M McMillan, Phi	21
W Williams, Pit	20
B Maxie, Car	20
5 tied with	19

Touchdowns

Player, Team	TDs
O Thomas, Min	**2**
T Dorn, StL	**2**
L Brown, Dal	**2**
S Gayle, SD	**2**
A Williams, Ari	**2**
T McDonald, SF	**2**
K Norton, SF	**2**
73 tied with	1

Stuffs

Player, Team	Stuff
E McDaniel, Min	**18.5**
C Slade, NE	11.5
D Farr, StL	11.0
C McGlockton, Oak	11.0
J Seau, SD	10.5
T Wooden, Sea	10.5
M Brock, NYA	10.0
M Jones, NYA	10.0
3 tied with	9.5

Stuff Yards

Player, Team	Stuffs	Yards
E McDaniel, Min	18.5	**39.5**
G Lloyd, Pit	8.0	35.5
T Wooden, Sea	10.5	29.0
K Harvey, Was	7.0	29.0
E Swann, Ari	8.0	29.0
A Smith, Oak	8.0	29.0
V Booker, KC	9.5	28.5
D Brooks, TB	8.0	27.5
M Washington, NYA	9.5	27.0
2 tied with		26.5

Forced Fumbles

Player, Team	FF
G Lloyd, Pit	6
A Pleasant, Cle	6
C Simmons, Ari	6
E McDaniel, Min	6
S Mills, Car	5
D Farr, StL	5
K Harvey, Was	5
P Swilling, Oak	5
M Washington, NYA	5
W Fuller, Phi	5

Fumbles Recovered

Player, Team	Fumbles
B Bishop, Hou	4
V Buck, NO	4
R Fredrickson, Oak	4
H Hasselbach, Den	4
M Johnson, Det	4
S Mills, Car	4
A Parker, StL	4
J Thierry, Chi	4
O Thomas, Min	4
14 tied with	3

Blocked FGs/Punts/PAT's

Player, Team	Blocks
E Swann, Ari	**3**
H Thomas, Det	2
C Buckley, TB	2
R Turnbull, NO	2
T Barnett, NE	2
R Burnett, Cle	2
A Marshall, Chi	2
F Smith, Min	2
24 tied with	1

1995 NFL Special Teams Statistics

Return Touchdowns

Player, Team	TDs
A Coleman, SD	**3**
T Vanover, KC	3
13 tied with	1

Tackles

Player, Team	Tackles
C Widmer, NYN	**19**
R Rivers, Det	18
S Pahukoa, NO	18
D Jones, Pit	17
G Manusky, KC	17
D Brownlow, Was	17
7 tied with	16

Assists

Player, Team	Assists
E Sutter, Cle	**8**
D Gray, Ind	6
M Wilson, GB	6
S Shanks, Ari	6
T Mickens, GB	6
O Harris, Hou	6
J Schwantz, Dal	6
K Elias, NYN	6
6 tied with	5

Field Goals

Player, Team	FGs
N Johnson, Pit	**34**
S Christie, Buf	31
J Elam, Den	31
M Andersen, Atl	31
G Davis, Ari	30
D Pelfrey, Cin	29
M Stover, Cle	29
J Hanson, Det	28
3 tied with	27

Field-Goal Pct
(Minimum 16 Attempts)

Player, Team	Made	Att	Pct
C Boniol, Dal	**27**	**28**	**96.4**
M Stover, Cle	29	33	87.9
A Del Greco, Hou	27	31	87.1
M Andersen, Atl	31	37	83.8
N Johnson, Pit	34	41	82.9
J Hanson, Det	28	34	82.4
T Peterson, Sea	23	28	82.1
J Elam, Den	31	38	81.6
N Lowery, NYA	17	21	81.0
J Carney, SD	21	26	80.8

1-39 Yd FG Pct
(Minimum 10 Attempts)

Player, Team	Made	Att	Pct
M Andersen, Atl	**20**	**20**	**100.0**
A Del Greco, Hou	14	14	100.0
J Wilkins, SF	11	11	100.0
M Stover, Cle	22	23	95.7
J Hanson, Det	22	23	95.7
J Carney, SD	18	19	94.7
B Daluiso, NYN	16	17	94.1
T Peterson, Sea	15	16	93.8
G Anderson, Phi	14	15	93.3
N Johnson, Pit	25	27	92.6

40+ Yd FG Pct
(Minimum 4 Attempts)

Player, Team	Made	Att	Pct
C Jacke, GB	**11**	**14**	**78.6**
J Kasay, Car	10	13	76.9
A Del Greco, Hou	13	17	76.5
C Blanchard, Ind	8	11	72.7
J Elam, Den	10	14	71.4
L Elliott, KC	7	10	70.0
M Stover, Cle	7	10	70.0
D Pelfrey, Cin	11	16	68.8
3 tied with			67.0

Net Kickoff Avg
(Minimum 40 Kickoffs)

Player, Team	Avg
M Andersen Atl	**46.7**
M Husted, TB	45.7
J Hanson, Det	44.5
B Deluiso, NYN	43.9
M Stover, Cle	43.6
C Boniol, Dal	42.9
D Silvestri, NYA	42.8
C Hentrich, GB	42.3
L Elliot, KC	41.9
J Carney, SD	41.9

Gross Punt Avg
(Minimum 40 Punts)

Player, Team	Yards	Punts	Avg
R Tuten, Sea	**3735**	**83**	**45.0**
D Bennett, SD	3221	72	44.7
S Landeta, StL	3679	83	44.3
L Aguiar, KC	3990	91	43.8
B Barker, Jac	3591	82	43.8
J Feagles, Ari	3150	72	43.8
T Tupa, Cle	2831	65	43.6
T Hutton, Phi	3682	85	43.3
R Roby, TB	3296	77	42.8
J Kidd, Mia	2433	57	42.7

Net Punt Avg
(Minimum 40 Punts)

Player, Team	Yards	Punts	Avg
B Barker, Jac	**3168**	**82**	**38.6**
L Johnson, Cin	2627	68	38.6
J Feagles, Ari	2748	72	38.2
M Turk, Was	2787	74	37.7
T Rouen, Den	1995	53	37.6
S Landeta, StL	3046	83	36.7
D Bennett, SD	2632	72	36.6
R Tuten, Sea	3026	83	36.5
L Aguiar, KC	3317	91	36.5
J Kidd, Mia	2068	57	36.3

Inside-20 Pct
(Minimum 40 Punts)

Player, Team	Punts	In20	Pct
T Rouen, Den	**52**	**22**	**42.3**
C Hentrich, GB	65	26	40.0
M Turk, Was	74	29	39.2
D Bennett, SD	72	28	38.9
L Johnson, Cin	68	26	38.2
R Stark, Pit	59	20	33.9
R Camarillo, Hou	77	26	33.8
J Jett, Dal	53	17	32.1
L Aguiar, KC	91	29	31.9
P O'Neill, NYA	44	14	31.8

Touchback Pct
(Minimum 40 Punts)

Player, Team	Punts	TB	Pct
T Rouen, Den	**52**	**3**	**5.8**
L Johnson, Cin	68	4	5.9
B Barker, Jac	82	5	6.1
K Wilmsmeyer, NO	73	5	6.8
P O'Neill, NE-Chi	44	3	6.8
D Stryzinski, Atl	67	5	7.5
C Mohr, Buf	86	7	8.1
M Saxon, Min	72	6	8.3
J Kidd, Mia	57	5	8.8
T Thompson, SF	57	5	8.8

NFL Active Career Leaders - Primary Statistics

Points

Player	Pts
Nick Lowery	**1634**
Eddie Murray	1473
Gary Anderson	1441
Morten Andersen	1440
Matt Bahr	1422
Norm Johnson	1346
Kevin Butler	1116
Al Del Greco	980
Jerry Rice	936
Fuad Reveiz	931

Total Touchdowns

Player	TDs
Jerry Rice	**156**
Marcus Allen	125
Emmitt Smith	100
Herschel Walker	81
Barry Sanders	80
Thurman Thomas	74
Andre Reed	70
Art Monk	68
Cris Carter	67
Earnest Byner	67

Rushing Yards

Player	Yds
Marcus Allen	**10908**
Barry Sanders	10172
Thurman Thomas	9729
Emmitt Smith	8956
Herschel Walker	8122
Earnest Byner	7314
Rodney Hampton	5989
Marion Butts	5185
John L. Williams	5006
Chris Warren	5004

Yards/Carry
(Minimum 750 Carries)

Player	Yds	Carries	Y/C
Barry Sanders	10172	2077	**4.9**
Emmitt Smith	8956	2007	4.5
Chris Warren	5004	1156	4.3
Thurman Thomas	9729	2285	4.3
Craig Heyward	3881	919	4.2
Terry Allen	4104	979	4.2
Herschel Walker	8122	1938	4.2
Ricky Watters	4113	990	4.2
Marcus Allen	10908	2692	4.1
John L. Williams	5006	1245	4.0

Rushing Touchdowns

Player	TDs
Marcus Allen	**103**
Emmitt Smith	96
Barry Sanders	73
Herschel Walker	60
Thurman Thomas	54
Earnest Byner	52
Rodney Hampton	47
Marion Butts	43
Ricky Watters	36
2 tied with	35

Carries

Player	Carries
Marcus Allen	**2692**
Thurman Thomas	2285
Barry Sanders	2077
Emmitt Smith	2007
Herschel Walker	1938
Earnest Byner	1852
Rodney Hampton	1547
Marion Butts	1345
John L. Williams	1245
Chris Warren	1156

Receptions

Player	Rec
Jerry Rice	**942**
Art Monk	940
Henry Ellard	723
Andre Reed	700
Gary Clark	699
Cris Carter	571
Ernest Givins	571
Bill Brooks	566
Irving Fryar	562
Marcus Allen	549

Receiving Yards

Player	Yds
Jerry Rice	**15123**
Art Monk	12721
Henry Ellard	12163
Gary Clark	10856
Andre Reed	9848
Irving Fryar	8916
Michael Irvin	8538
Ernest Givins	8215
Bill Brooks	7777
Anthony Miller	7768

Receiving Touchdowns

Player	TDs
Jerry Rice	**146**
Andre Reed	69
Art Monk	68
Cris Carter	66
Gary Clark	65
Andre Rison	63
Henry Ellard	59
Irving Fryar	58
Anthony Miller	56
Anthony Carter	55

Yards/Catch
(Minimum 200 Catches)

Player	Yards	Catch	Y/C
Flipper Anderson	5357	267	**20.1**
Henry Ellard	12163	723	16.8
Michael Irvin	8538	527	16.2
John Taylor	5598	347	16.1
Jerry Rice	15123	942	16.1
Anthony Carter	7733	486	15.9
Irving Fryar	8916	562	15.9
Anthony Miller	7768	493	15.8
Mark Carrier	7218	459	15.7
Jessie Hester	5850	373	15.7

Fumbles

Player	Fum
Dave Krieg	**144**
Warren Moon	138
Boomer Esiason	117
John Elway	113
Randall Cunningham	89
Dan Marino	84
Jim Kelly	67
Marcus Allen	59
Don Majkowski	54
Rodney Peete	53

Games Played

Player	Games
Clay Matthews	**263**
Jackie Slater	259
Nick Lowery	244
Matt Bahr	235
Stan Brock	234
Eddie Murray	228
Ray Donaldson	228
Rickey Jackson	227
Art Monk	224
Jim Ritcher	217

NFL Active Career Passing Leaders

Passing Yards

Player	Yds
Dan Marino	**48841**
Warren Moon	42177
John Elway	41706
Dave Krieg	35668
Boomer Esiason	34149
Jim Kelly	32657
Jim Everett	31583
Bernie Kosar	23093
Steve Young	23069
Randall Cunningham	22877

Attempts

Player	Att
Dan Marino	**6531**
John Elway	5926
Warren Moon	5753
Dave Krieg	4911
Boomer Esiason	4680
Jim Kelly	4400
Jim Everett	4384
Randall Cunningham	3362
Bernie Kosar	3333
Vinny Testaverde	3158

Quarterback Rating
(Minimum 1500 Attempts)

Player	Att	Rating
Steve Young	2876	**96.1**
Dan Marino	6531	88.4
Brett Favre	2150	86.8
Jim Kelly	4400	85.4
Troy Aikman	2713	83.5
Dave Krieg	4911	81.9
Jeff Hostetler	1792	81.8
Neil O'Donnell	1871	81.8
Bernie Kosar	3333	81.6
Warren Moon	5753	81.5

Passing Yards/Game
(Minimum 1500 Attempts)

Player	Yards	Games	Y/G
Dan Marino	48841	186	**262.6**
Warren Moon	42177	172	245.2
Drew Bledsoe	10556	44	239.9
Brett Favre	14825	65	228.1
Jim Everett	31583	139	227.2
Jim Kelly	32657	147	222.2
John Elway	41706	190	219.5
Jeff George	17428	84	207.5
Boomer Esiason	34149	170	200.9
Troy Aikman	19607	98	200.1

TD Passes

Player	TDs
Dan Marino	**352**
Warren Moon	247
Dave Krieg	247
John Elway	225
Jim Kelly	223
Boomer Esiason	223
Jim Everett	190
Steve Young	160
Randall Cunningham	150
Vinny Testaverde	124

Completions

Player	Comp
Dan Marino	**3913**
Warren Moon	3380
John Elway	3346
Dave Krieg	2866
Boomer Esiason	2661
Jim Kelly	2652
Jim Everett	2538
Bernie Kosar	1970
Randall Cunningham	1874
Steve Young	1845

Passes Intercepted

Player	Ints
Dan Marino	**200**
Warren Moon	199
John Elway	191
Dave Krieg	187
Boomer Esiason	168
Jim Kelly	156
Jim Everett	155
Vinny Testaverde	149
Randall Cunningham	105
Chris Miller	101

Times Sacked

Player	Sacks
Dave Krieg	**478**
John Elway	438
Randall Cunningham	422
Warren Moon	382
Boomer Esiason	294
Jim Kelly	286
Bernie Kosar	267
Vinny Testaverde	243
Jim Everett	234
Steve Young	233

Yards/Attempt
(Minimum 1500 Attempts)

Player	Att	Yds	Y/A
Steve Young	2876	23069	**8.02**
Dan Marino	6531	48841	7.48
Jim Kelly	4400	32657	7.42
Warren Moon	5753	42177	7.33
Boomer Esiason	4680	34149	7.30
Dave Krieg	4911	35668	7.26
Jeff Hostetler	1792	12983	7.24
Troy Aikman	2713	19607	7.23
Jim Everett	4384	31583	7.20
Wade Wilson	2301	16521	7.18

Completion Pct
(Minimum 1500 Attempts)

Player	Att	Comp	Pct
Steve Young	2876	1845	**64.2**
Troy Aikman	2713	1704	62.8
Brett Favre	2150	1342	62.4
Jim Kelly	4400	2652	60.3
Dan Marino	6531	3913	59.9
Jim Harbaugh	2275	1348	59.3
Bernie Kosar	3333	1970	59.1
Warren Moon	5753	3380	58.8
Bobby Hebert	2633	1545	58.7
Jeff George	2613	1532	58.6

Interception Pct
(Minimum 1500 Attempts)

Player	Att	Int	Pct
Neil O'Donnell	1871	39	**2.1**
Bernie Kosar	3333	87	2.6
Jeff Hostetler	1792	47	2.6
Steve Young	2876	79	2.7
Jeff George	2613	75	2.9
Jim Harbaugh	2275	67	2.9
Dan Marino	6531	200	3.1
Brett Favre	2150	66	3.1
Randall Cunningham	3362	105	3.1
Troy Aikman	2713	85	3.1

Sack Pct
(Minimum 1500 Attempts)

Player	Plays	Sacks	Pct
Dan Marino	6731	200	**3.0**
Drew Bledsoe	1817	61	3.4
Mark Rypien	2647	95	3.6
Mike Tomczak	1705	81	4.8
Jim Everett	4618	234	5.1
Stan Humphries	1981	106	5.4
Bobby Hebert	2784	151	5.4
Brett Favre	2279	129	5.7
Troy Aikman	2880	167	5.8
Jack Trudeau	1747	103	5.9

NFL Active Career Special Teams Leaders

Field Goals

Player	FGs
Nick Lowery	**366**
Morten Andersen	333
Gary Anderson	331
Eddie Murray	325
Matt Bahr	300
Norm Johnson	277
Kevin Butler	243
Al Del Greco	204
Fuad Reveiz	188
Tony Zendejas	186

Field Goal Pct
(Minimum 100 FG Made)

Player	Made	Att	Pct
Matt Stover	108	134	**80.6**
Nick Lowery	366	455	80.4
John Carney	152	191	79.6
Pete Stoyanovich	176	222	79.3
Steve Christie	140	177	79.1
John Kasay	108	138	78.3
Morten Andersen	333	426	78.2
Gary Anderson	331	425	77.9
Jason Hanson	101	130	77.7
Chris Jacke	152	197	77.2

1-39 Yd FG Pct
(Minimum 100 FG Made)

Player	Made	Att	Pct
Jason Hanson	74	76	**97.4**
Morten Andersen	219	238	92.0
Matt Stover	78	86	90.7
John Carney	116	128	90.6
Fuad Reveiz	130	144	90.3
Nick Lowery	246	273	90.1
Gary Anderson	229	258	88.8
Kevin Butler	188	214	87.9
Pete Stoyanovich	125	143	87.4
Norm Johnson	187	215	87.0

40-49 Yd FG Pct
(Minimum 100 FG Made)

Player	Made	Att	Pct
Nick Lowery	98	133	**73.7**
Pete Stoyanovich	37	51	72.5
Steve Christie	28	39	71.8
Matt Stover	26	37	70.3
Gary Anderson	94	137	68.6
John Kasay	27	40	67.5
Morten Andersen	85	127	66.9
Eddie Murray	86	130	66.2
Chris Jacke	35	53	66.0
Norm Johnson	71	111	64.0

50+ Yd FG Pct
(Minimum 100 FG Made)

Player	Made	Att	Pct
Tony Zendejas	17	23	**73.9**
Chris Jacke	16	25	64.0
Jeff Jaeger	13	25	52.0
Eddie Murray	21	42	50.0
Pete Stoyanovich	14	28	50.0
Steve Christie	10	20	50.0
Al Del Greco	16	33	48.5
Morten Andersen	30	62	48.4
Norm Johnson	19	40	47.5
John Carney	7	15	46.7

Gross Punt Avg
(Minimum 250 Punts)

Player	Yards	Punts	Avg
Sean Landeta	31804	729	**43.6**
Rohn Stark	45530	1044	43.6
Reggie Roby	34418	792	43.5
Rick Tuten	20876	481	43.4
Rich Camarillo	43895	1027	42.7
Tommy Barnhardt	23388	549	42.6
Mike Horan	32034	758	42.3
Brian Hansen	36744	872	42.1
Lee Johnson	31711	754	42.1
Bryan Barker	17554	420	41.8

Net Punt Avg
(Minimum 250 Punts)

Player	Yards	Punts	Avg
Rick Tuten	17796	482	**36.9**
Reggie Roby	28836	796	36.2
Mike Horan	27675	765	36.2
Rich Camarillo	37073	1033	35.9
Bryan Barker	15107	422	35.8
Tommy Barnhardt	19685	551	35.7
Dan Stryzinski	15980	448	35.7
Louis Aguiar	13724	386	35.6
Chris Mohr	15105	427	35.4
Rohn Stark	37152	1051	35.3

Inside 20 Pct
(Minimum 250 Punts)

Player	Punts	In20	Pct
Jeff Feagles	648	196	**30.2**
Reggie Roby	792	234	29.5
Mike Saxon	813	240	29.5
Chris Gardocki	298	86	28.9
Mark Royals	483	133	27.5
Tommy Barnhardt	549	150	27.3
Rich Camarillo	1027	278	27.1
Sean Landeta	729	194	26.6
Mike Horan	758	201	26.5
Bryan Wagner	506	134	26.5

Touchback Pct
(Minimum 250 Punts)

Player	Punts	TB	Pct
Chris Mohr	425	28	**6.6**
Dan Stryzinski	445	33	7.4
Mark Royals	477	36	7.5
Rick Tuten	481	38	7.9
Mike Horan	758	61	8.0
Bryan Wagner	506	41	8.1
Jeff Feagles	648	53	8.2
Chris Gardocki	298	27	9.1
John Kidd	786	72	9.2
Louis Aguiar	386	36	9.3

Kickoff Ret Avg
(Minimum 75 Returns)

Player	Ret	Yds	Avg
Tyrone Hughes	159	3926	**24.7**
Mel Gray	362	8833	24.4
Andre Coleman	111	2704	24.4
Kevin Williams	123	2945	23.9
Glyn Milburn	96	2250	23.4
Brian Mitchell	216	5004	23.2
Qadry Ismail	119	2746	23.1
Deion Sanders	148	3403	23.0
O.J. McDuffie	91	2086	22.9
Nate Lewis	168	3825	22.8

Punt Return Average
(Minimum 75 Returns)

Player	Ret	Yds	Avg
Mel Gray	211	2387	**11.3**
Henry Ellard	135	1527	11.3
Brian Mitchell	172	1938	11.3
Bobby Joe Edmonds	134	1471	11.0
David Meggett	247	2613	10.6
Tyrone Hughes	86	908	10.6
Tim Brown	269	2811	10.4
Eric Metcalf	166	1724	10.4
Glyn Milburn	112	1158	10.3
Dexter Carter	102	1041	10.2

Return Touchdowns

Player	TD
Mel Gray	**9**
Eric Metcalf	8
David Meggett	7
Brian Mitchell	6
Deion Sanders	5
Tyrone Hughes	5
Andre Coleman	5
4 tied with	4

NFL Active Career Defense Leaders

Interceptions

Player	Int
Eugene Robinson	**42**
Darrell Green	40
Albert Lewis	38
Kevin Ross	36
Eric Allen	36
Vencie Glenn	35
Lionel Washington	33
4 tied with	32

Yards/Int Return
(Minimum 20 Interceptions)

Player	Int	Yds	Y/R
Deion Sanders	32	857	**26.8**
Louis Oliver	24	495	20.6
Rod Woodson	32	658	20.6
Tim McDonald	29	552	19.0
Kevin Ross	36	647	18.0
Brian Washington	24	410	17.1
Darren Carrington	21	356	17.0
Leroy Butler	21	352	16.8
Terry McDaniel	28	457	16.3
Vencie Glenn	35	544	15.5

Sacks

Player	Sacks
Reggie White	**157.0**
Rickey Jackson	128.0
Bruce Smith	126.5
Richard Dent	126.5
Kevin Greene	108.0
Sean Jones	108.0
Leslie O'Neal	105.5
Chris Doleman	104.5
Pat Swilling	99.5
Simon Fletcher	97.5

Fumbles Recovered

Player	Fumbles
Rickey Jackson	**25**
Sam Mills	20
James Hasty	19
Ray Childress	18
Cornelius Bennett	18
Kevin Greene	17
Dan Saleaumua	17
Chris Spielman	17
Derrick Thomas	15
3 tied with	14

Interception Return Yards

Player	Ret Yds
Deion Sanders	**857**
Rod Woodson	658
Kevin Ross	647
Eugene Robinson	586
Tim McDonald	552
Vencie Glenn	544
Eddie Anderson	531
Eric Allen	510
Louis Oliver	495

Int Return Touchdowns

Player	TDs
Deion Sanders	**6**
Eric Allen	5
Brian Washington	4
Rod Woodson	4
Tim McDonald	4
Terry McDaniel	4
Darrell Green	4
13 tied with	3

Forced Fumbles

Player	FF
Rickey Jackson	**40**
Pat Swilling	34
Richard Dent	34
Chris Doleman	31
Greg Lloyd	31
Derrick Thomas	30
Neil Smith	27
Mike Johnson	26
5 tied with	25

Defensive TDs

Player	TDs
Deion Sanders	**6**
Terry McDaniel	**6**
Darrell Green	**6**
Jessie Tuggle	5
Tim McDonald	5
Eric Allen	5
Seth Joyner	5
10 tied with	4

Glossary

Big Pass Play

Any pass completion that gains 25 or more yards.

Big Running Play

Any running play that gains 10 or more yards.

Dropped Pass

Any incomplete pass which was catchable with normal effort. To determine if a pass was dropped, STATS compares and reviews the judgement of multiple reporters.

First Down

A play on which the player in question gained a first down.

First Down Percentage

The percentage of relevant plays which resulted in first downs. For example, if a receiver's First Down Percentage is 20 percent, that means one-fifth of his catches resulted in first downs.

Inside 20 Punt

According to the NFL, "Credit a player with an inside-20 when his punt is not returned to the receivers' 20-yard line or beyond. Also credit an inside-20 when a punt does not penetrate the 20, but the returner carries the ball back inside the 20 and his return ends there. A touchback is *not* an inside-20."

Inside 20 Percentage

Inside-20 punts divided by Net Punts.

Net Kickoff Average

Kickoff Yards, minus Return Yards, minus 20 yards for every Touchback, divided by Kickoffs.

Net Punts

Punt attempts which were not blocked.

Net Punting Average

Gross Punting Yards, minus Return Yards, minus 20 yards for every Touchback, divided by Total Punts.

Other

In the Offensive Profiles, refers to incomplete passes not covered under the primary categories, and includes instances when a receiver caught a pass out of bounds, when the QB spiked the ball to stop the clock, when he threw the ball away intentionally, and assorted other rare occurrences.

Pass Defensed

Any pass which a defender, through contact with the football, causes to be incomplete.

Passer (QB) Rating

The NFL formula used to rate quarterbacks. The formula goes like this:

Step 1: Complete passes divided by pass attempts. Subtract 0.3, then divide by 0.2.
Step 2: Passing yards divided by pass attempts. Subtract 3, then divide by 4.
Step 3: Touchdown passes divided by pass attempts, then divide by .05.
Step 4: Start with .095, and subtract interceptions divided by attempts. Divide the product by .04.

The sum of each step cannot be greater than 2.375 or less than zero. Add the sum of Steps 1 through 4, multiply by 100 and divide by 6. There you have it, the NFL's Passer Rating system. And no, we didn't just make that up.

Poor Pass

Any forward pass deemed uncatchable. This includes underthrows, overthrows, interceptions, passes thrown wide of the receiver, passes caught out of the bounds and passes thrown away intentionally.

Stuff

Any tackle of a ball carrier behind the line of scrimmage during a rushing attempt.

Target

The receiver for whom a pass was intended.

Total Punts

Net Punts plus blocked punts.

Yards After Catch (YAC)

The number of yards a receiver gains from the spot on the field at which he establishes possession of a passed football to the play's end. Example: A receiver catches a pass at his 10-yard line and is tackled (or run out of bounds) at his 24-yard line. He is credited with 14 yards after catch.

Yards at Catch (Y@C)

This is simply the number of yards beyond the line of scrimmage at which a receiver caught the pass. Yards at Catch plus Yards After Catch equals total receiving yards.

About STATS, Inc.

STATS, Inc. is the nation's leading independent sports information and statistical analysis company, providing detailed sports services for a wide array of clients.

One of the fastest-growing sports companies in the country, STATS provides the most up-to-the-minute sports information to professional teams, print and broadcast media, software developers and interactive service providers around the country. Some our major clients are ESPN, Turner Sports, the Associated Press, *The Sporting News*, Electronic Arts, and Motorola. Much of the information we provide is available to the public via STATS On-Line.

STATS Publishing, a division of STATS, Inc., produces 11 annual books, including the *STATS Major League Handbook*, the *STATS Pro Basketball Handbook*, and (new this summer) the *STATS Hockey Handbook*. These and other publications deliver STATS expertise to fans, scouts, general managers and media around the country.

In addition, STATS offers the most innovative—and fun—fantasy sports games around, from *Bill James Fantasy Baseball* and *Bill James Classic Baseball* to *STATS Fantasy Football* and *STATS Fantasy Hoops*.

Information technology continues to increase its importance in our lives, seemingly from day to day. You can bet that STATS will be in the vanguard as both a vendor and supplier of the most up-to-date, in-depth sports information available.

For more information on our products, or on joining our reporter network, write to us at:

STATS, Inc.
8131 Monticello Ave.
Skokie, IL 60076-3300

. . . or call us at 1-800-63-STATS. Outside the U.S., dial 1- 847-676-3383.

Unbeatable Gridiron Analysis...

STATS Presents...

PRO FOOTBALL REVEALED:
The 100 Yard War
(1996 Edition)

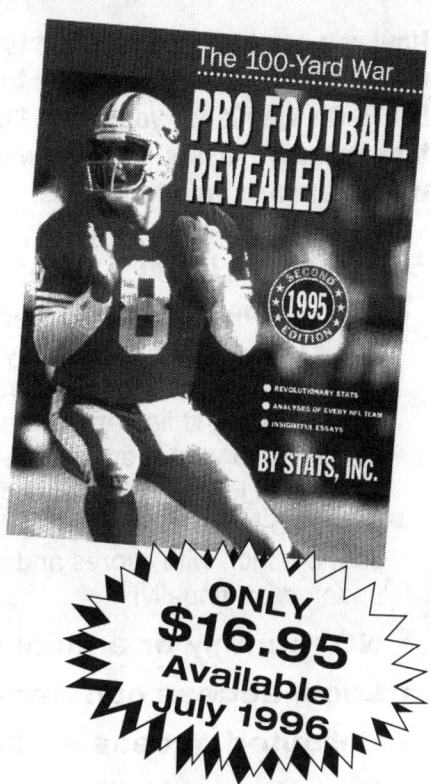

Pro Football Revealed provides the most comprehensive look at NFL teams, offering in-depth analyses guaranteed to appeal to all football enthusiasts. STATS takes a revolutionary approach in its examination of the NFL which has changed the way fans look at and enjoy the game. Whether you want to review what happened in 1995 or prepare for the 1996 season, *Pro Football Revealed* is the book you want!

ONLY $16.95 Available July 1996

Unique Features Include:

☆ In-depth essays on every team, complete with statistics, analysis, and much more!

☆ Detailed statistical breakdowns on teams, players and coaches

☆ Original essays on the best offenses of all time, review of 1995's rule changes, etc.

"Football statistics have never been as understandable and meaningful as STATS, Inc. has made them."

Don Pierson, *Chicago Tribune*

Order from STATS INC. Today!

Use Order Form in This Book, or Call 1-800-63-STATS or 847-676-3383 or e-mail: info@stats.com!

STATS On-Line

Now you can have a direct line to a world of sports information just like the pros use with STATS On-Line. If you love to keep up with your favorite teams and players, STATS On-Line is for you. From Shaquille O'Neal's fast-breaking dunks to Ken Griffey's tape-measure blasts — if you want baseball, basketball, football and   hockey stats, we put them at your fingertips!

STATS On-Line

- **Player Profiles and Team Profiles** — The #1 resource for scouting your favorite professional teams and players with information you simply can't find anywhere else! The most detailed info you've ever seen, including real-time stats. Follow baseball pitch-by-pitch, football snap-by-snap, and basketball and hockey shot-by-shot, with scores and player stats updated continually!

- **NO monthly or annual fees**

- **Local access numbers** — avoid costly long-distance charges!

- **Unlimited access** — 24 hours a day, seven days a week

- **Downloadable files** — get year-to-date stats in an ASCII format for baseball, football, basketball, and hockey

- **In-progress box scores** — You'll have access to the most up-to-the-second scoring stats for every team and player. When you log into STATS On-Line, you'll get detailed updates, including player stats and scoring plays while the games are in progress!

- **Other exclusive features** — transactions and injury information, team and player profiles and updates, standings, leader and trailer boards, game-by-game logs, fantasy game features, and much more!

Sign-up fee of $30 (applied towards future use), 24-hour access with usage charges of $.75/min. Mon.-Fri., 8am-6pm CST; $.25/min. all other hours and weekends.

Order from *STATS* INC. Today!

Use Order Form in This Book, or Call 1-800-63-STATS or 847-676-3383 or e-mail: info@stats.com!

STATS Fantasy Hoops

Soar into the 1995-96 season with STATS Fantasy Hoops! SFH puts YOU in charge. Don't just sit back and watch Grant Hill, Shawn Kemp, and Alonzo Mourning - get in the game and coach your team to the top!

How to Play SFH:
1. Sign up to coach a team.
2. You'll receive a full set of rules and a draft form with SFH point values for all eligible players - anyone who played in the NBA in 1994-95, plus all 1995 NBA draft picks.
3. Complete the draft form and return it to STATS.
4. You will take part in the draft with nine other owners, and we will send you league rosters.
5. You make unlimited weekly transactions including trades, free agent signings, activations, and benchings.
6. Six of the 10 teams in your league advance to postseason play, with two teams ultimately advancing to the Finals.

SFH points values are tested against actual NBA results, mirroring the real thing. Weekly reports will tell you everything you need to know to lead your team to the SFH Championship!

STATS Fantasy Football

STATS Fantasy Football puts YOU in charge! You draft, trade, cut, bench, activate players and even sign free agents each week. SFF pits you head-to-head against 11 other owners.

STATS' scoring system applies realistic values, tested against actual NFL results. Each week, you'll receive a superb in-depth report telling you all about both team and league performances.

How to Play SFF:
1. Sign up today!
2. STATS sends you a draft form listing all eligible NFL players.
3. Fill out the draft form and return it to STATS, and you will take part in the draft along with 11 other team owners.
4. Go head-to-head against the other owners in your league. You'll make week-by-week roster moves and transactions through STATS' Fantasy Football experts, via phone, fax, or on-line!

Order from *STATS* INC. Today!

Use Order Form in This Book, or Call 1-800-63-STATS or 847-676-3383 or e-mail: info@stats.com!

Bill James Classic Baseball

Joe Jackson, Walter Johnson, and Roberto Clemente are back on the field of your dreams!

If you're not ready to give up baseball in the fall, or if you're looking to relive its glorious past, then Bill James Classic Baseball is the game for you!

The Classic Game features players from all eras of Major League Baseball at all performance levels - not just the stars. You could see Honus Wagner, Josh Gibson, Carl Yastrzemski, Bob Uecker, Billy Grabarkewitz, and Dick Fowler...on the SAME team!

As owner, GM and manager all in one, you'll be able to...

- "Buy" your team of up to 25 players from our catalog of over 2,000 historical players (You'll receive $1 million to buy your favorite players)
- Choose the park your team will call home—current or historical, 63 in all!
- Rotate batting lineups for a right- or left-handed starting pitcher
- Change your pitching rotation for each series. Determine your set-up man, closer, and long reliever
- Alter in-game strategies, including stealing frequency, holding runners on base, hit-and-run, and much more!
- Select your best pinch hitter and late-inning defensive replacements (For example, Curt Flood will get to more balls than Hack Wilson!)

How to Play The Classic Game:

1. Sign up to be a team owner TODAY! Leagues forming year-round
2. STATS, Inc. will supply you with a catalog of eligible players and a rule book
3. You'll receive $1 million to buy your favorite major leaguers
4. Take part in a player and ballpark draft with 11 other owners
5. Set your pitching rotation, batting lineup, and managerial strategies
6. STATS runs the game simulation...a 154-game schedule, 14 weeks!
7. You'll receive customized in-depth weekly reports, featuring game summaries, stats, and boxscores

Order from STATS INC. Today!

Use Order Form in This Book, or Call 1-800-63-STATS or 847-676-3383 or e-mail: info@stats.com!

Bill James Fantasy Baseball

Bill James Fantasy Baseball enters its eighth season of offering baseball fans the most unique, realistic and exciting game fantasy sports has to offer.

You draft a 25-player roster and can expand to as many as 28. Players aren't ranked like in rotisserie leagues—you'll get credit for everything a player does, like hitting homers, driving in runs, turning double plays, pitching quality outings and more!

Also, the team which scores the most points among all leagues, plus wins the World Series, will receive the John McGraw Award, which includes a one-week trip to the Grapefruit League in spring training, a day at the ballpark with Bill James, and a new fantasy league named in his/her honor!

Unique Features Include:

• **Live fantasy experts** — available seven days a week

• **The best weekly reports in the business** — detailing who is in the lead, win-loss records, MVPs, and team strengths and weaknesses

• **On-Line computer system** — a world of information, including daily updates of fantasy standings and stats

• **Over twice as many statistics as rotisserie**

• **Transactions that are effective the very next day!**

"My goal was to develop a fantasy league based on the simplest yet most realistic principle possible. A league in which the values are as nearly as possible what they ought to be, without being distorted by artificial category values or rankings...."

- Bill James

All this, all summer long...for less than $5 per week!

Order from STATS INC. Today!

Use Order Form in This Book, or Call 1-800-63-STATS or 847-676-3383 or e-mail: info@stats.com!

STATS INC.
Meet the Winning Lineup...

Bill James Presents:
STATS Major League Handbook 1996

- Bill James' exclusive 1996 player projections
- Career data for every 1995 Major League Baseball player
- Leader boards, fielding stats and stadium data
- **Price: $17.95, Item #HB96, Available NOW!**

Bill James Presents:
STATS Minor League Handbook 1996

- Year-by-year career statistical data for AA and AAA players
- Bill James' exclusive Major League Equivalencies
- Complete 1995 Single-A player statistics
- **Price: $17.95, Item #MH96, Available NOW!**

STATS Player Profiles 1996

- Exclusive 1995 breakdowns for pitchers and hitters, over 30 in all: lefty/righty, home/road, clutch situations, ahead/behind in the count, month-by-month, etc.
- Complete breakdowns by player for the last five seasons
- **Price: $17.95, Item #PP96, Available NOW!**

STATS Scouting Notebook: 1996

- Extensive scouting reports on over 700 major league players
- Evaluations of nearly 200 minor league prospects
- **Price: $16.95, Item #SN96, Available NOW!**

STATS Minor League Scouting Notebook 1996

- Evaluation of each organization's top prospects
- Essays, stat lines and grades for more than 400 prospects
- **Price: $16.95, Item #MN96, Available NOW!**

Bill James Presents:
STATS 1996 Batter Versus Pitcher Match-Ups!

- Complete stats for pitchers vs. batters (5+ career AB against them)
- Leader boards and stats for all 1995 Major League players
- **Price: $12.95, Item #BP96, Available NOW!**

STATS Baseball Scoreboard 1996

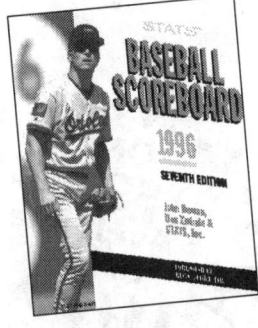

- Entertaining essays interpreting baseball stats
- Easy-to-understand statistical charts
- Specific coverage of every major team
- Appendices that invite further reader analysis
- **Price: $16.95, Item #SB96, Available 3/1/96**

STATS Pro Basketball Handbook 1995-96

- Career stats for every player who logged minutes during 1994-95
- Team game logs with points, rebounds, assists and much more
- Leader boards from points per game to triple doubles
- **Price: $17.95, Item #BH96, Available NOW!**

STATS Hockey Handbook 1996-97

- A complete season-by-season register for every active 1995 player
- Numerous statistical breakdowns for hundreds of NHL players
- Leader boards in a number of innovative and traditional categories
- **Price: $17.95, Item #HH97, Available 8/1/96**

Pro Football Revealed: The 100-Yard War (1996 Edition)

- Profiles each NFL team, complete with essays, charts and play diagrams
- Detailed statistical breakdowns on players, teams and coaches
- Essays about NFL trends and happenings by leading experts
- **Price: $16.95, Item #PF96 , Available 7/1/96**
- **1995 EDITION AVAILABLE NOW for ONLY $15.95!**

Order from STATS INC. Today!

Use Order Form in This Book, or Call 1-800-63-STATS or 847-676-3383 or e-mail: info@stats.com!

Exclusive Player Projections

STATS Presents...
The Projections Update 1996

ONLY $9.95 Available 3/1/96

The Projections Update 1996 is the most up-to-date, amazingly accurate set of projections ever assembled, perfect for your March fantasy draft! The updates for every 1995 major league player take into account all winter and spring trades, free agent signings, and much more! Projections Update is a must for those who live to win! The Projections Update 1996 is the perfect complement to your Major League Handbook 1996, giving you an updated set of projections for all hitters and pitchers.

Developed Exclusively for STATS, Inc. by Bill James and John Dewan

Includes projections updated for all players based on:

- ☆ Players in new ballparks
- ☆ Injury developments
- ☆ More accurate playing time projections
- ☆ Releases
- ☆ Trades
- ☆ Free agency

"There is no better source on the planet for preparing for your fantasy draft. This report is my drafting bible!"

- John Dewan
President and CEO

BE SURE TO MENTION OR INCLUDE THIS SPECIAL OFFER WHEN ORDERING!

Order from STATS INC. Today!
Use Order Form in This Book, or Call 1-800-63-STATS or 847-676-3383!

STATS INC Order Form

Name_____ Phone_____
Address_____ Fax_____
City_____ State_____ Zip_____

Method of Payment (U.S. Funds Only):
❑ Check/Money Order ❑ Visa ❑ MasterCard

Cardholder Name_____
Credit Card Number_____ Exp. _____
Signature_____

BOOKS

Qty	Product Name	Item #	Price	Total
	STATS 1996 Major League Handbook	HB96	$17.95	
	1996 Major League Hndbk. (Comb-bnd)	HC96	$19.95	
	STATS 1996 Projections Update	PJUP	$9.95	
	The Scouting Notebook: 1996	SN96	$16.95	
	STATS 1996 Player Profiles	PP96	$17.95	
	1996 Player Profiles (Comb-bound)	PC96	$19.95	
	STATS 1996 Minor Lg. Scouting Ntbk.	MN96	$16.95	
	STATS 1996 Minor League Handbook	MH96	$17.95	
	1996 Minor League Hndbk. (Comb-bnd)	MC96	$19.95	
	STATS 1996 BVSP Match-Ups!	BP96	$12.95	
	STATS 1996 Baseball Scoreboard	SB96	$16.95	
	STATS 1995-96 Pro Basketball Hndbk.	BH96	$17.95	
	Pro Football Revealed (1996 Edition)	PF96	$16.95	
	STATS 1996 Pro Football Handbook	FH96	$17.95	

For previous editions, circle appropriate years:

Major League Handbook 91 92 93 94 95			$9.95	
Scouting Report/Notebook 92 94 95			$9.95	
Player Profiles 93 94 95			$9.95	
Minor League Handbook 92 93 94 95			$9.95	
Baseball Scoreboard 92 93 94 95			$9.95	
Basketball Scoreboard 94 95			$9.95	
Pro Football Handbook 95			$9.95	
Pro Football Revealed 94 95			$9.95	

FANTASY GAMES & STATSfax

Qty	Product Name	Item #	Price	Total
	Bill James Classic Baseball	BJCG	$129.00	
	How to Win The Classic Game (book)	CGBK	$16.95	
	The Classic Game STATSfax	CGX5	$20.00	
	Bill James Fantasy Baseball	BJFB	$89.00	
	BJFB STATSfax/5-day	SFX5	$20.00	
	BJFB STATSfax/7-day	SFX7	$25.00	
	STATS Fantasy Hoops	SFH	$85.00	
	SFH STATSfax/5-day	SFH5	$20.00	
	SFH STATSfax/7-day	SFH7	$25.00	
	STATS Fantasy Football	SFF	$69.00	
	SFF STATSfax/3-day	SFF3	$15.00	

STATS ON-LINE

Qty	Product Name	Item #	Price	Total
	STATS On-Line	ONLE	$30.00	

**For faster service call
1-800-63-STATS or 847-676-3383,
fax this form to us at 847-676-0821,
or send e-mail to: info@stats.com**

1st Fantasy Team Name (ex. Colt 45's):_____ _____
  What Fantasy Game is this team for?_____
2nd Fantasy Team Name (ex. Colt 45's):_____ _____
  What Fantasy Game is this team for?_____

NOTE: $1.00/player is charged for all roster moves and transactions.

For Bill James Fantasy Baseball
Would you like to play in a league drafted by Bill James? ❑ Yes ❑ No

TOTALS

	Price	Total
Product Total (excl. Fantasy Games and On-Line)		
For first class mailing in U.S. add:	+$2.50/book	
Canada—all orders—add:	+$3.50/book	
Order 2 or more books—subtract:	-$1.00/book	
IL residents add 8.5% sales tax		
Subtotal		
Fantasy Games & On-Line Total		
GRAND TOTAL		

FREE Information Kits:

❑ STATS Reporter Networks
❑ Bill James Classic Baseball
❑ Bill James Fantasy Baseball
❑ STATS On-Line
❑ STATS Fantasy Hoops
❑ STATS Fantasy Football
❑ STATS Year-end Reports
❑ STATSfax

BOOK

Mail to: STATS, Inc., 8131 Monticello Ave., Skokie, IL 60076-3300